Blackstone's

EU Treaties & Legislation

Blackstone's

EU Treaties & Legislation

2013–2014

24th edition

edited by

Professor Nigel Foster, FRSA

Visiting Professor of European Law at the Europa-Institut, Universität des Saarlandes, Saarbrücken, Germany and at Law Schools of the University of the West of England and the University of Buckingham.

OXFORD
UNIVERSITY PRESS

OXFORD
UNIVERSITY PRESS

Great Clarendon Street, Oxford, OX2 6DP,
United Kingdom

Oxford University Press is a department of the University of Oxford.
It furthers the University's objective of excellence in research, scholarship,
and education by publishing worldwide. Oxford is a registered trade mark of
Oxford University Press in the UK and in certain other countries

First published by Blackstone Press 1990

Twenty-first edition 2010
Twenty-second edition 2011
Twenty-third edition 2012
Twenty-fourth edition 2013

Impression: 1

Published in the United States of America by Oxford University Press
198 Madison Avenue, New York, NY 10016, United States of America

British Library Cataloguing in Publication Data
Data available

ISBN 978–0–19–967852–5

Printed in Great Britain by
Bell & Bain Ltd, Glasgow

Contents

Editor's preface to the twenty-fourth edition

Dear lecturer, student buying this book, reviewer, or reader

This twenty-fourth edition has been constructed on the foundations of the editions before with a number of changes to the contents, subject, as ever, to space constraints, and helpful advice from the editorial support team in OUP.

A minor Treaty change is the inclusion of the amendments to Protocol 36 on transitional measures. To the Institutions section, I've added what is really a small but milestone Regulation which heralds the changing of the order or passing of the baton from the printed version of the OJ being for 61 years 'the only official version of the OJ' to the electronic version being the only official version as from 1 July 2013. This is, of course, a perfectly understandable, logical, and inevitable change. It does though remind me of the days and weeks I used to spend from 1989 when compiling the first edition and updating it for a number of years, sitting in a European Documentation Centre leafing through more than a year's supply of volumes of the Official Journal for new and amending EC laws. It's when I discovered numerous Regulations on the organization of the market in lupins! I wondered why on earth????...which was sufficient excuse for a much needed diversion from thousands of pages of OJ to find that out. I discovered rather than being regarded as an interesting flower, sweet lupins were extensively used as goat feed. Rather than waste that knowledge, lupins became the subject matter of many of my early problem questions in EC and EU law. One still survives and can be found at p. 106 in Chapter 5 of *EU Law, Questions and Answers*, 8th edition (2013–2014), OUP, 2013. So, now you know and so, no more idle and chance discoveries of obscure Eurobilia, no more occupying a choice seat in an EDC. Instead, efficient fast internet searches! The times, they are a-changin'! Back to this edition:

The Court of Justice 'Information note on references from national courts for a preliminary ruling' has had been amended further and renamed: Recommendations to national courts and tribunals in relation to the initiation of preliminary ruling proceedings and published in 2012. The Court of Justice Rules of Procedure have also been replaced in 2012. Other changes, as follows, have been made to the secondary legislation collection.

In equality law, I have added an Annex to Directive 2006/54 showing the Articles' numbers Correlation with the repealed Directives.

In competition law, because I still receive advice that it has been repealed, I wish to repeat my advice from previous years again that Article 8(3) of the largely repealed Regulation 17 has not been repealed and remains in force because it continues the Commission's powers in respect of being able to review past Decisions. If you don't believe me, look it up in 'EU Legislation in force'. I have removed the expired and repealed Block exemptions and added Commission Regulation 1217/2010 on Research and Development agreements and Commission Regulation 1218/2010 on Specialisation agreements.

As usual, I have made various corrections and amendments to the existing stock as required, as are noted throughout the volume.

I acknowledge with thanks the permission of the European Communities to reproduce material taken historically from the OJ printed volumes. More recent provisions and additions have been taken from the online EUR-Lex website and, likewise, permission to reproduce these is gratefully acknowledged but with the clear proviso that until 1 July 2013 'Only European Union legislation printed in the paper edition of the *Official Journal of the European Union* is deemed authentic' but that from that date 'only the Official Journal published in electronic form shall be authentic and shall produce legal effects' (Art 1 Regulation 216/2013). UK legislation is reproduced with the permission of HMSO (legislation.gov.uk) under the following terms: 'You may use and re-use the information featured on this website (not including logos) free of charge in any format or medium, under the terms of the Open Government Licence'. I am grateful for both those permissions.

I am really thankful for the extensive support work and close attention to detail undertaken by the staff of OUP, in particular Joanna Williams, for another year of important and necessary behind-the-editor work and for enthusiastic support, and again for conducting a specialized review of part of the volume and its contents. Thanks also to Heather Smyth and Joy Ruskin-Tompkins for their input in the production of this volume.

As ever, I would be most grateful to receive any comments, suggestions, hints, criticisms, or advice on the content, style, or indeed any other aspect of this publication or just to point out plain errors where they are noticed. Suggestions for additional material to be included are also most welcome. Whilst for each edition I am able to spot a few errors in the OJ and eradicate them, it is perfectly possible that I introduce, inadvertently, some of my own. Thanks to those of you who have made such comments or provided much appreciated advice. I do reflect on each piece of advice provided.

Nigel Foster
Cardiff
May 2013

New to this edition

The twenty-fourth edition of *Blackstone's EU Treaties & Legislation* has been fully revised and updated to include all relevant developments through to April 2013 including:

- Council Regulation 216/2013 on the electronic publication of the Official Journal of the European Union
- Recommendations to national courts and tribunals in relation to the initiation of preliminary ruling proceedings 2012
- Court of Justice Rules of Procedure 2012 Version
- Annex II of Directive 2006/54
- Commission Regulation 1217/2010 on Research and Development agreements
- Commission Regulation 1218/2010 on Specialisation agreements

Extracts from the editor's preface to the first edition

This collection of European Community legislation has been compiled with two main considerations in mind.

First, to compile an up-to-date selection of the Community primary and secondary legislation which is the subject of frequent reference and is therefore appropriate to include in an accessible reference work which will be useful to both students of Community law and the many others who now come into contact with it.

Secondly, to furnish a basic set of unannotated legislative provisions for those students of Community law who are permitted to take materials into examinations.

In attempting to fulfil these twin tasks, I have been acutely aware of the growing mass of Community law and the danger of trying to incorporate everything which may be considered relevant. Therefore, as demanded by a compilation attempting to achieve specific aims, I have been very selective in the material chosen, particularly with regard to the primary source material of the European Communities.

The first part of the compilation contains Community Treaty and other primary materials. The second part of the book includes secondary Community legislation taken from a number of areas of substantive law. Once again I have been necessarily selective and confined the scope to areas most commonly covered in Community law courses, although I am certain that I shall be unable to entirely satisfy all courses or perhaps even any course.

Finally I have included as a matter of necessity extracts from the European Communities Act 1972. For the latter item, I gratefully acknowledge HMSO.

The Community source material was taken predominantly from the Official Journal of the European Communities unless where otherwise stated and likewise I gratefully acknowledge the permission of the European Commission to reproduce those materials. Wherever they were noticed, errors in this material have been corrected, all other errors and omissions are my responsibility.

Nigel Foster
Cardiff
February 1990

Tables of equivalences*

Treaty on European Union

Old numbering of the Treaty on European Union	New numbering of the Treaty on European Union
TITLE I – COMMON PROVISIONS	TITLE I – COMMON PROVISIONS
Article 1	Article 1
	Article 2
Article 2	Article 3
Article 3 (repealed)[1]	
	Article 4
	Article 5[2]
Article 4 (repealed)[3]	
Article 5 (repealed)[4]	
Article 6	Article 6
Article 7	Article 7
	Article 8
TITLE II – PROVISIONS AMENDING THE TREATY ESTABLISHING THE EUROPEAN ECONOMIC COMMUNITY WITH A VIEW TO ESTABLISHING THE EUROPEAN COMMUNITY	TITLE II – PROVISIONS ON DEMOCRATIC PRINCIPLES
Article 8 (repealed)[5]	Article 9
	Article 10[6]
	Article 11
	Article 12
TITLE III – PROVISIONS AMENDING THE TREATY ESTABLISHING THE EUROPEAN COAL AND STEEL COMMUNITY	TITLE III – PROVISIONS ON THE INSTITUTIONS
Article 9 (repealed)[7]	Article 13
	Article 14[8]
	Article 15[9]

(cont.)

* **Editor's Note:** Tables of equivalences as referred to in Article 5 of the Treaty of Lisbon. The original centre column, which set out the intermediate numbering as used in that Treaty, has been omitted. Editor's further note: Changes have been made to the footnotes and footnote numbering with the Commission corrections also included as to publication of the new consolidated version of 30 March 2010.

[1] Replaced, in substance, by Article 7 of the Treaty on the Functioning of the European Union ('TFEU') and by Articles 13 and 21, paragraph 3, second subparagraph of the Treaty on European Union ('TEU').

[2] Replaces Article 5 of the Treaty establishing the European Community ('TEC').

[3] Replaced, in substance, by Article 15.

[4] Replaced, in substance, by Article 13, paragraph 2.

[5] Article 8 TEU, which was in force until the entry into force of the Treaty of Lisbon (hereinafter 'current'), amended the TEC. Those amendments are incorporated into the latter Treaty and Article 8 is repealed. Its number is used to insert a new provision.

[6] Paragraph 4 replaces, in substance, the first subparagraph of Article 191 TEC.

[7] The previous Article 9 TEU amended the Treaty establishing the European Coal and Steel Community. This latter expired on 23 July 2002. Article 9 is repealed and the number thereof is used to insert another provision.

[8] – Paragraphs 1 and 2 replace, in substance, Article 189 TEC;
– paragraphs 1 to 3 replace, in substance, paragraphs 1 to 3 of Article 190 TEC;
– paragraph 1 replaces, in substance, the first subparagraph of Article 192 TEC;
– paragraph 4 replaces, in substance, the first subparagraph of Article 197 TEC.

[9] Replaces, in substance, Article 4.

Old numbering of the Treaty on European Union	New numbering of the Treaty on European Union
	Article 16[10]
	Article 17[11]
	Article 18
	Article 19[12]
TITLE IV – PROVISIONS AMENDING THE TREATY ESTABLISHING THE EUROPEAN ATOMIC ENERGY COMMUNITY	TITLE IV – PROVISIONS ON ENHANCED COOPERATION
Article 10 (repealed)[13]	
Articles 27 A to 27 E (replaced)	
Articles 40 to 40 B (replaced)	
Articles 43 to 45 (replaced)	Article 20[14]
TITLE V – PROVISIONS ON A COMMON FOREIGN AND SECURITY POLICY	TITLE V – GENERAL PROVISIONS ON THE UNION'S EXTERNAL ACTION AND SPECIFIC PROVISIONS ON THE COMMON FOREIGN AND SECURITY POLICY
	Chapter 1 – General provisions on the Union's external action
	Article 21
	Article 22
	Chapter 2 – Specific provisions on the common foreign and security policy
	Section 1 – Common provisions
	Article 23
Article 11	Article 24
Article 12	Article 25
Article 13	Article 26
	Article 27
Article 14	Article 28
Article 15	Article 29
Article 22 (moved)	Article 30
Article 23 (moved)	Article 31
Article 16	Article 32
Article 17 (moved)	*Article 42*
Article 18	Article 33
Article 19	Article 34
Article 20	Article 35

[10] – Paragraph 1 replaces, in substance, the first and second indents of Article 202 TEC;
– paragraphs 2 and 9 replace, in substance, Article 203 TEC;
– paragraphs 4 and 5 replace, in substance, paragraphs 2 and 4 of Article 205 TEC.

[11] – Paragraph 1 replaces, in substance, Article 211 TEC;
– paragraphs 3 and 7 replace, in substance, Article 214 TEC.
– paragraph 6 replaces, in substance, paragraphs 1, 3 and 4 of Article 217 TEC.

[12] – Replaces, in substance, Article 220 TEC.
– the second subparagraph of paragraph 2 replaces, in substance, the first subparagraph of Article 221 TEC.

[13] The previous Article 10 TEU amended the Treaty establishing the European Atomic Energy Community. Those amendments are incorporated into the Treaty of Lisbon. Article 10 is repealed and the number thereof is used to insert another provision.

[14] Also replaces Articles 11 and 11a TEC.

Old numbering of the Treaty on European Union	New numbering of the Treaty on European Union
Article 21	Article 36
Article 22 (moved)	*Article 30*
Article 23 (moved)	*Article 31*
Article 24	Article 37
Article 25	Article 38
	Article 39
Article 47 (moved)	Article 40
Article 26 (repealed)	
Article 27 (repealed)	
Article 27 A (replaced)[15]	*Article 20*
Article 27 B (replaced)[1]	*Article 20*
Article 27 C (replaced)[1]	*Article 20*
Article 27 D (replaced)[1]	*Article 20*
Article 27 E (replaced)[1]	*Article 20*
Article 28	Article 41
	Section 2 – Provisions on the common security and defence policy
Article 17 (moved)	Article 42
	Article 43
	Article 44
	Article 45
	Article 46
TITLE VI – PROVISIONS ON POLICE AND JUDICIAL COOPERATION IN CRIMINAL MATTERS (repealed)[16]	
Article 29 (replaced)[17]	
Article 30 (replaced)[18]	
Article 31 (replaced)[19]	
Article 32 (replaced)[20]	
Article 33 (replaced)[21]	
Article 34 (repealed)	
Article 35 (repealed)	
Article 36 (replaced)[22]	
Article 37 (repealed)	
Article 38 (repealed)	
Article 39 (repealed)	

(cont.)

[15] The previous Articles 27 A to 27 E, on enhanced cooperation, are also replaced by Articles 326 to 334 TFEU.

[16] The previous provisions of Title VI of the TEU, on police and judicial cooperation in criminal matters, are replaced by the provisions of Chapters 1, 5 and 5 of Title IV of Part Three of the TFEU.

[17] Replaced by Article 67 TFEU.

[18] Replaced by Articles 87 and 88 TFEU.

[19] Replaced by Articles 82, 83 and 85 TFEU.

[20] Replaced by Article 89 TFEU.

[21] Replaced by Article 72 TFEU.

[22] Replaced by Article 71 TFEU.

Old numbering of the Treaty on European Union	New numbering of the Treaty on European Union
Article 40 (replaced)	*Article 20*
Article 40 A (replaced)[23]	*Article 20*
Article 40 B (replaced)	*Article 20*
Article 41 (repealed)	
Article 42 (repealed)	
TITLE VII – PROVISIONS ON ENHANCED COOPERATION (replaced)	*TITLE IV – PROVISIONS ON ENHANCED COOPERATION*
Article 43 (replaced)[24]	*Article 20*
Article 43 A (replaced)	*Article 20*
Article 43 B (replaced)	*Article 20*
Article 44 (replaced)[2]	*Article 20*
Article 44 A (replaced)	*Article 20*
Article 45 (replaced)	*Article 20*
TITLE VIII – FINAL PROVISIONS	TITLE VI – FINAL PROVISIONS
Article 46 (repealed)	
	Article 47
Article 47 (replaced)	*Article 40*
Article 48	Article 48
Article 49	Article 49
	Article 50
	Article 51
	Article 52
Article 50 (repealed)	
Article 51	Article 53
Article 52	Article 54
Article 53	Article 55

[23] The previous Articles 40 to 40 B TEU, on enhanced cooperation, are also replaced by Articles 326 to 334 TFEU.

[24] The previous Articles 43 to 45 and Title VII of the TEU, on enhanced cooperation, are also replaced by Articles 326 to 334 TFEU.

Treaty on the Functioning of the European Union

Old numbering of the Treaty establishing the European Community	New numbering of the Treaty on the Functioning of the European Union
PART ONE – PRINCIPLES	PART ONE – PRINCIPLES
Article 1 (repealed)	
	Article 1
Article 2 (repealed)[25]	
	Title I – Categories and areas of Union competence
	Article 2
	Article 3
	Article 4
	Article 5
	Article 6
	Title II – Provisions having general application
	Article 7
Article 3, paragraph 1 (repealed)[26]	
Article 3, paragraph 2	Article 8
Article 4 (moved)	*Article 119*
Article 5 (replaced)[27]	
	Article 9
	Article 10
Article 6	Article 11
Article 153, paragraph 2 (moved)	Article 12
	Article 13[28]
Article 7 (repealed)[29]	
Article 8 (repealed)[30]	
Article 9 (repealed)	
Article 10 (repealed)[31]	
Article 11 (replaced)[32]	*Articles 326 to 334*
Article 11a (replaced)[33]	*Articles 326 to 334*
Article 12 (repealed)	*Article 18*
Article 13 (moved)	*Article 19*
Article 14 (moved)	*Article 26*
Article 15 (moved)	*Article 27*
Article 16	Article 14
Article 255 (moved)	Article 15
Article 286 (moved)	Article 16
	Article 17

(cont.)

[25] Replaced, in substance, by Article 3 TEU.
[26] Replaced, in substance, by Articles 3 to 6 TFEU.
[27] Replaced, in substance, by Article 5 TEU.
[28] Insertion of the operative part of the protocol on protection and welfare of animals.
[29] Replaced, in substance, by Article 13 TEU.
[30] Replaced, in substance, by Article 13 TEU and Article 282, paragraph 1, TFEU.
[31] Replaced, in substance, by Article 4, paragraph 3, TEU.
[32] Also replaced by Article 20 TEU.
[33] Also replaces previous Article 29 TEU.

Old numbering of the Treaty establishing the European Community	New numbering of the Treaty on the Functioning of the European Union
PART TWO – CITIZENSHIP OF THE UNION	PART TWO – NON-DISCRIMINATION AND CITIZENSHIP OF THE UNION
Article 12 (moved)	Article 18
Article 13 (moved)	Article 19
Article 17	Article 20
Article 18	Article 21
Article 19	Article 22
Article 20	Article 23
Article 21	Article 24
Article 22	Article 25
PART THREE – COMMUNITY POLICIES	PART THREE – POLICIES AND INTERNAL ACTIONS OF THE UNION
	Title I – The internal market
Article 14 (moved)	Article 26
Article 15 (moved)	Article 27
Title I – Free movement of goods	Title II – Free movement of goods
Article 23	Article 28
Article 24	Article 29
Chapter 1 – The customs union	Chapter 1 – The customs union
Article 25	Article 30
Article 26	Article 31
Article 27	Article 32
Part Three, Title X, Customs cooperation (moved)	Chapter 2 – Customs cooperation
Article 135 (moved)	Article 33
Chapter 2 – Prohibition of quantitative restrictions between Member States	Chapter 3 – Prohibition of quantitative restrictions between Member States
Article 28	Article 34
Article 29	Article 35
Article 30	Article 36
Article 31	Article 37
Title II – Agriculture	Title III – Agriculture and fisheries
Article 32	Article 38
Article 33	Article 39
Article 34	Article 40
Article 35	Article 41
Article 36	Article 42
Article 37	Article 43
Article 38	Article 44
Title III – Free movement of persons, services and capital	Title IV – Free movement of persons, services and capital
Chapter 1 – Workers	Chapter 1 – Workers
Article 39	Article 45
Article 40	Article 46

Old numbering of the Treaty establishing the European Community	New numbering of the Treaty on the Functioning of the European Union
Article 41	Article 47
Article 42	Article 48
Chapter 2 – Right of establishment	Chapter 2 – Right of establishment
Article 43	Article 49
Article 44	Article 50
Article 45	Article 51
Article 46	Article 52
Article 47	Article 53
Article 48	Article 54
Article 294 (moved)	Article 55
Chapter 3 – Services	Chapter 3 – Services
Article 49	Article 56
Article 50	Article 57
Article 51	Article 58
Article 52	Article 59
Article 53	Article 60
Article 54	Article 61
Article 55	Article 62
Chapter 4 – Capital and payments	Chapter 4 – Capital and payments
Article 56	Article 63
Article 57	Article 64
Article 58	Article 65
Article 59	Article 66
Article 60 (moved)	*Article 75*
Title IV – Visas, asylum, immigration and other policies related to free movement of persons	Title V – Area of freedom, security and justice
	Chapter 1 – General provisions
Article 61	Article 67[33]
	Article 68
	Article 69
	Article 70
	Article 71[34]
Article 64, paragraph 1 (replaced)	Article 72[35]
	Article 73
Article 66 (replaced)	Article 74
Article 60 (moved)	Article 75
	Article 76
	Chapter 2 – Policies on border checks, asylum and immigration

(cont.)

[34] Also replaces previous Article 36 TEU.
[35] Also replaces previous Article 33 TEU.

Old numbering of the Treaty establishing the European Community	New numbering of the Treaty on the Functioning of the European Union
Article 62	Article 77
Article 63, points 1 and 2, and Article 64, paragraph 2[36]	Article 78
Article 63, points 3 and 4	Article 79
	Article 80
Article 64, paragraph 1 (replaced)	Article 72
	Chapter 3 – Judicial cooperation in civil matters
Article 65	Article 81
Article 66 (replaced)	Article 74
Article 67 (repealed)	
Article 68 (repealed)	
Article 69 (repealed)	
	Chapter 4 – Judicial cooperation in criminal matters
	Article 82[37]
	Article 83[38]
	Article 84
	Article 85[38]
	Article 86
	Chapter 5 – Police cooperation
	Article 87[38]
	Article 88[39]
	Article 89[39]
Title V – Transport	Title VI – Transport
Article 70	Article 90
Article 71	Article 91
Article 72	Article 92
Article 73	Article 93
Article 74	Article 94
Article 75	Article 95
Article 76	Article 96
Article 77	Article 97
Article 78	Article 98
Article 79	Article 99
Article 80	Article 100
Title VI – Common rules on competition, taxation and approximation of laws	Title VII – Common rules on competition, taxation and approximation of laws
Chapter 1 – Rules on competition	Chapter 1 – Rules on competition
Section 1 – Rules applying to undertakings	Section 1 – Rules applying to undertakings
Article 81	Article 101

[36] Points 1 and 2 of Article 63 EC are replaced by paragraphs 1 and 2 of Article 78 TFEU, and paragraph 2 of Article 64 is replaced by paragraph 3 of Article 78 TFEU.
[37] Replaces previous Article 31 TEU.
[38] Replaces previous Article 30 TEU.
[39] Replaces previous Article 32 TEU.

Old numbering of the Treaty establishing the European Community	New numbering of the Treaty on the Functioning of the European Union
Article 82	Article 102
Article 83	Article 103
Article 84	Article 104
Article 85	Article 105
Article 86	Article 106
Section 2 – Aids granted by States	Section 2 – Aids granted by States
Article 87	Article 107
Article 88	Article 108
Article 89	Article 109
Chapter 2 – Tax provisions	Chapter 2 – Tax provisions
Article 90	Article 110
Article 91	Article 111
Article 92	Article 112
Article 93	Article 113
Chapter 3 – Approximation of laws	Chapter 3 – Approximation of laws
Article 95 (moved)	Article 114
Article 94 (moved)	Article 115
Article 96	Article 116
Article 97	Article 117
	Article 118
Title VII – Economic and monetary policy	Title VIII – Economic and monetary policy
Article 4 (moved)	Article 119
Chapter 1 – Economic policy	Chapter 1 – Economic policy
Article 98	Article 120
Article 99	Article 121
Article 100	Article 122
Article 101	Article 123
Article 102	Article 124
Article 103	Article 125
Article 104	Article 126
Chapter 2 – Monetary policy	Chapter 2 – Monetary policy
Article 105	Article 127
Article 106	Article 128
Article 107	Article 129
Article 108	Article 130
Article 109	Article 131
Article 110	Article 132
Article 111, paragraphs 1 to 3 and 5 (moved)	*Article 219*
Article 111, paragraph 4 (moved)	*Article 138*
	Article 133
Chapter 3 – Institutional provisions	Chapter 3 – Institutional provisions
Article 112 (moved)	*Article 283*

(cont.)

Old numbering of the Treaty establishing the European Community	New numbering of the Treaty on the Functioning of the European Union
Article 113 (moved)	*Article 284*
Article 114	Article 134
Article 115	Article 135
	Chapter 4 – Provisions specific to Member States whose currency is the euro
	Article 136
	Article 137
Article 111, paragraph 4 (moved)	Article 138
Chapter 4 – Transitional provisions	Chapter 5 – Transitional provisions
Article 116 (repealed)	
	Article 139
Article 117, paragraphs 1, 2, sixth indent, and 3 to 9 (repealed)	
Article 117, paragraph 2, first five indents (moved)	*Article 141, paragraph 2*
Article 121, paragraph 1 (moved)	
Article 122, paragraph 2, second sentence (moved)	
Article 123, paragraph 5 (moved)	Article 140[40]
Article 118 (repealed)	
Article 123, paragraph 3 (moved)	
Article 117, paragraph 2, first five indents (moved)	Article 141[41]
Article 124, paragraph 1 (moved)	Article 142
Article 119	Article 143
Article 120	Article 144
Article 121, paragraph 1 (moved)	*Article 140, paragraph 1*
Article 121, paragraphs 2 to 4 (repealed)	
Article 122, paragraphs 1, 2, first sentence, 3, 4, 5 and 6 (repealed)	
Article 122, paragraph 2, second sentence (moved)	*Article 140, paragraph 2, first subparagraph*
Article 123, paragraphs 1, 2 and 4 (repealed)	
Article 123, paragraph 3 (moved)	*Article 141, paragraph 1*
Article 123, paragraph 5 (moved)	*Article 140, paragraph 3*
Article 124, paragraph 1 (moved)	*Article 142*
Article 124, paragraph 2 (repealed)	
Title VIII – Employment	Title IX – Employment
Article 125	Article 145
Article 126	Article 146
Article 127	Article 147
Article 128	Article 148

[40] – Article 140, paragraph 1 takes over the wording of paragraph 1 of Article 121.
– Article 140, paragraph 2 takes over the second sentence of paragraph 2 of Article 122.
– Article 140, paragraph 3 takes over paragraph 5 of Article 123.

[41] – Article 141, paragraph 1 takes over paragraph 3 of Article 123.
– Article 141, paragraph 2 takes over the first five indents of paragraph 2 of Article 117.

Old numbering of the Treaty establishing the European Community	New numbering of the Treaty on the Functioning of the European Union
Article 129	Article 149
Article 130	Article 150
Title IX – Common commercial policy (moved)	*Part Five, Title II, Common commercial policy*
Article 131 (moved)	*Article 206*
Article 132 (repealed)	
Article 133 (moved)	*Article 207*
Article 134 (repealed)	
Title X – Customs cooperation (moved)	*Part Three, Title II, Chapter 2, Customs cooperation*
Article 135 (moved)	*Article 33*
Title XI – Social policy, education, vocational training and youth	Title X – Social policy
Chapter 1 – Social provisions (repealed)	
Article 136	Article 151
	Article 152
Article 137	Article 153
Article 138	Article 154
Article 139	Article 155
Article 140	Article 156
Article 141	Article 157
Article 142	Article 158
Article 143	Article 159
Article 144	Article 160
Article 145	Article 161
Chapter 2 – The European Social Fund	Title XI – The European Social Fund
Article 146	Article 162
Article 147	Article 163
Article 148	Article 164
Chapter 3 – Education, vocational training and youth	Title XII – Education, vocational training, youth and sport
Article 149	Article 165
Article 150	Article 166
Title XII – Culture	Title XIII – Culture
Article 151	Article 167
Title XIII – Public health	Title XIV – Public health
Article 152	Article 168
Title XIV – Consumer protection	Title XV – Consumer protection
Article 153, paragraphs 1, 3, 4 and 5	Article 169
Article 153, paragraph 2 (moved)	*Article 12*
Title XV – Trans–European networks	Title XVI – Trans–European networks
Article 154	Article 170
Article 155	Article 171

(cont.)

Old numbering of the Treaty establishing the European Community	New numbering of the Treaty on the Functioning of the European Union
Article 156	Article 172
Title XVI – Industry	Title XVII – Industry
Article 157	Article 173
Title XVII – Economic and social cohesion	Title XVIII – Economic, social and territorial cohesion
Article 158	Article 174
Article 159	Article 175
Article 160	Article 176
Article 161	Article 177
Article 162	Article 178
Title XVIII – Research and technological development	Title XIX – Research and technological development and space
Article 163	Article 179
Article 164	Article 180
Article 165	Article 181
Article 166	Article 182
Article 167	Article 183
Article 168	Article 184
Article 169	Article 185
Article 170	Article 186
Article 171	Article 187
Article 172	Article 188
	Article 189
Article 173	Article 190
Title XIX – Environment	Title XX – Environment
Article 174	Article 191
Article 175	Article 192
Article 176	Article 193
	Title XXI – Energy
	Article 194
	Title XXII – Tourism
	Article 195
	Title XXIII – Civil protection
	Article 196
	Title XXIV – Administrative cooperation
	Article 197
Title XX – Development cooperation (moved)	*Part Five, Title III, Chapter 1, Development cooperation*
Article 177 (moved)	*Article 208*
Article 178 (repealed)[42]	
Article 179 (moved)	*Article 209*

[42] Replaced, in substance, by the second sentence of the second subparagraph of paragraph 1 of Article 208 TFEU.

Old numbering of the Treaty establishing the European Community	New numbering of the Treaty on the Functioning of the European Union
Article 180 (moved)	*Article 210*
Article 181 (moved)	*Article 211*
Title XXI – Economic, financial and technical cooperation with third countries (moved)	*Part Five, Title III, Chapter 2, Economic, financial and technical cooperation with third countries*
Article 181a (moved)	Article 212
PART FOUR – ASSOCIATION OF THE OVERSEAS COUNTRIES AND TERRITORIES	PART FOUR – ASSOCIATION OF THE OVERSEAS COUNTRIES AND TERRITORIES
Article 182	Article 198
Article 183	Article 199
Article 184	Article 200
Article 185	Article 201
Article 186	Article 202
Article 187	Article 203
Article 188	Article 204
	PART FIVE – EXTERNAL ACTION BY THE UNION
	Title I – General provisions on the Union's external action
	Article 205
Part Three, Title IX, Common commercial policy (moved)	Title II – Common commercial policy
Article 131 (moved)	Article 206
Article 133 (moved)	Article 207
	Title III – Cooperation with third countries and humanitarian aid
Part Three, Title XX, Development cooperation (moved)	Chapter 1 – Development cooperation
Article 177 (moved)	Article 208[43]
Article 179 (moved)	Article 209
Article 180 (moved)	Article 210
Article 181 (moved)	Article 211
Part Three, Title XXI, Economic, financial and technical cooperation with third countries (moved)	Chapter 2 – Economic, financial and technical cooperation with third countries
Article 181a (moved)	Article 212
	Article 213
	Chapter 3 – Humanitarian aid
	Article 214
	Title IV – Restrictive measures
Article 301 (replaced)	Article 215
	Title V – International agreements
	Article 216
Article 310 (moved)	Article 217

(cont.)

[43] The second sentence of the second subparagraph of paragraph 1 replaces, in substance, Article 178 TEC.

Old numbering of the Treaty establishing the European Community	New numbering of the Treaty on the Functioning of the European Union
Article 300 (replaced)	Article 218
Article 111, paragraphs 1 to 3 and 5 (moved)	Article 219
	Title VI – The Union's relations with international organisations and third countries and Union delegations
Articles 302 to 304 (replaced)	Article 220
	Article 221
	Title VII – Solidarity clause
	Article 222
PART FIVE – INSTITUTIONS OF THE COMMUNITY	PART SIX – INSTITUTIONAL AND FINANCIAL PROVISIONS
Title I – Institutional provisions	Title I – Institutional provisions
Chapter 1 – The institutions	Chapter 1 – The institutions
Section 1 – The European Parliament	Section 1 – The European Parliament
Article 189 (repealed)[44]	
Article 190, paragraphs 1 to 3 (repealed)[45]	
Article 190, paragraphs 4 and 5	Article 223
Article 191, first paragraph (repealed)[46]	
Article 191, second paragraph	Article 224
Article 192, first paragraph (repealed)[47]	
Article 192, second paragraph	Article 225
Article 193	Article 226
Article 194	Article 227
Article 195	Article 228
Article 196	Article 229
Article 197, first paragraph (repealed)[48]	
Article 197, second, third and fourth paragraphs	Article 230
Article 198	Article 231
Article 199	Article 232
Article 200	Article 233
Article 201	Article 234
	Section 2 – The European Council
	Article 235
	Article 236
Section 2 – The Council	Section 3 – The Council
Article 202 (repealed)[49]	
Article 203 (repealed)[50]	

[44] Replaced, in substance, by Article 14, paragraphs 1 and 2, TEU.
[45] Replaced, in substance, by Article 14, paragraphs 1 to 3, TEU.
[46] Replaced, in substance, by Article 11, paragraph 4, TEU.
[47] Replaced, in substance, by Article 14, paragraph 1, TEU.
[48] Replaced, in substance, by Article 14, paragraph 4, TEU.
[49] Replaced, in substance, by Article 16, paragraph 1, TEU and by Articles 290 and 291 TFEU.
[50] Replaced, in substance, by Article 16, paragraphs 2 and 9 TEU.

Old numbering of the Treaty establishing the European Community	New numbering of the Treaty on the Functioning of the European Union
Article 204	Article 237
Article 205, paragraphs 2 and 4 (repealed)	
Article 205, paragraphs 1 and 3[51]	Article 238
Article 206	Article 239
Article 207	Article 240
Article 208	Article 241
Article 209	Article 242
Article 210	Article 243
Section 3 – The Commission	Section 4 – The Commission
Article 211 (repealed)[52]	
	Article 244
Article 212 (moved)	*Article 249, paragraph 2*
Article 213	Article 245
Article 214 (repealed)[53]	
Article 215	Article 246
Article 216	Article 247
Article 217, paragraphs 1, 3 and 4 (repealed)[54]	
Article 217, paragraph 2	Article 248
Article 218, paragraph 1 (re-pealed)[55]	
Article 218, paragraph 2	Article 249
Article 219	Article 250
Section 4 – The Court of Justice	Section 5 – The Court of Justice of the European Union
Article 220 (repealed)[56]	
Article 221, first paragraph (repealed)[57]	
Article 221, second and third paragraphs	Article 251
Article 222	Article 252
Article 223	Article 253
Article 224[58]	Article 254
	Article 255
Article 225	Article 256
Article 225a	Article 257
Article 226	Article 258
Article 227	Article 259
Article 228	Article 260

(cont.)

[51] Replaced, in substance, by Article 16, paragraphs 4 and 5 TEU.
[52] Replaced, in substance, by Article 17, paragraph 1 TEU.
[53] Replaced, in substance, by Article 17, paragraphs 3 and 7 TEU.
[54] Replaced, in substance, by Article 17, paragraph 6, TEU.
[55] Replaced, in substance, by Article 295 TFEU.
[56] Replaced, in substance, by Article 19 TEU.
[57] Replaced, in substance, by Article 19, paragraph 2, first subparagraph, of the TEU.
[58] The first sentence of the first subparagraph is replaced, in substance, by Article 19, paragraph 2, second subparagraph of the TEU.

Old numbering of the Treaty establishing the European Community	New numbering of the Treaty on the Functioning of the European Union
Article 229	Article 261
Article 229a	Article 262
Article 230	Article 263
Article 231	Article 264
Article 232	Article 265
Article 233	Article 266
Article 234	Article 267
Article 235	Article 268
	Article 269
Article 236	Article 270
Article 237	Article 271
Article 238	Article 272
Article 239	Article 273
Article 240	Article 274
	Article 275
	Article 276
Article 241	Article 277
Article 242	Article 278
Article 243	Article 279
Article 244	Article 280
Article 245	Article 281
	Section 6 – The European Central Bank
	Article 282
Article 112 (moved)	Article 283
Article 113 (moved)	Article 284
Section 5 – The Court of Auditors	Section 7 – The Court of Auditors
Article 246	Article 285
Article 247	Article 286
Article 248	Article 287
Chapter 2 – Provisions common to several institutions	Chapter 2 – Legal acts of the Union, adoption procedures and other provisions
	Section 1 – The legal acts of the Union
Article 249	Article 288
	Article 289
	Article 290[59]
	Article 291[1]
	Article 292
	Section 2 – Procedures for the adoption of acts and other provisions
Article 250	Article 293
Article 251	Article 294

[59] Replaces, in substance, the third indent of Article 202 TEC.

Old numbering of the Treaty establishing the European Community	New numbering of the Treaty on the Functioning of the European Union
Article 252 (repealed)	
	Article 295
Article 253	Article 296
Article 254	Article 297
	Article 298
Article 255 (moved)	Article 15
Article 256	Article 299
	Chapter 3 – The Union's advisory bodies
	Article 300
Chapter 3 – The Economic and Social Committee	Section 1 – The Economic and Social Committee
Article 257 (repealed)[60]	
Article 258, first, second and fourth paragraphs	Article 301
Article 258, third paragraph (repealed)[61]	
Article 259	Article 302
Article 260	Article 303
Article 261 (repealed)	
Article 262	Article 304
Chapter 4 – The Committee of the Regions	Section 2 – The Committee of the Regions
Article 263, first and fifth paragraphs (repealed)[62]	
Article 263, second to fourth paragraphs	Article 305
Article 264	Article 306
Article 265	Article 307
Chapter 5 – The European Investment Bank	Chapter 4 – The European Investment Bank
Article 266	Article 308
Article 267	Article 309
Title II – Financial provisions	Title II – Financial provisions
Article 268	Article 310
	Chapter 1 – The Union's own resources
Article 269	Article 311
Article 270 (repealed)[63]	
	Chapter 2 – The multiannual financial framework
	Article 312
	Chapter 3 – The Union's annual budget
Article 272, paragraph 1 (moved)	Article 313
Article 271 (moved)	*Article 316*
Article 272, paragraph 1 (moved)	*Article 313*
Article 272, paragraphs 2 to 10	Article 314

(cont.)

[60] Replaced, in substance, by Article 300, paragraph 2 of the TFEU.
[61] Replaced, in substance, by Article 300, paragraph 4 of the TFEU.
[62] Replaced, in substance, by Article 300, paragraphs 3 and 4, TFEU.
[63] Replaced, in substance, by Article 310, paragraph 4, TFEU.

Old numbering of the Treaty establishing the European Community	New numbering of the Treaty on the Functioning of the European Union
Article 273	Article 315
Article 271 (moved)	Article 316
	Chapter 4 – Implementation of the budget and discharge
Article 274	Article 317
Article 275	Article 318
Article 276	Article 319
	Chapter 5 – Common provisions
Article 277	Article 320
Article 278	Article 321
Article 279	Article 322
	Article 323
	Article 324
	Chapter 6 – Combating fraud
Article 280	Article 325
	Title III – Enhanced cooperation
Articles 11 and 11 A (replaced)	Article 326[64]
Articles 11 and 11 A (replaced)	Article 327[1]
Articles 11 and 11 A (replaced)	Article 328[1]
Articles 11 and 11 A (replaced)	Article 329[1]
Articles 11 and 11 A (replaced)	Article 330[1]
Articles 11 and 11 A (replaced)	Article 331[1]
Articles 11 and 11 A (replaced)	Article 332[1]
Articles 11 and 11 A (replaced)	Article 333[1]
Articles 11 and 11 A (replaced)	Article 334[1]
PART SIX – GENERAL AND FINAL PROVISIONS	PART SEVEN – GENERAL AND FINAL PROVISIONS
Article 281 (repealed)[65]	
Article 282	Article 335
Article 283	Article 336
Article 284	Article 337
Article 285	Article 338
Article 286 (replaced)	*Article 16*
Article 287	Article 339
Article 288	Article 340
Article 289	Article 341
Article 290	Article 342
Article 291	Article 343
Article 292	Article 344

[64] Also replaces the previous Articles 27 A to 27 E, 40 to 40 B, and 43 to 45 TEU.

[65] Replaced, in substance, by Article 47 TEU.

Old numbering of the Treaty establishing the European Community	New numbering of the Treaty on the Functioning of the European Union
Article 293 (repealed)	
Article 294 (moved)	*Article 55*
Article 295	Article 345
Article 296	Article 346
Article 297	Article 347
Article 298	Article 348
Article 299, paragraph 1 (repealed)[66]	
Article 299, paragraph 2, second, third and fourth subparagraphs	Article 349
Article 299, paragraph 2, first subparagraph, and paragraphs 3 to 6 (moved)	*Article 355*
Article 300 (replaced)	*Article 218*
Article 301 (replaced)	*Article 215*
Article 302 (replaced)	*Article 220*
Article 303 (replaced)	*Article 220*
Article 304 (replaced)	*Article 220*
Article 305 (repealed)	
Article 306	Article 350
Article 307	Article 351
Article 308	Article 352
	Article 353
Article 309	Article 354
Article 310 (moved)	Article 217
Article 311 (repealed)[67]	
Article 299, paragraph 2, first subparagraph, and paragraphs 3 to 6 (moved)	Article 355
Article 312	Article 356
Final Provisions	
Article 313	Article 357
	Article 358
Article 314 (repealed)[68]	

[66] Replaced, in substance by Article 52 TEU.
[67] Replaced, in substance by Article 51 TEU.
[68] Replaced, in substance by Article 55 TEU.

Part I

Primary Legislation

Consolidated Version of the Treaty on European Union*

Preamble

HIS MAJESTY THE KING OF THE BELGIANS, HER MAJESTY THE QUEEN OF DENMARK, THE PRESIDENT OF THE FEDERAL REPUBLIC OF GERMANY, THE PRESIDENT OF IRELAND, THE PRESIDENT OF THE HELLENIC REPUBLIC, HIS MAJESTY THE KING OF SPAIN, THE PRESIDENT OF THE FRENCH REPUBLIC, THE PRESIDENT OF THE ITALIAN REPUBLIC, HIS ROYAL HIGHNESS THE GRAND DUKE OF LUXEMBOURG, HER MAJESTY THE QUEEN OF THE NETHERLANDS, THE PRESIDENT OF THE PORTUGUESE REPUBLIC, HER MAJESTY THE QUEEN OF THE UNITED KINGDOM OF GREAT BRITAIN AND NORTHERN IRELAND,[1]

RESOLVED to mark a new stage in the process of European integration undertaken with the establishment of the European Communities,

DRAWING INSPIRATION from the cultural, religious and humanist inheritance of Europe, from which have developed the universal values of the inviolable and inalienable rights of the human person, freedom, democracy, equality and the rule of law,

RECALLING the historic importance of the ending of the division of the European continent and the need to create firm bases for the construction of the future Europe,

CONFIRMING their attachment to the principles of liberty, democracy and respect for human rights and fundamental freedoms and of the rule of law,

CONFIRMING their attachment to fundamental social rights as defined in the European Social Charter signed at Turin on 18 October 1961 and in the 1989 Community Charter of the Fundamental Social Rights of Workers,

DESIRING to deepen the solidarity between their peoples while respecting their history, their culture and their traditions,

DESIRING to enhance further the democratic and efficient functioning of the institutions so as to enable them better to carry out, within a single institutional framework, the tasks entrusted to them,

RESOLVED to achieve the strengthening and the convergence of their economies and to establish an economic and monetary union including, in accordance with the provisions of this Treaty and of the Treaty on the Functioning of the European Union, a single and stable currency,

DETERMINED to promote economic and social progress for their peoples, taking into account the principle of sustainable development and within the context of the accomplishment of the internal market and of reinforced cohesion and environmental protection, and to implement policies ensuring that advances in economic integration are accompanied by parallel progress in other fields,

RESOLVED to establish a citizenship common to nationals of their countries,

* **Editor's Note:** Incorporating Lisbon Treaty changes. Signatures and contents omitted. This is the version as reproduced on 30 March 2010 (OJ 2010 C83/01).

[1] The Republic of Bulgaria, the Czech Republic, the Republic of Estonia, the Republic of Cyprus, the Republic of Latvia, the Republic of Lithuania, the Republic of Hungary, the Republic of Malta, the Republic of Austria, the Republic of Poland, Romania, the Republic of Slovenia, the Slovak Republic, the Republic of Finland and the Kingdom of Sweden have since become members of the European Union.

RESOLVED to implement a common foreign and security policy including the progressive framing of a common defence policy, which might lead to a common defence in accordance with the provisions of Article 42, thereby reinforcing the European identity and its independence in order to promote peace, security and progress in Europe and in the world,

RESOLVED to facilitate the free movement of persons, while ensuring the safety and security of their peoples, by establishing an area of freedom, security and justice, in accordance with the provisions of this Treaty and of the Treaty on the Functioning of the European Union,

RESOLVED to continue the process of creating an ever closer union among the peoples of Europe, in which decisions are taken as closely as possible to the citizen in accordance with the principle of subsidiarity,

IN VIEW of further steps to be taken in order to advance European integration,

HAVE DECIDED to establish a European Union and to this end have designated as their Plenipotentiaries:

(List of plenipotentiaries not reproduced)

WHO, having exchanged their full powers, found in good and due form, have agreed as follows:

Title I Common provisions

Article 1 (ex Article 1 TEU)[2]

By this Treaty, the HIGH CONTRACTING PARTIES establish among themselves a EUROPEAN UNION, hereinafter called 'the Union' on which the Member States confer competences to attain objectives they have in common.

This Treaty marks a new stage in the process of creating an ever closer union among the peoples of Europe, in which decisions are taken as openly as possible and as closely as possible to the citizen.

The Union shall be founded on the present Treaty and on the Treaty on the Functioning of the European Union (hereinafter referred to as 'the Treaties'). Those two Treaties shall have the same legal value. The Union shall replace and succeed the European Community.

Article 2

The Union is founded on the values of respect for human dignity, freedom, democracy, equality, the rule of law and respect for human rights, including the rights of persons belonging to minorities. These values are common to the Member States in a society in which pluralism, non-discrimination, tolerance, justice, solidarity and equality between women and men prevail.

Article 3 (ex Article 2 TEU)

1. The Union's aim is to promote peace, its values and the well-being of its peoples.

2. The Union shall offer its citizens an area of freedom, security and justice without internal frontiers, in which the free movement of persons is ensured in conjunction with appropriate measures with respect to external border controls, asylum, immigration and the prevention and combating of crime.

3. The Union shall establish an internal market. It shall work for the sustainable development of Europe based on balanced economic growth and price stability, a highly competitive social market economy, aiming at full employment and social progress, and a high level of protection and improvement of the quality of the environment. It shall promote scientific and technological advance.

It shall combat social exclusion and discrimination, and shall promote social justice and protection, equality between women and men, solidarity between generations and protection of the rights of the child.

It shall promote economic, social and territorial cohesion, and solidarity among Member States.

[2] These References are merely indicative. For more ample information, please refer to the tables of equivalences between the old and the new numbering of the Treaties in this volume, in prelims, page xv.

It shall respect its rich cultural and linguistic diversity, and shall ensure that Europe's cultural heritage is safeguarded and enhanced.

4. The Union shall establish an economic and monetary union whose currency is the euro.

5. In its relations with the wider world, the Union shall uphold and promote its values and interests and contribute to the protection of its citizens. It shall contribute to peace, security, the sustainable development of the Earth, solidarity and mutual respect among peoples, free and fair trade, eradication of poverty and the protection of human rights, in particular the rights of the child, as well as to the strict observance and the development of international law, including respect for the principles of the United Nations Charter.

6. The Union shall pursue its objectives by appropriate means commensurate with the competences which are conferred upon it in the Treaties.

Article 4

1. In accordance with Article 5, competences not conferred upon the Union in the Treaties remain with the Member States.

2. The Union shall respect the equality of Member States before the Treaties as well as their national identities, inherent in their fundamental structures, political and constitutional, inclusive of regional and local self-government. It shall respect their essential State functions, including ensuring the territorial integrity of the State, maintaining law and order and safeguarding national security. In particular, national security remains the sole responsibility of each Member State.

3. Pursuant to the principle of sincere cooperation, the Union and the Member States shall, in full mutual respect, assist each other in carrying out tasks which flow from the Treaties.

The Member States shall take any appropriate measure, general or particular, to ensure fulfilment of the obligations arising out of the Treaties or resulting from the acts of the institutions of the Union.

The Member States shall facilitate the achievement of the Union's tasks and refrain from any measure which could jeopardise the attainment of the Union's objectives.

Article 5 (ex Article 5 TEC)

1. The limits of Union competences are governed by the principle of conferral. The use of Union competences is governed by the principles of subsidiarity and proportionality.

2. Under the principle of conferral, the Union shall act only within the limits of the competences conferred upon it by the Member States in the Treaties to attain the objectives set out therein. Competences not conferred upon the Union in the Treaties remain with the Member States.

3. Under the principle of subsidiarity, in areas which do not fall within its exclusive competence, the Union shall act only if and in so far as the objectives of the proposed action cannot be sufficiently achieved by the Member States, either at central level or at regional and local level, but can rather, by reason of the scale or effects of the proposed action, be better achieved at Union level.

The institutions of the Union shall apply the principle of subsidiarity as laid down in the Protocol on the application of the principles of subsidiarity and proportionality. National Parliaments ensure compliance with the principle of subsidiarity in accordance with the procedure set out in that Protocol.

4. Under the principle of proportionality, the content and form of Union action shall not exceed what is necessary to achieve the objectives of the Treaties.

The institutions of the Union shall apply the principle of proportionality as laid down in the Protocol on the application of the principles of subsidiarity and proportionality.

Article 6 (ex Article 6 TEU)

1. The Union recognises the rights, freedoms and principles set out in the Charter of Fundamental Rights of the European Union of 7 December 2000, as adapted at Strasbourg, on 12 December 2007, which shall have the same legal value as the Treaties.

The provisions of the Charter shall not extend in any way the competences of the Union as defined in the Treaties.

The rights, freedoms and principles in the Charter shall be interpreted in accordance with the general provisions in Title VII of the Charter governing its interpretation and application and with due regard to the explanations referred to in the Charter, that set out the sources of those provisions.

2. The Union shall accede to the European Convention for the Protection of Human Rights and Fundamental Freedoms. Such accession shall not affect the Union's competences as defined in the Treaties.

3. Fundamental rights, as guaranteed by the European Convention for the Protection of Human Rights and Fundamental Freedoms and as they result from the constitutional traditions common to the Member States, shall constitute general principles of the Union's law.

Article 7 (ex Article 7 TEU)

1. On a reasoned proposal by one-third of the Member States, by the European Parliament or by the European Commission, the Council, acting by a majority of four-fifths of its members after obtaining the consent of the European Parliament, may determine that there is a clear risk of a serious breach by a Member State of the values referred to in Article 2. Before making such a determination, the Council shall hear the Member State in question and may address recommendations to it, acting in accordance with the same procedure.

The Council shall regularly verify that the grounds on which such a determination was made continue to apply.

2. The European Council, acting by unanimity on a proposal by one-third of the Member States or by the Commission and after obtaining the consent of the European Parliament, may determine the existence of a serious and persistent breach by a Member State of the values referred to in Article 2, after inviting the Member State in question to submit its observations.

3. Where a determination under paragraph 2 has been made, the Council, acting by a qualified majority, may decide to suspend certain of the rights deriving from the application of the Treaties to the Member State in question, including the voting rights of the representative of the government of that Member State in the Council. In doing so, the Council shall take into account the possible consequences of such a suspension on the rights and obligations of natural and legal persons.

The obligations of the Member State in question under this Treaty shall in any case continue to be binding on that State.

4. The Council, acting by a qualified majority, may decide subsequently to vary or revoke measures taken under paragraph 3 in response to changes in the situation which led to their being imposed.

5. The voting arrangements applying to the European Parliament, the European Council and the Council for the purposes of this Article are laid down in Article 354 of the Treaty on the Functioning of the European Union.

Article 8

1. The Union shall develop a special relationship with neighbouring countries, aiming to establish an area of prosperity and good neighbourliness, founded on the values of the Union and characterised by close and peaceful relations based on cooperation.

2. For the purposes of paragraph 1, the Union may conclude specific agreements with the countries concerned. These agreements may contain reciprocal rights and obligations as well as the possibility of undertaking activities jointly. Their implementation shall be the subject of periodic consultation.

Title II Provisions on democratic principles

Article 9

In all its activities, the Union shall observe the principle of the equality of its citizens, who shall receive equal attention from its institutions, bodies, offices and agencies. Every national of a Member State shall be a citizen of the Union. Citizenship of the Union shall be additional to national citizenship and shall not replace it.

Article 10

1. The functioning of the Union shall be founded on representative democracy.

2. Citizens are directly represented at Union level in the European Parliament.

Member States are represented in the European Council by their Heads of State or Government and in the Council by their governments, themselves democratically accountable either to their national Parliaments, or to their citizens.

3. Every citizen shall have the right to participate in the democratic life of the Union. Decisions shall be taken as openly and as closely as possible to the citizen.

4. Political parties at European level contribute to forming European political awareness and to expressing the will of citizens of the Union.

Article 11

1. The institutions shall, by appropriate means, give citizens and representative associations the opportunity to make known and publicly exchange their views in all areas of Union action.

2. The institutions shall maintain an open, transparent and regular dialogue with representative associations and civil society.

3. The European Commission shall carry out broad consultations with parties concerned in order to ensure that the Union's actions are coherent and transparent.

4. Not less than one million citizens who are nationals of a significant number of Member States may take the initiative of inviting the European Commission, within the framework of its powers, to submit any appropriate proposal on matters where citizens consider that a legal act of the Union is required for the purpose of implementing the Treaties.

The procedures and conditions required for such a citizens' initiative shall be determined in accordance with the first paragraph of Article 24 of the Treaty on the Functioning of the European Union.

Article 12

National Parliaments contribute actively to the good functioning of the Union:

(a) through being informed by the institutions of the Union and having draft legislative acts of the Union forwarded to them in accordance with the Protocol on the role of national Parliaments in the European Union;

(b) by seeing to it that the principle of subsidiarity is respected in accordance with the procedures provided for in the Protocol on the application of the principles of subsidiarity and proportionality;

(c) by taking part, within the framework of the area of freedom, security and justice, in the evaluation mechanisms for the implementation of the Union policies in that area, in accordance with Article 70 of the Treaty on the Functioning of the European Union, and through being involved in the political monitoring of Europol and the evaluation of Eurojust's activities in accordance with Articles 88 and 85 of that Treaty;

(d) by taking part in the revision procedures of the Treaties, in accordance with Article 48 of this Treaty;

(e) by being notified of applications for accession to the Union, in accordance with Article 49 of this Treaty;

(f) by taking part in the inter-parliamentary cooperation between national Parliaments and with the European Parliament, in accordance with the Protocol on the role of national Parliaments in the European Union.

Title III Provisions on the institutions

Article 13

1. The Union shall have an institutional framework which shall aim to promote its values, advance its objectives, serve its interests, those of its citizens and those of the Member States, and ensure the consistency, effectiveness and continuity of its policies and actions.

The Union's institutions shall be:

- the European Parliament,
- the European Council,
- the Council,

- the European Commission (hereinafter referred to as 'the Commission'),
- the Court of Justice of the European Union,
- the European Central Bank,
- the Court of Auditors.

2. Each institution shall act within the limits of the powers conferred on it in the Treaties, and in conformity with the procedures, conditions and objectives set out in them. The institutions shall practice mutual sincere cooperation.

3. The provisions relating to the European Central Bank and the Court of Auditors and detailed provisions on the other institutions are set out in the Treaty on the Functioning of the European Union.

4. The European Parliament, the Council and the Commission shall be assisted by an Economic and Social Committee and a Committee of the Regions acting in an advisory capacity.

Article 14

1. The European Parliament shall, jointly with the Council, exercise legislative and budgetary functions. It shall exercise functions of political control and consultation as laid down in the Treaties. It shall elect the President of the Commission.

2. The European Parliament shall be composed of representatives of the Union's citizens. They shall not exceed seven hundred and fifty in number, plus the President. Representation of citizens shall be degressively proportional, with a minimum threshold of six members per Member State. No Member State shall be allocated more than ninety-six seats.

The European Council shall adopt by unanimity, on the initiative of the European Parliament and with its consent, a decision establishing the composition of the European Parliament, respecting the principles referred to in the first subparagraph.

3. The members of the European Parliament shall be elected for a term of five years by direct universal suffrage in a free and secret ballot.

4. The European Parliament shall elect its President and its officers from among its members.

Article 15

1. The European Council shall provide the Union with the necessary impetus for its development and shall define the general political directions and priorities thereof. It shall not exercise legislative functions.

2. The European Council shall consist of the Heads of State or Government of the Member States, together with its President and the President of the Commission. The High Representative of the Union for Foreign Affairs and Security Policy shall take part in its work.

3. The European Council shall meet twice every six months, convened by its President. When the agenda so requires, the members of the European Council may decide each to be assisted by a minister and, in the case of the President of the Commission, by a member of the Commission. When the situation so requires, the President shall convene a special meeting of the European Council.

4. Except where the Treaties provide otherwise, decisions of the European Council shall be taken by consensus.

5. The European Council shall elect its President, by a qualified majority, for a term of two and a half years, renewable once. In the event of an impediment or serious misconduct, the European Council can end the President's term of office in accordance with the same procedure.

6. The President of the European Council:
   (a) shall chair it and drive forward its work;
   (b) shall ensure the preparation and continuity of the work of the European Council in cooperation with the President of the Commission, and on the basis of the work of the General Affairs Council;
   (c) shall endeavour to facilitate cohesion and consensus within the European Council;
   (d) shall present a report to the European Parliament after each of the meetings of the European Council.

The President of the European Council shall, at his level and in that capacity, ensure the external representation of the Union on issues concerning its common foreign and security policy, without prejudice to the powers of the High Representative of the Union for Foreign Affairs and Security Policy.

The President of the European Council shall not hold a national office.

Article 16

1. The Council shall, jointly with the European Parliament, exercise legislative and budgetary functions. It shall carry out policy-making and coordinating functions as laid down in the Treaties.

2. The Council shall consist of a representative of each Member State at ministerial level, who may commit the government of the Member State in question and cast its vote.

3. The Council shall act by a qualified majority except where the Treaties provide otherwise.

4. As from 1 November 2014, a qualified majority shall be defined as at least 55 % of the members of the Council, comprising at least fifteen of them and representing Member States comprising at least 65 % of the population of the Union.

A blocking minority must include at least four Council members, failing which the qualified majority shall be deemed attained.

The other arrangements governing the qualified majority are laid down in Article 238(2) of the Treaty on the Functioning of the European Union.

5. The transitional provisions relating to the definition of the qualified majority which shall be applicable until 31 October 2014 and those which shall be applicable from 1 November 2014 to 31 March 2017 are laid down in the Protocol on transitional provisions.

6. The Council shall meet in different configurations, the list of which shall be adopted in accordance with Article 236 of the Treaty on the Functioning of the European Union.

The General Affairs Council shall ensure consistency in the work of the different Council configurations. It shall prepare and ensure the follow-up to meetings of the European Council, in liaison with the President of the European Council and the Commission.

The Foreign Affairs Council shall elaborate the Union's external action on the basis of strategic guidelines laid down by the European Council and ensure that the Union's action is consistent.

7. A Committee of Permanent Representatives of the Governments of the Member States shall be responsible for preparing the work of the Council.

8. The Council shall meet in public when it deliberates and votes on a draft legislative act. To this end, each Council meeting shall be divided into two parts, dealing respectively with deliberations on Union legislative acts and non-legislative activities.

9. The Presidency of Council configurations, other than that of Foreign Affairs, shall be held by Member State representatives in the Council on the basis of equal rotation, in accordance with the conditions established in accordance with Article 236 of the Treaty on the Functioning of the European Union.

Article 17

1. The Commission shall promote the general interest of the Union and take appropriate initiatives to that end. It shall ensure the application of the Treaties, and of measures adopted by the institutions pursuant to them. It shall oversee the application of Union law under the control of the Court of Justice of the European Union. It shall execute the budget and manage programmes. It shall exercise coordinating, executive and management functions, as laid down in the Treaties. With the exception of the common foreign and security policy, and other cases provided for in the Treaties, it shall ensure the Union's external representation. It shall initiate the Union's annual and multiannual programming with a view to achieving interinstitutional agreements.

2. Union legislative acts may only be adopted on the basis of a Commission proposal, except where the Treaties provide otherwise. Other acts shall be adopted on the basis of a Commission proposal where the Treaties so provide.

3. The Commission's term of office shall be five years.

The members of the Commission shall be chosen on the ground of their general competence and European commitment from persons whose independence is beyond doubt.

In carrying out its responsibilities, the Commission shall be completely independent. Without prejudice to Article 18(2), the members of the Commission shall neither seek nor take instructions from any Government or other institution, body, office or entity. They shall refrain from any action incompatible with their duties or the performance of their tasks.

4. The Commission appointed between the date of entry into force of the Treaty of Lisbon and 31 October 2014, shall consist of one national of each Member State, including its President and the High Representative of the Union for Foreign Affairs and Security Policy who shall be one of its Vice-Presidents.

5. As from 1 November 2014, the Commission shall consist of a number of members, including its President and the High Representative of the Union for Foreign Affairs and Security Policy, corresponding to two-thirds of the number of Member States, unless the European Council, acting unanimously, decides to alter this number.

The members of the Commission shall be chosen from among the nationals of the Member States on the basis of a system of strictly equal rotation between the Member States, reflecting the demographic and geographical range of all the Member States. This system shall be established unanimously by the European Council in accordance with Article 244 of the Treaty on the Functioning of the European Union.

6. The President of the Commission shall:

(a) lay down guidelines within which the Commission is to work;

(b) decide on the internal organisation of the Commission, ensuring that it acts consistently, efficiently and as a collegiate body;

(c) appoint Vice-Presidents, other than the High Representative of the Union for Foreign Affairs and Security Policy, from among the members of the Commission.

A member of the Commission shall resign if the President so requests. The High Representative of the Union for Foreign Affairs and Security Policy shall resign, in accordance with the procedure set out in Article 18(1), if the President so requests.

7. Taking into account the elections to the European Parliament and after having held the appropriate consultations, the European Council, acting by a qualified majority, shall propose to the European Parliament a candidate for President of the Commission. This candidate shall be elected by the European Parliament by a majority of its component members. If he does not obtain the required majority, the European Council, acting by a qualified majority, shall within one month propose a new candidate who shall be elected by the European Parliament following the same procedure.

The Council, by common accord with the President-elect, shall adopt the list of the other persons whom it proposes for appointment as members of the Commission. They shall be selected, on the basis of the suggestions made by Member States, in accordance with the criteria set out in paragraph 3, second subparagraph, and paragraph 5, second subparagraph.

The President, the High Representative of the Union for Foreign Affairs and Security Policy and the other members of the Commission shall be subject as a body to a vote of consent by the European Parliament. On the basis of this consent the Commission shall be appointed by the European Council, acting by a qualified majority.

8. The Commission, as a body, shall be responsible to the European Parliament. In accordance with Article 234 of the Treaty on the Functioning of the European Union, the European Parliament may vote on a motion of censure of the Commission. If such a motion is carried, the members of the Commission shall resign as a body and the High Representative of the Union for Foreign Affairs and Security Policy shall resign from the duties that he carries out in the Commission.

Article 18

1. The European Council, acting by a qualified majority, with the agreement of the President of the Commission, shall appoint the High Representative of the Union for Foreign Affairs and Security Policy. The European Council may end his term of office by the same procedure.

2. The High Representative shall conduct the Union's common foreign and security policy. He shall contribute by his proposals to the development of that policy, which he shall carry out as mandated by the Council. The same shall apply to the common security and defence policy.

3. The High Representative shall preside over the Foreign Affairs Council.

4. The High Representative shall be one of the Vice-Presidents of the Commission. He shall ensure the consistency of the Union's external action. He shall be responsible within the Commission for responsibilities incumbent on it in external relations and for coordinating other aspects of the Union's external action. In exercising these responsibilities within the Commission, and only for these responsibilities, the High Representative shall be bound by Commission procedures to the extent that this is consistent with paragraphs 2 and 3.

Article 19

1. The Court of Justice of the European Union shall include the Court of Justice, the General Court and specialised courts. It shall ensure that in the interpretation and application of the Treaties the law is observed.

Member States shall provide remedies sufficient to ensure effective legal protection in the fields covered by Union law.

2. The Court of Justice shall consist of one judge from each Member State. It shall be assisted by Advocates-General.

The General Court shall include at least one judge per Member State.

The Judges and the Advocates-General of the Court of Justice and the Judges of the General Court shall be chosen from persons whose independence is beyond doubt and who satisfy the conditions set out in Articles 253 and 254 of the Treaty on the Functioning of the European Union. They shall be appointed by common accord of the governments of the Member States for six years. Retiring Judges and Advocates-General may be reappointed.

3. The Court of Justice of the European Union shall, in accordance with the Treaties:

(a) rule on actions brought by a Member State, an institution or a natural or legal person;
(b) give preliminary rulings, at the request of courts or tribunals of the Member States, on the interpretation of Union law or the validity of acts adopted by the institutions;
(c) rule in other cases provided for in the Treaties.

Title IV Provisions on enhanced cooperation

Article 20 (ex Articles 27a to 27e, 40 to 40b and 43 to 45 TEU and ex Articles 11 and 11a TEC)

1. Member States which wish to establish enhanced cooperation between themselves within the framework of the Union's non-exclusive competences may make use of its institutions and exercise those competences by applying the relevant provisions of the Treaties, subject to the limits and in accordance with the detailed arrangements laid down in this Article and in Articles 326 to 334 of the Treaty on the Functioning of the European Union.

Enhanced cooperation shall aim to further the objectives of the Union, protect its interests and reinforce its integration process. Such cooperation shall be open at any time to all Member States, in accordance with Article 328 of the Treaty on the Functioning of the European Union.

2. The decision authorising enhanced cooperation shall be adopted by the Council as a last resort, when it has established that the objectives of such cooperation cannot be attained within a reasonable period by the Union as a whole, and provided that at least nine Member States participate in it. The Council shall act in accordance with the procedure laid down in Article 329 of the Treaty on the Functioning of the European Union.

3. All members of the Council may participate in its deliberations, but only members of the Council representing the Member States participating in enhanced cooperation shall take part in the vote. The voting rules are set out in Article 330 of the Treaty on the Functioning of the European Union.

4. Acts adopted in the framework of enhanced cooperation shall bind only participating Member States. They shall not be regarded as part of the *acquis* which has to be accepted by candidate States for accession to the Union.

Title V General provisions on the Union's external action and specific provisions on the common foreign and security policy

Chapter 1 General provisions on the Union's external action

Article 21

1. The Union's action on the international scene shall be guided by the principles which have inspired its own creation, development and enlargement, and which it seeks to advance in the wider world: democracy, the rule of law, the universality and indivisibility of human rights and fundamental freedoms, respect for human dignity, the principles of equality and solidarity, and respect for the principles of the United Nations Charter and international law.

The Union shall seek to develop relations and build partnerships with third countries, and international, regional or global organisations which share the principles referred to in the first subparagraph. It shall promote multilateral solutions to common problems, in particular in the framework of the United Nations.

2. The Union shall define and pursue common policies and actions, and shall work for a high degree of cooperation in all fields of international relations, in order to:

(a) safeguard its values, fundamental interests, security, independence and integrity;
(b) consolidate and support democracy, the rule of law, human rights and the principles of international law;
(c) preserve peace, prevent conflicts and strengthen international security, in accordance with the purposes and principles of the United Nations Charter, with the principles of the Helsinki Final Act and with the aims of the Charter of Paris, including those relating to external borders;
(d) foster the sustainable economic, social and environmental development of developing countries, with the primary aim of eradicating poverty;
(e) encourage the integration of all countries into the world economy, including through the progressive abolition of restrictions on international trade;
(f) help develop international measures to preserve and improve the quality of the environment and the sustainable management of global natural resources, in order to ensure sustainable development;
(g) assist populations, countries and regions confronting natural or man-made disasters; and
(h) promote an international system based on stronger multilateral cooperation and good global governance.

3. The Union shall respect the principles and pursue the objectives set out in paragraphs 1 and 2 in the development and implementation of the different areas of the Union's external action covered by this Title and by Part Five of the Treaty on the Functioning of the European Union, and of the external aspects of its other policies.

The Union shall ensure consistency between the different areas of its external action and between these and its other policies. The Council and the Commission, assisted by the High Representative of the Union for Foreign Affairs and Security Policy, shall ensure that consistency and shall cooperate to that effect.

Article 22

1. On the basis of the principles and objectives set out in Article 21, the European Council shall identify the strategic interests and objectives of the Union.

Decisions of the European Council on the strategic interests and objectives of the Union shall relate to the common foreign and security policy and to other areas of the external action of the Union. Such decisions may concern the relations of the Union with a specific country or region or may be thematic in approach. They shall define their duration, and the means to be made available by the Union and the Member States.

The European Council shall act unanimously on a recommendation from the Council, adopted by the latter under the arrangements laid down for each area. Decisions of the European Council shall be implemented in accordance with the procedures provided for in the Treaties.

2. The High Representative of the Union for Foreign Affairs and Security Policy, for the area of common foreign and security policy, and the Commission, for other areas of external action, may submit joint proposals to the Council.

Chapter 2 Specific provisions on the common foreign and security policy

Section 1 Common provisions

Article 23

The Union's action on the international scene, pursuant to this Chapter, shall be guided by the principles, shall pursue the objectives of, and be conducted in accordance with, the general provisions laid down in Chapter 1.

Article 24 (ex Article 11 TEU)

1. The Union's competence in matters of common foreign and security policy shall cover all areas of foreign policy and all questions relating to the Union's security, including the progressive framing of a common defence policy that might lead to a common defence.

The common foreign and security policy is subject to specific rules and procedures. It shall be defined and implemented by the European Council and the Council acting unanimously, except where the Treaties provide otherwise. The adoption of legislative acts shall be excluded. The common foreign and security policy shall be put into effect by the High Representative of the Union for Foreign Affairs and Security Policy and by Member States, in accordance with the Treaties. The specific role of the European Parliament and of the Commission in this area is defined by the Treaties. The Court of Justice of the European Union shall not have jurisdiction with respect to these provisions, with the exception of its jurisdiction to monitor compliance with Article 40 of this Treaty and to review the legality of certain decisions as provided for by the second paragraph of Article 275 of the Treaty on the Functioning of the European Union.

2. Within the framework of the principles and objectives of its external action, the Union shall conduct, define and implement a common foreign and security policy, based on the development of mutual political solidarity among Member States, the identification of questions of general interest and the achievement of an ever-increasing degree of convergence of Member States' actions.

3. The Member States shall support the Union's external and security policy actively and unreservedly in a spirit of loyalty and mutual solidarity and shall comply with the Union's action in this area.

The Member States shall work together to enhance and develop their mutual political solidarity. They shall refrain from any action which is contrary to the interests of the Union or likely to impair its effectiveness as a cohesive force in international relations.

The Council and the High Representative shall ensure compliance with these principles.

Article 25 (ex Article 12 TEU)

The Union shall conduct the common foreign and security policy by:

(a) defining the general guidelines;

(b) adopting decisions defining:

(i) actions to be undertaken by the Union;

(ii) positions to be taken by the Union;

(iii) arrangements for the implementation of the decisions referred to in points (i) and (ii);

and by

(c) strengthening systematic cooperation between Member States in the conduct of policy.

Article 26 (ex Article 13 TEU)

1. The European Council shall identify the Union's strategic interests, determine the objectives of and define general guidelines for the common foreign and security policy, including for matters with defence implications. It shall adopt the necessary decisions.

If international developments so require, the President of the European Council shall convene an extraordinary meeting of the European Council in order to define the strategic lines of the Union's policy in the face of such developments.

2. The Council shall frame the common foreign and security policy and take the decisions necessary for defining and implementing it on the basis of the general guidelines and strategic lines defined by the European Council.

The Council and the High Representative of the Union for Foreign Affairs and Security Policy shall ensure the unity, consistency and effectiveness of action by the Union.

3. The common foreign and security policy shall be put into effect by the High Representative and by the Member States, using national and Union resources.

Article 27

1. The High Representative of the Union for Foreign Affairs and Security Policy, who shall chair the Foreign Affairs Council, shall contribute through his proposals towards the preparation of the common foreign and security policy and shall ensure implementation of the decisions adopted by the European Council and the Council.

2. The High Representative shall represent the Union for matters relating to the common foreign and security policy. He shall conduct political dialogue with third parties on the Union's behalf and shall express the Union's position in international organisations and at international conferences.

3. In fulfilling his mandate, the High Representative shall be assisted by a European External Action Service. This service shall work in cooperation with the diplomatic services of the Member States and shall comprise officials from relevant departments of the General Secretariat of the Council and of the Commission as well as staff seconded from national diplomatic services of the Member States. The organisation and functioning of the European External Action Service shall be established by a decision of the Council. The Council shall act on a proposal from the High Representative after consulting the European Parliament and after obtaining the consent of the Commission.

Article 28 (ex Article 14 TEU)

1. Where the international situation requires operational action by the Union, the Council shall adopt the necessary decisions. They shall lay down their objectives, scope, the means to be made available to the Union, if necessary their duration, and the conditions for their implementation.

If there is a change in circumstances having a substantial effect on a question subject to such a decision, the Council shall review the principles and objectives of that decision and take the necessary decisions.

2. Decisions referred to in paragraph 1 shall commit the Member States in the positions they adopt and in the conduct of their activity.

3. Whenever there is any plan to adopt a national position or take national action pursuant to a decision as referred to in paragraph 1, information shall be provided by the Member State concerned in time to allow, if necessary, for prior consultations within the Council. The obligation to provide prior information shall not apply to measures which are merely a national transposition of Council decisions.

4. In cases of imperative need arising from changes in the situation and failing a review of the Council decision as referred to in paragraph 1, Member States may take the necessary measures as a matter of urgency having regard to the general objectives of that decision. The Member State concerned shall inform the Council immediately of any such measures.

5. Should there be any major difficulties in implementing a decision as referred to in this Article, a Member State shall refer them to the Council which shall discuss them and seek appropriate solutions. Such solutions shall not run counter to the objectives of the decision referred to in paragraph 1 or impair its effectiveness.

Article 29 (ex Article 15 TEU)
The Council shall adopt decisions which shall define the approach of the Union to a particular matter of a geographical or thematic nature. Member States shall ensure that their national policies conform to the Union positions.

Article 30 (ex Article 22 TEU)
1. Any Member State, the High Representative of the Union for Foreign Affairs and Security Policy, or the High Representative with the Commission's support, may refer any question relating to the common foreign and security policy to the Council and may submit to it initiatives or proposals as appropriate.

2. In cases requiring a rapid decision, the High Representative, of his own motion, or at the request of a Member State, shall convene an extraordinary Council meeting within 48 hours or, in an emergency, within a shorter period.

Article 31 (ex Article 23 TEU)
1. Decisions under this Chapter shall be taken by the European Council and the Council acting unanimously, except where this Chapter provides otherwise. The adoption of legislative acts shall be excluded.

When abstaining in a vote, any member of the Council may qualify its abstention by making a formal declaration under the present subparagraph. In that case, it shall not be obliged to apply the decision, but shall accept that the decision commits the Union. In a spirit of mutual solidarity, the Member State concerned shall refrain from any action likely to conflict with or impede Union action based on that decision and the other Member States shall respect its position. If the members of the Council qualifying their abstention in this way represent at least one third of the Member States comprising at least one-third of the population of the Union, the decision shall not be adopted.

2. By derogation from the provisions of paragraph 1, the Council shall act by qualified majority:

- when adopting a decision defining a Union action or position on the basis of a decision of the European Council relating to the Union's strategic interests and objectives, as referred to in Article 22(1),
- when adopting a decision defining a Union action or position, on a proposal which the High Representative of the Union for Foreign Affairs and Security Policy has presented following a specific request from the European Council, made on its own initiative or that of the High Representative,
- when adopting any decision implementing a decision defining a Union action or position,
- when appointing a special representative in accordance with Article 33.

If a member of the Council declares that, for vital and stated reasons of national policy, it intends to oppose the adoption of a decision to be taken by qualified majority, a vote shall not be taken. The High Representative will, in close consultation with the Member State involved, search for a solution acceptable to it. If he does not succeed, the Council may, acting by a qualified majority, request that the matter be referred to the European Council for a decision by unanimity.

3. The European Council may unanimously adopt a decision stipulating that the Council shall act by a qualified majority in cases other than those referred to in paragraph 2.

4. Paragraphs 2 and 3 shall not apply to decisions having military or defence implications.

5. For procedural questions, the Council shall act by a majority of its members.

Article 32 (ex Article 16 TEU)
Member States shall consult one another within the European Council and the Council on any matter of foreign and security policy of general interest in order to determine a common approach. Before undertaking any action on the international scene or entering into any commitment which could affect the Union's interests, each Member State shall consult the others within the European Council or the Council. Member States shall ensure, through the convergence of their actions, that the Union is able to assert its interests and values on the international scene. Member States shall show mutual solidarity.

When the European Council or the Council has defined a common approach of the Union within the meaning of the first paragraph, the High Representative of the Union for Foreign Affairs and Security Policy and the Ministers for Foreign Affairs of the Member States shall coordinate their activities within the Council.

The diplomatic missions of the Member States and the Union delegations in third countries and at international organisations shall cooperate and shall contribute to formulating and implementing the common approach.

Article 33 (ex Article 18 TEU)

The Council may, on a proposal from the High Representative of the Union for Foreign Affairs and Security Policy, appoint a special representative with a mandate in relation to particular policy issues. The special representative shall carry out his mandate under the authority of the High Representative.

Article 34 (ex Article 19 TEU)

1. Member States shall coordinate their action in international organisations and at international conferences. They shall uphold the Union's positions in such forums. The High Representative of the Union for Foreign Affairs and Security Policy shall organise this coordination.

In international organisations and at international conferences where not all the Member States participate, those which do take part shall uphold the Union's positions.

2. In accordance with Article 24(3), Member States represented in international organisations or international conferences where not all the Member States participate shall keep the other Member States and the High Representative informed of any matter of common interest.

Member States which are also members of the United Nations Security Council will concert and keep the other Member States and the High Representative fully informed. Member States which are members of the Security Council will, in the execution of their functions, defend the positions and the interests of the Union, without prejudice to their responsibilities under the provisions of the United Nations Charter.

When the Union has defined a position on a subject which is on the United Nations Security Council agenda, those Member States which sit on the Security Council shall request that the High Representative be invited to present the Union's position.

Article 35 (ex Article 20 TEU)

The diplomatic and consular missions of the Member States and the Union delegations in third countries and international conferences, and their representations to international organisations, shall cooperate in ensuring that decisions defining Union positions and actions adopted pursuant to this Chapter are complied with and implemented.

They shall step up cooperation by exchanging information and carrying out joint assessments.

They shall contribute to the implementation of the right of citizens of the Union to protection in the territory of third countries as referred to in Article 20(2)(c) of the Treaty on the Functioning of the European Union and of the measures adopted pursuant to Article 23 of that Treaty.

Article 36 (ex Article 21 TEU)

The High Representative of the Union for Foreign Affairs and Security Policy shall regularly consult the European Parliament on the main aspects and the basic choices of the common foreign and security policy and the common security and defence policy and inform it of how those policies evolve. He shall ensure that the views of the European Parliament are duly taken into consideration. Special representatives may be involved in briefing the European Parliament.

The European Parliament may ask questions of the Council or make recommendations to it and to the High Representative. Twice a year it shall hold a debate on progress in implementing the common foreign and security policy, including the common security and defence policy.

Article 37 (ex Article 24 TEU)

The Union may conclude agreements with one or more States or international organisations in areas covered by this Chapter.

Article 38 (ex Article 25 TEU)

Without prejudice to Article 240 of the Treaty on the Functioning of the European Union, a Political and Security Committee shall monitor the international situation in the areas covered by the common foreign and security policy and contribute to the definition of policies by delivering opinions to the Council at the request of the Council or of the High Representative of the Union for Foreign Affairs and Security Policy or on its own initiative. It shall also monitor the implementation of agreed policies, without prejudice to the powers of the High Representative.

Within the scope of this Chapter, the Political and Security Committee shall exercise, under the responsibility of the Council and of the High Representative, the political control and strategic direction of the crisis management operations referred to in Article 43.

The Council may authorise the Committee, for the purpose and for the duration of a crisis management operation, as determined by the Council, to take the relevant decisions concerning the political control and strategic direction of the operation.

Article 39

In accordance with Article 16 of the Treaty on the Functioning of the European Union and by way of derogation from paragraph 2 thereof, the Council shall adopt a decision laying down the rules relating to the protection of individuals with regard to the processing of personal data by the Member States when carrying out activities which fall within the scope of this Chapter, and the rules relating to the free movement of such data. Compliance with these rules shall be subject to the control of independent authorities.

Article 40 (ex Article 47 TEU)

The implementation of the common foreign and security policy shall not affect the application of the procedures and the extent of the powers of the institutions laid down by the Treaties for the exercise of the Union competences referred to in Articles 3 to 6 of the Treaty on the Functioning of the European Union.

Similarly, the implementation of the policies listed in those Articles shall not affect the application of the procedures and the extent of the powers of the institutions laid down by the Treaties for the exercise of the Union competences under this Chapter.

Article 41 (ex Article 28 TEU)

1. Administrative expenditure to which the implementation of this Chapter gives rise for the institutions shall be charged to the Union budget.

2. Operating expenditure to which the implementation of this Chapter gives rise shall also be charged to the Union budget, except for such expenditure arising from operations having military or defence implications and cases where the Council acting unanimously decides otherwise.

In cases where expenditure is not charged to the Union budget, it shall be charged to the Member States in accordance with the gross national product scale, unless the Council acting unanimously decides otherwise. As for expenditure arising from operations having military or defence implications, Member States whose representatives in the Council have made a formal declaration under Article 31(1), second subparagraph, shall not be obliged to contribute to the financing thereof.

3. The Council shall adopt a decision establishing the specific procedures for guaranteeing rapid access to appropriations in the Union budget for urgent financing of initiatives in the framework of the common foreign and security policy, and in particular for preparatory activities for the tasks referred to in Article 42(1) and Article 43. It shall act after consulting the European Parliament.

Preparatory activities for the tasks referred to in Article 42(1) and Article 43 which are not charged to the Union budget shall be financed by a start-up fund made up of Member States' contributions.

The Council shall adopt by a qualified majority, on a proposal from the High Representative of the Union for Foreign Affairs and Security Policy, decisions establishing:

(a) the procedures for setting up and financing the start-up fund, in particular the amounts allocated to the fund;
(b) the procedures for administering the start-up fund;
(c) the financial control procedures.

When the task planned in accordance with Article 42(1) and Article 43 cannot be charged to the Union budget, the Council shall authorise the High Representative to use the fund. The High Representative shall report to the Council on the implementation of this remit.

Section 2 Provisions on the common security and defence policy

Article 42 (ex Article 17 TEU)

1. The common security and defence policy shall be an integral part of the common foreign and security policy. It shall provide the Union with an operational capacity drawing on civilian and military assets. The Union may use them on missions outside the Union for peace-keeping, conflict prevention and strengthening international security in accordance with the principles of the United Nations Charter. The performance of these tasks shall be undertaken using capabilities provided by the Member States.

2. The common security and defence policy shall include the progressive framing of a common Union defence policy. This will lead to a common defence, when the European Council, acting unanimously, so decides. It shall in that case recommend to the Member States the adoption of such a decision in accordance with their respective constitutional requirements.

The policy of the Union in accordance with this Section shall not prejudice the specific character of the security and defence policy of certain Member States and shall respect the obligations of certain Member States, which see their common defence realised in the North Atlantic Treaty Organisation (NATO), under the North Atlantic Treaty and be compatible with the common security and defence policy established within that framework.

3. Member States shall make civilian and military capabilities available to the Union for the implementation of the common security and defence policy, to contribute to the objectives defined by the Council. Those Member States which together establish multinational forces may also make them available to the common security and defence policy.

Member States shall undertake progressively to improve their military capabilities. The Agency in the field of defence capabilities development, research, acquisition and armaments (hereinafter referred to as 'the European Defence Agency') shall identify operational requirements, shall promote measures to satisfy those requirements, shall contribute to identifying and, where appropriate, implementing any measure needed to strengthen the industrial and technological base of the defence sector, shall participate in defining a European capabilities and armaments policy, and shall assist the Council in evaluating the improvement of military capabilities.

4. Decisions relating to the common security and defence policy, including those initiating a mission as referred to in this Article, shall be adopted by the Council acting unanimously on a proposal from the High Representative of the Union for Foreign Affairs and Security Policy or an initiative from a Member State. The High Representative may propose the use of both national resources and Union instruments, together with the Commission where appropriate.

5. The Council may entrust the execution of a task, within the Union framework, to a group of Member States in order to protect the Union's values and serve its interests. The execution of such a task shall be governed by Article 44.

6. Those Member States whose military capabilities fulfil higher criteria and which have made more binding commitments to one another in this area with a view to the most demanding missions shall establish permanent structured cooperation within the Union framework. Such cooperation shall be governed by Article 46. It shall not affect the provisions of Article 43.

7. If a Member State is the victim of armed aggression on its territory, the other Member States shall have towards it an obligation of aid and assistance by all the means in their power, in accordance

with Article 51 of the United Nations Charter. This shall not prejudice the specific character of the security and defence policy of certain Member States.

Commitments and cooperation in this area shall be consistent with commitments under the North Atlantic Treaty Organisation, which, for those States which are members of it, remains the foundation of their collective defence and the forum for its implementation.

Article 43

1. The tasks referred to in Article 42(1), in the course of which the Union may use civilian and military means, shall include joint disarmament operations, humanitarian and rescue tasks, military advice and assistance tasks, conflict prevention and peace-keeping tasks, tasks of combat forces in crisis management, including peace-making and post-conflict stabilisation. All these tasks may contribute to the fight against terrorism, including by supporting third countries in combating terrorism in their territories.

2. The Council shall adopt decisions relating to the tasks referred to in paragraph 1, defining their objectives and scope and the general conditions for their implementation. The High Representative of the Union for Foreign Affairs and Security Policy, acting under the authority of the Council and in close and constant contact with the Political and Security Committee, shall ensure coordination of the civilian and military aspects of such tasks.

Article 44

1. Within the framework of the decisions adopted in accordance with Article 43, the Council may entrust the implementation of a task to a group of Member States which are willing and have the necessary capability for such a task. Those Member States, in association with the High Representative of the Union for Foreign Affairs and Security Policy, shall agree among themselves on the management of the task.

2. Member States participating in the task shall keep the Council regularly informed of its progress on their own initiative or at the request of another Member State. Those States shall inform the Council immediately should the completion of the task entail major consequences or require amendment of the objective, scope and conditions determined for the task in the decisions referred to in paragraph 1. In such cases, the Council shall adopt the necessary decisions.

Article 45

1. The European Defence Agency referred to in Article 42(3), subject to the authority of the Council, shall have as its task to:

(a) contribute to identifying the Member States' military capability objectives and evaluating observance of the capability commitments given by the Member States;

(b) promote harmonisation of operational needs and adoption of effective, compatible procurement methods;

(c) propose multilateral projects to fulfil the objectives in terms of military capabilities, ensure coordination of the programmes implemented by the Member States and management of specific cooperation programmes;

(d) support defence technology research, and coordinate and plan joint research activities and the study of technical solutions meeting future operational needs;

(e) contribute to identifying and, if necessary, implementing any useful measure for strengthening the industrial and technological base of the defence sector and for improving the effectiveness of military expenditure.

2. The European Defence Agency shall be open to all Member States wishing to be part of it. The Council, acting by a qualified majority, shall adopt a decision defining the Agency's statute, seat and operational rules. That decision should take account of the level of effective participation in the Agency's activities. Specific groups shall be set up within the Agency bringing together Member States engaged in joint projects. The Agency shall carry out its tasks in liaison with the Commission where necessary.

Article 46

1. Those Member States which wish to participate in the permanent structured cooperation referred to in Article 42(6), which fulfil the criteria and have made the commitments on military

capabilities set out in the Protocol on permanent structured cooperation, shall notify their intention to the Council and to the High Representative of the Union for Foreign Affairs and Security Policy.

2. Within three months following the notification referred to in paragraph 1 the Council shall adopt a decision establishing permanent structured cooperation and determining the list of participating Member States. The Council shall act by a qualified majority after consulting the High Representative.

3. Any Member State which, at a later stage, wishes to participate in the permanent structured cooperation shall notify its intention to the Council and to the High Representative.

The Council shall adopt a decision confirming the participation of the Member State concerned which fulfils the criteria and makes the commitments referred to in Articles 1 and 2 of the Protocol on permanent structured cooperation. The Council shall act by a qualified majority after consulting the High Representative. Only members of the Council representing the participating Member States shall take part in the vote.

A qualified majority shall be defined in accordance with Article 238(3)(a) of the Treaty on the Functioning of the European Union.

4. If a participating Member State no longer fulfils the criteria or is no longer able to meet the commitments referred to in Articles 1 and 2 of the Protocol on permanent structured cooperation, the Council may adopt a decision suspending the participation of the Member State concerned.

The Council shall act by a qualified majority. Only members of the Council representing the participating Member States, with the exception of the Member State in question, shall take part in the vote.

A qualified majority shall be defined in accordance with Article 238(3)(a) of the Treaty on the Functioning of the European Union.

5. Any participating Member State which wishes to withdraw from permanent structured cooperation shall notify its intention to the Council, which shall take note that the Member State in question has ceased to participate.

6. The decisions and recommendations of the Council within the framework of permanent structured cooperation, other than those provided for in paragraphs 2 to 5, shall be adopted by unanimity. For the purposes of this paragraph, unanimity shall be constituted by the votes of the representatives of the participating Member States only.

Title VI Final provisions

Article 47

The Union shall have legal personality.

Article 48 (ex Article 48 TEU)

1. The Treaties may be amended in accordance with an ordinary revision procedure. They may also be amended in accordance with simplified revision procedures.

Ordinary revision procedure

2. The Government of any Member State, the European Parliament or the Commission may submit to the Council proposals for the amendment of the Treaties. These proposals may, inter alia, serve either to increase or to reduce the competences conferred on the Union in the Treaties. These proposals shall be submitted to the European Council by the Council and the national Parliaments shall be notified.

3. If the European Council, after consulting the European Parliament and the Commission, adopts by a simple majority a decision in favour of examining the proposed amendments, the President of the European Council shall convene a Convention composed of representatives of the national Parliaments, of the Heads of State or Government of the Member States, of the European Parliament and of the Commission. The European Central Bank shall also be consulted in the case of institutional changes in the monetary area. The Convention shall examine the proposals for amendments and shall

adopt by consensus a recommendation to a conference of representatives of the governments of the Member States as provided for in paragraph 4.

The European Council may decide by a simple majority, after obtaining the consent of the European Parliament, not to convene a Convention should this not be justified by the extent of the proposed amendments. In the latter case, the European Council shall define the terms of reference for a conference of representatives of the governments of the Member States.

4. A conference of representatives of the governments of the Member States shall be convened by the President of the Council for the purpose of determining by common accord the amendments to be made to the Treaties.

The amendments shall enter into force after being ratified by all the Member States in accordance with their respective constitutional requirements.

5. If, two years after the signature of a treaty amending the Treaties, four fifths of the Member States have ratified it and one or more Member States have encountered difficulties in proceeding with ratification, the matter shall be referred to the European Council.

Simplified revision procedures

6. The Government of any Member State, the European Parliament or the Commission may submit to the European Council proposals for revising all or part of the provisions of Part Three of the Treaty on the Functioning of the European Union relating to the internal policies and action of the Union.

The European Council may adopt a decision amending all or part of the provisions of Part Three of the Treaty on the Functioning of the European Union. The European Council shall act by unanimity after consulting the European Parliament and the Commission, and the European Central Bank in the case of institutional changes in the monetary area. That decision shall not enter into force until it is approved by the Member States in accordance with their respective constitutional requirements.

The decision referred to in the second subparagraph shall not increase the competences conferred on the Union in the Treaties.

7. Where the Treaty on the Functioning of the European Union or Title V of this Treaty provides for the Council to act by unanimity in a given area or case, the European Council may adopt a decision authorising the Council to act by a qualified majority in that area or in that case. This subparagraph shall not apply to decisions with military implications or those in the area of defence.

Where the Treaty on the Functioning of the European Union provides for legislative acts to be adopted by the Council in accordance with a special legislative procedure, the European Council may adopt a decision allowing for the adoption of such acts in accordance with the ordinary legislative procedure.

Any initiative taken by the European Council on the basis of the first or the second subparagraph shall be notified to the national Parliaments. If a national Parliament makes known its opposition within six months of the date of such notification, the decision referred to in the first or the second subparagraph shall not be adopted. In the absence of opposition, the European Council may adopt the decision.

For the adoption of the decisions referred to in the first and second subparagraphs, the European Council shall act by unanimity after obtaining the consent of the European Parliament, which shall be given by a majority of its component members.

Article 49 (ex Article 49 TEU)

Any European State which respects the values referred to in Article 2 and is committed to promoting them may apply to become a member of the Union. The European Parliament and national Parliaments shall be notified of this application. The applicant State shall address its application to the Council, which shall act unanimously after consulting the Commission and after receiving the consent of the European Parliament, which shall act by a majority of its component members. The conditions of eligibility agreed upon by the European Council shall be taken into account.

The conditions of admission and the adjustments to the Treaties on which the Union is founded, which such admission entails, shall be the subject of an agreement between the Member States and the applicant State. This agreement shall be submitted for ratification by all the contracting States in accordance with their respective constitutional requirements.

Article 50

1. Any Member State may decide to withdraw from the Union in accordance with its own constitutional requirements.

2. A Member State which decides to withdraw shall notify the European Council of its intention. In the light of the guidelines provided by the European Council, the Union shall negotiate and conclude an agreement with that State, setting out the arrangements for its withdrawal, taking account of the framework for its future relationship with the Union. That agreement shall be negotiated in accordance with Article 218(3) of the Treaty on the Functioning of the European Union. It shall be concluded on behalf of the Union by the Council, acting by a qualified majority, after obtaining the consent of the European Parliament.

3. The Treaties shall cease to apply to the State in question from the date of entry into force of the withdrawal agreement or, failing that, two years after the notification referred to in paragraph 2, unless the European Council, in agreement with the Member State concerned, unanimously decides to extend this period.

4. For the purposes of paragraphs 2 and 3, the member of the European Council or of the Council representing the withdrawing Member State shall not participate in the discussions of the European Council or Council or in decisions concerning it.

A qualified majority shall be defined in accordance with Article 238(3)(b) of the Treaty on the Functioning of the European Union.

5. If a State which has withdrawn from the Union asks to rejoin, its request shall be subject to the procedure referred to in Article 49.

Article 51

The Protocols and Annexes to the Treaties shall form an integral part thereof.

Article 52

1. The Treaties shall apply to the Kingdom of Belgium, the Republic of Bulgaria, the Czech Republic, the Kingdom of Denmark, the Federal Republic of Germany, the Republic of Estonia, Ireland, the Hellenic Republic, the Kingdom of Spain, the French Republic, the Italian Republic, the Republic of Cyprus, the Republic of Latvia, the Republic of Lithuania, the Grand Duchy of Luxembourg, the Republic of Hungary, the Republic of Malta, the Kingdom of the Netherlands, the Republic of Austria, the Republic of Poland, the Portuguese Republic, Romania, the Republic of Slovenia, the Slovak Republic, the Republic of Finland, the Kingdom of Sweden and the United Kingdom of Great Britain and Northern Ireland.

2. The territorial scope of the Treaties is specified in Article 355 of the Treaty on the Functioning of the European Union.

Article 53 (ex Article 51 TEU)

This Treaty is concluded for an unlimited period.

Article 54 (ex Article 52 TEU)

1. This Treaty shall be ratified by the High Contracting Parties in accordance with their respective constitutional requirements. The instruments of ratification shall be deposited with the Government of the Italian Republic.

2. This Treaty shall enter into force on 1 January 1993, provided that all the Instruments of ratification have been deposited, or, failing that, on the first day of the month following the deposit of the Instrument of ratification by the last signatory State to take this step.

Article 55 (ex Article 53 TEU)

1. This Treaty, drawn up in a single original in the Bulgarian, Czech, Danish, Dutch, English, Estonian, Finnish, French, German, Greek, Hungarian, Irish, Italian, Latvian, Lithuanian, Maltese,

Polish, Portuguese, Romanian, Slovak, Slovenian, Spanish and Swedish languages, the texts in each of these languages being equally authentic, shall be deposited in the archives of the Government of the Italian Republic, which will transmit a certified copy to each of the governments of the other signatory States.

2. This Treaty may also be translated into any other languages as determined by Member States among those which, in accordance with their constitutional order, enjoy official status in all or part of their territory. A certified copy of such translations shall be provided by the Member States concerned to be deposited in the archives of the Council.

IN WITNESS WHEREOF the undersigned Plenipotentiaries have signed this Treaty.

Done at Maastricht on the seventh day of February in the year one thousand and ninety-two.

(List of signatories not reproduced)

Consolidated Version of the Treaty on the Functioning of the European Union*

Preamble

HIS MAJESTY THE KING OF THE BELGIANS, THE PRESIDENT OF THE FEDERAL REPUBLIC OF GERMANY, THE PRESIDENT OF THE FRENCH REPUBLIC,

THE PRESIDENT OF THE ITALIAN REPUBLIC, HER ROYAL HIGHNESS THE GRAND DUCHESS OF LUXEMBOURG, HER MAJESTY THE QUEEN OF THE NETHERLANDS,[1]

DETERMINED to lay the foundations of an ever closer union among the peoples of Europe,

RESOLVED to ensure the economic and social progress of their States by common action to eliminate the barriers which divide Europe,

AFFIRMING as the essential objective of their efforts the constant improvements of the living and working conditions of their peoples,

RECOGNISING that the removal of existing obstacles calls for concerted action in order to guarantee steady expansion, balanced trade and fair competition,

ANXIOUS to strengthen the unity of their economies and to ensure their harmonious development by reducing the differences existing between the various regions and the backwardness of the less favoured regions,

DESIRING to contribute, by means of a common commercial policy, to the progressive abolition of restrictions on international trade,

INTENDING to confirm the solidarity which binds Europe and the overseas countries and desiring to ensure the development of their prosperity, in accordance with the principles of the Charter of the United Nations,

RESOLVED by thus pooling their resources to preserve and strengthen peace and liberty, and calling upon the other peoples of Europe who share their ideal to join in their efforts,

DETERMINED to promote the development of the highest possible level of knowledge for their peoples through a wide access to education and through its continuous updating,

and to this end HAVE DESIGNATED as their Plenipotentiaries:

(List of plenipotentiaries not reproduced)

WHO, having exchanged their full powers, found in good and due form, have agreed as follows.

* **Editor's Note:** Incorporating Lisbon Treaty changes. Signatures and contents omitted. This is the version as re-produced on 30 March 2010 (OJ 2010 C83/01).

[1] The Republic of Bulgaria, the Czech Republic, the Kingdom of Denmark, the Republic of Estonia, Ireland, the Hellenic Republic, the Kingdom of Spain, the Republic of Cyprus, the Republic of Latvia, the Republic of Lithuania, the Republic of Hungary, the Republic of Malta, the Republic of Austria, the Republic of Poland, the Portuguese Republic, Romania, the Republic of Slovenia, the Slovak Republic, the Republic of Finland, the Kingdom of Sweden and the United Kingdom of Great Britain and Northern Ireland have since become members of the European Union.

PART ONE PRINCIPLES

Article 1

1. This Treaty organises the functioning of the Union and determines the areas of, delimitation of, and arrangements for exercising its competences.

2. This Treaty and the Treaty on European Union constitute the Treaties on which the Union is founded. These two Treaties, which have the same legal value, shall be referred to as 'the Treaties'.

Title I Categories and areas of Union competence

Article 2

1. When the Treaties confer on the Union exclusive competence in a specific area, only the Union may legislate and adopt legally binding acts, the Member States being able to do so themselves only if so empowered by the Union or for the implementation of Union acts.

2. When the Treaties confer on the Union a competence shared with the Member States in a specific area, the Union and the Member States may legislate and adopt legally binding acts in that area. The Member States shall exercise their competence to the extent that the Union has not exercised its competence. The Member States shall again exercise their competence to the extent that the Union has decided to cease exercising its competence.

3. The Member States shall coordinate their economic and employment policies within arrangements as determined by this Treaty, which the Union shall have competence to provide.

4. The Union shall have competence, in accordance with the provisions of the Treaty on European Union, to define and implement a common foreign and security policy, including the progressive framing of a common defence policy.

5. In certain areas and under the conditions laid down in the Treaties, the Union shall have competence to carry out actions to support, coordinate or supplement the actions of the Member States, without thereby superseding their competence in these areas.

Legally binding acts of the Union adopted on the basis of the provisions of the Treaties relating to these areas shall not entail harmonisation of Member States' laws or regulations.

6. The scope of and arrangements for exercising the Union's competences shall be determined by the provisions of the Treaties relating to each area.

Article 3

1. The Union shall have exclusive competence in the following areas:

(a) customs union;

(b) the establishing of the competition rules necessary for the functioning of the internal market;

(c) monetary policy for the Member States whose currency is the euro;

(d) the conservation of marine biological resources under the common fisheries policy;

(e) common commercial policy.

2. The Union shall also have exclusive competence for the conclusion of an international agreement when its conclusion is provided for in a legislative act of the Union or is necessary to enable the Union to exercise its internal competence, or in so far as its conclusion may affect common rules or alter their scope.

Article 4

1. The Union shall share competence with the Member States where the Treaties confer on it a competence which does not relate to the areas referred to in Articles 3 and 6.

2. Shared competence between the Union and the Member States applies in the following principal areas:

(a) internal market;

(b) social policy, for the aspects defined in this Treaty;

(c) economic, social and territorial cohesion;
(d) agriculture and fisheries, excluding the conservation of marine biological resources;
(e) environment;
(f) consumer protection;
(g) transport;
(h) trans-European networks;
(i) energy;
(j) area of freedom, security and justice;
(k) common safety concerns in public health matters, for the aspects defined in this Treaty.

3. In the areas of research, technological development and space, the Union shall have competence to carry out activities, in particular to define and implement programmes; however, the exercise of that competence shall not result in Member States being prevented from exercising theirs.

4. In the areas of development cooperation and humanitarian aid, the Union shall have competence to carry out activities and conduct a common policy; however, the exercise of that competence shall not result in Member States being prevented from exercising theirs.

Article 5

1. The Member States shall coordinate their economic policies within the Union. To this end, the Council shall adopt measures, in particular broad guidelines for these policies.

Specific provisions shall apply to those Member States whose currency is the euro.

2. The Union shall take measures to ensure coordination of the employment policies of the Member States, in particular by defining guidelines for these policies.

3. The Union may take initiatives to ensure coordination of Member States' social policies.

Article 6

The Union shall have competence to carry out actions to support, coordinate or supplement the actions of the Member States. The areas of such action shall, at European level, be:

(a) protection and improvement of human health;
(b) industry;
(c) culture;
(d) tourism;
(e) education, vocational training, youth and sport;
(f) civil protection;
(g) administrative cooperation.

Title II Provisions having general application

Article 7

The Union shall ensure consistency between its policies and activities, taking all of its objectives into account and in accordance with the principle of conferral of powers.

Article 8 (ex Article 3(2) TEC)[2]

In all its activities, the Union shall aim to eliminate inequalities, and to promote equality, between men and women.

Article 9

In defining and implementing its policies and activities, the Union shall take into account requirements linked to the promotion of a high level of employment, the guarantee of adequate social protection, the fight against social exclusion, and a high level of education, training and protection of human health.

[2] These references are merely indicative. For more ample information, please refer to the tables of equivalences between the old and the new numbering of the Treaties in this volume, in prelims, page xix.

Article 10

In defining and implementing its policies and activities, the Union shall aim to combat discrimination based on sex, racial or ethnic origin, religion or belief, disability, age or sexual orientation.

Article 11 (ex Article 6 TEC)

Environmental protection requirements must be integrated into the definition and implementation of the Union policies and activities, in particular with a view to promoting sustainable development.

Article 12 (ex Article 153(2) TEC)

Consumer protection requirements shall be taken into account in defining and implementing other Union policies and activities.

Article 13

In formulating and implementing the Union's agriculture, fisheries, transport, internal market, research and technological development and space policies, the Union and the Member States shall, since animals are sentient beings, pay full regard to the welfare requirements of animals, while respecting the legislative or administrative provisions and customs of the Member States relating in particular to religious rites, cultural traditions and regional heritage.

Article 14 (ex Article 16 TEC)

Without prejudice to Article 4 of the Treaty on European Union or to Articles 93, 106 and 107 of this Treaty, and given the place occupied by services of general economic interest in the shared values of the Union as well as their role in promoting social and territorial cohesion, the Union and the Member States, each within their respective powers and within the scope of application of the Treaties, shall take care that such services operate on the basis of principles and conditions, particularly economic and financial conditions, which enable them to fulfil their missions. The European Parliament and the Council, acting by means of regulations in accordance with the ordinary legislative procedure, shall establish these principles and set these conditions without prejudice to the competence of Member States, in compliance with the Treaties, to provide, to commission and to fund such services.

Article 15 (ex Article 255 TEC)

1. In order to promote good governance and ensure the participation of civil society, the Union institutions, bodies, offices and agencies shall conduct their work as openly as possible.

2. The European Parliament shall meet in public, as shall the Council when considering and voting on a draft legislative act.

3. Any citizen of the Union, and any natural or legal person residing or having its registered office in a Member State, shall have a right of access to documents of the Union institutions, bodies, offices and agencies, whatever their medium, subject to the principles and the conditions to be defined in accordance with this paragraph.

General principles and limits on grounds of public or private interest governing this right of access to documents shall be determined by the European Parliament and the Council, by means of regulations, acting in accordance with the ordinary legislative procedure.

Each institution, body, office or agency shall ensure that its proceedings are transparent and shall elaborate in its own Rules of Procedure specific provisions regarding access to its documents, in accordance with the regulations referred to in the second subparagraph.

The Court of Justice of the European Union, the European Central Bank and the European Investment Bank shall be subject to this paragraph only when exercising their administrative tasks.

The European Parliament and the Council shall ensure publication of the documents relating to the legislative procedures under the terms laid down by the regulations referred to in the second subparagraph.

Article 16 (ex Article 286 TEC)

1. Everyone has the right to the protection of personal data concerning them.

2. The European Parliament and the Council, acting in accordance with the ordinary legislative procedure, shall lay down the rules relating to the protection of individuals with regard to the

processing of personal data by Union institutions, bodies, offices and agencies, and by the Member States when carrying out activities which fall within the scope of Union law, and the rules relating to the free movement of such data.

Compliance with these rules shall be subject to the control of independent authorities.

The rules adopted on the basis of this Article shall be without prejudice to the specific rules laid down in Article 39 of the Treaty on European Union.

Article 17

1. The Union respects and does not prejudice the status under national law of churches and religious associations or communities in the Member States.

2. The Union equally respects the status under national law of philosophical and non-confessional organisations.

3. Recognising their identity and their specific contribution, the Union shall maintain an open, transparent and regular dialogue with these churches and organisations.

PART TWO NON-DISCRIMINATION AND CITIZENSHIP OF THE UNION

Article 18 (ex Article 12 TEC)

Within the scope of application of the Treaties, and without prejudice to any special provisions contained therein, any discrimination on grounds of nationality shall be prohibited.

The European Parliament and the Council, acting in accordance with the ordinary legislative procedure, may adopt rules designed to prohibit such discrimination.

Article 19 (ex Article 13 TEC)

1. Without prejudice to the other provisions of the Treaties and within the limits of the powers conferred by them upon the Union, the Council, acting unanimously in accordance with a special legislative procedure and after obtaining the consent of the European Parliament, may take appropriate action to combat discrimination based on sex, racial or ethnic origin, religion or belief, disability, age or sexual orientation.

2. By way of derogation from paragraph 1, the European Parliament and the Council, acting in accordance with the ordinary legislative procedure, may adopt the basic principles of Union incentive measures, excluding any harmonisation of the laws and regulations of the Member States, to support action taken by the Member States in order to contribute to the achievement of the objectives referred to in paragraph 1.

Article 20 (ex Article 17 TEC)

1. Citizenship of the Union is hereby established. Every person holding the nationality of a Member State shall be a citizen of the Union. Citizenship of the Union shall be additional to and not replace national citizenship.

2. Citizens of the Union shall enjoy the rights and be subject to the duties provided for in the Treaties. They shall have, *inter alia*:

(a) the right to move and reside freely within the territory of the Member States;

(b) the right to vote and to stand as candidates in elections to the European Parliament and in municipal elections in their Member State of residence, under the same conditions as nationals of that State;

(c) the right to enjoy, in the territory of a third country in which the Member State of which they are nationals is not represented, the protection of the diplomatic and consular authorities of any Member State on the same conditions as the nationals of that State;

(d) the right to petition the European Parliament, to apply to the European Ombudsman, and to address the institutions and advisory bodies of the Union in any of the Treaty languages and to obtain a reply in the same language.

These rights shall be exercised in accordance with the conditions and limits defined by the Treaties and by the measures adopted thereunder.

Article 21 (ex Article 18 TEC)

1. Every citizen of the Union shall have the right to move and reside freely within the territory of the Member States, subject to the limitations and conditions laid down in the Treaties and by the measures adopted to give them effect.

2. If action by the Union should prove necessary to attain this objective and the Treaties have not provided the necessary powers, the European Parliament and the Council, acting in accordance with the ordinary legislative procedure, may adopt provisions with a view to facilitating the exercise of the rights referred to in paragraph 1.

3. For the same purposes as those referred to in paragraph 1 and if the Treaties have not provided the necessary powers, the Council, acting in accordance with a special legislative procedure, may adopt measures concerning social security or social protection. The Council shall act unanimously after consulting the European Parliament.

Article 22 (ex Article 19 TEC)

1. Every citizen of the Union residing in a Member State of which he is not a national shall have the right to vote and to stand as a candidate at municipal elections in the Member State in which he resides, under the same conditions as nationals of that State. This right shall be exercised subject to detailed arrangements adopted by the Council, acting unanimously in accordance with a special legislative procedure and after consulting the European Parliament; these arrangements may provide for derogations where warranted by problems specific to a Member State.

2. Without prejudice to Article 223(1) and to the provisions adopted for its implementation, every citizen of the Union residing in a Member State of which he is not a national shall have the right to vote and to stand as a candidate in elections to the European Parliament in the Member State in which he resides, under the same conditions as nationals of that State. This right shall be exercised subject to detailed arrangements adopted by the Council, acting unanimously in accordance with a special legislative procedure and after consulting the European Parliament; these arrangements may provide for derogations where warranted by problems specific to a Member State.

Article 23 (ex Article 20 TEC)

Every citizen of the Union shall, in the territory of a third country in which the Member State of which he is a national is not represented, be entitled to protection by the diplomatic or consular authorities of any Member State, on the same conditions as the nationals of that State. Member States shall adopt the necessary provisions and start the international negotiations required to secure this protection.

The Council, acting in accordance with a special legislative procedure and after consulting the European Parliament, may adopt directives establishing the coordination and cooperation measures necessary to facilitate such protection.

Article 24 (ex Article 21 TEC)

The European Parliament and the Council, acting by means of regulations in accordance with the ordinary legislative procedure, shall adopt the provisions for the procedures and conditions required for a citizens' initiative within the meaning of Article 11 of the Treaty on European Union, including the minimum number of Member States from which such citizens must come.

Every citizen of the Union shall have the right to petition the European Parliament in accordance with Article 227.

Every citizen of the Union may apply to the Ombudsman established in accordance with Article 228.

Every citizen of the Union may write to any of the institutions, bodies, offices or agencies referred to in this Article or in Article 13 of the Treaty on European Union in one of the languages mentioned in Article 55(1) of the Treaty on European Union and have an answer in the same language.

Article 25 (ex Article 22 TEC)

The Commission shall report to the European Parliament, to the Council and to the Economic and Social Committee every three years on the application of the provisions of this Part. This report shall take account of the development of the Union.

On this basis, and without prejudice to the other provisions of the Treaties, the Council, acting unanimously in accordance with a special legislative procedure and after obtaining the consent of the European Parliament, may adopt provisions to strengthen or to add to the rights listed in Article 20(2). These provisions shall enter into force after their approval by the Member States in accordance with their respective constitutional requirements.

PART THREE UNION POLICIES AND INTERNAL ACTIONS

Title I The internal market

Article 26 (ex Article 14 TEC)

1. The Union shall adopt measures with the aim of establishing or ensuring the functioning of the internal market, in accordance with the relevant provisions of the Treaties.

2. The internal market shall comprise an area without internal frontiers in which the free movement of goods, persons, services and capital is ensured in accordance with the provisions of the Treaties.

3. The Council, on a proposal from the Commission, shall determine the guidelines and conditions necessary to ensure balanced progress in all the sectors concerned.

Article 27 (ex Article 15 TEC)

When drawing up its proposals with a view to achieving the objectives set out in Article 26, the Commission shall take into account the extent of the effort that certain economies showing differences in development will have to sustain for the establishment of the internal market and it may propose appropriate provisions.

If these provisions take the form of derogations, they must be of a temporary nature and must cause the least possible disturbance to the functioning of the internal market.

Title II Free movement of goods

Article 28 (ex Article 23 TEC)

1. The Union shall comprise a customs union which shall cover all trade in goods and which shall involve the prohibition between Member States of customs duties on imports and exports and of all charges having equivalent effect, and the adoption of a common customs tariff in their relations with third countries.

2. The provisions of Article 30 and of Chapter 2 of this Title shall apply to products originating in Member States and to products coming from third countries which are in free circulation in Member States.

Article 29 (ex Article 24 TEC)

Products coming from a third country shall be considered to be in free circulation in a Member State if the import formalities have been complied with and any customs duties or charges having equivalent effect which are payable have been levied in that Member State, and if they have not benefited from a total or partial drawback of such duties or charges.

Chapter 1 The customs union

Article 30 (ex Article 25 TEC)

Customs duties on imports and exports and charges having equivalent effect shall be prohibited between Member States. This prohibition shall also apply to customs duties of a fiscal nature.

Article 31 (ex Article 26 TEC)

Common Customs Tariff duties shall be fixed by the Council on a proposal from the Commission.

Article 32 (ex Article 27 TEC)

In carrying out the tasks entrusted to it under this Chapter the Commission shall be guided by:

(a) the need to promote trade between Member States and third countries;

(b) developments in conditions of competition within the Union in so far as they lead to an improvement in the competitive capacity of undertakings;

(c) the requirements of the Union as regards the supply of raw materials and semi-finished goods; in this connection the Commission shall take care to avoid distorting conditions of competition between Member States in respect of finished goods;

(d) the need to avoid serious disturbances in the economies of Member States and to ensure rational development of production and an expansion of consumption within the Union.

Chapter 2 Customs cooperation

Article 33 (ex Article 135 TEC)

Within the scope of application of the Treaties, the European Parliament and the Council, acting in accordance with the ordinary legislative procedure, shall take measures in order to strengthen customs cooperation between Member States and between the latter and the Commission.

Chapter 3 Prohibition of quantitative restrictions between Member States

Article 34 (ex Article 28 TEC)

Quantitative restrictions on imports and all measures having equivalent effect shall be prohibited between Member States.

Article 35 (ex Article 29 TEC)

Quantitative restrictions on exports, and all measures having equivalent effect, shall be prohibited between Member States.

Article 36 (ex Article 30 TEC)

The provisions of Articles 34 and 35 shall not preclude prohibitions or restrictions on imports, exports or goods in transit justified on grounds of public morality, public policy or public security; the protection of health and life of humans, animals or plants; the protection of national treasures possessing artistic, historic or archaeological value; or the protection of industrial and commercial property. Such prohibitions or restrictions shall not, however, constitute a means of arbitrary discrimination or a disguised restriction on trade between Member States.

Article 37 (ex Article 31 TEC)

1. Member States shall adjust any State monopolies of a commercial character so as to ensure that no discrimination regarding the conditions under which goods are procured and marketed exists between nationals of Member States.

The provisions of this Article shall apply to any body through which a Member State, in law or in fact, either directly or indirectly supervises, determines or appreciably influences imports or exports between Member States. These provisions shall likewise apply to monopolies delegated by the State to others.

2. Member States shall refrain from introducing any new measure which is contrary to the principles laid down in paragraph 1 or which restricts the scope of the articles dealing with the prohibition of customs duties and quantitative restrictions between Member States.

3. If a State monopoly of a commercial character has rules which are designed to make it easier to dispose of agricultural products or obtain for them the best return, steps should be taken in applying

the rules contained in this Article to ensure equivalent safeguards for the employment and standard of living of the producers concerned.

Title III Agriculture and fisheries

Article 38 (ex Article 32 TEC)

1. The Union shall define and implement a common agriculture and fisheries policy.

'The internal market' shall extend to agriculture, fisheries and trade in agricultural products. 'Agricultural products' means the products of the soil, of stockfarming and of fisheries and products of first-stage processing directly related to these products. References to the common agricultural policy or to agriculture, and the use of the term 'agricultural', shall be understood as also referring to fisheries, having regard to the specific characteristics of this sector.

2. Save as otherwise provided in Articles 39 to 44, the rules laid down for the establishment and functioning of the internal market shall apply to agricultural products.

3. The products subject to the provisions of Articles 39 to 44 are listed in Annex I.

4. The operation and development of the internal market for agricultural products must be accompanied by the establishment of a common agricultural policy.

Article 39 (ex Article 33 TEC)

1. The objectives of the common agricultural policy shall be:
   - (a) to increase agricultural productivity by promoting technical progress and by ensuring the rational development of agricultural production and the optimum utilisation of the factors of production, in particular labour;
   - (b) thus to ensure a fair standard of living for the agricultural community, in particular by increasing the individual earnings of persons engaged in agriculture;
   - (c) to stabilise markets;
   - (d) to assure the availability of supplies;
   - (e) to ensure that supplies reach consumers at reasonable prices.

2. In working out the common agricultural policy and the special methods for its application, account shall be taken of:
   - (a) the particular nature of agricultural activity, which results from the social structure of agriculture and from structural and natural disparities between the various agricultural regions;
   - (b) the need to effect the appropriate adjustments by degrees;
   - (c) the fact that in the Member States agriculture constitutes a sector closely linked with the economy as a whole.

Article 40 (ex Article 34 TEC)

1. In order to attain the objectives set out in Article 39, a common organisation of agricultural markets shall be established.

This organisation shall take one of the following forms, depending on the product concerned:
   - (a) common rules on competition;
   - (b) compulsory coordination of the various national market organisations;
   - (c) a European market organisation.

2. The common organisation established in accordance with paragraph 1 may include all measures required to attain the objectives set out in Article 39, in particular regulation of prices, aids for the production and marketing of the various products, storage and carryover arrangements and common machinery for stabilising imports or exports.

The common organisation shall be limited to pursuit of the objectives set out in Article 39 and shall exclude any discrimination between producers or consumers within the Union.

Any common price policy shall be based on common criteria and uniform methods of calculation.

3. In order to enable the common organisation referred to in paragraph 1 to attain its objectives, one or more agricultural guidance and guarantee funds may be set up.

Article 41 (ex Article 35 TEC)

To enable the objectives set out in Article 39 to be attained, provision may be made within the framework of the common agricultural policy for measures such as:

(a) an effective coordination of efforts in the spheres of vocational training, of research and of the dissemination of agricultural knowledge; this may include joint financing of projects or institutions;

(b) joint measures to promote consumption of certain products.

Article 42 (ex Article 36 TEC)

The provisions of the Chapter relating to rules on competition shall apply to production of and trade in agricultural products only to the extent determined by the European Parliament and the Council within the framework of Article 43(2) and in accordance with the procedure laid down therein, account being taken of the objectives set out in Article 39.

The Council, on a proposal from the Commission, may authorise the granting of aid:

(a) for the protection of enterprises handicapped by structural or natural conditions;

(b) within the framework of economic development programmes.

Article 43 (ex Article 37 TEC)

1. The Commission shall submit proposals for working out and implementing the common agricultural policy, including the replacement of the national organisations by one of the forms of common organisation provided for in Article 40(1), and for implementing the measures specified in this Title.

These proposals shall take account of the interdependence of the agricultural matters mentioned in this Title.

2. The European Parliament and the Council, acting in accordance with the ordinary legislative procedure and after consulting the Economic and Social Committee, shall establish the common organisation of agricultural markets provided for in Article 40(1) and the other provisions necessary for the pursuit of the objectives of the common agricultural policy and the common fisheries policy.

3. The Council, on a proposal from the Commission, shall adopt measures on fixing prices, levies, aid and quantitative limitations and on the fixing and allocation of fishing opportunities.

4. In accordance with paragraph 1, the national market organisations may be replaced by the common organisation provided for in Article 40(1) if:

(a) the common organisation offers Member States which are opposed to this measure and which have an organisation of their own for the production in question equivalent safeguards for the employment and standard of living of the producers concerned, account being taken of the adjustments that will be possible and the specialisation that will be needed with the passage of time;

(b) such an organisation ensures conditions for trade within the Union similar to those existing in a national market.

5. If a common organisation for certain raw materials is established before a common organisation exists for the corresponding processed products, such raw materials as are used for processed products intended for export to third countries may be imported from outside the Union.

Article 44 (ex Article 38 TEC)

Where in a Member State a product is subject to a national market organisation or to internal rules having equivalent effect which affect the competitive position of similar production in another Member State, a countervailing charge shall be applied by Member States to imports of this product coming from the Member State where such organisation or rules exist, unless that State applies a countervailing charge on export.

The Commission shall fix the amount of these charges at the level required to redress the balance; it may also authorise other measures, the conditions and details of which it shall determine.

Title IV Free movement of persons, services and capital

Chapter 1 Workers

Article 45 (ex Article 39 TEC)

1. Freedom of movement for workers shall be secured within the Union.

2. Such freedom of movement shall entail the abolition of any discrimination based on nationality between workers of the Member States as regards employment, remuneration and other conditions of work and employment.

3. It shall entail the right, subject to limitations justified on grounds of public policy, public security or public health:

(a) to accept offers of employment actually made;
(b) to move freely within the territory of Member States for this purpose;
(c) to stay in a Member State for the purpose of employment in accordance with the provisions governing the employment of nationals of that State laid down by law, regulation or administrative action;
(d) to remain in the territory of a Member State after having been employed in that State, subject to conditions which shall be embodied in regulations to be drawn up by the Commission.

4. The provisions of this Article shall not apply to employment in the public service.

Article 46 (ex Article 40 TEC)

The European Parliament and the Council shall, acting in accordance with the ordinary legislative procedure and after consulting the Economic and Social Committee, issue directives or make regulations setting out the measures required to bring about freedom of movement for workers, as defined in Article 45, in particular:

(a) by ensuring close cooperation between national employment services;
(b) by abolishing those administrative procedures and practices and those qualifying periods in respect of eligibility for available employment, whether resulting from national legislation or from agreements previously concluded between Member States, the maintenance of which would form an obstacle to liberalisation of the movement of workers;
(c) by abolishing all such qualifying periods and other restrictions provided for either under national legislation or under agreements previously concluded between Member States as imposed on workers of other Member States conditions regarding the free choice of employment other than those imposed on workers of the State concerned;
(d) by setting up appropriate machinery to bring offers of employment into touch with applications for employment and to facilitate the achievement of a balance between supply and demand in the employment market in such a way as to avoid serious threats to the standard of living and level of employment in the various regions and industries.

Article 47 (ex Article 41 TEC)

Member States shall, within the framework of a joint programme, encourage the exchange of young workers.

Article 48 (ex Article 42 TEC)

The European Parliament and the Council shall, acting in accordance with the ordinary legislative procedure, adopt such measures in the field of social security as are necessary to provide freedom of movement for workers; to this end, they shall make arrangements to secure for employed and self-employed migrant workers and their dependants:

(a) aggregation, for the purpose of acquiring and retaining the right to benefit and of calculating the amount of benefit, of all periods taken into account under the laws of the several countries;

(b) payment of benefits to persons resident in the territories of Member States.

Where a member of the Council declares that a draft legislative act referred to in the first subparagraph would affect important aspects of its social security system, including its scope, cost or financial structure, or would affect the financial balance of that system, it may request that the matter be referred to the European Council. In that case, the ordinary legislative procedure shall be suspended. After discussion, the European Council shall, within four months of this suspension, either:

(a) refer the draft back to the Council, which shall terminate the suspension of the ordinary legislative procedure; or

(b) take no action or request the Commission to submit a new proposal; in that case, the act originally proposed shall be deemed not to have been adopted.

Chapter 2 Right of establishment

Article 49 (ex Article 43 TEC)

Within the framework of the provisions set out below, restrictions on the freedom of establishment of nationals of a Member State in the territory of another Member State shall be prohibited. Such prohibition shall also apply to restrictions on the setting-up of agencies, branches or subsidiaries by nationals of any Member State established in the territory of any Member State.

Freedom of establishment shall include the right to take up and pursue activities as self-employed persons and to set up and manage undertakings, in particular companies or firms within the meaning of the second paragraph of Article 54, under the conditions laid down for its own nationals by the law of the country where such establishment is effected, subject to the provisions of the Chapter relating to capital.

Article 50 (ex Article 44 TEC)

1. In order to attain freedom of establishment as regards a particular activity, the European Parliament and the Council, acting in accordance with the ordinary legislative procedure and after consulting the Economic and Social Committee, shall act by means of directives.

2. The European Parliament, the Council and the Commission shall carry out the duties devolving upon them under the preceding provisions, in particular:

(a) by according, as a general rule, priority treatment to activities where freedom of establishment makes a particularly valuable contribution to the development of production and trade;

(b) by ensuring close cooperation between the competent authorities in the Member States in order to ascertain the particular situation within the Union of the various activities concerned;

(c) by abolishing those administrative procedures and practices, whether resulting from national legislation or from agreements previously concluded between Member States, the maintenance of which would form an obstacle to freedom of establishment;

(d) by ensuring that workers of one Member State employed in the territory of another Member State may remain in that territory for the purpose of taking up activities therein as self-employed persons, where they satisfy the conditions which they would be required to satisfy if they were entering that State at the time when they intended to take up such activities;

(e) by enabling a national of one Member State to acquire and use land and buildings situated in the territory of another Member State, in so far as this does not conflict with the principles laid down in Article 39(2);

(f) by effecting the progressive abolition of restrictions on freedom of establishment in every branch of activity under consideration, both as regards the conditions for setting up agencies, branches or subsidiaries in the territory of a Member State and as regards the subsidiaries in the territory of a Member State and as regards the conditions governing the entry of personnel belonging to the main establishment into managerial or supervisory posts in such agencies, branches or subsidiaries;

(g) by coordinating to the necessary extent the safeguards which, for the protection of the interests of members and others, are required by Member States of companies or firms within the meaning of the second paragraph of Article 54 with a view to making such safeguards equivalent throughout the Union;

(h) by satisfying themselves that the conditions of establishment are not distorted by aids granted by Member States.

Article 51 (ex Article 45 TEC)

The provisions of this Chapter shall not apply, so far as any given Member State is concerned, to activities which in that State are connected, even occasionally, with the exercise of official authority.

The European Parliament and the Council, acting in accordance with the ordinary legislative procedure, may rule that the provisions of this Chapter shall not apply to certain activities.

Article 52 (ex Article 46 TEC)

1. The provisions of this Chapter and measures taken in pursuance thereof shall not prejudice the applicability of provisions laid down by law, regulation or administrative action providing for special treatment for foreign nationals on grounds of public policy, public security or public health.

2. The European Parliament and the Council shall, acting in accordance with the ordinary legislative procedure, issue directives for the coordination of the abovementioned provisions.

Article 53 (ex Article 47 TEC)

1. In order to make it easier for persons to take up and pursue activities as self-employed persons, the European Parliament and the Council shall, acting in accordance with the ordinary legislative procedure, issue directives for the mutual recognition of diplomas, certificates and other evidence of formal qualifications and for the coordination of the provisions laid down by law, regulation or administrative action in Member States concerning the taking-up and pursuit of activities as self-employed persons.

2. In the case of the medical and allied and pharmaceutical professions, the progressive abolition of restrictions shall be dependent upon coordination of the conditions for their exercise in the various Member States.

Article 54 (ex Article 48 TEC)

Companies or firms formed in accordance with the law of a Member State and having their registered office, central administration or principal place of business within the Union shall, for the purposes of this Chapter, be treated in the same way as natural persons who are nationals of Member States.,

'Companies or firms' means companies or firms constituted under civil or commercial law, including cooperative societies, and other legal persons governed by public or private law, save for those which are non-profit-making.

Article 55 (ex Article 294 TEC)

Member States shall accord nationals of the other Member States the same treatment as their own nationals as regards participation in the capital of companies or firms within the meaning of Article 54, without prejudice to the application of the other provisions of the Treaties.

Chapter 3 Services

Article 56 (ex Article 49 TEC)

Within the framework of the provisions set out below, restrictions on freedom to provide services within the Union shall be prohibited in respect of nationals of Member States who are established in a Member State other than that of the person for whom the services are intended.

The European Parliament and the Council, acting in accordance with the ordinary legislative procedure, may extend the provisions of the Chapter to nationals of a third country who provide services and who are established within the Union.

Article 57 (ex Article 50 TEC)

Services shall be considered to be 'services' within the meaning of the Treaties where they are normally provided for remuneration, in so far as they are not governed by the provisions relating to freedom of movement for goods, capital and persons.

'Services' shall in particular include:

(a) activities of an industrial character;

(b) activities of a commercial character;

(c) activities of craftsmen;

(d) activities of the professions.

Without prejudice to the provisions of the Chapter relating to the right of establishment, the person providing a service may, in order to do so, temporarily pursue his activity in the Member State where the service is provided, under the same conditions as are imposed by that State on its own nationals.

Article 58 (ex Article 51 TEC)

1. Freedom to provide services in the field of transport shall be governed by the provisions of the Title relating to transport.

2. The liberalisation of banking and insurance services connected with movements of capital shall be effected in step with the liberalisation of movement of capital.

Article 59 (ex Article 52 TEC)

1. In order to achieve the liberalisation of a specific service, the European Parliament and the Council, acting in accordance with the ordinary legislative procedure and after consulting the Economic and Social Committee, shall issue directives.

2. As regards the directives referred to in paragraph 1, priority shall as a general rule be given to those services which directly affect production costs or the liberalisation of which helps to promote trade in goods.

Article 60 (ex Article 53 TEC)

The Member States shall endeavour to undertake the liberalisation of services beyond the extent required by the directives issued pursuant to Article 59(1), if their general economic situation and the situation of the economic sector concerned so permit.

To this end, the Commission shall make recommendations to the Member States concerned.

Article 61 (ex Article 54 TEC)

As long as restrictions on freedom to provide services have not been abolished, each Member State shall apply such restrictions without distinction on grounds of nationality or residence to all persons providing services within the meaning of the first paragraph of Article 56.

Article 62 (ex Article 55 TEC)

The provisions of Articles 51 to 54 shall apply to the matters covered by this Chapter.

Chapter 4 Capital and payments

Article 63 (ex Article 56 TEC)

1. Within the framework of the provisions set out in this Chapter, all restrictions on the movement of capital between Member States and between Member States and third countries shall be prohibited.

2. Within the framework of the provisions set out in this Chapter, all restrictions on payments between Member States and between Member States and third countries shall be prohibited.

Article 64 (ex Article 57 TEC)

1. The provisions of Article 63 shall be without prejudice to the application to third countries of any restrictions which exist on 31 December 1993 under national or Union law adopted in respect of the movement of capital to or from third countries involving direct investment—including in

real estate—establishment, the provision of financial services or the admission of securities to capital markets. In respect of restrictions existing under national law in Bulgaria, Estonia and Hungary, the relevant date shall be 31 December 1999.

2. Whilst endeavouring to achieve the objective of free movement of capital between Member States and third countries to the greatest extent possible and without prejudice to the other Chapters of the Treaties, the European Parliament and the Council, acting in accordance with the ordinary legislative procedure, shall adopt the measures on the movement of capital to or from third countries involving direct investment—including investment in real estate—establishment, the provision of financial services or the admission of securities to capital markets.

3. Notwithstanding paragraph 2, only the Council, acting in accordance with a special legislative procedure, may unanimously, and after consulting the European Parliament, adopt measures which constitute a step backwards in Union law as regards the liberalisation of the movement of capital to or from third countries.

Article 65 (ex Article 58 TEC)

1. The provisions of Article 63 shall be without prejudice to the right of Member States:
   (a) to apply the relevant provisions of their tax law which distinguish between taxpayers who are not in the same situation with regard to their place of residence or with regard to the place where their capital is invested;
   (b) to take all requisite measures to prevent infringements of national law and regulations, in particular in the field of taxation and the prudential supervision of financial institutions, or to lay down procedures for the declaration of capital movements for purposes of administrative or statistical information, or to take measures which are justified on grounds of public policy or public security.

2. The provisions of this Chapter shall be without prejudice to the applicability of restrictions on the right of establishment which are compatible with the Treaties.

3. The measures and procedures referred to in paragraphs 1 and 2 shall not constitute a means of arbitrary discrimination or a disguised restriction on the free movement of capital and payments as defined in Article 63.

4. In the absence of measures pursuant to Article 64(3), the Commission or, in the absence of a Commission decision within three months from the request of the Member State concerned, the Council, may adopt a decision stating that restrictive tax measures adopted by a Member State concerning one or more third countries are to be considered compatible with the Treaties in so far as they are justified by one of the objectives of the Union and compatible with the proper functioning of the internal market. The Council shall act unanimously on application by a Member State.

Article 66 (ex Article 59 TEC)

Where, in exceptional circumstances, movements of capital to or from third countries cause, or threaten to cause, serious difficulties for the operation of economic and monetary union, the Council, on a proposal from the Commission and after consulting the European Central Bank, may take safeguard measures with regard to third countries for a period not exceeding six months if such measures are strictly necessary.

Title V Area of freedom, security and justice

Chapter 1 General provisions

Article 67 (ex Article 61 TEC and ex Article 29 TEU)

1. The Union shall constitute an area of freedom, security and justice with respect for fundamental rights and the different legal systems and traditions of the Member States.

2. It shall ensure the absence of internal border controls for persons and shall frame a common policy on asylum, immigration and external border control, based on solidarity between Member

States, which is fair towards third-country nationals. For the purpose of this Title, stateless persons shall be treated as third-country nationals.

3. The Union shall endeavour to ensure a high level of security through measures to prevent and combat crime, racism and xenophobia, and through measures for coordination and cooperation between police and judicial authorities and other competent authorities, as well as through the mutual recognition of judgments in criminal matters and, if necessary, through the approximation of criminal laws.

4. The Union shall facilitate access to justice, in particular through the principle of mutual recognition of judicial and extrajudicial decisions in civil matters.

Article 68

The European Council shall define the strategic guidelines for legislative and operational planning within the area of freedom, security and justice.

Article 69

National Parliaments ensure that the proposals and legislative initiatives submitted under Chapters 4 and 5 comply with the principle of subsidiarity, in accordance with the arrangements laid down by the Protocol on the application of the principles of subsidiarity and proportionality.

Article 70

Without prejudice to Articles 258, 259 and 260, the Council may, on a proposal from the Commission, adopt measures laying down the arrangements whereby Member States, in collaboration with the Commission, conduct objective and impartial evaluation of the implementation of the Union policies referred to in this Title by Member States' authorities, in particular in order to facilitate full application of the principle of mutual recognition. The European Parliament and national Parliaments shall be informed of the content and results of the evaluation.

Article 71 (ex Article 36 TEU)

A standing committee shall be set up within the Council in order to ensure that operational cooperation on internal security is promoted and strengthened within the Union. Without prejudice to Article 240, it shall facilitate coordination of the action of Member States' competent authorities. Representatives of the Union bodies, offices and agencies concerned may be involved in the proceedings of this committee. The European Parliament and national Parliaments shall be kept informed of the proceedings.

Article 72 (ex Article 64(1) TEC and ex Article 33 TEU)

This Title shall not affect the exercise of the responsibilities incumbent upon Member States with regard to the maintenance of law and order and the safeguarding of internal security.

Article 73

It shall be open to Member States to organise between themselves and under their responsibility such forms of cooperation and coordination as they deem appropriate between the competent departments of their administrations responsible for safeguarding national security.

Article 74 (ex Article 66 TEC)

The Council shall adopt measures to ensure administrative cooperation between the relevant departments of the Member States in the areas covered by this Title, as well as between those departments and the Commission. It shall act on a Commission proposal, subject to Article 76, and after consulting the European Parliament.

Article 75 (ex Article 60 TEC)

Where necessary to achieve the objectives set out in Article 67, as regards preventing and combating terrorism and related activities, the European Parliament and the Council, acting by means of regulations in accordance with the ordinary legislative procedure, shall define a framework for administrative measures with regard to capital movements and payments, such as the freezing of funds, financial assets or economic gains belonging to, or owned or held by, natural or legal persons, groups or non-State entities.

The Council, on a proposal from the Commission, shall adopt measures to implement the framework referred to in the first paragraph.

The acts referred to in this Article shall include necessary provisions on legal safeguards.

Article 76

The acts referred to in Chapters 4 and 5, together with the measures referred to in Article 74 which ensure administrative cooperation in the areas covered by these Chapters, shall be adopted:

(a) on a proposal from the Commission, or

(b) on the initiative of a quarter of the Member States.

Chapter 2 Policies on border checks, asylum and immigration

Article 77 (ex Article 62 TEC)

1. The Union shall develop a policy with a view to:

(a) ensuring the absence of any controls on persons, whatever their nationality, when crossing internal borders;

(b) carrying out checks on persons and efficient monitoring of the crossing of external borders;

(c) the gradual introduction of an integrated management system for external borders.

2. For the purposes of paragraph 1, the European Parliament and the Council, acting in accordance with the ordinary legislative procedure, shall adopt measures concerning:

(a) the common policy on visas and other short-stay residence permits;

(b) the checks to which persons crossing external borders are subject;

(c) the conditions under which nationals of third countries shall have the freedom to travel within the Union for a short period;

(d) any measure necessary for the gradual establishment of an integrated management system for external borders;

(e) the absence of any controls on persons, whatever their nationality, when crossing internal borders.

3. If action by the Union should prove necessary to facilitate the exercise of the right referred to in Article 20(2)(a), and if the Treaties have not provided the necessary powers, the Council, acting in accordance with a special legislative procedure, may adopt provisions concerning passports, identity cards, residence permits or any other such document. The Council shall act unanimously after consulting the European Parliament.

4. This Article shall not affect the competence of the Member States concerning the geographical demarcation of their borders, in accordance with international law.

Article 78 (ex Articles 63, points 1 and 2, and 64(2) TEC)

1. The Union shall develop a common policy on asylum, subsidiary protection and temporary protection with a view to offering appropriate status to any third-country national requiring international protection and ensuring compliance with the principle of *non-refoulement*. This policy must be in accordance with the Geneva Convention of 28 July 1951 and the Protocol of 31 January 1967 relating to the status of refugees, and other relevant treaties.

2. For the purposes of paragraph 1, the European Parliament and the Council, acting in accordance with the ordinary legislative procedure, shall adopt measures for a common European asylum system comprising:

(a) a uniform status of asylum for nationals of third countries, valid throughout the Union;

(b) a uniform status of subsidiary protection for nationals of third countries who, without obtaining European asylum, are in need of international protection;

(c) a common system of temporary protection for displaced persons in the event of a massive inflow;

(d) common procedures for the granting and withdrawing of uniform asylum or subsidiary protection status;
(e) criteria and mechanisms for determining which Member State is responsible for considering an application for asylum or subsidiary protection;
(f) standards concerning the conditions for the reception of applicants for asylum or subsidiary protection;
(g) partnership and cooperation with third countries for the purpose of managing inflows of people applying for asylum or subsidiary or temporary protection.

3. In the event of one or more Member States being confronted by an emergency situation characterised by a sudden inflow of nationals of third countries, the Council, on a proposal from the Commission, may adopt provisional measures for the benefit of the Member State(s) concerned. It shall act after consulting the European Parliament.

Article 79 (ex Article 63, points 3 and 4, TEC)

1. The Union shall develop a common immigration policy aimed at ensuring, at all stages, the efficient management of migration flows, fair treatment of third-country nationals residing legally in Member States, and the prevention of, and enhanced measures to combat, illegal immigration and trafficking in human beings.

2. For the purposes of paragraph 1, the European Parliament and the Council, acting in accordance with the ordinary legislative procedure, shall adopt measures in the following areas:
(a) the conditions of entry and residence, and standards on the issue by Member States of long-term visas and residence permits, including those for the purpose of family reunification;
(b) the definition of the rights of third-country nationals residing legally in a Member State, including the conditions governing freedom of movement and of residence in other Member States;
(c) illegal immigration and unauthorised residence, including removal and repatriation of persons residing without authorisation;
(d) combating trafficking in persons, in particular women and children.

3. The Union may conclude agreements with third countries for the readmission to their countries of origin or provenance of third-country nationals who do not or who no longer fulfil the conditions for entry, presence or residence in the territory of one of the Member States.

4. The European Parliament and the Council, acting in accordance with the ordinary legislative procedure, may establish measures to provide incentives and support for the action of Member States with a view to promoting the integration of third-country nationals residing legally in their territories, excluding any harmonisation of the laws and regulations of the Member States.

5. This Article shall not affect the right of Member States to determine volumes of admission of third-country nationals coming from third countries to their territory in order to seek work, whether employed or self-employed.

Article 80

The policies of the Union set out in this Chapter and their implementation shall be governed by the principle of solidarity and fair sharing of responsibility, including its financial implications, between the Member States. Whenever necessary, the Union acts adopted pursuant to this Chapter shall contain appropriate measures to give effect to this principle.

Chapter 3 Judicial cooperation in civil matters

Article 81 (ex Article 65 TEC)

1. The Union shall develop judicial cooperation in civil matters having cross-border implications, based on the principle of mutual recognition of judgments and of decisions in extrajudicial cases. Such cooperation may include the adoption of measures for the approximation of the laws and regulations of the Member States.

2. For the purposes of paragraph 1, the European Parliament and the Council, acting in accordance with the ordinary legislative procedure, shall adopt measures, particularly when necessary for the proper functioning of the internal market, aimed at ensuring:

(a) the mutual recognition and enforcement between Member States of judgments and of decisions in extrajudicial cases;
(b) the cross-border service of judicial and extrajudicial documents;
(c) the compatibility of the rules applicable in the Member States concerning conflict of laws and of jurisdiction;
(d) cooperation in the taking of evidence;
(e) effective access to justice;
(f) the elimination of obstacles to the proper functioning of civil proceedings, if necessary by promoting the compatibility of the rules on civil procedure applicable in the Member States;
(g) the development of alternative methods of dispute settlement;
(h) support for the training of the judiciary and judicial staff.

3. Notwithstanding paragraph 2, measures concerning family law with cross-border implications shall be established by the Council, acting in accordance with a special legislative procedure. The Council shall act unanimously after consulting the European Parliament.

The Council, on a proposal from the Commission, may adopt a decision determining those aspects of family law with cross-border implications which may be the subject of acts adopted by the ordinary legislative procedure. The Council shall act unanimously after consulting the European Parliament.

The proposal referred to in the second subparagraph shall be notified to the national Parliaments. If a national Parliament makes known its opposition within six months of the date of such notification, the decision shall not be adopted. In the absence of opposition, the Council may adopt the decision.

Chapter 4 Judicial cooperation in criminal matters

Article 82 (ex Article 31 TEU)

1. Judicial cooperation in criminal matters in the Union shall be based on the principle of mutual recognition of judgments and judicial decisions and shall include the approximation of the laws and regulations of the Member States in the areas referred to in paragraph 2 and in Article 83.

The European Parliament and the Council, acting in accordance with the ordinary legislative procedure, shall adopt measures to:

(a) lay down rules and procedures for ensuring recognition throughout the Union of all forms of judgments and judicial decisions;
(b) prevent and settle conflicts of jurisdiction between Member States;
(c) support the training of the judiciary and judicial staff;
(d) facilitate cooperation between judicial or equivalent authorities of the Member States in relation to proceedings in criminal matters and the enforcement of decisions.

2. To the extent necessary to facilitate mutual recognition of judgments and judicial decisions and police and judicial cooperation in criminal matters having a cross-border dimension, the European Parliament and the Council may, by means of directives adopted in accordance with the ordinary legislative procedure, establish minimum rules. Such rules shall take into account the differences between the legal traditions and systems of the Member States.

They shall concern:

(a) mutual admissibility of evidence between Member States;
(b) the rights of individuals in criminal procedure;
(c) the rights of victims of crime;
(d) any other specific aspects of criminal procedure which the Council has identified in advance by a decision; for the adoption of such a decision, the Council shall act unanimously after obtaining the consent of the European Parliament.

Adoption of the minimum rules referred to in this paragraph shall not prevent Member States from maintaining or introducing a higher level of protection for individuals.

3. Where a member of the Council considers that a draft directive as referred to in paragraph 2 would affect fundamental aspects of its criminal justice system, it may request that the draft directive be referred to the European Council. In that case, the ordinary legislative procedure shall be suspended. After discussion, and in case of a consensus, the European Council shall, within four months of this suspension, refer the draft back to the Council, which shall terminate the suspension of the ordinary legislative procedure.

Within the same timeframe, in case of disagreement, and if at least nine Member States wish to establish enhanced cooperation on the basis of the draft directive concerned, they shall notify the European Parliament, the Council and the Commission accordingly. In such a case, the authorisation to proceed with enhanced cooperation referred to in Article 20(2) of the Treaty on European Union and Article 329(1) of this Treaty shall be deemed to be granted and the provisions on enhanced cooperation shall apply.

Article 83 (ex Article 31 TEU)

1. The European Parliament and the Council may, by means of directives adopted in accordance with the ordinary legislative procedure, establish minimum rules concerning the definition of criminal offences and sanctions in the areas of particularly serious crime with a cross-border dimension resulting from the nature or impact of such offences or from a special need to combat them on a common basis.

These areas of crime are the following: terrorism, trafficking in human beings and sexual exploitation of women and children, illicit drug trafficking, illicit arms trafficking, money laundering, corruption, counterfeiting of means of payment, computer crime and organised crime.

On the basis of developments in crime, the Council may adopt a decision identifying other areas of crime that meet the criteria specified in this paragraph. It shall act unanimously after obtaining the consent of the European Parliament.

2. If the approximation of criminal laws and regulations of the Member States proves essential to ensure the effective implementation of a Union policy in an area which has been subject to harmonisation measures, directives may establish minimum rules with regard to the definition of criminal offences and sanctions in the area concerned.

Such directives shall be adopted by the same ordinary or special legislative procedure as was followed for the adoption of the harmonisation measures in question, without prejudice to Article 76.

3. Where a member of the Council considers that a draft directive as referred to in paragraph 1 or 2 would affect fundamental aspects of its criminal justice system, it may request that the draft directive be referred to the European Council. In that case, the ordinary legislative procedure shall be suspended. After discussion, and in case of a consensus, the European Council shall, within four months of this suspension, refer the draft back to the Council, which shall terminate the suspension of the ordinary legislative procedure.

Within the same timeframe, in case of disagreement, and if at least nine Member States wish to establish enhanced cooperation on the basis of the draft directive concerned, they shall notify the European Parliament, the Council and the Commission accordingly. In such a case, the authorisation to proceed with enhanced cooperation referred to in Article 20(2) of the Treaty on European Union and Article 329(1) of this Treaty shall be deemed to be granted and the provisions on enhanced cooperation shall apply.

Article 84

The European Parliament and the Council, acting in accordance with the ordinary legislative procedure, may establish measures to promote and support the action of Member States in the field of crime prevention, excluding any harmonisation of the laws and regulations of the Member States.

Article 85 (ex Article 31 TEU)

1. Eurojust's mission shall be to support and strengthen coordination and cooperation between national investigating and prosecuting authorities in relation to serious crime affecting two or more Member States or requiring a prosecution on common bases, on the basis of operations conducted and information supplied by the Member States' authorities and by Europol.

In this context, the European Parliament and the Council, by means of regulations adopted in accordance with the ordinary legislative procedure, shall determine Eurojust's structure, operation, field of action and tasks. These tasks may include:

(a) the initiation of criminal investigations, as well as proposing the initiation of prosecutions conducted by competent national authorities, particularly those relating to offences against the financial interests of the Union;

(b) the coordination of investigations and prosecutions referred to in point (a);

(c) the strengthening of judicial cooperation, including by resolution of conflicts of jurisdiction and by close cooperation with the European Judicial Network.

These regulations shall also determine arrangements for involving the European Parliament and national Parliaments in the evaluation of Eurojust's activities.

2. In the prosecutions referred to in paragraph 1, and without prejudice to Article 86, formal acts of judicial procedure shall be carried out by the competent national officials.

Article 86

1. In order to combat crimes affecting the financial interests of the Union, the Council, by means of regulations adopted in accordance with a special legislative procedure, may establish a European Public Prosecutor's Office from Eurojust. The Council shall act unanimously after obtaining the consent of the European Parliament.

In the absence of unanimity in the Council, a group of at least nine Member States may request that the draft regulation be referred to the European Council. In that case, the procedure in the Council shall be suspended. After discussion, and in case of a consensus, the European Council shall, within four months of this suspension, refer the draft back to the Council for adoption.

Within the same timeframe, in case of disagreement, and if at least nine Member States wish to establish enhanced cooperation on the basis of the draft regulation concerned, they shall notify the European Parliament, the Council and the Commission accordingly. In such a case, the authorisation to proceed with enhanced cooperation referred to in Article 20(2) of the Treaty on European Union and Article 329(1) of this Treaty shall be deemed to be granted and the provisions on enhanced cooperation shall apply.

2. The European Public Prosecutor's Office shall be responsible for investigating, prosecuting and bringing to judgment, where appropriate in liaison with Europol, the perpetrators of, and accomplices in, offences against the Union's financial interests, as determined by the regulation provided for in paragraph 1. It shall exercise the functions of prosecutor in the competent courts of the Member States in relation to such offences.

3. The regulations referred to in paragraph 1 shall determine the general rules applicable to the European Public Prosecutor's Office, the conditions governing the performance of its functions, the rules of procedure applicable to its activities, as well as those governing the admissibility of evidence, and the rules applicable to the judicial review of procedural measures taken by it in the performance of its functions.

4. The European Council may, at the same time or subsequently, adopt a decision amending paragraph 1 in order to extend the powers of the European Public Prosecutor's Office to include serious crime having a cross-border dimension and amending accordingly paragraph 2 as regards the perpetrators of, and accomplices in, serious crimes affecting more than one Member State. The European Council shall act unanimously after obtaining the consent of the European Parliament and after consulting the Commission.

Chapter 5 Police cooperation

Article 87 (ex Article 30 TEU)

1. The Union shall establish police cooperation involving all the Member States' competent authorities, including police, customs and other specialised law enforcement services in relation to the prevention, detection and investigation of criminal offences.

2. For the purposes of paragraph 1, the European Parliament and the Council, acting in accordance with the ordinary legislative procedure, may establish measures concerning:

(a) the collection, storage, processing, analysis and exchange of relevant information;

(b) support for the training of staff, and cooperation on the exchange of staff, on equipment and on research into crime-detection;

(c) common investigative techniques in relation to the detection of serious forms of organised crime.

3. The Council, acting in accordance with a special legislative procedure, may establish measures concerning operational cooperation between the authorities referred to in this Article. The Council shall act unanimously after consulting the European Parliament.

In case of the absence of unanimity in the Council, a group of at least nine Member States may request that the draft measures be referred to the European Council. In that case, the procedure in the Council shall be suspended. After discussion, and in case of a consensus, the European Council shall, within four months of this suspension, refer the draft back to the Council for adoption.

Within the same timeframe, in case of disagreement, and if at least nine Member States wish to establish enhanced cooperation on the basis of the draft measures concerned, they shall notify the European Parliament, the Council and the Commission accordingly. In such a case, the authorisation to proceed with enhanced cooperation referred to in Article 20(2) of the Treaty on European Union and Article 329(1) of this Treaty shall be deemed to be granted and the provisions on enhanced cooperation shall apply.

The specific procedure provided for in the second and third subparagraphs shall not apply to acts which constitute a development of the Schengen *acquis*.

Article 88 (ex Article 30 TEU)

1. Europol's mission shall be to support and strengthen action by the Member States' police authorities and other law enforcement services and their mutual cooperation in preventing and combating serious crime affecting two or more Member States, terrorism and forms of crime which affect a common interest covered by a Union policy.

2. The European Parliament and the Council, by means of regulations adopted in accordance with the ordinary legislative procedure, shall determine Europol's structure, operation, field of action and tasks. These tasks may include:

(a) the collection, storage, processing, analysis and exchange of information, in particular that forwarded by the authorities of the Member States or third countries or bodies;

(b) the coordination, organisation and implementation of investigative and operational action carried out jointly with the Member States' competent authorities or in the context of joint investigative teams, where appropriate in liaison with Eurojust.

These regulations shall also lay down the procedures for scrutiny of Europol's activities by the European Parliament, together with national Parliaments.

3. Any operational action by Europol must be carried out in liaison and in agreement with the authorities of the Member State or States whose territory is concerned. The application of coercive measures shall be the exclusive responsibility of the competent national authorities.

Article 89 (ex Article 32 TEU)

The Council, acting in accordance with a special legislative procedure, shall lay down the conditions and limitations under which the competent authorities of the Member States referred to in Articles 82 and 87 may operate in the territory of another Member State in liaison and in agreement with the authorities of that State. The Council shall act unanimously after consulting the European Parliament.

Title VI Transport

Article 90 (ex Article 70 TEC)

The objectives of the Treaties shall, in matters governed by this Title, be pursued within the framework of a common transport policy.

Article 91 (ex Article 71 TEC)

1. For the purpose of implementing Article 90, and taking into account the distinctive features of transport, the European Parliament and the Council shall, acting in accordance with the ordinary legislative procedure and after consulting the Economic and Social Committee and the Committee of the Regions, lay down:

(a) common rules applicable to international transport to or from the territory of a Member State or passing across the territory of one or more Member States;

(b) the conditions under which non-resident carriers may operate transport services within a Member State;

(c) measures to improve transport safety;

(d) any other appropriate provisions.

2. When the measures referred to in paragraph 1 are adopted, account shall be taken of cases where their application might seriously affect the standard of living and level of employment in certain regions, and the operation of transport facilities.

Article 92 (ex Article 72 TEC)

Until the provisions referred to in Article 91(1) have been laid down, no Member State may, unless the Council has unanimously adopted a measure granting a derogation, make the various provisions governing the subject on 1 January 1958 or, for acceding States, the date of their accession less favourable in their direct or indirect effect on carriers of other Member States as compared with carriers who are nationals of that State.

Article 93 (ex Article 73 TEC)

Aids shall be compatible with the Treaties if they meet the needs of coordination of transport or if they represent reimbursement for the discharge of certain obligations inherent in the concept of a public service.

Article 94 (ex Article 74 TEC)

Any measures taken within the framework of the Treaties in respect of transport rates and conditions shall take account of the economic circumstances of carriers.

Article 95 (ex Article 75 TEC)

1. In the case of transport within the Union, discrimination which takes the form of carriers charging different rates and imposing different conditions for the carriage of the same goods over the same transport links on grounds of the country of origin or of destination of the goods in question shall be prohibited.

2. Paragraph 1 shall not prevent the European Parliament and the Council from adopting other measures pursuant to Article 91(1).

3. The Council shall, on a proposal from the Commission and after consulting the European Parliament and the Economic and Social Committee, lay down rules for implementing the provisions of paragraph 1.

The Council may in particular lay down the provisions needed to enable the institutions of the Union to secure compliance with the rule laid down in paragraph 1 and to ensure that users benefit from it to the full.

4. The Commission shall, acting on its own initiative or on application by a Member State, investigate any cases of discrimination falling within paragraph 1 and, after consulting any Member State concerned, shall take the necessary decisions within the framework of the rules laid down in accordance with the provisions of paragraph 3.

Article 96 (ex Article 76 TEC)

1. The imposition by a Member State, in respect of transport operations carried out within the Union, of rates and conditions involving any element of support or protection in the interest of one or more particular undertakings or industries shall be prohibited, unless authorised by the Commission.

2. The Commission shall, acting on its own initiative or on application by a Member State, examine the rates and conditions referred to in paragraph 1, taking account in particular of the requirements of an appropriate regional economic policy, the needs of underdeveloped areas and the problems of areas seriously affected by political circumstances on the one hand, and of the effects of such rates and conditions on competition between the different modes of transport on the other.

After consulting each Member State concerned, the Commission shall take the necessary decisions.

3. The prohibition provided for in paragraph 1 shall not apply to tariffs fixed to meet competition.

Article 97 (ex Article 77 TEC)

Charges or dues in respect of the crossing of frontiers which are charged by a carrier in addition to the transport rates shall not exceed a reasonable level after taking the costs actually incurred thereby into account.

Member States shall endeavour to reduce these costs progressively.

The Commission may make recommendations to Member States for the application of this Article.

Article 98 (ex Article 78 TEC)

The provisions of this Title shall not form an obstacle to the application of measures taken in the Federal Republic of Germany to the extent that such measures are required in order to compensate for the economic disadvantages caused by the division of Germany to the economy of certain areas of the Federal Republic affected by that division. Five years after the entry into force of the Treaty of Lisbon, the Council, acting on a proposal from the Commission, may adopt a decision repealing this Article.

Article 99 (ex Article 79 TEC)

An Advisory Committee consisting of experts designated by the governments of Member States shall be attached to the Commission. The Commission, whenever it considers it desirable, shall consult the Committee on transport matters.

Article 100 (ex Article 80 TEC)

1. The provisions of this Title shall apply to transport by rail, road and inland waterway.

2. The European Parliament and the Council, acting in accordance with the ordinary legislative procedure, may lay down appropriate provisions for sea and air transport. They shall act after consulting the Economic and Social Committee and the Committee of the Regions.

Title VII Common rules on competition, taxation and approximation of laws

Chapter 1 Rules on competition

Section 1 Rules applying to undertakings

Article 101 (ex Article 81 TEC)

1. The following shall be prohibited as incompatible with the internal market: all agreements between undertakings, decisions by associations of undertakings and concerted practices which may affect trade between Member States and which have as their object or effect the prevention, restriction or distortion of competition within the internal market, and in particular those which:

(a) directly or indirectly fix purchase or selling prices or any other trading conditions;
(b) limit or control production, markets, technical development, or investment;
(c) share markets or sources of supply;
(d) apply dissimilar conditions to equivalent transactions with other trading parties, thereby placing them at a competitive disadvantage;
(e) make the conclusion of contracts subject to acceptance by the other parties of supplementary obligations which, by their nature or according to commercial usage, have no connection with the subject of such contracts.

2. Any agreements or decisions prohibited pursuant to this Article shall be automatically void.
3. The provisions of paragraph 1 may, however, be declared inapplicable in the case of:
- any agreement or category of agreements between undertakings,
- any decision or category of decisions by associations of undertakings,
- any concerted practice or category of concerted practices,

which contributes to improving the production or distribution of goods or to promoting technical or economic progress, while allowing consumers a fair share of the resulting benefit, and which does not:

(a) impose on the undertakings concerned restrictions which are not indispensable to the attainment of these objectives;
(b) afford such undertakings the possibility of eliminating competition in respect of a substantial part of the products in question.

Article 102 (ex Article 82 TEC)

Any abuse by one or more undertakings of a dominant position within the internal market or in a substantial part of it shall be prohibited as incompatible with the internal market in so far as it may affect trade between Member States.

Such abuse may, in particular, consist in:

(a) directly or indirectly imposing unfair purchase or selling prices or other unfair trading conditions;
(b) limiting production, markets or technical development to the prejudice of consumers;
(c) applying dissimilar conditions to equivalent transactions with other trading parties, thereby placing them at a competitive disadvantage;
(d) making the conclusion of contracts subject to acceptance by the other parties of supplementary obligations which, by their nature or according to commercial usage, have no connection with the subject of such contracts.

Article 103 (ex Article 83 TEC)

1. The appropriate regulations or directives to give effect to the principles set out in Articles 101 and 102 shall be laid down by the Council, on a proposal from the Commission and after consulting the European Parliament.

2. The regulations or directives referred to in paragraph 1 shall be designed in particular:

(a) to ensure compliance with the prohibitions laid down in Article 101(1) and in Article 102 by making provision for fines and periodic penalty payments;
(b) to lay down detailed rules for the application of Article 101(3), taking into account the need to ensure effective supervision on the one hand, and to simplify administration to the greatest possible extent on the other;
(c) to define, if need be, in the various branches of the economy, the scope of the provisions of Articles 101 and 102;
(d) to define the respective functions of the Commission and of the Court of Justice of the European Union in applying the provisions laid down in this paragraph;
(e) to determine the relationship between national laws and the provisions contained in this Section or adopted pursuant to this Article.

Article 104 (ex Article 84 TEC)

Until the entry into force of the provisions adopted in pursuance of Article 103, the authorities in Member States shall rule on the admissibility of agreements, decisions and concerted practices and on abuse of a dominant position in the internal market in accordance with the law of their country and with the provisions of Article 101, in particular paragraph 3, and of Article 102.

Article 105 (ex Article 85 TEC)

1. Without prejudice to Article 104, the Commission shall ensure the application of the principles laid down in Articles 101 and 102. On application by a Member State or on its own initiative, and in cooperation with the competent authorities in the Member States, which shall give it their assistance,

the Commission shall investigate cases of suspected infringement of these principles. If it finds that there has been an infringement, it shall propose appropriate measures to bring it to an end.

2. If the infringement is not brought to an end, the Commission shall record such infringement of the principles in a reasoned decision. The Commission may publish its decision and authorise Member States to take the measures, the conditions and details of which it shall determine, needed to remedy the situation.

3. The Commission may adopt regulations relating to the categories of agreement in respect of which the Council has adopted a regulation or a directive pursuant to Article 103(2)(b).

Article 106 (ex Article 86 TEC)

1. In the case of public undertakings and undertakings to which Member States grant special or exclusive rights, Member States shall neither enact nor maintain in force any measure contrary to the rules contained in the Treaties, in particular to those rules provided for in Article 18 and Articles 101 to 109.

2. Undertakings entrusted with the operation of services of general economic interest or having the character of a revenue-producing monopoly shall be subject to the rules contained in the Treaties, in particular to the rules on competition, in so far as the application of such rules does not obstruct the performance, in law or in fact, of the particular tasks assigned to them. The development of trade must not be affected to such an extent as would be contrary to the interests of the Union.

3. The Commission shall ensure the application of the provisions of this Article and shall, where necessary, address appropriate directives or decisions to Member States.

Section 2 Aids granted by States

Article 107 (ex Article 87 TEC)

1. Save as otherwise provided in the Treaties, any aid granted by a Member State or through State resources in any form whatsoever which distorts or threatens to distort competition by favouring certain undertakings or the production of certain goods shall, in so far as it affects trade between Member States, be incompatible with the internal market.

2. The following shall be compatible with the internal market:
   (a) aid having a social character, granted to individual consumers, provided that such aid is granted without discrimination related to the origin of the products concerned;
   (b) aid to make good the damage caused by natural disasters or exceptional occurrences;
   (c) aid granted to the economy of certain areas of the Federal Republic of Germany affected by the division of Germany, in so far as such aid is required in order to compensate for the economic disadvantages caused by that division. Five years after the entry into force of the Treaty of Lisbon, the Council, acting on a proposal from the Commission, may adopt a decision repealing this point.

3. The following may be considered to be compatible with the internal market:
   (a) aid to promote the economic development of areas where the standard of living is abnormally low or where there is serious underemployment, and of the regions referred to in Article 349, in view of their structural, economic and social situation;
   (b) aid to promote the execution of an important project of common European interest or to remedy a serious disturbance in the economy of a Member State;
   (c) aid to facilitate the development of certain economic activities or of certain economic areas, where such aid does not adversely affect trading conditions to an extent contrary to the common interest;
   (d) aid to promote culture and heritage conservation where such aid does not affect trading conditions and competition in the Union to an extent that is contrary to the common interest;
   (e) such other categories of aid as may be specified by decision of the Council on a proposal from the Commission.

Article 108 (ex Article 88 TEC)

1. The Commission shall, in cooperation with Member States, keep under constant review all systems of aid existing in those States. It shall propose to the latter any appropriate measures required by the progressive development or by the functioning of the internal market.

2. If, after giving notice to the parties concerned to submit their comments, the Commission finds that aid granted by a State or through State resources is not compatible with the internal market having regard to Article 107, or that such aid is being misused, it shall decide that the State concerned shall abolish or alter such aid within a period of time to be determined by the Commission.

If the State concerned does not comply with this decision within the prescribed time, the Commission or any other interested State may, in derogation from the provisions of Articles 258 and 259, refer the matter to the Court of Justice of the European Union direct.

On application by a Member State, the Council may, acting unanimously, decide that aid which that State is granting or intends to grant shall be considered to be compatible with the internal market, in derogation from the provisions of Article 107 or from the regulations provided for in Article 109, if such a decision is justified by exceptional circumstances. If, as regards the aid in question, the Commission has already initiated the procedure provided for in the first subparagraph of this paragraph, the fact that the State concerned has made its application to the Council shall have the effect of suspending that procedure until the Council has made its attitude known.

If, however, the Council has not made its attitude known within three months of the said application being made, the Commission shall give its decision on the case.

3. The Commission shall be informed, in sufficient time to enable it to submit its comments, of any plans to grant or alter aid. If it considers that any such plan is not compatible with the internal market having regard to Article 107, it shall without delay initiate the procedure provided for in paragraph 2. The Member State concerned shall not put its proposed measures into effect until this procedure has resulted in a final decision.

4. The Commission may adopt regulations relating to the categories of State aid that the Council has, pursuant to Article 109, determined may be exempted from the procedure provided for by paragraph 3 of this Article.

Article 109 (ex Article 89 TEC)

The Council, on a proposal from the Commission and after consulting the European Parliament, may make any appropriate regulations for the application of Articles 107 and 108 and may in particular determine the conditions in which Article 108(3) shall apply and the categories of aid exempted from this procedure.

Chapter 2 Tax provisions

Article 110 (ex Article 90 TEC)

No Member State shall impose, directly or indirectly, on the products of other Member States any internal taxation of any kind in excess of that imposed directly or indirectly on similar domestic products.

Furthermore, no Member State shall impose on the products of other Member States any internal taxation of such a nature as to afford indirect protection to other products.

Article 111 (ex Article 91 TEC)

Where products are exported to the territory of any Member State, any repayment of internal taxation shall not exceed the internal taxation imposed on them whether directly or indirectly.

Article 112 (ex Article 92 TEC)

In the case of charges other than turnover taxes, excise duties and other forms of indirect taxation, remissions and repayments in respect of exports to other Member States may not be granted and countervailing charges in respect of imports from Member States may not be imposed unless the measures contemplated have been previously approved for a limited period by the Council on a proposal from the Commission.

Article 113 (ex Article 93 TEC)

The Council shall, acting unanimously in accordance with a special legislative procedure and after consulting the European Parliament and the Economic and Social Committee, adopt provisions for the harmonisation of legislation concerning turnover taxes, excise duties and other forms of indirect taxation to the extent that such harmonisation is necessary to ensure the establishment and the functioning of the internal market and to avoid distortion of competition.

Chapter 3 Approximation of laws

Article 114 (ex Article 95 TEC)

1. Save where otherwise provided in the Treaties, the following provisions shall apply for the achievement of the objectives set out in Article 26. The European Parliament and the Council shall, acting in accordance with the ordinary legislative procedure and after consulting the Economic and Social Committee, adopt the measures for the approximation of the provisions laid down by law, regulation or administrative action in Member States which have as their object the establishment and functioning of the internal market.

2. Paragraph 1 shall not apply to fiscal provisions, to those relating to the free movement of persons nor to those relating to the rights and interests of employed persons.

3. The Commission, in its proposals envisaged in paragraph 1 concerning health, safety, environmental protection and consumer protection, will take as a base a high level of protection, taking account in particular of any new development based on scientific facts. Within their respective powers, the European Parliament and the Council will also seek to achieve this objective.

4. If, after the adoption of a harmonisation measure by the European Parliament and the Council, by the Council or by the Commission, a Member State deems it necessary to maintain national provisions on grounds of major needs referred to in Article 36, or relating to the protection of the environment or the working environment, it shall notify the Commission of these provisions as well as the grounds for maintaining them.

5. Moreover, without prejudice to paragraph 4, if, after the adoption of a harmonisation measure by the European Parliament and the Council, by the Council or by the Commission, a Member State deems it necessary to introduce national provisions based on new scientific evidence relating to the protection of the environment or the working environment on grounds of a problem specific to that Member State arising after the adoption of the harmonisation measure, it shall notify the Commission of the envisaged provisions as well as the grounds for introducing them.

6. The Commission shall, within six months of the notifications as referred to in paragraphs 4 and 5, approve or reject the national provisions involved after having verified whether or not they are a means of arbitrary discrimination or a disguised restriction on trade between Member States and whether or not they shall constitute an obstacle to the functioning of the internal market.

In the absence of a decision by the Commission within this period the national provisions referred to in paragraphs 4 and 5 shall be deemed to have been approved.

When justified by the complexity of the matter and in the absence of danger for human health, the Commission may notify the Member State concerned that the period referred to in this paragraph may be extended for a further period of up to six months.

7. When, pursuant to paragraph 6, a Member State is authorised to maintain or introduce national provisions derogating from a harmonisation measure, the Commission shall immediately examine whether to propose an adaptation to that measure.

8. When a Member State raises a specific problem on public health in a field which has been the subject of prior harmonisation measures, it shall bring it to the attention of the Commission which shall immediately examine whether to propose appropriate measures to the Council.

9. By way of derogation from the procedure laid down in Articles 258 and 259, the Commission and any Member State may bring the matter directly before the Court of Justice of the European Union if it considers that another Member State is making improper use of the powers provided for in this Article.

10. The harmonisation measures referred to above shall, in appropriate cases, include a safeguard clause authorising the Member States to take, for one or more of the non-economic reasons referred to in Article 36, provisional measures subject to a Union control procedure.

Article 115 (ex Article 94 TEC)

Without prejudice to Article 114, the Council shall, acting unanimously in accordance with a special legislative procedure and after consulting the European Parliament and the Economic and Social Committee, issue directives for the approximation of such laws, regulations or administrative provisions of the Member States as directly affect the establishment or functioning of the internal market.

Article 116 (ex Article 96 TEC)

Where the Commission finds that a difference between the provisions laid down by law, regulation or administrative action in Member States is distorting the conditions of competition in the internal market and that the resultant distortion needs to be eliminated, it shall consult the Member States concerned.

If such consultation does not result in an agreement eliminating the distortion in question, the European, Parliament and the Council, acting in accordance with the ordinary legislative procedure, shall issue the necessary directives. Any other appropriate measures provided for in the Treaties may be adopted.

Article 117 (ex Article 97 TEC)

1. Where there is a reason to fear that the adoption or amendment of a provision laid down by law, regulation or administrative action may cause distortion within the meaning of Article 116, a Member State desiring to proceed therewith shall consult the Commission. After consulting the Member States, the Commission shall recommend to the States concerned such measures as may be appropriate to avoid the distortion in question.

2. If a State desiring to introduce or amend its own provisions does not comply with the recommendation addressed to it by the Commission, other Member States shall not be required, pursuant to Article 116, to amend their own provisions in order to eliminate such distortion. If the Member State which has ignored the recommendation of the Commission causes distortion detrimental only to itself, the provisions of Article 116 shall not apply.

Article 118

In the context of the establishment and functioning of the internal market, the European Parliament and the Council, acting in accordance with the ordinary legislative procedure, shall establish measures for the creation of European intellectual property rights to provide uniform protection of intellectual property rights throughout the Union and for the setting up of centralised Union-wide authorisation, coordination and supervision arrangements.

The Council, acting in accordance with a special legislative procedure, shall by means of regulations establish language arrangements for the European intellectual property rights. The Council shall act unanimously after consulting the European Parliament.

Title VIII Economic and monetary policy

Article 119 (ex Article 4 TEC)

1. For the purposes set out in Article 3 of the Treaty on European Union, the activities of the Member States and the Union shall include, as provided in the Treaties, the adoption of an economic policy which is based on the close coordination of Member States' economic policies, on the internal market and on the definition of common objectives, and conducted in accordance with the principle of an open market economy with free competition.

2. Concurrently with the foregoing, and as provided in the Treaties and in accordance with the procedures set out therein, these activities shall include a single currency, the euro, and the definition and conduct of a single monetary policy and exchange-rate policy the primary objective of both of which shall be to maintain price stability and, without prejudice to this objective, to support the

general economic policies in the Union, in accordance with the principle of an open market economy with free competition.

3. These activities of the Member States and the Union shall entail compliance with the following guiding principles: stable prices, sound public finances and monetary conditions and a sustainable balance of payments.

Chapter 1 Economic policy

Article 120 (ex Article 98 TEC)

Member States shall conduct their economic policies with a view to contributing to the achievement of the objectives of the Union, as defined in Article 3 of the Treaty on European Union, and in the context of the broad guidelines referred to in Article 121(2). The Member States and the Union shall act in accordance with the principle of an open market economy with free competition, favouring an efficient allocation of resources, and in compliance with the principles set out in Article 119.

Article 121 (ex Article 99 TEC)

1. Member States shall regard their economic policies as a matter of common concern and shall coordinate them within the Council, in accordance with the provisions of Article 120.

2. The Council shall, on a recommendation from the Commission, formulate a draft for the broad guidelines of the economic policies of the Member States and of the Union, and shall report its findings to the European Council.

The European Council shall, acting on the basis of the report from the Council, discuss a conclusion on the broad guidelines of the economic policies of the Member States and of the Union.

On the basis of this conclusion, the Council shall adopt a recommendation setting out these broad guidelines. The Council shall inform the European Parliament of its recommendation.

3. In order to ensure closer coordination of economic policies and sustained convergence of the economic performances of the Member States, the Council shall, on the basis of reports submitted by the Commission, monitor economic developments in each of the Member States and in the Union as well as the consistency of economic policies with the broad guidelines referred to in paragraph 2, and regularly carry out an overall assessment.

For the purpose of this multilateral surveillance, Member States shall forward information to the Commission about important measures taken by them in the field of their economic policy and such other information as they deem necessary.

4. Where it is established, under the procedure referred to in paragraph 3, that the economic policies of a Member State are not consistent with the broad guidelines referred to in paragraph 2 or that they risk jeopardising the proper functioning of economic and monetary union, the Commission may address a warning to the Member State concerned. The Council, on a recommendation from the Commission, may address the necessary recommendations to the Member State concerned. The Council may, on a proposal from the Commission, decide to make its recommendations public.

Within the scope of this paragraph, the Council shall act without taking into account the vote of the member of the Council representing the Member State concerned.

A qualified majority of the other members of the Council shall be defined in accordance with Article 238(3)(a).

5. The President of the Council and the Commission shall report to the European Parliament on the results of multilateral surveillance. The President of the Council may be invited to appear before the competent committee of the European Parliament if the Council has made its recommendations public.

6. The European Parliament and the Council, acting by means of regulations in accordance with the ordinary legislative procedure, may adopt detailed rules for the multilateral surveillance procedure referred to in paragraphs 3 and 4.

Article 122 (ex Article 100 TEC)

1. Without prejudice to any other procedures provided for in the Treaties, the Council, on a proposal from the Commission, may decide, in a spirit of solidarity between Member States, upon the

measures appropriate to the economic situation, in particular if severe difficulties arise in the supply of certain products, notably in the area of energy.

2. Where a Member State is in difficulties or is seriously threatened with severe difficulties caused by natural disasters or exceptional occurrences beyond its control, the Council, on a proposal from the Commission, may grant, under certain conditions, Union financial assistance to the Member State concerned. The President of the Council shall inform the European Parliament of the decision taken.

Article 123 (ex Article 101 TEC)

1. Overdraft facilities or any other type of credit facility with the European Central Bank or with the central banks of the Member States (hereinafter referred to as 'national central banks') in favour of Union institutions, bodies, offices or agencies, central governments, regional, local or other public authorities, other bodies governed by public law, or public undertakings of Member States shall be prohibited, as shall the purchase directly from them by the European Central Bank or national central banks of debt instruments.

2. Paragraph 1 shall not apply to publicly owned credit institutions which, in the context of the supply of reserves by central banks, shall be given the same treatment by national central banks and the European Central Bank as private credit institutions.

Article 124 (ex Article 102 TEC)

Any measure, not based on prudential considerations, establishing privileged access by Union institutions, bodies, offices or agencies, central governments, regional, local or other public authorities, other bodies governed by public law, or public undertakings of Member States to financial institutions, shall be prohibited.

Article 125 (ex Article 103 TEC)

1. The Union shall not be liable for or assume the commitments of central governments, regional, local or other public authorities, other bodies governed by public law, or public undertakings of any Member State, without prejudice to mutual financial guarantees for the joint execution of a specific project. A Member State shall not be liable for or assume the commitments of central governments, regional, local or other public authorities, other bodies governed by public law, or public undertakings of another Member State, without prejudice to mutual financial guarantees for the joint execution of a specific project.

2. The Council, on a proposal from the Commission and after consulting the European Parliament, may, as required, specify definitions for the application of the prohibitions referred to in Articles 123 and 124 and in this Article.

Article 126 (ex Article 104 TEC)

1. Member States shall avoid excessive government deficits.

2. The Commission shall monitor the development of the budgetary situation and of the stock of government debt in the Member States with a view to identifying gross errors. In particular it shall examine compliance with budgetary discipline on the basis of the following two criteria:

(a) whether the ratio of the planned or actual government deficit to gross domestic product exceeds a reference value, unless:
   - either the ratio has declined substantially and continuously and reached a level that comes close to the reference value,
   - or, alternatively, the excess over the reference value is only exceptional and temporary and the ratio remains close to the reference value;

(b) whether the ratio of government debt to gross domestic product exceeds a reference value, unless the ratio is sufficiently diminishing and approaching the reference value at a satisfactory pace.

The reference values are specified in the Protocol on the excessive deficit procedure annexed to the Treaties.

3. If a Member State does not fulfil the requirements under one or both of these criteria, the Commission shall prepare a report. The report of the Commission shall also take into account

whether the government deficit exceeds government investment expenditure and take into account all other relevant factors, including the medium-term economic and budgetary position of the Member State.

The Commission may also prepare a report if, notwithstanding the fulfilment of the requirements under the criteria, it is of the opinion that there is a risk of an excessive deficit in a Member State.

4. The Economic and Financial Committee shall formulate an opinion on the report of the Commission.

5. If the Commission considers that an excessive deficit in a Member State exists or may occur, it shall address an opinion to the Member State concerned and shall inform the Council accordingly.

6. The Council shall, on a proposal from the Commission, and having considered any observations which the Member State concerned may wish to make, decide after an overall assessment whether an excessive deficit exists.

7. Where the Council decides, in accordance with paragraph 6, that an excessive deficit exists, it shall adopt, without undue delay, on a recommendation from the Commission, recommendations addressed to the Member State concerned with a view to bringing that situation to an end within a given period. Subject to the provisions of paragraph 8, these recommendations shall not be made public.

8. Where it establishes that there has been no effective action in response to its recommendations within the period laid down, the Council may make its recommendations public.

9. If a Member State persists in failing to put into practice the recommendations of the Council, the Council may decide to give notice to the Member State to take, within a specified time limit, measures for the deficit reduction which is judged necessary by the Council in order to remedy the situation.

In such a case, the Council may request the Member State concerned to submit reports in accordance with a specific timetable in order to examine the adjustment efforts of that Member State.

10. The rights to bring actions provided for in Articles 258 and 259 may not be exercised within the framework of paragraphs 1 to 9 of this Article.

11. As long as a Member State fails to comply with a decision taken in accordance with paragraph 9, the Council may decide to apply or, as the case may be, intensify one or more of the following measures:

- to require the Member State concerned to publish additional information, to be specified by the Council, before issuing bonds and securities,
- to invite the European Investment Bank to reconsider its lending policy towards the Member State concerned,
- to require the Member State concerned to make a non-interest-bearing deposit of an appropriate size with the Union until the excessive deficit has, in the view of the Council, been corrected,
- to impose fines of an appropriate size.

The President of the Council shall inform the European Parliament of the decisions taken.

12. The Council shall abrogate some or all of its decisions or recommendations referred to in paragraphs 6 to 9 and 11 to the extent that the excessive deficit in the Member State concerned has, in the view of the Council, been corrected. If the Council has previously made public recommendations, it shall, as soon as the decision under paragraph 8 has been abrogated, make a public statement that an excessive deficit in the Member State concerned no longer exists.

13. When taking the decisions or recommendations referred to in paragraphs 8, 9, 11 and 12, the Council shall act on a recommendation from the Commission.

When the Council adopts the measures referred to in paragraphs 6 to 9, 11 and 12, it shall act without taking into account the vote of the member of the Council representing the Member State concerned.

A qualified majority of the other members of the Council shall be defined in accordance with Article 238(3)(a).

14. Further provisions relating to the implementation of the procedure described in this Article are set out in the Protocol on the excessive deficit procedure annexed to the Treaties.

The Council shall, acting unanimously in accordance with a special legislative procedure and after consulting the European Parliament and the European Central Bank, adopt the appropriate provisions which shall then replace the said Protocol.

Subject to the other provisions of this paragraph, the Council shall, on a proposal from the Commission and after consulting the European Parliament, lay down detailed rules and definitions for the application of the provisions of the said Protocol.

Chapter 2 Monetary policy

Article 127 (ex Article 105 TEC)

1. The primary objective of the European System of Central Banks (hereinafter referred to as 'the ESCB') shall be to maintain price stability. Without prejudice to the objective of price stability, the ESCB shall support the general economic policies in the Union with a view to contributing to the achievement of the objectives of the Union as laid down in Article 3 of the Treaty on European Union. The ESCB shall act in accordance with the principle of an open market economy with free competition, favouring an efficient allocation of resources, and in compliance with the principles set out in Article 119.

2. The basic tasks to be carried out through the ESCB shall be:
   - to define and implement the monetary policy of the Union,
   - to conduct foreign-exchange operations consistent with the provisions of Article 219,
   - to hold and manage the official foreign reserves of the Member States,
   - to promote the smooth operation of payment systems.

3. The third indent of paragraph 2 shall be without prejudice to the holding and management by the governments of Member States of foreign-exchange working balances.

4. The European Central Bank shall be consulted:
   - on any proposed Union act in its fields of competence,
   - by national authorities regarding any draft legislative provision in its fields of competence, but within the limits and under the conditions set out by the Council in accordance with the procedure laid down in Article 129(4).

The European Central Bank may submit opinions to the appropriate Union institutions, bodies, offices or agencies or to national authorities on matters in its fields of competence.

5. The ESCB shall contribute to the smooth conduct of policies pursued by the competent authorities relating to the prudential supervision of credit institutions and the stability of the financial system.

6. The Council, acting by means of regulations in accordance with a special legislative procedure, may unanimously, and after consulting the European Parliament and the European Central Bank, confer specific tasks upon the European Central Bank concerning policies relating to the prudential supervision of credit institutions and other financial institutions with the exception of insurance undertakings.

Article 128 (ex Article 106 TEC)

1. The European Central Bank shall have the exclusive right to authorise the issue of euro banknotes within the Union. The European Central Bank and the national central banks may issue such notes. The banknotes issued by the European Central Bank and the national central banks shall be the only such notes to have the status of legal tender within the Union.

2. Member States may issue euro coins subject to approval by the European Central Bank of the volume of the issue. The Council, on a proposal from the Commission and after consulting the European Parliament and the European Central Bank, may adopt measures to harmonise the denominations and technical specifications of all coins intended for circulation to the extent necessary to permit their smooth circulation within the Union.

Article 129 (ex Article 107 TEC)

1. The ESCB shall be governed by the decision-making bodies of the European Central Bank which shall be the Governing Council and the Executive Board.

2. The Statute of the European System of Central Banks and of the European Central Bank (hereinafter referred to as 'the Statute of the ESCB and of the ECB') is laid down in a Protocol annexed to the Treaties.

3. Articles 5.1, 5.2, 5.3, 17, 18, 19.1, 22, 23, 24, 26, 32.2, 32.3, 32.4, 32.6, 33.1(a) and 36 of the Statute of the ESCB and of the ECB may be amended by the European Parliament and the Council, acting in accordance with the ordinary legislative procedure. They shall act either on a recommendation from the European Central Bank and after consulting the Commission or on a proposal from the Commission and after consulting the European Central Bank.

4. The Council, either on a proposal from the Commission and after consulting the European Parliament and the European Central Bank or on a recommendation from the European Central Bank and after consulting the European Parliament and the Commission, shall adopt the provisions referred to in Articles 4, 5.4, 19.2, 20, 28.1, 29.2, 30.4 and 34.3 of the Statute of the ESCB and of the ECB.

Article 130 (ex Article 108 TEC)

When exercising the powers and carrying out the tasks and duties conferred upon them by the Treaties and the Statute of the ESCB and of the ECB, neither the European Central Bank, nor a national central bank, nor any member of their decision-making bodies shall seek or take instructions from Union institutions, bodies, offices or agencies, from any government of a Member State or from any other body. The Union institutions, bodies, offices or agencies and the governments of the Member States undertake to respect this principle and not to seek to influence the members of the decision-making bodies of the European Central Bank or of the national central banks in the performance of their tasks.

Article 131 (ex Article 109 TEC)

Each Member State shall ensure that its national legislation including the statutes of its national central bank is compatible with the Treaties and the Statute of the ESCB and of the ECB.

Article 132 (ex Article 110 TEC)

1. In order to carry out the tasks entrusted to the ESCB, the European Central Bank shall, in accordance with the provisions of the Treaties and under the conditions laid down in the Statute of the ESCB and of the ECB:

- make regulations to the extent necessary to implement the tasks defined in Article 3.1, first indent, Articles 19.1, 22 and 25.2 of the Statute of the ESCB and of the ECB in cases which shall be laid down in the acts of the Council referred to in Article 129(4),
- take decisions necessary for carrying out the tasks entrusted to the ESCB under the Treaties and the Statute of the ESCB and of the ECB,
- make recommendations and deliver opinions.

2. The European Central Bank may decide to publish its decisions, recommendations and opinions.

3. Within the limits and under the conditions adopted by the Council under the procedure laid down in Article 129(4), the European Central Bank shall be entitled to impose fines or periodic penalty payments on undertakings for failure to comply with obligations under its regulations and decisions.

Article 133

Without prejudice to the powers of the European Central Bank, the European Parliament and the Council, acting in accordance with the ordinary legislative procedure, shall lay down the measures necessary for the use of the euro as the single currency. Such measures shall be adopted after consultation of the European Central Bank.

Chapter 3 Institutional provisions

Article 134 (ex Article 114 TEC)

1. In order to promote coordination of the policies of Member States to the full extent needed for the functioning of the internal market, an Economic and Financial Committee is hereby set up.

2. The Economic and Financial Committee shall have the following tasks:
- to deliver opinions at the request of the Council or of the Commission, or on its own initiative for submission to those institutions,
- to keep under review the economic and financial situation of the Member States and of the Union and to report regularly thereon to the Council and to the Commission, in particular on financial relations with third countries and international institutions,
- without prejudice to Article 240, to contribute to the preparation of the work of the Council referred to in Articles 66, 75, 121(2), (3), (4) and (6), 122, 124, 125, 126, 127(6), 128(2), 129(3) and (4), 138, 140(2) and (3), 143, 144(2) and (3), and in Article 219, and to carry out other advisory and preparatory tasks assigned to it by the Council,
- to examine, at least once a year, the situation regarding the movement of capital and the freedom of payments, as they result from the application of the Treaties* and of measures adopted by the Council; the examination shall cover all measures relating to capital movements and payments; the Committee shall report to the Commission and to the Council on the outcome of this examination.

The Member States, the Commission and the European Central Bank shall each appoint no more than two members of the Committee.

3. The Council shall, on a proposal from the Commission and after consulting the European Central Bank and the Committee referred to in this Article, lay down detailed provisions concerning the composition of the Economic and Financial Committee. The President of the Council shall inform the European Parliament of such a decision.

4. In addition to the tasks set out in paragraph 2, if and as long as there are Member States with a derogation as referred to in Article 139, the Committee shall keep under review the monetary and financial situation and the general payments system of those Member States and report regularly thereon to the Council and to the Commission.

Article 135 (ex Article 115 TEC)

For matters within the scope of Articles 121(4), 126 with the exception of paragraph 14, 138, 140(1), 140(2), first subparagraph, 140(3) and 219, the Council or a Member State may request the Commission to make a recommendation or a proposal, as appropriate. The Commission shall examine this request and submit its conclusions to the Council without delay.

Chapter 4 Provisions specific to Member States whose currency is the euro

Article 136

1. In order to ensure the proper functioning of economic and monetary union, and in accordance with the relevant provisions of the Treaties, the Council shall, in accordance with the relevant procedure from among those referred to in Articles 121 and 126, with the exception of the procedure set out in Article 126(14), adopt measures specific to those Member States whose currency is the euro:

(a) to strengthen the coordination and surveillance of their budgetary discipline;

(b) to set out economic policy guidelines for them, while ensuring that they are compatible with those adopted for the whole of the Union and are kept under surveillance.

2. For those measures set out in paragraph 1, only members of the Council representing Member States whose currency is the euro shall take part in the vote.

A qualified majority of the said members shall be defined in accordance with Article 238(3)(a).

Article 137

Arrangements for meetings between ministers of those Member States whose currency is the euro are laid down by the Protocol on the Euro Group.

Article 138 (ex Article 111(4), TEC)

1. In order to secure the euro's place in the international monetary system, the Council, on a proposal from the Commission, shall adopt a decision establishing common positions on matters of particular interest for economic and monetary union within the competent international financial institutions and conferences. The Council shall act after consulting the European Central Bank.

2. The Council, on a proposal from the Commission, may adopt appropriate measures to ensure unified representation within the international financial institutions and conferences. The Council shall act after consulting the European Central Bank.

3. For the measures referred to in paragraphs 1 and 2, only members of the Council representing Member States whose currency is the euro shall take part in the vote.

A qualified majority of the said members shall be defined in accordance with Article 238(3)(a).

Chapter 5 Transitional provisions

Article 139

1. Member States in respect of which the Council has not decided that they fulfil the necessary conditions for the adoption of the euro shall hereinafter be referred to as 'Member States with a derogation'.

2. The following provisions of the Treaties shall not apply to Member States with a derogation:
   - (a) adoption of the parts of the broad economic policy guidelines which concern the euro area generally (Article 121(2));
   - (b) coercive means of remedying excessive deficits (Article 126(9) and (11));
   - (c) the objectives and tasks of the ESCB (Article 127(1) to (3) and (5));
   - (d) issue of the euro (Article 128);
   - (e) acts of the European Central Bank (Article 132);
   - (f) measures governing the use of the euro (Article 133);
   - (g) monetary agreements and other measures relating to exchange-rate policy (Article 219);
   - (h) appointment of members of the Executive Board of the European Central Bank (Article 283(2));
   - (i) decisions establishing common positions on issues of particular relevance for economic and monetary union within the competent international financial institutions and conferences (Article 138(1));
   - (j) measures to ensure unified representation within the international financial institutions and conferences (Article 138(2)).

In the Articles referred to in points (a) to (j), 'Member States' shall therefore mean Member States whose currency is the euro.

3. Under Chapter IX of the Statute of the ESCB and of the ECB, Member States with a derogation and their national central banks are excluded from rights and obligations within the ESCB.

4. The voting rights of members of the Council representing Member States with a derogation shall be suspended for the adoption by the Council of the measures referred to in the Articles listed in paragraph 2, and in the following instances:
   - (a) recommendations made to those Member States whose currency is the euro in the framework of multilateral surveillance, including on stability programmes and warnings (Article 121(4));
   - (b) measures relating to excessive deficits concerning those Member States whose currency is the euro (Article 126(6), (7), (8), (12) and (13)).

A qualified majority of the other members of the Council shall be defined in accordance with Article 238(3)(a).

Article 140 (ex Articles 121(1), 122(2), second sentence, and 123(5) TEC)

1. At least once every two years, or at the request of a Member State with a derogation, the Commission and the European Central Bank shall report to the Council on the progress made by the Member States with a derogation in fulfilling their obligations regarding the achievement of economic

and monetary union. These reports shall include an examination of the compatibility between the national legislation of each of these Member States, including the statutes of its national central bank, and Articles 130 and 131 and the Statute of the ESCB and of the ECB. The reports shall also examine the achievement of a high degree of sustainable convergence by reference to the fulfilment by each Member State of the following criteria:

- the achievement of a high degree of price stability; this will be apparent from a rate of inflation which is close to that of, at most, the three best performing Member States in terms of price stability,
- the sustainability of the government financial position; this will be apparent from having achieved a government budgetary position without a deficit that is excessive as determined in accordance with Article 126(6),
- the observance of the normal fluctuation margins provided for by the exchange-rate mechanism of the European Monetary System, for at least two years, without devaluing against the euro,
- the durability of convergence achieved by the Member State with a derogation and of its participation in the exchange-rate mechanism being reflected in the long-term interest-rate levels.

The four criteria mentioned in this paragraph and the relevant periods over which they are to be respected are developed further in a Protocol annexed to the Treaties. The reports of the Commission and the European Central Bank shall also take account of the results of the integration of markets, the situation and development of the balances of payments on current account and an examination of the development of unit labour costs and other price indices.

2. After consulting the European Parliament and after discussion in the European Council, the Council shall, on a proposal from the Commission, decide which Member States with a derogation fulfil the necessary conditions on the basis of the criteria set out in paragraph 1, and abrogate the derogations of the Member States concerned.

The Council shall act having received a recommendation of a qualified majority of those among its members representing Member States whose currency is the euro. These members shall act within six months of the Council receiving the Commission's proposal.

The qualified majority of the said members, as referred to in the second subparagraph, shall be defined in accordance with Article 238(3)(a).

3. If it is decided, in accordance with the procedure set out in paragraph 2, to abrogate a derogation, the Council shall, acting with the unanimity of the Member States whose currency is the euro and the Member State concerned, on a proposal from the Commission and after consulting the European Central Bank, irrevocably fix the rate at which the euro shall be substituted for the currency of the Member State concerned, and take the other measures necessary for the introduction of the euro as the single currency in the Member State concerned.

Article 141 (ex Articles 123(3) and 117(2) first five indents, TEC)

1. If and as long as there are Member States with a derogation, and without prejudice to Article 129(1), the General Council of the European Central Bank referred to in Article 44 of the Statute of the ESCB and of the ECB shall be constituted as a third decision-making body of the European Central Bank.

2. If and as long as there are Member States with a derogation, the European Central Bank shall, as regards those Member States:

- strengthen cooperation between the national central banks,
- strengthen the coordination of the monetary policies of the Member States, with the aim of ensuring price stability,
- monitor the functioning of the exchange-rate mechanism,
- hold consultations concerning issues falling within the competence of the national central banks and affecting the stability of financial institutions and markets,
- carry out the former tasks of the European Monetary Cooperation Fund which had subsequently been taken over by the European Monetary Institute.

Article 142 (ex Article 124(1) TEC)

Each Member State with a derogation shall treat its exchange-rate policy as a matter of common interest. In so doing, Member States shall take account of the experience acquired in cooperation within the framework of the exchange-rate mechanism.

Article 143 (ex Article 119 TEC)

1. Where a Member State with a derogation is in difficulties or is seriously threatened with difficulties as regards its balance of payments either as a result of an overall disequilibrium in its balance of payments, or as a result of the type of currency at its disposal, and where such difficulties are liable in particular to jeopardise the functioning of the internal market or the implementation of the common commercial policy, the Commission shall immediately investigate the position of the State in question and the action which, making use of all the means at its disposal, that State has taken or may take in accordance with the provisions of the Treaties. The Commission shall state what measures it recommends the State concerned to take.

If the action taken by a Member State with a derogation and the measures suggested by the Commission do not prove sufficient to overcome the difficulties which have arisen or which threaten, the Commission shall, after consulting the Economic and Financial Committee, recommend to the Council the granting of mutual assistance and appropriate methods therefore.

The Commission shall keep the Council regularly informed of the situation and of how it is developing.

2. The Council shall grant such mutual assistance; it shall adopt directives or decisions laying down the conditions and details of such assistance, which may take such forms as:

(a) a concerted approach to or within any other international organisations to which Member States with a derogation may have recourse;

(b) measures needed to avoid deflection of trade where the Member State with a derogation which is in difficulties maintains or reintroduces quantitative restrictions against third countries;

(c) the granting of limited credits by other Member States, subject to their agreement.

3. If the mutual assistance recommended by the Commission is not granted by the Council or if the mutual assistance granted and the measures taken are insufficient, the Commission shall authorise the Member State with a derogation which is in difficulties to take protective measures, the conditions and details of which the Commission shall determine.

Such authorisation may be revoked and such conditions and details may be changed by the Council.

Article 144 (ex Article 120 TEC)

1. Where a sudden crisis in the balance of payments occurs and a decision within the meaning of Article 143(2) is not immediately taken, a Member State with a derogation may, as a precaution, take the necessary protective measures. Such measures must cause the least possible disturbance in the functioning of the internal market and must not be wider in scope than is strictly necessary to remedy the sudden difficulties which have arisen.

2. The Commission and the other Member States shall be informed of such protective measures not later than when they enter into force. The Commission may recommend to the Council the granting of mutual assistance under Article 143.

3. After the Commission has delivered a recommendation and the Economic and Financial Committee has been consulted, the Council may decide that the Member State concerned shall amend, suspend or abolish the protective measures referred to above.

Title IX Employment

Article 145 (ex Article 125 TEC)

Member States and the Union shall, in accordance with this Title, work towards developing a coordinated strategy for employment and particularly for promoting a skilled, trained and adaptable workforce and labour markets responsive to economic change with a view to achieving the objectives defined in Article 3 of the Treaty on European Union.

Article 146 (ex Article 126 TEC)

1. Member States, through their employment policies, shall contribute to the achievement of the objectives referred to in Article 145 in a way consistent with the broad guidelines of the economic policies of the Member States and of the Union adopted pursuant to Article 121(2).

2. Member States, having regard to national practices related to the responsibilities of management and labour, shall regard promoting employment as a matter of common concern and shall coordinate their action in this respect within the Council, in accordance with the provisions of Article 148.

Article 147 (ex Article 127 TEC)

1. The Union shall contribute to a high level of employment by encouraging cooperation between Member States and by supporting and, if necessary, complementing their action. In doing so, the competences of the Member States shall be respected.

2. The objective of a high level of employment shall be taken into consideration in the formulation and implementation of Union policies and activities.

Article 148 (ex Article 128 TEC)

1. The European Council shall each year consider the employment situation in the Union and adopt conclusions thereon, on the basis of a joint annual report by the Council and the Commission.

2. On the basis of the conclusions of the European Council, the Council, on a proposal from the Commission and after consulting the European Parliament, the Economic and Social Committee, the Committee of the Regions and the Employment Committee referred to in Article 150, shall each year draw up guidelines which the Member States shall take into account in their employment policies. These guidelines shall be consistent with the broad guidelines adopted pursuant to Article 121(2).

3. Each Member State shall provide the Council and the Commission with an annual report on the principal measures taken to implement its employment policy in the light of the guidelines for employment as referred to in paragraph 2.

4. The Council, on the basis of the reports referred to in paragraph 3 and having received the views of the Employment Committee, shall each year carry out an examination of the implementation of the employment policies of the Member States in the light of the guidelines for employment. The Council, on a recommendation from the Commission, may, if it considers it appropriate in the light of that examination, make recommendations to Member States.

5. On the basis of the results of that examination, the Council and the Commission shall make a joint annual report to the European Council on the employment situation in the Union and on the implementation of the guidelines for employment.

Article 149 (ex Article 129 TEC)

The European Parliament and the Council, acting in accordance with the ordinary legislative procedure and after consulting the Economic and Social Committee and the Committee of the Regions, may adopt incentive measures designed to encourage cooperation between Member States and to support their action in the field of employment through initiatives aimed at developing exchanges of information and best practices, providing comparative analysis and advice as well as promoting innovative approaches and evaluating experiences, in particular by recourse to pilot projects.

Those measures shall not include harmonisation of the laws and regulations of the Member States.

Article 150 (ex Article 130 TEC)

The Council, acting by a simple majority after consulting the European Parliament, shall establish an Employment Committee with advisory status to promote coordination between Member States on employment and labour market policies. The tasks of the Committee shall be:

- to monitor the employment situation and employment policies in the Member States and the Union,

– without prejudice to Article 240, to formulate opinions at the request of either the Council or the Commission or on its own initiative, and to contribute to the preparation of the Council proceedings referred to in Article 148.

In fulfilling its mandate, the Committee shall consult management and labour.

Each Member State and the Commission shall appoint two members of the Committee.

Title X Social policy

Article 151 (ex Article 136 TEC)

The Union and the Member States, having in mind fundamental social rights such as those set out in the European Social Charter signed at Turin on 18 October 1961 and in the 1989 Community Charter of the Fundamental Social Rights of Workers, shall have as their objectives the promotion of employment, improved living and working conditions, so as to make possible their harmonisation while the improvement is being maintained, proper social protection, dialogue between management and labour, the development of human resources with a view to lasting high employment and the combating of exclusion.

To this end the Union and the Member States shall implement measures which take account of the diverse forms of national practices, in particular in the field of contractual relations, and the need to maintain the competitiveness of the Union economy.

They believe that such a development will ensue not only from the functioning of the internal market, which will favour the harmonisation of social systems, but also from the procedures provided for in the Treaties and from the approximation of provisions laid down by law, regulation or administrative action.

Article 152

The Union recognises and promotes the role of the social partners at its level, taking into account the diversity of national systems. It shall facilitate dialogue between the social partners, respecting their autonomy.

The Tripartite Social Summit for Growth and Employment shall contribute to social dialogue.

Article 153 (ex Article 137 TEC)

1. With a view to achieving the objectives of Article 151, the Union shall support and complement the activities of the Member States in the following fields:
   (a) improvement in particular of the working environment to protect workers' health and safety;
   (b) working conditions;
   (c) social security and social protection of workers;
   (d) protection of workers where their employment contract is terminated;
   (e) the information and consultation of workers;
   (f) representation and collective defence of the interests of workers and employers, including co-determination, subject to paragraph 5;
   (g) conditions of employment for third-country nationals legally residing in Union territory;
   (h) the integration of persons excluded from the labour market, without prejudice to Article 166;
   (i) equality between men and women with regard to labour market opportunities and treatment at work;
   (j) the combating of social exclusion;
   (k) the modernisation of social protection systems without prejudice to point (c).
2. To this end, the European Parliament and the Council:
   (a) may adopt measures designed to encourage cooperation between Member States through initiatives aimed at improving knowledge, developing exchanges of information and best practices, promoting innovative approaches and evaluating experiences, excluding any harmonisation of the laws and regulations of the Member States;

(b) may adopt, in the fields referred to in paragraph 1(a) to (i), by means of directives, minimum requirements for gradual implementation, having regard to the conditions and technical rules obtaining in each of the Member States. Such directives shall avoid imposing administrative, financial and legal constraints in a way which would hold back the creation and development of small and medium-sized undertakings.

The European Parliament and the Council shall act in accordance with the ordinary legislative procedure after consulting the Economic and Social Committee and the Committee of the Regions.

In the fields referred to in paragraph 1(c), (d), (f) and (g), the Council shall act unanimously, in accordance with a special legislative procedure, after consulting the European Parliament and the said Committees.

The Council, acting unanimously on a proposal from the Commission, after consulting the European Parliament, may decide to render the ordinary legislative procedure applicable to paragraph 1(d), (f) and (g).

3. A Member State may entrust management and labour, at their joint request, with the implementation of directives adopted pursuant to paragraph 2, or, where appropriate, with the implementation of a Council decision adopted in accordance with Article 155.

In this case, it shall ensure that, no later than the date on which a directive or a decision must be transposed or implemented, management and labour have introduced the necessary measures by agreement, the Member State concerned being required to take any necessary measure enabling it at any time to be in a position to guarantee the results imposed by that directive or that decision.

4. The provisions adopted pursuant to this Article:

- shall not affect the right of Member States to define the fundamental principles of their social security systems and must not significantly affect the financial equilibrium thereof,
- shall not prevent any Member State from maintaining or introducing more stringent protective measures compatible with the Treaties.

5. The provisions of this Article shall not apply to pay, the right of association, the right to strike or the right to impose lock-outs.

Article 154 (ex Article 138 TEC)

1. The Commission shall have the task of promoting the consultation of management and labour at Union level and shall take any relevant measure to facilitate their dialogue by ensuring balanced support for the parties.

2. To this end, before submitting proposals in the social policy field, the Commission shall consult management and labour on the possible direction of Union action.

3. If, after such consultation, the Commission considers Union action advisable, it shall consult management and labour on the content of the envisaged proposal.

Management and labour shall forward to the Commission an opinion or, where appropriate, a recommendation.

4. On the occasion of the consultation referred to in paragraphs 2 and 3, management and labour may inform the Commission of their wish to initiate the process provided for in Article 155. The duration of this process shall not exceed nine months, unless the management and labour concerned and the Commission decide jointly to extend it.

Article 155 (ex Article 139 TEC)

1. Should management and labour so desire, the dialogue between them at Union level may lead to contractual relations, including agreements.

2. Agreements concluded at Union level shall be implemented either in accordance with the procedures and practices specific to management and labour and the Member States or, in matters covered by Article 153, at the joint request of the signatory parties, by a Council decision on a proposal from the Commission. The European Parliament shall be informed.

The Council shall act unanimously where the agreement in question contains one or more provisions relating to one of the areas for which unanimity is required pursuant to Article 153(2).

Article 156 (ex Article 140 TEC)

With a view to achieving the objectives of Article 151 and without prejudice to the other provisions of the Treaties, the Commission shall encourage cooperation between the Member States and facilitate the coordination of their action in all social policy fields under this Chapter, particularly in matters relating to:

- employment,
- labour law and working conditions,
- basic and advanced vocational training,
- social security,
- prevention of occupational accidents and diseases,
- occupational hygiene,
- the right of association and collective bargaining between employers and workers.

To this end, the Commission shall act in close contact with Member States by making studies, delivering opinions and arranging consultations both on problems arising at national level and on those of concern to international organisations, in particular initiatives aiming at the establishment of guidelines and indicators, the organisation of exchange of best practice, and the preparation of the necessary elements for periodic monitoring and evaluation. The European Parliament shall be kept fully informed.

Before delivering the opinions provided for in this Article, the Commission shall consult the Economic and Social Committee.

Article 157 (ex Article 141 TEC)

1. Each Member State shall ensure that the principle of equal pay for male and female workers for equal work or work of equal value is applied.

2. For the purpose of this Article, 'pay' means the ordinary basic or minimum wage or salary and any other consideration, whether in cash or in kind, which the worker receives directly or indirectly, in respect of his employment, from his employer.

Equal pay without discrimination based on sex means:

(a) that pay for the same work at piece rates shall be calculated on the basis of the same unit of measurement;

(b) that pay for work at time rates shall be the same for the same job.

3. The European Parliament and the Council, acting in accordance with the ordinary legislative procedure, and after consulting the Economic and Social Committee, shall adopt measures to ensure the application of the principle of equal opportunities and equal treatment of men and women in matters of employment and occupation, including the principle of equal pay for equal work or work of equal value.

4. With a view to ensuring full equality in practice between men and women in working life, the principle of equal treatment shall not prevent any Member State from maintaining or adopting measures providing for specific advantages in order to make it easier for the underrepresented sex to pursue a vocational activity or to prevent or compensate for disadvantages in professional careers.

Article 158 (ex Article 142 TEC)

Member States shall endeavour to maintain the existing equivalence between paid holiday schemes.

Article 159 (ex Article 143 TEC)

The Commission shall draw up a report each year on progress in achieving the objectives of Article 151, including the demographic situation in the Union. It shall forward the report to the European Parliament, the Council and the Economic and Social Committee.

Article 160 (ex Article 144 TEC)

The Council, acting by a simple majority after consulting the European Parliament, shall establish a Social Protection Committee with advisory status to promote cooperation on social protection policies between Member States and with the Commission. The tasks of the Committee shall be:

- to monitor the social situation and the development of social protection policies in the Member States and the Union,

- to promote exchanges of information, experience and good practice between Member States and with the Commission,
- without prejudice to Article 240, to prepare reports, formulate opinions or undertake other work within its fields of competence, at the request of either the Council or the Commission or on its own initiative.

In fulfilling its mandate, the Committee shall establish appropriate contacts with management and labour.

Each Member State and the Commission shall appoint two members of the Committee.

Article 161 (ex Article 145 TEC)

The Commission shall include a separate chapter on social developments within the Union in its annual report to the European Parliament.

The European Parliament may invite the Commission to draw up reports on any particular problems concerning social conditions.

Title XI The European Social Fund

Article 162 (ex Article 146 TEC)

In order to improve employment opportunities for workers in the internal market and to contribute thereby to raising the standard of living, a European Social Fund is hereby established in accordance with the provisions set out below; it shall aim to render the employment of workers easier and to increase their geographical and occupational mobility within the Union, and to facilitate their adaptation to industrial changes and to changes in production systems, in particular through vocational training and retraining.

Article 163 (ex Article 147 TEC)

The Fund shall be administered by the Commission.

The Commission shall be assisted in this task by a Committee presided over by a Member of the Commission and composed of representatives of governments, trade unions and employers' organisations.

Article 164 (ex Article 148 TEC)

The European Parliament and the Council, acting in accordance with the ordinary legislative procedure and after consulting the Economic and Social Committee and the Committee of the Regions, shall adopt implementing regulations relating to the European Social Fund.

Title XII Education, vocational training, youth and sport

Article 165 (ex Article 149 TEC)

1. The Union shall contribute to the development of quality education by encouraging cooperation between Member States and, if necessary, by supporting and supplementing their action, while fully respecting the responsibility of the Member States for the content of teaching and the organisation of education systems and their cultural and linguistic diversity.

The Union shall contribute to the promotion of European sporting issues, while taking account of the specific nature of sport, its structures based on voluntary activity and its social and educational function.

2. Union action shall be aimed at:
   - developing the European dimension in education, particularly through the teaching and dissemination of the languages of the Member States,
   - encouraging mobility of students and teachers, by encouraging *inter alia*, the academic recognition of diplomas and periods of study,
   - promoting cooperation between educational establishments,

- developing exchanges of information and experience on issues common to the education systems of the Member States,
- encouraging the development of youth exchanges and of exchanges of socio-educational instructors, and encouraging the participation of young people in democratic life in Europe,
- encouraging the development of distance education,
- developing the European dimension in sport, by promoting fairness and openness in sporting competitions and cooperation between bodies responsible for sports, and by protecting the physical and moral integrity of sportsmen and sportswomen, especially the youngest sportsmen and sportswomen.

3. The Union and the Member States shall foster cooperation with third countries and the competent international organisations in the field of education and sport, in particular the Council of Europe.

4. In order to contribute to the achievement of the objectives referred to in this Article:

- the European Parliament and the Council, acting in accordance with the ordinary legislative procedure, after consulting the Economic and Social Committee and the Committee of the Regions, shall adopt incentive measures, excluding any harmonisation of the laws and regulations of the Member States,
- the Council, on a proposal from the Commission, shall adopt recommendations.

Article 166 (ex Article 150 TEC)

1. The Union shall implement a vocational training policy which shall support and supplement the action of the Member States, while fully respecting the responsibility of the Member States for the content and organisation of vocational training.

2. Union action shall aim to:

- facilitate adaptation to industrial changes, in particular through vocational training and retraining,
- improve initial and continuing vocational training in order to facilitate vocational integration and reintegration into the labour market,
- facilitate access to vocational training and encourage mobility of instructors and trainees and particularly young people,
- stimulate cooperation on training between educational or training establishments and firms,
- develop exchanges of information and experience on issues common to the training systems of the Member States.

3. The Union and the Member States shall foster cooperation with third countries and the competent international organisations in the sphere of vocational training.

4. The European Parliament and the Council, acting in accordance with the ordinary legislative procedure and after consulting the Economic and Social Committee and the Committee of the Regions, shall adopt measures to contribute to the achievement of the objectives referred to in this Article, excluding any harmonisation of the laws and regulations of the Member States, and the Council, on a proposal from the Commission, shall adopt recommendations.

Title XIII Culture

Article 167 (ex Article 151 TEC)

1. The Union shall contribute to the flowering of the cultures of the Member States, while respecting their national and regional diversity and at the same time bringing the common cultural heritage to the fore.

2. Action by the Union shall be aimed at encouraging cooperation between Member States and, if necessary, supporting and supplementing their action in the following areas:

- improvement of the knowledge and dissemination of the culture and history of the European peoples,

- conservation and safeguarding of cultural heritage of European significance,
- non-commercial cultural exchanges,
- artistic and literary creation, including in the audiovisual sector.

3. The Union and the Member States shall foster cooperation with third countries and the competent international organisations in the sphere of culture, in particular the Council of Europe.

4. The Union shall take cultural aspects into account in its action under other provisions of the Treaties, in particular in order to respect and to promote the diversity of its cultures.

5. In order to contribute to the achievement of the objectives referred to in this Article:

- the European Parliament and the Council acting in accordance with the ordinary legislative procedure and after consulting the Committee of the Regions, shall adopt incentive measures, excluding any harmonisation of the laws and regulations of the Member States.
- the Council, on a proposal from the Commission, shall adopt recommendations.

Title XIV Public health

Article 168 (ex Article 152 TEC)

1. A high level of human health protection shall be ensured in the definition and implementation of all Union policies and activities.

Union action, which shall complement national policies, shall be directed towards improving public health, preventing physical and mental illness and diseases, and obviating sources of danger to physical and mental health. Such action shall cover the fight against the major health scourges, by promoting research into their causes, their transmission and their prevention, as well as health information and education, and monitoring, early warning of and combating serious cross-border threats to health.

The Union shall complement the Member States' action in reducing drugs-related health damage, including information and prevention.

2. The Union shall encourage cooperation between the Member States in the areas referred to in this Article and, if necessary, lend support to their action. It shall in particular encourage cooperation between the Member States to improve the complementarity of their health services in cross-border areas.

Member States shall, in liaison with the Commission, coordinate among themselves their policies and programmes in the areas referred to in paragraph 1. The Commission may, in close contact with the Member States, take any useful initiative to promote such coordination, in particular initiatives aiming at the establishment of guidelines and indicators, the organisation of exchange of best practice, and the preparation of the necessary elements for periodic monitoring and evaluation. The European Parliament shall be kept fully informed.

3. The Union and the Member States shall foster cooperation with third countries and the competent international organisations in the sphere of public health.

4. By way of derogation from Article 2(5) and Article 6(a) and in accordance with Article 4(2)(k) the European Parliament and the Council, acting in accordance with the ordinary legislative procedure and after consulting the Economic and Social Committee and the Committee of the Regions, shall contribute to the achievement of the objectives referred to in this Article through adopting in order to meet common safety concerns:

(a) measures setting high standards of quality and safety of organs and substances of human origin, blood and blood derivatives; these measures shall not prevent any Member State from maintaining or introducing more stringent protective measures;

(b) measures in the veterinary and phytosanitary fields which have as their direct objective the protection of public health;

(c) measures setting high standards of quality and safety for medicinal products and devices for medical use.

5. The European Parliament and the Council, acting in accordance with the ordinary legislative procedure and after consulting the Economic and Social Committee and the Committee of the Regions, may also adopt incentive measures designed to protect and improve human health and in

particular to combat the major cross-border health scourges, measures concerning monitoring, early warning of and combating serious cross-border threats to health, and measures which have as their direct objective the protection of public health regarding tobacco and the abuse of alcohol, excluding any harmonisation of the laws and regulations of the Member States.

6. The Council, on a proposal from the Commission, may also adopt recommendations for the purposes set out in this Article.

7. Union action shall respect the responsibilities of the Member States for the definition of their health policy and for the organisation and delivery of health services and medical care. The responsibilities of the Member States shall include the management of health services and medical care and the allocation of the resources assigned to them. The measures referred to in paragraph 4(a) shall not affect national provisions on the donation or medical use of organs and blood.

Title XV Consumer protection

Article 169 (ex Article 153 TEC)

1. In order to promote the interests of consumers and to ensure a high level of consumer protection, the Union shall contribute to protecting the health, safety and economic interests of consumers, as well as to promoting their right to information, education and to organise themselves in order to safeguard their interests.

2. The Union shall contribute to the attainment of the objectives referred to in paragraph 1 through:

(a) measures adopted pursuant to Article 114 in the context of the completion of the internal market;

(b) measures which support, supplement and monitor the policy pursued by the Member States.

3. The European Parliament and the Council, acting in accordance with the ordinary legislative procedure and after consulting the Economic and Social Committee, shall adopt the measures referred to in paragraph 2(b).

4. Measures adopted pursuant to paragraph 3 shall not prevent any Member State from maintaining or introducing more stringent protective measures. Such measures must be compatible with the Treaties. The Commission shall be notified of them.

Title XVI Trans-European networks

Article 170 (ex Article 154 TEC)

1. To help achieve the objectives referred to in Articles 26 and 174 and to enable citizens of the Union, economic operators and regional and local communities to derive full benefit from the setting-up of an area without internal frontiers, the Union shall contribute to the establishment and development of trans-European networks in the areas of transport, telecommunications and energy infrastructures.

2. Within the framework of a system of open and competitive markets, action by the Union shall aim at promoting the interconnection and interoperability of national networks as well as access to such networks. It shall take account in particular of the need to link island, landlocked and peripheral regions with the central regions of the Union.

Article 171 (ex Article 155 TEC)

1. In order to achieve the objectives referred to in Article 170, the Union:

– shall establish a series of guidelines covering the objectives, priorities and broad lines of measures envisaged in the sphere of trans-European networks; these guidelines shall identify projects of common interest,

- shall implement any measures that may prove necessary to ensure the interoperability of the networks, in particular in the field of technical standardisation,
- may support projects of common interest supported by Member States, which are identified in the framework of the guidelines referred to in the first indent, particularly through feasibility studies, loan guarantees or interest-rate subsidies; the Union may also contribute, through the Cohesion Fund set up pursuant to Article 177, to the financing of specific projects in Member States in the area of transport infrastructure.

The Union's activities shall take into account the potential economic viability of the projects.

2. Member States shall, in liaison with the Commission, coordinate among themselves the policies pursued at national level which may have a significant impact on the achievement of the objectives referred to in Article 170. The Commission may, in close cooperation with the Member State, take any useful initiative to promote such coordination.

3. The Union may decide to cooperate with third countries to promote projects of mutual interest and to ensure the interoperability of networks.

Article 172 (ex Article 156 TEC)

The guidelines and other measures referred to in Article 171(1) shall be adopted by the European Parliament and the Council, acting in accordance with the ordinary legislative procedure and after consulting the Economic and Social Committee and the Committee of the Regions.

Guidelines and projects of common interest which relate to the territory of a Member State shall require the approval of the Member State concerned.

Title XVII Industry

Article 173 (ex Article 157 TEC)

1. The Union and the Member States shall ensure that the conditions necessary for the competitiveness of the Union's industry exist.

For that purpose, in accordance with a system of open and competitive markets, their action shall be aimed at:

- speeding up the adjustment of industry to structural changes,
- encouraging an environment favourable to initiative and to the development of undertakings throughout the Union, particularly small and medium-sized undertakings,
- encouraging an environment favourable to cooperation between undertakings,
- fostering better exploitation of the industrial potential of policies of innovation, research and technological development.

2. The Member States shall consult each other in liaison with the Commission and, where necessary, shall coordinate their action. The Commission may take any useful initiative to promote such coordination, in particular initiatives aiming at the establishment of guidelines and indicators, the organisation of exchange of best practice, and the preparation of the necessary elements for periodic monitoring and evaluation. The European Parliament shall be kept fully informed.

3. The Union shall contribute to the achievement of the objectives set out in paragraph 1 through the policies and activities it pursues under other provisions of the Treaties. The European Parliament and the Council, acting in accordance with the ordinary legislative procedure and after consulting the Economic and Social Committee, may decide on specific measures in support of action taken in the Member States to achieve the objectives set out in paragraph 1, excluding any harmonisation of the laws and regulations of the Member States.

This Title shall not provide a basis for the introduction by the Union of any measure which could lead to a distortion of competition or contains tax provisions or provisions relating to the rights and interests of employed persons.

Title XVIII Economic, social and territorial cohesion

Article 174 (ex Article 158 TEC)

In order to promote its overall harmonious development, the Union shall develop and pursue its actions leading to the strengthening of its economic, social and territorial cohesion.

In particular, the Union shall aim at reducing disparities between the levels of development of the various regions and the backwardness of the least favoured regions.

Among the regions concerned, particular attention shall be paid to rural areas, areas affected by industrial transition, and regions which suffer from severe and permanent natural or demographic handicaps such as the northernmost regions with very low population density and island, cross-border and mountain regions.

Article 175 (ex Article 159 TEC)

Member States shall conduct their economic policies and shall coordinate them in such a way as, in addition, to attain the objectives set out in Article 174. The formulation and implementation of the Union's policies and actions and the implementation of the internal market shall take into account the objectives set out in Article 174 and shall contribute to their achievement. The Union shall also support the achievement of these objectives by the action it takes through the Structural Funds (European Agricultural Guidance and Guarantee Fund, Guidance Section; European Social Fund; European Regional Development Fund), the European Investment Bank and the other existing Financial Instruments.

The Commission shall submit a report to the European Parliament, the Council, the Economic and Social Committee and the Committee of the Regions every three years on the progress made towards achieving economic, social and territorial cohesion and on the manner in which the various means provided for in this Article have contributed to it. This report shall, if necessary, be accompanied by appropriate proposals.

If specific actions prove necessary outside the Funds and without prejudice to the measures decided upon within the framework of the other Union policies, such actions may be adopted by the Council acting in accordance with the ordinary legislative procedure and after consulting the Economic and Social Committee and the Committee of the Regions.

Article 176 (ex Article 160 TEC)

The European Regional Development Fund is intended to help to redress the main regional imbalances in the Union through participation in the development and structural adjustment of regions whose development is lagging behind and in the conversion of declining industrial regions.

Article 177 (ex Article 161 TEC)

Without prejudice to Article 178, the European Parliament and the Council, acting by means of regulations in accordance with the ordinary legislative procedure and consulting the Economic and Social Committee and the Committee of the Regions, shall define the tasks, priority objectives and the organisation of the Structural Funds, which may involve grouping the Funds. The general rules applicable to them and the provisions necessary to ensure their effectiveness and the coordination of the Funds with one another and with the other existing Financial Instruments shall also be defined by the same procedure.

A Cohesion Fund set up in accordance with the same procedure shall provide a financial contribution to projects in the fields of environment and trans-European networks in the area of transport infrastructure.

Article 178 (ex Article 162 TEC)

Implementing regulations relating to the European Regional Development Fund shall be taken by the European Parliament and the Council, acting in accordance with the ordinary legislative procedure and after consulting the Economic and Social Committee and the Committee of the Regions.

With regard to the European Agricultural Guidance and Guarantee Fund, Guidance Section, and the European Social Fund, Articles 43 and 164 respectively shall continue to apply.

Title XIX Research and technological development and space

Article 179 (ex Article 163 TEC)

1. The Union shall have the objective of strengthening its scientific and technological bases by achieving a European research area in which researchers, scientific knowledge and technology circulate freely, and encouraging it to become more competitive, including in its industry, while promoting all the research activities deemed necessary by virtue of other Chapters of the Treaties.

2. For this purpose the Union shall, throughout the Union, encourage undertakings, including small and medium-sized undertakings, research centres and universities in their research and technological development activities of high quality; it shall support their efforts to cooperate with one another, aiming, notably, at permitting researchers to cooperate freely across borders and at enabling undertakings to exploit the internal market potential to the full, in particular through the opening-up of national public contracts, the definition of common standards and the removal of legal and fiscal obstacles to that cooperation.

3. All Union activities under the Treaties in the area of research and technological development, including demonstration projects, shall be decided on and implemented in accordance with the provisions of this Title.

Article 180 (ex Article 164 TEC)

In pursuing these objectives, the Union shall carry out the following activities, complementing the activities carried out in the Member States:

(a) implementation of research, technological development and demonstration programmes, by promoting cooperation with and between undertakings, research centres and universities;
(b) promotion of cooperation in the field of Union research, technological development and demonstration with third countries and international organisations;
(c) dissemination and optimisation of the results of activities in Union research, technological development and demonstration;
(d) stimulation of the training and mobility of researchers in the Union.

Article 181 (ex Article 165 TEC)

1. The Union and the Member States shall coordinate their research and technological development activities so as to ensure that national policies and Union policy are mutually consistent.

2. In close cooperation with the Member State, the Commission may take any useful initiative to promote the coordination referred to in paragraph 1, in particular initiatives aiming at the establishment of guidelines and indicators, the organisation of exchange of best practice, and the preparation of the necessary elements for periodic monitoring and evaluation. The European Parliament shall be kept fully informed.

Article 182 (ex Article 166 TEC)

1. A multiannual framework programme, setting out all the activities of the Union, shall be adopted by the European Parliament and the Council, acting in accordance with the ordinary legislative procedure after consulting the Economic and Social Committee.

The framework programme shall:

- establish the scientific and technological objectives to be achieved by the activities provided for in Article 180 and fix the relevant priorities,
- indicate the broad lines of such activities,
- fix the maximum overall amount and the detailed rules for Union financial participation in the framework programme and the respective shares in each of the activities provided for.

2. The framework programme shall be adapted or supplemented as the situation changes.

3. The framework programme shall be implemented through specific programmes developed within each activity. Each specific programme shall define the detailed rules for implementing it, fix its duration and provide for the means deemed necessary. The sum of the amounts deemed necessary, fixed in the specific programmes, may not exceed the overall maximum amount fixed for the framework programme and each activity.

4. The Council, acting in accordance with a special legislative procedure and after consulting the European Parliament and the Economic and Social Committee, shall adopt the specific programmes.

5. As a complement to the activities planned in the multiannual framework programme, the European Parliament and the Council, acting in accordance with the ordinary legislative procedure and after consulting the Economic and Social Committee, shall establish the measures necessary for the implementation of the European research area.

Article 183 (ex Article 167 TEC)

For the implementation of the multiannual framework programme the Union shall:

– determine the rules for the participation of undertakings, research centres and universities,
– lay down the rules governing the dissemination of research results.

Article 184 (ex Article 168 TEC)

In implementing the multiannual framework programme, supplementary programmes may be decided on involving the participation of certain Member States only, which shall finance them subject to possible Union participation.

The Union shall adopt the rules applicable to supplementary programmes, particularly as regards the dissemination of knowledge and access by other Member States.

Article 185 (ex Article 169 TEC)

In implementing the multiannual framework programme, the Union may make provision, in agreement with the Member States concerned, for participation in research and development programmes undertaken by several Member States, including participation in the structures created for the execution of those programmes.

Article 186 (ex Article 170 TEC)

In implementing the multiannual framework programme the Union may make provision for cooperation in Union research, technological development and demonstration with third countries or international organisations.

The detailed arrangements for such cooperation may be the subject of agreements between the Union and the third parties concerned.

Article 187 (ex Article 171 TEC)

The Union may set up joint undertakings or any other structure necessary for the efficient execution of Union research, technological development and demonstration programmes.

Article 188 (ex Article 172 TEC)

The Council, on a proposal from the Commission and after consulting the European Parliament and the Economic and Social Committee, shall adopt the provisions referred to in Article 187.

The European Parliament and the Council, acting in accordance with the ordinary legislative procedure and after consulting the Economic and Social Committee, shall adopt the provisions referred to in Articles 183, 184 and 185. Adoption of the supplementary programmes shall require the agreement of the Member States concerned.

Article 189

1. To promote scientific and technical progress, industrial competitiveness and the implementation of its policies, the Union shall draw up a European space policy. To this end, it may promote joint

initiatives, support research and technological development and coordinate the efforts needed for the exploration and exploitation of space.

2. To contribute to attaining the objectives referred to in paragraph 1, the European Parliament and the Council, acting in accordance with the ordinary legislative procedure, shall establish the necessary measures, which may take the form of a European space programme, excluding any harmonisation of the laws and regulations of the Member States.

3. The Union shall establish any appropriate relations with the European Space Agency.

4. This Article shall be without prejudice to the other provisions of this Title.

Article 190 (ex Article 173 TEC)

At the beginning of each year the Commission shall send a report to the European Parliament and to the Council. The report shall include information on research and technological development activities and the dissemination of results during the previous year, and the work programme for the current year.

Title XX Environment

Article 191 (ex Article 174 TEC)

1. Union policy on the environment shall contribute to pursuit of the following objectives:
   - preserving, protecting and improving the quality of the environment,
   - protecting human health,
   - prudent and rational utilisation of natural resources,
   - promoting measures at international level to deal with regional or worldwide environmental problems, and in particular combating climate change.

2. Union policy on the environment shall aim at a high level of protection taking into account the diversity of situations in the various regions of the Union. It shall be based on the precautionary principle and on the principles that preventive action should be taken, that environmental damage should as a priority be rectified at source and that the polluter should pay.

In this context, harmonisation measures answering environmental protection requirements shall include, where appropriate, a safeguard clause allowing Member States to take provisional measures, for non-economic environmental reasons, subject to a procedure of inspection by the Union.

3. In preparing its policy on the environment, the Union shall take account of:
   - available scientific and technical data,
   - environmental conditions in the various regions of the Union,
   - the potential benefits and costs of action or lack of action,
   - the economic and social development of the Union as a whole and the balanced development of its regions.

4. Within their respective spheres of competence, the Union and the Member States shall cooperate with third countries and with the competent international organisations. The arrangements for Union cooperation may be the subject of agreements between the Union and the third parties concerned.

The previous subparagraph shall be without prejudice to Member States' competence to negotiate in international bodies and to conclude international agreements.

Article 192 (ex Article 175 TEC)

1. The European Parliament and the Council, acting in accordance with the ordinary legislative procedure and after consulting the Economic and Social Committee and the Committee of the Regions, shall decide what action is to be taken by the Union in order to achieve the objectives referred to in Article 191.

2. By way of derogation from the decision-making procedure provided for in paragraph 1 and without prejudice to Article 114, the Council acting unanimously in accordance with a special legislative

procedure and after consulting the European Parliament, the Economic and Social Committee and the Committee of the Regions, shall adopt:

(a) provisions primarily of a fiscal nature;

(b) measures affecting:

- town and country planning,
- quantitative management of water resources or affecting, directly or indirectly, the availability of those resources,
- land use, with the exception of waste management;

(c) measures significantly affecting a Member State's choice between different energy sources and the general structure of its energy supply.

The Council, acting unanimously on a proposal from the Commission and after consulting the European Parliament, the Economic and Social Committee and the Committee of the Regions, may make the ordinary legislative procedure applicable to the matters referred to in the first subparagraph.

3. General action programmes setting out priority objectives to be attained shall be adopted by the European Parliament and the Council, acting in accordance with the ordinary legislative procedure and after consulting the Economic and Social Committee and the Committee of the Regions.

The measures necessary for the implementation of these programmes shall be adopted under the terms of paragraph 1 or 2, as the case may be.

4. Without prejudice to certain measures adopted by the Union, the Member States shall finance and implement the environment policy.

5. Without prejudice to the principle that the polluter should pay, if a measure based on the provisions of paragraph 1 involves costs deemed disproportionate for the public authorities of a Member State, such measure shall lay down appropriate provisions in the form of:

- temporary derogations, and/or
- financial support from the Cohesion Fund set up pursuant to Article 177.

Article 193 (ex Article 176 TEC)

The protective measures adopted pursuant to Article 192 shall not prevent any Member State from maintaining or introducing more stringent protective measures. Such measures must be compatible with the Treaties. They shall be notified to the Commission.

Title XXI Energy

Article 194

1. In the context of the establishment and functioning of the internal market and with regard for the need to preserve and improve the environment, Union policy on energy shall aim, in a spirit of solidarity between Member States, to:

(a) ensure the functioning of the energy market;

(b) ensure security of energy supply in the Union;

(c) promote energy efficiency and energy saving and the development of new and renewable forms of energy; and

(d) promote the interconnection of energy networks.

2. Without prejudice to the application of other provisions of the Treaties, the European Parliament and the Council, acting in accordance with the ordinary legislative procedure, shall establish the measures necessary to achieve the objectives in paragraph 1. Such measures shall be adopted after consultation of the Economic and Social Committee and the Committee of the Regions.

Such measures shall not affect a Member State's right to determine the conditions for exploiting its energy resources, its choice between different energy sources and the general structure of its energy supply, without prejudice to Article 192(2)(c).

3. By way of derogation from paragraph 2, the Council, acting in accordance with a special legislative procedure, shall unanimously and after consulting the European Parliament, establish the measures referred to therein when they are primarily of a fiscal nature.

Title XXII Tourism

Article 195

1. The Union shall complement the action of the Member States in the tourism sector, in particular by promoting the competitiveness of Union undertakings in that sector.

To that end, Union action shall be aimed at:

(a) encouraging the creation of a favourable environment for the development of undertakings in this sector;

(b) promoting cooperation between the Member States, particularly by the exchange of good practice.

2. The European Parliament and the Council, acting in accordance with the ordinary legislative procedure, shall establish specific measures to complement actions within the Member States to achieve the objectives referred to in this Article, excluding any harmonisation of the laws and regulations of the Member States.

Title XXIII Civil protection

Article 196

1. The Union shall encourage cooperation between Member States in order to improve the effectiveness of systems for preventing and protecting against natural or man-made disasters.

Union action shall aim to:

(a) support and complement Member States' action at national, regional and local level in risk prevention, in preparing their civil-protection personnel and in responding to natural or man-made disasters within the Union;

(b) promote swift, effective operational cooperation within the Union between national civil-protection services;

(c) promote consistency in international civil-protection work.

2. The European Parliament and the Council, acting in accordance with the ordinary legislative procedure shall establish the measures necessary to help achieve the objectives referred to in paragraph 1, excluding any harmonisation of the laws and regulations of the Member States.

Title XXIV Administrative cooperation

Article 197

1. Effective implementation of Union law by the Member States, which is essential for the proper functioning of the Union, shall be regarded as a matter of common interest.

2. The Union may support the efforts of Member States to improve their administrative capacity to implement Union law. Such action may include facilitating the exchange of information and of civil servants as well as supporting training schemes. No Member State shall be obliged to avail itself of such support. The European Parliament and the Council, acting by means of regulations in accordance with the ordinary legislative procedure, shall establish the necessary measures to this end, excluding any harmonisation of the laws and regulations of the Member States.

3. This Article shall be without prejudice to the obligations of the Member States to implement Union law or to the prerogatives and duties of the Commission. It shall also be without prejudice to other provisions of the Treaties providing for administrative cooperation among the Member States and between them and the Union.

PART FOUR ASSOCIATION OF THE OVERSEAS COUNTRIES AND TERRITORIES

Article 198 (ex Article 182 TEC)

The Member States agree to associate with the Union the non-European countries and territories which have special relations with Denmark, France, the Netherlands and the United Kingdom. These countries and territories (hereinafter called the 'countries and territories') are listed in Annex II.

The purpose of association shall be to promote the economic and social development of the countries and territories and to establish close economic relations between them and the Union as a whole.

In accordance with the principles set out in the preamble to this Treaty, association shall serve primarily to further the interests and prosperity of the inhabitants of these countries and territories in order to lead them to the economic, social and cultural development to which they aspire.

Article 199 (ex Article 183 TEC)

Association shall have the following objectives.

1. Member States shall apply to their trade with the countries and territories the same treatment as they accord each other pursuant to the Treaties.

2. Each country or territory shall apply to its trade with Member States and with the other countries and territories the same treatment as that which it applies to the European State with which it has special relations.

3. The Member States shall contribute to the investments required for the progressive development of these countries and territories.

4. For investments financed by the Union, participation in tenders and supplies shall be open on equal terms to all natural and legal persons who are nationals of a Member State or of one of the countries and territories.

5. In relations between Member States and the countries and territories the right of establishment of nationals and companies or firms shall be regulated in accordance with the provisions and procedures laid down in the Chapter relating to the right of establishment and on a non-discriminatory basis, subject to any special provisions laid down pursuant to Article 203.

Article 200 (ex Article 184 TEC)

1. Customs duties on imports into the Member States of goods originating in the countries and territories shall be prohibited in conformity with the prohibition of customs duties between Member States in accordance with the provisions of the Treaties.

2. Customs duties on imports into each country or territory from Member States or from the other countries or territories shall be prohibited in accordance with the provisions of Article 30.

3. The countries and territories may, however, levy customs duties which meet the needs of their development and industrialisation or produce revenue for their budgets.

The duties referred to in the preceding subparagraph may not exceed the level of those imposed on imports of products from the Member State with which each country or territory has special relations.

4. Paragraph 2 shall not apply to countries and territories which, by reason of the particular international obligations by which they are bound, already apply a non-discriminatory customs tariff.

5. The introduction of or any change in customs duties imposed on goods imported into the countries and territories shall not, either in law or in fact, give rise to any direct or indirect discrimination between imports from the various Member States.

Article 201 (ex Article 185 TEC)

If the level of the duties applicable to goods from a third country on entry into a country or territory is liable, when the provisions of Article 200(1) have been applied, to cause deflections of trade to the detriment of any Member State, the latter may request the Commission to propose to the other Member States the measures needed to remedy the situation.

Article 202 (ex Article 186 TEC)

Subject to the provisions relating to public health, public security or public policy, freedom of movement within Member States for workers from the countries and territories, and within the countries and territories for workers from Member States, shall be regulated by acts adopted in accordance with Article 203.

Article 203 (ex Article 187 TEC)

The Council, acting unanimously on a proposal from the Commission, shall, on the basis of the experience acquired under the association of the countries and territories with the Union and of the principles set out in the Treaties, lay down provisions as regards the detailed rules and the procedure for the association of the countries and territories with the Union. Where the provisions in question are adopted by the Council in accordance with a special legislative procedure, it shall act unanimously on a proposal from the Commission and after consulting the European Parliament.

Article 204 (ex Article 188 TEC)

The provisions of Articles 198 to 203 shall apply to Greenland, subject to the specific provisions for Greenland set out in the Protocol on special arrangements for Greenland, annexed to the Treaties.

PART FIVE EXTERNAL ACTION BY THE UNION

Title I General provisions on the Union's external action

Article 205

The Union's action on the international scene, pursuant to this Part, shall be guided by the principles, pursue the objectives and be conducted in accordance with the general provisions laid down in Chapter 1 of Title V of the Treaty on European Union.

Title II Common commercial policy

Article 206 (ex Article 131 TEC)

By establishing a customs union in accordance with Articles 28 to 32, the Union shall contribute, in the common interest, to the harmonious development of world trade, the progressive abolition of restrictions on international trade and on foreign direct investment, and the lowering of customs and other barriers.

Article 207 (ex Article 133 TEC)

1. The common commercial policy shall be based on uniform principles, particularly with regard to changes in tariff rates, the conclusion of tariff and trade agreements relating to trade in goods and services, and the commercial aspects of intellectual property, foreign direct investment, the achievement of uniformity in measures of liberalisation, export policy and measures to protect trade such as those to be taken in the event of dumping or subsidies. The common commercial policy shall be conducted in the context of the principles and objectives of the Union's external action.

2. The European Parliament and the Council, acting by means of regulations in accordance with the ordinary legislative procedure, shall adopt the measures defining the framework for implementing the common commercial policy.

3. Where agreements with one or more third countries or international organisations need to be negotiated and concluded, Article 218 shall apply, subject to the special provisions of this Article.

The Commission shall make recommendations to the Council, which shall authorise it to open the necessary negotiations. The Council and the Commission shall be responsible for ensuring that the agreements negotiated are compatible with internal Union policies and rules.

The Commission shall conduct these negotiations in consultation with a special committee appointed by the Council to assist the Commission in this task and within the framework of such directives as the Council may issue to it. The Commission shall report regularly to the special committee and to the European Parliament on the progress of negotiations.

4. For the negotiation and conclusion of the agreements referred to in paragraph 3, the Council shall act by a qualified majority.

For the negotiation and conclusion of agreements in the fields of trade in services and the commercial aspects of intellectual property, as well as foreign direct investment, the Council shall act unanimously where such agreements include provisions for which unanimity is required for the adoption of internal rules.

The Council shall also act unanimously for the negotiation and conclusion of agreements:

(a) in the field of trade in cultural and audiovisual services, where these agreements risk prejudicing the Union's cultural and linguistic diversity;

(b) in the field of trade in social, education and health services, where these agreements risk seriously disturbing the national organisation of such services and prejudicing the responsibility of Member States to deliver them.

5. The negotiation and conclusion of international agreements in the field of transport shall be subject to Title VI of Part Three and to Article 218.

6. The exercise of the competences conferred by this Article in the field of the common commercial policy shall not affect the delimitation of competences between the Union and the Member States, and shall not lead to harmonisation of legislative or regulatory provisions of the Member States in so far as the Treaties exclude such harmonisation.

Title III Cooperation with third countries and humanitarian aid

Chapter 1 Development cooperation

Article 208 (ex Article 177 TEC)

1. Union policy in the field of development cooperation shall be conducted within the framework of the principles and objectives of the Union's external action. The Union's development cooperation policy and that of the Member States complement and reinforce each other.

Union development cooperation policy shall have as its primary objective the reduction and, in the long term, the eradication of poverty. The Union shall take account of the objectives of development cooperation in the policies that it implements which are likely to affect developing countries.

2. The Union and the Member States shall comply with the commitments and take account of the objectives they have approved in the context of the United Nations and other competent international organisations.

Article 209 (ex Article 179 TEC)

1. The European Parliament and the Council, acting in accordance with the ordinary legislative procedure, shall adopt the measures necessary for the implementation of development cooperation policy, which may relate to multiannual cooperation programmes with developing countries or programmes with a thematic approach.

2. The Union may conclude with third countries and competent international organisations any agreement helping to achieve the objectives referred to in Article 21 of the Treaty on European Union and in Article 208 of this Treaty.

The first subparagraph shall be without prejudice to Member States' competence to negotiate in international bodies and to conclude agreements.

3. The European Investment Bank shall contribute, under the terms laid down in its Statute, to the implementation of the measures referred to in paragraph 1.

Article 210 (ex Article 180 TEC)

1. In order to promote the complementarity and efficiency of their action, the Union and the Member States shall coordinate their policies on development cooperation and shall consult each other on their aid programmes, including in international organisations and during international conferences. They may undertake joint action. Member States shall contribute if necessary to the implementation of Union aid programmes.

2. The Commission may take any useful initiative to promote the coordination referred to in paragraph 1.

Article 211 (ex Article 181 TEC)

Within their respective spheres of competence, the Union and the Member States shall cooperate with third countries and with the competent international organisations.

Chapter 2 Economic, financial and technical cooperation with third countries

Article 212 (ex Article 181 a TEC)

1. Without prejudice to the other provisions of the Treaties, and in particular Articles 208 to 211, the Union shall carry out economic, financial and technical cooperation measures, including assistance, in particular financial assistance, with third countries other than developing countries. Such measures shall be consistent with the development policy of the Union and shall be carried out within the framework of the principles and objectives of its external action. The Union's operations and those of the Member States shall complement and reinforce each other.

2. The European Parliament and the Council, acting in accordance with the ordinary legislative procedure, shall adopt the measures necessary for the implementation of paragraph 1.

3. Within their respective spheres of competence, the Union and the Member States shall cooperate with third countries and the competent international organisations. The arrangements for Union cooperation may be the subject of agreements between the Union and the third parties concerned.

The first subparagraph shall be without prejudice to the Member States' competence to negotiate in international bodies and to conclude international agreements.

Article 213

When the situation in a third country requires urgent financial assistance from the Union, the Council shall adopt the necessary decisions on a proposal from the Commission.

Chapter 3 Humanitarian aid

Article 214

1. The Union's operations in the field of humanitarian aid shall be conducted within the framework of the principles and objectives of the external action of the Union. Such operations shall be intended to provide *ad hoc* assistance and relief and protection for people in third countries who are victims of natural or man-made disasters, in order to meet the humanitarian needs resulting from these different situations. The Union's measures and those of the Member States shall complement and reinforce each other.

2. Humanitarian aid operations shall be conducted in compliance with the principles of international law and with the principles of impartiality, neutrality and non-discrimination.

3. The European Parliament and the Council, acting in accordance with the ordinary legislative procedure, shall establish the measures defining the framework within which the Union's humanitarian aid operations shall be implemented.

4. The Union may conclude with third countries and competent international organisations any agreement helping to achieve the objectives referred to in paragraph 1 and in Article 21 of the Treaty on European Union.

The first subparagraph shall be without prejudice to Member States' competence to negotiate in international bodies and to conclude agreements.

5. In order to establish a framework for joint contributions from young Europeans to the humanitarian aid operations of the Union, a European Voluntary Humanitarian Aid Corps shall be set up. The European Parliament and the Council, acting by means of regulations in accordance with the ordinary legislative procedure, shall determine the rules and procedures for the operation of the Corps.

6. The Commission may take any useful initiative to promote coordination between actions of the Union and those of the Member States, in order to enhance the efficiency and complementarity of Union and national humanitarian aid measures.

7. The Union shall ensure that its humanitarian aid operations are coordinated and consistent with those of international organisations and bodies, in particular those forming part of the United Nations system.

Title IV Restrictive measures

Article 215 (ex Article 301 TEC)

1. Where a decision, adopted in accordance with Chapter 2 of Title V of the Treaty on European Union, provides for the interruption or reduction, in part or completely, of economic and financial relations with one or more third countries, the Council, acting by a qualified majority on a joint proposal from the High Representative of the Union for Foreign Affairs and Security Policy and the Commission, shall adopt the necessary measures. It shall inform the European Parliament thereof.

2. Where a decision adopted in accordance with Chapter 2 of Title V of the Treaty on European Union so provides, the Council may adopt restrictive measures under the procedure referred to in paragraph 1 against natural or legal persons and groups or non-State entities.

3. The acts referred to in this Article shall include necessary provisions on legal safeguards.

Title V International agreements

Article 216

1. The Union may conclude an agreement with one or more third countries or international organisations where the Treaties so provide or where the conclusion of an agreement is necessary in order to achieve, within the framework of the Union's policies, one of the objectives referred to in the Treaties, or is provided for in a legally binding Union act or is likely to affect common rules or alter their scope.

2. Agreements concluded by the Union are binding upon the institutions of the Union and on its Member States.

Article 217 (ex Article 310 TEC)

The Union may conclude with one or more third countries or international organisations agreements establishing an association involving reciprocal rights and obligations, common action and special procedure.

Article 218 (ex Article 300 TEC)

1. Without prejudice to the specific provisions laid down in Article 207, agreements between the Union and third countries or international organisations shall be negotiated and concluded in accordance with the following procedure.

2. The Council shall authorise the opening of negotiations, adopt negotiating directives, authorise the signing of agreements and conclude them.

3. The Commission, or the High Representative of the Union for Foreign Affairs and Security Policy where the agreement envisaged relates exclusively or principally to the common foreign and security policy, shall submit recommendations to the Council, which shall adopt a decision authorising

the opening of negotiations and, depending on the subject of the agreement envisaged, nominating the Union negotiator or the head of the Union's negotiating team.

4. The Council may address directives to the negotiator and designate a special committee in consultation with which the negotiations must be conducted.

5. The Council, on a proposal by the negotiator, shall adopt a decision authorising the signing of the agreement and, if necessary, its provisional application before entry into force.

6. The Council, on a proposal by the negotiator, shall adopt a decision concluding the agreement.

Except where agreements relate exclusively to the common foreign and security policy, the Council shall adopt the decision concluding the agreement:

(a) after obtaining the consent of the European Parliament in the following cases:
   (i) association agreements;
   (ii) agreement on Union accession to the European Convention for the Protection of Human Rights and Fundamental Freedoms;
   (iii) agreements establishing a specific institutional framework by organising cooperation procedures;
   (iv) agreements with important budgetary implications for the Union;
   (v) agreements covering fields to which either the ordinary legislative procedure applies, or the special legislative procedure where consent by the European Parliament is required.

   The European Parliament and the Council may, in an urgent situation, agree upon a time-limit for consent.

(b) after consulting the European Parliament in other cases. The European Parliament shall deliver its opinion within a time-limit which the Council may set depending on the urgency of the matter. In the absence of an opinion within that time-limit, the Council may act.

7. When concluding an agreement, the Council may, by way of derogation from paragraphs 5, 6 and 9, authorise the negotiator to approve on the Union's behalf modifications to the agreement where it provides for them to be adopted by a simplified procedure or by a body set up by the agreement. The Council may attach specific conditions to such authorisation.

8. The Council shall act by a qualified majority throughout the procedure.

However, it shall act unanimously when the agreement covers a field for which unanimity is required for the adoption of a Union act as well as for association agreements and the agreements referred to in Article 212 with the States which are candidates for accession. The Council shall also act unanimously for the agreement on accession of the Union to the European Convention for the Protection of Human Rights and Fundamental Freedoms; the decision concluding this agreement shall enter into force after it has been approved by the Member States in accordance with their respective constitutional requirements.

9. The Council, on a proposal from the Commission or the High Representative of the Union for Foreign Affairs and Security Policy, shall adopt a decision suspending application of an agreement and establishing the positions to be adopted on the Union's behalf in a body set up by an agreement, when that body is called upon to adopt acts having legal effects, with the exception of acts supplementing or amending the institutional framework of the agreement.

10. The European Parliament shall be immediately and fully informed at all stages of the procedure.

11. A Member State, the European Parliament, the Council or the Commission may obtain the opinion of the Court of Justice as to whether an agreement envisaged is compatible with the Treaties. Where the opinion of the Court is adverse, the agreement envisaged may not enter into force unless it is amended or the Treaties are revised.

Article 219 (ex Article 111(1) to (3) and (5) TEC)

1. By way of derogation from Article 218, the Council, either on a recommendation from the European Central Bank or on a recommendation from the Commission and after consulting the European Central Bank, in an endeavour to reach a consensus consistent with the objective of price

stability, may conclude formal agreements on an exchange-rate system for the euro in relation to the currencies of third States. The Council shall act unanimously after consulting the European Parliament and in accordance with the procedure provided for in paragraph 3.

The Council may, either on a recommendation from the European Central Bank or on a recommendation from the Commission, and after consulting the European Central Bank, in an endeavour to reach a consensus consistent with the objective of price stability, adopt, adjust or abandon the central rates of the euro within the exchange-rate system. The President of the Council shall inform the European Parliament of the adoption, adjustment or abandonment of the euro central rates.

2. In the absence of an exchange-rate system in relation to one or more currencies of third States as referred to in paragraph 1, the Council, either on a recommendation from the Commission and after consulting the European Central Bank or on a recommendation from the European Central Bank, may formulate general orientations for exchange-rate policy in relation to these currencies. These general orientations shall be without prejudice to the primary objective of the ESCB to maintain price stability.

3. By way of derogation from Article 218, where agreements concerning monetary or foreign exchange regime matters need to be negotiated by the Union with one or more third States or international organisations, the Council, on a recommendation from the Commission and after consulting the European Central Bank, shall decide the arrangements for the negotiation and for the conclusion of such agreements. These arrangements shall ensure that the Union expresses a single position. The Commission shall be fully associated with the negotiations.

4. Without prejudice to Union competence and Union agreements as regards economic and monetary union, Member States may negotiate in international bodies and conclude international agreements.

Title VI The Union's relations with international organisations and third countries and Union delegations

Article 220 (ex Articles 302 to 304 TEC)

1. The Union shall establish all appropriate forms of cooperation with the organs of the United Nations and its specialised agencies, the Council of Europe, the Organisation for Security and Cooperation in Europe and the Organisation for Economic Cooperation and Development.

The Union shall also maintain such relations as are appropriate with other international organisations.

2. The High Representative of the Union for Foreign Affairs and Security Policy and the Commission shall be instructed to implement this Article.

Article 221

1. Union delegations in third countries and at international organisations shall represent the Union.

2. Union delegations shall be placed under the authority of the High Representative of the Union for Foreign Affairs and Security Policy. They shall act in close cooperation with Member States' diplomatic and consular missions.

Title VII Solidarity clause

Article 222

1. The Union and its Member States shall act jointly in a spirit of solidarity if a Member State is the object of a terrorist attack or the victim of a natural or man-made disaster. The Union shall mobilise all the instruments at its disposal, including the military resources made available by the Member States, to:

(a) – prevent the terrorist threat in the territory of the Member States;
– protect democratic institutions and the civilian population from any terrorist attack;

– assist a Member State in its territory, at the request of its political authorities, in the event of a terrorist attack;

(b) assist a Member State in its territory, at the request of its political authorities, in the event of a natural or man-made disaster.

2. Should a Member State be the object of a terrorist attack or the victim of a natural or man-made disaster, the other Member States shall assist it at the request of its political authorities. To that end, the Member States shall coordinate between themselves in the Council.

3. The arrangements for the implementation by the Union of the solidarity clause shall be defined by a decision adopted by the Council acting on a joint proposal by the Commission and the High Representative of the Union for Foreign Affairs and Security Policy. The Council shall act in accordance with Article 31(1) of the Treaty on European Union where this decision has defence implications. The European Parliament shall be informed.

For the purposes of this paragraph and without prejudice to Article 240, the Council shall be assisted by the Political and Security Committee with the support of the structures developed in the context of the common security and defence policy and by the Committee referred to in Article 71; the two committees shall, if necessary, submit joint opinions.

4. The European Council shall regularly assess the threats facing the Union in order to enable the Union and its Member States to take effective action.

PART SIX INSTITUTIONAL AND FINANCIAL PROVISIONS

Title I Institutional provisions

Chapter 1 The institutions

Section 1 The European Parliament

Article 223 (ex Article 190(4) and (5) TEC)

1. The European Parliament shall draw up a proposal to lay down the provisions necessary for the election of its Members by direct universal suffrage in accordance with a uniform procedure in all Member States or in accordance with principles common to all Member States.

The Council, acting unanimously in accordance with a special legislative procedure and after obtaining the consent of the European Parliament, which shall act by a majority of its component Members, shall lay down the necessary provisions. These provisions shall enter into force following their approval by the Member States in accordance with their respective constitutional requirements.

2. The European Parliament, acting by means of regulations on its own initiative in accordance with a special legislative procedure after seeking an opinion from the Commission and with the approval of the Council, shall lay down the regulations and general conditions governing the performance of the duties of its Members. All rules or conditions relating to the taxation of Members or former Members shall require unanimity within the Council.

Article 224 (ex Article 191, second subparagraph, TEC)

The European Parliament and the Council, acting in accordance with the ordinary legislative procedure, by means of regulations, shall lay down the regulations governing political parties at European level referred to in Article 10(4) of the Treaty on European Union and in particular the rules regarding their funding.

Article 225 (ex Article 192, second subparagraph, TEC)

The European Parliament may, acting by a majority of its component Members, request the Commission to submit any appropriate proposal on matters on which it considers that a Union act is required for the purpose of implementing the Treaties. If the Commission does not submit a proposal, it shall inform the European Parliament of the reasons.

Article 226 (ex Article 193 TEC)

In the course of its duties, the European Parliament may, at the request of a quarter of its component Members, set up a temporary Committee of Inquiry to investigate, without prejudice to the powers conferred by the Treaties on other institutions or bodies, alleged contraventions or maladministration in the implementation of Union law, except where the alleged facts are being examined before a court and while the case is still subject to legal proceedings.

The temporary Committee of Inquiry shall cease to exist on the submission of its report.

The detailed provisions governing the exercise of the right of inquiry shall be determined by the European Parliament, acting by means of regulations on its own initiative in accordance with a special legislative procedure, after obtaining the consent of the Council and the Commission.

Article 227 (ex Article 194 TEC)

Any citizen of the Union, and any natural or legal person residing or having its registered office in a Member State, shall have the right to address, individually or in association with other citizens or persons, a petition to the European Parliament on a matter which comes within the Union's fields of activity and which affects him, her or it directly.

Article 228 (ex Article 195 TEC)

1. A European Ombudsman, elected by the European Parliament, shall be empowered to receive complaints from any citizen of the Union or any natural or legal person residing or having its registered office in a Member State concerning instances of maladministration in the activities of the Union institutions, bodies, offices or agencies, with the exception of the Court of Justice of the European Union acting in its judicial role. He or she shall examine such complaints and report on them.

In accordance with his duties, the Ombudsman shall conduct inquiries for which he finds grounds, either on his own initiative or on the basis of complaints submitted to him direct or through a Member of the European Parliament, except where the alleged facts are or have been the subject of legal proceedings. Where the Ombudsman establishes an instance of maladministration, he shall refer the matter to the institution, body, office or agency concerned, which shall have a period of three months in which to inform him of its views. The Ombudsman shall then forward a report to the European Parliament and the institution, body, office or agency concerned. The person lodging the complaint shall be informed of the outcome of such inquiries.

The Ombudsman shall submit an annual report to the European Parliament on the outcome of his inquiries.

2. The Ombudsman shall be elected after each election of the European Parliament for the duration of its term of office. The Ombudsman shall be eligible for reappointment.

The Ombudsman may be dismissed by the Court of Justice at the request of the European Parliament if he no longer fulfils the conditions required for the performance of his duties or if he is guilty of serious misconduct.

3. The Ombudsman shall be completely independent in the performance of his duties. In the performance of those duties he shall neither seek nor take instructions from any Government, institution, body, office or entity. The Ombudsman may not, during his term of office, engage in any other occupation, whether gainful or not.

4. The European Parliament acting by means of regulations on its own initiative in accordance with a special legislative procedure shall, after seeking an opinion from the Commission and with the approval of the Council, lay down the regulations and general conditions governing the performance of the Ombudsman's duties.

Article 229 (ex Article 196 TEC)

The European Parliament shall hold an annual session. It shall meet, without requiring to be convened, on the second Tuesday in March.

The European Parliament may meet in extraordinary part-session at the request of a majority of its component Members or at the request of the Council or of the Commission.

Article 230 (ex Article 197, second, third and fourth paragraph, TEC)

The Commission may attend all the meetings and shall, at its request, be heard.

The Commission shall reply orally or in writing to questions put to it by the European Parliament or by its Members.

The European Council and the Council shall be heard by the European Parliament in accordance with the conditions laid down in the Rules of Procedure of the European Council and those of the Council.

Article 231 (ex Article 198 TEC)

Save as otherwise provided in the Treaties, the European Parliament shall act by a majority of the votes cast.

The Rules of Procedure shall determine the quorum.

Article 232 (ex Article 199 TEC)

The European Parliament shall adopt its Rules of Procedure, acting by a majority of its Members.

The proceedings of the European Parliament shall be published in the manner laid down in the Treaties and in its Rules of Procedure.

Article 233 (ex Article 200 TEC)

The European Parliament shall discuss in open session the annual general report submitted to it by the Commission.

Article 234 (ex Article 201 TEC)

If a motion of censure on the activities of the Commission is tabled before it, the European Parliament shall not vote thereon until at least three days after the motion has been tabled and only by open vote.

If the motion of censure is carried by a two-thirds majority of the votes cast, representing a majority of the component Members of the European Parliament, the members of the Commission shall resign as a body and the High Representative of the Union for Foreign Affairs and Security Policy shall resign from duties that he or she carries out in the Commission. They shall remain in office and continue to deal with current business until they are replaced in accordance with Article 17 of the Treaty on European Union. In this case, the term of office of the members of the Commission appointed to replace them shall expire on the date on which the term of office of the members of the Commission obliged to resign as a body would have expired.

Section 2 The European Council

Article 235

1. Where a vote is taken, any member of the European Council may also act on behalf of not more than one other member.

Article 16(4) of the Treaty on European Union and Article 238(2) of this Treaty shall apply to the European Council when it is acting by a qualified majority. Where the European Council decides by vote, its President and the President of the Commission shall not take part in the vote.

Abstentions by members present in person or represented shall not prevent the adoption by the European Council of acts which require unanimity.

2. The President of the European Parliament may be invited to be heard by the European Council.
3. The European Council shall act by a simple majority for procedural questions and for the adoption of its Rules of Procedure.
4. The European Council shall be assisted by the General Secretariat of the Council.

Article 236

The European Council shall adopt by a qualified majority:

(a) a decision establishing the list of Council configurations, other than those of the General Affairs Council and of the Foreign Affairs Council, in accordance with Article 16(6) of the Treaty on European Union;

(b) a decision on the Presidency of Council configurations, other than that of Foreign Affairs, in accordance with Article 16(9) of the Treaty on European Union.

Section 3 The Council

Article 237 (ex Article 204 TEC)

The Council shall meet when convened by its President on his own initiative or at the request of one of its Members or of the Commission.

Article 238 (ex Article 205(1) and (2), TEC)*

1. Where it is required to act by a simple majority, the Council shall act by a majority of its component members.

2. By way of derogation from Article 16(4) of the Treaty on European Union, as from 1 November 2014 and subject to the provisions laid down in the Protocol on transitional provisions, where the Council does not act on a proposal from the Commission or from the High Representative of the Union for Foreign Affairs and Security Policy, the qualified majority shall be defined as at least 72 % of the members of the Council, representing Member States comprising at least 65 % of the population of the Union.

3. As from 1 November 2014 and subject to the provisions laid down in the Protocol on transitional provisions, in cases where, under the Treaties, not all the members of the Council participate in voting, a qualified majority shall be defined as follows:

(a) A qualified majority shall be defined as at least 55 % of the members of the Council representing the participating Member States, comprising at least 65 % of the population of these States.

A blocking minority must include at least the minimum number of Council members representing more than 35 % of the population of the participating Member States, plus one member, failing which the qualified majority shall be deemed attained;

(b) By way of derogation from point (a), where the Council does not act on a proposal from the Commission or from the High Representative of the Union for Foreign Affairs and Security Policy, the qualified majority shall be defined as at least 72 % of the members of the Council representing the participating Member States, comprising at least 65 % of the population of these States.

4. Abstentions by Members present in person or represented shall not prevent the adoption by the Council of acts which require unanimity.

Article 239 (ex Article 206 TEC)

Where a vote is taken, any Member of the Council may also act on behalf of not more than one other member.

Article 240 (ex Article 207 TEC)

1. A committee consisting of the Permanent Representatives of the Governments of the Member States shall be responsible for preparing the work of the Council and for carrying out the tasks assigned to it by the latter. The Committee may adopt procedural decisions in cases provided for in the Council's Rules of Procedure.

2. The Council shall be assisted by a General Secretariat, under the responsibility of a Secretary-General appointed by the Council.

The Council shall decide on the organisation of the General Secretariat by a simple majority.

3. The Council shall act by a simple majority regarding procedural matters and for the adoption of its Rules of Procedure.

Article 241 (ex Article 208 TEC)

The Council acting by a simple majority may request the Commission to undertake any studies the Council considers desirable for the attainment of the common objectives, and to submit to it any

* **Editor's Note:** The voting numbers per country are now contained in Protocol 36 attached to the Treaties reproduced below in this book at p. 144.

appropriate proposals. If the Commission does not submit a proposal, it shall inform the Council of the reasons.

Article 242 (ex Article 209 TEC)

The Council, acting by a simple majority shall, after consulting the Commission, determine the rules governing the committees provided for in the Treaties.

Article 243 (ex Article 210 TEC)

The Council shall determine the salaries, allowances and pensions of the President of the European Council, the President of the Commission, the High Representative of the Union for Foreign Affairs and Security Policy, the Members of the Commission, the Presidents, Members and Registrars of the Court of Justice of the European Union, and the Secretary-General of the Council. It shall also determine any payment to be made instead of remuneration.

Section 4 The Commission

Article 244

In accordance with Article 17(5) of the Treaty on European Union, the Members of the Commission shall be chosen on the basis of a system of rotation established unanimously by the European Council and on the basis of the following principles:

(a) Member States shall be treated on a strictly equal footing as regards determination of the sequence of, and the time spent by, their nationals as members of the Commission; consequently, the difference between the total number of terms of office held by nationals of any given pair of Member States may never be more than one;

(b) subject to point (a), each successive Commission shall be so composed as to reflect satisfactorily the demographic and geographical range of all the Member States.

Article 245 (ex Article 213 TEC)

The Members of the Commission shall refrain from any action incompatible with their duties. Member States shall respect their independence and shall not seek to influence them in the performance of their tasks.

The Members of the Commission may not, during their term of office, engage in any other occupation, whether gainful or not. When entering upon their duties they shall give a solemn undertaking that, both during and after their term of office, they will respect the obligations arising therefrom and in particular their duty to behave with integrity and discretion as regards the acceptance, after they have ceased to hold office, of certain appointments or benefits. In the event of any breach of these obligations, the Court of Justice may, on application by the Council acting by a simple majority or the Commission, rule that the Member concerned be, according to the circumstances, either compulsorily retired in accordance with Article 247 or deprived of his right to a pension or other benefits in its stead.

Article 246 (ex Article 215 TEC)

Apart from normal replacement, or death, the duties of a Member of the Commission shall end when he resigns or is compulsorily retired.

A vacancy caused by resignation, compulsory retirement or death shall be filled for the remainder of the Member's term of office by a new Member of the same nationality appointed by the Council, by common accord with the President of the Commission, after consulting the European Parliament and in accordance with the criteria set out in the second subparagraph of Article 17(3) of the Treaty on European Union.

The Council may, acting unanimously on a proposal from the President of the Commission, decide that such a vacancy need not be filled, in particular when the remainder of the Member's term of office is short.

In the event of resignation, compulsory retirement or death, the President shall be replaced for the remainder of his term of office. The procedure laid down in the first subparagraph of Article 17(7) of the Treaty on European Union shall be applicable for the replacement of the President.

In the event of resignation, compulsory retirement or death, the High Representative of the Union for Foreign Affairs and Security Policy shall be replaced, for the remainder of his or her term of office, in accordance with Article 18(1) of the Treaty on European Union.

In the case of the resignation of all the Members of the Commission, they shall remain in office and continue to deal with current business until they have been replaced, for the remainder of their term of office, in accordance with Article 17 of the Treaty on European Union.

Article 247 (ex Article 216 TEC)

If any Member of the Commission no longer fulfils the conditions required for the performance of his duties or if he has been guilty of serious misconduct, the Court of Justice may, on application by the Council acting by a simple majority or the Commission, compulsorily retire him.

Article 248 (ex Article 217(2), TEC)

Without prejudice to Article 18(4) of the Treaty on European Union, the responsibilities incumbent upon the Commission shall be structured and allocated among its members by its President, in accordance with Article 17(6) of that Treaty. The President may reshuffle the allocation of those responsibilities during the Commission's term of office. The Members of the Commission shall carry out the duties devolved upon them by the President under his authority.

Article 249 (ex Articles 218(2) and 212 TEC)

1. The Commission shall adopt its Rules of Procedure so as to ensure that both it and its departments operate. It shall ensure that these Rules are published.

2. The Commission shall publish annually, not later than one month before the opening of the session of the European Parliament, a general report on the activities of the Union.

Article 250 (ex Article 219 TEC)

The Commission shall act by a majority of its Members.

Its Rules of Procedure shall determine the quorum.

Section 5 The Court of Justice of the European Union

Article 251 (ex Article 221 TEC)

The Court of Justice shall sit in chambers or in a Grand Chamber, in accordance with the rules laid down for that purpose in the Statute of the Court of Justice of the European Union.

When provided for in the Statute, the Court of Justice may also sit as a full Court.

Article 252 (ex Article 222 TEC)

The Court of Justice shall be assisted by eight Advocates-General. Should the Court of Justice so request, the Council, acting unanimously, may increase the number of Advocates-General.

It shall be the duty of the Advocate-General, acting with complete impartiality and independence, to make, in open court, reasoned submissions on cases which, in accordance with the Statute of the Court of Justice of the European Union, require his involvement.

Article 253 (ex Article 223 TEC)

The Judges and Advocates-General of the Court of Justice shall be chosen from persons whose independence is beyond doubt and who possess the qualifications required for appointment to the highest judicial offices in their respective countries or who are jurisconsults of recognised competence; they shall be appointed by common accord of the governments of the Member States for a term of six years, after consultation of the panel provided for in Article 255.

Every three years there shall be a partial replacement of the Judges and Advocates-General, in accordance with the conditions laid down in the Statute of the Court of Justice of the European Union.

The Judges shall elect the President of the Court of Justice from among their number for a term of three years. He may be re-elected.

Retiring Judges and Advocates-General may be reappointed.

The Court of Justice shall appoint its Registrar and lay down the rules governing his service.

The Court of Justice shall establish its Rules of Procedure. Those Rules shall require the approval of the Council.

Article 254 (ex Article 224 TEC)

The number of Judges of the General Court shall be determined by the Statute of the Court of Justice of the European Union. The Statute may provide for the General Court to be assisted by Advocates-General.

The members of the General Court shall be chosen from persons whose independence is beyond doubt and who possess the ability required for appointment to high judicial office. They shall be appointed by common accord of the governments of the Member States for a term of six years, after consultation of the panel provided for in Article 255. The membership shall be partially renewed every three years. Retiring members shall be eligible for reappointment.

The Judges shall elect the President of the General Court from among their number for a term of three years. He may be re-elected.

The General Court shall appoint its Registrar and lay down the rules governing his service.

The General Court shall establish its Rules of Procedure in agreement with the Court of Justice. Those Rules shall require the approval of the Council.

Unless the Statute of the Court of Justice of the European Union provides otherwise, the provisions of the Treaties relating to the Court of Justice shall apply to the General Court.

Article 255

A panel shall be set up in order to give an opinion on candidates' suitability to perform the duties of Judge and Advocate-General of the Court of Justice and the General Court before the governments of the Member States make the appointments referred to in Articles 253 and 254.

The panel shall comprise seven persons chosen from among former members of the Court of Justice and the General Court, members of national supreme courts and lawyers of recognised competence, one of whom shall be proposed by the European Parliament. The Council shall adopt a decision establishing the panel's operating rules and a decision appointing its members. It shall act on the initiative of the President of the Court of Justice.

Article 256 (ex Article 225 TEC)

1. The General Court shall have jurisdiction to hear and determine at first instance actions or proceedings referred to in Articles 263, 265, 268, 270 and 272, with the exception of those assigned to a specialised court set up under Article 257 and those reserved in the Statute for the Court of Justice. The Statute may provide for the General Court to have jurisdiction for other classes of action or proceeding.

Decisions given by the General Court under this paragraph may be subject to a right of appeal to the Court of Justice on points of law only, under the conditions and within the limits laid down by the Statute.

2. The General Court shall have jurisdiction to hear and determine actions or proceedings brought against decisions of the specialised courts.

Decisions given by the General Court under this paragraph may exceptionally be subject to review by the Court of Justice, under the conditions and within the limits laid down by the Statute, where there is a serious risk of the unity or consistency of Union law being affected.

3. The General Court shall have jurisdiction to hear and determine questions referred for a preliminary ruling under Article 267, in specific areas laid down by the Statute.

Where the General Court considers that the case requires a decision of principle likely to affect the unity or consistency of Union law, it may refer the case to the Court of Justice for a ruling.

Decisions given by the General Court on questions referred for a preliminary ruling may exceptionally be subject to review by the Court of Justice, under the conditions and within the limits laid down by the Statute, where there is a serious risk of the unity or consistency of Union law being affected.

Article 257 (ex Article 225 A TEC)

The European Parliament and the Council, acting in accordance with the ordinary legislative procedure, may establish specialised courts attached to the General Court to hear and determine at first instance certain classes of action or proceeding brought in specific areas. The European Parliament and the Council shall act by means of regulations either on a proposal from the Commission after consultation of the Court of Justice or at the request of the Court of Justice after consultation of the Commission.

The regulation establishing a specialised court shall lay down the rules on the organisation of the court and the extent of the jurisdiction conferred upon it.

Decisions given by specialised courts may be subject to a right of appeal on points of law only or, when provided for in the regulation establishing the specialised court, a right of appeal also on matters of fact, before the General Court.

The members of the specialised courts shall be chosen from persons whose independence is beyond doubt and who possess the ability required for appointment to judicial office. They shall be appointed by the Council, acting unanimously.

The specialised courts shall establish their Rules of Procedure in agreement with the Court of Justice. Those Rules shall require the approval of the Council.

Unless the regulation establishing the specialised court provides otherwise, the provisions of the Treaties relating to the Court of Justice of the European Union and the provisions of the Statute of the Court of Justice of the European Union shall apply to the specialised courts. Title I of the Statute and Article 64 thereof shall in any case apply to the specialised courts.

Article 258 (ex Article 226 TEC)

If the Commission considers that a Member State has failed to fulfil an obligation under the Treaties, it shall deliver a reasoned opinion on the matter after giving the State concerned the opportunity to submit its observations.

If the State concerned does not comply with the opinion within the period laid down by the Commission, the latter may bring the matter before the Court of Justice of the European Union.

Article 259 (ex Article 227 TEC)

A Member State which considers that another Member State has failed to fulfil an obligation under the Treaties may bring the matter before the Court of Justice of the European Union.

Before a Member State brings an action against another Member State for an alleged infringement of an obligation under the Treaties, it shall bring the matter before the Commission.

The Commission shall deliver a reasoned opinion after each of the States concerned has been given the opportunity to submit its own case and its observations on the other party's case both orally and in writing.

If the Commission has not delivered an opinion within three months of the date on which the matter was brought before it, the absence of such opinion shall not prevent the matter from being brought before the Court.

Article 260 (ex Article 228 TEC)

1. If the Court of Justice of the European Union finds that a Member State has failed to fulfil an obligation under the Treaties, the State shall be required to take the necessary measures to comply with the judgment of the Court.

2. If the Commission considers that the Member State concerned has not taken the necessary measures to comply with the judgment of the Court, it may bring the case before the Court after giving that State the opportunity to submit its observations. It shall specify the amount of the lump sum or penalty payment to be paid by the Member State concerned which it considers appropriate in the circumstances.

If the Court finds that the Member State concerned has not complied with its judgment it may impose a lump sum or penalty payment on it.

This procedure shall be without prejudice to Article 259.

3. When the Commission brings a case before the Court pursuant to Article 258 on the grounds that the Member State concerned has failed to fulfil its obligation to notify measures transposing

a directive adopted under a legislative procedure, it may, when it deems appropriate, specify the amount of the lump sum or penalty payment to be paid by the Member State concerned which it considers appropriate in the circumstances.

If the Court finds that there is an infringement it may impose a lump sum or penalty payment on the Member State concerned not exceeding the amount specified by the Commission. The payment obligation shall take effect on the date set by the Court in its judgment.

Article 261 (ex Article 229 TEC)

Regulations adopted jointly by the European Parliament and the Council, and by the Council, pursuant to the provisions of the Treaties, may give the Court of Justice of the European Union unlimited jurisdiction with regard to the penalties provided for in such regulations.

Article 262 (ex Article 229 A TEC)

Without prejudice to the other provisions of the Treaties, the Council, acting unanimously in accordance with a special legislative procedure and after consulting the European Parliament, may adopt provisions to confer jurisdiction, to the extent that it shall determine, on the Court of Justice of the European Union in disputes relating to the application of acts adopted on the basis of the Treaties which create European intellectual property rights. These provisions shall enter into force after their approval by the Member States in accordance with their respective constitutional requirements.

Article 263 (ex Article 230 TEC)

The Court of Justice of the European Union shall review the legality of legislative acts, of acts of the Council, of the Commission and of the European Central Bank, other than recommendations and opinions, and of acts of the European Parliament and of the European Council intended to produce legal effects *vis-à-vis* third parties. It shall also review the legality of acts of bodies, offices or agencies of the Union intended to produce legal effects *vis-à-vis* third parties.

It shall for this purpose have jurisdiction in actions brought by a Member State, the European Parliament, the Council or the Commission on grounds of lack of competence, infringement of an essential procedural requirement, infringement of the Treaties or of any rule of law relating to their application, or misuse of powers.

The Court shall have jurisdiction under the same conditions in actions brought by the Court of Auditors, by the European Central Bank and by the Committee of the Regions for the purpose of protecting their prerogatives.

Any natural or legal person may, under the conditions laid down in the first and second paragraphs, institute proceedings against an act addressed to that person or which is of direct and individual concern to them, and against a regulatory act which is of direct concern to them and does not entail implementing measures.

Acts setting up bodies, offices and agencies of the Union may lay down specific conditions and arrangements concerning actions brought by natural or legal persons against acts of these bodies, offices or agencies intended to produce legal effects in relation to them.

The proceedings provided for in this Article shall be instituted within two months of the publication of the measure, or of its notification to the plaintiff, or, in the absence thereof, of the day on which it came to the knowledge of the latter, as the case may be.

Article 264 (ex Article 231 TEC)

If the action is well founded, the Court of Justice of the European Union shall declare the act concerned to be void.

However, the Court shall, if it considers this necessary, state which of the effects of the act which it has declared void shall be considered as definitive.

Article 265 (ex Article 232 TEC)

Should the European Parliament, the European Council, the Council, the Commission or the European Central Bank, in infringement of the Treaties, fail to act, the Member States and the other institutions of the Union may bring an action before the Court of Justice of the European Union to have the infringement established. This Article shall apply, under the same conditions, to bodies, offices and agencies of the Union which fail to act.

The action shall be admissible only if the institution, body, office or agency concerned has first been called upon to act. If, within two months of being so called upon, the institution, body, office or agency concerned has not defined its position, the action may be brought within a further period of two months.

Any natural or legal person may, under the conditions laid down in the preceding paragraphs, complain to the Court that an institution, body, office or agency of the Union has failed to address to that person any act other than a recommendation or an opinion.

Article 266 (ex Article 233 TEC)

The institution whose act has been declared void or whose failure to act has been declared contrary to the Treaties shall be required to take the necessary measures to comply with the judgment of the Court of Justice of the European Union.

This obligation shall not affect any obligation which may result from the application of the second paragraph of Article 340.

Article 267 (ex Article 234 TEC)

The Court of Justice of the European Union shall have jurisdiction to give preliminary rulings concerning:

(a) the interpretation of the Treaties;

(b) the validity and interpretation of acts of the institutions, bodies, offices or agencies of the Union;

Where such a question is raised before any court or tribunal of a Member State, that court or tribunal may, if it considers that a decision on the question is necessary to enable it to give judgment, request the Court to give a ruling thereon.

Where any such question is raised in a case pending before a court or tribunal of a Member State against whose decisions there is no judicial remedy under national law, that court or tribunal shall bring the matter before the Court.

If such a question is raised in a case pending before a court or tribunal of a Member State with regard to a person in custody, the Court of Justice of the European Union shall act with the minimum of delay.

Article 268 (ex Article 235 TEC)

The Court of Justice of the European Union shall have jurisdiction in disputes relating to compensation for damage provided for in the second and third paragraphs of Article 340.

Article 269

The Court of Justice shall have jurisdiction to decide on the legality of an act adopted by the European Council or by the Council pursuant to Article 7 of the Treaty on European Union solely at the request of the Member State concerned by a determination of the European Council or of the Council and in respect solely of the procedural stipulations contained in that Article.

Such a request must be made within one month from the date of such determination.

The Court shall rule within one month from the date of the request.

Article 270 (ex Article 236 TEC)

The Court of Justice of the European Union shall have jurisdiction in any dispute between the Union and its servants within the limits and under the conditions laid down in the Staff Regulations of Officials and the Conditions of Employment of other servants of the Union.

Article 271 (ex Article 237 TEC)

The Court of Justice of the European Union shall, within the limits hereinafter laid down, have jurisdiction in disputes concerning:

(a) the fulfilment by Member States of obligations under the Statute of the European Investment Bank. In this connection, the Board of Directors of the Bank shall enjoy the powers conferred upon the Commission by Article 258;
(b) measures adopted by the Board of Governors of the European Investment Bank. In this connection, any Member State, the Commission or the Board of Directors of the Bank may institute proceedings under the conditions laid down in Article 263;
(c) measures adopted by the Board of Directors of the European Investment Bank. Proceedings against such measures may be instituted only by Member States or by the Commission, under the conditions laid down in Article 263, and solely on the grounds of non-compliance with the procedure provided for in Article 19(2), (5), (6) and (7) of the Statute of the Bank;
(d) the fulfilment by national central banks of obligations under the Treaties and the Statute of the ESCB and of the ECB. In this connection the powers of the Governing Council of the European Central Bank in respect of national central banks shall be the same as those conferred upon the Commission in respect of Member States by Article 258. If the Court finds that a national central bank has failed to fulfil an obligation under the Treaties, that bank shall be required to take the necessary measures to comply with the judgment of the Court.

Article 272 (ex Article 238 TEC)

The Court of Justice of the European Union shall have jurisdiction to give judgment pursuant to any arbitration clause contained in a contract concluded by or on behalf of the Union, whether that contract be governed by public or private law.

Article 273 (ex Article 239 TEC)

The Court of Justice shall have jurisdiction in any dispute between Member States which relates to the subject matter of the Treaties if the dispute is submitted to it under a special agreement between the parties.

Article 274 (ex Article 240 TEC)

Save where jurisdiction is conferred on the Court of Justice of the European Union by the Treaties, disputes to which the Union is a party shall not on that ground be excluded from the jurisdiction of the courts or tribunals of the Member States.

Article 275

The Court of Justice of the European Union shall not have jurisdiction with respect to the provisions relating to the common foreign and security policy nor with respect to acts adopted on the basis of those provisions.

However, the Court shall have jurisdiction to monitor compliance with Article 40 of the Treaty on European Union and to rule on proceedings, brought in accordance with the conditions laid down in the fourth paragraph of Article 263 of this Treaty, reviewing the legality of decisions providing for restrictive measures against natural or legal persons adopted by the Council on the basis of Chapter 2 of Title V of the Treaty on European Union.

Article 276

In exercising its powers regarding the provisions of Chapters 4 and 5 of Title V of Part Three relating to the area of freedom, security and justice, the Court of Justice of the European Union shall have no jurisdiction to review the validity or proportionality of operations carried out by the police or other law-enforcement services of a Member State or the exercise of the responsibilities incumbent upon Member States with regard to the maintenance of law and order and the safeguarding of internal security.

Article 277 (ex Article 241 TEC)

Notwithstanding the expiry of the period laid down in Article 263, sixth paragraph, any party may, in proceedings in which an act of general application adopted by an institution, body, office or agency of the Union is at issue, plead the grounds specified in Article 263, second paragraph, in order to invoke before the Court of Justice of the European Union the inapplicability of that act.

Article 278 (ex Article 242 TEC)

Actions brought before the Court of Justice of the European Union shall not have suspensory effect. The Court may, however, if it considers that circumstances so require, order that application of the contested act be suspended.

Article 279 (ex Article 243 TEC)

The Court of Justice of the European Union may in any cases before it prescribe any necessary interim measures.

Article 280 (ex Article 244 TEC)

The judgments of the Court of Justice of the European Union shall be enforceable under the conditions laid down in Article 299.

Article 281 (ex Article 245 TEC)

The Statute of the Court of Justice of the European Union shall be laid down in a separate Protocol.

The European Parliament and the Council, acting in accordance with the ordinary legislative procedure, may amend the provisions of the Statute, with the exception of Title I and Article 64. The European Parliament and the Council shall act either at the request of the Court of Justice and after consultation of the Commission, or on a proposal from the Commission and after consultation of the Court of Justice.

Section 6 The European Central Bank

Article 282

1. The European Central Bank, together with the national central banks, shall constitute the European System of Central Banks (ESCB). The European Central Bank, together with the national central banks of the Member States whose currency is the euro, which constitute the Eurosystem, shall conduct the monetary policy of the Union.

2. The ESCB shall be governed by the decision-making bodies of the European Central Bank. The primary objective of the ESCB shall be to maintain price stability. Without prejudice to that objective, it shall support the general economic policies in the Union in order to contribute to the achievement of the latter's objectives.

3. The European Central Bank shall have legal personality. It alone may authorise the issue of the euro. It shall be independent in the exercise of its powers and in the management of its finances. Union institutions, bodies, offices and agencies and the governments of the Member States shall respect that independence.

4. The European Central Bank shall adopt such measures as are necessary to carry out its tasks in accordance with Articles 127 to 133, with Article 138, and with the conditions laid down in the Statute of the ESCB and of the ECB. In accordance with these same Articles, those Member States whose currency is not the euro, and their central banks, shall retain their powers in monetary matters.

5. Within the areas falling within its responsibilities, the European Central Bank shall be consulted on all proposed Union acts , and all proposals for regulation at national level, and may give an opinion.

Article 283 (ex Article 112 TEC)

1. The Governing Council of the European Central Bank shall comprise the members of the Executive Board of the European Central Bank and the Governors of the national central banks of the Member States whose currency is the euro.

2. The Executive Board shall comprise the President, the Vice-President and four other members.

The President, the Vice-President and the other members of the Executive Board shall be appointed by the European Council, acting by a qualified majority, from among persons of recognised standing and professional experience in monetary or banking matters, on a recommendation from the Council, after it has consulted the European Parliament and the Governing Council of the European Central Bank.

Their term of office shall be eight years and shall not be renewable.

Only nationals of Member States may be members of the Executive Board.

Article 284 (ex Article 113 TEC)

1. The President of the Council and a Member of the Commission may participate, without having the right to vote, in meetings of the Governing Council of the European Central Bank.

The President of the Council may submit a motion for deliberation to the Governing Council of the European Central Bank.

2. The President of the European Central Bank shall be invited to participate in Council meetings when the Council is discussing matters relating to the objectives and tasks of the ESCB.

3. The European Central Bank shall address an annual report on the activities of the ESCB and on the monetary policy of both the previous and current year to the European Parliament, the Council and the Commission, and also to the European Council. The President of the European Central Bank shall present this report to the Council and to the European Parliament, which may hold a general debate on that basis.

The President of the European Central Bank and the other members of the Executive Board may, at the request of the European Parliament or on their own initiative, be heard by the competent committees of the European Parliament.

Section 7 The Court of Auditors

Article 285 (ex Article 246 TEC)

The Court of Auditors shall carry out the Union's audit.

It shall consist of one national of each Member State. Its Members shall be completely independent in the performance of their duties, in the Union's general interest.

Article 286 (ex Article 247 TEC)

1. The Members of the Court of Auditors shall be chosen from among persons who belong or have belonged in their respective States to external audit bodies or who are especially qualified for this office. Their independence must be beyond doubt.

2. The Members of the Court of Auditors shall be appointed for a term of six years. The Council, after consulting the European Parliament, shall adopt the list of Members drawn up in accordance with the proposals made by each Member State. The term of office of the Members of the Court of Auditors shall be renewable.

They shall elect the President of the Court of Auditors from among their number for a term of three years. The President may be re-elected.

3. In the performance of these duties, the Members of the Court of Auditors shall neither seek nor take instructions from any government or from any other body. The Members of the Court of Auditors shall refrain from any action incompatible with their duties.

4. The Members of the Court of Auditors may not, during their term of office, engage in any other occupation, whether gainful or not. When entering upon their duties they shall give a solemn undertaking that, both during and after their term of office, they will respect the obligations arising therefrom and in particular their duty to behave with integrity and discretion as regards the acceptance, after they have ceased to hold office, of certain appointments or benefits.

5. Apart from normal replacement, or death, the duties of a Member of the Court of Auditors shall end when he resigns, or is compulsorily retired by a ruling of the Court of Justice pursuant to paragraph 6.

The vacancy thus caused shall be filled for the remainder of the Member's term of office.

Save in the case of compulsory retirement, Members of the Court of Auditors shall remain in office until they have been replaced.

6. A Member of the Court of Auditors may be deprived of his office or of his right to a pension or other benefits in its stead only if the Court of Justice, at the request of the Court of Auditors, finds that he no longer fulfils the requisite conditions or meets the obligations arising from his office.

7. The Council shall determine the conditions of employment of the President and the Members of the Court of Auditors and in particular their salaries, allowances and pensions. It shall also determine any payment to be made instead of remuneration.

8. The provisions of the Protocol on the privileges and immunities of the European Union applicable to the Judges of the Court of Justice of the European Union shall also apply to the Members of the Court of Auditors.

Article 287 (ex Article 248 TEC)

1. The Court of Auditors shall examine the accounts of all revenue and expenditure of the Union. It shall also examine the accounts of all revenue and expenditure of all bodies, offices or agencies set up by the Union in so far as the relevant constituent instrument does not preclude such examination.

The Court of Auditors shall provide the European Parliament and the Council with a statement of assurance as to the reliability of the accounts and the legality and regularity of the underlying transactions which shall be published in the *Official Journal of the European Union*. This statement may be supplemented by specific assessments for each major area of Union activity.

2. The Court of Auditors shall examine whether all revenue has been received and all expenditure incurred in a lawful and regular manner and whether the financial management has been sound. In doing so, it shall report in particular on any cases of irregularity.

The audit of revenue shall be carried out on the basis both of the amounts established as due and the amounts actually paid to the Union.

The audit of expenditure shall be carried out on the basis both of commitments undertaken and payments made.

These audits may be carried out before the closure of accounts for the financial year in question.

3. The audit shall be based on records and, if necessary, performed on the spot in the other institutions of the Union, on the premises of any body, office or agency which manages revenue or expenditure on behalf of the Union and in the Member States, including on the premises of any natural or legal person in receipt of payments from the budget. In the Member States the audit shall be carried out in liaison with national audit bodies or, if these do not have the necessary powers, with the competent national departments. The Court of Auditors and the national audit bodies of the Member States shall cooperate in a spirit of trust while maintaining their independence. These bodies or departments shall inform the Court of Auditors whether they intend to take part in the audit.

The other institutions of the Union, any bodies, offices or agencies managing revenue or expenditure on behalf of the Union, any natural or legal person in receipt of payments from the budget, and the national audit bodies or, if these do not have the necessary powers, the competent national departments, shall forward to the Court of Auditors, at its request, any document or information necessary to carry out its task.

In respect of the European Investment Bank's activity in managing Union expenditure and revenue, the Court's rights of access to information held by the Bank shall be governed by an agreement between the Court, the Bank and the Commission. In the absence of an agreement, the Court shall nevertheless have access to information necessary for the audit of Union expenditure and revenue managed by the Bank.

4. The Court of Auditors shall draw up an annual report after the close of each financial year. It shall be forwarded to the other institutions of the Union and shall be published, together with the replies of these institutions to the observations of the Court of Auditors, in the *Official Journal of the European Union*.

The Court of Auditors may also, at any time, submit observations, particularly in the form of special reports, on specific questions and deliver opinions at the request of one of the other institutions of the Union.

It shall adopt its annual reports, special reports or opinions by a majority of its Members. However, it may establish internal chambers in order to adopt certain categories of reports or opinions under the conditions laid down by its Rules of Procedure.

It shall assist the European Parliament and the Council in exercising their powers of control over the implementation of the budget.

The Court of Auditors shall draw up its Rules of Procedure. Those rules shall require the approval of the Council.

Chapter 2 Legal acts of the Union, adoption procedures and other provisions

Section 1 The legal acts of the Union

Article 288 (ex Article 249 TEC)

To exercise the Union's competences, the institutions shall adopt regulations, directives, decisions, recommendations and opinions.

A regulation shall have general application. It shall be binding in its entirety and directly applicable in all Member States.

A directive shall be binding, as to the result to be achieved, upon each Member State to which it is addressed, but shall leave to the national authorities the choice of form and methods.

A decision shall be binding in its entirety. A decision which specifies those to whom it is addressed shall be binding only on them.

Recommendations and opinions shall have no binding force.

Article 289

1. The ordinary legislative procedure shall consist in the joint adoption by the European Parliament and the Council of a regulation, directive or decision on a proposal from the Commission. This procedure is defined in Article 294.

2. In the specific cases provided for by the Treaties, the adoption of a regulation, directive or decision by the European Parliament with the participation of the Council, or by the latter with the participation of the European Parliament, shall constitute a special legislative procedure.

3. Legal acts adopted by legislative procedure shall constitute legislative acts.

4. In the specific cases provided for by the Treaties, legislative acts may be adopted on the initiative of a group of Member States or of the European Parliament, on a recommendation from the European Central Bank or at the request of the Court of Justice or the European Investment Bank.

Article 290

1. A legislative act may delegate to the Commission the power to adopt non-legislative acts of general application to supplement or amend certain non-essential elements of the legislative act.

The objectives, content, scope and duration of the delegation of power shall be explicitly defined in the legislative acts. The essential elements of an area shall be reserved for the legislative act and accordingly shall not be the subject of a delegation of power.

2. Legislative acts shall explicitly lay down the conditions to which the delegation is subject; these conditions may be as follows:

(a) the European Parliament or the Council may decide to revoke the delegation;

(b) the delegated act may enter into force only if no objection has been expressed by the European Parliament or the Council within a period set by the legislative act.

For the purposes of (a) and (b), the European Parliament shall act by a majority of its component members, and the Council by a qualified majority.

3. The adjective 'delegated' shall be inserted in the title of delegated acts.

Article 291

1. Member States shall adopt all measures of national law necessary to implement legally binding Union acts.

2. Where uniform conditions for implementing legally binding Union acts are needed, those acts shall confer implementing powers on the Commission, or, in duly justified specific cases and in the cases provided for in Articles 24 and 26 of the Treaty on European Union, on the Council.

3. For the purposes of paragraph 2, the European Parliament and the Council, acting by means of regulations in accordance with the ordinary legislative procedure, shall lay down in advance the rules and general principles concerning mechanisms for control by Member States of the Commission's exercise of implementing powers.

4. The word 'implementing' shall be inserted in the title of implementing acts.

Article 292

The Council shall adopt recommendations. It shall act on a proposal from the Commission in all cases where the Treaties provide that it shall adopt acts on a proposal from the Commission. It shall act unanimously in those areas in which unanimity is required for the adoption of a Union act. The Commission, and the European Central Bank in the specific cases provided for in the Treaties, shall adopt recommendations.

Section 2 Procedures for the adoption of acts and other provisions

Article 293 (ex Article 250 TEC)

1. Where, pursuant to the Treaties, the Council acts on a proposal from the Commission, it may amend that proposal only by acting unanimously, except in the cases referred to in paragraphs 10 and 13 of Article 294, in Articles 310, 312 and 314 and in the second paragraph of Article 315.

2. As long as the Council has not acted, the Commission may alter its proposal at any time during the procedures leading to the adoption of a Union act.

Article 294 (ex Article 251 TEC)

1. Where reference is made in the Treaties to the ordinary legislative procedure for the adoption of an act, the following procedure shall apply.

2. The Commission shall submit a proposal to the European Parliament and the Council.

First reading

3. The European Parliament shall adopt its position at first reading and communicate it to the Council.

4. If the Council approves the European Parliament's position, the act concerned shall be adopted in the wording which corresponds to the position of the European Parliament.

5. If the Council does not approve the European Parliament's position, it shall adopt its position at first reading and communicate it to the European Parliament.

6. The Council shall inform the European Parliament fully of the reasons which led it to adopt its position at first reading. The Commission shall inform the European Parliament fully of its position.

Second reading

7. If, within three months of such communication, the European Parliament:
   - (a) approves the Council's position at first reading or has not taken a decision, the act concerned shall be deemed to have been adopted in the wording which corresponds to the position of the Council;
   - (b) rejects, by a majority of its component members, the Council's position at first reading, the proposed act shall be deemed not to have been adopted;
   - (c) proposes, by a majority of its component members, amendments to the Council's position at first reading, the text thus amended shall be forwarded to the Council and to the Commission, which shall deliver an opinion on those amendments.

8. If, within three months of receiving the European Parliament's amendments, the Council, acting by a qualified majority:

(a) approves all those amendments, the act in question shall be deemed to have been adopted;

(b) does not approve all the amendments, the President of the Council, in agreement with the President of the European Parliament, shall within six weeks convene a meeting of the Conciliation Committee.

9. The Council shall act unanimously on the amendments on which the Commission has delivered a negative opinion.

Conciliation

10. The Conciliation Committee, which shall be composed of the members of the Council or their representatives and an equal number of members representing the European Parliament, shall have the task of reaching agreement on a joint text, by a qualified majority of the members of the Council or their representatives and by a majority of the members representing the European Parliament within six weeks of its being convened, on the basis of the positions of the European Parliament and the Council at second reading.

11. The Commission shall take part in the Conciliation Committee's proceedings and shall take all necessary initiatives with a view to reconciling the positions of the European Parliament and the Council.

12. If, within six weeks of its being convened, the Conciliation Committee does not approve the joint text, the proposed act shall be deemed not to have been adopted.

Third reading

13. If, within that period, the Conciliation Committee approves a joint text, the European Parliament, acting by a majority of the votes cast, and the Council, acting by a qualified majority, shall each have a period of six weeks from that approval in which to adopt the act in question in accordance with the joint text. If they fail to do so, the proposed act shall be deemed not to have been adopted.

14. The periods of three months and six weeks referred to in this Article shall be extended by a maximum of one month and two weeks respectively at the initiative of the European Parliament or the Council.

Special provisions

15. Where, in the cases provided for in the Treaties, a legislative act is submitted to the ordinary legislative procedure on the initiative of a group of Member States, on a recommendation by the European Central Bank, or at the request of the Court of Justice, paragraph 2, the second sentence of paragraph 6, and paragraph 9 shall not apply.

In such cases, the European Parliament and the Council shall communicate the proposed act to the Commission with their positions at first and second readings. The European Parliament or the Council may request the opinion of the Commission throughout the procedure, which the Commission may also deliver on its own initiative. It may also, if it deems it necessary, take part in the Conciliation Committee in accordance with paragraph 11.

Article 295

The European Parliament, the Council and the Commission shall consult each other and by common agreement make arrangements for their cooperation. To that end, they may, in compliance with the Treaties, conclude interinstitutional agreements which may be of a binding nature.

Article 296 (ex Article 253 TEC)

Where the Treaties do not specify the type of act to be adopted, the institutions shall select it on a case-by-case basis, in compliance with the applicable procedures and with the principle of proportionality.

Legal acts shall state the reasons on which they are based and shall refer to any proposals, initiatives, recommendations, requests or opinions required by the Treaties.

When considering draft legislative acts, the European Parliament and the Council shall refrain from adopting acts not provided for by the relevant legislative procedure in the area in question.

Article 297 (ex Article 254 TEC)

1. Legislative acts adopted under the ordinary legislative procedure shall be signed by the President of the European Parliament and by the President of the Council.

Legislative acts adopted under a special legislative procedure shall be signed by the President of the institution which adopted them.

Legislative acts shall be published in the *Official Journal of the European Union*. They shall enter into force on the date specified in them or, in the absence thereof, on the twentieth day following that of their publication.

2. Non-legislative acts adopted in the form of regulations, directives or decisions, when the latter do not specify to whom they are addressed, shall be signed by the President of the institution which adopted them.

Regulations and directives which are addressed to all Member States, as well as decisions which do not specify to whom they are addressed, shall be published in the *Official Journal of the European Union*. They shall enter into force on the date specified in them or, in the absence thereof, on the twentieth day following that of their publication.

Other directives, and decisions which specify to whom they are addressed, shall be notified to those to whom they are addressed and shall take effect upon such notification.

Article 298

1. In carrying out their missions, the institutions, bodies, offices and agencies of the Union shall have the support of an open, efficient and independent European administration.

2. In compliance with the Staff Regulations and the Conditions of Employment adopted on the basis of Article 336, the European Parliament and the Council, acting by means of regulations in accordance with the ordinary legislative procedure, shall establish provisions to that end.

Article 299 (ex Article 256 TEC)

Acts of the Council, the Commission or the European Central Bank which impose a pecuniary obligation on persons other than States, shall be enforceable.

Enforcement shall be governed by the rules of civil procedure in force in the State in the territory of which it is carried out. The order for its enforcement shall be appended to the decision, without other formality than verification of the authenticity of the decision, by the national authority which the government of each Member State shall designate for this purpose and shall make known to the Commission and to the Court of Justice of the European Union.

When these formalities have been completed on application by the party concerned, the latter may proceed to enforcement in accordance with the national law, by bringing the matter directly before the competent authority.

Enforcement may be suspended only by a decision of the Court. However, the courts of the country concerned shall have jurisdiction over complaints that enforcement is being carried out in an irregular manner.

Chapter 3 The Union's advisory bodies

Article 300

1. The European Parliament, the Council and the Commission shall be assisted by an Economic and Social Committee and a Committee of the Regions, exercising advisory functions.

2. The Economic and Social Committee shall consist of representatives of organisations of employers, of the employed, and of other parties representative of civil society, notably in socio-economic, civic, professional and cultural areas.

3. The Committee of the Regions shall consist of representatives of regional and local bodies who either hold a regional or local authority electoral mandate or are politically accountable to an elected assembly.

4. The members of the Economic and Social Committee and of the Committee of the Regions shall not be bound by any mandatory instructions. They shall be completely independent in the performance of their duties, in the Union's general interest.

5. The rules referred to in paragraphs 2 and 3 governing the nature of the composition of the Committees shall be reviewed at regular intervals by the Council to take account of economic, social and demographic developments within the Union. The Council, on a proposal from the Commission, shall adopt decisions to that end.

Section 1 The Economic and Social Committee

Article 301 (ex Article 258 TEC)

The number of members of the Economic and Social Committee shall not exceed 350.

The Council, acting unanimously on a proposal from the Commission, shall adopt a decision determining the Committee's composition.

The Council shall determine the allowances of members of the Committee.

Article 302 (ex Article 259 TEC)

1. The members of the Committee shall be appointed for five years The Council shall adopt the list of members drawn up in accordance with the proposals made by each Member State. The term of office of the members of the Committee shall be renewable.

2. The Council shall act after consulting the Commission. It may obtain the opinion of European bodies which are representative of the various economic and social sectors and of civil society to which the Union's activities are of concern.

Article 303 (ex Article 260 TEC)

The Committee shall elect its chairman and officers from among its members for a term of two and a half years.

It shall adopt its Rules of Procedure.

The Committee shall be convened by its chairman at the request of the European Parliament, the Council or of the Commission. It may also meet on its own initiative.

Article 304 (ex Article 262 TEC)

The Committee shall be consulted by the European Parliament, by the Council or by the Commission where the Treaties so provide. The Committee may be consulted by these institutions in all cases in which they consider it appropriate. It may issue an opinion on its own initiative in cases in which it considers such action appropriate.

The European Parliament, the Council or the Commission shall, if it considers it necessary, set the Committee, for the submission of its opinion, a time limit which may not be less than one month from the date on which the chairman receives notification to this effect. Upon expiry of the time limit, the absence of an opinion shall not prevent further action.

The opinion of the Committee, together with a record of the proceedings, shall be forwarded to the European Parliament, to the Council and to the Commission.

Section 2 The Committee of the Regions

Article 305 (ex Article 263, second, third and fourth paragraphs, TEC)

The number of members of the Committee of the Regions shall not exceed 350.

The Council, acting unanimously on a proposal from the Commission, shall adopt a decision determining the Committee's composition.

The members of the Committee and an equal number of alternate members shall be appointed for five years. Their term of office shall be renewable. The Council shall adopt the list of members and alternate members drawn up in accordance with the proposals made by each Member State. When the mandate referred to in Article 300(3) on the basis of which they were proposed comes to an end, the term of office of members of the Committee shall terminate automatically and they shall then be replaced for the remainder of the said term of office in accordance with the same procedure. No member of the Committee shall at the same time be a Member of the European Parliament.

Article 306 (ex Article 264 TEC)

The Committee of the Regions shall elect its chairman and officers from among its members for a term of two and a half years.

It shall adopt its Rules of Procedure.

The Committee shall be convened by its chairman at the request of the European Parliament, the Council or of the Commission. It may also meet on its own initiative.

Article 307 (ex Article 265 TEC)

The Committee of the Regions shall be consulted by the European Parliament, by the Council or by the Commission where the Treaties so provide and in all other cases, in particular those which concern cross-border cooperation, in which one of these institutions considers it appropriate.

The European Parliament, the Council or the Commission shall, if it considers it necessary, set the Committee, for the submission of its opinion, a time limit which may not be less than one month from the date on which the chairman receives notification to this effect. Upon expiry of the time limit, the absence of an opinion shall not prevent further action.

Where the Economic and Social Committee is consulted pursuant to Article 304, the Committee of the Regions shall be informed by the European Parliament, the Council or the Commission of the request for an opinion. Where it considers that specific regional interests are involved, the Committee of the Regions may issue an opinion on the matter.

It may issue an opinion on its own initiative in cases in which it considers such action appropriate.

The opinion of the Committee, together with a record of the proceedings, shall be forwarded to the European Parliament, to the Council and to the Commission.

Chapter 4 The European Investment Bank

Article 308 (ex Article 266 TEC)

The European Investment Bank shall have legal personality.

The members of the European Investment Bank shall be the Member States.

The Statute of the European Investment Bank is laid down in a Protocol annexed to the Treaties. The Council acting unanimously in accordance with a special legislative procedure, at the request of the European Investment Bank and after consulting the European Parliament and the Commission, or on a proposal from the Commission and after consulting the European Parliament and the European Investment Bank, may amend the Statute of the Bank.

Article 309 (ex Article 267 TEC)

The task of the European Investment Bank shall be to contribute, by having recourse to the capital market and utilising its own resources, to the balanced and steady development of the internal market in the interest of the Union. For this purpose the Bank shall, operating on a non-profit-making basis, grant loans and give guarantees which facilitate the financing of the following projects in all sectors of the economy:

(a) projects for developing less-developed regions;

(b) projects for modernising or converting undertakings or for developing fresh activities called for by the establishment or functioning of the internal market, where these projects are of such a size or nature that they cannot be entirely financed by the various means available in the individual Member States;

(c) projects of common interest to several Member States which are of such a size or nature that they cannot be entirely financed by the various means available in the individual Member States.

In carrying out its task, the Bank shall facilitate the financing of investment programmes in conjunction with assistance from the Structural Funds and other Union Financial Instruments.

Title II Financial provisions

Article 310 (ex Article 268 TEC)

1. All items of revenue and expenditure of the Union shall be included in estimates to be drawn up for each financial year and shall be shown in the budget.

The Union's annual budget shall be established by the European Parliament and the Council in accordance with Article 314.

The revenue and expenditure shown in the budget shall be in balance.

2. The expenditure shown in the budget shall be authorised for the annual budgetary period in accordance with the regulation referred to in Article 322.

3. The implementation of expenditure shown in the budget shall require the prior adoption of a legally binding Union act providing a legal basis for its action and for the implementation of the corresponding expenditure in accordance with the regulation referred to in Article 322, except in cases for which that law provides.

4. With a view to maintaining budgetary discipline, the Union shall not adopt any act which is likely to have appreciable implications for the budget without providing an assurance that the expenditure arising from such an act is capable of being financed within the limit of the Union's own resources and in compliance with the multiannual financial framework referred to in Article 312.

5. The budget shall be implemented in accordance with the principle of sound financial management. Member States shall cooperate with the Union to ensure that the appropriations entered in the budget are used in accordance with this principle.

6. The Union and the Member States, in accordance with Article 325, shall counter fraud and any other illegal activities affecting the financial interests of the Union.

Chapter 1 The Union's own resources

Article 311 (ex Article 269 TEC)

The Union shall provide itself with the means necessary to attain its objectives and carry through its policies.

Without prejudice to other revenue, the budget shall be financed wholly from own resources.

The Council, acting in accordance with a special legislative procedure, shall unanimously and after consulting the European Parliament adopt a decision laying down the provisions relating to the system of own resources of the Union. In this context it may establish new categories of own resources or abolish an existing category. That decision shall not enter into force until it is approved by the Member States in accordance with their respective constitutional requirements.

The Council, acting by means of regulations in accordance with a special legislative procedure, shall lay down implementing measures for the Union's own resources system in so far as this is provided for in the decision adopted on the basis of the third paragraph. The Council shall act after obtaining the consent of the European Parliament.

Chapter 2 The multiannual financial framework

Article 312

1. The multiannual financial framework shall ensure that Union expenditure develops in an orderly manner and within the limits of its own resources.

It shall be established for a period of at least five years.

The annual budget of the Union shall comply with the multiannual financial framework.

2. The Council, acting in accordance with a special legislative procedure, shall adopt a regulation laying down the multiannual financial framework. The Council shall act unanimously after obtaining the consent of the European Parliament, which shall be given by a majority of its component members.

The European Council may, unanimously, adopt a decision authorising the Council to act by a qualified majority when adopting the regulation referred to in the first subparagraph.

3. The financial framework shall determine the amounts of the annual ceilings on commitment appropriations by category of expenditure and of the annual ceiling on payment appropriations. The categories of expenditure, limited in number, shall correspond to the Union's major sectors of activity.

The financial framework shall lay down any other provisions required for the annual budgetary procedure to run smoothly.

4. Where no Council regulation determining a new financial framework has been adopted by the end of the previous financial framework, the ceilings and other provisions corresponding to the last year of that framework shall be extended until such time as that act is adopted.

5. Throughout the procedure leading to the adoption of the financial framework, the European Parliament, the Council and the Commission shall take any measure necessary to facilitate its adoption.

Chapter 3 The Union's annual budget

Article 313 (ex Article 272(1), TEC)

The financial year shall run from 1 January to 31 December.

Article 314 (ex Article 272(2) to (10), TEC)

The European Parliament and the Council, acting in accordance with a special legislative procedure, shall establish the Union's annual budget in accordance with the following provisions.

1. With the exception of the European Central Bank, each institution shall, before 1 July, draw up estimates of its expenditure for the following financial year. The Commission shall consolidate these estimates in a draft budget. which may contain different estimates.

The draft budget shall contain an estimate of revenue and an estimate of expenditure.

2. The Commission shall submit a proposal containing the draft budget to the European Parliament and to the Council not later than 1 September of the year preceding that in which the budget is to be implemented.

The Commission may amend the draft budget during the procedure until such time as the Conciliation Committee, referred to in paragraph 5, is convened.

3. The Council shall adopt its position on the draft budget and forward it to the European Parliament not later than 1 October of the year preceding that in which the budget is to be implemented. The Council shall inform the European Parliament in full of the reasons which led it to adopt its position.

4. If, within forty-two days of such communication, the European Parliament:

(a) approves the position of the Council, the budget shall be adopted;

(b) has not taken a decision, the budget shall be deemed to have been adopted;

(c) adopts amendments by a majority of its component members, the amended draft shall be forwarded to the Council and to the Commission. The President of the European Parliament, in agreement with the President of the Council, shall immediately convene a meeting of the Conciliation Committee. However, if within ten days of the draft being forwarded the Council informs the European Parliament that it has approved all its amendments, the Conciliation Committee shall not meet.

5. The Conciliation Committee, which shall be composed of the members of the Council or their representatives and an equal number of members representing the European Parliament, shall have the task of reaching agreement on a joint text, by a qualified majority of the members of the Council or their representatives and by a majority of the representatives of the European Parliament within twenty-one days of its being convened, on the basis of the positions of the European Parliament and the Council.

The Commission shall take part in the Conciliation Committee's proceedings and shall take all the necessary initiatives with a view to reconciling the positions of the European Parliament and the Council.

6. If, within the twenty-one days referred to in paragraph 5, the Conciliation Committee agrees on a joint text, the European Parliament and the Council shall each have a period of fourteen days from the date of that agreement in which to approve the joint text.

7. If, within the period of fourteen days referred to in paragraph 6:

(a) the European Parliament and the Council both approve the joint text or fail to take a decision, or if one of these institutions approves the joint text while the other one fails to take a decision, the budget shall be deemed to be definitively adopted in accordance with the joint text; or

(b) the European Parliament, acting by a majority of its component members, and the Council both reject the joint text, or if one of these institutions rejects the joint text while the other one fails to take a decision, a new draft budget shall be submitted by the Commission; or

(c) the European Parliament, acting by a majority of its component members, rejects the joint text while the Council approves it, a new draft budget shall be submitted by the Commission; or

(d) the European Parliament approves the joint text whilst the Council rejects it, the European Parliament may, within fourteen days from the date of the rejection by the Council and acting by a majority of its component members and three-fifths of the votes cast, decide to confirm all or some of the amendments referred to in paragraph 4(c). Where a European Parliament amendment is not confirmed, the position agreed in the Conciliation Committee on the budget heading which is the subject of the amendment shall be retained. The budget shall be deemed to be definitively adopted on this basis.

8. If, within the twenty-one days referred to in paragraph 5, the Conciliation Committee does not agree on a joint text, a new draft budget shall be submitted by the Commission.

9. When the procedure provided for in this Article has been completed, the President of the European Parliament shall declare that the budget has been definitively adopted.

10. Each institution shall exercise the powers conferred upon it under this Article in compliance with the Treaties and the acts adopted thereunder, with particular regard to the Union's own resources and the balance between revenue and expenditure.

Article 315 (ex Article 273 TEC)

If, at the beginning of a financial year, the budget has not yet been definitively adopted, a sum equivalent to not more than one-twelfth of the budget appropriations for the preceding financial year may be spent each month in respect of any chapter of the budget in accordance with the provisions of the Regulations made pursuant to Article 322; that sum shall not, however, exceed one-twelfth of the appropriations provided for in the same chapter of the draft budget.

The Council on a proposal by the Commission, may, provided that the other conditions laid down in the first paragraph are observed, authorise expenditure in excess of one-twelfth in accordance with the regulations made pursuant to Article 322. The Council shall forward the decision immediately to the European Parliament.

The decision referred to in the second paragraph shall lay down the necessary measures relating to resources to ensure application of this Article, in accordance with the acts referred to in Article 311.

It shall enter into force thirty days following its adoption if the European Parliament, acting by a majority of its component Members, has not decided to reduce this expenditure within that time limit.

Article 316 (ex Article 271 TEC)

In accordance with conditions to be laid down pursuant to Article 322, any appropriations, other than those relating to staff expenditure, that are unexpended at the end of the financial year may be carried forward to the next financial year only.

Appropriations shall be classified under different chapters grouping items of expenditure according to their nature or purpose and subdivided in accordance with the regulations made pursuant to Article 322.

The expenditure of the European Parliament, the European Council and the Council, the Commission and the Court of Justice of the European Union shall be set out in separate parts of the budget, without prejudice to special arrangements for certain common items of expenditure.

Chapter 4 Implementation of the budget and discharge

Article 317 (ex Article 274 TEC)

The Commission shall implement the budget in cooperation with the Member States, in accordance with the provisions of the regulations made pursuant to Article 322, on its own responsibility and within the limits of the appropriations, having regard to the principles of sound financial management. Member States shall cooperate with the Commission to ensure that the appropriations are used in accordance with the principles of sound financial management.

The regulations shall lay down the control and audit obligations of the Member States in the implementation of the budget and the resulting responsibilities. They shall also lay down the responsibilities and detailed rules for each institution concerning its part in effecting its own expenditure.

Within the budget, the Commission may, subject to the limits and conditions laid down in the regulations made pursuant to Article 322, transfer appropriations from one chapter to another or from one subdivision to another.

Article 318 (ex Article 275 TEC)

The Commission shall submit annually to the European Parliament and to the Council the accounts of the preceding financial year relating to the implementation of the budget. The Commission shall also forward to them a financial statement of the assets and liabilities of the Union.

The Commission shall also submit to the European Parliament and to the Council an evaluation report on the Union's finances based on the results achieved, in particular in relation to the indications given by the European Parliament and the Council pursuant to Article 319.

Article 319 (ex Article 276 TEC)

1. The European Parliament, acting on a recommendation from the Council, shall give a discharge to the Commission in respect of the implementation of the budget. To this end, the Council and the European Parliament in turn shall examine the accounts, the financial statement and the evaluation report referred to in Article 318, the annual report by the Court of Auditors together with the replies of the institutions under audit to the observations of the Court of Auditors, the statement of assurance referred to in Article 287(1), second subparagraph and any relevant special reports by the Court of Auditors.

2. Before giving a discharge to the Commission, or for any other purpose in connection with the exercise of its powers over the implementation of the budget, the European Parliament may ask to hear the Commission give evidence with regard to the execution of expenditure or the operation of financial control systems. The Commission shall submit any necessary information to the European Parliament at the latter's request.

3. The Commission shall take all appropriate steps to act on the observations in the decisions giving discharge and on other observations by the European Parliament relating to the execution of expenditure, as well as on comments accompanying the recommendations on discharge adopted by the Council.

At the request of the European Parliament or the Council, the Commission shall report on the measures taken in the light of these observations and comments and in particular on the instructions given to the departments which are responsible for the implementation of the budget. These reports shall also be forwarded to the Court of Auditors.

Chapter 5 Common provisions

Article 320 (ex Article 277 TEC)

The multiannual financial framework and the annual budget shall be drawn up in euro.

Article 321 (ex Article 278 TEC)

The Commission may, provided it notifies the competent authorities of the Member States concerned, transfer into the currency of one of the Member States its holdings in the currency of another Member State, to the extent necessary to enable them to be used for purposes which come within the scope of the Treaties. The Commission shall as far as possible avoid making such transfers if it possesses cash or liquid assets in the currencies which it needs.

The Commission shall deal with each Member State through the authority designated by the State concerned. In carrying out financial operations the Commission shall employ the services of the bank of issue of the Member State concerned or of any other financial institution approved by that State.

Article 322 (ex Article 279 TEC)

1. The European Parliament and the Council, acting in accordance with the ordinary legislative procedure, and after consulting the Court of Auditors, shall adopt by means of regulations:

(a) the financial rules which determine in particular the procedure to be adopted for establishing and implementing the budget and for presenting and auditing accounts;

(b) rules providing for checks on the responsibility of financial actors, in particular authorising officers and accounting officers.

2. The Council, acting on a proposal from the Commission and after consulting the European Parliament and the Court of Auditors, shall determine the methods and procedure whereby the budget revenue provided under the arrangements relating to the Union's own resources shall be made available to the Commission, and determine the measures to be applied, if need be, to meet cash requirements.

Article 323

The European Parliament, the Council and the Commission shall ensure that the financial means are made available to allow the Union to fulfil its legal obligations in respect of third parties.

Article 324

Regular meetings between the Presidents of the European Parliament, the Council and the Commission shall be convened, on the initiative of the Commission, under the budgetary procedures referred to in this Title. The Presidents shall take all the necessary steps to promote consultation and the reconciliation of the positions of the institutions over which they preside in order to facilitate the implementation of this Title.

Chapter 6 Combating fraud

Article 325 (ex Article 280 TEC)

1. The Union and the Member States shall counter fraud and any other illegal activities affecting the financial interests of the Union through measures to be taken in accordance with this Article, which shall act as a deterrent and be such as to afford effective protection in the Member States, and in all the Union's institutions, bodies, offices and agencies.

2. Member States shall take the same measures to counter fraud affecting the financial interests of the Union as they take to counter fraud affecting their own financial interests.

3. Without prejudice to other provisions of the Treaties, the Member States shall coordinate their action aimed at protecting the financial interests of the Union against fraud. To this end they shall organise, together with the Commission, close and regular cooperation between the competent authorities.

4. The European Parliament and the Council, acting in accordance with the ordinary legislative procedure, after consulting the Court of Auditors, shall adopt the necessary measures in the fields of

the prevention of and fight against fraud affecting the financial interests of the Union with a view to affording effective and equivalent protection in the Member States and in all the Union's institutions, bodies, offices and agencies.

5. The Commission, in cooperation with Member States, shall each year submit to the European Parliament and to the Council a report on the measures taken for the implementation of this Article.

Title III Enhanced cooperation

Article 326 (ex Articles 27a to 27e, 40 to 40b and 43 to 45 TEU and ex Articles 11 and 11a TEC)

Any enhanced cooperation shall comply with the Treaties and Union law.

Such cooperation shall not undermine the internal market or economic, social and territorial cohesion. It shall not constitute a barrier to or discrimination in trade between Member States, nor shall it distort competition between them.

Article 327 (ex Articles 27a to 27e, 40 to 40b and 43 to 45 TEU and ex Articles 11 and 11a TEC)

Any enhanced cooperation shall respect the competences, rights and obligations of those Member States which do not participate in it. Those Member States shall not impede its implementation by the participating Member States.

Article 328 (ex Articles 27a to 27e, 40 to 40b and 43 to 45 TEU and ex Articles 11 and 11a TEC)

1. When enhanced cooperation is being established, it shall be open to all Member States, subject to compliance with any conditions of participation laid down by the authorising decision. It shall also be open to them at any other time, subject to compliance with the acts already adopted within that framework, in addition to those conditions.

The Commission and the Member States participating in enhanced cooperation shall ensure that they promote participation by as many Member States as possible.

2. The Commission and, where appropriate, the High Representative of the Union for Foreign Affairs and Security Policy shall keep the European Parliament and the Council regularly informed regarding developments in enhanced cooperation.

Article 329 (ex Articles 27a to 27e, 40 to 40b and 43 to 45 TEU and ex Articles 11 and 11a TEC)

1. Member States which wish to establish enhanced cooperation between themselves in one of the areas covered by the Treaties, with the exception of fields of exclusive competence and the common foreign and security policy, shall address a request to the Commission, specifying the scope and objectives of the enhanced cooperation proposed. The Commission may submit a proposal to the Council to that effect. In the event of the Commission not submitting a proposal, it shall inform the Member States concerned of the reasons for not doing so.

Authorisation to proceed with the enhanced cooperation referred to in the first subparagraph shall be granted by the Council, on a proposal from the Commission and after obtaining the consent of the European Parliament.

2. The request of the Member States which wish to establish enhanced cooperation between themselves within the framework of the common foreign and security policy shall be addressed to the Council. It shall be forwarded to the High Representative of the Union for Foreign Affairs and Security Policy, who shall give an opinion on whether the enhanced cooperation proposed is consistent with the Union's common foreign and security policy, and to the Commission, which shall give its opinion in particular on whether the enhanced cooperation proposed is consistent with other Union policies. It shall also be forwarded to the European Parliament for information.

Authorisation to proceed with enhanced cooperation shall be granted by a decision of the Council acting unanimously.

Article 330 (ex Articles 27a to 27e, 40 to 40b and 43 to 45 TEU and ex Articles 11 and 11a TEC)

All members of the Council may participate in its deliberations, but only members of the Council representing the Member States participating in enhanced cooperation shall take part in the vote.

Unanimity shall be constituted by the votes of the representatives of the participating Member States only.

A qualified majority shall be defined in accordance with Article 238(3).

Article 331 (ex Articles 27a to 27e, 40 to 40b and 43 to 45 TEU and ex Articles 11 and 11a TEC)

1. Any Member State which wishes to participate in enhanced cooperation in progress in one of the areas referred to in Article 329(1) shall notify its intention to the Council and the Commission.

The Commission shall, within four months of the date of receipt of the notification, confirm the participation of the Member State concerned. It shall note where necessary that the conditions of participation have been fulfilled and shall adopt any transitional measures necessary with regard to the application of the acts already adopted within the framework of enhanced cooperation.

However, if the Commission considers that the conditions of participation have not been fulfilled, it shall indicate the arrangements to be adopted to fulfil those conditions and shall set a deadline for re-examining the request. On the expiry of that deadline, it shall re-examine the request, in accordance with the procedure set out in the second subparagraph. If the Commission considers that the conditions of participation have still not been met, the Member State concerned may refer the matter to the Council, which shall decide on the request. The Council shall act in accordance with Article 330. It may also adopt the transitional measures referred to in the second subparagraph on a proposal from the Commission.

2. Any Member State which wishes to participate in enhanced cooperation in progress in the framework of the common foreign and security policy shall notify its intention to the Council, the High Representative of the Union for Foreign Affairs and Security Policy and the Commission.

The Council shall confirm the participation of the Member State concerned, after consulting the High Representative of the Union for Foreign Affairs and Security Policy and after noting, where necessary, that the conditions of participation have been fulfilled. The Council, on a proposal from the High Representative, may also adopt any transitional measures necessary with regard to the application of the acts already adopted within the framework of enhanced cooperation. However, if the Council considers that the conditions of participation have not been fulfilled, it shall indicate the arrangements to be adopted to fulfil those conditions and shall set a deadline for re-examining the request for participation.

For the purposes of this paragraph, the Council shall act unanimously and in accordance with Article 330.

Article 332 (ex Articles 27a to 27e, 40 to 40b and 43 to 45 TEU and ex Articles 11 and 11a TEC)

Expenditure resulting from implementation of enhanced cooperation, other than administrative costs entailed for the institutions, shall be borne by the participating Member States, unless all members of the Council, acting unanimously after consulting the European Parliament, decide otherwise.

Article 333 (ex Articles 27a to 27e, 40 to 40b and 43 to 45 TEU and ex Articles 11 and 11a TEC)

1. Where a provision of the Treaties which may be applied in the context of enhanced cooperation stipulates that the Council shall act unanimously, the Council, acting unanimously in accordance with the arrangements laid down in Article 330, may adopt a decision stipulating that it will act by a qualified majority.

2. Where a provision of the Treaties which may be applied in the context of enhanced cooperation stipulates that the Council shall adopt acts under a special legislative procedure, the Council, acting unanimously in accordance with the arrangements laid down in Article 330, may adopt a decision stipulating that it will act under the ordinary legislative procedure. The Council shall act after consulting the European Parliament.

3. Paragraphs 1 and 2 shall not apply to decisions having military or defence implications.

Article 334 (ex Articles 27a to 27e, 40 to 40b and 43 to 45 TEU and ex Articles 11 and 11a TEC)

The Council and the Commission shall ensure the consistency of activities undertaken in the context of enhanced cooperation and the consistency of such activities with the policies of the Union, and shall cooperate to that end.

PART SEVEN GENERAL AND FINAL PROVISIONS

Article 335 (ex Article 282 TEC)

In each of the Member States, the Union shall enjoy the most extensive legal capacity accorded to legal persons under their laws; it may, in particular, acquire or dispose of movable and immovable property and may be a party to legal proceedings. To this end, the Union shall be represented by the Commission. However, the Union shall be represented by each of the institutions, by virtue of their administrative autonomy, in matters relating to their respective operation.

Article 336 (ex Article 283 TEC)

The European Parliament and the Council shall, acting by means of regulations in accordance with the ordinary legislative procedure on a proposal from the Commission and after consulting the other institutions concerned, lay down the Staff Regulations of Officials of the European Union and the Conditions of Employment of other servants of the Union.

Article 337 (ex Article 284 TEC)

The Commission may, within the limits and under conditions laid down by the Council acting by a simple majority in accordance with the provisions of the Treaties, collect any information and carry out any checks required for the performance of the tasks entrusted to it.

Article 338 (ex Article 285 TEC)

1. Without prejudice to Article 5 of the Protocol on the Statute of the European System of Central Banks and of the European Central Bank, the European Parliament and the Council, acting in accordance with the ordinary legislative procedure, shall adopt measures for the production of statistics where necessary for the performance of the activities of the Union.

2. The production of Union statistics shall conform to impartiality, reliability, objectivity, scientific independence, cost-effectiveness and statistical confidentiality; it shall not entail excessive burdens on economic operators.

Article 339 (ex Article 287 TEC)

The members of the institutions of the Union, the members of committees, and the officials and other servants of the Union shall be required, even after their duties have ceased, not to disclose information of the kind covered by the obligation of professional secrecy, in particular information about undertakings, their business relations or their cost components.

Article 340 (ex Article 288 TEC)

The contractual liability of the Union shall be governed by the law applicable to the contract in question.

In the case of non-contractual liability, the Union shall, in accordance with the general principles common to the laws of the Member States, make good any damage caused by its institutions or by its servants in the performance of their duties.

Notwithstanding the second paragraph, the European Central Bank shall, in accordance with the general principles common to the laws of the Member States, make good any damage caused by it or by its servants in the performance of their duties.

The personal liability of its servants towards the Union shall be governed by the provisions laid down in their Staff Regulations or in the Conditions of Employment applicable to them.

Article 341 (ex Article 289 TEC)

The seat of the institutions of the Union shall be determined by common accord of the governments of the Member States.

Article 342 (ex Article 290 TEC)

The rules governing the languages of the institutions of the Union shall, without prejudice to the provisions contained in the Statute of the Court of Justice of the European Union, be determined by the Council, acting unanimously by means of regulations.

Article 343 (ex Article 291 TEC)

The Union shall enjoy in the territories of the Member States such privileges and immunities as are necessary for the performance of its tasks, under the conditions laid down in the Protocol of 8 April 1965 on the privileges and immunities of the European Union. The same shall apply to the European Central Bank and the European Investment Bank.

Article 344 (ex Article 292 TEC)

Member States undertake not to submit a dispute concerning the interpretation or application of the Treaties to any method of settlement other than those provided for therein.

Article 345 (ex Article 295 TEC)

The Treaties shall in no way prejudice the rules in Member States governing the system of property ownership.

Article 346 (ex Article 296 TEC)

1. The provisions of the Treaties shall not preclude the application of the following rules:
   (a) no Member State shall be obliged to supply information the disclosure of which it considers contrary to the essential interests of its security;
   (b) any Member State may take such measures as it considers necessary for the protection of the essential interests of its security which are connected with the production of or trade in arms, munitions and war material; such measures shall not adversely affect the conditions of competition in the internal market regarding products which are not intended for specifically military purposes.

2. The Council may, acting unanimously on a proposal from the Commission, make changes to the list, which it drew up on 15 April 1958, of the products to which the provisions of paragraph 1(b) apply.

Article 347 (ex Article 297 TEC)

Member States shall consult each other with a view to taking together the steps needed to prevent the functioning of the internal market being affected by measures which a Member State may be called upon to take in the event of serious internal disturbances affecting the maintenance of law and order, in the event of war, serious international tension constituting a threat of war, or in order to carry out obligations it has accepted for the purpose of maintaining peace and international security.

Article 348 (ex Article 298 TEC)

If measures taken in the circumstances referred to in Articles 346 and 347 have the effect of distorting the conditions of competition in the internal market, the Commission shall, together with the State concerned, examine how these measures can be adjusted to the rules laid down in the Treaties.

By way of derogation from the procedure laid down in Articles 258 and 259, the Commission or any Member State may bring the matter directly before the Court of Justice if it considers that another Member State is making improper use of the powers provided for in Articles 346 and 347. The Court of Justice shall give its ruling in camera.

Article 349 (ex Article 299(2), second, third and fourth subparagraphs, TEC)

Taking account of the structural social and economic situation of Guadeloupe, French Guiana, Martinique, Réunion, Saint-Barthélemy, Saint-Martin, the Azores, Madeira and the Canary Islands, which is compounded by their remoteness, insularity, small size, difficult topography and climate, economic dependence on a few products, the permanence and combination of which severely restrain their development, the Council, on a proposal from the Commission and after consulting the European Parliament, shall adopt specific measures aimed, in particular, at laying down the conditions of application of the Treaties to those regions, including common policies. Where the specific measures in question are adopted by the Council in accordance with a special legislative procedure, it shall also act on a proposal from the Commission and after consulting the European Parliament.

The measures referred to in the first paragraph concern in particular areas such as customs and trade policies, fiscal policy, free zones, agriculture and fisheries policies, conditions for supply of raw materials and essential consumer goods, State aids and conditions of access to structural funds and to horizontal Union programmes.

The Council shall adopt the measures referred to in the first paragraph taking into account the special characteristics and constraints of the outermost regions without undermining the integrity and the coherence of the Union legal order, including the internal market and common policies.

Article 350 (ex Article 306 TEC)

The provisions of the Treaties shall not preclude the existence or completion of regional unions between Belgium and Luxembourg, or between Belgium, Luxembourg and the Netherlands, to the extent that the objectives of these regional unions are not attained by application of the Treaties.

Article 351 (ex Article 307 TEC)

The rights and obligations arising from agreements concluded before 1 January 1958 or, for acceding States, before the date of their accession, between one or more Member States on the one hand, and one or more third countries on the other, shall not be affected by the provisions of the Treaties.

To the extent that such agreements are not compatible with the Treaties, the Member State or States concerned shall take all appropriate steps to eliminate the incompatibilities established. Member States shall, where necessary, assist each other to this end and shall, where appropriate, adopt a common attitude.

In applying the agreements referred to in the first paragraph, Member States shall take into account the fact that the advantages accorded under the Treaties by each Member State form an integral part of the establishment of the Union and are thereby inseparably linked with the creation of common institutions, the conferring of powers upon them and the granting of the same advantages by all the other Member States.

Article 352 (ex Article 308 TEC)

1. If action by the Union should prove necessary, within the framework of the policies defined in the Treaties, to attain one of the objectives set out in the Treaties, and the Treaties have not provided the necessary powers, the Council, acting unanimously on a proposal from the Commission and after obtaining the consent of the European Parliament, shall adopt the appropriate measures. Where the measures in question are adopted by the Council in accordance with a special legislative procedure, it shall also act unanimously on a proposal from the Commission and after obtaining the consent of the European Parliament.

2. Using the procedure for monitoring the subsidiarity principle referred to in Article 5(3) of the Treaty on European Union, the Commission shall draw national Parliaments' attention to proposals based on this Article.

3. Measures based on this Article shall not entail harmonisation of Member States' laws or regulations in cases where the Treaties exclude such harmonisation.

4. This Article cannot serve as a basis for attaining objectives pertaining to the common foreign and security policy and any acts adopted pursuant to this Article shall respect the limits set out in Article 40, second paragraph, of the Treaty on European Union.

Article 353

Article 48(7) of the Treaty on European Union shall not apply to the following Articles:

- Article 311, third and fourth paragraphs,
- Article 312(2), first subparagraph,
- Article 352, and
- Article 354.

Article 354 (ex Article 309 TEC)

For the purposes of Article 7 of the Treaty on European Union on the suspension of certain rights resulting from Union membership, the member of the European Council or of the Council representing the Member State in question shall not take part in the vote and the Member State in question shall not be counted in the calculation of the one-third or four-fifths of Member States referred to in paragraphs 1 and 2 of that Article. Abstentions by members present in person or represented shall not prevent the adoption of decisions referred to in paragraph 2 of that Article.

For the adoption of the decisions referred to in paragraphs 3 and 4 of Article 7 of the Treaty on European Union, a qualified majority shall be defined in accordance with Article 238(3)(b) of this Treaty.

Where, following a decision to suspend voting rights adopted pursuant to paragraph 3 of Article 7 of the Treaty on European Union, the Council acts by a qualified majority on the basis of a provision of the Treaties, that qualified majority shall be defined in accordance with Article 238(3)(b) of this Treaty, or, where the Council acts on a proposal from the Commission or from the High Representative of the Union for Foreign Affairs and Security Policy, in accordance with Article 238(3)(a).

For the purposes of Article 7 of the Treaty on European Union, the European Parliament shall act by a two-thirds majority of the votes cast, representing the majority of its component Members.

Article 355 (ex Article 299(2), first subparagraph, and Article 299(3) to (6) TEC)

In addition to the provisions of Article 52 of the Treaty on European Union relating to the territorial scope of the Treaties, the following provisions shall apply:

1. The provisions of the Treaties shall apply to Guadeloupe, French Guiana, Martinique, Réunion, Saint-Barthélemy, Saint-Martin, the Azores, Madeira and the Canary Islands in accordance with Article 349.

2. The special arrangements for association set out in Part Four shall apply to the overseas countries and territories listed in Annex II.

The Treaties shall not apply to those overseas countries and territories having special relations with the United Kingdom of Great Britain and Northern Ireland which are not included in the aforementioned list.

3. The provisions of the Treaties shall apply to the European territories for whose external relations a Member State is responsible.

4. The provisions of the Treaties shall apply to the Åland Islands in accordance with the provisions set out in Protocol 2 to the Act concerning the conditions of accession of the Republic of Austria, the Republic of Finland and the Kingdom of Sweden.

5. Notwithstanding Article 52 of the Treaty on European Union and paragraphs 1 to 4 of this Article:

(a) the Treaties shall not apply to the Faeroe Islands;

(b) the Treaties shall not apply to the United Kingdom Sovereign Base Areas of Akrotiri and Dhekelia in Cyprus except to the extent necessary to ensure the implementation of the arrangements set out in the Protocol on the Sovereign Base Areas of the United Kingdom of Great Britain and Northern Ireland in Cyprus annexed to the Act concerning the conditions of accession of the Czech Republic, the Republic of Estonia, the Republic of Cyprus, the Republic of Latvia, the Republic of Lithuania, the Republic of Hungary, the Republic of Malta, the Republic of Poland, the Republic of Slovenia and the Slovak Republic to the European Union and in accordance with the terms of that Protocol;

(c) the Treaties shall apply to the Channel Islands and the Isle of Man only to the extent necessary to ensure the implementation of the arrangements for those islands set out in the Treaty concerning the accession of new Member States to the European Economic Community and to the European Atomic Energy Community signed on 22 January 1972.

6. The European Council may, on the initiative of the Member State concerned, adopt a decision amending the status, with regard to the Union, of a Danish, French or Netherlands country or territory

referred to in paragraphs 1 and 2. The European Council shall act unanimously after consulting the Commission.

Article 356 (ex Article 312 TEC)
This Treaty is concluded for an unlimited period.

Article 357 (ex Article 313 TEC)
This Treaty shall be ratified by the High Contracting Parties in accordance with their respective constitutional requirements. The Instruments of ratification shall be deposited with the Government of the Italian Republic.

This Treaty shall enter into force on the first day of the month following the deposit of the Instrument of ratification by the last signatory State to take this step. If, however, such deposit is made less than 15 days before the beginning of the following month, this Treaty shall not enter into force until the first day of the second month after the date of such deposit.

Article 358
The provisions of Article 55 of the Treaty on European Union shall apply to this Treaty.

IN WITNESS WHEREOF, the undersigned Plenipotentiaries have signed this Treaty.

Done at Rome this twenty-fifth day of March in the year one thousand nine hundred and fifty-seven.

(List of signatories not reproduced)

Tables of equivalences (pre Lisbon for information)

Tables of equivalences referred to in Article 12 of the Treaty of Amsterdam†

A. Treaty on European Union

Previous numbering	New numbering
Title I	Title I
Article A	Article 1
Article B	Article 2
Article C	Article 3
Article D	Article 4
Article E	Article 5
Article F	Article 6
Article F.1(*)	Article 7
Title II	Title II
Article G	Article 8
Title III	Title III
Article H	Article 9
Title IV	Title IV
Article I	Article 10
Title V(***)	Title V
Article J.1	Article 11
Article J.2	Article 12

† **Editor's Note:** This table is provided for information for those who wish to trace back to the original Treaty numbering of the EEC and EU Treaties; the table of equivalences between the EC & EU Treaties and the TEU & TFEU can be found at the front of this volume in prelim p. xv.

Previous numbering	New numbering
Article J.3	Article 13
Article J.4	Article 14
Article J.5	Article 15
Article J.6	Article 16
Article J.7	Article 17
Article J.8	Article 18
Article J.9	Article 19
Article J.10	Article 20
Article J.11	Article 21
Article J.12	Article 22
Article J.13	Article 23
Article J.14	Article 24
Article J.15	Article 25
Article J.16	Article 26
Article J.17	Article 27
Article J.18	Article 28
Title VI(***)	Title VI
Article K.1	Article 29
Article K.2	Article 30
Article K.3	Article 31
Article K.4	Article 32
Article K.5	Article 33
Article K.6	Article 34
Article K.7	Article 35
Article K.8	Article 36
Article K.9	Article 37
Article K.10	Article 38
Article K.11	Article 39
Article K.12	Article 40
Article K.13	Article 41
Article K.14	Article 42
Title VIa(**)	Title VII
Article K.15(*)	Article 43
Article K.16(*)	Article 44
Article K.17(*)	Article 45
Title VII	Title VIII
Article L	Article 46
Article M	Article 47
Article N	Article 48
Article O	Article 49
Article P	Article 50
Article Q	Article 51

(cont.)

Previous numbering	New numbering
Article R	Article 52
Article S	Article 53

(*) New Article introduced by the Treaty of Amsterdam.
(**) New Title introduced by the Treaty of Amsterdam.
(***) Title restructured by the Treaty of Amsterdam.

B. Treaty establishing the European Community

Previous numbering	New numbering
Part One	Part One
Article 1	Article 1
Article 2	Article 2
Article 3	Article 3
Article 3a	Article 4
Article 3b	Article 5
Article 3c(*)	Article 6
Article 4	Article 7
Article 4a	Article 8
Article 4b	Article 9
Article 5	Article 10
Article 5a(*)	Article 11
Article 6	Article 12
Article 6a(*)	Article 13
Article 7 (repealed)	–
Article 7a	Article 14
Article 7b (repealed)	–
Article 7c	Article 15
Article 7d(*)	Article 16
Part Two	Part Two
Article 8	Article 17
Article 8a	Article 18
Article 8b	Article 19
Article 8c	Article 20
Article 8d	Article 21
Article 8e	Article 22
Part Three	Part Three
Title 1	Title 1
Article 9	Article 23
Article 10	Article 24
Article 11 (repealed)	–

Previous numbering	New numbering
Chapter 1	Chapter 1
Section 1 (deleted)	–
Article 12	Article 25
Article 13 (repealed)	–
Article 14 (repealed)	–
Article 15 (repealed)	–
Article 16 (repealed)	–
Article 17 (repealed)	–
Section 2 (deleted)	–
Article 18 (repealed)	–
Article 19 (repealed)	–
Article 20 (repealed)	–
Article 22 (repealed)	–
Article 23 (repealed)	–
Article 24 (repealed)	–
Article 25 (repealed)	–
Article 26 (repealed)	–
Article 27 (repealed)	Article 26
Article 28	Article 27
Article 29	
Chapter 2	Chapter 2
Article 30	Article 28
Article 31 (repealed)	–
Article 32 (repealed)	–
Article 33 (repealed)	–
Article 34	Article 29
Article 35 (repealed)	–
Article 36	Article 30
Article 37	Article 31
Title II	Title II
Article 38	Article 32
Article 39	Article 33
Article 40	Article 34
Article 41	Article 35
Article 42	Article 36
Article 43	Article 37
Article 44 (repealed)	–
Article 45 (repealed)	–
Article 46	Article 38
Article 47 (repealed)	–

(cont.)

Previous numbering	New numbering
Title III	Title III
Chapter 1	Chapter 1
Article 48	Article 39
Article 49	Article 40
Article 50	Article 41
Article 51	Article 42
Chapter 2	Chapter 2
Article 52	Article 43
Article 53 (repealed)	–
Article 54	Article 44
Article 55	Article 45
Article 56	Article 46
Article 57	Article 47
Article 58	Article 48
Chapter 3	Chapter 3
Article 59	Article 49
Article 60	Article 50
Article 61	Article 51
Article 62 (repealed)	–
Article 63	Article 52
Article 64	Article 53
Article 65	Article 54
Article 66	Article 55
Chapter 4	Chapter 4
Article 67 (repealed)	–
Article 68 (repealed)	–
Article 69 (repealed)	–
Article 70 (repealed)	–
Article 71 (repealed)	–
Article 72 (repealed)	–
Article 73 (repealed)	–
Article 73a (repealed)	–
Article 73b	Article 56
Article 73c	Article 57
Article 73d	Article 58
Article 73e (repealed)	–
Article 73f	Article 59
Article 73h (repealed)	–
Title IIIa(**)	Title IV
Article 73i(*)	Article 61
Article 73j(*)	Article 62
Article 73k(*)	Article 63
Article 73l(*)	Article 64

Previous numbering	New numbering
Article 73m(*)	Article 65
Article 73n(*)	Article 66
Article 73o(*)	Article 67
Article 73p(*)	Article 68
Article 73q (*)	Article 69
Title IV	Title V
Article 74	Article 70
Article 75	Article 71
Article 76	Article 72
Article 77	Article 73
Article 78	Article 74
Article 79	Article 75
Article 80	Article 76
Article 81	Article 77
Article 82	Article 78
Article 83	Article 79
Article 84	Article 80
Title V	Title VI
Chapter 1	Chapter 1
Section 1	Section 1
Article 85	Article 81
Article 86	Article 82
Article 104c	Article 104
Chapter 2	Chapter 2
Article 105	Article 105
Article 105a	Article 106
Article 106	Article 107
Article 107	Article 108
Article 108	Article 109
Article 108a	Article 110
Article 109	Article 111
Chapter 3	Chapter 3
Article 109a	Article 112
Article 109b	Article 113
Article 109c	Article 114
Article 109d	Article 115
Chapter 4	Chapter 4
Article 109e	Article 116
Article 109f	Article 117
Article 109g	Article 118
Article 109h	Article 119
Article 109i	Article 120

(cont.)

Previous numbering	New numbering
Article 109j	Article 121
Article 109k	Article 122
Article 109l	Article 123
Article 109m	Article 124
Title VIa(**)	Title VIII
Article 109n(*)	Article 125
Article 109o(*)	Article 126
Article 109p(*)	Article 127
Article 109q(*)	Article 128
Article 109r(*)	Article 129
Article 109s(*)	Article 130
Title VII	Title IX
Article 110	Article 131
Article 111 (repealed)	–
Article 112	Article 132
Title VIIa(**)	Title X
Article 113	Article 133
Article 114 (repealed)	–
Article 115	Article 134
Article 116(*)	Article 135
Title VIII	Title XI
Chapter 1(***)	Chapter 1
Article 117	Article 136
Article 118	Article 137
Article 118a	Article 138
Article 118b	Article 139
Article 118c	Article 140
Article 119	Article 141
Article 119a	Article 142
Article 120	Article 143
Article 121	Article 144
Article 122	Article 145
Chapter 2	Chapter 2
Article 123	Article 146
Article 124	Article 147
Article 125	Article 148
Chapter 3	Chapter 3
Article 126	Article 149
Article 127	Article 150
Title IX	Title XII
Article 128	Article 151

Previous numbering	New numbering
Title X	Title XIII
Article 129	Article 152
Title XI	Title XIV
Article 129a	Article 153
Title XII	Title XV
Article 129b	Article 154
Article 129c	Article 155
Article 129d	Article 156
Title XIII	Title XVI
Article 130	Article 157
Title XIV	Title XVII
Article 130a	Article 158
Article 130b	Article 159
Article 130c	Article 160
Article 130d	Article 161
Article 130e	Article 162
Title XV	Title XVIII
Article 130f	Article 163
Article 130g	Article 164
Article 130h	Article 165
Article 130i	Article 166
Article 130j	Article 167
Article 130k	Article 168
Article 130l	Article 169
Article 130m	Article 170
Article 130n	Article 171
Article 130o	Article 172
Article 130p	Article 173
Article 130q (repealed)	–
Title XVI	Title XIX
Article 130r	Article 174
Article 130s	Article 175
Article 130t	Article 176
Title XVII	Title XX
Article 130u	Article 177
Article 130u	Article 177
Article 130v	Article 178
Article 130w	Article 179
Article 130x	Article 180
Article 130y	Article 181
Part Four	Part Four
Article 131	Article 182

(cont.)

Previous numbering	New numbering
Article 132	Article 183
Article 133	Article 184
Article 134	Article 185
Article 135	Article 186
Article 136	Article 187
Article 136a	Article 188
Part Five	Part Five
Title I	Title I
Chapter 1	Chapter 1
Section 1	Section 1
Article 137	Article 189
Article 138	Article 190
Article 138a	Article 191
Article 138b	Article 192
Article 138c	Article 193
Article 138d	Article 194
Article 138e	Article 195
Article 139	Article 196
Article 140	Article 197
Article 141	Article 198
Article 142	Article 199
Article 143	Article 200
Article 144	Article 201
Section 2	Section 2
Article 145	Article 202
Article 146	Article 203
Article 147	Article 204
Article 148	Article 205
Article 149 (repealed)	–
Article 150	Article 206
Article 151	Article 207
Article 152	Article 208
Article 153	Article 209
Article 154	Article 210
Section 3	Section 3
Article 155	Article 211
Article 156	Article 212
Article 157	Article 213
Article 158	Article 214
Article 159	Article 215
Article 160	Article 216
Article 161	Article 217

Previous numbering	New numbering
Article 162	Article 218
Article 163	Article 219
Section 4	Section 4
Article 164	Article 220
Article 165	Article 221
Article 166	Article 222
Article 167	Article 223
Article 168	Article 224
Article 168a	Article 225
Article 169	Article 226
Article 170	Article 227
Article 171	Article 228
Article 172	Article 229
Article 173	Article 230
Article 174	Article 231
Article 175	Article 232
Article 176	Article 233
Article 177	Article 234
Article 178	Article 235
Article 179	Article 236
Article 180	Article 237
Article 181	Article 238
Article 182	Article 239
Article 183	Article 240
Article 184	Article 241
Article 185	Article 242
Article 186	Article 243
Article 187	Article 244
Article 188	Article 245
Section 5	Section 5
Article 188a	Article 246
Article 188b	Article 247
Article 188c	Article 248
Chapter 2	Chapter 2
Article 189	Article 249
Article 189a	Article 250
Article 189b	Article 251
Article 189c	Article 252
Article 190	Article 253
Article 191	Article 254
Article 191a(*)	Article 255
Article 192	Article 256

(cont.)

Previous numbering	New numbering
Chapter 3	Chapter 3
Article 193	Article 257
Article 194	Article 258
Article 195	Article 259
Article 196	Article 260
Article 197	Article 261
Article 198	Article 262
Chapter 4	Chapter 4
Article 198a	Article 263
Article 198b	Article 264
Article 198c	Article 265
Chapter 5	Chapter 5
Article 198d	Article 266
Article 198e	Article 267
Title II	Title II
Article 199	Article 268
Article 200 (repealed)	–
Article 201	Article 269
Article 201a	Article 270
Article 202	Article 271
Article 203	Article 272
Article 204	Article 273
Article 205	Article 274
Article 205a	Article 275
Article 206	Article 276
Article 206a (repealed)	–
Article 207	Article 277
Article 208	Article 278
Article 209	Article 279
Article 209a	Article 280
Part Six	Part Six
Article 210	Article 281
Article 211	Article 282
Article 212(*)	Article 283
Article 213	Article 284
Article 213a(*)	Article 285
Article 213b(*)	Article 286
Article 214	Article 287
Article 215	Article 288
Article 216	Article 289

Previous numbering	New numbering
Article 217	Article 290
Article 218(*)	Article 291
Article 219	Article 292
Article 220	Article 293
Article 221	Article 294
Article 222	Article 295
Article 223	Article 296
Article 224	Article 297
Article 225	Article 298
Article 226 (repealed)	–
Article 227	Article 299
Article 228	Article 300
Article 228a	Article 301
Article 229	Article 302
Article 230	Article 303
Article 231	Article 304
Article 232	Article 305
Article 233	Article 306
Article 234	Article 307
Article 235	Article 308
Article 236(*)	Article 309
Article 237 (repealed)	–
Article 238	Article 310
Article 239	Article 311
Article 240	Article 312
Article 241 (repealed)	–
Article 242 (repealed)	–
Article 243 (repealed)	–
Article 244 (repealed)	–
Article 245 (repealed)	–
Article 246 (repealed)	–
Final Provisions	Final Provisions
Article 247	Article 313
Article 248	Article 314

(*) New Article introduced by the Treaty of Amsterdam.
(**) New Title introduced by the Treaty of Amsterdam.
(***) Chapter or Title restructured by the Treaty of Amsterdam.

Selected Protocols attached to the Treaties by the Lisbon Treaty

Protocol (No 1) on the Role of National Parliaments in the European Union

THE HIGH CONTRACTING PARTIES

RECALLING that the way in which national Parliaments scrutinise their governments in relation to the activities of the Union is a matter for the particular constitutional organisation and practice of each Member State,

DESIRING to encourage greater involvement of national Parliaments in the activities of the European Union and to enhance their ability to express their views on draft legislative acts of the Union as well as on other matters which may be of particular interest to them,

HAVE AGREED UPON the following provisions, which shall be annexed to the Treaty on European Union, to the Treaty on the Functioning of the European Union and to the Treaty establishing the European Atomic Energy Community:

Title I Information for national Parliaments

Article 1

Commission consultation documents (green and white papers and communications) shall be forwarded directly by the Commission to national Parliaments upon publication. The Commission shall also forward the annual legislative programme as well as any other instrument of legislative planning or policy to national Parliaments, at the same time as to the European Parliament and the Council.

Article 2

Draft legislative acts sent to the European Parliament and to the Council shall be forwarded to national Parliaments.

For the purposes of this Protocol, "draft legislative acts" shall mean proposals from the Commission, initiatives from a group of Member States, initiatives from the European Parliament, requests from the Court of Justice, recommendations from the European Central Bank and requests from the European Investment Bank for the adoption of a legislative act.

Draft legislative acts originating from the Commission shall be forwarded to national Parliaments directly by the Commission, at the same time as to the European Parliament and the Council.

Draft legislative acts originating from the European Parliament shall be forwarded to national Parliaments directly by the European Parliament.

Draft legislative acts originating from a group of Member States, the Court of Justice, the European Central Bank or the European Investment Bank shall be forwarded to national Parliaments by the Council.

Article 3

National Parliaments may send to the Presidents of the European Parliament, the Council and the Commission a reasoned opinion on whether a draft legislative act complies with the principle of subsidiarity, in accordance with the procedure laid down in the Protocol on the application of the principles of subsidiarity and proportionality.

If the draft legislative act originates from a group of Member States, the President of the Council shall forward the reasoned opinion or opinions to the governments of those Member States.

If the draft legislative act originates from the Court of Justice, the European Central Bank or the European Investment Bank, the President of the Council shall forward the reasoned opinion or opinions to the institution or body concerned.

Article 4

An eight-week period shall elapse between a draft legislative act being made available to national Parliaments in the official languages of the Union and the date when it is placed on a provisional agenda for the Council for its adoption or for adoption of a position under a legislative procedure. Exceptions shall be possible in cases of urgency, the reasons for which shall be stated in the act or position of the Council. Save in urgent cases for which due reasons have been given, no agreement may be reached on a draft legislative act during those eight weeks. Save in urgent cases for which due reasons have been given, a ten-day period shall elapse between the placing of a draft legislative act on the provisional agenda for the Council and the adoption of a position.

Article 5

The agendas for and the outcome of meetings of the Council, including the minutes of meetings where the Council is deliberating on draft legislative acts, shall be forwarded directly to national Parliaments, at the same time as to Member States' governments.

Article 6

When the European Council intends to make use of the first or second subparagraphs of Article 48(7) of the Treaty on European Union, national Parliaments shall be informed of the initiative of the European Council at least six months before any decision is adopted.

Article 7

The Court of Auditors shall forward its annual report to national Parliaments, for information, at the same time as to the European Parliament and to the Council.

Article 8

Where the national Parliamentary system is not unicameral, Articles 1 to 7 shall apply to the component chambers.

Title II Interparliamentary cooperation

Article 9

The European Parliament and national Parliaments shall together determine the organisation and promotion of effective and regular interparliamentary cooperation within the Union.

Article 10

A conference of Parliamentary Committees for Union Affairs may submit any contribution it deems appropriate for the attention of the European Parliament, the Council and the Commission. That conference shall in addition promote the exchange of information and best practice between national Parliaments and the European Parliament, including their special committees. It may also organise interparliamentary conferences on specific topics, in particular to debate matters of common foreign and security policy, including common security and defence policy. Contributions from the conference shall not bind national Parliaments and shall not prejudge their positions.

Protocol (No 2) on the Application of the Principles of Subsidiarity and Proportionality

THE HIGH CONTRACTING PARTIES,

WISHING to ensure that decisions are taken as closely as possible to the citizens of the Union,

RESOLVED to establish the conditions for the application of the principles of subsidiarity and proportionality, as laid down in Article 5 of the Treaty on European Union, and to establish a system for monitoring the application of those principles,

HAVE AGREED UPON the following provisions, which shall be annexed to the Treaty on European Union and to the Treaty on the Functioning of the European Union:

Article 1

Each institution shall ensure constant respect for the principles of subsidiarity and proportionality, as laid down in Article 5 of the Treaty on European Union.

Article 2

Before proposing legislative acts, the Commission shall consult widely. Such consultations shall, where appropriate, take into account the regional and local dimension of the action envisaged. In cases of exceptional urgency, the Commission shall not conduct such consultations. It shall give reasons for its decision in its proposal.

Article 3

For the purposes of this Protocol, "draft legislative acts" shall mean proposals from the Commission, initiatives from a group of Member States, initiatives from the European Parliament, requests from the Court of Justice, recommendations from the European Central Bank and requests from the European Investment Bank for the adoption of a legislative act.

Article 4

The Commission shall forward its draft legislative acts and its amended drafts to national Parliaments at the same time as to the Union legislator.

The European Parliament shall forward its draft legislative acts and its amended drafts to national Parliaments.

The Council shall forward draft legislative acts originating from a group of Member States, the Court of Justice, the European Central Bank or the European Investment Bank and amended drafts to national Parliaments.

Upon adoption, legislative resolutions of the European Parliament and positions of the Council shall be forwarded by them to national Parliaments.

Article 5

Draft legislative acts shall be justified with regard to the principles of subsidiarity and proportionality. Any draft legislative act should contain a detailed statement making it possible to appraise compliance with the principles of subsidiarity and proportionality. This statement should contain some assessment of the proposal's financial impact and, in the case of a directive, of its implications for the rules to be put in place by Member States, including, where necessary, the regional legislation. The reasons for concluding that a Union objective can be better achieved at Union level shall be substantiated by qualitative and, wherever possible, quantitative indicators. Draft legislative acts shall take account of the need for any burden, whether financial or administrative, falling upon the Union, national governments, regional or local authorities, economic operators and citizens, to be minimised and commensurate with the objective to be achieved.

Article 6

Any national Parliament or any chamber of a national Parliament may, within eight weeks from the date of transmission of a draft legislative act, in the official languages of the Union, send to the Presidents of the European Parliament, the Council and the Commission a reasoned opinion stating why it considers that the draft in question does not comply with the principle of subsidiarity. It will be for each national Parliament or each chamber of a national Parliament to consult, where appropriate, regional parliaments with legislative powers.

If the draft legislative act originates from a group of Member States, the President of the Council shall forward the opinion to the governments of those Member States.

If the draft legislative act originates from the Court of Justice, the European Central Bank or the European Investment Bank, the President of the Council shall forward the opinion to the institution or body concerned.

Article 7

1. The European Parliament, the Council and the Commission, and, where appropriate, the group of Member States, the Court of Justice, the European Central Bank or the European Investment Bank, if the draft legislative act originates from them, shall take account of the reasoned opinions issued by national Parliaments or by a chamber of a national Parliament.

Each national Parliament shall have two votes, shared out on the basis of the national Parliamentary system. In the case of a bicameral Parliamentary system, each of the two chambers shall have one vote.

2. Where reasoned opinions on a draft legislative act's non-compliance with the principle of subsidiarity represent at least one third of all the votes allocated to the national Parliaments in accordance with the second subparagraph of paragraph 1, the draft must be reviewed. This threshold shall be a quarter in the case of a draft legislative act submitted on the basis of Article 76 of the Treaty on the Functioning of the European Union on the area of freedom, security and justice.

After such review, the Commission or, where appropriate, the group of Member States, the European Parliament, the Court of Justice, the European Central Bank or the European Investment Bank, if the draft legislative act originates from them, may decide to maintain, amend or withdraw the draft. Reasons must be given for this decision.

3. Furthermore, under the ordinary legislative procedure, where reasoned opinions on the non-compliance of a proposal for a legislative act with the principle of subsidiarity represent at least a simple majority of the votes allocated to the national Parliaments in accordance with the second subparagraph of paragraph 1, the proposal must be reviewed. After such review, the Commission may decide to maintain, amend or withdraw the proposal.

If it chooses to maintain the proposal, the Commission will have, in a reasoned opinion, to justify why it considers that the proposal complies with the principle of subsidiarity. This reasoned opinion, as well as the reasoned opinions of the national Parliaments, will have to be submitted to the Union legislator, for consideration in the procedure:

(a) before concluding the first reading, the legislator (the European Parliament and the Council) shall consider whether the legislative proposal is compatible with the principle of subsidiarity, taking particular account of the reasons expressed and shared by the majority of national Parliaments as well as the reasoned opinion of the Commission;

(b) if, by a majority of 55 % of the members of the Council or a majority of the votes cast in the European Parliament, the legislator is of the opinion that the proposal is not compatible with the principle of subsidiarity, the legislative proposal shall not be given further consideration.

Article 8

The Court of Justice of the European Union shall have jurisdiction in actions on grounds of infringement of the principle of subsidiarity by a legislative act, brought in accordance with the rules laid down in Article 263 of the Treaty on the Functioning of the European Union by Member States, or notified by them in accordance with their legal order on behalf of their national Parliament or a chamber thereof.

In accordance with the rules laid down in the said Article, the Committee of the Regions may also bring such actions against legislative acts for the adoption of which the Treaty on the Functioning of the European Union provides that it be consulted.

Article 9

The Commission shall submit each year to the European Council, the European Parliament, the Council and national Parliaments a report on the application of Article 5 of the Treaty on European Union. This annual report shall also be forwarded to the Economic and Social Committee and the Committee of the Regions.

Protocol (No 3) on the Statute of the Court of Justice of the European Union*

THE HIGH CONTRACTING PARTIES,

DESIRING to lay down the Statute of the Court of Justice of the European Union provided for in Article 281 of the Treaty on the Functioning of the European Union,

HAVE AGREED UPON the following provisions, which shall be annexed to the Treaty on European Union, the Treaty on the Functioning of the European Union and the Treaty establishing the European Atomic Energy Community:

Article 1

The Court of Justice of the European Union shall be constituted and shall function in accordance with the provisions of the Treaties, of the Treaty establishing the European Atomic Energy Community (EAEC Treaty) and of this Statute.

Title I Judges and Advocates-General

Article 2

Before taking up his duties each Judge shall, before the Court of Justice sitting in open court, take an oath to perform his duties impartially and conscientiously and to preserve the secrecy of the deliberations of the Court.

Article 3

The Judges shall be immune from legal proceedings. After they have ceased to hold office, they shall continue to enjoy immunity in respect of acts performed by them in their official capacity, including words spoken or written.

The Court of Justice, sitting as a full Court, may waive the immunity. If the decision concerns a member of the General Court or of a specialised court, the Court shall decide after consulting the court concerned.

Where immunity has been waived and criminal proceedings are instituted against a Judge, he shall be tried, in any of the Member States, only by the court competent to judge the members of the highest national judiciary.

Articles 11 to 14 and Article 17 of the Protocol on the privileges and immunities of the European Union shall apply to the Judges, Advocates-General, Registrar and Assistant Rapporteurs of the Court of Justice of the European Union, without prejudice to the provisions relating to immunity from legal proceedings of Judges which are set out in the preceding paragraphs.

Article 4

The Judges may not hold any political or administrative office.

They may not engage in any occupation, whether gainful or not, unless exemption is exceptionally granted by the Council, acting by a simple majority.

When taking up their duties, they shall give a solemn undertaking that, both during and after their term of office, they will respect the obligations arising therefrom, in particular the duty to behave with integrity and discretion as regards the acceptance, after they have ceased to hold office, of certain appointments or benefits.

Any doubt on this point shall be settled by decision of the Court of Justice. If the decision concerns a member of the General Court or of a specialised court, the Court shall decide after consulting the court concerned.

Article 5

Apart from normal replacement, or death, the duties of a Judge shall end when he resigns.

Where a Judge resigns, his letter of resignation shall be addressed to the President of the Court of Justice for transmission to the President of the Council. Upon this notification a vacancy shall arise on the bench.

* **Editor's Note:** Version from 30.3.2010 (OJ 2010 C83/2010) as amended by Regulation 741/2012 of 11 August 2012 (OJ 2012 L228/1).

Save where Article 6 applies, a Judge shall continue to hold office until his successor takes up his duties.

Article 6

A Judge may be deprived of his office or of his right to a pension or other benefits in its stead only if, in the unanimous opinion of the Judges and Advocates-General of the Court of Justice, he no longer fulfils the requisite conditions or meets the obligations arising from his office. The Judge concerned shall not take part in any such deliberations. If the person concerned is a member of the General Court or of a specialised court, the Court shall decide after consulting the court concerned.

The Registrar of the Court shall communicate the decision of the Court to the President of the European Parliament and to the President of the Commission and shall notify it to the President of the Council.

In the case of a decision depriving a Judge of his office, a vacancy shall arise on the bench upon this latter notification.

Article 7

A Judge who is to replace a member of the Court whose term of office has not expired shall be appointed for the remainder of his predecessor's term.

Article 8

The provisions of Articles 2 to 7 shall apply to the Advocates-General.

Title II Organisation of the Court of Justice

Article 9

When, every three years, the Judges are partially replaced, 14 and 13 Judges shall be replaced alternately.

When, every three years, the Advocates-General are partially replaced, four Advocates-General shall be replaced on each occasion.

Article 9a

The Judges shall elect the President and the Vice-President of the Court of Justice from among their number for a term of three years. They may be re-elected.

The Vice-President shall assist the President in accordance with the conditions laid down in the Rules of Procedure. He shall take the President's place when the latter is prevented from attending or when the office of President is vacant.

Article 10

The Registrar shall take an oath before the Court of Justice to perform his duties impartially and conscientiously and to preserve the secrecy of the deliberations of the Court of Justice.

Article 11

The Court of Justice shall arrange for replacement of the Registrar on occasions when he is prevented from attending the Court of Justice.

Article 12

Officials and other servants shall be attached to the Court of Justice to enable it to function. They shall be responsible to the Registrar under the authority of the President.

Article 13

At the request of the Court of Justice, the European Parliament and the Council may, acting in accordance with the ordinary legislative procedure, provide for the appointment of Assistant Rapporteurs and lay down the rules governing their service. The Assistant Rapporteurs may be required, under conditions laid down in the Rules of Procedure, to participate in preparatory inquiries in cases pending before the Court and to cooperate with the Judge who acts as Rapporteur.

The Assistant Rapporteurs shall be chosen from persons whose independence is beyond doubt and who possess the necessary legal qualifications; they shall be appointed by the Council, acting by a simple majority. They shall take an oath before the Court to perform their duties impartially and conscientiously and to preserve the secrecy of the deliberations of the Court.

Article 14

The Judges, the Advocates-General and the Registrar shall be required to reside at the place where the Court of Justice has its seat.

Article 15

The Court of Justice shall remain permanently in session. The duration of the judicial vacations shall be determined by the Court with due regard to the needs of its business.

Article 16

The Court of Justice shall form chambers consisting of three and five Judges. The Judges shall elect the Presidents of the chambers from among their number. The Presidents of the chambers of five Judges shall be elected for three years. They may be re-elected once.

The Grand Chamber shall consist of 15 Judges. It shall be presided over by the President of the Court. The Vice-President of the Court and, in accordance with the conditions laid down in the Rules of Procedure, three of the Presidents of the chambers of five Judges and other Judges shall also form part of the Grand Chamber.

The Court shall sit in a Grand Chamber when a Member State or an institution of the Union that is party to the proceedings so requests.

The Court shall sit as a full Court where cases are brought before it pursuant to Article 228(2), Article 245(2), Article 247 or Article 286(7) of the Treaty on the Functioning of the European Union.

Moreover, where it considers that a case before it is of exceptional importance, the Court may decide, after hearing the Advocate-General, to refer the case to the full Court.

Article 17

Decisions of the Court of Justice shall be valid only when an uneven number of its members is sitting in the deliberations.

Decisions of the chambers consisting of either three or five Judges shall be valid only if they are taken by three Judges.

Decisions of the Grand Chamber shall be valid only if 11 Judges are sitting.

Decisions of the full Court shall be valid only if 17 Judges are sitting.

In the event of one of the Judges of a chamber being prevented from attending, a Judge of another chamber may be called upon to sit in accordance with conditions laid down in the Rules of Procedure.

Article 18

No Judge or Advocate-General may take part in the disposal of any case in which he has previously taken part as agent or adviser or has acted for one of the parties, or in which he has been called upon to pronounce as a member of a court or tribunal, of a commission of inquiry or in any other capacity.

If, for some special reason, any Judge or Advocate-General considers that he should not take part in the judgment or examination of a particular case, he shall so inform the President. If, for some special reason, the President considers that any Judge or Advocate-General should not sit or make submissions in a particular case, he shall notify him accordingly.

Any difficulty arising as to the application of this Article shall be settled by decision of the Court of Justice.

A party may not apply for a change in the composition of the Court or of one of its chambers on the grounds of either the nationality of a Judge or the absence from the Court or from the chamber of a Judge of the nationality of that party.

Title III Procedure before the Court of Justice

Article 19

The Member States and the institutions of the Union shall be represented before the Court of Justice by an agent appointed for each case; the agent may be assisted by an adviser or by a lawyer.

The States, other than the Member States, which are parties to the Agreement on the European Economic Area and also the EFTA Surveillance Authority referred to in that Agreement shall be represented in same manner.

Other parties must be represented by a lawyer.

Only a lawyer authorised to practise before a court of a Member State or of another State which is a party to the Agreement on the European Economic Area may represent or assist a party before the Court.

Such agents, advisers and lawyers shall, when they appear before the Court, enjoy the rights and immunities necessary to the independent exercise of their duties, under conditions laid down in the Rules of Procedure.

As regards such advisers and lawyers who appear before it, the Court shall have the powers normally accorded to courts of law, under conditions laid down in the Rules of Procedure.

University teachers being nationals of a Member State whose law accords them a right of audience shall have the same rights before the Court as are accorded by this Article to lawyers.

Article 20

The procedure before the Court of Justice shall consist of two parts: written and oral.

The written procedure shall consist of the communication to the parties and to the institutions of the Union whose decisions are in dispute, of applications, statements of case, defences and observations, and of replies, if any, as well as of all papers and documents in support or of certified copies of them.

Communications shall be made by the Registrar in the order and within the time laid down in the Rules of Procedure.

The oral procedure shall consist of the hearing by the Court of agents, advisers and lawyers and of the submissions of the Advocate-General, as well as the hearing, if any, of witnesses and experts.

Where it considers that the case raises no new point of law, the Court may decide, after hearing the Advocate-General, that the case shall be determined without a submission from the Advocate-General.

Article 21

A case shall be brought before the Court of Justice by a written application addressed to the Registrar. The application shall contain the applicant's name and permanent address and the description of the signatory, the name of the party or names of the parties against whom the application is made, the subject-matter of the dispute, the form of order sought and a brief statement of the pleas in law on which the application is based.

The application shall be accompanied, where appropriate, by the measure the annulment of which is sought or, in the circumstances referred to in Article 265 of the Treaty on the Functioning of the European Union, by documentary evidence of the date on which an institution was, in accordance with those Articles, requested to act. If the documents are not submitted with the application, the Registrar shall ask the party concerned to produce them within a reasonable period, but in that event the rights of the party shall not lapse even if such documents are produced after the time limit for bringing proceedings.

Article 22

A case governed by Article 18 of the EAEC Treaty shall be brought before the Court of Justice by an appeal addressed to the Registrar. The appeal shall contain the name and permanent address of the applicant and the description of the signatory, a reference to the decision against which the appeal is brought, the names of the respondents, the subject-matter of the dispute, the submissions and a brief statement of the grounds on which the appeal is based.

The appeal shall be accompanied by a certified copy of the decision of the Arbitration Committee which is contested.

If the Court rejects the appeal, the decision of the Arbitration Committee shall become final.

If the Court annuls the decision of the Arbitration Committee, the matter may be re-opened, where appropriate, on the initiative of one of the parties in the case, before the Arbitration Committee. The latter shall conform to any decisions on points of law given by the Court.

Article 23

In the cases governed by Article 267 of the Treaty on the Functioning of the European Union, the decision of the court or tribunal of a Member State which suspends its proceedings and refers a case to the Court of Justice shall be notified to the Court by the court or tribunal concerned. The decision shall then be notified by the Registrar of the Court to the parties, to the Member States and to the Commission, and to the institution, body, office or agency of the Union which adopted the act the validity or interpretation of which is in dispute.

Within two months of this notification, the parties, the Member States, the Commission and, where appropriate, the institution, body, office or agency which adopted the act the validity or interpretation of which is in dispute, shall be entitled to submit statements of case or written observations to the Court.

In the cases governed by Article 267 of the Treaty on the Functioning of the European Union, the decision of the national court or tribunal shall, moreover, be notified by the Registrar of the Court to the States, other than the Member States, which are parties to the Agreement on the European Economic Area and also to the EFTA Surveillance Authority referred to in that Agreement which may, within two months of notification, where one of the fields of application of that Agreement is concerned, submit statements of case or written observations to the Court.

Where an agreement relating to a specific subject matter, concluded by the Council and one or more non-member States, provides that those States are to be entitled to submit statements of case or written observations where a court or tribunal of a Member State refers to the Court of Justice for a preliminary ruling a question falling within the scope of the agreement, the decision of the national court or tribunal containing that question shall also be notified to the non-member States concerned. Within two months from such notification, those States may lodge at the Court statements of case or written observations.

Article 23a[1]

The Rules of Procedure may provide for an expedited or accelerated procedure and, for references for a preliminary ruling relating to the area of freedom, security and justice, an urgent procedure.

Those procedures may provide, in respect of the submission of statements of case or written observations, for a shorter period than that provided for by Article 23, and, in derogation from the fourth paragraph of Article 20, for the case to be determined without a submission from the Advocate General.

In addition, the urgent procedure may provide for restriction of the parties and other interested persons mentioned in Article 23, authorised to submit statements of case or written observations and, in cases of extreme urgency, for the written stage of the procedure to be omitted.

Article 24

The Court of Justice may require the parties to produce all documents and to supply all information which the Court considers desirable. Formal note shall be taken of any refusal.

The Court may also require the Member States and institutions, bodies, offices and agencies not being parties to the case to supply all information which the Court considers necessary for the proceedings.

[1] Article inserted by Decision 2008/79/EC, Euratom (OJ L 24, 29.1.2008, p. 42).

Article 25

The Court of Justice may at any time entrust any individual, body, authority, committee or other organisation it chooses with the task of giving an expert opinion.

Article 26

Witnesses may be heard under conditions laid down in the Rules of Procedure.

Article 27

With respect to defaulting witnesses the Court of Justice shall have the powers generally granted to courts and tribunals and may impose pecuniary penalties under conditions laid down in the Rules of Procedure.

Article 28

Witnesses and experts may be heard on oath taken in the form laid down in the Rules of Procedure or in the manner laid down by the law of the country of the witness or expert.

Article 29

The Court of Justice may order that a witness or expert be heard by the judicial authority of his place of permanent residence.

The order shall be sent for implementation to the competent judicial authority under conditions laid down in the Rules of Procedure. The documents drawn up in compliance with the letters rogatory shall be returned to the Court under the same conditions.

The Court shall defray the expenses, without prejudice to the right to charge them, where appropriate, to the parties.

Article 30

A Member State shall treat any violation of an oath by a witness or expert in the same manner as if the offence had been committed before one of its courts with jurisdiction in civil proceedings. At the instance of the Court of Justice, the Member State concerned shall prosecute the offender before its competent court.

Article 31

The hearing in court shall be public, unless the Court of Justice, of its own motion or on application by the parties, decides otherwise for serious reasons.

Article 32

During the hearings the Court of Justice may examine the experts, the witnesses and the parties themselves. The latter, however, may address the Court of Justice only through their representatives.

Article 33

Minutes shall be made of each hearing and signed by the President and the Registrar.

Article 34

The case list shall be established by the President.

Article 35

The deliberations of the Court of Justice shall be and shall remain secret.

Article 36

Judgments shall state the reasons on which they are based. They shall contain the names of the Judges who took part in the deliberations.

Article 37

Judgments shall be signed by the President and the Registrar. They shall be read in open court.

Article 38

The Court of Justice shall adjudicate upon costs.

Article 39

The President of the Court of Justice may, by way of summary procedure, which may, in so far as necessary, differ from some of the rules contained in this Statute and which shall be laid down in the Rules of Procedure, adjudicate upon applications to suspend execution, as provided for in Article 278 of the Treaty on the Functioning of the European Union and Article 157 of the EAEC Treaty, or to prescribe interim measures pursuant to Article 279 of the Treaty on the Functioning of the European Union, or to suspend enforcement in accordance with the fourth paragraph of Article 299 of the Treaty on the Functioning of the European Union or the third paragraph of Article 164 of the EAEC Treaty.

The powers referred to in the first paragraph may, under the conditions laid down in the Rules of Procedure, be exercised by the Vice-President of the Court of Justice.

Should the President and the Vice-President be prevented from attending, another Judge shall take their place under the conditions laid down in the Rules of Procedure.

The ruling of the President or of the Judge replacing him shall be provisional and shall in no way prejudice the decision of the Court on the substance of the case.

Article 40

Member States and institutions of the Union may intervene in cases before the Court of Justice.

The same right shall be open to the bodies, offices and agencies of the Union and to any other person which can establish an interest in the result of a case submitted to the Court. Natural or legal persons shall not intervene in cases between Member States, between institutions of the Union or between Member States and institutions of the Union.

Without prejudice to the second paragraph, the States, other than the Member States, which are parties to the Agreement on the European Economic Area, and also the EFTA Surveillance Authority referred to in that Agreement, may intervene in cases before the Court where one of the fields of application of that Agreement is concerned.

An application to intervene shall be limited to supporting the form of order sought by one of the parties.

Article 41

Where the defending party, after having been duly summoned, fails to file written submissions in defence, judgment shall be given against that party by default. An objection may be lodged against the judgment within one month of it being notified. The objection shall not have the effect of staying enforcement of the judgment by default unless the Court of Justice decides otherwise.

Article 42

Member States, institutions, bodies, offices and agencies of the Union and any other natural or legal persons may, in cases and under conditions to be determined by the Rules of Procedure, institute third-party proceedings to contest a judgment rendered without their being heard, where the judgment is prejudicial to their rights.

Article 43

If the meaning or scope of a judgment is in doubt, the Court of Justice shall construe it on application by any party or any institution of the Union establishing an interest therein.

Article 44

An application for revision of a judgment may be made to the Court of Justice only on discovery of a fact which is of such a nature as to be a decisive factor, and which, when the judgment was given, was unknown to the Court and to the party claiming the revision.

The revision shall be opened by a judgment of the Court expressly recording the existence of a new fact, recognising that it is of such a character as to lay the case open to revision and declaring the application admissible on this ground.

No application for revision may be made after the lapse of 10 years from the date of the judgment.

Article 45

Periods of grace based on considerations of distance shall be determined by the Rules of Procedure.

No right shall be prejudiced in consequence of the expiry of a time limit if the party concerned proves the existence of unforeseeable circumstances or of *force majeure*.

Article 46

Proceedings against the Union in matters arising from non-contractual liability shall be barred after a period of five years from the occurrence of the event giving rise thereto. The period of limitation shall be interrupted if proceedings are instituted before the Court of Justice or if prior to such proceedings an application is made by the aggrieved party to the relevant institution of the Union. In the latter event the proceedings must be instituted within the period of two months provided for in Article 263 of the Treaty on the Functioning of the European Union; the provisions of the second paragraph of Article 265 of the Treaty on the Functioning of the European Union shall apply where appropriate.

This Article shall also apply to proceedings against the European Central Bank regarding non-contractual liability.

Title IV General Court

Article 47

The first paragraph of Article 9, Article 9a, Articles 14 and 15, the first, second, fourth and fifth paragraphs of Article 17 and Article 18 shall apply to the General Court and its members.

The fourth paragraph of Article 3 and Articles 10, 11 and 14 shall apply to the Registrar of the General Court *mutatis mutandis*.

Article 48

The General Court shall consist of 27 Judges.

Article 49

The Members of the General Court may be called upon to perform the task of an Advocate-General.

It shall be the duty of the Advocate-General, acting with complete impartiality and independence, to make, in open court, reasoned submissions on certain cases brought before the General Court in order to assist the General Court in the performance of its task.

The criteria for selecting such cases, as well as the procedures for designating the Advocates-General, shall be laid down in the Rules of Procedure of the General Court.

A Member called upon to perform the task of Advocate-General in a case may not take part in the judgment of the case.

Article 50

The General Court shall sit in chambers of three or five Judges. The Judges shall elect the Presidents of the chambers from among their number. The Presidents of the chambers of five Judges shall be elected for three years. They may be re-elected once.

The composition of the chambers and the assignment of cases to them shall be governed by the Rules of Procedure. In certain cases governed by the Rules of Procedure, the General Court may sit as a full court or be constituted by a single Judge.

The Rules of Procedure may also provide that the General Court may sit in a Grand Chamber in cases and under the conditions specified therein.

Article 51

By way of derogation from the rule laid down in Article 256(1) of the Treaty on the Functioning of the European Union, jurisdiction shall be reserved to the Court of Justice in the actions referred to in Articles 263 and 265 of the Treaty on the Functioning of the European Union when they are brought by a Member State against:

(a) an act of or failure to act by the European Parliament or the Council, or by those institutions acting jointly, except for:

- decisions taken by the Council under the third subparagraph of Article 108(2) of the Treaty on the Functioning of the European Union;
- acts of the Council adopted pursuant to a Council regulation concerning measures to protect trade within the meaning of Article 207 of the Treaty on the Functioning of the European Union;
- acts of the Council by which the Council exercises implementing powers in accordance with the second paragraph of Article 291 of the Treaty on the Functioning of the European Union;

(b) against an act of or failure to act by the Commission under the first paragraph of Article 331 of the Treaty on the Functioning of the European Union.

Jurisdiction shall also be reserved to the Court of Justice in the actions referred to in the same Articles when they are brought by an institution of the Union against an act of or failure to act by the European Parliament, the Council, both those institutions acting jointly, or the Commission, or brought by an institution of the Union against an act of or failure to act by the European Central Bank.

Article 52

The President of the Court of Justice and the President of the General Court shall determine, by common accord, the conditions under which officials and other servants attached to the Court of Justice shall render their services to the General Court to enable it to function. Certain officials or other servants shall be responsible to the Registrar of the General Court under the authority of the President of the General Court.

Article 53

The procedure before the General Court shall be governed by Title III.

Such further and more detailed provisions as may be necessary shall be laid down in its Rules of Procedure. The Rules of Procedure may derogate from the fourth paragraph of Article 40 and from Article 41 in order to take account of the specific features of litigation in the field of intellectual property.

Notwithstanding the fourth paragraph of Article 20, the Advocate-General may make his reasoned submissions in writing.

Article 54

Where an application or other procedural document addressed to the General Court is lodged by mistake with the Registrar of the Court of Justice, it shall be transmitted immediately by that Registrar to the Registrar of the General Court; likewise, where an application or other procedural document addressed to the Court of Justice is lodged by mistake with the Registrar of the General Court, it shall be transmitted immediately by that Registrar to the Registrar of the Court of Justice.

Where the General Court finds that it does not have jurisdiction to hear and determine an action in respect of which the Court of Justice has jurisdiction, it shall refer that action to the Court of Justice; likewise, where the Court of Justice finds that an action falls within the jurisdiction of the General Court, it shall refer that action to the General Court, whereupon that Court may not decline jurisdiction.

Where the Court of Justice and the General Court are seised of cases in which the same relief is sought, the same issue of interpretation is raised or the validity of the same act is called in question, the General Court may, after hearing the parties, stay the proceedings before it until such time as the Court of Justice has delivered judgment or, where the action is one brought pursuant to Article 263 of the Treaty on the Functioning of the European Union, may decline jurisdiction so as to allow the Court of Justice to rule on such actions. In the same circumstances, the Court of Justice may also decide to stay the proceedings before it; in that event, the proceedings before the General Court shall continue.

Where a Member State and an institution of the Union are challenging the same act, the General Court shall decline jurisdiction so that the Court of Justice may rule on those applications.

Article 55

Final decisions of the General Court, decisions disposing of the substantive issues in part only or disposing of a procedural issue concerning a plea of lack of competence or inadmissibility, shall be notified by the Registrar of the General Court to all parties as well as all Member States and the institutions of the Union even if they did not intervene in the case before the General Court.

Article 56

An appeal may be brought before the Court of Justice, within two months of the notification of the decision appealed against, against final decisions of the General Court and decisions of that Court disposing of the substantive issues in part only or disposing of a procedural issue concerning a plea of lack of competence or inadmissibility.

Such an appeal may be brought by any party which has been unsuccessful, in whole or in part, in its submissions. However, interveners other than the Member States and the institutions of the Union may bring such an appeal only where the decision of the General Court directly affects them.

With the exception of cases relating to disputes between the Union and its servants, an appeal may also be brought by Member States and institutions of the Union which did not intervene in the proceedings before the General Court. Such Member States and institutions shall be in the same position as Member States or institutions which intervened at first instance.

Article 57

Any person whose application to intervene has been dismissed by the General Court may appeal to the Court of Justice within two weeks from the notification of the decision dismissing the application.

The parties to the proceedings may appeal to the Court of Justice against any decision of the General Court made pursuant to Article 278 or Article 279 or the fourth paragraph of Article 299 of the Treaty on the Functioning of the European Union or Article 157 or the third paragraph of Article 164 of the EAEC Treaty within two months from their notification.

The appeal referred to in the first two paragraphs of this Article shall be heard and determined under the procedure referred to in Article 39.

Article 58

An appeal to the Court of Justice shall be limited to points of law. It shall lie on the grounds of lack of competence of the General Court, a breach of procedure before it which adversely affects the interests of the appellant as well as the infringement of Union law by the General Court.

No appeal shall lie regarding only the amount of the costs or the party ordered to pay them.

Article 59

Where an appeal is brought against a decision of the General Court, the procedure before the Court of Justice shall consist of a written part and an oral part. In accordance with conditions laid down in the Rules of Procedure, the Court of Justice, having heard the Advocate-General and the parties, may dispense with the oral procedure.

Article 60

Without prejudice to Articles 278 and 279 of the Treaty on the Functioning of the European Union or Article 157 of the EAEC Treaty, an appeal shall not have suspensory effect.

By way of derogation from Article 280 of the Treaty on the Functioning of the European Union, decisions of the General Court declaring a regulation to be void shall take effect only as from the date of expiry of the period referred to in the first paragraph of Article 56 of this Statute or, if an appeal shall have been brought within that period, as from the date of dismissal of the appeal, without prejudice, however, to the right of a party to apply to the Court of Justice, pursuant to Articles 278 and 279 of the Treaty on the Functioning of the European Union or Article 157 of the EAEC Treaty, for the suspension of the effects of the regulation which has been declared void or for the prescription of any other interim measure.

Article 61

If the appeal is well founded, the Court of Justice shall quash the decision of the General Court. It may itself give final judgment in the matter, where the state of the proceedings so permits, or refer the case back to the General Court for judgment.

Where a case is referred back to the General Court, that Court shall be bound by the decision of the Court of Justice on points of law.

When an appeal brought by a Member State or an institution of the Union, which did not intervene in the proceedings before the General Court, is well founded, the Court of Justice may, if it considers this necessary, state which of the effects of the decision of the General Court which has been quashed shall be considered as definitive in respect of the parties to the litigation.

Article 62

In the cases provided for in Article 256(2) and (3) of the Treaty on the Functioning of the European Union, where the First Advocate-General considers that there is a serious risk of the unity or consistency of Union law being affected, he may propose that the Court of Justice review the decision of the General Court.

The proposal must be made within one month of delivery of the decision by the General Court. Within one month of receiving the proposal made by the First Advocate-General, the Court of Justice shall decide whether or not the decision should be reviewed.

Article 62a

The Court of Justice shall give a ruling on the questions which are subject to review by means of an urgent procedure on the basis of the file forwarded to it by the General Court.

Those referred to in Article 23 of this Statute and, in the cases provided for in Article 256(2) of the EC Treaty, the parties to the proceedings before the General Court shall be entitled to lodge statements or written observations with the Court of Justice relating to questions which are subject to review within a period prescribed for that purpose.

The Court of Justice may decide to open the oral procedure before giving a ruling.

Article 62b

In the cases provided for in Article 256(2) of the Treaty on the Functioning of the European Union, without prejudice to Articles 278 and 279 of the Treaty on the Functioning of the European Union, proposals for review and decisions to open the review procedure shall not have suspensory effect. If the Court of Justice finds that the decision of the General Court affects the unity or consistency of Union law, it shall refer the case back to the General Court which shall be bound by the points of law decided by the Court of Justice; the Court of Justice may state which of the effects of the decision of the General Court are to be considered as definitive in respect of the parties to the litigation. If, however, having regard to the result of the review, the outcome of the proceedings flows from the findings of fact on which the decision of the General Court was based, the Court of Justice shall give final judgment.

In the cases provided for in Article 256(3) of the Treaty on the Functioning of the European Union, in the absence of proposals for review or decisions to open the review procedure, the answer(s) given by the General Court to the questions submitted to it shall take effect upon expiry of the periods prescribed for that purpose in the second paragraph of Article 62. Should a review procedure be opened, the answer(s) subject to review shall take effect following that procedure, unless the Court of Justice decides otherwise. If the Court of Justice finds that the decision of the General Court affects the unity or consistency of Union law, the answer given by the Court of Justice to the questions subject to review shall be substituted for that given by the General Court.

Title IVa Specialised courts

Article 62c

The provisions relating to the jurisdiction, composition, organisation and procedure of the specialised courts established under Article 257 of the Treaty on the Functioning of the European Union are set out in an Annex to this Statute.

The European Parliament and the Council, acting in accordance with Article 257 of the Treaty on the Functioning of the European Union, may attach temporary Judges to the specialised courts in order to cover the absence of Judges who, while not suffering from disablement deemed to be total, are prevented from participating in the disposal of cases for a lengthy period of time. In that event, the European Parliament and the Council shall lay down the conditions under which the temporary Judges shall be appointed, their rights and duties, the detailed rules governing the performance of their duties and the circumstances in which they shall cease to perform those duties.

Title V Final provisions

Article 63

The Rules of Procedure of the Court of Justice and of the General Court shall contain any provisions necessary for applying and, where required, supplementing this Statute.

Article 64

The rules governing the language arrangements applicable at the Court of Justice of the European Union shall be laid down by a regulation of the Council acting unanimously. This regulation shall be adopted either at the request of the Court of Justice and after consultation of the Commission and the European Parliament, or on a proposal from the Commission and after consultation of the Court of Justice and of the European Parliament.

Until those rules have been adopted, the provisions of the Rules of Procedure of the Court of Justice and of the Rules of Procedure of the General Court governing language arrangements shall continue to apply. By way of derogation from Articles 253 and 254 of the Treaty on the Functioning of the European Union, those provisions may only be amended or repealed with the unanimous consent of the Council.

Annex I The European Union Civil Service Tribunal

Article 1

The European Union Civil Service Tribunal (hereafter "the Civil Service Tribunal") shall exercise at first instance jurisdiction in disputes between the Union and its servants referred to in Article 270 of the Treaty on the Functioning of the European Union, including disputes between all bodies or agencies and their servants in respect of which jurisdiction is conferred on the Court of Justice of the European Union.

Article 2

1. The Civil Service Tribunal shall consist of seven judges. Should the Court of Justice so request, the Council, acting by a qualified majority, may increase the number of judges. The judges shall be appointed for a period of six years. Retiring judges may be reappointed.

Any vacancy shall be filled by the appointment of a new judge for a period of six years.

2. Temporary Judges shall be appointed, in addition to the Judges referred to in the first subparagraph of paragraph 1, in order to cover the absence of Judges who, while not suffering from disablement deemed to be total, are prevented from participating in the disposal of cases for a lengthy period of time.

Article 3

1. The judges shall be appointed by the Council, acting in accordance with the fourth paragraph of Article 257 of the Treaty on the Functioning of the European Union, after consulting the committee provided for by this Article. When appointing judges, the Council shall ensure a balanced composition of the Civil Service Tribunal on as broad a geographical basis as possible from among nationals of the Member States and with respect to the national legal systems represented.

2. Any person who is a Union citizen and fulfils the conditions laid down in the fourth paragraph of Article 257 of the Treaty on the Functioning of the European Union may submit an application. The Council, acting on a recommendation from the Court of Justice, shall determine the conditions and the arrangements governing the submission and processing of such applications.

3. A committee shall be set up comprising seven persons chosen from among former members of the Court of Justice and the General Court and lawyers of recognised competence. The committee's membership and operating rules shall be determined by the Council, acting on a recommendation by the President of the Court of Justice.

4. The committee shall give an opinion on candidates' suitability to perform the duties of judge at the Civil Service Tribunal. The committee shall append to its opinion a list of candidates having the most suitable high-level experience. Such list shall contain the names of at least twice as many candidates as there are judges to be appointed by the Council.

Article 4

1. The judges shall elect the President of the Civil Service Tribunal from among their number for a term of three years. He may be re-elected.

2. The Civil Service Tribunal shall sit in chambers of three judges. It may, in certain cases determined by its rules of procedure, sit in full court or in a chamber of five judges or of a single judge.

3. The President of the Civil Service Tribunal shall preside over the full court and the chamber of five judges. The Presidents of the chambers of three judges shall be designated as provided in paragraph 1. If the President of the Civil Service Tribunal is assigned to a chamber of three judges, he shall preside over that chamber.

4. The jurisdiction of and quorum for the full court as well as the composition of the chambers and the assignment of cases to them shall be governed by the rules of procedure.

Article 5

Articles 2 to 6, 14, 15, the first, second and fifth paragraphs of Article 17, and Article 18 of the Statute of the Court of Justice of the European Union shall apply to the Civil Service Tribunal and its members.

The oath referred to in Article 2 of the Statute shall be taken before the Court of Justice, and the decisions referred to in Articles 3, 4 and 6 thereof shall be adopted by the Court of Justice after consulting the Civil Service Tribunal.

Article 6

1. The Civil Service Tribunal shall be supported by the departments of the Court of Justice and of the General Court. The President of the Court of Justice or, in appropriate cases, the President of the General Court, shall determine by common accord with the President of the Civil Service Tribunal the conditions under which officials and other servants attached to the Court of Justice or the General Court shall render their services to the Civil Service Tribunal to enable it to function. Certain officials or other servants shall be responsible to the Registrar of the Civil Service Tribunal under the authority of the President of that Tribunal.

2. The Civil Service Tribunal shall appoint its Registrar and lay down the rules governing his service. The fourth paragraph of Article 3 and Articles 10, 11 and 14 of the Statute of the Court of Justice of the European Union shall apply to the Registrar of the Tribunal.

Article 7

1. The procedure before the Civil Service Tribunal shall be governed by Title III of the Statute of the Court of Justice of the European Union, with the exception of Articles 22 and 23. Such further and more detailed provisions as may be necessary shall be laid down in the rules of procedure.

2. The provisions concerning the General Court's language arrangements shall apply to the Civil Service Tribunal.

3. The written stage of the procedure shall comprise the presentation of the application and of the statement of defence, unless the Civil Service Tribunal decides that a second exchange of written pleadings is necessary. Where there is such second exchange, the Civil Service Tribunal may, with the agreement of the parties, decide to proceed to judgment without an oral procedure.

4. At all stages of the procedure, including the time when the application is filed, the Civil Service Tribunal may examine the possibilities of an amicable settlement of the dispute and may try to facilitate such settlement.

5. The Civil Service Tribunal shall rule on the costs of a case. Subject to the specific provisions of the Rules of Procedure, the unsuccessful party shall be ordered to pay the costs should the court so decide.

Article 8

1. Where an application or other procedural document addressed to the Civil Service Tribunal is lodged by mistake with the Registrar of the Court of Justice or General Court, it shall be transmitted immediately by that Registrar to the Registrar of the Civil Service Tribunal. Likewise, where an application or other procedural document addressed to the Court of Justice or to the General Court is lodged by mistake with the Registrar of the Civil Service Tribunal, it shall be transmitted immediately by that Registrar to the Registrar of the Court of Justice or General Court.

2. Where the Civil Service Tribunal finds that it does not have jurisdiction to hear and determine an action in respect of which the Court of Justice or the General Court has jurisdiction, it shall refer that action to the Court of Justice or to the General Court. Likewise, where the Court of Justice or the General Court finds that an action falls within the jurisdiction of the Civil Service Tribunal, the Court seised shall refer that action to the Civil Service Tribunal, whereupon that Tribunal may not decline jurisdiction.

3. Where the Civil Service Tribunal and the General Court are seised of cases in which the same issue of interpretation is raised or the validity of the same act is called in question, the Civil Service Tribunal, after hearing the parties, may stay the proceedings until the judgment of the General Court has been delivered.

Where the Civil Service Tribunal and the General Court are seised of cases in which the same relief is sought, the Civil Service Tribunal shall decline jurisdiction so that the General Court may act on those cases.

Article 9

An appeal may be brought before the General Court, within two months of notification of the decision appealed against, against final decisions of the Civil Service Tribunal and decisions of that Tribunal disposing of the substantive issues in part only or disposing of a procedural issue concerning a plea of lack of jurisdiction or inadmissibility.

Such an appeal may be brought by any party which has been unsuccessful, in whole or in part, in its submissions. However, interveners other than the Member States and the institutions of the Union may bring such an appeal only where the decision of the Civil Service Tribunal directly affects them.

Article 10

1. Any person whose application to intervene has been dismissed by the Civil Service Tribunal may appeal to the General Court within two weeks of notification of the decision dismissing the application.

2. The parties to the proceedings may appeal to the General Court against any decision of the Civil Service Tribunal made pursuant to Article 278 or Article 279 or the fourth paragraph of Article 299 of the Treaty on the Functioning of the European Union or Article 157 or the third paragraph of Article 164 of the EAEC Treaty within two months of its notification.

3. The President of the General Court may, by way of summary procedure, which may, in so far as necessary, differ from some of the rules contained in this Annex and which shall be laid down in the rules of procedure of the General Court, adjudicate upon appeals brought in accordance with paragraphs 1 and 2.

Article 11

1. An appeal to the General Court shall be limited to points of law. It shall lie on the grounds of lack of jurisdiction of the Civil Service Tribunal, a breach of procedure before it which adversely affects the interests of the appellant, as well as the infringement of Union law by the Tribunal.

2. No appeal shall lie regarding only the amount of the costs or the party ordered to pay them.

Article 12

1. Without prejudice to Articles 278 and 279 of the Treaty on the Functioning of the European Union or Article 157 of the EAEC Treaty, an appeal before the General Court shall not have suspensory effect.

2. Where an appeal is brought against a decision of the Civil Service Tribunal, the procedure before the General Court shall consist of a written part and an oral part. In accordance with conditions laid down in the rules of procedure, the General Court, having heard the parties, may dispense with the oral procedure.

Article 13

1. If the appeal is well founded, the General Court shall quash the decision of the Civil Service Tribunal and itself give judgment in the matter. It shall refer the case back to the Civil Service Tribunal for judgment where the state of the proceedings does not permit a decision by the Court.

2. Where a case is referred back to the Civil Service Tribunal, the Tribunal shall be bound by the decision of the General Court on points of law.

Protocol (No 8) Relating to Article 6(2) of the Treaty on European Union on the Accession of the Union to the European Convention on the Protection of Human Rights and Fundamental Freedoms

THE HIGH CONTRACTING PARTIES,

HAVE AGREED UPON the following provisions, which shall be annexed to the Treaty on European Union and to the Treaty on the Functioning of the European Union:

Article 1

The agreement relating to the accession of the Union to the European Convention on the Protection of Human Rights and Fundamental Freedoms (hereinafter referred to as the "European Convention") provided for in Article 6(2) of the Treaty on European Union shall make provision for preserving the specific characteristics of the Union and Union law, in particular with regard to:

(a) the specific arrangements for the Union's possible participation in the control bodies of the European Convention;

(b) the mechanisms necessary to ensure that proceedings by non-Member States and individual applications are correctly addressed to Member States and/or the Union as appropriate.

Article 2

The agreement referred to in Article 1 shall ensure that accession of the Union shall not affect the competences of the Union or the powers of its institutions. It shall ensure that nothing therein affects the situation of Member States in relation to the European Convention, in particular in relation to the Protocols thereto, measures taken by Member States derogating from the European Convention in accordance with Article 15 thereof and reservations to the European Convention made by Member States in accordance with Article 57 thereof.

Article 3

Nothing in the agreement referred to in Article 1 shall affect Article 344 of the Treaty on the Functioning of the European Union.

Protocol (No 9) on the Decision of the Council Relating to the Implementation of Article 16(4) of the Treaty on European Union and Article 238(2) of the Treaty on the Functioning of the European Union between 1 November 2014 and 31 March 2017 on the one hand, and as from 1 April 2017 on the other

THE HIGH CONTRACTING PARTIES,

TAKING INTO ACCOUNT the fundamental importance that agreeing on the Decision of the Council relating to the implementation of Article 16(4) of the Treaty on European Union and Article 238(2) of the Treaty on the Functioning of the European Union between 1 November 2014 and 31 March

2017 on the one hand, and as from 1 April 2017 on the other (hereinafter "the Decision"), had when approving the Treaty of Lisbon,

HAVE AGREED UPON the following provisions, which shall be annexed to the Treaty on European Union and to the Treaty on the Functioning of the European Union:

Sole Article

Before the examination by the Council of any draft which would aim either at amending or abrogating the Decision or any of its provisions, or at modifying indirectly its scope or its meaning through the modification of another legal act of the Union, the European Council shall hold a preliminary deliberation on the said draft, acting by consensus in accordance with Article 15(4) of the Treaty on European Union.

Protocol (No 25) on the Exercise of Shared Competence

THE HIGH CONTRACTING PARTIES,

HAVE AGREED UPON the following provisions, which shall be annexed to the Treaty on European Union and to the Treaty on the Functioning of the European Union:

Sole Article

With reference to Article 2 (2) of the Treaty on the Functioning of the European Union on shared competence, when the Union has taken action in a certain area, the scope of this exercise of competence only covers those elements governed by the Union act in question and therefore does not cover the whole area.

Protocol (No 30) on the Application of the Charter of Fundamental Rights of the European Union to Poland and to the United Kingdom

THE HIGH CONTRACTING PARTIES,

WHEREAS in Article 6 of the Treaty on European Union, the Union recognises the rights, freedoms and principles set out in the Charter of Fundamental Rights of the European Union,

WHEREAS the Charter is to be applied in strict accordance with the provisions of the aforementioned Article 6 and Title VII of the Charter itself,

WHEREAS the aforementioned Article 6 requires the Charter to be applied and interpreted by the courts of Poland and of the United Kingdom strictly in accordance with the explanations referred to in that Article,

WHEREAS the Charter contains both rights and principles,

WHEREAS the Charter contains both provisions which are civil and political in character and those which are economic and social in character,

WHEREAS the Charter reaffirms the rights, freedoms and principles recognised in the Union and makes those rights more visible, but does not create new rights or principles,

RECALLING the obligations devolving upon Poland and the United Kingdom under the Treaty on European Union, the Treaty on the Functioning of the European Union, and Union law generally,

NOTING the wish of Poland and the United Kingdom to clarify certain aspects of the application of the Charter,

DESIROUS therefore of clarifying the application of the Charter in relation to the laws and administrative action of Poland and of the United Kingdom and of its justiciability within Poland and within the United Kingdom,

REAFFIRMING that references in this Protocol to the operation of specific provisions of the Charter are strictly without prejudice to the operation of other provisions of the Charter,

REAFFIRMING that this Protocol is without prejudice to the application of the Charter to other Member States,

REAFFIRMING that this Protocol is without prejudice to other obligations devolving upon Poland and the United Kingdom under the Treaty on European Union, the Treaty on the Functioning of the European Union, and Union law generally,

HAVE AGREED UPON the following provisions, which shall be annexed to the Treaty on European Union and to the Treaty on the Functioning of the European Union:

Article 1

1. The Charter does not extend the ability of the Court of Justice of the European Union, or any court or tribunal of Poland or of the United Kingdom, to find that the laws, regulations or administrative provisions, practices or action of Poland or of the United Kingdom are inconsistent with the fundamental rights, freedoms and principles that it reaffirms.

2. In particular, and for the avoidance of doubt, nothing in Title IV of the Charter creates justiciable rights applicable to Poland or the United Kingdom except in so far as Poland or the United Kingdom has provided for such rights in its national law.

Article 2

To the extent that a provision of the Charter refers to national laws and practices, it shall only apply to Poland or the United Kingdom to the extent that the rights or principles that it contains are recognised in the law or practices of Poland or of the United Kingdom.

Protocol (No 33) Concerning Article 157 of the Treaty on the Functioning of the European Union

THE HIGH CONTRACTING PARTIES,

HAVE AGREED upon the following provision, which shall be annexed to the Treaty on European Union and to the Treaty on the Functioning of the European Union:

For the purposes of Article 157 of the Treaty on the Functioning of the European Union, benefits under occupational social security schemes shall not be considered as remuneration if and in so far as they are attributable to periods of employment prior to 17 May 1990, except in the case of workers or those claiming under them who have before that date initiated legal proceedings or introduced an equivalent claim under the applicable national law.

Protocol (No 36) on Transitional Provisions*

THE HIGH CONTRACTING PARTIES,

WHEREAS, in order to organise the transition from the institutional provisions of the Treaties applicable prior to the entry into force of the Treaty of Lisbon to the provisions contained in that Treaty, it is necessary to lay down transitional provisions,

HAVE AGREED UPON the following provisions, which shall be annexed to the Treaty on European Union, to the Treaty on the Functioning of the European Union and to the Treaty establishing the European Atomic Energy Community:

Article 1

In this Protocol, the words 'the Treaties' shall mean the Treaty on European Union, the Treaty on the Functioning of the European Union and the Treaty establishing the European Atomic Energy Community.

* **Editor's Note:** This replaced the original Protocol 36 (OJ 2012 C263/01 reproduced in OJ 2012 C326/322).

Title I Provisions concerning the European Parliament

Article 2

1. For the period of the 2009–2014 parliamentary term remaining at the date of entry into force of this Article, and by way of derogation from Articles 189, second paragraph, and 190(2) of the Treaty establishing the European Community and Articles 107, second paragraph, and 108(2) of the Treaty establishing the European Atomic Energy Community, which were in force at the time of the European Parliament elections in June 2009, and by way of derogation from the number of seats provided for in the first subparagraph of Article 14(2) of the Treaty on European Union, the following 18 seats shall be added to the existing 736 seats, thus provisionally bringing the total number of members of the European Parliament to 754 until the end of the 2009–2014 parliamentary term:

Bulgaria	1	Netherlands	1
Spain	4	Austria	2
France	2	Poland	1
Italy	1	Slovenia	1
Latvia	1	Sweden	2
Malta	1	United Kingdom	1

2. By way of derogation from Article 14(3) of the Treaty on European Union, the Member States concerned shall designate the persons who will fill the additional seats referred to in paragraph 1, in accordance with the legislation of the Member States concerned and provided that the persons in question have been elected by direct universal suffrage:

(a) in ad hoc elections by direct universal suffrage in the Member State concerned, in accordance with the provisions applicable for elections to the European Parliament;

(b) by reference to the results of the European Parliament elections from 4 to 7 June 2009; or

(c) by designation, by the national parliament of the Member State concerned from among its members, of the requisite number of members, according to the procedure determined by each of those Member States.

3. In accordance with the second subparagraph of Article 14(2) of the Treaty on European Union, the European Council shall adopt a decision determining the composition of the European Parliament in good time before the 2014 European Parliament elections.

Title II Provisions concerning the qualified majority

Article 3

1. In accordance with Article 16(4) of the Treaty on European Union, the provisions of that paragraph and of Article 238(2) of the Treaty on the Functioning of the European Union relating to the definition of the qualified majority in the European Council and the Council shall take effect on 1 November 2014.

2. Between 1 November 2014 and 31 March 2017, when an act is to be adopted by qualified majority, a member of the Council may request that it be adopted in accordance with the qualified majority as defined in paragraph 3. In that case, paragraphs 3 and 4 shall apply.

3. Until 31 October 2014, the following provisions shall remain in force, without prejudice to the second subparagraph of Article 235(1) of the Treaty on the Functioning of the European Union. For acts of the European Council and of the Council requiring a qualified majority, members' votes shall be weighted as follows:

Belgium	12	Luxembourg	4
Bulgaria	10	Hungary	12
Czech Republic	12	Malta	3
Denmark	7	Netherlands	13
Germany	29	Austria	10
Estonia	4	Poland	27
Ireland	7	Portugal	12
Greece	12	Romania	14
Spain	27	Slovenia	4
France	29	Slovakia	7
Italy	29	Finland	7
Cyprus	4	Sweden	10
Latvia	4	United Kingdom	29
Lithuania	7		

Acts shall be adopted if there are at least 255 votes in favour representing a majority of the members where, under the Treaties, they must be adopted on a proposal from the Commission. In other cases decisions shall be adopted if there are at least 255 votes in favour representing at least two thirds of the members.

A member of the European Council or the Council may request that, where an act is adopted by the European Council or the Council by a qualified majority, a check is made to ensure that the Member States comprising the qualified majority represent at least 62 % of the total population of the Union. If that proves not to be the case, the act shall not be adopted.

4. Until 31 October 2014, the qualified majority shall, in cases where, under the Treaties, not all the members of the Council participate in voting, namely in the cases where reference is made to the qualified majority as defined in Article 238(3) of the Treaty on the Functioning of the European Union, be defined as the same proportion of the weighted votes and the same proportion of the number of the Council members and, if appropriate, the same percentage of the population of the Member States concerned as laid down in paragraph 3 of this Article.

Title III Provisions concerning the configurations of the Council

Article 4

Until the entry into force of the decision referred to in the first subparagraph of Article 16(6) of the Treaty on European Union, the Council may meet in the configurations laid down in the second and third subparagraphs of that paragraph and in the other configurations on the list established by a decision of the General Affairs Council, acting by a simple majority.

Title IV Provisions concerning the Commission, including the High Representative of the Union for Foreign Affairs and Security Policy

Article 5

The members of the Commission in office on the date of entry into force of the Treaty of Lisbon shall remain in office until the end of their term of office. However, on the day of the appointment of the

High Representative of the Union for Foreign Affairs and Security Policy, the term of office of the member having the same nationality as the High Representative shall end.

Title V Provisions concerning the Secretary-General of the Council, High Representative for the Common Foreign and Security Policy, and the Deputy Secretary-General of the Council

Article 6

The terms of office of the Secretary-General of the Council, High Representative for the common foreign and security policy, and the Deputy Secretary-General of the Council shall end on the date of entry into force of the Treaty of Lisbon. The Council shall appoint a Secretary-General in conformity with Article 240(2) of the Treaty on the Functioning of the European Union.

Title VI Provisions concerning advisory bodies

Article 7

Until the entry into force of the decision referred to in Article 301 of the Treaty on the Functioning of the European Union, the allocation of members of the Economic and Social Committee shall be as follows:

Belgium	12	Luxembourg	6
Bulgaria	12	Hungary	12
Czech Republic	12	Malta	5
Denmark	9	Netherlands	12
Germany	24	Austria	12
Estonia	7	Poland	21
Ireland	9	Portugal	12
Greece	12	Romania	15
Spain	21	Slovenia	7
France	24	Slovakia	9
Italy	24	Finland	9
Cyprus	6	Sweden	12
Latvia	7	United Kingdom	24
Lithuania	9		

Article 8

Until the entry into force of the decision referred to in Article 305 of the Treaty on the Functioning of the European Union, the allocation of members of the Committee of the Regions shall be as follows:

Belgium	12	Luxembourg	6
Bulgaria	12	Hungary	12
Czech Republic	12	Malta	5
Denmark	9	Netherlands	12
Germany	24	Austria	12

Estonia	7	Poland	21
Ireland	9	Portugal	12
Greece	12	Romania	15
Spain	21	Slovenia	7
France	24	Slovakia	9
Italy	24	Finland	9
Cyprus	6	Sweden	12
Latvia	7	United Kingdom	24
Lithuania	9		

Title VII Transitional provisions concerning acts adopted on the basis of Titles V and VI of the Treaty on European Union prior to the entry into force of the Treaty of Lisbon

Article 9

The legal effects of the acts of the institutions, bodies, offices and agencies of the Union adopted on the basis of the Treaty on European Union prior to the entry into force of the Treaty of Lisbon shall be preserved until those acts are repealed, annulled or amended in implementation of the Treaties. The same shall apply to agreements concluded between Member States on the basis of the Treaty on European Union.

Article 10

1. As a transitional measure, and with respect to acts of the Union in the field of police cooperation and judicial cooperation in criminal matters which have been adopted before the entry into force of the Treaty of Lisbon, the powers of the institutions shall be the following at the date of entry into force of that Treaty: the powers of the Commission under Article 258 of the Treaty on the Functioning of the European Union shall not be applicable and the powers of the Court of Justice of the European Union under Title VI of the Treaty on European Union, in the version in force before the entry into force of the Treaty of Lisbon, shall remain the same, including where they have been accepted under Article 35(2) of the said Treaty on European Union.

2. The amendment of an act referred to in paragraph 1 shall entail the applicability of the powers of the institutions referred to in that paragraph as set out in the Treaties with respect to the amended act for those Member States to which that amended act shall apply.

3. In any case, the transitional measure mentioned in paragraph 1 shall cease to have effect five years after the date of entry into force of the Treaty of Lisbon.

4. At the latest six months before the expiry of the transitional period referred to in paragraph 3, the United Kingdom may notify to the Council that it does not accept, with respect to the acts referred to in paragraph 1, the powers of the institutions referred to in paragraph 1 as set out in the Treaties. In case the United Kingdom has made that notification, all acts referred to in paragraph 1 shall cease to apply to it as from the date of expiry of the transitional period referred to in paragraph 3. This subparagraph shall not apply with respect to the amended acts which are applicable to the United Kingdom as referred to in paragraph 2.

The Council, acting by a qualified majority on a proposal from the Commission, shall determine the necessary consequential and transitional arrangements. The United Kingdom shall not participate in the adoption of this decision. A qualified majority of the Council shall be defined in accordance with Article 238(3)(a) of the Treaty on the Functioning of the European Union.

The Council, acting by a qualified majority on a proposal from the Commission, may also adopt a decision determining that the United Kingdom shall bear the direct financial consequences, if any, necessarily and unavoidably incurred as a result of the cessation of its participation in those acts.

5. The United Kingdom may, at any time afterwards, notify the Council of its wish to participate in acts which have ceased to apply to it pursuant to paragraph 4, first subparagraph. In that case, the relevant provisions of the Protocol on the Schengen acquis integrated into the framework of the European Union or of the Protocol on the position of the United Kingdom and Ireland in respect of the area of freedom, security and justice, as the case may be, shall apply. The powers of the institutions with regard to those acts shall be those set out in the Treaties. When acting under the relevant Protocols, the Union institutions and the United Kingdom shall seek to re-establish the widest possible measure of participation of the United Kingdom in the acquis of the Union in the area of freedom, security and justice without seriously affecting the practical operability of the various parts thereof, while respecting their coherence.

Selected Declarations concerning provisions of the Treaties

1. Declaration concerning the Charter of Fundamental Rights of the European Union

The Charter of Fundamental Rights of the European Union, which has legally binding force, confirms the fundamental rights guaranteed by the European Convention for the Protection of Human Rights and Fundamental Freedoms and as they result from the constitutional traditions common to the Member States.

The Charter does not extend the field of application of Union law beyond the powers of the Union or establish any new power or task for the Union, or modify powers and tasks as defined by the Treaties.

2. Declaration on Article 6(2) of the Treaty on European Union

The Conference agrees that the Union's accession to the European Convention for the Protection of Human Rights and Fundamental Freedoms should be arranged in such a way as to preserve the specific features of Union law. In this connection, the Conference notes the existence of a regular dialogue between the Court of Justice of the European Union and the European Court of Human Rights; such dialogue could be reinforced when the Union accedes to that Convention.

7. Declaration on Article 16(4) of the Treaty on European Union and Article 238(2) of the Treaty on the Functioning of the European Union

The Conference declares that the decision relating to the implementation of Article 16(4) of the Treaty on European Union and Article 238(2) of the Treaty on the Functioning of the European Union will be adopted by the Council on the date of the signature of the Treaty of Lisbon and will enter into force on the day that Treaty enters into force. The draft decision is set out below:

Draft decision of the Council relating to the implementation of Article 16(4) of the Treaty on European Union and Article 238(2) of the Treaty on the Functioning of the European Union between 1 November 2014 and 31 March 2017 on the one hand, and as from 1 April 2017 on the other

THE COUNCIL OF THE EUROPEAN UNION,

Whereas:

(1) Provisions should be adopted allowing for a smooth transition from the system for decision-making in the Council by a qualified majority as defined in Article 3(3) of the Protocol on the transitional provisions, which will continue to apply until 31 October 2014, to the voting system provided for in Article 16(4) of the Treaty on European Union and Article 238(2) of the Treaty on the Functioning of the European Union, which will apply with effect from 1 November 2014, including, during a transitional period until 31 March 2017, specific provisions laid down in Article 3(2) of that Protocol.

(2) It is recalled that it is the practice of the Council to devote every effort to strengthening the democratic legitimacy of decisions taken by a qualified majority,

HAS DECIDED AS FOLLOWS:

Section 1 Provisions to be applied from 1 November 2014 to 31 March 2017

Article 1

From 1 November 2014 to 31 March 2017, if members of the Council, representing:

(a) at least three quarters of the population, or

(b) at least three quarters of the number of Member States

necessary to constitute a blocking minority resulting from the application of Article 16(4), first subparagraph, of the Treaty on European Union or Article 238(2) of the Treaty on the Functioning of the European Union, indicate their opposition to the Council adopting an act by a qualified majority, the Council shall discuss the issue.

Article 2

The Council shall, in the course of these discussions, do all in its power to reach, within a reasonable time and without prejudicing obligatory time limits laid down by Union law, a satisfactory solution to address concerns raised by the members of the Council referred to in Article 1.

Article 3

To this end, the President of the Council, with the assistance of the Commission and in compliance with the Rules of Procedure of the Council, shall undertake any initiative necessary to facilitate a wider basis of agreement in the Council. The members of the Council shall lend him or her their assistance.

Section 2 Provisions to be applied as from 1 April 2017

Article 4

As from 1 April 2017, if members of the Council, representing:

(a) at least 55 % of the population, or

(b) at least 55 % of the number of Member States

necessary to constitute a blocking minority resulting from the application of Article 16(4), first subparagraph, of the Treaty on European Union or Article 238(2) of the Treaty on the Functioning of the European Union, indicate their opposition to the Council adopting an act by a qualified majority, the Council shall discuss the issue.

Article 5

The Council shall, in the course of these discussions, do all in its power to reach, within a reasonable time and without prejudicing obligatory time limits laid down by Union law, a satisfactory solution to address concerns raised by the members of the Council referred to in Article 4.

Article 6

To this end, the President of the Council, with the assistance of the Commission and in compliance with the Rules of Procedure of the Council, shall undertake any initiative necessary to facilitate a wider basis of agreement in the Council. The members of the Council shall lend him or her their assistance.

Section 3 Entry into force

Article 7
This Decision shall enter into force on the date of the entry into force of the Treaty of Lisbon.

17. Declaration concerning primacy

The Conference recalls that, in accordance with well settled case law of the Court of Justice of the European Union, the Treaties and the law adopted by the Union on the basis of the Treaties have primacy over the law of Member States, under the conditions laid down by the said case law.

The Conference has also decided to attach as an Annex to this Final Act the Opinion of the Council Legal Service on the primacy of EC law as set out in 11197/07 (JUR 260):

"Opinion of the Council Legal Service of 22 June 2007

It results from the case-law of the Court of Justice that primacy of EC law is a cornerstone principle of Community law. According to the Court, this principle is inherent to the specific nature of the European Community. At the time of the first judgment of this established case law (Costa/ENEL, 15 July 1964, Case 6/641[1]) there was no mention of primacy in the treaty. It is still the case today. The fact that the principle of primacy will not be included in the future treaty shall not in any way change the existence of the principle and the existing case-law of the Court of Justice."

18. Declaration in relation to the delimitation of competences

The Conference underlines that, in accordance with the system of division of competences between the Union and the Member States as provided for in the Treaty on European Union and the Treaty on the Functioning of the European Union, competences not conferred upon the Union in the Treaties remain with the Member States.

When the Treaties confer on the Union a competence shared with the Member States in a specific area, the Member States shall exercise their competence to the extent that the Union has not exercised, or has decided to cease exercising, its competence. The latter situation arises when the relevant EU institutions decide to repeal a legislative act, in particular better to ensure constant respect for the principles of subsidiarity and proportionality. The Council may, at the initiative of one or several of its members (representatives of Member States) and in accordance with Article 241 of the Treaty on the Functioning of the European Union, request the Commission to submit proposals for repealing a legislative act. The Conference welcomes the Commission's declaration that it will devote particular attention to these requests.

Equally, the representatives of the governments of the Member States, meeting in an Intergovernmental Conference, in accordance with the ordinary revision procedure provided for in Article 48(2) to (5) of the Treaty on European Union, may decide to amend the Treaties upon which the Union is founded, including either to increase or to reduce the competences conferred on the Union in the said Treaties.

[1] *"It follows (...) that the law stemming from the treaty, an independent source of law, could not, because of its special and original nature, be overridden by domestic legal provisions, however framed, without being deprived of its character as Community law and without the legal basis of the Community itself being called into question."*

24. Declaration concerning the legal personality of the European Union

The Conference confirms that the fact that the European Union has a legal personality will not in any way authorise the Union to legislate or to act beyond the competences conferred upon it by the Member States in the Treaties.

38. Declaration on Article 252 of the Treaty on the Functioning of the European Union regarding the number of Advocates-General in the Court of Justice

The Conference declares that if, in accordance with Article 252, first paragraph, of the Treaty on the Functioning of the European Union, the Court of Justice requests that the number of Advocates-General be increased by three (eleven instead of eight), the Council will, acting unanimously, agree on such an increase.

In that case, the Conference agrees that Poland will, as is already the case for Germany, France, Italy, Spain and the United Kingdom, have a permanent Advocate-General and no longer take part in the rotation system, while the existing rotation system will involve the rotation of five Advocates-General instead of three.

41. Declaration on Article 352 of the Treaty on the Functioning of the European Union

The Conference declares that the reference in Article 352(1) of the Treaty on the Functioning of the European Union to objectives of the Union refers to the objectives as set out in Article 3(2) and (3) of the Treaty on European Union and to the objectives of Article 3(5) of the said Treaty with respect to external action under Part Five of the Treaty on the Functioning of the European Union. It is therefore excluded that an action based on Article 352 of the Treaty on the Functioning of the European Union would only pursue objectives set out in Article 3(1) of the Treaty on European Union. In this connection, the Conference notes that in accordance with Article 31(1) of the Treaty on European Union, legislative acts may not be adopted in the area of the Common Foreign and Security Policy.

42. Declaration on Article 352 of the Treaty on the Functioning of the European Union

The Conference underlines that, in accordance with the settled case law of the Court of Justice of the European Union, Article 352 of the Treaty on the Functioning of the European Union, being an integral part of an institutional system based on the principle of conferred powers, cannot serve as a basis for widening the scope of Union powers beyond the general framework created by the provisions of the Treaties as a whole and, in particular, by those that define the tasks and the activities of the Union. In any event, this Article cannot be used as a basis for the adoption of provisions whose effect would, in substance, be to amend the Treaties without following the procedure which they provide for that purpose.

Charter of Fundamental Rights of the European Union

[OJ 2010 C83/02]*

Preamble

The peoples of Europe, in creating an ever closer union among them, are resolved to share a peaceful future based on common values.

Conscious of its spiritual and moral heritage, the Union is founded on the indivisible, universal values of human dignity, freedom, equality and solidarity; it is based on the principles of democracy and the rule of law. It places the individual at the heart of its activities, by establishing the citizenship of the Union and by creating an area of freedom, security and justice.

The Union contributes to the preservation and to the development of these common values while respecting the diversity of the cultures and traditions of the peoples of Europe as well as the national identities of the Member States and the organisation of their public authorities at national, regional and local levels; it seeks to promote balanced and sustainable development and ensures free movement of persons, goods, services and capital, and the freedom of establishment.

To this end, it is necessary to strengthen the protection of fundamental rights in the light of changes in society, social progress and scientific and technological developments by making those rights more visible in a Charter.

This Charter reaffirms, with due regard for the powers and tasks of the Community and the Union and the principle of subsidiarity, the rights as they result, in particular, from the constitutional traditions and international obligations common to the Member States, the Treaty on European Union, the Community Treaties, the European Convention for the Protection of Human Rights and Fundamental Freedoms, the Social Charters adopted by the Community and by the Council of Europe and the case-law of the Court of Justice of the European Communities and of the European Court of Human Rights. In this context the Charter will be interpreted by the courts of the Union and the Member States with due regard to the explanations prepared under the authority of the Praesidium of the Convention which drafted the Charter and updated under the responsibility of the Praesidium of the European Convention.

Enjoyment of these rights entails responsibilities and duties with regard to other persons, to the human community and to future generations.

The Union therefore recognises the rights, freedoms and principles set out hereafter.

Chapter I Dignity

Article 1 Human dignity

Human dignity is inviolable. It must be respected and protected.

Article 2 Right to life

1. Everyone has the right to life.
2. No one shall be condemned to the death penalty, or executed.

Article 3 Right to the integrity of the person

1. Everyone has the right to respect for his or her physical and mental integrity.
2. In the fields of medicine and biology, the following must be respected in particular:
   - the free and informed consent of the person concerned, according to the procedures laid down by law,
   - the prohibition of eugenic practices, in particular those aiming at the selection of persons,
   - the prohibition on making the human body and its parts as such a source of financial gain,
   - the prohibition of the reproductive cloning of human beings.

* **Editor's Note:** Proclamations and signatures omitted. This is the version reproclaimed in 2007 and subsequently reproduced in the OJ in 2010. It remains however, largely the text of 2000. Reproduced again unaltered in OJ 2012 C326/391.

Article 4 Prohibition of torture and inhuman or degrading treatment or punishment

No one shall be subjected to torture or to inhuman or degrading treatment or punishment.

Article 5 Prohibition of slavery and forced labour

1. No one shall be held in slavery or servitude.
2. No one shall be required to perform forced or compulsory labour.
3. Trafficking in human beings is prohibited.

Chapter II Freedoms

Article 6 Right to liberty and security

Everyone has the right to liberty and security of person.

Article 7 Respect for private and family life

Everyone has the right to respect for his or her private and family life, home and communications.

Article 8 Protection of personal data

1. Everyone has the right to the protection of personal data concerning him or her.

2. Such data must be processed fairly for specified purposes and on the basis of the consent of the person concerned or some other legitimate basis laid down by law. Everyone has the right of access to data which has been collected concerning him or her, and the right to have it rectified.

3. Compliance with these rules shall be subject to control by an independent authority.

Article 9 Right to marry and right to found a family

The right to marry and the right to found a family shall be guaranteed in accordance with the national laws governing the exercise of these rights.

Article 10 Freedom of thought, conscience and religion

1. Everyone has the right to freedom of thought, conscience and religion. This right includes freedom to change religion or belief and freedom, either alone or in community with others and in public or in private, to manifest religion or belief, in worship, teaching, practice and observance.

2. The right to conscientious objection is recognised, in accordance with the national laws governing the exercise of this right.

Article 11 Freedom of expression and information

1. Everyone has the right to freedom of expression. This right shall include freedom to hold opinions and to receive and impart information and ideas without interference by public authority and regardless of frontiers.

2. The freedom and pluralism of the media shall be respected.

Article 12 Freedom of assembly and of association

1. Everyone has the right to freedom of peaceful assembly and to freedom of association at all levels, in particular in political, trade union and civic matters, which implies the right of everyone to form and to join trade unions for the protection of his or her interests.

2. Political parties at Union level contribute to expressing the political will of the citizens of the Union.

Article 13 Freedom of the arts and sciences

The arts and scientific research shall be free of constraint. Academic freedom shall be respected.

Article 14 Right to education

1. Everyone has the right to education and to have access to vocational and continuing training.

2. This right includes the possibility to receive free compulsory education.

3. The freedom to found educational establishments with due respect for democratic principles and the right of parents to ensure the education and teaching of their children in conformity with

their religious, philosophical and pedagogical convictions shall be respected, in accordance with the national laws governing the exercise of such freedom and right.

Article 15 Freedom to choose an occupation and right to engage in work

1. Everyone has the right to engage in work and to pursue a freely chosen or accepted occupation.

2. Every citizen of the Union has the freedom to seek employment, to work, to exercise the right of establishment and to provide services in any Member State.

3. Nationals of third countries who are authorised to work in the territories of the Member States are entitled to working conditions equivalent to those of citizens of the Union.

Article 16 Freedom to conduct a business

The freedom to conduct a business in accordance with Union law and national laws and practices is recognised.

Article 17 Right to property

1. Everyone has the right to own, use, dispose of and bequeath his or her lawfully acquired possessions. No one may be deprived of his or her possessions, except in the public interest and in the cases and under the conditions provided for by law, subject to fair compensation being paid in good time for their loss. The use of property may be regulated by law in so far as is necessary for the general interest.

2. Intellectual property shall be protected.

Article 18 Right to asylum

The right to asylum shall be guaranteed with due respect for the rules of the Geneva Convention of 28 July 1951 and the Protocol of 31 January 1967 relating to the status of refugees and in accordance with the Treaty on European Union and the Treaty on the Functioning of the European Union (hereinafter referred to as "the Treaties").

Article 19 Protection in the event of removal, expulsion or extradition

1. Collective expulsions are prohibited.

2. No one may be removed, expelled or extradited to a State where there is a serious risk that he or she would be subjected to the death penalty, torture or other inhuman or degrading treatment or punishment.

Chapter III Equality

Article 20 Equality before the law

Everyone is equal before the law.

Article 21 Non-discrimination

1. Any discrimination based on any ground such as sex, race, colour, ethnic or social origin, genetic features, language, religion or belief, political or any other opinion, membership of a national minority, property, birth, disability, age or sexual orientation shall be prohibited.

2. Within the scope of application of the Treaties and without prejudice to the special provisions of those Treaties, any discrimination on grounds of nationality shall be prohibited.

Article 22 Cultural, religious and linguistic diversity

The Union shall respect cultural, religious and linguistic diversity.

Article 23 Equality between men and women

Equality between men and women must be ensured in all areas, including employment, work and pay.

The principle of equality shall not prevent the maintenance or adoption of measures providing for specific advantages in favour of the under-represented sex.

Article 24 The rights of the child

1. Children shall have the right to such protection and care as is necessary for their well-being. They may express their views freely. Such views shall be taken into consideration on matters which concern them in accordance with their age and maturity.

2. In all actions relating to children, whether taken by public authorities or private institutions, the child's best interests must be a primary consideration.

3. Every child shall have the right to maintain on a regular basis a personal relationship and direct contact with both his or her parents, unless that is contrary to his or her interests.

Article 25 The rights of the elderly

The Union recognises and respects the rights of the elderly to lead a life of dignity and independence and to participate in social and cultural life.

Article 26 Integration of persons with disabilities

The Union recognises and respects the right of persons with disabilities to benefit from measures designed to ensure their independence, social and occupational integration and participation in the life of the community.

Chapter IV Solidarity

Article 27 Workers' right to information and consultation within the undertaking

Workers or their representatives must, at the appropriate levels, be guaranteed information and consultation in good time in the cases and under the conditions provided for by Community law and national laws and practices.

Article 28 Right of collective bargaining and action

Workers and employers, or their respective organisations, have, in accordance with Community law and national laws and practices, the right to negotiate and conclude collective agreements at the appropriate levels and, in cases of conflicts of interest, to take collective action to defend their interests, including strike action.

Article 29 Right of access to placement services

Everyone has the right of access to a free placement service.

Article 30 Protection in the event of unjustified dismissal

Every worker has the right to protection against unjustified dismissal, in accordance with Union law and national laws and practices.

Article 31 Fair and just working conditions

1. Every worker has the right to working conditions which respect his or her health, safety and dignity.

2. Every worker has the right to limitation of maximum working hours, to daily and weekly rest periods and to an annual period of paid leave.

Article 32 Prohibition of child labour and protection of young people at work

The employment of children is prohibited. The minimum age of admission to employment may not be lower than the minimum school-leaving age, without prejudice to such rules as may be more favourable to young people and except for limited derogations.

Young people admitted to work must have working conditions appropriate to their age and be protected against economic exploitation and any work likely to harm their safety, health or physical, mental, moral or social development or to interfere with their education.

Article 33 Family and professional life

1. The family shall enjoy legal, economic and social protection.

2. To reconcile family and professional life, everyone shall have the right to protection from dismissal for a reason connected with maternity and the right to paid maternity leave and to parental leave following the birth or adoption of a child.

Article 34 Social security and social assistance

1. The Union recognises and respects the entitlement to social security benefits and social services providing protection in cases such as maternity, illness, industrial accidents, dependency or old age, and in the case of loss of employment, in accordance with the rules laid down by Union law and national laws and practices.

2. Everyone residing and moving legally within the European Union is entitled to social security benefits and social advantages in accordance with Union law and national laws and practices.

3. In order to combat social exclusion and poverty, the Union recognises and respects the right to social and housing assistance so as to ensure a decent existence for all those who lack sufficient resources, in accordance with the rules laid down by Union law and national laws and practices.

Article 35 Health care

Everyone has the right of access to preventive health care and the right to benefit from medical treatment under the conditions established by national laws and practices. A high level of human health protection shall be ensured in the definition and implementation of all Union policies and activities.

Article 36 Access to services of general economic interest

The Union recognises and respects access to services of general economic interest as provided for in national laws and practices, in accordance with the Treaties, in order to promote the social and territorial cohesion of the Union.

Article 37 Environmental protection

A high level of environmental protection and the improvement of the quality of the environment must be integrated into the policies of the Union and ensured in accordance with the principle of sustainable development.

Article 38 Consumer protection

Union policies shall ensure a high level of consumer protection.

Chapter V Citizens' rights

Article 39 Right to vote and to stand as a candidate at elections to the European Parliament

1. Every citizen of the Union has the right to vote and to stand as a candidate at elections to the European Parliament in the Member State in which he or she resides, under the same conditions as nationals of that State.

2. Members of the European Parliament shall be elected by direct universal suffrage in a free and secret ballot.

Article 40 Right to vote and to stand as a candidate at municipal elections

Every citizen of the Union has the right to vote and to stand as a candidate at municipal elections in the Member State in which he or she resides under the same conditions as nationals of that State.

Article 41 Right to good administration

1. Every person has the right to have his or her affairs handled impartially, fairly and within a reasonable time by the institutions, bodies, offices and agencies of the Union.

2. This right includes:

- the right of every person to be heard, before any individual measure which would affect him or her adversely is taken;

- the right of every person to have access to his or her file, while respecting the legitimate interests of confidentiality and of professional and business secrecy;
- the obligation of the administration to give reasons for its decisions.

3. Every person has the right to have the Community make good any damage caused by its institutions or by its servants in the performance of their duties, in accordance with the general principles common to the laws of the Member States.

4. Every person may write to the institutions of the Union in one of the languages of the Treaties and must have an answer in the same language.

Article 42 Right of access to documents

Any citizen of the Union, and any natural or legal person residing or having its registered office in a Member State, has a right of access to documents of the institutions, bodies, offices and agencies of the Union, whatever their medium.

Article 43 Ombudsman

Any citizen of the Union and any natural or legal person residing or having its registered office in a Member State has the right to refer to the European Ombudsman cases of maladministration in the activities of the institutions, bodies, offices or agencies of the Union, with the exception of the Court of Justice of the European Union acting in its judicial role.

Article 44 Right to petition

Any citizen of the Union and any natural or legal person residing or having its registered office in a Member State has the right to petition the European Parliament.

Article 45 Freedom of movement and of residence

1. Every citizen of the Union has the right to move and reside freely within the territory of the Member States.

2. Freedom of movement and residence may be granted, in accordance with the Treaties, to nationals of third countries legally resident in the territory of a Member State.

Article 46 Diplomatic and consular protection

Every citizen of the Union shall, in the territory of a third country in which the Member State of which he or she is a national is not represented, be entitled to protection by the diplomatic or consular authorities of any Member State, on the same conditions as the nationals of that Member State.

Chapter VI Justice

Article 47 Right to an effective remedy and to a fair trial

Everyone whose rights and freedoms guaranteed by the law of the Union are violated has the right to an effective remedy before a tribunal in compliance with the conditions laid down in this Article.

Everyone is entitled to a fair and public hearing within a reasonable time by an independent and impartial tribunal previously established by law. Everyone shall have the possibility of being advised, defended and represented.

Legal aid shall be made available to those who lack sufficient resources in so far as such aid is necessary to ensure effective access to justice.

Article 48 Presumption of innocence and right of defence

1. Everyone who has been charged shall be presumed innocent until proved guilty according to law.
2. Respect for the rights of the defence of anyone who has been charged shall be guaranteed.

Article 49 Principles of legality and proportionality of criminal offences and penalties

1. No one shall be held guilty of any criminal offence on account of any act or omission which did not constitute a criminal offence under national law or international law at the time when it was committed. Nor shall a heavier penalty be imposed than that which was applicable at the time the criminal

offence was committed. If, subsequent to the commission of a criminal offence, the law provides for a lighter penalty, that penalty shall be applicable.

2. This Article shall not prejudice the trial and punishment of any person for any act or omission which, at the time when it was committed, was criminal according to the general principles recognised by the community of nations.

3. The severity of penalties must not be disproportionate to the criminal offence.

Article 50 Right not to be tried or punished twice in criminal proceedings for the same criminal offence

No one shall be liable to be tried or punished again in criminal proceedings for an offence for which he or she has already been finally acquitted or convicted within the Union in accordance with the law.

Chapter VII General provisions

Article 51 Scope

1. The provisions of this Charter are addressed to the institutions, bodies, offices and agencies of the Union with due regard for the principle of subsidiarity and to the Member States only when they are implementing Union law. They shall therefore respect the rights, observe the principles and promote the application thereof in accordance with their respective powers and respecting the limits of the powers of the Union as conferred on it in the Treaties.

2. The Charter does not extend the field of application of Union law beyond the powers of the Union or establish any new power or task for the Union, or modify powers and tasks as defined in the Treaties.

Article 52 Scope of guaranteed rights

1. Any limitation on the exercise of the rights and freedoms recognised by this Charter must be provided for by law and respect the essence of those rights and freedoms. Subject to the principle of proportionality, limitations may be made only if they are necessary and genuinely meet objectives of general interest recognised by the Union or the need to protect the rights and freedoms of others.

2. Rights recognised by this Charter for which provision is made in the Treaties shall be exercised under the conditions and within the limits defined by those Treaties.

3. In so far as this Charter contains rights which correspond to rights guaranteed by the Convention for the Protection of Human Rights and Fundamental Freedoms, the meaning and scope of those rights shall be the same as those laid down by the said Convention. This provision shall not prevent Union law providing more extensive protection.

4. In so far as this Charter recognises fundamental rights as they result from the constitutional traditions common to the Member States, those rights shall be interpreted in harmony with those traditions.

5. The provisions of this Charter which contain principles may be implemented by legislative and executive acts taken by institutions, bodies, offices and agencies of the Union, and by acts of Member States when they are implementing Union law, in the exercise of their respective powers. They shall be judicially cognisable only in the interpretation of such acts and in the ruling on their legality.

6. Full account shall be taken of national laws and practices as specified in this Charter.

7. The explanations drawn up as a way of providing guidance in the interpretation of this Charter shall be given due regard by the courts of the Union and of the Member States.

Article 53 Level of protection

Nothing in this Charter shall be interpreted as restricting or adversely affecting human rights and fundamental freedoms as recognised, in their respective fields of application, by Union law and international law and by international agreements to which the Union, the Community or all the Member States are party, including the European Convention for the Protection of Human Rights and Fundamental Freedoms, and by the Member States' constitutions.

Article 54 Prohibition of abuse of rights

Nothing in this Charter shall be interpreted as implying any right to engage in any activity or to perform any act aimed at the destruction of any of the rights and freedoms recognised in this Charter or at their limitation to a greater extent than is provided for herein.

The above text adapts the wording of the Charter proclaimed on 7 December 2000, and will replace it as from the date of entry into force of the Treaty of Lisbon.

Additional legislation and agreements affecting the institutions

Majority voting procedure extract from the Luxembourg Accords

[EEC Bulletin 1966 No 3, p. 9]*

I. Where, in the case of decisions which may be taken by majority vote on a proposal of the Commission, very important interests of one or more partners are at stake, the Members of the Council will endeavour, within a reasonable time, to reach solutions which can be adopted by all the Members of the Council while respecting their mutual interests and those of the Community, in accordance with Article 2 of the Treaty.

II. With regard to the preceding paragraph, the French delegation considers that where very important interests are at stake the discussion must be continued until unanimous agreement is reached.

III. The six delegations note that there is a divergence of views on what should be done in the event of a failure to reach complete agreement.

IV. The six delegations nevertheless consider that this divergence does not prevent the Community's work being resumed in accordance with the normal procedure.

Regulation (EC) No 1049/2001 of the European Parliament and of the Council of 30 May 2001 regarding public access to European Parliament, Council and Commission documents

[OJ 2001 L145/43]

THE EUROPEAN PARLIAMENT AND THE COUNCIL OF THE EUROPEAN UNION,

Having regard to the Treaty establishing the European Community, and in particular Article 255(2) thereof,

Having regard to the proposal from the Commission[1],

Acting in accordance with the procedure referred to in Article 251 of the Treaty[2],

Whereas:

* **Editor's Note:** Permission to reproduce gratefully acknowledged but please note that 'Only European Community legislation printed in the paper edition of the Official Journal of the European Union is deemed authentic'.

[1] OJ C 177 E, 27.6.2000, p. 70.

[2] Opinion of the European Parliament of 3 May 2001 (not yet published in the Official Journal) and Council Decision of 28 May 2001.

(1) The second subparagraph of Article 1 of the Treaty on European Union enshrines the concept of openness, stating that the Treaty marks a new stage in the process of creating an ever closer union among the peoples of Europe, in which decisions are taken as openly as possible and as closely as possible to the citizen.

(2) Openness enables citizens to participate more closely in the decision-making process and guarantees that the administration enjoys greater legitimacy and is more effective and more accountable to the citizen in a democratic system. Openness contributes to strengthening the principles of democracy and respect for fundamental rights as laid down in Article 6 of the EU Treaty and in the Charter of Fundamental Rights of the European Union.

(3) The conclusions of the European Council meetings held at Birmingham, Edinburgh and Copenhagen stressed the need to introduce greater transparency into the work of the Union institutions. This Regulation consolidates the initiatives that the institutions have already taken with a view to improving the transparency of the decision-making process.

(4) The purpose of this Regulation is to give the fullest possible effect to the right of public access to documents and to lay down the general principles and limits on such access in accordance with Article 255(2) of the EC Treaty.

(5) Since the question of access of documents is not covered by provisions of the Treaty establishing the European Coal and Steel Community and the Treaty establishing the European Atomic Energy Community, the European Parliament, the Council and the Commission should, in accordance with Declaration No 41 attached to the Final Act of the Treaty of Amsterdam, draw guidance from this Regulation as regards documents concerning the activities covered by those two Treaties.

(6) Wider access should be granted to documents in cases where the institutions are acting in their legislative capacity, including under delegated powers, while at the same time preserving the effectiveness of the institutions' decision-making process. Such documents should be made directly accessible to the greatest possible extent.

(7) In accordance with Articles 28(1) and 41(1) of the EU Treaty, the right of access also applies to documents relating to the common foreign and security policy and to police and judicial cooperation in criminal matters. Each institution should respect its security rules.

(8) In order to ensure the full application of this Regulation to all activities of the Union, all agencies established by the institutions should apply the principles laid down in this Regulation.

(9) On account of their highly sensitive content, certain documents should be given special treatment. Arrangements for informing the European Parliament of the content of such documents should be made through interinstitutional agreement.

(10) In order to bring about greater openness in the work of the institutions, access to documents should be granted by the European Parliament, the Council and the Commission not only to documents drawn up by the institutions, but also to documents received by them. In this context, it is recalled that Declaration No 35 attached to the Final Act of the Treaty of Amsterdam provides that a Member State may request the Commission or the Council not to communicate to third parties a document originating from that State without its prior agreement.

(11) In principle, all documents of the institutions should be accessible to the public. However, certain public and private interests should be protected by way of exceptions. The institutions should be entitled to protect their internal consultations and deliberations where necessary to safeguard their ability to carry out their tasks. In assessing the exceptions, the institutions should take account of the principles in Community legislation concerning the protection of personal data, in all areas of Union activities.

(12) All rules concerning access to documents of the institutions should be in conformity with this Regulation.

(13) In order to ensure that the right of access is fully respected, a two-stage administrative procedure should apply, with the additional possibility of court proceedings or complaints to the Ombudsman.

(14) Each institution should take the measures necessary to inform the public of the new provisions in force and to train its staff to assist citizens exercising their rights under this Regulation. In order to make it easier for citizens to exercise their rights, each institution should provide access to a register of documents.

(15) Even though it is neither the object nor the effect of this Regulation to amend national legislation on access to documents, it is nevertheless clear that, by virtue of the principle of loyal cooperation which governs relations between the institutions and the Member States, Member States should take care not to hamper the proper application of this Regulation and should respect the security rules of the institutions.

(16) This Regulation is without prejudice to existing rights of access to documents for Member States, judicial authorities or investigative bodies.

(17) In accordance with Article 255(3) of the EC Treaty, each institution lays down specific provisions regarding access to its documents in its rules of procedure. Council Decision 93/731/EC of 20 December 1993 on public access to Council documents[3], Commission Decision 94/90/ECSC, EC, Euratom of 8 February 1994 on public access to Commission documents[4], European Parliament Decision 97/632/EC, ECSC, Euratom of 10 July 1997 on public access to European Parliament documents[5], and the rules on confidentiality of Schengen documents should therefore, if necessary, be modified or be repealed,

HAVE ADOPTED THIS REGULATION:

Article 1 Purpose

The purpose of this Regulation is:

(a) to define the principles, conditions and limits on grounds of public or private interest governing the right of access to European Parliament, Council and Commission (hereinafter referred to as 'the institutions') documents provided for in Article 255 of the EC Treaty in such a way as to ensure the widest possible access to documents,
(b) to establish rules ensuring the easiest possible exercise of this right, and
(c) to promote good administrative practice on access to documents.

Article 2 Beneficiaries and scope

1. Any citizen of the Union, and any natural or legal person residing or having its registered office in a Member State, has a right of access to documents of the institutions, subject to the principles, conditions and limits defined in this Regulation.

2. The institutions may, subject to the same principles, conditions and limits, grant access to documents to any natural or legal person not residing or not having its registered office in a Member State.

3. This Regulation shall apply to all documents held by an institution, that is to say, documents drawn up or received by it and in its possession, in all areas of activity of the European Union.

4. Without prejudice to Articles 4 and 9, documents shall be made accessible to the public either following a written application or directly in electronic form or through a register. In particular, documents drawn up or received in the course of a legislative procedure shall be made directly accessible in accordance with Article 12.

5. Sensitive documents as defined in Article 9(1) shall be subject to special treatment in accordance with that Article.

6. This Regulation shall be without prejudice to rights of public access to documents held by the institutions which might follow from instruments of international law or acts of the institutions implementing them.

[3] OJ L 340, 31.12.1993, p. 43. Decision as last amended by Decision 2000/527/EC (OJ L 212, 23.8.2000, p. 9).
[4] OJ L 46, 18.2.1994, p. 58. Decision as amended by Decision 96/567/EC, ECSC, Euratom (OJ L 247, 28.9.1996, p. 45).
[5] OJ L 263, 25.9.1997, p. 27

Article 3 Definitions

For the purpose of this Regulation:

(a) 'document' shall mean any content whatever its medium (written on paper or stored in electronic form or as a sound, visual or audiovisual recording) concerning a matter relating to the policies, activities and decisions falling within the institution's sphere of responsibility;

(b) 'third party' shall mean any natural or legal person, or any entity outside the institution concerned, including the Member States, other Community or non-Community institutions and bodies and third countries.

Article 4 Exceptions

1. The institutions shall refuse access to a document where disclosure would undermine the protection of:

(a) the public interest as regards:
- public security,
- defence and military matters,
- international relations,
- the financial, monetary or economic policy of the Community or a Member State;

(b) privacy and the integrity of the individual, in particular in accordance with Community legislation regarding the protection of personal data.

2. The institutions shall refuse access to a document where disclosure would undermine the protection of:
- commercial interests of a natural or legal person, including intellectual property,
- court proceedings and legal advice,
- the purpose of inspections, investigations and audits,

unless there is an overriding public interest in disclosure.

3. Access to a document, drawn up by an institution for internal use or received by an institution, which relates to a matter where the decision has not been taken by the institution, shall be refused if disclosure of the document would seriously undermine the institution's decision-making process, unless there is an overriding public interest in disclosure. Access to a document containing opinions for internal use as part of deliberations and preliminary consultations within the institution concerned shall be refused even after the decision has been taken if disclosure of the document would seriously undermine the institution's decision-making process, unless there is an overriding public interest in disclosure.

4. As regards third-party documents, the institution shall consult the third party with a view to assessing whether an exception in paragraph 1 or 2 is applicable, unless it is clear that the document shall or shall not be disclosed.

5. A Member State may request the institution not to disclose a document originating from that Member State without its prior agreement.

6. If only parts of the requested document are covered by any of the exceptions, the remaining parts of the document shall be released.

7. The exceptions as laid down in paragraphs 1 to 3 shall only apply for the period during which protection is justified on the basis of the content of the document. The exceptions may apply for a maximum period of 30 years. In the case of documents covered by the exceptions relating to privacy or commercial interests and in the case of sensitive documents, the exceptions may, if necessary, continue to apply after this period.

Article 5 Documents in the Member States

Where a Member State receives a request for a document in its possession, originating from an institution, unless it is clear that the document shall or shall not be disclosed, the Member State shall consult with the institution concerned in order to take a decision that does not jeopardise the attainment of the objectives of this Regulation. The Member State may instead refer the request to the institution.

Article 6 Applications

1. Applications for access to a document shall be made in any written form, including electronic form, in one of the languages referred to in Article 314 of the EC Treaty and in a sufficiently precise manner to enable the institution to identify the document. The applicant is not obliged to state reasons for the application.

2. If an application is not sufficiently precise, the institution shall ask the applicant to clarify the application and shall assist the applicant in doing so, for example, by providing information on the use of the public registers of documents.

3. In the event of an application relating to a very long document or to a very large number of documents, the institution concerned may confer with the applicant informally, with a view to finding a fair solution.

4. The institutions shall provide information and assistance to citizens on how and where applications for access to documents can be made.

Article 7 Processing of initial applications

1. An application for access to a document shall be handled promptly. An acknowledgement of receipt shall be sent to the applicant. Within 15 working days from registration of the application, the institution shall either grant access to the document requested and provide access in accordance with Article 10 within that period or, in a written reply, state the reasons for the total or partial refusal and inform the applicant of his or her right to make a confirmatory application in accordance with paragraph 2 of this Article.

2. In the event of a total or partial refusal, the applicant may, within 15 working days of receiving the institution's reply, make a confirmatory application asking the institution to reconsider its position.

3. In exceptional cases, for example, in the event of an application relating to a very long document or to a very large number of documents, the time-limit provided for in paragraph 1 may be extended by 15 working days, provided that the applicant is notified in advance and that detailed reasons are given.

4. Failure by the institution to reply within the prescribed time-limit shall entitle the applicant to make a confirmatory application.

Article 8 Processing of confirmatory applications

1. A confirmatory application shall be handled promptly. Within 15 working days from registration of such an application, the institution shall either grant access to the document requested and provide access in accordance with Article 10 within that period or, in a written reply, state the reasons for the total or partial refusal. In the event of a total or partial refusal, the institution shall inform the applicant of the remedies open to him or her, namely instituting court proceedings against the institution and/or making a complaint to the Ombudsman, under the conditions laid down in Articles 230 and 195 of the EC Treaty, respectively.

2. In exceptional cases, for example, in the event of an application relating to a very long document or to a very large number of documents, the time limit provided for in paragraph 1 may be extended by 15 working days, provided that the applicant is notified in advance and that detailed reasons are given.

3. Failure by the institution to reply within the prescribed time limit shall be considered as a negative reply and entitle the applicant to institute court proceedings against the institution and/or make a complaint to the Ombudsman, under the relevant provisions of the EC Treaty.

Article 9 Treatment of sensitive documents

1. Sensitive documents are documents originating from the institutions or the agencies established by them, from Member States, third countries or International Organisations, classified as 'TRÉS SECRET/TOP SECRET', 'SECRET' or 'CONFIDENTIEL' in accordance with the rules of the institution concerned, which protect essential interests of the European Union or of one or more of its Member States in the areas covered by Article 4(1)(a), notably public security, defence and military matters.

2. Applications for access to sensitive documents under the procedures laid down in Articles 7 and 8 shall be handled only by those persons who have a right to acquaint themselves with those documents. These persons shall also, without prejudice to Article 11(2), assess which references to sensitive documents could be made in the public register.

3. Sensitive documents shall be recorded in the register or released only with the consent of the originator.

4. An institution which decides to refuse access to a sensitive document shall give the reasons for its decision in a manner which does not harm the interests protected in Article 4.

5. Member States shall take appropriate measures to ensure that when handling applications for sensitive documents the principles in this Article and Article 4 are respected.

6. The rules of the institutions concerning sensitive documents shall be made public.

7. The Commission and the Council shall inform the European Parliament regarding sensitive documents in accordance with arrangements agreed between the institutions.

Article 10 Access following an application

1. The applicant shall have access to documents either by consulting them on the spot or by receiving a copy, including, where available, an electronic copy, according to the applicant's preference. The cost of producing and sending copies may be charged to the applicant. This charge shall not exceed the real cost of producing and sending the copies. Consultation on the spot, copies of less than 20 A4 pages and direct access in electronic form or through the register shall be free of charge.

2. If a document has already been released by the institution concerned and is easily accessible to the applicant, the institution may fulfil its obligation of granting access to documents by informing the applicant how to obtain the requested document.

3. Documents shall be supplied in an existing version and format (including electronically or in an alternative format such as Braille, large print or tape) with full regard to the applicant's preference.

Article 11 Registers

1. To make citizens' rights under this Regulation effective, each institution shall provide public access to a register of documents. Access to the register should be provided in electronic form. References to documents shall be recorded in the register without delay.

2. For each document the register shall contain a reference number (including, where applicable, the interinstitutional reference), the subject matter and/or a short description of the content of the document and the date on which it was received or drawn up and recorded in the register. References shall be made in a manner which does not undermine protection of the interests in Article 4.

3. The institutions shall immediately take the measures necessary to establish a register which shall be operational by 3 June 2002.

Article 12 Direct access in electronic form or through a register

1. The institutions shall as far as possible make documents directly accessible to the public in electronic form or through a register in accordance with the rules of the institution concerned.

2. In particular, legislative documents, that is to say, documents drawn up or received in the course of procedures for the adoption of acts which are legally binding in or for the Member States, should, subject to Articles 4 and 9, be made directly accessible.

3. Where possible, other documents, notably documents relating to the development of policy or strategy, should be made directly accessible.

4. Where direct access is not given through the register, the register shall as far as possible indicate where the document is located.

Article 13 Publication in the Official Journal

1. In addition to the acts referred to in Article 254(1) and (2) of the EC Treaty and the first paragraph of Article 163 of the Euratom Treaty, the following documents shall, subject to Articles 4 and 9 of this Regulation, be published in the Official Journal:

(a) Commission proposals;

(b) common positions adopted by the Council in accordance with the procedures referred to in Articles 251 and 252 of the EC Treaty and the reasons underlying those common positions, as well as the European Parliament's positions in these procedures;
(c) framework decisions and decisions referred to in Article 34(2) of the EU Treaty;
(d) conventions established by the Council in accordance with Article 34(2) of the EU Treaty;
(e) conventions signed between Member States on the basis of Article 293 of the EC Treaty;
(f) international agreements concluded by the Community or in accordance with Article 24 of the EU Treaty.

2. As far as possible, the following documents shall be published in the Official Journal:
(a) initiatives presented to the Council by a Member State pursuant to Article 67(1) of the EC Treaty or pursuant to Article 34(2) of the EU Treaty;
(b) common positions referred to in Article 34(2) of the EU Treaty;
(c) directives other than those referred to in Article 254(1) and (2) of the EC Treaty, decisions other than those referred to in Article 254(1) of the EC Treaty, recommendations and opinions.

3. Each institution may in its rules of procedure establish which further documents shall be published in the Official Journal.

Article 14 Information

1. Each institution shall take the requisite measures to inform the public of the rights they enjoy under this Regulation.

2. The Member States shall cooperate with the institutions in providing information to the citizens.

Article 15 Administrative practice in the institutions

1. The institutions shall develop good administrative practices in order to facilitate the exercise of the right of access guaranteed by this Regulation.

2. The institutions shall establish an interinstitutional committee to examine best practice, address possible conflicts and discuss future developments on public access to documents.

Article 16 Reproduction of documents

This Regulation shall be without prejudice to any existing rules on copyright which may limit a third party's right to reproduce or exploit released documents.

Article 17 Reports

1. Each institution shall publish annually a report for the preceding year including the number of cases in which the institution refused to grant access to documents, the reasons for such refusals and the number of sensitive documents not recorded in the register.

2. At the latest by 31 January 2004, the Commission shall publish a report on the implementation of the principles of this Regulation and shall make recommendations, including, if appropriate, proposals for the revision of this Regulation and an action programme of measures to be taken by the institutions.

Article 18 Application measures

1. Each institution shall adapt its rules of procedure to the provisions of this Regulation. The adaptations shall take effect from 3 December 2001.

2. Within six months of the entry into force of this Regulation, the Commission shall examine the conformity of Council Regulation (EEC, Euratom) No 354/83 of 1 February 1983 concerning the opening to the public of the historical archives of the European Economic Community and the European Atomic Energy Community[6] with this Regulation in order to ensure the preservation and archiving of documents to the fullest extent possible.

[6] OJ L 43, 15.2.1983, p. 1.

3. Within six months of the entry into force of this Regulation, the Commission shall examine the conformity of the existing rules on access to documents with this Regulation.

Article 19 Entry into force

This Regulation shall enter into force on the third day following that of its publication in the Official Journal of the European Communities. It shall be applicable from 3 December 2001.

This Regulation shall be binding in its entirety and directly applicable in all Member States.

Done at Brussels, 30 May 2001.

Joint declaration relating to Regulation 1049/2001 of the European Parliament and of the Council regarding public access to European Parliament, Council and Commission documents

[OJ 2001 L173/5]

1. The European Parliament, the Council and the Commission agree that the agencies and similar bodies created by the legislator should have rules on access to their documents which conform to those of this Regulation. To this effect, the European Parliament and the Council welcome the Commission's intention to propose, as soon as possible, amendments to the acts establishing the existing agencies and bodies and to include provisions in future proposals concerning the establishment of such agencies and bodies. They undertake to adopt the necessary acts rapidly.

2. The European Parliament, the Council and the Commission call on the institutions and bodies not covered by paragraph 1 to adopt internal rules on public access to documents which take account of the principles and limits in this Regulation.

Joint declaration on practical arrangements for the codecision procedure (Article 251 of the EC Treaty)

[OJ 2007 C145/02]

General principles

1. The European Parliament, the Council and the Commission, hereinafter referred to collectively as 'the institutions', note that current practice involving talks between the Council Presidency, the Commission and the chairs of the relevant committees and/or rapporteurs of the European Parliament and between the co-chairs of the Conciliation Committee has proved its worth.

2. The institutions confirm that this practice, which has developed at all stages of the codecision procedure, must continue to be encouraged. The institutions undertake to examine their working methods with a view to making even more effective use of the full scope of the codecision procedure as established by the EC Treaty.

3. This Joint Declaration clarifies these working methods, and the practical arrangements for pursuing them. It complements the Interinstitutional Agreement on Better Lawmaking[1] and notably its provisions relating to the co-decision procedure. The institutions undertake fully to respect such commitments in line with the principles of transparency, accountability and efficiency. In this respect,

[1] OJ C 321, 31.12.2003, p. 1.

the institutions should pay particular attention to making progress on simplification proposals while respecting the acquis communautaire.

4. The institutions shall cooperate in good faith throughout the procedure with a view to reconciling their positions as far as possible and thereby clearing the way, where appropriate, for the adoption of the act concerned at an early stage of the procedure.

5. With that aim in view, they shall cooperate through appropriate interinstitutional contacts to monitor the progress of the work and analyse the degree of convergence at all stages of the codecision procedure.

6. The institutions, in accordance with their internal rules of procedure, undertake to exchange information regularly on the progress of codecision files. They shall ensure that their respective calendars of work are coordinated as far as possible in order to enable proceedings to be conducted in a coherent and convergent fashion. They will therefore seek to establish an indicative timetable for the various stages leading to the final adoption of different legislative proposals, while fully respecting the political nature of the decision-making process.

7. Cooperation between the institutions in the context of codecision often takes the form of tripartite meetings ('trilogues'). This trilogue system has demonstrated its vitality and flexibility in increasing significantly the possibilities for agreement at first and second reading stages, as well as contributing to the preparation of the work of the Conciliation Committee.

8. Such trilogues are usually conducted in an informal framework. They may be held at all stages of the procedure and at different levels of representation, depending on the nature of the expected discussion. Each institution, in accordance with its own rules of procedure, will designate its participants for each meeting, define its mandate for the negotiations and inform the other institutions of arrangements for the meetings in good time.

9. As far as possible, any draft compromise texts submitted for discussion at a forthcoming meeting shall be circulated in advance to all participants. In order to enhance transparency, trilogues taking place within the European Parliament and Council shall be announced, where practicable.

10. The Council Presidency will endeavour to attend the meetings of the parliamentary committees. It will carefully consider any request it receives to provide information related to the Council position, as appropriate.

FIRST READING

11. The institutions shall cooperate in good faith with a view to reconciling their positions as far as possible so that, wherever possible, acts can be adopted at first reading.

Agreement at the stage of first reading in the European Parliament

12. Appropriate contacts shall be established to facilitate the conduct of proceedings at first reading.

13. The Commission shall facilitate such contacts and shall exercise its right of initiative in a constructive manner with a view to reconciling the positions of the European Parliament and the Council, with due regard for the balance between the institutions and the role conferred on it by the Treaty.

14. Where an agreement is reached through informal negotiations in trilogues, the chair of Coreper shall forward, in a letter to the chair of the relevant parliamentary committee, details of the substance of the agreement, in the form of amendments to the Commission proposal. That letter shall indicate the Council's willingness to accept that outcome, subject to legal-linguistic verification, should it be confirmed by the vote in plenary. A copy of that letter shall be forwarded to the Commission.

15. In this context, where conclusion of a dossier at first reading is imminent, information on the intention to conclude an agreement should be made readily available as early as possible.

Agreement at the stage of Council common position

16. Where no agreement is reached at the European Parliament's first reading, contacts may be continued with a view to concluding an agreement at the common position stage.

17. The Commission shall facilitate such contacts and shall exercise its right of initiative in a constructive manner with a view to reconciling the positions of the European Parliament and the Council, with due regard for the balance between the institutions and the role conferred on it by the Treaty.

18. Where an agreement is reached at this stage, the chair of the relevant parliamentary committee shall indicate, in a letter to the chair of Coreper, his recommendation to the plenary to accept the Council common position without amendment, subject to confirmation of the common position by the Council and to legal-linguistic verification. A copy of the letter shall be forwarded to the Commission.

SECOND READING

19. In its statement of reasons, the Council shall explain as clearly as possible the reasons that led it to adopt its common position. During its second reading, the European Parliament shall take the greatest possible account of those reasons and of the Commission's position.

20. Before transmitting the common position, the Council shall endeavour to consider in consultation with the European Parliament and the Commission the date for its transmission in order to ensure the maximum efficiency of the legislative procedure at second reading.

Agreement at the stage of second reading in the European Parliament

21. Appropriate contacts will continue as soon as the Council common position is forwarded to the European Parliament, with a view to achieving a better understanding of the respective positions and thus to bringing the legislative procedure to a conclusion as quickly as possible.

22. The Commission shall facilitate such contacts and give its opinion with a view to reconciling the positions of the European Parliament and the Council, with due regard for the balance between the institutions and the role conferred on it by the Treaty.

23. Where an agreement is reached through informal negotiations in trilogues, the chair of Coreper shall forward, in a letter to the chair of the relevant parliamentary committee, details of the substance of the agreement, in the form of amendments to the Council common position. That letter shall indicate the Council's willingness to accept that outcome, subject to legal-linguistic verification, should it be confirmed by the vote in plenary. A copy of that letter shall be forwarded to the Commission.

CONCILIATION

24. If it becomes clear that the Council will not be in a position to accept all the amendments of the European Parliament at second reading and when the Council is ready to present its position, a first trilogue will be organised. Each institution, in accordance with its own rules of procedure, will designate its participants for each meeting and define its mandate for the negotiations. The Commission will indicate to both delegations at the earliest possible stage its intentions with regard to its opinion on the European Parliament's second reading amendments.

25. Trilogues shall take place throughout the conciliation procedure with the aim of resolving outstanding issues and preparing the ground for an agreement to be reached in the Conciliation Committee. The results of the trilogues shall be discussed and possibly approved at the meetings of the respective institutions.

26. The Conciliation Committee shall be convened by the President of the Council, with the agreement of the President of the European Parliament and with due regard to the provisions of the Treaty.

27. The Commission shall take part in the conciliation proceedings and shall take all the necessary initiatives with a view to reconciling the positions of the European Parliament and the Council. Such initiatives may include, draft compromise texts having regard to the positions of the European

Parliament and of the Council and with due regard for the role conferred upon the Commission by the Treaty.

28. The Conciliation Committee shall be chaired jointly by the President of the European Parliament and the President of the Council. Committee meetings shall be chaired alternately by each co-chair.

29. The dates and the agendas for the Conciliation Committee's meetings shall be set jointly by the co-chairs with a view to the effective functioning of the Conciliation Committee throughout the conciliation procedure. The Commission shall be consulted on the dates envisaged. The European Parliament and the Council shall set aside, for guidance, appropriate dates for conciliation proceedings and shall notify the Commission thereof.

30. The co-chairs may put several dossiers on the agenda of any one meeting of the Conciliation Committee. As well as the principal topic ('B-item'), where agreement has not yet been reached, conciliation procedures on other topics may be opened and/or closed without discussion on these items ('A-item').

31. While respecting the Treaty provisions regarding time-limits, the European Parliament and the Council shall, as far as possible, take account of scheduling requirements, in particular those resulting from breaks in the institutions' activities and from the European Parliament's elections. At all events, the break in activities shall be as short as possible.

32. The Conciliation Committee shall meet alternately at the premises of the European Parliament and the Council, with a view to an equal sharing of facilities, including interpretation facilities.

33. The Conciliation Committee shall have available to it the Commission proposal, the Council common position and the Commission's opinion thereon, the amendments proposed by the European Parliament and the Commission's opinion thereon, and a joint working document by the European Parliament and Council delegations. This working document should enable users to identify the issues at stake easily and to refer to them efficiently. The Commission shall, as a general rule, submit its opinion within three weeks of official receipt of the outcome of the European Parliament's vote and at the latest by the commencement of conciliation proceedings.

34. The co-chairs may submit texts for the Conciliation Committee's approval.

35. Agreement on a joint text shall be established at a meeting of the Conciliation Committee or, subsequently, by an exchange of letters between the co-chairs. Copies of such letters shall be forwarded to the Commission.

36. If the Conciliation Committee reaches agreement on a joint text, the text shall, after legal-linguistic finalisation, be submitted to the co-chairs for formal approval. However, in exceptional cases in order to respect the deadlines, a draft joint text may be submitted to the co-chairs for approval.

37. The co-chairs shall forward the approved joint text to the Presidents of the European Parliament and of the Council by means of a jointly signed letter. Where the Conciliation Committee is unable to agree on a joint text, the co-chairs shall notify the Presidents of the European Parliament and of the Council thereof in a jointly signed letter. Such letters shall serve as an official record. Copies of such letters shall be forwarded to the Commission for information. The working documents used during the conciliation procedure will be accessible in the Register of each institution once the procedure has been concluded.

38. The Secretariat of the European Parliament and the General-Secretariat of the Council shall act jointly as the Conciliation Committee's secretariat, in association with the Secretariat-General of the Commission.

GENERAL PROVISIONS

39. Should the European Parliament or the Council deem it essential to extend the time-limits referred to in Article 251 of the Treaty, they shall notify the President of the other institution and the Commission accordingly.

40. Where an agreement is reached at first or second reading, or during conciliation, the agreed text shall be finalised by the legal-linguistic services of the European Parliament and of the Council acting in close cooperation and by mutual agreement.

41. No changes shall be made to any agreed texts without the explicit agreement, at the appropriate level, of both the European Parliament and the Council.

42. Finalisation shall be carried out with due regard to the different procedures of the European Parliament and the Council, in particular with respect to deadlines for conclusion of internal procedures. The institutions undertake not to use the time-limits laid down for the legal-linguistic finalisation of acts to reopen discussions on substantive issues.

43. The European Parliament and the Council shall agree on a common presentation of the texts prepared jointly by those institutions.

44. As far as possible, the institutions undertake to use mutually acceptable standard clauses to be incorporated in the acts adopted under codecision in particular as regards provisions concerning the exercise of implementing powers (in accordance with the 'comitology' decision[2], entry into force, transposition and the application of acts and respect for the Commission's right of initiative.

45. The institutions will endeavour to hold a joint press conference to announce the successful outcome of the legislative process at first or second reading or during conciliation. They will also endeavour to issue joint press releases.

46. Following adoption of a legislative act under the codecision procedure by the European Parliament and the Council, the text shall be submitted, for signature, to the President of the European Parliament and the President of the Council and to the Secretaries-General of those institutions.

47. The Presidents of the European Parliament and the Council shall receive the text for signature in their respective languages and shall, as far as possible, sign the text together at a joint ceremony to be organised on a monthly basis with a view to signing important acts in the presence of the media.

48. The jointly signed text shall be forwarded for publication in the *Official Journal of the European Union*. Publication shall normally follow within two months of the adoption of the legislative act by the European Parliament and the Council.

49. If one of the institutions identifies a clerical or obvious error in a text (or in one of the language versions thereof), it shall immediately notify the other institutions. If the error concerns an act that has not yet been adopted by either the European Parliament or the Council, the legal-linguistic services of the European Parliament and the Council shall prepare the necessary corrigendum in close cooperation.

Where this error concerns an act that has already been adopted by one or both of those institutions, whether published or not, the European Parliament and the Council shall adopt, by common agreement, a corrigendum drawn up under their respective procedures.

Done at Brussels, on the thirteenth day of June in the year two thousand and seven.
(Signatures omitted)

[2] Council Decision 1999/468/EC of 28 June 1999 laying down the procedures for the exercise of implementing powers conferred on the Commission (OJ L 184, 17.7.1999, p. 23. Decision as amended by Decision 2006/512/EC (OJ L 200, 27.7.2006, p. 11).

Regulation (EU) No 182/2011 of the European Parliament and of the Council of 16 February 2011 laying down the rules and general principles concerning mechanisms for control by Member States of the Commission's exercise of implementing powers

[OJ 2011 L55/13]

THE EUROPEAN PARLIAMENT AND THE COUNCIL OF THE EUROPEAN UNION,

Having regard to the Treaty on the Functioning of the European Union, and in particular Article 291(3) thereof,

Having regard to the proposal from the Commission,

After transmission of the draft legislative act to the national parliaments,

Acting in accordance with the ordinary legislative procedure[1],

Whereas:

(1) Where uniform conditions for the implementation of legally binding Union acts are needed, those acts (hereinafter "basic acts") are to confer implementing powers on the Commission, or, in duly justified specific cases and in the cases provided for in Articles 24 and 26 of the Treaty on European Union, on the Council.

(2) It is for the legislator, fully respecting the criteria laid down in the Treaty on the Functioning of the European Union ("TFEU"), to decide in respect of each basic act whether to confer implementing powers on the Commission in accordance with Article 291(2) of that Treaty.

(3) Hitherto, the exercise of implementing powers by the Commission has been governed by Council Decision 1999/468/EC[2].

(4) The TFEU now requires the European Parliament and the Council to lay down the rules and general principles concerning mechanisms for control by Member States of the Commission's exercise of implementing powers.

(5) It is necessary to ensure that the procedures for such control are clear, effective and proportionate to the nature of the implementing acts and that they reflect the institutional requirements of the TFEU as well as the experience gained and the common practice followed in the implementation of Decision 1999/468/EC.

(6) In those basic acts which require the control of the Member States for the adoption by the Commission of implementing acts, it is appropriate, for the purposes of such control, that committees composed of the representatives of the Member States and chaired by the Commission be set up.

(7) Where appropriate, the control mechanism should include referral to an appeal committee which should meet at the appropriate level.

(8) In the interests of simplification, the Commission should exercise implementing powers in accordance with one of only two procedures, namely the advisory procedure or the examination procedure.

(9) In order to simplify further, common procedural rules should apply to the committees, including the key provisions relating to their functioning and the possibility of delivering an opinion by written procedure.

(10) Criteria should be laid down to determine the procedure to be used for the adoption of implementing acts by the Commission. In order to achieve greater consistency, the procedural requirements should be proportionate to the nature and impact of the implementing acts to be adopted.

(11) The examination procedure should in particular apply for the adoption of acts of general scope designed to implement basic acts and specific implementing acts with a potentially important impact. That procedure should ensure that implementing acts cannot be adopted by the Commission if they are not in accordance with the opinion of the committee, except in very exceptional

[1] Position of the European Parliament of 16 December 2010 (not yet published in the Official Journal) and decision of the Council of 14 February 2011.

[2] OJ L 184, 17.7.1999, p. 23.

circumstances, where they may apply for a limited period of time. The procedure should also ensure that the Commission is able to review the draft implementing acts where no opinion is delivered by the committee, taking into account the views expressed within the committee.

(12) Provided that the basic act confers implementing powers on the Commission relating to programmes with substantial budgetary implications or directed to third countries, the examination procedure should apply.

(13) The chair of a committee should endeavour to find solutions which command the widest possible support within the committee or the appeal committee and should explain the manner in which the discussions and suggestions for amendments have been taken into account. For that purpose, the Commission should pay particular attention to the views expressed within the committee or the appeal committee as regards draft definitive anti-dumping or countervailing measures.

(14) When considering the adoption of other draft implementing acts concerning particularly sensitive sectors, notably taxation, consumer health, food safety and protection of the environment, the Commission, in order to find a balanced solution, will, as far as possible, act in such a way as to avoid going against any predominant position which might emerge within the appeal committee against the appropriateness of an implementing act.

(15) The advisory procedure should, as a general rule, apply in all other cases or where it is considered more appropriate.

(16) It should be possible, where this is provided for in a basic act, to adopt implementing acts which are to apply immediately on imperative grounds of urgency.

(17) The European Parliament and the Council should be promptly informed of committee proceedings on a regular basis.

(18) Either the European Parliament or the Council should be able at any time to indicate to the Commission that, in its view, a draft implementing act exceeds the implementing powers provided for in the basic act, taking into account their rights relating to the review of the legality of Union acts.

(19) Public access to information on committee proceedings should be ensured in accordance with Regulation (EC) No 1049/2001 of the European Parliament and of the Council of 30 May 2001 regarding public access to European Parliament, Council and Commission documents[3].

(20) A register containing information on committee proceedings should be kept by the Commission. Consequently, rules relating to the protection of classified documents applicable to the Commission should also apply to the use of the register.

(21) Decision 1999/468/EC should be repealed. In order to ensure the transition between the regime provided for in Decision 1999/468/EC and this Regulation, any reference in existing legislation to the procedures provided for in that Decision should, with the exception of the regulatory procedure with scrutiny provided for in Article 5a thereof, be understood as a reference to the corresponding procedures provided for in this Regulation. The effects of Article 5a of Decision 1999/468/EC should be provisionally maintained for the purposes of existing basic acts which refer to that Article.

(22) The Commission's powers, as laid down by the TFEU, concerning the implementation of the competition rules are not affected by this Regulation,

HAVE ADOPTED THIS REGULATION:

Article 1 Subject-matter

This Regulation lays down the rules and general principles governing the mechanisms which apply where a legally binding Union act (hereinafter a "basic act") identifies the need for uniform conditions of implementation and requires that the adoption of implementing acts by the Commission be subject to the control of Member States.

Article 2 Selection of procedures

1. A basic act may provide for the application of the advisory procedure or the examination procedure, taking into account the nature or the impact of the implementing act required.
2. The examination procedure applies, in particular, for the adoption of:
   (a) implementing acts of general scope;

[3] OJ L 145, 31.5.2001, p. 43.

(b) other implementing acts relating to:
  (i) programmes with substantial implications;
  (ii) the common agricultural and common fisheries policies;
  (iii) the environment, security and safety, or protection of the health or safety, of humans, animals or plants;
  (iv) the common commercial policy;
  (v) taxation.

3. The advisory procedure applies, as a general rule, for the adoption of implementing acts not falling within the ambit of paragraph 2. However, the advisory procedure may apply for the adoption of the implementing acts referred to in paragraph 2 in duly justified cases.

Article 3 Common provisions

1. The common provisions set out in this Article shall apply to all the procedures referred to in Articles 4 to 8.

2. The Commission shall be assisted by a committee composed of representatives of the Member States. The committee shall be chaired by a representative of the Commission. The chair shall not take part in the committee vote.

3. The chair shall submit to the committee the draft implementing act to be adopted by the Commission.

Except in duly justified cases, the chair shall convene a meeting not less than 14 days from submission of the draft implementing act and of the draft agenda to the committee. The committee shall deliver its opinion on the draft implementing act within a time limit which the chair may lay down according to the urgency of the matter. Time limits shall be proportionate and shall afford committee members early and effective opportunities to examine the draft implementing act and express their views.

4. Until the committee delivers an opinion, any committee member may suggest amendments and the chair may present amended versions of the draft implementing act.

The chair shall endeavour to find solutions which command the widest possible support within the committee. The chair shall inform the committee of the manner in which the discussions and suggestions for amendments have been taken into account, in particular as regards those suggestions which have been largely supported within the committee.

5. In duly justified cases, the chair may obtain the committee's opinion by written procedure. The chair shall send the committee members the draft implementing act and shall lay down a time limit for delivery of an opinion according to the urgency of the matter. Any committee member who does not oppose the draft implementing act or who does not explicitly abstain from voting thereon before the expiry of that time limit shall be regarded as having tacitly agreed to the draft implementing act.

Unless otherwise provided in the basic act, the written procedure shall be terminated without result where, within the time limit referred to in the first subparagraph, the chair so decides or a committee member so requests. In such a case, the chair shall convene a committee meeting within a reasonable time.

6. The committee's opinion shall be recorded in the minutes. Committee members shall have the right to ask for their position to be recorded in the minutes. The chair shall send the minutes to the committee members without delay.

7. Where applicable, the control mechanism shall include referral to an appeal committee.

The appeal committee shall adopt its own rules of procedure by a simple majority of its component members, on a proposal from the Commission.

Where the appeal committee is seised, it shall meet at the earliest 14 days, except in duly justified cases, and at the latest 6 weeks, after the date of referral. Without prejudice to paragraph 3, the appeal committee shall deliver its opinion within 2 months of the date of referral.

A representative of the Commission shall chair the appeal committee.

The chair shall set the date of the appeal committee meeting in close cooperation with the members of the committee, in order to enable Member States and the Commission to ensure an appropriate level of representation. By 1 April 2011, the Commission shall convene the first meeting of the appeal committee in order to adopt its rules of procedure.

Article 4 Advisory procedure

1. Where the advisory procedure applies, the committee shall deliver its opinion, if necessary by taking a vote. If the committee takes a vote, the opinion shall be delivered by a simple majority of its component members.

2. The Commission shall decide on the draft implementing act to be adopted, taking the utmost account of the conclusions drawn from the discussions within the committee and of the opinion delivered.

Article 5 Examination procedure

1. Where the examination procedure applies, the committee shall deliver its opinion by the majority laid down in Article 16(4) and (5) of the Treaty on European Union and, where applicable, Article 238(3) TFEU, for acts to be adopted on a proposal from the Commission. The votes of the representatives of the Member States within the committee shall be weighted in the manner set out in those Articles.

2. Where the committee delivers a positive opinion, the Commission shall adopt the draft implementing act.

3. Without prejudice to Article 7, if the committee delivers a negative opinion, the Commission shall not adopt the draft implementing act. Where an implementing act is deemed to be necessary, the chair may either submit an amended version of the draft implementing act to the same committee within 2 months of delivery of the negative opinion, or submit the draft implementing act within 1 month of such delivery to the appeal committee for further deliberation.

4. Where no opinion is delivered, the Commission may adopt the draft implementing act, except in the cases provided for in the second subparagraph. Where the Commission does not adopt the draft implementing act, the chair may submit to the committee an amended version thereof.

Without prejudice to Article 7, the Commission shall not adopt the draft implementing act where:

(a) that act concerns taxation, financial services, the protection of the health or safety of humans, animals or plants, or definitive multilateral safeguard measures;

(b) the basic act provides that the draft implementing act may not be adopted where no opinion is delivered; or

(c) a simple majority of the component members of the committee opposes it.

In any of the cases referred to in the second subparagraph, where an implementing act is deemed to be necessary, the chair may either submit an amended version of that act to the same committee within 2 months of the vote, or submit the draft implementing act within 1 month of the vote to the appeal committee for further deliberation.

5. By way of derogation from paragraph 4, the following procedure shall apply for the adoption of draft definitive anti-dumping or countervailing measures, where no opinion is delivered by the committee and a simple majority of its component members opposes the draft implementing act.

The Commission shall conduct consultations with the Member States. 14 days at the earliest and 1 month at the latest after the committee meeting, the Commission shall inform the committee members of the results of those consultations and submit a draft implementing act to the appeal committee. By way of derogation from Article 3(7), the appeal committee shall meet 14 days at the earliest and 1 month at the latest after the submission of the draft implementing act. The appeal committee shall deliver its opinion in accordance with Article 6. The time limits laid down in this paragraph shall be without prejudice to the need to respect the deadlines laid down in the relevant basic acts.

Article 6 Referral to the appeal committee

1. The appeal committee shall deliver its opinion by the majority provided for in Article 5(1).

2. Until an opinion is delivered, any member of the appeal committee may suggest amendments to the draft implementing act and the chair may decide whether or not to modify it.

The chair shall endeavour to find solutions which command the widest possible support within the appeal committee.

The chair shall inform the appeal committee of the manner in which the discussions and suggestions for amendments have been taken into account, in particular as regards suggestions for amendments which have been largely supported within the appeal committee.

3. Where the appeal committee delivers a positive opinion, the Commission shall adopt the draft implementing act.

Where no opinion is delivered, the Commission may adopt the draft implementing act.

Where the appeal committee delivers a negative opinion, the Commission shall not adopt the draft implementing act.

4. By way of derogation from paragraph 3, for the adoption of definitive multilateral safeguard measures, in the absence of a positive opinion voted by the majority provided for in Article 5(1), the Commission shall not adopt the draft measures.

5. By way of derogation from paragraph 1, until 1 September 2012, the appeal committee shall deliver its opinion on draft definitive anti-dumping or countervailing measures by a simple majority of its component members.

Article 7 Adoption of implementing acts in exceptional cases

By way of derogation from Article 5(3) and the second subparagraph of Article 5(4), the Commission may adopt a draft implementing act where it needs to be adopted without delay in order to avoid creating a significant disruption of the markets in the area of agriculture or a risk for the financial interests of the Union within the meaning of Article 325 TFEU.

In such a case, the Commission shall immediately submit the adopted implementing act to the appeal committee. Where the appeal committee delivers a negative opinion on the adopted implementing act, the Commission shall repeal that act immediately. Where the appeal committee delivers a positive opinion or no opinion is delivered, the implementing act shall remain in force.

Article 8 Immediately applicable implementing acts

1. By way of derogation from Articles 4 and 5, a basic act may provide that, on duly justified imperative grounds of urgency, this Article is to apply.

2. The Commission shall adopt an implementing act which shall apply immediately, without its prior submission to a committee, and shall remain in force for a period not exceeding 6 months unless the basic act provides otherwise.

3. At the latest 14 days after its adoption, the chair shall submit the act referred to in paragraph 2 to the relevant committee in order to obtain its opinion.

4. Where the examination procedure applies, in the event of the committee delivering a negative opinion, the Commission shall immediately repeal the implementing act adopted in accordance with paragraph 2.

5. Where the Commission adopts provisional anti-dumping or countervailing measures, the procedure provided for in this Article shall apply. The Commission shall adopt such measures after consulting or, in cases of extreme urgency, after informing the Member States. In the latter case, consultations shall take place 10 days at the latest after notification to the Member States of the measures adopted by the Commission.

Article 9 Rules of procedure

1. Each committee shall adopt by a simple majority of its component members its own rules of procedure on the proposal of its chair, on the basis of standard rules to be drawn up by the Commission following consultation with Member States. Such standard rules shall be published by the Commission in the *Official Journal of the European Union*.

In so far as may be necessary, existing committees shall adapt their rules of procedure to the standard rules.

2. The principles and conditions on public access to documents and the rules on data protection applicable to the Commission shall apply to the committees.

Article 10 Information on committee proceedings

1. The Commission shall keep a register of committee proceedings which shall contain:

(a) a list of committees;

(b) the agendas of committee meetings;
(c) the summary records, together with the lists of the authorities and organisations to which the persons designated by the Member States to represent them belong;
(d) the draft implementing acts on which the committees are asked to deliver an opinion;
(e) the voting results;
(f) the final draft implementing acts following delivery of the opinion of the committees;
(g) information concerning the adoption of the final draft implementing acts by the Commission; and
(h) statistical data on the work of the committees.

2. The Commission shall also publish an annual report on the work of the committees.

3. The European Parliament and the Council shall have access to the information referred to in paragraph 1 in accordance with the applicable rules.

4. At the same time as they are sent to the committee members, the Commission shall make available to the European Parliament and the Council the documents referred to in points (b), (d) and (f) of paragraph 1 whilst also informing them of the availability of such documents.

5. The references of all documents referred to in points (a) to (g) of paragraph 1 as well as the information referred to in paragraph 1(h) shall be made public in the register.

Article 11 Right of scrutiny for the European Parliament and the Council

Where a basic act is adopted under the ordinary legislative procedure, either the European Parliament or the Council may at any time indicate to the Commission that, in its view, a draft implementing act exceeds the implementing powers provided for in the basic act. In such a case, the Commission shall review the draft implementing act, taking account of the positions expressed, and shall inform the European Parliament and the Council whether it intends to maintain, amend or withdraw the draft implementing act.

Article 12 Repeal of Decision 1999/468/EC

Decision 1999/468/EC is hereby repealed.

The effects of Article 5a of Decision 1999/468/EC shall be maintained for the purposes of existing basic acts making reference thereto.

Article 13 Transitional provisions: adaptation of existing basic acts

1. Where basic acts adopted before the entry into force of this Regulation provide for the exercise of implementing powers by the Commission in accordance with Decision 1999/468/EC, the following rules shall apply:

(a) where the basic act makes reference to Article 3 of Decision 1999/468/EC, the advisory procedure referred to in Article 4 of this Regulation shall apply;
(b) where the basic act makes reference to Article 4 of Decision 1999/468/EC, the examination procedure referred to in Article 5 of this Regulation shall apply, with the exception of the second and third subparagraphs of Article 5(4);
(c) where the basic act makes reference to Article 5 of Decision 1999/468/EC, the examination procedure referred to in Article 5 of this Regulation shall apply and the basic act shall be deemed to provide that, in the absence of an opinion, the Commission may not adopt the draft implementing act, as envisaged in point (b) of the second subparagraph of Article 5(4);
(d) where the basic act makes reference to Article 6 of Decision 1999/468/EC, Article 8 of this Regulation shall apply;
(e) where the basic act makes reference to Articles 7 and 8 of Decision 1999/468/EC, Articles 10 and 11 of this Regulation shall apply.

2. Articles 3 and 9 of this Regulation shall apply to all existing committees for the purposes of paragraph 1.

3. Article 7 of this Regulation shall apply only to existing procedures which make reference to Article 4 of Decision 1999/468/EC.

4. The transitional provisions laid down in this Article shall not prejudge the nature of the acts concerned.

Article 14 Transitional arrangement

This Regulation shall not affect pending procedures in which a committee has already delivered its opinion in accordance with Decision 1999/468/EC.

Article 15 Review

By 1 March 2016, the Commission shall present a report to the European Parliament and the Council on the implementation of this Regulation, accompanied, if necessary, by appropriate legislative proposals.

Article 16 Entry into force

This Regulation shall enter into force on 1 March 2011.

This Regulation is binding in its entirety and directly applicable in all Member States.

Done at Strasbourg, 16 February 2011.
For the European Parliament
The President
J. BUZEK
For the Council
The President
MARTONYI J.

Council Regulation (EU) No 216/2013 of 7 March 2013 on the electronic publication of the Official Journal of the European Union

[OJ 2013 L69/1]

THE COUNCIL OF THE EUROPEAN UNION,

Having regard to the Treaty on the Functioning of the European Union, and in particular Article 352 thereof,

Having regard to the proposal from the European Commission,

After transmission of the draft legislative act to the national parliaments,

Having regard to the consent of the European Parliament,

Acting in accordance with a special legislative procedure,

Whereas:

(1) Article 297 of the Treaty on the Functioning of the European Union (TFEU) deals with the publication in the *Official Journal of the European Union* (hereinafter "the Official Journal") and the entry into force of legal acts of the Union.

(2) Regulation (EC) No 1/1958[1], including any subsequent amendments thereto, determines the official languages of the institutions of the European Union.

(3) The printed edition of the Official Journal, available in all official languages of the institutions of the Union, is at present the only legally binding publication, although it is also made available online.

(4) Decision 2009/496/EC, Euratom of the European Parliament, the Council, the Commission, the Court of Justice, the Court of Auditors, the European Economic and Social Committee and the Committee of the Regions of 26 June 2009 on the organisation and operation of the Publications Office of the European Union[2] ensures that the Publications Office enables the institutions to fulfil their obligation to publish legislative texts.

(5) The Court of Justice of the European Union has held, in Case C-161/06 Skoma-Lux sro v Celní ředitelství Olomouc[3], that legal acts of the Union are not enforceable against individuals if they

[1] Regulation No 1 determining the languages to be used by the European Economic Community (OJ 017, 6.10.1958, p. 385/58).
[2] OJ L 168, 30.6.2009, p. 41.
[3] ECR 2007, p. I-10841.

have not been properly published in the Official Journal and that making such acts available online does not equate to valid publication in the Official Journal in the absence of any rules in that regard in Union law.

(6) If publication in the Official Journal in electronic form were to constitute valid publication, access to Union law would be faster and more economical. Citizens should, nevertheless, continue to have the possibility to obtain a printed version of the Official Journal from the Publications Office.

(7) The Commission Communication entitled "A Digital Agenda for Europe" highlights that access to online legal content favours the development of a digital internal market, which leads to economic and social benefits.

(8) Rules ensuring the authenticity, integrity and inalterability of the electronic publication of the Official Journal should therefore be laid down.

(9) This Regulation should also lay down rules applicable in cases where, due to unforeseen and exceptional circumstances, it is not possible to publish and to make available the electronic edition of the Official Journal.

(10) Directive 1999/93/EC of the European Parliament and of the Council of 13 December 1999 on a Community framework for electronic signatures[4] establishes the legal effects of electronic signatures as a means for authentication. For the purposes of ensuring the authenticity, integrity and inalterability of the electronic edition of the Official Journal, an advanced electronic signature based on a qualified certificate and created by a secure-signature-creation device in accordance with that Directive provides sufficient guarantees to the public. It should be possible to verify the electronically signed Official Journal by readily available means.

(11) Access to the EUR-Lex website is to be ensured in compliance with the commitments for the protection of persons with disabilities in accordance with Council Decision 2010/48/EC of 26 November 2009 concerning the conclusion, by the European Community, of the United Nations Convention on the Rights of Persons with Disabilities[5].

(12) In accordance with the principle of proportionality, as set out in Article 5 of the Treaty on European Union, this Regulation does not go beyond what is necessary in order to achieve the objective of enabling all European citizens to rely on the electronic publication of the Official Journal, as its scope is limited to making such publication authentic, in the same way as the printed publication is today.

(13) The TFEU does not provide, for the adoption of this Regulation, powers other than those under Article 352,

HAS ADOPTED THIS REGULATION:

Article 1

1. The Official Journal shall be published in electronic form, in accordance with this Regulation, in the official languages of the institutions of the European Union.

2. Without prejudice to Article 3, only the Official Journal published in electronic form (hereinafter "the electronic edition of the Official Journal") shall be authentic and shall produce legal effects.

Article 2

1. The electronic edition of the Official Journal shall bear an advanced electronic signature based on a qualified certificate and created with a secure-signature-creation device, in accordance with Directive 1999/93/EC. The qualified certificate and renewals thereof shall be published on the EUR-Lex website in order to make it possible for the public to verify the advanced electronic signature and the authentic character of the electronic edition of the Official Journal.

2. The electronic edition of the Official Journal shall display information regarding its publication date.

3. The electronic edition of the Official Journal shall be made available to the public on the EUR-Lex website in a non-obsolete format and for an unlimited period. Its consultation shall be free of charge.

[4] OJ L 13, 19.1.2000, p. 12.
[5] OJ L 23, 27.1.2010, p. 35.

Article 3

1. Where it is not possible to publish the electronic edition of the Official Journal due to an unforeseen and exceptional disruption of the information system of the Publications Office, the information system shall be restored as soon as possible.

The moment at which such a disruption occurs shall be established by the Publications Office.

2. Where it is necessary to publish the Official Journal when the information system of the Publications Office is not operational pursuant to a disruption as referred to in paragraph 1, only the printed edition of the Official Journal shall be authentic and shall produce legal effects.

Once the information system of the Publications Office is restored, the corresponding electronic version of the printed edition referred to in the first subparagraph shall be made available to the public on the EUR-Lex website for information purposes only and shall contain a notice to that effect.

3. Once the information system of the Publications Office is restored, the EUR-Lex website shall provide information on all printed editions that are authentic and that produce legal effects in accordance with the first subparagraph of paragraph 2.

Article 4

1. With regard to the electronic edition of the Official Journal, the Publications Office shall be responsible for:

(a) publishing it and guaranteeing its authenticity;

(b) implementing, managing and maintaining the information system producing the electronic edition of the Official Journal, and upgrading that system in line with future technical developments;

(c) implementing and extending the technical facilities to ensure accessibility for all users to the electronic edition of the Official Journal;

(d) setting up internal security and access rules with regard to the information system producing the electronic edition of the Official Journal;

(e) preserving and archiving the electronic files and handling them in line with future technological developments.

2. The Publications Office shall exercise the responsibilities set out in paragraph 1 in accordance with Decision 2009/496/EC, Euratom.

Article 5

This Regulation shall enter into force on the first day of the fourth calendar month following its adoption.

This Regulation shall be binding in its entirety and directly applicable in all Member States.

Done at Brussels, 7 March 2013.
For the Council
The President
A. Shatter

Recommendations to national courts and tribunals in relation to the initiation of preliminary ruling proceedings (2012)

[OJ 2012 C338/01]*

I General provisions

The Court's jurisdiction in preliminary rulings

1. The reference for a preliminary ruling is a fundamental mechanism of European Union law aimed at enabling the courts and tribunals of the Member States to ensure uniform interpretation and application of that law within the European Union.

2. Under Article 19(3)(b) of the Treaty on European Union ("TEU") and Article 267 of the Treaty on the Functioning of the European Union ("TFEU"), the Court of Justice of the European Union has jurisdiction to give preliminary rulings on the interpretation of Union law and on the validity of acts adopted by the institutions, bodies, offices or agencies of the Union.

3. Article 256(3) TFEU provides that the General Court is to have jurisdiction to hear and determine questions referred for a preliminary ruling under Article 267 TFEU, in specific areas laid down by the Statute. However, since no provisions have been introduced into the Statute in that regard, the Court of Justice alone currently has jurisdiction to give preliminary rulings.

4. While Article 267 TFEU confers on the Court of Justice a general jurisdiction in that regard, a number of primary law provisions exist which lay down exceptions to or temporary restrictions on that jurisdiction. This is true, in particular, of Articles 275 TFEU and 276 TFEU and Article 10 of Protocol (No 36) on Transitional Provisions of the Treaty of Lisbon (OJEU 2010 C 83, p. 1)[1].

5. Since the preliminary ruling procedure is based on cooperation between the Court of Justice and the courts and tribunals of the Member States, it may be helpful, in order to ensure that that procedure is fully effective, to provide those courts and tribunals with the following recommendations.

6. While in no way binding, these recommendations are intended to supplement Title III of the Rules of Procedure of the Court of Justice (Articles 93 to 118) and to provide guidance to the courts and tribunals of the Member States as to whether it is appropriate to make a reference for a preliminary ruling, as well as practical information concerning the form and effect of such a reference.

The role of the Court of Justice in the preliminary ruling procedure

7. As stated above, under the preliminary ruling procedure the Court's role is to give an interpretation of European Union law or to rule on its validity, not to apply that law to the factual situation underlying the main proceedings. That is the task of the national court or tribunal and it is not, therefore, for the Court either to decide issues of fact raised in the main proceedings or to resolve any differences of opinion on the interpretation or application of rules of national law.

8. When ruling on the interpretation or validity of European Union law, the Court makes every effort to give a reply which will be of assistance in resolving the dispute in the main proceedings, but

* **Editor's Note:** The following statement precedes the Court of Justice Recommendations note: These recommendations follow on from the adoption on 25 September 2012 in Luxembourg of the new Rules of Procedure of the Court of Justice (OJ L 265, 29.9.2012, p. 1). They replace the information note on references from national courts for a preliminary ruling (OJ C 160, 28.5.2011, p. 1) and reflect innovations introduced by those Rules which may affect both the principle of a reference for a preliminary ruling to the Court of Justice and the procedure for making such a reference.

[1] Article 10(1) to (3) of Protocol No 36 provides that the powers of the Court of Justice in relation to acts of the Union adopted in the field of police cooperation and judicial cooperation in criminal matters before the entry into force of the Treaty of Lisbon, and which have not since been amended, are to remain the same for a maximum period of five years from the date of entry into force of the Treaty of Lisbon (1 December 2009). During that period, such acts may, therefore, form the subject-matter of a reference for a preliminary ruling only where the order for reference is made by a court or tribunal of a Member State which has accepted the jurisdiction of the Court of Justice, it being a matter for each of those States to determine whether the right to refer a question to the Court is to be available to all of its national courts and tribunals or is to be reserved to the courts or tribunals of last instance.

it is for the referring court or tribunal to draw specific conclusions from that reply, if necessary by disapplying the rule of national law in question.

The decision to make a reference for a preliminary ruling

The originator of the request for a preliminary ruling

9. Under Article 267 TFEU, any court or tribunal of a Member State, in so far as it is called upon to give a ruling in proceedings intended to arrive at a decision of a judicial nature, may as a rule submit a request for a preliminary ruling to the Court of Justice. Status as a court or tribunal is interpreted by the Court of Justice as a self-standing concept of European Union law, the Court taking account of a number of factors such as whether the body making the reference is established by law, whether it is permanent, whether its jurisdiction is compulsory, whether its procedure is *inter partes*, whether it applies rules of law and whether it is independent.

10. Whether or not the parties to the main proceedings have expressed the wish that it do so, it is for the national court or tribunal alone to decide whether to refer a question to the Court of Justice for a preliminary ruling.

References on interpretation

11. Article 267 TFEU provides that any court or tribunal may submit a request for a preliminary ruling to the Court of Justice on the interpretation of a rule of European Union law if it considers it necessary to do so in order to resolve the dispute brought before it.

12. However, courts or tribunals against whose decisions there is no judicial remedy under national law must bring such a request before the Court, unless the Court has already ruled on the point (and there is no new context that raises any serious doubt as to whether that case-law may be applied in that instance), or unless the correct interpretation of the rule of law in question is obvious.

13. Thus, a national court or tribunal may, in particular when it considers that sufficient guidance is given by the case-law of the Court of Justice, itself decide on the correct interpretation of European Union law and its application to the factual situation before it. However, a reference for a preliminary ruling may prove particularly useful when there is a new question of interpretation of general interest for the uniform application of European Union law, or where the existing case-law does not appear to be applicable to a new set of facts.

14. In order to enable the Court of Justice properly to identify the subject-matter of the main proceedings and the questions that arise, it is helpful if, in respect of each question referred, the national court or tribunal explains why the interpretation sought is necessary to enable it to give judgment.

References on determination of validity

15. Although the courts and tribunals of the Member States may reject pleas raised before them challenging the validity of acts of an institution, body, office or agency of the Union, the Court of Justice has exclusive jurisdiction to declare such an act invalid.

16. All national courts or tribunals must therefore submit a request for a preliminary ruling to the Court when they have doubts about the validity of such an act, stating the reasons for which they consider that the act may be invalid.

17. However, if a national court or tribunal has serious doubts about the validity of an act of an institution, body, office or agency of the Union on which a national measure is based, it may exceptionally suspend application of that measure temporarily or grant other interim relief with respect to it. It must then refer the question of validity to the Court of Justice, stating the reasons for which it considers the act to be invalid.

The appropriate stage at which to make a reference for a preliminary ruling

18. A national court or tribunal may submit a request for a preliminary ruling to the Court as soon as it finds that a ruling on the interpretation or validity of European Union law is necessary to enable it to give judgment. It is that court or tribunal which is in fact in the best position to decide at what stage of the proceedings such a request should be made.

19. It is, however, desirable that a decision to make a reference for a preliminary ruling should be taken when the national proceedings have reached a stage at which the referring court or tribunal

is able to define the legal and factual context of the case, so that the Court of Justice has available to it all the information necessary to check, where appropriate, that European Union law applies to the main proceedings. In the interests of the proper administration of justice, it may also be desirable for the reference to be made only after both sides have been heard.

The form and content of the request for a preliminary ruling

20. The decision by which a court or tribunal of a Member State refers one or more questions to the Court of Justice for a preliminary ruling may be in any form allowed by national law as regards procedural steps. However, it must be borne in mind that it is that document which will serve as the basis of the proceedings before the Court and that it must therefore contain such information as will enable the Court to give a reply which is of assistance to the referring court or tribunal. Moreover, it is only the request for a preliminary ruling which is notified to the parties to the main proceedings and to the other interested persons referred to in Article 23 of the Statute, including the Member States, in order to obtain any written observations.

21. Owing to the need to translate it into all the official languages of the European Union, the request for a preliminary ruling should therefore be drafted simply, clearly and precisely, avoiding superfluous detail.

22. About 10 pages is often sufficient to set out in a proper manner the context of a request for a preliminary ruling. That request must be succinct but sufficiently complete and must contain all the relevant information to give the Court and the interested persons entitled to submit observations a clear understanding of the factual and legal context of the main proceedings. In accordance with Article 94 of the Rules of Procedure, the request for a preliminary ruling must contain, in addition to the text of the questions referred to the Court for a preliminary ruling:

- a summary of the subject-matter of the dispute and the relevant findings of fact as determined by the referring court or tribunal, or, at least, an account of the facts on which the questions referred are based;
- the tenor of any national provisions applicable in the case and, where appropriate, the relevant national case-law[2];
- a statement of the reasons which prompted the referring court or tribunal to inquire about the interpretation or validity of certain provisions of European Union law, and the relationship between those provisions and the national legislation applicable to the main proceedings.

23. The European Union law provisions relevant to the case should be identified as accurately as possible in the request for a preliminary ruling, which should include, if need be, a brief summary of the relevant arguments of the parties to the main proceedings.

24. If it considers itself able to do so, the referring court or tribunal may, finally, briefly state its view on the answer to be given to the questions referred for a preliminary ruling. That information may be useful to the Court, particularly where it is called upon to give a preliminary ruling in an expedited or urgent procedure.

25. In order to make the request for a preliminary ruling easier to read, it is essential that the Court receive it in typewritten form. To enable the Court to refer to the request it is also very helpful if the pages and paragraphs of the order for reference—which must be dated and signed—are numbered.

26. The questions themselves should appear in a separate and clearly identified section of the order for reference, preferably at the beginning or the end. It must be possible to understand them on their own terms, without referring to the statement of the grounds for the request, which will however provide the necessary background for a proper understanding of the implications of the case.

27. Under the preliminary ruling procedure, the Court will, as a rule, use the information contained in the order for reference, including nominative or personal data. It is therefore for the referring court or tribunal itself, if it considers it necessary, to delete certain details in its request for a preliminary ruling or to render anonymous one or more persons or entities concerned by the dispute in the main proceedings.

[2] The referring court or tribunal is requested to provide precise references for those texts and their publication, such as a page of an official journal or a specific law report, or a reference to an internet site.

28. After the request for a preliminary ruling has been lodged, the Court may also render such persons or entities anonymous of its own motion, or at the request of the referring court or tribunal or of a party to the main proceedings. In order to maintain its effectiveness, such a request for anonymity must, however, be made at the earliest possible stage of the proceedings, and in any event prior to publication in the *Official Journal of the European Union* of the notice relating to the case concerned, and to service of the request for a preliminary ruling on the interested persons referred to in Article 23 of the Statute.

The effects of the reference for a preliminary ruling on the national proceedings

29. Although the national court or tribunal may still order protective measures, particularly in connection with a reference on determination of validity (see point 17 above), the lodging of a request for a preliminary ruling nevertheless calls for the national proceedings to be stayed until the Court of Justice has given its ruling.

30. In the interests of the proper conduct of the preliminary ruling proceedings before the Court and in order to maintain their effectiveness, it is incumbent on the referring court or tribunal to inform the Court of Justice of any procedural step that may affect the referral and, in particular, if any new parties are admitted to the national proceedings.

Costs and legal aid

31. Preliminary ruling proceedings before the Court of Justice are free of charge and the Court does not rule on the costs of the parties to the proceedings pending before the referring court or tribunal; it is for the referring court or tribunal to rule on those costs.

32. If a party to the main proceedings has insufficient means and where it is possible under national rules, the referring court or tribunal may grant that party legal aid to cover the costs, including those of lawyers' fees, which it incurs before the Court. The Court itself may also grant legal aid where the party in question is not already in receipt of aid under national rules or to the extent to which that aid does not cover, or covers only partly, costs incurred before the Court.

Communication between the Court of Justice and the national courts and tribunals

33. The request for a preliminary ruling and the relevant documents (including, where applicable, the case file or a copy of it) are to be sent by the national court or tribunal making the reference directly to the Court of Justice. They must be sent by registered post to the Registry of the Court of Justice (Rue du Fort Niedergrünewald, L-2925 Luxembourg).

34. Until the decision containing the Court's ruling on the referring court's or tribunal's request for a preliminary ruling is served on that court or tribunal, the Court Registry will stay in contact with the referring court or tribunal, and will send it copies of the procedural documents.

35. The Court of Justice will send its ruling to the referring court or tribunal. It would welcome information from that court or tribunal on the action taken upon its ruling in the main proceedings, and communication of the referring court's or tribunal's final decision.

II Special provisions in relation to urgent references for a preliminary ruling

36. As provided in Article 23a of the Statute and Articles 105 to 114 of the Rules of Procedure, a reference for a preliminary ruling may, in certain circumstances, be determined pursuant to an expedited procedure or an urgent procedure.

Conditions for the application of the expedited and urgent procedures

37. The Court of Justice decides whether these procedures are to be applied. Such a decision is generally taken only on a reasoned request from the referring court or tribunal. Exceptionally, the Court may, however, decide of its own motion to determine a reference for a preliminary ruling under an expedited procedure or an urgent procedure where that appears to be required by the nature or the particular circumstances of the case.

38. Article 105 of the Rules of Procedure provides that a reference for a preliminary ruling may be determined pursuant to an expedited procedure derogating from the provisions of those Rules, where the nature of the case requires that it be dealt with within a short time. Since that procedure imposes significant constraints on all those involved in it, and, in particular, on all the Member States called upon to lodge their observations, whether written or oral, within much shorter time-limits than would ordinarily apply, its application should be sought only in particular circumstances that warrant the Court giving its ruling quickly on the questions referred. The large number of persons or legal situations potentially affected by the decision that the referring court or tribunal has to deliver after bringing a matter before the Court for a preliminary ruling does not, in itself, constitute an exceptional circumstance that would justify the use of the expedited procedure[3].

39. The same applies a fortiori to the urgent preliminary ruling procedure, provided for in Article 107 of the Rules of Procedure. That procedure, which applies only in the areas covered by Title V of Part Three of the TFEU, relating to the area of freedom, security and justice, imposes even greater constraints on those concerned, since it limits in particular the number of parties authorised to lodge written observations and, in cases of extreme urgency, allows the written part of the procedure before the Court to be omitted altogether. The application of the urgent procedure should therefore be requested only where it is absolutely necessary for the Court to give its ruling very quickly on the questions submitted by the referring court or tribunal.

40. Although it is not possible to provide an exhaustive list of such circumstances, particularly because of the varied and evolving nature of the rules of European Union law governing the area of freedom, security and justice, a national court or tribunal might, for example, consider submitting a request for the urgent preliminary ruling procedure to be applied in the case, referred to in the fourth paragraph of Article 267 TFEU, of a person in custody or deprived of his liberty, where the answer to the question raised is decisive as to the assessment of that person's legal situation, or in proceedings concerning parental authority or custody of children, where the identity of the court having jurisdiction under European Union law depends on the answer to the question referred for a preliminary ruling.

The request for application of the expedited procedure or the urgent procedure

41. To enable the Court to decide quickly whether the expedited procedure or the urgent preliminary ruling procedure should be applied, the request must set out precisely the matters of fact and law which establish the urgency and, in particular, the risks involved in following the ordinary procedure.

42. In so far as it is able to do so, the referring court should briefly state its view on the answer to be given to the questions referred. Such a statement makes it easier for the parties to the main proceedings and the other interested persons participating in the procedure to define their positions and facilitates the Court's decision, thereby contributing to the rapidity of the procedure.

43. The request for the application of the expedited procedure or the urgent procedure must be submitted in an unambiguous form that enables the Court Registry to establish immediately that the file has to be dealt with in a particular way. Accordingly, the referring court or tribunal is asked to specify which of the two procedures is required in that particular case, and to mention in its request the relevant article of the Rules of Procedure (Article 105 for the expedited procedure or Article 107 for the urgent procedure). That mention must be included in a clearly identifiable place in its order for reference (for example, at the head of the page or in a separate judicial document). Where appropriate, a covering letter from the referring court or tribunal can usefully refer to that request.

44. As regards the order for reference itself, it is particularly important that it should be succinct where the matter is urgent, as this will help to ensure the rapidity of the procedure.

[3] For an insight into circumstances that have resulted in the approval or refusal of requests for the application of the accelerated procedure, made on the basis of Article 104a of the Rules of Procedure of the Court of Justice of 19 June 1991, as amended, see the orders made by the President of the Court of Justice, available at www.curia.europa.eu (the orders can be found under "Case-law", by selecting each of the following in turn in the search form: Documents—Documents not published in the ECR—Orders—Expedited procedure).

Communication between the Court of Justice, the referring court or tribunal and the parties to the main proceedings

45. In order to expedite and facilitate communication with the referring court or tribunal and the parties before it, a court or tribunal submitting a request for the expedited procedure or the urgent procedure to be applied is asked to state the e-mail address and any fax number which may be used by the Court of Justice, together with the e-mail addresses and any fax numbers of the representatives of the parties to the proceedings.

46. A copy of the signed order for reference together with a request for the expedited procedure or the urgent procedure to be applied can initially be sent to the Court by e-mail (ECJ-Registry@curia.europa.eu) or by fax (+352 43 37 66). Processing of the reference and of the request can then begin upon receipt of the e-mailed or faxed copy. The originals of those documents must, however, be sent to the Court Registry as soon as possible.

Rules of Procedure of the Court of Justice

THE COURT OF JUSTICE*

Having regard to the Treaty on European Union, and in particular Article 19 thereof,

Having regard to the Treaty on the Functioning of the European Union, and in particular the sixth paragraph of Article 253 thereof,

Having regard to the Treaty establishing the European Atomic Energy Community, and in particular Article 106a(1) thereof,

Having regard to the Protocol on the Statute of the Court of Justice of the European Union, and in particular Article 63 and the second paragraph of Article 64 thereof,

Whereas:

(1) Despite having been amended on several occasions over the years, the Rules of Procedure of the Court of Justice have remained fundamentally unchanged in structure since their original adoption on 4 March 1953. The Rules of Procedure of 19 June 1991, which are currently in force, still reflect the initial preponderance of direct actions, whereas in fact the majority of such actions now fall within the jurisdiction of the General Court, and references for a preliminary ruling from the courts and tribunals of the Member States represent, quantitatively, the primary category of cases brought before the Court. That fact should be taken into account and the structure and content of the Rules of Procedure of the Court adapted, in consequence, to changes in its caseload.

(2) While references for a preliminary ruling should be given their proper place in the Rules of Procedure, it is also appropriate to draw a clearer distinction between the rules that apply to all types of action and those that are specific to each type, to be contained in separate titles. In the interests of clarification, procedural provisions common to all cases brought before the Court should, therefore, all be contained in an initial title.

(3) In the light of experience gained in the course of implementing the various procedures, it is also necessary to supplement or to clarify, for the benefit of litigants as well as of national courts and tribunals, the rules that apply to each procedure. The rules in question concern, in particular, the concepts of party to the main proceedings, intervener and party to the proceedings before the General Court, or, in preliminary rulings, the rules governing the bringing of matters before the Court and the content of the order for reference. With regard to appeals against decisions of the General Court, a clearer distinction must also be drawn between appeals and cross-appeals in consequence of the service of an appeal on the cross-appellant.

(4) Conversely, the excessive complexity of certain procedures, such as the review procedure, has come to light on their implementation. Accordingly, they should be simplified by providing, inter alia, for a Chamber of five Judges to be designated for a period of one year to be responsible for ruling both on the First Advocate General's proposal to review and on the questions to be reviewed.

* **Editor's Note:** Of 25 September 2012 (OJ 2012 L265/1) which replace entirely the previously much amended rules of procedure from 1991.

(5) Similarly, the procedural arrangements for dealing with requests for Opinions should be eased by aligning them with those that apply to other cases and by providing, in consequence, for a single Advocate General to be involved in dealing with the request for an Opinion. In the interests of making the Rules easier to understand, all the particular procedures currently to be found in a number of separate titles and chapters of the Rules of Procedure should also be brought together in a single title.

(6) In order to maintain the Court's capacity, in the face of an ever-increasing caseload, to dispose within a reasonable period of time of the cases brought before it, it is also necessary to continue the efforts made to reduce the duration of proceedings before the Court, in particular by extending the opportunities for the Court to rule by reasoned order, simplifying the rules relating to the intervention of the States and institutions referred to in the first and third paragraphs of Article 40 of the Statute and providing for the Court to be able to rule without a hearing if it considers that it has sufficient information on the basis of all the written observations lodged in a case.

(7) In the interests of making the Rules applied by the Court easier to understand, lastly, certain rules which are outdated or not applied should be deleted, every paragraph of the present Rules numbered, each article given a specific heading summarising its content and the terminology harmonised.

With the Council's approval given on 24 September 2012.

HAS ADOPTED THESE RULES OF PROCEDURE:

Introductory provisions

Article 1 Definitions

1. In these Rules:
   (a) provisions of the Treaty on European Union are referred to by the number of the article concerned followed by "TEU",
   (b) provisions of the Treaty on the Functioning of the European Union are referred to by the number of the article concerned followed by "TFEU",
   (c) provisions of the Treaty establishing the European Atomic Energy Community are referred to by the number of the article concerned followed by "TEAEC",
   (d) "Statute" means the Protocol on the Statute of the Court of Justice of the European Union,
   (e) "EEA Agreement" means the Agreement on the European Economic Area,[1]
   (f) "Council Regulation No 1" means Council Regulation No 1 of 15 April 1958 determining the languages to be used by the European Economic Community.[2]
2. For the purposes of these Rules:
   (a) "institutions" means the institutions of the European Union referred to in Article 13(1) TEU and bodies, offices and agencies established by the Treaties, or by an act adopted in implementation thereof, which may be parties before the Court,
   (b) "EFTA Surveillance Authority" means the surveillance authority referred to in the EEA Agreement,
   (c) "interested persons referred to in Article 23 of the Statute" means all the parties, States, institutions, bodies, offices and agencies authorised, pursuant to that Article, to submit statements of case or observations in the context of a reference for a preliminary ruling.

Article 2 Purport of these Rules

These Rules implement and supplement, so far as necessary, the relevant provisions of the EU, FEU and EAEC Treaties, and the Statute.

[1] OJ L 1, 3.1.1994, p. 27.
[2] OJ, English Special Edition 1952–1958 (I), p. 59.

Title I Organisation of the Court

Chapter 1 Judges and Advocates General

Article 3 Commencement of the term of office of Judges and Advocates General

The term of office of a Judge or Advocate General shall begin on the date fixed for that purpose in the instrument of appointment. In the absence of any provisions in that instrument regarding the date of commencement of the term of office, that term shall begin on the date of publication of the instrument in the *Official Journal of the European Union*.

Article 4 Taking of the oath

Before taking up his duties, a Judge or Advocate General shall, at the first public sitting of the Court which he attends after his appointment, take the following oath provided for in Article 2 of the Statute:

"I swear that I will perform my duties impartially and conscientiously; I swear that I will preserve the secrecy of the deliberations of the Court."

Article 5 Solemn undertaking

Immediately after taking the oath, a Judge or Advocate General shall sign a declaration by which he gives the solemn undertaking provided for in the third paragraph of Article 4 of the Statute.

Article 6 Depriving a Judge or Advocate General of his office

1. Where the Court is called upon, pursuant to Article 6 of the Statute, to decide whether a Judge or Advocate General no longer fulfils the requisite conditions or no longer meets the obligations arising from his office, the President shall invite the Judge or Advocate General concerned to make representations.
2. The Court shall give a decision in the absence of the Registrar.

Article 7 Order of seniority

1. The seniority of Judges and Advocates General shall be calculated without distinction according to the date on which they took up their duties.
2. Where there is equal seniority on that basis, the order of seniority shall be determined by age.
3. Judges and Advocates General whose terms of office are renewed shall retain their former seniority.

Chapter 2 Presidency of the Court, constitution of the Chambers and designation of the first Advocate General

Article 8 Election of the President and of the Vice-President of the Court

1. The Judges shall, immediately after the partial replacement provided for in the second paragraph of Article 253 TFEU, elect one of their number as President of the Court for a term of three years.
2. If the office of the President falls vacant before the normal date of expiry of the term thereof, the Court shall elect a successor for the remainder of the term.
3. The elections provided for in this Article shall be by secret ballot. The Judge obtaining the votes of more than half the Judges of the Court shall be elected. If no Judge obtains that majority, further ballots shall be held until that majority is attained.
4. The Judges shall then elect one of their number as Vice-President of the Court for a term of three years, in accordance with the procedures laid down in the preceding paragraph. Paragraph 2 shall apply if the office of the Vice-President of the Court falls vacant before the normal date of expiry of the term thereof.

5. The names of the President and Vice-President elected in accordance with this Article shall be published in the *Official Journal of the European Union*.

Article 9 Responsibilities of the President of the Court

1. The President shall represent the Court.

2. The President shall direct the judicial business of the Court. He shall preside at general meetings of the Members of the Court and at hearings before and deliberations of the full Court and the Grand Chamber.

3. The President shall ensure the proper functioning of the services of the Court.

Article 10 Responsibilities of the Vice-President of the Court

1. The Vice-President shall assist the President of the Court in the performance of his duties and shall take the President's place when the latter is prevented from acting.

2. He shall take the President's place, at his request, in performing the duties referred to in Article 9(1) and (3) of these Rules.

3. The Court shall, by decision, specify the conditions under which the Vice-President shall take the place of the President of the Court in the performance of his judicial duties. That decision shall be published in the *Official Journal of the European Union*.

Article 11 Constitution of Chambers

1. The Court shall set up Chambers of five and three Judges in accordance with Article 16 of the Statute and shall decide which Judges shall be attached to them.

2. The Court shall designate the Chambers of five Judges which, for a period of one year, shall be responsible for cases of the kind referred to in Article 107 and Articles 193 and 194.

3. In respect of cases assigned to a formation of the Court in accordance with Article 60, the word "Court" in these Rules shall mean that formation.

4. In respect of cases assigned to a Chamber of five or three Judges, the powers of the President of the Court shall be exercised by the President of the Chamber.

5. The composition of the Chambers and the designation of the Chambers responsible for cases of the kind referred to in Article 107 and Articles 193 and 194 shall be published in the *Official Journal of the European Union*.

Article 12 Election of Presidents of Chambers

1. The Judges shall, immediately after the election of the President and Vice-President of the Court, elect the Presidents of the Chambers of five Judges for a term of three years.

2. The Judges shall then elect the Presidents of the Chambers of three Judges for a term of one year.

3. The provisions of Article 8(2) and (3) shall apply.

4. The names of the Presidents of Chambers elected in accordance with this Article shall be published in the *Official Journal of the European Union*.

Article 13 Where the President and Vice-President of the Court are prevented from acting

When the President and the Vice-President of the Court are prevented from acting, the functions of President shall be exercised by one of the Presidents of the Chambers of five Judges or, failing that, by one of the Presidents of the Chambers of three Judges or, failing that, by one of the other Judges, according to the order of seniority laid down in Article 7.

Article 14 Designation of the First Advocate General

1. The Court shall, after hearing the Advocates General, designate a First Advocate General for a period of one year.

2. If the office of the First Advocate General falls vacant before the normal date of expiry of the term thereof, the Court shall designate a successor for the remainder of the term.

3. The name of the First Advocate General designated in accordance with this Article shall be published in the *Official Journal of the European Union*.

Chapter 3 Assignment of cases to Judge-Rapporteurs and Advocates General

Article 15 Designation of the Judge-Rapporteur

1. As soon as possible after the document initiating proceedings has been lodged, the President of the Court s hall designate a Judge to act as Rapporteur in the case.

2. For cases of the kind referred to in Article 107 and Articles 193 and 194, the Judge-Rapporteur shall be selected from among the Judges of the Chamber designated in accordance with Article 11(2), on a proposal from the President of that Chamber. If, pursuant to Article 109, the Chamber decides that the reference is not to be dealt with under the urgent procedure, the President of the Court may reassign the case to a Judge-Rapporteur attached to another Chamber.

3. The President of the Court shall take the necessary steps if a Judge-Rapporteur is prevented from acting.

Article 16 Designation of the Advocate General

1. The First Advocate General shall assign each case to an Advocate General.

2. The First Advocate General shall take the necessary steps if an Advocate General is prevented from acting.

Chapter 4 Assistant Rapporteurs

Article 17 Assistant Rapporteurs

1. Where the Court is of the opinion that the consideration of and preparatory inquiries in cases before it so require, it shall, pursuant to Article 13 of the Statute, propose the appointment of Assistant Rapporteurs.

2. Assistant Rapporteurs shall in particular:
   (a) assist the President of the Court in interim proceedings and
   (b) assist the Judge-Rapporteurs in their work.

3. In the performance of their duties the Assistant Rapporteurs shall be responsible to the President of the Court, the President of a Chamber or a Judge-Rapporteur, as the case may be.

4. Before taking up his duties, an Assistant Rapporteur shall take before the Court the oath set out in Article 4 of these Rules.

Chapter 5 Registry

Article 18 Appointment of the Registrar

1. The Court shall appoint the Registrar.

2. When the post of Registrar is vacant, an advertisement shall be published in the *Official Journal of the European Union*. Interested persons shall be invited to submit their applications within a time-limit of not less than three weeks, accompanied by full details of their nationality, university degrees, knowledge of languages, present and past occupations, and experience, if any, in judicial and international fields.

3. The vote, in which the Judges and the Advocates General shall take part, shall take place in accordance with the procedure laid down in Article 8(3) of these Rules.

4. The Registrar shall be appointed for a term of six years. He may be reappointed. The Court may decide to renew the term of office of the incumbent Registrar without availing itself of the procedure laid down in paragraph 2 of this Article.

5. The Registrar shall take the oath set out in Article 4 and sign the declaration provided for in Article 5.

6. The Registrar may be deprived of his office only if he no longer fulfils the requisite conditions or no longer meets the obligations arising from his office. The Court shall take its decision after giving the Registrar an opportunity to make representations.

7. If the office of Registrar falls vacant before the normal date of expiry of the term thereof, the Court shall appoint a new Registrar for a term of six years.

8. The name of the Registrar elected in accordance with this Article shall be published in the *Official Journal of the European Union*.

Article 19 Deputy Registrar

The Court may, in accordance with the procedure laid down in respect of the Registrar, appoint a Deputy Registrar to assist the Registrar and to take his place if he is prevented from acting.

Article 20 Responsibilities of the Registrar

1. The Registrar shall be responsible, under the authority of the President of the Court, for the acceptance, transmission and custody of all documents and for effecting service as provided for by these Rules.

2. The Registrar shall assist the Members of the Court in all their official functions.

3. The Registrar shall have custody of the seals and shall be responsible for the records. He shall be in charge of the publications of the Court and, in particular, the European Court Reports.

4. The Registrar shall direct the services of the Court under the authority of the President of the Court. He shall be responsible for the management of the staff and the administration, and for the preparation and implementation of the budget.

Article 21 Keeping of the register

1. There shall be kept in the Registry, under the responsibility of the Registrar, a register in which all procedural documents and supporting items and documents lodged shall be entered in the order in which they are submitted.

2. When a document has been registered, the Registrar shall make a note to that effect on the original and, if a party so requests, on any copy submitted for the purpose.

3. Entries in the register and the notes provided for in the preceding paragraph shall be authentic.

4. A notice shall be published in the *Official Journal of the European Union* indicating the date of registration of an application initiating proceedings, the names of the parties, the form of order sought by the applicant and a summary of the pleas in law and of the main supporting arguments or, as the case may be, the date of lodging of a request for a preliminary ruling, the identity of the referring court or tribunal and the parties to the main proceedings, and the questions referred to the Court.

Article 22 Consultation of the register and of judgments and orders

1. Anyone may consult the register at the Registry and may obtain copies or extracts on payment of a charge on a scale fixed by the Court on a proposal from the Registrar.

2. The parties to a case may, on payment of the appropriate charge, obtain certified copies of procedural documents.

3. Anyone may, on payment of the appropriate charge, also obtain certified copies of judgments and orders.

Chapter 6 The working of the Court

Article 23 Location of the sittings of the Court

The Court may choose to hold one or more specific sittings in a place other than that in which it has its seat.

Article 24 Calendar of the Court's judicial business

1. The judicial year shall begin on 7 October of each calendar year and end on 6 October of the following year.

2. The judicial vacations shall be determined by the Court.

3. In a case of urgency, the President may convene the Judges and the Advocates General during the judicial vacations.

4. The Court shall observe the official holidays of the place in which it has its seat.

5. The Court may, in proper circumstances, grant leave of absence to any Judge or Advocate General.

6. The dates of the judicial vacations and the list of official holidays shall be published annually in the *Official Journal of the European Union*.

Article 25 General meeting

Decisions concerning administrative issues or the action to be taken upon the proposals contained in the preliminary report referred to in Article 59 of these Rules shall be taken by the Court at the general meeting in which all the Judges and Advocates General shall take part and have a vote. The Registrar shall be present, unless the Court decides to the contrary.

Article 26 Drawing-up of minutes

Where the Court sits without the Registrar being present it shall, if necessary, instruct the most junior Judge for the purposes of Article 7 of these Rules to draw up minutes, which shall be signed by that Judge and by the President.

Chapter 7 Formations of the Court

Section 1 Composition of the formations of the Court

Article 27 Composition of the Grand Chamber

1. The Grand Chamber shall, for each case, be composed of the President and the Vice-President of the Court, three Presidents of Chambers of five Judges, the Judge-Rapporteur and the number of Judges necessary to reach 15. The last-mentioned Judges and the three Presidents of Chambers of five Judges shall be designated from the lists referred to in paragraphs 3 and 4 of this Article, following the order laid down therein. The starting-point on each of those lists, in every case assigned to the Grand Chamber, shall be the name of the Judge immediately following the last Judge designated from the list concerned for the preceding case assigned to that formation of the Court.

2. After the election of the President and the Vice-President of the Court, and then of the Presidents of the Chambers of five Judges, a list of the Presidents of Chambers of five Judges and a list of the other Judges shall be drawn up for the purposes of determining the composition of the Grand Chamber.

3. The list of the Presidents of Chambers of five Judges shall be drawn up according to the order laid down in Article 7 of these Rules.

4. The list of the other Judges shall be drawn up according to the order laid down in Article 7 of these Rules, alternating with the reverse order: the first Judge on that list shall be the first according to the order laid down in that Article, the second Judge shall be the last according to that order, the third Judge shall be the second according to that order, the fourth Judge the penultimate according to that order, and so on.

5. The lists referred to in paragraphs 3 and 4 shall be published in the *Official Journal of the European Union*.

6. In cases which are assigned to the Grand Chamber between the beginning of a calendar year in which there is a partial replacement of Judges and the moment when that replacement has taken place, two substitute Judges may be designated to complete the formation of the Court for so long as the attainment of the quorum referred to in the third paragraph of Article 17 of the Statute is in doubt. Those substitute Judges shall be the two Judges appearing on the list referred to in paragraph 4 immediately after the last Judge designated for the composition of the Grand Chamber in the case.

7. The substitute Judges shall replace, in the order of the list referred to in paragraph 4, such Judges as are unable to take part in the determination of the case.

Article 28 Composition of the Chambers of five and of three Judges

1. The Chambers of five Judges and of three Judges shall, for each case, be composed of the President of the Chamber, the Judge-Rapporteur and the number of Judges required to attain the number of five and three Judges respectively. Those last-mentioned Judges shall be designated from the lists referred to in paragraphs 2 and 3, following the order laid down therein. The starting-point on those lists, in every case assigned to a Chamber, shall be the name of the Judge immediately following the last Judge designated from the list for the preceding case assigned to the Chamber concerned.

2. For the composition of the Chambers of five Judges, after the election of the Presidents of those Chambers lists shall be drawn up including all the Judges attached to the Chamber concerned, with the exception of its President. The lists shall be drawn up in the same way as the list referred to in Article 27(4).

3. For the composition of the Chambers of three Judges, after the election of the Presidents of those Chambers lists shall be drawn up including all the Judges attached to the Chamber concerned, with the exception of its President. The lists shall be drawn up according to the order laid down in Article 7.

4. The lists referred to in paragraphs 2 and 3 shall be published in the *Official Journal of the European Union*.

Article 29 Composition of Chambers where cases are related or referred back

1. Where the Court considers that a number of cases must be heard and determined together by one and the same formation of the Court, the composition of that formation shall be that fixed for the case in respect of which the preliminary report was examined first.

2. Where a Chamber to which a case has been assigned requests the Court, pursuant to Article 60(3) of these Rules, to assign the case to a formation composed of a greater number of Judges, that formation shall include the members of the Chamber which has referred the case back.

Article 30 Where a President of a Chamber is prevented from acting

1. When the President of a Chamber of five Judges is prevented from acting, the functions of President of the Chamber shall be exercised by a President of a Chamber of three Judges, where necessary according to the order laid down in Article 7 of these Rules, or, if that formation of the Court does not include a President of a Chamber of three Judges, by one of the other Judges according to the order laid down in Article 7.

2. When the President of a Chamber of three Judges is prevented from acting, the functions of President of the Chamber shall be exercised by a Judge of that formation of the Court according to the order laid down in Article 7.

Article 31 Where a member of the formation of the Court is prevented from acting

1. When a member of the Grand Chamber is prevented from acting, he shall be replaced by another Judge according to the order of the list referred to in Article 27(4).

2. When a member of a Chamber of five Judges is prevented from acting, he shall be replaced by another Judge of that Chamber, according to the order of the list referred to in Article 28(2). If it is not possible to replace the Judge prevented from acting by a Judge of the same Chamber, the President of that Chamber shall so inform the President of the Court who may designate another Judge to complete the Chamber.

3. When a member of a Chamber of three Judges is prevented from acting, he shall be replaced by another Judge of that Chamber, according to the order of the list referred to in Article 28(3). If it is not possible to replace the Judge prevented from acting by a Judge of the same Chamber, the President of that Chamber shall so inform the President of the Court who may designate another Judge to complete the Chamber.

Section 2 Deliberations

Article 32 Procedures concerning deliberations

1. The deliberations of the Court shall be and shall remain secret.

2. When a hearing has taken place, only those Judges who participated in that hearing and, where relevant, the Assistant Rapporteur responsible for the consideration of the case shall take part in the deliberations.

3. Every Judge taking part in the deliberations shall state his opinion and the reasons for it.

4. The conclusions reached by the majority of the Judges after final discussion shall determine the decision of the Court.

Article 33 Number of Judges taking part in the deliberations

Where, by reason of a Judge being prevented from acting, there is an even number of Judges, the most junior Judge for the purposes of Article 7 of these Rules shall abstain from taking part in the deliberations unless he is the Judge-Rapporteur. In that case the Judge immediately senior to him shall abstain from taking part in the deliberations.

Article 34 Quorum of the Grand Chamber

1. If, for a case assigned to the Grand Chamber, it is not possible to attain the quorum referred to in the third paragraph of Article 17 of the Statute, the President of the Court shall designate one or more other Judges according to the order of the list referred to in Article 27(4) of these Rules.

2. If a hearing has taken place before that designation, the Court shall rehear oral argument from the parties and the Opinion of the Advocate General.

Article 35 Quorum of the Chambers of five and of three Judges

1. If, for a case assigned to a Chamber of five or of three Judges, it is not possible to attain the quorum referred to in the second paragraph of Article 17 of the Statute, the President of the Court shall designate one or more other Judges according to the order of the list referred to in Article 28(2) or (3), respectively, of these Rules. If it is not possible to replace the Judge prevented from acting by a Judge of the same Chamber, the President of that Chamber shall so inform the President of the Court forthwith who shall designate another Judge to complete the Chamber.

2. Article 34(2) shall apply, *mutatis mutandis*, to the Chambers of five and of three Judges.

Chapter 8 Languages

Article 36 Language of a case

The language of a case shall be Bulgarian, Czech, Danish, Dutch, English, Estonian, Finnish, French, German, Greek, Hungarian, Irish, Italian, Latvian, Lithuanian, Maltese, Polish, Portuguese, Romanian, Slovak, Slovene, Spanish or Swedish.

Article 37 Determination of the language of a case

1. In direct actions, the language of a case shall be chosen by the applicant, except that:

(a) where the defendant is a Member State, the language of the case shall be the official language of that State; where that State has more than one official language, the applicant may choose between them;

(b) at the joint request of the parties, the use of another of the languages mentioned in Article 36 for all or part of the proceedings may be authorised;

(c) at the request of one of the parties, and after the opposite party and the Advocate General have been heard, the use of another of the languages mentioned in Article 36 may be authorised as the language of the case for all or part of the proceedings by way of derogation from subparagraphs (a) and (b); such a request may not be submitted by one of the institutions of the European Union.

2. Without prejudice to the provisions of paragraph 1(b) and (c), and of Article 38(4) and (5) of these Rules,

(a) in appeals against decisions of the General Court as referred to in Articles 56 and 57 of the Statute, the language of the case shall be the language of the decision of the General Court against which the appeal is brought;
(b) where, in accordance with the second paragraph of Article 62 of the Statute, the Court decides to review a decision of the General Court, the language of the case shall be the language of the decision of the General Court which is the subject of review;
(c) in the case of challenges concerning the costs to be recovered, applications to set aside judgments by default, third-party proceedings and applications for interpretation or revision of a judgment or for the Court to remedy a failure to adjudicate, the language of the case shall be the language of the decision to which those applications or challenges relate.

3. In preliminary ruling proceedings, the language of the case shall be the language of the referring court or tribunal. At the duly substantiated request of one of the parties to the main proceedings, and after the other party to the main proceedings and the Advocate General have been heard, the use of another of the languages mentioned in Article 36 may be authorised for the oral part of the procedure. Where granted, such authorisation shall apply in respect of all the interested persons referred to in Article 23 of the Statute.

4. Requests as above may be decided on by the President; the latter may, and where he wishes to accede to a request without the agreement of all the parties must, refer the request to the Court.

Article 38 Use of the language of the case

1. The language of the case shall in particular be used in the written and oral pleadings of the parties, including the items and documents produced or annexed to them, and also in the minutes and decisions of the Court.

2. Any item or document produced or annexed that is expressed in another language must be accompanied by a translation into the language of the case.

3. However, in the case of substantial items or lengthy documents, translations may be confined to extracts. At any time the Court may, of its own motion or at the request of one of the parties, call for a complete or fuller translation.

4. Notwithstanding the foregoing provisions, a Member State shall be entitled to use its official language when taking part in preliminary ruling proceedings, when intervening in a case before the Court or when bringing a matter before the Court pursuant to Article 259 TFEU. This provision shall apply both to written documents and to oral statements. The Registrar shall arrange in each instance for translation into the language of the case.

5. The States, other than the Member States, which are parties to the EEA Agreement, and also the EFTA Surveillance Authority, may be authorised to use one of the languages mentioned in Article 36, other than the language of the case, when they take part in preliminary ruling proceedings or intervene in a case before the Court. This provision shall apply both to written documents and to oral statements. The Registrar shall arrange in each instance for translation into the language of the case.

6. Non-Member States taking part in preliminary ruling proceedings pursuant to the fourth paragraph of Article 23 of the Statute may be authorised to use one of the languages mentioned in Article 36 other than the language of the case. This provision shall apply both to written documents and to oral statements. The Registrar shall arrange in each instance for translation into the language of the case.

7. Where a witness or expert states that he is unable adequately to express himself in one of the languages referred to in Article 36, the Court may authorise him to give his evidence in another language. The Registrar shall arrange for translation into the language of the case.

8. The President and the Vice-President of the Court and also the Presidents of Chambers in conducting oral proceedings, Judges and Advocates General in putting questions and Advocates General in delivering their Opinions may use one of the languages referred to in Article 36 other than the language of the case. The Registrar shall arrange for translation into the language of the case.

Article 39 Responsibility of the Registrar concerning language arrangements
The Registrar shall, at the request of any Judge, of the Advocate General or of a party, arrange for anything said or written in the course of the proceedings before the Court to be translated into the languages chosen from those referred to in Article 36.

Article 40 Languages of the publications of the Court
Publications of the Court shall be issued in the languages referred to in Article 1 of Council Regulation No 1.

Article 41 Authentic texts
The texts of documents drawn up in the language of the case or, where applicable, in another language authorised pursuant to Articles 37 or 38 of these Rules shall be authentic.

Article 42 Language service of the Court
The Court shall set up a language service staffed by experts with adequate legal training and a thorough knowledge of several official languages of the European Union.

Title II Common procedural provisions

Chapter 1 Rights and obligations of agents, advisers and lawyers

Article 43 Privileges, immunities and facilities

1. Agents, advisers and lawyers who appear before the Court or before any judicial authority to which the Court has addressed letters rogatory shall enjoy immunity in respect of words spoken or written by them concerning the case or the parties.

2. Agents, advisers and lawyers shall also enjoy the following privileges and facilities:
   (a) any papers and documents relating to the proceedings shall be exempt from both search and seizure. In the event of a dispute, the customs officials or police may seal those papers and documents; they shall then be immediately forwarded to the Court for inspection in the presence of the Registrar and of the person concerned;
   (b) agents, advisers and lawyers shall be entitled to travel in the course of duty without hindrance.

Article 44 Status of the parties' representatives

1. In order to qualify for the privileges, immunities and facilities specified in Article 43, persons entitled to them shall furnish proof of their status as follows:
   (a) agents shall produce an official document issued by the party for whom they act, who shall immediately serve a copy thereof on the Registrar;
   (b) lawyers shall produce a certificate that they are authorised to practise before a court of a Member State or of another State which is a party to the EEA Agreement, and, where the party which they represent is a legal person governed by private law, an authority to act issued by that person;
   (c) advisers shall produce an authority to act issued by the party whom they are assisting.

2. The Registrar of the Court shall issue them with a certificate, as required. The validity of this certificate shall be limited to a specified period, which may be extended or curtailed according to the duration of the proceedings.

Article 45 Waiver of immunity

1. The privileges, immunities and facilities specified in Article 43 of these Rules are granted exclusively in the interests of the proper conduct of proceedings.

2. The Court may waive immunity where it considers that the proper conduct of proceedings will not be hindered thereby.

Article 46 Exclusion from the proceedings

1. If the Court considers that the conduct of an agent, adviser or lawyer before the Court is incompatible with the dignity of the Court or with the requirements of the proper administration of justice, or that such agent, adviser or lawyer is using his rights for purposes other than those for which they were granted, it shall inform the person concerned. If the Court informs the competent authorities to whom the person concerned is answerable, a copy of the letter sent to those authorities shall be forwarded to the person concerned.

2. On the same grounds, the Court may at any time, having heard the person concerned and the Advocate General, decide to exclude an agent, adviser or lawyer from the proceedings by reasoned order. That order shall have immediate effect.

3. Where an agent, adviser or lawyer is excluded from the proceedings, the proceedings shall be suspended for a period fixed by the President in order to allow the party concerned to appoint another agent, adviser or lawyer.

4. Decisions taken under this Article may be rescinded.

Article 47 University teachers and parties to the main proceedings

1. The provisions of this Chapter shall apply to university teachers who have a right of audience before the Court in accordance with Article 19 of the Statute.

2. They shall also apply, in the context of references for a preliminary ruling, to the parties to the main proceedings where, in accordance with the national rules of procedure applicable, those parties are permitted to bring or defend court proceedings without being represented by a lawyer, and to persons authorised under those rules to represent them.

Chapter 2 Service

Article 48 Methods of service

1. Where these Rules require that a document be served on a person, the Registrar shall ensure that service is effected at that person's address for service either by the dispatch of a copy of the document by registered post with a form for acknowledgement of receipt or by personal delivery of the copy against a receipt. The Registrar shall prepare and certify the copies of documents to be served, save where the parties themselves supply the copies in accordance with Article 57(2) of these Rules.

2. Where the addressee has agreed that service is to be effected on him by telefax or any other technical means of communication, any procedural document, including a judgment or order of the Court, may be served by the transmission of a copy of the document by such means.

3. Where, for technical reasons or on account of the nature or length of the document, such transmission is impossible or impracticable, the document shall be served, if the addressee has not specified an address for service, at his address in accordance with the procedures laid down in paragraph 1 of this Article. The addressee shall be so informed by telefax or any other technical means of communication. Service shall then be deemed to have been effected on the addressee by registered post on the 10th day following the lodging of the registered letter at the post office of the place in which the Court has its seat, unless it is shown by the acknowledgement of receipt that the letter was received on a different date or the addressee informs the Registrar, within three weeks of being informed by telefax or any other technical means of communication, that the document to be served has not reached him.

4. The Court may, by decision, determine the criteria for a procedural document to be served by electronic means. That decision shall be published in the *Official Journal of the European Union*.

Chapter 3 Time-limits

Article 49 Calculation of time-limits

1. Any procedural time-limit prescribed by the Treaties, the Statute or these Rules shall be calculated as follows:

(a) where a time-limit expressed in days, weeks, months or years is to be calculated from the moment at which an event occurs or an action takes place, the day during which that event occurs or that action takes place shall not be counted as falling within the time-limit in question;

(b) a time-limit expressed in weeks, months or years shall end with the expiry of whichever day in the last week, month or year is the same day of the week, or falls on the same date, as the day during which the event or action from which the time-limit is to be calculated occurred or took place. If, in a time-limit expressed in months or years, the day on which it should expire does not occur in the last month, the time-limit shall end with the expiry of the last day of that month;

(c) where a time-limit is expressed in months and days, it shall first be calculated in whole months, then in days;

(d) time-limits shall include Saturdays, Sundays and the official holidays referred to in Article 24(6) of these Rules;

(e) time-limits shall not be suspended during the judicial vacations.

2. If the time-limit would otherwise end on a Saturday, Sunday or an official holiday, it shall be extended until the end of the first subsequent working day.

Article 50 Proceedings against a measure adopted by an institution

Where the time-limit allowed for initiating proceedings against a measure adopted by an institution runs from the publication of that measure, that time-limit shall be calculated, for the purposes of Article 49(1)(a), from the end of the 14th day after publication of the measure in the *Official Journal of the European Union*.

Article 51 Extension on account of distance

The procedural time-limits shall be extended on account of distance by a single period of 10 days.

Article 52 Setting and extension of time-limits

1. Any time-limit prescribed by the Court pursuant to these Rules may be extended.

2. The President and the Presidents of Chambers may delegate to the Registrar power of signature for the purposes of setting certain time-limits which, pursuant to these Rules, it falls to them to prescribe, or of extending such time-limits.

Chapter 4 Different procedures for dealing with cases

Article 53 Procedures for dealing with cases

1. Without prejudice to the special provisions laid down in the Statute or in these Rules, the procedure before the Court shall consist of a written part and an oral part.

2. Where it is clear that the Court has no jurisdiction to hear and determine a case or where a request or an application is manifestly inadmissible, the Court may, after hearing the Advocate General, at any time decide to give a decision by reasoned order without taking further steps in the proceedings.

3. The President may in special circumstances decide that a case be given priority over others.

4. A case may be dealt with under an expedited procedure in accordance with the conditions provided by these Rules.

5. A reference for a preliminary ruling may be dealt with under an urgent procedure in accordance with the conditions provided by these Rules.

Article 54 Joinder

1. Two or more cases of the same type concerning the same subject-matter may at any time be joined, on account of the connection between them, for the purposes of the written or oral part of the procedure or of the judgment which closes the proceedings.

2. A decision on whether cases should be joined shall be taken by the President after hearing the Judge-Rapporteur and the Advocate General, if the cases concerned have already been assigned, and,

save in the case of references for a preliminary ruling, after also hearing the parties. The President may refer the decision on this matter to the Court.

3. Joined cases may be disjoined, in accordance with the provisions of paragraph 2.

Article 55 Stay of proceedings

1. The proceedings may be stayed:
   (a) in the circumstances specified in the third paragraph of Article 54 of the Statute, by order of the Court, made after hearing the Advocate General;
   (b) in all other cases, by decision of the President adopted after hearing the Judge-Rapporteur and the Advocate General and, save in the case of references for a preliminary ruling, the parties.

2. The proceedings may be resumed by order or decision, following the same procedure.

3. The orders or decisions referred to in paragraphs 1 and 2 shall be served on the parties or interested persons referred to in Article 23 of the Statute.

4. The stay of proceedings shall take effect on the date indicated in the order or decision of stay or, in the absence of such indication, on the date of that order or decision.

5. While proceedings are stayed time shall cease to run for the parties or interested persons referred to in Article 23 of the Statute for the purposes of procedural time-limits.

6. Where the order or decision of stay does not fix the length of stay, it shall end on the date indicated in the order or decision of resumption or, in the absence of such indication, on the date of the order or decision of resumption.

7. From the date of resumption of proceedings following a stay, the suspended procedural time-limits shall be replaced by new time-limits and time shall begin to run from the date of that resumption.

Article 56 Deferment of the determination of a case

After hearing the Judge-Rapporteur, the Advocate General and the parties, the President may in special circumstances, either of his own motion or at the request of one of the parties, defer a case to be dealt with at a later date.

Chapter 5 Written part of the procedure

Article 57 Lodging of procedural documents

1. The original of every procedural document must bear the handwritten signature of the party's agent or lawyer or, in the case of observations submitted in the context of preliminary ruling proceedings, that of the party to the main proceedings or his representative, if the national rules of procedure applicable to those main proceedings so permit.

2. The original, accompanied by all annexes referred to therein, shall be submitted together with five copies for the Court and, in the case of proceedings other than preliminary ruling proceedings, a copy for every other party to the proceedings. Copies shall be certified by the party lodging them.

3. The institutions shall in addition produce, within time-limits laid down by the Court, translations of any procedural document into the other languages provided for by Article 1 of Council Regulation No 1. The preceding paragraph of this Article shall apply.

4. To every procedural document there shall be annexed a file containing the items and documents relied on in support of it, together with a schedule listing them.

5. Where in view of the length of an item or document only extracts from it are annexed to the procedural document, the whole item or document or a full copy of it shall be lodged at the Registry.

6. All procedural documents shall bear a date. In the calculation of procedural time-limits, only the date and time of lodgment of the original at the Registry shall be taken into account.

7. Without prejudice to the provisions of paragraphs 1 to 6, the date on and time at which a copy of the signed original of a procedural document, including the schedule of items and documents referred to in paragraph 4, is received at the Registry by telefax or any other technical means of communication available to the Court shall be deemed to be the date and time of lodgment for the purposes of

compliance with the procedural time-limits, provided that the signed original of the procedural document, accompanied by the annexes and copies referred to in paragraph 2, is lodged at the Registry no later than 10 days thereafter.

8. Without prejudice to paragraphs 3 to 6, the Court may, by decision, determine the criteria for a procedural document sent to the Registry by electronic means to be deemed to be the original of that document. That decision shall be published in the *Official Journal of the European Union*.

Article 58 Length of procedural documents

Without prejudice to any special provisions laid down in these Rules, the Court may, by decision, set the maximum length of written pleadings or observations lodged before it. That decision shall be published in the *Official Journal of the European Union*.

Chapter 6 The preliminary report and assignment of cases to formations of the Court

Article 59 Preliminary report

1. When the written part of the procedure is closed, the President shall fix a date on which the Judge-Rapporteur is to present a preliminary report to the general meeting of the Court.

2. The preliminary report shall contain proposals as to whether particular measures of organisation of procedure, measures of inquiry or, if appropriate, requests to the referring court or tribunal for clarification should be undertaken, and as to the formation to which the case should be assigned. It shall also contain the Judge-Rapporteur's proposals, if any, as to whether to dispense with a hearing and as to whether to dispense with an Opinion of the Advocate General pursuant to the fifth paragraph of Article 20 of the Statute.

3. The Court shall decide, after hearing the Advocate General, what action to take on the proposals of the Judge-Rapporteur.

Article 60 Assignment of cases to formations of the Court

1. The Court shall assign to the Chambers of five and of three Judges any case brought before it in so far as the difficulty or importance of the case or particular circumstances are not such as to require that it should be assigned to the Grand Chamber, unless a Member State or an institution of the European Union participating in the proceedings has requested that the case be assigned to the Grand Chamber, pursuant to the third paragraph of Article 16 of the Statute.

2. The Court shall sit as a full Court where cases are brought before it pursuant to the provisions referred to in the fourth paragraph of Article 16 of the Statute. It may assign a case to the full Court where, in accordance with the fifth paragraph of Article 16 of the Statute, it considers that the case is of exceptional importance.

3. The formation to which a case has been assigned may, at any stage of the proceedings, request the Court to assign the case to a formation composed of a greater number of Judges.

4. Where the oral part of the procedure is opened without an inquiry, the President of the formation determining the case shall fix the opening date.

Chapter 7 Measures of organisation of procedure and measures of inquiry

Section 1 Measures of organisation of procedure

Article 61 Measures of organisation prescribed by the Court

1. In addition to the measures which may be prescribed in accordance with Article 24 of the Statute, the Court may invite the parties or the interested persons referred to in Article 23 of the Statute to answer certain questions in writing, within the time-limit laid down by the Court, or at the hearing. The written replies shall be communicated to the other parties or the interested persons referred to in Article 23 of the Statute.

2. Where a hearing is organised, the Court shall, in so far as possible, invite the participants in that hearing to concentrate in their oral pleadings on one or more specified issues.

Article 62 Measures of organisation prescribed by the Judge-Rapporteur or the Advocate General

1. The Judge-Rapporteur or the Advocate General may request the parties or the interested persons referred to in Article 23 of the Statute to submit within a specified time-limit all such information relating to the facts, and all such documents or other particulars, as they may consider relevant. The replies and documents provided shall be communicated to the other parties or the interested persons referred to in Article 23 of the Statute.

2. The Judge-Rapporteur or the Advocate General may also send to the parties or the interested persons referred to in Article 23 of the Statute questions to be answered at the hearing.

Section 2 Measures of inquiry

Article 63 Decision on measures of inquiry

1. The Court shall decide in its general meeting whether a measure of inquiry is necessary.

2. Where the case has already been assigned to a formation of the Court, the decision shall be taken by that formation.

Article 64 Determination of measures of inquiry

1. The Court, after hearing the Advocate General, shall prescribe the measures of inquiry that it considers appropriate by means of an order setting out the facts to be proved.

2. Without prejudice to Articles 24 and 25 of the Statute, the following measures of inquiry may be adopted:

(a) the personal appearance of the parties;
(b) a request for information and production of documents;
(c) oral testimony;
(d) the commissioning of an expert's report;
(e) an inspection of the place or thing in question.

3. Evidence may be submitted in rebuttal and previous evidence may be amplified.

Article 65 Participation in measures of inquiry

1. Where the formation of the Court does not undertake the inquiry itself, it shall entrust the task of so doing to the Judge-Rapporteur.

2. The Advocate General shall take part in the measures of inquiry.

3. The parties shall be entitled to attend the measures of inquiry.

Article 66 Oral testimony

1. The Court may, either of its own motion or at the request of one of the parties, and after hearing the Advocate General, order that certain facts be proved by witnesses.

2. A request by a party for the examination of a witness shall state precisely about what facts and for what reasons the witness should be examined.

3. The Court shall rule by reasoned order on the request referred to in the preceding paragraph. If the request is granted, the order shall set out the facts to be established and state which witnesses are to be heard in respect of each of those facts.

4. Witnesses shall be summoned by the Court, where appropriate after lodgment of the security provided for in Article 73(1) of these Rules.

Article 67 Examination of witnesses

1. After the identity of the witness has been established, the President shall inform him that he will be required to vouch the truth of his evidence in the manner laid down in these Rules.

2. The witness shall give his evidence to the Court, the parties having been given notice to attend. After the witness has given his evidence the President may, at the request of one of the parties or of his own motion, put questions to him.

3. The other Judges and the Advocate General may do likewise.

4. Subject to the control of the President, questions may be put to witnesses by the representatives of the parties.

Article 68 Witnesses' oath

1. After giving his evidence, the witness shall take the following oath:

"I swear that I have spoken the truth, the whole truth and nothing but the truth."

2. The Court may, after hearing the parties, exempt a witness from taking the oath.

Article 69 Pecuniary penalties

1. Witnesses who have been duly summoned shall obey the summons and attend for examination.

2. If, without good reason, a witness who has been duly summoned fails to appear before the Court, the Court may impose upon him a pecuniary penalty not exceeding EUR 5000 and may order that a further summons be served on the witness at his own expense.

3. The same penalty may be imposed upon a witness who, without good reason, refuses to give evidence or to take the oath.

Article 70 Expert's report

1. The Court may order that an expert's report be obtained. The order appointing the expert shall define his task and set a time-limit within which he is to submit his report.

2. After the expert has submitted his report and that report has been served on the parties, the Court may order that the expert be examined, the parties having been given notice to attend. At the request of one of the parties or of his own motion, the President may put questions to the expert.

3. The other Judges and the Advocate General may do likewise.

4. Subject to the control of the President, questions may be put to the expert by the representatives of the parties.

Article 71 Expert's oath

1. After making his report, the expert shall take the following oath:

"I swear that I have conscientiously and impartially carried out my task."

2. The Court may, after hearing the parties, exempt the expert from taking the oath.

Article 72 Objection to a witness or expert

1. If one of the parties objects to a witness or an expert on the ground that he is not a competent or proper person to act as a witness or expert or for any other reason, or if a witness or expert refuses to give evidence or to take the oath, the matter shall be resolved by the Court.

2. An objection to a witness or an expert shall be raised within two weeks after service of the order summoning the witness or appointing the expert; the statement of objection must set out the grounds of objection and indicate the nature of any evidence offered.

Article 73 Witnesses' and experts' costs

1. Where the Court orders the examination of witnesses or an expert's report, it may request the parties or one of them to lodge security for the witnesses' costs or the costs of the expert's report.

2. Witnesses and experts shall be entitled to reimbursement of their travel and subsistence expenses. The cashier of the Court may make an advance payment towards these expenses.

3. Witnesses shall be entitled to compensation for loss of earnings, and experts to fees for their services. The cashier of the Court shall pay witnesses and experts these sums after they have carried out their respective duties or tasks.

Article 74 Minutes of inquiry hearings

1. The Registrar shall draw up minutes of every inquiry hearing. The minutes shall be signed by the President and by the Registrar. They shall constitute an official record.

2. In the case of the examination of witnesses or experts, the minutes shall be signed by the President or by the Judge-Rapporteur responsible for conducting the examination of the witness or

expert, and by the Registrar. Before the minutes are thus signed, the witness or expert must be given an opportunity to check the content of the minutes and to sign them.

3. The minutes shall be served on the parties.

Article 75 Opening of the oral part of the procedure after the inquiry

1. Unless the Court decides to prescribe a time-limit within which the parties may submit written observations, the President shall fix the date for the opening of the oral part of the procedure after the measures of inquiry have been completed.

2. Where a time-limit has been prescribed for the submission of written observations, the President shall fix the date for the opening of the oral part of the procedure after that time-limit has expired.

Chapter 8 Oral part of the procedure

Article 76 Hearing

1. Any reasoned requests for a hearing shall be submitted within three weeks after service on the parties or the interested persons referred to in Article 23 of the Statute of notification of the close of the written part of the procedure. That time-limit may be extended by the President.

2. On a proposal from the Judge-Rapporteur and after hearing the Advocate General, the Court may decide not to hold a hearing if it considers, on reading the written pleadings or observations lodged during the written part of the procedure, that it has sufficient information to give a ruling.

3. The preceding paragraph shall not apply where a request for a hearing, stating reasons, has been submitted by an interested person referred to in Article 23 of the Statute who did not participate in the written part of the procedure.

Article 77 Joint hearing

If the similarities between two or more cases of the same type so permit, the Court may decide to organise a joint hearing of those cases.

Article 78 Conduct of oral proceedings

Oral proceedings shall be opened and directed by the President, who shall be responsible for the proper conduct of the hearing.

Article 79 Cases heard in camera

1. For serious reasons related, in particular, to the security of the Member States or to the protection of minors, the Court may decide to hear a case *in camera*.

2. The oral proceedings in cases heard *in camera* shall not be published.

Article 80 Questions

The members of the formation of the Court and the Advocate General may in the course of the hearing put questions to the agents, advisers or lawyers of the parties and, in the circumstances referred to in Article 47(2) of these Rules, to the parties to the main proceedings or to their representatives.

Article 81 Close of the hearing

After the parties or the interested persons referred to in Article 23 of the Statute have presented oral argument, the President shall declare the hearing closed.

Article 82 Delivery of the Opinion of the Advocate General

1. Where a hearing takes place, the Opinion of the Advocate General shall be delivered after the close of that hearing.

2. The President shall declare the oral part of the procedure closed after the Advocate General has delivered his Opinion.

Article 83 Opening or reopening of the oral part of the procedure

The Court may at any time, after hearing the Advocate General, order the opening or reopening of the oral part of the procedure, in particular if it considers that it lacks sufficient information or where a party has, after the close of that part of the procedure, submitted a new fact which is of such a nature as to be a decisive factor for the decision of the Court, or where the case must be decided on the basis of an argument which has not been debated between the parties or the interested persons referred to in Article 23 of the Statute.

Article 84 Minutes of hearings

1. The Registrar shall draw up minutes of every hearing. The minutes shall be signed by the President and by the Registrar. They shall constitute an official record.

2. The parties and interested persons referred to in Article 23 of the Statute may inspect the minutes at the Registry and obtain copies.

Article 85 Recording of the hearing

The President may, on a duly substantiated request, authorise a party or an interested person referred to in Article 23 of the Statute who has participated in the written or oral part of the proceedings to listen, on the Court's premises, to the soundtrack of the hearing in the language used by the speaker during that hearing.

Chapter 9 Judgments and orders

Article 86 Date of delivery of a judgment

The parties or interested persons referred to in Article 23 of the Statute shall be informed of the date of delivery of a judgment.

Article 87 Content of a judgment

A judgment shall contain:

(a) a statement that it is the judgment of the Court,
(b) an indication as to the formation of the Court,
(c) the date of delivery,
(d) the names of the President and of the Judges who took part in the deliberations, with an indication as to the name of the Judge-Rapporteur,
(e) the name of the Advocate General,
(f) the name of the Registrar,
(g) a description of the parties or of the interested persons referred to in Article 23 of the Statute who participated in the proceedings,
(h) the names of their representatives,
(i) in the case of direct actions and appeals, a statement of the forms of order sought by the parties,
(j) where applicable, the date of the hearing,
(k) a statement that the Advocate General has been heard and, where applicable, the date of his Opinion,
(l) a summary of the facts,
(m) the grounds for the decision,
(n) the operative part of the judgment, including, where appropriate, the decision as to costs.

Article 88 Delivery and service of the judgment

1. The judgment shall be delivered in open court.

2. The original of the judgment, signed by the President, by the Judges who took part in the deliberations and by the Registrar, shall be sealed and deposited at the Registry; certified copies of the judgment shall be served on the parties and, where applicable, the referring court or tribunal, the interested persons referred to in Article 23 of the Statute and the General Court.

Article 89 Content of an order

1. An order shall contain:

(a) a statement that it is the order of the Court,
(b) an indication as to the formation of the Court,
(c) the date of its adoption,
(d) an indication as to the legal basis of the order,
(e) the names of the President and, where applicable, the Judges who took part in the deliberations, with an indication as to the name of the Judge-Rapporteur,
(f) the name of the Advocate General,
(g) the name of the Registrar,
(h) a description of the parties or of the parties to the main proceedings,
(i) the names of their representatives,
(j) a statement that the Advocate General has been heard,
(k) the operative part of the order, including, where appropriate, the decision as to costs.

2. Where, in accordance with these Rules, an order must be reasoned, it shall in addition contain:

(a) in the case of direct actions and appeals, a statement of the forms of order sought by the parties,
(b) a summary of the facts,
(c) the grounds for the decision.

Article 90 Signature and service of the order

The original of the order, signed by the President and by the Registrar, shall be sealed and deposited at the Registry; certified copies of the order shall be served on the parties and, where applicable, the referring court or tribunal, the interested persons referred to in Article 23 of the Statute and the General Court.

Article 91 Binding nature of judgments and orders

1. A judgment shall be binding from the date of its delivery.
2. An order shall be binding from the date of its service.

Article 92 Publication in the Official Journal of the European Union

A notice containing the date and the operative part of the judgment or order of the Court which closes the proceedings shall be published in the *Official Journal of the European Union*.

Title III References for a preliminary ruling

Chapter 1 General provisions

Article 93 Scope

The procedure shall be governed by the provisions of this Title:

(a) in the cases covered by Article 23 of the Statute,
(b) as regards references for interpretation which may be provided for by agreements to which the European Union or the Member States are parties.

Article 94 Content of the request for a preliminary ruling

In addition to the text of the questions referred to the Court for a preliminary ruling, the request for a preliminary ruling shall contain:

(a) a summary of the subject-matter of the dispute and the relevant findings of fact as determined by the referring court or tribunal, or, at least, an account of the facts on which the questions are based;
(b) the tenor of any national provisions applicable in the case and, where appropriate, the relevant national case-law;
(c) a statement of the reasons which prompted the referring court or tribunal to inquire about the interpretation or validity of certain provisions of European Union law, and the

relationship between those provisions and the national legislation applicable to the main proceedings.

Article 95 Anonymity

1. Where anonymity has been granted by the referring court or tribunal, the Court shall respect that anonymity in the proceedings pending before it.

2. At the request of the referring court or tribunal, at the duly reasoned request of a party to the main proceedings or of its own motion, the Court may also, if it considers it necessary, render anonymous one or more persons or entities concerned by the case.

Article 96 Participation in preliminary ruling proceedings

1. Pursuant to Article 23 of the Statute, the following shall be authorised to submit observations to the Court:

(a) the parties to the main proceedings,
(b) the Member States,
(c) the European Commission,
(d) the institution which adopted the act the validity or interpretation of which is in dispute,
(e) the States, other than the Member States, which are parties to the EEA Agreement, and also the EFTA Surveillance Authority, where a question concerning one of the fields of application of that Agreement is referred to the Court for a preliminary ruling,
(f) non-Member States which are parties to an agreement relating to a specific subject-matter, concluded with the Council, where the agreement so provides and where a court or tribunal of a Member State refers to the Court of Justice for a preliminary ruling a question falling within the scope of that agreement.

2. Non-participation in the written part of the procedure does not preclude participation in the oral part of the procedure.

Article 97 Parties to the main proceedings

1. The parties to the main proceedings are those who are determined as such by the referring court or tribunal in accordance with national rules of procedure.

2. Where the referring court or tribunal informs the Court that a new party has been admitted to the main proceedings, when the proceedings before the Court are already pending, that party must accept the case as he finds it at the time when the Court was so informed. That party shall receive a copy of every procedural document already served on the interested persons referred to in Article 23 of the Statute.

3. As regards the representation and attendance of the parties to the main proceedings, the Court shall take account of the rules of procedure in force before the court or tribunal which made the reference. In the event of any doubt as to whether a person may under national law represent a party to the main proceedings, the Court may obtain information from the referring court or tribunal on the rules of procedure applicable.

Article 98 Translation and service of the request for a preliminary ruling

1. The requests for a preliminary ruling referred to in this Title shall be served on the Member States in the original version, accompanied by a translation into the official language of the State to which they are being addressed. Where appropriate, on account of the length of the request, such translation shall be replaced by the translation into the official language of the State to which it is addressed of a summary of that request, which will serve as a basis for the position to be adopted by that State. The summary shall include the full text of the question or questions referred for a preliminary ruling. That summary shall contain, in particular, in so far as that information appears in the request for a preliminary ruling, the subject-matter of the main proceedings, the essential arguments of the parties to those proceedings, a succinct presentation of the reasons for the reference for a preliminary ruling and the case-law and the provisions of national law and European Union law relied on.

2. In the cases covered by the third paragraph of Article 23 of the Statute, the requests for a preliminary ruling shall be served on the States, other than the Member States, which are parties to the EEA Agreement and also on the EFTA Surveillance Authority in the original version, accompanied by a translation of the request, or where appropriate of a summary, into one of the languages referred to in Article 36, to be chosen by the addressee.

3. Where a non-Member State has the right to take part in preliminary ruling proceedings pursuant to the fourth paragraph of Article 23 of the Statute, the original version of the request for a preliminary ruling shall be served on it accompanied by a translation of the request, or where appropriate of a summary, into one of the languages referred to in Article 36, to be chosen by the non-Member State concerned.

Article 99 Reply by reasoned order

Where a question referred to the Court for a preliminary ruling is identical to a question on which the Court has already ruled, where the reply to such a question may be clearly deduced from existing case-law or where the answer to the question referred for a preliminary ruling admits of no reasonable doubt, the Court may at any time, on a proposal from the Judge-Rapporteur and after hearing the Advocate General, decide to rule by reasoned order.

Article 100 Circumstances in which the Court remains seised

1. The Court shall remain seised of a request for a preliminary ruling for as long as it is not withdrawn by the court or tribunal which made that request to the Court. The withdrawal of a request may be taken into account until notice of the date of delivery of the judgment has been served on the interested persons referred to in Article 23 of the Statute.

2. However, the Court may at any time declare that the conditions of its jurisdiction are no longer fulfilled.

Article 101 Request for clarification

1. Without prejudice to the measures of organisation of procedure and measures of inquiry provided for in these Rules, the Court may, after hearing the Advocate General, request clarification from the referring court or tribunal within a time-limit prescribed by the Court.

2. The reply of the referring court or tribunal to that request shall be served on the interested persons referred to in Article 23 of the Statute.

Article 102 Costs of the preliminary ruling proceedings

It shall be for the referring court or tribunal to decide as to the costs of the preliminary ruling proceedings.

Article 103 Rectification of judgments and orders

1. Clerical mistakes, errors in calculation and obvious inaccuracies affecting judgments or orders may be rectified by the Court, of its own motion or at the request of an interested person referred to in Article 23 of the Statute made within two weeks after delivery of the judgment or service of the order.

2. The Court shall take its decision after hearing the Advocate General.

3. The original of the rectification order shall be annexed to the original of the rectified decision. A note of this order shall be made in the margin of the original of the rectified decision.

Article 104 Interpretation of preliminary rulings

1. Article 158 of these Rules relating to the interpretation of judgments and orders shall not apply to decisions given in reply to a request for a preliminary ruling.

2. It shall be for the national courts or tribunals to assess whether they consider that sufficient guidance is given by a preliminary ruling, or whether it appears to them that a further reference to the Court is required.

Chapter 2 Expedited preliminary ruling procedure

Article 105 Expedited procedure

1. At the request of the referring court or tribunal or, exceptionally, of his own motion, the President of the Court may, where the nature of the case requires that it be dealt with within a short time, after hearing the Judge-Rapporteur and the Advocate General, decide that a reference for a preliminary ruling is to be determined pursuant to an expedited procedure derogating from the provisions of these Rules.

2. In that event, the President shall immediately fix the date for the hearing, which shall be communicated to the interested persons referred to in Article 23 of the Statute when the request for a preliminary ruling is served.

3. The interested persons referred to in the preceding paragraph may lodge statements of case or written observations within a time-limit prescribed by the President, which shall not be less than 15 days. The President may request those interested persons to restrict the matters addressed in their statement of case or written observations to the essential points of law raised by the request for a preliminary ruling.

4. The statements of case or written observations, if any, shall be communicated to all the interested persons referred to in Article 23 of the Statute prior to the hearing.

5. The Court shall rule after hearing the Advocate General.

Article 106 Transmission of procedural documents

1. The procedural documents referred to in the preceding Article shall be deemed to have been lodged on the transmission to the Registry, by telefax or any other technical means of communication available to the Court, of a copy of the signed original and the items and documents relied on in support of it, together with the schedule referred to in Article 57(4). The original of the document and the annexes referred to above shall be sent to the Registry immediately.

2. Where the preceding Article requires that a document be served on or communicated to a person, such service or communication may be effected by transmission of a copy of the document by telefax or any other technical means of communication available to the Court and the addressee.

Chapter 3 Urgent preliminary ruling procedure

Article 107 Scope of the urgent preliminary ruling procedure

1. A reference for a preliminary ruling which raises one or more questions in the areas covered by Title V of Part Three of the Treaty on the Functioning of the European Union may, at the request of the referring court or tribunal or, exceptionally, of the Court's own motion, be dealt with under an urgent procedure derogating from the provisions of these Rules.

2. The referring court or tribunal shall set out the matters of fact and law which establish the urgency and justify the application of that exceptional procedure and shall, in so far as possible, indicate the answer that it proposes to the questions referred.

3. If the referring court or tribunal has not submitted a request for the urgent procedure to be applied, the President of the Court may, if the application of that procedure appears, prima facie, to be required, ask the Chamber referred to in Article 108 to consider whether it is necessary to deal with the reference under that procedure.

Article 108 Decision as to urgency

1. The decision to deal with a reference for a preliminary ruling under the urgent procedure shall be taken by the designated Chamber, acting on a proposal from the Judge-Rapporteur and after hearing the Advocate General. The composition of that Chamber shall be determined in accordance with Article 28(2) on the day on which the case is assigned to the Judge-Rapporteur if the application of the urgent procedure is requested by the referring court or tribunal, or, if the application of that procedure is considered at the request of the President of the Court, on the day on which that request is made.

2. If the case is connected with a pending case assigned to a Judge-Rapporteur who is not a member of the designated Chamber, that Chamber may propose to the President of the Court that the case be assigned to that Judge-Rapporteur. Where the case is reassigned to that Judge-Rapporteur, the Chamber of five Judges which includes him shall carry out the duties of the designated Chamber in respect of that case. Article 29(1) shall apply.

Article 109 Written part of the urgent procedure

1. A request for a preliminary ruling shall, where the referring court or tribunal has requested the application of the urgent procedure or where the President has requested the designated Chamber to consider whether it is necessary to deal with the reference under that procedure, be served forthwith by the Registrar on the parties to the main proceedings, on the Member State from which the reference is made, on the European Commission and on the institution which adopted the act the validity or interpretation of which is in dispute.

2. The decision as to whether or not to deal with the reference for a preliminary ruling under the urgent procedure shall be served immediately on the referring court or tribunal and on the parties, Member State and institutions referred to in the preceding paragraph. The decision to deal with the reference under the urgent procedure shall prescribe the time-limit within which those parties or entities may lodge statements of case or written observations. The decision may specify the matters of law to which such statements of case or written observations must relate and may specify the maximum length of those documents.

3. Where a request for a preliminary ruling refers to an administrative procedure or judicial proceedings conducted in a Member State other than that from which the reference is made, the Court may invite that first Member State to provide all relevant information in writing or at the hearing.

4. As soon as the service referred to in paragraph 1 above has been effected, the request for a preliminary ruling shall also be communicated to the interested persons referred to in Article 23 of the Statute, other than the persons served, and the decision whether or not to deal with the reference for a preliminary ruling under the urgent procedure shall be communicated to those interested persons as soon as the service referred to in paragraph 2 has been effected.

5. The interested persons referred to in Article 23 of the Statute shall be informed as soon as possible of the likely date of the hearing.

6. Where the reference is not to be dealt with under the urgent procedure, the proceedings shall continue in accordance with the provisions of Article 23 of the Statute and the applicable provisions of these Rules.

Article 110 Service and information following the close of the written part of the procedure

1. Where a reference for a preliminary ruling is to be dealt with under the urgent procedure, the request for a preliminary ruling and the statements of case or written observations which have been lodged shall be served on the interested persons referred to in Article 23 of the Statute other than the parties and entities referred to in Article 109(1). The request for a preliminary ruling shall be accompanied by a translation, where appropriate of a summary, in accordance with Article 98.

2. The statements of case or written observations which have been lodged shall also be served on the parties and other interested persons referred to in Article 109(1).

3. The date of the hearing shall be communicated to the interested persons referred to in Article 23 of the Statute at the same time as the documents referred to in the preceding paragraphs are served.

Article 111 Omission of the written part of the procedure

The designated Chamber may, in cases of extreme urgency, decide to omit the written part of the procedure referred to in Article 109(2).

Article 112 Decision on the substance

The designated Chamber shall rule after hearing the Advocate General.

Article 113 Formation of the Court

1. The designated Chamber may decide to sit in a formation of three Judges. In that event, it shall be composed of the President of the designated Chamber, the Judge-Rapporteur and the first Judge or, as the case may be, the first two Judges designated from the list referred to in Article 28(2) on the date on which the composition of the designated Chamber is determined in accordance with Article 108(1).

2. The designated Chamber may also request the Court to assign the case to a formation composed of a greater number of Judges. The urgent procedure shall continue before the new formation of the Court, where necessary after the reopening of the oral part of the procedure.

Article 114 Transmission of procedural documents

Procedural documents shall be transmitted in accordance with Article 106.

Chapter 4 Legal aid

Article 115 Application for legal aid

1. A party to the main proceedings who is wholly or in part unable to meet the costs of the proceedings before the Court may at any time apply for legal aid.

2. The application shall be accompanied by all information and supporting documents making it possible to assess the applicant's financial situation, such as a certificate issued by a competent national authority attesting to his financial situation.

3. If the applicant has already obtained legal aid before the referring court or tribunal, he shall produce the decision of that court or tribunal and specify what is covered by the sums already granted.

Article 116 Decision on the application for legal aid

1. As soon as the application for legal aid has been lodged it shall be assigned by the President to the Judge-Rapporteur responsible for the case in the context of which the application has been made.

2. The decision to grant legal aid, in full or in part, or to refuse it shall be taken, on a proposal from the Judge-Rapporteur and after hearing the Advocate General, by the Chamber of three Judges to which the Judge-Rapporteur is assigned. The formation of the Court shall, in that event, be composed of the President of that Chamber, the Judge-Rapporteur and the first Judge or, as the case may be, the first two Judges designated from the list referred to in Article 28(3) on the date on which the application for legal aid is brought before that Chamber by the Judge-Rapporteur.

3. If the Judge-Rapporteur is not a member of a Chamber of three Judges, the decision shall be taken, under the same conditions, by the Chamber of five Judges to which he is assigned. In addition to the Judge-Rapporteur, the formation of the Court shall be composed of four Judges designated from the list referred to in Article 28(2) on the date on which the application for legal aid is brought before that Chamber by the Judge-Rapporteur.

4. The formation of the Court shall give its decision by way of order. Where the application for legal aid is refused in whole or in part, the order shall state the reasons for that refusal.

Article 117 Sums to be advanced as legal aid

Where legal aid is granted, the cashier of the Court shall be responsible, where applicable within the limits set by the formation of the Court, for costs involved in the assistance and representation of the applicant before the Court. At the request of the applicant or his representative, an advance on those costs may be paid.

Article 118 Withdrawal of legal aid

The formation of the Court which gave a decision on the application for legal aid may at any time, either of its own motion or on request, withdraw that legal aid if the circumstances which led to its being granted alter during the proceedings.

Title IV Direct actions

Chapter 1 Representation of the parties

Article 119 Obligation to be represented

1. A party may be represented only by his agent or lawyer.

2. Agents and lawyers must lodge at the Registry an official document or an authority to act issued by the party whom they represent.

3. The lawyer acting for a party must also lodge at the Registry a certificate that he is authorised to practise before a court of a Member State or of another State which is a party to the EEA Agreement.

4. If those documents are not lodged, the Registrar shall prescribe a reasonable time-limit within which the party concerned is to produce them. If the applicant fails to produce the required documents within the time-limit prescribed, the Court shall, after hearing the Judge-Rapporteur and the Advocate General, decide whether the non-compliance with that procedural requirement renders the application or written pleading formally inadmissible.

Chapter 2 Written part of the procedure

Article 120 Content of the application

An application of the kind referred to in Article 21 of the Statute shall state:

(a) the name and address of the applicant;
(b) the name of the party against whom the application is made;
(c) the subject-matter of the proceedings, the pleas in law and arguments relied on and a summary of those pleas in law;
(d) the form of order sought by the applicant;
(e) where appropriate, any evidence produced or offered.

Article 121 Information relating to service

1. For the purpose of the proceedings, the application shall state an address for service. It shall indicate the name of the person who is authorised and has expressed willingness to accept service.

2. In addition to, or instead of, specifying an address for service as referred to in paragraph 1, the application may state that the lawyer or agent agrees that service is to be effected on him by telefax or any other technical means of communication.

3. If the application does not comply with the requirements referred to in paragraphs 1 or 2, all service on the party concerned for the purpose of the proceedings shall be effected, for so long as the defect has not been cured, by registered letter addressed to the agent or lawyer of that party. By way of derogation from Article 48, service shall then be deemed to be duly effected by the lodging of the registered letter at the post office of the place in which the Court has its seat.

Article 122 Annexes to the application

1. The application shall be accompanied, where appropriate, by the documents specified in the second paragraph of Article 21 of the Statute.

2. An application submitted under Article 273 TFEU shall be accompanied by a copy of the special agreement concluded between the Member States concerned.

3. If an application does not comply with the requirements set out in paragraphs 1 or 2 of this Article, the Registrar shall prescribe a reasonable time-limit within which the applicant is to produce the abovementioned documents. If the applicant fails to put the application in order, the Court shall, after hearing the Judge-Rapporteur and the Advocate General, decide whether the non-compliance with these conditions renders the application formally inadmissible.

Article 123 Service of the application

The application shall be served on the defendant. In cases where Article 119(4) or Article 122(3) applies, service shall be effected as soon as the application has been put in order or the Court has declared it admissible notwithstanding the failure to observe the requirements set out in those two Articles.

Article 124 Content of the defence

1. Within two months after service on him of the application, the defendant shall lodge a defence, stating:

(a) the name and address of the defendant;

(b) the pleas in law and arguments relied on;

(c) the form of order sought by the defendant;

(d) where appropriate, any evidence produced or offered.

2. Article 121 shall apply to the defence.

3. The time-limit laid down in paragraph 1 may exceptionally be extended by the President at the duly reasoned request of the defendant.

Article 125 Transmission of documents

Where the European Parliament, the Council or the European Commission is not a party to a case, the Court shall send to them copies of the application and of the defence, without the annexes thereto, to enable them to assess whether the inapplicability of one of their acts is being invoked under Article 277 TFEU.

Article 126 Reply and rejoinder

1. The application initiating proceedings and the defence may be supplemented by a reply from the applicant and by a rejoinder from the defendant.

2. The President shall prescribe the time-limits within which those procedural documents are to be produced. He may specify the matters to which the reply or the rejoinder should relate.

Chapter 3 Pleas in law and evidence

Article 127 New pleas in law

1. No new plea in law may be introduced in the course of proceedings unless it is based on matters of law or of fact which come to light in the course of the procedure.

2. Without prejudice to the decision to be taken on the admissibility of the plea in law, the President may, on a proposal from the Judge-Rapporteur and after hearing the Advocate General, prescribe a time-limit within which the other party may respond to that plea.

Article 128 Evidence produced or offered

1. In reply or rejoinder a party may produce or offer further evidence in support of his arguments. The party must give reasons for the delay in submitting such evidence.

2. The parties may, exceptionally, produce or offer further evidence after the close of the written part of the procedure. They must give reasons for the delay in submitting such evidence. The President may, on a proposal from the Judge-Rapporteur and after hearing the Advocate General, prescribe a time-limit within which the other party may comment on such evidence.

Chapter 4 Intervention

Article 129 Object and effects of the intervention

1. The intervention shall be limited to supporting, in whole or in part, the form of order sought by one of the parties. It shall not confer the same procedural rights as those conferred on the parties and, in particular, shall not give rise to any right to request that a hearing be held.

2. The intervention shall be ancillary to the main proceedings. It shall become devoid of purpose if the case is removed from the register of the Court as a result of a party's discontinuance or withdrawal from the proceedings or of an agreement between the parties, or where the application is declared inadmissible.

3. The intervener must accept the case as he finds it at the time of his intervention.

4. Consideration may be given to an application to intervene which is made after the expiry of the time-limit prescribed in Article 130 but before the decision to open the oral part of the procedure provided for in Article 60(4). In that event, if the President allows the intervention, the intervener may submit his observations during the hearing, if it takes place.

Article 130 Application to intervene

1. An application to intervene must be submitted within six weeks of the publication of the notice referred to in Article 21(4).

2. The application to intervene shall contain:
   (a) a description of the case;
   (b) a description of the main parties;
   (c) the name and address of the intervener;
   (d) the form of order sought, in support of which the intervener is applying for leave to intervene;
   (e) a statement of the circumstances establishing the right to intervene, where the application is submitted pursuant to the second or third paragraph of Article 40 of the Statute.

3. The intervener shall be represented in accordance with Article 19 of the Statute.

4. Articles 119, 121 and 122 of these Rules shall apply.

Article 131 Decision on applications to intervene

1. The application to intervene shall be served on the parties in order to obtain any written or oral observations they may wish to make on that application.

2. Where the application is submitted pursuant to the first or third paragraph of Article 40 of the Statute, the intervention shall be allowed by decision of the President and the intervener shall receive a copy of every procedural document served on the parties, provided that those parties have not, within 10 days after the service referred to in paragraph 1 has been effected, put forward observations on the application to intervene or identified secret or confidential items or documents which, if communicated to the intervener, the parties claim would be prejudicial to them.

3. In any other case, the President shall decide on the application to intervene by order or shall refer the application to the Court.

4. If the application to intervene is granted, the intervener shall receive a copy of every procedural document served on the parties, save, where applicable, for the secret or confidential items or documents excluded from such communication pursuant to paragraph 3.

Article 132 Submission of statements

1. The intervener may submit a statement in intervention within one month after communication of the procedural documents referred to in the preceding Article. That time-limit may be extended by the President at the duly reasoned request of the intervener.

2. The statement in intervention shall contain:
   (a) the form of order sought by the intervener in support, in whole or in part, of the form of order sought by one of the parties;
   (b) the pleas in law and arguments relied on by the intervener;
   (c) where appropriate, any evidence produced or offered.

3. After the statement in intervention has been lodged, the President shall, where necessary, prescribe a time-limit within which the parties may reply to that statement.

Chapter 5 Expedited procedure

Article 133 Decision relating to the expedited procedure

1. At the request of the applicant or the defendant, the President of the Court may, where the nature of the case requires that it be dealt with within a short time, after hearing the other party, the Judge-Rapporteur and the Advocate General, decide that a case is to be determined pursuant to an expedited procedure derogating from the provisions of these Rules.

2. The request for a case to be determined pursuant to an expedited procedure must be made by a separate document submitted at the same time as the application initiating proceedings or the defence, as the case may be, is lodged.

3. Exceptionally the President may also take such a decision of his own motion, after hearing the parties, the Judge-Rapporteur and the Advocate General.

Article 134 Written part of the procedure

1. Under the expedited procedure, the application initiating proceedings and the defence may be supplemented by a reply and a rejoinder only if the President, after hearing the Judge-Rapporteur and the Advocate General, considers this to be necessary.

2. An intervener may submit a statement in intervention only if the President, after hearing the Judge-Rapporteur and the Advocate General, considers this to be necessary.

Article 135 Oral part of the procedure

1. Once the defence has been submitted or, if the decision to determine the case pursuant to an expedited procedure is not made until after that pleading has been lodged, once that decision has been taken, the President shall fix a date for the hearing, which shall be communicated forthwith to the parties. He may postpone the date of the hearing where it is necessary to undertake measures of inquiry or where measures of organisation of procedure so require.

2. Without prejudice to Articles 127 and 128, a party may supplement his arguments and produce or offer evidence during the oral part of the procedure. The party must, however, give reasons for the delay in producing such further arguments or evidence.

Article 136 Decision on the substance

The Court shall give its ruling after hearing the Advocate General.

Chapter 6 Costs

Article 137 Decision as to costs

A decision as to costs shall be given in the judgment or order which closes the proceedings.

Article 138 General rules as to allocation of costs

1. The unsuccessful party shall be ordered to pay the costs if they have been applied for in the successful party's pleadings.

2. Where there is more than one unsuccessful party the Court shall decide how the costs are to be shared.

3. Where each party succeeds on some and fails on other heads, the parties shall bear their own costs. However, if it appears justified in the circumstances of the case, the Court may order that one party, in addition to bearing its own costs, pay a proportion of the costs of the other party.

Article 139 Unreasonable or vexatious costs

The Court may order a party, even if successful, to pay costs which the Court considers that party to have unreasonably or vexatiously caused the opposite party to incur.

Article 140 Costs of interveners

1. The Member States and institutions which have intervened in the proceedings shall bear their own costs.

2. The States, other than the Member States, which are parties to the EEA Agreement, and also the EFTA Surveillance Authority, shall similarly bear their own costs if they have intervened in the proceedings.

3. The Court may order an intervener other than those referred to in the preceding paragraphs to bear his own costs.

Article 141 Costs in the event of discontinuance or withdrawal

1. A party who discontinues or withdraws from proceedings shall be ordered to pay the costs if they have been applied for in the other party's observations on the discontinuance.

2. However, at the request of the party who discontinues or withdraws from proceedings, the costs shall be borne by the other party if this appears justified by the conduct of that party.

3. Where the parties have come to an agreement on costs, the decision as to costs shall be in accordance with that agreement.

4. If costs are not claimed, the parties shall bear their own costs.

Article 142 Costs where a case does not proceed to judgment

Where a case does not proceed to judgment the costs shall be in the discretion of the Court.

Article 143 Costs of proceedings

Proceedings before the Court shall be free of charge, except that:

(a) where a party has caused the Court to incur avoidable costs the Court may, after hearing the Advocate General, order that party to refund them;

(b) where copying or translation work is carried out at the request of a party, the cost shall, in so far as the Registrar considers it excessive, be paid for by that party on the Registry's scale of charges referred to in Article 22.

Article 144 Recoverable costs

Without prejudice to the preceding Article, the following shall be regarded as recoverable costs:

(a) sums payable to witnesses and experts under Article 73 of these Rules;

(b) expenses necessarily incurred by the parties for the purpose of the proceedings, in particular the travel and subsistence expenses and the remuneration of agents, advisers or lawyers.

Article 145 Dispute concerning the costs to be recovered

1. If there is a dispute concerning the costs to be recovered, the Chamber of three Judges to which the Judge-Rapporteur who dealt with the case is assigned shall, on application by the party concerned and after hearing the opposite party and the Advocate General, make an order. In that event, the formation of the Court shall be composed of the President of that Chamber, the Judge-Rapporteur and the first Judge or, as the case may be, the first two Judges designated from the list referred to in Article 28(3) on the date on which the dispute is brought before that Chamber by the Judge-Rapporteur.

2. If the Judge-Rapporteur is not a member of a Chamber of three Judges, the decision shall be taken, under the same conditions, by the Chamber of five Judges to which he is assigned. In addition to the Judge-Rapporteur, the formation of the Court shall be composed of four Judges designated from the list referred to in Article 28(2) on the date on which the dispute is brought before that Chamber by the Judge-Rapporteur.

3. The parties may, for the purposes of enforcement, apply for an authenticated copy of the order.

Article 146 Procedure for payment

1. Sums due from the cashier of the Court and from its debtors shall be paid in euro.

2. Where costs to be recovered have been incurred in a currency other than the euro or where the steps in respect of which payment is due were taken in a country of which the euro is not the currency, the conversion shall be effected at the European Central Bank's official rates of exchange on the day of payment.

Chapter 7 Amicable settlement, discontinuance, cases that do not proceed to judgment and preliminary issues

Article 147 Amicable settlement

1. If, before the Court has given its decision, the parties reach a settlement of their dispute and inform the Court of the abandonment of their claims, the President shall order the case to be removed from the register and shall give a decision as to costs in accordance with Article 141, having regard to any proposals made by the parties on the matter.

2. This provision shall not apply to proceedings under Articles 263 TFEU and 265 TFEU.

Article 148 Discontinuance

If the applicant informs the Court in writing or at the hearing that he wishes to discontinue the proceedings, the President shall order the case to be removed from the register and shall give a decision as to costs in accordance with Article 141.

Article 149 Cases that do not proceed to judgment

If the Court declares that the action has become devoid of purpose and that there is no longer any need to adjudicate on it, the Court may at any time of its own motion, on a proposal from the Judge-Rapporteur and after hearing the parties and the Advocate General, decide to rule by reasoned order. It shall give a decision as to costs.

Article 150 Absolute bar to proceeding with a case

On a proposal from the Judge-Rapporteur, the Court may at any time of its own motion, after hearing the parties and the Advocate General, decide to rule by reasoned order on whether there exists any absolute bar to proceeding with a case.

Article 151 Preliminary objections and issues

1. A party applying to the Court for a decision on a preliminary objection or issue not going to the substance of the case shall submit the application by a separate document.

2. The application must state the pleas of law and arguments relied on and the form of order sought by the applicant; any supporting items and documents must be annexed to it.

3. As soon as the application has been submitted, the President shall prescribe a time-limit within which the opposite party may submit in writing his pleas in law and the form of order which he seeks.

4. Unless the Court decides otherwise, the remainder of the proceedings on the application shall be oral.

5. The Court shall, after hearing the Advocate General, decide on the application as soon as possible or, where special circumstances so justify, reserve its decision until it rules on the substance of the case.

6. If the Court refuses the application or reserves its decision, the President shall prescribe new time-limits for the further steps in the proceedings.

Chapter 8 Judgments by default

Article 152 Judgments by default

1. If a defendant on whom an application initiating proceedings has been duly served fails to respond to the application in the proper form and within the time-limit prescribed, the applicant may apply to the Court for judgment by default.

2. The application for judgment by default shall be served on the defendant. The Court may decide to open the oral part of the procedure on the application.

3. Before giving judgment by default the Court shall, after hearing the Advocate General, consider whether the application initiating proceedings is admissible, whether the appropriate formalities have been complied with, and whether the applicant's claims appear well founded. The Court may adopt measures of organisation of procedure or order measures of inquiry.

4. A judgment by default shall be enforceable. The Court may, however, grant a stay of execution until the Court has given its decision on any application under Article 156 to set aside the judgment, or it may make execution subject to the provision of security of an amount and nature to be fixed in the light of the circumstances; this security shall be released if no such application is made or if the application fails.

Chapter 9 Requests and applications relating to judgments and orders

Article 153 Competent formation of the Court

1. With the exception of applications referred to in Article 159, the requests and applications referred to in this Chapter shall be assigned to the Judge-Rapporteur who was responsible for the case to which the request or application relates, and shall be assigned to the formation of the Court which gave a decision in that case.

2. If the Judge-Rapporteur is prevented from acting, the President of the Court shall assign the request or application referred to in this Chapter to a Judge who was a member of the formation of the Court which gave a decision in the case to which that request or application relates.

3. If the quorum referred to in Article 17 of the Statute can no longer be attained, the Court shall, on a proposal from the Judge-Rapporteur and after hearing the Advocate General, assign the request or application to a new formation of the Court.

Article 154 Rectification

1. Without prejudice to the provisions relating to the interpretation of judgments and orders, clerical mistakes, errors in calculation and obvious inaccuracies may be rectified by the Court, of its own motion or at the request of a party made within two weeks after delivery of the judgment or service of the order.

2. Where the request for rectification concerns the operative part or one of the grounds constituting the necessary support for the operative part, the parties, whom the Registrar shall duly inform, may submit written observations within a time-limit prescribed by the President.

3. The Court shall take its decision after hearing the Advocate General.

4. The original of the rectification order shall be annexed to the original of the rectified decision. A note of this order shall be made in the margin of the original of the rectified decision.

Article 155 Failure to adjudicate

1. If the Court has failed to adjudicate on a specific head of claim or on costs, any party wishing to rely on that may, within a month after service of the decision, apply to the Court to supplement its decision.

2. The application shall be served on the opposite party and the President shall prescribe a time-limit within which that party may submit written observations.

3. After these observations have been submitted, the Court shall, after hearing the Advocate General, decide both on the admissibility and on the substance of the application.

Article 156 Application to set aside

1. Application may be made pursuant to Article 41 of the Statute to set aside a judgment delivered by default.

2. The application to set aside the judgment must be made within one month from the date of service of the judgment and must be submitted in the form prescribed by Articles 120 to 122 of these Rules.

3. After the application has been served, the President shall prescribe a time-limit within which the other party may submit his written observations.

4. The proceedings shall be conducted in accordance with Articles 59 to 92 of these Rules.

5. The Court shall decide by way of a judgment which may not be set aside.

6. The original of this judgment shall be annexed to the original of the judgment by default. A note of the judgment on the application to set aside shall be made in the margin of the original of the judgment by default.

Article 157 Third-party proceedings

1. Articles 120 to 122 of these Rules shall apply to an application initiating third-party proceedings made pursuant to Article 42 of the Statute. In addition such an application shall:

(a) specify the judgment or order contested;
(b) state how the contested decision is prejudicial to the rights of the third party;
(c) indicate the reasons for which the third party was unable to take part in the original case.

2. The application must be made against all the parties to the original case.

3. The application must be submitted within two months of publication of the decision in the *Official Journal of the European Union*.

4. The Court may, on application by the third party, order a stay of execution of the contested decision. The provisions of Chapter 10 of this Title shall apply.

5. The contested decision shall be varied on the points on which the submissions of the third party are upheld.

6. The original of the judgment in the third-party proceedings shall be annexed to the original of the contested decision. A note of the judgment in the third-party proceedings shall be made in the margin of the original of the contested decision.

Article 158 Interpretation

1. In accordance with Article 43 of the Statute, if the meaning or scope of a judgment or order is in doubt, the Court shall construe it on application by any party or any institution of the European Union establishing an interest therein.

2. An application for interpretation must be made within two years after the date of delivery of the judgment or service of the order.

3. An application for interpretation shall be made in accordance with Articles 120 to 122 of these Rules. In addition it shall specify:

(a) the decision in question;
(b) the passages of which interpretation is sought.

4. The application must be made against all the parties to the case in which the decision of which interpretation is sought was given.

5. The Court shall give its decision after having given the parties an opportunity to submit their observations and after hearing the Advocate General.

6. The original of the interpreting decision shall be annexed to the original of the decision interpreted. A note of the interpreting decision shall be made in the margin of the original of the decision interpreted.

Article 159 Revision

1. In accordance with Article 44 of the Statute, an application for revision of a decision of the Court may be made only on discovery of a fact which is of such a nature as to be a decisive factor and which, when the judgment was delivered or the order served, was unknown to the Court and to the party claiming the revision.

2. Without prejudice to the time-limit of 10 years prescribed in the third paragraph of Article 44 of the Statute, an application for revision shall be made within three months of the date on which the facts on which the application is founded came to the applicant's knowledge.

3. Articles 120 to 122 of these Rules shall apply to an application for revision. In addition such an application shall:

(a) specify the judgment or order contested;
(b) indicate the points on which the decision is contested;
(c) set out the facts on which the application is founded;
(d) indicate the nature of the evidence to show that there are facts justifying revision, and that the time-limits laid down in paragraph 2 have been observed.

4. The application for revision must be made against all parties to the case in which the contested decision was given.

5. Without prejudice to its decision on the substance, the Court shall, after hearing the Advocate General, give in the form of an order its decision on the admissibility of the application, having regard to the written observations of the parties.

6. If the Court declares the application admissible, it shall proceed to consider the substance of the application and shall give its decision in the form of a judgment in accordance with these Rules.

7. The original of the revising judgment shall be annexed to the original of the decision revised. A note of the revising judgment shall be made in the margin of the original of the decision revised.

Chapter 10 Suspension of operation or enforcement and other interim measures

Article 160 Application for suspension or for interim measures

1. An application to suspend the operation of any measure adopted by an institution, made pursuant to Article 278 TFEU or Article 157 TEAEC, shall be admissible only if the applicant has challenged that measure in an action before the Court.

2. An application for the adoption of one of the other interim measures referred to in Article 279 TFEU shall be admissible only if it is made by a party to a case before the Court and relates to that case.

3. An application of a kind referred to in the preceding paragraphs shall state the subject-matter of the proceedings, the circumstances giving rise to urgency and the pleas of fact and law establishing a prima facie case for the interim measure applied for.

4. The application shall be made by a separate document and in accordance with the provisions of Articles 120 to 122 of these Rules.

5. The application shall be served on the opposite party, and the President shall prescribe a short time-limit within which that party may submit written or oral observations.

6. The President may order a preparatory inquiry.

7. The President may grant the application even before the observations of the opposite party have been submitted. This decision may be varied or cancelled even without any application being made by any party.

Article 161 Decision on the application

1. The President shall either decide on the application himself or refer it immediately to the Court.

2. If the President is prevented from acting, Articles 10 and 13 of these Rules shall apply.

3. Where the application is referred to it, the Court shall give a decision immediately, after hearing the Advocate General.

Article 162 Order for suspension of operation or for interim measures

1. The decision on the application shall take the form of a reasoned order, from which no appeal shall lie. The order shall be served on the parties forthwith.

2. The execution of the order may be made conditional on the lodging by the applicant of security, of an amount and nature to be fixed in the light of the circumstances.

3. Unless the order fixes the date on which the interim measure is to lapse, the measure shall lapse when the judgment which closes the proceedings is delivered.

4. The order shall have only an interim effect, and shall be without prejudice to the decision of the Court on the substance of the case.

Article 163 Change in circumstances

On application by a party, the order may at any time be varied or cancelled on account of a change in circumstances.

Article 164 New application

Rejection of an application for an interim measure shall not bar the party who made it from making a further application on the basis of new facts.

Article 165 Applications pursuant to Articles 280 TFEU and 299 TFEU and Article 164 TEAEC

1. The provisions of this Chapter shall apply to applications to suspend the enforcement of a decision of the Court or of any measure adopted by the Council, the European Commission or the European Central Bank, submitted pursuant to Articles 280 TFEU and 299 TFEU or Article 164 TEAEC.

2. The order granting the application shall fix, where appropriate, a date on which the interim measure is to lapse.

Article 166 Application pursuant to Article 81 TEAEC

1. An application of a kind referred to in the third and fourth paragraphs of Article 81 TEAEC shall contain:

(a) the names and addresses of the persons or undertakings to be inspected;

(b) an indication of what is to be inspected and of the purpose of the inspection.

2. The President shall give his decision in the form of an order. Article 162 of these Rules shall apply.

3. If the President is prevented from acting, Articles 10 and 13 of these Rules shall apply.

Title V Appeals against decisions of the General Court

Chapter 1 Form and content of the appeal, and form of order sought

Article 167 Lodging of the appeal

1. An appeal shall be brought by lodging an application at the Registry of the Court of Justice or of the General Court.

2. The Registry of the General Court shall forthwith transmit to the Registry of the Court of Justice the file in the case at first instance and, where necessary, the appeal.

Article 168 Content of the appeal

1. An appeal shall contain:

(a) the name and address of the appellant;

(b) a reference to the decision of the General Court appealed against;

(c) the names of the other parties to the relevant case before the General Court;

(d) the pleas in law and legal arguments relied on, and a summary of those pleas in law;

(e) the form of order sought by the appellant.

2. Articles 119, 121 and 122(1) of these Rules shall apply to appeals.

3. The appeal shall state the date on which the decision appealed against was served on the appellant.

4. If an appeal does not comply with paragraphs 1 to 3 of this Article, the Registrar shall prescribe a reasonable time-limit within which the appellant is to put the appeal in order. If the appellant fails to put the appeal in order within the time-limit prescribed, the Court of Justice shall, after hearing the Judge-Rapporteur and the Advocate General, decide whether the non-compliance with that formal requirement renders the appeal formally inadmissible.

Article 169 Form of order sought, pleas in law and arguments of the appeal

1. An appeal shall seek to have set aside, in whole or in part, the decision of the General Court as set out in the operative part of that decision.

2. The pleas in law and legal arguments relied on shall identify precisely those points in the grounds of the decision of the General Court which are contested.

Article 170 Form of order sought in the event that the appeal is allowed

1. An appeal shall seek, in the event that it is declared well founded, the same form of order, in whole or in part, as that sought at first instance and shall not seek a different form of order. The subject-matter of the proceedings before the General Court may not be changed in the appeal.

2. Where the appellant requests that the case be referred back to the General Court if the decision appealed against is set aside, he shall set out the reasons why the state of the proceedings does not permit a decision by the Court of Justice.

Chapter 2 Responses, replies and rejoinders

Article 171 Service of the appeal

1. The appeal shall be served on the other parties to the relevant case before the General Court.

2. In a case where Article 168(4) of these Rules applies, service shall be effected as soon as the appeal has been put in order or the Court of Justice has declared it admissible notwith-standing the failure to observe the formal requirements laid down by that Article.

Article 172 Parties authorised to lodge a response

Any party to the relevant case before the General Court having an interest in the appeal being allowed or dismissed may submit a response within two months after service on him of the appeal. The time-limit for submitting a response shall not be extended.

Article 173 Content of the response

1. A response shall contain:
   (a) the name and address of the party submitting it;
   (b) the date on which the appeal was served on him;
   (c) the pleas in law and legal arguments relied on;
   (d) the form of order sought.
2. Articles 119 and 121 of these Rules shall apply to responses.

Article 174 Form of order sought in the response

A response shall seek to have the appeal allowed or dismissed, in whole or in part.

Article 175 Reply and rejoinder

1. The appeal and the response may be supplemented by a reply and a rejoinder only where the President, on a duly reasoned application submitted by the appellant within seven days of service of the response, considers it necessary, after hearing the Judge-Rapporteur and the Advocate General, in particular to enable the appellant to present his views on a plea of inadmissibility or on new matters relied on in the response.

2. The President shall fix the date by which the reply is to be produced and, upon service of that pleading, the date by which the rejoinder is to be produced. He may limit the number of pages and the subject-matter of those pleadings.

Chapter 3 Form and content of the cross-appeal, and form of order sought

Article 176 Cross-appeal

1. The parties referred to in Article 172 of these Rules may submit a cross-appeal within the same time-limit as that prescribed for the submission of a response.

2. A cross-appeal must be introduced by a document separate from the response.

Article 177 Content of the cross-appeal

1. A cross-appeal shall contain:
   (a) the name and address of the party bringing the cross-appeal;

(b) the date on which the appeal was served on him;
(c) the pleas in law and legal arguments relied on;
(d) the form of order sought.

2. Articles 119, 121 and 122(1) and (3) of these Rules shall apply to cross-appeals.

Article 178 Form of order sought, pleas in law and arguments of the cross-appeal

1. A cross-appeal shall seek to have set aside, in whole or in part, the decision of the General Court.

2. It may also seek to have set aside an express or implied decision relating to the admissibility of the action before the General Court.

3. The pleas in law and legal arguments relied on shall identify precisely those points in the grounds of the decision of the General Court which are contested. The pleas in law and arguments must be separate from those relied on in the response.

Chapter 4 Pleadings consequent on the cross-appeal

Article 179 Response to the cross-appeal

Where a cross-appeal is brought, the applicant at first instance or any other party to the relevant case before the General Court having an interest in the cross-appeal being allowed or dismissed may submit a response, which must be limited to the pleas in law relied on in that cross-appeal, within two months after its being served on him. That time-limit shall not be extended.

Article 180 Reply and rejoinder on a cross-appeal

1. The cross-appeal and the response thereto may be supplemented by a reply and a rejoinder only where the President, on a duly reasoned application submitted by the party who brought the cross-appeal within seven days of service of the response to the cross-appeal, considers it necessary, after hearing the Judge-Rapporteur and the Advocate General, in particular to enable that party to present his views on a plea of inadmissibility or on new matters relied on in the response to the cross-appeal.

2. The President shall fix the date by which that reply is to be produced and, upon service of that pleading, the date by which the rejoinder is to be produced. He may limit the number of pages and the subject-matter of those pleadings.

Chapter 5 Appeals determined by order

Article 181 Manifestly inadmissible or manifestly unfounded appeal or cross-appeal

Where the appeal or cross-appeal is, in whole or in part, manifestly inadmissible or manifestly unfounded, the Court may at any time, acting on a proposal from the Judge-Rapporteur and after hearing the Advocate General, decide by reasoned order to dismiss that appeal or cross-appeal in whole or in part.

Article 182 Manifestly well-founded appeal or cross-appeal

Where the Court has already ruled on one or more questions of law identical to those raised by the pleas in law of the appeal or cross-appeal and considers the appeal or cross-appeal to be manifestly well founded, it may, acting on a proposal from the Judge-Rapporteur and after hearing the parties and the Advocate General, decide by reasoned order in which reference is made to the relevant case-law to declare the appeal or cross-appeal manifestly well founded.

Chapter 6 Effect on a cross-appeal of the removal of the appeal from the register

Article 183 Effect on a cross-appeal of the discontinuance or manifest inadmissibility of the appeal

A cross-appeal shall be deemed to be devoid of purpose:

(a) if the appellant discontinues his appeal;

(b) if the appeal is declared manifestly inadmissible for non-compliance with the time-limit for lodging an appeal;

(c) if the appeal is declared manifestly inadmissible on the sole ground that it is not directed against a final decision of the General Court or against a decision disposing of the substantive issues in part only or disposing of a procedural issue concerning a plea of lack of competence or inadmissibility within the meaning of the first paragraph of Article 56 of the Statute.

Chapter 7 Costs and legal aid in appeals

Article 184 Costs in appeals

1. Subject to the following provisions, Articles 137 to 146 of these Rules shall apply, *mutatis mutandis*, to the procedure before the Court of Justice on an appeal against a decision of the General Court.

2. Where the appeal is unfounded or where the appeal is well founded and the Court itself gives final judgment in the case, the Court shall make a decision as to the costs.

3. When an appeal brought by a Member State or an institution of the European Union which did not intervene in the proceedings before the General Court is well founded, the Court of Justice may order that the parties share the costs or that the successful appellant pay the costs which the appeal has caused an unsuccessful party to incur.

4. Where the appeal has not been brought by an intervener at first instance, he may not be ordered to pay costs in the appeal proceedings unless he participated in the written or oral part of the proceedings before the Court of Justice. Where an intervener at first instance takes part in the proceedings, the Court may decide that he shall bear his own costs.

Article 185 Legal aid

1. A party who is wholly or in part unable to meet the costs of the proceedings may at any time apply for legal aid.

2. The application shall be accompanied by all information and supporting documents making it possible to assess the applicant's financial situation, such as a certificate issued by a competent national authority attesting to his financial situation.

Article 186 Prior application for legal aid

1. If the application is made prior to the appeal which the applicant for legal aid intends to commence, it shall briefly state the subject of the appeal.

2. The application for legal aid need not be made through a lawyer.

3. The introduction of an application for legal aid shall, with regard to the person who made that application, suspend the time-limit prescribed for the bringing of the appeal until the date of service of the order making a decision on that application.

4. The President shall assign the application for legal aid, as soon as it is lodged, to a Judge-Rapporteur who shall put forward, promptly, a proposal as to the action to be taken on it.

Article 187 Decision on the application for legal aid

1. The decision to grant legal aid, in whole or in part, or to refuse it shall be taken, on a proposal from the Judge-Rapporteur and after hearing the Advocate General, by the Chamber of three Judges to which the Judge-Rapporteur is assigned. In that event, the formation of the Court shall be

composed of the President of that Chamber, the Judge-Rapporteur and the first Judge or, as the case may be, the first two Judges designated from the list referred to in Article 28(3) on the date on which the application for legal aid is brought before that Chamber by the Judge-Rapporteur. It shall consider, if appropriate, whether the appeal is manifestly unfounded.

2. If the Judge-Rapporteur is not a member of a Chamber of three Judges, the decision shall be taken, under the same conditions, by the Chamber of five Judges to which he is assigned. In addition to the Judge-Rapporteur, the formation of the Court shall be composed of four Judges designated from the list referred to in Article 28(2) on the date on which the application for legal aid is brought before that Chamber by the Judge-Rapporteur.

3. The formation of the Court shall give its decision by way of order. Where the application for legal aid is refused in whole or in part, the order shall state the reasons for that refusal.

Article 188 Sums to be advanced as legal aid

1. Where legal aid is granted, the cashier of the Court shall be responsible, where applicable within the limits set by the formation of the Court, for costs involved in the assistance and representation of the applicant before the Court. At the request of the applicant or his representative, an advance on those costs may be paid.

2. In its decision as to costs the Court may order the payment to the cashier of the Court of sums advanced as legal aid.

3. The Registrar shall take steps to obtain the recovery of these sums from the party ordered to pay them.

Article 189 Withdrawal of legal aid

The formation of the Court which gave a decision on the application for legal aid may at any time, either of its own motion or on request, withdraw that legal aid if the circumstances which led to its being granted alter during the proceedings.

Chapter 8 Other provisions applicable to appeals

Article 190 Other provisions applicable to appeals

1. Articles 127, 129 to 136, 147 to 150, 153 to 155 and 157 to 166 of these Rules shall apply to the procedure before the Court of Justice on an appeal against decisions of the General Court.

2. By way of derogation from Article 130(1), an application to intervene shall, however, be made within one month of the publication of the notice referred to in Article 21(4).

3. Article 95 shall apply, *mutatis mutandis*, to the procedure before the Court of Justice on an appeal against decisions of the General Court.

Title VI Review of decisions of the General Court

Article 191 Reviewing Chamber

A Chamber of five Judges shall be designated for a period of one year for the purpose of deciding, in accordance with Articles 193 and 194 of these Rules, whether a decision of the General Court is to be reviewed in accordance with Article 62 of the Statute.

Article 192 Information and communication of decisions which may be reviewed

1. As soon as the date for the delivery or signature of a decision to be given under Article 256(2) or (3) TFEU is fixed, the Registry of the General Court shall inform the Registry of the Court of Justice.

2. The decision shall be communicated to the Registry of the Court of Justice immediately upon its delivery or signature, as shall the file in the case, which shall be made available forthwith to the First Advocate General.

Article 193 Review of decisions given on appeal

1. The proposal of the First Advocate General to review a decision of the General Court given under Article 256(2) TFEU shall be forwarded to the President of the Court of Justice and to the President of the reviewing Chamber. Notice of that transmission shall be given to the Registrar at the same time.

2. As soon as he is informed of the existence of a proposal, the Registrar shall communicate the file in the case before the General Court to the members of the reviewing Chamber.

3. As soon as the proposal to review has been received, the President of the Court shall designate the Judge-Rapporteur from among the Judges of the reviewing Chamber on a proposal from the President of that Chamber. The composition of the formation of the Court shall be determined in accordance with Article 28(2) of these Rules on the day on which the case is assigned to the Judge-Rapporteur.

4. That Chamber, acting on a proposal from the Judge-Rapporteur, shall decide whether the decision of the General Court is to be reviewed. The decision to review the decision of the General Court shall indicate only the questions which are to be reviewed.

5. The General Court, the parties to the proceedings before it and the other interested persons referred to in the second paragraph of Article 62a of the Statute shall forthwith be informed by the Registrar of the decision of the Court of Justice to review the decision of the General Court.

6. Notice of the date of the decision to review the decision of the General Court and of the questions which are to be reviewed shall be published in the *Official Journal of the European Union*.

Article 194 Review of preliminary rulings

1. The proposal of the First Advocate General to review a decision of the General Court given under Article 256(3) TFEU shall be forwarded to the President of the Court of Justice and to the President of the reviewing Chamber. Notice of that transmission shall be given to the Registrar at the same time.

2. As soon as he is informed of the existence of a proposal, the Registrar shall communicate the file in the case before the General Court to the members of the reviewing Chamber.

3. The Registrar shall also inform the General Court, the referring court or tribunal, the parties to the main proceedings and the other interested persons referred to in the second paragraph of Article 62a of the Statute of the existence of a proposal to review.

4. As soon as the proposal to review has been received, the President of the Court shall designate the Judge-Rapporteur from among the Judges of the reviewing Chamber on a proposal from the President of that Chamber. The composition of the formation of the Court shall be determined in accordance with Article 28(2) of these Rules on the day on which the case is assigned to the Judge-Rapporteur.

5. That Chamber, acting on a proposal from the Judge-Rapporteur, shall decide whether the decision of the General Court is to be reviewed. The decision to review the decision of the General Court shall indicate only the questions which are to be reviewed.

6. The General Court, the referring court or tribunal, the parties to the main proceedings and the other interested persons referred to in the second paragraph of Article 62a of the Statute shall forthwith be informed by the Registrar of the decision of the Court of Justice as to whether or not the decision of the General Court is to be reviewed.

7. Notice of the date of the decision to review the decision of the General Court and of the questions which are to be reviewed shall be published in the *Official Journal of the European Union*.

Article 195 Judgment on the substance of the case after a decision to review

1. The decision to review a decision of the General Court shall be served on the parties and other interested persons referred to in the second paragraph of Article 62a of the Statute. The decision served on the Member States, and the States, other than the Member States, which are parties to the

EEA Agreement, as well as the EFTA Surveillance Authority, shall be accompanied by a translation of the decision of the Court of Justice in accordance with the provisions of Article 98 of these Rules. The decision of the Court of Justice shall also be communicated to the General Court and, if applicable, to the referring court or tribunal.

2. Within one month of the date of service referred to in paragraph 1, the parties and other interested persons on whom the decision of the Court of Justice has been served may lodge statements or written observations on the questions which are subject to review.

3. As soon as a decision to review a decision of the General Court has been taken, the First Advocate General shall assign the review to an Advocate General.

4. The reviewing Chamber shall rule on the substance of the case, after hearing the Advocate General.

5. It may, however, request the Court of Justice to assign the case to a formation of the Court composed of a greater number of Judges.

6. Where the decision of the General Court which is subject to review was given under Article 256(2) TFEU, the Court of Justice shall make a decision as to costs.

Title VII Opinions

Article 196 Written part of the procedure

1. In accordance with Article 218(11) TFEU, a request for an Opinion may be made by a Member State, by the European Parliament, by the Council or by the European Commission.

2. A request for an Opinion may relate both to whether the envisaged agreement is compatible with the provisions of the Treaties and to whether the European Union or any institution of the European Union has the power to enter into that agreement.

3. It shall be served on the Member States and on the institutions referred to in paragraph 1, and the President shall prescribe a time-limit within which they may submit written observations.

Article 197 Designation of the Judge-Rapporteur and of the Advocate General

As soon as the request for an Opinion has been submitted, the President shall designate a Judge-Rapporteur and the First Advocate General shall assign the case to an Advocate General.

Article 198 Hearing

The Court may decide that the procedure before it shall also include a hearing.

Article 199 Time-limit for delivering the Opinion

The Court shall deliver its Opinion as soon as possible, after hearing the Advocate General.

Article 200 Delivery of the Opinion

The Opinion, signed by the President, the Judges who took part in the deliberations and the Registrar, shall be delivered in open court. It shall be served on all the Member States and on the institutions referred to in Article 196(1).

Title VIII Particular forms of procedure

Article 201 Appeals against decisions of the arbitration committee

1. An application initiating an appeal under the second paragraph of Article 18 TEAEC shall state:

(a) the name and permanent address of the applicant;
(b) the description of the signatory;
(c) a reference to the arbitration committee's decision against which the appeal is made;
(d) the names of the respondents;
(e) a summary of the facts;

(f) the grounds on which the appeal is based and arguments relied on, and a brief statement of those grounds;

(g) the form of order sought by the applicant.

2. Articles 119 and 121 of these Rules shall apply to the application.

3. A certified copy of the contested decision shall be annexed to the application.

4. As soon as the application has been lodged, the Registrar of the Court shall request the arbitration committee registry to transmit to the Court the file in the case.

5. Articles 123 and 124 of these Rules shall apply to this procedure. The Court may decide that the procedure before it shall also include a hearing.

6. The Court shall give its decision in the form of a judgment. Where the Court sets aside the decision of the arbitration committee it may refer the case back to the committee.

Article 202 Procedure under Article 103 TEAEC

1. Four certified copies shall be lodged of an application under the third paragraph of Article 103 TEAEC. The application shall be accompanied by the draft of the agreement or contract concerned, by the observations of the European Commission addressed to the State concerned and by all other supporting documents.

2. The application and annexes thereto shall be served on the European Commission, which shall have a time-limit of 10 days from such service to submit its written observations. This time-limit may be extended by the President after the State concerned has been heard.

3. Following the lodging of such observations, which shall be served on the State concerned, the Court shall give its decision promptly, after hearing the Advocate General and, if they so request, the State concerned and the European Commission.

Article 203 Procedures under Articles 104 TEAEC and 105 TEAEC

Applications under the third paragraph of Article 104 TEAEC and the second paragraph of Article 105 TEAEC shall be governed by the provisions of Titles II and IV of these Rules. Such applications shall also be served on the State to which the respondent person or undertaking belongs.

Article 204 Procedure provided for by Article 111(3) of the EEA Agreement

1. In the case governed by Article 111(3) of the EEA Agreement, the matter shall be brought before the Court by a request submitted by the Contracting Parties which are parties to the dispute. The request shall be served on the other Contracting Parties, on the European Commission, on the EFTA Surveillance Authority and, where appropriate, on the other interested persons on whom a request for a preliminary ruling raising the same question of interpretation of European Union legislation would be served.

2. The President shall prescribe a time-limit within which the Contracting Parties and the other interested persons on whom the request has been served may submit written observations.

3. The request shall be made in one of the languages referred to in Article 36 of these Rules. Article 38 shall apply. The provisions of Article 98 shall apply mutatis mutandis.

4. As soon as the request referred to in paragraph 1 of this Article has been submitted, the President shall designate a Judge-Rapporteur. The First Advocate General shall, immediately afterwards, assign the request to an Advocate General.

5. The Court shall, after hearing the Advocate General, give a reasoned decision on the request.

6. The decision of the Court, signed by the President, the Judges who took part in the deliberations and the Registrar, shall be served on the Contracting Parties and on the other interested persons referred to in paragraphs 1 and 2.

Article 205 Settlement of the disputes referred to in Article 35 TEU in the version in force before the entry into force of the Treaty of Lisbon

1. In the case of disputes between Member States as referred to in Article 35(7) TEU in the version in force before the entry into force of the Treaty of Lisbon, as maintained in force by Protocol No 36 annexed to the Treaties, the matter shall be brought before the Court by an application by a

party to the dispute. The application shall be served on the other Member States and on the European Commission.

2. In the case of disputes between Member States and the European Commission as referred to in Article 35(7) TEU in the version in force before the entry into force of the Treaty of Lisbon, as maintained in force by Protocol No 36 annexed to the Treaties, the matter shall be brought before the Court by an application by a party to the dispute. The application shall be served on the other Member States, the Council and the European Commission if it was submitted by a Member State. The application shall be served on the Member States and on the Council if it was submitted by the European Commission.

3. The President shall prescribe a time-limit within which the institutions and the Member States on which the application has been served may submit written observations.

4. As soon as the application referred to in paragraphs 1 and 2 has been submitted, the President shall designate a Judge-Rapporteur. The First Advocate General shall, immediately afterwards, assign the application to an Advocate General.

5. The Court may decide that the procedure before it shall also include a hearing.

6. The Court shall, after the Advocate General has delivered his Opinion, give its ruling on the dispute by way of judgment.

7. The same procedure as that laid down in the preceding paragraphs shall apply where an agreement concluded between the Member States confers jurisdiction on the Court to rule on a dispute between Member States or between Member States and an institution.

Article 206 Requests under Article 269 TFEU

1. Four certified copies shall be submitted of a request under Article 269 TFEU. The request shall be accompanied by any relevant document and, in particular, any observations and recommendations made pursuant to Article 7 TEU.

2. The request and annexes thereto shall be served on the European Council or on the Council, as appropriate, each of which shall have a time-limit of 10 days from such service to submit its written observations. This time-limit shall not be extended.

3. The request and annexes thereto shall also be communicated to the Member States other than the State in question, to the European Parliament and to the European Commission.

4. Following the lodging of the observations referred to in paragraph 2, which shall be served on the Member State concerned and on the States and institutions referred to in paragraph 3, the Court shall give its decision within a time-limit of one month from the lodging of the request and after hearing the Advocate General. At the request of the Member State concerned, the European Council or the Council, or of its own motion, the Court may decide that the procedure before it shall also include a hearing, which all the States and institutions referred to in this Article shall be given notice to attend.

Final provisions

Article 207 Supplementary rules

Subject to the provisions of Article 253 TFEU and after consultation with the Governments concerned, the Court shall adopt supplementary rules concerning its practice in relation to:

(a) letters rogatory;
(b) applications for legal aid;
(c) reports by the Court of perjury by witnesses or experts, delivered pursuant to Article 30 of the Statute.

Article 208 Implementing rules

The Court may, by a separate act, adopt practice rules for the implementation of these Rules.

Article 209 Repeal

These Rules replace the Rules of Procedure of the Court of Justice of the European Communities adopted on 19 June 1991, as last amended on 24 May 2011 (*Official Journal of the European Union*, L 162 of 22 June 2011, p. 17).

Article 210 Publication and entry into force of these Rules

These Rules, which are authentic in the languages referred to in Article 36 of these Rules, shall be published in the *Official Journal of the European Union* and shall enter into force on the first day of the second month following their publication.

Done at Luxembourg, 25 September 2012.

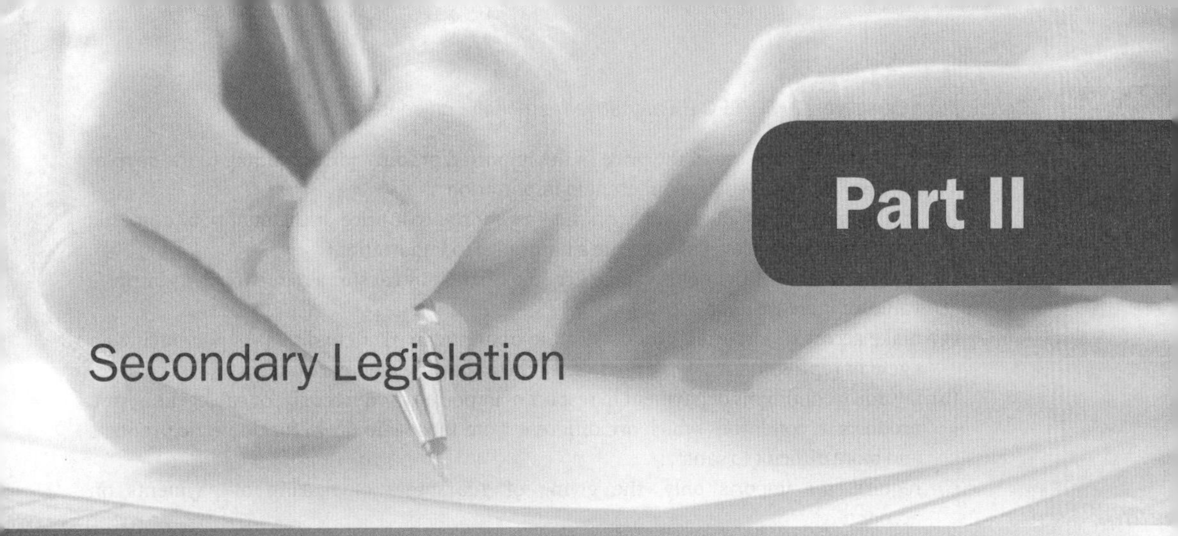

Part II

Secondary Legislation

Free movement of goods

Commission Directive of 22 December 1969 based on the provisions of Article 33(7), on the abolition of measures which have an effect equivalent to quantitative restrictions on imports and are not covered by other provisions adopted in pursuance of the EEC Treaty (70/50/EEC)

[OJ Sp. Ed. 1970, I No L13/29, p. 17]

(Preamble omitted.)

Article 1

The purpose of this Directive is to abolish the measures referred to in Articles 2 and 3, which were operative at the date of entry into force of the EEC Treaty.

Article 2

1. This Directive covers measures, other than those applicable equally to domestic or imported products, which hinder imports which could otherwise take place, including measures which make importation more difficult or costly than the disposal of domestic production.

2. In particular, it covers measures which make imports or the disposal, at any marketing stage, of imported products subject to a condition—other than a formality—which is required in respect of imported products only, or a condition differing from that required for domestic products and more difficult to satisfy. Equally, it covers, in particular, measures which favour domestic products or grant them a preference, other than an aid, to which conditions may or may not be attached.

3. The measures referred to must be taken to include those measures which:
   - (a) lay down, for imported products only, minimum or maximum prices below or above which imports are prohibited, reduced or made subject to conditions liable to hinder importation;
   - (b) lay down less favourable prices for imported products than for domestic products;
   - (c) fix profit margins or any other price components for imported products only or fix these differently for domestic products and for imported products, to the detriment of the latter;

(d) preclude any increase in the price of the imported product corresponding to the supplementary costs and charges inherent in importation;
(e) fix the prices of products solely on the basis of the cost price or the quality of domestic products at such a level as to create a hindrance to importation;
(f) lower the value of an imported product, in particular by causing a reduction in its intrinsic value, or increase its costs;
(g) make access of imported products to the domestic market conditional upon having an agent or representative in the territory of the importing Member State;
(h) lay down conditions of payment in respect of imported products only, or subject imported products to conditions which are different from those laid down for domestic products and more difficult to satisfy;
(i) require, for imports only, the giving of guarantees or making of payments on account;
(j) subject imported products only to conditions, in respect, in particular of shape, size, weight, composition, presentation, identification or putting up, or subject imported products to conditions which are different from those for domestic products and more difficult to satisfy;
(k) hinder the purchase by private individuals of imported products only, or encourage, require or give preference to the purchase of domestic products only;
(l) totally or partially preclude the use of national facilities or equipment in respect of imported products only, or totally or partially confine the use of such facilities or equipment to domestic products only;
(m) prohibit or limit publicity in respect of imported products only, or totally or partially confine publicity to domestic products only;
(n) prohibit, limit or require stocking in respect of imported products only; totally or partially confine the use of stocking facilities to domestic products only, or make the stocking of imported products subject to conditions which are different from those required for domestic products and more difficult to satisfy;
(o) make importation subject to the granting of reciprocity by one or more Member States;
(p) prescribe that imported products are to conform, totally or partially, to rules other than those of the importing country;
(q) specify time limits for imported products which are insufficient or excessive in relation to the normal course of the various transactions to which these time limits apply;
(r) subject imported products to controls or, other than those inherent in the customs clearance procedure, to which domestic products are not subject or which are stricter in respect of imported products than they are in respect of domestic products, without this being necessary in order to ensure equivalent protection;
(s) confine names which are not indicative of origin or source to domestic products only.

Article 3

This Directive also covers measures governing the marketing of products which deal, in particular, with shape, size, weight, composition, presentation, identification or putting up and which are equally applicable to domestic and imported products, where the restrictive effect of such measures on the free movement of goods exceeds the effects intrinsic to trade rules.

This is the case, in particular, where:

- the restrictive effects on the free movement of goods are out of proportion to their purpose;
- the same objective can be attained by other means which are less of a hindrance to trade.

(All remaining provisions omitted.)

Commission Practice Note on Import Prohibitions

Communication from the Commission concerning the consequences of the judgment given by the Court of Justice on 20 February 1979 in Case 120/78 ('Cassis de Dijon')

[OJ 1980 C256/2]

The following is the text of a letter which has been sent to the Member States; the European Parliament and the Council have also been notified of it.

In the Commission's Communication of 6 November 1978 on 'Safeguarding free trade within the Community', it was emphasised that the free movement of goods is being affected by a growing number of restrictive measures.

The judgment delivered by the Court of Justice on 20 February 1979 in Case 120/78 (the 'Cassis de Dijon' case), and recently reaffirmed in the judgment of 26 June 1980 in Case 788/79, has given the Commission some interpretative guidance enabling it to monitor more strictly the application of the Treaty rules on the free movement of goods, particularly Articles 30 to 36 of the EEC Treaty.

The Court gives a very general definition of the barriers to free trade which are prohibited by the provisions of Article 30 et seq. of the EEC Treaty. These are taken to include 'any national measure capable of hindering, directly or indirectly, actually or potentially, intra-Community trade'.

In its judgment of 20 February 1979 the Court indicates the scope of this definition as it applies to technical and commercial rules.

Any product lawfully produced and marketed in one Member State must, in principle, be admitted to the market of any other Member State.

Technical and commercial rules, even those equally applicable to national and imported products, may create barriers to trade only where those rules are necessary to satisfy mandatory requirements and to serve a purpose which is in the general interest and for which they are an essential guarantee. This purpose must be such as to take precedence over the requirements of the free movement of goods, which constitutes one of the fundamental rules of the Community.

The conclusions in terms of policy which the Commission draws from this new guidance are set out below.

- Whereas Member States may, with respect to domestic products and in the absence of relevant Community provisions, regulate the terms on which such products are marketed, the case is different for products imported from other Member States.

Any product imported from another Member State must in principle be admitted to the territory of the importing Member State if it has been lawfully produced, that is, conforms to the rules and processes of manufacture that are customarily and traditionally accepted in the exporting country, and is marketed in the territory of the latter.

This principle implies that Member States, when drawing up commercial or technical rules liable to affect the free movement of goods, may not take an exclusively national viewpoint and take account only of requirements confined to domestic products. The proper functioning of the common market demands that each Member State also give consideration to the legitimate requirements of the other Member States.

- Only under very strict conditions does the Court accept exceptions to this principle; barriers to trade resulting from differences between commercial and technical rules are only admissible:

- if the rules are necessary, that is appropriate and not excessive, in order to satisfy mandatory requirements (public health, protection of consumers or the environment, the fairness of commercial transactions, etc.);
- if the rules serve a purpose in the general interest which is compelling enough to justify an exception to a fundamental rule of the Treaty such as the free movement of goods;
- if the rules are essential for such a purpose to be attained, i.e. are the means which are the most appropriate and at the same time least hinder trade.

The Court's interpretation has induced the Commission to set out a number of guidelines.

- The principles deduced by the Court imply that a Member State may not in principle prohibit the sale in its territory of a product lawfully produced and marketed in another Member State even if the product is produced according to technical or quality requirements which differ from those imposed on its domestic products. Where a product 'suitably and satisfactorily' fulfils the legitimate objective of a Member State's own rules (public safety, protection of the consumer or the environment, etc.), the importing country cannot justify prohibiting its sale in its territory by claiming that the way it fulfils the objective is different from that imposed on domestic products.

In such a case, an absolute prohibition of sale could not be considered 'necessary' to satisfy a 'mandatory requirement' because it would not be an 'essential guarantee' in the sense defined in the Court's judgment.

The Commission will therefore have to tackle a whole body of commercial rules which lay down that products manufactured and marketed in one Member State must fulfil technical or qualitative conditions in order to be admitted to the market of another and specifically in all cases where the trade barriers occasioned by such rules are inadmissible according to the very strict criteria set out by the Court.

The Commission is referring in particular to rules covering the composition, designation, presentation and packaging of products as well as rules requiring compliance with certain technical standards.

The Commission's work of harmonisation will henceforth have to be directed mainly at national laws having an impact on the functioning of the common market where barriers to trade to be removed arise from national provisions which are admissible under the criteria set by the Court.

The Commission will be concentrating on sectors deserving priority because of their economic relevance to the creation of a single internal market.

To forestall later difficulties, the Commission will be informing Member States of potential objections, under the terms of Community law, to provisions they may be considering introducing which come to the attention of the Commission.

It will be producing suggestions soon on the procedures to be followed in such cases.

The Commission is confident that this approach will secure greater freedom of trade for the Community's manufacturers, so strengthening the industrial base of the Community, while meeting the expectations of consumers.

Council Regulation 2679/98 of 7 December 1998 on the functioning of the internal market in relation to the free movement of goods among the Member States

[OJ 1998 L337/8]

THE COUNCIL OF THE EUROPEAN UNION,

Having regard to the Treaty establishing the European Community, and in particular Article 235 thereof,

Having regard to the proposal from the Commission,[1]
Having regard to the opinion of the European Parliament,[2]
Having regard to the opinion of the Economic and Social Committee,[3]

(1) Whereas, as provided for in Article 7a of the Treaty, the internal market comprises an area without internal frontiers in which, in particular, the free movement of goods is ensured in accordance with Articles 30 to 36 of the Treaty;

(2) Whereas breaches of this principle, such as occur when in a given Member State the free movement of goods is obstructed by actions of private individuals, may cause grave disruption to the proper functioning of the internal market and inflict serious losses on the individuals affected;

(3) Whereas, in order to ensure fulfilment of the obligations arising from the Treaty, and, in particular, to ensure the proper functioning of the internal market, Member States should, on the one hand, abstain from adopting measures or engaging in conduct liable to constitute an obstacle to trade and, on the other hand, take all necessary and proportionate measures with a view to facilitating the free movement of goods in their territory;

(4) Whereas such measures must not affect the exercise of fundamental rights, including the right or freedom to strike;

(5) Whereas this Regulation does not prevent any actions which may be necessary in certain cases at Community level to respond to problems in the functioning of the internal market, taking into account, where appropriate, the application of this Regulation;

(6) Whereas Member States have exclusive competence as regards the maintenance of public order and the safeguarding of internal security as well as in determining whether, when and which measures are necessary and proportionate in order to facilitate the free movement of goods in their territory in a given situation;

(7) Whereas there should be adequate and rapid exchange of information between the Member States and the Commission on obstacles to the free movement of goods;

(8) Whereas a Member State on the territory of which obstacles to the free movement of goods occur should take all necessary and proportionate measures to restore as soon as possible the free movement of goods in their territory in order to avoid the risk that the disruption or loss in question will continue, increase or intensify and that there may be a breakdown in trade and in the contractual relations which underlie it; whereas such Member State should inform the Commission and, if requested, other Member States of the measures it has taken or intends to take in order to fulfil this objective;

(9) Whereas the Commission, in fulfilment of its duty under the Treaty, should notify the Member State concerned of its view that a breach has occurred and the Member State should respond to that notification;

(10) Whereas the Treaty provides for no powers, other than those in Article 235 thereof, for the adoption of this Regulation,

HAS ADOPTED THIS REGULATION:

Article 1

For the purpose of this Regulation:

1. the term 'obstacle' shall mean an obstacle to the free movement of goods among Member States which is attributable to a Member State, whether it involves action or inaction on its part, which may constitute a breach of Articles 30 to 36 of the Treaty and which:
   - (a) leads to serious disruption of the free movement of goods by physically or otherwise preventing, delaying or diverting their import into, export from or transport across a Member State,
   - (b) causes serious loss to the individuals affected, and

[1] OJ C 10, 15.1.1998, p. 14.
[2] OJ C 359, 23.11.1998.
[3] OJ C 214, 10.7.1998, p. 90.

(c) requires immediate action in order to prevent any continuation, increase or intensification of the disruption or loss in question;

2. the term 'inaction' shall cover the case when the competent authorities of a Member State, in the presence of an obstacle caused by actions taken by private individuals, fail to take all necessary and proportionate measures within their powers with a view to removing the obstacle and ensuring the free movement of goods in their territory.

Article 2

This Regulation may not be interpreted as affecting in any way the exercise of fundamental rights as recognised in Member States, including the right or freedom to strike. These rights may also include the right or freedom to take other actions covered by the specific industrial relations systems in Member States.

Article 3

1. When an obstacle occurs or when there is a threat thereof

(a) any Member State (whether or not it is the Member State concerned) which has relevant information shall immediately transmit it to the Commission, and

(b) the Commission shall immediately transmit to the Member States that information and any information from any other source which it may consider relevant.

2. The Member State concerned shall respond as soon as possible to requests for information from the Commission and from other Member States concerning the nature of the obstacle or threat and the action which it has taken or proposes to take. Information exchange between Member States shall also be transmitted to the Commission.

Article 4

1. When an obstacle occurs, and subject to Article 2, the Member State concerned shall

(a) take all necessary and proportionate measures so that the free movement of goods is assured in the territory of the Member State in accordance with the Treaty, and

(b) inform the Commission of the actions which its authorities have taken or intend to take.

2. The Commission shall immediately transmit the information received under paragraph 1(b) to the other Member States.

Article 5

1. Where the Commission considers that an obstacle is occurring in a Member State, it shall notify the Member State concerned of the reasons that have led the Commission to such a conclusion and shall request the Member State to take all necessary and proportionate measures to remove the said obstacle within a period which it shall determine with reference to the urgency of the case.

2. In reaching its conclusion, the Commission shall have regard to Article 2.

3. The Commission may publish in the Official Journal of the European Communities the text of the notification which it has sent to the Member State concerned and shall immediately transmit the text to any party which requests it.

4. The Member State shall, within five working days of receipt of the text, either:

- inform the Commission of the steps which it has taken or intends to take to implement paragraph 1, or
- communicate a reasoned submission as to why there is no obstacle constituting a breach of Articles 30 to 36 of the Treaty.

5. In exceptional cases, the Commission may allow an extension of the deadline mentioned in paragraph 4 if the Member State submits a duly substantiated request and the grounds cited are deemed acceptable.

This Regulation shall be binding in its entirety and directly applicable in all Member States.

Done at Brussels, 7 December 1998.
For the Council
The President
J. FARNLEITNER

Directive 98/34/EC of the European Parliament and of the Council of 22 June 1998 laying down a procedure for the provision of information in the field of technical standards and regulations and of rules on Information Society services*

[OJ 1998 L204/37]

THE EUROPEAN PARLIAMENT AND THE COUNCIL OF THE EUROPEAN UNION,

Having regard to the Treaty establishing the European Community, and in particular Articles 100a, 213 and 43 thereof,

Having regard to the proposal from the Commission[1],

Having regard to the opinion of the Economic and Social Committee[2],

Acting in accordance with the procedure laid down in Article 189b of the Treaty[3],

(1) Whereas Council Directive 83/189/EEC of 28 March 1983 laying down a procedure for the provision of information in the field of technical standards and regulations[4] has been variously and substantially amended; whereas for reasons of clarity and rationality the said Directive should be consolidated;

(2) Whereas the internal market comprises an area without internal frontiers in which the free movement of goods, persons, services and capital is ensured; whereas, therefore, the prohibition of quantitative restrictions on the movement of goods and of measures having an equivalent effect is one of the basic principles of the Community;

(3) Whereas in order to promote the smooth functioning of the internal market, as much transparency as possible should be ensured as regards national initiatives for the establishment of technical standards or regulations;

(4) Whereas barriers to trade resulting from technical regulations relating to products may be allowed only where they are necessary in order to meet essential requirements and have an objective in the public interest of which they constitute the main guarantee;

(5) Whereas it is essential for the Commission to have the necessary information at its disposal before the adoption of technical provisions; whereas, consequently, the Member States which are required to facilitate the achievement of its task pursuant to Article 5 of the Treaty must notify it of their projects in the field of technical regulations;

(6) Whereas all the Member States must also be informed of the technical regulations contemplated by any one Member State;

(7) Whereas the aim of the internal market is to create an environment that is conducive to the competitiveness of undertakings; whereas increased provision of information is one way of helping undertakings to make more of the advantages inherent in this market; whereas it is therefore necessary to enable economic operators to give their assessment of the impact of the national technical regulations proposed by other Member States, by providing for the regular publication of the titles of notified drafts and by means of the provisions relating to the confidentiality of such drafts;

(8) Whereas it is appropriate, in the interests of legal certainty, that Member States publicly announce that a national technical regulation has been adopted in accordance with the formalities laid down in this Directive;

(9) Whereas, as far as technical regulations for products are concerned, the measures designed to ensure the proper functioning or the continued development of the market include greater

* **Editor's Note**: As amended to Regulation 1025/2012 (OJ 2012 L 316/12). Annexes omitted.

[1] OJ C 78, 12.3.1997, p. 4.

[2] OJ C 133, 28.4.1997, p. 5.

[3] Opinion of the European Parliament of 17 September 1997 (OJ C 304, 6.10.1997, p. 79), Council Common Position of 23 February 1998 (OJ C 110, 8.4.1998, p. 1) and Decision of the European Parliament of 30 April 1998 (OJ C 152, 18.5.1998). Decision of the Council of 28 May 1998.

[4] OJ L 109, 26.4.1983, p. 8. Directive as last amended by Commission Decision 96/139/EC (OJ L 32, 10.2.1996, p. 31).

transparency of national intentions and a broadening of the criteria and conditions for assessing the potential effect of the proposed regulations on the market;

(10) Whereas it is therefore necessary to assess all the requirements laid down in respect of a product and to take account of developments in national practices for the regulation of products;

(11) Whereas requirements, other than technical specifications, referring to the life cycle of a product after it has been placed on the market are liable to affect the free movement of that product or to create obstacles to the proper functioning of the internal market;

(12) Whereas it is necessary to clarify the concept of a de facto technical regulation; whereas, in particular, the provisions by which the public authority refers to technical specifications or other requirements, or encourages the observance thereof, and the provisions referring to products with which the public authority is associated, in the public interest, have the effect of conferring on such requirements or specifications a more binding value than they would otherwise have by virtue of their private origin;

(13) Whereas the Commission and the Member States must also be allowed sufficient time in which to propose amendments to a contemplated measure, in order to remove or reduce any barriers which it might create to the free movement of goods;

(14) Whereas the Member State concerned must take account of these amendments when formulating the definitive text of the measure envisaged;

(15) Whereas it is inherent in the internal market that, in particular where the principle of mutual recognition cannot be implemented by the Member States, the Commission adopts or proposes the adoption of binding Community acts; whereas a specific temporary standstill period has been established in order to prevent the introduction of national measures from compromising the adoption of binding Community acts by the Council or the Commission in the same field;

(16) Whereas the Member State in question must, pursuant to the general obligations laid down in Article 5 of the Treaty, defer implementation of the contemplated measure for a period sufficient to allow either a joint examination of the proposed amendments or the preparation of a proposal for a binding act of the Council or the adoption of a binding act of the Commission; whereas the time limits laid down in the Agreement of the representatives of the Governments of the Member States meeting within the Council of 28 May 1969 providing for standstill and notification to the Commission[5], as amended by the Agreement of 5 March 1973[6], have proved inadequate in the cases concerned and should accordingly be extended;

(17) Whereas the procedure concerning the standstill arrangement and notification of the Commission contained in the abovementioned agreement of 28 May 1969 remains applicable to products subject to that procedure which are not covered by this Directive;

(18) Whereas, with a view to facilitating the adoption of Community measures by the Council, Member States should refrain from adopting technical regulations once the Council has adopted a common position on a Commission proposal concerning that sector;

(19) Whereas, in practice, national technical standards may have the same effects on the free movement of goods as technical regulations;

(20) Whereas it would therefore appear necessary to inform the Commission of draft standards under similar conditions to those which apply to technical regulations; whereas, pursuant to Article 213 of the Treaty, the Commission may, within the limits and under the conditions laid down by the Council in accordance with the provisions of the Treaty, collect any information and carry out any checks required for the performance of the tasks entrusted to it;

(21) Whereas it is also necessary for the Member States and the standards institutions to be informed of standards contemplated by standards institutions in the other Member States;

(22) Whereas systematic notification is actually necessary only in the case of new subjects for standardisation and in so far as the treatment of these subjects at national level may give rise to

[5] OJ C 76, 17.6.1969, p. 9.
[6] OJ C 9, 15.3.1973, p. 3.

differences in national standards which are liable to disturb the functioning of the market as a result; whereas any subsequent notification or communication relating to the progress of national activities must depend on the interest in such activities expressed by those to whom this new subject has already been communicated;

(23) Whereas the Commission must nevertheless be able to request the communication of all or part of the national standardisation programmes so that it can review the development of standardisation activity in particular economic sectors;

(24) Whereas the European standardisation system must be organised by and for the parties concerned, on a basis of coherence, transparency, openness, consensus, independence of special interests, efficiency and decision-making based on national representation;

(25) Whereas the functioning of standardisation in the Community must be based on fundamental rights for the national standardisation bodies, such as the possibility of obtaining draft standards, being informed of the action taken in response to comments submitted, being associated with national standardisation activities or requesting the preparation of European standards in place of national standards; whereas it is for the Member States to take the appropriate measures in their power to ensure that their standardisation bodies observe these rights;

(26) Whereas the provisions concerning the standstill arrangements applicable to national standardisation bodies when a European standard is in preparation must be brought into line with the relevant provisions adopted by the standardisation bodies within the framework of the European standardisation bodies;

(27) Whereas it is necessary to set up a Standing Committee, the members of which will be appointed by the Member States with the task of helping the Commission to examine draft national standards and cooperating in its efforts to lessen any adverse effects thereof on the free movement of goods;

(28) Whereas the Standing Committee should be consulted on the draft standardisation requests referred to in this Directive;

(29) Whereas this Directive must not affect the obligations of the Member States concerning the deadlines for transposition of the Directives set out in Annex III, Part B,

HAVE ADOPTED THIS DIRECTIVE:

Article 1

For the purposes of this Directive, the following meanings shall apply:

1. 'product', any industrially manufactured product and any agricultural product, including fish products;

2. 'service', any Information Society service, that is to say, any service normally provided for remuneration, at a distance, by electronic means and at the individual request of a recipient of services.

For the purposes of this definition:

- 'at a distance' means that the service is provided without the parties being simultaneously present,
- 'by electronic means' means that the service is sent initially and received at its destination by means of electronic equipment for the processing (including digital compression) and storage of data, and entirely transmitted, conveyed and received by wire, by radio, by optical means or by other electromagnetic means,
- 'at the individual request of a recipient of services' means that the service is provided through the transmission of data on individual request.

An indicative list of services not covered by this definition is set out in Annex V.

This Directive shall not apply to:

- radio broadcasting services,
- television broadcasting services covered by point (a) of Article 1 of Directive 89/552/EEC[7].

[7] OJ L 298, 17.10.1989, p. 23. Directive as last amended by Directive 97/36/EC (OJ L 202, 30.7.1997, p. 1.

3. 'technical specification', a specification contained in a document which lays down the characteristics required of a product such as levels of quality, performance, safety or dimensions, including the requirements applicable to the product as regards the name under which the product is sold, terminology, symbols, testing and test methods, packaging, marking or labelling and conformity assessment procedures.

The term 'technical specification' also covers production methods and processes used in respect of agricultural products as referred to Article 38(1) of the Treaty, products intended for human and animal consumption, and medicinal products as defined in Article 1 of Directive 65/65/EEC[8], as well as production methods and processes relating to other products, where these have an effect on their characteristics;

4. 'other requirements', a requirement, other than a technical specification, imposed on a product for the purpose of protecting, in particular, consumers or the environment, and which affects its life cycle after it has been placed on the market, such as conditions of use, recycling, reuse or disposal, where such conditions can significantly influence the composition or nature of the product or its marketing;

5. 'rule on services', requirement of a general nature relating to the taking-up and pursuit of service activities within the meaning of point 2, in particular provisions concerning the service provider, the services and the recipient of services, excluding any rules which are not specifically aimed at the services defined in that point.

This Directive shall not apply to rules relating to matters which are covered by Community legislation in the field of telecommunications services, as defined by Directive 90/387/EEC[9].

This Directive shall not apply to rules relating to matters which are covered by Community legislation in the field of financial services, as listed non-exhaustively in Annex VI to this Directive.

With the exception of Article 8(3), this Directive shall not apply to rules enacted by or for regulated markets within the meaning of Directive 93/22/EEC or by or for other markets or bodies carrying out clearing or settlement functions for those markets.

For the purposes of this definition:

- a rule shall be considered to be specifically aimed at Information Society services where, having regard to its statement of reasons and its operative part, the specific aim and object of all or some of its individual provisions is to regulate such services in an explicit and targeted manner,
- a rule shall not be considered to be specifically aimed at Information Society services if it affects such services only in an implicit or incidental manner;

11. 'technical regulation', technical specifications and other requirements or rules on services, including the relevant administrative provisions, the observance of which is compulsory, de jure or de facto, in the case of marketing, provision of a service, establishment of a service operator or use in a Member State or a major part thereof, as well as laws, regulations or administrative provisions of Member States, except those provided for in Article 10, prohibiting the manufacture, importation, marketing or use of a product or prohibiting the provision or use of a service, or establishment as a service provider.

De facto technical regulations include:

- laws, regulations or administrative provisions of a Member State which refer either to technical specifications or to other requirements or to rules on services, or to professional codes or codes of practice which in turn refer to technical specifications or to other requirements or to rules on services, compliance with which confers a presumption of conformity with the obligations imposed by the aforementioned laws, regulations or administrative provisions,

[8] Council Directive 65/65/EEC of 26 January 1965 on the approximation of provisions laid down by law, regulation or administrative action relating to medicinal products (OJ 22, 9.2.1965, p. 369/65), Directive as last amended by Directive 93/39/EEC (OJ L 214, 24.8.1993, p. 22).

[9] OJ L 192, 24.7.1990, p. 1. Directive as amended by Directive 97/51/EC (OJ L 295, 29.10.1997, p. 23).

- voluntary agreements to which a public authority is a contracting party and which provide, in the general interest, for compliance with technical specifications or other requirements or rules on services, excluding public procurement tender specifications,
- technical specifications or other requirements or rules on services which are linked to fiscal or financial measures affecting the consumption of products or services by encouraging compliance with such technical specifications or other requirements or rules on services; technical specifications or other requirements or rules on services linked to national social security systems are not included.
- This comprises technical regulations imposed by the authorities designated by the Member States and appearing on a list to be drawn up by the Commission before 5 August 1999 (*), in the framework of the Committee referred to in Article 5.
- The same procedure shall be used for amending this list;

12. 'draft technical regulation', the text of a technical specification or other requirement or of a rule on services, including administrative provisions, formulated with the aim of enacting it or of ultimately having it enacted as a technical regulation, the text being at a stage of preparation at which substantial amendments can still be made;

This Directive shall not apply to those measures Member States consider necessary under the Treaty for the protection of persons, in particular workers, when products are used, provided that such measures do not affect the products.

Article 5

A Standing Committee shall be set up consisting of representatives appointed by the Member States who may call on the assistance of experts or advisers; its chairman shall be a representative of the Commission.

The Committee shall draw up its own rules of procedure.

Article 6

1. The Committee shall meet at least twice a year.

The Committee shall meet in a specific composition to examine questions concerning Information Society services.

2. The Commission shall submit to the Committee a report on the implementation and application of the procedures set out in this Directive, and shall present proposals aimed at eliminating existing or foreseeable barriers to trade.

3. The Committee shall express its opinion on the communications and proposals referred to in paragraph 2 and may in this connection propose, in particular, that the Commission:

- ensure where necessary, in order to avoid the risk of barriers to trade, that initially the Member States concerned decide amongst themselves on appropriate measures,
- take all appropriate measures,
- identify the areas where harmonisation appears necessary, and, should the case arise, undertake appropriate harmonisation in a given sector.

4. The Committee must be consulted by the Commission:

(c) when deciding on the actual system whereby the exchange of information provided for in this Directive is to be effected and on any change to it;

(d) when reviewing the operation of the system set up by this Directive.

5. The Committee may be consulted by the Commission on any preliminary draft technical regulation received by the latter.

6. Any question regarding the implementation of this Directive may be submitted to the Committee at the request of its chairman or of a Member State.

7. The proceedings of the Committee and the information to be submitted to it shall be confidential.

However, the Committee and the national authorities may, provided that the necessary precautions are taken, consult, for an expert opinion, natural or legal persons, including persons in the private sector.

8. With respect to rules on services, the Commission and the Committee may consult natural or legal persons from industry or academia, and where possible representative bodies, capable of delivering an expert opinion on the social and societal aims and consequences of any draft rule on services, and take notice of their advice whenever requested to do so.

Article 7

Member States shall communicate to the Commission, in accordance with Article 8(1), all requests made to standards institutions to draw up technical specifications or a standard for specific products for the purpose of enacting a technical regulation for such products as draft technical regulations, and shall state the grounds for their enactment.

Article 8

1. Subject to Article 10, Member States shall immediately communicate to the Commission any draft technical regulation, except where it merely transposes the full text of an international or European standard, in which case information regarding the relevant standard shall suffice; they shall also let the Commission have a statement of the grounds which make the enactment of such a technical regulation necessary, where these have not already been made clear in the draft.

Where appropriate, and unless it has already been sent with a prior communication, Member States shall simultaneously communicate the text of the basic legislative or regulatory provisions principally and directly concerned, should knowledge of such text be necessary to assess the implications of the draft technical regulation.

Member States shall communicate the draft again under the above conditions if they make changes to the draft that have the effect of significantly altering its scope, shortening the timetable originally envisaged for implementation, adding specifications or requirements, or making the latter more restrictive.

Where, in particular, the draft seeks to limit the marketing or use of a chemical substance, preparation or product on grounds of public health or of the protection of consumers or the environment, Member States shall also forward either a summary or the references of all relevant data relating to the substance, preparation or product concerned and to known and available substitutes, where such information may be available, and communicate the anticipated effects of the measure on public health and the protection of the consumer and the environment, together with an analysis of the risk carried out as appropriate in accordance with the general principles for the risk evaluation of chemical substances as referred to in Article 10(4) of Regulation (EEC) No 793/93[10] in the case of an existing substance or in Article 3(2) of Directive 67/548/EEC[11], in the case of a new substance.

The Commission shall immediately notify the other Member States of the draft and all documents which have been forwarded to it; it may also refer this draft, for an opinion, to the Committee referred to in Article 5 and, where appropriate, to the committee responsible for the field in question.

With respect to the technical specifications or other requirements or rules on services referred to in the third indent of the second subparagraph of point 11 of Article 1, the comments or detailed opinions of the Commission or Member States may concern only aspects which may hinder trade or, in respect of rules on services, the free movement of services or the freedom of establishment of service operators and not the fiscal or financial aspects of the measure.

2. The Commission and the Member States may make comments to the Member State which has forwarded a draft technical regulation; that Member State shall take such comments into account as far as possible in the subsequent preparation of the technical regulation.

3. Member States shall communicate the definitive text of a technical regulation to the Commission without delay.

[10] Council Regulation (EEC) No 793/93 of 23 March 1993 on the evaluation and control of the risks of existing substances (OJ L 84, 5.4.1993, p. 1).

[11] Council Directive 67/548/EEC of 27 June 1967 on the approximation of the laws, regulations and administrative provisions relating to the classification, packaging and labelling of dangerous sub-stances (OJ L 196, 16.8.1967, p. 1). Directive, as amended by Directive 92/32/EEC (OJ L 154, 5.6.1992, p. 1).

4. Information supplied under this Article shall not be confidential except at the express request of the notifying Member State. Any such request shall be supported by reasons.

In cases of this kind, if necessary precautions are taken, the Committee referred to in Article 5 and the national authorities may seek expert advice from physical or legal persons in the private sector.

5. When draft technical regulations form part of measures which are required to be communicated to the Commission at the draft stage under another Community act, Member States may make a communication within the meaning of paragraph 1 under that other act, provided that they formally indicate that the said communication also constitutes a communication for the purposes of this Directive.

The absence of a reaction from the Commission under this Directive to a draft technical regulation shall not prejudice any decision which might be taken under other Community acts.

Article 9

1. Member States shall postpone the adoption of a draft technical regulation for three months from the date of receipt by the Commission of the communication referred to in Article 8(1).

2. Member States shall postpone:

- for four months the adoption of a draft technical regulation in the form of a voluntary agreement within the meaning of the second indent of the second subparagraph of point 11 of Article 1,
- without prejudice to paragraphs 3, 4 and 5, for six months the adoption of any other draft technical regulation (except for draft rules on services),

2. from the date of receipt by the Commission of the communication referred to in Article 8(1) if the Commission or another Member State delivers a detailed opinion, within three months of that date, to the effect that the measure envisaged may create obstacles to the free movement of goods within the internal market;

- without prejudice to paragraphs 4 and 5, for four months the adoption of any draft rule on services, from the date of receipt by the Commission of the communication referred to in Article 8(1) if the Commission or another Member State delivers a detailed opinion, within three months of that date, to the effect that the measure envisaged may create obstacles to the free movement of services or to the freedom of establishment of service operators within the internal market.

With regard to draft rules on services, detailed opinions from the Commission or Member States may not affect any cultural policy measures, in particular in the audiovisual sphere, which Member States might adopt in accordance with Community law, taking account of their linguistic diversity, their specific national and regional characteristics and their cultural heritage.

The Member State concerned shall report to the Commission on the action it proposes to take on such detailed opinions. The Commission shall comment on this reaction.

With respect to rules on services, the Member State concerned shall indicate, where appropriate, the reasons why the detailed opinions cannot be taken into account.

3. With the exclusion of draft rules relating to services, Member States shall postpone the adoption of a draft technical regulation for twelve months from the date of receipt by the Commission of the communication referred to in Article 8(1) if, within three months of that date, the Commission announces its intention of proposing or adopting a directive, regulation or decision on the matter in accordance with Article 189 of the Treaty.

4. Member States shall postpone the adoption of a draft technical regulation for 12 months from the date of receipt by the Commission of the communication referred to in Article 8(1) if, within the three months following that date, the Commission announces its finding that the draft technical regulation concerns a matter which is covered by a proposal for a directive, regulation or decision presented to the Council in accordance with Article 189 of the Treaty.

5. If the Council adopts a common position during the standstill period referred to in paragraphs 3 and 4, that period shall, subject to paragraph 6, be extended to 18 months.

6. The obligations referred to in paragraphs 3, 4 and 5 shall lapse:
   - when the Commission informs the Member States that it no longer intends to propose or adopt a binding Community act,
   - when the Commission informs the Member States of the withdrawal of its draft or proposal,
   - when the Commission or the Council has adopted a binding Community act.
7. Paragraphs 1 to 5 shall not apply in cases where:
   - for urgent reasons, occasioned by serious and unforeseeable circumstances relating to the protection of public health or safety, the protection of animals or the preservation of plants, and for rules on services, also for public policy, notably the protection of minors, a Member State is obliged to prepare technical regulations in a very short space of time in order to enact and introduce them immediately without any consultations being possible or
   - for urgent reasons occasioned by serious circumstances relating to the protection of the security and the integrity of the financial system, notably the protection of depositors, investors and insured persons, a Member State is obliged to enact and implement rules on financial services immediately.

In the communication referred to in Article 8, the Member State shall give reasons for the urgency of the measures taken. The Commission shall give its views on the communication as soon as possible. It shall take appropriate action in cases where improper use is made of this procedure. The European Parliament shall be kept informed by the Commission.

Article 10

1. Articles 8 and 9 shall not apply to those laws, regulations and administrative provisions of the Member States or voluntary agreements by means of which Member States:
   - comply with binding Community acts which result in the adoption of technical specifications or rules on services,
   - fulfil the obligations arising out of international agreements which result in the adoption of common technical specifications or rules on services in the Community,
   - make use of safeguard clauses provided for in binding Community acts,
   - apply Article 8(1) of Directive 92/59/EEC[12],
   - restrict themselves to implementing a judgment of the Court of Justice of the European Communities,
   - restrict themselves to amending a technical regulation within the meaning of point 11 of Article 1, in accordance with a Commission request, with a view to removing an obstacle to trade or, in the case of rules on services, to the free movement of services or the freedom of establishment of service operators.
2. Article 9 shall not apply to the laws, regulations and administrative provisions of the Member States prohibiting manufacture insofar as they do not impede the free movement of products.
3. Paragraphs 3 to 6 of Article 9 shall not apply to the voluntary agreements referred to in the second indent of the second subparagraph of point 11 of Article 1.
4. Article 9 shall not apply to the technical specifications or other requirements or the rules on services referred to in the third indent of the second subparagraph of point 11 of Article 1.

Article 12

When Member States adopt a technical regulation, it shall contain a reference to this Directive or shall be accompanied by such reference on the occasion of its official publication. The methods of making such reference shall be laid down by Member States.

Article 13

1. The Directives and Decisions listed in Annex III, Part A are hereby repealed without prejudice to the obligations of the Member States concerning the deadlines for transposition of the said Directives, set out in Annex III, Part B.

[12] Council Directive 92/59/EEC of 29 June 1992 on general product safety (OJ L 228, 11.8.1992, p. 24).

2. References to the repealed directives and decisions shall be construed as references to this Directive and shall be read in accordance with the correlation table set out in Annex IV.

Article 14

This Directive shall enter into force on the 20th day following that of its publication in the *Official Journal of the European Communities*.

Article 15

This Directive is addressed to the Member States.

Done at Luxembourg, 22 June 1998.
For the European Parliament
The President
J. M. GIL-ROBLES
For the Council
The President
J. CUNNINGHAM

Regulation (EC) No 764/2008 of the European Parliament and of the Council of 9 July 2008 laying down procedures relating to the application of certain national technical rules to products lawfully marketed in another Member State and repealing Decision No 3052/95/EC

[OJ 2008 L218/21]

THE EUROPEAN PARLIAMENT AND THE COUNCIL OF THE EUROPEAN UNION,

Having regard to the Treaty establishing the European Community, and in particular Articles 37 and 95 thereof,

Having regard to the proposal from the Commission,

Having regard to the opinion of the European Economic and Social Committee,[1]

After consulting the Committee of the Regions,

Acting in accordance with the procedure laid down in Article 251 of the Treaty,[2]

Whereas:

(1) The internal market comprises an area without internal frontiers, in which the free movement of goods is ensured under the Treaty, which prohibits measures having effects equivalent to quantitative restrictions on imports. That prohibition covers any national measure which is capable of hindering, directly or indirectly, actually or potentially, intra-Community trade in goods.

(2) Obstacles to the free movement of goods between Member States may be unlawfully created by the Member States' competent authorities applying, in the absence of harmonisation of legislation, to products lawfully marketed in other Member States, technical rules laying down requirements to be met by those products, such as rules relating to designation, form, size, weight, composition, presentation, labelling and packaging. The application of such rules to products lawfully marketed in another Member State can be contrary to Articles 28 and 30 of the Treaty, even if they apply without distinction to all products.

(3) The principle of mutual recognition, which derives from the case-law of the Court of Justice of the European Communities, is one of the means of ensuring the free movement of goods within the

[1] OJ C 120, 16.5.2008, p. 1.

[2] Opinion of the European Parliament of 21 February 2008 (not yet published in the Official Journal) and Council Decision of 23 June 2008.

internal market. Mutual recognition applies to products which are not subject to Community harmonisation legislation, or to aspects of products falling outside the scope of such legislation. According to that principle, a Member State may not prohibit the sale on its territory of products which are lawfully marketed in another Member State, even where those products were manufactured in accordance with technical rules different from those to which domestic products are subject. The only exceptions to that principle are restrictions which are justified on the grounds set out in Article 30 of the Treaty, or on the basis of other overriding reasons of public interest and which are proportionate to the aim pursued.

(4) Many problems still exist regarding the correct application of the principle of mutual recognition by the Member States. It is therefore necessary to establish procedures to minimise the possibility of technical rules creating unlawful obstacles to the free movement of goods between Member States. The absence of such procedures in the Member States creates additional obstacles to the free movement of goods, since it discourages enterprises from selling their products, lawfully marketed in another Member State, on the territory of the Member State applying technical rules. Surveys have shown that many enterprises, in particular small and medium-sized enterprises (SMEs), either adapt their products in order to comply with the technical rules of Member States, or refrain from marketing them in those Member States.

(5) Competent authorities also lack appropriate procedures for the application of their technical rules to specific products lawfully marketed in another Member State. The lack of such procedures compromises their ability to assess the conformity of products in accordance with the Treaty.

(6) The Council Resolution of 28 October 1999 on mutual recognition[3] noted that economic operators and citizens did not always make full and proper use of the principle of mutual recognition because they were not sufficiently aware of the principle and its operational consequences. It called upon the Member States to develop appropriate measures in order to provide economic operators and citizens with an effective framework for mutual recognition, inter alia, by dealing effectively with requests from economic operators and citizens and by replying rapidly to those requests.

(7) The European Council of 8 and 9 March 2007 underlined the importance of giving fresh impetus to the internal market in goods by strengthening mutual recognition, while guaranteeing a high level of safety and consumer protection. The European Council of 21 and 22 June 2007 stressed that the further strengthening of the four freedoms of the internal market (the free movement of goods, persons, services and capital) and improving its functioning remain of paramount importance for growth, competitiveness and employment.

(8) The smooth functioning of the internal market in goods requires adequate and transparent means of solving the problems that result from applying technical rules of a Member State to specific products lawfully marketed in another Member State.

(9) This Regulation should not prejudice further harmonisation of technical rules, where appropriate, with a view to improving the functioning of the internal market.

(10) Trade barriers may also result from other types of measures falling within the scope of Articles 28 and 30 of the Treaty. Those measures may, for example, include technical specifications drawn up for public procurement procedures or obligations to use official languages in the Member States. However, such measures should not constitute technical rules within the meaning of this Regulation and should not therefore fall within its scope.

(11) Technical rules within the meaning of this Regulation are sometimes applied during and by means of mandatory prior authorisation procedures, established by the law of a Member State and in accordance with which, before a product or type of product may be placed on that Member State's market or on a part thereof, the competent authority of that Member State should give its formal approval following an application. The existence of such procedures in itself restricts the free movement

[3] OJ C 141, 19.5.2000, p. 5.

of goods. Therefore, in order to be justified with regard to the fundamental principle of the free movement of goods within the internal market, a mandatory prior authorisation procedure should pursue a public-interest objective recognised by Community law, and should be non-discriminatory and proportionate; that is to say, it should be appropriate to ensure achievement of the aim pursued but not go beyond what is necessary in order to achieve that aim. The compliance of such a procedure with the principle of proportionality should be assessed in the light of the considerations set out in the case-law of the Court of Justice.

(12) A requirement that the placing of a product on the market be subject to prior authorisation should, as such, not constitute a technical rule within the meaning of this Regulation, so that a decision to exclude or remove a product from the market exclusively on the grounds that it does not have valid prior authorisation should not constitute a decision to which this Regulation applies. When, however, an application for such mandatory prior authorisation of a product is made, any intended decision to reject the application on the basis of a technical rule should be taken in accordance with this Regulation, so that the applicant could benefit from the procedural protection which this Regulation provides.

(13) Decisions of national courts or tribunals assessing the legality of cases in which, on account of the application of a technical rule, products lawfully marketed in one Member State are not granted access to the market of another Member State, or applying penalties, should be excluded from the scope of this Regulation.

(14) Weapons are products that can constitute a serious risk to the health and safety of persons and to the public security of Member States. Several specific types of weapons lawfully marketed in one Member State might, on grounds of the protection of the health and safety of persons and the prevention of crime, be subject to restrictive measures in another Member State. Such measures might consist of specific controls and authorisations before weapons lawfully marketed in one Member State are placed on the market of another Member State. Member States should therefore be permitted to prevent weapons being placed on their markets until their national procedural requirements are fully met.

(15) Directive 2001/95/EC of the European Parliament and of the Council of 3 December 2001 on general product safety[4] specifies that only safe products may be placed on the market and lays down the obligations of producers and distributors with respect to the safety of products. It entitles the authorities to ban any dangerous product with immediate effect or, for the period needed for the various safety evaluations, checks and controls, to ban temporarily a product that could be dangerous. It also entitles the authorities to take the necessary action to apply with due dispatch appropriate measures such as those referred to in Article 8(1)(b) to (f) thereof, in the case of products posing a serious risk. Therefore, measures taken by the competent authorities of the Member States pursuant to national laws adopted in implementation of Article 8(1)(d) to (f) and Article 8(3) of that Directive should be excluded from the scope of this Regulation.

(16) Regulation (EC) No 178/2002 of the European Parliament and of the Council of 28 January 2002 laying down the general principles and requirements of food law, establishing the European Food Safety Authority and laying down procedures in matters of food safety[5] establishes, inter alia, a rapid alert system for the notification of a direct or indirect risk to human health deriving from food or feed. It obliges the Member States to notify the Commission immediately under the rapid alert system of any measure they adopt which is aimed at restricting the placing on the market of, withdrawing from the market or recalling food or feed in order to protect human health, and which requires rapid action. Measures taken by the competent authorities of the Member States pursuant to Article 50(3)(a) and Article 54 of that Regulation should therefore be excluded from the scope of this Regulation.

[4] OJ L 11, 15.1.2002, p. 4.
[5] OJ L 31, 1.2.2002, p. 1. Regulation as last amended by Commission Regulation (EC) No 202/2008 (OJ L 60, 5.3.2008, p. 17).

(17) Regulation (EC) No 882/2004 of the European Parliament and of the Council of 29 April 2004 on official controls performed to ensure the verification of compliance with feed and food law, animal health and animal welfare rules[6] lays down general rules for the performance of official controls to verify compliance with rules intended, in particular, to prevent, eliminate or reduce to acceptable levels risks to humans and animals, either directly or through the environment, guaranteeing fair practices in feed and food trade and protecting consumer interests, including feed and food labelling and other forms of consumer information. It lays down a specific procedure to ensure that economic operators remedy a situation of non-compliance with feed and food law, animal health and animal welfare rules. Measures taken by the competent authorities of the Member States pursuant to Article 54 of that Regulation should therefore be excluded from the scope of this Regulation. However, measures taken or intended to be taken by competent authorities on the basis of national technical rules, insofar as they do not concern the objectives of Regulation (EC) No 882/2004, should be subject to this Regulation.

(18) Directive 2004/49/EC of the European Parliament and of the Council of 29 April 2004 on safety on the Community's railways (Railway Safety Directive)[7] provides for a procedure for authorisation of the placing in service of existing rolling stock, leaving scope for the application of certain national rules. Measures taken by the competent authorities pursuant to Article 14 of that Directive should therefore be excluded from the scope of this Regulation.

(19) Council Directive 96/48/EC of 23 July 1996 on the interoperability of the trans-European high-speed rail system[8] and Directive 2001/16/EC of the European Parliament and of the Council of 19 March 2001 on the interoperability of the trans-European conventional rail system[9] provide for the gradual harmonisation of systems and operations through the progressive adoption of Technical Specifications for Interoperability. Systems and interoperability constituents that fall within the scope of those Directives should therefore be excluded from the scope of this Regulation.

(20) Regulation (EC) No 765/2008 of the European Parliament and of the Council of 9 July 2008 setting out the requirements for accreditation and market surveillance relating to the marketing of products[10] establishes a system of accreditation which ensures the mutual acceptance of the level of competence of conformity-assessment bodies. The competent authorities of the Member States should therefore no longer refuse test reports and certificates issued by an accredited conformity-assessment body on grounds related to the competence of that body. Furthermore, Member States may also accept test reports and certificates issued by other conformity-assessment bodies in accordance with Community law.

(21) Directive 98/34/EC of the European Parliament and of the Council of 22 June 1998 laying down a procedure for the provision of information in the field of technical standards and regulations and of rules on Information Society services[11] obliges Member States to communicate to the Commission and the other Member States any draft technical regulation concerning any product, including agricultural and fish products, and a statement of the grounds which make the enactment of that regulation necessary. It is necessary, however, to ensure that, following the adoption of such a technical regulation, the principle of mutual recognition is correctly applied in individual cases to specific products. This Regulation lays down a procedure for the application of the principle of mutual recognition in individual cases, by means of the obligation on the competent authority to indicate the technical or scientific grounds on which the specific product in its current form cannot be marketed in its Member State, in accordance with Articles 28 and 30 of the Treaty. In the context of this Regulation, evidence should not be understood as meaning legal proof. The authorities of the Member States are not obliged, in the context of this Regulation, to justify the technical rule itself.

[6] OJ L 165, 30.4.2004; corrected version in OJ L 191, 28.5.2004, p. 1. Regulation as amended by Council Regulation (EC) No 1791/2006 (OJ L 363, 20.12.2006, p. 1).
[7] OJ L 164, 30.4.2004, p. 44; corrected version in OJ L 220, 21.6.2004, p. 16.
[8] OJ L 235, 17.9.1996, p. 6. Directive as last amended by Commission Directive 2007/32/EC (OJ L 141, 2.6.2007, p. 63).
[9] OJ L 110, 20.4.2001, p. 1. Directive as last amended by Commission Directive 2007/32/EC.
[10] See page 30 of this Official Journal.
[11] OJ L 204, 21.7.1998, p. 37. Directive as last amended by Council Directive 2006/96/EC (OJ L 363, 20.12.2006, p. 81).

However, they should justify, as laid down in this Regulation, the possible application of the technical rule to a product lawfully marketed in another Member State.

(22) In accordance with the principle of mutual recognition, the procedure laid down in this Regulation should provide for the competent authorities to communicate in each case to the economic operator, on the basis of the relevant technical or scientific elements available, that there are overriding reasons of public interest for imposing national technical rules on the product or type of product in question and that less restrictive measures cannot be used. The written notice should allow the economic operator to comment on all relevant aspects of the intended decision restricting access to the market. Nothing prevents the competent authority from taking action after the deadline for the receipt of those comments in the absence of a reply from the economic operator.

(23) The concept of overriding reasons of public interest to which reference is made in certain provisions of this Regulation is an evolving concept developed by the Court of Justice in its case law in relation to Articles 28 and 30 of the Treaty. This concept covers, inter alia, the effectiveness of fiscal supervision, the fairness of commercial transactions, the protection of consumers, the protection of the environment, the maintenance of press diversity and the risk of seriously undermining the financial balance of the social security system. Such overriding reasons may justify the application of technical rules by the competent authorities. However, no such application should constitute a means of arbitrary discrimination or a disguised restriction of trade between Member States. Furthermore, the principle of proportionality should always be respected, with regard to whether the competent authority has in fact made use of the least restrictive measure.

(24) While applying the procedure laid down in this Regulation, the competent authority of a Member State should not withdraw or restrict the placing on its market of a product or type of product lawfully marketed in another Member State. However, it is appropriate that a competent authority be able to adopt provisional measures where rapid intervention is required to prevent harm to safety and health of users. Such provisional measures may also be adopted by a competent authority to prevent the placing on its market of a product the marketing of which is generally prohibited on grounds of public morality or public security, including the prevention of crime. Therefore, Member States should be allowed, at any stage of the procedure laid down in this Regulation, to suspend temporarily the marketing on their territories of products or types of product under those circumstances.

(25) Any decision to which this Regulation applies should specify the remedies available so that an economic operator can bring proceedings before the competent national court or tribunal.

(26) It is appropriate that the economic operator also be informed of the availability of non-judicial problem-solving mechanisms, such as the SOLVIT system, in order to prevent legal uncertainty and legal costs.

(27) Once a competent authority has taken a decision to exclude a product on the basis of a technical rule in accordance with the procedural requirements of this Regulation, no further action taken in relation to that product which is based on that decision and on the same technical rule should be subject to the requirements of this Regulation.

(28) It is important for the internal market in goods that the accessibility of national technical rules be ensured, so that enterprises, and in particular SMEs, can gather reliable and precise information concerning the law in force.

(29) It is therefore necessary to implement principles of administrative simplification, inter alia, through the establishment of a system of Product Contact Points. This should be designed to ensure that enterprises can gain access to information in a transparent and correct manner, so that the delays, costs and dissuasive effects which result from national technical rules can be prevented.

(30) In order to facilitate the free movement of goods, Product Contact Points should provide, free of charge, information concerning their national technical rules and the application of the principle of mutual recognition with regard to products. Product Contact Points should be adequately equipped and resourced and encouraged also to make the information available through a website and in other Community languages. Product Contact Points could also provide economic operators with additional information or observations during the procedure laid down in this Regulation. For

additional information, Product Contact Points may charge fees that are proportionate to the costs of this information.

(31) Since the creation of Product Contact Points should not interfere with the allocation of functions among competent authorities within the regulatory systems of the Member States, it should be possible for Member States to set up Product Contact Points according to regional or local competences. Member States should be able to entrust the role of Product Contact Points to existing contact points established in accordance with other Community instruments, in order to prevent the unnecessary proliferation of contact points and to simplify administrative procedures. Member States should also be able to entrust the role of Product Contact Points not only to existing services within the public administration, but also to national SOLVIT centres, chambers of commerce, professional organisations and private bodies, in order not to increase administrative costs for enterprises and competent authorities.

(32) Member States and the Commission should be encouraged to work closely together to facilitate the training of staff employed in Product Contact Points.

(33) In view of the development and establishment of a pan-European eGovernment service and the underlying interoperable telematic networks, the possibility of establishing an electronic system for the exchange of information between Product Contact Points should be envisaged, in accordance with Decision 2004/387/EC of the European Parliament and of the Council of 21 April 2004 on the interoperable delivery of pan-European eGovernment services to public administrations, businesses and citizens (IDABC).[12]

(34) Reliable and efficient monitoring and evaluation mechanisms should be established in order to provide information on the application of this Regulation so as to enhance knowledge concerning the functioning of the internal market in goods in sectors not subject to harmonisation and to ensure that the principle of mutual recognition is duly applied by the competent authorities of the Member States. Such mechanisms should not go beyond what is necessary to achieve those objectives.

(35) This Regulation applies only to products, or particular features of products, which are not subject to Community harmonisation measures intended to eliminate obstacles to trade between Member States resulting from the existence of divergent national technical rules. The provisions of such harmonisation measures are often exhaustive, in which case Member States may not prohibit, restrict or impede the placing on the market in their territories of products complying with those measures. Some Community harmonisation measures, however, permit Member States to impose additional technical conditions on the placing of a product on their market. Such additional conditions should be subject to Articles 28 and 30 of the Treaty and to the provisions of this Regulation. It is therefore appropriate, with a view to the efficient application of this Regulation, that the Commission should establish an indicative and non-exhaustive list of products which are not subject to harmonisation at Community level.

(36) The monitoring scheme established by Decision No 3052/95/EC of the European Parliament and of the Council of 13 December 1995 establishing a procedure for the exchange of information on national measures derogating from the principle of the free movement of goods within the Community[13] has proved largely unsuccessful in that its implementation has not provided the Commission with sufficient information to identify sectors where harmonisation might be appropriate. Nor has it brought about a rapid resolution of certain free-movement problems. Decision No 3052/95/EC should therefore be repealed.

(37) It is appropriate to introduce a transitional period for the application of this Regulation, in order to enable the competent authorities to adapt to the requirements laid down herein.

(38) Since the objective of this Regulation, namely the elimination of technical obstacles to the free movement of goods between Member States, cannot be sufficiently achieved by the Member States and can therefore, by reason of its scale and effects, be better achieved at Community level,

[12] OJ L 144, 30.4.2004; corrected version in OJ L 181, 18.5.2004, p. 25.
[13] OJ L 321, 30.12.1995, p. 1.

the Community may adopt measures, in accordance with the principle of subsidiarity as set out in Article 5 of the Treaty. In accordance with the principle of proportionality, as set out in that Article, this Regulation does not go beyond what is necessary in order to achieve that objective.

(39) The measures necessary for the implementation of this Regulation should be adopted in accordance with Council Decision 1999/468/EC of 28 June 1999 laying down the procedures for the exercise of implementing powers conferred on the Commission.[14]

HAVE ADOPTED THIS REGULATION:

Chapter 1 Subject matter and scope

Article 1 Subject matter

1. The aim of this Regulation is to strengthen the functioning of the internal market by improving the free movement of goods.

2. This Regulation lays down the rules and procedures to be followed by the competent authorities of a Member State when taking or intending to take a decision, as referred to in Article 2(1), which would hinder the free movement of a product lawfully marketed in another Member State and subject to Article 28 of the Treaty.

3. It also provides for the establishment of Product Contact Points in the Member States to contribute to the achievement of the aim of this Regulation, as set out in paragraph 1.

Article 2 Scope

1. This Regulation shall apply to administrative decisions addressed to economic operators, whether taken or intended, on the basis of a technical rule as defined in paragraph 2, in respect of any product, including agricultural and fish products, lawfully marketed in another Member State, where the direct or indirect effect of that decision is any of the following:

(a) the prohibition of the placing on the market of that product or type of product;

(b) the modification or additional testing of that product or type of product before it can be placed or kept on the market;

(c) the withdrawal of that product or type of product from the market.

For the purposes of point (b) of the first subparagraph, modification of the product or type of product shall mean any modification of one or more of the characteristics of a product or a type of product as listed in point (b)(i) of paragraph 2.

2. For the purposes of this Regulation, a technical rule is any provision of a law, regulation or other administrative provision of a Member State:

(a) which is not the subject of harmonisation at Community level; and

(b) which prohibits the marketing of a product or type of product in the territory of that Member State or compliance with which is compulsory when a product or type of product is marketed in the territory of that Member State, and which lays down either:

(i) the characteristics required of that product or type of product, such as levels of quality, performance or safety, or dimensions, including the requirements applicable to the product or product type as regards the name under which it is sold, terminology, symbols, testing and test methods, packaging, marking or labelling; or

(ii) any other requirement which is imposed on the product or type of product for the purposes of protecting consumers or the environment, and which affects the life-cycle of the product after it has been placed on the market, such as conditions of use, recycling, reuse or disposal, where such conditions can significantly influence the composition, nature or marketing of the product or type of product.

[14] OJ L 184, 17.7.1999, p. 23. Decision as amended by Decision 2006/512/EC (OJ L 200, 22.7.2006, p. 11).

3. This Regulation shall not apply to:
   (a) decisions of a judicial nature taken by national courts or tribunals;
   (b) decisions of a judicial nature taken by law enforcement authorities in the course of the investigation or prosecution of a criminal offence as regards the terminology, symbols or any material reference to unconstitutional or criminal organisations or offences of a racist or xenophobic nature.

Article 3 Relationship with other provisions of Community law

1. This Regulation shall not apply to systems or interoperability constituents falling within the scope of Directives 96/48/EC and 2001/16/EC.

2. This Regulation shall not apply in the case of measures taken by the authorities of the Member States pursuant to:
   (a) Article 8(1)(d) to (f) and Article 8(3) of Directive 2001/95/EC;
   (b) Article 50(3)(a) and Article 54 of Regulation (EC) No 178/2002;
   (c) Article 54 of Regulation (EC) No 882/2004;
   (d) Article 14 of Directive 2004/49/EC.

Chapter 2 Procedure for the application of a technical rule

Article 4 Information on the product

Where a competent authority submits a product or type of product to an evaluation to determine whether or not to adopt a decision as referred to in Article 2(1), it may request from the economic operator identified in accordance with Article 8, with due regard to the principle of proportionality, any of the following in particular:
   (a) relevant information concerning the characteristics of the product or type of product in question;
   (b) relevant and readily available information on the lawful marketing of the product in another Member State.

Article 5 Mutual recognition of the level of competence of accredited conformity-assessment bodies

Member States shall not refuse certificates or test reports issued by a conformity-assessment body accredited for the appropriate field of conformity-assessment activity in accordance with Regulation (EC) No 765/2008 on grounds related to the competence of that body.

Article 6 Assessment of the need to apply a technical rule

1. Where a competent authority intends to adopt a decision as referred to in Article 2(1), it shall send the economic operator identified in accordance with Article 8 written notice of that intention, specifying the technical rule on which the decision is to be based and setting out technical or scientific evidence to the effect that:
   (a) the intended decision is justified on one of the grounds of public interest set out in Article 30 of the Treaty or by reference to other overriding reasons of public interest; and
   (b) the intended decision is appropriate for the purpose of achieving the objective pursued and does not go beyond what is necessary in order to attain that objective.

Any intended decision shall be based on the characteristics of the product or type of product in question.

The economic operator concerned shall, following receipt of such notice, be allowed at least 20 working days in which to submit comments. The notice shall specify the time limit within which comments may be submitted.

2. Any decision as referred to in Article 2(1) shall be taken and notified to the economic operator concerned and to the Commission within a period of 20 working days from the expiry of the time limit for the receipt of comments from the economic operator referred to in paragraph 1 of this Article. It shall take due account of those comments and shall state the grounds on which it is based, including the reasons for rejecting the arguments, if any, put forward by the operator, and the technical or scientific evidence as referred to in paragraph 1 of this Article.

Where duly justified by the complexity of the issue, the competent authority may, once only, extend the period specified in the first subparagraph by a maximum of 20 working days. That extension shall be duly reasoned and shall be notified to the economic operator before the expiry of the initial period.

Any decision as referred to in Article 2(1) shall also specify the remedies available under the law in force in the Member State concerned and the time limits applying to such remedies. Such a decision may be challenged before national courts or tribunals or other instances of appeal.

3. Where, after giving written notice in accordance with paragraph 1, the competent authority decides not to adopt a decision as referred to in Article 2(1), it shall immediately inform the economic operator concerned accordingly.

4. When the competent authority fails to notify the economic operator of a decision as referred to in Article 2(1) within the period specified in paragraph 2 of this Article, the product shall be deemed to be lawfully marketed in that Member State insofar as the application of its technical rule as referred to in paragraph 1 of this Article is concerned.

Article 7 Temporary suspension of the marketing of a product

1. The competent authority shall not temporarily suspend the marketing of the product or type of product in question, during the procedure laid down in this Chapter, except where either:

(a) under normal or reasonably foreseeable conditions of use, the product or type of product in question poses a serious risk to the safety and health of the users; or

(b) the marketing of the product or type of product in question is generally prohibited in a Member State on grounds of public morality or public security.

2. The competent authority shall immediately notify the economic operator identified in accordance with Article 8 and the Commission of any suspension as referred to in paragraph 1 of this Article. In the cases referred to in paragraph 1(a) of this Article, that notification shall be accompanied by a technical or scientific justification.

3. Any suspension of the marketing of a product pursuant to this Article may be challenged before national courts or tribunals or other instances of appeal.

Article 8 Information to the economic operator

References to the economic operators in Articles 4, 6 and 7 shall be considered references:

(a) to the manufacturer of the product, if established in the Community, or the person who has placed the product on the market or requests to the competent authority that the product be placed on the market;

(b) where the competent authority cannot establish the identity and contact details of any of the economic operators referred to in point (a), to the manufacturer's representative, when the manufacturer is not established in the Community or, if there is no representative established in the Community, to the importer of the product;

(c) where the competent authority cannot establish the identity and contact details of any of the economic operators referred to in points (a) and (b), to any professional in the supply chain whose activity may affect any property of the product regulated by the technical rule which is being applied to it;

(d) where the competent authority cannot establish the identity and contact details of any of the economic operators referred to in points (a), (b) and (c), to any professional in the supply chain whose activity does not affect any property of the product regulated by the technical rule which is being applied to it.

Chapter 3 Product Contact Points

Article 9 Establishment of Product Contact Points

1. Member States shall designate Product Contact Points in their territories and shall communicate their contact details to the other Member States and to the Commission.

2. The Commission shall draw up and regularly update a list of Product Contact Points and publish it in the Official Journal of the European Union. The Commission shall also make that information available through a website.

Article 10 Tasks

1. Product Contact Points shall, at the request of, inter alia, an economic operator or a competent authority of another Member State, provide the following information:

(a) the technical rules applicable to a specific type of product in the territory in which those Product Contact Points are established and information as to whether that type of product is subject to a requirement for prior authorisation under the laws of their Member State, together with information concerning the principle of mutual recognition and the application of this Regulation in the territory of that Member State;

(b) the contact details of the competent authorities within that Member State by means of which they may be contacted directly, including the particulars of the authorities responsible for supervising the implementation of the technical rules in question in the territory of that Member State;

(c) the remedies generally available in the territory of that Member State in the event of a dispute between the competent authorities and an economic operator.

2. Product Contact Points shall respond within 15 working days of receiving any request as referred to in paragraph 1.

3. Product Contact Points in the Member State in which the economic operator concerned has lawfully marketed the product in question may provide the economic operator or the competent authority as referred to in Article 6 with any relevant information or observations.

4. Product Contact Points shall not charge any fee for the provision of the information referred to in paragraph 1.

Article 11 Telematic network

The Commission may, in accordance with the advisory procedure referred to in Article 13(2), establish a telematic network for the implementation of the provisions of this Regulation concerning the exchange of information between Product Contact Points and/or the competent authorities of the Member States.

Chapter 4 Final provisions

Article 12 Reporting obligations

1. Each Member State shall send the Commission on a yearly basis a report on the application of this Regulation. That report shall include the following information at least:

(a) the number of written notices sent pursuant to Article 6(1) and the type of products concerned;

(b) sufficient information concerning any decisions taken pursuant to Article 6(2), including the grounds on which those decisions were based and the type of products concerned;

(c) the number of decisions taken pursuant to Article 6(3) and the type of products concerned.

2. In the light of the information provided by Member States pursuant to paragraph 1, the Commission shall analyse the decisions taken pursuant to Article 6(2) and assess the grounds on which they were based.

3. By 13 May 2012, and every five years thereafter, the Commission shall review the application of this Regulation and shall submit a report thereon to the European Parliament and to the Council. The Commission may, where appropriate, accompany the report with proposals with a view to improving the free movement of goods.

4. The Commission shall draw up, publish and regularly update a non-exhaustive list of products which are not subject to Community harmonisation legislation. It shall make that list accessible through a website.

Article 13 Committee procedure

1. The Commission shall be assisted by a committee composed of representatives of the Member States and chaired by a representative of the Commission.

2. Where reference is made to this paragraph, the advisory procedure laid down in Article 3 of Decision 1999/468/EC shall apply, in accordance with Article 7(3) and Article 8 thereof.

Article 14 Repeal

Decision No 3052/95/EC is hereby repealed with effect from 13 May 2009.

Article 15 Entry into force and application

This Regulation shall enter into force on the 20th day following its publication in the *Official Journal of the European Union*.

It shall apply from 13 May 2009.

This Regulation shall be binding in its entirety and directly applicable in all Member States.

Done at Strasbourg, 9 July 2008.
For the European Parliament The President H.-G. PÖTTERING
For the Council The President J.-P. JOUYET

Free movement of persons

Council Directive of 22 March 1977 to facilitate the effective exercise by lawyers of freedom to provide services (77/249/EEC)*

[OJ 1977 L78/17]

THE COUNCIL OF THE EUROPEAN COMMUNITIES,

Having regard to the Treaty establishing the European Economic Community, and in particular Articles 57 and 66 thereof,

Having regard to the proposal from the Commission,

Having regard to the opinion of the European Parliament,[1]

* **Editor's Note**: As amended up to and including OJ 2006 L363/141.

[1] OJ No C 103, 5. 10. 1972, p. 19 and OJ No C 53, 8. 3. 1976, p. 33.

Having regard to the opinion of the Economic and Social Committee,[2]

Whereas, pursuant to the Treaty, any restriction on the provision of services which is based on nationality or on conditions of residence has been prohibited since the end of the transitional period;

Whereas this Directive deals only with measures to facilitate the effective pursuit of the activities of lawyers by way of provision of services;

Whereas more detailed measures will be necessary to facilitate the effective exercise of the right of establishment;

Whereas if lawyers are to exercise effectively the freedom to provide services host Member States must recognize as lawyers those persons practising the profession in the various Member States;

Whereas, since this Directive solely concerns provision of services and does not contain provisions on the mutual recognition of diplomas, a person to whom the Directive applies must adopt the professional title used in the Member State in which he is established, hereinafter referred to as 'the Member State from which he comes',

HAS ADOPTED THIS DIRECTIVE:

Article 1

1. This Directive shall apply, within the limits and under the conditions laid down herein, to the activities of lawyers pursued by way of provision of services.

Notwithstanding anything contained in this Directive, Member States may reserve to prescribed categories of lawyers the preparation of formal documents for obtaining title to administer estates of deceased persons, and the drafting of formal documents creating or transferring interests in land.

2. 'Lawyers' means any person entitled to pursue his professional activities under one of the following designations:**

Belgium:	Avocat/Advocaat
Bulgaria:	Апвокат
Czech Republic:	Advokáat
Denmark:	Advokat
Germany:	Rechtsanwalt
Estonia:	Vandeadvokaat
Greece:	Dikigoros
France:	Avocat
Ireland:	Barrister
	Solicitor
Italy:	Avvocato
Cyprus:	Δικηγορος
Latvia:	Zvēerinā/Advokats
Lithuania:	Advokāts
Luxembourg:	Avocat-avoue
Hungary:	Ügyvéd
Malta:	Avukat/Prokuratur Legali
Netherlands:	Advocaat
Austria:	Rechtsanwalt
Poland:	Adwokat/Radca prawny
Portugal:	Advogado

[2] OJ No C 36, 28. 3. 1970, p. 37 and OJ No C .SO, 4. 3. 1976, p. 17.

** **Editor's Note**: As amended by the Accession Acts.

Romania:	Avocat
Slovenia:	Odvetnik/Odvetnica
Slovakia	Advokát/Komerčný právnik
Finland:	Asianajaja—Advokat
Spain:	Abogado
Sweden:	Advokat
United Kingdom:	Advocate Barrister Solicitor

Article 2

Each Member State shall recognise as a lawyer for the purpose of pursuing the activities specified in Article 1(1) any person listed in paragraph 2 of that Article.

Article 3

A person referred to in Article 1 shall adopt the professional title used in the Member State from which he comes, expressed in the language or one of the languages, of that State, with an indication of the professional organisation by which he is authorised to practise or the court of law before which he is entitled to practise pursuant to the laws of that State.

Article 4

1. Activities relating to the representation of a client in legal proceedings or before public authorities shall be pursued in each host Member State under the conditions laid down for lawyers established in that State, with the exception of any conditions requiring residence, or registration with a professional organisation, in that State.

2. A lawyer pursuing these activities shall observe the rules of professional conduct of the host Member State, without prejudice to his obligations in the Member State from which he comes.

3. When these activities are pursued in the United Kingdom, 'rules of professional conduct of the host Member State' means the rules of professional conduct applicable to solicitors, where such activities are not reserved for barristers and advocates. Otherwise the rules of professional conduct applicable to the latter shall apply. However, barristers from Ireland shall always be subject to the rules of professional conduct applicable in the United Kingdom to barristers and advocates.

When these activities are pursued in Ireland 'rules of professional conduct of the host Member State' means, in so far as they govern the oral presentation of a case in court, the rules of professional conduct applicable to barristers. In all other cases the rules of professional conduct applicable to solicitors shall apply. However, barristers and advocates from the United Kingdom shall always be subject to the rules of professional conduct applicable in Ireland to barristers.

4. A lawyer pursuing activities other than those referred to in paragraph 1 shall remain subject to the conditions and rules of professional conduct of the Member State from which he comes without prejudice to respect for the rules, whatever their source, which govern the profession in the host Member State, especially those concerning the incompatibility of the exercise of the activities of a lawyer with the exercise of other activities in that State, professional secrecy, relation with other lawyers, the prohibition on the same lawyer acting for parties with mutually conflicting interests, and publicity. The latter rules are applicable only if they are capable of being observed by a lawyer who is not established in the host Member State and to the extent to which their observance is objectively justified to ensure, in that State, the proper exercise of a lawyer's activities, the standing of the profession and respect for the rules concerning incompatibility.

Article 5

For the pursuit of activities relating to the representation of a client in legal proceedings, a Member State may require lawyers to whom Article 1 applies:

- to be introduced, in accordance with local rules or customs, to the presiding judge and, where appropriate, to the President of the relevant Bar in the host Member State;

– to work in conjunction with a lawyer who practises before the judicial authority in question and who would, where necessary, be answerable to that authority, or with an 'avoué' or 'procuratore' practising before it.

Article 6

Any Member State may exclude lawyers who are in the salaried employment of a public or private undertaking from pursuing activities relating to the representation of that undertaking in legal proceedings in so far as lawyers established in that State are not permitted to pursue those activities.

Article 7

1. The competent authority of the host Member State may request the person providing the services to establish his qualifications as a lawyer.

2. In the event of non-compliance with the obligations referred to in Article 4 and in force in the host Member State, the competent authority of the latter shall determine in accordance with its own rules and procedures the consequences of such non-compliance, and to this end may obtain an appropriate professional information concerning the person providing services. It shall notify the competent authority of the Member State from which the person comes of any decision taken. Such exchanges shall not affect the confidential nature of the information supplied.

(All remaining provisions omitted.)

Directive 96/71/EC of the European Parliament and of the Council of 16 December 1996 concerning the posting of workers in the framework of the provision of services

[OJ 1997 L18/1]

THE EUROPEAN PARLIAMENT AND THE COUNCIL OF THE EUROPEAN UNION,

Having regard to the Treaty establishing the European Community, and in particular Articles 57 (2) and 66 thereof,

Having regard to the proposal from the Commission[1],

Having regard to the opinion of the Economic and Social Committee[2],

Acting in accordance with the procedure laid down in Article 189b of the Treaty[3],

(1) Whereas, pursuant to Article 3 (c) of the Treaty, the abolition, as between Member States, of obstacles to the free movement of persons and services constitutes one of the objectives of the Community;

(2) Whereas, for the provision of services, any restrictions based on nationality or residence requirements are prohibited under the Treaty with effect from the end of the transitional period;

(3) Whereas the completion of the internal market offers a dynamic environment for the transnational provision of services, prompting a growing number of undertakings to post employees abroad temporarily to perform work in the territory of a Member State other than the State in which they are habitually employed;

(4) Whereas the provision of services may take the form either of performance of work by an undertaking on its account and under its direction, under a contract concluded between that undertaking and the party for whom the services are intended, or of the hiring-out of workers for use by an undertaking in the framework of a public or a private contract;

[1] OJ No C 225, 30. 8. 1991, p. 6 and OJ No C 187, 9. 7. 1993, p. 5.

[2] OJ No C 49, 24. 2. 1992, p. 41.

[3] Opinion of the European Parliament of 10 February 1993 (OJ No C 72, 15. 3. 1993, p. 78), Council common position of 3 June 1996 (OJ No C 220, 29. 7. 1996, p. 1) and Decision of the European Parliament of 18 September 1996 (not yet published in the Official Journal). Council Decision of 24 September 1996.

(5) Whereas any such promotion of the transnational provision of services requires a climate of fair competition and measures guaranteeing respect for the rights of workers;

(6) Whereas the transnationalization of the employment relationship raises problems with regard to the legislation applicable to the employment relationship; whereas it is in the interests of the parties to lay down the terms and conditions governing the employment relationship envisaged;

(7) Whereas the Rome Convention of 19 June 1980 on the law applicable to contractual obligations[4], signed by 12 Member States, entered into force on 1 April 1991 in the majority of Member States;

(8) Whereas Article 3 of that Convention provides, as a general rule, for the free choice of law made by the parties; whereas, in the absence of choice, the contract is to be governed, according to Article 6 (2), by the law of the country, in which the employee habitually carries out his work in performance of the contract, even if he is temporarily employed in another country, or, if the employee does not habitually carry out his work in any one country, by the law of the country in which the place of business through which he was engaged is situated, unless it appears from the circumstances as a whole that the contract is more closely connected with another country, in which case the contract is to be governed by the law of that country;

(9) Whereas, according to Article 6 (1) of the said Convention, the choice of law made by the parties is not to have the result of depriving the employee of the protection afforded to him by the mandatory rules of the law which would be applicable under paragraph 2 of that Article in the absence of choice;

(10) Whereas Article 7 of the said Convention lays down, subject to certain conditions, that effect may be given, concurrently with the law declared applicable, to the mandatory rules of the law of another country, in particular the law of the Member State within whose territory the worker is temporarily posted;

(11) Whereas, according to the principle of precedence of Community law laid down in its Article 20, the said Convention does not affect the application of provisions which, in relation to a particular matter, lay down choice-of-law rules relating to contractual obligations and which are or will be contained in acts of the institutions of the European Communities or in national laws harmonized in implementation of such acts;

(12) Whereas Community law does not preclude Member States from applying their legislation, or collective agreements entered into by employers and labour, to any person who is employed, even temporarily, within their territory, although his employer is established in another Member State; whereas Community law does not forbid Member States to guarantee the observance of those rules by the appropriate means;

(13) Whereas the laws of the Member States must be coordinated in order to lay down a nucleus of mandatory rules for minimum protection to be observed in the host country by employers who post workers to perform temporary work in the territory of a Member State where the services are provided; whereas such coordination can be achieved only by means of Community law;

(14) Whereas a 'hard core' of clearly defined protective rules should be observed by the provider of the services notwithstanding the duration of the worker's posting;

(15) Whereas it should be laid down that, in certain clearly defined cases of assembly and/or installation of goods, the provisions on minimum rates of pay and minimum paid annual holidays do not apply;

(16) Whereas there should also be some flexibility in application of the provisions concerning minimum rates of pay and the minimum length of paid annual holidays; whereas, when the length of the posting is not more than one month, Member States may, under certain conditions, derogate from the provisions concerning minimum rates of pay or provide for the possibility of derogation by means of collective agreements; whereas, where the amount of work to be done is not significant, Member

[4] OJ No L 266, 9. 10. 1980, p. 1.

States may derogate from the provisions concerning minimum rates of pay and the minimum length of paid annual holidays;

(17) Whereas the mandatory rules for minimum protection in force in the host country must not prevent the application of terms and conditions of employment which are more favourable to workers;

(18) Whereas the principle that undertakings established outside the Community must not receive more favourable treatment than undertakings established in the territory of a Member State should be upheld;

(19) Whereas, without prejudice to other provisions of Community law, this Directive does not entail the obligation to give legal recognition to the existence of temporary employment undertakings, nor does it prejudice the application by Member States of their laws concerning the hiring-out of workers and temporary employment undertakings to undertakings not established in their territory but operating therein in the framework of the provision of services;

(20) Whereas this Directive does not affect either the agreements concluded by the Community with third countries or the laws of Member States concerning the access to their territory of third-country providers of services; whereas this Directive is also without prejudice to national laws relating to the entry, residence and access to employment of third-country workers;

(21) Whereas Council Regulation (EEC) No 1408/71 of 14 June 1971 on the application of social security schemes to employed persons and their families moving within the Community[5] lays down the provisions applicable with regard to social security benefits and contributions;

(22) Whereas this Directive is without prejudice to the law of the Member States concerning collective action to defend the interests of trades and professions;

(23) Whereas competent bodies in different Member States must cooperate with each other in the application of this Directive;

whereas Member States must provide for appropriate remedies in the event of failure to comply with this Directive;

(24) Whereas it is necessary to guarantee proper application of this Directive and to that end to make provision for close collaboration between the Commission and the Member States;

(25) Whereas five years after adoption of this Directive at the latest the Commission must review the detailed rules for implementing this Directive with a view to proposing, where appropriate, the necessary amendments,

HAVE ADOPTED THIS DIRECTIVE:

Article 1 Scope

1. This Directive shall apply to undertakings established in a Member State which, in the framework of the transnational provision of services, post workers, in accordance with paragraph 3, to the territory of a Member State.

2. This Directive shall not apply to merchant navy undertakings as regards seagoing personnel.

3. This Directive shall apply to the extent that the undertakings referred to in paragraph 1 take one of the following transnational measures:

(a) post workers to the territory of a Member State on their account and under their direction, under a contract concluded between the undertaking making the posting and the party for whom the services are intended, operating in that Member State, provided there is an employment relationship between the undertaking making the36961 posting and the worker during the period of posting; or

(b) post workers to an establishment or to an undertaking owned by the group in the territory of a Member State, provided there is an employment relationship between the undertaking making the posting and the worker during the period of posting; or

[5] OJ No L 149, 5. 7. 1971, p. 2; Special Edition 1971 (II), p. 416. Regulation as last amended by Regulation (EC) No 3096/95 (OJ No L 335, 30. 12. 1995, p. 10).

(c) being a temporary employment undertaking or placement agency, hire out a worker to a user undertaking established or operating in the territory of a Member State, provided there is an employment relationship between the temporary employment undertaking or placement agency and the worker during the period of posting.

4. Undertakings established in a non-member State must not be given more favourable treatment than undertakings established in a Member State.

Article 2 Definition

1. For the purposes of this Directive, 'posted worker' means a worker who, for a limited period, carries out his work in the territory of a Member State other than the State in which he normally works.

2. For the purposes of this Directive, the definition of a worker is that which applies in the law of the Member State to whose territory the worker is posted.

Article 3 Terms and conditions of employment

1. Member States shall ensure that, whatever the law applicable to the employment relationship, the undertakings referred to in Article 1 (1) guarantee workers posted to their territory the terms and conditions of employment covering the following matters which, in the Member State where the work is carried out, are laid down:

- by law, regulation or administrative provision, and/or
- by collective agreements or arbitration awards which have been declared universally applicable within the meaning of paragraph 8, insofar as they concern the activities referred to in the Annex:

(a) maximum work periods and minimum rest periods;
(b) minimum paid annual holidays;
(c) the minimum rates of pay, including overtime rates; this point does not apply to supplementary occupational retirement pension schemes;
(d) the conditions of hiring-out of workers, in particular the supply of workers by temporary employment undertakings;
(e) health, safety and hygiene at work;
(f) protective measures with regard to the terms and conditions of employment of pregnant women or women who have recently given birth, of children and of young people;
(g) equality of treatment between men and women and other provisions on non-discrimination.

For the purposes of this Directive, the concept of minimum rates of pay referred to in paragraph 1 (c) is defined by the national law and/or practice of the Member State to whose territory the worker is posted.

2. In the case of initial assembly and/or first installation of goods where this is an integral part of a contract for the supply of goods and necessary for taking the goods supplied into use and carried out by the skilled and/or specialist workers of the supplying undertaking, the first subparagraph of paragraph 1 (b) and (c) shall not apply, if the period of posting does not exceed eight days.

This provision shall not apply to activities in the field of building work listed in the Annex.

3. Member States may, after consulting employers and labour, in accordance with the traditions and practices of each Member State, decide not to apply the first subparagraph of paragraph 1 (c) in the cases referred to in Article 1 (3) (a) and (b) when the length of the posting does not exceed one month.

4. Member States may, in accordance with national laws and/or practices, provide that exemptions may be made from the first subparagraph of paragraph 1 (c) in the cases referred to in Article 1 (3) (a) and (b) and from a decision by a Member State within the meaning of paragraph 3 of this Article, by

means of collective agreements within the meaning of paragraph 8 of this Article, concerning one or more sectors of activity, where the length of the posting does not exceed one month.

5. Member States may provide for exemptions to be granted from the first subparagraph of paragraph 1 (b) and (c) in the cases referred to in Article 1 (3) (a) and (b) on the grounds that the amount of work to be done is not significant.

Member States availing themselves of the option referred to in the first subparagraph shall lay down the criteria which the work to be performed must meet in order to be considered as 'non-significant'.

6. The length of the posting shall be calculated on the basis of a reference period of one year from the beginning of the posting.

For the purpose of such calculations, account shall be taken of any previous periods for which the post has been filled by a posted worker.

7. Paragraphs 1 to 6 shall not prevent application of terms and conditions of employment which are more favourable to workers.

Allowances specific to the posting shall be considered to be part of the minimum wage, unless they are paid in reimbursement of expenditure actually incurred on account of the posting, such as expenditure on travel, board and lodging.

8. 'Collective agreements or arbitration awards which have been declared universally applicable' means collective agreements or arbitration awards which must be observed by all undertakings in the geographical area and in the profession or industry concerned.

In the absence of a system for declaring collective agreements or arbitration awards to be of universal application within the meaning of the first subparagraph, Member States may, if they so decide, base themselves on:

- collective agreements or arbitration awards which are generally applicable to all similar undertakings in the geographical area and in the profession or industry concerned, and/or
- collective agreements which have been concluded by the most representative employers and labour organizations at national level and which are applied throughout national territory,

provided that their application to the undertakings referred to in Article 1 (1) ensures equality of treatment on matters listed in the first subparagraph of paragraph 1 of this Article between those undertakings and the other undertakings referred to in this subparagraph which are in a similar position.

Equality of treatment, within the meaning of this Article, shall be deemed to exist where national undertakings in a similar position:

- are subject, in the place in question or in the sector concerned, to the same obligations as posting undertakings as regards the matters listed in the first subparagraph of paragraph 1, and
- are required to fulfil such obligations with the same effects.

9. Member States may provide that the undertakings referred to in Article 1 (1) must guarantee workers referred to in Article 1 (3) (c) the terms and conditions which apply to temporary workers in the Member State where the work is carried out.

10. This Directive shall not preclude the application by Member States, in compliance with the Treaty, to national undertakings and to the undertakings of other States, on a basis of equality of treatment, of:

- terms and conditions of employment on matters other than those referred to in the first subparagraph of paragraph 1 in the case of public policy provisions,
- terms and conditions of employment laid down in the collective agreements or arbitration awards within the meaning of paragraph 8 and concerning activities other than those referred to in the Annex.

Article 4 Cooperation on information

1. For the purposes of implementing this Directive, Member States shall, in accordance with national legislation and/or practice, designate one or more liaison offices or one or more competent national bodies.

2. Member States shall make provision for cooperation between the public authorities which, in accordance with national legislation, are responsible for monitoring the terms and conditions of employment referred to in Article 3. Such cooperation shall in particular consist in replying to reasoned requests from those authorities for information on the transnational hiring-out of workers, including manifest abuses or possible cases of unlawful transnational activities.

The Commission and the public authorities referred to in the first subparagraph shall cooperate closely in order to examine any difficulties which might arise in the application of Article 3 (10).

Mutual administrative assistance shall be provided free of charge.

3. Each Member State shall take the appropriate measures to make the information on the terms and conditions of employment referred to in Article 3 generally available.

4. Each Member State shall notify the other Member States and the Commission of the liaison offices and/or competent bodies referred to in paragraph 1.

Article 5 Measures

Member States shall take appropriate measures in the event of failure to comply with this Directive.

They shall in particular ensure that adequate procedures are available to workers and/or their representatives for the enforcement of obligations under this Directive.

Article 6 Jurisdiction

In order to enforce the right to the terms and conditions of employment guaranteed in Article 3, judicial proceedings may be instituted in the Member State in whose territory the worker is or was posted, without prejudice, where applicable, to the right, under existing international conventions on jurisdiction, to institute proceedings in another State.

Article 7 Implementation

Member States shall adopt the laws, regulations and administrative provisions necessary to comply with this Directive by 16 December 1999 at the latest. They shall forthwith inform the Commission thereof.

When Member States adopt these provisions, they shall contain a reference to this Directive or shall be accompanied by such reference on the occasion of their official publication. The methods of making such reference shall be laid down by Member States.

Article 8 Commission review

By 16 December 2001 at the latest, the Commission shall review the operation of this Directive with a view to proposing the necessary amendments to the Council where appropriate.

Article 9

This Directive is addressed to the Member States.

Done at Brussels, 16 December 1996.
For the European Parliament
The President
K. HÄNSCH
For the Council
The President
I. YATES

ANNEX

The activities mentioned in Article 3 (1), second indent, include all building work relating to the construction, repair, upkeep, alteration or demolition of buildings, and in particular the following work:

1. excavation
2. earthmoving
3. actual building work
4. assembly and dismantling of prefabricated elements
5. fitting out or installation
6. alterations
7. renovation
8. repairs
9. dismantling
10. demolition
11. maintenance
12. upkeep, painting and cleaning work
13. improvements.

Directive 98/5/EC of the European Parliament and of the Council of 16 February 1998 to facilitate practice of the profession of lawyer on a permanent basis in a Member State other than that in which the qualification was obtained*

[OJ 1998 L77/36]

THE EUROPEAN PARLIAMENT AND THE COUNCIL OF THE EUROPEAN UNION,

Having regard to the Treaty establishing the European Community, and in particular Article 49, Article 57(1) and the first and third sentences of Article 57(2) thereof,

Having regard to the proposal from the Commission,[1]

Having regard to the Opinion of the Economic and Social Committee,[2]

Acting in accordance with the procedure laid down in Article 189b of the Treaty,[3]

(1) Whereas, pursuant to Article 7a of the Treaty, the internal market is to comprise an area without internal frontiers; whereas, pursuant to Article 3(c) of the Treaty, the abolition, as between Member States, of obstacles to freedom of movement for persons and services constitutes one of the objectives of the Community; whereas, for nationals of the Member States, this means among other things the possibility of practising a profession, whether in a self-employed or a salaried capacity, in a Member State other than that in which they obtained their professional qualifications;

(2) Whereas, pursuant to Council Directive 89/48/EEC of 21 December 1988 on a general system for the recognition of higher-education diplomas awarded on completion of professional

* **Editor's Note**: As amended up to and including OJ 2006 L363/141.

[1] OJ No C128, 24.5.1995, p. 6 and OJ No C355, 25.11.1996, p. 19.

[2] OJ No C256, 2.10.1995, p. 14.

[3] Opinion of the European Parliament of 19 June 1996 (OJ No C198, 8.7.1996, p. 85), Council Common Position of 24 July 1997 (OJ No C297, 29.9.1997, p. 6), Decision of the European Parliament of 19 November 1997 (Council Decision of 15 December 1997).

education and training of at least three years' duration,[4] a lawyer who is fully qualified in one Member State may already ask to have his diploma recognised with a view to establishing himself in another Member State in order to practise the profession of lawyer there under the professional title used in that State; whereas the objective of Directive 89/48/EEC is to ensure that a lawyer is integrated into the profession in the host Member State, and the Directive seeks neither to modify the rules regulating the profession in that State nor to remove such a lawyer from the ambit of those rules;

(3) Whereas while some lawyers may become quickly integrated into the profession in the host Member State, inter alia by passing an aptitude test as provided for in Directive 89/48/EEC, other fully qualified lawyers should be able to achieve such integration after a certain period of professional practice in the host Member State under their home-country professional titles or else continue to practise under their home-country professional titles;

(4) Whereas at the end of that period the lawyer should be able to integrate into the profession in the host Member States after verification that he possesses professional experience in that Member State;

(5) Whereas action along these lines is justified at Community level not only because, compared with the general system for the recognition of diplomas, it provides lawyers with an easier means whereby they can integrate into the profession in a host Member State, but also because, by enabling lawyers to practise under their home-country professional titles on a permanent basis in a host Member State, it meets the needs of consumers of legal services who, owing to the increasing trade flows resulting, in particular, from the internal market, seek advice when carrying out cross-border transactions in which international law, Community law and domestic laws often overlap;

(6) Whereas action is also justified at Community level because only a few Member States already permit in their territory the pursuit of activities of lawyers, otherwise than by way of provision of services, by lawyers from other Member States practising under their home-country professional titles; whereas, however, in the Member States where this possibility exists, the practical details concerning, for example, the area of activity and the obligation to register with the competent authorities differ considerably; whereas such a diversity of situations leads to inequalities and distortions in competition between lawyers from the Member States and constitutes an obstacle to freedom of movement; whereas only a directive laying down the conditions governing practice of the profession, otherwise than by way of provision of services, by lawyers practising under their home-country professional titles is capable of resolving these difficulties and of affording the same opportunities to lawyers and consumers of legal services in all Member States;

(7) Whereas, in keeping with its objective, this Directive does not lay down any rules concerning purely domestic situations, and where it does affect national rules regulating the legal profession it does so no more than is necessary to achieve its purpose effectively; whereas it is without prejudice in particular to national legislation governing access to and practice of the profession of lawyer under the professional title used in the host Member States;

(8) Whereas lawyers covered by the Directive should be required to register with the competent authority in the host Member State in order that that authority may ensure that they comply with the rules of professional conduct in force in that state; whereas the effect of such registration as regards the jurisdictions in which, and the levels and types of court before which lawyers may practise is determined by the law applicable to lawyers in the host Member States;

(9) Whereas lawyers who are not integrated into the profession in the host Member State should practise in that State under their home-country professional titles so as to ensure that consumers are properly informed and to distinguish between such lawyers and lawyers from the host Member State practising under the professional title used there;

[4] OJ No L19, 24.1.1989, p. 16.

(10) Whereas lawyers covered by this Directive should be permitted to give legal advice in particular on the law of their home Member States, on Community law, on international law and on the law of the host Member State; whereas this is already allowed as regards the provision of services under Council Directive 77/249/EEC of 22 March 1977 to facilitate the effective exercise by lawyers of freedom to provide services;[5] whereas, however, provision should be made, as in Directive 77/249/EEC, for the option of excluding from the activities of lawyers practising under their home-country professional titles in the United Kingdom and Ireland the preparation of certain formal documents in the conveyancing and probate spheres; whereas this Directive in no way affects the provisions under which, in every Member State, certain activities are reserved for professions other than the legal profession; whereas the provision in Directive 77/249/EEC concerning the possibility of the host Member State to require a lawyer practising under his home-country professional title to work in conjunction with a local lawyer when representing or defending a client in legal proceedings should also be incorporated in this Directive; whereas the requirement must be interpreted in the light of the case law of the Court of Justice of the European Communities, in particular its judgment of 25 February 1988 in Case 427/85, Commission v. Germany;[6]

(11) Whereas to ensure the smooth operation of the justice system Member States should be allowed, by means of specific rules, to reserve access to their highest courts to specialist lawyers, without hindering the integration of Member States' lawyers fulfilling the necessary requirements;

(12) Whereas a lawyer registered under his home-country professional title in the host Member State must remain registered with the competent authority in his home Member State if he is to retain his status of lawyer and be covered by this Directive; whereas for that reason close collaboration between the competent authorities is indispensable, in particular in connection with any disciplinary proceedings;

(13) Whereas lawyers covered by this Directive, whether salaried or self-employed in their home Member States, may practise as salaried lawyers in the host Member State, where that Member State offers that possibility to its own lawyers;

(14) Whereas the purpose pursued by this Directive in enabling lawyers to practise in another Member State under their home-country professional titles is also to make it easier for them to obtain the professional title of that host Member State; whereas under Articles 48 and 52 of the Treaty as interpreted by the Court of Justice the host Member State must take into consideration any professional experience gained in its territory; whereas after effectively and regularly pursuing in the host Member State an activity in the law of that State including Community law for a period of three years, a lawyer may reasonably be assumed to have gained the aptitude necessary to become fully integrated into the legal profession there; whereas at the end of that period the lawyer who can, subject to verification, furnish evidence of his professional competence in the host Member State should be able to obtain the professional title of that Member State; whereas if the period of effective and regular professional activity of at least three years includes a shorter period of practice in the law of the host Member State, the authority shall also take into consideration any other knowledge of that State's law, which it may verify during an interview; whereas if evidence of fulfilment of these conditions is not provided, the decision taken by the competent authority of the host State not to grant the State's professional title under the facilitation arrangements linked to those conditions must be substantiated and subject to appeal under national law;

(15) Whereas, for economic and professional reasons, the growing tendency for lawyers in the Community to practise jointly, including in the form of associations, has become a reality; whereas the fact that lawyers belong to a grouping in their home Member State should not be used as a pretext to prevent or deter them from establishing themselves in the host Member States; whereas Member States should be allowed, however, to take appropriate measures with the legitimate aim of safeguarding the profession's independence; whereas certain guarantees should be provided in those Member States which permit joint practice,

[5] OJ No L78, 26.3.1977, p. 17. Directive as last amended by the 1994 Act of Accession.

[6] [1988] ECR 1123.

Have adopted this Directive:

Article 1 Object, scope and definitions

1. The purpose of this Directive is to facilitate practice of the profession of lawyer on a permanent basis in a self-employed or salaried capacity in a Member State other than that in which the professional qualification was obtained.

2. For the purposes of this Directive:

(a) 'lawyer' means any person who is a national of a Member State and who is authorised to pursue his professional activities under one of the following professional titles:

Belgium:	Avocat/Advocaat
Bulgaria:	Адвокат
Czech Republic:	Advokát
Denmark:	Advokat
Germany:	Rechtsanwalt
Estonia:	Vandeadvokaat
Greece:	Dikigoros
France:	Avocat
Ireland:	Barrister Solicitor
Italy:	Avvocato
Cyprus:	Δικηγορος
Latvia:	Zvērinats/Advokaāts
Lithuania:	Advokatas
Luxembourg:	Avocat-avoue
Hungary:	Ügyvéd
Malta:	Avukat/Prokuratur Legali
Netherlands:	Advocaat
Austria:	Rechtsanwalt
Poland:	Adwokat/Radca prawny
Portugal:	Advogado
Romania:	Avocat
Slovenia:	Odvetnik/Odvetnica
Slovakia:	Advokát/Komerčný právnik
Finland:	Asianajaja—Advokat
Spain:	Abogado
Sweden:	Advokat
United Kingdom:	Advocate Barrister Solicitor.

(b) 'home Member State' means the Member State in which a lawyer acquired the right to use one of the professional titles referred to in (a) before practising the profession of lawyer in another Member State;

(c) 'host Member State' means the Member State in which a lawyer practises pursuant to this Directive;

(d) 'home-country professional title' means the professional title used in the Member State in which a lawyer acquired the right to use that title before practising the profession of lawyer in the host Member State;

(e) 'grouping' means any entity, with or without legal personality, formed under the law of a Member State, within which lawyers pursue their professional activities jointly under a joint name;

(f) 'relevant professional title' or 'relevant profession' means the professional title or profession governed by the competent authority with whom a lawyer has registered under Article 3, and 'competent authority' means that authority.

3. This Directive shall apply both to lawyers practising in a self-employed capacity and to lawyers practising in a salarial capacity in the home Member State and, subject to Article 8, in the host Member State.

4. Practice of the profession of lawyer within the meaning of this Directive shall not include the provision of services, which is covered by Directive 77/249/EEC.

Article 2 Right to practise under the home-country professional title

Any lawyer shall be entitled to pursue on a permanent basis, in any other Member State under his home-country professional title, the activities specified in Article 5.

Integration into the profession of lawyer in the host Member State shall be subject to Article 10.

Article 3 Registration with the competent authority

1. A lawyer who wishes to practise in a Member State other than that in which he obtained his professional qualification shall register with the competent authority in that State.

2. The competent authority in the host Member State shall register the lawyer upon presentation of a certificate attesting to his registration with the competent authority in the home Member State. It may require that, when presented by the competent authority of the home Member State, the certificate be not more than three months old. It shall inform the competent authority in the home Member State of the registration.

3. For the purpose of applying paragraph 1:

- in the United Kingdom and Ireland, lawyers practising under a professional title other than those used in the United Kingdom or Ireland shall register either with the authority responsible for the profession of barrister or advocate or with the authority responsible for the profession of solicitor,
- in the United Kingdom, the authority responsible for a barrister from Ireland shall be that responsible for the profession of barrister or advocate, and the authority responsible for a solicitor from Ireland shall be that responsible for the profession of solicitor,
- in Ireland, the authority responsible for a barrister or an advocate from the United Kingdom shall be that responsible for the profession of barrister, and the authority responsible for a solicitor from the United Kingdom shall be that responsible for the profession of solicitor.

4. Where the relevant competent authority in a host Member State publishes the names of lawyers registered with it, it shall also publish the names of lawyers registered pursuant to this Directive.

Article 4 Practice under the home-country professional title

1. A lawyer practising in a host Member State under his home-country professional title shall do so under that title, which must be expressed in the official language or one of the official languages of his home Member State, in an intelligible manner and in such a way as to avoid confusion with the professional title of the host Member State.

2. For the purpose of applying paragraph 1, a host Member State may require a lawyer practising under his home-country professional title to indicate the professional body of which he is a member in his home Member State or the judicial authority before which he is entitled to practise pursuant to the laws of his home Member State. A host Member State may also require a lawyer practising under his home-country professional title to include a reference to his registration with the competent authority in that State.

Article 5 Area of activity

1. Subject to paragraphs 2 and 3, a lawyer practising under his home-country professional title carries on the same professional activities as a lawyer practising under the relevant processional title used in the host Member State and may, inter alia, give advice on the law of his home Member State,

on Community law, on international law and on the law of the host Member State. He shall in any event comply with the rules of procedure applicable in the national courts.

2. Member States which authorise in their territory a prescribed category of lawyers to prepare deeds for obtaining title to administer estates of deceased persons and for creating or transferring interests in land which, in other Member States, are reserved for professions other than that of lawyer may exclude from such activities lawyers practising under a home-country professional title conferred in one of the latter Member States.

3. For the pursuit of activities relating to the representation or defence of a client in legal proceedings and insofar as the law of the host Member State reserves such activities to lawyers practising under the professional title of that State, the latter may require lawyers practising under their home-country professional titles to work in conjunction with a lawyer who practises before the judicial authority in question and who would, where necessary, be answerable to that authority or with an 'avoué' practising before it.

Nevertheless, in order to ensure the smooth operation of the justice system, Member States may lay down specific rules for access to supreme courts, such as the use of specialist lawyers.

Article 6 Rules of professional conduct applicable

1. Irrespective of the rules of professional conduct to which he is subject in his home Member State, a lawyer practising under his home-country professional title shall be subject to the same rules of professional conduct as lawyers practising under the relevant professional title of the host Member State in respect of all the activities he pursues in its territory.

2. Lawyers practising under their home-country professional titles shall be granted appropriate representation in the professional associations of the host Member State. Such representation shall involve at least the right to vote in elections to those associations' governing bodies.

3. The host Member State may require a lawyer practising under his home country professional title either to take out professional indemnity insurance or to become a member of a professional guarantee fund in accordance with the rules which that State lays down for professional activities pursued in its territory. Nevertheless, a lawyer practising under his home-country professional title shall be exempted from that requirement if he can prove that he is covered by insurance taken out or a guarantee provided in accordance with the rules of his home Member State, insofar as such insurance or guarantee is equivalent in terms of the conditions and extent of cover. Where the equivalence is only partial, the competent authority in the host Member State may require that additional insurance or an additional guarantee be contacted to cover the elements which are not already covered by the insurance or guarantee contracted in accordance with the rules of the home Member States.

Article 7 Disciplinary proceedings

1. In the event of failure by a lawyer practising under his home-country professional title to fulfil the obligations in force in the host Member State, the rules of procedure, penalties and remedies provided for in the host Member State shall apply.

2. Before initiating disciplinary proceedings against a lawyer practising under his home-country professional title, the competent authority in the host Member State shall inform the competent authority in the home Member State as soon as possible, furnishing it with all the relevant details.

The first subparagraph shall apply mutatis mutandis where disciplinary proceedings are initiated by the competent authority of the home Member State, which shall inform the competent authority of the host Member State(s) accordingly.

3. Without prejudice to the decision-making power of the competent authority in the host Member State, that authority shall cooperate throughout the disciplinary proceedings with the competent authority in the home Member State. In particular, the host Member State shall take the measures necessary to ensure that the competent authority in the home Member State can make submissions to the bodies responsible for hearing any appeal.

4. The competent authority in the home Member State shall decide what action to take, under its own procedural and substantive rules, in the light of a decision of the competent authority in the host Member State concerning a lawyer practising under his home-country professional title.

5. Although it is not a prerequisite for the decision of the competent authority in the host Member State, the temporary or permanent withdrawal by the competent authority in the home Member State of the authorisation to practise the profession shall automatically lead to the lawyer concerned being temporarily or permanently prohibited from practising under his home-country professional title in the host Member State.

Article 8 Salaried practice

A lawyer registered in a host Member State under his home-country professional title may practise as a salaried lawyer in the employ of another lawyer, an association or firm of lawyers, or a public or private enterprise to the extent that the host Member State so permits for lawyers registered under the professional title used in that State.

Article 9 Statement of reasons and remedies

Decisions not to effect the registration referred to in Article 3 or to cancel such registration and decisions imposing disciplinary measures shall state the reasons on which they are based.

A remedy shall be available against such decisions before a court or tribunal in accordance with the provisions of domestic law.

Article 10 Like treatment as a lawyer of the host Member State

1. A lawyer practising under his home-country professional title who has effectively and regularly pursued for a period of at least three years an activity in the host Member State in the law of that State including Community law shall, with a view to gaining admission to the profession of lawyer in the host Member State, be exempted from the conditions set out in Article 4(1)(b) of Directive 89/48/EEC, 'Effective and regular pursuit' means actual exercise of the activity without any interruption other than that resulting from the events of everyday life.

It shall be for the lawyer concerned to furnish the competent authority in the host Member State with proof of such effective regular pursuit for a period of at least three years of an activity in the law of the host Member State. To that end:

(a) the lawyer shall provide the competent authority in the host Member State with any relevant information and documentation, notably on the number of matters he has dealt with and their nature;

(b) the competent authority of the host Member State may verify the effective and regular nature of the activity pursued and may, if need be, request the lawyer to provide, orally or in writing, clarification of or further details on the information and documentation mentioned in point (a).

Reasons shall be given for a decision by the competent authority in the host Member State not to grant an exemption where proof is not provided that the requirements laid down in the first subparagraph have been fulfilled, and the decision shall be subject to appeal under domestic law.

2. A lawyer practising under his home-country professional title in a host Member State may, at any time, apply to have his diploma recognised in accordance with Directive 89/48/ EEC with a view to gaining admission to the profession of lawyer in the host Member State and practising it under the professional title corresponding to the profession in that Member State.

3. A lawyer practising under his home-country professional title who has effectively and regularly pursued a professional activity in the host Member State for a period of at least three years but for a lesser period in the law of that Member State may obtain from the competent authority of that State admission to the profession of lawyer in the host Member State and the right to practise it under the professional title corresponding to the profession in that Member State, without having to meet the conditions referred to in Article 4(1)(b) of Directive 89/48/ EEC, under the conditions and in accordance with the procedures set out below:

(a) The competent authority of the host Member State shall take into account the effective and regular professional activity pursued during the abovementioned period and any knowledge and professional experience of the law of the host Member State, and any attendance at lectures or seminars on the law of the host Member State, including the rules regulating professional practice and conduct.

(b) The lawyer shall provide the competent authority of the host Member State with any relevant information and documentation, in particular on the matters he has dealt with. Assessment of the lawyer's effective and regular activity in the host Member State and assessment of his capacity to continue the activity he has pursued there shall be carried out by means of an interview with the competent authority of the host Member State in order to verify the regular and effective nature of the activity pursued.

Reasons shall be given for a decision by the competent authority in the host Member State not to grant authorisation where proof is not provided that the requirements laid down in the first subparagraph have been fulfilled, and the decision shall be subject to appeal under domestic law.

4. The competent authority of the host Member State may, by reasoned decision subject to appeal under domestic law, refuse to allow the lawyer the benefit of the provisions of this Article if it considers that this would be against public policy, in particular because of disciplinary proceedings, complaints or incidents of any kind.

5. The representatives of the competent authority entrusted with consideration of the application shall preserve the confidentiality of any information received.

6. A lawyer who gains admission to the profession of lawyer in the host Member State in accordance with paragraphs 1, 2 and 3 shall be entitled to use his home-country professional title, expressed in the official language or one of the official languages of his home Member State, alongside the professional title corresponding to the profession of lawyer in the host Member State.

Article 11 Joint practice

Where joint practice is authorised in respect of lawyers carrying on their activities under the relevant professional title in the host Member State, the following provisions shall apply in respect of lawyers wishing to carry on activities under that title or registering with the competent authority:

(1) One or more lawyers who belong to the same grouping in their home Member State and who practise under their home-country professional title in a host Member State may pursue their professional activities in a branch or agency of their grouping in the host Member State. However, where the fundamental rules governing that grouping in the home Member State are incompatible with the fundamental rules laid down by law, regulation or administrative action in the host Member State, the latter rules shall prevail insofar as compliance therewith is justified by the public interest in protecting clients and third parties.

(2) Each Member State shall afford two or more lawyers from the same grouping or the same home Member State who practise in its territory under their home-country professional titles access to a form of joint practice. If the host Member State gives its lawyers a choice between several forms of joint practice, those same forms shall also be made available to the aforementioned lawyers. The manner in which such lawyers practise jointly in the host Member State shall be governed by the laws, regulations and administrative provisions of that State.

(3) The host Member State shall take the measures necessary to permit joint practice also between:

(a) several lawyers from different Member States practising under their home-country professional titles;

(b) one or more lawyers covered by point (a) and one or more lawyers from the host Member State.

The manner in which such lawyers practise jointly in the host Member State shall be governed by the laws, regulations and administrative provisions of that State.

(4) A lawyer who wishes to practise under his home-country professional title shall inform the competent authority in the host Member State of the fact that he is a member of a grouping in his home Member State and furnish any relevant information on that grouping.

(5) Notwithstanding points 1 to 4, a host Member State, insofar as it prohibits lawyers practising under its own relevant professional title from practising the profession of lawyer within a grouping

in which some persons are not members of the profession, may refuse to allow a lawyer registered under his home-country professional title to practice in its territory in his capacity as a member of his grouping. The grouping is deemed to include persons who are not members of the profession if

- the capital of the grouping is held entirely or partly, or
- the name under which it practises is used, or
- the decision-making power in that grouping is exercised, *de facto* or *de jure*,

by persons who do not have the status of lawyer within the meaning of Article 1(2).

Where the fundamental rules governing a grouping of lawyers in the home Member State are incompatible with the rules in force in the host Member State or with the provisions of the first subparagraph, the host Member State may oppose the opening of a branch or agency within its territory without the restrictions laid down in point (1).

Article 12 Name of the grouping

Whatever the manner in which lawyers practise under their home-country professional titles in the host Member State, they may employ the name of any grouping to which they belong in their home Member State.

The host Member State may require that, in addition to the name referred to in the first subparagraph, mention be made of the legal form of the grouping in the home Member State and/or of the names of any members of the grouping practising in the host Member State.

Article 13 Cooperation between the competent authorities in the home and host Member States and confidentiality

In order to facilitate the application of this Directive and to prevent its provisions from being misapplied for the sole purpose of circumventing the rules applicable in the host Member State, the competent authority in the host Member State and the competent authority in the home Member State shall collaborate closely and afford each other mutual assistance.

They shall preserve the confidentiality of the information they exchange.

Article 14 Designation of the competent authorities

Member States shall designate the competent authorities empowered to receive the applications and to take the decisions referred to in this Directive by 14 March 2000. They shall communicate this information to the other Member States and to the Commission.

Article 15 Report by the Commission

Ten years at the latest from the entry into force of this Directive, the Commission shall report to the European Parliament and to the Council on progress in the implementation of the Directive.

After having held all the necessary consultations, it shall on that occasion present its conclusions and any amendments which could be made to the existing system.

Article 16 Implementation

1. Member States shall bring into force the laws, regulations and administrative provisions necessary to comply with this Directive by 14 March 2000. They shall forthwith inform the Commission thereof.

When Member States adopt these measures, they shall contain a reference to this Directive or shall be accompanied by such reference on the occasion of their official publication. The methods of making such reference shall be adopted by Member States.

2. Member States shall communicate to the Commission the texts of the main provisions of domestic law which they adopt in the field covered by this Directive.

Article 17

This Directive shall enter into force on the date of its publication in the *Official Journal of the European Communities*.

Article 18 Addressees

This Directive is addressed to the Member States.

Done at Brussels, 16 February 1998.
For the European Parliament
The President
J. M. GIL-ROBLES

For the Council
The President
J. CUNNINGHAM

Directive 2004/38/EC of the European Parliament and of the Council of 29 April 2004 on the right of citizens of the Union and their family members to move and reside freely within the territory of the Member States*

[OJ 2004 L158/77]

(Entry into force 30/4/2006 at which time Regulation (EEC) No 1612/68 is amended and Directives 64/221/EEC, 68/360/EEC, 72/194/EEC, 73/148/EEC, 75/34/EEC, 75/35/EEC, 90/364/EEC, 90/365/EEC and 93/96/EEC are repealed)

THE EUROPEAN PARLIAMENT AND THE COUNCIL OF THE EUROPEAN UNION,

Having regard to the Treaty establishing the European Community, and in particular Articles 12, 18, 40, 44 and 52 thereof,

Having regard to the proposal from the Commission,[1]

Having regard to the Opinion of the European Economic and Social Committee,[2]

Having regard to the Opinion of the Committee of the Regions,[3]

Acting in accordance with the procedure laid down in Article 251 of the Treaty,[4]

Whereas:

(1) Citizenship of the Union confers on every citizen of the Union a primary and individual right to move and reside freely within the territory of the Member States, subject to the limitations and conditions laid down in the Treaty and to the measures adopted to give it effect.

(2) The free movement of persons constitutes one of the fundamental freedoms of the internal market, which comprises an area without internal frontiers, in which freedom is ensured in accordance with the provisions of the Treaty.

(3) Union citizenship should be the fundamental status of nationals of the Member States when they exercise their right of free movement and residence. It is therefore necessary to codify and review the existing Community instruments dealing separately with workers, self-employed persons, as well as students and other inactive persons in order to simplify and strengthen the right of free movement and residence of all Union citizens.

(4) With a view to remedying this sector-by-sector, piecemeal approach to the right of free movement and residence and facilitating the exercise of this right, there needs to be a single legislative act to amend Council Regulation (EEC) No 1612/68 of 15 October 1968 on freedom of movement for workers within the Community,[5] and to repeal the following acts: Council Directive 68/360/EEC of 15 October 1968 on the abolition of restrictions on movement and residence within the Community for workers of Member States and their families,[6] Council Directive 73/148/EEC of 21 May 1973 on the

* **Editor's Note:** As corrected by OJ 2007, L 204/28 and amended by Regulation 492/2011 (OJ 2011 L141/1).

1 OJ C 270 E, 25.9.2001, p. 150.

2 OJ C 149, 21.6.2002, p. 46.

3 OJ C 192, 12.8.2002, p. 17.

4 Opinion of the European Parliament of 11 February 2003 (OJ C 43 E, 19.2.2004, p. 42), Council Common Position of 5 December 2003 (OJ C 54 E, 2.3.2004, p. 12) and Position of the European Parliament of 10 March 2004 (not yet published in the Official Journal).

5 OJ L 257, 19.10.1968, p. 2. Regulation as last amended by Regulation (EEC) No 2434/92 (OJ L 245, 26.8.1992, p. 1).

6 OJ L 257, 19.10.1968, p. 13. Directive as last amended by the 2003 Act of Accession.

abolition of restrictions on movement and residence within the Community for nationals of Member States with regard to establishment and the provision of services,[7] Council Directive 90/364/EEC of 28 June 1990 on the right of residence,[8] Council Directive 90/365/EEC of 28 June 1990 on the right of residence for employees and self-employed persons who have ceased their occupational activity[9] and Council Directive 93/96/EEC of 29 October 1993 on the right of residence for students.[10]

(5) The right of all Union citizens to move and reside freely within the territory of the Member States should, if it is to be exercised under objective conditions of freedom and dignity, be also granted to their family members, irrespective of nationality. For the purposes of this Directive, the definition of 'family member' should also include the registered partner if the legislation of the host Member State treats registered partnership as equivalent to marriage.

(6) In order to maintain the unity of the family in a broader sense and without prejudice to the prohibition of discrimination on grounds of nationality, the situation of those persons who are not included in the definition of family members under this Directive, and who therefore do not enjoy an automatic right of entry and residence in the host Member State, should be examined by the host Member State on the basis of its own national legislation, in order to decide whether entry and residence could be granted to such persons, taking into consideration their relationship with the Union citizen or any other circumstances, such as their financial or physical dependence on the Union citizen.

(7) The formalities connected with the free movement of Union citizens within the territory of Member States should be clearly defined, without prejudice to the provisions applicable to national border controls.

(8) With a view to facilitating the free movement of family members who are not nationals of a Member State, those who have already obtained a residence card should be exempted from the requirement to obtain an entry visa within the meaning of Council Regulation (EC) No 539/2001 of 15 March 2001 listing the third countries whose nationals must be in possession of visas when crossing the external borders and those whose nationals are exempt from that requirement[11] or, where appropriate, of the applicable national legislation.

(9) Union citizens should have the right of residence in the host Member State for a period not exceeding three months without being subject to any conditions or any formalities other than the requirement to hold a valid identity card or passport, without prejudice to a more favourable treatment applicable to job-seekers as recognised by the case-law of the Court of Justice.

(10) Persons exercising their right of residence should not, however, become an unreasonable burden on the social assistance system of the host Member State during an initial period of residence. Therefore, the right of residence for Union citizens and their family members for periods in excess of three months should be subject to conditions.

(11) The fundamental and personal right of residence in another Member State is conferred directly on Union citizens by the Treaty and is not dependent upon their having fulfilled administrative procedures.

(12) For periods of residence of longer than three months, Member States should have the possibility to require Union citizens to register with the competent authorities in the place of residence, attested by a registration certificate issued to that effect.

(13) The residence card requirement should be restricted to family members of Union citizens who are not nationals of a Member State for periods of residence of longer than three months.

(14) The supporting documents required by the competent authorities for the issuing of a registration certificate or of a residence card should be comprehensively specified in order to avoid divergent administrative practices or interpretations constituting an undue obstacle to the exercise of the right of residence by Union citizens and their family members.

[7] OJ L 172, 28.6.1973, p. 14.
[8] OJ L 180, 13.7.1990, p. 26.
[9] OJ L 180, 13.7.1990, p. 28.
[10] OJ L 317, 18.12.1993, p. 59.
[11] OJ L 81, 21.3.2001, p. 1. Regulation as last amended by Regulation (EC) No 453/2003 (OJ L 69, 13.3.2003, p. 10).

(15) Family members should be legally safeguarded in the event of the death of the Union citizen, divorce, annulment of marriage or termination of a registered partnership. With due regard for family life and human dignity, and in certain conditions to guard against abuse, measures should therefore be taken to ensure that in such circumstances family members already residing within the territory of the host Member State retain their right of residence exclusively on a personal basis.

(16) As long as the beneficiaries of the right of residence do not become an unreasonable burden on the social assistance system of the host Member State they should not be expelled. Therefore, an expulsion measure should not be the automatic consequence of recourse to the social assistance system. The host Member State should examine whether it is a case of temporary difficulties and take into account the duration of residence, the personal circumstances and the amount of aid granted in order to consider whether the beneficiary has become an unreasonable burden on its social assistance system and to proceed to his expulsion. In no case should an expulsion measure be adopted against workers, self-employed persons or job-seekers as defined by the Court of Justice save on grounds of public policy or public security.

(17) Enjoyment of permanent residence by Union citizens who have chosen to settle long term in the host Member State would strengthen the feeling of Union citizenship and is a key element in promoting social cohesion, which is one of the fundamental objectives of the Union. A right of permanent residence should therefore be laid down for all Union citizens and their family members who have resided in the host Member State in compliance with the conditions laid down in this Directive during a continuous period of five years without becoming subject to an expulsion measure.

(18) In order to be a genuine vehicle for integration into the society of the host Member State in which the Union citizen resides, the right of permanent residence, once obtained, should not be subject to any conditions.

(19) Certain advantages specific to Union citizens who are workers or self-employed persons and to their family members, which may allow these persons to acquire a right of permanent residence before they have resided five years in the host Member State, should be maintained, as these constitute acquired rights, conferred by Commission Regulation (EEC) No 1251/70 of 29 June 1970 on the right of workers to remain in the territory of a Member State after having been employed in that State[12] and Council Directive 75/34/EEC of 17 December 1974 concerning the right of nationals of a Member State to remain in the territory of another Member State after having pursued therein an activity in a self-employed capacity.[13]

(20) In accordance with the prohibition of discrimination on grounds of nationality, all Union citizens and their family members residing in a Member State on the basis of this Directive should enjoy, in that Member State, equal treatment with nationals in areas covered by the Treaty, subject to such specific provisions as are expressly provided for in the Treaty and secondary law.

(21) However, it should be left to the host Member State to decide whether it will grant social assistance during the first three months of residence, or for a longer period in the case of job-seekers, to Union citizens other than those who are workers or self-employed persons or who retain that status or their family members, or maintenance assistance for studies, including vocational training, prior to acquisition of the right of permanent residence, to these same persons.

(22) The Treaty allows restrictions to be placed on the right of free movement and residence on grounds of public policy, public security or public health. In order to ensure a tighter definition of the circumstances and procedural safeguards subject to which Union citizens and their family members may be denied leave to enter or may be expelled, this Directive should replace Council Directive 64/221/EEC of 25 February 1964 on the coordination of special measures concerning the movement and residence of foreign nationals, which are justified on grounds of public policy, public security or public health.[14]

(23) Expulsion of Union citizens and their family members on grounds of public policy or public security is a measure that can seriously harm persons who, having availed themselves of the rights and

[12] OJ L 142, 30.6.1970, p. 24. [13] OJ L 14, 20.1.1975, p. 10.

[14] OJ 56, 4.4.1964, p. 850. Directive as last amended by Directive 75/35/EEC (OJ 14, 20.1.1975, p. 14).

freedoms conferred on them by the Treaty, have become genuinely integrated into the host Member State. The scope for such measures should therefore be limited in accordance with the principle of proportionality to take account of the degree of integration of the persons concerned, the length of their residence in the host Member State, their age, state of health, family and economic situation and the links with their country of origin.

(24) Accordingly, the greater the degree of integration of Union citizens and their family members in the host Member State, the greater the degree of protection against expulsion should be. Only in exceptional circumstances, where there are imperative grounds of public security, should an expulsion measure be taken against Union citizens who have resided for many years in the territory of the host Member State, in particular when they were born and have resided there throughout their life. In addition, such exceptional circumstances should also apply to an expulsion measure taken against minors, in order to protect their links with their family, in accordance with the United Nations Convention on the Rights of the Child, of 20 November 1989.

(25) Procedural safeguards should also be specified in detail in order to ensure a high level of protection of the rights of Union citizens and their family members in the event of their being denied leave to enter or reside in another Member State, as well as to uphold the principle that any action taken by the authorities must be properly justified.

(26) In all events, judicial redress procedures should be available to Union citizens and their family members who have been refused leave to enter or reside in another Member State.

(27) In line with the case-law of the Court of Justice prohibiting Member States from issuing orders excluding for life persons covered by this Directive from their territory, the right of Union citizens and their family members who have been excluded from the territory of a Member State to submit a fresh application after a reasonable period, and in any event after a three year period from enforcement of the final exclusion order, should be confirmed.

(28) To guard against abuse of rights or fraud, notably marriages of convenience or any other form of relationships contracted for the sole purpose of enjoying the right of free movement and residence, Member States should have the possibility to adopt the necessary measures.

(29) This Directive should not affect more favourable national provisions.

(30) With a view to examining how further to facilitate the exercise of the right of free movement and residence, a report should be prepared by the Commission in order to evaluate the opportunity to present any necessary proposals to this effect, notably on the extension of the period of residence with no conditions.

(31) This Directive respects the fundamental rights and freedoms and observes the principles recognised in particular by the Charter of Fundamental Rights of the European Union. In accordance with the prohibition of discrimination contained in the Charter, Member States should implement this Directive without discrimination between the beneficiaries of this Directive on grounds such as sex, race, colour, ethnic or social origin, genetic characteristics, language, religion or beliefs, political or other opinion, membership of an ethnic minority, property, birth, disability, age or sexual orientation,

HAVE ADOPTED THIS DIRECTIVE:

Chapter I General provisions

Article 1 Subject

This Directive lays down:

(a) the conditions governing the exercise of the right of free movement and residence within the territory of the Member States by Union citizens and their family members;
(b) the right of permanent residence in the territory of the Member States for Union citizens and their family members;
(c) the limits placed on the rights set out in (a) and (b) on grounds of public policy, public security or public health.

Article 2 Definitions

For the purposes of this Directive:

(1) 'Union citizen' means any person having the nationality of a Member State;

(2) 'Family member' means:

(a) the spouse;

(b) the partner with whom the Union citizen has contracted a registered partnership, on the basis of the legislation of a Member State, if the legislation of the host Member State treats registered partnerships as equivalent to marriage and in accordance with the conditions laid down in the relevant legislation of the host Member State;

(c) the direct descendants who are under the age of 21 or are dependants and those of the spouse or partner as defined in point (b);

(d) the dependent direct relatives in the ascending line and those of the spouse or partner as defined in point (b);

(3) 'Host Member State' means the Member State to which a Union citizen moves in order to exercise his/her right of free movement and residence.

Article 3 Beneficiaries

1. This Directive shall apply to all Union citizens who move to or reside in a Member State other than that of which they are a national, and to their family members as defined in point 2 of Article 2 who accompany or join them.

2. Without prejudice to any right to free movement and residence the persons concerned may have in their own right, the host Member State shall, in accordance with its national legislation, facilitate entry and residence for the following persons:

(a) any other family members, irrespective of their nationality, not falling under the definition in point 2 of Article 2 who, in the country from which they have come, are dependants or members of the household of the Union citizen having the primary right of residence, or where serious health grounds strictly require the personal care of the family member by the Union citizen;

(b) the partner with whom the Union citizen has a durable relationship, duly attested. The host Member State shall undertake an extensive examination of the personal circumstances and shall justify any denial of entry or residence to these people.

Chapter II Right of exit and entry

Article 4 Right of exit

1. Without prejudice to the provisions on travel documents applicable to national border controls, all Union citizens with a valid identity card or passport and their family members who are not nationals of a Member State and who hold a valid passport shall have the right to leave the territory of a Member State to travel to another Member State.

2. No exit visa or equivalent formality may be imposed on the persons to whom paragraph 1 applies.

3. Member States shall, acting in accordance with their laws, issue to their own nationals, and renew, an identity card or passport stating their nationality.

4. The passport shall be valid at least for all Member States and for countries through which the holder must pass when travelling between Member States. Where the law of a Member State does not provide for identity cards to be issued, the period of validity of any passport on being issued or renewed shall be not less than five years.

Article 5 Right of entry

1. Without prejudice to the provisions on travel documents applicable to national border controls, Member States shall grant Union citizens leave to enter their territory with a valid identity card or passport and shall grant family members who are not nationals of a Member State leave to enter their territory with a valid passport. No entry visa or equivalent formality may be imposed on Union citizens.

2. Family members who are not nationals of a Member State shall only be required to have an entry visa in accordance with Regulation (EC) No 539/2001 or, where appropriate, with national law. For the purposes of this Directive, possession of the valid residence card referred to in Article 10 shall exempt such family members from the visa requirement. Member States shall grant such persons every facility to obtain the necessary visas. Such visas shall be issued free of charge as soon as possible and on the basis of an accelerated procedure.

3. The host Member State shall not place an entry or exit stamp in the passport of family members who are not nationals of a Member State provided that they present the residence card provided for in Article 10.

4. Where a Union citizen, or a family member who is not a national of a Member State, does not have the necessary travel documents or, if required, the necessary visas, the Member State concerned shall, before turning them back, give such persons every reasonable opportunity to obtain the necessary documents or have them brought to them within a reasonable period of time or to corroborate or prove by other means that they are covered by the right of free movement and residence.

5. The Member State may require the person concerned to report his/her presence within its territory within a reasonable and non-discriminatory period of time. Failure to comply with this requirement may make the person concerned liable to proportionate and non-discriminatory sanctions.

Chapter III Right of residence

Article 6 Right of residence for up to three months

1. Union citizens shall have the right of residence on the territory of another Member State for a period of up to three months without any conditions or any formalities other than the requirement to hold a valid identity card or passport.

2. The provisions of paragraph 1 shall also apply to family members in possession of a valid passport who are not nationals of a Member State, accompanying or joining the Union citizen.

Article 7 Right of residence for more than three months

1. All Union citizens shall have the right of residence on the territory of another Member State for a period of longer than three months if they:

(a) are workers or self-employed persons in the host Member State; or

(b) have sufficient resources for themselves and their family members not to become a burden on the social assistance system of the host Member State during their period of residence and have comprehensive sickness insurance cover in the host Member State; or

(c) – are enrolled at a private or public establishment, accredited or financed by the host Member State on the basis of its legislation or administrative practice, for the principal purpose of following a course of study, including vocational training; and
- have comprehensive sickness insurance cover in the host Member State and assure the relevant national authority, by means of a declaration or by such equivalent means as they may choose, that they have sufficient resources for themselves and their family members not to become a burden on the social assistance system of the host Member State during their period of residence; or

(d) are family members accompanying or joining a Union citizen who satisfies the conditions referred to in points (a), (b) or (c).

2. The right of residence provided for in paragraph 1 shall extend to family members who are not nationals of a Member State, accompanying or joining the Union citizen in the host Member State, provided that such Union citizen satisfies the conditions referred to in paragraph 1(a), (b) or (c).

3. For the purposes of paragraph 1(a), a Union citizen who is no longer a worker or self-employed person shall retain the status of worker or self-employed person in the following circumstances:

(a) he/she is temporarily unable to work as the result of an illness or accident;

(b) he/she is in duly recorded involuntary unemployment after having been employed for more than one year and has registered as a job-seeker with the relevant employment office;

(c) he/she is in duly recorded involuntary unemployment after completing a fixed-term employment contract of less than a year or after having become involuntarily unemployed during the first twelve months and has registered as a job-seeker with the relevant employment office. In this case, the status of worker shall be retained for no less than six months;

(d) he/she embarks on vocational training. Unless he/she is involuntarily unemployed, the retention of the status of worker shall require the training to be related to the previous employment.

4. By way of derogation from paragraphs 1(d) and 2 above, only the spouse, the registered partner provided for in Article 2(2)(b) and dependent children shall have the right of residence as family members of a Union citizen meeting the conditions under 1(c) above. Article 3(2) shall apply to his/her dependent direct relatives in the ascending lines and those of his/her spouse or registered partner.

Article 8 Administrative formalities for Union citizens

1. Without prejudice to Article 5(5), for periods of residence longer than three months, the host Member State may require Union citizens to register with the relevant authorities.

2. The deadline for registration may not be less than three months from the date of arrival. A registration certificate shall be issued immediately, stating the name and address of the person registering and the date of the registration. Failure to comply with the registration requirement may render the person concerned liable to proportionate and non-discriminatory sanctions.

3. For the registration certificate to be issued, Member States may only require that

- Union citizens to whom point (a) of Article 7(1) applies present a valid identity card or passport, a confirmation of engagement from the employer or a certificate of employment, or proof that they are self-employed persons;
- Union citizens to whom point (b) of Article 7(1) applies present a valid identity card or passport and provide proof that they satisfy the conditions laid down therein;
- Union citizens to whom point (c) of Article 7(1) applies present a valid identity card or passport, provide proof of enrolment at an accredited establishment and of comprehensive sickness insurance cover and the declaration or equivalent means referred to in point (c) of Article 7(1). Member States may not require this declaration to refer to any specific amount of resources.

4. Member States may not lay down a fixed amount which they regard as 'sufficient resources', but they must take into account the personal situation of the person concerned. In all cases this amount shall not be higher than the threshold below which nationals of the host Member State become eligible for social assistance, or, where this criterion is not applicable, higher than the minimum social security pension paid by the host Member State.

5. For the registration certificate to be issued to family members of Union citizens, who are themselves Union citizens, Member States may require the following documents to be presented:

(a) a valid identity card or passport;

(b) a document attesting to the existence of a family relationship or of a registered partnership;

(c) where appropriate, the registration certificate of the Union citizen whom they are accompanying or joining;

(d) in cases falling under points (c) and (d) of Article 2(2), documentary evidence that the conditions laid down therein are met;

(e) in cases falling under Article 3(2)(a), a document issued by the relevant authority in the country of origin or country from which they are arriving certifying that they are dependants or members of the household of the Union citizen, or proof of the existence of serious health grounds which strictly require the personal care of the family member by the Union citizen;

(f) in cases falling under Article 3(2)(b), proof of the existence of a durable relationship with the Union citizen.

Article 9 Administrative formalities for family members who are not nationals of a Member State

1. Member States shall issue a residence card to family members of a Union citizen who are not nationals of a Member State, where the planned period of residence is for more than three months.

2. The deadline for submitting the residence card application may not be less than three months from the date of arrival.

3. Failure to comply with the requirement to apply for a residence card may make the person concerned liable to proportionate and non-discriminatory sanctions.

Article 10 Issue of residence cards

1. The right of residence of family members of a Union citizen who are not nationals of a Member State shall be evidenced by the issuing of a document called 'Residence card of a family member of a Union citizen' no later than six months from the date on which they submit the application. A certificate of application for the residence card shall be issued immediately.

2. For the residence card to be issued, Member States shall require presentation of the following documents:

(a) a valid passport;

(b) a document attesting to the existence of a family relationship or of a registered partnership;

(c) the registration certificate or, in the absence of a registration system, any other proof of residence in the host Member State of the Union citizen whom they are accompanying or joining;

(d) in cases falling under points (c) and (d) of Article 2(2), documentary evidence that the conditions laid down therein are met;

(e) in cases falling under Article 3(2)(a), a document issued by the relevant authority in the country of origin or country from which they are arriving certifying that they are dependants or members of the household of the Union citizen, or proof of the existence of serious health grounds which strictly require the personal care of the family member by the Union citizen;

(f) in cases falling under Article 3(2)(b), proof of the existence of a durable relationship with the Union citizen.

Article 11 Validity of the residence card

1. The residence card provided for by Article 10(1) shall be valid for five years from the date of issue or for the envisaged period of residence of the Union citizen, if this period is less than five years.

2. The validity of the residence card shall not be affected by temporary absences not exceeding six months a year, or by absences of a longer duration for compulsory military service or by one absence of a maximum of twelve consecutive months for important reasons such as pregnancy and childbirth, serious illness, study or vocational training, or a posting in another Member State or a third country.

Article 12 Retention of the right of residence by family members in the event of death or departure of the Union citizen

1. Without prejudice to the second subparagraph, the Union citizen's death or departure from the host Member State shall not affect the right of residence of his/her family members who are nationals of a Member State.

Before acquiring the right of permanent residence, the persons concerned must meet the conditions laid down in points (a), (b), (c) or (d) of Article 7(1).

2. Without prejudice to the second subparagraph, the Union citizen's death shall not entail loss of the right of residence of his/her family members who are not nationals of a Member State and who have been residing in the host Member State as family members for at least one year before the Union citizen's death.

Before acquiring the right of permanent residence, the right of residence of the persons concerned shall remain subject to the requirement that they are able to show that they are workers or self-employed persons or that they have sufficient resources for themselves and their family members not to become a burden on the social assistance system of the host Member State during their period of residence and have comprehensive sickness insurance cover in the host Member State, or that they are members of the family, already constituted in the host Member State, of a person satisfying these requirements. 'Sufficient resources' shall be as defined in Article 8(4).

Such family members shall retain their right of residence exclusively on a personal basis.

3. The Union citizen's departure from the host Member State or his/her death shall not entail loss of the right of residence of his/her children or of the parent who has actual custody of the children, irrespective of nationality, if the children reside in the host Member State and are enrolled at an educational establishment, for the purpose of studying there, until the completion of their studies.

Article 13 Retention of the right of residence by family members in the event of divorce, annulment of marriage or termination of registered partnership

1. Without prejudice to the second subparagraph, divorce, annulment of the Union citizen's marriage or termination of his/her registered partnership, as referred to in point 2(b) of Article 2 shall not affect the right of residence of his/her family members who are nationals of a Member State.

Before acquiring the right of permanent residence, the persons concerned must meet the conditions laid down in points (a), (b), (c) or (d) of Article 7(1).

2. Without prejudice to the second subparagraph, divorce, annulment of marriage or termination of the registered partnership referred to in point 2(b) of Article 2 shall not entail loss of the right of residence of a Union citizen's family members who are not nationals of a Member State where:

(a) prior to initiation of the divorce or annulment proceedings or termination of the registered partnership referred to in point 2(b) of Article 2, the marriage or registered partnership has lasted at least three years, including one year in the host Member State; or

(b) by agreement between the spouses or the partners referred to in point 2(b) of Article 2 or by court order, the spouse or partner who is not a national of a Member State has custody of the Union citizen's children; or

(c) this is warranted by particularly difficult circumstances, such as having been a victim of domestic violence while the marriage or registered partnership was subsisting; or

(d) by agreement between the spouses or partners referred to in point 2(b) of Article 2 or by court order, the spouse or partner who is not a national of a Member State has the right of access to a minor child, provided that the court has ruled that such access must be in the host Member State, and for as long as is required.

Before acquiring the right of permanent residence, the right of residence of the persons concerned shall remain subject to the requirement that they are able to show that they are workers or self-employed persons or that they have sufficient resources for themselves and their family members not to become a burden on the social assistance system of the host Member State during their period of residence and have comprehensive sickness insurance cover in the host Member State, or that they are members of the family, already constituted in the host Member State, of a person satisfying these requirements. 'Sufficient resources' shall be as defined in Article 8(4).

Such family members shall retain their right of residence exclusively on personal basis.

Article 14 Retention of the right of residence

1. Union citizens and their family members shall have the right of residence provided for in Article 6, as long as they do not become an unreasonable burden on the social assistance system of the host Member State.

2. Union citizens and their family members shall have the right of residence provided for in Articles 7, 12 and 13 as long as they meet the conditions set out therein. In specific cases where there is a reasonable doubt as to whether a Union citizen or his/her family members satisfies the conditions set out in Articles 7, 12 and 13, Member States may verify if these conditions are fulfilled. This verification shall not be carried out systematically.

3. An expulsion measure shall not be the automatic consequence of a Union citizen's or his or her family member's recourse to the social assistance system of the host Member State.

4. By way of derogation from paragraphs 1 and 2 and without prejudice to the provisions of Chapter VI, an expulsion measure may in no case be adopted against Union citizens or their family members if:

(a) the Union citizens are workers or self-employed persons, or

(b) the Union citizens entered the territory of the host Member State in order to seek employment. In this case, the Union citizens and their family members may not be expelled for as long as the Union citizens can provide evidence that they are continuing to seek employment and that they have a genuine chance of being engaged.

Article 15 Procedural safeguards

1. The procedures provided for by Articles 30 and 31 shall apply by analogy to all decisions restricting free movement of Union citizens and their family members on grounds other than public policy, public security or public health.

2. Expiry of the identity card or passport on the basis of which the person concerned entered the host Member State and was issued with a registration certificate or residence card shall not constitute a ground for expulsion from the host Member State.

3. The host Member State may not impose a ban on entry in the context of an expulsion decision to which paragraph 1 applies.

Chapter IV Right of permanent residence

Section I Eligibility

Article 16 General rule for Union citizens and their family members

1. Union citizens who have resided legally for a continuous period of five years in the host Member State shall have the right of permanent residence there. This right shall not be subject to the conditions provided for in Chapter III.

2. Paragraph 1 shall apply also to family members who are not nationals of a Member State and have legally resided with the Union citizen in the host Member State for a continuous period of five years.

3. Continuity of residence shall not be affected by temporary absences not exceeding a total of six months a year, or by absences of a longer duration for compulsory military service, or by one absence of a maximum of twelve consecutive months for important reasons such as pregnancy and childbirth, serious illness, study or vocational training, or a posting in another Member State or a third country.

4. Once acquired, the right of permanent residence shall be lost only through absence from the host Member State for a period exceeding two consecutive years.

Article 17 Exemptions for persons no longer working in the host Member State and their family members

1. By way of derogation from Article 16, the right of permanent residence in the host Member State shall be enjoyed before completion of a continuous period of five years of residence by:

(a) workers or self-employed persons who, at the time they stop working, have reached the age laid down by the law of that Member State for entitlement to an old age pension or workers who cease paid employment to take early retirement, provided that they have been working in that Member State for at least the preceding twelve months and have resided there continuously for more than three years.

If the law of the host Member State does not grant the right to an old age pension to certain categories of self-employed persons, the age condition shall be deemed to have been met once the person concerned has reached the age of 60;

(b) workers or self-employed persons who have resided continuously in the host Member State for more than two years and stop working there as a result of permanent incapacity to work.

If such incapacity is the result of an accident at work or an occupational disease entitling the person concerned to a benefit payable in full or in part by an institution in the host Member State, no condition shall be imposed as to length of residence;

(c) workers or self-employed persons who, after three years of continuous employment and residence in the host Member State, work in an employed or self-employed capacity in another Member State, while retaining their place of residence in the host Member State, to which they return, as a rule, each day or at least once a week.

For the purposes of entitlement to the rights referred to in points (a) and (b), periods of employment spent in the Member State in which the person concerned is working shall be regarded as having been spent in the host Member State.

Periods of involuntary unemployment duly recorded by the relevant employment office, periods not worked for reasons not of the person's own making and absences from work or cessation of work due to illness or accident shall be regarded as periods of employment.

2. The conditions as to length of residence and employment laid down in point (a) of paragraph 1 and the condition as to length of residence laid down in point (b) of paragraph 1 shall not apply if the worker's or the self-employed person's spouse or partner as referred to in point 2(b) of Article 2 is a national of the host Member State or has lost the nationality of that Member State by marriage to that worker or self-employed person.

3. Irrespective of nationality, the family members of a worker or a self-employed person who are residing with him in the territory of the host Member State shall have the right of permanent residence in that Member State, if the worker or self-employed person has acquired himself the right of permanent residence in that Member State on the basis of paragraph 1.

4. If, however, the worker or self-employed person dies while still working but before acquiring permanent residence status in the host Member State on the basis of paragraph 1, his family members who are residing with him in the host Member State shall acquire the right of permanent residence there, on condition that:

(a) the worker or self-employed person had, at the time of death, resided continuously on the territory of that Member State for two years; or
(b) the death resulted from an accident at work or an occupational disease; or
(c) the surviving spouse lost the nationality of that Member State following marriage to the worker or self-employed person.

Article 18 Acquisition of the right of permanent residence by certain family members who are not nationals of a Member State

Without prejudice to Article 17, the family members of a Union citizen to whom Articles 12(2) and 13(2) apply, who satisfy the conditions laid down therein, shall acquire the right of permanent residence after residing legally for a period of five consecutive years in the host Member State.

Section II Administrative formalities

Article 19 Document certifying permanent residence for Union citizens

1. Upon application Member States shall issue Union citizens entitled to permanent residence, after having verified duration of residence, with a document certifying permanent residence.

2. The document certifying permanent residence shall be issued as soon as possible.

Article 20 Permanent residence card for family members who are not nationals of a Member State

1. Member States shall issue family members who are not nationals of a Member State entitled to permanent residence with a permanent residence card within six months of the

submission of the application. The permanent residence card shall be renewable automatically every ten years.

2. The application for a permanent residence card shall be submitted before the residence card expires. Failure to comply with the requirement to apply for a permanent residence card may render the person concerned liable to proportionate and non-discriminatory sanctions.

3. Interruption in residence not exceeding two consecutive years shall not affect the validity of the permanent residence card.

Article 21 Continuity of residence

For the purposes of this Directive, continuity of residence may be attested by any means of proof in use in the host Member State. Continuity of residence is broken by any expulsion decision duly enforced against the person concerned.

Chapter V Provisions common to the right of residence and the right of permanent residence

Article 22 Territorial scope

The right of residence and the right of permanent residence shall cover the whole territory of the host Member State. Member States may impose territorial restrictions on the right of residence and the right of permanent residence only where the same restrictions apply to their own nationals.

Article 23 Related rights

Irrespective of nationality, the family members of a Union citizen who have the right of residence or the right of permanent residence in a Member State shall be entitled to take up employment or self-employment there.

Article 24 Equal treatment

1. Subject to such specific provisions as are expressly provided for in the Treaty and secondary law, all Union citizens residing on the basis of this Directive in the territory of the host Member State shall enjoy equal treatment with the nationals of that Member State within the scope of the Treaty. The benefit of this right shall be extended to family members who are not nationals of a Member State and who have the right of residence or permanent residence.

2. By way of derogation from paragraph 1, the host Member State shall not be obliged to confer entitlement to social assistance during the first three months of residence or, where appropriate, the longer period provided for in Article 14(4)(b), nor shall it be obliged, prior to acquisition of the right of permanent residence, to grant maintenance aid for studies, including vocational training, consisting in student grants or student loans to persons other than workers, self-employed persons, persons who retain such status and members of their families.

Article 25 General provisions concerning residence documents

1. Possession of a registration certificate as referred to in Article 8, of a document certifying permanent residence, of a certificate attesting submission of an application for a family member residence card, of a residence card or of a permanent residence card, may under no circumstances be made a precondition for the exercise of a right or the completion of an administrative formality, as entitlement to rights may be attested by any other means of proof.

2. All documents mentioned in paragraph 1 shall be issued free of charge or for a charge not exceeding that imposed on nationals for the issuing of similar documents.

Article 26 Checks

Member States may carry out checks on compliance with any requirement deriving from their national legislation for non-nationals always to carry their registration certificate or residence card, provided that the same requirement applies to their own nationals as regards their identity card. In the event of failure to comply with this requirement, Member States may impose the same sanctions as those imposed on their own nationals for failure to carry their identity card.

Chapter VI Restrictions on the right of entry and the right of residence on grounds of public policy, public security or public health

Article 27 General principles

1. Subject to the provisions of this Chapter, Member States may restrict the freedom of movement and residence of Union citizens and their family members, irrespective of nationality, on grounds of public policy, public security or public health. These grounds shall not be invoked to serve economic ends.

2. Measures taken on grounds of public policy or public security shall comply with the principle of proportionality and shall be based exclusively on the personal conduct of the individual concerned.

Previous criminal convictions shall not in themselves constitute grounds for taking such measures.

The personal conduct of the individual concerned must represent a genuine, present and sufficiently serious threat affecting one of the fundamental interests of society. Justifications that are isolated from the particulars of the case or that rely on considerations of general prevention shall not be accepted.

3. In order to ascertain whether the person concerned represents a danger for public policy or public security, when issuing the registration certificate or, in the absence of a registration system, not later than three months from the date of arrival of the person concerned on its territory or from the date of reporting his/her presence within the territory, as provided for in Article 5(5), or when issuing the residence card, the host Member State may, should it consider this essential, request the Member State of origin and, if need be, other Member States to provide information concerning any previous police record the person concerned may have. Such enquiries shall not be made as a matter of routine. The Member State consulted shall give its reply within two months.

4. The Member State which issued the passport or identity card shall allow the holder of the document who has been expelled on grounds of public policy, public security, or public health from another Member State to re-enter its territory without any formality even if the document is no longer valid or the nationality of the holder is in dispute.

Article 28 Protection against expulsion

1. Before taking an expulsion decision on grounds of public policy or public security, the host Member State shall take account of considerations such as how long the individual concerned has resided on its territory, his/her age, state of health, family and economic situation, social and cultural integration into the host Member State and the extent of his/her links with the country of origin.

2. The host Member State may not take an expulsion decision against Union citizens or their family members, irrespective of nationality, who have the right of permanent residence on its territory, except on serious grounds of public policy or public security.

3. An expulsion decision may not be taken against Union citizens, except if the decision is based on imperative grounds of public security, as defined by Member States, if they:

(a) have resided in the host Member State for the previous ten years; or

(b) are a minor, except if the expulsion is necessary for the best interests of the child, as provided for in the United Nations Convention on the Rights of the Child of 20 November 1989.

Article 29 Public health

1. The only diseases justifying measures restricting freedom of movement shall be the diseases with epidemic potential as defined by the relevant instruments of the World Health Organisation and other infectious diseases or contagious parasitic diseases if they are the subject of protection provisions applying to nationals of the host Member State.

2. Diseases occurring after a three-month period from the date of arrival shall not constitute grounds for expulsion from the territory.

3. Where there are serious indications that it is necessary, Member States may, within three months of the date of arrival, require persons entitled to the right of residence to undergo, free of

charge, a medical examination to certify that they are not suffering from any of the conditions referred to in paragraph 1. Such medical examinations may not be required as a matter of routine.

Article 30 Notification of decisions

1. The persons concerned shall be notified in writing of any decision taken under Article 27(1), in such a way that they are able to comprehend its content and the implications for them.

2. The persons concerned shall be informed, precisely and in full, of the public policy, public security or public health grounds on which the decision taken in their case is based, unless this is contrary to the interests of State security.

3. The notification shall specify the court or administrative authority with which the person concerned may lodge an appeal, the time limit for the appeal and, where applicable, the time allowed for the person to leave the territory of the Member State. Save in duly substantiated cases of urgency, the time allowed to leave the territory shall be not less than one month from the date of notification.

Article 31 Procedural safeguards

1. The persons concerned shall have access to judicial and, where appropriate, administrative redress procedures in the host Member State to appeal against or seek review of any decision taken against them on the grounds of public policy, public security or public health.

2. Where the application for appeal against or judicial review of the expulsion decision is accompanied by an application for an interim order to suspend enforcement of that decision, actual removal from the territory may not take place until such time as the decision on the interim order has been taken, except:

- where the expulsion decision is based on a previous judicial decision; or
- where the persons concerned have had previous access to judicial review; or
- where the expulsion decision is based on imperative grounds of public security under Article 28(3).

3. The redress procedures shall allow for an examination of the legality of the decision, as well as of the facts and circumstances on which the proposed measure is based. They shall ensure that the decision is not disproportionate, particularly in view of the requirements laid down in Article 28.

4. Member States may exclude the individual concerned from their territory pending the redress procedure, but they may not prevent the individual from submitting his/her defence in person, except when his/her appearance may cause serious troubles to public policy or public security or when the appeal or judicial review concerns a denial of entry to the territory.

Article 32 Duration of exclusion orders

1. Persons excluded on grounds of public policy or public security may submit an application for lifting of the exclusion order after a reasonable period, depending on the circumstances, and in any event after three years from enforcement of the final exclusion order which has been validly adopted in accordance with Community law, by putting forward arguments to establish that there has been a material change in the circumstances which justified the decision ordering their exclusion.

The Member State concerned shall reach a decision on this application within six months of its submission.

2. The persons referred to in paragraph 1 shall have no right of entry to the territory of the Member State concerned while their application is being considered.

Article 33 Expulsion as a penalty or legal consequence

1. Expulsion orders may not be issued by the host Member State as a penalty or legal consequence of a custodial penalty, unless they conform to the requirements of Articles 27, 28 and 29.

2. If an expulsion order, as provided for in paragraph 1, is enforced more than two years after it was issued, the Member State shall check that the individual concerned is currently and genuinely a threat to public policy or public security and shall assess whether there has been any material change in the circumstances since the expulsion order was issued.

Chapter VII Final provisions

Article 34 Publicity

Member States shall disseminate information concerning the rights and obligations of Union citizens and their family members on the subjects covered by this Directive, particularly by means of awareness-raising campaigns conducted through national and local media and other means of communication.

Article 35 Abuse of rights

Member States may adopt the necessary measures to refuse, terminate or withdraw any right conferred by this Directive in the case of abuse of rights or fraud, such as marriages of convenience. Any such measure shall be proportionate and subject to the procedural safeguards provided for in Articles 30 and 31.

Article 36 Sanctions

Member States shall lay down provisions on the sanctions applicable to breaches of national rules adopted for the implementation of this Directive and shall take the measures required for their application. The sanctions laid down shall be effective and proportionate. Member States shall notify the Commission of these provisions not later than 30 April 2006 and as promptly as possible in the case of any subsequent changes.

Article 37 More favourable national provisions

The provisions of this Directive shall not affect any laws, regulations or administrative provisions laid down by a Member State which would be more favourable to the persons covered by this Directive.

Article 38 Repeals

(Paragraph 1 has been repealed.)

2. Directives 64/221/EEC, 68/360/EEC, 72/194/EEC, 73/148/EEC, 75/34/EEC, 75/35/EEC, 90/364/EEC, 90/365/EEC and 93/96/EEC shall be repealed with effect from 30 April 2006.

3. References made to the repealed provisions and Directives shall be construed as being made to this Directive.

Article 39 Report

No later than 30 April 2008 the Commission shall submit a report on the application of this Directive to the European Parliament and the Council, together with any necessary proposals, notably on the opportunity to extend the period of time during which Union citizens and their family members may reside in the territory of the host Member State without any conditions. The Member States shall provide the Commission with the information needed to produce the report.

Article 40 Transposition

1. Member States shall bring into force the laws, regulations and administrative provisions necessary to comply with this Directive by 30 April 2006.

When Member States adopt those measures, they shall contain a reference to this Directive or shall be accompanied by such a reference on the occasion of their official publication. The methods of making such reference shall be laid down by the Member States.

2. Member States shall communicate to the Commission the text of the provisions of national law which they adopt in the field covered by this Directive together with a table showing how the provisions of this Directive correspond to the national provisions adopted.

Article 41 Entry into force

This Directive shall enter into force on the day of its publication in the Official Journal of the European Union.

Article 42 Addressees

This Directive is addressed to the Member States.

Done at Brussels, 29 April 2004.
For the European Parliament
The President
M. McDOWELL
For the Council
The President
P. COX

Directive 2005/36/EC of the European Parliament and of the Council of 7 September 2005 on the recognition of professional qualifications*

[OJ 2005 L255/22]

THE EUROPEAN PARLIAMENT AND THE COUNCIL OF THE EUROPEAN UNION,

Having regard to the Treaty establishing the European Community, and in particular Article 40, Article 47(1), the first and third sentences of Article 47(2), and Article 55 thereof,

Having regard to the proposal from the Commission,[1]

Having regard to the opinion of the European Economic and Social Committee,[2]

Acting in accordance with the procedure laid down in Article 251 of the Treaty,[3]

Whereas:

(1) Pursuant to Article 3(1)(c) of the Treaty, the abolition, as between Member States, of obstacles to the free movement of persons and services is one of the objectives of the Community. For nationals of the Member States, this includes, in particular, the right to pursue a profession, in a self-employed or employed capacity, in a Member State other than the one in which they have obtained their professional qualifications. In addition, Article 47(1) of the Treaty lays down that directives shall be issued for the mutual recognition of diplomas, certificates and other evidence of formal qualifications.

(2) Following the European Council of Lisbon on 23 and 24 March 2000, the Commission adopted a Communication on 'An Internal Market Strategy for Services', aimed in particular at making the free provision of services within the Community as simple as within an individual Member State. Further to the Communication from the Commission entitled 'New European Labour Markets, Open to All, with Access to All', the European Council of Stockholm on 23 and 24 March 2001 entrusted the Commission with presenting for the 2002 Spring European Council specific proposals for a more uniform, transparent and flexible regime of recognition of qualifications.

(3) The guarantee conferred by this Directive on persons having acquired their professional qualifications in a Member State to have access to the same profession and pursue it in another Member State with the same rights as nationals is without prejudice to compliance by the migrant professional with any non-discriminatory conditions of pursuit which might be laid down by the latter Member State, provided that these are objectively justified and proportionate.

(4) In order to facilitate the free provision of services, there should be specific rules aimed at extending the possibility of pursuing professional activities under the original professional title. In the case of information society services provided at a distance, the provisions of Directive 2000/31/EC

* **Editor's Note:** As amended following Bulgarian and Romanian entry to the EU (OJ 2006 L363/141) and corrected by OJ 2007 L271/18 and OJ 2008 L 93/28. Further amended to OJ 2012 L 180/9 (Regulation 632/2012).

[1] OJ C 181 E, 30.7.2002, p. 183. [2] OJ C 61, 14.3.2003, p. 67.

[3] Opinion of the European Parliament of 11 February 2004 (OJ C 97 E, 22.4.2004, p. 230), Council Common Position of 21 December 2004 (OJ C 58 E, 8.3.2005, p. 1) and Position of the European Parliament of 11 May 2005 (not yet published in the Official Journal). Council Decision of 6 June 2005.

of the European Parliament and of the Council of 8 June 2000 on certain legal aspects of information society services, in particular electronic commerce, in the Internal Market[4], should also apply.

(5) In view of the different systems established for the cross-border provision of services on a temporary and occasional basis on the one hand, and for establishment on the other, the criteria for distinguishing between these two concepts in the event of the movement of the service provider to the territory of the host Member State should be clarified.

(6) The facilitation of service provision has to be ensured in the context of strict respect for public health and safety and consumer protection. Therefore, specific provisions should be envisaged for regulated professions having public health or safety implications, which provide cross-frontier services on a temporary or occasional basis.

(7) Host Member States may, where necessary and in accordance with Community law, provide for declaration requirements. These requirements should not lead to a disproportionate burden on service providers nor hinder or render less attractive the exercise of the freedom to provide services. The need for such requirements should be reviewed periodically in the light of the progress made in establishing a Community framework for administrative cooperation between Member States.

(8) The service provider should be subject to the application of disciplinary rules of the host Member State having a direct and specific link with the professional qualifications, such as the definition of the profession, the scope of activities covered by a profession or reserved to it, the use of titles and serious professional malpractice which is directly and specifically linked to consumer protection and safety.

(9) While maintaining, for the freedom of establishment, the principles and safeguards underlying the different systems for recognition in force, the rules of such systems should be improved in the light of experience. Moreover, the relevant directives have been amended on several occasions, and their provisions should be reorganised and rationalised by standardising the principles applicable. It is therefore necessary to replace Council Directives 89/48/EEC[5] and 92/51/ EEC,[6] as well as Directive 1999/42/EC of the European Parliament and of the Council[7] on the general system for the recognition of professional qualifications, and Council Directives 77/452/ EEC,[8] 77/453/EEC,[9] 78/686/EEC,[10] 78/687/EEC,[11] 78/1026/EEC,[12] 78/1027/EEC,[13] 80/154/EEC,[14] 80/155/EEC,[15] 85/384/EEC,[16] 85/432/EEC,[17] 85/433/EEC[18] and 93/16/EEC[19] concerning the professions of nurse responsible for general care, dental practitioner, veterinary surgeon, midwife, architect, pharmacist and doctor, by combining them in a single text.

(10) This Directive does not create an obstacle to the possibility of Member States recognising, in accordance with their rules, the professional qualifications acquired outside the territory of the European Union by third country nationals. All recognition should respect in any case minimum training conditions for certain professions.

(11) In the case of the professions covered by the general system for the recognition of qualifications, hereinafter referred to as 'the general system', Member States should retain the right to lay

[4] OJ L 178, 17.7.2000, p. 1.
[5] OJ L 19, 24.1.1989, p. 16. Directive as amended by Directive 2001/19/EC of the European Parliament and of the Council (OJ L 206, 31.7.2001, p. 1).
[6] OJ L 209, 24.7.1992, p. 25. Directive as last amended by Commission Decision 2004/108/EC (OJ L 32, 5.2.2004, p. 15).
[7] OJ L 201, 31.7.1999, p. 77.
[8] OJ L 176, 15.7.1977, p. 1. Directive as last amended by the 2003 Act of Accession.
[9] OJ L 176, 15.7.1977, p. 8. Directive as last amended by Directive 2001/19/EC.
[10] OJ L 233, 24.8.1978, p. 1. Directive as last amended by the 2003 Act of Accession.
[11] OJ L 233, 24.8.1978, p. 10. Directive as last amended by the 2003 Act of Accession.
[12] OJ L 362, 23.12.1978, p. 1. Directive as last amended by Directive 2001/19/EC.
[13] OJ L 362, 23.12.1978, p. 7. Directive as last amended by Directive 2001/19/EC.
[14] OJ L 33, 11.2.1980, p. 1. Directive as last amended by the 2003 Act of Accession.
[15] OJ L 33, 11.2.1980, p. 8. Directive as last amended by Directive 2001/19/EC.
[16] OJ L 223, 21.8.1985, p. 15. Directive as last amended by the 2003 Act of Accession.
[17] OJ L 253, 24.9.1985, p. 34. Directive as amended by Directive 2001/19/EC.
[18] OJ L 253, 24.9.1985, p. 37. Directive as last amended by the 2003 Act of Accession.
[19] OJ L 165, 7.7.1993, p. 1. Directive as last amended by Regulation (EC) No 1882/2003 of the European Parliament and of the Council (OJ L 284, 31.10.2003, p. 1).

down the minimum level of qualification required to ensure the quality of the services provided on their territory. However, pursuant to Articles 10, 39 and 43 of the Treaty, they should not require a national of a Member State to obtain qualifications, which they generally lay down only in terms of the diplomas awarded under their national educational system, where the person concerned has already obtained all or part of those qualifications in another Member State. As a result, it should be laid down that any host Member State in which a profession is regulated must take account of the qualifications obtained in another Member State and assess whether they correspond to those which it requires. The general system for recognition, however, does not prevent a Member State from making any person pursuing a profession on its territory subject to specific requirements due to the application of professional rules justified by the general public interest. Rules of this kind relate, for example, to organisation of the profession, professional standards, including those concerning ethics, and supervision and liability. Lastly, this Directive is not intended to interfere with Member States' legitimate interest in preventing any of their citizens from evading enforcement of the national law relating to professions.

(12) This Directive concerns the recognition by Member States of professional qualifications acquired in other Member States. It does not, however, concern the recognition by Member States of recognition decisions adopted by other Member States pursuant to this Directive. Consequently, individuals holding professional qualifications which have been recognised pursuant to this Directive may not use such recognition to obtain in their Member State of origin rights different from those conferred by the professional qualification obtained in that Member State, unless they provide evidence that they have obtained additional professional qualifications in the host Member State.

(13) In order to define the mechanism of recognition under the general system, it is necessary to group the various national education and training schemes into different levels. These levels, which are established only for the purpose of the operation of the general system, have no effect upon the national education and training structures nor upon the competence of Member States in this field.

(14) The mechanism of recognition established by Directives 89/48/EEC and 92/51/EEC remains unchanged. As a consequence, the holder of a diploma certifying successful completion of training at post-secondary level of a duration of at least one year should be permitted access to a regulated profession in a Member State where access is contingent upon possession of a diploma certifying successful completion of higher or university education of four years' duration, regardless of the level to which the diploma required in the host Member State belongs. Conversely, where access to a regulated profession is contingent upon successful completion of higher or university education of more than four years, such access should be permitted only to holders of a diploma certifying successful completion of higher or university education of at least three years' duration.

(15) In the absence of harmonisation of the minimum training conditions for access to the professions governed by the general system, it should be possible for the host Member State to impose a compensation measure. This measure should be proportionate and, in particular, take account of the applicant's professional experience. Experience shows that requiring the migrant to choose between an aptitude test or an adaptation period offers adequate safeguards as regards the latter's level of qualification, so that any derogation from that choice should in each case be justified by an imperative requirement in the general interest.

(16) In order to promote the free movement of professionals, while ensuring an adequate level of qualification, various professional associations and organisations or Member States should be able to propose common platforms at European level. This Directive should take account, under certain conditions, in compliance with the competence of Member States to decide the qualifications required for the pursuit of professions in their territory as well as the contents and the organisation of their systems of education and professional training and in compliance with Community law, and in particular Community law on competition, of those initiatives, while promoting, in this context, a more automatic character of recognition under the general system. Professional associations which are in a position to submit common platforms should be representative at national and European level. A common platform is a set of criteria which make it possible to compensate for the widest range of

substantial differences which have been identified between the training requirements in at least two-thirds of the Member States including all the Member States which regulate that profession. These criteria could, for example, include requirements such as additional training, an adaptation period under supervised practice, an aptitude test, or a prescribed minimum level of professional practice, or combinations thereof.

(17) In order to take into account all situations for which there is still no provision relating to the recognition of professional qualifications, the general system should be extended to those cases which are not covered by a specific system, either where the profession is not covered by one of those systems or where, although the profession is covered by such a specific system, the applicant does not for some particular and exceptional reason meet the conditions to benefit from it.

(18) There is a need to simplify the rules allowing access to a number of industrial, commercial and craft activities, in Member States where those professions are regulated, in so far as those activities have been pursued for a reasonable and sufficiently recent period of time in another Member State, while maintaining for those activities a system of automatic recognition based on professional experience.

(19) Freedom of movement and the mutual recognition of the evidence of formal qualifications of doctors, nurses responsible for general care, dental practitioners, veterinary surgeons, midwives, pharmacists and architects should be based on the fundamental principle of automatic recognition of the evidence of formal qualifications on the basis of coordinated minimum conditions for training. In addition, access in the Member States to the professions of doctor, nurse responsible for general care, dental practitioner, veterinary surgeon, midwife and pharmacist should be made conditional upon the possession of a given qualification ensuring that the person concerned has undergone training which meets the minimum conditions laid down. This system should be supplemented by a number of acquired rights from which qualified professionals benefit under certain conditions.

(20) To allow for the characteristics of the qualification system for doctors and dental practitioners and the related acquis communautaire in the area of mutual recognition, the principle of automatic recognition of medical and dental specialities common to at least two Member States should continue to apply to all specialities recognised on the date of adoption of this Directive. To simplify the system, however, automatic recognition should apply after the date of entry into force of this Directive only to those new medical specialities common to at least two-fifths of Member States. Moreover, this Directive does not prevent Member States from agreeing amongst themselves on automatic recognition for certain medical and dental specialities common to them but not automatically recognised within the meaning of this Directive, according to their own rules.

(21) Automatic recognition of formal qualifications of doctor with basic training should be without prejudice to the competence of Member States to associate this qualification with professional activities or not.

(22) All Member States should recognise the profession of dental practitioner as a specific profession distinct from that of medical practitioner, whether or not specialised in odontostomatology. Member States should ensure that the training given to dental practitioners equips them with the skills needed for prevention, diagnosis and treatment relating to anomalies and illnesses of the teeth, mouth, jaws and associated tissues. The professional activity of the dental practitioner should be carried out by holders of a qualification as dental practitioner set out in this Directive.

(23) It did not appear desirable to lay down standardised training for midwives for all the Member States. Rather, the latter should have the greatest possible freedom to organise their training.

(24) With a view to simplifying this Directive, reference should be made to the concept of 'pharmacist' in order to delimit the scope of the provisions relating to the automatic recognition of the qualifications, without prejudice to the special features of the national regulations governing those activities.

(25) Holders of qualifications as a pharmacist are specialists in the field of medicines and should, in principle, have access in all Member States to a minimum range of activities in this field. In defining

this minimum range, this Directive should neither have the effect of limiting the activities accessible to pharmacists in the Member States, in particular as regards medical biology analyses, nor create a monopoly for those professionals, as this remains a matter solely for the Member States. The provisions of this Directive are without prejudice to the possibility for the Member States to impose supplementary training conditions for access to activities not included in the coordinated minimum range of activities. This means that the host Member State should be able to impose these conditions on the nationals who hold qualifications which are covered by automatic recognition within the meaning of this Directive.

(26) This Directive does not coordinate all the conditions for access to activities in the field of pharmacy and the pursuit of these activities. In particular, the geographical distribution of pharmacies and the monopoly for dispensing medicines should remain a matter for the Member States. This Directive leaves unchanged the legislative, regulatory and administrative provisions of the Member States forbidding companies from pursuing certain pharmacists' activities or subjecting the pursuit of such activities to certain conditions.

(27) Architectural design, the quality of buildings, their harmonious incorporation into their surroundings, respect for natural and urban landscapes and for the public and private heritage are a matter of public interest. Mutual recognition of qualifications should therefore be based on qualitative and quantitative criteria which ensure that the holders of recognised qualifications are in a position to understand and translate the needs of individuals, social groups and authorities as regards spatial planning, the design, organisation and realisation of structures, conservation and the exploitation of the architectural heritage, and protection of natural balances.

(28) National regulations in the field of architecture and on access to and the pursuit of the professional activities of an architect vary widely in scope. In most Member States, activities in the field of architecture are pursued, de jure or de facto, by persons bearing the title of architect alone or accompanied by another title, without those persons having a monopoly on the pursuit of such activities, unless there are legislative provisions to the contrary. These activities, or some of them, may also be pursued by other professionals, in particular by engineers who have undergone special training in the field of construction or the art of building. With a view to simplifying this Directive, reference should be made to the concept of 'architect' in order to delimit the scope of the provisions relating to the automatic recognition of the qualifications in the field of architecture, without prejudice to the special features of the national regulations governing those activities.

(29) Where a national and European-level professional organisation or association for a regulated profession makes a reasoned request for specific provisions for the recognition of qualifications on the basis of coordination of minimum training conditions, the Commission shall assess the appropriateness of adopting a proposal for the amendment of this Directive.

(30) In order to ensure the effectiveness of the system for the recognition of professional qualifications, uniform formalities and rules of procedure should be defined for its implementation, as well as certain details of the pursuit of the profession.

(31) Since collaboration among the Member States and between them and the Commission is likely to facilitate the implementation of this Directive and compliance with the obligations deriving from it, the means of collaboration should be organised.

(32) The introduction, at European level, of professional cards by professional associations or organisations could facilitate the mobility of professionals, in particular by speeding up the exchange of information between the host Member State and the Member State of origin. This professional card should make it possible to monitor the career of professionals who establish themselves in various Member States. Such cards could contain information, in full respect of data protection provisions, on the professional's professional qualifications (university or institution attended, qualifications obtained, professional experience), his legal establishment, penalties received relating to his profession and the details of the relevant competent authority.

(33) The establishment of a network of contact points with the task of providing the citizens of the Member States with information and assistance will make it possible to ensure that the system

of recognition is transparent. These contact points will provide any citizen who so requests and the Commission with all the information and addresses relevant to the recognition procedure. The designation of a single contact point by each Member State within this network does not affect the organisation of competencies at national level. In particular, it does not prevent the designation at national level of several offices, the contact point designated within the aforementioned network being in charge of coordinating with the other offices and informing the citizen, where necessary, of the details of the relevant competent office.

(34) Administering the various systems of recognition set up by the sectoral directives and the general system has proved cumbersome and complex. There is therefore a need to simplify the administration and updating of this Directive to take account of scientific and technical progress, in particular where the minimum conditions of training are coordinated with a view to automatic recognition of qualifications. A single committee for the recognition of professional qualifications should be set up for this purpose, and suitable involvement of representatives of the professional organisations, also at European level, should be ensured.

(35) The measures necessary for the implementation of this Directive should be adopted in accordance with Council Decision 1999/468/EC of 28 June 1999 laying down the procedures for the exercise of implementing powers conferred on the Commission.[20]

(36) The preparation by the Member States of a periodic report on the implementation of this Directive, containing statistical data, will make it possible to determine the impact of the system for the recognition of professional qualifications.

(37) There should be a suitable procedure for adopting temporary measures if the application of any provision of this Directive were to encounter major difficulties in a Member State.

(38) The provisions of this Directive do not affect the powers of the Member States as regards the organisation of their national social security system and determining the activities which must be pursued under that system.

(39) In view of the speed of technological change and scientific progress, life-long learning is of particular importance for a large number of professions. In this context, it is for the Member States to adopt the detailed arrangements under which, through suitable ongoing training, professionals will keep abreast of technical and scientific progress.

(40) Since the objectives of this Directive, namely the rationalisation, simplification and improvement of the rules for the recognition of professional qualifications, cannot be sufficiently achieved by the Member States and can therefore be better achieved at Community level, the Community may adopt measures, in accordance with the principle of subsidiarity as set out in Article 5 of the Treaty. In accordance with the principle of proportionality, as set out in that Article, this Directive does not go beyond what is necessary in order to achieve those objectives.

(41) This Directive is without prejudice to the application of Articles 39(4) and 45 of the Treaty concerning notably notaries.

(42) This Directive applies, concerning the right of establishment and the provision of services, without prejudice to other specific legal provisions regarding the recognition of professional qualifications, such as those existing in the field of transport, insurance intermediaries and statutory auditors. This Directive does not affect the operation of Council Directive 77/249/EEC of 22 March 1977 to facilitate the effective exercise by lawyers of freedom to provide services,[21] or of Directive 98/5/EC of the European Parliament and of the Council of 16 February 1998 to facilitate practice of the profession of lawyer on a permanent basis in a Member State other than that in which the qualification was obtained.[22] The recognition of professional qualifications for lawyers for the purpose of immediate establishment under the professional title of the host Member State should be covered by this Directive.

[20] OJ L 184, 17.7.1999, p.23.
[21] OJ L 78, 26.3.1977, p. 17. Directive as last amended by the 2003 Act of Accession.
[22] OJ L 77, 14.3.1998, p. 36. Directive as amended by the 2003 Act of Accession.

(43) To the extent that they are regulated, this Directive includes also liberal professions, which are, according to this Directive, those practised on the basis of relevant professional qualifications in a personal, responsible and professionally independent capacity by those providing intellectual and conceptual services in the interest of the client and the public. The exercise of the profession might be subject in the Member States, in conformity with the Treaty, to specific legal constraints based on national legislation and on the statutory provisions laid down autonomously, within that framework, by the respective professional representative bodies, safeguarding and developing their professionalism and quality of service and the confidentiality of relations with the client.

(44) This Directive is without prejudice to measures necessary to ensure a high level of health and consumer protection,

HAVE ADOPTED THIS DIRECTIVE:

Title I General provisions

Article 1 Purpose

This Directive establishes rules according to which a Member State which makes access to or pursuit of a regulated profession in its territory contingent upon possession of specific professional qualifications (referred to hereinafter as the host Member State) shall recognise professional qualifications obtained in one or more other Member States (referred to hereinafter as the home Member State) and which allow the holder of the said qualifications to pursue the same profession there, for access to and pursuit of that profession.

Article 2 Scope

1. This Directive shall apply to all nationals of a Member State wishing to pursue a regulated profession in a Member State, including those belonging to the liberal professions, other than that in which they obtained their professional qualifications, on either a self-employed or employed basis.

2. Each Member State may permit Member State nationals in possession of evidence of professional qualifications not obtained in a Member State to pursue a regulated profession within the meaning of Article 3(1)(a) on its territory in accordance with its rules. In the case of professions covered by Title III, Chapter III, this initial recognition shall respect the minimum training conditions laid down in that Chapter.

3. Where, for a given regulated profession, other specific arrangements directly related to the recognition of professional qualifications are established in a separate instrument of Community law, the corresponding provisions of this Directive shall not apply.

Article 3 Definitions

1. For the purposes of this Directive, the following definitions apply:

(a) 'regulated profession': a professional activity or group of professional activities, access to which, the pursuit of which, or one of the modes of pursuit of which is subject, directly or indirectly, by virtue of legislative, regulatory or administrative provisions to the possession of specific professional qualifications; in particular, the use of a professional title limited by legislative, regulatory or administrative provisions to holders of a given professional qualification shall constitute a mode of pursuit. Where the first sentence of this definition does not apply, a profession referred to in paragraph 2 shall be treated as a regulated profession;

(b) 'professional qualifications': qualifications attested by evidence of formal qualifications, an attestation of competence referred to in Article 11, point (a)(i) and/or professional experience;

(c) 'evidence of formal qualifications': diplomas, certificates and other evidence issued by an authority in a Member State designated pursuant to legislative, regulatory or administrative provisions of that Member State and certifying successful completion of professional training obtained mainly in the Community. Where the first sentence of this definition does not apply, evidence of formal qualifications referred to in paragraph 3 shall be treated as evidence of formal qualifications;

(d) 'competent authority': any authority or body empowered by a Member State specifically to issue or receive training diplomas and other documents or information and to receive the applications, and take the decisions, referred to in this Directive;

(e) 'regulated education and training': any training which is specifically geared to the pursuit of a given profession and which comprises a course or courses complemented, where appropriate, by professional training, or probationary or professional practice.

The structure and level of the professional training, probationary or professional practice shall be determined by the laws, regulations or administrative provisions of the Member State concerned or monitored or approved by the authority designated for that purpose;

(f) 'professional experience': the actual and lawful pursuit of the profession concerned in a Member State;

(g) 'adaptation period': the pursuit of a regulated profession in the host Member State under the responsibility of a qualified member of that profession, such period of supervised practice possibly being accompanied by further training. This period of supervised practice shall be the subject of an assessment. The detailed rules governing the adaptation period and its assessment as well as the status of a migrant under supervision shall be laid down by the competent authority in the host Member State.

The status enjoyed in the host Member State by the person undergoing the period of supervised practice, in particular in the matter of right of residence as well as obligations, social rights and benefits, allowances and remuneration, shall be established by the competent authorities in that Member State in accordance with applicable Community law;

(h) 'aptitude test': a test limited to the professional knowledge of the applicant, made by the competent authorities of the host Member State with the aim of assessing the ability of the applicant to pursue a regulated profession in that Member State. In order to permit this test to be carried out, the competent authorities shall draw up a list of subjects which, on the basis of a comparison of the education and training required in the Member State and that received by the applicant, are not covered by the diploma or other evidence of formal qualifications possessed by the applicant.

The aptitude test must take account of the fact that the applicant is a qualified professional in the home Member State or the Member State from which he comes. It shall cover subjects to be selected from those on the list, knowledge of which is essential in order to be able to pursue the profession in the host Member State. The test may also include knowledge of the professional rules applicable to the activities in question in the host Member State.

The detailed application of the aptitude test and the status, in the host Member State, of the applicant who wishes to prepare himself for the aptitude test in that State shall be determined by the competent authorities in that Member State;

(i) 'manager of an undertaking': any person who in an undertaking in the occupational field in question has pursued an activity:
   (i) as a manager of an undertaking or a manager of a branch of an undertaking; or
   (ii) as a deputy to the proprietor or the manager of an undertaking where that post involves responsibility equivalent to that of the proprietor or manager represented; or
   (iii) in a managerial post with duties of a commercial and/or technical nature and with responsibility for one or more departments of the undertaking.

2. A profession practised by the members of an association or organisation listed in Annex I shall be treated as a regulated profession.

The purpose of the associations or organisations referred to in the first subparagraph is, in particular, to promote and maintain a high standard in the professional field concerned. To that end they are recognised in a special form by a Member State and award evidence of formal qualifications to their members, ensure that their members respect the rules of professional conduct which they prescribe, and confer on them the right to use a title or designatory letters or to benefit from a status corresponding to those formal qualifications.

On each occasion that a Member State grants recognition to an association or organisation referred to in the first subparagraph, it shall inform the Commission, which shall publish an appropriate notification in the Official Journal of the European Union.

3. Evidence of formal qualifications issued by a third country shall be regarded as evidence of formal qualifications if the holder has three years' professional experience in the profession concerned on the territory of the Member State which recognised that evidence of formal qualifications in accordance with Article 2(2), certified by that Member State.

Article 4 Effects of recognition

1. The recognition of professional qualifications by the host Member State allows the beneficiary to gain access in that Member State to the same profession as that for which he is qualified in the home Member State and to pursue it in the host Member State under the same conditions as its nationals.

2. For the purposes of this Directive, the profession which the applicant wishes to pursue in the host Member State is the same as that for which he is qualified in his home Member State if the activities covered are comparable.

Title II Free provision of services

Article 5 Principle of the free provision of services

1. Without prejudice to specific provisions of Community law, as well as to Articles 6 and 7 of this Directive, Member States shall not restrict, for any reason relating to professional qualifications, the free provision of services in another Member State:

(a) if the service provider is legally established in a Member State for the purpose of pursuing the same profession there (hereinafter referred to as the Member State of establishment), and

(b) where the service provider moves, if he has pursued that profession in the Member State of establishment for at least two years during the 10 years preceding the provision of services when the profession is not regulated in that Member State. The condition requiring two years' pursuit shall not apply when either the profession or the education and training leading to the profession is regulated.

2. The provisions of this title shall only apply where the service provider moves to the territory of the host Member State to pursue, on a temporary and occasional basis, the profession referred to in paragraph 1.

The temporary and occasional nature of the provision of services shall be assessed case by case, in particular in relation to its duration, its frequency, its regularity and its continuity.

3. Where a service provider moves, he shall be subject to professional rules of a professional, statutory or administrative nature which are directly linked to professional qualifications, such as the definition of the profession, the use of titles and serious professional malpractice which is directly and specifically linked to consumer protection and safety, as well as disciplinary provisions which are applicable in the host Member State to professionals who pursue the same profession in that Member State.

Article 6 Exemptions

Pursuant to Article 5(1), the host Member State shall exempt service providers established in another Member State from the requirements which it places on professionals established in its territory relating to:

(a) authorisation by, registration with or membership of a professional organisation or body. In order to facilitate the application of disciplinary provisions in force on their territory according to Article 5(3), Member States may provide either for automatic temporary registration with or for pro forma membership of such a professional organisation or body, provided that such registration or membership does not delay or complicate in any way the provision of services and does not entail any additional costs for the service provider. A copy of the declaration and, where applicable, of the renewal referred to in Article 7(1), accompanied, for professions which have implications for public health and safety referred to in Article 7(4) or which benefit from automatic recognition under Title III Chapter III, by a copy of the documents referred to in Article 7(2) shall be sent by the competent authority to the relevant professional organisation or body, and this shall constitute automatic temporary registration or pro forma membership for this purpose;

(b) registration with a public social security body for the purpose of settling accounts with an insurer relating to activities pursued for the benefit of insured persons.

The service provider shall, however, inform in advance or, in an urgent case, afterwards, the body referred to in point (b) of the services which he has provided.

Article 7 Declaration to be made in advance, if the service provider moves

1. Member States may require that, where the service provider first moves from one Member State to another in order to provide services, he shall inform the competent authority in the host Member State in a written declaration to be made in advance including the details of any insurance cover or other means of personal or collective protection with regard to professional liability. Such declaration shall be renewed once a year if the service provider intends to provide temporary or occasional services in that Member State during that year. The service provider may supply the declaration by any means.

2. Moreover, for the first provision of services or if there is a material change in the situation substantiated by the documents, Member States may require that the declaration be accompanied by the following documents:

(a) proof of the nationality of the service provider;

(b) an attestation certifying that the holder is legally established in a Member State for the purpose of pursuing the activities concerned and that he is not prohibited from practising, even temporarily, at the moment of delivering the attestation;

(c) evidence of professional qualifications;

(d) for cases referred to in Article 5(1)(b), any means of proof that the service provider has pursued the activity concerned for at least two years during the previous ten years;

(e) for professions in the security sector, where the Member State so requires for its own nationals, evidence of no criminal convictions.

3. The service shall be provided under the professional title of the Member State of establishment, in so far as such a title exists in that Member State for the professional activity in question. That title shall be indicated in the official language or one of the official languages of the Member State of establishment in such a way as to avoid any confusion with the professional title of the host Member State. Where no such professional title exists in the Member State of establishment, the service provider shall indicate his formal qualification in the official language or one of the official languages of that Member State. By way of exception, the service shall be provided under the professional title of the host Member State for cases referred to in Title III Chapter III.

4. For the first provision of services, in the case of regulated professions having public health or safety implications, which do not benefit from automatic recognition under Title III Chapter III, the competent authority of the host Member State may check the professional qualifications of the service provider prior to the first provision of services. Such a prior check shall be possible only where the purpose of the check is to avoid serious damage to the health or safety of the service recipient due to a lack of professional qualification of the service provider and where this does not go beyond what is necessary for that purpose.

Within a maximum of one month of receipt of the declaration and accompanying documents, the competent authority shall endeavour to inform the service provider either of its decision not to check his qualifications or of the outcome of such check. Where there is a difficulty which would result in delay, the competent authority shall notify the service provider within the first month of the reason for the delay and the timescale for a decision, which must be finalised within the second month of receipt of completed documentation.

Where there is a substantial difference between the professional qualifications of the service provider and the training required in the host Member State, to the extent that that difference is such as to be harmful to public health or safety, the host Member State shall give the service provider the opportunity to show, in particular by means of an aptitude test, that he has acquired the knowledge or competence lacking. In any case, it must be possible to provide the service within one month of a decision being taken in accordance with the previous subparagraph.

In the absence of a reaction of the competent authority within the deadlines set in the previous subparagraphs, the service may be provided.

In cases where qualifications have been verified under this paragraph, the service shall be provided under the professional title of the host Member State.

Article 8 Administrative cooperation

1. The competent authorities of the host Member State may ask the competent authorities of the Member State of establishment, for each provision of services, to provide any information relevant to the legality of the service provider's establishment and his good conduct, as well as the absence of any disciplinary or criminal sanctions of a professional nature. The competent authorities of the Member State of establishment shall provide this information in accordance with the provisions of Article 56.

2. The competent authorities shall ensure the exchange of all information necessary for complaints by a recipient of a service against a service provider to be correctly pursued. Recipients shall be informed of the outcome of the complaint.

Article 9 Information to be given to the recipients of the service

In cases where the service is provided under the professional title of the Member State of establishment or under the formal qualification of the service provider, in addition to the other requirements relating to information contained in Community law, the competent authorities of the host Member State may require the service provider to furnish the recipient of the service with any or all of the following information:

(a) if the service provider is registered in a commercial register or similar public register, the register in which he is registered, his registration number, or equivalent means of identification contained in that register;

(b) if the activity is subject to authorisation in the Member State of establishment, the name and address of the competent supervisory authority;

(c) any professional association or similar body with which the service provider is registered;

(d) the professional title or, where no such title exists, the formal qualification of the service provider and the Member State in which it was awarded;

(e) if the service provider performs an activity which is subject to VAT, the VAT identification number referred to in Article 22(1) of the sixth Council Directive 77/388/EEC of 17 May 1977 on the harmonisation of the laws of the Member States relating to turnover taxes—Common system of value added tax: uniform basis of assessment;[23]

(f) details of any insurance cover or other means of personal or collective protection with regard to professional liability.

[23] OJ L 145, 13.6.1977, p. 1. Directive as last amended by Directive 2004/66/EC (OJ L 168, 1.5.2004, p. 35).

Title III Freedom of establishment

Chapter I General system for the recognition of evidence of training

Article 10 Scope

This Chapter applies to all professions which are not covered by Chapters II and III of this Title and in the following cases in which the applicant, for specific and exceptional reasons, does not satisfy the conditions laid down in those Chapters:

(a) for activities listed in Annex IV, when the migrant does not meet the requirements set out in Articles 17, 18 and 19;

(b) for doctors with basic training, specialised doctors, nurses responsible for general care, dental practitioners, specialised dental practitioners, veterinary surgeons, midwives, pharmacists and architects, when the migrant does not meet the requirements of effective and lawful professional practice referred to in Articles 23, 27, 33, 37, 39, 43 and 49;

(c) for architects, when the migrant holds evidence of formal qualification not listed in Annex V, point 5.7;

(d) without prejudice to Articles 21(1), 23 and 27, for doctors, nurses, dental practitioners, veterinary surgeons, midwives, pharmacists and architects holding evidence of formal qualifications as a specialist, who must have taken part in the training leading to the possession of a title listed in Annex V, points 5.1.1, 5.2.2, 5.3.2, 5.4.2, 5.5.2, 5.6.2 and 5.7.1, and solely for the purpose of the recognition of the relevant specialty;

(e) for nurses responsible for general care and specialised nurses holding evidence of formal qualifications as a specialist who must have taken part in the training leading to the possession of a title listed in Annex V, point 5.2.2, when the migrant seeks recognition in another Member State where the relevant professional activities are pursued by specialised nurses without training as general care nurse;

(f) for specialised nurses without training as general care nurse, when the migrant seeks recognition in another Member State where the relevant professional activities are pursued by nurses responsible for general care, specialised nurses without training as general care nurse or specialised nurses holding evidence of formal qualifications as a specialist who must have taken part in the training leading to the possession of the titles listed in Annex V, point 5.2.2;

(g) for migrants meeting the requirements set out in Article 3(3).

Article 11 Levels of qualification

For the purpose of applying Article 13, the professional qualifications are grouped under the following levels as described below:

(a) an attestation of competence issued by a competent authority in the home Member State designated pursuant to legislative, regulatory or administrative provisions of that Member State, on the basis of:

  (i) either a training course not forming part of a certificate or diploma within the meaning of points (b), (c), (d) or (e), or a specific examination without prior training, or full-time pursuit of the profession in a Member State for three consecutive years or for an equivalent duration on a part-time basis during the previous 10 years,

  (ii) or general primary or secondary education, attesting that the holder has acquired general knowledge;

(b) a certificate attesting to a successful completion of a secondary course,

  (i) either general in character, supplemented by a course of study or professional training other than those referred to in point (c) and/or by the probationary or professional practice required in addition to that course,

(ii) or technical or professional in character, supplemented where appropriate by a course of study or professional training as referred to in point (i), and/or by the probationary or professional practice required in addition to that course;

(c) a diploma certifying successful completion of

(i) either training at post-secondary level other than that referred to in points (d) and (e) of a duration of at least one year or of an equivalent duration on a part-time basis, one of the conditions of entry of which is, as a general rule, the successful completion of the secondary course required to obtain entry to university or higher education or the completion of equivalent school education of the second secondary level, as well as the professional training which may be required in addition to that post-secondary course; or

(ii) in the case of a regulated profession, training with a special structure, included in Annex II, equivalent to the level of training provided for under (i), which provides a comparable professional standard and which prepares the trainee for a comparable level of responsibilities and functions. The Commission may adapt the list in Annex II to take account of training which meets the requirements provided for in point (c)(ii) of the first paragraph. Those measures, designed to amend non-essential elements of this Directive, shall be adopted in accordance with the regulatory procedure with scrutiny referred to in Article 58(3);

(d) a diploma certifying successful completion of training at post-secondary level of at least three and not more than four years' duration, or of an equivalent duration on a part-time basis, at a university or establishment of higher education or another establishment providing the same level of training, as well as the professional training which may be required in addition to that post-secondary course;

(e) a diploma certifying that the holder has successfully completed a post-secondary course of at least four years' duration, or of an equivalent duration on a part-time basis, at a university or establishment of higher education or another establishment of equivalent level and, where appropriate, that he has successfully completed the professional training required in addition to the post-secondary course.

Article 12 Equal treatment of qualifications

Any evidence of formal qualifications or set of evidence of formal qualifications issued by a competent authority in a Member State, certifying successful completion of training in the Community which is recognised by that Member State as being of an equivalent level and which confers on the holder the same rights of access to or pursuit of a profession or prepares for the pursuit of that profession, shall be treated as evidence of formal qualifications of the type covered by Article 11, including the level in question.

Any professional qualification which, although not satisfying the requirements contained in the legislative, regulatory or administrative provisions in force in the home Member State for access to or the pursuit of a profession, confers on the holder acquired rights by virtue of these provisions, shall also be treated as such evidence of formal qualifications under the same conditions as set out in the first subparagraph. This applies in particular if the home Member State raises the level of training required for admission to a profession and for its exercise, and if an individual who has undergone former training, which does not meet the requirements of the new qualification, benefits from acquired rights by virtue of national legislative, regulatory or administrative provisions; in such case this former training is considered by the host Member State, for the purposes of the application of Article 13, as corresponding to the level of the new training.

Article 13 Conditions for recognition

1. If access to or pursuit of a regulated profession in a host Member State is contingent upon possession of specific professional qualifications, the competent authority of that Member State shall permit access to and pursuit of that profession, under the same conditions as apply to its nationals, to

applicants possessing the attestation of competence or evidence of formal qualifications required by another Member State in order to gain access to and pursue that profession on its territory.

Attestations of competence or evidence of formal qualifications shall satisfy the following conditions:

(a) they shall have been issued by a competent authority in a Member State, designated in accordance with the legislative, regulatory or administrative provisions of that Member State;

(b) they shall attest a level of professional qualification at least equivalent to the level immediately prior to that which is required in the host Member State, as described in Article 11.

2. Access to and pursuit of the profession, as described in paragraph 1, shall also be granted to applicants who have pursued the profession referred to in that paragraph on a full-time basis for two years during the previous 10 years in another Member State which does not regulate that profession, providing they possess one or more attestations of competence or documents providing evidence of formal qualifications.

Attestations of competence and evidence of formal qualifications shall satisfy the following conditions:

(a) they shall have been issued by a competent authority in a Member State, designated in accordance with the legislative, regulatory or administrative provisions of that Member State;

(b) they shall attest a level of professional qualification at least equivalent to the level immediately prior to that required in the host Member State, as described in Article 11;

(c) they shall attest that the holder has been prepared for the pursuit of the profession in question.

The two years' professional experience referred to in the first subparagraph may not, however, be required if the evidence of formal qualifications which the applicant possesses certifies regulated education and training within the meaning of Article 3(1)(e) at the levels of qualifications described in Article 11, points (b), (c), (d) or (e). The regulated education and training listed in Annex III shall be considered as such regulated education and training at the level described in Article 11, point (c). The Commission may adapt the list in Annex III to take account of regulated education and training which provides a comparable professional standard and which prepares the trainee for a comparable level of responsibilities and functions. Those measures, designed to amend non-essential elements of this Directive, shall be adopted in accordance with the regulatory procedure with scrutiny referred to in Article 58(3).

3. By way of derogation from paragraph 1, point (b) and to paragraph 2, point (b), the host Member State shall permit access and pursuit of a regulated profession where access to this profession is contingent in its territory upon possession of a qualification certifying successful completion of higher or university education of four years' duration, and where the applicant possesses a qualification referred to in Article 11, point (c).

Article 14 Compensation measures

1. Article 13 does not preclude the host Member State from requiring the applicant to complete an adaptation period of up to three years or to take an aptitude test if:

(a) the duration of the training of which he provides evidence under the terms of Article 13, paragraph 1 or 2, is at least one year shorter than that required by the host Member State;

(b) the training he has received covers substantially different matters than those covered by the evidence of formal qualifications required in the host Member State;

(c) the regulated profession in the host Member State comprises one or more regulated professional activities which do not exist in the corresponding profession in the applicant's home Member State within the meaning of Article 4(2), and that difference consists in specific training which is required in the host Member State and which covers substantially different matters from those covered by the applicant's attestation of competence or evidence of formal qualifications.

2. If the host Member State makes use of the option provided for in paragraph 1, it must offer the applicant the choice between an adaptation period and an aptitude test.

Where a Member State considers, with respect to a given profession, that it is necessary to derogate from the requirement, set out in the previous subparagraph, that it give the applicant a choice between an adaptation period and an aptitude test, it shall inform the other Member States and the Commission in advance and provide sufficient justification for the derogation.

If, after receiving all necessary information, the Commission considers that the derogation referred to in the second subparagraph is inappropriate or that it is not in accordance with Community law, it shall, within three months, ask the Member State in question to refrain from taking the envisaged measure. In the absence of a response from the Commission within the abovementioned deadline, the derogation may be applied.

3. By way of derogation from the principle of the right of the applicant to choose, as laid down in paragraph 2, for professions whose pursuit requires precise knowledge of national law and in respect of which the provision of advice and/or assistance concerning national law is an essential and constant aspect of the professional activity, the host Member State may stipulate either an adaptation period or an aptitude test.

This applies also to the cases provided for in Article 10 points (b) and (c), in Article 10 point (d) concerning doctors and dental practitioners, in Article 10 point (f) when the migrant seeks recognition in another Member State where the relevant professional activities are pursued by nurses responsible for general care or specialised nurses holding evidence of formal qualifications as a specialist who must have taken part in the training leading to the possession of the titles listed in Annex V, point 5.2.2 and in Article 10 point (g).

In the cases covered by Article 10 point (a), the host Member State may require an adaptation period or an aptitude test if the migrant envisages pursuing professional activities in a self-employed capacity or as a manager of an undertaking which require the knowledge and the application of the specific national rules in force, provided that knowledge and application of those rules are required by the competent authorities of the host Member State for access to such activities by its own nationals.

4. For the purpose of applying paragraph 1 points (b) and (c), 'substantially different matters' means matters of which knowledge is essential for pursuing the profession and with regard to which the training received by the migrant shows important differences in terms of duration or content from the training required by the host Member State.

5. Paragraph 1 shall be applied with due regard to the principle of proportionality. In particular, if the host Member State intends to require the applicant to complete an adaptation period or take an aptitude test, it must first ascertain whether the knowledge acquired by the applicant in the course of his professional experience in a Member State or in a third country, is of a nature to cover, in full or in part, the substantial difference referred to in paragraph 4.

Article 15 Waiving of compensation measures on the basis of common platforms

1. For the purpose of this Article, 'common platforms' is defined as a set of criteria of professional qualifications which are suitable for compensating for substantial differences which have been identified between the training requirements existing in the various Member States for a given profession. These substantial differences shall be identified by comparison between the duration and contents of the training in at least two-thirds of the Member States, including all Member States which regulate this profession. The differences in the contents of the training may result from substantial differences in the scope of the professional activities.

2. Common platforms as defined in paragraph 1 may be submitted to the Commission by Member States or by professional associations or organisations which are representative at national

and European level. If the Commission, after consulting the Member States, is of the opinion that a draft common platform facilitates the mutual recognition of professional qualifications, it may present draft measures with a view to their adoption. Those measures, designed to amend non-essential elements of this Directive by supplementing it, shall be adopted in accordance with the regulatory procedure with scrutiny referred to in Article 58(3).

3. Where the applicant's professional qualifications satisfy the criteria established in the measure adopted in accordance with paragraph 2, the host Member State shall waive the application of compensation measures under Article 14.

4. Paragraphs 1 to 3 shall not affect the competence of Member States to decide the professional qualifications required for the pursuit of professions in their territory as well as the contents and the organisation of their systems of education and professional training.

5. If a Member State considers that the criteria established in a measure adopted in accordance with paragraph 2 no longer offer adequate guarantees with regard to professional qualifications, it shall inform the Commission accordingly. The Commission shall, if appropriate, present a draft measure for adoption. That measure, designed to amend non-essential elements of this Directive by supplementing it, shall be adopted in accordance with the regulatory procedure with scrutiny referred to in Article 58(3).

6. The Commission shall, by 20 October 2010, submit to the European Parliament and the Council a report on the operation of this Article and, if necessary, appropriate proposals for amending this Article.

Chapter II Recognition of professional experience

Article 16 Requirements regarding professional experience

If, in a Member State, access to or pursuit of one of the activities listed in Annex IV is contingent upon possession of general, commercial or professional knowledge and aptitudes, that Member State shall recognise previous pursuit of the activity in another Member State as sufficient proof of such knowledge and aptitudes. The activity must have been pursued in accordance with Articles 17, 18 and 19.

Article 17 Activities referred to in list I of Annex IV

1. For the activities in list I of Annex IV, the activity in question must have been previously pursued:

(a) for six consecutive years on a self-employed basis or as a manager of an undertaking; or

(b) for three consecutive years on a self-employed basis or as a manager of an undertaking, where the beneficiary proves that he has received previous training of at least three years for the activity in question, evidenced by a certificate recognised by the Member State or judged by a competent professional body to be fully valid; or

(c) for four consecutive years on a self-employed basis or as a manager of an undertaking, where the beneficiary can prove that he has received, for the activity in question, previous training of at least two years' duration, attested by a certificate recognised by the Member State or judged by a competent professional body to be fully valid; or

(d) for three consecutive years on a self-employed basis, if the beneficiary can prove that he has pursued the activity in question on an employed basis for at least five years; or

(e) for five consecutive years in an executive position, of which at least three years involved technical duties and responsibility for at least one department of the company, if the beneficiary can prove that he has received, for the activity in question, previous training of at least three years' duration, as attested by a certificate recognised by the Member State or judged by a competent professional body to be fully valid.

2. In cases (a) and (d), the activity must not have finished more than 10 years before the date on which the complete application was submitted by the person concerned to the competent authority referred to in Article 56.

3. Paragraph 1(e) shall not apply to activities in Group ex 855, hairdressing establishments, of the ISIC Nomenclature.

Article 18 Activities referred to in list II of Annex IV

1. For the activities in list II of Annex IV, the activity in question must have been previously pursued:

(a) for five consecutive years on a self-employed basis or as a manager of an undertaking, or
(b) for three consecutive years on a self-employed basis or as a manager of an undertaking, where the beneficiary proves that he has received previous training of at least three years for the activity in question, evidenced by a certificate recognised by the Member State or judged by a competent professional body to be fully valid, or
(c) for four consecutive years on a self-employed basis or as a manager of an undertaking, where the beneficiary can prove that he has received, for the activity in question, previous training of at least two years' duration, attested by a certificate recognised by the Member State or judged by a competent professional body to be fully valid, or
(d) for three consecutive years on a self-employed basis or as a manager of an undertaking, if the beneficiary can prove that he has pursued the activity in question on an employed basis for at least five years, or
(e) for five consecutive years on an employed basis, if the beneficiary can prove that he has received, for the activity in question, previous training of at least three years' duration, as attested by a certificate recognised by the Member State or judged by a competent professional body to be fully valid, or
(f) for six consecutive years on an employed basis, if the beneficiary can prove that he has received previous training in the activity in question of at least two years' duration, as attested by a certificate recognised by the Member State or judged by a competent professional body to be fully valid.

2. In cases (a) and (d), the activity must not have finished more than 10 years before the date on which the complete application was submitted by the person concerned to the competent authority referred to in Article 56.

Article 19 Activities referred to in list III of Annex IV

1. For the activities in list III of Annex IV, the activity in question must have been previously pursued:

(a) for three consecutive years, either on a self-employed basis or as a manager of an undertaking, or
(b) for two consecutive years, either on a self-employed basis or as a manager of an undertaking, if the beneficiary can prove that he has received previous training for the activity in question, as attested by a certificate recognised by the Member State or judged by a competent professional body to be fully valid, or
(c) for two consecutive years, either on a self-employed basis or as a manager of an undertaking, if the beneficiary can prove that he has pursued the activity in question on an employed basis for at least three years, or
(d) for three consecutive years, on an employed basis, if the beneficiary can prove that he has received previous training for the activity in question, as attested by a certificate recognised by the Member State or judged by a competent professional body to be fully valid.

2. In cases (a) and (c), the activity must not have finished more than 10 years before the date on which the complete application was submitted by the person concerned to the competent authority referred to in Article 56.

Article 20 Adaptation of the lists of activities in Annex IV

The Commission may adapt the lists of activities in Annex IV which are the subject of recognition of professional experience pursuant to Article 16 with a view to updating or clarifying the nomenclature, provided that this does not involve any change in the activities related to the individual categories. Those measures, designed to amend non-essential elements of this Directive, shall be adopted in accordance with the regulatory procedure with scrutiny referred to in Article 58(3).

Chapter III Recognition on the basis of coordination of minimum training conditions

Section 1 General provisions

Article 21 Principle of automatic recognition

1. Each Member State shall recognise evidence of formal qualifications as doctor giving access to the professional activities of doctor with basic training and specialised doctor, as nurse responsible for general care, as dental practitioner, as specialised dental practitioner, as veterinary surgeon, as pharmacist and as architect, listed in Annex V, points 5.1.1, 5.1.2, 5.2.2, 5.3.2, 5.3.3, 5.4.2, 5.6.2 and 5.7.1 respectively, which satisfy the minimum training conditions referred to in Articles 24, 25, 31, 34, 35, 38, 44 and 46 respectively, and shall, for the purposes of access to and pursuit of the professional activities, give such evidence the same effect on its territory as the evidence of formal qualifications which it itself issues.

Such evidence of formal qualifications must be issued by the competent bodies in the Member States and accompanied, where appropriate, by the certificates listed in Annex V, points 5.1.1, 5.1.2, 5.2.2, 5.3.2, 5.3.3, 5.4.2, 5.6.2 and 5.7.1 respectively.

The provisions of the first and second subparagraphs do not affect the acquired rights referred to in Articles 23, 27, 33, 37, 39 and 49.

2. Each Member State shall recognise, for the purpose of pursuing general medical practice in the framework of its national social security system, evidence of formal qualifications listed in Annex V, point 5.1.4 and issued to nationals of the Member States by the other Member States in accordance with the minimum training conditions laid down in Article 28.

The provisions of the previous subparagraph do not affect the acquired rights referred to in Article 30.

3. Each Member State shall recognise evidence of formal qualifications as a midwife, awarded to nationals of Member States by the other Member States, listed in Annex V, point 5.5.2, which complies with the minimum training conditions referred to in Article 40 and satisfies the criteria set out in Article 41, and shall, for the purposes of access to and pursuit of the professional activities, give such evidence the same effect on its territory as the evidence of formal qualifications which it itself issues. This provision does not affect the acquired rights referred to in Articles 23 and 43.

4. Member States shall not be obliged to give effect to evidence of formal qualifications referred to in Annex V, point 5.6.2, for the setting up of new pharmacies open to the public. For the purposes of this paragraph, pharmacies which have been open for less than three years shall also be considered as new pharmacies.

5. Evidence of formal qualifications as an architect referred to in Annex V, point 5.7.1, which is subject to automatic recognition pursuant to paragraph 1, proves completion of a course of training which began not earlier than during the academic reference year referred to in that Annex.

6. Each Member State shall make access to and pursuit of the professional activities of doctors, nurses responsible for general care, dental practitioners, veterinary surgeons, midwives and pharmacists subject to possession of evidence of formal qualifications referred to in Annex V, points 5.1.1, 5.1.2, 5.1.4, 5.2.2, 5.3.2, 5.3.3, 5.4.2, 5.5.2 and 5.6.2 respectively, attesting that the person concerned has acquired, over the duration of his training, and where appropriate, the knowledge and skills referred to in Articles 24(3), 31(6), 34(3), 38(3), 40(3) and 44(3).

The Commission may adapt the knowledge and skills referred to in Articles 24(3), 31(6), 34(3), 38(3), 40(3) and 44(3) to scientific and technical progress. Those measures, designed to amend non-essential elements of this Directive, shall be adopted in accordance with the regulatory procedure with scrutiny referred to in Article 58(3).

Such updates shall not entail, for any Member State, an amendment of its existing legislative principles regarding the structure of professions as regards training and conditions of access by natural persons.

7. Each Member State shall notify the Commission of the legislative, regulatory and administrative provisions which it adopts with regard to the issuing of evidence of formal qualifications in the area covered by this Chapter. In addition, for evidence of formal qualifications in the area referred to in Section 8, this notification shall be addressed to the other Member States.

The Commission shall publish an appropriate communication in the Official Journal of the European Union, indicating the titles adopted by the Member States for evidence of formal qualifications and, where appropriate, the body which issues the evidence of formal qualifications, the certificate which accompanies it and the corresponding professional title referred to in Annex V, points 5.1.1, 5.1.2, 5.1.3, 5.1.4, 5.2.2, 5.3.2, 5.3.3, 5.4.2, 5.5.2, 5.6.2 and 5.7.1 respectively.

Article 22 Common provisions on training

With regard to the training referred to in Articles 24, 25, 28, 31, 34, 35, 38, 40, 44 and 46:

(a) Member States may authorise part-time training under conditions laid down by the competent authorities; those authorities shall ensure that the overall duration, level and quality of such training is not lower than that of continuous full-time training;

(b) in accordance with the procedures specific to each Member State, continuing education and training shall ensure that persons who have completed their studies are able to keep abreast of professional developments to the extent necessary to maintain safe and effective practice.

Article 23 Acquired rights

1. Without prejudice to the acquired rights specific to the professions concerned, in cases where the evidence of formal qualifications as doctor giving access to the professional activities of doctor with basic training and specialised doctor, as nurse responsible for general care, as dental practitioner, as specialised dental practitioner, as veterinary surgeon, as midwife and as pharmacist held by Member States nationals does not satisfy all the training requirements referred to in Articles 24, 25, 31, 34, 35, 38, 40 and 44, each Member State shall recognise as sufficient proof evidence of formal qualifications issued by those Member States insofar as such evidence attests successful completion of training which began before the reference dates laid down in Annex V, points 5.1.1, 5.1.2, 5.2.2, 5.3.2, 5.3.3, 5.4.2, 5.5.2 and 5.6.2 and is accompanied by a certificate stating that the holders have been effectively and lawfully engaged in the activities in question for at least three consecutive years during the five years preceding the award of the certificate.

2. The same provisions shall apply to evidence of formal qualifications as doctor giving access to the professional activities of doctor with basic training and specialised doctor, as nurse responsible for general care, as dental practitioner, as specialised dental practitioner, as veterinary surgeon, as midwife and as pharmacist, obtained in the territory of the former German Democratic Republic, which does not satisfy all the minimum training requirements laid down in Articles 24, 25, 31, 34, 35, 38, 40 and 44 if such evidence certifies successful completion of training which began before:

(a) 3 October 1990 for doctors with basic training, nurses responsible for general care, dental practitioners with basic training, specialised dental practitioners, veterinary surgeons, midwives and pharmacists, and

(b) 3 April 1992 for specialised doctors.

The evidence of formal qualifications referred to in the first subparagraph confers on the holder the right to pursue professional activities throughout German territory under the same conditions as evidence of formal qualifications issued by the competent German authorities referred to in Annex V, points 5.1.1, 5.1.2, 5.2.2, 5.3.2, 5.3.3, 5.4.2, 5.5.2 and 5.6.2.

3. Without prejudice to the provisions of Article 37(1), each Member State shall recognise evidence of formal qualifications as doctor giving access to the professional activities of doctor with basic training and specialised doctor, as nurse responsible for general care, as veterinary surgeon, as midwife, as pharmacist and as architect held by Member States nationals and issued by the former Czechoslovakia, or whose training commenced, for the Czech Republic and Slovakia, before 1 January 1993, where the authorities of either of the two aforementioned Member States attest that such evidence of formal qualifications has the same legal validity within their territory as the evidence of formal qualifications which they issue and, with respect to architects, as the evidence of formal qualifications specified for those Member States in Annex VI, point 6, as regards access to the professional activities of doctor with basic training, specialised doctor, nurse responsible for general care, veterinary surgeon, midwife, pharmacist with respect to the activities referred to in Article 45 (2), and architect with respect to the activities referred to in Article 48, and the pursuit of such activities.

Such an attestation must be accompanied by a certificate issued by those same authorities stating that such persons have effectively and lawfully been engaged in the activities in question within their territory for at least three consecutive years during the five years prior to the date of issue of the certificate.

4. Each Member State shall recognise evidence of formal qualifications as doctor giving access to the professional activities of doctor with basic training and specialised doctor, as nurse responsible for general care, as dental practitioner, as specialised dental practitioner, as veterinary surgeon, as midwife, as pharmacist and as architect held by nationals of the Member States and issued by the former Soviet Union, or whose training commenced

(a) for Estonia, before 20 August 1991,
(b) for Latvia, before 21 August 1991,
(c) for Lithuania, before 11 March 1990,

where the authorities of any of the three aforementioned Member States attest that such evidence has the same legal validity within their territory as the evidence which they issue and, with respect to architects, as the evidence of formal qualifications specified for those Member States in Annex VI, point 6, as regards access to the professional activities of doctor with basic training, specialised doctor, nurse responsible for general care, dental practitioner, specialised dental practitioner, veterinary surgeon, midwife, pharmacist with respect to the activities referred to in Article 45(2), and architect with respect to the activities referred to in Article 48, and the pursuit of such activities.

Such an attestation must be accompanied by a certificate issued by those same authorities stating that such persons have effectively and lawfully been engaged in the activities in question within their territory for at least three consecutive years during the five years prior to the date of issue of the certificate.

With regard to evidence of formal qualifications as veterinary surgeons issued by the former Soviet Union or in respect of which training commenced, for Estonia, before 20 August 1991, the attestation referred to in the preceding subparagraph must be accompanied by a certificate issued by the Estonian authorities stating that such persons have effectively and lawfully been engaged in the activities in question within their territory for at least five consecutive years during the seven years prior to the date of issue of the certificate.

5. Without prejudice to Article 43b, each Member State shall recognise evidence of formal qualifications as doctor giving access to the professional activities of doctor with basic training and specialised doctor, as nurse responsible for general care, as dental practitioner, as specialised dental practitioner, as veterinary surgeon, as midwife, as pharmacist and as architect held by nationals of the Member States and issued by the former Yugoslavia, or whose training commenced,

(a) for Slovenia, before 25 June 1991; and
(b) for Croatia, before 8 October 1991;

where the authorities of the aforementioned Member States attest that such evidence has the same legal validity within their territory as the evidence which they issue and, with respect to architects, as the evidence of formal qualifications specified for those Member States in Annex VI, point 6, as regards access to the professional activities of doctor with basic training, specialised doctor, nurse responsible for general care, dental practitioner, specialised dental practitioner, veterinary surgeon, midwife, pharmacist with respect to the activities referred to in Article 45(2), and architect with respect to the activities referred to in Article 48, and the pursuit of such activities.

Such an attestation must be accompanied by a certificate issued by those same authorities stating that such persons have effectively and lawfully been engaged in the activities in question within their territory for at least three consecutive years during the five years prior to the date of issue of the certificate.

6. Each Member State shall recognise as sufficient proof for Member State nationals whose evidence of formal qualifications as a doctor, nurse responsible for general care, dental practitioner, veterinary surgeon, midwife and pharmacist does not correspond to the titles given for that Member State in Annex V, points 5.1.1, 5.1.2, 5.1.3, 5.1.4, 5.2.2, 5.3.2, 5.3.3, 5.4.2, 5.5.2 and 5.6.2, evidence of formal qualifications issued by those Member States accompanied by a certificate issued by the competent authorities or bodies.

The certificate referred to in the first subparagraph shall state that the evidence of formal qualifications certifies successful completion of training in accordance with Articles 24, 25, 28, 31, 34, 35,

38, 40 and 44 respectively and is treated by the Member State which issued it in the same way as the qualifications whose titles are listed in Annex V, points 5.1.1, 5.1.2, 5.1.3, 5.1.4, 5.2.2, 5.3.2, 5.3.3, 5.4.2, 5.5.2 and 5.6.2.

Article 23a Specific circumstances

1. By way of derogation from the present Directive, Bulgaria may authorise the holders of the qualification of 'Фелдшер' (feldsher) awarded in Bulgaria before 31 December 1999 and exercising this profession under the Bulgarian national social security scheme on 1 January 2000 to continue to exercise the said profession, even if parts of their activity fall under the provisions of the present Directive concerning doctors of medicine and nurses responsible for general care respectively.

2. The holders of the Bulgarian qualification of 'Фелдшер' (feldsher) referred to in paragraph 1 are not entitled to obtain professional recognition in other Member States as doctors of medicine nor as nurses responsible for general care under this Directive.

Section 2 Doctors of medicine

Article 24 Basic medical training

1. Admission to basic medical training shall be contingent upon possession of a diploma or certificate providing access, for the studies in question, to universities.

2. Basic medical training shall comprise a total of at least six years of study or 5,500 hours of theoretical and practical training provided by, or under the supervision of, a university.

For persons who began their studies before 1 January 1972, the course of training referred to in the first subparagraph may comprise six months of full-time practical training at university level under the supervision of the competent authorities.

3. Basic medical training shall provide an assurance that the person in question has acquired the following knowledge and skills:

(a) adequate knowledge of the sciences on which medicine is based and a good understanding of the scientific methods including the principles of measuring biological functions, the evaluation of scientifically established facts and the analysis of data;

(b) sufficient understanding of the structure, functions and behaviour of healthy and sick persons, as well as relations between the state of health and physical and social surroundings of the human being;

(c) adequate knowledge of clinical disciplines and practices, providing him with a coherent picture of mental and physical diseases, of medicine from the points of view of prophylaxis, diagnosis and therapy and of human reproduction;

(d) suitable clinical experience in hospitals under appropriate supervision.

Article 25 Specialist medical training

1. Admission to specialist medical training shall be contingent upon completion and validation of six years of study as part of a training programme referred to in Article 24 in the course of which the trainee has acquired the relevant knowledge of basic medicine.

2. Specialist medical training shall comprise theoretical and practical training at a university or medical teaching hospital or, where appropriate, a medical care establishment approved for that purpose by the competent authorities or bodies.

The Member States shall ensure that the minimum duration of specialist medical training courses referred to in Annex V, point 5.1.3 is not less than the duration provided for in that point. Training shall be given under the supervision of the competent authorities or bodies. It shall include personal participation of the trainee specialised doctor in the activity and responsibilities entailed by the services in question.

3. Training shall be given on a full-time basis at specific establishments which are recognised by the competent authorities. It shall entail participation in the full range of medical activities of the department where the training is given, including duty on call, in such a way that the trainee specialist devotes all his professional activity to his practical and theoretical training throughout the

entire working week and throughout the year, in accordance with the procedures laid down by the competent authorities. Accordingly, these posts shall be the subject of appropriate remuneration.

4. The Member States shall make the issuance of evidence of specialist medical training contingent upon possession of evidence of basic medical training referred to in Annex V, point 5.1.1.

5. The Commission may adapt the minimum periods of training referred to in Annex V, point 5.1.3, to scientific and technical progress. Those measures, designed to amend non-essential elements of this Directive, shall be adopted in accordance with the regulatory procedure with scrutiny referred to in Article 58(3).

Article 26 Types of specialist medical training

Evidence of formal qualifications as a specialised doctor referred to in Article 21 is such evidence awarded by the competent authorities or bodies referred to in Annex V, point 5.1.2 as corresponds, for the specialised training in question, to the titles in use in the various Member States and referred to in Annex V, point 5.1.3.

The Commission may include in Annex V, point 5.1.3, new medical specialties common to at least two-fifths of the Member States with a view to updating this Directive in the light of changes in national legislation. That measure, designed to amend non-essential elements of this Directive, shall be adopted in accordance with the regulatory procedure with scrutiny referred to in Article 58(3).

Article 27 Acquired rights specific to specialised doctors

1. A host Member State may require of specialised doctors whose part-time specialist medical training was governed by legislative, regulatory and administrative provisions in force as of 20 June 1975 and who began their specialist training no later than 31 December 1983 that their evidence of formal qualifications be accompanied by a certificate stating that they have been effectively and lawfully engaged in the relevant activities for at least three consecutive years during the five years preceding the award of that certificate.

2. Every Member State shall recognise the qualification of specialised doctors awarded in Spain to doctors who completed their specialist training before 1 January 1995, even if that training does not satisfy the minimum training requirements provided for in Article 25, in so far as that qualification is accompanied by a certificate issued by the competent Spanish authorities and attesting that the person concerned has passed the examination in specific professional competence held in the context of exceptional measures concerning recognition laid down in Royal Decree 1497/99, with a view to ascertaining that the person concerned possesses a level of knowledge and skill comparable to that of doctors who possess a qualification as a specialised doctor defined for Spain in Annex V, points 5.1.2 and 5.1.3.

3. Every Member State which has repealed its legislative, regulatory or administrative provisions relating to the award of evidence of formal qualifications as a specialised doctor referred to in Annex V, points 5.1.2 and 5.1.3 and which has adopted measures relating to acquired rights benefiting its nationals, shall grant nationals of other Member States the right to benefit from those measures, in so far as such evidence of formal qualifications was issued before the date on which the host Member State ceased to issue such evidence for the specialty in question.

The dates on which these provisions were repealed are set out in Annex V, point 5.1.3.

Article 28 Specific training in general medical practice

1. Admission to specific training in general medical practice shall be contingent on the completion and validation of six years of study as part of a training programme referred to in Article 24.

2. The specific training in general medical practice leading to the award of evidence of formal qualifications issued before 1 January 2006 shall be of a duration of at least two years on a full-time basis. In the case of evidence of formal qualifications issued after that date, the training shall be of a duration of at least three years on a full-time basis.

Where the training programme referred to in Article 24 comprises practical training given by an approved hospital possessing appropriate general medical equipment and services or as part of an approved general medical practice or an approved centre in which doctors provide primary medical care, the duration of that practical training may, up to a maximum of one year, be included in the duration provided for in the first subparagraph for certificates of training issued on or after 1 January 2006.

The option provided for in the second subparagraph shall be available only for Member States in which the specific training in general medical practice lasted two years as of 1 January 2001.

3. The specific training in general medical practice shall be carried out on a full-time basis, under the supervision of the competent authorities or bodies. It shall be more practical than theoretical.

The practical training shall be given, on the one hand, for at least six months in an approved hospital possessing appropriate equipment and services and, on the other hand, for at least six months as part of an approved general medical practice or an approved centre at which doctors provide primary health care.

The practical training shall take place in conjunction with other health establishments or structures concerned with general medicine. Without prejudice to the minimum periods laid down in the second subparagraph, however, the practical training may be given during a period of not more than six months in other approved establishments or health structures concerned with general medicine.

The training shall require the personal participation of the trainee in the professional activity and responsibilities of the persons with whom he is working.

4. Member States shall make the issuance of evidence of formal qualifications in general medical practice subject to possession of evidence of formal qualifications in basic medical training referred to in Annex V, point 5.1.1.

5. Member States may issue evidence of formal qualifications referred to in Annex V, point 5.1.4 to a doctor who has not completed the training provided for in this Article but who has completed a different, supplementary training, as attested by evidence of formal qualifications issued by the competent authorities in a Member State. They may not, however, award evidence of formal qualifications unless it attests knowledge of a level qualitatively equivalent to the knowledge acquired from the training provided for in this Article.

Member States shall determine, inter alia, the extent to which the complementary training and professional experience already acquired by the applicant may replace the training provided for in this Article.

The Member States may only issue the evidence of formal qualifications referred to in Annex V, point 5.1.4 if the applicant has acquired at least six months' experience of general medicine in a general medical practice or a centre in which doctors provide primary health care of the types referred to in paragraph 3.

Article 29 Pursuit of the professional activities of general practitioners

Each Member State shall, subject to the provisions relating to acquired rights, make the pursuit of the activities of a general practitioner in the framework of its national social security system contingent upon possession of evidence of formal qualifications referred to in Annex V, point 5.1.4.

Member States may exempt persons who are currently undergoing specific training in general medicine from this condition.

Article 30 Acquired rights specific to general practitioners

1. Each Member State shall determine the acquired rights. It shall, however, confer as an acquired right the right to pursue the activities of a general practitioner in the framework of its national social security system, without the evidence of formal qualifications referred to in Annex V, point 5.1.4, on all doctors who enjoy this right as of the reference date stated in that point by virtue of provisions applicable to the medical profession giving access to the professional activities of doctor with basic training and who are established as of that date on its territory, having benefited from the provisions of Articles 21 or 23.

The competent authorities of each Member State shall, on demand, issue a certificate stating the holder's right to pursue the activities of general practitioner in the framework of their national social security systems, without the evidence of formal qualifications referred to in Annex V, point 5.1.4, to doctors who enjoy acquired rights pursuant to the first subparagraph.

2. Every Member State shall recognise the certificates referred to in paragraph 1, second subparagraph, awarded to nationals of Member States by the other Member States, and shall give such certificates the same effect on its territory as evidence of formal qualifications which it awards and which permit the pursuit of the activities of a general practitioner in the framework of its national social security system.

Section 3 Nurses responsible for general care

Article 31 Training of nurses responsible for general care

1. Admission to training for nurses responsible for general care shall be contingent upon completion of general education of 10 years, as attested by a diploma, certificate or other evidence issued by the competent authorities or bodies in a Member State or by a certificate attesting success in an examination, of an equivalent level, for admission to a school of nursing.

2. Training of nurses responsible for general care shall be given on a full-time basis and shall include at least the programme described in Annex V, point 5.2.1.

The Commission may adapt the content listed in Annex V, point 5.2.1, to scientific and technical progress. That measure, designed to amend non-essential elements of this Directive, shall be adopted in accordance with the regulatory procedure with scrutiny referred to in Article 58(3).

Such updates may not entail, for any Member State, any amendment of its existing legislative principles relating to the structure of professions as regards training and the conditions of access by natural persons.

3. The training of nurses responsible for general care shall comprise at least three years of study or 4600 hours of theoretical and clinical training, the duration of the theoretical training representing at least one-third and the duration of the clinical training at least one half of the minimum duration of the training. Member States may grant partial exemptions to persons who have received part of their training on courses which are of at least an equivalent level.

The Member States shall ensure that institutions providing nursing training are responsible for the coordination of theoretical and clinical training throughout the entire study programme.

4. Theoretical training is that part of nurse training from which trainee nurses acquire the professional knowledge, insights and skills necessary for organising, dispensing and evaluating overall health care. The training shall be given by teachers of nursing care and by other competent persons, in nursing schools and other training establishments selected by the training institution.

5. Clinical training is that part of nurse training in which trainee nurses learn, as part of a team and in direct contact with a healthy or sick individual and/or community, to organise, dispense and evaluate the required comprehensive nursing care, on the basis of the knowledge and skills which they have acquired. The trainee nurse shall learn not only how to work in a team, but also how to lead a team and organise overall nursing care, including health education for individuals and small groups, within the health institute or in the community.

This training shall take place in hospitals and other health institutions and in the community, under the responsibility of nursing teachers, in cooperation with and assisted by other qualified nurses. Other qualified personnel may also take part in the teaching process.

Trainee nurses shall participate in the activities of the department in question insofar as those activities are appropriate to their training, enabling them to learn to assume the responsibilities involved in nursing care.

6. Training for nurses responsible for general care shall provide an assurance that the person in question has acquired the following knowledge and skills:

(a) adequate knowledge of the sciences on which general nursing is based, including sufficient understanding of the structure, physiological functions and behaviour of healthy and sick persons, and of the relationship between the state of health and the physical and social environment of the human being;

(b) sufficient knowledge of the nature and ethics of the profession and of the general principles of health and nursing;

(c) adequate clinical experience; such experience, which should be selected for its training value, should be gained under the supervision of qualified nursing staff and in places where the number of qualified staff and equipment are appropriate for the nursing care of the patient;

(d) the ability to participate in the practical training of health personnel and experience of working with such personnel;

(e) experience of working with members of other professions in the health sector.

Article 32 Pursuit of the professional activities of nurses responsible for general care

For the purposes of this Directive, the professional activities of nurses responsible for general care are the activities pursued on a professional basis and referred to in Annex V, point 5.2.2.

Article 33 Acquired rights specific to nurses responsible for general care

1. Where the general rules of acquired rights apply to nurses responsible for general care, the activities referred to in Article 23 must have included full responsibility for the planning, organisation and administration of nursing care delivered to the patient.

2. As regards the Polish qualification of nurse responsible for general care, only the following acquired rights provisions shall apply. In the case of nationals of the Member States whose evidence of formal qualifications as nurse responsible for general care was awarded by, or whose training started in, Poland before 1 May 2004 and who do not satisfy the minimum training requirements laid down in Article 31, Member States shall recognise the following evidence of formal qualifications as nurse responsible for general care as being sufficient proof if accompanied by a certificate stating that those Member State nationals have effectively and lawfully been engaged in the activities of a nurse responsible for general care in Poland for the period specified below:

(a) evidence of formal qualifications as a nurse at degree level (dyplom licencjata pielęgniarstwa)—at least three consecutive years during the five years prior to the date of issue of the certificate,

(b) evidence of formal qualifications as a nurse certifying completion of post-secondary education obtained from a medical vocational school (dyplom pielęgniarki albo pielęgniarki dyplomowanej)—at least five consecutive years during the seven years prior to the date of issue of the certificate.

The said activities must have included taking full responsibility for the planning, organisation and administration of nursing care delivered to the patient.

3. Member States shall recognise evidence of formal qualifications in nursing awarded in Poland, to nurses who completed training before 1 May 2004, which did not comply with the minimum training requirements laid down in Article 31, attested by the diploma 'bachelor' which has been obtained on the basis of a special upgrading programme contained in Article 11 of the Act of 20 April 2004 on the amendment of the Act on professions of nurse and midwife and on some other legal acts (Official Journal of the Republic of Poland of 30 April 2004 No 92, pos. 885), and the Regulation of the Minister of Health of 11 May 2004 on the detailed conditions of delivering studies for nurses and midwives, who hold a certificate of secondary school (final examination—matura) and are graduates of medical lyceum and medical vocational schools teaching in a profession of a nurse and a midwife (Official Journal of the Republic of Poland of 13 May 2004 No 110, pos. 1170), with the aim of verifying that the person concerned has a level of knowledge and competence comparable to that of nurses holding the qualifications which, in the case of Poland, are defined in Annex V, point 5.2.2.

Article 33(a)

As regards the Romanian qualification of nurse responsible for general care, only the following acquired rights provisions will apply:

In the case of nationals of the Member States whose evidence of formal qualifications as nurse responsible for general care were awarded by, or whose training started in, Romania before the date of accession and which does not satisfy the minimum training requirements laid down in Article 31,

Member States shall recognise the evidence of formal qualification as nurse responsible for general care (Certificat de competenţe profesionale de asistent medical generalist) with post-secondary education obtained from a şcoală postliceală, as being sufficient proof if accompanied by a certificate stating that those Member State nationals have effectively and lawfully been engaged in the activities of a nurse responsible for general care in Romania for a period of at least five consecutive years during the seven years prior to the date of issue of the certificate.

The said activities must have included taking full responsibility for the planning, organisation and carrying out of the nursing care of the patient.

Section 4 Dental practitioners

Article 34 Basic dental training

1. Admission to basic dental training presupposes possession of a diploma or certificate giving access, for the studies in question, to universities or higher institutes of a level recognised as equivalent, in a Member State.

2. Basic dental training shall comprise a total of at least five years of full-time theoretical and practical study, comprising at least the programme described in Annex V, point 5.3.1 and given in a university, in a higher institute providing training recognised as being of an equivalent level or under the supervision of a university.

The Commission may adapt the content listed in Annex V, point 5.3.1, to scientific and technical progress. That measure, designed to amend non-essential elements of this Directive, shall be adopted in accordance with the regulatory procedure with scrutiny referred to in Article 58(3).

Such updates may not entail, for any Member State, any amendment of its existing legislative principles relating to the system of professions as regards training and the conditions of access by natural persons.

3. Basic dental training shall provide an assurance that the person in question has acquired the following knowledge and skills:

(a) adequate knowledge of the sciences on which dentistry is based and a good understanding of scientific methods, including the principles of measuring biological functions, the evaluation of scientifically established facts and the analysis of data;

(b) adequate knowledge of the constitution, physiology and behaviour of healthy and sick persons as well as the influence of the natural and social environment on the state of health of the human being, in so far as these factors affect dentistry;

(c) adequate knowledge of the structure and function of the teeth, mouth, jaws and associated tissues, both healthy and diseased, and their relationship to the general state of health and to the physical and social well-being of the patient;

(d) adequate knowledge of clinical disciplines and methods, providing the dentist with a coherent picture of anomalies, lesions and diseases of the teeth, mouth, jaws and associated tissues and of preventive, diagnostic and therapeutic dentistry;

(e) suitable clinical experience under appropriate supervision.

This training shall provide him with the skills necessary for carrying out all activities involving the prevention, diagnosis and treatment of anomalies and diseases of the teeth, mouth, jaws and associated tissues.

Article 35 Specialist dental training

1. Admission to specialist dental training shall entail the completion and validation of five years of theoretical and practical instruction within the framework of the training referred to in Article 34, or possession of the documents referred to in Articles 23 and 37.

2. Specialist dental training shall comprise theoretical and practical instruction in a university centre, in a treatment teaching and research centre or, where appropriate, in a health establishment approved for that purpose by the competent authorities or bodies.

Full-time specialist dental courses shall be of a minimum of three years' duration supervised by the competent authorities or bodies. It shall involve the personal participation of the dental practitioner training to be a specialist in the activity and in the responsibilities of the establishment concerned.

The Commission may adapt the minimum period of training referred to in the second subparagraph to scientific and technical progress. That measure, designed to amend non-essential elements of this Directive, shall be adopted in accordance with the regulatory procedure with scrutiny referred to in Article 58(3).

3. The Member States shall make the issuance of evidence of specialist dental training contingent upon possession of evidence of basic dental training referred to in Annex V, point 5.3.2.

Article 36 Pursuit of the professional activities of dental practitioners

1. For the purposes of this Directive, the professional activities of dental practitioners are the activities defined in paragraph 3 and pursued under the professional qualifications listed in Annex V, point 5.3.2.

2. The profession of dental practitioner shall be based on dental training referred to in Article 34 and shall constitute a specific profession which is distinct from other general or specialised medical professions. Pursuit of the activities of a dental practitioner requires the possession of evidence of formal qualifications referred to in Annex V, point 5.3.2. Holders of such evidence of formal qualifications shall be treated in the same way as those to whom Articles 23 or 37 apply.

3. The Member States shall ensure that dental practitioners are generally able to gain access to and pursue the activities of prevention, diagnosis and treatment of anomalies and diseases affecting the teeth, mouth, jaws and adjoining tissue, having due regard to the regulatory provisions and rules of professional ethics on the reference dates referred to in Annex V, point 5.3.2.

Article 37 Acquired rights specific to dental practitioners

1. Every Member State shall, for the purposes of the pursuit of the professional activities of dental practitioners under the qualifications listed in Annex V, point 5.3.2, recognise evidence of formal qualifications as a doctor issued in Italy, Spain, Austria, the Czech Republic, Slovakia and Romania to persons who began their medical training on or before the reference date stated in that Annex for the Member State concerned, accompanied by a certificate issued by the competent authorities of that Member State.

The certificate must show that the two following conditions are met:

(a) that the persons in question have been effectively, lawfully and principally engaged in that Member State in the activities referred to in Article 36 for at least three consecutive years during the five years preceding the award of the certificate;

(b) that those persons are authorised to pursue the said activities under the same conditions as holders of evidence of formal qualifications listed for that Member State in Annex V, point 5.3.2.

Persons who have successfully completed at least three years of study, certified by the competent authorities in the Member State concerned as being equivalent to the training referred to in Article 34, shall be exempt from the three-year practical work experience referred to in the second subparagraph, point (a).

With regard to the Czech Republic and Slovakia, evidence of formal qualifications obtained in the former Czechoslovakia shall be accorded the same level of recognition as Czech and Slovak evidence of formal qualifications and under the same conditions as set out in the preceding sub-paragraphs.

2. Each Member State shall recognise evidence of formal qualifications as a doctor issued in Italy to persons who began their university medical training after 28 January 1980 and no later than 31 December 1984, accompanied by a certificate issued by the competent Italian authorities.

The certificate must show that the three following conditions are met:

(a) that the persons in question passed the relevant aptitude test held by the competent Italian authorities with a view to establishing that those persons possess a level of knowledge and skills comparable to that of persons possessing evidence of formal qualifications listed for Italy in Annex V, point 5.3.2;

(b) that they have been effectively, lawfully and principally engaged in the activities referred to in Article 36 in Italy for at least three consecutive years during the five years preceding the award of the certificate;

(c) that they are authorised to engage in or are effectively, lawfully and principally engaged in the activities referred to in Article 36, under the same conditions as the holders of evidence of formal qualifications listed for Italy in Annex V, point 5.3.2.

Persons who have successfully completed at least three years of study certified by the competent authorities as being equivalent to the training referred to in Article 34 shall be exempt from the aptitude test referred to in the second subparagraph, point (a).

Persons who began their university medical training after 31 December 1984 shall be treated in the same way as those referred to above, provided that the abovementioned three years of study began before 31 December 1994.

Section 5 Veterinary surgeons

Article 38 The training of veterinary surgeons

1. The training of veterinary surgeons shall comprise a total of at least five years of full-time theoretical and practical study at a university or at a higher institute providing training recognised as being of an equivalent level, or under the supervision of a university, covering at least the study programme referred to in Annex V, point 5.4.1.

The Commission may adapt the content listed in Annex V, point 5.4.1, to scientific and technical progress. That measure, designed to amend non-essential elements of this Directive, shall be adopted in accordance with the regulatory procedure with scrutiny referred to in Article 58(3).

Such updates may not entail, for any Member State, any amendment of its existing legislative principles relating to the structure of professions as regards training and conditions of access by natural persons.

2. Admission to veterinary training shall be contingent upon possession of a diploma or certificate entitling the holder to enter, for the studies in question, university establishments or institutes of higher education recognised by a Member State to be of an equivalent level for the purpose of the relevant study.

3. Training as a veterinary surgeon shall provide an assurance that the person in question has acquired the following knowledge and skills:

(a) adequate knowledge of the sciences on which the activities of the veterinary surgeon are based;

(b) adequate knowledge of the structure and functions of healthy animals, of their husbandry, reproduction and hygiene in general, as well as their feeding, including the technology involved in the manufacture and preservation of foods corresponding to their needs;

(c) adequate knowledge of the behaviour and protection of animals;

(d) adequate knowledge of the causes, nature, course, effects, diagnosis and treatment of the diseases of animals, whether considered individually or in groups, including a special knowledge of the diseases which may be transmitted to humans;

(e) adequate knowledge of preventive medicine;

(f) adequate knowledge of the hygiene and technology involved in the production, manufacture and putting into circulation of animal foodstuffs or foodstuffs of animal origin intended for human consumption;

(g) adequate knowledge of the laws, regulations and administrative provisions relating to the subjects listed above;

(h) adequate clinical and other practical experience under appropriate supervision.

Article 39 Acquired rights specific to veterinary surgeons

Without prejudice to Article 23(4), with regard to nationals of Member States whose evidence of formal qualifications as a veterinary surgeon was issued by, or whose training commenced in, Estonia before 1 May 2004, Member States shall recognise such evidence of formal qualifications as a veterinary surgeon if it is accompanied by a certificate stating that such persons have effectively and lawfully been engaged in the activities in question in Estonia for at least five consecutive years during the seven years prior to the date of issue of the certificate.

Section 6 Midwives

Article 40 The training of midwives

1. The training of midwives shall comprise a total of at least:
   (a) specific full-time training as a midwife comprising at least three years of theoretical and practical study (route I) comprising at least the programme described in Annex V, point 5.5.1, or
   (b) specific full-time training as a midwife of 18 months' duration (route II), comprising at least the study programme described in Annex V, point 5.5.1, which was not the subject of equivalent training of nurses responsible for general care.

The Member States shall ensure that institutions providing midwife training are responsible for coordinating theory and practice throughout the programme of study.

The Commission may adapt the content listed in Annex V, point 5.5.1, to scientific and technical progress. That measure, designed to amend non-essential elements of this Directive, shall be adopted in accordance with the regulatory procedure with scrutiny referred to in Article 58(3).

Such updates must not entail, for any Member State, any amendment of existing legislative principles relating to the structure of professions as regards training and the conditions of access by natural persons.

2. Access to training as a midwife shall be contingent upon one of the following conditions:
   (a) completion of at least the first 10 years of general school education for route I, or
   (b) possession of evidence of formal qualifications as a nurse responsible for general care referred to in Annex V, point 5.2.2 for route II.

3. Training as a midwife shall provide an assurance that the person in question has acquired the following knowledge and skills:
   (a) adequate knowledge of the sciences on which the activities of midwives are based, particularly obstetrics and gynaecology;
   (b) adequate knowledge of the ethics of the profession and the professional legislation;
   (c) detailed knowledge of biological functions, anatomy and physiology in the field of obstetrics and of the newly born, and also a knowledge of the relationship between the state of health and the physical and social environment of the human being, and of his behaviour;
   (d) adequate clinical experience gained in approved institutions under the supervision of staff qualified in midwifery and obstetrics;
   (e) adequate understanding of the training of health personnel and experience of working with such.

Article 41 Procedures for the recognition of evidence of formal qualifications as a midwife

1. The evidence of formal qualifications as a midwife referred to in Annex V, point 5.5.2 shall be subject to automatic recognition pursuant to Article 21 in so far as they satisfy one of the following criteria:
   (a) full-time training of at least three years as a midwife:
      (i) either made contingent upon possession of a diploma, certificate or other evidence of qualification giving access to universities or higher education institutes, or otherwise guaranteeing an equivalent level of knowledge; or
      (ii) followed by two years of professional practice for which a certificate has been issued in accordance with paragraph 2;
   (b) full-time training as a midwife of at least two years or 3,600 hours, contingent upon possession of evidence of formal qualifications as a nurse responsible for general care referred to in Annex V, point 5.2.2;
   (c) full-time training as a midwife of at least 18 months or 3,000 hours, contingent upon possession of evidence of formal qualifications as a nurse responsible for general care referred to in Annex V, point 5.2.2 and followed by one year's professional practice for which a certificate has been issued in accordance with paragraph 2.

2. The certificate referred to in paragraph 1 shall be issued by the competent authorities in the home Member State. It shall certify that the holder, after obtaining evidence of formal qualifications as a midwife, has satisfactorily pursued all the activities of a midwife for a corresponding period in a hospital or a health care establishment approved for that purpose.

Article 42 Pursuit of the professional activities of a midwife

1. The provisions of this section shall apply to the activities of midwives as defined by each Member State, without prejudice to paragraph 2, and pursued under the professional titles set out in Annex V, point 5.5.2.

2. The Member States shall ensure that midwives are able to gain access to and pursue at least the following activities:

(a) provision of sound family planning information and advice;
(b) diagnosis of pregnancies and monitoring normal pregnancies; carrying out the examinations necessary for the monitoring of the development of normal pregnancies;
(c) prescribing or advising on the examinations necessary for the earliest possible diagnosis of pregnancies at risk;
(d) provision of programmes of parenthood preparation and complete preparation for childbirth including advice on hygiene and nutrition;
(e) caring for and assisting the mother during labour and monitoring the condition of the foetus in utero by the appropriate clinical and technical means;
(f) conducting spontaneous deliveries including where required episiotomies and in urgent cases breech deliveries;
(g) recognising the warning signs of abnormality in the mother or infant which necessitate referral to a doctor and assisting the latter where appropriate; taking the necessary emergency measures in the doctor's absence, in particular the manual removal of the placenta, possibly followed by manual examination of the uterus;
(h) examining and caring for the new-born infant; taking all initiatives which are necessary in case of need and carrying out where necessary immediate resuscitation;
(i) caring for and monitoring the progress of the mother in the post-natal period and giving all necessary advice to the mother on infant care to enable her to ensure the optimum progress of the new-born infant;
(j) carrying out treatment prescribed by doctors;
(k) drawing up the necessary written reports.

Article 43 Acquired rights specific to midwives

1. Every Member State shall, in the case of Member State nationals whose evidence of formal qualifications as a midwife satisfies all the minimum training requirements laid down in Article 40 but, by virtue of Article 41, is not recognised unless it is accompanied by a certificate of professional practice referred to in Article 41(2), recognise as sufficient proof evidence of formal qualifications issued by those Member States before the reference date referred to in Annex V, point 5.5.2, accompanied by a certificate stating that those nationals have been effectively and lawfully engaged in the activities in question for at least two consecutive years during the five years preceding the award of the certificate.

2. The conditions laid down in paragraph 1 shall apply to the nationals of Member States whose evidence of formal qualifications as a midwife certifies completion of training received in the territory of the former German Democratic Republic and satisfying all the minimum training requirements laid down in Article 40 but where the evidence of formal qualifications, by virtue of Article 41, is not recognised unless it is accompanied by the certificate of professional experience referred to in Article 41(2), where it attests a course of training which began before 3 October 1990.

3. As regards the Polish evidence of formal qualifications as a midwife, only the following acquired rights provisions shall apply.

In the case of Member States nationals whose evidence of formal qualifications as a midwife was awarded by, or whose training commenced in, Poland before 1 May 2004, and who do not satisfy the minimum training requirements as set out in Article 40, Member States shall recognise the following evidence of formal qualifications as a midwife if accompanied by a certificate stating that such persons have effectively and lawfully been engaged in the activities of a midwife for the period specified below:

(a) evidence of formal qualifications as a midwife at degree level (dyplom licencjata położnictwa): at least three consecutive years during the five years prior to the date of issue of the certificate,

(b) evidence of formal qualifications as a midwife certifying completion of post-secondary education obtained from a medical vocational school (dyplom położnej): at least five consecutive years during the seven years prior to the date of issue of the certificate.

4. Member States shall recognise evidence of formal qualifications in midwifery awarded in Poland, to midwives who completed training before 1 May 2004, which did not comply with the minimum training requirements laid down in Article 40, attested by the diploma 'bachelor' which has been obtained on the basis of a special upgrading programme contained in Article 11 of the Act of 20 April 2004 on the amendment of the Act on professions of nurse and midwife and on some other legal acts (Official Journal of the Republic of Poland of 30 April 2004 No 92, pos. 885), and the Regulation of the Minister of Health of 11 May 2004 on the detailed conditions of delivering studies for nurses and midwives, who hold a certificate of secondary school (final examination—matura) and are graduates of medical lyceum and medical vocational schools teaching in a profession of a nurse and a midwife (Official Journal of the Republic of Poland of 13 May 2004 No 110, pos 1170), with the aim of verifying that the person concerned has a level of knowledge and competence comparable to that of midwives holding the qualifications which, in the case of Poland, are defined in Annex V, point 5.5.2.

Article 43(a)

As regards the Romanian qualifications in midwifery, only the following acquired rights provisions will apply:

In the case of nationals of the Member States whose evidence of formal qualifications as a midwife (asistent medical obstetrică-ginecologie/obstetrics-gynaecology nurse) were awarded by Romania before the date of accession and which do not satisfy the minimum training requirements laid down in Article 40, Member States shall recognise the said evidence of formal qualifications as being sufficient proof for the purposes of carrying out the activities of midwife, if they are accompanied by a certificate stating that those Member State nationals have effectively and lawfully been engaged in the activities of midwife in Romania, for at least five consecutive years during the seven years prior to the issue of the certificate.

Article 43b

Acquired rights in midwifery shall not apply to the following qualifications which were obtained in Croatia before 1 July 2013: viša medicinska sestra ginekološko-opstetričkog smjera (High Gynaecology-Obstetrical Nurse), medicinska sestra ginekološko-opstetričkog smjera (Gynaecology-Obstetrical Nurse), viša medicinska sestra primaljskog smjera (High Nurse with Midwifery Degree), medicinska sestra primaljskog smjera (Nurse with Midwifery Degree), ginekološko-opstetrička primalja (Gynaecology-Obstetrical Midwife) and primalja (Midwife).

Section 7 Pharmacist

Article 44 Training as a pharmacist

1. Admission to a course of training as a pharmacist shall be contingent upon possession of a diploma or certificate giving access, in a Member State, to the studies in question, at universities or higher institutes of a level recognised as equivalent.

2. Evidence of formal qualifications as a pharmacist shall attest to training of at least five years' duration, including at least:

(a) four years of full-time theoretical and practical training at a university or at a higher institute of a level recognised as equivalent, or under the supervision of a university;

(b) six-month traineeship in a pharmacy which is open to the public or in a hospital, under the supervision of that hospital's pharmaceutical department.

That training cycle shall include at least the programme described in Annex V, point 5.6.1. The Commission may adapt the content listed in Annex V, point 5.6.1, to scientific and technical progress. That measure, designed to amend non-essential elements of this Directive, shall be adopted in accordance with the regulatory procedure with scrutiny referred to in Article 58(3).

Such updates must not entail, for any Member State, any amendment of existing legislative principles relating to the structure of professions as regards training and the conditions of access by natural persons.

3. Training for pharmacists shall provide an assurance that the person concerned has acquired the following knowledge and skills:

(a) adequate knowledge of medicines and the substances used in the manufacture of medicines;
(b) adequate knowledge of pharmaceutical technology and the physical, chemical, biological and microbiological testing of medicinal products;
(c) adequate knowledge of the metabolism and the effects of medicinal products and of the action of toxic substances, and of the use of medicinal products;
(d) adequate knowledge to evaluate scientific data concerning medicines in order to be able to supply appropriate information on the basis of this knowledge;
(e) adequate knowledge of the legal and other requirements associated with the pursuit of pharmacy.

Article 45 Pursuit of the professional activities of a pharmacist

1. For the purposes of this Directive, the activities of a pharmacist are those, access to which and pursuit of which are contingent, in one or more Member States, upon professional qualifications and which are open to holders of evidence of formal qualifications of the types listed in Annex V, point 5.6.2.

2. The Member States shall ensure that the holders of evidence of formal qualifications in pharmacy at university level or a level deemed to be equivalent, which satisfies the provisions of Article 44, are able to gain access to and pursue at least the following activities, subject to the requirement, where appropriate, of supplementary professional experience:

(a) preparation of the pharmaceutical form of medicinal products;
(b) manufacture and testing of medicinal products;
(c) testing of medicinal products in a laboratory for the testing of medicinal products;
(d) storage, preservation and distribution of medicinal products at the wholesale stage;
(e) preparation, testing, storage and supply of medicinal products in pharmacies open to the public;
(f) preparation, testing, storage and dispensing of medicinal products in hospitals;
(g) provision of information and advice on medicinal products.

3. If a Member State makes access to or pursuit of one of the activities of a pharmacist contingent upon supplementary professional experience, in addition to possession of evidence of formal qualifications referred to in Annex V, point 5.6.2, that Member State shall recognise as sufficient proof in this regard a certificate issued by the competent authorities in the home Member State stating that the person concerned has been engaged in those activities in the home Member State for a similar period.

4. The recognition referred to in paragraph 3 shall not apply with regard to the two-year period of professional experience required by the Grand Duchy of Luxembourg for the grant of a State public pharmacy concession.

5. If, on 16 September 1985, a Member State had a competitive examination in place designed to select from among the holders referred to in paragraph 2, those who are to be authorised to become owners of new pharmacies whose creation has been decided on as part of a national system of geographical division, that Member State may, by way of derogation from paragraph 1, proceed with that examination and require nationals of Member States who possess evidence of formal qualifications as a pharmacist referred to in Annex V, point 5.6.2 or who benefit from the provisions of Article 23 to take part in it.

Section 8 Architect

Article 46 Training of architects

1. Training as an architect shall comprise a total of at least four years of full-time study or six years of study, at least three years of which on a full-time basis, at a university or comparable teaching institution. The training must lead to successful completion of a university-level examination.

That training, which must be of university level, and of which architecture is the principal component, must maintain a balance between theoretical and practical aspects of architectural training and guarantee the acquisition of the following knowledge and skills:

(a) ability to create architectural designs that satisfy both aesthetic and technical requirements;
(b) adequate knowledge of the history and theories of architecture and the related arts, technologies and human sciences;
(c) knowledge of the fine arts as an influence on the quality of architectural design;
(d) adequate knowledge of urban design, planning and the skills involved in the planning process;
(e) understanding of the relationship between people and buildings, and between buildings and their environment, and of the need to relate buildings and the spaces between them to human needs and scale;
(f) understanding of the profession of architecture and the role of the architect in society, in particular in preparing briefs that take account of social factors;
(g) understanding of the methods of investigation and preparation of the brief for a design project;
(h) understanding of the structural design, constructional and engineering problems associated with building design;
(i) adequate knowledge of physical problems and technologies and of the function of buildings so as to provide them with internal conditions of comfort and protection against the climate;
(j) the necessary design skills to meet building users' requirements within the constraints imposed by cost factors and building regulations;
(k) adequate knowledge of the industries, organisations, regulations and procedures involved in translating design concepts into buildings and integrating plans into overall planning.

2. The Commission may adapt the knowledge and skills listed in paragraph 1 to scientific and technical progress. That measure, designed to amend non-essential elements of this Directive, shall be adopted in accordance with the regulatory procedure with scrutiny referred to in Article 58(3).

Such updates must not entail, for any Member State, any amendment of existing legislative principles relating to the structure of professions as regards training and the conditions of access by natural persons.

Article 47 Derogations from the conditions for the training of architects

1. By way of derogation from Article 46, the following shall also be recognised as satisfying Article 21: training existing as of 5 August 1985, provided by 'Fachhochschulen' in the Federal Republic of Germany over a period of three years, satisfying the requirements referred to in Article 46 and giving access to the activities referred to in Article 48 in that Member State under the professional title of 'architect', in so far as the training was followed by a four-year period of professional experience in the Federal Republic of Germany, as attested by a certificate issued by the professional association in whose roll the name of the architect wishing to benefit from the provisions of this Directive appears.

The professional association must first ascertain that the work performed by the architect concerned in the field of architecture represents convincing application of the full range of knowledge and skills listed in Article 46(1). That certificate shall be awarded in line with the same procedure as that applying to registration in the professional association's roll.

2. By way of derogation from Article 46, the following shall also be recognised as satisfying Article 21: training as part of social betterment schemes or part-time university studies which satisfies the requirements referred to in Article 46, as attested by an examination in architecture passed by a person who has been working for seven years or more in the field of architecture under the supervision of an architect or architectural bureau. The examination must be of university level and be equivalent to the final examination referred to in Article 46(1), first subparagraph.

Article 48 Pursuit of the professional activities of architects

1. For the purposes of this Directive, the professional activities of an architect are the activities regularly carried out under the professional title of 'architect'.

2. Nationals of a Member State who are authorised to use that title pursuant to a law which gives the competent authority of a Member State the power to award that title to Member States nationals who are especially distinguished by the quality of their work in the field of architecture shall be deemed to satisfy the conditions required for the pursuit of the activities of an architect, under the professional title of 'architect'. The architectural nature of the activities of the persons concerned shall be attested by a certificate awarded by their home Member State.

Article 49 Acquired rights specific to architects

1. Each Member State shall accept evidence of formal qualifications as an architect listed in Annex VI, point 6, awarded by the other Member States, and attesting a course of training which began no later than the reference academic year referred to in that Annex, even if they do not satisfy the minimum requirements laid down in Article 46, and shall, for the purposes of access to and pursuit of the professional activities of an architect, give such evidence the same effect on its territory as evidence of formal qualifications as an architect which it itself issues.

Under these circumstances, certificates issued by the competent authorities of the Federal Republic of Germany attesting that evidence of formal qualifications issued on or after 8 May 1945 by the competent authorities of the German Democratic Republic is equivalent to such evidence listed in that Annex, shall be recognised.

2. Without prejudice to paragraph 1, every Member State shall recognise the following evidence of formal qualifications and shall, for the purposes of access to and pursuit of the professional activities of an architect performed, give them the same effect on its territory as evidence of formal qualifications which it itself issues: certificates issued to nationals of Member States by the Member States which have enacted rules governing the access to and pursuit of the activities of an architect as of the following dates:

(a) 1 January 1995 for Austria, Finland and Sweden;

(b) 1 May 2004 for the Czech Republic, Estonia, Cyprus, Latvia, Lithuania, Hungary, Malta, Poland, Slovenia and Slovakia;

(c) 5 August 1987 for the other Member States.

The certificates referred to in paragraph 1 shall certify that the holder was authorised, no later than the respective date, to use the professional title of architect, and that he has been effectively engaged, in the context of those rules, in the activities in question for at least three consecutive years during the five years preceding the award of the certificate.

Chapter IV Common provisions on establishment

Article 50 Documentation and formalities

1. Where the competent authorities of the host Member State decide on an application for authorisation to pursue the regulated profession in question by virtue of this Title, those authorities may demand the documents and certificates listed in Annex VII.

The documents referred to in Annex VII, point 1(d), (e) and (f), shall not be more than three months old by the date on which they are submitted.

The Member States, bodies and other legal persons shall guarantee the confidentiality of the information which they receive.

2. In the event of justified doubts, the host Member State may require from the competent authorities of a Member State confirmation of the authenticity of the attestations and evidence of formal qualifications awarded in that other Member State, as well as, where applicable, confirmation of the fact that the beneficiary fulfils, for the professions referred to in Chapter III of this Title, the minimum training conditions set out respectively in Articles 24, 25, 28, 31, 34, 35, 38, 40, 44 and 46.

3. In cases of justified doubt, where evidence of formal qualifications, as defined in Article 3(1)(c), has been issued by a competent authority in a Member State and includes training received in whole or in part in an establishment legally established in the territory of another Member State, the host Member State shall be entitled to verify with the competent body in the Member State of origin of the award:

(a) whether the training course at the establishment which gave the training has been formally certified by the educational establishment based in the Member State of origin of the award;

(b) whether the evidence of formal qualifications issued is the same as that which would have been awarded if the course had been followed entirely in the Member State of origin of the award; and

(c) whether the evidence of formal qualifications confers the same professional rights in the territory of the Member State of origin of the award.

4. Where a host Member State requires its nationals to swear a solemn oath or make a sworn statement in order to gain access to a regulated profession, and where the wording of that oath or statement cannot be used by nationals of the other Member States, the host Member State shall ensure that the persons concerned can use an appropriate equivalent wording.

Article 51

Procedure for the mutual recognition of professional qualifications

1. The competent authority of the host Member State shall acknowledge receipt of the application within one month of receipt and inform the applicant of any missing document.

2. The procedure for examining an application for authorisation to practise a regulated profession must be completed as quickly as possible and lead to a duly substantiated decision by the competent authority in the host Member State in any case within three months after the date on which the applicant's complete file was submitted. However, this deadline may be extended by one month in cases falling under Chapters I and II of this Title.

3. The decision, or failure to reach a decision within the deadline, shall be subject to appeal under national law.

Article 52 Use of professional titles

1. If, in a host Member State, the use of a professional title relating to one of the activities of the profession in question is regulated, nationals of the other Member States who are authorised to practise a regulated profession on the basis of Title III shall use the professional title of the host Member State, which corresponds to that profession in that Member State, and make use of any associated initials.

2. Where a profession is regulated in the host Member State by an association or organisation within the meaning of Article 3(2), nationals of Member States shall not be authorised to use the professional title issued by that organisation or association, or its abbreviated form, unless they furnish proof that they are members of that association or organisation.

If the association or organisation makes membership contingent upon certain qualifications, it may do so, only under the conditions laid down in this Directive, in respect of nationals of other Member States who possess professional qualifications.

Title IV Detailed rules for pursuing the profession

Article 53 Knowledge of languages

Persons benefiting from the recognition of professional qualifications shall have a knowledge of languages necessary for practising the profession in the host Member State.

Article 54 Use of academic titles

Without prejudice to Articles 7 and 52, the host Member State shall ensure that the right shall be conferred on the persons concerned to use academic titles conferred on them in the home Member State, and possibly an abbreviated form thereof, in the language of the home Member State. The host Member State may require that title to be followed by the name and address of the establishment or examining board which awarded it. Where an academic title of the home Member State is liable to be confused in the host Member State with a title which, in the latter Member State, requires supplementary training not acquired by the beneficiary, the host Member State may require the beneficiary to use the academic title of the home Member State in an appropriate form, to be laid down by the host Member State.

Article 55 Approval by health insurance funds

Without prejudice to Article 5(1) and Article 6, first subparagraph, point (b), Member States which require persons who acquired their professional qualifications in their territory to complete a preparatory period of in-service training and/or a period of professional experience in order to be approved by a health insurance fund, shall waive this obligation for the holders of evidence of professional qualifications of doctor and dental practitioner acquired in other Member States.

Title V Administrative cooperation and responsibility for implementation

Article 56 Competent authorities

1. The competent authorities of the host Member State and of the home Member State shall work in close collaboration and shall provide mutual assistance in order to facilitate application of this Directive. They shall ensure the confidentiality of the information which they exchange.

2. The competent authorities of the host and home Member States shall exchange information regarding disciplinary action or criminal sanctions taken or any other serious, specific circumstances which are likely to have consequences for the pursuit of activities under this Directive, respecting personal data protection legislation provided for in Directives 95/46/EC of the European Parliament and of the Council of 24 October 1995 on the protection of individuals with regard to the processing of personal data and on the free movement of such data[24] and 2002/58/EC of the European Parliament and of the Council of 12 July 2002 concerning the processing of personal data and the protection of privacy in the electronic communications sector (Directive on privacy and electronic communications).[25]

The home Member State shall examine the veracity of the circumstances and its authorities shall decide on the nature and scope of the investigations which need to be carried out and shall inform the host Member State of the conclusions which it draws from the information available to it.

3. Each Member State shall, no later than 20 October 2007, designate the authorities and bodies competent to award or receive evidence of formal qualifications and other documents or information, and those competent to receive applications and take the decisions referred to in this Directive, and shall forthwith inform the other Member States and the Commission thereof.

4. Each Member State shall designate a coordinator for the activities of the authorities referred to in paragraph 1 and shall inform the other Member States and the Commission thereof.

The coordinators' remit shall be:

(a) to promote uniform application of this Directive;

(b) to collect all the information which is relevant for application of this Directive, such as on the conditions for access to regulated professions in the Member States.

[24] OJ L 281, 23.11.1995, p. 31. Directive as amended by Regulation (EC) No 1882/2003.

[25] OJ L 201, 31.07.2002, p. 37.

For the purpose of fulfilling the remit described in point (b), the coordinators may solicit the help of the contact points referred to in Article 57.

Article 57 Contact points

Each Member State shall designate, no later than 20 October 2007, a contact point whose remit shall be:

(a) to provide the citizens and contact points of the other Member States with such information as is necessary concerning the recognition of professional qualifications provided for in this Directive, such as information on the national legislation governing the professions and the pursuit of those professions, including social legislation, and, where appropriate, the rules of ethics;

(b) to assist citizens in realising the rights conferred on them by this Directive, in cooperation, where appropriate, with the other contact points and the competent authorities in the host Member State.

At the Commission's request, the contact points shall inform the Commission of the result of enquiries with which they are dealing pursuant to the provisions of point (b) within two months of receiving them.

Article 58 Committee procedure

1. The Commission shall be assisted by a Committee on the recognition of professional qualifications.

2. Where reference is made to this paragraph, Articles 5 and 7 of Decision 1999/468/EC shall apply, having regard to the provisions of Article 8 thereof. thereof.

The period provided for in Article 5(6) of Decision 1999/468/EC shall be set at two months.

3. Where reference is made to this paragraph, Article 5a(1) to (4) and Article 7 of Decision 1999/468/EC shall apply, having regard to the provisions of Article 8 thereof.

Article 59 Consultation

The Commission shall ensure the consultation of experts from the professional groups concerned in an appropriate manner in particular in the context of the work of the committee referred to in Article 58 and shall provide a reasoned report on these consultations to that committee.

Title VI Other provisions

Article 60 Reports

1. As from 20 October 2007, Member States shall, every two years, send a report to the Commission on the application of the system. In addition to general observations, the report shall contain a statistical summary of decisions taken and a description of the main problems arising from the application of this Directive.

2. As from 20 October 2007, the Commission shall draw up every five years a report on the implementation of this Directive.

Article 61 Derogation clause

If, for the application of one of the provisions of this Directive, a Member State encounters major difficulties in a particular area, the Commission shall examine those difficulties in collaboration with the Member State concerned.

Where appropriate, the Commission shall decide, in accordance with the procedure referred to in Article 58(2), to permit the Member State in question to derogate from the provision in question for a limited period.

Article 62 Repeal

Directives 77/452/EEC, 77/453/EEC, 78/686/EEC, 78/687/EEC, 78/1026/EEC, 78/1027/EEC, 80/154/EEC, 80/155/EEC, 85/384/EEC, 85/432/EEC, 85/433/EEC, 89/48/EEC, 92/51/EEC, 93/16/EEC and 1999/42/EC are repealed with effect from 20 October 2007. References to the repealed Directives shall be understood as references to this Directive and the acts adopted on the basis of those Directives shall not be affected by the repeal.

Article 63 Transposition

Member States shall bring into force the laws, regulations and administrative provisions necessary to comply with this Directive by 20 October 2007 at the latest. They shall forthwith inform the Commission thereof.

When Member States adopt these measures, they shall contain a reference to this Directive or be accompanied by such a reference on the occasion of their official publication. Member States shall determine how such reference is to be made.

Article 64 Entry into force

This Directive shall enter into force on the 20th day following its publication in the *Official Journal of the European Union*.

Article 65 Addressees

This Directive is addressed to the Member States.

Done at Strasbourg, 7 September 2005.
For the European Parliament
The President
J. BORRELL FONTELLES
For the Council
The President
C. CLARKE

Annex I*

List of professional associations or organisations fulfilling the conditions of Article 3(2)

Ireland[26]

1. The Institute of Chartered Accountants in Ireland
2. The Institute of Certified Public Accountants in Ireland
3. The Association of Certified Accountants
4. Institution of Engineers of Ireland
5. Irish Planning Institute

United Kingdom[27]

1. Institute of Chartered Accountants in England and Wales
2. Institute of Chartered Accountants of Scotland
3. Institute of Chartered Accountants in Ireland

* **Editor's Note:** All other Annexes omitted.

[26] Only for the activity of auditing accounts.

[27] Irish nationals are also members of the following associations or organisations in the United Kingdom:
- Institute of Chartered Accountants of Scotland
- Institute of Actuaries
- Faculty of Actuaries
- The Chartered Institute of Management Accountants
- Institute of Chartered Secretaries and Administrators
- Royal Town Planning Institute
- Royal Institution of Chartered Surveyors
- Chartered Institute of Building.
- Institute of Chartered Accountants in England and Wales

4. Chartered Association of Certified Accountants
5. Chartered Institute of Loss Adjusters
6. Chartered Institute of Management Accountants
7. Institute of Chartered Secretaries and Administrators
8. Chartered Insurance Institute
9. Institute of Actuaries
10. Faculty of Actuaries
11. Chartered Institute of Bankers
12. Institute of Bankers in Scotland
13. Royal Institution of Chartered Surveyors
14. Royal Town Planning Institute
15. Chartered Society of Physiotherapy
16. Royal Society of Chemistry
17. British Psychological Society
18. Library Association
19. Institute of Chartered Foresters
20. Chartered Institute of Building
21. Engineering Council
22. Institute of Energy
23. Institution of Structural Engineers
24. Institution of Civil Engineers
25. Institution of Mining Engineers
26. Institution of Mining and Metallurgy
27. Institution of Electrical Engineers
28. Institution of Gas Engineers
29. Institution of Mechanical Engineers
30. Institution of Chemical Engineers
31. Institution of Production Engineers
32. Institution of Marine Engineers
33. Royal Institution of Naval Architects
34. Royal Aeronautical Society
35. Institute of Metals
36. Chartered Institution of Building Services Engineers
37. Institute of Measurement and Control
38. British Computer Society

Directive 2006/123/EC of the European Parliament and of the Council of 12 December 2006 on services in the internal market

[OJ 2006 L376/36]

THE EUROPEAN PARLIAMENT AND THE COUNCIL OF THE EUROPEAN UNION,

Having regard to the Treaty establishing the European Community, and in particular the first and third sentence of Article 47(2) and Article 55 thereof,

Having regard to the proposal from the Commission,

Having regard to the Opinion of the European Economic and Social Committee,[1]

Having regard to the opinion of the Committee of the Regions,[2]

Acting in accordance with the procedure laid down in Article 251 of the Treaty.[3]

Whereas:

(1) The European Community is seeking to forge ever closer links between the States and peoples of Europe and to ensure economic and social progress. In accordance with Article 14(2) of the Treaty, the internal market comprises an area without internal frontiers in which the free movement of services is ensured. In accordance with Article 43 of the Treaty the freedom of establishment is ensured. Article 49 of the Treaty establishes the right to provide services within the Community. The elimination of barriers to the development of service activities between Member States is essential in order to strengthen the integration of the peoples of Europe and to promote balanced and sustainable economic and social progress. In eliminating such barriers it is essential to ensure that the development of service activities contributes to the fulfilment of the task laid down in Article 2 of the Treaty of promoting throughout the Community a harmonious, balanced and sustainable development of economic activities, a high level of employment and of social protection, equality between men and women, sustainable and non-inflationary growth, a high degree of competitiveness and convergence of economic performance, a high level of protection and improvement of the quality of the environment, the raising of the standard of living and quality of life and economic and social cohesion and solidarity among Member States.

(2) A competitive market in services is essential in order to promote economic growth and create jobs in the European Union. At present numerous barriers within the internal market prevent providers, particularly small and medium-sized enterprises (SMEs), from extending their operations beyond their national borders and from taking full advantage of the internal market. This weakens the worldwide competitiveness of European Union providers. A free market which compels the Member States to eliminate restrictions on cross-border provision of services while at the same time increasing transparency and information for consumers would give consumers wider choice and better services at lower prices.

(3) The report from the Commission on 'The State of the Internal Market for Services' drew up an inventory of a large number of barriers which are preventing or slowing down the development of services between Member States, in particular those provided by SMEs, which are predominant in the field of services. The report concludes that a decade after the envisaged completion of the internal market, there is still a huge gap between the vision of an integrated European Union economy and the reality as experienced by European citizens and providers. The barriers affect a wide variety of service activities across all stages of the provider's activity and have a number of common features, including the fact that they often arise from administrative burdens, the legal uncertainty associated with cross-border activity and the lack of mutual trust between Member States.

(4) Since services constitute the engine of economic growth and account for 70 % of GDP and employment in most Member States, this fragmentation of the internal market has a negative impact on the entire European economy, in particular on the competitiveness of SMEs and the movement of workers, and prevents consumers from gaining access to a greater variety of competitively priced services. It is important to point out that the services sector is a key employment sector for women in particular, and that they therefore stand to benefit greatly from new opportunities offered by the completion of the internal market for services. The European Parliament and the Council have emphasised that the removal of legal barriers to the establishment of a genuine internal market is a matter of priority for achieving the goal set by the European Council in Lisbon of 23 and 24 March 2000 of improving employment and social cohesion and achieving sustainable economic growth so as to make the European Union the most competitive and dynamic knowledge-based economy in the world by 2010, with more and better jobs. Removing those barriers, while ensuring an advanced European

[1] OJ C 221, 8.9.2005, p. 113.

[2] OJ C 43, 18.2.2005, p. 18.

[3] Opinion of the European Parliament of 16 February 2006 (not yet published in the Official Journal), Council Common Position of 24 July 2006 (OJ C 270 E, 7.11.2006, p. 1) and Position of the European Parliament of 15 November 2006. Council Decision of 11 December 2006.

social model, is thus a basic condition for overcoming the difficulties encountered in implementing the Lisbon Strategy and for reviving the European economy, particularly in terms of employment and investment. It is therefore important to achieve an internal market for services, with the right balance between market opening and preserving public services and social and consumer rights.

(5) It is therefore necessary to remove barriers to the freedom of establishment for providers in Member States and barriers to the free movement of services as between Member States and to guarantee recipients and providers the legal certainty necessary for the exercise in practice of those two fundamental freedoms of the Treaty. Since the barriers in the internal market for services affect operators who wish to become established in other Member States as well as those who provide a service in another Member State without being established there, it is necessary to enable providers to develop their service activities within the internal market either by becoming established in a Member State or by making use of the free movement of services. Providers should be able to choose between those two freedoms, depending on their strategy for growth in each Member State.

(6) Those barriers cannot be removed solely by relying on direct application of Articles 43 and 49 of the Treaty, since, on the one hand, addressing them on a case-by-case basis through infringement procedures against the Member States concerned would, especially following enlargement, be extremely complicated for national and Community institutions, and, on the other hand, the lifting of many barriers requires prior coordination of national legal schemes, including the setting up of administrative cooperation. As the European Parliament and the Council have recognised, a Community legislative instrument makes it possible to achieve a genuine internal market for services.

(7) This Directive establishes a general legal framework which benefits a wide variety of services while taking into account the distinctive features of each type of activity or profession and its system of regulation. That framework is based on a dynamic and selective approach consisting in the removal, as a matter of priority, of barriers which may be dismantled quickly and, for the others, the launching of a process of evaluation, consultation and complementary harmonisation of specific issues, which will make possible the progressive and coordinated modernisation of national regulatory systems for service activities which is vital in order to achieve a genuine internal market for services by 2010. Provision should be made for a balanced mix of measures involving targeted harmonisation, administrative cooperation, the provision on the freedom to provide services and encouragement of the development of codes of conduct on certain issues. That coordination of national legislative regimes should ensure a high degree of Community legal integration and a high level of protection of general interest objectives, especially protection of consumers, which is vital in order to establish trust between Member States. This Directive also takes into account other general interest objectives, including the protection of the environment, public security and public health as well as the need to comply with labour law.

(8) It is appropriate that the provisions of this Directive concerning the freedom of establishment and the free movement of services should apply only to the extent that the activities in question are open to competition, so that they do not oblige Member States either to liberalise services of general economic interest or to privatise public entities which provide such services or to abolish existing monopolies for other activities or certain distribution services.

(9) This Directive applies only to requirements which affect the access to, or the exercise of, a service activity. Therefore, it does not apply to requirements, such as road traffic rules, rules concerning the development or use of land, town and country planning, building standards as well as administrative penalties imposed for non-compliance with such rules which do not specifically regulate or specifically affect the service activity but have to be respected by providers in the course of carrying out their economic activity in the same way as by individuals acting in their private capacity.

(10) This Directive does not concern requirements governing access to public funds for certain providers. Such requirements include notably those laying down conditions under which providers are entitled to receive public funding, including specific contractual conditions, and in particular quality standards which need to be observed as a condition for receiving public funds, for example for social services.

(11) This Directive does not interfere with measures taken by Member States, in accordance with Community law, in relation to the protection or promotion of cultural and linguistic diversity

and media pluralism, including the funding thereof. This Directive does not prevent Member States from applying their fundamental rules and principles relating to the freedom of press and freedom of expression. This Directive does not affect Member State laws prohibiting discrimination on grounds of nationality or on grounds such as those set out in Article 13 of the Treaty.

(12) This Directive aims at creating a legal framework to ensure the freedom of establishment and the free movement of services between the Member States and does not harmonise or prejudice criminal law. However, Member States should not be able to restrict the freedom to provide services by applying criminal law provisions which specifically affect the access to or the exercise of a service activity in circumvention of the rules laid down in this Directive.

(13) It is equally important that this Directive fully respect Community initiatives based on Article 137 of the Treaty with a view to achieving the objectives of Article 136 thereof concerning the promotion of employment and improved living and working conditions.

(14) This Directive does not affect terms and conditions of employment, including maximum work periods and minimum rest periods, minimum paid annual holidays, minimum rates of pay as well as health, safety and hygiene at work, which Member States apply in compliance with Community law, nor does it affect relations between social partners, including the right to negotiate and conclude collective agreements, the right to strike and to take industrial action in accordance with national law and practices which respect Community law, nor does it apply to services provided by temporary work agencies. This Directive does not affect Member States' social security legislation.

(15) This Directive respects the exercise of fundamental rights applicable in the Member States and as recognised in the Charter of fundamental Rights of the European Union and the accompanying explanations, reconciling them with the fundamental freedoms laid down in Articles 43 and 49 of the Treaty. Those fundamental rights include the right to take industrial action in accordance with national law and practices which respect Community law.

(16) This Directive concerns only providers established in a Member State and does not cover external aspects. It does not concern negotiations within international organisations on trade in services, in particular in the framework of the General Agreement on Trade in Services (GATS).

(17) This Directive covers only services which are performed for an economic consideration. Services of general interest are not covered by the definition in Article 50 of the Treaty and therefore do not fall within the scope of this Directive. Services of general economic interest are services that are performed for an economic consideration and therefore do fall within the scope of this Directive. However, certain services of general economic interest, such as those that may exist in the field of transport, are excluded from the scope of this Directive and certain other services of general economic interest, for example, those that may exist in the area of postal services, are the subject of a derogation from the provision on the freedom to provide services set out in this Directive. This Directive does not deal with the funding of services of general economic interest and does not apply to systems of aids granted by Member States, in particular in the social field, in accordance with Community rules on competition. This Directive does not deal with the follow-up to the Commission White Paper on Services of General Interest.

(18) Financial services should be excluded from the scope of this Directive since these activities are the subject of specific Community legislation aimed, as is this Directive, at achieving a genuine internal market for services. Consequently, this exclusion should cover all financial services such as banking, credit, insurance, including reinsurance, occupational or personal pensions, securities, investment funds, payments and investment advice, including the services listed in Annex I to Directive 2006/48/EC of the European Parliament and of the Council of 14 June 2006 relating to the taking up and pursuit of the business of credit institutions.[4]

(19) In view of the adoption in 2002 of a package of legislative instruments relating to electronic communications networks and services, as well as to associated resources and services, which has established a regulatory framework facilitating access to those activities within the internal market,

[4] OJ L 177, 30.6.2006, p. 1.

notably through the elimination of most individual authorisation schemes, it is necessary to exclude issues dealt with by those instruments from the scope of this Directive.

(20) The exclusion from the scope of this Directive as regards matters of electronic communications services as covered by Directives 2002/19/EC of the European Parliament and of the Council of 7 March 2002 on access to, and interconnection of, electronic communications networks and associated facilities (Access Directive),[5] 2002/20/EC of the European Parliament and of the Council of 7 March 2002 on the authorisation of electronic communications networks and services (Authorisation Directive),[6] 2002/21/EC of the European Parliament and of the Council of 7 March 2002 on a common regulatory framework for electronic communications networks and services (Framework Directive),[7] 2002/22/EC of the European Parliament and of the Council of 7 March 2002 on universal service and users' rights relating to electronic communications networks and services (Universal Service Directive)[8] and 2002/58/EC of the European Parliament and of the Council of 12 July 2002 concerning the processing of personal data and the protection of privacy in the electronic communications sector (Directive on privacy and electronic communications)[9] should apply not only to questions specifically dealt with in these Directives but also to matters for which the Directives explicitly leave to Member States the possibility of adopting certain measures at national level.

(21) Transport services, including urban transport, taxis and ambulances as well as port services, should be excluded from the scope of this Directive.

(22) The exclusion of healthcare from the scope of this Directive should cover healthcare and pharmaceutical services provided by health professionals to patients to assess, maintain or restore their state of health where those activities are reserved to a regulated health profession in the Member State in which the services are provided.

(23) This Directive does not affect the reimbursement of healthcare provided in a Member State other than that in which the recipient of the care is resident. This issue has been addressed by the Court of Justice on numerous occasions, and the Court has recognised patients' rights. It is important to address this issue in another Community legal instrument in order to achieve greater legal certainty and clarity to the extent that this issue is not already addressed in Council Regulation (EEC) No 1408/71 of 14 June 1971 on the application of social security schemes to employed persons, to self-employed persons and to members of their families moving within the Community.[10]

(24) Audiovisual services, whatever their mode of transmission, including within cinemas, should also be excluded from the scope of this Directive. Furthermore, this Directive should not apply to aids granted by Member States in the audiovisual sector which are covered by Community rules on competition.

(25) Gambling activities, including lottery and betting transactions, should be excluded from the scope of this Directive in view of the specific nature of these activities, which entail implementation by Member States of policies relating to public policy and consumer protection.

(26) This Directive is without prejudice to the application of Article 45 of the Treaty.

(27) This Directive should not cover those social services in the areas of housing, childcare and support to families and persons in need which are provided by the State at national, regional or local level by providers mandated by the State or by charities recognised as such by the State with the objective of ensuring support for those who are permanently or temporarily in a particular state of need because of their insufficient family income or total or partial lack of independence and for those who risk being marginalised. These services are essential in order to guarantee the fundamental right to human dignity and integrity and are a manifestation of the principles of social cohesion and solidarity and should not be affected by this Directive.

[5] OJ L 108, 24.4.2002, p. 7.
[6] OJ L 108, 24.4.2002, p. 21.
[7] OJ L 108, 24.4.2002, p. 33.
[8] OJ L 108, 24.4.2002, p. 51.
[9] OJ L 201, 31.7.2002, p. 37. Directive as amended by Directive 2006/24/EC (OJ L 105, 13.4.2006, p. 54).
[10] OJ L 149, 5.7.1971, p. 2. Regulation as last amended by Regulation (EC) No 629/2006 of the European Parliament and of the Council (OJ L 114, 27.4.2006, p. 1).

(28) This Directive does not deal with the funding of, or the system of aids linked to, social services. Nor does it affect the criteria or conditions set by Member States to ensure that social services effectively carry out a function to the benefit of the public interest and social cohesion. In addition, this Directive should not affect the principle of universal service in Member States' social services.

(29) Given that the Treaty provides specific legal bases for taxation matters and given the Community instruments already adopted in that field, it is necessary to exclude the field of taxation from the scope of this Directive.

(30) There is already a considerable body of Community law on service activities. This Directive builds on, and thus complements, the Community acquis. Conflicts between this Directive and other Community instruments have been identified and are addressed by this Directive, including by means of derogations. However, it is necessary to provide a rule for any residual and exceptional cases where there is a conflict between a provision of this Directive and a provision of another Community instrument. The existence of such a conflict should be determined in compliance with the rules of the Treaty on the right of establishment and the free movement of services.

(31) This Directive is consistent with and does not affect Directive 2005/36/EC of the European Parliament and of the Council of 7 September 2005 on the recognition of professional qualifications.[11] It deals with questions other than those relating to professional qualifications, for example professional liability insurance, commercial communications, multidisciplinary activities and administrative simplification. With regard to temporary cross-border service provision, a derogation from the provision on the freedom to provide services in this Directive ensures that Title II on the free provision of services of Directive 2005/36/EC is not affected. Therefore, none of the measures applicable under that Directive in the Member State where the service is provided is affected by the provision on the freedom to provide services.

(32) This Directive is consistent with Community legislation on consumer protection, such as Directive 2005/29/EC of the European Parliament and of the Council of 11 May 2005 concerning unfair business-to-consumer commercial practices in the internal market (the Unfair Commercial Practices Directive)[12] and Regulation (EC) No 2006/2004 of the European Parliament and of the Council of 27 October 2004 on cooperation between national authorities responsible for the enforcement of consumer protection laws (the Regulation on consumer protection cooperation).[13]

(33) The services covered by this Directive concern a wide variety of ever-changing activities, including business services such as management consultancy, certification and testing; facilities management, including office maintenance; advertising; recruitment services; and the services of commercial agents. The services covered are also services provided both to businesses and to consumers, such as legal or fiscal advice; real estate services such as estate agencies; construction, including the services of architects; distributive trades; the organisation of trade fairs; car rental; and travel agencies. Consumer services are also covered, such as those in the field of tourism, including tour guides; leisure services, sports centres and amusement parks; and, to the extent that they are not excluded from the scope of application of the Directive, household support services, such as help for the elderly. Those activities may involve services requiring the proximity of provider and recipient, services requiring travel by the recipient or the provider and services which may be provided at a distance, including via the Internet.

(34) According to the case-law of the Court of Justice, the assessment of whether certain activities, in particular activities which are publicly funded or provided by public entities, constitute a 'service' has to be carried out on a case by case basis in the light of all their characteristics, in particular the way they are provided, organised and financed in the Member State concerned. The Court of Justice has held that the essential characteristic of remuneration lies in the fact that it constitutes consideration for the services in question and has recognised that the characteristic of remuneration is absent

[11] OJ L 255, 30.9.2005, p. 22.
[12] OJ L 149, 11.6.2005, p. 22.
[13] OJ L 364, 9.12.2004, p. 1. Regulation as amended by Directive 2005/29/EC.

in the case of activities performed, for no consideration, by the State or on behalf of the State in the context of its duties in the social, cultural, educational and judicial fields, such as courses provided under the national education system, or the management of social security schemes which do not engage in economic activity. The payment of a fee by recipients, for example, a tuition or enrolment fee paid by students in order to make a certain contribution to the operating expenses of a system, does not in itself constitute remuneration because the service is still essentially financed by public funds. These activities are, therefore, not covered by the definition of service in Article 50 of the Treaty and do not therefore fall within the scope of this Directive.

(35) Non-profit making amateur sporting activities are of considerable social importance. They often pursue wholly social or recreational objectives. Thus, they might not constitute economic activities within the meaning of Community law and should fall outside the scope of this Directive.

(36) The concept of 'provider' should cover any natural person who is a national of a Member State or any legal person engaged in a service activity in a Member State, in exercise either of the freedom of establishment or of the free movement of services. The concept of provider should thus not be limited solely to cross-border service provision within the framework of the free movement of services but should also cover cases in which an operator establishes itself in a Member State in order to develop its service activities there. On the other hand, the concept of a provider should not cover the case of branches in a Member State of companies from third countries because, under Article 48 of the Treaty, the freedom of establishment and free movement of services may benefit only companies constituted in accordance with the laws of a Member State and having their registered office, central administration or principal place of business within the Community. The concept of 'recipient' should also cover third country nationals who already benefit from rights conferred upon them by Community acts such as Regulation (EEC) No 1408/71, Council Directive 2003/109/EC of 25 November 2003 concerning the status of third-country nationals who are long-term residents,[14] Council Regulation (EC) No 859/2003 of 14 May 2003 extending the provisions of Regulation (EEC) No 1408/71 and Regulation (EEC) No 574/72 to nationals of third countries who are not already covered by those provisions solely on the ground of their nationality[15] and Directive 2004/38/ECof the European Parliament and of the Council of 29 April 2004 on the right of citizens of the Union and their family members to move and reside freely within the territory of the Member States.[16] Furthermore, Member States may extend the concept of recipient to other third country nationals that are present within their territory.

(37) The place at which a provider is established should be determined in accordance with the case-law of the Court of Justice according to which the concept of establishment involves the actual pursuit of an economic activity through a fixed establishment for an indefinite period. This requirement may also be fulfilled where a company is constituted for a given period or where it rents the building or installation through which it pursues its activity. It may also be fulfilled where a Member State grants authorisations for a limited duration only in relation to particular services. An establishment does not need to take the form of a subsidiary, branch or agency, but may consist of an office managed by a provider's own staff or by a person who is independent but authorised to act on a permanent basis for the undertaking, as would be the case with an agency. According to this definition, which requires the actual pursuit of an economic activity at the place of establishment of the provider, a mere letter box does not constitute an establishment. Where a provider has several places of establishment, it is important to determine the place of establishment from which the actual service concerned is provided. Where it is difficult to determine from which of several places of establishment a given service is provided, the location of the provider's centre of activities relating to this particular service should be that place of establishment.

[14] OJ L 16, 23.1.2004, p. 44.
[15] OJ L 124, 20.5.2003, p. 1.
[16] OJ L 158, 30.4.2004, p. 77.

(38) The concept of 'legal persons', according to the Treaty provisions on establishment, leaves operators free to choose the legal form which they deem suitable for carrying out their activity. Accordingly, 'legal persons', within the meaning of the Treaty, means all entities constituted under, or governed by, the law of a Member State, irrespective of their legal form.

(39) The concept of 'authorisation scheme' should cover, inter alia, the administrative procedures for granting authorisations, licences, approvals or concessions, and also the obligation, in order to be eligible to exercise the activity, to be registered as a member of a profession or entered in a register, roll or database, to be officially appointed to a body or to obtain a card attesting to membership of a particular profession. Authorisation may be granted not only by a formal decision but also by an implicit decision arising, for example, from the silence of the competent authority or from the fact that the interested party must await acknowledgement of receipt of a declaration in order to commence the activity in question or for the latter to become lawful.

(40) The concept of 'overriding reasons relating to the public interest' to which reference is made in certain provisions of this Directive has been developed by the Court of Justice in its case law in relation to Articles 43 and 49 of the Treaty and may continue to evolve. The notion as recognised in the case law of the Court of Justice covers at least the following grounds: public policy, public security and public health, within the meaning of Articles 46 and 55 of the Treaty; the maintenance of order in society; social policy objectives; the protection of the recipients of services; consumer protection; the protection of workers, including the social protection of workers; animal welfare; the preservation of the financial balance of the social security system; the prevention of fraud; the prevention of unfair competition; the protection of the environment and the urban environment, including town and country planning; the protection of creditors; safeguarding the sound administration of justice; road safety; the protection of intellectual property; cultural policy objectives, including safeguarding the freedom of expression of various elements, in particular social, cultural, religious and philosophical values of society; the need to ensure a high level of education, the maintenance of press diversity and the promotion of the national language; the preservation of national historical and artistic heritage; and veterinary policy.

(41) The concept of 'public policy', as interpreted by the Court of Justice, covers the protection against a genuine and sufficiently serious threat affecting one of the fundamental interests of society and may include, in particular, issues relating to human dignity, the protection of minors and vulnerable adults and animal welfare. Similarly, the concept of public security includes issues of public safety.

(42) The rules relating to administrative procedures should not aim at harmonising administrative procedures but at removing overly burdensome authorisation schemes, procedures and formalities that hinder the freedom of establishment and the creation of new service undertakings therefrom.

(43) One of the fundamental difficulties faced, in particular by SMEs, in accessing service activities and exercising them is the complexity, length and legal uncertainty of administrative procedures. For this reason, following the example of certain modernising and good administrative practice initiatives undertaken at Community and national level, it is necessary to establish principles of administrative simplification, inter alia through the limitation of the obligation of prior authorisation to cases in which it is essential and the introduction of the principle of tacit authorisation by the competent authorities after a certain period of time elapsed. Such modernising action, while maintaining the requirements on transparency and the updating of information relating to operators, is intended to eliminate the delays, costs and dissuasive effects which arise, for example, from unnecessary or excessively complex and burdensome procedures, the duplication of procedures, the 'red tape' involved in submitting documents, the arbitrary use of powers by the competent authorities, indeterminate or excessively long periods before a response is given, the limited duration of validity of authorisations granted and disproportionate fees and penalties. Such practices have particularly significant dissuasive effects on providers wishing to develop their activities in other Member States and require coordinated modernisation within an enlarged internal market of twenty-five Member States.

(44) Member States should introduce, where appropriate, forms harmonised at Community level, as established by the Commission, which will serve as an equivalent to certificates, attestations or any other document in relation to establishment.

(45) In order to examine the need for simplifying procedures and formalities, Member States should be able, in particular, to take into account their necessity, number, possible duplication, cost, clarity and accessibility, as well as the delay and practical difficulties to which they could give rise for the provider concerned.

(46) In order to facilitate access to service activities and the exercise thereof in the internal market, it is necessary to establish an objective, common to all Member States, of administrative simplification and to lay down provisions concerning, inter alia, the right to information, procedures by electronic means and the establishment of a framework for authorisation schemes. Other measures adopted at national level to meet that objective could involve reduction of the number of procedures and formalities applicable to service activities and the restriction of such procedures and formalities to those which are essential in order to achieve a general interest objective and which do not duplicate each other in terms of content or purpose.

(47) With the aim of administrative simplification, general formal requirements, such as presentation of original documents, certified copies or a certified translation, should not be imposed, except where objectively justified by an overriding reason relating to the public interest, such as the protection of workers, public health, the protection of the environment or the protection of consumers. It is also necessary to ensure that an authorisation as a general rule permits access to, or exercise of, a service activity throughout the national territory, unless a new authorisation for each establishment, for example for each new hypermarket, or an authorisation that is restricted to a specific part of the national territory is objectively justified by an overriding reason relating to the public interest.

(48) In order to further simplify administrative procedures, it is appropriate to ensure that each provider has a single point through which he can complete all procedures and formalities (hereinafter referred to as 'points of single contact'). The number of points of single contact per Member State may vary according to regional or local competencies or according to the activities concerned. The creation of points of single contact should not interfere with the allocation of functions among competent authorities within each national system. Where several authorities at regional or local level are competent, one of them may assume the role of point of single contact and coordinator. Points of single contact may be set up not only by administrative authorities but also by chambers of commerce or crafts, or by the professional organisations or private bodies to which a Member State decides to entrust that function. Points of single contact have an important role to play in providing assistance to providers either as the authority directly competent to issue the documents necessary to access a service activity or as an intermediary between the provider and the authorities which are directly competent.

(49) The fee which may be charged by points of single contact should be proportionate to the cost of the procedures and formalities with which they deal. This should not prevent Member States from entrusting the points of single contact with the collection of other administrative fees, such as the fee of supervisory bodies.

(50) It is necessary for providers and recipients of services to have easy access to certain types of information It should be for each Member State to determine, within the framework of this Directive, the way in which providers and recipients are provided with information. In particular, the obligation on Member States to ensure that relevant information is easily accessible to providers and recipients and that it can be accessed by the public without obstacle could be fulfilled by making this information accessible through a website. Any information given should be provided in a clear and unambiguous manner.

(51) The information provided to providers and recipients of services should include, in particular, information on procedures and formalities, contact details of the competent authorities, conditions for access to public registers and data bases and information concerning available remedies and the contact details of associations and organisations from which providers or recipients can obtain practical assistance. The obligation on competent authorities to assist providers and recipients should not include the provision of legal advice in individual cases. Nevertheless, general information on the way in which requirements are usually interpreted or applied should be given. Issues such as liability for providing incorrect or misleading information should be determined by Member States.

(52) The setting up, in the reasonably near future, of electronic means of completing procedures and formalities will be vital for administrative simplification in the field of service activities, for the benefit of providers, recipients and competent authorities. In order to meet that obligation as to results, national laws and other rules applicable to services may need to be adapted. This obligation should not prevent Member States from providing other means of completing such procedures and formalities, in addition to electronic means. The fact that it must be possible to complete those procedures and formalities at a distance means, in particular, that Member States must ensure that they may be completed across borders. The obligation as to results does not cover procedures or formalities which by their very nature are impossible to complete at a distance. Furthermore, this does not interfere with Member States' legislation on the use of languages.

(53) The granting of licences for certain service activities may require an interview with the applicant by the competent authority in order to assess the applicant's personal integrity and suitability for carrying out the service in question. In such cases, the completion of formalities by electronic means may not be appropriate.

(54) The possibility of gaining access to a service activity should be made subject to authorisation by the competent authorities only if that decision satisfies the criteria of non-discrimination, necessity and proportionality. That means, in particular, that authorisation schemes should be permissible only where an a posteriori inspection would not be effective because of the impossibility of ascertaining the defects of the services concerned a posteriori, due account being taken of the risks and dangers which could arise in the absence of a prior inspection. However, the provision to that effect made by this Directive cannot be relied upon in order to justify authorisation schemes which are prohibited by other Community instruments such as Directive 1999/93/EC of the European Parliament and the Council of 13 December 1999 on a Community framework for electronic signatures,[17] or Directive 2000/31/EC of the European Parliament and of the Council of 8 June 2000 on certain legal aspects of information society services, in particular electronic commerce, in the internal market (Directive on electronic commerce).[18] The results of the process of mutual evaluation will make it possible to determine, at Community level, the types of activity for which authorisation schemes should be eliminated.

(55) This Directive should be without prejudice to the possibility for Member States to withdraw authorisations after they have been issued, if the conditions for the granting of the authorisation are no longer fulfilled.

(56) According to the case law of the Court of Justice, public health, consumer protection, animal health and the protection of the urban environment constitute overriding reasons relating to the public interest. Such overriding reasons may justify the application of authorisation schemes and other restrictions. However, no such authorisation scheme or restriction should discriminate on grounds of nationality. Further, the principles of necessity and proportionality should always be respected.

(57) The provisions of this Directive relating to authorisation schemes should concern cases where the access to or exercise of a service activity by operators requires a decision by a competent authority. This concerns neither decisions by competent authorities to set up a public or private entity for the provision of a particular service nor the conclusion of contracts by competent authorities for the provision of a particular service which is governed by rules on public procurement, since this Directive does not deal with rules on public procurement.

(58) In order to facilitate access to and exercise of service activities, it is important to evaluate and report on authorisation schemes and their justification. This reporting obligation concerns only the existence of authorisation schemes and not the criteria and conditions for the granting of an authorisation.

(59) The authorisation should as a general rule enable the provider to have access to the service activity, or to exercise that activity, throughout the national territory, unless a territorial limit

[17] OJ L 13, 19.1.2000, p. 12.
[18] OJ L 178, 17.7.2000, p. 1.

is justified by an overriding reason relating to the public interest. For example, environmental protection may justify the requirement to obtain an individual authorisation for each installation on the national territory. This provision should not affect regional or local competences for the granting of authorisations within the Member States.

(60) This Directive, and in particular the provisions concerning authorisation schemes and the territorial scope of an authorisation, should not interfere with the division of regional or local competences within the Member States, including regional and local self-government and the use of official languages.

(61) The provision relating to the non-duplication of conditions for the granting of an authorisation should not prevent Member States from applying their own conditions as specified in the authorisation scheme. It should only require that competent authorities, when considering whether these conditions are met by the applicant, take into account the equivalent conditions which have already been satisfied by the applicant in another Member State. This provision should not require the application of the conditions for the granting of an authorisation provided for in the authorisation scheme of another Member State.

(62) Where the number of authorisations available for an activity is limited because of scarcity of natural resources or technical capacity, a procedure for selection from among several potential candidates should be adopted with the aim of developing through open competition the quality and conditions for supply of services available to users. Such a procedure should provide guarantees of transparency and impartiality and the authorisation thus granted should not have an excessive duration, be subject to automatic renewal or confer any advantage on the provider whose authorisation has just expired. In particular, the duration of the authorisation granted should be fixed in such a way that it does not restrict or limit free competition beyond what is necessary in order to enable the provider to recoup the cost of investment and to make a fair return on the capital invested. This provision should not prevent Member States from limiting the number of authorisations for reasons other than scarcity of natural resources or technical capacity. These authorisations should remain in any case subject to the other provisions of this Directive relating to authorisation schemes.

(63) In the absence of different arrangements, failing a response within a time period, an authorisation should be deemed to have been granted. However, different arrangements may be put in place in respect of certain activities, where objectively justified by overriding reasons relating to the public interest, including a legitimate interest of third parties. Such different arrangements could include national rules according to which, in the absence of a response of the competent authority, the application is deemed to have been rejected, this rejection being open to challenge before the courts.

(64) In order to establish a genuine internal market for services, it is necessary to abolish any restrictions on the freedom of establishment and the free movement of services which are still enshrined in the laws of certain Member States and which are incompatible with Articles 43 and 49 of the Treaty respectively. The restrictions to be prohibited particularly affect the internal market for services and should be systematically dismantled as soon as possible.

(65) Freedom of establishment is predicated, in particular, upon the principle of equal treatment, which entails the prohibition not only of any discrimination on grounds of nationality but also of any indirect discrimination based on other grounds but capable of producing the same result. Thus, access to a service activity or the exercise thereof in a Member State, either as a principal or secondary activity, should not be made subject to criteria such as place of establishment, residence, domicile or principal provision of the service activity. However, these criteria should not include requirements according to which a provider or one of his employees or a representative must be present during the exercise of the activity when this is justified by an overriding reason relating to the public interest. Furthermore, a Member State should not restrict the legal capacity or the right of companies, incorporated in accordance with the law of another Member State on whose territory they have their primary establishment, to bring legal proceedings. Moreover, a Member State should not be able to confer any advantages on providers having a particular national or local socio-economic link; nor should it be able to restrict, on grounds of place of establishment, the provider's freedom to acquire, exploit or

dispose of rights and goods or to access different forms of credit or accommodation in so far as those choices are useful for access to his activity or for the effective exercise thereof.

(66) Access to or the exercise of a service activity in the territory of a Member State should not be subject to an economic test. The prohibition of economic tests as a prerequisite for the grant of authorisation should cover economic tests as such, but not requirements which are objectively justified by overriding reasons relating to the public interest, such as the protection of the urban environment, social policy or public health. The prohibition should not affect the exercise of the powers of the authorities responsible for applying competition law.

(67) With respect to financial guarantees or insurance, the prohibition of requirements should concern only the obligation that the requested financial guarantees or insurance must be obtained from a financial institution established in the Member State concerned.

(68) With respect to pre-registration, the prohibition of requirements should concern only the obligation that the provider, prior to the establishment, be pre-registered for a given period in a register held in the Member State concerned.

(69) In order to coordinate the modernisation of national rules and regulations in a manner consistent with the requirements of the internal market, it is necessary to evaluate certain non-discriminatory national requirements which, by their very nature, could severely restrict or even prevent access to an activity or the exercise thereof under the freedom of establishment. This evaluation process should be limited to the compatibility of these requirements with the criteria already established by the Court of Justice on the freedom of establishment. It should not concern the application of Community competition law. Where such requirements are discriminatory or not objectively justified by an overriding reason relating to the public interest, or where they are disproportionate, they must be abolished or amended. The outcome of this assessment will be different according to the nature of the activity and the public interest concerned. In particular, such requirements could be fully justified when they pursue social policy objectives.

(70) For the purposes of this Directive, and without prejudice to Article 16 of the Treaty, services may be considered to be services of general economic interest only if they are provided in application of a special task in the public interest entrusted to the provider by the Member State concerned. This assignment should be made by way of one or more acts, the form of which is determined by the Member State concerned, and should specify the precise nature of the special task.

(71) The mutual evaluation process provided for in this Directive should not affect the freedom of Member States to set in their legislation a high level of protection of the public interest, in particular in relation to social policy objectives. Furthermore, it is necessary that the mutual evaluation process take fully into account the specificity of services of general economic interest and of the particular tasks assigned to them. This may justify certain restrictions on the freedom of establishment, in particular where such restrictions pursue the protection of public health and social policy objectives and where they satisfy the conditions set out in Article 15(3)(a), (b) and (c). For example, with regard to the obligation to take a specific legal form in order to exercise certain services in the social field, the Court of Justice has already recognised that it may be justified to subject the provider to a requirement to be non-profit making.

(72) Services of a general economic interest are entrusted with important tasks relating to social and territorial cohesion. The performance of these tasks should not be obstructed as a result of the evaluation process provided for in this Directive. Requirements which are necessary for the fulfilment of such tasks should not be affected by this process while, at the same time, unjustified restrictions on the freedom of establishment should be addressed.

(73) The requirements to be examined include national rules which, on grounds other than those relating to professional qualifications, reserve access to certain activities to particular providers. These requirements also include obligations on a provider to take a specific legal form, in particular to be a legal person, to be a company with individual ownership, to be a non-profit making organisation or a company owned exclusively by natural persons, and requirements which relate to the shareholding of a company, in particular obligations to hold a minimum amount of capital for certain service activities or to have a specific qualification in order to hold share capital in or to manage

certain companies. The evaluation of the compatibility of fixed minimum and/or maximum tariffs with the freedom of establishment concerns only tariffs imposed by competent authorities specifically for the provision of certain services and not, for example, general rules on price determination, such as for the renting of houses.

(74) The mutual evaluation process means that during the transposition period Member States will first have to conduct a screening of their legislation in order to ascertain whether any of the above mentioned requirements exists in their legal systems. At the latest by the end of the transposition period, Member States should draw up a report on the results of this screening. Each report will be submitted to all other Member States and interested parties. Member States will then have six months in which to submit their observations on these reports. At the latest by one year after the date of transposition of this Directive, the Commission should draw up a summary report, accompanied where appropriate by proposals for further initiatives. If necessary the Commission, in cooperation with the Member States, could assist them to design a common method.

(75) The fact that this Directive specifies a number of requirements to be abolished or evaluated by the Member States during the transposition period is without prejudice to any infringement proceedings against a Member State for failure to fulfil its obligations under Articles 43 or 49 of the Treaty.

(76) This Directive does not concern the application of Articles 28 to 30 of the Treaty relating to the free movement of goods. The restrictions prohibited pursuant to the provision on the freedom to provide services cover the requirements applicable to access to service activities or to the exercise thereof and not those applicable to goods as such.

(77) Where an operator travels to another Member State to exercise a service activity there, a distinction should be made between situations covered by the freedom of establishment and those covered, due to the temporary nature of the activities concerned, by the free movement of services. As regards the distinction between the freedom of establishment and the free movement of services, according to the case law of the Court of Justice the key element is whether or not the operator is established in the Member State where it provides the service concerned. If the operator is established in the Member State where it provides its services, it should come under the scope of application of the freedom of establishment. If, by contrast, the operator is not established in the Member State where the service is provided, its activities should be covered by the free movement of services. The Court of Justice has consistently held that the temporary nature of the activities in question should be determined in the light not only of the duration of the provision of the service, but also of its regularity, periodical nature or continuity. The fact that the activity is temporary should not mean that the provider may not equip itself with some forms of infrastructure in the Member State where the service is provided, such as an office, chambers or consulting rooms, in so far as such infrastructure is necessary for the purposes of providing the service in question.

(78) In order to secure effective implementation of the free movement of services and to ensure that recipients and providers can benefit from and supply services throughout the Community regardless of borders, it is necessary to clarify the extent to which requirements of the Member State where the service is provided can be imposed. It is indispensable to provide that the provision on the freedom to provide services does not prevent the Member State where the service is provided from imposing, in compliance with the principles set out in Article 16(1)(a) to (c), its specific requirements for reasons of public policy or public security or for the protection of public health or the environment.

(79) The Court of Justice has consistently held that Member States retain the right to take measures in order to prevent providers from abusively taking advantage of the internal market principles. Abuse by a provider should be established on a case by case basis.

(80) It is necessary to ensure that providers are able to take equipment which is integral to the provision of their service with them when they travel to provide services in another Member State. In particular, it is important to avoid cases in which the service could not be provided without the equipment or situations in which providers incur additional costs, for example, by hiring or purchasing

different equipment to that which they habitually use or by needing to deviate significantly from the way they habitually carry out their activity.

(81) The concept of equipment does not refer to physical objects which are either supplied by the provider to the client or become part of a physical object as a result of the service activity, such as building materials or spare parts, or which are consumed or left in situ in the course of the service provision, such as combustible fuels, explosives, fireworks, pesticides, poisons or medicines.

(82) The provisions of this Directive should not preclude the application by a Member State of rules on employment conditions. Rules laid down by law, regulation or administrative provisions should, in accordance with the Treaty, be justified for reasons relating to the protection of workers and be non-discriminatory, necessary, and proportionate, as interpreted by the Court of Justice, and comply with other relevant Community law.

(83) It is necessary to ensure that the provision on the freedom to provide services may be departed from only in the areas covered by derogations. Those derogations are necessary in order to take into account the level of integration of the internal market or certain Community instruments relating to services pursuant to which a provider is subject to the application of a law other than that of the Member State of establishment. Moreover, by way of exception, measures against a given provider should also be adopted in certain individual cases and under certain strict procedural and substantive conditions. In addition, any restriction of the free movement of services should be permitted, by way of exception, only if it is consistent with fundamental rights which form an integral part of the general principles of law enshrined in the Community legal order.

(84) The derogation from the provision on the freedom to provide services concerning postal services should cover both activities reserved to the universal service provider and other postal services.

(85) The derogation from the provision on the freedom to provide services relating to the judicial recovery of debts and the reference to a possible future harmonisation instrument should concern only the access to and the exercise of activities which consist, notably, in bringing actions before a court relating to the recovery of debts.

(86) This Directive should not affect terms and conditions of employment which, pursuant to Directive 96/71/ECof the European Parliament and of the Council of 16 December 1996 concerning the posting of workers in the framework of the provision of services,[19] apply to workers posted to provide a service in the territory of another Member State. In such cases, Directive 96/71/EC stipulates that providers have to comply with terms and conditions of employment in a listed number of areas applicable in the Member State where the service is provided. These are: maximum work periods and minimum rest periods, minimum paid annual holidays, minimum rates of pay, including overtime rates, the conditions of hiring out of workers, in particular the protection of workers hired out by temporary employment undertakings, health, safety and hygiene at work, protective measures with regard to the terms and conditions of employment of pregnant women or women who have recently given birth and of children and young people and equality of treatment between men and women and other provisions on non-discrimination. This not only concerns terms and conditions of employment which are laid down by law but also those laid down in collective agreements or arbitration awards that are officially declared or de facto universally applicable within the meaning of Directive 96/71/EC. Moreover, this Directive should not prevent Member States from applying terms and conditions of employment on matters other than those listed in Article 3(1) of Directive 96/71/EC on the grounds of public policy.

(87) Neither should this Directive affect terms and conditions of employment in cases where the worker employed for the provision of a cross-border service is recruited in the Member State where the service is provided. Furthermore, this Directive should not affect the right for the Member

[19] OJ L 18, 21.1.1997, p. 1.

State where the service is provided to determine the existence of an employment relationship and the distinction between self-employed persons and employed persons, including 'false self-employed persons'. In that respect the essential characteristic of an employment relationship within the meaning of Article 39 of the Treaty should be the fact that for a certain period of time a person provides services for and under the direction of another person in return for which he receives remuneration. Any activity which a person performs outside a relationship of subordination must be classified as an activity pursued in a self-employed capacity for the purposes of Articles 43 and 49 of the Treaty.

(88) The provision on the freedom to provide services should not apply in cases where, in conformity with Community law, an activity is reserved in a Member State to a particular profession, for example requirements which reserve the provision of legal advice to lawyers.

(89) The derogation from the provision on the freedom to provide services concerning matters relating to the registration of vehicles leased in a Member State other than that in which they are used follows from the case law of the Court of Justice, which has recognised that a Member State may impose such an obligation, in accordance with proportionate conditions, in the case of vehicles used on its territory. That exclusion does not cover occasional or temporary rental.

(90) Contractual relations between the provider and the client as well as between an employer and employee should not be subject to this Directive. The applicable law regarding the contractual or non contractual obligations of the provider should be determined by the rules of private international law.

(91) It is necessary to afford Member States the possibility, exceptionally and on a case-by-case basis, of taking measures which derogate from the provision on the freedom to provide services in respect of a provider established in another Member State on grounds of the safety of services. However, it should be possible to take such measures only in the absence of harmonisation at Community level.

(92) Restrictions on the free movement of services, contrary to this Directive, may arise not only from measures applied to providers, but also from the many barriers to the use of services by recipients, especially consumers. This Directive mentions, by way of illustration, certain types of restriction applied to a recipient wishing to use a service performed by a provider established in another Member State. This also includes cases where recipients of a service are under an obligation to obtain authorisation from or to make a declaration to their competent authorities in order to receive a service from a provider established in another Member State. This does not concern general authorisation schemes which also apply to the use of a service supplied by a provider established in the same Member State.

(93) The concept of financial assistance provided for the use of a particular service should not apply to systems of aids granted by Member States, in particular in the social field or in the cultural sector, which are covered by Community rules on competition, nor to general financial assistance not linked to the use of a particular service, for example grants or loans to students.

(94) In accordance with the Treaty rules on the free movement of services, discrimination on grounds of the nationality of the recipient or national or local residence is prohibited. Such discrimination could take the form of an obligation, imposed only on nationals of another Member State, to supply original documents, certified copies, a certificate of nationality or official translations of documents in order to benefit from a service or from more advantageous terms or prices. However, the prohibition of discriminatory requirements should not preclude the reservation of advantages, especially as regards tariffs, to certain recipients, if such reservation is based on legitimate and objective criteria.

(95) The principle of non-discrimination within the internal market means that access by a recipient, and especially by a consumer, to a service on offer to the public may not be denied or restricted by application of a criterion, included in general conditions made available to the public, relating to the recipient's nationality or place of residence. It does not follow that it will be unlawful discrimination if provision were made in such general conditions for different tariffs and conditions to apply to the provision of a service, where those tariffs, prices and conditions are justified for objective

reasons that can vary from country to country, such as additional costs incurred because of the distance involved or the technical characteristics of the provision of the service, or different market conditions, such as higher or lower demand influenced by seasonality, different vacation periods in the Member States and pricing by different competitors, or extra risks linked to rules differing from those of the Member State of establishment. Neither does it follow that the non-provision of a service to a consumer for lack of the required intellectual property rights in a particular territory would constitute unlawful discrimination.

(96) It is appropriate to provide that, as one of the means by which the provider may make the information which he is obliged to supply easily accessible to the recipient, he supply his electronic address, including that of his website. Furthermore, the obligation to make available certain information in the provider's information documents which present his services in detail should not cover commercial communications of a general nature, such as advertising, but rather documents giving a detailed description of the services proposed, including documents on a website.

(97) It is necessary to provide in this Directive for certain rules on high quality of services, ensuring in particular information and transparency requirements. These rules should apply both in cases of cross border provision of services between Member States and in cases of services provided in a Member State by a provider established there, without imposing unnecessary burdens on SMEs. They should not in any way prevent Member States from applying, in conformity with this Directive and other Community law, additional or different quality requirements.

(98) Any operator providing services involving a direct and particular health, safety or financial risk for the recipient or a third person should, in principle, be covered by appropriate professional liability insurance, or by another form of guarantee which is equivalent or comparable, which means, in particular, that such an operator should as a general rule have adequate insurance cover for services provided in one or more Member States other than the Member State of establishment.

(99) The insurance or guarantee should be appropriate to the nature and extent of the risk. Therefore it should be necessary for the provider to have cross-border cover only if that provider actually provides services in other Member States. Member States should not lay down more detailed rules concerning the insurance cover and fix for example minimum thresholds for the insured sum or limits on exclusions from the insurance cover. Providers and insurance companies should maintain the necessary flexibility to negotiate insurance policies precisely targeted to the nature and extent of the risk. Furthermore, it is not necessary for an obligation of appropriate insurance to be laid down by law. It should be sufficient if an insurance obligation is part of the ethical rules laid down by professional bodies. Finally, there should be no obligation for insurance companies to provide insurance cover.

(100) It is necessary to put an end to total prohibitions on commercial communications by the regulated professions, not by removing bans on the content of a commercial communication but rather by removing those bans which, in a general way and for a given profession, forbid one or more forms of commercial communication, such as a ban on all advertising in one or more given media. As regards the content and methods of commercial communication, it is necessary to encourage professionals to draw up, in accordance with Community law, codes of conduct at Community level.

(101) It is necessary and in the interest of recipients, in particular consumers, to ensure that it is possible for providers to offer multidisciplinary services and that restrictions in this regard be limited to what is necessary to ensure the impartiality, independence and integrity of the regulated professions. This does not affect restrictions or prohibitions on carrying out particular activities which aim at ensuring independence in cases in which a Member State entrusts a provider with a particular task, notably in the area of urban development, nor should it affect the application of competition rules.

(102) In order to increase transparency and promote assessments based on comparable criteria with regard to the quality of the services offered and supplied to recipients, it is important

that information on the meaning of quality labels and other distinctive marks relating to these services be easily accessible. That obligation of transparency is particularly important in areas such as tourism, especially the hotel business, in which the use of a system of classification is widespread. Moreover, it is appropriate to examine the extent to which European standardisation could facilitate compatibility and quality of services. European standards are drawn up by the European standards-setting bodies, the European Committee for Standardisation (CEN), the European Committee for Electrotechnical Standardisation (CENELEC) and the European Telecommunications Standards Institute (ETSI). Where appropriate, the Commission may, in accordance with the procedures laid down in Directive 98/34/EC of the European Parliament and of the Council of 22 June 1998 laying down a procedure for the provision of information in the field of technical standards and regulations[20] and of rules on Information Society services, issue a mandate for the drawing up of specific European standards.

(103) In order to solve potential problems with compliance with judicial decisions, it is appropriate to provide that Member States recognise equivalent guarantees lodged with institutions or bodies such as banks, insurance providers or other financial services providers established in another Member State.

(104) The development of a network of Member States' consumer protection authorities, which is the subject of Regulation (EC) No 2006/2004, complements the cooperation provided for in this Directive. The application of consumer protection legislation in cross-border cases, in particular with regard to new marketing and selling practices, as well as the need to remove certain specific obstacles to cooperation in this field, necessitates a greater degree of cooperation between Member States. In particular, it is necessary in this area to ensure that Member States require the cessation of illegal practices by operators in their territory who target consumers in another Member State.

(105) Administrative cooperation is essential to make the internal market in services function properly. Lack of cooperation between Member States results in proliferation of rules applicable to providers or duplication of controls for cross-border activities, and can also be used by rogue traders to avoid supervision or to circumvent applicable national rules on services. It is, therefore, essential to provide for clear, legally binding obligations for Member States to cooperate effectively.

(106) For the purposes of the Chapter on administrative cooperation, 'supervision' should cover activities such as monitoring and fact finding, problem solving, enforcement and imposition of sanctions and subsequent follow-up activities.

(107) In normal circumstances mutual assistance should take place directly between competent authorities. The liaison points designated by Member States should be required to facilitate this process only in the event of difficulties being encountered, for instance if assistance is required to identify the relevant competent authority.

(108) Certain obligations of mutual assistance should apply to all matters covered by this Directive, including those relating to cases where a provider establishes in another Member State. Other obligations of mutual assistance should apply only in cases of cross-border provision of services, where the provision on the freedom to provide services applies. A further set of obligations should apply in all cases of cross-border provision of services, including areas not covered by the provision on the freedom to provide services. Cross-border provision of services should include cases where services are provided at a distance and where the recipient travels to the Member State of establishment of the provider in order to receive services.

(109) In cases where a provider moves temporarily to a Member State other than the Member State of establishment, it is necessary to provide for mutual assistance between those two Member States so that the former can carry out checks, inspections and enquiries at the request of the Member State of establishment or carry out such checks on its own initiative if these are merely factual checks.

[20] OJ L 204, 21.7.1998, p. 37. Directive as last amended by the 2003 Act of Accession.

(110) It should not be possible for Member States to circumvent the rules laid down in this Directive, including the provision on the freedom to provide services, by conducting checks, inspections or investigations which are discriminatory or disproportionate.

(111) The provisions of this Directive concerning exchange of information regarding the good repute of providers should not pre-empt initiatives in the area of police and judicial cooperation in criminal matters, in particular on the exchange of information between law enforcement authorities of the Member States and on criminal records.

(112) Cooperation between Member States requires a well-functioning electronic information system in order to allow competent authorities easily to identify their relevant interlocutors in other Member States and to communicate in an efficient way.

(113) It is necessary to provide that the Member States, in cooperation with the Commission, are to encourage interested parties to draw up codes of conduct at Community level, aimed, in particular, at promoting the quality of services and taking into account the specific nature of each profession. Those codes of conduct should comply with Community law, especially competition law. They should be compatible with legally binding rules governing professional ethics and conduct in the Member States.

(114) Member States should encourage the setting up of codes of conduct, in particular, by professional bodies, organisations and associations at Community level. These codes of conduct should include, as appropriate to the specific nature of each profession, rules for commercial communications relating to the regulated professions and rules of professional ethics and conduct of the regulated professions which aim, in particular, at ensuring independence, impartiality and professional secrecy. In addition, the conditions to which the activities of estate agents are subject should be included in such codes of conduct. Member States should take accompanying measures to encourage professional bodies, organisations and associations to implement at national level the codes of conduct adopted at Community level.

(115) Codes of conduct at Community level are intended to set minimum standards of conduct and are complementary to Member States' legal requirements. They do not preclude Member States, in accordance with Community law, from taking more stringent measures in law or national professional bodies from providing for greater protection in their national codes of conduct.

(116) Since the objectives of this Directive, namely the elimination of barriers to the freedom of establishment for providers in the Member States and to the free provision of services between Member States, cannot be sufficiently achieved by the Member States and can therefore, by reason of the scale of the action, be better achieved at Community level, the Community may adopt measures, in accordance with the principle of subsidiarity as set out in Article 5 of the Treaty. In accordance with the principle of proportionality, as set out in that Article, this Directive does not go beyond what is necessary in order to achieve those objectives.

(117) The measures necessary for the implementation of this Directive should be adopted in accordance with Council Decision 1999/468/EC of 28 June 1999 laying down the procedures for the exercise of implementing powers conferred on the Commission.[21]

(118) In accordance with paragraph 34 of the Interinstitutional Agreement on better law-making,[22] Member States are encouraged to draw up, for themselves and in the interest of the Community, their own tables, which will, as far as possible, illustrate the correlation between the Directive and the transposition measures, and to make them public,

HAVE ADOPTED THIS DIRECTIVE:

[21] OJ L 184, 17.7.1999, p. 23. Decision as amended by Decision 2006/512/EC (OJ L 200, 22.7.2006, p. 11).

[22] OJ C 321, 31.12.2003, p. 1.

Chapter I General provisions

Article 1 Subject matter

1. This Directive establishes general provisions facilitating the exercise of the freedom of establishment for service providers and the free movement of services, while maintaining a high quality of services.

2. This Directive does not deal with the liberalisation of services of general economic interest, reserved to public or private entities, nor with the privatisation of public entities providing services.

3. This Directive does not deal with the abolition of monopolies providing services nor with aids granted by Member States which are covered by Community rules on competition.

This Directive does not affect the freedom of Member States to define, in conformity with Community law, what they consider to be services of general economic interest, how those services should be organised and financed, in compliance with the State aid rules, and what specific obligations they should be subject to.

4. This Directive does not affect measures taken at Community level or at national level, in conformity with Community law, to protect or promote cultural or linguistic diversity or media pluralism.

5. This Directive does not affect Member States' rules of criminal law. However, Member States may not restrict the freedom to provide services by applying criminal law provisions which specifically regulate or affect access to or exercise of a service activity in circumvention of the rules laid down in this Directive.

6. This Directive does not affect labour law, that is any legal or contractual provision concerning employment conditions, working conditions, including health and safety at work and the relationship between employers and workers, which Member States apply in accordance with national law which respects Community law. Equally, this Directive does not affect the social security legislation of the Member States.

7. This Directive does not affect the exercise of fundamental rights as recognised in the Member States and by Community law. Nor does it affect the right to negotiate, conclude and enforce collective agreements and to take industrial action in accordance with national law and practices which respect Community law.

Article 2 Scope

1. This Directive shall apply to services supplied by providers established in a Member State.
2. This Directive shall not apply to the following activities:
   - (a) non-economic services of general interest;
   - (b) financial services, such as banking, credit, insurance and re-insurance, occupational or personal pensions, securities, investment funds, payment and investment advice, including the services listed in Annex I to Directive 2006/48/EC;
   - (c) electronic communications services and networks, and associated facilities and services, with respect to matters covered by Directives 2002/19/EC, 2002/20/EC, 2002/21/EC, 2002/22/EC and 2002/58/EC;
   - (d) services in the field of transport, including port services, falling within the scope of Title V of the Treaty;
   - (e) services of temporary work agencies;
   - (f) healthcare services whether or not they are provided via healthcare facilities, and regardless of the ways in which they are organised and financed at national level or whether they are public or private;
   - (g) audiovisual services, including cinematographic services, whatever their mode of production, distribution and transmission, and radio broadcasting;
   - (h) gambling activities which involve wagering a stake with pecuniary value in games of chance, including lotteries, gambling in casinos and betting transactions;

(i) activities which are connected with the exercise of official authority as set out in Article 45 of the Treaty;

(j) social services relating to social housing, childcare and support of families and persons permanently or temporarily in need which are provided by the State, by providers mandated by the State or by charities recognised as such by the State;

(k) private security services;

(l) services provided by notaries and bailiffs, who are appointed by an official act of government.

3. This Directive shall not apply to the field of taxation.

Article 3 Relationship with other provisions of Community law

1. If the provisions of this Directive conflict with a provision of another Community act governing specific aspects of access to or exercise of a service activity in specific sectors or for specific professions, the provision of the other Community act shall prevail and shall apply to those specific sectors or professions. These include:

(a) Directive 96/71/EC;

(b) Regulation (EEC) No 1408/71;

(c) Council Directive 89/552/EEC of 3 October 1989 on the coordination of certain provisions laid down by law, regulation or administrative action in Member States concerning the pursuit of television broadcasting activities;[23]

(d) Directive 2005/36/EC.

2. This Directive does not concern rules of private international law, in particular rules governing the law applicable to contractual and non contractual obligations, including those which guarantee that consumers benefit from the protection granted to them by the consumer protection rules laid down in the consumer legislation in force in their Member State.

3. Member States shall apply the provisions of this Directive in compliance with the rules of the Treaty on the right of establishment and the free movement of services.

Article 4 Definitions

For the purposes of this Directive, the following definitions shall apply:

1) 'service' means any self-employed economic activity, normally provided for remuneration, as referred to in Article 50 of the Treaty;

2) 'provider' means any natural person who is a national of a Member State, or any legal person as referred to in Article 48 of the Treaty and established in a Member State, who offers or provides a service;

3) 'recipient' means any natural person who is a national of a Member State or who benefits from rights conferred upon him by Community acts, or any legal person as referred to in Article 48 of the Treaty and established in a Member State, who, for professional or non-professional purposes, uses, or wishes to use, a service;

4) 'Member State of establishment' means the Member State in whose territory the provider of the service concerned is established;

5) 'establishment' means the actual pursuit of an economic activity, as referred to in Article 43 of the Treaty, by the provider for an indefinite period and through a stable infrastructure from where the business of providing services is actually carried out;

6) 'authorisation scheme' means any procedure under which a provider or recipient is in effect required to take steps in order to obtain from a competent authority a formal decision, or an implied decision, concerning access to a service activity or the exercise thereof;

7) 'requirement' means any obligation, prohibition, condition or limit provided for in the laws, regulations or administrative provisions of the Member States or in consequence of case-law,

[23] OJ L 298, 17.10.1989, p. 23. Directive as amended by Directive 97/36/EC of the European Parliament and of the Council (OJ L 202, 30.7.1997, p. 60).

administrative practice, the rules of professional bodies, or the collective rules of professional associations or other professional organisations, adopted in the exercise of their legal autonomy; rules laid down in collective agreements negotiated by the social partners shall not as such be seen as requirements within the meaning of this Directive;

8) 'overriding reasons relating to the public interest' means reasons recognised as such in the case law of the Court of Justice, including the following grounds: public policy; public security; public safety; public health; preserving the financial equilibrium of the social security system; the protection of consumers, recipients of services and workers; fairness of trade transactions; combating fraud; the protection of the environment and the urban environment; the health of animals; intellectual property; the conservation of the national historic and artistic heritage; social policy objectives and cultural policy objectives;

9) 'competent authority' means any body or authority which has a supervisory or regulatory role in a Member State in relation to service activities, including, in particular, administrative authorities, including courts acting as such, professional bodies, and those professional associations or other professional organisations which, in the exercise of their legal autonomy, regulate in a collective manner access to service activities or the exercise thereof;

10) 'Member State where the service is provided' means the Member State where the service is supplied by a provider established in another Member State;

11) 'regulated profession' means a professional activity or a group of professional activities as referred to in Article 3(1)(a) of Directive 2005/36/EC;

12) 'commercial communication' means any form of communication designed to promote, directly or indirectly, the goods, services or image of an undertaking, organisation or person engaged in commercial, industrial or craft activity or practising a regulated profession. The following do not in themselves constitute commercial communications:

(a) information enabling direct access to the activity of the undertaking, organisation or person, including in particular a domain name or an electronic-mailing address;
(b) communications relating to the goods, services or image of the undertaking, organisation or person, compiled in an independent manner, particularly when provided for no financial consideration.

Chapter II Administrative simplification

Article 5 Simplification of procedures

1. Member States shall examine the procedures and formalities applicable to access to a service activity and to the exercise thereof. Where procedures and formalities examined under this paragraph are not sufficiently simple, Member States shall simplify them.

2. The Commission may introduce harmonised forms at Community level, in accordance with the procedure referred to in Article 40(2). These forms shall be equivalent to certificates, attestations and any other documents required of a provider.

3. Where Member States require a provider or recipient to supply a certificate, attestation or any other document proving that a requirement has been satisfied, they shall accept any document from another Member State which serves an equivalent purpose or from which it is clear that the requirement in question has been satisfied. They may not require a document from another Member State to be produced in its original form, or as a certified copy or as a certified translation, save in the cases provided for in other Community instruments or where such a requirement is justified by an overriding reason relating to the public interest, including public order and security.

The first subparagraph shall not affect the right of Member States to require non-certified translations of documents in one of their official languages.

4. Paragraph 3 shall not apply to the documents referred to in Article 7(2) and 50 of Directive 2005/36/EC, in Articles 45(3), 46, 49 and 50 of Directive 2004/18/EC of the European Parliament and of the Council of 31 March 2004 on the coordination of procedures for the award of public works

contracts, public supply contracts and public service contracts,[24] in Article 3(2) of Directive 98/5/EC of the European Parliament and of the Council of 16 February 1998 to facilitate practice of the profession of lawyer on a permanent basis in a Member State other than that in which the qualification was obtained,[25] in the First Council Directive 68/151/EEC of 9 March 1968 on coordination of safeguards which, for the protection of the interests of members and others, are required by Member States of companies within the meaning of the second paragraph of Article 58 of the Treaty, with a view to making such safeguards equivalent throughout the Community[26] and in the Eleventh Council Directive 89/666/EEC of 21 December 1989 concerning disclosure requirements in respect of branches opened in a Member State by certain types of company governed by the law of another State.[27]

Article 6 Points of single contact

1. Member States shall ensure that it is possible for providers to complete the following procedures and formalities through points of single contact:

(a) all procedures and formalities needed for access to his service activities, in particular, all declarations, notifications or applications necessary for authorisation from the competent authorities, including applications for inclusion in a register, a roll or a database, or for registration with a professional body or association;

(b) any applications for authorisation needed to exercise his service activities.

2. The establishment of points of single contact shall be without prejudice to the allocation of functions and powers among the authorities within national systems.

Article 7 Right to information

1. Member States shall ensure that the following information is easily accessible to providers and recipients through the points of single contact:

(a) requirements applicable to providers established in their territory, in particular those requirements concerning the procedures and formalities to be completed in order to access and to exercise service activities;

(b) the contact details of the competent authorities enabling the latter to be contacted directly, including the details of those authorities responsible for matters concerning the exercise of service activities;

(c) the means of, and conditions for, accessing public registers and databases on providers and services;

(d) the means of redress which are generally available in the event of dispute between the competent authorities and the provider or the recipient, or between a provider and a recipient or between providers;

(e) the contact details of the associations or organisations, other than the competent authorities, from which providers or recipients may obtain practical assistance.

2. Member States shall ensure that it is possible for providers and recipients to receive, at their request, assistance from the competent authorities, consisting in information on the way in which the requirements referred to in point (a) of paragraph 1 are generally interpreted and applied. Where appropriate, such advice shall include a simple step-by-step guide. The information shall be provided in plain and intelligible language.

3. Member States shall ensure that the information and assistance referred to in paragraphs 1 and 2 are provided in a clear and unambiguous manner, that they are easily accessible at a distance and by electronic means and that they are kept up to date.

[24] OJ L 134, 30.4.2004, p. 114. Directive as last amended by Commission Regulation (EC) No 2083/2005 (OJ L 333, 20.12.2005, p. 28).

[25] OJ L 77, 14.3.1998, p. 36. Directive as amended by the 2003 Act of Accession.

[26] OJ L 65, 14.3.1968, p. 8. Directive as last amended by Directive 2003/58/EC of the European Parliament and of the Council (OJ L 221, 4.9.2003, p. 13).

[27] OJ L 395, 30.12.1989, p. 36.

4. Member States shall ensure that the points of single contact and the competent authorities respond as quickly as possible to any request for information or assistance as referred to in paragraphs 1 and 2 and, in cases where the request is faulty or unfounded, inform the applicant accordingly without delay.

5. Member States and the Commission shall take accompanying measures in order to encourage points of single contact to make the information provided for in this Article available in other Community languages. This does not interfere with Member States' legislation on the use of languages.

6. The obligation for competent authorities to assist providers and recipients does not require those authorities to provide legal advice in individual cases but concerns only general information on the way in which requirements are usually interpreted or applied.

Article 8 Procedures by electronic means

1. Member States shall ensure that all procedures and formalities relating to access to a service activity and to the exercise thereof may be easily completed, at a distance and by electronic means, through the relevant point of single contact and with the relevant competent authorities.

2. Paragraph 1 shall not apply to the inspection of premises on which the service is provided or of equipment used by the provider or to physical examination of the capability or of the personal integrity of the provider or of his responsible staff.

3. The Commission shall, in accordance with the procedure referred to in Article 40(2), adopt detailed rules for the implementation of paragraph 1 of this Article with a view to facilitating the interoperability of information systems and use of procedures by electronic means between Member States, taking into account common standards developed at Community level.

Chapter III Freedom of establishment for providers

Section 1 Authorisations

Article 9 Authorisation schemes

1. Member States shall not make access to a service activity or the exercise thereof subject to an authorisation scheme unless the following conditions are satisfied:

(a) the authorisation scheme does not discriminate against the provider in question;

(b) the need for an authorisation scheme is justified by an overriding reason relating to the public interest;

(c) the objective pursued cannot be attained by means of a less restrictive measure, in particular because an a posteriori inspection would take place too late to be genuinely effective.

2. In the report referred to in Article 39(1), Member States shall identify their authorisation schemes and give reasons showing their compatibility with paragraph 1 of this Article.

3. This section shall not apply to those aspects of authorisation schemes which are governed directly or indirectly by other Community instruments.

Article 10 Conditions for the granting of authorisation

1. Authorisation schemes shall be based on criteria which preclude the competent authorities from exercising their power of assessment in an arbitrary manner.

2. The criteria referred to in paragraph 1 shall be:

(a) non-discriminatory;

(b) justified by an overriding reason relating to the public interest;

(c) proportionate to that public interest objective;

(d) clear and unambiguous;

(e) objective;

(f) made public in advance;

(g) transparent and accessible.

3. The conditions for granting authorisation for a new establishment shall not duplicate requirements and controls which are equivalent or essentially comparable as regards their purpose to which the provider is already subject in another Member State or in the same Member State. The liaison points referred to in Article 28(2) and the provider shall assist the competent authority by providing any necessary information regarding those requirements.

4. The authorisation shall enable the provider to have access to the service activity, or to exercise that activity, throughout the national territory, including by means of setting up agencies, subsidiaries, branches or offices, except where an authorisation for each individual establishment or a limitation of the authorisation to a certain part of the territory is justified by an overriding reason relating to the public interest.

5. The authorisation shall be granted as soon as it is established, in the light of an appropriate examination, that the conditions for authorisation have been met.

6. Except in the case of the granting of an authorisation, any decision from the competent authorities, including refusal or withdrawal of an authorisation, shall be fully reasoned and shall be open to challenge before the courts or other instances of appeal.

7. This Article shall not call into question the allocation of the competences, at local or regional level, of the Member States' authorities granting authorisations.

Article 11 Duration of authorisation

1. An authorisation granted to a provider shall not be for a limited period, except where:
   (a) the authorisation is being automatically renewed or is subject only to the continued fulfilment of requirements;
   (b) the number of available authorisations is limited by an overriding reason relating to the public interest; or
   (c) a limited authorisation period can be justified by an overriding reason relating to the public interest.

2. Paragraph 1 shall not concern the maximum period before the end of which the provider must actually commence his activity after receiving authorisation.

3. Member States shall require a provider to inform the relevant point of single contact provided for in Article 6 of the following changes:
   (a) the creation of subsidiaries whose activities fall within the scope of the authorisation scheme;
   (b) changes in his situation which result in the conditions for authorisation no longer being met.

4. This Article shall be without prejudice to the Member States' ability to revoke authorisations, when the conditions for authorisation are no longer met.

Article 12 Selection from among several candidates

1. Where the number of authorisations available for a given activity is limited because of the scarcity of available natural resources or technical capacity, Member States shall apply a selection procedure to potential candidates which provides full guarantees of impartiality and transparency, including, in particular, adequate publicity about the launch, conduct and completion of the procedure.

2. In the cases referred to in paragraph 1, authorisation shall be granted for an appropriate limited period and may not be open to automatic renewal nor confer any other advantage on the provider whose authorisation has just expired or on any person having any particular links with that provider.

3. Subject to paragraph 1 and to Articles 9 and 10, Member States may take into account, in establishing the rules for the selection procedure, considerations of public health, social policy objectives, the health and safety of employees or self-employed persons, the protection of the environment, the preservation of cultural heritage and other overriding reasons relating to the public interest, in conformity with Community law.

Article 13 Authorisation procedures

1. Authorisation procedures and formalities shall be clear, made public in advance and be such as to provide the applicants with a guarantee that their application will be dealt with objectively and impartially.

2. Authorisation procedures and formalities shall not be dissuasive and shall not unduly complicate or delay the provision of the service. They shall be easily accessible and any charges which the applicants may incur from their application shall be reasonable and proportionate to the cost of the authorisation procedures in question and shall not exceed the cost of the procedures.

3. Authorisation procedures and formalities shall provide applicants with a guarantee that their application will be processed as quickly as possible and, in any event, within a reasonable period which is fixed and made public in advance. The period shall run only from the time when all documentation has been submitted. When justified by the complexity of the issue, the time period may be extended once, by the competent authority, for a limited time. The extension and its duration shall be duly motivated and shall be notified to the applicant before the original period has expired.

4. Failing a response within the time period set or extended in accordance with paragraph 3, authorisation shall be deemed to have been granted. Different arrangements may nevertheless be put in place, where justified by overriding reasons relating to the public interest, including a legitimate interest of third parties.

5. All applications for authorisation shall be acknowledged as quickly as possible. The acknowledgement must specify the following:

(a) the period referred to in paragraph 3;

(b) the available means of redress;

(c) where applicable, a statement that in the absence of a response within the period specified, the authorisation shall be deemed to have been granted.

6. In the case of an incomplete application, the applicant shall be informed as quickly as possible of the need to supply any additional documentation, as well as of any possible effects on the period referred to in paragraph 3.

7. When a request is rejected because it fails to comply with the required procedures or formalities, the applicant shall be informed of the rejection as quickly as possible.

Section 2 Requirements prohibited or subject to evaluation

Article 14 Prohibited requirements

Member States shall not make access to, or the exercise of, a service activity in their territory subject to compliance with any of the following:

1) discriminatory requirements based directly or indirectly on nationality or, in the case of companies, the location of the registered office, including in particular:

(a) nationality requirements for the provider, his staff, persons holding the share capital or members of the provider's management or supervisory bodies;

(b) a requirement that the provider, his staff, persons holding the share capital or members of the provider's management or supervisory bodies be resident within the territory;

2) a prohibition on having an establishment in more than one Member State or on being entered in the registers or enrolled with professional bodies or associations of more than one Member State;

3) restrictions on the freedom of a provider to choose between a principal or a secondary establishment, in particular an obligation on the provider to have its principal establishment in their territory, or restrictions on the freedom to choose between establishment in the form of an agency, branch or subsidiary;

4) conditions of reciprocity with the Member State in which the provider already has an establishment, save in the case of conditions of reciprocity provided for in Community instruments concerning energy;

5) the case-by-case application of an economic test making the granting of authorisation subject to proof of the existence of an economic need or market demand, an assessment of the potential or current economic effects of the activity or an assessment of the appropriateness of the activity in relation to the economic planning objectives set by the competent authority; this prohibition shall not concern planning requirements which do not pursue economic aims but serve overriding reasons relating to the public interest;

6) the direct or indirect involvement of competing operators, including within consultative bodies, in the granting of authorisations or in the adoption of other decisions of the competent authorities, with the exception of professional bodies and associations or other organisations acting as the competent authority; this prohibition shall not concern the consultation of organisations, such as chambers of commerce or social partners, on matters other than individual applications for authorisation, or a consultation of the public at large;

7) an obligation to provide or participate in a financial guarantee or to take out insurance from a provider or body established in their territory. This shall not affect the possibility for Member States to require insurance or financial guarantees as such, nor shall it affect requirements relating to the participation in a collective compensation fund, for instance for members of professional bodies or organisations;

8) an obligation to have been pre-registered, for a given period, in the registers held in their territory or to have previously exercised the activity for a given period in their territory.

Article 15 Requirements to be evaluated

1. Member States shall examine whether, under their legal system, any of the requirements listed in paragraph 2 are imposed and shall ensure that any such requirements are compatible with the conditions laid down in paragraph 3. Member States shall adapt their laws, regulations or administrative provisions so as to make them compatible with those conditions.

2. Member States shall examine whether their legal system makes access to a service activity or the exercise of it subject to compliance with any of the following non-discriminatory requirements:

(a) quantitative or territorial restrictions, in particular in the form of limits fixed according to population or of a minimum geographical distance between providers;
(b) an obligation on a provider to take a specific legal form;
(c) requirements which relate to the shareholding of a company;
(d) requirements, other than those concerning matters covered by Directive 2005/36/EC or provided for in other Community instruments, which reserve access to the service activity in question to particular providers by virtue of the specific nature of the activity;
(e) a ban on having more than one establishment in the territory of the same State;
(f) requirements fixing a minimum number of employees;
(g) fixed minimum and/or maximum tariffs with which the provider must comply;
(h) an obligation on the provider to supply other specific services jointly with his service.

3. Member States shall verify that the requirements referred to in paragraph 2 satisfy the following conditions:

(a) non-discrimination: requirements must be neither directly nor indirectly discriminatory according to nationality nor, with regard to companies, according to the location of the registered office;
(b) necessity: requirements must be justified by an overriding reason relating to the public interest;

(c) proportionality: requirements must be suitable for securing the attainment of the objective pursued; they must not go beyond what is necessary to attain that objective and it must not be possible to replace those requirements with other, less restrictive measures which attain the same result.

4. Paragraphs 1, 2 and 3 shall apply to legislation in the field of services of general economic interest only insofar as the application of these paragraphs does not obstruct the performance, in law or in fact, of the particular task assigned to them.

5. In the mutual evaluation report provided for in Article 39(1), Member States shall specify the following:

(a) the requirements that they intend to maintain and the reasons why they consider that those requirements comply with the conditions set out in paragraph 3;
(b) the requirements which have been abolished or made less stringent.

6. From 28 December 2006 Member States shall not introduce any new requirement of a kind listed in paragraph 2, unless that requirement satisfies the conditions laid down in paragraph 3.

7. Member States shall notify the Commission of any new laws, regulations or administrative provisions which set requirements as referred to in paragraph 6, together with the reasons for those requirements. The Commission shall communicate the provisions concerned to the other Member States. Such notification shall not prevent Member States from adopting the provisions in question.

Within a period of 3 months from the date of receipt of the notification, the Commission shall examine the compatibility of any new requirements with Community law and, where appropriate, shall adopt a decision requesting the Member State in question to refrain from adopting them or to abolish them.

The notification of a draft national law in accordance with Directive 98/34/EC shall fulfil the obligation of notification provided for in this Directive.

Chapter IV Free movement of services

Section 1 Freedom to provide services and related derogations

Article 16 Freedom to provide services

1. Member States shall respect the right of providers to provide services in a Member State other than that in which they are established.

The Member State in which the service is provided shall ensure free access to and free exercise of a service activity within its territory.

Member States shall not make access to or exercise of a service activity in their territory subject to compliance with any requirements which do not respect the following principles:

(a) non-discrimination: the requirement may be neither directly nor indirectly discriminatory with regard to nationality or, in the case of legal persons, with regard to the Member State in which they are established;
(b) necessity: the requirement must be justified for reasons of public policy, public security, public health or the protection of the environment;
(c) proportionality: the requirement must be suitable for attaining the objective pursued, and must not go beyond what is necessary to attain that objective.

2. Member States may not restrict the freedom to provide services in the case of a provider established in another Member State by imposing any of the following requirements:

(a) an obligation on the provider to have an establishment in their territory;

(b) an obligation on the provider to obtain an authorisation from their competent authorities including entry in a register or registration with a professional body or association in their territory, except where provided for in this Directive or other instruments of Community law;

(c) a ban on the provider setting up a certain form or type of infrastructure in their territory, including an office or chambers, which the provider needs in order to supply the services in question;

(d) the application of specific contractual arrangements between the provider and the recipient which prevent or restrict service provision by the self-employed;

(e) an obligation on the provider to possess an identity document issued by its competent authorities specific to the exercise of a service activity;

(f) requirements, except for those necessary for health and safety at work, which affect the use of equipment and material which are an integral part of the service provided;

(g) restrictions on the freedom to provide the services referred to in Article 19.

3. The Member State to which the provider moves shall not be prevented from imposing requirements with regard to the provision of a service activity, where they are justified for reasons of public policy, public security, public health or the protection of the environment and in accordance with paragraph 1. Nor shall that Member State be prevented from applying, in accordance with Community law, its rules on employment conditions, including those laid down in collective agreements.

4. By 28 December 2011 the Commission shall, after consultation of the Member States and the social partners at Community level, submit to the European Parliament and the Council a report on the application of this Article, in which it shall consider the need to propose harmonisation measures regarding service activities covered by this Directive.

Article 17 Additional derogations from the freedom to provide services

Article 16 shall not apply to:

1) services of general economic interest which are provided in another Member State, inter alia:

(a) in the postal sector, services covered by Directive 97/67/EC of the European Parliament and of the Council of 15 December 1997 on common rules for the development of the internal market of Community postal services and the improvement of quality of service;[28]

(b) in the electricity sector, services covered by Directive 2003/54/EC[29] of the European Parliament and of the Council of 26 June 2003 concerning common rules for the internal market in electricity;

(c) in the gas sector, services covered by Directive 2003/55/EC of the European Parliament and of the Council of 26 June 2003 concerning common rules for the internal market in natural gas;[30]

(d) water distribution and supply services and waste water services;

(e) treatment of waste;

2) matters covered by Directive 96/71/EC;

3) matters covered by Directive 95/46/EC of the European Parliament and of the Council of 24 October 1995 on the protection of individuals with regard to the processing of personal data and on the free movement of such data;[31]

4) matters covered by Council Directive 77/249/EEC of 22 March 1977 to facilitate the effective exercise by lawyers of freedom to provide services;[32]

5) the activity of judicial recovery of debts;

[28] OJ L 15, 21.1.1998, p. 14. Directive as last amended by Regulation (EC) No 1882/2003 (OJ L 284, 31.10.2003, p. 1).

[29] OJ L 176, 15.7.2003, p. 37. Directive as last amended by Commission Decision 2006/653/EC (OJ L 270, 29.9.2006, p. 72).

[30] OJ L 176, 15.7.2003, p. 57.

[31] OJ L 281, 23.11.1995, p. 31. Directive as amended by Regulation (EC) No 1882/2003.

[32] OJ L 78, 26.3.1977, p. 17. Directive as last amended by the 2003 Act of Accession.

6) matters covered by Title II of Directive 2005/36/EC, as well as requirements in the Member State where the service is provided which reserve an activity to a particular profession;

7) matters covered by Regulation (EEC) No 1408/71;

8) as regards administrative formalities concerning the free movement of persons and their residence, matters covered by the provisions of Directive 2004/38/EC that lay down administrative formalities of the competent authorities of the Member State where the service is provided with which beneficiaries must comply;

9) as regards third country nationals who move to another Member State in the context of the provision of a service, the possibility for Member States to require visa or residence permits for third country nationals who are not covered by the mutual recognition regime provided for in Article 21 of the Convention implementing the Schengen Agreement of 14 June 1985 on the gradual abolition of checks at the common borders[33] or the possibility to oblige third country nationals to report to the competent authorities of the Member State in which the service is provided on or after their entry;

10) as regards the shipment of waste, matters covered by Council Regulation (EEC) No 259/93 of 1 February 1993 on the supervision and control of shipments of waste within, into and out of the European Community;[34]

11) copyright, neighbouring rights and rights covered by Council Directive 87/54/EEC of 16 December 1986 on the legal protection of topographies of semiconductor products[35] and by Directive 96/9/EC of the European Parliament and of the Council of 11 March 1996 on the legal protection of databases,[36] as well as industrial property rights;

12) acts requiring by law the involvement of a notary;

13) matters covered by Directive 2006/43/EC of the European Parliament and of the Council of 17 May 2006 on statutory audit of annual accounts and consolidated accounts;[37]

14) the registration of vehicles leased in another Member State;

15) provisions regarding contractual and non-contractual obligations, including the form of contracts, determined pursuant to the rules of private international law.

Article 18 Case-by-case derogations

1. By way of derogation from Article 16, and in exceptional circumstances only, a Member State may, in respect of a provider established in another Member State, take measures relating to the safety of services.

2. The measures provided for in paragraph 1 may be taken only if the mutual assistance procedure laid down in Article 35 is complied with and the following conditions are fulfilled:

(a) the national provisions in accordance with which the measure is taken have not been subject to Community harmonisation in the field of the safety of services;

(b) the measures provide for a higher level of protection of the recipient than would be the case in a measure taken by the Member State of establishment in accordance with its national provisions;

(c) the Member State of establishment has not taken any measures or has taken measures which are insufficient as compared with those referred to in Article 35(2);

(d) the measures are proportionate.

3. Paragraphs 1 and 2 shall be without prejudice to provisions, laid down in Community instruments, which guarantee the freedom to provide services or which allow derogations therefrom.

[33] OJ L 239, 22.9.2000, p. 19. Convention as last amended by Regulation (EC) No 1160/2005 of the European Parliament and of the Council (OJ L 191, 22.7.2005, p. 18).

[34] OJ L 30, 6.2.1993, p. 1. Regulation as last amended by Commission Regulation (EC) No 2557/2001 (OJ L 349, 31.12.2001, p. 1).

[35] OJ L 24, 27.1.1987, p. 36.

[36] OJ L 77, 27.3.1996, p. 20.

[37] OJ L 157, 9.6.2006, p. 87.

Section 2 Rights of recipients of services

Article 19 Prohibited restrictions

Member States may not impose on a recipient requirements which restrict the use of a service supplied by a provider established in another Member State, in particular the following requirements:

(a) an obligation to obtain authorisation from or to make a declaration to their competent authorities;

(b) discriminatory limits on the grant of financial assistance by reason of the fact that the provider is established in another Member State or by reason of the location of the place at which the service is provided.

Article 20 Non-discrimination

1. Member States shall ensure that the recipient is not made subject to discriminatory requirements based on his nationality or place of residence.

2. Member States shall ensure that the general conditions of access to a service, which are made available to the public at large by the provider, do not contain discriminatory provisions relating to the nationality or place of residence of the recipient, but without precluding the possibility of providing for differences in the conditions of access where those differences are directly justified by objective criteria.

Article 21 Assistance for recipients

1. Member States shall ensure that recipients can obtain, in their Member State of residence, the following information:

(a) general information on the requirements applicable in other Member States relating to access to, and exercise of, service activities, in particular those relating to consumer protection;

(b) general information on the means of redress available in the case of a dispute between a provider and a recipient;

(c) the contact details of associations or organisations, including the centres of the European Consumer Centres Network, from which providers or recipients may obtain practical assistance.

Where appropriate, advice from the competent authorities shall include a simple step-by-step guide. Information and assistance shall be provided in a clear and unambiguous manner, shall be easily accessible at a distance, including by electronic means, and shall be kept up to date.

2. Member States may confer responsibility for the task referred to in paragraph 1 on points of single contact or on any other body, such as the centres of the European Consumer Centres Network, consumer associations or Euro Info Centres.

Member States shall communicate to the Commission the names and contact details of the designated bodies. The Commission shall transmit them to all Member States.

3. In fulfilment of the requirements set out in paragraphs 1 and 2, the body approached by the recipient shall, if necessary, contact the relevant body for the Member State concerned. The latter shall send the information requested as soon as possible to the requesting body which shall forward the information to the recipient. Member States shall ensure that those bodies give each other mutual assistance and shall put in place all possible measures for effective cooperation. Together with the Commission, Member States shall put in place practical arrangements necessary for the implementation of paragraph 1.

4. The Commission shall, in accordance with the procedure referred to in Article 40(2), adopt measures for the implementation of paragraphs 1, 2 and 3 of this Article, specifying the technical mechanisms for the exchange of information between the bodies of the various Member States and, in particular, the interoperability of information systems, taking into account common standards.

Chapter V Quality of services

Article 22 Information on providers and their services

1. Member States shall ensure that providers make the following information available to the recipient:

(a) the name of the provider, his legal status and form, the geographic address at which he is established and details enabling him to be contacted rapidly and communicated with directly and, as the case may be, by electronic means;

(b) where the provider is registered in a trade or other similar public register, the name of that register and the provider's registration number, or equivalent means of identification in that register;

(c) where the activity is subject to an authorisation scheme, the particulars of the relevant competent authority or the single point of contact;

(d) where the provider exercises an activity which is subject to VAT, the identification number referred to in Article 22(1) of Sixth Council Directive 77/388/EEC of 17 May 1977 on the harmonisation of the laws of the Member States relating to turnover taxes – Common system of value added tax: uniform basis of assessment;[38]

(e) in the case of the regulated professions, any professional body or similar institution with which the provider is registered, the professional title and the Member State in which that title has been granted;

(f) the general conditions and clauses, if any, used by the provider;

(g) the existence of contractual clauses, if any, used by the provider concerning the law applicable to the contract and/or the competent courts;

(h) the existence of an after-sales guarantee, if any, not imposed by law;

(i) the price of the service, where a price is pre-determined by the provider for a given type of service;

(j) the main features of the service, if not already apparent from the context;

(k) the insurance or guarantees referred to in Article 23(1), and in particular the contact details of the insurer or guarantor and the territorial coverage.

2. Member States shall ensure that the information referred to in paragraph 1, according to the provider's preference:

(a) is supplied by the provider on his own initiative;

(b) is easily accessible to the recipient at the place where the service is provided or the contract concluded;

(c) can be easily accessed by the recipient electronically by means of an address supplied by the provider;

(d) appears in any information documents supplied to the recipient by the provider which set out a detailed description of the service he provides.

3. Member States shall ensure that, at the recipient's request, providers supply the following additional information:

(a) where the price is not pre-determined by the provider for a given type of service, the price of the service or, if an exact price cannot be given, the method for calculating the price so that it can be checked by the recipient, or a sufficiently detailed estimate;

(b) as regards the regulated professions, a reference to the professional rules applicable in the Member State of establishment and how to access them;

(c) information on their multidisciplinary activities and partnerships which are directly linked to the service in question and on the measures taken to avoid conflicts of interest. That information shall be included in any information document in which providers give a detailed description of their services;

[38] OJ L 145, 13.6.1977, p. 1. Directive as last amended by Directive 2006/18/EC (OJ L 51, 22.2.2006, p. 12).

(d) any codes of conduct to which the provider is subject and the address at which these codes may be consulted by electronic means, specifying the language version available;

(e) where a provider is subject to a code of conduct, or member of a trade association or professional body which provides for recourse to a non-judicial means of dispute settlement, information in this respect. The provider shall specify how to access detailed information on the characteristics of, and conditions for, the use of non-judicial means of dispute settlement.

4. Member States shall ensure that the information which a provider must supply in accordance with this Chapter is made available or communicated in a clear and unambiguous manner, and in good time before conclusion of the contract or, where there is no written contract, before the service is provided.

5. The information requirements laid down in this Chapter are in addition to requirements already provided for in Community law and do not prevent Member States from imposing additional information requirements applicable to providers established in their territory.

6. The Commission may, in accordance with the procedure referred to in Article 40(2), specify the content of the information provided for in paragraphs 1 and 3 of this Article according to the specific nature of certain activities and may specify the practical means of implementing paragraph 2 of this Article.

Article 23 Professional liability insurance and guarantees

1. Member States may ensure that providers whose services present a direct and particular risk to the health or safety of the recipient or a third person, or to the financial security of the recipient, subscribe to professional liability insurance appropriate to the nature and extent of the risk, or provide a guarantee or similar arrangement which is equivalent or essentially comparable as regards its purpose.

2. When a provider establishes himself in their territory, Member States may not require professional liability insurance or a guarantee from the provider where he is already covered by a guarantee which is equivalent, or essentially comparable with regard to its purpose and the cover it provides in terms of the insured risk, the insured sum or a ceiling for the guarantee and possible exclusions from the cover, in another Member State in which the provider is already established. Where equivalence is only partial, Member States may require a supplementary guarantee to cover those aspects not already covered.

When a Member State requires a provider established in its territory to subscribe to professional liability insurance or to provide another guarantee, that Member State shall accept as sufficient evidence attestations of such insurance cover issued by credit institutions and insurers established in other Member States.

3. Paragraphs 1 and 2 shall not affect professional insurance or guarantee arrangements provided for in other Community instruments.

4. For the implementation of paragraph 1, the Commission may, in accordance with the regulatory procedure referred to in Article 40(2), establish a list of services which exhibit the characteristics referred to in paragraph 1 of this Article. The Commission may also, in accordance with the procedure referred to in Article 40(3), adopt measures designed to amend non-essential elements of this Directive by supplementing it by establishing common criteria for defining, for the purposes of the insurance or guarantees referred to in paragraph 1 of this Article, what is appropriate to the nature and extent of the risk.

5. For the purpose of this Article

- 'direct and particular risk' means a risk arising directly from the provision of the service,
- 'health and safety' means, in relation to a recipient or a third person, the prevention of death or serious personal injury,

- 'financial security' means, in relation to a recipient, the prevention of substantial losses of money or of value of property,
- 'professional liability insurance' means insurance taken out by a provider in respect of potential liabilities to recipients and, where applicable, third parties arising out of the provision of the service.

Article 24 Commercial communications by the regulated professions

1. Member States shall remove all total prohibitions on commercial communications by the regulated professions.

2. Member States shall ensure that commercial communications by the regulated professions comply with professional rules, in conformity with Community law, which relate, in particular, to the independence, dignity and integrity of the profession, as well as to professional secrecy, in a manner consistent with the specific nature of each profession. Professional rules on commercial communications shall be non-discriminatory, justified by an overriding reason relating to the public interest and proportionate.

Article 25 Multidisciplinary activities

1. Member States shall ensure that providers are not made subject to requirements which oblige them to exercise a given specific activity exclusively or which restrict the exercise jointly or in partnership of different activities.

However, the following providers may be made subject to such requirements:

(a) the regulated professions, in so far as is justified in order to guarantee compliance with the rules governing professional ethics and conduct, which vary according to the specific nature of each profession, and is necessary in order to ensure their independence and impartiality;

(b) providers of certification, accreditation, technical monitoring, test or trial services, in so far as is justified in order to ensure their independence and impartiality.

2. Where multidisciplinary activities between providers referred to in points (a) and (b) of paragraph 1 are authorised, Member States shall ensure the following:

(a) that conflicts of interest and incompatibilities between certain activities are prevented;

(b) that the independence and impartiality required for certain activities is secured;

(c) that the rules governing professional ethics and conduct for different activities are compatible with one another, especially as regards matters of professional secrecy.

3. In the report referred to in Article 39(1), Member States shall indicate which providers are subject to the requirements laid down in paragraph 1 of this Article, the content of those requirements and the reasons for which they consider them to be justified.

Article 26 Policy on quality of services

1. Member States shall, in cooperation with the Commission, take accompanying measures to encourage providers to take action on a voluntary basis in order to ensure the quality of service provision, in particular through use of one of the following methods:

(a) certification or assessment of their activities by independent or accredited bodies;

(b) drawing up their own quality charter or participation in quality charters or labels drawn up by professional bodies at Community level.

2. Member States shall ensure that information on the significance of certain labels and the criteria for applying labels and other quality marks relating to services can be easily accessed by providers and recipients.

3. Member States shall, in cooperation with the Commission, take accompanying measures to encourage professional bodies, as well as chambers of commerce and craft associations and consumer associations, in their territory to cooperate at Community level in order to promote the quality of service provision, especially by making it easier to assess the competence of a provider.

4. Member States shall, in cooperation with the Commission, take accompanying measures to encourage the development of independent assessments, notably by consumer associations, in relation to the quality and defects of service provision, and, in particular, the development at Community level of comparative trials or testing and the communication of the results.

5. Member States, in cooperation with the Commission, shall encourage the development of voluntary European standards with the aim of facilitating compatibility between services supplied by providers in different Member States, information to the recipient and the quality of service provision.

Article 27 Settlement of disputes

1. Member States shall take the general measures necessary to ensure that providers supply contact details, in particular a postal address, fax number or e-mail address and telephone number to which all recipients, including those resident in another Member State, can send a complaint or a request for information about the service provided. Providers shall supply their legal address if this is not their usual address for correspondence.

Member States shall take the general measures necessary to ensure that providers respond to the complaints referred to in the first subparagraph in the shortest possible time and make their best efforts to find a satisfactory solution.

2. Member States shall take the general measures necessary to ensure that providers are obliged to demonstrate compliance with the obligations laid down in this Directive as to the provision of information and to demonstrate that the information is accurate.

3. Where a financial guarantee is required for compliance with a judicial decision, Member States shall recognise equivalent guarantees lodged with a credit institution or insurer established in another Member State. Such credit institutions must be authorised in a Member State in accordance with Directive 2006/48/EC and such insurers in accordance, as appropriate, with First Council Directive 73/239/EEC of 24 July 1973 on the coordination of laws, regulations and administrative provisions relating to the taking-up and pursuit of the business of direct insurance other than life assurance[39] and Directive 2002/83/EC of the European Parliament and of the Council of 5 November 2002 concerning life assurance.[40]

4. Member States shall take the general measures necessary to ensure that providers who are subject to a code of conduct, or are members of a trade association or professional body, which provides for recourse to a non-judicial means of dispute settlement inform the recipient thereof and mention that fact in any document which presents their services in detail, specifying how to access detailed information on the characteristics of, and conditions for, the use of such a mechanism.

Chapter VI Administrative cooperation

Article 28 Mutual assistance—general obligations

1. Member States shall give each other mutual assistance, and shall put in place measures for effective cooperation with one another, in order to ensure the supervision of providers and the services they provide.

2. For the purposes of this Chapter, Member States shall designate one or more liaison points, the contact details of which shall be communicated to the other Member States and the Commission. The Commission shall publish and regularly update the list of liaison points.

3. Information requests and requests to carry out any checks, inspections and investigations under this Chapter shall be duly motivated, in particular by specifying the reason for the request. Information exchanged shall be used only in respect of the matter for which it was requested.

[39] OJ L 228, 16.8.1973, p. 3. Directive as last amended by Directive 2005/68/EC of the European Parliament and of the Council (OJ L 323, 9.12.2005, p. 1).

[40] OJ L 345, 19.12.2002, p. 1. Directive as last amended by Directive 2005/68/EC

4. In the event of receiving a request for assistance from competent authorities in another Member State, Member States shall ensure that providers established in their territory supply their competent authorities with all the information necessary for supervising their activities in compliance with their national laws.

5. In the event of difficulty in meeting a request for information or in carrying out checks, inspections or investigations, the Member State in question shall rapidly inform the requesting Member State with a view to finding a solution.

6. Member States shall supply the information requested by other Member States or the Commission by electronic means and within the shortest possible period of time.

7. Member States shall ensure that registers in which providers have been entered, and which may be consulted by the competent authorities in their territory, may also be consulted, in accordance with the same conditions, by the equivalent competent authorities of the other Member States.

8. Member States shall communicate to the Commission information on cases where other Member States do not fulfil their obligation of mutual assistance. Where necessary, the Commission shall take appropriate steps, including proceedings provided for in Article 226 of the Treaty, in order to ensure that the Member States concerned comply with their obligation of mutual assistance. The Commission shall periodically inform Member States about the functioning of the mutual assistance provisions.

Article 29 Mutual assistance—general obligations for the Member State of establishment

1. With respect to providers providing services in another Member State, the Member State of establishment shall supply information on providers established in its territory when requested to do so by another Member State and, in particular, confirmation that a provider is established in its territory and, to its knowledge, is not exercising his activities in an unlawful manner.

2. The Member State of establishment shall undertake the checks, inspections and investigations requested by another Member State and shall inform the latter of the results and, as the case may be, of the measures taken. In so doing, the competent authorities shall act to the extent permitted by the powers vested in them in their Member State. The competent authorities can decide on the most appropriate measures to be taken in each individual case in order to meet the request by another Member State.

3. Upon gaining actual knowledge of any conduct or specific acts by a provider established in its territory which provides services in other Member States, that, to its knowledge, could cause serious damage to the health or safety of persons or to the environment, the Member State of establishment shall inform all other Member States and the Commission within the shortest possible period of time.

Article 30 Supervision by the Member State of establishment in the event of the temporary movement of a provider to another Member State

1. With respect to cases not covered by Article 31(1), the Member State of establishment shall ensure that compliance with its requirements is supervised in conformity with the powers of supervision provided for in its national law, in particular through supervisory measures at the place of establishment of the provider.

2. The Member State of establishment shall not refrain from taking supervisory or enforcement measures in its territory on the grounds that the service has been provided or caused damage in another Member State.

3. The obligation laid down in paragraph 1 shall not entail a duty on the part of the Member State of establishment to carry out factual checks and controls in the territory of the Member State where the service is provided. Such checks and controls shall be carried out by the authorities of the Member State where the provider is temporarily operating at the request of the authorities of the Member State of establishment, in accordance with Article 31.

Article 31 Supervision by the Member State where the service is provided in the event of the temporary movement of the provider

1. With respect to national requirements which may be imposed pursuant to Articles 16 or 17, the Member State where the service is provided is responsible for the supervision of the activity of the provider in its territory. In conformity with Community law, the Member State where the service is provided:

(a) shall take all measures necessary to ensure the provider complies with those requirements as regards the access to and the exercise of the activity;

(b) shall carry out the checks, inspections and investigations necessary to supervise the service provided.

2. With respect to requirements other than those referred to in paragraph 1, where a provider moves temporarily to another Member State in order to provide a service without being established there, the competent authorities of that Member State shall participate in the supervision of the provider in accordance with paragraphs 3 and 4.

3. At the request of the Member State of establishment, the competent authorities of the Member State where the service is provided shall carry out any checks, inspections and investigations necessary for ensuring the effective supervision by the Member State of establishment. In so doing, the competent authorities shall act to the extent permitted by the powers vested in them in their Member State. The competent authorities may decide on the most appropriate measures to be taken in each individual case in order to meet the request by the Member State of establishment.

4. On their own initiative, the competent authorities of the Member State where the service is provided may conduct checks, inspections and investigations on the spot, provided that those checks, inspections or investigations are not discriminatory, are not motivated by the fact that the provider is established in another Member State and are proportionate.

Article 32 Alert mechanism

1. Where a Member State becomes aware of serious specific acts or circumstances relating to a service activity that could cause serious damage to the health or safety of persons or to the environment in its territory or in the territory of other Member States, that Member State shall inform the Member State of establishment, the other Member States concerned and the Commission within the shortest possible period of time.

2. The Commission shall promote and take part in the operation of a European network of Member States' authorities in order to implement paragraph 1.

3. The Commission shall adopt and regularly update, in accordance with the procedure referred to in Article 40(2), detailed rules concerning the management of the network referred to in paragraph 2 of this Article.

Article 33 Information on the good repute of providers

1. Member States shall, at the request of a competent authority in another Member State, supply information, in conformity with their national law, on disciplinary or administrative actions or criminal sanctions and decisions concerning insolvency or bankruptcy involving fraud taken by their competent authorities in respect of the provider which are directly relevant to the provider's competence or professional reliability. The Member State which supplies the information shall inform the provider thereof.

A request made pursuant to the first subparagraph must be duly substantiated, in particular as regards the reasons for the request for information.

2. Sanctions and actions referred to in paragraph 1 shall only be communicated if a final decision has been taken. With regard to other enforceable decisions referred to in paragraph 1, the Member State which supplies the information shall specify whether a particular decision is final or whether an appeal has been lodged in respect of it, in which case the Member State in question should provide an indication of the date when the decision on appeal is expected.

Moreover, that Member State shall specify the provisions of national law pursuant to which the provider was found guilty or penalised.

3. Implementation of paragraphs 1and 2 must comply with rules on the provision of personal data and with rights guaranteed to persons found guilty or penalised in the Member States concerned, including by professional bodies. Any information in question which is public shall be accessible to consumers.

Article 34 Accompanying measures

1. The Commission, in cooperation with Member States, shall establish an electronic system for the exchange of information between Member States, taking into account existing information systems.

2. Member States shall, with the assistance of the Commission, take accompanying measures to facilitate the exchange of officials in charge of the implementation of mutual assistance and training of such officials, including language and computer training.

3. The Commission shall assess the need to establish a multi-annual programme in order to organise relevant exchanges of officials and training.

Article 35 Mutual assistance in the event of case-by-case derogations

1. Where a Member State intends to take a measure pursuant to Article 18, the procedure laid down in paragraphs 2 to 6 of this Article shall apply without prejudice to court proceedings, including preliminary proceedings and acts carried out in the framework of a criminal investigation.

2. The Member State referred to in paragraph 1 shall ask the Member State of establishment to take measures with regard to the provider, supplying all relevant information on the service in question and the circumstances of the case.

The Member State of establishment shall check, within the shortest possible period of time, whether the provider is operating lawfully and verify the facts underlying the request. It shall inform the requesting Member State within the shortest possible period of time of the measures taken or envisaged or, as the case may be, the reasons why it has not taken any measures.

3. Following communication by the Member State of establishment as provided for in the second subparagraph of paragraph 2, the requesting Member State shall notify the Commission and the Member State of establishment of its intention to take measures, stating the following:

(a) the reasons why it believes the measures taken or envisaged by the Member State of establishment are inadequate;

(b) the reasons why it believes the measures it intends to take fulfil the conditions laid down in Article 18.

4. The measures may not be taken until fifteen working days after the date of notification provided for in paragraph 3.

5. Without prejudice to the possibility for the requesting Member State to take the measures in question upon expiry of the period specified in paragraph 4, the Commission shall, within the shortest possible period of time, examine the compatibility with Community law of the measures notified.

Where the Commission concludes that the measure is incompatible with Community law, it shall adopt a decision asking the Member State concerned to refrain from taking the proposed measures or to put an end to the measures in question as a matter of urgency.

6. In the case of urgency, a Member State which intends to take a measure may derogate from paragraphs 2, 3 and 4. In such cases, the measures shall be notified within the shortest possible period of time to the Commission and the Member State of establishment, stating the reasons for which the Member State considers that there is urgency.

Article 36 Implementing measures

In accordance with the procedure referred to in Article 40(3), the Commission shall adopt the implementing measures designed to amend non-essential elements of this Chapter by supplementing it by specifying the time-limits provided for in Articles 28 and 35. The Commission shall also adopt, in accordance with the procedure referred to in Article 40(2), the practical arrangements for the exchange of information by electronic means between Member States, and in particular the interoperability provisions for information systems.

Chapter VII Convergence programme

Article 37 Codes of conduct at Community level

1. Member States shall, in cooperation with the Commission, take accompanying measures to encourage the drawing up at Community level, particularly by professional bodies, organisations and associations, of codes of conduct aimed at facilitating the provision of services or the establishment of a provider in another Member State, in conformity with Community law.

2. Member States shall ensure that the codes of conduct referred to in paragraph 1 are accessible at a distance, by electronic means.

Article 38 Additional harmonisation

The Commission shall assess, by 28 December 2010 the possibility of presenting proposals for harmonisation instruments on the following subjects:

(a) access to the activity of judicial recovery of debts;

(b) private security services and transport of cash and valuables.

Article 39 Mutual evaluation

1. By 28 December 2009 at the latest, Member States shall present a report to the Commission, containing the information specified in the following provisions:

(a) Article 9(2), on authorisation schemes;

(b) Article 15(5), on requirements to be evaluated;

(c) Article 25(3), on multidisciplinary activities.

2. The Commission shall forward the reports provided for in paragraph 1 to the Member States, which shall submit their observations on each of the reports within six months of receipt. Within the same period, the Commission shall consult interested parties on those reports.

3. The Commission shall present the reports and the Member States' observations to the Committee referred to in Article 40(1), which may make observations.

4. In the light of the observations provided for in paragraphs 2 and 3, the Commission shall, by 28 December 2010 at the latest, present a summary report to the European Parliament and to the Council, accompanied where appropriate by proposals for additional initiatives.

5. By 28 December 2009 at the latest, Member States shall present a report to the Commission on the national requirements whose application could fall under the third subparagraph of Article 16(1) and the first sentence of Article 16(3), providing reasons why they consider that the application of those requirements fulfil the criteria referred to in the third subparagraph of Article 16(1) and the first sentence of Article 16(3).

Thereafter, Member States shall transmit to the Commission any changes in their requirements, including new requirements, as referred to above, together with the reasons for them.

The Commission shall communicate the transmitted requirements to other Member States. Such transmission shall not prevent the adoption by Member States of the provisions in question. The Commission shall on an annual basis thereafter provide analyses and orientations on the application of these provisions in the context of this Directive.

Article 40 Committee procedure

1. The Commission shall be assisted by a Committee.

2. Where reference is made to this paragraph, Articles 5 and 7 of Decision 1999/468/EC shall apply, having regard to the provisions of Article 8 thereof. The period laid down in Article 5(6) of Decision 1999/468/EC shall be set at three months.

3. Where reference is made to this paragraph, Article 5a(1) to (4), and Article 7 of Decision 1999/468/EC shall apply, having regard to the provisions of Article 8 thereof.

Article 41 Review clause

The Commission, by 28 December 2011 and every three years thereafter, shall present to the European Parliament and to the Council a comprehensive report on the application of this Directive. This report shall, in accordance with Article 16(4), address in particular the application of Article 16. It shall also consider the need for additional measures for matters excluded from the scope of application of this Directive. It shall be accompanied, where appropriate, by proposals for amendment of this Directive with a view to completing the Internal Market for services.

Article 42 Amendment of Directive 98/27/EC

In the Annex to Directive 98/27/EC of the European Parliament and of the Council of 19 May 1998 on injunctions for the protection of consumers' interests,[41] the following point shall be added:

[41] OJ L 166, 11.6.1998, p. 51. Directive as last amended by Directive 2005/29/EC.

'13. Directive 2006/123/EC of the European Parliament and of the Council of 12 December 2006 on services in the internal market (OJ L 376, 27.12.2006, p. 36)'.

Article 43 Protection of personal data

The implementation and application of this Directive and, in particular, the provisions on supervision shall respect the rules on the protection of personal data as provided for in Directives 95/46/EC and 2002/58/EC.

Chapter VIII Final provisions

Article 44 Transposition

1. Member States shall bring into force the laws, regulations and administrative provisions necessary to comply with this Directive before 28 December 2009.

They shall forthwith communicate to the Commission the text of those measures.

When Member States adopt these measures, they shall contain a reference to this Directive or shall be accompanied by such a reference on the occasion of their official publication. The methods of making such reference shall be laid down by Member States.

2. Member States shall communicate to the Commission the text of the main provisions of national law which they adopt in the field covered by this Directive.

Article 45 Entry into force

This Directive shall enter into force on the day following that of its publication in the *Official Journal of the European Union*.

Article 46 Addressees

This Directive is addressed to the Member States.

Done at Strasbourg, 12 December 2006.
For the European Parliament,
The President,
J. BORRELL FONTELLES
For the Council,
The President,
M. PEKKARINEN

Regulation (EU) No 492/2011 of the European Parliament and of the Council of 5 April 2011 on freedom of movement for workers within the Union

[OJ 2011 L141/1]

THE EUROPEAN PARLIAMENT AND THE COUNCIL OF THE EUROPEAN UNION,

Having regard to the Treaty on the Functioning of the European Union, and in particular Article 46 thereof,

Having regard to the proposal from the European Commission,

After transmission of the draft legislative act to the national parliaments,

Having regard to the opinion of the European Economic and Social Committee[1],

Acting in accordance with the ordinary legislative procedure[2],

[1] OJ C 44, 11.2.2011, p. 170.

[2] Position of the European Parliament of 7 September 2010 (not yet published in the Official Journal) and decision of the Council of 21 March 2011.

Whereas:

(1) Regulation (EEC) No 1612/68 of the Council of 15 October 1968 on freedom of movement for workers within the Community[3] has been substantially amended several times[4]. In the interests of clarity and rationality the said Regulation should be codified.

(2) Freedom of movement for workers should be secured within the Union. The attainment of this objective entails the abolition of any discrimination based on nationality between workers of the Member States as regards employment, remuneration and other conditions of work and employment, as well as the right of such workers to move freely within the Union in order to pursue activities as employed persons subject to any limitations justified on grounds of public policy, public security or public health.

(3) Provisions should be laid down to enable the objectives laid down in Articles 45 and 46 of the Treaty on the Functioning of the European Union in the field of freedom of movement to be achieved.

(4) Freedom of movement constitutes a fundamental right of workers and their families. Mobility of labour within the Union must be one of the means by which workers are guaranteed the possibility of improving their living and working conditions and promoting their social advancement, while helping to satisfy the requirements of the economies of the Member States. The right of all workers in the Member States to pursue the activity of their choice within the Union should be affirmed.

(5) Such right should be enjoyed without discrimination by permanent, seasonal and frontier workers and by those who pursue their activities for the purpose of providing services.

(6) The right of freedom of movement, in order that it may be exercised, by objective standards, in freedom and dignity, requires that equality of treatment be ensured in fact and in law in respect of all matters relating to the actual pursuit of activities as employed persons and to eligibility for housing, and also that obstacles to the mobility of workers be eliminated, in particular as regards the conditions for the integration of the worker's family into the host country.

(7) The principle of non-discrimination between workers in the Union means that all nationals of Member States have the same priority as regards employment as is enjoyed by national workers.

(8) The machinery for vacancy clearance, in particular by means of direct cooperation between the central employment services and also between the regional services, as well as by coordination of the exchange of information, ensures in a general way a clearer picture of the labour market. Workers wishing to move should also be regularly informed of living and working conditions.

(9) Close links exist between freedom of movement for workers, employment and vocational training, particularly where the latter aims at putting workers in a position to take up concrete offers of employment from other regions of the Union. Such links make it necessary that the problems arising in this connection should no longer be studied in isolation but viewed as interdependent, account also being taken of the problems of employment at the regional level. It is therefore necessary to direct the efforts of Member States toward coordinating their employment policies,

HAVE ADOPTED THIS REGULATION:

Chapter I Employment, equal treatment and workers' families

Section 1 Eligibility for employment

Article 1

1. Any national of a Member State shall, irrespective of his place of residence, have the right to take up an activity as an employed person, and to pursue such activity, within the territory of another Member State in accordance with the provisions laid down by law, regulation or administrative action governing the employment of nationals of that State.

[3] OJ L 257, 19.10.1968, p. 2.
[4] See Annex I.

2. He shall, in particular, have the right to take up available employment in the territory of another Member State with the same priority as nationals of that State.

Article 2

Any national of a Member State and any employer pursuing an activity in the territory of a Member State may exchange their applications for and offers of employment, and may conclude and perform contracts of employment in accordance with the provisions in force laid down by law, regulation or administrative action, without any discrimination resulting therefrom.

Article 3

1. Under this Regulation, provisions laid down by law, regulation or administrative action or administrative practices of a Member State shall not apply:

(a) where they limit application for and offers of employment, or the right of foreign nationals to take up and pursue employment or subject these to conditions not applicable in respect of their own nationals; or

(b) where, though applicable irrespective of nationality, their exclusive or principal aim or effect is to keep nationals of other Member States away from the employment offered.

The first subparagraph shall not apply to conditions relating to linguistic knowledge required by reason of the nature of the post to be filled.

2. There shall be included in particular among the provisions or practices of a Member State referred to in the first subparagraph of paragraph 1 those which:

(a) prescribe a special recruitment procedure for foreign nationals;

(b) limit or restrict the advertising of vacancies in the press or through any other medium or subject it to conditions other than those applicable in respect of employers pursuing their activities in the territory of that Member State;

(c) subject eligibility for employment to conditions of registration with employment offices or impede recruitment of individual workers, where persons who do not reside in the territory of that State are concerned.

Article 4

1. Provisions laid down by law, regulation or administrative action of the Member States which restrict by number or percentage the employment of foreign nationals in any undertaking, branch of activity or region, or at a national level, shall not apply to nationals of the other Member States.

2. When in a Member State the granting of any benefit to undertakings is subject to a minimum percentage of national workers being employed, nationals of the other Member States shall be counted as national workers, subject to Directive 2005/36/EC of the European Parliament and of the Council of 7 September 2005 on the recognition of professional qualifications[5].

Article 5

A national of a Member State who seeks employment in the territory of another Member State shall receive the same assistance there as that afforded by the employment offices in that State to their own nationals seeking employment.

Article 6

1. The engagement and recruitment of a national of one Member State for a post in another Member State shall not depend on medical, vocational or other criteria which are discriminatory on grounds of nationality by comparison with those applied to nationals of the other Member State who wish to pursue the same activity.

2. A national who holds an offer in his name from an employer in a Member State other than that of which he is a national may have to undergo a vocational test, if the employer expressly requests this when making his offer of employment.

[5] OJ L 255, 30.9.2005, p. 22.

Section 2 Employment and equality of treatment

Article 7

1. A worker who is a national of a Member State may not, in the territory of another Member State, be treated differently from national workers by reason of his nationality in respect of any conditions of employment and work, in particular as regards remuneration, dismissal, and, should he become unemployed, reinstatement or re-employment.

2. He shall enjoy the same social and tax advantages as national workers.

3. He shall also, by virtue of the same right and under the same conditions as national workers, have access to training in vocational schools and retraining centres.

4. Any clause of a collective or individual agreement or of any other collective regulation concerning eligibility for employment, remuneration and other conditions of work or dismissal shall be null and void in so far as it lays down or authorises discriminatory conditions in respect of workers who are nationals of the other Member States.

Article 8

A worker who is a national of a Member State and who is employed in the territory of another Member State shall enjoy equality of treatment as regards membership of trade unions and the exercise of rights attaching thereto, including the right to vote and to be eligible for the administration or management posts of a trade union. He may be excluded from taking part in the management of bodies governed by public law and from holding an office governed by public law. Furthermore, he shall have the right of eligibility for workers' representative bodies in the undertaking.

The first paragraph of this Article shall not affect laws or regulations in certain Member States which grant more extensive rights to workers coming from the other Member States.

Article 9

1. A worker who is a national of a Member State and who is employed in the territory of another Member State shall enjoy all the rights and benefits accorded to national workers in matters of housing, including ownership of the housing he needs.

2. A worker referred to in paragraph 1 may, with the same right as nationals, put his name down on the housing lists in the region in which he is employed, where such lists exist, and shall enjoy the resultant benefits and priorities.

If his family has remained in the country whence he came, they shall be considered for this purpose as residing in the said region, where national workers benefit from a similar presumption.

Section 3 Workers' families

Article 10

The children of a national of a Member State who is or has been employed in the territory of another Member State shall be admitted to that State's general educational, apprenticeship and vocational training courses under the same conditions as the nationals of that State, if such children are residing in its territory.

Member States shall encourage all efforts to enable such children to attend these courses under the best possible conditions.

Chapter II Clearance of vacancies and applications for employment

Section 1 Cooperation between the Member States and with the Commission

Article 11

1. The Member States or the Commission shall instigate or together undertake any study of employment or unemployment which they consider necessary for freedom of movement for workers within the Union.

The central employment services of the Member States shall cooperate closely with each other and with the Commission with a view to acting jointly as regards the clearing of vacancies and applications for employment within the Union and the resultant placing of workers in employment.

2. To this end the Member States shall designate specialist services which shall be entrusted with organising work in the fields referred to in the second subparagraph of paragraph 1 and cooperating with each other and with the departments of the Commission.

The Member States shall notify the Commission of any change in the designation of such services and the Commission shall publish details thereof for information in the Official Journal of the European Union.

Article 12

1. The Member States shall send to the Commission information on problems arising in connection with the freedom of movement and employment of workers and particulars of the state and development of employment.

2. The Commission, taking the utmost account of the opinion of the Technical Committee referred to in Article 29 ("the Technical Committee"), shall determine the manner in which the information referred to in paragraph 1 of this Article is to be drawn up.

3. In accordance with the procedure laid down by the Commission taking the utmost account of the opinion of the Technical Committee, the specialist service of each Member State shall send to the specialist services of the other Member States and to the European Coordination Office referred to in Article 18 such information concerning living and working conditions and the state of the labour market as is likely to be of guidance to workers from the other Member States. Such information shall be brought up to date regularly.

The specialist services of the other Member States shall ensure that wide publicity is given to such information, in particular by circulating it among the appropriate employment services and by all suitable means of communication for informing the workers concerned.

Section 2 Machinery for vacancy clearance

Article 13

1. The specialist service of each Member State shall regularly send to the specialist services of the other Member States and to the European Coordination Office referred to in Article 18:

(a) details of vacancies which could be filled by nationals of other Member States;

(b) details of vacancies addressed to third countries;

(c) details of applications for employment by those who have formally expressed a wish to work in another Member State;

(d) information, by region and by branch of activity, on applicants who have declared themselves actually willing to accept employment in another country.

The specialist service of each Member State shall forward this information to the appropriate employment services and agencies as soon as possible.

2. The details of vacancies and applications referred to in paragraph 1 shall be circulated according to a uniform system to be established by the European Coordination Office referred to in Article 18 in collaboration with the Technical Committee.

This system may be adapted if necessary.

Article 14

1. Any vacancy within the meaning of Article 13 communicated to the employment services of a Member State shall be notified to and processed by the competent employment services of the other Member States concerned.

Such services shall forward to the services of the first Member State the details of suitable applications.

2. The applications for employment referred to in point (c) of the first subparagraph of Article 13(1) shall be responded to by the relevant services of the Member States within a reasonable period, not exceeding 1 month.

3. The employment services shall grant workers who are nationals of the Member States the same priority as the relevant measures grant to nationals vis-à-vis workers from third countries.

Article 15

1. The provisions of Article 14 shall be implemented by the specialist services. However, in so far as they have been authorised by the central services and in so far as the organisation of the employment services of a Member State and the placing techniques employed make it possible:

(a) the regional employment services of the Member States shall:

(i) on the basis of the information referred to in Article 13, on which appropriate action will be taken, directly bring together and clear vacancies and applications for employment;

(ii) establish direct relations for clearance:

– of vacancies offered to a named worker,
– of individual applications for employment sent either to a specific employment service or to an employer pursuing his activity within the area covered by such a service,
– where the clearing operations concern seasonal workers who must be recruited as quickly as possible;

(b) the services territorially responsible for the border regions of two or more Member States shall regularly exchange data relating to vacancies and applications for employment in their area and, acting in accordance with their arrangements with the other employment services of their countries, shall directly bring together and clear vacancies and applications for employment.

If necessary, the services territorially responsible for border regions shall also set up cooperation and service structures to provide:

– users with as much practical information as possible on the various aspects of mobility, and
– management and labour, social services (in particular public, private or those of public interest) and all institutions concerned, with a framework of coordinated measures relating to mobility,

(c) official employment services which specialise in certain occupations or specific categories of persons shall cooperate directly with each other.

2. The Member States concerned shall forward to the Commission the list, drawn up by common accord, of services referred to in paragraph 1 and the Commission shall publish such list for information, and any amendment thereto, in the Official Journal of the European Union.

Article 16

Adoption of recruiting procedures as applied by the implementing bodies provided for under agreements concluded between two or more Member States shall not be obligatory.

Section 3 Measures for controlling the balance of the labour market

Article 17

1. On the basis of a report from the Commission drawn up from information supplied by the Member States, the latter and the Commission shall at least once a year analyse jointly the results of Union arrangements regarding vacancies and applications.

2. The Member States shall examine with the Commission all the possibilities of giving priority to nationals of Member States when filling employment vacancies in order to achieve a balance between vacancies and applications for employment within the Union. They shall adopt all measures necessary for this purpose.

3. Every 2 years the Commission shall submit a report to the European Parliament, the Council and the European Economic and Social Committee on the implementation of Chapter II, summarising the information required and the data obtained from the studies and research carried out and highlighting any useful points with regard to developments on the Union's labour market.

Section 4 European Coordination Office

Article 18

The European Office for Coordinating the Clearance of Vacancies and Applications for Employment ("the European Coordination Office"), established within the Commission, shall have the general task of promoting vacancy clearance at Union level. It shall be responsible in particular for all the technical duties in this field which, under the provisions of this Regulation, are assigned to the Commission, and especially for assisting the national employment services.

It shall summarise the information referred to in Articles 12 and 13 and the data arising out of the studies and research carried out pursuant to Article 11, so as to bring to light any useful facts about foreseeable developments on the Union labour market; such facts shall be communicated to the specialist services of the Member States and to the Advisory Committee referred to in Article 21 and the Technical Committee.

Article 19

1. The European Coordination Office shall be responsible, in particular, for:
   (a) coordinating the practical measures necessary for vacancy clearance at Union level and for analysing the resulting movements of workers;
   (b) contributing to such objectives by implementing, in cooperation with the Technical Committee, joint methods of action at administrative and technical levels;
   (c) carrying out, where a special need arises, and in agreement with the specialist services, the bringing together of vacancies and applications for employment for clearance by those specialist services.

2. It shall communicate to the specialist services vacancies and applications for employment sent directly to the Commission, and shall be informed of the action taken thereon.

Article 20

The Commission may, in agreement with the competent authority of each Member State, and in accordance with the conditions and procedures which it shall determine on the basis of the opinion of the Technical Committee, organise visits and assignments for officials of other Member States, and also advanced programmes for specialist personnel.

Chapter III Committees for ensuring close cooperation between the Member States in matters concerning the freedom of movement of workers and their employment

Section 1 The Advisory Committee

Article 21

The Advisory Committee shall be responsible for assisting the Commission in the examination of any questions arising from the application of the Treaty on the Functioning of the European Union and measures taken in pursuance thereof, in matters concerning the freedom of movement of workers and their employment.

Article 22

The Advisory Committee shall be responsible in particular for:

(a) examining problems concerning freedom of movement and employment within the framework of national manpower policies, with a view to coordinating the employment policies of the Member States at Union level, thus contributing to the development of the economies and to an improved balance of the labour market;

(b) making a general study of the effects of implementing this Regulation and any supplementary measures;

(c) submitting to the Commission any reasoned proposals for revising this Regulation;

(d) delivering, either at the request of the Commission or on its own initiative, reasoned opinions on general questions or on questions of principle, in particular on exchange of information concerning developments in the labour market, on the movement of workers between Member States, on programmes or measures to develop vocational guidance and vocational training which are likely to increase the possibilities of freedom of movement and employment, and on all forms of assistance to workers and their families, including social assistance and the housing of workers.

Article 23

1. The Advisory Committee shall be composed of six members for each Member State, two of whom shall represent the Government, two the trade unions and two the employers' associations.

2. For each of the categories referred to in paragraph 1, one alternate member shall be appointed by each Member State.

3. The term of office of the members and their alternates shall be 2 years. Their appointments shall be renewable.

On expiry of their term of office, the members and their alternates shall remain in office until replaced or until their appointments are renewed.

Article 24

The members of the Advisory Committee and their alternates shall be appointed by the Council, which shall endeavour, when selecting representatives of trade unions and employers' associations, to achieve adequate representation on the Committee of the various economic sectors concerned.

The list of members and their alternates shall be published by the Council for information in the Official Journal of the European Union.

Article 25

The Advisory Committee shall be chaired by a member of the Commission or his representative. The Chairman shall not vote. The Committee shall meet at least twice a year. It shall be convened by its Chairman, either on his own initiative, or at the request of at least one third of the members.

Secretarial services shall be provided for the Committee by the Commission.

Article 26

The Chairman may invite individuals or representatives of bodies with wide experience in the field of employment or movement of workers to take part in meetings as observers or as experts. The Chairman may be assisted by expert advisers.

Article 27

1. An opinion delivered by the Advisory Committee shall not be valid unless two thirds of the members are present.

2. Opinions shall state the reasons on which they are based; they shall be delivered by an absolute majority of the votes validly cast; they shall be accompanied by a written statement of the views expressed by the minority, when the latter so requests.

Article 28

The Advisory Committee shall establish its working methods by rules of procedure which shall enter into force after the Council, having received an opinion from the Commission, has given its approval. The entry into force of any amendment that the Committee decides to make thereto shall be subject to the same procedure.

Section 2 The Technical Committee

Article 29

The Technical Committee shall be responsible for assisting the Commission in the preparation, promotion and follow-up of all technical work and measures for giving effect to this Regulation and any supplementary measures.

Article 30

The Technical Committee shall be responsible in particular for:

(a) promoting and advancing cooperation between the public authorities concerned in the Member States on all technical questions relating to freedom of movement of workers and their employment;

(b) formulating procedures for the organisation of the joint activities of the public authorities concerned;

(c) facilitating the gathering of information likely to be of use to the Commission and the undertaking of the studies and research provided for in this Regulation, and encouraging exchange of information and experience between the administrative bodies concerned;

(d) investigating at a technical level the harmonisation of the criteria by which Member States assess the state of their labour markets.

Article 31

1. The Technical Committee shall be composed of representatives of the Governments of the Member States. Each Government shall appoint as member of the Technical Committee one of the members who represent it on the Advisory Committee.

2. Each Government shall appoint an alternate from among its other representatives—members or alternates—on the Advisory Committee.

Article 32

The Technical Committee shall be chaired by a member of the Commission or his representative. The Chairman shall not vote. The Chairman and the members of the Committee may be assisted by expert advisers.

Secretarial services shall be provided for the Committee by the Commission.

Article 33

The proposals and opinions formulated by the Technical Committee shall be submitted to the Commission, and the Advisory Committee shall be informed thereof. Any such proposals and opinions shall be accompanied by a written statement of the views expressed by the various members of the Technical Committee, when the latter so request.

Article 34

The Technical Committee shall establish its working methods by rules of procedure which shall enter into force after the Council, having received an opinion from the Commission, has given its approval. The entry into force of any amendment which the Committee decides to make thereto shall be subject to the same procedure.

Chapter IV Final provisions

Article 35

The rules of procedure of the Advisory Committee and of the Technical Committee in force on 8 November 1968 shall continue to apply.

Article 36

1. This Regulation shall not affect the provisions of the Treaty establishing the European Atomic Energy Community which deal with eligibility for skilled employment in the field of nuclear energy, nor any measures taken in pursuance of that Treaty.

Nevertheless, this Regulation shall apply to the category of workers referred to in the first subparagraph and to members of their families in so far as their legal position is not governed by the above-mentioned Treaty or measures.

2. This Regulation shall not affect measures taken in accordance with Article 48 of the Treaty on the Functioning of the European Union.

3. This Regulation shall not affect the obligations of Member States arising out of special relations or future agreements with certain non-European countries or territories, based on institutional ties existing on 8 November 1968, or agreements in existence on 8 November 1968 with certain non-European countries or territories, based on institutional ties between them.

Workers from such countries or territories who, in accordance with this provision, are pursuing activities as employed persons in the territory of one of those Member States may not invoke the benefit of the provisions of this Regulation in the territory of the other Member States.

Article 37

Member States shall, for information purposes, communicate to the Commission the texts of agreements, conventions or arrangements concluded between them in the manpower field between the date of their being signed and that of their entry into force.

Article 38

The Commission shall adopt measures pursuant to this Regulation for its implementation. To this end it shall act in close cooperation with the central public authorities of the Member States.

Article 39

The administrative expenditure of the Advisory Committee and of the Technical Committee shall be included in the general budget of the European Union in the section relating to the Commission.

Article 40

This Regulation shall apply to the Member States and to their nationals, without prejudice to Articles 2 and 3.

Article 41

Regulation (EEC) No 1612/68 is hereby repealed.

References to the repealed Regulation shall be construed as references to this Regulation and shall be read in accordance with the correlation table in Annex II.

Article 42

This Regulation shall enter into force on the 20th day following its publication in the Official Journal of the European Union.

This Regulation shall be binding in its entirety and directly applicable in all Member States.

Done at Strasbourg, 5 April 2011.
For the European Parliament
The President
J. BUZEK
For the Council
The President
GYÖRI E.

Social security

Council Regulation (EEC) No 1408/71 of 14 June 1971

This is now to be found on the Online Resource Centre: **www.oxfordtextbooks.co.uk/orc/statutes/.**

Council Directive of 19 December 1978 on the progressive implementation of the principle of equal treatment for men and women in matters of social security (79/7/EEC)

[OJ 1979 L6/24]

(Preamble omitted.)

Article 1

The purpose of this Directive is the progressive implementation, in the field of social security and other elements of social protection provided for in Article 3, of the principle of equal treatment for men and women in matters of social security, hereinafter referred to as 'the principle of equal treatment'.

Article 2

This Directive shall apply to the working population—including self-employed persons, workers and self-employed persons whose activity is interrupted by illness, accident or involuntary unemployment and persons seeking employment—and to retired or invalided workers and self-employed persons.

Article 3

1. This Directive shall apply to:
   (a) statutory schemes which provide protection against the following risks:
   - sickness,
   - invalidity,
   - old age,
   - accidents at work and occupational diseases,
   - unemployment;

   (b) social assistance, in so far as it is intended to supplement or replace the schemes referred to in (a).

2. This Directive shall not apply to the provisions concerning survivors' benefits nor to those concerning family benefits, except in the case of family benefits granted by way of increases of benefits due in respect of the risks referred to in paragraph 1(a).

3. With a view to ensuring implementation of the principle of equal treatment in occupational schemes, the Council, acting on a proposal from the Commission, will adopt provisions defining its substance, its scope and the arrangements for its application.

Article 4

1. The principle of equal treatment means that there shall be no discrimination whatsoever on ground of sex either directly, or indirectly by reference in particular to marital or family status, in particular as concerns:
   - the scope of the schemes and the conditions of access thereto,
   - the obligation to contribute and the calculation of contributions,
   - the calculation of benefits including increases due in respect of a spouse and for dependants and the conditions governing the duration and retention of entitlement to benefits.

2. The principle of equal treatment shall be without prejudice to the provisions relating to the protection of women on the grounds of maternity.

Article 5

Member States shall take the measures necessary to ensure that any laws, regulations and administrative provisions contrary to the principle of equal treatment are abolished.

Article 6

Member States shall introduce into their national legal systems such measures as are necessary to enable all persons who consider themselves wronged by failure to apply the principle of equal treatment to pursue their claims by judicial process, possibly after recourse to other competent authorities.

Article 7

1. This Directive shall be without prejudice to the right of Member States to exclude from its scope:
   (a) the determination of pensionable age for the purposes of granting old-age and retirement pensions and the possible consequences thereof for other benefits;
   (b) advantages in respect of old-age pension schemes granted to persons who have brought up children; the acquisition of benefit entitlements following periods of interruption of employment due to the bringing up of children;
   (c) the granting of old-age or invalidity benefit entitlements by virtue of the derived entitlements of a wife;
   (d) the granting of increases of long-term invalidity, old-age, accidents at work and occupational disease benefits for a dependent wife;
   (e) the consequences of the exercise, before the adoption of this Directive, of a right of option not to acquire rights or incur obligations under a statutory scheme.

2. Member States shall periodically examine matters excluded under paragraph 1 in order to ascertain, in the light of social developments in the matter concerned, whether there is justification for maintaining the exclusions concerned.

Article 8

1. Member States shall bring into force the laws, regulations and administrative provisions necessary to comply with this Directive within six years of its notification. They shall immediately inform the Commission thereof.

2. Member States shall communicate to the Commission the text of laws, regulations and administrative provisions which they adopt in the field covered by this Directive, including measures adopted pursuant to Article 7(2).

They shall inform the Commission of their reasons for maintaining any existing provisions on the matters referred to in Article 7(1) and of the possibilities for reviewing them at a later date.

Article 9

Within seven years of notification of this Directive, Member States shall forward all information necessary to the Commission to enable it to draw up a report on the application of this Directive for submission to the Council and to propose such further measures as may be required for the implementation of the principle of equal treatment.

Article 10

This Directive is addressed to the Member States.

Done at Brussels, 19 December 1978.

Council Directive 86/613 was repealed with effect from 5 August 2012 and replaced by Directive 2011/41 reproduced at the end of this section

Council Directive 2000/43/EC of 29 June 2000 implementing the principle of equal treatment between persons irrespective of racial or ethnic origin

[OJ 2000 L180/22]

THE COUNCIL OF THE EUROPEAN UNION,

Having regard to the Treaty establishing the European Community and in particular Article 13 thereof,

Having regard to the proposal from the Commission,[1]

Having regard to the opinion of the European Parliament,[2]

Having regard to the opinion of the Economic and Social Committee,[3]

Having regard to the opinion of the Committee of the Regions,[4]

Whereas:

(1) The Treaty on European Union marks a new stage in the process of creating an ever closer union among the peoples of Europe.

(2) In accordance with Article 6 of the Treaty on European Union, the European Union is founded on the principles of liberty, democracy, respect for human rights and fundamental freedoms, and the rule of law, principles which are common to the Member States, and should respect fundamental rights as guaranteed by the European Convention for the protection of Human Rights and Fundamental Freedoms and as they result from the constitutional traditions common to the Member States, as general principles of Community Law.

(3) The right to equality before the law and protection against discrimination for all persons constitutes a universal right recognised by the Universal Declaration of Human Rights, the United Nations Convention on the Elimination of all forms of Discrimination Against Women, the International Convention on the Elimination of all forms of Racial Discrimination and the United Nations Covenants on Civil and Political Rights and on Economic, Social and Cultural Rights and by the European Convention for the Protection of Human Rights and Fundamental Freedoms, to which all Member States are signatories.

(4) It is important to respect such fundamental rights and freedoms, including the right to freedom of association. It is also important, in the context of the access to and provision of goods and services, to respect the protection of private and family life and transactions carried out in this context.

(5) The European Parliament has adopted a number of Resolutions on the fight against racism in the European Union.

(6) The European Union rejects theories which attempt to determine the existence of separate human races. The use of the term 'racial origin' in this Directive does not imply an acceptance of such theories.

(7) The European Council in Tampere, on 15 and 16 October 1999, invited the Commission to come forward as soon as possible with proposals implementing Article 13 of the EC Treaty as regards the fight against racism and xenophobia.

(8) The Employment Guidelines 2000 agreed by the European Council in Helsinki, on 10 and 11 December 1999, stress the need to foster conditions for a socially inclusive labour market by formulating a coherent set of policies aimed at combating discrimination against groups such as ethnic minorities.

(9) Discrimination based on racial or ethnic origin may undermine the achievement of the objectives of the EC Treaty, in particular the attainment of a high level of employment and of social protection, the raising of the standard of living and quality of life, economic and social cohesion and solidarity. It may also undermine the objective of developing the European Union as an area of freedom, security and justice.

(10) The Commission presented a communication on racism, xenophobia and anti-Semitism in December 1995.

(11) The Council adopted on 15 July 1996 Joint Action (96/443/JHA) concerning action to combat racism and xenophobia[5] under which the Member States undertake to ensure effective judicial cooperation in respect of offences based on racist or xenophobic behaviour.

[1] Not yet published in the Official Journal.
[2] Opinion delivered on 18.5.2000 (not yet published in the Official Journal).
[3] Opinion delivered on 12.4.2000 (not yet published in the Official Journal).
[4] Opinion delivered on 31.5.2000 (not yet published in the Official Journal).
[5] OJ L 185, 24.7.1996, p. 5.

(12) To ensure the development of democratic and tolerant societies which allow the participation of all persons irrespective of racial or ethnic origin, specific action in the field of discrimination based on racial or ethnic origin should go beyond access to employed and self-employed activities and cover areas such as education, social protection including social security and health-care, social advantages and access to and supply of goods and services.

(13) To this end, any direct or indirect discrimination based on racial or ethnic origin as regards the areas covered by this Directive should be prohibited throughout the Community. This prohibition of discrimination should also apply to nationals of third countries, but does not cover differences of treatment based on nationality and is without prejudice to provisions governing the entry and residence of third-country nationals and their access to employment and to occupation.

(14) In implementing the principle of equal treatment irrespective of racial or ethnic origin, the Community should, in accordance with Article 3(2) of the EC Treaty, aim to eliminate inequalities, and to promote equality between men and women, especially since women are often the victims of multiple discrimination.

(15) The appreciation of the facts from which it may be inferred that there has been direct or indirect discrimination is a matter for national judicial or other competent bodies, in accordance with rules of national law or practice. Such rules may provide in particular for indirect discrimination to be established by any means including on the basis of statistical evidence.

(16) It is important to protect all natural persons against discrimination on grounds of racial or ethnic origin. Member States should also provide, where appropriate and in accordance with their national traditions and practice, protection for legal persons where they suffer discrimination on grounds of the racial or ethnic origin of their members.

(17) The prohibition of discrimination should be without prejudice to the maintenance or adoption of measures intended to prevent or compensate for disadvantages suffered by a group of persons of a particular racial or ethnic origin, and such measures may permit organisations of persons of a particular racial or ethnic origin where their main object is the promotion of the special needs of those persons.

(18) In very limited circumstances, a difference of treatment may be justified where a characteristic related to racial or ethnic origin constitutes a genuine and determining occupational requirement, when the objective is legitimate and the requirement is proportionate. Such circumstances should be included in the information provided by the Member States to the Commission.

(19) Persons who have been subject to discrimination based on racial and ethnic origin should have adequate means of legal protection. To provide a more effective level of protection, associations or legal entities should also be empowered to engage, as the Member States so determine, either on behalf or in support of any victim, in proceedings, without prejudice to national rules of procedure concerning representation and defence before the courts.

(20) The effective implementation of the principle of equality requires adequate judicial protection against victimisation.

(21) The rules on the burden of proof must be adapted when there is a prima facie case of discrimination and, for the principle of equal treatment to be applied effectively, the burden of proof must shift back to the respondent when evidence of such discrimination is brought.

(22) Member States need not apply the rules on the burden of proof to proceedings in which it is for the court or other competent body to investigate the facts of the case. The procedures thus referred to are those in which the plaintiff is not required to prove the facts, which it is for the court or competent body to investigate.

(23) Member States should promote dialogue between the social partners and with nongovernmental organisations to address different forms of discrimination and to combat them.

(24) Protection against discrimination based on racial or ethnic origin would itself be strengthened by the existence of a body or bodies in each Member State, with competence to analyse the problems involved, to study possible solutions and to provide concrete assistance for the victims.

(25) This Directive lays down minimum requirements, thus giving the Member States the option of introducing or maintaining more favourable provisions. The implementation of this Directive should not serve to justify any regression in relation to the situation which already prevails in each Member State.

(26) Member States should provide for effective, proportionate and dissuasive sanctions in case of breaches of the obligations under this Directive.

(27) The Member States may entrust management and labour, at their joint request, with the implementation of this Directive as regards provisions falling within the scope of collective agreements, provided that the Member States take all the necessary steps to ensure that they can at all times guarantee the results imposed by this Directive.

(28) In accordance with the principles of subsidiarity and proportionality as set out in Article 5 of the EC Treaty, the objective of this Directive, namely ensuring a common high level of protection against discrimination in all the Member States, cannot be sufficiently achieved by the Member States and can therefore, by reason of the scale and impact of the proposed action, be better achieved by the Community. This Directive does not go beyond what is necessary in order to achieve those objectives,

HAS ADOPTED THIS DIRECTIVE:

Chapter I General provisions

Article 1 Purpose

The purpose of this Directive is to lay down a framework for combating discrimination on the grounds of racial or ethnic origin, with a view to putting into effect in the Member States the principle of equal treatment.

Article 2 Concept of discrimination

1. For the purposes of this Directive, the principle of equal treatment shall mean that there shall be no direct or indirect discrimination based on racial or ethnic origin.

2. For the purposes of paragraph 1:

   (a) direct discrimination shall be taken to occur where one person is treated less favourably than another is, has been or would be treated in a comparable situation on grounds of racial or ethnic origin;

   (b) indirect discrimination shall be taken to occur where an apparently neutral provision, criterion or practice would put persons of a racial or ethnic origin at a particular disadvantage compared with other persons, unless that provision, criterion or practice is objectively justified by a legitimate aim and the means of achieving that aim are appropriate and necessary.

3. Harassment shall be deemed to be discrimination within the meaning of paragraph 1, when an unwanted conduct related to racial or ethnic origin takes place with the purpose or effect of violating the dignity of a person and of creating an intimidating, hostile, degrading, humiliating or offensive environment. In this context, the concept of harassment may be defined in accordance with the national laws and practice of the Member States.

4. An instruction to discriminate against persons on grounds of racial or ethnic origin shall be deemed to be discrimination within the meaning of paragraph 1.

Article 3 Scope

1. Within the limits of the powers conferred upon the Community, this Directive shall apply to all persons, as regards both the public and private sectors, including public bodies, in relation to:

   (a) conditions for access to employment, to self-employment and to occupation, including selection criteria and recruitment conditions, whatever the branch of activity and at all levels of the professional hierarchy, including promotion;

(b) access to all types and to all levels of vocational guidance, vocational training, advanced vocational training and retraining, including practical work experience;
(c) employment and working conditions, including dismissals and pay;
(d) membership of and involvement in an organisation of workers or employers, or any organisation whose members carry on a particular profession, including the benefits provided for by such organisations;
(e) social protection, including social security and healthcare;
(f) social advantages;
(g) education;
(h) access to and supply of goods and services which are available to the public, including housing.

2. This Directive does not cover difference of treatment based on nationality and is without prejudice to provisions and conditions relating to the entry into and residence of third-country nationals and stateless persons on the territory of Member States, and to any treatment which arises from the legal status of the third-country nationals and stateless persons concerned.

Article 4 Genuine and determining occupational requirements

Notwithstanding Article 2(1) and (2), Member States may provide that a difference of treatment which is based on a characteristic related to racial or ethnic origin shall not constitute discrimination where, by reason of the nature of the particular occupational activities concerned or of the context in which they are carried out, such a characteristic constitutes a genuine and determining occupational requirement, provided that the objective is legitimate and the requirement is proportionate.

Article 5 Positive action

With a view to ensuring full equality in practice, the principle of equal treatment shall not prevent any Member State from maintaining or adopting specific measures to prevent or compensate for disadvantages linked to racial or ethnic origin.

Article 6 Minimum requirements

1. Member States may introduce or maintain provisions which are more favourable to the protection of the principle of equal treatment than those laid down in this Directive.

2. The implementation of this Directive shall under no circumstances constitute grounds for a reduction in the level of protection against discrimination already afforded by Member States in the fields covered by this Directive.

Chapter II Remedies and enforcement

Article 7 Defence of rights

1. Member States shall ensure that judicial and/or administrative procedures, including where they deem it appropriate conciliation procedures, for the enforcement of obligations under this Directive are available to all persons who consider themselves wronged by failure to apply the principle of equal treatment to them, even after the relationship in which the discrimination is alleged to have occurred has ended.

2. Member States shall ensure that associations, organisations or other legal entities, which have, in accordance with the criteria laid down by their national law, a legitimate interest in ensuring that the provisions of this Directive are complied with, may engage, either on behalf or in support of the complainant, with his or her approval, in any judicial and/or administrative procedure provided for the enforcement of obligations under this Directive.

3. Paragraphs 1 and 2 are without prejudice to national rules relating to time limits for bringing actions as regards the principle of equality of treatment.

Article 8 Burden of proof

1. Member States shall take such measures as are necessary, in accordance with their national judicial systems, to ensure that, when persons who consider themselves wronged because the principle

of equal treatment has not been applied to them establish, before a court or other competent authority, facts from which it may be presumed that there has been direct or indirect discrimination, it shall be for the respondent to prove that there has been no breach of the principle of equal treatment.

2. Paragraph 1 shall not prevent Member States from introducing rules of evidence which are more favourable to plaintiffs.

3. Paragraph 1 shall not apply to criminal procedures.

4. Paragraphs 1, 2 and 3 shall also apply to any proceedings brought in accordance with Article 7 (2).

5. Member States need not apply paragraph 1 to proceedings in which it is for the court or competent body to investigate the facts of the case.

Article 9 Victimisation

Member States shall introduce into their national legal systems such measures as are necessary to protect individuals from any adverse treatment or adverse consequence as a reaction to a complaint or to proceedings aimed at enforcing compliance with the principle of equal treatment.

Article 10 Dissemination of information

Member States shall take care that the provisions adopted pursuant to this Directive, together with the relevant provisions already in force, are brought to the attention of the persons concerned by all appropriate means throughout their territory.

Article 11 Social dialogue

1. Member States shall, in accordance with national traditions and practice, take adequate measures to promote the social dialogue between the two sides of industry with a view to fostering equal treatment, including through the monitoring of workplace practices, collective agreements, codes of conduct, research or exchange of experiences and good practices.

2. Where consistent with national traditions and practice, Member States shall encourage the two sides of the industry without prejudice to their autonomy to conclude, at the appropriate level, agreements laying down anti-discrimination rules in the fields referred to in Article 3 which fall within the scope of collective bargaining. These agreements shall respect the minimum requirements laid down by this Directive and the relevant national implementing measures.

Article 12 Dialogue with non-governmental organisations

Member States shall encourage dialogue with appropriate non-governmental organisations which have, in accordance with their national law and practice, a legitimate interest in contributing to the fight against discrimination on grounds of racial and ethnic origin with a view to promoting the principle of equal treatment.

Chapter III Bodies for the promotion of equal treatment

Article 13

1. Member States shall designate a body or bodies for the promotion of equal treatment of all persons without discrimination on the grounds of racial or ethnic origin. These bodies may form part of agencies charged at national level with the defence of human rights or the safeguard of individuals' rights.

2. Member States shall ensure that the competences of these bodies include:

- without prejudice to the right of victims and of associations, organisations or other legal entities referred to in Article 7(2), providing independent assistance to victims of discrimination in pursuing their complaints about discrimination,
- conducting independent surveys concerning discrimination,
- publishing independent reports and making recommendations on any issue relating to such discrimination.

Chapter IV Final provisions

Article 14 Compliance

Member States shall take the necessary measures to ensure that:

(a) any laws, regulations and administrative provisions contrary to the principle of equal treatment are abolished;

(b) any provisions contrary to the principle of equal treatment which are included in individual or collective contracts or agreements, internal rules of undertakings, rules governing profit-making or non-profit-making associations, and rules governing the independent professions and workers' and employers' organisations, are or may be declared, null and void or are amended.

Article 15 Sanctions

Member States shall lay down the rules on sanctions applicable to infringements of the national provisions adopted pursuant to this Directive and shall take all measures necessary to ensure that they are applied. The sanctions, which may comprise the payment of compensation to the victim, must be effective, proportionate and dissuasive. The Member States shall notify those provisions to the Commission by 19 July 2003 at the latest and shall notify it without delay of any subsequent amendment affecting them.

Article 16 Implementation

Member States shall adopt the laws, regulations and administrative provisions necessary to comply with this Directive by 19 July 2003 or may entrust management and labour, at their joint request, with the implementation of this Directive as regards provisions falling within the scope of collective agreements. In such cases, Member States shall ensure that by 19 July 2003, management and labour introduce the necessary measures by agreement, Member States being required to take any necessary measures to enable them at any time to be in a position to guarantee the results imposed by this Directive. They shall forthwith inform the Commission thereof.

When Member States adopt these measures, they shall contain a reference to this Directive or be accompanied by such a reference on the occasion of their official publication. The methods of making such a reference shall be laid down by the Member States.

Article 17 Report

1. Member States shall communicate to the Commission by 19 July 2005, and every five years thereafter, all the information necessary for the Commission to draw up a report to the European Parliament and the Council on the application of this Directive.

2. The Commission's report shall take into account, as appropriate, the views of the European Monitoring Centre on Racism and Xenophobia, as well as the viewpoints of the social partners and relevant non-governmental organisations. In accordance with the principle of gender mainstreaming, this report shall, inter alia, provide an assessment of the impact of the measures taken on women and men. In the light of the information received, this report shall include, if necessary, proposals to revise and update this Directive.

Article 18 Entry into force

This Directive shall enter into force on the day of its publication in the *Official Journal of the European Communities*.

Article 19 Addressees

This Directive is addressed to the Member States.

Done at Luxembourg, 29 June 2000.
For the Council
The President
M. ARCANJO

Council Directive 2000/78/EC of 27 November 2000 establishing a general framework for equal treatment in employment and occupation

[OJ 2000 L303/16]

THE COUNCIL OF THE EUROPEAN UNION,

Having regard to the Treaty establishing the European Community, and in particular Article 13 thereof,

Having regard to the proposal from the Commission,[1]

Having regard to the Opinion of the European Parliament,[2]

Having regard to the Opinion of the Economic and Social Committee,[3]

Having regard to the Opinion of the Committee of the Regions,[4]

Whereas:

(1) In accordance with Article 6 of the Treaty on European Union, the European Union is founded on the principles of liberty, democracy, respect for human rights and fundamental freedoms, and the rule of law, principles which are common to all Member States and it respects fundamental rights, as guaranteed by the European Convention for the Protection of Human Rights and Fundamental Freedoms and as they result from the constitutional traditions common to the Member States, as general principles of Community law.

(2) The principle of equal treatment between women and men is well established by an important body of Community law, in particular in Council Directive 76/207/EEC of 9 February 1976 on the implementation of the principle of equal treatment for men and women as regards access to employment, vocational training and promotion, and working conditions.[5]

(3) In implementing the principle of equal treatment, the Community should, in accordance with Article 3(2) of the EC Treaty, aim to eliminate inequalities, and to promote equality between men and women, especially since women are often the victims of multiple discrimination.

(4) The right of all persons to equality before the law and protection against discrimination constitutes a universal right recognised by the Universal Declaration of Human Rights, the United Nations Convention on the Elimination of All Forms of Discrimination against Women, United Nations Covenants on Civil and Political Rights and on Economic, Social and Cultural Rights and by the European Convention for the Protection of Human Rights and Fundamental Freedoms, to which all Member States are signatories. Convention No 111 of the International Labour Organisation (ILO) prohibits discrimination in the field of employment and occupation.

(5) It is important to respect such fundamental rights and freedoms. This Directive does not prejudice freedom of association, including the right to establish unions with others and to join unions to defend one's interests.

(6) The Community Charter of the Fundamental Social Rights of Workers recognises the importance of combating every form of discrimination, including the need to take appropriate action for the social and economic integration of elderly and disabled people.

(7) The EC Treaty includes among its objectives the promotion of coordination between employment policies of the Member States. To this end, a new employment chapter was incorporated in the EC Treaty as a means of developing a coordinated European strategy for employment to promote a skilled, trained and adaptable workforce.

(8) The Employment Guidelines for 2000 agreed by the European Council at Helsinki on 10 and 11 December 1999 stress the need to foster a labour market favourable to social integration by

[1] OJ C 177 E, 27.6.2000, p. 42.
[2] Opinion delivered on 12 October 2000 (not yet published in the Official Journal).
[3] OJ C 204, 18.7.2000, p. 82.
[4] OJ C 226, 8.8.2000, p. 1.
[5] OJ L 39, 14.2.1976, p. 40.

formulating a coherent set of policies aimed at combating discrimination against groups such as persons with disability. They also emphasise the need to pay particular attention to supporting older workers, in order to increase their participation in the labour force.

(9) Employment and occupation are key elements in guaranteeing equal opportunities for all and contribute strongly to the full participation of citizens in economic, cultural and social life and to realising their potential.

(10) On 29 June 2000 the Council adopted Directive 2000/43/EC[6] implementing the principle of equal treatment between persons irrespective of racial or ethnic origin. That Directive already provides protection against such discrimination in the field of employment and occupation.

(11) Discrimination based on religion or belief, disability, age or sexual orientation may undermine the achievement of the objectives of the EC Treaty, in particular the attainment of a high level of employment and social protection, raising the standard of living and the quality of life, economic and social cohesion and solidarity, and the free movement of persons.

(12) To this end, any direct or indirect discrimination based on religion or belief, disability, age or sexual orientation as regards the areas covered by this Directive should be prohibited throughout the Community. This prohibition of discrimination should also apply to nationals of third countries but does not cover differences of treatment based on nationality and is without prejudice to provisions governing the entry and residence of third-country nationals and their access to employment and occupation.

(13) This Directive does not apply to social security and social protection schemes whose benefits are not treated as income within the meaning given to that term for the purpose of applying Article 141 of the EC Treaty, nor to any kind of payment by the State aimed at providing access to employment or maintaining employment.

(14) This Directive shall be without prejudice to national provisions laying down retirement ages.

(15) The appreciation of the facts from which it may be inferred that there has been direct or indirect discrimination is a matter for national judicial or other competent bodies, in accordance with rules of national law or practice. Such rules may provide, in particular, for indirect discrimination to be established by any means including on the basis of statistical evidence.

(16) The provision of measures to accommodate the needs of disabled people at the workplace plays an important role in combating discrimination on grounds of disability.

(17) This Directive does not require the recruitment, promotion, maintenance in employment or training of an individual who is not competent, capable and available to perform the essential functions of the post concerned or to undergo the relevant training, without prejudice to the obligation to provide reasonable accommodation for people with disabilities.

(18) This Directive does not require, in particular, the armed forces and the police, prison or emergency services to recruit or maintain in employment persons who do not have the required capacity to carry out the range of functions that they may be called upon to perform with regard to the legitimate objective of preserving the operational capacity of those services.

(19) Moreover, in order that the Member States may continue to safeguard the combat effectiveness of their armed forces, they may choose not to apply the provisions of this Directive concerning disability and age to all or part of their armed forces. The Member States which make that choice must define the scope of that derogation.

(20) Appropriate measures should be provided, i.e. effective and practical measures to adapt the workplace to the disability, for example adapting premises and equipment, patterns of working time, the distribution of tasks or the provision of training or integration resources.

(21) To determine whether the measures in question give rise to a disproportionate burden, account should be taken in particular of the financial and other costs entailed, the scale and financial resources of the organisation or undertaking and the possibility of obtaining public funding or any other assistance.

[6] OJL 180, 19.7.2000, p. 22.

(22) This Directive is without prejudice to national laws on marital status and the benefits dependent thereon.

(23) In very limited circumstances, a difference of treatment may be justified where a characteristic related to religion or belief, disability, age or sexual orientation constitutes a genuine and determining occupational requirement, when the objective is legitimate and the requirement is proportionate. Such circumstances should be included in the information provided by the Member States to the Commission.

(24) The European Union in its Declaration No 11 on the status of churches and nonconfessional organisations, annexed to the Final Act of the Amsterdam Treaty, has explicitly recognised that it respects and does not prejudice the status under national law of churches and religious associations or communities in the Member States and that it equally respects the status of philosophical and non-confessional organisations. With this in view, Member States may maintain or lay down specific provisions on genuine, legitimate and justified occupational requirements which might be required for carrying out an occupational activity.

(25) The prohibition of age discrimination is an essential part of meeting the aims set out in the Employment Guidelines and encouraging diversity in the workforce. However, differences in treatment in connection with age may be justified under certain circumstances and therefore require specific provisions which may vary in accordance with the situation in Member States. It is therefore essential to distinguish between differences in treatment which are justified, in particular by legitimate employment policy, labour market and vocational training objectives, and discrimination which must be prohibited.

(26) The prohibition of discrimination should be without prejudice to the maintenance or adoption of measures intended to prevent or compensate for disadvantages suffered by a group of persons of a particular religion or belief, disability, age or sexual orientation, and such measures may permit organisations of persons of a particular religion or belief, disability, age or sexual orientation where their main object is the promotion of the special needs of those persons.

(27) In its Recommendation 86/379/EEC of 24 July 1986 on the employment of disabled people in the Community,[7] the Council established a guideline framework setting out examples of positive action to promote the employment and training of disabled people, and in its Resolution of 17 June 1999 on equal employment opportunities for people with disabilities,[8] affirmed the importance of giving specific attention inter alia to recruitment, retention, training and lifelong learning with regard to disabled persons.

(28) This Directive lays down minimum requirements, thus giving the Member States the option of introducing or maintaining more favourable provisions. The implementation of this Directive should not serve to justify any regression in relation to the situation which already prevails in each Member State.

(29) Persons who have been subject to discrimination based on religion or belief, disability, age or sexual orientation should have adequate means of legal protection. To provide a more effective level of protection, associations or legal entities should also be empowered to engage in proceedings, as the Member States so determine, either on behalf or in support of any victim, without prejudice to national rules of procedure concerning representation and defence before the courts.

(30) The effective implementation of the principle of equality requires adequate judicial protection against victimisation.

(31) The rules on the burden of proof must be adapted when there is a prima facie case of discrimination and, for the principle of equal treatment to be applied effectively, the burden of proof must shift back to the respondent when evidence of such discrimination is brought. However, it is not for the respondent to prove that the plaintiff adheres to a particular religion or belief, has a particular disability, is of a particular age or has a particular sexual orientation.

[7] OJ L 180, 19.7.2000, p. 22.

[8] OJ L 225, 12.8.1986, p. 43.

(32) Member States need not apply the rules on the burden of proof to proceedings in which it is for the court or other competent body to investigate the facts of the case. The procedures thus referred to are those in which the plaintiff is not required to prove the facts, which it is for the court or competent body to investigate.

(33) Member States should promote dialogue between the social partners and, within the framework of national practice, with non-governmental organisations to address different forms of discrimination at the workplace and to combat them.

(34) The need to promote peace and reconciliation between the major communities in Northern Ireland necessitates the incorporation of particular provisions into this Directive.

(35) Member States should provide for effective, proportionate and dissuasive sanctions in case of breaches of the obligations under this Directive.

(36) Member States may entrust the social partners, at their joint request, with the implementation of this Directive, as regards the provisions concerning collective agreements, provided they take any necessary steps to ensure that they are at all times able to guarantee the results required by this Directive.

(37) In accordance with the principle of subsidiarity set out in Article 5 of the EC Treaty, the objective of this Directive, namely the creation within the Community of a level playing-field as regards equality in employment and occupation, cannot be sufficiently achieved by the Member States and can therefore, by reason of the scale and impact of the action, be better achieved at Community level. In accordance with the principle of proportionality, as set out in that Article, this Directive does not go beyond what is necessary in order to achieve that objective,

HAS ADOPTED THIS DIRECTIVE:

Chapter I General provisions

Article 1 Purpose

The purpose of this Directive is to lay down a general framework for combating discrimination on the grounds of religion or belief, disability, age or sexual orientation as regards employment and occupation, with a view to putting into effect in the Member States the principle of equal treatment.

Article 2 Concept of discrimination

1. For the purposes of this Directive, the 'principle of equal treatment' shall mean that there shall be no direct or indirect discrimination whatsoever on any of the grounds referred to in Article 1.

2. For the purposes of paragraph 1:

(a) direct discrimination shall be taken to occur where one person is treated less favourably than another is, has been or would be treated in a comparable situation, on any of the grounds referred to in Article 1;

(b) indirect discrimination shall be taken to occur where an apparently neutral provision, criterion or practice would put persons having a particular religion or belief, a particular disability, a particular age, or a particular sexual orientation at a particular disadvantage compared with other persons unless:

(i) that provision, criterion or practice is objectively justified by a legitimate aim and the means of achieving that aim are appropriate and necessary, or

(ii) as regards persons with a particular disability, the employer or any person or organisation to whom this Directive applies, is obliged, under national legislation, to take appropriate measures in line with the principles contained in Article 5 in order to eliminate disadvantages entailed by such provision, criterion or practice.

3. Harassment shall be deemed to be a form of discrimination within the meaning of paragraph 1, when unwanted conduct related to any of the grounds referred to in Article 1 takes place with the purpose or effect of violating the dignity of a person and of creating an intimidating, hostile, degrading, humiliating or offensive environment. In this context, the concept of harassment may be defined in accordance with the national laws and practice of the Member States.

4. An instruction to discriminate against persons on any of the grounds referred to in Article 1 shall be deemed to be discrimination within the meaning of paragraph 1.

5. This Directive shall be without prejudice to measures laid down by national law which, in a democratic society, are necessary for public security, for the maintenance of public order and the prevention of criminal offences, for the protection of health and for the protection of the rights and freedoms of others.

Article 3 Scope

1. Within the limits of the areas of competence conferred on the Community, this Directive shall apply to all persons, as regards both the public and private sectors, including public bodies, in relation to:

(a) conditions for access to employment, to self-employment or to occupation, including selection criteria and recruitment conditions, whatever the branch of activity and at all levels of the professional hierarchy, including promotion;

(b) access to all types and to all levels of vocational guidance, vocational training, advanced vocational training and retraining, including practical work experience;

(c) employment and working conditions, including dismissals and pay;

(d) membership of, and involvement in, an organisation of workers or employers, or any organisation whose members carry on a particular profession, including the benefits provided for by such organisations.

2. This Directive does not cover differences of treatment based on nationality and is without prejudice to provisions and conditions relating to the entry into and residence of third-country nationals and stateless persons in the territory of Member States, and to any treatment which arises from the legal status of the third-country nationals and stateless persons concerned.

3. This Directive does not apply to payments of any kind made by state schemes or similar, including state social security or social protection schemes.

4. Member States may provide that this Directive, in so far as it relates to discrimination on the grounds of disability and age, shall not apply to the armed forces.

Article 4 Occupational requirements

1. Notwithstanding Article 2(1) and (2), Member States may provide that a difference of treatment which is based on a characteristic related to any of the grounds referred to in Article 1 shall not constitute discrimination where, by reason of the nature of the particular occupational activities concerned or of the context in which they are carried out, such a characteristic constitutes a genuine and determining occupational requirement, provided that the objective is legitimate and the requirement is proportionate.

2. Member States may maintain national legislation in force at the date of adoption of this Directive or provide for future legislation incorporating national practices existing at the date of adoption of this Directive pursuant to which, in the case of occupational activities within churches and other public or private organisations the ethos of which is based on religion or belief, a difference of treatment based on a person's religion or belief shall not constitute discrimination where, by reason of the nature of these activities or of the context in which they are carried out, a person's religion or belief constitute a genuine, legitimate and justified occupational requirement, having regard to the organisation's ethos. This difference of treatment shall be implemented taking account of Member States' constitutional provisions and principles, as well as the general principles of Community law, and should not justify discrimination on another ground.

Provided that its provisions are otherwise complied with, this Directive shall thus not prejudice the right of churches and other public or private organisations, the ethos of which is based on religion or belief, acting in conformity with national constitutions and laws, to require individuals working for them to act in good faith and with loyalty to the organisation's ethos.

Article 5 Reasonable accommodation for disabled persons

In order to guarantee compliance with the principle of equal treatment in relation to persons with disabilities, reasonable accommodation shall be provided. This means that employers shall take appropriate measures, where needed in a particular case, to enable a person with a disability to have access to, participate in, or advance in employment, or to undergo training, unless such measures would impose a disproportionate burden on the employer. This burden shall not be disproportionate when it is sufficiently remedied by measures existing within the framework of the disability policy of the Member State concerned.

Article 6 Justification of differences of treatment on grounds of age

1. Notwithstanding Article 2(2), Member States may provide that differences of treatment on grounds of age shall not constitute discrimination, if, within the context of national law, they are objectively and reasonably justified by a legitimate aim, including legitimate employment policy, labour market and vocational training objectives, and if the means of achieving that aim are appropriate and necessary.

Such differences of treatment may include, among others:

(a) the setting of special conditions on access to employment and vocational training, employment and occupation, including dismissal and remuneration conditions, for young people, older workers and persons with caring responsibilities in order to promote their vocational integration or ensure their protection;

(b) the fixing of minimum conditions of age, professional experience or seniority in service for access to employment or to certain advantages linked to employment;

(c) the fixing of a maximum age for recruitment which is based on the training requirements of the post in question or the need for a reasonable period of employment before retirement.

2. Notwithstanding Article 2(2), Member States may provide that the fixing for occupational social security schemes of ages for admission or entitlement to retirement or invalidity benefits, including the fixing under those schemes of different ages for employees or groups or categories of employees, and the use, in the context of such schemes, of age criteria in actuarial calculations, does not constitute discrimination on the grounds of age, provided this does not result in discrimination on the grounds of sex.

Article 7 Positive action

1. With a view to ensuring full equality in practice, the principle of equal treatment shall not prevent any Member State from maintaining or adopting specific measures to prevent or compensate for disadvantages linked to any of the grounds referred to in Article 1.

2. With regard to disabled persons, the principle of equal treatment shall be without prejudice to the right of Member States to maintain or adopt provisions on the protection of health and safety at work or to measures aimed at creating or maintaining provisions or facilities for safeguarding or promoting their integration into the working environment.

Article 8 Minimum requirements

1. Member States may introduce or maintain provisions which are more favourable to the protection of the principle of equal treatment than those laid down in this Directive.

2. The implementation of this Directive shall under no circumstances constitute grounds for a reduction in the level of protection against discrimination already afforded by Member States in the fields covered by this Directive.

Chapter II Remedies and enforcement

Article 9 Defence of rights

1. Member States shall ensure that judicial and/or administrative procedures, including where they deem it appropriate conciliation procedures, for the enforcement of obligations under this Directive are available to all persons who consider themselves wronged by failure to apply the principle of equal treatment to them, even after the relationship in which the discrimination is alleged to have occurred has ended.

2. Member States shall ensure that associations, organisations or other legal entities which have, in accordance with the criteria laid down by their national law, a legitimate interest in ensuring that the provisions of this Directive are complied with, may engage, either on behalf or in support of the complainant, with his or her approval, in any judicial and/or administrative procedure provided for the enforcement of obligations under this Directive.

3. Paragraphs 1 and 2 are without prejudice to national rules relating to time limits for bringing actions as regards the principle of equality of treatment.

Article 10 Burden of proof

1. Member States shall take such measures as are necessary, in accordance with their national judicial systems, to ensure that, when persons who consider themselves wronged because the principle of equal treatment has not been applied to them establish, before a court or other competent authority, facts from which it may be presumed that there has been direct or indirect discrimination, it shall be for the respondent to prove that there has been no breach of the principle of equal treatment.

2. Paragraph 1 shall not prevent Member States from introducing rules of evidence which are more favourable to plaintiffs.

3. Paragraph 1 shall not apply to criminal procedures.

4. Paragraphs 1, 2 and 3 shall also apply to any legal proceedings commenced in accordance with Article 9(2).

5. Member States need not apply paragraph 1 to proceedings in which it is for the court or competent body to investigate the facts of the case.

Article 11 Victimisation

Member States shall introduce into their national legal systems such measures as are necessary to protect employees against dismissal or other adverse treatment by the employer as a reaction to a complaint within the undertaking or to any legal proceedings aimed at enforcing compliance with the principle of equal treatment.

Article 12 Dissemination of information

Member States shall take care that the provisions adopted pursuant to this Directive, together with the relevant provisions already in force in this field, are brought to the attention of the persons concerned by all appropriate means, for example, at the workplace, throughout their territory.

Article 13 Social dialogue

1. Member States shall, in accordance with their national traditions and practice, take adequate measures to promote dialogue between the social partners with a view to fostering equal treatment, including through the monitoring of workplace practices, collective agreements, codes of conduct and through research or exchange of experiences and good practices.

2. Where consistent with their national traditions and practice, Member States shall encourage the social partners, without prejudice to their autonomy, to conclude at the appropriate level agreements laying down anti-discrimination rules in the fields referred to in Article 3 which fall within the scope of collective bargaining. These agreements shall respect the minimum requirements laid down by this Directive and by the relevant national implementing measures.

Article 14 Dialogue with non-governmental organisations

Member States shall encourage dialogue with appropriate non-governmental organisations which have, in accordance with their national law and practice, a legitimate interest in contributing to the fight against discrimination on any of the grounds referred to in Article 1 with a view to promoting the principle of equal treatment.

Chapter III Particular provisions

Article 15 Northern Ireland

1. In order to tackle the under-representation of one of the major religious communities in the police service of Northern Ireland, differences in treatment regarding recruitment into that service,

including its support staff, shall not constitute discrimination insofar as those differences in treatment are expressly authorised by national legislation.

2. In order to maintain a balance of opportunity in employment for teachers in Northern Ireland while furthering the reconciliation of historical divisions between the major religious communities there, the provisions on religion or belief in this Directive shall not apply to the recruitment of teachers in schools in Northern Ireland in so far as this is expressly authorised by national legislation.

Chapter IV Final provisions

Article 16 Compliance

Member States shall take the necessary measures to ensure that:

(a) any laws, regulations and administrative provisions contrary to the principle of equal treatment are abolished;

(b) any provisions contrary to the principle of equal treatment which are included in contracts or collective agreements, internal rules of undertakings or rules governing the independent occupations and professions and workers' and employers' organisations are, or may be, declared null and void or are amended.

Article 17 Sanctions

Member States shall lay down the rules on sanctions applicable to infringements of the national provisions adopted pursuant to this Directive and shall take all measures necessary to ensure that they are applied. The sanctions, which may comprise the payment of compensation to the victim, must be effective, proportionate and dissuasive. Member States shall notify those provisions to the Commission by 2 December 2003 at the latest and shall notify it without delay of any subsequent amendment affecting them.

Article 18 Implementation

Member States shall adopt the laws, regulations and administrative provisions necessary to comply with this Directive by 2 December 2003 at the latest or may entrust the social partners, at their joint request, with the implementation of this Directive as regards provisions concerning collective agreements. In such cases, Member States shall ensure that, no later than 2 December 2003, the social partners introduce the necessary measures by agreement, the Member States concerned being required to take any necessary measures to enable them at any time to be in a position to guarantee the results imposed by this Directive. They shall forthwith inform the Commission thereof.

In order to take account of particular conditions, Member States may, if necessary, have an additional period of 3 years from 2 December 2003, that is to say a total of 6 years, to implement the provisions of this Directive on age and disability discrimination. In that event they shall inform the Commission forthwith. Any Member State which chooses to use this additional period shall report annually to the Commission on the steps it is taking to tackle age and disability discrimination and on the progress it is making towards implementation. The Commission shall report annually to the Council.

When Member States adopt these measures, they shall contain a reference to this Directive or be accompanied by such reference on the occasion of their official publication. The methods of making such reference shall be laid down by Member States.

Article 19 Report

1. Member States shall communicate to the Commission, by 2 December 2005 at the latest and every five years thereafter, all the information necessary for the Commission to draw up a report to the European Parliament and the Council on the application of this Directive.

2. The Commission's report shall take into account, as appropriate, the viewpoints of the social partners and relevant non-governmental organisations. In accordance with the principle of gender mainstreaming, this report shall, inter alia, provide an assessment of the impact of the measures taken on women and men. In the light of the information received, this report shall include, if necessary, proposals to revise and update this Directive.

Article 20 Entry into force

This Directive shall enter into force on the day of its publication in the *Official Journal of the European Communities*.

Article 21 Addressees

This Directive is addressed to the Member States.

Done at Brussels, 27 November 2000.
For the Council
The President
E. GUIGOU

Council Directive 2004/113/EC of 13 December 2004 implementing the principle of equal treatment between men and women in the access to and supply of goods and services

[OJ 2004 L373/37]

THE COUNCIL OF THE EUROPEAN UNION,

Having regard to the Treaty establishing the European Community and in particular Article 13(1) thereof,

Having regard to the proposal from the Commission,

Having regard to the Opinion of the European Parliament[1],

Having regard to the Opinion of the European Economic and Social Committee[2],

Having regard to the opinion of the Committee of the Regions[3],

Whereas:

(1) In accordance with Article 6 of the Treaty on European Union, the Union is founded on the principles of liberty, democracy, respect for human rights and fundamental freedoms and the rule of law, principles which are common to the Member States, and respects fundamental rights as guaranteed by the European Convention for the Protection of Human Rights and Fundamental Freedoms and as they result from the constitutional traditions common to the Member States as general principles of Community law.

(2) The right to equality before the law and protection against discrimination for all persons constitutes a universal right recognised by the Universal Declaration of Human Rights, the United Nations Convention on the Elimination of all forms of Discrimination Against Women, the International Convention on the Elimination of all forms of Racial Discrimination and the United Nations Covenants on Civil and Political Rights and on Economic, Social and Cultural Rights and by the Rights and Fundamental Freedoms, to which all Member States are signatories.

(3) While prohibiting discrimination, it is important to respect other fundamental rights and freedoms, including the protection of private and family life and transactions carried out in that context and the freedom of religion.

(4) Equality between men and women is a fundamental principle of the European Union. Articles 21 and 23 of the Charter of Fundamental Rights of the European Union prohibit any discrimination on grounds of sex and require equality between men and women to be ensured in all areas.

[1] Opinion delivered on 30 March 2004 (not yet published in the Official Journal)
[2] OJ C 241, 28.9.2004, p. 44.,
[3] OJ C 121, 30.4.2004, p. 27.

(5) Article 2 of the Treaty establishing the European Community provides that promoting such equality is one of the Community's essential tasks. Similarly, Article 3(2) of the Treaty requires the Community to aim to eliminate inequalities and to promote equality between men and women in all its activities.

(6) The Commission announced its intention of proposing a directive on sex discrimination outside of the labour market in its Communication on the Social Policy Agenda. Such a proposal is fully consistent with Council Decision 2001/51/EC of 20 December 2000 establishing a Programme relating to the Community framework strategy on gender equality (2001-2005),[4] covering all Community policies and aimed at promoting equality for men and women by adjusting these policies and implementing practical measures to improve the situation of men and women in society.

(7) At its meeting in Nice of 7 and 9 December 2000, the European Council called on the Commission to reinforce equality-related rights by adopting a proposal for a directive on promoting gender equality in areas other than employment and professional life.

(8) The Community has adopted a range of legal instruments to prevent and combat sex discrimination in the labour market. These instruments have demonstrated the value of legislation in the fight against discrimination.

(9) Discrimination based on sex, including harassment and sexual harassment, also takes place in areas outside of the labour market. Such discrimination can be equally damaging, acting as a barrier to the full and successful integration of men and women into economic and social life.

(10) Problems are particularly apparent in the area of the access to and supply of goods and services. Discrimination based on sex, should therefore be prevented and eliminated in this area. As in the case of Council Directive 2000/43/EC of 29 June 2000 implementing the principle of equal treatment between persons irrespective of racial and ethnic origin[5], this objective can be better achieved by means of Community legislation.

(11) Such legislation should prohibit discrimination based on sex in the access to and supply of goods and services. Goods should be taken to be those within the meaning of the provisions of the Treaty establishing the European Community relating to the free movement of goods. Services should be taken to be those within the meaning of Article 50 of that Treaty.

(12) To prevent discrimination based on sex, this Directive should apply to both direct discrimination and indirect discrimination. Direct discrimination occurs only when one person is treated less favourably, on grounds of sex, than another person in a comparable situation. Accordingly, for example, differences between men and women in the provision of healthcare services, which result from the physical differences between men and women, do not relate to comparable situations and therefore, do not constitute discrimination.

(13) The prohibition of discrimination should apply to persons providing goods and services, which are available to the public and which are offered outside the area of private and family life and the transactions carried out in this context. It should not apply to the content of media or advertising nor to public or private education.

(14) All individuals enjoy the freedom to contract, including the freedom to choose a contractual partner for a transaction. An individual who provides goods or services may have a number of subjective reasons for his or her choice of contractual partner. As long as the choice of partner is not based on that person's sex, this Directive should not prejudice the individual's freedom to choose a contractual partner.

(15) There are already a number of existing legal instruments for the implementation of the principle of equal treatment between men and women in matters of employment and occupation. Therefore, this Directive should not apply in this field. The same reasoning applies to matters of self-employment insofar as they are covered by existing legal instruments. The Directive should apply

[4] OJ L 17, 19.1.2001, p. 22.
[5] OJ L 180, 19.7.2000, p. 22.

only to insurance and pensions which are private, voluntary and separate from the employment relationship.

(16) Differences in treatment may be accepted only if they are justified by a legitimate aim. A legitimate aim may, for example, be the protection of victims of sex-related violence (in cases such as the establishment of single-sex shelters), reasons of privacy and decency (in cases such as the provision of accommodation by a person in a part of that person's home), the promotion of gender equality or of the interests of men or women (for example single-sex voluntary bodies), the freedom of association (in cases of membership of single-sex private clubs), and the organisation of sporting activities (for example single-sex sports events). Any limitation should nevertheless be appropriate and necessary in accordance with the criteria derived from case law of the Court of Justice of the European Communities.

(17) The principle of equal treatment in the access to goods and services does not require that facilities should always be provided to men and women on a shared basis, as long as they are not provided more favourably to members of one sex.

(18) The use of actuarial factors related to sex is widespread in the provision of insurance and other related financial services. In order to ensure equal treatment between men and women, the use of sex as an actuarial factor should not result in differences in individuals' premiums and benefits. To avoid a sudden readjustment of the market, the implementation of this rule should apply only to new contracts concluded after the date of transposition of this Directive.

(19) Certain categories of risks may vary between the sexes. In some cases, sex is one but not necessarily the only determining factor in the assessment of risks insured. For contracts insuring those types of risks, Member States may decide to permit exemptions from the rule of unisex premiums and benefits, as long as they can ensure that underlying actuarial and statistical data on which the calculations are based, are reliable, regularly updated and available to the public. Exemptions are allowed only where national legislation has not already applied the unisex rule. Five years after transposition of this Directive, Member States should re-examine the justification for these exemptions, taking into account the most recent actuarial and statistical data and a report by the Commission three years after the date of transposition of this Directive.

(20) Less favourable treatment of women for reasons of pregnancy and maternity should be considered a form of direct discrimination based on sex and therefore prohibited in insurance and related financial services. Costs related to risks of pregnancy and maternity should therefore not be attributed to the members of one sex only.

(21) Persons who have been subject to discrimination based on sex should have adequate means of legal protection. To provide a more effective level of protection, associations, organisations and other legal entities should also be empowered to engage in proceedings, as the Member States so determine, either on behalf or in support of any victim, without prejudice to national rules of procedure concerning representation and defence before the courts.

(22) The rules on the burden of proof should be adapted when there is a prima facie case of discrimination and for the principle of equal treatment to be applied effectively, the burden of proof should shift back to the defendant when evidence of such discrimination is brought.

(23) The effective implementation of the principle of equal treatment requires adequate judicial protection against victimisation.

(24) With a view to promoting the principle of equal treatment, Member States should encourage dialogue with relevant stakeholders, which have, in accordance with national law and practice, a legitimate interest in contributing to the fight against discrimination on grounds of sex in the area of access to and supply of goods and services.

(25) Protection against discrimination based on sex should itself be strengthened by the existence of a body or bodies in each Member State, with competence to analyse the problems involved, to study possible solutions and to provide concrete assistance for the victims. The body or bodies may be the same as those with responsibility at national level for the defence of human rights or the safeguarding of individuals' rights, or the implementation of the principle of equal treatment.

(26) This Directive lays down minimum requirements, thus giving the Member States the option of introducing or maintaining more favourable provisions. The implementation of this Directive should not serve to justify any regression in relation to the situation, which already prevails in each Member State.

(27) Member States should provide for effective, proportionate and dissuasive penalties in cases of breaches of the obligations under this Directive.

(28) Since the objectives of this Directive, namely to ensure a common high level of protection against discrimination in all the Member States, cannot be sufficiently achieved by the Member States and can, therefore, by reason of the scale and effects of the action, be better achieved at Community level, the Community may adopt measures, in accordance with the principle of subsidiarity as set out in Article 5 of the Treaty. In accordance with the principle of proportionality, as set out in that Article, this Directive does not go beyond what is necessary in order to achieve those objectives.

(29) In accordance with paragraph 34 of the interinstitutional agreement on better law-making,[6] Member States are encouraged to draw up, for themselves and in the interest of the Community, their own tables, which will, as far as possible, illustrate the correlation between the Directive and the transposition measures and to make them public,

HAS ADOPTED THIS DIRECTIVE:

Chapter I General provisions

Article 1 Purpose

The purpose of this Directive is to lay down a framework for combating discrimination based on sex in access to and supply of goods and services, with a view to putting into effect in the Member States the principle of equal treatment between men and women.

Article 2 Definitions

For the purposes of this Directive, the following definitions shall apply:

(a) direct discrimination: where one person is treated less favourably, on grounds of sex, than another is, has been or would be treated in a comparable situation;

(b) indirect discrimination: where an apparently neutral provision, criterion or practice would put persons of one sex at a particular disadvantage compared with persons of the other sex, unless that provision, criterion or practice is objectively justified by a legitimate aim and the means of achieving that aim are appropriate and necessary;

(c) harassment: where an unwanted conduct related to the sex of a person occurs with the purpose or effect of violating the dignity of a person and of creating an intimidating, hostile, degrading, humiliating or offensive environment;

(d) sexual harassment: where any form of unwanted physical, verbal, non-verbal or physical conduct of a sexual nature occurs, with the purpose or effect of violating the dignity of a person, in particular when creating an intimidating, hostile, degrading, humiliating or offensive environment.

Article 3 Scope

1. Within the limits of the powers conferred upon the Community, this Directive shall apply to all persons who provide goods and services, which are available to the public irrespective of the person concerned as regards both the public and private sectors, including public bodies, and which are offered outside the area of private and family life and the transactions carried out in this context.

2. This Directive does not prejudice the individual's freedom to choose a contractual partner as long as an individual's choice of contractual partner is not based on that person's sex.

3. This Directive shall not apply to the content of media and advertising nor to education.

[6] OJ C 321, 31.12.2003, p. 1.

4. This Directive shall not apply to matters of employment and occupation. This Directive shall not apply to matters of self-employment, insofar as these matters are covered by other Community legislative acts.

Article 4 Principle of equal treatment

1. For the purposes of this Directive, the principle of equal treatment between men and women shall mean that

(a) there shall be no direct discrimination based on sex, including less favourable treatment of women for reasons of pregnancy and maternity;

(b) there shall be no indirect discrimination based on sex.

2. This Directive shall be without prejudice to more favourable provisions concerning the protection of women as regards pregnancy and maternity.

3. Harassment and sexual harassment within the meaning of this Directive shall be deemed to be discrimination on the grounds of sex and therefore prohibited. A person's rejection of, or submission to, such conduct may not be used as a basis for a decision affecting that person.

4. Instruction to direct or indirect discrimination on the grounds of sex shall be deemed to be discrimination within the meaning of this Directive.

5. This Directive shall not preclude differences in treatment, if the provision of the goods and services exclusively or primarily to members of one sex is justified by a legitimate aim and the means of achieving that aim are appropriate and necessary.

Article 5 Actuarial factors

1. Member States shall ensure that in all new contracts concluded after 21 December 2007 at the latest, the use of sex as a factor in the calculation of premiums and benefits for the purposes of insurance and related financial services shall not result in differences in individuals' premiums and benefits.

2. Notwithstanding paragraph 1, Member States may decide before 21 December 2007 to permit proportionate differences in individuals' premiums and benefits where the use of sex is a determining factor in the assessment of risk based on relevant and accurate actuarial and statistical data. The Member States concerned shall inform the Commission and ensure that accurate data relevant to the use of sex as a determining actuarial factor are compiled, published and regularly updated. These Member States shall review their decision five years after 21 December 2007, taking into account the Commission report referred to in Article 16, and shall forward the results of this review to the Commission.

3. In any event, costs related to pregnancy and maternity shall not result in differences in individuals' premiums and benefits. Member States may defer implementation of the measures necessary to comply with this paragraph until two years after 21 December 2007 at the latest. In that case the Member States concerned shall immediately inform the Commission.

Article 6 Positive action

With a view to ensuring full equality in practice between men and women, the principle of equal treatment shall not prevent any Member State from maintaining or adopting specific measures to prevent or compensate for disadvantages linked to sex.

Article 7 Minimum requirements

1. Member States may introduce or maintain provisions which are more favourable to the protection of the principle of equal treatment between men and women than those laid down in this Directive.

2. The implementation of this Directive shall in no circumstances constitute grounds for a reduction in the level of protection against discrimination already afforded by Member States in the fields covered by this Directive.

Chapter II Remedies and enforcement

Article 8 Defence of rights

1. Member States shall ensure that judicial and/or administrative procedures, including where they deem it appropriate conciliation procedures, for the enforcement of the obligations under this Directive are available to all persons who consider themselves wronged by failure to apply the principle of equal treatment to them, even after the relationship in which the discrimination is alleged to have occurred has ended.

2. Member States shall introduce into their national legal systems such measures as are necessary to ensure real and effective compensation or reparation, as the Member States so determine, for the loss and damage sustained by a person injured as a result of discrimination within the meaning of this Directive, in a way which is dissuasive and proportionate to the damage suffered. The fixing of a prior upper limit shall not restrict such compensation or reparation.

3. Member States shall ensure that associations, organisations or other legal entities, which have, in accordance with the criteria laid down by their national law, a legitimate interest in ensuring that the provisions of this Directive are complied with, may engage, on behalf or in support of the complainant, with his or her approval, in any judicial and/or administrative procedure provided for the enforcement of obligations under this Directive.

4. Paragraphs 1 and 3 shall be without prejudice to national rules on time limits for bringing actions relating to the principle of equal treatment.

Article 9 Burden of proof

1. Member States shall take such measures as are necessary, in accordance with their national judicial systems, to ensure that, when persons who consider themselves wronged because the principle of equal treatment has not been applied to them establish, before a court or other competent authority, facts from which it may be presumed that there has been direct or indirect discrimination, it shall be for the respondent to prove that there has been no breach of the principle of equal treatment.

2. Paragraph 1 shall not prevent Member States from introducing rules of evidence, which are more favourable to plaintiffs.

3. Paragraph 1 shall not apply to criminal procedures.

4. Paragraphs 1, 2 and 3 shall also apply to any proceedings brought in accordance with Article 8(3).

5. Member States need not apply paragraph 1 to proceedings in which it is for the court or other competent authority to investigate the facts of the case.

Article 10 Victimisation

Member States shall introduce into their national legal systems such measures as are necessary to protect persons from any adverse treatment or adverse consequence as a reaction to a complaint or to legal proceedings aimed at enforcing compliance with the principle of equal treatment.

Article 11 Dialogue with relevant stakeholders

With a view to promoting the principle of equal treatment, Member States shall encourage dialogue with relevant stakeholders which have, in accordance with national law and practice, a legitimate interest in contributing to the fight against discrimination on grounds of sex in the area of access to and supply of goods and services.

Chapter III Bodies for the promotion of equal treatment

Article 12

1. Member States shall designate and make the necessary arrangements for a body or bodies for the promotion, analysis, monitoring and support of equal treatment of all persons without discrimination on the grounds of sex. These bodies may form part of agencies charged at national level with the

defence of human rights or the safeguard of individuals' rights, or the implementation of the principle of equal treatment.

2. Member States shall ensure that the competencies of the bodies referred to in paragraph 1 include:

(a) without prejudice to the rights of victims and of associations, organisations or other legal entities referred to in Article 8(3), providing independent assistance to victims of discrimination in pursuing their complaints about discrimination;
(b) conducting independent surveys concerning discrimination;
(c) publishing independent reports and making recommendations on any issue relating to such discrimination.

Chapter IV Final provisions

Article 13 Compliance

Member States shall take the necessary measures to ensure that the principle of equal treatment is respected in relation to the access to and supply of goods and services within the scope of this Directive, and in particular that:

(a) any laws, regulations and administrative provisions contrary to the principle of equal treatment are abolished;
(b) any contractual provisions, internal rules of undertakings, and rules governing profit-making or non-profit-making associations contrary to the principle of equal treatment are, or may be, declared null and void or are amended.

Article 14 Penalties

Member States shall lay down the rules on penalties applicable to infringements of the national provisions adopted pursuant to this Directive and shall take all measures necessary to ensure that they are applied. The penalties, which may comprise the payment of compensation to the victim, shall be effective, proportionate and dissuasive. Member States shall notify those provisions to the Commission by 21 December 2007 at the latest and shall notify it without delay of any subsequent amendment affecting them.

Article 15 Dissemination of information

Member States shall take care that the provisions adopted pursuant to this Directive, together with the relevant provisions already in force, are brought to the attention of the persons concerned by all appropriate means throughout their territory.

Article 16 Reports

1. Member States shall communicate all available information concerning the application of this Directive to the Commission, by 21 December 2009. and every five years thereafter. The Commission shall draw up a summary report, which shall include a review of the current practices of Member States in relation to Article 5 with regard to the use of sex as a factor in the calculation of premiums and benefits. It shall submit this report to the European Parliament and to the Council no later 21 December 2010. Where appropriate, the Commission shall accompany its report with proposals to modify the Directive.

2. The Commission's report shall take into account the viewpoints of relevant stakeholders.

Article 17 Transposition

1. Member States shall bring into force the laws, regulations and administrative provisions necessary to comply with this Directive by 21 December 2007 at the latest. They shall forthwith communicate to the Commission the text of those provisions. When Member States adopt these measures, they shall contain a reference to this Directive or be accompanied by such a reference on the occasion of their official publication. The methods of making such publication of reference shall be laid down by the Member States.

2. Member States shall communicate to the Commission the text of the main provisions of national law which they adopt in the field covered by this Directive.

Article 18 Entry into force
This Directive shall enter into force on the day of its publication in the *Official Journal of the European Union*.

Article 19 Addressees
This Directive is addressed to the Member States.

Done at Brussels, 13 December 2004.
For the Council
The President
B. R. BOT

Directive 2006/54/EC of the European Parliament and of the Council of 5 July 2006 on the implementation of the principle of equal opportunities and equal treatment of men and women in matters of employment and occupation (recast)

[OJ 2006 L204/23]

THE EUROPEAN PARLIAMENT AND THE COUNCIL OF THE EUROPEAN UNION,

HAVING REGARD TO THE TREATY ESTABLISHING THE EUROPEAN COMMUNITY, AND IN particular Article 141(3) thereof,

Having regard to the proposal from the Commission,

Having regard to the opinion of the European Economic and Social Committee,[1]

Acting in accordance with the procedure laid down in Article 251 of the Treaty,[2]

Whereas:

(1) Council Directive 76/207/EEC of 9 February 1976 on the implementation of the principle of equal treatment for men and women as regards access to employment, vocational training and promotion, and working conditions[3] and Council Directive 86/378/EEC of 24 July 1986 on the implementation of the principle of equal treatment for men and women in occupational social security schemes[4] have been significantly amended.[5] Council Directive 75/117/EEC of 10 February 1975 on the approximation of the laws of the Member States relating to the application of the principle of equal pay for men and women[6] and Council Directive 97/80/EC of 15 December 1997 on the burden of proof in cases of discrimination based on sex[7] also contain provisions which have as their purpose the implementation of the principle of equal treatment between men and women. Now that new amendments are being made to the said Directives, it is desirable, for reasons of clarity, that the provisions in question should be recast by bringing together in a single text the main provisions existing in this field as well as certain developments arising out of the case-law of the Court of Justice of the European Communities (hereinafter referred to as the Court of Justice).

[1] OJ C 157, 28.6.2005, p. 83.

[2] Opinion of the European Parliament of 6 July 2005 (not yet published in the Official Journal), Council Common Position of 10 March 2006(OJ C 126 E, 30.5.2006, p. 33) and Position of the European Parliament of 1 June 2006 (not yet published in the Official Journal).

[3] OJ L 39, 14.2.1976, p. 40. Directive as amended by Directive 2002/73/EC of the European Parliament and of the Council (OJ L 269, 5.10.2002, p. 15).

[4] OJ L 225, 12.8.1986, p. 40. Directive as amended by Directive 96/97/EC (OJ L 46, 17.2.1997, p. 20).

[5] See Annex I Part A.

[6] OJ L 45, 19.2.1975, p. 19.

[7] OJ L 14, 20.1.1998, p. 6. Directive as amended by Directive 98/52/EC (OJ L 205, 22.7.1998, p. 66).

(2) Equality between men and women is a fundamental principle of Community law under Article 2 and Article 3(2) of the Treaty and the case-law of the Court of Justice. Those Treaty provisions proclaim equality between men and women as a 'task' and an 'aim' of the Community and impose a positive obligation to promote it in all its activities.

(3) The Court of Justice has held that the scope of the principle of equal treatment for men and women cannot be confined to the prohibition of discrimination based on the fact that a person is of one or other sex. In view of its purpose and the nature of the rights which it seeks to safeguard, it also applies to discrimination arising from the gender reassignment of a person.

(4) Article 141(3) of the Treaty now provides a specific legal basis for the adoption of Community measures to ensure the application of the principle of equal opportunities and equal treatment in matters of employment and occupation, including the principle of equal pay for equal work or work of equal value.

(5) Articles 21 and 23 of the Charter of Fundamental Rights of the European Union also prohibit any discrimination on grounds of sex and enshrine the right to equal treatment between men and women in all areas, including employment, work and pay.

(6) Harassment and sexual harassment are contrary to the principle of equal treatment between men and women and constitute discrimination on grounds of sex for the purposes of this Directive. These forms of discrimination occur not only in the workplace, but also in the context of access to employment, vocational training and promotion. They should therefore be prohibited and should be subject to effective, proportionate and dissuasive penalties.

(7) In this context, employers and those responsible for vocational training should be encouraged to take measures to combat all forms of discrimination on grounds of sex and, in particular, to take preventive measures against harassment and sexual harassment in the workplace and in access to employment, vocational training and promotion, in accordance with national law and practice.

(8) The principle of equal pay for equal work or work of equal value as laid down by Article 141 of the Treaty and consistently upheld in the case-law of the Court of Justice constitutes an important aspect of the principle of equal treatment between men and women and an essential and indispensable part of the acquis communautaire, including the case-law of the Court concerning sex discrimination. It is therefore appropriate to make further provision for its implementation.

(9) In accordance with settled case-law of the Court of Justice, in order to assess whether workers are performing the same work or work of equal value, it should be determined whether, having regard to a range of factors including the nature of the work and training and working conditions, those workers may be considered to be in a comparable situation.

(10) The Court of Justice has established that, in certain circumstances, the principle of equal pay is not limited to situations in which men and women work for the same employer.

(11) The Member States, in collaboration with the social partners, should continue to address the problem of the continuing gender-based wage differentials and marked gender segregation on the labour market by means such as flexible working time arrangements which enable both men and women to combine family and work commitments more successfully. This could also include appropriate parental leave arrangements which could be taken up by either parent as well as the provision of accessible and affordable child-care facilities and care for dependent persons.

(12) Specific measures should be adopted to ensure the implementation of the principle of equal treatment in occupational social security schemes and to define its scope more clearly.

(13) In its judgment of 17 May 1990 in Case C-262/88,[8] the Court of Justice determined that all forms of occupational pension constitute an element of pay within the meaning of Article 141 of the Treaty.

(14) Although the concept of pay within the meaning of Article 141 of the Treaty does not encompass social security benefits, it is now clearly established that a pension scheme for public servants falls within the scope of the principle of equal pay if the benefits payable under the scheme are paid to

[8] C-262/88: Barber v Guardian Royal Exchange Assurance Group (1990 ECR I-1889).

the worker by reason of his/her employment relationship with the public employer, notwithstanding the fact that such scheme forms part of a general statutory scheme. According to the judgments of the Court of Justice in Cases C-7/93[9] and C-351/00,[10] that condition will be satisfied if the pension scheme concerns a particular category of workers and its benefits are directly related to the period of service and calculated by reference to the public servant's final salary. For reasons of clarity, it is therefore appropriate to make specific provision to that effect.

(15) The Court of Justice has confirmed that whilst the contributions of male and female workers to a defined-benefit pension scheme are covered by Article 141 of the Treaty, any inequality in employers' contributions paid under funded defined-benefit schemes which is due to the use of actuarial factors differing according to sex is not to be assessed in the light of that same provision.

(16) By way of example, in the case of funded defined benefit schemes, certain elements, such as conversion into a capital sum of part of a periodic pension, transfer of pension rights, a reversionary pension payable to a dependant in return for the surrender of part of a pension or a reduced pension where the worker opts to take earlier retirement, may be unequal where the inequality of the amounts results from the effects of the use of actuarial factors differing according to sex at the time when the scheme's funding is implemented.

(17) It is well established that benefits payable under occupational social security schemes are not to be considered as remuneration insofar as they are attributable to periods of employment prior to 17 May 1990, except in the case of workers or those claiming under them who initiated legal proceedings or brought an equivalent claim under the applicable national law before that date. It is therefore necessary to limit the implementation of the principle of equal treatment accordingly.

(18) The Court of Justice has consistently held that the Barber Protocol[11] does not affect the right to join an occupational pension scheme and that the limitation of the effects in time of the judgment in Case C-262/88 does not apply to the right to join an occupational pension scheme. The Court of Justice also ruled that the national rules relating to time limits for bringing actions under national law may be relied on against workers who assert their right to join an occupational pension scheme, provided that they are not less favourable for that type of action than for similar actions of a domestic nature and that they do not render the exercise of rights conferred by Community law impossible in practice. The Court of Justice has also pointed out that the fact that a worker can claim retroactively to join an occupational pension scheme does not allow the worker to avoid paying the contributions relating to the period of membership concerned.

(19) Ensuring equal access to employment and the vocational training leading thereto is fundamental to the application of the principle of equal treatment of men and women in matters of employment and occupation. Any exception to this principle should therefore be limited to those occupational activities which necessitate the employment of a person of a particular sex by reason of their nature or the context in which they are carried out, provided that the objective sought is legitimate and complies with the principle of proportionality.

(20) This Directive does not prejudice freedom of association, including the right to establish unions with others and to join unions to defend one's interests. Measures within the meaning of Article 141(4) of the Treaty may include membership or the continuation of the activity of organisations or unions whose main objective is the promotion, in practice, of the principle of equal treatment between men and women.

(21) The prohibition of discrimination should be without prejudice to the maintenance or adoption of measures intended to prevent or compensate for disadvantages suffered by a group of persons of one sex. Such measures permit organisations of persons of one sex where their main object is the promotion of the special needs of those persons and the promotion of equality between men and women.

[9] C-7/93: Bestuur van het Algemeen Burgerlijk Pensioenfonds v G. A. Beune (1994 ECR I-4471).
[10] C-351/00: Pirkko Niemi (2002 ECR I-7007).
[11] Protocol 17 concerning Article 141 of the Treaty establishing the European Community (1992).

(22) In accordance with Article 141(4) of the Treaty, with a view to ensuring full equality in practice between men and women in working life, the principle of equal treatment does not prevent Member States from maintaining or adopting measures providing for specific advantages in order to make it easier for the under-represented sex to pursue a vocational activity or to prevent or compensate for disadvantages in professional careers. Given the current situation and bearing in mind Declaration No 28 to the Amsterdam Treaty, Member States should, in the first instance, aim at improving the situation of women in working life.

(23) It is clear from the case-law of the Court of Justice that unfavourable treatment of a woman related to pregnancy or maternity constitutes direct discrimination on grounds of sex. Such treatment should therefore be expressly covered by this Directive.

(24) The Court of Justice has consistently recognised the legitimacy, as regards the principle of equal treatment, of protecting a woman's biological condition during pregnancy and maternity and of introducing maternity protection measures as a means to achieve substantive equality. This Directive should therefore be without prejudice to Council Directive 92/85/EEC of 19 October 1992 on the introduction of measures to encourage improvements in the safety and health at work of pregnant workers and workers who have recently given birth or are breastfeeding.[12] This Directive should further be without prejudice to Council Directive 96/34/EC of 3 June 1996 on the framework agreement on parental leave concluded by UNICE, CEEP and the ETUC.[13]

(25) For reasons of clarity, it is also appropriate to make express provision for the protection of the employment rights of women on maternity leave and in particular their right to return to the same or an equivalent post, to suffer no detriment in their terms and conditions as a result of taking such leave and to benefit from any improvement in working conditions to which they would have been entitled during their absence.

(26) In the Resolution of the Council and of the Ministers for Employment and Social Policy, meeting within the Council, of 29 June 2000 on the balanced participation of women and men in family and working life,[14] Member States were encouraged to consider examining the scope for their respective legal systems to grant working men an individual and non-transferable right to paternity leave, while maintaining their rights relating to employment.

(27) Similar considerations apply to the granting by Member States to men and women of an individual and non-transferable right to leave subsequent to the adoption of a child. It is for the Member States to determine whether or not to grant such a right to paternity and/or adoption leave and also to determine any conditions, other than dismissal and return to work, which are outside the scope of this Directive.

(28) The effective implementation of the principle of equal treatment requires appropriate procedures to be put in place by the Member States.

(29) The provision of adequate judicial or administrative procedures for the enforcement of the obligations imposed by this Directive is essential to the effective implementation of the principle of equal treatment.

(30) The adoption of rules on the burden of proof plays a significant role in ensuring that the principle of equal treatment can be effectively enforced. As the Court of Justice has held, provision should therefore be made to ensure that the burden of proof shifts to the respondent when there is a prima facie case of discrimination, except in relation to proceedings in which it is for the court or other competent national body to investigate the facts. It is however necessary to clarify that the appreciation of the facts from which it may be presumed that there has been direct or indirect discrimination remains a matter for the relevant national body in accordance with national law or practice. Further, it is for the Member States to introduce, at any appropriate stage of the proceedings, rules of evidence which are more favourable to plaintiffs.

[12] OJ L 348, 28.11.1992, p. 1.
[13] OJ L 145, 19.6.1996, p. 4. Directive as amended by Directive 97/75/EC (OJ L 10, 16.1.1998, p. 24).
[14] OJ C 218, 31.7.2000, p. 5.

(31) With a view to further improving the level of protection offered by this Directive, associations, organisations and other legal entities should also be empowered to engage in proceedings, as the Member States so determine, either on behalf or in support of a complainant, without prejudice to national rules of procedure concerning representation and defence.

(32) Having regard to the fundamental nature of the right to effective legal protection, it is appropriate to ensure that workers continue to enjoy such protection even after the relationship giving rise to an alleged breach of the principle of equal treatment has ended. An employee defending or giving evidence on behalf of a person protected under this Directive should be entitled to the same protection.

(33) It has been clearly established by the Court of Justice that in order to be effective, the principle of equal treatment implies that the compensation awarded for any breach must be adequate in relation to the damage sustained. It is therefore appropriate to exclude the fixing of any prior upper limit for such compensation, except where the employer can prove that the only damage suffered by an applicant as a result of discrimination within the meaning of this Directive was the refusal to take his/her job application into consideration.

(34) In order to enhance the effective implementation of the principle of equal treatment, Member States should promote dialogue between the social partners and, within the framework of national practice, with non-governmental organisations.

(35) Member States should provide for effective, proportionate and dissuasive penalties for breaches of the obligations under this Directive.

(36) Since the objectives of this Directive cannot be sufficiently achieved by the Member States and can therefore be better achieved at Community level, the Community may adopt measures in accordance with the principle of subsidiarity as set out in Article 5 of the Treaty. In accordance with the principle of proportionality, as set out in that Article, this Directive does not go beyond what is necessary in order to achieve those objectives.

(37) For the sake of a better understanding of the different treatment of men and women in matters of employment and occupation, comparable statistics disaggregated by sex should continue to be developed, analysed and made available at the appropriate levels.

(38) Equal treatment of men and women in matters of employment and occupation cannot be restricted to legislative measures. Instead, the European Union and the Member States should continue to promote the raising of public awareness of wage discrimination and the changing of public attitudes, involving all parties concerned at public and private level to the greatest possible extent. The dialogue between the social partners could play an important role in this process.

(39) The obligation to transpose this Directive into national law should be confined to those provisions which represent a substantive change as compared with the earlier Directives. The obligation to transpose the provisions which are substantially unchanged arises under the earlier Directives.

(40) This Directive should be without prejudice to the obligations of the Member States relating to the time limits for transposition into national law and application of the Directives set out in Annex I, Part B.

(41) In accordance with paragraph 34 of the Interinstitutional agreement on better law-making,[15] Member States are encouraged to draw up, for themselves and in the interest of the Community, their own tables, which will, as far as possible, illustrate the correlation between this Directive and the transposition measures and to make them public,

HAVE ADOPTED THIS DIRECTIVE:

[15] OJ C 321, 31.12.2003, p. 1.

Title I General provisions

Article 1 Purpose

The purpose of this Directive is to ensure the implementation of the principle of equal opportunities and equal treatment of men and women in matters of employment and occupation.

To that end, it contains provisions to implement the principle of equal treatment in relation to:

(a) access to employment, including promotion, and to vocational training;

(b) working conditions, including pay;

(c) occupational social security schemes.

It also contains provisions to ensure that such implementation is made more effective by the establishment of appropriate procedures.

Article 2 Definitions

1. For the purposes of this Directive, the following definitions shall apply:

(a) 'direct discrimination': where one person is treated less favourably on grounds of sex than another is, has been or would be treated in a comparable situation;

(b) 'indirect discrimination': where an apparently neutral provision, criterion or practice would put persons of one sex at a particular disadvantage compared with persons of the other sex, unless that provision, criterion or practice is objectively justified by a legitimate aim, and the means of achieving that aim are appropriate and necessary;

(c) 'harassment': where unwanted conduct related to the sex of a person occurs with the purpose or effect of violating the dignity of a person, and of creating an intimidating, hostile, degrading, humiliating or offensive environment;

(d) 'sexual harassment': where any form of unwanted verbal, non-verbal or physical conduct of a sexual nature occurs, with the purpose or effect of violating the dignity of a person, in particular when creating an intimidating, hostile, degrading, humiliating or offensive environment;

(e) 'pay': the ordinary basic or minimum wage or salary and any other consideration, whether in cash or in kind, which the worker receives directly or indirectly, in respect of his/her employment from his/her employer;

(f) 'occupational social security schemes': schemes not governed by Council Directive 79/7/EEC of 19 December 1978 on the progressive implementation of the principle of equal treatment for men and women in matters of social security[16] whose purpose is to provide workers, whether employees or self-employed, in an undertaking or group of undertakings, area of economic activity, occupational sector or group of sectors with benefits intended to supplement the benefits provided by statutory social security schemes or to replace them, whether membership of such schemes is compulsory or optional.

2. For the purposes of this Directive, discrimination includes:

(a) harassment and sexual harassment, as well as any less favourable treatment based on a person's rejection of or submission to such conduct;

(b) instruction to discriminate against persons on grounds of sex;

(c) any less favourable treatment of a woman related to pregnancy or maternity leave within the meaning of Directive 92/85/EEC.

Article 3 Positive action

Member States may maintain or adopt measures within the meaning of Article 141(4) of the Treaty with a view to ensuring full equality in practice between men and women in working life.

[16] OJ L 6, 10.1.1979, p. 24.

Title II Specific provisions

Chapter 1 Equal pay

Article 4 Prohibition of discrimination

For the same work or for work to which equal value is attributed, direct and indirect discrimination on grounds of sex with regard to all aspects and conditions of remuneration shall be eliminated.

In particular, where a job classification system is used for determining pay, it shall be based on the same criteria for both men and women and so drawn up as to exclude any discrimination on grounds of sex.

Chapter 2 Equal treatment in occupational social security schemes

Article 5 Prohibition of discrimination

Without prejudice to Article 4, there shall be no direct or indirect discrimination on grounds of sex in occupational social security schemes, in particular as regards:

(a) the scope of such schemes and the conditions of access to them;

(b) the obligation to contribute and the calculation of contributions;

(c) the calculation of benefits, including supplementary benefits due in respect of a spouse or dependants, and the conditions governing the duration and retention of entitlement to benefits.

Article 6 Personal scope

This Chapter shall apply to members of the working population, including self-employed persons, persons whose activity is interrupted by illness, maternity, accident or involuntary unemployment and persons seeking employment and to retired and disabled workers, and to those claiming under them, in accordance with national law and/or practice.

Article 7 Material scope

1. This Chapter applies to:

(a) occupational social security schemes which provide protection against the following risks:

(i) sickness,

(ii) invalidity,

(iii) old age, including early retirement,

(iv) industrial accidents and occupational diseases,

(v) unemployment;

(b) occupational social security schemes which provide for other social benefits, in cash or in kind, and in particular survivors' benefits and family allowances, if such benefits constitute a consideration paid by the employer to the worker by reason of the latter's employment.

2. This Chapter also applies to pension schemes for a particular category of worker such as that of public servants if the benefits payable under the scheme are paid by reason of the employment relationship with the public employer. The fact that such a scheme forms part of a general statutory scheme shall be without prejudice in that respect.

Article 8 Exclusions from the material scope

1. This Chapter does not apply to:

(a) individual contracts for self-employed persons;

(b) single-member schemes for self-employed persons;

(c) insurance contracts to which the employer is not a party, in the case of workers;

(d) optional provisions of occupational social security schemes offered to participants individually to guarantee them:

(i) either additional benefits,

(ii) or a choice of date on which the normal benefits for self-employed persons will start, or a choice between several benefits;

(e) occupational social security schemes in so far as benefits are financed by contributions paid by workers on a voluntary basis.

2. This Chapter does not preclude an employer granting to persons who have already reached the retirement age for the purposes of granting a pension by virtue of an occupational social security scheme, but who have not yet reached the retirement age for the purposes of granting a statutory retirement pension, a pension supplement, the aim of which is to make equal or more nearly equal the overall amount of benefit paid to these persons in relation to the amount paid to persons of the other sex in the same situation who have already reached the statutory retirement age, until the persons benefiting from the supplement reach the statutory retirement age.

Article 9 Examples of discrimination

1. Provisions contrary to the principle of equal treatment shall include those based on sex, either directly or indirectly, for:

(a) determining the persons who may participate in an occupational social security scheme;

(b) fixing the compulsory or optional nature of participation in an occupational social security scheme;

(c) laying down different rules as regards the age of entry into the scheme or the minimum period of employment or membership of the scheme required to obtain the benefits thereof;

(d) laying down different rules, except as provided for in points (h) and (j), for the reimbursement of contributions when a worker leaves a scheme without having fulfilled the conditions guaranteeing a deferred right to long-term benefits;

(e) setting different conditions for the granting of benefits or restricting such benefits to workers of one or other of the sexes;

(f) fixing different retirement ages;

(g) suspending the retention or acquisition of rights during periods of maternity leave or leave for family reasons which are granted by law or agreement and are paid by the employer;

(h) setting different levels of benefit, except in so far as may be necessary to take account of actuarial calculation factors which differ according to sex in the case of defined-contribution schemes; in the case of funded defined-benefit schemes, certain elements may be unequal where the inequality of the amounts results from the effects of the use of actuarial factors differing according to sex at the time when the scheme's funding is implemented;

(i) setting different levels for workers' contributions;

(j) setting different levels for employers' contributions, except:

(i) in the case of defined-contribution schemes if the aim is to equalise the amount of the final benefits or to make them more nearly equal for both sexes,

(ii) in the case of funded defined-benefit schemes where the employer's contributions are intended to ensure the adequacy of the funds necessary to cover the cost of the benefits defined;

(k) laying down different standards or standards applicable only to workers of a specified sex, except as provided for in points (h) and (j), as regards the guarantee or retention of entitlement to deferred benefits when a worker leaves a scheme.

2. Where the granting of benefits within the scope of this Chapter is left to the discretion of the scheme's management bodies, the latter shall comply with the principle of equal treatment.

Article 10 Implementation as regards self-employed persons

1. Member States shall take the necessary steps to ensure that the provisions of occupational social security schemes for self-employed persons contrary to the principle of equal treatment are

revised with effect from 1 January 1993 at the latest or for Member States whose accession took place after that date, at the date that Directive 86/378/EEC became applicable in their territory.

2. This Chapter shall not preclude rights and obligations relating to a period of membership of an occupational social security scheme for self-employed persons prior to revision of that scheme from remaining subject to the provisions of the scheme in force during that period.

Article 11 Possibility of deferral as regards self-employed persons

As regards occupational social security schemes for self-employed persons, Member States may defer compulsory application of the principle of equal treatment with regard to:

(a) determination of pensionable age for the granting of old-age or retirement pensions, and the possible implications for other benefits:
   (i) either until the date on which such equality is achieved in statutory schemes,
   (ii) or, at the latest, until such equality is prescribed by a directive;

(b) survivors' pensions until Community law establishes the principle of equal treatment in statutory social security schemes in that regard;

(c) the application of Article 9(1)(i) in relation to the use of actuarial calculation factors, until 1 January 1999 or for Member States whose accession took place after that date until the date that Directive 86/378/EEC became applicable in their territory.

Article 12 Retroactive effect

1. Any measure implementing this Chapter, as regards workers, shall cover all benefits under occupational social security schemes derived from periods of employment subsequent to 17 May 1990 and shall apply retroactively to that date, without prejudice to workers or those claiming under them who have, before that date, initiated legal proceedings or raised an equivalent claim under national law. In that event, the implementation measures shall apply retroactively to 8 April 1976 and shall cover all the benefits derived from periods of employment after that date. For Member States which acceded to the Community after 8 April 1976, and before 17 May 1990, that date shall be replaced by the date on which Article 141 of the Treaty became applicable in their territory.

2. The second sentence of paragraph 1 shall not prevent national rules relating to time limits for bringing actions under national law from being relied on against workers or those claiming under them who initiated legal proceedings or raised an equivalent claim under national law before 17 May 1990, provided that they are not less favourable for that type of action than for similar actions of a domestic nature and that they do not render the exercise of rights conferred by Community law impossible in practice.

3. For Member States whose accession took place after 17 May 1990 and which were on 1 January 1994 Contracting Parties to the Agreement on the European Economic Area, the date of 17 May 1990 in the first sentence of paragraph 1 shall be replaced by 1 January 1994.

4. For other Member States whose accession took place after 17 May 1990, the date of 17 May 1990 in paragraphs 1 and 2 shall be replaced by the date on which Article 141 of the Treaty became applicable in their territory.

Article 13 Flexible pensionable age

Where men and women may claim a flexible pensionable age under the same conditions, this shall not be deemed to be incompatible with this Chapter.

Chapter 3 Equal treatment as regards access to employment, vocational training and promotion and working conditions

Article 14 Prohibition of discrimination

1. There shall be no direct or indirect discrimination on grounds of sex in the public or private sectors, including public bodies, in relation to:

(a) conditions for access to employment, to self-employment or to occupation, including selection criteria and recruitment conditions, whatever the branch of activity and at all levels of the professional hierarchy, including promotion;

(b) access to all types and to all levels of vocational guidance, vocational training, advanced vocational training and retraining, including practical work experience;

(c) employment and working conditions, including dismissals, as well as pay as provided for in Article 141 of the Treaty;

(d) membership of, and involvement in, an organisation of workers or employers, or any organisation whose members carry on a particular profession, including the benefits provided for by such organisations.

2. Member States may provide, as regards access to employment including the training leading thereto, that a difference of treatment which is based on a characteristic related to sex shall not constitute discrimination where, by reason of the nature of the particular occupational activities concerned or of the context in which they are carried out, such a characteristic constitutes a genuine and determining occupational requirement, provided that its objective is legitimate and the requirement is proportionate.

Article 15 Return from maternity leave

A woman on maternity leave shall be entitled, after the end of her period of maternity leave, to return to her job or to an equivalent post on terms and conditions which are no less favourable to her and to benefit from any improvement in working conditions to which she would have been entitled during her absence.

Article 16 Paternity and adoption leave

This Directive is without prejudice to the right of Member States to recognise distinct rights to paternity and/or adoption leave. Those Member States which recognise such rights shall take the necessary measures to protect working men and women against dismissal due to exercising those rights and ensure that, at the end of such leave, they are entitled to return to their jobs or to equivalent posts on terms and conditions which are no less favourable to them, and to benefit from any improvement in working conditions to which they would have been entitled during their absence.

Title III Horizontal provisions

Chapter 1 Remedies and enforcement

Section 1 Remedies

Article 17 Defence of rights

1. Member States shall ensure that, after possible recourse to other competent authorities including where they deem it appropriate conciliation procedures, judicial procedures for the enforcement of obligations under this Directive are available to all persons who consider themselves wronged by failure to apply the principle of equal treatment to them, even after the relationship in which the discrimination is alleged to have occurred has ended.

2. Member States shall ensure that associations, organisations or other legal entities which have, in accordance with the criteria laid down by their national law, a legitimate interest in ensuring that the provisions of this Directive are complied with, may engage, either on behalf or in support of the complainant, with his/her approval, in any judicial and/or administrative procedure provided for the enforcement of obligations under this Directive.

3. Paragraphs 1 and 2 are without prejudice to national rules relating to time limits for bringing actions as regards the principle of equal treatment.

Article 18 Compensation or reparation

Member States shall introduce into their national legal systems such measures as are necessary to ensure real and effective compensation or reparation as the Member States so determine for the loss and damage sustained by a person injured as a result of discrimination on grounds of sex, in a way which is dissuasive and proportionate to the damage suffered. Such compensation or reparation may not be restricted by the fixing of a prior upper limit, except in cases where the employer can prove that the only damage suffered by an applicant as a result of discrimination within the meaning of this Directive is the refusal to take his/her job application into consideration.

Section 2 Burden of proof

Article 19 Burden of proof

1. Member States shall take such measures as are necessary, in accordance with their national judicial systems, to ensure that, when persons who consider themselves wronged because the principle of equal treatment has not been applied to them establish, before a court or other competent authority, facts from which it may be presumed that there has been direct or indirect discrimination, it shall be for the respondent to prove that there has been no breach of the principle of equal treatment.

2. Paragraph 1 shall not prevent Member States from introducing rules of evidence which are more favourable to plaintiffs.

3. Member States need not apply paragraph 1 to proceedings in which it is for the court or competent body to investigate the facts of the case.

4. Paragraphs 1, 2 and 3 shall also apply to:

(a) the situations covered by Article 141 of the Treaty and, insofar as discrimination based on sex is concerned, by Directives 92/85/EEC and 96/34/EC;

(b) any civil or administrative procedure concerning the public or private sector which provides for means of redress under national law pursuant to the measures referred to in (a) with the exception of out-of-court procedures of a voluntary nature or provided for in national law.

5. This Article shall not apply to criminal procedures, unless otherwise provided by the Member States.

Chapter 2 Promotion of equal treatment—Dialogue

Article 20 Equality bodies

1. Member States shall designate and make the necessary arrangements for a body or bodies for the promotion, analysis, monitoring and support of equal treatment of all persons without discrimination on grounds of sex. These bodies may form part of agencies with responsibility at national level for the defence of human rights or the safeguard of individuals' rights.

2. Member States shall ensure that the competences of these bodies include:

(a) without prejudice to the right of victims and of associations, organisations or other legal entities referred to in Article 17(2), providing independent assistance to victims of discrimination in pursuing their complaints about discrimination;

(b) conducting independent surveys concerning discrimination;

(c) publishing independent reports and making recommendations on any issue relating to such discrimination;

(d) at the appropriate level exchanging available information with corresponding European bodies such as any future European Institute for Gender Equality.

Article 21 Social dialogue

1. Member States shall, in accordance with national traditions and practice, take adequate measures to promote social dialogue between the social partners with a view to fostering equal treatment, including, for example, through the monitoring of practices in the workplace, in access to employment, vocational training and promotion, as well as through the monitoring of collective agreements, codes of conduct, research or exchange of experience and good practice.

2. Where consistent with national traditions and practice, Member States shall encourage the social partners, without prejudice to their autonomy, to promote equality between men and women, and flexible working arrangements, with the aim of facilitating the reconciliation of work and private life, and to conclude, at the appropriate level, agreements laying down anti-discrimination rules in the fields referred to in Article 1 which fall within the scope of collective bargaining. These agreements shall respect the provisions of this Directive and the relevant national implementing measures.

3. Member States shall, in accordance with national law, collective agreements or practice, encourage employers to promote equal treatment for men and women in a planned and systematic way in the workplace, in access to employment, vocational training and promotion.

4. To this end, employers shall be encouraged to provide at appropriate regular intervals employees and/or their representatives with appropriate information on equal treatment for men and women in the undertaking.

Such information may include an overview of the proportions of men and women at different levels of the organisation; their pay and pay differentials; and possible measures to improve the situation in cooperation with employees' representatives.

Article 22 Dialogue with non-governmental organisations

Member States shall encourage dialogue with appropriate non-governmental organisations which have, in accordance with their national law and practice, a legitimate interest in contributing to the fight against discrimination on grounds of sex with a view to promoting the principle of equal treatment.

Chapter 3 General horizontal provisions

Article 23 Compliance

Member States shall take all necessary measures to ensure that:

(a) any laws, regulations and administrative provisions contrary to the principle of equal treatment are abolished;

(b) provisions contrary to the principle of equal treatment in individual or collective contracts or agreements, internal rules of undertakings or rules governing the independent occupations and professions and workers' and employers' organisations or any other arrangements shall be, or may be, declared null and void or are amended;

(c) occupational social security schemes containing such provisions may not be approved or extended by administrative measures.

Article 24 Victimisation

Member States shall introduce into their national legal systems such measures as are necessary to protect employees, including those who are employees' representatives provided for by national laws and/or practices, against dismissal or other adverse treatment by the employer as a reaction to a complaint within the undertaking or to any legal proceedings aimed at enforcing compliance with the principle of equal treatment.

Article 25 Penalties

Member States shall lay down the rules on penalties applicable to infringements of the national provisions adopted pursuant to this Directive, and shall take all measures necessary to ensure that they are applied. The penalties, which may comprise the payment of compensation to the victim, must be effective, proportionate and dissuasive. The Member States shall notify those provisions to the Commission by 5 October 2005 at the latest and shall notify it without delay of any subsequent amendment affecting them.

Article 26 Prevention of discrimination

Member States shall encourage, in accordance with national law, collective agreements or practice, employers and those responsible for access to vocational training to take effective measures to prevent all forms of discrimination on grounds of sex, in particular harassment and sexual harassment in the workplace, in access to employment, vocational training and promotion.

Article 27 Minimum requirements

1. Member States may introduce or maintain provisions which are more favourable to the protection of the principle of equal treatment than those laid down in this Directive.

2. Implementation of this Directive shall under no circumstances be sufficient grounds for a reduction in the level of protection of workers in the areas to which it applies, without prejudice to the Member States' right to respond to changes in the situation by introducing laws, regulations and administrative provisions which differ from those in force on the notification of this Directive, provided that the provisions of this Directive are complied with.

Article 28 Relationship to Community and national provisions

1. This Directive shall be without prejudice to provisions concerning the protection of women, particularly as regards pregnancy and maternity.

2. This Directive shall be without prejudice to the provisions of Directive 96/34/EC and Directive 92/85/EEC.

Article 29 Gender mainstreaming

Member States shall actively take into account the objective of equality between men and women when formulating and implementing laws, regulations, administrative provisions, policies and activities in the areas referred to in this Directive.

Article 30 Dissemination of information

Member States shall ensure that measures taken pursuant to this Directive, together with the provisions already in force, are brought to the attention of all the persons concerned by all suitable means and, where appropriate, at the workplace.

Title IV Final provisions

Article 31 Reports

1. By 15 February 2011, the Member States shall communicate to the Commission all the information necessary for the Commission to draw up a report to the European Parliament and the Council on the application of this Directive.

2. Without prejudice to paragraph 1, Member States shall communicate to the Commission, every four years, the texts of any measures adopted pursuant to Article 141(4) of the Treaty, as well as reports on these measures and their implementation. On the basis of that information, the Commission will adopt and publish every four years a report establishing a comparative assessment of any measures in the light of Declaration No 28 annexed to the Final Act of the Treaty of Amsterdam.

3. Member States shall assess the occupational activities referred to in Article 14(2), in order to decide, in the light of social developments, whether there is justification for maintaining the exclusions concerned. They shall notify the Commission of the results of this assessment periodically, but at least every 8 years.

Article 32 Review

By 15 February 2011 at the latest, the Commission shall review the operation of this Directive and if appropriate, propose any amendments it deems necessary.

Article 33 Implementation

Member States shall bring into force the laws, regulations and administrative provisions necessary to comply with this Directive by 15 August 2008 at the latest or shall ensure, by that date, that management and labour introduce the requisite provisions by way of agreement. Member States may, if necessary to take account of particular difficulties, have up to one additional year to comply with this

Directive. Member States shall take all necessary steps to be able to guarantee the results imposed by this Directive. They shall forthwith communicate to the Commission the texts of those measures.

When Member States adopt these measures, they shall contain a reference to this Directive or be accompanied by such reference on the occasion of their official publication. They shall also include a statement that references in existing laws, regulations and administrative provisions to the Directives repealed by this Directive shall be construed as references to this Directive. Member States shall determine how such reference is to be made and how that statement is to be formulated.

The obligation to transpose this Directive into national law shall be confined to those provisions which represent a substantive change as compared with the earlier Directives. The obligation to transpose the provisions which are substantially unchanged arises under the earlier Directives.

Member States shall communicate to the Commission the text of the main provisions of national law which they adopt in the field covered by this Directive.

Article 34 Repeal

1. With effect from 15 August 2009 Directives 75/117/EEC, 76/207/EEC, 86/378/EEC and 97/80/EC shall be repealed without prejudice to the obligations of the Member States relating to the time-limits for transposition into national law and application of the Directives set out in Annex I, Part B.

2. References made to the repealed Directives shall be construed as being made to this Directive and should be read in accordance with the correlation table in Annex II.

Article 35 Entry into force

This Directive shall enter into force on the 20th day following its publication in the *Official Journal of the European Union*.

Article 36 Addressees

This Directive is addressed to the Member States.

Done at Strasbourg, 5 July 2006.
For the European Parliament
The President
J. BORRELL FONTELLES
For the Council
The President P. LEHTOMÄKI

Annex II

Correlation table

Directive 75/117/EEC	Directive 76/207/EEC	Directive 86/378/EEC	Directive 97/80/EC	This Directive
—	Article 1(1)	Article 1	Article 1	Article 1
—	Article 1(2)	—	—	—
—	Article 2(2), first indent	—	—	Article 2(1), (a)
—	Article 2(2), second indent	—	Article 2(2)	Article 2(1), (b)
—	Article 2(2), third and fourth indents	—	—	Article 2(1), (c) and (d)
—	—	—	—	Article 2(1), (e)

Directive 75/117/EEC	Directive 76/207/EEC	Directive 86/378/EEC	Directive 97/80/EC	This Directive
—	—	Article 2(1)	—	Article 2(1), (f)
—	Article 2(3) and (4) and Article 2(7) third subparagraph	—	—	Article 2(2)
—	Article 2(8)	—	—	Article 3
Article 1	—	—	—	Article 4
—	—	Article 5(1)	—	Article 5
—	—	Article 3	—	Article 6
—	—	Article 4	—	Article 7(1)
—	—	—	—	Article 7(2)
		Article 2(2)		Article 8(1)
—	—	Article 2(3)	—	Article 8(2)
—	—	Article 6	—	Article 9
—	—	Article 8	—	Article 10
—	—	Article 9	—	Article 11
—	—	(Article 2 of Directive 96/97/EE)	—	Article 12
—	—	Article 9a	—	Article 13
—	Articles 2(1) and 3(1)	—	Article 2(1)	Article 14(1)
—	Article 2(6)	—	—	Article 14(2)
—	Article 2(7), second subparagraph	—	—	Article 15
—	Article 2(7), fourth subparagraph, second and third sentence	—	—	Article 16
Article 2	Article 6(1)	Article 10	—	Article 17(1)
—	Article 6(3)	—	—	Article 17(2)
—	Article 6(4)	—	—	Article 17(3)
—	Article 6(2)	—	—	Article 18
—	—	—	Articles 3 and 4	Article 19
—	Article 8a	—	—	Article 20
—	Article 8b	—	—	Article 21
—	Article 8c	—	—	Article 22
Articles 3 and 6	Article 3 (2)(a)	—	—	Article 23(a)
Article 4	Article 3(2)(b)	Article 7(a)	—	Article 23(b)
—	—	Article 7(b)	—	Article 23(c)
Article 5	Article 7	Article 11	—	Article 24
Article 6	—	—	—	—
—	Article 8d	—	—	Article 25
	Article 2(5)			Article 26
—	Article 8e(1)	—	Article 4(2)	Article 27(1)
—	Article 8e(2)	—	Article 6	Article 27(2)
—	Article 2(7) first subparagraph	Article 5(2)	—	Article 28(1)

Directive 75/117/EEC	Directive 76/207/EEC	Directive 86/378/EEC	Directive 97/80/EC	This Directive
—	Article 2(7) fourth subparagraph first sentence			Article 28(2)
—	Article 1(1a)			Article 29
Article 7	Article 8	—	Article 5	Article 30
Article 9	Article 10	Article 12(2)	Article 7, fourth subparagraph	Article 31(1) and (2)
—	Article 9(2)	—	—	Article 31(3)
—	—	—	—	Article 32
Article 8	Article 9(1), first subparagraph and 9 (2) and (3)	Article 12(1)	Article 7, first, second and third subparagraphs	Article 33
—	Article 9(1), second subparagraph	—	—	—
—	—	—	—	Article 34
—	—	—	—	Article 35
—	—	—	—	Article 36
—	—	Annex	—	—

Council Directive 2010/18/EU of 8 March 2010 implementing the revised Framework Agreement on parental leave concluded by BUSINESSEUROPE, UEAPME, CEEP and ETUC

[OJ 2010 L68/13]

THE COUNCIL OF THE EUROPEAN UNION,

Having regard to the Treaty on the Functioning of the European Union, and in particular Article 155(2) thereof,

Having regard to the proposal from the European Commission,

Whereas:

(1) Article 153 of the Treaty on the Functioning of the European Union (the "TFEU") enables the Union to support and complement the activities of the Member States, inter alia in the field of equality between men and women with regard to labour market opportunities and treatment at work.

(2) Social dialogue at Union level may, in accordance with Article 155(1) of the TFEU, lead to contractual relations, including agreements, should management and labour (the "social partners") so desire. The social partners may, in accordance with Article 155(2) of the TFEU, request jointly that agreements concluded by them at Union level in matters covered by Article 153 of the TFEU be implemented by a Council decision on a proposal from the Commission.

(3) A Framework Agreement on parental leave was concluded by the European cross-industry social partner organisations (ETUC, UNICE and CEEP) on 14 December 1995 and was given legal

effect by Council Directive 96/34/EC of 3 June 1996 on the framework agreement on parental leave concluded by UNICE, CEEP and the ETUC[1]. That Directive was amended and extended to the United Kingdom of Great Britain and Northern Ireland by Council Directive 97/75/EC[2]. Directive 96/34/EC contributed greatly to improving the opportunities available to working parents in the Member States to better reconcile their work and family responsibilities through leave arrangements.

(4) In accordance with Article 138(2) and (3) of the Treaty establishing the European Community (the "EC Treaty")*, the Commission consulted the European social partners in 2006 and 2007 on ways of further improving the reconciliation of work, private and family life and, in particular, the existing Community legislation on maternity protection and parental leave, and on the possibility of introducing new types of family-related leave, such as paternity leave, adoption leave and leave to care for family members.

(5) The three European general cross-industry social partner organisations (ETUC, CEEP and BUSINESSEUROPE, formerly named UNICE) and the European cross-industry social partner organisation representing a certain category of undertakings (UEAPME) informed the Commission on 11 September 2008 of their wish to enter into negotiations, in accordance with Article 138(4) and Article 139 of the EC Treaty**, with a view to revising the Framework Agreement on parental leave concluded in 1995.

(6) On 18 June 2009, those organisations signed the revised Framework Agreement on parental leave (the "revised Framework Agreement") and addressed a joint request to the Commission to submit a proposal for a Council decision implementing that revised Framework Agreement.

(7) In the course of their negotiations, the European social partners completely revised the 1995 Framework Agreement on parental leave. Therefore Directive 96/34/EC should be repealed and replaced by a new directive rather than being simply amended.

(8) Since the objectives of the Directive, namely to improve the reconciliation of work, private and family life for working parents and equality between men and women with regard to labour market opportunities and treatment at work across the Union, cannot be sufficiently achieved by the Member States and can therefore be better achieved at Union level, the Union may adopt measures, in accordance with the principle of subsidiarity as set out in Article 5 of the Treaty on European Union. In accordance with the principle of proportionality, as set out in that Article, this Directive does not go beyond what is necessary in order to achieve those objectives.

(9) When drafting its proposal for a Directive, the Commission took account of the representative status of the signatory parties to the revised Framework Agreement, their mandate and the legality of the clauses in that revised Framework Agreement and its compliance with the relevant provisions concerning small and medium-sized undertakings.

(10) The Commission informed the European Parliament and the European Economic and Social Committee of its proposal.

(11) Clause 1(1) of the revised Framework Agreement, in line with the general principles of Union law in the social policy area, states that the Agreement lays down minimum requirements.

(12) Clause 8(1) of the revised Framework Agreement states that the Member States may apply or introduce more favourable provisions than those set out in the Agreement.

(13) Clause 8(2) of the revised Framework Agreement states that the implementation of the provisions of the Agreement shall not constitute valid grounds for reducing the general level of protection afforded to workers in the field covered by the Agreement.

(14) Member States should provide for effective, proportionate and dissuasive penalties in the event of any breach of the obligations under this Directive.

[1] OJ L 145, 19.6.1996, p. 4.
[2] OJ L 10, 16.1.1998, p. 24.
* Renumbered: Article 154(2) and (3) of the TFEU.
** Renumbered: Articles 154(4) and 155 of the TFEU.

(15) Member States may entrust the social partners, at their joint request, with the implementation of this Directive, as long as such Member States take all the steps necessary to ensure that they can at all times guarantee the results imposed by this Directive.

(16) In accordance with point 34 of the Interinstitutional agreement on better law-making[3], Member States are encouraged to draw up, for themselves and in the interests of the Union, their own tables which will, as far as possible, illustrate the correlation between this Directive and the transposition measures, and to make them public,

HAS ADOPTED THIS DIRECTIVE:

Article 1

This Directive puts into effect the revised Framework Agreement on parental leave concluded on 18 June 2009 by the European cross-industry social partner organisations (BUSINESSEUROPE, UEAPME, CEEP and ETUC), as set out in the Annex.

Article 2

Member States shall determine what penalties are applicable when national provisions enacted pursuant to this Directive are infringed. The penalties shall be effective, proportionate and dissuasive.

Article 3

1. Member States shall bring into force the laws, regulations and administrative provisions necessary to comply with this Directive or shall ensure that the social partners have introduced the necessary measures by agreement by 8 March 2012 at the latest. They shall forthwith inform the Commission thereof.

When those provisions are adopted by Member States, they shall contain a reference to this Directive or shall be accompanied by such reference on the occasion of their official publication. The methods of making such reference shall be laid down by Member States.

2. Member States may have a maximum additional period of one year to comply with this Directive, if this is necessary to take account of particular difficulties or implementation by collective agreement. They shall inform the Commission thereof by 8 March 2012 at the latest, stating the reasons for which an additional period is required.

3. Member States shall communicate to the Commission the text of the main provisions of national law which they adopt in the field covered by this Directive.

Article 4

Directive 96/34/EC shall be repealed with effect from 8 March 2012. References to Directive 96/34/EC shall be construed as references to this Directive.

Article 5

This Directive shall enter into force on the 20th day following its publication in the *Official Journal of the European Union*.

Article 6

This Directive is addressed to the Member States.

Done at Brussels, 8 March 2010.
For the Council
The President
C. Corbacho

[3] OJ C 321, 31.12.2003, p. 1.

Annex
Framework agreement on parental leave (revised)

18 June 2009

Preamble

This framework agreement between the European social partners, BUSINESSEUROPE, UEAPME, CEEP and ETUC (and the liaison committee Eurocadres/CEC) revises the framework agreement on parental leave, concluded on 14 December 1995, setting out the minimum requirements on parental leave, as an important means of reconciling professional and family responsibilities and promoting equal opportunities and treatment between men and women.

The European social partners request the Commission to submit this framework agreement to the Council for a Council decision making these requirements binding in the Member States of the European Union.

I. General considerations

1. Having regard to the EC Treaty and in particular Articles 138 and 139 thereof*;

2. Having regard to Articles 137(1)(c) and 141 of the EC Treaty** and the principle of equal treatment (Articles 2, 3 and 13 of the EC Treaty***) and the secondary legislation based on this, in particular Council Directive 75/117/EEC on the approximation of the laws of the Member States relating to the application of the principle of equal pay for men and women[4]; Council Directive 92/85/EEC on the introduction of measures to encourage improvements in the safety and health at work of pregnant workers and workers who have recently given birth or are breastfeeding[5]; Council Directive 96/97/EC amending Directive 86/378/EEC on the implementation of the principle of equal treatment for men and women in occupational social security schemes[6]; and Directive 2006/54/EC on the implementation of the principle of equal opportunities and equal treatment of men and women in matters of employment and occupation (recast)[7];

3. Having regard to the Charter of Fundamental Rights of the European Union of 7 December 2000 and Articles 23 and 33 thereof relating to equality between men and women and reconciliation of professional, private and family life;

4. Having regard to the 2003 Report from the Commission on the Implementation of Council Directive 96/34/EC of 3 June 1996 on the framework agreement on parental leave concluded by UNICE, CEEP and the ETUC;

5. Having regard to the objective of the Lisbon strategy on growth and jobs of increasing overall employment rates to 70 %, women's employment rates to 60 % and the employment rates of older workers to 50 %; to the Barcelona targets on the provision of childcare facilities; and to the contribution of policies to improve reconciliation of professional, private and family life in achieving these targets;

6. Having regard to the European social partners' Framework of Actions on Gender Equality of 22 March 2005 in which supporting work-life balance is addressed as a priority area for action, while recognising that, in order to continue to make progress on the issue of reconciliation, a balanced, integrated and coherent policy mix must be put in place, comprising of leave arrangements, working arrangements and care infrastructures;

* Renumbered: Articles 154 and 155 of the TFEU.

** Renumbered: Articles 153(1)c and 157 of the TFEU.

*** Article 2 of the EC Treaty is repealed and replaced, in substance, by Article 3 of the Treaty on the European Union. Article 3(1) of the EC Treaty is repealed and replaced, in substance, by Articles 3 to 6 of the TFEU. Article 3(2) of the EC Treaty is renumbered as Article 8 of the TFEU. Article 13 of the EC Treaty is renumbered as Article 19 of the TFEU.

4 OJ L 45, 19.2.1975, p. 19–20.

5 OJ L 348, 28.11.1992, p. 1–8.

6 OJ L 46, 17.2.1997, p. 20–24.

7 OJ L 204, 26.7.2006, p. 23–36.

7. Whereas measures to improve reconciliation are part of a broader policy agenda to address the needs of employers and workers and improve adaptability and employability, as part of a flexicurity approach;

8. Whereas family policies should contribute to the achievement of gender equality and be looked at in the context of demographic changes, the effects of an ageing population, closing the generation gap, promoting women's participation in the labour force and the sharing of care responsibilities between women and men;

9. Whereas the Commission has consulted the European social partners in 2006 and 2007 in a first and second stage consultation on reconciliation of professional, private and family life, and, among other things, has addressed the issue of updating the regulatory framework at Community level, and has encouraged the European social partners to assess the provisions of their framework agreement on parental leave with a view to its review;

10. Whereas the Framework agreement of the European social partners of 1995 on parental leave has been a catalyst for positive change, ensured common ground on work life balance in the Member States and played a significant role in helping working parents in Europe to achieve better reconciliation; however, on the basis of a joint evaluation, the European social partners consider that certain elements of the agreement need to be adapted or revised in order to better achieve its aims;

11. Whereas certain aspects need to be adapted, taking into account the growing diversity of the labour force and societal developments including the increasing diversity of family structures, while respecting national law, collective agreements and/or practice;

12. Whereas in many Member States encouraging men to assume an equal share of family responsibilities has not led to sufficient results; therefore, more effective measures should be taken to encourage a more equal sharing of family responsibilities between men and women;

13. Whereas many Member States already have a wide variety of policy measures and practices relating to leave facilities, childcare and flexible working arrangements, tailored to the needs of workers and employers and aiming to support parents in reconciling their professional, private and family life; these should be taken into account when implementing this agreement;

14. Whereas this framework agreement provides one element of European social partners' actions in the field of reconciliation;

15. Whereas this agreement is a framework agreement setting out minimum requirements and provisions for parental leave, distinct from maternity leave, and for time off from work on grounds of force majeure, and refers back to Member States and social partners for the establishment of conditions for access and modalities of application in order to take account of the situation in each Member State;

16. Whereas the right of parental leave in this agreement is an individual right and in principle non-transferable, and Member States are allowed to make it transferable. Experience shows that making the leave non-transferable can act as a positive incentive for the take up by fathers, the European social partners therefore agree to make a part of the leave non-transferable;

17. Whereas it is important to take into account the special needs of parents with children with disabilities or long term illness;

18. Whereas Member States should provide for the maintenance of entitlements to benefits in kind under sickness insurance during the minimum period of parental leave;

19. Whereas Member States should also, where appropriate under national conditions and taking into account the budgetary situation, consider the maintenance of entitlements to relevant social security benefits as they stand during the minimum period of parental leave as well as the role of income among other factors in the take-up of parental leave when implementing this agreement;

20. Whereas experiences in Member States have shown that the level of income during parental leave is one factor that influences the take up by parents, especially fathers;

21. Whereas the access to flexible working arrangements makes it easier for parents to combine work and parental responsibilities and facilitates the reintegration into work, especially after returning from parental leave;

22. Whereas parental leave arrangements are meant to support working parents during a specific period of time, aimed at maintaining and promoting their continued labour market participation; therefore, greater attention should be paid to keeping in contact with the employer during the leave or by making arrangements for return to work;

23. Whereas this agreement takes into consideration the need to improve social policy requirements, to enhance the competitiveness of the European Union economy and to avoid imposing administrative, financial and legal constraints in a way which would hold back the creation and development of small and medium sized undertakings;

24. Whereas the social partners are best placed to find solutions that correspond to the needs of both employers and workers and shall therefore play a special role in the implementation, application, monitoring and evaluation of this agreement, in the broader context of other measures to improve the reconciliation of professional and family responsibilities and to promote equal opportunities and treatment between men and women.

THE SIGNATORY PARTIES HAVE AGREED THE FOLLOWING:

II. Content

Clause 1: Purpose and scope

1. This agreement lays down minimum requirements designed to facilitate the reconciliation of parental and professional responsibilities for working parents, taking into account the increasing diversity of family structures while respecting national law, collective agreements and/or practice.

2. This agreement applies to all workers, men and women, who have an employment contract or employment relationship as defined by the law, collective agreements and/or practice in force in each Member State.

3. Member States and/or social partners shall not exclude from the scope and application of this agreement workers, contracts of employment or employment relationships solely because they relate to part-time workers, fixed-term contract workers or persons with a contract of employment or employment relationship with a temporary agency.

Clause 2: Parental leave

1. This agreement entitles men and women workers to an individual right to parental leave on the grounds of the birth or adoption of a child to take care of that child until a given age up to eight years to be defined by Member States and/or social partners.

2. The leave shall be granted for at least a period of four months and, to promote equal opportunities and equal treatment between men and women, should, in principle, be provided on a non-transferable basis. To encourage a more equal take-up of leave by both parents, at least one of the four months shall be provided on a non-transferable basis. The modalities of application of the non-transferable period shall be set down at national level through legislation and/or collective agreements taking into account existing leave arrangements in the Member States.

Clause 3: Modalities of application

1. The conditions of access and detailed rules for applying parental leave shall be defined by law and/or collective agreements in the Member States, as long as the minimum requirements of this agreement are respected. Member States and/or social partners may, in particular:

(a) decide whether parental leave is granted on a full-time or part-time basis, in a piecemeal way or in the form of a time-credit system, taking into account the needs of both employers and workers;

(b) make entitlement to parental leave subject to a period of work qualification and/or a length of service qualification which shall not exceed one year; Member States and/or social partners shall ensure, when making use of this provision, that in case of successive fixed term contracts, as defined in Council Directive 1999/70/EC on fixed-term work, with the same employer the sum of these contracts shall be taken into account for the purpose of calculating the qualifying period;

(c) define the circumstances in which an employer, following consultation in accordance with national law, collective agreements and/or practice, is allowed to postpone the granting of parental leave for justifiable reasons related to the operation of the organisation. Any problem arising from the application of this provision should be dealt with in accordance with national law, collective agreements and/or practice;

(d) in addition to (c), authorise special arrangements to meet the operational and organisational requirements of small undertakings.

2. Member States and/or social partners shall establish notice periods to be given by the worker to the employer when exercising the right to parental leave, specifying the beginning and the end of the period of leave. Member States and/or social partners shall have regard to the interests of workers and of employers in specifying the length of such notice periods.

3. Member States and/or social partners should assess the need to adjust the conditions for access and modalities of application of parental leave to the needs of parents of children with a disability or a long-term illness.

Clause 4: Adoption

1. Member States and/or social partners shall assess the need for additional measures to address the specific needs of adoptive parents.

Clause 5: Employment rights and non-discrimination

1. At the end of parental leave, workers shall have the right to return to the same job or, if that is not possible, to an equivalent or similar job consistent with their employment contract or employment relationship.

2. Rights acquired or in the process of being acquired by the worker on the date on which parental leave starts shall be maintained as they stand until the end of parental leave. At the end of parental leave, these rights, including any changes arising from national law, collective agreements and/or practice, shall apply.

3. Member States and/or social partners shall define the status of the employment contract or employment relationship for the period of parental leave.

4. In order to ensure that workers can exercise their right to parental leave, Member States and/or social partners shall take the necessary measures to protect workers against less favourable treatment or dismissal on the grounds of an application for, or the taking of, parental leave in accordance with national law, collective agreements and/or practice.

5. All matters regarding social security in relation to this agreement are for consideration and determination by Member States and/or social partners according to national law and/or collective agreements, taking into account the importance of the continuity of the entitlements to social security cover under the different schemes, in particular health care.

All matters regarding income in relation to this agreement are for consideration and determination by Member States and/or social partners according to national law, collective agreements and/or practice, taking into account the role of income—among other factors—in the take-up of parental leave.

Clause 6: Return to work

1. In order to promote better reconciliation, Member States and/or social partners shall take the necessary measures to ensure that workers, when returning from parental leave, may request changes to their working hours and/or patterns for a set period of time. Employers shall consider and respond to such requests, taking into account both employers' and workers' needs.

The modalities of this paragraph shall be determined in accordance with national law, collective agreements and/or practice.

2. In order to facilitate the return to work following parental leave, workers and employers are encouraged to maintain contact during the period of leave and may make arrangements for any appropriate reintegration measures, to be decided between the parties concerned, taking into account national law, collective agreements and/or practice.

Clause 7: Time off from work on grounds of force majeure

1. Member States and/or social partners shall take the necessary measures to entitle workers to time off from work, in accordance with national legislation, collective agreements and/or practice, on grounds of force majeure for urgent family reasons in cases of sickness or accident making the immediate presence of the worker indispensable.

2. Member States and/or social partners may specify the conditions of access and detailed rules for applying clause 7.1 and limit this entitlement to a certain amount of time per year and/or per case.

Clause 8: Final provisions

1. Member States may apply or introduce more favourable provisions than those set out in this agreement.

2. Implementation of the provisions of this agreement shall not constitute valid grounds for reducing the general level of protection afforded to workers in the field covered by this agreement. This shall not prejudice the right of Member States and/or social partners to develop different legislative, regulatory or contractual provisions, in the light of changing circumstances (including the introduction of non-transferability), as long as the minimum requirements provided for in the present agreement are complied with.

3. This agreement shall not prejudice the right of social partners to conclude, at the appropriate level including European level, agreements adapting and/or complementing the provisions of this agreement in order to take into account particular circumstances.

4. Member States shall adopt the laws, regulations and administrative provisions necessary to comply with the Council decision within a period of two years from its adoption or shall ensure that social partners introduce the necessary measures by way of agreement by the end of this period. Member States may, if necessary to take account of particular difficulties or implementation by collective agreements, have up to a maximum of one additional year to comply with this decision.

5. The prevention and settlement of disputes and grievances arising from the application of this agreement shall be dealt with in accordance with national law, collective agreements and/or practice.

6. Without prejudice to the respective role of the Commission, national courts and the European Court of Justice, any matter relating to the interpretation of this agreement at European level should, in the first instance, be referred by the Commission to the signatory parties who will give an opinion.

7. The signatory parties shall review the application of this agreement five years after the date of the Council decision if requested by one of the parties to this agreement.

Done at Brussels, 18 June 2009.
For ETUC
John Monks
General Secretary
On behalf of the trade union delegation
For BUSINESSEUROPE
Philippe de Buck
Director General
For UEAPME
Andrea Benassi
Secretary General
For CEEP
Ralf Resch
General Secretary

Directive 2010/41/EU of the European Parliament and of the Council of 7 July 2010 on the application of the principle of equal treatment between men and women engaged in an activity in a self-employed capacity.

[OJ 2010 L180/1]

THE EUROPEAN PARLIAMENT AND THE COUNCIL OF THE EUROPEAN UNION,

Having regard to the Treaty on the Functioning of the European Union, and in particular Article 157(3) thereof,

Having regard to the proposal from the European Commission,

Having regard to the opinion of the European Economic and Social Committee[1],

Acting in accordance with the ordinary legislative procedure[2],

Whereas:

(1) Council Directive 86/613/EEC of 11 December 1986 on the application of the principle of equal treatment between men and women engaged in an activity, including agriculture, in a self-employed capacity, and on the protection of self-employed women during pregnancy and motherhood[3] ensures application in Member States of the principle of equal treatment as between men and women engaged in an activity in a self-employed capacity, or contributing to the pursuit of such activity. As far as self-employed workers and spouses of self-employed workers are concerned, Directive 86/613/EEC has not been very effective and its scope should be reconsidered, as discrimination based on sex and harassment also occur in areas outside salaried work. In the interest of clarity, Directive 86/613/EEC should be replaced by this Directive.

(2) In its Communication of 1 March 2006 entitled “Roadmap for equality between women and men”, the Commission announced that in order to improve governance of gender equality, it would review the existing Union gender equality legislation not included in the 2005 recast exercise with a view to updating, modernising and recasting where necessary. Directive 86/613/EEC was not included in the recasting exercise.

(3) In its conclusions of 5 and 6 December 2007 on “Balanced roles of women and men for jobs, growth and social cohesion”, the Council called on the Commission to consider the need to revise, if necessary, Directive 86/613/EEC in order to safeguard the rights related to motherhood and fatherhood of self-employed workers and their helping spouses.

(4) The European Parliament has consistently called on the Commission to review Directive 86/613/EEC, in particular so as to boost maternity protection for self-employed women and to improve the situation of spouses of self-employed workers.

(5) The European Parliament has already stated its position on these matters in its resolution of 21 February 1997 on the situation of the assisting spouses of the self-employed[4].

(6) In its Communication of 2 July 2008 entitled “Renewed Social Agenda: Opportunities, access and solidarity in 21st century Europe2, the Commission has affirmed the need to take action on the gender gap in entrepreneurship as well as to improve the reconciliation of private and professional life.

(7) There are already a number of existing legal instruments for the implementation of the principle of equal treatment which cover self-employment activities, in particular Council Directive 79/7/EEC of 19 December 1978 on the progressive implementation of the principle of equal treatment for men and women in matters of social security[5] and Directive 2006/54/EC of the European Parliament and of the Council of 5 July 2006 on the implementation of the principle of equal opportunities and

[1] OJ C 228, 22.9.2009, p. 107.

[2] Position of the European Parliament of 6 May 2009 (not yet published in the Official Journal), Position of the Council at first reading of 8 March 2010 (OJ C 123 E, 12.5.2010, p. 5), Position of the European Parliament of 18 May 2010.

[3] OJ L 359, 19.12.1986, p. 56.

[4] OJ C 85, 17.3.1997, p. 186.

[5] OJ L 6, 10.1.1979, p. 24.

equal treatment of men and women in matters of employment and occupation[6]. This Directive should therefore not apply to the areas already covered by other directives.

(8) This Directive is without prejudice to the powers of the Member States to organise their social protection systems. The exclusive competence of the Member States with regard to the organisation of their social protection systems includes, inter alia decisions on the setting up, financing and management of such systems and related institutions as well as on the substance and delivery of benefits, the level of contributions and the conditions for access.

(9) This Directive should apply to self-employed workers and to their spouses or, when and in so far as recognised by national law, their life partners, where they, under the conditions laid down by national law, habitually participate in the activities of the business. In order to improve the situation for these spouses and, when and in so far as recognised by national law, the life partners of self-employed workers, their work should be recognised.

(10) This Directive should not apply to matters covered by other Directives implementing the principle of equal treatment between men and women, notably Council Directive 2004/113/EC of 13 December 2004 implementing the principle of equal treatment between men and women in the access to and supply of goods and services[7], inter alia, Article 5 of Directive 2004/113/EC on insurance and related financial services remains applicable.

(11) To prevent discrimination based on sex, this Directive should apply to both direct and indirect discrimination. Harassment and sexual harassment should be considered discrimination and therefore prohibited.

(12) This Directive should be without prejudice to the rights and obligations deriving from marital or family status as defined in national law.

(13) The principle of equal treatment should cover the relationships between the self-employed worker and third parties within the remit of this Directive, but not relationships between the self-employed worker and his or her spouse or life partner.

(14) In the area of self-employment, the application of the principle of equal treatment means that there must be no discrimination on grounds of sex, for instance in relation to the establishment, equipment or extension of a business or the launching or extension of any other form of self-employed activity.

(15) Member States may, under Article 157(4) of the Treaty on the Functioning of the European Union, maintain or adopt measures providing for specific advantages in order to make it easier for the under-represented sex to engage in self-employed activities or to prevent or compensate for disadvantages in their professional careers. In principle, measures such as positive action aimed at achieving gender equality in practice should not be seen as being in breach of the legal principle of equal treatment between men and women.

(16) It is necessary to ensure that the conditions for setting up a company between spouses or, when and in so far as recognised by national law, life partners, are not more restrictive than the conditions for setting up a company between other persons.

(17) In view of their participation in the activities of the family business, the spouses or, when and in so far as recognised by national law, the life partners of self-employed workers who have access to a system for social protection, should also be entitled to benefit from social protection. Member States should be required to take the necessary measures to organise this social protection in accordance with national law. In particular, it is up to Member States to decide whether this social protection should be implemented on a mandatory or voluntary basis. Member States may provide that this social protection may be proportional to the participation in the activities of the self-employed worker and/or the level of contribution.

(18) The economic and physical vulnerability of pregnant self-employed workers and pregnant spouses and, when and in so far as recognised by national law, pregnant life partners of self-employed workers, makes it necessary for them to be granted the right to maternity benefits. The Member States

[6] OJ L 204, 26.7.2006, p. 23.
[7] OJ L 373, 21.12.2004, p. 37.

remain competent to organise such benefits, including establishing the level of contributions and all the arrangements concerning benefits and payments, provided the minimum requirements of this Directive are complied with. In particular, they may determine in which period before and/or after confinement the right to maternity benefits is granted.

(19) The length of the period during which female self-employed workers and female spouses or, when and in so far as recognised by national law, female life partners of self-employed workers, are granted maternity benefits is similar to the duration of maternity leave for employees currently in place at Union level. In case the duration of maternity leave provided for employees is modified at Union level, the Commission should report to the European Parliament and the Council assessing whether the duration of maternity benefits for female self-employed workers and female spouses and life partners referred to in Article 2 should also be modified.

(20) In order to take the specificities of self-employed activities into account, female self-employed workers and female spouses or, when and in so far as recognised by national law, female life partners of self-employed workers should be given access to any existing services supplying temporary replacement enabling interruptions in their occupational activity owing to pregnancy or motherhood, or to any existing national social services. Access to those services can be an alternative to or a part of the maternity allowance.

(21) Persons who have been subject to discrimination based on sex should have suitable means of legal protection. To provide more effective protection, associations, organisations and other legal entities should be empowered to engage in proceedings, as Member States so determine, either on behalf or in support of any victim, without prejudice to national rules of procedure concerning representation and defence before the courts.

(22) Protection of self-employed workers and spouses of self-employed workers and, when and in so far as recognised by national law, the life partners of self-employed workers, from discrimination based on sex should be strengthened by the existence of a body or bodies in each Member State with competence to analyse the problems involved, to study possible solutions and to provide practical assistance to the victims. The body or bodies may be the same as those with responsibility at national level for the implementation of the principle of equal treatment.

(23) This Directive lays down minimum requirements, thus giving the Member States the option of introducing or maintaining more favourable provisions.

(24) Since the objective of the action to be taken, namely to ensure a common high level of protection from discrimination in all the Member States, cannot be sufficiently achieved by the Member States and can be better achieved at Union level, the Union may adopt measures, in accordance with the principle of subsidiarity as set out in Article 5 of the Treaty on European Union. In accordance with the principle of proportionality, as set out in that Article, this Directive does not go beyond what is necessary in order to achieve that objective,

HAVE ADOPTED THIS DIRECTIVE:

Article 1 Subject matter

1. This Directive lays down a framework for putting into effect in the Member States the principle of equal treatment between men and women engaged in an activity in a self-employed capacity, or contributing to the pursuit of such an activity, as regards those aspects not covered by Directives 2006/54/EC and 79/7/EEC.

2. The implementation of the principle of equal treatment between men and women in the access to and supply of goods and services remains covered by Directive 2004/113/EC.

Article 2 Scope

This Directive covers:

(a) self-employed workers, namely all persons pursuing a gainful activity for their own account, under the conditions laid down by national law;

(b) the spouses of self-employed workers or, when and in so far as recognised by national law, the life partners of self-employed workers, not being employees or business partners, where they habitually, under the conditions laid down by national law, participate in the activities of the self-employed worker and perform the same tasks or ancillary tasks.

Article 3 Definitions

For the purposes of this Directive, the following definitions shall apply:

(a) "direct discrimination": where one person is treated less favourably on grounds of sex than another is, has been or would be, treated in a comparable situation;

(b) "indirect discrimination": where an apparently neutral provision, criterion or practice would put persons of one sex at a particular disadvantage compared with persons of the other sex, unless that provision, criterion or practice is objectively justified by a legitimate aim, and the means of achieving that aim are appropriate and necessary;

(c) "harassment": where unwanted conduct related to the sex of a person occurs with the purpose, or effect, of violating the dignity of that person, and of creating an intimidating, hostile, degrading, humiliating or offensive environment;

(d) "sexual harassment": where any form of unwanted verbal, non-verbal, or physical, conduct of a sexual nature occurs, with the purpose or effect of violating the dignity of a person, in particular when creating an intimidating, hostile, degrading, humiliating or offensive environment.

Article 4 Principle of equal treatment

1. The principle of equal treatment means that there shall be no discrimination whatsoever on grounds of sex in the public or private sectors, either directly or indirectly, for instance in relation to the establishment, equipment or extension of a business or the launching or extension of any other form of self-employed activity.

2. In the areas covered by paragraph 1, harassment and sexual harassment shall be deemed to be discrimination on grounds of sex and therefore prohibited. A person's rejection of, or submission to, such conduct may not be used as a basis for a decision affecting that person.

3. In the areas covered by paragraph 1, an instruction to discriminate against persons on grounds of sex shall be deemed to be discrimination.

Article 5 Positive action

Member States may maintain or adopt measures within the meaning of Article 157(4) of the Treaty on the Functioning of the European Union with a view to ensuring full equality in practice between men and women in working life, for instance aimed at promoting entrepreneurship initiatives among women.

Article 6 Establishment of a company

Without prejudice to the specific conditions for access to certain activities which apply equally to both sexes, the Member States shall take the measures necessary to ensure that the conditions for the establishment of a company between spouses, or between life partners when and in so far as recognised by national law, are not more restrictive than the conditions for the establishment of a company between other persons.

Article 7 Social protection

1. Where a system for social protection for self-employed workers exists in a Member State, that Member State shall take the necessary measures to ensure that spouses and life partners referred to in Article 2(b) can benefit from a social protection in accordance with national law.

2. The Member States may decide whether the social protection referred to in paragraph 1 is implemented on a mandatory or voluntary basis.

Article 8 Maternity benefits

1. The Member States shall take the necessary measures to ensure that female self-employed workers and female spouses and life partners referred to in Article 2 may, in accordance with national law, be granted a sufficient maternity allowance enabling interruptions in their occupational activity owing to pregnancy or motherhood for at least 14 weeks.

2. The Member States may decide whether the maternity allowance referred to in paragraph 1 is granted on a mandatory or voluntary basis.

3. The allowance referred to in paragraph 1 shall be deemed sufficient if it guarantees an income at least equivalent to:

(a) the allowance which the person concerned would receive in the event of a break in her activities on grounds connected with her state of health and/or;
(b) the average loss of income or profit in relation to a comparable preceding period subject to any ceiling laid down under national law and/or;
(c) any other family related allowance established by national law, subject to any ceiling laid down under national law.

4. The Member States shall take the necessary measures to ensure that female self-employed workers and female spouses and life partners referred to in Article 2 have access to any existing services supplying temporary replacements or to any existing national social services. The Member States may provide that access to those services is an alternative to or a part of the allowance referred to in paragraph 1 of this Article.

Article 9 Defence of rights

1. The Member States shall ensure that judicial or administrative proceedings, including, where Member States consider it appropriate, conciliation procedures, for the enforcement of the obligations under this Directive are available to all persons who consider they have sustained loss or damage as a result of a failure to apply the principle of equal treatment to them, even after the relationship in which the discrimination is alleged to have occurred has ended.

2. The Member States shall ensure that associations, organisations and other legal entities which have, in accordance with the criteria laid down by their national law, a legitimate interest in ensuring that this Directive is complied with may engage, either on behalf or in support of the complainant, with his or her approval, in any judicial or administrative proceedings provided for the enforcement of obligations under this Directive.

3. Paragraphs 1 and 2 shall be without prejudice to national rules on time limits for bringing actions relating to the principle of equal treatment.

Article 10 Compensation or reparation

The Member States shall introduce such measures into their national legal systems as are necessary to ensure real and effective compensation or reparation, as Member States so determine, for the loss or damage sustained by a person as a result of discrimination on grounds of sex, such compensation or reparation being dissuasive and proportionate to the loss or damage suffered. Such compensation or reparation shall not be limited by the fixing of a prior upper limit.

Article 11 Equality bodies

1. The Member States shall take the necessary measures to ensure that the body or bodies designated in accordance with Article 20 of Directive 2006/54/EC are also competent for the promotion, analysis, monitoring and support of equal treatment of all persons covered by this Directive without discrimination on grounds of sex.

2. The Member States shall ensure that the tasks of the bodies referred to in paragraph 1 include:

(a) providing independent assistance to victims of discrimination in pursuing their complaints of discrimination, without prejudice to the rights of victims and of associations, organisations and other legal entities referred to in Article 9(2);
(b) conducting independent surveys on discrimination;
(c) publishing independent reports and making recommendations on any issue relating to such discrimination;
(d) exchanging, at the appropriate level, the information available with the corresponding European bodies, such as the European Institute for Gender Equality.

Article 12 Gender mainstreaming

The Member States shall actively take into account the objective of equality between men and women when formulating and implementing laws, regulations, administrative provisions, policies and activities in the areas referred to in this Directive.

Article 13 Dissemination of information

The Member States shall ensure that the provisions adopted pursuant to this Directive, together with the relevant provisions already in force, are brought by all appropriate means to the attention of the persons concerned throughout their territory.

Article 14 Level of protection

The Member States may introduce or maintain provisions which are more favourable to the protection of the principle of equal treatment between men and women than those laid down in this Directive.

The implementation of this Directive shall under no circumstances constitute grounds for a reduction in the level of protection against discrimination already afforded by Member States in the fields covered by this Directive.

Article 15 Reports

1. Member States shall communicate all available information concerning the application of this Directive to the Commission by 5 August 2015.

The Commission shall draw up a summary report for submission to the European Parliament and to the Council no later than 5 August 2016. That report should take into account any legal change concerning the duration of maternity leave for employees. Where appropriate, that report shall be accompanied by proposals for amending this Directive.

2. The Commission's report shall take the viewpoints of the stakeholders into account.

Article 16 Implementation

1. The Member States shall bring into force the laws, regulations and administrative provisions necessary to comply with this Directive by 5 August 2012 at the latest. They shall forthwith communicate to the Commission the text of those provisions.

When the Member States adopt those provisions, they shall contain a reference to this Directive or be accompanied by such a reference on the occasion of their official publication. Member States shall determine how such reference is to be made.

2. Where justified by particular difficulties, the Member States may, if necessary, have an additional period of two years until 5 August 2014 in order to comply with Article 7, and in order to comply with Article 8 as regards female spouses and life partners referred to in Article 2(b).

3. The Member States shall communicate to the Commission the text of the main provisions of national law which they adopt in the field covered by this Directive.

Article 17 Repeal

Directive 86/613/EEC shall be repealed, with effect from 5 August 2012.

References to the repealed Directive shall be construed as references to this Directive.

Article 18 Entry into force

This Directive shall enter into force on the 20th day following its publication in the *Official Journal of the European Union*.

Article 19 Addressees

This Directive is addressed to the Member States.

Done at Strasbourg, 7 July 2010
For the European Parliament
The President
J. BUZEK
For the Council
The President
O. CHASTEL

Council Directive 2001/23/EC of 12 March 2001 on the approximation of the laws of the Member States relating to the safeguarding of employees' rights in the event of transfers of undertakings, businesses or parts of undertakings or businesses*

[OJ 2001 L82/16]

THE COUNCIL OF THE EUROPEAN UNION,

Having regard to the Treaty establishing the European Community, and in particular Article 94 thereof,

Having regard to the proposal from the Commission,

Having regard to the opinion of the European Parliament,[1]

Having regard to the opinion of the Economic and Social Committee,[2]

Whereas:

(1) Council Directive 77/1877/EEC of 14 February 1977 on the approximation of the laws of the Member States relating to the safeguarding of employees' rights in the event of transfers of undertakings, businesses or parts of undertakings or businesses[3] has been substantially amended.[4] In the interests of clarity and rationality, it should therefore be codified.

(2) Economic trends are bringing in their wake, at both national and Community level, changes in the structure of undertakings, through transfers of undertakings, businesses or parts of undertakings or businesses to other employers as a result of legal transfers or mergers.

(3) It is necessary to provide for the protection of employees in the event of a change of employer, in particular, to ensure that their rights are safeguarded.

(4) Differences still remain in the Member States as regards the extent of the protection of employees in this respect and these differences should be reduced.

(5) The Community Charter of the Fundamental Social Rights of Workers adopted on 9 December 1989 ('Social Charter') states, in points 7, 17 and 18 in particular that: 'The completion of the internal market must lead to an improvement in the living and working conditions of workers in the European Community. The improvement must cover, where necessary, the development of certain aspects of employment regulations such as procedures for collective redundancies and those regarding bankruptcies. Information, consultation and participation for workers must be developed along appropriate lines, taking account of the practice in force in the various Member States. Such information, consultation and participation must be implemented in due time, particularly in connection with restructuring operations in undertakings or in cases of mergers having an impact on the employment of workers'.

* **Editor's Note:** This Directive repeals and replaces Council Directive 77/187/EEC (OJ L61, 5.3.1977, p. 26) and Council Directive 98/50/EC (OJ L201, 17.7.1998, p. 88).

[1] Opinion delivered on 25 October 2000 (not yet published in the Official Journal).

[2] OJ C 367, 20.12.2000, p. 21.

[3] OJ L 61, 5.3.1977, p. 26.

[4] See Annex I, Part A.

(6) In 1977 the Council adopted Directive 77/187/EEC to promote the harmonisation of the relevant national laws ensuring the safeguarding of the rights of employees and requiring transferors and transferees to inform and consult employees' representatives in good time.

(7) That Directive was subsequently amended in the light of the impact of the internal market, the legislative tendencies of the Member States with regard to the rescue of undertakings in economic difficulties, the case-law of the Court of Justice of the European Communities, Council Directive 75/129/EEC of 17 February 1975 on the approximation of the laws of the Member States relating to collective redundancies[5] and the legislation already in force in most Member States.

(8) Considerations of legal security and transparency required that the legal concept of transfer be clarified in the light of the case-law of the Court of Justice. Such clarification has not altered the scope of Directive 77/187/EEC as interpreted by the Court of Justice.

(9) The Social Charter recognises the importance of the fight against all forms of discrimination, especially based on sex, colour, race, opinion and creed.

(10) This Directive should be without prejudice to the time limits set out in Annex I Part B within which the Member States are to comply with Directive 77/187/EEC, and the act amending it,

HAS ADOPTED THIS DIRECTIVE:

Chapter I Scope and definitions

Article 1

1. (a) This Directive shall apply to any transfer of an undertaking, business, or part of an undertaking or business to another employer as a result of a legal transfer or merger.
   (b) Subject to subparagraph (a) and the following provisions of this Article, there is a transfer within the meaning of this Directive where there is a transfer of an economic entity which retains its identity, meaning an organised grouping of resources which has the objective of pursuing an economic activity, whether or not that activity is central or ancillary.
   (c) This Directive shall apply to public and private undertakings engaged in economic activities whether or not they are operating for gain. An administrative reorganisation of public administrative authorities, or the transfer of administrative functions between public administrative authorities, is not a transfer within the meaning of this Directive.

2. This Directive shall apply where and in so far as the undertaking, business or part of the undertaking or business to be transferred is situated within the territorial scope of the Treaty.

3. This Directive shall not apply to seagoing vessels.

Article 2

1. For the purposes of this Directive:
   (a) 'transferor' shall mean any natural or legal person who, by reason of a transfer within the meaning of Article 1(1), ceases to be the employer in respect of the undertaking, business or part of the undertaking or business;
   (b) 'transferee' shall mean any natural or legal person who, by reason of a transfer within the meaning of Article 1(1), becomes the employer in respect of the undertaking, business or part of the undertaking or business;
   (c) 'representatives of employees' and related expressions shall mean the representatives of the employees provided for by the laws or practices of the Member States;
   (d) 'employee' shall mean any person who, in the Member State concerned, is protected as an employee under national employment law.

2. This Directive shall be without prejudice to national law as regards the definition of contract of employment or employment relationship. However, Member States shall not exclude from the scope of this Directive contracts of employment or employment relationships solely because:
   (a) of the number of working hours performed or to be performed,

[5] OJ L 48, 22.2.1975, p. 29. Directive replaced by Directive 98/59/EC (OJ L 225, 12.8.1998, p. 6).

(b) they are employment relationships governed by a fixed-duration contract of employment within the meaning of Article 1(1) of Council Directive 91/383/EEC of 25 June 1991 supplementing the measures to encourage improvements in the safety and health at work of workers with a fixed-duration employment relationship or a temporary employment relationship,[6] or

(c) they are temporary employment relationships within the meaning of Article 1(2) of Directive 91/383/EEC, and the undertaking, business or part of the undertaking or business transferred is, or is part of, the temporary employment business which is the employer.

Chapter II Safeguarding of employees' rights

Article 3

1. The transferor's rights and obligations arising from a contract of employment or from an employment relationship existing on the date of a transfer shall, by reason of such transfer, be transferred to the transferee.

Member States may provide that, after the date of transfer, the transferor and the transferee shall be jointly and severally liable in respect of obligations which arose before the date of transfer from a contract of employment or an employment relationship existing on the date of the transfer.

2. Member States may adopt appropriate measures to ensure that the transferor notifies the transferee of all the rights and obligations which will be transferred to the transferee under this Article, so far as those rights and obligations are or ought to have been known to the transferor at the time of the transfer. A failure by the transferor to notify the transferee of any such right or obligation shall not affect the transfer of that right or obligation and the rights of any employees against the transferee and/or transferor in respect of that right or obligation.

3. Following the transfer, the transferee shall continue to observe the terms and conditions agreed in any collective agreement on the same terms applicable to the transferor under that agreement, until the date of termination or expiry of the collective agreement or the entry into force or application of another collective agreement. Member States may limit the period for observing such terms and conditions with the proviso that it shall not be less than one year.

4. (a) Unless Member States provide otherwise, paragraphs 1 and 3 shall not apply in relation to employees' rights to old-age, invalidity or survivors' benefits under supplementary company or intercompany pension schemes outside the statutory social security schemes in Member States.

(b) Even where they do not provide in accordance with sub-paragraph (a) that paragraphs 1 and 3 apply in relation to such rights, Member States shall adopt the measures necessary to protect the interests of employees and of persons no longer employed in the transferor's business at the time of the transfer in respect of rights conferring on them immediate or prospective entitlement to old age benefits, including survivors' benefits, under supplementary schemes referred to in subparagraph (a).

Article 4

1. The transfer of the undertaking, business or part of the undertaking or business shall not in itself constitute grounds for dismissal by the transferor or the transferee. This provision shall not stand in the way of dismissals that may take place for economic, technical or organisational reasons entailing changes in the workforce. Member States may provide that the first sub-paragraph shall not apply to certain specific categories of employees who are not covered by the laws or practice of the Member States in respect of protection against dismissal.

[6] OJ L 206, 29.7.1991, p. 19.

2. If the contract of employment or the employment relationship is terminated because the transfer involves a substantial change in working conditions to the detriment of the employee, the employer shall be regarded as having been responsible for termination of the contract of employment or of the employment relationship.

Article 5

1. Unless Member States provide otherwise, Articles 3 and 4 shall not apply to any transfer of an undertaking, business or part of an undertaking or business where the transferor is the subject of bankruptcy proceedings or any analogous insolvency proceedings which have been instituted with a view to the liquidation of the assets of the transferor and are under the supervision of a competent public authority (which may be an insolvency practitioner authorised by a competent public authority).

2. Where Articles 3 and 4 apply to a transfer during insolvency proceedings which have been opened in relation to a transferor (whether or not those proceedings have been instituted with a view to the liquidation of the assets of the transferor) and provided that such proceedings are under the supervision of a competent public authority (which may be an insolvency practitioner determined by national law) a Member State may provide that:

(a) notwithstanding Article 3(1), the transferor's debts arising from any contracts of employment or employment relationships and payable before the transfer or before the opening of the insolvency proceedings shall not be transferred to the transferee, provided that such proceedings give rise, under the law of that Member State, to protection at least equivalent to that provided for in situations covered by Council Directive 80/987/EEC of 20 October 1980 on the approximation of the laws of the Member States relating to the protection of employees in the event of the insolvency of their employer,[7] and, or alternatively, that,

(b) the transferee, transferor or person or persons exercising the transferor's functions, on the one hand, and the representatives of the employees on the other hand may agree alterations, in so far as current law or practice permits, to the employees' terms and conditions of employment designed to safeguard employment opportunities by ensuring the survival of the undertaking, business or part of the undertaking or business.

3. A Member State may apply paragraph 20(b) to any transfers where the transferor is in a situation of serious economic crisis, as defined by national law, provided that the situation is declared by a competent public authority and open to judicial supervision, on condition that such provisions already existed in national law on 17 July 1998.

The Commission shall present a report on the effects of this provision before 17 July 2003 and shall submit any appropriate proposals to the Council.

4. Member States shall take appropriate measures with a view to preventing misuse of insolvency proceedings in such a way as to deprive employees of the rights provided for in this Directive.

Article 6

1. If the undertaking, business or part of an undertaking or business preserves its autonomy, the status and function of the representatives or of the representation of the employees affected by the transfer shall be preserved on the same terms and subject to the same conditions as existed before the date of the transfer by virtue of law, regulation, administrative provision or agreement, provided that the conditions necessary for the constitution of the employee's representation are fulfilled.

The first subparagraph shall not apply if, under the laws, regulations, administrative provisions or practice in the Member States, or by agreement with the representatives of the employees,

[7] OJ L 283, 20.10.1980, p. 23. Directive as last amended by the 1994 Act of Accession.

the conditions necessary for the reappointment of the representatives of the employees or for the reconstitution of the representation of the employees are fulfilled.

Where the transferor is the subject of bankruptcy proceedings or any analogous insolvency proceedings which have been instituted with a view to the liquidation of the assets of the transferor and are under the supervision of a competent public authority (which may be an insolvency practitioner authorised by a competent public authority), Member States may take the necessary measures to ensure that the transferred employees are properly represented until the new election or designation of representatives of the employees.

If the undertaking, business or part of an undertaking or business does not preserve its autonomy, the Member States shall take the necessary measures to ensure that the employees transferred who were represented before the transfer continue to be properly represented during the period necessary for the reconstitution or reappointment of the representation of employees in accordance with national law or practice.

2. If the term of office of the representatives of the employees affected by the transfer expires as a result of the transfer, the representatives shall continue to enjoy the protection provided by the laws, regulations, administrative provisions or practice of the Member States.

Chapter III Information and consultation

Article 7

1. The transferor and transferee shall be required to inform the representatives of their respective employees affected by the transfer of the following:

- the date or proposed date of the transfer,
- the reasons for the transfer,
- the legal, economic and social implications of the transfer for the employees,
- any measures envisaged in relation to the employees.

The transferor must give such information to the representatives of his employees in good time, before the transfer is carried out.

The transferee must give such information to the representatives of his employees in good time, and in any event before his employees are directly affected by the transfer as regards their conditions of works and employment.

2. Where the transferor or the transferee envisages measures in relation to his employees, he shall consult the representatives of his employees in good time on such measures with a view to reaching an agreement.

3. Member States whose laws, regulations or administrative provisions provide that representatives of the employees may have recourse to an arbitration board to obtain a decision on the measures to be taken in relation to employees may limit the obligations laid down in paragraphs 1 and 2 to cases where the transfer carried out gives rise to a change in the business likely to entail serious disadvantages for a considerable number of the employees. The information and consultations shall cover at least the measures envisaged in relation to the employees.

The information must be provided and consultations take place in good time before the change in the business as referred to in the first subparagraph is effected.

4. The obligations laid down in this Article shall apply irrespective of whether the decision resulting in the transfer is taken by the employer or an undertaking controlling the employer.

In considering alleged breaches of the information and consultation requirements laid down by this Directive, the argument that such a breach occurred because the information was not provided by an undertaking controlling the employer shall not be accepted as an excuse.

5. Member States may limit the obligations laid down in paragraphs 1, 2 and 3 to undertakings or businesses which, in terms of the number of employees, meet the conditions for the election or nomination of a collegiate body representing the employees.

6. Member States shall provide that, where there are no representatives of the employees in an undertaking or business through no fault of their own, the employees concerned must be informed in advance of:

- the date or proposed date of the transfer,
- the reason for the transfer,
- the legal, economic and social implications of the transfer for the employees,
- any measures envisaged in relation to the employees.

Chapter IV Final provisions

Article 8
This Directive shall not affect the right of Member States to apply or introduce laws, regulations or administrative provisions which are more favourable to employees or to promote or permit collective agreements or agreements between social partners more favourable to employees.

Article 9
Member States shall introduce into their national legal systems such measures as are necessary to enable all employees and representatives of employees who consider themselves wronged by failure to comply with the obligations arising from this Directive to pursue their claims by judicial process after possible recourse to other competent authorities.

Article 10
The Commission shall submit to the Council an analysis of the effect of the provisions of this Directive before 17 July 2006. It shall propose any amendment which may seem necessary.

Article 11
Member States shall communicate to the Commission the texts of the laws, regulations and administrative provisions which they adopt in the field covered by this Directive.

Article 12
Directive 77/187/EEC, as amended by the Directive referred to in Annex I, Part A, is repealed, without prejudice to the obligations of the Member States concerning the time limits for implementation set out in Annex I, Part B.

References to the repealed Directive shall be construed as references to this Directive and shall be read in accordance with the correlation table in Annex II.

Article 13
This Directive shall enter into force on the 20th day following its publication in the *Official Journal of the European Communities*.

Article 14
This Directive is addressed to the Member States.

Done at Brussels, 12 March 2001.
For the Council
The President
B. RINGHOLM

Annex I

Part A

Repealed Directive and its amending Directive (referred to in Article 12)

Council Directive 77/ 187/EEC (OJ L61, 5.3.1977, p. 26)
Council Directive 98/50/EC (OJ L201, 17.7.1998, p. 88)

Part B

Deadlines for transposition into national law (referred to in Article 12)

Directive	Deadline for transposition
77/187/EEC	16 February 1979
98/50/EC	17 July 2001

Annex II Correlation table

Directive 77/187/EEC	This Directive
Article 1	Article 1
Article 2	Article 2
Article 3	Article 3
Article 4	Article 4
Article 4a	Article 5
Article 5	Article 6
Article 6	Article 7
Article 7	Article 8
Article 7a	Article 9
Article 7b	Article 10
Article 8	Article 11
–	Article 12
–	Article 13
–	Article 14
–	Annex I
–	Annex II

Council Directive of 12 June 1989 on the introduction of measures to encourage improvements in the safety and health of workers at work (89/391/EEC)*

[OJ 1989 L183/1]

THE COUNCIL OF THE EUROPEAN COMMUNITIES,

Having regard to the Treaty establishing the European Economic Community, and in particular Article 118a thereof,

(Recitals and Preamble omitted.)

HAS ADOPTED THIS DIRECTIVE:

Section I General provisions

Article 1 Object

1. The object of this Directive is to introduce measures to encourage improvements in the safety and health of workers at work.

2. To that end it contains general principles concerning the prevention of occupational risks, the protection of safety and health, the elimination of risk and accident factors, the informing, consultation, balanced participation in accordance with national laws and/or practices and training of workers and their representatives, as well as general guidelines for the implementation of the said principles.

3. This Directive shall be without prejudice to existing or future national and Community provisions which are more favourable to protection of the safety and health of workers at work.

Article 2 Scope

1. This Directive shall apply to all sectors of activity, both public and private (industrial, agricultural, commercial, administrative, service, educational, cultural, leisure, etc.).

2. This Directive shall not be applicable where characteristics peculiar to certain specific public service activities, such as the armed forces or the police, or to certain specific activities in the civil protection services inevitably conflict with it.

In that event, the safety and health of workers must be ensured as far as possible in the light of the objectives of this Directive.

Article 3 Definitions

For the purposes of this Directive, the following terms shall have the following meanings:

(a) worker: any person employed by an employer, including trainees and apprentices but excluding domestic servants;

(b) employer: any natural or legal person who has an employment relationship with the worker and has responsibility for the undertaking and/or establishment;

(c) workers' representative with specific responsibility for the safety and health of workers: any person elected, chosen or designated in accordance with national laws and/or practices to represent workers where problems arise relating to the safety and health protection of workers at work;

(d) prevention: all the steps or measures taken or planned at all stages of work in the undertaking to prevent or reduce occupational risks.

Article 4

1. Member States shall take the necessary steps to ensure that employers, workers and workers' representatives are subject to the legal provisions necessary for the implementation of this Directive.

2. In particular, Member States shall ensure adequate controls and supervision.

* **Editor's Note:** Amended by Regulation 2003/1882, OJ 2003 L284/1 and Directive 2007/30, OJ 2007 L165/21 and Regulation 1137/2008 OJ 2008 L311/1.

Section II Employers' obligations

Article 5 General provision

1. The employer shall have a duty to ensure the safety and health of workers in every aspect related to the work.

2. Where, pursuant to Article 7(3), an employer enlists competent external services or persons, this shall not discharge him from his responsibilities in this area.

3. The workers' obligations in the field of safety and health at work shall not affect the principle of the responsibility of the employer.

4. This Directive shall not restrict the option of Member States to provide for the exclusion or the limitation of employers' responsibility where occurrences are due to unusual and unforeseeable circumstances, beyond the employers' control, or to exceptional events, the consequences of which could not have been avoided despite the exercise of all due care.

Member States need not exercise the option referred to in the first subparagraph.

Article 6 General obligations on employers

1. Within the context of his responsibilities, the employer shall take the measures necessary for the safety and health protection of workers, including prevention of occupational risks and provision of information and training, as well as provision of the necessary organisation and means.

The employer shall be alert to the need to adjust these measures to take account of changing circumstances and aim to improve existing situations.

2. The employer shall implement the measures referred to in the first sub-paragraph of paragraph 1 on the basis of the following general principles of prevention:

(a) avoiding risks;
(b) evaluating the risks which cannot be avoided;
(c) combating the risks at source;
(d) adapting the work to the individual, especially as regards the design of work places, the choice of work equipment and the choice of working and production methods, with a view, in particular, to alleviating monotonous work and work at a predetermined work-rate and to reducing their effect on health;
(e) adapting to technical progress;
(f) replacing the dangerous by the non-dangerous or the less dangerous;
(g) developing a coherent overall prevention policy which covers technology, organisation of work, working conditions, social relationships and the influence of factors related to the working environment;
(h) giving collective protective measures priority over individual protective measures;
(i) giving appropriate instructions to the workers.

3. Without prejudice to the other provisions of this Directive, the employer shall, taking into account the nature of the activities of the enterprise and/or establishment:

(a) evaluate the risks to the safety and health of workers, inter alia in the choice of work equipment, the chemical substances or preparations used, and the fitting out of work places.

Subsequent to this evaluation and as necessary, the preventive measures and the working and production methods implemented by the employer must:

- assure an improvement in the level of protection afforded to workers with regard to safety and health,
- be integrated into all the activities of the undertaking and/or establishment and at all hierarchical levels;

(b) where he entrusts tasks to a worker, take into consideration the worker's capabilities as regards health and safety;
(c) ensure that the planning and introduction of new technologies are the subject of consultation with the workers and/or their representatives, as regards the consequences of the choice of equipment, the working conditions and the working environment for the safety and health of workers;

(d) take appropriate steps to ensure that only workers who have received adequate instructions may have access to areas where there is serious and specific danger.

4. Without prejudice to the other provisions of this Directive, where several undertakings share a work place, the employers shall cooperate in implementing the safety, health and occupational hygiene provisions and, taking into account the nature of the activities, shall coordinate their actions in matters of the protection and prevention of occupational risks, and shall inform one another and their respective workers and/or workers' representatives of those risks.

5. Measures related to safety, hygiene and health at work may in no circumstances involve the workers in financial cost.

Article 7 Protective and preventive services

1. Without prejudice to the obligations referred to in Articles 5 and 6, the employer shall designate one or more workers to carry out activities related to the protection and prevention of occupational risks for the undertaking and/or establishment.

2. Designated workers may not be placed at any disadvantage because of their activities related to the protection and prevention of occupational risks.

Designated workers shall be allowed adequate time to enable them to fulfil their obligations arising from this Directive.

3. If such protective and preventive measures cannot be organised for lack of competent personnel in the undertaking and/or establishment, the employer shall enlist competent external services or persons.

4. Where the employer enlists such services or persons, he shall inform them of the factors known to affect, or suspected of affecting, the safety and health of the workers and they must have access to the information referred to in Article 10(2).

5. In all cases:

- the workers designated must have the necessary capabilities and the necessary means,
- the external services or persons consulted must have the necessary aptitudes and the necessary personal and professional means, and
- the workers designated and the external services or persons consulted must be sufficient in number

to deal with the organisation of protective and preventive measures, taking into account the size of the undertaking and/or establishment and/or the hazards to which the workers are exposed and their distribution throughout the entire undertaking and/or establishment.

6. The protection from, and prevention of, the health and safety risks which form the subject of this Article shall be the responsibility of one or more workers, of one service or of separate services whether from inside or outside the undertaking and/or establishment.

The worker(s) and/or agency(ies) must work together whenever necessary.

7. Member States may define, in the light of the nature of the activities and size of the undertakings, the categories of undertakings in which the employer, provided he is competent, may himself take responsibility for the measures referred to in paragraph 1.

8. Member States shall define the necessary capabilities and aptitudes referred to in paragraph 5. They may determine the sufficient number referred to in paragraph 5.

Article 8 First aid, fire-fighting and evacuation of workers, serious and imminent danger

1. The employer shall:

- take the necessary measures for first aid, fire-fighting and evacuation of workers, adapted to the nature of the activities and the size of the undertaking and/or establishment and taking into account other persons present,
- arrange any necessary contacts with external services, particularly as regards first aid, emergency medical care, rescue work and fire-fighting.

2. Pursuant to paragraph 1, the employer shall, inter alia, for first aid, fire-fighting and the evacuation of workers, designate the workers required to implement such measures.

The number of such workers, their training and the equipment available to them shall be adequate, taking account of the size and/or specific hazards of the undertaking and/or establishment.

3. The employer shall:

(a) as soon as possible, inform all workers who are, or may be, exposed to serious and imminent danger of the risk involved and of the steps taken or to be taken as regards protection;

(b) take action and give instructions to enable workers in the event of serious, imminent and unavoidable danger to stop work and/or immediately to leave the work place and proceed to a place of safety;

(c) save in exceptional cases for reasons duly substantiated, refrain from asking workers to resume work in a working situation where there is still a serious and imminent danger.

4. Workers who, in the event of serious, imminent and unavoidable danger, leave their workstation and/or a dangerous area may not be placed at any disadvantage because of their action and must be protected against any harmful and unjustified consequences, in accordance with national laws and/or practices.

5. The employer shall ensure that all workers are able, in the event of serious and imminent danger to their own safety and/or that of other persons, and where the immediate superior responsible cannot be contacted, to take the appropriate steps in the light of their knowledge and the technical means at their disposal, to avoid the consequences of such danger.

Their actions shall not place them at any disadvantage, unless they acted carelessly or there was negligence on their part.

Article 9 Various obligations on employers

1. The employer shall:

(a) be in possession of an assessment of the risks to safety and health at work, including those facing groups of workers exposed to particular risks;

(b) decide on the protective measures to be taken and, if necessary, the protective equipment to be used;

(c) keep a list of occupational accidents resulting in a worker being unfit for work for more than three working days;

(d) draw up, for the responsible authorities and in accordance with national laws and/or practices, reports on occupational accidents suffered by his workers.

2. Member States shall define, in the light of the nature of the activities and size of the undertakings, the obligations to be met by the different categories of undertakings in respect of the drawing-up of the documents provided for in paragraph 1(a) and (b) and when preparing the documents provided for in paragraph 1(c) and (d).

Article 10 Worker information

1. The employer shall take appropriate measures so that workers and/or their representatives in the undertaking and/or establishment receive, in accordance with national laws and/or practices which may take account, *inter alia*, of the size of the undertaking and/or establishment, all the necessary information concerning:

(a) the safety and health risks and protective and preventive measures and activities in respect of both the undertaking and/or establishment in general and each type of workstation and/or job;

(b) the measures taken pursuant to Article 8(2).

2. The employer shall take appropriate measures so that employers of workers from any outside undertakings and/or establishments engaged in work in his undertaking and/or establishment receive, in accordance with national laws and/or practices, adequate information concerning the points referred to in paragraph 1(a) and (b) which is to be provided to the workers in question.

3. The employer shall take appropriate measures so that workers with specific functions in protecting the safety and health of workers, and workers' representatives with specific responsibility for

the safety and health of workers shall have access, to carry out their functions and in accordance with national laws and/or practices, to:

(a) the risk assessment and protective measures referred to in Article 9(1)(a) and (b);
(b) the list and reports referred to in Article 9(1)(c) and (d);
(c) the information yielded by protective and preventive measures, inspection agencies and bodies responsible for safety and health.

Article 11 Consultation and participation of workers

1. Employers shall consult workers and/or their representatives and allow them to take part in discussions on all questions relating to safety and health at work.

(a) This presupposes:
- the consultation of workers,
- the right of workers and/or their representatives to make proposals,
- balanced participation in accordance with national laws and/or practices.

2. Workers or workers' representatives with specific responsibility for the safety and health of workers shall take part in a balanced way, in accordance with national laws and/or practices, or shall be consulted in advance and in good time by the employer with regard to:

(a) any measure which may substantially affect safety and health;
(b) the designation of workers referred to in Articles 7(1) and 8(2) and the activities referred to in Article 7(1);
(c) the information referred to in Articles 9(1) and 10;
(d) the enlistment, where appropriate, of the competent services or persons outside the undertaking and/or establishment, as referred to in Article 7(3);
(e) the planning and organisation of the training referred to in Article 12.

3. Workers' representatives with specific responsibility for the safety and health of workers shall have the right to ask the employer to take appropriate measures and to submit proposals to him to that end to mitigate hazards for workers and/or to remove sources of danger.

4. The workers referred to in paragraph 2 and the workers' representatives referred to in paragraphs 2 and 3 may not be placed at a disadvantage because of their respective activities referred to in paragraphs 2 and 3.

5. Employers must allow workers' representatives with specific responsibility for the safety and health of workers adequate time off work, without loss of pay, and provide them with the necessary means to enable such representatives to exercise their rights and functions deriving from this Directive.

6. Workers and/or their representatives are entitled to appeal, in accordance with national law and/or practice, to the authority responsible for safety and health protection at work if they consider that the measures taken and the means employed by the employer are inadequate for the purposes of ensuring safety and health at work.

Workers' representatives must be given the opportunity to submit their observations during inspection visits by the competent authority.

Article 12 Training of workers

1. The employer shall ensure that each worker receives adequate safety and health training, in particular in the form of information and instructions specific to his workstation or job:

- on recruitment,
- in the event of a transfer or a change of job,
- in the event of the introduction of new work equipment or a change in equipment,
- in the event of the introduction of any new technology.

The training shall be:

- adapted to take account of new or changed risks, and
- repeated periodically if necessary.

2. The employer shall ensure that workers from outside undertakings and/or establishments engaged in work in his undertaking and/or establishment have in fact received appropriate instructions regarding health and safety risks during their activities in his undertaking and/or establishment.

3. Workers' representatives with a specific role in protecting the safety and health of workers shall be entitled to appropriate training.

4. The training referred to in paragraphs 1 and 3 may not be at the workers' expense or at that of the workers' representatives.

The training referred to in paragraph 1 must take place during working hours.

The training referred to in paragraph 3 must take place during working hours or in accordance with national practice either within or outside the undertaking and/or the establishment.

Section III Workers' obligations

Article 13

1. It shall be the responsibility of each worker to take care as far as possible of his own safety and health and that of other persons affected by his acts or omissions at work in accordance with his training and the instructions given by his employer.

2. To this end, workers must in particular, in accordance with their training and the instructions given by their employer:

(a) make correct use of machinery, apparatus, tools, dangerous substances, transport equipment and other means of production;

(b) make correct use of the personal protective equipment supplied to them and, after use, return it to its proper place;

(c) refrain from disconnecting, changing or removing arbitrarily safety devices fitted, e.g., to machinery, apparatus, tools, plant and buildings, and use such safety devices correctly;

(d) immediately inform the employer and/or the workers with specific responsibility for the safety and health of workers of any work situation they have reasonable grounds for considering represents a serious and immediate danger to safety and health and of any shortcomings in the protection arrangements;

(e) cooperate, in accordance with national practice, with the employer and/or workers with specific responsibility for the safety and health of workers, for as long as may be necessary to enable any tasks or requirements imposed by the competent authority to protect the safety and health of workers at work to be carried out;

(f) cooperate, in accordance with national practice, with the employer and/or workers with specific responsibility for the safety and health of workers, for as long as may be necessary to enable the employer to ensure that the working environment and working conditions are safe and pose no risk to safety and health within their field of activity.

Section IV Miscellaneous provisions

Article 14 Health surveillance

1. To ensure that workers receive health surveillance appropriate to the health and safety risks they incur at work, measures shall be introduced in accordance with national law and/or practices.

2. The measures referred to in paragraph 1 shall be such that each worker, if he so wishes, may receive health surveillance at regular intervals.

3. Health surveillance may be provided as part of a national health system.

Article 15 Risk groups

Particularly sensitive risk groups must be protected against the dangers which specifically affect them.

Article 16 Individual Directives—amendments—general scope of this Directive

1. The Council, acting on a proposal from the Commission based on Article 118a of the Treaty, shall adopt individual Directives, inter alia, in the areas listed in the Annex.

2. This Directive and, without prejudice to the procedure referred to in Article 17 concerning technical adjustments, the individual Directives may be amended in accordance with the procedure provided for in Article 118a of the Treaty.

3. The provisions of this Directive shall apply in full to all the areas covered by the individual Directives, without prejudice to more stringent and/or specific provisions contained in these individual Directives.

Article 17 Committee procedure

1. The Commission shall be assisted by a committee to make purely technical adjustments to the individual directives provided for in Article 16(1) in order to take account of:

(a) the adoption of directives in the field of technical harmonisation and standardisation;

(b) technical progress, changes in international regulations or specifications and new findings.

Those measures, designed to amend non-essential elements of the individual directives, shall be adopted in accordance with the regulatory procedure with scrutiny referred to in paragraph 2. On imperative grounds of urgency, the Commission may have recourse to the urgency procedure referred to in paragraph 3.

2. Where reference is made to this paragraph, Article 5a(1) to (4) and Article 7 of Decision 1999/468/EC shall apply, having regard to the provisions of Article 8 thereof.

3. Where reference is made to this paragraph, Article 5a(1), (2), (4) and (6) and Article 7 of Decision 1999/468 EC shall apply, having regard to the provisions of Article 8 thereof.

Article 17a Implementation reports

1. Every five years, the Member States shall submit a single report to the Commission on the practical implementation of this Directive and individual Directives within the meaning of Article 16(1), indicating the points of view of the social partners. The report shall assess the various points related to the practical implementation of the different Directives and, where appropriate and available, provide data disaggregated by gender.

2. The structure of the report, together with a questionnaire specifying its content, shall be defined by the Commission, in cooperation with the Advisory Committee on Safety and Health at Work.

The report shall include a general part on the provisions of this Directive relating to the common principles and points applicable to all of the Directives referred to in paragraph 1.

To complement the general part, specific chapters shall deal with implementation of the particular aspects of each Directive, including specific indicators, where available.

3. The Commission shall submit the structure of the report, together with the above-mentioned questionnaire specifying its content, to the Member States at least six months before the end of the period covered by the report. The report shall be transmitted to the Commission within 12 months of the end of the five-year period that it covers.

4. Using these reports as a basis, the Commission shall evaluate the implementation of the Directives concerned in terms of their relevance, of research and of new scientific knowledge in the various fields in question. It shall, within 36 months of the end of the five-year period, inform the European Parliament, the Council, the European Economic and Social Committee and the Advisory Committee on Safety and Health at Work of the results of this evaluation and, if necessary, of any initiatives to improve the operation of the regulatory framework.

5. The first report shall cover the period 2007 to 2012.

Article 18 Final provisions

1. Member States shall bring into force the laws, regulations and administrative provisions necessary to comply with this Directive by 31 December 1992.

They shall forthwith inform the Commission thereof.

2. Member States shall communicate to the Commission the texts of the provisions of national law which they have already adopted or adopt in the field covered by this Directive.

Article 19

This Directive is addressed to the Member States.

Done at Luxembourg, 12 June 1989.

(Signature omitted.)

Annex

List of areas referred to in Article 16(1) Work places[1]

- Work equipment
- Personal protective equipment
- Work with visual display units
- Handling of heavy loads involving risk of back injury
- Temporary or mobile work sites[2]
- Fisheries and agriculture

Council Directive 92/85/EEC of 19 October 1992 on the introduction of measures to encourage improvements in the safety and health at work of pregnant workers and workers who have recently given birth or are breastfeeding (tenth individual Directive within the meaning of Article 16(1) of Directive 89/391/EEC)*

[OJ 1992 L348/1]

The Council of the European Communities,

Having regard to the Treaty establishing the European Economic Community, and in particular Article 118a thereof,

Having regard to the proposal from the Commission, drawn up after consultation with the Advisory Committee on Safety, Hygiene and Health Protection at work,[1]

In cooperation with the European Parliament,[2]

Having regard to the opinion of the Economic and Social Committee,[3]

Whereas Article 118a of the Treaty provides that the Council shall adopt, by means of directives, minimum requirements for encouraging improvements, especially in the working environment, to protect the safety and health of workers;

Whereas this Directive does not justify any reduction in levels of protection already achieved in individual Member States, the Member States being committed, under the Treaty, to encouraging improvements in conditions in this area and to harmonising conditions while maintaining the improvements made;

Whereas, under the terms of Article 118a of the Treaty, the said directives are to avoid imposing administrative, financial and legal constraints in a way which would hold back the creation and development of small and medium-sized undertakings;

Whereas, pursuant to Decision 74/325/EEC,[4] as last amended by the 1985 Act of Accession, the Advisory Committee on Safety, Hygiene and Health protection at Work is consulted by the Commission on the drafting of proposals in this field;

Whereas the Community Charter of the fundamental social rights of workers, adopted at the Strasbourg European Council on 9 December 1989 by the Heads of State or Government of 11 Member States, lays down, in paragraph 19 in particular, that:

[1] Council Directive of 19 October 1992 (92/85/EEC) [No L348/1] in the area of pregnant workers and workers who have recently given birth or are breastfeeding.

[2] Council Directive of 24 June 1992 (92/57/EEC) [No L245/6] implementing minimum health and safety requirements in this area.

* **Editor's Note:** As amended by Directive 2007/30, OJ 2007 L165/21.

[1] OJ No C281, 9 November 1990, p. 3 and OJ No C25 1 February 1991, p. 9.

[2] OJ No C19, 28 January 1992, p. 177 and OJ No C150, 15 June 1992, p. 99.

[3] OJ No C41, 18 February 1991, p. 29.

[4] OJ No L185, 9 July 1974, p. 15.

'Every worker must enjoy satisfactory health and safety conditions in his working environment. Appropriate measures must be taken in order to achieve further harmonisation of conditions in this area while maintaining the improvements made';

Whereas the Commission, in its action programme for the implementation of the Community Charter of the fundamental social rights of workers, has included among its aims the adoption by the Council of a Directive on the protection of pregnant women at work;

Whereas Article 15 of Council Directive 89/391/EEC of 12 June 1989 on the introduction of measures to encourage improvements in the safety and health of workers at work[5] provides that particularly sensitive risk groups must be protected against the dangers which specifically affect them;

Whereas pregnant workers, workers who have recently given birth or who are breastfeeding must be considered a specific risk group in many respects, measures must be taken with regard to their safety and health;

Whereas the protection of the safety and health of pregnant workers, workers who have recently given birth or workers who are breastfeeding should not treat women on the labour market unfavourably nor work to the detriment of directives concerning equal treatment for men and women;

Whereas some types of activities may pose a specific risk, for pregnant workers, workers who have recently given birth or workers who are breastfeeding, of exposure to dangerous agents, processes or working conditions; whereas such risks must therefore be assessed and the result of such assessment communicated to female workers and/or their representatives;

Whereas, further, should the result of this assessment reveal the existence of a risk to the safety or health of the female worker, provision must be made for such worker to be protected;

Whereas pregnant workers and workers who are breastfeeding must not engage in activities which have been assessed as revealing a risk of exposure, jeopardizing safety and health, to certain particularly dangerous agents or working conditions;

Whereas provision should be made for pregnant workers, workers who have recently given birth or workers who are breastfeeding not to be required to work at night where such provision is necessary from the point of view of their safety and health;

Whereas the vulnerability of pregnant workers, workers who have recently given birth or who are breastfeeding makes it necessary for them to be granted the right to maternity leave of at least 14 continuous weeks, allocated before and/or after confinement, and renders necessary the compulsory nature of maternity leave of at least two weeks, allocated before and/or after confinement;

Whereas the risk of dismissal for reasons associated with their condition may have harmful effects on the physical and mental state of pregnant workers, workers who have recently given birth or who are breastfeeding; whereas provision should be made for such dismissal to be prohibited;

Whereas measures for the organisation of work concerning the protection of the health of pregnant workers, workers who have recently given birth or workers who are breastfeeding would serve no purpose unless accompanied by the maintenance of rights linked to the employment contract, including maintenance of payment and/or entitlement to an adequate allowance;

Whereas, moreover, provision concerning maternity leave would also serve no purpose unless accompanied by the maintenance of rights linked to the employment contract and/or entitlement to an adequate allowance;

Whereas the concept of an adequate allowance in the case of maternity leave must be regarded as a technical point of reference with a view to fixing the minimum level of protection and should in no circumstances be interpreted as suggesting an analogy between pregnancy and illness,

Has adopted this Directive:

Section I Purpose and definitions

Article 1 Purpose

1. The purpose of this Directive, which is the tenth individual Directive within the meaning of Article 16(1) of Directive 89/391/EEC, is to implement measures to encourage improvements in the

[5] OJ No L183, 29 June 1989, p. 1.

safety and health at work of pregnant workers and workers who have recently given birth or who are breastfeeding.

2. The provisions of Directive 89/391/EEC, except for Article 2(2) thereof, shall apply in full to the whole area covered by paragraph 1, without prejudice to any more stringent and/or specific provisions contained in this Directive.

3. This Directive may not have the effect of reducing the level of protection afforded to pregnant workers, workers who have recently given birth or who are breastfeeding as compared with the situation which exists in each Member State on the date on which this Directive is adopted.

Article 2 Definitions

For the purposes of this Directive:

(a) *pregnant worker* shall mean a pregnant worker who informs her employer of her condition, in accordance with national legislation and/or national practice;

(b) *worker who has recently given birth* shall mean a worker who has recently given birth within the meaning of national legislation and/or national practice and who informs her employer of her condition, in accordance with that legislation and/or practice;

(c) *worker who is breastfeeding* shall mean a worker who is breastfeeding within the meaning of national legislation and/or national practice and who informs her employer of her condition, in accordance with that legislation and/or practice.

Section II General provisions

Article 3 Guidelines

1. In consultation with the Member States and assisted by the Advisory Committee on Safety, Hygiene and Health Protection at Work, the Commission shall draw up guidelines on the assessment of the chemical, physical and biological agents and industrial processes considered hazardous for the safety or health of workers within the meaning of Article 2.

The guidelines referred to in the first sub-paragraph shall also cover movements and postures, mental and physical fatigue and other types of physical and mental stress connected with the work done by workers within the meaning of Article 2.

2. The purpose of the guidelines referred to in paragraph 1 is to serve as a basis for the assessment referred to in Article 4(1).

To this end, Member States shall bring these guidelines to the attention of all employers and all female workers and/or their representatives in the respective Member State.

Article 4 Assessment and information

1. For all activities liable to involve a specific risk of exposure to the agents, processes or working conditions of which a non-exhaustive list is given in Annex I, the employer shall assess the nature, degree and duration of exposure, in the undertaking and/or establishment concerned, of workers within the meaning of Article 2, either directly or by way of the protective and preventive services referred to in Article 7 of Directive 89/391/EEC, in order to:

- assess any risks to the safety or health and any possible effect on the pregnancy or breastfeeding of workers within the meaning of Article 2,
- decide what measures should be taken.

2. Without prejudice to Article 10 of Directive 89/391/EEC, workers within the meaning of Article 2 and workers likely to be in one of the situations referred to in Article 2 in the undertaking and/or establishment concerned and/or their representatives shall be informed of the results of the assessment referred to in paragraph 1 and of all measures to be taken concerning health and safety at work.

Article 5 Action further to the results of the assessment

1. Without prejudice to Article 6 of Directive 89/391/EEC, if the results of the assessment referred to in Article 4(1) reveal risk to the safety or health or an effect on the pregnancy or breastfeeding of a worker within the meaning of Article 2, the employer shall take the necessary measures to

ensure that, by temporarily adjusting the working conditions and/or the working hours of the worker concerned, the exposure of that worker to such risks is avoided.

2. If the adjustment of her working conditions and/or working hours is not technically and/or objectively feasible, or cannot reasonably be required on duly substantiated grounds, the employer shall take the necessary measures to move the worker concerned to another job.

3. If moving her to another job is not technically and/or objectively feasible or cannot reasonably be required on duly substantiated grounds, the worker concerned shall be granted leave in accordance with national legislation and/or national practice for the whole of the period necessary to protect her safety or health.

4. The provisions of this Article shall apply mutatis mutandis to the case where a worker pursuing an activity which is forbidden pursuant to Article 6 becomes pregnant or starts breastfeeding and informs her employer thereof.

Article 6 Cases in which exposure is prohibited

In addition to the general provisions concerning the protection of workers, in particular those relating to the limit values for occupational exposure:

1. pregnant workers within the meaning of Article 2(a) may under no circumstances be obliged to perform duties for which the assessment has revealed a risk of exposure, which would jeopardise safety or health, to the agents and working conditions listed in Annex II, Section A;

2. workers who are breastfeeding, within the meaning of Article 2(c), may under no circumstances be obliged to perform duties for which the assessment has revealed a risk of exposure, which would jeopardise safety or health, to the agents and working conditions listed in Annex II, Section B.

Article 7 Night work

1. Member States shall take the necessary measures to ensure that workers referred to in Article 2 are not obliged to perform night work during their pregnancy and for a period following childbirth which shall be determined by the national authority competent for safety and health, subject to submission, in accordance with the procedures laid down by the Member States, of a medical certificate stating that this is necessary for the safety or health of the worker concerned.

2. The measures referred to in paragraph 1 must entail the possibility, in accordance with national legislation and/or national practice, of:

(a) transfer to daytime work; or
(b) leave from work or extension of maternity leave where such a transfer is not technically and/or objectively feasible or cannot reasonably be required on duly substantiated grounds.

Article 8 Maternity leave

1. Member States shall take the necessary measures to ensure that workers within the meaning of Article 2 are entitled to a continuous period of maternity leave of at least 14 weeks allocated before and/or after confinement in accordance with national legislation and/or practice.

2. The maternity leave stipulated in paragraph 1 must include compulsory maternity leave of at least two weeks allocated before and/or after confinement in accordance with national legislation and/or practice.

Article 9 Time off for ante-natal examinations

Member States shall take the necessary measures to ensure that pregnant workers within the meaning of Article 2(a) are entitled to, in accordance with national legislation and/or practice, time off, without loss of pay, in order to attend ante-natal examinations, if such examinations have to take place during working hours.

Article 10 Prohibition of dismissal

In order to guarantee workers, within the meaning of Article 2, the exercise of their health and safety protection rights as recognised under this Article, it will be provided that:

1. Member States shall take the necessary measures to prohibit the dismissal of workers, within the meaning of Article 2, during the period from the beginning of their pregnancy to the end of the maternity leave referred to in Article 8(1), save in exceptional cases not connected with their condition which are permitted under national legislation and/or practice and, where applicable, provided that the competent authority has given its consent;

2. if a worker, within the meaning of Article 2, is dismissed during the period referred to in point 1, the employer must cite duly substantiated grounds for her dismissal in writing;

3. Member States shall take the necessary measures to protect workers, within the meaning of Article 2, from consequences of dismissal which is unlawful by virtue of point 1.

Article 11 Employment rights

In order to guarantee workers within the meaning of Article 2 the exercise of their health and safety protection rights as recognised in this Article, it shall be provided that:

1. in the cases referred to in Articles 5, 6 and 7, the employment rights relating to the employment contract, including the maintenance of a payment to, and/or entitlement to an adequate allowance for, workers within the meaning of Article 2, must be ensured in accordance with national legislation and/or national practice;

2. in the case referred to in Article 8, the following must be ensured:
   (a) the rights connected with the employment contract of workers within the meaning of Article 2, other than those referred to in point (b) below;
   (b) maintenance of a payment to, and/or entitlement to an adequate allowance for, workers within the meaning of Article 2;

3. the allowance referred to in point 2(b) shall be deemed adequate if it guarantees income at least equivalent to that which the worker concerned would receive in the event of a break in her activities on grounds connected with her state of health, subject to any ceiling laid down under national legislation;

4. Member States may make entitlement to pay or the allowance referred to in points 1 and 2 (b) conditional upon the worker concerned fulfilling the conditions of eligibility for such benefits laid down under national legislation.

These conditions may under no circumstances provide for periods of previous employment in excess of 12 months immediately prior to the presumed date of confinement.

Article 12 Defence of rights

Member States shall introduce into their national legal systems such measures as are necessary to enable all workers who should themselves wronged by failure to comply with the obligations arising from the Directive to pursue their claims by judicial process (and/or, in accordance with national laws and/or practice) by recourse to other competent authorities.

Article 13 Amendments to the Annexes

1. Strictly technical adjustments to Annex I as a result of technical progress, changes in international regulations or specifications and new findings in the area covered by this Directive shall be adopted in accordance with the procedure laid down in Article 17 of Directive 89/391/EEC.

2. Annex II may be amended only in accordance with the procedure laid down in Article 118a of the Treaty.

Article 14 Final provisions

1. Member States shall bring into force the laws, regulations and administrative provisions necessary to comply with this Directive not later than two years after the adoption thereof or ensure, at the latest two years after adoption of this Directive, that the two sides of industry introduce the requisite provisions by means of collective agreements, with Member States being required to make all the necessary provisions to enable them at all times to guarantee the results laid down by this Directive. They shall forthwith inform the Commission thereof.

2. When Member States adopt the measures referred to in paragraph 1, they shall contain a reference of this Directive or shall be accompanied by such reference on the occasion of their official publication. The methods of making such a reference shall be laid down by the Member States.

3. Member States shall communicate to the Commission the texts of the essential provisions of national law which they have already adopted or adopt in the field governed by this Directive.

Article 15

This Directive is addressed to the Member States.

Done at Luxembourg, 19 October 1992.

For the Council

The President

D. CURRY

Annex I

Non-exhaustive list of agents, processes and working conditions referred to in Article 4(1)

A. Agents

1. Physical agents where these are regarded as agents causing foetal lesions and/or likely to disrupt placental attachment, and in particular:

(a) shocks, vibration or movement;
(b) handling of loads entailing risks, particularly of a dorsolumbar nature;
(c) noise;
(d) ionizing radiation;
(e) non-ionizing radiation;
(f) extremes of cold or heat;
(g) movements and postures, travelling—either inside or outside the establishment—mental and physical fatigue and other physical burdens connected with the activity of the worker within the meaning of Article 2 of the Directive.

2. Biological agents

Biological agents of risk groups 2, 3 and 3 within the meaning of Article 2(d) numbers 2, 3 and 4 of Directive 90/679/EEC, in so far as it is known that these agents or the therapeutic measures necessitated by such agents endanger the health of pregnant women and the unborn child and in so far as they do not yet appear in Annex II.

3. Chemical agents

The following chemical agents in so far as it is known that they endanger the health of pregnant women and the unborn child and in so far as they do not yet appear in Annex II:

(a) substances labelled R 40, R 45, R 46, and R 47 under Directive 67/548/EEC in so far as they do not yet appear in Annex II;
(b) chemical agents in Annex I to Directive 90/394/EEC;
(c) mercury and mercury derivatives;
(d) antimitotic drugs;
(e) carbon monoxide;
(f) chemical agents of known and dangerous percutaneous absorption.

B. Processes

Industrial processes listed in Annex I to Directive 90/394/EEC.

C. Working conditions

Underground mining work.

Annex II

Non-exhaustive list of agents and working conditions referred to in Article 6

A. Pregnant workers within the meaning of Article 2(a)

1. *Agents*
   (a) Physical agents
   Work in hyperbaric atmosphere, e.g., pressurised enclosures and underwater diving.

   (b) Biological agents
   The following biological agents:
   - toxoplasma,
   - rubella virus,

   unless the pregnant workers are proved to be adequately protected against such agents by immunisation.

   (c) Chemical agents
   Lead and lead derivatives in so far as these agents are capable of being absorbed by the human organism.
2. *Working conditions*
   Underground mining work.

B. Workers who are breastfeeding within the meaning of Article 2(c)

1. *Agents*
   (a) Chemical agents
   Lead and lead derivatives in so far as these agents are capable of being absorbed by the human organism.
2. *Working conditions*
   Underground mining work.

Council Directive 94/33/EC of 22 June 1994 on the protection of young people at work*

[OJ 1994 L216/12]

THE COUNCIL OF THE EUROPEAN UNION,

Having regard to the Treaty establishing the European Community, and in particular Article 118a thereof,

Having regard to the proposal from the Commission,[1]

Having regard to the opinion of the Economic and Social Committee,[2]

Acting in accordance with the procedure referred to in Article 189c of the Treaty,[3]

Whereas Article 118a of the Treaty provides that the Council shall adopt, by means of directives, minimum requirements to encourage improvements, especially in the working environment, as regards the health and safety of workers;

* **Editor's Note:** As amended by Directive 2007/30. OJ 2007 L 165/21.

1 OJ No C84, 4.4.1992, p. 7.

2 OJ No C313, 30.11.1992, p. 70.

3 Opinion of the European Parliament of 17 December 1992 (OJ No C21, 25.1.1993, p. 167). Council Common Position of 23 November 1993 (not yet published in the Official Journal) and Decision of the European Parliament of 9 March 1994 (OJ No C91, 28.3.1994, p. 89).

Whereas, under that Article, such directives must avoid imposing administrative, financial and legal constraints in a way which would hold back the creation and development of small and medium-sized undertakings;

Whereas points 20 and 22 of the Community Charter of the Fundamental Social Rights of Workers, adopted by the European Council in Strasbourg on 9 December 1989, state that:

'20. Without prejudice to such rules as may be more favourable to young people, in particular those ensuring their preparation for work through vocational training, and subject to derogations limited to certain light work, the minimum employment age must not be lower than the minimum school-leaving age and, in any case, not lower than 15 years;

22. Appropriate measures must be taken to adjust labour regulations applicable to young workers so that their specific development and vocational training and access to employment needs are met.

The duration of work must, in particular, be limited—without it being possible to circumvent this limitation through recourse to overtime—and night work prohibited in the case of workers of under eighteen years of age, save in the case of certain jobs laid down in national legislation or regulations.';

Whereas account should be taken of the principles of the International Labour Organisation regarding the protection of young people at work, including those relating to the minimum age for access to employment or work;

Whereas, in this Resolution on child labour,[4] the European Parliament summarised the various aspects of work by young people and stressed its effects on their health, safety and physical and intellectual development, and pointed to the need to adopt a Directive harmonising national legislation in the field;

Whereas Article 15 of Council Directive 89/391/EEC of 12 June 1989 on the introduction of measures to encourage improvements in the safety and health of workers at work[5] provides that particularly sensitive risk groups must be protected against the dangers which specifically affect them;

Whereas children and adolescents must be considered specific risk groups, and measures must be taken with regard to their safety and health;

Whereas the vulnerability of children calls for Member States to prohibit their employment and ensure that the minimum working or employment age is not lower than the minimum age at which compulsory schooling as imposed by national law ends or 15 years in any event; whereas derogations from the prohibition on child labour may be admitted only in special cases and under the conditions stipulated in this Directive; Whereas, under no circumstances, may such derogations be detrimental to regular school attendance or prevent children benefiting fully from their education;

Whereas, in view of the nature of the transition from childhood to adult life, work by adolescents should be strictly regulated and protected;

Whereas every employer should guarantee young people working conditions appropriate to their age;

Whereas employers should implement the measures necessary to protect the safety and health of young people on the basis of an assessment of work-related hazards to the young;

Whereas Member States should protect young people against any specific risks arising from their lack of experience, absence of awareness of existing or potential risks, or from their immaturity;

Whereas Member States should therefore prohibit the employment of young people for the work specified by this Directive;

Whereas the adoption of specific minimal requirements in respect of the organisation of working time is likely to improve working conditions for young people;

Whereas the maximum working time of young people should be strictly limited and night work by young people should be prohibited, with the exception of certain jobs specified by national legislation or rules;

Whereas Member States should take the appropriate measures to ensure that the working time of adolescents receiving school education does not adversely affect their ability to benefit from that education;

[4] OJ No C190, 20.7.1987, p. 44.

[5] OJ No L183, 29.6.1989, p. 1.

Whereas time spent on training by young persons working under a theoretical and/or practical combined work/training scheme or an in-plant work-experience should be counted as working time;

Whereas, in order to ensure the safety and health of young people, the latter should be granted minimum daily, weekly and annual periods of rest and adequate breaks;

Whereas, with respect to the weekly rest period, due account should be taken of the diversity of cultural, ethnic, religious and other factors prevailing in the Member States;

Whereas in particular, it is ultimately for each Member State to decide whether Sunday should be included in the weekly rest period, and if so to what extent;

Whereas appropriate work experience may contribute to the aim of preparing young people for adult working and social life, provided it is ensured that any harm to their safety, health and development is avoided;

Whereas, although derogations from the bans and limitations imposed by this Directive would appear indispensable for certain activities or particular situations, applications thereof must not prejudice the principles underlying the established protection system;

Whereas this Directive constitutes a tangible step towards developing the social dimension of the internal market;

Whereas the application in practice of the system of protection laid down by this Directive will require that Member States implement a system of effective and proportionate measures;

Whereas the implementation of some provisions of this Directive poses particular problems for one Member State with regard to its system of protection for young people at work; whereas that Member State should therefore be allowed to refrain from implementing the relevant provisions for a suitable period,

HAS ADOPTED THIS DIRECTIVE:

Section I

Article 1 Purpose

1. Member States shall take the necessary measures to prohibit work by children. They shall ensure, under the conditions laid down by this Directive, that the minimum working or employment age is not lower than the minimum age at which compulsory full-time schooling as imposed by national law ends or 15 years in any event.

2. Member States ensure that work by adolescents is strictly regulated and protected under the conditions laid down in this Directive.

3. Member States shall ensure in general that employers guarantee that young people have working conditions which suit their age.

They shall ensure that young people are protected against economic exploitation and against any work likely to harm their safety, health or physical, mental, moral or social development or to jeopardise their education.

Article 2 Scope

1. This Directive shall apply to any person under 18 years of age having an employment contract or an employment relationship defined by the law in force in a Member State and/or governed by the law in force in a Member State.

2. Member States may make legislative or regulatory provision for this Directive not to apply, within the limits and under the conditions which they set by legislative or regulatory provision, to occasional work or short-term work involving:

(a) domestic service in a private household, or

(b) work regarded as not being harmful, damaging or dangerous to young people in a family undertaking.

Article 3 Definitions

For the purposes of this Directive:

(a) 'young person' shall mean any person under 18 years of age referred to in Article 2(1);

(b) 'child' shall mean any young person of less than 15 years of age or who is still subject to compulsory full-time schooling under national law;
(c) 'adolescent' shall mean any young person of at least 15 years of age but less than 18 years of age who is no longer subject to compulsory full-time schooling under national law;
(d) 'light work' shall mean all work which, on account of the inherent nature of the tasks which it involves and the particular conditions under which they are performed:
 (i) is not likely to be harmful to the safety, health or development of children, and
 (ii) is not such as to be harmful to their attendance at school, their participation in vocational guidance or training programmes approved by the competent authority or their capacity to benefit from the instruction received;
(e) 'working time' shall mean any period during which the young person is at work, at the employer's disposal and carrying out his activity or duties in accordance with national legislation and/or practice;
(f) 'rest period' shall mean any period which is not working time.

Article 4 Prohibition of work by children

1. Member States shall adopt the measures necessary to prohibit work by children.

2. Taking into account the objectives set out in Article 1, Member States may make legislative or regulatory provision for the prohibition of work by children not to apply to:
(a) children pursuing the activities set out in Article 5;
(b) children of at least 14 years of age working under a combined work/training scheme or an in-plant work-experience scheme, provided that such work is done in accordance with the conditions laid down by the competent authority;
(c) children of at least 14 years of age performing light work other than that covered by Article 5; light work other than that covered by Article 5 may, however, be performed by children of 13 years of age for a limited number of hours per week in the case of categories of work determined by national legislation.

3. Member States that make use of the opinion referred to in paragraph 2(c) shall determine, subject to the provisions of this Directive, the working conditions relating to the light work in question.

Article 5 Cultural or similar activities

1. The employment of children for the purposes of performance in cultural, artistic, sports or advertising activities shall be subject to prior authorisation to be given by the competent authority in individual cases.

2. Member States shall by legislative or regulatory provision lay down the working conditions for children in the cases referred to in paragraph 1 and the details of the prior authorisation procedure, on condition that the activities:
 (i) are not likely to be harmful to the safety, health or development of children, and
 (ii) are not such as to be harmful to their attendance at school, their participation in vocational guidance or training programmes approved by the competent authority or their capacity to benefit from the instruction received.

3. By way of derogation from the procedure laid down in paragraph 1, in the case of children of at least 13 years of age, Member States may authorise, by legislative or regulatory provision, in accordance with conditions which they shall determine, the employment of children for the purposes of performance in cultural, artistic, sports or advertising activities.

4. The Member States which have a specific authorisation system for modelling agencies with regard to the activities of children may retain that system.

Section II

Article 6 General obligations on employers

1. Without prejudice to Article 4(1), the employer shall adopt the measures necessary to protect the safety and health of young people, taking particular account of the specific risks referred to in Article 7(1).

2. The employer shall implement the measures provided for in paragraph 1 on the basis of an assessment of the hazards to young people in connection with their work. The assessment must be made before young people begin work and when there is any major change in working conditions and must pay particular attention to the following points:

(a) the fitting-out and layout of the workplace and the workstation;
(b) the nature, degree and duration of exposure to physical, biological and chemical agents;
(c) the form, range and use of work equipment, in particular agents, machines, apparatus and devices, and the way in which they are handled;
(d) the arrangement of work processes and operations and the way in which these are combined (organisation of work);
(e) the level of training and instruction given to young people.

Where this assessment shows that there is a risk to the safety, the physical or mental health or development of young people, an appropriate free assessment and monitoring of their health shall be provided at regular intervals without prejudice to Directive 89/391/EEC. The free health assessment and monitoring may form part of a national health system.

3. The employer shall inform young people of possible risks and of all measures adopted concerning their safety and health.

Furthermore, he shall inform the legal representatives of children of possible risks and of all measures adopted concerning children's safety and health.

4. The employer shall involve the protective and preventive services referred to in Article 7 of Directive 89/391/EEC in the planning, implementation and monitoring of the safety and health conditions applicable to young people.

Article 7 Vulnerability of young people—prohibition of work

1. Member States shall ensure that young people are protected from any specific risks to their safety, health and development which are a consequence of their lack of experience, of absence of awareness of existing or potential risks or of the fact that young people have not yet fully matured.

2. Without prejudice to Article 4(1), Member States shall to this end prohibit the employment of young people for:

(a) work which is objectively beyond their physical or psychological capacity;
(b) work involving harmful exposure to agents which are toxic, carcinogenic, cause heritable genetic damage, or harm to the unborn child or which in any other way chronically affect human health;
(c) work involving harmful exposure to radiation;
(d) work involving the risk of accidents which it may be assumed cannot be recognised or avoided by young persons owing to their insufficient attention to safety or lack of experience or training; or
(e) work in which there is a risk to health from extreme cold or heat, or from noise or vibration.

Work which is likely to entail specific risks for young people within the meaning of paragraph 1 includes:

- work involving harmful exposure to the physical, biological and chemical agents referred to in point I of the Annex, and
- processes and work referred to in point II of the Annex.

3. Member States may, by legislative or regulatory provision, authorise derogations from paragraph 2 in the case of adolescents where such derogations are indispensable for their vocational training, provided that protection of their safety and health is ensured by the fact that the work is performed under the supervision of a competent person within the meaning of Article 7 of Directive 89/391/EEC and provided that the protection afforded by that Directive is guaranteed.

Section III

Article 8 Working time

1. Member States which make use of the option in Article 4(2)(b) or (c) shall adopt the measures necessary to limit the working time of children to:

(a) eight hours a day and 40 hours a week for work performed under a combined work/training scheme or an in-plant work-experience scheme;
(b) two hours on a school day and 12 hours a week for work performed in term-time outside the hours fixed for school attendance, provided that this is not prohibited by national legislation and/or practice; in no circumstances may the daily working time exceed seven hours; this limit may be raised to eight hours in the case of children who have reached the age of 15;
(c) seven hours a day and 35 hours a week for work performed during a period of at least a week when school is not operating; these limits may be raised to eight hours a day and 40 hours a week in the case of children who have reached the age of 15;
(d) seven hours a day and 35 hours a week for light work performed by children no longer subject to compulsory full-time schooling under national law.

2. Member States shall adopt the measures necessary to limit the working time of adolescents to eight hours a day and 40 hours a week.

3. The time spent on training by a young person working under a theoretical and/or practical combined work/training scheme or an in-plant work-experience scheme shall be counted as working time.

4. Where a young person is employed by more than one employer, working days and working time shall be cumulative.

5. Member States may, by legislative or regulatory provision, authorise derogations from paragraph 1(a) and paragraph 2 either by way of exception or where there are objective grounds for so doing. Member States shall, by legislative or regulatory provision, determine the conditions, limits and procedure for implementing such derogations.

Article 9 Night work

1. (a) Member States which make use of the option in Article 4(2)(b) or (c) shall adopt the measures necessary to prohibit work by children between 8 p.m. and 6 a.m.
(b) Member States shall adopt the measures necessary to prohibit work by adolescents either between 10 p.m. and 6 a.m. or between 11 p.m. and 7 a.m.

2. (a) Member States may, by legislative or regulatory provision, authorise work by adolescents in specific areas of activity during the period in which night work is prohibited as referred to in paragraph 1(b). In that event, Member States shall take appropriate measures to ensure that the adolescent is supervised by an adult where such supervision is necessary for the adolescent's protection.
(b) If point (a) is applied, work shall continue to be prohibited between midnight and 4 a.m.

However, Member States may, by legislative or regulatory provision, authorise work by adolescents during the period in which night work is prohibited in the following cases, where there are objective grounds for so doing and provided that adolescents are allowed suitable compensatory rest time and that the objectives set out in Article 1 are not called into question:

- work performed in the shipping or fisheries sectors;
- work performed in the context of the armed forces or the police;
- work performed in hospitals or similar establishments;
- cultural, artistic, sports or advertising activities.

3. Prior to any assignment to night work and at regular intervals thereafter, adolescents shall be entitled to a free assessment of their health and capacities, unless the work they do during the period during which work is prohibited is of an exceptional nature.

Article 10 Rest period

1. (a) Member States which make use of the option in Article 4(2)(b) or (c) shall adopt the measures necessary to ensure that, for each 24-hour period, children are entitled to a minimum rest period of 14 consecutive hours.

(b) Member States shall adopt the measures necessary to ensure that, for each 24-hour period, adolescents are entitled to a minimum rest period of 12 consecutive hours.

2. Member States shall adopt the measures necessary to ensure that, for each seven-day period:

- children in respect of whom they have made use of the option in Article 4(2)(b) or (c), and
- adolescents

are entitled to a minimum rest period of two days, which shall be consecutive if possible. Where justified by technical or organisation reasons, the minimum rest period may be reduced, but may in no circumstances be less than 36 consecutive hours. The minimum rest period referred to in the first and second sub-paragraphs shall in principle include Sunday.

3. Member States may, by legislative or regulatory provision, provide for the minimum rest periods referred to in paragraphs 1 and 2 to be interrupted in the case of activities involving periods of work that are split up over the day or are of short duration.

4. Member States may make legislative or regulatory provision for derogations from paragraph 1(b) and paragraph 2 in respect of adolescents in the following cases, where there are objective grounds for so doing and provided that they are granted appropriate compensatory rest time and that the objectives set out in Article 1 are not called into question:

(a) work performed in the shipping or fisheries sectors;
(b) work performed in the context of the armed forces or the police;
(c) work performed in hospitals or similar establishments;
(d) work performed in agriculture;
(e) work performed in the tourism industry or in the hotel, restaurant and café sector;
(f) activities involving periods of work split up over the day.

Article 11 Annual rest

Member States which make use of the option referred to in Article 4(2)(b) or (c) shall see to it that a period free of any work is included, as far as possible, in the school holidays of children subject to compulsory full-time schooling under national law.

Article 12 Breaks

Member States shall adopt the measures necessary to ensure that, where daily working time is more than four and a half hours, young people are entitled to a break of at least 30 minutes, which shall be consecutive if possible.

Article 13 Work by adolescents in the event of force majeure

Member States may, by legislative or regulatory provision, authorise derogations from Article 8(2), Article 9(1)(b), Article 10(1)(b) and, in the case of adolescents, Article 12, for work in the circumstances referred to in Article 5(4) of Directive 89/391/EEC, provided that such work is of a temporary nature and must be performed immediately, that adult workers are not available and that the adolescents are allowed equivalent compensatory rest time within the following three weeks.

Section IV

Article 14 Measures

Each Member State shall lay down any necessary measures to be applied in the event of failure to comply with the provisions adopted in order to implement this Directive; such measures must be effective and proportionate.

Article 15 Adaptation of the Annex

Adaptations of a strictly technical nature to the Annex in the light of technical progress, changes in international rules or specifications and advances in knowledge in the field covered by this Directive shall be adopted in accordance with the procedure provided for in Article 17 of Directive 89/391/EEC.

Article 16 Non-reducing clause

Without prejudice to the right of Member States to develop, in the light of changing circumstances, different provisions on the protection of young people, as long as the minimum requirements provided for by this Directive are complied with, the implementation of this Directive shall not constitute valid grounds for reducing the general level of protection afforded to young people.

Article 17 Final provisions

1. (a) Member States shall bring into force the laws, regulations and administrative provisions necessary to comply with this Directive not later than 22 June 1996 or ensure, by that date at the latest, that the two sides of industry introduce the requisite provisions by means of collective agreements, with Member States being required to make all the necessary provisions to enable them at all times to guarantee the results laid down by this Directive.

(b) The United Kingdom may refrain from implementing the first subparagraph of Article 8(1)(b) with regard to the provision relating to the maximum weekly working time, and also Article 8(2) and Article 9(1)(b) and (2) for a period of four years from the date specified in subparagraph (a).

The Commission shall submit a report on the effects of this provision.

The Council, acting in accordance with the conditions laid down by the Treaty, shall decide whether this period should be extended.

(c) Member States shall forthwith inform the Commission thereof.

2. When Member States adopt the measures referred to in paragraph 1, such measures shall contain a reference to this Directive or shall be accompanied by such reference on the occasion of their official publication. The methods of making such reference shall be laid down by Member States.

3. Member States shall communicate to the Commission the texts of the main provisions of national law which they have already adopted or adopt in the field governed by this Directive.

Article 17a Implementation report

Every five years, the Member States shall submit to the Commission a report on the practical implementation of this Directive in the form of a specific chapter of the single report referred to in Article 17a(1), (2) and (3) of Directive 89/391/EEC, which serves as a basis for the Commission's evaluation, in accordance with Article 17a(4) of that Directive.

Article 18

This Directive is addressed to the Member States.

Done at Luxembourg, 22 June 1994.
For the Council
The President
E. YIANNOPOULOS

Annex

Non-exhaustive list of agents, processes and work (Article 7(2), second sub-paragraph)

I Agents

1. Physical agents:
   (a) Ionizing radiation;
   (b) Work in a high-pressure atmosphere, e.g., in pressurised containers, diving.
2. Biological agents
   (a) Biological agents belonging to groups 3 and 4 within the meaning of Article 2(d) of Council Directive 90/679/EEC of 26 November 1990 on the protection of workers from risks related to exposure to biological agents at work (Seventh individual Directive within the meaning of Article 16(1) of Directive 89/391/EEC).[6]
3. Chemical agents
   (a) Substances and preparations classified according to Council Directive 67/548/EEC of 27 June 1967 on the approximation of laws, regulations and administrative provisions

[6] OJ No L374, 31.12.1990, p. 1.

relating to the classification, packaging and labelling of dangerous substances[7] with amendments and Council Directive 88/379/EEC of 7 June 1988 on the approximation of the laws, regulations and administrative provisions of the Member States relating to the classification, packaging and labelling of dangerous preparations[8] as toxic (T), very toxic (Tx), corrosive (C) or explosive (E);

(b) Substances and preparations classified according to Directives 67/548/EEC and 88/379/EEC as harmful (Xn) and with one or more of the following risk phrases:
- danger of very serious irreversible effects (R39),
- possible risk of irreversible effects (R40),
- may cause sensitisation by inhalation (R42),
- may cause sensitisation by skin contact (R43),
- may cause cancer (R45),
- may cause heritable genetic damage (R46),
- danger of serious damage to health by prolonged exposure (R48),
- may impair fertility (R60),
- may cause harm to the unborn child (R61);

(c) Substances and preparations classified according to Directives 67/548/EEC and 88/ 379/EEC as irritant (Xi) and with one or more of the following risk phrases:
- highly flammable (R12),
- may cause sensitisation by inhalation (R42),
- may cause sensitisation by skin contact (R43),

(d) Substances and preparations referred to Article 2(c) of Council Directive 90/394/EEC of 28 June 1990 on the protection of workers from the risks related to exposure to carcinogens at work (Sixth individual Directive within the meaning of Article 16(1) of Directive 89/391/EEC;[9]

(e) Lead and compounds thereof, inasmuch as the agents in question are absorbable by the human organism;

(f) Asbestos.

II Processes and work

1. Processes at work referred to in Annex I to Directive 90/394/EEC.
2. Manufacture and handling of devices, fireworks or other objects containing explosives.
3. Work with fierce or poisonous animals.
4. Animal slaughtering on an industrial scale.
5. Work involving the handling of equipment for the production, storage or application of compressed, liquified or dissolved gases.
6. Work with vats, tanks, reservoirs or carboys containing chemical agents referred to in 1.3.
7. Work involving a risk of structural collapse.
8. Work involving high-voltage electrical hazards.
9. Work the pace of which is determined by machinery and involving payment by results.

Council Directive 97/81/EC of 15 December 1997 concerning the framework agreement on part-time work concluded by UNICE, CEEP and the ETUC*

[OJ 1998 L14/9]

THE COUNCIL OF THE EUROPEAN UNION,

Having regard to the Agreement on social policy annexed to the Protocol (No 14) on social policy, annexed to the Treaty establishing the European Community, and in particular Article 4(2) thereof,

[7] OJ No L196, 16.8.1967, p. 1. Directive as last amended by Directive 93/679/EEC (OJ No L268, 29.10.1993, p. 71).
[8] OJ No L187, 16.7.1988, p. 14. Directive as last amended by Directive 93/18/EEC (OJ No L104, 29.4.1993, p. 46).
[9] OJ No L196, 26.7.1990, p. 1.
* **Editor's Note:** As extended to the UK by Council Directive 98/23/EC.

Having regard to the proposal from the Commission,

(1) Whereas on the basis of the Protocol on social policy annexed to the Treaty establishing the European Community, the Member States, with the exception of the United Kingdom of Great Britain and Northern Ireland (hereinafter referred to as 'the Member States'), wishing to continue along the path laid down in the 1989 Social Charter, have concluded an agreement on social policy;

(2) Whereas management and labour (the social partners) may, in accordance with Article 4(2) of the Agreement on social policy, request jointly that agreements at Community level be implemented by a Council decision on a proposal from the Commission;

(3) Whereas point 7 of the Community Charter of the Fundamental Social Rights of Workers provides, inter alia, that 'the completion of the internal market must lead to an improvement in the living and working conditions of workers in the European Community. This process must result from an approximation of these conditions while the improvement is being maintained, as regards in particular... forms of employment other than open-ended contracts, such as fixed-term contracts, part-time working, temporary work and seasonal work';

(4) Whereas the Council has not reached a decision on the proposal for a Directive on certain employment relationships with regard to distortions of competition,[1] as amended,[2] nor on the proposal for a Directive on certain employment relationships with regard to working conditions;[3]

(5) Whereas the conclusions of the Essen European Council stressed the need to take measures to promote employment and equal opportunities for women and men, and called for measures with a view to increasing the employment-intensiveness of growth, in particular by a more flexible organisation of work in a way which fulfils both the wishes of employees and the requirements of competition;

(6) Whereas the Commission, in accordance with Article 3(2) of the Agreement on social policy, has consulted management and labour on the possible direction of Community action with regard to flexible working time and job security;

(7) Whereas the Commission, considering after such consultation that Community action was desirable, once again consulted management and labour at Community level on the substance of the envisaged proposal in accordance with Article 3(3) of the said Agreement;

(8) Whereas the general cross-industry organisations, the Union of Industrial and Employer's Confederations of Europe (UNICE), the European Centre of Enterprises with Public Participation (CEEP) and the European Trade Union Confederation (ETUC) informed the Commission in their joint letter of 19 June 1996 of their desire to initiate the procedure provided for in Article 4 of the Agreement on social policy; whereas they asked the Commission, in a joint letter dated 12 March 1997, for a further three months; whereas the Commission complied with this request;

(9) Whereas the said cross-industry organisations concluded, on 6 June 1997, a Framework Agreement on part-time work; whereas they forwarded to the Commission their joint request to implement this Framework Agreement by a Council decision on a proposal from the Commission, in accordance with Article 4(2) of the said Agreement;

(10) Whereas the Council, in its Resolution of 6 December 1994 on prospects for a European Union social policy: contribution to economic and social convergence in the Union,[4] asked management and labour to make use of the opportunities for concluding agreements, since they are as a rule closer to social reality and to social problems;

(11) Whereas the signatory parties wished to conclude a framework agreement on part-time work setting out the general principles and minimum requirements for part-time working; whereas they have demonstrated their desire to establish a general framework for eliminating discrimination against part-time workers and to contribute to developing the potential for part-time work on a basis which is acceptable for employers and workers alike;

[1] OJ C 224, 8.9.1990, p. 6.
[2] OJ C 305, 5.12.1990, p. 8.
[3] OJ C 224, 8.9.1990, p. 4.
[4] OJ C 368, 23.12.1994, p. 6.

(12) Whereas the social partners wished to give particular attention to part-time work, while at the same time indicating that it was their intention to consider the need for similar agreements for other flexible forms of work;

(13) Whereas, in the conclusions of the Amsterdam European Council, the Heads of State and Government of the European Union strongly welcomed the agreement concluded by the social partners on part-time work;

(14) Whereas the proper instrument for implementing the Framework Agreement is a Directive within the meaning of Article 189 of the Treaty; whereas it therefore binds the Member States as to the result to be achieved, whilst leaving national authorities the choice of form and methods;

(15) Whereas, in accordance with the principles of subsidiarity and proportionality as set out in Article 3(b) of the Treaty, the objectives of this Directive cannot be sufficiently achieved by the Member States and can therefore be better achieved by the Community; whereas this Directive does not go beyond what is necessary for the attainment of those objectives;

(16) Whereas, with regard to terms used in the Framework Agreement which are not specifically defined therein, this Directive leaves Member States free to define those terms in accordance with national law and practice, as is the case for other social policy Directives using similar terms, providing that the said definitions respect the content of the Framework Agreement;

(17) Whereas the Commission has drafted its proposal for a Directive, in accordance with its Communication of 14 December 1993 concerning the application of the Protocol (No 14) on social policy and its Communication of 18 September 1996 concerning the development of the social dialogue at Community level, taking into account the representative status of the signatory parties and the legality of each clause of the Framework Agreement;

(18) Whereas the Commission has drafted its proposal for a Directive in compliance with Article 2 (2) of the Agreement on social policy which provides that Directives in the social policy domain 'shall avoid imposing administrative, financial and legal constraints in a way which would hold back the creation and development of small and medium-sized undertakings';

(19) Whereas the Commission, in accordance with its Communication of 14 December 1993 concerning the application of the Protocol (No 14) on social policy, informed the European Parliament by sending it the text of its proposal for a Directive containing the Framework Agreement;

(20) Whereas the Commission also informed the Economic and Social Committee;

(21) Whereas Clause 6.1 of the Framework Agreement provides that Member States and/or the social partners may maintain or introduce more favourable provisions;

(22) Whereas Clause 6.2 of the Framework Agreement provides that implementation of this Directive may not serve to justify any regression in relation to the situation which already exists in each Member State;

(23) Whereas the Community Charter of the Fundamental Social Rights of Workers recognises the importance of the fight against all forms of discrimination, especially based on sex, colour, race, opinion and creed;

(24) Whereas Article F(2) of the Treaty on European Union states that the Union shall respect fundamental rights, as guaranteed by the European Convention for the Protection of Human Rights and Fundamental Freedoms and as they result from the constitutional traditions common to the Member States, as general principles of Community law;

(25) Whereas the Member States may entrust the social partners, at their joint request, with the implementation of this Directive, provided that the Member States take all the necessary steps to ensure that they can at all times guarantee the results imposed by this Directive;

(26) Whereas the implementation of the Framework Agreement contributes to achieving the objectives under Article 1 of the Agreement on social policy,

HAS ADOPTED THIS DIRECTIVE:

Article 1

The purpose of this Directive is to implement the Framework Agreement on part-time work concluded on 6 June 1997 between the general cross-industry organisations (UNICE, CEEP and the ETUC) annexed hereto.

Article 2

1. Member States shall bring into force the laws, regulations and administrative provisions necessary to comply with this Directive not later than 20 January 2000, or shall ensure that, by that date at the latest, the social partners have introduced the necessary measures by agreement, the Member States being required to take any necessary measures to enable them at any time to be in a position to guarantee the results imposed by this Directive. They shall forthwith inform the Commission thereof.

Member States may have a maximum of one more year, if necessary, to take account of special difficulties or implementation by a collective agreement.

They shall inform the Commission forthwith in such circumstances. When Member States adopt the measures referred to in the first sub-paragraph, they shall contain a reference to this Directive or shall be accompanied by such reference on the occasion of their official publication. The methods of making such a reference shall be laid down by the Member States.

1a. As regards the United Kingdom of Great Britain and Northern Ireland, the date of 20 January 2000 in paragraph 1 shall be replaced by the date of 7 April 2000.

2. Member States shall communicate to the Commission the text of the main provisions of domestic law which they have adopted or which they adopt in the field governed by this Directive.

Article 3

This Directive shall enter into force on the day of its publication in the *Official Journal of the European Communities*.

Article 4

This Directive is addressed to the Member States.

Done at Brussels, 15 December 1997.
For the Council
The President
J.-C. JUNCKER

Annex

Union of Industrial and Employers' Confederations of Europe, European Trade Union Confederation, European Centre of Enterprises with Public Participation Framework Agreement on Part-time Work

Preamble

This Framework Agreement is a contribution to the overall European strategy on employment. Part-time work has had an important impact on employment in recent years. For this reason, the parties to this agreement have given priority attention to this form of work. It is the intention of the parties to consider the need for similar agreements relating to other forms of flexible work.

Recognising the diversity of situations in Member States and acknowledging that part-time work is a feature of employment in certain sectors and activities, this Agreement sets out the general principles and minimum requirements relating to part-time work. It illustrates the willingness of the social partners to establish a general framework for the elimination of discrimination against part-time workers and to assist the development of opportunities for part-time working on a basis acceptable to employers and workers.

This Agreement relates to employment conditions of part-time workers recognising that matters concerning statutory social security are for decision by the Member States. In the context of the principle of non-discrimination, the parties to this Agreement have noted the Employment Declaration of the Dublin European Council of December 1996, wherein the Council inter alia emphasised the need to make social security systems more employment-friendly by 'developing social protection systems capable of adapting to new patterns of work and of providing appropriate protection to people engaged in such work'. The parties to this Agreement consider that effect should be given to this Declaration.

ETUC, UNICE and CEEP request the Commission to submit this Framework Agreement to the Council for a decision making these requirements binding in the Member States which are party to the Agreement on social policy annexed to the Protocol (No 14) on social policy annexed to the Treaty establishing the European Community.

The parties to this Agreement ask the Commission, in its proposal to implement this Agreement, to request that Member States adopt the laws, regulations and administrative provisions necessary to comply with the Council decision within a period of two years from its adoption or ensure[5] that the social partners establish the necessary measures by way of agreement by the end of this period. Member States may, if necessary to take account of particular difficulties or implementation by collective agreement, have up to a maximum of one additional year to comply with this provision.

Without prejudice to the role of national courts and the Court of Justice, the parties to this agreement request that any matter relating to the interpretation of this agreement at European level should, in the first instance, be referred by the Commission to them for an opinion.

General considerations

1. Having regard to the Agreement on social policy annexed to the Protocol (No 14) on social policy annexed to the Treaty establishing the European Community, and in particular Articles 3(4) and 4(2) thereof;

2. Whereas Article 4(2) of the Agreement on social policy provides that agreements concluded at Community level may be implemented, at the joint request of the signatory parties, by a Council decision on a proposal from the Commission.

3. Whereas, in its second consultation document on flexibility of working time and security for workers, the Commission announced its intention to propose a legally binding Community measure;

4. Whereas the conclusions of the European Council meeting in Essen emphasised the need for measures to promote both employment and equal opportunities for women and men, and called for measures aimed at 'increasing the employment intensiveness of growth, in particular by more flexible organisation of work in a way which fulfils both the wishes of employees and the requirements of competition';

5. Whereas the parties to this agreement attach importance to measures which would facilitate access to part-time work for men and women in order to prepare for retirement, reconcile professional and family life, and take up education and training opportunities to improve their skills and career opportunities for the mutual benefit of employers and workers and in a manner which would assist the development of enterprises;

6. Whereas this Agreement refers back to Member States and social partners for the arrangements for the application of these general principles, minimum requirements and provisions, in order to take account of the situation in each Member State;

7. Whereas this Agreement takes into consideration the need to improve social policy requirements, to enhance the competitiveness of the Community economy and to avoid imposing administrative, financial and legal constraints in a way which would hold back the creation and development of small and medium-sized undertakings;

8. Whereas the social partners are best placed to find solutions that correspond to the needs of both employers and workers and must therefore be given a special role in the implementation and application of this Agreement.

[5] Within the meaning of Article 2(4) of the Agreement on social policy of the Treaty establishing the European Community.

THE SIGNATORY PARTIES HAVE AGREED THE FOLLOWING:

Clause 1: Purpose

The purpose of this Framework Agreement is:

(a) to provide for the removal of discrimination against part-time workers and to improve the quality of part-time work;

(b) to facilitate the development of part-time work on a voluntary basis and to contribute to the flexible organisation of working time in a manner which takes into account the needs of employers and workers.

Clause 2: Scope

1. This Agreement applies to part-time workers who have an employment contract or employment relationship as defined by the law, collective agreement or practice in force in each Member State.

2. Member States, after consultation with the social partners in accordance with national law, collective agreements or practice, and/or the social partners at the appropriate level in conformity with national industrial relations practice may, for objective reasons, exclude wholly or partly from the terms of this Agreement part-time workers who work on a casual basis. Such exclusions should be reviewed periodically to establish if the objective reasons for making them remain valid.

Clause 3: Definitions

For the purpose of this agreement:

1. The term 'part-time worker' refers to an employee whose normal hours of work, calculated on a weekly basis or on average over a period of employment of up to one year, are less than the normal hours of work of a comparable full-time worker.

2. The term 'comparable full-time worker' means a full-time worker in the same establishment having the same type of employment contract or relationship, who is engaged in the same or a similar work/occupation, due regard being given to other considerations which may include seniority and qualification/skills.

Where there is no comparable full-time worker in the same establishment, the comparison shall be made by reference to the applicable collective agreement or, where there is no applicable collective agreement, in accordance with national law, collective agreements or practice.

Clause 4: Principle of non-discrimination

1. In respect of employment conditions, part-time workers shall not be treated in a less favourable manner than comparable full-time workers solely because they work part time unless different treatment is justified on objective grounds.

2. Where appropriate, the principle of pro rata temporis shall apply.

3. The arrangements for the application of this clause shall be defined by the Member States and/or social partners, having regard to European legislation, national law, collective agreements and practice.

4. Where justified by objective reasons, Member States after consultation of the social partners in accordance with national law, collective agreements or practice and/or social partners may, where appropriate, make access to particular conditions of employment subject to a period of service, time worked or earnings qualification. Qualifications relating to access by part-time workers to particular conditions of employment should be reviewed periodically having regard to the principle of non-discrimination as expressed in Clause 4.1.

Clause 5: Opportunities for part-time work

1. In the context of Clause 1 of this Agreement and of the principle of non-discrimination between part-time and full-time workers:

(a) Member States, following consultations with the social partners in accordance with national law or practice, should identify and review obstacles of a legal or administrative nature which may limit the opportunities for part-time work and, where appropriate, eliminate them;

(b) the social partners, acting within their sphere of competence and through the procedures set out in collective agreements, should identify and review obstacles which may limit opportunities for part-time work and, where appropriate, eliminate them.

2. A worker's refusal to transfer from full-time to part-time work or vice-versa should not in itself constitute a valid reason for termination of employment, without prejudice to termination in accordance with national law, collective agreements and practice, for other reasons such as may arise from the operational requirements of the establishment concerned.

3. As far as possible, employers should give consideration to:

(a) requests by workers to transfer from full-time to part-time work that becomes available in the establishment;

(b) requests by workers to transfer from part-time to full-time work or to increase their working time should the opportunity arise;

(c) the provision of timely information on the availability of part-time and full-time positions in the establishment in order to facilitate transfers from full-time to part-time or vice versa;

(d) measures to facilitate access to part-time work at all levels of the enterprise, including skilled and managerial positions, and where appropriate, to facilitate access by part-time workers to vocational training to enhance career opportunities and occupational mobility;

(e) the provision of appropriate information to existing bodies representing workers about part-time working in the enterprise.

Clause 6: Provisions on implementation

1. Member States and/or social partners may maintain or introduce more favourable provisions than set out in this agreement.

2. Implementation of the provisions of this Agreement shall not constitute valid grounds for reducing the general level of protection afforded to workers in the field of this agreement. This does not prejudice the right of Member States and/or social partners to develop different legislative, regulatory or contractual provisions, in the light of changing circumstances, and does not prejudice the application of Clause 5.1 as long as the principle of non-discrimination as expressed in Clause 4.1 is complied with.

3. This Agreement does not prejudice the right of the social partners to conclude, at the appropriate level, including European level, agreements adapting and/or complementing the provisions of this Agreement in a manner which will take account of the specific needs of the social partners concerned.

4. This Agreement shall be without prejudice to any more specific Community provisions, and in particular Community provisions concerning equal treatment or opportunities for men and women.

5. The prevention and settlement of disputes and grievances arising from the application of this Agreement shall be dealt with in accordance with national law, collective agreements and practice.

6. The signatory parties shall review this Agreement, five years after the date of the Council decision, if requested by one of the parties to this Agreement.

Council Directive 98/59/EC of 20 July 1998 on the approximation of the laws of the Member States relating to collective redundancies*

[OJ 1998 L225/16]

THE COUNCIL OF THE EUROPEAN UNION,

Having regard to the Treaty establishing the European Community, and in particular Article 100 thereof,

* **Editor's Note:** This repeals Directive 75/129 as amended by Directive 92/56. As corrected by OJ 2007 L59/84.

Having regard to the proposal from the Commission,

Having regard to the opinion of the European Parliament,[1]

Having regard to the opinion of the Economic and Social Committee,[2]

(1) Whereas for reasons of clarity and rationality Council Directive 75/129/EEC of 17 February 1975 on the approximation of the laws of the Member States relating to collective redundancies[3] should be consolidated;

(2) Whereas it is important that greater protection should be afforded to workers in the event of collective redundancies while taking into account the need for balanced economic and social development within the Community;

(3) Whereas, despite increasing convergence, differences still remain between the provisions in force in the Member States concerning the practical arrangements and procedures for such redundancies and the measures designed to alleviate the consequences of redundancy for workers;

(4) Whereas these differences can have a direct effect on the functioning of the internal market;

(5) Whereas the Council resolution of 21 January 1974 concerning a social action programme[4] made provision for a directive on the approximation of Member States' legislation on collective redundancies;

(6) Whereas the Community Charter of the fundamental social rights of workers, adopted at the European Council meeting held in Strasbourg on 9 December 1989 by the Heads of State or Government of 11 Member States, states, inter alia, in point 7, first paragraph, first sentence, and second paragraph; in point 17, first paragraph; and in point 18, third indent:

'7. The completion of the internal market must lead to an improvement in the living and working conditions of workers in the European Community.

The improvement must cover, where necessary, the development of certain aspects of employment regulations such as procedures for collective redundancies and those regarding bankruptcies.

17. Information, consultation and participation for workers must be developed along appropriate lines, taking account of the practices in force in the various Member States.

18. Such information, consultation and participation must be implemented in due time, particularly in the following cases:

– in cases of collective redundancy procedures';

(7) Whereas this approximation must therefore be promoted while the improvement is being maintained within the meaning of Article 117 of the Treaty;

(8) Whereas, in order to calculate the number of redundancies provided for in the definition of collective redundancies within the meaning of this Directive, other forms of termination of employment contracts on the initiative of the employer should be equated to redundancies, provided that there are at least five redundancies;

(9) Whereas it should be stipulated that this Directive applies in principle also to collective redundancies resulting where the establishment's activities are terminated as a result of a judicial decision;

(10) Whereas the Member States should be given the option of stipulating that workers' representatives may call on experts on grounds of the technical complexity of the matters which are likely to be the subject of the informing and consulting;

(11) Whereas it is necessary to ensure that employers' obligations as regards information, consultation and notification apply independently of whether the decision on collective redundancies emanates from the employer or from an undertaking which controls that employer;

[1] OJ C 210, 6.7.1998.

[2] OJ C 158, 26.5.1997, p. 11.

[3] OJ L 48, 22.2.1975, p. 29. Directive as amended by Directive 92/56/EEC (OJ L 245, 26.8.1992, p. 3).

[4] OJ C 13, 12.2.1974, p. 1.

(12) Whereas Member States should ensure that workers' representatives and/or workers have at their disposal administrative and/or judicial procedures in order to ensure that the obligations laid down in this Directive are fulfilled;

(13) Whereas this Directive must not affect the obligations of the Member States concerning the deadlines for transposition of the Directives set out in Annex I, Part B.

HAS ADOPTED THIS DIRECTIVE:

Section I Definitions and scope

Article 1

1. For the purposes of this Directive:
   - (a) 'collective redundancies' means dismissals effected by an employer for one or more reasons not related to the individual workers concerned where, according to the choice of the Member States, the number of redundancies is:
     - (i) either, over a period of 30 days:
       - at least 10 in establishments normally employing more than 20 and less than 100 workers,
       - at least 10% of the number of workers in establishments normally employing at least 100 but less than 300 workers,
       - at least 30 in establishments normally employing 300 workers or more,
     - (ii) or, over a period of 90 days, at least 20, whatever the number of workers normally employed in the establishments in question;
   - (b) 'workers' representatives means the workers' representatives provided for by the laws or practices of the Member States.

For the purpose of calculating the number of redundancies provided for in the first subparagraph of point (a), terminations of an employment contract which occur on the employer's initiative for one or more reasons not related to the individual workers concerned shall be assimilated to redundancies, provided that there are at least five redundancies.

2. This Directive shall not apply to:
   - (a) collective redundancies effected under contracts of employment concluded for limited periods of time or for specific tasks except where such redundancies take place prior to the date of expiry or the completion of such contracts;
   - (b) workers employed by public administrative bodies or by establishments governed by public law (or, in Member States where this concept is unknown, by equivalent bodies);
   - (c) the crews of seagoing vessels.

Section II Information and consultation

Article 2

1. Where an employer is contemplating collective redundancies, he shall begin consultations with the workers' representatives in good time with a view to reaching an agreement.

2. These consultations shall, at least, cover ways and means of avoiding collective redundancies or reducing the number of workers affected, and of mitigating the consequences by recourse to accompanying social measures aimed, inter alia, at aid for redeploying or retraining workers made redundant.

Member States may provide that the workers' representatives may call on the services of experts in accordance with national legislation and/or practice.

3. To enable workers' representatives to make constructive proposals, the employers shall in good time during the course of the consultations:
   - (a) supply them with all relevant information and
   - (b) in any event notify them in writing of:
     - (i) the reasons for the projected redundancies;
     - (ii) the number of categories of workers to be made redundant;

(iii) the number and categories of workers normally employed;
(iv) the period over which the projected redundancies are to be effected;
(v) the criteria proposed for the selection of the workers to be made redundant in so far as national legislation and/or practice confers the power therefore upon the employer;
(vi) the method for calculating any redundancy payments other than those arising out of national legislation and/or practice.

The employer shall forward to the competent public authority a copy of, at least, the elements of the written communication which are provided for in the first subparagraph, point (b), subpoints (i) to (v).

4. The obligations laid down in paragraphs 1, 2 and 3 shall apply irrespective of whether the decision regarding collective redundancies is being taken by the employer or by an undertaking controlling the employer.

In considering alleged breaches of the information, consultation and notification requirements laid down by this Directive, account shall not be taken of any defence on the part of the employer on the ground that the necessary information has not been provided to the employer by the undertaking which took the decision leading to collective redundancies.

Section III Procedure for collective redundancies

Article 3

1. Employers shall notify the competent public authority in writing of any projected collective redundancies.

However, Member States may provide that in the case of planned collective redundancies arising from termination of the establishment's activities as a result of a judicial decision, the employer shall be obliged to notify the competent public authority in writing only if the latter so requests.

This notification shall contain all relevant information concerning the projected collective redundancies and the consultations with workers' representatives provided for in Article 2, and particularly the reasons for the redundancies, the number of workers to be made redundant, the number of workers normally employed and the period over which the redundancies are to be effected.

2. Employers shall forward to the workers' representatives a copy of the notification provided for in paragraph 1.

The workers' representatives may send any comments they may have to the competent public authority.

Article 4

1. Projected collective redundancies notified to the competent public authority shall take effect not earlier than 30 days after the notification referred to in Article 3(1) without prejudice to any provisions governing individual rights with regard to notice of dismissal.

Member States may grant the competent public authority the power to reduce the period provided for in the preceding subparagraph.

2. The period provided for in paragraph 1 shall be used by the competent public authority to seek solutions to the problems raised by the projected collective redundancies.

3. Where the initial period provided for in paragraph 1 is shorter than 60 days, Member States may grant the competent public authority the power to extend the initial period to 60 days following notification where the problems raised by the projected collective redundancies are not likely to be solved within the initial period.

Member States may grant the competent public authority wider powers of extension. The employer must be informed of the extension and the grounds for it before expiry of the initial period provided for in paragraph 1.

4. Member States need not apply this Article to collective redundancies arising from termination of the establishment's activities where this is the result of a judicial decision.

Section IV Final provisions

Article 5

This Directive shall not affect the right of Member States to apply or to introduce laws, regulations or administrative provisions which are more favourable to workers or to promote or to allow the application of collective agreements more favourable to workers.

Article 6

Member States shall ensure that judicial and/or administrative procedures for the enforcement of obligations under this Directive are available to the workers' representatives and/or workers.

Article 7

Member States shall forward to the Commission the text of any fundamental provisions of national law already adopted or being adopted in the area governed by this Directive.

Article 8

1. The Directives listed in Annex I, Part A, are hereby repealed without prejudice to the obligations of the Member States concerning the deadlines for transposition of the said Directive set out in Annex I, Part B.

2. References to the repealed Directives shall be construed as references to this Directive and shall be read in accordance with the correlation table in Annex II.

Article 9

This Directive shall enter into force on the 20th day following its publication in the *Official Journal of the European Communities*.

Article 10

This Directive is addressed to the Member States.

Done at Brussels, 20 July 1998.
For the Council
The President
W. MOLTERER

Annex I

Part A

Repealed Directives (referred to by Article 8) Council Directive 75/129/EEC and its following amendment: Council Directive 92/56/EEC.

Part B Deadlines for transposition into national law

(referred to by Article 8)

Directive	Deadline for transposition
75/129/EEC (OJ L48, 22.2.1975, p. 29)	19 February 1977
92/56/EEC (OJ L245, 26.8.1992, p. 3)	24 June 1994
Article 1(1), first sub-paragraph, point (a), first indent, point 1	Article 1(1), first sub-paragraph, point (a), first indent
Article 1(1), first sub-paragraph, point (a), first indent, point 2	Article 1(1), first sub-paragraph, point (a)(i), second indent
Article 1(1), first sub-paragraph, point (a), first indent, point 3	Article 1(1), first sub-paragraph, point (a)(i), third indent

Directive	Deadline for transposition
Article 1(1), first sub-paragraph, point (b)	Article 1(1), first sub-paragraph, point (b)
Article 1(1), second sub-paragraph	Article 1(1), second sub-paragraph
Article 1(2)	Article 1(2)
Article 2	Article 2
Article 3	Article 3
Article 4	Article 4
Article 5	Article 5
Article 5a	Article 6
Article 6(1)	–
Article 6(2)	Article 7
Article 7	–
–	Article 8
–	Article 9
–	Article 10
–	Annex I
–	Annex II

Council Directive 1999/70/EC of 28 June 1999 concerning the framework agreement on fixed-term work concluded by ETUC, UNICE and CEEP*

[OJ 1999 L175/43]

THE COUNCIL OF THE EUROPEAN UNION,

Having regard to the Treaty establishing the European Community, and in particular Article 139(2) thereof,

Having regard to the proposal from the Commission,

Whereas:

(1) Following the entry into force of the Treaty of Amsterdam the provisions of the Agreement on social policy annexed to the Protocol on social policy, annexed to the Treaty establishing the European Community have been incorporated into Articles 136 to 139 of the Treaty establishing the European Community;

(2) Management and labour (the social partners) may, in accordance with Article 139(2) of the Treaty, request jointly that agreements at Community level be implemented by a Council decision on a proposal from the Commission;

(3) Point 7 of the Community Charter of the Fundamental Social Rights of Workers provides, inter alia, that 'the completion of the internal market must lead to an improvement in the living and working conditions of workers in the European Community. This process must result from an approximation of these conditions while the improvement is being maintained, as regards in particular forms of employment other than open-ended contracts, such as fixed-term contracts, part-time working, temporary work and seasonal work';

* **Editor's Note:** As corrected by OJ 1999 L224/64.

(4) The Council has been unable to reach a decision on the proposal for a Directive on certain employment relationships with regard to distortions of competition[1], nor on the proposal for a Directive on certain employment relationships with regard to working conditions[2];

(5) The conclusions of the Essen European Council stressed the need to take measures with a view to 'increasing the employment-intensiveness of growth, in particular by a more flexible organisation of work in a way which fulfils both the wishes of employees and the requirements of competition';

(6) The Council Resolution of 9 February 1999 on the 1999 Employment Guidelines invites the social partners at all appropriate levels to negotiate agreements to modernise the organisation of work, including flexible working arrangements, with the aim of making undertakings productive and competitive and achieving the required balance between flexibility and security;

(7) The Commission, in accordance with Article 3(2) of the Agreement on social policy, has consulted management and labour on the possible direction of Community action with regard to flexible working time and job security;

(8) The Commission, considering after such consultation that Community action was desirable, once again consulted management and labour on the substance of the envisaged proposal in accordance with Article 3(3) of the said Agreement;

(9) The general cross-industry organisations, namely the Union of Industrial and Employers' Confederations of Europe (UNICE), the European Centre of Enterprises with Public Participation (CEEP) and the European Trade Union Confederation (ETUC), informed the Commission in a joint letter dated 23 March 1998 of their desire to initiate the procedure provided for in Article 4 of the said Agreement; they asked the Commission, in a joint letter, for a further period of three months; the Commission complied with this request extending the negotiation period to 30 March 1999;

(10) The said cross-industry organisations on 18 March 1999 concluded a framework agreement on fixed-term work; they forwarded to the Commission their joint request to implement the framework agreement by a Council Decision on a proposal from the Commission, in accordance with Article 4(2) of the Agreement on social policy;

(11) The Council, in its Resolution of 6 December 1994 on 'certain aspects for a European Union social policy: a contribution to economic and social convergence in the Union',[3] asked management and labour to make use of the opportunities for concluding agreements, since they are as a rule closer to social reality and to social problems;

(12) The signatory parties, in the preamble to the framework agreement on part-time work concluded on 6 June 1997, announced their intention to consider the need for similar agreements relating to other forms of flexible work;

(13) Management and labour wished to give particular attention to fixed-term work, while at the same time indicating that it was their intention to consider the need for a similar agreement relating to temporary agency work;

(14) The signatory parties wished to conclude a framework agreement on fixed-term work setting out the general principles and minimum requirements for fixed-term employment contracts and employment relationships; they have demonstrated their desire to improve the quality of fixed-term work by ensuring the application of the principle of non-discrimination, and to establish a framework to prevent abuse arising from the use of successive fixed-term employment contracts or relationships;

(15) The proper instrument for implementing the framework agreement is a directive within the meaning of Article 249 of the Treaty; it therefore binds the Member States as to the result to be achieved, whilst leaving them the choice of form and methods;

(16) In accordance with the principles of subsidiarity and proportionality as set out in Article 5 of the Treaty, the objectives of this Directive cannot be sufficiently achieved by the Member States and can therefore be better achieved by the Community; this Directive limits itself to the minimum required for the attainment of those objectives and does not go beyond what is necessary for that purpose;

[1] OJ C 224, 8.9.1990, p. 6 and OJ C 305, 5.12.1990, p. 8.
[2] OJ C 224, 8.9.1990, p. 4.
[3] OJ C 368, 23.12.1994, p. 6.

(17) As regards terms used in the framework agreement but not specifically defined therein, this Directive allows Member States to define such terms in conformity with national law or practice as is the case for other Directives on social matters using similar terms, provided that the definitions in question respect the content of the framework agreement;

(18) The Commission has drafted its proposal for a Directive, in accordance with its Communication of 14 December 1993 concerning the application of the agreement on social policy and its Communication of 20 May 1998 on adapting and promoting the social dialogue at Community level, taking into account the representative status of the contracting parties, their mandate and the legality of each clause of the framework agreement; the contracting parties together have a sufficiently representative status;

(19) The Commission informed the European Parliament and the Economic and Social Committee by sending them the text of the agreement, accompanied by its proposal for a Directive and the explanatory memorandum, in accordance with its communication concerning the implementation of the Protocol on social policy;

(20) On 6 May 1999 the European Parliament adopted a Resolution on the framework agreement between the social partners;

(21) The implementation of the framework agreement contributes to achieving the objectives in Article 136 of the Treaty,

HAS ADOPTED THIS DIRECTIVE:

Article 1

The purpose of the Directive is to put into effect the framework agreement on fixed-term contracts concluded on 18 March 1999 between the general cross-industry organisations (ETUC, UNICE and CEEP) annexed hereto.

Article 2

Member States shall bring into force the laws, regulations and administrative provisions necessary to comply with this Directive by 10 July 2001, or shall ensure that, by that date at the latest, management and labour have introduced the necessary measures by agreement, the Member States being required to take any necessary measures to enable them at any time to be in a position to guarantee the results imposed by this Directive. They shall forthwith inform the Commission thereof. Member States may have a maximum of one more year, if necessary, and following consultation with management and labour, to take account of special difficulties or implementation by a collective agreement. They shall inform the Commission forthwith in such circumstances.

When Member States adopt the provisions referred to in the first paragraph, these shall contain a reference to this Directive or shall be accompanied by such reference at the time of their official publication. The procedure for such reference shall be adopted by the Member States.

Article 3

This Directive shall enter into force on the day of its publication in the *Official Journal of the European Communities*.

Article 4

This Directive is addressed to the Member States.

Done at Luxembourg, 28 June 1999.

For the Council

The President

M. NAUMANN

Annex
ETUC-UNICE-CEEP framework agreement on fixed-term work

Preamble

This framework agreement illustrates the role that the social partners can play in the European employment strategy agreed at the 1997 Luxembourg extraordinary summit and, following the framework agreement on part-time work, represents a further contribution towards achieving a better balance between 'flexibility in working time and security for workers'.

The parties to this agreement recognise that contracts of an indefinite duration are, and will continue to be, the general form of employment relationship between employers and workers. They also recognise that fixed-term employment contracts respond, in certain circumstances, to the needs of both employers and workers.

This agreement sets out the general principles and minimum requirements relating to fixed-term work, recognising that their detailed application needs to take account of the realities of specific national, sectoral and seasonal situations. It illustrates the willingness of the Social Partners to establish a general framework for ensuring equal treatment for fixed-term workers by protecting them against discrimination and for using fixed-term employment contracts on a basis acceptable to employers and workers.

This agreement applies to fixed-term workers with the exception of those placed by a temporary work agency at the disposition of a user enterprise. It is the intention of the parties to consider the need for a similar agreement relating to temporary agency work.

This agreement relates to the employment conditions of fixed-term workers, recognising that matters relating to statutory social security are for decision by the Member States. In this respect the Social Partners note the Employment Declaration of the Dublin European Council in 1996 which emphasised inter alia, the need to develop more employment-friendly social security systems by 'developing social protection systems capable of adapting to new patterns of work and providing appropriate protection to those engaged in such work'. The parties to this agreement reiterate the view expressed in the 1997 part-time agreement that Member States should give effect to this Declaration without delay.

In addition, it is also recognised that innovations in occupational social protection systems are necessary in order to adapt them to current conditions, and in particular to provide for the transferability of rights.

The ETUC, UNICE and CEEP request the Commission to submit this framework agreement to the Council for a decision making these requirements binding in the Member States which are party to the Agreement on social policy annexed to the Protocol (No 14) on social policy annexed to the Treaty establishing the European Community.

The parties to this agreement ask the Commission, in its proposal to implement the agreement, to request Member States to adopt the laws, regulations and administrative provisions necessary to comply with the Council Decision within two years from its adoption or ensure[4] that the social partners establish the necessary measures by way of agreement by the end of this period. Member States may, if necessary and following consultation with the social partners, and in order to take account of particular difficulties or implementation by collective agreement, have up to a maximum of one additional year to comply with this provision.

The parties to this agreement request that the social partners are consulted prior to any legislative, regulatory or administrative initiative taken by a Member State to conform to the present agreement.

Without prejudice to the role of national courts and the Court of Justice, the parties to this agreement request that any matter relating to the interpretation of this agreement at European level should in the first instance be referred by the Commission to them for an opinion.

[4] Within the meaning of Article 2.4 of the Agreement on social policy annexed to the Protocol (No 14) on social policy annexed to the Treaty establishing the European Community.

General considerations

1. Having regard to the Agreement on social policy annexed to the Protocol (No 14) on social policy annexed to the Treaty establishing the European Community, and in particular Article 3.4 and 4.2 thereof;

2. Whereas Article 4.2 of the Agreement on social policy provides that agreements concluded at Community level may be implemented, at the joint request of the signatory parties, by a Council decision on a proposal from the Commission;

3. Whereas, in its second consultation document on flexibility in working time and security for workers, the Commission announced its intention to propose a legally-binding Community measure;

4. Whereas in its opinion on the proposal for a Directive on part-time work, the European Parliament invited the Commission to submit immediately proposals for directives on other forms of flexible work, such as fixed-term work and temporary agency work;

5. Whereas in the conclusions of the extraordinary summit on employment adopted in Luxembourg, the European Council invited the social partners to negotiate agreements to 'modernise the organisation of work, including flexible working arrangements, with the aim of making undertakings productive and competitive and achieving the required balance between flexibility and security';

6. Whereas employment contracts of an indefinite duration are the general form of employment relationships and contribute to the quality of life of the workers concerned and improve performance;

7. Whereas the use of fixed-term employment contracts based on objective reasons is a way to prevent abuse;

8. Whereas fixed-term employment contracts are a feature of employment in certain sectors, occupations and activities which can suit both employers and workers;

9. Whereas more than half of fixed-term workers in the European Union are women and this agreement can therefore contribute to improving equality of opportunities between women and men;

10. Whereas this agreement refers back to Member States and social partners for the arrangements for the application of its general principles, minimum requirements and provisions, in order to take account of the situation in each Member State and the circumstances of particular sectors and occupations, including the activities of a seasonal nature;

11. Whereas this agreement takes into consideration the need to improve social policy requirements, to enhance the competitiveness of the Community economy and to avoid imposing administrative, financial and legal constraints in a way which would hold back the creation and development of small and medium-sized undertakings;

12. Whereas the social partners are best placed to find solutions that correspond to the needs of both employers and workers and shall therefore be given a special role in the implementation and application of this agreement.

THE SIGNATORY PARTIES HAVE AGREED THE FOLLOWING

Purpose (clause 1)

The purpose of this framework agreement is to:

(a) improve the quality of fixed-term work by ensuring the application of the principle of non-discrimination;

(b) establish a framework to prevent abuse arising from the use of successive fixed-term employment contracts or relationships.

Scope (clause 2)

1. This agreement applies to fixed-term workers who have an employment contract or employment relationship as defined in law, collective agreements or practice in each Member State.

2. Member States after consultation with the social partners and/or the social partners may provide that this agreement does not apply to:

(a) initial vocational training relationships and apprenticeship schemes;

(b) employment contracts and relationships which have been concluded within the framework of a specific public or publicly-supported training, integration and vocational retraining programme.

Definitions (clause 3)

1. For the purpose of this agreement the term 'fixed-term worker' means a person having an employment contract or relationship entered into directly between an employer and a worker where the end of the employment contract or relationship is determined by objective conditions such as reaching a specific date, completing a specific task, or the occurrence of a specific event.

2. For the purpose of this agreement, the term 'comparable permanent worker' means a worker with an employment contract or relationship of indefinite duration, in the same establishment, engaged in the same or similar work/occupation, due regard being given to qualifications/skills. Where there is no comparable permanent worker in the same establishment, the comparison shall be made by reference to the applicable collective agreement, or where there is no applicable collective agreement, in accordance with national law, collective agreements or practice.

Principle of non-discrimination (clause 4)

1. In respect of employment conditions, fixed-term workers shall not be treated in a less favourable manner than comparable permanent workers solely because they have a fixed-term contract or relation unless different treatment is justified on objective grounds.

2. Where appropriate, the principle of pro rata temporis shall apply.

3. The arrangements for the application of this clause shall be defined by the Member States after consultation with the social partners and/or the social partners, having regard to Community law and national law, collective agreements and practice.

4. Period-of service qualifications relating to particular conditions of employment shall be the same for fixed-term workers as for permanent workers except where different length-of service qualifications are justified on objective grounds.

Measures to prevent abuse (clause 5)

1. To prevent abuse arising from the use of successive fixed-term employment contracts or relationships, Member States, after consultation with social partners in accordance with national law, collective agreements or practice, and/or the social partners, shall, where there are no equivalent legal measures to prevent abuse, introduce in a manner which takes account of the needs of specific sectors and/or categories of workers, one or more of the following measures:

   (a) objective reasons justifying the renewal of such contracts or relationships;
   (b) the maximum total duration of successive fixed-term employment contracts or relationships;
   (c) the number of renewals of such contracts or relationships.

2. Member States after consultation with the social partners and/or the social partners shall, where appropriate, determine under what conditions fixed-term employment contracts or relationships:

   (a) shall be regarded as 'successive'
   (b) shall be deemed to be contracts or relationships of indefinite duration.

Information and employment opportunities (clause 6)

1. Employers shall inform fixed-term workers about vacancies which become available in the undertaking or establishment to ensure that they have the same opportunity to secure permanent positions as other workers. Such information may be provided by way of a general announcement at a suitable place in the undertaking or establishment.

2. As far as possible, employers should facilitate access by fixed-term workers to appropriate training opportunities to enhance their skills, career development and occupational mobility.

Information and consultation (clause 7)

1. Fixed-term workers shall be taken into consideration in calculating the threshold above which workers' representative bodies provided for in national and Community law may be constituted in the undertaking as required by national provisions.

2. The arrangements for the application of clause 7.1 shall be defined by Member States after consultation with the social partners and/or the social partners in accordance with national law, collective agreements or practice and having regard to clause 4.1.

3. As far as possible, employers should give consideration to the provision of appropriate information to existing workers' representative bodies about fixed-term work in the undertaking.

Provisions on implementation (clause 8)

1. Member States and/or the social partners can maintain or introduce more favourable provisions for workers than set out in this agreement.

2. This agreement shall be without prejudice to any more specific Community provisions, and in particular Community provisions concerning equal treatment or opportunities for men and women.

3. Implementation of this agreement shall not constitute valid grounds for reducing the general level of protection afforded to workers in the field of the agreement.

4. The present agreement does not prejudice the right of the social partners to conclude at the appropriate level, including European level, agreements adapting and/or complementing the provisions of this agreement in a manner which will take note of the specific needs of the social partners concerned.

5. The prevention and settlement of disputes and grievances arising from the application of this agreement shall be dealt with in accordance with national law, collective agreements and practice.

6. The signatory parties shall review the application of this agreement five years after the date of the Council decision if requested by one of the parties to this agreement.

Fritz VERZETNITSCH
President of the ETUC
Georges JACOBS
President of UNICE
Antonio CASTELLANO AUYANET
President of CEEP
Emilio GABAGLIO.
General-Secretary of the ETUC
Dirk F. HUDIG
Secretary-General of UNICE
Jytte FREDENSBORG
Secretary-General of CEEP
18 March 1999

Directive 2002/14/EC of the European Parliament and of the Council of 11 March 2002 establishing a general framework for informing and consulting employees in the European Community

[OJ 2000 L80/29]

THE EUROPEAN PARLIAMENT AND THE COUNCIL OF THE EUROPEAN UNION,

Having regard to the Treaty establishing the European Community, and in particular Article 137(2) thereof,

Having regard to the proposal from the Commission[1],

Having regard to the opinion of the Economic and Social Committee[2],

[1] OJ C 2, 5.1.1999, p. 3.
[2] OJ C 258, 10.9.1999, p. 24.

Having regard to the opinion of the Committee of the Regions[3],

Acting in accordance with the procedure referred to in Article 251[4], and in the light of the joint text approved by the Conciliation Committee on 23 January 2002,

Whereas:

(1) Pursuant to Article 136 of the Treaty, a particular objective of the Community and the Member States is to promote social dialogue between management and labour.

(2) Point 17 of the Community Charter of Fundamental Social Rights of Workers provides, inter alia, that information, consultation and participation for workers must be developed along appropriate lines, taking account of the practices in force in different Member States.

(3) The Commission consulted management and labour at Community level on the possible direction of Community action on the information and consultation of employees in undertakings within the Community.

(4) Following this consultation, the Commission considered that Community action was advisable and again consulted management and labour on the contents of the planned proposal; management and labour have presented their opinions to the Commission.

(5) Having completed this second stage of consultation, management and labour have not informed the Commission of their wish to initiate the process potentially leading to the conclusion of an agreement.

(6) The existence of legal frameworks at national and Community level, intended to ensure that employees are involved in the affairs of the undertaking employing them and in decisions which affect them, has not always prevented serious decisions affecting employees from being taken and made public without adequate procedures having been implemented beforehand to inform and consult them.

(7) There is a need to strengthen dialogue and promote mutual trust within undertakings in order to improve risk anticipation, make work organisation more flexible and facilitate employee access to training within the undertaking while maintaining security, make employees aware of adaptation needs, increase employees' availability to undertake measures and activities to increase their employability, promote employee involvement in the operation and future of the undertaking and increase its competitiveness.

(8) There is a need, in particular, to promote and enhance information and consultation on the situation and likely development of employment within the undertaking and, where the employer's evaluation suggests that employment within the undertaking may be under threat, the possible anticipatory measures envisaged, in particular in terms of employee training and skill development, with a view to offsetting the negative developments or their consequences and increasing the employability and adaptability of the employees likely to be affected.

(9) Timely information and consultation is a prerequisite for the success of the restructuring and adaptation of undertakings to the new conditions created by globalisation of the economy, particularly through the development of new forms of organisation of work.

(10) The Community has drawn up and implemented an employment strategy based on the concepts of 'anticipation', 'prevention' and 'employability', which are to be incorporated as key elements into all public policies likely to benefit employment, including the policies of individual undertakings, by strengthening the social dialogue with a view to promoting change compatible with preserving the priority objective of employment.

(11) Further development of the internal market must be properly balanced, maintaining the essential values on which our societies are based and ensuring that all citizens benefit from economic development.

[3] OJ C 144, 16.5.2001, p. 58.

[4] Opinion of the European Parliament of 14 April 1999 (OJ C 219, 30.7.1999, p. 223), confirmed on 16 September 1999 (OJ C 54, 25.2.2000, p. 55), Council Common Position of 27 July 2001 (OJ C 307, 31.10.2001, p. 16) and Decision of the European Parliament of 23 October 2001 (not yet published in the Official Journal). Decision of the European Parliament of 5 February 2002 and Decision of the Council of 18 February 2002.

(12) Entry into the third stage of economic and monetary union has extended and accelerated the competitive pressures at European level. This means that more supportive measures are needed at national level.

(13) The existing legal frameworks for employee information and consultation at Community and national level tend to adopt an excessively a posteriori approach to the process of change, neglect the economic aspects of decisions taken and do not contribute either to genuine anticipation of employment developments within the undertaking or to risk prevention.

(14) All of these political, economic, social and legal developments call for changes to the existing legal framework providing for the legal and practical instruments enabling the right to be informed and consulted to be exercised.

(15) This Directive is without prejudice to national systems regarding the exercise of this right in practice where those entitled to exercise it are required to indicate their wishes collectively.

(16) This Directive is without prejudice to those systems which provide for the direct involvement of employees, as long as they are always free to exercise the right to be informed and consulted through their representatives.

(17) Since the objectives of the proposed action, as outlined above, cannot be adequately achieved by the Member States, in that the object is to establish a framework for employee information and consultation appropriate for the new European context described above, and can therefore, in view of the scale and impact of the proposed action, be better achieved at Community level, the Community may adopt measures in accordance with the principle of subsidiarity as set out in Article 5 of the Treaty. In accordance with the principle of proportionality, as set out in that Article, this Directive does not go beyond what is necessary in order to achieve these objectives.

(18) The purpose of this general framework is to establish minimum requirements applicable throughout the Community while not preventing Member States from laying down provisions more favourable to employees.

(19) The purpose of this general framework is also to avoid any administrative, financial or legal constraints which would hinder the creation and development of small and medium-sized undertakings. To this end, the scope of this Directive should be restricted, according to the choice made by Member States, to undertakings with at least 50 employees or establishments employing at least 20 employees.

(20) This takes into account and is without prejudice to other national measures and practices aimed at fostering social dialogue within companies not covered by this Directive and within public administrations.

(21) However, on a transitional basis, Member States in which there is no established statutory system of information and consultation of employees or employee representation should have the possibility of further restricting the scope of the Directive as regards the numbers of employees.

(22) A Community framework for informing and consulting employees should keep to a minimum the burden on undertakings or establishments while ensuring the effective exercise of the rights granted.

(23) The objective of this Directive is to be achieved through the establishment of a general framework comprising the principles, definitions and arrangements for information and consultation, which it will be for the Member States to comply with and adapt to their own national situation, ensuring, where appropriate, that management and labour have a leading role by allowing them to define freely, by agreement, the arrangements for informing and consulting employees which they consider to be best suited to their needs and wishes.

(24) Care should be taken to avoid affecting some specific rules in the field of employee information and consultation existing in some national laws, addressed to undertakings or establishments which pursue political, professional, organisational, religious, charitable, educational, scientific or artistic aims, as well as aims involving information and the expression of opinions.

(25) Undertakings and establishments should be protected against disclosure of certain particularly sensitive information.

(26) The employer should be allowed not to inform and consult where this would seriously damage the undertaking or the establishment or where he has to comply immediately with an order issued to him by a regulatory or supervisory body.

(27) Information and consultation imply both rights and obligations for management and labour at undertaking or establishment level.

(28) Administrative or judicial procedures, as well as sanctions that are effective, dissuasive and proportionate in relation to the seriousness of the offence, should be applicable in cases of infringement of the obligations based on this Directive.

(29) This Directive should not affect the provisions, where these are more specific, of Council Directive 98/59/EC of 20 July 1998 on the approximation of the laws of the Member States relating to collective redundancies[5] and of Council Directive 2001/23/EC of 12 March 2001 on the approximation of the laws of the Member States relating to the safeguarding of employees' rights in the event of transfers of undertakings, businesses or parts of undertakings or businesses.[6]

(30) Other rights of information and consultation, including those arising from Council Directive 94/45/EEC of 22 September 1994 on the establishment of a European Works Council or a procedure in Community-scale undertakings and Community-scale groups of undertakings for the purposes of informing and consulting employees,[7] should not be affected by this Directive.

(31) Implementation of this Directive should not be sufficient grounds for a reduction in the general level of protection of workers in the areas to which it applies,

HAVE ADOPTED THIS DIRECTIVE:

Article 1 Object and principles

1. The purpose of this Directive is to establish a general framework setting out minimum requirements for the right to information and consultation of employees in undertakings or establishments within the Community.

2. The practical arrangements for information and consultation shall be defined and implemented in accordance with national law and industrial relations practices in individual Member States in such a way as to ensure their effectiveness.

3. When defining or implementing practical arrangements for information and consultation, the employer and the employees' representatives shall work in a spirit of cooperation and with due regard for their reciprocal rights and obligations, taking into account the interests both of the undertaking or establishment and of the employees.

Article 2 Definitions

For the purposes of this Directive:

(a) 'undertaking' means a public or private undertaking carrying out an economic activity, whether or not operating for gain, which is located within the territory of the Member States;

(b) 'establishment' means a unit of business defined in accordance with national law and practice, and located within the territory of a Member State, where an economic activity is carried out on an ongoing basis with human and material resources;

(c) 'employer' means the natural or legal person party to employment contracts or employment relationships with employees, in accordance with national law and practice;

(d) 'employee' means any person who, in the Member State concerned, is protected as an employee under national employment law and in accordance with national practice;

(e) 'employees' representatives' means the employees' representatives provided for by national laws and/or practices;

(f) 'information' means transmission by the employer to the employees' representatives of data in order to enable them to acquaint themselves with the subject matter and to examine it;

(g) 'consultation' means the exchange of views and establishment of dialogue between the employees' representatives and the employer.

Article 3 Scope

1. This Directive shall apply, according to the choice made by Member States, to:

(a) undertakings employing at least 50 employees in any one Member State, or

[5] OJ L 225, 12.8.1998, p. 16.

[6] OJ L 82, 22.3.2001, p. 16.

[7] OJ L 254, 30.9.1994, p. 64. Directive as amended by Directive 97/74/EC (OJ L 10, 16.1.1998, p. 22).

(b) establishments employing at least 20 employees in any one Member State.

Member States shall determine the method for calculating the thresholds of employees employed.

2. In conformity with the principles and objectives of this Directive, Member States may lay down particular provisions applicable to undertakings or establishments which pursue directly and essentially political, professional organisational, religious, charitable, educational, scientific or artistic aims, as well as aims involving information and the expression of opinions, on condition that, at the date of entry into force of this Directive, provisions of that nature already exist in national legislation.

3. Member States may derogate from this Directive through particular provisions applicable to the crews of vessels plying the high seas.

Article 4 Practical arrangements for information and consultation

1. In accordance with the principles set out in Article 1 and without prejudice to any provisions and/or practices in force more favourable to employees, the Member States shall determine the practical arrangements for exercising the right to information and consultation at the appropriate level in accordance with this Article.

2. Information and consultation shall cover:

(a) information on the recent and probable development of the undertaking's or the establishment's activities and economic situation;

(b) information and consultation on the situation, structure and probable development of employment within the undertaking or establishment and on any anticipatory measures envisaged, in particular where there is a threat to employment;

(c) information and consultation on decisions likely to lead to substantial changes in work organisation or in contractual relations, including those covered by the Community provisions referred to in Article 9(1).

3. Information shall be given at such time, in such fashion and with such content as are appropriate to enable, in particular, employees' representatives to conduct an adequate study and, where necessary, prepare for consultation.

4. Consultation shall take place:

(a) while ensuring that the timing, method and content thereof are appropriate;

(b) at the relevant level of management and representation, depending on the subject under discussion;

(c) on the basis of information supplied by the employer in accordance with Article 2(f) and of the opinion which the employees' representatives are entitled to formulate;

(d) in such a way as to enable employees' representatives to meet the employer and obtain a response, and the reasons for that response, to any opinion they might formulate;

(e) with a view to reaching an agreement on decisions within the scope of the employer's powers referred to in paragraph 2(c).

Article 5 Information and consultation deriving from an agreement

Member States may entrust management and labour at the appropriate level, including at undertaking or establishment level, with defining freely and at any time through negotiated agreement the practical arrangements for informing and consulting employees. These agreements, and agreements existing on the date laid down in Article 11, as well as any subsequent renewals of such agreements, may establish, while respecting the principles set out in Article 1 and subject to conditions and limitations laid down by the Member States, provisions which are different from those referred to in Article 4.

Article 6 Confidential information

1. Member States shall provide that, within the conditions and limits laid down by national legislation, the employees' representatives, and any experts who assist them, are not authorised to reveal to employees or to third parties, any information which, in the legitimate interest of the undertaking or establishment, has expressly been provided to them in confidence. This obligation shall continue to apply, wherever the said representatives or experts are, even after expiry of their terms of

office. However, a Member State may authorise the employees' representatives and anyone assisting them to pass on confidential information to employees and to third parties bound by an obligation of confidentiality.

2. Member States shall provide, in specific cases and within the conditions and limits laid down by national legislation, that the employer is not obliged to communicate information or undertake consultation when the nature of that information or consultation is such that, according to objective criteria, it would seriously harm the functioning of the undertaking or establishment or would be prejudicial to it.

3. Without prejudice to existing national procedures, Member States shall provide for administrative or judicial review procedures for the case where the employer requires confidentiality or does not provide the information in accordance with paragraphs 1 and 2. They may also provide for procedures intended to safeguard the confidentiality of the information in question.

Article 7 Protection of employees' representatives

Member States shall ensure that employees' representatives, when carrying out their functions, enjoy adequate protection and guarantees to enable them to perform properly the duties which have been assigned to them.

Article 8 Protection of rights

1. Member States shall provide for appropriate measures in the event of non-compliance with this Directive by the employer or the employees' representatives. In particular, they shall ensure that adequate administrative or judicial procedures are available to enable the obligations deriving from this Directive to be enforced.

2. Member States shall provide for adequate sanctions to be applicable in the event of infringement of this Directive by the employer or the employees' representatives. These sanctions must be effective, proportionate and dissuasive.

Article 9 Link between this Directive and other Community and national provisions

1. This Directive shall be without prejudice to the specific information and consultation procedures set out in Article 2 of Directive 98/59/EC and Article 7 of Directive 2001/23/EC.

2. This Directive shall be without prejudice to provisions adopted in accordance with Directives 94/45/EC and 97/74/EC.

3. This Directive shall be without prejudice to other rights to information, consultation and participation under national law.

4. Implementation of this Directive shall not be sufficient grounds for any regression in relation to the situation which already prevails in each Member State and in relation to the general level of protection of workers in the areas to which it applies.

Article 10 Transitional provisions

Notwithstanding Article 3, a Member State in which there is, at the date of entry into force of this Directive, no general, permanent and statutory system of information and consultation of employees, nor a general, permanent and statutory system of employee representation at the workplace allowing employees to be represented for that purpose, may limit the application of the national provisions implementing this Directive to:

(a) undertakings employing at least 150 employees or establishments employing at least 100 employees until 23 March 2007, and

(b) undertakings employing at least 100 employees or establishments employing at least 50 employees during the year following the date in point (a).

Article 11 Transposition

1. Member States shall adopt the laws, regulations and administrative provisions necessary to comply with this Directive not later than 23 March 2005 or shall ensure that management and labour introduce by that date the required provisions by way of agreement, the Member States being obliged

to take all necessary steps enabling them to guarantee the results imposed by this Directive at all times. They shall forthwith inform the Commission thereof.

2. Where Member States adopt these measures, they shall contain a reference to this Directive or shall be accompanied by such reference on the occasion of their official publication. The methods of making such reference shall be laid down by the Member States.

Article 12 Review by the Commission

Not later than 23 March 2007, the Commission shall, in consultation with the Member States and the social partners at Community level, review the application of this Directive with a view to proposing any necessary amendments.

Article 13 Entry into force

This Directive shall enter into force on the day of its publication in the *Official Journal of the European Communities*.

Article 14 Addressees

This Directive is addressed to the Member States.

Done at Brussels, 11 March 2002.
For the European Parliament
The President
P. COX

For the Council
The President
J. PIQUÉ i CAMPS

Joint Declaration of the European Parliament, the Council and the Commission on Employee Representation

'With regard to employee representation, the European Parliament, the Council and the Commission recall the judgements of the European Court of Justice of 8 June 1994 in Cases C-382/92 (Safeguarding of employees rights in the event of transfers of undertakings) and C-383/92 (Collective redundancies).'

Directive 2003/88/EC of the European Parliament and of the Council of 4 November 2003 concerning certain aspects of the organisation of working time*

[OJ 2003 L299/9]

THE EUROPEAN PARLIAMENT AND THE COUNCIL OF THE EUROPEAN UNION,

Having regard to the Treaty establishing the European Community, and in particular Article 137(2) thereof,

Having regard to the proposal from the Commission,

Having regard to the opinion of the European Economic and Social Committee,[1]

Having consulted the Committee of the Regions,

Acting in accordance with the procedure referred to in Article 251 of the Treaty,[2]

* **Editor's Note:** This Directive repeals and replaces Directives 93/104 and 2000/34.

[1] OJ C 61, 14.3.2003, p. 123.

[2] Opinion of the European Parliament of 17 December 2002 (not yet published in the Official Journal) and Council Decision of 22 September 2003.

Whereas:

(1) Council Directive 93/104/EC of 23 November 1993, concerning certain aspects of the organisation of working time,[3] which lays down minimum safety and health requirements for the organisation of working time, in respect of periods of daily rest, breaks, weekly rest, maximum weekly working time, annual leave and aspects of night work, shift work and patterns of work, has been significantly amended. In order to clarify matters, a codification of the provisions in question should be drawn up.

(2) Article 137 of the Treaty provides that the Community is to support and complement the activities of the Member States with a view to improving the working environment to protect workers' health and safety. Directives adopted on the basis of that Article are to avoid imposing administrative, financial and legal constraints in a way which would hold back the creation and development of small and medium-sized undertakings.

(3) The provisions of Council Directive 89/391/EEC of 12 June 1989 on the introduction of measures to encourage improvements in the safety and health of workers at work[4] remain fully applicable to the areas covered by this Directive without prejudice to more stringent and/or specific provisions contained herein.

(4) The improvement of workers' safety, hygiene and health at work is an objective which should not be subordinated to purely economic considerations.

(5) All workers should have adequate rest periods. The concept of 'rest' must be expressed in units of time, i.e. in days, hours and/or fractions thereof. Community workers must be granted minimum daily, weekly and annual periods of rest and adequate breaks. It is also necessary in this context to place a maximum limit on weekly working hours.

(6) Account should be taken of the principles of the International Labour Organisation with regard to the organisation of working time, including those relating to night work.

(7) Research has shown that the human body is more sensitive at night to environmental disturbances and also to certain burdensome forms of work organisation and that long periods of night work can be detrimental to the health of workers and can endanger safety at the workplace.

(8) There is a need to limit the duration of periods of night work, including overtime, and to provide for employers who regularly use night workers to bring this information to the attention of the competent authorities if they so request.

(9) It is important that night workers should be entitled to a free health assessment prior to their assignment and thereafter at regular intervals and that whenever possible they should be transferred to day work for which they are suited if they suffer from health problems.

(10) The situation of night and shift workers requires that the level of safety and health protection should be adapted to the nature of their work and that the organisation and functioning of protection and prevention services and resources should be efficient.

(11) Specific working conditions may have detrimental effects on the safety and health of workers. The organisation of work according to a certain pattern must take account of the general principle of adapting work to the worker.

(12) A European Agreement in respect of the working time of seafarers has been put into effect by means of Council Directive 1999/63/EC of 21 June 1999 concerning the Agreement on the organisation of working time of seafarers concluded by the European Community Ship-owners' Association (ECSA) and the Federation of Transport Workers' Unions in the European Union (FST)[5] based on Article 139(2) of the Treaty. Accordingly, the provisions of this Directive should not apply to seafarers.

(13) In the case of those 'share-fishermen' who are employees, it is for the Member States to determine, pursuant to this Directive, the conditions for entitlement to, and granting of, annual leave, including the arrangements for payments.

[3] OJ L 307, 13.12.1993, p. 18. Directive as amended by Directive 2000/34/EC of the European Parliament and of the Council (OJ L 195, 1.8.2000, p. 41).

[4] OJ L 183, 29.6.1989, p. 1.

[5] OJ L 167, 2.7.1999, p. 33.

(14) Specific standards laid down in other Community instruments relating, for example, to rest periods, working time, annual leave and night work for certain categories of workers should take precedence over the provisions of this Directive.

(15) In view of the question likely to be raised by the organisation of working time within an undertaking, it appears desirable to provide for flexibility in the application of certain provisions of this Directive, whilst ensuring compliance with the principles of protecting the safety and health of workers.

(16) It is necessary to provide that certain provisions may be subject to derogations implemented, according to the case, by the Member States or the two sides of industry. As a general rule, in the event of a derogation, the workers concerned must be given equivalent compensatory rest periods.

(17) This Directive should not affect the obligations of the Member States concerning the deadlines for transposition of the Directives set out in Annex I, part B,

HAVE ADOPTED THIS DIRECTIVE:

Chapter 1 Scope and definitions

Article 1 Purpose and scope

1. This Directive lays down minimum safety and health requirements for the organisation of working time.

2. This Directive applies to:

(a) minimum periods of daily rest, weekly rest and annual leave, to breaks and maximum weekly working time; and

(b) certain aspects of night work, shift work and patterns of work.

3. This Directive shall apply to all sectors of activity, both public and private, within the meaning of Article 2 of Directive 89/391/EEC, without prejudice to Articles 14, 17, 18 and 19 of this Directive.

This Directive shall not apply to seafarers, as defined in Directive 1999/63/EC without prejudice to Article 2(8) of this Directive.

4. The provisions of Directive 89/391/EEC are fully applicable to the matters referred to in paragraph 2, without prejudice to more stringent and/or specific provisions contained in this Directive.

Article 2 Definitions

For the purposes of this Directive, the following definitions shall apply:

1. 'working time' means any period during which the worker is working, at the employer's disposal and carrying out his activity or duties, in accordance with national laws and/or practice;

2. 'rest period' means any period which is not working time;

3. 'night time' means any period of not less than seven hours, as defined by national law, and which must include, in any case, the period between midnight and 5.00;

4. 'night worker' means:

(a) on the one hand, any worker, who, during night time, works at least three hours of his daily working time as a normal course; and

(b) on the other hand, any worker who is likely during night time to work a certain proportion of his annual working time, as defined at the choice of the Member State concerned:

(i) by national legislation, following consultation with the two sides of industry; or

(ii) by collective agreements or agreements concluded between the two sides of industry at national or regional level;

5. 'shift work' means any method of organising work in shifts whereby workers succeed each other at the same work stations according to a certain pattern, including a rotating pattern, and which may be continuous or discontinuous, entailing the need for workers to work at different times over a given period of days or weeks;

6. 'shift worker' means any worker whose work schedule is part of shift work;

7. 'mobile worker' means any worker employed as a member of travelling or flying personnel by an undertaking which operates transport services for passengers or goods by road, air or inland waterway;

8. 'offshore work' means work performed mainly on or from offshore installations (including drilling rigs), directly or indirectly in connection with the exploration, extraction or exploitation of mineral resources, including hydrocarbons, and diving in connection with such activities, whether performed from an offshore installation or a vessel;

9. 'adequate rest' means that workers have regular rest periods, the duration of which is expressed in units of time and which are sufficiently long and continuous to ensure that, as a result of fatigue or other irregular working patterns, they do not cause injury to themselves, to fellow workers or to others and that they do not damage their health, either in the short term or in the longer term.

Chapter 2 Minimum rest periods—Other aspects of the organisation of working time

Article 3 Daily rest

Member States shall take the measures necessary to ensure that every worker is entitled to a minimum daily rest period of 11 consecutive hours per 24-hour period.

Article 4 Breaks

Member States shall take the measures necessary to ensure that, where the working day is longer than six hours, every worker is entitled to a rest break, the details of which, including duration and the terms on which it is granted, shall be laid down in collective agreements or agreements between the two sides of industry or, failing that, by national legislation.

Article 5 Weekly rest period

Member States shall take the measures necessary to ensure that, per each seven-day period, every worker is entitled to a minimum uninterrupted rest period of 24 hours plus the 11 hours' daily rest referred to in Article 3.

If objective, technical or work organisation conditions so justify, a minimum rest period of 24 hours may be applied.

Article 6 Maximum weekly working time

Member States shall take the measures necessary to ensure that, in keeping with the need to protect the safety and health of workers:

(a) the period of weekly working time is limited by means of laws, regulations or administrative provisions or by collective agreements or agreements between the two sides of industry;

(b) the average working time for each seven-day period, including overtime, does not exceed 48 hours.

Article 7 Annual leave

1. Member States shall take the measures necessary to ensure that every worker is entitled to paid annual leave of at least four weeks in accordance with the conditions for entitlement to, and granting of, such leave laid down by national legislation and/or practice.

2. The minimum period of paid annual leave may not be replaced by an allowance in lieu, except where the employment relationship is terminated.

Chapter 3 Night work—Shift work—Patterns of work

Article 8 Length of night work

Member States shall take the measures necessary to ensure that:

(a) normal hours of work for night workers do not exceed an average of eight hours in any 24-hour period;

(b) night workers whose work involves special hazards or heavy physical or mental strain do not work more than eight hours in any period of 24 hours during which they perform night work.

For the purposes of point (b), work involving special hazards or heavy physical or mental strain shall be defined by national legislation and/or practice or by collective agreements or agreements concluded between the two sides of industry, taking account of the specific effects and hazards of night work.

Article 9 Health assessment and transfer of night workers to day work

1. Member States shall take the measures necessary to ensure that:

(a) night workers are entitled to a free health assessment before their assignment and thereafter at regular intervals;

(b) night workers suffering from health problems recognised as being connected with the fact that they perform night work are transferred whenever possible to day work to which they are suited.

2. The free health assessment referred to in paragraph 1(a) must comply with medical confidentiality.

3. The free health assessment referred to in paragraph 1(a) may be conducted within the national health system.

Article 10 Guarantees for night-time working

Member States may make the work of certain categories of night workers subject to certain guarantees, under conditions laid down by national legislation and/or practice, in the case of workers who incur risks to their safety or health linked to night-time working.

Article 11 Notification of regular use of night workers

Member States shall take the measures necessary to ensure that an employer who regularly uses night workers brings this information to the attention of the competent authorities if they so request.

Article 12 Safety and health protection

Member States shall take the measures necessary to ensure that:

(a) night workers and shift workers have safety and health protection appropriate to the nature of their work;

(b) appropriate protection and prevention services or facilities with regard to the safety and health of night workers and shift workers are equivalent to those applicable to other workers and are available at all times.

Article 13 Pattern of work

Member States shall take the measures necessary to ensure that an employer who intends to organise work according to a certain pattern takes account of the general principle of adapting work to the worker, with a view, in particular, to alleviating monotonous work and work at a predetermined work-rate, depending on the type of activity, and of safety and health requirements, especially as regards breaks during working time.

Chapter 4 Miscellaneous provisions

Article 14 More specific Community provisions

This Directive shall not apply where other Community instruments contain more specific requirements relating to the organisation of working time for certain occupations or occupational activities.

Article 15 More favourable provisions

This Directive shall not affect Member States' right to apply or introduce laws, regulations or administrative provisions more favourable to the protection of the safety and health of workers or to facilitate or permit the application of collective agreements or agreements concluded between the two sides of industry which are more favourable to the protection of the safety and health of workers.

Article 16 Reference periods

Member States may lay down:

(a) for the application of Article 5 (weekly rest period), a reference period not exceeding 14 days;

(b) for the application of Article 6 (maximum weekly working time), a reference period not exceeding four months.

The periods of paid annual leave, granted in accordance with Article 7, and the periods of sick leave shall not be included or shall be neutral in the calculation of the average;

(c) for the application of Article 8 (length of night work), a reference period defined after consultation of the two sides of industry or by collective agreements or agreements concluded between the two sides of industry at national or regional level.

If the minimum weekly rest period of 24 hours required by Article 5 falls within that reference period, it shall not be included in the calculation of the average.

Chapter 5 Derogations and exceptions

Article 17 Derogations

1. With due regard for the general principles of the protection of the safety and health of workers, Member States may derogate from Articles 3 to 6, 8 and 16 when, on account of the specific characteristics of the activity concerned, the duration of the working time is not measured and/or predetermined or can be determined by the workers themselves, and particularly in the case of:

(a) managing executives or other persons with autonomous decision-taking powers;

(b) family workers; or

(c) workers officiating at religious ceremonies in churches and religious communities.

2. Derogations provided for in paragraphs 3, 4 and 5 may be adopted by means of laws, regulations or administrative provisions or by means of collective agreements or agreements between the two sides of industry provided that the workers concerned are afforded equivalent periods of compensatory rest or that, in exceptional cases in which it is not possible, for objective reasons, to grant such equivalent periods of compensatory rest, the workers concerned are afforded appropriate protection.

3. In accordance with paragraph 2 of this Article derogations may be made from Articles 3, 4, 5, 8 and 16:

(a) in the case of activities where the worker's place of work and his place of residence are distant from one another, including offshore work, or where the worker's different places of work are distant from one another;

(b) in the case of security and surveillance activities requiring a permanent presence in order to protect property and persons, particularly security guards and caretakers or security firms;

(c) in the case of activities involving the need for continuity of service or production, particularly:

(i) services relating to the reception, treatment and/or care provided by hospitals or similar establishments, including the activities of doctors in training, residential institutions and prisons;

(ii) dock or airport workers;

(iii) press, radio, television, cinematographic production, postal and telecommunications services, ambulance, fire and civil protection services;

(iv) gas, water and electricity production, transmission and distribution, household refuse collection and incineration plants;

(v) industries in which work cannot be interrupted on technical grounds;

(vi) research and development activities;

(vii) agriculture;

(viii) workers concerned with the carriage of passengers on regular urban transport services;

(d) where there is a foreseeable surge of activity, particularly in:

(i) agriculture;

(ii) tourism;
(iii) postal services;

(e) in the case of persons working in railway transport:
(i) whose activities are intermittent;
(ii) who spend their working time on board trains; or
(iii) whose activities are linked to transport timetables and to ensuring the continuity and regularity of traffic;

(f) in the circumstances described in Article 5(4) of Directive 89/391/EEC;

(g) in cases of accident or imminent risk of accident.

4. In accordance with paragraph 2 of this Article derogations may be made from Articles 3 and 5:

(a) in the case of shift work activities, each time the worker changes shift and cannot take daily and/or weekly rest periods between the end of one shift and the start of the next one;

(b) in the case of activities involving periods of work split up over the day, particularly those of cleaning staff.

5. In accordance with paragraph 2 of this Article, derogations may be made from Article 6 and Article 16(b), in the case of doctors in training, in accordance with the provisions set out in the second to the seventh subparagraphs of this paragraph.

With respect to Article 6 derogations referred to in the first subparagraph shall be permitted for a transitional period of five years from 1 August 2004.

Member States may have up to two more years, if necessary, to take account of difficulties in meeting the working time provisions with respect to their responsibilities for the organisation and delivery of health services and medical care. At least six months before the end of the transitional period, the Member State concerned shall inform the Commission giving its reasons, so that the Commission can give an opinion, after appropriate consultations, within the three months following receipt of such information. If the Member State does not follow the opinion of the Commission, it will justify its decision. The notification and justification of the Member State and the opinion of the Commission shall be published in the *Official Journal of the European Union* and forwarded to the European Parliament.

Member States may have an additional period of up to one year, if necessary, to take account of special difficulties in meeting the responsibilities referred to in the third subparagraph. They shall follow the procedure set out in that subparagraph.

Member States shall ensure that in no case will the number of weekly working hours exceed an average of 58 during the first three years of the transitional period, an average of 56 for the following two years and an average of 52 for any remaining period.

The employer shall consult the representatives of the employees in good time with a view to reaching an agreement, wherever possible, on the arrangements applying to the transitional period. Within the limits set out in the fifth subparagraph, such an agreement may cover:

(a) the average number of weekly hours of work during the transitional period; and

(b) the measures to be adopted to reduce weekly working hours to an average of 48 by the end of the transitional period.

With respect to Article 16(b) derogations referred to in the first subparagraph shall be permitted provided that the reference period does not exceed 12 months, during the first part of the transitional period specified in the fifth subparagraph, and six months thereafter.

Article 18 Derogations by collective agreements

Derogations may be made from Articles 3, 4, 5, 8 and 16 by means of collective agreements or agreements concluded between the two sides of industry at national or regional level or, in conformity with the rules laid down by them, by means of collective agreements or agreements concluded between the two sides of industry at a lower level.

Member States in which there is no statutory system ensuring the conclusion of collective agreements or agreements concluded between the two sides of industry at national or regional level, on the matters covered by this Directive, or those Member States in which there is a specific legislative framework for this purpose and within the limits thereof, may, in accordance with national legislation and/or practice, allow derogations from Articles 3, 4, 5, 8 and 16 by way of collective agreements or agreements concluded between the two sides of industry at the appropriate collective level.

The derogations provided for in the first and second subparagraphs shall be allowed on condition that equivalent compensating rest periods are granted to the workers concerned or, in exceptional cases where it is not possible for objective reasons to grant such periods, the workers concerned are afforded appropriate protection.

Member States may lay down rules:

(a) for the application of this Article by the two sides of industry; and

(b) for the extension of the provisions of collective agreements or agreements concluded in conformity with this Article to other workers in accordance with national legislation and/or practice.

Article 19 Limitations to derogations from reference periods

The option to derogate from Article 16(b), provided for in Article 17(3) and in Article 18, may not result in the establishment of a reference period exceeding six months.

However, Member States shall have the option, subject to compliance with the general principles relating to the protection of the safety and health of workers, of allowing, for objective or technical reasons or reasons concerning the organisation of work, collective agreements or agreements concluded between the two sides of industry to set reference periods in no event exceeding 12 months.

Before 23 November 2003, the Council shall, on the basis of a Commission proposal accompanied by an appraisal report, re-examine the provisions of this Article and decide what action to take.

Article 20 Mobile workers and offshore work

1. Articles 3, 4, 5 and 8 shall not apply to mobile workers.

Member States shall, however, take the necessary measures to ensure that such mobile workers are entitled to adequate rest, except in the circumstances laid down in Article 17(3)(f) and (g).

2. Subject to compliance with the general principles relating to the protection of the safety and health of workers, and provided that there is consultation of representatives of the employer and employees concerned and efforts to encourage all relevant forms of social dialogue, including negotiation if the parties so wish, Member States may, for objective or technical reasons or reasons concerning the organisation of work, extend the reference period referred to in Article 16(b) to 12 months in respect of workers who mainly perform offshore work.

3. Not later than 1 August 2005 the Commission shall, after consulting the Member States and management and labour at European level, review the operation of the provisions with regard to offshore workers from a health and safety perspective with a view to presenting, if need be, the appropriate modifications.

Article 21 Workers on board seagoing fishing vessels

1. Articles 3 to 6 and 8 shall not apply to any worker on board a seagoing fishing vessel flying the flag of a Member State.

Member States shall, however, take the necessary measures to ensure that any worker on board a seagoing fishing vessel flying the flag of a Member State is entitled to adequate rest and to limit the number of hours of work to 48 hours a week on average calculated over a reference period not exceeding 12 months.

2. Within the limits set out in paragraph 1, second subparagraph, and paragraphs 3 and 4 Member States shall take the necessary measures to ensure that, in keeping with the need to protect the safety and health of such workers:

(a) the working hours are limited to a maximum number of hours which shall not be exceeded in a given period of time; or

(b) a minimum number of hours of rest are provided within a given period of time.

The maximum number of hours of work or minimum number of hours of rest shall be specified by law, regulations, administrative provisions or by collective agreements or agreements between the two sides of the industry.

3. The limits on hours of work or rest shall be either:

(a) maximum hours of work which shall not exceed:

(i) 14 hours in any 24-hour period; and

(ii) 72 hours in any seven-day period;

or

(b) minimum hours of rest which shall not be less than:

(i) 10 hours in any 24-hour period; and

(ii) 77 hours in any seven-day period.

4. Hours of rest may be divided into no more than two periods, one of which shall be at least six hours in length, and the interval between consecutive periods of rest shall not exceed 14 hours.

5. In accordance with the general principles of the protection of the health and safety of workers, and for objective or technical reasons or reasons concerning the organisation of work, Member States may allow exceptions, including the establishment of reference periods, to the limits laid down in paragraph 1, second subparagraph, and paragraphs 3 and 4. Such exceptions shall, as far as possible, comply with the standards laid down but may take account of more frequent or longer leave periods or the granting of compensatory leave for the workers. These exceptions may be laid down by means of:

(a) laws, regulations or administrative provisions provided there is consultation, where possible, of the representatives of the employers and workers concerned and efforts are made to encourage all relevant forms of social dialogue; or

(b) collective agreements or agreements between the two sides of industry.

6. The master of a seagoing fishing vessel shall have the right to require workers on board to perform any hours of work necessary for the immediate safety of the vessel, persons on board or cargo, or for the purpose of giving assistance to other vessels or persons in distress at sea.

7. Members States may provide that workers on board seagoing fishing vessels for which national legislation or practice determines that these vessels are not allowed to operate in a specific period of the calendar year exceeding one month, shall take annual leave in accordance with Article 7 within that period.

Article 22 Miscellaneous provisions

1. A Member State shall have the option not to apply Article 6, while respecting the general principles of the protection of the safety and health of workers, and provided it takes the necessary measures to ensure that:

(a) no employer requires a worker to work more than 48 hours over a seven-day period, calculated as an average for the reference period referred to in Article 16(b), unless he has first obtained the worker's agreement to perform such work;

(b) no worker is subjected to any detriment by his employer because he is not willing to give his agreement to perform such work;

(c) the employer keeps up-to-date records of all workers who carry out such work;

(d) the records are placed at the disposal of the competent authorities, which may, for reasons connected with the safety and/or health of workers, prohibit or restrict the possibility of exceeding the maximum weekly working hours;

(e) the employer provides the competent authorities at their request with information on cases in which agreement has been given by workers to perform work exceeding 48 hours over a period of seven days, calculated as an average for the reference period referred to in Article 16(b).

Before 23 November 2003, the Council shall, on the basis of a Commission proposal accompanied by an appraisal report, re-examine the provisions of this paragraph and decide on what action to take.

2. Member States shall have the option, as regards the application of Article 7, of making use of a transitional period of not more than three years from 23 November 1996, provided that during that transitional period:

(a) every worker receives three weeks' paid annual leave in accordance with the conditions for the entitlement to, and granting of, such leave laid down by national legislation and/or practice; and

(b) the three-week period of paid annual leave may not be replaced by an allowance in lieu, except where the employment relationship is terminated.

3. If Member States avail themselves of the options provided for in this Article, they shall forthwith inform the Commission thereof.

Chapter 6 Final provisions

Article 23 Level of protection

Without prejudice to the right of Member States to develop, in the light of changing circumstances, different legislative, regulatory or contractual provisions in the field of working time, as long as the minimum requirements provided for in this Directive are complied with, implementation of this Directive shall not constitute valid grounds for reducing the general level of protection afforded to workers.

Article 24 Reports

1. Member States shall communicate to the Commission the texts of the provisions of national law already adopted or being adopted in the field governed by this Directive.

2. Member States shall report to the Commission every five years on the practical implementation of the provisions of this Directive, indicating the viewpoints of the two sides of industry.

The Commission shall inform the European Parliament, the Council, the European Economic and Social Committee and the Advisory Committee on Safety, Hygiene and Health Protection at Work thereof.

3. Every five years from 23 November 1996 the Commission shall submit to the European Parliament, the Council and the European Economic and Social Committee a report on the application of this Directive taking into account Articles 22 and 23 and paragraphs 1 and 2 of this Article.

Article 25 Review of the operation of the provisions with regard to workers on board seagoing fishing vessels

Not later than 1 August 2009 the Commission shall, after consulting the Member States and management and labour at European level, review the operation of the provisions with regard to workers on board seagoing fishing vessels, and, in particular examine whether these provisions remain appropriate, in particular, as far as health and safety are concerned with a view to proposing suitable amendments, if necessary.

Article 26 Review of the operation of the provisions with regard to workers concerned with the carriage of passengers

Not later than 1 August 2005 the Commission shall, after consulting the Member States and management and labour at European level, review the operation of the provisions with regard to workers concerned with the carriage of passengers on regular urban transport services, with a view to presenting, if need be, the appropriate modifications to ensure a coherent and suitable approach in the sector.

Article 27 Repeal

1. Directive 93/104/EC, as amended by the Directive referred to in Annex I, part A, shall be repealed, without prejudice to the obligations of the Member States in respect of the deadlines for transposition laid down in Annex I, part B.

2. The references made to the said repealed Directive shall be construed as references to this Directive and shall be read in accordance with the correlation table set out in Annex II.

Article 28 Entry into force

This Directive shall enter into force on 2 August 2004.

Article 29 Addressees

This Directive is addressed to the Member States.

Done at Brussels, 4 November 2003.
For the European Parliament
The President
P. COX

For the Council
The President
G. TREMONTI

Annex I

Part A Repealed Directive and its amendment (Article 27)

Council Directive 93/104/EC (OJ L 307, 13.12.1993, p. 18)
Directive 2000/34/EC of the European Parliament and of the Council (OJ L 195, 1.8.2000, p. 41)

Part B Deadlines for transposition into national law (Article 27)

Directive	Deadline for transposition
93/104/EC	23 November 1996
2000/34/EC	1 August 2003[6]

Annex II

Correlation table

Directive 93/104/EC	This Directive
Articles 1 to 5	Articles 1 to 5
Article 6, introductory words	Article 6, introductory words
Article 6(1)	Article 6(a)
Article 6(2)	Article 6(b)
Article 7	Article 7
Article 8, introductory words	Article 8, introductory words
Article 8(1)	Article 8(a)
Article 8(2)	Article 8(b)
Articles 9, 10 and 11	Articles 9, 10 and 11
Article 12, introductory words	Article 12, introductory words
Article 12(1)	Article 12(a)
Article 12(2)	Article 12(b)
Articles 13, 14 and 15	Articles 13, 14 and 15
Article 16, introductory words	Article 16, introductory words
Article 16(1)	Article 16(a)
Article 16(2)	Article 16(b)
Article 16(3)	Article 16(c)
Article 17(1)	Article 17(1)
Article 17(2), introductory words	Article 17(2)
Article 17(2)(1)	Article 17(3)(a) to (e)

(cont.)

[6] August 2004 in the case of doctors in training. See Article 2 of Directive 2000/34/EC.

Directive 93/104/EC	This Directive
Article 17(2)(2)	Article 17(3)(f) to (g)
Article 17(2)(3)	Article 17(4)
Article 17(2)(4)	Article 17(5)
Article 17(3)	Article 18
Article 17(4)	Article 19
Article 17a(1)	Article 20(1), first subparagraph
Article 17a(2)	Article 20(1), second subparagraph
Article 17a(3)	Article 20(2)
Article 17a(4)	Article 20(3)
Article 17b(1)	Article 21(1), first subparagraph
Article 17b(2)	Article 21(1), second subparagraph
Article 17b(3)	Article 21(2)
Article 17b(4)	Article 21(3)
Article 17b(5)	Article 21(4)
Article 17b(6)	Article 21(5)
Article 17b(7)	Article 21(6)
Article 17b(8)	Article 21(7)
Article 18(1)(a)	—
Article 18(1)(b)(i)	Article 22(1)
Article 18(1)(b)(ii)	Article 22(2)
Article 18(1)(c)	Article 22(3)
Article 18(2)	—
Article 18(3)	Article 23
Article 18(4)	Article 24(1)
Article 18(5)	Article 24(2)
Article 18(6)	Article 24(3)
—	Article 25[7]
—	Article 26[8]
—	Article 27
Article 19	Article 28
—	Article 29
—	Annex 1

Directive 2008/94/EC of the European Parliament and of the Council of 22 October 2008 on the protection of employees in the event of the insolvency of their employer

[OJ 2008 L283/36]

THE EUROPEAN PARLIAMENT AND THE COUNCIL OF THE EUROPEAN UNION,

Having regard to the Treaty establishing the European Community, and in particular Article 137(2) thereof,

Having regard to the proposal from the Commission,

Having regard to the opinion of the European Economic and Social Committee,[1]

[7] Directive 2000/34/EC, Article 3.
[8] Directive 2000/34/EC, Article 4.
[1] OJ C 161, 13.7.2007, p. 75.

After consultation of the Committee of the Regions,

Acting in accordance with the procedure laid down in Article 251 of the Treaty,[2]

Whereas:

(1) Council Directive 80/987/EEC of 20 October 1980 on the protection of employees in the event of the insolvency of their employer[3] has been substantially amended several times.[4] In the interests of clarity and rationality the said Directive should be codified.

(2) The Community Charter of Fundamental Social Rights for Workers adopted on 9 December 1989 states, in point 7, that the completion of the internal market must lead to an improvement in the living and working conditions of workers in the Community and that this improvement must cover, where necessary, the development of certain aspects of employment regulations such as procedures for collective redundancies and those regarding bankruptcies.

(3) It is necessary to provide for the protection of employees in the event of the insolvency of their employer and to ensure a minimum degree of protection, in particular in order to guarantee payment of their outstanding claims, while taking account of the need for balanced economic and social development in the Community. To this end, the Member States should establish a body which guarantees payment of the outstanding claims of the employees concerned.

(4) In order to ensure equitable protection for the employees concerned, the state of insolvency should be defined in the light of the legislative trends in the Member States and that concept should also include insolvency proceedings other than liquidation. In this context, Member States should, in order to determine the liability of the guarantee institution, be able to lay down that where an insolvency situation results in several insolvency proceedings, the situation is to be treated as a single insolvency procedure.

(5) It should be ensured that the employees referred to in Council Directive 97/81/EC of 15 December 1997 concerning the Framework Agreement on part-time work concluded by UNICE, CEEP and the ETUC,[5] Council Directive 1999/70/EC of 28 June 1999 concerning the framework agreement on fixed-term work concluded by the ETUC, UNICE and CEEP[6] and Council Directive 91/383/EEC of 25 June 1991 supplementing the measures to encourage improvements in the safety and health at work of workers with a fixed-duration employment relationship or a temporary employment relationship[7] are not excluded from the scope of this Directive.

(6) In order to ensure legal certainty for employees in the event of insolvency of undertakings pursuing their activities in a number of Member States, and to strengthen employees' rights in line with the established case-law of the Court of Justice of the European Communities, provisions should be laid down which expressly state which institution is responsible for meeting pay claims in these cases and establish as the aim of cooperation between the competent administrative authorities of the Member States the early settlement of employees' outstanding claims. Furthermore it is necessary to ensure that the relevant arrangements are properly implemented by making provision for collaboration between the competent administrative authorities in the Member States.

(7) Member States may set limitations on the responsibility of the guarantee institutions. Those limitations must be compatible with the social objective of the Directive and may take into account the different levels of claims.

(8) In order to make it easier to identify insolvency proceedings, in particular in situations with a cross-border dimension, provision should be made for the Member States to notify the Commission and the other Member States about the types of insolvency proceedings which give rise to intervention by the guarantee institution.

[2] Opinion of the European Parliament of 19 June 2007 (OJ C 146 E, 12.6.2008, p. 71) and Council Decision of 25 September 2008.
[3] OJ L 283, 28.10.1980, p. 23.
[4] See Annex I, Parts A and B.
[5] OJ L 14, 20.1.1998, p. 9.
[6] OJ L 175, 10.7.1999, p. 43.
[7] OJ L 206, 29.7.1991, p. 19.

(9) Since the objective of the action to be taken cannot be sufficiently achieved by the Member States and can therefore be better achieved at Community level, the Community may adopt measures, in accordance with the principle of subsidiarity as set out in Article 5 of the Treaty. In accordance with the principle of proportionality, as set out in that Article, this Directive does not go beyond what is necessary in order to achieve that objective.

(10) The Commission should submit to the European Parliament and the Council a report on the implementation and application of this Directive in particular as regards the new forms of employment emerging in the Member States.

(11) This Directive should be without prejudice to the obligations of the Member States relating to the time-limits for transposition into national law and application of the Directives set out in Annex I, Part C,

HAVE ADOPTED THIS DIRECTIVE:

Chapter I Scope and definitions

Article 1

1. This Directive shall apply to employees' claims arising from contracts of employment or employment relationships and existing against employers who are in a state of insolvency within the meaning of Article 2(1).

2. Member States may, by way of exception, exclude claims by certain categories of employee from the scope of this Directive, by virtue of the existence of other forms of guarantee if it is established that these offer the persons concerned a degree of protection equivalent to that resulting from this Directive.

3. Where such provision already applies in their national legislation, Member States may continue to exclude from the scope of this Directive:

(a) domestic servants employed by a natural person;

(b) share-fishermen.

Article 2

1. For the purposes of this Directive, an employer shall be deemed to be in a state of insolvency where a request has been made for the opening of collective proceedings based on insolvency of the employer, as provided for under the laws, regulations and administrative provisions of a Member State, and involving the partial or total divestment of the employer's assets and the appointment of a liquidator or a person performing a similar task, and the authority which is competent pursuant to the said provisions has:

(a) either decided to open the proceedings; or

(b) established that the employer's undertaking or business has been definitively closed down and that the available assets are insufficient to warrant the opening of the proceedings.

2. This Directive is without prejudice to national law as regards the definition of the terms 'employee', 'employer', 'pay', 'right conferring immediate entitlement' and 'right conferring prospective entitlement'.

However, the Member States may not exclude from the scope of this Directive:

(a) part-time employees within the meaning of Directive 97/81/EC;

(b) employees with a fixed-term contract within the meaning of Directive 1999/70/EC;

(c) employees with a temporary employment relationship within the meaning of Article 1(2) of Directive 91/383/EEC.

3. Member States may not set a minimum duration for the contract of employment or the employment relationship in order for employees to qualify for claims under this Directive.

4. This Directive does not prevent Member States from extending employee protection to other situations of insolvency, for example where payments have been de facto stopped on a permanent basis, established by proceedings different from those mentioned in paragraph 1 as provided for under national law.

Such procedures shall not however create a guarantee obligation for the institutions of the other Member States in the cases referred to in Chapter IV.

Chapter II Provisions concerning guarantee institutions

Article 3

Member States shall take the measures necessary to ensure that guarantee institutions guarantee, subject to Article 4, payment of employees' outstanding claims resulting from contracts of employment or employment relationships, including, where provided for by national law, severance pay on termination of employment relationships.

The claims taken over by the guarantee institution shall be the outstanding pay claims relating to a period prior to and/or, as applicable, after a given date determined by the Member States.

Article 4

1. Member States shall have the option to limit the liability of the guarantee institutions referred to in Article 3.

2. If Member States exercise the option referred to in paragraph 1, they shall specify the length of the period for which outstanding claims are to be met by the guarantee institution. However, this may not be shorter than a period covering the remuneration of the last three months of the employment relationship prior to and/or after the date referred to in the second paragraph of Article 3.

Member States may include this minimum period of three months in a reference period with a duration of not less than six months.

Member States having a reference period of not less than 18 months may limit the period for which outstanding claims are met by the guarantee institution to eight weeks. In this case, those periods which are most favourable to the employee shall be used for the calculation of the minimum period.

3. Member States may set ceilings on the payments made by the guarantee institution. These ceilings must not fall below a level which is socially compatible with the social objective of this Directive.

If Member States exercise this option, they shall inform the Commission of the methods used to set the ceiling.

Article 5

Member States shall lay down detailed rules for the organisation, financing and operation of the guarantee institutions, complying with the following principles in particular:

(a) the assets of the institutions must be independent of the employers' operating capital and be inaccessible to proceedings for insolvency;
(b) employers must contribute to financing, unless it is fully covered by the public authorities;
(c) the institutions' liabilities must not depend on whether or not obligations to contribute to financing have been fulfilled.

Chapter III Provisions concerning social security

Article 6

Member States may stipulate that Articles 3, 4 and 5 shall not apply to contributions due under national statutory social security schemes or under supplementary occupational or inter-occupational pension schemes outside the national statutory social security schemes.

Article 7

Member States shall take the measures necessary to ensure that non-payment of compulsory contributions due from the employer, before the onset of his insolvency, to their insurance institutions under national statutory social security schemes does not adversely affect employees' benefit entitlement in respect of these insurance institutions in so far as the employees' contributions have been deducted at source from the remuneration paid.

Article 8

Member States shall ensure that the necessary measures are taken to protect the interests of employees and of persons having already left the employer's undertaking or business at the date of the onset of the employer's insolvency in respect of rights conferring on them immediate or prospective entitlement to old-age benefits, including survivors' benefits, under supplementary occupational or inter-occupational pension schemes outside the national statutory social security schemes.

Chapter IV Provisions concerning transnational situations

Article 9

1. If an undertaking with activities in the territories of at least two Member States is in a state of insolvency within the meaning of Article 2(1), the institution responsible for meeting employees' outstanding claims shall be that in the Member State in whose territory they work or habitually work.

2. The extent of employees' rights shall be determined by the law governing the competent guarantee institution.

3. Member States shall take the measures necessary to ensure that, in the cases referred to in paragraph 1 of this Article, decisions taken in the context of insolvency proceedings referred to in Article 2(1), which have been requested in another Member State, are taken into account when determining the employer's state of insolvency within the meaning of this Directive.

Article 10

1. For the purposes of implementing Article 9, Member States shall make provision for the sharing of relevant information between their competent administrative authorities and/or the guarantee institutions mentioned in the first paragraph of Article 3, making it possible in particular to inform the guarantee institution responsible for meeting the employees' outstanding claims.

2. Member States shall notify the Commission and the other Member States of the contact details of their competent administrative authorities and/or guarantee institutions. The Commission shall make that information publicly accessible.

Chapter V General and final provisions

Article 11

This Directive shall not affect the option of Member States to apply or introduce laws, regulations or administrative provisions which are more favourable to employees.

Implementation of this Directive shall not under any circumstances be sufficient grounds for a regression in relation to the current situation in the Member States and in relation to the general level of protection of employees in the area covered by it.

Article 12

This Directive shall not affect the option of Member States:

(a) to take the measures necessary to avoid abuses;

(b) to refuse or reduce the liability referred to in the first paragraph of Article 3 or the guarantee obligation referred to in Article 7 if it appears that fulfilment of the obligation is unjustifiable because of the existence of special links between the employee and the employer and of common interests resulting in collusion between them;

(c) to refuse or reduce the liability referred to in the first paragraph of Article 3 or the guarantee obligation referred to in Article 7 in cases where the employee, on his or her own or together with his or her close relatives, was the owner of an essential part of the employer's undertaking or business and had a considerable influence on its activities.

Article 13

Member States shall notify the Commission and the other Member States of the types of national insolvency proceedings falling within the scope of this Directive, and of any amendments relating thereto.

The Commission shall publish these communications in the Official Journal of the European Union.

Article 14
Member States shall communicate to the Commission the text of the laws, regulations and administrative provisions which they adopt in the field covered by this Directive.

Article 15
By 8 October 2010 at the latest, the Commission shall submit to the European Parliament and to the Council a report on the implementation and application in the Member States of Articles 1 to 4, 9 and 10, Article 11, second paragraph, Article 12, point (c), and Articles 13 and 14.

Article 16
Directive 80/987/EEC, as amended by the acts listed in Annex I, is repealed, without prejudice to the obligations of the Member States relating to the time limits for transposition into national law and application of the Directives set out in Annex I, Part C.

References to the repealed Directive shall be construed as references to this Directive and shall be read in accordance with the correlation table in Annex II.

Article 17
This Directive shall enter into force on the 20th day following its publication in the *Official Journal of the European Union*.

Article 18
This Directive is addressed to the Member States.

Done at Strasbourg, 22 October 2008.
For the European Parliament The President H.-G. PÖTTERING
For the Council The President J.-P. JOUYET

Annex I

Part A Repealed Directive with its successive amendments (referred to in Article 16)

Council Directive 80/987/EEC	(OJ L 283, 28.10.1980, p. 23)
Council Directive 87/164/EEC	(OJ L 66, 11.3.1987, p. 11)
Directive 2002/74/EC of the European Parliament and of the Council	(OJ L 270, 8.10.2002, p. 10)

Part B Non-repealed amending act (referred to in Article 16)

1994 Act of Accession

Part C Time-limits for transposition into national law and application (referred to in Article 16)

Directive	Time limit for transposition	Date of application
Directive 80/987/EEC	23 October 1983	29 June 1994
Directive 87/164/EEC	1 January 1986	7 October 2005

Annex II

Correlation table

Directive 80/987/EEC	This Directive
Article 1	Article 1
Article 2	Article 2
Article 3	Article 3
Article 4	Article 4
Article 5	Article 5
Article 6	Article 6
Article 7	Article 7
Article 8	Article 8
Article 8a	Article 9
Article 8b	Article 10
Article 9	Article 11
Article 10	Article 12
Article 10a	Article 13
Article 11(1)	—
Article 11(2)	Article 14
Article 12	—
—	Article 15
—	Article 16
—	Article 17
Article 13	Article 18
—	Annex I
—	Annex II

Competition

Regulation No 17—First Regulation implementing Articles 81 and 82 of the Treaty*

[OJ Sp. Ed. 1962, No 204/62, p. 87]

Article 8 Duration and revocation of decisions under Article 85(3)

3. The Commission may revoke or amend its decision or prohibit specified acts by the parties:
    (a) where there has been a change in any of the facts which were basic to the making of the decision;
    (b) where the parties commit a breach of any obligation attached to the decision;
    (c) where the decision is based on incorrect information or was induced by deceit;

* **Editor's Note:** Following the entry into force of Regulation No 1/2003, included below, Article 8(3) is the only Article which remains, temporarily, in force and which is still the case as of 30 March 2013.

(d) where the parties abuse the exemption from the provisions of Article 85(1) of the Treaty granted to them by the decision.

In cases to which subparagraphs (b), (c) or (d) apply, the decision may be revoked with retroactive effect.

Commission Notice on agreements of minor importance which do not appreciably restrict competition under Article 81(1) of the Treaty Establishing the European Community (*de minimis*)[*1]

[OJ 2001 C368/13]

I

1. Article 81(1) prohibits agreements between undertakings which may affect trade between Member States and which have as their object or effect the prevention, restriction or distortion of competition within the common market. The Court of Justice of the European Communities has clarified that this provision is not applicable where the impact of the agreement on intra-Community trade or on competition is not appreciable.

2. In this notice the Commission quantifies, with the help of market share thresholds, what is not an appreciable restriction of competition under Article 81 of the EC Treaty. This negative definition of appreciability does not imply that agreements between undertakings which exceed the thresholds set out in this notice appreciably restrict competition. Such agreements may still have only a negligible effect on competition and may therefore not be prohibited by Article 81(1).[2]

3. Agreements may in addition not fall under Article 81(1) because they are not capable of appreciably affecting trade between Member States. This notice does not deal with this issue. It does not quantify what does not constitute an appreciable effect on trade. It is however acknowledged that agreements between small and medium-sized undertakings, as defined in the Annex to Commission Recommendation 96/280/EC[3] are rarely capable of appreciably affecting trade between Member States. Small and medium-sized undertakings are currently defined in that recommendation as undertakings which have fewer than 250 employees and have either an annual turnover not exceeding EUR 40 million or an annual balance-sheet total not exceeding EUR 27 million.

4. In cases covered by this notice the Commission will not institute proceedings either upon application or on its own initiative. Where undertakings assume in good faith that an agreement is covered by this notice, the Commission will not impose fines. Although not binding on them, this notice also intends to give guidance to the courts and authorities of the Member States in their application of Article 81.

5. This notice also applies to decisions by associations of undertakings and to concerted practices.

6. This notice is without prejudice to any interpretation of Article 81 which may be given by the Court of Justice or the Court of First Instance of the European Communities.

* **Editor's Note:** Permission to reproduce this document is gratefully acknowledged but please note that 'Only European Community legislation printed in the paper edition of the *Official Journal of the European Union* is deemed authentic' but as from 1 July 2013 only the Official Journal published in electronic form shall be authentic and shall produce legal effects.

[1] This notice replaces the notice on agreements of minor importance published in OJ C 372, 9.12.1997.

[2] See, for instance, the judgment of the Court of Justice in Joined Cases C-215/96 and C-216/96 *Bagnasco (Carlos)* v *Banca Popolare di Novara and Casa di Risparmio di Genova e Imperia* (1999) ECR I-135, points 34–35. This notice is also without prejudice to the principles for assessment under Article 81(1) as expressed in the Commission notice 'Guidelines on the applicability of Article 81 of the EC Treaty to horizontal cooperation agreements', OJ C 3, 6.1.2001, in particular points 17–31 inclusive, and in the Commission notice 'Guidelines on vertical restraints', OJ C 291, 13.10.2000, in particular points 5–20 inclusive.

[3] OJ L 107, 30.4.1996, p. 4. This recommendation will be revised. It is envisaged to increase the annual turnover threshold from EUR 40 million to EUR 50 million and the annual balance-sheet total threshold from EUR 27 million to EUR 43 million.

II

7. The Commission holds the view that agreements between undertakings which affect trade between Member States do not appreciably restrict competition within the meaning of Article 81(1):

(a) if the aggregate market share held by the parties to the agreement does not exceed 10% on any of the relevant markets affected by the agreement, where the agreement is made between undertakings which are actual or potential competitors on any of these markets (agreements between competitors);[4] or

(b) if the market share held by each of the parties to the agreement does not exceed 15% on any of the relevant markets affected by the agreement, where the agreement is made between undertakings which are not actual or potential competitors on any of these markets (agreements between non-competitors).

In cases where it is difficult to classify the agreement as either an agreement between competitors or an agreement between non-competitors the 10% threshold is applicable.

8. Where in a relevant market competition is restricted by the cumulative effect of agreements for the sale of goods or services entered into by different suppliers or distributors (cumulative foreclosure effect of parallel networks of agreements having similar effects on the market), the market share thresholds under point 7 are reduced to 5%, both for agreements between competitors and for agreements between non-competitors. Individual suppliers or distributors with a market share not exceeding 5% are in general not considered to contribute significantly to a cumulative foreclosure effect.[5] A cumulative foreclosure effect is unlikely to exist if less than 30% of the relevant market is covered by parallel (networks of) agreements having similar effects.

9. The Commission also holds the view that agreements are not restrictive of competition if the market shares do not exceed the thresholds of respectively 10%, 15% and 5% set out in point 7 and 8 during two successive calendar years by more than 2 percentage points.

10. In order to calculate the market share, it is necessary to determine the relevant market. This consists of the relevant product market and the relevant geographic market. When defining the relevant market, reference should be had to the notice on the definition of the relevant market for the purposes of Community competition law.[6] The market shares are to be calculated on the basis of sales value data or, where appropriate, purchase value data. If value data are not available, estimates based on other reliable market information, including volume data, may be used.

11. Points 7, 8 and 9 do not apply to agreements containing any of the following hardcore restrictions:

(1) as regards agreements between competitors as defined in point 7, restrictions which, directly or indirectly, in isolation or in combination with other factors under the control of the parties, have as their object[7]

(a) the fixing of prices when selling the products to third parties;

(b) the limitation of output or sales;

(c) the allocation of markets or customers;

[4] On what are actual or potential competitors, see the Commission notice 'Guidelines on the applicability of Article 81 of the EC Treaty to horizontal cooperation agreements', OJ C 3, 6.1.2001, paragraph 9. A firm is treated as an actual competitor if it is either active on the same relevant market or if, in the absence of the agreement, it is able to switch production to the relevant products and market them in the short term without incurring significant additional costs or risks in response to a small and permanent increase in relative prices (immediate supply- side substitutability). A firm is treated as a potential competitor if there is evidence that, absent the agreement, this firm could and would be likely to undertake the necessary additional investments or other necessary switching costs so that it could enter the relevant market in response to a small and permanent increase in relative prices.

[5] See also the Commission notice 'Guidelines on vertical restraints', OJ C 291, 13.10.2000, in particular paragraphs 73, 142, 143 and 189. While in the guidelines on vertical restraints in relation to certain restrictions reference is made not only to the total but also to the tied market share of a particular supplier or buyer, in this notice all market share thresholds refer to total market shares.

[6] OJ C 372, 9.12.1997, p. 5.

[7] Without prejudice to situations of joint production with or without joint distribution as defined in Article 5, paragraph 2, of Commission Regulation (EC) No 2658/2000 and Article 5, paragraph 2, of Commission Regulation (EC) No 2659/2000, OJ L 304, 5.12.2000, pp. 3 and 7 respectively.

(2) as regards agreements between non-competitors as defined in point 7, restrictions which, directly or indirectly, in isolation or in combination with other factors under the control of the parties, have as their object:

(a) the restriction of the buyer's ability to determine its sale price, without prejudice to the possibility of the supplier imposing a maximum sale price or recommending a sale price, provided that they do not amount to a fixed or minimum sale price as a result of pressure from, or incentives offered by, any of the parties;

(b) the restriction of the territory into which, or of the customers to whom, the buyer may sell the contract goods or services, except the following restrictions which are not hardcore:

- the restriction of active sales into the exclusive territory or to an exclusive customer group reserved to the supplier or allocated by the supplier to another buyer, where such a restriction does not limit sales by the customers of the buyer,
- the restriction of sales to end users by a buyer operating at the wholesale level of trade,
- the restriction of sales to unauthorised distributors by the members of a selective distribution system, and
- the restriction of the buyer's ability to sell components, supplied for the purposes of incorporation, to customers who would use them to manufacture the same type of goods as those produced by the supplier;

(c) the restriction of active or passive sales to end users by members of a selective distribution system operating at the retail level of trade, without prejudice to the possibility of prohibiting a member of the system from operating out of an unauthorised place of establishment;

(d) the restriction of cross-supplies between distributors within a selective distribution system, including between distributors operating at different levels of trade;

(e) the restriction agreed between a supplier of components and a buyer who incorporates those components, which limits the supplier's ability to sell the components as spare parts to end users or to repairers or other service providers not entrusted by the buyer with the repair or servicing of its goods;

(3) as regards agreements between competitors as defined in point 7, where the competitors operate, for the purposes of the agreement, at a different level of the production or distribution chain, any of the hardcore restrictions listed in paragraph (1) and (2) above.

12. (1) For the purposes of this notice, the terms 'undertaking', 'party to the agreement', 'distributor', 'supplier' and 'buyer' shall include their respective connected undertakings.

(2) 'Connected undertakings' are:

(a) undertakings in which a party to the agreement, directly or indirectly:

- has the power to exercise more than half the voting rights, or
- has the power to appoint more than half the members of the supervisory board, board of management or bodies legally representing the undertaking, or
- has the right to manage the undertaking's affairs;

(b) undertakings which directly or indirectly have, over a party to the agreement, the rights or powers listed in (a);

(c) undertakings in which an undertaking referred to in (b) has, directly or indirectly, the rights or powers listed in (a);

(d) undertakings in which a party to the agreement together with one or more of the undertakings referred to in (a), (b) or (c), or in which two or more of the latter undertakings, jointly have the rights or powers listed in (a);

(e) undertakings in which the rights or the powers listed in (a) are jointly held by:

- parties to the agreement or their respective connected undertakings referred to in (a) to (d), or
- one or more of the parties to the agreement or one or more of their connected undertakings referred to in (a) to (d) and one or more third parties.

(3) For the purposes of paragraph 2(e), the market share held by these jointly held undertakings shall be apportioned equally to each undertaking having the rights or the powers listed in paragraph 2(a).

Commission Notice on the definition of relevant market for the purposes of Community competition law (97/C 372/03)*

[OJ 1997 C372/5]

I. INTRODUCTION

1. The purpose of this notice is to provide guidance as to how the Commission applies the concept of relevant product and geographic market in its ongoing enforcement of Community competition law, in particular the application of Council Regulation No 17 and (EEC) No 4064/89, their equivalents in other sectoral applications such as transport, coal and steel, and agriculture, and the relevant provisions of the EEA Agreement.[1] Throughout this notice, references to Articles 85 and 86 of the Treaty and to merger control are to be understood as referring to the equivalent provisions in the EEA Agreement and the ECSC Treaty.

2. Market definition is a tool to identify and define the boundaries of competition between firms. It serves to establish the framework within which competition policy is applied by the Commission. The main purpose of market definition is to identify in a systematic way the competitive constraints that the undertakings involved[2] face. The objective of defining a market in both its product and geographic dimension is to identify those actual competitors of the undertakings involved that are capable of constraining those undertakings' behaviour and of preventing them from behaving independently of effective competitive pressure. It is from this perspective that the market definition makes it possible inter alia to calculate market shares that would convey meaningful information regarding market power for the purposes of assessing dominance or for the purposes of applying Article 85.

3. It follows from point 2 that the concept of 'relevant market' is different from other definitions of market often used in other contexts. For instance, companies often use the term 'market' to refer to the area where it sells its products or to refer broadly to the industry or sector where it belongs.

4. The definition of the relevant market in both its product and its geographic dimensions often has a decisive influence on the assessment of a competition case. By rendering public the procedures which the Commission follows when considering market definition and by indicating the criteria and evidence on which it relies to reach a decision, the Commission expects to increase the transparency of its policy and decision-making in the area of competition policy.

5. Increased transparency will also result in companies and their advisers being able to better anticipate the possibility that the Commission may raise competition concerns in an individual case. Companies could, therefore, take such a possibility into account in their own internal decision- making when contemplating, for instance, acquisitions, the creation of joint ventures, or the establishment of certain agreements. It is also intended that companies should be in a better position to understand what sort of information the Commission considers relevant for the purposes of market definition.

* **Editor's Note:** Permission to reproduce this document is gratefully acknowledged but please note that 'Only European Community legislation printed in the paper edition of the *Official Journal of the European Union* is deemed authentic' but from 1 July 2013 only the Official Journal published in electronic form shall be authentic and shall produce legal effects.

[1] The focus of assessment in State aid cases is the aid recipient and the industry/sector concerned rather than identification of competitive constraints faced by the aid recipient. When consideration of market power and therefore of the relevant market are raised in any particular case, elements of the approach outlined here might serve as a basis for the assessment of State aid cases.

[2] For the purposes of this notice, the undertakings involved will be, in the case of a concentration, the parties to the concentration; in investigations within the meaning of Article 86 of the Treaty, the undertaking being investigated or the complainants; for investigations within the meaning of Article 85, the parties to the Agreement.

6. The Commission's interpretation of 'relevant market' is without prejudice to the interpretation which may be given by the Court of Justice or the Court of First Instance of the European Communities.

II. DEFINITION OF RELEVANT MARKET

Definition of relevant product market and relevant geographic market

7. The Regulations based on Article 85 and 86 of the Treaty, in particular in section 6 of Form A/B with respect to Regulation No 17, as well as in section 6 of Form CO with respect to Regulation (EEC) No 4064/89 on the control of concentrations having a Community dimension have laid down the following definitions, 'Relevant product markets' are defined as follows:

'A relevant product market comprises all those products and/or services which are regarded as interchangeable or substitutable by the consumer, by reason of the products' characteristics, their prices and their intended use'.

8. 'Relevant geographic markets' are defined as follows:

'The relevant geographic market comprises the area in which the undertakings concerned are involved in the supply and demand of products or services, in which the conditions of competition are sufficiently homogeneous and which can be distinguished from neighbouring areas because the conditions of competition are appreciably different in those area'.

9. The relevant market within which to assess a given competition issue is therefore established by the combination of the product and geographic markets. The Commission interprets the definitions in paragraphs 7 and 8 (which reflect the case-law of the Court of Justice and the Court of First Instance as well as its own decision-making practice) according to the orientations defined in this notice.

Concept of relevant market and objectives of Community competition policy

10. The concept of relevant market is closely related to the objectives pursued under Community competition policy. For example, under the Community's merger control, the objective in controlling structural changes in the supply of a product/service is to prevent the creation or reinforcement of a dominant position as a result of which effective competition would be significantly impeded in a substantial part of the common market. Under the Community's competition rules, a dominant position is such that a firm or group of firms would be in a position to behave to an appreciable extent independently of its competitors, customers and ultimately of its consumers.[3] Such a position would usually arise when a firm or group of firms accounted for a large share of the supply in any given market, provided that other factors analysed in the assessment (such as entry barriers, customers' capacity to react, etc.) point in the same direction.

11. The same approach is followed by the Commission in its application of Article 86 of the Treaty to firms that enjoy a single or collective dominant position. Within the meaning of Regulation No 17, the Commission has the power to investigate and bring to an end abuses of such a dominant position, which must also be defined by reference to the relevant market. Markets may also need to be defined in the application of Article 85 of the Treaty, in particular, in determining whether an appreciable restriction of competition exists or in establishing if the condition pursuant to Article 85(3)(b) for an exemption from the application of Article 85(1) is met.

12. The criteria for defining the relevant market are applied generally for the analysis of certain types of behaviour in the market and for the analysis of structural changes in the supply of products. This methodology, though, might lead to different results depending on the nature of the competition issue being examined. For instance, the scope of the geographic market might be different when analysing a concentration, where the analysis is essentially prospective, from an analysis of past behaviour. The different time horizon considered in each case might lead to the result that different geographic markets are defined for the same products depending on whether the Commission is

[3] Definition given by the Court of Justice in its judgment of 13 February 1979 in Case 85/76, Hoffmann-La Roche [1979] ECR 461, and confirmed in subsequent judgments.

examining a change in the structure of supply, such as a concentration or a cooperative joint venture, or examining issues relating to certain past behaviour.

Basic principles for market definition

Competitive constraints

13. Firms are subject to three main sources or competitive constraints: demand substitutability, supply substitutability and potential competition. From an economic point of view, for the definition of the relevant market, demand substitution constitutes the most immediate and effective disciplinary force on the suppliers of a given product, in particular in relation to their pricing decisions. A firm or a group of firms cannot have a significant impact on the prevailing conditions of sale, such as prices, if its customers are in a position to switch easily to available substitute products or to suppliers located elsewhere. Basically, the exercise of market definition consists in identifying the effective alternative sources of supply for the customers of the undertakings involved, in terms both of products/services and of geographic location of suppliers.

14. The competitive constraints arising from supply side substitutability other then those described in paragraphs 20 to 23 and from potential competition are in general less immediate and in any case require an analysis of additional factors. As a result such constraints are taken into account at the assessment stage of competition analysis.

Demand substitution

15. The assessment of demand substitution entails a determination of the range of products which are viewed as substitutes by the consumer. One way of making this determination can be viewed as a speculative experiment, postulating a hypothetical small, lasting change in relative prices and evaluating the likely reactions of customers to that increase. The exercise of market definition focuses on prices for operational and practical purposes, and more precisely on demand substitution arising from small, permanent changes in relative prices. This concept can provide clear indications as to the evidence that is relevant in defining markets.

16. Conceptually, this approach means that, starting from the type of products that the undertakings involved sell and the area in which they sell them, additional products and areas will be included in, or excluded from, the market definition depending on whether competition from these other products and areas affect or restrain sufficiently the pricing of the parties' products in the short term.

17. The question to be answered is whether the parties' customers would switch to readily available substitutes or to suppliers located elsewhere in response to a hypothetical small (in the range 5% to 10%) but permanent relative price increase in the products and areas being considered. If substitution were enough to make the price increase unprofitable because of the resulting loss of sales, additional substitutes and areas are included in the relevant market. This would be done until the set of products and geographical areas is such that small, permanent increases in relative prices would be profitable. The equivalent analysis is applicable in cases concerning the concentration of buying power, where the starting point would then be the supplier and the price test serves to identify the alternative distribution channels or outlets for the supplier's products. In the application of these principles, careful account should be taken of certain particular situations as described within paragraphs 56 and 58.

18. A practical example of this test can be provided by its application to a merger of, for instance, soft-drink bottlers. An issue to examine in such a case would be to decide whether different flavours of soft drinks belong to the same market. In practice, the question to address would be whether consumers of flavour A would switch to other flavours when confronted with a permanent price increase of 5% to 10% for flavour A. If a sufficient number of consumers would switch to, say, flavour B, to such an extent that the price increase for flavour A would not be profitable owing to the resulting loss of sales, then the market would comprise at least flavours A and B. The process would have to be extended in addition to other available flavours until a set of products is identified for which a price rise would not induce a sufficient substitution in demand.

19. Generally, and in particular for the analysis of merger cases, the price to take into account will be the prevailing market price. This may not be the case where the prevailing price has been determined in the absence of sufficient competition. In particular for the investigation of abuses of dominant positions, the fact that the prevailing price might already have been substantially increased will be taken into account.

Supply substitution

20. Supply-side substitutability may also be taken into account when defining markets in those situations in which its effects are equivalent to those of demand substitution in terms of effectiveness and immediacy. This means that suppliers are able to switch production to the relevant products and market them in the short term[4] without incurring significant additional costs or risks in response to small and permanent changes in relative prices. When these conditions are met, the additional production that is put on the market will have a disciplinary effect on the competitive behaviour of the companies involved. Such an impact in terms of effectiveness and immediacy is equivalent to the demand substitution effect.

21. These situations typically arise when companies market a wide range of qualities or grades of one product; even if, for a given final customer or group of consumers, the different qualities are not substitutable, the different qualities will be grouped into one product market, provided that most of the suppliers are able to offer and sell the various qualities immediately and without the significant increases in costs described above. In such cases, the relevant product market will encompass all products that are substitutable in demand and supply, and the current sales of those products will be aggregated so as to give the total value or volume of the market. The same reasoning may lead to group different geographic areas.

22. A practical example of the approach to supply-side substitutability when defining product markets is to be found in the case of paper. Paper is usually supplied in a range of different qualities, from standard writing paper to high quality papers to be used, for instance, to publish art books. From a demand point of view, different qualities of paper cannot be used for any given use, i.e. an art book or a high quality publication cannot be based on lower quality papers. However, paper plants are prepared to manufacture the different qualities, and production can be adjusted with negligible costs and in a short time-frame. In the absence of particular difficulties in distribution, paper manufacturers are able therefore, to compete for orders of the various qualities, in particular if orders are placed with sufficient lead time to allow for modification of production plans. Under such circumstances, the Commission would not define a separate market for each quality of paper and its respective use. The various qualities of paper are included in the relevant market, and their sales added up to estimate total market value and volume.

23. When supply-side substitutability would entail the need to adjust significantly existing tangible and intangible assets, additional investments, strategic decisions or time delays, it will not be considered at the stage of market definition. Examples where supply-side substitution did not induce the Commission to enlarge the market are offered in the area of consumer products, in particular for branded beverages. Although bottling plants may in principle bottle different beverages, there are costs and lead times involved (in terms of advertising, product testing and distribution) before the products can actually be sold. In these cases, the effects of supply-side substitutability and other forms of potential competition would then be examined at a later stage.

Potential competition

24. The third source of competitive constraint, potential competition, is not taken into account when defining markets, since the conditions under which potential competition will actually represent an effective competitive constraint depend on the analysis of specific factors and circumstances related to the conditions of entry. If required, this analysis is only carried out at a subsequent stage, in general once the position of the companies involved in the relevant market has already been ascertained, and when such position gives rise to concerns from a competition point of view.

[4] That is such a period that does not entail a significant adjustment of existing tangible and intangible assets (see paragraph 23).

III. EVIDENCE RELIED ON TO DEFINE RELEVANT MARKETS

The process of defining the relevant market in practice

Product dimension

25. There is a range of evidence permitting an assessment of the extent to which substitution would take place. In individual cases, certain types of evidence will be determinant, depending very much on the characteristics and specificity of the industry and products or services that are being examined. The same type of evidence may be of no importance in other cases. In most cases, a decision will have to be based on the consideration of a number of criteria and different items of evidence. The Commission follows an open approach to empirical evidence, aimed at making an effective use of all available information which may be relevant in individual cases. The Commission does not follow a rigid hierarchy of different sources of information or types of evidence.

26. The process of defining relevant markets may be summarized as follows: on the basis of the preliminary information available or information submitted by the undertakings involved, the Commission will usually be in a position to broadly establish the possible relevant markets within which, for instance, a concentration or a restriction of competition has to be assessed. In general, and for all practical purposes when handling individual cases, the question will usually be to decide on a few alternative possible relevant markets. For instance, with respect to the product market, the issue will often be to establish whether product A and product B belong or do not belong to the same product market. it is often the case that the inclusion of product B would be enough to remove any competition concerns.

27. In such situations it is not necessary to consider whether the market includes additional products, or to reach a definitive conclusion on the precise product market. If under the conceivable alternative market definitions the operation in question does not raise competition concerns, the question of market definition will be left open, reducing thereby the burden on companies to supply information.

Geographic dimension

28. The Commission's approach to geographic market definition might be summarized as follows: it will take a preliminary view of the scope of the geographic market on the basis of broad indications as to the distribution of market shares between the parties and their competitors, as well as a preliminary analysis of pricing and price differences at national and Community or EEA level. This initial view is used basically as a working hypothesis to focus the Commission's enquiries for the purposes of arriving at a precise geographic market definition.

29. The reasons behind any particular configuration of prices and market shares need to be explored. Companies might enjoy high market shares in their domestic markets just because of the weight of the past, and conversely, a homogeneous presence of companies throughout the EEA might be consistent with national or regional geographic markets. The initial working hypothesis will therefore be checked against an analysis of demand characteristics (importance of national or local preferences, current patterns of purchases of customers, product differentiation/brands, other) in order to establish whether companies in different areas do indeed constitute a real alternative source of supply for consumers. The theoretical experiment is again based on substitution arising from changes in relative prices, and the question to answer is again whether the customers of the parties would switch their orders to companies located elsewhere in the short term and at a negligible cost.

30. If necessary, a further check on supply factors will be carried out to ensure that those companies located in differing areas do not face impediments in developing their sales on competitive terms throughout the whole geographic market. This analysis will include an examination of requirements for a local presence in order to sell in that area the conditions of access to distribution channels, costs associated with setting up a distribution network, and the presence or absence of regulatory barriers arising from public procurement, price regulations, quotas and tariffs limiting trade or production, technical standards, monopolies, freedom of establishment, requirements for administrative authorizations, packaging regulations, etc. In short, the Commission will identify possible obstacles

and barriers isolating companies located in a given area from the competitive pressure of companies located outside that area, so as to determine the precise degree of market interpenetration at national, European or global level.

31. The actual pattern and evolution of trade flows offers useful supplementary indications as to the economic importance of each demand or supply factor mentioned above, and the extent to which they may or may not constitute actual barriers creating different geographic markets. The analysis of trade flows will generally address the question of transport costs and the extent to which these may hinder trade between different areas, having regard to plant location, costs of production and relative price levels.

Market integration in the Community

32. Finally, the Commission also takes into account the continuing process of market integration, in particular in the Community, when defining geographic markets, especially in the area of concentrations and structural joint ventures. The measures adopted and implemented in the internal market programme to remove barriers to trade and further integrate the Community markets cannot be ignored when assessing the effects on competition of a concentration or a structural joint venture. A situation where national markets have been artificially isolated from each other because of the existence of legislative barriers that have now been removed will generally lead to a cautious assessment of past evidence regarding prices, market shares or trade patterns. A process of market integration that would, in the short term, lead to wider geographic markets may therefore be taken into consideration when defining the geographic market for the purposes of assessing concentrations and joint ventures.

The process of gathering evidence

33. When a precise market definition is deemed necessary, the Commission will often contact the main customers and the main companies in the industry to enquire into their views about the boundaries of product and geographic markets and to obtain the necessary factual evidence to reach a conclusion. The Commission might also contact the relevant professional associations, and companies active in upstream markets, so as to be able to define, in so far as necessary, separate product and geographic markets, for different levels of production or distribution of the products/services in question. It might also request additional information to the undertakings involved.

34. Where appropriate, the Commission will address written requests for information to the market players mentioned above. These requests will usually include questions relating to the perceptions of companies about reactions to hypothetical price increases and their views of the boundaries of the relevant market. They will also ask for provision of the factual information the Commission deems necessary to reach a conclusion on the extent of the relevant market. The Commission might also discuss with marketing directors or other officers of those companies to gain a better understanding on how negotiations between suppliers and customers take place and better understand issues relating to the definition of the relevant market. Where appropriate, they might also carry out visits or inspections to the premises of the parties, their customers and/or their competitors, in order to better understand how products are manufactured and sold.

35. The type of evidence relevant to reach a conclusion as to the product market can be categorized as follows:

Evidence to define markets—product dimension

36. An analysis of the product characteristics and its intended use allows the Commission, as a first step, to limit the field of investigation of possible substitutes. However, product characteristics and intended use are insufficient to show whether two products are demand substitutes. Functional interchangeability or similarity in characteristics may not, in themselves, provide sufficient criteria, because the responsiveness of customers to relative price changes may be determined by other considerations as well. For example, there may be different competitive constraints in the original equipment market for car components and in spare parts, thereby leading to a separate delineation of two relevant markets. Conversely, differences in product characteristics are not in themselves sufficient to exclude demand substitutability, since this will depend to a large extent on how customers value different characteristics.

37. The type of evidence the Commission considers relevant to assess whether two products are demand substitutes can be categorized as follows:

38. Evidence of substitution in the recent past. In certain cases, it is possible to analyse evidence relating to recent past events or shocks in the market that offer actual examples of substitution between two products. When available, this sort of information will normally be fundamental for market definition. If there have been changes in relative prices in the past (all else being equal), the reactions in terms of quantities demanded will be determinant in establishing substitutability. Launches of new products in the past can also offer useful information, when it is possible to precisely analyse which products have lost sales to the new product.

39. There are a number of quantitative tests that have specifically been designed for the purpose of delineating markets. These tests consist of various econometric and statistical approaches estimates of elasticities and cross-price elasticities[5] for the demand of a product, tests based on similarity of price movements over time, the analysis of causality between price series and similarity of price levels and/or their convergence. The Commission takes into account the available quantitative evidence capable of withstanding rigorous scrutiny for the purposes of establishing patterns of substitution in the past.

40. Views of customers and competitors. The Commission often contacts the main customers and competitors of the companies involved in its enquiries, to gather their views on the boundaries of the product market as well as most of the factual information it requires to reach a conclusion on the scope of the market. Reasoned answers of customers and competitors as to what would happen if relative prices for the candidate products were to increase in the candidate geographic area by a small amount (for instance of 5% to 10%) are taken into account when they are sufficiently backed by factual evidence.

41. Consumer preferences. In the case of consumer goods, it may be difficult for the Commission to gather the direct views of end consumers about substitute products. Marketing studies that companies have commissioned in the past and that are used by companies in their own decision-making as to pricing of their products and/or marketing actions may provide useful information for the Commission's delineation of the relevant market. Consumer surveys on usage patterns and attitudes, data from consumer's purchasing patterns, the views expressed by retailers and more generally, market research studies submitted by the parties and their competitors are taken into account to establish whether an economically significant proportion of consumers consider two products as substitutable, also taking into account the importance of brands for the products in question. The methodology followed in consumer surveys carried out ad hoc by the undertakings involved or their competitors for the purposes of a merger procedure or a procedure pursuant to Regulation No 17 will usually be scrutinized with utmost care. Unlike pre-existing studies, they have not been prepared in the normal course of business for the adoption of business decisions.

42. Barriers and costs associated with switching demand to potential substitutes. There are a number of barriers and costs that might prevent the Commission from considering two prima facie demand substitutes as belonging to one single product market. It is not possible to provide an exhaustive list of all the possible barriers to substitution and of switching costs. These barriers or obstacles might have a wide range of origins, and in its decisions, the Commission has been confronted with regulatory barriers or other forms of State intervention, constraints arising in downstream markets, need to incur specific capital investment or loss in current output in order to switch to alternative inputs, the location of customers, specific investment in production process, learning and human capital investment, retooling costs or other investments, uncertainty about quality and reputation of unknown suppliers, and others.

43. Different categories of customers and price discrimination. The extent of the product market might be narrowed in the presence of distinct groups of customers. A distinct group of customers for the relevant product may constitute a narrower, distinct market when such a group could be subject

[5] Own-price elasticity of demand for product X is a measure of the responsiveness of demand for X to percentage change in its own price. Cross-price elasticity between products X and Y is the responsiveness of demand for product X to percentage change in the price of product Y.

to price discrimination. This will usually be the case when two conditions are met: (a) it is possible to identify clearly which group an individual customer belongs to at the moment of selling the relevant products to him, and (b) trade among customers or arbitrage by third parties should not be feasible.

Evidence for defining markets—geographic dimension

44. The type of evidence the Commission considers relevant to reach a conclusion as to the geographic market can be categorized as follows:

45. Past evidence of diversion of orders to other areas. In certain cases, evidence on changes in prices between different areas and consequent reactions by customers might be available. Generally, the same quantitative tests used for product market definition might as well be used in geographic market definition, bearing in mind that international comparisons of prices might be more complex due to a number of factors such as exchange rate movements, taxation and product differentiation.

46. Basic demand characteristics. The nature of demand for the relevant product may in itself determine the scope of the geographical market. Factors such as national preferences or preferences for national brands, language, culture and life style, and the need for a local presence have a strong potential to limit the geographic scope of competition.

47. Views of customers and competitors. Where appropriate, the Commission will contact the main customers and competitors of the parties in its enquiries, to gather their views on the boundaries of the geographic market as well as most of the factual information it requires to reach a conclusion on the scope of the market when they are sufficiently backed by factual evidence.

48. Current geographic pattern of purchases. An examination of the customers' current geographic pattern of purchases provides useful evidence as to the possible scope of the geographic market. When customers purchase from companies located anywhere in the Community or the EEA on similar terms, or they procure their supplies through effective tendering procedures in which companies from anywhere in the Community or the EEA submit bids, usually the geographic market will be considered to be Community-wide.

49. Trade flows/pattern of shipments. When the number of customers is so large that it is not possible to obtain through them a clear picture of geographic purchasing patterns, information on trade flows might be used alternatively, provided that the trade statistics are available with a sufficient degree of detail for the relevant products. Trade flows, and above all, the rationale behind trade flows provide useful insights and information for the purpose of establishing the scope of the geographic market but are not in themselves conclusive.

50. Barriers and switching costs associated to divert orders to companies located in other areas. The absence of trans-border purchases or trade flows, for instance, does not necessarily mean that the market is at most national in scope. Still, barriers isolating the national market have to identified before it is concluded that the relevant geographic market in such a case is national. Perhaps the clearest obstacle for a customer to divert its orders to other areas is the impact of transport costs and transport restrictions arising from legislation or from the nature of the relevant products. The impact of transport costs will usually limit the scope of the geographic market for bulky, low-value products, bearing in mind that a transport disadvantage might also be compensated by a comparative advantage in other costs (labour costs or raw materials). Access to distribution in a given area, regulatory barriers still existing in certain sectors, quotas and custom tariffs might also constitute barriers isolating a geographic area from the competitive pressure of companies located outside that area. Significant switching costs in procuring supplies from companies located in other countries constitute additional sources of such barriers.

51. On the basis of the evidence gathered, the Commission will then define a geographic market that could range from a local dimension to a global one, and there are examples of both local and global markets in past decisions of the Commission.

52. The paragraphs above describe the different factors which might be relevant to define markets. This does not imply that in each individual case it will be necessary to obtain evidence and assess each of these factors. Often in practice the evidence provided by a subset of these factors will be sufficient to reach a conclusion, as shown in the past decisional practice of the Commission.

IV. CALCULATION OF MARKET SHARE

53. The definition of the relevant market in both its product and geographic dimensions allows the identification the suppliers and the customers/consumers active on that market. On that basis, a total market size and market shares for each supplier can be calculated on the basis of their sales of the relevant products in the relevant area. In practice, the total market size and market shares are often available from market sources, i.e. companies' estimates, studies commissioned from industry consultants and/or trade associations. When this is not the case, or when available estimates are not reliable, the Commission will usually ask each supplier in the relevant market to provide its own sales in order to calculate total market size and market shares.

54. If sales are usually the reference to calculate market shares, there are nevertheless other indications that, depending on the specific products or industry in question, can offer useful information such as, in particular, capacity, the number of players in bidding markets, units of fleet as in aerospace, or the reserves held in the case of sectors such as mining.

55. As a rule of thumb, both volume sales and value sales provide useful information. In cases of differentiated products, sales in value and their associated market share will usually be considered to better reflect the relative position and strength of each supplier.

V. ADDITIONAL CONSIDERATIONS

56. There are certain areas where the application of the principles above has to be undertaken with care. This is the case when considering primary and secondary markets, in particular, when the behaviour of undertakings at a point in time has to be analysed pursuant to Article 86. The method of defining markets in these cases is the same, i.e. assessing the responses of customers based on their purchasing decisions to relative price changes, but taking into account as well, constraints on substitution imposed by conditions in the connected markets. A narrow definition of market for secondary products, for instance, spare parts, may result when compatibility with the primary product is important. Problems of finding compatible secondary products together with the existence of high prices and a long lifetime of the primary products may render relative price increases of secondary products profitable. A different market definition may result if significant substitution between secondary products is possible or if the characteristics of the primary products make quick and direct consumer responses to relative price increases of the secondary products feasible.

57. In certain cases, the existence of chains of substitution might lead to the definition of a relevant market where products or areas at the extreme of the market are not directly substitutable. An example might be provided by the geographic dimension of a product with significant transport costs. In such cases, deliveries from a given plant are limited to a certain area around each plant by the impact of transport costs. In principle, such an area could constitute the relevant geographic market. However, if the distribution of plants is such that there are considerable overlaps between the areas around different plants, it is possible that the pricing of those products will be constrained by a chain substitution effect, and lead to the definition of a broader geographic market. The same reasoning may apply if product B is a demand substitute for products A and C. Even if products A and C are not direct demand substitutes, they might be found to be in the same relevant product market since their respective pricing might be constrained by substitution to B.

58. From a practical perspective, the concept of chains of substitution has to be corroborated by actual evidence, for instance related to price interdependence at the extremes of the chains of substitution, in order to lead to an extension of the relevant market in an individual case. Price levels at the extremes of the chains would have to be of the same magnitude as well.

Council Regulation (EC) No 1/2003 of 16 December 2002 on the implementation of the rules on competition laid down in Articles 81 and 82 of the Treaty*

[OJ 2003 L1/1]

THE COUNCIL OF THE EUROPEAN UNION,

Having regard to the Treaty establishing the European Community, and in particular Article 83 thereof,

Having regard to the proposal from the Commission,[1]

Having regard to the opinion of the European Parliament,[2]

Having regard to the opinion of the European Economic and Social Committee,[3]

Whereas:

(1) In order to establish a system which ensures that competition in the common market is not distorted, Articles 81 and 82 of the Treaty must be applied effectively and uniformly in the Community. Council Regulation No 17 of 6 February 1962, First Regulation implementing Articles 81 and 82[4] of the Treaty,[5] has allowed a Community competition policy to develop that has helped to disseminate a competition culture within the Community. In the light of experience, however, that Regulation should now be replaced by legislation designed to meet the challenges of an integrated market and a future enlargement of the Community.

(2) In particular, there is a need to rethink the arrangements for applying the exception from the prohibition on agreements, which restrict competition, laid down in Article 81(3) of the Treaty. Under Article 83(2)(b) of the Treaty, account must be taken in this regard of the need to ensure effective supervision, on the one hand, and to simplify administration to the greatest possible extent, on the other.

(3) The centralised scheme set up by Regulation No 17 no longer secures a balance between those two objectives. It hampers application of the Community competition rules by the courts and competition authorities of the Member States, and the system of notification it involves prevents the Commission from concentrating its resources on curbing the most serious infringements. It also imposes considerable costs on undertakings.

(4) The present system should therefore be replaced by a directly applicable exception system in which the competition authorities and courts of the Member States have the power to apply not only Article 81(1) and Article 82 of the Treaty, which have direct applicability by virtue of the case-law of the Court of Justice of the European Communities, but also Article 81(3) of the Treaty.

(5) In order to ensure an effective enforcement of the Community competition rules and at the same time the respect of fundamental rights of defence, this Regulation should regulate the burden of proof under Articles 81 and 82 of the Treaty. It should be for the party or the authority alleging an infringement of Article 81(1) and Article 82 of the Treaty to prove the existence thereof to the required legal standard. It should be for the undertaking or association of undertakings invoking the benefit of a defence against a finding of an infringement to demonstrate to the required legal standard

* **Editor's Note:** This Regulation replaced Regulation 17 with effect from 1 May 2004, with the exception of Art 8 which remains in force. As amended by Regulation 411/2004 (OJ 2004 L68/1), Regulation 1419/2006 (OJ 2006 L269/1) and Regulations 169, 246 & 487/2009 (OJ 2009 L61/1, L79/1 & L148/1).

[1] OJ C 365 E, 19.12.2000, p. 284.

[2] OJ C 72 E, 21.3.2002, p. 305.

[3] OJ C 155, 29.5.2001, p. 73.

[4] The title of Regulation No 17 has been adjusted to take account of the renumbering of the Articles of the EC Treaty, in accordance with Article 12 of the Treaty of Amsterdam; the original reference was to Articles 85 and 86 of the Treaty.

[5] OJ 13, 21.2.1962, p. 204/62. Regulation as last amended by Regulation (EC) No 1216/1999 (OJ L 148, 15.6.1999, p. 5).

that the conditions for applying such defence are satisfied. This Regulation affects neither national rules on the standard of proof nor obligations of competition authorities and courts of the Member States to ascertain the relevant facts of a case, provided that such rules and obligations are compatible with general principles of Community law.

(6) In order to ensure that the Community competition rules are applied effectively, the competition authorities of the Member States should be associated more closely with their application. To this end, they should be empowered to apply Community law.

(7) National courts have an essential part to play in applying the Community competition rules. When deciding disputes between private individuals, they protect the subjective rights under Community law, for example, by awarding damages to the victims of infringements. The role of the national courts here complements that of the competition authorities of the Member States. They should therefore be allowed to apply Articles 81 and 82 of the Treaty in full.

(8) In order to ensure the effective enforcement of the Community competition rules and the proper functioning of the cooperation mechanisms contained in this Regulation, it is necessary to oblige the competition authorities and courts of the Member States to also apply Articles 81 and 82 of the Treaty where they apply national competition law to agreements and practices which may affect trade between Member States. In order to create a level playing field for agreements, decisions by associations of undertakings and concerted practices within the internal market, it is also necessary to determine pursuant to Article 83(2)(e) of the Treaty the relationship between national laws and Community competition law. To that effect it is necessary to provide that the application of national competition laws to agreements, decisions or concerted practices within the meaning of Article 81(1) of the Treaty may not lead to the prohibition of such agreements, decisions and concerted practices if they are not also prohibited under Community competition law. The notions of agreements, decisions and concerted practices are autonomous concepts of Community competition law covering the coordination of behaviour of undertakings on the market as interpreted by the Community Courts. Member States should not under this Regulation be precluded from adopting and applying on their territory stricter national competition laws which prohibit or impose sanctions on unilateral conduct engaged in by undertakings. These stricter national laws may include provisions which prohibit or impose sanctions on abusive behaviour toward economically dependent undertakings. Furthermore, this Regulation does not apply to national laws which impose criminal sanctions on natural persons except to the extent that such sanctions are the means whereby competition rules applying to undertakings are enforced.

(9) Articles 81 and 82 of the Treaty have as their objective the protection of competition on the market. This Regulation, which is adopted for the implementation of these Treaty provisions, does not preclude Member States from implementing on their territory national legislation, which protects other legitimate interests provided that such legislation is compatible with general principles and other provisions of Community law. Insofar as such national legislation pursues predominantly an objective different from that of protecting competition on the market, the competition authorities and courts of the Member States may apply such legislation on their territory. Accordingly, Member States may under this Regulation implement on their territory national legislation that prohibits or imposes sanctions on acts of unfair trading practice, be they unilateral or contractual. Such legislation pursues a specific objective, irrespective of the actual or presumed effects of such acts on competition on the market. This is particularly the case of legislation which prohibits undertakings from imposing on their trading partners, obtaining or attempting to obtain from them terms and conditions that are unjustified, disproportionate or without consideration.

(10) Regulations such as 19/65/EEC,[6] (EEC) No 2821/71,[7] (EEC) No 3976/87,[8] (EEC) No 1534/91,[9] or (EEC) No 479/92[10] empower the Commission to apply Article 81(3) of the Treaty by Regulation to certain categories of agreements, decisions by associations of undertakings and concerted practices. In the areas defined by such Regulations, the Commission has adopted and may continue to adopt so called 'block' exemption Regulations by which it declares Article 81(1) of the Treaty inapplicable to categories of agreements, decisions and concerted practices. Where agreements, decisions and concerted practices to which such Regulations apply nonetheless have effects that are incompatible with Article 81(3) of the Treaty, the Commission and the competition authorities of the Member States should have the power to withdraw in a particular case the benefit of the block exemption Regulation.

(11) For it to ensure that the provisions of the Treaty are applied, the Commission should be able to address decisions to undertakings or associations of undertakings for the purpose of bringing to an end infringements of Articles 81 and 82 of the Treaty. Provided there is a legitimate interest in doing so, the Commission should also be able to adopt decisions which find that an infringement has been committed in the past even if it does not impose a fine. This Regulation should also make explicit provision for the Commission's power to adopt decisions ordering interim measures, which has been acknowledged by the Court of Justice.

(12) This Regulation should make explicit provision for the Commission's power to impose any remedy, whether behavioural or structural, which is necessary to bring the infringement effectively to an end, having regard to the principle of proportionality. Structural remedies should only be imposed either where there is no equally effective behavioural remedy or where any equally effective behavioural remedy would be more burdensome for the undertaking concerned than the structural remedy. Changes to the structure of an undertaking as it existed before the infringement was committed would only be proportionate where there is a substantial risk of a lasting or repeated infringement that derives from the very structure of the undertaking.

(13) Where, in the course of proceedings which might lead to an agreement or practice being prohibited, undertakings offer the Commission commitments such as to meet its concerns, the Commission should be able to adopt decisions which make those commitments binding on the undertakings concerned. Commitment decisions should find that there are no longer grounds for action by the Commission without concluding whether or not there has been or still is an infringement. Commitment decisions are without prejudice to the powers of competition authorities and courts of

[6] Council Regulation No 19/65/EEC of 2 March 1965 on the application of Article 81(3) (the titles of the Regulations have been adjusted to take account of the renumbering of the Articles of the EC Treaty, in accordance with Article 12 of the Treaty of Amsterdam; the original reference was to Article 85(3) of the Treaty) of the Treaty to certain categories of agreements and concerted practices (OJ 36, 6.3.1965, p. 533). Regulation as last amended by Regulation (EC) No 1215/1999 (OJ L 148, 15.6.1999, p. 1).

[7] Council Regulation (EEC) No 2821/71 of 20 December 1971 on the application of Article 81(3) (the titles of the Regulations have been adjusted to take account of the renumbering of the Articles of the EC Treaty, in accordance with Article 12 of the Treaty of Amsterdam; the original reference was to Article 85(3) of the Treaty) of the Treaty to categories of agreements, decisions and concerted practices (OJ L 285, 29.12.1971, p. 46). Regulation as last amended by the Act of Accession of 1994.

[8] Council Regulation (EEC) No 3976/87 of 14 December 1987 on the application of Article 81(3) (the titles of the Regulations have been adjusted to take account of the renumbering of the Articles of the EC Treaty, in accordance with Article 12 of the Treaty of Amsterdam; the original reference was to Article 85(3) of the Treaty) of the Treaty to certain categories of agreements and concerted practices in the air transport sector (OJ L 374, 31.12.1987, p. 9). Regulation as last amended by the Act of Accession of 1994.

[9] Council Regulation (EEC) No 1534/91 of 31 May 1991 on the application of Article 81(3) (the titles of the Regulations have been adjusted to take account of the renumbering of the Articles of the EC Treaty, in accordance with Article 12 of the Treaty of Amsterdam; the original reference was to Article 85(3) of the Treaty) of the Treaty to certain categories of agreements, decisions and concerted practices in the insurance sector (OJ L 143, 7.6.1991, p. 1).

[10] Council Regulation (EEC) No 479/92 of 25 February 1992 on the application of Article 81(3) (the titles of the Regulations have been adjusted to take account of the renumbering of the Articles of the EC Treaty, in accordance with Article 12 of the Treaty of Amsterdam; the original reference was to Article 85(3) of the Treaty) of the Treaty to certain categories of agreements, decisions and concerted practices between liner shipping companies (Consortia) (OJ L 55, 29.2.1992, p. 3). Regulation amended by the Act of Accession of 1994.

the Member States to make such a finding and decide upon the case. Commitment decisions are not appropriate in cases where the Commission intends to impose a fine.

(14) In exceptional cases where the public interest of the Community so requires, it may also be expedient for the Commission to adopt a decision of a declaratory nature finding that the prohibition in Article 81 or Article 82 of the Treaty does not apply, with a view to clarifying the law and ensuring its consistent application throughout the Community, in particular with regard to new types of agreements or practices that have not been settled in the existing case-law and administrative practice.

(15) The Commission and the competition authorities of the Member States should form together a network of public authorities applying the Community competition rules in close cooperation. For that purpose it is necessary to set up arrangements for information and consultation. Further modalities for the cooperation within the network will be laid down and revised by the Commission, in close cooperation with the Member States.

(16) Notwithstanding any national provision to the contrary, the exchange of information and the use of such information in evidence should be allowed between the members of the network even where the information is confidential. This information may be used for the application of Articles 81 and 82 of the Treaty as well as for the parallel application of national competition law, provided that the latter application relates to the same case and does not lead to a different outcome. When the information exchanged is used by the receiving authority to impose sanctions on undertakings, there should be no other limit to the use of the information than the obligation to use it for the purpose for which it was collected given the fact that the sanctions imposed on undertakings are of the same type in all systems. The rights of defence enjoyed by undertakings in the various systems can be considered as sufficiently equivalent. However, as regards natural persons, they may be subject to substantially different types of sanctions across the various systems. Where that is the case, it is necessary to ensure that information can only be used if it has been collected in a way which respects the same level of protection of the rights of defence of natural persons as provided for under the national rules of the receiving authority.

(17) If the competition rules are to be applied consistently and, at the same time, the network is to be managed in the best possible way, it is essential to retain the rule that the competition authorities of the Member States are automatically relieved of their competence if the Commission initiates its own proceedings. Where a competition authority of a Member State is already acting on a case and the Commission intends to initiate proceedings, it should endeavour to do so as soon as possible. Before initiating proceedings, the Commission should consult the national authority concerned.

(18) To ensure that cases are dealt with by the most appropriate authorities within the network, a general provision should be laid down allowing a competition authority to suspend or close a case on the ground that another authority is dealing with it or has already dealt with it, the objective being that each case should be handled by a single authority. This provision should not prevent the Commission from rejecting a complaint for lack of Community interest, as the case-law of the Court of Justice has acknowledged it may do, even if no other competition authority has indicated its intention of dealing with the case.

(19) The Advisory Committee on Restrictive Practices and Dominant Positions set up by Regulation No 17 has functioned in a very satisfactory manner. It will fit well into the new system of decentralised application. It is necessary, therefore, to build upon the rules laid down by Regulation No 17, while improving the effectiveness of the organisational arrangements. To this end, it would be expedient to allow opinions to be delivered by written procedure. The Advisory Committee should also be able to act as a forum for discussing cases that are being handled by the competition authorities of the Member States, so as to help safeguard the consistent application of the Community competition rules.

(20) The Advisory Committee should be composed of representatives of the competition authorities of the Member States. For meetings in which general issues are being discussed, Member States should be able to appoint an additional representative. This is without prejudice to members of the Committee being assisted by other experts from the Member States.

(21) Consistency in the application of the competition rules also requires that arrangements be established for cooperation between the courts of the Member States and the Commission. This is relevant for all courts of the Member States that apply Articles 81 and 82 of the Treaty, whether applying these rules in lawsuits between private parties, acting as public enforcers or as review courts. In particular, national courts should be able to ask the Commission for information or for its opinion on points concerning the application of Community competition law. The Commission and the competition authorities of the Member States should also be able to submit written or oral observations to courts called upon to apply Article 81 or Article 82 of the Treaty. These observations should be submitted within the framework of national procedural rules and practices including those safeguarding the rights of the parties. Steps should therefore be taken to ensure that the Commission and the competition authorities of the Member States are kept sufficiently well informed of proceedings before national courts.

(22) In order to ensure compliance with the principles of legal certainty and the uniform application of the Community competition rules in a system of parallel powers, conflicting decisions must be avoided. It is therefore necessary to clarify, in accordance with the case-law of the Court of Justice, the effects of Commission decisions and proceedings on courts and competition authorities of the Member States. Commitment decisions adopted by the Commission do not affect the power of the courts and the competition authorities of the Member States to apply Articles 81 and 82 of the Treaty.

(23) The Commission should be empowered throughout the Community to require such information to be supplied as is necessary to detect any agreement, decision or concerted practice prohibited by Article 81 of the Treaty or any abuse of a dominant position prohibited by Article 82 of the Treaty. When complying with a decision of the Commission, undertakings cannot be forced to admit that they have committed an infringement, but they are in any event obliged to answer factual questions and to provide documents, even if this information may be used to establish against them or against another undertaking the existence of an infringement.

(24) The Commission should also be empowered to undertake such inspections as are necessary to detect any agreement, decision or concerted practice prohibited by Article 81 of the Treaty or any abuse of a dominant position prohibited by Article 82 of the Treaty. The competition authorities of the Member States should cooperate actively in the exercise of these powers.

(25) The detection of infringements of the competition rules is growing ever more difficult, and, in order to protect competition effectively, the Commission's powers of investigation need to be supplemented. The Commission should in particular be empowered to interview any persons who may be in possession of useful information and to record the statements made. In the course of an inspection, officials authorised by the Commission should be empowered to affix seals for the period of time necessary for the inspection. Seals should normally not be affixed for more than 72 hours. Officials authorised by the Commission should also be empowered to ask for any information relevant to the subject matter and purpose of the inspection.

(26) Experience has shown that there are cases where business records are kept in the homes of directors or other people working for an undertaking. In order to safeguard the effectiveness of inspections, therefore, officials and other persons authorised by the Commission should be empowered to enter any premises where business records may be kept, including private homes. However, the exercise of this latter power should be subject to the authorisation of the judicial authority.

(27) Without prejudice to the case-law of the Court of Justice, it is useful to set out the scope of the control that the national judicial authority may carry out when it authorises, as foreseen by national law including as a precautionary measure, assistance from law enforcement authorities in order to overcome possible opposition on the part of the undertaking or the execution of the decision to carry out inspections in non-business premises. It results from the case-law that the national judicial authority may in particular ask the Commission for further information which it needs to carry out its control and in the absence of which it could refuse the authorisation. The case-law also confirms the competence of the national courts to control the application of national rules governing the implementation of coercive measures.

(28) In order to help the competition authorities of the Member States to apply Articles 81 and 82 of the Treaty effectively, it is expedient to enable them to assist one another by carrying out inspections and other fact-finding measures.

(29) Compliance with Articles 81 and 82 of the Treaty and the fulfilment of the obligations imposed on undertakings and associations of undertakings under this Regulation should be enforceable by means of fines and periodic penalty payments. To that end, appropriate levels of fine should also be laid down for infringements of the procedural rules.

(30) In order to ensure effective recovery of fines imposed on associations of undertakings for infringements that they have committed, it is necessary to lay down the conditions on which the Commission may require payment of the fine from the members of the association where the association is not solvent. In doing so, the Commission should have regard to the relative size of the undertakings belonging to the association and in particular to the situation of small and medium sized enterprises. Payment of the fine by one or several members of an association is without prejudice to rules of national law that provide for recovery of the amount paid from other members of the association.

(31) The rules on periods of limitation for the imposition of fines and periodic penalty payments were laid down in Council Regulation (EEC) No 2988/74,[11] which also concerns penalties in the field of transport. In a system of parallel powers, the acts, which may interrupt a limitation period, should include procedural steps taken independently by the competition authority of a Member State. To clarify the legal framework, Regulation (EEC) No 2988/74 should therefore be amended to prevent it applying to matters covered by this Regulation, and this Regulation should include provisions on periods of limitation.

(32) The undertakings concerned should be accorded the right to be heard by the Commission, third parties whose interests may be affected by a decision should be given the opportunity of submitting their observations beforehand, and the decisions taken should be widely publicised. While ensuring the rights of defence of the undertakings concerned, in particular, the right of access to the file, it is essential that business secrets be protected. The confidentiality of information exchanged in the network should likewise be safeguarded.

(33) Since all decisions taken by the Commission under this Regulation are subject to review by the Court of Justice in accordance with the Treaty, the Court of Justice should, in accordance with Article 229 thereof be given unlimited jurisdiction in respect of decisions by which the Commission imposes fines or periodic penalty payments.

(34) The principles laid down in Articles 81 and 82 of the Treaty, as they have been applied by Regulation No 17, have given a central role to the Community bodies. This central role should be retained, whilst associating the Member States more closely with the application of the Community competition rules. In accordance with the principles of subsidiarity and proportionality as set out in Article 5 of the Treaty, this Regulation does not go beyond what is necessary in order to achieve its objective, which is to allow the Community competition rules to be applied effectively.

(35) In order to attain a proper enforcement of Community competition law, Member States should designate and empower authorities to apply Articles 81 and 82 of the Treaty as public enforcers. They should be able to designate administrative as well as judicial authorities to carry out the various functions conferred upon competition authorities in this Regulation. This Regulation recognises the wide variation which exists in the public enforcement systems of Member States. The effects of Article 11(6) of this Regulation should apply to all competition authorities. As an exception to this general rule, where a prosecuting authority brings a case before a separate judicial authority, Article 11(6) should apply to the prosecuting authority subject to the conditions in Article 35(4) of this Regulation. Where these conditions are not fulfilled, the general rule should apply. In any case, Article 11(6) should not apply to courts insofar as they are acting as review courts.

(36) As the case-law has made it clear that the competition rules apply to transport, that sector should be made subject to the procedural provisions of this Regulation. Council Regulation No 141 of 26 November 1962 exempting transport from the application of Regulation No 17[12] should therefore

[11] Council Regulation (EEC) No 2988/74 of 26 November 1974 concerning limitation periods in proceedings and the enforcement of sanctions under the rules of the European Economic Community relating to transport and competition (OJ L 319, 29.11.1974, p. 1).

[12] OJ 124, 28.11.1962, p. 2751/62; Regulation as last amended by Regulation No 1002/67/EEC (OJ 306, 16.12.1967, p. 1).

be repealed and Regulations (EEC) No 1017/68,[13] (EEC) No 4056/86[14] and (EEC) No 3975/87[15] should be amended in order to delete the specific procedural provisions they contain.

(37) This Regulation respects the fundamental rights and observes the principles recognised in particular by the Charter of Fundamental Rights of the European Union. Accordingly, this Regulation should be interpreted and applied with respect to those rights and principles.

(38) Legal certainty for undertakings operating under the Community competition rules contributes to the promotion of innovation and investment. Where cases give rise to genuine uncertainty because they present novel or unresolved questions for the application of these rules, individual undertakings may wish to seek informal guidance from the Commission. This Regulation is without prejudice to the ability of the Commission to issue such informal guidance,

HAS ADOPTED THIS REGULATION:

Chapter I Principles

Article 1 Application of Articles 81 and 82 of the Treaty

1. Agreements, decisions and concerted practices caught by Article 81(1) of the Treaty which do not satisfy the conditions of Article 81(3) of the Treaty shall be prohibited, no prior decision to that effect being required.

2. Agreements, decisions and concerted practices caught by Article 81(1) of the Treaty which satisfy the conditions of Article 81(3) of the Treaty shall not be prohibited, no prior decision to that effect being required.

3. The abuse of a dominant position referred to in Article 82 of the Treaty shall be prohibited, no prior decision to that effect being required.

Article 2 Burden of proof

In any national or Community proceedings for the application of Articles 81 and 82 of the Treaty, the burden of proving an infringement of Article 81(1) or of Article 82 of the Treaty shall rest on the party or the authority alleging the infringement. The undertaking or association of undertakings claiming the benefit of Article 81(3) of the Treaty shall bear the burden of proving that the conditions of that paragraph are fulfilled.

Article 3 Relationship between Articles 81 and 82 of the Treaty and national competition laws

1. Where the competition authorities of the Member States or national courts apply national competition law to agreements, decisions by associations of undertakings or concerted practices within the meaning of Article 81(1) of the Treaty which may affect trade between Member States within the meaning of that provision, they shall also apply Article 81 of the Treaty to such agreements, decisions or concerted practices. Where the competition authorities of the Member States or national courts apply national competition law to any abuse prohibited by Article 82 of the Treaty, they shall also apply Article 82 of the Treaty.

2. The application of national competition law may not lead to the prohibition of agreements, decisions by associations of undertakings or concerted practices which may affect trade between Member States but which do not restrict competition within the meaning of Article 81(1) of the Treaty, or which fulfil the conditions of Article 81(3) of the Treaty or which are covered by a Regulation for the application of Article 81(3) of the Treaty. Member States shall not under this Regulation be precluded from adopting and applying on their territory stricter national laws which prohibit or sanction unilateral conduct engaged in by undertakings.

[13] Council Regulation (EEC) No 1017/68 of 19 July 1968 applying rules of competition to transport by rail, road and inland waterway (OJ L 175, 23.7.1968, p. 1). Regulation as last amended by the Act of Accession of 1994.

[14] Council Regulation (EEC) No 4056/86 of 22 December 1986 laying down detailed rules for the application of Articles 81 and 82 (the title of the Regulation has been adjusted to take account of the renumbering of the Articles of the EC Treaty, in accordance with Article 12 of the Treaty of Amsterdam; the original reference was to Articles 85 and 86 of the Treaty) of the Treaty to maritime transport (OJ L 378, 31.12.1986, p. 4). Regulation as last amended by the Act of Accession of 1994.

[15] Council Regulation (EEC) No 3975/87 of 14 December 1987 laying down the procedure for the application of the rules on competition to undertakings in the air transport sector (OJ L 374, 31.12.1987, p. 1). Regulation as last amended by Regulation (EEC) No 2410/92 (OJ L 240, 24.8.1992, p. 18).

3. Without prejudice to general principles and other provisions of Community law, paragraphs 1 and 2 do not apply when the competition authorities and the courts of the Member States apply national merger control laws nor do they preclude the application of provisions of national law that predominantly pursue an objective different from that pursued by Articles 81 and 82 of the Treaty.

Chapter II Powers

Article 4 Powers of the Commission

For the purpose of applying Articles 81 and 82 of the Treaty, the Commission shall have the powers provided for by this Regulation.

Article 5 Powers of the competition authorities of the Member States

The competition authorities of the Member States shall have the power to apply Articles 81 and 82 of the Treaty in individual cases. For this purpose, acting on their own initiative or on a complaint, they may take the following decisions:

- requiring that an infringement be brought to an end,
- ordering interim measures,
- accepting commitments,
- imposing fines, periodic penalty payments or any other penalty provided for in their national law.

Where on the basis of the information in their possession the conditions for prohibition are not met they may likewise decide that there are no grounds for action on their part.

Article 6 Powers of the national courts

National courts shall have the power to apply Articles 81 and 82 of the Treaty.

Chapter III Commission decisions

Article 7 Finding and termination of infringement

1. Where the Commission, acting on a complaint or on its own initiative, finds that there is an infringement of Article 81 or of Article 82 of the Treaty, it may by decision require the undertakings and associations of undertakings concerned to bring such infringement to an end. For this purpose, it may impose on them any behavioural or structural remedies which are proportionate to the infringement committed and necessary to bring the infringement effectively to an end. Structural remedies can only be imposed either where there is no equally effective behavioural remedy or where any equally effective behavioural remedy would be more burdensome for the undertaking concerned than the structural remedy. If the Commission has a legitimate interest in doing so, it may also find that an infringement has been committed in the past.

2. Those entitled to lodge a complaint for the purposes of paragraph 1 are natural or legal persons who can show a legitimate interest and Member States.

Article 8 Interim measures

1. In cases of urgency due to the risk of serious and irreparable damage to competition, the Commission, acting on its own initiative may by decision, on the basis of a prima facie finding of infringement, order interim measures.

2. A decision under paragraph 1 shall apply for a specified period of time and may be renewed in so far this is necessary and appropriate.

Article 9 Commitments

1. Where the Commission intends to adopt a decision requiring that an infringement be brought to an end and the undertakings concerned offer commitments to meet the concerns expressed to them by the Commission in its preliminary assessment, the Commission may by decision make those commitments binding on the undertakings. Such a decision may be adopted for a specified period and shall conclude that there are no longer grounds for action by the Commission.

2. The Commission may, upon request or on its own initiative, reopen the proceedings:
   (a) where there has been a material change in any of the facts on which the decision was based;
   (b) where the undertakings concerned act contrary to their commitments; or
   (c) where the decision was based on incomplete, incorrect or misleading information provided by the parties.

Article 10 Finding of inapplicability

Where the Community public interest relating to the application of Articles 81 and 82 of the Treaty so requires, the Commission, acting on its own initiative, may by decision find that Article 81 of the Treaty is not applicable to an agreement, a decision by an association of undertakings or a concerted practice, either because the conditions of Article 81(1) of the Treaty are not fulfilled, or because the conditions of Article 81(3) of the Treaty are satisfied.

The Commission may likewise make such a finding with reference to Article 82 of the Treaty.

Chapter IV Cooperation

Article 11

Cooperation between the Commission and the competition authorities of the Member States

1. The Commission and the competition authorities of the Member States shall apply the Community competition rules in close cooperation.

2. The Commission shall transmit to the competition authorities of the Member States copies of the most important documents it has collected with a view to applying Articles 7, 8, 9, 10 and Article 29(1). At the request of the competition authority of a Member State, the Commission shall provide it with a copy of other existing documents necessary for the assessment of the case.

3. The competition authorities of the Member States shall, when acting under Article 81 or Article 82 of the Treaty, inform the Commission in writing before or without delay after commencing the first formal investigative measure. This information may also be made available to the competition authorities of the other Member States.

4. No later than 30 days before the adoption of a decision requiring that an infringement be brought to an end, accepting commitments or withdrawing the benefit of a block exemption Regulation, the competition authorities of the Member States shall inform the Commission. To that effect, they shall provide the Commission with a summary of the case, the envisaged decision or, in the absence thereof, any other document indicating the proposed course of action. This information may also be made available to the competition authorities of the other Member States. At the request of the Commission, the acting competition authority shall make available to the Commission other documents it holds which are necessary for the assessment of the case. The information supplied to the Commission may be made available to the competition authorities of the other Member States. National competition authorities may also exchange between themselves information necessary for the assessment of a case that they are dealing with under Article 81 or Article 82 of the Treaty.

5. The competition authorities of the Member States may consult the Commission on any case involving the application of Community law.

6. The initiation by the Commission of proceedings for the adoption of a decision under Chapter III shall relieve the competition authorities of the Member States of their competence to apply Articles 81 and 82 of the Treaty. If a competition authority of a Member State is already acting on a case, the Commission shall only initiate proceedings after consulting with that national competition authority.

Article 12 Exchange of information

1. For the purpose of applying Articles 81 and 82 of the Treaty the Commission and the competition authorities of the Member States shall have the power to provide one another with and use in evidence any matter of fact or of law, including confidential information.

2. Information exchanged shall only be used in evidence for the purpose of applying Article 81 or Article 82 of the Treaty and in respect of the subject-matter for which it was collected by the transmitting authority. However, where national competition law is applied in the same case and in parallel to Community competition law and does not lead to a different outcome, information exchanged under this Article may also be used for the application of national competition law.

3. Information exchanged pursuant to paragraph 1 can only be used in evidence to impose sanctions on natural persons where:

- the law of the transmitting authority foresees sanctions of a similar kind in relation to an infringement of Article 81 or Article 82 of the Treaty or, in the absence thereof,
- the information has been collected in a way which respects the same level of protection of the rights of defence of natural persons as provided for under the national rules of the receiving authority. However, in this case, the information exchanged cannot be used by the receiving authority to impose custodial sanctions.

Article 13 Suspension or termination of proceedings

1. Where competition authorities of two or more Member States have received a complaint or are acting on their own initiative under Article 81 or Article 82 of the Treaty against the same agreement, decision of an association or practice, the fact that one authority is dealing with the case shall be sufficient grounds for the others to suspend the proceedings before them or to reject the complaint. The Commission may likewise reject a complaint on the ground that a competition authority of a Member State is dealing with the case.

2. Where a competition authority of a Member State or the Commission has received a complaint against an agreement, decision of an association or practice which has already been dealt with by another competition authority, it may reject it.

Article 14 Advisory Committee

1. The Commission shall consult an Advisory Committee on Restrictive Practices and Dominant Positions prior to the taking of any decision under Articles 7, 8, 9, 10, 23, Article 24(2) and Article 29(1).

2. For the discussion of individual cases, the Advisory Committee shall be composed of representatives of the competition authorities of the Member States. For meetings in which issues other than individual cases are being discussed, an additional Member State representative competent in competition matters may be appointed. Representatives may, if unable to attend, be replaced by other representatives.

3. The consultation may take place at a meeting convened and chaired by the Commission, held not earlier than 14 days after dispatch of the notice convening it, together with a summary of the case, an indication of the most important documents and a preliminary draft decision. In respect of decisions pursuant to Article 8, the meeting may be held seven days after the dispatch of the operative part of a draft decision. Where the Commission dispatches a notice convening the meeting which gives a shorter period of notice than those specified above, the meeting may take place on the proposed date in the absence of an objection by any Member State. The Advisory Committee shall deliver a written opinion on the Commission's preliminary draft decision. It may deliver an opinion even if some members are absent and are not represented. At the request of one or several members, the positions stated in the opinion shall be reasoned.

4. Consultation may also take place by written procedure. However, if any Member State so requests, the Commission shall convene a meeting. In case of written procedure, the Commission shall determine a time-limit of not less than 14 days within which the Member States are to put forward their observations for circulation to all other Member States. In case of decisions to be taken pursuant to Article 8, the time-limit of 14 days is replaced by seven days. Where the Commission determines a time-limit for the written procedure which is shorter than those specified above, the proposed time-limit shall be applicable in the absence of an objection by any Member State.

5. The Commission shall take the utmost account of the opinion delivered by the Advisory Committee. It shall inform the Committee of the manner in which its opinion has been taken into account.

6. Where the Advisory Committee delivers a written opinion, this opinion shall be appended to the draft decision. If the Advisory Committee recommends publication of the opinion, the Commission shall carry out such publication taking into account the legitimate interest of undertakings in the protection of their business secrets.

7. At the request of a competition authority of a Member State, the Commission shall include on the agenda of the Advisory Committee cases that are being dealt with by a competition authority of a Member State under Article 81 or Article 82 of the Treaty. The Commission may also do so on its own initiative. In either case, the Commission shall inform the competition authority concerned.

A request may in particular be made by a competition authority of a Member State in respect of a case where the Commission intends to initiate proceedings with the effect of Article 11(6).

The Advisory Committee shall not issue opinions on cases dealt with by competition authorities of the Member States. The Advisory Committee may also discuss general issues of Community competition law.

Article 15 Cooperation with national courts

1. In proceedings for the application of Article 81 or Article 82 of the Treaty, courts of the Member States may ask the Commission to transmit to them information in its possession or its opinion on questions concerning the application of the Community competition rules.

2. Member States shall forward to the Commission a copy of any written judgment of national courts deciding on the application of Article 81 or Article 82 of the Treaty. Such copy shall be forwarded without delay after the full written judgment is notified to the parties.

3. Competition authorities of the Member States, acting on their own initiative, may submit written observations to the national courts of their Member State on issues relating to the application of Article 81 or Article 82 of the Treaty. With the permission of the court in question, they may also submit oral observations to the national courts of their Member State. Where the coherent application of Article 81 or Article 82 of the Treaty so requires, the Commission, acting on its own initiative, may submit written observations to courts of the Member States. With the permission of the court in question, it may also make oral observations.

For the purpose of the preparation of their observations only, the competition authorities of the Member States and the Commission may request the relevant court of the Member State to transmit or ensure the transmission to them of any documents necessary for the assessment of the case.

4. This Article is without prejudice to wider powers to make observations before courts conferred on competition authorities of the Member States under the law of their Member State.

Article 16 Uniform application of Community competition law

1. When national courts rule on agreements, decisions or practices under Article 81 or Article 82 of the Treaty which are already the subject of a Commission decision, they cannot take decisions running counter to the decision adopted by the Commission. They must also avoid giving decisions which would conflict with a decision contemplated by the Commission in proceedings it has initiated. To that effect, the national court may assess whether it is necessary to stay its proceedings. This obligation is without prejudice to the rights and obligations under Article 234 of the Treaty.

2. When competition authorities of the Member States rule on agreements, decisions or practices under Article 81 or Article 82 of the Treaty which are already the subject of a Commission decision, they cannot take decisions which would run counter to the decision adopted by the Commission.

Chapter V Powers of investigation

Article 17 Investigations into sectors of the economy and into types of agreements

1. Where the trend of trade between Member States, the rigidity of prices or other circumstances suggest that competition may be restricted or distorted within the common market, the Commission may conduct its inquiry into a particular sector of the economy or into a particular type of agreements across various sectors. In the course of that inquiry, the Commission may request the undertakings

or associations of undertakings concerned to supply the information necessary for giving effect to Articles 81 and 82 of the Treaty and may carry out any inspections necessary for that purpose.

The Commission may in particular request the undertakings or associations of undertakings concerned to communicate to it all agreements, decisions and concerted practices.

The Commission may publish a report on the results of its inquiry into particular sectors of the economy or particular types of agreements across various sectors and invite comments from interested parties.

2. Articles 14, 18, 19, 20, 22, 23 and 24 shall apply *mutatis mutandis*.

Article 18 Requests for information

1. In order to carry out the duties assigned to it by this Regulation, the Commission may, by simple request or by decision, require undertakings and associations of undertakings to provide all necessary information.

2. When sending a simple request for information to an undertaking or association of undertakings, the Commission shall state the legal basis and the purpose of the request, specify what information is required and fix the time-limit within which the information is to be provided, and the penalties provided for in Article 23 for supplying incorrect or misleading information.

3. Where the Commission requires undertakings and associations of undertakings to supply information by decision, it shall state the legal basis and the purpose of the request, specify what information is required and fix the time-limit within which it is to be provided. It shall also indicate the penalties provided for in Article 23 and indicate or impose the penalties provided for in Article 24. It shall further indicate the right to have the decision reviewed by the Court of Justice.

4. The owners of the undertakings or their representatives and, in the case of legal persons, companies or firms, or associations having no legal personality, the persons authorised to represent them by law or by their constitution shall supply the information requested on behalf of the undertaking or the association of undertakings concerned. Lawyers duly authorised to act may supply the information on behalf of their clients. The latter shall remain fully responsible if the information supplied is incomplete, incorrect or misleading.

5. The Commission shall without delay forward a copy of the simple request or of the decision to the competition authority of the Member State in whose territory the seat of the undertaking or association of undertakings is situated and the competition authority of the Member State whose territory is affected.

6. At the request of the Commission the governments and competition authorities of the Member States shall provide the Commission with all necessary information to carry out the duties assigned to it by this Regulation.

Article 19 Power to take statements

1. In order to carry out the duties assigned to it by this Regulation, the Commission may interview any natural or legal person who consents to be interviewed for the purpose of collecting information relating to the subject-matter of an investigation.

2. Where an interview pursuant to paragraph 1 is conducted in the premises of an undertaking, the Commission shall inform the competition authority of the Member State in whose territory the interview takes place. If so requested by the competition authority of that Member State, its officials may assist the officials and other accompanying persons authorised by the Commission to conduct the interview.

Article 20 The Commission's powers of inspection

1. In order to carry out the duties assigned to it by this Regulation, the Commission may conduct all necessary inspections of undertakings and associations of undertakings.

2. The officials and other accompanying persons authorised by the Commission to conduct an inspection are empowered:

(a) to enter any premises, land and means of transport of undertakings and associations of undertakings;

(b) to examine the books and other records related to the business, irrespective of the medium on which they are stored;

(c) to take or obtain in any form copies of or extracts from such books or records;

(d) to seal any business premises and books or records for the period and to the extent necessary for the inspection;

(e) to ask any representative or member of staff of the undertaking or association of undertakings for explanations on facts or documents relating to the subject-matter and purpose of the inspection and to record the answers.

3. The officials and other accompanying persons authorised by the Commission to conduct an inspection shall exercise their powers upon production of a written authorisation specifying the subject matter and purpose of the inspection and the penalties provided for in Article 23 in case the production of the required books or other records related to the business is incomplete or where the answers to questions asked under paragraph 2 of the present Article are incorrect or misleading. In good time before the inspection, the Commission shall give notice of the inspection to the competition authority of the Member State in whose territory it is to be conducted.

4. Undertakings and associations of undertakings are required to submit to inspections ordered by decision of the Commission. The decision shall specify the subject matter and purpose of the inspection, appoint the date on which it is to begin and indicate the penalties provided for in Articles 23 and 24 and the right to have the decision reviewed by the Court of Justice. The Commission shall take such decisions after consulting the competition authority of the Member State in whose territory the inspection is to be conducted.

5. Officials of as well as those authorised or appointed by the competition authority of the Member State in whose territory the inspection is to be conducted shall, at the request of that authority or of the Commission, actively assist the officials and other accompanying persons authorised by the Commission. To this end, they shall enjoy the powers specified in paragraph 2.

6. Where the officials and other accompanying persons authorised by the Commission find that an undertaking opposes an inspection ordered pursuant to this Article, the Member State concerned shall afford them the necessary assistance, requesting where appropriate the assistance of the police or of an equivalent enforcement authority, so as to enable them to conduct their inspection.

7. If the assistance provided for in paragraph 6 requires authorisation from a judicial authority according to national rules, such authorisation shall be applied for. Such authorisation may also be applied for as a precautionary measure.

8. Where authorisation as referred to in paragraph 7 is applied for, the national judicial authority shall control that the Commission decision is authentic and that the coercive measures envisaged are neither arbitrary nor excessive having regard to the subject matter of the inspection. In its control of the proportionality of the coercive measures, the national judicial authority may ask the Commission, directly or through the Member State competition authority, for detailed explanations in particular on the grounds the Commission has for suspecting infringement of Articles 81 and 82 of the Treaty, as well as on the seriousness of the suspected infringement and on the nature of the involvement of the undertaking concerned. However, the national judicial authority may not call into question the necessity for the inspection nor demand that it be provided with the information in the Commission's file. The lawfulness of the Commission decision shall be subject to review only by the Court of Justice.

Article 21 Inspection of other premises

1. If a reasonable suspicion exists that books or other records related to the business and to the subject-matter of the inspection, which may be relevant to prove a serious violation of Article 81 or Article 82 of the Treaty, are being kept in any other premises, land and means of transport, including the homes of directors, managers and other members of staff of the undertakings and associations of undertakings concerned, the Commission can by decision order an inspection to be conducted in such other premises, land and means of transport.

2. The decision shall specify the subject matter and purpose of the inspection, appoint the date on which it is to begin and indicate the right to have the decision reviewed by the Court of Justice. It shall in particular state the reasons that have led the Commission to conclude that a suspicion in the sense of paragraph 1 exists. The Commission shall take such decisions after

consulting the competition authority of the Member State in whose territory the inspection is to be conducted.

3. A decision adopted pursuant to paragraph 1 cannot be executed without prior authorisation from the national judicial authority of the Member State concerned. The national judicial authority shall control that the Commission decision is authentic and that the coercive measures envisaged are neither arbitrary nor excessive having regard in particular to the seriousness of the suspected infringement, to the importance of the evidence sought, to the involvement of the undertaking concerned and to the reasonable likelihood that business books and records relating to the subject matter of the inspection are kept in the premises for which the authorisation is requested. The national judicial authority may ask the Commission, directly or through the Member State competition authority, for detailed explanations on those elements which are necessary to allow its control of the proportionality of the coercive measures envisaged.

However, the national judicial authority may not call into question the necessity for the inspection nor demand that it be provided with information in the Commission's file. The lawfulness of the Commission decision shall be subject to review only by the Court of Justice.

4. The officials and other accompanying persons authorised by the Commission to conduct an inspection ordered in accordance with paragraph 1 of this Article shall have the powers set out in Article 20(2)(a), (b) and (c). Article 20(5) and (6) shall apply mutatis mutandis.

Article 22 Investigations by competition authorities of Member States

1. The competition authority of a Member State may in its own territory carry out any inspection or other fact-finding measure under its national law on behalf and for the account of the competition authority of another Member State in order to establish whether there has been an infringement of Article 81 or Article 82 of the Treaty. Any exchange and use of the information collected shall be carried out in accordance with Article 12.

2. At the request of the Commission, the competition authorities of the Member States shall undertake the inspections which the Commission considers to be necessary under Article 20(1) or which it has ordered by decision pursuant to Article 20(4). The officials of the competition authorities of the Member States who are responsible for conducting these inspections as well as those authorised or appointed by them shall exercise their powers in accordance with their national law.

If so requested by the Commission or by the competition authority of the Member State in whose territory the inspection is to be conducted, officials and other accompanying persons authorised by the Commission may assist the officials of the authority concerned.

Chapter VI Penalties

Article 23 Fines

1. The Commission may by decision impose on undertakings and associations of undertakings fines not exceeding 1% of the total turnover in the preceding business year where, intentionally or negligently:

(a) they supply incorrect or misleading information in response to a request made pursuant to Article 17 or Article 18(2);

(b) in response to a request made by decision adopted pursuant to Article 17 or Article 18(3), they supply incorrect, incomplete or misleading information or do not supply information within the required time-limit;

(c) they produce the required books or other records related to the business in incomplete form during inspections under Article 20 or refuse to submit to inspections ordered by a decision adopted pursuant to Article 20(4);

(d) in response to a question asked in accordance with Article 20(2)(e),

- they give an incorrect or misleading answer,
- they fail to rectify within a time-limit set by the Commission an incorrect, incomplete or misleading answer given by a member of staff, or

– they fail or refuse to provide a complete answer on facts relating to the subject- matter and purpose of an inspection ordered by a decision adopted pursuant to Article 20(4);

(e) seals affixed in accordance with Article 20(2)(d) by officials or other accompanying persons authorised by the Commission have been broken.

2. The Commission may by decision impose fines on undertakings and associations of undertakings where, either intentionally or negligently:

(a) they infringe Article 81 or Article 82 of the Treaty; or

(b) they contravene a decision ordering interim measures under Article 8; or

(c) they fail to comply with a commitment made binding by a decision pursuant to Article 9.

For each undertaking and association of undertakings participating in the infringement, the fine shall not exceed 10% of its total turnover in the preceding business year.

Where the infringement of an association relates to the activities of its members, the fine shall not exceed 10% of the sum of the total turnover of each member active on the market affected by the infringement of the association.

3. In fixing the amount of the fine, regard shall be had both to the gravity and to the duration of the infringement.

4. When a fine is imposed on an association of undertakings taking account of the turnover of its members and the association is not solvent, the association is obliged to call for contributions from its members to cover the amount of the fine.

Where such contributions have not been made to the association within a time-limit fixed by the Commission, the Commission may require payment of the fine directly by any of the undertakings whose representatives were members of the decision-making bodies concerned of the association.

After the Commission has required payment under the second subparagraph, where necessary to ensure full payment of the fine, the Commission may require payment of the balance by any of the members of the association which were active on the market on which the infringement occurred.

However, the Commission shall not require payment under the second or the third sub paragraph from undertakings which show that they have not implemented the infringing decision of the association and either were not aware of its existence or have actively distanced themselves from it before the Commission started investigating the case.

The financial liability of each undertaking in respect of the payment of the fine shall not exceed 10% of its total turnover in the preceding business year.

5. Decisions taken pursuant to paragraphs 1 and 2 shall not be of a criminal law nature.

Article 24 Periodic penalty payments

1. The Commission may, by decision, impose on undertakings or associations of undertakings periodic penalty payments not exceeding 5% of the average daily turnover in the preceding business year per day and calculated from the date appointed by the decision, in order to compel them:

(a) to put an end to an infringement of Article 81 or Article 82 of the Treaty, in accordance with a decision taken pursuant to Article 7;

(b) to comply with a decision ordering interim measures taken pursuant to Article 8;

(c) to comply with a commitment made binding by a decision pursuant to Article 9;

(d) to supply complete and correct information which it has requested by decision taken pursuant to Article 17 or Article 18(3);

(e) to submit to an inspection which it has ordered by decision taken pursuant to Article 20(4).

2. Where the undertakings or associations of undertakings have satisfied the obligation which the periodic penalty payment was intended to enforce, the Commission may fix the definitive amount of the periodic penalty payment at a figure lower than that which would arise under the original decision. Article 23(4) shall apply correspondingly.

Chapter VII Limitation periods

Article 25 Limitation periods for the imposition of penalties

1. The powers conferred on the Commission by Articles 23 and 24 shall be subject to the following limitation periods:

(a) three years in the case of infringements of provisions concerning requests for information or the conduct of inspections;

(b) five years in the case of all other infringements.

2. Time shall begin to run on the day on which the infringement is committed. However, in the case of continuing or repeated infringements, time shall begin to run on the day on which the infringement ceases.

3. Any action taken by the Commission or by the competition authority of a Member State for the purpose of the investigation or proceedings in respect of an infringement shall interrupt the limitation period for the imposition of fines or periodic penalty payments. The limitation period shall be interrupted with effect from the date on which the action is notified to at least one undertaking or association of undertakings which has participated in the infringement. Actions which interrupt the running of the period shall include in particular the following:

(a) written requests for information by the Commission or by the competition authority of a Member State;

(b) written authorisations to conduct inspections issued to its officials by the Commission or by the competition authority of a Member State;

(c) the initiation of proceedings by the Commission or by the competition authority of a Member State;

(d) notification of the statement of objections of the Commission or of the competition authority of a Member State.

4. The interruption of the limitation period shall apply for all the undertakings or associations of undertakings which have participated in the infringement.

5. Each interruption shall start time running afresh. However, the limitation period shall expire at the latest on the day on which a period equal to twice the limitation period has elapsed without the Commission having imposed a fine or a periodic penalty payment. That period shall be extended by the time during which limitation is suspended pursuant to paragraph 6.

6. The limitation period for the imposition of fines or periodic penalty payments shall be suspended for as long as the decision of the Commission is the subject of proceedings pending before the Court of Justice.

Article 26 Limitation period for the enforcement of penalties

1. The power of the Commission to enforce decisions taken pursuant to Articles 23 and 24 shall be subject to a limitation period of five years.

2. Time shall begin to run on the day on which the decision becomes final.

3. The limitation period for the enforcement of penalties shall be interrupted:

(a) by notification of a decision varying the original amount of the fine or periodic penalty payment or refusing an application for variation;

(b) by any action of the Commission or of a Member State, acting at the request of the Commission, designed to enforce payment of the fine or periodic penalty payment.

4. Each interruption shall start time running afresh.

5. The limitation period for the enforcement of penalties shall be suspended for so long as:

(a) time to pay is allowed;

(b) enforcement of payment is suspended pursuant to a decision of the Court of Justice.

Chapter VIII Hearings and professional secrecy

Article 27 Hearing of the parties, complainants and others

1. Before taking decisions as provided for in Articles 7, 8, 23 and Article 24(2), the Commission shall give the undertakings or associations of undertakings which are the subject of the proceedings

conducted by the Commission the opportunity of being heard on the matters to which the Commission has taken objection. The Commission shall base its decisions only on objections on which the parties concerned have been able to comment. Complainants shall be associated closely with the proceedings.

2. The rights of defence of the parties concerned shall be fully respected in the proceedings. They shall be entitled to have access to the Commission's file, subject to the legitimate interest of undertakings in the protection of their business secrets. The right of access to the file shall not extend to confidential information and internal documents of the Commission or the competition authorities of the Member States. In particular, the right of access shall not extend to correspondence between the Commission and the competition authorities of the Member States, or between the latter, including documents drawn up pursuant to Articles 11 and 14. Nothing in this paragraph shall prevent the Commission from disclosing and using information necessary to prove an infringement.

3. If the Commission considers it necessary, it may also hear other natural or legal persons. Applications to be heard on the part of such persons shall, where they show a sufficient interest, be granted. The competition authorities of the Member States may also ask the Commission to hear other natural or legal persons.

4. Where the Commission intends to adopt a decision pursuant to Article 9 or Article 10, it shall publish a concise summary of the case and the main content of the commitments or of the proposed course of action. Interested third parties may submit their observations within a time limit which is fixed by the Commission in its publication and which may not be less than one month. Publication shall have regard to the legitimate interest of undertakings in the protection of their business secrets.

Article 28 Professional secrecy

1. Without prejudice to Articles 12 and 15, information collected pursuant to Articles 17 to 22 shall be used only for the purpose for which it was acquired.

2. Without prejudice to the exchange and to the use of information foreseen in Articles 11, 12, 14, 15 and 27, the Commission and the competition authorities of the Member States, their officials, servants and other persons working under the supervision of these authorities as well as officials and civil servants of other authorities of the Member States shall not disclose information acquired or exchanged by them pursuant to this Regulation and of the kind covered by the obligation of professional secrecy. This obligation also applies to all representatives and experts of Member States attending meetings of the Advisory Committee pursuant to Article 14.

Chapter IX Exemption regulations

Article 29 Withdrawal in individual cases

1. Where the Commission, empowered by a Council Regulation, such as Regulations 19/65/EEC, (EEC) No 2821/71, (EEC) No 3976/87, (EEC) No 1534/91 or (EEC) No 479/92, to apply Article 81(3) of the Treaty by regulation, has declared Article 81(1) of the Treaty inapplicable to certain categories of agreements, decisions by associations of undertakings or concerted practices, it may, acting on its own initiative or on a complaint, withdraw the benefit of such an exemption Regulation when it finds that in any particular case an agreement, decision or concerted practice to which the exemption Regulation applies has certain effects which are incompatible with Article 81(3) of the Treaty.

2. Where, in any particular case, agreements, decisions by associations of undertakings or concerted practices to which a Commission Regulation referred to in paragraph 1 applies have effects which are incompatible with Article 81(3) of the Treaty in the territory of a Member State, or in a part thereof, which has all the characteristics of a distinct geographic market, the competition authority of that Member State may withdraw the benefit of the Regulation in question in respect of that territory.

Chapter X General provisions

Article 30 Publication of decisions

1. The Commission shall publish the decisions, which it takes pursuant to Articles 7 to 10, 23 and 24.

2. The publication shall state the names of the parties and the main content of the decision, including any penalties imposed. It shall have regard to the legitimate interest of undertakings in the protection of their business secrets.

Article 31 Review by the Court of Justice

The Court of Justice shall have unlimited jurisdiction to review decisions whereby the Commission has fixed a fine or periodic penalty payment. It may cancel, reduce or increase the fine or periodic penalty payment imposed.

Article 32 (Deleted by Regulation 1419/2006 OJ 2006 L269/1)

Article 33 Implementing provisions

1. The Commission shall be authorised to take such measures as may be appropriate in order to apply this Regulation. The measures may concern, inter alia:

(a) the form, content and other details of complaints lodged pursuant to Article 7 and the procedure for rejecting complaints;

(b) the practical arrangements for the exchange of information and consultations provided for in Article 11;

(c) the practical arrangements for the hearings provided for in Article 27.

2. Before the adoption of any measures pursuant to paragraph 1, the Commission shall publish a draft thereof and invite all interested parties to submit their comments within the time-limit it lays down, which may not be less than one month. Before publishing a draft measure and before adopting it, the Commission shall consult the Advisory Committee on Restrictive Practices and Dominant Positions.

Chapter XI Transitional, amending and final provisions

Article 34 Transitional provisions

1. Applications made to the Commission under Article 2 of Regulation No 17, notifications made under Articles 4 and 5 of that Regulation and the corresponding applications and notifications made under Regulations (EEC) No 1017/68, (EEC) No 4056/86 and (EEC) No 3975/87 shall lapse as from the date of application of this Regulation.

2. Procedural steps taken under Regulation No 17 and Regulations (EEC) No 1017/68, (EEC) No 4056/86 and (EEC) No 3975/87 shall continue to have effect for the purposes of applying this Regulation.

Article 35 Designation of competition authorities of Member States

1. The Member States shall designate the competition authority or authorities responsible for the application of Articles 81 and 82 of the Treaty in such a way that the provisions of this regulation are effectively complied with. The measures necessary to empower those authorities to apply those Articles shall be taken before 1 May 2004. The authorities designated may include courts.

2. When enforcement of Community competition law is entrusted to national administrative and judicial authorities, the Member States may allocate different powers and functions to those different national authorities, whether administrative or judicial.

3. The effects of Article 11(6) apply to the authorities designated by the Member States including courts that exercise functions regarding the preparation and the adoption of the types of decisions foreseen in Article 5. The effects of Article 11(6) do not extend to courts insofar as they act as review courts in respect of the types of decisions foreseen in Article 5.

4. Notwithstanding paragraph 3, in the Member States where, for the adoption of certain types of decisions foreseen in Article 5, an authority brings an action before a judicial authority that is separate and different from the prosecuting authority and provided that the terms of this paragraph are complied with, the effects of Article 11(6) shall be limited to the authority prosecuting the case which

shall withdraw its claim before the judicial authority when the Commission opens proceedings and this withdrawal shall bring the national proceedings effectively to an end.

Article 36 (Repealed)

Article 37 Amendment of Regulation (EEC) No 2988/74

In Regulation (EEC) No 2988/74, the following Article is inserted:

'Article 7a Exclusion

This Regulation shall not apply to measures taken under Council Regulation (EC) No 1/2003 of 16 December 2002 on the implementation of the rules on competition laid down in Articles 81 and 82 of the Treaty.'[16]

Article 38 Amendment of Regulation (EEC) No 4056/86

Regulation (EEC) No 4056/86 is amended as follows:

1. Article 7 is amended as follows:
    (a) Paragraph 1 is replaced by the following:

'1. Breach of an obligation

Where the persons concerned are in breach of an obligation which, pursuant to Article 5, attaches to the exemption provided for in Article 3, the Commission may, in order to put an end to such breach and under the conditions laid down in Council Regulation (EC) No 1/2003 of 16 December 2002 on the implementation of the rules on competition laid down in Articles 81 and 82 of the Treaty[17] adopt a decision that either prohibits them from carrying out or requires them to perform certain specific acts, or withdraws the benefit of the block exemption which they enjoyed.'

    (b) Paragraph 2 is amended as follows:
        (i) In point (a), the words 'under the conditions laid down in Section II' are replaced by the words 'under the conditions laid down in Regulation (EC) No 1/ 2003';
        (ii) The second sentence of the second subparagraph of point (c)(i) is replaced by the following:

'At the same time it shall decide, in accordance with Article 9 of Regulation (EC) No 1/2003, whether to accept commitments offered by the undertakings concerned with a view, inter alia, to obtaining access to the market for non-conference lines.'

2. Article 8 is amended as follows:
    (a) Paragraph 1 is deleted.
    (b) In paragraph 2 the words 'pursuant to Article 10' are replaced by the words 'pursuant to Regulation (EC) No 1/2003.'
    (c) Paragraph 3 is deleted;
3. Article 9 is amended as follows:
    (a) In paragraph 1, the words 'Advisory Committee referred to in Article 15' are replaced by the words 'Advisory Committee referred to in Article 14 of Regulation (EC) No 1/2003';
    (b) In paragraph 2, the words 'Advisory Committee as referred to in Article 15' are replaced by the words 'Advisory Committee referred to in Article 14 of Regulation (EC) No 1/2003';
4. Articles 10 to 25 are repealed with the exception of Article 13(3) which continues to apply to decisions adopted pursuant to Article 81(3) of the Treaty prior to the date of application of this Regulation until the date of expiration of those decisions;
5. in Article 26, the words 'the form, content and other details of complaints pursuant to Article 10, applications pursuant to Article 12 and the hearings provided for in Article 23(1) and (2)' are deleted.

Article 39 Amendment of Regulation (EEC) No 3975/87

Articles 3 to 19 of Regulation (EEC) No 3975/87 are repealed with the exception of Article 6(3) which continues to apply to decisions adopted pursuant to Article 81(3) of the Treaty prior to the date of application of this Regulation until the date of expiration of those decisions.

[16] OJ L 1, 4.1.2003, p. 1.

[17] OJL 1, 4.1.2003, p. 1.

Article 40 Amendment of Regulations No 19/65/EEC, (EEC) No 2821/71 and (EEC) No 1534/91

Article 7 of Regulation No 19/65/EEC, Article 7 of Regulation (EEC) No 2821/71 and Article 7 of Regulation (EEC) No 1534/91 are repealed.

Article 41 (Repealed)

Article 42 (Repealed)

Article 43 Repeal of Regulations No 17 and No 141

1. Regulation No 17 is repealed with the exception of Article 8(3) which continues to apply to decisions adopted pursuant to Article 81(3) of the Treaty prior to the date of application of this Regulation until the date of expiration of those decisions.
2. Regulation No 141 is repealed.
3. References to the repealed Regulations shall be construed as references to this Regulation.

Article 44 Report on the application of the present Regulation

Five years from the date of application of this Regulation, the Commission shall report to the European Parliament and the Council on the functioning of this Regulation, in particular on the application of Article 11(6) and Article 17.

On the basis of this report, the Commission shall assess whether it is appropriate to propose to the Council a revision of this Regulation.

Article 45 Entry into force

This Regulation shall enter into force on the 20th day following that of its publication in the *Official Journal of the European Communities*.

It shall apply from 1 May 2004.

This Regulation shall be binding in its entirety and directly applicable in all Member States.

Done at Brussels, 16 December 2002.
For the Council
The President
M. FISCHER BOEL

Council Regulation (EC) No 139/2004 of 20 January 2004 on the control of concentrations between undertakings (the EC Merger Regulation)*

[OJ 2004 L24/22]

THE COUNCIL OF THE EUROPEAN UNION,

Having regard to the Treaty establishing the European Community, and in particular Articles 83 and 308 thereof,

Having regard to the proposal from the Commission,[1]

Having regard to the opinion of the European Parliament,[2]

Having regard to the opinion of the European Economic and Social Committee,[3]

Whereas:

* **Editor's Note:** This Regulation replaces and repeals Regulations 4064/89 and 1310/97.

[1] OJ C20, 28.1.2003, p. 4.

[2] Opinion delivered on 9.10.2003 (not yet published in the Official Journal).

[3] Opinion delivered on 24.10.2003 (not yet published in the Official Journal).

(1) Council Regulation (EEC) No 4064/89 of 21 December 1989 on the control of concentrations between undertakings[4] has been substantially amended. Since further amendments are to be made, it should be recast in the interest of clarity.

(2) For the achievement of the aims of the Treaty, Article 3(1)(g) gives the Community the objective of instituting a system ensuring that competition in the internal market is not distorted. Article 4(1) of the Treaty provides that the activities of the Member States and the Community are to be conducted in accordance with the principle of an open market economy with free competition. These principles are essential for the further development of the internal market.

(3) The completion of the internal market and of economic and monetary union, the enlargement of the European Union and the lowering of international barriers to trade and investment will continue to result in major corporate reorganisations, particularly in the form of concentrations.

(4) Such reorganisations are to be welcomed to the extent that they are in line with the requirements of dynamic competition and capable of increasing the competitiveness of European industry, improving the conditions of growth and raising the standard of living in the Community.

(5) However, it should be ensured that the process of reorganisation does not result in lasting damage to competition; Community law must therefore include provisions governing those concentrations which may significantly impede effective competition in the common market or in a substantial part of it.

(6) A specific legal instrument is therefore necessary to permit effective control of all concentrations in terms of their effect on the structure of competition in the Community and to be the only instrument applicable to such concentrations. Regulation (EEC) No 4064/89 has allowed a Community policy to develop in this field. In the light of experience, however, that Regulation should now be recast into legislation designed to meet the challenges of a more integrated market and the future enlargement of the European Union. In accordance with the principles of subsidiarity and of proportionality as set out in Article 5 of the Treaty, this Regulation does not go beyond what is necessary in order to achieve the objective of ensuring that competition in the common market is not distorted, in accordance with the principle of an open market economy with free competition.

(7) Articles 81 and 82, while applicable, according to the case-law of the Court of Justice, to certain concentrations, are not sufficient to control all operations which may prove to be incompatible with the system of undistorted competition envisaged in the Treaty. This Regulation should therefore be based not only on Article 83 but, principally, on Article 308 of the Treaty, under which the Community may give itself the additional powers of action necessary for the attainment of its objectives, and also powers of action with regard to concentrations on the markets for agricultural products listed in Annex I to the Treaty.

(8) The provisions to be adopted in this Regulation should apply to significant structural changes, the impact of which on the market goes beyond the national borders of any one Member State. Such concentrations should, as a general rule, be reviewed exclusively at Community level, in application of a 'one-stop shop' system and in compliance with the principle of subsidiarity. Concentrations not covered by this Regulation come, in principle, within the jurisdiction of the Member States.

(9) The scope of application of this Regulation should be defined according to the geographical area of activity of the undertakings concerned and be limited by quantitative thresholds in order to cover those concentrations which have a Community dimension. The Commission should report to the Council on the implementation of the applicable thresholds and criteria so that the Council, acting in accordance with Article 202 of the Treaty, is in a position to review them regularly, as well as the rules regarding pre-notification referral, in the light of the experience gained; this requires statistical data to be provided by the Member States to the Commission to enable it to prepare such reports and possible proposals for amendments. The Commission's reports and proposals should be based on relevant information regularly provided by the Member States.

(10) A concentration with a Community dimension should be deemed to exist where the aggregate turnover of the undertakings concerned exceeds given thresholds; that is the case irrespective of

[4] OJ L 395, 30.12.1989, p. 1. Corrected version in OJ L 257, 21.9.1990, p. 13. regulation as last amended by Regulation (EC) No 1310/97 (OJ L 180, 9.7.1997, p. 1). Corrigendum in OJ L 40, 13.2.1998, p. 17.

whether or not the undertakings effecting the concentration have their seat or their principal fields of activity in the Community, provided they have substantial operations there.

(11) The rules governing the referral of concentrations from the Commission to Member States and from Member States to the Commission should operate as an effective corrective mechanism in the light of the principle of subsidiarity; these rules protect the competition interests of the Member States in an adequate manner and take due account of legal certainty and the 'one-stop shop' principle.

(12) Concentrations may qualify for examination under a number of national merger control systems if they fall below the turnover thresholds referred to in this Regulation. Multiple notification of the same transaction increases legal uncertainty, effort and cost for undertakings and may lead to conflicting assessments. The system whereby concentrations may be referred to the Commission by the Member States concerned should therefore be further developed.

(13) The Commission should act in close and constant liaison with the competent authorities of the Member States from which it obtains comments and information.

(14) The Commission and the competent authorities of the Member States should together form a network of public authorities, applying their respective competences in close cooperation, using efficient arrangements for information-sharing and consultation, with a view to ensuring that a case is dealt with by the most appropriate authority, in the light of the principle of subsidiarity and with a view to ensuring that multiple notifications of a given concentration are avoided to the greatest extent possible. Referrals of concentrations from the Commission to Member States and from Member States to the Commission should be made in an efficient manner avoiding, to the greatest extent possible, situations where a concentration is subject to a referral both before and after its notification.

(15) The Commission should be able to refer to a Member State notified concentrations with a Community dimension which threaten significantly to affect competition in a market within that Member State presenting all the characteristics of a distinct market. Where the concentration affects competition on such a market, which does not constitute a substantial part of the common market, the Commission should be obliged, upon request, to refer the whole or part of the case to the Member State concerned. A Member State should be able to refer to the Commission a concentration which does not have a Community dimension but which affects trade between Member States and threatens to significantly affect competition within its territory. Other Member States which are also competent to review the concentration should be able to join the request. In such a situation, in order to ensure the efficiency and predictability of the system, national time limits should be suspended until a decision has been reached as to the referral of the case. The Commission should have the power to examine and deal with a concentration on behalf of a requesting Member State or requesting Member States.

(16) The undertakings concerned should be granted the possibility of requesting referrals to or from the Commission before a concentration is notified so as to further improve the efficiency of the system for the control of concentrations within the Community. In such situations, the Commission and national competition authorities should decide within short, clearly defined time limits whether a referral to or from the Commission ought to be made, thereby ensuring the efficiency of the system. Upon request by the undertakings concerned, the Commission should be able to refer to a Member State a concentration with a Community dimension which may significantly affect competition in a market within that Member State presenting all the characteristics of a distinct market; the undertakings concerned should not, however, be required to demonstrate that the effects of the concentration would be detrimental to competition. A concentration should not be referred from the Commission to a Member State which has expressed its disagreement to such a referral. Before notification to national authorities, the undertakings concerned should also be able to request that a concentration without a Community dimension which is capable of being reviewed under the national competition laws of at least three Member States be referred to the Commission. Such requests for pre-notification referrals to the Commission would be particularly pertinent in situations where the concentration would affect competition beyond the territory of one Member State. Where a concentration capable of being reviewed under the competition laws of three or more Member States is referred to the Commission prior to any national notification, and no Member State competent to review the case expresses its disagreement, the Commission should acquire exclusive competence to review the concentration and

such a concentration should be deemed to have a Community dimension. Such pre-notification referrals from Member States to the Commission should not, however, be made where at least one Member State competent to review the case has expressed its disagreement with such a referral.

(17) The Commission should be given exclusive competence to apply this Regulation, subject to review by the Court of Justice.

(18) The Member States should not be permitted to apply their national legislation on competition to concentrations with a Community dimension, unless this Regulation makes provision therefore. The relevant powers of national authorities should be limited to cases where, failing intervention by the Commission, effective competition is likely to be significantly impeded within the territory of a Member State and where the competition interests of that Member State cannot be sufficiently protected otherwise by this Regulation. The Member States concerned must act promptly in such cases; this Regulation cannot, because of the diversity of national law, fix a single time limit for the adoption of final decisions under national law.

(19) Furthermore, the exclusive application of this Regulation to concentrations with a Community dimension is without prejudice to Article 296 of the Treaty, and does not prevent the Member States from taking appropriate measures to protect legitimate interests other than those pursued by this Regulation, provided that such measures are compatible with the general principles and other provisions of Community law.

(20) It is expedient to define the concept of concentration in such a manner as to cover operations bringing about a lasting change in the control of the undertakings concerned and therefore in the structure of the market. It is therefore appropriate to include, within the scope of this Regulation, all joint ventures performing on a lasting basis all the functions of an autonomous economic entity. It is moreover appropriate to treat as a single concentration transactions that are closely connected in that they are linked by condition or take the form of a series of transactions in securities taking place within a reasonably short period of time.

(21) This Regulation should also apply where the undertakings concerned accept restrictions directly related to, and necessary for, the implementation of the concentration. Commission decisions declaring concentrations compatible with the common market in application of this Regulation should automatically cover such restrictions, without the Commission having to assess such restrictions in individual cases. At the request of the undertakings concerned, however, the Commission should, in cases presenting novel or unresolved questions giving rise to genuine uncertainty, expressly assess whether or not any restriction is directly related to, and necessary for, the implementation of the concentration. A case presents a novel or unresolved question giving rise to genuine uncertainty if the question is not covered by the relevant Commission notice in force or a published Commission decision.

(22) The arrangements to be introduced for the control of concentrations should, without prejudice to Article 86(2) of the Treaty, respect the principle of non-discrimination between the public and the private sectors. In the public sector, calculation of the turnover of an undertaking concerned in a concentration needs, therefore, to take account of undertakings making up an economic unit with an independent power of decision, irrespective of the way in which their capital is held or of the rules of administrative supervision applicable to them.

(23) It is necessary to establish whether or not concentrations with a Community dimension are compatible with the common market in terms of the need to maintain and develop effective competition in the common market. In so doing, the Commission must place its appraisal within the general framework of the achievement of the fundamental objectives referred to in Article 2 of the Treaty establishing the European Community and Article 2 of the Treaty on European Union.

(24) In order to ensure a system of undistorted competition in the common market, in furtherance of a policy conducted in accordance with the principle of an open market economy with free competition, this Regulation must permit effective control of all concentrations from the point of view of their effect on competition in the Community. Accordingly, Regulation (EEC) No 4064/89 established the principle that a concentration with a Community dimension which creates or strengthens a dominant position as a result of which effective competition in the common market or in a substantial part of it would be significantly impeded should be declared incompatible with the common market.

(25) In view of the consequences that concentrations in oligopolistic market structures may have, it is all the more necessary to maintain effective competition in such markets. Many oligopolistic markets exhibit a healthy degree of competition. However, under certain circumstances, concentrations involving the elimination of important competitive constraints that the merging parties had exerted upon each other, as well as a reduction of competitive pressure on the remaining competitors, may, even in the absence of a likelihood of coordination between the members of the oligopoly, result in a significant impediment to effective competition. The Community courts have, however, not to date expressly interpreted Regulation (EEC) No 4064/89 as requiring concentrations giving rise to such non-coordinated effects to be declared incompatible with the common market. Therefore, in the interests of legal certainty, it should be made clear that this Regulation permits effective control of all such concentrations by providing that any concentration which would significantly impede effective competition, in the common market or in a substantial part of it, should be declared incompatible with the common market. The notion of 'significant impediment to effective competition' in Article 2(2) and (3) should be interpreted as extending, beyond the concept of dominance, only to the anti-competitive effects of a concentration resulting from the non-coordinated behaviour of undertakings which would not have a dominant position on the market concerned.

(26) A significant impediment to effective competition generally results from the creation or strengthening of a dominant position. With a view to preserving the guidance that may be drawn from past judgments of the European courts and Commission decisions pursuant to Regulation (EEC) No 4064/89, while at the same time maintaining consistency with the standards of competitive harm which have been applied by the Commission and the Community courts regarding the compatibility of a concentration with the common market, this Regulation should accordingly establish the principle that a concentration with a Community dimension which would significantly impede effective competition, in the common market or in a substantial part thereof, in particular as a result of the creation or strengthening of a dominant position, is to be declared incompatible with the common market.

(27) In addition, the criteria of Article 81(1) and (3) of the Treaty should be applied to joint ventures performing, on a lasting basis, all the functions of autonomous economic entities, to the extent that their creation has as its consequence an appreciable restriction of competition between undertakings that remain independent.

(28) In order to clarify and explain the Commission's appraisal of concentrations under this Regulation, it is appropriate for the Commission to publish guidance which should provide a sound economic framework for the assessment of concentrations with a view to determining whether or not they may be declared compatible with the common market.

(29) In order to determine the impact of a concentration on competition in the common market, it is appropriate to take account of any substantiated and likely efficiencies put forward by the undertakings concerned. It is possible that the efficiencies brought about by the concentration counteract the effects on competition, and in particular the potential harm to consumers, that it might otherwise have and that, as a consequence, the concentration would not significantly impede effective competition, in the common market or in a substantial part of it, in particular as a result of the creation or strengthening of a dominant position. The Commission should publish guidance on the conditions under which it may take efficiencies into account in the assessment of a concentration.

(30) Where the undertakings concerned modify a notified concentration, in particular by offering commitments with a view to rendering the concentration compatible with the common market, the Commission should be able to declare the concentration, as modified, compatible with the common market. Such commitments should be proportionate to the competition problem and entirely eliminate it. It is also appropriate to accept commitments before the initiation of proceedings where the competition problem is readily identifiable and can easily be remedied. It should be expressly provided that the Commission may attach to its decision conditions and obligations in order to ensure that the undertakings concerned comply with their commitments in a timely and effective manner so as to render the concentration compatible with the common market. Transparency and effective consultation of Member States as well as of interested third parties should be ensured throughout the procedure.

(31) The Commission should have at its disposal appropriate instruments to ensure the enforcement of commitments and to deal with situations where they are not fulfilled. In cases of failure to fulfil a condition attached to the decision declaring a concentration compatible with the common market, the situation rendering the concentration compatible with the common market does not materialise and the concentration, as implemented, is therefore not authorised by the Commission. As a consequence, if the concentration is implemented, it should be treated in the same way as a non-notified concentration implemented without authorisation. Furthermore, where the Commission has already found that, in the absence of the condition, the concentration would be incompatible with the common market, it should have the power to directly order the dissolution of the concentration, so as to restore the situation prevailing prior to the implementation of the concentration. Where an obligation attached to a decision declaring the concentration compatible with the common market is not fulfilled, the Commission should be able to revoke its decision. Moreover, the Commission should be able to impose appropriate financial sanctions where conditions or obligations are not fulfilled.

(32) Concentrations which, by reason of the limited market share of the undertakings concerned, are not liable to impede effective competition may be presumed to be compatible with the common market. Without prejudice to Articles 81 and 82 of the Treaty, an indication to this effect exists, in particular, where the market share of the undertakings concerned does not exceed 25% either in the common market or in a substantial part of it.

(33) The Commission should have the task of taking all the decisions necessary to establish whether or not concentrations with a Community dimension are compatible with the common market, as well as decisions designed to restore the situation prevailing prior to the implementation of a concentration which has been declared incompatible with the common market.

(34) To ensure effective control, undertakings should be obliged to give prior notification of concentrations with a Community dimension following the conclusion of the agreement, the announcement of the public bid or the acquisition of a controlling interest. Notification should also be possible where the undertakings concerned satisfy the Commission of their intention to enter into an agreement for a proposed concentration and demonstrate to the Commission that their plan for that proposed concentration is sufficiently concrete, for example on the basis of an agreement in principle, a memorandum of understanding, or a letter of intent signed by all undertakings concerned, or, in the case of a public bid, where they have publicly announced an intention to make such a bid, provided that the intended agreement or bid would result in a concentration with a Community dimension. The implementation of concentrations should be suspended until a final decision of the Commission has been taken. However, it should be possible to derogate from this suspension at the request of the undertakings concerned, where appropriate. In deciding whether or not to grant a derogation, the Commission should take account of all pertinent factors, such as the nature and gravity of damage to the undertakings concerned or to third parties, and the threat to competition posed by the concentration. In the interest of legal certainty, the validity of transactions must nevertheless be protected as much as necessary.

(35) A period within which the Commission must initiate proceedings in respect of a notified concentration and a period within which it must take a final decision on the compatibility or incompatibility with the common market of that concentration should be laid down. These periods should be extended whenever the undertakings concerned offer commitments with a view to rendering the concentration compatible with the common market, in order to allow for sufficient time for the analysis and market testing of such commitment offers and for the consultation of Member States as well as interested third parties. A limited extension of the period within which the Commission must take a final decision should also be possible in order to allow sufficient time for the investigation of the case and the verification of the facts and arguments submitted to the Commission.

(36) The Community respects the fundamental rights and observes the principles recognised in particular by the Charter of Fundamental Rights of the European Union.[5] Accordingly, this Regulation should be interpreted and applied with respect to those rights and principles.

(37) The undertakings concerned must be afforded the right to be heard by the Commission when proceedings have been initiated; the members of the management and supervisory bodies and

[5] OJ C 364, 18.12.2000, p. 1.

the recognised representatives of the employees of the undertakings concerned, and interested third parties, must also be given the opportunity to be heard.

(38) In order properly to appraise concentrations, the Commission should have the right to request all necessary information and to conduct all necessary inspections throughout the Community. To that end, and with a view to protecting competition effectively, the Commission's powers of investigation need to be expanded. The Commission should, in particular, have the right to interview any persons who may be in possession of useful information and to record the statements made.

(39) In the course of an inspection, officials authorised by the Commission should have the right to ask for any information relevant to the subject matter and purpose of the inspection; they should also have the right to affix seals during inspections, particularly in circumstances where there are reasonable grounds to suspect that a concentration has been implemented without being notified; that incorrect, incomplete or misleading information has been supplied to the Commission; or that the undertakings or persons concerned have failed to comply with a condition or obligation imposed by decision of the Commission. In any event, seals should only be used in exceptional circumstances, for the period of time strictly necessary for the inspection, normally not for more than 48 hours.

(40) Without prejudice to the case-law of the Court of Justice, it is also useful to set out the scope of the control that the national judicial authority may exercise when it authorises, as provided by national law and as a precautionary measure, assistance from law enforcement authorities in order to overcome possible opposition on the part of the undertaking against an inspection, including the affixing of seals, ordered by Commission decision. It results from the case-law that the national judicial authority may in particular ask of the Commission further information which it needs to carry out its control and in the absence of which it could refuse the authorisation. The case-law also confirms the competence of the national courts to control the application of national rules governing the implementation of coercive measures. The competent authorities of the Member States should cooperate actively in the exercise of the Commission's investigative powers.

(41) When complying with decisions of the Commission, the undertakings and persons concerned cannot be forced to admit that they have committed infringements, but they are in any event obliged to answer factual questions and to provide documents, even if this information may be used to establish against themselves or against others the existence of such infringements.

(42) For the sake of transparency, all decisions of the Commission which are not of a merely procedural nature should be widely publicised. While ensuring preservation of the rights of defence of the undertakings concerned, in particular the right of access to the file, it is essential that business secrets be protected. The confidentiality of information exchanged in the network and with the competent authorities of third countries should likewise be safeguarded.

(43) Compliance with this Regulation should be enforceable, as appropriate, by means of fines and periodic penalty payments. The Court of Justice should be given unlimited jurisdiction in that regard pursuant to Article 229 of the Treaty.

(44) The conditions in which concentrations, involving undertakings having their seat or their principal fields of activity in the Community, are carried out in third countries should be observed, and provision should be made for the possibility of the Council giving the Commission an appropriate mandate for negotiation with a view to obtaining non-discriminatory treatment for such undertakings.

(45) This Regulation in no way detracts from the collective rights of employees, as recognised in the undertakings concerned, notably with regard to any obligation to inform or consult their recognised representatives under Community and national law.

(46) The Commission should be able to lay down detailed rules concerning the implementation of this Regulation in accordance with the procedures for the exercise of implementing powers conferred on the Commission. For the adoption of such implementing provisions, the Commission should be assisted by an Advisory Committee composed of the representatives of the Member States as specified in Article 23,

HAS ADOPTED THIS REGULATION:

Article 1 Scope

1. Without prejudice to Article 4(5) and Article 22, this Regulation shall apply to all concentrations with a Community dimension as defined in this Article.

2. A concentration has a Community dimension where:

(a) the combined aggregate worldwide turnover of all the undertakings concerned is more than EUR 5000 million; and

(b) the aggregate Community-wide turnover of each of at least two of the undertakings concerned is more than EUR 250 million,

unless each of the undertakings concerned achieves more than two-thirds of its aggregate Community-wide turnover within one and the same Member State.

3. A concentration that does not meet the thresholds laid down in paragraph 2 has a Community dimension where:

(a) the combined aggregate worldwide turnover of all the undertakings concerned is more than EUR 2500 million;

(b) in each of at least three Member States, the combined aggregate turnover of all the undertakings concerned is more than EUR 100 million;

(c) in each of at least three Member States included for the purpose of point (b), the aggregate turnover of each of at least two of the undertakings concerned is more than EUR 25 million; and

(d) the aggregate Community-wide turnover of each of at least two of the undertakings concerned is more than EUR 100 million,

unless each of the undertakings concerned achieves more than two-thirds of its aggregate Community-wide turnover within one and the same Member State.

4. On the basis of statistical data that may be regularly provided by the Member States, the Commission shall report to the Council on the operation of the thresholds and criteria set out in paragraphs 2 and 3 by 1 July 2009 and may present proposals pursuant to paragraph 5.

5. Following the report referred to in paragraph 4 and on a proposal from the Commission, the Council, acting by a qualified majority, may revise the thresholds and criteria mentioned in paragraph 3.

Article 2 Appraisal of concentrations

1. Concentrations within the scope of this Regulation shall be appraised in accordance with the objectives of this Regulation and the following provisions with a view to establishing whether or not they are compatible with the common market.

In making this appraisal, the Commission shall take into account:

(a) the need to maintain and develop effective competition within the common market in view of, among other things, the structure of all the markets concerned and the actual or potential competition from undertakings located either within or outwith the Community;

(b) the market position of the undertakings concerned and their economic and financial power, the alternatives available to suppliers and users, their access to supplies or markets, any legal or other barriers to entry, supply and demand trends for the relevant goods and services, the interests of the intermediate and ultimate consumers, and the development of technical and economic progress provided that it is to consumers' advantage and does not form an obstacle to competition.

2. A concentration which would not significantly impede effective competition in the common market or in a substantial part of it, in particular as a result of the creation or strengthening of a dominant position, shall be declared compatible with the common market.

3. A concentration which would significantly impede effective competition, in the common market or in a substantial part of it, in particular as a result of the creation or strengthening of a dominant position, shall be declared incompatible with the common market.

4. To the extent that the creation of a joint venture constituting a concentration pursuant to Article 3 has as its object or effect the coordination of the competitive behaviour of undertakings that remain independent, such coordination shall be appraised in accordance with the criteria of

Article 81(1) and (3) of the Treaty, with a view to establishing whether or not the operation is compatible with the common market.

5. In making this appraisal, the Commission shall take into account in particular:
   - whether two or more parent companies retain, to a significant extent, activities in the same market as the joint venture or in a market which is downstream or upstream from that of the joint venture or in a neighbouring market closely related to this market,
   - whether the coordination which is the direct consequence of the creation of the joint venture affords the undertakings concerned the possibility of eliminating competition in respect of a substantial part of the products or services in question.

Article 3 Definition of concentration

1. A concentration shall be deemed to arise where a change of control on a lasting basis results from:
   (a) the merger of two or more previously independent undertakings or parts of undertakings, or
   (b) the acquisition, by one or more persons already controlling at least one undertaking, or by one or more undertakings, whether by purchase of securities or assets, by contract or by any other means, of direct or indirect control of the whole or parts of one or more other undertakings.

2. Control shall be constituted by rights, contracts or any other means which, either separately or in combination and having regard to the considerations of fact or law involved, confer the possibility of exercising decisive influence on an undertaking, in particular by:
   (a) ownership or the right to use all or part of the assets of an undertaking;
   (b) rights or contracts which confer decisive influence on the composition, voting or decisions of the organs of an undertaking.

3. Control is acquired by persons or undertakings which:
   (a) are holders of the rights or entitled to rights under the contracts concerned; or
   (b) while not being holders of such rights or entitled to rights under such contracts, have the power to exercise the rights deriving therefrom.

4. The creation of a joint venture performing on a lasting basis all the functions of an autonomous economic entity shall constitute a concentration within the meaning of paragraph 1(b).

5. A concentration shall not be deemed to arise where:
   (a) credit institutions or other financial institutions or insurance companies, the normal activities of which include transactions and dealing in securities for their own account or for the account of others, hold on a temporary basis securities which they have acquired in an undertaking with a view to reselling them, provided that they do not exercise voting rights in respect of those securities with a view to determining the competitive behaviour of that undertaking or provided that they exercise such voting rights only with a view to preparing the disposal of all or part of that undertaking or of its assets or the disposal of those securities and that any such disposal takes place within one year of the date of acquisition; that period may be extended by the Commission on request where such institutions or companies can show that the disposal was not reasonably possible within the period set;
   (b) control is acquired by an office-holder according to the law of a Member State relating to liquidation, winding up, insolvency, cessation of payments, compositions or analogous proceedings;
   (c) the operations referred to in paragraph 1(b) are carried out by the financial holding companies referred to in Article 5(3) of Fourth Council Directive 78/660/ EEC of 25 July 1978 based on Article 54(3)(g) of the Treaty on the annual accounts of certain types of companies[6] provided however that the voting rights in respect of the holding are exercised, in particular in relation to the appointment of members of the management and supervisory bodies of the undertakings in which they have holdings, only to maintain the full value of those investments and not to determine directly or indirectly the competitive conduct of those undertakings.

[6] OJ L 222, 14.8.1978, p. 11. Directive as last amended by Directive 2003/51/EC of the European Parliament and of the Council (OJ L 178, 17.7.2003, p. 16).

Article 4 Prior notification of concentrations and pre-notification referral at the request of the notifying parties

1. Concentrations with a Community dimension defined in this Regulation shall be notified to the Commission prior to their implementation and following the conclusion of the agreement, the announcement of the public bid, or the acquisition of a controlling interest.

Notification may also be made where the undertakings concerned demonstrate to the Commission a good faith intention to conclude an agreement or, in the case of a public bid, where they have publicly announced an intention to make such a bid, provided that the intended agreement or bid would result in a concentration with a Community dimension.

For the purposes of this Regulation, the term 'notified concentration' shall also cover intended concentrations notified pursuant to the second subparagraph. For the purposes of paragraphs 4 and 5 of this Article, the term 'concentration' includes intended concentrations within the meaning of the second subparagraph.

2. A concentration which consists of a merger within the meaning of Article 3(1)(a) or in the acquisition of joint control within the meaning of Article 3(1)(b) shall be notified jointly by the parties to the merger or by those acquiring joint control as the case may be. In all other cases, the notification shall be effected by the person or undertaking acquiring control of the whole or parts of one or more undertakings.

3. Where the Commission finds that a notified concentration falls within the scope of this Regulation, it shall publish the fact of the notification, at the same time indicating the names of the undertakings concerned, their country of origin, the nature of the concentration and the economic sectors involved. The Commission shall take account of the legitimate interest of undertakings in the protection of their business secrets.

4. Prior to the notification of a concentration within the meaning of paragraph 1, the persons or undertakings referred to in paragraph 2 may inform the Commission, by means of a reasoned submission, that the concentration may significantly affect competition in a market within a Member State which presents all the characteristics of a distinct market and should therefore be examined, in whole or in part, by that Member State.

The Commission shall transmit this submission to all Member States without delay. The Member State referred to in the reasoned submission shall, within 15 working days of receiving the submission, express its agreement or disagreement as regards the request to refer the case. Where that Member State takes no such decision within this period, it shall be deemed to have agreed.

Unless that Member State disagrees, the Commission, where it considers that such a distinct market exists, and that competition in that market may be significantly affected by the concentration, may decide to refer the whole or part of the case to the competent authorities of that Member State with a view to the application of that State's national competition law.

The decision whether or not to refer the case in accordance with the third subparagraph shall be taken within 25 working days starting from the receipt of the reasoned submission by the Commission. The Commission shall inform the other Member States and the persons or undertakings concerned of its decision. If the Commission does not take a decision within this period, it shall be deemed to have adopted a decision to refer the case in accordance with the submission made by the persons or undertakings concerned.

If the Commission decides, or is deemed to have decided, pursuant to the third and fourth subparagraphs, to refer the whole of the case, no notification shall be made pursuant to paragraph 1 and national competition law shall apply. Article 9(6) to (9) shall apply mutatis mutandis.

5. With regard to a concentration as defined in Article 3 which does not have a Community dimension within the meaning of Article 1 and which is capable of being reviewed under the national competition laws of at least three Member States, the persons or undertakings referred to in paragraph 2 may, before any notification to the competent authorities, inform the Commission by means of a reasoned submission that the concentration should be examined by the Commission.

The Commission shall transmit this submission to all Member States without delay.

Any Member State competent to examine the concentration under its national competition law may, within 15 working days of receiving the reasoned submission, express its disagreement as regards the request to refer the case.

Where at least one such Member State has expressed its disagreement in accordance with the third subparagraph within the period of 15 working days, the case shall not be referred. The Commission shall, without delay, inform all Member States and the persons or undertakings concerned of any such expression of disagreement.

Where no Member State has expressed its disagreement in accordance with the third subparagraph within the period of 15 working days, the concentration shall be deemed to have a Community dimension and shall be notified to the Commission in accordance with paragraphs 1 and 2. In such situations, no Member State shall apply its national competition law to the concentration.

6. The Commission shall report to the Council on the operation of paragraphs 4 and 5 by 1 July 2009. Following this report and on a proposal from the Commission, the Council, acting by a qualified majority, may revise paragraphs 4 and 5.

Article 5 Calculation of turnover

1. Aggregate turnover within the meaning of this Regulation shall comprise the amounts derived by the undertakings concerned in the preceding financial year from the sale of products and the provision of services falling within the undertakings' ordinary activities after deduction of sales rebates and of value added tax and other taxes directly related to turnover. The aggregate turnover of an undertaking concerned shall not include the sale of products or the provision of services between any of the undertakings referred to in paragraph 4.

Turnover, in the Community or in a Member State, shall comprise products sold and services provided to undertakings or consumers, in the Community or in that Member State as the case may be.

2. By way of derogation from paragraph 1, where the concentration consists of the acquisition of parts, whether or not constituted as legal entities, of one or more undertakings, only the turnover relating to the parts which are the subject of the concentration shall be taken into account with regard to the seller or sellers.

However, two or more transactions within the meaning of the first subparagraph which take place within a two-year period between the same persons or undertakings shall be treated as one and the same concentration arising on the date of the last transaction.

3. In place of turnover the following shall be used:

(a) for credit institutions and other financial institutions, the sum of the following income items as defined in Council Directive 86/635/EEC,[7] after deduction of value added tax and other taxes directly related to those items, where appropriate:
   (i) interest income and similar income;
   (ii) income from securities:
      – income from shares and other variable yield securities,
      – income from participating interests,
      – income from shares in affiliated undertakings;
   (iii) commissions receivable;
   (iv) net profit on financial operations;
   (v) other operating income.

The turnover of a credit or financial institution in the Community or in a Member State shall comprise the income items, as defined above, which are received by the branch or division of that institution established in the Community or in the Member State in question, as the case may be;

(b) for insurance undertakings, the value of gross premiums written which shall comprise all amounts received and receivable in respect of insurance contracts issued by or on behalf of the insurance undertakings, including also outgoing reinsurance premiums, and after deduction of taxes and parafiscal contributions or levies charged by reference to the amounts of individual premiums or the total volume of premiums; as regards Article 1(2)(b) and (3)(b), (c) and (d) and the final part of Article 1(2) and (3), gross premiums received from

[7] OJ L 372, 31.12.1986, p. 1. Directive as last amended by Directive 2003/51/EC of the European Parliament and of the Council.

Community residents and from residents of one Member State respectively shall be taken into account.

4. Without prejudice to paragraph 2, the aggregate turnover of an undertaking concerned within the meaning of this Regulation shall be calculated by adding together the respective turnovers of the following:

(a) the undertaking concerned;
(b) those undertakings in which the undertaking concerned, directly or indirectly:
   (i) owns more than half the capital or business assets, or
   (ii) has the power to exercise more than half the voting rights, or
   (iii) has the power to appoint more than half the members of the supervisory board, the administrative board or bodies legally representing the undertakings, or
   (iv) has the right to manage the undertakings' affairs;
(c) those undertakings which have in the undertaking concerned the rights or powers listed in (b);
(d) those undertakings in which an undertaking as referred to in (c) has the rights or powers listed in (b);
(e) those undertakings in which two or more undertakings as referred to in (a) to (d) jointly have the rights or powers listed in (b).

5. Where undertakings concerned by the concentration jointly have the rights or powers listed in paragraph 4(b), in calculating the aggregate turnover of the undertakings concerned for the purposes of this Regulation:

(a) no account shall be taken of the turnover resulting from the sale of products or the provision of services between the joint undertaking and each of the undertakings concerned or any other undertaking connected with any one of them, as set out in paragraph 4(b) to (e);
(b) account shall be taken of the turnover resulting from the sale of products and the provision of services between the joint undertaking and any third undertakings. This turnover shall be apportioned equally amongst the undertakings concerned.

Article 6 Examination of the notification and initiation of proceedings

1. The Commission shall examine the notification as soon as it is received.

(a) Where it concludes that the concentration notified does not fall within the scope of this Regulation, it shall record that finding by means of a decision.
(b) Where it finds that the concentration notified, although falling within the scope of this Regulation, does not raise serious doubts as to its compatibility with the common market, it shall decide not to oppose it and shall declare that it is compatible with the common market.

   A decision declaring a concentration compatible shall be deemed to cover restrictions directly related and necessary to the implementation of the concentration.
(c) Without prejudice to paragraph 2, where the Commission finds that the concentration notified falls within the scope of this Regulation and raises serious doubts as to its compatibility with the common market, it shall decide to initiate proceedings. Without prejudice to Article 9, such proceedings shall be closed by means of a decision as provided for in Article 8(1) to (4), unless the undertakings concerned have demonstrated to the satisfaction of the Commission that they have abandoned the concentration.

2. Where the Commission finds that, following modification by the undertakings concerned, a notified concentration no longer raises serious doubts within the meaning of paragraph 1(c), it shall declare the concentration compatible with the common market pursuant to paragraph 1(b).

The Commission may attach to its decision under paragraph 1(b) conditions and obligations intended to ensure that the undertakings concerned comply with the commitments they have entered into vis-à-vis the Commission with a view to rendering the concentration compatible with the common market.

3. The Commission may revoke the decision it took pursuant to paragraph 1(a) or (b) where:

(a) the decision is based on incorrect information for which one of the undertakings is responsible or where it has been obtained by deceit,

or

(b) the undertakings concerned commit a breach of an obligation attached to the decision.

4. In the cases referred to in paragraph 3, the Commission may take a decision under paragraph 1, without being bound by the time limits referred to in Article 10(1).

5. The Commission shall notify its decision to the undertakings concerned and the competent authorities of the Member States without delay.

Article 7 Suspension of concentrations

1. A concentration with a Community dimension as defined in Article 1, or which is to be examined by the Commission pursuant to Article 4(5), shall not be implemented either before its notification or until it has been declared compatible with the common market pursuant to a decision under Articles 6(1)(b), 8(1) or 8(2), or on the basis of a presumption according to Article 10(6).

2. Paragraph 1 shall not prevent the implementation of a public bid or of a series of transactions in securities including those convertible into other securities admitted to trading on a market such as a stock exchange, by which control within the meaning of Article 3 is acquired from various sellers, provided that:

(a) the concentration is notified to the Commission pursuant to Article 4 without delay; and

(b) the acquirer does not exercise the voting rights attached to the securities in question or does so only to maintain the full value of its investments based on a derogation granted by the Commission under paragraph 3.

3. The Commission may, on request, grant a derogation from the obligations imposed in paragraphs 1 or 2. The request to grant a derogation must be reasoned. In deciding on the request, the Commission shall take into account inter alia the effects of the suspension on one or more undertakings concerned by the concentration or on a third party and the threat to competition posed by the concentration. Such a derogation may be made subject to conditions and obligations in order to ensure conditions of effective competition. A derogation may be applied for and granted at any time, be it before notification or after the transaction.

4. The validity of any transaction carried out in contravention of paragraph 1 shall be dependent on a decision pursuant to Article 6(1)(b) or Article 8(1), (2) or (3) or on a presumption pursuant to Article 10(6).

This Article shall, however, have no effect on the validity of transactions in securities including those convertible into other securities admitted to trading on a market such as a stock exchange, unless the buyer and seller knew or ought to have known that the transaction was carried out in contravention of paragraph 1.

Article 8 Powers of decision of the Commission

1. Where the Commission finds that a notified concentration fulfils the criterion laid down in Article 2(2) and, in the cases referred to in Article 2(4), the criteria laid down in Article 81(3) of the Treaty, it shall issue a decision declaring the concentration compatible with the common market.

A decision declaring a concentration compatible shall be deemed to cover restrictions directly related and necessary to the implementation of the concentration.

2. Where the Commission finds that, following modification by the undertakings concerned, a notified concentration fulfils the criterion laid down in Article 2(2) and, in the cases referred to in Article 2(4), the criteria laid down in Article 81(3) of the Treaty, it shall issue a decision declaring the concentration compatible with the common market.

The Commission may attach to its decision conditions and obligations intended to ensure that the undertakings concerned comply with the commitments they have entered into vis-à-vis the Commission with a view to rendering the concentration compatible with the common market. A decision declaring a concentration compatible shall be deemed to cover restrictions directly related and necessary to the implementation of the concentration.

3. Where the Commission finds that a concentration fulfils the criterion defined in Article 2(3) or, in the cases referred to in Article 2(4), does not fulfil the criteria laid down in Article 81(3) of the Treaty, it shall issue a decision declaring that the concentration is incompatible with the common market.

4. Where the Commission finds that a concentration:

(a) has already been implemented and that concentration has been declared incompatible with the common market, or

(b) has been implemented in contravention of a condition attached to a decision taken under paragraph 2, which has found that, in the absence of the condition, the concentration would fulfil the criterion laid down in Article 2(3) or, in the cases referred to in Article 2(4), would not fulfil the criteria laid down in Article 81(3) of the Treaty, the Commission may:

- require the undertakings concerned to dissolve the concentration, in particular through the dissolution of the merger or the disposal of all the shares or assets acquired, so as to restore the situation prevailing prior to the implementation of the concentration; in circumstances where restoration of the situation prevailing before the implementation of the concentration is not possible through dissolution of the concentration, the Commission may take any other measure appropriate to achieve such restoration as far as possible,
- order any other appropriate measure to ensure that the undertakings concerned dissolve the concentration or take other restorative measures as required in its decision.

In cases falling within point (a) of the first subparagraph, the measures referred to in that subparagraph may be imposed either in a decision pursuant to paragraph 3 or by separate decision.

5. The Commission may take interim measures appropriate to restore or maintain conditions of effective competition where a concentration:

(a) has been implemented in contravention of Article 7, and a decision as to the compatibility of the concentration with the common market has not yet been taken;

(b) has been implemented in contravention of a condition attached to a decision under Article 6(1)(b) or paragraph 2 of this Article;

(c) has already been implemented and is declared incompatible with the common market.

6. The Commission may revoke the decision it has taken pursuant to paragraphs 1 or 2 where:

(a) the declaration of compatibility is based on incorrect information for which one of the undertakings is responsible or where it has been obtained by deceit; or

(b) the undertakings concerned commit a breach of an obligation attached to the decision.

7. The Commission may take a decision pursuant to paragraphs 1 to 3 without being bound by the time limits referred to in Article 10(3), in cases where:

(a) it finds that a concentration has been implemented

(i) in contravention of a condition attached to a decision under Article 6(1)(b), or

(ii) in contravention of a condition attached to a decision taken under paragraph 2 and in accordance with Article 10(2), which has found that, in the absence of the condition, the concentration would raise serious doubts as to its compatibility with the common market; or

(b) a decision has been revoked pursuant to paragraph 6.

8. The Commission shall notify its decision to the undertakings concerned and the competent authorities of the Member States without delay.

Article 9 Referral to the competent authorities of the Member States

1. The Commission may, by means of a decision notified without delay to the undertakings concerned and the competent authorities of the other Member States, refer a notified concentration to the competent authorities of the Member State concerned in the following circumstances.

2. Within 15 working days of the date of receipt of the copy of the notification, a Member State, on its own initiative or upon the invitation of the Commission, may inform the Commission, which shall inform the undertakings concerned, that:

(a) a concentration threatens to affect significantly competition in a market within that Member State, which presents all the characteristics of a distinct market, or

(b) a concentration affects competition in a market within that Member State, which presents all the characteristics of a distinct market and which does not constitute a substantial part of the common market.

3. If the Commission considers that, having regard to the market for the products or services in question and the geographical reference market within the meaning of paragraph 7, there is such a distinct market and that such a threat exists, either:

(a) it shall itself deal with the case in accordance with this Regulation; or

(b) it shall refer the whole or part of the case to the competent authorities of the Member State concerned with a view to the application of that State's national competition law.

If, however, the Commission considers that such a distinct market or threat does not exist, it shall adopt a decision to that effect which it shall address to the Member State concerned, and shall itself deal with the case in accordance with this Regulation.

In cases where a Member State informs the Commission pursuant to paragraph 2(b) that a concentration affects competition in a distinct market within its territory that does not form a substantial part of the common market, the Commission shall refer the whole or part of the case relating to the distinct market concerned, if it considers that such a distinct market is affected.

4. A decision to refer or not to refer pursuant to paragraph 3 shall be taken:

(a) as a general rule within the period provided for in Article 10(1), second subparagraph, where the Commission, pursuant to Article 6(1)(b), has not initiated proceedings; or

(b) within 65 working days at most of the notification of the concentration concerned where the Commission has initiated proceedings under Article 6(1)(c), without taking the preparatory steps in order to adopt the necessary measures under Article 8(2), (3) or (4) to maintain or restore effective competition on the market concerned.

5. If within the 65 working days referred to in paragraph 4(b) the Commission, despite a reminder from the Member State concerned, has not taken a decision on referral in accordance with paragraph 3 nor has taken the preparatory steps referred to in paragraph 4(b), it shall be deemed to have taken a decision to refer the case to the Member State concerned in accordance with paragraph 3(b).

6. The competent authority of the Member State concerned shall decide upon the case without undue delay.

Within 45 working days after the Commission's referral, the competent authority of the Member State concerned shall inform the undertakings concerned of the result of the preliminary competition assessment and what further action, if any, it proposes to take. The Member State concerned may exceptionally suspend this time limit where necessary information has not been provided to it by the undertakings concerned as provided for by its national competition law.

Where a notification is requested under national law, the period of 45 working days shall begin on the working day following that of the receipt of a complete notification by the competent authority of that Member State.

7. The geographical reference market shall consist of the area in which the undertakings concerned are involved in the supply and demand of products or services, in which the conditions of competition are sufficiently homogeneous and which can be distinguished from neighbouring areas because, in particular, conditions of competition are appreciably different in those areas. This assessment should take account in particular of the nature and characteristics of the products or services concerned, of the existence of entry barriers or of consumer preferences, of appreciable differences of the undertakings' market shares between the area concerned and neighbouring areas or of substantial price differences.

8. In applying the provisions of this Article, the Member State concerned may take only the measures strictly necessary to safeguard or restore effective competition on the market concerned.

9. In accordance with the relevant provisions of the Treaty, any Member State may appeal to the Court of Justice, and in particular request the application of Article 243 of the Treaty, for the purpose of applying its national competition law.

Article 10 Time limits for initiating proceedings and for decisions

1. Without prejudice to Article 6(4), the decisions referred to in Article 6(1) shall be taken within 25 working days at most. That period shall begin on the working day following that of the receipt of a notification or, if the information to be supplied with the notification is incomplete, on the working day following that of the receipt of the complete information. That period shall be increased to 35 working days where the Commission receives a request from a Member State in accordance with Article 9(2)or where, the undertakings concerned offer commitments pursuant to Article 6(2) with a view to rendering the concentration compatible with the common market.

2. Decisions pursuant to Article 8(1) or (2) concerning notified concentrations shall be taken as soon as it appears that the serious doubts referred to in Article 6(1)(c) have been removed, particularly as a result of modifications made by the undertakings concerned, and at the latest by the time limit laid down in paragraph 3.

3. Without prejudice to Article 8(7), decisions pursuant to Article 8(1) to (3) concerning notified concentrations shall be taken within not more than 90 working days of the date on which the proceedings are initiated. That period shall be increased to 105 working days where the undertakings concerned offer commitments pursuant to Article 8(2), second subparagraph, with a view to rendering the concentration compatible with the common market, unless these commitments have been offered less than 55 working days after the initiation of proceedings. The periods set by the first subparagraph shall likewise be extended if the notifying parties make a request to that effect not later than 15 working days after the initiation of proceedings pursuant to Article 6 (1)(c). The notifying parties may make only one such request. Likewise, at any time following the initiation of proceedings, the periods set by the first subparagraph may be extended by the Commission with the agreement of the notifying parties. The total duration of any extension or extensions effected pursuant to this subparagraph shall not exceed 20 working days.

4. The periods set by paragraphs 1 and 3 shall exceptionally be suspended where, owing to circumstances for which one of the undertakings involved in the concentration is responsible, the Commission has had to request information by decision pursuant to Article 11 or to order an inspection by decision pursuant to Article 13.

The first subparagraph shall also apply to the period referred to in Article 9(4)(b).

5. Where the Court of Justice gives a judgment which annuls the whole or part of a Commission decision which is subject to a time limit set by this Article, the concentration shall be re-examined by the Commission with a view to adopting a decision pursuant to Article 6(1).

The concentration shall be re-examined in the light of current market conditions.

The notifying parties shall submit a new notification or supplement the original notification, without delay, where the original notification becomes incomplete by reason of intervening changes in market conditions or in the information provided. Where there are no such changes, the parties shall certify this fact without delay.

The periods laid down in paragraph 1 shall start on the working day following that of the receipt of complete information in a new notification, a supplemented notification, or a certification within the meaning of the third subparagraph.

The second and third subparagraphs shall also apply in the cases referred to in Article 6(4) and Article 8(7).

6. Where the Commission has not taken a decision in accordance with Article 6(1)(b), (c), 8(1), (2) or (3) within the time limits set in paragraphs 1 and 3 respectively, the concentration shall be deemed to have been declared compatible with the common market, without prejudice to Article 9.

Article 11 Requests for information

1. In order to carry out the duties assigned to it by this Regulation, the Commission may, by simple request or by decision, require the persons referred to in Article 3(1)(b), as well as undertakings and associations of undertakings, to provide all necessary information.

2. When sending a simple request for information to a person, an undertaking or an association of undertakings, the Commission shall state the legal basis and the purpose of the request, specify

what information is required and fix the time limit within which the information is to be provided, as well as the penalties provided for in Article 14 for supplying incorrect or misleading information.

3. Where the Commission requires a person, an undertaking or an association of undertakings to supply information by decision, it shall state the legal basis and the purpose of the request, specify what information is required and fix the time limit within which it is to be provided. It shall also indicate the penalties provided for in Article 14 and indicate or impose the penalties provided for in Article 15. It shall further indicate the right to have the decision reviewed by the Court of Justice.

4. The owners of the undertakings or their representatives and, in the case of legal persons, companies or firms, or associations having no legal personality, the persons authorised to represent them by law or by their constitution, shall supply the information requested on behalf of the undertaking concerned. Persons duly authorised to act may supply the information on behalf of their clients. The latter shall remain fully responsible if the information supplied is incomplete, incorrect or misleading.

5. The Commission shall without delay forward a copy of any decision taken pursuant to paragraph 3 to the competent authorities of the Member State in whose territory the residence of the person or the seat of the undertaking or association of undertakings is situated, and to the competent authority of the Member State whose territory is affected. At the specific request of the competent authority of a Member State, the Commission shall also forward to that authority copies of simple requests for information relating to a notified concentration.

6. At the request of the Commission, the governments and competent authorities of the Member States shall provide the Commission with all necessary information to carry out the duties assigned to it by this Regulation.

7. In order to carry out the duties assigned to it by this Regulation, the Commission may interview any natural or legal person who consents to be interviewed for the purpose of collecting information relating to the subject matter of an investigation. At the beginning of the interview, which may be conducted by telephone or other electronic means, the Commission shall state the legal basis and the purpose of the interview.

Where an interview is not conducted on the premises of the Commission or by telephone or other electronic means, the Commission shall inform in advance the competent authority of the Member State in whose territory the interview takes place. If the competent authority of that Member State so requests, officials of that authority may assist the officials and other persons authorised by the Commission to conduct the interview.

Article 12 Inspections by the authorities of the Member States

1. At the request of the Commission, the competent authorities of the Member States shall undertake the inspections which the Commission considers to be necessary under Article 13(1), or which it has ordered by decision pursuant to Article 13(4). The officials of the competent authorities of the Member States who are responsible for conducting these inspections as well as those authorised or appointed by them shall exercise their powers in accordance with their national law.

2. If so requested by the Commission or by the competent authority of the Member State within whose territory the inspection is to be conducted, officials and other accompanying persons authorised by the Commission may assist the officials of the authority concerned.

Article 13 The Commission's powers of inspection

1. In order to carry out the duties assigned to it by this Regulation, the Commission may conduct all necessary inspections of undertakings and associations of undertakings.

2. The officials and other accompanying persons authorised by the Commission to conduct an inspection shall have the power:

(a) to enter any premises, land and means of transport of undertakings and associations of undertakings;

(b) to examine the books and other records related to the business, irrespective of the medium on which they are stored;

(c) to take or obtain in any form copies of or extracts from such books or records;
(d) to seal any business premises and books or records for the period and to the extent necessary for the inspection;
(e) to ask any representative or member of staff of the undertaking or association of undertakings for explanations on facts or documents relating to the subject matter and purpose of the inspection and to record the answers.

3. Officials and other accompanying persons authorised by the Commission to conduct an inspection shall exercise their powers upon production of a written authorisation specifying the subject matter and purpose of the inspection and the penalties provided for in Article 14, in the production of the required books or other records related to the business which is incomplete or where answers to questions asked under paragraph 2 of this Article are incorrect or misleading. In good time before the inspection, the Commission shall give notice of the inspection to the competent authority of the Member State in whose territory the inspection is to be conducted.

4. Undertakings and associations of undertakings are required to submit to inspections ordered by decision of the Commission. The decision shall specify the subject matter and purpose of the inspection, appoint the date on which it is to begin and indicate the penalties provided for in Articles 14 and 15 and the right to have the decision reviewed by the Court of Justice. The Commission shall take such decisions after consulting the competent authority of the Member State in whose territory the inspection is to be conducted.

5. Officials of, and those authorised or appointed by, the competent authority of the Member State in whose territory the inspection is to be conducted shall, at the request of that authority or of the Commission, actively assist the officials and other accompanying persons authorised by the Commission. To this end, they shall enjoy the powers specified in paragraph 2.

6. Where the officials and other accompanying persons authorised by the Commission find that an undertaking opposes an inspection, including the sealing of business premises, books or records, ordered pursuant to this Article, the Member State concerned shall afford them the necessary assistance, requesting where appropriate the assistance of the police or of an equivalent enforcement authority, so as to enable them to conduct their inspection.

7. If the assistance provided for in paragraph 6 requires authorisation from a judicial authority according to national rules, such authorisation shall be applied for. Such authorisation may also be applied for as a precautionary measure.

8. Where authorisation as referred to in paragraph 7 is applied for, the national judicial authority shall ensure that the Commission decision is authentic and that the coercive measures envisaged are neither arbitrary nor excessive having regard to the subject matter of the inspection. In its control of proportionality of the coercive measures, the national judicial authority may ask the Commission, directly or through the competent authority of that Member State, for detailed explanations relating to the subject matter of the inspection. However, the national judicial authority may not call into question the necessity for the inspection nor demand that it be provided with the information in the Commission's file. The lawfulness of the Commission's decision shall be subject to review only by the Court of Justice.

Article 14 Fines

1. The Commission may by decision impose on the persons referred to in Article 3(1)b, undertakings or associations of undertakings, fines not exceeding 1% of the aggregate turnover of the undertaking or association of undertakings concerned within the meaning of Article 5 where, intentionally or negligently:

(a) they supply incorrect or misleading information in a submission, certification, notification or supplement thereto, pursuant to Article 4, Article 10(5) or Article 22(3);
(b) they supply incorrect or misleading information in response to a request made pursuant to Article 11(2);
(c) in response to a request made by decision adopted pursuant to Article 11(3), they supply incorrect, incomplete or misleading information or do not supply information within the required time limit;

(d) they produce the required books or other records related to the business in incomplete form during inspections under Article 13, or refuse to submit to an inspection ordered by decision taken pursuant to Article 13(4);

(e) in response to a question asked in accordance with Article 13(2)(e),
- they give an incorrect or misleading answer,
- they fail to rectify within a time limit set by the Commission an incorrect, incomplete or misleading answer given by a member of staff, or
- they fail or refuse to provide a complete answer on facts relating to the subject matter and purpose of an inspection ordered by a decision adopted pursuant to Article 13(4);

(f) seals affixed by officials or other accompanying persons authorised by the Commission in accordance with Article 13(2)(d) have been broken.

2. The Commission may by decision impose fines not exceeding 10% of the aggregate turnover of the undertaking concerned within the meaning of Article 5 on the persons referred to in Article 3(1)b or the undertakings concerned where, either intentionally or negligently, they:

(a) fail to notify a concentration in accordance with Articles 4 or 22(3) prior to its implementation, unless they are expressly authorised to do so by Article 7(2) or by a decision taken pursuant to Article 7(3);

(b) implement a concentration in breach of Article 7;

(c) implement a concentration declared incompatible with the common market by decision pursuant to Article 8(3) or do not comply with any measure ordered by decision pursuant to Article 8(4) or (5);

(d) fail to comply with a condition or an obligation imposed by decision pursuant to Articles 6(1)(b), Article 7(3) or Article 8(2), second subparagraph.

3. In fixing the amount of the fine, regard shall be had to the nature, gravity and duration of the infringement.

4. Decisions taken pursuant to paragraphs 1, 2 and 3 shall not be of a criminal law nature.

Article 15 Periodic penalty payments

1. The Commission may by decision impose on the persons referred to in Article 3(1)b, undertakings or associations of undertakings, periodic penalty payments not exceeding 5% of the average daily aggregate turnover of the undertaking or association of undertakings concerned within the meaning of Article 5 for each working day of delay, calculated from the date set in the decision, in order to compel them:

(a) to supply complete and correct information which it has requested by decision taken pursuant to Article 11(3);

(b) to submit to an inspection which it has ordered by decision taken pursuant to Article 13(4);

(c) to comply with an obligation imposed by decision pursuant to Article 6(1)(b), Article 7 (3) or Article 8(2), second subparagraph; or;

(d) to comply with any measures ordered by decision pursuant to Article 8(4) or (5).

2. Where the persons referred to in Article 3(1)(b), undertakings or associations of undertakings have satisfied the obligation which the periodic penalty payment was intended to enforce, the Commission may fix the definitive amount of the periodic penalty payments at a figure lower than that which would arise under the original decision.

Article 16 Review by the Court of Justice

The Court of Justice shall have unlimited jurisdiction within the meaning of Article 229 of the Treaty to review decisions whereby the Commission has fixed a fine or periodic penalty payments; it may cancel, reduce or increase the fine or periodic penalty payment imposed.

Article 17 Professional secrecy

1. Information acquired as a result of the application of this Regulation shall be used only for the purposes of the relevant request, investigation or hearing.

2. Without prejudice to Article 4(3), Articles 18 and 20, the Commission and the competent authorities of the Member States, their officials and other servants and other persons working under the

supervision of these authorities as well as officials and civil servants of other authorities of the Member States shall not disclose information they have acquired through the application of this Regulation of the kind covered by the obligation of professional secrecy.

3. Paragraphs 1 and 2 shall not prevent publication of general information or of surveys which do not contain information relating to particular undertakings or associations of undertakings.

Article 18 Hearing of the parties and of third persons

1. Before taking any decision provided for in Article 6(3), Article 7(3), Article 8(2) to (6), and Articles 14 and 15, the Commission shall give the persons, undertakings and associations of undertakings concerned the opportunity, at every stage of the procedure up to the consultation of the Advisory Committee, of making known their views on the objections against them.

2. By way of derogation from paragraph 1, a decision pursuant to Articles 7(3) and 8(5) may be taken provisionally, without the persons, undertakings or associations of undertakings concerned being given the opportunity to make known their views beforehand, provided that the Commission gives them that opportunity as soon as possible after having taken its decision.

3. The Commission shall base its decision only on objections on which the parties have been able to submit their observations. The rights of the defence shall be fully respected in the proceedings. Access to the file shall be open at least to the parties directly involved, subject to the legitimate interest of undertakings in the protection of their business secrets.

4. In so far as the Commission or the competent authorities of the Member States deem it necessary, they may also hear other natural or legal persons. Natural or legal persons showing a sufficient interest and especially members of the administrative or management bodies of the undertakings concerned or the recognised representatives of their employees shall be entitled, upon application, to be heard.

Article 19 Liaison with the authorities of the Member States

1. The Commission shall transmit to the competent authorities of the Member States copies of notifications within three working days and, as soon as possible, copies of the most important documents lodged with or issued by the Commission pursuant to this Regulation. Such documents shall include commitments offered by the undertakings concerned vis-à-vis the Commission with a view to rendering the concentration compatible with the common market pursuant to Article 6(2) or Article 8(2), second subparagraph.

2. The Commission shall carry out the procedures set out in this Regulation in close and constant liaison with the competent authorities of the Member States, which may express their views upon those procedures. For the purposes of Article 9 it shall obtain information from the competent authority of the Member State as referred to in paragraph 2 of that Article and give it the opportunity to make known its views at every stage of the procedure up to the adoption of a decision pursuant to paragraph 3 of that Article; to that end it shall give it access to the file.

3. An Advisory Committee on concentrations shall be consulted before any decision is taken pursuant to Article 8(1) to (6), Articles 14 or 15 with the exception of provisional decisions taken in accordance with Article 18(2).

4. The Advisory Committee shall consist of representatives of the competent authorities of the Member States. Each Member State shall appoint one or two representatives; if unable to attend, they may be replaced by other representatives. At least one of the representatives of a Member State shall be competent in matters of restrictive practices and dominant positions.

5. Consultation shall take place at a joint meeting convened at the invitation of and chaired by the Commission. A summary of the case, together with an indication of the most important documents and a preliminary draft of the decision to be taken for each case considered, shall be sent with the invitation. The meeting shall take place not less than 10 working days after the invitation has been sent. The Commission may in exceptional cases shorten that period as appropriate in order to avoid serious harm to one or more of the undertakings concerned by a concentration.

6. The Advisory Committee shall deliver an opinion on the Commission's draft decision, if necessary by taking a vote. The Advisory Committee may deliver an opinion even if some members

are absent and unrepresented. The opinion shall be delivered in writing and appended to the draft decision. The Commission shall take the utmost account of the opinion delivered by the Committee. It shall inform the Committee of the manner in which its opinion has been taken into account.

7. The Commission shall communicate the opinion of the Advisory Committee, together with the decision, to the addressees of the decision. It shall make the opinion public together with the decision, having regard to the legitimate interest of undertakings in the protection of their business secrets.

Article 20 Publication of decisions

1. The Commission shall publish the decisions which it takes pursuant to Article 8(1) to (6), Articles 14 and 15 with the exception of provisional decisions taken in accordance with Article 18(2) together with the opinion of the Advisory Committee in the Official Journal of the European Union.

2. The publication shall state the names of the parties and the main content of the decision; it shall have regard to the legitimate interest of undertakings in the protection of their business secrets.

Article 21 Application of the Regulation and jurisdiction

1. This Regulation alone shall apply to concentrations as defined in Article 3, and Council Regulations (EC) No 1/2003,[8] (EEC) No 1017/68,[9] (EEC) No 4056/86[10] and (EEC) No 3975/87[11] shall not apply, except in relation to joint ventures that do not have a Community dimension and which have as their object or effect the coordination of the competitive behaviour of undertakings that remain independent.

2. Subject to review by the Court of Justice, the Commission shall have sole jurisdiction to take the decisions provided for in this Regulation.

3. No Member State shall apply its national legislation on competition to any concentration that has a Community dimension.

The first subparagraph shall be without prejudice to any Member State's power to carry out any enquiries necessary for the application of Articles 4(4), 9(2) or after referral, pursuant to Article 9(3), first subparagraph, indent (b), or Article 9(5), to take the measures strictly necessary for the application of Article 9(8).

4. Notwithstanding paragraphs 2 and 3, Member States may take appropriate measures to protect legitimate interests other than those taken into consideration by this Regulation and compatible with the general principles and other provisions of Community law. Public security, plurality of the media and prudential rules shall be regarded as legitimate interests within the meaning of the first subparagraph.

Any other public interest must be communicated to the Commission by the Member State concerned and shall be recognised by the Commission after an assessment of its compatibility with the general principles and other provisions of Community law before the measures referred to above may be taken. The Commission shall inform the Member State concerned of its decision within 25 working days of that communication.

Article 22 Referral to the Commission

1. One or more Member States may request the Commission to examine any concentration as defined in Article 3 that does not have a Community dimension within the meaning of Article 1 but affects trade between Member States and threatens to significantly affect competition within the territory of the Member State or States making the request.

Such a request shall be made at most within 15 working days of the date on which the concentration was notified, or if no notification is required, otherwise made known to the Member State concerned.

2. The Commission shall inform the competent authorities of the Member States and the undertakings concerned of any request received pursuant to paragraph 1 without delay. Any other

[8] OJ L 1, 4. 1. 2003, p. 1.
[9] OJ L 175, 23. 7. 1968, p. 1. Regulation as last amended by Regulation (EC) No 1/2003 (OJ L 1, 4.1.2003, p. 1).
[10] OJ L 378, 31. 12. 1986, p. 4. Regulation as last amended by Regulation (EC) No 1/2003.
[11] OJ L 374. 31. 12. 1987, p. 1. Regulation as last amended by Regulation (EC) No 1/2003.

Member State shall have the right to join the initial request within a period of 15 working days of being informed by the Commission of the initial request.

All national time limits relating to the concentration shall be suspended until, in accordance with the procedure set out in this Article, it has been decided where the concentration shall be examined. As soon as a Member State has informed the Commission and the undertakings concerned that it does not wish to join the request, the suspension of its national time limits shall end.

3. The Commission may, at the latest 10 working days after the expiry of the period set in paragraph 2, decide to examine, the concentration where it considers that it affects trade between Member States and threatens to significantly affect competition within the territory of the Member State or States making the request. If the Commission does not take a decision within this period, it shall be deemed to have adopted a decision to examine the concentration in accordance with the request.

The Commission shall inform all Member States and the undertakings concerned of its decision. It may request the submission of a notification pursuant to Article 4.

The Member State or States having made the request shall no longer apply their national legislation on competition to the concentration.

4. Article 2, Article 4(2) to (3), Articles 5, 6, and 8 to 21 shall apply where the Commission examines a concentration pursuant to paragraph 3. Article 7 shall apply to the extent that the concentration has not been implemented on the date on which the Commission informs the undertakings concerned that a request has been made.

Regulation (EEC) No 4064/89	This Regulation
Article 1(1), (2) and (3)	Article 1(1), (2) and (3)
Article 1(4)	Article 1(4)
Article 1(5)	Article 1(5)
Article 2(1)	Article 2(1)
—	Article 2(2)
Article 2(2)	Article 2(3)
Article 2(3)	Article 2(4)
Article 2(4)	Article 2(5)
Article 3(1)	Article 3(1)
Article 3(1)	Article 3(4)
Article 3(4)	Article 3(3)
—	Article 3(4)
Article 3(5)	Article 3(5)
Article 4(1) first sentence	Article 4(1) first subparagraph
Article 4(1) second sentence	—
—	Article 4(1) second and third subparagraphs
Article 4(2) and (3)	Article 4(2) and (3)
—	Article 4(4) to (6)
Article 5(1) to (3)	Article 5(1) to (3)
Article 5(4), introductory words	Article 5(4), introductory words
Article 5(4) point (a)	Article 5(4) point (a)
Article 5(4) point (b), introductory words	Article 5(4) point (b), introductory words
Article 5(4) point (b), first indent	Article 5(4) point (b)(i)
Article 5(4) point (b), second indent	Article 5(4) point (b)(ii)
Article 5(4) point (b), third indent	Article 5(4) point (b)(iii)
Article 5(4) point (b), fourth indent	Article 5(4) point (b)(iv)
Article 5(4) points (c), (d) and (e)	Article 5(4) points (c), (d) and (e)

(cont.)

Regulation (EEC) No 4064/89	This Regulation
Article 5(5)	Article 5(5)
Article 6(1), introductory words	Article 6(1), introductory words
Article 6(1) points (a) and (b)	Article 6(1) points (a) and (b)
Article 6(1) point (c)	Article 6(1) point (c), first sentence
Article 6(2) to (5)	Article 6(2) to (5)
Article 7(1)	Article 7(1)
Article 7(3)	Article 7(2)
Article 7(4)	Article 7(3)
Article 7(5)	Article 7(4)
Article 8(1)	Article 6(1) point (c), second sentence
Article 8(2)	Article 8(1) and (2)
Article 8(3)	Article 8(3)
Article 8(4)	Article 8(4)
—	Article 8(5)
Article 8(5)	Article 8(6)
Article 8(6)	Article 8(7)
—	Article 8(8)
Article 9(1) to (9)	Article 9(1) to (9)
Article 9(10)	—
Article 10(1) and (2)	Article 10(1) and (2)
Article 10(3)	Article 10(3) first subparagraph, first sentence
—	Article 10(3) first subparagraph, second sentence
—	Article 10(3) second subparagraph
Article 10(4)	Article 10(4) first subparagraph
—	Article 10(4), second subparagraph
Article 10(5)	Article 10(5), first and fourth subparagraphs
—	Article 10(5), second, third and fifth subparagraphs
Article 10(6)	Article 10(6)
Article 11(1)	Article 11(1)
Article 11(2)	—
Article 11(3)	Article 11(2)
Article 11(4)	Article 11(4) first sentence
—	Article 11(4) second and third sentences
Article 11(5) first sentence	—
Article 11(5) second sentence	Article 11(3)
Article 11(6)	Article 11(5)
—	Article 11(6) and (7)
Article 12	Article 12
Article 13(1) first subparagraph	Article 13(1)
Article 13(1) second subparagraph, intro words	Article 13(2) introductory words
Article 13(1) second subparagraph, point (a)	Article 13(2) point (b)
Article 13(1) second subparagraph, point (b)	Article 13(2) point (c)
Article 13(1) second subparagraph, point (c)	Article 13(2) point (e)
Article 13(1) second subparagraph, point (d)	Article 13(2) point (a)
—	Article 13(2) point (d)
Article 13(2)	Article 13(3)
Article 13(3)	Article 13(4) first and second sentences
Article 13(4)	Article 13(4) third sentence
Article 13(5)	Article 13(5), first sentence
—	Article 13(5), second sentence

Regulation (EEC) No 4064/89	This Regulation
Article 13(6) first sentence	Article 13(6)
Article 13(6) second sentence	—
—	Article 13(7) and (8)
Article 14(1) introductory words	Article 14(1) introductory words
Article 14(1) point (a)	Article 14(2) point (a)
Article 14(1) point (b)	Article 14(1) point (a)
Article 14(1) point (c)	Article 14(1) points (b) and (c)
Article 14(1) point (d)	Article 14(1) point (d)
—	Article 14(1) points (e) and (f)
Article 14(2) introductory words	Article 14(2) introductory words
Article 14(2) point (a)	Article 14(2) point (d)
Article 14(2) points (b) and (c)	Article 14(2) points (b) and (c)
Article 14(3)	Article 14(3)
Article 14(4)	Article 14(4)
Article 15(1) introductory words	Article 15(1) introductory words
Article 15(1) points (a) and (b)	Article 15(1) points (a) and (b)
Article 15(2) introductory words	Article 15(1) introductory words
Article 15(2) point (a)	Article 15(1) point (c)
Article 15(2) point (b)	Article 15(1) point (d)
Article 15(3)	Article 15(2)
Articles 16 to 20	Articles 16 to 20
Article 21(1)	Article 21(2)
Article 21(2)	Article 21(3)
Article 21(3)	Article 21(4)
Article 22(1)	Article 21(1)
Article 22(3)	—
—	Article 22(1) to (3)
Article 22(4)	Article 22(4)
Article 22(5)	—
—	Article 22(5)
Article 23	Article 23(1)
—	Article 23(2)
Article 24	Article 24
—	Article 25
Article 25(1)	Article 26(1), first subparagraph

Where a notification pursuant to Article 4 is not required, the period set in Article 10(1) within which proceedings may be initiated shall begin on the working day following that on which the Commission informs the undertakings concerned that it has decided to examine the concentration pursuant to paragraph 3.

5. The Commission may inform one or several Member States that it considers a concentration fulfils the criteria in paragraph 1. In such cases, the Commission may invite that Member State or those Member States to make a request pursuant to paragraph 1.

Article 23 Implementing provisions

1. The Commission shall have the power to lay down in accordance with the procedure referred to in paragraph 2:
   - (a) implementing provisions concerning the form, content and other details of notifications and submissions pursuant to Article 4;
   - (b) implementing provisions concerning time limits pursuant to Article 4(4), (5) Articles 7, 9, 10 and 22;
   - (c) the procedure and time limits for the submission and implementation of commitments pursuant to Article 6(2) and Article 8(2);

(d) implementing provisions concerning hearings pursuant to Article 18.

2. The Commission shall be assisted by an Advisory Committee, composed of representatives of the Member States.

(a) Before publishing draft implementing provisions and before adopting such provisions, the Commission shall consult the Advisory Committee.

(b) Consultation shall take place at a meeting convened at the invitation of and chaired by the Commission. A draft of the implementing provisions to be taken shall be sent with the invitation. The meeting shall take place not less than 10 working days after the invitation has been sent.

(c) The Advisory Committee shall deliver an opinion on the draft implementing provisions, if necessary by taking a vote. The Commission shall take the utmost account of the opinion delivered by the Committee.

Article 24 Relations with third countries

1. The Member States shall inform the Commission of any general difficulties encountered by their undertakings with concentrations as defined in Article 3 in a third country.

2. Initially not more than one year after the entry into force of this Regulation and, thereafter periodically, the Commission shall draw up a report examining the treatment accorded to undertakings having their seat or their principal fields of activity in the Community, in the terms referred to in paragraphs 3 and 4, as regards concentrations in third countries. The Commission shall submit those reports to the Council, together with any recommendations.

3. Whenever it appears to the Commission, either on the basis of the reports referred to in paragraph 2 or on the basis of other information, that a third country does not grant undertakings having their seat or their principal fields of activity in the Community, treatment comparable to that granted by the Community to undertakings from that country, the Commission may submit proposals to the Council for an appropriate mandate for negotiation with a view to obtaining comparable treatment for undertakings having their seat or their principal fields of activity in the Community.

4. Measures taken under this Article shall comply with the obligations of the Community or of the Member States, without prejudice to Article 307 of the Treaty, under international agreements, whether bilateral or multilateral.

Article 25 Repeal

1. Without prejudice to Article 26(2), Regulations (EEC) No 4064/89 and (EC) No 1310/97 shall be repealed with effect from 1 May 2004.

2. References to the repealed Regulations shall be construed as references to this Regulation and shall be read in accordance with the correlation table in the Annex.

Article 26 Entry into force and transitional provisions

1. This Regulation shall enter into force on the 20th day following that of its publication in the Official Journal of the European Union.

It shall apply from 1 May 2004.

2. Regulation (EEC) No 4064/89 shall continue to apply to any concentration which was the subject of an agreement or announcement or where control was acquired within the meaning of Article 4(1) of that Regulation before the date of application of this Regulation, subject, in particular, to the provisions governing applicability set out in Article 25(2) and (3) of Regulation (EEC) No 4064/89 and Article 2 of Regulation (EEC) No 1310/97.

3. As regards concentrations to which this Regulation applies by virtue of accession, the date of accession shall be substituted for the date of application of this Regulation.

This Regulation shall be binding in its entirety and directly applicable in all Member States.

Done at Brussels, 20 January 2004.

For the Council

The President

C. McCREEVY

Commission Regulation (EC) No 773/2004 of 7 April 2004 relating to the conduct of proceedings by the Commission pursuant to Articles 81 and 82 of the EC Treaty*

[OJ 2004 L123/18]

THE COMMISSION OF THE EUROPEAN COMMUNITIES,

Having regard to the Treaty establishing the European Community,

Having regard to the Agreement on the European Economic Area,

Having regard to Council Regulation (EC) No 1/2003 of 16 December 2002 on the implementation of the rules on competition laid down in Articles 81 and 82 of the Treaty,[1] and in particular Article 33 thereof,

After consulting the Advisory Committee on Restrictive Practices and Dominant Positions, Whereas:

(1) Regulation (EC) No 1/2003 empowers the Commission to regulate certain aspects of proceedings for the application of Articles 81 and 82 of the Treaty. It is necessary to lay down rules concerning the initiation of proceedings by the Commission as well as the handling of complaints and the hearing of the parties concerned.

(2) According to Regulation (EC) No 1/2003, national courts are under an obligation to avoid taking decisions which could run counter to decisions envisaged by the Commission in the same case. According to Article 11(6) of that Regulation, national competition authorities are relieved from their competence once the Commission has initiated proceedings for the adoption of a decision under Chapter III of Regulation (EC) No 1/2003. In this context, it is important that courts and competition authorities of the Member States are aware of the initiation of proceedings by the Commission. The Commission should therefore be able to make public its decisions to initiate proceedings.

(3) Before taking oral statements from natural or legal persons who consent to be interviewed, the Commission should inform those persons of the legal basis of the interview and its voluntary nature. The persons interviewed should also be informed of the purpose of the interview and of any record which may be made. In order to enhance the accuracy of the statements, the persons interviewed should also be given an opportunity to correct the statements recorded. Where information gathered from oral statements is exchanged pursuant to Article 12 of Regulation (EC) No 1/2003, that information should only be used in evidence to impose sanctions on natural persons where the conditions set out in that Article are fulfilled.

(4) Pursuant to Article 23(1)(d) of Regulation (EC) No 1/2003 fines may be imposed on undertakings and associations of undertakings where they fail to rectify within the time limit fixed by the Commission an incorrect, incomplete or misleading answer given by a member of their staff to questions in the course of inspections. It is therefore necessary to provide the undertaking concerned with a record of any explanations given and to establish a procedure enabling it to add any rectification, amendment or supplement to the explanations given by the member of staff who is not or was not authorised to provide explanations on behalf of the undertaking. The explanations given by a member of staff should remain in the Commission file as recorded during the inspection.

(5) Complaints are an essential source of information for detecting infringements of competition rules. It is important to define clear and efficient procedures for handling complaints lodged with the Commission.

(6) In order to be admissible for the purposes of Article 7 of Regulation (EC) No 1/2003, a complaint must contain certain specified information.

(7) In order to assist complainants in submitting the necessary facts to the Commission, a form should be drawn up. The submission of the information listed in that form should be a condition for a complaint to be treated as a complaint as referred to in Article 7 of Regulation (EC) No 1/2003.

* **Editor's Note:** As amended by Regulations 1792/2006 (OJ 2006 L362/1) and 622/2008 (OJ 2008 L171/3).

[1] OJ L 1, 4.1.2003, p. 1. Regulation as amended by Regulation (EC) No 411/2004 (OJ L 68, 6.3.2004, p. 1) and Regulation 1792/2006 OJ 2006 L362/1.

(8) Natural or legal persons having chosen to lodge a complaint should be given the possibility to be associated closely with the proceedings initiated by the Commission with a view to finding an infringement. However, they should not have access to business secrets or other confidential information belonging to other parties involved in the proceedings.

(9) Complainants should be granted the opportunity of expressing their views if the Commission considers that there are insufficient grounds for acting on the complaint. Where the Commission rejects a complaint on the grounds that a competition authority of a Member State is dealing with it or has already done so, it should inform the complainant of the identity of that authority.

(10) In order to respect the rights of defence of undertakings, the Commission should give the parties concerned the right to be heard before it takes a decision.

(11) Provision should also be made for the hearing of persons who have not submitted a complaint as referred to in Article 7 of Regulation (EC) No 1/2003 and who are not parties to whom a statement of objections has been addressed but who can nevertheless show a sufficient interest. Consumer associations that apply to be heard should generally be regarded as having a sufficient interest, where the proceedings concern products or services used by the end-consumer or products or services that constitute a direct input into such products or services. Where it considers this to be useful for the proceedings, the Commission should also be able to invite other persons to express their views in writing and to attend the oral hearing of the parties to whom a statement of objections has been addressed. Where appropriate, it should also be able to invite such persons to express their views at that oral hearing.

(12) To improve the effectiveness of oral hearings, the Hearing Officer should have the power to allow the parties concerned, complainants, other persons invited to the hearing, the Commission services and the authorities of the Member States to ask questions during the hearing.

(13) When granting access to the file, the Commission should ensure the protection of business secrets and other confidential information. The category of 'other confidential information' includes information other than business secrets, which may be considered as confidential, insofar as its disclosure would significantly harm an undertaking or person. The Commission should be able to request undertakings or associations of undertakings that submit or have submitted documents or statements to identify confidential information.

(14) Where business secrets or other confidential information are necessary to prove an infringement, the Commission should assess for each individual document whether the need to disclose is greater than the harm which might result from disclosure.

(15) In the interest of legal certainty, a minimum time-limit for the various submissions provided for in this Regulation should be laid down.

(16) This Regulation replaces Commission Regulation (EC) No 2842/98 of 22 December 1998 on the hearing of parties in certain proceedings under Articles 85 and 86 of the EC Treaty,[2] which should therefore be repealed.

(17) This Regulation aligns the procedural rules in the transport sector with the general rules of procedure in all sectors. Commission Regulation (EC) No 2843/98 of 22 December 1998 on the form, content and other details of applications and notifications provided for in Council Regulations (EEC) No 1017/68, (EEC) No 4056/86 and (EEC) No 3975/87 applying the rules on competition to the transport sector[3] should therefore be repealed.

(18) Regulation (EC) No 1/2003 abolishes the notification and authorisation system. Commission Regulation (EC) No 3385/94 of 21 December 1994 on the form, content and other details of applications and notifications provided for in Council Regulation No 17[4] should therefore be repealed,

HAS ADOPTED THIS REGULATION:

[2] OJ L 354, 30.12.1998, p. 18.
[3] OJ L 354, 30.12.1998, p. 22.
[4] OJ L 354, 31.12.1994, p. 28.

Chapter I Scope

Article 1 Subject-matter and scope

This regulation applies to proceedings conducted by the Commission for the application of Articles 81 and 82 of the Treaty.

Chapter II Initiation of proceedings

Article 2 Initiation of proceedings

1. The Commission may decide to initiate proceedings with a view to adopting a decision pursuant to Chapter III of Regulation (EC) No 1/2003 at any point in time, but no later than the date on which it issues a preliminary assessment as referred to in Article 9(1) of that Regulation, a statement of objections or a request for the parties to express their interest in engaging in settlement discussions, or the date on which a notice pursuant to Article 27(4) of that Regulation is published, whichever is the earlier.

2. The Commission may make public the initiation of proceedings, in any appropriate way. Before doing so, it shall inform the parties concerned.

3. The Commission may exercise its powers of investigation pursuant to Chapter V of Regulation (EC) No 1/2003 before initiating proceedings.

4. The Commission may reject a complaint pursuant to Article 7 of Regulation (EC) No 1/2003 without initiating proceedings.

Chapter III Investigations by the Commission

Article 3 Power to take statements

1. Where the Commission interviews a person with his consent in accordance with Article 19 of Regulation (EC) No 1/2003, it shall, at the beginning of the interview, state the legal basis and the purpose of the interview, and recall its voluntary nature. It shall also inform the person interviewed of its intention to make a record of the interview.

2. The interview may be conducted by any means including by telephone or electronic means.

3. The Commission may record the statements made by the persons interviewed in any form.

A copy of any recording shall be made available to the person interviewed for approval. Where necessary, the Commission shall set a time-limit within which the person interviewed may communicate to it any correction to be made to the statement.

Article 4 Oral questions during inspections

1. When, pursuant to Article 20(2)(e) of Regulation (EC) No 1/2003, officials or other accompanying persons authorised by the Commission ask representatives or members of staff of an undertaking or of an association of undertakings for explanations, the explanations given may be recorded in any form.

2. A copy of any recording made pursuant to paragraph 1 shall be made available to the undertaking or association of undertakings concerned after the inspection.

3. In cases where a member of staff of an undertaking or of an association of undertakings who is not or was not authorised by the undertaking or by the association of undertakings to provide explanations on behalf of the undertaking or association of undertakings has been asked for explanations, the Commission shall set a time-limit within which the undertaking or the association of undertakings may communicate to the Commission any rectification, amendment or supplement to the explanations given by such member of staff. The rectification, amendment or supplement shall be added to the explanations as recorded pursuant to paragraph 1.

Chapter IV Handling of complaints

Article 5 Admissibility of complaints

1. Natural and legal persons shall show a legitimate interest in order to be entitled to lodge a complaint for the purposes of Article 7 of Regulation (EC) No 1/2003.

Such complaints shall contain the information required by Form C, as set out in the Annex. The Commission may dispense with this obligation as regards part of the information, including documents, required by Form C.

2. Three paper copies as well as, if possible, an electronic copy of the complaint shall be submitted to the Commission. The complainant shall also submit a non-confidential version of the complaint, if confidentiality is claimed for any part of the complaint.

3. Complaints shall be submitted in one of the official languages of the Community.

Article 6 Participation of complainants in proceedings

1. Where the Commission issues a statement of objections relating to a matter in respect of which it has received a complaint, it shall provide the complainant with a copy of the non-confidential version of the statement of objections, except in cases where the settlement procedure applies, where it shall inform the complainant in writing of the nature and subject matter of the procedure. The Commission shall also set a time limit within which the complainant may make known its views in writing.

2. The Commission may, where appropriate, afford complainants the opportunity of expressing their views at the oral hearing of the parties to which a statement of objections has been issued, if complainants so request in their written comments.

Article 7 Rejection of complaints

1. Where the Commission considers that on the basis of the information in its possession there are insufficient grounds for acting on a complaint, it shall inform the complainant of its reasons and set a time-limit within which the complainant may make known its views in writing. The Commission shall not be obliged to take into account any further written submission received after the expiry of that time-limit.

2. If the complainant makes known its views within the time-limit set by the Commission and the written submissions made by the complainant do not lead to a different assessment of the complaint, the Commission shall reject the complaint by decision.

3. If the complainant fails to make known its views within the time-limit set by the Commission, the complaint shall be deemed to have been withdrawn.

Article 8 Access to information

1. Where the Commission has informed the complainant of its intention to reject a complaint pursuant to Article 7(1) the complainant may request access to the documents on which the Commission bases its provisional assessment. For this purpose, the complainant may however not have access to business secrets and other confidential information belonging to other parties involved in the proceedings.

2. The documents to which the complainant has had access in the context of proceedings conducted by the Commission under Articles 81 and 82 of the Treaty may only be used by the complainant for the purposes of judicial or administrative proceedings for the application of those Treaty provisions.

Article 9 Rejections of complaints pursuant to Article 13 of Regulation (EC) No 1/2003

Where the Commission rejects a complaint pursuant to Article 13 of Regulation (EC) No 1/2003, it shall inform the complainant without delay of the national competition authority which is dealing or has already dealt with the case.

Chapter V Exercise of the right to be heard

Article 10 Statement of objections and reply

1. The Commission shall inform the parties concerned of the objections raised against them. The statement of objections shall be notified in writing to each of the parties against whom objections are raised.

2. The Commission shall, when notifying the statement of objections to the parties concerned, set a time-limit within which these parties may inform it in writing of their views. The Commission shall not be obliged to take into account written submissions received after the expiry of that time-limit.

3. The parties may, in their written submissions, set out all facts known to them which are relevant to their defence against the objections raised by the Commission. They shall attach any relevant documents as proof of the facts set out. They shall provide a paper original as well as an electronic copy or, where they do not provide an electronic copy, 30 paper copies of their submission and of the documents attached to it. They may propose that the Commission hear persons who may corroborate the facts set out in their submission.

Article 10a Settlement procedure in cartel cases

1. After the initiation of proceedings pursuant to Article 11(6) of Regulation (EC) No 1/2003, the Commission may set a time limit within which the parties may indicate in writing that they are prepared to engage in settlement discussions with a view to possibly introducing settlement submissions. The Commission shall not be obliged to take into account replies received after the expiry of that time limit.

If two or more parties within the same undertaking indicate their willingness to engage in settlement discussions pursuant to the first subparagraph, they shall appoint a joint representation to engage in discussions with the Commission on their behalf. When setting the time limit referred to in the first subparagraph, the Commission shall indicate to the relevant parties that they are identified within the same undertaking, for the sole purpose of enabling them to comply with this provision.

2. Parties taking part in settlement discussions may be informed by the Commission of:

(a) the objections it envisages to raise against them;
(b) the evidence used to determine the envisaged objections;
(c) non-confidential versions of any specified accessible document listed in the case file at that point in time, in so far as a request by the party is justified for the purpose of enabling the party to ascertain its position regarding a time period or any other particular aspect of the cartel; and
(d) the range of potential fines.

This information shall be confidential vis-à-vis third parties, save where the Commission has given a prior explicit authorisation for disclosure.

Should settlement discussions progress, the Commission may set a time limit within which the parties may commit to follow the settlement procedure by introducing settlement submissions reflecting the results of the settlement discussions and acknowledging their participation in an infringement of Article 81 of the Treaty as well as their liability. Before the Commission sets a time limit to introduce their settlement submissions, the parties concerned shall be entitled to have the information specified in Article 10a(2), first subparagraph disclosed to them, upon request, in a timely manner. The Commission shall not be obliged to take into account settlement submissions received after the expiry of that time limit.

3. When the statement of objections notified to the parties reflects the contents of their settlement submissions, the written reply to the statement of objections by the parties concerned shall, within a time limit set by the Commission, confirm that the statement of objections addressed to them reflects the contents of their settlement submissions. The Commission may then proceed to the adoption of a Decision pursuant to Article 7 and Article 23 of Regulation (EC) No 1/2003 after consultation of the Advisory Committee on Restrictive Practices and Dominant Positions pursuant to Article 14 of Regulation (EC) No 1/2003.

4. The Commission may decide at any time during the procedure to discontinue settlement discussions altogether in a specific case or with respect to one or more of the parties involved, if it considers that procedural efficiencies are not likely to be achieved.

Article 11 Right to be heard

1. The Commission shall give the parties to whom it addresses a statement of objections the opportunity to be heard before consulting the Advisory Committee referred to in Article 14(1) of Regulation (EC) No 1/2003.

2. The Commission shall, in its decisions, deal only with objections in respect of which the parties referred to in paragraph 1 have been able to comment.

Article 12 Right to an oral hearing

1. The Commission shall give the parties to whom it addresses a statement of objections the opportunity to develop their arguments at an oral hearing, if they so request in their written submissions.

2. However, when introducing their settlement submissions the parties shall confirm to the Commission that they would only require having the opportunity to develop their arguments at an oral hearing, if the statement of objections does not reflect the contents of their settlement submissions.

Article 13 Hearing of other persons

1. If natural or legal persons other than those referred to in Articles 5 and 11 apply to be heard and show a sufficient interest, the Commission shall inform them in writing of the nature and subject matter of the procedure and shall set a time-limit within which they may make known their views in writing.

2. The Commission may, where appropriate, invite persons referred to in paragraph 1 to develop their arguments at the oral hearing of the parties to whom a statement of objections has been addressed, if the persons referred to in paragraph 1 so request in their written comments.

3. The Commission may invite any other person to express its views in writing and to attend the oral hearing of the parties to whom a statement of objections has been addressed. The Commission may also invite such persons to express their views at that oral hearing.

Article 14 Conduct of oral hearings

1. Hearings shall be conducted by a Hearing Officer in full independence.

2. The Commission shall invite the persons to be heard to attend the oral hearing on such date as it shall determine.

3. The Commission shall invite the competition authorities of the Member States to take part in the oral hearing. It may likewise invite officials and civil servants of other authorities of the Member States.

4. Persons invited to attend shall either appear in person or be represented by legal representatives or by representatives authorised by their constitution as appropriate. Undertakings and associations of undertakings may also be represented by a duly authorised agent appointed from among their permanent staff.

5. Persons heard by the Commission may be assisted by their lawyers or other qualified persons admitted by the Hearing Officer.

6. Oral hearings shall not be public. Each person may be heard separately or in the presence of other persons invited to attend, having regard to the legitimate interest of the undertakings in the protection of their business secrets and other confidential information.

7. The Hearing Officer may allow the parties to whom a statement of objections has been addressed, the complainants, other persons invited to the hearing, the Commission services and the authorities of the Member States to ask questions during the hearing.

8. The statements made by each person heard shall be recorded. Upon request, the recording of the hearing shall be made available to the persons who attended the hearing. Regard shall be had to the legitimate interest of the parties in the protection of their business secrets and other confidential information.

Chapter VI Access to the file and treatment of confidential information

Article 15 Access to the file and use of documents

1. If so requested, the Commission shall grant access to the file to the parties to whom it has addressed a statement of objections. Access shall be granted after the notification of the statement of objections.

1a. After the initiation of proceedings pursuant to Article 11(6) of Regulation (EC) No 1/2003 and in order to enable the parties willing to introduce settlement submissions to do so, the Commission shall disclose to them the evidence and documents described in Article 10a(2) upon request and subject to the conditions established in the relevant subparagraphs. In view thereof, when introducing their settlement submissions, the parties shall confirm to the Commission that they will only require access to the file after the receipt of the statement of objections, if the statement of objections does not reflect the contents of their settlement submissions.

2. The right of access to the file shall not extend to business secrets, other confidential information and internal documents of the Commission or of the competition authorities of the Member States. The right of access to the file shall also not extend to correspondence between the Commission and the competition authorities of the Member States or between the latter where such correspondence is contained in the file of the Commission.

3. Nothing in this Regulation prevents the Commission from disclosing and using information necessary to prove an infringement of Articles 81 or 82 of the Treaty.

4. Documents obtained through access to the file pursuant to this Article shall only be used for the purposes of judicial or administrative proceedings for the application of Articles 81 and 82 of the Treaty.

Article 16 Identification and protection of confidential information

1. Information, including documents, shall not be communicated or made accessible by the Commission in so far as it contains business secrets or other confidential information of any person.

2. Any person which makes known its views pursuant to Article 6(1), Article 7(1), Article 10 (2) and Article 13(1) and (3) or subsequently submits further information to the Commission in the course of the same procedure, shall clearly identify any material which it considers to be confidential, giving reasons, and provide a separate non-confidential version by the date set by the Commission for making its views known.

3. Without prejudice to paragraph 2 of this Article, the Commission may require undertakings and associations of undertakings which produce documents or statements pursuant to Regulation (EC) No 1/2003 to identify the documents or parts of documents which they consider to contain business secrets or other confidential information belonging to them and to identify the undertakings with regard to which such documents are to be considered confidential. The Commission may likewise require undertakings or associations of undertakings to identify any part of a statement of objections, a case summary drawn up pursuant to Article 27(4) of Regulation (EC) No 1/2003 or a decision adopted by the Commission which in their view contains business secrets.

The Commission may set a time-limit within which the undertakings and associations of undertakings are to:

(a) substantiate their claim for confidentiality with regard to each individual document or part of document, statement or part of statement;

(b) provide the Commission with a non-confidential version of the documents or statements, in which the confidential passages are deleted;

(c) provide a concise description of each piece of deleted information.

4. If undertakings or associations of undertakings fail to comply with paragraphs 2 and 3, the Commission may assume that the documents or statements concerned do not contain confidential information.

Chapter VII General and final provisions

Article 17 Time-limits

1. In setting the time limits provided for in Article 3(3), Article 4(3), Article 6(1), Article 7(1), Article 10(2), Article 10a(1), Article 10a(2), Article 10a(3) and Article 16(3), the Commission shall have regard both to the time required for preparation of the submission and to the urgency of the case.

2. The time-limits referred to in Article 6(1), Article 7(1) and Article 10(2) shall be at least four weeks. However, for proceedings initiated with a view to adopting interim measures pursuant to Article 8 of Regulation (EC) No 1/2003, the time-limit may be shortened to one week.

3. The time limits referred to in Article 4(3), Article 10a(1), Article 10a(2) and Article 16(3) shall be at least two weeks. The time limit referred to in Article 3(3) shall be at least two weeks, except for settlement submissions, for which corrections shall be made within one week. The time limit referred to in Article 10a(3) shall be at least two weeks.

4. Where appropriate and upon reasoned request made before the expiry of the original time-limit, time-limits may be extended.

Article 18 Repeals

Regulations (EC) No 2842/98, (EC) No 2843/98 and (EC) No 3385/94 are repealed.

References to the repealed regulations shall be construed as references to this regulation.

Article 19 Transitional provisions

Procedural steps taken under Regulations (EC) No 2842/98 and (EC) No 2843/98 shall continue to have effect for the purpose of applying this Regulation.

Article 20 Entry into force

This Regulation shall enter into force on 1 May 2004.

This Regulation shall be binding in its entirety and directly applicable in all Member States.

Done at Brussels, 7 April 2004.
For the Commission
Mario MONTI
Member of the Commission

Annex

Form C Complaint pursuant to Article 7 of Regulation (EC) No 1/2003

I. Information regarding the complainant and the undertaking(s) or association of undertakings giving rise to the complaint

1. Give full details on the identity of the legal or natural person submitting the complaint. Where the complainant is an undertaking, identify the corporate group to which it belongs and provide a concise overview of the nature and scope of its business activities. Provide a contact person (with telephone number, postal and e-mail-address) from which supplementary explanations can be obtained.

2. Identify the undertaking(s) or association of undertakings whose conduct the complaint relates to, including, where applicable, all available information on the corporate group to which the undertaking(s) complained of belong and the nature and scope of the business activities pursued by them. Indicate the position of the complainant vis-à-vis the undertaking(s) or association of undertakings complained of (e.g. customer, competitor).

II. Details of the alleged infringement and evidence

3. Set out in detail the facts from which, in your opinion, it appears that there exists an infringement of Article 81 or 82 of the Treaty and/or Article 53 or 54 of the EEA agreement. Indicate in particular the nature of the products (goods or services) affected by the alleged infringements and explain, where necessary, the commercial relationships concerning these products. Provide all available details on the agreements or practices of the undertakings or associations of undertakings to which

this complaint relates. Indicate, to the extent possible, the relative market positions of the undertakings concerned by the complaint.

4. Submit all documentation in your possession relating to or directly connected with the facts set out in the complaint (for example, texts of agreements, minutes of negotiations or meetings, terms of transactions, business documents, circulars, correspondence, notes of telephone conversations . . .). State the names and address of the persons able to testify to the facts set out in the complaint, and in particular of persons affected by the alleged infringement. Submit statistics or other data in your possession which relate to the facts set out, in particular where they show developments in the marketplace (for example information relating to prices and price trends, barriers to entry to the market for new suppliers etc.).

5. Set out your view about the geographical scope of the alleged infringement and explain, where that is not obvious, to what extent trade between Member States or between the Community and one or more EFTA States that are contracting parties of the EEA Agreement may be affected by the conduct complained of.

III. Finding sought from the Commission and legitimate interest

6. Explain what finding or action you are seeking as a result of proceedings brought by the Commission.

7. Set out the grounds on which you claim a legitimate interest as complainant pursuant to Article 7 of Regulation (EC) No 1/2003. State in particular how the conduct complained of affects you and explain how, in your view, intervention by the Commission would be liable to remedy the alleged grievance.

IV. Proceedings before national competition authorities or national courts

8. Provide full information about whether you have approached, concerning the same or closely related subject-matters, any other competition authority and/or whether a lawsuit has been brought before a national court. If so, provide full details about the administrative or judicial authority contacted and your submissions to such authority.

Declaration that the information given in this form and in the Annexes thereto is given entirely in good faith.

Date and signature.

Commission Regulation (EC) No 772/2004 of 7 April 2004 on the application of Article 81(3) of the Treaty to categories of technology transfer agreements*

[OJ 2004 L123/11]

THE COMMISSION OF THE EUROPEAN COMMUNITIES,

Having regard to the Treaty establishing the European Community,

Having regard to Council Regulation No 19/65/EEC of 2 March 1965 on application of Article 85(3) of the Treaty to certain categories of agreements and concerted practices,[1] and in particular Article 1 thereof,

Having published a draft of this Regulation,[2]

After consulting the Advisory Committee on Restrictive Practices and Dominant Positions,

Whereas:

(1) Regulation No 19/65/EEC empowers the Commission to apply Article 81(3) of the Treaty by Regulation to certain categories of technology transfer agreements and corresponding concerted practices to which only two undertakings are party which fall within Article 81(1).

(2) Pursuant to Regulation No 19/65/EEC, the Commission has, in particular, adopted Regulation (EC) No 240/96 of 31 January 1996 on the application of Article 85(3) of the Treaty to certain categories of technology transfer agreements.[3]

* **Editor's Note:** As corrected by OJ 2004 L127/158.

[1] OJ 36, 6.3.1965, p. 533/65. Regulation as last amended by Regulation (EC) No 1/2003 (OJ L 1, 4.1.2003, p. 1).

[2] OJ C 235, 1.10.2003, p. 10.

[3] OJ L 31, 9.2.1996, p. 2. Regulation as amended by the 2003 Act of Accession.

(3) On 20 December 2001 the Commission published an evaluation report on the transfer of technology block exemption Regulation (EC) No 240/96.[4] This generated a public debate on the application of Regulation (EC) No 240/96 and on the application in general of Article 81(1) and (3) of the Treaty to technology transfer agreements. The response to the evaluation report from Member States and third parties has been generally in favour of reform of Community competition policy on technology transfer agreements. It is therefore appropriate to repeal Regulation (EC) No 240/96.

(4) This Regulation should meet the two requirements of ensuring effective competition and providing adequate legal security for undertakings. The pursuit of these objectives should take account of the need to simplify the regulatory framework and its application. It is appropriate to move away from the approach of listing exempted clauses and to place greater emphasis on defining the categories of agreements which are exempted up to a certain level of market power and on specifying the restrictions or clauses which are not to be contained in such agreements. This is consistent with an economics-based approach which assesses the impact of agreements on the relevant market. It is also consistent with such an approach to make a distinction between agreements between competitors and agreements between non-competitors.

(5) Technology transfer agreements concern the licensing of technology. Such agreements will usually improve economic efficiency and be pro-competitive as they can reduce duplication of research and development, strengthen the incentive for the initial research and development, spur incremental innovation, facilitate diffusion and generate product market competition.

(6) The likelihood that such efficiency-enhancing and pro-competitive effects will outweigh any anti-competitive effects due to restrictions contained in technology transfer agreements depends on the degree of market power of the undertakings concerned and, therefore, on the extent to which those undertakings face competition from undertakings owning substitute technologies or undertakings producing substitute products.

(7) This Regulation should only deal with agreements where the licensor permits the licensee to exploit the licensed technology, possibly after further research and development by the licensee, for the production of goods or services. It should not deal with licensing agreements for the purpose of subcontracting research and development. It should also not deal with licensing agreements to set up technology pools, that is to say, agreements for the pooling of technologies with the purpose of licensing the created package of intellectual property rights to third parties.

(8) For the application of Article 81(3) by regulation, it is not necessary to define those technology transfer agreements that are capable of falling within Article 81(1). In the individual assessment of agreements pursuant to Article 81(1), account has to be taken of several factors, and in particular the structure and the dynamics of the relevant technology and product markets.

(9) The benefit of the block exemption established by this Regulation should be limited to those agreements which can be assumed with sufficient certainty to satisfy the conditions of Article 81(3). In order to attain the benefits and objectives of technology transfer, the benefit of this Regulation should also apply to provisions contained in technology transfer agreements that do not constitute the primary object of such agreements, but are directly related to the application of the licensed technology.

(10) For technology transfer agreements between competitors it can be presumed that, where the combined share of the relevant markets accounted for by the parties does not exceed 20% and the agreements do not contain certain severely anti-competitive restraints, they generally lead to an improvement in production or distribution and allow consumers a fair share of the resulting benefits.

(11) For technology transfer agreements between non-competitors it can be presumed that, where the individual share of the relevant markets accounted for by each of the parties does not exceed 30% and the agreements do not contain certain severely anti-competitive restraints, they generally lead to an improvement in production or distribution and allow consumers a fair share of the resulting benefits.

(12) There can be no presumption that above these market-share thresholds technology transfer agreements do fall within the scope of Article 81(1). For instance, an exclusive licensing agreement between non-competing undertakings does often not fall within the scope of Article 81(1). There can

[4] COM(2001) 786 final.

also be no presumption that, above these market-share thresholds, technology transfer agreements falling within the scope of Article 81(1) will not satisfy the conditions for exemption. However, it can also not be presumed that they will usually give rise to objective advantages of such a character and size as to compensate for the disadvantages which they create for competition.

(13) This Regulation should not exempt technology transfer agreements containing restrictions which are not indispensable to the improvement of production or distribution. In particular, technology transfer agreements containing certain severely anti-competitive restraints such as the fixing of prices charged to third parties should be excluded from the benefit of the block exemption established by this Regulation irrespective of the market shares of the undertakings concerned. In the case of such hard-core restrictions the whole agreement should be excluded from the benefit of the block exemption.

(14) In order to protect incentives to innovate and the appropriate application of intellectual property rights, certain restrictions should be excluded from the block exemption. In particular exclusive grant back obligations for severable improvements should be excluded. Where such a restriction is included in a licence agreement only the restriction in question should be excluded from the benefit of the block exemption.

(15) The market-share thresholds, the non-exemption of technology transfer agreements containing severely anti-competitive restraints and the excluded restrictions provided for in this Regulation will normally ensure that the agreements to which the block exemption applies do not enable the participating undertakings to eliminate competition in respect of a substantial part of the products in question.

(16) In particular cases in which the agreements falling under this Regulation nevertheless have effects incompatible with Article 81(3), the Commission should be able to withdraw the benefit of the block exemption. This may occur in particular where the incentives to innovate are reduced or where access to markets is hindered.

(17) Council Regulation (EC) No 1/2003 of 16 December 2002 on the implementation of the rules on competition laid down in Articles 81 and 82 of the Treaty[5] empowers the competent authorities of Member States to withdraw the benefit of the block exemption in respect of technology transfer agreements having effects incompatible with Article 81(3), where such effects are felt in their respective territory, or in a part thereof, and where such territory has the characteristics of a distinct geographic market. Member States must ensure that the exercise of this power of withdrawal does not prejudice the uniform application throughout the common market of the Community competition rules or the full effect of the measures adopted in implementation of those rules.

(18) In order to strengthen supervision of parallel networks of technology transfer agreements which have similar restrictive effects and which cover more than 50% of a given market, the Commission should be able to declare this Regulation inapplicable to technology transfer agreements containing specific restraints relating to the market concerned, thereby restoring the full application of Article 81 to such agreements.

(19) This Regulation should cover only technology transfer agreements between a licensor and a licensee. It should cover such agreements even if conditions are stipulated for more than one level of trade, by, for instance, requiring the licensee to set up a particular distribution system and specifying the obligations the licensee must or may impose on resellers of the products produced under the licence. However, such conditions and obligations should comply with the competition rules applicable to supply and distribution agreements. Supply and distribution agreements concluded between a licensee and its buyers should not be exempted by this Regulation.

(20) This Regulation is without prejudice to the application of Article 82 of the Treaty,

HAS ADOPTED THIS REGULATION:

Article 1 Definitions

1. For the purposes of this Regulation, the following definitions shall apply:
   (a) 'agreement' means an agreement, a decision of an association of undertakings or a concerted practice;

[5] OJ L 1, 4.1.2003, p. 1. Regulation as amended by Regulation (EC) No 411/2004 (OJ L 68, 6.3.2004, p. 1).

(b) 'technology transfer agreement' means a patent licensing agreement, a know-how licensing agreement, a software copyright licensing agreement or a mixed patent, know-how or software copyright licensing agreement, including any such agreement containing provisions which relate to the sale and purchase of products or which relate to the licensing of other intellectual property rights or the assignment of intellectual property rights, provided that those provisions do not constitute the primary object of the agreement and are directly related to the production of the contract products; assignments of patents, know-how, software copyright or a combination thereof where part of the risk associated with the exploitation of the technology remains with the assignor, in particular where the sum payable in consideration of the assignment is dependent on the turnover obtained by the assignee in respect of products produced with the assigned technology, the quantity of such products produced or the number of operations carried out employing the technology, shall also be deemed to be technology transfer agreements;

(c) 'reciprocal agreement' means a technology transfer agreement where two undertakings grant each other, in the same or separate contracts, a patent licence, a know-how licence, a software copyright licence or a mixed patent, know-how or software copyright licence and where these licences concern competing technologies or can be used for the production of competing products;

(d) 'non-reciprocal agreement' means a technology transfer agreement where one undertaking grants another undertaking a patent licence, a know-how licence, a software copyright licence or a mixed patent, know-how or software copyright licence, or where two undertakings grant each other such a licence but where these licences do not concern competing technologies and cannot be used for the production of competing products;

(e) 'product' means a good or a service, including both intermediary goods and services and final goods and services;

(f) 'contract products' means products produced with the licensed technology;

(g) 'intellectual property rights' includes industrial property rights, know-how, copyright and neighbouring rights;

(h) 'patents' means patents, patent applications, utility models, applications for registration of utility models, designs, topographies of semiconductor products, supplementary protection certificates for medicinal products or other products for which such supplementary protection certificates may be obtained and plant breeder's certificates;

(i) 'know-how' means a package of non-patented practical information, resulting from experience and testing, which is:
   (i) secret, that is to say, not generally known or easily accessible,
   (ii) substantial, that is to say, significant and useful for the production of the contract products, and
   (iii) identified, that is to say, described in a sufficiently comprehensive manner so as to make it possible to verify that it fulfils the criteria of secrecy and substantiality;

(j) 'competing undertakings' means undertakings which compete on the relevant technology market and/or the relevant product market, that is to say:
   (i) competing undertakings on the relevant technology market, being undertakings which license out competing technologies without infringing each others' intellectual property rights (actual competitors on the technology market); the relevant technology market includes technologies which are regarded by the licensees as interchangeable with or substitutable for the licensed technology, by reason of the technologies' characteristics, their royalties and their intended use,
   (ii) competing undertakings on the relevant product market, being undertakings which, in the absence of the technology transfer agreement, are both active on the relevant product and geographic market(s) on which the contract products are sold without infringing each others' intellectual property rights (actual

competitors on the product market) or would, on realistic grounds, undertake the necessary additional investments or other necessary switching costs so that they could timely enter, without infringing each others' intellectual property rights, the (se) relevant product and geographic market(s) in response to a small and permanent increase in relative prices (potential competitors on the product market); the relevant product market comprises products which are regarded by the buyers as interchangeable with or substitutable for the contract products, by reason of the products' characteristics, their prices and their intended use;

(k) 'selective distribution system' means a distribution system where the licensor undertakes to license the production of the contract products only to licensees selected on the basis of specified criteria and where these licensees undertake not to sell the contract products to unauthorised distributors;

(l) 'exclusive territory' means a territory in which only one undertaking is allowed to produce the contract products with the licensed technology, without prejudice to the possibility of allowing within that territory another licensee to produce the contract products only for a particular customer where this second licence was granted in order to create an alternative source of supply for that customer;

(m) 'exclusive customer group' means a group of customers to which only one undertaking is allowed actively to sell the contract products produced with the licensed technology;

(n) 'severable improvement' means an improvement that can be exploited without infringing the licensed technology.

2. The terms 'undertaking', 'licensor' and 'licensee' shall include their respective connected undertakings.

'Connected undertakings' means:

(a) undertakings in which a party to the agreement, directly or indirectly:
   (i) has the power to exercise more than half the voting rights, or
   (ii) has the power to appoint more than half the members of the supervisory board, board of management or bodies legally representing the undertaking, or
   (iii) has the right to manage the undertaking's affairs;

(b) undertakings which directly or indirectly have, over a party to the agreement, the rights or powers listed in (a);

(c) undertakings in which an undertaking referred to in (b) has, directly or indirectly, the rights or powers listed in (a);

(d) undertakings in which a party to the agreement together with one or more of the undertakings referred to in (a), (b) or (c), or in which two or more of the latter undertakings, jointly have the rights or powers listed in (a);

(e) undertakings in which the rights or the powers listed in (a) are jointly held by:
   (i) parties to the agreement or their respective connected undertakings referred to in (a) to (d), or
   (ii) one or more of the parties to the agreement or one or more of their connected undertakings referred to in (a) to (d) and one or more third parties.

Article 2 Exemption

Pursuant to Article 81(3) of the Treaty and subject to the provisions of this Regulation, it is hereby declared that Article 81(1) of the Treaty shall not apply to technology transfer agreements entered into between two undertakings permitting the production of contract products.

This exemption shall apply to the extent that such agreements contain restrictions of competition falling within the scope of Article 81(1). The exemption shall apply for as long as the intellectual property right in the licensed technology has not expired, lapsed or been declared invalid or, in the case of know-how, for as long as the know-how remains secret, except in the event where the know-how becomes publicly known as a result of action by the licensee, in which case the exemption shall apply for the duration of the agreement.

Article 3 Market-share thresholds

1. Where the undertakings party to the agreement are competing undertakings, the exemption provided for in Article 2 shall apply on condition that the combined market share of the parties does not exceed 20% on the affected relevant technology and product market.

2. Where the undertakings party to the agreement are not competing undertakings, the exemption provided for in Article 2 shall apply on condition that the market share of each of the parties does not exceed 30% on the affected relevant technology and product market.

3. For the purposes of paragraphs 1 and 2, the market share of a party on the relevant technology market(s) is defined in terms of the presence of the licensed technology on the relevant product market(s). A licensor's market share on the relevant technology market shall be the combined market share on the relevant product market of the contract products produced by the licensor and its licensees.

Article 4 Hardcore restrictions

1. Where the undertakings party to the agreement are competing undertakings, the exemption provided for in Article 2 shall not apply to agreements which, directly or indirectly, in isolation or in combination with other factors under the control of the parties, have as their object:

(a) the restriction of a party's ability to determine its prices when selling products to third parties;

(b) the limitation of output, except limitations on the output of contract products imposed on the licensee in a non-reciprocal agreement or imposed on only one of the licensees in a reciprocal agreement;

(c) the allocation of markets or customers except:

(i) the obligation on the licensee(s) to produce with the licensed technology only within one or more technical fields of use or one or more product markets,

(ii) the obligation on the licensor and/or the licensee, in a non-reciprocal agreement, not to produce with the licensed technology within one or more technical fields of use or one or more product markets or one or more exclusive territories reserved for the other party,

(iii) the obligation on the licensor not to license the technology to another licensee in a particular territory,

(iv) the restriction, in a non-reciprocal agreement, of active and/or passive sales by the licensee and/or the licensor into the exclusive territory or to the exclusive customer group reserved for the other party,

(v) the restriction, in a non-reciprocal agreement, of active sales by the licensee into the exclusive territory or to the exclusive customer group allocated by the licensor to another licensee provided the latter was not a competing undertaking of the licensor at the time of the conclusion of its own licence,

(vi) the obligation on the licensee to produce the contract products only for its own use provided that the licensee is not restricted in selling the contract products actively and passively as spare parts for its own products,

(vii) the obligation on the licensee, in a non-reciprocal agreement, to produce the contract products only for a particular customer, where the licence was granted in order to create an alternative source of supply for that customer;

(d) the restriction of the licensee's ability to exploit its own technology or the restriction of the ability of any of the parties to the agreement to carry out research and development, unless such latter restriction is indispensable to prevent the disclosure of the licensed know-how to third parties.

2. Where the undertakings party to the agreement are not competing undertakings, the exemption provided for in Article 2 shall not apply to agreements which, directly or indirectly, in isolation or in combination with other factors under the control of the parties, have as their object:

(a) the restriction of a party's ability to determine its prices when selling products to third parties, without prejudice to the possibility of imposing a maximum sale price or recommending a sale price, provided that it does not amount to a fixed or minimum sale price as a result of pressure from, or incentives offered by, any of the parties;

(b) the restriction of the territory into which, or of the customers to whom, the licensee may passively sell the contract products, except:

(i) the restriction of passive sales into an exclusive territory or to an exclusive customer group reserved for the licensor,

(ii) the restriction of passive sales into an exclusive territory or to an exclusive customer group allocated by the licensor to another licensee during the first two years that this other licensee is selling the contract products in that territory or to that customer group,

(iii) the obligation to produce the contract products only for its own use provided that the licensee is not restricted in selling the contract products actively and passively as spare parts for its own products,

(iv) the obligation to produce the contract products only for a particular customer, where the licence was granted in order to create an alternative source of supply for that customer,

(v) the restriction of sales to end-users by a licensee operating at the wholesale level of trade,

(vi) the restriction of sales to unauthorised distributors by the members of a selective distribution system;

(c) the restriction of active or passive sales to end-users by a licensee which is a member of a selective distribution system and which operates at the retail level, without prejudice to the possibility of prohibiting a member of the system from operating out of an unauthorised place of establishment.

3. Where the undertakings party to the agreement are not competing undertakings at the time of the conclusion of the agreement but become competing undertakings afterwards, paragraph 2 and not paragraph 1 shall apply for the full life of the agreement unless the agreement is subsequently amended in any material respect.

Article 5 Excluded restrictions

1. The exemption provided for in Article 2 shall not apply to any of the following obligations contained in technology transfer agreements:

(a) any direct or indirect obligation on the licensee to grant an exclusive licence to the licensor or to a third party designated by the licensor in respect of its own severable improvements to or its own new applications of the licensed technology;

(b) any direct or indirect obligation on the licensee to assign, in whole or in part, to the licensor or to a third party designated by the licensor, rights to its own severable improvements to or its own new applications of the licensed technology;

(c) any direct or indirect obligation on the licensee not to challenge the validity of intellectual property rights which the licensor holds in the common market, without prejudice to the possibility of providing for termination of the technology transfer agreement in the event that the licensee challenges the validity of one or more of the licensed intellectual property rights.

2. Where the undertakings party to the agreement are not competing undertakings, the exemption provided for in Article 2 shall not apply to any direct or indirect obligation limiting the licensee's ability to exploit its own technology or limiting the ability of any of the parties to the agreement to carry out research and development, unless such latter restriction is indispensable to prevent the disclosure of the licensed know-how to third parties.

Article 6 Withdrawal in individual cases

1. The Commission may withdraw the benefit of this Regulation, pursuant to Article 29(1) of Regulation (EC) No 1/2003, where it finds in any particular case that a technology transfer agreement to which the exemption provided for in Article 2 applies nevertheless has effects which are incompatible with Article 81(3) of the Treaty, and in particular where:

(a) access of third parties' technologies to the market is restricted, for instance by the cumulative effect of parallel networks of similar restrictive agreements prohibiting licensees from using third parties' technologies;

(b) access of potential licensees to the market is restricted, for instance by the cumulative effect of parallel networks of similar restrictive agreements prohibiting licensors from licensing to other licensees;

(c) without any objectively valid reason, the parties do not exploit the licensed technology.

2. Where, in any particular case, a technology transfer agreement to which the exemption provided for in Article 2 applies has effects which are incompatible with Article 81(3) of the Treaty in the territory of a Member State, or in a part thereof, which has all the characteristics of a distinct geographic market, the competition authority of that Member State may withdraw the benefit of this Regulation, pursuant to Article 29(2) of Regulation (EC) No 1/2003, in respect of that territory, under the same circumstances as those set out in paragraph 1 of this Article.

Article 7 Non-application of this Regulation

1. Pursuant to Article 1a of Regulation No 19/65/EEC, the Commission may by regulation declare that, where parallel networks of similar technology transfer agreements cover more than 50% of a relevant market, this Regulation is not to apply to technology transfer agreements containing specific restraints relating to that market.

2. A regulation pursuant to paragraph 1 shall not become applicable earlier than six months following its adoption.

Article 8 Application of the market-share thresholds

1. For the purposes of applying the market-share thresholds provided for in Article 3 the rules set out in this paragraph shall apply. The market share shall be calculated on the basis of market sales value data. If market sales value data are not available, estimates based on other reliable market information, including market sales volumes, may be used to establish the market share of the undertaking concerned. The market share shall be calculated on the basis of data relating to the preceding calendar year. The market share held by the undertakings referred to in point (e) of the second subparagraph of Article 1(2) shall be apportioned equally to each undertaking having the rights or the powers listed in point (a) of the second subparagraph of Article 1(2).

2. If the market share referred to in Article 3(1) or (2) is initially not more than 20% respectively 30% but subsequently rises above those levels, the exemption provided for in Article 2 shall continue to apply for a period of two consecutive calendar years following the year in which the 20% threshold or 30% threshold was first exceeded.

Article 9 Repeal

Regulation (EC) No 240/96 is repealed.

References to the repealed Regulation shall be construed as references to this Regulation.

Article 10 Transitional period

The prohibition laid down in Article 81(1) of the Treaty shall not apply during the period from 1 May 2004 to 31 March 2006 in respect of agreements already in force on 30 April 2004 which do not satisfy the conditions for exemption provided for in this Regulation but which, on 30 April 2004, satisfied the conditions for exemption provided for in Regulation (EC) No 240/96.

Article 11 Period of validity

This Regulation shall enter into force on 1 May 2004.

It shall expire on 30 April 2014.

This Regulation shall be binding in its entirety and directly applicable in all Member States.

Done at Brussels, 7 April 2004.
For the Commission
Mario MONTI
Member of the Commission

Commission Regulation (EU) No 330/2010 of 20 April 2010 on the application of Article 101(3) of the Treaty on the Functioning of the European Union to categories of vertical agreements and concerted practices

THE EUROPEAN COMMISSION,

Having regard to the Treaty on the Functioning of the European Union,

Having regard to Regulation No 19/65/EEC of the Council of 2 March 1965 on the application of Article 85(3) of the Treaty to certain categories of agreements and concerted practices[1], and in particular Article 1 thereof,

Having published a draft of this Regulation,

After consulting the Advisory Committee on Restrictive Practices and Dominant Positions,

Whereas:

(1) Regulation No 19/65/EEC empowers the Commission to apply Article 101(3) of the Treaty on the Functioning of the European Union* by regulation to certain categories of vertical agreements and corresponding concerted practices falling within Article 101(1) of the Treaty.

(2) Commission Regulation (EC) No 2790/1999 of 22 December 1999 on the application of Article 81(3) of the Treaty to categories of vertical agreements and concerted practices[2] defines a category of vertical agreements which the Commission regarded as normally satisfying the conditions laid down in Article 101(3) of the Treaty. In view of the overall positive experience with the application of that Regulation, which expires on 31 May 2010, and taking into account further experience acquired since its adoption, it is appropriate to adopt a new block exemption regulation.

(3) The category of agreements which can be regarded as normally satisfying the conditions laid down in Article 101(3) of the Treaty includes vertical agreements for the purchase or sale of goods or services where those agreements are concluded between non-competing undertakings, between certain competitors or by certain associations of retailers of goods. It also includes vertical agreements containing ancillary provisions on the assignment or use of intellectual property rights. The term "vertical agreements" should include the corresponding concerted practices.

(4) For the application of Article 101(3) of the Treaty by regulation, it is not necessary to define those vertical agreements which are capable of falling within Article 101(1) of the Treaty. In the individual assessment of agreements under Article 101(1) of the Treaty, account has to be taken of several factors, and in particular the market structure on the supply and purchase side.

(5) The benefit of the block exemption established by this Regulation should be limited to vertical agreements for which it can be assumed with sufficient certainty that they satisfy the conditions of Article 101(3) of the Treaty.

(6) Certain types of vertical agreements can improve economic efficiency within a chain of production or distribution by facilitating better coordination between the participating undertakings. In particular, they can lead to a reduction in the transaction and distribution costs of the parties and to an optimisation of their sales and investment levels.

(7) The likelihood that such efficiency-enhancing effects will outweigh any anti-competitive effects due to restrictions contained in vertical agreements depends on the degree of market power of

[1] OJ 36, 6.3.1965, p. 533.

* With effect from 1 December 2009, Article 81 of the EC Treaty has become Article 101 of the Treaty on the Functioning of the European Union. The two Articles are, in substance, identical. For the purposes of this Regulation, references to Article 101 of the Treaty on the Functioning of the European Union should be understood as references to Article 81 of the EC Treaty where appropriate.

[2] OJ L 336, 29.12.1999, p. 21.

the parties to the agreement and, therefore, on the extent to which those undertakings face competition from other suppliers of goods or services regarded by their customers as interchangeable or substitutable for one another, by reason of the products' characteristics, their prices and their intended use.

(8) It can be presumed that, where the market share held by each of the undertakings party to the agreement on the relevant market does not exceed 30%, vertical agreements which do not contain certain types of severe restrictions of competition generally lead to an improvement in production or distribution and allow consumers a fair share of the resulting benefits.

(9) Above the market share threshold of 30%, there can be no presumption that vertical agreements falling within the scope of Article 101(1) of the Treaty will usually give rise to objective advantages of such a character and size as to compensate for the disadvantages which they create for competition. At the same time, there is no presumption that those vertical agreements are either caught by Article 101(1) of the Treaty or that they fail to satisfy the conditions of Article 101(3) of the Treaty.

(10) This Regulation should not exempt vertical agreements containing restrictions which are likely to restrict competition and harm consumers or which are not indispensable to the attainment of the efficiency-enhancing effects. In particular, vertical agreements containing certain types of severe restrictions of competition such as minimum and fixed resale-prices, as well as certain types of territorial protection, should be excluded from the benefit of the block exemption established by this Regulation irrespective of the market share of the undertakings concerned.

(11) In order to ensure access to or to prevent collusion on the relevant market, certain conditions should be attached to the block exemption. To this end, the exemption of non-compete obligations should be limited to obligations which do not exceed a defined duration. For the same reasons, any direct or indirect obligation causing the members of a selective distribution system not to sell the brands of particular competing suppliers should be excluded from the benefit of this Regulation.

(12) The market-share limitation, the non-exemption of certain vertical agreements and the conditions provided for in this Regulation normally ensure that the agreements to which the block exemption applies do not enable the participating undertakings to eliminate competition in respect of a substantial part of the products in question.

(13) The Commission may withdraw the benefit of this Regulation, pursuant to Article 29(1) of Council Regulation (EC) No 1/2003 of 16 December 2002 on the implementation of the rules on competition laid down in Articles 81 and 82 of the Treaty[3], where it finds in a particular case that an agreement to which the exemption provided for in this Regulation applies nevertheless has effects which are incompatible with Article 101(3) of the Treaty.

(14) The competition authority of a Member State may withdraw the benefit of this Regulation pursuant to Article 29(2) of Regulation (EC) No 1/2003 in respect of the territory of that Member State, or a part thereof where, in a particular case, an agreement to which the exemption provided for in this Regulation applies nevertheless has effects which are incompatible with Article 101(3) of the Treaty in the territory of that Member State, or in a part thereof, and where such territory has all the characteristics of a distinct geographic market.

(15) In determining whether the benefit of this Regulation should be withdrawn pursuant to Article 29 of Regulation (EC) No 1/2003, the anti-competitive effects that may derive from the existence of parallel networks of vertical agreements that have similar effects which significantly restrict access to a relevant market or competition therein are of particular importance. Such cumulative effects may for example arise in the case of selective distribution or non compete obligations.

(16) In order to strengthen supervision of parallel networks of vertical agreements which have similar anti-competitive effects and which cover more than 50% of a given market, the Commission may by regulation declare this Regulation inapplicable to vertical agreements containing specific restraints relating to the market concerned, thereby restoring the full application of Article 101 of the Treaty to such agreements,

HAS ADOPTED THIS REGULATION:

[3] OJ L 1, 4.1.2003, p. 1.

Article 1 Definitions

1. For the purposes of this Regulation, the following definitions shall apply:

(a) "vertical agreement" means an agreement or concerted practice entered into between two or more undertakings each of which operates, for the purposes of the agreement or the concerted practice, at a different level of the production or distribution chain, and relating to the conditions under which the parties may purchase, sell or resell certain goods or services;

(b) "vertical restraint" means a restriction of competition in a vertical agreement falling within the scope of Article 101(1) of the Treaty;

(c) "competing undertaking" means an actual or potential competitor; "actual competitor" means an undertaking that is active on the same relevant market; "potential competitor" means an undertaking that, in the absence of the vertical agreement, would, on realistic grounds and not just as a mere theoretical possibility, in case of a small but permanent increase in relative prices be likely to undertake, within a short period of time, the necessary additional investments or other necessary switching costs to enter the relevant market;

(d) "non-compete obligation" means any direct or indirect obligation causing the buyer not to manufacture, purchase, sell or resell goods or services which compete with the contract goods or services, or any direct or indirect obligation on the buyer to purchase from the supplier or from another undertaking designated by the supplier more than 80% of the buyer's total purchases of the contract goods or services and their substitutes on the relevant market, calculated on the basis of the value or, where such is standard industry practice, the volume of its purchases in the preceding calendar year;

(e) "selective distribution system" means a distribution system where the supplier undertakes to sell the contract goods or services, either directly or indirectly, only to distributors selected on the basis of specified criteria and where these distributors undertake not to sell such goods or services to unauthorised distributors within the territory reserved by the supplier to operate that system;

(f) "intellectual property rights" includes industrial property rights, know how, copyright and neighbouring rights;

(g) "know-how" means a package of non-patented practical information, resulting from experience and testing by the supplier, which is secret, substantial and identified: in this context, "secret" means that the know-how is not generally known or easily accessible; "substantial" means that the know-how is significant and useful to the buyer for the use, sale or resale of the contract goods or services; "identified" means that the know-how is described in a sufficiently comprehensive manner so as to make it possible to verify that it fulfils the criteria of secrecy and substantiality;

(h) "buyer" includes an undertaking which, under an agreement falling within Article 101(1) of the Treaty, sells goods or services on behalf of another undertaking;

(i) "customer of the buyer" means an undertaking not party to the agreement which purchases the contract goods or services from a buyer which is party to the agreement.

2. For the purposes of this Regulation, the terms "undertaking", "supplier" and "buyer" shall include their respective connected undertakings.

"Connected undertakings" means:

(a) undertakings in which a party to the agreement, directly or indirectly:

(i) has the power to exercise more than half the voting rights, or

(ii) has the power to appoint more than half the members of the supervisory board, board of management or bodies legally representing the undertaking, or

(iii) has the right to manage the undertaking's affairs;

(b) undertakings which directly or indirectly have, over a party to the agreement, the rights or powers listed in point (a);

(c) undertakings in which an undertaking referred to in point (b) has, directly or indirectly, the rights or powers listed in point (a);

(d) undertakings in which a party to the agreement together with one or more of the undertakings referred to in points (a), (b) or (c), or in which two or more of the latter undertakings, jointly have the rights or powers listed in point (a);

(e) undertakings in which the rights or the powers listed in point (a) are jointly held by:

(i) parties to the agreement or their respective connected undertakings referred to in points (a) to (d), or

(ii) one or more of the parties to the agreement or one or more of their connected undertakings referred to in points (a) to (d) and one or more third parties.

Article 2 Exemption

1. Pursuant to Article 101(3) of the Treaty and subject to the provisions of this Regulation, it is hereby declared that Article 101(1) of the Treaty shall not apply to vertical agreements.
This exemption shall apply to the extent that such agreements contain vertical restraints.

2. The exemption provided for in paragraph 1 shall apply to vertical agreements entered into between an association of undertakings and its members, or between such an association and its suppliers, only if all its members are retailers of goods and if no individual member of the association, together with its connected undertakings, has a total annual turnover exceeding EUR 50 million. Vertical agreements entered into by such associations shall be covered by this Regulation without prejudice to the application of Article 101 of the Treaty to horizontal agreements concluded between the members of the association or decisions adopted by the association.

3. The exemption provided for in paragraph 1 shall apply to vertical agreements containing provisions which relate to the assignment to the buyer or use by the buyer of intellectual property rights, provided that those provisions do not constitute the primary object of such agreements and are directly related to the use, sale or resale of goods or services by the buyer or its customers. The exemption applies on condition that, in relation to the contract goods or services, those provisions do not contain restrictions of competition having the same object as vertical restraints which are not exempted under this Regulation.

4. The exemption provided for in paragraph 1 shall not apply to vertical agreements entered into between competing undertakings. However, it shall apply where competing undertakings enter into a non-reciprocal vertical agreement and:

(a) the supplier is a manufacturer and a distributor of goods, while the buyer is a distributor and not a competing undertaking at the manufacturing level; or

(b) the supplier is a provider of services at several levels of trade, while the buyer provides its goods or services at the retail level and is not a competing undertaking at the level of trade where it purchases the contract services.

5. This Regulation shall not apply to vertical agreements the subject matter of which falls within the scope of any other block exemption regulation, unless otherwise provided for in such a regulation.

Article 3 Market share threshold

1. The exemption provided for in Article 2 shall apply on condition that the market share held by the supplier does not exceed 30% of the relevant market on which it sells the contract goods or services and the market share held by the buyer does not exceed 30% of the relevant market on which it purchases the contract goods or services.

2. For the purposes of paragraph 1, where in a multi party agreement an undertaking buys the contract goods or services from one undertaking party to the agreement and sells the contract goods or services to another undertaking party to the agreement, the market share of the first undertaking must respect the market share threshold provided for in that paragraph both as a buyer and a supplier in order for the exemption provided for in Article 2 to apply.

Article 4 Restrictions that remove the benefit of the block exemption—hardcore restrictions

The exemption provided for in Article 2 shall not apply to vertical agreements which, directly or indirectly, in isolation or in combination with other factors under the control of the parties, have as their object:

(a) the restriction of the buyer's ability to determine its sale price, without prejudice to the possibility of the supplier to impose a maximum sale price or recommend a sale price, provided that they do not amount to a fixed or minimum sale price as a result of pressure from, or incentives offered by, any of the parties;
(b) the restriction of the territory into which, or of the customers to whom, a buyer party to the agreement, without prejudice to a restriction on its place of establishment, may sell the contract goods or services, except:
   (i) the restriction of active sales into the exclusive territory or to an exclusive customer group reserved to the supplier or allocated by the supplier to another buyer, where such a restriction does not limit sales by the customers of the buyer,
   (ii) the restriction of sales to end users by a buyer operating at the wholesale level of trade,
   (iii) the restriction of sales by the members of a selective distribution system to unauthorised distributors within the territory reserved by the supplier to operate that system, and
   (iv) the restriction of the buyer's ability to sell components, supplied for the purposes of incorporation, to customers who would use them to manufacture the same type of goods as those produced by the supplier;
(c) the restriction of active or passive sales to end users by members of a selective distribution system operating at the retail level of trade, without prejudice to the possibility of prohibiting a member of the system from operating out of an unauthorised place of establishment;
(d) the restriction of cross-supplies between distributors within a selective distribution system, including between distributors operating at different level of trade;
(e) the restriction, agreed between a supplier of components and a buyer who incorporates those components, of the supplier's ability to sell the components as spare parts to end-users or to repairers or other service providers not entrusted by the buyer with the repair or servicing of its goods.

Article 5 Excluded restrictions

1. The exemption provided for in Article 2 shall not apply to the following obligations contained in vertical agreements:
(a) any direct or indirect non-compete obligation, the duration of which is indefinite or exceeds five years;
(b) any direct or indirect obligation causing the buyer, after termination of the agreement, not to manufacture, purchase, sell or resell goods or services;
(c) any direct or indirect obligation causing the members of a selective distribution system not to sell the brands of particular competing suppliers.

For the purposes of point (a) of the first subparagraph, a non-compete obligation which is tacitly renewable beyond a period of five years shall be deemed to have been concluded for an indefinite duration.

2. By way of derogation from paragraph 1(a), the time limitation of five years shall not apply where the contract goods or services are sold by the buyer from premises and land owned by the supplier or leased by the supplier from third parties not connected with the buyer, provided that the duration of the non-compete obligation does not exceed the period of occupancy of the premises and land by the buyer.

3. By way of derogation from paragraph 1(b), the exemption provided for in Article 2 shall apply to any direct or indirect obligation causing the buyer, after termination of the agreement, not to manufacture, purchase, sell or resell goods or services where the following conditions are fulfilled:
(a) the obligation relates to goods or services which compete with the contract goods or services;
(b) the obligation is limited to the premises and land from which the buyer has operated during the contract period;

(c) the obligation is indispensable to protect know-how transferred by the supplier to the buyer;

(d) the duration of the obligation is limited to a period of one year after termination of the agreement.

Paragraph 1(b) is without prejudice to the possibility of imposing a restriction which is unlimited in time on the use and disclosure of know-how which has not entered the public domain.

Article 6 Non-application of this Regulation

Pursuant to Article 1a of Regulation No 19/65/EEC, the Commission may by regulation declare that, where parallel networks of similar vertical restraints cover more than 50% of a relevant market, this Regulation shall not apply to vertical agreements containing specific restraints relating to that market.

Article 7 Application of the market share threshold

For the purposes of applying the market share thresholds provided for in Article 3 the following rules shall apply:

(a) the market share of the supplier shall be calculated on the basis of market sales value data and the market share of the buyer shall be calculated on the basis of market purchase value data. If market sales value or market purchase value data are not available, estimates based on other reliable market information, including market sales and purchase volumes, may be used to establish the market share of the undertaking concerned;

(b) the market shares shall be calculated on the basis of data relating to the preceding calendar year;

(c) the market share of the supplier shall include any goods or services supplied to vertically integrated distributors for the purposes of sale;

(d) if a market share is initially not more than 30% but subsequently rises above that level without exceeding 35%, the exemption provided for in Article 2 shall continue to apply for a period of two consecutive calendar years following the year in which the 30% market share threshold was first exceeded;

(e) if a market share is initially not more than 30% but subsequently rises above 35%, the exemption provided for in Article 2 shall continue to apply for one calendar year following the year in which the level of 35% was first exceeded;

(f) the benefit of points (d) and (e) may not be combined so as to exceed a period of two calendar years;

(g) the market share held by the undertakings referred to in point (e) of the second subparagraph of Article 1(2) shall be apportioned equally to each undertaking having the rights or the powers listed in point (a) of the second subparagraph of Article 1(2).

Article 8 Application of the turnover threshold

1. For the purpose of calculating total annual turnover within the meaning of Article 2(2), the turnover achieved during the previous financial year by the relevant party to the vertical agreement and the turnover achieved by its connected undertakings in respect of all goods and services, excluding all taxes and other duties, shall be added together. For this purpose, no account shall be taken of dealings between the party to the vertical agreement and its connected undertakings or between its connected undertakings.

2. The exemption provided for in Article 2 shall remain applicable where, for any period of two consecutive financial years, the total annual turnover threshold is exceeded by no more than 10%.

Article 9 Transitional period

The prohibition laid down in Article 101(1) of the Treaty shall not apply during the period from 1 June 2010 to 31 May 2011 in respect of agreements already in force on 31 May 2010 which do not satisfy the conditions for exemption provided for in this Regulation but which, on 31 May 2010, satisfied the conditions for exemption provided for in Regulation (EC) No 2790/1999.

Article 10 Period of validity

This Regulation shall enter into force on 1 June 2010.

It shall expire on 31 May 2022.

This Regulation shall be binding in its entirety and directly applicable in all Member States.

Done at Brussels, 20 April 2010.
For the Commission
The President
José Manuel Barroso

Commission Regulation (EU) No 1217/2010 of 14 December 2010 on the application of Article 101(3) of the Treaty on the Functioning of the European Union to certain categories of research and development agreements

[OJ 2010 L335/36]

THE EUROPEAN COMMISSION,

Having regard to the Treaty on the Functioning of the European Union,

Having regard to Regulation (EEC) No 2821/71 of the Council of 20 December 1971 on application of Article 85(3) of the Treaty to categories of agreements, decisions and concerted practices[1],

Having published a draft of this Regulation,

After consulting the Advisory Committee on Restrictive Practices and Dominant Positions,

Whereas:

(1) Regulation (EEC) No 2821/71 empowers the Commission to apply Article 101(3) of the Treaty on the Functioning of the European Union* by regulation to certain categories of agreements, decisions and concerted practices falling within the scope of Article 101(1) of the Treaty which have as their object the research and development of products, technologies or processes up to the stage of industrial application, and exploitation of the results, including provisions regarding intellectual property rights.

(2) Article 179(2) of the Treaty calls upon the Union to encourage undertakings, including small and medium-sized undertakings, in their research and technological development activities of high quality, and to support their efforts to cooperate with one another. This Regulation is intended to facilitate research and development while at the same time effectively protecting competition.

(3) Commission Regulation (EC) No 2659/2000 of 29 November 2000 on the application of Article 81(3) of the Treaty to categories of research and development agreements[2] defines categories of research and development agreements which the Commission regarded as normally satisfying the conditions laid down in Article 101(3) of the Treaty. In view of the overall positive experience with the application of that Regulation, which expires on 31 December 2010, and taking into account further experience acquired since its adoption, it is appropriate to adopt a new block exemption regulation.

(4) This Regulation should meet the two requirements of ensuring effective protection of competition and providing adequate legal security for undertakings. The pursuit of those objectives should take account of the need to simplify administrative supervision and the legislative framework to as great an extent as possible. Below a certain level of market power it can in general be presumed, for the application of Article 101(3) of the Treaty, that the positive effects of research and development agreements will outweigh any negative effects on competition.

[1] OJ L 285, 29.12.1971, p. 46.

* With effect from 1 December 2009, Article 81 of the EC Treaty has become Article 101 of the Treaty on the Functioning of the European Union (TFEU). The two articles are, in substance, identical. For the purposes of this Regulation, references to Article 101 of the TFEU should be understood as references to Article 81 of the EC Treaty where appropriate. The TFEU also introduced certain changes in terminology, such as the replacement of "Community" by "Union" and "common market" by "internal market". The terminology of the TFEU will be used throughout this Regulation.

[2] OJ L 304, 5.12.2000, p. 7.

(5) For the application of Article 101(3) of the Treaty by regulation, it is not necessary to define those agreements which are capable of falling within Article 101(1) of the Treaty. In the individual assessment of agreements under Article 101(1) of the Treaty, account has to be taken of several factors, and in particular the market structure on the relevant market.

(6) Agreements on the joint execution of research work or the joint development of the results of the research, up to but not including the stage of industrial application, generally do not fall within the scope of Article 101(1) of the Treaty. In certain circumstances, however, such as where the parties agree not to carry out other research and development in the same field, thereby forgoing the opportunity of gaining competitive advantages over the other parties, such agreements may fall within Article 101(1) of the Treaty and should therefore be included within the scope of this Regulation.

(7) The benefit of the exemption established by this Regulation should be limited to those agreements for which it can be assumed with sufficient certainty that they satisfy the conditions of Article 101(3) of the Treaty.

(8) Cooperation in research and development and in the exploitation of the results is most likely to promote technical and economic progress if the parties contribute complementary skills, assets or activities to the cooperation. This also includes scenarios where one party merely finances the research and development activities of another party.

(9) The joint exploitation of results can be considered as the natural consequence of joint research and development. It can take different forms such as manufacture, the exploitation of intellectual property rights that substantially contribute to technical or economic progress, or the marketing of new products.

(10) Consumers can generally be expected to benefit from the increased volume and effectiveness of research and development through the introduction of new or improved products or services, a quicker launch of those products or services, or the reduction of prices brought about by new or improved technologies or processes.

(11) In order to justify the exemption, the joint exploitation should relate to products, technologies or processes for which the use of the results of the research and development is decisive. Moreover, all the parties should agree in the research and development agreement that they will all have full access to the final results of the joint research and development, including any arising intellectual property rights and know-how, for the purposes of further research and development and exploitation, as soon as the final results become available. Access to the results should generally not be limited as regards the use of the results for the purposes of further research and development. However, where the parties, in accordance with this Regulation, limit their rights of exploitation, in particular where they specialise in the context of exploitation, access to the results for the purposes of exploitation may be limited accordingly. Moreover, where academic bodies, research institutes or undertakings which supply research and development as a commercial service without normally being active in the exploitation of results participate in research and development, they may agree to use the results of research and development solely for the purpose of further research. Depending on their capabilities and commercial needs, the parties may make unequal contributions to their research and development cooperation. Therefore, in order to reflect, and to make up for, the differences in the value or the nature of the parties' contributions, a research and development agreement benefiting from this Regulation may provide that one party is to compensate another for obtaining access to the results for the purposes of further research or exploitation. However, the compensation should not be so high as to effectively impede such access.

(12) Similarly, where the research and development agreement does not provide for any joint exploitation of the results, the parties should agree in the research and development agreement to grant each other access to their respective pre-existing know-how, as long as this know-how is indispensable for the purposes of the exploitation of the results by the other parties. The rates of any licence fee charged should not be so high as to effectively impede access to the know-how by the other parties.

(13) The exemption established by this Regulation should be limited to research and development agreements which do not afford the undertakings the possibility of eliminating competition in respect of a substantial part of the products, services or technologies in question. It is necessary to

exclude from the block exemption agreements between competitors whose combined share of the market for products, services or technologies capable of being improved or replaced by the results of the research and development exceeds a certain level at the time the agreement is entered into. However, there is no presumption that research and development agreements are either caught by Article 101(1) of the Treaty or that they fail to satisfy the conditions of Article 101(3) of the Treaty once the market share threshold set out in this Regulation is exceeded or other conditions of this Regulation are not met. In such cases, an individual assessment of the research and development agreement needs to be conducted under Article 101 of the Treaty.

(14) In order to ensure the maintenance of effective competition during joint exploitation of the results, provision should be made for the block exemption to cease to apply if the parties' combined share of the market for the products, services or technologies arising out of the joint research and development becomes too great. The exemption should continue to apply, irrespective of the parties' market shares, for a certain period after the commencement of joint exploitation, so as to await stabilisation of their market shares, particularly after the introduction of an entirely new product, and to guarantee a minimum period of return on the investments involved.

(15) This Regulation should not exempt agreements containing restrictions which are not indispensable to the attainment of the positive effects generated by a research and development agreement. In principle, agreements containing certain types of severe restrictions of competition such as limitations on the freedom of parties to carry out research and development in a field unconnected to the agreement, the fixing of prices charged to third parties, limitations on output or sales, and limitations on effecting passive sales for the contract products or contract technologies in territories or to customers reserved for other parties should be excluded from the benefit of the exemption established by this Regulation irrespective of the market share of the parties. In this context, field of use restrictions do not constitute limitations of output or sales, and also do not constitute territorial or customer restrictions.

(16) The market share limitation, the non-exemption of certain agreements and the conditions provided for in this Regulation normally ensure that the agreements to which the block exemption applies do not enable the parties to eliminate competition in respect of a substantial part of the products or services in question.

(17) The possibility cannot be ruled out that anti-competitive foreclosure effects may arise where one party finances several research and development projects carried out by competitors with regard to the same contract products or contract technologies, in particular where it obtains the exclusive right to exploit the results vis-à-vis third parties. Therefore the benefit of this Regulation should be conferred on such paid-for research and development agreements only if the combined market share of all the parties involved in the connected agreements, that is to say, the financing party and all the parties carrying out the research and development, does not exceed 25 %.

(18) Agreements between undertakings which are not competing manufacturers of products, technologies or processes capable of being improved, substituted or replaced by the results of the research and development will only eliminate effective competition in research and development in exceptional circumstances. It is therefore appropriate to enable such agreements to benefit from the exemption established by this Regulation irrespective of market share and to address any exceptional cases by way of withdrawal of its benefit.

(19) The Commission may withdraw the benefit of this Regulation, pursuant to Article 29(1) of Council Regulation (EC) No 1/2003 of 16 December 2002 on the implementation of the rules on competition laid down in Articles 81 and 82 of the Treaty[3], where it finds in a particular case that an agreement to which the exemption provided for in this Regulation applies nevertheless has effects which are incompatible with Article 101(3) of the Treaty.

(20) The competition authority of a Member State may withdraw the benefit of this Regulation pursuant to Article 29(2) of Regulation (EC) No 1/2003 in respect of the territory of that Member State, or a part thereof where, in a particular case, an agreement to which the exemption established by this Regulation applies nevertheless has effects which are incompatible with Article 101(3) of the

[3] OJ L 1, 4.1.2003, p. 1.

Treaty in the territory of that Member State, or in a part thereof, and where such territory has all the characteristics of a distinct geographic market.

(21) The benefit of this Regulation could be withdrawn pursuant to Article 29 of Regulation (EC) No 1/2003, for example, where the existence of a research and development agreement substantially restricts the scope for third parties to carry out research and development in the relevant field because of the limited research capacity available elsewhere, where because of the particular structure of supply, the existence of the research and development agreement substantially restricts the access of third parties to the market for the contract products or contract technologies, where without any objectively valid reason, the parties do not exploit the results of the joint research and development vis-à-vis third parties, where the contract products or contract technologies are not subject in the whole or a substantial part of the internal market to effective competition from products, technologies or processes considered by users as equivalent in view of their characteristics, price and intended use, or where the existence of the research and development agreement would restrict competition in innovation or eliminate effective competition in research and development on a particular market.

(22) As research and development agreements are often of a long-term nature, especially where the cooperation extends to the exploitation of the results, the period of validity of this Regulation should be fixed at 12 years,

HAS ADOPTED THIS REGULATION:

Article 1 Definitions

1. For the purposes of this Regulation, the following definitions shall apply:
   (a) "research and development agreement" means an agreement entered into between two or more parties which relate to the conditions under which those parties pursue:
      (i) joint research and development of contract products or contract technologies and joint exploitation of the results of that research and development;
      (ii) joint exploitation of the results of research and development of contract products or contract technologies jointly carried out pursuant to a prior agreement between the same parties;
      (iii) joint research and development of contract products or contract technologies excluding joint exploitation of the results;
      (iv) paid-for research and development of contract products or contract technologies and joint exploitation of the results of that research and development;
      (v) joint exploitation of the results of paid-for research and development of contract products or contract technologies pursuant to a prior agreement between the same parties; or
      (vi) paid-for research and development of contract products or contract technologies excluding joint exploitation of the results;
   (b) "agreement" means an agreement, a decision by an association of undertakings or a concerted practice;
   (c) "research and development" means the acquisition of know-how relating to products, technologies or processes and the carrying out of theoretical analysis, systematic study or experimentation, including experimental production, technical testing of products or processes, the establishment of the necessary facilities and the obtaining of intellectual property rights for the results;
   (d) "product" means a good or a service, including both intermediary goods or services and final goods or services;
   (e) "contract technology" means a technology or process arising out of the joint research and development;
   (f) "contract product" means a product arising out of the joint research and development or manufactured or provided applying the contract technologies;

(g) "exploitation of the results" means the production or distribution of the contract products or the application of the contract technologies or the assignment or licensing of intellectual property rights or the communication of know-how required for such manufacture or application;

(h) "intellectual property rights" means intellectual property rights, including industrial property rights, copyright and neighbouring rights;

(i) "know-how" means a package of non-patented practical information, resulting from experience and testing, which is secret, substantial and identified;

(j) "secret", in the context of know-how, means that the know-how is not generally known or easily accessible;

(k) "substantial", in the context of know-how, means that the know-how is significant and useful for the manufacture of the contract products or the application of the contract technologies;

(l) "identified", in the context of know-how, means that the know-how is described in a sufficiently comprehensive manner so as to make it possible to verify that it fulfils the criteria of secrecy and substantiality;

(m) "joint", in the context of activities carried out under a research and development agreement, means activities where the work involved is:

- (i) carried out by a joint team, organisation or undertaking;
- (ii) jointly entrusted to a third party; or
- (iii) allocated between the parties by way of specialisation in the context of research and development or exploitation;

(n) "specialisation in the context of research and development" means that each of the parties is involved in the research and development activities covered by the research and development agreement and they divide the research and development work between them in any way that they consider most appropriate; this does not include paid-for research and development;

(o) "specialisation in the context of exploitation" means that the parties allocate between them individual tasks such as production or distribution, or impose restrictions upon each other regarding the exploitation of the results such as restrictions in relation to certain territories, customers or fields of use; this includes a scenario where only one party produces and distributes the contract products on the basis of an exclusive licence granted by the other parties;

(p) "paid-for research and development" means research and development that is carried out by one party and financed by a financing party;

(q) "financing party" means a party financing paid-for research and development while not carrying out any of the research and development activities itself;

(r) "competing undertaking" means an actual or potential competitor;

(s) "actual competitor" means an undertaking that is supplying a product, technology or process capable of being improved, substituted or replaced by the contract product or the contract technology on the relevant geographic market;

(t) "potential competitor" means an undertaking that, in the absence of the research and development agreement, would, on realistic grounds and not just as a mere theoretical possibility, in case of a small but permanent increase in relative prices be likely to undertake, within not more than 3 years, the necessary additional investments or other necessary switching costs to supply a product, technology or process capable of being improved, substituted or replaced by the contract product or contract technology on the relevant geographic market;

(u) "relevant product market" means the relevant market for the products capable of being improved, substituted or replaced by the contract products;

(v) "relevant technology market" means the relevant market for the technologies or processes capable of being improved, substituted or replaced by the contract technologies.

2. For the purposes of this Regulation, the terms "undertaking" and "party" shall include their respective connected undertakings.

"Connected undertakings" means:

(a) undertakings in which a party to the research and development agreement, directly or indirectly:
   (i) has the power to exercise more than half the voting rights;
   (ii) has the power to appoint more than half the members of the supervisory board, board of management or bodies legally representing the undertaking; or
   (iii) has the right to manage the undertaking's affairs;

(b) undertakings which directly or indirectly have, over a party to the research and development agreement, the rights or powers listed in point (a);

(c) undertakings in which an undertaking referred to in point (b) has, directly or indirectly, the rights or powers listed in point (a);

(d) undertakings in which a party to the research and development agreement together with one or more of the undertakings referred to in points (a), (b) or (c), or in which two or more of the latter undertakings, jointly have the rights or powers listed in point (a);

(e) undertakings in which the rights or the powers listed in point (a) are jointly held by:
   (i) parties to the research and development agreement or their respective connected undertakings referred to in points (a) to (d); or
   (ii) one or more of the parties to the research and development agreement or one or more of their connected undertakings referred to in points (a) to (d) and one or more third parties.

Article 2 Exemption

1. Pursuant to Article 101(3) of the Treaty and subject to the provisions of this Regulation, it is hereby declared that Article 101(1) of the Treaty shall not apply to research and development agreements.

This exemption shall apply to the extent that such agreements contain restrictions of competition falling within the scope of Article 101(1) of the Treaty.

2. The exemption provided for in paragraph 1 shall apply to research and development agreements containing provisions which relate to the assignment or licensing of intellectual property rights to one or more of the parties or to an entity the parties establish to carry out the joint research and development, paid-for research and development or joint exploitation, provided that those provisions do not constitute the primary object of such agreements, but are directly related to and necessary for their implementation.

Article 3 Conditions for exemption

1. The exemption provided for in Article 2 shall apply subject to the conditions set out in paragraphs 2 to 5.

2. The research and development agreement must stipulate that all the parties have full access to the final results of the joint research and development or paid-for research and development, including any resulting intellectual property rights and know-how, for the purposes of further research and development and exploitation, as soon as they become available. Where the parties limit their rights of exploitation in accordance with this Regulation, in particular where they specialise in the context of exploitation, access to the results for the purposes of exploitation may be limited accordingly. Moreover, research institutes, academic bodies, or undertakings which supply research and development as a commercial service without normally being active in the exploitation of results may agree to confine their use of the results for the purposes of further research. The research and development agreement may foresee that the parties compensate each other for giving access to the results for the purposes of further research or exploitation, but the compensation must not be so high as to effectively impede such access.

3. Without prejudice to paragraph 2, where the research and development agreement provides only for joint research and development or paid-for research and development, the research and development agreement must stipulate that each party must be granted access to any pre-existing know-how of the other parties, if this know-how is indispensable for the purposes of its exploitation of the results. The research and development agreement may foresee that the parties compensate each other for giving access to their pre-existing know-how, but the compensation must not be so high as to effectively impede such access.

4. Any joint exploitation may only pertain to results which are protected by intellectual property rights or constitute know-how and which are indispensable for the manufacture of the contract products or the application of the contract technologies.

5. Parties charged with the manufacture of the contract products by way of specialisation in the context of exploitation must be required to fulfil orders for supplies of the contract products from the other parties, except where the research and development agreement also provides for joint distribution within the meaning of point (m)(i) or (ii) of Article 1(1) or where the parties have agreed that only the party manufacturing the contract products may distribute them.

Article 4 Market share threshold and duration of exemption

1. Where the parties are not competing undertakings, the exemption provided for in Article 2 shall apply for the duration of the research and development. Where the results are jointly exploited, the exemption shall continue to apply for 7 years from the time the contract products or contract technologies are first put on the market within the internal market.

2. Where two or more of the parties are competing undertakings, the exemption provided for in Article 2 shall apply for the period referred to in paragraph 1 of this Article only if, at the time the research and development agreement is entered into:

(a) in the case of research and development agreements referred to in point (a)(i), (ii) or (iii) of Article 1(1), the combined market share of the parties to a research and development agreement does not exceed 25 % on the relevant product and technology markets; or

(b) in the case of research and agreements referred to in point (a)(iv), (v) or (vi) of Article 1(1), the combined market share of the financing party and all the parties with which the financing party has entered into research and development agreements with regard to the same contract products or contract technologies, does not exceed 25 % on the relevant product and technology markets.

3. After the end of the period referred to in paragraph 1, the exemption shall continue to apply as long as the combined market share of the parties does not exceed 25 % on the relevant product and technology markets.

Article 5 Hardcore restrictions

The exemption provided for in Article 2 shall not apply to research and development agreements which, directly or indirectly, in isolation or in combination with other factors under the control of the parties, have as their object any of the following:

(a) the restriction of the freedom of the parties to carry out research and development independently or in cooperation with third parties in a field unconnected with that to which the research and development agreement relates or, after the completion of the joint research and development or the paid-for research and development, in the field to which it relates or in a connected field;

(b) the limitation of output or sales, with the exception of:

  (i) the setting of production targets where the joint exploitation of the results includes the joint production of the contract products;

  (ii) the setting of sales targets where the joint exploitation of the results includes the joint distribution of the contract products or the joint licensing of the contract technologies within the meaning of point (m)(i) or (ii) of Article 1(1);

  (iii) practices constituting specialisation in the context of exploitation; and

(iv) the restriction of the freedom of the parties to manufacture, sell, assign or license products, technologies or processes which compete with the contract products or contract technologies during the period for which the parties have agreed to jointly exploit the results;

(c) the fixing of prices when selling the contract product or licensing the contract technologies to third parties, with the exception of the fixing of prices charged to immediate customers or the fixing of licence fees charged to immediate licensees where the joint exploitation of the results includes the joint distribution of the contract products or the joint licensing of the contract technologies within the meaning of point (m)(i) or (ii) of Article 1(1);

(d) the restriction of the territory in which, or of the customers to whom, the parties may passively sell the contract products or license the contract technologies, with the exception of the requirement to exclusively license the results to another party;

(e) the requirement not to make any, or to limit, active sales of the contract products or contract technologies in territories or to customers which have not been exclusively allocated to one of the parties by way of specialisation in the context of exploitation;

(f) the requirement to refuse to meet demand from customers in the parties' respective territories, or from customers otherwise allocated between the parties by way of specialisation in the context of exploitation, who would market the contract products in other territories within the internal market;

(g) the requirement to make it difficult for users or resellers to obtain the contract products from other resellers within the internal market.

Article 6 Excluded restrictions

The exemption provided for in Article 2 shall not apply to the following obligations contained in research and development agreements:

(a) the obligation not to challenge after completion of the research and development the validity of intellectual property rights which the parties hold in the internal market and which are relevant to the research and development or, after the expiry of the research and development agreement, the validity of intellectual property rights which the parties hold in the internal market and which protect the results of the research and development, without prejudice to the possibility to provide for termination of the research and development agreement in the event of one of the parties challenging the validity of such intellectual property rights;

(b) the obligation not to grant licences to third parties to manufacture the contract products or to apply the contract technologies unless the agreement provides for the exploitation of the results of the joint research and development or paid-for research and development by at least one of the parties and such exploitation takes place in the internal market vis-à-vis third parties.

Article 7 Application of the market share threshold

For the purposes of applying the market share threshold provided for in Article 4 the following rules shall apply:

(a) the market share shall be calculated on the basis of the market sales value; if market sales value data are not available, estimates based on other reliable market information, including market sales volumes, may be used to establish the market share of the parties;

(b) the market share shall be calculated on the basis of data relating to the preceding calendar year;

(c) the market share held by the undertakings referred to in point (e) of the second subparagraph of Article 1(2) shall be apportioned equally to each undertaking having the rights or the powers listed in point (a) of that subparagraph;

(d) if the market share referred to in Article 4(3) is initially not more than 25 % but subsequently rises above that level without exceeding 30 %, the exemption provided for in Article 2 shall continue to apply for a period of two consecutive calendar years following the year in which the 25 % threshold was first exceeded;

(e) if the market share referred to in Article 4(3) is initially not more than 25 % but subsequently rises above 30 %, the exemption provided for in Article 2 shall continue to apply for a period of one calendar year following the year in which the level of 30 % was first exceeded;

(f) the benefit of points (d) and (e) may not be combined so as to exceed a period of two calendar years.

Article 8 Transitional period

The prohibition laid down in Article 101(1) of the Treaty shall not apply during the period from 1 January 2011 to 31 December 2012 in respect of agreements already in force on 31 December 2010 which do not satisfy the conditions for exemption provided for in this Regulation but which satisfy the conditions for exemption provided for in Regulation (EC) No 2659/2000.

Article 9 Period of validity

This Regulation shall enter into force on 1 January 2011.

It shall expire on 31 December 2022.

This Regulation shall be binding in its entirety and directly applicable in all Member States.

Done at Brussels, 14 December 2010.
For the Commission
The President
José Manuel Barroso

Commission Regulation (EU) No 1218/2010 of 14 December 2010 on the application of Article 101(3) of the Treaty on the Functioning of the European Union to certain categories of specialisation agreements

[OJ 2010 L335/43]

THE EUROPEAN COMMISSION,

Having regard to the Treaty on the Functioning of the European Union,

Having regard to Regulation (EEC) No 2821/71 of the Council of 20 December 1971 on application of Article 85(3) of the Treaty to categories of agreements, decisions and concerted practices[1],

Having published a draft of this Regulation,

After consulting the Advisory Committee on Restrictive Practices and Dominant Positions,

Whereas:

(1) Regulation (EEC) No 2821/71 empowers the Commission to apply Article 101(3) of the Treaty on the Functioning of the European Union* by regulation to certain categories of agreements, decisions and concerted practices falling within the scope of Article 101(1) of the Treaty which have as their object specialisation, including agreements necessary for achieving it.

[1] OJ L 285, 29.12.1971, p. 46.

* With effect from 1 December 2009, Article 81 of the EC Treaty has become Article 101 of the Treaty on the Functioning of the European Union (TFEU). The two Articles are, in substance, identical. For the purposes of this Regulation, references to Article 101 of the TFEU should be understood as references to Article 81 of the EC Treaty where appropriate. The TFEU also introduced certain changes in terminology, such as the replacement of "Community" by "Union" and "common market" by "internal market". The terminology of the TFEU will be used throughout this Regulation.

(2) Commission Regulation (EC) No 2658/2000 of 29 November 2000 on the application of Article 81(3) of the Treaty to categories of specialisation agreements[2] defines categories of specialisation agreements which the Commission regarded as normally satisfying the conditions laid down in Article 101(3) of the Treaty. In view of the overall positive experience with the application of that Regulation, which expires on 31 December 2010, and taking into account further experience acquired since its adoption, it is appropriate to adopt a new block exemption regulation.

(3) This Regulation should meet the two requirements of ensuring effective protection of competition and providing adequate legal security for undertakings. The pursuit of those objectives should take account of the need to simplify administrative supervision and the legislative framework to as great an extent as possible. Below a certain level of market power it can in general be presumed, for the application of Article 101(3) of the Treaty, that the positive effects of specialisation agreements will outweigh any negative effects on competition.

(4) For the application of Article 101(3) of the Treaty by regulation, it is not necessary to define those agreements which are capable of falling within Article 101(1) of the Treaty. In the individual assessment of agreements under Article 101(1) of the Treaty, account has to be taken of several factors, and in particular the market structure on the relevant market.

(5) The benefit of the exemption established by this Regulation should be limited to those agreements for which it can be assumed with sufficient certainty that they satisfy the conditions of Article 101(3) of the Treaty.

(6) Agreements on specialisation in production are most likely to contribute to improving the production or distribution of goods if the parties have complementary skills, assets or activities, because they can concentrate on the manufacture of certain products and thus operate more efficiently and supply the products more cheaply. The same can generally be said about agreements on specialisation in the preparation of services. Given effective competition, it is likely that consumers will receive a fair share of the resulting benefits.

(7) Such advantages can arise from agreements whereby one party fully or partly gives up the manufacture of certain products or preparation of certain services in favour of another party (unilateral specialisation), from agreements whereby each party fully or partly gives up the manufacture of certain products or preparation of certain services in favour of another party (reciprocal specialisation) and from agreements whereby the parties undertake to jointly manufacture certain products or prepare certain services (joint production). In the context of this Regulation, the concepts of unilateral and reciprocal specialisation do not require a party to reduce capacity, as it is sufficient if they reduce their production volumes. The concept of joint production, however, does not require the parties to reduce their individual production activities outside the scope of their envisaged joint production arrangement.

(8) The nature of unilateral and reciprocal specialisation agreements presupposes that the parties are active on the same product market. It is not necessary for the parties to be active on the same geographic market. Consequently, the application of this Regulation to unilateral and reciprocal specialisation agreements should be limited to scenarios where the parties are active on the same product market. Joint production agreements can be entered into by parties who are already active on the same product market but also by parties who wish to enter a product market by way of the agreement. Therefore, joint production agreements should fall within the scope of this Regulation irrespective of whether the parties are already active in the same product market.

(9) To ensure that the benefits of specialisation will materialise without one party leaving the market downstream of production entirely, unilateral and reciprocal specialisation agreements should only be covered by this Regulation where they provide for supply and purchase obligations or joint distribution. Supply and purchase obligations may, but do not have to, be of an exclusive nature.

(10) It can be presumed that, where the parties' share of the relevant market for the products which are the subject matter of a specialisation agreement does not exceed a certain level, the agreements will, as a general rule, give rise to economic benefits in the form of economies of scale or scope or better production technologies, while allowing consumers a fair share of the resulting benefits.

[2] OJ L 304, 5.12.2000, p. 3.

However, where the products manufactured under a specialisation agreement are intermediary products which one or more of the parties fully or partly use as an input for their own production of certain downstream products which they subsequently sell on the market, the exemption conferred by this Regulation should also be conditional on the parties' share on the relevant market for these downstream products not exceeding a certain level. In such a case, merely looking at the parties' market share at the level of the intermediary product would ignore the potential risk of foreclosing or increasing the price of inputs for competitors at the level of the downstream products. However, there is no presumption that specialisation agreements are either caught by Article 101(1) of the Treaty or that they fail to satisfy the conditions of Article 101(3) of the Treaty once the market share threshold set out in this Regulation is exceeded or other conditions of this Regulation are not met. In such cases, an individual assessment of the specialisation agreement needs to be conducted under Article 101 of the Treaty.

(11) This Regulation should not exempt agreements containing restrictions which are not indispensable to the attainment of the positive effects generated by a specialisation agreement. In principle, agreements containing certain types of severe restrictions of competition relating to the fixing of prices charged to third parties, limitation of output or sales, and allocation of markets or customers should be excluded from the benefit of the exemption established by this Regulation irrespective of the market share of the parties.

(12) The market share limitation, the non-exemption of certain agreements and the conditions provided for in this Regulation normally ensure that the agreements to which the block exemption applies do not enable the parties to eliminate competition in respect of a substantial part of the products or services in question.

(13) The Commission may withdraw the benefit of this Regulation, pursuant to Article 29(1) of Council Regulation (EC) No 1/2003 of 16 December 2002 on the implementation of the rules on competition laid down in Articles 81 and 82 of the Treaty[3], where it finds in a particular case that an agreement to which the exemption provided for in this Regulation applies nevertheless has effects which are incompatible with Article 101(3) of the Treaty.

(14) The competition authority of a Member State may withdraw the benefit of this Regulation pursuant to Article 29(2) of Regulation (EC) No 1/2003 in respect of the territory of that Member State, or a part thereof where, in a particular case, an agreement to which the exemption established by this Regulation applies nevertheless has effects which are incompatible with Article 101(3) of the Treaty in the territory of that Member State, or in a part thereof, and where such territory has all the characteristics of a distinct geographic market.

(15) The benefit of this Regulation could be withdrawn pursuant to Article 29 of Regulation (EC) No 1/2003 where, for example, the relevant market is very concentrated and competition is already weak, in particular because of the individual market positions of other market participants or links between other market participants created by parallel specialisation agreements.

(16) In order to facilitate the conclusion of specialisation agreements, which can have a bearing on the structure of the parties, the period of validity of this Regulation should be fixed at 12 years,

HAS ADOPTED THIS REGULATION:

Article 1 Definitions

1. For the purposes of this Regulation, the following definitions shall apply:
   (a) "specialisation agreement" means a unilateral specialisation agreement, a reciprocal specialisation agreement or a joint production agreement;
   (b) "unilateral specialisation agreement" means an agreement between two parties which are active on the same product market by virtue of which one party agrees to fully or partly cease production of certain products or to refrain from producing those products and to purchase them from the other party, who agrees to produce and supply those products;
   (c) "reciprocal specialisation agreement" means an agreement between two or more parties which are active on the same product market, by virtue of which two or more parties on a reciprocal basis agree to fully or partly cease or refrain from producing certain but

[3] OJ L 1, 4.1.2003, p. 1.

different products and to purchase these products from the other parties, who agree to produce and supply them;

(d) "joint production agreement" means an agreement by virtue of which two or more parties agree to produce certain products jointly;

(e) "agreement" means an agreement, a decision by an association of undertakings or a concerted practice;

(f) "product" means a good or a service, including both intermediary goods or services and final goods or services, with the exception of distribution and rental services;

(g) "production" means the manufacture of goods or the preparation of services and includes production by way of subcontracting;

(h) "preparation of services" means activities upstream of the provision of services to customers;

(i) "relevant market" means the relevant product and geographic market to which the specialisation products belong, and, in addition, where the specialisation products are intermediary products which one or more of the parties fully or partly use captively for the production of downstream products, the relevant product and geographic market to which the downstream products belong;

(j) "specialisation product" means a product which is produced under a specialisation agreement;

(k) "downstream product" means a product for which a specialisation product is used by one or more of the parties as an input and which is sold by those parties on the market;

(l) "competing undertaking" means an actual or potential competitor;

(m) "actual competitor" means an undertaking that is active on the same relevant market;

(n) "potential competitor" means an undertaking that, in the absence of the specialisation agreement, would, on realistic grounds and not just as a mere theoretical possibility, in case of a small but permanent increase in relative prices be likely to undertake, within not more than 3 years, the necessary additional investments or other necessary switching costs to enter the relevant market;

(o) "exclusive supply obligation" means an obligation not to supply a competing undertaking other than a party to the agreement with the specialisation product;

(p) "exclusive purchase obligation" means an obligation to purchase the specialisation product only from a party to the agreement;

(q) "joint", in the context of distribution, means that the parties:
   (i) carry out the distribution of the products by way of a joint team, organisation or undertaking; or
   (ii) appoint a third party distributor on an exclusive or non-exclusive basis, provided that the third party is not a competing undertaking;

(r) "distribution" means distribution, including the sale of goods and the provision of services.

2. For the purposes of this Regulation, the terms "undertaking" and "party" shall include their respective connected undertakings.

"Connected undertakings" means:

(a) undertakings in which a party to the specialisation agreement, directly or indirectly:
   (i) has the power to exercise more than half the voting rights;
   (ii) has the power to appoint more than half the members of the supervisory board, board of management or bodies legally representing the undertaking; or
   (iii) has the right to manage the undertaking's affairs;

(b) undertakings which directly or indirectly have, over a party to the specialisation agreement, the rights or powers listed in point (a);

(c) undertakings in which an undertaking referred to in point (b) has, directly or indirectly, the rights or powers listed in point (a);

(d) undertakings in which a party to the specialisation agreement together with one or more of the undertakings referred to in points (a), (b) or (c), or in which two or more of the latter undertakings, jointly have the rights or powers listed in point (a);

(e) undertakings in which the rights or the powers listed in point (a) are jointly held by:

 (i) parties to the specialisation agreement or their respective connected undertakings referred to in points (a) to (d); or

 (ii) one or more of the parties to the specialisation agreement or one or more of their connected undertakings referred to in points (a) to (d) and one or more third parties.

Article 2 Exemption

1. Pursuant to Article 101(3) of the Treaty and subject to the provisions of this Regulation, it is hereby declared that Article 101(1) of the Treaty shall not apply to specialisation agreements.

This exemption shall apply to the extent that such agreements contain restrictions of competition falling within the scope of Article 101(1) of the Treaty.

2. The exemption provided for in paragraph 1 shall apply to specialisation agreements containing provisions which relate to the assignment or licensing of intellectual property rights to one or more of the parties, provided that those provisions do not constitute the primary object of such agreements, but are directly related to and necessary for their implementation.

3. The exemption provided for in paragraph 1 shall apply to specialisation agreements whereby:

(a) the parties accept an exclusive purchase or exclusive supply obligation; or

(b) the parties do not independently sell the specialisation products but jointly distribute those products.

Article 3 Market share threshold

The exemption provided for in Article 2 shall apply on condition that the combined market share of the parties does not exceed 20 % on any relevant market.

Article 4 Hardcore restrictions

The exemption provided for in Article 2 shall not apply to specialisation agreements which, directly or indirectly, in isolation or in combination with other factors under the control of the parties, have as their object any of the following:

(a) the fixing of prices when selling the products to third parties with the exception of the fixing of prices charged to immediate customers in the context of joint distribution;

(b) the limitation of output or sales with the exception of:

 (i) provisions on the agreed amount of products in the context of unilateral or reciprocal specialisation agreements or the setting of the capacity and production volume in the context of a joint production agreement; and

 (ii) the setting of sales targets in the context of joint distribution;

(c) the allocation of markets or customers.

Article 5 Application of the market share threshold

For the purposes of applying the market share threshold provided for in Article 3 the following rules shall apply:

(a) the market share shall be calculated on the basis of the market sales value; if market sales value data are not available, estimates based on other reliable market information, including market sales volumes, may be used to establish the market share of the parties;

(b) the market share shall be calculated on the basis of data relating to the preceding calendar year;

(c) the market share held by the undertakings referred to in point (e) of the second subparagraph of Article 1(2) shall be apportioned equally to each undertaking having the rights or the powers listed in point (a) of that subparagraph;

(d) if the market share referred to in Article 3 is initially not more than 20 % but subsequently rises above that level without exceeding 25 %, the exemption provided for in Article 2 shall continue to apply for a period of 2 consecutive calendar years following the year in which the 20 % threshold was first exceeded;

(e) if the market share referred to in Article 3 is initially not more than 20 % but subsequently rises above 25 %, the exemption provided for in Article 2 shall continue to apply for a period of 1 calendar year following the year in which the level of 25 % was first exceeded;

(f) the benefit of points (d) and (e) may not be combined so as to exceed a period of 2 calendar years.

Article 6 Transitional period

The prohibition laid down in Article 101(1) of the Treaty shall not apply during the period from 1 January 2011 to 31 December 2012 in respect of agreements already in force on 31 December 2010 which do not satisfy the conditions for exemption provided for in this Regulation but which satisfy the conditions for exemption provided for in Regulation (EC) No 2658/2000.

Article 7 Period of validity

This Regulation shall enter into force on 1 January 2011.

It shall expire on 31 December 2022.

This Regulation shall be binding in its entirety and directly applicable in all Member States.

Done at Brussels, 14 December 2010.
For the Commission
The President
José Manuel Barroso

Consumer protection

Council Directive of 25 July 1985 on the approximation of the laws, regulations and administrative provisions of the Member States concerning liability for defective products (85/374/EEC)*

[OJ 1985 L210/29]

THE COUNCIL OF THE EUROPEAN COMMUNITIES,

Having regard to the Treaty establishing the European Economic Community, and in particular Article 100 thereof,

Having regard to the proposal from the Commission,[1]

Having regard to the opinion of the European Parliament,[2]

Having regard to the opinion of the Economic and Social Committee,[3]

Whereas approximation of the laws of the Member States concerning the liability of the producer for damage caused by the defectiveness of his products is necessary because the existing divergences may distort competition and affect the movement of goods within the common market and entail a differing degree of protection of the consumer against damage caused by a defective product to his health or property;

* **Editor's Note:** Amended by Directive 99/34 (OJ 1999 L141/20).

[1] OJ No C241, 14. 10. 1976, p. 9 and OJ No C271, 26. 10. 1979, p. 3.

[2] OJ No C127, 21. 5. 1979, p. 61.

[3] OJ No C114, 7. 5. 1979, p. 15.

Whereas liability without fault on the part of the producer is the sole means of adequately solving the problem, peculiar to our age of increasing technicality, of a fair apportionment of the risks inherent in modern technological production;

Whereas liability without fault should apply only to movables which have been industrially produced; whereas, as a result, it is appropriate to exclude liability for agricultural products and game, except where they have undergone a processing of an industrial nature which could cause a defect in these products;

Whereas the liability provided for in this Directive should also apply to movables which are used in the construction of immovables or are installed in immovables;

Whereas protection of the consumer requires that all producers involved in the production process should be made liable, in so far as their finished product, component part or any raw material supplied by them was defective; whereas, for the same reason, liability should extend to importers of products into the Community and to persons who present themselves as producers by affixing their name, trade mark or other distinguishing feature or who supply a product the producer of which cannot be identified;

Whereas, in situations where several persons are liable for the same damage, the protection of the consumer requires that the injured person should be able to claim full compensation for the damage from any one of them;

Whereas, to protect the physical well-being and property of the consumer, the defectiveness of the product should be determined by reference not to its fitness for use but to the lack of the safety which the public at large is entitled to expect; whereas the safety is assessed by excluding any misuse of the product not reasonable under the circumstances;

Whereas a fair apportionment of risk between the injured person and the producer implies that the producer should be able to free himself from liability if he furnishes proof as to the existence of certain exonerating circumstances;

Whereas the protection of the consumer requires that the liability of the producer remains unaffected by acts or omissions of other persons having contributed to cause the damage; whereas, however, the contributory negligence of the injured person may be taken into account to reduce or disallow such liability;

Whereas the protection of the consumer requires compensation for death and personal injury as well as compensation for damage to property; whereas the latter should nevertheless be limited to goods for private use or consumption and be subject to a deduction of a lower threshold of a fixed amount in order to avoid litigation in an excessive number of cases; whereas this Directive should not prejudice compensation for pain and suffering and other non-material damages payable, where appropriate, under the law applicable to the case;

Whereas a uniform period of limitation for the bringing of action for compensation is in the interests both of the injured person and of the producer;

Whereas products age in the course of time, higher safety standards are developed and the state of science and technology progresses; whereas, therefore, it would not be reasonable to make the producer liable for an unlimited period for the defectiveness of his product; whereas, therefore, liability should expire after a reasonable length of time, without prejudice to claims pending at law;

Whereas, to achieve effective protection of consumers, no contractual derogation should be permitted as regards the liability of the producer in relation to the injured person;

Whereas under the legal systems of the Member States an injured party may have a claim for damages based on grounds of contractual liability or on grounds of non-contractual liability other than that provided for in this Directive; in so far as these provisions also serve to attain the objective of effective protection of consumers, they should remain unaffected by this Directive; whereas, in so far as effective protection of consumers in the sector of pharmaceutical products is already also attained in a Member State under a special liability system, claims based on this system should similarly remain possible;

Whereas, to the extent that liability for nuclear injury or damage is already covered in all Member States by adequate special rules, it has been possible to exclude damage of this type from the scope of this Directive;

Whereas, since the exclusion of primary agricultural products and game from the scope of this Directive may be felt, in certain Member States, in view of what is expected for the protection of consumers, to restrict unduly such protection, it should be possible for a Member State to extend liability to such products;

Whereas, for similar reasons, the possibility offered to a producer to free himself from liability if he proves that the state of scientific and technical knowledge at the time when he put the product into circulation was not such as to enable the existence of a defect to be discovered may be felt in certain Member States to restrict unduly the protection of the consumer; whereas it should therefore be possible for a Member State to maintain in its legislation or to provide by new legislation that this exonerating circumstance is not admitted; whereas, in the case of new legislation, making use of this derogation should, however, be subject to a Community stand-still procedure, in order to raise, if possible, the level of protection in a uniform manner throughout the Community;

Whereas, taking into account the legal traditions in most of the Member States, it is inappropriate to set any financial ceiling on the producer's liability without fault; whereas, in so far as there are, however, differing traditions, it seems possible to admit that a Member State may derogate from the principle of unlimited liability by providing a limit for the total liability of the producer for damage resulting from a death or personal injury and caused by identical items with the same defect, provided that this limit is established at a level sufficiently high to guarantee adequate protection of the consumer and the correct functioning of the common market;

Whereas the harmonization resulting from this cannot be total at the present stage, but opens the way towards greater harmonization; whereas it is therefore necessary that the Council receive at regular intervals, reports from the Commission on the application of this Directive, accompanied, as the case may be, by appropriate proposals;

Whereas it is particularly important in this respect that a re-examination be carried out of those parts of the Directive relating to the derogations open to the Member States, at the expiry of a period of sufficient length to gather practical experience on the effects of these derogations on the protection of consumers and on the functioning of the common market,

HAS ADOPTED THIS DIRECTIVE:

Article 1

The producer shall be liable for damage caused by a defect in his product.

Article 2

For the purpose of this Directive, 'product' means all movables even if incorporated into another movable or into an immovable. 'Product' includes electricity.

Article 3

1. 'Producer' means the manufacturer of a finished product, the producer of any raw material or the manufacturer of a component part and any person who, by putting his name, trade mark or other distinguishing feature on the product presents himself as its producer.

2. Without prejudice to the liability of the producer, any person who imports into the Community a product for sale, hire, leasing or any form of distribution in the course of his business shall be deemed to be a producer within the meaning of this Directive and shall be responsible as a producer.

3. Where the producer of the product cannot be identified, each supplier of the product shall be treated as its producer unless he informs the injured person, within a reasonable time, of the identity of the producer or of the person who supplied him with the product. The same shall apply, in the case of an imported product, if this product does not indicate the identity of the importer referred to in paragraph 2, even if the name of the producer is indicated.

Article 4

The injured person shall be required to prove the damage, the defect and the causal relationship between defect and damage.

Article 5

Where, as a result of the provisions of this Directive, two or more persons are liable for the same damage, they shall be liable jointly and severally, without prejudice to the provisions of national law concerning the rights of contribution or recourse.

Article 6

1. A product is defective when it does not provide the safety which a person is entitled to expect, taking all circumstances into account, including:
   (a) the presentation of the product;
   (b) the use to which it could reasonably be expected that the product would be put;
   (c) the time when the product was put into circulation.

2. A product shall not be considered defective for the sole reason that a better product is subsequently put into circulation.

Article 7

The producer shall not be liable as a result of this Directive if he proves:

(a) that he did not put the product into circulation; or
(b) that, having regard to the circumstances, it is probable that the defect which caused the damage did not exist at the time when the product was put into circulation by him or that this defect came into being afterwards; or
(c) that the product was neither manufactured by him for sale or any form of distribution for economic purpose nor manufactured or distributed by him in the course of his business; or
(d) that the defect is due to compliance of the product with mandatory regulations issued by the public authorities; or
(e) that the state of scientific and technical knowledge at the time when he put the product into circulation was not such as to enable the existence of the defect to be discovered; or
(f) in the case of a manufacturer of a component, that the defect is attributable to the design of the product in which the component has been fitted or to the instructions given by the manufacturer of the product.

Article 8

1. Without prejudice to the provisions of national law concerning the right of contribution or recourse, the liability of the producer shall not be reduced when the damage is caused both by a defect in product and by the act or omission of a third party.

2. The liability of the producer may be reduced or disallowed when, having regard to all the circumstances, the damage is caused both by a defect in the product and by the fault of the injured person or any person for whom the injured person is responsible.

Article 9

For the purpose of Article 1, 'damage' means:

(a) damage caused by death or by personal injuries;
(b) damage to, or destruction of, any item of property other than the defective product itself, with a lower threshold of 500 ECU, provided that the item of property:
    (i) is of a type ordinarily intended for private use or consumption, and
    (ii) was used by the injured person mainly for his own private use or consumption.

This Article shall be without prejudice to national provisions relating to non-material damage.

Article 10

1. Member States shall provide in their legislation that a limitation period of three years shall apply to proceedings for the recovery of damages as provided for in this Directive. The limitation period shall begin to run from the day on which the plaintiff became aware, or should reasonably have become aware, of the damage, the defect and the identity of the producer.

2. The laws of Member States regulating suspension or interruption of the limitation period shall not be affected by this Directive.

Article 11

Member States shall provide in their legislation that the rights conferred upon the injured person pursuant to this Directive shall be extinguished upon the expiry of a period of 10 years from the date on which the producer put into circulation the actual product which caused the damage, unless the injured person has in the meantime instituted proceedings against the producer.

Article 12

The liability of the producer arising from this Directive may not, in relation to the injured person, be limited or excluded by a provision limiting his liability or exempting him from liability.

Article 13

This Directive shall not affect any rights which an injured person may have according to the rules of the law of contractual or non-contractual liability or a special liability system existing at the moment when this Directive is notified.

Article 14

This Directive shall not apply to injury or damage arising from nuclear accidents and covered by international conventions ratified by the Member States.

Article 15

1. Each Member State may:

—

(b) by way of derogation from Article 7(e), maintain or, subject to the procedure set out in paragraph 2 of this Article, provide in this legislation that the producer shall be liable even if he proves that the state of scientific and technical knowledge at the time when he put the product into circulation was not such as to enable the existence of a defect to be discovered.

2. A Member State wishing to introduce the measure specified in paragraph 1(b) shall communicate the text of the proposed measure to the Commission. The Commission shall inform the other Member States thereof. The Member State concerned shall hold the proposed measure in abeyance for nine months after the Commission is informed and provided that in the meantime the Commission has not submitted to the Council a proposal amending this Directive on the relevant matter. However, if within three months of receiving the said information, the Commission does not advise the Member State concerned that it intends submitting such a proposal to the Council, the Member State may take the proposed measure immediately. If the Commission does submit to the Council such a proposal amending this Directive within the aforementioned nine months, the Member State concerned shall hold the proposed measure in abeyance for a further period of 18 months from the date on which the proposal is submitted.

3. Ten years after the date of notification of this Directive, the Commission shall submit to the Council a report on the effect that rulings by the courts as to the application of Article 7(e) and of paragraph 1(b) of this Article have on consumer protection and the functioning of the common market. In the light of this report the Council, acting on a proposal from the Commission and pursuant to the terms of Article 100 of the Treaty, shall decide whether to repeal Article 7(e).

Article 16

1. Any Member State may provide that a producer's total liability for damage resulting from a death or personal injury and caused by identical items with the same defect shall be limited to an amount which may not be less than 70 million ECU.

2. Ten years after the date of notification of this Directive, the Commission shall submit to the Council a report on the effect on consumer protection and the functioning of the common market of the implementation of the financial limit on liability by those Member States which have used the option provided for in paragraph 1. In the light of this report the Council, acting on a proposal from

the Commission and pursuant to the terms of Article 100 of the Treaty, shall decide whether to repeal paragraph 1.

Article 17

This Directive shall not apply to products put into circulation before the date on which the provisions referred to in Article 19 enter into force.

Article 18

1. For the purposes of this Directive, the ECU shall be that defined by Regulation (EEC) No 3180/78,[4] as amended by Regulation (EEC) No 2626/84[5] The equivalent in national currency shall initially be calculated at the rate obtaining on the date of adoption of this Directive.

2. Every five years the Council, acting on a proposal from the Commission, shall examine and, if need be, revise the amounts in this Directive, in the light of economic and monetary trends in the Community.

Article 19

1. Member States shall bring into force, not later than three years from the date of notification of this Directive, the laws, regulations and administrative provisions necessary to comply with this Directive. They shall forthwith inform the Commission thereof.[6]

2. The procedure set out in Article 15(2) shall apply from the date of notification of this Directive.

Article 20

Member States shall communicate to the Commission the texts of the main provisions of national law which they subsequently adopt in the field governed by this Directive.

Article 21

Every five years the Commission shall present a report to the Council on the application of this Directive and, if necessary, shall submit appropriate proposals to it.

Article 22

This Directive is addressed to the Member States.

Done at Brussels, 25 July 1985.
For the Council
The President
J. POOS

Council Directive of 20 December 1985 to protect the consumer in respect of contracts negotiated away from business premises (85/577/EEC)*

[OJ 1985, L 372/31]

THE COUNCIL OF THE EUROPEAN COMMUNITIES,

Having regard to the Treaty establishing the European Economic Community, and in particular Article 100 thereof,

Having regard to the proposal from the Commission,[1]

[4] OJ No L379, 30.12.1978, p. 1.
[5] OJ No L247, 16.9.1984, p. 1.
[6] This Directive was notified to the Member States on 30 July 1985.
* **Editor's Note:** This Directive will be repealed and replaced by Directive 2011/83 effective 13 June 2014, until which time Directive 85/577 remains in force.
[1] OJ No C22, 29.1.1977, p. 6; OJ No C127, 1.6.1978, p. 6.

Having regard to the opinion of the European Parliament,[2]

Having regard to the opinion of the Economic and Social Committee,[3]

Whereas it is a common form of commercial practice in the Member States for the conclusion of a contract or a unilateral engagement between a trader and consumer to be made away from the business premises of the trader, and whereas such contracts and engagements are the subject of legislation which differs from one Member State to another;

Whereas any disparity between such legislation may directly affect the functioning of the common market; whereas it is therefore necessary to approximate laws in this field;

Whereas the preliminary programme of the European Economic Community for a consumer protection and information policy[4] provides *inter alia*, under paragraphs 24 and 25, that appropriate measures be taken to protect consumers against unfair commercial practices in respect of doorstep selling; whereas the second programme of the European Economic Community for a consumer protection and information policy[5] confirmed that the action and priorities defined in the preliminary programme would be pursued;

Whereas the special feature of contracts concluded away from the business premises of the trader is that as a rule it is the trader who initiates the contract negotiations, for which the consumer is unprepared or which he does not except; whereas the consumer is often unable to compare the quality and price of the offer with other offers;

Whereas this surprise element generally exists not only in contracts made at the doorstep but also in other forms of contract concluded by the trader away from his business premises;

Whereas the consumer should be given a right of cancellation over a period of at least seven days in order to enable him to assess the obligations arising under the contract;

Whereas appropriate measures should be taken to ensure that the consumer is informed in writing of this period for reflection;

Whereas the freedom of Member States to maintain or introduce a total or partial prohibition on the conclusion of contracts away from business premises, inasmuch as they consider this to be in the interest of consumers, must not be affected;

HAS ADOPTED THIS DIRECTIVE:

Article 1

1. This Directive shall apply to contracts under which a trader supplies goods or services to a consumer and which are concluded:

- during an excursion organised by the trader away from his business premises, or
- during a visit by a trader
  - (i) to the consumer's home or to that of another consumer;
  - (ii) to the consumer's place of work;

  where the visit does not take place at the express request of the consumer.

2. This Directive shall also apply to contracts for the supply of goods or services other than those concerning which the consumer requested the visit of the trader, provided that when he requested the visit the consumer did not know, or could not reasonably have known, that the supply of those other goods or services formed part of the trader's commercial or professional activities.

3. This Directive shall also apply to contracts in respect of which an offer was made by the consumer under conditions similar to those described in paragraph 1 or paragraph 2 although the consumer was not bound by that offer before its acceptance by the trader.

4. This Directive shall also apply to offers made contractually by the consumer under conditions similar to those described in paragraph 1 or paragraph 2 where the consumer is bound by his offer.

[2] OJ No C241, 10.10.1977, p. 26.
[3] OJ No C180, 18.7.1977, p. 39.
[4] OJ No C92, 25.4.1975, p. 2.
[5] OJ No C133, 3.6.1981, p. 1.

Article 2

For the purposes of this Directive:

'consumer' means a natural person who, in transactions covered by this Directive, is acting for purposes which can be regarded as outside his trade or profession;

'trader' means a natural or legal person who, for the transaction in question, acts in his commercial or professional capacity, and anyone acting in the name or on behalf of a trader.

Article 3

1. The Member States may decide that this Directive shall apply only to contracts for which the payment to be made by the consumer exceeds a specified amount. This amount may not exceed 60 ECU. The Council, acting on a proposal from the Commission, shall examine and, if necessary, revise this amount for the first time no later than four years after notification of the Directive and thereafter every two years, taking into account economic and monetary developments in the Community.

2. This Directive shall not apply to:

(a) contracts for the construction, sale and rental of immovable property or contracts concerning other rights relating to immovable property. Contracts for the supply of goods and for their incorporation in immovable property or contracts for repairing immovable property shall fall within the scope of this Directive;

(b) contracts for the supply of foodstuffs or beverages or other goods intended for current consumption in the household and supplied by regular roundsmen;

(c) contracts for the supply of goods or services, provided that all three of the following conditions are met:

(i) the contract is concluded on the basis of a trader's catalogue which the consumer has a proper opportunity of reading in the absence of the trader's representative,

(ii) there is intended to be continuity of contact between the trader's representative and the consumer in relation to that or any subsequent transaction,

(iii) both the catalogue and the contract clearly inform the consumer of his right to return goods to the supplier within a period of not less than seven days of receipt or otherwise to cancel the contract within that period without obligation of any kind other than to take reasonable care of the goods;

(d) insurance contracts;

(e) contracts for securities.

3. By way of derogation from Article 1(2), Member States may refrain from applying this Directive to contracts for the supply of goods or services having a direct connection with the goods or services concerning which the consumer requested the visit of the trader.

Article 4

In the case of transactions within the scope of Article 1, traders shall be required to give consumers written notice of their right of cancellation within the period laid down in Article 5, together with the name and address of a person against whom that right may be exercised. Such notice shall be dated and shall state particulars enabling the contract to be identified. It shall be given to the consumer:

(a) in the case of Article 1(1), at the time of conclusion of the contract;

(b) in the case of Article 1(2), not later than the time of conclusion of the contract;

(c) in the case of Article 1(3) and 1(4), when the offer is made by the consumer.

Member States shall ensure that their national legislation lays down appropriate consumer protection measures in cases where the information referred to in this Article is not supplied.

Article 5

1. The consumer shall have the right to renounce the effects of his undertaking by sending notice within a period of not less than seven days from receipt by the consumer of the notice referred to in Article 4, in accordance with the procedure laid down by national law. It shall be sufficient if the notice is dispatched before the end of such period.

2. The giving of the notice shall have the effect of releasing the consumer from any obligations under the cancelled contract.

Article 6

The consumer may not waive the rights conferred on him by this Directive.

Article 7

If the consumer exercises his right of renunciation, the legal effects of such renunciation shall be governed by national laws, particularly regarding the reimbursement of payments for goods or services provided and the return of goods received.

Article 8

This Directive shall not prevent Member States from adopting or maintaining more favourable provisions to protect consumers in the field which it covers.

Article 9

1. Member States shall take the measures necessary to comply with this Directive within 24 months of its notification.[6] They shall forthwith inform the Commission thereof.

2. Member States shall ensure that the texts of the main provisions of national law which they adopt in the field covered by this Directive are communicated to the Commission.

Article 10

This Directive is addressed to the Member States.

Done at Brussels, 20 December 1985.
For the Council
The President
R. KRIEPS

Council Directive of 13 June 1990 on package travel, package holidays and package tours (90/314/EEC)

[OJ 1990 L158/59]

THE COUNCIL OF THE EUROPEAN COMMUNITIES,

Having regard to the Treaty establishing the European Economic Community, and in particular Article 100a thereof,

Having regard to the proposal from the Commission,[1]

In cooperation with the European Parliament,[2]

Having regard to the opinion of the Economic and Social Committee,[3]

Whereas one of the main objectives of the Community is to complete the internal market, of which the tourist sector is an essential part;

Whereas the national laws of Member States concerning package travel, package holidays and package tours, hereinafter referred to as 'packages', show many disparities and national practices in this field are markedly different, which gives rise to obstacles to the freedom to provide services in respect of packages and distortions of competition amongst operators established in different Member States;

Whereas the establishment of common rules on packages will contribute to the elimination of these obstacles and thereby to the achievement of a common market in services, thus enabling operators established in one Member State to offer their services in other Member States and Community consumers to benefit from comparable conditions when buying a package in any Member State;

[6] This Directive was notified to the Member States on 23 December 1985.
[1] OJ No C96, 12.4.1988, p. 5.
[2] OJ No C69, 20.3.1989, p. 102 and OJ No C149, 18.6.1990.
[3] OJ No C102, 24.4.1989, p. 27.

Whereas paragraph 36(b) of the Annex to the Council resolution of 19 May 1981 on a second programme of the European Economic Community for a consumer protection and information policy[4] invites the Commission to study, inter alia, tourism and, if appropriate, to put forward suitable proposals, with due regard for their significance for consumer protection and the effects of differences in Member States' legislation on the proper functioning of the common market;

Whereas in the resolution on a Community policy on tourism on 10 April 1984[5] the Council welcomed the Commission's initiative in drawing attention to the importance of tourism and took note of the Commission's initial guidelines for a Community policy on tourism;

Whereas the Commission communication to the Council entitled 'A New Impetus for Consumer Protection Policy', which was approved by resolution of the Council on 6 May 1986,[6] lists in paragraph 37, among the measures proposed by the Commission, the harmonization of legislation on packages;

Whereas tourism plays an increasingly important role in the economies of the Member States; whereas the package system is a fundamental part of tourism; whereas the package travel industry in Member States would be stimulated to greater growth and productivity if at least a minimum of common rules were adopted in order to give it a Community dimension; whereas this would not only produce benefits for Community citizens buying packages organised on the basis of those rules, but would attract tourists from outside the Community seeking the advantages of guaranteed standards in packages;

Whereas disparities in the rules protecting consumers in different Member States are a disincentive to consumers in one Member State from buying packages in another Member State;

Whereas this disincentive is particularly effective in deterring consumers from buying packages outside their own Member State, and more effective than it would be in relation to the acquisition of other services, having regard to the special nature of the services supplied in a package which generally involve the expenditure of substantial amounts of money in advance and the supply of the services in a State other than that in which the consumer is resident;

Whereas the consumer should have the benefit of the protection introduced by this Directive irrespective of whether he is a direct contracting party, a transferee or a member of a group on whose behalf another person has concluded a contract in respect of a package;

Whereas the organiser of the package and/or the retailer of it should be under obligation to ensure that in descriptive matter relating to packages which they respectively organise and sell, the information which is given is not misleading and brochures made available to consumers contain information which is comprehensible and accurate;

Whereas the consumer needs to have a record of the terms of contract applicable to the package; whereas this can conveniently be achieved by requiring that all the terms of the contract be stated in writing of such other documentary form as shall be comprehensible and accessible to him, and that he be given a copy thereof;

Whereas the consumer should be at liberty in certain circumstances to transfer to a willing third person a booking made by him for a package;

Whereas the price established under the contract should not in principle be subject to revision except where the possibility of upward or downward revision is expressly provided for in the contract; whereas that possibility should nonetheless be subject to certain conditions;

Whereas the consumer should in certain circumstances be free to withdraw before departure from a package travel contract;

Whereas there should be a clear definition of the rights available to the consumer in circumstances where the organiser of the package cancels it before the agreed date of departure;

Whereas if, after the consumer has departed, there occurs a significant failure of performance of the services for which he has contracted or the organiser perceives that he will be unable to procure a significant part of the services to be provided; the organiser should have certain obligations towards the consumer;

4 OJ No C165, 23.6.1981, p. 24.

5 OJ No C115, 30.4.1984, p. 1.

6 OJ No C118, 7.3.1986, p. 28.

Whereas the organiser and/or retailer party to the contract should be liable to the consumer for the proper performance of the obligations arising from the contract; whereas, moreover, the organiser and/or retailer should be liable for the damage resulting for the consumer from failure to perform or improper performance of the contract unless the defects in the performance of the contract are attributable neither to any fault of theirs nor to that of another supplier of services;

Whereas in cases where the organiser and/or retailer is liable for failure to perform or improper performance of the services involved in the package, such liability should be limited in accordance with the international conventions governing such services, in particular the Warsaw Convention of 1929 in International Carriage by Air, the Berne Convention of 1961 on Carriage by Rail, the Athens Convention of 1974 on Carriage by Sea and the Paris Convention of 1962 on the Liability of Hotel-keepers; whereas, moreover, with regard to damage other than personal injury, it should be possible for liability also to be limited under the package contract provided, however, that such limits are not unreasonable;

Whereas certain arrangements should be made for the information of consumers and the handling of complaints;

Whereas both the consumer and the package travel industry would benefit if organisers and/or retailers were placed under an obligation to provide sufficient evidence of security in the event of insolvency;

Whereas Member States should be at liberty to adopt, or retain, more stringent provisions relating to package travel for the purpose of protecting the consumer,

HAS ADOPTED THIS DIRECTIVE:

Article 1

The purpose of this Directive is to approximate the laws, regulations and administrative provisions of the Member States relating to packages sold or offered for sale in the territory of the Community.

Article 2

For the purposes of this Directive:

1. 'package' means the pre-arranged combination of not fewer than two of the following when sold or offered for sale at an inclusive price and when the service covers a period of more than twenty-four hours or includes overnight accommodation:
   (a) transport;
   (b) accommodation;
   (c) other tourist services not ancillary to transport or accommodation and accounting for a significant proportion of the package. The separate billing of various components of the same package shall not absolve the organiser or retailer from the obligations under this Directive;
2. 'organiser' means the person who, other than occasionally, organises packages and sells or offers them for sale, whether directly or through a retailer;
3. 'retailer' means the person who sells or offers for sale the package put together by the organiser;
4. 'consumer' means the person who takes or agrees to take the package ('the principal contractor'), or any person on whose behalf the principal contractor agrees to purchase the package ('the other beneficiaries') or any person to whom the principal contractor or any of the other beneficiaries transfers the package ('the transferee');
5. 'contract' means the agreement linking the consumer to the organiser and/or the retailer.

Article 3

1. Any descriptive matter concerning a package and supplied by the organiser or the retailer to the consumer, the price of the package and any other conditions applying to the contract must not contain any misleading information.

2. When a brochure is made available to the consumer, it shall indicate in a legible, comprehensible and accurate manner both the price and adequate information concerning:

(a) the destination and the means, characteristics and categories of transport used;
(b) the type of accommodation, its location, category or degree of comfort and its main features, its approval and tourist classification under the rules of the host Member State concerned;
(c) the meal plan;
(d) the itinerary;
(e) general information on passport and visa requirements for nationals of the Member State or States concerned and health formalities required for the journey and the stay;
(f) either the monetary amount or the percentage of the price which is to be paid on account, and the timetable for payment of the balance;
(g) whether a minimum number of persons is required for the package to take place and, if so, the deadline for informing the consumer in the event of cancellation. The particulars contained in the brochure are binding on the organiser or retailer, unless:
– changes in such particulars have been clearly communicated to the consumer before conclusion of the contract, in which case the brochure shall expressly state so,
– changes are made later following an agreement between the parties to the contract.

Article 4

1. (a) The organiser and/or the retailer shall provide the consumer, in writing or any other appropriate form, before the contract is concluded, with general information on passport and visa requirements applicable to nationals of the Member State or States concerned and in particular on the periods for obtaining them, as well as with information on the health formalities required for the journey and the stay;
(b) The organiser and/or retailer shall also provide the consumer, in writing or any other appropriate form, with the following information in good time before the start of the journey:
(i) the times and places of intermediate stops and transport connections as well as details of the place to be occupied by the traveller, e.g. cabin or berth on ship, sleeper compartment on train;
(ii) the name, address and telephone number of the organiser's and/or retailer's local representative or, failing that, of local agencies on whose assistance a consumer in difficulty could call. Where no such representatives or agencies exist, the consumer must in any case be provided with an emergency telephone number or any other information that will enable him to contract the organiser and/or the retailer;
(iii) in the case of journeys or stays abroad by minors, information enabling direct contact to be established with the child or the person responsible at the child's place of stay;
(iv) information on the optional conclusion of an insurance policy to cover the cost of cancellation by the consumer or the cost of assistance, including repatriation, in the event of accident or illness.

2. Member States shall ensure that in relation to the contract the following principles apply:
(a) depending on the particular package, the contract shall contain at least the elements listed in the Annex;
(b) all the terms of the contract are set out in writing or such other form as is comprehensible and accessible to the consumer and must be communicated to him before the conclusion of the contract; the consumer is given a copy of these terms;
(c) the provision under (b) shall not preclude the belated conclusion of last-minute reservations or contracts.

3. Where the consumer is prevented from proceeding with the package, he may transfer his booking, having first given the organiser or the retailer reasonable notice of his intention before departure, to a person who satisfies all the conditions applicable to the package. The transferor of the package and the transferee shall be jointly and severally liable to the organiser or retailer party to the contract for payment of the balance due and for any additional costs arising from such transfer.

4. (a) The prices laid down in the contract shall not be subject to revision unless the contract expressly provides for the possibility of upward or downward revision and states precisely how the revised price is to be calculated, and solely to allow for variations in:
- transportation costs, including the cost of fuel,
- dues, taxes or fees chargeable for certain services, such as landing taxes or embarkation or disembarkation fees at ports and airports,
- the exchange rates applied to the particular package.

(b) During the twenty days prior to the departure date stipulated, the price stated in the contract shall not be increased.

5. If the organiser finds that before the departure he is constrained to alter significantly any of the essential terms, such as the price, he shall notify the consumer as quickly as possible in order to enable him to take appropriate decisions and in particular:
- either to withdraw from the contract without penalty,
- or to accept a rider to the contract specifying the alterations made and their impact on the price.

The consumer shall inform the organiser or the retailer of his decision as soon as possible.

6. If the consumer withdraws from the contract pursuant to paragraph 5, or if, for whatever cause, other than the fault of the consumer, the organiser cancels the package before the agreed date of departure, the consumer shall be entitled:

(a) either to take a substitute package of equivalent or higher quality where the organiser and/or retailer is able to offer him such a substitute. If the replacement package offered is of lower quality, the organiser shall refund the difference in price to the consumer;

(b) or to be repaid as soon as possible all sums paid by him under the contract. In such a case, he shall be entitled, if appropriate, to be compensated by either the organiser or the retailer, whichever the relevant Member State's law requires, for non-performance of the contract, except where:

(i) cancellation is on the grounds that the number of persons enrolled for the package is less than the minimum number required and the consumer is informed of the cancellation, in writing, within the period indicated in the package description; or

(ii) cancellation, excluding overbooking, is for reasons of force majeure, i.e. unusual and unforeseeable circumstances beyond the control of the party by whom it is pleaded, the consequences of which could not have been avoided even if all due care had been exercised.

7. Where, after departure, a significant proportion of the services contracted for is not provided or the organiser perceives that he will be unable to procure a significant proportion of the services to be provided, the organiser shall make suitable alternative arrangements, at no extra cost to the consumer, for the continuation of the package, and where appropriate compensate the consumer for the difference between the services offered and those supplied. If it is impossible to make such arrangements or these are not accepted by the consumer for good reasons, the organiser shall, where appropriate, provide the consumer, at no extra cost, with equivalent transport back to the place of departure, or to another return-point to which the consumer has agreed and shall, where appropriate, compensate the consumer.

Article 5

1. Member States shall take the necessary steps to ensure that the organiser and/or retailer party to the contract is liable to the consumer for the proper performance of the obligations arising from the contract, irrespective of whether such obligations are to be performed by that organiser and/or retailer or by other suppliers of services without prejudice to the right of the organiser and/ or retailer to pursue those other suppliers of services.

2. With regard to the damage resulting for the consumer from the failure to perform or the improper performance of the contract, Member States shall take the necessary steps to ensure that the organiser and/or retailer is/are liable unless such failure to perform or improper performance is attributable neither to any fault of theirs nor to that of another supplier of services, because:

- the failures which occur in the performance of the contract are attributable to the consumer,
- such failures are attributable to a third party unconnected with the provision of the services contracted for, and are unforeseeable or unavoidable,
- such failures are due to a case of force majeure such as that defined in Article 4(6), second sub-paragraph (ii), or to an event which the organiser and/or retailer or the supplier of services, even with all due care, could not foresee or forestall.

In the cases referred to in the second and third indents, the organiser and/or retailer party to the contract shall be required to give prompt assistance to a consumer in difficulty. In the matter of damages arising from the non-performance or improper performance of the services involved in the package, the Member States may allow compensation to be limited in accordance with the international conventions governing such services. In the matter of damage other than personal injury resulting from the non-performance or improper performance of the services involved in the package, the Member States may allow compensation to be limited under the contract. Such limitation shall not be unreasonable.

3. Without prejudice to the fourth sub-paragraph of paragraph 2, there may be no exclusion by means of a contractual clause from the provisions of paragraphs 1 and 2.

4. The consumer must communicate any failure in the performance of a contract which he perceives on the spot to the supplier of the services concerned and to the organiser and/or retailer in writing or any other appropriate form at the earliest opportunity. This obligation must be stated clearly and explicitly in the contract.

Article 6

In cases of complaint, the organiser and/or retailer or his local representative, if there is one, must make prompt efforts to find appropriate solutions.

Article 7

The organiser and/or retailer party to the contract shall provide sufficient evidence of security for the refund of money paid over and for the repatriation of the consumer in the event of insolvency.

Article 8

Member States may adopt or return more stringent provisions in the field covered by this Directive to protect the consumer.

Article 9

1. Member States shall bring into force the measures necessary to comply with this Directive before 31 December 1992. They shall forthwith inform the Commission thereof.

2. Member States shall communicate to the Commission the texts of the main provisions of national law which they adopt in the field governed by this Directive. The Commission shall inform the other Member States thereof.

Article 10

This Directive is addressed to the Member States.

Done at Luxembourg, 13 June 1990.
For the Council
The President
D. J. O'MALLEY

Annex

Elements to be included in the contract if relevant to the particular package;

(a) the travel destination(s) and, where periods of stay are involved, the relevant periods, with dates;

(b) the means, characteristics and categories of transport to be used, the dates, times and points of departure and return;
(c) where the package includes accommodation, its location, its tourist category or degree of comfort, its main features, its compliance with the rules of the host Member State concerned and the meal plan;
(d) whether a minimum number of persons is required for the package to take place and, if so, the deadline for informing the consumer in the event of cancellation;
(e) the itinerary;
(f) visits, excursions or other services which are included in the total price agreed for the package;
(g) the name and address of the organiser, the retailer and, where appropriate, the insurer;
(h) the price of the package, an indication of the possibility of price revisions under Article 4(4) and an indication of any dues, taxes or fees chargeable for certain services (landing, embarkation or disembarkation fees at ports and airports, tourist taxes) where such costs are not included in the package;
(i) the payment schedule and method of payment;
(j) special requirements which the consumer has communicated to the organiser or retailer when making the booking, and which both have accepted;
(k) periods within which the consumer must make any complaint concerning failure to perform or improper performance of the contract.

Council Directive 93/13/EEC of 5 April 1993 on unfair terms in consumer contracts

[OJ 1993 L95/29]*

THE COUNCIL OF THE EUROPEAN COMMUNITIES,

Having regard to the Treaty establishing the European Economic Community, and in particular Article 100 A thereof,

Having regard to the proposal from the Commission,[1]

In cooperation with the European Parliament,[2]

Having regard to the opinion of the Economic and Social Committee,[3]

Whereas it is necessary to adopt measures with the aim of progressively establishing the internal market before 31 December 1992; whereas the internal market comprises an area without internal frontiers in which goods, persons, services and capital move freely;

Whereas the laws of Member States relating to the terms of contract between the seller of goods or supplier of services, on the one hand, and the consumer of them, on the other hand, show many disparities, with the result that the national markets for the sale of goods and services to consumers differ from each other and that distortions of competition may arise amongst the sellers and suppliers, notably when they sell and supply in other Member States;

Whereas, in particular, the laws of Member States relating to unfair terms in consumer contracts show marked divergences;

Whereas it is the responsibility of the Member States to ensure that contracts concluded with consumers do not contain unfair terms;

Whereas, generally speaking, consumers do not know the rules of law which, in Member States other than their own, govern contracts for the sale of goods or services; whereas this lack of awareness may deter them from direct transactions for the purchase of goods or services in another Member State;

* **Editor's Note**: Article 8a inserted by Directive 2011/83 (OJ L304/64).
[1] OJ No C73, 24.3.1992, p. 7.
[2] OJ No C326, 16.12.1991, p. 108 and OJ No C21, 25.1.1993.
[3] OJ No C159, 17.6.1991, p. 34.

Whereas, in order to facilitate the establishment of the internal market and to safeguard the citizen in his role as consumer when acquiring goods and services under contracts which are governed by the laws of Member States other than his own, it is essential to remove unfair terms from those contracts;

Whereas sellers of goods and suppliers of services will thereby be helped in their task of selling goods and supplying services, both at home and throughout the internal market; whereas competition will thus be stimulated, so contributing to increased choice for Community citizens as consumers;

Whereas the two Community programmes for a consumer protection and information policy[4] underlined the importance of safeguarding consumers in the matter of unfair terms of contract; whereas this protection ought to be provided by laws and regulations which are either harmonised at Community level or adopted directly at that level;

Whereas in accordance with the principle laid down under the heading 'Protection of the economic interests of the consumers', as stated in those programmes: 'acquirers of goods and services should be protected against the abuse of power by the seller or supplier, in particular against one-sided standard contracts and the unfair exclusion of essential rights in contracts';

Whereas more effective protection of the consumer can be achieved by adopting uniform rules of law in the matter of unfair terms; whereas those rules should apply to all contracts concluded between sellers or suppliers and consumers; whereas as a result inter alia contracts relating to employment, contracts relating to succession rights, contracts relating to rights under family law and contracts relating to the incorporation and organization of companies or partnership agreements must be excluded from this Directive;

Whereas the consumer must receive equal protection under contracts concluded by word of mouth and written contracts regardless, in the latter case, of whether the terms of the contract are contained in one or more documents;

Whereas, however, as they now stand, national laws allow only partial harmonization to be envisaged; whereas, in particular, only contractual terms which have not been individually negotiated are covered by this Directive; whereas Member States should have the option, with due regard for the Treaty, to afford consumers a higher level of protection through national provisions that are more stringent than those of this Directive;

Whereas the statutory or regulatory provisions of the Member States which directly or indirectly determine the terms of consumer contracts are presumed not to contain unfair terms; whereas, therefore, it does not appear to be necessary to subject the terms which reflect mandatory statutory or regulatory provisions and the principles or provisions of international conventions to which the Member States or the Community are party; whereas in that respect the wording 'mandatory statutory or regulatory provisions' in Article 1(2) also covers rules which, according to the law, shall apply between the contracting parties provided that no other arrangements have been established;

Whereas Member States must however ensure that unfair terms are not included, particularly because this Directive also applies to trades, business or professions of a public nature;

Whereas it is necessary to fix in a general way the criteria for assessing the unfair character of contract terms;

Whereas the assessment, according to the general criteria chosen, of the unfair character of terms, in particular in sale or supply activities of a public nature providing collective services which take account of solidarity among users, must be supplemented by a means of making an overall evaluation of the different interests involved; whereas this constitutes the requirement of good faith; whereas, in making an assessment of good faith, particular regard shall be had to the strength of the bargaining positions of the parties, whether the consumer had an inducement to agree to the term and whether the goods or services were sold or supplied to the special order of the consumer; whereas the requirement of good faith may be satisfied by the seller or supplier where he deals fairly and equitably with the other party whose legitimate interests he has to take into account;

Whereas, for the purposes of this Directive, the annexed list of terms can be of indicative value only and, because of the cause of the minimal character of the Directive, the scope of these terms may be the subject of amplification or more restrictive editing by the Member States in their national laws;

[4] OJ No C92, 25.4.1975, p. 1 and OJ No C133, 3.6.1981, p. 1.

Whereas the nature of goods or services should have an influence on assessing the unfairness of contractual terms;

Whereas, for the purposes of this Directive, assessment of unfair character shall not be made of terms which describe the main subject matter of the contract nor the quality/price ratio of the goods or services supplied; whereas the main subject matter of the contract and the price/quality ratio may nevertheless be taken into account in assessing the fairness of other terms; whereas it follows, inter alia, that in insurance contracts, the terms which clearly define or circumscribe the insured risk and the insurer's liability shall not be subject to such assessment since these restrictions are taken into account in calculating the premium paid by the consumer;

Whereas contracts should be drafted in plain, intelligible language, the consumer should actually be given an opportunity to examine all the terms and, if in doubt, the interpretation most favourable to the consumer should prevail;

Whereas Member States should ensure that unfair terms are not used in contracts concluded with consumers by a seller or supplier and that if, nevertheless, such terms are so used, they will not bind the consumer, and the contract will continue to bind the parties upon those terms if it is capable of continuing in existence without the unfair provisions;

Whereas there is a risk that, in certain cases, the consumer may be deprived of protection under this Directive by designating the law of a non-Member country as the law applicable to the contract; whereas provisions should therefore be included in this Directive designed to avert this risk;

Whereas persons or organisations, if regarded under the law of a Member State as having a legitimate interest in the matter, must have facilities for initiating proceedings concerning terms of contract drawn up for general use in contracts concluded with consumers, and in particular unfair terms, either before a court or before an administrative authority competent to decide upon complaints or to initiate appropriate legal proceedings; whereas this possibility does not, however, entail prior verification of the general conditions obtaining in individual economic sectors;

Whereas the courts or administrative authorities of the Member States must have at their disposal adequate and effective means of preventing the continued application of unfair terms in consumer contracts,

HAS ADOPTED THIS DIRECTIVE:

Article 1

1. The purpose of this Directive is to approximate the laws, regulations and administrative provisions of the Member States relating to unfair terms in contracts concluded between a seller or supplier and a consumer.

2. The contractual terms which reflect mandatory statutory or regulatory provisions and the provisions or principles of international conventions to which the Member States or the Community are party, particularly in the transport area, shall not be subject to the provisions of this Directive.

Article 2

For the purposes of this Directive:

(a) 'unfair terms' means the contractual terms defined in Article 3;

(b) 'consumer' means any natural person who, in contracts covered by this Directive, is acting for purposes which are outside his trade, business or profession;

(c) 'seller or supplier' means any natural or legal person who, in contracts covered by this Directive, is acting for purposes relating to his trade, business or profession, whether publicly owned or privately owned.

Article 3

1. A contractual term which has not been individually negotiated shall be regarded as unfair if, contrary to the requirement of good faith, it causes a significant imbalance in the parties' rights and obligations arising under the contract, to the detriment of the consumer.

2. A term shall always be regarded as not individually negotiated where it has been drafted in advance and the consumer has therefore not been able to influence the substance of the term,

particularly in the context of a pre-formulated standard contract. The fact that certain aspects of a term or one specific term have been individually negotiated shall not exclude the application of this Article to the rest of a contract if an overall assessment of the contract indicates that it is nevertheless a pre-formulated standard contract. Where any seller or supplier claims that a standard term has been individually negotiated, the burden of proof in this respect shall be incumbent on him.

3. The Annex shall contain an indicative and non-exhaustive list of the terms which may be regarded as unfair.

Article 4

1. Without prejudice to Article 7, the unfairness of a contractual term shall be assessed, taking into account the nature of the goods or services for which the contract was concluded and by referring, at the time of conclusion of the contract, to all the circumstances attending the conclusion of the contract and to all the other terms of the contract or of another contract on which it is dependent.

2. Assessment of the unfair nature of the terms shall relate neither to the definition of the main subject matter of the contract nor to the adequacy of the price and remuneration, on the one hand, as against the services or goods supplies in exchange, on the other, in so far as these terms are in plain intelligible language.

Article 5

In the case of contracts where all or certain terms offered to the consumer are in writing, these terms must always be drafted in plain, intelligible language. Where there is doubt about the meaning of a term, the interpretation most favourable to the consumer shall prevail. This rule on interpretation shall not apply in the context of the procedures laid down in Article 7(2).

Article 6

1. Member States shall lay down that unfair terms used in a contract concluded with a consumer by a seller or supplier shall, as provided for under their national law, not be binding on the consumer and that the contract shall continue to bind the parties upon those terms if it is capable of continuing in existence without the unfair terms.

2. Member States shall take the necessary measures to ensure that the consumer does not lose the protection granted by this Directive by virtue of the choice of the law of a non-Member country as the law applicable to the contract if the latter has a close connection with the territory of the Member States.

Article 7

1. Member States shall ensure that, in the interests of consumers and of competitors, adequate and effective means exist to prevent the continued use of unfair terms in contracts concluded with consumers by sellers or suppliers.

2. The means referred to in paragraph 1 shall include provisions whereby persons or organisations, having a legitimate interest under national law in protecting consumers, may take action according to the national law concerned before the courts or before competent administrative bodies for a decision as to whether contractual terms drawn up for general use are unfair, so that they can apply appropriate and effective means to prevent the continued use of such terms.

3. With due regard for national laws, the legal remedies referred to in paragraph 2 may be directed separately or jointly against a number of sellers or suppliers from the same economic sector or their associations which use or recommend the use of the same general contractual terms or similar terms.

Article 8

Member States may adopt or retain the most stringent provisions compatible with the Treaty in the area covered by this Directive, to ensure a maximum degree of protection for the consumer.

Article 8a

1. Where a Member State adopts provisions in accordance with Article 8, it shall inform the Commission thereof, as well as of any subsequent changes, in particular where those provisions:

- extend the unfairness assessment to individually negotiated contractual terms or to the adequacy of the price or remuneration; or,

– contain lists of contractual terms which shall be considered as unfair,

2. The Commission shall ensure that the information referred to in paragraph 1 is easily accessible to consumers and traders, inter alia, on a dedicated website.

3. The Commission shall forward the information referred to in paragraph 1 to the other Member States and the European Parliament. The Commission shall consult stakeholders on that information.

Article 9

The Commission shall present a report to the European Parliament and to the Council concerning the application of this Directive five years at the latest after the date in Article 10(1).

Article 10

1. Member States shall bring into force the laws, regulations and administrative provisions necessary to comply with this Directive no later than 31 December 1994. They shall forthwith inform the Commission thereof. These provisions shall be applicable to all contracts concluded after 31 December 1994.

2. When Member States adopt these measures, they shall contain a reference to this Directive or shall be accompanied by such reference on the occasion of their official publication. The methods of making such a reference shall be laid down by the Member States.

3. Member States shall communicate the main provisions of national law which they adopt in the field covered by this Directive to the Commission.

Article 11

This Directive is addressed to the Member States.

Done at Luxembourg, 5 April 1993.
For the Council
The President
N. HELVEG PETERSEN

Annex

Terms referred to in Article 3(3)

1. Terms which have the object or effect of:
   (a) excluding or limiting the legal liability of a seller or supplier in the event of the death of a consumer or personal injury to the latter resulting from an act or omission of that seller or supplier;
   (b) inappropriately excluding or limiting the legal rights of the consumer vis-à-vis the seller or supplier or another party in the event of total or partial non-performance or inadequate performance by the seller or supplier of any of the contractual obligations, including the option of offsetting a debt owed to the seller or supplier against any claim which the consumer may have against him;
   (c) making an agreement binding on the consumer whereas provision of services by the seller or supplier is subject to a condition whose realisation depends on his own will alone;
   (d) permitting the seller or supplier to retain sums paid by the consumer where the latter decides not to conclude or perform the contract, without providing for the consumer to receive compensation of an equivalent amount from the seller or supplier where the latter is the party cancelling the contract;
   (e) requiring any consumer who fails to fulfil his obligation to pay a disproportionately high sum in compensation;
   (f) authorising the seller or supplier to dissolve the contract on a discretionary basis where the same facility is not granted to the consumer, or permitting the seller or supplier to retain the sums paid for services not yet supplied by him where it is the seller or supplier himself who dissolves the contract;

(g) enabling the seller or supplier to terminate a contract of indeterminate duration without reasonable notice except where there are serious grounds for doing so;
(h) automatically extending a contract of fixed duration where the consumer does not indicate otherwise, when the deadline fixed for the consumer to express this desire not to extend the contract is unreasonably early;
(i) irrevocably binding the consumer to terms with which he had no real opportunity of becoming acquainted before the conclusion of the contract;
(j) enabling the seller or supplier to alter the terms of the contract unilaterally without a valid reason which is specified in the contract;
(k) enabling the seller or supplier to alter unilaterally without a valid reason any characteristics of the product or service to be provided;
(l) providing for the price of goods to be determined at the time of delivery or allowing a seller of goods or supplier of services to increase their price without in both cases giving the consumer the corresponding right to cancel the contract if the final price is too high in relation to the price agreed when the contract was concluded;
(m) giving the seller or supplier the right to determine whether the goods or services supplied are in conformity with the contract, or giving him the exclusive right to interpret any term of the contract;
(n) limiting the seller's or supplier's obligation to respect commitments undertaken by his agents or making his commitments subject to compliance with a particular formality;
(o) obliging the consumer to fulfil all his obligations where the seller or supplier does not perform his;
(p) giving the seller or supplier the possibility of transferring his rights and obligations under the contract, where this may serve to reduce the guarantees for the consumer, without the latter's agreement;
(q) excluding or hindering the consumer's right to take legal action or exercise any other legal remedy, particularly by requiring the consumer to take disputes exclusively to arbitration not covered by legal provisions, unduly restricting the evidence available to him or imposing on him a burden of proof which, according to the applicable law, should lie with another party to the contract.

2. Scope of subparagraphs (g), (j) and (l)
   (a) Subparagraph (g) is without hindrance to terms by which a supplier of financial services reserves the right to terminate unilaterally a contract of indeterminate duration without notice where there is a valid reason, provided that the supplier is required to inform the other contracting party or parties thereof immediately.
   (b) Subparagraph (j) is without hindrance to terms under which a supplier of financial services reserves the right to alter the rate of interest payable by the consumer or due to the latter, or the amount of other charges for financial services without notice where there is a valid reason, provided that the supplier is required to inform the other contracting party or parties thereof at the earliest opportunity and that the latter are free to dissolve the contract immediately. Subparagraph (j) is also without hindrance to terms under which a seller or supplier reserves the right to alter unilaterally the conditions of a contract of indeterminate duration, provided that he is required to inform the consumer with reasonable notice and that the consumer is free to dissolve the contract.
   (c) Subparagraphs (g), (j) and (l) do not apply to:
      - transactions in transferable securities, financial instruments and other products or services where the price is linked to fluctuations in a stock exchange quotation or index or a financial market rate that the seller or supplier does not control;
      - contracts for the purchase or sale of foreign currency, traveller's cheques or international money orders denominated in foreign currency;
   (d) Subparagraph (l) is without hindrance to price-indexation clauses, where lawful, provided that the method by which prices vary is explicitly described.

Directive 2001/95/EEC of the European Parliament and of the Council of 3 December 2001 on general product safety*

[OJ 2002 L11/4]**

THE EUROPEAN PARLIAMENT AND THE COUNCIL OF THE EUROPEAN UNION,

Having regard to the Treaty establishing the European Economic Community, and in particular Articles 95 thereof,

Having regard to the proposal from the Commission,[1]

Having regard to the opinion of the Economic and Social Committee,[2]

Acting in accordance with the procedure referred to in Article 251 of the Treaty,[3] in the light of the joint text approved by the Conciliation Committee on 2 August 2001,

Whereas:

(1) Under Article 16 of Council Directive 92/59/EEC of 29 June 1992 on general product safety,[4] the Council was to decide, four years after the date set for the implementation of the said Directive, on the basis of a report of the Commission on the experience acquired, together with appropriate proposals, whether to adjust Directive 92/59/EEC. It is necessary to amend Directive 92/59/EEC in several respects, in order to complete, reinforce or clarify some of its provisions in the light of experience as well as new and relevant developments on consumer product safety, together with the changes made to the Treaty, especially in Articles 152 concerning public health and 153 concerning consumer protection, and in the light of the precautionary principle. Directive 92/59/ EEC should therefore be recast in the interest of clarity. This recasting leaves the safety of services outside the scope of this Directive, since the Commission intends to identify the needs, possibilities and priorities for Community action on the safety of services and liability of service providers, with a view to presenting appropriate proposals.

(2) It is important to adopt measures with the aim of improving the functioning of the internal market, comprising an area without internal frontiers in which the free movement of goods, persons, services and capital is assured.

(3) In the absence of Community provisions, horizontal legislation of the Member States on product safety, imposing in particular a general obligation on economic operators to market only safe products, might differ in the level of protection afforded to consumers. Such disparities, and the absence of horizontal legislation in some Member States, would be liable to create barriers to trade and distortion of competition within the internal market.

(4) In order to ensure a high level of consumer protection, the Community must contribute to protecting the health and safety of consumers. Horizontal Community legislation introducing a general product safety requirement, and containing provisions on the general obligations of producers and distributors, on the enforcement of Community product safety requirements and on rapid exchange of information and action at Community level in certain cases, should contribute to that aim.

(5) It is very difficult to adopt Community legislation for every product which exists or which may be developed; there is a need for a broad-based, legislative framework of a horizontal nature to deal with such products, and also to cover lacunae, in particular pending revision of the existing specific legislation, and to complement provisions in existing or forthcoming specific legislation, in particular with a view to ensuring a high level of protection of safety and health of consumers, as required by Article 95 of the Treaty.

* **Editor's Note:** Article 8.3 replaced as from 1 January 2010 by Regulation 765/2008 (OJ 2008 L218/30) and amendments also by Regulation 596/2009 (OJ 2009 L188/14).

** **Editor's Note:** This Directive replaces Directive 92/59 with effect from 15 January 2004.

[1] OJ C 337 E, 28.11.2000, p. 109 and OJ C 154 E, 29.5.2000, p. 265.

[2] OJ C 367, 20.12.2000, p. 34.

[3] Opinion of the European Parliament of 15.11.2000 (OJ C 223, 8.8.2001, p. 154), Council Common Position of 12.2.2001 (OJ C 93, 23.3.2001, p. 24) and Decision of the European Parliament of 16.5.2001 (not yet published in the Official Journal). Decision of the European Parliament of 4.10.2001 and Council Decision of 27.9.2001.

[4] OJ L 228, 11.8.1992, p. 24.

(6) It is therefore necessary to establish at Community level a general safety requirement for any product placed on the market, or otherwise supplied or made available to consumers, intended for consumers, or likely to be used by consumers under reasonably foreseeable conditions even if not intended for them. In all these cases the products under consideration can pose risks for the health and safety of consumers which must be prevented. Certain second-hand goods should nevertheless be excluded by their very nature.

(7) This Directive should apply to products irrespective of the selling techniques, including distance and electronic selling.

(8) The safety of products should be assessed taking into account all the relevant aspects, in particular the categories of consumers which can be particularly vulnerable to the risks posed by the products under consideration, in particular children and the elderly.

(9) This Directive does not cover services, but in order to secure the attainment of the protection objectives in question, its provisions should also apply to products that are supplied or made available to consumers in the context of service provision for use by them. The safety of the equipment used by service providers themselves to supply a service to consumers does not come within the scope of this Directive since it has to be dealt with in conjunction with the safety of the service provided. In particular, equipment on which consumers ride or travel which is operated by a service provider is excluded from the scope of this Directive.

(10) Products which are designed exclusively for professional use but have subsequently migrated to the consumer market should be subject to the requirements of this Directive because they can pose risks to consumer health and safety when used under reasonably foreseeable conditions.

(11) In the absence of more specific provisions, within the framework of Community legislation covering safety of the products concerned, all the provisions of this Directive should apply in order to ensure consumer health and safety.

(12) If specific Community legislation sets out safety requirements covering only certain risks or categories of risks, with regard to the products concerned the obligations of economic operators in respect of these risks are those determined by the provisions of the specific legislation, while the general safety requirement of this Directive should apply to the other risks.

(13) The provisions of this Directive relating to the other obligations of producers and distributors, the obligations and powers of the Member States, the exchanges of information and rapid intervention situations and dissemination of information and confidentiality apply in the case of products covered by specific rules of Community law, if those rules do not already contain such obligations.

(14) In order to facilitate the effective and consistent application of the general safety requirement of this Directive, it is important to establish European voluntary standards covering certain products and risks in such a way that a product which conforms to a national standard transposing a European standard is to be presumed to be in compliance with the said requirement.

(15) With regard to the aims of this Directive, European standards should be established by European standardisation bodies, under mandates set by the Commission assisted by appropriate Committees. In order to ensure that products in compliance with the standards fulfil the general safety requirement, the Commission assisted by a committee composed of representatives of the Member States, should fix the requirements that the standards must meet. These requirements should be included in the mandates to the standardisation bodies.

(16) In the absence of specific regulations and when the European standards established under mandates set by the Commission are not available or recourse is not made to such standards, the safety of products should be assessed taking into account in particular national standards transposing any other relevant European or international standards, Commission recommendations or national standards, international standards, codes of good practice, the state of the art and the safety which consumers may reasonably expect. In this context, the Commission's recommendations may facilitate the consistent and effective application of this Directive pending the introduction of European standards or as regards the risks and/or products for which such standards are deemed not to be possible or appropriate.

(17) Appropriate independent certification recognised by the competent authorities may facilitate proof of compliance with the applicable product safety criteria.

(18) It is appropriate to supplement the duty to observe the general safety requirement by other obligations on economic operators because action by such operators is necessary to prevent risks to consumers under certain circumstances.

(19) The additional obligations on producers should include the duty to adopt measures commensurate with the characteristics of the products, enabling them to be informed of the risks that these products may present, to supply consumers with information enabling them to assess and prevent risks, to warn consumers of the risks posed by dangerous products already supplied to them, to withdraw those products from the market and, as a last resort, to recall them when necessary, which may involve, depending on the provisions applicable in the Member States, an appropriate form of compensation, for example, exchange or reimbursement.

(20) Distributors should help in ensuring compliance with the applicable safety requirements. The obligations placed on distributors apply in proportion to their respective responsibilities. In particular, it may prove impossible, in the context of charitable activities, to provide the competent authorities with information and documentation on possible risks and origin of the product in the case of isolated used objects provided by private individuals.

(21) Both producers and distributors should cooperate with the competent authorities in action aimed at preventing risks and inform them when they conclude that certain products supplied are dangerous. The conditions regarding the provision of such information should be set in this Directive to facilitate its effective application, while avoiding an excessive burden for economic operators and the authorities.

(22) In order to ensure the effective enforcement of the obligations incumbent on producers and distributors, the Member States should establish or designate authorities which are responsible for monitoring product safety and have powers to take appropriate measures, including the power to impose effective, proportionate and dissuasive penalties, and ensure appropriate coordination between the various designated authorities.

(23) It is necessary in particular for the appropriate measures to include the power for Member States to order or organise, immediately and efficiently, the withdrawal of dangerous products already placed on the market and as a last resort to order, coordinate or organise the recall from consumers of dangerous products already supplied to them. Those powers should be applied when producers and distributors fail to prevent risks to consumers in accordance with their obligations. Where necessary, the appropriate powers and procedures should be available to the authorities to decide and apply any necessary measures rapidly.

(24) The safety of consumers depends to a great extent on the active enforcement of Community product safety requirements. The Member States should, therefore, establish systematic approaches to ensure the effectiveness of market surveillance and other enforcement activities and should ensure their openness to the public and interested parties.

(25) Collaboration between the enforcement authorities of the Member States is necessary in ensuring the attainment of the protection objectives of this Directive. It is, therefore, appropriate to promote the operation of a European network of the enforcement authorities of the Member States to facilitate, in a coordinated manner with other Community procedures, in particular the Community Rapid Information System (RAPEX), improved collaboration at operational level on market surveillance and other enforcement activities, in particular risk assessment, testing of products, exchange of expertise and scientific knowledge, execution of joint surveillance projects and tracing, withdrawing or recalling dangerous products.

(26) It is necessary, for the purpose of ensuring a consistent, high level of consumer health and safety protection and preserving the unity of the internal market, that the Commission be informed of any measure restricting the placing on the market of a product or requiring its withdrawal or recall from the market. Such measures should be taken in compliance with the provisions of the Treaty, and in particular Articles 28, 29 and 30 thereof.

(27) Effective supervision of product safety requires the setting-up at national and Community levels of a system of rapid exchange of information in situations of serious risk requiring rapid intervention in respect of the safety of a product. It is also appropriate in this Directive to set out detailed procedures for the operation of the system and to give the Commission, assisted by an advisory committee, power to adapt them.

(28) This Directive provides for the establishment of non-binding guidelines aimed at indicating simple and clear criteria and practical rules which may change, in particular for the purpose of allowing efficient notification of measures restricting the placing on the market of products in the cases referred to in this Directive, whilst taking into account the range of situations dealt with by Member States and economic operators. The guidelines should in particular include criteria for the application of the definition of serious risks in order to facilitate consistent implementation of the relevant provisions in case of such risks.

(29) It is primarily for Member States, in compliance with the Treaty and in particular with Articles 28, 29 and 30 thereof, to take appropriate measures with regard to dangerous products located within their territory.

(30) However, if the Member States differ as regards the approach to dealing with the risk posed by certain products, such differences could entail unacceptable disparities in consumer protection and constitute a barrier to intra-Community trade.

(31) It may be necessary to deal with serious product-safety problems requiring rapid intervention which affect or could affect, in the immediate future, all or a significant part of the Community and which, in view of the nature of the safety problem posed by the product, cannot be dealt with effectively in a manner commensurate with the degree of urgency, under the procedures laid down in the specific rules of Community law applicable to the products or category of products in question.

(32) It is therefore necessary to provide for an adequate mechanism allowing, as a last resort, for the adoption of measures applicable throughout the Community, in the form of a decision addressed to the Member States, to cope with situations created by products presenting a serious risk. Such a decision should entail a ban on the export of the product in question, unless in the case in point exceptional circumstances allow a partial ban or even no ban to be decided upon, particularly when a system of prior consent is established. In addition, the banning of exports should be examined with a view to preventing risks to the health and safety of consumers. Since such a decision is not directly applicable to economic operators, Member States should take all necessary measures for its implementation. Measures adopted under such a procedure are interim measures, save when they apply to individually identified products or batches of products. In order to ensure the appropriate assessment of the need for, and the best preparation of such measures, they should be taken by the Commission, assisted by a committee, in the light of consultations with the Member States, and, if scientific questions are involved falling within the competence of a Community scientific committee, with the scientific committee competent for the risk concerned.

(33) The measures necessary for the implementation of this Directive should be adopted in accordance with Council Decision 1999/468/EC of 28 June 1999 laying down the procedures for the exercise of implementing powers conferred on the Commission.[5]

(34) In order to facilitate effective and consistent application of this Directive, the various aspects of its application may need to be discussed within a committee.

(35) Public access to the information available to the authorities on product safety should be ensured. However, professional secrecy, as referred to in Article 287 of the Treaty, must be protected in a way which is compatible with the need to ensure the effectiveness of market surveillance activities and of protection measures.

(36) This Directive should not affect victims' rights within the meaning of Council Directive 85/374/EEC of 25 July 1985 on the approximation of the laws, regulations and administrative provisions of the Member States concerning liability for defective products.[6]

(37) It is necessary for Member States to provide for appropriate means of redress before the competent courts in respect of measures taken by the competent authorities which restrict the placing on the market of a product or require its withdrawal or recall.

(38) In addition, the adoption of measures concerning imported products, like those concerning the banning of exports, with a view to preventing risks to the safety and health of consumers must comply with the Community's international obligations.

[5] OJ L 184, 17.7.1999, p. 23.

[6] OJ L 210, 7.8.1985, p. 29. Directive as amended by Directive 1999/34/EC of the European Parliament and of the Council (OJ L 141, 4.6.1999, p. 20).

(39) The Commission should periodically examine the manner in which this Directive is applied and the results obtained, in particular in relation to the functioning of market surveillance systems, the rapid exchange of information and measures adopted at Community level, together with other issues relevant for consumer product safety in the Community, and submit regular reports to the European Parliament and the Council on the subject.

(40) This Directive should not affect the obligations of Member States concerning the deadline for transposition and application of Directive 92/59/EEC,

HAVE ADOPTED THIS DIRECTIVE:

Chapter I Objective—Scope—Definitions

Article 1

1. The purpose of this Directive is to ensure that products placed on the market are safe.

2. This Directive shall apply to all the products defined in Article 2(a). Each of its provisions shall apply in so far as there are no specific provisions with the same objective in rules of Community law governing the safety of the products concerned.

Where products are subject to specific safety requirements imposed by Community legislation, this Directive shall apply only to the aspects and risks or categories of risks not covered by those requirements. This means that:

(a) Articles 2(b) and (c), 3 and 4 shall not apply to those products insofar as concerns the risks or categories of risks covered by the specific legislation;

(b) Articles 5 to 18 shall apply except where there are specific provisions governing the aspects covered by the said Articles with the same objective.

Article 2

For the purposes of this Directive:

(a) 'product' shall mean any product—including in the context of providing a service—which is intended for consumers or likely, under reasonably foreseeable conditions, to be used by consumers even if not intended for them, and is supplied or made available, whether for consideration or not, in the course of a commercial activity, and whether new, used or reconditioned.

This definition shall not apply to second-hand products supplied as antiques or as products to be repaired or reconditioned prior to being used, provided that the supplier clearly informs the person to whom he supplies the product to that effect;

(b) 'safe product' shall mean any product which, under normal or reasonably foreseeable conditions of use including duration and, where applicable, putting into service, installation and maintenance requirements, does not present any risk or only the minimum risks compatible with the product's use, considered to be acceptable and consistent with a high level of protection for the safety and health of persons, taking into account the following points in particular:

(i) the characteristics of the product, including its composition, packaging, instructions for assembly and, where applicable, for installation and maintenance;

(ii) the effect on other products, where it is reasonably foreseeable that it will be used with other products;

(iii) the presentation of the product, the labelling, any warnings and instructions for its use and disposal and any other indication or information regarding the product;

(iv) the categories of consumers at risk when using the product, in particular children and the elderly.

The feasibility of obtaining higher levels of safety or the availability of other products presenting a lesser degree of risk shall not constitute grounds for considering a product to be 'dangerous';

(c) 'dangerous product' shall mean any product which does not meet the definition of 'safe product' in (b);

(d) 'serious risk' shall mean any serious risk, including those the effects of which are not immediate, requiring rapid intervention by the public authorities;

(e) 'producer' shall mean:

(i) the manufacturer of the product, when he is established in the Community, and any other person presenting himself as the manufacturer by affixing to the product his name, trade mark or other distinctive mark, or the person who reconditions the product;

(ii) the manufacturer's representative, when the manufacturer is not established in the Community or, if there is no representative established in the Community, the importer of the product;

(iii) other professionals in the supply chain, insofar as their activities may affect the safety properties of a product;

(f) 'distributor' shall mean any professional in the supply chain whose activity does not affect the safety properties of a product;

(g) 'recall' shall mean any measure aimed at achieving the return of a dangerous product that has already been supplied or made available to consumers by the producer or distributor;

(h) 'withdrawal' shall mean any measure aimed at preventing the distribution, display and offer of a product dangerous to the consumer.

Chapter II General safety requirement, conformity assessment criteria and European standards

Article 3

1. Producers shall be obliged to place only safe products on the market.

2. A product shall be deemed safe, as far as the aspects covered by the relevant national legislation are concerned, when, in the absence of specific Community provisions governing the safety of the product in question, it conforms to the specific rules of national law of the Member State in whose territory the product is marketed, such rules being drawn up in conformity with the Treaty, and in particular Articles 28 and 30 thereof, and laying down the health and safety requirements which the product must satisfy in order to be marketed.

A product shall be presumed safe as far as the risks and risk categories covered by relevant national standards are concerned when it conforms to voluntary national standards transposing European standards, the references of which have been published by the Commission in the Official Journal of the European Communities in accordance with Article 4. The Member States shall publish the references of such national standards.

3. In circumstances other than those referred to in paragraph 2, the conformity of a product to the general safety requirement shall be assessed by taking into account the following elements in particular, where they exist:

(a) voluntary national standards transposing relevant European standards other than those referred to in paragraph 2;

(b) the standards drawn up in the Member State in which the product is marketed;

(c) Commission recommendations setting guidelines on product safety assessment;

(d) product safety codes of good practice in force in the sector concerned;

(e) the state of the art and technology;

(f) reasonable consumer expectations concerning safety.

4. Conformity of a product with the criteria designed to ensure the general safety requirement, in particular the provisions mentioned in paragraphs 2 or 3, shall not bar the competent authorities of the Member States from taking appropriate measures to impose restrictions on its being placed on the market or to require its withdrawal from the market or recall where there is evidence that, despite such conformity, it is dangerous.

Article 4

1. For the purposes of this Directive, the European standards referred to in the second subparagraph of Article 3(2) shall be drawn up as follows:

(a) the requirements intended to ensure that products which conform to those standards satisfy the general safety requirement shall be determined by the Commission. Those measures, designed to amend non-essential elements of this Directive by supplementing it, shall be adopted in accordance with the regulatory procedure with scrutiny referred to in Article 15(4);

(b) on the basis of those requirements, the Commission shall, in accordance with Directive 98/34/EC of the European Parliament and of the Council of 22 June 1998 laying down a procedure for the provision of information in the field of technical standards and regulations and of rules on information society services[7] call on the European standardisation bodies to draw up standards which satisfy these requirements;

(c) on the basis of those mandates, the European standardisation bodies shall adopt the standards in accordance with the principles contained in the general guidelines for cooperation between the Commission and those bodies;

(d) the Commission shall report every three years to the European Parliament and the Council, within the framework of the report referred to in Article 19(2), on its programmes for setting the requirements and the mandates for standardisation provided for in subparagraphs (a) and (b) above. This report will, in particular, include an analysis of the decisions taken regarding requirements and mandates for standardisation referred to in subparagraphs (a) and (b) and regarding the standards referred to in subparagraph (c). It will also include information on the products for which the Commission intends to set the requirements and the mandates in question, the product risks to be considered and the results of any preparatory work launched in this area.

2. The Commission shall publish in the Official Journal of the European Communities the references of the European standards adopted in this way and drawn up in accordance with the requirements referred to in paragraph 1.

If a standard adopted by the European standardisation bodies before the entry into force of this Directive ensures compliance with the general safety requirement, the Commission shall decide to publish its references in the Official Journal of the European Communities.

If a standard does not ensure compliance with the general safety requirement, the Commission shall withdraw reference to the standard from publication in whole or in part.

In the cases referred to in the second and third subparagraphs, the Commission shall, on its own initiative or at the request of a Member State, decide in accordance with the procedure laid down in Article 15(2) whether the standard in question meets the general safety requirement. The Commission shall decide to publish or withdraw after consulting the Committee established by Article 5 of Directive 98/34/EC. The Commission shall notify the Member States of its decision.

Chapter III Other obligations of producers and obligations of distributors

Article 5

1. Within the limits of their respective activities, producers shall provide consumers with the relevant information to enable them to assess the risks inherent in a product throughout the normal or reasonably foreseeable period of its use, where such risks are not immediately obvious without adequate warnings, and to take precautions against those risks.

The presence of warnings does not exempt any person from compliance with the other requirements laid down in this Directive.

Within the limits of their respective activities, producers shall adopt measures commensurate with the characteristics of the products which they supply, enabling them to:

[7] OJ L 204, 21.7.1998, p. 37. Directive amended by Directive 98/48/EC (OJ L 217, 5.8.1998, p. 18).

(a) be informed of risks which these products might pose;

(b) choose to take appropriate action including, if necessary to avoid these risks, withdrawal from the market, adequately and effectively warning consumers or recall from consumers.

The measures referred to in the third subparagraph shall include, for example:

(a) an indication, by means of the product or its packaging, of the identity and details of the producer and the product reference or, where applicable, the batch of products to which it belongs, except where not to give such indication is justified and

(b) in all cases where appropriate, the carrying out of sample testing of marketed products, investigating and, if necessary, keeping a register of complaints and keeping distributors informed of such monitoring.

Action such as that referred to in (b) of the third subparagraph shall be undertaken on a voluntary basis or at the request of the competent authorities in accordance with Article 8 (1)(f). Recall shall take place as a last resort, where other measures would not suffice to prevent the risks involved, in instances where the producers consider it necessary or where they are obliged to do so further to a measure taken by the competent authority. It may be effected within the framework of codes of good practice on the matter in the Member State concerned, where such codes exist.

2. Distributors shall be required to act with due care to help to ensure compliance with the applicable safety requirements, in particular by not supplying products which they know or should have presumed, on the basis of the information in their possession and as professionals, do not comply with those requirements. Moreover, within the limits of their respective activities, they shall participate in monitoring the safety of products placed on the market, especially by passing on information on product risks, keeping and providing the documentation necessary for tracing the origin of products, and cooperating in the action taken by producers and competent authorities to avoid the risks. Within the limits of their respective activities they shall take measures enabling them to cooperate efficiently.

3. Where producers and distributors know or ought to know, on the basis of the information in their possession and as professionals, that a product that they have placed on the market poses risks to the consumer that are incompatible with the general safety requirement, they shall immediately inform the competent authorities of the Member States thereof under the conditions laid down in Annex I, giving details, in particular, of action taken to prevent risk to the consumer.

The Commission shall adapt the specific requirements relating to the obligation to provide information laid down in Annex I. Those measures, designed to amend non-essential elements of this Directive by supplementing it, shall be adopted in accordance with the regulatory procedure with scrutiny referred to in Article 15(5).

4. Producers and distributors shall, within the limits of their respective activities, cooperate with the competent authorities, at the request of the latter, on action taken to avoid the risks posed by products which they supply or have supplied. The procedures for such cooperation, including procedures for dialogue with the producers and distributors concerned on issues related to product safety, shall be established by the competent authorities.

Chapter IV Specific obligations and powers of the Member States

Article 6

1. Member States shall ensure that producers and distributors comply with their obligations under this Directive in such a way that products placed on the market are safe.

2. Member States shall establish or nominate authorities competent to monitor the compliance of products with the general safety requirements and arrange for such authorities to have and use the necessary powers to take the appropriate measures incumbent upon them under this Directive.

3. Member States shall define the tasks, powers, organisation and cooperation arrangements of the competent authorities. They shall keep the Commission informed, and the Commission shall pass on such information to the other Member States.

Article 7

Member States shall lay down the rules on penalties applicable to infringements of the national provisions adopted pursuant to this Directive and shall take all measures necessary to ensure that they are implemented. The penalties provided for shall be effective, proportionate and dissuasive. Member States shall notify those provisions to the Commission by 15 January 2004 and shall also notify it, without delay, of any amendment affecting them.

Article 8

1. For the purposes of this Directive, and in particular of Article 6 thereof, the competent authorities of the Member States shall be entitled to take, inter alia, the measures in (a) and in (b) to (f) below, where appropriate:

(a) for any product:
  (i) to organise, even after its being placed on the market as being safe, appropriate checks on its safety properties, on an adequate scale, up to the final stage of use or consumption;
  (ii) to require all necessary information from the parties concerned;
  (iii) to take samples of products and subject them to safety checks;

(b) for any product that could pose risks in certain conditions:
  (i) to require that it be marked with suitable, clearly worded and easily comprehensible warnings, in the official languages of the Member State in which the product is marketed, on the risks it may present;
  (ii) to make its marketing subject to prior conditions so as to make it safe;

(c) for any product that could pose risks for certain persons: to order that they be given warning of the risk in good time and in an appropriate form, including the publication of special warnings;

(d) for any product that could be dangerous: for the period needed for the various safety evaluations, checks and controls, temporarily to ban its supply, the offer to supply it or its display;

(e) for any dangerous product: to ban its marketing and introduce the accompanying measures required to ensure the ban is complied with;

(f) for any dangerous product already on the market:
  (i) to order or organise its actual and immediate withdrawal, and alert consumers to the risks it presents;
  (ii) to order or coordinate or, if appropriate, to organise together with producers and distributors its recall from consumers and its destruction in suitable conditions.

2. When the competent authorities of the Member States take measures such as those provided for in paragraph 1, in particular those referred to in (d) to (f), they shall act in accordance with the Treaty, and in particular Articles 28 and 30 thereof, in such a way as to implement the measures in a manner proportional to the seriousness of the risk, and taking due account of the precautionary principle.

In this context, they shall encourage and promote voluntary action by producers and distributors, in accordance with the obligations incumbent on them under this Directive, and in particular Chapter III thereof, including where applicable by the development of codes of good practice.

If necessary, they shall organise or order the measures provided for in paragraph 1(f) if the action undertaken by the producers and distributors in fulfilment of their obligations is unsatisfactory or insufficient. Recall shall take place as a last resort. It may be effected within the framework of codes of good practice on the matter in the Member State concerned, where such codes exist.

3. In particular, the competent authorities shall have the power to take the necessary action to apply with due dispatch appropriate measures such as those mentioned in paragraph 1, (b) to (f), in the case of products posing a serious risk. These circumstances shall be determined by the Member States, assessing each individual case on its merits, taking into account the guidelines referred to in point 8 of Annex II.

(New Article 8(3) to take effect from 1 January 2010.)

3. In the case of products posing a serious risk, the competent authorities shall with due dispatch take the appropriate measures referred to in paragraph 1(b) to (f). The existence of a serious risk shall be determined by the Member States, assessing each individual case on its merits and taking into account the guidelines referred to in point 8 of Annex II.

4. The measures to be taken by the competent authorities under this Article shall be addressed, as appropriate, to:

(a) the producer;

(b) within the limits of their respective activities, distributors and in particular the party responsible for the first stage of distribution on the national market;

(c) any other person, where necessary, with a view to cooperation in action taken to avoid risks arising from a product.

Article 9

1. In order to ensure effective market surveillance, aimed at guaranteeing a high level of consumer health and safety protection, which entails cooperation between their competent authorities, Member States shall ensure that approaches employing appropriate means and procedures are put in place, which may include in particular:

(a) establishment, periodical updating and implementation of sectoral surveillance programmes by categories of products or risks and the monitoring of surveillance activities, findings and results;

(b) follow-up and updating of scientific and technical knowledge concerning the safety of products;

(c) periodical review and assessment of the functioning of the control activities and their effectiveness and, if necessary, revision of the surveillance approach and organisation put in place.

2. Member States shall ensure that consumers and other interested parties are given an opportunity to submit complaints to the competent authorities on product safety and on surveillance and control activities and that these complaints are followed up as appropriate. Member States shall actively inform consumers and other interested parties of the procedures established to that end.

Article 10

1. The Commission shall promote and take part in the operation in a European network of the authorities of the Member States competent for product safety, in particular in the form of administrative cooperation.

2. This network operation shall develop in a coordinated manner with the other existing Community procedures, particularly RAPEX. Its objective shall be, in particular, to facilitate:

(a) the exchange of information on risk assessment, dangerous products, test methods and results, recent scientific developments as well as other aspects relevant for control activities;

(b) the establishment and execution of joint surveillance and testing projects;

(c) the exchange of expertise and best practices and cooperation in training activities;

(d) improved cooperation at Community level with regard to the tracing, withdrawal and recall of dangerous products.

Chapter V Exchanges of information and rapid intervention situations

Article 11

1. Where a Member State takes measures which restrict the placing on the market of products—or require their withdrawal or recall—such as those provided for in Article 8(1)(b) to (f), the Member State shall, to the extent that such notification is not required under Article 12 or any specific Community legislation, inform the Commission of the measures, specifying its reasons for adopting them. It shall also inform the Commission of any modification or lifting of such measures.

If the notifying Member State considers that the effects of the risk do not or cannot go beyond its territory, it shall notify the measures concerned insofar as they involve information likely to be of interest to Member States from the product safety standpoint, and in particular if they are in response to a new risk which has not yet been reported in other notifications.

In accordance with the procedure laid down in Article 15(3) of this Directive, the Commission shall, while ensuring the effectiveness and proper functioning of the system, adopt the guidelines referred to in point 8 of Annex II. These shall propose the content and standard form for the notifications provided for in this Article, and, in particular, shall provide precise criteria for determining the conditions for which notification is relevant for the purposes of the second subparagraph.

2. The Commission shall forward the notification to the other Member States, unless it concludes, after examination on the basis of the information contained in the notification, that the measure does not comply with Community law. In such a case, it shall immediately inform the Member State which initiated the action.

Article 12

1. Where a Member State adopts or decides to adopt, recommend or agree with producers and distributors, whether on a compulsory or voluntary basis, measures or actions to prevent, restrict or impose specific conditions on the possible marketing or use, within its own territory, of products by reason of a serious risk, it shall immediately notify the Commission thereof through RAPEX. It shall also inform the Commission without delay of modification or withdrawal of any such measure or action.

If the notifying Member State considers that the effects of the risk do not or cannot go beyond its territory, it shall follow the procedure laid down in Article 11, taking into account the relevant criteria proposed in the guidelines referred to in point 8 of Annex II.

Without prejudice to the first subparagraph, before deciding to adopt such measures or to take such action, Member States may pass on to the Commission any information in their possession regarding the existence of a serious risk.

In the case of a serious risk, they shall notify the Commission of the voluntary measures laid down in Article 5 of this Directive taken by producers and distributors.

2. On receiving such notifications, the Commission shall check whether they comply with this Article and with the requirements applicable to the functioning of RAPEX, and shall forward them to the other Member States, which, in turn, shall immediately inform the Commission of any measures adopted.

3. Detailed procedures for RAPEX are set out in Annex II. They shall be adapted by the Commission. Those measures, designed to amend non-essential elements of this Directive by supplementing it, shall be adopted in accordance with the regulatory procedure with scrutiny referred to in Article 15(5).

4. Access to RAPEX shall be open to applicant countries, third countries or international organisations, within the framework of agreements between the Community and those countries or international organisations, according to arrangements defined in these agreements. Any such agreements shall be based on reciprocity and include provisions on confidentiality corresponding to those applicable in the Community.

Article 13

1. If the Commission becomes aware of a serious risk from certain products to the health and safety of consumers in various Member States, it may, after consulting the Member States, and, if scientific questions arise which fall within the competence of a Community Scientific Committee, the Scientific Committee competent to deal with the risk concerned, adopt a decision in the light of the result of those consultations, in accordance with the procedure laid down in Article 15(2), requiring Member States to take measures from among those listed in Article 8(1)(b) to (f) if, at one and the same time:

(a) it emerges from prior consultations with the Member States that they differ significantly on the approach adopted or to be adopted to deal with the risk; and

(b) the risk cannot be dealt with, in view of the nature of the safety issue posed by the product, in a manner compatible with the degree of urgency of the case, under other procedures laid down by the specific Community legislation applicable to the products concerned; and

(c) the risk can be eliminated effectively only by adopting appropriate measures applicable at Community level, in order to ensure a consistent and high level of protection of the health and safety of consumers and the proper functioning of the internal market.

2. The decisions referred to in paragraph 1 shall be valid for a period not exceeding one year and may be confirmed, under the same procedure, for additional periods none of which shall exceed one year.

However, decisions concerning specific, individually identified products or batches of products shall be valid without a time limit.

3. Export from the Community of dangerous products which have been the subject of a decision referred to in paragraph 1 shall be prohibited unless the decision provides otherwise.

4. Member States shall take all necessary measures to implement the decisions referred to in paragraph 1 within less than 20 days, unless a different period is specified in those decisions.

5. The competent authorities responsible for carrying out the measures referred to in paragraph 1 shall, within one month, give the parties concerned an opportunity to submit their views and shall inform the Commission accordingly.

Chapter VI Committee procedures

Article 14

1. The measures necessary for the implementation of this Directive relating to the matters referred to below shall be adopted in accordance with the regulatory procedure provided for in Article 15(2):

(a) the measures referred to in Article 4 concerning standards adopted by the European standardisation bodies;

(b) the decisions referred to in Article 13 requiring Member States to take measures as listed in Article 8(1)(b) to (f).

2. The measures necessary for the implementation of this Directive in respect of all other matters shall be adopted in accordance with the advisory procedure provided for in Article 15(3).

Article 15

1. The Commission shall be assisted by a Committee.

2. Where reference is made to this paragraph, Articles 5 and 7 of Decision 1999/468/EC shall apply, having regard to the provisions of Article 8 thereof.

The period laid down in Article 5(6) of Decision 1999/468/EC shall be set at 15 days.

3. Where reference is made to this paragraph, Articles 3 and 7 of Decision 1999/468/EC shall apply, having regard to the provisions of Article 8 thereof.

4. Where reference is made to this paragraph, Article 5a(1) to (4) and Article 7 of Decision 1999/468/EC shall apply, having regard to the provisions of Article 8 thereof.

5. Where reference is made to this paragraph, Article 5a(1) to (4) and (5)(b) and Article 7 of Decision 1999/468/EC shall apply, having regard to the provisions of Article 8 thereof.

The time-limits laid down in Article 5a(3)(c) and (4)(b) and (e) of Decision 1999/468/EC shall be set at two months, one month and two months respectively.

Chapter VII Final provisions

Article 16

1. Information available to the authorities of the Member States or the Commission relating to risks to consumer health and safety posed by products shall in general be available to the public, in accordance with the requirements of transparency and without prejudice to the restrictions required for monitoring and investigation activities. In particular the public shall have access to information on product identification, the nature of the risk and the measures taken.

However, Member States and the Commission shall take the steps necessary to ensure that their officials and agents are required not to disclose information obtained for the purposes of this Directive which, by its nature, is covered by professional secrecy in duly justified cases, except for information relating to the safety properties of products which must be made public if circumstances so require, in order to protect the health and safety of consumers.

2. Protection of professional secrecy shall not prevent the dissemination to the competent authorities of information relevant for ensuring the effectiveness of market monitoring and surveil-

lance activities. The authorities receiving information covered by professional secrecy shall ensure its protection.

Article 17

This Directive shall be without prejudice to the application of Directive 85/374/EEC.

Article 18

1. Any measure adopted under this Directive and involving restrictions on the placing of a product on the market or requiring its withdrawal or recall must state the appropriate reasons on which it is based. It shall be notified as soon as possible to the party concerned and shall indicate the remedies available under the provisions in force in the Member State in question and the time limits applying to such remedies.

The parties concerned shall, whenever feasible, be given an opportunity to submit their views before the adoption of the measure. If this has not been done in advance because of the urgency of the measures to be taken, they shall be given such opportunity in due course after the measure has been implemented.

Measures requiring the withdrawal of a product or its recall shall take into consideration the need to encourage distributors, users and consumers to contribute to the implementation of such measures.

2. Member States shall ensure that any measure taken by the competent authorities involving restrictions on the placing of a product on the market or requiring its withdrawal or recall can be challenged before the competent courts.

3. Any decision taken by virtue of this Directive and involving restrictions on the placing of a product on the market or requiring its withdrawal or its recall shall be without prejudice to assessment of the liability of the party concerned, in the light of the national criminal law applying in the case in question.

Article 19

1. The Commission may bring before the Committee referred to in Article 15 any matter concerning the application of this Directive and particularly those relating to market monitoring and surveillance activities.

2. Every three years, following 15 January 2004, the Commission shall submit a report on the implementation of this Directive to the European Parliament and the Council.

The report shall in particular include information on the safety of consumer products, in particular on improved traceability of products, the functioning of market surveillance, standardisation work, the functioning of RAPEX and Community measures taken on the basis of Article 13. To this end the Commission shall conduct assessments of the relevant issues, in particular the approaches, systems and practices put in place in the Member States, in the light of the requirements of this Directive and the other Community legislation relating to product safety. The Member States shall provide the Commission with all the necessary assistance and information for carrying out the assessments and preparing the reports.

Article 20

The Commission shall identify the needs, possibilities and priorities for Community action on the safety of services and submit to the European Parliament and the Council, before 1 January 2003, a report, accompanied by proposals on the subject as appropriate.

Article 21

1. Member States shall bring into force the laws, regulations and administrative provisions necessary in order to comply with this Directive with effect from 15 January 2004. They shall forthwith inform the Commission thereof.

When Member States adopt those measures, they shall contain a reference to this Directive or be accompanied by such reference on the occasion of their official publication. The methods of making such reference shall be laid down by Member States.

2. Member States shall communicate to the Commission the provisions of national law which they adopt in the field covered by this Directive.

Article 22

Directive 92/59/EEC is hereby repealed from 15 January 2004, without prejudice to the obligations of Member States concerning the deadlines for transposition and application of the said Directive as indicated in Annex III.

References to Directive 92/59/EEC shall be construed as references to this Directive and shall be read in accordance with the correlation table in Annex IV.

Article 23

This Directive shall enter into force on the day of its publication in the Official Journal of the European Communities.

Article 24

This Directive is addressed to the Member States.

Done at Brussels, 3 December 2001.
For the European Parliament
The President
N. FONTAINE

For the Council
The President
F. VANDENBROUCKE

Annex I

Requirements concerning information on products that do not comply with the general safety requirement to be provided to the competent authorities by producers and distributors

1. The information specified in Article 5(3), or where applicable by specific requirements of Community rules on the product concerned, shall be passed to the competent authorities appointed for the purpose in the Member States where the products in question are or have been marketed or otherwise supplied to consumers.

2. The Commission, assisted by the Committee referred to in Article 15, shall define the content and draw up the standard form of the notifications provided for in this Annex, while ensuring the effectiveness and proper functioning of the system. In particular, it shall put forward, possibly in the form of a guide, simple and clear criteria for determining the special conditions, particularly those concerning isolated circumstances or products, for which notification is not relevant in relation to this Annex.

3. In the event of serious risks, this information shall include at least the following:
   - (a) information enabling a precise identification of the product or batch of products in question;
   - (b) a full description of the risk that the products in question present;
   - (c) all available information relevant for tracing the product;
   - (d) a description of the action undertaken to prevent risks to consumers.

Annex II

Procedures for the application of RAPEX and guidelines for notifications

1. RAPEX covers products as defined in Article 2(a) that pose a serious risk to the health and safety of consumers.

Pharmaceuticals, which come under Directives 75/319/EEC[8] and 81/851/EEC,[9] are excluded from the scope of RAPEX.

2. RAPEX is essentially aimed at a rapid exchange of information in the event of a serious risk. The guidelines referred to in point 8 define specific criteria for identifying serious risks.

3. Member States notifying under Article 12 shall provide all available details. In particular, the notification shall contain the information stipulated in the guidelines referred to in point 8 and at least:

(a) information enabling the product to be identified;
(b) a description of the risk involved, including a summary of the results of any tests/ analyses and of their conclusions which are relevant to assessing the level of risk;
(c) the nature and the duration of the measures or action taken or decided on, if applicable;
(d) information on supply chains and distribution of the product, in particular on destination countries.

Such information must be transmitted using the special standard notification form and by the means stipulated in the guidelines referred to in point 8.

When the measure notified pursuant to Article 11 or Article 12 seeks to limit the marketing or use of a chemical substance or preparation, the Member States shall provide as soon as possible either a summary or the references of the relevant data relating to the substance or preparation considered and to known and available substitutes, where such information is available. They will also communicate the anticipated effects of the measure on consumer health and safety together with the assessment of the risk carried out in accordance with the general principles for the risk evaluation of chemical substances as referred to in Article 10(4) of Regulation (EEC) No 793/93[10] in the case of an existing substance or in Article 3(2) of Directive 67/548/EEC[11] in the case of a new substance. The guidelines referred to in point 8 shall define the details and procedures for the information requested in that respect.

4. When a Member State has informed the Commission, in accordance with Article 12(1), third subparagraph, of a serious risk before deciding to adopt measures, it must inform the Commission within 45 days whether it confirms or modifies this information.

5. The Commission shall, in the shortest time possible, verify the conformity with the provisions of the Directive of the information received under RAPEX and, may, when it considers it to be necessary and in order to assess product safety, carry out an investigation on its own initiative. In the case of such an investigation, Member States shall supply the Commission with the requested information to the best of their ability.

6. Upon receipt of a notification referred to in Article 12, the Member States are requested to inform the Commission, at the latest within the set period of time stipulated in the guidelines referred to in point 8, of the following:

(a) whether the product has been marketed in their territory;
(b) what measures concerning the product in question they may be adopting in the light of their own circumstances, stating the reasons, including any differing assessment of risk or any other special circumstance justifying their decision, in particular lack of action or of follow-up;
(c) any relevant supplementary information they have obtained on the risk involved, including the results of any tests or analyses carried out.

The guidelines referred to in point 8 shall provide precise criteria for notifying measures limited to national territory and shall specify how to deal with notifications concerning risks which are considered by the Member State not to go beyond its territory.

7. Member States shall immediately inform the Commission of any modification or lifting of the measure(s) or action(s) in question.

[8] OJ L 147, 9.6.1975, p. 13. Directive as last amended by Commission Directive 2000/38/EC (OJ L 139, 10.6.2000, p. 28).
[9] OJ L 317, 6.11.1981, p. 1. Directive as last amended by Commission Directive 2000/37/EC (OJ L 139, 10.6.2000, p. 25).
[10] OJ L 84, 5.4.1993, p. 1.
[11] OJ 196, 16.8.1967, p. 1/67. Directive as last amended by Commission Directive 2000/33/EC (OJ L 136, 8.6.2000, p. 90).

8. The Commission shall prepare and regularly update, in accordance with the procedure laid down in Article 15(3), guidelines concerning the management of RAPEX by the Commission and the Member States.

9. The Commission may inform the national contact points regarding products posing serious risks, imported into or exported from the Community and the European Economic Area.

10. Responsibility for the information provided lies with the notifying Member State.

11. The Commission shall ensure the proper functioning of the system, in particular classifying and indexing notifications according to the degree of urgency. Detailed procedures shall be laid down by the guidelines referred to in point 8.

Annex III

Period for the transposition and application of the repealed Directive

(Referred to in the First Subparagraph of Article 22)

Directive	*Period for transposition*	*Period for bringing into application*
Directive 92/59/EEC	29 June 1994	29 June 1994

Annex IV Correlation table

(Referred to in the second subparagraph of Article 22)

This Directive	Directive 92/59/EEC
Article 1	Article 1
Article 2	Article 2
Article 3	Article 4
Article 4	—
Article 5	Article 3
Article 6	Article 5
Article 7	Article 5(2)
Article 8	Article 6
Article 9	—
Article 10	—
Article 11	Article 7
Article 12	Article 8
Article 13	Article 9
Articles 14 and 15	Article 10
Article 16	Article 12
Article 17	Article 13
Article 18	Article 14
Article 19	Article 15
Article 20	—
Article 21	Article 17
Article 22	Article 18
Article 23	Article 19
Annex I	—
Annex II	Annex
Annex III	—
Annex IV	—

Directive 2005/29/EC of the European Parliament and of the Council of 11 May 2005 concerning unfair business-to-consumer commercial practices in the internal market and amending Council Directive 84/450/EEC, Directives 97/7/EC, 98/27/EC and 2002/65/EC of the European Parliament and of the Council and Regulation (EC) No 2006/2004 of the European Parliament and of the Council

THE EUROPEAN PARLIAMENT AND THE COUNCIL OF THE EUROPEAN UNION,

Having regard to the Treaty establishing the European Community, and in particular Article 95 thereof,

Having regard to the proposal from the Commission,

Having regard to the opinion of the European Economic and Social Committee[1],

Acting in accordance with the procedure laid down in Article 251 of the Treaty[2],

Whereas:

(1) Article 153(1) and (3)(a) of the Treaty provides that the Community is to contribute to the attainment of a high level of consumer protection by the measures it adopts pursuant to Article 95 thereof.

(2) In accordance with Article 14(2) of the Treaty, the internal market comprises an area without internal frontiers in which the free movement of goods and services and freedom of establishment are ensured. The development of fair commercial practices within the area without internal frontiers is vital for the promotion of the development of cross-border activities.

(3) The laws of the Member States relating to unfair commercial practices show marked differences which can generate appreciable distortions of competition and obstacles to the smooth functioning of the internal market. In the field of advertising, Council Directive 84/450/EEC of 10 September 1984 concerning misleading and comparative advertising[3] establishes minimum criteria for harmonising legislation on misleading advertising, but does not prevent the Member States from retaining or adopting measures which provide more extensive protection for consumers. As a result, Member States' provisions on misleading advertising diverge significantly.

(4) These disparities cause uncertainty as to which national rules apply to unfair commercial practices harming consumers' economic interests and create many barriers affecting business and consumers. These barriers increase the cost to business of exercising internal market freedoms, in particular when businesses wish to engage in cross border marketing, advertising campaigns and sales promotions. Such barriers also make consumers uncertain of their rights and undermine their confidence in the internal market.

(5) In the absence of uniform rules at Community level, obstacles to the free movement of services and goods across borders or the freedom of establishment could be justified in the light of the case-law of the Court of Justice of the European Communities as long as they seek to protect recognised public interest objectives and are proportionate to those objectives. In view of the Community's objectives, as set out in the provisions of the Treaty and in secondary Community law relating to freedom of movement, and in accordance with the Commission's policy on commercial communications as indicated in the Communication from the Commission entitled "The follow-up to the Green

[1] OJ C 108, 30.4.2004, p. 81.

[2] Opinion of the European Parliament of 20 April 2004 (OJ C 104 E, 30.4.2004, p. 260), Council Common Position of 15 November 2004 (OJ C 38 E, 15.2.2005, p. 1), Position of the European Parliament of 24 February 2005 (not yet published in the Official Journal) and Council Decision of 12 April 2005.

[3] OJ L 250, 19.9.1984, p. 17. Directive as amended by Directive 97/55/EC of the European Parliament and of the Council (OJ L 290, 23.10.1997, p. 18).

Paper on Commercial Communications in the Internal Market", such obstacles should be eliminated. These obstacles can only be eliminated by establishing uniform rules at Community level which establish a high level of consumer protection and by clarifying certain legal concepts at Community level to the extent necessary for the proper functioning of the internal market and to meet the requirement of legal certainty.

(6) This Directive therefore approximates the laws of the Member States on unfair commercial practices, including unfair advertising, which directly harm consumers' economic interests and thereby indirectly harm the economic interests of legitimate competitors. In line with the principle of proportionality, this Directive protects consumers from the consequences of such unfair commercial practices where they are material but recognises that in some cases the impact on consumers may be negligible. It neither covers nor affects the national laws on unfair commercial practices which harm only competitors' economic interests or which relate to a transaction between traders; taking full account of the principle of subsidiarity, Member States will continue to be able to regulate such practices, in conformity with Community law, if they choose to do so. Nor does this Directive cover or affect the provisions of Directive 84/450/EEC on advertising which misleads business but which is not misleading for consumers and on comparative advertising. Further, this Directive does not affect accepted advertising and marketing practices, such as legitimate product placement, brand differentiation or the offering of incentives which may legitimately affect consumers' perceptions of products and influence their behaviour without impairing the consumer's ability to make an informed decision.

(7) This Directive addresses commercial practices directly related to influencing consumers' transactional decisions in relation to products. It does not address commercial practices carried out primarily for other purposes, including for example commercial communication aimed at investors, such as annual reports and corporate promotional literature. It does not address legal requirements related to taste and decency which vary widely among the Member States. Commercial practices such as, for example, commercial solicitation in the streets, may be undesirable in Member States for cultural reasons. Member States should accordingly be able to continue to ban commercial practices in their territory, in conformity with Community law, for reasons of taste and decency even where such practices do not limit consumers' freedom of choice. Full account should be taken of the context of the individual case concerned in applying this Directive, in particular the general clauses thereof.

(8) This Directive directly protects consumer economic interests from unfair business-to-consumer commercial practices. Thereby, it also indirectly protects legitimate businesses from their competitors who do not play by the rules in this Directive and thus guarantees fair competition in fields coordinated by it. It is understood that there are other commercial practices which, although not harming consumers, may hurt competitors and business customers. The Commission should carefully examine the need for Community action in the field of unfair competition beyond the remit of this Directive and, if necessary, make a legislative proposal to cover these other aspects of unfair competition.

(9) This Directive is without prejudice to individual actions brought by those who have been harmed by an unfair commercial practice. It is also without prejudice to Community and national rules on contract law, on intellectual property rights, on the health and safety aspects of products, on conditions of establishment and authorisation regimes, including those rules which, in conformity with Community law, relate to gambling activities, and to Community competition rules and the national provisions implementing them. The Member States will thus be able to retain or introduce restrictions and prohibitions of commercial practices on grounds of the protection of the health and safety of consumers in their territory wherever the trader is based, for example in relation to alcohol, tobacco or pharmaceuticals. Financial services and immovable property, by reason of their complexity and inherent serious risks, necessitate detailed requirements, including positive obligations on traders. For this reason, in the field of financial services and immovable property, this Directive is without prejudice to the right of Member States to go beyond its provisions to protect the economic interests of consumers. It is not appropriate to regulate here the certification and indication of the standard of fineness of articles of precious metal.

(10) It is necessary to ensure that the relationship between this Directive and existing Community law is coherent, particularly where detailed provisions on unfair commercial practices apply to specific sectors. This Directive therefore amends Directive 84/450/EEC, Directive 97/7/EC of the European Parliament and of the Council of 20 May 1997 on the protection of consumers in respect of distance contracts[4], Directive 98/27/EC of the European Parliament and of the Council of 19 May 1998 on injunctions for the protection of consumers' interests[5] and Directive 2002/65/EC of the European Parliament and of the Council of 23 September 2002 concerning the distance marketing of consumer financial services[6]. This Directive accordingly applies only in so far as there are no specific Community law provisions regulating specific aspects of unfair commercial practices, such as information requirements and rules on the way the information is presented to the consumer. It provides protection for consumers where there is no specific sectoral legislation at Community level and prohibits traders from creating a false impression of the nature of products. This is particularly important for complex products with high levels of risk to consumers, such as certain financial services products. This Directive consequently complements the Community acquis, which is applicable to commercial practices harming consumers' economic interests.

(11) The high level of convergence achieved by the approximation of national provisions through this Directive creates a high common level of consumer protection. This Directive establishes a single general prohibition of those unfair commercial practices distorting consumers' economic behaviour. It also sets rules on aggressive commercial practices, which are currently not regulated at Community level.

(12) Harmonisation will considerably increase legal certainty for both consumers and business. Both consumers and business will be able to rely on a single regulatory framework based on clearly defined legal concepts regulating all aspects of unfair commercial practices across the EU. The effect will be to eliminate the barriers stemming from the fragmentation of the rules on unfair commercial practices harming consumer economic interests and to enable the internal market to be achieved in this area.

(13) In order to achieve the Community's objectives through the removal of internal market barriers, it is necessary to replace Member States' existing, divergent general clauses and legal principles. The single, common general prohibition established by this Directive therefore covers unfair commercial practices distorting consumers' economic behaviour. In order to support consumer confidence the general prohibition should apply equally to unfair commercial practices which occur outside any contractual relationship between a trader and a consumer or following the conclusion of a contract and during its execution. The general prohibition is elaborated by rules on the two types of commercial practices which are by far the most common, namely misleading commercial practices and aggressive commercial practices.

(14) It is desirable that misleading commercial practices cover those practices, including misleading advertising, which by deceiving the consumer prevent him from making an informed and thus efficient choice. In conformity with the laws and practices of Member States on misleading advertising, this Directive classifies misleading practices into misleading actions and misleading omissions. In respect of omissions, this Directive sets out a limited number of key items of information which the consumer needs to make an informed transactional decision. Such information will not have to be disclosed in all advertisements, but only where the trader makes an invitation to purchase, which is a concept clearly defined in this Directive. The full harmonisation approach adopted in this Directive does not preclude the Member States from specifying in national law the main characteristics of particular products such as, for example, collectors' items or electrical goods, the omission of which would be material when an invitation to purchase is made. It is not the intention of this Directive to reduce consumer choice by prohibiting the promotion of products which look similar to other products unless this similarity confuses consumers as to the commercial origin of the product and is therefore misleading. This Directive should

[4] OJ L 144, 4.6.1997, p. 19. Directive as amended by Directive 2002/65/EC (OJ L 271, 9.10.2002, p. 16).
[5] OJ L 166, 11.6.1998, p. 51. Directive as last amended by Directive 2002/65/EC.
[6] OJ L 271, 9.10.2002, p. 16.

be without prejudice to existing Community law which expressly affords Member States the choice between several regulatory options for the protection of consumers in the field of commercial practices. In particular, this Directive should be without prejudice to Article 13(3) of Directive 2002/58/EC of the European Parliament and of the Council of 12 July 2002 concerning the processing of personal data and the protection of privacy in the electronic communications sector[7].

(15) Where Community law sets out information requirements in relation to commercial communication, advertising and marketing that information is considered as material under this Directive. Member States will be able to retain or add information requirements relating to contract law and having contract law consequences where this is allowed by the minimum clauses in the existing Community law instruments. A non-exhaustive list of such information requirements in the acquis is contained in Annex II. Given the full harmonisation introduced by this Directive only the information required in Community law is considered as material for the purpose of Article 7(5) thereof. Where Member States have introduced information requirements over and above what is specified in Community law, on the basis of minimum clauses, the omission of that extra information will not constitute a misleading omission under this Directive. By contrast Member States will be able, when allowed by the minimum clauses in Community law, to maintain or introduce more stringent provisions in conformity with Community law so as to ensure a higher level of protection of consumers' individual contractual rights.

(16) The provisions on aggressive commercial practices should cover those practices which significantly impair the consumer's freedom of choice. Those are practices using harassment, coercion, including the use of physical force, and undue influence.

(17) It is desirable that those commercial practices which are in all circumstances unfair be identified to provide greater legal certainty. Annex I therefore contains the full list of all such practices. These are the only commercial practices which can be deemed to be unfair without a case-by-case assessment against the provisions of Articles 5 to 9. The list may only be modified by revision of the Directive.

(18) It is appropriate to protect all consumers from unfair commercial practices; however the Court of Justice has found it necessary in adjudicating on advertising cases since the enactment of Directive 84/450/EEC to examine the effect on a notional, typical consumer. In line with the principle of proportionality, and to permit the effective application of the protections contained in it, this Directive takes as a benchmark the average consumer, who is reasonably well-informed and reasonably observant and circumspect, taking into account social, cultural and linguistic factors, as interpreted by the Court of Justice, but also contains provisions aimed at preventing the exploitation of consumers whose characteristics make them particularly vulnerable to unfair commercial practices. Where a commercial practice is specifically aimed at a particular group of consumers, such as children, it is desirable that the impact of the commercial practice be assessed from the perspective of the average member of that group. It is therefore appropriate to include in the list of practices which are in all circumstances unfair a provision which, without imposing an outright ban on advertising directed at children, protects them from direct exhortations to purchase. The average consumer test is not a statistical test. National courts and authorities will have to exercise their own faculty of judgement, having regard to the case-law of the Court of Justice, to determine the typical reaction of the average consumer in a given case.

(19) Where certain characteristics such as age, physical or mental infirmity or credulity make consumers particularly susceptible to a commercial practice or to the underlying product and the economic behaviour only of such consumers is likely to be distorted by the practice in a way that the trader can reasonably foresee, it is appropriate to ensure that they are adequately protected by assessing the practice from the perspective of the average member of that group.

(20) It is appropriate to provide a role for codes of conduct, which enable traders to apply the principles of this Directive effectively in specific economic fields. In sectors where there are specific

[7] OJ L 201, 31.7.2002, p. 37.

mandatory requirements regulating the behaviour of traders, it is appropriate that these will also provide evidence as to the requirements of professional diligence in that sector. The control exercised by code owners at national or Community level to eliminate unfair commercial practices may avoid the need for recourse to administrative or judicial action and should therefore be encouraged. With the aim of pursuing a high level of consumer protection, consumers' organisations could be informed and involved in the drafting of codes of conduct.

(21) Persons or organisations regarded under national law as having a legitimate interest in the matter must have legal remedies for initiating proceedings against unfair commercial practices, either before a court or before an administrative authority which is competent to decide upon complaints or to initiate appropriate legal proceedings. While it is for national law to determine the burden of proof, it is appropriate to enable courts and administrative authorities to require traders to produce evidence as to the accuracy of factual claims they have made.

(22) It is necessary that Member States lay down penalties for infringements of the provisions of this Directive and they must ensure that these are enforced. The penalties must be effective, proportionate and dissuasive.

(23) Since the objectives of this Directive, namely to eliminate the barriers to the functioning of the internal market represented by national laws on unfair commercial practices and to provide a high common level of consumer protection, by approximating the laws, regulations and administrative provisions of the Member States on unfair commercial practices, cannot be sufficiently achieved by the Member States and can therefore be better achieved at Community level, the Community may adopt measures, in accordance with the principle of subsidiarity as set out in Article 5 of the Treaty. In accordance with the principle of proportionality, as set out in that Article, this Directive does not go beyond what is necessary in order to eliminate the internal market barriers and achieve a high common level of consumer protection.

(24) It is appropriate to review this Directive to ensure that barriers to the internal market have been addressed and a high level of consumer protection achieved. The review could lead to a Commission proposal to amend this Directive, which may include a limited extension to the derogation in Article 3(5), and/or amendments to other consumer protection legislation reflecting the Commission's Consumer Policy Strategy commitment to review the existing acquis in order to achieve a high, common level of consumer protection.

(25) This Directive respects the fundamental rights and observes the principles recognised in particular by the Charter of Fundamental Rights of the European Union,

HAVE ADOPTED THIS DIRECTIVE:

Chapter 1 General provisions

Article 1 Purpose

The purpose of this Directive is to contribute to the proper functioning of the internal market and achieve a high level of consumer protection by approximating the laws, regulations and administrative provisions of the Member States on unfair commercial practices harming consumers' economic interests.

Article 2 Definitions

For the purposes of this Directive:

(a) "consumer" means any natural person who, in commercial practices covered by this Directive, is acting for purposes which are outside his trade, business, craft or profession;

(b) "trader" means any natural or legal person who, in commercial practices covered by this Directive, is acting for purposes relating to his trade, business, craft or profession and anyone acting in the name of or on behalf of a trader;

(c) "product" means any goods or service including immovable property, rights and obligations;

(d) "business-to-consumer commercial practices" (hereinafter also referred to as commercial practices) means any act, omission, course of conduct or representation, commercial communication including advertising and marketing, by a trader, directly connected with the promotion, sale or supply of a product to consumers;

(e) "to materially distort the economic behaviour of consumers" means using a commercial practice to appreciably impair the consumer's ability to make an informed decision, thereby causing the consumer to take a transactional decision that he would not have taken otherwise;

(f) "code of conduct" means an agreement or set of rules not imposed by law, regulation or administrative provision of a Member State which defines the behaviour of traders who undertake to be bound by the code in relation to one or more particular commercial practices or business sectors;

(g) "code owner" means any entity, including a trader or group of traders, which is responsible for the formulation and revision of a code of conduct and/or for monitoring compliance with the code by those who have undertaken to be bound by it;

(h) "professional diligence" means the standard of special skill and care which a trader may reasonably be expected to exercise towards consumers, commensurate with honest market practice and/or the general principle of good faith in the trader's field of activity;

(i) "invitation to purchase" means a commercial communication which indicates characteristics of the product and the price in a way appropriate to the means of the commercial communication used and thereby enables the consumer to make a purchase;

(j) "undue influence" means exploiting a position of power in relation to the consumer so as to apply pressure, even without using or threatening to use physical force, in a way which significantly limits the consumer's ability to make an informed decision;

(k) "transactional decision" means any decision taken by a consumer concerning whether, how and on what terms to purchase, make payment in whole or in part for, retain or dispose of a product or to exercise a contractual right in relation to the product, whether the consumer decides to act or to refrain from acting;

(l) "regulated profession" means a professional activity or a group of professional activities, access to which or the pursuit of which, or one of the modes of pursuing which, is conditional, directly or indirectly, upon possession of specific professional qualifications, pursuant to laws, regulations or administrative provisions.

Article 3 Scope

1. This Directive shall apply to unfair business-to-consumer commercial practices, as laid down in Article 5, before, during and after a commercial transaction in relation to a product.

2. This Directive is without prejudice to contract law and, in particular, to the rules on the validity, formation or effect of a contract.

3. This Directive is without prejudice to Community or national rules relating to the health and safety aspects of products.

4. In the case of conflict between the provisions of this Directive and other Community rules regulating specific aspects of unfair commercial practices, the latter shall prevail and apply to those specific aspects.

5. For a period of six years from 12 June 2007, Member States shall be able to continue to apply national provisions within the field approximated by this Directive which are more restrictive or prescriptive than this Directive and which implement directives containing minimum harmonisation clauses. These measures must be essential to ensure that consumers are adequately protected against unfair commercial practices and must be proportionate to the attainment of this objective. The review referred to in Article 18 may, if considered appropriate, include a proposal to prolong this derogation for a further limited period.

6. Member States shall notify the Commission without delay of any national provisions applied on the basis of paragraph 5.

7. This Directive is without prejudice to the rules determining the jurisdiction of the courts.

8. This Directive is without prejudice to any conditions of establishment or of authorisation regimes, or to the deontological codes of conduct or other specific rules governing regulated professions in order to uphold high standards of integrity on the part of the professional, which Member States may, in conformity with Community law, impose on professionals.

9. In relation to "financial services", as defined in Directive 2002/65/EC, and immovable property, Member States may impose requirements which are more restrictive or prescriptive than this Directive in the field which it approximates.

10. This Directive shall not apply to the application of the laws, regulations and administrative provisions of Member States relating to the certification and indication of the standard of fineness of articles of precious metal.

Article 4 Internal market

Member States shall neither restrict the freedom to provide services nor restrict the free movement of goods for reasons falling within the field approximated by this Directive.

Chapter 2 Unfair commercial practices

Article 5 Prohibition of unfair commercial practices

1. Unfair commercial practices shall be prohibited.

2. A commercial practice shall be unfair if:

(a) it is contrary to the requirements of professional diligence,

and

(b) it materially distorts or is likely to materially distort the economic behaviour with regard to the product of the average consumer whom it reaches or to whom it is addressed, or of the average member of the group when a commercial practice is directed to a particular group of consumers.

3. Commercial practices which are likely to materially distort the economic behaviour only of a clearly identifiable group of consumers who are particularly vulnerable to the practice or the underlying product because of their mental or physical infirmity, age or credulity in a way which the trader could reasonably be expected to foresee, shall be assessed from the perspective of the average member of that group. This is without prejudice to the common and legitimate advertising practice of making exaggerated statements or statements which are not meant to be taken literally.

4. In particular, commercial practices shall be unfair which:

(a) are misleading as set out in Articles 6 and 7,

or

(b) are aggressive as set out in Articles 8 and 9.

5. Annex I contains the list of those commercial practices which shall in all circumstances be regarded as unfair. The same single list shall apply in all Member States and may only be modified by revision of this Directive.

Section 1 Misleading commercial practices

Article 6 Misleading actions

1. A commercial practice shall be regarded as misleading if it contains false information and is therefore untruthful or in any way, including overall presentation, deceives or is likely to deceive the average consumer, even if the information is factually correct, in relation to one or more of the following elements, and in either case causes or is likely to cause him to take a transactional decision that he would not have taken otherwise:

(a) the existence or nature of the product;

(b) the main characteristics of the product, such as its availability, benefits, risks, execution, composition, accessories, after-sale customer assistance and complaint handling, method and date of manufacture or provision, delivery, fitness for purpose, usage, quantity, specification, geographical or commercial origin or the results to be expected from its use, or the results and material features of tests or checks carried out on the product;

(c) the extent of the trader's commitments, the motives for the commercial practice and the nature of the sales process, any statement or symbol in relation to direct or indirect sponsorship or approval of the trader or the product;

(d) the price or the manner in which the price is calculated, or the existence of a specific price advantage;

(e) the need for a service, part, replacement or repair;

(f) the nature, attributes and rights of the trader or his agent, such as his identity and assets, his qualifications, status, approval, affiliation or connection and ownership of industrial, commercial or intellectual property rights or his awards and distinctions;

(g) the consumer's rights, including the right to replacement or reimbursement under Directive 1999/44/EC of the European Parliament and of the Council of 25 May 1999 on certain aspects of the sale of consumer goods and associated guarantees[8], or the risks he may face.

2. A commercial practice shall also be regarded as misleading if, in its factual context, taking account of all its features and circumstances, it causes or is likely to cause the average consumer to take a transactional decision that he would not have taken otherwise, and it involves:

(a) any marketing of a product, including comparative advertising, which creates confusion with any products, trade marks, trade names or other distinguishing marks of a competitor;

(b) non-compliance by the trader with commitments contained in codes of conduct by which the trader has undertaken to be bound, where:

(i) the commitment is not aspirational but is firm and is capable of being verified,

and

(ii) the trader indicates in a commercial practice that he is bound by the code.

Article 7 Misleading omissions

1. A commercial practice shall be regarded as misleading if, in its factual context, taking account of all its features and circumstances and the limitations of the communication medium, it omits material information that the average consumer needs, according to the context, to take an informed transactional decision and thereby causes or is likely to cause the average consumer to take a transactional decision that he would not have taken otherwise.

2. It shall also be regarded as a misleading omission when, taking account of the matters described in paragraph 1, a trader hides or provides in an unclear, unintelligible, ambiguous or untimely manner such material information as referred to in that paragraph or fails to identify the commercial intent of the commercial practice if not already apparent from the context, and where, in either case, this causes or is likely to cause the average consumer to take a transactional decision that he would not have taken otherwise.

3. Where the medium used to communicate the commercial practice imposes limitations of space or time, these limitations and any measures taken by the trader to make the information available to consumers by other means shall be taken into account in deciding whether information has been omitted.

4. In the case of an invitation to purchase, the following information shall be regarded as material, if not already apparent from the context:

(a) the main characteristics of the product, to an extent appropriate to the medium and the product;

(b) the geographical address and the identity of the trader, such as his trading name and, where applicable, the geographical address and the identity of the trader on whose behalf he is acting;

8 OJ L 171, 7.7.1999, p. 12.

(c) the price inclusive of taxes, or where the nature of the product means that the price cannot reasonably be calculated in advance, the manner in which the price is calculated, as well as, where appropriate, all additional freight, delivery or postal charges or, where these charges cannot reasonably be calculated in advance, the fact that such additional charges may be payable;
(d) the arrangements for payment, delivery, performance and the complaint handling policy, if they depart from the requirements of professional diligence;
(e) for products and transactions involving a right of withdrawal or cancellation, the existence of such a right.

5. Information requirements established by Community law in relation to commercial communication including advertising or marketing, a non-exhaustive list of which is contained in Annex II, shall be regarded as material.

Section 2 Aggressive commercial practices

Article 8 Aggressive commercial practices

A commercial practice shall be regarded as aggressive if, in its factual context, taking account of all its features and circumstances, by harassment, coercion, including the use of physical force, or undue influence, it significantly impairs or is likely to significantly impair the average consumer's freedom of choice or conduct with regard to the product and thereby causes him or is likely to cause him to take a transactional decision that he would not have taken otherwise.

Article 9 Use of harassment, coercion and undue influence

In determining whether a commercial practice uses harassment, coercion, including the use of physical force, or undue influence, account shall be taken of:

(a) its timing, location, nature or persistence;
(b) the use of threatening or abusive language or behaviour;
(c) the exploitation by the trader of any specific misfortune or circumstance of such gravity as to impair the consumer's judgement, of which the trader is aware, to influence the consumer's decision with regard to the product;
(d) any onerous or disproportionate non-contractual barriers imposed by the trader where a consumer wishes to exercise rights under the contract, including rights to terminate a contract or to switch to another product or another trader;
(e) any threat to take any action that cannot legally be taken.

Chapter 3 Codes of conduct

Article 10 Codes of conduct

This Directive does not exclude the control, which Member States may encourage, of unfair commercial practices by code owners and recourse to such bodies by the persons or organisations referred to in Article 11 if proceedings before such bodies are in addition to the court or administrative proceedings referred to in that Article.

Recourse to such control bodies shall never be deemed the equivalent of foregoing a means of judicial or administrative recourse as provided for in Article 11.

Chapter 4 Final provisions

Article 11 Enforcement

1. Member States shall ensure that adequate and effective means exist to combat unfair commercial practices in order to enforce compliance with the provisions of this Directive in the interest of consumers.

Such means shall include legal provisions under which persons or organisations regarded under national law as having a legitimate interest in combating unfair commercial practices, including competitors, may:

(a) take legal action against such unfair commercial practices;

and/or

(b) bring such unfair commercial practices before an administrative authority competent either to decide on complaints or to initiate appropriate legal proceedings.

It shall be for each Member State to decide which of these facilities shall be available and whether to enable the courts or administrative authorities to require prior recourse to other established means of dealing with complaints, including those referred to in Article 10. These facilities shall be available regardless of whether the consumers affected are in the territory of the Member State where the trader is located or in another Member State.

It shall be for each Member State to decide:

(a) whether these legal facilities may be directed separately or jointly against a number of traders from the same economic sector;

and

(b) whether these legal facilities may be directed against a code owner where the relevant code promotes non-compliance with legal requirements.

2. Under the legal provisions referred to in paragraph 1, Member States shall confer upon the courts or administrative authorities powers enabling them, in cases where they deem such measures to be necessary taking into account all the interests involved and in particular the public interest:

(a) to order the cessation of, or to institute appropriate legal proceedings for an order for the cessation of, unfair commercial practices;

or

(b) if the unfair commercial practice has not yet been carried out but is imminent, to order the prohibition of the practice, or to institute appropriate legal proceedings for an order for the prohibition of the practice,

even without proof of actual loss or damage or of intention or negligence on the part of the trader.

Member States shall also make provision for the measures referred to in the first subparagraph to be taken under an accelerated procedure:

- either with interim effect,

or

- with definitive effect,

on the understanding that it is for each Member State to decide which of the two options to select.

Furthermore, Member States may confer upon the courts or administrative authorities powers enabling them, with a view to eliminating the continuing effects of unfair commercial practices the cessation of which has been ordered by a final decision:

(a) to require publication of that decision in full or in part and in such form as they deem adequate;

(b) to require in addition the publication of a corrective statement.

3. The administrative authorities referred to in paragraph 1 must:

(a) be composed so as not to cast doubt on their impartiality;

(b) have adequate powers, where they decide on complaints, to monitor and enforce the observance of their decisions effectively;

(c) normally give reasons for their decisions.

Where the powers referred to in paragraph 2 are exercised exclusively by an administrative authority, reasons for its decisions shall always be given. Furthermore, in this case, provision must be made for procedures whereby improper or unreasonable exercise of its powers by the administrative authority or improper or unreasonable failure to exercise the said powers can be the subject of judicial review.

Article 12 Courts and administrative authorities: substantiation of claims

Member States shall confer upon the courts or administrative authorities powers enabling them in the civil or administrative proceedings provided for in Article 11:

(a) to require the trader to furnish evidence as to the accuracy of factual claims in relation to a commercial practice if, taking into account the legitimate interest of the trader and any other party to the proceedings, such a requirement appears appropriate on the basis of the circumstances of the particular case;

and

(b) to consider factual claims as inaccurate if the evidence demanded in accordance with (a) is not furnished or is deemed insufficient by the court or administrative authority.

Article 13 Penalties

Member States shall lay down penalties for infringements of national provisions adopted in application of this Directive and shall take all necessary measures to ensure that these are enforced. These penalties must be effective, proportionate and dissuasive.

Article 14 Amendments to Directive 84/450/EEC

Directive 84/450/EEC is hereby amended as follows:

1. Article 1 shall be replaced by the following:

"Article 1

The purpose of this Directive is to protect traders against misleading advertising and the unfair consequences thereof and to lay down the conditions under which comparative advertising is permitted.";

2. in Article 2:

– point 3 shall be replaced by the following:

"3. "trader" means any natural or legal person who is acting for purposes relating to his trade, craft, business or profession and any one acting in the name of or on behalf of a trader.",

– the following point shall be added:

"4. "code owner" means any entity, including a trader or group of traders, which is responsible for the formulation and revision of a code of conduct and/or for monitoring compliance with the code by those who have undertaken to be bound by it.";

3. Article 3a shall be replaced by the following:

"Article 3a

1. Comparative advertising shall, as far as the comparison is concerned, be permitted when the following conditions are met:

(a) it is not misleading within the meaning of Articles 2(2), 3 and 7(1) of this Directive or Articles 6 and 7 of Directive 2005/29/EC of the European Parliament and of the Council of 11 May 2005 concerning unfair business-to-consumer commercial practices in the internal market[9];

(b) it compares goods or services meeting the same needs or intended for the same purpose;

(c) it objectively compares one or more material, relevant, verifiable and representative features of those goods and services, which may include price;

(d) it does not discredit or denigrate the trade marks, trade names, other distinguishing marks, goods, services, activities, or circumstances of a competitor;

(e) for products with designation of origin, it relates in each case to products with the same designation;

(f) it does not take unfair advantage of the reputation of a trade mark, trade name or other distinguishing marks of a competitor or of the designation of origin of competing products;

(g) it does not present goods or services as imitations or replicas of goods or services bearing a protected trade mark or trade name;

(h) it does not create confusion among traders, between the advertiser and a competitor or between the advertiser's trade marks, trade names, other distinguishing marks, goods or services and those of a competitor.;"

[9] OJ L 149, 11.6.2005, p. 22.

4. Article 4(1) shall be replaced by the following:
"1. Member States shall ensure that adequate and effective means exist to combat misleading advertising in order to enforce compliance with the provisions on comparative advertising in the interest of traders and competitors. Such means shall include legal provisions under which persons or organisations regarded under national law as having a legitimate interest in combating misleading advertising or regulating comparative advertising may:
(a) take legal action against such advertising;
or
(b) bring such advertising before an administrative authority competent either to decide on complaints or to initiate appropriate legal proceedings.

It shall be for each Member State to decide which of these facilities shall be available and whether to enable the courts or administrative authorities to require prior recourse to other established means of dealing with complaints, including those referred to in Article 5.

It shall be for each Member State to decide:
(a) whether these legal facilities may be directed separately or jointly against a number of traders from the same economic sector;
and
(b) whether these legal facilities may be directed against a code owner where the relevant code promotes non-compliance with legal requirements.";

5. Article 7(1) shall be replaced by the following:
"1. This Directive shall not preclude Member States from retaining or adopting provisions with a view to ensuring more extensive protection, with regard to misleading advertising, for traders and competitors."

Article 15 Amendments to Directives 97/7/EC and 2002/65/EC

1. Article 9 of Directive 97/7/EC shall be replaced by the following:
"Article 9
Inertia selling
Given the prohibition of inertia selling practices laid down in Directive 2005/29/EC of 11 May 2005 of the European Parliament and of the Council concerning unfair business-to-consumer commercial practices in the internal market[10], Member States shall take the measures necessary to exempt the consumer from the provision of any consideration in cases of unsolicited supply, the absence of a response not constituting consent.;"

2. Article 9 of Directive 2002/65/EC shall be replaced by the following:
"Article 9
Given the prohibition of inertia selling practices laid down in Directive 2005/29/EC of 11 May 2005 of the European Parliament and of the Council concerning unfair business-to-consumer commercial practices in the internal market[11] and without prejudice to the provisions of Member States' legislation on the tacit renewal of distance contracts, when such rules permit tacit renewal, Member States shall take measures to exempt the consumer from any obligation in the event of unsolicited supplies, the absence of a reply not constituting consent."

Article 16 Amendments to Directive 98/27/EC and Regulation (EC) No 2006/2004

1. In the Annex to Directive 98/27/EC, point 1 shall be replaced by the following:

"1. Directive 2005/29/EC of the European Parliament and of the Council of 11 May 2005 concerning unfair business-to-consumer commercial practices in the internal market (OJ L 149, 11.6.2005, p. 22)."

2. In the Annex to Regulation (EC) No 2006/2004 of the European Parliament and of the Council of 27 October 2004 on cooperation between national authorities responsible for the enforcement of

[10] OJ L 149, 11.6.2005, p. 22.
[11] OJ L 149, 11.6.2005, p. 22.

the consumer protection law (the Regulation on consumer protection cooperation)[12] the following point shall be added:

"16. Directive 2005/29/EC of the European Parliament and of the Council of 11 May 2005 concerning unfair business-to-consumer commercial practices in the internal market (OJ L 149, 11.6.2005, p. 22)."

Article 17 Information

Member States shall take appropriate measures to inform consumers of the national law transposing this Directive and shall, where appropriate, encourage traders and code owners to inform consumers of their codes of conduct.

Article 18 Review

1. By 12 June 2011 the Commission shall submit to the European Parliament and the Council a comprehensive report on the application of this Directive, in particular of Articles 3(9) and 4 and Annex I, on the scope for further harmonisation and simplification of Community law relating to consumer protection, and, having regard to Article 3(5), on any measures that need to be taken at Community level to ensure that appropriate levels of consumer protection are maintained. The report shall be accompanied, if necessary, by a proposal to revise this Directive or other relevant parts of Community law.

2. The European Parliament and the Council shall endeavour to act, in accordance with the Treaty, within two years of the presentation by the Commission of any proposal submitted under paragraph 1.

Article 19 Transposition

Member States shall adopt and publish the laws, regulations and administrative provisions necessary to comply with this Directive by 12 June 2007. They shall forthwith inform the Commission thereof and inform the Commission of any subsequent amendments without delay.

They shall apply those measures by 12 December 2007. When Member States adopt those measures, they shall contain a reference to this Directive or be accompanied by such a reference on the occasion of their official publication. Member States shall determine how such reference is to be made.

Article 20 Entry into force

This Directive shall enter into force on the day following its publication in the Official Journal of the European Union.

Article 21 Addressees

This Directive is addressed to the Member States.

Done at Strasbourg, 11 May 2005.
For the European Parliament
The President
J. P. Borrell Fontelles

For the Council
The President
N. Schmit

[12] OJ L 364, 9.12.2004, p. 1.

ANNEX I

COMMERCIAL PRACTICES WHICH ARE IN ALL CIRCUMSTANCES CONSIDERED UNFAIR

Misleading commercial practices

1. Claiming to be a signatory to a code of conduct when the trader is not.

2. Displaying a trust mark, quality mark or equivalent without having obtained the necessary authorisation.

3. Claiming that a code of conduct has an endorsement from a public or other body which it does not have.

4. Claiming that a trader (including his commercial practices) or a product has been approved, endorsed or authorised by a public or private body when he/it has not or making such a claim without complying with the terms of the approval, endorsement or authorisation.

5. Making an invitation to purchase products at a specified price without disclosing the existence of any reasonable grounds the trader may have for believing that he will not be able to offer for supply or to procure another trader to supply, those products or equivalent products at that price for a period that is, and in quantities that are, reasonable having regard to the product, the scale of advertising of the product and the price offered (bait advertising).

6. Making an invitation to purchase products at a specified price and then:

(a) refusing to show the advertised item to consumers;

or

(b) refusing to take orders for it or deliver it within a reasonable time;

or

(c) demonstrating a defective sample of it,

with the intention of promoting a different product (bait and switch)

7. Falsely stating that a product will only be available for a very limited time, or that it will only be available on particular terms for a very limited time, in order to elicit an immediate decision and deprive consumers of sufficient opportunity or time to make an informed choice.

8. Undertaking to provide after-sales service to consumers with whom the trader has communicated prior to a transaction in a language which is not an official language of the Member State where the trader is located and then making such service available only in another language without clearly disclosing this to the consumer before the consumer is committed to the transaction.

9. Stating or otherwise creating the impression that a product can legally be sold when it cannot.

10. Presenting rights given to consumers in law as a distinctive feature of the trader's offer.

11. Using editorial content in the media to promote a product where a trader has paid for the promotion without making that clear in the content or by images or sounds clearly identifiable by the consumer (advertorial). This is without prejudice to Council Directive 89/552/EEC[1].

12. Making a materially inaccurate claim concerning the nature and extent of the risk to the personal security of the consumer or his family if the consumer does not purchase the product.

13. Promoting a product similar to a product made by a particular manufacturer in such a manner as deliberately to mislead the consumer into believing that the product is made by that same manufacturer when it is not.

14. Establishing, operating or promoting a pyramid promotional scheme where a consumer gives consideration for the opportunity to receive compensation that is derived primarily from the introduction of other consumers into the scheme rather than from the sale or consumption of products.

15. Claiming that the trader is about to cease trading or move premises when he is not.

[1] Council Directive 89/552/EEC of 3 October 1989 on the coordination of certain provisions laid down by Law, Regulation or Administrative Action in Member States concerning the pursuit of television broadcasting activities (OJ L 298, 17.10.1989, p. 23). Directive as amended by Directive 97/36/EC of the European Parliament and of the Council (OJ L 202, 30.7.1997, p. 60).

16. Claiming that products are able to facilitate winning in games of chance.

17. Falsely claiming that a product is able to cure illnesses, dysfunction or malformations.

18. Passing on materially inaccurate information on market conditions or on the possibility of finding the product with the intention of inducing the consumer to acquire the product at conditions less favourable than normal market conditions.

19. Claiming in a commercial practice to offer a competition or prize promotion without awarding the prizes described or a reasonable equivalent.

20. Describing a product as "gratis", "free", "without charge" or similar if the consumer has to pay anything other than the unavoidable cost of responding to the commercial practice and collecting or paying for delivery of the item.

21. Including in marketing material an invoice or similar document seeking payment which gives the consumer the impression that he has already ordered the marketed product when he has not.

22. Falsely claiming or creating the impression that the trader is not acting for purposes relating to his trade, business, craft or profession, or falsely representing oneself as a consumer.

23. Creating the false impression that after-sales service in relation to a product is available in a Member State other than the one in which the product is sold.

Aggressive commercial practices

24. Creating the impression that the consumer cannot leave the premises until a contract is formed.

25. Conducting personal visits to the consumer's home ignoring the consumer's request to leave or not to return except in circumstances and to the extent justified, under national law, to enforce a contractual obligation.

26. Making persistent and unwanted solicitations by telephone, fax, e-mail or other remote media except in circumstances and to the extent justified under national law to enforce a contractual obligation. This is without prejudice to Article 10 of Directive 97/7/EC and Directives 95/46/EC[2] and 2002/58/EC.

27. Requiring a consumer who wishes to claim on an insurance policy to produce documents which could not reasonably be considered relevant as to whether the claim was valid, or failing systematically to respond to pertinent correspondence, in order to dissuade a consumer from exercising his contractual rights.

28. Including in an advertisement a direct exhortation to children to buy advertised products or persuade their parents or other adults to buy advertised products for them. This provision is without prejudice to Article 16 of Directive 89/552/EEC on television broadcasting.

29. Demanding immediate or deferred payment for or the return or safekeeping of products supplied by the trader, but not solicited by the consumer except where the product is a substitute supplied in conformity with Article 7(3) of Directive 97/7/EC (inertia selling).

30. Explicitly informing a consumer that if he does not buy the product or service, the trader's job or livelihood will be in jeopardy.

31. Creating the false impression that the consumer has already won, will win, or will on doing a particular act win, a prize or other equivalent benefit, when in fact either:

– there is no prize or other equivalent benefit,

or

– taking any action in relation to claiming the prize or other equivalent benefit is subject to the consumer paying money or incurring a cost.

[2] Directive 95/46/EC of the European Parliament and of the Council of 24 October 1995 on the protection of individuals with regard to the processing of personal data and on the free movement of such data (OJ L 281, 23.11.1995, p. 31). Directive as amended by Regulation (EC) No 1882/2003 (OJ L 284, 31.10.2003, p. 1).

ANNEX II

COMMUNITY LAW PROVISIONS SETTING OUT RULES FOR ADVERTISING AND COMMERCIAL COMMUNICATION

Articles 4 and 5 of Directive 97/7/EC

Article 3 of Council Directive 90/314/EEC of 13 June 1990 on package travel, package holidays and package tours[1]

Article 3(3) of Directive 94/47/EC of the European Parliament and of the Council of 26 October 1994 on the protection of purchasers in respect of certain aspects of contracts relating to the purchase of a right to use immovable properties on a timeshare basis[2]

Article 3(4) of Directive 98/6/EC of the European Parliament and of the Council of 16 February 1998 on consumer protection in the indication of the prices of products offered to consumers[3]

Articles 86 to 100 of Directive 2001/83/EC of the European Parliament and of the Council of 6 November 2001 on the Community code relating to medicinal products for human use[4]

Articles 5 and 6 of Directive 2000/31/EC of the European Parliament and of the Council of 8 June 2000 on certain legal aspects of information society services, in particular electronic commerce, in the Internal Market (Directive on electronic commerce)[5]

Article 1(d) of Directive 98/7/EC of the European Parliament and of the Council of 16 February 1998 amending Council Directive 87/102/EEC for the approximation of the laws, regulations and administrative provisions of the Member States concerning consumer credit[6]

Articles 3 and 4 of Directive 2002/65/EC

Article 1(9) of Directive 2001/107/EC of the European Parliament and of the Council of 21 January 2002 amending Council Directive 85/611/EEC on the coordination of laws, regulations and administrative provisions relating to undertakings for collective investment in transferable securities (UCITS) with a view to regulating management companies and simplified prospectuses[7]

Articles 12 and 13 of Directive 2002/92/EC of the European Parliament and of the Council of 9 December 2002 on insurance mediation[8]

Article 36 of Directive 2002/83/EC of the European Parliament and of the Council of 5 November 2002 concerning life assurance[9]

Article 19 of Directive 2004/39/EC of the European Parliament and of the Council of 21 April 2004 on markets in financial instruments[10]

Articles 31 and 43 of Council Directive 92/49/EEC of 18 June 1992 on the coordination of laws, regulations and administrative provisions relating to direct insurance other than life assurance[11] (third non-life insurance Directive)

Articles 5, 7 and 8 of Directive 2003/71/EC of the European Parliament and of the Council of 4 November 2003 on the prospectus to be published when securities are offered to the public or admitted to trading[12]

[1] OJ L 158, 23.6.1990, p. 59.
[2] OJ L 280, 29.10.1994, p. 83.
[3] OJ L 80, 18.3.1998, p. 27.
[4] OJ L 311, 28.11.2001, p. 67. Directive as last amended by Directive 2004/27/EC (OJ L 136, 30.4.2004, p. 34).
[5] OJ L 178, 17.7.2000, p. 1.
[6] OJ L 101, 1.4.1998, p. 17.
[7] OJ L 41, 13.2.2002, p. 20.
[8] OJ L 9, 15.1.2003, p. 3.
[9] OJ L 345, 19.12.2002, p. 1. Directive as amended by Council Directive 2004/66/EC. (OJ L 168, 1.5.2004, p. 35).
[10] OJ L 145, 30.4.2004, p. 1.
[11] OJ L 228, 11.8.1992, p. 1. Directive as last amended by Directive 2002/87/EC of the European Parliament and of the Council (OJ L 35, 11.2.2003, p. 1).
[12] OJ L 345, 31.12.2003, p. 64.

Directive 2006/114/EC of the European Parliament and of the Council of 12 December 2006 concerning misleading and comparative advertising

[OJ 2006 L376/21]

THE EUROPEAN PARLIAMENT AND THE COUNCIL OF THE EUROPEAN UNION,

Having regard to the Treaty establishing the European Community, and in particular Article 95 thereof,

Having regard to the proposal from the Commission,

Having regard to the opinion of the European Economic and Social Committee,[1]

Acting in accordance with the procedure laid down in Article 251 of the Treaty,[2]

Whereas:

(1) Council Directive 84/450/EEC of 10 September 1984 concerning misleading and comparative advertising[3] has been substantially amended several times.[4] In the interests of clarity and rationality the said Directive should be codified.

(2) The laws against misleading advertising in force in the Member States differ widely. Since advertising reaches beyond the frontiers of individual Member States, it has a direct effect on the smooth functioning of the internal market.

(3) Misleading and unlawful comparative advertising can lead to distortion of competition within the internal market.

(4) Advertising, whether or not it induces a contract, affects the economic welfare of consumers and traders.

(5) The differences between the laws of the Member States on advertising which misleads business hinder the execution of advertising campaigns beyond national boundaries and thus affect the free circulation of goods and provision of services.

(6) The completion of the internal market means a wide range of choice. Given that consumers and traders can and must make the best possible use of the internal market, and that advertising is a very important means of creating genuine outlets for all goods and services throughout the Community, the basic provisions governing the form and content of comparative advertising should be uniform and the conditions of the use of comparative advertising in the Member States should be harmonised. If these conditions are met, this will help demonstrate objectively the merits of the various comparable products. Comparative advertising can also stimulate competition between suppliers of goods and services to the consumer's advantage.

(7) Minimum and objective criteria for determining whether advertising is misleading should be established.

(8) Comparative advertising, when it compares material, relevant, verifiable and representative features and is not misleading, may be a legitimate means of informing consumers of their advantage. It is desirable to provide a broad concept of comparative advertising to cover all modes of comparative advertising.

(9) Conditions of permitted comparative advertising, as far as the comparison is concerned, should be established in order to determine which practices relating to comparative advertising may distort competition, be detrimental to competitors and have an adverse effect on consumer choice. Such conditions of permitted advertising should include criteria of objective comparison of the features of goods and services.

[1] Opinion of 26 October 2006 (not yet published in the Official Journal).

[2] Opinion of the European Parliament of 12 October 2006 (not yet published in the Official Journal) and Council Decision of 30 November 2006.

[3] OJ L 250, 19.9.1984, p. 17. Directive as last amended by Directive 2005/29/EC of the European Parliament and of the Council (OJ L 149, 11.6.2005, p. 22).

[4] See Annex I, Part A.

(10) The international conventions on copyright as well as the national provisions on contractual and non-contractual liability should apply when the results of comparative tests carried out by third parties are referred to or reproduced in comparative advertising.

(11) The conditions of comparative advertising should be cumulative and respected in their entirety. In accordance with the Treaty, the choice of forms and methods for the implementation of these conditions should be left to the Member States, insofar as those forms and methods are not already determined by this Directive.

(12) These conditions should include, in particular, consideration of the provisions resulting from Council Regulation (EC) No 510/2006 of 20 March 2006 on the protection of geographical indications and designations of origin for agricultural products and foodstuffs,[5] and in particular Article 13 thereof, and of the other Community provisions adopted in the agricultural sphere.

(13) Article 5 of First Council Directive 89/104/EEC of 21 December 1988 to approximate the laws of the Member States relating to trade marks[6] confers exclusive rights on the proprietor of a registered trade mark, including the right to prevent all third parties from using, in the course of trade, any sign which is identical to, or similar to, the trade mark in relation to identical goods or services or even, where appropriate, other goods.

(14) It may, however, be indispensable, in order to make comparative advertising effective, to identify the goods or services of a competitor, making reference to a trade mark or trade name of which the latter is the proprietor.

(15) Such use of another's trade mark, trade name or other distinguishing marks does not breach this exclusive right in cases where it complies with the conditions laid down by this Directive, the intended target being solely to distinguish between them and thus to highlight differences objectively.

(16) Persons or organisations regarded under national law as having a legitimate interest in the matter should have facilities for initiating proceedings against misleading and unlawful comparative advertising, either before a court or before an administrative authority which is competent to decide upon complaints or to initiate appropriate legal proceedings.

(17) The courts or administrative authorities should have powers enabling them to order or obtain the cessation of misleading and unlawful comparative advertising. In certain cases it may be desirable to prohibit misleading and unlawful comparative advertising even before it is published. However, this in no way implies that Member States are under an obligation to introduce rules requiring the systematic prior vetting of advertising.

(18) The voluntary control exercised by self-regulatory bodies to eliminate misleading or unlawful comparative advertising may avoid recourse to administrative or judicial action and ought therefore to be encouraged.

(19) While it is for national law to determine the burden of proof, it is appropriate to enable courts and administrative authorities to require traders to produce evidence as to the accuracy of factual claims they have made.

(20) Regulating comparative advertising is necessary for the smooth functioning of the internal market. Action at Community level is therefore required. The adoption of a Directive is the appropriate instrument because it lays down uniform general principles while allowing the Member States to choose the form and appropriate method by which to attain these objectives. It is in accordance with the principle of subsidiarity.

(21) This Directive should be without prejudice to the obligations of the Member States relating to the time-limits for transposition into national law and application of the Directives as set out in Part B of Annex I,

HAVE ADOPTED THIS DIRECTIVE:

[5] OJ L 93, 31.3.2006, p. 12.
[6] OJ L 40, 11.2.1989, p. 1. Directive as amended by Decision 92/10/EEC (OJ L 6, 11.1.1992, p. 35).

Article 1

The purpose of this Directive is to protect traders against misleading advertising and the unfair consequences thereof and to lay down the conditions under which comparative advertising is permitted.

Article 2

For the purposes of this Directive:

(a) 'advertising' means the making of a representation in any form in connection with a trade, business, craft or profession in order to promote the supply of goods or services, including immovable property, rights and obligations;

(b) 'misleading advertising' means any advertising which in any way, including its presentation, deceives or is likely to deceive the persons to whom it is addressed or whom it reaches and which, by reason of its deceptive nature, is likely to affect their economic behaviour or which, for those reasons, injures or is likely to injure a competitor;

(c) 'comparative advertising' means any advertising which explicitly or by implication identifies a competitor or goods or services offered by a competitor;

(d) 'trader' means any natural or legal person who is acting for purposes relating to his trade, craft, business or profession and anyone acting in the name of or on behalf of a trader;

(e) 'code owner' means any entity, including a trader or group of traders, which is responsible for the formulation and revision of a code of conduct and/or for monitoring compliance with the code by those who have undertaken to be bound by it.

Article 3

In determining whether advertising is misleading, account shall be taken of all its features, and in particular of any information it contains concerning:

(a) the characteristics of goods or services, such as their availability, nature, execution, composition, method and date of manufacture or provision, fitness for purpose, uses, quantity, specification, geographical or commercial origin or the results to be expected from their use, or the results and material features of tests or checks carried out on the goods or services;

(b) the price or the manner in which the price is calculated, and the conditions on which the goods are supplied or the services provided;

(c) the nature, attributes and rights of the advertiser, such as his identity and assets, his qualifications and ownership of industrial, commercial or intellectual property rights or his awards and distinctions.

Article 4

Comparative advertising shall, as far as the comparison is concerned, be permitted when the following conditions are met:

(a) it is not misleading within the meaning of Articles 2(b), 3 and 8(1) of this Directive or Articles 6 and 7 of Directive 2005/29/EC of the European Parliament and of the Council of 11 May 2005 concerning unfair business-to-consumer commercial practices in the internal market ('Unfair Commercial Practices Directive');[7]

(b) it compares goods or services meeting the same needs or intended for the same purpose;

(c) it objectively compares one or more material, relevant, verifiable and representative features of those goods and services, which may include price;

(d) it does not discredit or denigrate the trade marks, trade names, other distinguishing marks, goods, services, activities or circumstances of a competitor;

(e) for products with designation of origin, it relates in each case to products with the same designation;

(f) it does not take unfair advantage of the reputation of a trade mark, trade name or other distinguishing marks of a competitor or of the designation of origin of competing products;

[7] OJ L 149, 11.6.2005, p. 22.

(g) it does not present goods or services as imitations or replicas of goods or services bearing a protected trade mark or trade name;

(h) it does not create confusion among traders, between the advertiser and a competitor or between the advertiser's trade marks, trade names, other distinguishing marks, goods or services and those of a competitor.

Article 5

1. Member States shall ensure that adequate and effective means exist to combat misleading advertising and enforce compliance with the provisions on comparative advertising in the interests of traders and competitors.

Such means shall include legal provisions under which persons or organisations regarded under national law as having a legitimate interest in combating misleading advertising or regulating comparative advertising may:

(a) take legal action against such advertising;

or

(b) bring such advertising before an administrative authority competent either to decide on complaints or to initiate appropriate legal proceedings.

2. It shall be for each Member State to decide which of the facilities referred to in the second subparagraph of paragraph 1 shall be available and whether to enable the courts or administrative authorities to require prior recourse to other established means of dealing with complaints, including those referred to in Article 6.

It shall be for each Member State to decide:

(a) whether these legal facilities may be directed separately or jointly against a number of traders from the same economic sector;

and

(b) whether these legal facilities may be directed against a code owner where the relevant code promotes non-compliance with legal requirements.

3. Under the provisions referred to in paragraphs 1 and 2, Member States shall confer upon the courts or administrative authorities powers enabling them, in cases where they deem such measures to be necessary taking into account all the interests involved and in particular the public interest:

(a) to order the cessation of, or to institute appropriate legal proceedings for an order for the cessation of, misleading advertising or unlawful comparative advertising;

or

(b) if the misleading advertising or unlawful comparative advertising has not yet been published but publication is imminent, to order the prohibition of, or to institute appropriate legal proceedings for an order for the prohibition of, such publication.

The first subparagraph shall apply even where there is no proof of actual loss or damage or of intention or negligence on the part of the advertiser.

Member States shall make provision for the measures referred to in the first subparagraph to be taken under an accelerated procedure either with interim effect or with definitive effect, at the Member States' discretion.

4. Member States may confer upon the courts or administrative authorities powers enabling them, with a view to eliminating the continuing effects of misleading advertising or unlawful comparative advertising, the cessation of which has been ordered by a final decision:

(a) to require publication of that decision in full or in part and in such form as they deem adequate;

(b) to require in addition the publication of a corrective statement.

5. The administrative authorities referred to in point (b) of the second subparagraph of paragraph 1 must:

(a) be composed so as not to cast doubt on their impartiality;

(b) have adequate powers, where they decide on complaints, to monitor and enforce the observance of their decisions effectively;

(c) normally give reasons for their decisions.

6. Where the powers referred to in paragraphs 3 and 4 are exercised exclusively by an administrative authority, reasons for its decisions shall always be given. In this case, provision must be made for procedures whereby improper or unreasonable exercise of its powers by the administrative authority or improper or unreasonable failure to exercise the said powers can be the subject of judicial review.

Article 6

This Directive does not exclude the voluntary control, which Member States may encourage, of misleading or comparative advertising by self-regulatory bodies and recourse to such bodies by the persons or organisations referred to in the second subparagraph of Article 5(1) on condition that proceedings before such bodies are additional to the court or administrative proceedings referred to in that Article.

Article 7

Member States shall confer upon the courts or administrative authorities powers enabling them in the civil or administrative proceedings referred to in Article 5:

(a) to require the advertiser to furnish evidence as to the accuracy of factual claims in advertising if, taking into account the legitimate interest of the advertiser and any other party to the proceedings, such a requirement appears appropriate on the basis of the circumstances of the particular case and in the case of comparative advertising to require the advertiser to furnish such evidence in a short period of time;

and

(b) to consider factual claims as inaccurate if the evidence demanded in accordance with point (a) is not furnished or is deemed insufficient by the court or administrative authority.

Article 8

1. This Directive shall not preclude Member States from retaining or adopting provisions with a view to ensuring more extensive protection, with regard to misleading advertising, for traders and competitors.

The first subparagraph shall not apply to comparative advertising as far as the comparison is concerned.

2. The provisions of this Directive shall apply without prejudice to Community provisions on advertising for specific products and/or services or to restrictions or prohibitions on advertising in particular media.

3. The provisions of this Directive concerning comparative advertising shall not oblige Member States which, in compliance with the provisions of the Treaty, maintain or introduce advertising bans regarding certain goods or services, whether imposed directly or by a body or organisation responsible, under the law of the Member States, for regulating the exercise of a commercial, industrial, craft or professional activity, to permit comparative advertising regarding those goods or services. Where these bans are limited to particular media, this Directive shall apply to the media not covered by these bans.

4. Nothing in this Directive shall prevent Member States, in compliance with the provisions of the Treaty, from maintaining or introducing bans or limitations on the use of comparisons in the advertising of professional services, whether imposed directly or by a body or organisation responsible, under the law of the Member States, for regulating the exercise of a professional activity.

Article 9

Member States shall communicate to the Commission the text of the main provisions of national law which they adopt in the field covered by this Directive.

Article 10

Directive 84/450/EEC is hereby repealed, without prejudice to the obligations of the Member States relating to the time-limits for transposition into national law and application of the Directives, as set out in Part B of Annex I.

References made to the repealed Directive shall be construed as being made to this Directive and should be read in accordance with the correlation table set out in Annex II.

Article 11

This Directive shall enter into force on 12 December 2007.

Article 12

This Directive is addressed to the Member States.

Done at Strasbourg, 12 December 2006.
For the European Parliament
The President
J. BORRELL FONTELLES
For the Council
The President
M. PEKKARINEN

Annex I

Part A

Repealed Directive with its successive amendments

Council Directive 84/450/EEC
(OJ L 250, 19.9.1984, p. 17)
Directive 97/55/EC of the European Parliament and of the Council
(OJ L 290, 23.10.1997, p. 18)
Directive 2005/29/EC of the European Parliament and of the Council only Article 14
(OJ L 149, 11.6.2005, p. 22)

Part B

List of time-limits for transposition into national law and application

(referred to in Article 10)

Directive	Time-limit for transposition	Date of application
84/450/EEC	1 October 1986	—
97/55/EC	23 April 2000	—
2005/29/EC	12 June 2007	12 December 2007

Annex II Correlation table

Directive 84/450/EEC	This Directive
Article 1	Article 1
Article 2, introductory words	Article 2, introductory words
Article 2, point 1	Article 2(a)
Article 2, point 2	Article 2(b)
Article 2, point 2a	Article 2(c)
Article 2, point 3	Article 2(d)
Article 2, point 4	Article 2(e)

(cont.)

Directive 84/450/EEC	This Directive
Article 3	Article 3
Article 3a(1)	Article 4
Article 4(1), first subparagraph, first sentence	Article 5(1), first subparagraph
Article 4(1), first subparagraph, second sentence	Article 5(1), second subparagraph
Article 4(1), second subparagraph	Article 5(2), first subparagraph
Article 4(1), third subparagraph	Article 5(2), second subparagraph
Article 4(2), first subparagraph, introductory words	Article 5(3), first subparagraph, introductory words
Article 4(2), first subparagraph, first indent	Article 5(3), first subparagraph, point (a)
Article 4(2), first subparagraph, second indent	Article 5(3), first subparagraph, point (b)
Article 4(2), first subparagraph, final words	Article 5(3), second subparagraph
Article 4(2), second subparagraph, introductory words	Article 5(3), third subparagraph
Article 4(2), second subparagraph, first indent	Article 5(3), third subparagraph
Article 4(2), second subparagraph, second indent	Article 5(3), third subparagraph
Article 4(2), second subparagraph, final words	Article 5(3), third subparagraph
Article 4(2), third subparagraph, introductory words	Article 5(4), introductory words
Article 4(2), third subparagraph, first indent	Article 5(4), point (a)
Article 4(2), third subparagraph, second indent	Article 5(4), point (b)
Article 4(3), first subparagraph	Article 5(5)
Article 4(3), second subparagraph	Article 5(6)
Article 5	Article 6
Article 6	Article 7
Article 7(1)	Article 8(1), first subparagraph
Article 7(2)	Article 8(1), second subparagraph
Article 7(3)	Article 8(2)
Article 7(4)	Article 8(3)
Article 7(5)	Article 8(4)
Article 8, first subparagraph	—
Article 8, second subparagraph	Article 9
—	Article 10
—	Article 11
Article 9	Article 12
—	Annex I
—	Annex II

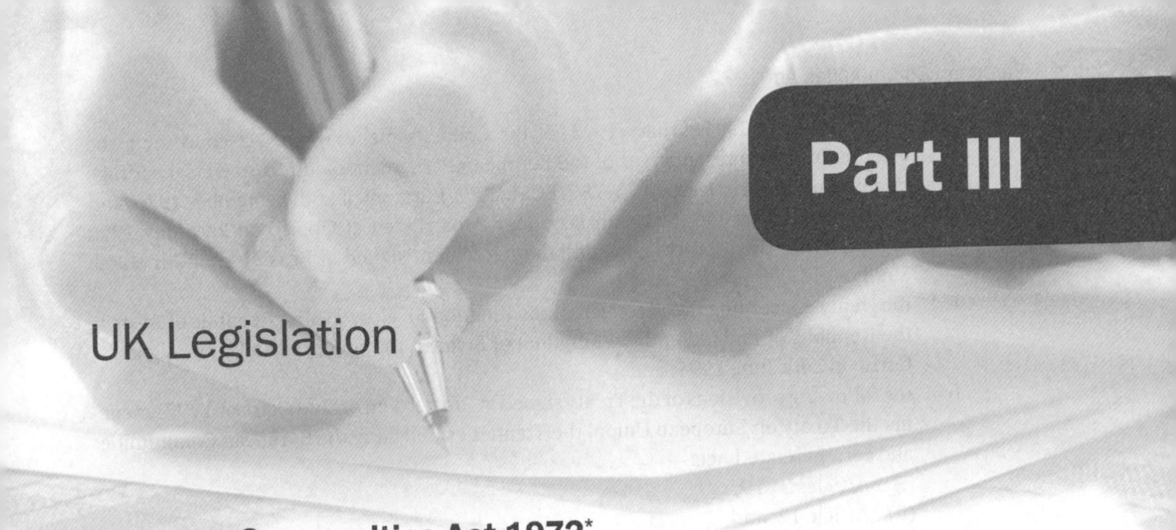

Part III

UK Legislation

European Communities Act 1972[*]

[1972 c.68]

1.—(1) This Act may be cited as the European Communities Act 1972.

(2) In this Act

'the Communities' means the European Economic Community, the European Coal and Steel Community and the European Atomic Energy Community,

'the Treaties' or 'the EU Treaties' means, subject to subsection (3) below, the pre-accession treaties, that is to say, those described in Part I of Schedule I to this Act, taken with

(a) the treaty relating to the accession of the United Kingdom to the European Economic Community and to the European Atomic Energy Community, signed at Brussels on the 22nd January 1972; and

(b) the decision, of the same date, of the Council of the European Communities relating to the accession of the United Kingdom to the European Coal and Steel Community; and

(c) the treaty relating to the accession of the Hellenic Republic to the European Economic Community and to the European Atomic Energy Community, signed at Athens on 28th May 1979; and

(d) the decision, of 24th May 1979, of the Council relating to the accession of the Hellenic Republic to the European Coal and Steel Community; and

(e) the decisions of the Council of 7th May 1985, 24th June 1988 and 31st October 1994, on the Communities' system of own resources; and

(g) the treaty relating to the accession of the Kingdom of Spain and the Portuguese Republic to the European Economic Community and to the European Atomic Energy Community, signed at Lisbon and Madrid on 12th June 1985; and

(h) the decision, of 11th June 1985, of the Council relating to the accession of the Kingdom of Spain and the Portuguese Republic to the European Coal and Steel Community; and

(j) the following provisions of the Single European Act signed at Luxembourg and The Hague on 17th and 28th February 1986, namely Title II (amendment of the treaties establishing the Communities) and, so far as they relate to any of the Communities or any Community institution, the preamble and Titles II (common provisions) and IV (general and final provisions); and

(k) Titles II, III and IV of the Treaty on European Union signed at Maastricht on 7th February 1992, together with the other provisions of the Treaty so far as they relate to those Titles, and the Protocols adopted at Maastricht on the date and annexed to the Treaty establishing the European Community with the exception of the Protocol on Social Policy on page 117 of Cm 1934; and

* **Editor's Note:** As amended up to the European Union Act 2011 (2011 c.12) and European Union (Croatian Accession and Irish Protocol) Act 2013.

(l) the decision, of 1st February 1993, of the Council amending the Act concerning the election of the representatives of the European Parliament by direct universal suffrage annexed to Council Decision 76/787/ECSC, EEC, Euratom of 20th September 1976; and

(m) the Agreement on the European Economic Area signed at Oporto on 2nd May 1992 together with the Protocol adjusting the Agreement signed at Brussels on 17th March 1993; and

(n) the treaty concerning the accession of the Kingdom of Norway, the Republic of Austria, the Republic of Finland and the Kingdom of Sweden to the European Union, signed at Corfu on 24th June 1994; and

(o) the following provisions of the Treaty signed at Amsterdam on 2nd October 1997 amending the Treaty on European Union, the Treaties establishing the European Communities and certain related Acts—

(i) Articles 2 to 9,

(ii) Article 12, and

(iii) the other provisions of the Treaty so far as they relate to those Articles, and the Protocols adopted on that occasion other than the Protocol on Article J.7 of the Treaty on European Union, and

(p) the following provisions of the Treaty signed at Nice on 26th February 2001 amending the Treaty on European Union, the Treaties establishing the European Communities and certain related Acts—

(i) Articles 2 to 10, and

(ii) the other provisions of the Treaty so far as they relate to those Articles, and the Protocols adopted on that occasion;

(q) the treaty concerning the accession of the Czech Republic, the Republic of Estonia, the Republic of Cyprus, the Republic of Latvia, the Republic of Lithuania, the Republic of Hungary, the Republic of Malta, the Republic of Poland, the Republic of Slovenia and the Slovak Republic to the European Union, signed at Athens on 16th April 2003;

(r) the treaty concerning the accession of the Republic of Bulgaria and Romania to the European Union, signed at Luxembourg on 25th April 2005; and any other treaty entered into by any of the Communities, with or without any of the Member States, or entered into, as a treaty ancillary to any of the Treaties, by the United Kingdom;

(s) the Treaty of Lisbon Amending the Treaty on European Union and the Treaty Establishing the European Community signed at Lisbon on 13th December 2007 (together with its Annex and protocols), excluding any provision that relates to, or in so far as it relates to or could be applied in relation to, the Common Foreign and Security Policy;

(t) the Protocol amending the Protocol (No. 36) on transitional provisions annexed to the Treaty on European Union, to the Treaty on the Functioning of the European Union and to the Treaty establishing the European Atomic Energy Community, signed at Brussels on 23 June 2010;

(u) the treaty concerning the accession of the Republic of Croatia to the European Union, signed at Brussels on 9 December 2011; and

(v) the Protocol on the concerns of the Irish people on the Treaty of Lisbon, adopted at Brussels on 16 May 2012;

and any other treaty entered into by the EU (except in so far as it relates to, or could be applied in relation to, the Common Foreign and Security Policy) , with or without any of the member States, or entered into, as a treaty ancillary to any of the Treaties, by the United Kingdom;

and any expression defined in Schedule I to this Act has the meaning there given to it.

(3) If Her Majesty by Order in Council declares that a treaty specified in the Order is to be regarded as one of the EU Treaties as herein defined, the Order shall be conclusive that it is to be so regarded; but a treaty entered into by the United Kingdom after the 22nd January 1972, other than a pre-accession treaty to which the United Kingdom accedes on terms settled on or before that date, shall not be so regarded unless it is so specified, nor be so specified unless a draft of the Order in Council has been approved by resolution of each House of Parliament.

(4) For purposes of subsections (2) and (3) above, 'treaty' includes any international agreement, and any protocol or annex to a treaty or international agreement.

2 General implementation of Treaties.

2.—(1) All such rights, powers, liabilities, obligations and restrictions from time to time created or arising by or under the Treaties, and all such remedies and procedures from time to time provided for by or under the Treaties, as in accordance with the Treaties are without further enactment to be given legal effect or used in the United Kingdom shall be recognised and available in law, and be enforced, allowed and followed accordingly; and the expression 'enforceable EU right' and similar expressions shall be read as referring to one to which this subsection applies.

(2) Subject to Schedule 2 to this Act, at any time after its passing Her Majesty may by Order in Council, and any designated Minister or department may by order, rules, regulations or scheme, make provision—

(a) for the purpose of implementing any EU obligation of the United Kingdom, or enabling any such obligation to be implemented, or of enabling any rights enjoyed or to be enjoyed by the United Kingdom under or by virtue of the Treaties to be exercised; or

(b) for the purpose of dealing with matters arising out of or related to any such obligation or rights or the coming into force, or the operation from time to time, of subsection (1) above;

and in the exercise of any statutory power or duty, including any power to give directions or to legislate by means of orders, rules, regulations or other subordinate instrument, the person entrusted with the power or duty may have regard to the objects of the EU and to any such obligation or rights as aforesaid.

In this subsection 'designated Minister or department' means such Minister of the Crown or government department as may from time to time be designated by Order in Council in relation to any matter or for any purpose, but subject to such restrictions or conditions (if any) as may be specified by the Order in Council.

(3) There shall be charged on and issued out of the Consolidated Fund or, if so determined by the Treasury, the National Loans Fund the amounts required to meet any EU obligation to make payments to any of the EU or a member State, or any EU obligation in respect of contributions to the capital or reserves of the European Investment Bank or in respect of loans to the Bank, or to redeem any notes or obligations issued or created in respect of any such EU obligation; and, except as otherwise provided by or under any enactment,—

(a) any other expenses incurred under or by virtue of the Treaties or this Act by any Minister of the Crown or government department may be paid out of moneys provided by Parliament and;

(b) any sums received under or by virtue of the Treaties or this Act by any Minister of the Crown or government department save for such sums as may be required for disbursements permitted by any other enactment, shall be paid into the Consolidated Fund or, if so determined by the Treasury, the National Loans Fund.

(4) The provision that may be made under subsection (2) above includes, subject to Schedule 2 to this Act, any such provision (of any such extent) as might be made by Act of Parliament, and any enactment passed or to be passed, other than one contained in this part of this Act, shall be construed and have effect subject to the foregoing provisions of this section; but, except as may be provided by any Act passed after this Act, Schedule 2 shall have effect in connection with the powers conferred by this and the following sections of this Act to make Orders in Council or orders, rules, regulations or schemes.

(5) …[1] and the references in that subsection to a Minister of the Crown or Government department and to a statutory power or duty shall include a Minister or department of the Government of Northern Ireland and a power or duty arising under or by virtue of an Act of the Parliament of Northern Ireland.

[1] Words repealed by the Northern Ireland Constitution Act 1973 (c. 36 SIF 29:3), Sch. 6 Pt. I.

(6) A law passed by the legislature of any of the Channel Islands or of the Isle of Man, or a colonial Law (within the meaning of the Colonial Laws Validity Act 1865) passed or made for Gibraltar, if expressed to be passed or made in the implementation of the Treaties and of the obligations of the United Kingdom thereunder, shall not be void or inoperative by reason of any inconsistency with or repugnancy to an Act of Parliament, passed or to be passed, that extends to the Island or Gibraltar or any provision having the force and effect of an Act there (but not including this section), nor by reason of its having some operation outside the Island or Gibraltar; and any such Act or provision that extends to the Island or Gibraltar shall be construed and have effect subject to the provisions of any such law.

3 Decisions on, and proof of, Treaties and EU instruments etc.

3.—(1) For the purposes of all legal proceedings any question as to the meaning or effect of any of the Treaties, or as to the validity, meaning or effect of any EU instrument, shall be treated as a question of law (and, if not referred to the European Court, be for determination as such in accordance with the principles laid down by and any relevant decision of the European Court).

Notes:

S. 2(2)(a)(b) excluded (N.I.) by Northern Ireland Constitution Act 1973 (c. 36, SIF 29:3), s. 2(2), Sch. 2 para. 3.

Reference in s. 2(5) to 'that subsection' means s. 2(2) of this Act. Reference to a Minister of the Government of Northern Ireland to be construed, as respects the discharge of functions, as a reference to the head of a Northern Ireland department: Northern Ireland Constitution Act 1973 (c. 36, SIF 29:3), Sch. 5 para. 7(2).

(2) Judicial notice shall be taken of the Treaties, of the Official Journal of the European Union and of any decision of, or expression of opinion by, the European Court on any such question as aforesaid; and the Official Journal shall be admissible as evidence of any instrument or other act thereby communicated of any of the EU or of any EU institution.

(3) Evidence of any instrument issued by a EU institution, including any judgment or order of the European Court, or of any document in the custody of a EU institution, or any entry in or extract from such a document, may be given in any legal proceedings by production of a copy certified as a true copy by an official of that institution; and any document purporting to be such a copy shall be received in evidence without proof of the official position or handwriting of the person signing the certificate.

(4) Evidence of any EU instrument may also be given in any legal proceedings—

(a) by production of a copy purporting to be printed by the Queen's Printer;

(b) where the instrument is in the custody of a government department (including a department of the Government of Northern Ireland), by production of a copy certified on behalf of the department to be a true copy by an officer of the department generally or specially authorised so to do;

and any document purporting to be such a copy as is mentioned in paragraph (b) above of an instrument in the custody of a department shall be received in evidence without proof of the official position or handwriting of the person signing the certificate, or of his authority to do so, or of the document being in the custody of the Department.

(5) In any legal proceedings in Scotland evidence of any matter given in a manner authorised by this section shall be sufficient evidence of it.

SCHEDULE 1

PART II OTHER DEFINITIONS

'Economic Community', 'Coal and Steel Community' and 'Euratom' mean respectively the European Economic Community, the European Coal and Steel Community and the European Atomic Energy Community.

'EU customs duty' means, in relation to any goods, such duty of customs as may from time to time be fixed for those goods by directly applicable EU provision as the duty chargeable on importation into Member States.

'EU institution' means any institution of the EU
'EU instrument' means any instrument issued by a EU institution.
'EU obligation' means any obligation created or arising by or under the Treaties, whether an enforceable EU obligation or not.
'Enforceable EU right' and similar expressions shall be construed in accordance with section 2(1) of this Act.
'Entry date' means the date on which the United Kingdom becomes a member of the Communities.
Note: Entry date: the United Kingdom became a member of the Communities on 1.1.1973.
'European Court' means the Court of Justice of the European Union.
'Member', in the expression 'Member State', refers to membership of the EU.

SCHEDULE 2 PROVISIONS AS TO SUBORDINATE LEGISLATION

1.—(1) The powers conferred by section 2(2) of this Act to make provision for the purposes mentioned in section 2(2)(a) and (b) shall not include power—

(a) to make any provision imposing or increasing taxation; or
(b) to make any provision taking effect from a date earlier than that of the making of the instrument containing the provision; or
(c) to confer any power to legislate by means of orders, rules, regulations or other subordinate instrument, other than rules of procedure for any court or tribunal; or
(d) to create any new criminal offence punishable with imprisonment for more than two years or punishable on summary conviction with imprisonment for more than three months or with a fine of more than [[2]level 5 on the standard scale] (if not calculated on a daily basis) or with a fine of more than [[3]£100 a day].

1A(1) Where—

(a) subordinate legislation makes provision for a purpose mentioned in section 2(2) of this Act,
(b) the legislation contains a reference to a EU instrument or any provision of a EU instrument, and
(c) it appears to the person making the legislation that it is necessary or expedient for the reference to be construed as a reference to that instrument or that provision as amended from time to time,

the subordinate legislation may make express provision to that effect.

(2) In this paragraph 'subordinate legislation' means any Order in Council, order, rules, regulations, scheme, warrant, byelaws or other instrument made after the coming into force of this paragraph under any Act, Act of the Scottish Parliament, Measure or Act of the National Assembly for Wales or Northern Ireland legislation passed or made before or after the coming into force of this paragraph.

2.—(1) Subject to paragraph 3 below, where a provision contained in any section of this Act confers power to make any order, rules, regulations or scheme (otherwise than by modification or extension of an existing power), the power shall be exercisable by statutory instrument.

(2) Any statutory instrument containing an Order in Council or any order, rules, regulations or scheme made in the exercise of a power so conferred, if made without a draft having been approved by resolution of each House of Parliament, shall be subject to annulment in pursuance of a resolution of either House.

3. Nothing in paragraph 2 above shall apply to any Order in Council made by the Governor of Northern Ireland or to any regulation made by a Minister or department of the Government of Northern

[2] Words substituted (E.W.S.) (N.I.) by virtue of (E.W.) Criminal Justice Act 1982 (c. 48, SIF 39:1), ss. 38, 46, (S.) Criminal Procedure (Scotland) Act 1975 (c. 21, SIF 39:1), ss. 289F, 289G and (N.I.) by SI 1984/703 (N.I.3), arts 5, 6.

[3] Words substituted by Criminal Law Act 1977 (c. 45, SIF 39:1). s. 32(3).

Ireland; but where a provision contained in any section of this Act confers power to make such an Order in Council or order, rules, regulations or scheme, then any Order in Council or order, rules, regulations or scheme made in the exercise of that power, if made without a draft having been approved by resolution of each House of the Parliament of Northern Ireland, shall be subject to negative resolution within the meaning of section 41(6) of the Interpretation Act (Northern Ireland) 1954 as if the Order or order, rules, regulations or scheme were a statutory instrument within the meaning of that Act.

European Union Act 2011*

[2011 c.12]

An Act to make provision about treaties relating to the European Union and decisions made under them, including provision implementing the Protocol signed at Brussels on 23 June 2010 amending the Protocol (No. 36) on transitional provisions annexed to the Treaty on European Union, to the Treaty on the Functioning of the European Union and to the Treaty establishing the European Atomic Energy Community; and to make provision about the means by which directly applicable or directly effective European Union law has effect in the United Kingdom.

[19th July 2011]

Be it enacted by the Queen's most Excellent Majesty, by and with the advice and consent of the Lords Spiritual and Temporal, and Commons, in this present Parliament assembled, and by the authority of the same, as follows:

PART 1 RESTRICTIONS ON TREATIES AND DECISIONS RELATING TO EU

Introductory

1 Interpretation of Part 1

(1) This section has effect for the interpretation of this Part.

(2) 'TEU' means the Treaty on European Union.

(3) 'TFEU' means the Treaty on the Functioning of the European Union.

(4) A reference to a treaty which amends TEU or TFEU includes a reference to—

(a) a treaty resulting from the application of Article 48(2) to (5) of TEU (ordinary revision procedure);

(b) an agreement under Article 49 of TEU (admission of new members).

(5) An 'Article 48(6) decision' means a decision under Article 48(6) of TEU (simplified revision procedure).

(6) Except in a reference to 'the European Council', 'the Council' means the Council of the European Union.

(7) A reference to a Minister of the Crown voting in favour of or otherwise supporting a decision is a reference to a Minister of the Crown—

(a) voting in favour of the decision in the European Council or the Council, or

(b) allowing the decision to be adopted by consensus or unanimity by the European Council or the Council.

Restrictions relating to amendments of TEU or TFEU

2 Treaties amending or replacing TEU or TFEU

(1) A treaty which amends or replaces TEU or TFEU is not to be ratified unless—

(a) a statement relating to the treaty was laid before Parliament in accordance with section 5,

(b) the treaty is approved by Act of Parliament, and

* **Editor's Note:** Extracts omitting ss 15–17 concerned with temporary measures to elect an additional MEP.

(c) the referendum condition or the exemption condition is met.

(2) The referendum condition is that—

(a) the Act providing for the approval of the treaty provides that the provision approving the treaty is not to come into force until a referendum about whether the treaty should be ratified has been held throughout the United Kingdom or, where the treaty also affects Gibraltar, throughout the United Kingdom and Gibraltar,

(b) the referendum has been held, and

(c) the majority of those voting in the referendum are in favour of the ratification of the treaty.

(3) The exemption condition is that the Act providing for the approval of the treaty states that the treaty does not fall within section 4.

3 Amendment of TFEU under simplified revision procedure

(1) Where the European Council has adopted an Article 48(6) decision subject to its approval by the member States, a Minister of the Crown may not confirm the approval of the decision by the United Kingdom unless—

(a) a statement relating to the decision was laid before Parliament in accordance with section 5,

(b) the decision is approved by Act of Parliament, and

(c) the referendum condition, the exemption condition or the significance condition is met.

(2) The referendum condition is that—

(a) the Act providing for the approval of the decision provides that the provision approving the decision is not to come into force until a referendum about whether the decision should be approved has been held throughout the United Kingdom or, where the decision also affects Gibraltar, throughout the United Kingdom and Gibraltar,

(b) the referendum has been held, and

(c) the majority of those voting in the referendum are in favour of the approval of the decision.

(3) The exemption condition is that the Act providing for the approval of the decision states that the decision does not fall within section 4.

(4) The significance condition is that the Act providing for the approval of the decision states that—

(a) the decision falls within section 4 only because of provision of the kind mentioned in subsection (1)(i) or (j) of that section, and

(b) the effect of that provision in relation to the United Kingdom is not significant.

4 Cases where treaty or Article 48(6) decision attracts a referendum

(1) Subject to subsection (4), a treaty or an Article 48(6) decision falls within this section if it involves one or more of the following—

(a) the extension of the objectives of the EU as set out in Article 3 of TEU;

(b) the conferring on the EU of a new exclusive competence;

(c) the extension of an exclusive competence of the EU;

(d) the conferring on the EU of a new competence shared with the member States;

(e) the extension of any competence of the EU that is shared with the member States;

(f) the extension of the competence of the EU in relation to—

(i) the co-ordination of economic and employment policies, or

(ii) common foreign and security policy;

(g) the conferring on the EU of a new competence to carry out actions to support, co-ordinate or supplement the actions of member States;

(h) the extension of a supporting, co-ordinating or supplementing competence of the EU;

(i) the conferring on an EU institution or body of power to impose a requirement or obligation on the United Kingdom, or the removal of any limitation on any such power of an EU institution or body;

(j) the conferring on an EU institution or body of new or extended power to impose sanctions on the United Kingdom;

(k) any amendment of a provision listed in Schedule 1 that removes a requirement that anything should be done unanimously, by consensus or by common accord;

(l) any amendment of Article 31(2) of TEU (decisions relating to common foreign and security policy to which qualified majority voting applies) that removes or amends the provision enabling a member of the Council to oppose the adoption of a decision to be taken by qualified majority voting;

(m) any amendment of any of the provisions specified in subsection (3) that removes or amends the provision enabling a member of the Council, in relation to a draft legislative act, to ensure the suspension of the ordinary legislative procedure.

(2) Any reference in subsection (1) to the extension of a competence includes a reference to the removal of a limitation on a competence.

(3) The provisions referred to in subsection (1)(m) are—

(a) Article 48 of TFEU (social security),

(b) Article 82(3) of TFEU (judicial co-operation in criminal matters), and

(c) Article 83(3) of TFEU (particularly serious crime with a cross-border dimension).

(4) A treaty or Article 48(6) decision does not fall within this section merely because it involves one or more of the following—

(a) the codification of practice under TEU or TFEU in relation to the previous exercise of an existing competence;

(b) the making of any provision that applies only to member States other than the United Kingdom;

(c) in the case of a treaty, the accession of a new member State.

5 Statement to be laid before Parliament

(1) If a treaty amending TEU or TFEU is agreed in an inter-governmental conference, a Minister of the Crown must lay the required statement before Parliament before the end of the 2 months beginning with the date on which the treaty is agreed.

(2) If an Article 48(6) decision is adopted by the European Council subject to its approval by the member States, a Minister of the Crown must lay the required statement before Parliament before the end of the 2 months beginning with the date on which the decision is adopted.

(3) The required statement is a statement as to whether, in the Minister's opinion, the treaty or Article 48(6) decision falls within section 4.

(4) If the Minister is of the opinion that an Article 48(6) decision falls within section 4 only because of provision of the kind mentioned in subsection (1)(i) or (j) of that section, the statement must indicate whether in the Minister's opinion the effect of that provision in relation to the United Kingdom is significant.

(5) The statement must give reasons for the Minister's opinion under subsection (3) and, if relevant, subsection (4).

(6) In relation to an Article 48(6) decision adopted by the European Council before the day on which this section comes into force ('the commencement date'), the condition in section 3(1)(a) is to be taken to be complied with if a statement under this section is laid before Parliament before the end of the 2 months beginning with the commencement date.

Restrictions relating to other decisions under TEU or TFEU

6 Decisions requiring approval by Act and by referendum

(1) A Minister of the Crown may not vote in favour of or otherwise support a decision to which this subsection applies unless—

(a) the draft decision is approved by Act of Parliament, and

(b) the referendum condition is met.

(2) Where the European Council has recommended to the member States the adoption of a decision under Article 42(2) of TEU in relation to a common EU defence, a Minister of the Crown may not notify the European Council that the decision is adopted by the United Kingdom unless—

(a) the decision is approved by Act of Parliament, and
(b) the referendum condition is met.

(3) A Minister of the Crown may not give a notification under Article 4 of Protocol (No. 21) on the position of the United Kingdom and Ireland in respect of the area of freedom, security and justice annexed to TEU and TFEU which relates to participation by the United Kingdom in a European Public Prosecutor's Office or an extension of the powers of that Office unless—
(a) the notification has been approved by Act of Parliament, and
(b) the referendum condition is met.

(4) The referendum condition is that set out in section 3(2), with references to a decision being read for the purposes of subsection (1) as references to a draft decision and for the purposes of subsection (3) as references to a notification.

(5) The decisions to which subsection (1) applies are—
(a) a decision under the provision of Article 31(3) of TEU that permits the adoption of qualified majority voting;
(b) a decision under Article 48(7) of TEU which in relation to any provision listed in Schedule 1—
(i) adopts qualified majority voting, or
(ii) applies the ordinary legislative procedure in place of a special legislative procedure requiring the Council to act unanimously;
(c) a decision under Article 86(1) of TFEU involving participation by the United Kingdom in a European Public Prosecutor's Office;
(d) where the United Kingdom has become a participant in a European Public Prosecutor's Office, a decision under Article 86(4) of TFEU to extend the powers of that Office;
(e) a decision under Article 140(3) of TFEU which would make the euro the currency of the United Kingdom;
(f) a decision under the provision of Article 153(2) of TFEU (social policy) that permits the application of the ordinary legislative procedure in place of a special legislative procedure;
(g) a decision under the provision of Article 192(2) of TFEU (environment) that permits the application of the ordinary legislative procedure in place of a special legislative procedure;
(h) a decision under the provision of Article 312(2) of TFEU (EU finance) that permits the adoption of qualified majority voting;
(i) a decision under the provision of Article 333(1) of TFEU (enhanced co-operation) that permits the adoption of qualified majority voting, where the decision relates to a provision listed in Schedule 1 and the United Kingdom is a participant in the enhanced co-operation to which the decision relates;
(j) a decision under the provision of Article 333(2) of TFEU (enhanced co-operation) that permits the adoption of the ordinary legislative procedure in place of a special legislative procedure, where—
(i) the decision relates to a provision listed in Schedule 1,
(ii) the special legislative procedure requires the Council to act unanimously, and
(iii) the United Kingdom is a participant in the enhanced co-operation to which the decision relates;
(k) a decision under Article 4 of the Schengen Protocol that removes any border control of the United Kingdom.

(6) In subsection (5)(k) 'the Schengen Protocol' means the Protocol (No. 19) on the Schengen acquis integrated into the framework of the European Union, annexed to TEU and TFEU.

7 Decisions requiring approval by Act

(1) A Minister of the Crown may not confirm the approval by the United Kingdom of a decision to which this subsection applies unless the decision is approved by Act of Parliament.

(2) The decisions to which subsection (1) applies are—

(a) a decision under the provision of Article 25 of TFEU that permits the adoption of provisions to strengthen or add to the rights listed in Article 20(2) of that Treaty (rights of citizens of the European Union);
(b) a decision under the provision of Article 223(1) of TFEU that permits the laying down of the provisions necessary for the election of the members of the European Parliament in accordance with that Article;
(c) a decision under the provision of Article 262 of TFEU that permits the conferring of jurisdiction on the Court of Justice of the European Union in disputes relating to the application of acts adopted on the basis of the EU Treaties which create European intellectual property rights;
(d) a decision under the third paragraph of Article 311 of TFEU to adopt a decision laying down provisions relating to the system of own resources of the European Union.

(3) A Minister of the Crown may not vote in favour of or otherwise support a decision to which this subsection applies unless the draft decision is approved by Act of Parliament.

(4) The decisions to which subsection (3) applies are—
(a) a decision under the provision of Article 17(5) of TEU that permits the alteration of the number of members of the European Commission;
(b) a decision under Article 48(7) of TEU which in relation to any provision not listed in Schedule 1—
(i) adopts qualified majority voting, or
(ii) applies the ordinary legislative procedure in place of a special legislative procedure requiring the Council to act unanimously;
(c) a decision under the provision of Article 64(3) of TFEU that permits the adoption of measures which constitute a step backwards in European Union law as regards the liberalisation of the movement of capital to or from third countries;
(d) a decision under the provision of Article 126(14) of TFEU that permits the adoption of provisions to replace the Protocol (No. 12) on the excessive deficit procedure annexed to TEU and TFEU;
(e) a decision under the provision of Article 333(1) of TFEU (enhanced co-operation) that permits the adoption of qualified majority voting, where the decision relates to a provision not listed in Schedule 1 and the United Kingdom is a participant in the enhanced co-operation to which the decision relates;
(f) a decision under the provision of Article 333(2) of TFEU (enhanced co-operation) that permits the adoption of the ordinary legislative procedure in place of a special legislative procedure, where—
(i) the decision relates to a provision not listed in Schedule 1,
(ii) the special legislative procedure requires the Council to act unanimously, and
(iii) the United Kingdom is a participant in the enhanced co-operation to which the decision relates.

8 Decisions under Article 352 of TFEU

(1) A Minister of the Crown may not vote in favour of or otherwise support an Article 352 decision unless one of subsections (3) to (5) is complied with in relation to the draft decision.

(2) An Article 352 decision is a decision under the provision of Article 352 of TFEU that permits the adoption of measures to attain one of the objectives set out in the EU Treaties (but for which those Treaties have not provided the necessary powers).

(3) This subsection is complied with if a draft decision is approved by Act of Parliament.

(4) This subsection is complied with if—
(a) in each House of Parliament a Minister of the Crown moves a motion that the House approves Her Majesty's Government's intention to support a specified draft decision and is of the opinion that the measure to which it relates is required as a matter of urgency, and
(b) each House agrees to the motion without amendment.

(5) This subsection is complied with if a Minister of the Crown has laid before Parliament a statement specifying a draft decision and stating that in the opinion of the Minister the decision relates only to one or more exempt purposes.

(6) The exempt purposes are—

(a) to make provision equivalent to that made by a measure previously adopted under Article 352 of TFEU, other than an excepted measure;

(b) to prolong or renew a measure previously adopted under that Article, other than an excepted measure;

(c) to extend a measure previously adopted under that Article to another member State or other country;

(d) to repeal existing measures adopted under that Article;

(e) to consolidate existing measures adopted under that Article without any change of substance.

(7) In subsection (6)(a) and (b), 'excepted measure' means a measure adopted after the commencement of this section and resulting from a decision in relation to which a Minister of the Crown had relied on compliance with subsection (4).

9 Approval required in connection with Title V of Part 3 of TFEU

(1) A Minister of the Crown may not give a notification to which this subsection applies unless Parliamentary approval has been given in accordance with subsection (3).

(2) Subsection (1) applies in relation to a notification under Article 3 of Protocol (No. 21) on the position of the United Kingdom and Ireland in respect of the area of freedom, security and justice annexed to TEU and TFEU (the 'AFSJ Protocol') that the United Kingdom wishes to take part in the adoption and application of a measure proposed under any of the following—

(a) the provision of Article 81(3) of TFEU (family law) that permits the application of the ordinary legislative procedure in place of a special legislative procedure;

(b) the provision of Article 82(2)(d) of TFEU (criminal procedure) that permits the identification of further specific aspects of criminal procedure to which directives adopted under the ordinary legislative procedure may relate;

(c) the provision of Article 83(1) of TFEU (particularly serious crime with a cross-border dimension) that permits the identification of further areas of crime to which directives adopted under the ordinary legislative procedure may relate.

(3) Parliamentary approval is given if—

(a) in each House of Parliament a Minister of the Crown moves a motion that the House approves Her Majesty's Government's intention to give a notification in respect of a specified measure, and

(b) each House agrees to the motion without amendment.

(4) Despite any Parliamentary approval given for the purposes of subsection (1), a Minister may not vote in favour of or otherwise support a decision under a provision falling within any of paragraphs (a) to (c) of subsection (2) unless the draft decision is approved by Act of Parliament.

(5) A Minister of the Crown may not give a notification under Article 4 of the AFSJ Protocol that the United Kingdom wishes to accept a measure to which this subsection applies unless the notification in respect of the measure has been approved by Act of Parliament.

(6) The measures to which subsection (5) applies are—

(a) a measure adopted under a provision described in any of paragraphs (a) to (c) of subsection (2), or

(b) a measure established under Article 81(3), 82(2)(d) or 83(1) of TFEU by virtue of a previous decision adopted, without the participation of the United Kingdom, under a provision falling within any of those paragraphs.

10 Parliamentary control of certain decisions not requiring approval by Act

(1) A Minister of the Crown may not vote in favour of or otherwise support a decision under any of the following unless Parliamentary approval has been given in accordance with this section—

(a) the provision of Article 56 of TFEU that permits the extension of the provisions of Chapter 3 of Title IV of Part 3 of that Treaty (free movement of services) to nationals of a third country;

(b) Article 129(3) of TFEU (amendment of provisions of the Statute of the European System of Central Banks or of the European Central Bank);

(c) the provision of Article 252 of TFEU that permits an increase in the number of Advocates-General;

(d) the provision of Article 257 of TFEU that permits the establishment of specialised courts attached to the General Court;

(e) the provision of Article 281 of TFEU that permits the amendment of the Statute of the Court of Justice of the European Union;

(f) the provision of Article 308 of TFEU that permits the amendment of the Statute of the European Investment Bank.

(2) A Minister of the Crown may not vote in favour of or otherwise support a decision to which this subsection applies unless Parliamentary approval has been given in accordance with this section.

(3) Subsection (2) applies to a decision under Article 48(7) of TEU which in relation to a provision of TFEU applies the ordinary legislative procedure in place of a special legislative procedure not requiring the Council to act unanimously.

(4) A Minister of the Crown may not confirm the approval by the United Kingdom of a decision under Article 218(8) of TFEU for the accession of the European Union to the European Convention for the Protection of Human Rights and Fundamental Freedoms in accordance with Article 6(2) of TEU unless Parliamentary approval has been given in accordance with this section.

(5) Parliamentary approval is given if—

(a) in each House of Parliament a Minister of the Crown moves a motion that the House approves Her Majesty's Government's intention to support the adoption of a specified draft decision, and

(b) each House agrees to the motion without amendment.

Further provisions about referendums held in pursuance of section 2, 3 or 6E+W+S+N.I.

11 Persons entitled to vote in referendum

(1) The persons entitled to vote in any referendum held in pursuance of section 2, 3 or 6 are to be as follows—

(a) the persons who, on the date of the referendum, would be entitled to vote as an elector at a parliamentary election in a constituency in the United Kingdom;

(b) the persons who, on that date, are disqualified by reason of being peers from voting as electors in parliamentary elections but—

(i) would be entitled to vote as electors at a local government election in any electoral area in Great Britain,

(ii) would be entitled to vote as electors at a local election in any district electoral area in Northern Ireland, or

(iii) would be entitled to vote as electors at a European Parliamentary election in any electoral region by virtue of section 3 of the Representation of the People Act 1985 (peers resident outside the United Kingdom);

(c) if the referendum is also held in Gibraltar, the Commonwealth citizens who, on the date of the referendum, would be entitled to vote in Gibraltar at a European Parliamentary election in the combined electoral region in which Gibraltar is comprised.

(2) In subsection (1)(b)(i) 'local government election' includes a municipal election in the City of London (that is, an election to the office of mayor, alderman, common councilman or sheriff and also the election of any officer elected by the mayor, aldermen and liverymen in common hall).

12 Separate questions

If a referendum is to be held in pursuance of any of sections 2, 3 and 6 in relation to two or more treaties or decisions, or in relation to one or more treaties and one or more decisions, a separate question must be included on the ballot paper in relation to each treaty or decision.

13 Role of Electoral Commission

Where an Act provides for a referendum to be held in pursuance of section 2, 3 or 6, the Electoral Commission—

(a) must take whatever steps they think appropriate to promote public awareness of the referendum and how to vote in it, and

(b) may take whatever steps they think appropriate to promote public awareness of the subject-matter of the referendum.

Supplementary

14 Consequential amendments and repeals relating to Part 1

(1) In section 5 of the European Union (Amendment) Act 2008 (amendment of founding treaties)—

(a) in subsection (2), for the words from 'amends' onwards substitute 'amends the Treaty establishing the European Atomic Energy Community (signed at Rome on 25th March 1957).', and

(b) accordingly, in the heading, for 'founding treaties' substitute 'Euratom Treaty'.

(2) In section 23 of the Constitutional Reform and Governance Act 2010 (section 20 of that Act not to apply to certain descriptions of treaties), in subsection (1)—

(a) omit paragraph (a),

(b) in paragraph (b), for 'founding Treaties' substitute 'Treaty establishing European Atomic Energy Community', and

(c) at the end insert—

'(c) a treaty that is subject to a requirement imposed by Part 1 of the European Union Act 2011 (restrictions on treaties and decisions relating to EU).'

(3) The following enactments (which are superseded by the provisions of this Part) are repealed—

(a) section 2 of the European Communities (Amendment) Act 1993,

(b) section 1(2) and (3) of the European Communities (Amendment) Act 2002,

(c) section 12 of the European Parliamentary Elections Act 2002, and

(d) section 6 of the European Union (Amendment) Act 2008.

(Sections 15–17 omitted.)

PART 3 GENERAL

Status of EU law

18 Status of EU law dependent on continuing statutory basis

Directly applicable or directly effective EU law (that is, the rights, powers, liabilities, obligations, restrictions, remedies and procedures referred to in section 2(1) of the European Communities Act 1972) falls to be recognised and available in law in the United Kingdom only by virtue of that Act or where it is required to be recognised and available in law by virtue of any other Act.

Final provisions

19 Financial provisions

(1) There is to be paid out of money provided by Parliament any increase attributable to this Act in the sums payable under any other Act out of money so provided.

(2) There is to be charged on and paid out of the Consolidated Fund any increase attributable to this Act in the sums charged on and paid out of that Fund under any other Act.

20 Extent

(1) This Act extends to the whole of the United Kingdom.

(2) Part 2 (and this section and sections 21 and 22 so far as relating to that Part) extend also to Gibraltar.

21 Commencement

(1) The following provisions come into force on the day on which this Act is passed—

(a) section 15;

(b) this Part.

(2) The other provisions of this Act come into force on such day as the Secretary of State may by order made by statutory instrument appoint.

(3) Different days may be appointed for different purposes.

22 Short title

This Act may be cited as the European Union Act 2011.

SCHEDULES

SCHEDULE 1 TREATY PROVISIONS WHERE AMENDMENT REMOVING NEED FOR UNANIMITY, CONSENSUS OR COMMON ACCORD WOULD ATTRACT REFERENDUM

PART 1 PROVISIONS OF THE TREATY ON EUROPEAN UNION

Article 7(2) (determination by European Council of existence of serious and persistent breach by member State of values referred to in Article 2).
Article 14(2) (composition of European Parliament).
Article 15(4) (decisions of European Council require consensus).
Article 17(5) (number of, and system for appointing, Commissioners).
Article 19(2) (appointment of Judges and Advocates-General of European Court of Justice).
Article 22(1) (identification of strategic interests and objectives of the EU).
Chapter 2 of Title V (specific provisions on the common foreign and security policy).
Article 48(3), (4), (6) and (7) (treaty revision procedures).
Article 49 (application for EU membership).
Article 50(3) (decision of European Council extending time during which treaties apply to state withdrawing from EU).

PART 2 PROVISIONS OF THE TREATY ON THE FUNCTIONING OF THE EUROPEAN UNION

Article 19(1) (measures to combat discrimination based on sex, racial or ethnic origin, religion or belief, age or sexual orientation).
Article 21(3) (measures concerning social security or social protection).
Article 22(1) (arrangements to enable EU citizens living in another member State to stand and vote in local elections in the State in which they reside).
Article 22(2) (arrangements to enable such persons to stand and vote in elections to the European Parliament in the State in which they reside).
Article 25 (provisions to strengthen or add to the rights of EU citizens listed in Article 20(2) of TFEU).
Article 77(3) (provisions concerning passports, identity cards, residence permits etc.).
Article 82(2)(d) (minimum rules on criminal procedure).
Article 83(1) (decision identifying other areas of crime to which provision is to apply).
Article 86(1) and (4) (European Public Prosecutor's Office).
Article 87(3) (police co-operation).
Article 89 (cross-border operation by competent authorities).
Article 113 (harmonisation of indirect taxes).
Article 115 (approximation of national laws affecting internal market).

Article 121(2) (broad guidelines of economic policies), so far as relating to a conclusion of the European Council.
Article 126(14) (adoption of provisions replacing the protocol on the excessive deficit procedure).
Article 127(6) (conferral on European Central Bank of specific tasks relating to prudential supervision).
Article 153(2)(b) (measures on working conditions, social security etc.).
Article 155(2) (agreements at EU level between management and labour).
Article 192(2) (adoption of certain environmental measures).
Article 194(3) (energy measures that are primarily of a fiscal nature).
Article 203 (decisions establishing procedure for association of countries and territories with the EU).
Article 218(8) (certain international agreements).
Article 222(3) (decisions on implementation of solidarity clause having defence implications).
Article 223(1) (uniform procedures for elections to European Parliament).
Article 311 (own resources decisions).
Article 312(2) (laying down of multi-annual financial framework).
Article 332 (decisions to allow expenditure on enhanced co-operation to be borne by member States other than those participating).
Article 333(1) and (2) (enhanced co-operation).
Article 346(2) (changes to list of military products exempt from internal market provisions).
Article 352(1) (measures to attain objectives of EU in cases where treaties have not provided the necessary powers).

SCHEDULE 2 ELECTION OF ADDITIONAL MEP

(Omitted.)

Index

Statistics for the Behavioral Sciences

Statistics for the Behavioral Sciences

Ninth Edition

Frederick J Gravetter
The College at Brockport, State University of New York

Larry B. Wallnau
The College at Brockport, State University of New York

WADSWORTH
CENGAGE Learning™

Australia • Brazil • Japan • Korea • Mexico • Singapore • Spain • United Kingdom • United States

WADSWORTH
CENGAGE Learning

Statistics for the Behavioral Sciences, Ninth Edition
Frederick J Gravetter and Larry B. Wallnau

Publisher: Jon-David Hague
Psychology Editor: Tim Matray
Developmental Editor: Tangelique Williams
Freelance Developmental Editor: Liana Sarkisian
Assistant Editor: Kelly Miller
Editorial Assistant: Lauren K. Moody
Media Editor: Mary Noel
Marketing Program Manager: Sean Foy
Marketing Communications Manager: Laura Localio
Content Project Manager: Charlene M. Carpentier
Design Director: Rob Hugel
Art Director: Pam Galbreath
Manufacturing Planner: Judy Inouye
Rights Acquisitions Specialist: Tom McDonough
Production Service: Graphic World Inc.
Text Designer: Cheryl Carrington
Text Researcher: Karyn Morrison
Copy Editor: Graphic World Inc.
Illustrator: Graphic World Inc.
Cover Designer: Denise Davidson
Cover Image: Edouard Benedictus, Dover Publications
Compositor: Graphic World Inc.

Printed in the Canada
2 3 4 5 6 7 15 14 13 12

Library of Congress Control Number: 2011934937

International Edition:
ISBN-13: 978-1-111-83955-0
ISBN-10: 1-111-83955-7
Cengage Learning International Offices

Asia
www.cengageasia.com
tel: (65) 6410 1200

Australia/New Zealand
www.cengage.com.au
tel: (61) 3 9685 4111

Brazil
www.cengage.com.br
tel: (55) 11 3665 9900

India
www.cengage.co.in
tel: (91) 11 4364 1111

Latin America
www.cengage.com.mx
tel: (52) 55 1500 6000

UK/Europe/Middle East/Africa
www.cengage.co.uk
tel: (44) 0 1264 332 424

Represented in Canada by
Nelson Education, Ltd.
www.nelson.com
tel: (416) 752 9100 / (800) 668 0671

Cengage Learning is a leading provider of customized learning solutions with office locations around the globe, including Singapore, the United Kingdom, Australia, Mexico, Brazil, and Japan. Locate your local office at:
www.cengage.com/global

For product information and free companion resources: **www.cengage.com/international**
Visit your local office: **www.cengage.com/global**
Visit our corporate **website: www.cengage.com**

Contents in Brief

PART V Correlations and Nonparametric Tests

Contents

PART I Introduction and Descriptive Statistics

Preface

Many students in the behavioral sciences view the required statistics course as an intimidating obstacle that has been placed in the middle of an otherwise interesting curriculum. They want to learn about human behavior—not about math and science. As a result, they see the statistics course as irrelevant to their education and career goals. However, as long as the behavioral sciences are founded in science, knowledge of statistics will be necessary. Statistical procedures provide researchers with objective and systematic methods for describing and interpreting their research results. Scientific research is the system that we use to gather information, and statistics are the tools that we use to distill the information into sensible and justified conclusions. The goal of this book is not only to teach the methods of statistics, but also to convey the basic principles of objectivity and logic that are essential for science and valuable in everyday life.

Those familiar with previous editions of *Statistics for the Behavioral Sciences* will notice that some changes have been made. These changes are summarized in the section titled "To the Instructor." In revising this text, our students have been foremost in our minds. Over the years, they have provided honest and useful feedback. Their hard work and perseverance has made our writing and teaching most rewarding. We sincerely thank them. Students who are using this edition should please read the section of the preface titled "To the Student."

ANCILLARIES

Ancillaries for this edition include the following:

- *Study Guide:* Contains chapter summaries, learning objectives, new terms and concepts with definitions, new formulas, step-by-step procedures for problem solving, study hints and cautions, self-tests, and review. The Study Guide contains answers to the self-test questions.
- *Instructor's Manual with Test Bank:* Contains a detailed table of contents, chapter outlines, annotated learning objectives, lecture suggestions, test items, and solutions to all end-of-chapter problems in the text. Test items are also available as a Microsoft Word® download or for ExamView® computerized test bank software with multiple-choice, true/false, and short-answer questions. An answer key is provided for all questions, and each question is cross-referenced to a page in the textbook.
- *PowerPoint and ExamView:* Book-specific Microsoft PowerPoint® lectures and class tools are available to enhance the educational experience. ExamView allows you to create, deliver, and customize tests and study guides (both print and online) in minutes.
- *Psychology CourseMate®:* Psychology CourseMate, with Engagement Tracker, a first-of-its-kind tool that monitors student engagement in the course, includes:
    - An interactive eBook
    - Interactive teaching and learning tools including:
        - Quizzes
        - Glossary

- Flashcards
- and more

ACKNOWLEDGMENTS

It takes a lot of good, hard-working people to produce a book. Our friends at Wadsworth/Cengage have made enormous contributions to this textbook. We thank: Linda Schreiber-Ganster, Publisher/Executive Editor; Timothy Matray, Acquisitions Editor; Tangelique Williams, Managing Developmental Editor; Kelly Miller, Assistant Editor; Lauren K. Moody, Editorial Assistant/Associate; Charlene M. Carpentier, Content Project Manager; Mary Noel, Media Editor; and Pam Galbreath, Art Director. Special thanks go to Liana Sarkisian, our Development Editor, and to Mike Ederer who led us through production at Graphic World.

Reviewers play a very important role in the development of a manuscript. Accordingly, we offer our appreciation to the following colleagues for their assistance with the ninth edition: Patricia Case, University of Toledo; Kevin David, Northeastern State University; Adia Garrett, University of Maryland, Baltimore County; Carrie E. Hall, Miami University; Deletha Hardin, University of Tampa; Angela Heads, Prairie View A&M University; Roberto Heredia, Texas A&M International University; Alisha Janowski, University of Central Florida; Matthew Mulvaney, The College at Brockport (SUNY); Nicholas Von Glahn, California State Polytechnic University, Pomona; and Ronald Yockey, Fresno State University.

TO THE INSTRUCTOR

Those of you familiar with the previous edition of *Statistics for the Behavioral Sciences* will notice a number of changes in the ninth edition. Throughout the book, research examples have been updated, real-world examples have been added, and the end-of-chapter problems have been extensively revised. The book has been separated into five sections to emphasize the similarities among groups of statistical methods. Each section contains two to four chapters, and begins with an introduction and concludes with a review, including review exercises.

Major revisions for this edition include:

1. The former Chapter 12 on Estimation has been eliminated. In its place, sections on confidence intervals have been added to the three *t*-statistic chapters.
2. The former Chapter 20 covering hypothesis tests for ordinal data has been converted into an appendix.
3. A new final chapter discusses the process of selecting the correct statistics to be used with different categories of data and replaces the Statistics Organizer, which appeared as an appendix in earlier editions.

Other examples of specific and noteworthy revisions include:

Chapter 1 A separate section explains how statistical methods can be classified using the same categories that are used to group data structures and research methods. A new heading clarifies the concept that different scales of measurement require different statistical methods.

Chapter 2 The discussion of histograms has been modified to differentiate discrete and continuous variables. The section on stem-and-leaf displays has been heavily edited to simplify.

Chapter 3 A modified definition of the median acknowledges that this value is not algebraically defined, and that determining the median, especially for discrete variables, can be somewhat subjective. A new Box demonstrates that precisely locating the median for a continuous variable is equivalent to using interpolation to find the 50th percentile (as was demonstrated in Chapter 2).

Chapter 4 Alternative definitions of the range have been added, and discussion of the interquartile range has been deleted. Greater emphasis has been placed on conceptual definitions of standard deviation and the sum of squared deviations *(SS)*. The section on variance and inferential statistics has been simplified and the section comparing measures of variability has been deleted.

Chapter 5 Relatively minor editing for clarity.

Chapter 6 The concepts of *random sample* and *independent random sample* are clarified with separate definitions. A new figure helps demonstrate the process of using the unit normal table to find proportions for negative z-scores. The section on the binomial distribution has been shortened and simplified.

Chapter 7 Relatively minor editing for clarity.

Chapter 8 The chapter has been shortened by substantial editing that eliminated several pages of unnecessary text, particularly in the sections on errors (Type I and II) and power. The distinction between reporting one-tailed and two-tailed tests was clarified.

Chapter 9 The section describing how sample size and sample variance influence the outcome of a hypothesis test has been moved so that it appears immediately after the hypothesis test example. A new section introduces confidence intervals in the context of describing effect size, describes how confidence intervals are reported in the literature, and discusses factors affecting the width of a confidence interval.

Chapter 10 An expanded section discusses how sample variance and sample size influence the outcome of an independent-measures hypothesis test and measures of effect size. A new section introduces confidence intervals as an alternative for describing effect size. The relationship between a confidence interval and a hypothesis test is also discussed. We also note that the Mann-Whitney test (presented in Appendix E) can be used as an alternative to the independent-measures t test if high variance causes problems or if an assumption is violated.

Chapter 11 The description of repeated-measures and matched-subjects designs was clarified and we increased emphasis on the concept that all calculations for the related-samples test are done with the difference scores. A new section introduces confidence intervals as an alternative for describing effect size and discusses the relationship between a confidence interval and a hypothesis test. We also note that the Wilcoxon test (presented in Appendix E) can be used as an alternative to the repeated-measures t test if high variance causes problems or if an assumption is violated.

The former Chapter 12 has been deleted. The content from this chapter covering confidence intervals has been added to Chapters 9, 10, and 11.

Chapter 12 (former Chapter 13, introducing ANOVA) The discussion of testwise alpha levels versus experimentwise alpha levels was moved from a Box into the text, and definitions of the two terms were added. To emphasize the concepts of ANOVA rather than the formulas, $SS_{\text{between treatments}}$ is routinely found by subtraction instead of being computed directly. Two alternative equations for $SS_{\text{between treatments}}$ were moved from the text into a Box. We also note that the Kruskal-Wallis test (presented in Appendix E) can be used as an alternative to the independent-measures ANOVA if high variance causes problems or if an assumption is violated.

Chapter 13 (former Chapter 14, introducing repeated-measures ANOVA) A new section demonstrates the relationship between ANOVA and the *t* test when a repeated-measures study is comparing only two treatments. Major editing shortened the chapter and simplified the presentation. We also note that the Friedman test (presented in Appendix E) can be used as an alternative to the repeated-measures ANOVA if high variance causes problems or if an assumption is violated.

Chapter 14 (formerly Chapter 15, introducing two-factor ANOVA) A new section demonstrates how using a participant characteristic as a second factor can reduce the variance caused by individual differences. Major editing shortened the chapter and simplified the presentation.

Chapter 15 (formerly Chapter 16, introducing correlations) The introduction to partial correlations was simplified and moved from the regression chapter into the section discussing the Pearson correlation.

Chapter 16 (formerly Chapter 17, introducing regression) Major editing shortened and simplified the section on multiple regression. A printout showing the results of multiple regression from SPSS was added as a figure to illustrate the different elements of the process.

Chapter 17 (formerly Chapter 18, introducing chi-square tests) Relatively minor editing to shorten and clarify.

Chapter 18 (formerly Chapter 19, introducing the binomial test) Relatively minor editing for clarity.

Chapter 19 A completely new chapter outlining the process of selecting the correct statistical procedures to use with different sets of data.

The former Chapter 20 covering hypothesis tests for ordinal data has been substantially shortened and converted into an Appendix.

Matching the Text to Your Syllabus The book chapters are organized in the sequence that we use for our own statistics courses. However, different instructors may prefer different organizations and probably will choose to omit or deemphasize specific topics. We have tried to make separate chapters, and even sections of chapters, completely self-contained, so they can be deleted or reorganized to fit the syllabus for nearly any instructor. Some common examples are as follows:

- It is common for instructors to choose between emphasizing analysis of variance (Chapters 12, 13, and 14) or emphasizing correlation/regression (Chapters 15 and 16). It is rare for a one-semester course to complete coverage of both topics.
- Although we choose to complete all the hypothesis tests for means and mean differences before introducing correlation (Chapter 15), many instructors prefer to place correlation much earlier in the sequence of course topics. To accommodate this, sections 15.1, 15.2, and 15.3 present the calculation and interpretation of the Pearson correlation and can be introduced immediately following Chapter 4

(variability). Other sections of Chapter 15 refer to hypothesis testing and should be delayed until the process of hypothesis testing (Chapter 8) has been introduced.

- It is also possible for instructors to present the chi-square tests (Chapter 17) much earlier in the sequence of course topics. Chapter 17, which presents hypothesis tests for proportions, can be presented immediately after Chapter 8, which introduces the process of hypothesis testing. If this is done, we also recommend that the Pearson correlation (Sections 15.1, 15.2, and 15.3) be presented early to provide a foundation for the chi-square test for independence.

TO THE STUDENT

A primary goal of this book is to make the task of learning statistics as easy and painless as possible. Among other things, you will notice that the book provides you with a number of opportunities to practice the techniques you will be learning in the form of Learning Checks, Examples, Demonstrations, and end-of-chapter problems. We encourage you to take advantage of these opportunities. Read the text rather than just memorizing the formulas. We have taken care to present each statistical procedure in a conceptual context that explains why the procedure was developed and when it should be used. If you read this material and gain an understanding of the basic concepts underlying a statistical formula, you will find that learning the formula and how to use it will be much easier. In the "Study Hints," that follow, we provide advice that we give our own students. Ask your instructor for advice as well; we are sure that other instructors will have ideas of their own.

Over the years, the students in our classes and other students using our book have given us valuable feedback. If you have any suggestions or comments about this book, you can write to either Professor Emeritus Frederick Gravetter or Professor Emeritus Larry Wallnau at the Department of Psychology, SUNY College at Brockport, 350 New Campus Drive, Brockport, New York 14420. You can also contact Professor Emeritus Gravetter directly at fgravett@brockport.edu.

Study Hints You may find some of these tips helpful, as our own students have reported.

- The key to success in a statistics course is to keep up with the material. Each new topic builds on previous topics. If you have learned the previous material, then the new topic is just one small step forward. Without the proper background, however, the new topic can be a complete mystery. If you find that you are falling behind, get help immediately.
- You will learn (and remember) much more if you study for short periods several times per week rather than try to condense all of your studying into one long session. For example, it is far more effective to study half an hour every night than to have a single $3\frac{1}{2}$-hour study session once a week. We cannot even work on *writing* this book without frequent rest breaks.
- Do some work before class. Keep a little ahead of the instructor by reading the appropriate sections before they are presented in class. Although you may not fully understand what you read, you will have a general idea of the topic, which will make the lecture easier to follow. Also, you can identify material that is particularly confusing and then be sure the topic is clarified in class.
- Pay attention and think during class. Although this advice seems obvious, often it is not practiced. Many students spend so much time trying to write down every example presented or every word spoken by the instructor that they do not actually understand and process what is being said. Check with your instructor—there may not be a need to copy every example presented in class, especially if

there are many examples like it in the text. Sometimes, we tell our students to put their pens and pencils down for a moment and just listen.

- Test yourself regularly. Do not wait until the end of the chapter or the end of the week to check your knowledge. After each lecture, work some of the end-of-chapter problems and do the Learning Checks. Review the Demonstration Problems, and be sure you can define the Key Terms. If you are having trouble, get your questions answered *immediately*—reread the section, go to your instructor, or ask questions in class. By doing so, you will be able to move ahead to new material.
- Do not kid yourself! Avoid denial. Many students observe their instructor solve problems in class and think to themselves, "This looks easy, I understand it." Do you really understand it? Can you really do the problem on your own without having to leaf through the pages of a chapter? Although there is nothing wrong with using examples in the text as models for solving problems, you should try working a problem with your book closed to test your level of mastery.
- We realize that many students are embarrassed to ask for help. It is our biggest challenge as instructors. You must find a way to overcome this aversion. Perhaps contacting the instructor directly would be a good starting point, if asking questions in class is too anxiety-provoking. You could be pleasantly surprised to find that your instructor does not yell, scold, or bite! Also, your instructor might know of another student who can offer assistance. Peer tutoring can be very helpful.

Frederick J Gravetter
Larry B. Wallnau

About the Authors

Frederick J Gravetter is Professor Emeritus of Psychology at the State University of New York College at Brockport. While teaching at Brockport, Dr. Gravetter specialized in statistics, experimental design, and cognitive psychology. He received his bachelor's degree in mathematics from M.I.T. and his Ph.D. in psychology from Duke University. In addition to publishing this textbook and several research articles, Dr. Gravetter co-authored *Research Methods for the Behavioral Sciences* and *Essentials of Statistics for the Behavioral Sciences.*

Fred

Larry B. Wallnau is Professor Emeritus of Psychology at the State University of New York College at Brockport. While teaching at Brockport, he published numerous research articles, primarily on the behavioral effects of psychotropic drugs. With Dr. Gravetter, he co-authored *Essentials of Statistics for the Behavioral Sciences*. He also has provided editorial consulting for numerous publishers and journals. He routinely gives lectures and demonstrations on service dogs for those with disabilities.

Ed Berns

Ben and Larry

PART

I

Introduction and Descriptive Statistics

We have divided this book into five sections, each covering a general topic area of statistics. The first section, consisting of Chapters 1 to 4, provides a broad overview of statistical methods and a more focused presentation of those methods that are classified as *descriptive statistics.*

By the time you finish the four chapters in this part, you should have a good understanding of the general goals of statistics and you should be familiar with the basic terminology and notation used in statistics. In addition, you should be familiar with the techniques of descriptive statistics that help researchers organize and summarize the results they obtain from their research. Specifically, you should be able to take a set of scores and present them in a table or in a graph that provides an overall picture of the complete set. Also, you should be able to summarize a set of scores by calculating one or two values (such as the average) that describe the entire set.

At the end of this section there is a brief summary and a set of review problems that should help integrate the elements from the separate chapters.

CHAPTER

1

Introduction to Statistics

Preview

Before we begin our discussion of statistics, we ask you to read the following paragraph taken from the philosophy of Wrong Shui (Candappa, 2000).

> The Journey to Enlightenment
>
> In Wrong Shui, life is seen as a cosmic journey, a struggle to overcome unseen and unexpected obstacles at the end of which the traveler will find illumination and enlightenment. Replicate this quest in your home by moving light switches away from doors and over to the far side of each room.*

Why did we begin a statistics book with a bit of twisted philosophy? Actually, the paragraph is an excellent (and humorous) counterexample for the purpose of this book. Specifically, our goal is to help you avoid stumbling around in the dark by providing lots of easily available light switches and plenty of illumination as you journey through the world of statistics. To accomplish this, we try to present sufficient background and a clear statement of purpose as we introduce each new statistical procedure. Remember that all statistical procedures were developed to serve a purpose. If you understand why a new procedure is needed, you will find it much easier to learn.

The objectives for this first chapter are to provide an introduction to the topic of statistics and to give you some background for the rest of the book. We discuss the role of statistics within the general field of scientific inquiry, and we introduce some of the vocabulary and notation that are necessary for the statistical methods that follow.

As you read through the following chapters, keep in mind that the general topic of statistics follows a well-organized, logically developed progression that leads from basic concepts and definitions to increasingly sophisticated techniques. Thus, the material presented in the early chapters of this book serves as a foundation for the material that follows. The content of the first nine chapters, for example, provides an essential background and context for the statistical methods presented in Chapter 10. If you turn directly to Chapter 10 without reading the first nine chapters, you will find the material confusing and incomprehensible. However, if you learn and use the background material, you will have a good frame of reference for understanding and incorporating new concepts as they are presented.

*Candappa, R. (2000). *The little book of wrong shui.* Kansas City: Andrews McMeel Publishing. Reprinted by permission.

1.1 STATISTICS, SCIENCE, AND OBSERVATIONS

DEFINITIONS OF STATISTICS

By one definition, *statistics* consist of facts and figures such as average income, crime rate, birth rate, baseball batting averages, and so on. These statistics are usually informative and time saving because they condense large quantities of information into a few simple figures. Later in this chapter we return to the notion of calculating statistics (facts and figures) but, for now, we concentrate on a much broader definition of statistics. Specifically, we use the term statistics to refer to a set of mathematical procedures. In this case, we are using the term *statistics* as a shortened version of *statistical procedures*. For example, you are probably using this book for a statistics course in which you will learn about the statistical techniques that are used for research in the behavioral sciences.

Research in psychology (and other fields) involves gathering information. To determine, for example, whether violence on TV has any effect on children's behavior, you would need to gather information about children's behaviors and the TV programs they watch. When researchers finish the task of gathering information, they typically find themselves with pages and pages of measurements such as IQ scores, personality scores, reaction time scores, and so on. In this book, we present the statistics that researchers use to analyze and interpret the information that they gather. Specifically, statistics serve two general purposes:

1. Statistics are used to organize and summarize the information so that the researcher can see what happened in the research study and can communicate the results to others.
2. Statistics help the researcher to answer the questions that initiated the research by determining exactly what general conclusions are justified based on the specific results that were obtained.

DEFINITION

The term **statistics** refers to a set of mathematical procedures for organizing, summarizing, and interpreting information.

Statistical procedures help to ensure that the information or observations are presented and interpreted in an accurate and informative way. In somewhat grandiose terms, statistics help researchers bring order out of chaos. In addition, statistics provide researchers with a set of standardized techniques that are recognized and understood throughout the scientific community. Thus, the statistical methods used by one researcher are familiar to other researchers, who can accurately interpret the statistical analyses with a full understanding of how the analysis was done and what the results signify.

1.2 POPULATIONS AND SAMPLES

WHAT ARE THEY?

Research in the behavioral sciences typically begins with a general question about a specific group (or groups) of individuals. For example, a researcher may be interested in the effect of divorce on the self-esteem of preteen children. Or a researcher may want to examine the amount of time spent in the bathroom for men compared to women. In the first example, the researcher is interested in the group of *preteen children*. In the second example, the researcher wants to compare the group of *men* with the group of *women*. In statistical terminology, the entire group that a researcher wishes to study is called a *population*.

DEFINITION

A **population** is the set of all the individuals of interest in a particular study.

As you can well imagine, a population can be quite large—for example, the entire set of women on the planet Earth. A researcher might be more specific, limiting the population for study to women who are registered voters in the United States. Perhaps the investigator would like to study the population consisting of women who are heads of state. Populations can obviously vary in size from extremely large to very small, depending on how the researcher defines the population. The population being studied should always be identified by the researcher. In addition, the population need not consist of people—it could be a population of rats, corporations, parts produced in a factory, or anything else a researcher wants to study. In practice, populations are typically very large, such as the population of college sophomores in the United States or the population of small businesses.

Because populations tend to be very large, it usually is impossible for a researcher to examine every individual in the population of interest. Therefore, researchers typically select a smaller, more manageable group from the population and limit their studies to the individuals in the selected group. In statistical terms, a set of individuals selected from a population is called a *sample*. A sample is intended to be representative of its population, and a sample should always be identified in terms of the population from which it was selected.

DEFINITION

A **sample** is a set of individuals selected from a population, usually intended to represent the population in a research study.

Just as we saw with populations, samples can vary in size. For example, one study might examine a sample of only 10 students in a graduate program, and another study might use a sample of more than 1,000 registered voters representing the population of a major city.

So far we have talked about a sample being selected from a population. However, this is actually only half of the full relationship between a sample and its population. Specifically, when a researcher finishes examining the sample, the goal is to generalize the results back to the entire population. Remember that the research started with a general question about the population. To answer the question, a researcher studies a sample and then generalizes the results from the sample to the population. The full relationship between a sample and a population is shown in Figure 1.1.

VARIABLES AND DATA

Typically, researchers are interested in specific characteristics of the individuals in the population (or in the sample), or they are interested in outside factors that may influence the individuals. For example, a researcher may be interested in the influence of the weather on people's moods. As the weather changes, do people's moods also change? Something that can change or have different values is called a *variable*.

DEFINITION

A **variable** is a characteristic or condition that changes or has different values for different individuals.

FIGURE 1.1
The relationship between a population and a sample.

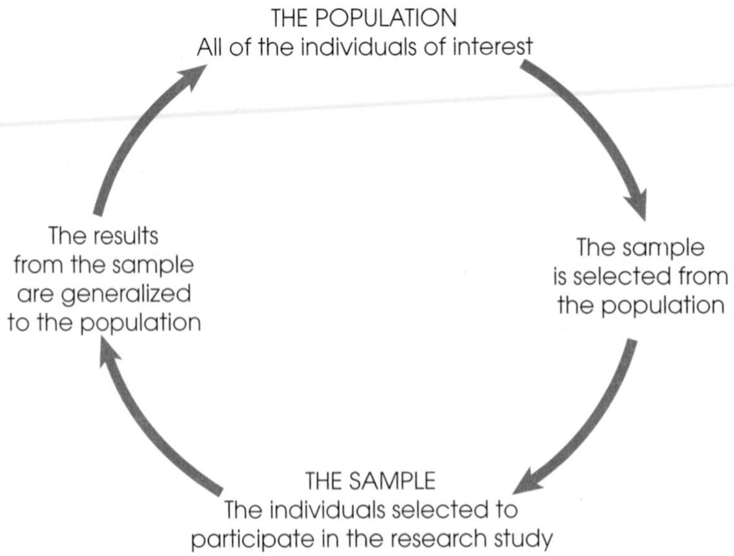

Once again, variables can be characteristics that differ from one individual to another, such as height, weight, gender, or personality. Also, variables can be environmental conditions that change, such as temperature, time of day, or the size of the room in which the research is being conducted.

To demonstrate changes in variables, it is necessary to make measurements of the variables being examined. The measurement obtained for each individual is called a *datum* or, more commonly, a *score* or *raw score*. The complete set of scores is called the *data set* or simply the *data*.

DEFINITIONS

Data (plural) are measurements or observations. A **data set** is a collection of measurements or observations. A **datum** (singular) is a single measurement or observation and is commonly called a **score** or **raw score**.

Before we move on, we should make one more point about samples, populations, and data. Earlier, we defined populations and samples in terms of *individuals*. For example, we discussed a population of college sophomores and a sample of preschool children. Be forewarned, however, that we will also refer to populations or samples of *scores*. Because research typically involves measuring each individual to obtain a score, every sample (or population) of individuals produces a corresponding sample (or population) of scores.

PARAMETERS AND STATISTICS

When describing data, it is necessary to distinguish whether the data come from a population or a sample. A characteristic that describes a population—for example, the average score for the population—is called a *parameter*. A characteristic that describes a sample is called a *statistic*. Thus, the average score for a sample is an example of a statistic. Typically, the research process begins with a question about a population parameter. However, the actual data come from a sample and are used to compute sample statistics.

DEFINITIONS

A **parameter** is a value, usually a numerical value, that describes a population. A parameter is usually derived from measurements of the individuals in the population.

A **statistic** is a value, usually a numerical value, that describes a sample. A statistic is usually derived from measurements of the individuals in the sample.

Every population parameter has a corresponding sample statistic, and most research studies involve using statistics from samples as the basis for answering questions about population parameters. As a result, much of this book is concerned with the relationship between sample statistics and the corresponding population parameters. In Chapter 7, for example, we examine the relationship between the mean obtained for a sample and the mean for the population from which the sample was obtained.

DESCRIPTIVE AND INFERENTIAL STATISTICAL METHODS

Although researchers have developed a variety of different statistical procedures to organize and interpret data, these different procedures can be classified into two general categories. The first category, *descriptive statistics*, consists of statistical procedures that are used to simplify and summarize data.

DEFINITION

Descriptive statistics are statistical procedures used to summarize, organize, and simplify data.

Descriptive statistics are techniques that take raw scores and organize or summarize them in a form that is more manageable. Often the scores are organized in a table or a graph so that it is possible to see the entire set of scores. Another common technique is to summarize a set of scores by computing an average. Note that even if the data set has hundreds of scores, the average provides a single descriptive value for the entire set.

The second general category of statistical techniques is called *inferential statistics*. Inferential statistics are methods that use sample data to make general statements about a population.

DEFINITION

Inferential statistics consist of techniques that allow us to study samples and then make generalizations about the populations from which they were selected.

Because populations are typically very large, it usually is not possible to measure everyone in the population. Therefore, a sample is selected to represent the population. By analyzing the results from the sample, we hope to make general statements about the population. Typically, researchers use sample statistics as the basis for drawing conclusions about population parameters.

One problem with using samples, however, is that a sample provides only limited information about the population. Although samples are generally *representative* of their populations, a sample is not expected to give a perfectly accurate picture of the whole population. There usually is some discrepancy between a sample statistic and the corresponding population parameter. This discrepancy is called *sampling error*, and it creates the fundamental problem that inferential statistics must always address (Box 1.1).

DEFINITION

Sampling error is the naturally occurring discrepancy, or error, that exists between a sample statistic and the corresponding population parameter.

The concept of sampling error is illustrated in Figure 1.2. The figure shows a population of 1,000 college students and two samples, each with 5 students, that have been selected from the population. Notice that each sample contains different individuals who have different characteristics. Because the characteristics of each sample depend on the specific people in the sample, statistics vary from one sample to another. For example, the five students in sample 1 have an average age of 19.8 years and the students in sample 2 have an average age of 20.4 years.

BOX 1.1

THE MARGIN OF ERROR BETWEEN STATISTICS AND PARAMETERS

One common example of sampling error is the error associated with a sample proportion. For example, in newspaper articles reporting results from political polls, you frequently find statements such as this:

> Candidate Brown leads the poll with 51% of the vote. Candidate Jones has 42% approval, and the remaining 7% are undecided. This poll was taken from a sample of registered voters and has a margin of error of plus-or-minus 4 percentage points.

The *margin of error* is the sampling error. In this case, the percentages that are reported were obtained from a sample and are being generalized to the whole population. As always, you do not expect the statistics from a sample to be perfect. There is always some margin of error when sample statistics are used to represent population parameters.

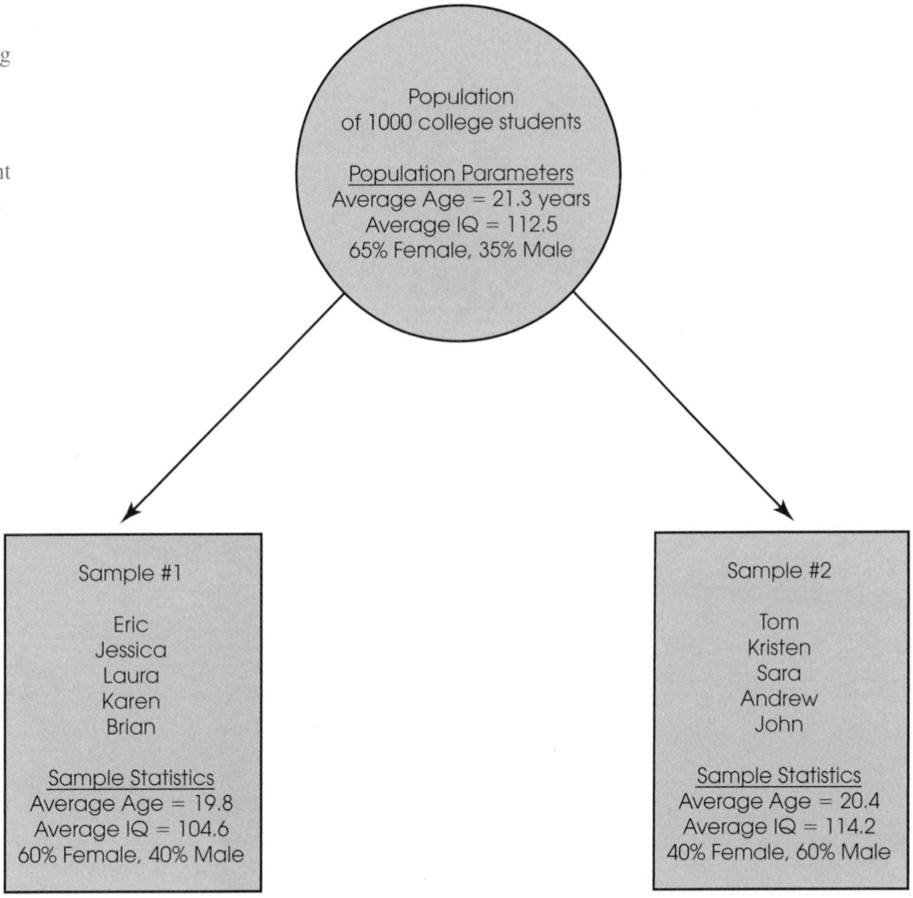

FIGURE 1.2

A demonstration of sampling error. Two samples are selected from the same population. Notice that the sample statistics are different from one sample to another, and all of the sample statistics are different from the corresponding population parameters. The natural differences that exist, by chance, between a sample statistic and a population parameter are called sampling error.

It is also very unlikely that the statistics obtained for a sample are identical to the parameters for the entire population. In Figure 1.2, for example, neither sample has statistics that are exactly the same as the population parameters. You should also realize that Figure 1.2 shows only two of the hundreds of possible samples. Each sample would contain different individuals and would produce different statistics. This is the basic concept of sampling error: sample statistics vary from one sample to another and typically are different from the corresponding population parameters.

As a further demonstration of sampling error, imagine that your statistics class is separated into two groups by drawing a line from front to back through the middle of the room. Now imagine that you compute the average age (or height, or IQ) for each group. Will the two groups have exactly the same average? Almost certainly they will not. No matter what you chose to measure, you will probably find some difference between the two groups.

However, the difference you obtain does not necessarily mean that there is a systematic difference between the two groups. For example, if the average age for students on the right-hand side of the room is higher than the average for students on the left, it is unlikely that some mysterious force has caused the older people to gravitate to the right side of the room. Instead, the difference is probably the result of random factors such as chance. The unpredictable, unsystematic differences that exist from one sample to another are an example of sampling error.

STATISTICS IN THE CONTEXT OF RESEARCH

The following example shows the general stages of a research study and demonstrates how descriptive statistics and inferential statistics are used to organize and interpret the data. At the end of the example, note how sampling error can affect the interpretation of experimental results, and consider why inferential statistical methods are needed to deal with this problem.

EXAMPLE 1.1

Figure 1.3 shows an overview of a general research situation and demonstrates the roles that descriptive and inferential statistics play. The purpose of the research study

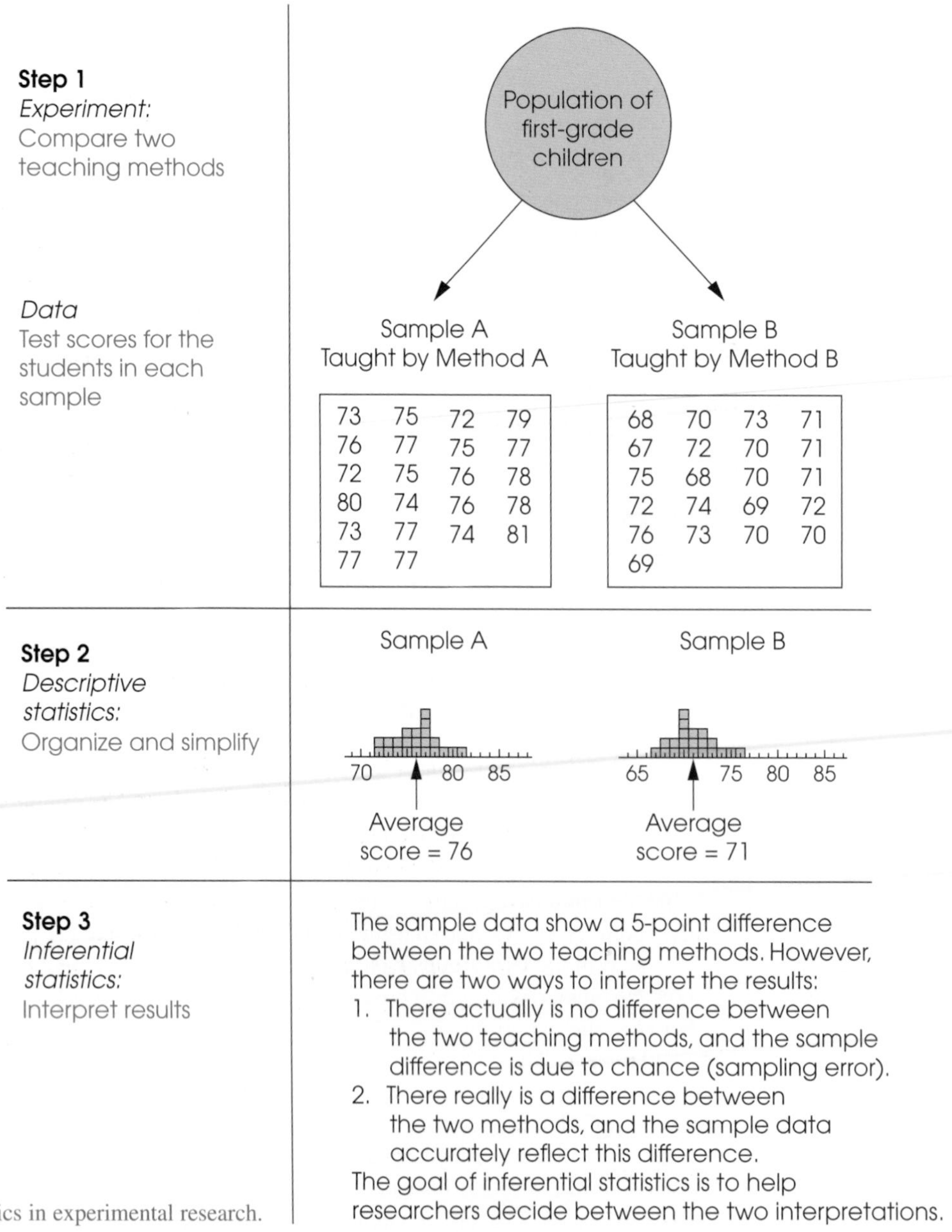

FIGURE 1.3

The role of statistics in experimental research.

is to evaluate the difference between two methods for teaching reading to first-grade children. Two samples are selected from the population of first-grade children. The children in sample A are assigned to teaching method A and the children in sample B are assigned to method B. After 6 months, all of the students are given a standardized reading test. At this point, the researcher has two sets of data: the scores for sample A and the scores for sample B (see Figure 1.3). Now is the time to begin using statistics.

First, descriptive statistics are used to simplify the pages of data. For example, the researcher could draw a graph showing the scores for each sample or compute the average score for each sample. Note that descriptive methods provide a simplified, organized description of the scores. In this example, the students taught by method A averaged 76 on the standardized test, and the students taught by method B averaged only 71.

Once the researcher has described the results, the next step is to interpret the outcome. This is the role of inferential statistics. In this example, the researcher has found a difference of 5 points between the two samples (sample A averaged 76 and sample B averaged 71). The problem for inferential statistics is to differentiate between the following two interpretations:

1. There is no real difference between the two teaching methods, and the 5-point difference between the samples is just an example of sampling error (like the samples in Figure 1.2).
2. There really is a difference between the two teaching methods, and the 5-point difference between the samples was caused by the different methods of teaching.

In simple English, does the 5-point difference between samples provide convincing evidence of a difference between the two teaching methods, or is the 5-point difference just chance? The purpose of inferential statistics is to answer this question.

LEARNING CHECK

1. A researcher is interested in the texting habits of high school students in the United States. If the researcher measures the number of text messages that each individual sends each day and calculates the average number for the entire group of high school students, the average number would be an example of a ___________.
2. A researcher is interested in how watching a reality television show featuring fashion models influences the eating behavior of 13-year-old girls.
   a. A group of 30 13-year-old girls is selected to participate in a research study. The group of 30 13-year-old girls is an example of a ___________.
   b. In the same study, the amount of food eaten in one day is measured for each girl and the researcher computes the average score for the 30 13-year-old girls. The average score is an example of a __________.
3. Statistical techniques are classified into two general categories. What are the two categories called, and what is the general purpose for the techniques in each category?
4. Briefly define the concept of sampling error.

ANSWERS

1. parameter
2. a. sample
   b. statistic

3. The two categories are descriptive statistics and inferential statistics. Descriptive techniques are intended to organize, simplify, and summarize data. Inferential techniques use sample data to reach general conclusions about populations.

4. Sampling error is the error, or discrepancy, between the value obtained for a sample statistic and the value for the corresponding population parameter.

1.3 DATA STRUCTURES, RESEARCH METHODS, AND STATISTICS

INDIVIDUAL VARIABLES

Some research studies are conducted simply to describe individual variables as they exist naturally. For example, a college official may conduct a survey to describe the eating, sleeping, and study habits of a group of college students. When the results consist of numerical scores, such as the number of hours spent studying each day, they are typically described by the statistical techniques that are presented in Chapters 3 and 4. Non-numerical scores are typically described by computing the proportion or percentage in each category. For example, a recent newspaper article reported that 61% of the adults in the United States currently drink alcohol.

RELATIONSHIPS BETWEEN VARIABLES

Most research, however, is intended to examine relationships between two or more variables. For example, is there a relationship between the amount of violence that children see on television and the amount of aggressive behavior they display? Is there a relationship between the quality of breakfast and level of academic performance for elementary school children? Is there a relationship between the number of hours of sleep and grade point average for college students? To establish the existence of a relationship, researchers must make observations—that is, measurements of the two variables. The resulting measurements can be classified into two distinct data structures that also help to classify different research methods and different statistical techniques. In the following section we identify and discuss these two data structures.

I. Measuring Two Variables for Each Individual: The Correlational Method
One method for examining the relationship between variables is to observe the two variables as they exist naturally for a set of individuals. That is, simply measure the two variables for each individual. For example, research has demonstrated a relationship between sleep habits, especially wake-up time, and academic performance for college students (Trockel, Barnes, and Egget, 2000). The researchers used a survey to measure wake-up time and school records to measure academic performance for each student. Figure 1.4 shows an example of the kind of data obtained in the study. The researchers then look for consistent patterns in the data to provide evidence for a relationship between variables. For example, as wake-up time changes from one student to another, is there also a tendency for academic performance to change?

Consistent patterns in the data are often easier to see if the scores are presented in a graph. Figure 1.4 also shows the scores for the eight students in a graph called a scatter plot. In the scatter plot, each individual is represented by a point so that the horizontal position corresponds to the student's wake-up time and the vertical position corresponds to the student's academic performance score. The scatter plot shows a clear relationship between wake-up time and academic performance: as wake-up time increases, academic performance decreases.

(a)

Student	Wake-up Time	Academic Performance
A	11	2.4
B	9	3.6
C	9	3.2
D	12	2.2
E	7	3.8
F	10	2.2
G	10	3.0
H	8	3.0

(b)

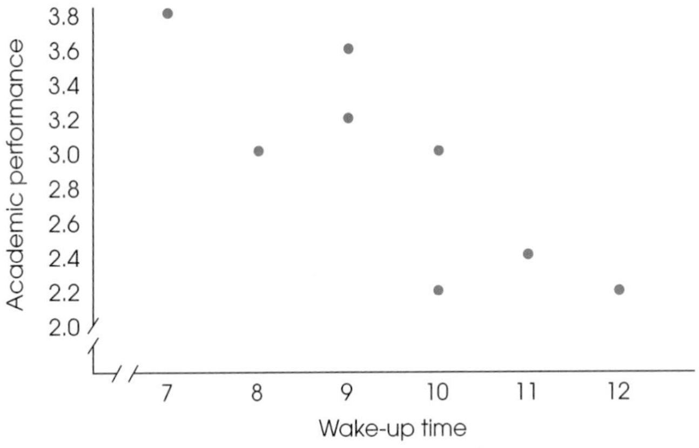

FIGURE 1.4

One of two data structures for studies evaluating the relationship between variables. Note that there are two separate measurements for each individual (wake-up time and academic performance). The same scores are shown in a table (a) and in a graph (b).

A research study that simply measures two different variables for each individual and produces the kind of data shown in Figure 1.4 is an example of the *correlational method*, or the *correlational research strategy.*

DEFINITION

In the **correlational method**, two different variables are observed to determine whether there is a relationship between them.

Limitations of the Correlational Method The results from a correlational study can demonstrate the existence of a relationship between two variables, but they do not provide an explanation for the relationship. In particular, a correlational study cannot demonstrate a cause-and-effect relationship. For example, the data in Figure 1.4 show a systematic relationship between wake-up time and academic performance for a group of college students; those who sleep late tend to have lower performance scores than those who wake early. However, there are many possible explanations for the relationship and we do not know exactly what factor (or factors) is responsible for late sleepers having lower grades. In particular, we cannot conclude that waking students up earlier would cause their academic performance to improve, or that studying more would cause students to wake up earlier. To demonstrate a cause-and-effect relationship between two variables, researchers must use the experimental method, which is discussed next.

II. Comparing Two (or More) Groups of Scores: Experimental and Nonexperimental Methods The second method for examining the relationship between two variables involves the comparison of two or more groups of scores. In this situation, the relationship between variables is examined by using one of the variables to define the groups, and then measuring the second variable to obtain scores for each group. For example, one group of elementary school children is shown a 30-minute action/adventure television program involving numerous instances of violence, and a second group is shown a 30-minute comedy that includes no violence. Both groups are

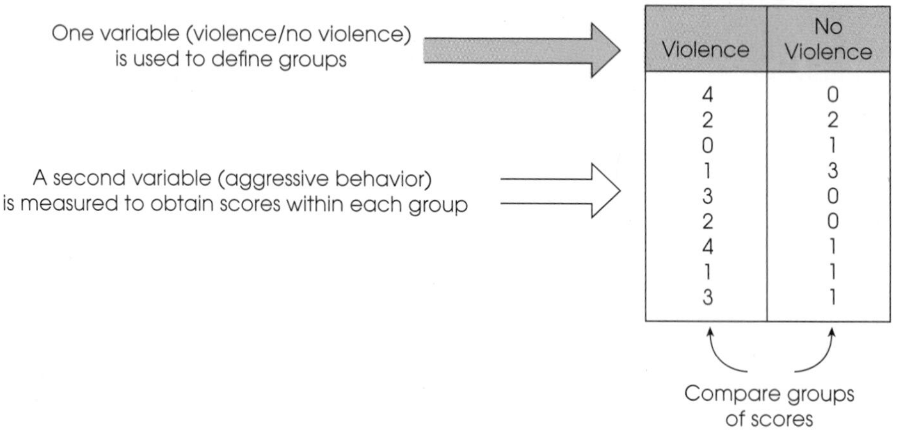

FIGURE 1.5
The second data structure for studies evaluating the relationship between variables. Note that one variable is used to define the groups and the second variable is measured to obtain scores within each group.

then observed on the playground and a researcher records the number of aggressive acts committed by each child. An example of the resulting data is shown in Figure 1.5. The researcher compares the scores for the violence group with the scores for the no-violence group. A systematic difference between the two groups provides evidence for a relationship between viewing television violence and aggressive behavior for elementary school children.

THE EXPERIMENTAL METHOD

One specific research method that involves comparing groups of scores is known as the *experimental method* or the *experimental research strategy.* The goal of an experimental study is to demonstrate a cause-and-effect relationship between two variables. Specifically, an experiment attempts to show that changing the value of one variable causes changes to occur in the second variable. To accomplish this goal, the experimental method has two characteristics that differentiate experiments from other types of research studies:

1. **Manipulation** The researcher manipulates one variable by changing its value from one level to another. A second variable is observed (measured) to determine whether the manipulation causes changes to occur.
2. **Control** The researcher must exercise control over the research situation to ensure that other, extraneous variables do not influence the relationship being examined.

In more complex experiments, a researcher may systematically manipulate more than one variable and may observe more than one variable. Here we are considering the simplest case, in which only one variable is manipulated and only one variable is observed.

To demonstrate these two characteristics, consider an experiment in which researchers demonstrate the pain-killing effects of handling money (Zhou & Vohs, 2009). In the experiment, a group of college students was told that they were participating in a manual dexterity study. The researcher then manipulated the treatment conditions by giving half of the students a stack of money to count and the other half a stack of blank pieces of paper. After the counting task, the participants were asked to dip their hands into bowls of painfully hot water (122° F) and rate how uncomfortable it was. Participants who had counted money rated the pain significantly lower than those who had counted paper. The structure of the experiment is shown in Figure 1.6.

To be able to say that the difference in pain is caused by the money, the researcher must rule out any other possible explanation for the difference. That is, any other

FIGURE 1.6

The structure of an experiment. Participants are randomly assigned to one of two treatment conditions: counting money or counting blank pieces of paper. Later, each participant is tested by placing one hand in a bowl of hot (122° F) water and rating the level of pain. A difference between the ratings for the two groups is attributed to the treatment (paper versus money).

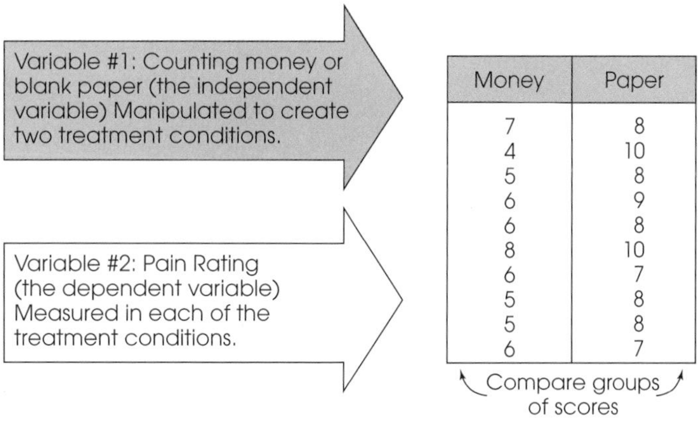

Money	Paper
7	8
4	10
5	8
6	9
6	8
8	10
6	7
5	8
5	8
6	7

variables that might affect pain tolerance must be controlled. There are two general categories of variables that researchers must consider:

1. **Participant Variables** These are characteristics such as age, gender, and intelligence that vary from one individual to another. Whenever an experiment compares different groups of participants (one group in treatment A and a different group in treatment B), researchers must ensure that participant variables do not differ from one group to another. For the experiment shown in Figure 1.6, for example, the researchers would like to conclude that handling money instead of plain paper causes a change in the participants' perceptions of pain. Suppose, however, that the participants in the money condition were primarily females and those in the paper condition were primarily males. In this case, there is an alternative explanation for any difference in the pain ratings that exists between the two groups. Specifically, it is possible that the difference in pain was caused by the money, but it also is possible that the difference was caused by the participants' gender (females can tolerate more pain than males can). Whenever a research study allows more than one explanation for the results, the study is said to be *confounded* because it is impossible to reach an unambiguous conclusion.
2. **Environmental Variables** These are characteristics of the environment such as lighting, time of day, and weather conditions. A researcher must ensure that the individuals in treatment A are tested in the same environment as the individuals in treatment B. Using the money-counting experiment (see Figure 1.6) as an example, suppose that the individuals in the money condition were all tested in the morning and the individuals in the paper condition were all tested in the evening. Again, this would produce a confounded experiment because the researcher could not determine whether the differences in the pain ratings were caused by the money or caused by the time of day.

Researchers typically use three basic techniques to control other variables. First, the researcher could use *random assignment*, which means that each participant has an equal chance of being assigned to each of the treatment conditions. The goal of random assignment is to distribute the participant characteristics evenly between the two groups so that neither group is noticeably smarter (or older, or faster) than the other. Random assignment can also be used to control environmental variables. For example, participants could be assigned randomly for testing either in the morning or in the afternoon. Second, the researcher can use *matching* to ensure equivalent groups or equivalent environments. For example, the researcher could match groups by ensuring that every group has exactly 60% females and 40% males. Finally, the researcher can control variables by *holding them constant.* For example, if an experiment uses only 10-year-old children as participants (holding age constant), then the researcher can be certain that one group is not noticeably older than another.

DEFINITION

In the **experimental method**, one variable is manipulated while another variable is observed and measured. To establish a cause-and-effect relationship between the two variables, an experiment attempts to control all other variables to prevent them from influencing the results.

Terminology in the Experimental Method Specific names are used for the two variables that are studied by the experimental method. The variable that is manipulated by the experimenter is called the *independent variable*. It can be identified as the treatment conditions to which participants are assigned. For the example in Figure 1.6, money versus paper is the independent variable. The variable that is observed and measured to obtain scores within each condition is the *dependent variable*. For the example in Figure 1.6, the level of pain is the dependent variable.

DEFINITIONS

The **independent variable** is the variable that is manipulated by the researcher. In behavioral research, the independent variable usually consists of the two (or more) treatment conditions to which subjects are exposed. The independent variable consists of the *antecedent* conditions that were manipulated *prior* to observing the dependent variable.

The **dependent variable** is the variable that is observed to assess the effect of the treatment.

Control conditions in an experiment An experimental study evaluates the relationship between two variables by manipulating one variable (the independent variable) and measuring one variable (the dependent variable). Note that in an experiment only one variable is actually measured. You should realize that this is different from a correlational study, in which both variables are measured and the data consist of two separate scores for each individual.

Often an experiment will include a condition in which the participants do not receive any treatment. The scores from these individuals are then compared with scores from participants who do receive the treatment. The goal of this type of study is to demonstrate that the treatment has an effect by showing that the scores in the treatment condition are substantially different from the scores in the no-treatment condition. In this kind of research, the no-treatment condition is called the *control condition*, and the treatment condition is called the *experimental condition*.

DEFINITIONS

Individuals in a **control condition** do not receive the experimental treatment. Instead, they either receive no treatment or they receive a neutral, placebo treatment. The purpose of a control condition is to provide a baseline for comparison with the experimental condition.

Individuals in the **experimental condition** do receive the experimental treatment.

Note that the independent variable always consists of at least two values. (Something must have at least two different values before you can say that it is "variable.") For the money-counting experiment (see Figure 1.6), the independent variable is money versus plain paper. For an experiment with an experimental group and a control group, the independent variable is treatment versus no treatment.

NONEXPERIMENTAL METHODS: NONEQUIVALENT GROUPS AND PRE–POST STUDIES

In informal conversation, there is a tendency for people to use the term *experiment* to refer to any kind of research study. You should realize, however, that the term only applies to studies that satisfy the specific requirements outlined earlier. In particular, a real experiment must include manipulation of an independent variable and rigorous control of other, extraneous variables. As a result, there are a number of other research designs that are not true experiments but still examine the relationship between variables by comparing groups of scores. Two examples are shown in Figure 1.7 and are discussed in the following paragraphs. This type of research study is classified as nonexperimental.

The top part of Figure 1.7 shows an example of a *nonequivalent groups* study comparing boys and girls. Notice that this study involves comparing two groups of scores (like an experiment). However, the researcher has no ability to control which

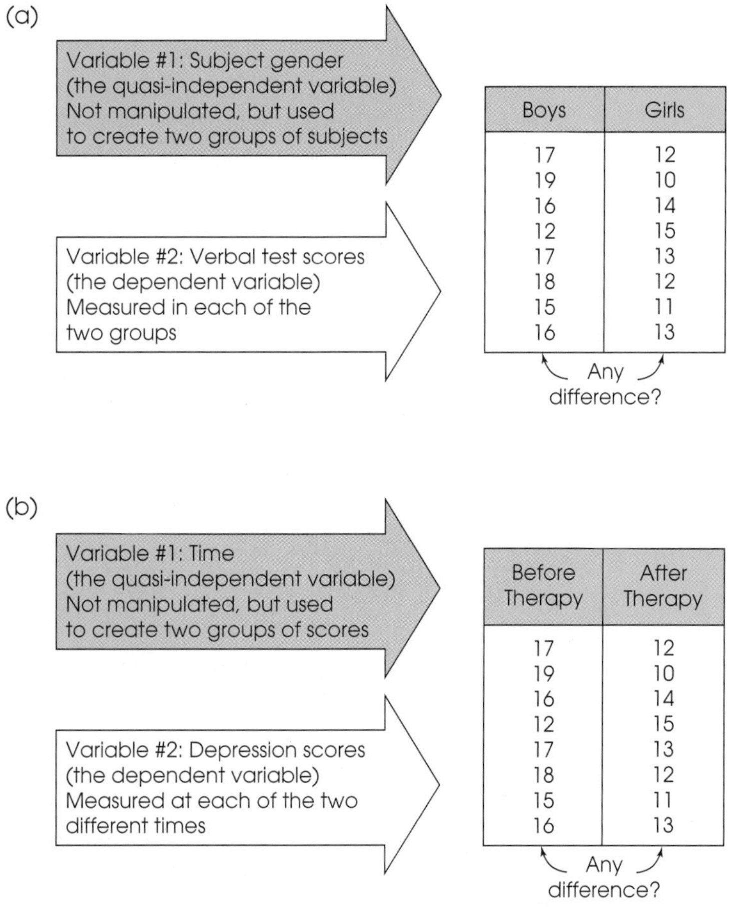

FIGURE 1.7

Two examples of nonexperimental studies that involve comparing two groups of scores. In (a) the study uses two preexisting groups (boys/girls) and measures a dependent variable (verbal scores) in each group. In (b) the study uses time (before/after) to define the two groups and measures a dependent variable (depression) in each group.

participants go into which group—all the males must be in the boy group and all the females must be in the girl group. Because this type of research compares preexisting groups, the researcher cannot control the assignment of participants to groups and cannot ensure equivalent groups. Other examples of nonequivalent group studies include comparing 8-year-old children and 10-year-old children, people with an eating disorder and those with no disorder, and comparing children from a single-parent home and those from a two-parent home. Because it is impossible to use techniques like random assignment to control participant variables and ensure equivalent groups, this type of research is not a true experiment.

Correlational studies are also examples of nonexperimental research. In this section, however, we are discussing non-experimental studies that compare two or more groups of scores.

The bottom part of Figure 1.7 shows an example of a *pre–post* study comparing depression scores before therapy and after therapy. The two groups of scores are obtained by measuring the same variable (depression) twice for each participant; once before therapy and again after therapy. In a pre–post study, however, the researcher has no control over the passage of time. The "before" scores are always measured earlier than the "after" scores. Although a difference between the two groups of scores may be caused by the treatment, it is always possible that the scores simply change as time goes by. For example, the depression scores may decrease over time in the same way that the symptoms of a cold disappear over time. In a pre–post study, the researcher also has no control over other variables that change with time. For example, the weather could change from dark and gloomy before therapy to bright and sunny after therapy. In this case, the depression scores could improve because of the weather and not because of the therapy. Because the researcher cannot control the passage of time or other variables related to time, this study is not a true experiment.

Terminology in nonexperimental research Although the two research studies shown in Figure 1.7 are not true experiments, you should notice that they produce the same kind of data that are found in an experiment (see Figure 1.6). In each case, one variable is used to create groups, and a second variable is measured to obtain scores within each group. In an experiment, the groups are created by manipulation of the independent variable, and the participants' scores are the dependent variable. The same terminology is often used to identify the two variables in nonexperimental studies. That is, the variable that is used to create groups is the independent variable and the scores are the dependent variable. For example, the top part of Figure 1.7, gender (boy/girl), is the independent variable and the verbal test scores are the dependent variable. However, you should realize that gender (boy/girl) is not a true independent variable because it is not manipulated. For this reason, the "independent variable" in a nonexperimental study is often called a *quasi-independent variable.*

DEFINITION

In a nonexperimental study, the "independent variable" that is used to create the different groups of scores is often called the **quasi-independent variable**.

DATA STRUCTURES AND STATISTICAL METHODS

The two general data structures that we used to classify research methods can also be used to classify statistical methods.

I. One Group with Two Variables Measured for each Individual Recall that the data from a correlational study consist of two scores, representing two different variables, for each individual. The scores can be listed in a table or displayed in a scatter plot as in Figure 1.5. The relationship between the two variables is usually measured and described using a statistic called a *correlation*. Correlations and the correlational method are discussed in detail in Chapters 15 and 16.

Occasionally, the measurement process used for a correlational study simply classifies individuals into categories that do not correspond to numerical values. For example, a researcher could classify a group of college students by gender (male or female) and by cell-phone preference (talk or text). Note that the researcher has two scores for each individual but neither of the scores is a numerical value. This type of data is typically summarized in a table showing how many individuals are classified into each of the possible categories. Table 1.1 shows an example of this kind of summary table. The table shows, for example, that 30 of the males in the sample preferred texting to talking. This type of data can be coded with numbers (for example, male = 0 and female = 1) so that it is possible to compute a correlation. However, the relationship between variables for non-numerical data, such as the data in Table 1.1, is usually evaluated using a statistical technique known as a *chi-square test.* Chi-square tests are presented in Chapter 17.

II. Comparing Two or More Groups of Scores Most of the statistical procedures presented in this book are designed for research studies that compare groups of scores, like the experimental study in Figure 1.6 and the nonexperimental studies in Figure 1.7. Specifically, we examine descriptive statistics that summarize and describe the scores in each group, and we examine inferential statistics that allow us to use the groups, or samples, to generalize to the entire population.

When the measurement procedure produces numerical scores, the statistical evaluation typically involves computing the average score for each group and then comparing the averages. The process of computing averages is presented in Chapter 3, and a variety of statistical techniques for comparing averages are presented in Chapters 8–14. If the measurement process simply classifies individuals into non-numerical categories, the statistical evaluation usually consists of computing proportions for each group and then comparing proportions. In Table 1.1 we present an example of non-numerical data examining the relationship between gender and cell-phone preference. The same data can be used to compare the proportions for males with the proportions for females. For example, using text is preferred by 60% of the males compared to 50% of the females. As mentioned before, these data are evaluated using a chi-square test, which is presented in Chapter 17.

TABLE 1.1

Correlational data consisting of non-numerical scores. Note that there are two measurements for each individual: gender and cell phone preference. The numbers indicate how many people are in each category. For example, out of the 50 males, 30 prefer text over talk.

	Cell Phone Preference		
	Text	Talk	
Males	30	20	50
Females	25	25	50

LEARNING CHECK

1. Researchers have observed that high school students who watched educational television programs as young children tend to have higher grades than their peers who did not watch educational television. Is this study an example of an experiment? Explain why or why not.
2. What two elements are necessary for a research study to be an experiment?
3. Loftus and Palmer (1974) conducted an experiment in which participants were shown a video of an automobile accident. After the video, some participants were

asked to estimate the speed of the cars when they "smashed into" each other. Others were asked to estimate the speed when the cars "hit" each other. The "smashed into" group produced significantly higher estimates than the "hit" group. Identify the independent and dependent variables for this study.

ANSWERS

1. This study could be correlational or nonexperimental, but it is definitely not an example of a true experiment. The researcher is simply observing, not manipulating, the amount of educational television.
2. First, the researcher must manipulate one of the two variables being studied. Second, all other variables that might influence the results must be controlled.
3. The independent variable is the phrasing of the question and the dependent variable is the speed estimated by each participant.

1.4 VARIABLES AND MEASUREMENT

The scores that make up the data from a research study are the result of observing and measuring variables. For example, a researcher may finish a study with a set of IQ scores, personality scores, or reaction-time scores. In this section, we take a closer look at the variables that are being measured and the process of measurement.

CONSTRUCTS AND OPERATIONAL DEFINITIONS

Some variables, such as height, weight, and eye color are well-defined, concrete entities that can be observed and measured directly. On the other hand, many variables studied by behavioral scientists are internal characteristics that people use to help describe and explain behavior. For example, we say that a student does well in school because he or she is *intelligent*. Or we say that someone is *anxious* in social situations, or that someone seems to be *hungry*. Variables like intelligence, anxiety, and hunger are called *constructs*, and because they are intangible and cannot be directly observed, they are often called *hypothetical constructs*.

Although constructs such as intelligence are internal characteristics that cannot be directly observed, it is possible to observe and measure behaviors that are representative of the construct. For example, we cannot "see" intelligence but we can see examples of intelligent behavior. The external behaviors can then be used to create an operational definition for the construct. An *operational definition* defines a construct in terms of external behaviors that can be observed and measured. For example, your intelligence is measured and defined by your performance on an IQ test, or hunger can be measured and defined by the number of hours since last eating.

DEFINITIONS

Constructs are internal attributes or characteristics that cannot be directly observed but are useful for describing and explaining behavior.

An **operational definition** identifies a measurement procedure (a set of operations) for measuring an external behavior and uses the resulting measurements as a definition and a measurement of a hypothetical construct. Note that an operational definition has two components: First, it describes a set of operations for measuring a construct. Second, it defines the construct in terms of the resulting measurements.

DISCRETE AND CONTINUOUS VARIABLES

The variables in a study can be characterized by the type of values that can be assigned to them. A *discrete variable* consists of separate, indivisible categories. For this type of variable, there are no intermediate values between two adjacent categories. Consider the values displayed when dice are rolled. Between neighboring values—for example, five dots and six dots—no other values can ever be observed.

DEFINITION

A **discrete variable** consists of separate, indivisible categories. No values can exist between two neighboring categories.

Discrete variables are commonly restricted to whole, countable numbers—for example, the number of children in a family or the number of students attending class. If you observe class attendance from day to day, you may count 18 students one day and 19 students the next day. However, it is impossible ever to observe a value between 18 and 19. A discrete variable may also consist of observations that differ qualitatively. For example, people can be classified by gender (male or female), by occupation (nurse, teacher, lawyer, etc.), and college students can be classified by academic major (art, biology, chemistry, etc.). In each case, the variable is discrete because it consists of separate, indivisible categories.

On the other hand, many variables are not discrete. Variables such as time, height, and weight are not limited to a fixed set of separate, indivisible categories. You can measure time, for example, in hours, minutes, seconds, or fractions of seconds. These variables are called *continuous* because they can be divided into an infinite number of fractional parts.

DEFINITION

For a **continuous variable**, there are an infinite number of possible values that fall between any two observed values. A continuous variable is divisible into an infinite number of fractional parts.

Suppose, for example, that a researcher is measuring weights for a group of individuals participating in a diet study. Because weight is a continuous variable, it can be pictured as a continuous line (Figure 1.8). Note that there are an infinite number of possible points on the line without any gaps or separations between neighboring points. For

FIGURE 1.8

When measuring weight to the nearest whole pound, 149.6 and 150.3 are assigned the value of 150 (top). Any value in the interval between 149.5 and 150.5 is given the value of 150.

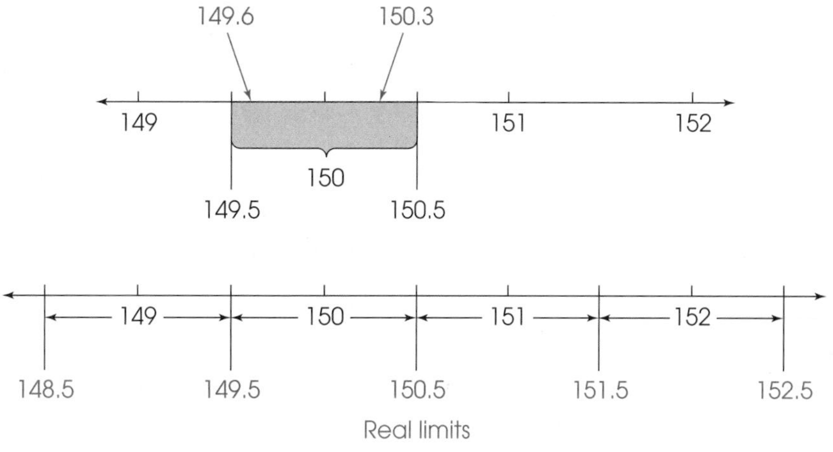

any two different points on the line, it is always possible to find a third value that is between the two points.

Two other factors apply to continuous variables:

1. When measuring a continuous variable, it should be very rare to obtain identical measurements for two different individuals. Because a continuous variable has an infinite number of possible values, it should be almost impossible for two people to have exactly the same score. If the data show a substantial number of tied scores, then you should suspect that the measurement procedure is very crude or that the variable is not really continuous.
2. When measuring a continuous variable, each measurement category is actually an *interval* that must be defined by boundaries. For example, two people who both claim to weigh 150 pounds are probably not *exactly* the same weight. However, they are both around 150 pounds. One person may actually weigh 149.6 and the other 150.3. Thus, a score of 150 is not a specific point on the scale but instead is an interval (see Figure 1.8). To differentiate a score of 150 from a score of 149 or 151, we must set up boundaries on the scale of measurement. These boundaries are called *real limits* and are positioned exactly halfway between adjacent scores. Thus, a score of $X = 150$ pounds is actually an interval bounded by a *lower real limit* of 149.5 at the bottom and an *upper real limit* of 150.5 at the top. Any individual whose weight falls between these real limits will be assigned a score of $X = 150$.

DEFINITIONS

Real limits are the boundaries of intervals for scores that are represented on a continuous number line. The real limit separating two adjacent scores is located exactly halfway between the scores. Each score has two real limits. The **upper real limit** is at the top of the interval, and the **lower real limit** is at the bottom.

Technical Note: Students often ask whether a value of exactly 150.5 should be assigned to the $X = 150$ interval or the $X = 151$ interval. The answer is that 150.5 is the *boundary* between the two intervals and is not necessarily in one or the other. Instead, the placement of 150.5 depends on the rule that you are using for rounding numbers. If you are rounding up, then 150.5 goes in the higher interval ($X = 151$) but if you are rounding down, then it goes in the lower interval ($X = 150$).

The concept of real limits applies to any measurement of a continuous variable, even when the score categories are not whole numbers. For example, if you were measuring time to the nearest tenth of a second, the measurement categories would be 31.0, 31.1, 31.2, and so on. Each of these categories represents an interval on the scale that is bounded by real limits. For example, a score of $X = 31.1$ seconds indicates that the actual measurement is in an interval bounded by a lower real limit of 31.05 and an upper real limit of 31.15. Remember that the real limits are always halfway between adjacent categories.

Later in this book, real limits are used for constructing graphs and for various calculations with continuous scales. For now, however, you should realize that real limits are a necessity whenever you make measurements of a continuous variable.

Finally, we should warn you that the terms *continuous* and *discrete* apply to the variables that are being measured and not to the scores that are obtained from the measurement. For example, measuring people's heights to the nearest inch produces scores of 60, 61, 62, and so on. Although the scores may appear to be discrete numbers, the underlying variable is continuous. One key to determining whether a variable is continuous or discrete is that a continuous variable can be divided into any number of fractional parts. Height can be measured to the nearest inch, the nearest 0.5 inch, or the nearest 0.1 inch. Similarly, a professor evaluating students' knowledge could use a pass/fail system that classifies students into two broad categories. However, the professor could choose to use a 10-point quiz that divides student knowledge into 11 categories corresponding to quiz scores from 0 to 10. Or the professor could use a 100-point exam that potentially divides student knowledge into 101 categories from 0 to 100. Whenever you are free to choose the degree of precision or the number of categories for measuring a variable, the variable must be continuous.

SCALES OF MEASUREMENT

It should be obvious by now that data collection requires that we make measurements of our observations. Measurement involves assigning individuals or events to categories. The categories can simply be names such as male/female or employed/unemployed, or they can be numerical values such as 68 inches or 175 pounds. The categories used to measure a variable make up a *scale of measurement*, and the relationships between the categories determine different types of scales. The distinctions among the scales are important because they identify the limitations of certain types of measurements and because certain statistical procedures are appropriate for scores that have been measured on some scales but not on others. If you were interested in people's heights, for example, you could measure a group of individuals by simply classifying them into three categories: tall, medium, and short. However, this simple classification would not tell you much about the actual heights of the individuals, and these measurements would not give you enough information to calculate an average height for the group. Although the simple classification would be adequate for some purposes, you would need more sophisticated measurements before you could answer more detailed questions. In this section, we examine four different scales of measurement, beginning with the simplest and moving to the most sophisticated.

THE NOMINAL SCALE

The word *nominal* means "having to do with names." Measurement on a nominal scale involves classifying individuals into categories that have different names but are not related to each other in any systematic way. For example, if you were measuring the academic majors for a group of college students, the categories would be art, biology, business, chemistry, and so on. Each student would be classified in one category according to his or her major. The measurements from a nominal scale allow us to determine whether two individuals are different, but they do not identify either the direction or the size of the difference. If one student is an art major and another is a biology major we can say that they are different, but we cannot say that art is "more than" or "less than" biology and we cannot specify how much difference there is between art and biology. Other examples of nominal scales include classifying people by race, gender, or occupation.

DEFINITION

A **nominal scale** consists of a set of categories that have different names. Measurements on a nominal scale label and categorize observations, but do not make any quantitative distinctions between observations.

Although the categories on a nominal scale are not quantitative values, they are occasionally represented by numbers. For example, the rooms or offices in a building may be identified by numbers. You should realize that the room numbers are simply names and do not reflect any quantitative information. Room 109 is not necessarily bigger than Room 100 and certainly not 9 points bigger. It also is fairly common to use numerical values as a code for nominal categories when data are entered into computer programs. For example, the data from a survey may code males with a 0 and females with a 1. Again, the numerical values are simply names and do not represent any quantitative difference. The scales that follow do reflect an attempt to make quantitative distinctions.

THE ORDINAL SCALE

The categories that make up an *ordinal scale* not only have different names (as in a nominal scale) but also are organized in a fixed order corresponding to differences of magnitude.

DEFINITION

An **ordinal scale** consists of a set of categories that are organized in an ordered sequence. Measurements on an ordinal scale rank observations in terms of size or magnitude.

Often, an ordinal scale consists of a series of ranks (first, second, third, and so on) like the order of finish in a horse race. Occasionally, the categories are identified by verbal labels like small, medium, and large drink sizes at a fast-food restaurant. In either case, the fact that the categories form an ordered sequence means that there is a directional relationship between categories. With measurements from an ordinal scale, you can determine whether two individuals are different and you can determine the direction of difference. However, ordinal measurements do not allow you to determine the size of the difference between two individuals. For example, if Billy is placed in the low-reading group and Tim is placed in the high-reading group, you know that Tim is a better reader, but you do not know how much better. Other examples of ordinal scales include socioeconomic class (upper, middle, lower) and T-shirt sizes (small, medium, large). In addition, ordinal scales are often used to measure variables for which it is difficult to assign numerical scores. For example, people can rank their food preferences but might have trouble explaining "how much" they prefer chocolate ice cream to steak.

THE INTERVAL AND RATIO SCALES

Both an *interval scale* and a *ratio scale* consist of a series of ordered categories (like an ordinal scale) with the additional requirement that the categories form a series of intervals that are all exactly the same size. Thus, the scale of measurement consists of a series of equal intervals, such as inches on a ruler. Other examples of interval and ratio scales are the measurement of time in seconds, weight in pounds, and temperature in degrees Fahrenheit. Note that, in each case, one interval (1 inch, 1 second, 1 pound, 1 degree) is the same size, no matter where it is located on the scale. The fact that the intervals are all the same size makes it possible to determine both the size and the direction of the difference between two measurements. For example, you know that a measurement of 80° Fahrenheit is higher than a measure of 60°, and you know that it is exactly 20° higher.

The factor that differentiates an interval scale from a ratio scale is the nature of the zero point. An interval scale has an arbitrary zero point. That is, the value 0 is assigned to a particular location on the scale simply as a matter of convenience or reference. In particular, a value of zero does not indicate a total absence of the variable being measured. For example a temperature of 0° Fahrenheit does not mean that there is no temperature, and it does not prohibit the temperature from going even lower. Interval scales with an arbitrary zero point are relatively rare. The two most common examples are the Fahrenheit and Celsius temperature scales. Other examples include golf scores (above and below par) and relative measures such as above and below average rainfall.

A ratio scale is anchored by a zero point that is not arbitrary but rather is a meaningful value representing none (a complete absence) of the variable being measured. The existence of an absolute, nonarbitrary zero point means that we can measure the absolute amount of the variable; that is, we can measure the distance from 0. This makes it possible to compare measurements in terms of ratios. For example, an individual who requires 10 seconds to solve a problem (10 more than 0) has taken twice as much time as an individual who finishes in only 5 seconds (5 more than 0). With a ratio scale, we can measure the direction and the size of the difference between two measurements and we can describe the difference in terms of a ratio. Ratio scales are quite common and include physical measures such as height and weight, as well as variables such as reaction time or the number of errors on a test. The distinction between an interval scale and a ratio scale is demonstrated in Example 1.2.

DEFINITIONS

An **interval scale** consists of ordered categories that are all intervals of exactly the same size. Equal differences between numbers on a scale reflect equal differences in magnitude. However, the zero point on an interval scale is arbitrary and does not indicate a zero amount of the variable being measured.

A **ratio scale** is an interval scale with the additional feature of an absolute zero point. With a ratio scale, ratios of numbers do reflect ratios of magnitude.

EXAMPLE 1.2

A researcher obtains measurements of height for a group of 8-year-old boys. Initially, the researcher simply records each child's height in inches, obtaining values such as 44, 51, 49, and so on. These initial measurements constitute a ratio scale. A value of zero represents no height (absolute zero). Also, it is possible to use these measurements to form ratios. For example, a child who is 60 inches tall is one-and-a-half times taller than a child who is 40 inches tall.

Now suppose that the researcher converts the initial measurement into a new scale by calculating the difference between each child's actual height and the average height for this age group. A child who is 1 inch taller than average now gets a score of +1; a child 4 inches taller than average gets a score of +4. Similarly, a child who is 2 inches shorter than average gets a score of −2. On this scale, a score of zero corresponds to average height. Because zero no longer indicates a complete absence of height, the new scores constitute an interval scale of measurement.

Notice that original scores and the converted scores both involve measurement in inches, and you can compute differences, or distances, on either scale. For example, there is a 6-inch difference in height between two boys who measure 57 and 51 inches tall on the first scale. Likewise, there is a 6-inch difference between two boys who measure +9 and +3 on the second scale. However, you should also notice that ratio comparisons are not possible on the second scale. For example, a boy who measures +9 is not three times taller than a boy who measures +3.

STATISTICS AND SCALES OF MEASUREMENT

For our purposes, scales of measurement are important because they influence the kind of statistics that can and cannot be used. For example, if you measure IQ scores for a group of students, it is possible to add the scores together and calculate a mean score for the group. On the other hand, if you measure the academic major for each student, you cannot compute the mean. (What is the mean of three psychology majors, an English major, and two chemistry majors?) The vast majority of the statistical techniques presented in this book are designed for numerical scores from an interval or a ratio scale. For most statistical applications, the distinction between an interval scale and a ratio scale is not important because both scales produce numerical values that permit us to compute differences between scores, to add scores, and to calculate mean scores. On the other hand, measurements from nominal or ordinal scales are typically not numerical values and are not compatible with many basic arithmetic operations. Therefore, alternative statistical techniques are necessary for data from nominal or ordinal scales of measurement (for example, the median and the mode in Chapter 3, the Spearman correlation in Chapter 15, and the chi-square tests in Chapter 17). Additional statistical methods for measurements from ordinal scales are presented in Appendix E.

LEARNING CHECK

1. A survey asks people to identify their age, annual income, and marital status (single, married, divorced, etc.). For each of these three variables, identify the scale of measurement that probably is used and identify whether the variable is continuous or discrete.
2. An English professor uses letter grades (A, B, C, D, and F) to evaluate a set of student essays. What kind of scale is being used to measure the quality of the essays?
3. The teacher in a communications class asks students to identify their favorite reality television show. The different television shows make up a ______ scale of measurement.
4. A researcher studies the factors that determine the number of children that couples decide to have. The variable, number of children, is a ______________ (discrete/continuous) variable.
5. **a.** When measuring height to the nearest inch, what are the real limits for a score of 68 inches?
   b. When measuring height to the nearest half inch, what are the real limits for a score of 68 inches?

ANSWERS

1. Age and annual income are measured on ratio scales and are both continuous variables. Marital status is measured on a nominal scale and is a discrete variable.
2. ordinal
3. nominal
4. discrete
5. **a.** 67.5 and 68.5
   b. 67.75 and 68.25

1.5 STATISTICAL NOTATION

The measurements obtained in research studies provide the data for statistical analysis. Most of the statistical analyses use the same general mathematical operations, notation, and basic arithmetic that you have learned during previous years of school. In case you are unsure of your mathematical skills, there is a mathematics review section in Appendix A at the back of this book. The appendix also includes a skills-assessment exam (p. 678) to help you determine whether you need the basic mathematics review. In this section, we introduce some of the specialized notation that is used for statistical calculations. In later chapters, additional statistical notation is introduced as it is needed.

Measuring a variable in a research study typically yields a value or a score for each individual. Raw scores are the original, unchanged scores obtained in the study. Scores for a particular variable are represented by the letter X. For example, if performance in your statistics course is measured by tests and you obtain a 35 on the first test, then we could state that $X = 35$. A set of scores can be presented in a column that is headed by X. For example, a list of quiz scores from your class might be presented as shown in the margin (the single column on the left).

X
37
35
35
30
25
17
16

Scores	
X	Y
72	165
68	151
67	160
67	160
68	146
70	160
66	133

When observations are made for two variables, there will be two scores for each individual. The data can be presented as two lists labeled X and Y for the two variables. For example, observations for people's height in inches (variable X) and weight in pounds (variable Y) can be presented as shown in the double column in the margin. Each pair X, Y represents the observations made of a single participant.

The letter N is used to specify how many scores are in a set. An uppercase letter N identifies the number of scores in a population and a lowercase letter n identifies the number of scores in a sample. Throughout the remainder of the book you will notice that we often use notational differences to distinguish between samples and populations. For the height and weight data in the preceding table, $n = 7$ for both variables. Note that by using a lowercase letter n, we are implying that these data are a sample.

SUMMATION NOTATION

Many of the computations required in statistics involve adding a set of scores. Because this procedure is used so frequently, a special notation is used to refer to the sum of a set of scores. The Greek letter *sigma*, or Σ, is used to stand for summation. The expression ΣX means to add all the scores for variable X. The summation sign, Σ, can be read as "the sum of." Thus, ΣX is read "the sum of the scores." For the following set of quiz scores,

10, 6, 7, 4

$\Sigma X = 27$ and $N = 4$.

To use summation notation correctly, keep in mind the following two points:

1. The summation sign, Σ, is always followed by a symbol or mathematical expression. The symbol or expression identifies exactly which values are to be added. To compute ΣX, for example, the symbol following the summation sign is X, and the task is to find the sum of the X values. On the other hand, to compute $\Sigma(X - 1)^2$, the summation sign is followed by a relatively complex mathematical expression, so your first task is to calculate all of the $(X - 1)^2$ values and then add the results.
2. The summation process is often included with several other mathematical operations, such as multiplication or squaring. To obtain the correct answer, it is essential that the different operations be done in the correct sequence. Following is a list showing the correct *order of operations* for performing mathematical operations. Most of this list should be familiar, but you should note that we have inserted the summation process as the fourth operation in the list.

Order of Mathematical Operations

More information on the order of operations for mathematics is available in the Math Review appendix, page 679.

1. Any calculation contained within parentheses is done first.
2. Squaring (or raising to other exponents) is done second.
3. Multiplying and/or dividing is done third. A series of multiplication and/or division operations should be done in order from left to right.
4. Summation using the Σ notation is done next.
5. Finally, any other addition and/or subtraction is done.

The following examples demonstrate how summation notation is used in most of the calculations and formulas we present in this book.

EXAMPLE 1.3 A set of four scores consists of values 3, 1, 7, and 4. We will compute ΣX, ΣX^2, and $(\Sigma X)^2$ for these scores. To help demonstrate the calculations, we will use a computational table showing the original scores (the X values) in the first column. Additional columns can then be added to show additional steps in the series of operations. You should notice that the first three operations in the list (parentheses, squaring, and multiplying) all create a new column of values. The last two operations, however, produce a single value corresponding to the sum.

X	X^2
3	9
1	1
7	49
4	16

The table to the left shows the original scores (the X values) and the squared scores (the X^2 values) that are needed to compute ΣX^2.

The first calculation, ΣX, does not include any parentheses, squaring, or multiplication, so we go directly to the summation operation. The X values are listed in the first column of the table, and we simply add the values in this column:

$$\Sigma X = 3 + 1 + 7 + 4 = 15$$

To compute ΣX^2, the correct order of operations is to square each score and then find the sum of the squared values. The computational table shows the original scores and the results obtained from squaring (the first step in the calculation). The second step is to find the sum of the squared values, so we simply add the numbers in the X^2 column.

$$\Sigma X^2 = 9 + 1 + 49 + 16 = 75$$

The final calculation, $(\Sigma X)^2$, includes parentheses, so the first step is to perform the calculation inside the parentheses. Thus, we first find ΣX and then square this sum. Earlier, we computed $\Sigma X = 15$, so

$$(\Sigma X)^2 = (15)^2 = 225$$

EXAMPLE 1.4 Use the same set of four scores from Example 1.3 and compute $\Sigma(X - 1)$ and $\Sigma(X - 1)^2$. The following computational table will help demonstrate the calculations.

X	$(X - 1)$	$(X - 1)^2$
3	2	4
1	0	0
7	6	36
4	3	9

The first column lists the original scores. A second column lists the $(X - 1)$ values, and a third column shows the $(X - 1)^2$ values.

To compute $\Sigma(X - 1)$, the first step is to perform the operation inside the parentheses. Thus, we begin by subtracting one point from each of the X values. The resulting values are listed in the middle column of the table. The next step is to add the $(X - 1)$ values.

$$\Sigma(X - 1) = 2 + 0 + 6 + 3 + = 11$$

The calculation of $\Sigma(X + 1)^2$ requires three steps. The first step (inside parentheses) is to subtract 1 point from each X value. The results from this step are shown in the middle column of the computational table. The second step is to square each of the

$(X - 1)$ values. The results from this step are shown in the third column of the table. The final step is to add the $(X - 1)^2$ values to obtain

$$\Sigma(X - 1)^2 = 4 + 0 + 36 + 9 = 49$$

Notice that this calculation requires squaring before adding. A common mistake is to add the $(X - 1)$ values and then square the total. Be careful!

EXAMPLE 1.5 In both of the preceding examples, and in many other situations, the summation operation is the last step in the calculation. According to the order of operations, parentheses, exponents, and multiplication all come before summation. However, there are situations in which extra addition and subtraction are completed after the summation. For this example, use the same scores that appeared in the previous two examples, and compute $\Sigma X - 1$.

With no parentheses, exponents, or multiplication, the first step is the summation. Thus, we begin by computing ΣX. Earlier we found $\Sigma X = 15$. The next step is to subtract one point from the total. For these data,

$$\Sigma X - 1 = 15 - 1 = 14$$

EXAMPLE 1.6 For this example, each individual has two scores. The first score is identified as X, and the second score is Y. With the help of the following computational table, compute ΣX, ΣY, and ΣXY.

Person	X	Y	XY
A	3	5	15
B	1	3	3
C	7	4	28
D	4	2	8

To find ΣX, simply add the values in the X column.

$$\Sigma X = 3 + 1 + 7 + 4 = 15$$

Similarly, ΣY is the sum of the Y values.

$$\Sigma Y = 5 + 3 + 4 + 2 = 14$$

To compute ΣXY, the first step is to multiply X times Y for each individual. The resulting products (XY values) are listed in the third column of the table. Finally, we add the products to obtain

$$\Sigma XY = 15 + 3 + 28 + 8 = 54$$

LEARNING CHECK

1. Calculate each value requested for the following scores: 6, 2, 4, 2.
   a. ΣX
   b. ΣX^2
   c. $(\Sigma X)^2$
   d. $\Sigma(X - 2)$
   e. $\Sigma(X - 2)^2$
2. Identify the first step in each of the following calculations.
   a. ΣX^2 b. $(\Sigma X)^2$ c. $\Sigma(X - 2)^2$
3. Use summation notation to express each of the following.
   a. Add 4 points to each score and then add the resulting values.
   b. Add the scores and then square the total.
   c. Square each score, then add the squared values.

ANSWERS

1. a. 14
   b. 60
   c. 196
   d. 6
   e. 20
2. a. Square each score.
   b. Add the scores.
   c. Subtract 2 points from each score.
3. a. $\Sigma(X + 4)$
   b. $(\Sigma X)^2$
   c. ΣX^2

SUMMARY

1. The term *statistics* is used to refer to methods for organizing, summarizing, and interpreting data.
2. Scientific questions usually concern a population, which is the entire set of individuals one wishes to study. Usually, populations are so large that it is impossible to examine every individual, so most research is conducted with samples. A sample is a group selected from a population, usually for purposes of a research study.
3. A characteristic that describes a sample is called a statistic, and a characteristic that describes a population is called a parameter. Although sample statistics are usually representative of corresponding population parameters, there is typically some discrepancy between a statistic and a parameter. The naturally occurring difference between a statistic and a parameter is called sampling error.
4. Statistical methods can be classified into two broad categories: descriptive statistics, which organize and summarize data, and inferential statistics, which use sample data to draw inferences about populations.
5. The correlational method examines relationships between variables by measuring two different variables for each individual. This method allows researchers to measure and describe relationships, but cannot produce a cause-and-effect explanation for the relationship.
6. The experimental method examines relationships between variables by manipulating an independent variable to create different treatment conditions and then measuring a dependent variable to obtain a group of scores in each condition. The groups of scores are then compared. A systematic difference between groups provides evidence that changing the independent variable from one condition to another

also caused a change in the dependent variable. All other variables are controlled to prevent them from influencing the relationship. The intent of the experimental method is to demonstrate a cause-and-effect relationship between variables.

7. Nonexperimental studies also examine relationships between variables by comparing groups of scores, but they do not have the rigor of true experiments and cannot produce cause-and-effect explanations. Instead of manipulating a variable to create different groups, a nonexperimental study uses a preexisting participant characteristic (such as male/female) or the passage of time (before/after) to create the groups being compared.

8. A measurement scale consists of a set of categories that are used to classify individuals. A nominal scale consists of categories that differ only in name and are not differentiated in terms of magnitude or direction. In an ordinal scale, the categories are differentiated in terms of direction, forming an ordered series. An interval scale consists of an ordered series of categories that are all equal-sized intervals. With an interval scale, it is possible to differentiate direction and magnitude (or distance) between categories. Finally, a ratio scale is an interval scale for which the zero point indicates none of the variable being measured. With a ratio scale, ratios of measurements reflect ratios of magnitude.

9. A discrete variable consists of indivisible categories, often whole numbers that vary in countable steps. A continuous variable consists of categories that are infinitely divisible and each score corresponds to an interval on the scale. The boundaries that separate intervals are called real limits and are located exactly halfway between adjacent scores.

10. The letter X is used to represent scores for a variable. If a second variable is used, Y represents its scores. The letter N is used as the symbol for the number of scores in a population; n is the symbol for a number of scores in a sample.

11. The Greek letter sigma (Σ) is used to stand for summation. Therefore, the expression ΣX is read "the sum of the scores." Summation is a mathematical operation (like addition or multiplication) and must be performed in its proper place in the order of operations; summation occurs after parentheses, exponents, and multiplying/dividing have been completed.

KEY TERMS

statistics (5)
population (5)
sample (6)
variable (6)
data (7)
data set (7)
datum (7)
raw score (7)
parameter (7)
statistic (7)
descriptive statistics (7)
inferential statistics (8)
sampling error (8)
correlational method (13)
experimental method (14)
independent variable (16)
dependent variable (16)
control condition (16)
experimental condition (16)
nonequivalent groups study (17)
pre–post study (18)
quasi-independent variable (18)
construct (20)
operational definition (20)
discrete variable (21)
continuous variable (21)
real limits (22)
upper real limit (22)
lower real limit (22)
nominal scale (23)
ordinal scale (23)
interval scale (25)
ratio scale (25)

RESOURCES

Book Companion Website: www.cengage.com/psychology/gravetter

You can find practice quizzes and other learning aids for every chapter in this book on the book companion website, as well as a series of workshops and other resources corresponding to the main topic areas. In the left-hand column are a variety of learning exercises for Chapter 1, including a tutorial quiz. Also in the left-hand column, under

Book Resources, is a link to the workshops. For Chapter 1, there is a workshop that reviews the scales of measurement. To get there, click on the *Workshop* link, then click on *Scales of Measurement*. To find materials for other chapters, begin by selecting the desired chapter at the top of the page. Note that the workshops were not developed specifically for this book but are used by several different books written by different authors. As a result, you may find that some of the notation or terminology is different from that which you learned in this text.

At the end of each chapter we remind you about the Web resources. Again, there is a tutorial quiz for every chapter, and we notify you whenever there is a workshop that is related to the chapter content.

aplia

Improve your understanding of statistics with Aplia's auto-graded problem sets and immediate, detailed explanations for every question. To learn more, visit **www.aplia.com/statistics**.

CENGAGE**brain**.com

Psychology CourseMate brings course concepts to life with interactive learning, study, and exam preparation tools that support the printed textbook. A textbook-specific website, Psychology CourseMate includes an integrated interactive eBook and other interactive learning tools including quizzes, flashcards, and more.

Visit www.cengagebrain.com to access your account and purchase materials.

SPSS

The Statistical Package for the Social Sciences, known as SPSS, is a computer program that performs most of the statistical calculations that are presented in this book, and is commonly available on college and university computer systems. Appendix D contains a general introduction to SPSS. In the Resource section at the end of each chapter for which SPSS is applicable, there are step-by-step instructions for using SPSS to perform the statistical operations presented in the chapter.

FOCUS ON PROBLEM SOLVING

It may help to simplify summation notation if you observe that the summation sign is always followed by a symbol or symbolic expression—for example, ΣX or $\Sigma(X + 3)$. This symbol specifies which values you are to add. If you use the symbol as a column heading and list all the appropriate values in the column, your task is simply to add up the numbers in the column. To find $\Sigma(X + 3)$ for example, start a column headed with $(X + 3)$ next to the column of Xs. List all the $(X + 3)$ values; then find the total for the column.

Often, summation notation is part of a relatively complex mathematical expression that requires several steps of calculation. The series of steps must be performed according to the order of mathematical operations (see page 27). The best procedure is to use a computational table that begins with the original X values listed in the first column. Except for summation, each step in the calculation creates a new column of values. For example, computing $\Sigma(X + 1)^2$ involves three steps and produces a computational table with three columns. The final step is to add the values in the third column (see Example 1.4).

DEMONSTRATION 1.1

SUMMATION NOTATION

A set of scores consists of the following values:

7 3 9 5 4

For these scores, compute each of the following:

ΣX
$(\Sigma X)^2$
ΣX^2
$\Sigma X + 5$
$\Sigma(X - 2)$

Compute ΣX To compute ΣX, we simply add all of the scores in the group.

$$\Sigma X = 7 + 3 + 9 + 5 + 4 = 28$$

Compute $(\Sigma X)^2$ The first step, inside the parentheses, is to compute ΣX. The second step is to square the value for ΣX.

$$\Sigma X = 28 \text{ and } (\Sigma X)^2 = (28)^2 = 784$$

X	X^2
7	49
3	9
9	81
5	25
4	16

Compute ΣX^2 The first step is to square each score. The second step is to add the squared scores. The computational table shows the scores and squared scores. To compute ΣX^2 we add the values in the X^2 column.

$$\Sigma X^2 = 49 + 9 + 81 + 25 + 16 = 180$$

Compute $\Sigma X + 5$ The first step is to compute ΣX. The second step is to add 5 points to the total.

$$\Sigma X = 28 \text{ and } \Sigma X + 5 = 28 + 5 = 33$$

X	$X - 2$
7	5
3	1
9	7
5	3
4	2

Compute $\Sigma(X - 2)$ The first step, inside parentheses, is to subtract 2 points from each score. The second step is to add the resulting values. The computational table shows the scores and the $(X - 2)$ values. To compute $\Sigma(X - 2)$, add the values in the $(X - 2)$ column

$$\Sigma(X - 2) = 5 + 1 + 7 + 3 + 2 = 18$$

PROBLEMS

*1. A researcher is investigating the effectiveness of a treatment for adolescent boys who are taking medication for depression. A group of 30 boys is selected and half receive the new treatment in addition to their medication and the other half continue to take their medication without any treatment. For this study,
   a. Identify the population.
   b. Identify the sample.

2. Judge and Cable (2010) found that thin women had higher incomes than heavier women. Is this an example of an experimental or a nonexperimental study?

3. Statistical methods are classified into two major categories: descriptive and inferential. Describe the general purpose for the statistical methods in each category.

4. A researcher plans to compare two treatment conditions by measuring one sample in treatment 1 and a second sample in treatment 2. The researcher then compares the scores for the two treatments and finds a difference between the two groups.
   a. Briefly explain how the difference may have been caused by the treatments.
   b. Briefly explain how the difference simply may be sampling error.

5. Describe the data for a correlational research study. Explain how these data are different from the data obtained in experimental and nonexperimental studies, which also evaluate relationships between two variables.

6. Describe how the goal of an experimental research study is different from the goal for nonexperimental or correlational research. Identify the two elements that are necessary for an experiment to achieve its goal.

7. Strack, Martin, and Stepper (1988) found that people rated cartoons as funnier when holding a pen in their teeth (which forced them to smile) than when holding a pen in their lips (which forced them to frown). For this study, identify the independent variable and the dependent variable.

8. Define the terms parameter and statistic. Be sure that the concepts of population and sample are included in your definitions.

9. Two researchers are both interested in the relationship between caffeine consumption and activity level for elementary school children. Each obtains a sample of $n = 20$ children.
   a. The first researcher interviews each child to determine the level of caffeine consumption. The researcher then records the level of activity for each child during a 30-minute session on the playground. Is this an experimental or a nonexperimental study? Explain your answer.
   b. The second researcher separates the children into two roughly equivalent groups. The children in one group are given a drink containing 300 mg of caffeine and the other group gets a drink with no caffeine. The researcher then records the level of activity for each child during a 30-minute session on the playground. Is this an experimental or a nonexperimental study? Explain your answer.

10. Oxytocin is a naturally occurring brain chemical that is nicknamed the "love hormone" because it seems to play a role in the formation of social relationships such as mating pairs and parent-child bonding. A recent study demonstrated that oxytocin appears to increase people's tendency to trust others (Kosfeld, Heinrichs, Zak, Fischbacher, and Fehr, 2005). Using an investment game, the study demonstrated that people who inhaled oxytocin were more likely to give their money to a trustee compared to people who inhaled an inactive placebo. For this experimental study, identify the independent variable and the dependent variable.

11. A research study comparing alcohol use for college students in the United States and Canada reports that more Canadian students drink but American students drink more (Kuo, Adlaf, Lee, Gliksman, Demers, and Wechsler, 2002). Is this study an example of an experiment? Explain why or why not.

12. A researcher would like to evaluate the claim that large doses of vitamin C can help prevent the common cold. One group of participants is given a large dose of the vitamin (500 mg per day), and a second group is given a placebo (sugar pill). The researcher records the number of colds each individual experiences during the 3-month winter season.
   a. Identify the dependent variable for this study.
   b. Is the dependent variable discrete or continuous?
   c. What scale of measurement (nominal, ordinal, interval, or ratio) is used to measure the dependent variable?

13. For each of the following, determine whether the variable being measured is discrete or continuous and explain your answer.
   a. Social networking (number of daily minutes on Facebook)
   b. Family size (number of siblings)

*Solutions for odd-numbered problems are provided in Appendix C.

c. Preference between digital or analog watch
d. Number of correct answers on a statistics quiz

14. Four scales of measurement were introduced in this chapter: nominal, ordinal, interval, and ratio.
a. What additional information is obtained from measurements on an ordinal scale compared to measurements on a nominal scale?
b. What additional information is obtained from measurements on an interval scale compared to measurements on an ordinal scale?
c. What additional information is obtained from measurements on a ratio scale compared to measurements on an interval scale?

15. In an experiment examining the effects of humor on memory, Schmidt (1994) showed participants a list of sentences, half of which were humorous and half were nonhumorous. The participants consistently recalled more of the humorous sentences than the nonhumorous sentences.
a. Identify the independent variable for this study.
b. What scale of measurement is used for the independent variable?
c. Identify the dependent variable for this study.
d. What scale of measurement is used for the dependent variable?

16. Explain why *shyness* is a hypothetical construct instead of a concrete variable. Describe how shyness might be measured and defined using an operational definition.

17. Ford and Torok (2008) found that motivational signs were effective in increasing physical activity on a college campus. Signs such as "Step up to a healthier lifestyle" and "An average person burns 10 calories a minute walking up the stairs" were posted by the elevators and stairs in a college building. Students and faculty increased their use of the stairs during times that the signs were posted compared to times when there were no signs.
a. Identify the independent and dependent variables for this study.
b. What scale of measurement is used for the independent variable?

18. For the following scores, find the value of each expression:
a. ΣX
b. ΣX^2
c. $(\Sigma X)^2$
d. $\Sigma(X - 1)$

X
4
2
1
5

19. For the following set of scores, find the value of each expression:
a. ΣX
b. ΣX^2
c. $\Sigma(X + 1)$
d. $\Sigma(X + 1)^2$

X
4
6
0
3
2

20. Use summation notation to express each of the following calculations:
a. Add 1 point to each score, then add the resulting values.
b. Add 1 point to each score and square the result, then add the squared values.
c. Add the scores and square the sum, then subtract 3 points from the squared value.

21. Two scores, X and Y, are recorded for each of $n = 4$ subjects. For these scores, find the value of each expression.
a. ΣX
b. ΣY
c. ΣXY

Subject	X	Y
A	6	4
B	0	10
C	3	8
D	2	3

22. For the following set of scores, find the value of each expression:
a. ΣX
b. ΣX^2
c. $\Sigma(X + 4)$

X
−4
−2
0
−1
−1

23. For the following set of scores, find the value of each expression:
a. ΣX^2
b. $(\Sigma X)^2$
c. $\Sigma(X - 2)$
d. $\Sigma(X - 2)^2$

X
1
0
5
2

CHAPTER

2

Frequency Distributions

Tools You Will Need

The following items are considered essential background material for this chapter. If you doubt your knowledge of any of these items, you should review the appropriate chapter or section before proceeding.

- Proportions (math review, Appendix A)
  - Fractions
  - Decimals
  - Percentages
- Scales of measurement (Chapter 1): Nominal, ordinal, interval, and ratio
- Continuous and discrete variables (Chapter 1)
- Real limits (Chapter 1)

Preview

If at first you don't succeed, you are probably not related to the boss.

Did we make you chuckle or, at least, smile a little? The use of humor is a common technique to capture attention and to communicate ideas. Advertisers, for example, often try to make a commercial funny so that people notice it and, perhaps, remember the product. After-dinner speakers always put a few jokes into the speech in an effort to maintain the audience's interest. Although humor seems to capture our attention, does it actually affect our memory?

In an attempt to answer this question, Stephen Schmidt (1994) conducted a series of experiments examining the effects of humor on memory for sentences. Humorous sentences were collected from a variety of sources and then a nonhumorous version was constructed for each sentence. For example, the nonhumorous version of our opening sentence was:

People who are related to the boss often succeed the very first time.

Participants were then presented with a list containing half humorous and half nonhumorous sentences. Later, each person was asked to recall as many sentences as possible. The researcher measured the number of humorous sentences and the number of nonhumorous sentences recalled by each participant. Data similar to the results obtained by Schmidt are shown in Table 2.1.

TABLE 2.1

Memory scores for a sample of 16 participants. The scores represent the number of sentences recalled from each category.

Humorous Sentences				Nonhumorous Sentences			
4	5	2	4	5	2	4	2
6	7	6	6	2	3	1	6
2	5	4	3	3	2	3	3
1	3	5	5	4	1	5	3

The Problem: It is difficult to see any clear pattern simply by looking at the list of numbers. Can you tell whether the memory scores for one type of sentence are generally higher than those for the other type?

The Solution: A frequency distribution provides an overview of the entire group of scores making it easy to see the general level of performance for each type of sentence. For example, the same memory scores that are shown in Table 2.1 have been organized in a frequency distribution graph in Figure 2.1. In the figure, each individual is represented by a block that is placed above that individual's score. The resulting pile of blocks shows a picture of how the individual scores are distributed. For this example, it is now easy to see that the scores for the humorous sentences are generally higher than the scores for the nonhumorous sentences; on average, participants recalled around 5 humorous sentences but only about 3 of the nonhumorous sentences.

In this chapter we present techniques for organizing data into tables and graphs so that an entire set of scores can be presented in a relatively simple display or illustration.

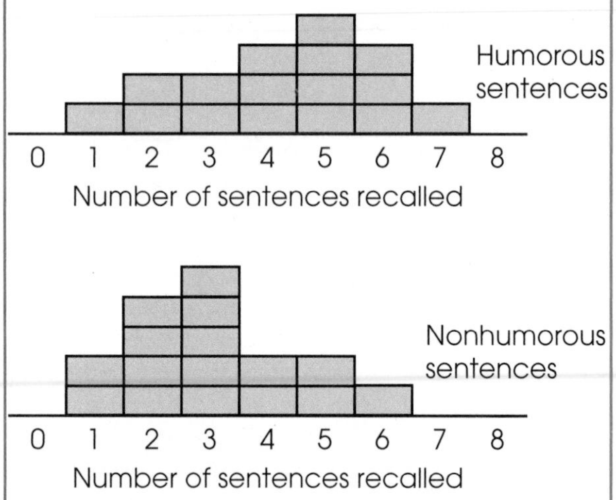

FIGURE 2.1

Hypothetical data showing the number of humorous sentences and the number of nonhumorous sentences recalled by participants in a memory experiment.

2.1 INTRODUCTION TO FREQUENCY DISTRIBUTIONS

The results from a research study usually consist of pages of numbers corresponding to the measurements, or scores, collected during the study. The immediate problem for the researcher is to organize the scores into some comprehensible form so that any patterns in the data can be seen easily and communicated to others. This is the job of descriptive statistics: to simplify the organization and presentation of data. One of the most common procedures for organizing a set of data is to place the scores in a *frequency distribution.*

DEFINITION

A **frequency distribution** is an organized tabulation of the number of individuals located in each category on the scale of measurement.

A frequency distribution takes a disorganized set of scores and places them in order from highest to lowest, grouping together individuals who all have the same score. If the highest score is $X = 10$, for example, the frequency distribution groups together all the 10s, then all the 9s, then the 8s, and so on. Thus, a frequency distribution allows the researcher to see "at a glance" the entire set of scores. It shows whether the scores are generally high or low, whether they are concentrated in one area or spread out across the entire scale, and generally provides an organized picture of the data. In addition to providing a picture of the entire set of scores, a frequency distribution allows you to see the location of any individual score relative to all of the other scores in the set.

A frequency distribution can be structured either as a table or as a graph, but in either case, the distribution presents the same two elements:

1. The set of categories that make up the original measurement scale.
2. A record of the frequency, or number of individuals in each category.

Thus, a frequency distribution presents a picture of how the individual scores are distributed on the measurement scale—hence the name *frequency distribution.*

2.2 FREQUENCY DISTRIBUTION TABLES

It is customary to list categories from highest to lowest, but this is an arbitrary arrangement. Many computer programs list categories from lowest to highest.

The simplest frequency distribution table presents the measurement scale by listing the different measurement categories (X values) in a column from highest to lowest. Beside each X value, we indicate the frequency, or the number of times that particular measurement occurred in the data. It is customary to use an X as the column heading for the scores and an f as the column heading for the frequencies. An example of a frequency distribution table follows.

EXAMPLE 2.1

The following set of $N = 20$ scores was obtained from a 10-point statistics quiz. We organize these scores by constructing a frequency distribution table. Scores:

8, 9, 8, 7, 10, 9, 6, 4, 9, 8,

7, 8, 10, 9, 8, 6, 9, 7, 8, 8

1. The highest score is $X = 10$, and the lowest score is $X = 4$. Therefore, the first column of the table lists the categories that make up the scale of measurement

X	f
10	2
9	5
8	7
7	3
6	2
5	0
4	1

(X values) from 10 down to 4. Notice that all of the possible values are listed in the table. For example, no one had a score of $X = 5$, but this value is included. With an ordinal, interval, or ratio scale, the categories are listed in order (usually highest to lowest). For a nominal scale, the categories can be listed in any order.

2. The frequency associated with each score is recorded in the second column. For example, two people had scores of $X = 10$, so there is a 2 in the f column beside $X = 10$.

Because the table organizes the scores, it is possible to see the general quiz results very quickly. For example, there were only two perfect scores, but most of the class had high grades (8s and 9s). With one exception (the score of $X = 4$), it appears that the class has learned the material fairly well.

Notice that the X values in a frequency distribution table represent the scale of measurement, *not* the actual set of scores. For example, the X column lists the value 10 only one time, but the frequency column indicates that there are actually two values of $X = 10$. Also, the X column lists a value of $X = 5$, but the frequency column indicates that no one actually had a score of $X = 5$.

You also should notice that the frequencies can be used to find the total number of scores in the distribution. By adding up the frequencies, you obtain the total number of individuals:

$$\Sigma f = N$$

OBTAINING ΣX FROM A FREQUENCY DISTRIBUTION TABLE

There may be times when you need to compute the sum of the scores, ΣX, or perform other computations for a set of scores that has been organized into a frequency distribution table. To complete these calculations correctly, you must use all the information presented in the table. That is, it is essential to use the information in the f column as well as the X column to obtain the full set of scores.

When it is necessary to perform calculations for scores that have been organized into a frequency distribution table, the safest procedure is to take the individual scores out of the table before you begin any computations. This process is demonstrated in the following example.

EXAMPLE 2.2

X	f
5	1
4	2
3	3
2	3
1	1

Consider the frequency distribution table shown in the margin. The table shows that the distribution has one 5, two 4s, three 3s, three 2s, and one 1, for a total of 10 scores. If you simply list all 10 scores, you can safely proceed with calculations such as finding ΣX or ΣX^2. For example, to compute ΣX you must add all 10 scores:

$$\Sigma X = 5 + 4 + 4 + 3 + 3 + 3 + 2 + 2 + 2 + 1$$

For the distribution in this table, you should obtain $\Sigma X = 29$. Try it yourself. Similarly, to compute ΣX^2 you square each of the 10 scores and then add the squared values.

$$\Sigma X^2 = 5^2 + 4^2 + 4^2 + 3^2 + 3^2 + 3^2 + 2^2 + 2^2 + 2^2 + 1^2$$

This time you should obtain $\Sigma X^2 = 97$.

An alternative way to get ΣX from a frequency distribution table is to multiply each X value by its frequency and then add these products. This sum may be expressed in symbols as ΣfX. The computation is summarized as follows for the data in Example 2.2:

Caution: Doing calculations within the table works well for ΣX but can lead to errors for more complex formulas.

X	f	fX	
5	1	5	(the one 5 totals 5)
4	2	8	(the two 4s total 8)
3	3	9	(the three 3s total 9)
2	3	6	(the three 2s total 6)
1	1	1	(the one 1 totals 1)
		$\Sigma X = 29$	

No matter which method you use to find ΣX, the important point is that you must use the information given in the frequency column in addition to the information in the X column.

PROPORTIONS AND PERCENTAGES

In addition to the two basic columns of a frequency distribution, there are other measures that describe the distribution of scores and can be incorporated into the table. The two most common are proportion and percentage.

Proportion measures the fraction of the total group that is associated with each score. In Example 2.2, there were two individuals with $X = 4$. Thus, 2 out of 10 people had $X = 4$, so the proportion would be $\frac{2}{10} = 0.20$. In general, the proportion associated with each score is

$$\text{proportion} = p = \frac{f}{N}$$

Because proportions describe the frequency (f) in relation to the total number (N), they often are called *relative frequencies.* Although proportions can be expressed as fractions (for example, $\frac{2}{10}$), they more commonly appear as decimals. A column of proportions, headed with a p, can be added to the basic frequency distribution table (see Example 2.3).

In addition to using frequencies (f) and proportions (p), researchers often describe a distribution of scores with percentages. For example, an instructor might describe the results of an exam by saying that 15% of the class earned *A*s, 23% earned *B*s, and so on. To compute the percentage associated with each score, you first find the proportion (p) and then multiply by 100:

$$\text{percentage} = p(100) = \frac{f}{N}(100)$$

Percentages can be included in a frequency distribution table by adding a column headed with % (see Example 2.3).

EXAMPLE 2.3

The frequency distribution table from Example 2.2 is repeated here. This time we have added columns showing the proportion (p) and the percentage (%) associated with each score.

X	f	$p = f/N$	$\% = p(100)$
5	1	1/10 = 0.10	10%
4	2	2/10 = 0.20	20%
3	3	3/10 = 0.30	30%
2	3	3/10 = 0.30	30%
1	1	1/10 = 0.10	10%

LEARNING CHECK

1. Construct a frequency distribution table for the following set of scores.

Scores: 3, 2, 3, 2, 4, 1, 3, 3, 5

2. Find each of the following values for the sample in the following frequency distribution table.

a. n
b. ΣX
c. ΣX^2

X	f
5	1
4	2
3	2
2	4
1	1

ANSWERS

1.

X	f
5	1
4	1
3	4
2	2
1	1

2. **a.** $n = 10$ **b.** $\Sigma X = 28$ **c.** $\Sigma X^2 = 92$ (square then add all 10 scores)

GROUPED FREQUENCY DISTRIBUTION TABLES

When a set of data covers a wide range of values, it is unreasonable to list all the individual scores in a frequency distribution table. Consider, for example, a set of exam scores that range from a low of $X = 41$ to a high of $X = 96$. These scores cover a *range* of more than 50 points.

When the scores are whole numbers, the total number of rows for a regular table can be obtained by finding the difference between the highest and the lowest scores and adding 1:

rows = highest − lowest + 1

If we were to list all of the individual scores from $X = 96$ down to $X = 41$, it would take 56 rows to complete the frequency distribution table. Although this would organize the data, the table would be long and cumbersome. Remember: The purpose for constructing a table is to obtain a relatively simple, organized picture of the data. This can be accomplished by grouping the scores into intervals and then listing the intervals in the table instead of listing each individual score. For example, we could construct a table showing the number of students who had scores in the 90s, the number with scores in the 80s, and so on. The result is called a *grouped frequency distribution table* because we are presenting groups of scores rather than individual values. The groups, or intervals, are called *class intervals*.

There are several guidelines that help guide you in the construction of a grouped frequency distribution table. Note that these are simply guidelines, rather than absolute requirements, but they do help produce a simple, well-organized, and easily understood table.

GUIDELINE 1

The grouped frequency distribution table should have about 10 class intervals. If a table has many more than 10 intervals, it becomes cumbersome and defeats the purpose of a frequency distribution table. On the other hand, if you have too few intervals, you begin to lose information about the distribution of the scores. At the extreme, with only one interval, the table would not tell you anything about how the scores are distributed. Remember that the purpose of a frequency distribution is to help a researcher see the data. With too few or too many intervals, the table will not provide a clear picture. You should note that 10 intervals is a general guide. If you are constructing a table on a blackboard, for example, you probably want only 5 or 6 intervals. If the table is to be printed in a scientific report, you may want 12 or 15 intervals. In each case, your goal is to present a table that is relatively easy to see and understand.

GUIDELINE 2 The width of each interval should be a relatively simple number. For example, 2, 5, 10, or 20 would be a good choice for the interval width. Notice that it is easy to count by 5s or 10s. These numbers are easy to understand and make it possible for someone to see quickly how you have divided the range of scores.

GUIDELINE 3 The bottom score in each class interval should be a multiple of the width. If you are using a width of 10 points, for example, the intervals should start with 10, 20, 30, 40, and so on. Again, this makes it easier for someone to understand how the table has been constructed.

GUIDELINE 4 All intervals should be the same width. They should cover the range of scores completely with no gaps and no overlaps, so that any particular score belongs in exactly one interval.

The application of these rules is demonstrated in Example 2.4.

EXAMPLE 2.4 An instructor has obtained the set of $N = 25$ exam scores shown here. To help organize these scores, we will place them in a frequency distribution table. The scores are:

82, 75, 88, 93, 53, 84, 87, 58, 72, 94, 69, 84, 61,
91, 64, 87, 84, 70, 76, 89, 75, 80, 73, 78, 60

Remember, when the scores are whole numbers, the number of rows is determined by

highest – lowest + 1

The first step is to determine the range of scores. For these data, the smallest score is $X = 53$ and the largest score is $X = 94$, so a total of 42 rows would be needed for a table that lists each individual score. Because 42 rows would not provide a simple table, we have to group the scores into class intervals.

The best method for finding a good interval width is a systematic trial-and-error approach that uses guidelines 1 and 2 simultaneously. Specifically, we want about 10 intervals and we want the interval width to be a simple number. For this example, the scores cover a range of 42 points, so we will try several different interval widths to see how many intervals are needed to cover this range. For example, if each interval is 2 points wide, it would take 21 intervals to cover a range of 42 points. This is too many, so we move on to an interval width of 5 or 10 points. The following table shows how many intervals would be needed for these possible widths:

Because the bottom interval usually extends below the lowest score and the top interval extends beyond the highest score, you often need slightly more than the computed number of intervals.

Width	Number of Intervals Needed to Cover a Range of 42 Points	
2	21	(too many)
5	9	(OK)
10	5	(too few)

Notice that an interval width of 5 will result in about 10 intervals, which is exactly what we want.

The next step is to actually identify the intervals. The lowest score for these data is $X = 53$, so the lowest interval should contain this value. Because the interval should have a multiple of 5 as its bottom score, the interval should begin at 50. The interval has a width of 5, so it should contain 5 values: 50, 51, 52, 53, and 54. Thus, the bottom interval is 50–54. The next interval would start at 55 and go to 59. Note that this interval also has a bottom score that is a multiple of 5, and contains exactly 5 scores (55, 56, 57, 58, and 59). The complete frequency distribution table showing all of the class intervals is presented in Table 2.2.

Once the class intervals are listed, you complete the table by adding a column of frequencies. The values in the frequency column indicate the number of individuals who have scores located in that class interval. For this example, there were three students with scores in the 60–64 interval, so the frequency for this class interval is $f = 3$ (see Table 2.2). The basic table can be extended by adding columns showing the proportion and percentage associated with each class interval.

Finally, you should note that after the scores have been placed in a grouped table, you lose information about the specific value for any individual score. For example, Table 2.2 shows that one person had a score between 65 and 69, but the table does not identify the exact value for the score. In general, the wider the class intervals are, the more information is lost. In Table 2.2 the interval width is 5 points, and the table shows that there are three people with scores in the lower 60s and one person with a score in the upper 60s. This information would be lost if the interval width were increased to 10 points. With an interval width of 10, all of the 60s would be grouped together into one interval labeled 60–69. The table would show a frequency of four people in the 60–69 interval, but it would not tell whether the scores were in the upper 60s or the lower 60s.

REAL LIMITS AND FREQUENCY DISTRIBUTIONS

Recall from Chapter 1 that a continuous variable has an infinite number of possible values and can be represented by a number line that is continuous and contains an infinite number of points. However, when a continuous variable is measured, the resulting measurements correspond to *intervals* on the number line rather than single points. If you are measuring time in seconds, for example, a score of $X = 8$ seconds actually represents an interval bounded by the real limits 7.5 seconds and 8.5 seconds. Thus, a frequency distribution table showing a frequency of $f = 3$ individuals all assigned a score of $X = 8$ does not mean that all three individuals had exactly the same measurement. Instead, you should realize that the three measurements are simply located in the same interval between 7.5 and 8.5.

The concept of real limits also applies to the class intervals of a grouped frequency distribution table. For example, a class interval of 40–49 contains scores from $X = 40$ to $X = 49$. These values are called the *apparent limits* of the interval because it appears

TABLE 2.2

This grouped frequency distribution table shows the data from Example 2.4. The original scores range from a high of $X = 94$ to a low of $X = 53$. This range has been divided into 9 intervals with each interval exactly 5 points wide. The frequency column (f) lists the number of individuals with scores in each of the class intervals.

X	f
90–94	3
85–89	4
80–84	5
75–79	4
70–74	3
65–69	1
60–64	3
55–59	1
50–54	1

that they form the upper and lower boundaries for the class interval. If you are measuring a continuous variable, however, a score of $X = 40$ is actually an interval from 39.5 to 40.5. Similarly, $X = 49$ is an interval from 48.5 to 49.5. Therefore, the real limits of the interval are 39.5 (the lower real limit) and 49.5 (the upper real limit). Notice that the next higher class interval is 50–59, which has a lower real limit of 49.5. Thus, the two intervals meet at the real limit 49.5, so there are no gaps in the scale. You also should notice that the width of each class interval becomes easier to understand when you consider the real limits of an interval. For example, the interval 50–59 has real limits of 49.5 and 59.5. The distance between these two real limits (10 points) is the width of the interval.

LEARNING CHECK

1. For each of the following situations, determine what interval width is most appropriate for a grouped frequency distribution and identify the apparent limits of the bottom interval.
   a. Scores range from $X = 7$ to $X = 21$.
   b. Scores range from $X = 52$ to $X = 98$.
   c. Scores range from $X = 16$ to $X = 93$.
2. Using only the frequency distribution table presented in Table 2.2, how many individuals had a score of $X = 73$?

ANSWERS

1. **a.** A width of 2 points would require 8 intervals. Bottom interval is 6−7.
   b. A width of 5 points would require 10 intervals. Bottom interval is 50−54.
   c. A width of 10 points would require 9 intervals. Bottom interval is 10−19.
3. After a set of scores has been summarized in a grouped table, you cannot determine the frequency for any specific score. There is no way to determine how many individuals had $X = 73$ from the table alone. (You can say that *at most* three people had $X = 73$.)

2.3 FREQUENCY DISTRIBUTION GRAPHS

A frequency distribution graph is basically a picture of the information available in a frequency distribution table. We consider several different types of graphs, but all start with two perpendicular lines called *axes*. The horizontal line is the X-axis, or the abscissa (ab-SIS-uh). The vertical line is the Y-axis, or the ordinate. The measurement scale (set of X values) is listed along the X-axis with values increasing from left to right. The frequencies are listed on the Y-axis with values increasing from bottom to top. As a general rule, the point where the two axes intersect should have a value of zero for both the scores and the frequencies. A final general rule is that the graph should be constructed so that its height (Y-axis) is approximately two-thirds to three-quarters of its length (X-axis). Violating these guidelines can result in graphs that give a misleading picture of the data (see Box 2.1).

GRAPHS FOR INTERVAL OR RATIO DATA

When the data consist of numerical scores that have been measured on an interval or ratio scale, there are two options for constructing a frequency distribution graph. The two types of graphs are called *histograms* and *polygons.*

Histograms To construct a histogram, you first list the numerical scores (the categories of measurement) along the *X*-axis. Then you draw a bar above each *X* value so that

a. The height of the bar corresponds to the frequency for that category.

b. For continuous variables, the width of the bar extends to the real limits of the category. For discrete variables, each bar extends exactly half the distance to the adjacent category on each side.

For both continuous and discrete variables, each bar in a histogram extends to the midpoint between adjacent categories. As a result, adjacent bars touch and there are no spaces or gaps between bars. An example of a histogram is shown in Figure 2.2.

When data have been grouped into class intervals, you can construct a frequency distribution histogram by drawing a bar above each interval so that the width of the bar extends exactly half the distance to the adjacent category on each side. This process is demonstrated in Figure 2.3.

For the two histograms shown in Figures 2.2 and 2.3, notice that the values on both the vertical and horizontal axes are clearly marked and that both axes are labeled. Also note that, whenever possible, the units of measurement are specified; for example, Figure 2.3 shows a distribution of heights measured in inches. Finally, notice that the horizontal axis in Figure 2.3 does not list all of the possible heights starting from zero and going up to 48 inches. Instead, the graph clearly shows a break between zero and 30, indicating that some scores have been omitted.

A modified histogram A slight modification to the traditional histogram produces a very easy to draw and simple to understand sketch of a frequency distribution. Instead

FIGURE 2.2

An example of a frequency distribution histogram. The same set of quiz scores is presented in a frequency distribution table and in a histogram.

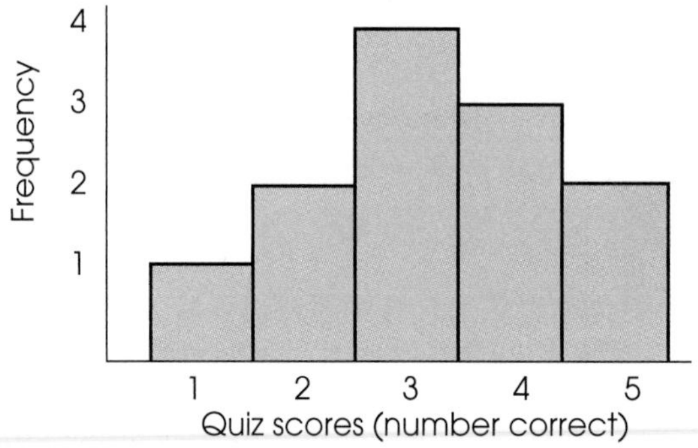

X	*f*
5	2
4	3
3	4
2	2
1	1

FIGURE 2.3

An example of a frequency distribution histogram for grouped data. The same set of children's heights is presented in a frequency distribution table and in a histogram.

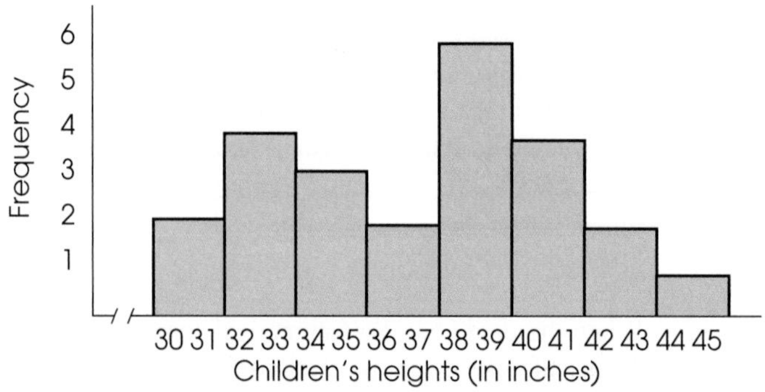

X	*f*
44–45	1
42–43	2
40–41	4
38–39	6
36–37	2
34–35	3
32–33	4
30–31	2

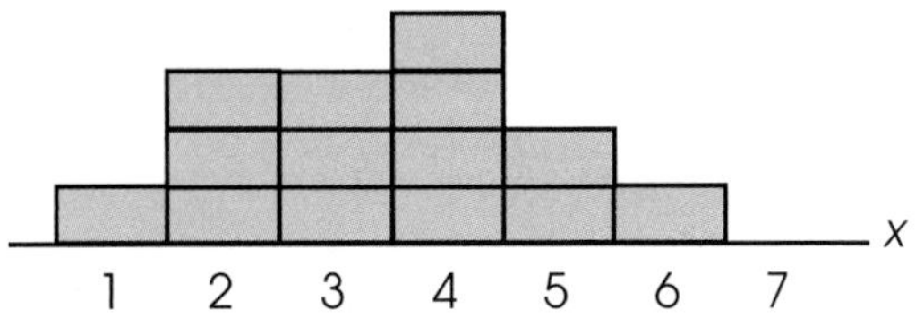

FIGURE 2.4
A frequency distribution in which each individual is represented by a block placed directly above the individual's score. For example, three people had scores of $X = 2$.

of drawing a bar above each score, the modification consists of drawing a stack of blocks. Each block represents one individual, so the number of blocks above each score corresponds to the frequency for that score. An example is shown in Figure 2.4.

Note that the number of blocks in each stack makes it very easy to see the absolute frequency for each category. In addition, it is easy to see the exact difference in frequency from one category to another. In Figure 2.4, for example, there are exactly two more people with scores of $X = 2$ than with scores of $X = 1$. Because the frequencies are clearly displayed by the number of blocks, this type of display eliminates the need for a vertical line (the Y-axis) showing frequencies. In general, this kind of graph provides a simple and concrete picture of the distribution for a sample of scores. Note that we often use this kind of graph to show sample data throughout the rest of the book. You should also note, however, that this kind of display simply provides a sketch of the distribution and is not a substitute for an accurately drawn histogram with two labeled axes.

Polygons The second option for graphing a distribution of numerical scores from an interval or ratio scale of measurement is called a polygon. To construct a polygon, you begin by listing the numerical scores (the categories of measurement) along the X-axis. Then,

a. A dot is centered above each score so that the vertical position of the dot corresponds to the frequency for the category.

b. A continuous line is drawn from dot to dot to connect the series of dots.

c. The graph is completed by drawing a line down to the X-axis (zero frequency) at each end of the range of scores. The final lines are usually drawn so that they reach the X-axis at a point that is one category below the lowest score on the left side and one category above the highest score on the right side. An example of a polygon is shown in Figure 2.5.

A polygon also can be used with data that have been grouped into class intervals. For a grouped distribution, you position each dot directly above the midpoint of the class interval. The midpoint can be found by averaging the highest and the lowest scores in the interval. For example, a class interval that is listed as 20–29 would have a midpoint of 24.5.

$$\text{midpoint} = \frac{20+29}{2} = \frac{49}{2} = 24.5$$

An example of a frequency distribution polygon with grouped data is shown in Figure 2.6.

GRAPHS FOR NOMINAL OR ORDINAL DATA

When the scores are measured on a nominal or ordinal scale (usually non-numerical values), the frequency distribution can be displayed in a *bar graph.*

FIGURE 2.5

An example of a frequency distribution polygon. The same set of data is presented in a frequency distribution table and in a polygon.

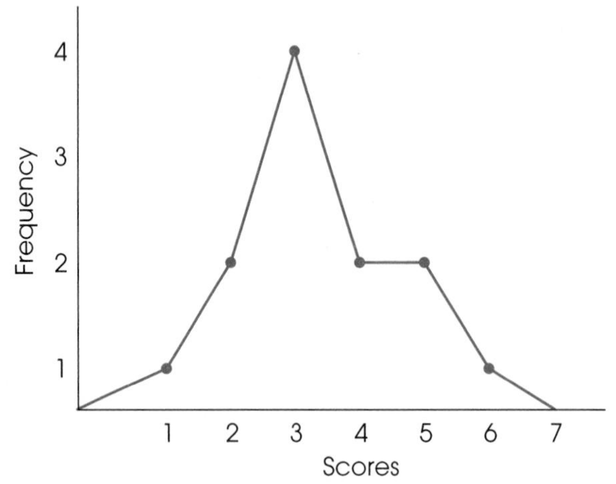

X	f
6	1
5	2
4	2
3	4
2	2
1	1

FIGURE 2.6

An example of a frequency distribution polygon for grouped data. The same set of data is presented in a grouped frequency distribution table and in a polygon.

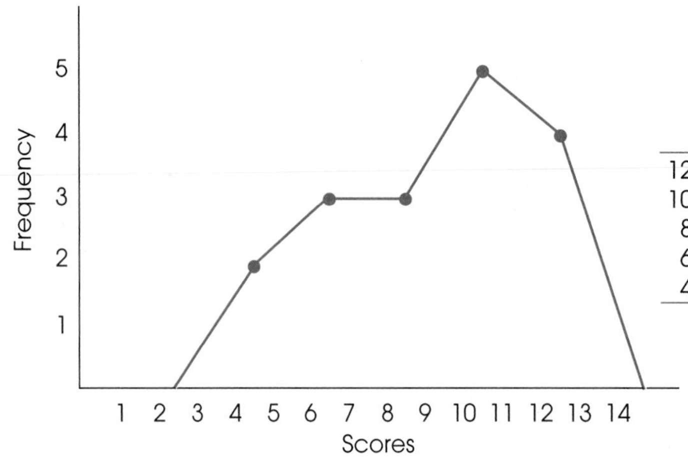

X	f
12–13	4
10–11	5
8–9	3
6–7	3
4–5	2

Bar graphs A bar graph is essentially the same as a histogram, except that spaces are left between adjacent bars. For a nominal scale, the space between bars emphasizes that the scale consists of separate, distinct categories. For ordinal scales, separate bars are used because you cannot assume that the categories are all the same size.

To construct a bar graph, list the categories of measurement along the X-axis and then draw a bar above each category so that the height of the bar equals the frequency for the category. An example of a bar graph is shown in Figure 2.7.

GRAPHS FOR POPULATION DISTRIBUTIONS

When you can obtain an exact frequency for each score in a population, you can construct frequency distribution graphs that are exactly the same as the histograms, polygons, and bar graphs that are typically used for samples. For example, if a population is defined as a specific group of $N = 50$ people, we could easily determine how many have IQs of $X = 110$. However, if we are interested in the entire population of adults

FIGURE 2.7

A bar graph showing the distribution of personality types in a sample of college students. Because personality type is a discrete variable measured on a nominal scale, the graph is drawn with space between the bars.

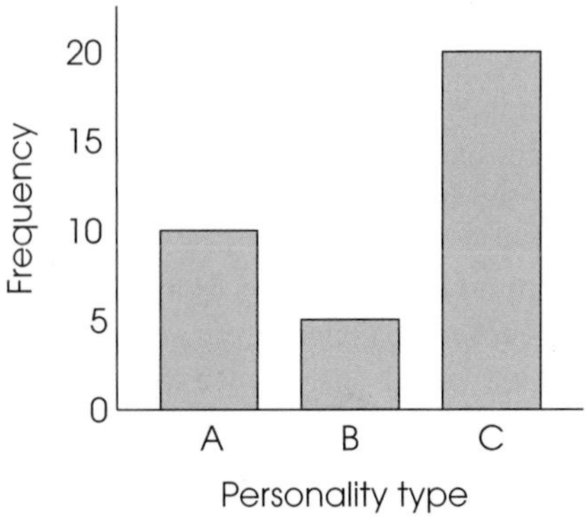

in the United States, it would be impossible to obtain an exact count of the number of people with an IQ of 110. Although it is still possible to construct graphs showing frequency distributions for extremely large populations, the graphs usually involve two special features: relative frequencies and smooth curves.

Relative frequencies Although you usually cannot find the absolute frequency for each score in a population, you very often can obtain *relative frequencies.* For example, you may not know exactly how many fish are in the lake, but after years of fishing you do know that there are twice as many bluegill as there are bass. You can represent these relative frequencies in a bar graph by making the bar above bluegill two times taller than the bar above bass (Figure 2.8). Notice that the graph does not show the absolute number of fish. Instead, it shows the relative number of bluegill and bass.

Smooth curves When a population consists of numerical scores from an interval or a ratio scale, it is customary to draw the distribution with a smooth curve instead of the jagged, step-wise shapes that occur with histograms and polygons. The smooth curve indicates that you are not connecting a series of dots (real frequencies) but instead are showing the relative changes that occur from one score to the next. One commonly occurring population distribution is the normal curve. The word *normal* refers to a specific shape that can be precisely defined by an equation. Less precisely, we can describe

FIGURE 2.8

A frequency distribution showing the relative frequency for two types of fish. Notice that the exact number of fish is not reported; the graph simply says that there are twice as many bluegill as there are bass.

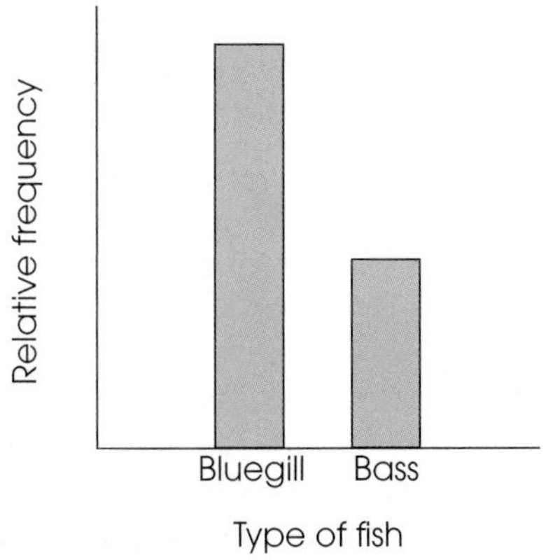

a normal distribution as being symmetrical, with the greatest frequency in the middle and relatively smaller frequencies as you move toward either extreme. A good example of a normal distribution is the population distribution for IQ scores shown in Figure 2.9. Because normal-shaped distributions occur commonly and because this shape is mathematically guaranteed in certain situations, we give it extensive attention throughout this book.

In the future, we will be referring to *distributions of scores*. Whenever the term *distribution* appears, you should conjure up an image of a frequency distribution graph. The graph provides a picture showing exactly where the individual scores are located. To make this concept more concrete, you might find it useful to think of the graph as showing a pile of individuals just like we showed a pile of blocks in Figure 2.4. For the population of IQ scores shown in Figure 2.9, the pile is highest at an IQ score around 100 because most people have average IQs. There are only a few individuals piled up at an IQ of 130; it must be lonely at the top.

2.4 THE SHAPE OF A FREQUENCY DISTRIBUTION

Rather than drawing a complete frequency distribution graph, researchers often simply describe a distribution by listing its characteristics. There are three characteristics that completely describe any distribution: shape, central tendency, and variability. In simple terms, central tendency measures where the center of the distribution is located. Variability tells whether the scores are spread over a wide range or are clustered together. Central tendency and variability will be covered in detail in Chapters 3 and 4. Technically, the shape of a distribution is defined by an equation that prescribes the exact relationship between each X and Y value on the graph. However, we rely on a few less-precise terms that serve to describe the shape of most distributions.

Nearly all distributions can be classified as being either *symmetrical* or *skewed*.

DEFINITIONS

In a **symmetrical distribution**, it is possible to draw a vertical line through the middle so that one side of the distribution is a mirror image of the other (Figure 2.11).

In a **skewed distribution**, the scores tend to pile up toward one end of the scale and taper off gradually at the other end (see Figure 2.11).

FIGURE 2.9

The population distribution of IQ scores: an example of a normal distribution.

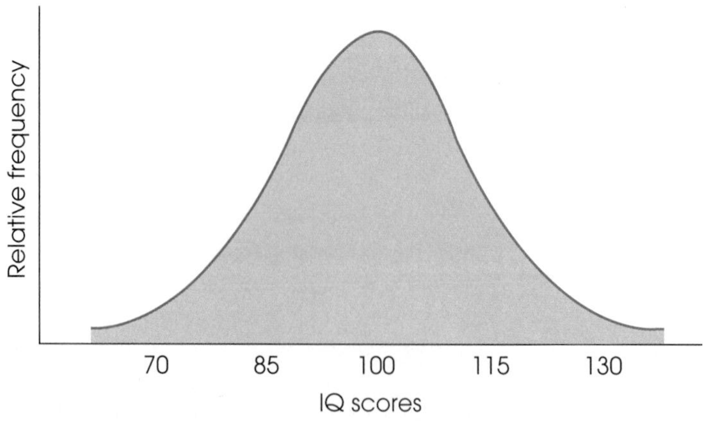

BOX 2.1 THE USE AND MISUSE OF GRAPHS

Although graphs are intended to provide an accurate picture of a set of data, they can be used to exaggerate or misrepresent a set of scores. These misrepresentations generally result from failing to follow the basic rules for graph construction. The following example demonstrates how the same set of data can be presented in two entirely different ways by manipulating the structure of a graph.

For the past several years, the city has kept records of the number of homicides. The data are summarized as follows:

Year	Number of Homicides
2007	42
2008	44
2009	47
2010	49

These data are shown in two different graphs in Figure 2.10. In the first graph, we have exaggerated the height and started numbering the *Y*-axis at 40 rather than at zero. As a result, the graph seems to indicate a rapid rise in the number of homicides over the 4-year period. In the second graph, we have stretched out the *X*-axis and used zero as the starting point for the *Y*-axis. The result is a graph that shows little change in the homicide rate over the 4-year period.

Which graph is correct? The answer is that neither one is very good. Remember that the purpose of a graph is to provide an accurate display of the data. The first graph in Figure 2.10 exaggerates the differences between years, and the second graph conceals the differences. Some compromise is needed. Also note that in some cases a graph may not be the best way to display information. For these data, for example, showing the numbers in a table would be better than either graph.

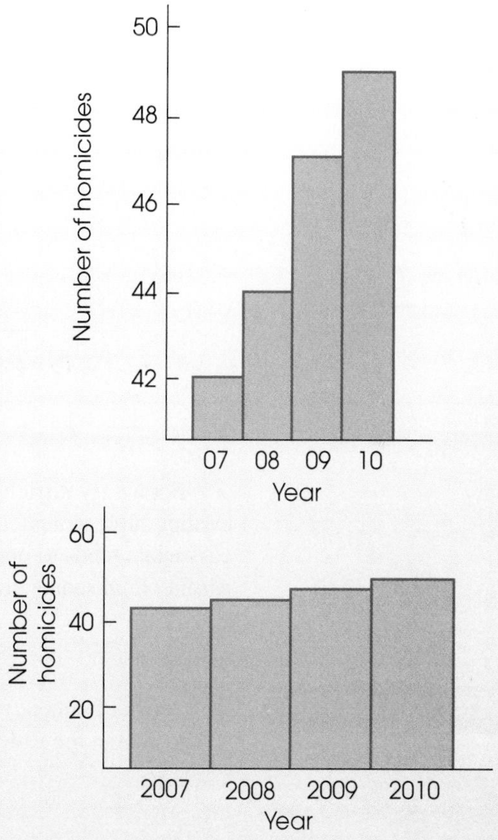

FIGURE 2.10

Two graphs showing the number of homicides in a city over a 4-year period. Both graphs show exactly the same data. However, the first graph gives the appearance that the homicide rate is high and rising rapidly. The second graph gives the impression that homicides rate is low and has not changed over the 4-year period.

The section where the scores taper off toward one end of a distribution is called the **tail** of the distribution.

A skewed distribution with the tail on the right-hand side is **positively skewed** because the tail points toward the positive (above-zero) end of the *X*-axis. If the tail points to the left, the distribution is **negatively skewed** (see Figure 2.11).

FIGURE 2.11
Examples of different shapes for distributions.

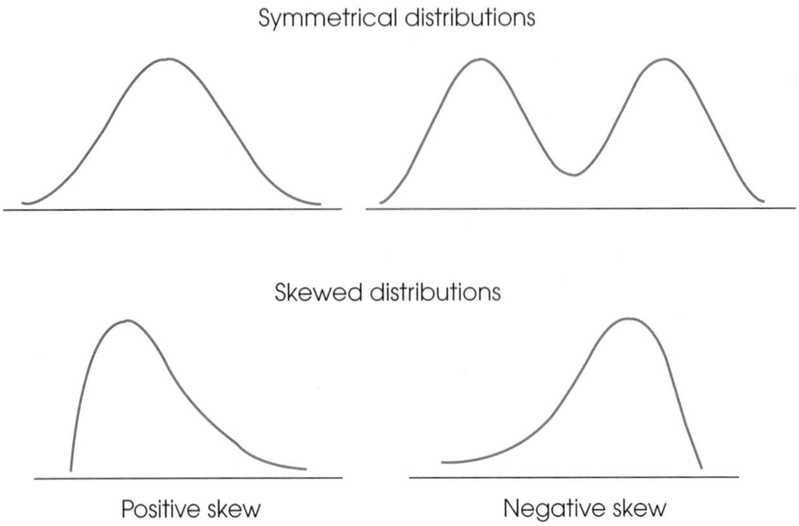

For a very difficult exam, most scores tend to be low, with only a few individuals earning high scores. This produces a positively skewed distribution. Similarly, a very easy exam tends to produce a negatively skewed distribution, with most of the students earning high scores and only a few with low values.

LEARNING CHECK

1. Sketch a frequency distribution histogram and a frequency distribution polygon for the data in the following table:

X	f
5	4
4	6
3	3
2	1
1	1

2. Describe the shape of the distribution in Exercise 1.
3. A researcher records the gender and academic major for each student at a college basketball game. If the distribution of majors is shown in a frequency distribution graph, what type of graph should be used?
4. If the results from a research study are presented in a frequency distribution histogram, would it also be appropriate to show the same results in a polygon? Explain your answer.
5. A college reports that the youngest registered student is 17 years old, and 20% of the registered students are older than 25. What is the shape of the distribution of ages for registered students?

ANSWERS

1. The graphs are shown in Figure 2.12.
2. The distribution is negatively skewed.
3. A bar graph is used for nominal data.
4. Yes. Histograms and polygons are both used for data from interval or ratio scales.
5. It is positively skewed with most of the distribution around 17–21 and a few scores scattered at 25 and higher.

2.5 PERCENTILES, PERCENTILE RANKS, AND INTERPOLATION

Although the primary purpose of a frequency distribution is to provide a description of an entire set of scores, it also can be used to describe the position of an individual within the set. Individual scores, or X values, are called *raw scores*. By themselves, raw scores do not provide much information. For example, if you are told that your score on an exam is $X = 43$, you cannot tell how well you did relative to other students in the class. To evaluate your score, you need more information, such as the average score or the number of people who had scores above and below you. With this additional information, you would be able to determine your relative position in the class. Because raw scores do not provide much information, it is desirable to transform them into a more meaningful form. One transformation that we consider changes raw scores into *percentiles*.

DEFINITIONS

The **rank** or **percentile rank** of a particular score is defined as the percentage of individuals in the distribution with scores equal to or less than the particular value.

When a score is identified by its percentile rank, the score is called a **percentile**.

Suppose, for example, that you have a score of $X = 43$ on an exam and that you know that exactly 60% of the class had scores of 43 or lower. Then your score $X = 43$ has a percentile rank of 60%, and your score would be called the 60th percentile. Notice that *percentile rank* refers to a percentage and that *percentile* refers to a score. Also notice that your rank or percentile describes your exact position within the distribution.

FIGURE 2.12
Answer to the Learning Check Exercise 1.

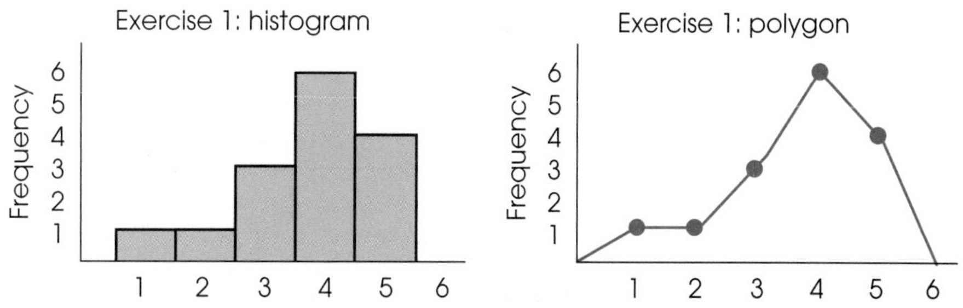

CUMULATIVE FREQUENCY AND CUMULATIVE PERCENTAGE

To determine percentiles or percentile ranks, the first step is to find the number of individuals who are located at or below each point in the distribution. This can be done most easily with a frequency distribution table by simply counting the number who are in or below each category on the scale. The resulting values are called *cumulative frequencies* because they represent the accumulation of individuals as you move up the scale.

EXAMPLE 2.5

In the following frequency distribution table, we have included a cumulative frequency column headed by *cf*. For each row, the cumulative frequency value is obtained by adding up the frequencies in and below that category. For example, the score $X = 3$ has a cumulative frequency of 14 because exactly 14 individuals had scores of $X = 3$ or less.

X	*f*	*cf*
5	1	20
4	5	19
3	8	14
2	4	6
1	2	2

The cumulative frequencies show the number of individuals located at or below each score. To find percentiles, we must convert these frequencies into percentages. The resulting values are called *cumulative percentages* because they show the percentage of individuals who are accumulated as you move up the scale.

EXAMPLE 2.6

This time we have added a cumulative percentage column (c%) to the frequency distribution table from Example 2.5. The values in this column represent the percentage of individuals who are located in and below each category. For example, 70% of the individuals (14 out of 20) had scores of $X = 3$ or lower. Cumulative percentages can be computed by

$$c\% = \frac{cf}{N}(100\%)$$

X	*f*	*cf*	c%
5	1	20	100%
4	5	19	95%
3	8	14	70%
2	4	6	30%
1	2	2	10%

The cumulative percentages in a frequency distribution table give the percentage of individuals with scores at or below each *X* value. However, you must remember that the *X* values in the table are usually measurements of a continuous variable and, therefore, represent intervals on the scale of measurement (see page 22). A score of $X = 2$, for example, means that the measurement was somewhere between the real limits of 1.5 and 2.5. Thus, when a table shows that a score of $X = 2$ has a cumulative percentage of 30%, you should interpret this as meaning that 30% of the individuals have been accumulated by the time you reach the top of the interval for $X = 2$. Notice that each cumulative percentage value is associated with the upper real limit of its interval. This point is demonstrated in Figure 2.13, which shows the same data that were used in Example 2.6. Figure 2.13 shows that two people, or 10%, had scores of $X = 1$; that is, two people had scores between 0.5 and 1.5. You cannot be sure that both individuals have been accumulated until you reach 1.5, the upper real limit of the interval. Similarly, a cumulative percentage of 30% is reached at 2.5 on the scale, a percentage of 70% is reached at 3.5, and so on.

INTERPOLATION

It is possible to determine some percentiles and percentile ranks directly from a frequency distribution table, provided that the percentiles are upper real limits and the ranks are percentages that appear in the table. Using the table in Example 2.6, for example, you should be able to answer the following questions:

1. What is the 95th percentile? (Answer: $X = 4.5$.)
2. What is the percentile rank for $X = 3.5$? (Answer: 70%.)

However, there are many values that do not appear directly in the table, and it is impossible to determine these values precisely. Referring to the table in Example 2.6 again,

1. What is the 50th percentile?
2. What is the percentile rank for $X = 4$?

Because these values are not specifically reported in the table, you cannot answer the questions. However, it is possible to estimate these intermediate values by using a standard procedure known as *interpolation.*

Before we apply the process of interpolation to percentiles and percentile ranks, we use a simple, commonsense example to introduce this method. Suppose that Bob walks

FIGURE 2.13
The relationship between cumulative frequencies (*cf* values) and upper real limits. Notice that two people have scores of $X = 1$. These two individuals are located between the real limits of 0.5 and 1.5. Although their exact locations are not known, you can be certain that both had scores below the upper limit of 1.

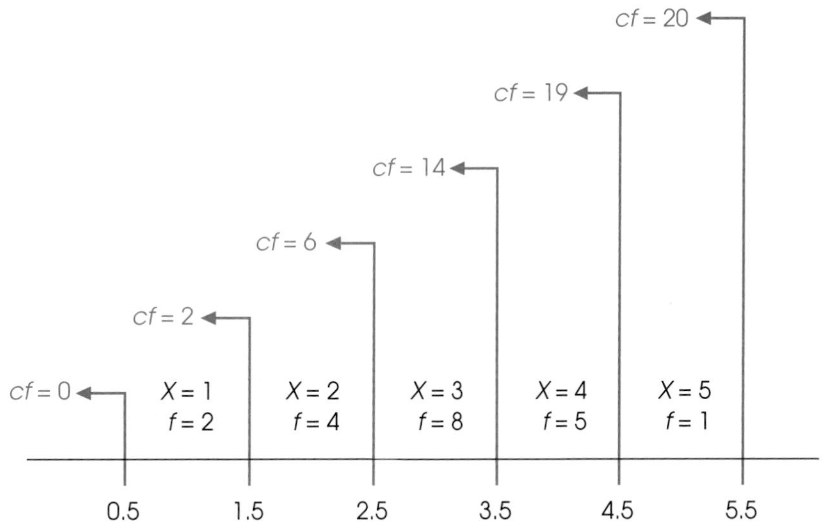

to work each day. The total distance is 2 miles and the trip takes Bob 40 minutes. What is your estimate of how far Bob has walked after 20 minutes? To help, we have created a table showing the time and distance for the start and finish of Bob's trip.

	Time	Distance
Start	0	0
Finish	40	2

If you estimated that Bob walked 1 mile in 20 minutes, you have done interpolation. You probably went through the following logical steps:

1. The total time is 40 minutes.
2. 20 minutes represents half of the total time.
3. Assuming that Bob walks at a steady pace, he should walk half of the total distance in half of the total time.
4. The total distance is 2 miles and half of the total distance is 1.

The process of interpolation is pictured in Figure 2.14. In the figure, the top line shows the time for Bob's walk, from 0 to 40 minutes, and the bottom line shows the time, from 0 to 2 miles. The middle line shows different fractions along the way. Using the figure, try answering the following questions about time and distance.

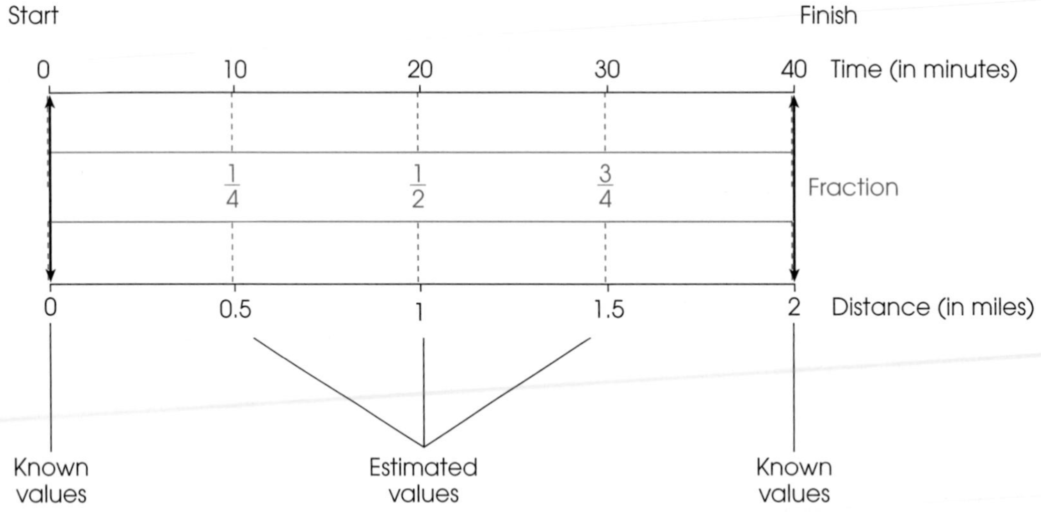

FIGURE 2.14

A graphic representation of the process of interpolation. The same interval is shown on two separate scales, time and distance. Only the endpoints of the scales are known—Bob starts at 0 for both time and distance, and he ends at 40 minutes and 2 miles. Interpolation is used to estimate values within the interval by assuming that fractional portions of one scale correspond to the same fractional portions of the other. For example, it is assumed that halfway through the time scale corresponds to halfway through the distance scale.

1. How much time does it take for Bob to walk 1.5 miles?
2. How far has Bob walked after 10 minutes?

If you got answers of 30 minutes and $\frac{1}{2}$ mile, you have mastered the process of interpolation.

Notice that interpolation provides a method for finding intermediate values—that is, values that are located between two specified numbers. This is exactly the problem we faced with percentiles and percentile ranks. Some values are given in the table, but others are not. Also notice that interpolation only *estimates* the intermediate values. The basic assumption underlying interpolation is that there is a constant rate of change from one end of the interval to the other. In Bob's walking example, we assume that he is walking at a constant rate for the entire trip. Because interpolation is based on this assumption, the values that we calculate are only estimates. The general process of interpolation can be summarized as follows:

1. A single interval is measured on two separate scales (for example, time and distance). The endpoints of the interval are known for each scale.
2. You are given an intermediate value on one of the scales. The problem is to find the corresponding intermediate value on the other scale.
3. The interpolation process requires four steps:
   a. Find the width of the interval on both scales.
   b. Locate the position of the intermediate value in the interval. This position corresponds to a fraction of the whole interval:

$$\text{fraction} = \frac{\text{distance from the top of the interval}}{\text{interval width}}$$

   c. Use the same fraction to determine the corresponding position on the other scale. First, determine the distance from the top of the interval:

$$\text{distance} = (\text{fraction}) \times (\text{width})$$

   d. Use the distance from the top to determine the position on the other scale.

You may notice that in each of these problems we use interpolation working from the *top* of the interval. However, this choice is arbitrary, and you should realize that interpolation can be done just as easily working from the bottom of the interval.

The following examples demonstrate the process of interpolation as it is applied to percentiles and percentile ranks. The key to success in solving these problems is that each cumulative percentage in the table is associated with the upper real limit of its score interval.

EXAMPLE 2.7 Using the following distribution of scores, we will find the percentile rank corresponding to $X = 7.0$:

X	f	cf	$c\%$
10	2	25	100%
9	8	23	92%
8	4	15	60%
7	6	11	44%
6	4	5	20%
5	1	1	4%

Notice that $X = 7.0$ is located in the interval bounded by the real limits of 6.5 and 7.5. The cumulative percentages corresponding to these real limits are 20% and 44%, respectively. These values are shown in the following table:

	Scores (*X*)	Percentages
Top	7.5	44%
Intermediate value	7.0	?
Bottom	6.5	20%

For interpolation problems, it is always helpful to create a table showing the range on both scales.

STEP 1 For the scores, the width of the interval is 1 point (from 6.5 to 7.5). For the percentages, the width is 24 points (from 20% to 44%).

STEP 2 Our particular score is located 0.5 point from the top of the interval. This is exactly halfway down in the interval.

STEP 3 On the percentage scale, halfway down is

$$\frac{1}{2}\text{(24 points)} = \text{12 points}$$

STEP 4 For the percentages, the top of the interval is 44%, so 12 points down would be

$$44\% - 12\% = 32\%$$

This is the answer. A score of $X = 7.0$ corresponds to a percentile rank of 32%

This same interpolation procedure can be used with data that have been grouped into class intervals. Once again, you must remember that the cumulative percentage values are associated with the upper real limits of each interval. The following example demonstrates the calculation of percentiles and percentile ranks using data in a grouped frequency distribution.

EXAMPLE 2.8 Using the following distribution of scores, we can use interpolation to find the 50th percentile:

X	*f*	*cf*	*c*%
20–24	2	20	100%
15–19	3	18	90%
10–14	3	15	75%
5–9	10	12	60%
0–4	2	2	10%

A percentage value of 50% is not given in the table; however, it is located between 10% and 60%, which are given. These two percentage values are associated with the upper real limits of 4.5 and 9.5, respectively. These values are shown in the following table:

	Scores (X)	Percentages	
Top	9.5	60%	
	?	50%	Intermediate value
Bottom	4.5	10%	

STEP 1 For the scores, the width of the interval is 5 points. For the percentages, the width is 50 points.

STEP 2 The value of 50% is located 10 points from the top of the percentage interval. As a fraction of the whole interval, this is 10 out of 50, or $\frac{1}{5}$ of the total interval.

STEP 3 Using this same fraction for the scores, we obtain a distance of

$$\frac{1}{5}\text{(5 points)} = 1 \text{ point}$$

The location we want is 1 point down from the top of the score interval.

STEP 4 Because the top of the interval is 9.5, the position we want is

$$9.5 - 1 = 8.5$$

This is the answer. The 50th percentile is $X = 8.5$.

LEARNING CHECK

1. On a statistics exam, would you rather score at the 80th percentile or at the 20th percentile?
2. For the distribution of scores presented in the following table,
   a. Find the 70th percentile.
   b. Find the percentile rank for $X = 9.5$.

X	f	cf	$c\%$
20–24	1	20	100%
15–19	5	19	95%
10–14	8	14	70%
5–9	4	6	20%
0–4	2	2	10%

3. Using the distribution of scores from Exercise 2 and interpolation,
   a. Find the 15th percentile.
   b. Find the percentile rank for $X = 13$.

ANSWERS

1. The 80th percentile is the higher score.
2. **a.** $X = 14.5$ is the 70th percentile. **b.** $X = 9.5$ has a rank of 20%.
3. **a.** Because 15% is between the values of 10% and 20% in the table, you must use interpolation. The score corresponding to a rank of 15% is $X = 7$.
   b. Because $X = 13$ is between the real limits of 9.5 and 14.5, you must use interpolation. The percentile rank for $X = 13$ is 55%.

2.6 STEM AND LEAF DISPLAYS

In 1977, J.W. Tukey presented a technique for organizing data that provides a simple alternative to a grouped frequency distribution table or graph (Tukey, 1977). This technique, called a *stem and leaf display*, requires that each score be separated into two parts: The first digit (or digits) is called the *stem*, and the last digit is called the *leaf*. For example, $X = 85$ would be separated into a stem of 8 and a leaf of 5. Similarly, $X = 42$ would have a stem of 4 and a leaf of 2. To construct a stem and leaf display for a set of data, the first step is to list all the stems in a column. For the data in Table 2.3, for example, the lowest scores are in the 30s and the highest scores are in the 90s, so the list of stems would be

Stems
3
4
5
6
7
8
9

The next step is to go through the data, one score at a time, and write the leaf for each score beside its stem. For the data in Table 2.3, the first score is $X = 83$, so you would write 3 in the leaf column beside the 8 in the column of stems. This process is continued for the entire set of scores. The complete stem and leaf display is shown with the original data in Table 2.3.

COMPARING STEM AND LEAF DISPLAYS WITH FREQUENCY DISTRIBUTIONS

Notice that the stem and leaf display is very similar to a grouped frequency distribution. Each of the stem values corresponds to a class interval. For example, the stem 3 represents all scores in the 30s—that is, all scores in the interval 30–39. The number of leaves in the display shows the frequency associated with each stem. It also should be clear that the stem and leaf display has one important advantage over a traditional grouped frequency distribution. Specifically, the stem and leaf display allows you to identify every individual score in the data. In the display shown in Table 2.3, for example, you know that there were three scores in the 60s and that the specific values were 62, 68, and 63. A frequency distribution would tell you only the frequency, not

TABLE 2.3

A set of $N = 24$ scores presented as raw data and organized in a stem and leaf display.

Data			Stem	Leaf
83	82	63	3	23
62	93	78	4	26
71	68	33	5	6279
76	52	97	6	283
85	42	46	7	1643846
32	57	59	8	3521
56	73	74	9	37
74	81	76		

the specific values. This advantage can be very valuable, especially if you need to do any calculations with the original scores. For example, if you need to add all the scores, you can recover the actual values from the stem and leaf display and compute the total. With a grouped frequency distribution, however, the individual scores are not available.

LEARNING CHECK

1. Use a stem and leaf display to organize the following set of scores:

   74, 103, 95, 98, 81, 117, 105, 99, 63, 86, 94, 107

   96, 100, 98, 118, 107, 82, 84, 71, 91, 107, 84, 77

2. Explain how a stem and leaf display contains more information than a grouped frequency distribution.

ANSWERS

1. The stem and leaf display for these data is as follows:

6	3
7	417
8	16244
9	5894681
10	357077
11	78

2. A grouped frequency distribution table tells only the number of scores in each interval; it does not identify the exact value for each score. The stem and leaf display identifies the individual scores as well as the number of scores in each interval.

SUMMARY

1. The goal of descriptive statistics is to simplify the organization and presentation of data. One descriptive technique is to place the data in a frequency distribution table or graph that shows exactly how many individuals (or scores) are located in each category on the scale of measurement.

2. A frequency distribution table lists the categories that make up the scale of measurement (the X values) in one column. Beside each X value, in a second column, is the frequency or number of individuals in that category. The table may include a proportion column showing the relative frequency for each category:

$$\text{proportion} = p = \frac{f}{n}$$

The table may include a percentage column showing the percentage associated with each X value:

$$\text{percentage} = p(100) = \frac{f}{n}(100)$$

3. It is recommended that a frequency distribution table have a maximum of 10 to 15 rows to keep it simple. If the scores cover a range that is wider than this suggested maximum, it is customary to divide the range into sections called *class intervals*. These intervals are then listed in the frequency distribution table along with the frequency or number of individuals with scores in each interval. The result is called a *grouped frequency distribution*. The guidelines for constructing a grouped frequency distribution table are as follows:
   a. There should be about 10 intervals.
   b. The width of each interval should be a simple number (e.g., 2, 5, or 10).
   c. The bottom score in each interval should be a multiple of the width.
   d. All intervals should be the same width, and they should cover the range of scores with no gaps.

4. A frequency distribution graph lists scores on the horizontal axis and frequencies on the vertical axis. The type of graph used to display a distribution depends on the scale of measurement used. For interval or ratio scales, you should use a histogram or a polygon. For a histogram, a bar is drawn above each score so that the height of the bar corresponds to the frequency. Each bar extends to the real limits of the score, so that adjacent bars touch. For a polygon, a dot is placed above the midpoint of each score or class interval so that the height of the dot corresponds to the frequency; then lines are drawn to connect the dots. Bar graphs are used with nominal or ordinal scales. Bar graphs are similar to histograms except that gaps are left between adjacent bars.

5. Shape is one of the basic characteristics used to describe a distribution of scores. Most distributions can be classified as either symmetrical or skewed. A skewed distribution with the tail on the right is said to be positively skewed. If it has the tail on the left, it is negatively skewed.

6. The cumulative percentage is the percentage of individuals with scores at or below a particular point in the distribution. The cumulative percentage values are associated with the upper real limits of the corresponding scores or intervals.

7. Percentiles and percentile ranks are used to describe the position of individual scores within a distribution. Percentile rank gives the cumulative percentage associated with a particular score. A score that is identified by its rank is called a *percentile*.

8. When a desired percentile or percentile rank is located between two known values, it is possible to estimate the desired value using the process of interpolation. Interpolation assumes a regular linear change between the two known values.

9. A stem and leaf display is an alternative procedure for organizing data. Each score is separated into a stem (the first digit or digits) and a leaf (the last digit or digits). The display consists of the stems listed in a column with the leaf for each score written beside its stem. A stem and leaf display combines the characteristics of a table and a graph and produces a concise, well-organized picture of the data.

KEY TERMS

frequency distribution (39)
range (42)
grouped frequency distribution (42)
class interval (42)
apparent limits (44)
histogram (46)
polygon (47)
bar graph (48)
relative frequency (49)
symmetrical distribution (50)
tail(s) of a distribution (51)
positively skewed distribution (51)
negatively skewed distribution (51)
percentile rank (53)
percentile (53)
cumulative frequency (*cf*) (54)
cumulative percentage (*c*%) (54)
interpolation (55)
stem and leaf display (60)

RESOURCES

Book Companion Website: www.cengage.com/psychology/gravetter

You can find a tutorial quiz and other learning exercises for Chapter 2 on the book companion website.

aplia

Improve your understanding of statistics with Aplia's auto-graded problem sets and immediate, detailed explanations for every question. To learn more, visit **www.aplia.com/statistics**.

CENGAGE brain.com

Psychology CourseMate brings course concepts to life with interactive learning, study, and exam preparation tools that support the printed textbook. A textbook-specific website, Psychology CourseMate includes an integrated interactive eBook and other interactive learning tools including quizzes, flashcards, and more.

Visit www.cengagebrain.com to access your account and purchase materials.

SPSS

General instructions for using SPSS are presented in Appendix D. Following are detailed instructions for using SPSS to produce **Frequency Distribution Tables or Graphs**.

Frequency Distribution Tables

Data Entry

1. Enter all the scores in one column of the data editor, probably VAR00001.

Data Analysis

1. Click **Analyze** on the tool bar, select **Descriptive Statistics,** and click on **Frequencies.**
2. Highlight the column label for the set of scores (VAR00001) in the left box and click the arrow to move it into the **Variable** box.
3. Be sure that the option to **Display Frequency Table** is selected.
4. Click **OK.**

SPSS Output

The frequency distribution table lists the score values in a column from smallest to largest, with the percentage and cumulative percentage also listed for each score. Score values that do not occur (zero frequencies) are not included in the table, and the program does not group scores into class intervals (all values are listed).

Frequency Distribution Histograms or Bar Graphs

Data Entry

1. Enter all the scores in one column of the data editor, probably VAR00001.

Data Analysis

1. Click **Analyze** on the tool bar, select **Descriptive Statistics,** and click on **Frequencies.**
2. Highlight the column label for the set of scores (VAR00001) in the left box and click the arrow to move it into the **Variable** box.
3. Click **Charts.**
4. Select either **Bar Graphs** or **Histogram.**
5. Click **Continue.**
6. Click **OK**.

SPSS Output

After a brief delay, SPSS displays a frequency distribution table and a graph. Note that SPSS often produces a histogram that groups the scores in unpredictable intervals. A bar graph usually produces a clearer picture of the actual frequency associated with each score.

FOCUS ON PROBLEM SOLVING

1. The reason for constructing frequency distributions is to put a disorganized set of raw data into a comprehensible, organized format. Because several different types of frequency distribution tables and graphs are available, one problem is deciding which type to use. Tables have the advantage of being easier to construct, but graphs generally give a better picture of the data and are easier to understand.

To help you decide which type of frequency distribution is best, consider the following points:

a. What is the range of scores? With a wide range, you need to group the scores into class intervals.

b. What is the scale of measurement? With an interval or a ratio scale, you can use a polygon or a histogram. With a nominal or an ordinal scale, you must use a bar graph.

2. When using a grouped frequency distribution table, a common mistake is to calculate the interval width by using the highest and lowest values that define each interval. For example, some students are tricked into thinking that an interval identified as 20–24 is only 4 points wide. To determine the correct interval width, you can:

a. Count the individual scores in the interval. For this example, the scores are 20, 21, 22, 23, and 24, for a total of 5 values. Thus, the interval width is 5 points.

b. Use the real limits to determine the real width of the interval. For example, an interval identified as 20–24 has a lower real limit of 19.5 and an upper real limit of 24.5 (halfway to the next score). Using the real limits, the interval width is

$$24.5 - 19.5 = 5 \text{ points}$$

3. Percentiles and percentile ranks are intended to identify specific locations within a distribution of scores. When solving percentile problems, especially with interpolation, it is helpful to sketch a frequency distribution graph. Use the graph to make a preliminary estimate of the answer before you begin any calculations. For example, to find the 60th percentile, draw a vertical line through the graph so that slightly more than half (60%) of the distribution is on the left-hand side of the line. Locating this position in your sketch gives you a rough estimate of what the final answer should be. When doing interpolation problems, you should keep several points in mind:

a. Remember that the cumulative percentage values correspond to the upper real limits of each score or interval.

b. You should always identify the interval with which you are working. The easiest way to do this is to create a table showing the endpoints on both scales (scores and cumulative percentages). This is illustrated in Example 2.7 on pages 57–58.

c. The word *interpolation* means *between two poles*. Remember: Your goal is to find an intermediate value between the two ends of the interval. Check your answer to be sure that it is located between the two endpoints. If it is not, then check your calculations.

DEMONSTRATION 2.1

A GROUPED FREQUENCY DISTRIBUTION TABLE

For the following set of $N = 20$ scores, construct a grouped frequency distribution table using an interval width of 5 points. The scores are:

14, 8, 27, 16, 10, 22, 9, 13, 16, 12,
10, 9, 15, 17, 6, 14, 11, 18, 14, 11

STEP 1 Set up the class intervals.

The largest score in this distribution is $X = 27$, and the lowest is $X = 6$. Therefore, a frequency distribution table for these data would have 22 rows and would be too large. A grouped frequency distribution table would be better. We have asked specifically for an interval width of 5 points, and the resulting table has five rows.

X
25–29
20–24
15–19
10–14
5–9

Remember that the interval width is determined by the real limits of the interval. For example, the class interval 25–29 has an upper real limit of 29.5 and a lower real limit of 24.5. The difference between these two values is the width of the interval—namely, 5.

STEP 2 Determine the frequencies for each interval.

Examine the scores, and count how many fall into the class interval of 25–29. Cross out each score that you have already counted. Record the frequency for this class interval. Now repeat this process for the remaining intervals. The result is the following table:

X	f	
25–29	1	(the score $X = 27$)
20–24	1	($X = 22$)
15–19	5	(the scores $X = 16, 16, 15, 17$, and 18)
10–14	9	($X = 14, 10, 13, 12, 10, 14, 11, 14$, and 11)
5–9	4	($X = 8, 9, 9$, and 6)

DEMONSTRATION 2.2

USING INTERPOLATION TO FIND PERCENTILES AND PERCENTILE RANKS

Find the 50th percentile for the set of scores in the grouped frequency distribution table that was constructed in Demonstration 2.1.

STEP 1 Find the cumulative frequency (*cf*) and cumulative percentage values, and add these values to the basic frequency distribution table.

Cumulative frequencies indicate the number of individuals located in or below each category (class interval). To find these frequencies, begin with the bottom interval, and then accumulate the frequencies as you move up the scale.

Cumulative percentages are determined from the cumulative frequencies by the relationship

$$c\% = \left(\frac{cf}{N}\right)100\%$$

For example, the *cf* column shows that 4 individuals (out of the total set of $N = 20$) have scores in or below the 5–9 interval. The corresponding cumulative percentage is

$$c\% = \left(\frac{4}{20}\right)100\% = \left(\frac{1}{5}\right)100\% = 20\%$$

The complete set of cumulative frequencies and cumulative percentages is shown in the following table:

X	f	cf	$c\%$
25–29	1	20	100%
20–24	1	19	95%
15–19	5	18	90%
10–14	9	13	65%
5–9	4	4	20%

STEP 2 Locate the interval that contains the value that you want to calculate.

We are looking for the 50th percentile, which is located between the values of 20% and 65% in the table. The scores (upper real limits) corresponding to these two percentages are 9.5 and 14.5, respectively. The interval, measured in terms of scores and percentages, is shown in the following table:

X	$c\%$
14.5	65%
??	50%
9.5	20%

STEP 3 Locate the intermediate value as a fraction of the total interval.

Our intermediate value is 50%, which is located in the interval between 65% and 20%. The total width of the interval is 45 points ($65 - 20 = 45$), and the value of 50% is located 15 points down from the top of the interval. As a fraction, the 50th percentile is located $\frac{15}{45} = \frac{1}{3}$ down from the top of the interval.

STEP 4 Use the fraction to determine the corresponding location on the other scale.

Our intermediate value, 50%, is located $\frac{1}{3}$ of the way down from the top of the interval. Our goal is to find the score, the X value, that also is located $\frac{1}{3}$ of the way down from the top of the interval.

On the score (X) side of the interval, the top value is 14.5, and the bottom value is 9.5, so the total interval width is 5 points ($14.5 - 9.5 = 5$). The position we are seeking is $\frac{1}{3}$ of the way from the top of the interval. One-third of the total interval is

$$\left(\frac{1}{3}\right)5 = \frac{5}{3} = 1.67 \text{ points}$$

To find this location, begin at the top of the interval, and come down 1.67 points:

$$14.5 - 1.67 = 12.83$$

This is our answer. The 50th percentile is $X = 12.83$.

PROBLEMS

1. Place the following sample of $n = 20$ scores in a frequency distribution table.

   6, 9, 9, 10, 8, 9, 4, 7, 10, 9
   5, 8, 10, 6, 9, 6, 8, 8, 7, 9

2. Construct a frequency distribution table for the following set of scores. Include columns for proportion and percentage in your table.

   Scores: 5, 7, 8, 4, 7, 9, 6, 6, 5, 3
   9, 6, 4, 7, 7, 8, 6, 7, 8, 5

3. Find each value requested for the distribution of scores in the following table.
   a. n
   b. ΣX
   c. ΣX^2

X	f
5	2
4	3
3	5
2	1
1	1

4. Find each value requested for the distribution of scores in the following table.
   a. n
   b. ΣX
   c. ΣX^2

X	f
5	1
4	2
3	3
2	5
1	3

5. For the following scores, the smallest value is $X = 8$ and the largest value is $X = 29$. Place the scores in a grouped frequency distribution table
   a. using an interval width of 2 points.
   b. using an interval width of 5 points.

   24, 19, 23, 10, 25, 27, 22, 26
   25, 20, 8, 24, 29, 21, 24, 13
   23, 27, 24, 16, 22, 18, 26, 25

6. What information can you obtain about the scores in a regular frequency distribution table that is not available from a grouped table?

7. For each of the following samples, determine the interval width that is most appropriate for a grouped frequency distribution and identify the approximate number of intervals needed to cover the range of scores.
   a. Sample scores range from $X = 24$ to $X = 41$
   b. Sample scores range from $X = 46$ to $X = 103$
   c. Sample scores range from $X = 46$ to $X = 133$

8. The following scores are the ages for a random sample of $n = 30$ drivers who were issued speeding tickets in New York during 2008. Determine the best interval width and place the scores in a grouped frequency distribution table. From looking at your table, does it appear that tickets are issued equally across age groups?

   17, 30, 45, 20, 39, 53, 28, 19,
   24, 21, 34, 38, 22, 29, 64,
   22, 44, 36, 16, 56, 20, 23, 58,
   32, 25, 28, 22, 51, 26, 43

9. Describe the difference in appearance between a bar graph and a histogram and describe the circumstances in which each type of graph is used.

10. A report from the college dean indicates that for the previous semester, the grade distribution for the Department of Psychology included 135 As, 158 Bs,

140 Cs, 94 Ds, and 53 Fs. Determine what kind of graph would be appropriate for showing this distribution and sketch the frequency distribution graph.

11. Sketch a histogram and a polygon showing the distribution of scores presented in the following table:

X	*f*
7	1
6	1
5	3
4	6
3	4
2	1

12. A survey given to a sample of 200 college students contained questions about the following variables. For each variable, identify the kind of graph that should be used to display the distribution of scores (histogram, polygon, or bar graph).
a. number of pizzas consumed during the previous week
b. size of T-shirt worn (S, M, L, XL)
c. gender (male/female)
d. grade point average for the previous semester
e. college class (freshman, sophomore, junior, senior)

13. Each year the college gives away T-shirts to new students during freshman orientation. The students are allowed to pick the shirt sizes that they want. To determine how many of each size shirt they should order, college officials look at the distribution from last year. The following table shows the distribution of shirt sizes selected last year.

Size	*f*
S	27
M	48
L	136
XL	120
XXL	39

a. What kind of graph would be appropriate for showing this distribution?
b. Sketch the frequency distribution graph.

14. For the following set of quiz scores:

3, 5, 4, 6, 2, 3, 4, 1, 4, 3
7, 7, 3, 4, 5, 8, 2, 4, 7, 10

a. Construct a frequency distribution table to organize the scores.
b. Draw a frequency distribution histogram for these data.

15. For the following set of scores

Scores: 5, 8, 5, 7, 6, 6, 5, 7, 4, 6
6, 9, 5, 5, 4, 6, 7, 5, 7, 5

a. Place the scores in a frequency distribution table.
b. Identify the shape of the distribution.

16. Place the following scores in a frequency distribution table. Based on the frequencies, what is the shape of the distribution?

5, 6, 4, 7, 7, 6, 8, 2, 5, 6
3, 1, 7, 4, 6, 8, 2, 6, 5, 7

17. For the following set of scores:

3, 7, 6, 5, 5, 9, 6, 4, 6, 8
10, 2, 7, 4, 9, 5, 6, 3, 8

a. Construct a frequency distribution table.
b. Sketch a polygon showing the distribution.
c. Describe the distribution using the following characteristics:
(1) What is the shape of the distribution?
(2) What score best identifies the center (average) for the distribution?
(3) Are the scores clustered together, or are they spread out across the scale?

18. Fowler and Christakis (2008) report that personal happiness tends to be associated with having a social network including many other happy friends. To test this claim, a researcher obtains a sample of $n = 16$ adults who claim to be happy people and a similar sample of $n = 16$ adults who describe themselves as neutral or unhappy. Each individual is then asked to identify the number of their close friends whom they consider to be happy people. The scores are as follows:

Happy:
8, 7, 4, 10, 6, 6, 8, 9, 8, 8,
7, 5, 6, 9, 8, 9

Unhappy:
5, 8, 4, 6, 6, 7, 9, 6, 2, 8,
5, 6, 4, 7, 5, 6

Sketch a polygon showing the frequency distribution for the happy people. In the same graph, sketch a polygon for the unhappy people. (Use two different colors, or use a solid line for one polygon and a dashed line for the other.) Does one group seem to have more happy friends?

19. Complete the final two columns in the following frequency distribution table and then find the percentiles and percentile ranks requested.

X	*f*	*cf*	*c*%
7	2		
6	3		
5	6		
4	9		
3	4		
2	1		

a. What is the percentile rank for $X = 2.5$?
b. What is the percentile rank for $X = 6.5$?
c. What is the 20th percentile?
d. What is the 80th percentile?

20. Find the requested percentiles and percentile ranks for the following distribution of quiz scores for a class of N = 40 students.

X	*f*	*cf*	*c*%
20	2	40	100.0
19	4	38	95.0
18	6	34	85.0
17	13	28	70.0
16	6	15	37.5
15	4	9	22.5
14	3	5	12.5
13	2	2	5.0

a. What is the percentile rank for X = 15?
b. What is the percentile rank for X = 18?
c. What is the 15th percentile?
d. What is the 90th percentile?

21. Complete the final two columns in the following frequency distribution table and then use interpolation to find the percentiles and percentile ranks requested.

X	*f*	*cf*	*c*%
10	2		
9	5		
8	8		
7	15		
6	10		
5	6		
4	4		

a. What is the percentile rank for $X = 6$?
b. What is the percentile rank for $X = 9$?
c. What is the 25th percentile?
d. What is the 90th percentile?

22. Complete the final two columns in the following frequency distribution table and then find the percentiles and percentile ranks requested.

X	*f*	*cf*	*c*%
50–59	1		
40–49	3		
30–39	6		
20–29	5		
10–19	3		
0–9	2		

a. What is the percentile rank for $X = 9.5$?
b. What is the percentile rank for $X = 39.5$?
c. What is the 25th percentile?
d. What is the 50th percentile?

23. Use interpolation to find the requested percentiles and percentile ranks requested for the following distribution of scores.

X	*f*	*cf*	*c*%
14–15	3	50	100
12–13	6	47	94
10–11	8	41	82
8–9	18	33	66
6–7	10	15	30
4–5	4	5	10
2–3	1	1	2

a. What is the percentile rank for $X = 5$?
b. What is the percentile rank for $X = 12$?
c. What is the 25th percentile?
d. What is the 70th percentile?

24. The following frequency distribution presents a set of exam scores for a class of $N = 20$ students.

X	*f*	*cf*	*c*%
90–99	4	20	100
80–89	7	16	80
70–79	4	9	45
60–69	3	5	25
50–59	2	2	10

a. Find the 30th percentile.
b. Find the 88th percentile.
c. What is the percentile rank for $X = 77$?
d. What is the percentile rank for $X = 90$?

25. Construct a stem and leaf display for the data in problem 6 using one stem for the scores in the 60s, one for scores in the 50s, and so on.

26. A set of scores has been organized into the following stem and leaf display. For this set of scores:
a. How many scores are in the 70s?
b. Identify the individual scores in the 70s.
c. How many scores are in the 40s?
d. Identify the individual scores in the 40s.

3	8
4	60
5	734
6	81469
7	2184
8	247

27. Use a stem and leaf display to organize the following distribution of scores. Use seven stems with each stem corresponding to a 10-point interval.

Scores:

28,	54,	65,	53,	81
45,	44,	51,	72,	34
43,	59,	65,	39,	20
53,	74,	24,	30,	49
36,	58,	60,	27,	47
22,	52,	46,	39,	65

CHAPTER

3

Central Tendency

Tools You Will Need

The following items are considered essential background material for this chapter. If you doubt your knowledge of any of these items, you should review the appropriate chapter or section before proceeding.

- Summation notation (Chapter 1)
- Frequency distributions (Chapter 2)

Preview

Research has now confirmed what you already suspected to be true—alcohol consumption increases the attractiveness of opposite-sex individuals (Jones, Jones, Thomas, & Piper, 2003). In the study, college-age participants were recruited from bars and restaurants near campus and asked to participate in a "market research" study. During the introductory conversation, they were asked to report their alcohol consumption for the day and were told that moderate consumption would not prevent them from taking part in the study. Participants were then shown a series of photographs of male and female faces and asked to rate the attractiveness of each face on a scale from 1 to 7. Figure 3.1 shows the general pattern of results obtained in the study. The two polygons in the figure show the distributions of attractiveness ratings for one female photograph obtained from two groups of males: those who had no alcohol and those with moderate alcohol consumption. Note that the attractiveness ratings from the alcohol group are noticeably higher than the ratings from the no-alcohol group. Incidentally, the same pattern of results was obtained for the female's ratings of male photographs.

The Problem: Although it seems obvious that the moderate-alcohol ratings are noticeably higher than the no-alcohol ratings, this conclusion is based on a general impression, or a subjective interpretation, of the figure. In fact, this conclusion is not always true. For example, there is overlap between the two groups so that some of the no-alcohol males actually rate the photograph as more attractive than some of the moderate-alcohol males. What we need is a method to summarize each group as a whole so that we can objectively describe how much difference exists between the two groups.

The Solution: A measure of *central tendency* identifies the average, or typical, score to serve as a representative value for each group. Then we can use the two averages to describe the two groups and to measure the difference between them. The results should show that average attractiveness rating from males consuming alcohol really is higher than the average rating from males who have not consumed alcohol.

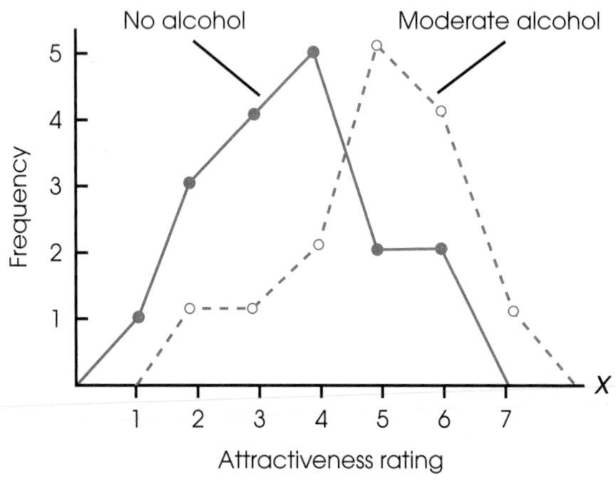

FIGURE 3.1

Frequency distributions for ratings of attractiveness of a female face shown in a photograph for two groups of male participants: those who had consumed no alcohol and those who had consumed moderate amounts of alcohol.

3.1 OVERVIEW

The general purpose of descriptive statistical methods is to organize and summarize a set of scores. Perhaps the most common method for summarizing and describing a distribution is to find a single value that defines the average score and can serve as a representative for the entire distribution. In statistics, the concept of an average, or representative, score is called *central tendency*. The goal in measuring central tendency is to describe a distribution of scores by determining a single value that identifies the center of the distribution. Ideally, this central value is the score that is the best representative value for all of the individuals in the distribution.

DEFINITION

Central tendency is a statistical measure to determine a single score that defines the center of a distribution. The goal of central tendency is to find the single score that is most typical or most representative of the entire group.

In everyday language, central tendency attempts to identify the "average" or "typical" individual. This average value can then be used to provide a simple description of an entire population or a sample. In addition to describing an entire distribution, measures of central tendency are also useful for making comparisons between groups of individuals or between sets of figures. For example, weather data indicate that for Seattle, Washington, the average yearly temperature is 53° and the average annual precipitation is 34 inches. By comparison, the average temperature in Phoenix, Arizona, is 71° and the average precipitation is 7.4 inches. The point of these examples is to demonstrate the great advantage of being able to describe a large set of data with a single, representative number. Central tendency characterizes what is typical for a large population and, in doing so, makes large amounts of data more digestible. Statisticians sometimes use the expression *number crunching* to illustrate this aspect of data description. That is, we take a distribution consisting of many scores and "crunch" them down to a single value that describes them all.

Unfortunately, there is no single, standard procedure for determining central tendency. The problem is that no single measure produces a central, representative value in every situation. The three distributions shown in Figure 3.2 should help demonstrate this fact. Before we discuss the three distributions, take a moment to look at the figure and try to identify the center or the most representative score for each distribution.

1. The first distribution [Figure 3.2(a)] is symmetrical, with the scores forming a distinct pile centered around $X = 5$. For this type of distribution, it is easy to identify the center, and most people would agree that the value $X = 5$ is an appropriate measure of central tendency.
2. In the second distribution [Figure 3.2(b)], however, problems begin to appear. Now the scores form a negatively skewed distribution, piling up at the high end of the scale around $X = 8$, but tapering off to the left all the way down to $X = 1$. Where is the center in this case? Some people might select $X = 8$ as the center because more individuals had this score than any other single value. However, $X = 8$ is clearly not in the middle of the distribution. In fact, the majority of the scores (10 out of 16) have values less than 8, so it seems reasonable that the center should be defined by a value that is less than 8.
3. Now consider the third distribution [Figure 3.2(c)]. Again, the distribution is symmetrical, but now there are two distinct piles of scores. Because the distribution is symmetrical with $X = 5$ as the midpoint, you may choose $X = 5$ as the center. However, none of the scores is located at $X = 5$ (or even close), so this value is not particularly good as a representative score. On the other hand, because there are two separate piles of scores with one group centered at $X = 2$ and the other centered at $X = 8$, it is tempting to say that this distribution has two centers. But can one distribution have two centers?

Clearly, there can be problems defining the center of a distribution. Occasionally, you will find a nice, neat distribution like the one shown in Figure 3.2(a), for which everyone agrees on the center. But you should realize that other distributions are possible and that there may be different opinions concerning the definition of the center. To deal with these problems, statisticians have developed three different methods for measuring central tendency: the mean, the median, and the mode. They are computed

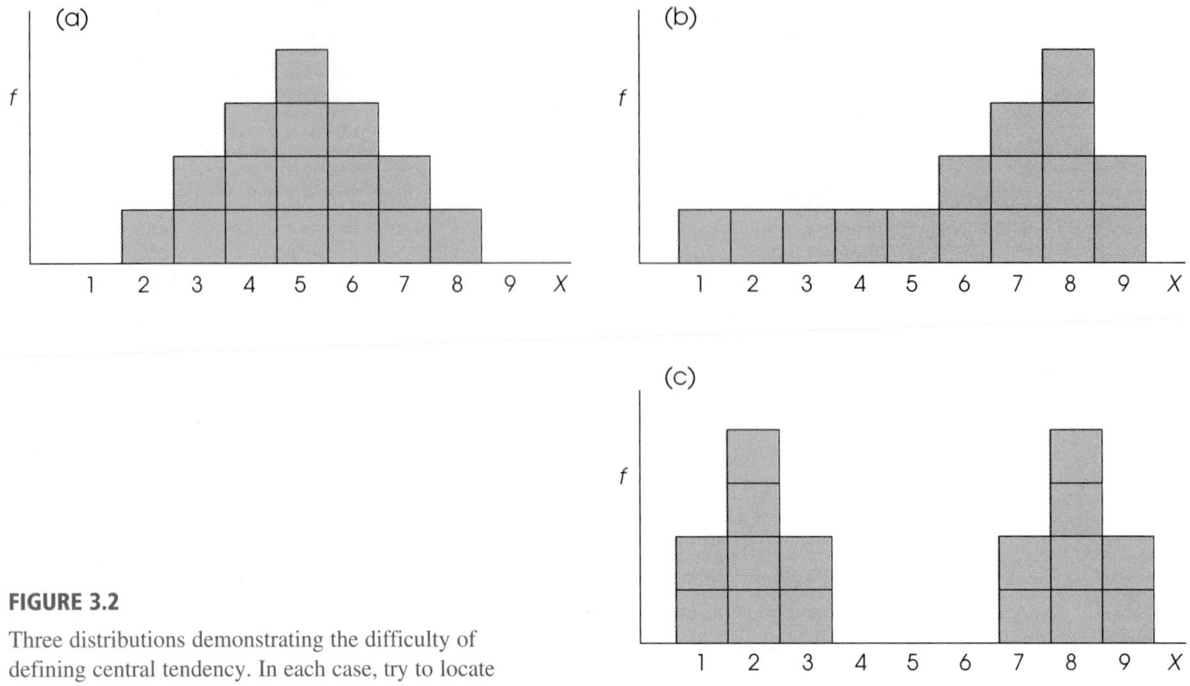

FIGURE 3.2
Three distributions demonstrating the difficulty of defining central tendency. In each case, try to locate the "center" of the distribution.

differently and have different characteristics. To decide which of the three measures is best for any particular distribution, you should keep in mind that the general purpose of central tendency is to find the single most representative score. Each of the three measures we present has been developed to work best in a specific situation. We examine this issue in more detail after we introduce the three measures.

3.2 THE MEAN

The *mean*, also known as the arithmetic average, is computed by adding all the scores in the distribution and dividing by the number of scores. The mean for a population is identified by the Greek letter mu, μ (pronounced "mew"), and the mean for a sample is identified by M or $\overline{X}$ (read "x-bar").

The convention in many statistics textbooks is to use $\overline{X}$ to represent the mean for a sample. However, in manuscripts and in published research reports the letter M is the standard notation for a sample mean. Because you will encounter the letter M when reading research reports and because you should use the letter M when writing research reports, we have decided to use the same notation in this text. Keep in mind that the $\overline{X}$ notation is still appropriate for identifying a sample mean, and you may find it used on occasion, especially in textbooks.

DEFINITION

The **mean** for a distribution is the sum of the scores divided by the number of scores.

The formula for the *population mean* is

$$\mu = \frac{\sum X}{N} \tag{3.1}$$

First, add all the scores in the population, and then divide by N. For a sample, the computation is exactly the same, but the formula for the *sample mean* uses symbols that signify sample values:

$$\text{sample mean} = M = \frac{\sum X}{n} \tag{3.2}$$

In general, we use Greek letters to identify characteristics of a population (parameters) and letters of our own alphabet to stand for sample values (statistics). If a mean is identified with the symbol M, you should realize that we are dealing with a sample. Also note that the equation for the sample mean uses a lowercase n as the symbol for the number of scores in the sample.

EXAMPLE 3.1

For a population of $N = 4$ scores,

3, 7, 4, 6

the mean is

$$\mu = \frac{\Sigma X}{N} = \frac{20}{4} = 5$$

ALTERNATIVE DEFINITIONS FOR THE MEAN

Although the procedure of adding the scores and dividing by the number of scores provides a useful definition of the mean, there are two alternative definitions that may give you a better understanding of this important measure of central tendency.

Dividing the total equally The first alternative is to think of the mean as the amount each individual receives when the total (ΣX) is divided equally among all of the individuals (N) in the distribution. This somewhat socialistic viewpoint is particularly useful in problems for which you know the mean and must find the total. Consider the following example.

EXAMPLE 3.2

A group of $n = 6$ boys buys a box of baseball cards at a garage sale and discovers that the box contains a total of 180 cards. If the boys divide the cards equally among themselves, how many cards will each boy get? You should recognize that this problem represents the standard procedure for computing the mean. Specifically, the total (ΣX) is divided by the number (n) to produce the mean, $\frac{180}{6} = 30$ cards for each boy.

The previous example demonstrates that it is possible to define the mean as the amount that each individual gets when the total is distributed equally. This new definition can be useful for some problems involving the mean. Consider the following example.

EXAMPLE 3.3 Now suppose that the 6 boys from Example 3.2 decide to sell their baseball cards on eBay. If they make an average of $M = \$5$ per boy, what is the total amount of money for the whole group? Although you do not know exactly how much money each boy has, the new definition of the mean tells you that if they pool their money together and then distribute the total equally, each boy will get \$5. For each of $n = 6$ boys to get \$5, the total must be 6(\$5) = \$30. To check this answer, use the formula for the mean:

$$M = \frac{\Sigma X}{n} = \frac{\$30}{6} = \$5$$

The mean as a balance point The second alternative definition of the mean describes the mean as a balance point for the distribution. Consider a population consisting of $N = 5$ scores (1, 2, 6, 6, 10). For this population, $\Sigma X = 25$ and $\mu = \frac{25}{5} = 5$. Figure 3.3 shows this population drawn as a histogram, with each score represented as a box that is sitting on a seesaw. If the seesaw is positioned so that it pivots at a point equal to the mean, then it will be balanced and will rest level.

The reason that the seesaw is balanced over the mean becomes clear when we measures the distance of each box (score) from the mean:

Score	Distance from the Mean
$X = 1$	4 points below the mean
$X = 2$	3 points below the mean
$X = 6$	1 point above the mean
$X = 6$	1 point above the mean
$X = 10$	5 points above the mean

Notice that the mean balances the distances. That is, the total distance below the mean is the same as the total distance above the mean:

below the mean: $4 + 3 = 7$ points

above the mean: $1 + 1 + 5 = 7$ points

Because the mean serves as a balance point, the value of the mean is always located somewhere between the highest score and the lowest score; that is, the mean can never be outside the range of scores. If the lowest score in a distribution is $X = 8$ and the highest is $X = 15$, then the mean *must* be between 8 and 15. If you calculate a value that is outside this range, then you have made an error.

FIGURE 3.3

The frequency distribution shown as a seesaw balanced at the mean.

(Based on G. H. Weinberg, J. A. Schumaker, & D. Oltman (1981). *Statistics: An Intuitive Approach* (p. 14). Belmont, Calif.: Wadsworth.

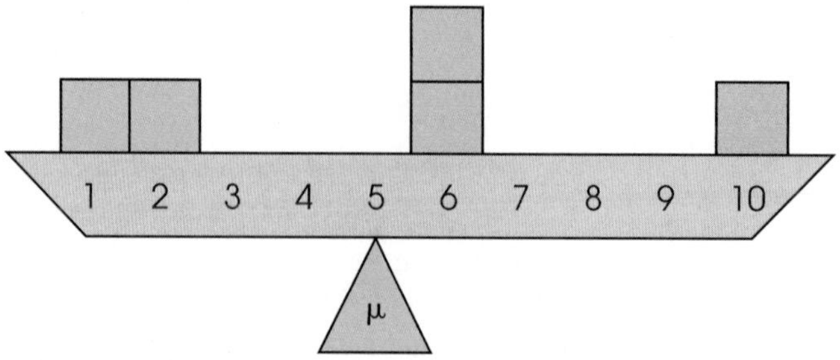

The image of a seesaw with the mean at the balance point is also useful for determining how a distribution is affected if a new score is added or if an existing score is removed. For the distribution in Figure 3.3, for example, what would happen to the mean (balance point) if a new score were added at $X = 10$?

THE WEIGHTED MEAN

Often it is necessary to combine two sets of scores and then find the overall mean for the combined group. Suppose that we begin with two separate samples. The first sample has $n = 12$ scores and a mean of $M = 6$. The second sample has $n = 8$ and $M = 7$. If the two samples are combined, what is the mean for the total group?

To calculate the overall mean, we need two values:

1. the overall sum of the scores for the combined group (ΣX), and
2. the total number of scores in the combined group (n).

The total number of scores in the combined group can be found easily by adding the number of scores in the first sample (n_1) and the number in the second sample (n_2). In this case, there are $12 + 8 = 20$ scores in the combined group. Similarly, the overall sum for the combined group can be found by adding the sum for the first sample (ΣX_1) and the sum for the second sample (ΣX_2). With these two values, we can compute the mean using the basic equation

$$\text{overall mean} = M = \frac{\Sigma X \text{ (overall sum for the combined group)}}{n \text{ (total number in the combined group)}}$$

$$= \frac{\Sigma X_1 + \Sigma X_2}{n_1 + n_2}$$

To find the sum of the scores for each sample, remember that the mean can be defined as the amount each person receives when the total (ΣX) is distributed equally. The first sample has $n = 12$ and $M = 6$. (Expressed in dollars instead of scores, this sample has $n = 12$ people and each person gets \$6 when the total is divided equally.) For each of 12 people to get $M = 6$, the total must be $\Sigma X = 12 \times 6 = 72$. In the same way, the second sample has $n = 8$ and $M = 7$ so the total must be $\Sigma X = 8 \times 7 = 56$. Using these values, we obtain an overall mean of

$$\text{overall mean} = M = \frac{\Sigma X_1 + \Sigma X_1}{n_1 + n_2} = \frac{72 + 56}{12 + 8} = \frac{128}{20} = 6.4$$

The following table summarizes the calculations.

First Sample	Second Sample	Combined Sample
$n = 12$	$n = 8$	$n = 20$ $(12 + 8)$
$\Sigma X = 72$	$\Sigma X = 56$	$\Sigma X = 128$ $(72 + 56)$
$M = 6$	$M = 7$	$M = 6.4$

Note that the overall mean is not halfway between the original two sample means. Because the samples are not the same size, one makes a larger contribution to the total group and, therefore, carries more weight in determining the overall mean. For this reason, the overall mean we have calculated is called the *weighted mean*. In this example, the overall mean of $M = 6.4$ is closer to the value of $M = 6$ (the larger sample) than it is to $M = 7$ (the smaller sample). An alternative method for finding the weighted mean is presented in Box 3.1.

BOX 3.1 AN ALTERNATIVE PROCEDURE FOR FINDING THE WEIGHTED MEAN

In the text, the weighted mean was obtained by first determining the total number of scores (n) for the two combined samples and then determining the overall sum (ΣX) for the two combined samples. The following example demonstrates how the same result can be obtained using a slightly different conceptual approach.

We begin with the same two samples that were used in the text: One sample has $M = 6$ for $n = 12$ students, and the second sample has $M = 7$ for $n = 8$ students. The goal is to determine the mean for the overall group when the two samples are combined.

Logically, when these two samples are combined, the larger sample (with $n = 12$ scores) will make a greater contribution to the combined group than the smaller sample (with $n = 8$ scores). Thus, the larger sample will carry more weight in determining the mean for the combined group. We accommodate this fact by assigning a weight to each sample mean so that the weight is determined by the size of the sample. To determine how much weight should be assigned to each sample mean, you simply consider the sample's contribution to the combined group. When the two samples are combined, the resulting group will have a total of 20 scores ($n = 12$ from the first sample and $n = 8$ from the second). The first sample contributes 12 out of 20 scores and, therefore, is assigned a weight of $\frac{12}{20}$. The second sample contributes 8 out of 20 scores, and its weight is $\frac{8}{20}$. Each sample mean is then multiplied by its weight, and the results are added to find the weighted mean for the combined sample. For this example,

$$\text{weighted mean} = \left(\frac{12}{20}\right)(6) + \left(\frac{8}{20}\right)(7)$$

$$= \frac{72}{20} + \frac{56}{20}$$

$$= 3.6 + 2.8$$

$$= 6.4$$

Note that this is the same result obtained using the method described in the text.

COMPUTING THE MEAN FROM A FREQUENCY DISTRIBUTION TABLE

When a set of scores has been organized in a frequency distribution table, the calculation of the mean is usually easier if you first remove the individual scores from the table. Table 3.1 shows a distribution of scores organized in a frequency distribution table. To compute the mean for this distribution you must be careful to use both the X values in the first column and the frequencies in the second column. The values in the table show that the distribution consists of one 10, two 9s, four 8s, and one 6, for a total of $n = 8$ scores. Remember that you can determine the number of scores by adding the frequencies, $n = \Sigma f$. To find the sum of the scores, you must be careful to add all eight scores:

$$\Sigma X = 10 + 9 + 9 + 8 + 8 + 8 + 8 + 6 = 66$$

Note that you can also find the sum of the scores by computing ΣfX as we demonstrated in Chapter 2 (pp. 40–41). Once you have found ΣX and n, you compute the mean as usual. For these data,

$$M = \frac{\sum X}{n} = \frac{66}{8} = 8.25$$

TABLE 3.1

Statistics quiz scores for a sample of $n = 8$ students.

Quiz Score (X)	f	fX
10	1	10
9	2	18
8	4	32
7	0	0
6	1	6

LEARNING CHECK

1. Find the mean for the following sample of $n = 5$ scores: 1, 8, 7, 5, 9
2. A sample of $n = 6$ scores has a mean of $M = 8$. What is the value of ΣX for this sample?
3. One sample has $n = 5$ scores with a mean of $M = 4$. A second sample has $n = 3$ scores with a mean of $M = 10$. If the two samples are combined, what is the mean for the combined sample?
4. A sample of $n = 6$ scores has a mean of $M = 40$. One new score is added to the sample and the new mean is found to be $M = 35$. What can you conclude about the value of the new score?
   a. It must be greater 40.
   b. It must be less than 40.
5. Find the values for n, ΣX, and M for the sample that is summarized in the following frequency distribution table.

X	f
5	1
4	2
3	3
2	5
1	1

ANSWERS

1. $\Sigma X = 30$ and $M = 6$
2. $\Sigma X = 48$
3. The combined sample has $n = 8$ scores that total $\Sigma X = 50$. The mean is $M = 6.25$.
4. b
5. For this sample, $n = 12$, $\Sigma X = 33$, and $M = \frac{33}{12} = 2.75$.

CHARACTERISTICS OF THE MEAN

The mean has many characteristics that will be important in future discussions. In general, these characteristics result from the fact that every score in the distribution contributes to the value of the mean. Specifically, every score adds to the total (ΣX) and every score contributes one point to the number of scores (n). These two values (ΣX and n) determine the value of the mean. We now discuss four of the more important characteristics of the mean.

Changing a score Changing the value of any score changes the mean. For example, a sample of quiz scores for a psychology lab section consists of 9, 8, 7, 5, and 1. Note that the sample consists of $n = 5$ scores with $\Sigma X = 30$. The mean for this sample is

$$M = \frac{\sum X}{n} = \frac{30}{5} = 6.00$$

Now suppose that the score of $X = 1$ is changed to $X = 8$. Note that we have added 7 points to this individual's score, which also adds 7 points to the total (ΣX). After changing the score, the new distribution consists of

9, 8, 7, 5, 8

There are still $n = 5$ scores, but now the total is $\Sigma X = 37$. Thus, the new mean is

$$M = \frac{\Sigma X}{n} = \frac{37}{5} = 7.40$$

Notice that changing a single score in the sample has produced a new mean. You should recognize that changing any score also changes the value of ΣX (the sum of the scores), and, thus, always changes the value of the mean.

Introducing a new score or removing a score Adding a new score to a distribution, or removing an existing score, usually changes the mean. The exception is when the new score (or the removed score) is exactly equal to the mean. It is easy to visualize the effect of adding or removing a score if you remember that the mean is defined as the balance point for the distribution. Figure 3.4 shows a distribution of scores represented as boxes on a seesaw that is balanced at the mean, $\mu = 7$. Imagine what would happen if we added a new score (a new box) at $X = 10$. Clearly, the seesaw would tip to the right and we would need to move the pivot point (the mean) to the right to restore balance.

Now imagine what would happen if we removed the score (the box) at $X = 9$. This time the seesaw would tip to the left and, once again, we would need to change the mean to restore balance.

Finally, consider what would happen if we added a new score of $X = 7$, exactly equal to the mean. It should be clear that the seesaw would not tilt in either direction, so the mean would stay in exactly the same place. Also note that if we removed the new score at $X = 7$, the seesaw would remain balanced and the mean would not change. In general, adding a new score or removing an existing score causes the mean to change unless the that score is located exactly at the mean.

The following example demonstrates exactly how the new mean is computed when a new score is added to an existing sample.

EXAMPLE 3.4 Adding a score (or removing a score) has the same effect on the mean whether the original set of scores is a sample or a population. To demonstrate the calculation of the new mean, we will use the set of scores that is shown in Figure 3.4. This time, however, we will treat the scores as a sample with $n = 5$ and $M = 7$. Note that this sample must have $\Sigma X = 35$. What happens to the mean if a new score of $X = 13$ is added to the sample?

To find the new sample mean, we must determine how the values for n and ΣX are be changed by a new score. We begin with the original sample and then consider the effect of adding the new score. The original sample had $n = 5$ scores, so adding one new score produces $n = 6$. Similarly, the original sample had $\Sigma X = 35$. Adding a score

FIGURE 3.4

A distribution of $N = 5$ scores that is balanced with a mean of $\mu = 7$.

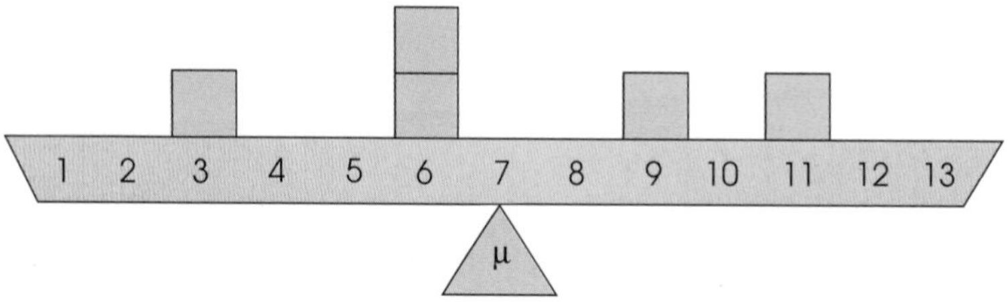

of $X = 13$ increases the sum by 13 points, producing a new sum of $\Sigma X = 35 + 13 = 48$. Finally, the new mean is computed using the new values for n and ΣX.

$$M = \frac{\Sigma X}{n} = \frac{48}{6} = 8$$

The entire process can be summarized as follows:

Original Sample	New Sample, Adding $X = 13$
$n = 5$	$n = 6$
$\Sigma X = 35$	$\Sigma X = 48$
$M = 35/5 = 7$	$M = 48/6 = 8$

Adding or subtracting a constant from each score If a constant value is added to every score in a distribution, the same constant is added to the mean. Similarly, if you subtract a constant from every score, the same constant is subtracted from the mean.

As mentioned in Chapter 2 (p. 38), Schmidt (1994) conducted a set of experiments examining how humor influences memory. In one study, participants were shown lists of sentences, of which half were humorous (I got a bill for my surgery—now I know why those doctors were wearing masks.) and half were nonhumorous (I got a bill for my surgery—those doctors were like robbers with the prices they charged.). The results showed that people consistently recalled more of the humorous sentences.

Table 3.2 shows the results for a sample of $n = 6$ participants. The first column shows their memory scores for nonhumorous sentences. Note that the total number of sentences recalled is $\Sigma X = 17$ for a sample of $n = 6$ participants, so the mean is $M = \frac{17}{6} = 2.83$. Now suppose that the effect of humor is to add a constant amount (2 points) to each individual's memory score. The resulting scores for humorous sentences are shown in the second column of the table. For these scores, the 6 participants recalled a total of $\Sigma X = 29$ sentences, so the mean is $M = \frac{29}{6} = 4.83$. Adding 2 points to each score has also added 2 points to the mean, from $M = 2.83$ to $M = 4.83$. (It is important to note that experimental effects are usually not as simple as adding or subtracting a constant amount. Nonetheless, the concept of adding a constant to every score is important and will be addressed in later chapters when we are using statistics to evaluate the effects of experimental manipulations.)

TABLE 3.2

Number of sentences recalled for humorous and nonhumorous sentences.

Participant	Nonhumorous Sentences	Humorous Sentences
A	4	6
B	2	4
C	3	5
D	3	5
E	2	4
F	3	5
	$\Sigma X = 17$	$\Sigma X = 29$
	$M = 2.83$	$M = 4.83$

Multiplying or dividing each score by a constant If every score in a distribution is multiplied by (or divided by) a constant value, the mean changes in the same way.

Multiplying (or dividing) each score by a constant value is a common method for changing the unit of measurement. To change a set of measurements from minutes to seconds, for example, you multiply by 60; to change from inches to feet, you divide by 12. One common task for researchers is converting measurements into metric units to conform to international standards. For example, publication guidelines of the American Psychological Association call for metric equivalents to be reported in parentheses when most nonmetric units are used. Table 3.3 shows how a sample of $n = 5$ scores measured in inches would be transformed to a set of scores measured in centimeters. (Note that 1 inch equals 2.54 centimeters.) The first column shows the original scores that total $\Sigma X = 50$ with $M = 10$ inches. In the second column, each of the original scores has been multiplied by 2.54 (to convert from inches to centimeters) and the resulting values total $\Sigma X = 127$, with $M = 25.4$. Multiplying each score by 2.54 has also caused the mean to be multiplied by 2.54. You should realize, however, that although the numerical values for the individual scores and the sample mean have changed, the actual measurements have not changed.

LEARNING CHECK

1. Adding a new score to a distribution always changes the mean. (True or false?)
2. Changing the value of a score in a distribution always changes the mean. (True or false?)
3. A population has a mean of $\mu = 40$.
   a. If 5 points were added to every score, what would be the value for the new mean?
   b. If every score were multiplied by 3, what would be the value for the new mean?
4. A sample of $n = 4$ scores has a mean of 9. If one person with a score of $X = 3$ is removed from the sample, what is the value for the new sample mean?

ANSWERS

1. False. If the score is equal to the mean, it does not change the mean.
2. True.
3. **a.** The new mean would be 45. **b.** The new mean would be 120.
4. The original sample has $n = 4$ and $\Sigma X = 36$. The new sample has $n = 3$ scores that total $\Sigma X = 33$. The new mean is $M = 11$.

TABLE 3.3

Measurements converted from inches to centimeters.

Original Measurement in Inches	Conversion to Centimeters (Multiply by 2.54)
10	25.40
9	22.86
12	30.48
8	20.32
11	27.94
$\Sigma X = 50$	$\Sigma X = 127.00$
$M = 10$	$M = 25.40$

3.3 THE MEDIAN

The second measure of central tendency we consider is called the *median*. The goal of the median is to locate the midpoint of the distribution. Unlike the mean, there are no specific symbols or notation to identify the median. Instead, the median is simply identified by the word *median*. In addition, the definition and the computations for the median are identical for a sample and for a population.

DEFINITION

If the scores in a distribution are listed in order from smallest to largest, the **median** is the midpoint of the list. More specifically, the median is the point on the measurement scale below which 50% of the scores in the distribution are located.

FINDING THE MEDIAN FOR MOST DISTRIBUTIONS

Defining the median as the *midpoint* of a distribution means that the scores are divided into two equal-sized groups. We are not locating the midpoint between the highest and lowest X values. To find the median, list the scores in order from smallest to largest. Begin with the smallest score and count the scores as you move up the list. The median is the first point you reach that is greater than 50% of the scores in the distribution. The median can be equal to a score in the list or it can be a point between two scores. Notice that the median is not algebraically defined (there is no equation for computing the median), which means that there is a degree of subjectivity in determining the exact value. However, the following two examples demonstrate the process of finding the median for most distributions.

EXAMPLE 3.5

This example demonstrates the calculation of the median when n is an odd number. With an odd number of scores, you list the scores in order (lowest to highest), and the median is the middle score in the list. Consider the following set of $N = 5$ scores, which have been listed in order:

3, 5, 8, 10, 11

The middle score is $X = 8$, so the median is equal to 8. Using the counting method, with $N = 5$ scores, the 50% point would be $2\frac{1}{2}$ scores. Starting with the smallest scores, we must count the 3, the 5, and the 8 before we reach the target of at least 50%. Again, for this distribution, the median is the middle score, $X = 8$.

EXAMPLE 3.6

This example demonstrates the calculation of the median when n is an even number. With an even number of scores in the distribution, you list the scores in order (lowest to highest) and then locate the median by finding the average of the middle two scores. Consider the following population:

1, 1, 4, 5, 7, 8

Now we select the middle pair of scores (4 and 5), add them together, and divide by 2:

$$\text{median} = \frac{4 + 5}{2} = \frac{9}{2} = 4.5$$

Using the counting procedure, with $N = 6$ scores, the 50% point is 3 scores. Starting with the smallest scores, we must count the first 1, the second 1, and the 4 before we reach the target of at least 50%. Again, the median for this distribution is 4.5, which is the first point on the scale beyond $X = 4$. For this distribution, exactly 3 scores (50%) are located below 4.5. Note: If there is a gap between the middle two scores, the convention is to define the median as the midpoint between the two scores. For example, if the middle two scores are $X = 4$ and $X = 6$, the median would be defined as 5.

The simple technique of listing and counting scores is sufficient to determine the median for most distributions and is always appropriate for discrete variables. Notice that this technique always produces a median that is either a whole number or is halfway between two whole numbers. With a continuous variable, however, it is possible to divide a distribution precisely in half so that *exactly* 50% of the distribution is located below (and above) a specific point. The procedure for locating the precise median is discussed in the following section.

FINDING THE PRECISE MEDIAN FOR A CONTINUOUS VARIABLE

Recall from Chapter 1 that a continuous variable consists of categories that can be split into an infinite number of fractional parts. For example, time can be measured in seconds, tenths of a second, hundredths of a second, and so on. When the scores in a distribution are measurements of a continuous variable, it is possible to split one of the categories into fractional parts and find the median by locating the precise point that separates the bottom 50% of the distribution from the top 50%. The following example demonstrates this process.

EXAMPLE 3.7

For this example, we will find the precise median for the following sample of $n = 8$ scores: 1, 2, 3, 4, 4, 4, 4, 6

The frequency distribution for this sample is shown in Figure 3.5(a). With an even number of scores, you normally would compute the average of the middle two scores to find the median. This process produces a median of $X = 4$. For a discrete variable,

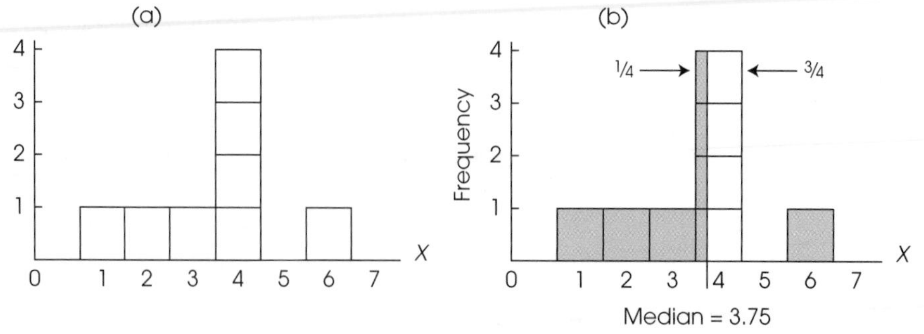

FIGURE 3.5
A distribution with several scores clustered at the median. The median for this distribution is positioned so that each of the four boxes above $X = 4$ is divided into two sections, with $\frac{1}{4}$ of each box below the median (to the left) and $\frac{3}{4}$ of each box above the median (to the right). As a result, there are exactly four boxes, 50% of the distribution, on each side of the median.

$X = 4$ is the correct value for the median. Recall from Chapter 1 that a discrete variable consists of indivisible categories, such as the number of children in a family. Some families have 4 children and some have 5, but none have 4.31 children. For a discrete variable, the category $X = 4$ cannot be divided and the whole number 4 is the median.

However, if you look at the distribution histogram, the value $X = 4$ does not appear to be the exact midpoint. The problem comes from the tendency to interpret a score of $X = 4$ as meaning exactly 4.00. However, if the scores are measurements of a continuous variable, then the score $X = 4$ actually corresponds to an interval from 3.5 to 4.5, and the median corresponds to a point within this interval.

To find the precise median, we first observe that the distribution contains $n = 8$ scores represented by 8 boxes in the graph. The median is the point that has exactly 4 boxes (50%) on each side. Starting at the left-hand side and moving up the scale of measurement, we accumulate a total of 3 boxes when we reach a value of 3.5 on the X-axis [see Figure 3.5(a)]. What is needed is 1 more box to reach the goal of 4 boxes (50%). The problem is that the next interval contains four boxes. The solution is to take a fraction of each box so that the fractions combine to give you one box. For this example, if we take $\frac{1}{4}$ of each box, the four quarters will combine to make one whole box. This solution is shown in Figure 3.5(b). The fraction is determined by the number of boxes needed to reach 50% and the number that exists in the interval.

$$\text{fraction} = \frac{\text{number needed to reach 50\%}}{\text{number in the interval}}$$

For this example, we needed 1 out of the 4 boxes in the interval, so the fraction is $\frac{1}{4}$. To obtain one-fourth of each box, the median is the point that is located exactly one-fourth of the way into the interval. The interval for $X = 4$ extends from 3.5 to 4.5. The interval width is 1 point, so one-fourth of the interval corresponds to 0.25 points. Starting at the bottom of the interval and moving up 0.25 points produces a value of $3.50 + 0.25 = 3.75$. This is the median, with exactly 50% of the distribution (4 boxes) on each side.

You may recognize that the process used to find the precise median in Example 3.7 is equivalent to the process of interpolation that was introduced in Chapter 2 (pp. 55–59). Specifically, the precise median is identical to the 50th percentile for a distribution, and interpolation can be used to locate the 50th percentile. The process of using interpolation is demonstrated in Box 3.2 using the same scores that were used in Example 3.7.

Remember, finding the precise midpoint by dividing scores into fractional parts is sensible for a continuous variable, however, it is not appropriate for a discrete variable. For example, a median time of 3.75 seconds is reasonable, but a median family size of 3.75 children is not.

THE MEDIAN, THE MEAN, AND THE MIDDLE

Earlier, we defined the mean as the "balance point" for a distribution because the distances above the mean must have the same total as the distances below the mean. One consequence of this definition is that the mean is always located inside the group of scores, somewhere between the smallest score and the largest score. You should notice, however, that the concept of a balance point focuses on distances rather than scores. In particular, it is possible to have a distribution in which the vast majority of the scores

BOX 3.2 USING INTERPOLATION TO LOCATE THE 50TH PERCENTILE (THE MEDIAN)

The precise median and the 50th percentile are both defined as the point that separates the top 50% of a distribution from the bottom 50%. In Chapter 2, we introduced interpolation as a technique for finding specific percentiles. We now use that same process to find the 50th percentile for the scores in Example 3.7.

Looking at the distribution of scores shown in Figure 3.5, exactly 3 of the $n = 8$ scores, or 37.5%, are located below the real limit of 3.5. Also, 7 of the $n = 8$ scores (87.5%) are located below the real limit of 4.5. This interval of scores and percentages is shown in the following table. Note that the median, the 50th percentile, is located within this interval.

	Scores (*X*)	Percentages	
Top	4.5	87.5%	
	?	50%	← Intermediate value
Bottom	3.5	37.5%	

We will find the 50th percentile (the median) using the 4-step interpolation process that was introduced in Chapter 2.

1. For the scores, the width of the interval is 1 point. For the percentages, the width is 50 points.
2. The value of 50% is located 37.5 points down from the top of the percentage interval. As a fraction of the whole interval, this is 37.5 out of 50, or 0.75 of the total interval.
3. For the scores, the interval width is 1 point and 0.75 of the interval corresponds to a distance of $0.75(1) = 0.75$ points.
4. Because the top of the interval is 4.5, the position we want is $4.5 - 0.75 = 3.75$

For this distribution, the 50% point (the 50th percentile) corresponds to a score of $X = 3.75$. Note that this is exactly the same value that we obtained for the median in Example 3.7.

are located on one side of the mean. Figure 3.6 shows a distribution of $N = 6$ scores in which 5 out of 6 scores have values less than the mean. In this figure, the total of the distances above the mean is 8 points and the total of the distances below the mean is 8 points. Thus, the mean is located in the middle of the distribution if you use the concept of distance to define the middle. However, you should realize that the mean is not necessarily located at the exact center of the group of scores.

The median, on the other hand, defines the middle of the distribution in terms of scores. In particular, the median is located so that half of the scores are on one side and half are on the other side. For the distribution in Figure 3.6, for example, the median is located at $X = 2.5$, with exactly 3 scores above this value and exactly 3 scores below. Thus, it is possible to claim that the median is located in the middle of the distribution, provided that the term *middle* is defined by the number of scores.

FIGURE 3.6

A population of $N = 6$ scores with a mean of $\mu = 4$. Notice that the mean does not necessarily divide the scores into two equal groups. In this example, 5 out of the 6 scores have values less than the mean.

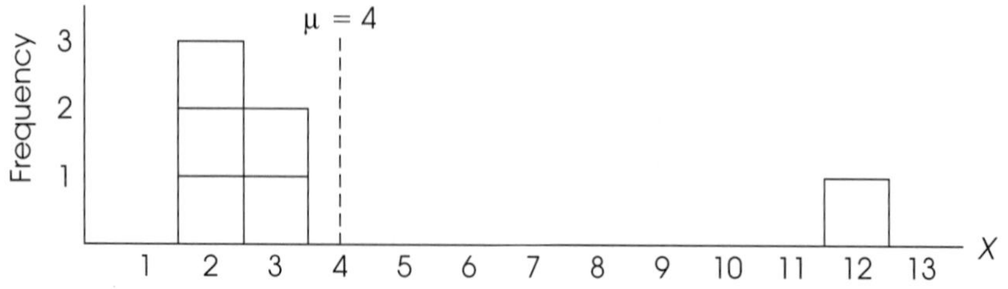

In summary, the mean and the median are both methods for defining and measuring central tendency. Although they both define the middle of the distribution, they use different definitions of the term *middle*.

LEARNING CHECK

1. Find the median for each distribution of scores:
   a. 3, 4, 6, 7, 9, 10, 11
   b. 8, 10, 11, 12, 14, 15
2. If you have a score of 52 on an 80-point exam, then you definitely scored above the median. (True or false?)
3. The following is a distribution of measurements for a continuous variable. Find the precise median that divides the distribution exactly in half.

   Scores: 1, 2, 2, 3, 4, 4, 4, 4, 4, 5

ANSWERS

1. **a.** The median is $X = 7$. **b.** The median is $X = 11.5$.
2. False. The value of the median would depend on where all of the scores are located.
3. The median is 3.70 (one-fifth of the way into the interval from 3.5 to 4.5).

3.4 THE MODE

The final measure of central tendency that we consider is called the *mode*. In its common usage, the word *mode* means "the customary fashion" or "a popular style." The statistical definition is similar in that the mode is the most common observation among a group of scores.

DEFINITION

In a frequency distribution, the **mode** is the score or category that has the greatest frequency.

As with the median, there are no symbols or special notation used to identify the mode or to differentiate between a sample mode and a population mode. In addition, the definition of the mode is the same for a population and for a sample distribution.

The mode is a useful measure of central tendency because it can be used to determine the typical or average value for any scale of measurement, including a nominal scale (see Chapter 1). Consider, for example, the data shown in Table 3.4. These data were obtained by asking a sample of 100 students to name their favorite restaurants in

TABLE 3.4

Favorite restaurants named by a sample of $n = 100$ students. *Caution:* The mode is a score or category, not a frequency. For this example, the mode is Luigi's, not $f = 42$.

Restaurant	f
College Grill	5
George & Harry's	16
Luigi's	42
Oasis Diner	18
Roxbury Inn	7
Sutter's Mill	12

town. The result is a sample of $n = 100$ scores with each score corresponding to the restaurant that the student named.

For these data, the mode is Luigi's, the restaurant (score) that was named most frequently as a favorite place. Although we can identify a modal response for these data, you should notice that it would be impossible to compute a mean or a median. For example, you cannot add the scores to determine a mean (How much is 5 College Grills plus 42 Luigi's?). Also, it is impossible to list the scores in order because the restaurants do not form any natural order. For example, the College Grill is not "more than" or "less than" the Oasis Diner, they are simply two different restaurants. Thus, it is impossible to obtain the median by finding the midpoint of the list. In general, the mode is the only measure of central tendency that can be used with data from a nominal scale of measurement.

The mode also can be useful because it is the only measure of central tendency that corresponds to an actual score in the data; by definition, the mode is the most frequently occurring score. The mean and the median, on the other hand, are both calculated values and often produce an answer that does not equal any score in the distribution. For example, in Figure 3.6 (p. 86) we presented a distribution with a mean of 4 and a median of 2.5. Note that none of the scores is equal to 4 and none of the scores is equal to 2.5. However, the mode for this distribution is $X = 2$; there are three individuals who actually have scores of $X = 2$.

In a frequency distribution graph, the greatest frequency appears as the tallest part of the figure. To find the mode, you simply identify the score located directly beneath the highest point in the distribution.

Although a distribution has only one mean and only one median, it is possible to have more than one mode. Specifically, it is possible to have two or more scores that have the same highest frequency. In a frequency distribution graph, the different modes correspond to distinct, equally high peaks. A distribution with two modes is said to be *bimodal,* and a distribution with more than two modes is called *multimodal.* Occasionally, a distribution with several equally high points is said to have no mode.

Incidentally, a bimodal distribution is often an indication that two separate and distinct groups of individuals exist within the same population (or sample). For example, if you measured height for each person in a set of 100 college students, the resulting distribution would probably have two modes, one corresponding primarily to the males in the group and one corresponding primarily to the females.

Technically, the mode is the score with the absolute highest frequency. However, the term *mode* is often used more casually to refer to scores with relatively high frequencies—that is, scores that correspond to peaks in a distribution even though the peaks are not the absolute highest points. For example, Athos, et al. (2007) asked people to identify the pitch for both pure tones and piano tones. Participants were presented with a series of tones and had to name the note corresponding to each tone. Nearly half the participants (44%) had extraordinary pitch-naming ability (absolute pitch), and were able to identify most of the tones correctly. Most of the other participants performed around chance level, apparently guessing the pitch names randomly. Figure 3.7 shows a distribution of scores that is consistent with the results of the study. There are two distinct peaks in the distribution, one located at $X = 2$ (chance performance) and the other located at $X = 10$ (perfect performance). Each of these values is a mode in the distribution. Note, however, that the two modes do not have identical frequencies. Eight people scored at $X = 2$ and only seven had scores of $X = 10$. Nonetheless, both of these points are called modes. When two modes have unequal frequencies, researchers occasionally differentiate the two values by calling the taller peak the *major mode,* and the shorter one the *minor mode.*

FIGURE 3.7

A frequency distribution for tone identification scores. An example of bimodal distributions.

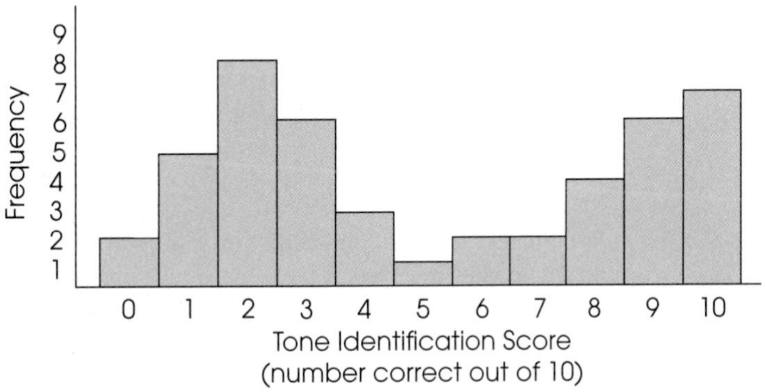

LEARNING CHECK

1. During the month of October, an instructor recorded the number of absences for each student in a class of $n = 20$ and obtained the following distribution.

Number of Absences	f
5	1
4	2
3	7
2	5
1	3
0	2

a. Using the mean, what is the average number of absences for the class?

b. Using the median, what is the average number of absences for the class?

c. Using the mode, what is the average number of absences for the class?

ANSWERS **1.**

a. The mean is 47/20 = 2.35.

b. The median is 2.5.

c. The mode is 3.

3.5 SELECTING A MEASURE OF CENTRAL TENDENCY

How do you decide which measure of central tendency to use? The answer to this question depends on several factors. Before we discuss these factors, however, note that you usually can compute two or even three measures of central tendency for the same set of data. Although the three measures often produce similar results, there are situations in which they are very different (see Section 3.6). Also note that the mean is usually the preferred measure of central tendency. Because the mean uses every score in the distribution, it typically produces a good representative value. Remember that the goal of central tendency is to find the single value that best represents the entire distribution. Besides being a good representative, the mean has the added advantage of being closely related to variance and standard deviation, the most common measures of variability (Chapter 4). This relationship makes the mean a valuable measure for purposes of inferential statistics. For these reasons, and others, the mean generally is considered to be the best of the three measures of central tendency. But there are specific situations in which it is impossible to compute a mean or in which the mean is not particularly representative. It is in these situations that the mode and the median are used.

WHEN TO USE THE MEDIAN

We consider four situations in which the median serves as a valuable alternative to the mean. In the first three cases, the data consist of numerical values (interval or ratio scales) for which you would normally compute the mean. However, each case also involves a special problem so that it is either impossible to compute the mean, or the calculation of the mean produces a value that is not central or not representative of the distribution. The fourth situation involves measuring central tendency for ordinal data.

Extreme scores or skewed distributions When a distribution has a few extreme scores, scores that are very different in value from most of the others, then the mean may not be a good representative of the majority of the distribution. The problem comes from the fact that one or two extreme values can have a large influence and cause the mean to be displaced. In this situation, the fact that the mean uses all of the scores equally can be a disadvantage. Consider, for example, the distribution of $n = 10$ scores in Figure 3.8. For this sample, the mean is

$$M = \frac{\Sigma X}{n} = \frac{203}{10} = 20.3$$

Notice that the mean is not very representative of any score in this distribution. Although most of the scores are clustered between 10 and 13, the extreme score of $X = 100$ inflates the value of ΣX and distorts the mean.

FIGURE 3.8

Frequency distribution of errors committed before reaching learning criterion. Notice that the graph shows two *breaks* in the X-axis. Rather than listing all the scores from 0 to 100, the graph jumps directly to the first score, which is $X = 10$, and then jumps directly from $X = 15$ to $X = 100$. The breaks shown in the X-axis are the conventional way of notifying the reader that some values have been omitted.

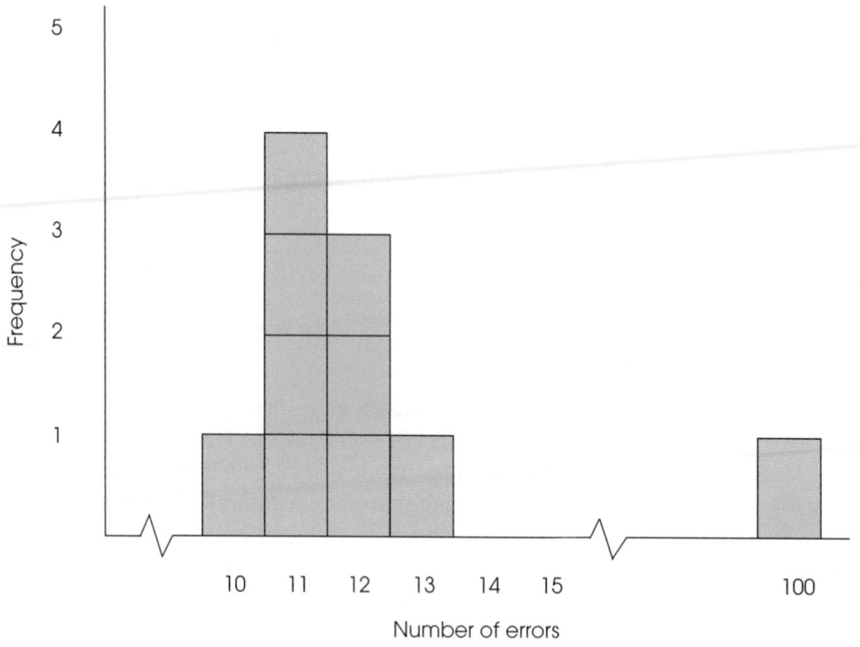

The median, on the other hand, is not easily affected by extreme scores. For this sample, $n = 10$, so there should be five scores on either side of the median. The median is 11.50. Notice that this is a very representative value. Also note that the median would be unchanged even if the extreme score were 1000 instead of only 100. Because it is relatively unaffected by extreme scores, the median commonly is used when reporting the average value for a skewed distribution. For example, the distribution of personal incomes is very skewed, with a small segment of the population earning incomes that are astronomical. These extreme values distort the mean, so that it is not very representative of the salaries that most of us earn. The median is the preferred measure of central tendency when extreme scores exist.

Undetermined values Occasionally, you encounter a situation in which an individual has an unknown or undetermined score. In psychology, this often occurs in learning experiments in which you are measuring the number of errors (or amount of time) required for an individual to solve a particular problem. For example, suppose that participants are asked to assemble a wooden puzzle as quickly as possible. The experimenter records how long (in minutes) it takes each individual to arrange all of the pieces to complete the puzzle. Table 3.5 presents results for a sample of $n = 6$ people.

TABLE 3.5

Number of minutes needed to assemble a wooden puzzle.

Person	Time (Min.)
1	8
2	11
3	12
4	13
5	17
6	Never finished

Notice that person 6 never completed the puzzle. After an hour, this person still showed no sign of solving the puzzle, so the experimenter stopped him or her. This person has an undetermined score. (There are two important points to be noted. First, the experimenter should not throw out this individual's score. The whole purpose for using a sample is to gain a picture of the population, and this individual tells us that part of the population cannot solve the puzzle. Second, this person should not be given a score of $X = 60$ minutes. Even though the experimenter stopped the individual after 1 hour, the person did not finish the puzzle. The score that is recorded is the amount of time needed to finish. For this individual, we do not know how long this is.)

It is impossible to compute the mean for these data because of the undetermined value. We cannot calculate the ΣX part of the formula for the mean. However, it is possible to determine the median. For these data, the median is 12.5. Three scores are below the median, and three scores (including the undetermined value) are above the median.

Number of Pizzas (X)	f
5 or more	3
4	2
3	2
2	3
1	6
0	4

Open-ended distributions A distribution is said to be *open-ended* when there is no upper limit (or lower limit) for one of the categories. The table in the margin provides an example of an open-ended distribution, showing the number of pizzas eaten during a 1 month period for a sample of $n = 20$ high school students. The top category in this distribution shows that three of the students consumed "5 or more" pizzas. This is an open-ended category. Notice that it is impossible to compute a mean for these data because you cannot find ΣX (the total number of pizzas for all 20 students). However, you can find the median. Listing the 20 scores in order produces $X = 1$ and $X = 2$ as the middle two scores. For these data, the median is 1.5.

Ordinal scale Many researchers believe that it is not appropriate to use the mean to describe central tendency for ordinal data. When scores are measured on an ordinal scale, the median is always appropriate and is usually the preferred measure of central tendency.

You should recall that ordinal measurements allow you to determine direction (greater than or less than) but do not allow you to determine distance. The median is compatible with this type of measurement because it is defined by direction: half of the scores are above the median and half are below the median. The mean, on the other hand, defines central tendency in terms of distance. Remember that the mean is the balance point for the distribution, so that the distances above the mean are exactly balanced by the distances below the mean. Because the mean is defined in terms of distances, and because ordinal scales do not measure distance, it is not appropriate to compute a mean for scores from an ordinal scale.

WHEN TO USE THE MODE

We consider three situations in which the mode is commonly used as an alternative to the mean, or is used in conjunction with the mean to describe central tendency.

Nominal scales The primary advantage of the mode is that it can be used to measure and describe central tendency for data that are measured on a nominal scale. Recall that the categories that make up a nominal scale are differentiated only by name. Because nominal scales do not measure quantity (distance or direction), it is impossible to compute a mean or a median for data from a nominal scale. Therefore, the mode is the only option for describing central tendency for nominal data.

Discrete variables Recall that discrete variables are those that exist only in whole, indivisible categories. Often, discrete variables are numerical values, such as the number of children in a family or the number of rooms in a house. When these variables produce numerical scores, it is possible to calculate means. In this situation, the calculated means are usually fractional values that cannot actually exist. For example, computing means generates results such as "the average family has 2.4 children and a house with 5.33 rooms." On the other hand, the mode always identifies the most typical case and, therefore, it produces more sensible measures of central tendency. Using the mode, our conclusion would be "the typical, or modal, family has 2 children and a house with 5 rooms." In many situations, especially with discrete variables, people are more comfortable using the realistic, whole-number values produced by the mode.

Describing shape Because the mode requires little or no calculation, it is often included as a supplementary measure along with the mean or median as a no-cost extra. The value of the mode (or modes) in this situation is that it gives an indication of the shape of the distribution as well as a measure of central tendency. Remember that the mode identifies the location of the peak (or peaks) in the frequency distribution graph. For example, if you are told that a set of exam scores has a mean of 72 and a mode of 80, you should have a better picture of the distribution than would be available from the mean alone (see Section 3.6).

IN THE LITERATURE
REPORTING MEASURES OF CENTRAL TENDENCY

Measures of central tendency are commonly used in the behavioral sciences to summarize and describe the results of a research study. For example, a researcher may report the sample means from two different treatments or the median score for a large sample. These values may be reported in verbal descriptions of the results, in tables, or in graphs.

In reporting results, many behavioral science journals use guidelines adopted by the American Psychological Association (APA), as outlined in the *Publication Manual of the American Psychological Association* (2010). We refer to the APA manual from time to time in describing how data and research results are reported in the scientific literature. The APA style uses the letter M as the symbol for the sample mean. Thus, a study might state:

> The treatment group showed fewer errors ($M = 2.56$) on the task than the control group ($M = 11.76$).

When there are many means to report, tables with headings provide an organized and more easily understood presentation. Table 3.6 illustrates this point.

The median can be reported using the abbreviation *Mdn,* as in "Mdn = 8.5 errors," or it can simply be reported in narrative text, as follows:

> The median number of errors for the treatment group was 8.5, compared to a median of 13 for the control group.

There is no special symbol or convention for reporting the mode. If mentioned at all, the mode is usually just reported in narrative text.

PRESENTING MEANS AND MEDIANS IN GRAPHS

Graphs also can be used to report and compare measures of central tendency. Usually, graphs are used to display values obtained for sample means, but occasionally sample medians are reported in graphs (modes are rarely, if ever, shown in a graph). The value of a graph is that it allows several means (or medians) to be shown simultaneously, so it is possible to make quick comparisons between groups or treatment conditions. When preparing a graph, it is customary to list the different groups or treatment conditions on the horizontal axis. Typically, these are the different values that make up the independent variable or the quasi-independent variable. Values for the dependent variable (the scores) are listed on the vertical axis. The means (or medians) are then displayed using a *line graph,* a *histogram,* or a *bar graph,* depending on the scale of measurement used for the independent variable.

Figure 3.9 shows an example of a *line graph* displaying the relationship between drug dose (the independent variable) and food consumption (the dependent variable). In this study, there were five different drug doses (treatment conditions) and they are listed along the horizontal axis. The five means appear as points in the graph. To construct this graph, a point was placed above each treatment condition so that the vertical position of the point corresponds to the mean score for the treatment condition. The points are then connected with straight lines. A line graph is used when the values on the horizontal axis are measured on an interval or a ratio scale. An alternative to the line graph is a *histogram.* For this example, the histogram would show a bar above each drug dose so that the height of each bar corresponds to the mean food consumption for that group, with no space between adjacent bars.

TABLE 3.6

The mean number of errors made on the task for treatment and control groups, divided by gender.

	Treatment	Control
Females	1.45	8.36
Males	3.83	14.77

FIGURE 3.9

The relationship between an independent variable (drug dose) and a dependent variable (food consumption). Because drug dose is a continuous variable, a continuous line is used to connect the different dose levels.

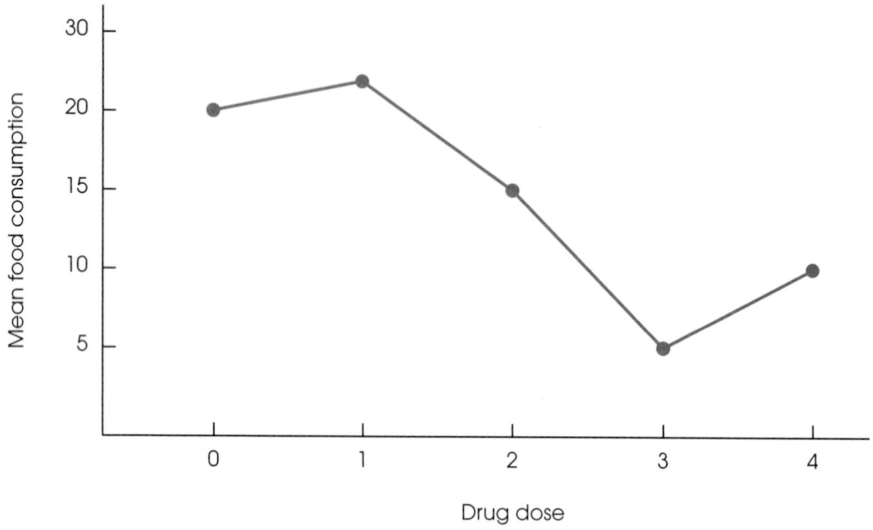

Figure 3.10 shows a bar graph displaying the median selling price for single-family homes in different regions of the United States. Bar graphs are used to present means (or medians) when the groups or treatments shown on the horizontal axis are measured on a nominal or an ordinal scale. To construct a bar graph, you simply draw a bar directly above each group or treatment so that the height of the bar corresponds to the mean (or median) for that group or treatment. For a bar graph, a space is left between adjacent bars to indicate that the scale of measurement is nominal or ordinal.

When constructing graphs of any type, you should recall the basic rules that we introduced in Chapter 2:

1. The height of a graph should be approximately two-thirds to three-quarters of its length.
2. Normally, you start numbering both the *X*-axis and the *Y*-axis with zero at the point where the two axes intersect. However, when a value of zero is part of the

FIGURE 3.10

Median cost of a new, single-family home by region.

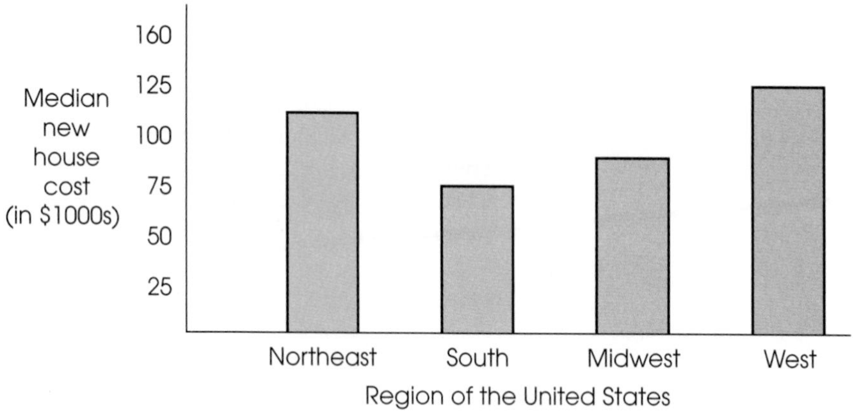

data, it is common to move the zero point away from the intersection so that the graph does not overlap the axes (see Figure 3.9).

Following these rules helps to produce a graph that provides an accurate presentation of the information in a set of data. Although it is possible to construct graphs that distort the results of a study (see Box 2.1), researchers have an ethical responsibility to present an honest and accurate report of their research results. ❑

3.6 CENTRAL TENDENCY AND THE SHAPE OF THE DISTRIBUTION

We have identified three different measures of central tendency, and often a researcher calculates all three for a single set of data. Because the mean, the median, and the mode are all trying to measure the same thing, it is reasonable to expect that these three values should be related. In fact, there are some consistent and predictable relationships among the three measures of central tendency. Specifically, there are situations in which all three measures have exactly the same value. On the other hand, there are situations in which the three measures are guaranteed to be different. In part, the relationships among the mean, median, and mode are determined by the shape of the distribution. We consider two general types of distributions.

SYMMETRICAL DISTRIBUTIONS

For a *symmetrical distribution,* the right-hand side of the graph is a mirror image of the left-hand side. If a distribution is perfectly symmetrical, the median is exactly at the center because exactly half of the area in the graph is on either side of the center. The mean also is exactly at the center of a perfectly symmetrical distribution because each score on the left side of the distribution is balanced by a corresponding score (the mirror image) on the right side. As a result, the mean (the balance point) is located at the center of the distribution. Thus, for a perfectly symmetrical distribution, the mean and the median are the same (Figure 3.11). If a distribution is roughly symmetrical, but not perfect, the mean and median are close together in the center of the distribution.

If a symmetrical distribution has only one mode, it is also in the center of the distribution. Thus, for a perfectly symmetrical distribution with one mode, all three measures of central tendency, the mean, the median, and the mode, have the same value. For a roughly symmetrical distribution, the three measures are clustered together in the center of the distribution. On the other hand, a bimodal distribution that is symmetrical [see Figure 3.11(b)] has the mean and median together in the center with the modes on each side. A rectangular distribution [see Figure 3.11(c)] has no mode because all X values occur with the same frequency. Still, the mean and the median are in the center of the distribution.

SKEWED DISTRIBUTIONS

The positions of the mean, median, and mode are not as consistently predictable in distributions of discrete variables (see Von Hippel, 2005).

In *skewed distributions,* especially distributions for continuous variables, there is a strong tendency for the mean, median, and mode to be located in predictably different positions. Figure 3.12(a), for example, shows a positively skewed distribution with the peak (highest frequency) on the left-hand side. This is the position of the mode. However, it should be clear that the vertical line drawn at the mode does not divide the distribution into two equal parts. To have exactly 50% of the distribution

FIGURE 3.11

Measures of central tendency for three symmetrical distributions: normal, bimodal, and rectangular.

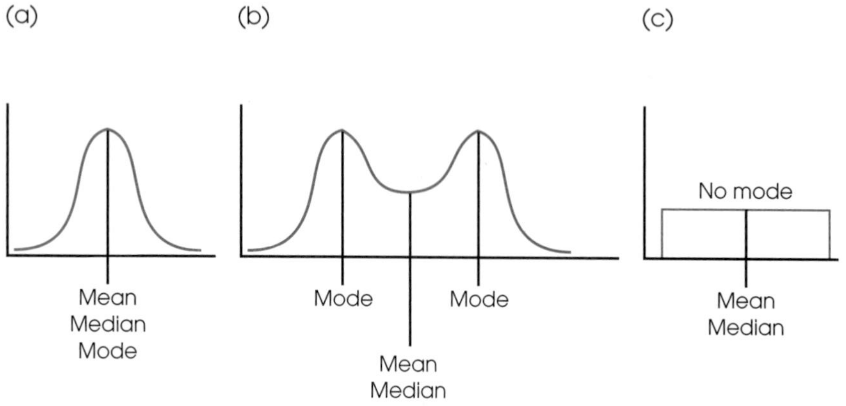

on each side, the median must be located to the right of the mode. Finally, the mean is located to the right of the median because it is the measure influenced most by the extreme scores in the tail and is displaced farthest to the right toward the tail of the distribution. Therefore, in a positively skewed distribution, the order of the three measures of central tendency from smallest to largest (left to right) is the mode, the median, and the mean.

Negatively skewed distributions are lopsided in the opposite direction, with the scores piling up on the right-hand side and the tail tapering off to the left. The grades on an easy exam, for example, tend to form a negatively skewed distribution [see Figure 3.12(b)]. For a distribution with negative skew, the mode is on the right-hand side (with the peak), whereas the mean is displaced toward the left by the extreme scores in the tail. As before, the median is located between the mean and the mode. In order from smallest value to largest value (left to right), the three measures of central tendency for a negatively skewed distribution are the mean, the median, and the mode.

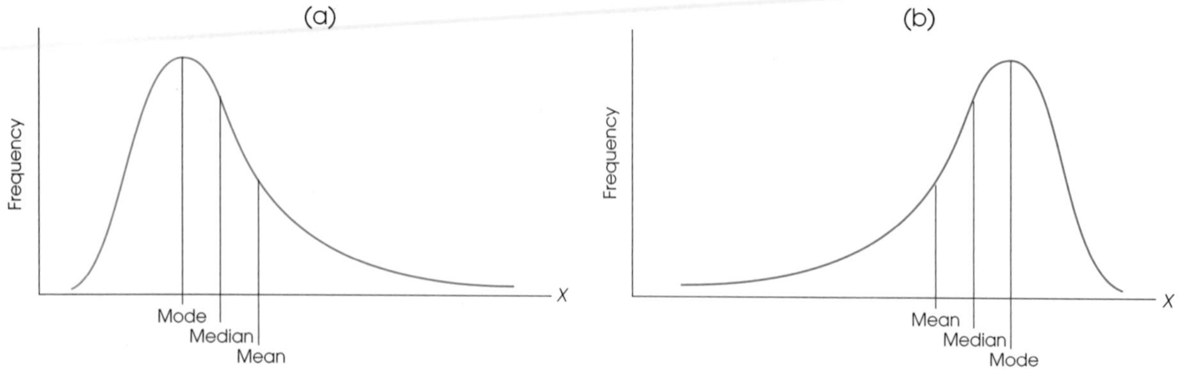

FIGURE 3.12

Measures of central tendency for skewed distributions.

LEARNING CHECK

1. Which measure of central tendency is most affected if one extremely large score is added to a distribution? (mean, median, mode)
2. Why is it usually considered inappropriate to compute a mean for scores measured on an ordinal scale?
3. In a perfectly symmetrical distribution, the mean, the median, and the mode will all have the same value. (True or false?)
4. A distribution with a mean of 70 and a median of 75 is probably positively skewed. (True or false?)

ANSWERS

1. mean
2. The definition of the mean is based on distances (the mean balances the distances) and ordinal scales do not measure distance.
3. False, if the distribution is bimodal.
4. False. The mean is displaced toward the tail on the left-hand side.

SUMMARY

1. The purpose of central tendency is to determine the single value that identifies the center of the distribution and best represents the entire set of scores. The three standard measures of central tendency are the mode, the median, and the mean.
2. The mean is the arithmetic average. It is computed by adding all of the scores and then dividing by the number of scores. Conceptually, the mean is obtained by dividing the total (ΣX) equally among the number of individuals (N or n). The mean can also be defined as the balance point for the distribution. The distances above the mean are exactly balanced by the distances below the mean. Although the calculation is the same for a population or a sample mean, a population mean is identified by the symbol μ, and a sample mean is identified by M. In most situations with numerical scores from an interval or a ratio scale, the mean is the preferred measure of central tendency.
3. Changing any score in the distribution causes the mean to be changed. When a constant value is added to (or subtracted from) every score in a distribution, the same constant value is added to (or subtracted from) the mean. If every score is multiplied by a constant, the mean is multiplied by the same constant.
4. The median is the midpoint of a distribution of scores. The median is the preferred measure of central tendency when a distribution has a few extreme scores that displace the value of the mean. The median also is used for open-ended distributions and when there are undetermined (infinite) scores that make it impossible to compute a mean. Finally, the median is the preferred measure of central tendency for data from an ordinal scale.
5. The mode is the most frequently occurring score in a distribution. It is easily located by finding the peak in a frequency distribution graph. For data measured on a nominal scale, the mode is the appropriate measure of central tendency. It is possible for a distribution to have more than one mode.
6. For symmetrical distributions, the mean is equal to the median. If there is only one mode, then it has the same value, too.
7. For skewed distributions, the mode is located toward the side where the scores pile up, and the mean is pulled toward the extreme scores in the tail. The median is usually located between these two values.

KEY TERMS

central tendency (73)
population mean (μ) (75)
sample mean (M) (75)
weighted mean (77)
median (83)
mode (87)
bimodal (88)
multimodal (88)
major mode (88)
minor mode (88)
line graph (93)
symmetrical distribution (95)
skewed distribution (95)
positive skew (95)
negative skew (96)

RESOURCES

Book Companion Website: www.cengage.com/psychology/gravetter

You can find a tutorial quiz and other learning exercises for Chapter 3 on the book companion website. The website also includes a workshop entitled *Central Tendency and Variability* that reviews the basic concept of the mean and introduces the concept of variability that is presented in Chapter 4.

aplia

Improve your understanding of statistics with Aplia's auto-graded problem sets and immediate, detailed explanations for every question. To learn more, visit **www.aplia.com/statistics**.

CENGAGEbrain.com

Psychology CourseMate brings course concepts to life with interactive learning, study, and exam preparation tools that support the printed textbook. A textbook-specific website, Psychology CourseMate includes an integrated interactive eBook and other interactive learning tools including quizzes, flashcards, and more.

Visit www.cengagebrain.com to access your account and purchase materials.

SPSS

General instructions for using SPSS are presented in Appendix D. Following are detailed instructions for using SPSS to compute the **Mean** and ΣX for a set of scores.

Data Entry

1. Enter all of the scores in one column of the data editor, probably VAR00001.

Data Analysis

1. Click **Analyze** on the tool bar, select **Descriptive Statistics,** and click on **Descriptives.**
2. Highlight the column label for the set of scores (VAR00001) in the left box and click the arrow to move it into the **Variable** box.
3. If you want ΣX as well as the mean, click on the **Options** box, select **Sum,** then click **Continue.**
4. Click **OK.**

SPSS Output

SPSS produces a summary table listing the number of scores (N), the maximum and minimum scores, the sum of the scores (if you selected this option), the mean, and the standard deviation. Note: The standard deviation is a measure of variability that is presented in Chapter 4.

FOCUS ON PROBLEM SOLVING

X	f
4	1
3	4
2	3
1	2

1. Although the three measures of central tendency appear to be very simple to calculate, there is always a chance for errors. The most common sources of error are listed next.
   a. Many students find it very difficult to compute the mean for data presented in a frequency distribution table. They tend to ignore the frequencies in the table and simply average the score values listed in the X column. You must use the frequencies *and* the scores! Remember that the number of scores is found by $N = \Sigma f$, and the sum of all N scores is found by ΣfX. For the distribution shown in the margin, the mean is $\frac{24}{10} = 2.40$.
   b. The median is the midpoint of the distribution of scores, not the midpoint of the scale of measurement. For a 100-point test, for example, many students incorrectly assume that the median must be $X = 50$. To find the median, you must have the *complete set* of individual scores. The median separates the individuals into two equal-sized groups.
   c. The most common error with the mode is for students to report the highest frequency in a distribution rather than the *score* with the highest frequency. Remember that the purpose of central tendency is to find the most representative score. For the distribution in the margin, the mode is $X = 3$, not $f = 4$.

DEMONSTRATION 3.1

COMPUTING MEASURES OF CENTRAL TENDENCY

For the following sample, find the mean, the median, and the mode. The scores are:

5, 6, 9, 11, 5, 11, 8, 14, 2, 11

Compute the mean The calculation of the mean requires two pieces of information: the sum of the scores, ΣX; and the number of scores, n. For this sample, $n = 10$ and

$$\Sigma X = 5 + 6 + 9 + 11 + 5 + 11 + 8 + 14 + 2 + 11 = 82$$

Therefore, the sample mean is

$$M = \frac{\Sigma X}{n} = \frac{82}{10} = 8.2$$

Find the median To find the median, first list the scores in order from smallest to largest. With an even number of scores, the median is the average of the middle two scores in the list. Listed in order, the scores are:

2, 5, 5, 6, 8, 9, 11, 11, 11, 14

The middle two scores are 8 and 9, and the median is 8.5.

Find the mode For this sample, $X = 11$ is the score that occurs most frequently. The mode is $X = 11$.

PROBLEMS

1. What general purpose is served by a good measure of central tendency?

2. A sample of $n = 7$ scores has a mean of $M = 9$. What is the value of ΣX for this sample?

3. Find the mean, median, and mode for the following sample of scores:

6, 2, 4, 1, 2, 2, 3, 4, 3, 2

4. Find the mean, median, and mode for the following sample of scores:

8, 7, 8, 8, 4, 9, 10, 7, 8, 8, 9, 8

5. Find the mean, median, and mode for the scores in the following frequency distribution table:

X	f
8	1
7	4
6	2
5	2
4	2
3	1

6. Find the mean, median, and mode for the scores in the following frequency distribution table:

X	f
10	1
9	2
8	3
7	3
6	4
5	2

7. For the following sample
a. Assume that the scores are measurements of a continuous variable and find the median by locating the precise midpoint of the distribution.
b. Assume that the scores are measurements of a discrete variable and find the median.

Scores: 1, 2, 3, 3, 3, 4

8. Why is it necessary to have more than one method for measuring central tendency?

9. A population with a mean of $\mu = 10$ has $\Sigma X = 250$. How many scores are in the population?

10. A sample of $n = 8$ scores has a mean of $M = 10$. If one new person with a score of $X = 1$ is added to the sample, what is the value for the new mean?

11. A sample of $n = 5$ scores has a mean of $M = 12$. If one person with a score of $X = 8$ is removed from the sample, what is the value for the new mean?

12. A sample of $n = 7$ scores has a mean of $M = 5$. After one new score is added to the sample, the new mean is found to be $M = 6$. What is the value of the new score? (Hint: Compare the values for ΣX before and after the score was added.)

13. A sample of $n = 9$ scores has a mean of $M = 10$. One person with a score of $X = 2$ is removed from the sample. What is the value for the new sample mean?

14. A population of $N = 20$ scores has a mean of $\mu = 15$. One score in the population is changed from $X = 8$ to $X = 28$. What is the value for the new population mean?

15. A sample of $n = 7$ scores has a mean of $M = 9$. One score in the sample is changed from $X = 19$ to $X = 5$. What is the value for the new sample mean?

16. A sample of $n = 11$ scores has a mean of $M = 4$. One person with a score of $X = 16$ is added to the sample. What is the value for the new sample mean?

17. A population of $N = 16$ scores has a mean of $\mu = 20$. After one score is removed from the population, the new mean is found to be $\mu = 19$. What is the value of the score that was removed? (Hint: Compare the values for ΣX before and after the score was removed.)

18. One sample has a mean of $M = 4$ and a second sample has a mean of $M = 8$. The two samples are combined into a single set of scores.
a. What is the mean for the combined set if both of the original samples have $n = 7$ scores?
b. What is the mean for the combined set if the first sample has $n = 3$ and the second sample has $n = 7$?
c. What is the mean for the combined set if the first sample has $n = 7$ and the second sample has $n = 3$?

19. One sample has a mean of $M = 5$ and a second sample has a mean of $M = 10$. The two samples are combined into a single set of scores.
a. What is the mean for the combined set if both of the original samples have $n = 5$ scores?
b. What is the mean for the combined set if the first sample has $n = 4$ scores and the second sample has $n = 6$?
c. What is the mean for the combined set if the first sample has $n = 6$ scores and the second sample has $n = 4$?

20. Explain why the mean is often not a good measure of central tendency for a skewed distribution.

21. Identify the circumstances in which the median rather than the mean is the preferred measure of central tendency.

22. A nutritionist studying weight gain for college freshmen obtains a sample of $n = 20$ first-year students at the state college. Each student is weighed on the first day of school and again on the last day of the semester. The following scores measure the change in weight, in pounds, for each student. A positive score indicates a weight gain during the semester.

+5, +6, +3, +1, +8, +5, +4, +4, +3, −1
+2, +7, +1, +5, +8, 0, +4, +6, +5, +3

a. Sketch a histogram showing the distribution of weight-change scores.
b. Calculate the mean weight-change score for this sample.
c. Does there appear to be a consistent trend in weight change during the semester?

23. One question on a student survey asks: In a typical week, how many times do you eat at a fast-food restaurant? The following frequency distribution table summarizes the results for a sample of $n = 20$ students.

Number of times per week	f
5 or more	2
4	2
3	3
2	6
1	4
0	3

a. Find the mode for this distribution.
b. Find the median for the distribution.
c. Explain why you cannot compute the mean using the data in the table.

24. For each of the following situations, identify the measure of central tendency (mean, median, or mode) that would provide the best description of the average score:

a. A news reporter interviewed people shopping in a local mall and asked how much they spent on summer vacations. Most people traveled locally and reported modest amounts but one couple had flown to Paris for a month and paid a small fortune.

b. A marketing researcher asked consumers to select their favorite from a set of four designs for a new product logo.

c. A driving instructor recorded the number of orange cones that each student ran over during the first attempt at parallel parking.

25. Does it ever seem to you that the weather is nice during the work week, but lousy on the weekend? Cerveny and Balling (1998) have confirmed that this is not your imagination—pollution accumulating during the work week most likely spoils the weekend weather for people on the Atlantic coast. Consider the following hypothetical data showing the daily amount of rainfall for 10 weeks during the summer.

Week	Average Daily Rainfall on Weekdays (Mon.–Fri.)	Average Daily Rainfall on Weekends (Sat.–Sun.)
1	1.2	1.5
2	0.6	2.0
3	0.0	1.8
4	1.6	1.5
5	0.8	2.2
6	2.1	2.4
7	0.2	0.8
8	0.9	1.6
9	1.1	1.2
10	1.4	1.7

a. Calculate the average daily rainfall (the mean) during the week, and the average daily rainfall for weekends.

b. Based on the two means, does there appear to be a pattern in the data?

CHAPTER

4

Variability

Tools You Will Need

The following items are considered essential background material for this chapter. If you doubt your knowledge of any of these items, you should review the appropriate chapter or section before proceeding.

- Summation notation (Chapter 1)
- Central tendency (Chapter 3)
  - Mean
  - Median

Preview

Although measures of central tendency, such as the mean and median, are handy ways to summarize large sets of data, these measures do not tell the whole story. Specifically, not everyone is average. Many people may perform near average, but others demonstrate performance that is far above (or below) average. In simple terms, people are different.

The differences that exist from one person to another are often called *diversity.* Researchers comparing cognitive skills for younger adults and older adults typically find that differences between people tend to increase as people age. For example, Morse (1993) reviewed hundreds of research studies published in *Psychology and Aging* and in the *Journal of Gerontology* from 1986 to 1990, and found increased diversity in older adults on measures of reaction time, memory, and some measures of intelligence. One possible explanation for the increased diversity is that different people respond differently to the aging process; some are essentially unchanged and others show a rapid decline. As a result, the differences from one person to another are larger for older people than for those who are younger.

It also is possible to measure differences in performance for the same person. These differences provide a measure of *consistency.* Often, large differences from trial to trial for the same person are viewed as evidence of poor performance. For example, the ability to consistently hit a target is an indication of skilled performance in many sports, whereas inconsistent performance indicates a lack of skill. Researchers in the field of aging have also found that older participants tend to have larger differences from trial to trial than younger participants. That is, older people seem to lose the ability to perform consistently on many tasks. For example, in a study comparing older and younger women, Wegesin and Stern (2004) found lower consistency for older women on a recognition memory task.

The Problem: To study phenomena such as diversity and consistency, it is necessary to devise a method to measure and objectively describe the differences that exist from one score to another within a distribution.

The Solution: A measure of *variability* provides an objective description of the differences between the scores in a distribution by measuring the degree to which the scores are spread out or are clustered together.

4.1 OVERVIEW

The term *variability* has much the same meaning in statistics as it has in everyday language; to say that things are variable means that they are not all the same. In statistics, our goal is to measure the amount of variability for a particular set of scores, a distribution. In simple terms, if the scores in a distribution are all the same, then there is no variability. If there are small differences between scores, then the variability is small, and if there are large differences between scores, then the variability is large.

DEFINITION

Variability provides a quantitative measure of the differences between scores in a distribution and describes the degree to which the scores are spread out or clustered together.

Figure 4.1 shows two distributions of familiar values for the population of adult males: Part (a) shows the distribution of men's heights (in inches), and part (b) shows the distribution of men's weights (in pounds). Notice that the two distributions differ in terms of central tendency. The mean height is 70 inches (5 feet, 10 inches) and the mean weight is 170 pounds. In addition, notice that the distributions differ in terms of variability. For example, most heights are clustered close together, within 5 or 6 inches of

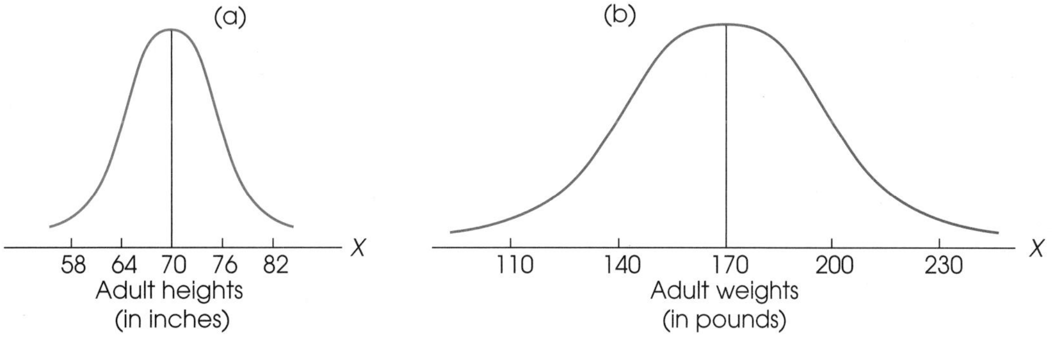

FIGURE 4.1

Population distributions of adult heights and adult weights.

the mean. On the other hand, weights are spread over a much wider range. In the weight distribution it is not unusual to find individuals who are located more than 30 pounds away from the mean, and it would not be surprising to find two individuals whose weights differ by more than 30 or 40 pounds. The purpose for measuring variability is to obtain an objective measure of how the scores are spread out in a distribution. In general, a good measure of variability serves two purposes:

1. Variability describes the distribution. Specifically, it tells whether the scores are clustered close together or are spread out over a large distance. Usually, variability is defined in terms of *distance.* It tells how much distance to expect between one score and another, or how much distance to expect between an individual score and the mean. For example, we know that the heights for most adult males are clustered close together, within 5 or 6 inches of the average. Although more extreme heights exist, they are relatively rare.
2. Variability measures how well an individual score (or group of scores) represents the entire distribution. This aspect of variability is very important for inferential statistics, in which relatively small samples are used to answer questions about populations. For example, suppose that you selected a sample of one person to represent the entire population. Because most adult males have heights that are within a few inches of the population average (the distances are small), there is a very good chance that you would select someone whose height is within 6 inches of the population mean. On the other hand, the scores are much more spread out (greater distances) in the distribution of weights. In this case, you probably would *not* obtain someone whose weight was within 6 pounds of the population mean. Thus, variability provides information about how much error to expect if you are using a sample to represent a population.

In this chapter, we consider three different measures of variability: the range, standard deviation, and the variance. Of these three, the standard deviation and the related measure of variance are by far the most important.

4.2 THE RANGE

The *range* is the distance covered by the scores in a distribution, from the smallest score to the largest score. When the scores are measurements of a continuous variable, the range can be defined as the difference between the upper real limit (URL) for the largest score (X_{max}) and the lower real limit (LRL) for the smallest score (X_{min}).

$$\text{range} = \text{URL for } X_{max} - \text{LRL for } X_{min}$$

If the scores have values from 1 to 5, for example, the range is 5.5 – 0.5 = 5 points. When the scores are whole numbers, the range is also a measure of the number of measurement categories. If every individual is classified as either 1, 2, 3, 4, or 5, then there are five measurement categories and the range is 5 points.

Continuous and discrete variables were discussed in Chapter 1 on pages 21–22.

Defining the range as the number of measurement categories also works for discrete variables that are measured with numerical scores. For example, if you are measuring the number of children in a family and the data produce values from 0 to 4, then there are five measurement categories (0, 1, 2, 3, and 4) and the range is 5 points. By this definition, when the scores are all whole numbers, the range can be obtained by

$$X_{max} - X_{min} + 1.$$

A commonly used alternative definition of the range simply measures the difference between the largest score (X_{max}) and the smallest score (X_{min}), without any reference to real limits.

$$\text{range} = X_{max} - X_{max}$$

By this definition, scores having values from 1 to 5 cover a range of only 4 points. Many computer programs, such as SPSS, use this definition. For discrete variables, which do not have real limits, this definition is often considered more appropriate. Also, this definition works well for variables with precisely defined upper and lower boundaries. For example, if you are measuring proportions of an object, like pieces of a pizza, you can obtain values such as $\frac{1}{8}, \frac{1}{4}, \frac{1}{2}, \frac{3}{4},$ and so on. Expressed as decimal values, the proportions range from 0 to 1. You can never have a value less than 0 (none of the pizza) and you can never have a value greater than 1 (all of the pizza). Thus, the complete set of proportions is bounded by 0 at one end and by 1 at the other. As a result, the proportions cover a range of 1 point.

Using either definition, the range is probably the most obvious way to describe how spread out the scores are—simply find the distance between the maximum and the minimum scores. The problem with using the range as a measure of variability is that it is completely determined by the two extreme values and ignores the other scores in the distribution. Thus, a distribution with one unusually large (or small) score has a large range even if the other scores are all clustered close together.

Because the range does not consider all of the scores in the distribution, it often does not give an accurate description of the variability for the entire distribution. For this reason, the range is considered to be a crude and unreliable measure of variability. Therefore, in most situations, it does not matter which definition you use to determine the range.

4.3 STANDARD DEVIATION AND VARIANCE FOR A POPULATION

The standard deviation is the most commonly used and the most important measure of variability. Standard deviation uses the mean of the distribution as a reference point and measures variability by considering the distance between each score and the mean.

In simple terms, the standard deviation provides a measure of the standard, or average, distance from the mean, and describes whether the scores are clustered closely around the mean or are widely scattered. The fundamental definition of the standard deviation is the same for both samples and populations, but the calculations differ slightly. We look first at the standard deviation as it is computed for a population, and then turn our attention to samples in Section 4.4.

Although the concept of standard deviation is straightforward, the actual equations appear complex. Therefore, we begin by looking at the logic that leads to these equations. If you remember that our goal is to measure the standard, or typical, distance from the mean, then this logic and the equations that follow should be easier to remember.

STEP 1 The first step in finding the standard distance from the mean is to determine the *deviation,* or distance from the mean, for each individual score. By definition, the deviation for each score is the difference between the score and the mean.

DEFINITION

Deviation is distance from the mean:

$$\text{deviation score} = X - \mu$$

A deviation score is often represented by a lowercase letter x.

For a distribution of scores with $\mu = 50$, if your score is $X = 53$, then your *deviation score* is

$$X - \mu = 53 - 50 = 3$$

If your score is $X = 45$, then your deviation score is

$$X - \mu = 45 - 50 = -5$$

Notice that there are two parts to a deviation score: the sign (+ or –) and the number. The sign tells the direction from the mean—that is, whether the score is located above (+) or below (–) the mean. The number gives the actual distance from the mean. For example, a deviation score of –6 corresponds to a score that is below the mean by a distance of 6 points.

STEP 2 Because our goal is to compute a measure of the standard distance from the mean, the obvious next step is to calculate the mean of the deviation scores. To compute this mean, you first add up the deviation scores and then divide by N. This process is demonstrated in the following example.

EXAMPLE 4.1 We start with the following set of $N = 4$ scores. These scores add up to $\Sigma X = 12$, so the mean is $\mu = \frac{12}{4} = 3$. For each score, we have computed the deviation.

X	$X - \mu$
8	+5
1	–2
3	0
0	–3
	$0 = \Sigma(X - \mu)$

Note that the deviation scores add up to zero. This should not be surprising if you remember that the mean serves as a balance point for the distribution. The total of the distances above the mean is exactly equal to the total of the distances below the mean (see page 76). Thus, the total for the positive deviations is exactly equal to the total for the negative deviations, and the complete set of deviations always adds up to zero.

Because the sum of the deviations is always zero, the mean of the deviations is also zero and is of no value as a measure of variability. The mean of the deviations is zero if the scores are closely clustered and it is zero if the scores are widely scattered. (You should note, however, that the constant value of zero can be useful in other ways. Whenever you are working with deviation scores, you can check your calculations by making sure that the deviation scores add up to zero.)

STEP 3 The average of the deviation scores does not work as a measure of variability because it is always zero. Clearly, this problem results from the positive and negative values canceling each other out. The solution is to get rid of the signs (+ and –). The standard procedure for accomplishing this is to square each deviation score. Using the squared values, you then compute the *mean squared deviation,* which is called *variance.*

DEFINITION

Population variance equals the mean squared deviation. Variance is the average squared distance from the mean.

Note that the process of squaring deviation scores does more than simply get rid of plus and minus signs. It results in a measure of variability based on *squared* distances. Although variance is valuable for some of the *inferential* statistical methods covered later, the concept of squared distance is not an intuitive or easy to understand *descriptive* measure. For example, it is not particularly useful to know that the squared distance from New York City to Boston is 26,244 miles squared. The squared value becomes meaningful, however, if you take the square root. Therefore, we continue the process with one more step.

STEP 4 Remember that our goal is to compute a measure of the standard distance from the mean. Variance, which measures the average squared distance from the mean, is not exactly what we want. The final step simply takes the square root of the variance to obtain the *standard deviation,* which measures the standard distance from the mean.

DEFINITION

Standard deviation is the square root of the variance and provides a measure of the standard, or average, distance from the mean.

$$\text{Standard deviation} = \sqrt{\text{variance}}$$

Figure 4.2 shows the overall process of computing variance and standard deviation. Remember that our goal is to measure variability by finding the standard distance from the mean. However, we cannot simply calculate the average of the distances because this value will always be zero. Therefore, we begin by squaring each distance, then we find the average of the squared distances, and finally we take the square root to obtain a measure of the standard distance. Technically, the standard deviation is the square root of the average squared deviation. Conceptually, however, the standard deviation provides a measure of the average distance from the mean.

Because the standard deviation and variance are defined in terms of distance from the mean, these measures of variability are used only with numerical scores that are obtained from measurements on an interval or a ratio scale. Recall from Chapter 1 (p. 24) that these two scales are the only ones that provide information about distance; nominal and ordinal scales do not. Also, recall from Chapter 3 (p. 92) that it is inappropriate to compute a mean for ordinal data and impossible to compute a mean for nominal data. Because the mean is a critical component in the calculation of standard deviation

FIGURE 4.2
The calculation of variance and standard deviation.

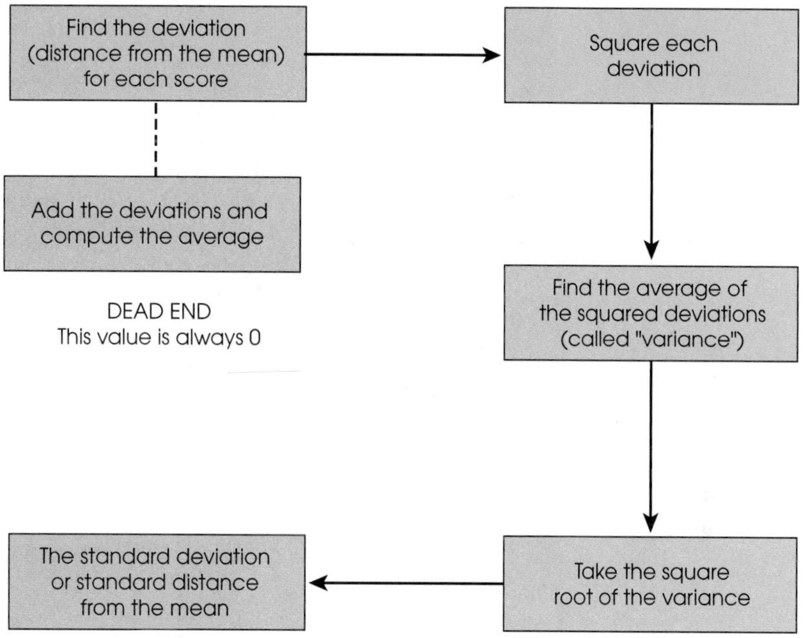

and variance, the same restrictions that apply to the mean also apply to these two measures of variability. Specifically, the mean, the standard deviation, and the variance should be used only with numerical scores from interval or ordinal scales of measurement.

Although we still have not presented any formulas for variance or standard deviation, you should be able to compute these two statistical values from their definitions. The following example demonstrates this process.

EXAMPLE 4.2 We will calculate the variance and standard deviation for the following population of $N = 5$ scores:

1, 9, 5, 8, 7

Remember that the purpose of standard deviation is to measure the standard distance from the mean, so we begin by computing the population mean. These five scores add up to $\Sigma X = 30$ so the mean is $\mu = \frac{30}{5} = 6$. Next, we find the deviation, (distance from the mean) for each score and then square the deviations. Using the population mean $\mu = 6$, these calculations are shown in the following table.

Score X	Deviation $X - \mu$	Squared Deviation $(X - \mu)^2$
1	–5	25
9	3	9
5	–1	1
8	2	4
7	1	1
		40 = the sum of the squared deviations

For this set of $N = 5$ scores, the squared deviations add up to 40. The mean of the squared deviations, the variance, is $\frac{40}{5} = 8$, and the standard deviation is $\sqrt{8} = 2.83$.

You should note that a standard deviation of 2.83 is a sensible answer for this distribution. The five scores in the population are shown in a histogram in Figure 4.3 so that you can see the distances more clearly. Note that the scores closest to the mean are only 1 point away. Also, the score farthest from the mean is 5 points away. For this distribution, the largest distance from the mean is 5 points and the smallest distance is 1 point. Thus, the standard distance should be somewhere between 1 and 5. By looking at a distribution in this way, you should be able to make a rough estimate of the standard deviation. In this case, the standard deviation should be between 1 and 5, probably around 3 points. The value we calculated for the standard deviation is in excellent agreement with this estimate.

Making a quick estimate of the standard deviation can help you avoid errors in calculation. For example, if you calculated the standard deviation for the scores in Figure 4.3 and obtained a value of 12, you should realize immediately that you have made an error. (If the biggest deviation is only 5 points, then it is impossible for the standard deviation to be 12.)

LEARNING CHECK

1. Briefly explain what is measured by the standard deviation and what is measured by the variance.
2. The deviation scores are calculated for each individual in a population of $N = 4$. The first three individuals have deviations of +2, +4, and –1. What is the deviation for the fourth individual?
3. What is the standard deviation for the following set of $N = 5$ scores: 10, 10, 10, 10, and 10? (*Note:* You should be able to answer this question directly from the definition of standard deviation, without doing any calculations.)
4. Calculate the variance for the following population of $N = 5$ scores: 4, 0, 7, 1, 3.

ANSWERS

1. Standard deviation measures the standard distance from the mean and variance measures the average squared distance from the mean.
2. The deviation scores for the entire set must add up to zero. The first four deviations add to +5 so the fifth deviation must be –5.
3. Because there is no variability (the scores are all the same), the standard deviation is zero.
4. For these scores, the sum of the squared deviations is 30 and the variance is 30/5 = 6.

FORMULAS FOR POPULATION VARIANCE AND STANDARD DEVIATION

The concepts of standard deviation and variance are the same for both samples and populations. However, the details of the calculations differ slightly, depending on whether you have data from a sample or from a complete population. We first consider the formulas for populations and then look at samples in Section 4.4.

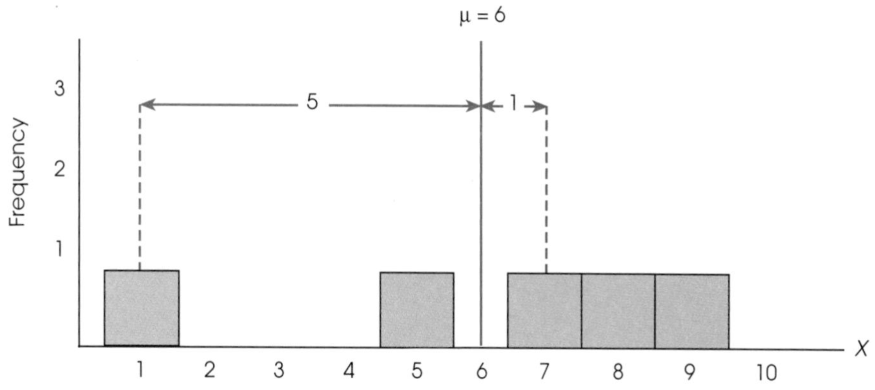

FIGURE 4.3
A frequency distribution histogram for a population of $N = 5$ scores. The mean for this population is $\mu = 6$. The smallest distance from the mean is 1 point, and the largest distance is 5 points. The standard distance (or standard deviation) should be between 1 and 5 points.

The sum of squared deviations (*SS*) Recall that variance is defined as the mean of the squared deviations. This mean is computed in exactly the same way you compute any mean: First find the sum, and then divide by the number of scores.

$$\text{variance} = \text{mean squared deviation} = \frac{\text{sum of squared deviations}}{\text{number of scores}}$$

The value in the numerator of this equation, the sum of the squared deviations, is a basic component of variability, and we focus on it. To simplify things, it is identified by the notation *SS* (for sum of squared deviations), and it generally is referred to as the *sum of squares*.

DEFINITION

SS, or sum of squares, is the sum of the squared deviation scores.

You need to know two formulas to compute *SS*. These formulas are algebraically equivalent (they always produce the same answer), but they look different and are used in different situations.

The first of these formulas is called the definitional formula because the symbols in the formula literally define the process of adding up the squared deviations:

$$\text{Definitional formula: } SS = \Sigma(X - \mu)^2 \quad (4.1)$$

To find the sum of the squared deviations, the formula instructs you to perform the following sequence of calculations:

1. Find each deviation score $(X - \mu)$.
2. Square each deviation score $(X - \mu)^2$.
3. Add the squared deviations.

The result is *SS*, the sum of the squared deviations. The following example demonstrates using this formula.

EXAMPLE 4.3

We compute *SS* for the following set of $N = 4$ scores. These scores have a sum of $\Sigma X = 8$, so the mean is $\mu = \frac{8}{4} = 2$. The following table shows the deviation and the squared deviation for each score. The sum of the squared deviation is $SS = 22$.

Score X	Deviation $X - \mu$	Squared Deviation $(X - \mu)^2$	
1	−1	1	$\Sigma X = 8$
0	−2	4	$\mu = 2$
6	+4	16	
1	−1	1	
		$22 = \Sigma(X - \mu)^2$	

Although the definitional formula is the most direct method for computing *SS*, it can be awkward to use. In particular, when the mean is not a whole number, the deviations all contain decimals or fractions, and the calculations become difficult. In addition, calculations with decimal values introduce the opportunity for rounding error, which can make the result less accurate. For these reasons, an alternative formula has been developed for computing *SS*. The alternative, known as the computational formula, performs calculations with the scores (not the deviations) and therefore minimizes the complications of decimals and fractions.

$$\text{computational formula: } SS = \Sigma X^2 - \frac{(\Sigma X)^2}{N} \tag{4.2}$$

The first part of this formula directs you to square each score and then add the squared values, ΣX^2. In the second part of the formula, you find the sum of the scores, ΣX, then square this total and divide the result by *N*. Finally, subtract the second part from the first. The use of this formula is shown in Example 4.4 with the same scores that we used to demonstrate the definitional formula.

EXAMPLE 4.4

The computational formula can be used to calculate *SS* for the same set of $N = 4$ scores we used in Example 4.3. Note that the formula requires the calculation of two sums: first, compute ΣX, and then square each score and compute ΣX^2. These calculations are shown in the following table. The two sums are used in the formula to compute *SS*.

X	X^2
1	1
0	0
6	36
1	1
$\Sigma X = 8$	$\Sigma X^2 = 38$

$$SS = \Sigma X^2 - \frac{(\Sigma X)^2}{N}$$

$$= 38 - \frac{(8)^2}{4}$$

$$= 38 - \frac{64}{4}$$

$$= 38 - 16$$

$$= 22$$

Note that the two formulas produce exactly the same value for *SS*. Although the formulas look different, they are in fact equivalent. The definitional formula provides the most direct representation of the concept of *SS*; however, this formula can be awkward to use, especially if the mean includes a fraction or decimal value. If you have a small group of scores and the mean is a whole number, then the definitional formula is fine; otherwise the computational formula is usually easier to use.

FINAL FORMULAS AND NOTATION

In the same way that sum of squares, or *SS*, is used to refer to the sum of squared deviations, the term *mean square*, or *MS*, is often used to refer to variance, which is the mean squared deviation.

With the definition and calculation of *SS* behind you, the equations for variance and standard deviation become relatively simple. Remember that variance is defined as the mean squared deviation. The mean is the sum of the squared deviations divided by *N*, so the equation for the *population variance* is

$$\text{variance} = \frac{SS}{N}$$

Standard deviation is the square root of variance, so the equation for the *population standard deviation* is

$$\text{standard deviation} = \sqrt{\frac{SS}{N}}$$

There is one final bit of notation before we work completely through an example computing *SS*, variance, and standard deviation. Like the mean (μ), variance and standard deviation are parameters of a population and are identified by Greek letters. To identify the standard deviation, we use the Greek letter sigma (the Greek letter *s*, standing for standard deviation). The capital letter sigma (Σ) has been used already, so we now use the lowercase sigma, σ, as the symbol for the population standard deviation. To emphasize the relationship between standard deviation and variance, we use σ^2 as the symbol for population variance (standard deviation is the square root of the variance). Thus,

$$\text{population standard deviation} = \sigma = \sqrt{\sigma^2} = \sqrt{\frac{SS}{N}} \quad (4.3)$$

$$\text{population variance} = \sigma^2 = \frac{SS}{N} \quad (4.4)$$

Earlier, in Examples 4.3 and 4.4, we computed the sum of squared deviations for a simple population of $N = 4$ scores (1, 0, 6, 1) and obtained $SS = 22$. For this population, the variance is

$$\sigma^2 = \frac{SS}{N} = \frac{22}{4} = 5.50$$

and the standard deviation is $\sigma = \sqrt{5.50} = 2.345$

LEARNING CHECK

1. Find the sum of the squared deviations, *SS*, for each of the following populations. Note that the definitional formula works well for one population but the computational formula is better for the other.

   Population 1: 3, 1, 5, 1
   Population 2: 6, 4, 2, 0, 9, 3

2. **a.** Sketch a histogram showing the frequency distribution for the following population of $N = 6$ scores: 12, 0, 1, 7, 4, 6. Locate the mean in your sketch, and estimate the value of the standard deviation.

   b. Calculate *SS*, variance, and the standard deviation for these scores. How well does your estimate compare with the actual standard deviation?

ANSWERS

1. For population 1, the mean is not a whole number ($M = 2.5$) and the computational formula is better and produces $SS = 11$. The mean is a whole number ($M = 4$) and definitional formula works well for population 2, which has $SS = 50$.

2. **a.** Your sketch should show a mean of $\mu = 5$. The scores closest to the mean are $X = 4$ and $X = 6$, both of which are only 1 point away. The score farthest from the mean is $X = 12$, which is 7 points away. The standard deviation should have a value between 1 and 7, probably around 4 points.

   b. For these scores, $SS = 96$, the variance is $96/6 = 16$, and the standard deviation is $\sigma = 4$.

4.4 STANDARD DEVIATION AND VARIANCE FOR SAMPLES

A sample statistic is said to be *biased* if, on average, it consistently overestimates or underestimates the corresponding population parameter.

The goal of inferential statistics is to use the limited information from samples to draw general conclusions about populations. The basic assumption of this process is that samples should be representative of the populations from which they come. This assumption poses a special problem for variability because samples consistently tend to be less variable than their populations. An example of this general tendency is shown in Figure 4.4. Notice that a few extreme scores in the population tend to make the population variability relatively large. However, these extreme values are unlikely to be obtained when you are selecting a sample, which means that the sample variability is relatively small. The fact that a sample tends to be less variable than its population means that sample variability gives a *biased* estimate of population variability. This bias is in the direction of underestimating the population value rather than being right on the mark. (The concept of a biased statistic is discussed in more detail in Section 4.5.)

Fortunately, the bias in sample variability is consistent and predictable, which means it can be corrected. For example, if the speedometer in your car consistently shows speeds that are 5 mph slower than you are actually going, it does not mean that

FIGURE 4.4

The population of adult heights forms a normal distribution. If you select a sample from this population, you are most likely to obtain individuals who are near average in height. As a result, the scores in the sample are less variable (spread out) than the scores in the population.

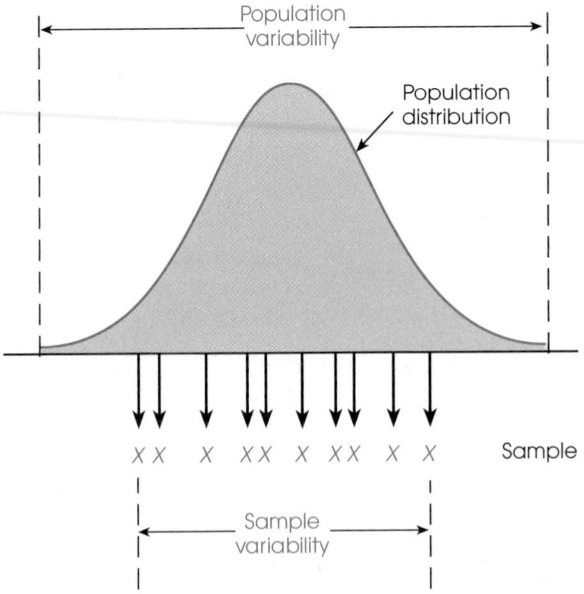

the speedometer is useless. It simply means that you must make an adjustment to the speedometer reading to get an accurate speed. In the same way, we make an adjustment in the calculation of sample variance. The purpose of the adjustment is to make the resulting value for sample variance an accurate and unbiased representative of the population variance.

The calculations of variance and standard deviation for a sample follow the same steps that were used to find population variance and standard deviation. Except for minor changes in notation, the first three steps in this process are exactly the same for a sample as they were for a population. That is, calculating the sum of the squared deviations, *SS*, is the same for a sample as it is for a population. The changes in notation involve using *M* for the sample mean instead of μ, and using *n* (instead of *N*) for the number of scores. Thus, to find the *SS* for a sample

1. Find the deviation from the mean for each score: deviation $= X - M$
2. Square each deviation: squared deviation $= (X - M)^2$
3. Add the squared deviations: $SS = \Sigma(X - M)^2$

These three steps can be summarized in a definitional formula for *SS*:

$$\text{Definitional formula: } SS = \Sigma(X - M)^2 \tag{4.5}$$

The value of *SS* also can be obtained using a computational formula. Except for one minor difference in notation (using *n* in place of *N*), the computational formula for *SS* is the same for a sample as it was for a population (see Equation 4.2). Using sample notation, this formula is:

$$\text{Computational formula: } SS = \Sigma X^2 - \frac{(\Sigma X)^2}{n} \tag{4.6}$$

Again, calculating *SS* for a sample is exactly the same as for a population, except for minor changes in notation. After you compute *SS*, however, it becomes critical to differentiate between samples and populations. To correct for the bias in sample variability, it is necessary to make an adjustment in the formulas for sample variance and standard deviation. With this in mind, *sample variance* (identified by the symbol s^2) is defined as

$$\text{sample variance} = s^2 = \frac{SS}{n - 1} \tag{4.7}$$

Sample standard deviation (identified by the symbol *s*) is simply the square root of the variance.

$$\text{sample standard deviation} = s = \sqrt{s^2} = \sqrt{\frac{SS}{n - 1}} \tag{4.8}$$

Notice that the sample formulas divide by $n - 1$, unlike the population formulas, which divide by *N* (see Equations 4.3 and 4.4). This is the adjustment that is necessary to correct for the bias in sample variability. The effect of the adjustment is to increase the value that you obtain. Dividing by a smaller number ($n - 1$ instead of *n*) produces a larger result and makes sample variance an accurate and unbiased estimator of population variance. The following example demonstrates the calculation of variance and standard deviation for a sample.

Remember, sample variability tends to underestimate population variability unless some correction is made.

EXAMPLE 4.5 We have selected a sample of $n = 7$ scores from a population. The scores are 1, 6, 4, 3, 8, 7, 6. The frequency distribution histogram for this sample is shown in Figure 4.5. Before we begin any calculations, you should be able to look at the sample distribution and make a preliminary estimate of the outcome. Remember that standard deviation measures the standard distance from the mean. For this sample, the mean is $M = \frac{35}{7} = 5$. The scores closest to the mean are $X = 4$ and $X = 6$, both of which are exactly 1 point away. The score farthest from the mean is $X = 1$, which is 4 points away. With the smallest distance from the mean equal to 1 and the largest distance equal to 4, we should obtain a standard distance somewhere between 1 and 4, probably around 2.5.

We begin the calculations by finding the value of *SS* for this sample. Because there are only a few scores and the mean is a whole number ($M = 5$), the definitional formula is easy to use. The scores, the deviations, and the squared deviations are shown in the following table.

Squared Score X	Deviation $X - M$	Deviation $(X - M)^2$
1	–4	16
6	1	1
4	–1	1
3	–2	4
8	3	9
7	2	4
6	1	1
		$36 = SS = \Sigma(X - M)^2$

The sum of squared deviations for this sample is $SS = 36$. Continuing the calculations,

$$\text{sample variance} = s^2 = \frac{SS}{n-1} = \frac{36}{7-1} = 6$$

Finally, the standard deviation is

$$s = \sqrt{s^2} = \sqrt{6} = 2.45$$

Note that the value we obtained is in excellent agreement with our preliminary prediction (see Figure 4.5).

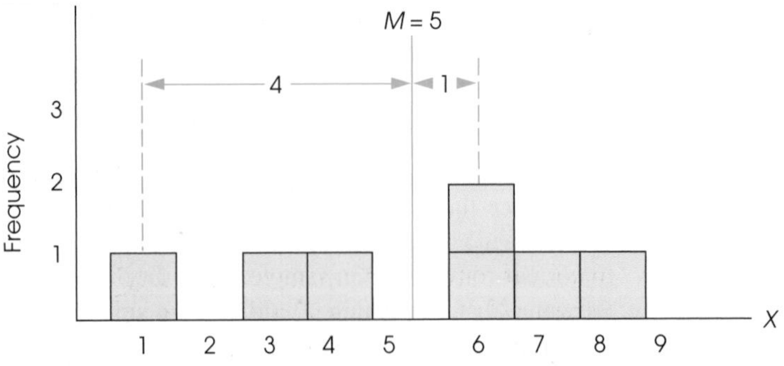

FIGURE 4.5
The frequency distribution histogram for a sample of $n = 7$ scores. The sample mean is $M = 5$. The smallest distance from the mean is 1 point, and the largest distance from the mean is 4 points. The standard distance (standard deviation) should be between 1 and 4 points, or about 2.5.

Remember that the formulas for sample variance and standard deviation were constructed so that the sample variability would provide a good estimate of population variability. For this reason, the sample variance is often called *estimated population variance,* and the sample standard deviation is called *estimated population standard deviation.* When you have only a sample to work with, the variance and standard deviation for the sample provide the best possible estimates of the population variability.

SAMPLE VARIABILITY AND DEGREES OF FREEDOM

Although the concept of a deviation score and the calculation of *SS* are almost exactly the same for samples and populations, the minor differences in notation are really very important. Specifically, with a population, you find the deviation for each score by measuring its distance from the population mean, μ. With a sample, on the other hand, the value of μ is unknown and you must measure distances from the sample mean. Because the value of the sample mean varies from one sample to another, you must first compute the sample mean before you can begin to compute deviations. However, calculating the value of M places a restriction on the variability of the scores in the sample. This restriction is demonstrated in the following example.

EXAMPLE 4.6

Suppose we select a sample of $n = 3$ scores and compute a mean of $M = 5$. The first two scores in the sample have no restrictions; they are independent of each other and they can have any values. For this demonstration, we assume that we obtained $X = 2$ for the first score and $X = 9$ for the second. At this point, however, the third score in the sample is restricted.

X	A sample of $n = 3$ scores with a mean of $M = 5$.
2	
9	
—	← What is the third score?

For this example, the third score must be $X = 4$. The reason that the third score is restricted to $X = 4$ is that the entire sample of $n = 3$ scores has a mean of $M = 5$. For 3 scores to have a mean of 5, the scores must have a total of $\Sigma X = 15$. Because the first two scores add up to 11 $(9 + 2)$, the third score must be $X = 4$.

In Example 4.6, the first two out of three scores were free to have any values, but the final score was dependent on the values chosen for the first two. In general, with a sample of n scores, the first $n - 1$ scores are free to vary, but the final score is restricted. As a result, the sample is said to have $n - 1$ *degrees of freedom.*

DEFINITION

For a sample of n scores, the **degrees of freedom,** or ***df,*** for the sample variance are defined as $df = n - 1$. The degrees of freedom determine the number of scores in the sample that are independent and free to vary.

The $n - 1$ degrees of freedom for a sample is the same $n - 1$ that is used in the formulas for sample variance and standard deviation. Remember that variance is defined as the mean squared deviation. As always, this mean is computed by finding the sum and dividing by the number of scores:

$$\text{mean} = \frac{\text{sum}}{\text{number}}$$

To calculate sample variance (mean squared deviation), we find the sum of the squared deviations (*SS*) and divide by the number of scores that are free to vary. This number is $n - 1 = df$. Thus, the formula for sample variance is

$$s^2 = \frac{\text{sum of squared deviations}}{\text{number of scores free to vary}} = \frac{SS}{df} = \frac{SS}{n-1}$$

Later in this book, we use the concept of degrees of freedom in other situations. For now, remember that knowing the sample mean places a restriction on sample variability. Only $n - 1$ of the scores are free to vary; $df = n - 1$.

LEARNING CHECK

1. **a.** Sketch a histogram showing the frequency distribution for the following sample of $n = 5$ scores: 3, 1, 9, 4, 3. Locate the mean in your sketch, and estimate the value of the sample standard deviation.
   b. Calculate *SS*, variance, and standard deviation for this sample. How well does your estimate from part a compare with the real standard deviation?
2. For the following set of scores: 1, 5, 7, 3, 4
   a. Assume that this is a population of $N = 5$ scores and compute *SS* and variance for the population.
   b. Assume that this is a sample of $n = 5$ scores and compute *SS* and variance for the sample.
3. Explain why the formula for sample variance divides *SS* by $n - 1$ instead of dividing by n.

ANSWERS

1. **a.** Your graph should show a sample mean of $M = 4$. The score farthest from the mean is $X = 9$ (which is 5 points away), and the closest score is $X = 4$ (which is 0 points away). You should estimate the standard deviation to be between 1 and 5 points, probably around 3 points.
   b. For this sample, $SS = 36$; the sample variance is $36/4 = 9$; the sample standard deviation is $\sqrt{9} = 3$.
2. **a.** $SS = 20$ and the population variance is $20/5 = 4$.
   b. $SS = 20$ and the sample variance is $20/4 = 5$.
3. Without some correction, sample variability consistently underestimates the population variability. Dividing by a smaller number ($n - 1$ instead of n) increases the value of the sample variance and makes it an unbiased estimate of the population variance.

4.5 MORE ABOUT VARIANCE AND STANDARD DEVIATION

PRESENTING THE MEAN AND STANDARD DEVIATION IN A FREQUENCY DISTRIBUTION GRAPH

In frequency distribution graphs, we identify the position of the mean by drawing a vertical line and labeling it with μ or M. Because the standard deviation measures distance from the mean, it is represented by a line or an arrow drawn from the mean outward for a distance equal to the standard deviation and labeled with a σ or an s. Figure 4.6(a) shows an example of a population distribution with a mean of $\mu = 80$ and a standard

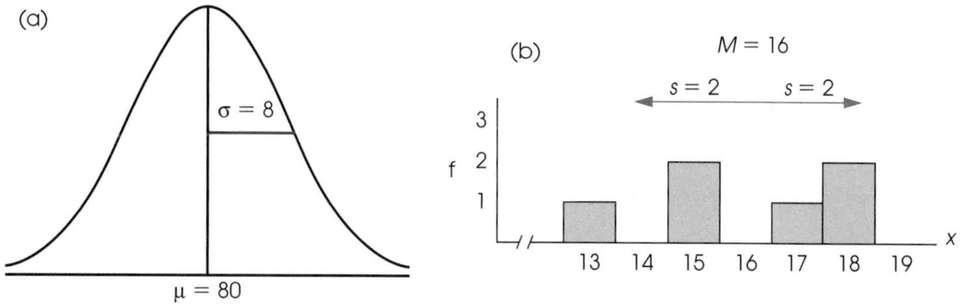

FIGURE 4.6

Showing means and standard deviations in frequency distribution graphs. (a) A population distribution with a mean of $\mu = 80$ and a standard deviation of $\sigma = 8$. (b) A sample with a mean of $M = 16$ and a standard deviation of $s = 2$.

deviation of $\sigma = 8$, and Figure 4.6(b) shows the frequency distribution for a sample with a mean of $M = 16$ and a standard deviation of $s = 2$. For rough sketches, you can identify the mean with a vertical line in the middle of the distribution. The standard deviation line should extend approximately halfway from the mean to the most extreme score. [*Note:* In Figure 4.6(a) we show the standard deviation as a line to the right of the mean. You should realize that we could have drawn the line pointing to the left, or we could have drawn two lines (or arrows), with one pointing to the right and one pointing to the left, as in Figure 4.6(b). In each case, the goal is to show the standard distance from the mean.]

SAMPLE VARIANCE AS AN UNBIASED STATISTIC

Earlier we noted that sample variability tends to underestimate the variability in the corresponding population. To correct for this problem we adjusted the formula for sample variance by dividing by $n - 1$ instead of dividing by n. The result of the adjustment is that sample variance provides a much more accurate representation of the population variance. Specifically, dividing by $n - 1$ produces a sample variance that provides an *unbiased* estimate of the corresponding population variance. This does not mean that each individual sample variance is exactly equal to its population variance. In fact, some sample variances overestimate the population value and some underestimate it. However, the average of all the sample variances produces an accurate estimate of the population variance. This is the idea behind the concept of an unbiased statistic.

DEFINITIONS

A sample statistic is **unbiased** if the average value of the statistic is equal to the population parameter. (The average value of the statistic is obtained from all the possible samples for a specific sample size, *n*.)

A sample statistic is **biased** if the average value of the statistic either underestimates or overestimates the corresponding population parameter.

The following example demonstrates the concept of biased and unbiased statistics.

EXAMPLE 4.7

We have structured this example to mimic "sampling with replacement," which is covered in Chapter 6.

We begin with a population that consists of exactly $N = 6$ scores: 0, 0, 3, 3, 9, 9. With a few calculations you should be able to verify that this population has a mean of $\mu = 4$ and a variance of $\sigma^2 = 14$.

Next, we select samples of $n = 2$ scores from this population. In fact, we obtain every single possible sample with $n = 2$. The complete set of samples is listed in Table 4.1. Notice that the samples are listed systematically to ensure that every possible sample is included. We begin by listing all the samples that have $X = 0$ as the first score, then all the samples with $X = 3$ as the first score, and so on. Notice that the table shows a total of 9 samples.

Finally, we have computed the mean and the variance for each sample. Note that the sample variance has been computed two different ways. First, we examine what happens if there is no correction for bias and the sample variance is computed by simply dividing *SS* by *n*. Second, we examine the correct sample variances for which *SS* is divided by $n - 1$ to produce an unbiased measure of variance. You should verify our calculations by computing one or two of the values for yourself. The complete set of sample means and sample variances is presented in Table 4.1.

First, consider the column of biased sample variances, which were calculated by dividing by *n*. These 9 sample variances add up to a total of 63, which produces an average value of $\frac{63}{9} = 7$. The original population variance, however, is $\sigma^2 = 14$. Note that the average of the sample variances is *not* equal to the population variance. If the sample variance is computed by dividing by *n*, the resulting values do not produce an accurate estimate of the population variance. On average, these sample variances underestimate the population variance and, therefore, are biased statistics.

Next, consider the column of sample variances that are computed using $n - 1$. Although the population has a variance of $\sigma^2 = 14$, you should notice that none of the samples has a variance exactly equal to 14. However, if you consider the complete set of sample variances, you will find that the 9 values add up to a total of 126, which produces an average value of $\frac{126}{9} = 14$. Thus, the average of the sample variances is exactly equal to the original population variance. On average, the sample variance (computed using $n - 1$) produces an accurate, unbiased estimate of the population variance.

Finally, direct your attention to the column of sample means. For this example, the original population has a mean of $\mu = 4$. Although none of the samples has a

TABLE 4.1

The set of all the possible samples for $n = 2$ selected from the population described in Example 4.7. The mean is computed for each sample, and the variance is computed two different ways: (1) dividing by *n*, which is incorrect and produces a biased statistic; and (2) dividing by $n - 1$, which is correct and produces an unbiased statistic.

				Sample Statistics	
Sample	First Score	Second Score	Mean *M*	Biased Variance (Using *n*)	Unbiased Variance (Using *n* – 1)
1	0	0	0.00	0.00	0.00
2	0	3	1.50	2.25	4.50
3	0	9	4.50	20.25	40.50
4	3	0	1.50	2.25	4.50
5	3	3	3.00	0.00	0.00
6	3	9	6.00	9.00	18.00
7	9	0	4.50	20.25	40.50
8	9	3	6.00	9.00	18.00
9	9	9	9.00	0.00	0.00
		Totals	36.00	63.00	126.00

mean exactly equal to 4, if you consider the complete set of sample means, you will find that the 9 sample means add up to a total of 36, so the average of the sample means is $\frac{36}{9} = 4$. Note that the average of the sample means is exactly equal to the population mean. Again, this is what is meant by the concept of an unbiased statistic. On average, the sample values provide an accurate representation of the population. In this example, the average of the 9 sample means is exactly equal to the population mean.

In summary, both the sample mean and the sample variance (using $n - 1$) are examples of unbiased statistics. This fact makes the sample mean and sample variance extremely valuable for use as inferential statistics. Although no individual sample is likely to have a mean and variance exactly equal to the population values, both the sample mean and the sample variance, on average, do provide accurate estimates of the corresponding population values.

STANDARD DEVIATION AND DESCRIPTIVE STATISTICS

Because standard deviation requires extensive calculations, there is a tendency to get lost in the arithmetic and forget what standard deviation is and why it is important. Standard deviation is primarily a descriptive measure; it describes how variable, or how spread out, the scores are in a distribution. Behavioral scientists must deal with the variability that comes from studying people and animals. People are not all the same; they have different attitudes, opinions, talents, IQs, and personalities. Although we can calculate the average value for any of these variables, it is equally important to describe the variability. Standard deviation describes variability by measuring *distance from the mean*. In any distribution, some individuals are close to the mean, and others are relatively far from the mean. Standard deviation provides a measure of the typical, or standard, distance from the mean.

Describing an entire distribution Rather than listing all of the individual scores in a distribution, research reports typically summarize the data by reporting only the mean and the standard deviation. When you are given these two descriptive statistics, however, you should be able to visualize the entire set of data. For example, consider a sample with a mean of $M = 36$ and a standard deviation of $s = 4$. Although there are several different ways to picture the data, one simple technique is to imagine (or sketch) a histogram in which each score is represented by a box in the graph. For this sample, the data can be pictured as a pile of boxes (scores) with the center of the pile located at a value of $M = 36$. The individual scores, or boxes, are scattered on both sides of the mean with some of the boxes relatively close to the mean and some farther away. As a rule of thumb, roughly 70% of the scores in a distribution are located within a distance of one standard deviation from the mean, and almost all of the scores (roughly 95%) are within two standard deviations of the mean. In this example, the standard distance from the mean is $s = 4$ points, so your image should have most of the boxes within 4 points of the mean, and nearly all of the boxes within 8 points. One possibility for the resulting image is shown in Figure 4.7.

Describing the location of individual scores Notice that Figure 4.7 not only shows the mean and the standard deviation, but also uses these two values to reconstruct the underlying scale of measurement (the X values along the horizontal line). The scale of measurement helps to complete the picture of the entire distribution and relate each individual score to the rest of the group. In this example, you should realize that a score of $X = 34$ is located near the center of the distribution, only slightly below the mean.

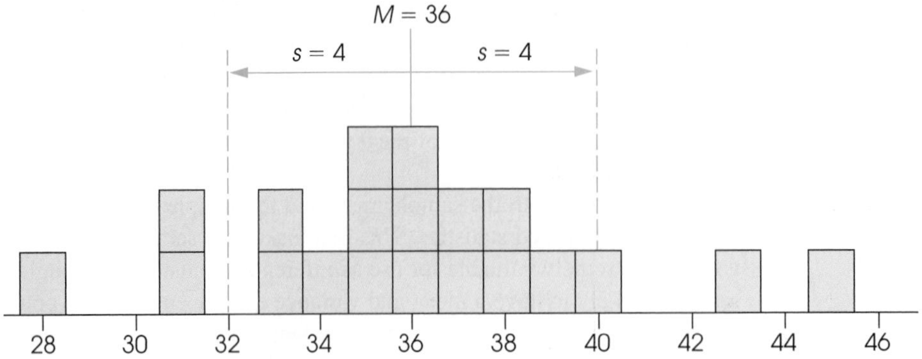

FIGURE 4.7
A sample of $n = 20$ scores with a mean of $M = 36$ and a standard deviation of $s = 4$.

On the other hand, a score of $X = 45$ is an extremely high score, located far out in the right-hand tail of the distribution.

Notice that the relative position of a score depends in part on the size of the standard deviation. In Figure 4.6 (p. 119), for example, we show a population distribution with a mean of $\mu = 80$ and a standard deviation of $\sigma = 8$, and a sample distribution with a mean of $M = 16$ and a standard deviation of $s = 2$. In the population distribution, a score that is 4 points above the mean is slightly above average but is certainly not an extreme value. In the sample distribution, however, a score that is 4 points above the mean is an extremely high score. In each case, the relative position of the score depends on the size of the standard deviation. For the population, a deviation of 4 points from the mean is relatively small, corresponding to only half of the standard deviation. For the sample, on the other hand, a 4-point deviation is very large, twice the size of the standard deviation.

The general point of this discussion is that the mean and standard deviation are not simply abstract concepts or mathematical equations. Instead, these two values should be concrete and meaningful, especially in the context of a set of scores. The mean and standard deviation are central concepts for most of the statistics that are presented in the following chapters. A good understanding of these two statistics will help you with the more complex procedures that follow. (Box 4.1.)

TRANSFORMATIONS OF SCALE

Occasionally a set of scores is transformed by adding a constant to each score or by multiplying each score by a constant value. This happens, for example, when exposure to a treatment adds a fixed amount to each participant's score or when you want to change the unit of measurement (to convert from minutes to seconds, multiply each score by 60). What happens to the standard deviation when the scores are transformed in this manner?

The easiest way to determine the effect of a transformation is to remember that the standard deviation is a measure of distance. If you select any two scores and see what happens to the distance between them, you also find out what happens to the standard deviation.

1. Adding a constant to each score does not change the standard deviation If you begin with a distribution that has $\mu = 40$ and $\sigma = 10$, what happens to σ if you add 5 points to every score? Consider any two scores in this distribution: Suppose, for

BOX 4.1 AN ANALOGY FOR THE MEAN AND THE STANDARD DEVIATION

Although the basic concepts of the mean and the standard deviation are not overly complex, the following analogy often helps students gain a more complete understanding of these two statistical measures.

In our local community, the site for a new high school was selected because it provides a central location. An alternative site on the western edge of the community was considered, but this site was rejected because it would require extensive busing for students living on the east side. In this example, the location of the high school is analogous to the concept of the mean; just as the high school is located in the center of the community, the mean is located in the center of the distribution of scores.

For each student in the community, it is possible to measure the distance between home and the new high school. Some students live only a few blocks from the new school and others live as much as 3 miles away. The average distance that a student must travel to school was calculated to be 0.80 miles. The average distance from the school is analogous to the concept of the standard deviation; that is, the standard deviation measures the standard distance from an individual score to the mean.

example, that these are exam scores and that you had a score of $X = 41$ and your friend had $X = 43$. The distance between these two scores is $43 - 41 = 2$ points. After adding the constant, 5 points, to each score, your score would be $X = 46$, and your friend would have $X = 48$. The distance between scores is still 2 points. Adding a constant to every score does not affect any of the distances and, therefore, does not change the standard deviation. This fact can be seen clearly if you imagine a frequency distribution graph. If, for example, you add 10 points to each score, then every score in the graph is moved 10 points to the right. The result is that the entire distribution is shifted to a new position 10 points up the scale. Note that the mean moves along with the scores and is increased by 10 points. However, the variability does not change because each of the deviation scores $(X - \mu)$ does not change.

2. Multiplying each score by a constant causes the standard deviation to be multiplied by the same constant Consider the same distribution of exam scores we looked at earlier. If $\mu = 40$ and $\sigma = 10$, what would happen to σ if each score were multiplied by 2? Again, we look at two scores, $X = 41$ and $X = 43$, with a distance between them equal to 2 points. After all of the scores have been multiplied by 2, these scores become $X = 82$ and $X = 86$. Now the distance between scores is 4 points, twice the original distance. Multiplying each score causes each distance to be multiplied, so the standard deviation also is multiplied by the same amount.

IN THE LITERATURE

REPORTING THE STANDARD DEVIATION

In reporting the results of a study, the researcher often provides descriptive information for both central tendency and variability. The dependent variables in psychology research are often numerical values obtained from measurements on interval or ratio scales. With numerical scores, the most common descriptive statistics are the mean (central tendency) and the standard deviation (variability), which are usually reported together. In many journals, especially those following APA style, the symbol SD is used for the sample standard deviation. For example, the results might state:

> Children who viewed the violent cartoon displayed more aggressive responses (M = 12.45, SD = 3.7) than those who viewed the control cartoon (M = 4.22, SD = 1.04).

When reporting the descriptive measures for several groups, the findings may be summarized in a table. Table 4.2 illustrates the results of hypothetical data.

TABLE 4.2

The number of aggressive responses in male and female children after viewing cartoons.

	Type of Cartoon	
	Violent	Control
Males	M = 15.72	M = 6.94
	SD = 4.43	SD = 2.26
Females	M = 3.47	M = 2.61
	SD = 1.12	SD = 0.98

Sometimes the table also indicates the sample size, n, for each group. You should remember that the purpose of the table is to present the data in an organized, concise, and accurate manner. ❑

VARIANCE AND INFERENTIAL STATISTICS

In very general terms, the goal of inferential statistics is to detect meaningful and significant patterns in research results. The basic question is whether the patterns observed in the sample data reflect corresponding patterns that exist in the population, or are simply random fluctuations that occur by chance. Variability plays an important role in the inferential process because the variability in the data influences how easy it is to see patterns. In general, low variability means that existing patterns can be seen clearly, whereas high variability tends to obscure any patterns that might exist. The following example provides a simple demonstration of how variance can influence the perception of patterns.

EXAMPLE 4.8

In most research studies the goal is to compare means for two (or more) sets of data. For example:

> Is the mean level of depression lower after therapy than it was before therapy?
>
> Is the mean attitude score for men different from the mean score for women?
>
> Is the mean reading achievement score higher for students in a special program than for students in regular classrooms?

In each of these situations, the goal is to find a clear difference between two means that would demonstrate a significant, meaningful pattern in the results. Variability plays an important role in determining whether a clear pattern exists. Consider the following data representing hypothetical results from two experiments, each comparing two treatment conditions. For both experiments, your task is to determine whether there appears to be any consistent difference between the scores in treatment 1 and the scores in treatment 2.

Experiment A		Experiment B	
Treatment 1	Treatment 2	Treatment 1	Treatment 2
35	39	31	46
34	40	15	21
36	41	57	61
35	40	37	32

For each experiment, the data have been constructed so that there is a 5-point mean difference between the two treatments: On average, the scores in treatment 2 are 5 points higher than the scores in treatment 1. The 5-point difference is relatively easy to see in experiment A, where the variability is low, but the same 5-point difference is difficult to see in experiment B, where the variability is large. Again, high variability tends to obscure any patterns in the data. This general fact is perhaps even more convincing when the data are presented in a graph. Figure 4.8 shows the two sets of data from experiments A and B. Notice that the results from experiment A clearly show the 5-point difference between treatments. One group of scores piles up around 35 and the second group piles up around 40. On the other hand, the scores from experiment B [Figure 4.8(b)] seem to be mixed together randomly with no clear difference between the two treatments.

In the context of inferential statistics, the variance that exists in a set of sample data is often classified as *error variance*. This term is used to indicate that the sample variance represents unexplained and uncontrolled differences between scores. As the error variance increases, it becomes more difficult to see any systematic differences or patterns that might exist in the data. An analogy is to think of variance as the static that appears on a radio station or a cell phone when you enter an area of poor reception. In general, variance makes it difficult to get a clear signal from the data. High variance can make it difficult or impossible to see a mean difference between two sets of scores, or to see any other meaningful patterns in the results from a research study.

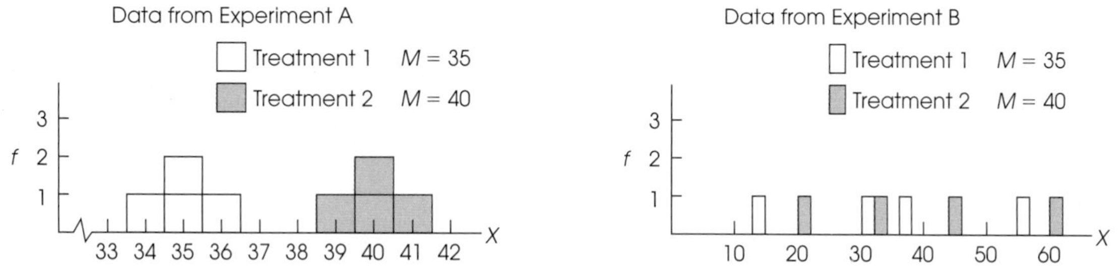

FIGURE 4.8

Graphs showing the results from two experiments. In experiment A, the variability is small and it is easy to see the 5-point mean difference between the two treatments. In experiment B, however, the 5-point mean difference between treatments is obscured by the large variability.

LEARNING CHECK

1. Explain the difference between a biased and an unbiased statistic.
2. In a population with a mean of $\mu = 50$ and a standard deviation of $\sigma = 10$, would a score of $X = 58$ be considered an extreme value (far out in the tail of the distribution)? What if the standard deviation were $\sigma = 3$?
3. A population has a mean of $\mu = 70$ and a standard deviation of $\sigma = 5$.
   a. If 10 points were added to every score in the population, what would be the new values for the population mean and standard deviation?
   b. If every score in the population were multiplied by 2, what would be the new values for the population mean and standard deviation?

ANSWERS

1. If a statistic is biased, it means that the average value of the statistic does not accurately represent the corresponding population parameter. Instead, the average value of the statistic either overestimates or underestimates the parameter. If a statistic is unbiased, it means that the average value of the statistic is an accurate representation of the corresponding population parameter.
2. With $\sigma = 10$, a score of $X = 58$ would be located in the central section of the distribution (within one standard deviation). With $\sigma = 3$, a score of $X = 58$ would be an extreme value, located more than two standard deviations above the mean.
3. a. The new mean would be $\mu = 80$ but the standard deviation would still be $\sigma = 5$.
   b. The new mean would be $\mu = 140$ and the new standard deviation would be $\sigma = 10$.

SUMMARY

1. The purpose of variability is to measure and describe the degree to which the scores in a distribution are spread out or clustered together. There are three basic measures of variability: the range, the variance, and the standard deviation.

   The range is the distance covered by the set of scores, from the smallest score to the largest score. The range is completely determined by the two extreme scores and is considered to be a relatively crude measure of variability.

   Standard deviation and variance are the most commonly used measures of variability. Both of these measures are based on the idea that each score can be described in terms of its deviation, or distance, from the mean. The variance is the mean of the squared deviations. The standard deviation is the square root of the variance and provides a measure of the standard distance from the mean.

2. To calculate variance or standard deviation, you first need to find the sum of the squared deviations, *SS*. Except for minor changes in notation, the calculation of *SS* is identical for samples and populations. There are two methods for calculating *SS*:

   I. By definition, you can find *SS* using the following steps:
   a. Find the deviation $(X - \mu)$ for each score.
   b. Square each deviation.
   c. Add the squared deviations.
   This process can be summarized in a formula as follows:

   $$\text{Definitional formula:} \quad SS = \Sigma(X - \mu)^2$$

   II. The sum of the squared deviations can also be found using a computational formula, which is especially useful when the mean is not a whole number:

   $$\text{Computational formula: } SS = \Sigma X^2 - \frac{(\Sigma X)^2}{N}$$

3. Variance is the mean squared deviation and is obtained by finding the sum of the squared deviations and then dividing by the number of scores. For a population, variance is

$$\sigma^2 = \frac{SS}{N}$$

For a sample, only $n - 1$ of the scores are free to vary (degrees of freedom or $df = n - 1$), so sample variance is

$$s^2 = \frac{SS}{n-1} = \frac{SS}{df}$$

Using $n - 1$ in the sample formula makes the sample variance an accurate and unbiased estimate of the population variance.

4. Standard deviation is the square root of the variance. For a population, this is

$$\sigma = \sqrt{\frac{SS}{N}}$$

Sample standard deviation is

$$s = \sqrt{\frac{SS}{n-1}} = \sqrt{\frac{SS}{df}}$$

5. Adding a constant value to every score in a distribution does not change the standard deviation. Multiplying every score by a constant, however, causes the standard deviation to be multiplied by the same constant.

KEY TERMS

variability (104)
range (106)
deviation score (107)
sum of squares (SS) (111)
population variance (σ^2) (113)
population standard deviation (σ) (113)
sample variance (s^2) (115)
sample standard deviation (s) (115)
degrees of freedom (df) (117)
unbiased statistic (119)
biased statistic (119)

RESOURCES

Book Companion Website: www.cengage.com/psychology/gravetter

You can find a tutorial quiz and other learning exercises for Chapter 4 on the book companion website. The website also includes a workshop entitled *Central Tendency and Variability,* which examines the basic concepts of variability and the standard deviation, and reviews the concept of central tendency, which was covered in Chapter 3.

SPSS

General instructions for using SPSS are presented in Appendix D. Following are detailed instructions for using SPSS to compute the **Range, Standard Deviation,** and **Variance** for a sample of scores.

Data Entry

1. Enter all of the scores in one column of the data editor, probably VAR00001.

Data Analysis

1. Click **Analyze** on the tool bar, select **Descriptive Statistics,** and click on **Descriptives.**
2. Highlight the column label for the set of scores (VAR00001) in the left box and click the arrow to move it into the **Variable** box.
3. If you want the variance and/or the range reported along with the standard deviation, click on the **Options** box, select **Variance** and/or **Range,** then click **Continue.**
4. Click **OK.**

SPSS Output

The SPSS output is shown in Figure 4.9. The summary table lists the number of scores, the maximum and minimum scores, the mean, the range, the standard deviation, and the variance. Note that the range and variance are included because these values were selected using the Options box during data analysis. Caution: SPSS computes the *sample* standard deviation and *sample* variance using $n - 1$. If your scores are intended to be a population, you can multiply the sample standard deviation by the square root of $(n - 1)/n$ to obtain the population standard deviation.

Note: You can also obtain the mean and standard deviation for a sample if you use SPSS to display the scores in a frequency distribution histogram (see the SPSS section at the end of Chapter 2). The mean and standard deviation are displayed beside the graph.

FOCUS ON PROBLEM SOLVING

1. The purpose of variability is to provide a measure of how spread out the scores in a distribution are. Usually this is described by the standard deviation. Because the calculations are relatively complicated, it is wise to make a preliminary estimate of

Descriptive Statistics

	N	Range	Minimum	Maximum	Mean	Std. Deviation	Variance
VAR00001	7	7.00	1.00	8.00	5.0000	2.44949	6.000
Valid N (listwise)	7						

FIGURE 4.9
The SPSS summary table showing descriptive statistics for a sample of $n = 7$ scores.

the standard deviation before you begin. Remember that standard deviation provides a measure of the typical, or standard, distance from the mean. Therefore, the standard deviation must have a value somewhere between the largest and the smallest deviation scores. As a rule of thumb, the standard deviation should be about one-fourth of the range.

2. Rather than trying to memorize all of the formulas for *SS*, variance, and standard deviation, you should focus on the definitions of these values and the logic that relates them to each other:

   SS is the sum of squared deviations.

   Variance is the mean squared deviation.

   Standard deviation is the square root of variance.

   The only formula you should need to memorize is the computational formula for *SS*.

3. A common error is to use $n - 1$ in the computational formula for *SS* when you have scores from a sample. Remember that the *SS* formula always uses n (or N). After you compute *SS* for a sample, you must correct for the sample bias by using $n - 1$ in the formulas for variance and standard deviation.

DEMONSTRATION 4.1

COMPUTING MEASURES OF VARIABILITY

For the following sample data, compute the variance and standard deviation. The scores are:

10, 7, 6, 10, 6, 15

STEP 1 **Compute *SS*, the sum of squared deviations** We use the computational formula. For this sample, $n = 6$ and

$$\Sigma X = 10 + 7 + 6 + 10 + 6 + 15 = 54$$

$$\Sigma X^2 = 10^2 + 7^2 + 6^2 + 10^2 + 6^2 + 15^2 = 546$$

$$SS = \Sigma X^2 - \frac{(\Sigma X)^2}{N} = 546 - \frac{(54)^2}{6}$$

$$= 546 - 486$$

$$= 60$$

STEP 2 **Compute the sample variance** For sample variance, *SS* is divided by the degrees of freedom, $df = n - 1$

$$s^2 = \frac{SS}{n-1} = \frac{60}{5} = 12$$

STEP 3 **Compute the sample standard deviation** Standard deviation is simply the square root of the variance.

PROBLEMS

1. In words, explain what is measured by each of the following:
  a. *SS*
  b. Variance
  c. Standard deviation

2. A population has a mean of $\mu = 80$ and a standard deviation of $\sigma = 20$.
  a. Would a score of $X = 70$ be considered an extreme value (out in the tail) in this sample?
  b. If the standard deviation were $\sigma = 5$, would a score of $X = 70$ be considered an extreme value?

3. Is it possible to obtain a negative value for the variance or the standard deviation?

4. What does it mean for a sample to have a standard deviation of zero? Describe the scores in such a sample.

5. Explain why the formulas for sample variance and population variance are different.

6. Can *SS* ever have a value less than zero? Explain your answer.

7. On an exam with a mean of $M = 78$, you obtain a score of $X = 84$.
  a. Would you prefer a standard deviation of $s = 2$ or $s = 10$? (*Hint:* Sketch each distribution and find the location of your score.)
  b. If your score were $X = 72$, would you prefer $s = 2$ or $s = 10$? Explain your answer.

8. A population has a mean of $\mu = 30$ and a standard deviation of $\sigma = 5$.
  a. If 5 points were added to every score in the population, what would be the new values for the mean and standard deviation?
  b. If every score in the population were multiplied by 3 what would be the new values for the mean and standard deviation?

9. a. After 3 points have been added to every score in a sample, the mean is found to be $M = 83$ and the standard deviation is $s = 8$. What were the values for the mean and standard deviation for the original sample?
  b. After every score in a sample has been multiplied by 4, the mean is found to be $M = 48$ and the standard deviation is $s = 12$. What were the values for the mean and standard deviation for the original sample?

10. A student was asked to compute the mean and standard deviation for the following sample of $n = 5$ scores: 81, 87, 89, 86, and 87. To simplify the arithmetic, the student first subtracted 80 points from each score to obtain a new sample consisting of 1, 7, 9, 6, and 7. The mean and standard deviation for the new sample were then calculated to be $M = 6$ and $s = 3$. What are the values of the mean and standard deviation for the original sample?

11. For the following population of $N = 6$ scores:

11, 0, 2, 9, 9, 5

  a. Calculate the range and the standard deviation. (Use either definition for the range.)
  b. Add 2 points to each score and compute the range and standard deviation again. Describe how adding a constant to each score influences measures of variability.

12. The range is completely determined by the two extreme scores in a distribution. The standard deviation, on the other hand, uses every score.
  a. Compute the range (choose either definition) and the standard deviation for the following sample of $n = 5$ scores. Note that there are three scores clustered around the mean in the center of the distribution, and two extreme values.

Scores: 0, 6, 7, 8, 14.

  b. Now we break up the cluster in the center of the distribution by moving two of the central scores out to the extremes. Once again compute the range and the standard deviation.

New scores: 0, 0, 7, 14, 14.

  c. According to the range, how do the two distributions compare in variability? How do they compare according to the standard deviation?

13. Calculate the mean and *SS* (sum of squared deviations) for each of the following samples. Based on the value for the mean, you should be able to decide which *SS* formula is better to use.

Sample A: 1, 4, 8, 5
Sample B: 3, 0, 9, 4

14. There are two different formulas or methods that can be used to calculate *SS*.
  a. Under what circumstances is the definitional formula easy to use?
  b. Under what circumstances is the computational formula preferred?

15. For the data in the following sample:

8, 1, 5, 1, 5

a. Find the mean and the standard deviation.
b. Now change the score of $X = 8$ to $X = 18$, and find the new mean and standard deviation.
c. Describe how one extreme score influences the mean and standard deviation.

16. Calculate *SS*, variance, and standard deviation for the following population of $N = 7$ scores: 8, 1, 4, 3, 5, 3, 4. (*Note:* The definitional formula works well with these scores.)

17. Calculate *SS*, variance, and standard deviation for the following population of $N = 8$ scores: 0, 0, 5, 0, 3, 0, 0, 4. (*Note:* The computational formula works well with these scores.)

18. Calculate *SS*, variance, and standard deviation for the following sample of $n = 4$ scores: 7, 4, 2, 1. (*Note:* The computational formula works well with these scores.)

19. Calculate *SS*, variance, and standard deviation for the following sample of $n = 5$ scores: 9, 6, 2, 2, 6. (Note: The definitional formula works well with these scores.)

20. For the following population of $N = 6$ scores:

3, 1, 4, 3, 3, 4

a. Sketch a histogram showing the population distribution.
b. Locate the value of the population mean in your sketch, and make an estimate of the standard deviation (as done in Example 4.2).
c. Compute *SS*, variance, and standard deviation for the population. (How well does your estimate compare with the actual value of σ?)

21. For the following sample of $n = 7$ scores:

8, 6, 5, 2, 6, 3, 5

a. Sketch a histogram showing the sample distribution.
b. Locate the value of the sample mean in your sketch, and make an estimate of the standard deviation (as done in Example 4.5).
c. Compute *SS*, variance, and standard deviation for the sample. (How well does your estimate compare with the actual value of *s*?)

22. In an extensive study involving thousands of British children, Arden and Plomin (2006) found significantly higher variance in the intelligence scores for males than for females. Following are hypothetical data, similar to the results obtained in the study. Note that the scores are not regular IQ scores but have been standardized so that the entire sample has a mean of $M = 10$ and a standard deviation of $s = 2$.
a. Calculate the mean and the standard deviation for the sample of $n = 8$ females and for the sample of $n = 8$ males.
b. Based on the means and the standard deviations, describe the differences in intelligence scores for males and females.

Female	Male
9	8
11	10
10	11
13	12
8	6
9	10
11	14
9	9

23. In the Preview section at the beginning of this chapter we reported a study by Wegesin and Stern (2004) that found greater consistency (less variability) in the memory performance scores for younger women than for older women. The following data represent memory scores obtained for two women, one older and one younger, over a series of memory trials.
a. Calculate the variance of the scores for each woman.
b. Are the scores for the younger woman more consistent (less variable)?

Younger	Older
8	7
6	5
6	8
7	5
8	7
7	6
8	8
8	5

PART I

REVIEW

By completing this part, you should understand and be able to perform basic descriptive statistical procedures. These include:

1. Familiarity with statistical terminology and notation (Chapter 1).
2. The ability to organize a set of scores in a frequency distribution table or a frequency distribution graph (Chapter 2).
3. The ability to summarize and describe a distribution of scores by computing a measure of central tendency (Chapter 3).
4. The ability to summarize and describe a distribution of scores by computing a measure of variability (Chapter 4).

The general goal of descriptive statistics is to simplify a set of data by organizing or summarizing a large set of scores. A frequency distribution table or graph organizes the entire set of scores so that it is possible to see the complete distribution all at once. Measures of central tendency describe the distribution by identifying its center. They also summarize the distribution by condensing all of the individual scores into one value that represents the entire group. Measures of variability describe whether the scores in a distribution are widely scattered or closely clustered. Variability also provides an indication of how accurately a measure of central tendency represents the entire group.

Of the basic skills presented in this part, the most commonly used are calculating the mean and standard deviation for a sample of numerical scores. The following exercises should provide an opportunity to use and reinforce these statistical skills.

REVIEW EXERCISES

1. a. What is the general goal for descriptive statistics?
   b. How is the goal served by putting scores in a frequency distribution?
   c. How is the goal served by computing a measure of central tendency?
   d. How is the goal served by computing a measure of variability?

2. In a classic study examining the relationship between heredity and intelligence, Robert Tryon (1940) used a selective breeding program to develop separate strains of "smart rats" and "dumb rats." Tryon started with a large sample of laboratory rats and tested each animal on a maze-learning problem. Based on their error scores for the maze, Tryon selected the brightest rats and the dullest rats from the sample. The brightest males were mated with the brightest females. Similarly, the dullest rats were interbred. This process of testing and selective breeding was continued for several generations until Tryon had established a line of maze-bright rats and a separate line of maze-dull rats. The following data represent results similar to those obtained by Tryon. The data consist of maze-learning error scores for the original sample of laboratory rats and the seventh generation of the maze-bright rats.

Errors Before Solving Maze					
Original Rats			Seventh Generation Maze-Bright Rats		
10	14	7	5	8	7
17	13	12	8	8	6
11	9	20	6	10	4
13	6	15	6	9	8
4	18	10	5	7	9
13	21	6	10	8	6
17	11	14	9	7	8

   a. Sketch a polygon showing the distribution of error scores for the sample of original rats. On the same graph, sketch a polygon for the sample of maze-bright rats. (Use two different colors or use a dashed line for one group and a solid line for the other.) Based on the appearance of your graph, describe the differences between the two samples.
   b. Calculate the mean error score for each sample. Does the mean difference support your description from part a?
   c. Calculate the variance and standard deviation for each sample. Based on the measures of variability, is one group more diverse than the other? Is one group more homogeneous than the other?

PART

II

Foundations of Inferential Statistics

You should recall from Chapter 1 that statistical methods are classified into two general categories: descriptive statistics, which attempt to organize and summarize data, and inferential statistics, which use the limited information from samples to answer general questions about populations. In most research situations, both kinds of statistics are used to gain a complete understanding of the research results. In Part I of this book we introduced the techniques of descriptive statistics. We now are ready to turn our attention to inferential statistics.

Before we proceed with inferential statistics, however, it is necessary to present some additional information about samples. We know that it is possible to obtain hundreds or even thousands of different samples from the same population. We need to determine how all the different samples are related to each other and how individual samples are related to the population from which they were obtained. Finally, we need a system for designating which samples are representative of their populations and which are not.

In the next four chapters we develop the concepts and skills that form the foundation for inferential statistics. In general, these chapters establish formal, quantitative relationships between samples and populations and introduce a standardized procedure for determining whether the data from a sample justify a conclusion about the population. After we have developed this foundation, we will be prepared to begin inferential statistics. That is, we can begin to look at statistical techniques that use the sample data obtained in research studies as the basis for answering questions about populations.

CHAPTER

5

z-Scores: Location of Scores and Standardized Distributions

Tools You Will Need

The following items are considered essential background material for this chapter. If you doubt your knowledge of any of these items, you should review the appropriate chapter and section before proceeding.

- The mean (Chapter 3)
- The standard deviation (Chapter 4)
- Basic algebra (math review, Appendix A)

Preview

A common test of cognitive ability requires participants to search through a visual display and respond to specific targets as quickly as possible. This kind of test is called a perceptual-speed test. Measures of perceptual speed are commonly used for predicting performance on jobs that demand a high level of speed and accuracy. Although many different tests are used, a typical example is shown in Figure 5.1. This task requires the participant to search through the display of digit pairs as quickly as possible and circle each pair that adds up 10. Your score is determined by the amount of time required to complete the task with a correction for the number of errors that you make. One complaint about this kind of paper-and-pencil test is that it is tedious and time consuming to score because a researcher must also search through the entire display to identify errors to determine the participant's level of accuracy. An alternative, proposed by Ackerman and Beier (2007), is a computerized version of the task. The computer version presents a series of digit pairs and participants respond on a touch-sensitive monitor. The computerized test is very reliable and the scores are equivalent to the paper-and-pencil tests in terms of assessing cognitive skill. The advantage of the computerized test is that the computer produces a test score immediately when a participant finishes the test.

Suppose that you took Ackerman and Beier's test and your combined time and errors produced a score of 92. How did you do? Are you faster than average, fairly normal in perceptual speed, or does your score indicate a serious deficit in cognitive skill?

FIGURE 5.1

An example of a perceptual speed task. The participant is asked to search through the display as quickly as possible and circle each pair of digits that add up to 10.

Circle every pair of adjacent numbers that add up to 10.

64	23	19	31	19	46	31	91	83	82	82	46	19	87
11	42	94	87	64	44	19	55	82	46	57	98	39	46
78	73	72	66	63	71	67	42	62	73	45	22	62	99
73	91	52	37	55	97	91	51	44	23	46	64	97	62
97	31	21	49	93	91	89	46	73	82	55	98	12	56
73	82	37	55	89	83	73	27	83	82	73	46	97	62
57	96	46	55	46	19	13	67	73	26	58	64	32	73
23	94	66	55	91	73	67	73	82	55	64	62	46	39
87	11	99	73	56	73	63	73	91	82	63	33	16	88
19	42	62	91	12	82	32	92	73	46	68	19	11	64
93	91	32	82	63	91	46	46	36	55	19	92	62	71

The Problem: Without any frame of reference, a simple raw score provides relatively little information. Specifically, you have no idea how your test score of 92 compares with others who took the same test.

The Solution: Transforming your test score into a *z-score* will identify exactly where you are located in the distribution of scores. In this case, the distribution of scores has a mean of 86.75 and a standard deviation of 10.50. With this additional information, you should realize that your score ($X = 92$) is somewhat higher than average but not extreme. The z-score combines all of this information (your score, the mean, and the standard deviation) into a single number that precisely describes your location relative to the other scores in the distribution.

5.1 INTRODUCTION TO z-SCORES

In the previous two chapters, we introduced the concepts of the mean and the standard deviation as methods for describing an entire distribution of scores. Now we shift attention to the individual scores within a distribution. In this chapter, we introduce a statistical technique that uses the mean and the standard deviation to transform each score (X value) into a *z-score,* or a *standard score*. The purpose of z-scores, or standard scores, is to identify and describe the exact location of each score in a distribution.

The following example demonstrates why z-scores are useful and introduces the general concept of transforming X values into z-scores.

EXAMPLE 5.1

Suppose you received a score of $X = 76$ on a statistics exam. How did you do? It should be clear that you need more information to predict your grade. Your score of $X = 76$ could be one of the best scores in the class, or it might be the lowest score in the distribution. To find the location of your score, you must have information about the other scores in the distribution. It would be useful, for example, to know the mean for the class. If the mean were $\mu = 70$, you would be in a much better position than if the mean were $\mu = 85$. Obviously, your position relative to the rest of the class depends on the mean. However, the mean by itself is not sufficient to tell you the exact location of your score. Suppose you know that the mean for the statistics exam is $\mu = 70$ and your score is $X = 76$. At this point, you know that your score is 6 points above the mean, but you still do not know exactly where it is located. Six points may be a relatively big distance and you may have one of the highest scores in the class, or 6 points may be a relatively small distance and you may be only slightly above the average. Figure 5.2 shows two possible distributions of exam scores. Both distributions have a mean of $\mu = 70$, but for one distribution, the standard deviation is $\sigma = 3$, and for the other, $\sigma = 12$. The location of $X = 76$ is highlighted in each of the two distributions. When the standard deviation is $\sigma = 3$, your score of $X = 76$ is in the extreme right-hand tail, the highest score in the distribution. However, in the other distribution, where $\sigma = 12$, your score is only slightly above average. Thus, the relative location of your score within the distribution depends on the standard deviation as well as the mean.

The purpose of the preceding example is to demonstrate that a score *by itself* does not necessarily provide much information about its position within a distribution. These original, unchanged scores that are the direct result of measurement are called *raw scores*. To make raw scores more meaningful, they are often transformed into new values that contain more information. This transformation is one purpose for z-scores. In particular, we transform X values into z-scores so that the resulting z-scores tell exactly where the original scores are located.

A second purpose for z-scores is to *standardize* an entire distribution. A common example of a standardized distribution is the distribution of IQ scores. Although there are several different tests for measuring IQ, the tests usually are standardized so that they have a mean of 100 and a standard deviation of 15. Because all the different tests are standardized, it is possible to understand and compare IQ scores even though they come from different tests. For example, we all understand that an IQ score of 95 is a little below average, *no matter which IQ test was used.* Similarly, an IQ of 145 is extremely high, *no matter which IQ test was used.* In general terms, the process of

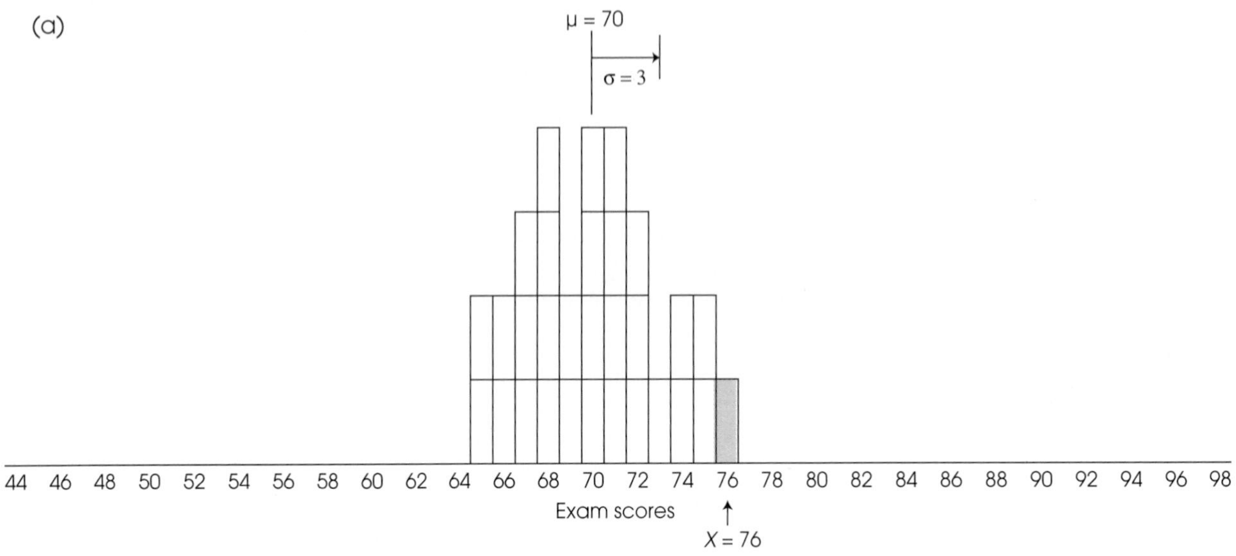

FIGURE 5.2

Two distributions of exam scores. For both distributions, $\mu = 70$, but for one distribution, $\sigma = 3$, and for the other, $\sigma = 12$. The relative position of $X = 76$ is very different for the two distributions.

standardizing takes different distributions and makes them equivalent. The advantage of this process is that it is possible to compare distributions even though they may have been quite different before standardization.

In summary, the process of transforming X values into z-scores serves two useful purposes:

1. Each z-score tells the exact location of the original X value within the distribution.

2. The z-scores form a standardized distribution that can be directly compared to other distributions that also have been transformed into z-scores.

Each of these purposes is discussed in the following sections.

5.2 z-SCORES AND LOCATION IN A DISTRIBUTION

One of the primary purposes of a z-score is to describe the exact location of a score within a distribution. The z-score accomplishes this goal by transforming each X value into a signed number (+ or –) so that

1. The *sign* tells whether the score is located above (+) or below (–) the mean, and
2. The *number* tells the distance between the score and the mean in terms of the number of standard deviations.

Thus, in a distribution of IQ scores with $\mu = 100$ and $\sigma = 15$, a score of $X = 130$ would be transformed into $z = +2.00$. The z value indicates that the score is located above the mean (+) by a distance of 2 standard deviations (30 points).

DEFINITION

A ***z*-score** specifies the precise location of each X value within a distribution. The sign of the z-score (+ or –) signifies whether the score is above the mean (positive) or below the mean (negative). The numerical value of the z-score specifies the distance from the mean by counting the number of standard deviations between X and μ.

Whenever you are working with z-scores, you should imagine or draw a picture similar to Figure 5.3. Although you should realize that not all distributions are normal, we use the normal shape as an example when showing z-scores for populations.

Notice that a z-score always consists of two parts: a sign (+ or –) and a magnitude. Both parts are necessary to describe completely where a raw score is located within a distribution.

Figure 5.3 shows a population distribution with various positions identified by their z-score values. Notice that all z-scores above the mean are positive and all z-scores below the mean are negative. The sign of a z-score tells you immediately whether the score is located above or below the mean. Also, note that a z-score of $z = +1.00$ corresponds to a position exactly 1 standard deviation above the mean. A z-score of

FIGURE 5.3

The relationship between z-score values and locations in a population distribution.

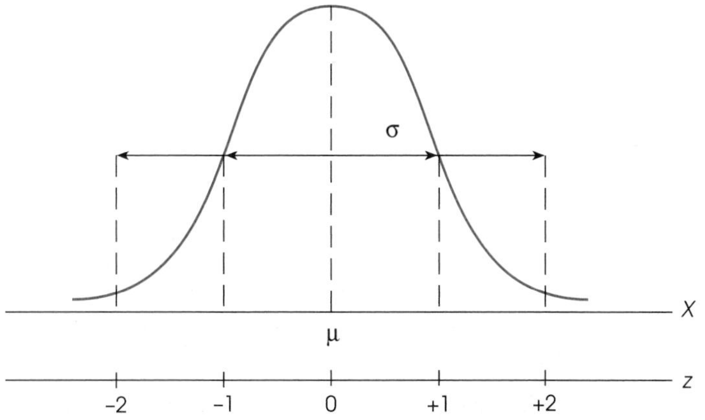

$z = +2.00$ is always located exactly 2 standard deviations above the mean. The numerical value of the z-score tells you the number of standard deviations it is from the mean. Finally, you should notice that Figure 5.3 does not give any specific values for the population mean or the standard deviation. The locations identified by z-scores are the same for *all distributions,* no matter what mean or standard deviation the distributions may have.

Now we can return to the two distributions shown in Figure 5.2 and use a z-score to describe the position of $X = 76$ within each distribution as follows:

> In Figure 5.2(a), with a standard deviation of $\sigma = 3$, the score $X = 76$ corresponds to a z-score of $z = +2.00$. That is, the score is located above the mean by exactly 2 standard deviations.
>
> In Figure 5.2(b), with $\sigma = 12$, the score $X = 76$ corresponds to a z-score of $z = +0.50$. In this distribution, the score is located above the mean by exactly $\frac{1}{2}$ standard deviation.

LEARNING CHECK

1. Identify the z-score value corresponding to each of the following locations in a distribution.

a. Below the mean by 2 standard deviations.

b. Above the mean by $\frac{1}{2}$ standard deviation.

c. Below the mean by 1.50 standard deviations.

2. Describe the location in the distribution for each of the following z-scores. (For example, $z = +1.00$ is located above the mean by 1 standard deviation.)

a. $z = -1.50$ **b.** $z = 0.25$ **c.** $z = -2.50$ **d.** $z = 0.50$

3. For a population with $\mu = 30$ and $\sigma = 8$, find the z-score for each of the following scores:

a. $X = 32$ **b.** $X = 26$ **c.** $X = 42$

4. For a population with $\mu = 50$ and $\sigma = 12$, find the X value corresponding to each of the following z-scores:

a. $z = -0.25$ **b.** $z = 2.00$ **c.** $z = 0.50$

ANSWERS

1. a. $z = -2.00$ **b.** $z = +0.50$ **c.** $z = -1.50$

2. a. Below the mean by $1\frac{1}{2}$ standard deviations.

b. Above the mean by $\frac{1}{4}$ standard deviation.

c. Below the mean by $2\frac{1}{2}$ standard deviations.

d. Above the mean by $\frac{1}{2}$ standard deviation.

3. a. $z = +0.25$ **b.** $z = -0.50$ **c.** $z = +1.50$

4. a. $X = 47$ **b.** $X = 74$ **c.** $X = 56$

THE z-SCORE FORMULA

The z-score definition is adequate for transforming back and forth from X values to z-scores as long as the arithmetic is easy to do in your head. For more complicated values, it is best to have an equation to help structure the calculations. Fortunately, the relationship between X values and z-scores is easily expressed in a formula. The formula for transforming scores into z-scores is

$$z = \frac{X - \mu}{\sigma} \qquad (5.1)$$

The numerator of the equation, $X - \mu$, is a *deviation score* (Chapter 4, page 107); it measures the distance in points between X and μ and indicates whether X is located above or below the mean. The deviation score is then divided by σ because we want the *z*-score to measure distance in terms of standard deviation units. The formula performs exactly the same arithmetic that is used with the *z*-score definition, and it provides a structured equation to organize the calculations when the numbers are more difficult. The following examples demonstrate the use of the *z*-score formula.

EXAMPLE 5.2

A distribution of scores has a mean of $\mu = 100$ and a standard deviation of $\sigma = 10$. What *z*-score corresponds to a score of $X = 130$ in this distribution?

According to the definition, the *z*-score has a value of +3 because the score is located above the mean by exactly 3 standard deviations. Using the *z*-score formula, we obtain

$$z = \frac{X - \mu}{\sigma} = \frac{130 - 100}{10} = \frac{30}{10} = 3.00$$

The formula produces exactly the same result that is obtained using the *z*-score definition.

EXAMPLE 5.3

A distribution of scores has a mean of $\mu = 86$ and a standard deviation of $\sigma = 7$. What *z*-score corresponds to a score of $X = 95$ in this distribution?

Note that this problem is not particularly easy, especially if you try to use the *z*-score definition and perform the calculations in your head. However, the *z*-score formula organizes the numbers and allows you to finish the final arithmetic with your calculator. Using the formula, we obtain

$$z = \frac{X - \mu}{\sigma} = \frac{95 - 86}{7} = \frac{9}{7} = 1.29$$

According to the formula, a score of $X = 95$ corresponds to $z = 1.29$. The *z*-score indicates a location that is above the mean (positive) by slightly more than 1 standard deviation.

When you use the *z*-score formula, it can be useful to pay attention to the definition of a *z*-score as well. For example, we used the formula in Example 5.3 to calculate the *z*-score corresponding to $X = 95$, and obtained $z = 1.29$. Using the *z*-score definition, we note that $X = 95$ is located above the mean by 9 points, which is slightly more than one standard deviation ($\sigma = 7$). Therefore, the *z*-score should be positive and have a value slightly greater than 1.00. In this case, the answer predicted by the definition is in perfect agreement with the calculation. However, if the calculations produce a different value, for example $z = 0.78$, you should realize that this answer is not consistent with the definition of a *z*-score. In this case, an error has been made and you should double check the calculations.

DETERMINING A RAW SCORE (*X*) FROM A *z*-SCORE

Although the *z*-score equation (Formula 5.1) works well for transforming X values into *z*-scores, it can be awkward when you are trying to work in the opposite direction and change *z*-scores back into X values. In general it is easier to use the definition of a *z*-score, rather than a formula, when you are changing *z*-scores into X values. Remember, the *z*-score describes exactly where the score is located by identifying the direction and distance from the mean. It is possible, however, to express this definition as a formula, and we use a sample problem to demonstrate how the formula can be created.

For a distribution with a mean of $\mu = 60$ and $\sigma = 5$, what X value corresponds to a z-score of $z = -3.00$?

To solve this problem, we use the z-score definition and carefully monitor the step-by-step process. The value of the z-score indicates that X is located below the mean by a distance equal to 3 standard deviations. Thus, the first step in the calculation is to determine the distance corresponding to 3 standard deviations. For this problem, the standard deviation is $\sigma = 5$ points, so 3 standard deviations is $3(5) = 15$ points. The next step is to find the value of X that is located below the mean by 15 points. With a mean of $\mu = 60$, the score is

$$X = \mu - 15 = 60 - 15 = 45$$

The two steps can be combined to form a single formula:

$$X = \mu + z\sigma \qquad (5.2)$$

In the formula, the value of $z\sigma$ is the *deviation* of X and determines both the direction and the size of the distance from the mean. In this problem, $z\sigma = (-3)(5) = -15$, or 15 points below the mean. Formula 5.2 simply combines the mean and the deviation from the mean to determine the exact value of X.

Finally, you should realize that Formula 5.1 and Formula 5.2 are actually two different versions of the same equation. If you begin with either formula and use algebra to shuffle the terms around, you soon end up with the other formula. We leave this as an exercise for those who want to try it.

OTHER RELATIONSHIPS BETWEEN z, X, μ, AND σ

In most cases, we simply transform scores (X values) into z-scores, or change z-scores back into X values. However, you should realize that a z-score establishes a relationship between the score, the mean, and the standard deviation. This relationship can be used to answer a variety of different questions about scores and the distributions in which they are located. The following two examples demonstrate some possibilities.

EXAMPLE 5.4

In a population with a mean of $\mu = 65$, a score of $X = 59$ corresponds to $z = -2.00$. What is the standard deviation for the population?

To answer the question, we begin with the z-score value. A z-score of -2.00 indicates that the corresponding score is located below the mean by a distance of 2 standard deviations. You also can determine that the score ($X = 59$) is located below the mean ($\mu = 65$) by a distance of 6 points. Thus, 2 standard deviations correspond to a distance of 6 points, which means that 1 standard deviation must be $\sigma = 3$ points.

EXAMPLE 5.5

In a population with a standard deviation of $\sigma = 4$, a score of $X = 33$ corresponds to $z = +1.50$. What is the mean for the population?

Again, we begin with the z-score value. In this case, a z-score of $+1.50$ indicates that the score is located above the mean by a distance corresponding to 1.50 standard deviations. With a standard deviation of $\sigma = 4$, this distance is $(1.50)(4) = 6$ points.

Thus, the score is located 6 points above the mean. The score is $X = 33$, so the mean must be $\mu = 27$.

Many students find problems like those in Examples 5.4 and 5.5 easier to understand if they draw a picture showing all of the information presented in the problem. For the problem in Example 5.4, the picture would begin with a distribution that has a mean of $\mu = 65$ (we use a normal distribution, which is shown in Figure 5.4). The value of the standard deviation is unknown, but you can add arrows to the sketch pointing outward from the mean for a distance corresponding to 1 standard deviation. Finally, use standard deviation arrows to identify the location of $z = -2.00$ (2 standard deviations below the mean) and add $X = 59$ at that location. All of these factors are shown in Figure 5.4. In the figure, it is easy to see that $X = 59$ is located 6 points below the mean, and that the 6-point distance corresponds to exactly 2 standard deviations. Again, if 2 standard deviations equal 6 points, then 1 standard deviation must be $\sigma = 3$ points.

LEARNING CHECK

1. For a distribution with $\mu = 40$ and $\sigma = 12$, find the z-score for each of the following scores.

   a. $X = 36$ **b.** $X = 46$ **c.** $X = 56$

2. For a distribution with $\mu = 40$ and $\sigma = 12$, find the X value corresponding to each of the following z-scores.

   a. $z = 1.50$ **b.** $z = -1.25$ **c.** $z = \frac{1}{3}$

3. In a distribution with $\mu = 50$, a score of $X = 42$ corresponds to $z = -2.00$. What is the standard deviation for this distribution?

4. In a distribution with $\sigma = 12$, a score of $X = 56$ corresponds to $z = -0.25$. What is the mean for this distribution?

ANSWERS

1. **a.** $z = -0.33$ (or $-\frac{1}{3}$) **b.** $z = 0.50$ **c.** $z = 1.33$ ($+1\frac{1}{3}$)
2. **a.** $X = 58$ **b.** $X = 25$ **c.** $X = 44$
3. $\sigma = 4$
4. $\mu = 59$

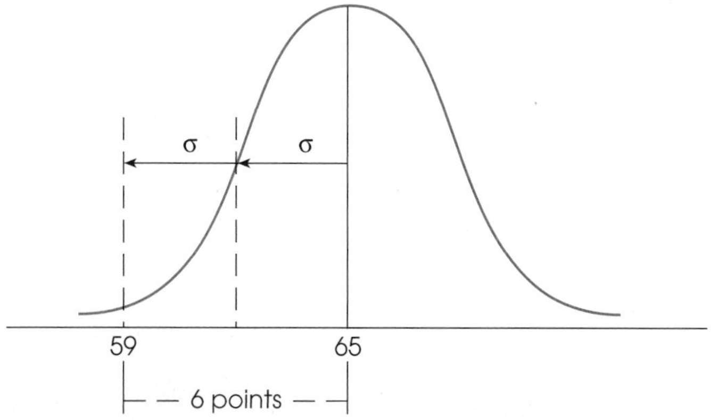

FIGURE 5.4

A visual presentation of the question in Example 5.4. If 2 standard deviations correspond to a 6-point distance, then 1 standard deviation must equal 3 points.

5.3 USING z-SCORES TO STANDARDIZE A DISTRIBUTION

It is possible to transform every X value in a distribution into a corresponding z-score. The result of this process is that the entire distribution of X values is transformed into a distribution of z-scores (Figure 5.5). The new distribution of z-scores has characteristics that make the *z-score transformation* a very useful tool. Specifically, if every X value is transformed into a z-score, then the distribution of z-scores will have the following properties:

1. Shape. The distribution of z-scores will have exactly the same shape as the original distribution of scores. If the original distribution is negatively skewed, for example, then the z-score distribution will also be negatively skewed. If the original distribution is normal, the distribution of z-scores will also be normal. Transforming raw scores into z-scores does not change anyone's position in the distribution. For example, any raw score that is above the mean by 1 standard deviation will be transformed to a z-score of $+1.00$, which is still above the mean by 1 standard deviation. Transforming a distribution from X values to z values does not move scores from one position to another; the procedure simply relabels each score (see Figure 5.5). Because each individual score stays in its same position within the distribution, the overall shape of the distribution does not change.

2. The mean. The z-score distribution will *always* have a mean of zero. In Figure 5.5, the original distribution of X values has a mean of $\mu = 100$. When this value, $X = 100$, is transformed into a z-score, the result is

$$z = \frac{X - \mu}{\sigma} = \frac{100 - 100}{10} = 0$$

Thus, the original population mean is transformed into a value of zero in the z-score distribution. The fact that the z-score distribution has a mean of zero makes the mean a convenient reference point. Recall from the definition of z-scores that all

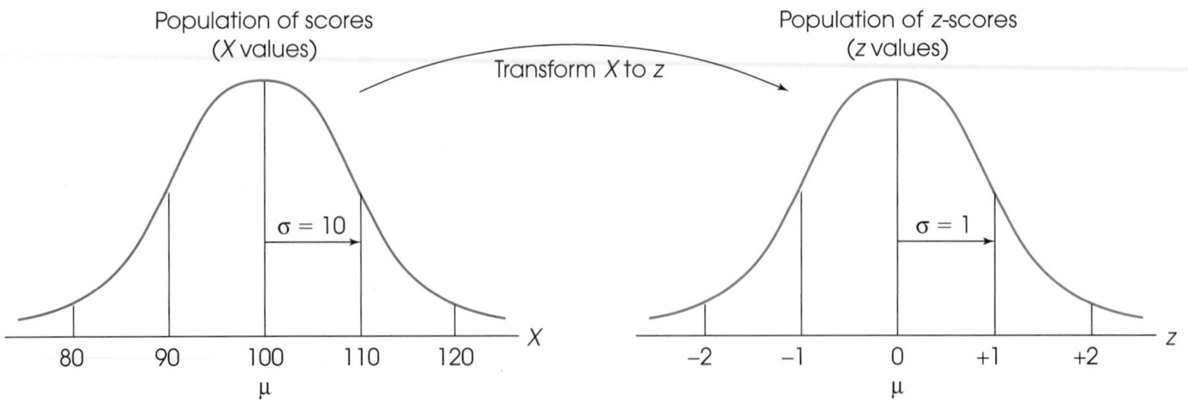

FIGURE 5.5

An entire population of scores is transformed into z-scores. The transformation does not change the shape of the population, but the mean is transformed into a value of 0 and the standard deviation is transformed to a value of 1.

positive *z*-scores are above the mean and all negative *z*-scores are below the mean. In other words, for *z*-scores, $\mu = 0$.

3. The standard deviation. The distribution of *z*-scores will *always* have a standard deviation of 1. In Figure 5.5, the original distribution of *X* values has $\mu = 100$ and $\sigma = 10$. In this distribution, a value of $X = 110$ is above the mean by exactly 10 points or 1 standard deviation. When $X = 110$ is transformed, it becomes $z = +1.00$, which is above the mean by exactly 1 point in the *z*-score distribution. Thus, the standard deviation corresponds to a 10-point distance in the *X* distribution and is transformed into a 1-point distance in the *z*-score distribution. The advantage of having a standard deviation of 1 is that the numerical value of a *z*-score is exactly the same as the number of standard deviations from the mean. For example, a *z*-score of $z = 1.50$ is exactly 1.50 standard deviations from the mean.

In Figure 5.5, we showed the *z*-score transformation as a process that changed a distribution of *X* values into a new distribution of *z*-scores. In fact, there is no need to create a whole new distribution. Instead, you can think of the *z*-score transformation as simply *relabeling* the values along the *X*-axis. That is, after a *z*-score transformation, you still have the same distribution, but now each individual is labeled with a *z*-score instead of an *X* value. Figure 5.6 demonstrates this concept with a single distribution that has two sets of labels: the *X* values along one line and the corresponding *z*-scores along another line. Notice that the mean for the distribution of *z*-scores is zero and the standard deviation is 1.

When *any* distribution (with any mean or standard deviation) is transformed into *z*-scores, the resulting distribution will always have a mean of $\mu = 0$ and a standard deviation of $\sigma = 1$. Because all *z*-score distributions have the same mean and the same standard deviation, the *z*-score distribution is called a *standardized distribution.*

DEFINITION

A **standardized distribution** is composed of scores that have been transformed to create predetermined values for μ and σ. Standardized distributions are used to make dissimilar distributions comparable.

FIGURE 5.6

Following a *z*-score transformation, the *X*-axis is relabeled in *z*-score units. The distance that is equivalent to 1 standard deviation on the *X*-axis ($\sigma = 10$ points in this example) corresponds to 1 point on the *z*-score scale.

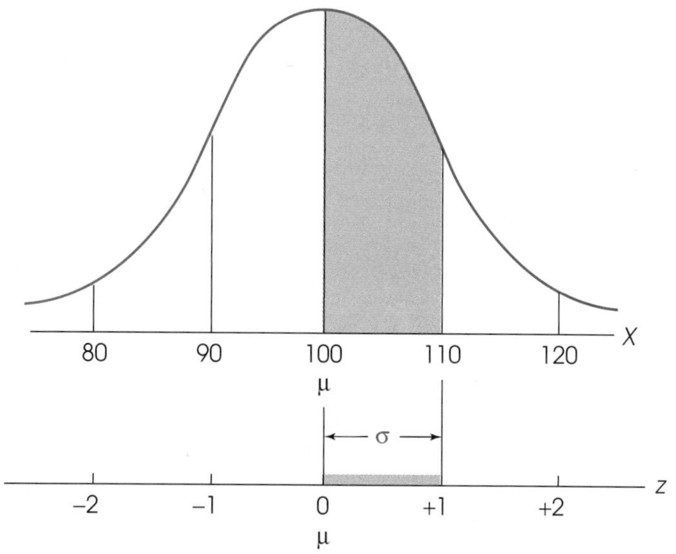

A z-score distribution is an example of a standardized distribution with $\mu = 0$ and $\sigma = 1$. That is, when any distribution (with any mean or standard deviation) is transformed into z-scores, the transformed distribution will always have $\mu = 0$ and $\sigma = 1$.

DEMONSTRATION OF A z-SCORE TRANSFORMATION

Although the basic characteristics of a z-score distribution have been explained logically, the following example provides a concrete demonstration that a z-score transformation creates a new distribution with a mean of zero, a standard deviation of 1, and the same shape as the original population.

EXAMPLE 5.6

We begin with a population of $N = 6$ scores consisting of the following values: 0, 6, 5, 2, 3, 2. This population has a mean of $\mu = \frac{18}{6} = 3$ and a standard deviation of $\sigma = 2$ (check the calculations for yourself).

Each of the X values in the original population is then transformed into a z-score as summarized in the following table.

$X = 0$	Below the mean by $1\frac{1}{2}$ standard deviations	$z = -1.50$
$X = 6$	Above the mean by $1\frac{1}{2}$ standard deviations	$z = +1.50$
$X = 5$	Above the mean by 1 standard deviation	$z = +1.00$
$X = 2$	Below the mean by $\frac{1}{2}$ standard deviation	$z = -0.50$
$X = 3$	Exactly equal to the mean—zero deviation	$z = 0$
$X = 2$	Below the mean by $\frac{1}{2}$ standard deviation	$z = -0.50$

The frequency distribution for the original population of X values is shown in Figure 5.7(a) and the corresponding distribution for the z-scores is shown in Figure 5.7(b). A simple comparison of the two distributions demonstrates the results of a z-score transformation.

FIGURE 5.7

Transforming a distribution of raw scores (a) into z-scores (b) will not change the shape of the distribution.

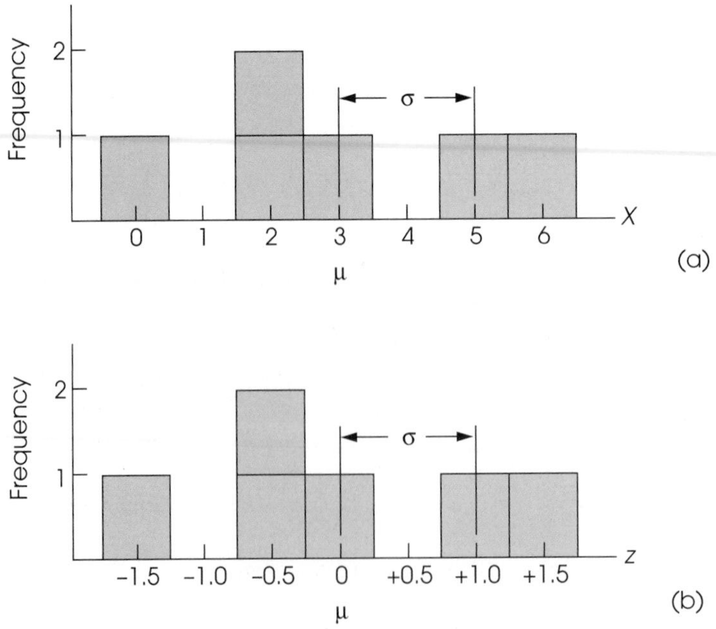

1. The two distributions have exactly the same shape. Each individual has exactly the same relative position in the X distribution and in the z-score distribution.
2. After the transformation to z-scores, the mean of the distribution becomes $\mu = 0$. For these z-scores values, $N = 6$ and $\Sigma z = -1.50 + 1.50 + 1.00 + -0.50 + 0 + -0.50 = 0$. Thus, the mean for the z-scores is $\mu = \Sigma z/N = 0/6 = 0$.

   Note that the individual with a score of $X = 3$ is located exactly at the mean in the X distribution and this individual is transformed into $z = 0$, exactly at the mean in the z-distribution.
3. After the transformation, the standard deviation becomes $\sigma = 1$. For these z-scores, $\Sigma z = 0$ and

$$\begin{aligned}\Sigma z^2 &= (-1.50)^2 + (1.50)^2 + (1.00)^2 + (-0.50)^2 + (0)^2 + (-0.50)^2 \\ &= 2.25 + 2.25 + 1.00 + 0.25 + 0 + 0.25 \\ &= 6.00\end{aligned}$$

Using the computational formula for SS, substituting z in place of X, we obtain

$$SS = \Sigma z^2 - \frac{(\Sigma z)^2}{N} = 6 - \frac{(0)^2}{6} = 6.00$$

For these z-scores, the variance is $\sigma^2 = \frac{SS}{N} = \frac{6}{6} = 1.00$ and the standard deviation is

$$\sigma = \sqrt{1.00} = 1.00$$

Note that the individual with $X = 5$ is located above the mean by 2 points, which is exactly one standard deviation in the X distribution. After transformation, this individual has a z-score that is located above the mean by 1 point, which is exactly one standard deviation in the z-score distribution.

USING z-SCORES TO MAKE COMPARISONS

One advantage of standardizing distributions is that it makes it possible to compare different scores or different individuals even though they come from completely different distributions. Normally, if two scores come from different distributions, it is impossible to make any direct comparison between them. Suppose, for example, Dave received a score of $X = 60$ on a psychology exam and a score of $X = 56$ on a biology test. For which course should Dave expect the better grade?

Because the scores come from two different distributions, you cannot make any direct comparison. Without additional information, it is even impossible to determine whether Dave is above or below the mean in either distribution. Before you can begin to make comparisons, you must know the values for the mean and standard deviation for each distribution. Suppose the biology scores had $\mu = 48$ and $\sigma = 4$, and the psychology scores had $\mu = 50$ and $\sigma = 10$. With this new information, you could sketch the two distributions, locate Dave's score in each distribution, and compare the two locations.

Instead of drawing the two distributions to determine where Dave's two scores are located, we simply can compute the two z-scores to find the two locations. For psychology, Dave's z-score is

$$z = \frac{X - \mu}{\sigma} = \frac{60 - 50}{10} = \frac{10}{10} = +1.0$$

Be sure to use the μ and σ values for the distribution to which X belongs.

For biology, Dave's z-score is

$$z = \frac{56 - 48}{4} = \frac{8}{4} = +2.0$$

Note that Dave's z-score for biology is +2.0, which means that his test score is 2 standard deviations above the class mean. On the other hand, his z-score is +1.0 for psychology, or 1 standard deviation above the mean. In terms of relative class standing, Dave is doing much better in the biology class.

Notice that we cannot compare Dave's two exam scores ($X = 60$ and $X = 56$) because the scores come from different distributions with different means and standard deviations. However, we can compare the two z-scores because all distributions of z-scores have the same mean ($\mu = 0$) and the same standard deviation ($\sigma = 1$).

LEARNING CHECK

1. A normal-shaped distribution with $\mu = 40$ and $\sigma = 8$ is transformed into z-scores. Describe the shape, the mean, and the standard deviation for the resulting distribution of z-scores.
2. What is the advantage of having a mean of $\mu = 0$ for a distribution of z-scores?
3. A distribution of English exam scores has $\mu = 70$ and $\sigma = 4$. A distribution of history exam scores has $\mu = 60$ and $\sigma = 20$. For which exam would a score of $X = 78$ have a higher standing? Explain your answer.
4. A distribution of English exam scores has $\mu = 50$ and $\sigma = 12$. A distribution of history exam scores has $\mu = 58$ and $\sigma = 4$. For which exam would a score of $X = 62$ have a higher standing? Explain your answer.

ANSWERS

1. The z-score distribution would be normal with a mean of 0 and a standard deviation of 1.
2. With a mean of zero, all positive scores are above the mean and all negative scores are below the mean.
3. For the English exam, $X = 78$ corresponds to $z = 2.00$, which is a higher standing than $z = 0.90$ for the history exam.
4. The score $X = 62$ corresponds to $z = +1.00$ in both distributions. The score has exactly the same standing for both exams.

5.4 OTHER STANDARDIZED DISTRIBUTIONS BASED ON z-SCORES

TRANSFORMING z-SCORES TO A DISTRIBUTION WITH A PREDETERMINED μ AND σ

Although z-score distributions have distinct advantages, many people find them cumbersome because they contain negative values and decimals. For this reason, it is common to standardize a distribution by transforming the scores into a new distribution with a predetermined mean and standard deviation that are whole round numbers. The goal is to create a new (standardized) distribution that has "simple" values for the mean and standard deviation but does not change any individual's location within the distribution. Standardized scores of this type are frequently used in psychological or educational testing. For example, raw scores of the Scholastic Aptitude Test (SAT) are transformed to a standardized distribution that has $\mu = 500$ and $\sigma = 100$. For intelligence tests, raw scores are frequently converted to standard scores that have a mean of 100 and a standard deviation of 15. Because most IQ tests are standardized so that they have the same mean and standard deviation, it is possible to compare IQ scores even though they may come from different tests.

The procedure for standardizing a distribution to create new values for μ and σ involves two-steps:

1. The original raw scores are transformed into z-scores.
2. The z-scores are then transformed into new X values so that the specific μ and σ are attained.

This procedure ensures that each individual has exactly the same z-score location in the new distribution as in the original distribution. The following example demonstrates the standardization procedure.

EXAMPLE 5.7 An instructor gives an exam to a psychology class. For this exam, the distribution of raw scores has a mean of $\mu = 57$ with $\sigma = 14$. The instructor would like to simplify the distribution by transforming all scores into a new, standardized distribution with $\mu = 50$ and $\sigma = 10$. To demonstrate this process, we consider what happens to two specific students: Maria, who has a raw score of $X = 64$ in the original distribution; and Joe, whose original raw score is $X = 43$.

STEP 1 Transform each of the original raw scores into z-scores. For Maria, $X = 64$, so her z-score is

$$z = \frac{X - \mu}{\sigma} = \frac{64 - 57}{14} = +0.5$$

For Joe, $X = 43$, and his z-score is

$$z = \frac{X - \mu}{\sigma} = \frac{43 - 57}{14} = -1.0$$

Remember: The values of μ and σ are for the distribution from which X was taken.

STEP 2 Change each z-score into an X value in the new standardized distribution that has a mean of $\mu = 50$ and a standard deviation of $\sigma = 10$.

Maria's z-score, $z = +0.50$, indicates that she is located above the mean by $\frac{1}{2}$ standard deviation. In the new, standardized distribution, this location corresponds to $X = 55$ (above the mean by 5 points).

Joe's z-score, $z = -1.00$, indicates that he is located below the mean by exactly 1 standard deviation. In the new distribution, this location corresponds to $X = 40$ (below the mean by 10 points).

The results of this two-step transformation process are summarized in Table 5.1. Note that Joe, for example, has exactly the same z-score ($z = -1.00$) in both the original distribution and the new standardized distribution. This means that Joe's position relative to the other students in the class has not changed.

Figure 5.8 provides another demonstration of the concept that standardizing a distribution does not change the individual positions within the distribution. The figure shows the original exam scores from Example 5.7, with a mean of $\mu = 57$ and a

TABLE 5.1

A demonstration of how two individual scores are changed when a distribution is standardized. See Example 5.7.

	Original Scores $\mu = 57$ and $\sigma = 14$		z-Score Location		Standardized Scores $\mu = 50$ and $\sigma = 10$
Maria	$X = 64$	⟶	$z = +0.50$	⟶	$X = 55$
Joe	$X = 43$	⟶	$z = -1.00$	⟶	$X = 40$

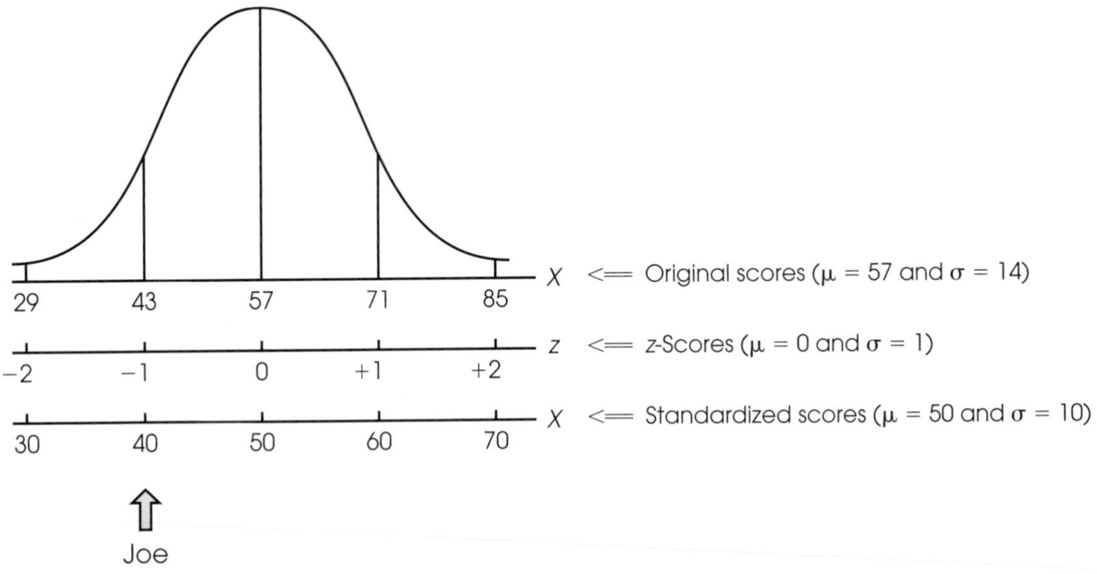

FIGURE 5.8

The distribution of exam scores from Example 5.7. The original distribution was standardized to produce a new distribution with $\mu = 50$ or $\sigma = 10$. Note that each individual is identified by an original score, a z-score, and a new, standardized score. For example, Joe has an original score of 43, a z-score of –1.00, and a standardized score of 40.

standard deviation of $\sigma = 14$. In the original distribution, Joe is located at a score of $X = 43$. In addition to the original scores, we have included a second scale showing the z-score value for each location in the distribution. In terms of z-scores, Joe is located at a value of $z = -1.00$. Finally, we have added a third scale showing the *standardized scores,* for which the mean is $\mu = 50$ and the standard deviation is $\sigma = 10$. For the standardized scores, Joe is located at $X = 40$. Note that Joe is always in the same place in the distribution. The only thing that changes is the number that is assigned to Joe: For the original scores, Joe is at 43; for the z-scores, Joe is at –1.00; and for the standardized scores, Joe is at 40.

LEARNING CHECK

1. A population of scores has $\mu = 73$ and $\sigma = 8$. If the distribution is standardized to create a new distribution with $\mu = 100$ and $\sigma = 20$, what are the new values for each of the following scores from the original distribution?

a. $X = 65$ **b.** $X = 71$ **c.** $X = 81$ **d.** $X = 83$

2. A population with a mean of $\mu = 44$ and a standard deviation of $\sigma = 6$ is standardized to create a new distribution with $\mu = 50$ and $\sigma = 10$.

a. What is the new standardized value for a score of $X = 47$ from the original distribution?

b. One individual has a new standardized score of $X = 65$. What was this person's score in the original distribution?

ANSWERS

1. **a.** $z = -1.00, X = 80$ **b.** $z = -0.25, X = 95$
   c. $z = 1.00, X = 120$ **d.** $z = 1.25, X = 125$

2. **a.** $X = 47$ corresponds to $z = +0.50$ in the original distribution. In the new distribution, the corresponding score is $X = 55$.
   b. In the new distribution, $X = 65$ corresponds to $z = +1.50$. The corresponding score in the original distribution is $X = 53$.

5.5 COMPUTING *z*-SCORES FOR A SAMPLE

Although *z*-scores are most commonly used in the context of a population, the same principles can be used to identify individual locations within a sample. The definition of a *z*-score is the same for a sample as for a population, provided that you use the sample mean and the sample standard deviation to specify each *z*-score location. Thus, for a sample, each *X* value is transformed into a *z*-score so that

1. The sign of the *z*-score indicates whether the *X* value is above (+) or below (–) the sample mean, and
2. The numerical value of the *z*-score identifies the distance from the sample mean by measuring the number of sample standard deviations between the score (*X*) and the sample mean (*M*).

See the population equations (5.1 and 5.2) on pages 142 and 144 for comparison.

Expressed as a formula, each *X* value in a sample can be transformed into a *z*-score as follows:

$$z = \frac{X - M}{s} \tag{5.3}$$

Similarly, each *z*-score can be transformed back into an *X* value, as follows:

$$X = M + zs \tag{5.4}$$

EXAMPLE 5.8

In a sample with a mean of $M = 40$ and a standard deviation of $s = 10$, what is the *z*-score corresponding to $X = 35$ and what is the *X* value corresponding to $z = +2.00$?

The score, $X = 35$, is located below the mean by 5 points, which is exactly half of the standard deviation. Therefore, the corresponding *z*-score is $z = -0.50$. The *z*-score, $z = +2.00$, corresponds to a location above the mean by 2 standard deviations. With a standard deviation of $s = 10$, this is distance of 20 points. The score that is located 20 points above the mean is $X = 60$. Note that it is possible to find these answers using either the z-score definition or one of the equations (5.3 or 5.4).

STANDARDIZING A SAMPLE DISTRIBUTION

If all the scores in a sample are transformed into *z*-scores, the result is a sample of *z*-scores. The transformed distribution of *z*-scores will have the same properties that exist when a population of *X* values is transformed into *z*-scores. Specifically,

1. The sample of *z*-scores will have the same shape as the original sample of scores.
2. The sample of *z*-scores will have a mean of $M_z = 0$.
3. The sample of *z*-scores will have a standard deviation of $s_z = 1$.

Note that the set of *z*-scores is still considered to be a sample (just like the set of *X* values) and the sample formulas must be used to compute variance and standard deviation. The following example demonstrates the process of transforming the scores from a sample into *z*-scores.

EXAMPLE 5.9

We begin with a sample of $n = 5$ scores: 0, 2, 4, 4, 5. With a few simple calculations, you should be able to verify that the sample mean is $M = 3$, the sample variance is $s^2 = 4$, and the sample standard deviation is $s = 2$. Using the sample mean and sample standard deviation, we can convert each *X* value into a *z*-score. For example, $X = 5$ is located above the mean by 2 points. Thus, $X = 5$ is above the mean by exactly 1 standard deviation and has a *z*-score of $z = +1.00$. The *z*-scores for the entire sample are shown in the following table.

X	*z*
0	−1.50
2	−0.50
4	+0.50
4	+0.50
5	+1.00

Again, a few simple calculations demonstrate that the sum of the *z*-score values is $\sigma z = 0$, so the mean is $M_z = 0$.

Because the mean is zero, each *z*-score value is its own deviation from the mean. Therefore, the sum of the squared deviations is simply the sum of the squared *z*-scores. For this sample of *z*-scores,

$$SS = \Sigma z^2 = (-1.50)^2 + (-0.50)^2 + (+0.50)^2 + (0.50)^2 + (+1.00)^2$$
$$= 2.25 + 0.25 + 0.25 + 0.25 + 1.00$$
$$= 4.00$$

The variance for the sample of *z*-scores is

$$s_z^2 = \frac{SS}{n-1} = \frac{4}{4} = 1.00$$

Notice that the set of *z*-scores is considered to be a sample and the variance is computed using the sample formula with $df = n - 1$.

Finally, the standard deviation for the sample of *z*-scores is. $s_z^2 = \sqrt{1.00} = 1.00$. As always, the distribution of *z*-scores has a mean of 0 and a standard deviation of 1.

5.6 LOOKING AHEAD TO INFERENTIAL STATISTICS

Recall that inferential statistics are techniques that use the information from samples to answer questions about populations. In later chapters, we use inferential statistics to help interpret the results from research studies. A typical research study begins with a question about how a treatment will affect the individuals in a population. Because it is usually impossible to study an entire population, the researcher selects a sample and administers the treatment to the individuals in the sample. This general research situation is shown in Figure 5.9. To evaluate the effect of the treatment, the researcher simply compares the treated sample with the original population. If the individuals in the sample are noticeably different from the individuals in the original population, the researcher has evidence that the treatment has had an effect. On the other hand, if the sample is not noticeably different from the original population, it would appear that the treatment has had no effect.

Notice that the interpretation of the research results depends on whether the sample is *noticeably different* from the population. One technique for deciding whether a sample is noticeably different is to use z-scores. For example, an individual with a z-score near 0 is located in the center of the population and would be considered to be a fairly typical or representative individual. However, an individual with an extreme z-score, beyond $+2.00$ or -2.00 for example, would be considered noticeably different from most of the individuals in the population. Thus, we can use z-scores to help decide whether the treatment has caused a change. Specifically, if the individuals who receive the treatment in a research study tend to have extreme z-scores, we can conclude that the treatment does appear to have an effect. The following example demonstrates this process.

EXAMPLE 5.10 A researcher is evaluating the effect of a new growth hormone. It is known that regular adult rats weigh an average of $\mu = 400$ grams. The weights vary from rat to rat, and the distribution of weights is normal with a standard deviation

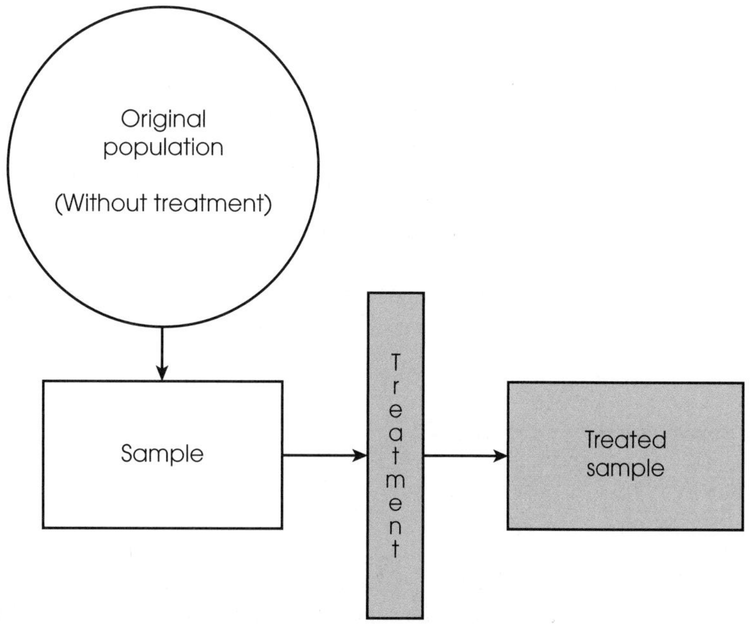

FIGURE 5.9
A diagram of a research study. The goal of the study is to evaluate the effect of a treatment. A sample is selected from the population and the treatment is administered to the sample. If, after treatment, the individuals in the sample are noticeably different from the individuals in the original population, then we have evidence that the treatment does have an effect.

FIGURE 5.10

The distribution of weights for the population of adult rats. Note that individuals with z-scores near 0 are typical or representative. However, individuals with z-scores beyond +2.00 or −2.00 are extreme and noticeably different from most of the others in the distribution.

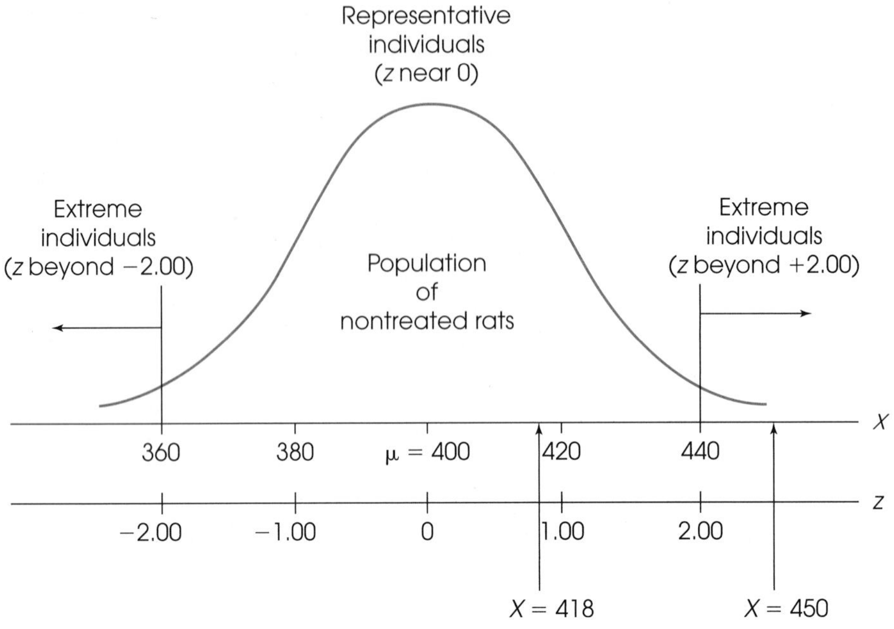

of σ = 20 grams. The population distribution is shown in Figure 5.10. The researcher selects one newborn rat and injects the rat with the growth hormone. When the rat reaches maturity, it is weighed to determine whether there is any evidence that the hormone has an effect.

First, assume that the hormone-injected rat weighs $X = 418$ grams. Although this is more than the average nontreated rat ($\mu = 400$ grams), is it convincing evidence that the hormone has an effect? If you look at the distribution in Figure 5.10, you should realize that a rat weighing 418 grams is not noticeably different from the regular rats that did not receive any hormone injection. Specifically, our injected rat would be located near the center of the distribution for regular rats with a z-score of

$$z = \frac{X - \mu}{\sigma} = \frac{418 - 400}{20} = \frac{18}{20} = 0.90$$

Because the injected rat still looks the same as a regular, nontreated rat, the conclusion is that the hormone does not appear to have an effect.

Now, assume that our injected rat weighs $X = 450$ grams. In the distribution of regular rats (see Figure 5.10), this animal would have a z-score of

$$z = \frac{X - \mu}{\sigma} = \frac{450 - 400}{20} = \frac{50}{20} = 2.50$$

In this case, the hormone-injected rat is substantially bigger than most ordinary rats, and it would be reasonable to conclude that the hormone does have an effect on weight.

In the preceding example, we used z-scores to help interpret the results obtained from a sample. Specifically, if the individuals who receive the treatment in a research study have extreme z-scores compared to those who do not receive the treatment, we can conclude that the treatment does appear to have an effect. The example, however, used an arbitrary definition to determine which z-score values are noticeably different. Although it is reasonable to describe individuals with z-scores near 0 as "highly representative" of the population, and individuals with z-scores beyond ±2.00 as "extreme," you should realize that these z-score boundaries were not determined by any mathematical rule. In the following chapter we introduce *probability*, which gives us a rationale for deciding exactly where to set the boundaries.

LEARNING CHECK

1. For a sample with a mean of $M = 40$ and a standard deviation of $s = 12$, find the z-score corresponding to each of the following X values.

$X = 43$	$X = 58$	$X = 49$
$X = 34$	$X = 28$	$X = 16$

2. For a sample with a mean of $M = 80$ and a standard deviation of $s = 20$, find the X value corresponding to each of the following z-scores.

$z = -1.00$	$z = -0.50$	$z = -0.20$
$z = 1.50$	$z = 0.80$	$z = 1.40$

3. For a sample with a mean of $M = 85$, a score of $X = 80$ corresponds to $z = -0.50$. What is the standard deviation for the sample?

4. For a sample with a standard deviation of $s = 12$, a score of $X = 83$ corresponds to $z = 0.50$. What is the mean for the sample?

5. A sample has a mean of $M = 30$ and a standard deviation of $s = 8$.

a. Would a score of $X = 36$ be considered a central score or an extreme score in the sample?

b. If the standard deviation were $s = 2$, would $X = 36$ be central or extreme?

ANSWERS

1.

$z = 0.25$	$z = 1.50$	$z = 0.75$
$z = -0.50$	$z = -1.00$	$z = -2.00$

2.

$X = 60$	$X = 70$	$X = 76$
$X = 110$	$X = 96$	$X = 108$

3. $s = 10$

4. $M = 77$

5. a. $X = 36$ is a central score corresponding to $z = 0.75$.

b. $X = 36$ would be an extreme score corresponding to $z = 3.00$.

SUMMARY

1. Each X value can be transformed into a z-score that specifies the exact location of X within the distribution. The sign of the z-score indicates whether the location is above (positive) or below (negative) the mean. The numerical value of the z-score specifies the number of standard deviations between X and μ.

2. The z-score formula is used to transform X values into z-scores. For a population:

$$z = \frac{X - \mu}{\sigma}$$

For a sample:

$$z = \frac{X - M}{s}$$

3. To transform z-scores back into X values, it usually is easier to use the z-score definition rather than a formula. However, the z-score formula can be transformed into a new equation. For a population:

$$X = \mu + z\sigma$$

For a sample: $X = M + zs$

4. When an entire distribution of X values is transformed into z-scores, the result is a distribution of z-scores. The z-score distribution will have the same shape as the distribution of raw scores, and it always will have a mean of 0 and a standard deviation of 1.

5. When comparing raw scores from different distributions, it is necessary to standardize the distributions with a z-score transformation. The distributions will then be comparable because they will have the same parameters ($\mu = 0$, $\sigma = 1$). In practice, it is necessary to transform only those raw scores that are being compared.

6. In certain situations, such as psychological testing, a distribution may be standardized by converting the original X values into z-scores and then converting the z-scores into a new distribution of scores with predetermined values for the mean and the standard deviation.

7. In inferential statistics, z-scores provide an objective method for determining how well a specific score represents its population. A z-score near 0 indicates that the score is close to the population mean and, therefore, is representative. A z-score beyond +2.00 (or –2.00) indicates that the score is extreme and is noticeably different from the other scores in the distribution.

KEY TERMS

raw score (139)
z-score (139)
deviation score (143)
z-score transformation (146)
standardized distribution (147)
standardized score (152)

RESOURCES

Book Companion Website: www.cengage.com/psychology/gravetter

You can find a tutorial quiz and other learning exercises for Chapter 5 on the book companion website. The website also includes a workshop entitled *z-Scores* that examines the basic concepts and calculations underlying z-scores.

aplia

Improve your understanding of statistics with Aplia's auto-graded problem sets and immediate, detailed explanations for every question. To learn more, visit **www.aplia.com/statistics.**

Psychology CourseMate brings course concepts to life with interactive learning, study, and exam preparation tools that support the printed textbook. A textbook-specific website, Psychology CourseMate includes an integrated interactive eBook and other interactive learning tools including quizzes, flashcards, and more.

Visit www.cengagebrain.com to access your account and purchase materials.

SPSS

General instructions for using SPSS are presented in Appendix D. Following are detailed instructions for using SPSS to **Transform** X **Values into** z**-Scores for a Sample.**

Data Entry

1. Enter all of the scores in one column of the data editor, probably VAR00001.

Data Analysis

1. Click **Analyze** on the tool bar, select **Descriptive Statistics,** and click on **Descriptives.**
2. Highlight the column label for the set of scores (VAR0001) in the left box and click the arrow to move it into the **Variable** box.
3. Click the box to **Save standardized values as variables** at the bottom of the **Descriptives** screen.
4. Click **OK.**

SPSS Output

The program produces the usual output display listing the number of scores (N), the maximum and minimum scores, the mean, and the standard deviation. However, if you go back to the Data Editor (use the tool bar at the bottom of the screen), you can see that SPSS has produced a new column showing the z-score corresponding to each of the original X values.

Caution: The SPSS program computes the z-scores using the sample standard deviation instead of the population standard deviation. If your set of scores is intended to be a population, SPSS does not produce the correct z-score values. You can convert the SPSS values into population z-scores by multiplying each z-score value by the square root of $n/(n - 1)$.

FOCUS ON PROBLEM SOLVING

1. When you are converting an X value to a z-score (or vice versa), do not rely entirely on the formula. You can avoid careless mistakes if you use the definition of a z-score (sign and numerical value) to make a preliminary estimate of the answer before you begin computations. For example, a z-score of $z = -0.85$ identifies a score located below the mean by almost 1 standard deviation. When computing the X value for this z-score, be sure that your answer is smaller than the mean, and check that the distance between X and μ is slightly less than the standard deviation.

2. When comparing scores from distributions that have different standard deviations, it is important to be sure that you use the correct value for σ in the z-score formula. Use the σ value for the distribution from which the raw score in question was taken.

3. Remember that a z-score specifies a relative position within the context of a specific distribution. A z-score is a relative value, not an absolute value. For example, a z-score of $z = -2.0$ does not necessarily suggest a very low raw score—it simply means that the raw score is among the lowest within that specific group.

DEMONSTRATION 5.1

TRANSFORMING *X* VALUES INTO *z*-SCORES

A distribution of scores has a mean of $\mu = 60$ with $\sigma = 12$. Find the z-score for $X = 75$.

STEP 1 **Determine the sign of the *z*-score.** First, determine whether X is above or below the mean. This determines the sign of the z-score. For this demonstration, X is larger than (above) μ, so the z-score is positive.

STEP 2 **Convert the distance between *X* and μ into standard deviation units.** For $X = 75$ and $\mu = 60$, the distance between X and μ is 15 points. With $\sigma = 12$ points, this distance corresponds to $\frac{15}{12} = 1.25$ standard deviations.

STEP 3 **Combine the sign from step 1 with the numerical value from step 2.** The score is above the mean (+) by a distance of 1.25 standard deviations. Thus, $z = +1.25$.

STEP 4 **Confirm the answer using the *z*-score formula.** For this example, $X = 75$, $\mu = 60$, and $\sigma = 12$.

$$z = \frac{X-\mu}{\sigma} = \frac{75-60}{12} = \frac{+15}{12} = +1.25$$

DEMONSTRATION 5.2

CONVERTING *z*-SCORES TO *X* VALUES

For a population with $\mu = 60$ and $\sigma = 12$, what is the X value corresponding to $z = -0.50$?

STEP 1 **Locate *X* in relation to the mean.** A z-score of -0.50 indicates a location below the mean by half of a standard deviation.

STEP 2 **Convert the distance from standard deviation units to points.** With $\sigma = 12$, half of a standard deviation is 6 points.

STEP 3 **Identify the *X* value.** The value we want is located below the mean by 6 points. The mean is $\mu = 60$, so the score must be $X = 54$.

PROBLEMS

1. What information is provided by the sign (+/–) of a z-score? What information is provided by the numerical value of the z-score?

2. A distribution has a standard deviation of $\sigma = 12$. Find the z-score for each of the following locations in the distribution.
   a. Above the mean by 3 points.
   b. Above the mean by 12 points.
   c. Below the mean by 24 points.
   d. Below the mean by 18 points.

3. A distribution has a standard deviation of $\sigma = 6$. Describe the location of each of the following z-scores in terms of position relative to the mean. For example, $z = +1.00$ is a location that is 6 points above the mean.
   a. $z = +2.00$
   b. $z = +0.50$
   c. $z = -2.00$
   d. $z = -0.50$

4. A sample has a mean of $M = 40$ and a standard deviation of $s = 6$. Find the z-score for each of the following X values from this sample.

   $X = 44$ $X = 42$ $X = 46$
   $X = 28$ $X = 50$ $X = 37$

5. For a population with $\mu = 40$ and $\sigma = 7$, find the z-score for each of the following X values. (*Note:* You probably will need to use a formula and a calculator to find these values.)

   $X = 45$ $X = 51$ $X = 41$
   $X = 30$ $X = 25$ $X = 38$

6. For a population with a mean of $\mu = 100$ and a standard deviation of $\sigma = 12$,
   a. Find the z-score for each of the following X values.

      $X = 106$ $X = 115$ $X = 130$
      $X = 91$ $X = 88$ $X = 64$

   b. Find the score (X value) that corresponds to each of the following z-scores.

      $z = -1.00$ $z = -0.50$ $z = 2.00$
      $z = 0.75$ $z = 1.50$ $z = -1.25$

7. A population has a mean of $\mu = 40$ and a standard deviation of $\sigma = 8$.
   a. For this population, find the z-score for each of the following X values.

      $X = 44$ $X = 50$ $X = 52$
      $X = 34$ $X = 28$ $X = 64$

   b. For the same population, find the score (X value) that corresponds to each of the following z-scores.

      $z = 0.75$ $z = 1.50$ $z = -2.00$
      $z = -0.25$ $z = -0.50$ $z = 1.25$

8. For a population with $\mu = 50$ and $\sigma = 8$,
   a. Find the z-score for each of the following X values. (*Note:* You should be able to find these values using the definition of a z-score. You should not need to use a formula or do any serious calculations.)

      $X = 54$ $X = 62$ $X = 52$
      $X = 42$ $X = 48$ $X = 34$

   b. Find the score (X value) that corresponds to each of the following z-scores. (Again, you should be able to find these values without any formula or serious calculations.)

      $z = 1.00$ $z = 0.75$ $z = 1.50$
      $z = -0.50$ $z = -0.25$ $z = -1.50$

9. A sample has a mean of $M = 80$ and a standard deviation of $s = 10$. For this sample, find the X value corresponding to each of the following z-scores.

   $z = 0.80$ $z = 1.20$ $z = 2.00$
   $z = -0.40$ $z = -0.60$ $z = -1.80$

10. Find the z-score corresponding to a score of $X = 60$ for each of the following distributions.
    a. $\mu = 50$ and $\sigma = 20$
    b. $\mu = 50$ and $\sigma = 10$
    c. $\mu = 50$ and $\sigma = 5$
    d. $\mu = 50$ and $\sigma = 2$

11. Find the X value corresponding to $z = 0.25$ for each of the following distributions.
    a. $\mu = 40$ and $\sigma = 4$
    b. $\mu = 40$ and $\sigma = 8$
    c. $\mu = 40$ and $\sigma = 12$
    d. $\mu = 40$ and $\sigma = 20$

12. For a population with a standard deviation of $\sigma = 8$, a score of $X = 44$ corresponds to $z = -0.50$. What is the population mean?

13. A score that is 12 points above the mean corresponds to a z-score of $z = 3.00$. What is the population standard deviation?

14. A score that is 6 points below the mean corresponds to a z-score of $z = -0.50$. What is the population standard deviation?

15. For a sample with a standard deviation of $s = 10$, a score of $X = 65$ corresponds to $z = 1.50$. What is the sample mean?

16. For a sample with a mean of $\mu = 45$, a score of $X = 59$ corresponds to $z = 2.00$. What is the sample standard deviation?

17. For a population with a mean of $\mu = 70$, a score of $X = 62$ corresponds to $z = -2.00$. What is the population standard deviation?

18. In a population of exam scores, a score of $X = 48$ corresponds to $z = +1.00$ and a score of $X = 36$ corresponds to $z = -0.50$. Find the mean and standard deviation for the population. (*Hint:* Sketch the distribution and locate the two scores on your sketch.)

19. In a distribution of scores, $X = 64$ corresponds to $z = 1.00$, and $X = 67$ corresponds to $z = 2.00$. Find the mean and standard deviation for the distribution.

20. A distribution with a mean of $\mu = 56$ and a standard deviation of $\sigma = 20$ is transformed into a standardized distribution with $\mu = 50$ and $\sigma = 10$. Find the new, standardized score for each of the following values from the original population.
a. $X = 46$
b. $X = 76$
c. $X = 40$
d. $X = 80$

21. A distribution of exam scores has a mean of $\mu = 80$.
a. If your score is $X = 86$, which standard deviation would give you a better grade: $\sigma = 4$ $\sigma = 8$?
b. If your score is $X = 74$, which standard deviation would give you a better grade: $\sigma = 4$ or $\sigma = 8$?

22. For each of the following, identify the exam score that should lead to the better grade. In each case, explain your answer.
a. A score of $X = 56$, on an exam with $\mu = 50$ and $\sigma = 4$; or a score of $X = 60$ on an exam with $\mu = 50$ and $\sigma = 20$.
b. A score of $X = 40$, on an exam with $\mu = 45$ and $\sigma = 2$; or a score of $X = 60$ on an exam with $\mu = 70$ and $\sigma = 20$.
c. A score of $X = 62$, on an exam with $\mu = 50$ and $\sigma = 8$; or a score of $X = 23$ on an exam with $\mu = 20$ and $\sigma = 2$.

23. A distribution with a mean of $\mu = 62$ and a standard deviation of $\sigma = 8$ is transformed into a standardized distribution with $\mu = 100$ and $\sigma = 20$. Find the new, standardized score for each of the following values from the original population.
a. $X = 60$
b. $X = 54$
c. $X = 72$
d. $X = 66$

24. For each of the following populations, would a score of $X = 50$ be considered a central score (near the middle of the distribution) or an extreme score (far out in the tail of the distribution)?
a. $\mu = 45$ and $\sigma = 10$
b. $\mu = 45$ and $\sigma = 2$
c. $\mu = 90$ and $\sigma = 20$
d. $\mu = 60$ and $\sigma = 20$

25. A population consists of the following $N = 5$ scores: 0, 6, 4, 3, and 12.
a. Compute μ and σ for the population.
b. Find the z-score for each score in the population.
c. Transform the original population into a new population of $N = 5$ scores with a mean of $\mu = 100$ and a standard deviation of $\sigma = 20$.

26. A sample consists of the following $n = 6$ scores: 2, 7, 4, 6, 4, and 7.
a. Compute the mean and standard deviation for the sample.
b. Find the z-score for each score in the sample.
c. Transform the original sample into a new sample with a mean of $M = 50$ and $s = 10$.

CHAPTER

6

Probability

Tools You Will Need

The following items are considered essential background material for this chapter. If you doubt your knowledge of any of these items, you should review the appropriate chapter or section before proceeding.

- Proportions (math review, Appendix A)
  - Fractions
  - Decimals
  - Percentages
- Basic algebra (math review, Appendix A)
  - *z*-Scores (Chapter 5)

Preview

Background: If you open a dictionary and randomly pick one word, which are you more likely to select:

1. A word beginning with the letter K?
2. A word with a *K* as its third letter?

If you think about this question and answer honestly, you probably will decide that words beginning with a *K* are more probable.

A similar question was asked a group of participants in an experiment reported by Tversky and Kahneman (1973). Their participants estimated that words beginning with *K* are twice as likely as words with a *K* as the third letter. In truth, the relationship is just the opposite. There are more than twice as many words with a *K* in the third position as there are words beginning with a *K*. How can people be so wrong? Do they completely misunderstand probability?

When you were deciding which type of *K* words are more likely, you probably searched your memory and tried to estimate which words are more common. How many words can you think of that start with the letter *K*? How many words can you think of that have a *K* as the third letter? Because you have had years of practice alphabetizing words according to their first letter, you should find it much easier to search your memory for words beginning with a *K* than to search for words with a *K* in the third position. Consequently, you are likely to conclude that first-letter *K* words are more common.

If you had searched for words in a dictionary (instead of those in your memory), you would have found more third-letter *K* words, and you would have concluded (correctly) that these words are more common.

The Problem: If you open a dictionary and randomly pick one word, it is impossible to predict exactly which word you will get. In the same way, when researchers recruit people to participate in research studies, it is impossible to predict exactly which individuals will be obtained.

The Solution: Although it is impossible to predict exactly which word will be picked from a dictionary, or which person will participate in a research study, you can use *probability* to demonstrate that some outcomes are more likely than others. For example, it is more likely that you will pick a third-letter *K* word than a first-letter *K* word. Similarly, it is more likely that you will obtain a person with an IQ around 100 than a person with an IQ around 150.

6.1 INTRODUCTION TO PROBABILITY

In Chapter 1, we introduced the idea that research studies begin with a general question about an entire population, but the actual research is conducted using a sample. In this situation, the role of inferential statistics is to use the sample data as the basis for answering questions about the population. To accomplish this goal, inferential procedures are typically built around the concept of probability. Specifically, the relationships between samples and populations are usually defined in terms of probability.

Suppose, for example, that you are selecting a single marble from a jar that contains 50 black and 50 white marbles. (In this example, the jar of marbles is the *population* and the single marble to be selected is the *sample*.) Although you cannot guarantee the exact outcome of your sample, it is possible to talk about the potential outcomes in terms of probabilities. In this case, you have a 50-50 chance of getting either color. Now consider another jar (population) that has 90 black and only 10 white marbles. Again, you cannot predict the exact outcome of a sample, but now you know that the sample probably will be a black marble. By knowing the makeup of a population, we can determine the probability of obtaining specific samples. In this way, probability gives us a connection between populations and samples, and this connection is the foundation for the inferential statistics that are presented in the chapters that follow.

You may have noticed that the preceding examples begin with a population and then use probability to describe the samples that could be obtained. This is exactly backward from what we want to do with inferential statistics. Remember that the goal of inferential statistics is to begin with a sample and then answer a general question about the population. We reach this goal in a two-stage process. In the first stage, we develop probability as a bridge from populations to samples. This stage involves identifying the types of samples that probably would be obtained from a specific population. Once this bridge is established, we simply reverse the probability rules to allow us to move from samples to populations (Figure 6.1). The process of reversing the probability relationship can be demonstrated by considering again the two jars of marbles we looked at earlier. (Jar 1 has 50 black and 50 white marbles; jar 2 has 90 black and only 10 white marbles.) This time, suppose you are blindfolded when the sample is selected, so you do not know which jar is being used. Your task is to look at the sample that you obtain and then decide which jar is most likely. If you select a sample of $n = 4$ marbles and all are black, which jar would you choose? It should be clear that it would be relatively unlikely (low probability) to obtain this sample from jar 1; in four draws, you almost certainly would get at least 1 white marble. On the other hand, this sample would have a high probability of coming from jar 2, where nearly all of the marbles are black. Your decision, therefore, is that the sample probably came from jar 2. Note that you now are using the sample to make an inference about the population.

DEFINING PROBABILITY

Probability is a huge topic that extends far beyond the limits of introductory statistics, and we do not attempt to examine it all here. Instead, we concentrate on the few concepts and definitions that are needed for an introduction to inferential statistics. We begin with a relatively simple definition of probability.

DEFINITION

For a situation in which several different outcomes are possible, the **probability** for any specific outcome is defined as a fraction or a proportion of all the possible outcomes. If the possible outcomes are identified as A, B, C, D, and so on, then

$$\text{probability of } A = \frac{\text{number of outcomes classified as } A}{\text{total number of possible outcomes}}$$

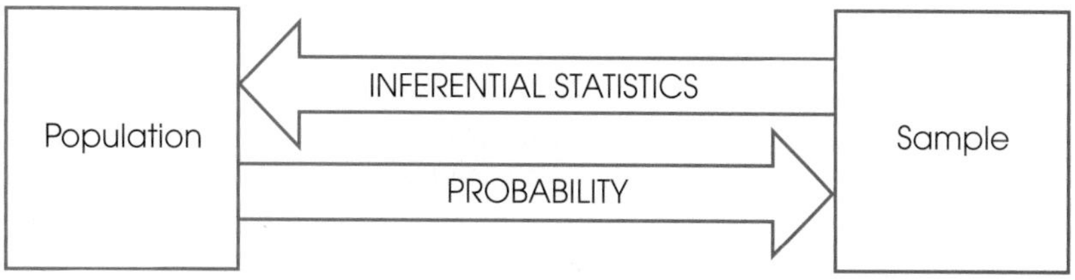

FIGURE 6.1
The role of probability in inferential statistics. Probability is used to predict what kind of samples are likely to be obtained from a population. Thus, probability establishes a connection between samples and populations. Inferential statistics rely on this connection when they use sample data as the basis for making conclusions about populations.

For example, if you are selecting a card from a complete deck, there are 52 possible outcomes. The probability of selecting the king of hearts is $p = \frac{1}{52}$. The probability of selecting an ace is $p = \frac{4}{52}$ because there are 4 aces in the deck.

To simplify the discussion of probability, we use a notation system that eliminates a lot of the words. The probability of a specific outcome is expressed with a *p* (for probability) followed by the specific outcome in parentheses. For example, the probability of selecting a king from a deck of cards is written as *p*(king). The probability of obtaining heads for a coin toss is written as *p*(heads).

Note that probability is defined as a proportion, or a part of the whole. This definition makes it possible to restate any probability problem as a proportion problem. For example, the probability problem "What is the probability of selecting a king from a deck of cards?" can be restated as "What proportion of the whole deck consists of kings?" In each case, the answer is $\frac{4}{52}$, or "4 out of 52." This translation from probability to proportion may seem trivial now, but it is a great aid when the probability problems become more complex. In most situations, we are concerned with the probability of obtaining a particular sample from a population. The terminology of *sample* and *population* do change the basic definition of probability. For example, the whole deck of cards can be considered as a population, and the single card we select is the sample.

Probability values The definition we are using identifies probability as a fraction or a proportion. If you work directly from this definition, the probability values you obtain are expressed as fractions. For example, if you are selecting a card at random,

$$p(\text{spade}) = \frac{13}{52} = \frac{1}{4}$$

Of if you are tossing a coin,

$$p(\text{heads}) = \frac{1}{2}$$

If you are unsure how to convert from fractions to decimals or percentages, you should review the section on proportions in the math review, Appendix A.

You should be aware that these fractions can be expressed equally well as either decimals or percentages:

$$p = \frac{1}{4} = 0.25 = 25\%$$

$$p = \frac{1}{2} = 0.50 = 50\%$$

By convention, probability values most often are expressed as decimal values. But you should realize that any of these three forms is acceptable.

You also should note that all of the possible probability values are contained in a limited range. At one extreme, when an event never occurs, the probability is zero, or 0% (Box 6.1). At the other extreme, when an event always occurs, the probability is 1, or 100%. Thus, all probability values are contained in a range from 0 to 1. For example, suppose that you have a jar containing 10 white marbles. The probability of randomly selecting a black marble is

$$p(\text{black}) = \frac{0}{10} = 0$$

The probability of selecting a white marble is

$$p(\text{white}) = \frac{10}{10} = 1$$

RANDOM SAMPLING

For the preceding definition of probability to be accurate, it is necessary that the outcomes be obtained by a process called *random sampling.*

DEFINITION

A **random sample** requires that each individual in the population has an *equal chance* of being selected.

A second requirement, necessary for many statistical formulas, states that if more than one individual is being selected, the probabilities must *stay constant* from one selection to the next. Adding this second requirement produces what is called *independent random sampling*. The term *independent* refers to the fact that the probability of selecting any particular individual is independent of those individuals who have already been selected for the sample. For example, the probability that you will be selected is constant and does not change even when other individuals are selected before you are.

DEFINITION

An **independent random sample** requires that each individual has an equal chance of being selected and that the probability of being selected stays constant from one selection to the next if more than one individual is selected.

Because independent random sample is a required component for most statistical applications, we always assume that this is the sampling method being used. To simplify discussion, we typically omit the word "independent" and simply refer to this sampling technique as *random sampling.* However, you should always assume that both requirements (equal chance and constant probability) are part of the process.

Each of the two requirements for random sampling has some interesting consequences. The first assures that there is no bias in the selection process. For a population with N individuals, each individual must have the same probability, $p = \frac{1}{N}$, of being selected. This means, for example, that you would not get a random sample of people in your city by selecting names from a yacht-club membership list. Similarly, you would not get a random sample of college students by selecting individuals from your psychology classes. You also should note that the first requirement of random sampling prohibits you from applying the definition of probability to situations in which the possible outcomes are not equally likely. Consider, for example, the question of whether you will win a million dollars in the lottery tomorrow. There are only two possible alternatives.

1. You will win.
2. You will not win.

According to our simple definition, the probability of winning would be one out of two, or $p = \frac{1}{2}$. However, the two alternatives are not equally likely, so the simple definition of probability does not apply.

The second requirement also is more interesting than may be apparent at first glance. Consider, for example, the selection of $n = 2$ cards from a complete deck. For the first draw, the probability of obtaining the jack of diamonds is

$$p(\text{jack of diamonds}) = \frac{1}{52}$$

After selecting one card for the sample, you are ready to draw the second card. What is the probability of obtaining the jack of diamonds this time? Assuming that you still are holding the first card, there are two possibilities:

$$p(\text{jack of diamonds}) = \frac{1}{51} \text{ if the first card was not the jack of diamonds}$$

or

$$p(\text{jack of diamonds}) = 0 \text{ if the first card was the jack of diamonds}$$

In either case, the probability is different from its value for the first draw. This contradicts the requirement for random sampling, which says that the probability must stay constant. To keep the probabilities from changing from one selection to the next, it is necessary to return each individual to the population before you make the next selection. This process is called *sampling with replacement.* The second requirement for random samples (constant probability) demands that you sample with replacement.

(*Note:* We are using a definition of random sampling that requires equal chance of selection and constant probabilities. This kind of sampling is also known as independent random sampling, and often is called *random sampling with replacement.* Many of the statistics we encounter later are founded on this kind of sampling. However, you should realize that other definitions exist for the concept of random sampling. In particular, it is very common to define random sampling without the requirement of constant probabilities—that is, *random sampling without replacement.* In addition, there are many different sampling techniques that are used when researchers are selecting individuals to participate in research studies.)

PROBABILITY AND FREQUENCY DISTRIBUTIONS

The situations in which we are concerned with probability usually involve a population of scores that can be displayed in a frequency distribution graph. If you think of the graph as representing the entire population, then different proportions of the graph represent different proportions of the population. Because probabilities and proportions are equivalent, a particular proportion of the graph corresponds to a particular probability in the population. Thus, whenever a population is presented in a frequency distribution graph, it is possible to represent probabilities as proportions of the graph. The relationship between graphs and probabilities is demonstrated in the following example.

EXAMPLE 6.1

We use a very simple population that contains only $N = 10$ scores with values 1, 1, 2, 3, 3, 4, 4, 4, 5, 6. This population is shown in the frequency distribution graph in Figure 6.2. If you are taking a random sample of $n = 1$ score from this population,

FIGURE 6.2

A frequency distribution histogram for a population that consists of $N = 10$ scores. The shaded part of the figure indicates the portion of the whole population that corresponds to scores greater than $X = 4$. The shaded portion is two-tenths ($p = \frac{2}{10}$) of the whole distribution.

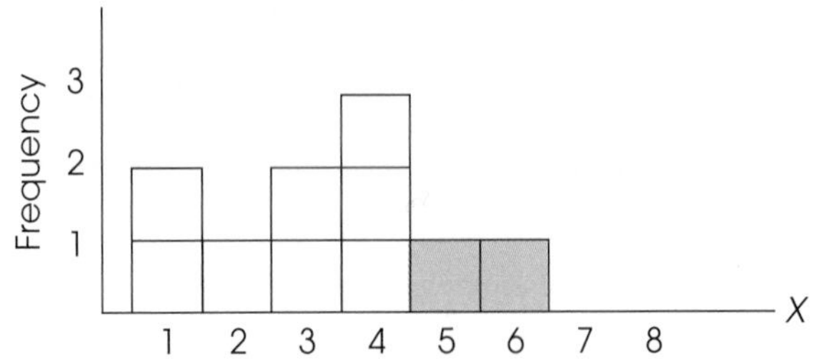

what is the probability of obtaining an individual with a score greater than 4? In probability notation,

$$p(X > 4) = ?$$

Using the definition of probability, there are 2 scores that meet this criterion out of the total group of $N = 10$ scores, so the answer would be $p = \frac{2}{10}$. This answer can be obtained directly from the frequency distribution graph if you recall that probability and proportion measure the same thing. Looking at the graph (see Figure 6.2), what proportion of the population consists of scores greater than 4? The answer is the shaded part of the distribution—that is, 2 squares out of the total of 10 squares in the distribution. Notice that we now are defining probability as a proportion of *area* in the frequency distribution graph. This provides a very concrete and graphic way of representing probability.

Using the same population once again, what is the probability of selecting an individual with a score less than 5? In symbols,

$$p(X < 5) = ?$$

Going directly to the distribution in Figure 6.2, we now want to know what part of the graph is not shaded. The unshaded portion consists of 8 out of the 10 blocks (eight-tenths of the area of the graph), so the answer is $p = \frac{8}{10}$.

LEARNING CHECK

1. A survey of the students in a psychology class revealed that there were 19 females and 8 males. Of the 19 females, only 4 had no brothers or sisters, and 3 of the males were also the only child in the household. If a student is randomly selected from this class,
   a. What is the probability of obtaining a male?
   b. What is the probability of selecting a student who has at least one brother or sister?
   c. What is the probability of selecting a female who has no siblings?
2. A jar contains 10 red marbles and 30 blue marbles.
   a. If you randomly select 1 marble from the jar, what is the probability of obtaining a red marble?
   b. If you take a *random sample* of $n = 3$ marbles from the jar and the first two marbles are both blue, what is the probability that the third marble will be red?
3. Suppose that you are going to select a random sample of $n = 1$ score from the distribution in Figure 6.2. Find the following probabilities:
   a. $p(X > 2)$
   b. $p(X > 5)$
   c. $p(X < 3)$

ANSWERS

1. **a.** $p = \frac{8}{27}$
   b. $p = \frac{20}{27}$
   c. $p = \frac{4}{27}$

2. a. $p = \frac{10}{40} = 0.25$

   b. $p = \frac{10}{40} = 0.25$. Remember that random sampling requires sampling with replacement.

3. a. $p = \frac{7}{10} = 0.70$

   b. $p = \frac{1}{10} = 0.10$

   c. $p = \frac{3}{10} = 0.30$

6.2 PROBABILITY AND THE NORMAL DISTRIBUTION

The normal distribution was first introduced in Chapter 2 as an example of a commonly occurring shape for population distributions. An example of a normal distribution is shown in Figure 6.3.

Note that the normal distribution is symmetrical, with the highest frequency in the middle and frequencies tapering off as you move toward either extreme. Although the exact shape for the normal distribution is defined by an equation (see Figure 6.3), the normal shape can also be described by the proportions of area contained in each section of the distribution. Statisticians often identify sections of a normal distribution by using *z*-scores. Figure 6.4 shows a normal distribution with several sections marked in *z*-score units. You should recall that *z*-scores measure positions in a distribution in terms of standard deviations from the mean. (Thus, $z = +1$ is 1 standard deviation above the mean, $z = +2$ is 2 standard deviations above the mean, and so on.) The graph shows the percentage of scores that fall in each of these sections. For example, the section between the mean ($z = 0$) and the point that is 1 standard deviation above the mean ($z = 1$) contains 34.13% of the scores. Similarly, 13.59% of the scores are located in the section between

FIGURE 6.3
The normal distribution. The exact shape of the normal distribution is specified by an equation relating each *X* value (score) with each *Y* value (frequency). The equation is

$$Y = \frac{1}{\sqrt{2\pi\sigma^2}} e^{-(X-\mu)^2/2\sigma^2}$$

(π and e are mathematical constants). In simpler terms, the normal distribution is symmetrical with a single mode in the middle. The frequency tapers off as you move farther from the middle in either direction.

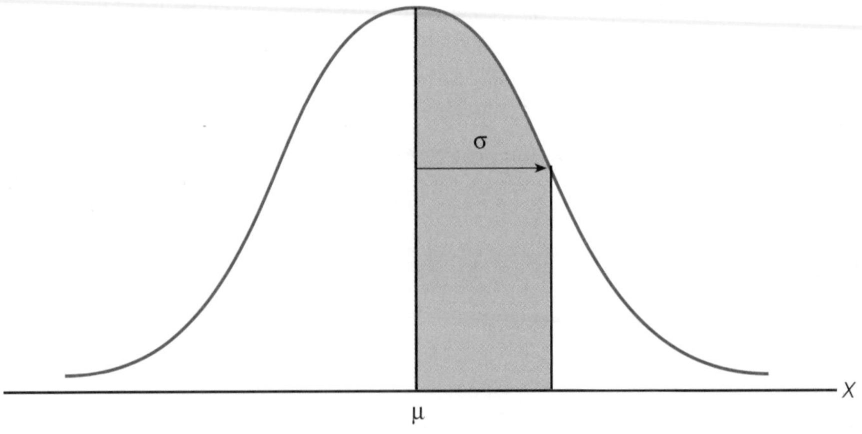

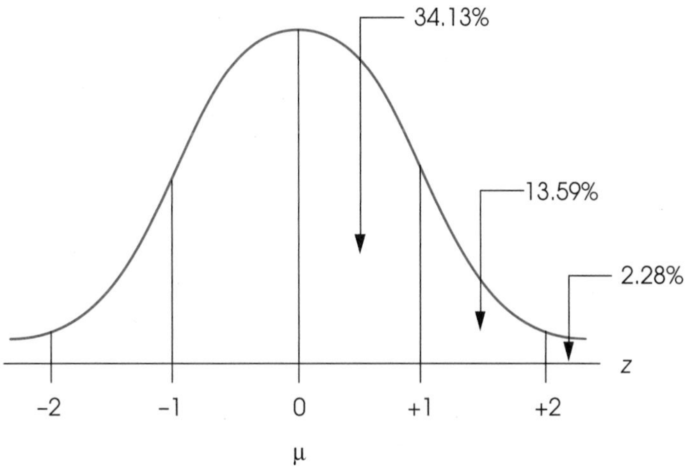

FIGURE 6.4
The normal distribution following a *z*-score transformation.

1 and 2 standard deviations above the mean. In this way it is possible to define a normal distribution in terms of its proportions; that is, a distribution is normal if and only if it has all the right proportions.

There are two additional points to be made about the distribution shown in Figure 6.4. First, you should realize that the sections on the left side of the distribution have exactly the same areas as the corresponding sections on the right side because the normal distribution is symmetrical. Second, because the locations in the distribution are identified by *z*-scores, the percentages shown in the figure apply to *any normal distribution* regardless of the values for the mean and the standard deviation. Remember: When any distribution is transformed into *z*-scores, the mean becomes zero and the standard deviation becomes one.

Because the normal distribution is a good model for many naturally occurring distributions and because this shape is guaranteed in some circumstances (as we see in Chapter 7), we devote considerable attention to this particular distribution. The process of answering probability questions about a normal distribution is introduced in the following example.

EXAMPLE 6.2

The population distribution of SAT scores is normal with a mean of $\mu = 500$ and a standard deviation of $\sigma = 100$. Given this information about the population and the known proportions for a normal distribution (see Figure 6.4), we can determine the probabilities associated with specific samples. For example, what is the probability of randomly selecting an individual from this population who has an SAT score greater than 700?

Restating this question in probability notation, we get

$$p(X > 700) = ?$$

We follow a step-by-step process to find the answer to this question.

1. First, the probability question is translated into a proportion question: Out of all possible SAT scores, what proportion is greater than 700?

2. The set of "all possible SAT scores" is simply the population distribution. This population is shown in Figure 6.5. The mean is $\mu = 500$, so the score $X = 700$ is to the right of the mean. Because we are interested in all scores greater than 700, we shade in the area to the right of 700. This area represents the proportion we are trying to determine.
3. Identify the exact position of $X = 700$ by computing a z-score. For this example,

$$z = \frac{X - \mu}{\sigma} = \frac{700 - 500}{100} = \frac{200}{100} = 2.00$$

That is, an SAT score of $X = 700$ is exactly 2 standard deviations above the mean and corresponds to a z-score of $z = +2.00$. We have also located this z-score in Figure 6.5.
4. The proportion we are trying to determine may now be expressed in terms of its z-score:

$$p(z > 2.00) = ?$$

According to the proportions shown in Figure 6.4, all normal distributions, regardless of the values for μ and σ, have 2.28% of the scores in the tail beyond $z = +2.00$. Thus, for the population of SAT scores,

$$p(X > 700) = p(z > +2.00) = 2.28\%$$

THE UNIT NORMAL TABLE

Before we attempt any more probability questions, we must introduce a more useful tool than the graph of the normal distribution shown in Figure 6.4. The graph shows proportions for only a few selected z-score values. A more complete listing of z-scores and proportions is provided in the *unit normal table*. This table lists proportions of the normal distribution for a full range of possible z-score values.

The complete unit normal table is provided in Appendix B Table B.1, and part of the table is reproduced in Figure 6.6. Notice that the table is structured in a four-column

FIGURE 6.5

The distribution of SAT scores described in Example 6.2.

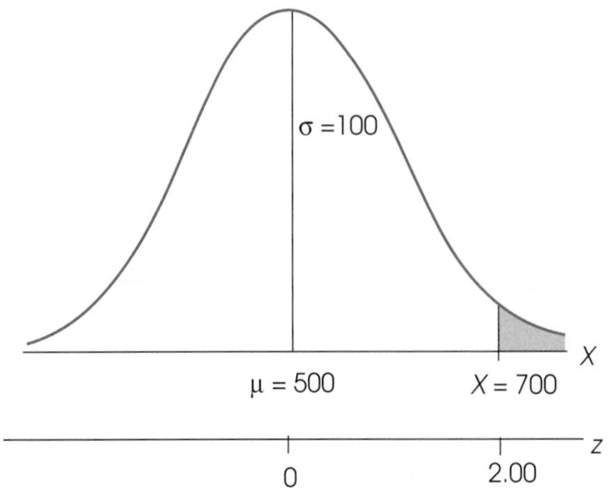

(A) z	(B) Proportion in body	(C) Proportion in tail	(D) Proportion between mean and z
0.00	.5000	.5000	.0000
0.01	.5040	.4960	.0040
0.02	.5080	.4920	.0080
0.03	.5120	.4880	.0120
0.21	.5832	.4168	.0832
0.22	.5871	.4129	.0871
0.23	.5910	.4090	.0910
0.24	.5948	.4052	.0948
0.25	.5987	.4013	.0987
0.26	.6026	.3974	.1026
0.27	.6064	.3936	.1064
0.28	.6103	.3897	.1103
0.29	.6141	.3859	.1141
0.30	.6179	.3821	.1179
0.31	.6217	.3783	.1217
0.32	.6255	.3745	.1255
0.33	.6293	.3707	.1293
0.34	.6331	.3669	.1331

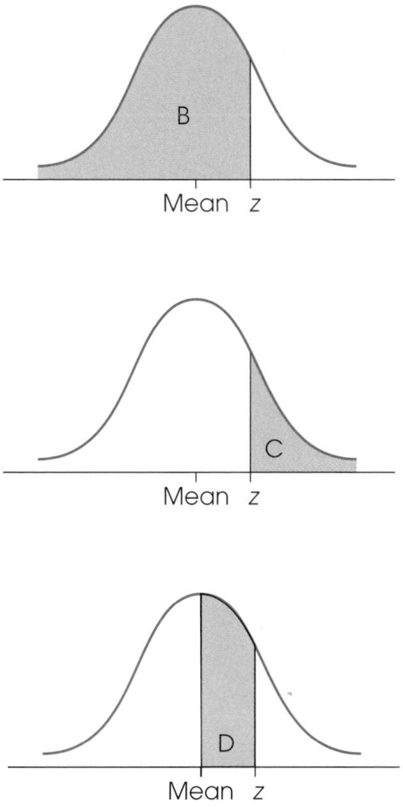

FIGURE 6.6

A portion of the unit normal table. This table lists proportions of the normal distribution corresponding to each z-score value. Column A of the table lists z-scores. Column B lists the proportion in the body of the normal distribution up to the z-score value. Column C lists the proportion of the normal distribution that is located in the tail of the distribution beyond the z-score value. Column D lists the proportion between the mean and the z-score value.

format. The first column (A) lists z-score values corresponding to different positions in a normal distribution. If you imagine a vertical line drawn through a normal distribution, then the exact location of the line can be described by one of the z-score values listed in column A. You should also realize that a vertical line separates the distribution into two sections: a larger section called the *body* and a smaller section called the *tail*. Columns B and C in the table identify the proportion of the distribution in each of the two sections. Column B presents the proportion in the body (the larger portion), and column C presents the proportion in the tail. Finally, we have added a fourth column, column D, that identifies the proportion of the distribution that is located *between* the mean and the z-score.

We use the distribution in Figure 6.7(a) to help introduce the unit normal table. The figure shows a normal distribution with a vertical line drawn at $z = +0.25$. Using the portion of the table shown in Figure 6.6, find the row in the table that contains $z = 0.25$ in column A. Reading across the row, you should find that the line drawn $z = +0.25$

separates the distribution into two sections with the larger section containing 0.5987 (59.87%) of the distribution and the smaller section containing 0.4013 (40.13%) of the distribution. Also, there is exactly 0.0987 (9.87%) of the distribution between the mean and $z = +0.25$.

To make full use of the unit normal table, there are a few facts to keep in mind:

1. The *body* always corresponds to the larger part of the distribution whether it is on the right-hand side or the left-hand side. Similarly, the *tail* is always the smaller section whether it is on the right or the left.
2. Because the normal distribution is symmetrical, the proportions on the right-hand side are exactly the same as the corresponding proportions on the left-hand side. Earlier, for example, we used the unit normal table to obtain proportions for $z = +0.25$. Figure 6.7(b) shows the same proportions for $z = -0.25$. For a negative z-score, however, notice that the tail of the distribution is on the left side and the body is on the right. For a positive z-score [Figure 6.7(a)], the positions are reversed. However, the proportions in each section are exactly the same, with 0.55987 in the body and 0.4013 in the tail. Once again, the table does not list negative z-score values. To find proportions for negative z-scores, you must look up the corresponding proportions for the positive value of z.
3. Although the z-score values change signs (+ and –) from one side to the other, the proportions are always positive. Thus, column C in the table always lists the proportion in the tail whether it is the right-hand tail or the left-hand tail.

PROBABILITIES, PROPORTIONS, AND Z-SCORES

The unit normal table lists relationships between z-score locations and proportions in a normal distribution. For any z-score location, you can use the table to look up the corresponding proportions. Similarly, if you know the proportions, you can use the table to find the specific z-score location. Because we have defined probability as equivalent to proportion, you can also use the unit normal table to look up probabilities for normal distributions. The following examples demonstrate a variety of different ways that the unit normal table can be used.

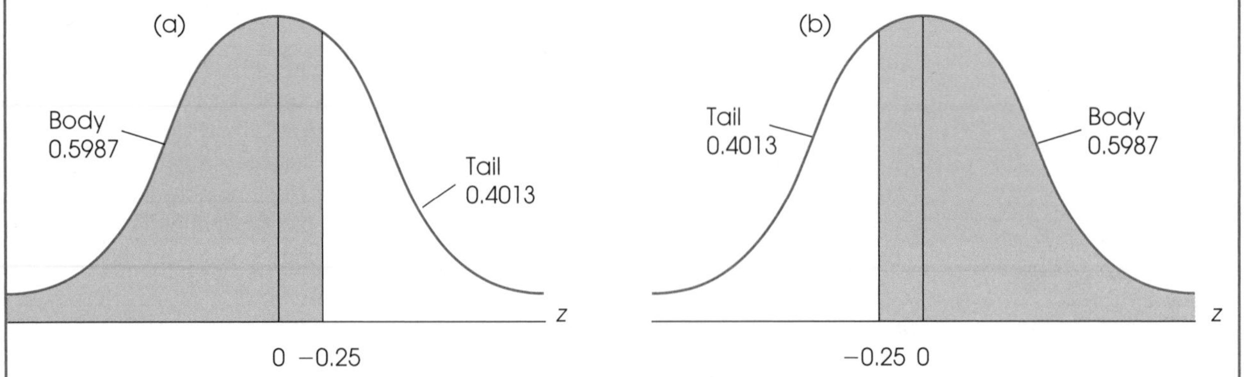

FIGURE 6.7

Proportions of a normal distribution corresponding to $z = +0.25$ (a) and -0.25 (b).

Finding proportions or probabilities for specific *z*-score values For each of the following examples, we begin with a specific *z*-score value and then use the unit normal table to find probabilities or proportions associated with the *z*-score.

EXAMPLE 6.3A

What proportion of the normal distribution corresponds to *z*-score values greater than $z = 1.00$? First, you should sketch the distribution and shade in the area you are trying to determine. This is shown in Figure 6.8(a). In this case, the shaded portion is the tail of the distribution beyond $z = 1.00$. To find this shaded area, you simply look for $z = 1.00$ in column A to find the appropriate row in the unit normal table. Then scan across the row to column C (tail) to find the proportion. Using the table in Appendix B, you should find that the answer is 0.1587.

You also should notice that this same problem could have been phrased as a probability question. Specifically, we could have asked, "For a normal distribution, what is the probability of selecting a *z*-score value greater than $z = +1.00$?" Again, the answer is $p(z > 1.00) = 0.1587$ (or 15.87%).

EXAMPLE 6.3B

For a normal distribution, what is the probability of selecting a *z*-score less than $z = 1.50$? In symbols, $p(z < 1.50) = ?$ Our goal is to determine what proportion of the normal distribution corresponds to *z*-scores less than 1.50. A normal distribution is shown in Figure 6.8(b) and $z = 1.50$ is marked in the distribution. Notice that we have shaded all the values to the left of (less than) $z = 1.50$. This is the portion we are trying to find. Clearly the shaded portion is more than 50%, so it corresponds to the body of the distribution. Therefore, find $z = 1.50$ in column A of the unit normal table and read across the row to obtain the proportion from column B. The answer is $p(z < 1.50) = 0.9332$ (or 93.32%).

EXAMPLE 6.3C

Moving to the left on the *X*-axis results in smaller *X* values and smaller *z*-scores. Thus, a *z*-score of –3.00 reflects a smaller value than a *z*-score of –1.

Many problems require that you find proportions for negative *z*-scores. For example, what proportion of the normal distribution is contained in the tail beyond $z = -0.50$? That is, $p(z < -0.50)$. This portion has been shaded in Figure 6.8(c). To answer questions with negative *z*-scores, simply remember that the normal distribution is symmetrical with a *z*-score of zero at the mean, positive values to the right, and negative values to the left. The proportion in the left tail beyond $z = -0.50$ is identical to the proportion

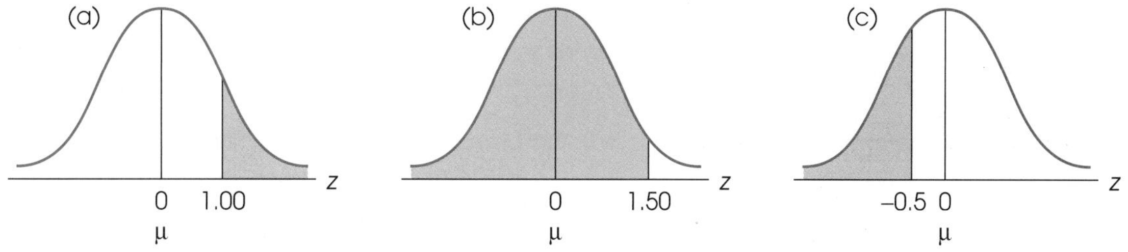

FIGURE 6.8
The distribution for Examples 6.3A to 6.3C.

in the right tail beyond $z = +0.50$. To find this proportion, look up $z = 0.50$ in column A, and read across the row to find the proportion in column C (tail). You should get an answer of 0.3085 (30.85%).

Finding the z-score location that corresponds to specific proportions The preceding examples all involved using a z-score value in column A to look up proportions in column B or C. You should realize, however, that the table also allows you to begin with a known proportion and then look up the corresponding z-score. The following examples demonstrate this process.

EXAMPLE 6.4A For a normal distribution, what z-score separates the top 10% from the remainder of the distribution? To answer this question, we have sketched a normal distribution [Figure 6.9(a)] and drawn a vertical line that separates the highest 10% (approximately) from the rest. The problem is to locate the exact position of this line. For this distribution, we know that the tail contains 0.1000 (10%) and the body contains 0.9000 (90%). To find the z-score value, you simply locate the row in the unit normal table that has 0.1000 in column C or 0.9000 in column B. For example, you can scan down the values in column C (tail) until you find a proportion of 0.1000. Note that you probably will not find the exact proportion, but you can use the closest value listed in the table. For this example, a proportion of 0.1000 is not listed in column C but you can use 0.1003, which is listed. Once you have found the correct proportion in the table, simply read across the row to find the corresponding z-score value in column A.

For this example, the z-score that separates the extreme 10% in the tail is $z = 1.28$. At this point you must be careful because the table does not differentiate between the right-hand tail and the left-hand tail of the distribution. Specifically, the final answer could be either $z = +1.28$, which separates 10% in the right-hand tail, or $z = -1.28$, which separates 10% in the left-hand tail. For this problem we want the right-hand tail (the highest 10%), so the z-score value is $z = +1.28$.

EXAMPLE 6.4B For a normal distribution, what z-score values form the boundaries that separate the middle 60% of the distribution from the rest of the scores?

Again, we have sketched a normal distribution [Figure 6.9(b)] and drawn vertical lines so that roughly 60% of the distribution in the central section, with the remainder

FIGURE 6.9
The distribution for Examples 6.4A and 6.4B.

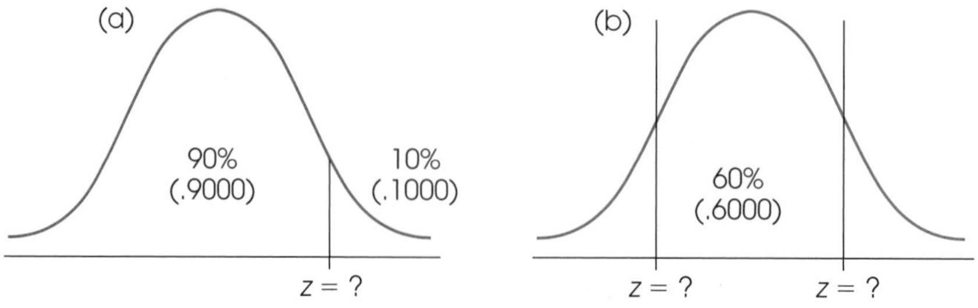

split equally between the two tails. The problem is to find the z-score values that define the exact locations for the lines. To find the z-score values, we begin with the known proportions: 0.6000 in the center and 0.4000 divided equally between the two tails. Although these proportions can be used in several different ways, this example provides an opportunity to demonstrate how column D in the table can be used to solve problems. For this problem, the 0.6000 in the center can be divided in half with exactly 0.3000 to the right of the mean and exactly 0.3000 to the left. Each of these sections corresponds to the proportion listed in column D. Begin by scanning down column D, looking for a value of 0.3000. Again, this exact proportion is not in the table, but the closest value is 0.2995. Reading across the row to column A, you should find a z-score value of $z = 0.84$. Looking again at the sketch [Figure 6.9(b)], the right-hand line is located at $z = +0.84$ and the left-hand line is located at $z = -0.84$.

You may have noticed that we have sketched distributions for each of the preceding problems. As a general rule, you should always sketch a distribution, locate the mean with a vertical line, and shade in the portion that you are trying to determine. Look at your sketch. It will help you to determine which columns to use in the unit normal table. If you make a habit of drawing sketches, you will avoid careless errors when using the table.

LEARNING CHECK

1. Find the proportion of a normal distribution that corresponds to each of the following sections:

a. $z < 0.25$

b. $z > 0.80$

c. $z < -1.50$

d. $z > -0.75$

2. For a normal distribution, find the z-score location that divides the distribution as follows:

a. Separate the top 20% from the rest.

b. Separate the top 60% from the rest.

c. Separate the middle 70% from the rest.

3. The tail will be on the right-hand side of a normal distribution for any positive z-score. (True or false?)

ANSWERS

1. a. $p = 0.5987$

b. $p = 0.2119$

c. $p = 0.0668$

d. $p = 0.7734$

2. a. $z = 0.84$

b. $z = -0.25$

c. $z = -1.04$ and $+ 1.04$

3. True

6.3 PROBABILITIES AND PROPORTIONS FOR SCORES FROM A NORMAL DISTRIBUTION

In the preceding section, we used the unit normal table to find probabilities and proportions corresponding to specific *z*-score values. In most situations, however, it is necessary to find probabilities for specific *X* values. Consider the following example:

> It is known that IQ scores form a normal distribution with $\mu = 100$ and $\sigma = 15$. Given this information, what is the probability of randomly selecting an individual with an IQ score less than 120?

This problem is asking for a specific probability or proportion of a normal distribution. However, before we can look up the answer in the unit normal table, we must first transform the IQ scores (*X* values) into *z*-scores. Thus, to solve this new kind of probability problem, we must add one new step to the process. Specifically, to answer probability questions about scores (*X* values) from a normal distribution, you must use the following two-step procedure:

Caution: The unit normal table can be used only with normal-shaped distributions. If a distribution is not normal, transforming to *z*-scores does not make it normal.

1. Transform the *X* values into *z*-scores.
2. Use the unit normal table to look up the proportions corresponding to the *z*-score values.

This process is demonstrated in the following examples. Once again, we suggest that you sketch the distribution and shade the portion you are trying to find to avoid careless mistakes.

EXAMPLE 6.5 We now answer the probability question about IQ scores that we presented earlier. Specifically, what is the probability of randomly selecting an individual with an IQ score less than 120? Restated in terms of proportions, we want to find the proportion of the IQ distribution that corresponds to scores less than 120. The distribution is drawn in Figure 6.10, and the portion we want has been shaded.

The first step is to change the *X* values into *z*-scores. In particular, the score of $X = 120$ is changed to

$$z = \frac{X - \mu}{\sigma} = \frac{120 - 100}{15} = \frac{20}{15} = 1.33$$

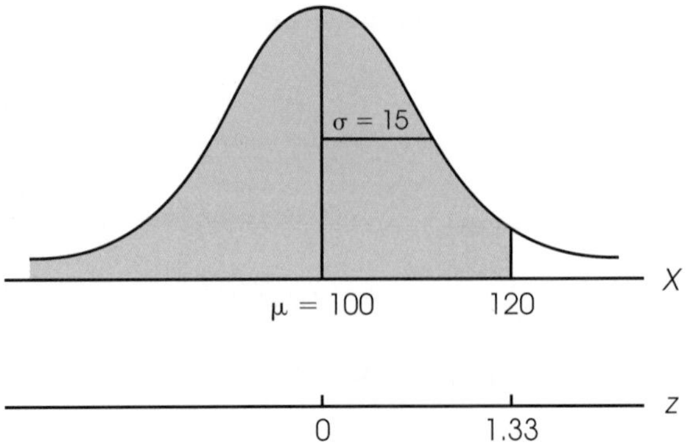

FIGURE 6.10
The distribution of IQ scores. The problem is to find the probability or proportion of the distribution corresponding to scores less than 120.

Thus, an IQ score of $X = 120$ corresponds to a z-score of $z = 1.33$, and IQ scores less than 120 correspond to z-scores less than 1.33.

Next, look up the z-score value in the unit normal table. Because we want the proportion of the distribution in the body to the left of $X = 120$ (see Figure 6.10), the answer is in column B. Consulting the table, we see that a z-score of 1.33 corresponds to a proportion of 0.9082. The probability of randomly selecting an individual with an IQ less than 120 is $p = 0.9082$. In symbols,

$$p(X < 120) = p(z < 1.33) = 0.9082 \text{ (or } 90.82\%)$$

Finally, notice that we phrased this question in terms of a *probability*. Specifically, we asked, "What is the probability of selecting an individual with an IQ less than 120?" However, the same question can be phrased in terms of a *proportion:* "What proportion of all of the individuals in the population have IQ scores less than 120?" Both versions ask exactly the same question and produce exactly the same answer. A third alternative for presenting the same question is introduced in Box 6.1.

Finding proportions/probabilities located between two scores The next example demonstrates the process of finding the probability of selecting a score that is located *between* two specific values. Although these problems can be solved using the proportions of columns B and C (body and tail), they are often easier to solve with the proportions listed in column D.

EXAMPLE 6.6 The highway department conducted a study measuring driving speeds on a local section of interstate highway. They found an average speed of $\mu = 58$ miles per hour with a standard deviation of $\sigma = 10$. The distribution was approximately normal.

BOX 6.1 PROBABILITIES, PROPORTIONS, AND PERCENTILE RANKS

Thus far we have discussed parts of distributions in terms of proportions and probabilities. However, there is another set of terminology that deals with many of the same concepts. Specifically, in Chapter 2 we defined the *percentile rank* for a specific score as the percentage of the individuals in the distribution who have scores that are less than or equal to the specific score. For example, if 70% of the individuals have scores of $X = 45$ or lower, then $X = 45$ has a percentile rank of 70%. When a score is referred to by its percentile rank, the score is called a *percentile*. For example, a score with a percentile rank of 70% is called the 70th percentile.

Using this terminology, it is possible to rephrase some of the probability problems that we have been working. In Example 6.5, the problem is presented as "What is the probability of randomly selecting an individual with an IQ of less than 120?" Exactly the same question could be phrased as "What is the percentile rank for an IQ score of 120?" In each case, we are drawing a line at $X = 120$ and looking for the proportion of the distribution on the left-hand side of the line. Similarly, Example 6.8 asks "How much time do you have to spend commuting each day to be in the highest 10% nationwide?" Because this score separates the top 10% from the bottom 90%, the same question could be rephrased as "What is the 90th percentile for the distribution of commuting times?"

Given this information, what proportion of the cars are traveling between 55 and 65 miles per hour? Using probability notation, we can express the problem as

$$p(55 < X < 65) = ?$$

The distribution of driving speeds is shown in Figure 6.11 with the appropriate area shaded. The first step is to determine the z-score corresponding to the X value at each end of the interval.

$$\text{For } X = 55: z = \frac{X - \mu}{\sigma} = \frac{55 - 58}{10} = \frac{-3}{10} = -0.30$$

$$\text{For } X = 65: z = \frac{X - \mu}{\sigma} = \frac{65 - 58}{10} = \frac{7}{10} = 0.70$$

Looking again at Figure 6.11, we see that the proportion we are seeking can be divided into two sections: (1) the area left of the mean, and (2) the area right of the mean. The first area is the proportion between the mean and $z = -0.30$, and the second is the proportion between the mean and $z = +0.70$. Using column D of the unit normal table, these two proportions are 0.1179 and 0.2580. The total proportion is obtained by adding these two sections:

$$p(55 < X < 65) = p(-0.30 < z < +0.70) = 0.1179 + 0.2580 = 0.3759$$

EXAMPLE 6.7 Using the same distribution of driving speeds from the previous example, what proportion of cars are traveling between 65 and 75 miles per hour?

$$p(65 < X < 75) = ?$$

The distribution is shown in Figure 6.12 with the appropriate area shaded. Again, we start by determining the z-score corresponding to each end of the interval.

$$\text{For } X = 75: \quad z = \frac{X - \mu}{\sigma} = \frac{75 - 58}{10} = \frac{17}{10} = 1.70$$

$$\text{For } X = 65: \quad z = \frac{X - \mu}{\sigma} = \frac{65 - 58}{10} = \frac{7}{10} = 0.70$$

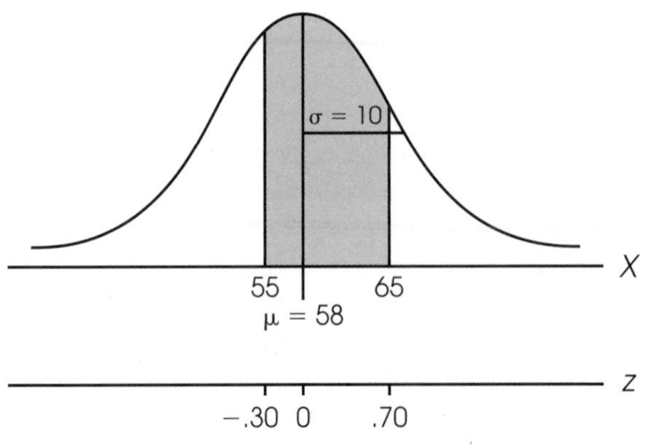

FIGURE 6.11
The distribution for Example 6.6.

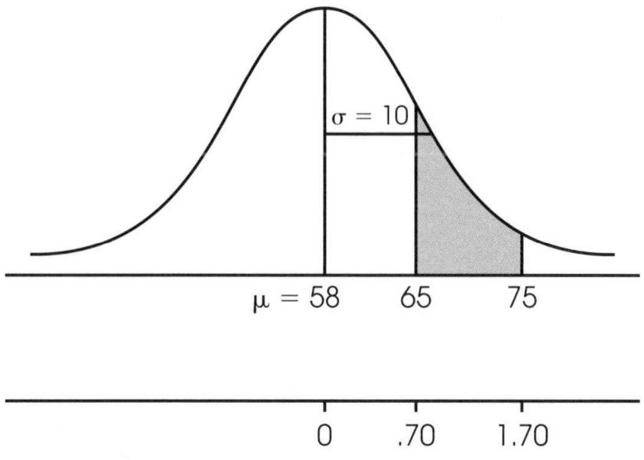

FIGURE 6.12
The distribution for Example 6.7.

There are several different ways to use the unit normal table to find the proportion between these two *z*-scores. For this example, we use the proportions in the tail of the distribution (column C). According to column C in the unit normal table, the proportion in the tail beyond $z = 0.70$ is $p = 0.2420$. Note that this proportion includes the section that we want, but it also includes an extra, unwanted section located in the tail beyond $z = 1.70$. Locating $z = 1.70$ in the table, and reading across the row to column C, we see that the unwanted section is $p = 0.0446$. To obtain the correct answer, we subtract the unwanted portion from the total proportion in the tail beyond $z = 0.70$.

$$p(65 < X < 75) = p(0.70 < z < 1.70) = 0.2420 - 0.0446 = 0.1974$$

Finding scores corresponding to specific proportions or probabilities In the previous three examples, the problem was to find the proportion or probability corresponding to specific *X* values. The two-step process for finding these proportions is shown in Figure 6.13. Thus far, we have only considered examples that move in a clockwise direction around the triangle shown in the figure; that is, we start with an *X* value that is transformed into a *z*-score, and then we use the unit normal table to look up the

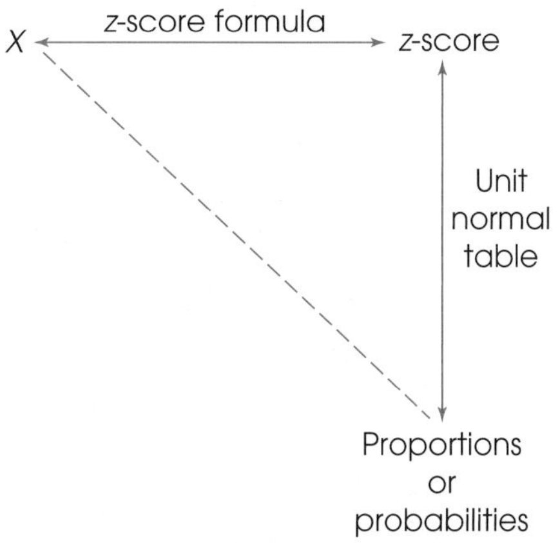

FIGURE 6.13
Determining probabilities or proportions for a normal distribution is shown as a two-step process with *z*-scores as an intermediate stop along the way. Note that you cannot move directly along the dashed line between *X* values and probabilities and proportions. Instead, you must follow the solid lines around the corner.

appropriate proportion. You should realize, however, that it is possible to reverse this two-step process so that we move backward, or counterclockwise, around the triangle. This reverse process allows us to find the score (*X* value) corresponding to a specific proportion in the distribution. Following the lines in Figure 6.13, we begin with a specific proportion, use the unit normal table to look up the corresponding *z*-score, and then transform the *z*-score into an *X* value. The following example demonstrates this process.

EXAMPLE 6.8

The U.S. Census Bureau (2005) reports that Americans spend an average of $\mu = 24.3$ minutes commuting to work each day. Assuming that the distribution of commuting times is normal with a standard deviation of $\sigma = 10$ minutes, how much time do you have to spend commuting each day to be in the highest 10% nationwide? (An alternative form of the same question is presented in Box 6.1.) The distribution is shown in Figure 6.14 with a portion representing approximately 10% shaded in the right-hand tail.

In this problem, we begin with a proportion (10% or 0.10), and we are looking for a score. According to the map in Figure 6.13, we can move from *p* (proportion) to *X* (score) via *z*-scores. The first step is to use the unit normal table to find the *z*-score that corresponds to a proportion of 0.10 in the tail. First, scan the values in column C to locate the row that has a proportion of 0.10 in the tail of the distribution. Note that you will not find 0.1000 exactly, but locate the closest value possible. In this case, the closest value is 0.1003. Reading across the row, we find $z = 1.28$ in column A.

The next step is to determine whether the *z*-score is positive or negative. Remember that the table does not specify the sign of the *z*-score. Looking at the distribution in Figure 6.14, you should realize that the score we want is above the mean, so the *z*-score is positive, $z = +1.28$.

The final step is to transform the *z*-score into an *X* value. By definition, a *z*-score of $+1.28$ corresponds to a score that is located above the mean by 1.28 standard deviations. One standard deviation is equal to 10 points ($\sigma = 10$), so 1.28 standard deviations is

$$1.28\sigma = 1.28(10) = 12.8 \text{ points}$$

FIGURE 6.14

The distribution of commuting times for American workers. The problem is to find the score that separates the highest 10% of commuting times from the rest.

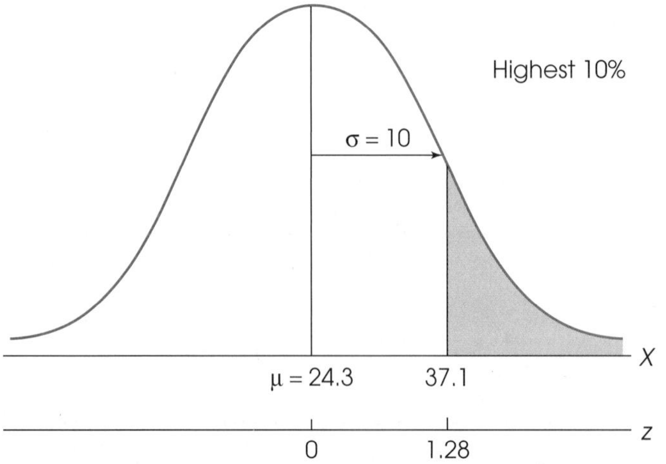

Thus, our score is located above the mean ($\mu = 24.3$) by a distance of 12.8 points. Therefore,

$$X = 24.3 + 12.8 = 37.1$$

The answer for our original question is that you must commute at least 37.1 minutes a day to be in the top 10% of American commuters.

EXAMPLE 6.9 Again, the distribution of commuting time for American workers is normal with a mean of $\mu = 24.3$ minutes and a standard deviation of $\sigma = 10$ minutes. For this example, we find the range of values that defines the middle 90% of the distribution. The entire distribution is shown in Figure 6.15 with the middle portion shaded.

The 90% (0.9000) in the middle of the distribution can be split in half with 45% (0.4500) on each side of the mean. Looking up 0.4500, in column D of the unit normal table, you will find that the exact proportion is not listed. However, you will find 0.4495 and 0.4505, which are equally close. Technically, either value is acceptable, but we use 0.4505 so that the total area in the middle is at least 90%. Reading across the row, you should find a *z*-score of $z = 1.65$ in column A. Thus, the *z*-score at the right boundary is $z = +1.65$ and the *z*-score at the left boundary is $z = -1.65$. In either case, a *z*-score of 1.65 indicates a location that is 1.65 standard deviations away from the mean. For the distribution of commuting times, one standard deviation is $\sigma = 10$, so 1.65 standard deviations is a distance of

$$1.65\sigma = 1.65(10) = 16.5 \text{ points}$$

Therefore, the score at the right-hand boundary is located above the mean by 16.5 points and corresponds to $X = 24.3 + 16.5 = 40.8$. Similarly, the score at the left-hand boundary is below the mean by 16.5 points and corresponds to $X = 24.3 - 16.5 = 7.8$. The middle 90% of the distribution corresponds to values between 7.8 and 40.8. Thus, 90% of American commuters spend between 7.8 and 40.8 minutes commuting to work each day. Only 10% of commuters spend either more time or less time.

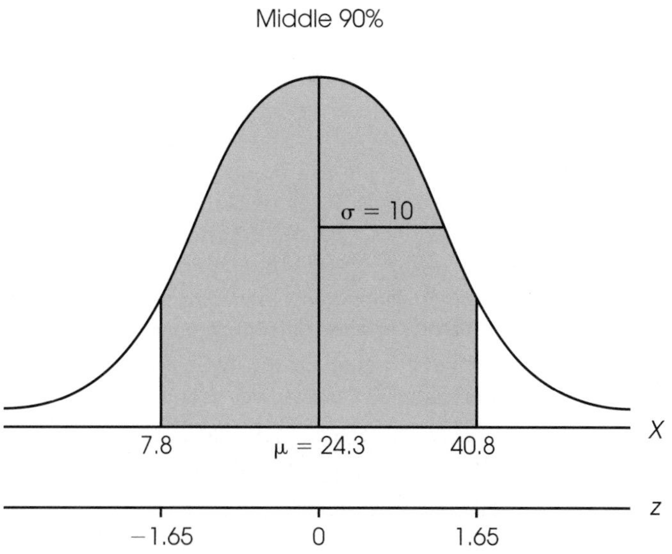

FIGURE 6.15
The distribution of commuting times for American workers. The problem is to find the middle 90% of the distribution.

LEARNING CHECK

1. For a normal distribution with a mean of $\mu = 60$ and a standard deviation of $\sigma = 12$, find each probability value requested.

a. $p(X > 66)$

b. $p(X < 75)$

c. $p(X < 57)$

d. $p(48 < X < 72)$

2. Scores on the Mathematics section of the SAT Reasoning Test form a normal distribution with a mean of $\mu = 500$ and a standard deviation of $\sigma = 100$.

a. If the state college only accepts students who score in the top 60% on this test, what is the minimum score needed for admission?

b. What is the minimum score necessary to be in the top 10% of the distribution?

c. What scores form the boundaries for the middle 50% of the distribution?

3. What is the probability of selecting a score greater than 45 from a positively skewed distribution with $\mu = 40$ and $\sigma = 10$? (Be careful.)

ANSWERS

1. **a.** $p = 0.3085$

b. $p = 0.8944$

c. $p = 0.4013$

d. $p = 0.6826$

2. **a.** $z = -0.25$; $X = 475$

b. $z = 1.28$; $X = 628$

c. $z = \pm 0.67$; $X = 433$ and $X = 567$

3. You cannot obtain the answer. The unit normal table cannot be used to answer this question because the distribution is not normal.

6.4 PROBABILITY AND THE BINOMIAL DISTRIBUTION

When a variable is measured on a scale consisting of exactly two categories, the resulting data are called binomial. The term *binomial* can be loosely translated as "two names," referring to the two categories on the measurement scale.

Binomial data can occur when a variable naturally exists with only two categories. For example, people can be classified as male or female, and a coin toss results in either heads or tails. It also is common for a researcher to simplify data by collapsing the scores into two categories. For example, a psychologist may use personality scores to classify people as either high or low in aggression.

In binomial situations, the researcher often knows the probabilities associated with each of the two categories. With a balanced coin, for example, $p(\text{heads}) = p(\text{tails}) = \frac{1}{2}$. The question of interest is the number of times each category occurs in a series of trials or in a sample of individuals. For example:

> What is the probability of obtaining 15 heads in 20 tosses of a balanced coin?
> What is the probability of obtaining more than 40 introverts in a sampling of 50 college freshmen?

As we shall see, the normal distribution serves as an excellent model for computing probabilities with binomial data.

THE BINOMIAL DISTRIBUTION

To answer probability questions about binomial data, we must examine the binomial distribution. To define and describe this distribution, we first introduce some notation.

1. The two categories are identified as A and B.
2. The probabilities (or proportions) associated with each category are identified as

$$p = p(A) = \text{the probability of } A$$
$$q = p(B) = \text{the probability of } B$$

   Notice that $p + q = 1.00$ because A and B are the only two possible outcomes.
3. The number of individuals or observations in the sample is identified by n.
4. The variable X refers to the number of times category A occurs in the sample.

Notice that X can have any value from 0 (none of the sample is in category A) to n (all of the sample is in category A).

DEFINITION

Using the notation presented here, the **binomial distribution** shows the probability associated with each value of X from $X = 0$ to $X = n$.

A simple example of a binomial distribution is presented next.

EXAMPLE 6.10

Figure 6.16 shows the binomial distribution for the number of heads obtained in 2 tosses of a balanced coin. This distribution shows that it is possible to obtain as many as 2 heads or as few as 0 heads in 2 tosses. The most likely outcome (highest probability) is to obtain exactly 1 head in 2 tosses. The construction of this binomial distribution is discussed in detail next.

For this example, the event we are considering is a coin toss. There are two possible outcomes, heads and tails. We assume the coin is balanced, so

$$p = p(\text{heads}) = \frac{1}{2}$$

FIGURE 6.16
The binomial distribution showing the probability for the number of heads in 2 tosses of a balanced coin.

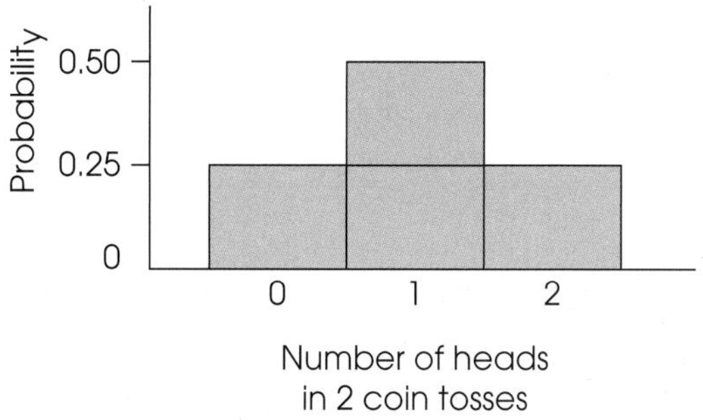

$$q = p(\text{tails}) = \frac{1}{2}$$

We are looking at a sample of $n = 2$ tosses, and the variable of interest is

X = the number of heads

To construct the binomial distribution, we look at all of the possible outcomes from tossing a coin 2 times. The complete set of 4 outcomes is listed in the following table.

1st Toss	2nd Toss	
Heads	Heads	(Both heads)
Heads	Tails	(Each sequence has exactly 1 head)
Tails	Heads	
Tails	Tails	(No heads)

Notice that there are 4 possible outcomes when you toss a coin 2 times. Only 1 of the 4 outcomes has 2 heads, so the probability of obtaining 2 heads is $p = \frac{1}{4}$. Similarly, 2 of the 4 outcomes have exactly 1 head, so the probability of 1 head is $p = \frac{2}{4} = \frac{1}{2}$. Finally, the probability of no heads ($X = 0$) is $p = \frac{1}{4}$. These are the probabilities shown in Figure 6.16.

Note that this binomial distribution can be used to answer probability questions. For example, what is the probability of obtaining at least 1 head in 2 tosses? According to the distribution shown in Figure 6.16, the answer is $\frac{3}{4}$.

Similar binomial distributions have been constructed for the number of heads in 4 tosses of a balanced coin and in 6 tosses of a coin (Figure 6.17). It should be obvious from the binomial distributions shown in Figures 6.16 and 6.17 that the binomial

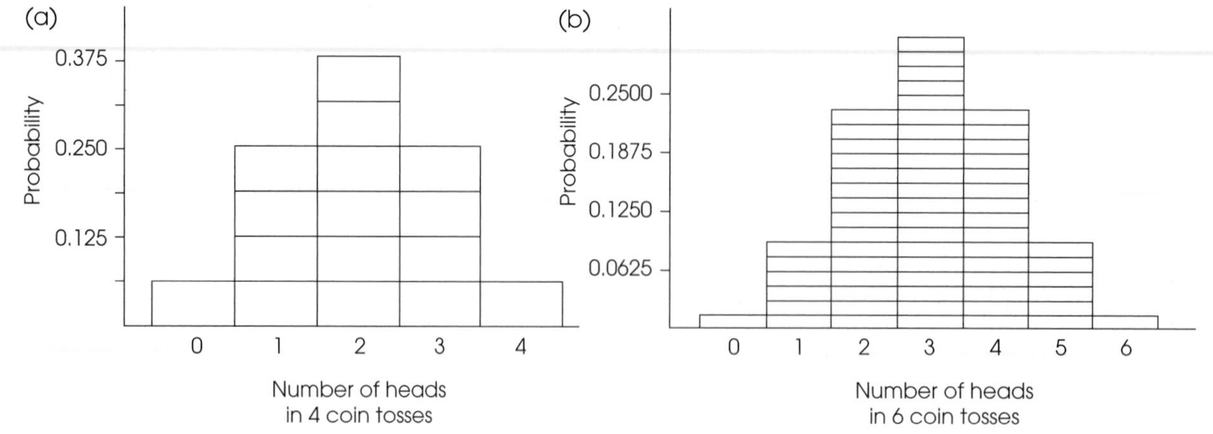

FIGURE 6.17

Binomial distributions showing probabilities for the number of heads (a) in 4 tosses of a balanced coin and (b) in 6 tosses of a balanced coin.

distribution tends toward a normal shape, especially when the sample size (n) is relatively large.

It should not be surprising that the binomial distribution tends to be normal. With $n = 10$ coin tosses, for example, the most likely outcome would be to obtain around $X = 5$ heads. On the other hand, values far from 5 would be very unlikely—you would not expect to get all 10 heads or all 10 tails (0 heads) in 10 tosses. Notice that we have described a normal-shaped distribution: The probabilities are highest in the middle (around $X = 5$), and they taper off as you move toward either extreme.

THE NORMAL APPROXIMATION TO THE BINOMIAL DISTRIBUTION

We have stated that the binomial distribution tends to approximate a normal distribution, particularly when n is large. To be more specific, the binomial distribution is a nearly perfect normal distribution when pn and qn are both equal to or greater than 10. Under these circumstances, the binomial distribution approximates a normal distribution with the following parameters:

The value of 10 for pn or qn is a general guide, not an absolute cutoff. Values slightly less than 10 still provide a good approximation. However, with smaller values the normal approximation becomes less accurate as a substitute for the binomial distribution.

$$\text{Mean: } \mu = pn \tag{6.1}$$

$$\text{standard deviation: } \sigma = \sqrt{npq} \tag{6.2}$$

Within this normal distribution, each value of X has a corresponding z-score,

$$z = \frac{X - \mu}{\sigma} = \frac{X - pn}{\sqrt{npq}} \tag{6.3}$$

The fact that the binomial distribution tends to be normal in shape means that we can compute probability values directly from z-scores and the unit normal table.

Coin tosses produce discrete events. In a series of coin tosses, you may observe 1 head, 2 heads, 3 heads, and so on, but no values between them are possible (p. 21).

It is important to remember that the normal distribution is only an approximation of a true binomial distribution. Binomial values, such as the number of heads in a series of coin tosses, are *discrete*. The normal distribution is *continuous*. However, the *normal approximation* provides an extremely accurate model for computing binomial probabilities in many situations. Figure 6.18 shows the difference between the true binomial distribution, the discrete histogram, and the normal curve that approximates the binomial distribution. Although the two distributions are slightly different, the area under the distributions is nearly equivalent. *Remember, it is the area under the distribution that is used to find probabilities.*

FIGURE 6.18

The relationship between the binomial distribution and the normal distribution. The binomial distribution is always a discrete histogram, and the normal distribution is a continuous, smooth curve. Each X value is represented by a bar in the histogram or a section of the normal distribution.

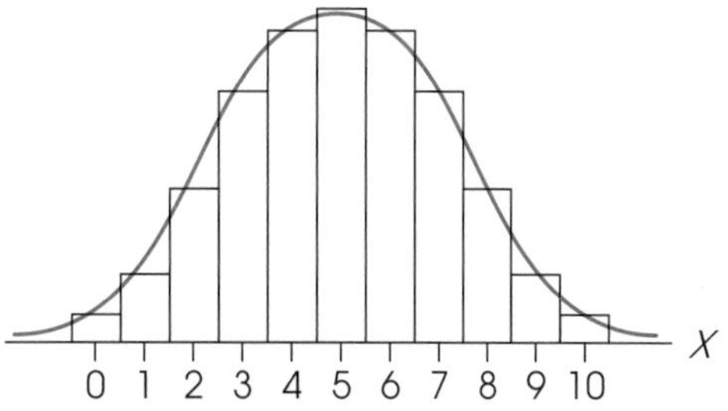

To gain maximum accuracy when using the normal approximation, you must remember that each X value in the binomial distribution actually corresponds to a bar in the histogram. In the histogram in Figure 6.18, for example, the score $X = 6$ is represented by a bar that is bounded by real limits of 5.5 and 6.5. The actual probability of $X = 6$ is determined by the area contained in this bar. To approximate this probability using the normal distribution, you should find the area that is contained between the two real limits. Similarly, if you are using the normal approximation to find the probability of obtaining a score greater than $X = 6$, you should use the area beyond the real limit boundary of 6.5. The following example demonstrates how the normal approximation to the binomial distribution is used to compute probability values.

EXAMPLE 6.11

Suppose that you plan to test for ESP (extra-sensory perception) by asking people to predict the suit of a card that is randomly selected from a complete deck. Before you begin your test, however, you need to know what kind of performance is expected from people who do not have ESP and are simply guessing. For these people, there are two possible outcomes, correct or incorrect, on each trial. Because there are four different suits, the probability of a correct prediction (assuming that there is no ESP) is $p = \frac{1}{4}$ and the probability of an incorrect prediction is $q = \frac{3}{4}$. With a series of $n = 48$ trials, this situation meets the criteria for the normal approximation to the binomial distribution:

$$pn = \tfrac{1}{4}(48) = 12 \quad qn = \tfrac{3}{4}(48) = 36 \text{ Both are greater than 10.}$$

Thus, the distribution of correct predictions forms a normal-shaped distribution with a mean of $\mu = pn = 12$ and a standard deviation of $\sigma = \sqrt{npq} = \sqrt{9} = 3$. We can use this distribution to determine probabilities for different levels of performance. For example, we can calculate the probability that a person without ESP would guess correctly more than 15 times in a series of 48 trials.

Figure 6.19 shows the binomial distribution that we are considering. Because we want the probability of obtaining *more than* 15 correct predictions, we must find the

FIGURE 6.19
The normal approximation of the binomial distribution discussed in Example 6.11.

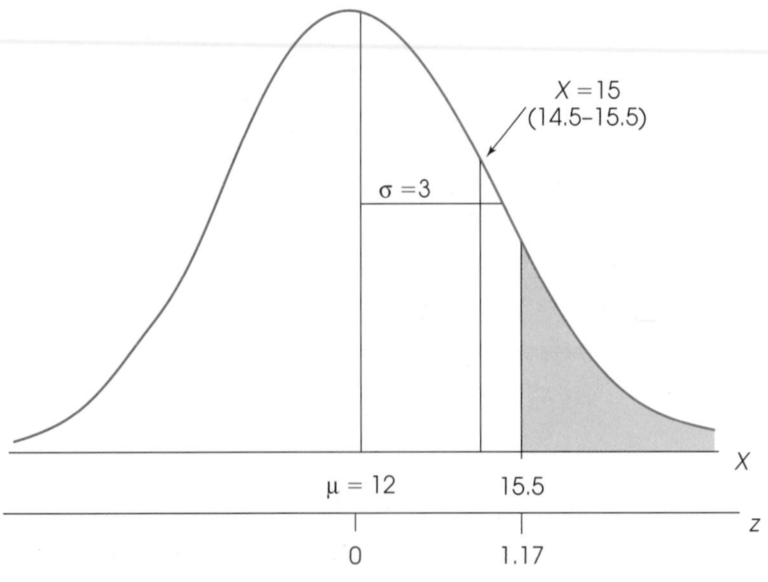

Caution: If the question had asked for the probability of *15 or more* correct predictions, we would find the area beyond $X = 14.5$. Read the question carefully.

shaded area in the tail of the distribution beyond $X = 15.5$. (Remember that a score of 15 corresponds to an interval from 14.5 to 15.5. We want scores beyond this interval.) The first step is to find the z-score corresponding to $X = 15.5$.

$$z = \frac{X - \mu}{\sigma} = \frac{15.5 - 12}{3} = 1.17$$

Next, look up the probability in the unit normal table. In this case, we want the proportion in the tail beyond $z = 1.17$. The value from the table is $p = 0.1210$. This is the answer we want. The probability of correctly predicting the suit of a card more than 15 times in a series of 48 trials is only $p = 0.1210$ or 12.10%. Thus, it is very unlikely for an individual without ESP to guess correctly more than 15 out of 48 trials.

LEARNING CHECK

1. Under what circumstances is the normal distribution an accurate approximation of the binomial distribution?
2. In the game Rock-Paper-Scissors, the probability that both players will select the same response and tie is $p = \frac{1}{3}$, and the probability that they will pick different responses is $p = \frac{2}{3}$. If two people play 72 rounds of the game and choose their responses randomly, what is the probability that they will choose the same response (tie) more than 28 times?
3. If you toss a balanced coin 36 times, you would expect, on the average, to get 18 heads and 18 tails. What is the probability of obtaining exactly 18 heads in 36 tosses?

ANSWERS

1. When pn and qn are both greater than 10
2. With $p = \frac{1}{3}$ and $q = \frac{2}{3}$, the binomial distribution is normal with $\mu = 24$ and $\sigma = 4$; $p(X > 28.5) = p(z > 1.13) = 0.1292$.
3. $X = 18$ is an interval with real limits of 17.5 and 18.5. The real limits correspond to $z = \pm 0.17$, and a probability of $p = 0.1350$.

6.5 LOOKING AHEAD TO INFERENTIAL STATISTICS

Probability forms a direct link between samples and the populations from which they come. As we noted at the beginning of this chapter, this link is the foundation for the inferential statistics in future chapters. The following example provides a brief preview of how probability is used in the context of inferential statistics.

We ended Chapter 5 with a demonstration of how inferential statistics are used to help interpret the results of a research study. A general research situation was shown in Figure 5.9 and is repeated here in Figure 6.20. The research begins with a population that forms a normal distribution with a mean of $\mu = 400$ and a standard deviation of $\sigma = 20$. A sample is selected from the population and a treatment is administered to the sample. The goal for the study is to evaluate the effect of the treatment.

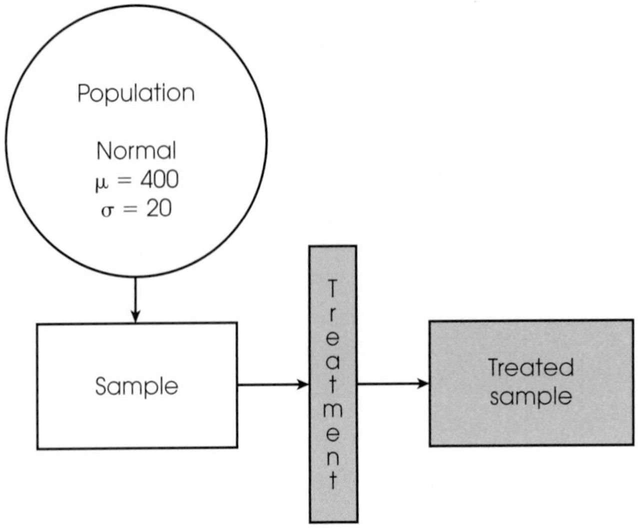

FIGURE 6.20
A diagram of a research study. A sample is selected from the population and receives a treatment. The goal is to determine whether the treatment has an effect.

To determine whether the treatment has an effect, the researcher simply compares the treated sample with the original population. If the individuals in the sample have scores around 400 (the original population mean), then we must conclude that the treatment appears to have no effect. On the other hand, if the treated individuals have scores that are noticeably different from 400, then the researcher has evidence that the treatment does have an effect. Notice that the study is using a sample to help answer a question about a population; this is the essence of inferential statistics.

The problem for the researcher is determining exactly what is meant by "noticeably different" from 400. If a treated individual has a score of $X = 415$, is that enough to say that the treatment has an effect? What about $X = 420$ or $X = 450$? In Chapter 5, we suggested that *z*-scores provide one method for solving this problem. Specifically, we suggested that a *z*-score value beyond $z = 2.00$ (or –2.00) was an extreme value and, therefore, noticeably different. However, the choice of $z = \pm 2.00$ was purely arbitrary. Now we have another tool, *probability*, to help us decide exactly where to set the boundaries.

Figure 6.21 shows the original population from our hypothetical research study. Note that most of the scores are located close to $\mu = 400$. Also note that we have added boundaries separating the middle 95% of the distribution from the extreme 5%, or 0.0500, in the two tails. Dividing the 0.0500 in half produces proportions of 0.0250 in the right-hand tail and 0.0250 in the left-hand tail. Using column C of the unit normal table, the *z*-score boundaries for the right and left tails are $z = +1.96$ and $z = -1.96$, respectively.

The boundaries set at $z = \pm 1.96$ provide objective criteria for deciding whether our sample provides evidence that the treatment has an effect. Specifically, we use the sample data to help decide between the following two alternatives:

1. The treatment has no effect. After treatment, the scores still average $\mu = 400$.
2. The treatment does have an effect. The treatment changes the scores so that, after treatment, they no longer average $\mu = 400$.

As a starting point, we assume that the first alternative is true and the treatment has no effect. In this case, treated individuals should be no different from the individuals in

FIGURE 6.21

Using probability to evaluate a treatment effect. Values that are extremely unlikely to be obtained from the original population are viewed as evidence of a treatment effect.

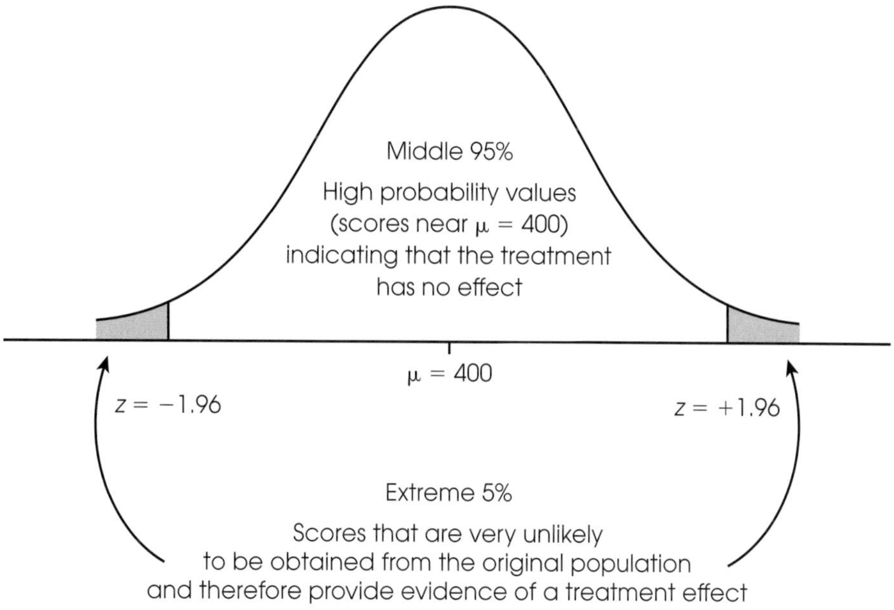

the original population, which is shown in Figure 6.21. Notice that, if our assumption is correct, it is extremely unlikely (probability less than 5%) for a treated individual to be outside the ± 1.96 boundaries. Therefore, if we obtain a treated individual who is outside the boundaries, we must conclude that the assumption is probably not correct. In this case, we are left with the second alternative (the treatment does have an effect) as the more likely explanation.

Notice that we are comparing the treated sample with the original population to see if the sample is noticeably different. If it is different, we can conclude that the treatment seems to have an effect. Now we are defining "noticeably different" as meaning "very unlikely." Specifically, if the sample is very unlikely to have come from a population of untreated individuals, then we must conclude that the treatment has an effect and has caused the sample to be different.

We are using the sample data and the ± 1.96 boundaries, which were determined by probabilities, to make a general decision about the treatment. If the sample falls outside the boundaries we make the following logical conclusion:

a. This kind of sample is very unlikely to occur if the treatment has no effect.

b. Therefore, the treatment must have an effect that changed the sample.

On the other hand, if the sample falls between the ± 1.96 boundaries, we conclude:

a. This is the kind of sample that is likely to occur if the treatment has no effect.

b. Therefore, the treatment does not appear to have had an effect.

SUMMARY

1. The probability of a particular event A is defined as a fraction or proportion:

$$p(A) = \frac{\text{number of outcomes classified as } A}{\text{total number of possible outcomes}}$$

2. Our definition of probability is accurate only for random samples. There are two requirements that must be satisfied for a random sample:
   a. Every individual in the population has an equal chance of being selected.
   b. When more than one individual is being selected, the probabilities must stay constant. This means that there must be sampling with replacement.

3. All probability problems can be restated as proportion problems. The "probability of selecting a king from a deck of cards" is equivalent to the "proportion of the deck that consists of kings." For frequency distributions, probability questions can be answered by determining proportions of area. The "probability of selecting an individual with an IQ greater than 108" is equivalent to the "proportion of the whole population that consists of IQs greater than 108."

4. For normal distributions, probabilities (proportions) can be found in the unit normal table. The table provides a listing of the proportions of a normal distribution that correspond to each z-score value. With the table, it is possible to move between X values and probabilities using a two-step procedure:
   a. The z-score formula (Chapter 5) allows you to transform X to z or to change z back to X.
   b. The unit normal table allows you to look up the probability (proportion) corresponding to each z-score or the z-score corresponding to each probability.

5. Percentiles and percentile ranks measure the relative standing of a score within a distribution (see Box 6.1). Percentile rank is the percentage of individuals with scores at or below a particular X value. A percentile is an X value that is identified by its rank. The percentile rank always corresponds to the proportion to the left of the score in question.

6. The binomial distribution is used whenever the measurement procedure classifies individuals into exactly two categories. The two categories are identified as A and B, with probabilities of

$$p(A) = p \quad \text{and} \quad p(B) = q$$

7. The binomial distribution gives the probability for each value of X, where X equals the number of occurrences of category A in a series of n events. For example, X equals the number of heads in $n = 10$ tosses of a coin.

   When pn and qn are both at least 10, the binomial distribution is closely approximated by a normal distribution with

$$\mu = pn \quad \sigma = \sqrt{npq}$$

8. In the normal approximation to the binomial distribution, each value of X has a corresponding z-score:

$$z = \frac{X - \mu}{\sigma} = \frac{X - pn}{\sqrt{npq}}$$

   With the z-score and the unit normal table, you can find probability values associated with any value of X. For maximum accuracy, you should use the appropriate real limits for X when computing z-scores and probabilities.

KEY TERMS

probability (165)
random sample (167)
independent random sample (167)
sampling with replacement (168)
unit normal table (172)
percentile rank (179)
percentile (179)
binomial distribution (185)
normal approximation (binomial) (187)

RESOURCES

Book Companion Website: www.cengage.com/psychology/gravetter

You can find a tutorial quiz and other learning exercises for Chapter 6 on the book companion website.

aplia

Improve your understanding of statistics with Aplia's auto-graded problem sets and immediate, detailed explanations for every question. To learn more, visit **www.aplia.com/statistics.**

CENGAGE**brain**.com

Psychology CourseMate brings course concepts to life with interactive learning, study, and exam preparation tools that support the printed textbook. A textbook-specific website, Psychology CourseMate includes an integrated interactive eBook and other interactive learning tools including quizzes, flashcards, and more.

Visit www.cengagebrain.com to access your account and purchase materials.

SPSS

The statistics computer package SPSS is not structured to compute probabilities. However, the program does report probability values as part of the inferential statistics that we examine later in this book. In the context of inferential statistics, the probabilities are called *significance levels,* and they warn researchers about the probability of misinterpreting their research results.

FOCUS ON PROBLEM SOLVING

1. We have defined probability as being equivalent to a proportion, which means that you can restate every probability problem as a proportion problem. This definition is particularly useful when you are working with frequency distribution graphs in which the population is represented by the whole graph and probabilities (proportions) are represented by portions of the graph. When working problems with the normal distribution, you always should start with a sketch of the distribution. You should shade the portion of the graph that reflects the proportion you are looking for.
2. Remember that the unit normal table shows only positive *z*-scores in column A. However, because the normal distribution is symmetrical, the proportions in the table apply to both positive and negative *z*-score values.

3. A common error for students is to use negative values for proportions on the left-hand side of the normal distribution. Proportions (or probabilities) are always positive: 10% is 10% whether it is in the left or right tail of the distribution.

4. The proportions in the unit normal table are accurate only for normal distributions. If a distribution is not normal, you cannot use the table.

5. For maximum accuracy when using the normal approximation to the binomial distribution, you must remember that each X value is an interval bounded by real limits. For example, a score of $X = 10$ is actually an interval from 9.5 to 10.5. To find the probability of obtaining an X value greater than 10, you should use the real limit 10.5 in the z-score formula. Similarly, to find the probability of obtaining an X value less than 10, you should use the real limit 9.5.

DEMONSTRATION 6.1

FINDING PROBABILITY FROM THE UNIT NORMAL TABLE

A population is normally distributed with a mean of $\mu = 45$ and a standard deviation of $\sigma = 4$. What is the probability of randomly selecting a score that is greater than 43? In other words, what proportion of the distribution consists of scores greater than 43?

STEP 1 **Sketch the distribution.** For this demonstration, the distribution is normal with $\mu = 45$ and $\sigma = 4$. The score of $X = 43$ is lower than the mean and therefore is placed to the left of the mean. The question asks for the proportion corresponding to scores greater than 43, so shade in the area to the right of this score. Figure 6.22 shows the sketch.

STEP 2 **Transform the X value to a z-score.**

$$z = \frac{X - \mu}{\sigma} = \frac{43 - 45}{4} = \frac{-2}{4} = -0.5$$

STEP 3 **Find the appropriate proportion in the unit normal table.** Ignoring the negative size, locate $z = -0.50$ in column A. In this case, the proportion we want corresponds to the body of the distribution and the value is found in column B. For this example,

$$p(X > 43) = p(z > -0.50) = 0.6915$$

FIGURE 6.22
A sketch of the distribution for Demonstration 6.1.

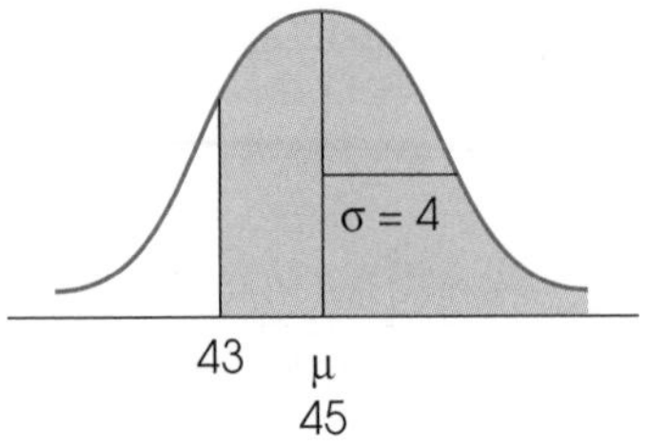

DEMONSTRATION 6.2

PROBABILITY AND THE BINOMIAL DISTRIBUTION

Suppose that you completely forgot to study for a quiz and now must guess on every question. It is a true/false quiz with $n = 40$ questions. What is the probability that you will get at least 26 questions correct just by chance? Stated in symbols,

$$p(X \geq 26) = ?$$

STEP 1 **Identify p and q.** This problem is a binomial situation, in which

$$p = \text{probability of guessing correctly} = 0.50$$

$$q = \text{probability of guessing incorrectly} = 0.50$$

With $n = 40$ quiz items, both pn and qn are greater than 10. Thus, the criteria for the normal approximation to the binomial distribution are satisfied:

$$pn = 0.50(40) = 20$$

$$qn = 0.50(40) = 20$$

STEP 2 **Identify the parameters, and sketch the binomial distribution.** For a true/false quiz, correct and incorrect guesses are equally likely, $p = q = \frac{1}{2}$. With pn and qn both greater than 10, the normal approximation is appropriate and has a mean and a standard deviation as follows:

$$\mu = pn = 0.5(40) = 20$$

$$\sigma = \sqrt{npq} = \sqrt{10} = 3.16$$

Figure 6.23 shows the distribution. We are looking for the probability of getting $X = 26$ or more questions correct, so we use the lower real limit for 26, which is 25.5.

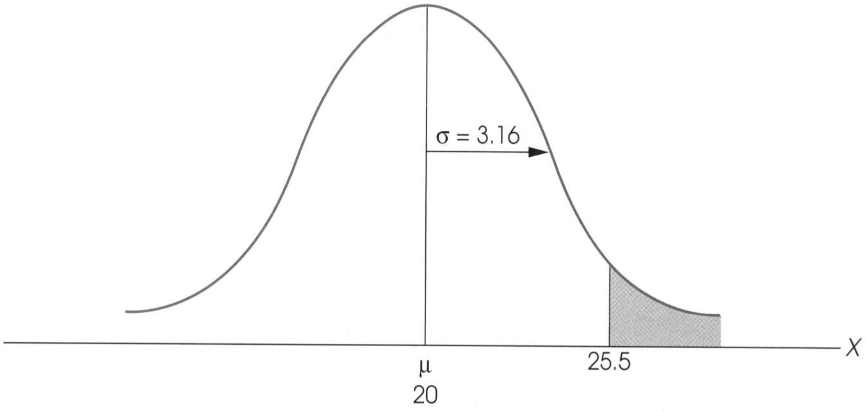

FIGURE 6.23

The normal approximation of a binomial distribution with $\mu = 20$ and $\sigma = 3.16$. The proportion of all scores equal to or greater than 26 is shaded. Notice that the real lower limit (25.5) for $X = 26$ is used.

STEP 3 The z-score for $X = 25.5$ is calculated as follows:

$$z = \frac{X - pn}{\sqrt{npq}} = \frac{25.5 - 20}{3.16} = +1.74$$

According to the unit normal table, the proportion we want is 0.0409. Thus, the probability of getting at least 26 questions right just by guessing is

$$p(X \geq 26) = 0.0409 \text{ (or 4.09\%)}$$

PROBLEMS

1. A local hardware store has a "Savings Wheel" at the checkout. Customers get to spin the wheel and, when the wheel stops, a pointer indicates how much they will save. The wheel can stop in any one of 50 sections. Of the sections, 10 produce 0% off, 20 sections are for 10% off, 10 sections for 20%, 5 for 30%, 3 for 40%, 1 for 50%, and 1 for 100% off. Assuming that all 50 sections are equally likely,
   a. What is the probability that a customer's purchase will be free (100% off)?
   b. What is the probability that a customer will get no savings from the wheel (0% off)?
   c. What is the probability that a customer will get at least 20% off?

2. Find the z-score location of a vertical line that separates a normal distribution as described in each of the following.
   a. 20% in the tail on the left
   b. 40% in the tail on the right
   c. 75% in the body on the left
   d. 99% in the body on the right

3. What are the two requirements that must be satisfied for a random sample?

4. What is sampling with replacement, and why is it used?

5. Draw a vertical line through a normal distribution for each of the following z-score locations. Determine whether the tail is on the right or left side of the line and find the proportion in the tail.
   a. $z = 2.00$
   b. $z = 0.60$
   c. $z = -1.30$
   d. $z = -0.30$

6. Draw a vertical line through a normal distribution for each of the following z-score locations. Determine whether the body is on the right or left side of the line and find the proportion in the body.
   a. $z = 2.20$
   b. $z = 1.60$
   c. $z = -1.50$
   d. $z = -0.70$

7. Find each of the following probabilities for a normal distribution.
   a. $p(z > 0.25)$
   b. $p(z > -0.75)$
   c. $p(z < 1.20)$
   d. $p(z < -1.20)$

8. What proportion of a normal distribution is located between each of the following z-score boundaries?
   a. $z = -0.50$ and $z = +0.50$
   b. $z = -0.90$ and $z = +0.90$
   c. $z = -1.50$ and $z = +1.50$

9. Find each of the following probabilities for a normal distribution.
   a. $p(-0.25 < z < 0.25)$
   b. $p(-2.00 < z < 2.00)$
   c. $p(-0.30 < z < 1.00)$
   d. $p(-1.25 < z < 0.25)$

10. A psychology class consists of 14 males and 36 females. If the professor selects names from the class list using *random sampling,*
    a. What is the probability that the first student selected will be a female?
    b. If a random sample of $n = 3$ students is selected and the first two are both females, what is the probability that the third student selected will be a male?

11. Find the z-score boundaries that separate a normal distribution as described in each of the following.
    a. The middle 20% from the 80% in the tails.
    b. The middle 50% from the 50% in the tails.
    c. The middle 95% from the 5% in the tails.
    d. The middle 99% from the 1% in the tails.

12. For a normal distribution with a mean of $\mu = 80$ and a standard deviation of $\sigma = 20$, find the proportion of the population corresponding to each of the following scores.
 a. Scores greater than 85.
 b. Scores less than 100.
 c. Scores between 70 and 90.

13. A normal distribution has a mean of $\mu = 50$ and a standard deviation of $\sigma = 12$. For each of the following scores, indicate whether the tail is to the right or left of the score and find the proportion of the distribution located in the tail.
 a. $X = 53$
 b. $X = 44$
 c. $X = 68$
 d. $X = 38$

14. Information from the Department of Motor Vehicles indicates that the average age of licensed drivers is $\mu = 45.7$ years with a standard deviation of $\sigma = 12.5$ years. Assuming that the distribution of drivers' ages is approximately normal,
 a. What proportion of licensed drivers are older than 50 years old?
 b. What proportion of licensed drivers are younger than 30 years old?

15. The distribution of scores on the SAT is approximately normal with a mean of $\mu = 500$ and a standard deviation of $\sigma = 100$. For the population of students who have taken the SAT,
 a. What proportion have SAT scores greater than 700?
 b. What proportion have SAT scores greater than 550?
 c. What is the minimum SAT score needed to be in the highest 10% of the population?
 d. If the state college only accepts students from the top 60% of the SAT distribution, what is the minimum SAT score needed to be accepted?

16. The distribution of SAT scores is normal with $\mu = 500$ and $\sigma = 100$.
 a. What SAT score, X value, separates the top 15% of the distribution from the rest?
 b. What SAT score, X value, separates the top 10% of the distribution from the rest?
 c. What SAT score, X value, separates the top 2% of the distribution from the rest?

17. A recent newspaper article reported the results of a survey of well-educated suburban parents. The responses to one question indicated that by age 2, children were watching an average of $\mu = 60$ minutes of television each day. Assuming that the distribution of television-watching times is normal with a standard deviation of $\sigma = 20$ minutes, find each of the following proportions.
 a. What proportion of 2-year-old children watch more than 90 minutes of television each day?
 b. What proportion of 2-year-old children watch less than 20 minutes a day?

18. IQ test scores are standardized to produce a normal distribution with a mean of $\mu = 100$ and a standard deviation of $\sigma = 15$. Find the proportion of the population in each of the following IQ categories.
 a. Genius or near genius: IQ greater than 140
 b. Very superior intelligence: IQ between 120 and 140
 c. Average or normal intelligence: IQ between 90 and 109

19. A consumer survey indicates that the average household spends $\mu = \$185$ on groceries each week. The distribution of spending amounts is approximately normal with a standard deviation of $\sigma = \$25$. Based on this distribution,
 a. What proportion of the population spends more than \$200 per week on groceries?
 b. What is the probability of randomly selecting a family that spends less than \$150 per week on groceries?
 c. How much money do you need to spend on groceries each week to be in the top 20% of the distribution?

20. Over the past 10 years, the local school district has measured physical fitness for all high school freshmen. During that time, the average score on a treadmill endurance task has been $\mu = 19.8$ minutes with a standard deviation of $\sigma = 7.2$ minutes. Assuming that the distribution is approximately normal, find each of the following probabilities.
 a. What is the probability of randomly selecting a student with a treadmill time greater than 25 minutes? In symbols, $p(X > 25) = ?$
 b. What is the probability of randomly selecting a student with a time greater than 30 minutes? In symbols, $p(X > 30) = ?$
 c. If the school required a minimum time of 10 minutes for students to pass the physical education course, what proportion of the freshmen would fail?

21. Rochester, New York, averages $\mu = 21.9$ inches of snow for the month of December. The distribution of snowfall amounts is approximately normal with a standard deviation of $\sigma = 6.5$ inches. This year, a local jewelry store is advertising a refund of 50% off of all purchases made in December, if Rochester finishes the month with more than 3 feet (36 inches) of total snowfall. What is the probability that the jewelry store will have to pay off on its promise?

22. A national health organization predicts that 20% of American adults will get the flu this season. If a sample of 100 adults is selected from the population,

a. What is the probability that at least 25 of the people will be diagnosed with the flu? (Be careful: "at least 25" means "25 or more.")

b. What is the probability that fewer than 15 of the people will be diagnosed with the flu? (Be careful: "fewer than 15" means "14 or less.")

23. A true/false test has 40 questions. If a students is simply guessing at the answers,

a. What is the probability of guessing correctly for any one question?

b. On average, how many questions would the student get correct for the entire test?

c. What is the probability that the student would get more than 25 answers correct simply by guessing?

d. What is the probability that the student would get 25 or more answers correct simply by guessing?

24. A roulette wheel has alternating red and black numbered slots into one of which the ball finally stops to determine the winner. If a gambler always bets on black to win, what is the probability of winning at least 24 times in a series of 36 spins? (Note that *at least* 24 wins means 24 or more.)

25. One test for ESP involves using Zener cards. Each card shows one of five different symbols (square, circle, star, cross, wavy lines), and the person being tested has to predict the shape on each card before it is selected. Find each of the probabilities requested for a person who has no ESP and is just guessing.

a. What is the probability of correctly predicting 20 cards in a series of 100 trials?

b. What is the probability of correctly predicting more than 30 cards in a series of 100 trials?

c. What is the probability of correctly predicting 50 or more cards in a series of 200 trials?

26. A trick coin has been weighted so that heads occurs with a probability of $p = \frac{2}{3}$, and $p(\text{tails}) = \frac{1}{3}$. If you toss this coin 72 times,

a. How many heads would you expect to get on average?

b. What is the probability of getting more than 50 heads?

c. What is the probability of getting exactly 50 heads?

27. For a balanced coin:

a. What is the probability of getting more than 30 heads in 50 tosses?

b. What is the probability of getting more than 60 heads in 100 tosses?

c. Parts a and b both asked for the probability of getting more than 60% heads in a series of coin tosses ($\frac{30}{50} = \frac{60}{100} = 60\%$). Why do you think the two probabilities are different?

28. A multiple-choice test has 48 questions, each with four response choices. If a student is simply guessing at the answers,

a. What is the probability of guessing correctly for any question?

b. On average, how many questions would a student get correct for the entire test?

c. What is the probability that a student would get more than 15 answers correct simply by guessing?

d. What is the probability that a student would get 15 or more answers correct simply by guessing?

CHAPTER

7

Probability and Samples: The Distribution of Sample Means

Tools You Will Need

The following items are considered essential background material for this chapter. If you doubt your knowledge of any of these items, you should review the appropriate chapter and section before proceeding.

- Random sampling (Chapter 6)
- Probability and the normal distribution (Chapter 6)
- *z*-Scores (Chapter 5)

Preview

In this chapter we extend the topic of probability to cover larger samples; specifically, samples that have more than one score. Fortunately, you already know the one basic fact governing probability for samples:

Samples tend to be similar to the populations from which they are taken.

For example, if you take a sample from a population that consists of 75% females and only 25% males, you probably will get a sample that has more females than males. Or, if you select a sample from a population for which the average age is $\mu = 21$ years, you probably will get a sample with an average age around 21 years. We are confident that you already know this basic fact because research indicates that even 8-month-old infants understand this basic law of sampling.

Xu and Garcia (2008) began one experiment by showing 8-month-old infants a large box filled with ping-pong balls. The box was brought onto a puppet stage and the front panel was opened to reveal the balls inside. The box contained either mostly red with a few white balls or mostly white with a few red balls. The experimenter alternated between the two boxes until the infants had seen both displays several times. After the infants were familiar with the boxes, the researchers began a series of test trials. On each trial, the box was brought on stage with the front panel closed. The researcher reached in the box and, one at a time, drew out a sample of five balls. The balls were placed in a transparent container next to the box. On half of the trials, the sample was rigged to have 1 red ball and 4 white balls. For the other half, the sample had 1 white ball and 4 red balls. The researchers then removed the front panel to reveal the contents of the box and recorded how long the infants continued to look at the box. The contents of the box were either consistent with the sample, and, therefore, expected, or inconsistent with the sample, and, therefore, unexpected. An *expected* outcome, for example, means that a sample with 4 red balls and 1 white ball should come from a box with mostly red balls. This same sample is *unexpected* from a box with mostly white balls. The results showed that the infants consistently looked longer at the unexpected outcome ($M = 9.9$ seconds) than at the expected outcome ($M = 7.5$ seconds), indicating that the infants considered the unexpected outcome surprising and more interesting than the expected outcome.

The Problem: Xu and Garcia's results strongly suggest that even 8-month-old infants understand the basic principles that determine which samples have high probability and which have low probability. Nevertheless, whenever you are picking ping pong balls from a box or recruiting people to participate in a research study, it usually is possible to obtain thousands or even millions of different samples from the same population. Under these circumstances, how can we determine the probability for obtaining any specific sample?

The Solution: In this chapter we introduce the *distribution of sample means,* which allows us to find the exact probability of obtaining a specific sample mean from a specific population. This distribution describes the entire set of all the possible sample means for any sized sample. Because we can describe the entire set, we can find probabilities associated with specific sample means. (Recall from Chapter 6 that probabilities are equivalent to proportions of the entire distribution.) Also, because the distribution of sample means tends to be normal, it is possible to find probabilities using *z*-scores and the unit normal table. Although it is impossible to predict exactly which sample will be obtained, the probabilities allow researchers to determine which samples are likely (and which are very unlikely).

7.1 SAMPLES AND POPULATIONS

The preceding two chapters presented the topics of *z*-scores and probability. Whenever a score is selected from a population, you should be able to compute a *z*-score that describes exactly where the score is located in the distribution. If the population is normal, you also should be able to determine the probability value for obtaining any individual score. In a normal distribution, for example, any score located in the tail of the distribution beyond $z = +2.00$ is an extreme value, and a score this large has a probability of only $p = 0.0228$.

However, the z-scores and probabilities that we have considered so far are limited to situations in which the sample consists of a single score. Most research studies involve much larger samples, such as $n = 25$ preschool children or $n = 100$ American Idol contestants. In these situations, the sample mean, rather than a single score, is used to answer questions about the population. In this chapter we extend the concepts of z-scores and probability to cover situations with larger samples. In particular, we introduce a procedure for transforming a sample mean into a z-score. Thus, a researcher is able to compute a z-score that describes an entire sample. As always, a z-score near zero indicates a central, representative sample; a z-score beyond +2.00 or –2.00 indicates an extreme sample. Thus, it is possible to describe how any specific sample is related to all the other possible samples. In addition, we can use the z-scores to look up probabilities for obtaining certain samples, no matter how many scores the sample contains.

In general, the difficulty of working with samples is that a sample provides an incomplete picture of the population. Suppose, for example, a researcher randomly selects a sample of $n = 25$ students from the state college. Although the sample should be representative of the entire student population, there are almost certainly some segments of the population that are not included in the sample. In addition, any statistics that are computed for the sample are not identical to the corresponding parameters for the entire population. For example, the average IQ for the sample of 25 students is not the same as the overall mean IQ for the entire population. This difference, or *error,* between sample statistics and the corresponding population parameters is called *sampling error* and was illustrated in Figure 1.2 (p. 201).

DEFINITION

Sampling error is the natural discrepancy, or amount of error, between a sample statistic and its corresponding population parameter.

Furthermore, samples are variable; they are not all the same. If you take two separate samples from the same population, the samples are different. They contain different individuals, they have different scores, and they have different sample means. How can you tell which sample gives the best description of the population? Can you even predict how well a sample describes its population? What is the probability of selecting a sample with specific characteristics? These questions can be answered once we establish the rules that relate samples and populations.

7.2 THE DISTRIBUTION OF SAMPLE MEANS

As noted, two separate samples probably are different even though they are taken from the same population. The samples have different individuals, different scores, different means, and so on. In most cases, it is possible to obtain thousands of different samples from one population. With all these different samples coming from the same population, it may seem hopeless to try to establish some simple rules for the relationships between samples and populations. Fortunately, however, the huge set of possible samples forms a relatively simple and orderly pattern that makes it possible to predict the characteristics of a sample with some accuracy. The ability to predict sample characteristics is based on the *distribution of sample means.*

DEFINITION

The **distribution of sample means** is the collection of sample means for all of the possible random samples of a particular size (n) that can be obtained from a population.

Notice that the distribution of sample means contains *all of the possible samples*. It is necessary to have all of the possible values to compute probabilities. For example, if the entire set contains exactly 100 samples, then the probability of obtaining any specific sample is 1 out of 100: $p = \frac{1}{100}$ (Box 7.1).

Also, you should notice that the distribution of sample means is different from the distributions that we have considered before. Until now we always have discussed distributions of scores; now the values in the distribution are not scores, but statistics (sample means). Because statistics are obtained from samples, a distribution of statistics is referred to as a *sampling distribution*.

DEFINITION

A **sampling distribution** is a distribution of statistics obtained by selecting all of the possible samples of a specific size from a population.

Thus, the distribution of sample means is an example of a sampling distribution. In fact, it often is called the sampling distribution of M.

If you actually wanted to construct the distribution of sample means, you would first select a random sample of a specific size (n) from a population, calculate the sample mean, and place the sample mean in a frequency distribution. Then you would select another random sample with the same number of scores. Again, you would calculate the sample mean and add it to your distribution. You would continue selecting samples and calculating means, over and over, until you had the complete set of all the possible random samples. At this point, your frequency distribution would show the distribution of sample means.

We demonstrate the process of constructing a distribution of sample means in Example 7.1, but first we use common sense and a little logic to predict the general characteristics of the distribution.

1. The sample means should pile up around the population mean. Samples are not expected to be perfect but they are representative of the population. As a result, most of the sample means should be relatively close to the population mean.

BOX 7.1 PROBABILITY AND THE DISTRIBUTION OF SAMPLE MEANS

I have a bad habit of losing playing cards. This habit is compounded by the fact that I always save the old deck in the hope that someday I will find the missing cards. As a result, I have a drawer filled with partial decks of playing cards. Suppose that I take one of these almost-complete decks, shuffle the cards carefully, and then randomly select one card. What is the probability that I will draw a king?

You should realize that it is impossible to answer this probability question. To find the probability of selecting a king, you must know how many cards are in the deck and exactly which cards are missing. (It is crucial that you know whether any kings are missing.) The point of this simple example is that any probability question requires that you have complete information about the population from which the sample is being selected. In this case, you must know all of the possible cards in the deck before you can find the probability for selecting any specific card.

In this chapter, we are examining probability and sample means. To find the probability for any specific sample mean, you first must know *all of the possible sample means*. Therefore, we begin by defining and describing the set of all possible sample means that can be obtained from a particular population. Once we have specified the complete set of all possible sample means (i.e., the distribution of sample means), we can find the probability of selecting any specific sample means.

2. The pile of sample means should tend to form a normal-shaped distribution. Logically, most of the samples should have means close to μ, and it should be relatively rare to find sample means that are substantially different from μ. As a result, the sample means should pile up in the center of the distribution (around μ) and the frequencies should taper off as the distance between M and μ increases. This describes a normal-shaped distribution.
3. In general, the larger the sample size, the closer the sample means should be to the population mean, μ. Logically, a large sample should be a better representative than a small sample. Thus, the sample means obtained with a large sample size should cluster relatively close to the population mean; the means obtained from small samples should be more widely scattered.

As you will see, each of these three commonsense characteristics is an accurate description of the distribution of sample means. The following example demonstrates the process of constructing the distribution of sample means by repeatedly selecting samples from a population.

EXAMPLE 7.1 Consider a population that consists of only 4 scores: 2, 4, 6, 8. This population is pictured in the frequency distribution histogram in Figure 7.1.

Remember that random sampling requires sampling with replacement.

We are going to use this population as the basis for constructing the distribution of sample means for $n = 2$. Remember: This distribution is the collection of sample means from all of the possible random samples of $n = 2$ from this population. We begin by looking at all of the possible samples. For this example, there are 16 different samples, and they are all listed in Table 7.1. Notice that the samples are listed systematically. First, we list all of the possible samples with $X = 2$ as the first score, then all of the possible samples with $X = 4$ as the first score, and so on. In this way, we can be sure that we have all of the possible random samples.

Next, we compute the mean, M, for each of the 16 samples (see the last column of Table 7.1). The 16 means are then placed in a frequency distribution histogram in Figure 7.2. This is the distribution of sample means. Note that the distribution in Figure 7.2 demonstrates two of the characteristics that we predicted for the distribution of sample means.

1. The sample means pile up around the population mean. For this example, the population mean is $\mu = 5$, and the sample means are clustered around a value of 5. It should not surprise you that the sample means tend to approximate the

FIGURE 7.1

Frequency distribution histogram for a population of 4 scores: 2, 4, 6, 8.

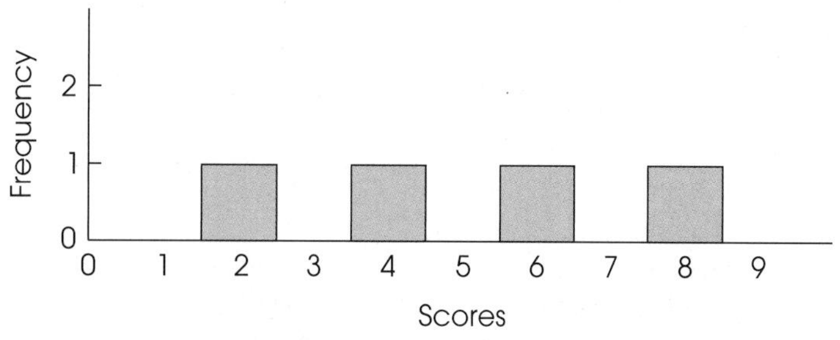

TABLE 7.1

All the possible samples of $n = 2$ scores that can be obtained from the population presented in Figure 7.1. Notice that the table lists *random samples*. This requires sampling with replacement, so it is possible to select the same score twice.

Sample	Scores: First	Scores: Second	Sample Mean (M)
1	2	2	2
2	2	4	3
3	2	6	4
4	2	8	5
5	4	2	3
6	4	4	4
7	4	6	5
8	4	8	6
9	6	2	4
10	6	4	5
11	6	6	6
12	6	8	7
13	8	2	5
14	8	4	6
15	8	6	7
16	8	8	8

population mean. After all, samples are supposed to be representative of the population.

2. The distribution of sample means is approximately normal in shape. This is a characteristic that is discussed in detail later and is extremely useful because we already know a great deal about probabilities and the normal distribution (Chapter 6).

Remember that our goal in this chapter is to answer probability questions about samples with $n > 1$.

Finally, you should notice that we can use the distribution of sample means to answer probability questions about sample means. For example, if you take a sample of $n = 2$ scores from the original population, what is the probability of obtaining a sample mean greater than 7? In symbols,

$$p(M > 7) = ?$$

FIGURE 7.2

The distribution of sample means for $n = 2$. The distribution shows the 16 sample means from Table 7.1.

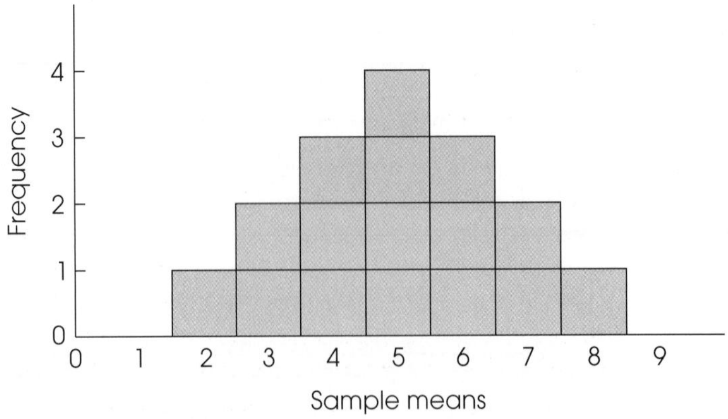

Because probability is equivalent to proportion, the probability question can be restated as follows: Of all of the possible sample means, what proportion have values greater than 7? In this form, the question is easily answered by looking at the distribution of sample means. All of the possible sample means are pictured (see Figure 7.2), and only 1 out of the 16 means has a value greater than 7. The answer, therefore, is 1 out of 16, or $p = \frac{1}{16}$.

THE CENTRAL LIMIT THEOREM

Example 7.1 demonstrated the construction of the distribution of sample means for an overly simplified situation with a very small population and samples that each contain only $n = 2$ scores. In more realistic circumstances, with larger populations and larger samples, the number of possible samples increases dramatically and it is virtually impossible to actually obtain every possible random sample. Fortunately, it is possible to determine exactly what the distribution of sample means looks like without taking hundreds or thousands of samples. Specifically, a mathematical proposition known as the *central limit theorem* provides a precise description of the distribution that would be obtained if you selected every possible sample, calculated every sample mean, and constructed the distribution of the sample mean. This important and useful theorem serves as a cornerstone for much of inferential statistics. Following is the essence of the theorem.

> **Central limit theorem:** For any population with mean μ and standard deviation σ, the distribution of sample means for sample size n will have a mean of μ and a standard deviation of $\sigma/\sqrt{n}$ and will approach a normal distribution as n approaches infinity.

The value of this theorem comes from two simple facts. First, it describes the distribution of sample means for *any population,* no matter what shape, mean, or standard deviation. Second, the distribution of sample means "approaches" a normal distribution very rapidly. By the time the sample size reaches $n = 30$, the distribution is almost perfectly normal.

Note that the central limit theorem describes the distribution of sample means by identifying the three basic characteristics that describe any distribution: shape, central tendency, and variability. We examine each of these.

THE SHAPE OF THE DISTRIBUTION OF SAMPLE MEANS

It has been observed that the distribution of sample means tends to be a normal distribution. In fact, this distribution is almost perfectly normal if either of the following two conditions is satisfied:

1. The population from which the samples are selected is a normal distribution.
2. The number of scores (n) in each sample is relatively large, around 30 or more.

(As n gets larger, the distribution of sample means more closely approximates a normal distribution. When $n > 30$, the distribution is almost normal, regardless of the shape of the original population.)

As we noted earlier, the fact that the distribution of sample means tends to be normal is not surprising. Whenever you take a sample from a population, you expect the sample mean to be near to the population mean. When you take lots of different samples, you expect the sample means to "pile up" around μ, resulting in a normal-shaped distribution. You can see this tendency emerging (although it is not yet normal) in Figure 7.2.

THE MEAN OF THE DISTRIBUTION OF SAMPLE MEANS: THE EXPECTED VALUE OF *M*

In Example 7.1, the distribution of sample means is centered around the mean of the population from which the samples were obtained. In fact, the average value of all the sample means is exactly equal to the value of the population mean. This fact should be intuitively reasonable; the sample means are expected to be close to the population mean, and they do tend to pile up around μ. The formal statement of this phenomenon is that the mean of the distribution of sample means always is identical to the population mean. This mean value is called the *expected value of* M.

In commonsense terms, a sample mean is "expected" to be near its population mean. When all of the possible sample means are obtained, the average value is identical to μ.

The fact that the average value of *M* is equal to μ was first introduced in Chapter 4 (p. 121) in the context of *biased* versus *unbiased* statistics. The sample mean is an example of an unbiased statistic, which means that, on average, the sample statistic produces a value that is exactly equal to the corresponding population parameter. In this case, the average value of all of the sample means is exactly equal to μ.

DEFINITION

The mean of the distribution of sample means is equal to the mean of the population of scores, μ, and is called the **expected value of *M***.

THE STANDARD ERROR OF *M*

So far, we have considered the shape and the central tendency of the distribution of sample means. To completely describe this distribution, we need one more characteristic, variability. The value we will be working with is the standard deviation for the distribution of sample means. This standard deviation is identified by the symbol σ_M and is called the *standard error of* M.

When the standard deviation was first introduced in Chapter 4, we noted that this measure of variability serves two general purposes. First, the standard deviation describes the distribution by telling whether the individual scores are clustered close together or scattered over a wide range. Second, the standard deviation measures how well any individual score represents the population by providing a measure of how much distance is reasonable to expect between a score and the population mean. The standard error serves the same two purposes for the distribution of sample means.

1. The standard error describes the distribution of sample means. It provides a measure of how much difference is expected from one sample to another. When the standard error is small, then all of the sample means are close together and have similar values. If the standard error is large, then the sample means are scattered over a wide range and there are big differences from one sample to another.
2. Standard error measures how well an individual sample mean represents the entire distribution. Specifically, it provides a measure of how much distance is reasonable to expect between a sample mean and the overall mean for the distribution of sample means. However, because the overall mean is equal to μ, the standard error also provides a measure of how much distance to expect between a sample mean (*M*) and the population mean (μ).

Remember that a sample is not expected to provide a perfectly accurate reflection of its population. Although a sample mean should be representative of the population mean, there typically is some error between the sample and the population. The standard error measures exactly how much difference is expected on average between a sample mean, M, and the population mean, μ.

DEFINITION

The standard deviation of the distribution of sample means, σ_M, is called the **standard error of M**. The standard error provides a measure of how much distance is expected on average between a sample mean (M) and the population mean (μ).

Once again, the symbol for the standard error is σ_M. The σ indicates that this value is a standard deviation, and the subscript M indicates that it is the standard deviation for the distribution of sample means. Similarly, it is common to use the symbol μ_M to represent the mean of the distribution of sample means. However, μ_M is always equal to μ and our primary interest in inferential statistics is to compare sample means (M) with their population means (μ). Therefore, we simply use the symbol μ to refer to the mean of the distribution of sample means.

The standard error is an extremely valuable measure because it specifies precisely how well a sample mean estimates its population mean—that is, how much error you should expect, on the average, between M and μ. Remember that one basic reason for taking samples is to use the sample data to answer questions about the population. However, you do not expect a sample to provide a perfectly accurate picture of the population. There always is some discrepancy, or error, between a sample statistic and the corresponding population parameter. Now we are able to calculate exactly how much error to expect. For any sample size (n), we can compute the standard error, which measures the average distance between a sample mean and the population mean.

The magnitude of the standard error is determined by two factors: (1) the size of the sample and (2) the standard deviation of the population from which the sample is selected. We examine each of these factors.

The sample size Earlier we predicted, based on common sense, that the size of a sample should influence how accurately the sample represents its population. Specifically, a large sample should be more accurate than a small sample. In general, as the sample size increases, the error between the sample mean and the population mean should decrease. This rule is also known as the *law of large numbers*.

DEFINITION

The **law of large numbers** states that the larger the sample size (n), the more probable it is that the sample mean is close to the population mean.

The population standard deviation As we noted earlier, there is an inverse relationship between the sample size and the standard error: bigger samples have smaller error, and smaller samples have bigger error. At the extreme, the smallest possible sample (and the largest standard error) occurs when the sample consists of $n = 1$ score. At this extreme, each sample is a single score and the distribution of sample means is identical to the original distribution of scores. In this case, the standard deviation for the distribution of sample means, which is the standard error, is identical to the standard deviation for the distribution of scores. In other words, when $n = 1$, the standard error $= \sigma_M$ is identical to the standard deviation $= \sigma$.

$$\text{When } n = 1, \sigma_M = \sigma \text{ (standard error = standard deviation).}$$

You can think of the standard deviation as the "starting point" for standard error. When $n = 1$, the standard error and the standard deviation are the same: $\sigma_M = \sigma$.

As sample size increases beyond $n = 1$, the sample becomes a more accurate representative of the population, and the standard error decreases. The formula for standard error expresses this relationship between standard deviation and sample size (n).

This formula is contained in the central limit theorem.

$$\text{standard error} = \sigma_M = \frac{\sigma}{\sqrt{n}} \qquad (7.1)$$

Note that the formula satisfies all of the requirements for the standard error. Specifically,

a. As sample size (n) increases, the size of the standard error decreases. (Larger samples are more accurate.)

b. When the sample consists of a single score ($n = 1$), the standard error is the same as the standard deviation ($\sigma_M = \sigma$).

In Equation 7.1 and in most of the preceding discussion, we defined standard error in terms of the population standard deviation. However, the population standard deviation (σ) and the population variance (σ^2) are directly related, and it is easy to substitute variance into the equation for standard error. Using the simple equality $\sigma = \sqrt{\sigma^2}$, the equation for standard error can be rewritten as follows:

$$\text{standard error} = \sigma_M = \frac{\sigma}{\sqrt{n}} = \frac{\sqrt{\sigma^2}}{\sqrt{n}} = \sqrt{\frac{\sigma^2}{n}} \qquad (7.2)$$

Throughout the rest of this chapter (and in Chapter 8), we continue to define standard error in terms of the standard deviation (Equation 7.1). However, in later chapters (starting in Chapter 9) the formula based on variance (Equation 7.2) will become more useful.

Figure 7.3 illustrates the general relationship between standard error and sample size. (The calculations for the data points in Figure 7.3 are presented in Table 7.2.) Again, the basic concept is that the larger a sample is, the more accurately it represents its population. Also note that the standard error decreases in relation to the *square root* of the sample size. As a result, researchers can substantially reduce error by increasing

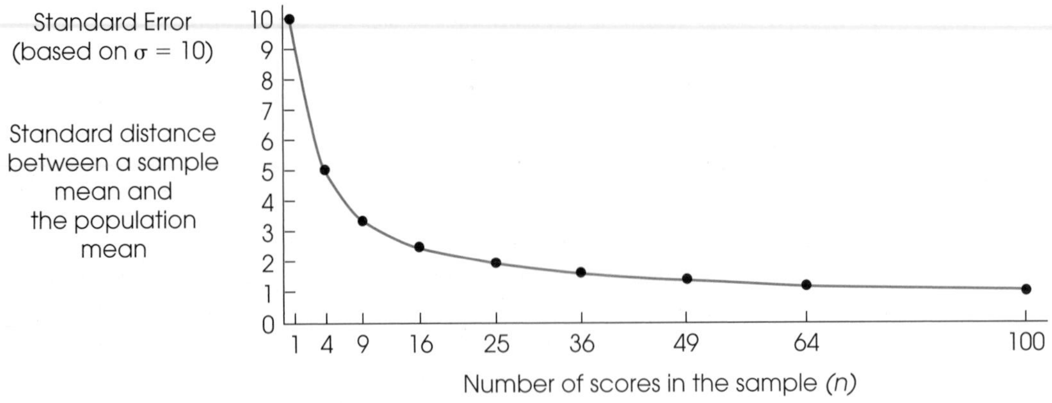

FIGURE 7.3

The relationship between standard error and sample size. As the sample size is increased, there is less error between the sample mean and the population mean.

TABLE 7.2

Calculations for the points shown in Figure 7.3. Again, notice that the size of the standard error decreases as the size of the sample increases.

Sample Size (n)	Standard Error	
1	$\sigma_M = \frac{10}{\sqrt{1}}$	= 10.00
4	$\sigma_M = \frac{10}{\sqrt{4}}$	= 5.00
9	$\sigma_M = \frac{10}{\sqrt{9}}$	= 3.33
16	$\sigma_M = \frac{10}{\sqrt{16}}$	= 2.50
25	$\sigma_M = \frac{10}{\sqrt{25}}$	= 2.00
49	$\sigma_M = \frac{10}{\sqrt{49}}$	= 1.43
64	$\sigma_M = \frac{10}{\sqrt{64}}$	= 1.25
100	$\sigma_M = \frac{10}{\sqrt{100}}$	= 1.00

sample size up to around $n = 30$. However, increasing sample size beyond $n = 30$ does not produce much additional improvement in how well the sample represents the population.

THREE DIFFERENT DISTRIBUTIONS

Before we move forward with our discussion of the distribution of sample means, we pause for a moment to emphasize the idea that we are now dealing with three different but interrelated distributions.

1. First, we have the original population of scores. This population contains the scores for thousands or millions of individual people, and it has its own shape, mean, and standard deviation. For example, the population of IQ scores consists of millions of individual IQ scores that form a normal distribution with a mean of $\mu = 100$ and a standard deviation of $\sigma = 15$. An example of a population is shown in Figure 7.4(a).
2. Next, we have a sample that is selected from the population. The sample consists of a small set of scores for a few people who have been selected to represent the entire population. For example, we could select a sample of $n = 25$ people and measure each individual's IQ score. The 25 scores could be organized in a frequency distribution and we could calculate the sample mean and the sample standard deviation. Note that the sample also has its own shape, mean, and standard deviation. An example of a sample is shown in Figure 7.4(b).
3. The third distribution is the distribution of sample means. This is a theoretical distribution consisting of the sample means obtained from all of the possible random samples of a specific size. For example, the distribution of sample means for samples of $n = 25$ IQ scores would be normal with a mean (expected value) of $\mu = 100$ and a standard deviation (standard error) of $\sigma_M = \frac{15}{\sqrt{25}} = 3$. This

FIGURE 7.4

The distribution. Part (a) shows the population of IQ scores. Part (b) shows a sample of $n = 25$ IQ scores. Part (c) shows the distribution of sample means for samples of $n = 25$ scores. Note that the sample mean from part (b) is one of the thousands of sample means in the part (c) distribution.

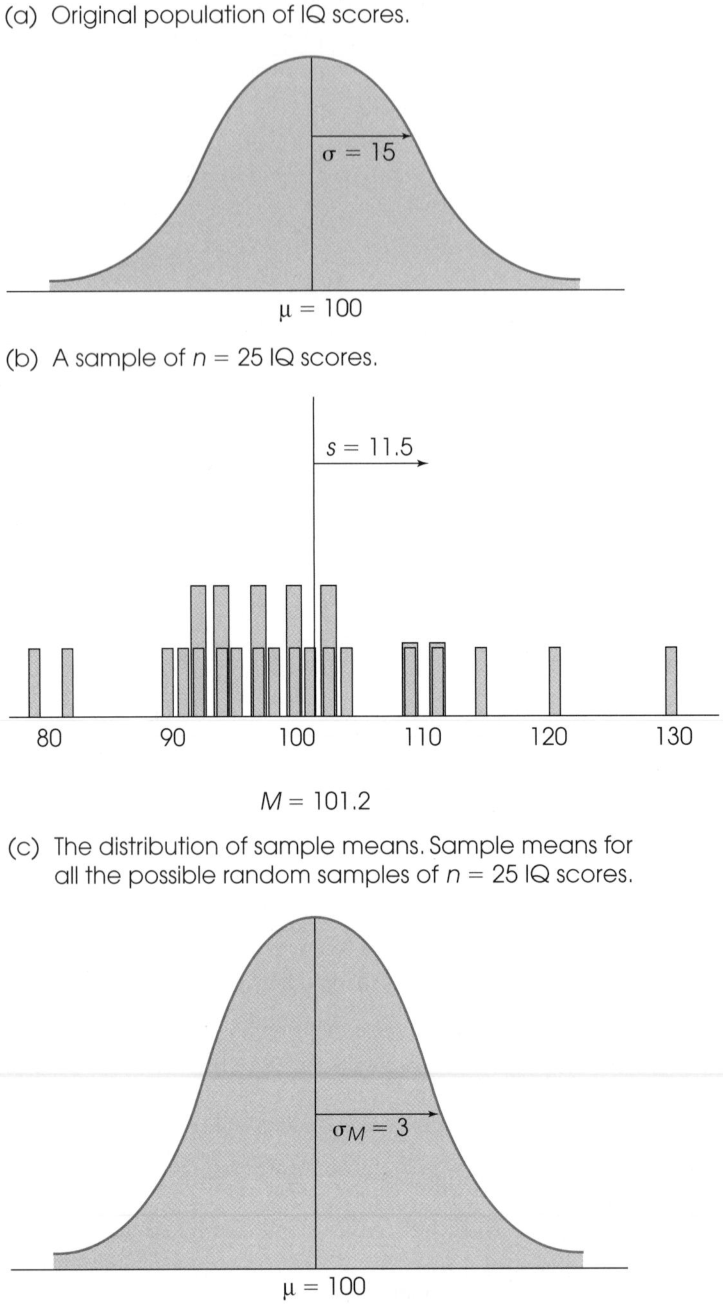

distribution, shown in Figure 7.4(c), also has its own shape, mean, and standard deviation.

Note that the scores for the sample [Figure 7.4(b)] were taken from the original population [Figure 7.4(a)] and that the mean for the sample is one of the values contained in the distribution of sample means [Figure 7.4(c)]. Thus, the three distributions are all connected, but they are all distinct.

LEARNING CHECK

1. A population has a mean of $\mu = 50$ and a standard deviation of $\sigma = 12$.
   a. For samples of size $n = 4$, what is the mean (expected value) and the standard deviation (standard error) for the distribution of sample means?
   b. If the population distribution is not normal, describe the shape of the distribution of sample means based on $n = 4$.
   c. For samples of size $n = 36$, what is the mean (expected value) and the standard deviation (standard error) for the distribution of sample means?
   d. If the population distribution is not normal, describe the shape of the distribution of sample means based on $n = 36$.
2. As sample size increases, the value of expected value also increases. (True or false?)
3. As sample size increases, the value of the standard error also increases. (True or false?)

ANSWERS

1. a. The distribution of sample means would have a mean of $\mu = 50$ and a standard error of $\sigma_M = 12/\sqrt{4} = 6$.
   b. The distribution of sample means does not satisfy either criterion to be normal. It would not be a normal distribution.
   c. The distribution of sample means is normal and would have a mean of $\mu = 50$ and a standard error of $\sigma_M = 12/\sqrt{36} = 2$.
   d. Because the sample size is greater than 30, the distribution of sample means is a normal distribution.
2. False. The expected value does not depend on sample size.
3. False. The standard error decreases as sample size increases.

7.3 PROBABILITY AND THE DISTRIBUTION OF SAMPLE MEANS

The primary use of the distribution of sample means is to find the probability associated with any specific sample. Recall that probability is equivalent to proportion. Because the distribution of sample means presents the entire set of all possible sample means, we can use proportions of this distribution to determine probabilities. The following example demonstrates this process.

EXAMPLE 7.2

The population of scores on the SAT forms a normal distribution with $\mu = 500$ and $\sigma = 100$. If you take a random sample of $n = 25$ students, what is the probability that the sample mean will be greater than $M = 540$?

Caution: Whenever you have a probability question about a sample mean, you must use the distribution of sample means.

First, you can restate this probability question as a proportion question: Out of all of the possible sample means, what proportion have values greater than 540? You know about "all of the possible sample means"; this is the distribution of sample means. The problem is to find a specific portion of this distribution.

Although we cannot construct the distribution of sample means by repeatedly taking samples and calculating means (as in Example 7.1), we know exactly what the distribution looks like based on the information from the central limit theorem. Specifically, the distribution of sample means has the following characteristics:

a. The distribution is normal because the population of SAT scores is normal.

b. The distribution has a mean of 500 because the population mean is $\mu = 500$.

c. For $n = 25$, the distribution has a standard error of $\sigma_M = 20$:

$$\sigma_M = \frac{\sigma}{\sqrt{n}} = \frac{100}{\sqrt{25}} = \frac{100}{5} = 20$$

This distribution of sample means is shown in Figure 7.5.

We are interested in sample means greater than 540 (the shaded area in Figure 7.5), so the next step is to use a z-score to locate the exact position of $M = 540$ in the distribution. The value 540 is located above the mean by 40 points, which is exactly 2 standard deviations (in this case, exactly 2 standard errors). Thus, the z-score for $M = 540$ is $z = +2.00$.

Because this distribution of sample means is normal, you can use the unit normal table to find the probability associated with $z = +2.00$. The table indicates that 0.0228 of the distribution is located in the tail of the distribution beyond $z = +2.00$. Our conclusion is that it is very unlikely, $p = 0.0228$ (2.28%), to obtain a random sample of $n = 25$ students with an average SAT score greater than 540.

A *z*-SCORE FOR SAMPLE MEANS

As demonstrated in Example 7.2, it is possible to use a z-score to describe the exact location of any specific sample mean within the distribution of sample means. The z-score tells exactly where the sample mean is located in relation to all of the other possible sample means that could have been obtained. As defined in Chapter 5, a z-score identifies the location with a signed number so that

1. The sign tells whether the location is above (+) or below (−) the mean.
2. The number tells the distance between the location and the mean in terms of the number of standard deviations.

FIGURE 7.5

The distribution of sample means for $n = 25$. Samples were selected from a normal population with $\mu = 500$ and $\sigma = 100$.

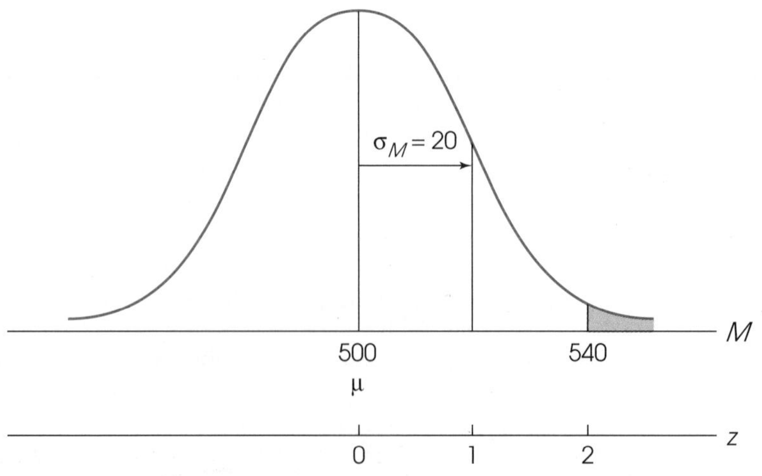

However, we are now finding a location within the distribution of sample means. Therefore, we must use the notation and terminology appropriate for this distribution. First, we are finding the location for a sample mean (M) rather than a score (X). Second, the standard deviation for the distribution of sample means is the standard error, σ_M. With these changes, the z-score formula for locating a sample mean is

$$z = \frac{M - \mu}{\sigma_M} \tag{7.3}$$

Caution: When computing z for a single score, use the standard deviation, σ. When computing z for a sample mean, you must use the standard error, σ_M (see Box 7.2).

Just as every score (X) has a z-score that describes its position in the distribution of scores, every sample mean (M) has a z-score that describes its position in the distribution of sample means. When the distribution of sample means is normal, it is possible to use z-scores and the unit normal table to find the probability associated with any specific sample mean (as in Example 7.2). The following example demonstrates that it also is possible to make quantitative predictions about the kinds of samples that should be obtained from any population.

EXAMPLE 7.3

Once again, the distribution of SAT scores forms a normal distribution with a mean of $\mu = 500$ and a standard deviation of $\sigma = 100$. For this example, we are going to determine what kind of sample mean is likely to be obtained as the average SAT score for a random sample of $n = 25$ students. Specifically, we determine the exact range of values that is expected for the sample mean 80% of the time.

We begin with the distribution of sample means for $n = 25$. As demonstrated in Example 7.2, this distribution is normal with an expected value of $\mu = 500$ and a standard error of $\sigma_M = 20$ (Figure 7.6). Our goal is to find the range of values that make up the middle 80% of the distribution. Because the distribution is normal, we can use the unit normal table. First, the 80% in the middle is split in half, with 40% (0.4000) on each side of the mean. Looking up 0.4000 in column D (the proportion between the mean and z), we find a corresponding z-score of $z = 1.28$. Thus, the z-score boundaries for the middle 80% are $z = +1.28$ and $z = -1.28$. By definition, a z-score of 1.28 represents a location that is 1.28 standard deviations (or standard

FIGURE 7.6

The middle 80% of the distribution of sample means for $n = 25$. Sample were selected from a normal population with $\mu = 500$ and $\sigma = 100$.

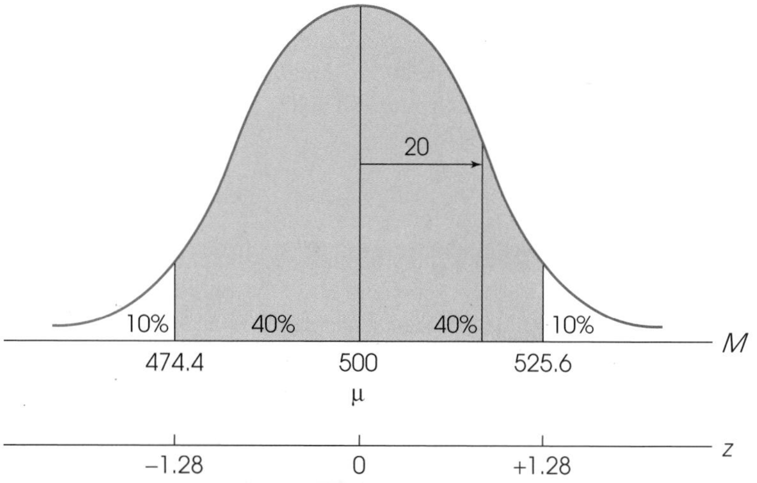

BOX 7.2

THE DIFFERENCE BETWEEN STANDARD DEVIATION AND STANDARD ERROR

A constant source of confusion for many students is the difference between standard deviation and standard error. Remember that standard deviation measures the standard distance between a *score* and the population mean, $X - \mu$. If you are working with a distribution of scores, the standard deviation is the appropriate measure of variability. Standard error, on the other hand, measures the standard distance between a *sample mean* and the population mean, $M - \mu$. Whenever you have a question concerning a sample, the standard error is the appropriate measure of variability.

If you still find the distinction confusing, there is a simple solution. Namely, if you always use standard error, you always will be right. Consider the formula for standard error:

$$\text{standard error} = \sigma_M = \frac{\sigma}{\sqrt{n}}$$

If you are working with a single score, then $n = 1$, and the standard error becomes

$$\text{standard error} = \sigma_M = \frac{\sigma}{\sqrt{n}} = \frac{\sigma}{\sqrt{1}}$$

$$= \sigma = \text{standard deviation}$$

Thus, standard error always measures the standard distance from the population mean for any sample size, including $n = 1$.

errors) from the mean. With a standard error of 20 points, the distance from the mean is 1.28(20) = 25.6 points. The mean is $\mu = 500$, so a distance of 25.6 in both directions produces a range of values from 474.4 to 525.6.

Thus, 80% of all the possible sample means are contained in a range between 474.4 and 525.6. If we select a sample of $n = 25$ students, we can be 80% confident that the mean SAT score for the sample will be in this range.

The point of Example 7.3 is that the distribution of sample means makes it possible to predict the value that ought to be obtained for a sample mean. We know, for example, that a sample of $n = 25$ students ought to have a mean SAT score around 500. More specifically, we are 80% confident that the value of the sample mean will be between 474.4 and 525.6. The ability to predict sample means in this way is a valuable tool for the inferential statistics that follow.

LEARNING CHECK

1. For a population with a mean of $\mu = 40$ and a standard deviation of $\sigma = 8$, find the z-score corresponding to a sample mean of $M = 44$ for each of the following sample sizes.
   a. $n = 4$
   b. $n = 16$
2. What is the probability of obtaining a sample mean greater than $M = 60$ for a random sample of $n = 16$ scores selected from a normal population with a mean of $\mu = 65$ and a standard deviation of $\sigma = 20$?
3. A positively skewed distribution has $\mu = 60$ and $\sigma = 8$.
   a. What is the probability of obtaining a sample mean greater than $M = 62$ for a sample of $n = 4$ scores? (Be careful. This is a trick question.)

b. What is the probability of obtaining a sample mean greater than $M = 62$ for a sample of $n = 64$ scores?

ANSWERS

1. **a.** The standard error is $\sigma_M = 4$, and $z = 1.00$.
   b. The standard error is $\sigma_M = 2$, and $z = 2.00$.
2. The standard error is $\sigma_M = 5$, and $M = 60$ corresponds to $z = -1.00$, $p(M > 60) = p(z > -1.00) = 0.8413$ (or 84.13%).
3. **a.** The distribution of sample means does not satisfy either of the criteria for being normal. Therefore, you cannot use the unit normal table, and it is impossible to find the probability.
   b. With $n = 64$, the distribution of sample means is nearly normal. The standard error is $8/\sqrt{64} = 1$, the z-score is $+2.00$, and the probability is 0.0228.

7.4 MORE ABOUT STANDARD ERROR

At the beginning of this chapter, we introduced the idea that it is possible to obtain thousands of different samples from a single population. Each sample has its own individuals, its own scores, and its own sample mean. The distribution of sample means provides a method for organizing all of the different sample means into a single picture. Figure 7.7 shows a prototypical distribution of sample means. To emphasize the fact that the distribution contains many different samples, we have constructed this figure so that the distribution is made up of hundreds of small boxes, each box representing a single sample mean. Also notice that the sample means tend to pile up around the population mean (μ), forming a normal-shaped distribution as predicted by the central limit theorem.

FIGURE 7.7

An example of a typical distribution of sample means. Each of the small boxes represents the mean obtained for one sample.

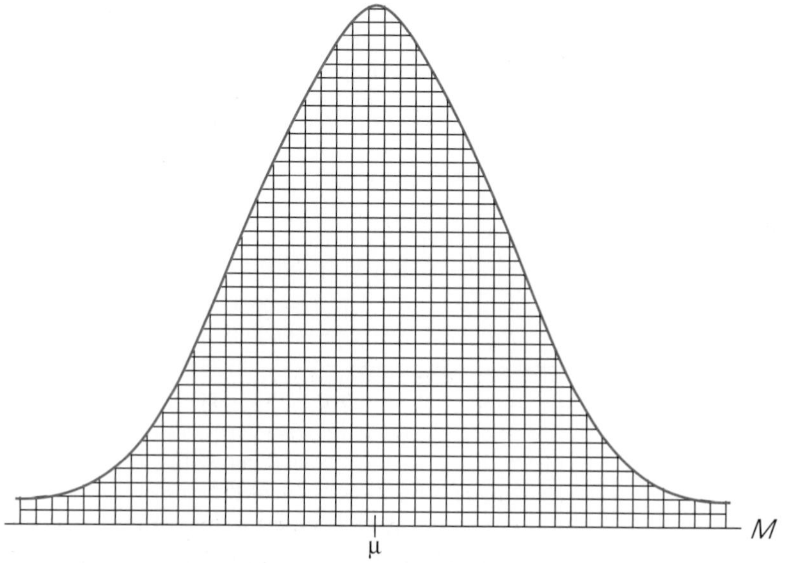

The distribution shown in Figure 7.7 provides a concrete example for reviewing the general concepts of sampling error and standard error. Although the following points may seem obvious, they are intended to provide you with a better understanding of these two statistical concepts.

1. Sampling Error. The general concept of sampling error is that a sample typically does not provide a perfectly accurate representation of its population. More specifically, there typically is some discrepancy (or error) between a statistic computed for a sample and the corresponding parameter for the population. As you look at Figure 7.7, notice that the individual sample means are not exactly equal to the population mean. In fact, 50% of the samples have means that are smaller than μ (the entire left-hand side of the distribution). Similarly, 50% of the samples produce means that overestimate the true population mean. In general, there is some discrepancy, or *sampling error,* between the mean for a sample and the mean for the population from which the sample was obtained.
2. Standard Error. Again looking at Figure 7.7, notice that most of the sample means are relatively close to the population mean (those in the center of the distribution). These samples provide a fairly accurate representation of the population. On the other hand, some samples produce means that are out in the tails of the distribution, relatively far from the population mean. These extreme sample means do not accurately represent the population. For each individual sample, you can measure the error (or distance) between the sample mean and the population mean. For some samples, the error is relatively small, but for other samples, the error is relatively large. The *standard error* provides a way to measure the "average," or standard, distance between a sample mean and the population mean.

Thus, the standard error provides a method for defining and measuring sampling error. Knowing the standard error gives researchers a good indication of how accurately their sample data represent the populations that they are studying. In most research situations, for example, the population mean is unknown, and the researcher selects a sample to help obtain information about the unknown population. Specifically, the sample mean provides information about the value of the unknown population mean. The sample mean is not expected to give a perfectly accurate representation of the population mean; there will be some error, and the standard error tells *exactly how much error,* on average, should exist between the sample mean and the unknown population mean. The following example demonstrates the use of standard error and provides additional information about the relationship between standard error and standard deviation.

EXAMPLE 7.4

A recent survey of students at a local college included the following question: How many minutes do you spend each day watching electronic video (e.g., online, TV, cell phone, iPod, etc.). The average response was $\mu = 80$ minutes, and the distribution of viewing times was approximately normal with a standard deviation of $\sigma = 20$ minutes. Next, we take a sample from this population and examine how accurately the sample mean represents the population mean. More specifically, we will examine how sample size affects accuracy by considering three different samples: one with $n = 1$ student, one with $n = 4$ students, and one with $n = 100$ students.

Figure 7.8 shows the distributions of sample means based on samples of $n = 1$, $n = 4$, and $n = 100$. Each distribution shows the collection of all possible sample means that could be obtained for that particular sample size. Notice that all three sampling distributions are normal (because the original population is normal), and

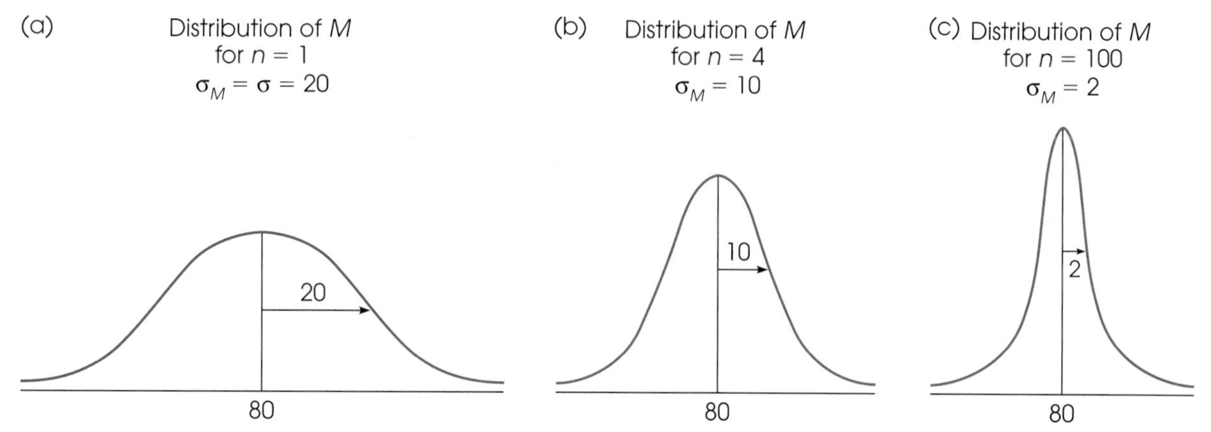

FIGURE 7.8

The distribution of sample means for random samples of size (a) $n = 1$, (b) $n = 4$, and (c) $n = 100$ obtained from a normal population with ($\mu = 80$) and ($\sigma = 20$). Notice that the size of the standard error decreases as the sample size increases.

all three have the same mean, $\mu = 80$, which is the expected value of M. However, the three distributions differ greatly with respect to variability. We will consider each one separately.

The smallest sample size is $n = 1$. When a sample consists of a single student, the mean for the sample equals the score for the student, $M = X$. Thus, when $n = 1$, the distribution of sample means is identical to the original population of scores. In this case, the standard error for the distribution of sample means is equal to the standard deviation for the original population. Equation 7.1 confirms this observation.

$$\sigma_M = \frac{\sigma}{\sqrt{n}} = \frac{20}{\sqrt{1}} = 20$$

When the sample consists of a single student, you expect, on average, a 20-point difference between the sample mean and the mean for the population. As we noted earlier, the population standard deviation is the "starting point" for the standard error. With the smallest possible sample, $n = 1$, the standard error is equal to the standard deviation [see Figure 7.8(a)].

As the sample size increases, however, the standard error gets smaller. For a sample of $n = 4$ students, the standard error is

$$\sigma_M = \frac{\sigma}{\sqrt{n}} = \frac{20}{\sqrt{4}} = \frac{20}{2} = 10$$

That is, the typical (or standard) distance between M and μ is 10 points. Figure 7.8(b) illustrates this distribution. Notice that the sample means in this distribution approximate the population mean more closely than in the previous distribution where $n = 1$.

With a sample of $n = 100$, the standard error is still smaller.

$$\sigma_M = \frac{\sigma}{\sqrt{n}} = \frac{20}{\sqrt{100}} = \frac{20}{10} = 2$$

A sample of $n = 100$ students should produce a sample mean that represents the population much more accurately than a sample of $n = 4$ or $n = 1$. As shown in Figure 7.8(c), there is very little error between M and μ when $n = 100$. Specifically, you would expect, on average, only a 2-point difference between the population mean and the sample mean.

In summary, this example illustrates that with the smallest possible sample ($n = 1$), the standard error and the population standard deviation are the same. When sample size is increased, the standard error gets smaller, and the sample means tend to approximate μ more closely. Thus, standard error defines the relationship between sample size and the accuracy with which M represents μ.

IN THE LITERATURE

REPORTING STANDARD ERROR

As we will see later, standard error plays a very important role in inferential statistics. Because of its crucial role, the standard error for a sample mean, rather than the sample standard deviation, is often reported in scientific papers. Scientific journals vary in how they refer to the standard error, but frequently the symbols *SE* and *SEM* (for standard error of the mean) are used. The standard error is reported in two ways. Much like the standard deviation, it may be reported in a table along with the sample means (Table 7.3). Alternatively, the standard error may be reported in graphs.

Figure 7.9 illustrates the use of a bar graph to display information about the sample mean and the standard error. In this experiment, two samples (groups A

TABLE 7.3

The mean self-consciousness scores for participants who were working in front of a video camera and those who were not (controls).

	n	Mean	*SE*
Control	17	32.23	2.31
Camera	15	45.17	2.78

FIGURE 7.9

The mean ($\pm SE$) score for treatment groups A and B.

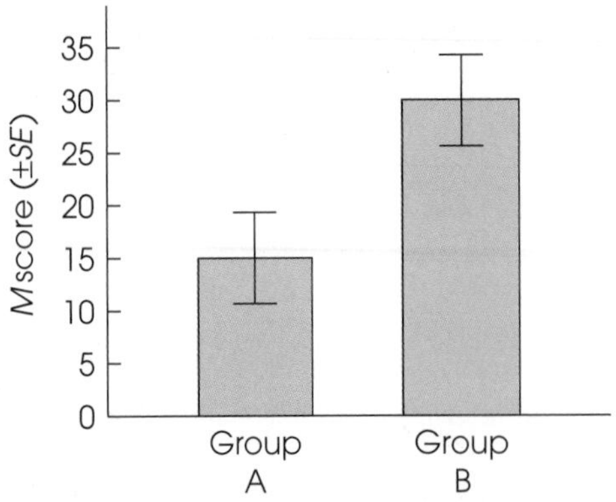

and B) are given different treatments, and then the subjects' scores on a dependent variable are recorded. The mean for group A is $M = 15$, and for group B, it is $M = 30$. For both samples, the standard error of M is $\sigma_M = 4$. Note that the mean is represented by the height of the bar, and the standard error is depicted by brackets at the top of each bar. Each bracket extends 1 standard error above and 1 standard error below the sample mean. Thus, the graph illustrates the mean for each group plus or minus 1 standard error ($M \pm SE$). When you glance at Figure 7.9, not only do you get a "picture" of the sample means, but also you get an idea of how much error you should expect for those means.

Figure 7.10 shows how sample means and standard error are displayed in a line graph. In this study, two samples representing different age groups are tested on a task for four trials. The number of errors committed on each trial is recorded for all participants. The graph shows the mean (M) number of errors committed for each group on each trial. The brackets show the size of the standard error for each sample mean. Again, the brackets extend 1 standard error above and below the value of the mean.

FIGURE 7.10

The mean ($\pm SE$) number of mistakes made for groups A and B on each trial.

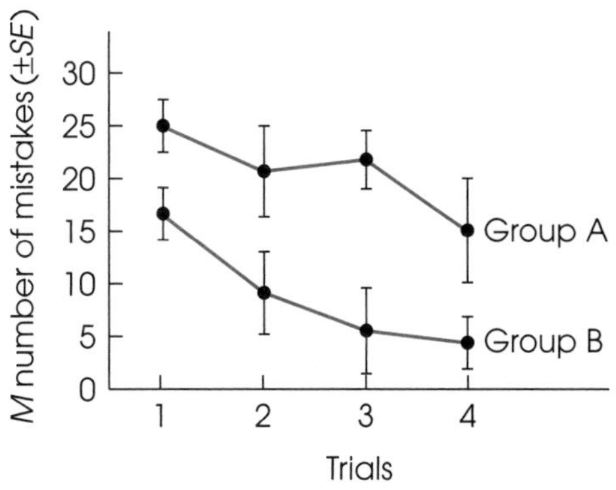

LEARNING CHECK

1. A population has a standard deviation of $\sigma = 10$.
   a. On average, how much difference should there be between the population mean and a single score selected from this population?
   b. On average, how much difference should there be between the population mean and the sample mean for $n = 4$ scores selected from this population?
   c. On average, how much difference should there be between the population mean and the sample mean for $n = 25$ scores selected from this population?
2. Can the value of the standard error ever be larger than the value of the population standard deviation? Explain your answer.
3. A researcher plans to select a random sample from a population with a standard deviation of $\sigma = 12$.
   a. How large a sample is needed to have a standard error of 6 points or less?
   b. How large a sample is needed to have a standard error of 4 points or less?

ANSWERS

1. **a.** $\sigma = 10$ points
   b. $\sigma_M = 5$ points
   c. $\sigma_M = 2$ points
2. No. The standard error is computed by dividing the standard deviation by the square root of n. The standard error is always less than or equal to the standard deviation.
3. **a.** A sample of $n = 4$ or larger.
   b. A sample of $n = 9$ or larger.

7.5 LOOKING AHEAD TO INFERENTIAL STATISTICS

Inferential statistics are methods that use sample data as the basis for drawing general conclusions about populations. However, we have noted that a sample is not expected to give a perfectly accurate reflection of its population. In particular, there will be some error or discrepancy between a sample statistic and the corresponding population parameter. In this chapter, we have observed that a sample mean is not exactly equal to the population mean. The standard error of M specifies how much difference is expected on average between the mean for a sample and the mean for the population.

The natural differences that exist between samples and populations introduce a degree of uncertainty and error into all inferential processes. Specifically, there is always a margin of error that must be considered whenever a researcher uses a sample mean as the basis for drawing a conclusion about a population mean. Remember that the sample mean is not perfect. In the next seven chapters we introduce a variety of statistical methods that all use sample means to draw inferences about population means.

In each case, the distribution of sample means and the standard error are critical elements in the inferential process. Before we begin this series of chapters, we pause briefly to demonstrate how the distribution of sample means, along with z-scores and probability, can help us use sample means to draw inferences about population means.

EXAMPLE 7.5

Suppose that a psychologist is planning a research study to evaluate the effect of a new growth hormone. It is known that regular adult rats (with no hormone) weigh an average of $\mu = 400$ grams. Of course, not all rats are the same size, and the distribution of their weights is normal with $\sigma = 20$. The psychologist plans to select a sample of $n = 25$ newborn rats, inject them with the hormone, and then measure their weights when they become adults. The structure of this research study is shown in Figure 7.11.

The psychologist makes a decision about the effect of the hormone by comparing the sample of treated rats with the regular untreated rats in the original population. If the treated rats in the sample are noticeably different from untreated rats, then the researcher has evidence that the hormone has an effect. The problem is to determine exactly how much difference is necessary before we can say that the sample is *noticeably different.*

The distribution of sample means and the standard error can help researchers make this decision. In particular, the distribution of sample means can be used to show exactly what would be expected for a sample of rats who do not receive any hormone injections. This allows researchers to make a simple comparison between

a. The sample of treated rats (from the research study)

b. Samples of untreated rats (from the distribution of sample means)

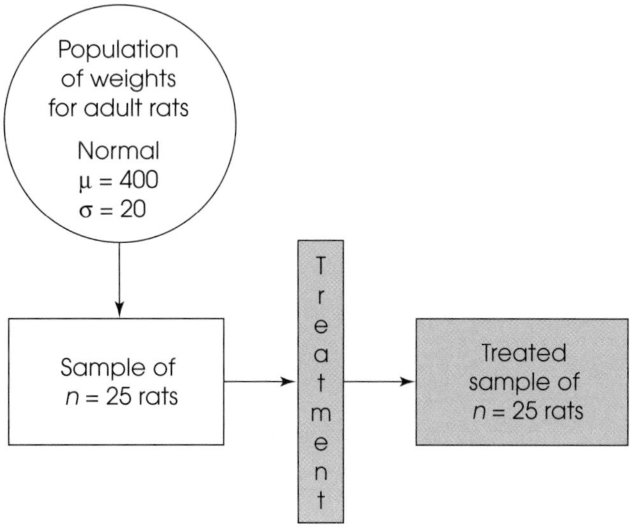

FIGURE 7.11
The structure of the research study described in Example 7.5. The purpose of the study is to determine whether the treatment (a growth hormone) has an effect on weight for rats.

If our treated sample is noticeably different from the untreated samples, then we have evidence that the treatment has an effect. On the other hand, if our treated sample still looks like one of the untreated samples, then we must conclude that the treatment does not appear to have any effect.

We begin with the original population of untreated rats and consider the distribution of sample means for all of the possible samples of $n = 25$ rats. The distribution of sample means has the following characteristics:

1. It is a normal distribution, because the population of rat weights is normal.
2. It has an expected value of 400, because the population mean for untreated rats is $\mu = 400$.
3. It has a standard error of $\sigma_M = \frac{20}{\sqrt{25}} = \frac{20}{5} = 4$, because the population standard deviation is $\sigma = 20$ and the sample size is $n = 25$.

The distribution of sample means is shown in Figure 7.12. Notice that a sample of $n = 25$ untreated rats (without the hormone) should have a mean weight around 400 grams. To be more precise, we can use z-scores to determine the middle 95% of all the possible sample means. As demonstrated in Chapter 6 (p. 190), the middle 95% of a normal distribution is located between z-score boundaries of $z = +1.96$ and $z = -1.96$ (check the unit normal table). These z-score boundaries are shown in Figure 7.12. With a standard error of $\sigma_M = 4$ points, a z-score of $z = 1.96$ corresponds to a distance of $1.96(4) = 7.84$ points from the mean. Thus, the z-score boundaries of ± 1.96 correspond to sample means of 392.16 and 407.84.

We have demonstrated that a sample of untreated rats is almost guaranteed (95% probability) to have a sample mean between 392.16 and 407.84. If our sample has a mean within this range, then we must conclude that our sample of treated rats is not noticeably different from samples of untreated rats. In this case, we conclude that the treatment does not appear to have any effect.

On the other hand, if the mean for the treated sample is outside the 95% range, then we can conclude that our sample of treated rats is noticeably different from the

FIGURE 7.12
The distribution of sample means for samples of $n = 25$ untreated rats. (from Example 7.5).

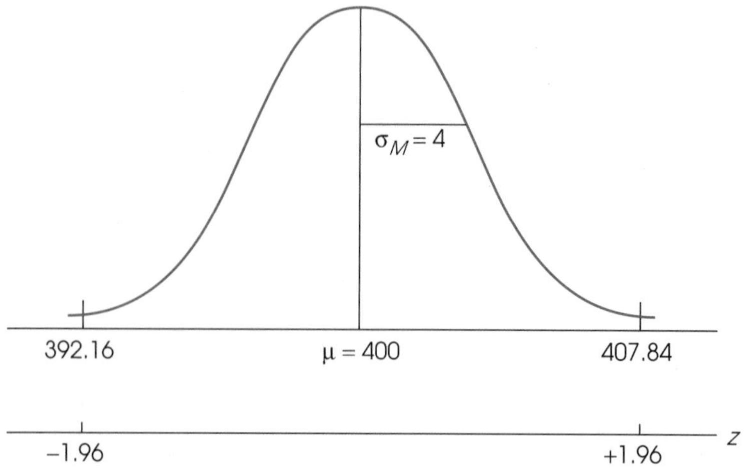

samples that would be obtained without any treatment. In this case, the research results provide evidence that the treatment has an effect.

In Example 7.5 we used the distribution of sample means, together with z-scores and probability, to provide a description of what is reasonable to expect for an untreated sample. Then, we evaluated the effect of a treatment by determining whether the treated sample was noticeably different from an untreated sample. This procedure forms the foundation for the inferential technique known as *hypothesis testing,* which is introduced in Chapter 8 and repeated throughout the remainder of this book.

STANDARD ERROR AS A MEASURE OF RELIABILITY

The research situation shown in Figure 7.11 introduces one final issue concerning sample means and standard error. In Figure 7.11, as in most research studies, the researcher must rely on a *single* sample to provide an accurate representation of the population being investigated. As we have noted, however, if you take two different samples from the same population, the samples will have different individuals with different scores and different sample means. Thus, every researcher must face the nagging question, "If I had taken a different sample, would I have obtained different results?"

The importance of this question is directly related to the degree of similarity among all the different samples. For example, if there is a high level of consistency from one sample to another, then a researcher can be reasonably confident that the specific sample being studied provides a good measurement of the population. That is, when all of the samples are similar, then it does not matter which one you have selected. On the other hand, if there are big differences from one sample to another, then the researcher is left with some doubts about the accuracy of his or her specific sample. In this case, a different sample could have produced vastly different results.

The relationship between the number of scores in the sample and the size of the standard error is shown in Figure 7.3 on page 208.

In this context, the standard error can be viewed as a measure of the *reliability* of a sample mean. The term *reliability* refers to the consistency of different measurements of the same thing. More specifically, a measurement procedure is said to be reliable if you make two different measurements of the same thing and obtain identical (or nearly identical) values. If you view a sample as a "measurement" of a population, then a sample mean is a "measurement" of the population mean.

If the standard error is small, then all of the possible sample means are clustered close together and a researcher can be confident that any individual sample mean provides a reliable measure of the population. On the other hand, a large standard error indicates that there are relatively large differences from one sample mean to another, and a researcher must be concerned that a different sample could produce a different conclusion. Fortunately, the size of the standard error can be controlled. In particular, if a researcher is concerned about a large standard error and the potential for big differences from one sample to another, then the researcher has the option of reducing the standard error by selecting a larger sample. Thus, the ability to compute the value of the standard error provides researchers with the ability to control the reliability of their samples.

The reliability of a sample mean is directly related to the degree of confidence that a specific sample mean is a stable and accurate representative of the population. If a researcher suspects that adding one or two new scores to a sample might produce a substantial change in the sample mean, then the sample is not reliable and the researcher has no confidence that it is stable and accurate. There are two factors that influence whether a few new scores might substantially change a sample mean.

1. The number of scores in the sample. If there are only 2 or 3 scores in a sample, then a few new scores can have a huge influence on the sample mean. On the other hand, if a sample already has 100 scores, then one or two new ones cannot have much effect.
2. The size of the population standard deviation. When the standard deviation is large, it means that the scores are spread over a wide range of values. In this situation it is possible to select one or two extreme scores that are very different from the others. As we noted in Chapter 3 (p. 90), adding one or two extreme scores to a sample can have a large influence on the sample mean. With a small standard deviation, however, all of the scores are close together and a few new scores should be similar to the ones already in the sample.

Notice that these two factors are the same values that are used to calculate the standard error. A large sample means that the standard error is small and the sample mean is reliable. Also, a small population standard deviation means that the standard error is small and the sample mean is reliable. In either case, a researcher can be confident that adding a few new scores to an existing sample will not have a significant influence on the sample mean.

LEARNING CHECK

1. A population forms a normal distribution with a mean of $\mu = 80$ and a standard deviation of $\sigma = 20$.
   a. If single score is selected from this population, how much distance would you expect, on average, between the score and the population mean?
   b. If a sample of $n = 100$ scores is selected from this population, how much distance would you expect, on average, between the sample mean and the population mean?
2. A population forms a normal shaped distribution with $\mu = 40$ and $\sigma = 8$.
   a. A sample of $n = 16$ scores from this population has a mean of $M = 36$. Would you describe this as a relatively typical sample, or is the sample mean an extreme value? Explain your answer.
   b. If the sample from part a had $n = 4$ scores, would it be considered typical or extreme?

3. The SAT scores for the entering freshman class at a local college form a normal distribution with a mean of $\mu = 530$ and a standard deviation of $\sigma = 80$.

a. For a random sample of $n = 16$ students, what range of values for the sample mean would be expected 95% of the time?

b. What range of values would be expected 95% of the time if the sample size were $n = 100$?

4. An automobile manufacturer claims that a new model will average $\mu = 45$ miles per gallon with $\sigma = 4$. A sample of $n = 16$ cars is tested and averages only $M = 43$ miles per gallon. Is this sample mean likely to occur if the manufacturer's claim is true? Specifically, is the sample mean within the range of values that would be expected 95% of the time? (Assume that the distribution of mileage scores is normal.)

ANSWERS

1. a. For a single score, the standard distance from the mean is the standard deviation, $\sigma = 20$.

b. For a sample of $n = 100$ scores, the average distance between the sample mean and the population mean is the standard error, $\sigma_M = 20/\sqrt{100} = 2$.

2. a. With $n = 16$ the standard error is 2, and the sample mean corresponds to $z = -2.00$. This is an extreme value.

b. With $n = 4$ the standard error is 4, and the sample mean corresponds to $z = -1.00$. This is a relatively typical value.

3. a. With $n = 16$ the standard error is $\sigma_M = 20$ points. Using $z = \pm 1.96$, the 95% range extends from 490.8 to 569.2.

b. With $n = 100$ the standard error is only 8 points and the range extends from 514.32 to 545.68.

4. With $n = 16$, the standard error is $\sigma_M = 1$. If the real mean is $\mu = 45$, then 95% of all sample means should be within 1.96(1) = 1.96 points of $\mu = 45$. This is a range of values from 43.04 to 46.96. Our sample mean is outside this range, so it is not the kind of sample that ought to be obtained if the manufacturer's claim is true.

SUMMARY

1. The distribution of sample means is defined as the set of *M*s for all the possible random samples for a specific sample size (n) that can be obtained from a given population. According to the *central limit theorem,* the parameters of the distribution of sample means are as follows:

a. *Shape*. The distribution of sample means is normal if either one of the following two conditions is satisfied:

(1) The population from which the samples are selected is normal.

(2) The size of the samples is relatively large ($n = 30$ or more).

b. *Central Tendency*. The mean of the distribution of sample means is identical to the mean of the population from which the samples are selected. The mean of the distribution of sample means is called the expected value of M.

c. *Variability*. The standard deviation of the distribution of sample means is called the standard error of M and is defined by the formula

$$\sigma_M = \frac{\sigma}{\sqrt{n}} \quad \text{or} \quad \sigma_M = \sqrt{\frac{\sigma^2}{n}}$$

Standard error measures the standard distance between a sample mean (M) and the population mean (μ).

2. One of the most important concepts in this chapter is standard error. The standard error is the standard deviation of the distribution of sample means. It measures the standard distance between a sample mean (M) and the population mean (μ). The standard error tells how much error to expect if you are using a sample mean to represent a population mean.

3. The location of each M in the distribution of sample means can be specified by a z-score:

$$z = \frac{M - \mu}{\sigma_M}$$

Because the distribution of sample means tends to be normal, we can use these z-scores and the unit normal table to find probabilities for specific sample means. In particular, we can identify which sample means are likely and which are very unlikely to be obtained from any given population. This ability to find probabilities for samples is the basis for the inferential statistics in the chapters ahead.

4. In general terms, the standard error measures how much discrepancy you should expect between a sample statistic and a population parameter. Statistical inference involves using sample statistics to make a general conclusion about a population parameter. Thus, standard error plays a crucial role in inferential statistics.

KEY TERMS

sampling error (201)
distribution of sample means (201)
sampling distribution (202)
central limit theorem (205)
expected value of M (206)
standard error of M (207)
law of large numbers (207)

RESOURCES

Book Companion Website: www.cengage.com/psychology/gravetter

You can find a tutorial quiz and other learning exercises for Chapter 7 on the book companion website. The website also provides access to two workshops entitled *Standard Error* and *Central Limit Theorem* that review the material covered in Chapter 7.

aplia

Improve your understanding of statistics with Aplia's auto-graded problem sets and immediate, detailed explanations for every question. To learn more, visit **www.aplia.com/statistics.**

CENGAGE**brain**.com

Psychology CourseMate brings course concepts to life with interactive learning, study, and exam preparation tools that support the printed textbook. A textbook-specific website, Psychology CourseMate includes an integrated interactive eBook and other interactive learning tools including quizzes, flashcards, and more.

Visit www.cengagebrain.com to access your account and purchase materials.

SPSS

The statistical computer package SPSS is not structured to compute the standard error or a *z*-score for a sample mean. In later chapters, however, we introduce new inferential statistics that are included in SPSS. When these new statistics are computed, SPSS typically includes a report of standard error that describes how accurately, on average, the sample represents its population.

FOCUS ON PROBLEM SOLVING

1. Whenever you are working probability questions about sample means, you must use the distribution of sample means. Remember that every probability question can be restated as a proportion question. Probabilities for sample means are equivalent to proportions of the distribution of sample means.

2. When computing probabilities for sample means, the most common error is to use standard deviation (σ) instead of standard error (σ_M) in the *z*-score formula. Standard deviation measures the typical deviation (or error) for a single score. Standard error measures the typical deviation (or error) for a sample. Remember: The larger the sample is, the more accurately the sample represents the population. Thus, sample size (n) is a critical part of the standard error.

$$\text{Standard error} = \sigma_M = \frac{\sigma}{\sqrt{n}}$$

Although the distribution of sample means is often normal, it is not always a normal distribution. Check the criteria to be certain that the distribution is normal before you use the unit normal table to find probabilities (see item 1a of the Summary). Remember that all probability problems with a normal distribution are easier to solve if you sketch the distribution and shade in the area of interest.

DEMONSTRATION 7.1

PROBABILITY AND THE DISTRIBUTION OF SAMPLE MEANS

A population forms a normal distribution with a mean of $\mu = 60$ and a standard deviation of $\sigma = 12$. For a sample of $n = 36$ scores from this population, what is the probability of obtaining a sample mean greater than 64?

$$p(M > 64) = ?$$

STEP 1 **Rephrase the probability question as a proportion question.** Out of all of the possible sample means for $n = 36$, what proportion has values greater than 64? *All of the possible sample means* is simply the distribution of sample means, which is normal, with a mean of $\mu = 60$ and a standard error of

$$\sigma_M = \frac{\sigma}{\sqrt{n}} = \frac{12}{\sqrt{36}} = \frac{12}{6} = 2$$

The distribution is shown in Figure 7.13(a). Because the problem is asking for the proportion greater than $M = 64$, this portion of the distribution is shaded in Figure 7.13(b).

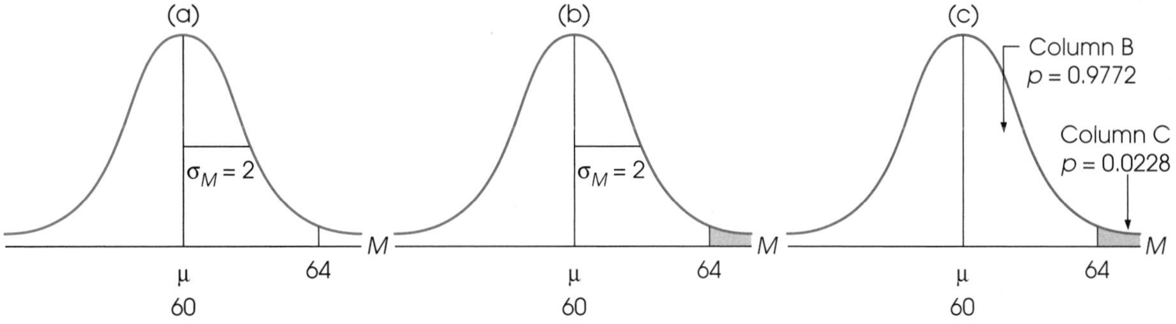

FIGURE 7.13

Sketches of the distributions for Demonstration 7.1.

STEP 2 **Compute the z-score for the sample mean.** A sample mean of $M = 64$ corresponds to a z-score of

$$z = \frac{M - \mu}{\sigma_M} = \frac{64 - 60}{2} = \frac{4}{2} = 2.00$$

Therefore, $p(M > 64) = p(z > 2.00)$

STEP 3 **Look up the proportion in the unit normal table.** Find $z = 2.00$ in column A and read across the row to find $p = 0.0228$ in column C. This is the answer as shown in Figure 7.13(c).

$$p(M > 64) = p(z > 2.00) = 0.0228 \text{ (or 2.28\%)}$$

PROBLEMS

1. Briefly define each of the following:
  a. Distribution of sample means
  b. Expected value of M
  c. Standard error of M

2. The distribution of sample means is not always a normal distribution. Under what circumstances is the distribution of sample means *not* normal?

3. A sample is selected from a population with a mean of $\mu = 40$ and a standard deviation of $\sigma = 8$.
  a. If the sample has $n = 4$ scores, what is the expected value of M and the standard error of M?
  b. If the sample has $n = 16$ scores, what is the expected value of M and the standard error of M?

4. Describe the distribution of sample means (shape, expected value, and standard error) for samples of $n = 36$ selected from a population with a mean of $\mu = 100$ and a standard deviation of $\sigma = 12$.

5. A population has a standard deviation of $\sigma = 30$.
  a. On average, how much difference should exist between the population mean and the sample mean for $n = 4$ scores randomly selected from the population?
  b. On average, how much difference should exist for a sample of $n = 25$ scores?
  c. On average, how much difference should exist for a sample of $n = 100$ scores?

6. For a population with a mean of $\mu = 70$ and a standard deviation of $\sigma = 20$, how much error, on average, would you expect between the sample mean (M) and the population mean for each of the following sample sizes?
  a. $n = 4$ scores
  b. $n = 16$ scores
  c. $n = 25$ scores

7. For a population with a standard deviation of $\sigma = 20$, how large a sample is necessary to have a standard error that is:
a. less than or equal to 5 points?
b. less than or equal to 2 points?
c. less than or equal to 1 point?

8. If the population standard deviation is $\sigma = 8$, how large a sample is necessary to have a standard error that is:
a. less than 4 points?
b. less than 2 points?
c. less than 1 point?

9. For a sample of $n = 25$ scores, what is the value of the population standard deviation (σ) necessary to produce each of the following a standard error values?
a. $\sigma_M = 10$ points?
b. $\sigma_M = 5$ points?
c. $\sigma_M = 2$ points?

10. The population of IQ scores forms a normal distribution with a mean of $\mu = 100$ and a standard deviation of $\sigma = 15$. What is the probability of obtaining a sample mean greater than $M = 97$,
a. for a random sample of $n = 9$ people?
b. for a random sample of $n = 25$ people?

11. A sample of $n = 4$ scores has a mean of $M = 75$. Find the *z*-score for this sample:
a. If it was obtained from a population with $\mu = 80$ and $\sigma = 10$.
b. If it was obtained from a population with $\mu = 80$ and $\sigma = 20$.
c. If it was obtained from a population with $\mu = 80$ and $\sigma = 40$.

12. A population forms a normal distribution with a mean of $\mu = 80$ and a standard deviation of $\sigma = 15$. For each of the following samples, compute the *z*-score for the sample mean and determine whether the sample mean is a typical, representative value or an extreme value for a sample of this size.
a. $M = 84$ for $n = 9$ scores
b. $M = 84$ for $n = 100$ scores

13. A random sample is obtained from a normal population with a mean of $\mu = 30$ and a standard deviation of $\sigma = 8$. The sample mean is $M = 33$.
a. Is this a fairly typical sample mean or an extreme value for a sample of $n = 4$ scores?
b. Is this a fairly typical sample mean or an extreme value for a sample of $n = 64$ scores?

14. For a population with a mean of $\mu = 80$ and a standard deviation of $\sigma = 12$, find the *z*-score corresponding to each of the following samples.
a. $M = 83$ for a sample of $n = 4$ scores
b. $M = 83$ for a sample of $n = 16$ scores
c. $M = 83$ for a sample of $n = 36$ scores

15. The scores on a standardized mathematics test for 8th-grade children in New York State form a normal distribution with a mean of $\mu = 70$ and a standard deviation of $\sigma = 10$.
a. What proportion of the students in the state have scores less than $X = 75$?
b. If samples of $n = 4$ are selected from the population, what proportion of the samples will have means less than $M = 75$?
c. If samples of $n = 25$ are selected from the population, what proportion of the samples will have means less than $M = 75$?

16. A population of scores forms a normal distribution with a mean of $\mu = 40$ and a standard deviation of $\sigma = 12$.
a. What is the probability of randomly selecting a score less than $X = 34$?
b. What is the probability of selecting a sample of $n = 9$ scores with a mean less than $M = 34$?
c. What is the probability of selecting a sample of $n = 36$ scores with a mean less than $M = 34$?

17. A population of scores forms a normal distribution with a mean of $\mu = 80$ and a standard deviation of $\sigma = 10$.
a. What proportion of the scores have values between 75 and 85?
b. For samples of $n = 4$, what proportion of the samples will have means between 75 and 85?
c. For samples of $n = 16$, what proportion of the samples will have means between 75 and 85?

18. Welsh, Davis, Burke, and Williams (2002) conducted a study to evaluate the effectiveness of a carbohydrate-electrolyte drink on sports performance and endurance. Experienced athletes were given either a carbohydrate-electrolyte drink or a placebo while they were tested on a series of high-intensity exercises. One measure was how much time it took for the athletes to run to fatigue. Data similar to the results obtained in the study are shown in the following table.

Time to Run to Fatigue (in minutes)		
	Mean	*SE*
Placebo	21.7	2.2
Carbohydrate-electrolyte	28.6	2.7

a. Construct a bar graph that incorporates all of the information in the table.
b. Looking at your graph, do you think that the carbohydrate-electrolyte drink helps performance?

19. The machinery at a food-packing plant is able to put exactly 12 ounces of juice in every bottle. However, some items such as apples come in variable sizes so it is almost impossible to get exactly 3 pounds of apples in a bag labeled "3 lbs." Therefore, the machinery is set to put an average of $\mu = 50$ ounces (3 pounds and 2 ounces) in each bag. The distribution of bag weights is approximately normal with a standard deviation of $\sigma = 4$ ounces.
a. What is the probability of randomly picking a bag of apples that weighs less than 48 ounces (3 pounds)?
b. What is the probability of randomly picking $n = 4$ bags of apples that have an average weight less than $M = 48$ ounces?

20. The average age for licensed drivers in the county is $\mu = 40.3$ years with a standard deviation of $\sigma = 13.2$ years.
a. A researcher obtained a random sample of $n = 16$ parking tickets and computed an average age of $M = 38.9$ years for the drivers. Compute the *z*-score for the sample mean and find the probability of obtaining an average age this young or younger for a random sample of licensed drivers. Is it reasonable to conclude that this set of $n = 16$ people is a representative sample of licensed drivers?
b. The same researcher obtained a random sample of $n = 36$ speeding tickets and computed an average age of $M = 36.2$ years for the drivers. Compute the *z*-score for the sample mean and find the probability of obtaining an average age this young or younger for a random sample of licensed drivers. Is it reasonable to conclude that this set of $n = 36$ people is a representative sample of licensed drivers?

21. People are selected to serve on juries by randomly picking names from the list of registered voters. The average age for registered voters in the county is $\mu = 44.3$ years with a standard deviation of $\sigma = 12.4$. A statistician computes the average age for a group of $n = 12$ people currently serving on a jury and obtains a mean of $M = 48.9$ years.
a. How likely is it to obtain a random sample of $n = 12$ jurors with an average age equal to or greater than 48.9?
b. Is it reasonable to conclude that this set of $n = 12$ people is not a representative random sample of registered voters?

22. At the end of the spring semester, the Dean of Students sent a survey to the entire freshman class. One question asked the students how much weight they had gained or lost since the beginning of the school year. The average was a gain of $\mu = 9$ pounds with a standard deviation of $\sigma = 6$. The distribution of scores was approximately normal. A sample of $n = 4$ students is selected and the average weight change is computed for the sample.
a. What is the probability that the sample mean will be greater than $M = 10$ pounds? In symbols, what is $p(M > 10)$?
b. Of all of the possible samples, what proportion will show an average weight loss? In symbols, what is $p(M < 0)$?
c. What is the probability that the sample mean will be a gain of between $M = 9$ and $M = 12$ pounds? In symbols, what is $p(9 < M < 12)$?

23. In the Preview section for this chapter, we discussed a research study demonstrating that 8-month-old infants appear to recognize which samples are likely to be obtained from a population and which are not. In the study, the infants watched as a sample of $n = 5$ ping pong balls was selected from a large box. In one condition, the sample consisted of 1 red ball and 4 white balls. After the sample was selected, the front panel of the box was removed to reveal the contents. In the *expected* condition, the box contained primarily white balls like the sample and the infants looked at it for an average of $M = 7.5$ seconds. In the *unexpected* condition, the box had primarily red balls, unlike the sample, and the infants looked at it for $M = 9.9$ seconds. Assuming that the standard error for both means is $(\sigma_M = 1$ second, draw a bar graph showing the two sample means using brackets to show the size of the standard error for each mean.

CHAPTER

8

Introduction to Hypothesis Testing

Tools You Will Need

The following items are considered essential background material for this chapter. If you doubt your knowledge of any of these items, you should review the appropriate chapter or section before proceeding.

- z-Scores (Chapter 5)
- Distribution of sample means (Chapter 7)
  - Expected value
  - Standard error
  - Probability and sample means

Preview

Most of us spend more time looking down at our mobile devices than we do looking up at the clouds. But if you do watch the clouds and have a little imagination, you occasionally see them form into familiar shapes. Figure 8.1 is a photograph of a cloud formation seen over Kansas City around Christmas in 2008. Do you recognize a familiar image?

The cloud pattern shown in Figure 8.1 was formed simply by chance. Specifically, it was the random forces of wind and air currents that produced a portrait of Santa Claus. The clouds did not conspire to form the image, and it was not deliberately created by a team of professional skywriters. The point we would like to make is that what appear to be meaningful patterns can be produced by random chance.

The Problem Researchers often find meaningful patterns in the sample data obtained in research studies. The problem is deciding whether the patterns found in a sample reflect real patterns that exist in the population or are simply random, chance occurrences.

The Solution To differentiate between real, systematic patterns and random, chance occurrences, researchers rely on a statistical technique known as *hypothesis testing,* which is introduced in this chapter. As you will see, a hypothesis test first determines the probability that the pattern could have been produced by chance alone. If this probability is large enough, then we conclude that the pattern can reasonably be explained by chance. However, if the probability is extremely small, then we can rule out chance as a plausible explanation and conclude that some meaningful, systematic force has created the pattern. For example, it is reasonable, once in a lifetime, to see a cloud formation that resembles Santa Claus. However, it would be extremely unlikely if the clouds also included the words "Merry Christmas" spelled out beneath Santa's face. If this happened, we would conclude that the pattern was not produced by the random forces of chance, but rather was created by a deliberate, systematic act.

FIGURE 8.1

A cloud formation seen over Kansas City.

Mark Gravetter

8.1 THE LOGIC OF HYPOTHESIS TESTING

It usually is impossible or impractical for a researcher to observe every individual in a population. Therefore, researchers usually collect data from a sample and then use the sample data to help answer questions about the population. Hypothesis testing is a statistical procedure that allows researchers to use sample data to draw inferences about the population of interest.

Hypothesis testing is one of the most commonly used inferential procedures. In fact, most of the remainder of this book examines hypothesis testing in a variety of different situations and applications. Although the details of a hypothesis test change from one situation to another, the general process remains constant. In this chapter, we introduce the general procedure for a hypothesis test. You should notice that we use the statistical techniques that have been developed in the preceding three chapters—that is, we combine the concepts of *z*-scores, probability, and the distribution of sample means to create a new statistical procedure known as a *hypothesis test*.

DEFINITION

A hypothesis test is a statistical method that uses sample data to evaluate a hypothesis about a population.

In very simple terms, the logic underlying the hypothesis-testing procedure is as follows:

1. First, we state a hypothesis about a population. Usually the hypothesis concerns the value of a population parameter. For example, we might hypothesize that American adults gain an average of $\mu = 7$ pounds between Thanksgiving and New Year's Day each year.
2. Before we select a sample, we use the hypothesis to predict the characteristics that the sample should have. For example, if we predict that the average weight gain for the population is $\mu = 7$ pounds, then we would predict that our sample should have a mean *around* 7 pounds. Remember: The sample should be similar to the population, but you always expect a certain amount of error.
3. Next, we obtain a random sample from the population. For example, we might select a sample of $n = 200$ American adults and measure the average weight change for the sample between Thanksgiving and New Year's Day.
4. Finally, we compare the obtained sample data with the prediction that was made from the hypothesis. If the sample mean is consistent with the prediction, then we conclude that the hypothesis is reasonable. But if there is a big discrepancy between the data and the prediction, then we decide that the hypothesis is wrong.

A hypothesis test is typically used in the context of a research study. That is, a researcher completes a research study and then uses a hypothesis test to evaluate the results. Depending on the type of research and the type of data, the details of the hypothesis test change from one research situation to another. In later chapters, we examine different versions of hypothesis testing that are used for different kinds of research. For now, however, we focus on the basic elements that are common to all hypothesis tests. To accomplish this general goal, we examine a hypothesis test as it applies to the simplest possible situation—using a sample mean to test a hypothesis about a population mean.

In the six chapters that follow, we consider hypothesis testing in more complex research situations involving sample means and mean differences. In Chapters 15 and 16, we look at correlational research and examine how the relationships obtained for sample data are used to evaluate hypotheses about relationships in the population. In Chapters 17 and 18, we examine how the proportions that exist in a sample are used to test hypotheses about the corresponding proportions in the population. Chapter 19 reviews the complete set of hypothesis tests and presents a guide to help you find the appropriate test for a specific set of data.

Once again, we introduce hypothesis testing with a situation in which a researcher is using one sample mean to evaluate a hypothesis about one unknown population mean.

The unknown population Figure 8.2 shows the general research situation that we use to introduce the process of hypothesis testing. Notice that the researcher begins with a known population. This is the set of individuals as they exist *before treatment.* For this example, we are assuming that the original set of scores forms a normal distribution with $\mu = 80$ and $\sigma = 20$. The purpose of the research is to determine the effect of a treatment on the individuals in the population. That is, the goal is to determine what happens to the population *after the treatment is administered.*

To simplify the hypothesis-testing situation, one basic assumption is made about the effect of the treatment: If the treatment has any effect, it is simply to add a constant amount to (or subtract a constant amount from) each individual's score. You should recall from Chapters 3 and 4 that adding (or subtracting) a constant changes the mean but does not change the shape of the population, nor does it change the standard deviation. Thus, we assume that the population after treatment has the same shape as the original population and the same standard deviation as the original population. This assumption is incorporated into the situation shown in Figure 8.2.

Note that the unknown population, after treatment, is the focus of the research question. Specifically, the purpose of the research is to determine what would happen if the treatment were administered to every individual in the population.

The sample in the research study The goal of the hypothesis test is to determine whether the treatment has any effect on the individuals in the population (see Figure 8.2). Usually, however, we cannot administer the treatment to the entire population, so the actual research study is conducted using a sample. Figure 8.3 shows the structure of the research study from the point of view of the hypothesis test. The original population, before treatment, is shown on the left-hand side. The unknown population, after treatment, is shown on the right-hand side. Note that the unknown population is actually *hypothetical* (the treatment is never administered to the entire population). Instead, we are asking *what would happen if* the treatment were administered to the entire population. The research

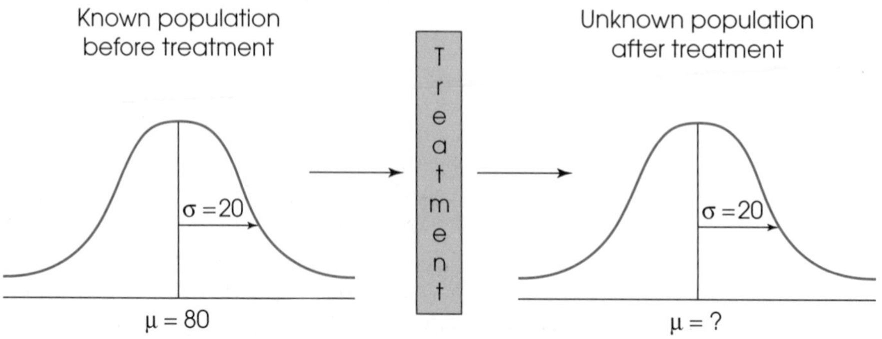

FIGURE 8.2
The basic experimental situation for hypothesis testing. It is assumed that the parameter μ is known for the population before treatment. The purpose of the experiment is to determine whether the treatment has an effect on the population mean.

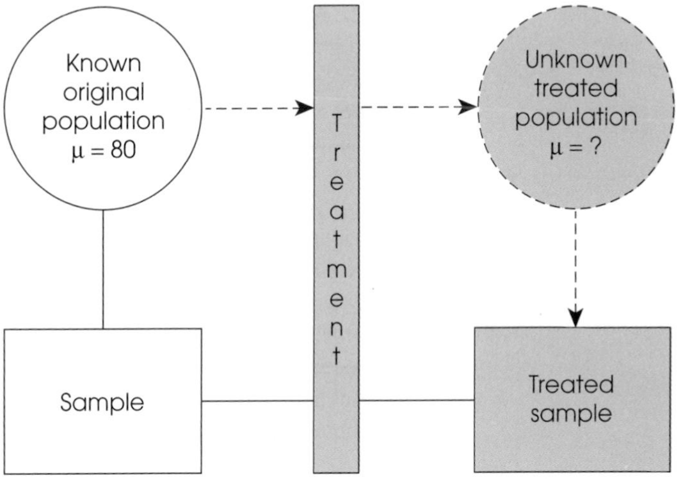

FIGURE 8.3
From the point of view of the hypothesis test, the entire population receives the treatment and then a sample is selected from the treated population. In the actual research study, a sample is selected from the original population and the treatment is administered to the sample. From either perspective, the result is a treated sample that represents the treated population.

study involves selecting a sample from the original population, administering the treatment to the sample, and then recording scores for the individuals in the treated sample. Notice that the research study produces a treated sample. Although this sample was obtained indirectly, it is equivalent to a sample that is obtained directly from the unknown treated population. The hypothesis test uses the treated sample on the right-hand side of Figure 8.3 to evaluate a hypothesis about the unknown treated population on the right side of the figure.

A hypothesis test is a formalized procedure that follows a standard series of operations. In this way, researchers have a standardized method for evaluating the results of their research studies. Other researchers recognize and understand exactly how the data were evaluated and how conclusions were reached. To emphasize the formal structure of a hypothesis test, we present hypothesis testing as a four-step process that is used throughout the rest of the book. The following example provides a concrete foundation for introducing the hypothesis-testing procedure.

EXAMPLE 8.1

Researchers have noted a decline in cognitive functioning as people age (Bartus, 1990). However, the results from other research suggest that the antioxidants in foods such as blueberries can reduce and even reverse these age-related declines, at least in laboratory rats (Joseph et al., 1999). Based on these results, one might theorize that the same antioxidants might also benefit elderly humans. Suppose a researcher is interested in testing this theory.

Standardized neuropsychological tests such as the Wisconsin Card Sorting Test can be used to measure conceptual thinking ability and mental flexibility (Heaton, Chelune, Talley, Kay, & Curtiss, 1993). Performance on this type of test declines gradually with age. Suppose that our researcher selects a test for which adults older than 65 have an average score of $\mu = 80$ with a standard deviation of $\sigma = 20$. The distribution of test scores is approximately normal. The researcher's plan is to obtain a sample of $n = 25$ adults who are older than 65, and give each participant a daily dose of a blueberry supplement that is very high in antioxidants. After taking the supplement for 6 months, the participants are given the neuropsychological test to measure their level of cognitive function. If the mean score for the sample is noticeably different from the mean for the general population of elderly adults, then the researcher can conclude that the supplement does appear to have an effect on cognitive function. On the other hand, if the sample mean is around 80 (the same as the general population mean), the researcher must conclude that the supplement does not appear to have any effect.

THE FOUR STEPS OF A HYPOTHESIS TEST

Figure 8.3 depicts the research situation that was described in the preceding example. Notice that the population after treatment is unknown. Specifically, we do not know what will happen to the mean score if the entire population of elderly adults is given the blueberry supplement. However, we do have a sample of $n = 25$ participants who have received the supplement and we can use this sample to help draw inferences about the unknown population. The following four steps outline the hypothesis-testing procedure that allows us to use sample data to answer questions about an unknown population.

STEP 1: STATE THE HYPOTHESIS

As the name implies, the process of hypothesis testing begins by stating a hypothesis about the unknown population. Actually, we state two opposing hypotheses. Notice that both hypotheses are stated in terms of population parameters.

The goal of inferential statistics is to make general statements about the population by using sample data. Therefore, when testing hypotheses, we make our predictions about the population parameters.

The first, and most important, of the two hypotheses is called the *null hypothesis*. The null hypothesis states that the treatment has no effect. In general, the null hypothesis states that there is no change, no effect, no difference—nothing happened, hence the name *null*. The null hypothesis is identified by the symbol H_0. (The H stands for *hypothesis*, and the zero subscript indicates that this is the *zero-effect* hypothesis.) For the study in Example 8.1, the null hypothesis states that the blueberry supplement has no effect on cognitive functioning for the population of adults who are more than 65 years old. In symbols, this hypothesis is

$$H_0: \mu_{\text{with supplement}} = 80$$ (Even with the supplement, the mean test score is still 80.)

DEFINITION

> The **null hypothesis** (H_0) states that in the general population there is no change, no difference, or no relationship. In the context of an experiment, H_0 predicts that the independent variable (treatment) *has no effect* on the dependent variable (scores) for the population.

The second hypothesis is simply the opposite of the null hypothesis, and it is called the *scientific*, or *alternative*, *hypothesis* (H_1). This hypothesis states that the treatment has an effect on the dependent variable.

DEFINITION

> The **alternative hypothesis** (H_1) states that there is a change, a difference, or a relationship for the general population. In the context of an experiment, H_1 predicts that the independent variable (treatment) *does have an effect* on the dependent variable.

The null hypothesis and the alternative hypothesis are mutually exclusive and exhaustive. They cannot both be true, and one of them must be true. The data determine which one should be rejected.

For this example, the alternative hypothesis states that the supplement does have an effect on cognitive functioning for the population and will cause a change in the mean score. In symbols, the alternative hypothesis is represented as

$$H_1: \mu_{\text{with supplement}} \neq 80$$ (With the supplement, the mean test score is different from 80.)

Notice that the alternative hypothesis simply states that there will be some type of change. It does not specify whether the effect will be increased or decreased test scores. In some circumstances, it is appropriate for the alternative hypothesis to specify the direction of the effect. For example, the researcher might hypothesize that the supplement will increase neuropsychological test scores ($\mu > 80$). This type of hypothesis results in a directional hypothesis test, which is examined in detail later in this chapter. For now we concentrate on nondirectional tests, for which the hypotheses simply state that the treatment has no effect (H_0) or has some effect (H_1).

STEP 2: SET THE CRITERIA FOR A DECISION

Eventually the researcher uses the data from the sample to evaluate the credibility of the null hypothesis. The data either provide support for the null hypothesis or tend to refute the null hypothesis. In particular, if there is a big discrepancy between the data and the null hypothesis, then we conclude that the null hypothesis is wrong.

To formalize the decision process, we use the null hypothesis to predict the kind of sample mean that ought to be obtained. Specifically, we determine exactly which sample means are consistent with the null hypothesis and which sample means are at odds with the null hypothesis.

For our example, the null hypothesis states that the supplement has no effect and the population mean is still $\mu = 80$. If this is true, then the sample mean should have a value around 80. Therefore, a sample mean near 80 is consistent with the null hypothesis. On the other hand, a sample mean that is very different from 80 is not consistent with the null hypothesis. To determine exactly which values are "near" 80 and which values are "very different from" 80, we examine all of the possible sample means that could be obtained if the null hypothesis is true. For our example, this is the distribution of sample means for $n = 25$. According to the null hypothesis, this distribution is centered at $\mu = 80$. The distribution of sample means is then divided into two sections:

1. Sample means that are likely to be obtained if H_0 is true; that is, sample means that are close to the null hypothesis
2. Sample means that are very unlikely to be obtained if H_0 is true; that is, sample means that are very different from the null hypothesis

Figure 8.4 shows the distribution of sample means divided into these two sections. Notice that the high-probability samples are located in the center of the distribution and have sample means close to the value specified in the null hypothesis. On the other hand, the low-probability samples are located in the extreme tails of the distribution. After the distribution has been divided in this way, we can compare our sample data with the values in the distribution. Specifically, we can determine whether our sample mean is consistent with the null hypothesis (like the values in the center of the distribution) or whether our sample mean is very different from the null hypothesis (like the values in the extreme tails).

The alpha level To find the boundaries that separate the high-probability samples from the low-probability samples, we must define exactly what is meant by "low" probability and "high" probability. This is accomplished by selecting a specific probability value, which is known as the *level of significance,* or the *alpha level,* for the hypothesis test. The alpha (α) value is a small probability that is used to identify the low-probability samples. By convention, commonly used alpha levels are $\alpha = .05$ (5%), $\alpha = .01$ (1%), and $\alpha = .001$ (0.1%). For example, with $\alpha = .05$, we separate the most unlikely 5% of the sample means (the extreme values) from the most likely 95% of the sample means (the central values).

With rare exceptions, an alpha level is never larger than .05.

FIGURE 8.4

The set of potential samples is divided into those that are likely to be obtained and those that are very unlikely to be obtained if the null hypothesis is true.

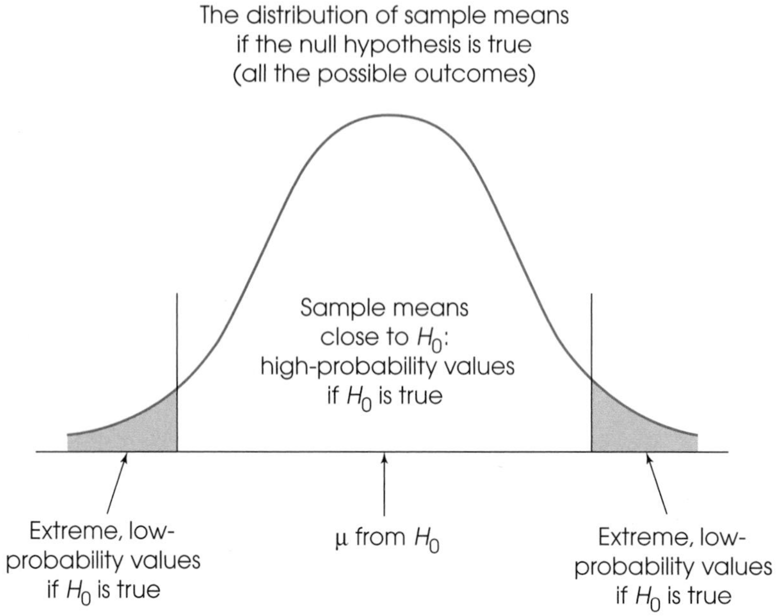

The extremely unlikely values, as defined by the alpha level, make up what is called the *critical region*. These extreme values in the tails of the distribution define outcomes that are not consistent with the null hypothesis; that is, they are very unlikely to occur if the null hypothesis is true. Whenever the data from a research study produce a sample mean that is located in the critical region, we conclude that the data are not consistent with the null hypothesis, and we reject the null hypothesis.

DEFINITIONS

The **alpha level,** or the **level of significance,** is a probability value that is used to define the concept of "very unlikely" in a hypothesis test.

The **critical region** is composed of the extreme sample values that are very unlikely (as defined by the alpha level) to be obtained if the null hypothesis is true. The boundaries for the critical region are determined by the alpha level. If sample data fall in the critical region, the null hypothesis is rejected.

Technically, the critical region is defined by sample outcomes that are *very unlikely* to occur if the treatment has no effect (that is, if the null hypothesis is true). Reversing the point of view, we can also define the critical region as sample values that provide *convincing evidence* that the treatment really does have an effect. For our example, the regular population of elderly adults has a mean test score of $\mu = 80$. We selected a sample from this population and administered a treatment (the blueberry supplement) to the individuals in the sample. What kind of sample mean would convince you that the treatment has an effect? It should be obvious that the most convincing evidence would be a sample mean that is really different from $\mu = 80$. In a hypothesis test, the critical region is determined by sample values that are "really different" from the original population.

The boundaries for the critical region To determine the exact location for the boundaries that define the critical region, we use the alpha-level probability and the unit normal table. In most cases, the distribution of sample means is normal, and the unit normal table provides the precise z-score location for the critical region boundaries. With $\alpha = .05$, for example, the boundaries separate the extreme 5% from the middle 95%. Because the extreme 5% is split between two tails of the distribution, there is exactly 2.5% (or 0.0250) in each tail. In the unit normal table, you can look up a proportion of 0.0250 in column C (the tail) and find that the z-score boundary is $z = 1.96$. Thus, for any normal distribution, the extreme 5% is in the tails of the distribution beyond $z = +1.96$ and $z = -1.96$. These values define the boundaries of the critical region for a hypothesis test using $\alpha = .05$ (Figure 8.5).

Similarly, an alpha level of $\alpha = .01$ means that 1%, or .0100, is split between the two tails. In this case, the proportion in each tail is .0050, and the corresponding z-score boundaries are $z = \pm 2.58$ (± 2.57 is equally good). For $\alpha = .001$, the boundaries are located at $z = \pm 3.30$. You should verify these values in the unit normal table and be sure that you understand exactly how they are obtained.

LEARNING CHECK

1. The city school district is considering increasing class size in the elementary schools. However, some members of the school board are concerned that larger classes may have a negative effect on student learning. In words, what would the null hypothesis say about the effect of class size on student learning?
2. If the alpha level is increased from $\alpha = .01$ to $\alpha = .05$, then the boundaries for the critical region move farther away from the center of the distribution. (True or false?)
3. If a researcher conducted a hypothesis test with an alpha level of $\alpha = .02$, what z-score values would form the boundaries for the critical region?

FIGURE 8.5
The critical region (very unlikely outcomes) for $\alpha = .05$.

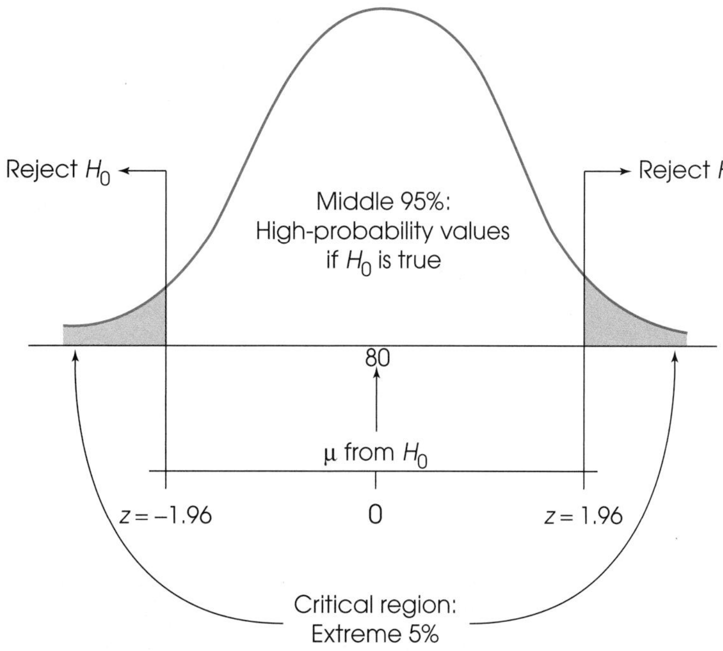

ANSWERS

1. The null hypothesis would say that class size has no effect on student learning.
2. False. A larger alpha means that the boundaries for the critical region move closer to the center of the distribution.
3. The .02 would be split between the two tails, with .01 in each tail. The z-score boundaries would be $z = +2.33$ and $z = -2.33$.

STEP 3: COLLECT DATA AND COMPUTE SAMPLE STATISTICS

At this time, we select a sample of adults who are more than 65 years old and give each one a daily dose of the blueberry supplement. After 6 months, the neuropsychological test is used to measure cognitive function for the sample of participants. Notice that the data are collected *after* the researcher has stated the hypotheses and established the criteria for a decision. This sequence of events helps to ensure that a researcher makes an honest, objective evaluation of the data and does not tamper with the decision criteria after the experimental outcome is known.

Next, the raw data from the sample are summarized with the appropriate statistics: For this example, the researcher would compute the sample mean. Now it is possible for the researcher to compare the sample mean (the data) with the null hypothesis. This is the heart of the hypothesis test: comparing the data with the hypothesis.

The comparison is accomplished by computing a z-score that describes exactly where the sample mean is located relative to the hypothesized population mean from H_0. In step 2, we constructed the distribution of sample means that would be expected if the null hypothesis were true—that is, the entire set of sample means that could be obtained if the treatment has no effect (see Figure 8.5). Now we calculate a z-score that identifies where our sample mean is located in this hypothesized distribution. The z-score formula for a sample mean is

$$z = \frac{M - \mu}{\sigma_M}$$

In the formula, the value of the sample mean (M) is obtained from the sample data, and the value of μ is obtained from the null hypothesis. Thus, the z-score formula can be expressed in words as follows:

$$z = \frac{\text{sample mean} - \text{hypothesized population mean}}{\text{standard error between } M \text{ and } \mu}$$

Notice that the top of the z-score formula measures how much difference there is between the data and the hypothesis. The bottom of the formula measures the standard distance that ought to exist between a sample mean and the population mean.

STEP 4: MAKE A DECISION

In the final step, the researcher uses the z-score value obtained in step 3 to make a decision about the null hypothesis according to the criteria established in step 2. There are two possible outcomes:

1. The sample data are located in the critical region. By definition, a sample value in the critical region is very unlikely to occur if the null hypothesis is true. Therefore, we conclude that the sample is not consistent with H_0 and our decision is to *reject the null hypothesis*. Remember, the null hypothesis states that there is no treatment effect, so rejecting H_0 means that we are concluding that the treatment did have an effect.

For the example we have been considering, suppose that the sample produced a mean of $M = 92$ after taking the supplement for 6 months. The null hypothesis states that the population mean is $\mu = 80$ and, with $n = 25$ and $\sigma = 20$, the standard error for the sample mean is

$$\sigma_M = \frac{\sigma}{\sqrt{n}} = \frac{20}{\sqrt{25}} = \frac{20}{5} = 4$$

Thus, a sample mean of $M = 92$ produces a z-score of

$$z = \frac{M - \mu}{\sigma_M} = \frac{92 - 80}{4} = \frac{12}{4} = 3.00$$

With an alpha level of $\alpha = .05$, this z-score is far beyond the boundary of 1.96. Because the sample z-score is in the critical region, we reject the null hypothesis and conclude that the blueberry supplement did have an effect on cognitive functioning.

2. The second possibility is that the sample data are not in the critical region. In this case, the sample mean is reasonably close to the population mean specified in the null hypothesis (in the center of the distribution). Because the data do not provide strong evidence that the null hypothesis is wrong, our conclusion is to *fail to reject the null hypothesis*. This conclusion means that the treatment does not appear to have an effect.

   For the research study examining the blueberry supplement, suppose our sample produced a mean test score of $M = 84$. As before, the standard error for a sample of $n = 25$ is $\sigma_M = 4$, and the null hypothesis states that $\mu = 80$. These values produce a z-score of

$$z = \frac{M - \mu}{\sigma_M} = \frac{84 - 80}{4} = \frac{4}{4} = 1.00$$

   The z-score of 1.00 is not in the critical region. Therefore, we would fail to reject the null hypothesis and conclude that the blueberry supplement does not appear to have an effect on cognitive functioning.

In general, the final decision is made by comparing our treated sample with the distribution of sample means that would be obtained for untreated samples. If our treated sample looks much the same as samples that do not receive the blueberry treatment, we conclude that the treatment does not appear to have any effect. On the other hand, if the treated sample is noticeably different from the majority of untreated samples, we conclude that the treatment does have an effect.

An Analogy for Hypothesis Testing It may seem awkward to phrase both of the two possible decisions in terms of rejecting the null hypothesis; either we reject H_0 or we fail to reject H_0. These two decisions may be easier to understand if you think of a research study as an attempt to gather evidence to prove that a treatment works. From this perspective, the process of conducting a hypothesis test is similar to the process that takes place during a jury trial. For example,

1. The test begins with a null hypothesis stating that there is no treatment effect. The trial begins with a null hypothesis that the defendant did not commit a crime (innocent until proven guilty).

2. The research study gathers evidence to show that the treatment actually does have an effect, and the police gather evidence to show that the defendant really did commit a crime. Note that both are trying to refute the null hypothesis.
3. If there is enough evidence, the researcher rejects the null hypothesis and concludes that there really is a treatment effect. If there is enough evidence, the jury rejects the hypothesis and concludes that the defendant is guilty of a crime.
4. If there is not enough evidence, the researcher fails to reject the null hypothesis. Note that the researcher does not conclude that there is no treatment effect, simply that there is not enough evidence to conclude that there is an effect. Similarly, if there is not enough evidence, the jury fails to find the defendant guilty. Note that the jury does not conclude that the defendant is innocent, simply that there is not enough evidence for a guilty verdict.

A CLOSER LOOK AT THE *z*-SCORE STATISTIC

The *z*-score statistic that is used in the hypothesis test is the first specific example of what is called a *test statistic*. The term *test statistic* simply indicates that the sample data are converted into a single, specific statistic that is used to test the hypotheses. In the chapters that follow, we introduce several other test statistics that are used in a variety of different research situations. However, most of the new test statistics have the same basic structure and serve the same purpose as the *z*-score. We have already described the *z*-score equation as a formal method for comparing the sample data and the population hypothesis. In this section, we discuss the *z*-score from two other perspectives that may give you a better understanding of hypothesis testing and the role that *z*-scores play in this inferential technique. In each case, keep in mind that the *z*-score serves as a general model for other test statistics that come in future chapters.

The *z*-score formula as a recipe The *z*-score formula, like any formula, can be viewed as a recipe. If you follow instructions and use all of the right ingredients, the formula produces a *z*-score. In the hypothesis-testing situation, however, you do not have all of the necessary ingredients. Specifically, you do not know the value for the population mean (μ), which is one component, or ingredient, in the formula.

This situation is similar to trying to follow a cake recipe in which one of the ingredients is not clearly listed. For example, the recipe may call for flour but there is a grease stain that makes it impossible to read how much flour. Faced with this situation, you might try the following steps:

1. Make a hypothesis about the amount of flour. For example, hypothesize that the correct amount is 2 cups.
2. To test your hypothesis, add the rest of the ingredients along with the hypothesized amount of flour and bake the cake.
3. If the cake turns out to be good, you can reasonably conclude that your hypothesis was correct. But if the cake is terrible, you conclude that your hypothesis was wrong.

In a hypothesis test with *z*-scores, we do essentially the same thing. We have a formula (recipe) for *z*-scores but one ingredient is missing. Specifically, we do not know the value for the population mean, μ. Therefore, we try the following steps:

1. Make a hypothesis about the value of μ. This is the null hypothesis.
2. Plug the hypothesized value in the formula along with the other values (ingredients).

3. If the formula produces a z-score near zero (which is where z-scores are supposed to be), we conclude that the hypothesis was correct. On the other hand, if the formula produces an extreme value (a very unlikely result), we conclude that the hypothesis was wrong.

The z-score formula as a ratio In the context of a hypothesis test, the z-score formula has the following structure:

$$z = \frac{M - \mu}{\sigma_M} = \frac{\text{sample mean} - \text{hypothesized population mean}}{\text{standard error between } M \text{ and } \mu}$$

Notice that the numerator of the formula involves a direct comparison between the sample data and the null hypothesis. In particular, the numerator measures the obtained difference between the sample mean and the hypothesized population mean. The standard error in the denominator of the formula measures the standard amount of distance that exists naturally between a sample mean and the population mean without any treatment effect causing the sample to be different. Thus, the z-score formula (and most other test statistics) forms a ratio

$$z = \frac{\text{actual difference between the sample } (M) \text{ and the hypothesis } (\mu)}{\text{standard difference between } M \text{ and } \mu \text{ with no treatment effect}}$$

Thus, for example, a z-score of $z = 3.00$ means that the obtained difference between the sample and the hypothesis is 3 times bigger than would be expected if the treatment had no effect.

In general, a large value for a test statistic like the z-score indicates a large discrepancy between the sample data and the null hypothesis. Specifically, a large value indicates that the sample data are very unlikely to have occurred by chance alone. Therefore, when we obtain a large value (in the critical region), we conclude that it must have been caused by a treatment effect.

LEARNING CHECK

1. A researcher selects a sample of $n = 16$ individuals from a normal population with a mean of $\mu = 40$ and $\sigma = 8$. A treatment is administered to the sample and, after treatment, the sample mean is $M = 43$. If the researcher uses a hypothesis test to evaluate the treatment effect, what z-score would be obtained for this sample?
2. A small value (near zero) for the z-score statistic is evidence that the sample data are consistent with the null hypothesis. (True or false?)
3. A z-score value in the critical region means that you should reject the null hypothesis. (True or false?)

ANSWERS

1. The standard error is 2 points and $z = 3/2 = 1.50$.
2. True. A z-score near zero indicates that the data support the null hypothesis.
3. True. A z-score value in the critical region means that the sample is not consistent with the null hypothesis.

8.2 UNCERTAINTY AND ERRORS IN HYPOTHESIS TESTING

Hypothesis testing is an *inferential process,* which means that it uses limited information as the basis for reaching a general conclusion. Specifically, a sample provides only limited or incomplete information about the whole population, and yet a hypothesis test uses a sample to draw a conclusion about the population. In this situation, there is always the possibility that an incorrect conclusion will be made. Although sample data are usually representative of the population, there is always a chance that the sample is misleading and will cause a researcher to make the wrong decision about the research results. In a hypothesis test, there are two different kinds of errors that can be made.

TYPE I ERRORS

It is possible that the data will lead you to reject the null hypothesis when in fact the treatment has no effect. Remember: Samples are not expected to be identical to their populations, and some extreme samples can be very different from the populations that they are supposed to represent. If a researcher selects one of these extreme samples by chance, then the data from the sample may give the appearance of a strong treatment effect, even though there is no real effect. In the previous section, for example, we discussed a research study examining how a food supplement that is high in antioxidants affects the cognitive functioning of elderly adults. Suppose that the researcher selects a sample of $n = 25$ people who already have cognitive functioning that is well above average. Even if the blueberry supplement (the treatment) has no effect at all, these people will still score higher than average on the neuropsychological test when they are tested after 6 months of taking the supplement. In this case, the researcher is likely to conclude that the treatment does have an effect, when in fact it really does not. This is an example of what is called a *Type I error.*

DEFINITION

A **Type I error** occurs when a researcher rejects a null hypothesis that is actually true. In a typical research situation, a Type I error means that the researcher concludes that a treatment does have an effect when, in fact, it has no effect.

You should realize that a Type I error is not a stupid mistake in the sense that a researcher is overlooking something that should be perfectly obvious. On the contrary, the researcher is looking at sample data that appear to show a clear treatment effect. The researcher then makes a careful decision based on the available information. The problem is that the information from the sample is misleading.

In most research situations, the consequences of a Type I error can be very serious. Because the researcher has rejected the null hypothesis and believes that the treatment has a real effect, it is likely that the researcher will report or even publish the research results. A Type I error, however, means that this is a false report. Thus, Type I errors lead to false reports in the scientific literature. Other researchers may try to build theories or develop other experiments based on the false results. A lot of precious time and resources may be wasted.

The Probability of a Type I Error A Type I error occurs when a researcher unknowingly obtains an extreme, nonrepresentative sample. Fortunately, the hypothesis test is structured to minimize the risk that this will occur. Figure 8.5 shows the distribution of sample means and the critical region for the research study we have been discussing. This distribution contains all of the possible sample means for samples of $n = 25$ if the null hypothesis is true. Notice that most of the sample means are near the hypothesized population mean, $\mu = 80$, and that means in the critical region are very unlikely to occur.

With an alpha level of $\alpha = .05$, only 5% of the samples have means in the critical region. Therefore, there is only a 5% probability ($p = .05$) that one of these samples will be obtained. Thus, the alpha level determines the probability of obtaining a sample mean in the critical region when the null hypothesis is true. In other words, the alpha level determines the probability of a Type I error.

DEFINITION

The **alpha level** for a hypothesis test is the probability that the test will lead to a Type I error. That is, the alpha level determines the probability of obtaining sample data in the critical region even though the null hypothesis is true.

In summary, whenever the sample data are in the critical region, the appropriate decision for a hypothesis test is to reject the null hypothesis. Normally this is the correct decision because the treatment has caused the sample to be different from the original population; that is, the treatment effect has pushed the sample mean into the critical region. In this case, the hypothesis test has correctly identified a real treatment effect. Occasionally, however, sample data are in the critical region just by chance, without any treatment effect. When this occurs, the researcher makes a Type I error; that is, the researcher concludes that a treatment effect exists when in fact it does not. Fortunately, the risk of a Type I error is small and is under the control of the researcher. Specifically, the probability of a Type I error is equal to the alpha level.

TYPE II ERRORS

Whenever a researcher rejects the null hypothesis, there is a risk of a Type I error. Similarly, whenever a researcher fails to reject the null hypothesis, there is a risk of a *Type II error*. By definition, a Type II error is the failure to reject a false null hypothesis. In more straightforward English, a Type II error means that a treatment effect really exists, but the hypothesis test fails to detect it.

DEFINITION

A **Type II error** occurs when a researcher fails to reject a null hypothesis that is really false. In a typical research situation, a Type II error means that the hypothesis test has failed to detect a real treatment effect.

A Type II error occurs when the sample mean is not in the critical region even though the treatment has had an effect on the sample. Often this happens when the effect of the treatment is relatively small. In this case, the treatment does influence the sample, but the magnitude of the effect is not big enough to move the sample mean into the critical region. Because the sample is not substantially different from the original population (it is not in the critical region), the statistical decision is to fail to reject the null hypothesis and to conclude that there is not enough evidence to say that there is a treatment effect.

The consequences of a Type II error are usually not as serious as those of a Type I error. In general terms, a Type II error means that the research data do not show the results that the researcher had hoped to obtain. The researcher can accept this outcome and conclude that the treatment either has no effect or has only a small effect that is not worth pursuing, or the researcher can repeat the experiment (usually with some improvement, such as a larger sample) and try to demonstrate that the treatment really does work.

Unlike a Type I error, it is impossible to determine a single, exact probability for a Type II error. Instead, the probability of a Type II error depends on a variety of factors and therefore is a function, rather than a specific number. Nonetheless, the probability of a Type II error is represented by the symbol β, the Greek letter *beta.*

In summary, a hypothesis test always leads to one of two decisions:

1. The sample data provide sufficient evidence to reject the null hypothesis and conclude that the treatment has an effect.
2. The sample data do not provide enough evidence to reject the null hypothesis. In this case, you fail to reject H_0 and conclude that the treatment does not appear to have an effect.

In either case, there is a chance that the data are misleading and the decision is wrong. The complete set of decisions and outcomes is shown in Table 8.1. The risk of an error is especially important in the case of a Type I error, which can lead to a false report. Fortunately, the probability of a Type I error is determined by the alpha level, which is completely under the control of the researcher. At the beginning of a hypothesis test, the researcher states the hypotheses and selects the alpha level, which immediately determines the risk that a Type I error will be made.

SELECTING AN ALPHA LEVEL

As you have seen, the alpha level for a hypothesis test serves two very important functions. First, the alpha level helps to determine the boundaries for the critical region by defining the concept of "very unlikely" outcomes. At the same time, the alpha level determines the probability of a Type I error. When you select a value for alpha at the beginning of a hypothesis test, your decision influences both of these functions.

The primary concern when selecting an alpha level is to minimize the risk of a Type I error. Thus, alpha levels tend to be very small probability values. By convention, the largest permissible value is $\alpha = .05$. When there is no treatment effect, an alpha level of .05 means that there is still a 5% risk, or a 1-in-20 probability, of rejecting the null hypothesis and committing a Type I error. Because the consequences of a Type I error can be relatively serious, many individual researchers and many scientific publications prefer to use a more conservative alpha level such as .01 or .001 to reduce the risk that a false report is published and becomes part of the scientific literature. (For more information on the origins of the .05 level of significance, see the excellent short article by Cowles and Davis, 1982.)

TABLE 8.1

Possible outcomes of a statistical decision

		Actual Situation	
		No Effect, H_0 True	Effect Exists, H_0 False
Experimenter's Decision	Reject H_0	Type I error	Decision correct
	Retain H_0	Decision correct	Type II error

At this point, it may appear that the best strategy for selecting an alpha level is to choose the smallest possible value to minimize the risk of a Type I error. However, there is a different kind of risk that develops as the alpha level is lowered. Specifically, a lower alpha level means less risk of a Type I error, but it also means that the hypothesis test demands more evidence from the research results.

The trade-off between the risk of a Type I error and the demands of the test is controlled by the boundaries of the critical region. For the hypothesis test to conclude that the treatment does have an effect, the sample data must be in the critical region. If the treatment really has an effect, it should cause the sample to be different from the original population; essentially, the treatment should push the sample into the critical region. However, as the alpha level is lowered, the boundaries for the critical region move farther out and become more difficult to reach. Figure 8.6 shows how the boundaries for the critical region move farther into the tails as the alpha level decreases. Notice that $z = 0$, in the center of the distribution, corresponds to the value of μ specified in the null hypothesis. The boundaries for the critical region determine how much distance between the sample mean and μ is needed to reject the null hypothesis. As the alpha level gets smaller, this distance gets larger.

Thus, an extremely small alpha level, such as .000001 (one in a million), would mean almost no risk of a Type I error but would push the critical region so far out that it would become essentially impossible to ever reject the null hypothesis; that is, it would require an enormous treatment effect before the sample data would reach the critical boundaries.

In general, researchers try to maintain a balance between the risk of a Type I error and the demands of the hypothesis test. Alpha levels of .05, .01, and .001 are considered reasonably good values because they provide a low risk of error without placing excessive demands on the research results.

FIGURE 8.6

The locations of the critical region boundaries for three different levels of significance: $\alpha = .05$, $\alpha = .01$, and $\alpha = .001$.

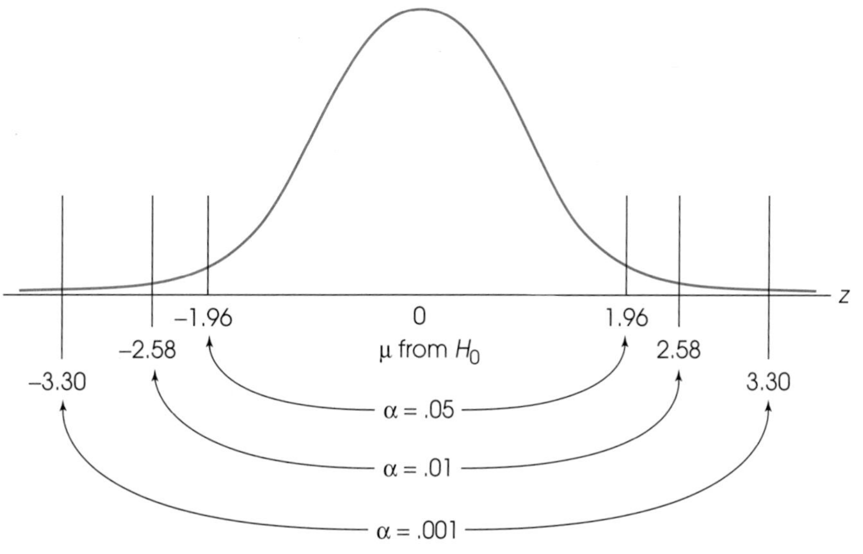

LEARNING CHECK

1. Define a Type I error.
2. Define a Type II error.
3. Under what circumstances is a Type II error likely to occur?
4. If a sample mean is in the critical region with $\alpha = .05$, it would still (always) be in the critical region if alpha were changed to $\alpha = .01$. (True or false?)
5. If a sample mean is in the critical region with $\alpha = .01$, it would still (always) be in the critical region if alpha were changed to $\alpha = .05$. (True or false?)

ANSWERS

1. A Type I error is rejecting a true null hypothesis—that is, saying that the treatment has an effect when, in fact, it does not.
2. A Type II error is the failure to reject a false null hypothesis. In terms of a research study, a Type II error occurs when a study fails to detect a treatment effect that really exists.
3. A Type II error is likely to occur when the treatment effect is very small. In this case, a research study is more likely to fail to detect the effect.
4. False. With $\alpha = .01$, the boundaries for the critical region move farther out into the tails of the distribution. It is possible that a sample mean could be beyond the .05 boundary but not beyond the .01 boundary.
5. True. With $\alpha = .01$, the boundaries for the critical region are farther out into the tails of the distribution than for $\alpha = .05$. If a sample mean is beyond the .01 boundary it is definitely beyond the .05 boundary.

8.3 AN EXAMPLE OF A HYPOTHESIS TEST

At this time, we have introduced all the elements of a hypothesis test. In this section, we present a complete example of the hypothesis-testing process and discuss how the results from a hypothesis test are presented in a research report. For purposes of demonstration, the following scenario is used to provide a concrete background for the hypothesis-testing process.

EXAMPLE 8.2

Alcohol appears to be involved in a variety of birth defects, including low birth weight and retarded growth. A researcher would like to investigate the effect of prenatal alcohol exposure on birth weight. A random sample of $n = 16$ pregnant rats is obtained. The mother rats are given daily doses of alcohol. At birth, one pup is selected from each litter to produce a sample of $n = 16$ newborn rats. The average weight for the sample is $M = 15$ grams. The researcher would like to compare the sample with the general population of rats. It is known that regular newborn rats (not exposed to alcohol) have an average weight of $\mu = 18$ grams. The distribution of weights is normal with $\sigma = 4$. Figure 8.7 shows the overall research situation. Notice that the researcher's question concerns the unknown population that is exposed to alcohol. Also notice that we have a sample representing the unknown population, and we have a hypothesis about the unknown population mean. Specifically, the null hypothesis says that the alcohol has no effect and the unknown mean is still $\mu = 18$. The goal of the hypothesis test is to determine whether the sample data are compatible with the hypothesis.

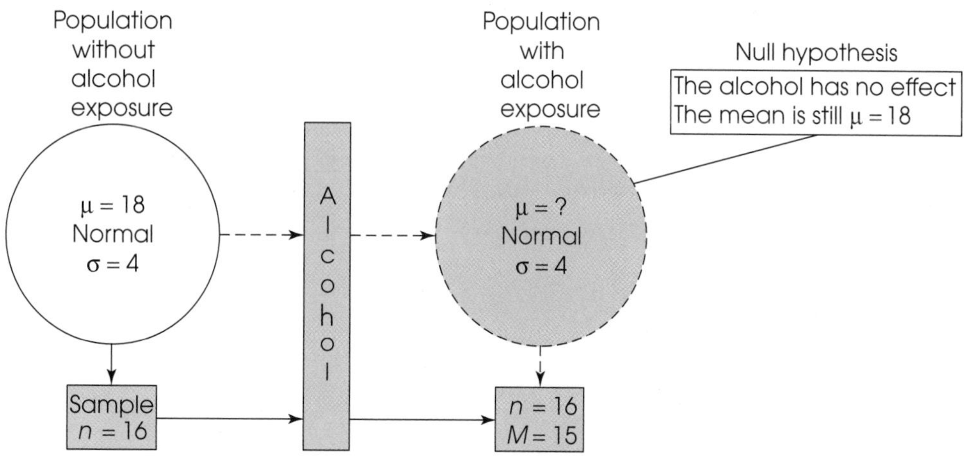

FIGURE 8.7

The structure of a research study to determine whether prenatal alcohol affects birth weight. A sample is selected from the original population and is exposed to alcohol. The question is what would happen if the entire population were exposed to alcohol. The treated sample provides information about the unknown treated population.

The following steps outline the hypothesis test that evaluates the effect of alcohol exposure on birth weight.

STEP 1 *State the hypotheses, and select the alpha level.* Both hypotheses concern the unknown population that is exposed to alcohol (the population on the right-hand side of Figure 8.7). The null hypothesis states that exposure to alcohol has no effect on birth weight. Thus, the population of rats with alcohol exposure should have the same mean birth weight as the regular, unexposed rats. In symbols,

H_0: $\mu_{\text{alcohol exposure}} = 18$ (Even with alcohol exposure, the rats still average 18 grams at birth.)

The alternative hypothesis states that alcohol exposure does affect birth weight, so the exposed population should be different from the regular rats. In symbols,

H_1: $\mu_{\text{alcohol exposure}} \neq 18$ (Alcohol exposure will change birth weight.)

Notice that both hypotheses concern the unknown population. For this test, we will use an alpha level of $\alpha = .05$. That is, we are taking a 5% risk of committing a Type I error.

STEP 2 *Set the decision criteria by locating the critical region.* By definition, the critical region consists of outcomes that are very unlikely if the null hypothesis is true. To locate the critical region we go through a three-stage process that is portrayed in Figure 8.8. We begin with the null hypothesis, which states that the alcohol has no effect on newborn rats. If H_0 is true, the population treated with alcohol is the same as the original population: that is, a normal distribution with $\mu = 18$ and $\sigma = 4$. Next, we consider all

FIGURE 8.8

Locating the critical region as a three-step process. You begin with the population of scores that is predicted by the null hypothesis. Then, you construct the distribution of sample means for the sample size that is being used. The distribution of sample means corresponds to all the possible outcomes that could be obtained if H_0 is true. Finally, you use z-scores to separate the extreme outcomes (as defined by the alpha level) from the high-probability outcomes. The extreme values determine the critical region.

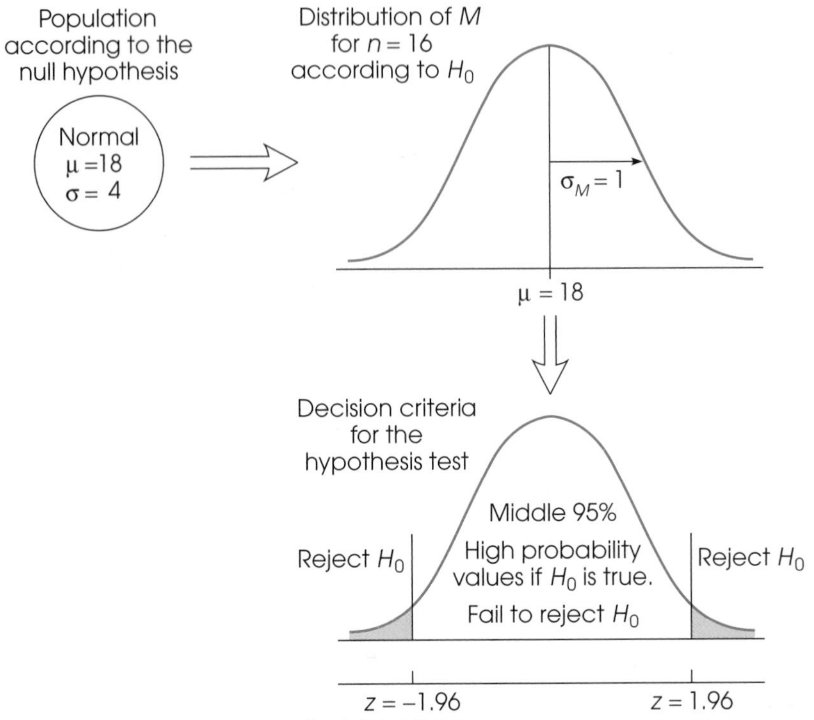

the possible outcomes for a sample of $n = 16$ newborn rats. This is the distribution of sample means for $n = 16$. For this example, the distribution of sample means is normal, is centered at $\mu = 18$ (according to H_0), and has a standard error of $\sigma_M = \frac{4}{\sqrt{16}} = 1$.

Finally, we use the distribution of sample means to identify the critical region, which consists of those outcomes that are very unlikely if the null hypothesis is true. With $\alpha = .05$, the critical region consists of the extreme 5% of the distribution. As we saw earlier, for any normal distribution, z-scores of $z = \pm1.96$ separate the middle 95% from the extreme 5% (a proportion of 0.0250 in each tail). Thus, we have identified the sample means that, according to the null hypothesis, are very unlikely to occur. It is the unlikely sample means, those with z-score values beyond ±1.96, that form the critical region for the test. If we obtain a sample mean that is in the critical region, we conclude that the sample is not compatible with the null hypothesis and we reject H_0.

STEP 3 *Collect the data, and compute the test statistic.* At this point, we would select one newborn pup from each of the $n = 16$ mothers that received alcohol during pregnancy. The birth weight is recorded for each pup and the sample mean is computed. For this example, we obtained a sample mean of $M = 15$ grams. The sample mean is then converted to a z-score, which is our test statistic.

$$z = \frac{M - \mu}{\sigma_M} = \frac{15 - 18}{1} = \frac{-3}{1} = -3.00$$

STEP 4 *Make a decision.* The z-score computed in step 3 has a value of -3.00, which is beyond the boundary of -1.96. Therefore, the sample mean is located in the critical region. This is a very unlikely outcome if the null hypothesis is true, so our decision is to reject the null hypothesis. In addition to this statistical decision concerning the null hypothesis, it is customary to state a conclusion about the results of the research study. For this example, we conclude that prenatal exposure to alcohol does have a significant effect on birth weight.

IN THE LITERATURE

REPORTING THE RESULTS OF THE STATISTICAL TEST

A special jargon and notational system are used in published reports of hypothesis tests. When you are reading a scientific journal, for example, you typically are not told explicitly that the researcher evaluated the data using a z-score as a test statistic with an alpha level of .05. Nor are you told that "the null hypothesis is rejected." Instead, you see a statement such as:

> The treatment with alcohol had a significant effect on the birth weight of newborn rats, $z = 3.00$, $p < .05$.

Let us examine this statement, piece by piece. First, what is meant by the word *significant*? In statistical tests, a *significant* result means that the null hypothesis has been rejected, which means that the result is very unlikely to have occurred merely by chance. For this example, the null hypothesis stated that the alcohol has no effect, however the data clearly indicate that the alcohol did have an effect. Specifically, it is very unlikely that the data would have been obtained if the alcohol did not have an effect.

DEFINITION

A result is said to be **significant,** or **statistically significant,** if it is very unlikely to occur when the null hypothesis is true. That is, the result is sufficient to reject the null hypothesis. Thus, a treatment has a significant effect if the decision from the hypothesis test is to reject H_0.

Next, what is the meaning of $z = 3.00$? The z indicates that a z-score was used as the test statistic to evaluate the sample data and that its value is 3.00. Finally, what is meant by $p < .05$? This part of the statement is a conventional way of specifying the alpha level that was used for the hypothesis test. It also acknowledges the possibility (and the probability) of a Type I error. Specifically, the researcher is reporting that the treatment had an effect but admits that this could be a false report. That is, it is possible that the sample mean was in the critical region even though the alcohol had no effect. However, the probability (p) of obtaining a sample mean in the critical region is extremely small (less than .05) if there is no treatment effect.

In circumstances in which the statistical decision is to *fail to reject* H_0, the report might state that.

> There was no evidence that the alcohol had an effect on birth weight, $z = 1.30$, $p > .05$.

The APA style does not use a leading zero in a probability value that refers to a level of significance.

In that case, we would be saying that the obtained result, $z = 1.30$, is not unusual (not in the critical region) and that it has a relatively high probability of occurring (greater than .05) even if the null hypothesis is true and there is no treatment effect.

Sometimes students become confused trying to differentiate between $p < .05$ and $p > .05$. Remember that you reject the null hypothesis with extreme, low-probability values, located in the critical region in the tails of the distribution. Thus, a significant result that rejects the null hypothesis corresponds to $p < .05$ (Figure 8.9).

When a hypothesis test is conducted using a computer program, the printout often includes not only a *z*-score value but also an exact value for *p*, the probability that the result occurred without any treatment effect. In this case, researchers are encouraged to report the exact *p* value instead of using the less-than or greater-than notation. For example, a research report might state that the treatment effect was significant, with $z = 2.45$, $p = .0142$. When using exact values for *p*, however, you must still satisfy the traditional criterion for significance; specifically, the *p* value must be smaller than .05 to be considered statistically significant. Remember: The *p* value is the probability that the result would occur if H_0 were true (without any treatment effect), which is also the probability of a Type I error. It is essential that this probability be very small.

FACTORS THAT INFLUENCE A HYPOTHESIS TEST

The final decision in a hypothesis test is determined by the value obtained for the *z*-score statistic. If the *z*-score is large enough to be in the critical region, then we reject the null hypothesis and conclude that there is a significant treatment effect. Otherwise, we fail to reject H_0 and conclude that the treatment does not have a significant effect. The most obvious factor influencing the size of the *z*-score is the difference between the sample mean and the hypothesized population mean from H_0. A big mean difference indicates that the treated sample is noticeably different from the untreated population and usually supports a conclusion that the treatment effect is significant. In addition to the mean difference, however, there are other factors that help determine whether the *z*-score is large enough to reject H_0. In this section we examine two factors that can influence the outcome of a hypothesis test.

1. The variability of the scores, which is measured by either the standard deviation or the variance. The variability influences the size of the standard error in the denominator of the *z*-score.
2. The number of scores in the sample. This value also influences the size of the standard error in the denominator.

We use the research study from Example 8.2, shown in Figure 8.7, to examine each of these factors. The study used a sample of $n = 16$ newborn rats and concluded that alcohol has a significant effect on birth weight, $z = -3.00$, $p < .05$.

FIGURE 8.9

Sample means that fall in the critical region (shaded areas) have a probability *less than* alpha ($p < \alpha$). In this case, H_0 should be rejected. Sample means that do not fall in the critical region have a probability *greater than* alpha ($p > \alpha$).

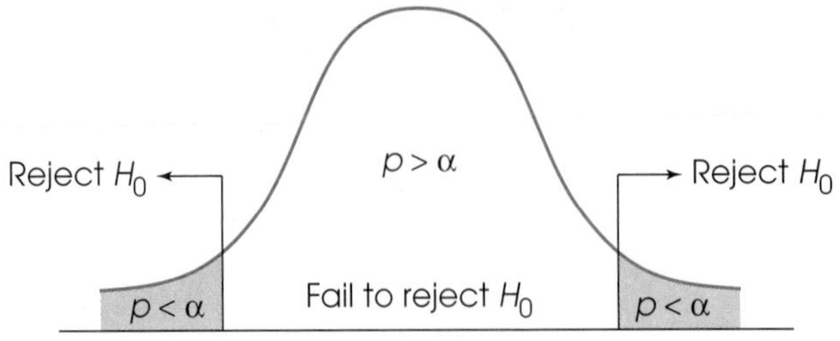

The variability of the scores In Chapter 4 (p. 124) we noted that high variability can make it very difficult to see any clear patterns in the results from a research study. In a hypothesis test, higher variability can reduce the chances of finding a significant treatment effect. For the study in Figure 8.7, the standard deviation is $\sigma = 4$. With a sample of $n = 16$, this produced a standard error of $\sigma_M = 1$ point and a significant z-score of $z = -300$. Now consider what happens if the standard deviation is increased to $\sigma = 12$. With the increased variability, the standard error becomes $\sigma_M = 12/\sqrt{16} = 3$ points. Using the same 3-points mean difference from the original example the new z-score becomes

$$z = \frac{M - \mu}{\sigma_M} = \frac{15 - 18}{3} = \frac{-3}{3} = -1.00$$

The z-score is no longer beyond the critical boundary of 1.96, so the statistical decision is to fail to reject the null hypothesis. The increased variability means that the sample data are no longer sufficient to conclude that the treatment has a significant effect. In general, increasing the variability of the scores produces a larger standard error and a smaller value (closer to zero) for the z-score. If other factors are held constant, then the larger the variability, the lower the likelihood of finding a significant treatment effect.

The number of scores in the sample The second factor that influences the outcome of a hypothesis test is the number of scores in the sample. The study in Figure 8.7 used a sample of $n = 16$ rats obtained a standard error of $\sigma_M = 4/\sqrt{16} = 1$ point and a significant z-score of $z = -3.00$. Now consider what happens if we increase the sample size to $n = 64$ rats. With $n = 64$, the standard error becomes $\sigma_M = 4/\sqrt{64} = 0.5$ points, and the z-score becomes

$$z = \frac{M - \mu}{\sigma_M} = \frac{15 - 18}{0.5} = \frac{-3}{0.5} = -6.00$$

Increasing the sample size from $n = 16$ to $n = 64$ has doubled the size of the z-score. In general, increasing the number of scores in the sample produces a smaller standard error and a larger value for the z-score. If all other factors are held constant, the larger the sample size, the greater the likelihood of finding a significant treatment effect. In simple terms, finding a 3-point treatment effect with large sample is more convincing than finding a 3-point effect with a small sample.

ASSUMPTIONS FOR HYPOTHESIS TESTS WITH *z*-SCORES

The mathematics used for a hypothesis test are based on a set of assumptions. When these assumptions are satisfied, you can be confident that the test produces a justified conclusion. However, if the assumptions are not satisfied, then the hypothesis test may be compromised. In practice, researchers are not overly concerned with the assumptions underlying a hypothesis test because the tests usually work well even when the assumptions are violated. However, you should be aware of the fundamental conditions that are associated with each type of statistical test to ensure that the test is being used appropriately. The assumptions for hypothesis tests with z-scores are summarized as follows.

Random sampling It is assumed that the participants used in the study were selected randomly. Remember, we wish to generalize our findings from the sample to the population. Therefore, the sample must be representative of the population from which it has been drawn. Random sampling helps to ensure that it is representative.

Independent observations The values in the sample must consist of *independent* observations. In everyday terms, two observations are independent if there is no consistent, predictable relationship between the first observation and the second. More precisely, two events (or observations) are independent if the occurrence of the first event has no effect on the probability of the second event. Specific examples of independence and non-independence are examined in Box 8.1. Usually, this assumption is satisfied by using a *random* sample, which also helps to ensure that the sample is representative of the population and that the results can be generalized to the population.

The value of σ is unchanged by the treatment A critical part of the z-score formula in a hypothesis test is the standard error, σ_M. To compute the value for the standard error, we must know the sample size (n) and the population standard deviation (σ). In a hypothesis test, however, the sample comes from an *unknown* population (see Figures 8.3 and 8.7). If the population is really unknown, it would suggest that we do not know the standard deviation and, therefore, we cannot calculate the standard error. To solve this dilemma, we have made an assumption. Specifically, we assume that the standard deviation for the unknown population (after treatment) is the same as it was for the population before treatment.

BOX 8.1 INDEPENDENT OBSERVATIONS

Independent observations are a basic requirement for nearly all hypothesis tests. The critical concern is that each observation or measurement is not influenced by any other observation or measurement. An example of independent observations is the set of outcomes obtained in a series of coin tosses. Assuming that the coin is balanced, each toss has a 50–50 chance of coming up either heads or tails. More important, each toss is *independent* of the tosses that came before. On the fifth toss, for example, there is a 50% chance of heads no matter what happened on the previous four tosses; the coin does not remember what happened earlier and is not influenced by the past. (*Note:* Many people fail to believe in the independence of events. For example, after a series of four tails in a row, it is tempting to think that the probability of heads must increase because the coin is overdue to come up heads. This is a mistake, called the "gambler's fallacy." Remember that the coin does not know what happened on the preceding tosses and cannot be influenced by previous outcomes.)

In most research situations, the requirement for independent observations is satisfied by using a random sample of separate, unrelated individuals. Thus, the measurement obtained for each individual is not influenced by other participants in the study. The following two situations demonstrate circumstances in which the observations are *not* independent.

1. A researcher is interested in examining television preferences for children. To obtain a sample of $n = 20$ children, the researcher selects 4 children from family A, 3 children from family B, 5 children from family C, 2 children from family D, and 6 children from family E.

   It should be obvious that the researcher does *not* have 20 independent observations. Within each family, the children probably share television preference (at least, they watch the same shows). Thus, the response, for each child is likely to be related to the responses of his or her siblings.

2. The principle of independent observations is violated if the sample is obtained using *sampling without replacement.* For example, if you are selecting from a group of 20 potential participants, each individual has a 1 in 20 chance of being selected first. After the first person is selected, however, there are only 19 people remaining and the probability of being selected changes to 1 in 19. Because the probability of the second selection depends on the first, the two selections are not independent.

Actually, this assumption is the consequence of a more general assumption that is part of many statistical procedures. This general assumption states that the effect of the treatment is to add a constant amount to (or subtract a constant amount from) every score in the population. You should recall that adding (or subtracting) a constant changes the mean but has no effect on the standard deviation. You also should note that this assumption is a theoretical ideal. In actual experiments, a treatment generally does not show a perfect and consistent additive effect.

Normal sampling distribution To evaluate hypotheses with z-scores, we have used the unit normal table to identify the critical region. This table can be used only if the distribution of sample means is normal.

LEARNING CHECK

1. After years of teaching driver's education, an instructor knows that students hit an average of $\mu = 10.5$ orange cones while driving the obstacle course in their final exam. The distribution of run-over cones is approximately normal with a standard deviation of $\sigma = 4.8$. To test a theory about text messaging and driving, the instructor recruits a sample of $n = 16$ student drivers to attempt the obstacle course while sending a text message. The individuals in this sample hit an average of $M = 15.9$ cones.
   a. Do the data indicate that texting has a significant effect on driving? Test with $\alpha = .01$.
   b. Write a sentence describing the outcome of the hypothesis test as it would appear in a research report.
2. In a research report, the term *significant* is used when the null hypothesis is rejected. (True or false?)
3. In a research report, the results of a hypothesis test include the phrase "$z = 3.15$, $p < .01$." This means that the test failed to reject the null hypothesis. (True or false?)
4. If other factors are held constant, increasing the size of the sample increases the likelihood of rejecting the null hypothesis. (True or false?)
5. If other factors are held constant, are you more likely to reject the null hypothesis with a standard deviation of $\sigma = 2$ or with $\sigma = 10$?

ANSWERS

1. **a.** With $\alpha = .01$, the critical region consists of z-scores in the tails beyond $z = \pm 2.58$. For these data, the standard error is 1.2 and $z = 4.50$. Reject the null hypothesis and conclude that texting has a significant effect on driving.
   b. Texting while driving had a significant effect on the number of cones hit by the participants, $z = 4.50$, $p < .01$.
2. True.
3. False. The probability is *less than* .01, which means it is very unlikely that the result occurred without any treatment effect. In this case, the data are in the critical region, and H_0 is rejected.
4. True. A larger sample produces a smaller standard error, which leads to a larger z-score.
5. $\sigma = 2$. A smaller standard deviation produces a smaller standard error, which leads to larger z-score.

8.4 DIRECTIONAL (ONE-TAILED) HYPOTHESIS TESTS

The hypothesis-testing procedure presented in Section 8.3 is the standard, or *two-tailed,* test format. The term *two-tailed* comes from the fact that the critical region is divided between the two tails of the distribution. This format is by far the most widely accepted procedure for hypothesis testing. Nonetheless, there is an alternative that is discussed in this section.

Usually a researcher begins an experiment with a specific prediction about the direction of the treatment effect. For example, a special training program is expected to *increase* student performance, or alcohol consumption is expected to *slow* reaction times. In these situations, it is possible to state the statistical hypotheses in a manner that incorporates the directional prediction into the statement of H_0 and H_1. The result is a directional test, or what commonly is called a *one-tailed test.*

DEFINITION

In a **directional hypothesis test,** or a **one-tailed test,** the statistical hypotheses (H_0 and H_1) specify either an increase or a decrease in the population mean. That is, they make a statement about the direction of the effect.

The following example demonstrates the elements of a one-tailed hypothesis test.

EXAMPLE 8.3 Earlier, in Example 8.1, we discussed a research study that examined the effect of antioxidants (such as those found in blueberries) on the cognitive skills of elderly adults. In the study, each participant in a sample of $n = 25$ received a blueberry supplement every day for 6 months and then was given a standardized test to measure cognitive skill. For the general population of elderly adults (without any supplement), the test scores form a normal distribution with a mean of $\mu = 80$ and a standard deviation of $\sigma = 20$. For this example, the expected effect is that the blueberry supplement will improve cognitive performance. If the researcher obtains a sample mean of $M = 87$ for the $n = 25$ participants, is the result sufficient to conclude that the supplement really works?

THE HYPOTHESIS FOR A DIRECTIONAL TEST

Because a specific direction is expected for the treatment effect, it is possible for the researcher to perform a directional test. The first step (and the most critical step) is to state the statistical hypotheses. Remember that the null hypothesis states that there is no treatment effect and the alternative hypothesis says that there is an effect. For this example, the predicted effect is that the blueberry supplement will increase test scores. Thus, the two hypotheses would state:

H_0: Test scores are not increased. (The treatment does not work.)

H_1: Test scores are increased. (The treatment works as predicted.)

To express directional hypotheses in symbols, it usually is easier to begin with the alternative hypothesis (H_1). Again, we know that the general population has an average test score of $\mu = 80$, and H_1 states that test scores will be increased by the blueberry supplement. Therefore, expressed in symbols, H_1 states,

H_1: $\mu > 80$ (With the supplement, the average score is greater than 80.)

The null hypothesis states that the supplement does not increase scores. In symbols,

H_0: $\mu \leq 80$ (With the supplement, the average score is not greater than 80.)

Note again that the two hypotheses are mutually exclusive and cover all of the possibilities.

THE CRITICAL REGION FOR DIRECTIONAL TESTS

The critical region is defined by sample outcomes that are very unlikely to occur if the null hypothesis is true (that is, if the treatment has no effect). Earlier (p. 238), we noted that the critical region can also be defined in terms of sample values that provide *convincing evidence* that the treatment really does have an effect. For a directional test, the concept of "convincing evidence" is the simplest way to determine the location of the critical region. We begin with all of the possible sample means that could be obtained if the null hypothesis is true. This is the distribution of sample means and it is normal (because the population of test scores is normal), has an expected value of $\mu = 80$ (from H_0), and, for a sample of $n = 25$, has a standard error of $\sigma_M = 20/\sqrt{25} = 4$. The distribution is shown in Figure 8.10.

If the prediction is that the treatment will produce a *decrease* in scores, then the critical region is located entirely in the left-hand tail of the distribution.

For this example, the treatment is expected to increase test scores. If untreated adults average $\mu = 80$ on the test, then a sample mean that is substantially more than 80 would provide convincing evidence that the treatment worked. Thus, the critical region is located entirely in the right-hand tail of the distribution corresponding to sample means much greater than $\mu = 80$ (see Figure 8.10). Because the critical region is contained in one tail of the distribution, a directional test is commonly called a *one-tailed* test. Also note that the proportion specified by the alpha level is not divided between two tails, but rather is contained entirely in one tail. Using $\alpha = .05$ for example, the whole 5% is located in one tail. In this case, the z-score boundary for the critical region is $z = 1.65$, which is obtained by looking up a proportion of .05 in column C (the tail) of the unit normal table.

Notice that a directional (one-tailed) test requires two changes in the step-by-step hypothesis-testing procedure.

1. In the first step of the hypothesis test, the directional prediction is incorporated into the statement of the hypotheses.
2. In the second step of the process, the critical region is located entirely in one tail of the distribution.

FIGURE 8.10

Critical region for Example 8.3.

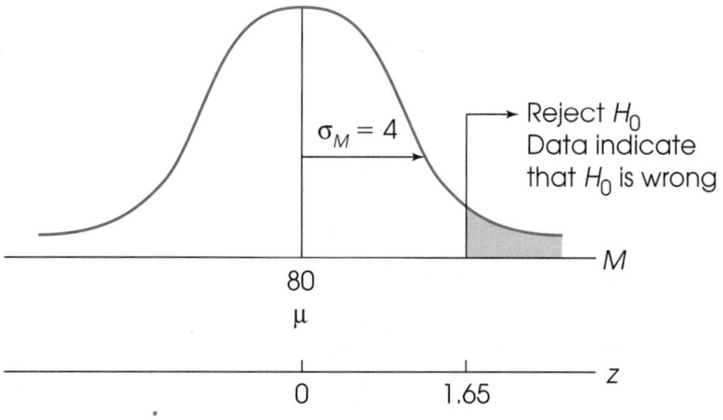

After these two changes, the remainder of a one-tailed test proceeds exactly the same as a regular two-tailed test. Specifically, you calculate the z-score statistic and then make a decision about H_0 depending on whether the z-score is in the critical region.

For this example, the researcher obtained a mean of $M = 87$ for the 25 participants who received the blueberry supplement. This sample mean corresponds to a z-score of

$$z = \frac{M - \mu}{\sigma_M} = \frac{87 - 80}{4} = \frac{7}{4} = 1.75$$

A z-score of $z = 1.75$ is in the critical region for a one-tailed test (see Figure 8.10). This is a very unlikely outcome if H_0 is true. Therefore, we reject the null hypothesis and conclude that the blueberry supplement produces a significant increase in cognitive performance scores. In the literature, this result would be reported as follows:

> The supplement produced a significant increase in scores, $z = 1.75$, $p < .05$, one tailed.

Note that the report clearly acknowledges that a one-tailed test was used.

COMPARISON OF ONE-TAILED VERSUS TWO-TAILED TESTS

The general goal of hypothesis testing is to determine whether a particular treatment has any effect on a population. The test is performed by selecting a sample, administering the treatment to the sample, and then comparing the result with the original population. If the treated sample is noticeably different from the original population, then we conclude that the treatment has an effect, and we reject H_0. On the other hand, if the treated sample is still similar to the original population, then we conclude that there is no convincing evidence for a treatment effect, and we fail to reject H_0. The critical factor in this decision is the *size of the difference* between the treated sample and the original population. A large difference is evidence that the treatment worked; a small difference is not sufficient to say that the treatment had any effect.

The major distinction between one-tailed and two-tailed tests is the criteria that they use for rejecting H_0. A one-tailed test allows you to reject the null hypothesis when the difference between the sample and the population is relatively small, provided that the difference is in the specified direction. A two-tailed test, on the other hand, requires a relatively large difference independent of direction. This point is illustrated in the following example.

EXAMPLE 8.4

Consider again the one-tailed test evaluating the effect of an antioxidant supplement. If we had used a standard two-tailed test, the hypotheses would be

H_0: $\mu = 80$ (The supplement has no effect on test scores.)

H_1: $\mu \neq 80$ (The supplement does have an effect on test scores.)

For a two-tailed test with $\alpha = .05$, the critical region consists of z-scores beyond ± 1.96. The data from Example 8.3 produced a sample mean of $M = 87$ and $z = 1.75$. For the two-tailed test, this z-score is not in the critical region, and we conclude that the supplement does not have a significant effect.

With the two-tailed test in Example 8.4, the 7-point difference between the sample mean and the hypothesized population mean ($M = 87$ and $\mu = 80$) is not big enough to reject the null hypothesis. However, with the one-tailed test introduced in

Example 8.3, the same 7-point difference is large enough to reject H_0 and conclude that the treatment had a significant effect.

All researchers agree that one-tailed tests are different from two-tailed tests. However, there are several ways to interpret the difference. One group of researchers contends that a two-tailed test is more rigorous and, therefore, more convincing than a one-tailed test. Remember that the two-tailed test demands more evidence to reject H_0 and thus provides a stronger demonstration that a treatment effect has occurred.

Other researchers feel that one-tailed tests are preferable because they are more sensitive. That is, a relatively small treatment effect may be significant with a one-tailed test but fail to reach significance with a two-tailed test. Also, there is the argument that one-tailed tests are more precise because they test hypotheses about a specific directional effect instead of an indefinite hypothesis about a general effect.

In general, two-tailed tests should be used in research situations when there is no strong directional expectation or when there are two competing predictions. For example, a two-tailed test would be appropriate for a study in which one theory predicts an increase in scores but another theory predicts a decrease. One-tailed tests should be used only in situations in which the directional prediction is made before the research is conducted and there is a strong justification for making the directional prediction. In particular, if a two-tailed test fails to reach significance, you should never follow up with a one-tailed test as a second attempt to salvage a significant result for the same data.

LEARNING CHECK

1. If a researcher predicts that a treatment will increase scores, then the critical region for a one-tailed test would be located in the right-hand tail of the distribution. (True or false?)
2. If the sample data are sufficient to reject the null hypothesis for a one-tailed test, then the same data would also reject H_0 for a two-tailed test. (True or false?)
3. A researcher obtains $z = 2.43$ for a hypothesis test. Using $\alpha = .01$, the researcher should reject the null hypothesis for a one-tailed test but fail to reject for a two-tailed test. (True or false?)

ANSWERS

1. True. A large sample mean, in the right-hand tail, would indicate that the treatment worked as predicted.
2. False. Because a two-tailed test requires a larger mean difference, it is possible for a sample to be significant for a one-tailed test but not for a two-tailed test.
3. True. The one-tailed critical value is $z = 2.33$ and the two-tailed value is $z = 2.58$.

8.5 CONCERNS ABOUT HYPOTHESIS TESTING: MEASURING EFFECT SIZE

Although hypothesis testing is the most commonly used technique for evaluating and interpreting research data, a number of scientists have expressed a variety of concerns about the hypothesis testing procedure (for example, see Loftus, 1996; Hunter, 1997; and Killeen, 2005).

There are two serious limitations with using a hypothesis test to establish the significance of a treatment effect. The first concern is that the focus of a hypothesis test is on the data rather than the hypothesis. Specifically, when the null hypothesis is rejected, we are actually making a strong probability statement about the sample data, not about the null hypothesis. A significant result permits the following conclusion: "This specific sample mean is very unlikely ($p < .05$) if the null hypothesis is true." Note that the conclusion does not make any definite statement about the probability of the null hypothesis being true or false. The fact that the data are very unlikely *suggests* that the null hypothesis is also very unlikely, but we do not have any solid grounds for making a probability statement about the null hypothesis. Specifically, you cannot conclude that the probability of the null hypothesis being true is less than 5% simply because you rejected the null hypothesis with $\alpha = .05$ (see Box 8.2).

A second concern is that demonstrating a *significant* treatment effect does not necessarily indicate a *substantial* treatment effect. In particular, statistical significance

BOX 8.2 A FLAW IN THE LOGIC OF HYPOTHESIS TESTING

Suppose that you do a hypothesis test and reject the null hypothesis with $\alpha = .05$. Can you conclude that there is a 5% probability that you are making a Type I error? Can you also conclude that there is a 95% probability that your decision is correct and the treatment does have an effect? For both questions, the answer is no.

The problem is that the probabilities for a hypothesis test are well defined only when the null hypothesis is true. Specifically, a hypothesis test using $\alpha = .05$ is structured so that the error rate is $p < .05$ and the accuracy rate is $p \geq .95$ *if the null hypothesis is true*. If H_0 is false, however, these probabilities start to fall apart. When there is a treatment effect (H_0 is false), the probability that a hypothesis test will detect it and reject H_0 depends on a variety of factors. For example, if the treatment effect is very small, then a hypothesis test is unlikely to detect it. With a large treatment effect, the hypothesis test is more likely to detect it and the probability of rejecting H_0 increases. Thus, whenever there is a treatment effect (H_0 is false), it becomes impossible to define precisely the probability of rejecting the null hypothesis.

Most researchers begin research studies believing that there is a good likelihood that the null hypothesis is false and there really is a treatment effect. They are hoping that the study will provide evidence of the effect so they can convince their colleagues. Thus, most research begins with some probability that the null hypothesis is false. For the sake of argument, let's assume that there is an 80% probability that the null hypothesis is true.

p(there is no treatment effect—H_0 is true) $= 0.80$ and
p(there is a treatment effect—H_0 is false) $= 0.20$

In this situation, suppose that 125 researchers are all doing hypothesis tests with $\alpha = .05$. Of these researchers, 80% ($n = 100$) are testing a true H_0. For these researchers, the probability of rejecting the null hypothesis (and making a Type I error) is $\alpha = .05$. Therefore, the 100 hypothesis tests for this group should produce, at most, 5 tests that reject H_0.

Meanwhile, the other 20% of the researchers ($n = 25$) are testing a false null hypothesis. For this group, the probability of rejecting the null hypothesis is unknown. For the sake of argument, however, let's assume that the probability of detecting the treatment effect and correctly rejecting H_0 is 60%. This means that the 25 hypothesis tests should result in 15 tests (60%) that reject H_0 and 10 that fail to reject H_0.

Notice that there could be as many as 20 hypothesis tests that reject the null hypothesis (5 from the first group and 15 from the second group). Thus, a total of 20 researchers will find a statistically significant effect. Of these 20 "significant" results, however, the 5 from the first group are making a Type I error. In this case, the probability of a Type I error is 5 out of 20, or $p = 5/20 = .25$, which is five times greater than the alpha level of .05.

Based on this kind of argument, many scientists suspect that a large number of the results and conclusions published in research journals are simply wrong. Specifically, the Type I error rate in published research is almost certainly higher than the alpha levels used in the hypothesis tests that support the results (Siegfried, 2010).

does not provide any real information about the absolute size of a treatment effect. Instead, the hypothesis test has simply established that the results obtained in the research study are very unlikely to have occurred if there is no treatment effect. The hypothesis test reaches this conclusion by (1) calculating the standard error, which measures how much difference is reasonable to expect between M and μ, and (2) demonstrating that the obtained mean difference is substantially bigger than the standard error.

Notice that the test is making a *relative* comparison: the size of the treatment effect is being evaluated relative to the standard error. If the standard error is very small, then the treatment effect can also be very small and still be large enough to be significant. Thus, a significant effect does not necessarily mean a big effect.

The idea that a hypothesis test evaluates the relative size of a treatment effect, rather than the absolute size, is illustrated in the following example.

EXAMPLE 8.5

We begin with a population of scores that forms a normal distribution with $\mu = 50$ and $\sigma = 10$. A sample is selected from the population and a treatment is administered to the sample. After treatment, the sample mean is found to be $M = 51$. Does this sample provide evidence of a statistically significant treatment effect?

Although there is only a 1-point difference between the sample mean and the original population mean, the difference may be enough to be significant. In particular, the outcome of the hypothesis test depends on the sample size.

For example, with a sample of $n = 25$ the standard error is

$$\sigma_M = \frac{\sigma}{\sqrt{n}} = \frac{10}{\sqrt{25}} = \frac{10}{5} = 2.00$$

and the z-score for $M = 51$ is

$$z = \frac{M - \mu}{\sigma_M} = \frac{51 - 50}{2} = \frac{1}{2} = 0.50$$

This z-score fails to reach the critical boundary of $z = 1.96$, so we fail to reject the null hypothesis. In this case, the 1-point difference between M and μ is not significant because it is being evaluated relative to a standard error of 2 points.

Now consider the outcome with a sample of $n = 400$. With a larger sample, the standard error is

$$\sigma_M = \frac{\sigma}{\sqrt{n}} = \frac{10}{\sqrt{400}} = \frac{10}{20} = 0.50$$

and the z-score for $M = 51$ is

$$z = \frac{M - \mu}{\sigma_M} = \frac{51 - 50}{0.5} = \frac{1}{0.5} = 2.00$$

Now the z-score is beyond the 1.96 boundary, so we reject the null hypothesis and conclude that there is a significant effect. In this case, the 1-point difference between M and μ is considered statistically significant because it is being evaluated relative to a standard error of only 0.5 points.

The point of Example 8.5 is that a small treatment effect can still be statistically significant. If the sample size is large enough, any treatment effect, no matter how small, can be enough for us to reject the null hypothesis.

MEASURING EFFECT SIZE

As noted in the previous section, one concern with hypothesis testing is that a hypothesis test does not really evaluate the absolute size of a treatment effect. To correct this problem, it is recommended that whenever researchers report a statistically significant effect, they also provide a report of the effect size (see the guidelines presented by L. Wilkinson and the APA Task Force on Statistical Inference, 1999). Therefore, as we present different hypothesis tests we also present different options for measuring and reporting *effect size.*

DEFINITION

A measure of **effect size** is intended to provide a measurement of the absolute magnitude of a treatment effect, independent of the size of the sample(s) being used.

One of the simplest and most direct methods for measuring effect size is *Cohen's d.* Cohen (1988) recommended that effect size can be standardized by measuring the mean difference in terms of the standard deviation. The resulting measure of effect size is computed as

$$\text{Cohen's } d = \frac{\text{mean difference}}{\text{standard deviation}} = \frac{\mu_{\text{treatment}} - \mu_{\text{no treatment}}}{\sigma} \tag{8.1}$$

For the z-score hypothesis test, the mean difference is determined by the difference between the population mean before treatment and the population mean after treatment. However, the population mean after treatment is unknown. Therefore, we must use the mean for the treated sample in its place. Remember, the sample mean is expected to be representative of the population mean and provides the best measure of the treatment effect. Thus, the actual calculations are really estimating the value of Cohen's d as follows:

Cohen's d measures the distance between two means and is typically reported as a positive number even when the formula produces a negative value.

$$\text{estimated Cohen's } d = \frac{\text{mean difference}}{\text{standard deviation}} = \frac{M_{\text{treatment}} - \mu_{\text{no treatment}}}{\sigma} \tag{8.2}$$

The standard deviation is included in the calculation to standardize the size of the mean difference in much the same way that z-scores standardize locations in a distribution. For example, a 15-point mean difference can be a relatively large treatment effect or a relatively small effect depending on the size of the standard deviation. This phenomenon is demonstrated in Figure 8.11. The top portion of the figure (part a) shows the results of a treatment that produces a 15-point mean difference in SAT scores; before treatment, the average SAT score is $\mu = 500$, and after treatment the average is 515. Notice that the standard deviation for SAT scores is $\sigma = 100$, so the 15-point difference appears to be small. For this example, Cohen's d is

$$\text{Cohen's } d = \frac{\text{mean difference}}{\text{standard deviation}} = \frac{15}{100} = 0.15$$

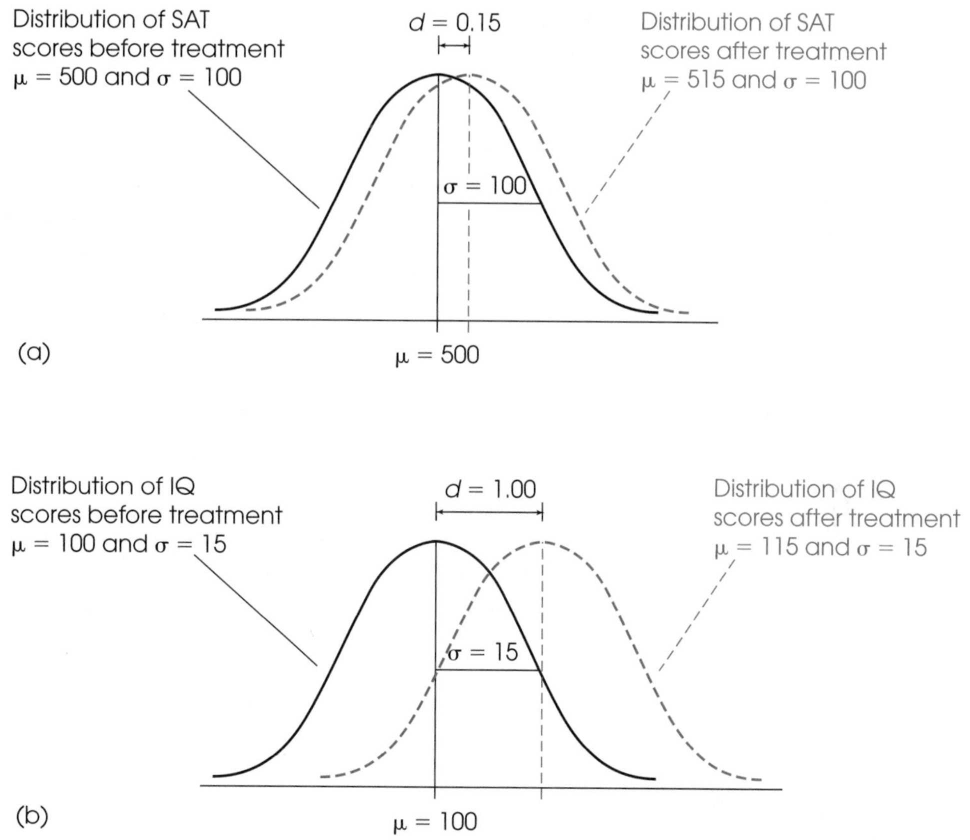

FIGURE 8.11

The appearance of a 15-point treatment effect in two different situations. In part (a), the standard deviation is $\sigma = 100$ and the 15-point effect is relatively small. In part (b), the standard deviation is $\sigma = 15$ and the 15-point effect is relatively large. Cohen's *d* uses the standard deviation to help measure effect size.

Now consider the treatment effect shown in Figure 8.11(b). This time, the treatment produces a 15-point mean difference in IQ scores; before treatment the average IQ is 100, and after treatment the average is 115. Because IQ scores have a standard deviation of $\sigma = 15$, the 15-point mean difference now appears to be large. For this example, Cohen's *d* is

$$\text{Cohen's } d = \frac{\text{mean difference}}{\text{standard deviation}} = \frac{15}{15} = 1.00$$

Notice that Cohen's *d* measures the size of the treatment effect in terms of the standard deviation. For example, a value of $d = 0.50$ indicates that the treatment changed the mean by half of a standard deviation; similarly, a value of $d = 1.00$ indicates that the size of the treatment effect is equal to one whole standard deviation. (See Box 8.3.)

Cohen (1988) also suggested criteria for evaluating the size of a treatment effect as shown in Table 8.2.

BOX 8.3 OVERLAPPING DISTRIBUTIONS

Figure 8.11(b) shows the results of a treatment with a Cohen's d of 1.00; that is, the effect of the treatment is to increase the mean by one full standard deviation. According to the guidelines in Table 8.2, a value of $d = 1.00$ is considered a large treatment effect. However, looking at the figure, you may get the impression that there really isn't that much difference between the distribution before treatment and the distribution after treatment. In particular, there is substantial overlap between the two distributions, so that many of the individuals who receive the treatment are not any different from the individuals who do not receive the treatment.

The overlap between distributions is a basic fact of life in most research situations; it is extremely rare for the scores after treatment to be *completely different* (no overlap) from the scores before treatment. Consider, for example, children's heights at different ages. Everyone knows that 8-year-old children are taller than 6-year-old children; on average, the difference is 3 or 4 inches. However, this does not mean that all 8-year-old children are taller than all 6-year-old children. In fact, there is considerable overlap between the two distributions, so that the tallest among the 6-year-old children are actually taller than most 8-year-old children. In fact, the height distributions for the two age groups would look a lot like the two distributions in Figure 8.10(b). Although there is a clear *mean difference* between the two distributions, there still can be substantial overlap.

Cohen's d measures the degree of separation between two distributions, and a separation of one standard deviation ($d = 1.00$) represents a large difference. Eight-year-old children really are bigger than 6-year-old children.

TABLE 8.2

Evaluating effect size with Cohen's *d*.

Magnitude of *d*	Evaluation of Effect Size
$d = 0.2$	Small effect (mean difference around 0.2 standard deviation)
$d = 0.5$	Medium effect (mean difference around 0.5 standard deviation)
$d = 0.8$	Large effect (mean difference around 0.8 standard deviation)

As one final demonstration of Cohen's d, consider the two hypothesis tests in Example 8.5. For each test, the original population had a mean of $\mu = 50$ with a standard deviation of $\sigma = 10$. For each test, the mean for the treated sample was $M = 51$. Although one test used a sample of $n = 25$ and the other test used a sample of $n = 400$, the sample size is not considered when computing Cohen's d. Therefore, both of the hypothesis tests would produce the same value:

$$\text{Cohen's } d = \frac{\text{mean difference}}{\text{standard deviation}} = \frac{15}{15} = 1.00$$

Notice that Cohen's d simply describes the size of the treatment effect and is not influenced by the number of scores in the sample. For both hypothesis tests, the original population mean was $\mu = 50$ and, after treatment, the sample mean was $M = 51$. Thus, treatment appears to have increased the scores by 1 point, which is equal to one-tenth of a standard deviation (Cohen's $d = 0.1$).

LEARNING CHECK

1. **a.** How does increasing sample size influence the outcome of a hypothesis test?
   b. How does increasing sample size influence the value of Cohen's *d*?

2. A researcher selects a sample from a population with $\mu = 45$ and $\sigma = 8$. A treatment is administered to the sample and, after treatment, the sample mean is found to be $M = 47$. Compute Cohen's *d* to measure the size of the treatment effect.

ANSWERS

1. **a.** Increasing sample size increases the likelihood of rejecting the null hypothesis.
   b. Cohen's *d* is not influenced at all by the sample size.

2. $d = 2/8 = 0.25$

8.6 STATISTICAL POWER

Instead of measuring effect size directly, an alternative approach to determining the size or strength of a treatment effect is to measure the power of the statistical test. The *power* of a test is defined as the probability that the test will reject the null hypothesis if the treatment really has an effect.

DEFINITION

The **power** of a statistical test is the probability that the test will correctly reject a false null hypothesis. That is, power is the probability that the test will identify a treatment effect if one really exists.

Whenever a treatment has an effect, there are only two possible outcomes for a hypothesis test: either fail to reject H_0 or reject H_0. Because there are only two possible outcomes, the probability for the first and the probability for the second must add up to 1.00. The first outcome, failing to reject H_0 when there is a real effect, was defined earlier (p. 245) as a Type II error with a probability identified as $p = \beta$. Therefore, the second outcome must have a probability of $1 - \beta$. However, the second outcome, rejecting H_0 when there is a real effect, is the power of the test. Thus, the power of a hypothesis test is equal to $1 - \beta$. In the examples that follow, we demonstrate the calculation of power for a hypothesis test; that is, the probability that the test will correctly reject the null hypothesis. At the same time, however, we are computing the probability that the test will result in a Type II error. For example, if the power of the test is 70% $(1 - \beta)$ then the probability of a Type II error must be 30% (β).

Researchers typically calculate power as a means of determining whether a research study is likely to be successful. Thus, researchers usually calculate the power of a hypothesis test *before* they actually conduct the research study. In this way, they can determine the probability that the results will be significant (reject H_0) before investing time and effort in the actual research. To calculate power, however, it is first necessary to make assumptions about a variety of factors that influence the outcome of a hypothesis test. Factors such as the sample size, the size of the treatment effect, and the value chosen for the alpha level can all influence a hypothesis test. The following example demonstrates the calculation of power for a specific research situation.

EXAMPLE 8.6

We start with a normal-shaped population with a mean of $\mu = 80$ and a standard deviation of $\sigma = 10$. A researcher plans to select a sample of $n = 25$ individuals from this population and administer a treatment to each individual. It is expected that the treatment will have an 8-point effect; that is, the treatment will add 8 points to each individual's score.

Figure 8.12 shows the original population distribution and two possible outcomes:

1. If the null hypothesis is true and there is no treatment effect.
2. If the researcher's expectation is correct and there is an 8-point effect.

The left-hand side of the figure shows what should happen according to the null hypothesis. In this case, the treatment has no effect and the population mean is still $\mu = 80$. On the right-hand side of the figure we show what would happen if the treatment has an 8-point effect. If the treatment adds 8 points to each person's score, then the population mean after treatment increases to $\mu = 88$.

Beneath each of the two populations, Figure 8.12 shows the distribution of sample means for $n = 25$. According to the null hypothesis, the sample means are centered

FIGURE 8.12

A demonstration of measuring power for a hypothesis test. The left-hand side shows the distribution of sample means that would occur if the null hypothesis is true. The critical region is defined for this distribution. The right-hand side shows the distribution of sample means that would be obtained if there were an 8-point treatment effect. Notice that if there is an 8-point effect, essentially all of the sample means would be in the critical region. Thus, the probability of rejecting H_0 (the power of the test) would be nearly 100% for an 8-point treatment effect.

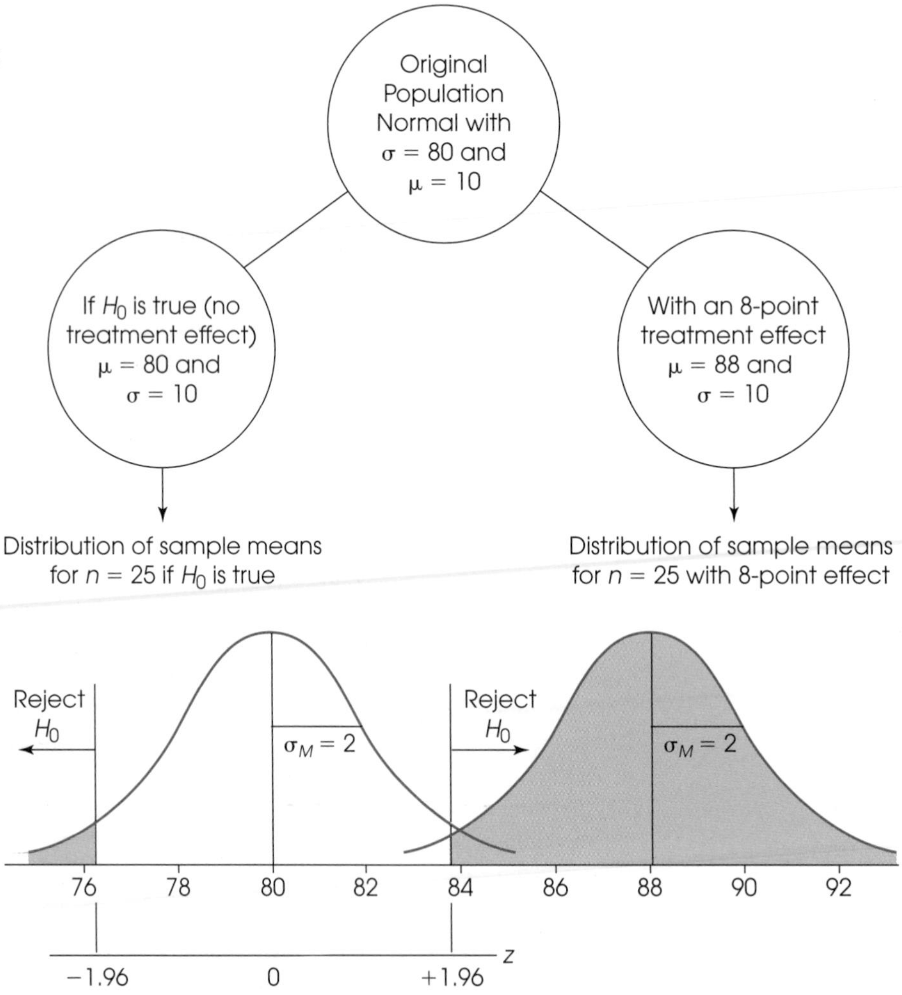

around $\mu = 80$. With an 8-point treatment effect, the sample means are centered around $\mu = 88$. Both distributions have a standard error of

$$\sigma_M = \frac{\sigma}{\sqrt{n}} = \frac{10}{\sqrt{25}} = \frac{10}{5} = 2$$

Notice that the distribution on the left shows all of the possible sample means if the null hypothesis is true. This is the distribution we use to locate the critical region for the hypothesis test. Using $\alpha = .05$, the critical region consists of extreme values in this distribution, specifically sample means beyond $z = 1.96$ or $z = -1.96$. These values are shown in Figure 8.12, and we have shaded all of the sample means located in the critical region.

Now turn your attention to the distribution on the right, which shows all of the possible sample means if there is an 8-point treatment effect. Notice that most of these sample means are located beyond the $z = 1.96$ boundary. This means that, if there is an 8-point treatment effect, you are almost guaranteed to obtain a sample mean in the critical region and reject the null hypothesis. Thus, the power of the test (the probability of rejecting H_0) is close to 100% if there is an 8-point treatment effect.

To calculate the exact value for the power of the test we must determine what portion of the distribution on the right-hand side is shaded. Thus, we must locate the exact boundary for the critical region, then find the probability value in the unit normal table. For the distribution on the left-hand side, the critical boundary of $z = +1.96$ corresponds to a location that is above $\mu = 80$ by a distance equal to

$$1.96\mu_M = 1.96(2) = 3.92 \text{ points}$$

Thus, the critical boundary of $z = +1.96$ corresponds to a sample mean of $M = 80 + 3.92 = 83.92$. Any sample mean greater than $M = 83.92$ is in the critical region and would lead to rejecting the null hypothesis. Next, we determine what proportion of the treated samples are greater than $M = 83.92$. For the treated distribution (right-hand side), the population mean is $\mu = 88$ and a sample mean of $M = 83.92$ corresponds to a z-score of

$$z = \frac{M - \mu}{\sigma_M} = \frac{83.92 - 88}{2} = \frac{-4.08}{2} = -2.04$$

Finally, look up $z = -2.04$ in the unit normal table and determine that the shaded area ($z > -2.04$) corresponds to $p = 0.9793$ (or 97.93%). Thus, if the treatment has an 8-point effect, 97.93% of all the possible sample means will be in the critical region and we will reject the null hypothesis. In other words, the power of the test is 97.93%. In practical terms, this means that the research study is almost guaranteed to be successful. If the researcher selects a sample of $n = 25$ individuals, and if the treatment really does have an 8-point effect, then 97.93% of the time the hypothesis test will conclude that there is a significant effect.

POWER AND EFFECT SIZE

Logically, it should be clear that power and effect size are related. Figure 8.12 shows the calculation of power for an 8-point treatment effect. Now consider what would happen if the treatment effect were only 4 points. With a 4-point treatment effect, the distribution on the right-hand side would shift to the left so that it is centered at $\mu = 84$.

In this new position, only about 50% of the treated sample means would be beyond the $z = 1.96$ boundary. Thus, with a 4-point treatment effect, there is only a 50% probability of selecting a sample that leads to rejecting the null hypothesis. In other words, the power of the test is only about 50% for a 4-point effect compared to nearly 98% with an 8-point effect (Example 8.6). Again, it is possible to find the z-score corresponding to the exact location of the critical boundary and to look up the probability value for power in the unit normal table. In this case, you should obtain $z = -0.04$ and the exact power of the test is $p = 0.5160$, or 51.60%.

In general, as the effect size increases, the distribution of sample means on the right-hand side moves even farther to the right so that more and more of the samples are beyond the $z = 1.96$ boundary. Thus, as the effect size increases, the probability of rejecting H_0 also increases, which means that the power of the test increases. Thus, measures of effect size such as Cohen's d and measures of power both provide an indication of the strength or magnitude of a treatment effect.

OTHER FACTORS THAT AFFECT POWER

Although the power of a hypothesis test is directly influenced by the size of the treatment effect, power is not meant to be a pure measure of effect size. Instead, power is influenced by several factors, other than effect size, that are related to the hypothesis test. Some of these factors are considered in the following section.

Sample size One factor that has a huge influence on power is the size of the sample. In Example 8.6 we demonstrated power for an 8-point treatment effect using a sample of $n = 25$. If the researcher decided to conduct the study using a sample of $n = 4$, then the power would be dramatically different. With $n = 4$, the standard error for the sample means would be

$$\sigma_M = \frac{\sigma}{\sqrt{n}} = \frac{10}{\sqrt{4}} = \frac{10}{2} = 5$$

Figure 8.13 shows the two distributions of sample means with $n = 4$ and a standard error of $\sigma_M = 5$ points. Again, the distribution on the left is centered at $\mu = 80$ and shows all of the possible sample means if H_0 is true. As always, this distribution is used to locate the critical boundaries for the hypothesis test, $z = -1.96$ and $z = +1.96$. The distribution on the right is centered at $\mu = 88$ and shows all of the possible sample means if there is an 8-point treatment effect. Note that less than half of the treated sample means in the right-hand distribution are now located beyond the 1.96 boundary. Thus, with a sample of $n = 4$, there is less than a 50% probability that the hypothesis test would reject H_0, even though the treatment has an 8-point effect. Earlier, in Example 8.6, we found power equal to 97.93% for a sample of $n = 25$. However, when the sample size is reduced to $n = 4$, power decreases to less than 50%. In general, a larger sample produces greater power for a hypothesis test.

Because power is directly related to sample size, one of the primary reasons for computing power is to determine what sample size is necessary to achieve a reasonable probability for a successful research study. Before a study is conducted, researchers can compute power to determine the probability that their research will successfully reject the null hypothesis. If the probability (power) is too small, they always have the option of increasing sample size to increase power.

Alpha level Reducing the alpha level for a hypothesis test also reduces the power of the test. For example, lowering α from .05 to .01 lowers the power of the hypothesis

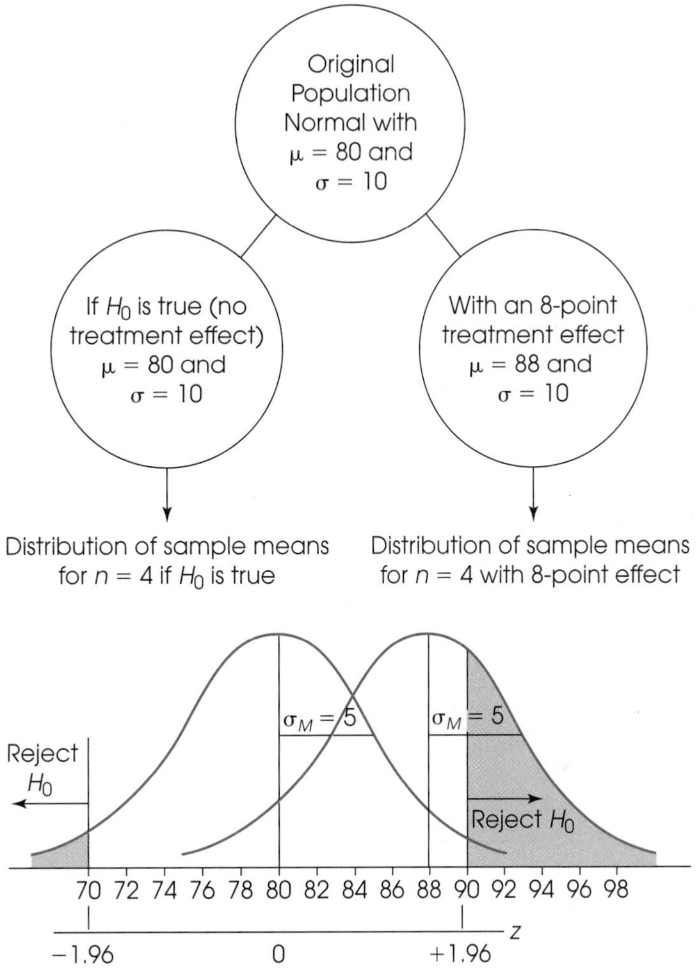

FIGURE 8.13

A demonstration of how sample size affects the power of a hypothesis test. As in Figure 8.12, the left-hand side shows the distribution of sample means if the null hypothesis were true. The critical region is defined for this distribution. The right-hand side shows the distribution of sample means that would be obtained if there were an 8-point treatment effect. Notice that reducing the sample size to $n = 4$ has reduced the power of the test to less than 50% compared to a power of nearly 100% with a sample of $n = 25$ in Figure 8.12.

test. The effect of reducing the alpha level can be seen by referring again to Figure 8.13. In this figure, the boundaries for the critical region are drawn using $\alpha = .05$. Specifically, the critical region on the right-hand side begins at $z = 1.96$. If α were changed to .01, the boundary would be moved farther to the right, out to $z = 2.58$. It should be clear that moving the critical boundary to the right means that a smaller portion of the treatment distribution (the distribution on the right-hand side) will be in the critical region. Thus, there would be a lower probability of rejecting the null hypothesis and a lower value for the power of the test.

One-tailed versus two-tailed tests Changing from a regular two-tailed test to a one-tailed test increases the power of the hypothesis test. Again, this effect can be seen by referring to Figure 8.13. The figure shows the boundaries for the critical region using a two-tailed test with $\alpha = .05$ so that the critical region on the right-hand side begins at $z = 1.96$. Changing to a one-tailed test would move the critical boundary to the left to a value of $z = 1.65$. Moving the boundary to the left would cause a larger proportion of the treatment distribution to be in the critical region and, therefore, would increase the power of the test.

LEARNING CHECK

1. For a particular hypothesis test, the power is .50 (50%) for a 5-point treatment effect. Will the power be greater or less than .50 for a 10-point treatment effect?
2. As the power of a test increases, what happens to the probability of a Type II error?
3. How does increasing sample size influence the power of a hypothesis test?
4. Find the exact value of the power for the hypothesis test shown in Figure 8.13.

ANSWERS

1. The hypothesis test is more likely to detect a 10-point effect, so power will be greater.
2. As power increases, the probability of a Type II error decreases.
3. Increasing sample size increases the power of a test.
4. With $n = 4$, the critical boundary of $z = 1.96$ corresponds to a sample mean of $M = 89.8$, and the exact value for power is $p = 0.3594$ or 35.945%.

SUMMARY

1. Hypothesis testing is an inferential procedure that uses the data from a sample to draw a general conclusion about a population. The procedure begins with a hypothesis about an unknown population. Then a sample is selected, and the sample data provide evidence that either supports or refutes the hypothesis.
2. In this chapter, we introduced hypothesis testing using the simple situation in which a sample mean is used to test a hypothesis about an unknown population mean; usually the mean for a population that has received a treatment. The question is to determine whether the treatment has an effect on the population mean (see Figure 8.2).
3. Hypothesis testing is structured as a four-step process that is used throughout the remainder of the book.
   - **a.** State the null hypothesis (H_0), and select an alpha level. The null hypothesis states that there is no effect or no change. In this case, H_0 states that the mean for the treated population is the same as the mean before treatment. The alpha level, usually $\alpha = .05$ or $\alpha = .01$, provides a definition of the term *very unlikely* and determines the risk of a Type I error. Also state an alternative hypothesis (H_1), which is the exact opposite of the null hypothesis.
   - **b.** Locate the critical region. The critical region is defined as extreme sample outcomes that would be very unlikely to occur if the null hypothesis is true. The alpha level defines "very unlikely."
   - **c.** Collect the data, and compute the test statistic. The sample mean is transformed into a z-score by the formula

     $$z = \frac{M - \mu}{\sigma_M}$$

     The value of μ is obtained from the null hypothesis. The z-score test statistic identifies the location of the sample mean in the distribution of sample means.
   - **d.** Make a decision. If the obtained z-score is in the critical region, reject H_0 because it is very unlikely that these data would be obtained if H_0 were true. In this case, conclude that the treatment has changed the population mean. If the z-score is not in the critical region, fail to reject H_0 because the data are not significantly different from the null hypothesis. In this case, the data do not provide sufficient evidence to indicate that the treatment has had an effect.
4. Whatever decision is reached in a hypothesis test, there is always a risk of making the incorrect decision. There are two types of errors that can be committed.

   A Type I error is defined as rejecting a true H_0. This is a serious error because it results in falsely reporting a treatment effect. The risk of a Type I error is determined by the alpha level and, therefore, is under the experimenter's control.

   A Type II error is defined as the failure to reject a false H_0. In this case, the experiment fails to detect an effect that actually occurred. The probability of a Type II error cannot be specified as a single value and depends in part on the size of the treatment effect. It is identified by the symbol β (beta).

5. When a researcher expects that a treatment will change scores in a particular direction (increase or decrease), it is possible to do a directional, or one-tailed, test. The first step in this procedure is to incorporate the directional prediction into the hypotheses. For example, if the prediction is that a treatment will increase scores, the null hypothesis says that there is no increase and the alternative hypothesis states that there is an increase. To locate the critical region, you must determine what kind of data would refute the null hypothesis by demonstrating that the treatment worked as predicted. These outcomes are located entirely in one tail of the distribution, so the entire critical region (5%, 1%, or 0.1% depending on α) will be in one tail.

6. A one-tailed test is used when there is prior justification for making a directional prediction. These *a priori* reasons may be previous reports and findings or theoretical considerations. In the absence of the *a priori* basis, a two-tailed test is appropriate. In this situation, you might be unsure of what to expect in the study, or you might be testing competing theories.

7. In addition to using a hypothesis test to evaluate the *significance* of a treatment effect, it is recommended that you also measure and report the *effect size*. One measure of effect size is Cohen's *d*, which is a standardized measure of the mean difference. Cohen's *d* is computed as

$$\text{Cohen's } d = \frac{\text{mean difference}}{\text{standard deviation}}$$

8. The power of a hypothesis test is defined as the probability that the test will correctly reject the null hypothesis.

9. To determine the power for a hypothesis test, you must first identify the treatment and null distributions. Also, you must specify the magnitude of the treatment effect. Next, you locate the critical region in the null distribution. The power of the hypothesis test is the portion of the treatment distribution that is located beyond the boundary (critical value) of the critical region.

10. As the size of the treatment effect increases, statistical power increases. Also, power is influenced by several factors that can be controlled by the experimenter:

    a. Increasing the alpha level increases power.
    b. A one-tailed test has greater power than a two-tailed test.
    c. A large sample results in more power than a small sample.

KEY TERMS

hypothesis test (233)
null hypothesis (236)
alternative hypothesis (236)
level of significance (237)
alpha level (237)
critical region (238)
test statistic (242)
Type I error (244)
Type II error (245)
beta (246)
significant (251)
directional test (256)
one-tailed test (256)
effect size (262)
Cohen's *d* (262)
power (265)

RESOURCES

Book Companion Website: www.cengage.com/psychology/gravetter

You can find a tutorial quiz and other learning exercises for Chapter 8 on the book companion website. The website also provides access to a workshop titled *Hypothesis Testing,* which reviews the concept and logic of hypothesis testing.

SPSS

The statistical computer package SPSS is not structured to conduct hypothesis tests using *z*-scores. In truth, the *z*-score test presented in this chapter is rarely used in actual research situations. The problem with the *z*-score test is that it requires that you know the value of the population standard deviation, and this information is usually not available. Researchers rarely have detailed information about the populations that they wish to study. Instead, they must obtain information entirely from samples. In the following chapters we introduce new hypothesis-testing techniques that are based entirely on sample data. These new techniques are included in SPSS.

FOCUS ON PROBLEM SOLVING

1. Hypothesis testing involves a set of logical procedures and rules that enable us to make general statements about a population when all we have are sample data. This logic is reflected in the four steps that have been used throughout this chapter. Hypothesis-testing problems are easier to tackle when you learn to follow the steps.

STEP 1 State the hypotheses and set the alpha level.

STEP 2 Locate the critical region.

STEP 3 Compute the test statistic (in this case, the *z*-score) for the sample.

STEP 4 Make a decision about H_0 based on the result of step 3.

2. Students often ask, "What alpha level should I use?" Or a student may ask, "Why is an alpha of .05 used?" as opposed to something else. There is no single correct answer to either of these questions. Keep in mind that the aim of setting an alpha level in the first place: *to reduce the risk of committing a Type I error.* Therefore, the maximum acceptable value is $\alpha = .05$. However, some researchers prefer to take even less risk and use alpha levels of .01 or smaller.

Most statistical tests are now done with computer programs that provide an exact probability (p value) for a Type I error. Because an exact value is available, most researchers simply report the p value from the computer printout rather than setting an alpha level at the beginning of the test. However, the same criterion still applies: A result is not significant unless the p value is less than .05.

3. Take time to consider the implications of your decision about the null hypothesis. The null hypothesis states that there is no effect. Therefore, if your decision is to reject H_0, you should conclude that the sample data provide evidence for a treatment effect. However, it is an entirely different matter if your decision is to fail to reject H_0. Remember that when you fail to reject the null hypothesis, the results are inconclusive. It is impossible to *prove* that H_0 is correct; therefore, you cannot state with certainty that "there is no effect" when H_0 is not rejected. At best, all you can state is that "there is insufficient evidence for an effect."
4. It is very important that you understand the structure of the z-score formula (p. 242). It will help you understand many of the other hypothesis tests that are covered later.
5. When you are doing a directional hypothesis test, read the problem carefully, and watch for key words (such as increase or decrease, raise or lower, and more or less) that tell you which direction the researcher is predicting. The predicted direction determines the alternative hypothesis (H_1) and the critical region. For example, if a treatment is expected to *increase* scores, H_1 would contain a *greater than* symbol, and the critical region would be in the tail associated with high scores.

DEMONSTRATION 8.1

HYPOTHESIS TEST WITH *Z*

A researcher begins with a known population—in this case, scores on a standardized test that are normally distributed with $\mu = 65$ and $\sigma = 15$. The researcher suspects that special training in reading skills will produce a change in the scores for the individuals in the population. Because it is not feasible to administer the treatment (the special training) to everyone in the population, a sample of $n = 25$ individuals is selected, and the treatment is given to this sample. Following treatment, the average score for this sample is $M = 70$. Is there evidence that the training has an effect on test scores?

STEP 1 **State the hypothesis and select an alpha level.** The null hypothesis states that the special training has no effect. In symbols,

H_0: $\mu = 65$ (After special training, the mean is still 65.)

The alternative hypothesis states that the treatment does have an effect.

H_1: $\mu \neq 65$ (After training, the mean is different from 65.)

At this time you also select the alpha level. For this demonstration, we will use $\alpha = .05$. Thus, there is a 5% risk of committing a Type I error if we reject H_0.

STEP 2 **Locate the critical region.** With $\alpha = .05$, the critical region consists of sample means that correspond to z-scores beyond the critical boundaries of $z = \pm 1.96$.

STEP 3 **Obtain the sample data, and compute the test statistic.** For this example, the distribution of sample means, according to the null hypothesis, is normal with an expected value of $\mu = 65$ and a standard error of

$$\sigma_M = \frac{\sigma}{\sqrt{n}} = \frac{15}{\sqrt{25}} = \frac{15}{5} = 3$$

In this distribution, our sample mean of $M = 70$ corresponds to a z-score of

$$z = \frac{M - \mu}{\sigma_M} = \frac{70 - 65}{3} = \frac{5}{3} = +1.67$$

STEP 4 **Make a decision about H_0, and state the conclusion.** The z-score we obtained is not in the critical region. This indicates that our sample mean of $M = 70$ is not an extreme or unusual value to be obtained from a population with $\mu = 65$. Therefore, our statistical decision is to *fail to reject* H_0. Our conclusion for the study is that the data do not provide sufficient evidence that the special training changes test scores.

DEMONSTRATION 8.2

EFFECT SIZE USING COHEN'S *D*

We will compute Cohen's d using the research situation and the data from Demonstration 8.1. Again, the original population mean was $\mu = 65$ and, after treatment (special training), the sample mean was $M = 70$. Thus, there is a 5-point mean difference. Using the population standard deviation, $\sigma = 15$, we obtain an effect size of

$$\text{Cohen's } d = \frac{\text{mean difference}}{\text{standard deviation}} = \frac{5}{15} = 0.33$$

According to Cohen's evaluation standards (see Table 8.2), this is a medium treatment effect.

PROBLEMS

1. In the z-score formula as it is used in a hypothesis test,
   a. Explain what is measured by $M - \mu$ in the numerator.
   b. Explain what is measured by the standard error in the denominator.
2. If the alpha level is changed from $\alpha = .05$ to $\alpha = .01$,
   a. What happens to the boundaries for the critical region?
   b. What happens to the probability of a Type I error?
3. In words, define the alpha level and the critical region for a hypothesis test.
4. The value of the z-score in a hypothesis test is influenced by a variety of factors. Assuming that all other variables are held constant, explain how the value of z is influenced by each of the following:
   a. Increasing the difference between the sample mean and the original population mean.
   b. Increasing the population standard deviation.
   c. Increasing the number of scores in the sample.
5. Although there is a popular belief that herbal remedies such as ginkgo biloba and ginseng may improve

learning and memory in healthy adults, these effects are usually not supported by well-controlled research (Persson, Bringlov, Nilsson, & Nyberg, 2004). In a typical study, a researcher obtains a sample of $n = 36$ participants and has each person take the herbal supplements every day for 90 days. At the end of the 90 days, each person takes a standardized memory test. For the general population, scores from the test are normally distributed with a mean of $\mu = 80$ and a standard deviation of $\sigma = 18$. The sample of research participants had an average of $M = 84$.

a. Assuming a two-tailed test, state the null hypothesis in a sentence that includes the two variables being examined.
b. Using symbols, state the hypotheses (H_0 and H_1) for the two-tailed test.
c. Sketch the appropriate distribution, and locate the critical region for $\alpha = .05$.
d. Calculate the test statistic (*z*-score) for the sample.
e. What decision should be made about the null hypothesis, and what decision should be made about the effect of the herbal supplements?

6. Childhood participation in sports, cultural groups, and youth groups appears to be related to improved self-esteem for adolescents (McGee, Williams, Howden-Chapman, Martin, & Kawachi, 2006). In a representative study, a sample of $n = 100$ adolescents with a history of group participation is given a standardized self-esteem questionnaire. For the general population of adolescents, scores on this questionnaire form a normal distribution with a mean of $\mu = 40$ and a standard deviation of $\sigma = 12$. The sample of group-participation adolescents had an average of $M = 43.84$.

a. Does this sample provide enough evidence to conclude that self-esteem scores for these adolescents are significantly different from those of the general population? Use a two-tailed test with $\alpha = .01$.
b. Compute Cohen's *d* to measure the size of the difference.
c. Write a sentence describing the outcome of the hypothesis test and the measure of effect size as it would appear in a research report.

7. A local college requires an English composition course for all freshmen. This year they are evaluating a new online version of the course. A random sample of $n = 16$ freshmen is selected and the students are placed in the online course. At the end of the semester, all freshmen take the same English composition exam. The average score for the sample is $M = 76$. For the general population of freshmen who took the traditional lecture class, the exam scores form a normal distribution with a mean of $\mu = 80$.

a. If the final exam scores for the population have a standard deviation of $\sigma = 12$, does the sample provide enough evidence to conclude that the new online course is significantly different from the traditional class? Assume a two-tailed test with $\alpha = .05$.
b. If the population standard deviation is $\sigma = 6$, is the sample sufficient to demonstrate a significant difference? Again, assume a two-tailed test with $\alpha = .05$.
c. Comparing your answers for parts a and b, explain how the magnitude of the standard deviation influences the outcome of a hypothesis test.

8. A random sample is selected from a normal population with a mean of $\mu = 50$ and a standard deviation of $\sigma = 12$. After a treatment is administered to the individuals in the sample, the sample mean is found to be $M = 55$.

a. If the sample consists of $n = 16$ scores, is the sample mean sufficient to conclude that the treatment has a significant effect? Use a two-tailed test with $\alpha = .05$.
b. If the sample consists of $n = 36$ scores, is the sample mean sufficient to conclude that the treatment has a significant effect? Use a two-tailed test with $\alpha = .05$.
c. Comparing your answers for parts a and b, explain how the size of the sample influences the outcome of a hypothesis test.

9. A random sample of $n = 36$ scores is selected from a normal population with a mean of $\mu = 60$. After a treatment is administered to the individuals in the sample, the sample mean is found to be $M = 52$.

a. If the population standard deviation is $\sigma = 18$, is the sample mean sufficient to conclude that the treatment has a significant effect? Use a two-tailed test with $\alpha = .05$.
b. If the population standard deviation is $\sigma = 30$, is the sample mean sufficient to conclude that the treatment has a significant effect? Use a two-tailed test with $\alpha = .05$.
c. Comparing your answers for parts a and b, explain how the magnitude of the standard deviation influences the outcome of a hypothesis test.

10. Miller (2008) examined the energy drink consumption of college undergraduates and found that males use energy drinks significantly more often than females. To further investigate this phenomenon, suppose that a researcher selects a random sample of $n = 36$ male undergraduates and a sample of $n = 25$ females. On average, the males reported consuming $M = 2.45$ drinks per month and females had an average of $M = 1.28$. Assume that the overall level of consumption for college undergraduates averages $\mu = 1.85$ energy drinks per month, and that the distribution of monthly consumption scores is approximately normal with a standard deviation of $\sigma = 1.2$.

a. Did this sample of males consume significantly more energy drinks than the overall population average? Use a one-tailed test with $\alpha = .01$.

b. Did this sample of females consume significantly fewer energy drinks than the overall population average? Use a one-tailed test with $\alpha = .01$

11. A random sample is selected from a normal population with a mean of $\mu = 40$ and a standard deviation of $\sigma = 10$. After a treatment is administered to the individuals in the sample, the sample mean is found to be $M = 42$.

a. How large a sample is necessary for this sample mean to be statistically significant? Assume a two-tailed test with $\alpha = .05$.

b. If the sample mean were $M = 41$, what sample size is needed to be significant for a two-tailed test with $\alpha = .05$?

12. A psychologist is investigating the hypothesis that children who grow up as the only child in the household develop different personality characteristics than those who grow up in larger families. A sample of $n = 30$ only children is obtained and each child is given a standardized personality test. For the general population, scores on the test from a normal distribution with a mean of $\mu = 50$ and a standard deviation of $\sigma = 15$. If the mean for the sample is $M = 58$, can the researcher conclude that there is a significant difference in personality between only children and the rest of the population? Use a two-tailed test with $\alpha = .05$.

13. There is some evidence indicating that people with visible tattoos are viewed more negatively than people without visible tattoos (Resenhoeft, Villa, & Wiseman, 2008). In a similar study, a researcher first obtained overall ratings of attractiveness for a woman with no tattoos shown in a color photograph. On a 7-point scale, the woman received an average rating of $\mu = 4.9$, and the distribution of ratings was normal with a standard deviation of $\sigma = 0.84$. The researcher then modified the photo by adding a tattoo of a butterfly on the woman's left arm. The modified photo was then shown to a sample of $n = 16$ students at a local community college and the students used the same 7-point scale to rate the attractiveness of the woman. The average score for the photo with the tattoo was $M = 4.2$.

a. Do the data indicate a significant difference in rated attractiveness when the woman appeared to have a tattoo? Use a two-tailed test with $\alpha = .05$.

b. Compute Cohen's *d* to measure the size of the effect.

c. Write a sentence describing the outcome of the hypothesis test and the measure of effect size as it would appear in a research report.

14. There is some evidence that REM sleep, associated with dreaming, may also play a role in learning and memory processing. For example, Smith and Lapp (1991) found increased REM activity for college students during exam periods. Suppose that REM activity for a sample of $n = 16$ students during the final exam period produced an average score of $M = 143$. Regular REM activity for the college population averages $\mu = 110$ with a standard deviation of $\sigma = 50$. The population distribution is approximately normal.

a. Do the data from this sample provide evidence for a significant increase in REM activity during exams? Use a one-tailed test with $\alpha = .01$.

b. Compute Cohen's *d* to estimate the size of the effect.

c. Write a sentence describing the outcome of the hypothesis test and the measure of effect size as it would appear in a research report.

15. A researcher is testing the hypothesis that consuming a sports drink during exercise improves endurance. A sample of $n = 50$ male college students is obtained and each student is given a series of three endurance tasks and asked to consume 4 ounces of the drink during each break between tasks. The overall endurance score for this sample is $M = 53$. For the general population of male college students, without any sports drink, the scores for this task average $\mu = 50$ with a standard deviation of $\sigma = 12$.

a. Can the researcher conclude that endurance scores with the sports drink are significantly higher than scores without the drink? Use a one-tailed test with $\alpha = .05$.

b. Can the researcher conclude that endurance scores with the sports drink are significantly different than scores without the drink? Use a two-tailed test with $\alpha = .05$.

c. You should find that the two tests lead to different conclusions. Explain why.

16. Montarello and Martins (2005) found that fifth-grade students completed more mathematics problems correctly when simple problems were mixed in with their regular math assignments. To further explore this phenomenon, suppose that a researcher selects a standardized mathematics achievement test that produces a normal distribution of scores with a mean of $\mu = 100$ and a standard deviation of $\sigma = 18$. The researcher modifies the test by inserting a set of very easy problems among the standardized questions, and gives the modified test to a sample of $n = 36$ students. If the average test score for the sample is $M = 104$, is this result sufficient to conclude that inserting the easy questions improves student performance? Use a one-tailed test with $\alpha = .01$.

17. Researchers have often noted increases in violent crimes when it is very hot. In fact, Reifman, Larrick, and Fein (1991) noted that this relationship even extends to baseball. That is, there is a much greater chance of a batter being hit by a pitch when the temperature increases. Consider the following hypothetical data. Suppose that over the past 30 years, during any given week of the major-league season, an average of $\mu = 12$ players are hit by wild pitches. Assume that the distribution is nearly normal with $\sigma = 3$. For a sample of $n = 4$ weeks in which the daily temperature was extremely hot, the weekly average of hit-by-pitch players was $M = 15.5$. Are players more likely to get hit by pitches during hot weeks? Set alpha to .05 for a one-tailed test.

18. A researcher is investigating the effectiveness of a new medication for lowering blood pressure for individuals with systolic pressure greater than 140. For this population, systolic scores average $\mu = 160$ with a standard deviation of $\sigma = 20$, and the scores form a normal-shaped distribution. The researcher plans to select a sample of $n = 25$ individuals, and measure their systolic blood pressure after they take the medication for 60 days. If the researcher uses a two-tailed test with $\alpha = .05$,

a. What is the power of the test if the medication has a 5-point effect?

b. What is the power of the test if the medication has a 10-point effect?

19. A sample of $n = 40$ is selected from a normal population with $\mu = 75$ msec. and $\sigma = 12$, and a treatment is administered to the sample. The treatment is expected to increase scores by an average of 4 points.

a. If the treatment effect is evaluated with a two-tailed hypothesis test using $\alpha = .05$, what is the power of the test?

b. What is the power of the test if the researcher uses a one-tailed test with $\alpha = .05$?

20. Briefly explain how increasing sample size influences each of the following. Assume that all other factors are held constant.

a. The size of the z-score in a hypothesis test.

b. The size of Cohen's d.

c. The power of a hypothesis test.

21. Explain how the power of a hypothesis test is influenced by each of the following. Assume that all other factors are held constant.

a. Increasing the alpha level from .01 to .05.

b. Changing from a one-tailed test to a two-tailed test.

22. A researcher plans to conduct an experiment testing the effect of caffeine on reaction time during a driving simulation task. A sample of $n = 9$ participants is selected and each person receives a standard dose of caffeine before being tested on the simulator. The caffeine is expected to lower reaction time by an average of 30 msec. Scores on the simulator task for the regular population (without caffeine) form a normal distribution with $\mu = 240$ msec. and $\sigma = 30$.

a. If the researcher uses a two-tailed test with $\alpha = .05$, what is the power of the hypothesis test?

b. Again assuming a two-tailed test with $\alpha = .05$, what is the power of the hypothesis test if the sample size is increased to $n = 25$?

23. A researcher is evaluating the influence of a treatment using a sample selected from a normally distributed population with a mean of $\mu = 80$ and a standard deviation of $\sigma = 20$. The researcher expects a 12-point treatment effect and plans to use a two-tailed hypothesis test with $\alpha = .05$.

a. Compute the power of the test if the researcher uses a sample of $n = 16$ individuals. (See Example 8.6.)

b. Compute the power of the test if the researcher uses a sample of $n = 25$ individuals.

PART II

REVIEW

After completing this part, you should understand the basic procedures that form the foundation of inferential statistics. These include:

1. The ability to transform scores into z-scores to describe locations within a distribution and to standardize entire distributions.
2. The ability to determine probabilities associated with individual scores selected from a distribution, especially for scores from normal distributions.
3. The ability to transform sample means into z-scores and to determine the probabilities associated with sample means.
4. The ability to use a sample mean to evaluate a hypothesis about an unknown population mean.

The general goal of inferential statistics is to use the limited information from a sample to answer general questions about an unknown population. In Chapter 8, we introduced hypothesis testing, one of the most commonly used inferential procedures. The hypothesis test presented in Chapter 8 integrates z-scores from Chapter 5, probability from Chapter 6, and the distribution of sample means from Chapter 7 into a single procedure that allows researchers to use a sample from an unknown population to evaluate a hypothesis about the population mean. The researcher first obtains a sample from the unknown population and computes the sample mean. The sample mean and a hypothesized value for the population mean are then used to compute a z-score. If the resulting z-score is a high-probability value, near the center of the distribution of sample means, then the researcher concludes that the sample data fit the hypothesis and the decision is to fail to reject the hypothesis. On the other hand, if the resulting z-score is a low-probability value, out in the tails of the distribution of sample means, then the researcher concludes that the sample data do not fit the hypothesis and the decision is to reject the hypothesis.

REVIEW EXERCISES

1. Find each of the requested values for a population with a mean of $\mu = 40$ and a standard deviation of $\sigma = 8$.
   a. What is the z-score corresponding to $X = 52$?
   b. What is the X value corresponding to $z = -0.50$?
   c. If all of the scores in the population are transformed into z-scores, what will be the values for the mean and standard deviation for the complete set of z-scores?
   d. What is the z-score corresponding to a sample mean of $M = 42$ for a sample of $n = 4$ scores?
   e. What is the z-score corresponding to a sample mean of $M = 42$ for a sample of $n = 16$ scores?

2. A survey of female high school seniors shows that the average amount of time spent on clothes, hair, and makeup each morning before school is $\mu = 35$ minutes. Assume that the distribution of preparation times is approximately normal with a standard deviation of $\sigma = 14$ minutes, and find each of the requested values.
   a. What proportion of female high school seniors spend more than 40 minutes preparing themselves for going to school each morning?
   b. What is the probability of randomly selecting a female high school senior who spends less than 10 minutes on her clothes, hair, and makeup each morning?
   c. What is the probability of obtaining a mean preparation time less than $M = 30$ minutes for a sample of $n = 49$ female high school students?

3. Brunt, Rhee, and Zhong (2008) surveyed 557 undergraduate college students to examine their weight status, health behaviors, and diet. Using body mass index (BMI), they classified the students into four categories: underweight, healthy weight, overweight, and obese. They also measured dietary variety by counting the number of different foods each student ate from several food groups. Note that the researchers are not measuring the amount of food eaten, but rather the number of different foods eaten (variety, not quantity). Nonetheless, it was somewhat surprising that the results showed no differences among the four weight categories that were related to eating fatty and/or sugary snacks.

   Suppose a researcher conducting a follow up study obtains a sample of $n = 25$ students classified as healthy weight and a sample of $n = 36$ students classified as overweight. Each student completes the food variety questionnaire, and the healthy-weight group produces a mean of $M = 4.01$ for the fatty, sugary snack category compared to a mean of $M = 4.48$ for the overweight group. The results from the Brunt, Rhee, and Zhong study showed an overall mean variety score of $\mu = 4.22$ for the discretionary sweets or fats food group. Assume that the distribution of scores is approximately normal with a standard deviation of $\sigma = 0.60$.
   a. Does the sample of $n = 36$ indicate that number of fatty, sugary snacks eaten by overweight students is significantly different from the overall population mean? Use a two-tailed test with $\alpha = .05$.
   b. Based on the sample of $n = 25$ healthy-weight students, can you conclude that healthy-weight students eat significantly fewer fatty, sugary snacks than the overall population? Use a one-tailed test with $\alpha = .05$.

PART

III

Using *t* Statistics for Inferences About Population Means and Mean Differences

In Part II we presented the foundation for inferential statistics. In this part, we begin to introduce some of the inferential procedures that are actually used in behavioral science research. Specifically, we look at a family of *t* statistics that use sample means and mean differences to draw inferences about the corresponding population means and mean differences. The *t* statistics are all modeled after the *z*-score for sample means that was introduced in Chapter 7 and used for hypothesis testing in Chapter 8. However, the *t* statistics do not require any prior knowledge about the population being evaluated. The three *t* statistics introduced in this part apply to three distinct research situations:

1. Using a single sample to draw an inference about the unknown mean for a single population.
2. Using two separate samples to draw an inference about the mean difference between two unknown populations.
3. Using one sample, with each individual tested in two different treatment conditions, to draw an inference about the population mean difference between the two conditions.

In addition to the hypothesis testing procedure introduced in Chapter 8, this part introduces a new inferential technique known as *confidence intervals*. Confidence intervals allow researchers to use sample data to estimate population means or mean differences by computing a range of values that is highly likely to contain the unknown parameter.

CHAPTER

9

Introduction to the t Statistic

Tools You Will Need

The following items are considered essential background material for this chapter. If you doubt your knowledge of any of these items, you should review the appropriate chapter or section before proceeding.

- Sample standard deviation (Chapter 4)
- Degrees of freedom (Chapter 4)
- Standard error (Chapter 7)
- Hypothesis testing (Chapter 8)

Preview

Numerous accounts suggest that for many animals, including humans, direct stare from another animal is aversive (e.g., Cook, 1977). Try it out for yourself. Make direct eye contact with a stranger in a cafeteria. Chances are the person will display avoidance by averting his or her gaze or turning away from you. Some insects, such as moths, have even developed eye-spot patterns on the wings or body to ward off predators (mostly birds) who may have a natural fear of eyes (Blest, 1957). Suppose that a comparative psychologist is interested in determining whether the birds that feed on these insects show an avoidance of eye-spot patterns.

Using methods similar to those of Scaife (1976), the researcher performed the following experiment. A sample of $n = 16$ moth-eating birds is selected. The animals are tested in an apparatus that consists of a two-chambered box. The birds are free to roam from one side of the box to the other through a doorway in the partition that separates the two chambers. In one chamber, there are two eye-spot patterns painted on the wall. The other side of the box has plain walls. One at a time, the researcher tests each bird by placing it in the doorway between the chambers. Each subject is left in the apparatus for 60 minutes, and the amount of time spent in the plain chamber is recorded.

The null hypothesis for this study would state that eye-spot patterns have no effect on the behavior of moth-eating birds. If this is true, then birds placed in the apparatus should wander randomly from side to side during the 60-minute period, averaging half of the time on each side. Therefore, for the general population of moth-eating birds, the null hypothesis states

$$H_0\text{: } \mu_{\text{plain side}} = 30 \text{ minutes}$$

The Problem: The researcher has most of the information needed to conduct a hypothesis test. In particular, the researcher has a hypothesis about the population ($\mu = 30$ minutes) and a sample of $n = 16$ scores that produces a sample mean (M). However, the researcher does not know the population standard deviation (σ). This value is needed to compute the standard error for the sample mean (σ_M) that appears in the denominator of the z-score equation. Recall that the standard error measures how much difference is reasonable to expect between a sample mean (M) and the population mean (μ). The value of the standard error is critical to deciding whether the sample data are consistent with the null hypothesis or refute the null hypothesis. Without the standard error, it is impossible to conduct a z-score hypothesis test.

The Solution: Because it is impossible to compute the standard error, a z-score cannot be used for the hypothesis test. However, it is possible to estimate the standard error using the sample data. The estimated standard error can then be used to compute a new statistic that is similar in structure to the z-score. The new statistic is called a *t statistic* and it can be used to conduct a new kind of hypothesis test.

9.1 THE *t* STATISTIC: AN ALTERNATIVE TO *z*

In the previous chapter, we presented the statistical procedures that permit researchers to use a sample mean to test hypotheses about an unknown population mean. These statistical procedures were based on a few basic concepts, which we summarize as follows:

Remember that the expected value of the distribution of sample means is μ, the population mean.

1. A sample mean (M) is expected to approximate its population mean (μ). This permits us to use the sample mean to test a hypothesis about the population mean.
2. The standard error provides a measure of how well a sample mean approximates the population mean. Specifically, the standard error determines how much difference is reasonable to expect between a sample mean (M) and the population mean (μ).

$$\sigma_M = \frac{\sigma}{\sqrt{n}} \quad \text{or} \quad \sigma_M = \sqrt{\frac{\sigma^2}{n}}$$

3. To quantify our inferences about the population, we compare the obtained sample mean (M) with the hypothesized population mean (μ) by computing a z-score test statistic.

$$z = \frac{M - \mu}{\sigma_M} = \frac{\text{obtained difference between data and hypothesis}}{\text{standard distance between } M \text{ and } \mu}$$

The goal of the hypothesis test is to determine whether the obtained difference between the data and the hypothesis is significantly greater than would be expected by chance. When the z-scores form a normal distribution, we are able to use the unit normal table (in Appendix B) to find the critical region for the hypothesis test.

THE PROBLEM WITH *z*-SCORES

The shortcoming of using a z-score for hypothesis testing is that the z-score formula requires more information than is usually available. Specifically, a z-score requires that we know the value of the population standard deviation (or variance), which is needed to compute the standard error. In most situations, however, the standard deviation for the population is not known. In fact, the whole reason for conducting a hypothesis test is to gain knowledge about an *unknown* population. This situation appears to create a paradox: You want to use a z-score to find out about an unknown population, but you must know about the population before you can compute a z-score. Fortunately, there is a relatively simple solution to this problem. When the variability for the population is not known, we use the sample variability in its place.

INTRODUCING THE *t* STATISTIC

In Chapter 4, the sample variance was developed specifically to provide an unbiased estimate of the corresponding population variance. Recall that the formulas for sample variance and sample standard deviation are as follows:

The concept of degrees of freedom, $df = n - 1$, was introduced in Chapter 4 (p. 117) and is discussed later in this chapter (p. 287).

$$\text{sample variance} = s^2 = \frac{SS}{n-1} = \frac{SS}{df}$$

$$\text{sample standard deviation} = s = \sqrt{\frac{SS}{n-1}} = \sqrt{\frac{SS}{df}}$$

Using the sample values, we can now *estimate* the standard error. Recall from Chapters 7 and 8 that the value of the standard error can be computed using either standard deviation or variance:

$$\text{standard error} = \sigma_M = \frac{\sigma}{\sqrt{n}} \quad \text{or} \quad \sigma_M = \sqrt{\frac{\sigma^2}{n}}$$

Now we estimate the standard error by simply substituting the sample variance or standard deviation in place of the unknown population value:

$$\text{estimated standard error} = s_M = \frac{s}{\sqrt{n}} \quad \text{or} \quad s_M = \sqrt{\frac{s^2}{n}} \qquad (9.1)$$

Notice that the symbol for the *estimated standard error of* M is s_M instead of σ_M, indicating that the estimated value is computed from sample data rather than from the actual population parameter.

DEFINITION

The **estimated standard error** (s_M) is used as an estimate of the real standard error, σ_M, when the value of σ is unknown. It is computed from the sample variance or sample standard deviation and provides an estimate of the standard distance between a sample mean, *M*, and the population mean, μ.

Finally, you should recognize that we have shown formulas for standard error (actual or estimated) using both the standard deviation and the variance. In the past (Chapters 7 and 8), we concentrated on the formula using the standard deviation. At this point, however, we shift our focus to the formula based on variance. Thus, throughout the remainder of this chapter, and in following chapters, the estimated standard error of *M* typically is presented and computed using

$$s_M = \sqrt{\frac{s^2}{n}}$$

There are two reasons for making this shift from standard deviation to variance:

1. In Chapter 4 (p. 119) we saw that the sample variance is an *unbiased* statistic; on average, the sample variance (s^2) provides an accurate and unbiased estimate of the population variance (σ^2). Therefore, the most accurate way to estimate the standard error is to use the sample variance to estimate the population variance.
2. In future chapters we encounter other versions of the *t* statistic that require variance (instead of standard deviation) in the formulas for estimated standard error. To maximize the similarity from one version to another, we use variance in the formula for *all* of the different *t* statistics. Thus, whenever we present a *t* statistic, the estimated standard error is computed as

$$\text{estimated standard error} = \sqrt{\frac{\text{sample variance}}{\text{sample size}}}$$

Now we can substitute the estimated standard error in the denominator of the *z*-score formula. The result is a new test statistic called a *t statistic*:

$$t = \frac{M - \mu}{s_M} \tag{9.2}$$

DEFINITION

The ***t* statistic** is used to test hypotheses about an unknown population mean, μ, when the value of σ is unknown. The formula for the *t* statistic has the same structure as the *z*-score formula, except that the *t* statistic uses the estimated standard error in the denominator.

The only difference between the *t* formula and the *z*-score formula is that the *z*-score uses the actual population variance, σ^2 (or the standard deviation), and the *t* formula uses the corresponding sample variance (or standard deviation) when the population value is not known.

$$z = \frac{M - \mu}{\sigma_M} = \frac{M - \mu}{\sqrt{\sigma^2 / n}} \qquad t = \frac{M - \mu}{s_M} = \frac{M - \mu}{\sqrt{s^2 / n}}$$

DEGREES OF FREEDOM AND THE *t* STATISTIC

In this chapter, we have introduced the *t* statistic as a substitute for a *z*-score. The basic difference between these two is that the *t* statistic uses sample variance (s^2) and the *z*-score uses the population variance (σ^2). To determine how well a *t* statistic approximates a *z*-score, we must determine how well the sample variance approximates the population variance.

In Chapter 4, we introduced the concept of degrees of freedom (p. 117). Reviewing briefly, you must know the sample mean before you can compute sample variance. This places a restriction on sample variability such that only $n - 1$ scores in a sample are independent and free to vary. The value $n - 1$ is called the *degrees of freedom* (or *df*) for the sample variance.

$$\text{degrees of freedom} = df = n - 1 \tag{9.3}$$

DEFINITION

> **Degrees of freedom** describe the number of scores in a sample that are independent and free to vary. Because the sample mean places a restriction on the value of one score in the sample, there are $n - 1$ degrees of freedom for a sample with *n* scores (see Chapter 4).

The greater the value of *df* for a sample, the better the sample variance, s^2, represents the population variance, σ^2, and the better the *t* statistic approximates the *z*-score. This should make sense because the larger the sample (*n*) is, the better the sample represents its population. Thus, the degrees of freedom associated with s^2 also describe how well *t* represents *z*.

THE *t* DISTRIBUTION

Every sample from a population can be used to compute a *z*-score or a *t* statistic. If you select all of the possible samples of a particular size (*n*), and compute the *z*-score for each sample mean, then the entire set of *z*-scores form a *z*-score distribution. In the same way, you can compute the *t* statistic for every sample and the entire set of *t* values form a *t distribution.* As we saw in Chapter 7, the distribution of *z*-scores for sample means tends to be a normal distribution. Specifically, if the sample size is large (around $n = 30$ or more) or if the sample is selected from a normal population, then the distribution of sample means is a nearly perfect normal distribution. In these same situations, the *t* distribution approximates a normal distribution, just as a *t* statistic approximates a *z*-score. How well a *t* distribution approximates a normal distributor is determined by degrees of freedom. In general, the greater the sample size (*n*) is, the larger the degrees of freedom ($n - 1$) are, and the better the *t* distribution approximates the normal distribution (Figure 9.1).

DEFINITION

> A ***t* distribution** is the complete set of *t* values computed for every possible random sample for a specific sample size (*n*) or a specific degrees of freedom (*df*). The *t* distribution approximates the shape of a normal distribution.

FIGURE 9.1

Distributions of the *t* statistic for different values of degrees of freedom are compared to a normal *z*-score distribution. Like the normal distribution, *t* distributions are bell-shaped and symmetrical and have a mean of zero. However, *t* distributions have more variability, indicated by the flatter and more spread-out shape. The larger the value of *df* is, the more closely the *t* distribution approximates a normal distribution.

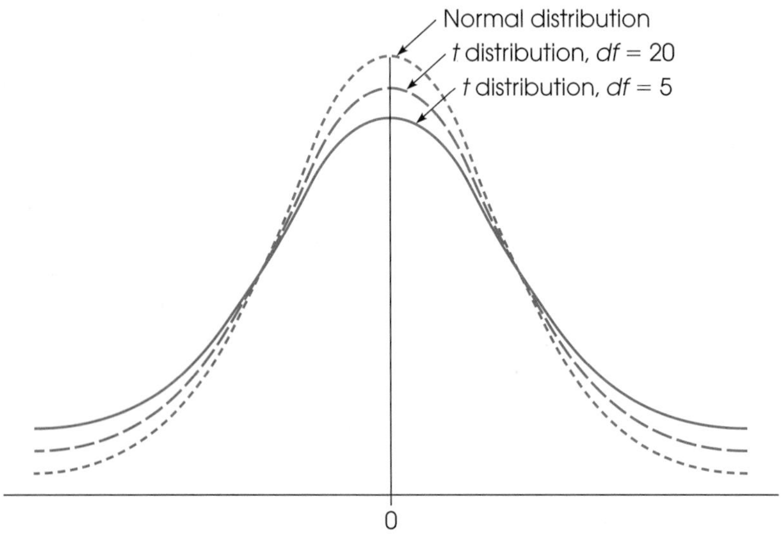

THE SHAPE OF THE *t* DISTRIBUTION

The exact shape of a *t* distribution changes with degrees of freedom. In fact, statisticians speak of a "family" of *t* distributions. That is, there is a different sampling distribution of *t* (a distribution of all possible sample *t* values) for each possible number of degrees of freedom. As *df* gets very large, the *t* distribution gets closer in shape to a normal *z*-score distribution. A quick glance at Figure 9.1 reveals that distributions of *t* are bell-shaped and symmetrical and have a mean of zero. However, the *t* distribution has more variability than a normal *z* distribution, especially when *df* values are small (see Figure 9.1). The *t* distribution tends to be flatter and more spread out, whereas the normal *z* distribution has more of a central peak.

The reason that the *t* distribution is flatter and more variable than the normal *z*-score distribution becomes clear if you look at the structure of the formulas for *z* and *t*. For both formulas, *z* and *t*, the top of the formula, $M - \mu$, can take on different values because the sample mean (M) varies from one sample to another. For *z*-scores, however, the bottom of the formula does not vary, provided that all of the samples are the same size and are selected from the same population. Specifically, all of the *z*-scores have the same standard error in the denominator, $\sigma_M = \sqrt{\sigma^2/n}$, because the population variance and the sample size are the same for every sample. For *t* statistics, on the other hand, the bottom of the formula varies from one sample to another. Specifically, the sample variance (s^2) changes from one sample to the next, so the estimated standard error also varies, $s_M = \sqrt{s^2/n}$. Thus, only the numerator of the *z*-score formula varies, but both the numerator and the denominator of the *t* statistic vary. As a result, *t* statistics are more variable than are *z*-scores, and the *t* distribution is flatter and more spread out. As sample size and *df* increase, however, the variability in the *t* distribution decreases, and it more closely resembles a normal distribution.

DETERMINING PROPORTIONS AND PROBABILITIES FOR *t* DISTRIBUTIONS

Just as we used the unit normal table to locate proportions associated with *z*-scores, we use a *t* distribution table to find proportions for *t* statistics. The complete *t* distribution table is presented in Appendix B, page 703, and a portion of this table is reproduced in

Table 9.1. The two rows at the top of the table show proportions of the *t* distribution contained in either one or two tails, depending on which row is used. The first column of the table lists degrees of freedom for the *t* statistic. Finally, the numbers in the body of the table are the *t* values that mark the boundary between the tails and the rest of the *t* distribution.

For example, with $df = 3$, exactly 5% of the *t* distribution is located in the tail beyond $t = 2.353$ (Figure 9.2). The process of finding this value is highlighted in Table 9.1. Begin by locating $df = 3$ in the first column of the table. Then locate a proportion of 0.05 (5%) in the one-tail proportion row. When you line up these two values in the table, you should find $t = 2.353$. Similarly, 5% of the *t* distribution is located in the tail beyond $t = -2.353$ (see Figure 9.2). Finally, notice that a total of 10% (or 0.10) is contained in the two tails beyond $t = \pm 2.353$ (check the proportion value in the "two-tails combined" row at the top of the table).

A close inspection of the *t* distribution table in Appendix B demonstrates a point we made earlier: As the value for *df* increases, the *t* distribution becomes more similar to a normal distribution. For example, examine the column containing *t* values for a 0.05 proportion in two tails. You will find that when $df = 1$, the *t* values that separate the extreme 5% (0.05) from the rest of the distribution are $t = \pm 12.706$. As

TABLE 9.1

A portion of the *t*-distribution table. The numbers in the table are the values of *t* that separate the tail from the main body of the distribution. Proportions for one or two tails are listed at the top of the table, and *df* values for *t* are listed in the first column.

	Proportion in One Tail					
	0.25	0.10	0.05	0.025	0.01	0.005
	Proportion in Two Tails Combined					
df	0.50	0.20	0.10	0.05	0.02	0.01
1	1.000	3.078	6.314	12.706	31.821	63.657
2	0.816	1.886	2.920	4.303	6.965	9.925
3	0.765	1.638	2.353	3.182	4.541	5.841
4	0.741	1.533	2.132	2.776	3.747	4.604
5	0.727	1.476	2.015	2.571	3.365	4.032
6	0.718	1.440	1.943	2.447	3.143	3.707

FIGURE 9.2

The *t* distribution with $df = 3$. Note that 5% of the distribution is located in the tail beyond $t = 2.353$. Also, 5% is in the tail beyond $t = -2.353$. Thus, a total proportion of 10% (0.10) is in the two tails beyond $t = \pm 2.353$.

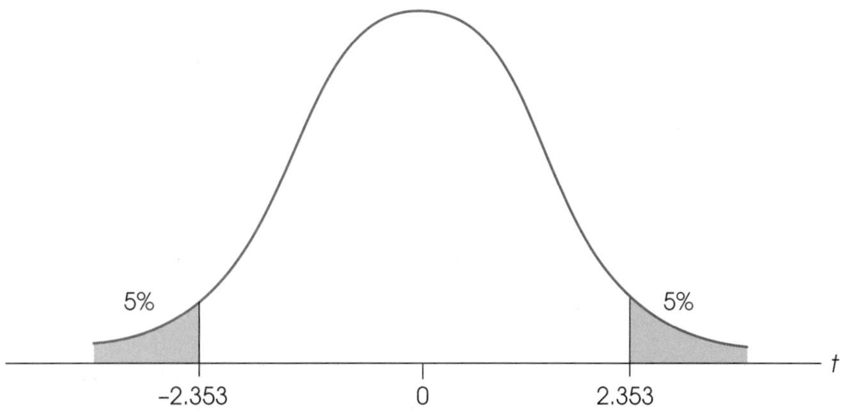

you read down the column, however, you will find that the critical *t* values become smaller and smaller, ultimately reaching ±1.96. You should recognize ±1.96 as the *z*-score values that separate the extreme 5% in a normal distribution. Thus, as *df* increases, the proportions in a *t* distribution become more like the proportions in a normal distribution. When the sample size (and degrees of freedom) is sufficiently large, the difference between a *t* distribution and the normal distribution becomes negligible.

Caution: The *t* distribution table printed in this book has been abridged and does not include entries for every possible *df* value. For example, the table lists *t* values for $df = 40$ and for $df = 60$, but does not list any entries for *df* values between 40 and 60. Occasionally, you will encounter a situation in which your *t* statistic has a *df* value that is not listed in the table. In these situations, you should look up the critical *t* for both of the surrounding *df* values listed and then use the *larger* value for *t*. If, for example, you have $df = 53$ (not listed), look up the critical *t* value for both $df = 40$ and $df = 60$ and *then use the larger t value.* If your sample *t* statistic is greater than the larger value listed, then you can be certain that the data are in the critical region, and you can confidently reject the null hypothesis.

LEARNING CHECK

1. Under what circumstances is a *t* statistic used instead of a *z*-score for a hypothesis test?
2. A sample of $n = 9$ scores has $SS = 288$.
   a. Compute the variance for the sample.
   b. Compute the estimated standard error for the sample mean.
3. In general, a distribution of *t* statistics is flatter and more spread out than the standard normal distribution. (True or false?)
4. A researcher reports a *t* statistic with $df = 20$. How many individuals participated in the study?
5. For $df = 15$, find the value(s) of *t* associated with each of the following:
   a. The top 5% of the distribution.
   b. The middle 95% of the distribution.
   c. The middle 99% of the distribution.

ANSWERS

1. A *t* statistic is used instead of a *z*-score when the population standard deviation and variance are not known.
2. **a.** $s^2 = 36$
   b. $s_M = 2$
3. True.
4. $n = 21$
5. **a.** $t = +1.753$
   b. $t = \pm 2.131$
   c. $t = \pm 2.947$

9.2 HYPOTHESIS TESTS WITH THE *t* STATISTIC

In the hypothesis-testing situation, we begin with a population with an unknown mean and an unknown variance, often a population that has received some treatment (Figure 9.3). The goal is to use a sample from the treated population (a treated sample) as the basis for determining whether the treatment has any effect.

As always, the null hypothesis states that the treatment has no effect; specifically, H_0 states that the population mean is unchanged. Thus, the null hypothesis provides a specific value for the unknown population mean. The sample data provide a value for the sample mean. Finally, the variance and estimated standard error are computed from the sample data. When these values are used in the t formula, the result becomes

$$t = \frac{\begin{matrix}\text{sample mean} \\ \text{(from the data)}\end{matrix} - \begin{matrix}\text{population mean} \\ \text{(hypothesized from } H_0\text{)}\end{matrix}}{\begin{matrix}\text{estimated standard error} \\ \text{(computed from the sample data)}\end{matrix}}$$

As with the z-score formula, the t statistic forms a ratio. The numerator measures the actual difference between the sample data (M) and the population hypothesis (μ). The estimated standard error in the denominator measures how much difference is reasonable to expect between a sample mean and the population mean. When the obtained difference between the data and the hypothesis (numerator) is much greater than expected (denominator), we obtain a large value for t (either large positive or large negative). In this case, we conclude that the data are not consistent with the hypothesis, and our decision is to "reject H_0." On the other hand, when the difference between the data and the hypothesis is small relative to the standard error, we obtain a t statistic near zero, and our decision is "fail to reject H_0."

The Unknown Population As mentioned earlier, the hypothesis test often concerns a population that has received a treatment. This situation is shown in Figure 9.3. Note

FIGURE 9.3

The basic experimental situation for using the t statistic or the z-score is presented. It is assumed that the parameter μ is known for the population before treatment. The purpose of the experiment is to determine whether the treatment has an effect. Note that the population after treatment has unknown values for the mean and the variance. We will use a sample to test a hypothesis about the population mean.

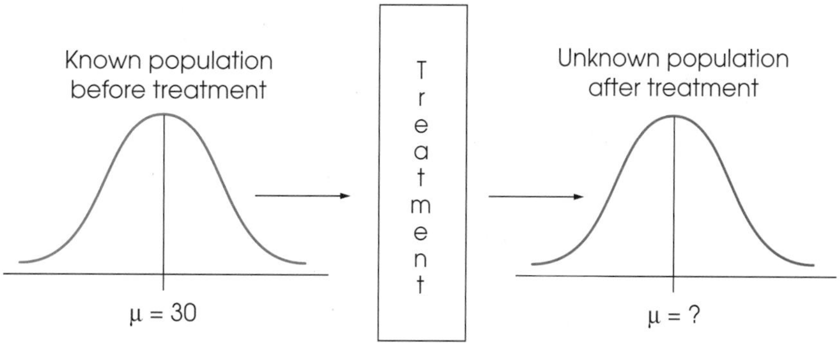

that the value of the mean is known for the population before treatment. The question is whether the treatment influences the scores and causes the mean to change. In this case, the unknown population is the one that exists after the treatment is administered, and the null hypothesis simply states that the value of the mean is not changed by the treatment.

Although the *t* statistic can be used in the "before and after" type of research shown in Figure 9.3, it also permits hypothesis testing in situations for which you do not have a known population mean to serve as a standard. Specifically, the *t* test does not require any prior knowledge about the population mean or the population variance. All you need to compute a *t* statistic is a null hypothesis and a sample from the unknown population. Thus, a *t* test can be used in situations for which the null hypothesis is obtained from a theory, a logical prediction, or just wishful thinking. For example, many surveys contain rating-scale questions to determine how people feel about controversial issues. Participants are presented with a statement and asked to express their opinion on a scale from 1 to 7, with 1 indicating "strongly agree" and 7 indicating "strongly disagree." A score of 4 indicates a neutral position, with no strong opinion one way or the other. In this situation, the null hypothesis would state that there is no preference in the population, H_0: $\mu = 4$. The data from a sample is then used to evaluate the hypothesis. Note that the researcher has no prior knowledge about the population mean and states a hypothesis that is based on logic.

HYPOTHESIS TESTING EXAMPLE

The following research situation demonstrates the procedures of hypothesis testing with the *t* statistic. Note that this is another example of a null hypothesis that is founded in logic rather than prior knowledge of a population mean.

EXAMPLE 9.1

Infants, even newborns, prefer to look at attractive faces compared to less attractive faces (Slater, et al., 1998). In the study, infants from 1 to 6 days old were shown two photographs of women's faces. Previously, a group of adults had rated one of the faces as significantly more attractive than the other. The babies were positioned in front of a screen on which the photographs were presented. The pair of faces remained on the screen until the baby accumulated a total of 20 seconds of looking at one or the other. The number of seconds looking at the attractive face was recorded for each infant. Suppose that the study used a sample of $n = 9$ infants and the data produced an average of $M = 13$ seconds for the attractive face with $SS = 72$. Note that all of the available information comes from the sample. Specifically, we do not know the population mean or the population standard deviation.

STEP 1 State the hypotheses and select an alpha level. Although we have no information about the population of scores, it is possible to form a logical hypothesis about the value of μ. In this case, the null hypothesis states that the infants have no preference for either face. That is, they should average half of the 20 seconds looking at each of the two faces. In symbols, the null hypothesis states

$$H_0: \mu_{\text{attractive}} = 10 \text{ seconds}$$

The alternative hypothesis states that there is a preference and one of the faces is preferred over the other. A directional, one-tailed test would specify which of the two faces is preferred, but the nondirectional alternative hypothesis is expressed as follows:

$$H_1: \mu_{\text{attractive}} \neq 10 \text{ seconds}$$

We set the level of significance at $\alpha = .05$ for two tails.

STEP 2 Locate the critical region. The test statistic is a t statistic because the population variance is not known. Therefore, the value for degrees of freedom must be determined before the critical region can be located. For this sample

$$df = n - 1 = 9 - 1 = 8$$

For a two-tailed test at the .05 level of significance and with 8 degrees of freedom, the critical region consists of t values greater than $+2.306$ or less than -2.306. Figure 9.4 depicts the critical region in this t distribution.

STEP 3 Calculate the test statistic. The t statistic typically requires much more computation than is necessary for a z-score. Therefore, we recommend that you divide the calculations into a three-stage process as follows:

a. First, calculate the sample variance. Remember that the population variance is unknown, and you must use the sample value in its place. (This is why we are using a t statistic instead of a z-score.)

$$s^2 = \frac{SS}{n-1} = \frac{SS}{df} = \frac{72}{8} = 9$$

b. Next, use the sample variance (s^2) and the sample size (n) to compute the estimated standard error. This value is the denominator of the t statistic and measures how much difference is reasonable to expect by chance between a sample mean and the corresponding population mean.

$$s_M = \sqrt{\frac{s^2}{n}} = \sqrt{\frac{9}{9}} = \sqrt{1} = 1$$

Finally, compute the t statistic for the sample data.

$$t = \frac{M - \mu}{s_M} = \frac{13 - 10}{1} = 3.00$$

STEP 4 Make a decision regarding H_0. The obtained t statistic of 3.00 falls into the critical region on the right-hand side of the t distribution (see Figure 9.4). Our statistical decision is to reject H_0 and conclude that babies do show a preference when given a

FIGURE 9.4

The critical region in the t distribution for $\alpha = .05$ and $df = 8$.

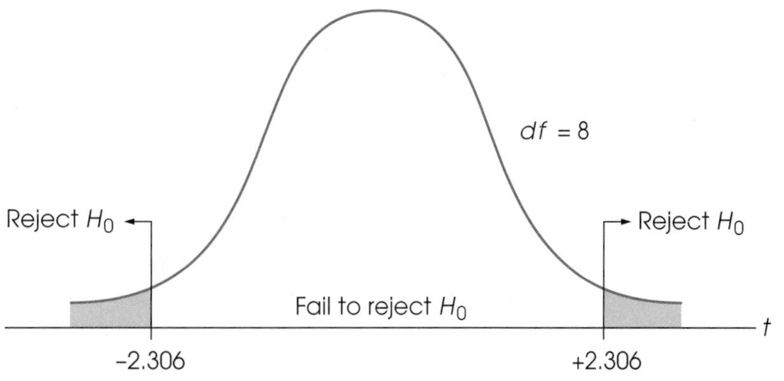

choice between an attractive and an unattractive face. Specifically, the average amount of time that the babies spent looking at the attractive face was significantly different from the 10 seconds that would be expected if there were no preference. As indicated by the sample mean, there is a tendency for the babies to spend more time looking at the attractive face.

ASSUMPTIONS OF THE *t* TEST

Two basic assumptions are necessary for hypothesis tests with the *t* statistic.

1. The values in the sample must consist of *independent* observations.
   In everyday terms, two observations are independent if there is no consistent, predictable relationship between the first observation and the second. More precisely, two events (or observations) are independent if the occurrence of the first event has no effect on the probability of the second event. We examined specific examples of independence and non-independence in Box 8.1 (p. 254).
2. The population that is sampled must be normal.
   This assumption is a necessary part of the mathematics underlying the development of the *t* statistic and the *t* distribution table. However, violating this assumption has little practical effect on the results obtained for a *t* statistic, especially when the sample size is relatively large. With very small samples, a normal population distribution is important. With larger samples, this assumption can be violated without affecting the validity of the hypothesis test. If you have reason to suspect that the population distribution is not normal, use a large sample to be safe.

THE INFLUENCE OF SAMPLE SIZE AND SAMPLE VARIANCE

As we noted in Chapter 8 (p. 252), a variety of factors can influence the outcome of a hypothesis test. In particular, the number of scores in the sample and the magnitude of the sample variance both have a large effect on the *t* statistic and thereby influence the statistical decision. The structure of the *t* formula makes these factors easier to understand.

$$t = \frac{M - \mu}{s_M} \quad \text{where } s_M = \sqrt{\frac{s^2}{n}}$$

Because the estimated standard error, s_M, appears in the denominator of the formula, a larger value for s_M produces a smaller value (closer to zero) for t. Thus, any factor that influences the standard error also affects the likelihood of rejecting the null hypothesis and finding a significant treatment effect. The two factors that determine the size of the standard error are the sample variance, s^2, and the sample size, n.

The estimated standard error is directly related to the sample variance so that the larger the variance, the larger the error. Thus, large variance means that you are less likely to obtain a significant treatment effect. In general, large variance is bad for inferential statistics. Large variance means that the scores are widely scattered, which makes it difficult to see any consistent patterns or trends in the data. In general, high variance reduces the likelihood of rejecting the null hypothesis.

On the other hand, the estimated standard error is inversely related to the number of scores in the sample. The larger the sample is, the smaller the error is. If all other factors are held constant, large samples tend to produce bigger *t* statistics and therefore are more likely to produce significant results. For example, a 2-point mean difference with a sample of $n = 4$ may not be convincing evidence of a treatment effect. However, the same 2-point difference with a sample of $n = 100$ is much more compelling.

LEARNING CHECK

1. A sample of $n = 4$ individuals is selected from a population with a mean of $\mu = 40$. A treatment is administered to the individuals in the sample and, after treatment, the sample has a mean of $M = 44$ and a variance of $s^2 = 16$.
   a. Is this sample sufficient to conclude that the treatment has a significant effect? Use a two-tailed test with $\alpha = .05$.
   b. If all other factors are held constant and the sample size is increased to $n = 16$, is the sample sufficient to conclude that the treatment has a significant effect? Again, use a two-tailed test with $\alpha = .05$.

ANSWER

1. **a.** H_0: $\mu = 40$ even after the treatment. With $n = 4$, the estimated standard error is 2, and $t = 4/2 = 2.00$. With $df = 3$, the critical boundaries are set at $t = \pm 3.182$. Fail to reject H_0 and conclude that the treatment does not have a significant effect.
   b. With $n = 16$, the estimated standard error is 1 and $t = 4.00$. With $df = 15$, the critical boundary is ± 2.131. The t value is beyond the critical boundary, so we reject H_0 and conclude that the treatment does have a significant effect.

9.3 MEASURING EFFECT SIZE FOR THE *t* STATISTIC

In Chapter 8, we noted that one criticism of a hypothesis test is that it does not really evaluate the size of the treatment effect. Instead, a hypothesis test simply determines whether the treatment effect is greater than chance, where "chance" is measured by the standard error. In particular, it is possible for a very small treatment effect to be "statistically significant," especially when the sample size is very large. To correct for this problem, it is recommended that the results from a hypothesis test be accompanied by a report of effect size, such as Cohen's *d*.

ESTIMATED COHEN'S *d*

When Cohen's *d* was originally introduced (p. 262), the formula was presented as

$$\text{Cohen's } d = \frac{\text{mean difference}}{\text{standard deviation}} = \frac{\mu_{\text{treatment}} - \mu_{\text{no treatment}}}{\sigma}$$

Cohen defined this measure of effect size in terms of the population mean difference and the population standard deviation. However, in most situations the population values are not known and you must substitute the corresponding sample values in their place. When this is done, many researchers prefer to identify the calculated value as an "*estimated* d" or name the value after one of the statisticians who first substituted sample statistics into Cohen's formula (e.g., Glass's *g* or Hedges's *g*). For hypothesis tests using the *t* statistic, the population mean with no treatment is the value specified by the null hypothesis. However, the population mean with treatment and the standard deviation are both unknown. Therefore, we use the mean for the treated sample and the standard deviation for the sample after treatment as estimates of the unknown parameters. With these substitutions, the formula for estimating Cohen's d becomes

$$\text{estimated } d = \frac{\text{mean difference}}{\text{sample standard deviation}} = \frac{M - \mu}{s} \quad (9.4)$$

The numerator measures that magnitude of the treatment effect by finding the difference between the mean for the treated sample and the mean for the untreated population (μ from H_0). The sample standard deviation in the denominator standardizes the mean difference into standard deviation units. Thus, an estimated d of 1.00 indicates that the size of the treatment effect is equivalent to one standard deviation. The following example demonstrates how the estimated d is used to measure effect size for a hypothesis test using a t statistic.

EXAMPLE 9.2

For the infant face-preference study in Example 9.1, the babies averaged $M = 13$ out of 20 seconds looking at the attractive face. If there were no preference (as stated by the null hypothesis), the population mean would be $\mu = 10$ seconds. Thus, the results show a 3-second difference between the mean with a preference ($M = 13$) and the mean with no preference ($\mu = 10$). Also, for this study the sample standard deviation is

$$s = \sqrt{\frac{SS}{df}} = \sqrt{\frac{72}{8}} = \sqrt{9} = 3$$

Thus, Cohen's d for this example is estimated to be

$$\text{Cohen's } d = \frac{M - \mu}{s} = \frac{13 - 10}{3} = 1.00$$

According to the standards suggested by Cohen (Table 8.2, p. 264), this is a large treatment effect.

To help you visualize what is measured by Cohen's d, we have constructed a set of $n = 9$ scores with a mean of $M = 13$ and a standard deviation of $s = 3$ (the same values as in Examples 9.1 and 9.2). The set of scores is shown in Figure 9.5. Notice that the figure also includes an arrow that locates $\mu = 10$. Recall that $\mu = 10$ is the value specified by the null hypothesis and identifies what the mean ought to be if the treatment has no effect. Clearly, our sample is not centered around $\mu = 10$. Instead, the scores have been shifted to the right so that the sample mean is $M = 13$. This shift, from 10 to 13, is the 3-point mean difference that was caused by the treatment effect. Also notice that the 3-point mean difference is exactly equal to the standard deviation. Thus, the size of the treatment effect is equal to 1 standard deviation. In other words, Cohen's $d = 1.00$.

MEASURING THE PERCENTAGE OF VARIANCE EXPLAINED, r^2

An alternative method for measuring effect size is to determine how much of the variability in the scores is explained by the treatment effect. The concept behind this measure is that the treatment causes the scores to increase (or decrease), which means that the treatment is causing the scores to vary. If we can measure how much of the variability is explained by the treatment, we can obtain a measure of the size of the treatment effect.

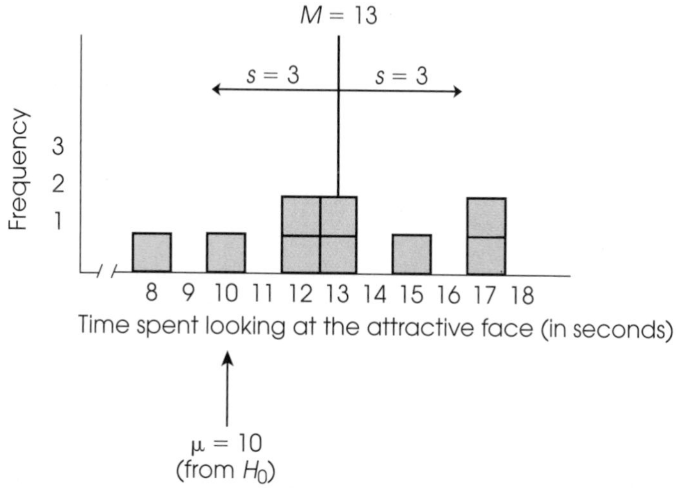

FIGURE 9.5

The sample distribution for the scores that were used in Examples 9.1 and 9.2. The population mean, $\mu = 10$ seconds, is the value that would be expected if attractiveness has no effect on the infants' behavior. Note that the sample mean is displaced away from $\mu = 10$ by a distance equal to one standard deviation.

To demonstrate this concept we use the data from the hypothesis test in Example 9.1. Recall that the null hypothesis stated that the treatment (the attractiveness of the faces) has no effect on the infants' behavior. According to the null hypothesis, the infants should show no preference between the two photographs, and therefore should spend an average of $\mu = 10$ out of 20 seconds looking at the attractive face.

However, if you look at the data in Figure 9.5, the scores are not centered around $\mu = 10$. Instead, the scores are shifted to the right so that they are centered around the sample mean, $M = 13$. This shift is the treatment effect. To measure the size of the treatment effect, we calculate deviations from the mean and the sum of squared deviations, *SS*, in two different ways.

Figure 9.6(a) shows the original set of scores. For each score, the deviation from $\mu = 10$ is shown as a colored line. Recall that $\mu = 10$ comes from the null hypothesis and represents the population mean if the treatment has no effect. Note that almost all of the scores are located on the right-hand side of $\mu = 10$. This shift to the right is the treatment effect. Specifically, the preference for the attractive face has caused the infants to spend more time looking at the attractive photograph, which means that their scores are generally greater than 10. Thus, the treatment has pushed the scores away from $\mu = 10$ and has increased the size of the deviations.

Next, we see what happens if the treatment effect is removed. In this example, the treatment has a 3-point effect (the average increases from $\mu = 10$ to $M = 13$). To remove the treatment effect, we simply subtract 3 points from each score. The adjusted scores are shown in Figure 9.6(b) and, once again, the deviations from $\mu = 10$ are shown as colored lines. First, notice that the adjusted scores are centered at $\mu = 10$, indicating that there is no treatment effect. Also notice that the deviations, the colored lines, are noticeably smaller when the treatment effect is removed.

To measure how much the variability is reduced when the treatment effect is removed, we compute the sum of squared deviations, *SS*, for each set of scores. The left-hand columns of Table 9.2 show the calculations for the original scores [Figure 9.6(a)], and the right-hand columns show the calculations for the adjusted scores [Figure 9.6(b)]. Note that the total variability, including the treatment effect, is $SS = 153$. However, when the treatment effect is removed, the variability is reduced to $SS = 72$. The difference

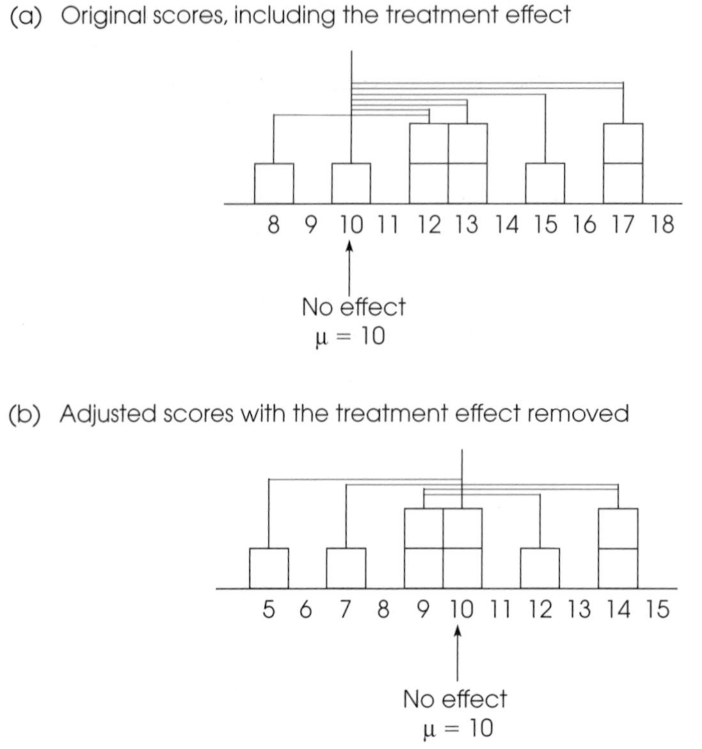

FIGURE 9.6

Deviations from $\mu = 10$ (no treatment effect) for the scores in Example 9.1. The colored lines in part (a) show the deviations for the original scores, including the treatment effect. In part (b) the colored lines show the deviations for the adjusted scores after the treatment effect has been removed.

between these two values, 153 – 72 = 81 points, is the amount of variability that is accounted for by the treatment effect. This value is usually reported as a proportion or percentage of the total variability:

$$\frac{\text{variability accounted for}}{\text{total variability}} = \frac{81}{153} = 0.5294 \quad (52.94\%)$$

TABLE 9.2

Calculation of *SS*, the sum of squared deviations, for the data in Figure 9.6. The first three columns show the calculations for the original scores, including the treatment effect. The last three columns show the calculations for the adjusted scores after the treatment effect has been removed.

Calculation of *SS* including the treatment effect			Calculation of *SS* after the treatment effect is removed		
Score	Deviation from $\mu = 10$	Squared Deviation	Adjusted Score	Deviation from $\mu = 10$	Squared Deviation
8	−2	4	8 − 3 = 5	−5	25
10	0	0	10 − 3 = 7	−3	9
12	2	4	12 − 3 = 9	−1	1
12	2	4	12 − 3 = 9	−1	1
13	3	9	13 − 3 = 10	0	0
13	3	9	13 − 3 = 10	0	0
15	5	25	15 − 3 = 12	2	4
17	7	49	17 − 3 = 14	4	16
17	7	49	17 − 3 = 14	4	16
		SS = 153			*SS* = 72

Thus, removing the treatment effect reduces the variability by 52.94%. This value is called the *percentage of variance accounted for by the treatment* and is identified as r^2.

Rather than computing r^2 directly by comparing two different calculations for *SS*, the value can be found from a single equation based on the outcome of the *t* test.

$$r^2 = \frac{t^2}{t^2 + df} \tag{9.5}$$

The letter *r* is the traditional symbol used for a correlation, and the concept of r^2 is discussed again when we consider correlations in Chapter 15. Also, in the context of *t* statistics, the percentage of variance that we are calling r^2 is often identified by the Greek letter omega squared (ω^2).

For the hypothesis test in Example 9.1, we obtained $t = 3.00$ with $df = 8$. These values produce

$$r^2 = \frac{3^2}{3^2 + 8} = \frac{9}{17} = 0.5294 \quad (52.94\%)$$

Note that this is exactly the same value we obtained with the direct calculation of the percentage of variability accounted for by the treatment.

Interpreting r^2 In addition to developing the Cohen's *d* measure of effect size, Cohen (1988) also proposed criteria for evaluating the size of a treatment effect that is measured by r^2. The criteria were actually suggested for evaluating the size of a correlation, *r*, but are easily extended to apply to r^2. Cohen's standards for interpreting r^2 are shown in Table 9.3.

According to these standards, the data we constructed for Examples 9.1 and 9.2 show a very large effect size with $r^2 = .5294$.

As a final note, we should remind you that, although sample size affects the hypothesis test, this factor has little or no effect on measures of effect size. In particular, estimates of Cohen's *d* are not influenced at all by sample size, and measures of r^2 are only slightly affected by changes in the size of the sample. The sample variance, on the other hand, influences hypothesis tests and measures of effect size. Specifically, high variance reduces both the likelihood of rejecting the null hypothesis and measures of effect size.

CONFIDENCE INTERVALS FOR ESTIMATING μ

An alternative technique for describing the size of a treatment effect is to compute an estimate of the population mean after treatment. For example, if the mean before treatment is known to be $\mu = 80$ and the mean after treatment is estimated to be $\mu = 86$, then we can conclude that the size of the treatment effect is around 6 points.

Estimating an unknown population mean involves constructing a *confidence interval*. A confidence interval is based on the observation that a sample mean tends to provide a reasonably accurate estimate of the population mean. The fact that a sample

TABLE 9.3

Criteria for interpreting the value of r^2 as proposed by Cohen (1988).

Percentage of Variance Explained, r^2	
$r^2 = 0.01$	Small effect
$r^2 = 0.09$	Medium effect
$r^2 = 0.25$	Large effect

mean tends to be near to the population mean implies that the population mean should be near to the sample mean. For example, if we obtain a sample mean of $M = 86$, we can be reasonably confident that the population mean is around 86. Thus, a confidence interval consists of an interval of values around a sample mean, and we can be reasonably confident that the unknown population mean is located somewhere in the interval.

DEFINITION

A **confidence interval** is an interval, or range of values, centered around a sample statistic. The logic behind a confidence interval is that a sample statistic, such as a sample mean, should be relatively near to the corresponding population parameter. Therefore, we can confidently estimate that the value of the parameter should be located in the interval.

CONSTRUCTING A CONFIDENCE INTERVAL

The construction of a confidence interval begins with the observation that every sample mean has a corresponding *t* value defined by the equation

$$t = \frac{M - \mu}{s_M}$$

Although the values for M and s_M are available from the sample data, we cannot use the equation to calculate t because the value for μ is unknown. Instead of calculating the t value, for a confidence interval we *estimate* the t value. For example, if the sample has $n = 9$ scores, then the t statistic has $df = 8$, and the distribution of all possible t values can be pictured as in Figure 9.7. Notice that the t values pile up around $t = 0$, so we can estimate that the t value for our sample should have a value around 0. Furthermore, the t distribution table lists a variety of different t values that correspond to specific proportions of the t distribution. With $df = 8$, for example, 80% of the t values are located between $t = +1.397$ and $t = -1.397$. To obtain these values, simply look up a two-tailed proportion of 0.20 (20%) for $df = 8$. Because 80% of all of the possible t values are located between ± 1.397, we can be 80% confident that our sample mean corresponds to a t value in this interval. Similarly, we can be 95% confident that the mean for a sample of $n = 9$ scores corresponds to a t value between $+2.306$ and -2.306. Notice that we are able to estimate the value of t with a specific level of

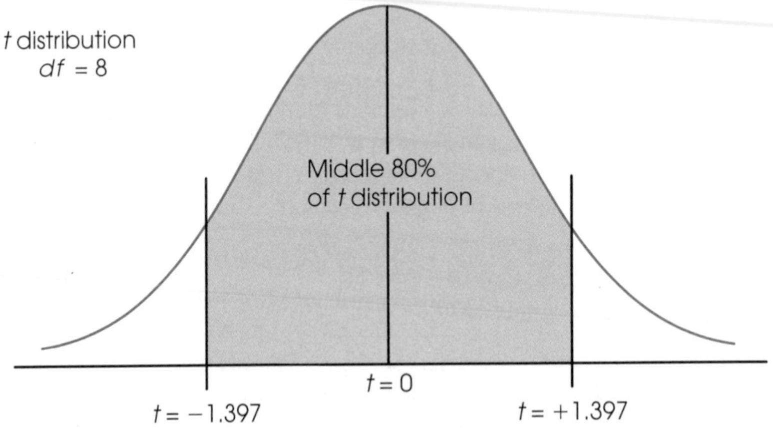

FIGURE 9.7

The distribution of t statistics with $df = 8$. The t values pile up around $t = 0$ and 80% of all of the possible values are located between $t = -1.397$ and $t = +1.397$.

confidence. To construct a confidence interval for μ, we plug the estimated t value into the t equation, and then we can calculate the value of μ.

Before we demonstrate the process of constructing a confidence interval for an unknown population mean, we simplify the calculations by regrouping the terms in the t equation. Because the goal is to compute the value of μ, we use simple algebra to solve the equation for μ. The result is

$$\mu = M \pm ts_M \qquad (9.6)$$

The process of using this equation to construct a confidence interval is demonstrated in the following example.

EXAMPLE 9.3

Example 9.1 describes a study in which infants displayed a preference for the more attractive face by looking at it, instead of the less attractive face, for the majority of a 20-second viewing period. Specifically, a sample of $n = 9$ infants spent an average of $M = 13$ seconds out of a 20-second period looking at the more attractive face. The data produced an estimated standard error of $s_M = 1$. We use this sample to construct a confidence interval to estimate the mean amount of time that the population of infants spends looking at the more attractive face. That is, we construct an interval of values that is likely to contain the unknown population mean.

Again, the estimation formula is

$$\mu = M \pm t(s_M)$$

To have 80% in the middle, there must be 20% (or .20) in the tails. To find the t values, look under two tails, .20 in the t table.

In the equation, the value of $M = 13$ and $s_M = 1$ are obtained from the sample data. The next step is to select a level of confidence that determines the value of t in the equation. The most commonly used confidence level is probably 95%, but values of 80%, 90%, and 99% are also common. For this example, we use a confidence level of 80%, which means that we construct the confidence interval so that we are 80% confident that the population mean is actually contained in the interval. Because we are using a confidence level of 80%, the resulting interval is called the *80% confidence interval for* μ.

To obtain the value for t in the equation, we simply estimate that the t statistic for our sample is located somewhere in the middle 80% of the t distribution. With $df = n - 1 = 8$, the middle 80% of the distribution is bounded by t values of $+1.397$ and -1.397 (see Figure 9.7). Using the sample data and the estimated range of t values, we obtain

$$\mu = M \pm t(s_M) = 13 \pm 1.397(1.00) = 13 \pm 1.397$$

At one end of the interval, we obtain $\mu = 13 + 1.397 = 14.397$, and at the other end we obtain $\mu = 13 - 1.397 = 11.603$. Our conclusion is that the average time looking at the more attractive fact for the population of infants is between $\mu = 11.603$ seconds and $\mu = 14.397$ seconds, and we are 80% confident that the true population mean is located within this interval. The confidence comes from the fact that the calculation was based on only one assumption. Specifically, we assumed that the t statistic was located between $+1.397$ and -1.397, and we are 80% confident that this assumption is correct because 80% of all of the possible t values are located in this interval. Finally, note that the confidence interval is constructed around the sample mean. As a result, the sample mean, $M = 13$, is located exactly in the center of the interval.

FACTORS AFFECTING THE WIDTH OF A CONFIDENCE INTERVAL

Two characteristics of the confidence interval should be noted. First, notice what happens to the width of the interval when you change the level of confidence (the percent confidence). To gain more confidence in your estimate, you must increase the width of the interval. Conversely, to have a smaller, more precise interval, you must give up confidence. In the estimation formula, the percentage of confidence influences the value of t. A larger level of confidence (the percentage), produces a larger t value and a wider interval. This relationship can be seen in Figure 9.7. In the figure, we identified the middle 80% of the t distribution to find an 80% confidence interval. It should be obvious that if we were to increase the confidence level to 95%, it would be necessary to increase the range of t values, and thereby increase the width of the interval.

Second, note what happens to the width of the interval if you change the sample size. This time the basic rule is as follows: The bigger the sample (n), the smaller the interval. This relationship is straightforward if you consider the sample size as a measure of the amount of information. A bigger sample gives you more information about the population and allows you to make a more precise estimate (a narrower interval). The sample size controls the magnitude of the standard error in the estimation formula. As the sample size increases, the standard error decreases, and the interval gets smaller. Because confidence intervals are influenced by sample size, they do not provide an unqualified measure of absolute effect size and are not an adequate substitute for Cohen's d or r^2. Nonetheless, they can be used in a research report to provide a description of the size of the treatment effect.

LEARNING CHECK

1. If all other factors are held constant, an 80% confidence interval is wider than a 90% confidence interval. (True or false?)
2. If all other factors are held constant, a confidence interval computed from a sample of $n = 25$ is wider than a confidence interval computed from a sample of $n = 100$. (True or false?)

ANSWERS

1. False. Greater confidence requires a wider interval.
2. True. The smaller sample produces a wider interval.

IN THE LITERATURE

REPORTING THE RESULTS OF A *t* TEST

In Chapter 8, we noted the conventional style for reporting the results of a hypothesis test, according to APA format. First, recall that a scientific report typically uses the term *significant* to indicate that the null hypothesis has been rejected and the term *not significant* to indicate failure to reject H_0. Additionally, there is a prescribed format for reporting the calculated value of the test statistic, degrees of freedom, and alpha level for a t test. This format parallels the style introduced in Chapter 8 (p. 251).

In Example 9.1 we calculated a t statistic of 3.00 with $df = 8$, and we decided to reject H_0 with alpha set at .05. Using the same data from Example 9.1, we obtained $r^2 = 0.5294$ (52.94%) for the percentage of variance explained by the treatment effect. In a scientific report, this information is conveyed in a concise statement, as follows:

> The infants spent an average of $M = 13$ out of 20 seconds looking at the attractive face, with $SD = 3.00$. Statistical analysis indicates that the time spent looking at the attractive face was significantly greater than would be expected if there were no preference, $t(8) = 3.00, p < .05, r^2 = 0.5294$.

The first statement reports the descriptive statistics, the mean ($M = 13$) and the standard deviation ($SD = 3$), as previously described (Chapter 4, p. 123). The next statement provides the results of the inferential statistical analysis. Note that the degrees of freedom are reported in parentheses immediately after the symbol t. The value for the obtained t statistic follows (3.00), and next is the probability of committing a Type I error (less than 5%). Finally, the effect size is reported, $r^2 = 52.94\%$. If the 80% confidence interval from Example 9.3 were included in the report as a description of effect size, it would be added after the results of the hypothesis test as follows:

$$t(8) = 3.00, p < .05, 80\% \text{ CI } [11.603, 14.397].$$

Often, researchers use a computer to perform a hypothesis test like the one in Example 9.1. In addition to calculating the mean, standard deviation, and the t statistic for the data, the computer usually calculates and reports the *exact probability* (or α level) associated with the t value. In Example 9.1 we determined that any t value beyond ± 2.306 has a probability of less than .05 (see Figure 9.4). Thus, the obtained t value, $t = 3.00$, is reported as being very unlikely, $p < .05$. A computer printout, however, would have included an exact probability for our specific t value.

The statement $p < .05$ was explained in Chapter 8, page 251.

Whenever a specific probability value is available, you are encouraged to use it in a research report. For example, the computer analysis of these data reports an exact p value of $p = .017$, and the research report would state "$t(8) = 3.00$, $p = .017$" instead of using the less specific "$p < .05$." As one final caution, we note that occasionally a t value is so extreme that the computer reports $p = 0.000$. The zero value does not mean that the probability is literally zero; instead, it means that the computer has rounded off the probability value to three decimal places and obtained a result of 0.000. In this situation, you do not know the exact probability value, but you can report $p < .001$.

LEARNING CHECK

1. A sample of $n = 16$ individuals is selected from a population with a mean of $\mu = 80$. A treatment is administered to the sample and, after treatment, the sample mean is found to be $M = 86$ with a standard deviation of $s = 8$.
   - **a.** Does the sample provide sufficient evidence to conclude that the treatment has a significant effect? Test with $\alpha = .05$.
   - **b.** Compute Cohen's d and r^2 to measure the effect size.
   - **c.** Find the 95% confidence interval for the population mean after treatment.
2. How does sample size influence the outcome of a hypothesis test and measures of effect size? How does the standard deviation influence the outcome of a hypothesis test and measures of effect size?

ANSWERS

1. **a.** The estimated standard error is 2 points and the data produce $t = 6/2 = 3.00$. With $df = 15$, the critical values are $t = \pm 2.131$, so the decision is to reject H_0 and conclude that there is a significant treatment effect.
   b. For these data, $d = 6/8 = 0.75$ and $r^2 = 9/24 = 0.375$ or 37.5%.
   c. For 95% confidence and $df = 15$, use $t = \pm 2.131$. The confidence interval is $\mu = 86 \pm 2.131(2)$ and extends from 81.738 to 90.262.
2. Increasing sample size increases the likelihood of rejecting the null hypothesis but has little or no effect on measures of effect size. Increasing the sample variance reduces the likelihood of rejecting the null hypothesis and reduces measures of effect size.

9.4 DIRECTIONAL HYPOTHESES AND ONE-TAILED TESTS

As noted in Chapter 8, the nondirectional (two-tailed) test is more commonly used than the directional (one-tailed) alternative. On the other hand, a directional test may be used in some research situations, such as exploratory investigations or pilot studies or when there is *a priori* justification (for example, a theory or previous findings). The following example demonstrates a directional hypothesis test with a *t* statistic, using the same experimental situation presented in Example 9.1.

EXAMPLE 9.4 The research question is whether attractiveness affects the behavior of infants looking at photographs of women's faces. The researcher is expecting the infants to prefer the more attractive face. Therefore, the researcher predicts that the infants will spend more than half of the 20-second period looking at the attractive face. For this example, we use the same sample data that were used in the original hypothesis test in Example 9.1. Specifically, the researcher tested a sample of $n = 9$ infants and obtained a mean of $M = 13$ seconds looking at the attractive face with $SS = 72$.

STEP 1 State the hypotheses, and select an alpha level. With most directional tests, it is usually easier to state the hypothesis in words, including the directional prediction, and then convert the words into symbols. For this example, the researcher is predicting that attractiveness will cause the infants to increase the amount of time they spend looking at the attractive face; that is, more than half of the 20 seconds should be spent looking at the attractive face. In general, the null hypothesis states that the predicted effect will not happen. For this study, the null hypothesis states that the infants will not spend more than half of the 20 seconds looking at the attractive face. In symbols,

H_0: $\mu_{attractive} \leq 10$ seconds (Not more than half of the 20 seconds looking at the attractive face)

Similarly, the alternative states that the treatment will work. In this case, H_1 states that the infants will spend more than half of the time looking at the attractive face. In symbols,

H_1: $\mu_{attractive} > 10$ seconds (More than half of the 20 seconds looking at the attractive face)

This time, we set the level of significance at $\alpha = .01$.

STEP 2 Locate the critical region. In this example, the researcher is predicting that the sample mean (*M*) will be greater than 10 seconds. Thus, if the infants average more than 10 seconds looking at the attractive face, the data will provide support for the researcher's prediction and will tend to refute the null hypothesis. Also note that a sample mean greater than 10 will produce a positive value for the *t* statistic. Thus, the critical region for the one-tailed test will consist of positive *t* values located in the right-hand tail of the distribution. To find the critical value, you must look in the *t* distribution table using the one-tail proportions. With a sample of $n = 9$, the *t* statistic has $df = 8$; using $\alpha = .01$, you should find a critical value of $t = 2.896$. Therefore, if we obtain a *t* statistic greater than 2.896, we will reject the null hypothesis and conclude that the infants show a significant preference for the attractive face. Figure 9.8 shows the one-tailed critical region for this test.

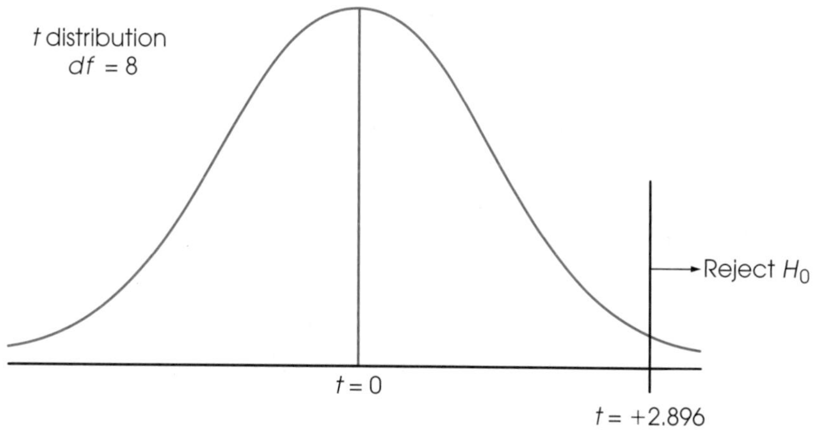

FIGURE 9.8

The one-tailed critical region for the hypothesis test in Example 9.4 with $df = 8$ and $\alpha = .01$.

STEP 3 Calculate the test statistic. The computation of the t statistic is the same for either a one-tailed or a two-tailed test. Earlier (in Example 9.1), we found that the data for this experiment produce a test statistic of $t = 3.00$.

STEP 4 Make a decision. The test statistic is in the critical region, so we reject H_0. In terms of the experimental variables, we have decided that the infants show a preference and spend significantly more time looking at the attractive face than they do looking at the unattractive face. In a research report, the results would be presented as follows:

> The time spent looking at the attractive face was significantly greater than would be expected if there were no preference, $t(8) = 3.00$, $p < .01$, one tailed.

Note that the report clearly acknowledges that a one-tailed test was used.

THE CRITICAL REGION FOR A ONE-TAILED TEST

In step 2 of Example 9.4, we determined that the critical region is in the right-hand tail of the distribution. However, it is possible to divide this step into two stages that eliminate the need to determine which tail (right or left) should contain the critical region. The first stage in this process is simply to determine whether the sample mean is in the direction predicted by the original research question. For this example, the researcher predicted that the infants would prefer the attractive face and spend more time looking at it. Specifically, the researcher expects the infants to spend more than 10 out of 20 seconds focused on the attractive face. The obtained sample mean, $M = 13$ seconds, is in the correct direction. This first stage eliminates the need to determine whether the critical region is in the left- or right-hand tail. Because we already have determined that the effect is in the correct direction, the sign of the t statistic (+ or –) no longer matters. The second stage of the process is to determine whether the effect is large enough to be significant. For this example, the requirement is that the sample produces a t statistic greater than 2.896. If the magnitude of the t statistic, independent of its sign, is greater than 2.896, then the result is significant and H_0 is rejected.

LEARNING CHECK

1. A new over-the-counter cold medication includes a warning label stating that it "may cause drowsiness." A researcher would like to evaluate this effect. It is known that under regular circumstances the distribution of reaction times is normal with $\mu = 200$. A sample of $n = 9$ participants is obtained. Each person is given the new cold medication, and, 1 hour later, reaction time is measured for each individual. The average reaction time for this sample is $M = 206$ with $SS = 648$. The researcher would like to use a hypothesis test with $\alpha = .05$ to evaluate the effect of the medication.
   a. Use a two-tailed test with $\alpha = .05$ to determine whether the medication has a significant effect on reaction time.
   b. Write a sentences that demonstrates how the outcome of the hypothesis test would appear in a research report.
   c. Use a one-tailed test with $\alpha = .05$ to determine whether the medication produces a significant increase in reaction time.
   d. Write a sentence that demonstrates how the outcome of the one-tailed hypothesis test would appear in a research report.

ANSWER

1. **a.** For the two-tailed test, H_0: $\mu = 200$. The sample variance is 81, the estimated standard error is 3, and $t = 6/3 = 2.00$. With $df = 8$, the critical boundaries are $\pm$ 2.306. Fail to reject the null hypothesis.
   b. The result indicates that the medication does not have a significant effect on reaction time, $t(8) = 2.00$, $p > .05$.
   c. For a one-tailed test, H_0: $\mu \leq 200$ (no increase). The data product $t = 6/3 = 2.00$. With $df = 8$, the critical boundary is 1.860. Reject the null hypothesis.
   d. The results indicate that the medication produces a significant increase in reaction time, $t(8) = 2.00$, $p < .05$, one tailed.

SUMMARY

1. The *t* statistic is used instead of a *z*-score for hypothesis testing when the population standard deviation (or variance) is unknown.
2. To compute the *t* statistic, you must first calculate the sample variance (or standard deviation) as a substitute for the unknown population value.

$$\text{sample variance} = s^2 = \frac{SS}{df}$$

Next, the standard error is *estimated* by substituting s^2 in the formula for standard error. The estimated standard error is calculated in the following manner:

$$\text{estimated standard error} = s_M = \sqrt{\frac{s^2}{n}}$$

Finally, a *t* statistic is computed using the estimated standard error. The *t* statistic is used as a substitute for a *z*-score that cannot be computed when the population variance or standard deviation is unknown.

$$t = \frac{M - \mu}{s_M}$$

The structure of the *t* formula is similar to that of the *z*-score in that

$$z \text{ or } t = \frac{\text{sample mean} - \text{population mean}}{\text{(estimated) standard error}}$$

For a hypothesis test, you hypothesize a value for the unknown population mean and plug the hypothesized value into the equation along with the sample mean and the estimated standard error, which are computed from the sample data. If the hypothesized mean produces an extreme value for t, then you conclude that the hypothesis was wrong.

4. The t distribution is an approximation of the normal z distribution. To evaluate a t statistic that is obtained for a sample mean, the critical region must be located in a t distribution. There is a family of t distributions, with the exact shape of a particular distribution of t values depending on degrees of freedom ($n - 1$). Therefore, the critical t values depend on the value for df associated with the t test. As df increases, the shape of the t distribution approaches a normal distribution.

5. When a t statistic is used for a hypothesis test, Cohen's d can be computed to measure effect size. In this situation, the sample standard deviation is used in the formula to obtain an estimated value for d:

$$\text{estimated } d = \frac{\text{mean difference}}{\text{standard deviation}} = \frac{M - \mu}{s}$$

6. A second measure of effect size is r^2, which measures the percentage of the variability that is accounted for by the treatment effect. This value is computed as follows:

$$r^2 = \frac{t^2}{t^2 + df}$$

7. An alternative method for describing the size of a treatment effect is to use a confidence interval for μ. A confidence interval is a range of values that estimates the unknown population mean. The confidence interval uses the t equation, solved for the unknown mean:

$$\mu = M \pm t(s_M)$$

First, select a level of confidence and then look up the corresponding t values to use in the equation. For example, for 95% confidence, use the range of t values that determine the middle 95% of the distribution.

KEY TERMS

estimated standard error (286)

t statistic (286)

degrees of freedom (287)

t distribution (287)

estimated d (295)

percentage of variance accounted for by the treatment (r^2) (299)

confidence interval (300)

RESOURCES

Book Companion Website: www.cengage.com/psychology/gravetter

You can find a tutorial quiz and other learning exercises for Chapter 9 on the book companion website. The website also provides access to a workshop entitled *Single-Sample* t *Test,* which reviews the concepts and logic of hypothesis testing with the t statistic.

aplia

Improve your understanding of statistics with Aplia's auto-graded problem sets and immediate, detailed explanations for every question. To learn more, visit **www.aplia.com/statistics.**

CENGAGEbrain.com

Psychology CourseMate brings course concepts to life with interactive learning, study, and exam preparation tools that support the printed textbook. A textbook-specific website, Psychology CourseMate includes an integrated interactive eBook and other interactive learning tools including quizzes, flashcards, and more.

Visit www.cengagebrain.com to access your account and purchase materials.

SPSS

General instructions for using SPSS are presented in Appendix D. Following are detailed instructions for using SPSS to perform the ***t* Test** presented in this chapter.

Data Entry

Enter all of the scores from the sample in one column of the data editor, probably VAR00001.

Data Analysis

1. Click Analyze on the tool bar, select **Compare Means,** and click on **One-Sample T Test.**
2. Highlight the column label for the set of scores (VAR0001) in the left box and click the arrow to move it into the **Test Variable(s)** box.
3. In the **Test Value** box at the bottom of the One-Sample *t* Test window, enter the hypothesized value for the population mean from the null hypothesis. *Note:* The value is automatically set at zero until you type in a new value.
4. In addition to performing the hypothesis test, the program computes a confidence interval for the population mean difference. The confidence level is automatically set at 95%, but you can select **Options** and change the percentage.
5. Click **OK.**

SPSS Output

We used the SPSS program to analyze the data from the infants-and-attractive-faces study in Example 9.1 and the program output is shown in Figure 9.9. The output includes a table of sample statistics with the mean, standard deviation, and standard error for the sample mean. A second table shows the results of the hypothesis test, including the values for *t*, *df*, and the level of significance (the *p* value for the test), as well as the mean difference from the hypothesized value of $\mu = 10$ and a 95% confidence interval for the mean difference. To obtain a 95% confidence interval for the mean, simply add $\mu = 10$ points to the values in the table.

FOCUS ON PROBLEM SOLVING

1. The first problem we confront in analyzing data is determining the appropriate statistical test. Remember that you can use a *z*-score for the test statistic only when the value for σ is known. If the value for σ is not provided, then you must use the *t* statistic.

One-Sample Statistics

	N	Mean	Std. Deviation	Std. Error Mean
VAR00001	9	13.0000	3.00000	1.00000

One-Sample Test

	Test Value = 10					
					95% Confidence Interval of the Difference	
	t	df	Sig. (2-tailed)	Mean Difference	Lower	Upper
VAR00001	3.000	8	.017	3.00000	.6940	5.3060

FIGURE 9.9

The SPSS output for the hypothesis test presented in Example 9.1.

2. For the t test, the sample variance is used to find the value for the estimated standard error. Remember to use $n - 1$ in the denominator when computing the sample variance (see Chapter 4). When computing estimated standard error, use n in the denominator.

DEMONSTRATION 9.1

A HYPOTHESIS TEST WITH THE *t* STATISTIC

A psychologist has prepared an "Optimism Test" that is administered yearly to graduating college seniors. The test measures how each graduating class feels about its future—the higher the score, the more optimistic the class. Last year's class had a mean score of $\mu = 15$. A sample of $n = 9$ seniors from this year's class was selected and tested. The scores for these seniors are 7, 12, 11, 15, 7, 8, 15, 9, and 6, which produce a sample mean of $M = 10$ with $SS = 94$.

On the basis of this sample, can the psychologist conclude that this year's class has a different level of optimism than last year's class?

Note that this hypothesis test uses a t statistic because the population variance (σ^2) is not known.

STEP 1 **State the hypotheses, and select an alpha level.** The statements for the null hypothesis and the alternative hypothesis follow the same form for the t statistic and the z-score test.

$$H_0: \mu = 15 \qquad \text{(There is no change.)}$$

$$H_1: \mu \neq 15 \qquad \text{(This year's mean is different.)}$$

For this demonstration, we use $\alpha = .05$, two tails.

STEP 2 **Locate the critical region.** With a sample of $n = 9$ students, the t statistic has $df = n - 1 = 8$. For a two-tailed test with $\alpha = .05$ and $df = 8$, the critical t values are $t = \pm 2.306$. These critical t values define the boundaries of the critical region. The obtained t value must be more extreme than either of these critical values to reject H_0.

STEP 3 **Compute the test statistic.** As we have noted, it is easier to separate the calculation of the t statistic into three stages.

Sample variance.

$$s^2 = \frac{SS}{n-1} = \frac{94}{8} = 11.75$$

Estimated standard error. The estimated standard error for these data is

$$s_M = \sqrt{\frac{s^2}{n}} = \sqrt{\frac{11.75}{9}} = 1.14$$

The t statistic. Now that we have the estimated standard error and the sample mean, we can compute the t statistic. For this demonstration,

$$t = \frac{M - \mu}{s_M} = \frac{10 - 15}{1.14} = \frac{-5}{1.14} = -4.39$$

STEP 4 **Make a decision about H_0, and state a conclusion.** The t statistic we obtained ($t = -4.39$) is in the critical region. Thus, our sample data are unusual enough to reject the null hypothesis at the .05 level of significance. We can conclude that there is a significant difference in level of optimism between this year's and last year's graduating classes, $t(8) = -4.39$, $p < .05$, two-tailed.

DEMONSTRATION 9.2

EFFECT SIZE: ESTIMATING COHEN'S *d* AND COMPUTING r^2

We will estimate Cohen's d for the same data used for the hypothesis test in Demonstration 9.1. The mean optimism score for the sample from this year's class was 5 points lower than the mean from last year ($M = 10$ versus $\mu = 15$). In Demonstration 9.1, we computed a sample variance of $s^2 = 11.75$, so the standard deviation is $\sqrt{11.75} = 3.43$. With these values,

$$\text{estimated } d = \frac{\text{mean difference}}{\text{standard deviation}} = \frac{5}{3.43} = 1.46$$

To calculate the percentage of variance explained by the treatment effect, r^2, we need the value of t and the df value from the hypothesis test. In Demonstration 9.1, we obtained $t = -4.39$ with $df = 8$. Using these values in Equation 9.5, we obtain

$$r^2 = \frac{t^2}{t^2 + df} = \frac{(-4.39)^2}{(-4.39)^2 + 8} = \frac{19.27}{27.27} = 0.71$$

PROBLEMS

1. Under what circumstances is a t statistic used instead of a z-score for a hypothesis test?

2. Explain why t distributions tend to be flatter and more spread out than the normal distribution.

3. Find the estimated standard error for the sample mean for each of the following samples.
   a. $n = 4$ with $SS = 48$
   b. $n = 6$ with $SS = 270$
   c. $n = 12$ with $SS = 132$

4. A sample of $n = 25$ scores has a mean of $M = 83$ and a standard deviation of $s = 15$.
   a. Explain what is measured by the sample standard deviation.
   b. Compute the estimated standard error for the sample mean and explain what is measured by the standard error.

5. Find the t values that form the boundaries of the critical region for a two-tailed test with $\alpha = .05$ for each of the following sample sizes:
   a. $n = 6$
   b. $n = 12$
   c. $n = 24$

6. The following sample of $n = 6$ scores was obtained from a population with unknown parameters.
   Scores: 7, 1, 6, 3, 6, 7
   a. Compute the sample mean and standard deviation. (Note that these are descriptive values that summarize the sample data.)
   b. Compute the estimated standard error for M. (Note that this is an inferential value that describes how accurately the sample mean represents the unknown population mean.)

7. The following sample was obtained from a population with unknown parameters.
   Scores: 6, 12, 0, 3, 4
   a. Compute the sample mean and standard deviation. (Note that these are descriptive values that summarize the sample data.)
   b. Compute the estimated standard error for M. (Note that this is an inferential value that describes how accurately the sample mean represents the unknown population mean.)

8. To evaluate the effect of a treatment, a sample is obtained from a population with a mean of $\mu = 75$, and the treatment is administered to the individuals in the sample. After treatment, the sample mean is found to be $M = 79.6$ with a standard deviation of $s = 12$.
   a. If the sample consists of $n = 16$ individuals, are the data sufficient to conclude that the treatment has a significant effect using a two-tailed test with $\alpha = .05$?
   b. If the sample consists of $n = 36$ individuals, are the data sufficient to conclude that the treatment has a significant effect using a two-tailed test with $\alpha = .05$?
   c. Comparing your answer for parts a and b, how does the size of the sample influence the outcome of a hypothesis test?

9. To evaluate the effect of a treatment, a sample of $n = 9$ is obtained from a population with a mean of $\mu = 40$, and the treatment is administered to the individuals in the sample. After treatment, the sample mean is found to be $M = 33$.
   a. If the sample has a standard deviation of $s = 9$, are the data sufficient to conclude that the treatment has a significant effect using a two-tailed test with $\alpha = .05$?
   b. If the sample standard deviation is $s = 15$, are the data sufficient to conclude that the treatment has a significant effect using a two-tailed test with $\alpha = .05$?
   c. Comparing your answer for parts a and b, how does the variability of the scores in the sample influence the outcome of a hypothesis test?

10. A random sample of $n = 16$ individuals is selected from a population with $\mu = 70$, and a treatment is administered to each individual in the sample. After treatment, the sample mean is found to be $M = 76$ with $SS = 960$.
    a. How much difference is there between the mean for the treated sample and the mean for the original population? (*Note:* In a hypothesis test, this value forms the numerator of the t statistic.)
    b. How much difference is expected just by chance between the sample mean and its population mean? That is, find the standard error for M. (*Note:* In a hypothesis test, this value is the denominator of the t statistic.)
    c. Based on the sample data, does the treatment have a significant effect? Use a two-tailed test with $\alpha = .05$.

11. The spotlight effect refers to overestimating the extent to which others notice your appearance or behavior, especially when you commit a social faux pas. Effectively, you feel as if you are suddenly standing in a spotlight with everyone looking. In one demonstration of this phenomenon, Gilovich, Medvec, and Savitsky (2000) asked college students to put on a Barry Manilow T-shirt that fellow students had previously judged to be embarrassing. The participants were

then led into a room in which other students were already participating in an experiment. After a few minutes, the participant was led back out of the room and was allowed to remove the shirt. Later, each participant was asked to estimate how many people in the room had noticed the shirt. The individuals who were in the room were also asked whether they noticed the shirt. In the study, the participants significantly overestimated the actual number of people who had noticed.

a. In a similar study using a sample of $n = 9$ participants, the individuals who wore the shirt produced an average estimate of $M = 6.4$ with $SS = 162$. The average number who said they noticed was 3.1. Is the estimate from the participants significantly different from the actual number? Test the null hypothesis that the true mean is $\mu = 3.1$ using a two-tailed test with $\alpha = .05$.

b. Is the estimate from the participants significantly higher than the actual number ($\mu = 3.1$)? Use a one-tailed test with $\alpha = .05$.

12. The librarian at the local elementary school claims that, on average, the books in the library are more than 20 years old. To test this claim, a student takes a sample of $n = 30$ books and records the publication date for each. The sample produces an average age of $M = 23.8$ years with a variance of $s^2 = 67.5$. Use this sample to conduct a one-tailed test with $\alpha = .01$ to determine whether the average age of the library books is significantly greater than 20 years ($\mu > 20$).

13. Standardized measures seem to indicate that the average level of anxiety has increased gradually over the past 50 years (Twenge, 2000). In the 1950s, the average score on the Child Manifest Anxiety Scale was $\mu = 15.1$. A sample of $n = 16$ of today's children produces a mean score of $M = 23.3$ with $SS = 240$.

a. Based on the sample, has there been a significant change in the average level of anxiety since the 1950s? Use a two-tailed test with $\alpha = .01$.

b. Make a 90% confidence interval estimate of today's population mean level of anxiety.

c. Write a sentence that demonstrates how the outcome of the hypothesis test and the confidence interval would appear in a research report.

14. Many animals, including humans, tend to avoid direct eye contact and even patterns that look like eyes. Some insects, including moths, have evolved eye-spot patterns on their wings to help ward off predators. Scaife (1976) reports a study examining how eye-spot patterns affect the behavior of birds. In the study, the birds were tested in a box with two chambers and were free to move from one chamber to another. In one chamber, two large eye-spots were painted on one wall. The other chamber had plain walls. The researcher recorded the amount of time each bird spent in the plain chamber during a 60-minute session. Suppose the study produced a mean of $M = 37$ minutes in the plain chamber with $SS = 288$ for a sample of $n = 9$ birds. (*Note:* If the eye-spots have no effect, then the birds should spend an average of $\mu = 30$ minutes in each chamber.)

a. Is this sample sufficient to conclude that the eye-spots have a significant influence on the birds' behavior? Use a two-tailed test with $\alpha = .05$.

b. Compute the estimated Cohen's *d* to measure the size of the treatment effect.

c. Construct the 95% confidence interval to estimate the mean amount of time spent on the plain side for the population of birds.

15. For several years researchers have noticed that there appears to be a regular, year-by-year increase in the average IQ for the general population. This phenomenon is called the Flynn effect after the researcher who first reported it (Flynn, 1984, 1999), and it means that psychologists must continuously update IQ tests to keep the population mean at $\mu = 100$. To evaluate the size of the effect, a researcher obtained a 10-year-old IQ test that was standardized to produce a mean IQ of $\mu = 100$ for the population 10 years ago. The test was then given to a sample of $n = 64$ of today's 20-year-old adults. The average score for the sample was $M = 107$ with a standard deviation of $s = 12$.

a. Based on the sample, is the average IQ for today's population significantly different from the average 10 years ago, when the test would have produces a mean of $\mu = 100$? Use a two-tailed test with $\alpha = .01$.

b. Make an 80% confidence interval estimate of today's population mean IQ for the 10-year-old test.

16. In a classic study of infant attachment, Harlow (1959) placed infant monkeys in cages with two artificial surrogate mothers. One "mother" was made from bare wire mesh and contained a baby bottle from which the infants could feed. The other mother was made from soft terry cloth and did not provide any access to food. Harlow observed the infant monkeys and recorded how much time per day was spent with each mother. In a typical day, the infants spent a total of 18 hours clinging to one of the two mothers. If there were no preference between the two, you would expect the time to be divided evenly, with an average of $\mu = 9$ hours for each of the mothers. However, the typical monkey spent around 15 hours per day with the terry-cloth mother, indicating a strong preference for the soft, cuddly mother. Suppose a sample of $n = 9$ infant monkeys averaged $M = 15.3$ hours per day with $SS = 216$ with the terry-cloth mother. Is this result sufficient to conclude that the monkeys spent significantly more time with the softer mother than would be expected if there were no preference? Use a two-tailed test with $\alpha = .05$.

17. Belsky, Weinraub, Owen, and Kelly (2001) reported on the effects of preschool childcare on the development of young children. One result suggests that children who spend more time away from their mothers are more likely to show behavioral problems in kindergarten. Using a standardized scale, the average rating of behavioral problems for kindergarten children is $\mu = 35$. A sample of $n = 16$ kindergarten children who had spent at least 20 hours per week in childcare during the previous year produced a mean score of $M = 42.7$ with a standard deviation of $s = 6$.

a. Are the data sufficient to conclude that children with a history of childcare show significantly more behavioral problems than the average kindergarten child? Use a one-tailed test with $\alpha = .01$.

b. Compute r^2, the percentage of variance accounted for, to measure the size of the preschool effect.

c. Write a sentence showing how the outcome of the hypothesis test and the measure of effect size would appear in a research report.

18. A random sample is obtained from a population with a mean of $\mu = 70$. A treatment is administered to the individuals in the sample and, after treatment, the sample mean is $M = 78$ with a standard deviation of $s = 20$.

a. Assuming that the sample consists of $n = 25$ scores, compute r^2 and the estimated Cohen's d to measure the size of treatment effect.

b. Assuming that the sample consists of $n = 16$ scores, compute r^2 and the estimated Cohen's d to measure the size of treatment effect.

c. Comparing your answers from parts a and b, how does the number of scores in the sample influence the measures of effect size?

19. A random sample of $n = 25$ scores is obtained from a population with a mean of $\mu = 45$. A treatment is administered to the individuals in the sample and, after treatment, the sample mean is $M = 48$.

a. Assuming that the sample standard deviation is $s = 6$ compute r^2 and the estimated Cohen's d to measure the size of the treatment effect.

b. Assuming that the sample standard deviation is $s = 15$, compute r^2 and the estimated Cohen's d to measure the size of the treatment effect.

c. Comparing your answers from parts a and b, how does the variability of the scores in the sample influence the measures of effect size?

20. Other research examining the effects of preschool childcare has found that children who spent time in day care, especially high-quality day care, perform better on math and language tests than children who stay home with their mothers (Broberg, Wessels, Lamb, & Hwang, 1997). Typical results, for example, show that a sample of $n = 25$ children who attended day care before starting school had an average score of $M = 87$ with $SS = 1536$ on a standardized math test for which the population mean is $\mu = 81$.

a. Is this sample sufficient to conclude that the children with a history of preschool day care are significantly different from the general population? Use a two-tailed test with $\alpha = .01$.

b. Compute Cohen's d to measure the size of the preschool effect.

c. Write a sentence showing how the outcome of the hypothesis test and the measure of effect size would appear in a research report.

21. An example of the vertical-horizontal illusion is shown in the figure below. Although the two lines are exactly the same length, the vertical line appears to be much longer. To examine the strength of this illusion, a researcher prepared an example in which both lines were exactly 10 inches long. The example was shown to individual participants who were told that the horizontal line was 10 inches long and then were asked to estimate the length of the vertical line. For a sample of $n = 25$ participants, the average estimate was $M = 12.2$ inches with a standard deviation of $s = 1.00$.

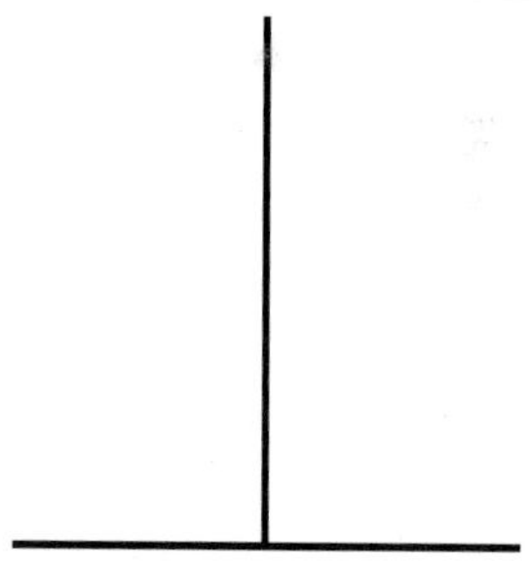

An example of the vertical-horizontal illusion

a. Use a one-tailed hypothesis test with $\alpha = .01$ to demonstrate that the individuals in the sample significantly overestimate the true length of the line. (*Note:* Accurate estimation would produce a mean of $\mu = 10$ inches.)

b. Calculate the estimated d and r^2, the percentage of variance accounted for, to measure the size of this effect.

c. Construct a 95% confidence interval for the population mean estimated length of the vertical line.

22. In studies examining the effect of humor on interpersonal attractions, McGee and Shevlin (2009) found that an individual's sense of humor had a significant effect on how the individual was perceived by others. In one part of the study, female college students were given brief descriptions of a potential romantic partner. The fictitious male was described positively as being single, ambitious, and having good job prospects. For one group of participants, the description also said that he had a great sense of humor. For another group, it said that he had no sense of humor. After reading the description, each participant was asked to rate the attractiveness of the man on a seven-point scale from 1 (very attractive) to 7 (very unattractive). A score of 4 indicates a neutral rating.

a. The females who read the "great sense of humor" description gave the potential partner an average attractiveness score of $M = 4.53$ with a standard deviation of $s = 1.04$. If the sample consisted of $n = 16$ participants, is the average rating significantly higher than neutral ($\mu = 4$)? Use a one-tailed test with $\alpha = .05$.

b. The females who read the description saying "no sense of humor" gave the potential partner an average attractiveness score of $M = 3.30$ with a standard deviation of $s = 1.18$. If the sample consisted of $n = 16$ participants, is the average rating significantly lower than neutral ($\mu = 4$)? Use a one-tailed test with $\alpha = .05$.

23. A psychologist would like to determine whether there is a relationship between depression and aging. It is known that the general population averages $\mu = 40$ on a standardized depression test. The psychologist obtains a sample of $n = 9$ individuals who are all more than 70 years old. The depression scores for this sample are as follows: 37, 50, 43, 41, 39, 45, 49, 44, 48.

a. On the basis of this sample, is depression for elderly people significantly different from depression in the general population? Use a two-tailed test with $\alpha = .05$.

b. Compute the estimated Cohen's d to measure the size of the difference.

c. Write a sentence showing how the outcome of the hypothesis test and the measure of effect size would appear in a research report.

CHAPTER

10

The *t* Test for Two Independent Samples

Tools You Will Need

The following items are considered essential background material for this chapter. If you doubt your knowledge of any of these items, you should review the appropriate chapter or section before proceeding.

- Sample variance (Chapter 4)
- Standard error formulas (Chapter 7)
- The *t* statistic (Chapter 9)
  - Distribution of *t* values
  - *df* for the *t* statistic
  - Estimated standard error

Preview

In a classic study in the area of problem solving, Katona (1940) compared the effectiveness of two methods of instruction. One group of participants was shown the exact, step-by-step procedure for solving a problem, and then these participants were required to memorize the solution. This method was called *learning by memorization* (later called the *expository* method). Participants in a second group were encouraged to study the problem and find the solution on their own. Although these participants were given helpful hints and clues, the exact solution was never explained. This method was called *learning by understanding* (later called the *discovery* method).

Katona's experiment included the problem shown in Figure 10.1. This figure shows a pattern of five squares made of matchsticks. The problem is to change the pattern into exactly four squares by moving only three matches. (All matches must be used, none can be removed, and all the squares must be the same size.) Two groups of participants learned the solution to this problem. One group learned by understanding, and the other group learned by memorization. After 3 weeks, both groups returned to be tested again. The two groups did equally well on the matchstick problem they had learned earlier. But when they were given two new problems (similar to the matchstick problem), the *understanding* group performed much better than the *memorization* group.

FIGURE 10.1

A pattern of five squares made of matchsticks. The problem is to change the pattern into exactly four squares by moving only three matchsticks.

The Problem: Although the data a show a mean difference between the two groups in Katona's study, you cannot automatically conclude that the difference was caused by the method they used to solve the first problem. Specifically, the two groups consist of different people with different backgrounds, different skills, different IQs, and so on. Because the two different groups consist of different individuals, you should expect them to have different scores and different means. This issue was first presented in Chapter 1 when we introduced the concept of sampling error (see Figure 1.2 on p. 9). Thus, there are two possible explanations for the difference between the two groups.

1. It is possible that there really is a difference between the two treatment conditions so that the method of understanding produces better learning than the method of memorization.
2. It is possible that there is no difference between the two treatment conditions and the mean difference obtained in the experiment is simply the result of sampling error.

A hypothesis test is necessary to determine which of the two explanations is most plausible. However, the hypothesis tests we have examined thus far are intended to evaluate the data from only one sample. In this study there are two separate samples.

The Solution: In this chapter we introduce the *independent-measures* t *test,* which is a hypothesis test that uses two separate samples to evaluate the mean difference between two treatment conditions or between two different populations. Like the t test introduced in Chapter 9, the independent-measures t test uses the sample variance to compute an estimated standard error. This test, however, combines the variance from the two separate samples to evaluate the difference between two separate sample means.

Incidentally, if you still have not discovered the solution to the matchstick problem, keep trying. According to Katona's results, it would be a very poor teaching strategy for us to give you the answer to the matchstick problem. If you still have not discovered the solution, however, check Appendix C at the beginning of the Chapter 10 problem solutions; there we show you how it is done.

10.1 INTRODUCTION TO THE INDEPENDENT-MEASURES DESIGN

Until this point, all the inferential statistics we have considered involve using one sample as the basis for drawing conclusions about one population. Although these *single-sample* techniques are used occasionally in real research, most research studies require the comparison of two (or more) sets of data. For example, a social psychologist may want to compare men and women in terms of their political attitudes, an educational psychologist may want to compare two methods for teaching mathematics, or a clinical psychologist may want to evaluate a therapy technique by comparing depression scores for patients before therapy with their scores after therapy. In each case, the research question concerns a mean difference between two sets of data.

There are two general research designs that can be used to obtain the two sets of data to be compared:

1. The two sets of data could come from two completely separate groups of participants. For example, the study could involve a sample of men compared with a sample of women. Or the study could compare grades for one group of freshmen who are given laptop computers with grades for a second group who are not given computers.
2. The two sets of data could come from the same group of participants. For example, the researcher could obtain one set of scores by measuring depression for a sample of patients before they begin therapy and then obtain a second set of data by measuring the same individuals after 6 weeks of therapy.

The first research strategy, using completely separate groups, is called an *independent-measures* research design or a *between-subjects* design. These terms emphasize the fact that the design involves separate and independent samples and makes a comparison between two groups of individuals. The structure of an independent-measures research design is shown in Figure 10.2. Notice that the research study uses two separate

FIGURE 10.2

Do the achievement scores for children taught by method A differ from the scores for children taught by method B? In statistical terms, are the two population means the same or different? Because neither of the two population means is known, it will be necessary to take two samples, one from each population. The first sample provides information about the mean for the first population, and the second sample provides information about the second population.

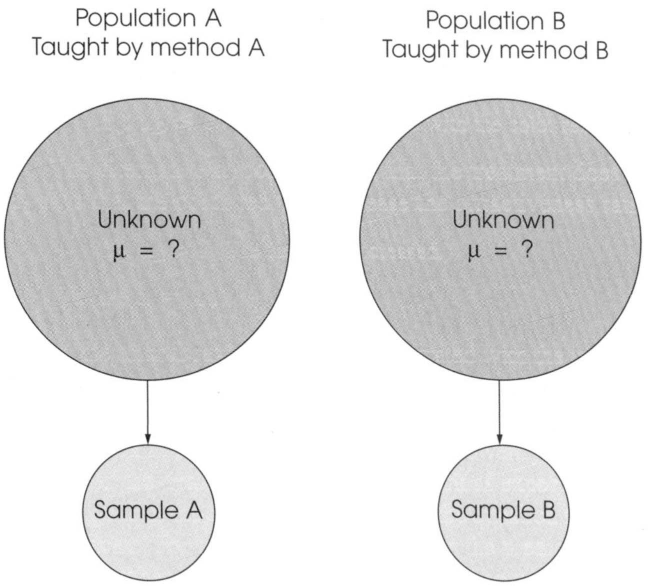

samples to represent the two different populations (or two different treatments) being compared.

DEFINITION

A research design that uses a separate group of participants for each treatment condition (or for each population) is called an **independent-measures research design** or a **between-subjects research design.**

In this chapter, we examine the statistical techniques used to evaluate the data from an independent-measures design. More precisely, we introduce the hypothesis test that allows researchers to use the data from two separate samples to evaluate the mean difference between two populations or between two treatment conditions.

The second research strategy, in which the two sets of data are obtained from the same group of participants, is called a *repeated-measures* research design or a *within-subjects* design. The statistics for evaluating the results from a repeated-measures design are introduced in Chapter 11. Also, at the end of Chapter 11, we discuss some of the advantages and disadvantages of independent-measures and repeated-measures designs.

10.2 THE *t* STATISTIC FOR AN INDEPENDENT-MEASURES RESEARCH DESIGN

Because an independent-measures study involves two separate samples, we need some special notation to help specify which data go with which sample. This notation involves the use of subscripts, which are small numbers written beside a sample statistic. For example, the number of scores in the first sample would be identified by n_1; for the second sample, the number of scores is n_2. The sample means would be identified by M_1 and M_2. The sums of squares would be SS_1 and SS_2.

THE HYPOTHESIS FOR AN INDEPENDENT-MEASURES TEST

The goal of an independent-measures research study is to evaluate the mean difference between two populations (or between two treatment conditions). Using subscripts to differentiate the two populations, the mean for the first population is μ_1, and the second population mean is μ_2. The difference between means is simply $\mu_1 - \mu_2$. As always, the null hypothesis states that there is no change, no effect, or, in this case, no difference. Thus, in symbols, the null hypothesis for the independent-measures test is

$$H_0: \mu_1 - \mu_2 = 0 \text{ (No difference between the population means)}$$

You should notice that the null hypothesis could also be stated as $\mu_1 = \mu_2$. However, the first version of H_0 produces a specific numerical value (zero) that is used in the calculation of the *t* statistic. Therefore, we prefer to phrase the null hypothesis in terms of the difference between the two population means.

The alternative hypothesis states that there is a mean difference between the two populations,

$$H_1: \mu_1 - \mu_2 \neq 0 \text{ (There is a mean difference.)}$$

Equivalently, the alternative hypothesis can simply state that the two population means are not equal: $\mu_1 \neq \mu_2$.

THE FORMULAS FOR AN INDEPENDENT-MEASURES HYPOTHESIS TEST

The independent-measures hypothesis test uses another version of the t statistic. The formula for this new t statistic has the same general structure as the t statistic formula that was introduced in Chapter 9. To help distinguish between the two t formulas, we refer to the original formula (Chapter 9) as the *single-sample* t *statistic* and we refer to the new formula as the *independent-measures* t *statistic*. Because the new independent-measures t includes data from two separate samples and hypotheses about two populations, the formulas may appear to be a bit overpowering. However, the new formulas are easier to understand if you view them in relation to the single-sample t formulas from Chapter 9. In particular, there are two points to remember:

1. The basic structure of the t statistic is the same for both the independent-measures and the single-sample hypothesis tests. In both cases,

$$t = \frac{\text{sample statistic} - \text{hypothesized population parameter}}{\text{estimated standard error}}$$

2. The independent-measures t is basically a *two-sample* t *that doubles all the elements of the single-sample* t *formulas.*

To demonstrate the second point, we examine the two t formulas piece by piece.

The overall *t* formula The single-sample t uses one sample mean to test a hypothesis about one population mean. The sample mean and the population mean appear in the numerator of the t formula, which measures how much difference there is between the sample data and the population hypothesis.

$$t = \frac{\text{sample mean} - \text{population mean}}{\text{estimated standard error}} = \frac{M - \mu}{s_M}$$

The independent-measures t uses the difference between *two* sample means to evaluate a hypothesis about the difference between *two* population means. Thus, the independent-measures t formula is

$$t = \frac{\text{sample mean difference} - \text{population mean difference}}{\text{estimated standard error}} = \frac{(M_1 - M_2) - (\mu_1 - \mu_2)}{s_{(M_1 - M_2)}}$$

In this formula, the value of $M_1 - M_2$ is obtained from the sample data and the value for $\mu_1 - \mu_2$ comes from the null hypothesis.

The estimated standard error In each of the t-score formulas, the standard error in the denominator measures how accurately the sample statistic represents the population parameter. In the single-sample t formula, the standard error measures the amount of error expected for a sample mean and is represented by the symbol s_M. For the independent-measures t formula, the standard error measures the amount of error that is expected when you use a sample mean difference ($M_1 - M_2$) to represent a population mean difference ($\mu_1 - \mu_2$). The standard error for the sample mean difference is represented by the symbol $s_{(M_1 - M_2)}$.

Caution: Do not let the notation for standard error confuse you. In general, standard error measures how accurately a statistic represents a parameter. The symbol for standard error takes the form $s_{\text{statistic}}$. When the statistic is a sample mean, M, the symbol for standard error is s_M. For the independent-measures test, the statistic is a sample mean difference ($M_1 - M_2$), and the symbol for standard error is $s_{(M_1-M_2)}$. In each case, the standard error tells how much discrepancy is reasonable to expect between the sample statistic and the corresponding population parameter.

Interpreting the estimated standard error The *estimated standard error of* $M_1 - M_2$ that appears in the bottom of the independent-measures t statistic can be interpreted in two ways. First, the standard error is defined as a measure of the standard, or average, distance between a sample statistic ($M_1 - M_2$) and the corresponding population parameter ($\mu_1 - \mu_2$). As always, samples are not expected to be perfectly accurate and the standard error measures how much difference is reasonable to expect between a sample statistic and the population parameter.

$$\begin{array}{ccc} \text{Sample mean} & & \text{Population mean} \\ \text{difference} & \xleftrightarrow[\text{(average distance)}]{\text{estimated standard error}} & \text{difference} \\ (M_1 - M_2) & & (\mu_1 - \mu_2) \end{array}$$

When the null hypothesis is true, however, the population mean difference is zero.

$$\begin{array}{ccc} \text{Sample mean} & & \\ \text{difference} & \xleftrightarrow[\text{(average distance)}]{\text{estimated standard error}} & 0(\text{If } H_0 \text{ is true}) \\ (M_1 - M_2) & & \end{array}$$

The standard error is measuring how close the sample mean difference is to zero, which is equivalent to measuring how much difference there is between the two sample means.

$$M_1 \xleftrightarrow[\text{(average distance)}]{\text{estimated standard error}} M_2$$

This produces a second interpretation for the estimated standard error. Specifically, the standard error can be viewed as a measure of how much difference is reasonable to expect between two sample means if the null hypothesis is true.

The second interpretation of the estimated standard error produces a simplified version of the independent-measures t statistic.

$$t = \frac{\text{sample mean difference}}{\text{estimated standard error}}$$

$$= \frac{\text{actual difference between } M_1 \text{ and } M_2}{\text{standard difference (If } H_0 \text{ is true) between } M_1 \text{ and } M_2}$$

In this version, the numerator of the t statistic measures how much difference *actually exists* between the two sample means, including any difference that is caused by the different treatments. The denominator measures how much difference *should exist* between the two sample means if there is no treatment effect that causes them to be different. A large value for the t statistic is evidence for the existence of a treatment effect.

CALCULATING THE ESTIMATED STANDARD ERROR

To develop the formula for $s_{(M_1-M_2)}$, we consider the following three points:

1. Each of the two sample means represents it own population mean, but in each case there is some error.

M_1 approximates μ_1 with some error.

M_2 approximates μ_2 with some error.

Thus, there are two sources of error.

2. The amount of error associated with each sample mean is measured by the estimated standard error of M. Using Equation 9.1 (p. 285), the estimated standard error for each sample mean is computed as follows:

$$\text{For } M_1 \quad s_M = \sqrt{\frac{s_1^2}{n_1}} \qquad \text{For } M_2 \quad s_M = \sqrt{\frac{s_2^2}{n_2}}$$

3. For the independent-measures t statistic, we want to know the total amount of error involved in using *two* sample means to approximate *two* population means. To do this, we find the error from each sample separately and then add the two errors together. The resulting formula for standard error is

$$s_{(M_1-M_2)} = \sqrt{\frac{s_1^2}{n_1} + \frac{s_2^2}{n_2}} \tag{10.1}$$

Because the independent-measures t statistic uses two sample means, the formula for the estimated standard error simply combines the error for the first sample mean and the error for the second sample mean (Box 10.1).

POOLED VARIANCE

Although Equation 10.1 accurately presents the concept of standard error for the independent-measures t statistic, this formula is limited to situations in which the

BOX 10.1 THE VARIABILITY OF DIFFERENCE SCORES

It may seem odd that the independent-measures t statistic *adds* together the two sample errors when it *subtracts* to find the difference between the two sample means. The logic behind this apparently unusual procedure is demonstrated here.

We begin with two populations, I and II (Figure 10.3). The scores in population I range from a high of 70 to a low of 50. The scores in population II range from 30 to 20. We use the range as a measure of how spread out (variable) each population is:

For population I, the scores cover a range of 20 points.
For population II, the scores cover a range of 10 points.

If we randomly select one score from population I and one score from population II and compute the difference between these two scores ($X_1 - X_2$), what range of values is possible for these differences? To answer this question, we need to find the biggest possible difference and the smallest possible difference. Look at Figure 10.3; the biggest difference occurs when $X_1 = 70$ and $X_2 = 20$. This is a difference of $X_1 - X_2 = 50$ points. The smallest difference occurs when $X_1 = 50$ and $X_2 = 30$. This is a difference of $X_1 - X_2 = 20$ points. Notice that the differences go from a high of 50 to a low of 20. This is a range of 30 points:

range for population I (X_1 scores) = 20 points
range for population II (X_2 scores) = 10 points
range for the differences ($X_1 - X_2$) = 30 points

The variability for the difference scores is found by *adding* together the variability for each of the two populations.

In the independent-measures t statistics, we compute the variability (standard error) for a sample mean difference. To compute this value, we add together the variability for each of the two sample means.

FIGURE 10.3

Two population distributions. The scores in population I vary from 50 to 70 (a 20-point spread), and the scores in population II range from 20 to 30 (a 10-point spread). If you select one score from each of these two populations, the closest two values are $X_1 = 50$ and $X_2 = 30$. The two values that are farthest apart are $X_1 = 70$ and $X_2 = 20$.

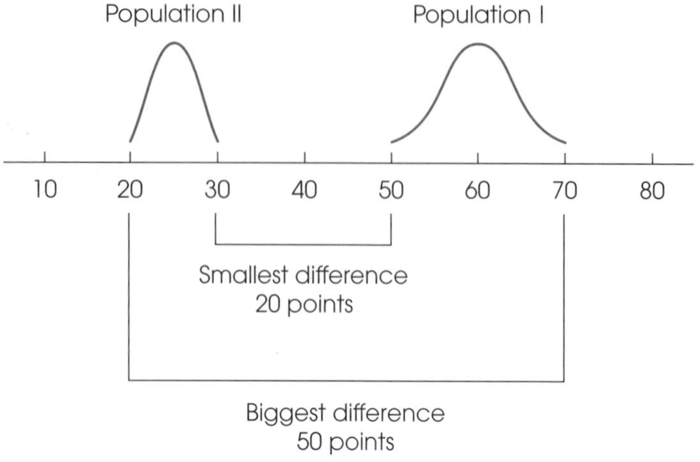

An alternative to computing pooled variance is presented in Box 10.2, p. 339.

two samples are exactly the same size (that is, $n_1 = n_2$). For situations in which the two sample sizes are different, the formula is *biased* and, therefore, inappropriate. The bias comes from the fact that Equation 10.1 treats the two sample variances equally. However, when the sample sizes are different, the two sample variances are not equally good and should not be treated equally. In Chapter 7, we introduced the law of large numbers, which states that statistics obtained from large samples tend to be better (more accurate) estimates of population parameters than statistics obtained from small samples. This same fact holds for sample variances: The variance obtained from a large sample is a more accurate estimate of σ^2 than the variance obtained from a small sample.

One method for correcting the bias in the standard error is to combine the two sample variances into a single value called the *pooled variance*. The pooled variance is obtained by averaging or "pooling" the two sample variances using a procedure that allows the bigger sample to carry more weight in determining the final value.

You should recall that when there is only one sample, the sample variance is computed as

$$s^2 = \frac{SS}{df}$$

For the independent-measures t statistic, there are two SS values and two df values (one from each sample). The values from the two samples are combined to compute what is called the *pooled variance*. The pooled variance is identified by the symbol s_p^2 and is computed as

$$\text{pooled variance} = s_p^2 = \frac{SS_1 + SS_2}{df_1 + df_2} \qquad (10.2)$$

With one sample, the variance is computed as SS divided by df. With two samples, the pooled variance is computed by combining the two SS values and then dividing by the combination of the two df values.

As we mentioned earlier, the pooled variance is actually an average of the two sample variances, but the average is computed so that the larger sample carries more weight in determining the final value. The following examples demonstrate this point.

Equal samples sizes We begin with two samples that are exactly the same size. The first sample has n = 6 scores with SS = 50, and the second sample has n = 6 scores with SS = 30. Individually, the two sample variances are

$$\text{Variance for sample 1: } s^2 = \frac{SS}{df} = \frac{50}{5} = 10$$

$$\text{Variance for sample 2: } s^2 = \frac{SS}{df} = \frac{30}{5} = 6$$

The pooled variance for these two samples is

$$s_p^2 = \frac{SS_1 + SS_2}{df_1 + df_2} = \frac{50+30}{5+5} = \frac{80}{10} = 8.00$$

Note that the pooled variance is exactly halfway between the two sample variances. Because the two samples are exactly the same size, the pooled variance is simply the average of the two sample variances.

Unequal samples sizes Now consider what happens when the samples are not the same size. This time the first sample has n = 3 scores with SS = 20, and the second sample has n = 9 scores with SS = 48. Individually, the two sample variances are

$$\text{Variance for sample 1: } s^2 = \frac{SS}{df} = \frac{20}{2} = 10$$

$$\text{Variance for sample 2: } s^2 = \frac{SS}{df} = \frac{48}{8} = 6$$

The pooled variance for these two samples is

$$s_p^2 = \frac{SS_1 + SS_2}{df_1 + df_2} = \frac{20+48}{2+8} = \frac{68}{10} = 6.80$$

This time the pooled variance is not located halfway between the two sample variances. Instead, the pooled value is closer to the variance for the larger sample (n = 9 and s^2 = 6) than to the variance for the smaller sample (n = 3 and s^2 = 10). The larger sample carries more weight when the pooled variance is computed.

When computing the pooled variance, the weight for each of the individual sample variances is determined by its degrees of freedom. Because the larger sample has a larger df value, it carries more weight when averaging the two variances. This produces an alternative formula for computing pooled variance.

$$\text{pooled variance} = s_p^2 = \frac{df_1 s_1^2 + df_2 s_2^2}{df_1 + df_2} \tag{10.3}$$

For example, if the first sample has df_1 = 3 and the second sample has df_2 = 7, then the formula instructs you to take 3 of the first sample variance and 7 of the second sample variance for a total of 10 variances. You then divide by 10 to obtain the average. The alternative formula is especially useful if the sample data are summarized as means and variances. Finally, you should note that because the pooled variance is an average of the two sample variances, the value obtained for the pooled variance is always located between the two sample variances.

ESTIMATED STANDARD ERROR

Using the pooled variance in place of the individual sample variances, we can now obtain an unbiased measure of the standard error for a sample mean difference. The resulting formula for the independent-measures estimated standard error is

$$\text{estimated standard error of } M_1 - M_2 = s_{(M_1-M_2)} = \sqrt{\frac{s_p^2}{n_1} + \frac{s_p^2}{n_2}} \qquad (10.4)$$

Conceptually, this standard error measures how accurately the difference between two sample means represents the difference between the two population means. In a hypothesis test, H_0 specifies that $\mu_1 - \mu_2 = 0$, and the standard error also measures how much difference is expected, on average, between the two sample means. In either case, the formula combines the error for the first sample mean with the error for the second sample mean. Also note that the pooled variance from the two samples is used to compute the standard error for the sample mean difference.

THE FINAL FORMULA AND DEGREES OF FREEDOM

The complete formula for the independent-measures *t* statistic is as follows:

$$t = \frac{(M_1 - M_2) - (\mu_1 - \mu_2)}{s_{(M_1-M_2)}}$$

$$= \frac{\text{sample mean difference} - \text{population mean difference}}{\text{estimated standard error}} \qquad (10.5)$$

In the formula, the estimated standard error in the denominator is calculated using Equation 10.4, and requires calculation of the pooled variance using either Equation 10.2 or 10.3.

The degrees of freedom for the independent-measures *t* statistic are determined by the *df* values for the two separate samples:

$$\begin{aligned} df \text{ for the } t \text{ statistic} &= df \text{ for the first sample} + df \text{ for the second sample} \\ &= df_1 + df_2 \\ &= (n_1 - 1) + (n_2 - 1) \end{aligned} \qquad (10.6)$$

Equivalently, the *df* value for the independent-measures *t* statistic can be expressed as

$$df = n_1 + n_2 - 2 \qquad (10.7)$$

Note that the *df* formula subtracts 2 points from the total number of scores; 1 point for the first sample and 1 for the second.

The independent-measures *t* statistic is used for hypothesis testing. Specifically, we use the difference between two sample means ($M_1 - M_2$) as the basis for testing hypotheses about the difference between two population means ($\mu_1 - \mu_2$). In this context, the overall structure of the *t* statistic can be reduced to the following:

$$t = \frac{\text{data} - \text{hypothesis}}{\text{error}}$$

This same structure is used for both the single-sample *t* from Chapter 9 and the new independent-measures *t* that was introduced in the preceding pages. Table 10.1 identifies each component of these two *t* statistics and should help reinforce the point that we made earlier in the chapter; that is, the independent-measures *t* statistic simply doubles each aspect of the single-sample *t* statistic.

TABLE 10.1

The basic elements of a *t* statistic for the single-sample *t* and the independent-measures *t*.

	Sample Data	Hypothesized Population Parameter	Estimated Standard Error	Sample Variance
Single-sample *t* statistic	M	μ	$\sqrt{\frac{s^2}{n}}$	$s^2 = \frac{SS}{df}$
Independent-measures *t* statistic	$(M_1 - M_2)$	$(\mu_1 - \mu_2)$	$\sqrt{\frac{s_p^2}{n_1} + \frac{s_p^2}{n_2}}$	$s_p^2 = \frac{SS_1 + SS_2}{df_1 + df_2}$

LEARNING CHECK

1. What is the defining characteristic of an independent-measures research study?
2. Explain what is measured by the estimated standard error in the denominator of the independent-measures *t* statistic.
3. One sample from an independent-measures study has $n = 4$ with $SS = 100$. The other sample has $n = 8$ and $SS = 140$.
   a. Compute the pooled variance. (*Note:* Equation 10.2 works well with these data.)
   b. Compute the estimated standard error for the mean difference.
4. One sample from an independent-measures study has $n = 9$ with a variance of $s^2 = 35$. The other sample has $n = 3$ and $s^2 = 40$.
   a. Compute the pooled variance. (*Note:* Equation 10.3 works well with these data.)
   b. Compute the estimated standard error for the mean difference.
5. An independent-measures *t* statistic is used to evaluate the mean difference between two treatments with $n = 8$ in one treatment and $n = 12$ in the other. What is the *df* value for the *t* statistic?

ANSWERS

1. An independent-measures study uses a separate group of participants to represent each of the populations or treatment conditions being compared.
2. The estimated standard error measures how much difference is expected, on average, between a sample mean difference and the population mean difference. In a hypothesis test, $\mu_1 - \mu_2$ is set to zero and the standard error measures how much difference is expected between the two sample means.
3. **a.** The pooled variance is 240/10 = 24.
   b. The estimated standard error is 3.
4. **a.** The pooled variance is 36.
   b. The estimated standard error is 4.
5. $df = df_1 + df_2 = 7 + 11 = 18$.

10.3 HYPOTHESIS TESTS AND EFFECT SIZE WITH THE INDEPENDENT-MEASURES *t* STATISTIC

The independent-measures *t* statistic uses the data from two separate samples to help decide whether there is a significant mean difference between two populations or between two treatment conditions. A complete example of a hypothesis test with two independent samples follows.

EXAMPLE 10.1 Research results suggest a relationship between the TV viewing habits of 5-year-old children and their future performance in high school. For example, Anderson, Huston, Wright, and Collins (1998) report that high school students who had regularly watched Sesame Street as children had better grades in high school than their peers who had not watched Sesame Street. Suppose that a researcher intends to examine this phenomenon using a sample of 20 high school students.

The researcher first surveys the students' parents to obtain information on the family's TV-viewing habits during the time that the students were 5 years old. Based on the survey results, the researcher selects a sample of $n = 10$ students with a history of watching Sesame Street and a sample of $n = 10$ students who did not watch the program. The average high school grade is recorded for each student and the data are as follows:

Average High School Grade			
Watched Sesame Street		Did Not Watch Sesame Street	
86	99	90	79
87	97	89	83
91	94	82	86
97	89	83	81
98	92	85	92
$n = 10$		$n = 10$	
$M = 93$		$M = 85$	
$SS = 200$		$SS = 160$	

Note that this is an independent-measures study using two separate samples representing two distinct populations of high school students. The researcher would like to know whether there is a significant difference between the two types of high school student.

STEP 1 State the hypotheses and select the alpha level.

H_0: $\mu_1 - \mu_2 = 0$ (No difference.)

H_1: $\mu_1 - \mu_2 \neq 0$ (There is a difference.)

We set $\alpha = .01$.

Directional hypotheses could be used and would specify whether the students who watched Sesame Street should have higher or lower grades.

STEP 2 This is an independent-measures design. The *t* statistic for these data has degrees of freedom determined by

$$
\begin{aligned}
df &= df_1 + df_2 \\
&= (n_1 - 1) + (n_2 - 1) \\
&= 9 + 9 \\
&= 18
\end{aligned}
$$

The *t* distribution for $df = 18$ is presented in Figure 10.4. For $\alpha = .01$, the critical region consists of the extreme 1% of the distribution and has boundaries of $t = +2.878$ and $t = -2.878$.

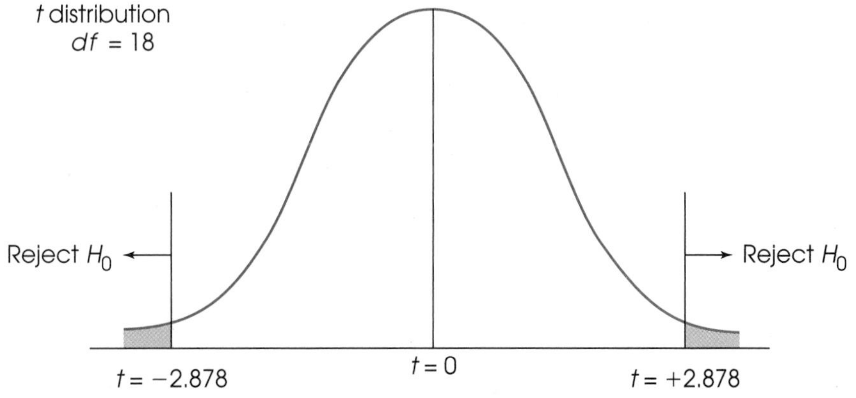

FIGURE 10.4
The critical region for the independent-measures hypothesis test in Example 10.1 with $df = 18$ and $\alpha = .01$.

STEP 3 Obtain the data and compute the test statistic. The data are given, so all that remains is to compute the *t* statistic. As with the single-sample *t* test in Chapter 9, we recommend that the calculations be divided into three parts.

First, find the pooled variance for the two samples:

Caution: The pooled variance combines the two samples to obtain a single estimate of variance. In the formula, the two samples are combined in a single fraction.

$$s_p^2 = \frac{SS_1 + SS_2}{df_1 + df_2} = \frac{200+160}{9+9} = \frac{360}{18} = 20$$

Second, use the pooled variance to compute the estimated standard error:

Caution: The standard error adds the errors from two separate samples. In the formula, these two errors are added as two separate fractions. In this case, the two errors are equal because the sample sizes are the same.

$$s_{(M_1-M_2)} = \sqrt{\frac{s_p^2}{n_1} + \frac{s_p^2}{n_2}} = \sqrt{\frac{20}{10} + \frac{20}{10}} = \sqrt{2+2} = \sqrt{4} = 2$$

Third, compute the *t* statistic:

$$t = \frac{(M_1 - M_2) - (\mu_1 - \mu_2)}{s_{(M_1-M_2)}} = \frac{(93-85)-0}{2} = \frac{8}{2} = 4$$

STEP 4 Make a decision. The obtained value ($t = 4.00$) is in the critical region. In this example, the obtained sample mean difference is four times greater than would be expected if there were no difference between the two populations. In other words, this result is very unlikely if H_0 is true. Therefore, we reject H_0 and conclude that there is a significant difference between the high school grades for students who watched Sesame Street and those who did not. Specifically, the students who watched Sesame Street had significantly higher grades than those who did not watch the program.

Note that the Sesame Street study in Example 10.1 is an example of nonexperimental research (see Chapter 1, p. 17). Specifically, the researcher did not manipulate the TV programs watched by the children and did not control a variety of variables that could influence high school grades. As a result, we cannot conclude that watching Sesame Street *causes* higher high school grades. In particular, many other, uncontrolled factors, such as the parents' level of education or family economic status, might explain the difference between the two groups. Thus, we do not know exactly why there is a relationship between watching Sesame Street and high school grades, but we do know that a relationship exists.

MEASURING EFFECT SIZE FOR THE INDEPENDENT-MEASURES *t* TEST

As noted in Chapters 8 and 9, a hypothesis test is usually accompanied by a report of effect size to provide an indication of the absolute magnitude of the treatment effect. One technique for measuring effect size is Cohen's *d*, which produces a standardized measure of mean difference. In its general form, Cohen's *d* is defined as

$$d = \frac{\text{mean difference}}{\text{standard deviation}} = \frac{\mu_1 - \mu_2}{\sigma}$$

In the context of an independent-measures research study, the difference between the two sample means ($M_1 - M_2$) is used as the best estimate of the mean difference between the two populations, and the pooled standard deviation (the square root of the pooled variance) is used to estimate the population standard deviation. Thus, the formula for estimating Cohen's *d* becomes

$$\text{estimated } d = \frac{\text{estimated mean difference}}{\text{estimated standard deviation}} = \frac{M_1 - M_2}{\sqrt{s_p^2}} \qquad (10.8)$$

For the data from Example 10.1, the two sample means are 93 and 85, and the pooled variance is 20. The estimated *d* for these data is

$$d = \frac{M_1 - M_2}{\sqrt{s_p^2}} = \frac{93 - 85}{\sqrt{20}} = \frac{8}{4.7} = 1.79$$

Using the criteria established to evaluate Cohen's *d* (see Table 8.2 on p. 264), this value indicates a very large treatment effect.

The independent-measures *t* test also allows for measuring effect size by computing the percentage of variance accounted for, r^2. As we saw in Chapter 9, r^2 measures how much of the variability in the scores can be explained by the treatment effects. For example, some of the variability in the high school grades from the Sesame Street study can be explained by knowing whether a particular student watched the program; students who watched Sesame Street tend to have higher grades and students who did not watch the show tend to have lower grades. By measuring exactly how much of the variability can be explained, we can obtain a measure of how big the treatment effect actually is. The calculation of r^2 for the independent-measures t test is exactly the same as it was for the single-sample t test in Chapter 9.

$$r^2 = \frac{t^2}{t^2 + df} \tag{10.9}$$

For the data in Example 10.1, we obtained $t = 4.00$ with $df = 18$. These values produce an r^2 of

$$r^2 = \frac{4^2}{4^2 + 18} = \frac{16}{16+18} = \frac{16}{34} = 0.47$$

According to the standards used to evaluate r^2 (see Table 9.3 on p. 299), this value also indicates a very large treatment effect.

Although the value of r^2 is usually obtained by using Equation 10.9, it is possible to determine the percentage of variability directly by computing SS values for the set of scores. The following example demonstrates this process using the data from the Sesame Street study in Example 10.1.

EXAMPLE 10.2

The Sesame Street study described in Example 10.1 compared high school grades for two groups of students; one group who had watched Sesame Street when they were children and one group who had not watched the program. If we assume that the null hypothesis is true and that there is no difference between the two populations of students, then there should be no systematic difference between the two samples. In this case, the two samples can be combined to form a single set of $n = 20$ scores with an overall mean of $M = 89$. The two samples are shown as a single distribution in Figure 10.5(a).

For this example, however, the conclusion from the hypothesis test is that there is a real difference between the two groups. The students who watched Sesame Street have a mean score of $M = 93$, which is 4 points above the overall average. Similarly, the students who did not watch the program had a mean score of $M = 85$, 4 points below the overall average. Thus, the Sesame Street effect causes one group of scores to move toward the right of the distribution, away from the middle, and causes the other group to move toward the left, away from the middle. The result is that the Sesame Street effect causes the scores to spread out and increases the variability.

To determine how much the treatment effect has increased the variability, we remove the treatment effect and examine the resulting scores. To remove the effect, we add 4 points to the score for each student who did not watch Sesame Street and we subtract 4 points from the score for each student who did watch. This adjustment causes both groups to have a mean of $M = 89$, so there is no longer any mean difference between the two groups. The adjusted scores are shown in Figure 10.5(b).

It should be clear that the adjusted scores in Figure 10.5(b) are less variable (more closely clustered) than the original scores in Figure 10.5(a). That is, removing the treatment effect has reduced the variability. To determine exactly how much the treatment influences variability, we have computed SS, the sum of squared deviations, for each set of scores. For the scores in Figure 10.5(a), including the treatment effect, we obtain $SS = 680$. When the treatment effect is removed, in Figure 10.5(b), the variability is reduced to $SS = 360$. The difference between these two values is 320 points. Thus, the treatment effect accounts for 320 points of the total variability in the original scores. When expressed as a proportion of the total variability, we obtain

$$\frac{\text{variability explained by the treatment}}{\text{total variability}} = \frac{320}{680} = 0.47 = 47\%$$

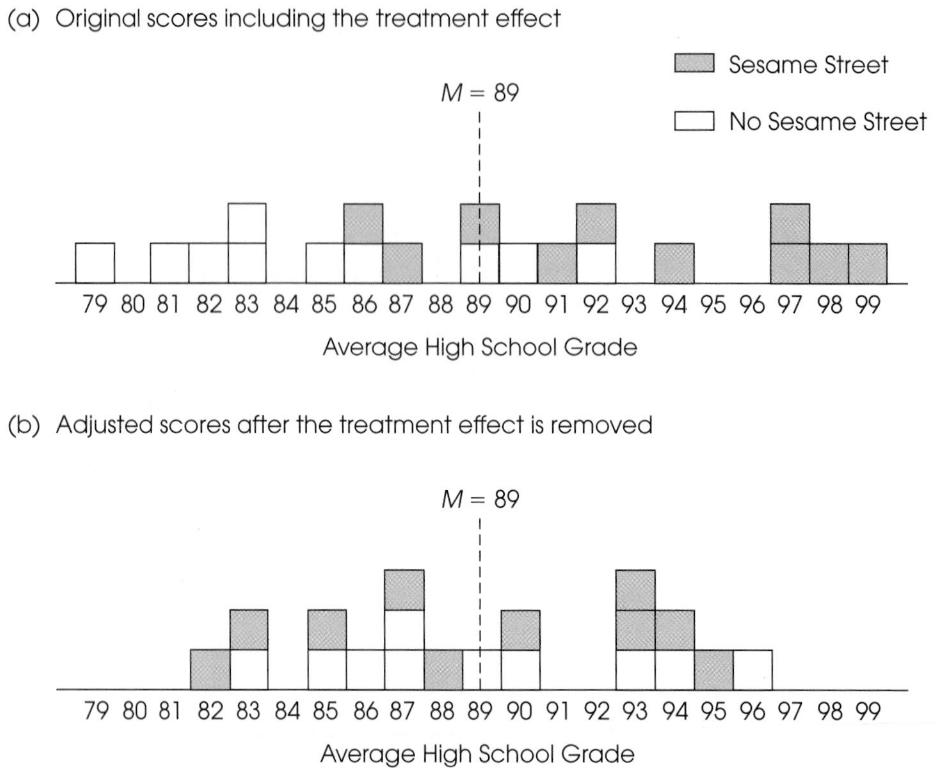

FIGURE 10.5

The two groups of scores from Example 10.1 combined into a single distribution. The original scores, including the treatment effect, are shown in part (a). Part (b) shows the adjusted scores, after the treatment effect has been removed.

You should recognize that this is exactly the same value we obtained for r^2 using Equation 10.9.

CONFIDENCE INTERVALS FOR ESTIMATING $\mu_1 - \mu_2$

As noted in Chapter 9, it is possible to compute a confidence interval as an alternative method for measuring and describing the size of the treatment effect. For the single-sample *t*, we used a single sample mean, *M*, to estimate a single population mean. For the independent-measures *t*, we use a sample mean difference, $M_1 - M_2$, to estimate the population mean difference, $\mu_1 - \mu_2$. In this case, the confidence interval literally estimates the size of the population mean difference between the two populations or treatment conditions.

As with the single-sample *t*, the first step is to solve the *t* equation for the unknown parameter. For the independent-measures *t* statistic, we obtain

$$\mu_1 - \mu_2 = M_1 - M_2 \pm ts_{(M_1-M_2)} \qquad (10.10)$$

In the equation, the values for $M_1 - M_2$ and for $s_{(M_1-M_2)}$ are obtained from the sample data. Although the value for the *t* statistic is unknown, we can use the degrees of freedom for the *t* statistic and the *t* distribution table to estimate the *t* value. Using the estimated t and the known values from the sample, we can then compute the value of $\mu_1 - \mu_2$. The following example demonstrates the process of constructing a confidence interval for a population mean difference.

EXAMPLE 10.3

Earlier we presented a research study comparing high school grades for students who had watched Sesame Street as children with the grades for students who had not watched the program (p. 326). The results of the hypothesis test indicated a significant mean difference between the two populations of students. Now, we construct a 95% confidence interval to estimate the size of the population mean difference.

The data from the study produced a mean grade of $M = 93$ for the Sesame Street group and a mean of $M = 85$ for the no-Sesame Street group, and the estimated standard error for the mean difference was $s_{(M_1-M_2)} = 2$. With $n = 10$ scores in each sample, the independent-measures t statistic has $df = 18$. To have 95% confidence, we simply estimate that the t statistic for the sample mean difference is located somewhere in the middle 95% of all the possible t values. According to the t distribution table, with $df = 18$, 95% of the t values are located between t = +2.101 and $t = -2.101$. Using these values in the estimation equation, we obtain

$$\begin{aligned}\mu_1 - \mu_2 &= M_1 - M_2 \pm ts_{(M_1-M_2)}\\ &= 93 - 85 \pm 2.101(2)\\ &= 8 \pm 4.202\end{aligned}$$

This produces an interval of values ranging from $8 - 4.202 = 3.798$ to $8 + 4.202 = 12.202$. Thus, our conclusion is that students who watched Sesame Street have higher grades that those who did not, and the mean difference between the two populations is somewhere between 3.798 points and 12.202 points. Furthermore, we are 95% confident that the true mean difference is in this interval because the only value estimated during the calculations was the t statistic, and we are 95% confident that the t value is located in the middle 95% of the distribution. Finally note that the confidence interval is constructed around the sample mean difference. As a result, the sample mean difference, $M_1 - M_2 = 93 - 83 = 8$ points, is located exactly in the center of the interval.

As with the confidence interval for the single-sample t (p. 302), the confidence interval for an independent-measures t is influenced by a variety of factors other than the actual size of the treatment effect. In particular, the width of the interval depends on the percentage of confidence used so that a larger percentage produces a wider interval. Also, the width of the interval depends on the sample size, so that a larger sample produces a narrower interval. Because the interval width is related to sample size, the confidence interval is not a pure measure of effect size like Cohen's d or r^2.

CONFIDENCE INTERVALS AND HYPOTHESIS TESTS

In addition to describing the size of a treatment effect, estimation can be used to get an indication of the *significance* of the effect. Example 10.3 presented an independent-measures research study examining the effect on high school grades of having watched Sesame Street as a child. Based on the results of the study, the 95% confidence interval estimated that the population mean difference for the two groups of students was between

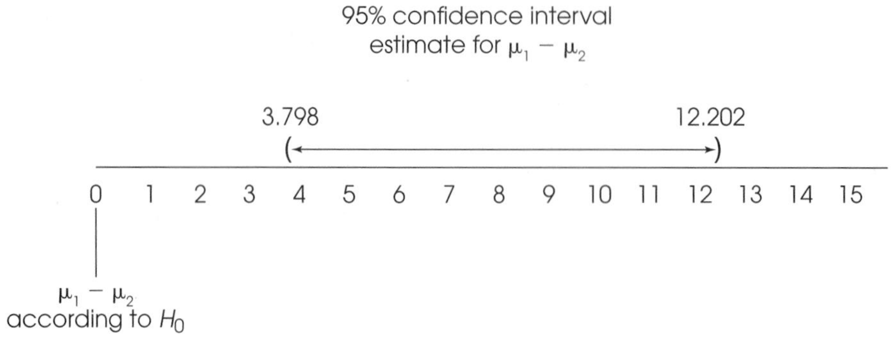

FIGURE 10.6

The 95% confidence interval for the population mean difference ($\mu_1 - \mu_2$) from Example 10.3. Note that $\mu_1 - \mu_2 = 0$ is excluded from the confidence interval, indicating that a zero difference is not an acceptable value (H_0 would be rejected in a hypothesis test with $\alpha = .05$).

3.798 and 12.202 points. The confidence interval estimate is shown in Figure 10.6. In addition to the confidence interval for $\mu_1 - \mu_2$, we have marked the spot where the mean difference is equal to zero. You should recognize that a mean difference of zero is exactly what would be predicted by the null hypothesis if we were doing a hypothesis test. You also should realize that a zero difference ($\mu_1 - \mu_2 = 0$) is *outside* of the 95% confidence interval. In other words, $\mu_1 - \mu_2 = 0$ is not an acceptable value if we want 95% confidence in our estimate. To conclude that a value of zero is *not acceptable* with 95% confidence is equivalent to concluding that a value of zero is *rejected* with 95% confidence. This conclusion is equivalent to rejecting H_0 with $\alpha = .05$. On the other hand, if a mean difference of zero were included within the 95% confidence interval, then we would have to conclude that $\mu_1 - \mu_2 = 0$ is an acceptable value, which is the same as failing to reject H_0.

The hypothesis test for these data was conducted in Example 10.1 (p. 326) and the decision was to reject H_0.

IN THE LITERATURE

REPORTING THE RESULTS OF AN INDEPENDENT-MEASURES *t* TEST

A research report typically presents the descriptive statistics followed by the results of the hypothesis test and measures of effect size (inferential statistics). In Chapter 4 (p. 123), we demonstrated how the mean and the standard deviation are reported in APA format. In Chapter 9 (p. 302), we illustrated the APA style for reporting the results of a *t* test. Now we use the APA format to report the results of Example 10.1, an independent-measures *t* test. A concise statement might read as follows:

> The students who watched Sesame Street as children had higher high school grades ($M = 93$, $SD = 4.71$) than the students who did not watch the program ($M = 85$, $SD = 4.22$). The mean difference was significant, $t(18) = 4.00$, $p < .01$, $d = 1.79$.

You should note that standard deviation is not a step in the computations for the independent-measures *t* test, yet it is useful when providing descriptive statistics for each treatment group. It is easily computed when doing the *t* test because you need *SS* and *df* for both groups to determine the pooled variance. Note that the format for reporting *t* is exactly the same as that described in Chapter 9 (p. 302) and that the measure of effect size is reported immediately after the results of the hypothesis test.

Also, as we noted in Chapter 9, if an exact probability is available from a computer analysis, it should be reported. For the data in Example 10.1, the computer analysis reports a probability value of $p = .001$ for $t = 4.00$ with $df = 18$. In the research report, this value would be included as follows:

The difference was significant, $t(18) = 4.00$, $p = .001$, $d = 1.79$.

Finally, if a confidence interval is reported to describe effect size, it appears immediately after the results from the hypothesis test. For the Sesame Street examples (Example 10.1 and Example 10.3), the report would be as follows:

The difference was significant, $t(18) = 4.00$, $p = .001$, 95% CI [3.798, 12.202].

LEARNING CHECK

1. An educational psychologist would like to determine whether access to computers has an effect on grades for high school students. One group of $n = 16$ students has home room each day in a computer classroom in which each student has a computer. A comparison group of $n = 16$ students has home room in a traditional classroom. At the end of the school year, the average grade is recorded for each student. The data are as follows:

Computer	Traditional
$M = 86$	$M = 82.5$
$SS = 1005$	$SS = 1155$

a. Is there a significant difference between the two groups? Use a two-tailed test with $\alpha = .05$.

b. Compute Cohen's d to measure the size of the difference.

c. Write a sentence that demonstrates how the outcome of the hypothesis test and the measure of effect size would appear in a research report.

d. Compute the 90% confidence interval for the population mean difference between a computer classroom and a regular classroom.

2. A researcher report states that there is a significant difference between treatments for an independent-measures design with $t(28) = 2.27$.

a. How many individuals participated in the research study? (*Hint:* Start with the *df* value.)

b. Should the report state that $p > .05$ or $p < .05$?

ANSWERS

1. a. The pooled variance is 72, the standard error is 3, and $t = 1.17$. With a critical value of $t = 2.042$, fail to reject the null hypothesis.

b. Cohen's $d = 3.5/\sqrt{72} = 0.412$

c. The results show no significant difference in grades for students with computers compared to students without computers, $t(30) = 1.17$, $p > .05$, $d = 0.412$.

d. With $df = 30$ and 90% confidence, the t values for the confidence interval are ± 1.697. The interval is $\mu_1 - \mu_2 = 3.5 \pm 1.697(3)$. Thus, the population mean difference is estimated to be between -1.591 and 8.591. The fact that zero is an acceptable value (inside the interval) is consistent with the decision that there is no significant difference between the two population means.

2. a. The $df = 28$, so the total number of participants is 30.

b. A significant result is indicated by $p < .05$.

DIRECTIONAL HYPOTHESES AND ONE-TAILED TESTS

When planning an independent-measures study, a researcher usually has some expectation or specific prediction for the outcome. For the Sesame Street study in Example 10.1, the researcher clearly expects the students who watched Sesame Street to have higher grades than the students who did not watch. This kind of directional prediction can be incorporated into the statement of the hypotheses, resulting in a directional, or one-tailed, test. Recall from Chapter 8 that one-tailed tests can lead to rejecting H_0 when the mean difference is relatively small compared to the magnitude required by a two-tailed test. As a result, one-tailed tests should be used when clearly justified by theory or previous findings. The following example demonstrates the procedure for stating hypotheses and locating the critical region for a one-tailed test using the independent-measures t statistic.

EXAMPLE 10.4

We use the same research situation that was described in Example 10.1. The researcher is using an independent-measures design to examine the relationship between watching educational TV as a child and academic performance as a high school student. The prediction is that high school students who watched Sesame Street regularly as 5-year-old children have higher grades.

STEP 1 State the hypotheses and select the alpha level. As always, the null hypothesis says that there is no effect, and the alternative hypothesis says that there is an effect. For this example, the predicted effect is that the students who watched Sesame Street have higher grades. Thus, the two hypotheses are as follows.

H_0: $\mu_{\text{Sesame Street}} \leq \mu_{\text{No Sesame Street}}$ (Grades are not higher with Sesame Street)

H_1: $\mu_{\text{Sesame Street}} > \mu_{\text{No Sesame Street}}$ (Grades are higher with Sesame Street)

Note that it is usually easier to state the hypotheses in words before you try to write them in symbols. Also, it usually is easier to begin with the alternative hypothesis (H_1), which states that the treatment works as predicted. Also note that the equal sign goes in the null hypothesis, indicating *no difference* between the two treatment conditions. The idea of zero difference is the essence of the null hypothesis, and the numerical value of zero is used for $(\mu_1 - \mu_2)$ during the calculation of the t statistic. For this test we use $\alpha = .01$.

STEP 2 Locate the critical region. For a directional test, the critical region is located entirely in one tail of the distribution. Rather than trying to determine which tail, positive or negative, is the correct location, we suggest that you identify the criteria for the critical region in a two-step process as follows. First, look at the data and determine whether the sample mean difference is in the direction that was predicted. If the answer is no, then the data obviously do not support the predicted treatment effect, and you can stop the analysis. On the other hand, if the difference is in the predicted direction, then the second step is to determine whether the difference is large enough to be significant. To test for significance, simply find the one-tailed critical value in the t distribution table. If the calculated t statistic is more extreme (either positive or negative) than the critical value, then the difference is significant.

For this example, the students who watched Sesame Street had higher grades, as predicted. With $df = 18$, the one-tailed critical value for $\alpha = .01$ is $t = 2.552$.

STEP 3 Collect the data and calculate the test statistic. The details of the calculations were shown in Example 10.1. The data produce a t statistic of $t = 4.00$.

STEP 4 Make a decision. The t statistic of $t = 4.00$ is well beyond the critical boundary of $t = 2.552$. Therefore, we reject the null hypothesis and conclude that grades for students who watched Sesame Street are significantly higher than grades for students who did not watch the program. In a research report, the one-tailed test would be clearly noted:

> Grades were significantly higher for students who watched Sesame Street, $t(18) = 4.00$, $p < .01$, one tailed.

THE ROLE OF SAMPLE VARIANCE AND SAMPLE SIZE IN THE INDEPENDENT-MEASURES *t* TEST

In Chapter 9 (p. 294), we identified several factors that can influence the outcome of a hypothesis test. Two factors that play important roles are the variability of the scores and the size of the samples. Both factors influence the magnitude of the estimated standard error in the denominator of the t statistic. However, the standard error is directly related to sample variance (larger variance leads to larger error) but it is inversely related to sample size (larger size leads to smaller error). As a result, larger variance produces a smaller value for the t statistic (closer to zero) and reduces the likelihood of finding a significant result. By contrast, a larger sample produces a larger value for the t statistic (farther from zero) and increases the likelihood of rejecting H_0.

Although variance and sample size both influence the hypothesis test, only variance has a large influence on measures of effect size such as Cohen's d and r^2; larger variance produces smaller measures of effect size. Sample size, on the other hand, has no effect on the value of Cohen's d and only a small influence on r^2.

The following example provides a visual demonstration of how large sample variance can obscure a mean difference between samples and lower the likelihood of rejecting H_0 for an independent-measures study.

EXAMPLE 10.5 We use the data in Figure 10.7 to demonstrate the influence of sample variance. The figure shows the results from a research study comparing two treatments. Notice that the study uses two separate samples, each with $n = 9$, and there is a 5-point mean difference

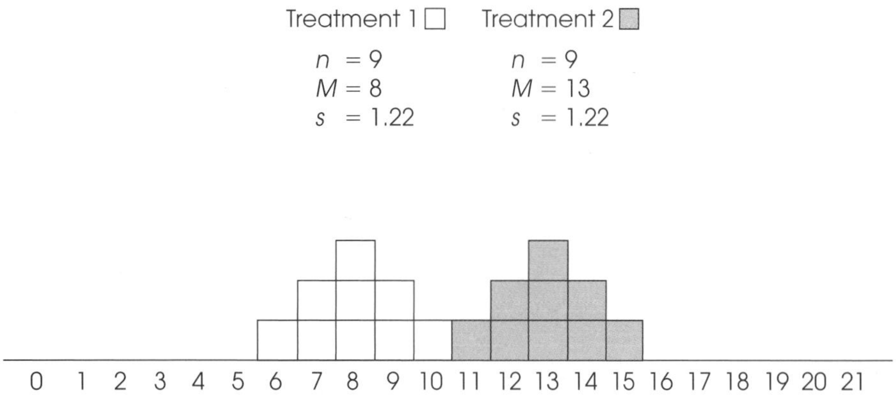

FIGURE 10.7

Two sample distributions representing two different treatments. These data show a significant difference between treatments, $t(16) = 8.62$, $p < .01$, and both measures of effect size indicate a very large treatment effect, $d = 4.10$ and $r^2 = 0.82$.

between the two samples: $M = 8$ for treatment 1 and $M = 13$ for treatment 2. Also notice that there is a clear difference between the two distributions; the scores for treatment 2 are clearly higher than the scores for treatment 1.

For the hypothesis test, the data produce a pooled variance of 1.50 and an estimated standard error of 0.58. The t statistic is

$$t = \frac{\text{mean difference}}{\text{estimated standard error}} = \frac{5}{0.58} = 8.62$$

With $df = 16$, this value is far into the critical region (for $\alpha = .05$ or $\alpha = .01$), so we reject the null hypothesis and conclude that there is a significant difference between the two treatments.

Now consider the effect of increasing sample variance. Figure 10.8 shows the results from a second research study comparing two treatments. Notice that there are still $n = 9$ scores in each sample, and the two sample means are still $M = 8$ and $M = 13$. However, the sample variances have been greatly increased: Each sample now has $s^2 = 44.25$ as compared with $s^2 = 1.5$ for the data in Figure 10.7. Notice that the increased variance means that the scores are now spread out over a wider range, with the result that the two samples are mixed together without any clear distinction between them.

The absence of a clear difference between the two samples is supported by the hypothesis test. The pooled variance is 44.25, the estimated standard error is 3.14, and the independent-measures t statistic is

$$t = \frac{\text{mean difference}}{\text{estimated standard error}} = \frac{5}{3.14} = 1.59$$

With $df = 16$ and $\alpha = .05$, this value is not in the critical region. Therefore, we fail to reject the null hypothesis and conclude that there is no significant difference between the two treatments. Although there is still a 5-point difference between sample means (as in Figure 10.7), the 5-point difference is not significant with the increased variance. In general, large sample variance can obscure any mean difference that exists in the data and reduces the likelihood of obtaining a significant difference in a hypothesis test.

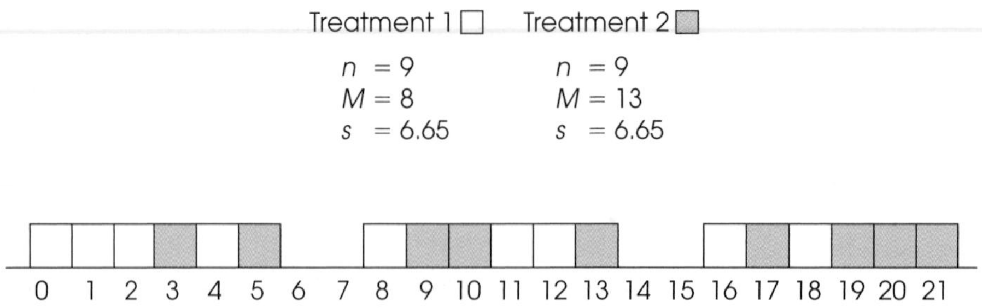

FIGURE 10.8

Two sample distributions representing two different treatments. These data show exactly the same mean difference as the scores in Figure 10.7; however, the variance has been greatly increased. With the increased variance, there is no longer a significant difference between treatments, $t(16) = 1.59$, $p > .05$, and both measures of effect size are substantially reduced, $d = 0.75$ and $r^2 = 0.14$.

Finally, we should note that the problems associated with high variance often can be minimized by transforming the original scores to ranks and then conducting an alternative statistical analysis known as the *Mann-Whitney test,* which is designed specifically for ordinal data. The Mann-Whitney test is presented in Appendix E, which also discusses the general purpose and process of converting numerical scores into ranks. The Mann-Whitney test also can be used if the data violate one of the assumptions for the independent-measures t test outlined in the next section.

10.4 ASSUMPTIONS UNDERLYING THE INDEPENDENT-MEASURES *t* FORMULA

There are three assumptions that should be satisfied before you use the independent-measures t formula for hypothesis testing:

1. The observations within each sample must be independent (see p. 254).
2. The two populations from which the samples are selected must be normal.
3. The two populations from which the samples are selected must have equal variances.

The first two assumptions should be familiar from the single-sample t hypothesis test presented in Chapter 9. As before, the normality assumption is the less important of the two, especially with large samples. When there is reason to suspect that the populations are far from normal, you should compensate by ensuring that the samples are relatively large.

Remember: Adding a constant to (or subtracting a constant from) each score does not change the standard deviation.

The third assumption is referred to as *homogeneity of variance* and states that the two populations being compared must have the same variance. You may recall a similar assumption for the z-score hypothesis test in Chapter 8. For that test, we assumed that the effect of the treatment was to add a constant amount to (or subtract a constant amount from) each individual score. As a result, the population standard deviation after treatment was the same as it had been before treatment. We now are making essentially the same assumption, but phrasing it in terms of variances.

Recall that the pooled variance in the t-statistic formula is obtained by averaging together the two sample variances. It makes sense to average these two values only if they both are estimating the same population variance—that is, if the homogeneity of variance assumption is satisfied. If the two sample variances are estimating different population variances, then the average is meaningless. (*Note*: If two people are asked to estimate the same thing—for example, what your IQ is—it is reasonable to average the two estimates. However, it is not meaningful to average estimates of two different things. If one person estimates your IQ and another estimates the number of grapes in a pound, it is meaningless to average the two numbers.)

Homogeneity of variance is most important when there is a large discrepancy between the sample sizes. With equal (or nearly equal) sample sizes, this assumption is less critical, but still important. Violating the homogeneity of variance assumption can negate any meaningful interpretation of the data from an independent-measures experiment. Specifically, when you compute the t statistic in a hypothesis test, all of the numbers in the formula come from the data except for the population mean difference, which you get from H_0. Thus, you are sure of all of the numbers in the formula except one. If you obtain an extreme result for the t statistic (a value in the critical region), then you conclude that the hypothesized value was wrong. But consider what happens when you violate the homogeneity of variance assumption. In this case, you have two questionable values in the formula (the hypothesized population value and the meaningless average of the two variances). Now if you obtain an extreme t statistic, you do not know which of these two values is responsible. Specifically, you cannot reject the hypothesis because it may have been the pooled variance that produced the extreme t statistic. Without satisfying the homogeneity of variance requirement, you cannot accurately interpret a t statistic, and the hypothesis test becomes meaningless.

HARTLEY'S *F*-MAX TEST

How do you know whether the homogeneity of variance assumption is satisfied? One simple test involves just looking at the two sample variances. Logically, if the two population variances are equal, then the two sample variances should be very similar. When the two sample variances are reasonably close, you can be reasonably confident that the homogeneity assumption has been satisfied and proceed with the test. However, if one sample variance is more than three or four times larger than the other, then there is reason for concern. A more objective procedure involves a statistical test to evaluate the homogeneity assumption. Although there are many different statistical methods for determining whether the homogeneity of variance assumption has been satisfied, Hartley's F-max test is one of the simplest to compute and to understand. An additional advantage is that this test can also be used to check homogeneity of variance with more than two independent samples. Later, in Chapter 12, we examine statistical methods for comparing several different samples, and Hartley's test is useful again. The following example demonstrates the F-max test for two independent samples.

EXAMPLE 10.6

The F-max test is based on the principle that a sample variance provides an unbiased estimate of the population variance. The null hypothesis for this test states that the population variances are equal, therefore, the sample variances should be very similar. The procedure for using the F-max test is as follows:

1. Compute the sample variance, $s^2 = \frac{SS}{df}$, for each of the separate samples.

2. Select the largest and the smallest of these sample variances and compute

$$F\text{-max} = \frac{s^2(\text{largest})}{s^2(\text{smallest})}$$

A relatively large value for F-max indicates a large difference between the sample variances. In this case, the data suggest that the population variances are different and that the homogeneity assumption has been violated. On the other hand, a small value of F-max (near 1.00) indicates that the sample variances are similar and that the homogeneity assumption is reasonable.

3. The F-max value computed for the sample data is compared with the critical value found in Table B.3 (Appendix B). If the sample value is larger than the table value, then you conclude that the variances are different and that the homogeneity assumption is not valid.

To locate the critical value in the table, you need to know:

a. k = number of separate samples. (For the independent-measures t test, $k = 2$.)

b. $df = n - 1$ for each sample variance. The Hartley test assumes that all samples are the same size.

c. The alpha level. The table provides critical values for $\alpha = .05$ and $\alpha = .01$. Generally a test for homogeneity would use the larger alpha level.

Suppose, for example, that two independent samples each have $n = 10$ with sample variances of 12.34 and 9.15. For these data,

$$F\text{-max} = \frac{s^2(\text{largest})}{s^2(\text{smallest})} = \frac{12.34}{9.15} = 1.35$$

With $\alpha = .05$, $k = 2$, and $df = n - 1 = 9$, the critical value from the table is 4.03. Because the obtained F-max is smaller than this critical value, you conclude that the data do not provide evidence that the homogeneity of variance assumption has been violated.

The goal for most hypothesis tests is to reject the null hypothesis to demonstrate a significant difference or a significant treatment effect. However, when testing for homogeneity of variance, the preferred outcome is to fail to reject H_0. Failing to reject H_0 with the F-max test means that there is no significant difference between the two population variances and the homogeneity assumption is satisfied. In this case, you may proceed with the independent-measures t test using pooled variance.

If the F-max test rejects the hypothesis of equal variances, or if you simply suspect that the homogeneity of variance assumption is not justified, you should not compute an independent-measures t statistic using pooled variance. However, there is an alternative formula for the t statistic that does not pool the two sample variances and does not require the homogeneity assumption. The alternative formula is presented in Box 10.2.

BOX 10.2

AN ALTERNATIVE TO POOLED VARIANCE

Computing the independent-measures t statistic using pooled variance requires that the data satisfy the homogeneity of variance assumption. Specifically, the two distributions from which the samples are obtained must have equal variances. To avoid this assumption, many statisticians recommend an alternative formula for computing the independent-measures t statistic that does not require pooled variance or the homogeneity assumption. The alternative procedure consists of two steps:

1. The standard error is computed using the two separate sample variances as in Equation 10.1.
2. The value of degrees of freedom for the t statistic is adjusted using the following equation:

$$df = \frac{(V_1 + V_2)^2}{\frac{V_1^2}{n_1 - 1} + \frac{V_2^2}{n_2 - 1}} \quad \text{where } V_1 = \frac{s_1^2}{n_1} \text{ and } V_2 = \frac{s_2^2}{n_2}$$

Decimal values for df should be rounded down to the next lower integer.

The adjustment to degrees of freedom lowers the value of df, which pushes the boundaries for the critical region farther out. Thus, the adjustment makes the test more demanding and therefore corrects for the same bias problem that the pooled variance attempts to avoid.

Note: Many computer programs that perform statistical analysis (such as SPSS) report two versions of the independent-measures t statistic; one using pooled variance (with equal variances assumed) and one using the adjustment shown here (with equal variances not assumed).

LEARNING CHECK

1. A researcher is using an independent-measures design to evaluate the difference between two treatment conditions with $n = 8$ in each treatment. The first treatment produces $M = 63$ with a variance of $s^2 = 18$, and the second treatment has $M = 58$ with $s^2 = 14$.
   a. Use a one-tailed test with $\alpha = .05$ to determine whether the scores in the first treatment are significantly greater than the scores in the second. (*Note*: Because the two samples are the same size, the pooled variance is simply the average of the two sample variances.)
   b. Predict how the value for the t statistic would be affected if the two sample variances were increased to $s^2 = 68$ and $s^2 = 60$. Compute the new t to confirm your answer.
   c. Predict how the value for the t statistic for the original samples would be affected if each sample had $n = 32$ scores (instead of $n = 8$). Compute the new t to confirm your answer.
2. The homogeneity of variance assumption requires that the two sample variances be equal. (True or false?)
3. When you are using an F-max test to evaluate the homogeneity of variance assumption, you usually do not want to find a significant difference between the variances. (True or false?)

ANSWERS

1. a. The pooled variance is 16, the estimated standard error is 2, and $t(14) = 2.50$. With a one-tailed critical value of 1.761, reject the null hypothesis. Scores in the first treatment are significantly higher than scores in the second.
   b. Increasing the variance should lower the value of t. The new pooled variance is 64, the estimated standard error is 4, and $t(14) = 1.25$.
   c. Increasing the sample sizes should increase the value of t. The pooled variance is still 16, but the new standard error is 1, and $t(62) = 5.00$.
2. False. The assumption is that the two *population* variances are equal.
3. True. If there is a significant difference between the two variances, you cannot do the t test with pooled variance.

SUMMARY

1. The independent-measures t statistic uses the data from two separate samples to draw inferences about the mean difference between two populations or between two different treatment conditions.
2. The formula for the independent-measures t statistic has the same structure as the original z-score or the single-sample t:

$$t = \frac{\text{sample statistic} - \text{population parameter}}{\text{estimated standard error}}$$

For the independent-measures t, the sample statistic is the sample mean difference ($M_1 - M_2$). The population parameter is the population mean difference, ($\mu_1 - \mu_2$). The estimated standard error for the sample mean difference is computed by combining the errors for the two sample means. The resulting formula is

$$t = \frac{(M_1 - M_2) - (\mu_1 - \mu_2)}{s_{(M_1 - M_2)}}$$

where the estimated standard error is

$$s_{(M_1 - M_2)} = \sqrt{\frac{s_p^2}{n_1} + \frac{s_p^2}{n_2}}$$

The pooled variance in the formula, s_p^2, is the weighted mean of the two sample variances:

$$s_p^2 = \frac{SS_1 + SS_2}{df_1 + df_2}$$

This t statistic has degrees of freedom determined by the sum of the df values for the two samples:

$$df = df_1 + df_2$$
$$= (n_1 - 1) + (n_2 - 1)$$

3. For hypothesis testing, the null hypothesis states that there is no difference between the two population means:

$$H_0\text{: } \mu_1 = \mu_2 \qquad \text{or} \qquad \mu_1 - \mu_2 = 0$$

4. When a hypothesis test with an independent-measures t statistic indicates a significant difference, you should also compute a measure of the effect size. One measure of effect size is Cohen's d, which is a standardized measure of the mean difference. For the independent-measures t statistic, Cohen's d is estimated as follows:

$$\text{estimated } d = \frac{M_1 - M_2}{\sqrt{s_p^2}}$$

A second common measure of effect size is the percentage of variance accounted for by the treatment effect. This measure is identified by r^2 and is computed as

$$r^2 = \frac{t^2}{t^2 + df}$$

5. An alternative method for describing the size of the treatment effect is to construct a confidence interval for the population mean difference, $\mu_1 - \mu_2$. The confidence interval uses the independent-measures t equation, solved for the unknown mean difference:

$$\mu_1 - \mu_2 = M_1 - M_2 \pm t s_{(M_1 - M_2)}$$

First, select a level of confidence and then look up the corresponding t values. For example, for 95% confidence, use the range of t values that determine the middle 95% of the distribution. The t values are then used in the equation along with the values for the sample mean difference and the standard error, which are computed from the sample data.

6. Appropriate use and interpretation of the t statistic using pooled variance require that the data satisfy the homogeneity of variance assumption. This assumption stipulates that the two populations have equal variances. An informal test of the assumption can be made by verifying that the two sample variances are approximately equal. Hartley's F-max test provides a statistical technique for determining whether the data satisfy the homogeneity assumption. An alternative technique that avoids pooling variances and eliminates the need for the homogeneity assumption is presented in Box 10.2.

KEY TERMS

independent-measures research design (318)
between-subjects research design (318)
repeated-measures research design (318)
within-subjects research design (318)
independent-measures t statistic (319)
estimated standard error of $M_1 - M_2$ (320)
pooled variance (322)
Mann-Whitney test (337)
homogeneity of variance (337)

RESOURCES

Book Companion Website: www.cengage.com/psychology/gravetter

You can find a tutorial quiz and other learning exercises for Chapter 10 on the book companion website. The website also provides access to a workshop entitled *Independent vs. Repeated t-tests,* which compares the t test presented in this chapter with the repeated-measures test presented in Chapter 11.

aplia

Improve your understanding of statistics with Aplia's auto-graded problem sets and immediate, detailed explanations for every question. To learn more, visit **www.aplia.com/statistics**.

CENGAGE**brain**.com

Psychology CourseMate brings course concepts to life with interactive learning, study, and exam preparation tools that support the printed textbook. A textbook-specific website, Psychology CourseMate includes an integrated interactive eBook and other interactive learning tools including quizzes, flashcards, and more.

Visit www.cengagebrain.com to access your account and purchase materials.

SPSS

General instructions for using SPSS are presented in Appendix D. Following are detailed instructions for using SPSS to perform **The Independent-Measures *t* Test** presented in this chapter.

Data Entry

1. The scores are entered in what is called *stacked format,* which means that all of the scores from *both samples* are entered in one column of the data editor (probably VAR00001). Enter the scores for sample #2 directly beneath the scores from sample #1 with no gaps or extra spaces.
2. Values are then entered into a second column (VAR00002) to identify the sample or treatment condition corresponding to each of the scores. For example, enter a 1 beside each score from sample #1 and enter a 2 beside each score from sample #2.

Data Analysis

1. Click **Analyze** on the tool bar, select **Compare Means,** and click on **Independent-Samples *t* Test.**
2. Highlight the column label for the set of scores (VAR0001) in the left box and click the arrow to move it into the **Test Variable(s)** box.
3. Highlight the label from the column containing the sample numbers (VAR0002) in the left box and click the arrow to move it into the **Group Variable** box.
4. Click on **Define Groups.**
5. Assuming that you used the numbers 1 and 2 to identify the two sets of scores, enter the values 1 and 2 into the appropriate group boxes.
6. Click **Continue.**
7. In addition to performing the hypothesis test, the program computes a confidence interval for the population mean difference. The confidence level is automatically set at 95% but you can select **Options** and change the percentage.
8. Click **OK.**

SPSS Output

We used the SPSS program to analyze the data from the Sesame Street study in Example 10.1 and the program output is shown in Figure 10.9. The output includes a table of sample statistics with the mean, standard deviation, and standard error of the mean for each group. A second table, which is split into two sections in Figure 10.9, begins with the results of Levene's test for homogeneity of variance. This test should *not* be significant (you do not want the two variances to be different), so you want the reported Sig. value to be greater than .05. Next, the results of the independent-measures t test are presented using two different assumptions. The top row shows the outcome assuming equal variances, using the pooled variance to compute t. The second row does not assume equal variances and computes the t statistic using the alternative method presented in Box 10.2. Each row reports the calculated t value, the degrees of freedom, the level of significance (the p value for the test), the size of the mean difference and the standard error for the mean difference (the denominator of the t statistic). Finally, the output includes a 95% confidence interval for the mean difference.

Group Statistics

	VAR00002	N	Mean	Std. Deviation	Std. Error Mean
VAR00001	1.00	10	93.0000	4.71405	1.49071
	2.00	10	85.0000	4.21637	1.33333

Independent Samples Test

		Levene's Test for Equality of Variances		t-test for Equality of Means	
		F	Sig.	t	df
VAR00001	Equal variances assumed	.384	.543	4.000	18
	Equal variances not assumed			4.000	17.780

Independent Samples Test

		t-test for Equality of Means				
					95% Confidence Interval of the Difference	
		Sig. (2-tailed)	Mean Difference	Std. Error Difference	Lower	Upper
VAR00001	Equal variances assumed	.001	8.00000	2.00000	3.79816	12.20184
	Equal variances not assumed	.001	8.00000	2.00000	3.79443	12.20557

FIGURE 10.9

The SPSS output for the independent-measures hypothesis test in Example 10.1.

FOCUS ON PROBLEM SOLVING

1. As you learn more about different statistical methods, one basic problem is deciding which method is appropriate for a particular set of data. Fortunately, it is easy to identify situations in which the independent-measures *t* statistic is used. First, the data always consist of two separate samples (two *n*s, two *M*s, two *SS*s, and so on). Second, this *t* statistic is always used to answer questions about a mean difference: On the average, is one group different (better, faster, smarter) than the other group? If you examine the data and identify the type of question that a researcher is asking, you should be able to decide whether an independent-measures *t* is appropriate.
2. When computing an independent-measures *t* statistic from sample data, we suggest that you routinely divide the formula into separate stages rather than trying to do all of the calculations at once. First, find the pooled variance. Second, compute the standard error. Third, compute the *t* statistic.
3. One of the most common errors for students involves confusing the formulas for pooled variance and standard error. When computing pooled variance, you are "pooling" the two samples together into a single variance. This variance is computed as a *single fraction,* with two *SS* values in the numerator and two *df* values in the denominator. When computing the standard error, you are adding the error from the first sample and the error from the second sample. These two separate errors are added as *two separate fractions* under the square root symbol.

DEMONSTRATION 10.1

THE INDEPENDENT-MEASURES *t* TEST

In a study of jury behavior, two samples of participants were provided details about a trial in which the defendant was obviously guilty. Although group 2 received the same details as group 1, the second group was also told that some evidence had been withheld from the jury by the judge. Later the participants were asked to recommend a jail sentence. The length of term suggested by each participant is presented here. Is there a significant difference between the two groups in their responses?

Group 1	Group 2
4	3
4	7
3	8
2	5
5	4
1	7
1	6
4	8

for Group 1: $M = 3$ and $SS = 16$

for Group 2: $M = 6$ and $SS = 24$

There are two separate samples in this study. Therefore, the analysis uses the independent-measures *t* test.

STEP 1 State the hypothesis, and select an alpha level.

H_0: $\mu_1 - \mu_2 = 0$ (For the population, knowing that evidence has been withheld has no effect on the suggested sentence.)

H_1: $\mu_1 \neq \mu_2 \neq 0$ (For the population, knowing that evidence has been withheld has an effect on the jury's response.)

We set the level of significance to $\alpha = .05$, two tails.

STEP 2 **Identify the critical region.** For the independent-measures *t* statistic, degrees of freedom are determined by

$$\begin{aligned} df &= n_1 + n_2 - 2 \\ &= 8 + 8 - 2 \\ &= 14 \end{aligned}$$

The *t* distribution table is consulted, for a two-tailed test with $\alpha = .05$ and $df = 14$. The critical *t* values are +2.145 and −2.145.

STEP 3 **Compute the test statistic.** As usual, we recommend that the calculation of the t statistic be separated into three stages.

Pooled variance: For these data, the pooled variance equals

$$s_p^2 = \frac{SS_1 + SS_2}{df_1 + df_2} = \frac{16+24}{7+7} = \frac{40}{14} = 2.86$$

Estimated standard error: Now we can calculate the estimated standard error for mean differences.

$$s_{(M_1-M_2)} = \sqrt{\frac{s_p^2}{n_1} + \frac{s_p^2}{n_2}} = \sqrt{\frac{2.86}{8} + \frac{2.86}{8}} = \sqrt{0.358+0.358} = \sqrt{0.716} = 0.85$$

The t *statistic:* Finally, the *t* statistic can be computed.

$$t = \frac{(M_1 - M_2) - (\mu_1 - \mu_2)}{s_{(M_1-M_2)}} = \frac{(3-6)-0}{0.85} = \frac{-3}{0.85} = -3.53$$

STEP 4 **Make a decision about H_0, and state a conclusion.** The obtained *t* value of −3.53 falls in the critical region of the left tail (critical $t = \pm 2.145$). Therefore, the null hypothesis is rejected. The participants who were informed about the withheld evidence gave significantly longer sentences, $t(14) = -3.53$, $p < .05$, two tails.

DEMONSTRATION 10.2

EFFECT SIZE FOR THE INDEPENDENT-MEASURES *t*

We estimate Cohen's *d* and compute r^2 for the jury decision data in Demonstration 10.1. For these data, the two sample means are $M_1 = 3$ and $M_2 = 6$, and the pooled variance is 2.86. Therefore, our estimate of Cohen's *d* is

$$\text{estimated } d = \frac{M_1 - M_2}{\sqrt{s_p^2}} = \frac{3 - 6}{\sqrt{2.86}} = \frac{3}{1.69} = 1.78$$

With a *t* value of $t = 3.53$ and $df = 14$, the percentage of variance accounted for is

$$r^2 = \frac{t^2}{t^2 + df} = \frac{(3.53)^2}{(3.53)^2 + 14} = \frac{12.46}{26.46} = 0.47 \text{ (or 47\%)}$$

PROBLEMS

1. Describe the basic characteristics of an independent-measures, or a between-subjects, research study.

2. Describe the homogeneity of variance assumption and explain why it is important for the independent-measures *t* test.

3. If other factors are held constant, explain how each of the following influences the value of the independent-measures *t* statistic and the likelihood of rejecting the null hypothesis:
   a. Increasing the number of scores in each sample.
   b. Increasing the variance for each sample.

4. Describe what is measured by the estimated standard error in the bottom of the independent-measures *t* statistic.

5. One sample has $SS = 48$ and a second sample has $SS = 32$.
   a. If $n = 5$ for both samples, find each of the sample variances and compute the pooled variance. Because the samples are the same size, you should find that the pooled variance is exactly halfway between the two sample variances.
   b. Now assume that $n = 5$ for the first sample and $n = 9$ for the second. Again, calculate the two sample variances and the pooled variance. You should find that the pooled variance is closer to the variance for the larger sample.

6. One sample has $SS = 70$ and a second sample has $SS = 42$.
   a. If $n = 8$ for both samples, find each of the sample variances, and calculate the pooled variance. Because the samples are the same size, you should find that the pooled variance is exactly halfway between the two sample variances.
   b. Now assume that $n = 8$ for the first sample and $n = 4$ for the second. Again, calculate the two sample variances and the pooled variance. You should find that the pooled variance is closer to the variance for the larger sample.

7. As noted on page 320, when the two population means are equal, the estimated standard error for the independent-measures *t* test provides a measure of how much difference to expect between two sample means. For each of the following situations, assume that $\mu_1 = \mu_2$ and calculate how much difference should be expected between the two sample means.
   a. One sample has $n = 8$ scores with $SS = 45$ and the second sample has $n = 4$ scores with $SS = 15$.
   b. One sample has $n = 8$ scores with $SS = 150$ and the second sample has $n = 4$ scores with $SS = 90$.
   c. In part b, the samples have larger variability (bigger *SS* values) than in part a, but the sample sizes are unchanged. How does larger variability affect the size of the standard error for the sample mean difference?

8. Two separate samples, each with $n = 12$ individuals, receive two different treatments. After treatment, the first sample has $SS = 1740$ and the second has $SS = 1560$.
   a. Find the pooled variance for the two samples.
   b. Compute the estimated standard error for the sample mean difference.
   c. If the sample mean difference is 8 points, is this enough to reject the null hypothesis and conclude that there is a significant difference for a two-tailed test at the .05 level?

d. If the sample mean difference is 12 points, is this enough to indicate a significant difference for a two-tailed test at the .05 level?
e. Calculate the percentage of variance accounted for (r^2) to measure the effect size for an 8-point mean difference and for a 12-point mean difference.

9. Two separate samples receive two different treatments. The first sample has $n = 9$ with $SS = 710$, and the second has $n = 6$ with $SS = 460$.
a. Compute the pooled variance for the two samples.
b. Calculate the estimated standard error for the sample mean difference.
c. If the sample mean difference is 10 points, is this enough to reject the null hypothesis using a two-tailed test with $\alpha = .05$?
d. If the sample mean difference is 13 points, is this enough to reject the null hypothesis using a two tailed test with $\alpha = .05$?

10. A researcher conducts an independent-measures study comparing two treatments and reports the t statistic as $t(30) = 2.085$.
a. How many individuals participated in the entire study?
b. Using a two-tailed test with $\alpha = .05$, is there a significant difference between the two treatments?
c. Compute r^2 to measure the percentage of variance accounted for by the treatment effect.

11. For each of the following, calculate the pooled variance and the estimated standard error for the sample mean difference
a. The first sample has $n = 4$ scores and a variance of $s^2 = 55$, and the second sample has $n = 6$ scores and a variance of $s^2 = 63$.
b. Now the sample variances are increased so that the first sample has $n = 4$ scores and a variance of $s^2 = 220$, and the second sample has $n = 6$ scores and a variance of $s^2 = 252$.
c. Comparing your answers for parts a and b, how does increased variance influence the size of the estimated standard error?

12. For each of the following, assume that the two samples are selected from populations with equal means and calculate how much difference should be expected, on average, between the two sample means.
a. Each sample has $n = 5$ scores with $s^2 = 38$ for the first sample and $s^2 = 42$ for the second. (*Note:* Because the two samples are the same size, the pooled variance is equal to the average of the two sample variances.)
b. Each sample has $n = 20$ scores with $s^2 = 38$ for the first sample and $s^2 = 42$ for the second.
c. In part b, the two samples are bigger than in part a, but the variances are unchanged. How does sample size affect the size of the standard error for the sample mean difference?

13. Hallam, Price, and Katsarou (2002) investigated the influence of background noise on classroom performance for children aged 10 to 12. In one part of the study, calming music led to better performance on an arithmetic task compared to a no-music condition. Suppose that a researcher selects one class of $n = 18$ students who listen to calming music each day while working on arithmetic problems. A second class of $n = 18$ serves as a control group with no music. Accuracy scores are measured for each child and the average for students in the music condition is $M = 86.4$ with $SS = 1550$ compared to an average of $M = 78.8$ with $SS = 1204$ for students in the no-music condition.
a. Is there a significant difference between the two music conditions? Use a two-tailed test with $\alpha = .05$.
b. Compute the 90% confidence interval for the population mean difference.
c. Write a sentence demonstrating how the results from the hypothesis test and the confidence interval would appear in a research report.

14. Do you view a chocolate bar as delicious or as fattening? Your attitude may depend on your gender. In a study of American college students, Rozin, Bauer, and Catanese (2003) examined the importance of food as a source of pleasure versus concerns about food associated with weight gain and health. The following results are similar to those obtained in the study. The scores are a measure of concern about the negative aspects of eating.

Males	Females
$n = 9$	$n = 15$
$M = 33$	$M = 42$
$SS = 740$	$SS = 1240$

a. Based on these results, is there a significant difference between the attitudes for males and for females? Use a two-tailed test with $\alpha = .05$.
b. Compute r^2, the percentage of variance accounted for by the gender difference, to measure effect size for this study.
c. Write a sentence demonstrating how the result of the hypothesis test and the measure of effect size would appear in a research report.

15. In a study examining overweight and obese college football players, Mathews and Wagner (2008) found that on average both offensive and defensive linemen exceeded the at-risk criterion for body mass index (BMI). BMI is a ratio of body weight to height squared and is commonly used to classify people as overweight or obese. Any value greater than 30 kg/m^2 is considered to be at risk. In the study, a sample of $n = 17$ offensive linemen averaged $M = 34.4$ with a

standard deviation of $s = 4.0$. A sample of $n = 19$ defensive linemen averaged $M = 31.9$ with $s = 3.5$.

a. Use a single-sample *t* test to determine whether the offensive linemen are significantly above the at-risk criterion for BMI. Use a one-tailed test with $\alpha = .01$.

b. Use a single-sample *t* test to determine whether the defensive linemen are significantly above the at-risk criterion for BMI. Use a one-tailed test with $\alpha = .01$.

c. Use an independent-measures *t* test to determine whether there is a significant difference between the offensive linemen and the defensive linemen. Use a two-tailed test with $\alpha = .01$.

16. Functional foods are those containing nutritional supplements in addition to natural nutrients. Examples include orange juice with calcium and eggs with omega-3. Kolodinsky, et al. (2008) examined attitudes toward functional foods for college students. For American students, the results indicated that females had a more positive attitude toward functional foods and were more likely to purchase them compared to males. In a similar study, a researcher asked students to rate their general attitude toward functional foods on a 7-point scale (higher score is more positive). The results are as follows:

Females	Male
$n = 8$	$n = 12$
$M = 4.69$	$M = 4.43$
$SS = 1.60$	$SS = 2.72$

a. Do the data indicate a significant difference in attitude for males and females? Use a two-tailed test with $\alpha = .05$.

b. Compute r^2, the amount of variance accounted for by the gender difference, to measure effect size.

c. Write a sentence demonstrating how the results of the hypothesis test and the measure of effect size would appear in a research report.

17. In 1974, Loftus and Palmer conducted a classic study demonstrating how the language used to ask a question can influence eyewitness memory. In the study, college students watched a film of an automobile accident and then were asked questions about what they saw. One group was asked, "About how fast were the cars going when they smashed into each other?" Another group was asked the same question except the verb was changed to "hit" instead of "smashed into." The "smashed into" group reported significantly higher estimates of speed than the "hit" group. Suppose a researcher repeats this study with a sample of today's college students and obtains the following results.

Estimated Speed	
Smashed into	Hit
$n = 15$	$n = 15$
$M = 40.8$	$M = 34.0$
$SS = 510$	$SS = 414$

a. Do the results indicate a significantly higher estimated speed for the "smashed into" group? Use a one-tailed test with $\alpha = .01$.

b. Compute the estimated value for Cohen's *d* to measure the size of the effect.

c. Write a sentence demonstrating how the results of the hypothesis test and the measure of effect size would appear in a research report.

18. Numerous studies have found that males report higher self-esteem than females, especially for adolescents (Kling, Hyde, Showers, & Buswell, 1999). Typical results show a mean self-esteem score of $M = 39.0$ with $SS = 60.2$ for a sample of $n = 10$ male adolescents and a mean of $M = 35.4$ with $SS = 69.4$ for a sample of $n = 10$ female adolescents.

a. Do the results indicate that self-esteem is significantly higher for males? Use a one-tailed test with $\alpha = .01$.

b. Use the data to make a 95% confidence interval estimate of the mean difference in self-esteem between male and female adolescents.

c. Write a sentence demonstrating how the results from the hypothesis test and the confidence interval would appear in a research report.

19. A researcher is comparing the effectiveness of two sets of instructions for assembling a child's bike. A sample of eight fathers is obtained. Half of the fathers are given one set of instructions and the other half receives the second set. The researcher measures how much time is needed for each father to assemble the bike. The scores are the number of minutes needed by each participant.

Instruction Set I	Instruction Set II
8	14
4	10
8	6
4	10

a. Is there a significant difference in time for the two sets of instructions? Use a two-tailed test at the .05 level of significance.

b. Calculate the estimated Cohen's *d* and r^2 to measure effect size for this study.

20. Downs and Abwender (2002) evaluated soccer players and swimmers to determine whether the routine blows to the head experienced by soccer players produced long-term neurological deficits. In the study, neurological tests were administered to mature soccer players and swimmers and the results indicated significant differences. In a similar study, a researcher obtained the following data.

Swimmers	Soccer players
10	7
8	4
7	9
9	3
13	7
7	
6	
12	

a. Are the neurological test scores significantly lower for the soccer players than for the swimmers in the control group? Use a one-tailed test with $\alpha = .05$.
b. Compute the value of r^2 (percentage of variance accounted for) for these data.

21. Steven Schmidt (1994) conducted a series of experiments examining the effects of humor on memory. In one study, participants were given a mix of humorous and nonhumorous sentences and significantly more humorous sentences were recalled. However, Schmidt argued that the humorous sentences were not necessarily easier to remember, they were simply preferred when participants had a choice between the two types of sentence. To test this argument, he switched to an independent-measures design in which one group got a set of exclusively humorous sentences and another group got a set of exclusively nonhumorous sentences. The following data are similar to the results from the independent-measures study.

Humorous Sentences				Nonhumorous Sentences			
4	5	2	4	6	3	5	3
6	7	6	6	3	4	2	6
2	5	4	3	4	3	4	4
3	3	5	3	5	2	6	4

Do the results indicate a significant difference in the recall of humorous versus nonhumorous sentences? Use a two-tailed test with $\alpha = .05$.

22. When people learn a new task, their performance usually improves when they are tested the next day, but only if they get at least 6 hours of sleep (Stickgold, Whidbee, Schirmer, Patel, & Hobson, 2000). The following data demonstrate this phenomenon. The participants learned a visual discrimination task on one day, and then were tested on the task the following day. Half of the participants were allowed to have at least 6 hours of sleep and the other half were kept awake all night. Is there a significant difference between the two conditions? Use a two-tailed test with $\alpha = .05$.

Performance Scores	
6 Hours of Sleep	No Sleep
$n = 14$	$n = 14$
$M = 72$	$M = 65$
$SS = 932$	$SS = 706$

23. Research has shown that people are more likely to show dishonest and self-interested behaviors in darkness than in a well-lit environment (Zhong, Bohns, & Gino, 2010). In one experiment, participants were given a set of 20 puzzles and were paid $0.50 for each one solved in a 5-minute period. However, the participants reported their own performance and there was no obvious method for checking their honesty. Thus, the task provided a clear opportunity to cheat and receive undeserved money. One group of participants was tested in a room with dimmed lighting and a second group was tested in a well-lit room. The reported number of solved puzzles was recorded for each individual. The following data represent results similar to those obtained in the study.

Well-Lit Room	Dimly Lit Room
7	9
8	11
10	13
6	10
8	11
5	9
7	15
12	14
5	10

a. Is there a significant difference in reported performance between the two conditions? Use a two-tailed test with $\alpha = .01$.
b. Compute Cohen's d to estimate the size of the treatment effect.

CHAPTER

11

The t Test for Two Related Samples

Tools You Will Need

The following items are considered essential background material for this chapter. If you doubt your knowledge of any of these items, you should review the appropriate chapter or section before proceeding.

- Introduction to the t statistic (Chapter 9)
  - Estimated standard error
  - Degrees of freedom
  - t Distribution
  - Hypothesis tests with the t statistic
- Independent-measures design (Chapter 10)

Preview

Swearing is a common, almost reflexive, response to pain. Whether you knock your shin into the edge of a coffee table or smash your thumb with a hammer, most of us respond with a streak of obscenities. One question, however, is whether swearing focuses attention on the pain and, thereby, increases its intensity, or serves as a distraction that reduces pain. To address this issue, Stephens, Atkins, and Kingston (2009) conducted an experiment comparing swearing with other responses to pain. In the study, participants were asked to place one hand in icy cold water for as long as they could bear the pain. Half of the participants were told to repeat their favorite swear word over and over for as long as their hands were in the water. The other half repeated a neutral word. The researchers recorded how long each participant was able to tolerate the ice water. After a brief rest, the two groups switched words and repeated the ice water plunge. Thus, all the participants experienced both conditions (swearing and neutral) with half swearing on their first plunge and half on their second. The results clearly showed that swearing significantly increased the average amount of time that participants could tolerate the pain.

The Problem: In the previous chapter, we introduced a statistical procedure for evaluating the mean difference between two sets of data (the independent-measures t statistic). However, the independent-measures t statistic is intended for research situations involving two separate and independent samples. You should realize that the two sets of scores in the swearing study are not independent samples. In fact, the same group individuals participated in both of the treatment conditions. What is needed is a new statistical analysis for comparing two means that are both obtained from the same group of participants.

The Solution: In this chapter, we introduce the *repeated-measures* t *statistic,* which is used for hypothesis tests evaluating the mean difference between two sets of scores obtained from the same group of individuals. As you will see, however, this new t statistic is very similar to the original t statistic that was introduced in Chapter 9.

Finally, we should note that researchers often have a choice when they are planning a research study that compares two different treatment conditions. Specifically, a researcher may choose to use two separate groups of participants, one for each of the treatments, or a researcher may choose to use one group and measure each individual in both of the treatment conditions. Later in this chapter, we take a closer look at the differences between these two research designs and discuss the advantages and disadvantages of each.

11.1 INTRODUCTION TO REPEATED-MEASURES DESIGNS

In the previous chapter, we introduced the independent-measures research design as one strategy for comparing two treatment conditions or two populations. The independent-measures design is characterized by the fact that two separate samples are used to obtain the two sets of scores that are to be compared. In this chapter, we examine an alternative strategy known as a *repeated-measures design,* or a *within-subjects design.* With a repeated-measures design, two separate scores are obtained for each individual in the sample. For example, a group of patients could be measured before therapy and then measured again after therapy. Or, response time could be measured in a driving simulation task for a group of individuals who are first tested when they are sober and then tested again after two alcoholic drinks. In each case, the same variable is being measured twice for the same set of individuals; that is, we are literally repeating measurements on the same sample.

DEFINITION

A **repeated-measures design,** or a **within-subject design,** is one in which the dependent variable is measured two or more times for each individual in a single sample. The same group of subjects is used in all of the treatment conditions.

The main advantage of a repeated-measures study is that it uses exactly the same individuals in all treatment conditions. Thus, there is no risk that the participants in one treatment are substantially different from the participants in another. With an independent-measures design, on the other hand, there is always a risk that the results are biased because the individuals in one sample are systematically different (smarter, faster, more extroverted, and so on) than the individuals in the other sample. At the end of this chapter, we present a more detailed comparison of repeated-measures studies and independent-measures studies, considering the advantages and disadvantages of both types of research.

THE MATCHED-SUBJECTS DESIGN

Occasionally, researchers try to approximate the advantages of a repeated-measures design by using a technique known as *matched subjects*. A matched-subjects design involves two separate samples, but each individual in one sample is matched one-to-one with an individual in the other sample. Typically, the individuals are matched on one or more variables that are considered to be especially important for the study. For example, a researcher studying verbal learning might want to be certain that the two samples are matched in terms of IQ and gender. In this case, a male participant with an IQ of 120 in one sample would be matched with another male with an IQ of 120 in the other sample. Although the participants in one sample are not *identical* to the participants in the other sample, the matched-subjects design at least ensures that the two samples are equivalent (or matched) with respect to some specific variables.

DEFINITION

In a **matched-subjects design,** each individual in one sample is matched with an individual in the other sample. The matching is done so that the two individuals are equivalent (or nearly equivalent) with respect to a specific variable that the researcher would like to control.

Of course, it is possible to match participants on more than one variable. For example, a researcher could match pairs of subjects on age, gender, race, and IQ. In this case, for example, a 22-year-old white female with an IQ of 115 who was in one sample would be matched with another 22-year-old white female with an IQ of 115 in the second sample. The more variables that are used, however, the more difficult it is to find matching pairs. The goal of the matching process is to simulate a repeated-measures design as closely as possible. In a repeated-measures design, the matching is perfect because the same individual is used in both conditions. In a matched-subjects design, however, the best you can get is a degree of match that is limited to the variable(s) that are used for the matching process.

In a repeated-measures design or a matched-subjects design comparing two treatment conditions, the data consist of two sets of scores, which are grouped into sets of two, corresponding to the two scores obtained for each individual or each matched pair of subjects (Table 11.1). Because the scores in one set are directly related, one-to-one, with the scores in the second set, the two research designs are statistically equivalent and share the common name *related-samples* designs (or correlated-samples designs). In this chapter, we focus our discussion on repeated-measures designs because they are overwhelmingly the more common example of related-samples designs. However, you should realize that the statistical techniques used for repeated-measures studies also can be applied directly to data from matched-subjects studies. We should also note that a matched-subjects study occasionally is called a *matched samples design*, but the subjects in the samples must be matched one-to-one before you can use the statistical techniques in this chapter.

TABLE 11.1

An example of the data from a repeated-measures or a matched-subjects study using $n = 5$ participants (or matched pairs).

Participant or Matched Pair	First Score	Second Score	
#1	12	15	←The 2 scores for
#2	10	14	one participant or
#3	15	17	one matched pair
#4	17	17	
#5	12	18	

Now we examine the statistical techniques that allow a researcher to use the sample data from a repeated-measures study to draw inferences about the general population.

11.2 THE *t* STATISTIC FOR A REPEATED-MEASURES RESEARCH DESIGN

The *t* statistic for a repeated-measures design is structurally similar to the other *t* statistics we have examined. As we shall see, it is essentially the same as the single-sample *t* statistic covered in Chapter 9. The major distinction of the related-samples *t* is that it is based on *difference scores* rather than raw scores (*X* values). In this section, we examine difference scores and develop the *t* statistic for related samples.

DIFFERENCE SCORES: THE DATA FOR A REPEATED-MEASURES STUDY

Many over-the-counter cold medications include the warning "may cause drowsiness." Table 11.2 shows an example of data from a study that examines this phenomenon. Note that there is one sample of $n = 4$ participants, and that each individual is measured twice. The first score for each person (X_1) is a measurement of reaction time before the medication was administered. The second score (X_2) measures reaction time 1 hour after taking the medication. Because we are interested in how the medication affects reaction time, we have computed the difference between the first score and the second score for each individual. The *difference scores*, or *D* values, are shown in the last column of the table. Notice that the difference scores measure the amount of change

TABLE 11.2

Reaction-time measurements taken before and after taking an over-the-counter cold medication.

Person	Before Medication (X_1)	After Medication (X_2)	Difference D
A	215	210	−5
B	221	242	21
C	196	219	23
D	203	228	25
			$\Sigma D = 64$

$$M_D = \frac{\Sigma D}{n} = \frac{64}{4} = 16$$

Note that M_D is the mean for the sample of *D* scores.

in reaction time for each person. Typically, the difference scores are obtained by subtracting the first score (before treatment) from the second score (after treatment) for each person:

$$\text{difference score} = D = X_2 - X_1 \quad (11.1)$$

Note that the sign of each D score tells you the direction of the change. Person A, for example, shows a decrease in reaction time after taking the medication (a negative change), but person B shows an increase (a positive change).

The sample of difference scores (D values) serves as the sample data for the hypothesis test and all calculations are done using the D scores. To compute the t statistic, for example, we use the number of D scores (n) as well as the sample mean (M_D) and the value of SS for the sample of D scores.

THE HYPOTHESES FOR A RELATED-SAMPLES STUDY

The researcher's goal is to use the sample of difference scores to answer questions about the general population. In particular, the researcher would like to know whether there is any difference between the two treatment conditions for the general population. Note that we are interested in a population of *difference scores*. That is, we would like to know what would happen if every individual in the population were measured in two treatment conditions (X_1 and X_2) and a difference score (D) were computed for everyone. Specifically, we are interested in the mean for the population of difference scores. We identify this population mean difference with the symbol μ_D (using the subscript letter D to indicate that we are dealing with D values rather than X scores).

As always, the null hypothesis states that, for the general population, there is no effect, no change, or no difference. For a repeated-measures study, the null hypothesis states that the mean difference for the general population is zero. In symbols,

$$H_0: \mu_D = 0$$

Again, this hypothesis refers to the mean for the entire population of difference scores. Figure 11.1(a) shows an example of a population of difference scores with a

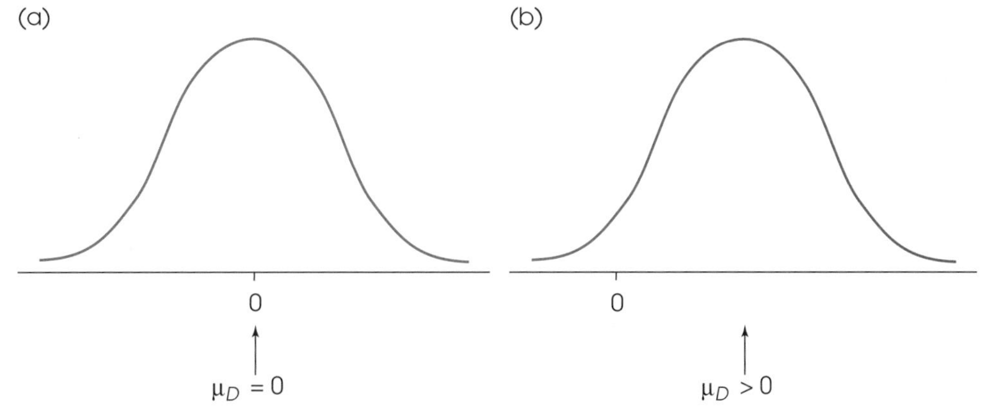

FIGURE 11.1

(a) A population of difference scores for which the mean is $\mu_D = 0$. Note that the typical difference score (D value) is not equal to zero. (b) A population of difference scores for which the mean is greater than zero. Note that most of the difference scores are also greater than zero.

mean of $\mu_D = 0$. Although the population mean is zero, the individual scores in the population are not all equal to zero. Thus, even when the null hypothesis is true, we still expect some individuals to have positive difference scores and some to have negative difference scores. However, the positives and negatives are unsystematic and in the long run balance out to $\mu_D = 0$. Also note that a sample selected from this population probably will not have a mean exactly equal to zero. As always, there will be some error between a sample mean and the population mean, so even if $\mu_D = 0$ (H_0 is true), we do not expect M_D to be exactly equal to zero.

The alternative hypothesis states that there is a treatment effect that causes the scores in one treatment condition to be systematically higher (or lower) than the scores in the other condition. In symbols,

$$H_1\colon \mu_D \neq 0$$

According to H_1, the difference scores for the individuals in the population tend to be systematically positive (or negative), indicating a consistent, predictable difference between the two treatments.

Figure 11.1(b) shows an example of a population of difference scores with a positive mean difference, $\mu_D > 0$. This time, most of the individuals in the population have difference scores that are greater than zero. A sample selected from this population will contain primarily positive difference scores and will probably have a mean difference that is greater than zero, $M_D > 0$. See Box 11.1 for further discussion of H_0 and H_1.

THE *t* STATISTIC FOR RELATED SAMPLES

Figure 11.2 shows the general situation that exists for a repeated-measures hypothesis test. You may recognize that we are facing essentially the same situation that we encountered in Chapter 9. In particular, we have a population for which the mean and the standard deviation are unknown, and we have a sample that will be used to test a hypothesis about the unknown population. In Chapter 9, we introduced the single-sample *t* statistic, which allowed us to use a sample mean as a basis for testing hypotheses about an unknown

BOX 11.1 ANALOGIES FOR H_0 AND H_1 IN THE REPEATED-MEASURES TEST

An Analogy for H_0: Intelligence is a fairly stable characteristic; that is, you do not get noticeably smarter or dumber from one day to the next. However, if we gave you an IQ test every day for a week, we probably would get seven different numbers. The day-to-day changes in your IQ score are caused by random factors such as your health, your mood, and your luck at guessing answers you do not know. Some days your IQ score is slightly higher, and some days it is slightly lower. On average, the day-to-day changes in IQ should balance out to zero. This is the situation that is predicted by the null hypothesis for a repeated-measures test. According to H_0, any changes that occur either for an individual or for a sample are just due to chance, and in the long run, they will average out to zero.

An Analogy for H_1: On the other hand, suppose that we evaluate your performance on a new video game by measuring your score every day for a week. Again, we probably will find small differences in your scores from one day to the next, just as we did with the IQ scores. However, the day-to-day changes in your game score will not be random. Instead, there should be a general trend toward higher scores as you gain more experience with the new game. Thus, most of the day-to-day changes should show an increase. This is the situation that is predicted by the alternative hypothesis for the repeated-measures test. According to H_1, the changes that occur are systematic and predictable and will not average out to zero.

FIGURE 11.2

A sample of $n = 4$ people is selected from the population. Each individual is measured twice, once in treatment I and once in treatment II, and a difference score, D, is computed for each individual. This sample of difference scores is intended to represent the population. Note that we are using a sample of difference scores to represent a population of difference scores. Note that the mean for the population of difference scores is unknown. The null hypothesis states that for the general population there is no consistent or systematic difference between the two treatments, so the population mean difference is $\mu_D = 0$.

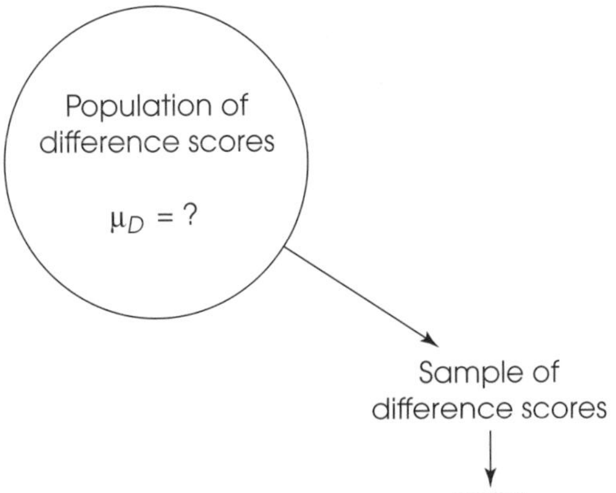

Subject	I	II	*D*
A	10	14	4
B	15	13	−2
C	12	15	3
D	11	12	1

population mean. This *t*-statistic formula is used again here to develop the repeated-measures *t* test. To refresh your memory, the single-sample *t* statistic (Chapter 9) is defined by the formula

$$t = \frac{M - \mu}{s_M}$$

In this formula, the sample mean, M, is calculated from the data, and the value for the population mean, μ, is obtained from the null hypothesis. The estimated standard error, s_M, is also calculated from the data and provides a measure of how much difference it is reasonable to expect between a sample mean and the population mean.

For the repeated-measures design, the sample data are difference scores and are identified by the letter D, rather than X. Therefore, we use Ds in the formula to emphasize that we are dealing with difference scores instead of X values. Also, the population mean that is of interest to us is the population mean difference (the mean amount of change for the entire population), and we identify this parameter with the symbol μ_D. With these simple changes, the *t* formula for the repeated-measures design becomes

As noted earlier, the repeated-measures *t* formula is also used for matched-subjects designs.

$$t = \frac{M_D - \mu_D}{s_{M_D}} \qquad (11.2)$$

In this formula, the *estimated standard error for* M_D, s_{M_D}, is computed in exactly the same way as it is computed for the single-sample *t* statistic. To calculate the estimated standard error, the first step is to compute the variance (or the standard deviation) for the sample of D scores.

$$s^2 = \frac{SS}{n-1} = \frac{SS}{df} \quad \text{or} \quad s = \sqrt{\frac{SS}{df}}$$

The estimated standard error is then computed using the sample variance (or sample standard deviation) and the sample size, n.

$$s_{M_D} = \sqrt{\frac{s^2}{n}} \quad \text{or} \quad s_{M_D} = \frac{s}{\sqrt{n}} \tag{11.3}$$

Notice that all of the calculations are done using the difference scores (the D scores) and that there is only one D score for each subject. With a sample of n subjects, there are exactly n D scores, and the t statistic has $df = n - 1$. Remember that n refers to the number of D scores, not the number of X scores in the original data.

You should also note that the *repeated-measures* t *statistic* is conceptually similar to the t statistics that we have previously examined:

$$t = \frac{\text{sample statistic} - \text{population parameter}}{\text{estimated standard error}}$$

In this case, the sample data are represented by the sample mean of the difference scores (M_D), the population parameter is the value predicted by H_0 ($\mu_D = 0$), and the estimated standard error is computed from the sample data using Equation 11.3.

LEARNING CHECK

1. For a research study comparing two treatment conditions, what characteristic differentiates a repeated-measures design from an independent-measures design?
2. Describe the data used to compute the sample mean and the sample variance for the repeated-measures t statistic.
3. In words and in symbols, what is the null hypothesis for a repeated-measures t test?

ANSWERS

1. For a repeated-measures design, the same group of individuals is tested in both of the treatments. An independent-measures design uses a separate group for each treatment.
2. The two scores obtained for each individual are used to compute a difference score. The sample of difference scores is used to compute the mean and variance.
3. The null hypothesis states that, for the general population, the average difference between the two conditions is zero. In symbols, $\mu_D = 0$.

11.3 HYPOTHESIS TESTS AND EFFECT SIZE FOR THE REPEATED-MEASURES DESIGN

In a repeated-measures study, each individual is measured in two different treatment conditions and we are interested in whether there is a systematic difference between the scores in the first treatment condition and the scores in the second treatment condition. A difference score (D value) is computed for each person and the hypothesis test uses the difference scores from the sample to evaluate the overall mean difference, μ_D, for the entire population. The hypothesis test with the repeated-measures t statistic follows the same four-step process that we have used for other tests. The complete hypothesis-testing procedure is demonstrated in Example 11.1.

EXAMPLE 11.1 Research indicates that the color red increases men's attraction to women (Elliot & Niesta, 2008). In the original study, men were shown women's photographs presented on either a white or a red background. Photographs presented on red were rated significantly more attractive than the same photographs mounted on white. In a similar study, a researcher prepares a set of 30 women's photographs, with 15 mounted on a white background and 15 mounted on red. One picture is identified as the test photograph, and appears twice in the set, once on white and once on red. Each male participant looks through the entire set of photographs and rates the attractiveness of each woman on a 12-point scale. Table 11.3 summarizes the ratings of the test photograph for a sample of $n = 9$ men. Are the ratings for the test photograph significantly different when it is presented on a red background compared to a white background?

STEP 1 State the hypotheses, and select the alpha level.

H_0: $\mu_D = 0$ (There is no difference between the two colors.)

H_1: $\mu_D \neq 0$ (There is a change.)

For this test, we use $\alpha = .01$.

STEP 2 Locate the critical region. For this example, $n = 9$, so the t statistic has $df = n - 1 = 8$. For $\alpha = .01$, the critical value listed in the t distribution table is $\pm$ 3.355. The critical region is shown in Figure 11.3.

TABLE 11.3

Attractiveness ratings for a woman shown in a photograph presented on a red and a white background.

Participant	White Background	Red Background	D	D^2
A	6	9	+3	9
B	8	9	+1	1
C	7	10	+3	9
D	7	11	+4	16
E	8	11	+3	9
F	6	9	+3	9
G	5	11	+6	36
H	10	11	+1	1
I	8	11	+3	9
			$\Sigma D = 27$	$\Sigma D^2 = 99$

$$M_D = \frac{27}{9} = 3.00$$

$$SS = \Sigma D^2 - \frac{(\Sigma D)^2}{n} = 99 - \frac{(27)^2}{9} = 99 - 81 = 18$$

FIGURE 11.3

The critical region for the t distribution with $df = 8$ and $\alpha = .01$.

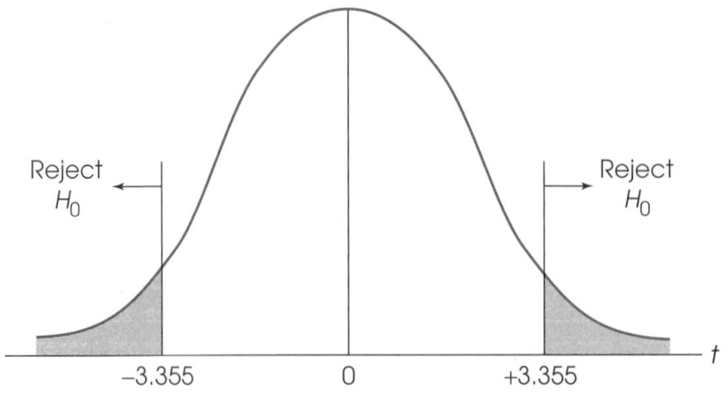

STEP 3 Calculate the t statistic. Table 11.3 shows the sample data and the calculations of $M_D = 3.00$ and $SS = 18$. Note that all calculations are done with the difference scores. As we have done with the other t statistics, we present the calculation of the t statistic as a three-step process.

First, compute the sample variance.

$$s^2 = \frac{SS}{n-1} = \frac{18}{8} = 2.25$$

Next, use the sample variance to compute the estimated standard error.

$$s_{M_D} = \sqrt{\frac{s^2}{n}} = \sqrt{\frac{2.25}{9}} = 0.50$$

Finally, use the sample mean (M_D) and the hypothesized population mean (μ_D) along with the estimated standard error to compute the value for the t statistic.

$$t = \frac{M_D - \mu_D}{s_{M_D}} = \frac{3.00 - 0}{0.50} = 6.00$$

STEP 4 Make a decision. The t value we obtained falls in the critical region (see Figure 11.3). The researcher rejects the null hypothesis and concludes that the background color has a significant effect on the judged attractiveness of the woman in the test photograph.

MEASURING EFFECT SIZE FOR THE REPEATED-MEASURES *t*

As we noted with other hypothesis tests, whenever a treatment effect is found to be statistically significant, it is recommended that you also report a measure of the absolute magnitude of the effect. The most commonly used measures of effect size are Cohen's d and r^2, the percentage of variance accounted for. The size of the treatment effect also can be described with a confidence interval estimating the population mean difference, μ_D. Using the data from Example 11.1, we demonstrate how these values are calculated to measure and describe effect size.

Cohen's *d* In Chapters 8 and 9, we introduced Cohen's *d* as a standardized measure of the mean difference between treatments. The standardization simply divides the population mean difference by the standard deviation. For a repeated-measures study, Cohen's *d* is defined as

$$d = \frac{\text{population mean difference}}{\text{standard deviation}} = \frac{\mu_D}{\sigma_D}$$

Because the population mean and standard deviation are unknown, we use the sample values instead. The sample mean, M_D, is the best estimate of the actual mean difference, and the sample standard deviation (square root of sample variance) provides the best estimate of the actual standard deviation. Thus, we are able to estimate the value of *d* as follows:

Because we are measuring the size of the effect and not the direction, it is customary to ignore the minus sign and report Cohen's *d* as a positive value.

$$\text{estimated } d = \frac{\text{sample mean difference}}{\text{sample standard deviation}} = \frac{M_D}{s} \quad (11.4)$$

For the repeated-measures study in Example 11.1, $M_D = 3$ and the sample variance is $s^2 = 2.25$, so the data produce

$$\text{estimated } d = \frac{M_D}{s} = \frac{3.00}{\sqrt{2.25}} = \frac{3.00}{1.5} = 2.00$$

Any value greater than 0.80 is considered to be a large effect, and these data are clearly in that category (see Table 8.2 on p. 264).

The percentage of variance accounted for, r^2 Percentage of variance is computed using the obtained *t* value and the *df* value from the hypothesis test, exactly as was done for the single-sample *t* (see p. 299) and for the independent-measures *t* (see p. 329). For the data in Example 11.1, we obtain

$$r^2 = \frac{t^2}{t^2 + df} = \frac{(6.00)^2}{(6.00)^2 + 8} = \frac{36}{44} = 0.818 \text{ or } 81.8\%$$

For these data, 81.8% of the variance in the scores is explained by the background color for the photograph. More specifically, the color red caused the difference scores to be consistently positive. Thus, the deviations from zero are largely explained by the treatment.

Confidence intervals for estimating μ_D As noted in the previous two chapters, it is possible to compute a confidence interval as an alternative method for measuring and describing the size of the treatment effect. For the repeated-measures *t*, we use a sample mean difference, M_D, to estimate the population mean difference, μ_D. In this case, the confidence interval literally estimates the size of the treatment effect by estimating the population mean difference between the two treatment conditions.

As with the other *t* statistics, the first step is to solve the *t* equation for the unknown parameter. For the repeated-measures *t* statistic, we obtain

$$\mu_D = M_D \pm t s_{M_D} \quad (11.5)$$

In the equation, the values for M_D and for s_{M_D} are obtained from the sample data. Although the value for the t statistic is unknown, we can use the degrees of freedom for the t statistic and the t distribution table to estimate the t value. Using the estimated t and the known values from the sample, we can then compute the value of μ_D. The following example demonstrates the process of constructing a confidence interval for a population mean difference.

EXAMPLE 11.2 In Example 11.1 we presented a research study demonstrating how men's attractiveness ratings for women are influenced by the color red. In the study, a sample of $n = 9$ men rated a woman shown in a photograph as significantly more attractive when the photo was presented on a red background than when it was on a white background. The mean difference between treatments was $M_D = 3$ points and the estimated standard error for the mean difference was $s_{M_D} = 0.50$. Now, we construct a 95% confidence interval to estimate the size of the population mean difference.

With a sample of $n = 9$ participants, the repeated-measures t statistic has $df = 8$. To have 95% confidence, we simply estimate that the t statistic for the sample mean difference is located somewhere in the middle 95% of all the possible t values. According to the t distribution table, with $df = 8$, 95% of the t values are located between $t = +2.306$ and $t = -2.306$. Using these values in the estimation equation, together with the values for the sample mean and the standard error, we obtain

$$\mu_D = M_D \pm t s_{M_D}$$

$$= 3 \pm 2.306(0.50)$$

$$= 3 \pm 1.153$$

This produces an interval of values ranging from $3 - 1.153 = 1.847$ to $3 + 1.153 = 4.153$. Our conclusion is that for general population of men, changing the background color from white to red increases the average attractiveness rating for the woman in the photograph between 1.847 and 4.153 points. We are 95% confident that the true mean difference is in this interval because the only value estimated during the calculations was the t statistic, and we are 95% confident that the t value is located in the middle 95% of the distribution. Finally note that the confidence interval is constructed around the sample mean difference. As a result, the sample mean difference, $M_D = 3$ points, is located exactly in the center of the interval.

As with the other confidence intervals presented in Chapters 9 and 10, the confidence interval for a repeated-measures t is influenced by a variety of factors other than the actual size of the treatment effect. In particular, the width of the interval depends on the percentage of confidence used, so that a larger percentage produces a wider interval. Also, the width of the interval depends on the sample size, so that a larger sample produces a narrower interval. Because the interval width is related to sample size, the confidence interval is not a pure measure of effect size like Cohen's d or r^2.

Finally, we should note that the 95% confidence interval computed in Example 11.2 does not include the value $\mu_D = 0$. In other words, we are 95% confident that the population mean difference is not $\mu_D = 0$. This is equivalent to concluding that a null hypothesis specifying that $\mu_D = 0$ would be rejected with a test using $\alpha = .05$. If $\mu_D = 0$ were included in the 95% confidence interval, it would indicate that a hypothesis test would fail to reject H_0 with $\alpha = .05$.

IN THE LITERATURE
REPORTING THE RESULTS OF A REPEATED-MEASURES *t* TEST

As we have seen in Chapters 9 and 10, the APA format for reporting the results of *t* tests consists of a concise statement that incorporates the *t* value, degrees of freedom, and alpha level. One typically includes values for means and standard deviations, either in a statement or a table (Chapter 4). For Example 11.1, we observed a mean difference of $M_D = 3.00$ with $s = 1.50$. Also, we obtained a *t* statistic of $t = 6.00$ with $df = 8$, and our decision was to reject the null hypothesis at the .01 level of significance. Finally, we measured effect size by computing the percentage of variance explained and obtained $r^2 = 0.818$. A published report of this study might summarize the results as follows:

> Changing the background color from white to red increased the attractiveness rating of the woman in the photograph by an average of $M = 3.00$ points with $SD = 1.50$. The treatment effect was statistically significant, $t(8) = 6.00$, $p < .01$, $r^2 = 0.818$.

When the hypothesis test is conducted with a computer program, the printout typically includes an exact probability for the level of significance. The *p*-value from the printout is then stated as the level of significance in the research report. However, the data from Example 11.1 produced a significance level of $p = .000$ in the computer printout. In this case, the probability was so small that the computer rounded it off to 3 decimal points and obtained a value of zero. In this situation you do not know the exact probability value and should report $p < .001$.

If the confidence interval from Example 11.2 is reported as a description of effect size together with the results from the hypothesis test, it would appear as follows:

> Changing the background color from white to red significantly increased the attractiveness rating, $t(8) = 6.00$, $p < .001$, 95% CI [1.817, 4.183].

DESCRIPTIVE STATISTICS AND THE HYPOTHESIS TEST

Often, a close look at the sample data from a research study makes it easier to see the size of the treatment effect and to understand the outcome of the hypothesis test. In Example 11.1, we obtained a sample of $n = 9$ men who produce a mean difference of $M_D = 3.00$ with a standard deviation of $s = 1.50$ points. The sample mean and standard deviation describe a set of scores centered at $M_D = 3.00$ with most of the scores located within 1.5 points of the mean. Figure 11.4 shows the actual set of difference scores that were obtained in Example 11.1. In addition to showing the scores in the sample, we have highlighted the position of $\mu_D = 0$; that is, the value specified in the null hypothesis. Notice that the scores in the sample are displaced away from zero. Specifically, the data are not consistent with a population mean of $\mu_D = 0$, which is why we rejected the null hypothesis. In addition, note that the sample mean is located 2 standard deviations above zero. This distance corresponds to the effect size measured by Cohen's $d = 2.00$. For these data, the picture of the sample distribution (see Figure 11.4) should help you to understand the measure of effect size and the outcome of the hypothesis test.

VARIABILITY AS A MEASURE OF CONSISTENCY FOR THE TREATMENT EFFECT

In a repeated-measures study, the variability of the difference scores becomes a relatively concrete and easy-to-understand concept. In particular, the sample variability describes the *consistency* of the treatment effect. For example, if a treatment consistently adds a few points to each individual's score, then the set of difference scores are clustered together with relatively small variability. This is the situation that we

FIGURE 11.4

The sample of difference scores from Example 11.1. The mean is $M_D = 3$ and the standard deviation is $s = 1.5$. The data show a consistent increase in scores (positive differences) and suggest that $\mu_D = 0$ is not a reasonable hypothesis.

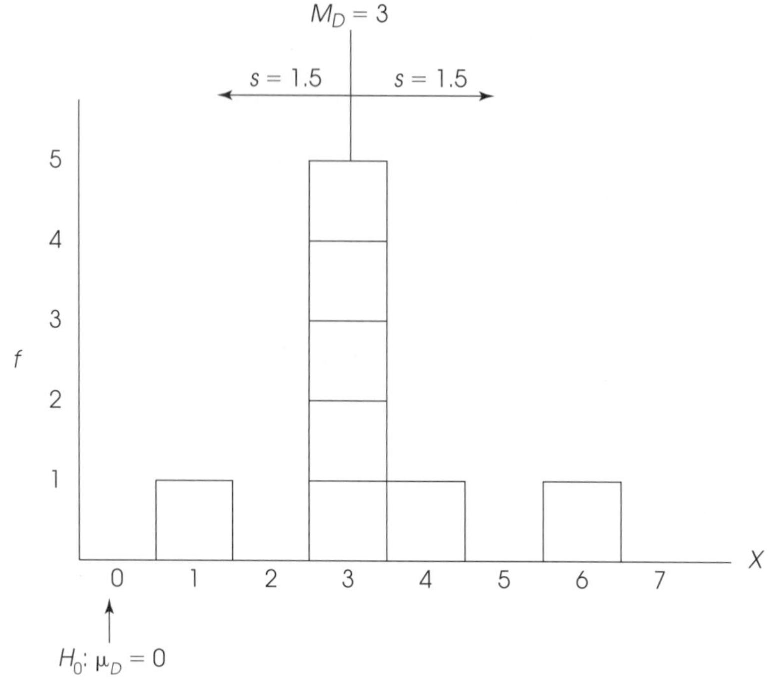

observed in Example 11.1 (see Figure 11.4) in which all of the participants produced higher attractiveness ratings for the photograph on a red background. In this situation, with small variability, it is easy to see the treatment effect and it is likely to be significant.

Now consider what happens when the variability is large. Suppose that the red/white study in Example 11.1 produced a sample of $n = 9$ difference scores consisting of –4, –3, –2, +1, +1, +3, +8, +11, and +12. These difference scores also have a mean of $M_D = 3.00$, but now the variability is substantially increased so that $SS = 288$ and the standard deviation is $s = 6.00$. Figure 11.5 shows the new set of difference scores. Again, we have highlighted the position of $\mu_D = 0$, which is the value specified in the null hypothesis. Notice that the high variability means that there is no consistent treatment effect. Some participants rate the photograph as more attractive when it is on a red background (the positive differences) and some rate it higher on a white background (the negative differences). In the hypothesis test, the high variability increases the size of the estimated standard error and results in a hypothesis test that produces $t = 1.50$, which is not in the critical region. With these data, we would fail to reject the null hypothesis and conclude that the color has no effect on the perceived attractiveness of the woman in the photograph.

With small variability (see Figure 11.4), the 3-point treatment effect is easy to see and is statistically significant. With large variability (see Figure 11.5), the 3-point effect is not easy to see and is not significant. As we have noted several times in the past, large variability can obscure patterns in the data and reduces the likelihood of finding a significant treatment effect.

DIRECTIONAL HYPOTHESIS AND ONE-TAILED TESTS

In many repeated-measures and matched-subjects studies, the researcher has a specific prediction concerning the direction of the treatment effect. For example, in the study described in Example 11.1, the researcher expects the woman to be judged as more

FIGURE 11.5

A sample of difference scores with a mean difference of $M_D = 3$ and a standard deviation of $s = 6$. The data do not show a consistent increase or decrease in scores. Because there is no consistent treatment effect, $\alpha_D = 0$ is a reasonable hypothesis.

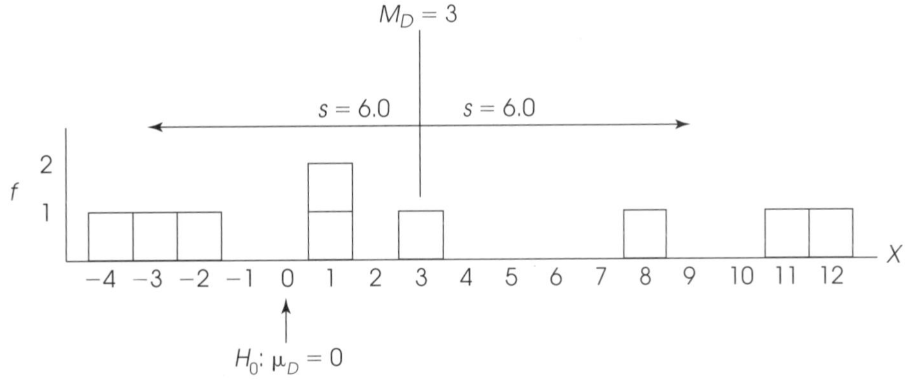

attractive when her photograph is presented on a red background. This kind of directional prediction can be incorporated into the statement of the hypotheses, resulting in a directional, or one-tailed, hypothesis test. The following example demonstrates how the hypotheses and critical region are determined for a directional test.

EXAMPLE 11.3 We reexamine the experiment presented in Example 11.1. The researcher is using a repeated-measures design to investigate the effect of the color red on the perceived attractiveness of a woman. The researcher predicts that the attractiveness ratings for the woman in a photograph will increase when the photograph is presented on a red background compared to a white background.

STEP 1 State the hypotheses and select the alpha level. For this example, the researcher predicts that attractiveness ratings will increase when the photograph is shown on the red background. The null hypothesis, on the other hand says that the attractiveness ratings will not increase but rather will be unchanged or even lowered with the red background. In symbols,

H_0: $\mu_D \leq 0$ (There is no increase with the color red.)

The alternative hypothesis says that the treatment does work. For this example, H_1 says that the color red will increase the attractiveness ratings.

H_1: $\mu_D > 0$ (The rating is increased.)

We use $\alpha = .01$.

STEP 2 Locate the critical region. As we demonstrated with the independent-measures t statistic (p. 305), the critical region for a one-tailed test can be located using a two-stage process. Rather than trying to determine which tail of the distribution contains the critical region, you first look at the sample mean difference to verify that it is in the predicted direction. If not, then the treatment clearly did not work as expected and you can stop the test. If the change is in the correct direction, then the question is whether it is large enough to be significant. For this example, change is in the predicted direction (the researcher predicted higher ratings and the sample mean shows an increase.) With $n = 9$, we obtain $df = 8$ and a critical value of $t = 2.896$ for a one-tailed test with $\alpha = .01$. Thus, any t statistic beyond 2.896 (positive or negative) is sufficient to reject the null hypothesis.

STEP 3 Compute the t statistic. We calculated the t statistic in Example 11.1, and obtained $t = 6.00$.

STEP 4 Make a decision. The obtained t statistic is well beyond the critical boundary. Therefore, we reject the null hypothesis and conclude that the color red significantly increased the attractiveness ratings for the woman in the photograph. In a research report, the use of a one-tailed test would be clearly noted as follows:

> Changing the background color from white to red significantly increased the attractiveness rating, $t(8) = 6.00$, $p < .01$, one tailed.

LEARNING CHECK

1. A researcher is investigating the effectiveness of acupuncture treatment for chronic back pain. A sample of $n = 4$ participants is obtained from a pain clinic. Each individual ranks the current level of pain and then begins a 6-week program of acupuncture treatment. At the end of the program, the pain level is rated again and the researcher records the amount of difference between the two ratings. For this sample, pain level decreased by an average of $M = 4.5$ points with $SS = 27$.
   a. Are the data sufficient to conclude that acupuncture has a significant effect on back pain? Use a two-tailed test with $\alpha = .05$.
   b. Can you conclude that acupuncture significantly reduces back pain? Use a one-tailed test with $\alpha = .05$.
2. Compute the effect size using both Cohen's d and r^2 acupuncture study in the previous question.
3. A computer printout for a repeated-measures t test reports a p value of $p = .021$.
   a. Can the researcher claim a significant effect with $\alpha = .01$?
   b. Is the effect significant with $\alpha = .05$?

ANSWERS

1. **a.** For these data, the sample variance is 9, the standard error is 1.50, and $t = 3.00$. With $df = 3$, the critical values are $t = \pm 3.182$. Fail to reject the null hypothesis.
   b. For a one-tailed test, the critical value is $t = 2.353$. Reject the null hypothesis and conclude that acupuncture treatment significantly reduces pain.
2. $d = 4.5/3 = 1.50$ and $r^2 = 9/12 = 0.75$.
3. **a.** The exact p value, $p = .021$, is not less than $\alpha = .01$. Therefore, the effect is not significant for $\alpha = .01$ ($p > .01$).
   b. The p value is less than .05, so the effect is significant with $\alpha = .05$.

11.4 USES AND ASSUMPTIONS FOR REPEATED-MEASURES *t* TESTS

REPEATED-MEASURES VERSUS INDEPENDENT-MEASURES DESIGNS

In many research situations, it is possible to use either a repeated-measures design or an independent-measures design to compare two treatment conditions. The independent-measures design would use two separate samples (one in each treatment condition) and the repeated-measures design would use only one sample with the same individuals participating in both treatments. The decision about which design to use is often made by considering the advantages and disadvantages of the two designs. In general, the repeated-measures design has most of the advantages.

Number of subjects A repeated-measures design typically requires fewer subjects than an independent-measures design. The repeated-measures design uses the subjects more efficiently because each individual is measured in both of the treatment conditions. This can be especially important when there are relatively few subjects available (for example, when you are studying a rare species or individuals in a rare profession).

Study changes over time The repeated-measures design is especially well suited for studying learning, development, or other changes that take place over time. Remember that this design involves measuring individuals at one time and then returning to measure the same individuals at a later time. In this way, a researcher can observe behaviors that change or develop over time.

Individual differences The primary advantage of a repeated-measures design is that it reduces or eliminates problems caused by individual differences. *Individual differences* are characteristics such as age, IQ, gender, and personality that vary from one individual to another. These individual differences can influence the scores obtained in a research study, and they can affect the outcome of a hypothesis test. Consider the data in Table 11.4. The first set of data represents the results from a typical independent-measures study and the second set represents a repeated-measures study. Note that we have identified each participant by name to help demonstrate the effects of individual differences.

For the independent-measures data, note that every score represents a different person. For the repeated-measures study, on the other hand, the same participants are measured in both of the treatment conditions. This difference between the two designs has some important consequences.

1. We have constructed the data so that both research studies have exactly the same scores and they both show the same 5-point mean difference between treatments. In each case, the researcher would like to conclude that the 5-point difference was caused by the treatments. However, with the independent-measures design, there is always the possibility that the participants in treatment 1 have different characteristics than those in treatment 2. For example, the three participants in treatment 1 may be more intelligent than those in treatment 2 and their higher intelligence caused them to have higher scores. Note that this problem disappears with the repeated-measures design. Specifically, with repeated measures there is no possibility that the participants in one treatment are different from those in another treatment because the same participants are used in all of the treatments.

TABLE 11.4

Hypothetical data showing the results from an independent-measures study and a repeated-measures study. The two sets of data use exactly the same numerical scores and they both show the same 5-point mean difference between treatments.

Independent-Measures Study (2 Separate Samples)		Repeated-Measures Study (Same Sample in Both Treatments)		
Treatment 1	Treatment 2	Treatment 1	Treatment 2	D
(John) $X = 18$	(Sue) $X = 15$	(John) $X = 18$	(John) $X = 15$	-3
(Mary) $X = 27$	(Tom) $X = 20$	(Mary) $X = 27$	(Mary) $X = 20$	-7
(Bill) $X = 33$	(Dave) $X = 28$	(Bill) $X = 33$	(Bill) $X = 28$	-5
$M = 26$	$M = 21$			$M_D = -5$
$SS = 114$	$SS = 86$			$SS = 8$

2. Although the two sets of data contain exactly the same scores and have exactly the same 5-point mean difference, you should realize that they are very different in terms of the variance used to compute standard error. For the independent-measures study, you calculate the *SS* or variance for the scores in each of the two separate samples. Note that in each sample there are big differences between participants. In treatment 1, for example, Bill has a score of 33 and John's score is only 18. These individual differences produce a relatively large sample variance and a large standard error. For the independent-measures study, the standard error is 5.77, which produces a t statistic of $t = 0.87$. For these data, the hypothesis test concludes that there is no significant difference between treatments.

   In the repeated-measures study, the *SS* and variance are computed for the difference scores. If you examine the repeated-measures data in Table 11.4, you will see that the big differences between John and Bill that exist in treatment 1 and in treatment 2 are eliminated when you get to the difference scores. Because the individual differences are eliminated, the variance and standard error are dramatically reduced. For the repeated-measures study, the standard error is 1.15 and the t statistic is $t = -4.35$. With the repeated-measures t, the data show a significant difference between treatments. Thus, one big advantage of a repeated-measures study is that it reduces variance by removing individual differences, which increases the chances of finding a significant result.

TIME-RELATED FACTORS AND ORDER EFFECTS

The primary disadvantage of a repeated-measures design is that the structure of the design allows for factors other than the treatment effect to cause a participant's score to change from one treatment to the next. Specifically, in a repeated-measures design, each individual is measured in two different treatment conditions, usually *at two different times.* In this situation, outside factors that change over time may be responsible for changes in the participants' scores. For example, a participant's health or mood may change over time and cause a difference in the participant's scores. Outside factors such as the weather can also change and may have an influence on participants' scores. Because a repeated-measures study typically takes place over time, it is possible that time-related factors (other than the two treatments) are responsible for causing changes in the participants' scores.

Also, it is possible that participation in the first treatment influences the individual's score in the second treatment. If the researcher is measuring individual performance, for example, the participants may gain experience during the first treatment condition, and this extra practice may help their performance in the second condition. In this situation, the researcher would find a mean difference between the two conditions; however, the difference would not be caused by the treatments, instead it would caused be by practice effects. Changes in scores that are caused by participation in an earlier treatment are called *order effects* and can distort the mean differences found in repeated-measures research studies.

Counterbalancing One way to deal with time-related factors and order effects is to counterbalance the order of presentation of treatments. That is, the participants are randomly divided into two groups, with one group receiving treatment 1 followed by treatment 2, and the other group receiving treatment 2 followed by treatment 1. The goal of counterbalancing is to distribute any outside effects evenly over the two treatments. For example, if practice effects are a problem, then half of the participants gain experience in treatment 1, which then helps their performance in treatment 2. However, the other half gain experience in treatment 2, which helps their performance in treatment 1. Thus, prior experience helps the two treatments equally.

Finally, if there is reason to expect strong time-related effects or strong order effects, your best strategy is not to use a repeated-measures design. Instead, use independent-measures (or a matched-subjects design) so that each individual participates in only one treatment and is measured only one time.

ASSUMPTIONS OF THE RELATED-SAMPLES *t* TEST

The related-samples *t* statistic requires two basic assumptions:

1. The observations within each treatment condition must be independent (see p. 254). Notice that the assumption of independence refers to the scores *within* each treatment. Inside each treatment, the scores are obtained from different individuals and should be independent of one another.
2. The population distribution of difference scores (D values) must be normal.

   As before, the normality assumption is not a cause for concern unless the sample size is relatively small. In the case of severe departures from normality, the validity of the t test may be compromised with small samples. However, with relatively large samples ($n > 30$), this assumption can be ignored.

If there is reason to suspect that one of the assumptions for the repeated-measures t test has been violated, an alternative analysis known as the *Wilcoxon test* is presented in Appendix E. The Wilcoxon test requires that the original scores be transformed into ranks before evaluating the difference between the two treatment conditions.

LEARNING CHECK

1. What assumptions must be satisfied for repeated-measures t tests to be valid?
2. Describe some situations for which a repeated-measures design is well suited.
3. How is a matched-subjects design similar to a repeated-measures design? How do they differ?
4. The data from a research study consist of 10 scores in each of two different treatment conditions. How many individual subjects would be needed to produce these data
   a. For an independent-measures design?
   b. For a repeated-measures design?
   c. For a matched-subjects design?

ANSWERS

1. The observations within a treatment are independent. The population distribution of D scores is assumed to be normal.
2. The repeated-measures design is suited to situations in which a particular type of subject is not readily available for study. This design is helpful because it uses fewer subjects (only one sample is needed). Certain questions are addressed more adequately by a repeated-measures design—for example, any time one would like to study changes across time in the same individuals. Also, when individual differences are large, a repeated-measures design is helpful because it reduces the amount of this type of error in the statistical analysis.
3. They are similar in that the role of individual differences in the experiment is reduced. They differ in that there are two samples in a matched-subjects design and only one in a repeated-measures study.
4. a. The independent-measures design would require 20 subjects (two separate samples with $n = 10$ in each).
   b. The repeated-measures design would require 10 subjects (the same 10 individuals are measured in both treatments).
   c. The matched-subjects design would require 20 subjects (10 matched pairs).

SUMMARY

1. In a related-samples research study, the individuals in one treatment condition are directly related, one-to-one, with the individuals in the other treatment condition(s). The most common related-samples study is a repeated-measures design, in which the same sample of individuals is tested in all of the treatment conditions. This design literally repeats measurements on the same subjects. An alternative is a matched-subjects design, in which the individuals in one sample are matched one-to-one with individuals in another sample. The matching is based on a variable relevant to the study.

2. The repeated-measures *t* test begins by computing a difference between the first and second measurements for each subject (or the difference for each matched pair). The difference scores, or *D* scores, are obtained by

$$D = X_2 - X_1$$

The sample mean, M_D, and sample variance, s^2, are used to summarize and describe the set of difference scores.

3. The formula for the repeated-measures *t* statistic is

$$t = \frac{M_D - \mu_D}{s_{M_D}}$$

In the formula, the null hypothesis specifies $\mu_D = 0$, and the estimated standard error is computed by

$$s_{M_D} = \sqrt{\frac{s^2}{n}}$$

4. A repeated-measures design may be preferred to an independent-measures study when one wants to observe changes in behavior in the same subjects, as in learning or developmental studies. An important advantage of the repeated-measures design is that it removes or reduces individual differences, which, in turn lowers sample variability and tends to increase the chances for obtaining a significant result.

5. For a repeated-measures design, effect size can be measured using either r^2 (the percentage of variance accounted for) or Cohen's *d* (the standardized mean difference). The value of r^2 is computed the same way for both independent- and repeated-measures designs.

$$r^2 = \frac{t^2}{t^2 + df}$$

Cohen's *d* is defined as the sample mean difference divided by standard deviation for both repeated- and independent-measures designs. For repeated-measures studies, Cohen's *d* is estimated as

$$\text{estimated } d = \frac{M_D}{s}$$

6. An alternative method for describing the size of the treatment effect is to construct a confidence interval for the population mean difference, μ_D. The confidence interval uses the repeated-measures *t* equation, solved for the unknown mean difference:

$$\mu_D = M_D \pm t s_{M_D}$$

First, select a level of confidence and then look up the corresponding *t* values. For example, for 95% confidence, use the range of *t* values that determine the middle 95% of the distribution. The *t* values are then used in the equation along with the values for the sample mean difference and the standard error, which are computed from the sample data.

KEY TERMS

repeated-measures design (352)
within-subjects design (352)
matched-subjects design (353)
related-samples design (353)
difference scores (354)
estimated standard error for M_D (357)
repeated-measures *t* statistic (358)
individual differences (367)
order effects (368)
Wilcoxon test (369)

RESOURCES

Book Companion Website: www.cengage.com/psychology/gravetter

You can find a tutorial quiz and other learning exercises for Chapter 11 on the book companion website. The website also provides access to a workshop entitled *Independent vs. Repeated t-tests* that compares the *t* test presented in this chapter with the independent-measures test that was presented in Chapter 10.

aplia

Improve your understanding of statistics with Aplia's auto-graded problem sets and immediate, detailed explanations for every question. To learn more, visit **www.aplia.com/statistics**.

CENGAGEbrain.com

Psychology CourseMate brings course concepts to life with interactive learning, study, and exam preparation tools that support the printed textbook. A textbook-specific website, Psychology CourseMate includes an integrated interactive eBook and other interactive learning tools including quizzes, flashcards, and more.

Visit www.cengagebrain.com to access your account and purchase materials.

SPSS

General instructions for using SPSS are presented in Appendix D. Following are detailed instructions for using SPSS to perform **The Repeated-Measures *t* Test** presented in this chapter.

Data Entry

Enter the data into two columns (VAR0001 and VAR0002) in the data editor with the first score for each participant in the first column and the second score in the second column. The two scores for each participant must be in the same row.

Data Analysis

1. Click **Analyze** on the tool bar, select **Compare Means**, and click on **Paired-Samples T Test.**
2. One at a time, highlight the column labels for the two data columns and click the arrow to move them into the **Paired Variables** box.

3. In addition to performing the hypothesis test, the program computes a confidence interval for the population mean difference. The confidence level is automatically set at 95%, but you can select **Options** and change the percentage.
4. Click **OK.**

SPSS Output

We used the SPSS program to analyze the data from the red/white photograph experiment in Example 11.1 and the program output is shown in Figure 11.6. The output includes a table of sample statistics with the mean and standard deviation for each treatment. A second table shows the correlation between the two sets of scores (correlations are presented in Chapter 15). The final table, which is split into two sections in Figure 11.6, shows the results of the hypothesis test, including the mean and standard deviation for the difference scores, the standard error for the mean, a 95% confidence interval for the mean difference, and the values for t, df, and the level of significance (the p value for the test).

Paired Samples Statistics

		Mean	N	Std. Deviation	Std. Error Mean
Pair 1	VAR00001	7.2222	9	1.48137	.49379
	VAR00002	10.2222	9	.97183	.32394

Paired Samples Correlations

		N	Correlation	Sig.
Pair 1	VAR00001 & VAR00002	9	.309	.419

Paired Samples Test

		Paired Differences		
		Mean	Std. Deviation	Std. Error Mean
Pair 1	VAR00001 - VAR00002	−3.00000	1.50000	.50000

Paired Samples Test

		Paired Differences				
		95% Confidence Interval of the Difference				
		Lower	Upper	t	df	Sig. (2-tailed)
Pair 1	VAR00001 - VAR00002	−4.15300	−1.84700	−6.000	8	.000

FIGURE 11.6

The SPSS output for the repeated-measures hypothesis test in Example 11.1.

FOCUS ON PROBLEM SOLVING

1. Once data have been collected, we must then select the appropriate statistical analysis. How can you tell whether the data call for a repeated-measures *t* test? Look at the experiment carefully. Is there only one sample of subjects? Are the same subjects tested a second time? If your answers are yes to both of these questions, then a repeated-measures *t* test should be done. There is only one situation in which the repeated-measures *t* can be used for data from two samples, and that is for *matched-subjects* studies (p. 353).

2. The repeated-measures *t* test is based on difference scores. In finding difference scores, be sure that you are consistent with your method. That is, you may use either $X_2 - X_1$ or $X_1 - X_2$ to find *D* scores, but you must use the same method for all subjects.

DEMONSTRATION 11.1

A REPEATED-MEASURES *t* TEST

A major oil company would like to improve its tarnished image following a large oil spill. Its marketing department develops a short television commercial and tests it on a sample of $n = 7$ participants. People's attitudes about the company are measured with a short questionnaire, both before and after viewing the commercial. The data are as follows:

Person	X_1 (Before)	X_2 (After)	D (Difference)
A	15	15	0
B	11	13	+2
C	10	18	+8
D	11	12	+1
E	14	16	+2
F	10	10	0
G	11	19	+8

$\Sigma D = 21$

$M_D = \frac{21}{7} = 3.00$

$SS = 74$

Was there a significant change? Note that participants are being tested twice—once before and once after viewing the commercial. Therefore, we have a repeated-measures design.

STEP 1 **State the hypotheses, and select an alpha level.** The null hypothesis states that the commercial has no effect on people's attitude, or, in symbols,

H_0: $\mu_D = 0$ (The mean difference is zero.)

The alternative hypothesis states that the commercial does alter attitudes about the company, or

H_1: $\mu_D \neq 0$ (There is a mean change in attitudes.)

For this demonstration, we use an alpha level of .05 for a two-tailed test.

STEP 2 **Locate the critical region.** Degrees of freedom for the repeated-measures *t* test are obtained by the formula

$df = n - 1$

For these data, degrees of freedom equal

$$df = 7 - 1 = 6$$

The t distribution table is consulted for a two-tailed test with $\alpha = .05$ for $df = 6$. The critical t values for the critical region are $t = \pm 2.447$.

STEP 3 **Compute the test statistic.** Once again, we suggest that the calculation of the t statistic be divided into a three-part process.

Variance for the D scores: The variance for the sample of D scores is

$$s^2 = \frac{SS}{n-1} = \frac{74}{6} = 12.33$$

Estimated standard error for M_D: The estimated standard error for the sample mean difference is computed as follows:

$$s_{M_D} = \sqrt{\frac{s^2}{n}} = \sqrt{\frac{12.33}{7}} = \sqrt{1.76} = 1.33$$

The repeated-measures t statistic: Now we have the information required to calculate the t statistic.

$$t = \frac{M_D - \mu_D}{s_{M_D}} = \frac{3-0}{1.33} = 2.26$$

STEP 4 **Make a decision about H_0, and state the conclusion.** The obtained t value is not extreme enough to fall in the critical region. Therefore, we fail to reject the null hypothesis. We conclude that there is not enough evidence to conclude that the commercial changes people's attitudes, $t(6) = 2.26$, $p > .05$, two-tailed. (Note that we state that p is *greater than* .05 because we failed to reject H_0.)

DEMONSTRATION 11.2

EFFECT SIZE FOR THE REPEATED-MEASURES *t*

We estimate Cohen's d and calculate r^2 for the data in Demonstration 11.1. The data produced a sample mean difference of $M_D = 3.00$ with a sample variance of $s^2 = 12.33$. Based on these values, Cohen's d is

$$\text{estimated } d = \frac{\text{mean difference}}{\text{standard deviation}} = \frac{M_D}{s} = \frac{3.00}{\sqrt{12.33}} = \frac{3.00}{3.51} = 0.86$$

The hypothesis test produced $t = 2.26$ with $df = 6$. Based on these values,

$$r^2 = \frac{t^2}{t^2 + df} = \frac{(2.26)^2}{(2.26)^2 + 6} = \frac{5.11}{11.11} = 0.46 \quad (\text{or } 46\%)$$

PROBLEMS

1. For the following studies, indicate whether a repeated-measures t test is the appropriate analysis. Explain your answers.
   a. A researcher is comparing the amount of time spent playing video games each week for college males versus college females.
   b. A researcher is comparing two new designs for cell phones by having a group of high school students send a scripted text message on each model and measuring the difference in speed for each student.
   c. A researcher is evaluating the effects of fatigue by testing people in the morning when they are well rested and testing again at midnight when they have been awake for at least 14 hours.

2. Participants enter a research study with unique characteristics that produce different scores from one person to another. For an independent-measures study, these individual differences can cause problems. Briefly explain how these problems are eliminated or reduced with a repeated-measures study.

3. Explain the difference between a matched-subjects design and a repeated-measures design.

4. A sample of difference scores from a repeated-measures experiment has a mean of $M_D = 4$ with a standard deviation of $s = 6$.
   a. If $n = 4$, is this sample sufficient to reject the null hypothesis using a two-tailed test with $\alpha = .05$?
   b. Would you reject H_0 if $n = 16$? Again, assume a two-tailed test with $\alpha = .05$.
   c. Explain how the size of the sample influences the likelihood of finding a significant mean difference.

5. A sample of $n = 9$ individuals participates in a repeated-measures study that produces a sample mean difference of $M_D = 6.5$ with $SS = 200$ for the difference scores.
   a. Calculate the standard deviation for the sample of difference scores. Briefly explain what is measured by the standard deviation.
   b. Calculate the estimated standard error for the sample mean difference. Briefly explain what is measured by the estimated standard error.

6. **a.** A repeated-measures study with a sample of $n = 25$ participants produces a mean difference of $M_D = 3$ with a standard deviation of $s = 4$. Based on the mean and standard deviation, you should be able to visualize (or sketch) the sample distribution. Use a two-tailed hypothesis test with $\alpha = .05$ to determine whether it is likely that this sample came from a population with $\mu_D = 0$.
   b. Now assume that the sample standard deviation is $s = 12$, and once again visualize the sample distribution. Use a two-tailed hypothesis test with $\alpha = .05$ to determine whether it is likely that this sample came from a population with $\mu_D = 0$.
   Explain how the size of the sample standard deviation influences the likelihood of finding a significant mean difference.

7. **a.** A repeated-measures study with a sample of $n = 9$ participants produces a mean difference of $M_D = 3$ with a standard deviation of $s = 6$. Based on the mean and standard deviation, you should be able to visualize (or sketch) the sample distribution. Use a two-tailed hypothesis test with $\alpha = .05$ to determine whether it is likely that this sample came from a population with $\mu_D = 0$.
   b. Now assume that the sample mean difference is $M_D = 12$, and once again visualize the sample distribution. Use a two-tailed hypothesis test with $\alpha = .05$ to determine whether it is likely that this sample came from a population with $\mu_D = 0$.
   c. Explain how the size of the sample mean difference influences the likelihood of finding a significant mean difference.

8. A researcher conducts an experiment comparing two treatment conditions and obtains data with 10 scores for each treatment condition.
   a. If the researcher used an independent-measures design, how many subjects participated in the experiment?
   b. If the researcher used a repeated-measures design, how many subjects participated in the experiment?
   c. If the researcher used a matched-subjects design, how many subjects participated in the experiment?

9. As mentioned in Chapters 2 and 3 (pp. 38 and 81), Steven Schmidt (1994) reported a series of studies examining the effect of humor on memory. In one part of the study, participants were presented with a list containing a mix of humorous and nonhumorous sentences, and were then asked to recall as many sentences as possible. Schmidt recorded the number of humorous and the number of nonhumorous sentences recalled by each individual. Notice that the data consist of two memory scores for each participant. Suppose that a difference score is computed for each individual in a sample of $n = 16$ and the resulting data show that participants recalled an average of $M_D = 3.25$ more humorous sentences than nonhumorous, with $SS = 135$. Are these results sufficient to conclude that humor has a significant effect on memory? Use a two-tailed test with $\alpha = .05$.

10. Research has shown that losing even one night's sleep can have a significant effect on performance of complex tasks such as problem solving (Linde & Bergstroem, 1992). To demonstrate this phenomenon, a sample of $n = 25$ college students was given a problem-solving task at noon on one day and again at noon on the following day. The students were not permitted any sleep between the two tests. For each student, the difference between the first and second score was recorded. For this sample, the students averaged $M_D = 4.7$ points better on the first test with a variance of $s^2 = 64$ for the difference scores.
  a. Do the data indicate a significant change in problem-solving ability? Use a two-tailed test with $\alpha = .05$.
  b. Compute an estimated Cohen's *d* to measure the size of the effect.

11. Strack, Martin, and Stepper (1988) reported that people rate cartoons as funnier when holding a pen in their teeth (which forced them to smile) than when holding a pen in their lips (which forced them to frown). A researcher attempted to replicate this result using a sample of $n = 25$ adults between the ages of 40 and 45. For each person, the researcher recorded the difference between the rating obtained while smiling and the rating obtained while frowning. On average the cartoons were rated as funnier when the participants were smiling, with an average difference of $M_D = 1.6$ with $SS = 150$.
  a. Do the data indicate that the cartoons are rated significantly funnier when the participants are smiling? Use a one-tailed test with $\alpha = .01$.
  b. Compute r^2 to measure the size of the treatment effect.
  c. Write a sentence describing the outcome of the hypothesis test and the measure of effect size as it would appear in a research report.

12. How would you react to doing much worse on an exam than you expected? There is some evidence to suggest that most individuals believe that they can cope with this kind of problem better than their fellow students (Igou, 2008). In the study, participants read a scenario of a negative event and were asked to use a 10-point scale to rate how it would affect their immediate well-being (−5 strongly worsen to +5 strongly improve). Then they were asked to imagine the event from the perspective of an ordinary fellow student and rate how it would affect that person. The difference between the two ratings was recorded. Suppose that a sample of $n = 25$ participants produced a mean difference of $M_D = 1.28$ points (self rated higher) with a standard deviation of $s = 1.50$ for the difference scores.
  a. Is this result sufficient to conclude that there is a significant difference in the ratings for self versus others? Use a two-tailed test with $\alpha = .05$.
  b. Compute r^2 and estimate Cohen's *d* to measure the size of the treatment effect.
  c. Write a sentence describing the outcome of the hypothesis test and the measure of effect size as it would appear in a research report.

13. Research results indicate that physically attractive people are also perceived as being more intelligent (Eagly, Ashmore, Makhijani, & Longo, 1991). As a demonstration of this phenomenon, a researcher obtained a set of 10 photographs, 5 showing men who were judged to be attractive and 5 showing men who were judged to be unattractive. The photographs were shown to a sample of $n = 25$ college students and the students were asked to rate the intelligence of the person in the photo on a scale from 1 to 10. For each student, the researcher determined the average rating for the 5 attractive photos and the average for the 5 unattractive photos, and then computed the difference between the two scores. For the entire sample, the average difference was $M_D = 2.7$ (attractive photos rated higher) with $s = 2.00$. Are the data sufficient to conclude that there was a significant difference in perceived intelligence for the two sets of photos? Use a two-tailed test at the .05 level of significance.

14. A researcher for a cereal company wanted to demonstrate the health benefits of eating oatmeal. A sample of 9 volunteers was obtained and each participant ate a fixed diet without any oatmeal for 30 days. At the end of the 30-day period, cholesterol was measured for each individual. Then the participants began a second 30-day period in which they repeated exactly the same diet except that they added 2 cups of oatmeal each day. After the second 30-day period, cholesterol levels were measured again and the researcher recorded the difference between the two scores for each participant. For this sample, cholesterol scores averaged $M_D = 16$ points lower with the oatmeal diet with $SS = 538$ for the difference scores.
  a. Are the data sufficient to indicate a significant change in cholesterol level? Use a two-tailed test with $\alpha = .01$.
  b. Compute r^2, the percentage of variance accounted for by the treatment, to measure the size of the treatment effect.
  c. Write a sentence describing the outcome of the hypothesis test and the measure of effect size as it would appear in a research report.

15. The following data are from a repeated-measures study examining the effect of a treatment by measuring a group of $n = 4$ participants before and after they receive the treatment.
  a. Calculate the difference scores and M_D.
  b. Compute *SS*, sample variance, and estimated standard error.

c. Is there a significant treatment effect? Use $\alpha = .05$, two tails.

Participant	Before Treatment	After Treatment
A	7	10
B	6	13
C	9	12
D	5	8

16. Researchers have noted a decline in cognitive functioning as people age (Bartus, 1990). However, the results from other research suggest that the antioxidants in foods such as blueberries may reduce and even reverse these age-related declines (Joseph et al., 1999). To examine this phenomenon, suppose that a researcher obtains a sample of $n = 16$ adults who are between the ages of 65 and 75. The researcher uses a standardized test to measure cognitive performance for each individual. The participants then begin a 2-month program in which they receive daily doses of a blueberry supplement. At the end of the 2-month period, the researcher again measures cognitive performance for each participant. The results show an average increase in performance of $M_D = 7.4$ with $SS = 1215$.

a. Does this result support the conclusion that the antioxidant supplement has a significant effect on cognitive performance? Use a two-tailed test with $\alpha = .05$.

b. Construct a 95% confidence interval to estimate the average cognitive performance improvement for the population of older adults.

17. A variety of research results suggest that visual images interfere with visual perception. In one study, Segal and Fusella (1970) had participants watch a screen, looking for brief presentations of a small blue arrow. On some trials, the participants were also asked to form a mental image (for example, imagine a volcano). The results for a sample of $n = 6$, show that participants made an average of $M_D = 4.3$ more errors while forming images than while not forming images. The difference scores had $SS = 63$. Do the data indicate a significant difference between the two conditions? Use a two-tailed test with $\alpha = .05$.

18. One of the primary advantages of a repeated-measures design, compared to independent-measures, is that it reduces the overall variability by removing variance caused by individual differences. The following data are from a research study comparing two treatment conditions.

a. Assume that the data are from an independent-measures study using two separate samples, each with $n = 6$ participants. Compute the pooled variance and the estimated standard error for the mean difference.

b. Now assume that the data are from a repeated-measures study using the same sample of $n = 6$ participants in both treatment conditions. Compute the variance for the sample of difference scores and the estimated standard error for the mean difference. (You should find that the repeated-measures design substantially reduces the variance and the standard error.)

Treatment 1	Treatment 2	Difference
10	13	3
12	12	0
8	10	2
6	10	4
5	6	1
7	9	2
$M = 8$	$M = 10$	$M_D = 2$
$SS = 34$	$SS = 30$	$SS = 10$

19. The previous problem demonstrates that removing individual differences can substantially reduce variance and lower the standard error. However, this benefit only occurs if the individual differences are consistent across treatment conditions. In problem 18, for example, the first two participants (top two rows) consistently had the highest scores in both treatment conditions. Similarly, the last two participants consistently had the lowest scores in both treatments. To construct the following data, we started with the scores in problem 18 and scrambled the scores in treatment 1 to eliminate the consistency of the individual differences.

a. Assume that the data are from an independent-measures study using two separate samples, each with $n = 6$ participants. Compute the pooled variance and the estimated standard error for the mean difference.

b. Now assume that the data are from a repeated-measures study using the same sample of $n = 6$ participants in both treatment conditions. Compute the variance for the sample of difference scores and the estimated standard error for the mean difference. (This time you should find that removing the individual differences does not reduce the variance or the standard error.)

Treatment 1	Treatment 2	Difference
6	13	7
7	12	5
8	10	2
10	10	0
5	6	0
12	9	−3
$M = 8$	$M = 10$	$M_D = 2$
$SS = 34$	$SS = 30$	$SS = 64$

20. The teacher from the previous problem also tried a different approach to answering the question of whether changing answers helps or hurts exam grades. In a separate class, students were encouraged to review their final exams and change any answers they wanted to before turning in their papers. However, the students had to indicate both the original answer and the changed answer for each question. The teacher then graded each exam twice, one using the set of original answers and once with the changes. In the class of $n = 22$ students, the average exam score improved by an average of $M_D = 2.5$ points with the changed answers. The standard deviation for the difference scores was $s = 3.1$. Are the data sufficient to conclude that rethinking and changing answers can significantly improve exam scores? Use a one-tailed test at the .01 level of significance.

21. There is some evidence suggesting that you are likely to improve your test score if you rethink and change answers on a multiple-choice exam (Johnston, 1975). To examine this phenomenon, a teacher gave the same final exam to two sections of a psychology course. The students in one section were told to turn in their exams immediately after finishing, without changing any of their answers. In the other section, students were encouraged to reconsider each question and to change answers whenever they felt it was appropriate. Before the final exam, the teacher had matched 9 students in the first section with 9 students in the second section based on their midterm grades. For example, a student in the no-change section with an 89 on the midterm exam was matched with student in the change section who also had an 89 on the midterm. The final exam grades for the 9 matched pairs of students are presented in the following table.

a. Do the data indicate a significant difference between the two conditions? Use a two-tailed test with $\alpha = .05$.

b. Construct a 95% confidence interval to estimate the size of the population mean difference.

c. Write a sentence demonstrating how the results of the hypothesis test and the confidence interval would appear in a research report.

Matched Pair	No-Change Section	Change Section
#1	71	86
#2	68	80
#3	91	88
#4	65	74
#5	73	82
#6	81	89
#7	85	85
#8	86	88
#9	65	76

22. A researcher uses a matched-subjects design to investigate whether single people who own pets are generally happier than singles without pets. A mood inventory questionnaire is administered to a group of 20- to 29-year-old non–pet owners and a similar age group of pet owners. The pet owners are matched one to one with the non–pet owners for income, number of close friendships, and general health. The data are as follows:

Matched Pair	Non-Pet Owner	Pet Owner
A	12	14
B	8	7
C	10	13
D	9	9
E	7	13
F	10	12

a. Is there a significant difference in the mood scores for non–pet owners versus pet owners? Test with $\alpha = .05$ for two tails.

b. Construct the 95% confidence interval to estimate the size of the mean difference in mood between the population of pet owners and the population of non–pet owners. (You should find that a mean difference of $\mu_D = 0$ is an acceptable value, which is consistent with the conclusion from the hypothesis test.)

23. At the Olympic level of competition, even the smallest factors can make the difference between winning and losing. For example, Pelton (1983) has shown that Olympic marksmen shoot much better if they fire between heartbeats, rather than squeezing the trigger during a heartbeat. The small vibration caused by a heartbeat seems to be sufficient to affect the marksman's aim. The following hypothetical data demonstrate this phenomenon. A sample of $n = 8$ Olympic marksmen fires a series of rounds while a researcher records heartbeats. For each marksman, a score is recorded for shots fired during heartbeats and for shots fired between heartbeats. Do these data indicate a significant difference? Test with $\alpha = .05$.

Participant	During Heartbeats	Between Heartbeats
A	93	98
B	90	94
C	95	96
D	92	91
E	95	97
F	91	97
G	92	95
H	93	97

24. The Preview section of this chapter presented a repeated-measures research study demonstrating that swearing can help reduce pain (Stephens, Atkins, & Kingston, 2009). In the study, each participant was asked to plunge a hand into icy water and keep it there as long as the pain would allow. In one condition, the participants repeated their favorite curse words while their hands were in the water. In the other condition, the participants repeated a neutral word. Data similar to the results obtained in the study are shown in the following table.

a. Do these data indicate a significant difference in pain tolerance between the two conditions? Use a two-tailed test with $\alpha = .05$.

b. Compute r^2, the percentage of variance accounted for, to measure the size of the treatment effect.

c. Write a sentence demonstrating how the results of the hypothesis test and the measure of effect size would appear in a research report.

	Amount of Time (in Seconds)	
Participant	Swear Words	Neutral Words
1	94	59
2	70	61
3	52	47
4	83	60
5	46	35
6	117	92
7	69	53
8	39	30
9	51	56
10	73	61

PART III

REVIEW

After completing this part, you should be able to perform hypothesis tests and compute confidence intervals using t statistics. These include:

1. The single-sample t introduced in Chapter 9.
2. The independent-measures t introduced in Chapter 10.
3. The repeated-measures t introduced in Chapter 11.

In this part, we considered a set of three t statistics that are used to draw inferences about the means and mean differences for unknown populations. Because the populations are completely unknown, we rely on sample data to provide all of the necessary information. In particular, each inferential procedure begins by computing sample means and sample variances (or the corresponding SS values or standard deviations). Therefore, a good understanding of the definitions and formulas from Chapters 3 and 4 is a critical foundation for this section.

With three different t statistics available, the first problem is often deciding which one is appropriate for a specific research situation. Perhaps the best approach is to begin with a close look at the sample data.

1. For the single-sample t (Chapter 9), there is only one group of participants and only one score for each individual. With a single sample mean and a single sample variance, the t statistic can be used to test a hypothesis about a single unknown population mean or construct a confidence interval to estimate the population mean.
2. For the independent-measures t, there are two separate groups of participants who produce two groups of scores. The mean and variance are computed for each group, producing two sample means and two sample variances. After pooling the two variances, the t statistic uses the difference between the two sample means to test a hypothesis about the corresponding difference between the two unknown population means or estimate the population mean difference with a confidence interval. The null hypothesis always states that there is no difference between the two population means; $\mu_1 - \mu_2 = 0$.
3. For the repeated-measures t, there is only one group of participants but each individual is measured twice, at two different times and/or under two different treatment conditions. The two scores are then used to find a difference score for each person, and the mean and variance are computed for the sample of difference scores. The t statistic uses the sample mean difference to test a hypothesis about the corresponding population mean difference or estimate the population mean difference with a confidence interval. The null hypothesis always states that the mean for the population of difference scores is zero; $\mu_D = 0$.

REVIEW EXERCISES

1. People tend to evaluate the quality of their lives relative to others around them. In a demonstration of this phenomenon, Frieswijk, Buunk, Steverink, and Slaets (2004) conducted interviews with frail elderly people. In the interview, each person was compared with fictitious others who were worse off. After the interviews, the participants completed a life-satisfaction survey and reported more satisfaction with their own lives. Following are hypothetical data similar to those obtained in the research study, representing satisfaction scores for a sample of $n = 9$ older people who completed the interview. Assume that the average score on the life-satisfaction scale is $\mu = 20$. The scores for the sample are 18, 23, 24, 22, 19, 27, 23, 26, 25.
   a. Calculate the mean and standard deviation for the sample.
   b. Are the data sufficient to conclude that the people in this sample are significantly more satisfied than others in the general population? Use a one-tailed test with $\alpha = .05$.
   c. Compute Cohen's d to estimate the size of the effect.
   d. Compute the 90% confidence interval for the mean life-satisfaction score for people who participate in this type of interview.
2. In the problems at the end of Chapter 8, we presented a study indicating that people with visible tattoos are viewed more negatively than people without visible tattoos (Resenhoeft, Villa, & Wiseman, 2008). Suppose that a researcher intends to examine this phenomenon by asking participants to rate the attractiveness of women in a series of ten photographs. For one group of participants, none of the women has any visible tattoos. For a second group, however, the researcher modified one of the photographs by adding a tattoo of a butterfly on the woman's left arm. Using a 7-point rating scale, the $n = 15$ participants who viewed the photograph with no tattoo gave the woman an average rating of $M = 4.9$ with $SS = 15.0$. The $n = 15$ participants who saw the photograph with a tattoo gave the same woman an average rating of $M = 4.2$ with $SS = 18.6$.
   a. Does the existence of a tattoo have a significant effect on the attractiveness rating of the woman in the photograph? Use a two-tailed test with $\alpha = .05$.
   b. Compute r^2, the percentage of variance accounted for by the treatment, to measure the effect size.
   c. Write a sentence describing the outcome of the hypothesis test and the measure of effect size as it would appear in a research report.

3. The stimulant Ritalin has been shown to increase attention span and improve academic performance in children with ADHD (Evans, Pelham, Smith, et al., 2001). To demonstrate the effectiveness of the drug, a researcher selects a sample of $n = 20$ children diagnosed with the disorder and measures each child's attention span before and after taking the drug. The data show an average increase of attention span of $M_D = 4.8$ minutes with a variance of $s^2 = 125$ for the sample of difference scores.

a. Is this result sufficient to conclude that Ritalin significantly improves attention span? Use a one-tailed test with $\alpha = .05$.

b. Compute the 80% confidence interval for the mean change in attention span for the population.

PART

IV

Analysis of Variance: Tests for Differences Among Two or More Population Means

In Part III we presented a set of t statistics that use sample means and mean differences to draw inferences about the corresponding population means and mean differences. However, the t statistics are limited to situations that compare no more than two population means. Often, a research question involves the differences among more than two means and, in these situations, t tests are not appropriate. In this part we introduce a new hypothesis testing technique known as analysis of variance (ANOVA). ANOVA permits researchers to evaluate the mean differences among *two or more* populations using sample data. We present three different applications of ANOVA that apply to three distinct research situations:

1. Independent-measures designs: Using two or more separate samples to draw an inference about the mean differences between two or more unknown populations.
2. Repeated-measures designs: Using one sample, with each individual tested in two or more different treatment conditions, to draw an inference about the population mean differences among the conditions.
3. Two-factor designs: Allowing two independent variables to change simultaneously within one study to create combinations of treatment conditions involving both variables. The ANOVA then evaluates the mean differences attributed to each variable acting independently and to combinations of the two variables interacting together.

In the next three chapters we continue to examine statistical methods that use sample means as the foundation for drawing inferences about population means. The primary application of these inferential methods is to help researchers interpret the outcome of their research studies. In a typical study, the goal is to demonstrate a difference between two or more treatment conditions. For example, a researcher hopes to demonstrate that a group of children who are exposed to violent TV programs behave more aggressively than children who are shown nonviolent TV programs. In this situation, the data consist of one sample mean representing the scores in one treatment condition and another sample mean representing the scores from a different treatment. The researcher hopes to find a difference between the sample means and would like to generalize the mean difference to the entire population.

The problem is that sample means can be different even when there are no differences whatsoever among the population means. As you saw in Chapter 1 (see Figure 1.2), two samples can have different means even when they are selected from the same population. Thus, even though a researcher may obtain a sample mean difference in a research study, it does not necessarily indicate that there is a mean difference in the population. As with the *t* tests presented in Part III, a hypothesis test is needed to determine whether the mean differences found in sample data are statistically significant. With more than two sample means, the appropriate hypothesis test is ANOVA.

CHAPTER

12

Introduction to Analysis of Variance

Tools You Will Need

The following items are considered essential background material for this chapter. If you doubt your knowledge of any of these items, you should review the appropriate chapter or section before proceeding.

- Variability (Chapter 4)
- Sum of squares
- Sample variance
- Degrees of freedom
- Introduction to hypothesis testing (Chapter 8)
- The logic of hypothesis testing
- Independent-measures *t* statistic (Chapter 10)

Preview

"But I read the chapter four times! How could I possibly have failed the exam?!"

Most of you probably have had the experience of reading a textbook and suddenly realizing that you have no idea of what was said on the past few pages. Although you have been reading the words, your mind has wandered off, and the meaning of the words has never reached memory. In an influential paper on human memory, Craik and Lockhart (1972) proposed a *levels of processing* theory of memory that can account for this phenomenon. In general terms, this theory says that all perceptual and mental processing leaves behind a memory trace. However, the quality of the memory trace depends on the level or the depth of the processing. If you superficially skim the words in a book, your memory also is superficial. On the other hand, when you think about the meaning of the words and try to understand what you are reading, the result is a good, substantial memory that should serve you well on exams. In general, deeper processing results in better memory.

Rogers, Kuiper, and Kirker (1977) conducted an experiment demonstrating the effect of levels of processing. Participants in this experiment were shown lists of words and asked to answer questions about each word. The questions were designed to require different levels of processing, from superficial to deep. In one experimental condition, participants were simply asked to judge the physical characteristics of each printed word ("Is it printed in capital letters or lowercase letters?"). A second condition asked about the sound of each word ("Does it rhyme with 'boat'?"). In a third condition, participants were required to process the meaning of each word ("Does it have the same meaning as 'attractive'?"). The final condition required participants to understand each word and relate its meaning to themselves ("Does this word describe you?"). After going through the complete list, all participants were given a surprise memory test. As you can see in Figure 12.1, deeper processing resulted in better memory. Remember that the participants were not trying to memorize the words; they were simply reading through the list answering questions. However, the more they processed and understood the words, the better they recalled the words on the test.

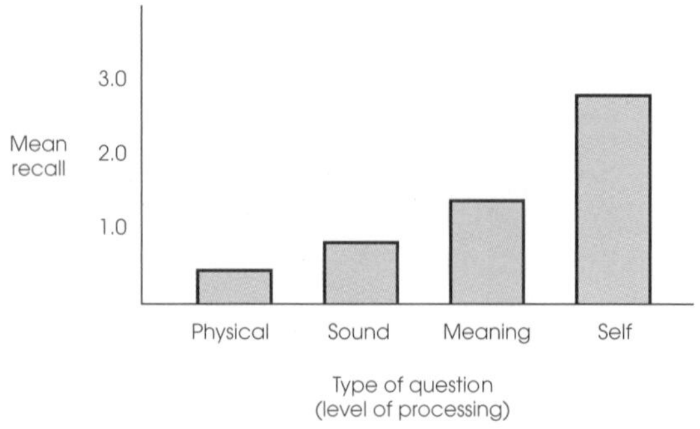

FIGURE 12.1

Mean recall as a function of the level of processing.

Rogers, T. B., Kuiper, N. A., & Kirker, W. S. (1977). Self-reference and the encoding of personal information. *Journal of personality and Social Psychology*, 35, 677–688. Copyright (1977) by the American Psychological Association. Adapted by permission of the author.

The Problem: In terms of human memory, the Rogers, Kuiper, and Kirker experiment is notable because it demonstrates the importance of "self" in memory. You are most likely to remember material that is directly related to you. In terms of statistics, however, this study is notable because it compares four different treatment conditions in a single experiment. We now have four different means and need a hypothesis test to evaluate the mean differences. Unfortunately, the t tests introduced in Chapter 10 and 11 are limited to comparing only two treatments. A new hypothesis test is needed for this kind of data.

The Solution: In this chapter we introduce a new hypothesis test known as *analysis of variance* that is designed to evaluate the mean differences from research studies producing two or more sample means. Although "two or more" may seem like a small step from "two," this new hypothesis testing procedure provides researchers with a tremendous gain in experimental sophistication. In this chapter, and the two that follow, we examine some of the many applications of analysis of variance.

12.1 INTRODUCTION

Analysis of variance (ANOVA) is a hypothesis-testing procedure that is used to evaluate mean differences between two or more treatments (or populations). As with all inferential procedures, ANOVA uses sample data as the basis for drawing general conclusions about populations. It may appear that ANOVA and *t* tests are simply two different ways of doing exactly the same job: testing for mean differences. In some respects, this is true—both tests use sample data to test hypotheses about population means. However, ANOVA has a tremendous advantage over *t* tests. Specifically, *t* tests are limited to situations in which there are only two treatments to compare. The major advantage of ANOVA is that it can be used to compare *two or more treatments*. Thus, ANOVA provides researchers with much greater flexibility in designing experiments and interpreting results.

Figure 12.2 shows a typical research situation for which ANOVA would be used. Note that the study involves three samples representing three populations. The goal of the analysis is to determine whether the mean differences observed among the samples provide enough evidence to conclude that there are mean differences among the three populations. Specifically, we must decide between two interpretations:

1. There really are no differences between the populations (or treatments). The observed differences between the sample means are caused by random, unsystematic factors (sampling error) that differentiate one sample from another.
2. The populations (or treatments) really do have different means, and these population mean differences are responsible for causing systematic differences between the sample means.

You should recognize that these two interpretations correspond to the two hypotheses (null and alternative) that are part of the general hypothesis-testing procedure.

TERMINOLOGY IN ANOVA

Before we continue, it is necessary to introduce some of the terminology that is used to describe the research situation shown in Figure 12.2. Recall (from Chapter 1) that when a researcher manipulates a variable to create the treatment conditions in an experiment, the variable is called an *independent variable*. For example, Figure 12.2 could represent

FIGURE 12.2
A typical situation in which ANOVA would be used. Three separate samples are obtained to evaluate the mean differences among three populations (or treatments) with unknown means.

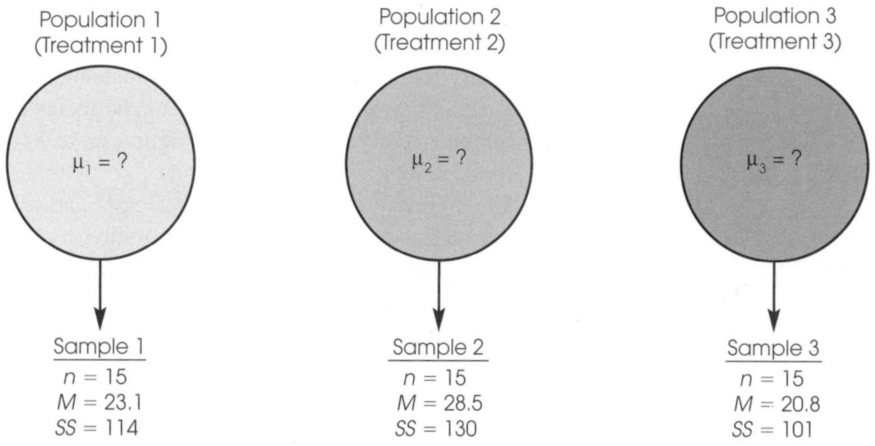

a study examining driving performance under three different telephone conditions: driving with no phone, talking on a hands-free phone, and talking on a hand-held phone. Note that the three conditions are created by the researcher. On the other hand, when a researcher uses a nonmanipulated variable to designate groups, the variable is called a *quasi-independent variable*. For example, the three groups in Figure 12.2 could represent 6-year-old, 8-year-old, and 10-year-old children. In the context of ANOVA, an independent variable or a quasi-independent variable is called a *factor*. Thus, Figure 12.2 could represent an experimental study in which the telephone condition is the factor being evaluated or it could represent a nonexperimental study in which age is the factor being examined.

DEFINITION

In ANOVA, the variable (independent or quasi-independent) that designates the groups being compared is called a **factor**.

In addition, the individual groups or treatment conditions that are used to make up a factor are called the *levels* of the factor. For example, a study that examined performance under three different telephone conditions would have three levels of the factor.

DEFINITION

The individual conditions or values that make up a factor are called the **levels** of the factor.

Like the t tests presented in Chapters 10 and 11, ANOVA can be used with either an independent-measures or a repeated-measures design. Recall that an independent-measures design means that there is a separate group of participants for each of the treatments (or populations) being compared. In a repeated-measures design, on the other hand, the same group is tested in all of the different treatment conditions. In addition, ANOVA can be used to evaluate the results from a research study that involves more than one factor. For example, a researcher may want to compare two different therapy techniques, examining their immediate effectiveness as well as the persistence of their effectiveness over time. In this situation, the research study could involve two different groups of participants, one for each therapy, and measure each group at several different points in time. The structure of this design is shown in Figure 12.3. Notice that the study uses two factors, one independent-measures factor and one repeated-measures factor:

1. Factor 1: Therapy technique. A separate group is used for each technique (independent measures).
2. Factor 2: Time. Each group is tested at three different times (repeated measures).

In this case, the ANOVA would evaluate mean differences between the two therapies as well as mean differences between the scores obtained at different times. A study that combines two factors, like the one in Figure 12.3, is called a *two-factor design* or a *factorial design*.

The ability to combine different factors and to mix different designs within one study provides researchers with the flexibility to develop studies that address scientific questions that could not be answered by a single design using a single factor.

Although ANOVA can be used in a wide variety of research situations, this chapter introduces ANOVA in its simplest form. Specifically, we consider only *single-factor* designs. That is, we examine studies that have only one independent variable (or only one quasi-independent variable). Second, we consider only *independent-measures* designs; that is, studies that use a separate group of participants for each treatment condition. The basic logic and procedures that are presented in this chapter form the foundation for more complex applications of

		TIME		
		Before Therapy	After Therapy	6 Months After Therapy
THERAPY TECHNIQUE	Therapy I (Group 1)	Scores for group 1 measured before Therapy I	Scores for group 1 measured after Therapy I	Scores for group 1 measured 6 months after Therapy I
	Therapy II (Group 2)	Scores for group 2 measured before Therapy II	Scores for group 2 measured after Therapy II	Scores for group 2 measured 6 months after Therapy II

FIGURE 12.3

A research design with two factors. The research study uses two factors: One factor uses two levels of therapy technique (I versus II), and the second factor uses three levels of time (before, after, and 6 months after). Also notice that the therapy factor uses two separate groups (independent measures) and the time factor uses the same group for all three levels (repeated measures).

ANOVA. For example, in Chapter 13, we extend the analysis to single-factor, repeated-measures designs and in Chapter 14, we introduce two-factor designs. But for now, in this chapter, we limit our discussion of ANOVA to *single-factor, independent-measures* research studies.

STATISTICAL HYPOTHESES FOR ANOVA

The following example introduces the statistical hypotheses for ANOVA. Suppose that a researcher examined driving performance under three different telephone conditions: no phone, a hands-free phone, and a hand-held phone. Three samples of participants are selected, one sample for each treatment condition. The purpose of the study is to determine whether using a telephone affects driving performance. In statistical terms, we want to decide between two hypotheses: the null hypothesis (H_0), which states that the telephone condition has no effect, and the alternative hypothesis (H_1), which states that the telephone condition does affect driving. In symbols, the null hypothesis states

$$H_0\colon \mu_1 = \mu_2 = \mu_3$$

In words, the null hypothesis states that the telephone condition has no effect on driving performance. That is, the population means for the three telephone conditions are all the same. In general, H_0 states that there is no treatment effect.

The alternative hypothesis states that the population means are not all the same:

H_1: There is at least one mean difference among the populations.

In general, H_1 states that the treatment conditions are not all the same; that is, there is a real treatment effect. As always, the hypotheses are stated in terms of population parameters, even though we use sample data to test them.

Notice that we are not stating a specific alternative hypothesis. This is because many different alternatives are possible, and it would be tedious to list them all.

One alternative, for example, is that the first two populations are identical, but that the third is different. Another alternative states that the last two means are the same, but that the first is different. Other alternatives might be

H_1: $\mu_1 \neq \mu_2 \neq \mu_3$ (All three means are different.)

H_1: $\mu_1 = \mu_3$, but μ_2 is different.

We should point out that a researcher typically entertains only one (or at most a few) of these alternative hypotheses. Usually a theory or the outcomes of previous studies dictate a specific prediction concerning the treatment effect. For the sake of simplicity, we state a general alternative hypothesis rather than try to list all of the possible specific alternatives.

THE TEST STATISTIC FOR ANOVA

The test statistic for ANOVA is very similar to the independent-measures t statistic used in Chapter 10. For the t statistic, we first computed the standard error, which measures how much difference is expected between two sample means if there is no treatment effect (that is, if H_0 is true). Then we computed the t statistic with the following structure:

$$t = \frac{\text{obtained difference between two sample means}}{\text{standard error (the difference expected with no treatment effect)}}$$

For ANOVA, however, we want to compare differences among two *or more* sample means. With more than two samples, the concept of "difference between sample means" becomes difficult to define or measure. For example, if there are only two samples and they have means of $M = 20$ and $M = 30$, then there is a 10-point difference between the sample means. Suppose, however, that we add a third sample with a mean of $M = 35$. Now how much difference is there between the sample means? It should be clear that we have a problem. The solution to this problem is to use variance to define and measure the size of the differences among the sample means. Consider the following two sets of sample means:

Set 1	Set 2
$M_1 = 20$	$M_1 = 28$
$M_2 = 30$	$M_2 = 30$
$M_3 = 35$	$M_3 = 31$

If you compute the variance for the three numbers in each set, then the variance is $s^2 = 58.33$ for set 1 and the variance is $s^2 = 2.33$ for set 2. Notice that the two variances provide an accurate representation of the size of the differences. In set 1, there are relatively large differences between sample means and the variance is relatively large. In set 2, the mean differences are small and the variance is small.

Thus, we can use variance to measure sample mean differences when there are two or more samples. The test statistic for ANOVA uses this fact to compute an F-*ratio* with the following structure:

$$F = \frac{\text{variance (differences) between sample means}}{\text{variance (differences) expected with no treatment effect}}$$

Note that the F-ratio has the same basic structure as the t statistic but is based on *variance* instead of sample mean *difference*. The variance in the numerator of the F-ratio provides a single number that measures the differences among all of the sample means. The variance in the denominator of the F-ratio, like the standard error in the denominator of the t statistic, measures the mean differences that would be expected if there were no treatment effect. Thus, the t statistic and the F-ratio provide the same basic information. In each case, a large value for the test statistic provides evidence that the sample mean differences (numerator) are larger than would be expected if there were no treatment effects (denominator).

TYPE I ERRORS AND MULTIPLE-HYPOTHESIS TESTS

If we already have t tests for comparing mean differences, you might wonder why ANOVA is necessary. Why create a whole new hypothesis-testing procedure that simply duplicates what the t tests can already do? The answer to this question is based in a concern about Type I errors.

Remember that each time you do a hypothesis test, you select an alpha level that determines the risk of a Type I error. With $\alpha = .05$, for example, there is a 5%, or a 1-in-20, risk of a Type I error. Often a single experiment requires several hypothesis tests to evaluate all the mean differences. However, each test has a risk of a Type I error, and the more tests you do, the more risk there is.

For this reason, researchers often make a distinction between the *testwise alpha level* and the *experimentwise alpha level*. The testwise alpha level is simply the alpha level that you select for each individual hypothesis test. The experimentwise alpha level is the total probability of a Type I error accumulated from all of the separate tests in the experiment. As the number of separate tests increases, so does the experimentwise alpha level.

DEFINITIONS

The **testwise alpha level** is the risk of a Type I error, or alpha level, for an individual hypothesis test.

When an experiment involves several different hypothesis tests, the **experimentwise alpha level** is the total probability of a Type I error that is accumulated from all of the individual tests in the experiment. Typically, the experimentwise alpha level is substantially greater than the value of alpha used for any one of the individual tests.

For example, an experiment involving three treatments would require three separate t tests to compare all of the mean differences:

Test 1 compares treatment I with treatment II.

Test 2 compares treatment I with treatment III.

Test 3 compares treatment II with treatment III.

If all tests use $\alpha = .05$, then there is a 5% risk of a Type I error for the first test, a 5% risk for the second test, and another 5% risk for the third test. The three separate tests accumulate to produce a relatively large experimentwise alpha level. The advantage of ANOVA is that it performs all three comparisons simultaneously in one hypothesis test. Thus, no matter how many different means are being compared, ANOVA uses one test with one alpha level to evaluate the mean differences, and thereby avoids the problem of an inflated experimentwise alpha level.

12.2 THE LOGIC OF ANOVA

The formulas and calculations required in ANOVA are somewhat complicated, but the logic that underlies the whole procedure is fairly straightforward. Therefore, this section gives a general picture of ANOVA before we start looking at the details. We introduce the logic of ANOVA with the help of the hypothetical data in Table 12.1.

TABLE 12.1

Hypothetical data from an experiment examining driving performance under three telephone conditions.*

Treatment 1: No Phone (Sample 1)	Treatment 2: Hand-Held (Sample 2)	Treatment 3: Hands-Free (Sample 3)
4	0	1
3	1	2
6	3	2
3	1	0
4	0	0
$M = 4$	$M = 1$	$M = 1$

*Note that there are three separate samples, with $n = 5$ in each sample. The dependent variable is a measure of performance in a driving simulator.

These data represent the results of an independent-measures experiment comparing performance in a driving simulator under three telephone conditions.

One obvious characteristic of the data in Table 12.1 is that the scores are not all the same. In everyday language, the scores are different; in statistical terms, the scores are variable. Our goal is to measure the amount of variability (the size of the differences) and to explain why the scores are different.

The first step is to determine the total variability for the entire set of data. To compute the total variability, we combine all of the scores from all of the separate samples to obtain one general measure of variability for the complete experiment. Once we have measured the total variability, we can begin to break it apart into separate components. The word *analysis* means dividing into smaller parts. Because we are going to analyze variability, the process is called *analysis of variance*. This analysis process divides the total variability into two basic components.

1. **Between-Treatments Variance.** Looking at the data in Table 12.1, we clearly see that much of the variability in the scores results from general differences between treatment conditions. For example, the scores in the no-phone condition tend to be much higher ($M = 4$) than the scores in the hand-held condition ($M = 1$). We calculate the variance between treatments to provide a measure of the overall differences between treatment conditions. Notice that the variance between treatments is really measuring the differences between sample means.
2. **Within-Treatment Variance.** In addition to the general differences between treatment conditions, there is variability within each sample. Looking again at Table 12.1, we see that the scores in the no-phone condition are not all the same; they are variable. The within-treatments variance provides a measure of the variability inside each treatment condition.

Analyzing the total variability into these two components is the heart of ANOVA. We now examine each of the components in more detail.

BETWEEN-TREATMENTS VARIANCE

Remember that calculating variance is simply a method for measuring how big the differences are for a set of numbers. When you see the term *variance,* you can automatically translate it into the term *differences.* Thus, the *between-treatments variance* simply measures how much difference exists between the treatment conditions. There are two possible explanations for these between-treatment differences:

1. The differences between treatments are not caused by any treatment effect but are simply the naturally occurring, random, and unsystematic differences that

exist between one sample and another. That is, the differences are the result of sampling error.

2. The differences between treatments have been caused by the *treatment effects*. For example, if using a telephone really does interfere with driving performance, then scores in the telephone conditions should be systematically lower than scores in the no-phone condition.

Thus, when we compute the between-treatments variance, we are measuring differences that could be caused by a systematic treatment effect or could simply be random and unsystematic mean differences caused by sampling error. To demonstrate that there really is a treatment effect, we must establish that the differences between treatments are bigger than would be expected by sampling error alone. To accomplish this goal, we determine how big the differences are when there is no systematic treatment effect; that is, we measure how much difference (or variance) can be explained by random and unsystematic factors. To measure these differences, we compute the variance within treatments.

WITHIN-TREATMENTS VARIANCE

Inside each treatment condition, we have a set of individuals who all receive exactly the same treatment; that is, the researcher does not do anything that would cause these individuals to have different scores. In Table 12.1, for example, the data show that five individuals were tested while talking on a hand-held phone (sample 2). Although these five individuals all received exactly the same treatment, their scores are different. Why are the scores different? The answer is that there is no specific cause for the differences. Instead, the differences that exist within a treatment represent random and unsystematic differences that occur when there are no treatment effects causing the scores to be different. Thus, the *within-treatments variance* provides a measure of how big the differences are when H_0 is true.

Figure 12.4 shows the overall ANOVA and identifies the sources of variability that are measured by each of the two basic components.

THE *F*-RATIO: THE TEST STATISTIC FOR ANOVA

Once we have analyzed the total variability into two basic components (between treatments and within treatments), we simply compare them. The comparison is made by

FIGURE 12.4

The independent-measures ANOVA partitions, or analyzes, the total variability into two components: variance between treatments and variance within treatments.

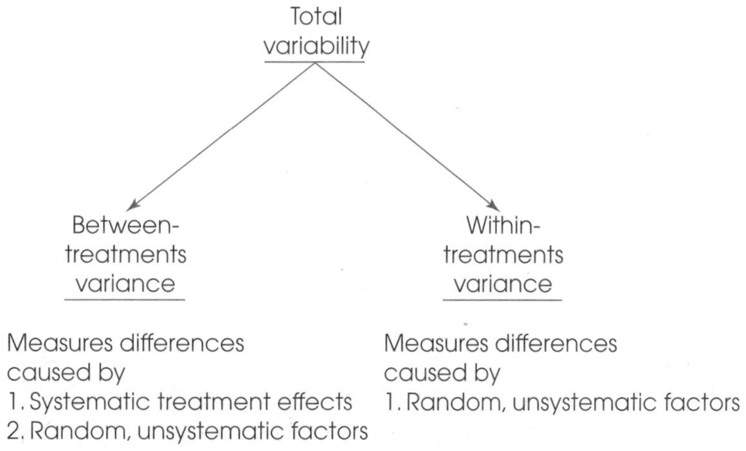

computing an F-*ratio*. For the independent-measures ANOVA, the F-ratio has the following structure:

$$F = \frac{\text{variance between treatments}}{\text{variance within treatments}} = \frac{\text{differences including any treatment effects}}{\text{differences with no treatment effects}} \quad (12.1)$$

When we express each component of variability in terms of its sources (see Figure 12.4), the structure of the F-ratio is

$$F = \frac{\text{systematic treatment effects} + \text{random, unsystematic differences}}{\text{random, unsystematic differences}} \quad (12.2)$$

The value obtained for the F-ratio helps determine whether any treatment effects exist. Consider the following two possibilities:

1. When there are no systematic treatment effects, the differences between treatments (numerator) are entirely caused by random, unsystematic factors. In this case, the numerator and the denominator of the F-ratio are both measuring random differences and should be roughly the same size. With the numerator and denominator roughly equal, the F-ratio should have a value around 1.00. In terms of the formula, when the treatment effect is zero, we obtain

$$F = \frac{0 + \text{random, unsystematic differences}}{\text{random, unsystematic differences}}$$

   Thus, an F-ratio near 1.00 indicates that the differences between treatments (numerator) are random and unsystematic, just like the differences in the denominator. With an F-ratio near 1.00, we conclude that there is no evidence to suggest that the treatment has any effect.

2. When the treatment does have an effect, causing systematic differences between samples, then the combination of systematic and random differences in the numerator should be larger than the random differences alone in the denominator. In this case, the numerator of the F-ratio should be noticeably larger than the denominator, and we should obtain an F-ratio that is substantially larger than 1.00. Thus, a large F-ratio is evidence for the existence of systematic treatment effects; that is, there are consistent differences between treatments.

Because the denominator of the F-ratio measures only random and unsystematic variability, it is called the *error term*. The numerator of the F-ratio always includes the same unsystematic variability as in the error term, but it also includes any systematic differences caused by the treatment effect. The goal of ANOVA is to find out whether a treatment effect exists.

DEFINITION

For ANOVA, the denominator of the F-ratio is called the **error term**. The error term provides a measure of the variance caused by random, unsystematic differences. When the treatment effect is zero (H_0 is true), the error term measures the same sources of variance as the numerator of the F-ratio, so the value of the F-ratio is expected to be nearly equal to 1.00.

LEARNING CHECK

1. ANOVA is a statistical procedure that compares two or more treatment conditions for differences in variance. (True or false?)
2. In ANOVA, what value is expected, on the average, for the F-ratio when the null hypothesis is true?
3. What happens to the value of the F-ratio if differences between treatments are increased? What happens to the F-ratio if variability inside the treatments is increased?
4. In ANOVA, the total variability is partitioned into two parts. What are these two variability components called, and how are they used in the F-ratio?

ANSWERS

1. False. Although ANOVA uses variance in the computations, the purpose of the test is to evaluate differences in *means* between treatments.
2. When H_0 is true, the expected value for the F-ratio is 1.00 because the top and bottom of the ratio are both measuring the same variance.
3. As differences between treatments increase, the F-ratio increases. As variability within treatments increases, the F-ratio decreases.
4. The two components are between-treatments variability and within-treatments variability. Between-treatments variance is the numerator of the F-ratio, and within-treatments variance is the denominator.

12.3 ANOVA NOTATION AND FORMULAS

Because ANOVA typically is used to examine data from more than two treatment conditions (and more than two samples), we need a notational system to keep track of all the individual scores and totals. To help introduce this notational system, we use the hypothetical data from Table 12.1 again. The data are reproduced in Table 12.2 along with some of the notation and statistics that are described in the following list.

1. The letter k is used to identify the number of treatment conditions—that is, the number of levels of the factor. For an independent-measures study, k also specifies the number of separate samples. For the data in Table 12.2, there are three treatments, so $k = 3$.
2. The number of scores in each treatment is identified by a lowercase letter n. For the example in Table 12.2, $n = 5$ for all the treatments. If the samples are of different sizes, you can identify a specific sample by using a subscript. For example, n_2 is the number of scores in treatment 2.
3. The total number of scores in the entire study is specified by a capital letter N. When all of the samples are the same size (n is constant), $N = kn$. For the data in Table 12.2, there are $n = 5$ scores in each of the $k = 3$ treatments, so we have a total of $N = 3(5) = 15$ scores in the entire study.
4. The sum of the scores (ΣX) for each treatment condition is identified by the capital letter T (for treatment total). The total for a specific treatment can be identified by adding a numerical subscript to the T. For example, the total for the second treatment in Table 12.2 is $T_2 = 5$.
5. The sum of all of the scores in the research study (the grand total) is identified by G. You can compute G by adding up all N scores or by adding up the treatment totals: $G = \Sigma T$.
6. Although there is no new notation involved, we also have computed SS and M for each sample, and we have calculated ΣX^2 for the entire set of $N = 15$ scores

TABLE 12.2
The same data that appeared in Table 12.1 with summary values and notation appropriate for an ANOVA.

Telephone Conditions			
Treatment 1 No Phone (Sample 1)	Treatment 2 Hand-Held Phone (Sample 2)	Treatment 3 Hands-Free Phone (Sample 3)	
4	0	1	$\Sigma X^2 = 106$
3	1	2	$G = 30$
6	3	2	$N = 15$
3	1	0	$k = 3$
4	0	0	
$T_1 = 20$	$T_2 = 5$	$T_3 = 5$	
$SS_1 = 6$	$SS_2 = 6$	$SS_3 = 4$	
$n_1 = 5$	$n_2 = 5$	$n_3 = 5$	
$M_1 = 4$	$M_2 = 1$	$M_3 = 1$	

in the study. These values are given in Table 12.2 and are important in the formulas and calculations for ANOVA.

Finally, we should note that there is no universally accepted notation for ANOVA. Although we are using *G*s and *T*s, for example, you may find that other sources use other symbols.

ANOVA FORMULAS

Because ANOVA requires extensive calculations and many formulas, one common problem for students is simply keeping track of the different formulas and numbers. Therefore, we examine the general structure of the procedure and look at the organization of the calculations before we introduce the individual formulas.

Because ANOVA formulas require ΣX for each treatment and ΣX for the entire set of scores, we have introduced new notation (T and G) to help identify which ΣX is being used. Remember: T stands for *treatment total*, and G stands for *grand total*.

1. The final calculation for ANOVA is the F-ratio, which is composed of two variances:

$$F = \frac{\text{variance between treatments}}{\text{variance within treatments}}$$

2. Each of the two variances in the F-ratio is calculated using the basic formula for sample variance.

$$\text{sample variance} = s^2 = \frac{SS}{df}$$

Therefore, we need to compute an *SS* and a *df* for the variance between treatments (numerator of F), and we need another *SS* and *df* for the variance within treatments (denominator of F). To obtain these *SS* and *df* values, we must go through two separate analyses: First, compute *SS* for the total study, and analyze it in two components (between and within). Then compute *df* for the total study, and analyze it in two components (between and within).

Thus, the entire process of ANOVA requires nine calculations: three values for *SS*, three values for *df*, two variances (between and within), and a final F-ratio. However, these nine calculations are all logically related and are all directed toward finding the final F-ratio. Figure 12.5 shows the logical structure of ANOVA calculations.

FIGURE 12.5

The structure and sequence of calculations for the ANOVA.

The final goal for the ANOVA is an *F*-ratio	$F = \dfrac{\text{Variance between treatments}}{\text{Variance within treatments}}$	
Each variance in the *F*-ratio is computed as *SS*/*df*	Variance between treatments $= \dfrac{SS \text{ between}}{df \text{ between}}$	Variance within treatments $= \dfrac{SS \text{ within}}{df \text{ within}}$
To obtain each of the *SS* and *df* values, the total variability is analyzed into the two components	*SS* total → *SS* between, *SS* within	*df* total → *df* between, *df* within

ANALYSIS OF THE SUM OF SQUARES (*SS*)

The ANOVA requires that we first compute a total sum of squares and then partition this value into two components: between treatments and within treatments. This analysis is outlined in Figure 12.6. We will examine each of the three components separately.

1. **Total Sum of Squares, SS_{total}.** As the name implies, SS_{total} is the sum of squares for the entire set of N scores. As described in Chapter 4 (pp. 111–112), this SS value can be computed using either a definitional or a computational formula. However, ANOVA typically involves a large number of scores and the mean is often not a whole number. Therefore, it is usually much easier to calculate SS_{total} using the computational formula:

$$SS = \Sigma X^2 - \frac{(\Sigma X)^2}{N}$$

FIGURE 12.6

Partitioning the sum of squares (*SS*) for the independent-measures ANOVA.

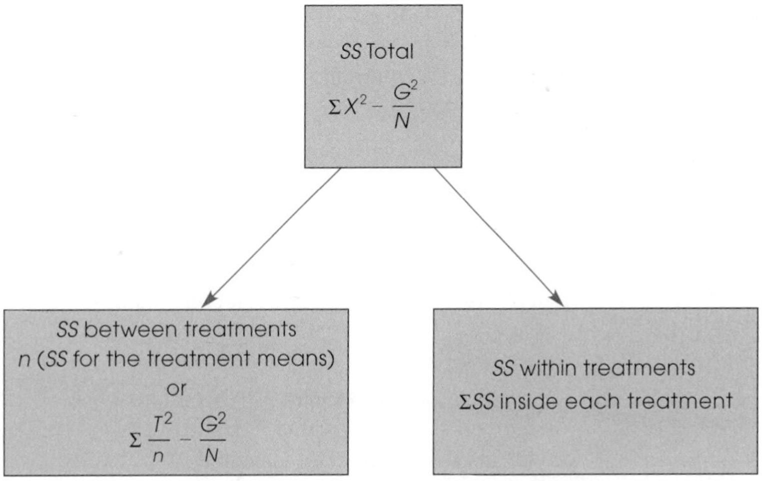

To make this formula consistent with the ANOVA notation, we substitute the letter G in place of ΣX and obtain

$$SS_{\text{total}} = \Sigma X^2 - \frac{G^2}{N} \tag{12.3}$$

Applying this formula to the set of data in Table 12.2, we obtain

$$\begin{aligned} SS_{\text{total}} &= 106 - \frac{30^2}{15} \\ &= 106 - 60 \\ &= 46 \end{aligned}$$

2. **Within-Treatments Sum of Squares, $SS_{\text{within treatments}}$.** Now we are looking at the variability inside each of the treatment conditions. We already have computed the SS within each of the three treatment conditions (Table 12.2): $SS_1 = 6$, $SS_2 = 6$, and $SS_3 = 4$. To find the overall within-treatment sum of squares, we simply add these values together:

$$SS_{\text{within treatments}} = \Sigma SS_{\text{inside each treatment}} \tag{12.4}$$

For the data in Table 12.2, this formula gives

$$\begin{aligned} SS_{\text{within treatments}} &= 6 + 6 + 4 \\ &= 16 \end{aligned}$$

3. **Between-Treatments Sum of Squares, $SS_{\text{between treatments}}$.** Before we introduce any equations for $SS_{\text{between treatments}}$, consider what we have found so far. The total variability for the data in Table 12.2 is $SS_{\text{total}} = 46$. We intend to partition this total into two parts (see Figure 12.5). One part, $SS_{\text{within treatments}}$, has been found to be equal to 16. This means that $SS_{\text{between treatments}}$ must be equal to 30 so that the two parts (16 and 30) add up to the total (46). Thus, the value for $SS_{\text{between treatments}}$ can be found simply by subtraction:

$$SS_{\text{between}} = SS_{\text{total}} - SS_{\text{within}} \tag{12.5}$$

To simplify the notation, we use the subscripts *between* and *within* in place of *between treatments* and *within treatments.*

However, it is also possible to compute SS_{between} independently, then check your calculations by ensuring that the two components, between and within, add up to the total. Box 12.1 presents two different formulas for calculating SS_{between} directly from the data.

Computing SS_{between} Including the two formulas in Box 12.1, we have presented three different equations for computing SS_{between}. Rather than memorizing all three, however, we suggest that you pick one formula and use it consistently. There are two reasonable alternatives to use. The simplest is Equation 12.5, which finds SS_{between} simply by subtraction: First you compute SS_{total} and SS_{within}, then subtract:

$$SS_{\text{between}} = SS_{\text{total}} - SS_{\text{within}}$$

The second alternative is to use Equation 12.7, which computes SS_{between} using the treatment totals (the T values). The advantage of this alternative is that it provides a way to check your arithmetic: Calculate SS_{total}, SS_{between}, and SS_{within} separately, and then check to be sure that the two components add up to equal SS_{total}.

BOX 12.1 ALTERNATIVE FORMULAS FOR SS_{between}

Recall that the variability between treatments is measuring the differences between treatment means. Conceptually, the most direct way of measuring the amount of variability among the treatment means is to compute the sum of squares for the set of sample means, SS_{means}. For the data in Table 12.2, the samples means are 4, 1, and 1. These three values produce $SS_{\text{means}} = 6$. However, each of the three means represents a group of $n = 5$ scores. Therefore, the final value for SS_{between} is obtained by multiplying SS_{means} by n.

$$SS_{\text{between}} = n(SS_{\text{means}}) \tag{12.6}$$

For the data in Table 12.2, we obtain

$$SS_{\text{between}} = n(SS_{\text{means}}) = 5(6) = 30$$

Unfortunately, Equation 12.6 can only be used when all of the samples are exactly the same size (equal ns), and the equation can be very awkward, especially when the treatment means are not whole numbers. Therefore, we also present a computational formula for SS_{between} that uses the treatment totals (T) instead of the treatment means.

$$SS_{\text{between}} = \Sigma\frac{T^2}{n} - \frac{G^2}{N} \tag{12.7}$$

For the data in Table 12.2, this formula produces:

$$\begin{aligned} SS_{\text{between}} &= \frac{20^2}{5} + \frac{5^2}{5} + \frac{5^2}{5} - \frac{30^2}{15} \\ &= 80 + 5 + 5 - 60 \\ &= 90 - 60 \\ &= 30 \end{aligned}$$

Note that all three techniques (Equations 12.5, 12.6, and 12.7) produce the same result, $SS_{\text{between}} = 30$.

Using Equation 12.6, which computes SS for the set of sample means, is usually not a good choice. Unless the sample means are all whole numbers, this equation can produce very tedious calculations. In most situations, one of the other two equations is a better alternative.

THE ANALYSIS OF DEGREES OF FREEDOM (*DF*)

The analysis of degrees of freedom (df) follows the same pattern as the analysis of SS. First, we find df for the total set of N scores, and then we partition this value into two components: degrees of freedom between treatments and degrees of freedom within treatments. In computing degrees of freedom, there are two important considerations to keep in mind:

1. Each df value is associated with a specific SS value.
2. Normally, the value of df is obtained by counting the number of items that were used to calculate SS and then subtracting 1. For example, if you compute SS for a set of n scores, then $df = n - 1$.

With this in mind, we examine the degrees of freedom for each part of the analysis.

1. **Total Degrees of Freedom, df_{total}.** To find the df associated with SS_{total}, you must first recall that this SS value measures variability for the entire set of N scores. Therefore, the df value is

$$df_{\text{total}} = N - 1 \tag{12.8}$$

For the data in Table 12.2, the total number of scores is $N = 15$, so the total degrees of freedom are

$$\begin{aligned} df_{\text{total}} &= 15 - 1 \\ &= 14 \end{aligned}$$

2. **Within-Treatments Degrees of Freedom, df_{within}.** To find the *df* associated with SS_{within}, we must look at how this *SS* value is computed. Remember, we first find *SS* inside of each of the treatments and then add these values together. Each of the treatment *SS* values measures variability for the *n* scores in the treatment, so each *SS* has $df = n - 1$. When all of these individual treatment values are added together, we obtain

$$df_{within} = \Sigma(n - 1) = \Sigma df_{in\ each\ treatment} \quad (12.9)$$

For the experiment we have been considering, each treatment has $n = 5$ scores. This means there are $n - 1 = 4$ degrees of freedom inside each treatment. Because there are three different treatment conditions, this gives a total of 12 for the within-treatments degrees of freedom. Notice that this formula for *df* simply adds up the number of scores in each treatment (the *n* values) and subtracts 1 for each treatment. If these two stages are done separately, you obtain

$$df_{within} = N - k \quad (12.10)$$

(Adding up all the *n* values gives *N*. If you subtract 1 for each treatment, then altogether you have subtracted *k* because there are *k* treatments.) For the data in Table 12.2, $N = 15$ and $k = 3$, so

$$df_{within} = 15 - 3$$
$$= 12$$

3. **Between-Treatments Degrees of Freedom, $df_{between}$.** The *df* associated with $SS_{between}$ can be found by considering how the *SS* value is obtained. This *SS* formulas measure the variability for the set of treatments (totals or means). To find $df_{between}$, simply count the number of treatments and subtract 1. Because the number of treatments is specified by the letter *k*, the formula for *df* is

$$df_{between} = k - 1 \quad (12.11)$$

For the data in Table 12.2, there are three different treatment conditions (three *T* values or three sample means), so the between-treatments degrees of freedom are computed as follows:

$$df_{between} = 3 - 1$$
$$= 2$$

Notice that the two parts we obtained from this analysis of degrees of freedom add up to equal the total degrees of freedom:

$$df_{total} = df_{within} + df_{between}$$
$$14 = 12 + 2$$

The complete analysis of degrees of freedom is shown in Figure 12.7.

As you are computing the *SS* and *df* values for ANOVA, keep in mind that the labels that are used for each value can help you understand the formulas. Specifically,

1. The term **total** refers to the entire set of scores. We compute *SS* for the whole set of *N* scores, and the *df* value is simply $N - 1$.

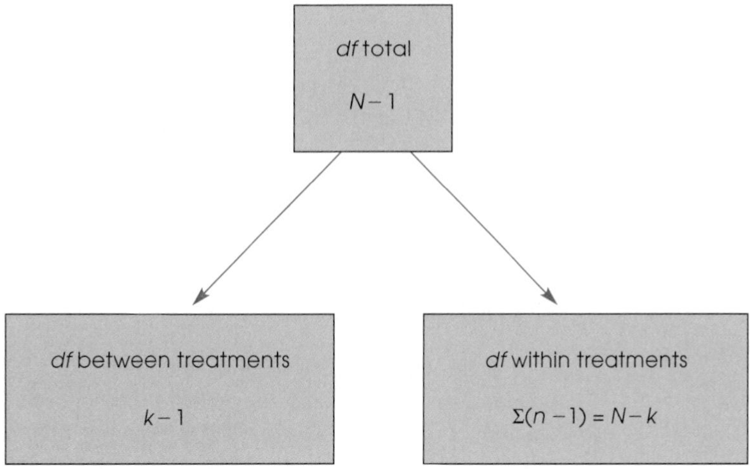

FIGURE 12.7
Partitioning degrees of freedom (*df*) for the independent-measures ANOVA.

2. The term **within treatments** refers to differences that exist inside the individual treatment conditions. Thus, we compute *SS* and *df* inside each of the separate treatments.
3. The term **between treatments** refers to differences from one treatment to another. With three treatments, for example, we are comparing three different means (or totals) and have $df = 3 - 1 = 2$.

CALCULATION OF VARIANCES (*MS*) AND THE *F*-RATIO

The next step in the ANOVA procedure is to compute the variance between treatments and the variance within treatments, which are used to calculate the *F*-ratio (see Figure 12.5).

In ANOVA, it is customary to use the term *mean square,* or simply *MS,* in place of the term *variance*. Recall (from Chapter 4) that variance is defined as the mean of the squared deviations. In the same way that we use *SS* to stand for the sum of the squared deviations, we now use *MS* to stand for the mean of the squared deviations. For the final *F*-ratio we need an *MS* (variance) between treatments for the numerator and an *MS* (variance) within treatments for the denominator. In each case

$$MS \text{ (variance)} = s^2 = \frac{SS}{df} \tag{12.12}$$

For the data we have been considering,

$$MS_{\text{between}} = s^2_{\text{between}} = \frac{SS_{\text{between}}}{df_{\text{between}}} = \frac{30}{2} = 15$$

and

$$MS_{\text{within}} = s^2_{\text{within}} = \frac{SS_{\text{within}}}{df_{\text{within}}} = \frac{16}{12} = 1.33$$

We now have a measure of the variance (or differences) between the treatments and a measure of the variance within the treatments. The F-ratio simply compares these two variances:

$$F = \frac{s^2_{\text{between}}}{s^2_{\text{within}}} = \frac{MS_{\text{between}}}{MS_{\text{within}}} \tag{12.13}$$

For the experiment we have been examining, the data give an F-ratio of

$$F = \frac{15}{1.33} = 11.28$$

For this example, the obtained value of $F = 11.28$ indicates that the numerator of the F-ratio is substantially bigger than the denominator. If you recall the conceptual structure of the F-ratio as presented in Equations 12.1 and 12.2, the F value we obtained indicates that the differences between treatments are more than 11 times bigger than what would be expected if there were no treatment effect. Stated in terms of the experimental variables: using a telephone while driving does appear to have an effect on driving performance. However, to properly evaluate the F-ratio, we must select an α level and consult the F-distribution table that is discussed in the next section.

ANOVA Summary Tables It is useful to organize the results of the analysis in one table called an *ANOVA summary table*. The table shows the source of variability (between treatments, within treatments, and total variability), *SS*, *df*, *MS*, and *F*. For the previous computations, the ANOVA summary table is constructed as follows:

Source	*SS*	*df*	*MS*	
Between treatments	30	2	15	$F = 11.28$
Within treatments	16	12	1.33	
Total	46	14		

Although these tables are no longer used in published reports, they are a common part of computer printouts, and they do provide a concise method for presenting the results of an analysis. (Note that you can conveniently check your work: Adding the first two entries in the *SS* column, 30 + 16, produces SS_{total}. The same applies to the *df* column.) When using ANOVA, you might start with a blank ANOVA summary table and then fill in the values as they are calculated. With this method, you are less likely to "get lost" in the analysis, wondering what to do next.

LEARNING CHECK

1. Calculate SS_{total}, SS_{between}, and SS_{within} for the following set of data:

Treatment 1	Treatment 2	Treatment 3	
$n = 10$	$n = 10$	$n = 10$	$N = 30$
$T = 10$	$T = 20$	$T = 30$	$G = 60$
$SS = 27$	$SS = 16$	$SS = 23$	$\Sigma X^2 = 206$

2. A researcher uses an ANOVA to compare three treatment conditions with a sample of $n = 8$ in each treatment. For this analysis, find df_{total}, df_{between}, and df_{within}.

3. A researcher reports an F-ratio with $df_{between} = 2$ and $df_{within} = 30$ for an independent-measures ANOVA. How many treatment conditions were compared in the experiment? How many subjects participated in the experiment?

4. A researcher conducts an experiment comparing four treatment conditions with a separate sample of $n = 6$ in each treatment. An ANOVA is used to evaluate the data, and the results of the ANOVA are presented in the following table. Complete all missing values in the table. *Hint:* Begin with the values in the *df* column.

Source	*SS*	*df*	*MS*	
Between treatments	__	__	__	$F =$ ____
Within treatments	__	__	2	
Total	58	__		

ANSWERS

1. $SS_{total} = 86$; $SS_{between} = 20$; $SS_{within} = 66$

2. $df_{total} = 23$; $df_{between} = 2$; $df_{within} = 21$

3. There were 3 treatment conditions ($df_{between} = k - 1 = 2$). A total of $N = 33$ individuals participated ($df_{within} = 30 = N - k$).

4.

Source	*SS*	*df*	*MS*	
Between treatments	18	3	6	$F = 3.00$
Within treatments	40	20	2	
Total	58	23		

12.4 THE DISTRIBUTION OF *F*-RATIOS

In ANOVA, the F-ratio is constructed so that the numerator and denominator of the ratio are measuring exactly the same variance when the null hypothesis is true (see Equation 12.2). In this situation, we expect the value of F to be around 1.00.

If the null hypothesis is false, then the F-ratio should be much greater than 1.00. The problem now is to define precisely which values are "around 1.00" and which are "much greater than 1.00." To answer this question, we need to look at all of the possible F values—that is, the *distribution of* F*-ratios.*

Before we examine this distribution in detail, you should note two obvious characteristics:

1. Because F-ratios are computed from two variances (the numerator and denominator of the ratio), F values always are positive numbers. Remember that variance is always positive.
2. When H_0 is true, the numerator and denominator of the F-ratio are measuring the same variance. In this case, the two sample variances should be about the same size, so the ratio should be near 1. In other words, the distribution of F-ratios should pile up around 1.00.

With these two factors in mind, we can sketch the distribution of F-ratios. The distribution is cut off at zero (all positive values), piles up around 1.00, and then tapers off to the right (Figure 12.8). The exact shape of the F distribution depends on the degrees

FIGURE 12.8

The distribution of F-ratios with $df = 2, 12$. Of all the values in the distribution, only 5% are larger than $F = 3.88$, and only 1% are larger than $F = 6.93$.

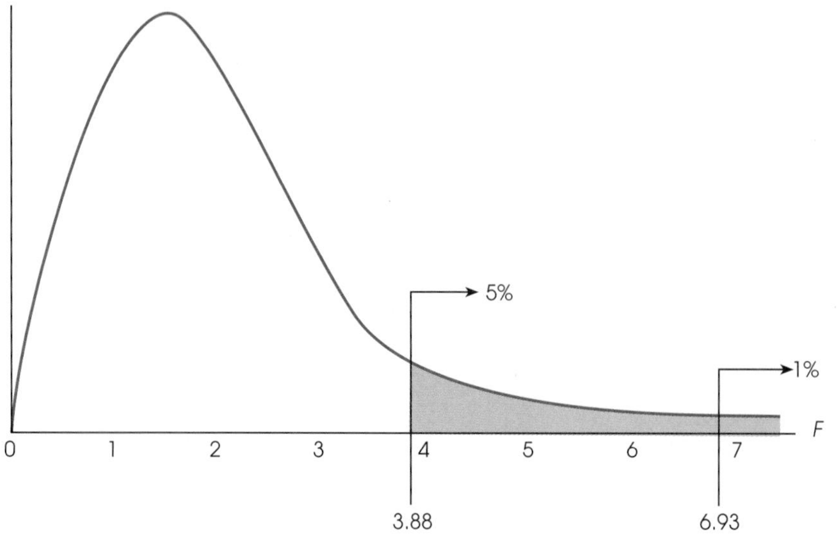

of freedom for the two variances in the F-ratio. You should recall that the precision of a sample variance depends on the number of scores or the degrees of freedom. In general, the variance for a large sample (large df) provides a more accurate estimate of the population variance. Because the precision of the MS values depends on df, the shape of the F distribution also depends on the df values for the numerator and denominator of the F-ratio. With very large df values, nearly all of the F-ratios are clustered very near to 1.00. With the smaller df values, the F distribution is more spread out.

THE *F* DISTRIBUTION TABLE

For ANOVA, we expect F near 1.00 if H_0 is true, and we expect a large value for F if H_0 is not true. In the F distribution, we need to separate those values that are reasonably near 1.00 from the values that are significantly greater than 1.00. These critical values are presented in an F distribution table in Appendix B, page 705. A portion of the F distribution table is shown in Table 12.3. To use the table, you must know the df values for the F-ratio (numerator and denominator), and you must know the alpha level for the hypothesis test. It is customary for an F table to have the df values for the numerator of the F-ratio printed across the top of the table. The df values for the denominator of F are printed in a column on the left-hand side. For the experiment we have been considering, the numerator of the F-ratio (between treatments) has $df = 2$, and the denominator of the F-ratio (within treatments) has $df = 12$. This F-ratio is said to have "degrees of freedom equal to 2 and 12." The degrees of freedom would be written as $df = 2, 12$. To use the table, you would first find $df = 2$ across the top of the table and $df = 12$ in the first column. When you line up these two values, they point to a pair of numbers in the middle of the table. These numbers give the critical cutoffs for $\alpha = .05$ and $\alpha = .01$. With $df = 2, 12$, for example, the numbers in the table are 3.88 and 6.93. Thus, only 5% of the distribution ($\alpha = .05$) corresponds to values greater than 3.88, and only1% of the distribution ($\alpha = .01$) corresponds to values greater than 6.93 (see Figure 12.8).

In the experiment comparing driving performance under different telephone conditions, we obtained an F-ratio of 11.28. According to the critical cutoffs in Figure 12.8, this value is extremely unlikely (it is in the most extreme 1%). Therefore, we would reject H_0 with an α level of either .05 or .01, and conclude that the different telephone conditions significantly affect driving performance.

TABLE 12.3

A portion of the F distribution table. Entries in roman type are critical values for the .05 level of significance, and bold type values are for the .01 level of significance. The critical values for $df = 2, 12$ have been highlighted (see text).

Degrees of Freedom: Denominator	Degrees of Freedom: Numerator					
	1	2	3	4	5	6
10	4.96	4.10	3.71	3.48	3.33	3.22
	10.04	**7.56**	**6.55**	**5.99**	**5.64**	**5.39**
11	4.84	3.98	3.59	3.36	3.20	3.09
	9.65	**7.20**	**6.22**	**5.67**	**5.32**	**5.07**
12	4.75	3.88	3.49	3.26	3.11	3.00
	9.33	**6.93**	**5.95**	**5.41**	**5.06**	**4.82**
13	4.67	3.80	3.41	3.18	3.02	2.92
	9.07	**6.70**	**5.74**	**5.20**	**4.86**	**4.62**
14	4.60	3.74	3.34	3.11	2.96	2.85
	8.86	**6.51**	**5.56**	**5.03**	**4.69**	**4.46**

LEARNING CHECK

1. A researcher obtains $F = 4.18$ with $df = 2, 15$. Is this value sufficient to reject H_0 with $\alpha = .05$? Is it big enough to reject H_0 if $\alpha = .01$?
2. With $\alpha = .05$, what value forms the boundary for the critical region in the distribution of F-ratios with $df = 2, 24$?

ANSWERS

1. For $\alpha = .05$, the critical value is 3.68 and you should reject H_0. For $\alpha = .01$, the critical value is 6.36 and you should fail to reject H_0.
2. The critical value is 3.40.

12.5 EXAMPLES OF HYPOTHESIS TESTING AND EFFECT SIZE WITH ANOVA

Although we have now seen all the individual components of ANOVA, the following example demonstrates the complete ANOVA process using the standard four-step procedure for hypothesis testing.

EXAMPLE 12.1

The data in Table 12.4 were obtained from an independent-measures experiment designed to examine people's preferences for viewing distance of a 42-inch, high-definition television. Four viewing distances were evaluated, 9 feet, 12 feet, 15 feet, and 18 feet, with a separate group of participants tested at each distance. Each individual watched a 30-minute television program from a specific distance and then completed a brief questionnaire measuring their satisfaction with the experience. One question asked them to rate the viewing distance on a scale from 1 (Very Bad—definitely need to move closer or farther away) to 7 (Excellent—perfect viewing distance). The purpose of the ANOVA is to determine whether there are any significant differences among the four viewing distances that were tested.

Before we begin the hypothesis test, note that we have already computed several summary statistics for the data in Table 12.4. Specifically, the treatment totals (T) and SS values are shown for each sample, and the grand total (G) as well as N and ΣX^2 are shown for the entire set of data. Having these summary values simplifies the

TABLE 12.4

Satisfaction with different viewing distances of a 42-inch high-definition television.

9 feet	12 feet	15 feet	18 feet	
3	4	7	6	$N = 20$
0	3	6	3	$G = 60$
2	1	5	4	$\Sigma X^2 = 262$
0	1	4	3	
0	1	3	4	
$T = 5$	$T = 10$	$T = 25$	$T = 20$	
$SS = 8$	$SS = 8$	$SS = 10$	$SS = 6$	

computations in the hypothesis test, and we suggest that you always compute these summary statistics before you begin an ANOVA.

STEP 1: State the hypotheses and select an alpha level.

H_0: $\mu_1 = \mu_2 = \mu_3 = \mu_4$ (There is no treatment effect.)

H_1: At least one of the treatment means is different.

We use $\alpha = .05$.

STEP 2: Locate the critical region.

We first must determine degrees of freedom for $MS_{\text{between treatments}}$ and $MS_{\text{within treatments}}$ (the numerator and denominator of the F-ratio), so we begin by analyzing the degrees of freedom. For these data, the total degrees of freedom are

Often it is easier to postpone finding the critical region until after step 3, where you compute the *df* values as part of the calculations for the F-ratio.

$$\begin{aligned} df_{\text{total}} &= N - 1 \\ &= 20 - 1 \\ &= 19 \end{aligned}$$

Analyzing this total into two components, we obtain

$$df_{\text{between}} = k - 1 = 4 - 1 = 3$$

$$df_{\text{within}} = \Sigma df_{\text{inside each treatment}} = 4 + 4 + 4 + 4 = 16$$

The F-ratio for these data has $df = 3, 16$. The distribution of all the possible F-ratios with $df = 3, 16$ is presented in Figure 12.9. Note that F-ratios larger than 3.24 are extremely rare ($p < .05$) if H_0 is true and, therefore, form the critical region for the test.

STEP 3: Compute the F-ratio.

The series of calculations for computing F is presented in Figure 12.5 and can be summarized as follows:

a. Analyze the *SS* to obtain SS_{between} and SS_{within}.

b. Use the *SS* values and the *df* values (from step 2) to calculate the two variances, MS_{between} and MS_{within}.

c. Finally, use the two *MS* values (variances) to compute the F-ratio.

Analysis of SS. First, we compute the total *SS* and then the two components, as indicated in Figure 12.6.

SS_{total} is simply the *SS* for the total set of $N = 20$ scores.

FIGURE 12.9
The distribution of F-ratios with $df = 3, 16$. The critical value for $\alpha = .05$ is $F = 3.24$.

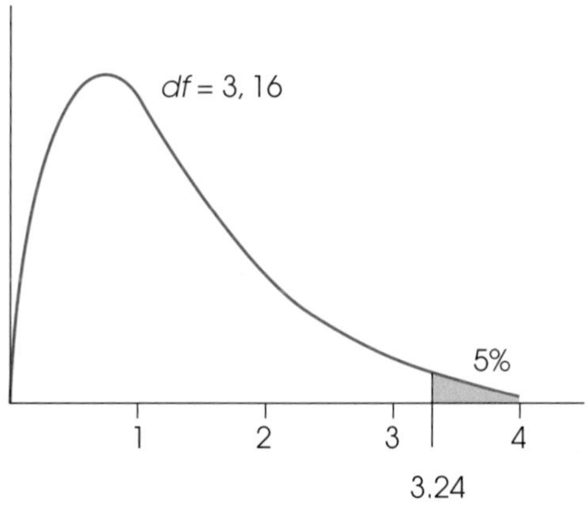

$$\begin{aligned} SS_{\text{total}} &= \Sigma X^2 - \frac{G^2}{N} \\ &= 262 - \frac{60^2}{20} \\ &= 262 - 180 \\ &= 82 \end{aligned}$$

SS_{within} combines the SS values from inside each of the treatment conditions.

$$SS_{\text{within}} = \Sigma SS_{\text{inside each treatment}} = 8 + 8 + 10 + 6 = 32$$

SS_{between} measures the differences among the four treatment means (or treatment totals). Because we have already calculated SS_{total} and SS_{within}, the simplest way to obtain SS_{between} is by subtraction (Equation 12.5).

$$\begin{aligned} SS_{\text{between}} &= SS_{\text{total}} - SS_{\text{within}} \\ &= 82 - 32 \\ &= 50 \end{aligned}$$

Calculation of mean squares. Because we already found $df_{\text{between}} = 3$ and $df_{\text{within}} = 16$ (Step 2), we now can compute the variance or MS value for each of the two components.

$$MS_{\text{between}} = \frac{SS_{\text{between}}}{df_{\text{between}}} = \frac{50}{3} = 16.67$$

$$MS_{\text{within}} = \frac{SS_{\text{within}}}{df_{\text{within}}} = \frac{32}{16} = 2.00$$

Calculation of F. We compute the F-ratio:

$$F = \frac{MS_{\text{between}}}{MS_{\text{within}}} = \frac{16.67}{2.00} = 8.33$$

STEP 4: Make a decision.

The F value we obtained, $F = 8.33$, is in the critical region (see Figure 12.9). It is very unlikely ($p < .05$) that we would obtain a value this large if H_0 is true. Therefore, we reject H_0 and conclude that there is a significant treatment effect.

Example 12.1 demonstrated the complete, step-by-step application of the ANOVA procedure. There are two additional points that can be made using this example.

First, you should look carefully at the statistical decision. We have rejected H_0 and concluded that not all the treatments are the same. But we have not determined which ones are different. Is a 9-foot distance different from 12 feet? Is 12 feet different from 15 feet? Unfortunately, these questions remain unanswered. We do know that at least one difference exists (we rejected H_0), but additional analysis is necessary to find out exactly where this difference is. We address this problem in Section 12.6.

Second, as noted earlier, all of the components of the analysis (the *SS*, *df*, *MS*, and *F*) can be presented together in one summary table. The summary table for the analysis in Example 12.1 is as follows:

Source	*SS*	*df*	*MS*	
Between treatments	50	3	16.67	$F = 8.33$
Within treatments	32	16	2.00	
Total	82	19		

Although these tables are very useful for organizing the components of an ANOVA, they are not commonly used in published reports. The current method for reporting the results from an ANOVA is presented on page 409.

MEASURING EFFECT SIZE FOR ANOVA

As we noted previously, a *significant* mean difference simply indicates that the difference observed in the sample data is very unlikely to have occurred just by chance. Thus, the term significant does not necessarily mean *large*, it simply means larger than expected by chance. To provide an indication of how large the effect actually is, researchers should report a measure of effect size in addition to the measure of significance.

For ANOVA, the simplest and most direct way to measure effect size is to compute the percentage of variance accounted for by the treatment conditions. Like the r^2 value used to measure effect size for the t tests in Chapters 9, 10, and 11, this percentage measures how much of the variability in the scores is accounted for by the differences between treatments. For ANOVA, the calculation and the concept of the percentage of variance is extremely straightforward. Specifically, we determine how much of the total *SS* is accounted for by the $SS_{\text{between treatments}}$.

$$\text{The percentage of variance accounted for} = \frac{SS_{\text{between treatments}}}{SS_{\text{total}}} \tag{12.14}$$

For the data in Example 12.1, the percentage of variance accounted for $= \frac{50}{82} = 0.61$ (or 61%).

In published reports of ANOVA results, the percentage of variance accounted for by the treatment effect is usually called η^2 (the Greek letter *eta squared*) instead of using r^2. Thus, for the study in Example 12.1, $\eta^2 = 0.61$.

IN THE LITERATURE

REPORTING THE RESULTS OF ANOVA

The APA format for reporting the results of ANOVA begins with a presentation of the treatment means and standard deviations in the narrative of the article, a table, or a graph. These descriptive statistics are not part of the calculations for the ANOVA, but you can easily determine the treatment means from n and T ($M = T/n$) and the standard deviations from the SS and $n-1$ values for each treatment. Next, report the results of the ANOVA. For the study described in Example 12.1, the report might state the following:

> The means and standard deviations are presented in Table 1. The analysis of variance indicates that there are significant differences among the four viewing distances, $F(3, 16) = 8.33$, $p < .05$, $\eta^2 = 0.61$.
>
> **TABLE 1**
>
> Ratings of satisfaction with different television viewing distances.

	9 Feet	12 Feet	15 Feet	18 Feet
M	1.00	2.00	5.00	4.00
SD	1.41	1.41	1.58	1.22

Note how the F-ratio is reported. In this example, degrees of freedom for between and within treatments are $df = 3, 16$, respectively. These values are placed in parentheses immediately following the symbol F. Next, the calculated value for F is reported, followed by the probability of committing a Type I error (the alpha level) and the measure of effect size.

When an ANOVA is done using a computer program, the F-ratio is usually accompanied by an exact value for p. The data from Example 12.1 were analyzed using the SPSS program (see Resources at the end of this chapter) and the computer output included a significance level of $p = .001$. Using the exact p value from the computer output, the research report would conclude, "The analysis of variance revealed significant differences among the four viewing distances, $F(3, 16) = 8.33$, $p = .001$, $\eta^2 = 0.61$."

A CONCEPTUAL VIEW OF ANOVA

Because ANOVA requires relatively complex calculations, students encountering this statistical technique for the first time often tend to be overwhelmed by the formulas and arithmetic and lose sight of the general purpose for the analysis. The following two examples are intended to minimize the role of the formulas and shift attention back to the conceptual goal of the ANOVA process.

EXAMPLE 12.2 The following data represent the outcome of an experiment using two separate samples to evaluate the mean difference between two treatment conditions. Take a minute to look at the data and, without doing any calculations, try to predict the outcome of an ANOVA for these values. Specifically, predict what values should be obtained for the between-treatments variance (*MS*) and the *F*-ratio. If you do not "see" the answer after 20 or 30 seconds, try reading the hints that follow the data.

Treatment I	Treatment II	
4	2	$N = 8$
0	1	$G = 16$
1	0	$\Sigma X^2 = 56$
3	5	
$T = 8$	$T = 8$	
$SS = 10$	$SS = 14$	

If you are having trouble predicting the outcome of the ANOVA, read the following hints, and then go back and look at the data.

Hint 1: Remember: SS_{between} and MS_{between} provide a measure of how much difference there is between treatment conditions.

Hint 2: Find the mean or total (T) for each treatment, and determine how much difference there is between the two treatments.

You should realize by now that the data have been constructed so that there is zero difference between treatments. The two sample means (and totals) are identical, so $SS_{\text{between}} = 0$, $MS_{\text{between}} = 0$, and the *F*-ratio is zero.

Conceptually, the numerator of the *F*-ratio always measures how much difference exists between treatments. In Example 12.2, we constructed an extreme set of scores with zero difference. However, you should be able to look at any set of data and quickly compare the means (or totals) to determine whether there are big differences or small differences between treatments.

Being able to estimate the magnitude of between-treatment differences is a good first step in understanding ANOVA and should help you to predict the outcome of an ANOVA. However, the *between-treatment* differences are only one part of the analysis. You must also understand the *within-treatment* differences that form the denominator of the *F*-ratio. The following example is intended to demonstrate the concepts underlying SS_{within} and MS_{within}. In addition, the example should give you a better understanding of how the between-treatment differences and the within-treatment differences act together within the ANOVA.

EXAMPLE 12.3 The purpose of this example is to present a visual image for the concepts of between-treatments variability and within-treatments variability. In this example, we compare two hypothetical outcomes for the same experiment. In each case, the experiment uses two separate samples to evaluate the mean difference between two treatments. The following data represent the two outcomes, which we call experiment A and experiment B.

Experiment A		Experiment B	
Treatment		Treatment	
I	II	I	II
8	12	4	12
8	13	11	9
7	12	2	20
9	11	17	6
8	13	0	16
9	12	8	18
7	11	14	3
$M = 8$	$M = 12$	$M = 8$	$M = 12$
$s = 0.82$	$s = 0.82$	$s = 6.35$	$s = 6.35$

The data from experiment A are displayed in a frequency distribution graph in Figure 12.10(a). Notice that there is a 4-point difference between the treatment means ($M_1 = 8$ and $M_2 = 12$). This is the *between-treatments* difference that contributes to the numerator of the F-ratio. Also notice that the scores in each treatment are clustered closely around the mean, indicating that the variance inside each treatment is relatively small. This is the *within-treatments* variance that contributes to the denominator of the F-ratio. Finally, you should realize that it is easy to see the mean difference between the two samples. The fact that there is a clear mean difference between the two treatments is confirmed by computing the F-ratio for experiment A.

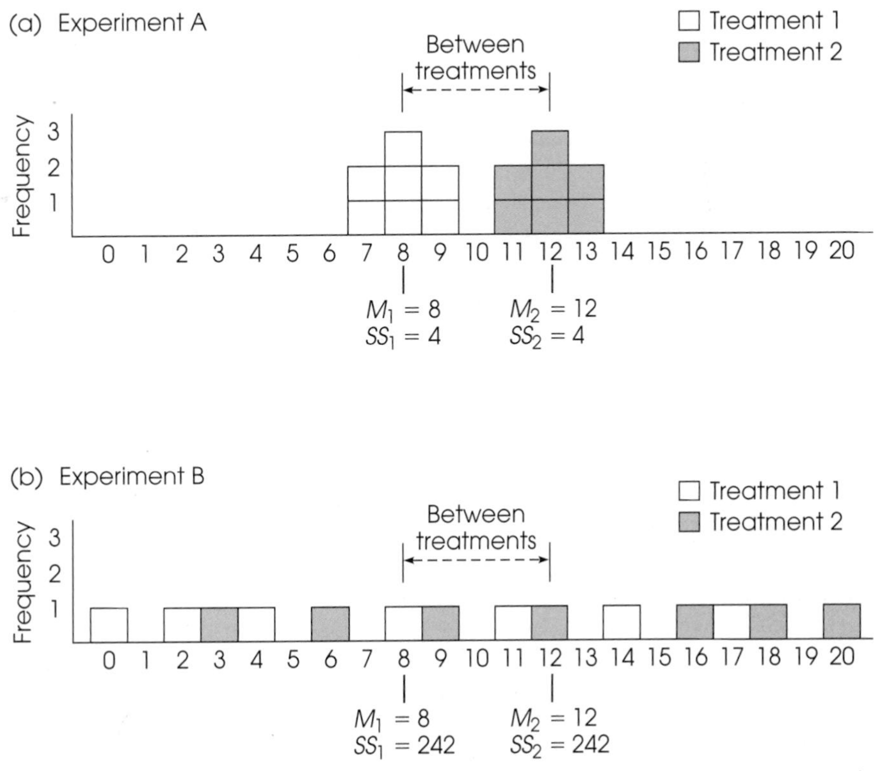

FIGURE 12.10

A visual representation of the between-treatments variability and the within-treatments variability that form the numerator and denominator, respectively, of the F-ratio. In (a), the difference between treatments is relatively large and easy to see. In (b), the same 4-point difference between treatments is relatively small and is overwhelmed by the within-treatments variability.

$$F = \frac{\text{between-treatments difference}}{\text{within-treatments differences}} = \frac{MS_{\text{between}}}{MS_{\text{within}}} = \frac{56}{0.667} = 83.96$$

An F-ratio of $F = 83.96$ is sufficient to reject the null hypothesis, so we conclude that there is a significant difference between the two treatments.

Now consider the data from experiment B, which are shown in Figure 12.10(b) and present a very different picture. This experiment has the same 4-point difference between treatment means that we found in experiment A ($M_1 = 8$ and $M_2 = 12$). However, for these data the scores in each treatment are scattered across the entire scale, indicating relatively large variance inside each treatment. In this case, the large variance within treatments overwhelms the relatively small mean difference between treatments. In the figure it is almost impossible to see the mean difference between treatments. For these data, the F-ratio confirms that there is no clear mean difference between treatments.

$$F = \frac{\text{between-treatments difference}}{\text{within-treatments differences}} = \frac{MS_{\text{between}}}{MS_{\text{within}}} = \frac{56}{40.33} = 1.39$$

For experiment B, the F-ratio is not large enough to reject the null hypothesis, so we conclude that there is no significant difference between the two treatments. Once again, the statistical conclusion is consistent with the appearance of the data in Figure 12.10(b). Looking at the figure, we see that the scores from the two samples appear to be intermixed randomly with no clear distinction between treatments.

As a final point, note that the denominator of the F-ratio, MS_{within}, is a measure of the variability (or variance) within each of the separate samples. As we have noted in previous chapters, high variability makes it difficult to see any patterns in the data. In Figure 12.10(a), the 4-point mean difference between treatments is easy to see because the sample variability is small. In Figure 12.10(b), the 4-point difference gets lost because the sample variability is large. In general, you can think of variance as measuring the amount of "noise" or "confusion" in the data. With large variance, there is a lot of noise and confusion and it is difficult to see any clear patterns.

Although Examples 12.2 and 12.3 present somewhat simplified demonstrations with exaggerated data, the general point of the examples is to help you *see* what happens when you perform an ANOVA. Specifically:

1. The numerator of the F-ratio (MS_{between}) measures how much difference exists between the treatment means. The bigger the mean differences, the bigger the F-ratio.
2. The denominator of the F-ratio (MS_{within}) measures the variance of the scores inside each treatment; that is, the variance for each of the separate samples. In general, larger sample variance produces a smaller F-ratio.

We should note that the number of scores in the samples also can influence the outcome of an ANOVA. As with most other hypothesis tests, if other factors are held constant, increasing the sample size tends to increase the likelihood of rejecting the null hypothesis. However, changes in sample size have little or no effect on measures of effect size such as η^2.

Finally, we should note that the problems associated with high variance often can be minimized by transforming the original scores to ranks and then conducting an alternative statistical analysis known as the *Kruskal-Wallis test,* which is designed specifically for ordinal data. The Kruskal-Wallis test is presented in Appendix E, which also discusses the general purpose and process of converting numerical scores into ranks. The Kruskal-Wallis test also can be used if the data violate one of the assumptions for the independent-measures *ANOVA*, which are outlined at the end of section 12.7.

MS_{within} AND POOLED VARIANCE

You may have recognized that the two research outcomes presented in Example 12.3 are similar to those presented earlier in Example 10.5 in Chapter 10. Both examples are intended to demonstrate the role of variance in a hypothesis test. Both examples show that large values for sample variance can obscure any patterns in the data and reduce the potential for finding significant differences between means.

For the independent-measures t statistic in Chapter 10, the sample variance contributed directly to the standard error in the bottom of the t formula. Now, the sample variance contributes directly to the value of MS_{within} in the bottom of the F-ratio. In the t-statistic and in the F-ratio the variances from the separate samples are pooled together to create one average value for sample variance. For the independent-measures t statistic, we pooled two samples together to compute

$$\text{pooled variance} = s_p^2 = \frac{SS_1 + SS_2}{df_1 + df_2}$$

Now, in ANOVA, we are combining two or more samples to calculate

$$MS_{\text{within}} = \frac{SS_{\text{within}}}{df_{\text{within}}} = \frac{\Sigma SS}{\Sigma df} = \frac{SS_1 + SS_2 + SS_3 + \cdots}{df_1 + df_2 + df_3 + \cdots}$$

Notice that the concept of pooled variance is the same whether you have exactly two samples or more than two samples. In either case, you simply add the *SS* values and divide by the sum of the *df* values. The result is an average of all of the different sample variances.

AN EXAMPLE WITH UNEQUAL SAMPLE SIZES

In the previous examples, all of the samples were exactly the same size (equal *n*s). However, the formulas for ANOVA can be used when the sample size varies within an experiment. You also should note, however, that the general ANOVA procedure is most accurate when used to examine experimental data with equal sample sizes. Therefore, researchers generally try to plan experiments with equal *n*s. However, there are circumstances in which it is impossible or impractical to have an equal number of subjects in every treatment condition. In these situations, ANOVA still provides a valid test, especially when the samples are relatively large and when the discrepancy between sample sizes is not extreme.

The following example demonstrates an ANOVA with samples of different sizes.

EXAMPLE 12.4

A researcher is interested in the amount of homework required by different academic majors. Students are recruited from Biology, English, and Psychology to participant in the study. The researcher randomly selects one course that each student is currently taking and asks the student to record the amount of out-of-class work required each week for the course. The researcher used all of the volunteer participants, which resulted in unequal sample sizes. The data are summarized in Table 12.5.

STEP 1: State the hypotheses, and select the alpha level.

$$H_0\colon \mu_1 = \mu_2 = \mu_3$$

H_1: At least one population is different.

$$\alpha = .05$$

STEP 2: Locate the critical region.

To find the critical region, we first must determine the *df* values for the *F*-ratio:

$$df_{\text{total}} = N - 1 = 20 - 1 = 19$$

$$df_{\text{between}} = k - 1 = 3 - 1 = 2$$

$$df_{\text{within}} = N - k = 20 - 3 = 17$$

The *F*-ratio for these data has $df = 2, 17$. With $\alpha = .05$, the critical value for the *F*-ratio is 3.59.

STEP 3: Compute the *F*-ratio.

First, compute the three *SS* values. As usual, SS_{total} is the *SS* for the total set of $N = 20$ scores, and SS_{within} combines the *SS* values from inside each of the treatment conditions.

$$SS_{\text{total}} = \Sigma X^2 - \frac{G^2}{N}$$

$$= 3377 - \frac{250^2}{20}$$

$$= 3377 - 3125$$

$$= 252$$

$$SS_{\text{within}} = \Sigma SS_{\text{inside each treatment}}$$

$$= 37 + 90 + 60$$

$$= 187$$

SS_{between} can be found by subtraction (Equation 12.5).

$$SS_{\text{between}} = SS_{\text{total}} - SS_{\text{within}}$$

$$= 252 - 187$$

$$= 65$$

TABLE 12.5

Average hours of homework per week for one course for students in three academic majors.

Biology	English	Psychology	
$n = 4$	$n = 10$	$n = 6$	$N = 20$
$M = 9$	$M = 13$	$M = 14$	$G = 250$
$T = 36$	$T = 130$	$T = 84$	$\Sigma X^2 = 3377$
$SS = 37$	$SS = 90$	$SS = 60$	

Or, SS_{between} can be calculated using the computation formula (Equation 12.7). If you use the computational formula, be careful to match each treatment total (T) with the appropriate sample size (n) as follows:

$$\begin{aligned} SS_{\text{between}} &= \Sigma\frac{T^2}{n} - \frac{G^2}{N} \\ &= \frac{36^2}{4} + \frac{130^2}{10} + \frac{84^2}{6} - \frac{250^2}{20} \\ &= 324 + 1690 + 1176 - 3125 \\ &= 65 \end{aligned}$$

Finally, compute the MS values and the F-ratio:

$$MS_{\text{between}} = \frac{SS}{df} = \frac{65}{2} = 32.5$$

$$MS_{\text{within}} = \frac{SS}{df} = \frac{187}{17} = 11$$

$$F = \frac{MS_{\text{between}}}{MS_{\text{within}}} = \frac{32.5}{11} = 2.95$$

STEP 4: Make a decision.

Because the obtained F-ratio is not in the critical region, we fail to reject the null hypothesis and conclude that there are no significant differences among the three populations of students in terms of the average amount of homework each week.

LEARNING CHECK

1. A researcher used ANOVA and computed $F = 4.25$ for the following data.

Treatments		
I	II	III
$n =$ 10	$n =$ 10	$n =$ 10
$M =$ 20	$M =$ 28	$M =$ 35
$SS =$ 1005	$SS =$ 1391	$SS =$ 1180

   a. If the mean for treatment III were changed to $M = 25$, what would happen to the size of the F-ratio (increase or decrease)? Explain your answer.

   b. If the SS for treatment I were changed to $SS = 1400$, what would happen to the size of the F-ratio (increase or decrease)? Explain your answer.

2. A research study comparing three treatment conditions produces $T = 20$ with $n = 4$ for the first treatment, $T = 10$ with $n = 5$ for the second treatment, and $T = 30$ with $n = 6$ for the third treatment. Calculate $SS_{\text{between treatments}}$ for these data.

ANSWERS

1. **a.** If the mean for treatment III were changed to $M = 25$, it would reduce the size of the mean differences (the three means would be closer together). This would reduce the size of MS_{between} and would reduce the size of the F-ratio.

   b. If the SS in treatment I were increased to $SS = 1400$, it would increase the size of the variability within treatments. This would increase MS_{within} and would reduce the size of the F-ratio.

2. With $G = 60$ and $N = 15$, $SS_{\text{between}} = 30$.

12.6 POST HOC TESTS

As noted earlier, the primary advantage of ANOVA (compared to t tests) is that it allows researchers to test for significant mean differences when there are *more than two* treatment conditions. ANOVA accomplishes this feat by comparing all the individual mean differences simultaneously within a single test. Unfortunately, the process of combining several mean differences into a single test statistic creates some difficulty when it is time to interpret the outcome of the test. Specifically, when you obtain a significant F-ratio (reject H_0), it simply indicates that somewhere among the entire set of mean differences there is at least one that is statistically significant. In other words, the overall F-ratio only tells you that a significant difference exists; it does not tell exactly which means are significantly different and which are not.

Consider, for example, a research study that uses three samples to compare three treatment conditions. Suppose that the three sample means are $M_1 = 3$, $M_2 = 5$, and $M_3 = 10$. In this hypothetical study there are three mean differences:

1. There is a 2-point difference between M_1 and M_2.
2. There is a 5-point difference between M_2 and M_3.
3. There is a 7-point difference between M_1 and M_3.

If an ANOVA were used to evaluate these data, a significant F-ratio would indicate that at least one of the sample mean differences is large enough to satisfy the criterion of statistical significance. In this example, the 7-point difference is the biggest of the three and, therefore, it must indicate a significant difference between the first treatment and the third treatment ($\mu_1 \neq \mu_3$). But what about the 5-point difference? Is it also large enough to be significant? And what about the 2-point difference between M_1 and M_2? Is it also significant? The purpose of *post hoc tests* is to answer these questions.

DEFINITION

Post hoc tests (or **posttests**) are additional hypothesis tests that are done after an ANOVA to determine exactly which mean differences are significant and which are not.

As the name implies, post hoc tests are done after an ANOVA. More specifically, these tests are done after ANOVA when

1. You reject H_0 and
2. There are three or more treatments ($k \geq 3$).

Rejecting H_0 indicates that at least one difference exists among the treatments. If there are only two treatments, then there is no question about which means are different and, therefore, no need for posttests. However, with three or more treatments ($k \geq 3$), the problem is to determine exactly which means are significantly different.

POSTTESTS AND TYPE I ERRORS

In general, a post hoc test enables you to go back through the data and compare the individual treatments two at a time. In statistical terms, this is called making *pairwise comparisons*. For example, with $k = 3$, we would compare μ_1 versus μ_2, then μ_2 versus μ_3, and then μ_1 versus μ_3. In each case, we are looking for a significant mean difference. The process of conducting pairwise comparisons involves performing a series of separate hypothesis tests, and each of these tests includes the risk of a Type I error. As you do more and more separate tests, the risk of a Type I error accumulates and is called the *experimentwise alpha level* (see p. 391).

We have seen, for example, that a research study with three treatment conditions produces three separate mean differences, each of which could be evaluated using a post hoc test. If each test uses $\alpha = .05$, then there is a 5% risk of a Type I error for the first posttest, another 5% risk for the second test, and one more 5% risk for the third test. Although the probability of error is not simply the sum across the three tests, it should be clear that increasing the number of separate tests definitely increases the total, experimentwise probability of a Type I error.

Whenever you are conducting posttests, you must be concerned about the experimentwise alpha level. Statisticians have worked with this problem and have developed several methods for trying to control Type I errors in the context of post hoc tests. We consider two alternatives.

TUKEY'S HONESTLY SIGNIFICANT DIFFERENCE (HSD) TEST

The first post hoc test we consider is *Tukey's HSD test.* We selected Tukey's HSD test because it is a commonly used test in psychological research. Tukey's test allows you to compute a single value that determines the minimum difference between treatment means that is necessary for significance. This value, called the *honestly significant difference,* or HSD, is then used to compare any two treatment conditions. If the mean difference exceeds Tukey's HSD, then you conclude that there is a significant difference between the treatments. Otherwise, you cannot conclude that the treatments are significantly different. The formula for Tukey's HSD is

$$HSD = q\sqrt{\frac{MS_{\text{within}}}{n}} \qquad (12.15)$$

The q value used in Tukey's HSD test is called a Studentized range statistic.

where the value of q is found in Table B.5 (Appendix B, p. 708), MS_{within} is the within-treatments variance from the ANOVA, and n is the number of scores in each treatment. Tukey's test requires that the sample size, n, be the same for all treatments. To locate the appropriate value of q, you must know the number of treatments in the overall experiment (k), the degrees of freedom for MS_{within} (the error term in the F-ratio), and you must select an alpha level (generally the same α used for the ANOVA).

EXAMPLE 12.5

To demonstrate the procedure for conducting post hoc tests with Tukey's HSD, we use the hypothetical data shown in Table 12.6. The data represent the results of a study comparing scores in three different treatment conditions. Note that the table displays summary statistics for each sample and the results from the overall ANOVA. With $k = 3$ treatments, $df_{\text{within}} = 24$, and $\alpha = .05$, you should find that the value of q for the test is $q = 3.53$ (see Table B.5). Therefore, Tukey's HSD is

$$HSD = q\sqrt{\frac{MS_{\text{within}}}{n}} = 3.53\sqrt{\frac{4.00}{9}} = 2.36$$

TABLE 12.6

Hypothetical results from a research study comparing three treatment conditions. Summary statistics are presented for each treatment along with the outcome from the ANOVA.

Treatment A	Treatment B	Treatment C
$n = 9$	$n = 9$	$n = 9$
$T = 27$	$T = 49$	$T = 63$
$M = 3.00$	$M = 5.44$	$M = 7.00$

Source	*SS*	*df*	*MS*
Between	73.19	2	36.60
Within	96.00	24	4.00
Total	169.19	26	
Overall $F(2, 24) = 9.15$			

Thus, the mean difference between any two samples must be at least 2.36 to be significant. Using this value, we can make the following conclusions:

1. Treatment A is significantly different from treatment B ($M_A - M_B = 2.44$).
2. Treatment A is also significantly different from treatment C ($M_A - M_C = 4.00$).
3. Treatment B is not significantly different from treatment C ($M_B - M_C = 1.56$).

THE SCHEFFÉ TEST

Because it uses an extremely cautious method for reducing the risk of a Type I error, the *Scheffé test* has the distinction of being one of the safest of all possible post hoc tests (smallest risk of a Type I error). The Scheffé test uses an F-ratio to evaluate the significance of the difference between any two treatment conditions. The numerator of the F-ratio is an MS_{between} that is calculated using *only the two treatments you want to compare*. The denominator is the same MS_{within} that was used for the overall ANOVA. The "safety factor" for the Scheffé test comes from the following two considerations:

1. Although you are comparing only two treatments, the Scheffé test uses the value of k from the original experiment to compute df between treatments. Thus, df for the numerator of the F-ratio is $k - 1$.
2. The critical value for the Scheffé F-ratio is the same as was used to evaluate the F-ratio from the overall ANOVA. Thus, Scheffé requires that every posttest satisfy the same criterion that was used for the complete ANOVA. The following example uses the data from Table 12.6 to demonstrate the Scheffé posttest procedure.

EXAMPLE 12.6

Remember that the Scheffé procedure requires a separate SS_{between}, MS_{between}, and F-ratio for each comparison being made. Although Scheffé computes SS_{between} using the regular computational formula (Equation 12.7), you must remember that all of the numbers in the formula are entirely determined by the two treatment conditions being compared. We begin by comparing treatment A (with $T = 27$ and $n = 9$) and treatment B (with $T = 49$ and $n = 9$). The first step is to compute SS_{between} for these two groups. In the formula for SS, notice that the grand total for the two groups is $G = 27 + 49 = 76$, and the total number of scores for the two groups is $N = 9 + 9 = 18$.

$$\begin{aligned} SS_{\text{between}} &= \Sigma\frac{T^2}{n} - \frac{G^2}{N} \\ &= \frac{27^2}{9} + \frac{49^2}{9} - \frac{76^2}{18} \\ &= 81 + 266.78 - 320.89 \\ &= 26.89 \end{aligned}$$

Although we are comparing only two groups, these two were selected from a study consisting of $k = 3$ samples. The Scheffé test uses the overall study to determine the degrees of freedom between treatments. Therefore, $df_{\text{between}} = 3 - 1 = 2$, and the MS_{between} is

$$MS_{\text{between}} = \frac{SS_{\text{between}}}{df_{\text{between}}} = \frac{26.89}{2} = 13.45$$

Finally, the Scheffé procedure uses the error term from the overall ANOVA to compute the F-ratio. In this case, $MS_{\text{within}} = 4.00$ with $df_{\text{within}} = 24$. Thus, the Scheffé test produces an F-ratio of

$$F_{\text{A verus B}} = \frac{MS_{\text{between}}}{MS_{\text{within}}} = \frac{13.45}{4.00} = 3.36$$

With $df = 2, 24$ and $\alpha = .05$, the critical value for F is 3.40 (see Table B.4). Therefore, our obtained F-ratio is not in the critical region, and we must conclude that these data show no significant difference between treatment A and treatment B.

The second comparison involves treatment B ($T = 49$) and treatment C ($T = 63$). This time the data produce $SS_{\text{between}} = 10.89$, $MS_{\text{between}} = 5.45$, and $F(2, 24) = 1.36$ (check the calculations for yourself). Once again the critical value for F is 3.40, so we must conclude that the data show no significant difference between treatment B and treatment C.

The final comparison is treatment A ($T = 27$) and treatment C ($T = 63$). This time the data produce $SS_{\text{between}} = 72$, $MS_{\text{between}} = 36$, and $F(2, 24) = 9.00$ (check the calculations for yourself). Once again the critical value for F is 3.40, and this time we conclude that the data show a significant difference.

Thus, the Scheffé posttest indicates that the only significant difference is between treatment A and treatment C.

There are two interesting points to be made from the posttest outcomes presented in the preceding two examples. First, the Scheffé test was introduced as being one of the safest of the posttest techniques because it provides the greatest protection from Type I errors. To provide this protection, the Scheffé test simply requires a larger difference between sample means before you may conclude that the difference is significant. For example, using Tukey's test in Example 12.5, we found that the difference between treatment A and treatment B was large enough to be significant. However, this same difference failed to reach significance according to the Scheffé test (Example 12.6). The discrepancy between the results is an example of the Scheffé test's extra demands: The Scheffé test simply requires more evidence and, therefore, it is less likely to lead to a Type I error.

The second point concerns the pattern of results from the three Scheffé tests in Example 12.6. You may have noticed that the posttests produce what are apparently contradictory results. Specifically, the tests show no significant difference between A and B and they show no significant difference between B and C. This combination of outcomes might lead you to suspect that there is no significant difference between A and C. However, the test did show a significant difference. The answer to this apparent contradiction lies in the criterion of statistical significance. The differences between A and B and between B and C are too small to satisfy the criterion of significance. However, when these differences are combined, the total difference between A and C is large enough to meet the criterion for significance.

LEARNING CHECK

1. With $k = 2$ treatments, are post hoc tests necessary when the null hypothesis is rejected? Explain why or why not.

2. An ANOVA comparing three treatments produces an overall F-ratio with $df = 2, 27$. If the Scheffé test was used to compare two of the three treatments, then the Scheffé F-ratio would also have $df = 2, 27$. (True or false?)

3. Using the data and the results from Example 12.1,
   a. Use Tukey's HSD test to determine whether there is a significant mean difference between a 12-foot and a 15-foot distance. Use $\alpha = .05$.
   b. Use the Scheffé test to determine whether there is a significant mean difference between 12 feet and 15 feet. Use $\alpha = .05$.

ANSWERS

1. No. Post hoc tests are used to determine which treatments are different. With only two treatment conditions, there is no uncertainty as to which two treatments are different.
2. True
3. a. For this test, $q = 4.05$ and HSD $= 2.55$. There is a 3-point mean difference between 12 feet and 15 feet, which is large enough to be significant.
   b. The Scheffé $F = 3.75$, which is greater than the critical value of 3.24. Conclude that the mean difference between 12 feet and 15 feet is significant.

12.7 THE RELATIONSHIP BETWEEN ANOVA AND *t* TESTS

When you are evaluating the mean difference from an independent-measures study comparing only two treatments (two separate samples), you can use either an independent-measures *t* test (Chapter 10) or the ANOVA presented in this chapter. In practical terms, it makes no difference which you choose. These two statistical techniques always result in the same statistical decision. In fact the two methods use many of the same calculations and are very closely related in several other respects. The basic relationship between *t* statistics and *F*-ratios can be stated in an equation:

$$F = t^2$$

This relationship can be explained by first looking at the structure of the formulas for *F* and *t*. The *t* statistic compares *distances*: the distance between two sample means (numerator) and the distance computed for the standard error (denominator). The *F*-ratio, on the other hand, compares *variances*. You should recall that variance is a measure of squared distance. Hence, the relationship: $F = t^2$.

There are several other points to consider in comparing the *t* statistic to the *F*-ratio.

1. It should be obvious that you are testing the same hypotheses whether you choose a *t* test or an ANOVA. With only two treatments, the hypotheses for either test are

$$H_0: \mu_1 = \mu_2$$

$$H_1: \mu_1 \neq \mu_2$$

2. The degrees of freedom for the *t* statistic and the *df* for the denominator of the *F*-ratio (df_{within}) are identical. For example, if you have two samples, each with six scores, the independent-measures *t* statistic has $df = 10$, and the *F*-ratio has $df = 1, 10$. In each case, you are adding the *df* from the first sample $(n - 1)$ and the *df* from the second sample $(n - 1)$.
3. The distribution of *t* and the distribution of *F*-ratios match perfectly if you take into consideration the relationship $F = t^2$. Consider the *t* distribution with $df = 18$ and the corresponding *F* distribution with $df = 1, 18$ that are presented in Figure 12.11. Notice the following relationships:
   a. If each of the *t* values is squared, then all of the negative values become positive. As a result, the whole left-hand side of the *t* distribution (below

FIGURE 12.11

The distribution of t statistics with $df = 18$ and the corresponding distribution of F-ratios with $df = 1, 18$. Notice that the critical values for $\alpha = .05$ are $t = \pm 2.101$ and that $F = 2.101^2 = 4.41$.

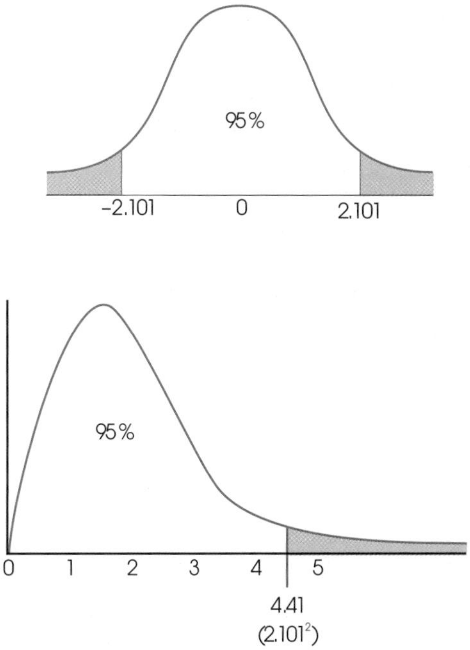

zero) is flipped over to the positive side. This creates an asymmetrical, positively skewed distribution—that is, the F distribution.

b. For $\alpha = .05$, the critical region for t is determined by values greater than $+2.101$ or less than -2.101. When these boundaries are squared, you get $\pm 2.101^2 = 4.41$

Notice that 4.41 is the critical value for $\alpha = .05$ in the F distribution. Any value that is in the critical region for t ends up in the critical region for F-ratios after it is squared.

ASSUMPTIONS FOR THE INDEPENDENT-MEASURES ANOVA

The independent-measures ANOVA requires the same three assumptions that were necessary for the independent-measures t hypothesis test:

1. The observations within each sample must be independent (see p. 254).
2. The populations from which the samples are selected must be normal.
3. The populations from which the samples are selected must have equal variances (homogeneity of variance).

Ordinarily, researchers are not overly concerned with the assumption of normality, especially when large samples are used, unless there are strong reasons to suspect that the assumption has not been satisfied. The assumption of homogeneity of variance is an important one. If a researcher suspects that it has been violated, it can be tested by Hartley's F-max test for homogeneity of variance (Chapter 10, p. 338).

Finally, if you suspect that one of the assumptions for the independent-measures ANOVA has been violated, you can still proceed by transforming the original scores into ranks and then using an alternative statistical analysis known as the Kruskal-Wallis test, which is designed specifically for ordinal data. The Kruskal-Wallis test is presented in Appendix E. As noted earlier, the Kruskal-Wallis test also can be useful if large sample variance prevents the independent-measures ANOVA from producing a significant result.

LEARNING CHECK

1. A researcher uses an independent-measures *t* test to evaluate the mean difference obtained in a research study, and obtains a *t* statistic of $t = 3.00$. If the researcher had used an ANOVA to evaluate the results, the *F*-ratio would be $F = 9.00$. (True or false?)
2. An ANOVA produces an *F*-ratio with $df = 1, 34$. Could the data have been analyzed with a *t* test? What would be the degrees of freedom for the *t* statistic?

ANSWERS

1. True. $F = t^2$
2. If the *F*-ratio has $df = 1, 34$, then the experiment compared only two treatments, and you could use a *t* statistic to evaluate the data. The *t* statistic would have $df = 34$.

SUMMARY

1. Analysis of variance (ANOVA) is a statistical technique that is used to test the significance of mean differences among two or more treatment conditions. The null hypothesis for this test states that, in the general population, there are no mean differences among the treatments. The alternative states that at least one mean is different from another.
2. The test statistic for ANOVA is a ratio of two variances called an *F*-ratio. The variances in the *F*-ratio are called mean squares, or *MS* values. Each *MS* is computed by

$$MS = \frac{SS}{df}$$

3. For the independent-measures ANOVA, the *F*-ratio is

$$F = \frac{MS_{\text{between}}}{MS_{\text{within}}}$$

The MS_{between} measures differences between the treatments by computing the variability of the treatment means or totals. These differences are assumed to be produced by

a. Treatment effects (if they exist)
b. Random, unsystematic differences (chance)

The MS_{within} measures variability inside each of the treatment conditions. Because individuals inside a treatment condition are all treated exactly the same, any differences within treatments cannot be caused by treatment effects. Thus, the within-treatments *MS* is produced only by random, unsystematic differences. With these factors in mind, the *F*-ratio has the following structure:

$$F = \frac{\text{treatment effect} + \text{differences due to chance}}{\text{differences due to chance}}$$

When there is no treatment effect (H_0 is true), the numerator and the denominator of the *F*-ratio are measuring the same variance, and the obtained ratio should be near 1.00. If there is a significant treatment effect, then the numerator of the ratio should be larger than the denominator, and the obtained *F* value should be much greater than 1.00.

4. The formulas for computing each *SS*, *df*, and *MS* value are presented in Figure 12.12, which also shows the general structure for the ANOVA.
5. The *F*-ratio has two values for degrees of freedom, one associated with the *MS* in the numerator and one associated with the *MS* in the denominator. These *df* values are used to find the critical value for the *F*-ratio in the *F* distribution table.
6. Effect size for the independent-measures ANOVA is measured by computing eta squared, the percentage of variance accounted for by the treatment effect.

FIGURE 12.12
Formulas for ANOVA.

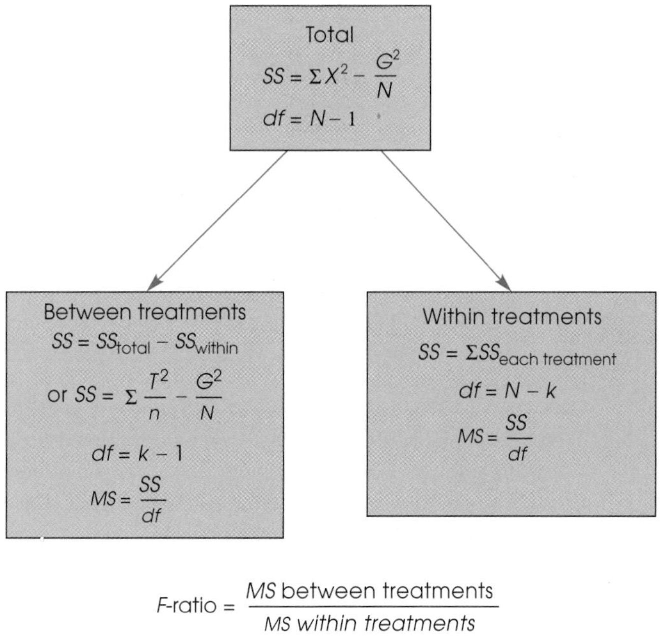

$$\eta^2 = \frac{SS_{\text{between}}}{SS_{\text{between}} + SS_{\text{within}}} = \frac{SS_{\text{between}}}{SS_{\text{total}}}$$

7. When the decision from an ANOVA is to reject the null hypothesis and when the experiment contains more than two treatment conditions, it is necessary to continue the analysis with a post hoc test, such as Tukey's HSD test or the Scheffé test. The purpose of these tests is to determine exactly which treatments are significantly different and which are not.

KEY TERMS

analysis of variance (ANOVA) (386)
factor (388)
levels (388)
testwise alpha level (391)
experimentwise alpha level (391)
between-treatments variance (392)
treatment effect (393)
within-treatments variance (393)
F-ratio (394)
error term (394)
mean square (*MS*) (401)
ANOVA summary table (402)
distribution of *F*-ratios (403)
eta squared (η^2) (408)
Kruskal-Wallis test (413)
post hoc tests (416)
pairwise comparisons (416)
Tukey's HSD test (417)
Scheffé test (418)

RESOURCES

Book Companion Website: www.cengage.com/psychology/gravetter.
You can find a tutorial quiz and other learning exercises for Chapter 12 on the book companion website.

aplia

Improve your understanding of statistics with Aplia's auto-graded problem sets and immediate, detailed explanations for every question. To learn more, visit **www.aplia.com/statistics**.

CENGAGE brain.com

Psychology CourseMate brings course concepts to life with interactive learning, study, and exam preparation tools that support the printed textbook. A textbook-specific website, Psychology CourseMate includes an integrated interactive eBook and other interactive learning tools including quizzes, flashcards, and more.

Visit www.cengagebrain.com to access your account and purchase materials.

SPSS

General instructions for using SPSS are presented in Appendix D. Following are detailed instructions for using SPSS to perform **The Single-Factor, Independent-Measures Analysis of Variance (ANOVA)** presented in this chapter.

Data Entry

1. The scores are entered in a *stacked format* in the data editor, which means that all of the scores from all of the different treatments are entered in a single column (VAR00001). Enter the scores for treatment #2 directly beneath the scores from treatment #1 with no gaps or extra spaces. Continue in the same column with the scores from treatment #3, and so on.
2. In the second column (VAR00002), enter a number to identify the treatment condition for each score. For example, enter a 1 beside each score from the first treatment, enter a 2 beside each score from the second treatment, and so on.

Data Analysis

1. Click **Analyze** on the tool bar, select **Compare Means,** and click on **One-Way ANOVA.**
2. Highlight the column label for the set of scores (VAR0001) in the left box and click the arrow to move it into the **Dependent List** box.
3. Highlight the label for the column containing the treatment numbers (VAR0002) in the left box and click the arrow to move it into the **Factor** box.
4. If you want descriptive statistics for each treatment, click on the **Options** box, select **Descriptives,** and click **Continue.**
5. Click **OK.**

SPSS Output

We used the SPSS program to analyze the data from the television viewing study in Example 12.1 and the program output is shown in Figure 12.13. The output begins with a table showing descriptive statistics (number of scores, mean, standard deviation, standard error for the mean, a 95% confidence interval for the mean, maximum and minimum scores) for each sample. The second part of the output presents a summary table showing the results from the ANOVA.

FOCUS ON PROBLEM SOLVING

1. It can be helpful to compute all three *SS* values separately, then check to verify that the two components (between and within) add up to the total. However, you can

Descriptives

VAR00001

	N	Mean	Std. Deviation	Std. Error	95% Confidence Interval for Mean		Minimum	Maximum
					Lower Bound	Upper Bound		
1.00	5	1.0000	1.41421	.63246	−.7560	2.7560	.00	3.00
2.00	5	2.0000	1.41421	.63246	.2440	3.7560	1.00	4.00
3.00	5	5.0000	1.58114	.70711	3.0368	6.9632	3.00	7.00
4.00	5	4.0000	1.22474	.54772	2.4793	5.5207	3.00	6.00
Total	20	3.0000	2.07745	.46453	2.0277	3.9723	.00	7.00

ANOVA

VAR00001

	Sum of Squares	df	Mean Square	F	Sig.
Between Groups	50.000	3	16.667	8.333	.001
Within Groups	32.000	16	2.000		
Total	82.000	19			

FIGURE 12.13

SPSS output of the ANOVA for the television-viewing distance study in Example 12.1.

greatly simplify the calculations if you simply find SS_{total} and SS_{within}, then obtain $SS_{between}$ by subtraction.

2. Remember that an F-ratio has two separate values for df: a value for the numerator and one for the denominator. Properly reported, the $df_{between}$ value is stated first. You will need both df values when consulting the F distribution table for the critical F value. You should recognize immediately that an error has been made if you see an F-ratio reported with a single value for df.

3. When you encounter an F-ratio and its df values reported in the literature, you should be able to reconstruct much of the original experiment. For example, if you see "$F(2, 36) = 4.80$," you should realize that the experiment compared $k = 3$ treatment groups (because $df_{between} = k - 1 = 2$), with a total of $N = 39$ subjects participating in the experiment (because $df_{within} = N - k = 36$).

DEMONSTRATION 12.1

ANALYSIS OF VARIANCE

A human-factors psychologist studied three computer keyboard designs. Three samples of individuals were given material to type on a particular keyboard, and the number of errors committed by each participant was recorded. The data are as follows:

Keyboard A	Keyboard B	Keyboard C	
0	6	6	$N = 15$
4	8	5	$G = 60$
0	5	9	$\Sigma X^2 = 356$
1	4	4	
0	2	6	
$T = 5$	$T = 25$	$T = 30$	
$SS = 12$	$SS = 20$	$SS = 14$	

Are these data sufficient to conclude that there are significant differences in typing performance among the three keyboard designs?

STEP 1 **State the hypotheses, and specify the alpha level.** The null hypothesis states that there is no difference among the keyboards in terms of number of errors committed. In symbols, we would state

$$H_0: \mu_1 = \mu_2 = \mu_3 \qquad \text{(Type of keyboard used has no effect.)}$$

As noted previously in this chapter, there are a number of possible statements for the alternative hypothesis. Here we state the general alternative hypothesis:

H_1: At least one of the treatment means is different.

We set alpha at $\alpha = .05$.

STEP 2 **Locate the critical region.** To locate the critical region, we must obtain the values for $df_{between}$ and df_{within}.

$$df_{\text{between}} = k - 1 = 3 - 1 = 2$$

$$df_{\text{within}} = N - k = 15 - 3 = 12$$

The F-ratio for this problem has $df = 2, 12$, and the critical F value for $\alpha = .05$ is $F = 3.88$.

STEP 3 **Perform the analysis.** The analysis involves the following steps:

1. Perform the analysis of SS.
2. Perform the analysis of df.
3. Calculate mean squares.
4. Calculate the F-ratio.

Perform the analysis of SS. We compute SS_{total} followed by its two components.

$$SS_{\text{total}} = \Sigma X^2 - \frac{G^2}{N} = 356 - \frac{60^2}{15} = 356 - \frac{3600}{15}$$
$$= 356 - 240 = 116$$

$$SS_{\text{within}} = \Sigma SS_{\text{inside each treatment}}$$
$$= 12 + 20 + 14$$
$$= 46$$

$$SS_{\text{between}} = \Sigma\frac{T^2}{n} - \frac{G^2}{N}$$
$$= \frac{5^2}{5} + \frac{25^2}{5} + \frac{30^2}{5} - \frac{60^2}{15}$$
$$= \frac{25}{5} + \frac{625}{5} + \frac{900}{5} - \frac{3600}{15}$$
$$= 5 + 125 + 180 - 240$$
$$= 70$$

Analyze degrees of freedom. We compute df_{total}. Its components, df_{between} and df_{within}, were previously calculated (see step 2).

$$df_{\text{total}} = N - 1 = 15 - 1 = 14$$

$$df_{\text{between}} = 2$$

$$df_{\text{within}} = 12$$

Calculate the MS values. We determine the values for MS_{between} and MS_{within}.

$$MS_{\text{between}} = \frac{SS_{\text{between}}}{df_{\text{between}}} = \frac{70}{2} = 35$$

$$MS_{\text{within}} = \frac{SS_{\text{within}}}{df_{\text{within}}} = \frac{46}{12} = 3.83$$

Compute the F-ratio. Finally, we can compute F.

$$F = \frac{MS_{\text{between}}}{MS_{\text{within}}} = \frac{35}{3.83} = 9.14$$

STEP 4 **Make a decision about H_0, and state a conclusion.** The obtained F of 9.14 exceeds the critical value of 3.88. Therefore, we can reject the null hypothesis. The type of keyboard used has a significant effect on the number of errors committed, $F(2, 12) = 9.14, p < .05$. The following table summarizes the results of the analysis:

Source	*SS*	*df*	*MS*	
Between treatments	70	2	35	$F = 9.14$
Within treatments	46	12	3.83	
Total	116	14		

DEMONSTRATION 12.2

COMPUTING EFFECT SIZE FOR ANOVA

We compute eta squared (η^2), the percentage of variance explained, for the data that were analyzed in Demonstration 12.1. The data produced a between-treatments *SS* of 70 and a total *SS* of 116. Thus,

$$\eta^2 = \frac{SS_{\text{between}}}{SS_{\text{total}}} = \frac{70}{116} = 0.60 \text{ (or 60\%)}$$

PROBLEMS

1. Explain why the F-ratio is expected to be near 1.00 when the null hypothesis is true.
2. Why should you use ANOVA instead of several t tests to evaluate mean differences when an experiment consists of three or more treatment conditions?
3. Several factors influence the size of the F-ratio. For each of the following, indicate whether it would influence the numerator or the denominator of the F-ratio, and indicate whether the size of the F-ratio would increase or decrease.
   a. Increase the differences between the sample means.
   b. Increase the size of the sample variances.
4. Describe the similarities between an F-ratio and a t statistic.
5. Posttests are done after an ANOVA.
   a. What is the purpose of posttests?
   b. Explain why you do not need posttests if the analysis is comparing only two treatments.
   c. Explain why you do not need posttests if the decision from the ANOVA is to fail to reject the null hypothesis.
6. An independent-measures research study compares three treatment conditions with a sample of $n = 10$ in each condition. The sample means are $M_1 = 2$, $M_2 = 3$, and $M_3 = 7$.
   a. Compute *SS* for the set of 3 treatment means. (Use the three means as a set of $n = 3$ scores and compute *SS*.)
   b. Using the result from part a, compute $n(SS_{\text{means}})$. Note that this value is equal to SS_{between} (see Equation 12.6).
   c. Now, compute SS_{between} with the computational formula using the T values (Equation 12.7). You should obtain the same result as in part b.
7. The following data summarize the results from an independent-measures study comparing three treatment conditions.

I	II	III	
$n = 6$	$n = 6$	$n = 6$	
$M = 1$	$M = 5$	$M = 6$	$N = 18$
$T = 6$	$T = 30$	$T = 36$	$G = 72$
$SS = 30$	$SS = 35$	$SS = 40$	$\Sigma X^2 = 477$

a. Use an ANOVA with $\alpha = .05$ to determine whether there are any significant differences among the three treatment means.
b. Calculate η^2 to measure the effect size for this study.
c. Write a sentence demonstrating how a research report would present the results of the hypothesis test and the measure of effect size.

8. There is some evidence that high school students justify cheating in class on the basis of poor teacher skills or low levels of teacher caring (Murdock, Miller, and Kohlhardt, 2004). Students appear to rationalize their illicit behavior based on perceptions of how their teachers view cheating. Poor teachers are thought not to know or care whether students cheat, so cheating in their classes is okay. Good teachers, on the other hand, do care and are alert to cheating, so students tend not to cheat in their classes. Following are hypothetical data similar to the actual research results. The scores represent judgments of the acceptability of cheating for the students in each sample.

Poor Teacher	Average Teacher	Good Teacher	
$n = 6$	$n = 8$	$n = 10$	$N = 24$
$M = 6$	$M = 2$	$M = 2$	$G = 72$
$SS = 30$	$SS = 33$	$SS = 42$	$\Sigma X^2 = 393$

a. Use an ANOVA with $\alpha = .05$ to determine whether there are significant differences in student judgments depending on how they see their teachers.
b. Calculate η^2 to measure the effect size for this study.
c. Write a sentence demonstrating how a research report would present the results of the hypothesis test and the measure of effect size.

9. The following data summarize the results from an independent-measures study comparing three treatment conditions.

I	II	III	
$n = 5$	$n = 5$	$n = 5$	
$M = 2$	$M = 5$	$M = 8$	$N = 15$
$T = 10$	$T = 25$	$T = 40$	$G = 75$
$SS = 16$	$SS = 20$	$SS = 24$	$\Sigma X^2 = 525$

a. Calculate the sample variance for each of the three samples.
b. Use an ANOVA with $\alpha = .05$ to determine whether there are any significant differences among the three treatment means.

10. For the preceding problem you should find that there are significant differences among the three treatments. One reason for the significance is that the sample variances are relatively small. To create the following data, we started with the values from problem 9 and increased the variability (the *SS* values) within each sample.

I	II	III	
$n = 5$	$n = 5$	$n = 5$	
$M = 2$	$M = 5$	$M = 8$	$N = 15$
$T = 10$	$T = 25$	$T = 40$	$G = 75$
$SS = 64$	$SS = 80$	$SS = 96$	$\Sigma X^2 = 705$

a. Calculate the sample variance for each of the three samples. Describe how these sample variances compare with those from problem 9.
b. Predict how the increase in sample variance should influence the outcome of the analysis. That is, how will the *F*-ratio for these data compare with the value obtained in problem 9?
c. Use an ANOVA with $\alpha = .05$ to determine whether there are any significant differences among the three treatment means. (Does your answer agree with your prediction in part b?)

11. Binge drinking on college campuses has been a hot topic in the popular media and in scholarly research. Flett, Goldstein, Wall, Hewitt, Wekerle, and Azzi (2008) report the results of a study relating perfectionism to binge drinking. In the study, students were classified into three groups based on the number of binge drinking episodes they experienced during the past month (0, 1, 2 or more). The students then completed a perfectionism questionnaire including one scale measuring parental criticism. One sample item is "I never felt that I could meet my parents' standards." Students rated their level of agreement with each item, and the total score was calculated for each student. The following results are similar to those obtained by the researchers.

Binge Drinking Episodes in Past Month			
0	1	2 or more	
8	10	13	$N = 15$
8	12	14	
10	8	12	$G = 165$
9	9	15	
10	11	16	$\Sigma X^2 = 1909$
$M = 9$	$M = 10$	$M = 14$	
$T = 45$	$T = 50$	$T = 70$	
$SS = 4$	$SS = 10$	$SS = 10$	

a. Use an ANOVA with $\alpha = .05$ to determine whether there are any significant differences among the three treatment means.

b. Calculate η^2 to measure the effect size for this study.
c. Write a sentence demonstrating how a research report would present the results of the hypothesis test and the measure of effect size.

12. A researcher reports an F-ratio with $df = 3, 36$ from an independent-measures research study.
a. How many treatment conditions were compared in the study?
b. What was the total number of participants in the study?

13. A research report from an independent-measures study states that there are significant differences between treatments, $F(2, 54) = 3.58, p < .05$.
a. How many treatment conditions were compared in the study?
b. What was the total number of participants in the study?

14. For the preceding problem you should find that there are significant differences among the three treatments. The primary reason for the significance is that the mean for treatment I is substantially smaller than the means for the other two treatments. To create the following data, we started with the values from problem 7 and added 3 points to each score in treatment I. Recall that adding a constant causes the mean to change but has no influence on the variability of the sample. In the resulting data, the mean differences are much smaller than those in problem 7.

I	II	III	
$n = 6$	$n = 6$	$n = 6$	
$M = 4$	$M = 5$	$M = 6$	$N = 18$
$T = 24$	$T = 30$	$T = 36$	$G = 90$
$SS = 30$	$SS = 35$	$SS = 40$	$\Sigma X^2 = 567$

a. Before you begin any calculations, predict how the change in the data should influence the outcome of the analysis. That is, how will the F-ratio and the value of η^2 for these data compare with the values obtained in problem 7?
b. Use an ANOVA with $\alpha = .05$ to determine whether there are any significant differences among the three treatment means. (Does your answer agree with your prediction in part a?)
c. Calculate η^2 to measure the effect size for this study. (Does your answer agree with your prediction in part a?)

15. The following summary table presents the results from an ANOVA comparing three treatment conditions with $n = 8$ participants in each condition. Complete all missing values. (*Hint:* Start with the *df* column.)

Source	*SS*	*df*	*MS*	
Between treatments	____	____	15	$F =$ ____
Within treatments	____	____	____	
Total	93	____		

16. A pharmaceutical company has developed a drug that is expected to reduce hunger. To test the drug, two samples of rats are selected with $n = 20$ in each sample. The rats in the first sample receive the drug every day and those in the second sample are given a placebo. The dependent variable is the amount of food eaten by each rat over a 1-month period. An ANOVA is used to evaluate the difference between the two sample means and the results are reported in the following summary table. Fill in all missing values in the table. (*Hint:* Start with the *df* column.)

Source	*SS*	*df*	*MS*	
Between treatments	____	____	20	$F = 4.00$
Within treatments	____	____	____	
Total	____	____		

17. A developmental psychologist is examining the development of language skills from age 2 to age 4. Three different groups of children are obtained, one for each age, with $n = 16$ children in each group. Each child is given a language-skills assessment test. The resulting data were analyzed with an ANOVA to test for mean differences between age groups. The results of the ANOVA are presented in the following table. Fill in all missing values.

Source	*SS*	*df*	*MS*	
Between treatments	20	____	____	$F =$ ____
Within treatments	____	____	____	
Total	200	____		

18. The following data represent the results from an independent-measures study comparing two treatment conditions.

a. Use an independent-measures t test with $\alpha = .05$ to determine whether there is a significant mean difference between the two treatments.

b. Use an ANOVA with $\alpha = .05$ to determine whether there is a significant mean difference between the two treatments.

Treatment I	Treatment II	
8	2	$N = 10$
7	3	$G = 50$
6	3	$\Sigma X^2 = 306$
5	5	
9	2	
$M = 7$	$M = 3$	
$T = 35$	$T = 15$	
$SS = 10$	$SS = 6$	

19. The following values summarize the results from an independent-measures study comparing two treatment conditions.

a. Use an independent-measures t test with $\alpha = .05$ to determine whether there is a significant mean difference between the two treatments.

b. Use an ANOVA with $\alpha = .05$ to determine whether there is a significant mean difference between the two treatments.

Treatment I	Treatment II	
$n = 8$	$n = 4$	
$M = 4$	$M = 10$	$N = 12$
$T = 32$	$T = 40$	$G = 72$
$SS = 45$	$SS = 15$	$\Sigma X^2 = 588$

20. The following data were obtained from an independent-measures research study comparing three treatment conditions. Use an ANOVA with $\alpha = .05$ to determine whether there are any significant mean differences among the treatments.

Treatment I	Treatment II	Treatment III	
2	5	7	$N = 14$
5	2	3	$G = 42$
0	1	6	$\Sigma X^2 = 182$
1	2	4	
2			
2			
$T = 12$	$T = 10$	$T = 20$	
$SS = 14$	$SS = 9$	$SS = 10$	

21. One possible explanation for why some birds migrate and others maintain year round residency in a single location is intelligence. Specifically, birds with small brains, relative to their body size, are simply not smart enough to find food during the winter and must migrate to warmer climates where food is easily available (Sol, Lefebvre, & Rodriguez-Teijeiro, 2005). Birds with bigger brains, on the other hand, are more creative and can find food even when the weather turns harsh. Following are hypothetical data similar to the actual research results. The numbers represent relative brain size for the individual birds in each sample.

Non-Migrating	Short-Distance Migrants	Long-Distance Migrants	
18	6	4	$N = 18$
13	11	9	$G = 180$
19	7	5	$\Sigma X^2 = 2150$
12	9	6	
16	8	5	
12	13	7	
$M = 15$	$M = 9$	$M = 6$	
$T = 90$	$T = 54$	$T = 36$	
$SS = 48$	$SS = 34$	$SS = 16$	

a. Use an ANOVA with $\alpha = .05$ to determine whether there are any significant mean differences among the three groups of birds.

b. Compute η^2, the percentage of variance explained by the group differences, for these data.

c. Write a sentence demonstrating how a research report would present the results of the hypothesis test and the measure of effect size.
d. Use the Tukey HSD posttest to determine which groups are significantly different.

22. There is some research indicating that college students who use Facebook while studying tend to have lower grades than non-users (Kirschner & Karpinski, 2010). A representative study surveys students to determine the amount of Facebook use during the time they are studying or doing homework. Based on the amount of time spent on Facebook, students are classified into three groups and their grade point averages are recorded. The following data show the typical pattern of results.

Facebook Use While Studying		
Non-User	Rarely Use	Regularly Use
3.70	3.51	3.02
3.45	3.42	2.84
2.98	3.81	3.42
3.94	3.15	3.10
3.82	3.64	2.74
3.68	3.20	3.22
3.90	2.95	2.58
4.00	3.55	3.07
3.75	3.92	3.31
3.88	3.45	2.80

a. Use an ANOVA with $\alpha = .05$ to determine whether there are significant mean differences among the three groups.
b. Compute η^2 to measure the size of the effect.
c. Write a sentence demonstrating how the result from the hypothesis test and the measure of effect size would appear in a research report.

23. New research suggests that watching television, especially medical shows such as *Grey's Anatomy* and *House* can result in more concern about personal health (Ye, 2010). Surveys administered to college students measure television viewing habits and health concerns such as fear of developing the diseases and disorders seen on television. For the following data, students are classified into three categories based on their television viewing patterns and health concerns are measured on a 10-point scale with 0 indicating "none."

Television Viewing		
Little or None	Moderate	Substantial
4	5	5
2	7	7
5	3	6
1	4	6
3	8	8
7	6	9
4	2	6
4	7	4
8	3	6
2	5	8

a. Use an ANOVA with $\alpha = .05$ to determine whether there are significant mean differences among the three groups.
b. Compute η^2 to measure the size of the effect.
c. Use Tukey's HSD test with $\alpha = .05$ to determine which groups are significantly different.

CHAPTER

13

Repeated-Measures Analysis of Variance

Tools You Will Need

The following items are considered essential background material for this chapter. If you doubt your knowledge of any of these items, you should review the appropriate chapter or section before proceeding.

- Independent-measures analysis of variance (Chapter 12)
- Repeated-measures designs (Chapter 11)
- Individual differences

Preview

Suppose that you were offered a choice between receiving $1000 in 5 years or a smaller amount today. How much would you be willing to take today to avoid waiting 5 years to get the full $1000 payment?

The general result for this kind of decision is that the longer the $1000 payment is delayed, the smaller the amount that people will accept today. For example, you may be willing to take $300 today rather than waiting 5 years for the $1000. However, you might be willing to settle for $100 today if you have to wait 10 years for the $1000. This phenomenon is known as delayed discounting because people discount the value of a future reward depending on how long it is delayed (Green, Fry, & Myerson, 1994). In a typical study examining delayed discounting, people are asked to place a value on a future reward for several different delay periods. For example, how much would you accept today instead of waiting for a future reward of $1000 if you had to wait 1 month before receiving the payment? How about waiting 6 months? 12 months? 24 months? 60 months?

Typical results for a sample of college students are shown in Figure 13.1. Note that the average value declines regularly as the delay period increases. The statistical question is whether the mean differences from one delay period to another are significant.

FIGURE 13.1

Mean amount of immediate payment selected as equivalent to receiving a $1000 payment at each delay.

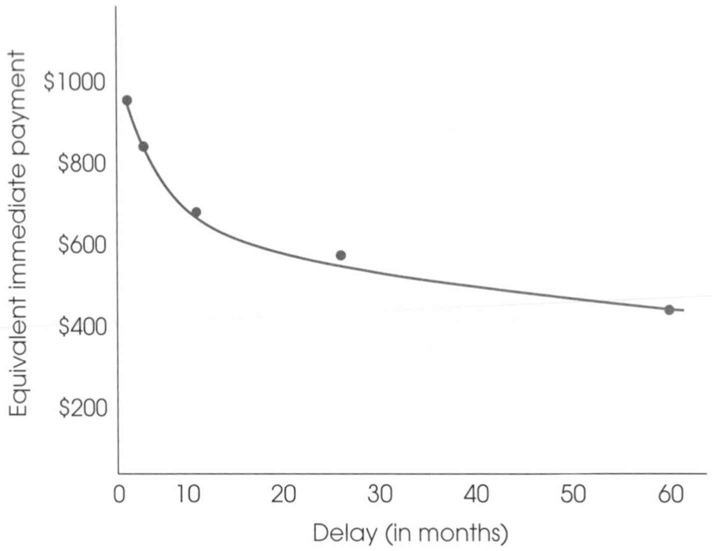

The Problem: You should recognize that evaluating mean differences for more than two sample means is a job for analysis of variance (ANOVA). However, the discounting study is a repeated-measures design with five scores for each individual, and the ANOVA introduced in Chapter 12 is intended for independent-measures studies. Once again, a new hypothesis test is needed.

The Solution: In this chapter we introduce the *repeated-measures ANOVA*. As the name implies, this new procedure is used to evaluate the differences between two or more sample means obtained from a repeated-measures research study. As you will see, many of the notational symbols and computations are the same as those used for the independent-measures ANOVA. In fact, your best preparation for this chapter is a good understanding of the basic ANOVA procedure presented in Chapter 12.

13.1 OVERVIEW OF REPEATED-MEASURES DESIGNS

In the preceding chapter, we introduced ANOVA as a hypothesis-testing procedure for evaluating differences among two or more sample means. The specific advantage of ANOVA, especially in contrast to t tests, is that ANOVA can be used to evaluate the significance of mean differences in situations in which there are more than two sample means being compared. However, the presentation of ANOVA in Chapter 12 was limited to single-factor, independent-measures research designs. Recall that *single factor* indicates that the research study involves only one independent variable (or only one quasi-independent variable), and the term *independent-measures* indicates that the study uses a separate sample for each of the different treatment conditions being compared.

In this chapter, we extend the ANOVA procedure to single-factor, repeated-measures designs. The defining characteristic of a repeated-measures design is that one group of individuals participates in all of the different treatment conditions. The repeated-measures ANOVA is used to evaluate mean differences in two general research situations:

1. An experimental study in which the researcher manipulates an independent variable to create two or more treatment conditions, with the same group of individuals tested in all of the conditions.
2. A nonexperimental study in which the same group of individuals is simply observed at two or more different times.

Examples of these two research situations are presented in Table 13.1. Table 13.1(a) shows data from a study in which the researcher changes the type of distraction to

TABLE 13.1

Two sets of data representing typical examples of single-factor, repeated-measures research designs.

(a) Data from an experimental study evaluating the effects of different types of distraction on the performance of a visual detection task.

	Visual Detection Scores		
Participant	No Distraction	Visual Distraction	Auditory Distraction
A	47	22	41
B	57	31	52
C	38	18	40
D	45	32	43

(b) Data from a nonexperimental design evaluating the effectiveness of a clinical therapy for treating depression.

	Depression Scores		
Participant	Before Therapy	After Therapy	6-Month Follow-Up
A	71	53	55
B	62	45	44
C	82	56	61
D	77	50	46
E	81	54	55

create three treatment conditions. One group of participants is then tested in all three conditions. In this study, the factor being examined is the type of distraction.

Table 13.1(b) shows a study in which a researcher observes depression scores for the same group of individuals at three different times. In this study, the time of measurement is the factor being examined. Another common example of this type of design is found in developmental psychology when the participants' age is the factor being studied. For example, a researcher could study the development of vocabulary skill by measuring vocabulary for a sample of 3-year-old children, then measuring the same children again at ages 4 and 5.

13.2 THE REPEATED-MEASURES ANOVA

HYPOTHESES FOR THE REPEATED-MEASURES ANOVA

The hypotheses for the repeated-measures ANOVA are exactly the same as those for the independent-measures ANOVA presented in Chapter 12. Specifically, the null hypothesis states that, for the general population, there are no mean differences among the treatment conditions being compared. In symbols,

$$H_0: \mu_1 = \mu_2 = \mu_3 = \ldots$$

The null hypothesis states that, on average, all of the treatments have exactly the same effect. According to the null hypothesis, any differences that may exist among the sample means are not caused by systematic treatment effects but rather are the result of random and unsystematic factors.

The alternative hypothesis states that there are mean differences among the treatment conditions. Rather than specifying exactly which treatments are different, we use a generic version of H_1, which simply states that differences exist:

H_1: At least one treatment mean (μ) is different from another.

Notice that the alternative says that, on average, the treatments do have different effects. Thus, the treatment conditions may be responsible for causing mean differences among the samples. As always, the goal of the ANOVA is to use the sample data to determine which of the two hypotheses is more likely to be correct.

THE *F*-RATIO FOR REPEATED-MEASURES ANOVA

The F-ratio for the repeated-measures ANOVA has the same structure that was used for the independent-measures ANOVA in Chapter 12. In each case, the F-ratio compares the actual mean differences between treatments with the amount of difference that would be expected if there were no treatment effect. The numerator of the F-ratio measures the actual mean differences between treatments. The denominator measures how big the differences should be if there is no treatment effect. As always, the F-ratio uses variance to measure the size of the differences. Thus, the F-ratio for both ANOVAs has the general structure

$$F = \frac{\text{variance (differences) between treatments}}{\text{variance (differences) expected if there is no treatment effect}}$$

A large value for the F-ratio indicates that the differences between treatments are greater than would be expected without any treatment effect. If the F-ratio is larger than the critical value in the F distribution table, then we can conclude that the differences between treatments are *significantly* larger than would be caused by chance.

Individual Differences in the F-ratio Although the structure of the F-ratio is the same for independent-measures and repeated-measures designs, there is a fundamental difference between the two designs that produces a corresponding difference in the two F-ratios. Specifically, individual differences are a part of one ratio but are eliminated from the other.

You should recall that the term *individual differences* refers to participant characteristics such as age, personality, and gender that vary from one person to another and may influence the measurements that you obtain for each person. Suppose, for example, that you are measuring reaction time. The first participant in your study is a 19-year-old female with an IQ of 136 who is on the college varsity volleyball team. The next participant is a 42-year-old male with an IQ of 111 who returned to college after losing his job and comes to the research study with a head cold. Would you expect to obtain the same reaction time score for these two individuals?

Individual differences are a part of the variance in the numerator and in the denominator of the F-ratio for the independent-measures ANOVA. However, individual difference are eliminated or removed from the variances in the F-ratio for the repeated measures ANOVA. The idea of removing individual differences was first presented in Chapter 11 when we introduced the repeated-measures design (p. 367), but we review it briefly now.

In a repeated-measures study, exactly the same individuals participate in all of the treatment conditions. Therefore, if there are any mean differences between treatments, they cannot be explained by individual differences. Thus, individual differences are automatically eliminated from the numerator of the repeated-measures F-ratio.

A repeated-measures design also allows you to remove individual differences from the variance in the denominator of the F-ratio. Because the same individuals are measured in every treatment condition, it is possible to measure the size of the individual differences. In Table 13.1(a), for example, participant A has scores that are consistently 10 points lower than the scores for participant B. Because the individual differences are systematic and predictable, they can be measured and separated from the random, unsystematic differences in the denominator of the F-ratio.

Thus, individual differences are automatically eliminated from the numerator of the repeated-measures F-ratio. In addition, they can be measured and removed from the denominator. As a result, the structure of the final F-ratio is as follows:

$$F = \frac{\substack{\text{variance/differences between treatments} \\ \text{(without individual differences)}}}{\substack{\text{variance/differences with no treatment effect} \\ \text{(with individual differences removed)}}}$$

The process of removing individual differences is an important part of the procedure for a repeated-measures ANOVA.

THE LOGIC OF THE REPEATED-MEASURES ANOVA

The general purpose of the repeated-measures ANOVA is to determine whether the differences that are found between treatment conditions are significantly greater than would be expected if there is no treatment effect. In the numerator of the F-ratio, the *between-treatments variance* measures the actual mean differences between the treatment conditions. The variance in the denominator is intended to measure how much difference is reasonable to expect if there are no systematic treatment effects and no systematic individual differences. In other words, the denominator measures variability caused entirely by random and unsystematic factors. For this reason, the variance in the denominator is called the *error variance*. In this section we examine the elements that make up the two variances in the repeated-measures F-ratio.

The numerator of the F-ratio: between-treatments variance Logically, any differences that are found between treatments can be explained by only two factors:

1. **Systematic Differences Caused by the Treatments.** It is possible that the different treatment conditions really do have different effects and, therefore, cause the individuals' scores in one condition to be higher (or lower) than in another. Remember that the purpose for the research study is to determine whether a *treatment effect* exists.
2. **Random, Unsystematic Differences.** Even if there is no treatment effect, it is possible for the scores in one treatment condition to be different from the scores in another. For example, suppose that I measure your IQ score on a Monday morning. A week later I come back and measure your IQ again under exactly the same conditions. Will you get exactly the same IQ score both times? In fact, minor differences between the two measurement situations would probably cause you to end up with two different scores. For example, for one of the IQ tests you might be more tired, or hungry, or worried, or distracted than you were on the other test. These differences can cause your scores to vary. The same thing can happen in a repeated-measures research study. The same individuals are measured at two or more different times and, even though there may be no difference between the two treatment conditions, you can still end up with different scores. However, these differences are random and unsystematic and are classified as error variance.

Thus, it is possible that any differences (or variance) found between treatments could be caused by treatment effects, and it is possible that the differences could simply be the result of chance. On the other hand, it is *impossible* that the differences between treatments are caused by individual differences. Because the repeated-measures design uses exactly the same individuals in every treatment condition, individual differences are *automatically eliminated* from the variance between treatments in the numerator of the F-ratio.

The denominator of the F-ratio: error variance The goal of the ANOVA is to determine whether the differences that are observed in the data are greater than would be expected without any systematic treatment effects. To accomplish this goal, the denominator of the F-ratio is intended to measure how much difference (or variance) is reasonable to expect from random and unsystematic factors. This means that we must measure the variance that exists when there are no treatment effects or any other systematic differences.

We begin exactly as we did with the independent-measures F-ratio; specifically, we calculate the variance that exists within treatments. Recall from Chapter 12 that within each treatment all of the individuals are treated in exactly the same way. Therefore, any differences that exist within treatments cannot be caused by treatment effects.

In a repeated-measures design, however, it is also possible that individual differences can cause systematic differences between the scores within treatments. For example, one individual may score consistently higher than another. To eliminate the individual differences from the denominator of the F-ratio, we measure the individual differences and then subtract them from the rest of the variability. The variance that remains is a measure of pure *error* without any systematic differences that can be explained by treatment effects or by individual differences.

In summary, the F-ratio for a repeated-measures ANOVA has the same basic structure as the F-ratio for independent measures (Chapter 12) except that it includes no variability caused by individual differences. The individual differences are automatically eliminated from the variance between treatments (numerator) because the repeated-measures design uses the same individuals in all treatments. In the denominator, the individual differences are subtracted during the analysis. As a result, the repeated-measures F-ratio has the following structure:

$$F = \frac{\text{between-treatments variance}}{\text{error variance}}$$

$$= \frac{\text{treatment effects + random, unsystematic differences}}{\text{random, unsystematic differences}} \qquad (13.1)$$

Note that this F-ratio is structured so that there are no individual differences contributing to either the numerator or the denominator. When there is no treatment effect, the F-ratio is balanced because the numerator and denominator are both measuring exactly the same variance. In this case, the F-ratio should have a value near 1.00. When research results produce an F-ratio near 1.00, we conclude that there is no evidence of a treatment effect and we fail to reject the null hypothesis. On the other hand, when a treatment effect does exist, it contributes only to the numerator and should produce a large value for the F-ratio. Thus, a large value for F indicates that there is a real treatment effect and, therefore, we should reject the null hypothesis.

LEARNING CHECK

1. Explain why individual differences do not contribute to the between-treatments variability in a repeated-measures study.
2. What sources of variability contribute to the within-treatment variability for a repeated-measures study?
3. Describe the structure of the F-ratio for the repeated-measures ANOVA.

ANSWERS

1. Because the individuals in one treatment are exactly the same as the individuals in every other treatment, there are no individual differences from one treatment to another.
2. Variability (differences) within treatments is caused by individual differences and random, unsystematic differences.
3. The numerator of the F-ratio measures between-treatments variability, which consists of treatment effects and random, unsystematic differences. The denominator measures variability that is exclusively caused by random, unsystematic differences.

13.3 HYPOTHESIS TESTING AND EFFECT SIZE WITH THE REPEATED-MEASURES ANOVA

The overall structure of the repeated-measures ANOVA is shown in Figure 13.2. Note that the ANOVA can be viewed as a two-stage process. In the first stage, the total variance is partitioned into two components: *between-treatments variance* and *within-treatments*

FIGURE 13.2
The partitioning of variance for a repeated-measures experiment.

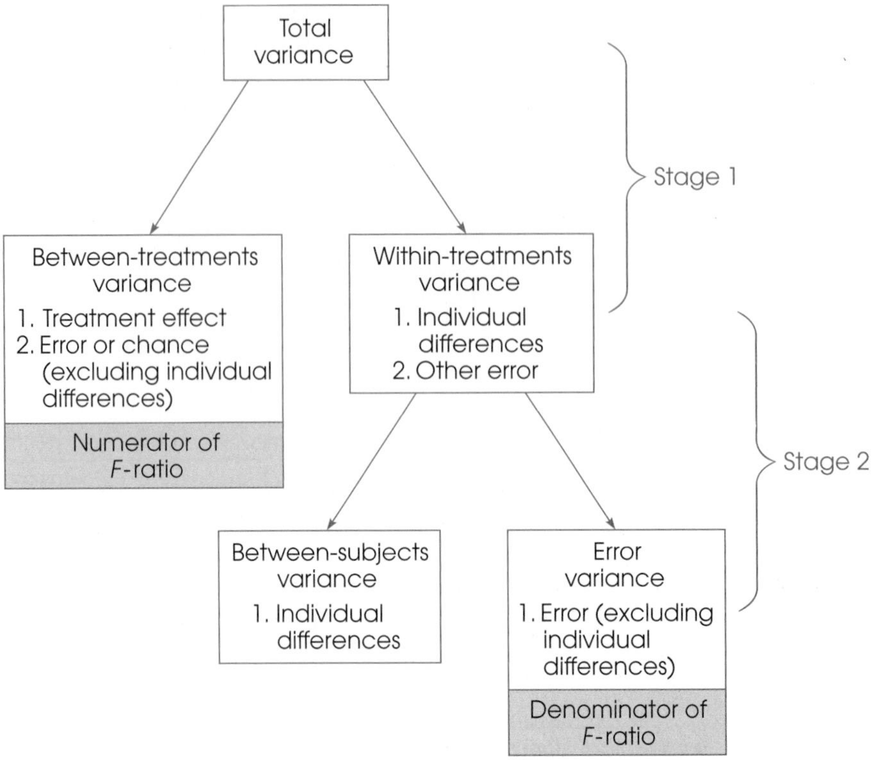

variance. This stage is identical to the analysis that we conducted for an independent-measures design in Chapter 12.

The second stage of the analysis is intended to remove the individual differences from the denominator of the *F*-ratio. In the second stage, we begin with the variance within treatments and then measure and subtract out the *between-subject variance,* which measures the size of the individual differences. The remaining variance, often called the *residual variance,* or *error variance,* provides a measure of how much variance is reasonable to expect after the treatment effects and individual differences have been removed. The second stage of the analysis is what differentiates the repeated-measures ANOVA from the independent-measures ANOVA. Specifically, the repeated-measures design requires that the individual differences be removed.

DEFINITION

In a repeated-measures ANOVA, the denominator of the *F*-ratio is called the **residual variance,** or the **error variance,** and measures how much variance is expected if there are no systematic treatment effects and no individual differences contributing to the variability of the scores.

NOTATION FOR THE REPEATED-MEASURES ANOVA

We use the data in Table 13.2 to introduce the notation for the repeated-measures ANOVA. The data represent the results of a study comparing different viewing distances for a 42-inch high-definition television. Four viewing distances were evaluated,

TABLE 13.2

Satisfaction with different viewing distances of a 42-inch, high-definition television.
Note: For comparison, the scores are identical to the values in Example 12.1 on page 405.

	Viewing Distance					
Person	9 Feet	12 Feet	15 Feet	18 Feet	Person Totals	
A	3	4	7	6	$P = 20$	$n = 5$
B	0	3	6	3	$P = 12$	$k = 4$
C	2	1	5	4	$P = 12$	$N = 20$
D	0	1	4	3	$P = 8$	$G = 60$
E	0	1	3	4	$P = 8$	$\Sigma X^2 = 262$
	$T = 5$	$T = 10$	$T = 25$	$T = 20$		
	$SS = 8$	$SS = 8$	$SS = 10$	$SS = 6$		

9 feet, 12 feet, 15 feet, and 18 feet. Each participant was free to move back and forth among the four distances while watching a 30-minute video on the television. The only restriction was that each person had to spend at least 2 minutes watching from each of the four distances. At the end of the video, each participant rated the all of the viewing distances on a scale from 1 (Very Bad, definitely need to move closer or farther away) to 7 (excellent, perfect viewing distance). You may notice that this research study and the numerical values in the table are identical to those used to demonstrate the independent-measures ANOVA in the previous chapter (Example 12.1, page 405). In this case, however, the data represent a repeated-measures study in which the same group of $n = 5$ individuals is tested in all four treatment conditions.

You should recognize that most of the notation in Table 13.2 is identical to the notation used in an independent-measures analysis (Chapter 12). For example, there are $n = 5$ participants who are tested in $k = 4$ treatment conditions, producing a total of $N = 20$ scores that add up to a grand total of $G = 60$. Note, however, that $N = 20$ now refers to the total number of scores in the study, not the number of participants.

The repeated-measures ANOVA introduces only one new notational symbol. The letter P is used to represent the total of all of the scores for each individual in the study. You can think of the P values as "Person totals" or "Participant totals." In Table 13.2, for example, participant A had scores of 3, 4, 6, and 7 for a total of $P = 20$. The P values are used to define and measure the magnitude of the individual differences in the second stage of the analysis.

EXAMPLE 13.1

We use the data in Table 13.2 to demonstrate the repeated-measures ANOVA. Again, the goal of the test is to determine whether there are any significant differences among the four distances being compared. Specifically, are any of the mean differences in the data greater than would be expected if there are no systematic differences among the four viewing distances?

STAGE 1 OF THE REPEATED-MEASURES ANOVA

The first stage of the repeated-measures analysis is identical to the independent-measures ANOVA that was presented in Chapter 12. Specially, the *SS* and *df* for the total set of scores are analyzed into within-treatments and between-treatments components.

Because the numerical values in Table 13.2 are the same as the values used in Example 12.1 (p. 405), the computations for the first stage of the repeated-measures analysis are identical to those in Example 12.1. Rather than repeating the same arithmetic, the results of the first stage of the repeated-measures analysis can be summarized as follows:

Total:

$$SS_{\text{total}} = \Sigma X^2 - \frac{G^2}{N} = 262 - \frac{(60)^2}{20} = 262 - 180 = 82$$

$$df_{\text{total}} = N - 1 = 19$$

Within treatments:

$$SS_{\text{within treatments}} = \Sigma SS_{\text{inside each treatment}} = 8 + 8 + 10 + 6 = 32$$

$$df_{\text{within treatments}} = \Sigma df_{\text{inside each treatment}} = 4 + 4 + 4 + 4 = 16$$

Between treatments: For this example we use the computational formula for $SS_{\text{between treatments}}$.

$$SS_{\text{between treatments}} = \Sigma\frac{T^2}{n} - \frac{G^2}{N} = \frac{5^2}{5} + \frac{10^2}{5} + \frac{25^2}{5} + \frac{20^2}{5} - \frac{60^2}{20} = 50$$

$$df_{\text{between treatments}} = k - 1 = 3$$

For more details on the formulas and calculations, see Example 12.1, pages 405–407.

This completes the first stage of the repeated-measures ANOVA. Note that the two components, between and within, add up to the total for the *SS* values and for the *df* values. Also note that the between-treatments *SS* and *df* values provide a measure of the mean differences between treatments and are used to compute the variance in the numerator of the final *F*-ratio.

STAGE 2 OF THE REPEATED-MEASURES ANOVA

The second stage of the analysis involves removing the individual differences from the denominator of the *F*-ratio. Because the same individuals are used in every treatment, it is possible to measure the size of the individual differences. For the data in Table 13.2, for example, participant A tends to have the highest scores and participants D and E tend to have the lowest scores. These individual differences are reflected in the *P* values, or person totals, in the right-hand column. We use these *P* values to create a computational formula for $SS_{\text{between subjects}}$ in much the same way that we used the treatment totals, the *T* values, in the computational formula for $SS_{\text{between treatments}}$. Specifically, the formula for the between-subjects *SS* is

$$SS_{\text{between subjects}} = \Sigma\frac{P^2}{k} - \frac{G^2}{N} \tag{13.2}$$

Notice that the formula for the between-subjects *SS* has exactly the same structure as the computational formula for the between-treatments *SS* (see the calculation above). In this case we use the person totals (*P* values) instead of the treatment totals (*T* values). Each *P* value is squared and divided by the number of scores that were added to obtain the total. In this case, each person has *k* scores, one for each treatment. Box 13.1 presents another demonstration of the similarity of the formulas for SS between subjects and SS between treatments. For the data in Table 13.2,

$$SS_{\text{between subjects}} = \frac{20^2}{4} + \frac{12^2}{4} + \frac{12^2}{4} + \frac{8^2}{4} + \frac{8^2}{4} - \frac{60^2}{20}$$

$$= 100 + 36 + 36 + 16 + 16 - 180$$

$$= 24$$

The value of $SS_{\text{between subjects}}$ provides a measure of the size of the individual differences—that is, the differences between subjects. In the second stage of the analysis, we simply subtract the individual differences to obtain the measure of error that forms the denominator of the F-ratio. Thus, the final step in the analysis of SS is

$$SS_{\text{error}} = SS_{\text{within treatments}} - SS_{\text{between subjects}} \quad (13.3)$$

We have already computed $SS_{\text{within treatments}} = 32$ and $SS_{\text{between subjects}} = 24$, therefore

$$SS_{\text{error}} = 32 - 24 = 8$$

The analysis of degrees of freedom follows exactly the same pattern that was used to analyze SS. Remember that we are using the P values to measure the magnitude of the individual differences. The number of P values corresponds to the number of subjects, n, so the corresponding df is

$$df_{\text{between subjects}} = n - 1 \quad (13.4)$$

For the data in Table 13.2, there are $n = 5$ subjects and

$$df_{\text{between subjects}} = 5 - 1 = 4$$

BOX 13.1 $SS_{\text{between subjects}}$ AND $SS_{\text{between treatments}}$

The data for a repeated-measures study are normally presented in a matrix, with the treatment conditions determining the columns and the participants defining the rows. The data in Table 13.2 demonstrate this normal presentation. The calculation of $SS_{\text{between treatments}}$ provides a measure of the differences between treatment conditions—that is, a measure of the mean differences between the *columns* in the data matrix. For the data in Table 13.2, the column totals are 5, 10, 20, and 25. These values are variable, and $SS_{\text{between treatments}}$ measures the amount of variability.

The following table reproduces the data from Table 13.2, but now we have turned the data matrix on its side so that the participants define the columns and the treatment conditions define the rows.

In this new format, the differences between the columns represent the between-subjects variability. The column totals are now P values (instead of T values) and the number of scores in each column is now identified by k (instead of n). With these changes in notation, the formula for $SS_{\text{between subjects}}$ has exactly the same structure as the formula for $SS_{\text{between treatments}}$. If you examine the two equations, the similarity should be clear.

	Participant					
	A	B	C	D	E	
9 feet	3	0	2	0	0	$T = 5$
12 feet	4	3	1	1	1	$T = 10$
15 feet	7	6	5	4	3	$T = 25$
18 feet	6	3	4	3	4	$T = 20$
	$P = 20$	$P = 12$	$P = 12$	$P = 8$	$P = 8$	

Next, we subtract the individual differences from the within-subjects component to obtain a measure of error. In terms of degrees of freedom,

$$df_{\text{error}} = df_{\text{within treatments}} - df_{\text{between subjects}} \tag{13.5}$$

For the data in Table 13.2,

$$df_{\text{error}} = 16 - 4 = 12$$

An algebraically equivalent formula for df_{error} uses only the number of treatment conditions (k) and the number of participants (n):

$$df_{\text{error}} = (k - 1)(n - 1) \tag{13.6}$$

The usefulness of equation 13.6 is discussed in Box 13.2.

Remember: The purpose for the second stage of the analysis is to measure the individual differences and then remove the individual differences from the denominator of the F-ratio. This goal is accomplished by computing SS and df between subjects (the individual differences) and then subtracting these values from the within-treatments values. The result is a measure of variability resulting from error with the individual differences removed. This error variance (SS and df) is used in the denominator of the F-ratio.

CALCULATION OF THE VARIANCES (*MS* VALUES) AND THE *F*-RATIO

The final calculation in the analysis is the F-ratio, which is a ratio of two variances. Each variance is called a *mean square,* or MS, and is obtained by dividing the appropriate SS by its corresponding df value. The MS in the numerator of the F-ratio measures the size of the differences between treatments and is calculated as

$$MS_{\text{between treatments}} = \frac{SS_{\text{between treatments}}}{df_{\text{between treatments}}} \tag{13.7}$$

For the data in Table 13.2,

$$MS_{\text{between treatments}} = \frac{50}{3} = 16.67$$

BOX 13.2 USING THE ALTERNATIVE FORMULA FOR df_{error}

The statistics presented in a research report not only describe the significance of the results but typically provide enough information to reconstruct the research design. The alternative formula for df_{error} is particularly useful for this purpose. Suppose, for example, that a research report for a repeated-measures study includes an F-ratio with $df = 2, 10$. How many treatment conditions were compared in the study, and how many individuals participated?

To answer these questions, begin with the first df value, which is $df_{\text{between treatments}} = 2 = k - 1$. From this value, it is clear that $k = 3$ treatments. Next, use the second df value, which is $df_{\text{error}} = 10$. Using this value and the fact that $k - 1 = 2$, use equation 13.6 to find the number of participants.

$$df_{\text{error}} = 10 = (k - 1)(n - 1) = 2(n - 1)$$

If $2(n - 1) = 10$, then $n - 1$ must equal 5. Therefore, $n = 6$.

Therefore, we conclude that a repeated-measures study producing an F-ratio with $df = 2, 10$ must have compared 3 treatment conditions using a sample of 6 participants.

The denominator of the F-ratio measures how much difference is reasonable to expect if there are no systematic treatment effects and the individual differences have been removed. This is the error variance, or the residual variance, obtained in stage 2 of the analysis.

$$MS_{\text{error}} = \frac{SS_{\text{error}}}{df_{\text{error}}} \tag{13.8}$$

For the data in Table 13.2,

$$MS_{\text{error}} = \frac{8}{12} = 0.67$$

Finally, the F-ratio is computed as

$$F = \frac{MS_{\text{between treatments}}}{MS_{\text{error}}} \tag{13.9}$$

For the data in Table 13.2,

$$F = \frac{16.67}{0.67} = 24.88$$

Once again, notice that the repeated-measures ANOVA uses MS_{error} in the denominator of the F-ratio. This MS value is obtained in the second stage of the analysis, after the individual differences have been removed. As a result, individual differences are completely eliminated from the repeated-measures F-ratio, so that the general structure is

$$F = \frac{\text{treatment effects} + \text{unsystematic differences (without individual diffs)}}{\text{unsystematic differences (without individual diffs)}}$$

For the data we have been examining, the F-ratio is $F = 24.88$, indicating that the differences between treatments (numerator) are almost 25 times bigger than you would expect without any treatment effects (denominator). A ratio this large provides clear evidence that there is a real treatment effect. To verify this conclusion you must consult the F distribution table to determine the appropriate critical value for the test. The degrees of freedom for the F-ratio are determined by the two variances that form the numerator and the denominator. For a repeated-measures ANOVA, the df values for the F-ratio are reported as

$$df = df_{\text{between treatments}},\ df_{\text{error}}$$

For the example we are considering, the F-ratio has $df = 2, 12$ ("degrees of freedom equal two and twelve"). Using the F distribution table (p. 705) with $\alpha = .05$, the critical value is $F = 3.88$, and with $\alpha = .01$ the critical value is $F = 6.93$. Our obtained F-ratio, $F = 24.88$, is well beyond either of the critical values, so we can conclude that the differences between treatments are *significantly* greater than expected by chance using either $\alpha = .05$ or $\alpha = .01$.

The summary table for the repeated-measures ANOVA from Example 13.1 is presented in Table 13.3. Although these tables are no longer commonly used in research reports, they provide a concise format for displaying all of the elements of the analysis.

MEASURING EFFECT SIZE FOR THE REPEATED-MEASURES ANOVA

The most common method for measuring effect size with ANOVA is to compute the percentage of variance that is explained by the treatment differences. In the context of ANOVA, the percentage of variance is commonly identified as η^2 (eta squared). In Chapter 12, for the independent-measures analysis, we computed η^2 as

$$\eta^2 = \frac{SS_{\text{between treatments}}}{SS_{\text{between treatments}} + SS_{\text{within treatments}}} = \frac{SS_{\text{between treatments}}}{SS_{\text{total}}}$$

The intent is to measure how much of the total variability is explained by the differences between treatments. With a repeated-measures design, however, there is another component that can explain some of the variability in the data. Specifically, part of the variability is caused by differences between individuals. In Table 13.2, for example, person A consistently scored higher than person B. This consistent difference explains some of the variability in the data. When computing the size of the treatment effect, it is customary to remove any variability that can be explained by other factors, and then compute the percentage of the remaining variability that can be explained by the treatment effects. Thus, for a repeated-measures ANOVA, the variability from the individual differences is removed before computing η^2. As a result, η^2 is computed as

$$\eta^2 = \frac{SS_{\text{between treatments}}}{SS_{\text{total}} - SS_{\text{between subjects}}} \tag{13.10}$$

Because Equation 13.10 computes a percentage that is not based on the total variability of the scores (one part, $SS_{\text{between subjects}}$, is removed), the result is often called a *partial* eta squared.

The general goal of Equation 13.10 is to calculate a percentage of the variability that has not already been explained by other factors. Thus, the denominator of Equation 13.10 is limited to variability from the treatment differences and variability that is exclusively from random, unsystematic factors. With this in mind, an equivalent version of the η^2 formula is

$$\eta^2 = \frac{SS_{\text{between treatments}}}{SS_{\text{between treatments}} + SS_{\text{error}}} \tag{13.11}$$

TABLE 13.3

A summary table for the repeated-measures ANOVA for the data from Example 13.1.

Source	*SS*	*df*	*MS*	*F*
Between treatments	50	3	16.67	$F(3,12) = 24.88$
Within treatments	32	16		
Between subjects	24	4		
Error	8	12	0.67	
Total	82	19		

In this new version of the eta-squared formula, the denominator consists of the variability that is explained by the treatment differences plus the other *unexplained* variability. Using either formula, the data from Example 13.1 produce

$$\eta^2 = \frac{50}{58} = 0.862 \ (\text{or } 86.2\%)$$

This result means that 86.2% of the variability in the data (except for the individual differences) is accounted for by the differences between treatments.

IN THE LITERATURE

REPORTING THE RESULTS OF A REPEATED-MEASURES ANOVA

As described in Chapter 12 (p. 409), the format for reporting ANOVA results in journal articles consists of

1. A summary of descriptive statistics (at least treatment means and standard deviations, and tables or graphs as needed)
2. A concise statement of the outcome of the ANOVA

For the study in Example 13.1, the report could state:

> The means and variances for the four television viewing distances are shown in Table 1. A repeated-measures analysis of variance indicated significant mean differences in the participants' ratings of the four distances, $F(3, 12) = 24.88$, $p < .01$, $\eta^2 = 0.862$.

TABLE 1

Ratings of satisfaction with different television-viewing distances

	9 Feet	12 Feet	15 Feet	18 Feet
M	1.00	2.00	5.00	4.00
SD	1.41	1.41	1.58	1.22

POST HOC TESTS WITH REPEATED-MEASURES ANOVA

Recall that ANOVA provides an overall test of significance for the mean differences between treatments. When the null hypothesis is rejected, it indicates only that there is a difference between at least two of the treatment means. If $k = 2$, it is obvious which two treatments are different. However, when k is greater than 2, the situation becomes more complex. To determine exactly where significant differences exist, the researcher must follow the ANOVA with post hoc tests. In Chapter 12, we used Tukey's HSD and the Scheffé test to make these multiple comparisons among treatment means. These two procedures attempt to control the overall alpha level by making adjustments for the number of potential comparisons.

For a repeated-measures ANOVA, Tukey's HSD and the Scheffé test can be used in the exact same manner as was done for the independent-measures ANOVA, *provided* that you substitute MS_{error} in place of $MS_{\text{within treatments}}$ in the formulas and use df_{error} in place of $df_{\text{within treatments}}$ when locating the critical value in a statistical table. Note that statisticians are not in complete agreement about the appropriate error term in post hoc tests for repeated-measures designs (for a discussion, see Keppel, 1973, or Keppel & Zedeck, 1989).

ASSUMPTIONS OF THE REPEATED-MEASURES ANOVA

The basic assumptions for the repeated-measures ANOVA are identical to those required for the independent-measures ANOVA.

1. The observations within each treatment condition must be independent (see p. 254).
2. The population distribution within each treatment must be normal. (As before, the assumption of normality is important only with small samples.)
3. The variances of the population distributions for each treatment should be equivalent.

For the repeated-measures ANOVA, there is an additional assumption, called homogeneity of covariance. Basically, it refers to the requirement that the relative standing of each subject be maintained in each treatment condition. This assumption is violated if the effect of the treatment is not consistent for all of the subjects or if order effects exist for some, but not other, subjects. This issue is very complex and is beyond the scope of this book. However, methods do exist for dealing with violations of this assumption (for a discussion, see Keppel, 1973).

If there is reason to suspect that one of the assumptions for the repeated-measures ANOVA has been violated, an alternative analysis known as the Friedman test can be used. The Friedman test is presented in Appendix E. It requires that the original scores be transformed into ranks before evaluating the differences between treatment conditions.

LEARNING CHECK

1. Explain how SS_{error} is computed in the repeated-measures ANOVA.
2. A repeated-measures study is used to evaluate the mean differences among three treatment conditions using a sample of $n = 8$ participants. What are the *df* values for the *F*-ratio?
3. For the following data, compute $SS_{\text{between treatments}}$ and $SS_{\text{between subjects}}$.

	Treatment				
Subject	1	2	3	4	
A	2	2	2	2	$G = 32$
B	4	0	0	4	$\Sigma X^2 = 96$
C	2	0	2	0	
D	4	2	2	4	
	$T = 12$	$T = 4$	$T = 6$	$T = 10$	
	$SS = 4$	$SS = 4$	$SS = 3$	$SS = 11$	

4. A research report includes a repeated-measures *F*-ratio with $df = 3, 24$. How many treatment conditions were compared, and how many individuals participated in the study? (See Box 13.2.)

ANSWERS

1. $SS_{\text{error}} = SS_{\text{within}} - SS_{\text{between subjects}}$ Variability from individual differences is subtracted from the within-treatments variability.
2. $df = 2, 14$
3. $SS_{\text{between treatments}} = 10$, $SS_{\text{between subjects}} = 8$
4. There were 4 treatment conditions ($k - 1 = 3$) and 9 participants ($n - 1 = 8$).

13.4 ADVANTAGES AND DISADVANTAGES OF THE REPEATED-MEASURES DESIGN

When we first encountered the repeated-measure design (Chapter 11), we noted that this type of research study has certain advantages and disadvantages (pp. 366–369). On the bright side, a repeated-measures study may be desirable if the supply of participants is limited. A repeated-measures study is economical in that the research requires relatively few participants. Also, a repeated-measures design eliminates or minimizes most of the problems associated with individual differences. However, disadvantages also exist. These take the form of order effects, such as fatigue, that can make the interpretation of the data difficult.

Now that we have introduced the repeated-measures ANOVA, we can examine one of the primary advantages of this design—namely, the elimination of variability caused by individual differences. Consider the structure of the F-ratio for both the independent-and the repeated-measures designs.

$$F = \frac{\text{treatment effects} + \text{random, unsystematic differences}}{\text{random, unsystematic differences}}$$

In each case, the goal of the analysis is to determine whether the data provide evidence for a treatment effect. If there is no treatment effect, then the numerator and denominator are both measuring the same random, unsystematic variance and the F-ratio should produce a value near 1.00. On the other hand, the existence of a treatment effect should make the numerator substantially larger than the denominator and result in a large value for the F-ratio.

For the independent-measures design, the unsystematic differences include individual differences as well as other random sources of error. Thus, for the independent-measures ANOVA, the F-ratio has the following structure:

$$F = \frac{\text{treatment effect} + \text{individual differences and other error}}{\text{individual differences and other error}}$$

For the repeated-measures design, the individual differences are eliminated or subtracted out, and the resulting F-ratio is structured as follows:

$$F = \frac{\text{treatment effect} + \text{error (excluding individual differences)}}{\text{error (excluding individual differences)}}$$

The removal of individual differences from the analysis becomes an advantage in situations in which very large individual differences exist among the participants being studied.

When individual differences are large, the presence of a treatment effect may be masked if an independent-measures study is performed. In this case, a repeated-measures design would be more sensitive in detecting a treatment effect because individual differences do not influence the value of the F-ratio.

This point will become evident in the following example. Suppose that we know how much variability is accounted for by the different sources of variance. For example,

$$\text{treatment effect} = 10 \text{ units of variance}$$

$$\text{individual differences} = 10 \text{ units of variance}$$

$$\text{other error} = 1 \text{ unit of variance}$$

Notice that a large amount of the variability in the experiment is caused by individual differences. By comparing the F-ratios for an independent- and a repeated-measures analysis, we are able to see a fundamental difference between the two types of experimental designs. For an independent-measures experiment, we obtain

$$F = \frac{\text{treatment effect} + \text{individual differences} + \text{error}}{\text{individual differences} + \text{error}}$$

$$= \frac{10+10+1}{10+1} = \frac{21}{11} = 1.91$$

Thus, the independent-measures ANOVA produces an F-ratio of $F = 1.91$. Recall that the F-ratio is structured to produce $F = 1.00$ if there is no treatment effect whatsoever. In this case, the F-ratio is near to 1.00 and strongly suggests that there is little or no treatment effect. If you check the F-distribution table in Appendix B, you will find that it is almost impossible for an F-ratio as small as 1.91 to be significant. For the independent-measures ANOVA, the 10-point treatment effect is overwhelmed by all of the other variance.

Now consider what happens with a repeated-measures ANOVA. With the individual differences removed, the F-ratio becomes:

$$F = \frac{\text{treatment effect} + \text{error}}{\text{error}}$$

$$= \frac{10 + 1}{1} = \frac{11}{1} = 11$$

For the repeated-measures ANOVA, the numerator of the F-ratio (which includes the treatment effect) is 11 times larger than the denominator (which has no treatment effect). This result strongly indicates that there is a substantial treatment effect. In this example, the F-ratio is much larger for the repeated-measures study because the individual differences, which are extremely large, have been removed. In the independent-measures ANOVA, the presence of a treatment effect is obscured by the influence of individual differences. This problem is eliminated by the repeated-measures design, in which variability caused by individual differences is partitioned out of the analysis. When the individual differences are large, a repeated-measures experiment may provide a more sensitive test for a treatment effect. In statistical terms, a repeated-measures test has more *power* than an independent-measures test; that is, it is more likely to detect a real treatment effect.

INDIVIDUAL DIFFERENCES AND THE CONSISTENCY OF THE TREATMENT EFFECTS

As we have demonstrated, one major advantage of a repeated-measures design is that it removes individual differences from the denominator of the F-ratio, which usually increases the likelihood of obtaining a significant result. However, removing individual differences is an advantage only when the treatment effects are reasonably consistent for all of the participants. If the treatment effects are not consistent across participants, the individual differences tend to disappear and value in the denominator is not noticeably reduced by removing them. This phenomenon is demonstrated in the following example.

EXAMPLE 13.2

Table 13.4 presents hypothetical data from a repeated-measures research study. We constructed the data specifically to demonstrate the relationship between consistent treatment effects and large individual differences.

TABLE 13.4

Data from a repeated-measures study comparing three treatments. The data show consistent treatment effects from one participant to another, which produce consistent and relatively large differences in the individual P totals.

	Treatment			
Person	I	II	III	
A	0	1	2	$P = 3$
B	1	2	3	$P = 6$
C	2	4	6	$P = 12$
D	3	5	7	$P = 15$
	$T = 6$	$T = 12$	$T = 18$	
	$SS = 5$	$SS = 10$	$SS = 17$	

First, notice the consistency of the treatment effects. Treatment II has the same effect on every participant, increasing everyone's score by 1 or 2 points compared to treatment I. Also, treatment III produces a consistent increase of 1 or 2 points compared to treatment II. One consequence of the consistent treatment effects is that the individual differences are maintained in all of the treatment conditions. For example, participant A has the lowest score in all three treatments, and participant D always has the highest score. The participant totals (P values) reflect the consistent differences. For example, participant D has the largest score in every treatment and, therefore, has the largest P value. Also notice that there are big differences between the P totals from one individual to the next. For these data, $SS_{\text{between subjects}} = 30$ points.

Now consider the data in Table 13.5. To construct these data we started with the same numbers within each treatment that were used in Table 13.4. However, we scrambled the numbers within each column to eliminate the consistency of the treatment effects. In Table 13.5, for example, two participants show an increase in scores as they go from treatment I to treatment II, and two show a decrease. The data also show an inconsistent treatment effect as the participants go from treatment II to treatment III. One consequence of the inconsistent treatment effects is that there are no consistent individual differences between participants. Participant C, for example, has the lowest score in treatment II and the highest score in treatment III. As a result, there are no longer consistent differences between the individual participants. All of the P totals are about the same. For these data, $SS_{\text{between subjects}} = 3.33$ points. Because the two sets of data (Tables 13.4 and 13.5) have the same treatment totals (T values) and SS values, they have the same $SS_{\text{between treatments}}$ and $SS_{\text{within treatments}}$. For both sets of data,

$$SS_{\text{between treatments}} = 18 \text{ and } SS_{\text{within treatments}} = 32$$

However, there is a huge difference between the two sets of data when you compute SS_{error} for the denominator of the F-ratio. For the data in Table 13.4, with consistent treatment effects and large individual differences,

$$\begin{aligned} SS_{\text{error}} &= SS_{\text{within treatments}} - SS_{\text{between subjects}} \\ &= 32 - 30 \\ &= 2 \end{aligned}$$

For the data in Table 13.5, with no consistent treatment effects and relatively small differences between the individual P totals,

$$\begin{aligned} SS_{\text{error}} &= SS_{\text{within treatments}} - SS_{\text{between subjects}} \\ &= 32 - 3.33 \\ &= 28.67 \end{aligned}$$

TABLE 13.5

Data from a repeated-measures study comparing three treatments. The data show treatment effects that are inconsistent from one participant to another and, as a result, produce relatively small differences in the individual P totals. Note that the data have exactly the same scores within each treatment as the data in Table 13.5, however, the scores have been scrambled to eliminate the consistency of the treatment effects.

	Treatment			
Person	I	II	III	
A	0	4	3	$P = 7$
B	1	5	2	$P = 8$
C	2	1	7	$P = 10$
D	3	2	6	$P = 11$
	$T = 6$	$T = 12$	$T = 18$	
	$SS = 5$	$SS = 10$	$SS = 17$	

Thus, consistent treatment effects tend to produce a relatively small error term for the F-ratio. As a result, consistent treatment effects are more likely to be statistically significant (reject the null hypothesis). For the examples we have been considering, the data in Table 13.4 produce an F-ratio of $F = 27.0$. With $df = 2, 6$, this F-ratio is well into the critical region for $\alpha = .05$ or $.01$ and we conclude that there are significant differences among the three treatments. On the other hand, the same mean differences in Table 13.5 produce $F = 1.88$. With $df = 2, 6$, this value is not in the critical region for $\alpha = .05$ or $.01$, and we conclude that there are no significant differences.

In summary, when treatment effects are consistent from one individual to another, the individual differences also tend to be consistent and relatively large. The large individual differences get subtracted from the denominator of the F-ratio producing a larger value for F and increasing the likelihood that the F-ratio will be in the critical region.

13.5 REPEATED-MEASURES ANOVA AND REPEATED-MEASURES *t* TEST

As we noted in Chapter 12 (pp. 420–421), whenever you are evaluating the difference between two sample means, you can use either a t test or ANOVA. In Chapter 12, we demonstrated that the two tests are related in many respects, including:

1. The two tests always reach the same conclusion about the null hypothesis.
2. The basic relationship between the two test statistics is $F = t^2$.
3. The df value for the t statistic is identical to the df value for the denominator of the F-ratio.
4. If you square the critical value for the two-tailed t test, you obtain the critical value for the F-ratio. Again, the basic relationship is $F = t^2$.

In Chapter 12, these relationships were demonstrated for the independent-measures tests, but they are also true for repeated-measures designs comparing two treatment conditions. The following example demonstrates the relationships.

EXAMPLE 13.3 The following table shows the data from a repeated-measures study comparing two treatment conditions. We have structured the data in a format that is compatible with the repeated-measures *t* test. Note that the calculations for the *t* test are based on the difference scores (*D* values) in the final column.

	Treatment			
Participant	I	II	D	
A	3	5	2	
B	4	14	10	
C	5	7	2	
D	4	6	2	
				$M_D = 4$
				$SS_D = 48$

The repeated-measures *t* test The null hypothesis for the *t* test states that, for the general population, there is no mean difference between the two treatment conditions.

$$H_0\colon \mu_D = 0$$

With $n = 4$ participants, the test has $df = 3$ and the critical boundaries for a two-tailed test with $\alpha = .05$ are $t = \pm 3.182$.

For these data, the sample mean difference is $M_D = 4$, the variance for the difference scores is $s^2 = 16$, and the standard error is $s_{M_D} = 2$ points. These values produce a *t* statistic of

$$t = \frac{M_D - \mu_D}{s_{M_D}} = \frac{4-0}{2} = 2.00$$

The *t* value is not in the critical region so we fail to reject H_0 and conclude that there is no significant difference between the two treatments.

The repeated-measures ANOVA Now we reorganize the data into a format that is compatible with a repeated-measures ANOVA. Notice that the ANOVA uses the original scores (not the difference scores) and requires the *P* totals for each participant.

	Treatment			
Participant	I	II	*P*	
A	3	5	8	$G = 48$
B	4	14	18	$\Sigma X^2 = 372$
C	5	7	12	$N = 8$
D	4	6	10	

Again, the null hypothesis states that, for the general population, there is no mean difference between the two treatment conditions.

$$H_0\colon \mu_1 = \mu_2$$

For this study, $df_{\text{between treatments}} = 1$, $df_{\text{within treatments}} = 6$, $df_{\text{between subjects}} = 3$, which produce $df_{\text{error}} = (6 - 3) = 3$. Thus, the F-ratio has $df = 1, 3$ and the critical value for $\alpha = .05$ is $F = 10.13$. Note that the denominator of the F-ratio has the same df value as the t statistic ($df = 3$) and that the critical value for F is equal to the squared critical value for t ($10.13 = 3.182^2$).

$$\text{For these data, } SS_{\text{total}} = 84,$$
$$SS_{\text{within}} = 52$$
$$SS_{\text{between treatments}} = (84 - 52) = 32$$
$$SS_{\text{between subjects}} = 28$$
$$SS_{\text{error}} = (52 - 28) = 24$$

The two variances in the F-ratio are

$$MS_{\text{between treatments}} = \frac{SS_{\text{between treatments}}}{df_{\text{between treatments}}} = \frac{32}{1} = 32$$

$$\text{and } MS_{\text{error}} = \frac{SS_{\text{error}}}{df_{\text{error}}} = \frac{24}{3} = 8$$

$$\text{and the } F\text{-ratio is } F = \frac{MS_{\text{between treatments}}}{MS_{\text{error}}} = \frac{32}{8} = 4.00$$

Notice that the F-ratio and the t statistic are related by the equation $F = t^2$ ($4 = 2^2$). The F-ratio (like the t statistic) is not in the critical region so, once again, we fail to reject H_0 and conclude that there is no significant difference between the two treatments.

SUMMARY

1. The repeated-measures ANOVA is used to evaluate the mean differences obtained in a research study comparing two or more treatment conditions using the same sample of individuals in each condition. The test statistic is an F-ratio, in which the numerator measures the variance (differences) between treatments and the denominator measures the variance (differences) that is expected without any treatment effects or individual differences.

$$F = \frac{MS_{\text{between treatments}}}{MS_{\text{error}}}$$

2. The first stage of the repeated-measures ANOVA is identical to the independent-measures ANOVA and separates the total variability into two components: between-treatments and within-treatments. Because a repeated-measures design uses the same subjects in every treatment condition, the differences between treatments cannot be caused by individual differences. Thus, individual differences are automatically eliminated from the between-treatments variance in the numerator of the F-ratio.

3. In the second stage of the repeated-measures analysis, individual differences are computed and removed from the denominator of the F-ratio. To remove the individual differences, you first compute the variability between subjects (SS and df) and then subtract these values from the corresponding within-treatments values. The residual provides a measure of error excluding individual differences, which is the appropriate denominator for the repeated-measures F-ratio. The equations for analyzing SS and df for the repeated-measures ANVOA are presented in Figure 13.3.

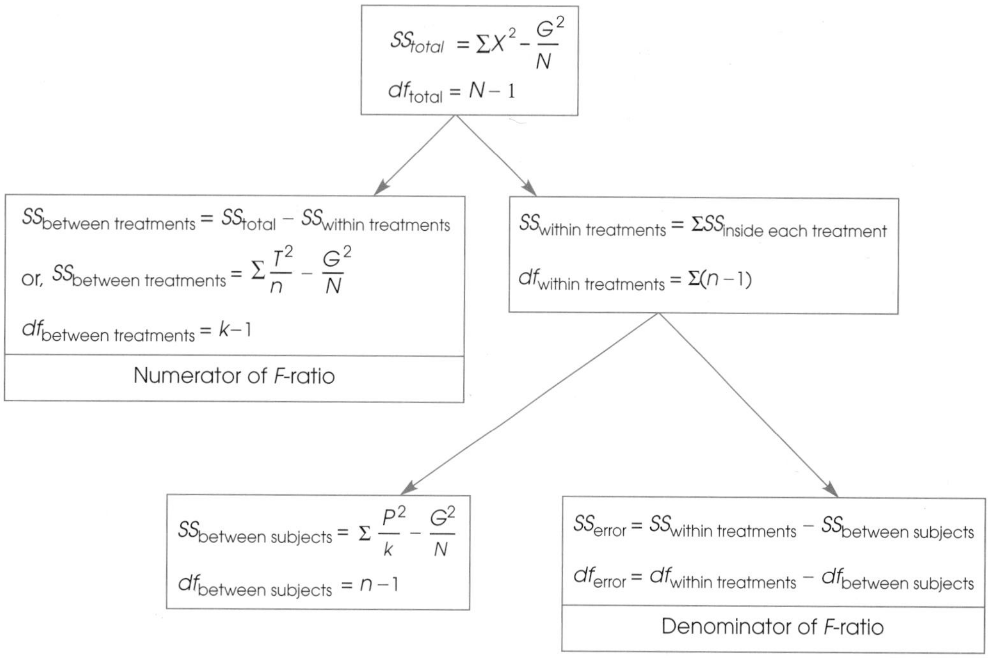

FIGURE 13.3

Formulas for the repeated-measures ANOVA.

4. Effect size for the repeated-measures ANOVA is measured by computing eta squared, the percentage of variance accounted for by the treatment effect. For the repeated-measures ANOVA

$$\eta^2 = \frac{SS_{\text{between treatments}}}{SS_{\text{total}} - SS_{\text{between subjects}}}$$

$$= \frac{SS_{\text{between treatments}}}{SS_{\text{between treatments}} + SS_{\text{error}}}$$

Because part of the variability (the *SS* caused by individual differences) is removed before computing η^2, this measure of effect size is often called a partial eta squared.

5. When the obtained *F*-ratio is significant (that is, H_0 is rejected), it indicates that a significant difference lies between at least two of the treatment conditions. To determine exactly where the difference lies, post hoc comparisons may be made. Post hoc tests, such as Tukey's HSD, use MS_{error} rather than $MS_{\text{within treatments}}$ and df_{error} instead of $df_{\text{within treatments}}$.

6. A repeated-measures ANOVA eliminates the influence of individual differences from the analysis. If individual differences are extremely large, then a treatment effect might be masked in an independent-measures experiment. In this case, a repeated-measures design might be a more sensitive test for a treatment effect.

KEY TERMS

individual differences (437)

between-treatments variance(437)

error variance (438)

between-subjects variance (440)

RESOURCES

Book Companion Website: www.cengage.com/psychology/gravetter

You can find a tutorial quiz and other learning exercises for Chapter 13 on the book companion website.

Improve your understanding of statistics with Aplia's auto-graded problem sets and immediate, detailed explanations for every question. To learn more, visit **www.aplia.com/statistics.**

Log in to CengageBrain to access the resources your instructor requires. For this book, you can access:

Psychology CourseMate brings course concepts to life with interactive learning, study, and exam preparation tools that support the printed textbook. A textbook-specific website, Psychology CourseMate includes an integrated interactive eBook and other interactive learning tools including quizzes, flashcards, and more.

Visit www.cengagebrain.com to access your account and purchase materials.

General instructions for using SPSS are presented in Appendix D. Following are detailed instructions for using SPSS to perform the Single-Factor, **Repeated-Measures Analysis of Variance (ANOVA)** presented in this chapter.

Data Entry

Enter the scores for each treatment condition in a separate column, with the scores for each individual in the same row. All of the scores for the first treatment go in the VAR00001 column, the second treatment scores go in the VAR00002 column, and so on.

Data Analysis

1. Click **Analyze** on the tool bar, select **General Linear Model,** and click on **Repeated-Measures.**
2. SPSS presents a box entitled **Repeated-Measures Define Factors.** Within the box, the Within-Subjects Factor Name should already contain **Factor 1.** If not, type in Factor 1.
3. Enter the **Number of levels** (number of different treatment conditions) in the next box.
4. Click **Add.**
5. Click **Define.**
6. One by one, move the column labels for your treatment conditions into the **Within Subjects Variables** box. (Highlight the column label on the left and click the arrow to move it into the box.)
7. If you want descriptive statistics for each treatment, click on the **Options** box, select **Descriptives,** and click **Continue.**
8. Click **OK.**

SPSS Output

We used the SPSS program to analyze the data from the television viewing study in Example 13.1 and portions of the program output are shown in Figure 13.4. Note that large portions of the SPSS output are not relevant for our purposes and are not included in Figure 13.1. The first item of interest is the table of **Descriptive Statistics,** which presents the mean, standard deviation, and number of scores for each treatment. Next, we skip to the table showing **Tests of Within-Subjects Effects.** The top line of the factor 1 box (Sphericity Assumed) shows the between-treatments sum of squares, degrees of freedom, and mean square that form the numerator of the F-ratio. The same line reports the value of the F-ratio and the level of significance (the p value or alpha level). Similarly, the top line of the Error (factor 1) box shows the sum of squares, the degrees of freedom, and the mean square for the error term (the denominator of the F-ratio). The final box in the output (not shown in Figure 13.4) is labeled **Tests of Between-Subjects Effects** and the bottom line (Error) reports the between-subjects sum of squares and degrees of freedom (ignore the mean square and F-ratio, which are not part of the repeated-measures ANOVA).

Descriptive Statistics

	Mean	Std. Deviation	N
VAR00001	1.0000	1.41421	5
VAR00002	2.0000	1.41421	5
VAR00003	5.0000	1.58114	5
VAR00004	4.0000	1.22474	5

Tests of Within-Subjects Effects

Measure: MEASURE_1

Source		Type III Sum of Squares	df	Mean Square	F	Sig.
factor 1	Sphericity Assumed	50.000	3	16.667	25.000	.000
	Greenhouse-Geisser	50.000	1.600	31.250	25.000	.001
	Huynh-Feldt	50.000	2.500	20.000	25.000	.000
	Lower-bound	50.000	1.000	50.000	25.000	.007
Error (factor 1)	Sphericity Assumed	8.000	12	.667		
	Greenhouse-Geisser	8.000	6.400	1.250		
	Huynh-Feldt	8.000	10.000	.800		
	Lower-bound	8.000	4.000	2.000		

FIGURE 13.4

Portions of the SPSS output for the repeated-measures ANOVA for the television viewing study in Example 13.1.

FOCUS ON PROBLEM SOLVING

1. Before you begin a repeated-measures ANOVA, complete all of the preliminary calculations needed for the ANOVA formulas. This requires that you find the total for each treatment (*T*s), the total for each person (*P*s), the grand total (*G*), the *SS* for each treatment condition, and ΣX^2 for the entire set of *N* scores. As a partial check on these calculations, be sure that the *T* values add up to *G* and that the *P* values have a sum of *G*.

2. To help remember the structure of repeated-measures ANOVA, keep in mind that a repeated-measures experiment eliminates the contribution of individual differences. There are no individual differences contributing to the numerator of the *F*-ratio ($MS_{\text{between treatments}}$) because the same individuals are used for all treatments. Therefore, you must also eliminate individual differences in the denominator. This is accomplished by partitioning within-treatments variability into two components: between-subjects variability and error variability. It is the *MS* value for error variability that is used in the denominator of the *F*-ratio.

DEMONSTRATION 13.1

REPEATED-MEASURES ANOVA

The following data were obtained from a research study examining the effect of sleep deprivation on motor-skills performance. A sample of five participants was tested on a motor-skills task after 24 hours of sleep deprivation, tested again after 36 hours, and tested once more after 48 hours. The dependent variable is the number of errors made on the motor-skills task. Do these data indicate that the number of hours of sleep deprivation has a significant effect on motor skills performance?

Participant	24 Hours	36 Hours	48 Hours	P totals	
A	0	0	6	6	$N = 15$
B	1	3	5	9	$G = 45$
C	0	1	5	6	$\Sigma X^2 = 245$
D	4	5	9	18	
E	0	1	5	6	
	$T = 5$	$T = 10$	$T = 30$		
	$SS = 12$	$SS = 16$	$SS = 12$		

STEP 1 **State the hypotheses, and specify alpha.** The null hypothesis states that, for the general population, there are no differences among the three deprivation conditions. Any differences that exist among the samples are simply the result of chance or error. In symbols,

$$H_0: \mu_1 = \mu_2 = \mu_3$$

The alternative hypothesis states that there are differences among the conditions.

H_1: At least one of the treatment means is different.

We use $\alpha = .05$.

STEP 2 **The repeated-measures analysis.** Rather than compute the *df* values and look for a critical value for F at this time, we proceed directly to the ANOVA.

STAGE 1 The first stage of the analysis is identical to the independent-measures ANOVA presented in Chapter 12.

$$SS_{\text{total}} = \Sigma X^2 - \frac{G^2}{N} = 245 - \frac{45^2}{15} = 110$$

$$SS_{\text{within}} = \Sigma SS_{\text{inside each treatment}} = 12 + 16 + 12 = 40$$

$$SS_{\text{between}} = \Sigma\frac{T^2}{n} - \frac{G^2}{N} = \frac{5^2}{5} + \frac{10^2}{5} + \frac{30^2}{5} - \frac{45^2}{15} = 70$$

and the corresponding degrees of freedom are

$$df_{\text{total}} = N = -1 = 14$$

$$df_{\text{within}} = \Sigma df = 4 + 4 + 4 = 12$$

$$df_{\text{between}} = k - 1 = 2$$

STAGE 2 The second stage of the repeated-measures analysis measures and removes the individual differences from the denominator of the F-ratio.

$$SS_{\text{between subjects}} = \Sigma\frac{P^2}{k} - \frac{G^2}{N}$$

$$= \frac{6^2}{3} + \frac{9^2}{3} + \frac{6^2}{3} + \frac{18^2}{3} + \frac{6^2}{3} - \frac{45^2}{15}$$

$$= 36$$

$$SS_{\text{error}} = SS_{\text{within}} = SS_{\text{between subjects}}$$

$$= 40 - 36$$

$$= 4$$

and the corresponding *df* values are

$$df_{\text{between subjects}} = n - 1 = 4$$

$$df_{\text{error}} = df_{\text{within}} - df_{\text{between subjects}}$$

$$= 12 - 4$$

$$= 8$$

The mean square values that form the F-ratio are as follows:

$$MS_{\text{between}} = \frac{SS_{\text{between}}}{df_{\text{between}}} = \frac{70}{2} = 35$$

$$MS_{\text{error}} = \frac{SS_{\text{error}}}{df_{\text{error}}} = \frac{4}{8} = 0.50$$

Finally, the F-ratio is

$$F = \frac{MS_{\text{between}}}{MS_{\text{error}}} = \frac{35}{0.50} = 70.00$$

STEP 3 **Make a decision and state a conclusion.** With $df = 2, 8$ and $\alpha = .05$, the critical value is $F = 4.46$. Our obtained F-ratio ($F = 70.00$) is well into the critical region, so our decision is to reject the null hypothesis and conclude that there are significant differences among the three levels of sleep deprivation.

DEMONSTRATION 13.2

EFFECT SIZE FOR THE REPEATED-MEASURES ANOVA

We compute η^2, the percentage of variance explained by the treatment differences, for the data in Demonstration 13.1. Using Equation 13.11 we obtain

$$\eta^2 = \frac{SS_{\text{between treatments}}}{SS_{\text{between treatments}} + SS_{\text{error}}} = \frac{70}{70 + 4} = \frac{70}{74} = 0.95 \quad \text{(or 95\%)}$$

PROBLEMS

1. How does the denominator of the F-ratio (the error term) differ for a repeated-measures ANOVA compared to an independent-measures ANOVA?
2. The repeated-measures ANOVA can be viewed as a two-stage process. What is the purpose of the second stage?
3. A researcher conducts an experiment comparing three treatment conditions with $n = 10$ scores in each condition.
   a. If the researcher uses an independent-measures design, how many individuals are needed for the study and what are the df values for the F-ratio?
   b. If the researcher uses a repeated-measures design, how many individuals are needed for the study and what are the df values for the F-ratio?
4. A published report of a repeated-measures research study includes the following description of the statistical analysis. "The results show significant differences among the treatment conditions, $F(2, 20) = 6.10, p < .01$."
   a. How many treatment conditions were compared in the study?
   b. How many individuals participated in the study?
5. A researcher uses a repeated-measures ANOVA to evaluate the results from a research study and reports an F-ratio with $df = 2, 30$.
   a. How many treatment conditions were compared in the study?
   b. How many individuals participated in the study?
6. A researcher conducts a repeated-measures experiment using a sample of $n = 8$ subjects to evaluate the differences among four treatment conditions. If the results are examined with an ANOVA, what are the df values for the F-ratio?
7. The following data were obtained from a repeated-measures study comparing three treatment conditions. Use a repeated-measures ANOVA with $\alpha = .05$ to determine whether there are significant mean differences among the three treatments.

	Treatments				
Person	I	II	III	Person Totals	
A	0	4	2	$P = 6$	
B	1	5	6	$P = 12$	$N = 18$
C	3	3	3	$P = 9$	$G = 48$
D	0	1	5	$P = 6$	$\Sigma X^2 = 184$
E	0	2	4	$P = 6$	
F	2	3	4	$P = 9$	
	$M = 1$	$M = 3$	$M = 4$		
	$T = 6$	$T = 18$	$T = 24$		
	$SS = 8$	$SS = 10$	$SS = 10$		

8. In Problem 11 the data show large and consistent differences between subjects. For example, subject A has the largest score in every treatment and subject D always has the smallest score. In the second stage of the ANOVA, the large individual differences are subtracted out of the denominator of the *F*-ratio, which results in a larger value for *F*.

The following data were created by using the same numbers that appeared in Problem 11. However, we eliminated the consistent individual differences by scrambling the scores within each treatment.

	Treatment				
Subject	I	II	III	*P*	
A	6	2	3	11	$G = 48$
B	5	1	5	11	$\Sigma X^2 = 294$
C	0	5	10	15	
D	1	8	2	11	
	$T = 12$	$T = 16$	$T = 20$		
	$SS = 26$	$SS = 30$	$SS = 38$		

a. Use a repeated-measures ANOVA with $\alpha = .05$ to determine whether these data are sufficient to demonstrate significant differences between the treatments.

b. Explain how the results of this analysis compare with the results from Problem 11.

9. The following data were obtained from a repeated-measures study comparing three treatment conditions.

a. Use a repeated-measures ANOVA with $\alpha = .05$ to determine whether there are significant mean differences among the three treatments.

b. Compute η^2, the percentage of variance accounted for by the mean differences, to measure the size of the treatment effects.

c. Write a sentence demonstrating how a research report would present the results of the hypothesis test and the measure of effect size.

	Treatments				
Person	I	II	III	Person Totals	
A	1	1	4	$P = 6$	
B	3	4	8	$P = 15$	$N = 15$
C	0	2	7	$P = 9$	$G = 45$
D	0	0	6	$P = 6$	$\Sigma X^2 = 231$
E	1	3	5	$P = 9$	
	$M = 1$	$M = 2$	$M = 6$		
	$T = 5$	$T = 10$	$T = 30$		
	$SS = 6$	$SS = 10$	$SS = 10$		

10. For the data in problem 9,

a. Compute SS_{total} and $SS_{between\ treatments}$.

b. Eliminate the mean differences between treatments by adding 2 points to each score in treatment I, adding 1 point to each score in treatment II, and subtracting 3 points from each score in treatment III. (All three treatments should end up with $M = 3$ and $T = 15$.)

c. Calculate SS_{total} for the modified scores. (*Caution:* You first must find the new value for ΣX^2.)

d. Because the treatment effects were eliminated in part b, you should find that SS_{total} for the modified scores is smaller than SS_{total} for the original scores. The difference between the two *SS* values should be exactly equal to the value of $SS_{between\ treatments}$ for the original scores.

11. The following data were obtained from a repeated-measures study comparing three treatment conditions.

	Treatment				
Subject	I	II	III	*P*	
A	6	8	10	24	$G = 48$
B	5	5	5	15	$\Sigma X^2 = 294$
C	1	2	3	6	
D	0	1	2	3	
	$T = 12$	$T = 16$	$T = 20$		
	$SS = 26$	$SS = 30$	$SS = 38$		

Use a repeated-measures ANOVA with $\alpha = .05$ to determine whether these data are sufficient to demonstrate significant differences between the treatments.

12. The following data were obtained from a repeated-measures study comparing two treatment conditions. Use a repeated-measures ANOVA with $\alpha = .05$ to determine whether there are significant mean differences between the two treatments.

	Treatments			
Person	I	II	Person Totals	
A	3	5	$P = 8$	
B	5	9	$P = 14$	$N = 16$
C	1	5	$P = 6$	$G = 80$
D	1	7	$P = 8$	$\Sigma X^2 = 500$
E	5	9	$P = 14$	
F	3	7	$P = 10$	
G	2	6	$P = 8$	
H	4	8	$P = 12$	
	$M = 3$	$M = 7$		
	$T = 24$	$T = 56$		
	$SS = 18$	$SS = 18$		

13. One of the primary advantages of a repeated-measures design, compared to an independent-measures design, is that it reduces the overall variability by removing variance caused by individual differences. The following data are from a research study comparing three treatment conditions.

a. Assume that the data are from an independent-measures study using three separate samples, each with $n = 6$ participants. Ignore the column of P totals and use an independent-measures ANOVA with $\alpha = .05$ to test the significance of the mean differences.

b. Now assume that the data are from a repeated-measures study using the same sample of $n = 6$ participants in all three treatment conditions. Use a repeated-measures ANOVA with $\alpha = .05$ to test the significance of the mean differences.

c. Explain why the two analyses lead to different conclusions.

Treatment 1	Treatment 2	Treatment 3	P	
6	9	12	27	
8	8	8	24	$N = 18$
5	7	9	21	$G = 108$
0	4	8	12	$\Sigma X^2 = 800$
2	3	4	9	
3	5	7	15	
$M = 4$	$M = 6$	$M = 8$		
$T = 24$	$T = 36$	$T = 48$		
$SS = 42$	$SS = 28$	$SS = 34$		

14. The following data are from an experiment comparing three different treatment conditions:

A	B	C	
0	1	2	$N = 15$
2	5	5	$\Sigma X^2 = 354$
1	2	6	
5	4	9	
2	8	8	
$T = 10$	$T = 20$	$T = 30$	
$SS = 14$	$SS = 30$	$SS = 30$	

a. If the experiment uses an *independent-measures design,* can the researcher conclude that the treatments are significantly different? Test at the .05 level of significance.

b. If the experiment is done with a *repeated-measures design,* should the researcher conclude that the treatments are significantly different? Set alpha at .05 again.

c. Explain why the analyses in parts a and b lead to different conclusions.

15. A researcher is evaluating customer satisfaction with the service and coverage of two phone carriers. Each individual in a sample of $n = 25$ uses one carrier for two weeks and then switches to the other. Each participant then rates the two carriers. The following table presents the results from the repeated-measures ANOVA comparing the average ratings. Fill in the missing values in the table. (*Hint:* Start with the *df* values.)

Source	SS	df	MS	
Between treatments	____	____	2	$F =$ ____
Within treatments	____	____		
Between subjects	____	____		
Error	12	____	____	
Total	23	____		

16. The following summary table presents the results from a repeated-measures ANOVA comparing three treatment conditions with a sample of $n = 11$ subjects. Fill in the missing values in the table. (*Hint:* Start with the *df* values.)

Source	SS	df	MS	
Between treatments	____	____	____	$F = 5.00$
Within treatments	80	____		
Between subjects	____	____		
Error	60	____	____	
Total	____	____		

17. The following summary table presents the results from a repeated-measures ANOVA comparing four treatment conditions, each with a sample of $n = 12$ participants. Fill in the missing values in the table. (*Hint:* Start with the *df* values.)

Source	SS	df	MS	
Between treatments	54	____	20	$F =$ ____
Within treatments	____	____		
Between subjects	____	____		
Error	____	____	3	
Total	194	____		

18. For either independent-measures or repeated-measures designs comparing two treatments, the mean difference can be evaluated with either a *t* test or an ANOVA. The two tests are related by the equation $F = t^2$. For the following data,

a. Use a repeated-measures *t* test with $\alpha = .05$ to determine whether the mean difference between treatments is statistically significant.

b. Use a repeated-measures ANOVA with $\alpha = .05$ to determine whether the mean difference between treatments is statistically significant. (You should find that $F = t^2$.)

Person	Treatment 1	Treatment 2	Difference
A	4	7	3
B	2	11	9
C	3	6	3
D	7	10	3
	$M = 4$	$M = 8.5$	$M_D = 4.5$
	$T = 16$	$T = 34$	
	$SS = 14$	$SS = 17$	$SS = 27$

19. A repeated-measures experiment comparing only two treatments can be evaluated with either a *t* statistic or an ANOVA. As we found with the independent-measures design, the *t* test and the ANOVA produce equivalent conclusions, and the two test statistics are related by the equation $F = t^2$. The following data are from a repeated-measures study:

Subject	Treatment 1	Treatment 2	Difference
1	2	4	+2
2	1	3	+2
3	0	10	+10
4	1	3	+2

a. Use a repeated-measures *t* statistic with $\alpha = .05$ to determine whether the data provide evidence of a significant difference between the two treatments. (*Caution:* ANOVA calculations are done with the *X* values, but for *t* you use the difference scores.)

b. Use a repeated-measures ANOVA with $\alpha = .05$ to evaluate the data. (You should find $F = t^2$.)

20. A recent study indicates that simply giving college students a pedometer can result in increased walking (Jackson & Howton, 2008). Students were given pedometers for a 12-week period, and asked to record the average number of steps per day during weeks 1, 6, and 12. The following data are similar to the results obtained in the study.

	Number of steps (x1000)				
	Week				
Participant	1	6	12	*P*	
A	6	8	10	24	
B	4	5	6	15	
C	5	5	5	15	$G = 72$
D	1	2	3	6	$\Sigma X^2 = 400$
E	0	1	2	3	
F	2	3	4	9	
	$T = 18$	$T = 24$	$T = 30$		
	$SS = 28$	$SS = 32$	$SS = 40$		

a. Use a repeated-measures ANOVA with $\alpha = .05$ to determine whether the mean number of steps changes significantly from one week to another.

b. Compute η^2 to measure the size of the treatment effect.

c. Write a sentence demonstrating how a research report would present the results of the hypothesis test and the measure of effect size.

21. In the Preview section for this chapter, we presented an example of a delayed discounting study in which people are willing to settle for a smaller reward today in exchange for a larger reward in the future. The following data represent the typical results from one of these studies. The participants are asked how much they would take today instead of waiting for a specific delay period to receive $1000. Each participant responds to all 5 of the delay periods. Use a repeated-measures ANOVA with $\alpha = .01$ to determine whether there are significant differences among the 5 delay periods for the following data:

Participant	1 month	6 months	1 year	2 years	5 years
A	950	850	800	700	550
B	800	800	750	700	600
C	850	750	650	600	500
D	750	700	700	650	550
E	950	900	850	800	650
F	900	900	850	750	650

22. The endorphins released by the brain act as natural painkillers. For example, Gintzler (1970) monitored endorphin activity and pain thresholds in pregnant rats during the days before they gave birth. The data showed an increase in pain threshold as the pregnancy progressed. The change was gradual until 1 or 2 days before birth, at which point there was an abrupt increase in pain threshold. Apparently a natural painkilling mechanism was preparing the animals for the stress of giving birth. The following data represent pain-threshold scores similar to the results obtained by Gintzler. Do these data indicate a significant change in pain threshold? Use a repeated-measures ANOVA with $\alpha = .01$.

	Days Before Giving Birth			
Subject	7	5	3	1
A	39	40	49	52
B	38	39	44	55
C	44	46	50	60
D	40	42	46	56
E	34	33	41	52

CHAPTER

14

Two-Factor Analysis of Variance (Independent Measures)

Tools You Will Need

The following items are considered essential background material for this chapter. If you doubt your knowledge of any of these items, you should review the appropriate chapter or section before proceeding.

- Introduction to analysis of variance (Chapter 12)
  - The logic of analysis of variance
  - ANOVA notation and formulas
  - Distribution of *F*-ratios

Preview

Imagine that you are seated at your desk, ready to take the final exam in statistics. Just before the exams are handed out, a television crew appears and sets up a camera and lights aimed directly at you. They explain that they are filming students during exams for a television special. You are told to ignore the camera and go ahead with your exam.

Would the presence of a TV camera affect your performance on an exam? For some of you, the answer to this question is "definitely yes" and for others, "probably not." In fact, both answers are right; whether the TV camera affects performance depends on your personality. Some of you would become terribly distressed and self-conscious, while others really could ignore the camera and go on as if everything were normal.

In an experiment that duplicates the situation we have described, Shrauger (1972) tested participants on a concept-formation task. Half of the participants worked alone (no audience), and half worked with an audience of people who claimed to be interested in observing the experiment. Shrauger also divided the participants into two groups on the basis of personality: those high in self-esteem and those low in self-esteem. The dependent variable for this experiment was the number of errors on the concept formation task. Data similar to those obtained by Shrauger are shown in Figure 14.1. Notice that the audience had no effect on the high-self-esteem participants. However, the low-self-esteem participants made nearly twice as many errors with an audience as when working alone.

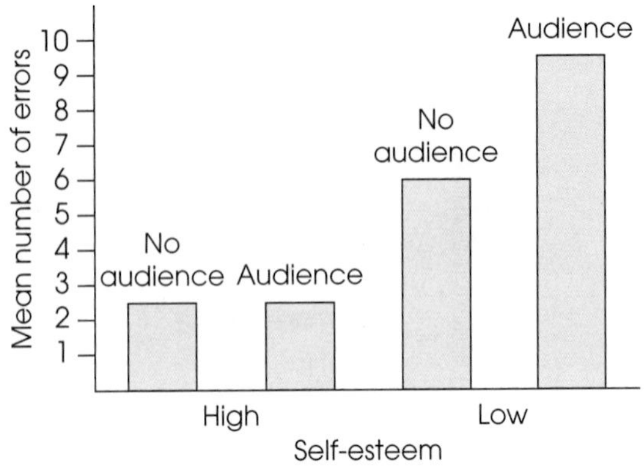

FIGURE 14.1

Results of an experiment examining the effect of an audience on the number of errors made on a concept formation task for participants who are rated either high or low in self-esteem. Notice that the effect of the audience depends on the self-esteem of the participants.

Shrauger, J. S. (1972). Self-esteem and reactions to being observed by others. *Journal of Personality and Social Psychology*, *23*, 192–200. Copyright 1972 by the American Psychological Association. Adapted by permission of the author.

The Problem: Shrauger's study is an example of research that involves two independent variables in the same study. The independent variables are:

1. Audience (present or absent)
2. Self-esteem (high or low)

The results of the study indicate that the effect of one variable (audience) *depends on* another variable (self-esteem).

You should realize that it is quite common to have two variables that interact in this way. For example, a drug may have a profound effect on some patients and have no effect whatsoever on others. Some children survive abusive environments and live normal, productive lives, while others show serious difficulties. To observe how one variable interacts with another, it is necessary to study both variables simultaneously in one study. However, the analysis of variance (ANOVA) procedures introduced in Chapters 12 and 13 are limited to evaluating mean differences produced by one independent variable and are not appropriate for mean differences involving two (or more) independent variables.

The Solution: ANOVA is a very flexible hypothesis testing procedure and can be modified again to evaluate the mean differences produced in a research study with two (or more) independent variables. In this chapter we introduce the *two-factor* ANOVA, which tests the significance of each independent variable acting alone as well as the interaction between variables.

14.1 AN OVERVIEW OF THE TWO-FACTOR, INDEPENDENT-MEASURES ANOVA

In most research situations, the goal is to examine the relationship between two variables. Typically, the research study attempts to isolate the two variables to eliminate or reduce the influence of any outside variables that may distort the relationship being studied. A typical experiment, for example, focuses on one independent variable (which is expected to influence behavior) and one dependent variable (which is a measure of the behavior). In real life, however, variables rarely exist in isolation. That is, behavior usually is influenced by a variety of different variables acting and interacting simultaneously. To examine these more complex, real-life situations, researchers often design research studies that include more than one independent variable. Thus, researchers systematically change two (or more) variables and then observe how the changes influence another (dependent) variable.

An independent variable is a manipulated variable in an experiment. A quasi-independent variable is not manipulated but defines the groups of scores in a nonexperimental study.

In Chapters 12 and 13, we examined ANOVA for *single-factor* research designs—that is, designs that included only one independent variable or only one quasi-independent variable. When a research study involves more than one factor, it is called a *factorial design*. In this chapter, we consider the simplest version of a factorial design. Specifically, we examine ANOVA as it applies to research studies with exactly two factors. In addition, we limit our discussion to studies that use a separate sample for each treatment condition—that is, independent-measures designs. Finally, we consider only research designs for which the sample size (n) is the same for all treatment conditions. In the terminology of ANOVA, this chapter examines *two-factor, independent-measures, equal* n *designs.*

We use Shrauger's audience and self-esteem study described in the Chapter Preview to introduce the two-factor research design. Table 14.1 shows the structure of Shrauger's study. Note that the study involves two separate factors: One factor is manipulated by the researcher, changing from no-audience to audience, and the second factor is self-esteem, which varies from high to low. The two factors are used to create a *matrix* with the different levels of self-esteem defining the rows and the different audience conditions defining the columns. The resulting two-by-two matrix shows four different combinations of the variables, producing four different conditions. Thus, the research study would require four separate samples, one for each *cell*, or box, in the matrix. The dependent variable for the study is the number of errors on the concept-formation task for people observed in each of the four conditions.

TABLE 14.1

The structure of a two-factor experiment presented as a matrix. The two factors are self-esteem and presence/absence of an audience, with two levels for each factor.

		Factor *B*: Audience Condition	
		No Audience	Audience
Factor *A*: Self-Esteem	Low	Scores for a group of participants who are classified as low self-esteem and are tested with no audience.	Scores for a group of participants who are classified as low self-esteem and are tested with an audience.
	High	Scores for a group of participants who are classified as high self-esteem and are tested with no audience.	Scores for a group of participants who are classified as high self-esteem and are tested with an audience.

The two-factor ANOVA tests for mean differences in research studies that are structured like the audience-and-self-esteem example in Table 14.1. For this example, the two-factor ANOVA evaluates three separate sets of mean differences:

1. What happens to the mean number of errors when the audience is added or taken away?
2. Is there a difference in the mean number of errors for participants with high self-esteem compared to those with low self-esteem?
3. Is the mean number of errors affected by specific combinations of self-esteem and audience? (For example, an audience may have a large effect on participants with low self-esteem but only a small effect for those with high self-esteem.)

Thus, the two-factor ANOVA allows us to examine three types of mean differences within one analysis. In particular, we conduct three separate hypotheses tests for the same data, with a separate F-ratio for each test. The three F-ratios have the same basic structure:

$$F = \frac{\text{variance (differences) between treatments}}{\text{variance (differences) expected if there is no treatment effect}}$$

In each case, the numerator of the F-ratio measures the actual mean differences in the data, and the denominator measures the differences that would be expected if there is no treatment effect. As always, a large value for the F-ratio indicates that the sample mean differences are greater than would be expected by chance alone, and, therefore, provides evidence of a treatment effect. To determine whether the obtained F-ratios are *significant*, we need to compare each F-ratio with the critical values found in the F-distribution table in Appendix B.

14.2 MAIN EFFECTS AND INTERACTIONS

As noted in the previous section, a two-factor ANOVA actually involves three distinct hypothesis tests. In this section, we examine these three tests in more detail.

Traditionally, the two independent variables in a two-factor experiment are identified as factor A and factor B. For the study presented in Table 14.1, self-esteem is factor A, and the presence or absence of an audience is factor B. The goal of the study is to evaluate the mean differences that may be produced by either of these factors acting independently or by the two factors acting together.

MAIN EFFECTS

One purpose of the study is to determine whether differences in self-esteem (factor A) result in differences in performance. To answer this question, we compare the mean score for all of the participants with low self-esteem with the mean for those with high self-esteem. Note that this process evaluates the mean difference between the top row and the bottom row in Table 14.1.

To make this process more concrete, we present a set of hypothetical data in Table 14.2. The table shows the mean score for each of the treatment conditions (cells) as well as the overall mean for each column (each audience condition) and the overall mean for each row (each self-esteem group). These data indicate that the low self-esteem participants (the top row) had an overall mean of $M = 8$ errors. This overall mean was obtained by computing the average of the two means in the top row. In

TABLE 14.2

Hypothetical data for an experiment examining the effect of an audience on participants with different levels of self-esteem.

	No Audience	Audience	
Low	$M = 7$	$M = 9$	$M = 8$
High	$M = 3$	$M = 5$	$M = 4$
	$M = 5$	$M = 7$	

contrast, the high self-esteem participants had an overall mean of $M = 4$ errors (the mean for the bottom row). The difference between these means constitutes what is called the *main effect* for self-esteem, or the *main effect for factor* A.

Similarly, the main effect for factor B (audience condition) is defined by the mean difference between the columns of the matrix. For the data in Table 14.2, the two groups of participants tested with no audience had an overall mean score of $M = 5$ errors. Participants tested with an audience committed an overall average of $M = 7$ errors. The difference between these means constitutes the *main effect* for the audience conditions, or the *main effect for factor* B.

DEFINITION

The mean differences among the levels of one factor are referred to as the **main effect** of that factor. When the design of the research study is represented as a matrix with one factor determining the rows and the second factor determining the columns, then the mean differences among the rows describe the main effect of one factor, and the mean differences among the columns describe the main effect for the second factor.

The mean differences between columns or rows simply *describe* the main effects for a two-factor study. As we have observed in earlier chapters, the existence of sample mean differences does not necessarily imply that the differences are *statistically significant*. In general, two samples are not expected to have exactly the same means. There are always small differences from one sample to another, and you should not automatically assume that these differences are an indication of a systematic treatment effect. In the case of a two-factor study, any main effects that are observed in the data must be evaluated with a hypothesis test to determine whether they are statistically significant effects. Unless the hypothesis test demonstrates that the main effects are significant, you must conclude that the observed mean differences are simply the result of sampling error.

The evaluation of main effects accounts for two of the three hypothesis tests in a two-factor ANOVA. We state hypotheses concerning the main effect of factor A and the main effect of factor B and then calculate two separate F-ratios to evaluate the hypotheses.

For the example we are considering, factor A involves the comparison of two different levels of self-esteem. The null hypothesis would state that there is no difference between the two levels; that is, self-esteem has no effect on performance. In symbols,

$$H_0: \quad \mu_{A_1} = \mu_{A_2}$$

The alternative hypothesis is that the two different levels of self-esteem do produce different scores:

$$H_1: \quad \mu_{A_1} \neq \mu_{A_2}$$

To evaluate these hypotheses, we compute an F-ratio that compares the actual mean differences between the two self-esteem levels versus the amount of difference that would be expected without any systematic treatment effects.

$$F = \frac{\text{variance (differences) between the means for factor } A}{\text{variance (differences) expected if there is no treatment effect}}$$

$$F = \frac{\text{variance (differences) between the row means}}{\text{variance (differences) expected if there is no treatment effect}}$$

Similarly, factor B involves the comparison of the two different audience conditions. The null hypothesis states that there is no difference in the mean number of errors between the two conditions. In symbols,

$$H_0\colon \quad \mu_{B_1} = \mu_{B_2}$$

As always, the alternative hypothesis states that the means are different:

$$H_1\colon \quad \mu_{B_1} \neq \mu_{B_2}$$

Again, the F-ratio compares the obtained mean difference between the two audience conditions versus the amount of difference that would be expected if there is no systematic treatment effect.

$$F = \frac{\text{variance (differences) between the means for factor } B}{\text{variance (differences) expected if there is no treatment effect}}$$

$$F = \frac{\text{variance (differences) between the column means}}{\text{variance (differences) expected if there is no treatment effect}}$$

INTERACTIONS

In addition to evaluating the main effect of each factor individually, the two-factor ANOVA allows you to evaluate other mean differences that may result from unique combinations of the two factors. For example, specific combinations of self-esteem and an audience acting together may have effects that are different from the effects of self-esteem or an audience acting alone. Any "extra" mean differences that are not explained by the main effects are called an *interaction,* or an *interaction between factors*. The real advantage of combining two factors within the same study is the ability to examine the unique effects caused by an interaction.

DEFINITION

An **interaction** between two factors occurs whenever the mean differences between individual treatment conditions, or cells, are different from what would be predicted from the overall main effects of the factors.

To make the concept of an interaction more concrete, we reexamine the data shown in Table 14.2. For these data, there is no interaction; that is, there are no extra mean differences that are not explained by the main effects. For example, within each audience condition (each column of the matrix) the average number of errors for the low self-esteem participants is 4 points higher than the average for the high self-esteem participants. This 4-point mean difference is exactly what is predicted by the overall main effect for self-esteem.

Now consider a different set of data shown in Table 14.3. These new data show exactly the same main effects that existed in Table 14.2 (the column means and the row

TABLE 14.3

Hypothetical data for an experiment examining the effect of an audience on participants with different levels of self-esteem. The data show the same main effects as the values in Table 14.5 but the individual treatment means have been modified to create an interaction.

	No Audience	Audience	
Low	$M = 6$	$M = 10$	$M = 8$
High	$M = 4$	$M = 4$	$M = 4$
	$M = 5$	$M = 7$	

The data in Table 14.3 show the same pattern of results that was obtained in Shrauger's research study.

means have not been changed). But now there is an interaction between the two factors. For example, for the low self-esteem participants (top row), there is a 4-point difference in the number of errors committed with an audience and without an audience. This 4-point difference cannot be explained by the 2-point main effect for the audience factor. Also, for the high self-esteem participants (bottom row), the data show no difference between the two audience conditions. Again, the zero difference is not what would be expected based on the 2-point main effect for the audience factor. Mean differences that are not explained by the main effects are an indication of an interaction between the two factors.

To evaluate the interaction, the two-factor ANOVA first identifies mean differences that are not explained by the main effects. The extra mean differences are then evaluated by an F-ratio with the following structure:

$$F = \frac{\text{variance (mean differences) not explained by main effects}}{\text{variance (differences) expected if there is no treatment effects}}$$

The null hypothesis for this F-ratio simply states that there is no interaction:

> H_0: There is no interaction between factors A and B. All of the mean differences between treatment conditions are explained by the main effects of the two factors.

The alternative hypothesis is that there is an interaction between the two factors:

> H_1: There is an interaction between factors. The mean differences between treatment conditions are not what would be predicted from the overall main effects of the two factors.

MORE ABOUT INTERACTIONS

In the previous section, we introduced the concept of an interaction as the unique effect produced by two factors working together. This section presents two alternative definitions of an interaction. These alternatives are intended to help you understand the concept of an interaction and to help you identify an interaction when you encounter one in a set of data. You should realize that the new definitions are equivalent to the original and simply present slightly different perspectives on the same concept.

The first new perspective on the concept of an interaction focuses on the notion of independence for the two factors. More specifically, if the two factors are independent, so that one factor does not influence the effect of the other, then there is no interaction. On the other hand, when the two factors are not independent, so that the effect of one factor *depends on* the other, then there is an interaction. The notion of dependence between factors is consistent with our earlier discussion of interactions. If one factor influences the effect of the other, then unique combinations of the factors produce unique effects.

DEFINITION

When the effect of one factor depends on the different levels of a second factor, then there is an **interaction** between the factors.

This definition of an interaction should be familiar in the context of a "drug interaction." Your doctor and pharmacist are always concerned that the effect of one medication may be altered or distorted by a second medication that is being taken at the same time. Thus, the effect of one drug (factor A) depends on a second drug (factor B), and you have an interaction between the two drugs.

Returning to Table 14.2, notice that the size of the audience effect (first column versus second column) *does not depend* on the self-esteem of the participants. For these data, adding an audience produces the same 2-point increase in errors for both groups of participants. Thus, the audience effect does not depend on self-esteem, and there is no interaction. Now consider the data in Table 14.3. This time, the effect of adding an audience *depends on* the self-esteem of the participants. For example, there is a 4-point increase in errors for the low-self-esteem participants but adding an audience has no effect on the errors for the high-self-esteem participants. Thus, the audience effect depends on the level of self-esteem, which means that there is an interaction between the two factors.

The second alternative definition of an interaction is obtained when the results of a two-factor study are presented in a line graph. In this case, the concept of an interaction can be defined in terms of the pattern displayed in the graph. Figure 14.2 shows the two sets of data we have been considering. The original data from Table 14.2, where there is no interaction, are presented in Figure 14.2(a). To construct this figure, we selected one of the factors to be displayed on the horizontal axis; in this case, the different levels of the audience factor. The dependent variable, the number of errors, is shown on the vertical axis. Note that the figure actually contains two separate graphs: The top line shows the relationship between the audience factor and errors for the low-self-esteem

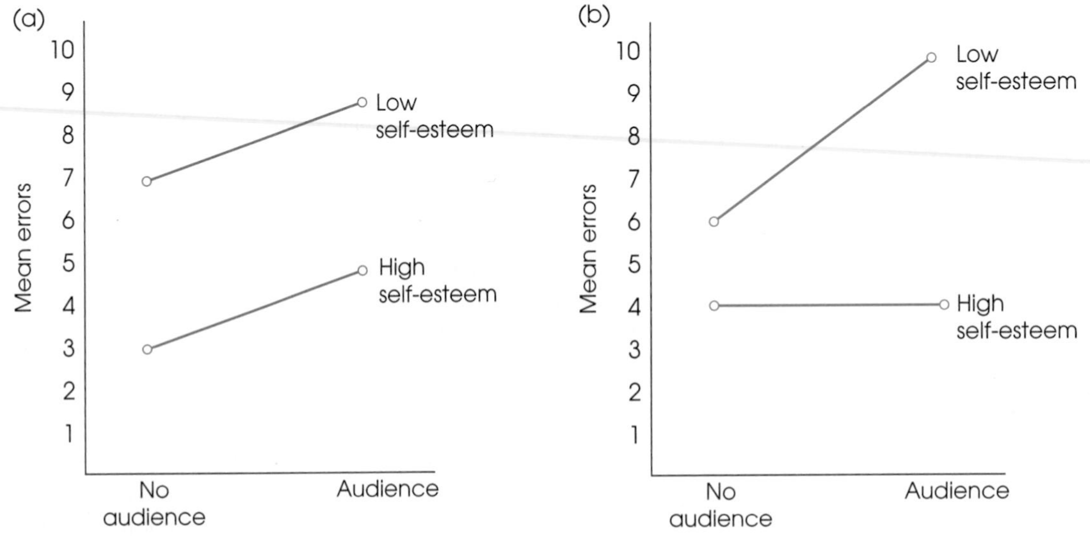

FIGURE 14.2

(a) Graph showing the treatment means from Table 14.2, for which there is no reaction. (b) Graph for Table 14.3, for which there is an interaction.

participants, and the bottom line shows the relationship for the high-self-esteem participants. In general, the picture in the graph matches the structure of the data matrix; the columns of the matrix appear as values along the X-axis, and the rows of the matrix appear as separate lines in the graph (Box 14.1).

For the original set of data, Figure 14.2(a), note that the two lines are parallel; that is, the distance between lines is constant. In this case, the distance between lines reflects the 2-point difference in mean errors between low- and high-self-esteem participants, and this 2-point difference is the same for both audience conditions.

Now look at a graph that is obtained when there is an interaction in the data. Figure 14.2(b) shows the data from Table 14.3. This time, note that the lines in the graph are not parallel. The distance between the lines changes as you scan from left to right. For these data, the distance between the lines corresponds to the self-esteem effect—that is, the mean difference in errors for low- versus high-self-esteem participants. The fact that this difference depends on the audience condition is an indication of an interaction between the two factors.

DEFINITION

When the results of a two-factor study are presented in a graph, the existence of nonparallel lines (lines that cross or converge) indicates an **interaction** between the two factors.

The $A \times B$ interaction typically is called the "A by B" interaction. If there is an interaction between an audience and self-esteem, it may be called the "audience by self-esteem" interaction.

For many students, the concept of an interaction is easiest to understand using the perspective of interdependency; that is, an interaction exists when the effects of one variable *depend* on another factor. However, the easiest way to identify an interaction within a set of data is to draw a graph showing the treatment means. The presence of nonparallel lines is an easy way to spot an interaction.

BOX 14.1 GRAPHING RESULTS FROM A TWO-FACTOR DESIGN

One of the best ways to get a quick overview of the results from a two-factor study is to present the data in a line graph. Because the graph must display the means obtained for *two* independent variables (two factors), constructing the graph can be a bit more complicated than constructing the single-factor graphs we presented in Chapter 3 (pp. 93–95).

Figure 14.3 shows a line graph presenting the results from a two-factor study with 2 levels of factor A and 3 levels of factor B. With a 2×3 design, there are a total of 6 different treatment means, which are shown in the following matrix.

		Factor B		
		$B1$	$B2$	$B3$
Factor A	A_1	10	40	20
	A_2	30	50	30

In the graph, note that values for the dependent variable (the treatment means) are shown on the vertical axis. Also note that the levels for one factor (we selected factor B) are displayed on the horizontal axis. Directly above the B_1 value on the horizontal axis, we have placed two dots corresponding to the two means in the B_1 column of the data matrix. Similarly, we have placed two dots above B_2 and another two dots above B_3. Finally, we have drawn a line connecting the three dots corresponding to level 1 of factor A (the three means in the top row of the data matrix). We have also drawn a second line that connects the three dots corresponding to level 2 of factor A. These lines are labeled A_1 and A_2 in the figure.

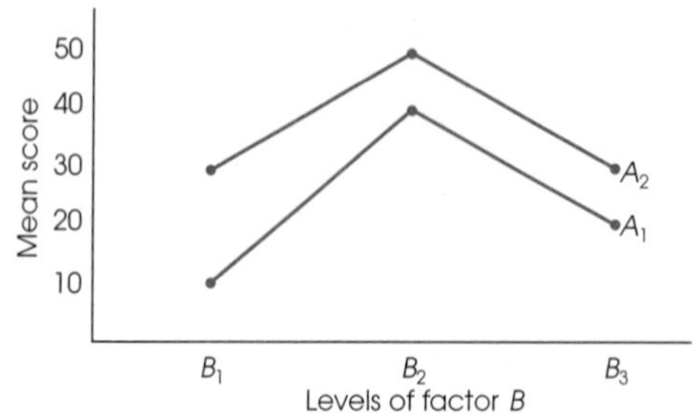

FIGURE 14.3
A line graph showing the results from a two-factor experiment.

INDEPENDENCE OF MAIN EFFECTS AND INTERACTIONS

The two-factor ANOVA consists of three hypothesis tests, each evaluating specific mean differences: the A effect, the B effect, and the $A \times B$ interaction. As we have noted, these are three *separate* tests, but you should also realize that the three tests are *independent*. That is, the outcome for any one of the three tests is totally unrelated to the outcome for either of the other two. Thus, it is possible for data from a two-factor study to display any possible combination of significant and/or nonsignificant main effects and interactions. The data sets in Table 14.4 show several possibilities.

Table 14.4(a) shows data with mean differences between levels of factor A (an A effect) but no mean differences for factor B and no interaction. To identify the A effect, notice that the overall mean for A_1 (the top row) is 10 points higher than the overall mean for A_2 (the bottom row). This 10-point difference is the main effect for factor A. To evaluate the B effect, notice that both columns have exactly the same overall mean, indicating no difference between levels of factor B; hence, there is no B effect. Finally, the absence of an interaction is indicated by the fact that the overall A effect (the 10-point difference) is constant within each column; that is, the A effect *does not depend* on the levels of factor B. (Another indication is that the data indicate that the overall B effect is constant within each row.)

Table 14.4(b) shows data with an A effect and a B effect but no interaction. For these data, the A effect is indicated by the 10-point mean difference between rows, and the B effect is indicated by the 20-point mean difference between columns. The fact that the 10-point A effect is constant within each column indicates no interaction.

Finally, Table 14.4(c) shows data that display an interaction but no main effect for factor A or for factor B. For these data, there is no mean difference between rows (no A effect) and no mean difference between columns (no B effect). However, within each row (or within each column), there are mean differences. The "extra" mean differences within the rows and columns cannot be explained by the overall main effects and, therefore, indicate an interaction.

TABLE 14.4
Three sets of data showing different combinations of main effects and interaction for a two-factor study. (The numerical value in each cell of the matrices represents the mean value obtained for the sample in that treatment condition.)

(a) Data showing a main effect for factor A but no B effect and no interaction

	B_1	B_2		
A_1	20	20	A_1 mean = 20	↕ 10-point difference
A_2	10	10	A_2 mean = 10	
	B_1 mean = 15	B_2 mean = 15		

↔ No difference

(b) Data showing main effects for both factor A and factor B but no interaction

	B_1	B_2	
A_1	10	30	A_1 mean = 20
A_2	20	40	A_2 mean = 30
	B_1 mean = 15	B_2 mean = 35	

10-point difference (between A_1 mean and A_2 mean)

20-point difference (between B_1 mean and B_2 mean)

(c) Data showing no main effect for either factor but an interaction

	B_1	B_2	
A_1	10	20	A_1 mean = 15
A_2	20	10	A_2 mean = 15
	B_1 mean = 15	B_2 mean = 15	

No difference (between A_1 mean and A_2 mean)

No difference (between B_1 mean and B_2 mean)

LEARNING CHECK

1. Each of the following matrices represents a possible outcome of a two-factor experiment. For each experiment:
   a. Describe the main effect for factor A.
   b. Describe the main effect for factor B.
   c. Does there appear to be an interaction between the two factors?

Experiment I

	B_1	B_2
A_1	$M = 10$	$M = 20$
A_2	$M = 30$	$M = 40$

Experiment II

	B_1	B_2
A_1	$M = 10$	$M = 30$
A_2	$M = 20$	$M = 20$

2. In a graph showing the means from a two-factor experiment, parallel lines indicate that there is no interaction. (True or false?)
3. A two-factor ANOVA consists of three hypothesis tests. What are they?
4. It is impossible to have an interaction unless you also have main effects for at least one of the two factors. (True or false?)

ANSWERS

1. For Experiment I:
   a. There is a main effect for factor A; the scores in A_2 average 20 points higher than in A_1.
   b. There is a main effect for factor B; the scores in B_2 average 10 points higher than in B_1.
   c. There is no interaction; there is a constant 20-point difference between A_1 and A_2 that does not depend on the levels of factor B.

For Experiment II:

a. There is no main effect for factor A; the scores in A_1 and in A_2 both average 20.

b. There is a main effect for factor B; on average, the scores in B_2 are 10 points higher than in B_1.

c. There is an interaction. The difference between A_1 and A_2 depends on the level of factor B. (There is a $+10$ difference in B_1 and a -10 difference in B_2.)

2. True.

3. The two-factor ANOVA evaluates the main effect for factor A, the main effect for factor B, and the interaction between the two factors.

4. False. Main effects and interactions are completely independent.

14.3 NOTATION AND FORMULAS FOR THE TWO-FACTOR ANOVA

The two-factor ANOVA is composed of three distinct hypothesis tests:

1. The main effect for factor A (often called the A-effect). Assuming that factor A is used to define the rows of the matrix, the main effect for factor A evaluates the mean differences between rows.
2. The main effect for factor B (called the B-effect). Assuming that factor B is used to define the columns of the matrix, the main effect for factor B evaluates the mean differences between columns.
3. The interaction (called the $A \times B$ interaction). The interaction evaluates mean differences between treatment conditions that are not predicted from the overall main effects from factor A and factor B.

For each of these three tests, we are looking for mean differences between treatments that are larger than would be expected if there are no treatment effects. In each case, the significance of the treatment effect is evaluated by an F-ratio. All three F-ratios have the same basic structure:

$$F = \frac{\text{variance (mean differences) between treatments}}{\text{variance (mean differences) expected if there are no treatment effects}} \qquad (14.1)$$

The general structure of the two-factor ANOVA is shown in Figure 14.4. Note that the overall analysis is divided into two stages. In the first stage, the total variability is separated into two components: between-treatments variability and within-treatments variability. This first stage is identical to the single-factor ANOVA introduced in Chapter 12, with each cell in the two-factor matrix viewed as a separate treatment condition. The within-treatments variability that is obtained in stage 1 of the analysis is used to compute the denominator for the F-ratios. As we noted in Chapter 12, within each treatment, all of the participants are treated exactly the same. Thus, any differences that exist within the treatments cannot be caused by treatment effects. As a result,

FIGURE 14.4
Structure of the analysis for a two-factor ANOVA.

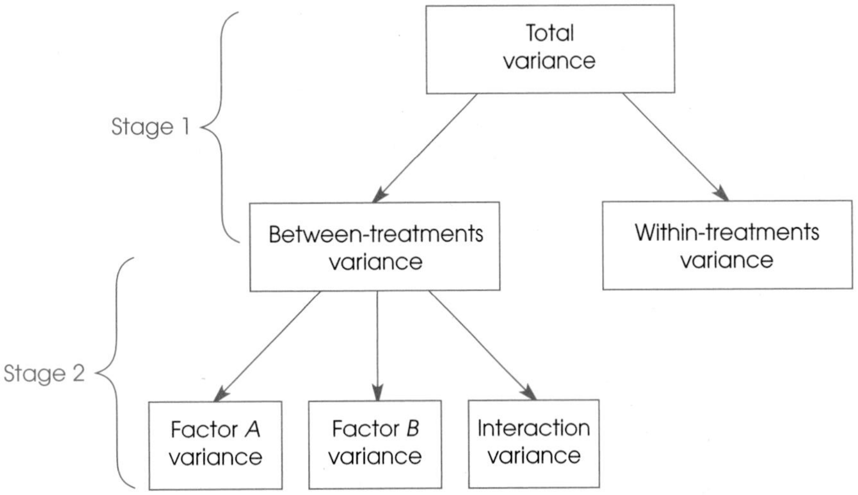

the within-treatments variability provides a measure of the differences that exist when there are no systematic treatment effects influencing the scores (see Equation 14.1).

The between-treatments variability obtained in stage 1 of the analysis combines all of the mean differences produced by factor *A*, factor *B*, and the interaction. The purpose of the second stage is to partition the differences into three separate components: differences attributed to factor *A*, differences attributed to factor *B*, and any remaining mean differences that define the interaction. These three components form the numerators for the three *F*-ratios in the analysis.

The goal of this analysis is to compute the variance values needed for the three *F*-ratios. We need three between-treatments variances (one for factor *A*, one for factor *B*, and one for the interaction), and we need a within-treatments variance. Each of these variances (or mean squares) is determined by a sum of squares value (*SS*) and a degrees of freedom value (*df*):

Remember that in ANOVA a variance is called a mean square, or *MS*.

$$\text{mean square} = MS = \frac{SS}{df}$$

EXAMPLE 14.1 We use the data shown in Table 14.5 to demonstrate the two-factor ANOVA. The data are representative of many studies examining the relationship between arousal and performance. The general result of these studies is that increasing the level of arousal (or motivation) tends to improve the level of performance. (You probably have tried to "psych yourself up" to do well on a task.) For very difficult tasks, however, increasing arousal beyond a certain point tends to lower the level of performance. (Your friends have probably advised you to "calm down and stay focused" when you get overanxious about doing well.) This relationship between arousal and performance is known as the Yerkes-Dodson law.

The data are displayed in a matrix with the two levels of task difficulty (factor *A*) making up the rows and the three levels of arousal (factor *B*) making up

TABLE 14.5

Data for a two-factor research study comparing two levels of task difficulty (easy and hard) and three levels of arousal (low, medium, and high). The study involves a total of six different treatment conditions with $n = 5$ participants in each condition.

		Factor *B* Arousal Level			
		Low	Medium	High	
Factor *A* Task Difficulty	Easy	3	1	10	
		1	4	10	
		1	8	14	
		6	6	7	$T_{ROW1} = 90$
		4	6	9	
		$M = 3$	$M = 5$	$M = 10$	
		$T = 15$	$T = 25$	$T = 50$	
		$SS = 18$	$SS = 28$	$SS = 26$	$N = 30$
					$G = 120$
					$\Sigma X^2 = 860$
	Difficult	0	2	1	
		2		7q	
		0	2	1	
		0	2	6	$T_{ROW2} = 30$
		3	2	1	
		$M = 1$	$M = 3$	$M = 2$	
		$T = 5$	$T = 15$	$T = 10$	
		$SS = 8$	$SS = 20$	$SS = 20$	
		$T_{COL1} = 20$	$T_{COL2} = 40$	$T_{COL3} = 60$	

the columns. For the easy task, note that performance scores increase consistently as arousal increases. For the difficult task, on the other hand, performance peaks at a medium level of arousal and drops when arousal is increased to a high level. Note that the data matrix has a total of six *cells,* or treatment conditions, with a separate sample of $n = 5$ subjects in each condition. Most of the notation should be familiar from the single-factor ANOVA presented in Chapter 12. Specifically, the treatment totals are identified by T values, the total number of scores in the entire study is $N = 30$, and the grand total (sum) of all 30 scores is $G = 120$. In addition to these familiar values, we have included the totals for each row and for each column in the matrix. The goal of the ANOVA is to determine whether the mean differences observed in the data are significantly greater than would be expected if there are no treatment effects.

STAGE 1 OF THE TWO-FACTOR ANOVA

The first stage of the two-factor ANOVA separates the total variability into two components: between-treatments and within-treatments. The formulas for this stage are identical to the formulas used in the single-factor ANOVA in Chapter 12 with the provision that each cell in the two-factor matrix is treated as a separate treatment condition. The formulas and the calculations for the data in Table 14.5 are as follows:

Total variability

$$SS_{total} = \Sigma X^2 - \frac{G^2}{N} \qquad (14.2)$$

For these data,

$$SS_{total} = 860 - \frac{120^2}{30}$$
$$= 860 - 480$$
$$= 380$$

This SS value measures the variability for all $N = 30$ scores and has degrees of freedom given by

$$df_{total} = N - 1 \qquad (14.3)$$

For the data in Table 14.5, $df_{total} = 29$.

Within-treatments variability To compute the variance within treatments, we first compute SS and $df = n - 1$ for each of the individual treatment conditions. Then the within-treatments SS is defined as

$$SS_{\text{within treatments}} = \Sigma SS_{\text{each treatment}} \qquad (14.4)$$

And the within-treatments df is defined as

$$df_{\text{within treatments}} = \Sigma df_{\text{each treatment}} \qquad (14.5)$$

For the six treatment conditions in Table 14.4,

$$SS_{\text{within treatments}} = 18 + 28 + 26 + 8 + 20 + 20$$
$$= 120$$
$$df_{\text{within treatments}} = 4 + 4 + 4 + 4 + 4 + 4$$
$$= 24$$

Between-treatments variability Because the two components in stage 1 must add up to the total, the easiest way to find $SS_{\text{between treatments}}$ is by subtraction.

$$SS_{\text{between treatments}} = SS_{total} - SS_{within} \qquad (14.6)$$

For the data in Table 14.4, we obtain

$$SS_{\text{between treatments}} = 380 - 120 = 260$$

However, you can also use the computational formula to calculate $SS_{\text{between treatments}}$ directly.

$$SS_{\text{between treatments}} = \Sigma\frac{T^2}{n} - \frac{G^2}{N} \qquad (14.7)$$

For the data in Table 14.4, there are six treatments (six T values), each with $n = 5$ scores, and the between-treatments SS is

$$SS_{\text{between treatments}} = \frac{15^2}{5} + \frac{25^2}{5} + \frac{50^2}{5} + \frac{5^2}{5} + \frac{15^2}{5} + \frac{10^2}{5} - \frac{120^2}{30}$$
$$= 45+125+500+5+45+20-480$$
$$= 260$$

The between-treatments *df* value is determined by the number of treatments (or the number of *T* values) minus one. For a two-factor study, the number of treatments is equal to the number of cells in the matrix. Thus,

$$df_{\text{between treatments}} = \text{number of cells} - 1 \tag{14.8}$$

For these data, $df_{\text{between treatments}} = 5$.

This completes the first stage of the analysis. Note that the two components, when added, equal the total for both *SS* values and *df* values.

$$SS_{\text{between treatments}} + SS_{\text{within treatments}} = SS_{\text{total}}$$

$$240 + 120 = 360$$

$$df_{\text{between treatments}} + df_{\text{within treatments}} = df_{\text{total}}$$

$$5 + 24 = 29$$

STAGE 2 OF THE TWO-FACTOR ANOVA

The second stage of the analysis determines the numerators for the three *F*-ratios. Specifically, this stage determines the between-treatments variance for factor *A*, factor *B*, and the interaction.

1. Factor *A*. The main effect for factor *A* evaluates the mean differences between the levels of factor *A*. For this example, factor *A* defines the rows of the matrix, so we are evaluating the mean differences between rows. To compute the *SS* for factor *A*, we calculate a between-treatment *SS* using the row totals in exactly the same way that we computed $SS_{\text{between treatments}}$ using the treatment totals (*T* values) earlier. For factor *A*, the row totals are 90 and 30, and each total was obtained by adding 15 scores.

   Therefore,

$$SS_A = \Sigma\frac{T^2_{ROW}}{n_{ROW}} - \frac{G^2}{N} \tag{14.9}$$

   For our data,

$$SS_A = \frac{90^2}{15} + \frac{30^2}{15} - \frac{120^2}{30}$$

$$= 540 + 60 - 480$$

$$= 120$$

   Factor *A* involves two treatments (or two rows), easy and difficult, so the *df* value is

$$df_A = \text{number of rows} - 1 \tag{14.10}$$

$$= 2 - 1$$

$$= 1$$

2. Factor *B*. The calculations for factor *B* follow exactly the same pattern that was used for factor *A*, except for substituting columns in place of rows. The main

effect for factor *B* evaluates the mean differences between the levels of factor *B*, which define the columns of the matrix.

$$SS_B = \Sigma \frac{T_{COL}^2}{n_{COL}} - \frac{G^2}{N} \tag{14.11}$$

For our data, the column totals are 20, 40, and 60, and each total was obtained by adding 10 scores. Thus,

$$\begin{aligned} SS_B &= \frac{20^2}{10} + \frac{40^2}{10} + \frac{60^2}{10} - \frac{120^2}{30} \\ &= 40 + 160 + 360 - 480 \\ &= 80 \end{aligned}$$

$$\begin{aligned} df_B &= \text{number of columns} - 1 \\ &= 3 - 1 \\ &= 2 \end{aligned} \tag{14.12}$$

3. The $A \times B$ Interaction. The $A \times B$ interaction is defined as the "extra" mean differences not accounted for by the main effects of the two factors. We use this definition to find the *SS* and *df* values for the interaction by simple subtraction. Specifically, the between-treatments variability is partitioned into three parts: the *A* effect, the *B* effect, and the interaction (see Figure 14.4). We have already computed the *SS* and *df* values for *A* and *B*, so we can find the interaction values by subtracting to find out how much is left. Thus,

$$SS_{A \times B} = SS_{\text{between treatments}} - SS_A - SS_B \tag{14.13}$$

For our data,

$$\begin{aligned} SS_{A \times B} &= 260 - 120 - 80 \\ &= 60 \end{aligned}$$

Similarly,

$$\begin{aligned} df_{A \times B} &= df_{\text{between treatments}} - df_A - df_B \\ &= 5 - 1 - 2 \\ &= 2 \end{aligned} \tag{14.14}$$

The two-factor ANOVA consists of three separate hypothesis tests with three separate *F*-ratios. The denominator for each *F*-ratio is intended to measure the variance (differences) that would be expected if there are no treatment effects. As we saw in Chapter 12, the within-treatments variance is the appropriate denominator for an independent-measures design. Remember that inside each treatment all of the individuals are treated exactly the same, which means that the differences that exist were not caused by any systematic treatment effects (see Chapter 12, p. 393). The within-treatments variance is called a *mean square,* or *MS*, and is computed as follows:

$$MS_{\text{within treatments}} = \frac{SS_{\text{within treatments}}}{df_{\text{within treatments}}}$$

For the data in Table 14.4,

$$MS_{\text{within treatments}} = \frac{120}{24} = 5.00$$

This value forms the denominator for all three F-ratios.

The numerators of the three F-ratios all measured variance or differences between treatments: differences between levels of factor A, differences between levels of factor B, and extra differences that are attributed to the $A \times B$ interaction. These three variances are computed as follows:

$$MS_A = \frac{SS_A}{df_A} \quad MS_B = \frac{SS_B}{df_B} \quad MS_{A\times B} = \frac{SS_{A\times B}}{df_{A\times B}}$$

For the data in Table 14.5, the three MS values are

$$MS_A = \frac{SS_A}{df_A} = \frac{120}{1} = 120 \qquad MS_B = \frac{SS_B}{df_B} = \frac{80}{2} = 40$$

$$MS_{A\times B} = \frac{SS_{A\times B}}{df_{A\times B}} = \frac{60}{2} = 30$$

Finally, the three F-ratios are

$$F_A = \frac{MS_A}{MS_{\text{within treatments}}} = \frac{120}{5} = 24.00$$

$$F_B = \frac{MS_B}{MS_{\text{within treatments}}} = \frac{40}{5} = 8.00$$

$$F_{A\times B} = \frac{MS_{A\times B}}{MS_{\text{within treatments}}} = \frac{30}{5} = 6.00$$

To determine the significance of each F-ratio, we must consult the F distribution table using the df values for each of the individual F-ratios. For this example, the F-ratio for factor A has $df = 1$ for the numerator and $df = 24$ for the denominator. Checking the table with $df = 1, 24$, we find a critical value of 4.26 for $\alpha = .05$ and a critical value of 7.82 for $\alpha = .01$. Our obtained F-ratio, $F = 24.00$ exceeds both of these values, so we conclude that there is a significant difference between the levels of factor A. That is, performance on the easy task (top row) is significantly different from performance on the difficult task (bottom row).

The F-ratio for factor B has $df = 2, 24$. The critical values obtained from the table are 3.40 for $\alpha = .05$ and 5.61 for $\alpha = .01$. Again, our obtained F-ratio, $F = 8.00$, exceeds both values, so we can conclude that there are significant differences among the levels of factor B. For this study, the three levels of arousal result in significantly different levels of performance.

Finally, the F-ratio for the $A \times B$ interaction has $df = 2, 24$ (the same as factor B). With critical values of 3.40 for $\alpha = .05$ and 5.61 for $\alpha = .01$, our obtained F-ratio of $F = 6.00$ is sufficient to conclude that there is a significant interaction between task difficulty and level of arousal.

Table 14.6 is a summary table for the complete two-factor ANOVA from Example 14.1. Although these tables are no longer commonly used in research reports, they provide a concise format for displaying all of the elements of the analysis.

LEARNING CHECK

1. Explain why the within-treatment variability is the appropriate denominator for the two-factor independent-measures F-ratios.
2. The following data summarize the results from a two-factor independent-measures experiment:

		Factor B		
		B_1	B_2	B_3
Factor A	A_1	$n = 10$ $T = 0$ $SS = 30$	$n = 10$ $T = 10$ $SS = 40$	$n = 10$ $T = 20$ $SS = 50$
	A_2	$n = 10$ $T = 40$ $SS = 60$	$n = 10$ $T = 30$ $SS = 50$	$n = 10$ $T = 20$ $SS = 40$

   a. Calculate the totals for each level of factor A, and compute SS for factor A.
   b. Calculate the totals for factor B, and compute SS for this factor. (*Note:* You should find that the totals for B are all the same, so there is no variability for this factor.)
   c. Given that the between-treatments (or between-cells) SS is equal to 100, what is the SS for the interaction?

ANSWERS

1. Within each treatment condition, all individuals are treated exactly the same. Therefore, the within-treatment variability measures the differences that exist between one score and another when there is no treatment effect causing the scores to be different. This is exactly the variance that is needed for the denominator of the F-ratios.
2. **a.** The totals for factor A are 30 and 90, and each total is obtained by adding 30 scores. $SS_A = 60$.
   b. All three totals for factor B are equal to 40. Because they are all the same, there is no variability, and $SS_B = 0$.
   c. The interaction is determined by differences that remain after the main effects have been accounted for. For these data,

$$\begin{aligned} SS_{A\times B} &= SS_{\text{between treatments}} - SS_A - SS_B \\ &= 100 - 60 - 0 \\ &= 40 \end{aligned}$$

TABLE 14.6
A summary table for the two-factor ANOVA for the data from Example 14.1.

Source	SS	df	MS	F
Between treatments	260	5		
Factor A (difficulty)	120	1	120	$F(1, 24) = 24.00$
Factor B (arousal)	80	2	40	$F(2, 24) = 8.00$
$A \times B$	60	2	30	$F(2, 24) = 6.00$
Within treatments	120	24	5	
Total	380	29		

MEASURING EFFECT SIZE FOR THE TWO-FACTOR ANOVA

The general technique for measuring effect size with an ANOVA is to compute a value for η^2, the percentage of variance that is explained by the treatment effects. For a two-factor ANOVA, we compute three separate values for eta squared: one measuring how much of the variance is explained by the main effect for factor *A*, one for factor *B*, and a third for the interaction. As we did with the repeated-measures ANOVA (p. 446), we remove any variability that can be explained by other sources before we calculate the percentage for each of the three specific effects. Thus, for example, before we compute the η^2 for factor *A*, we remove the variability that is explained by factor *B* and the variability explained by the interaction. The resulting equation is,

$$\text{for factor } A,\ \eta^2 = \frac{SS_A}{SS_{\text{total}} - SS_B - SS_{A\times B}} \qquad (14.15)$$

Note that the denominator of Equation 14.15 consists of the variability that is explained by factor *A* and the other *unexplained* variability. Thus, an equivalent version of the equation is,

$$\text{for factor } A,\ \eta^2 = \frac{SS_A}{SS_A + SS_{\text{within treatments}}} \qquad (14.16)$$

Similarly, the η^2 formulas for factor *B* and for the interaction are as follows:

$$\text{for factor } B,\ \eta^2 = \frac{SS_B}{SS_{\text{total}} - SS_A - SS_{A\times B}} = \frac{SS_B}{SS_B + SS_{\text{within treatments}}} \qquad (14.17)$$

$$\text{for } A \times B,\ \eta^2 = \frac{SS_{A\times B}}{SS_{\text{total}} - SS_A - SS_B} = \frac{SS_{A\times B}}{SS_{A\times B} + SS_{\text{within treatments}}} \qquad (14.18)$$

Because each of the η^2 equations computes a percentage that is not based on the total variability of the scores, the results are often called *partial* eta squares. For the data in Example 14.1, the equations produce the following values:

$$\eta^2 \text{ for factor } A \text{ (difficulty)} = \frac{120}{380-80-60} = \frac{120}{240} = 0.50\ (50\%)$$

$$\eta^2 \text{ for factor } B \text{ (arousal)} = \frac{80}{380-120-60} = \frac{80}{200} = 0.40\ (40\%)$$

$$\eta^2 \text{ for the interaction} = \frac{60}{380-120-80} = \frac{60}{180} = 0.33\ (33\%)$$

IN THE LITERATURE

REPORTING THE RESULTS OF A TWO-FACTOR ANOVA

The APA format for reporting the results of a two-factor ANOVA follows the same basic guidelines as the single-factor report. First, the means and standard deviations are reported. Because a two-factor design typically involves several treatment conditions, these descriptive statistics usually are presented in a table or a graph.

Next, the results of all three hypothesis tests (F-ratios) are reported. The results for the study in Example 14.1 could be reported as follows:

> The means and standard deviations for all treatment conditions are shown in Table 1. The two-factor analysis of variance showed a significant main effect for task difficulty, $F(1, 24) = 24.00$, $p < .01$, $\eta^2 = 0.50$; a significant main effect for arousal, $F(2, 24) = 8.00$, $p < .01$, $\eta^2 = 0.40$; and a significant interaction between difficulty and arousal, $F(2, 24) = 6.00$, $p < .01$, $\eta^2 = 0.33$.
>
> **TABLE 1**
>
> Mean performance score for each treatment condition.

		Level of Arousal		
		Low	Medium	High
Difficulty	Easy	$M = 3$ $SD = 2.12$	$M = 5$ $SD = 2.65$	$M = 10$ $SD = 2.55$
	Hard	$M = 1$ $SD = 1.41$	$M = 3$ $SD = 2.24$	$M = 2$ $SD = 2.24$

INTERPRETING THE RESULT FROM A TWO-FACTOR ANOVA

Because the two-factor ANOVA involves three separate tests, you must consider the overall pattern of results rather than focusing on the individual main effects or the interaction. In particular, whenever there is a significant interaction, you should be cautious about accepting the main effects at face value (whether they are significant or not). Remember, an interaction means that the effect of one factor *depends on* the level of the second factor. Because the effect changes from one level to the next, there is no consistent "main effect."

Figure 14.5 shows the sample means obtained from the task difficulty and arousal study. Recall that the analysis showed that both main effects and the interaction were

FIGURE 14.5

Sample means for the data in Example 14.1. The data are hypothetical results for a two-factor study examining how performance is related to task difficulty and level of arousal.

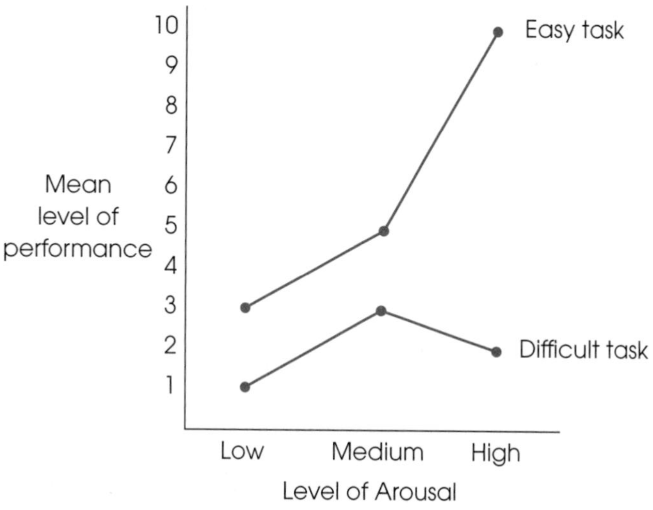

significant. The main effect for factor A (task difficulty) can be seen by the fact that the scores on the easy task are generally higher than scores on the difficult task.

The main effect for factor B (arousal) is based on the general tendency for the scores to increase as the level of arousal increases. However, this is not a completely consistent trend. In fact, the scores on the difficult task show a sharp *decrease* when arousal is increased from moderate to high. This is an example of the complications that can occur when you have a significant interaction. Remember that an interaction means that a factor does not have a consistent effect. Instead, the effect of one factor *depends on* the other factor. For the data in Figure 14.5, the effect of increasing arousal depends on the task difficulty. For the easy task, increasing arousal produces increased performance. For the difficult task, however, increasing arousal beyond a moderate level produces decreased performance. Thus, the consequences of increasing arousal *depend on* the difficulty of the task. This interdependence between factors is the source of the significant interaction.

TESTING SIMPLE MAIN EFFECTS

The existence of a significant interaction indicates that the effect (mean differences) for one factor depends on the levels of the second factor. When the data are presented in a matrix showing treatment means, a significant interaction indicates that the mean differences within one column (or row) show a different pattern than the mean differences within another column (or row). In this case, a researcher may want to perform a separate analysis for each of the individual columns (or rows). In effect, the researcher is separating the two-factor experiment into a series of separate single-factor experiments. The process of testing the significance of mean differences within one column (or one row) of a two-factor design is called testing *simple main effects.* To demonstrate this process, we once again use the data from the task-difficulty and arousal study (Example 14.1), which are summarized in Figure 14.5.

EXAMPLE 14.2

For this demonstration, we test for significant mean differences within each column of the two-factor data matrix. That is, we test for significant mean differences between the two levels of task difficulty for the low level of arousal, then repeat the test for the medium level of arousal, and once more for the high level. In terms of the two-factor notation system, we test the simple main effect of factor A for each level of factor B.

For the low level of arousal We begin by considering only the low level of arousal. Because we are restricting the data to the first column of the data matrix, the data effectively have been reduced to a single-factor study comparing only two treatment conditions. Therefore, the analysis is essentially a single-factor ANOVA duplicating the procedure presented in Chapter 12. To facilitate the change from a two-factor to a

Low Level of Arousal		
Easy Task	Difficult Task	
$n = 5$	$n = 5$	$N = 10$
$M = 3$	$M = 1$	$G = 20$
$T = 15$	$T = 5$	

single-factor ANOVA, the data for the low level of arousal (first column of the matrix) are reproduced using the notation for a single-factor study.

STEP 1 State the hypothesis. For this restricted set of the data, the null hypothesis would state that there is no difference between the mean for the easy task condition and the mean for the difficult task condition. In symbols,

$$H_0\colon \mu_{\text{easy}} = \mu_{\text{difficult}} \quad \text{for the low level of arousal}$$

STEP 2 To evaluate this hypothesis, we use an F-ratio for which the numerator, $MS_{\text{between treatments}}$, is determined by the mean differences between these two groups and the denominator consists of $MS_{\text{within treatments}}$ from the original ANOVA. Thus, the F-ratio has the structure

$$F = \frac{\text{variance (differences) for the means in column 1}}{\text{variance (differences) expected if there are no treatment effects}}$$

$$= \frac{MS_{\text{between treatments}} \text{ for the two treatments in column 1}}{MS_{\text{within treatments}} \text{ from the original ANOVA}}$$

To compute the $MS_{\text{between treatments}}$, we begin with the two treatment totals $T = 15$ and $T = 5$. Each of these totals is based on $n = 5$ scores, and the two totals add up to a grand total of $G = 20$. The $SS_{\text{between treatments}}$ for the two treatments is

$$SS_{\text{between treatments}} = \Sigma\frac{T^2}{n} - \frac{G^2}{N}$$

$$= \frac{15^2}{5} + \frac{5^2}{5} - \frac{20^2}{10}$$

$$= 45 + 5 - 40$$

$$= 10$$

$$MS_{\text{between treatments}} = \frac{SS}{df} = \frac{10}{1} = 10$$

Remember that the F-ratio uses $MS_{\text{within treatments}}$ from the original ANOVA. This $MS = 5$ with $df = 24$. Because this SS value is based on only two treatments, it has $df = 1$. Therefore,

Using $MS_{\text{within treatments}} = 5$ from the original two-factor analysis, the final F-ratio is

$$F = \frac{MS_{\text{between treatments}}}{MS_{\text{within treatments}}} = \frac{10}{5} = 2.00$$

Note that this F-ratio has the same df values (1, 24) as the test for factor A main effects (easy versus difficult) in the original ANOVA. Therefore, the critical value for the F-ratio is the same as that in the original ANOVA. With $df = 1, 24$ the critical value is 4.26. In this case, our F-ratio fails to reach the critical value, so we conclude that there is no significant difference between the two tasks, easy and difficult, at a low level of arousal.

For the medium level of arousal The test for the medium level of arousal follows the same process. The data for the medium level are as follows:

Medium Level of Arousal		
Easy Task	Difficult Task	
$n = 5$	$n = 5$	$N = 10$
$M = 5$	$M = 3$	$G = 40$
$T = 25$	$T = 15$	

Note that these data show a 2-point mean difference between the two conditions ($M = 5$ and $M = 3$), which is exactly the same as the 2-point difference that we evaluated for the low level of arousal ($M = 3$ and $M = 1$). Because the mean difference is the same for these two levels of arousal, the F-ratios are also identical. For the low level of arousal, we obtained $F(1, 24) = 2.00$, which was not significant. This test also produces $F(1, 24) = 2.00$ and again we conclude that there is no significant difference. (*Note:* You should be able to complete the test to verify this decision.)

For the high level of arousal The data for the high level are as follows:

High Level of Arousal		
Easy Task	Difficult Task	
$n = 5$	$n = 5$	$N = 10$
$M = 10$	$M = 2$	$G = 60$
$T = 50$	$Y = 10$	

For these data,

$$SS_{\text{between treatments}} = \Sigma\frac{T^2}{n} - \frac{G^2}{N}$$

$$= \frac{50^2}{5} + \frac{10^2}{5} + \frac{60^2}{10}$$

$$= 500 + 20 - 360$$

$$= 160$$

Again, we are comparing only two treatment conditions, so $df = 1$ and

$$MS_{\text{between treatments}} = \frac{SS}{df} = \frac{160}{1} = 160$$

Thus, for the high level of arousal, the final F-ratio is

$$F = \frac{MS_{\text{between treatments}}}{MS_{\text{within treatments}}} = \frac{160}{5} = 32.00$$

As before, this F-ratio has $df = 1, 24$ and is compared with the critical value $F = 4.26$. This time the F-ratio is far into the critical region and we conclude that there is a significant difference between the easy task and the difficult task for the high level of arousal.

As a final note, we should point out that the evaluation of simple main effects accounts for the interaction as well as the overall main effect for one factor. In Example 14.1, the significant interaction indicates that the effect of task difficulty (factor A) depends on the level of arousal (factor B). The evaluation of the simple main effects demonstrates this dependency. Specifically, task difficulty has no significant effect on performance when arousal level is low or medium, but does have a significant effect when arousal level is high. Thus, the analysis of simple main effects provides a detailed evaluation of the effects of one factor *including its interaction with a second factor.*

The fact that the simple main effects for one factor encompass both the interaction and the overall main effect of the factor can be seen if you consider the *SS* values. For this demonstration,

Simple Main Effects for Arousal	Interaction and Main Effect for Arousal
$SS_{\text{low arousal}} = 10$	$SS_{A\times B} = 60$
$SS_{\text{medium arousal}} = 10$	$SS_A = 120$
$SS_{\text{high arousal}} = 160$	
Total $SS = 180$	Total $SS = 180$

Notice that the total variability from the simple main effects of difficulty (factor A) completely accounts for the total variability of factor A and the $A \times B$ interaction.

14.4 USING A SECOND FACTOR TO REDUCE VARIANCE CAUSED BY INDIVIDUAL DIFFERENCES

As we noted in Chapters 10 and 12, a concern for independent-measures designs is the variance that exists within each treatment condition. Specifically, large variance tends to reduce the size of the t statistic or F-ratio and, therefore, reduces the likelihood of finding significant mean differences. Much of the variance in an independent-measures study comes from individual differences. Recall that individual differences are the characteristics, such as age or gender, that differ from one participant to the next and can influence the scores obtained in the study.

Occasionally, there are consistent individual differences for one specific participant characteristic. For example, the males in a study may consistently have lower scores than the females. Or, the older participants may have consistently higher scores than the younger participants. For example, suppose that a researcher compares two treatment conditions using a separate group of children for each condition. Each group of participants contains a mix of boys and girls. Hypothetical data for this study are shown in Table 14.7(a), with each child's gender noted with an M or an F. While examining the results, the researcher notices that the girls tend to have higher scores than the boys, which produces big individual differences and high variance within each group. Fortunately, there is a relatively simple solution to the problem of high variance. The solution involves using the specific variable, in this case gender,

TABLE 14.7

A single-factor study comparing two treatments (a) can be transformed into a two-factor study (b) by using a participant characteristic (gender) as a second factor. This process creates smaller, more homogeneous groups, which reduces the variance within groups.

(a)

Treatment I	Treatment II
3 (M)	8 (F)
4 (F)	4 (F)
4 (F)	1 (M)
0 (M)	10 (F)
6 (F)	5 (M)
1 (M)	5 (M)
2 (F)	10 (F)
4 (M)	5 (M)
$M = 3$	$M = 6$
$SS = 50$	$SS = 68$

(b)

	Treatment I	Treatment II
Males	3	1
	0	5
	1	5
	4	5
	$M = 2$	$M = 4$
	$SS = 10$	$SS = 12$
Females	4	8
	4	4
	6	10
	2	10
	$M = 4$	$M = 8$
	$SS = 8$	$SS = 24$

as a second factor. Instead of one group in each treatment, the researcher divides the participants into two separate groups within each treatment: a group of boys and a group of girls. This process creates the two-factor study shown in Table 14.7(b), with one factor consisting of the two treatments (I and II) and the second factor consisting of the gender (male and female).

By adding a second factor and creating four groups of participants instead of only two, the researcher has greatly reduced the individual differences (gender differences) within each group. This should produce a smaller variance within each group and, therefore, increase the likelihood of obtaining a significant mean difference. This process is demonstrated in the following example.

EXAMPLE 14.3

We use the data in Table 14.7 to demonstrate how the variance caused by individual differences can be reduced by adding a participant characteristic, such as age or gender, as a second factor. For the single-factor study in Table 14.7(a), the two treatments produce $SS_{\text{within treatments}} = 50 + 68 = 118$. With $n = 8$ in each treatment, we obtain $df_{\text{within treatments}} = 7 + 7 = 14$. These values produce $MS_{\text{within treatments}} = \frac{118}{14} = 8.43$, which is the denominator of the F-ratio evaluating the mean difference between treatments. For the two-factor study in Table 14.7(b), the four treatments produce $SS_{\text{within treatments}} = 10 + 12 + 8 + 24 = 54$. With $n = 4$ in each treatment, we obtain $df_{\text{within treatments}} = 3 + 3 + 3 + 3 = 12$. These value produce $MS_{\text{within treatments}} = \frac{54}{12} = 4.50$, which is the denominator of the F-ratio evaluating the main effect for the treatments. Notice that the error term for the single-factor F is nearly twice as big as the error term for the two-factor F. Reducing the individual differences within each group has greatly reduced the within-treatment variance that forms the denominator of the F-ratio.

Both designs, single-factor and two-factor, evaluate the difference between the two treatment means, $M = 3$ and $M = 6$, with $n = 8$ in each treatment. These values produce $SS_{\text{between treatments}} = 36$ and, with $k = 2$ treatments, we obtain $df_{\text{between treatments}} = 1$. Thus, $MS_{\text{between treatments}} = \frac{36}{1} = 36$. (For the two-factor design, this is the MS for the main effect of the treatment factor.) With different denominators, however, the two designs produce very different F-ratios. For the single-factor design, we obtain

$$F = \frac{MS_{\text{between treatments}}}{MS_{\text{within treatments}}} = \frac{36}{8.43} = 4.27$$

With $df = 1, 14$, the critical value for $\alpha = .05$ is $F = 4.60$. Our F-ratio is not in the critical region, so we fail to reject the null hypothesis and must conclude that there is no significant difference between the two treatments.

For the two-factor design, however, we obtain

$$F = \frac{MS_{\text{between treatments}}}{MS_{\text{within treatments}}} = \frac{36}{4.50} = 8.88$$

With $df = 1, 14$, the critical value for $\alpha = .05$ is $F = 4.75$. Our F-ratio is well beyond this value, so we reject the null hypothesis and conclude that there is a significant difference between the two treatments.

For the single-factor study in Example 14.3, the individual differences caused by gender are part of the variance within each treatment condition. This increased variance reduces the F-ratio and results in a conclusion of no significant difference between treatments. In the two-factor analysis, the individual differences caused by gender are measured by the main effect for gender, which is a between-groups factor. Because the gender differences are now between-groups rather than within-groups, they no longer contribute to the variance.

The two-factor ANOVA has other advantages beyond reducing the variance. Specifically, it allows you to evaluate mean differences between genders as well as differences between treatments, and it reveals any interaction between treatment and gender.

14.5 ASSUMPTIONS FOR THE TWO-FACTOR ANOVA

The validity of the ANOVA presented in this chapter depends on the same three assumptions we have encountered with other hypothesis tests for independent-measures designs (the t test in Chapter 10 and the single-factor ANOVA in Chapter 12):

1. The observations within each sample must be independent (see p. 254).
2. The populations from which the samples are selected must be normal.
3. The populations from which the samples are selected must have equal variances (homogeneity of variance).

As before, the assumption of normality generally is not a cause for concern, especially when the sample size is relatively large. The homogeneity of variance assumption is more important, and if it appears that your data fail to satisfy this requirement, you should conduct a test for homogeneity before you attempt the ANOVA. Hartley's F-max test (see p. 338) allows you to use the sample variances from your data to determine whether there is evidence for any differences among the population variances. Remember, for the two-factor ANOVA, there is a separate sample for each cell in the data matrix. The test for homogeneity applies to all of these samples and the populations that they represent.

SUMMARY

1. A research study with two independent variables is called a two-factor design. Such a design can be diagramed as a matrix with the levels of one factor defining the rows and the levels of the other factor defining the columns. Each cell in the matrix corresponds to a specific combination of the two factors.
2. Traditionally, the two factors are identified as factor *A* and factor *B*. The purpose of the ANOVA is to determine whether there are any significant mean differences among the treatment conditions or cells in the experimental matrix. These treatment effects are classified as follows:
   a. The *A*-effect: Overall mean differences among the levels of factor *A*.
   b. The *B*-effect: Overall mean differences among the levels of factor *B*.
   c. The $A \times B$ interaction: Extra mean differences that are not accounted for by the main effects.
3. The two-factor ANOVA produces three *F*-ratios: one for factor *A*, one for factor *B*, and one for the $A \times B$ interaction. Each *F*-ratio has the same basic structure:

$$F = \frac{MS_{\text{treatment effect}}(\text{either } A \text{ or } B \text{ or } A \times B)}{MS_{\text{within treatments}}}$$

The formulas for the *SS*, *df*, and *MS* values for the two-factor ANOVA are presented in Figure 14.6.

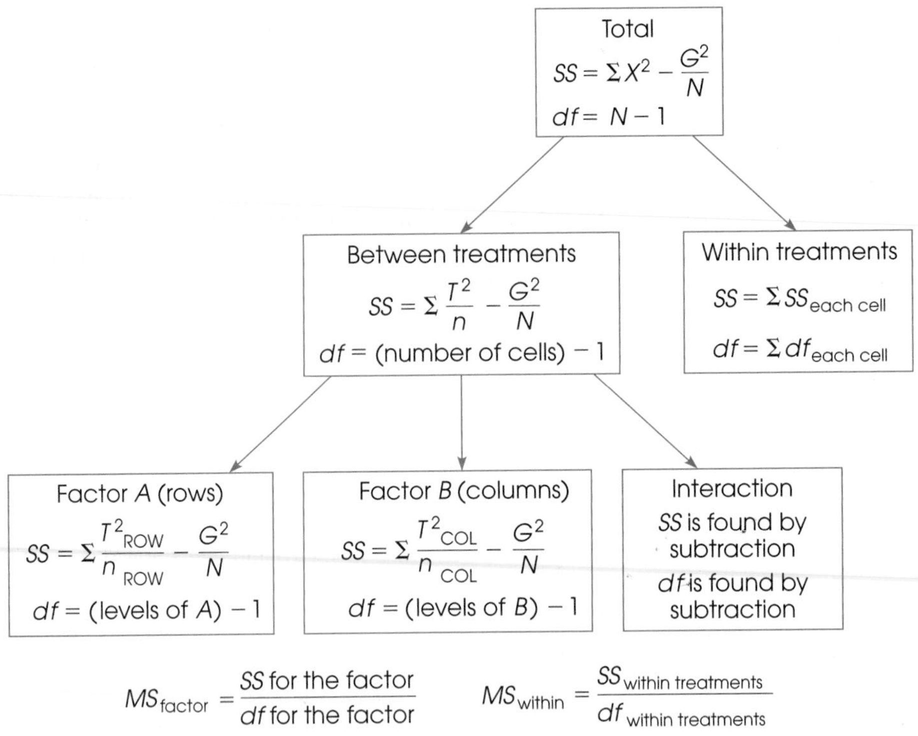

FIGURE 14.6
The ANOVA for an independent-measures two-factor design.

KEY TERMS

two-factor design (467)
matrix (467)
cells (467)
main effect (469)
interaction (470)

RESOURCES

Book Companion Website: www.cengage.com/psychology/gravetter

You can find a tutorial quiz and other learning exercises for Chapter 14 on the book companion website. The website also provides access to two workshops entitled *Two Way ANOVA* and *Factorial ANOVA* that both review the two-factor analysis presented in this chapter.

aplia

Improve your understanding of statistics with Aplia's auto-graded problem sets and immediate, detailed explanations for every question. To learn more, visit **www.aplia.com/statistics.**

CENGAGEbrain.com

Log in to CengageBrain to access the resources your instructor requires. For this book, you can access:

Psychology CourseMate brings course concepts to life with interactive learning, study, and exam preparation tools that support the printed textbook. A textbook-specific website, Psychology CourseMate includes an integrated interactive eBook and other interactive learning tools including quizzes, flashcards, and more.

Visit www.cengagebrain.com to access your account and purchase materials.

SPSS

General instructions for using SPSS are presented in Appendix D. Following are detailed instructions for using SPSS to perform the **Two-Factor, Independent-Measures Analysis of Variance (ANOVA)** presented in this chapter.

Data Entry

1. The scores are entered into the SPSS data editor in a *stacked format,* which means that all of the scores from all of the different treatment conditions are entered in a single column (VAR00001).
2. In a second column (VAR00002), enter a code number to identify the level of factor *A* for each score. If factor *A* defines the rows of the data matrix, enter a 1 beside each score from the first row, enter a 2 beside each score from the second row, and so on.
3. In a third column (VAR00003), enter a code number to identify the level of factor *B* for each score. If factor *B* defines the columns of the data matrix, enter a 1 beside each score from the first column, enter a 2 beside each score from the second column, and so on.

   Thus, each row of the SPSS data editor has one score and two code numbers, with the score in the first column, the code for factor *A* in the second column, and the code for factor *B* in the third column.

Data Analysis

1. Click **Analyze** on the tool bar, select **General Linear Model,** and click on **Univariant.**
2. Highlight the column label for the set of scores (VAR0001) in the left box and click the arrow to move it into the **Dependent Variable** box.
3. One by one, highlight the column labels for the two factor codes and click the arrow to move them into the **Fixed Factors** box.
4. If you want descriptive statistics for each treatment, click on the **Options** box, select **Descriptives,** and click **Continue.**
5. Click **OK.**

SPSS Output

We used the SPSS program to analyze the data from the arousal-and-task-difficulty study in Example 14.1 and part of the program output is shown in Figure 14.7. The output begins with a table listing the factors (not shown in Figure 14.7), followed by a table showing descriptive statistics, including the mean and standard deviation for each cell, or treatment condition. The results of the ANOVA are shown in the table labeled **Tests of Between-Subjects Effects.** The top row (*Corrected Model*) presents the between-treatments *SS* and *df* values. The second row (*Intercept*) is not relevant for our purposes. The next three rows present the two main effects and the interaction (the *SS*, *df*, and *MS* values, as well as the *F*-ratio and the level of significance), with each factor identified by its column number from the SPSS data editor. The next row (*Error*) describes the error term (denominator of the *F*-ratio), and the final row (*Corrected Total*) describes the total variability for the entire set of scores. (Ignore the row labeled *Total.*)

FOCUS ON PROBLEM SOLVING

1. Before you begin a two-factor ANOVA, take time to organize and summarize the data. It is best if you summarize the data in a matrix with rows corresponding to the levels of one factor and columns corresponding to the levels of the other factor. In each cell of the matrix, show the number of scores (n), the total and mean for the cell, and the *SS* within the cell. Also compute the row totals and column totals that are needed to calculate main effects.

2. For a two-factor ANOVA, there are three separate *F*-ratios. These three *F*-ratios use the same error term in the denominator (MS_{within}). On the other hand, these *F*-ratios have different numerators and may have different *df* values associated with each of these numerators. Therefore, you must be careful when you look up the critical *F* values in the table. The two factors and the interaction may have different critical *F* values.

DEMONSTRATION 14.1

TWO-FACTOR ANOVA

The following data are representative of the results obtained in a research study examining the relationship between eating behavior and body weight (Schachter, 1968). The two factors in this study were:

1. The participant's weight (normal or obese)
2. The participant's state of hunger (full stomach or empty stomach)

Descriptive Statistics

Dependent Variable: VAR00001

VAR00002	VAR00003	Mean	Std. Deviation	N
1.00	1.00	3.0000	2.12132	5
	2.00	5.0000	2.64575	5
	3.00	10.0000	2.54951	5
	Total	6.0000	3.79850	15
2.00	1.00	1.0000	1.41421	5
	2.00	3.0000	2.23607	5
	3.00	2.0000	2.23607	5
	Total	2.0000	2.03540	15
1.00	1.00	2.0000	2.00000	10
	2.00	4.0000	2.53859	10
	3.00	6.0000	4.78423	10
	Total	4.0000	3.61987	30

Tests of Between-Subjects Effects

Dependent Variable: VAR00001

Source	Type III Sum of Squares	df	Mean Square	F	Sig.
Corrected Model	260.000	5	52.000	10.400	.000
Intercept	480.000	1	480.000	96.000	.000
VAR00002	120.000	1	120.000	24.000	.000
VAR00003	80.000	2	40.000	8.000	.002
VAR00002 * VAR00003	60.000	2	30.000	6.000	.008
Error	120.000	24	5.000		
Total	860.000	30			
Corrected Total	380.000	29			

FIGURE 14.7

Portions of the SPSS output for the two-factor ANOVA for the arousal-and-task-difficulty study in Example 14.1.

All participants were led to believe that they were taking part in a taste test for several types of crackers, and they were allowed to eat as many crackers as they wanted. The dependent variable was the number of crackers eaten by each participant. There were two specific predictions for this study. First, it was predicted that normal participants' eating behavior would be determined by their state of hunger. That is, people with empty stomachs would eat more and people with full stomachs would eat less. Second, it was predicted that eating behavior for obese participants would not be related to their state of hunger. Specifically, it was predicted that obese participants would eat the same amount whether their stomachs were full or empty. Note that the researchers are predicting an interaction: The effect of hunger will be different for the normal participants and the obese participants. The data are as follows:

		Factor *B*: Hunger			
		Empty stomach	Full stomach		
Factor *A*: Weight	Normal	$n = 20$ $M = 22$ $T = 440$ $SS = 1540$	$n = 20$ $M = 15$ $T = 300$ $SS = 1270$	$T_{normal} = 740$	$G = 1440$ $N = 80$ $\Sigma X^2 = 31,836$
	Obese	$n = 20$ $M = 17$ $T = 340$ $SS = 1320$	$n = 20$ $M = 18$ $T = 360$ $SS = 1266$	$T_{normal} = 700$	
		$T_{empty} = 780$	$T_{full} = 660$		

STEP 1 **State the hypotheses, and select alpha.** For a two-factor study, there are three separate hypotheses, the two main effects and the interaction.

For factor *A*, the null hypothesis states that there is no difference in the amount eaten for normal participants versus obese participants. In symbols,

$$H_0: \mu_{normal} = \mu_{obese}$$

For factor *B*, the null hypothesis states that there is no difference in the amount eaten for full-stomach versus empty-stomach conditions. In symbols,

$$H_0: \mu_{full} = \mu_{empty}$$

For the $A \times B$ interaction, the null hypothesis can be stated two different ways. First, the difference in eating between the full-stomach and empty-stomach conditions will be the same for normal and obese participants. Second, the difference in eating between the normal and obese participants will be the same for the full-stomach and empty-stomach conditions. In more general terms,

> H_0: The effect of factor *A* does not depend on the levels of factor *B* (and *B* does not depend on *A*).

We use $\alpha = .05$ for all tests.

STEP 2 **The two-factor analysis.** Rather than compute the *df* values and look up critical values for *F* at this time, we proceed directly to the ANOVA.

STAGE 1 The first stage of the analysis is identical to the independent-measures ANOVA presented in Chapter 12, where each cell in the data matrix is considered a separate treatment condition.

$$SS_{\text{total}} = \Sigma X^2 - \frac{G^2}{N}$$
$$= 31{,}836 - \frac{1440^2}{80} = 5916$$

$$SS_{\text{within treatments}} = \Sigma SS_{\text{inside each treatment}} = 1540 + 1270 + 1320 + 1266 = 5396$$

$$SS_{\text{between treatments}} = \Sigma\frac{T^2}{n} - \frac{G^2}{N}$$
$$= \frac{440^2}{20} + \frac{300^2}{20} + \frac{340^2}{20} + \frac{360^2}{20} - \frac{1440^2}{80}$$
$$= 520$$

The corresponding degrees of freedom are

$$df_{\text{total}} = N - 1 = 79$$
$$df_{\text{within treatments}} = \Sigma df = 19 + 19 + 19 + 19 = 76$$
$$df_{\text{between treatments}} = \text{number of treatments} - 1 = 3$$

STAGE 2 The second stage of the analysis partitions the between-treatments variability into three components: the main effect for factor *A*, the main effect for factor *B*, and the $A \times B$ interaction.

For factor *A* (normal/obese),

$$SS_A = \Sigma\frac{T^2_{\text{ROWS}}}{n_{\text{ROWS}}} - \frac{G^2}{N}$$
$$= \frac{740^2}{40} + \frac{700^2}{40} - \frac{1440^2}{80}$$
$$= 20$$

For factor *B* (full/empty),

$$SS_B = \Sigma\frac{T^2_{\text{COLS}}}{n_{\text{COLS}}} - \frac{G^2}{N}$$
$$= \frac{780^2}{40} + \frac{660^2}{40} - \frac{1440^2}{80}$$
$$= 180$$

For the $A \times B$ interaction,

$$SS_{A\times B} = SS_{\text{between treatments}} - SS_A \times SS_B$$
$$= 520 - 20 - 180$$
$$= 320$$

The corresponding degrees of freedom are

$$df_A = \text{number of rows} - 1 = 1$$

$$df_B = \text{number of columns} - 1 = 1$$

$$\begin{aligned} df_{A \times B} &= df_{\text{between treatments}} - df_A - df_B \\ &= 3 - 1 - 1 \\ &= 1 \end{aligned}$$

The MS values needed for the F-ratios are

$$MS_A = \frac{SS_A}{df_A} = \frac{20}{1} = 20$$

$$MS_B = \frac{SS_B}{df_B} = \frac{180}{1} = 180$$

$$MS_{A \times B} = \frac{SS_{A \times B}}{df_{A \times B}} = \frac{320}{1} = 320$$

$$MS_{\text{within treatments}} = \frac{SS_{\text{within treatments}}}{df_{\text{within treatments}}} = \frac{5396}{76} = 71$$

Finally, the F-ratios are

$$F_A = \frac{MS_A}{MS_{\text{within treatments}}} = \frac{20}{71} = 0.28$$

$$F_B = \frac{MS_B}{MS_{\text{within treatments}}} = \frac{180}{71} = 2.54$$

$$F_{A \times B} = \frac{MS_{A \times B}}{MS_{\text{within treatments}}} = \frac{320}{71} = 4.51$$

STEP 3 **Make a decision and state a conclusion.** All three F-ratios have $df = 1, 76$. With $\alpha = .05$, the critical F value is 3.98 for all three tests.

For these data, factor A (weight) has no significant effect; $F(1, 76) = 0.28$. Statistically, there is no difference in the number of crackers eaten by normal versus obese participants.

Similarly, factor B (fullness) has no significant effect; $F(1, 76) = 2.54$. Statistically, the number of crackers eaten by full participants is no different from the number eaten by hungry participants. (*Note:* This conclusion concerns the combined group of normal and obese participants. The interaction concerns these two groups separately.)

These data produce a significant interaction; $F(1, 76) = 4.51$, $p < .05$. This means that the effect of fullness does depend on weight. A closer look at the original data shows that the degree of fullness did affect the normal participants, but it had no effect on the obese participants.

DEMONSTRATION 14.2

MEASURING EFFECT SIZE FOR THE TWO-FACTOR ANOVA

Effect size for each main effect and for the interaction is measured by eta squared (η^2), the percentage of variance explained by the specific main effect or interaction. In each case, the variability that is explained by other sources is removed before the percentage is computed. For the two-factor ANOVA in Demonstration 14.1,

$$\text{For factor } A,\ \eta^2 = \frac{SS_A}{SS_{\text{total}} - SS_B - SS_{A\times B}} = \frac{20}{5916-180-320} = 0.004 \text{ (or 0.4\%)}$$

$$\text{For factor } B,\ \eta^2 = \frac{SS_B}{SS_{\text{total}} - SS_A - SS_{A\times B}} = \frac{180}{5916-20-320} = 0.032 \text{ (or 3.2\%)}$$

$$\text{For } A\times B,\ \eta^2 = \frac{SS_{A\times B}}{SS_{\text{total}} - SS_A - SS_B} = \frac{320}{5916-20-180} = 0.056 \text{ (or 5.6\%)}$$

PROBLEMS

1. Define each of the following terms:
  a. Factor
  b. Level
  c. Two-factor study

2. For the data in the following matrix:

	No Treatment	Treatment	
Male	$M = 5$	$M = 3$	Overall $M = 4$
Female	$M = 9$	$M = 13$	Overall $M = 11$
	overall $M = 7$	overall $M = 8$	

  a. Which two means are compared to describe the treatment main effect?
  b. Which two means are compared to describe the gender main effect?
  c. Is there an interaction between gender and treatment? Explain your answer.

3. Briefly explain what happens during the second stage of the two-factor ANOVA.

4. The structure of a two-factor study can be presented as a matrix with the levels of one factor determining the rows and the levels of the second factor determining the columns. With this structure in mind, describe the mean differences that are evaluated by each of the three hypothesis tests that make up a two-factor ANOVA.

5. The following matrix presents the results from an independent-measures, two-factor study with a sample of $n = 10$ participants in each treatment condition. Note that one treatment mean is missing.

		Factor B	
		B_1	B_2
Factor A	A_1	$M = 20$	$M = 30$
	A_2	$M = 40$	

  a. What value for the missing mean would result in no main effect for factor A?
  b. What value for the missing mean would result in no main effect for factor B?
  c. What value for the missing mean would result in no interaction?

6. The following matrix presents the results of a two-factor study with $n = 10$ scores in each of the six treatment conditions. Note that one of the treatment means is missing.

		Factor B		
		B_1	B_2	B_3
Factor A	A_1	$M = 10$	$M = 20$	$M = 40$
	A_2	$M = 20$	$M = 30$	

a. What value for the missing mean would result in no main effect for factor *A*?
b. What value for the missing mean would result in no interaction?

7. For the data in the following graph:
a. Is there a main effect for the treatment factor?
b. Is there a main effect for the age factor?
c. Is there an interaction between age and treatment?

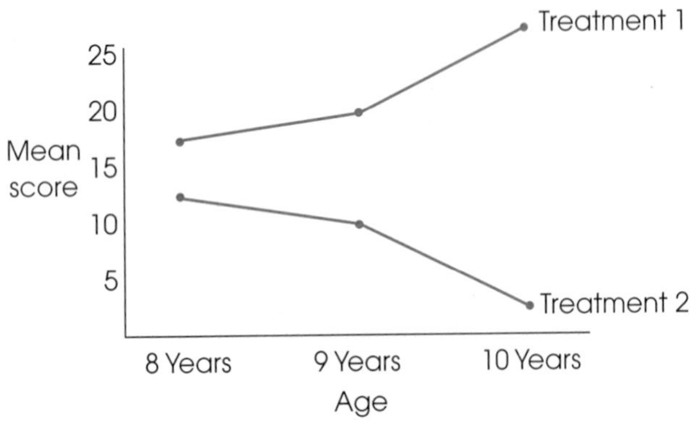

8. A researcher conducts an independent-measures, two-factor study using a separate sample of $n = 15$ participants in each treatment condition. The results are evaluated using an ANOVA and the researcher reports an *F*-ratio with $df = 1, 84$ for factor *A*, and an *F*-ratio with $df = 2, 84$ for factor *B*.
a. How many levels of factor *A* were used in the study?
b. How many levels of factor *B* were used in the study?
c. What are the *df* values for the *F*-ratio evaluating the interaction?

9. The following results are from an independent-measures, two-factor study with $n = 10$ participants in each treatment condition.

		Factor B	
		B_1	B_2
Factor A	A_1	T = 40 $M = 4$ $SS = 50$	$T = 10$ $M = 1$ $SS = 30$
	A_2	$T = 50$ $M = 5$ $SS = 60$	$T = 20$ $M = 2$ $SS = 40$

$N = 40$
$G = 120$
$\Sigma X^2 = 640$

a. Use a two-factor ANOVA with $\alpha = .05$ to evaluate the main effects and the interaction.
b. Compute η^2 to measure the effect size for each of the main effects and the interaction.

10. The following results are from an independent-measures, two-factor study with $n = 5$ participants in each treatment condition.

		Factor B		
		B_1	B_2	B_3
Factor A	A_1	T = 25 $M = 5$ $SS = 30$	$T = 40$ $M = 8$ $SS = 38$	$T = 70$ $M = 14$ $SS = 46$
	A_2	$T = 15$ $M = 3$ $SS = 22$	$T = 20$ $M = 4$ $SS = 26$	$T = 40$ $M = 8$ $SS = 30$

$N = 30$
$G = 210$
$\Sigma X^2 = 2062$

a. Use a two-factor ANOVA with $\alpha = .05$ to evaluate the main effects and the interaction.
b. Test the simple main effects using $\alpha = .05$ to evaluate the mean difference between treatment A_1 and A_2 for each level of factor *B*.

11. A researcher conducts an independent-measures, two-factor study with two levels of factor *A* and three levels of factor *B*, using a sample of $n = 12$ participants in each treatment condition.
a. What are the *df* values for the *F*-ratio evaluating the main effect of factor *A*?
b. What are the *df* values for the *F*-ratio evaluating the main effect of factor *B*?
c. What are the *df* values for the *F*-ratio evaluating the interaction?

12. The Preview section for this chapter described a two-factor study examining performance under two audience conditions (factor *B*) for high and low self-esteem participants (factor *A*). The following summary table presents possible results from the analysis of that study. Assuming that the study used a separate sample of $n = 15$ participants in each treatment condition (each cell), fill in the missing values in the table. (*Hint*: Start with the *df* values.)

Source	SS	df	MS	
Between treatments	67	——		
Audience	——	——	——	F = ——
Self-esteem	29	——	——	F = ——
Interaction	——	——	——	F = 5.50
Within treatments	——	——	4	
Total	——	——		

13. Some people like to pour beer gently down the side of the glass to preserve bubbles. Others splash it down the center to release the bubbles into a foamy head and free the aromas. Champagne, however is best when the bubbles remain concentrated in the wine. A group of French scientists recently verified the difference between the two pouring methods by measuring the amount of bubbles in each glass of champagne poured two different ways and at three different temperatures (Liger-Belair, 2010). The following data present the pattern of results obtained in the study.

	Champagne Temperature (°F)		
	40°	46°	52°
Gentle Pour	$n = 10$ $M = 7$ $SS = 64$	$n = 10$ $M = 3$ $SS = 57$	$n = 10$ $M = 2$ $SS = 47$
Splashing Pour	$n = 10$ $M = 5$ $SS = 56$	$n = 10$ $M = 1$ $SS = 54$	$n = 10$ $M = 0$ $SS = 46$

a. Use a two-factor ANOVA with $\alpha = .05$ to evaluate the mean differences.

b. Briefly explain how temperature and pouring influence the bubbles in champagne according to this pattern of results.

14. The following table summarizes the results from a two-factor study with 2 levels of factor *A* and 3 levels of factor *B* using a separate sample of $n = 8$ participants in each treatment condition. Fill in the missing values. (*Hint:* Start with the *df* values.)

Source	SS	df	MS	
Between treatments	60	——		
Factor A	——	——	5	F = ——
Factor B	——	——	——	F = ——
A × B Interaction	25	——	——	F = ——
Within treatments	——	——	2.5	
Total	——	——		

15. The following table summarizes the results from a two-factor study with 3 levels of factor *A* and 3 levels of factor *B* using a separate sample of $n = 9$ participants in each treatment condition. Fill in the missing values. (*Hint:* Start with the *df* values.)

Source	SS	df	MS	
Between treatments	144	——		
Factor A	——	——	18	F = ——
Factor B	——	——	——	F = ——
A × B Interaction	——	——	——	F = 7.0
Within treatments	——	——	——	
Total	360	——		

16. Most sports injuries are immediate and obvious, like a broken leg. However, some can be more subtle, like the neurological damage that may occur when soccer players repeatedly head a soccer ball. To examine long-term effects of repeated heading, Downs and Abwender (2002) examined two different age groups of soccer players and swimmers. The dependent variable was performance on a conceptual thinking task. Following are hypothetical data, similar to the research results.

a. Use a two-factor ANOVA with $\alpha = .05$ to evaluate the main effects and interaction.

b. Calculate the effects size (η^2) for the main effects and the interaction.

c. Briefly describe the outcome of the study.

		Factor B: Age	
		College	Older
Factor A: Sport	Soccer	$n = 20$ $M = 9$ $T = 180$ $SS = 380$	$n = 20$ $M = 4$ $T = 80$ $SS = 390$
	Swimming	$n = 20$ $M = 9$ $T = 180$ $SS = 350$	$n = 20$ $M = 8$ $T = 160$ $SS = 400$

$\Sigma X^2 = 6360$

17. The following table summarizes the results from a two-factor study with 2 levels of factor *A* and 3 levels of factor *B* using a separate sample of $n = 11$ participants in each treatment condition. Fill in the missing values. (*Hint:* Start with the *df* values.)

Source	*SS*	*df*	*MS*	
Between treatments	___	___		
Factor *A*	___	___	___	$F = 7$
Factor *B*	___	___	___	$F = 8$
$A \times B$ Interaction	___	___	___	$F = 3$
Within treatments	240	___	___	
Total	___	___		

18. In Chapter 11, we described a research study in which the color red appeared to increase men's attraction to women (Elliot & Niesta, 2008). The same researchers have published other results showing that red also increases women's attraction to men but does not appear to affect judgments of same sex individuals (Elliot, et al., 2010). Combining these results into one study produces a two-factor design in which men judge photographs of both women and men, which are shown on both red and white backgrounds. The dependent variable is a rating of attractiveness for the person shown in the photograph. The study uses a separate group of participants for each condition. The following table presents data similar to the results from previous research.

a. Use a two-factor ANOVA with $\alpha = .05$ to evaluate the main effects and the interaction.

		Person Shown in Photograph	
		Female	Male
Background Color for Photograph	White	$n = 10$ $M = 4.5$ $SS = 6$	$n = 10$ $M = 4.4$ $SS = 7$
	Red	$n = 10$ $M = 7.5$ $SS = 9$	$n = 10$ $M = 4.6$ $SS = 8$

b. Describe the effect of background color on judgments of males and females.

19. The following data are from a two-factor study examining the effects of three treatment conditions on males and females.

a. Use an ANOVA with $\alpha = .05$ for all tests to evaluate the significance of the main effects and the interaction.

b. Test the simple main effects using $\alpha = .05$ to evaluate the mean difference between males and females for each of the three treatments.

		Factor *B* Treatments			
		I	II	III	
Factor *A*: Gender	Male	1 2 6 $M = 3$ $T = 9$ $SS = 14$	7 2 9 $M = 6$ $T = 18$ $SS = 26$	9 11 7 $M = 9$ $T = 27$ $SS = 8$	$T_{male} = 54$
	Female	3 1 5 $M = 3$ $T = 9$ $SS = 8$	10 11 15 $M = 12$ $T = 36$ $SS = 14$	16 18 11 $M = 15$ $T = 45$ $SS = 26$	$T_{female} = 90$

$N = 18$
$G = 144$
$\Sigma X^2 = 1608$

20. Mathematics word problems can be particularly difficult, especially for primary-grade children. A recent study investigated a combination of techniques for teaching students to master these problems (Fuchs, Fuchs, Craddock, Hollenbeck, Hamlett, & Schatschneider, 2008). The study investigated the effectiveness of small-group tutoring and the effectiveness of a classroom instruction technique known as "hot math." The hot-math program teaches students to recognize types or categories of problems so that they can generalize skills from one problem to another. The following data are similar to the results obtained in the study. The dependent variable is a math test score for each student after 16 weeks in the study.

	No Tutoring	With Tutoring
Traditional Instruction	3 6 2 2 4 7	9 4 5 8 4 6
Hot-Math Instruction	7 7 2 6 8 6	8 12 9 13 9 9

a. Use a two-factor ANOVA with $\alpha = .05$ to evaluate the significance of the main effects and the interaction.

b. Calculate the η^2 values to measure the effect size for the two main effects.

c. Describe the pattern of results. (Is tutoring significantly better than no tutoring? Is traditional classroom instruction significantly different from hot math? Does the effect of tutoring depend on the type of classroom instruction?)

21. In Chapter 12 (p. 432), we described a study reporting that college students who are on Facebook (or have it running in the background) while studying had lower grades than students who did not use the social network (Kirschner & Karpinski, 2010). A researcher would like to know if the same result extends to students in lower grade levels. The researcher planned a two-factor study comparing Facebook users with non-users for middle school students, high school students, and college students. For consistency across groups, grades were converted into six categories, numbered 0 to 5 from low to high. The results are presented in the following matrix.

a. Use a two-factor ANOVA with $\alpha = .05$ to evaluate the mean differences.

b. Describe the pattern of results.

	Middle School	High School	College
User	3 5 5 3	5 5 2 4	5 4 2 5
Non-user	5 3 2 2	1 2 3 2	1 0 0 3

22. The following data are from a two-factor study examining the effects of two treatment conditions on males and females.

a. Use an ANOVA with $\alpha = .05$ for all tests to evaluate the significance of the main effects and the interaction.

b. Compute η^2 to measure the size of the effect for each main effect and the interaction.

Factor A: Gender	Treatments I	Treatments II	
Male	3 8 9 4 $M = 6$ $T = 24$ $SS = 26$	2 8 7 7 $M = 6$ $T = 24$ $SS = 22$	$T_{male} = 48$
Female	0 0 2 6 $M = 2$ $T = 8$ $SS = 24$	12 6 9 13 $M = 10$ $T = 40$ $SS = 30$	$T_{female} = 48$
	$T_I = 32$	$T_{II} = 64$	

$N = 16$
$G = 96$
$\Sigma X^2 = 806$

23. In the Preview section of this chapter, we presented an experiment that examined the effect of an audience on the performance of two different personality types. Data from this experiment are as follows. The dependent variable is the number of errors made by each participant.

Self-Esteem	No Audience	Audience
High	3 6 2 2 4 7	9 4 5 8 4 6
Low	7 7 2 6 8 6	10 14 11 15 11 11

a. Use an ANOVA with $\alpha = .05$ to evaluate the data. Describe the effect of the audience and the effect of self-esteem on performance.

b. Calculate the effect size (η^2) for each main effect and for the interaction.

PART IV
REVIEW

After completing this part, you should be able to perform an ANOVA to evaluate the significance of mean differences in three research situations. These include:

1. The single-factor independent-measures design introduced in Chapter 12.
2. The single-factor repeated-measures design introduced in Chapter 13.
3. The two-factor independent-measures design introduced in Chapter 14.

In this part we introduce three applications of ANOVA that use an F-ratio statistic to evaluate the mean differences among two or more populations. In each case, the F-ratio has the following structure:

$$F = \frac{\text{variance between treatments}}{\text{variance from random unsystematic sources}}$$

The numerator of the F-ratio measures the mean differences that exist from one treatment condition to another, including any systematic differences caused by the treatments. The denominator measures the differences that exist when there are no systematic factors that cause one score to be different from another. The F-ratio is structured so that the numerator and denominator are measuring exactly the same variance when the null hypothesis is true and there are no systematic treatment effects. In this case, the F-ratio should have a value near 1.00. Thus, an F-ratio near 1.00 is evidence that the null hypothesis is true. Similarly, an F-ratio that is much larger than 1.00 provides evidence that a systematic treatment effect does exist and the null hypothesis should be rejected.

For independent-measures designs, either single-factor or two-factor, the denominator of the F-ratio is obtained by computing the variance within treatments. Inside each treatment condition all participants are treated exactly the same, so there are no systematic treatment effects that cause the scores to vary.

For a repeated-measures design, the same individuals are used in every treatment condition, so any differences between treatments cannot be caused by individual differences. Thus, the numerator of the F-ratio does not include any individual differences. Therefore, individual differences must also be eliminated from the denominator to balance the F-ratio. As a result, the repeated-measures ANOVA is a two-stage process. The first stage separates the between-treatments variance (numerator) and the within-treatments variance. The second stage removes the systematic individual differences from the within-treatments variance to produce the appropriate denominator for the F-ratio.

For a two-factor design, the mean differences between treatments can be caused by either of the two factors or by specific combinations of factors. The goal of the ANOVA is to separate these possible treatment effects so that each can be evaluated independent of the others. To accomplish this, the two-factor ANOVA is a two-stage process. The first stage separates the between-treatments variance and the within-treatments variance (denominator). The second stage analyzes the between-treatments variance into three components: the main effect from the first factor, the main effect from the second factor, and the interaction.

Note that the repeated-measures ANOVA and the two-factor ANOVA are both two-stage processes. Both begin by separating the total variance into between-treatments and within-treatments variance. However, the second stages of these two ANOVAs serve different purposes and focus on different components. The repeated-measures ANOVA focuses on the within-treatments variance and removes the individual differences to obtain the error variance. The two-factor ANOVA separates the between-treatments variance into the two main effects and the interaction.

REVIEW EXERCISES

1. Recent research indicates that the effectiveness of antidepressant medication is directly related to the severity of the depression (Khan, Brodhead, Kolts, & Brown, 2005). Based on pre-treatment depression scores, patients were divided into four groups by level of depression. After receiving the antidepressant medication, depression scores were measured again and the amount of improvement was recorded for each patient. The following data are similar to the results of the study.
   a. Do the data indicate significant differences among the four levels of severity? Test with $\alpha = .05$.
   b. Compute η^2, the percentage of variance explained by the group differences.
   c. Write a sentence demonstrating how the outcome of the hypothesis test and the measure of effect size would appear in a research report.

Low Moderate	High Moderate	Moderately Severe	Severe	
0	1	4	5	$N = 16$
2	3	6	6	$G = 48$
2	2	2	6	$\Sigma X^2 = 204$
0	2	4	3	
$M = 1$	$M = 2$	$M = 4$	$M = 5$	
$T = 4$	$T = 8$	$T = 16$	$T = 20$	
$SS = 4$	$SS = 2$	$SS = 8$	$SS = 6$	

2. Loss of hearing can be a significant problem for older adults. Although hearing aids can correct the physical

problem, people who have lived with hearing impairment often develop poor communication strategies and social skills. To address this problem, a home education program has been developed to help people who are receiving hearing aids for the first time. The program emphasizes communication skills. To evaluate the program, overall quality of life and satisfaction were measured before treatment, again at the end of the training program, and once more at a 6-month follow-up (Kramer, Allessie, Dondorp, Zekveld, & Kapteyn, 2005). Data similar to the results obtained in the study are shown below.

	Quality-of-Life Scores			
Person	Before	After	6 Months	
A	3	7	8	$N = 12$
B	0	5	7	$G = 60$
C	4	9	5	$\Sigma X^2 = 384$
D	1	7	4	
	$T = 8$	$T = 28$	$T = 24$	
	$SS = 10$	$SS = 8$	$SS = 10$	

a. Do the data indicate a significant improvement in the quality of life following the training program? Test at the .05 level of significance.
b. Calculate η^2 to measure the size of the effect.
c. Write a sentence demonstrating how the outcome of the hypothesis test and the measure of effect size would appear in a research report.

3. Briefly describe what is meant by an interaction between factors in a two-factor research study.
4. A recent study of driving behavior suggests that self-reported measures of high driving skills and low ratings of safety skills create a dangerous combination (Sümer, Özkan, & Lajunen, 2006). (*Note:* Those who rate themselves as highly skilled drivers are probably overly confident.) Drivers were classified as high or low in self-rated skill based on responses to a driver-skill inventory, then classified as high or low in safety skill based on responses to a driver-aggression scale. An overall measure of driving risk was obtained by combining several variables such as number of accidents, tickets, tendency to speed, and tendency to pass other cars. The following data represent results similar to those obtained in the study. Use a two-factor ANOVA with $\alpha = .05$ to evaluate the results.

		Self-Rated Driving Skill		
		Low	High	
Driving Safety	Low	$n = 8$ $M = 5$ $T = 40$ $SS = 52$	$n = 8$ $M = 8.5$ $T = 68$ $SS = 71$	$N = 32$ $G = 160$ $\Sigma X^2 = 1151$
	High	$n = 8$ $M = 3$ $T = 24$ $SS = 34$	$n = 8$ $M = 3.5$ $T = 28$ $SS = 46$	

PART

V

Correlations and Nonparametric Tests

Back in Chapter 1 we stated that the primary goal of science is to establish relationships between variables. Until this point, the statistics we have presented all attempt to accomplish this goal by comparing *groups of scores* using *means and variances* as the basic statistical measures. Typically, one variable is used to define the groups, and a second variable is measured to obtain a set of scores within each group. Means and variances are then computed for the scores, and the sample means are used to test hypotheses about population means. If the hypothesis test indicates a significant mean difference, then we conclude that there is a relationship between the variables.

However, many research situations do not involve comparing groups, and many do not produce data that allow you to calculate means and variances. For example, a researcher can investigate the relationship between two variables (for example, IQ and creativity) by measuring both variables within a single group of individuals. Also, the measurement procedure may not produce numerical scores. For example, participants can indicate their color preferences by simply picking a favorite color or by ranking several choices. Without numerical scores, it is impossible to calculate means and variances. Instead, the data consist of proportions or frequencies. For example, a research study may investigate what proportion of people select red as their favorite color and whether this proportion is different for introverted people compared with extroverted people.

Notice that these new research situations are still asking questions about the relationships between variables, and they are still using sample data to make inferences about populations. However, they are no longer comparing groups and they are no longer based on means and variances. In this part, we introduce the statistical methods that have been developed for these other kinds of research.

CHAPTER

15

Correlation

Tools You Will Need

The following items are considered essential background material for this chapter. If you doubt your knowledge of any of these items, you should review the appropriate chapter or section before proceeding.

- Sum of squares (SS) (Chapter 4)
  - Computational formula
  - Definitional formula
- *z*-scores (Chapter 5)
- Hypothesis testing (Chapter 8)

Preview

Having been a student and taken exams for much of your life, you probably have noticed a curious phenomenon. In every class, there are some students who zip through exams and turn in their papers while everyone else is still on page 1. Other students cling to their exams and are still working frantically when the instructor announces that time is up and demands that all papers be turned in. Have you wondered what grades these students receive? Are the students who finish first the best in the class, or are they completely unprepared and simply accepting their failure? Are the *A* students the last to finish because they are compulsively checking and rechecking their answers? To help answer these questions, we carefully observed a recent exam and recorded the amount of time each student spent on the exam and the grade each student received. These data are shown in Figure 15.1. Note that we have listed time along the *X*-axis and grade on the *Y*-axis. Each student is identified by a point on the graph that is located directly above the student's time and directly across from the student's grade. Also note that we have drawn a line through the middle of the data points in Figure 15.1. The line helps make the relationship between time and grade more obvious. The graph shows that the highest grades tend to go to the students who finished their exams early. Students who held their papers to the bitter end tended to have low grades.

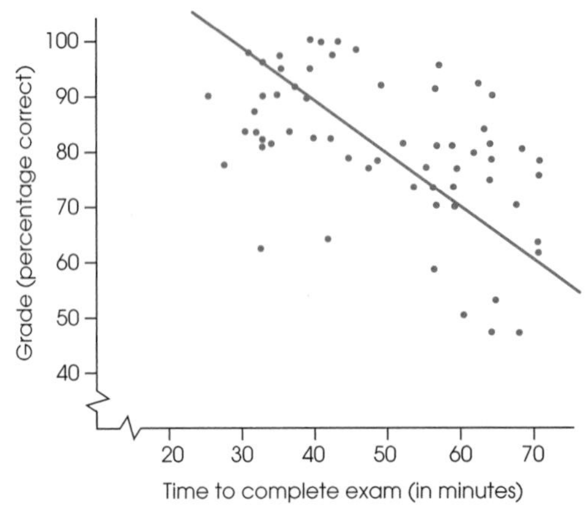

FIGURE 15.1

The relationship between exam grade and time needed to complete the exam. Notice the general trend in these data: Students who finish the exam early tend to have better grades.

The Problem: Although the data in Figure 15.1 appear to show a clear relationship, we need some procedure to measure the relationship and a hypothesis test to determine whether it is significant. In the preceding five chapters, we described relationships between variables in terms of mean differences between two or more groups of scores, and we used hypothesis tests that evaluate the significance of mean differences. For the data in Figure 15.1, there is only one group of scores, and calculating a mean is not going to help describe the relationship. To evaluate these data, a completely different approach is needed for both descriptive and inferential statistics.

The Solution: The data in Figure 15.1 are an example of the results from a correlational research study. In Chapter 1, the correlational design was introduced as a method for examining the relationship between two variables by measuring two different variables for each individual in one group of participants. The relationship obtained in a correlational study is typically described and evaluated with a statistical measure known as a *correlation*. Just as a sample mean provides a concise description of an entire sample, a correlation provides a concise description of a relationship. We look at how correlations are used and interpreted. For example, now that you have seen the relationship between time and grades, do you think it might be a good idea to start turning in your exam papers a little sooner? Wait and see.

15.1 INTRODUCTION

Correlation is a statistical technique that is used to measure and describe the relationship between two variables. Usually the two variables are simply observed as they exist naturally in the environment—there is no attempt to control or manipulate the variables. For example, a researcher could check high school records (with permission) to obtain a measure of each student's academic performance, and then survey each family to obtain a measure of income. The resulting data could be used to determine whether there is relationship between high school grades and family income. Notice that the researcher is not manipulating any student's grade or any family's income, but is simply observing what occurs naturally. You also should notice that a correlation requires two scores for each individual (one score from each of the two variables). These scores normally are identified as *X* and *Y*. The pairs of scores can be listed in a table, or they can be presented graphically in a scatter plot (Figure 15.2). In the scatter plot, the values for the *X* variable are listed on the horizontal axis and the *Y* values are listed on the vertical axis. Each individual is then represented by a single point in the graph so that the horizontal position corresponds to the individual's *X* value and the vertical position corresponds to the *Y* value. The value of a scatter plot is that it allows you to see any patterns or trends that exist in the data. The scores in Figure 15.2, for example, show a clear relationship between family income and student grades; as income increases, grades also increase.

Person	Family Income (in $1000)	Student's Average Grade
A	31	72
B	38	86
C	42	81
D	44	78
E	49	85
F	56	80
G	58	91
H	65	89
I	70	94
J	90	83
K	92	90
L	106	97
M	135	89
N	174	95

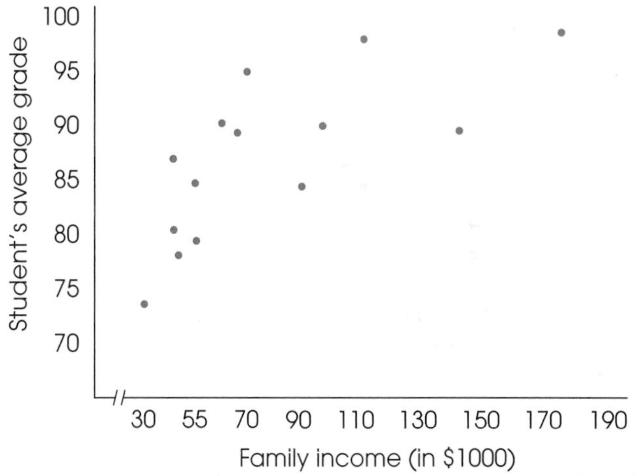

FIGURE 15.2

Correlational data showing the relationship between family income (*X*) and student grades (*Y*) for a sample of $n = 14$ high school students. The scores are listed in order from lowest to highest family income and are shown in a scatter plot.

THE CHARACTERISTICS OF A RELATIONSHIP

A correlation is a numerical value that describes and measures three characteristics of the relationship between *X* and *Y*. These three characteristics are as follows:

1. **The Direction of the Relationship.** The sign of the correlation, positive or negative, describes the direction of the relationship.

DEFINITIONS

In a **positive correlation,** the two variables tend to change in the same direction: As the value of the *X* variable increases from one individual to another, the *Y* variable also tends to increase; when the *X* variable decreases, the *Y* variable also decreases.

In a **negative correlation,** the two variables tend to go in opposite directions. As the *X* variable increases, the *Y* variable decreases. That is, it is an inverse relationship.

The following examples illustrate positive and negative relationships.

EXAMPLE 15.1

Suppose you run the drink concession at the football stadium. After several seasons, you begin to notice a relationship between the temperature at game time and the beverages you sell. Specifically, you have noted that when the temperature is low, you sell relatively little beer. However, as the temperature goes up, beer sales also go up (Figure 15.3). This is an example of a positive correlation. You also have noted a relationship between temperature and coffee sales: On cold days you sell a lot of coffee, but coffee sales go down as the temperature goes up. This is an example of a negative relationship.

2. **The Form of the Relationship.** In the preceding coffee and beer examples, the relationships tend to have a linear form; that is, the points in the scatter plot tend to cluster around a straight line. We have drawn a line through the middle

FIGURE 15.3

Examples of positive and negative relationships. (a) Beer sales are positively related to temperature. (b) Coffee sales are negatively related to temperature.

of the data points in each figure to help show the relationship. The most common use of correlation is to measure straight-line relationships. However, other forms of relationships do exist and there are special correlations used to measure them. (We examine alternatives in Section 15.5.)

3. **The Strength or Consistency of the Relationship**. Finally, the correlation measures the consistency of the relationship. For a linear elationship, for example, the data points could fit perfectly on a straight line. Every time *X* increases by one point, the value of *Y* also changes by a consistent and predictable amount. Figure 15.4(a) shows an example of a perfect linear relationship. However, relationships are usually not perfect. Although there may be a tendency for the value of *Y* to increase whenever *X* increases, the amount that *Y* changes is not always the same, and occasionally, *Y* decreases when *X* increases. In this situation, the data points do not fall perfectly on a straight line. The consistency of the relationship is measured by the numerical value of the correlation. A *perfect correlation* always is identified by a correlation of 1.00 and indicates a perfectly consistent relationship. For a correlation of 1.00 (or –1.00), each change in *X* is accompanied by a perfectly predictable change in *Y*. At the other extreme, a correlation of 0 indicates no consistency at all. For a correlation of 0, the data points are scattered randomly with no clear trend [see Figure 15.4(b)]. Intermediate values between 0 and 1 indicate the degree of consistency.

   Examples of different values for linear correlations are shown in Figure 15.4. In each example we have sketched a line around the data points. This line, called an *envelope* because it encloses the data, often helps you to see the overall trend in the data. As a rule of thumb, when the envelope is shaped roughly like a football, the correlation is around 0.7. Envelopes that are fatter than a football indicate correlations closer to 0, and narrower shapes indicate correlations closer to 1.00.

You should also note that the sign (+ or −) and the strength of a correlation are independent. For example, a correlation of 1.00 indicates a perfectly consistent relationship whether it is positive (+1.00) or negative (−1.00). Similarly, correlations of +0.80 and −0.80 are equally consistent relationships.

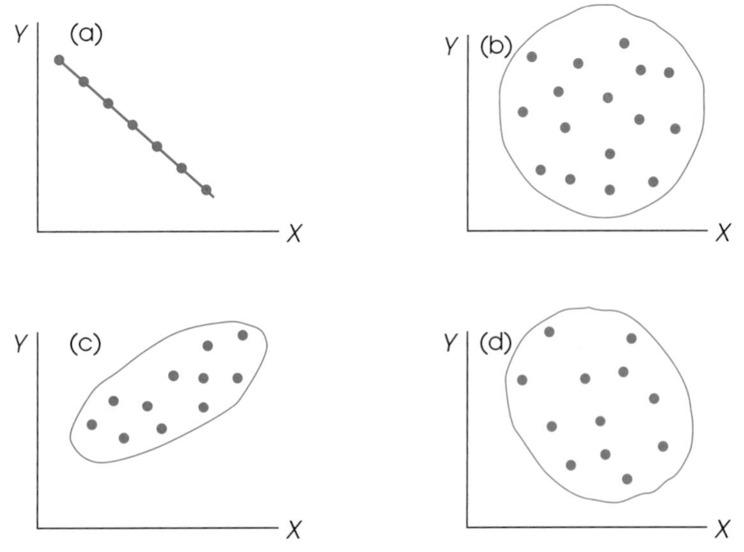

FIGURE 15.4

Examples of different values for linear correlations: (a) a perfect negative correlation, −1.00; (b) no linear trend, 0.00; (c) a strong positive relationship, approximately +0.90; (d) a relatively weak negative correlation, approximately −0.40.

LEARNING CHECK

1. For each of the following, indicate whether you would expect a positive or a negative correlation.
   a. Model year and price for a used Honda
   b. IQ and grade point average for high school students
   c. Daily high temperature and daily energy consumption for 30 winter days in New York City
2. The data points would be clustered more closely around a straight line for a correlation of –0.80 than for a correlation of +0.05. (True or false?)
3. If the data points are clustered close to a line that slopes up from left to right, then a good estimate of the correlation would be +0.90. (True or false?)
4. If a scatter plot shows a set of data points that form a circular pattern, the correlation should be near zero. (True or false?)

ANSWERS

1. a. Positive: Higher model years tend to have higher prices.
   b. Positive: More intelligent students tend to get higher grades.
   c. Negative: Higher temperature tends to decrease the need for heating.
2. True. The numerical value indicates the strength of the relationship. The sign only indicates direction.
3. True.
4. True.

15.2 THE PEARSON CORRELATION

By far the most common correlation is the *Pearson correlation* (or the Pearson product–moment correlation) which measures the degree of straight-line relationship.

DEFINITION

The **Pearson correlation** measures the degree and the direction of the linear relationship between two variables.

The Pearson correlation is identified by the letter r. Conceptually, this correlation is computed by

$$r = \frac{\text{degree to which } X \text{ and } Y \text{ vary together}}{\text{degree to which } X \text{ and } Y \text{ vary separately}}$$

$$= \frac{\text{covariability of } X \text{ and } Y}{\text{variability of } X \text{ and } Y \text{ separately}}$$

When there is a perfect linear relationship, every change in the X variable is accompanied by a corresponding change in the Y variable. In Figure 15.4(a), for example, every time the value of X increases, there is a perfectly predictable decrease in the value of Y. The result is a perfect linear relationship, with X and Y always varying together. In this case, the covariability (X and Y together) is identical to the variability of X and Y separately, and the formula produces a correlation with a magnitude of 1.00 or –1.00. At the other extreme, when there is no linear relationship, a change in the

X variable does not correspond to any predictable change in the Y variable. In this case, there is no covariability, and the resulting correlation is zero.

THE SUM OF PRODUCTS OF DEVIATIONS

To calculate the Pearson correlation, it is necessary to introduce one new concept: the *sum of products* of deviations, or *SP*. This new value is similar to *SS* (the sum of squared deviations), which is used to measure variability for a single variable. Now, we use *SP* to measure the amount of covariability between two variables. The value for *SP* can be calculated with either a definitional formula or a computational formula.

The *definitional formula* for the sum of products is

$$SP = \Sigma(X - M_X)(Y - M_Y) \tag{15.1}$$

where M_X is the mean for the X scores and M_Y is the mean for the Ys.

The definitional formula instructs you to perform the following sequence of operations:

1. Find the X deviation and the Y deviation for each individual.
2. Find the product of the deviations for each individual.
3. Add the products.

Notice that this process "defines" the value being calculated: the sum of the products of the deviations.

The *computational formula* for the sum of products of deviations is

$$SP = \Sigma XY - \frac{\Sigma X \Sigma Y}{n} \tag{15.2}$$

Caution: The n in this formula refers to the number of pairs of scores.

Because the computational formula uses the original scores (X and Y values), it usually results in easier calculations than those required with the definitional formula, especially if M_X or M_Y is not a whole number. However, both formulas always produce the same value for *SP*.

You may have noted that the formulas for *SP* are similar to the formulas you have learned for *SS* (sum of squares). The relationship between the two sets of formulas is described in Box 15.1. The following example demonstrates the calculation of *SP* with both formulas.

EXAMPLE 15.2

The same set of $n = 4$ pairs of scores is used to calculate *SP*, first using the definitional formula and then using the computational formula.

For the definitional formula, you need deviation scores for each of the X values and each of the Y values. Note that the mean for the Xs is $M_X = 3$ and the mean for the Ys is $M_Y = 5$. The deviations and the products of deviations are shown in the following table:

Caution: The signs (+ and −) are critical in determining the sum of products, *SP*.

Scores		Deviations		Products
X	Y	$X - M_X$	$Y - M_Y$	$(X - M_X)(Y - M_Y)$
1	3	−2	−2	+4
2	6	−1	+1	−1
4	4	+1	−1	−1
5	7	+2	+2	+4
				$+6 = SP$

For these scores, the sum of the products of the deviations is $SP = +6$.

For the computational formula, you need the X value, the Y value, and the XY product for each individual. Then you find the sum of the Xs, the sum of the Ys, and the sum of the XY products. These values are as follows:

X	Y	XY	
1	3	3	
2	6	12	
4	4	16	
5	7	35	
12	20	66	Totals

Substituting the totals in the formula gives

$$SP = \Sigma XY - \frac{\Sigma X \Sigma Y}{n}$$

$$= 66 - \frac{12(20)}{4}$$

$$= 66 - 60$$

$$= 6$$

Both formulas produce the same result, $SP = 6$.

BOX 15.1 COMPARING THE *SP* AND *SS* FORMULAS

ΣX^2 = Square each No. of X & add all together.

It will help you to learn the formulas for *SP* if you note the similarity between the two *SP* formulas and the corresponding formulas for *SS* that were presented in Chapter 4. The definitional formula for *SS* is

$$SS = \Sigma(X - M)^2$$

In this formula, you must square each deviation, which is equivalent to multiplying it by itself. With this in mind, the formula can be rewritten as

$$SS = \Sigma(X - M)(X - M)$$

The similarity between the *SS* formula and the *SP* formula should be obvious—the *SS* formula uses squares and the *SP* formula uses products. This same relationship exists for the computational formulas. For *SS*, the computational formula is

$$SS = \Sigma X^2 - \frac{(\Sigma X)^2}{n}$$

As before, each squared value can be rewritten so that the formula becomes

$$SS = \Sigma XX - \frac{\Sigma X \Sigma X}{n}$$

Again, note the similarity in structure between the *SS* formula and the *SP* formula. If you remember that *SS* uses squares and *SP* uses products, the two new formulas for the sum of products should be easy to learn.

CALCULATION OF THE PEARSON-CORRELATION

As noted earlier, the Pearson correlation consists of a ratio comparing the covariability of X and Y (the numerator) with the variability of X and Y separately (the denominator). In the formula for the Pearson r, we use SP to measure the covariability of X and Y. The variability of X is measured by computing SS for the X scores and the variability of Y is measured by SS for the Y scores. With these definitions, the formula for the Pearson correlation becomes

Note that you *multiply SS* for X by SS for Y in the denominator of the Pearson formula.

$$r = \frac{SP}{\sqrt{SS_X SS_Y}} \tag{15.3}$$

The following example demonstrates the use of this formula with a simple set of scores.

EXAMPLE 15.3

X	Y
0	2
10	6
4	2
8	4
8	6

The Pearson correlation is computed for the set of $n = 5$ pairs of scores shown in the margin.

Before starting any calculations, it is useful to put the data in a scatter plot and make a preliminary estimate of the correlation. These data have been graphed in Figure 15.5. Looking at the scatter plot, it appears that there is a very good (but not perfect) positive correlation. You should expect an approximate value of $r = +0.8$ or $+0.9$. To find the Pearson correlation, we need SP, SS for X, and SS for Y. The calculations for each of these values, using the definitional formulas, are presented in Table 15.1. (Note that the mean for the X values is $M_X = 6$ and the mean for the Y scores is $M_Y = 4$.)

Using the values from Table 15.1, the Pearson correlation is

$$r = \frac{SP}{\sqrt{(SS_X)(SS_Y)}} = \frac{28}{\sqrt{(64)(16)}} = \frac{28}{32} = +0.875$$

Note that the value we obtained for the correlation is perfectly consistent with the pattern shown in Figure 15.5. First, the positive value of the correlation indicates

FIGURE 15.5
Scatter plot of the data from Example 15.3.

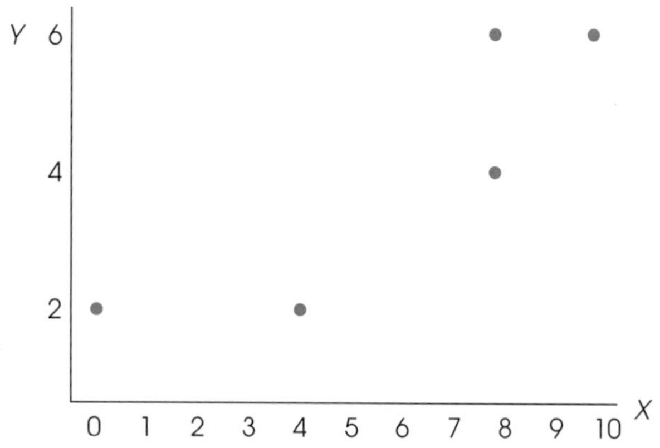

TABLE 15.1

Calculation of SS_X, SS_Y, and SP for a sample of $n = 5$ pairs of scores.

Scores		Deviations		Squared Deviations		Products
X	Y	$X - M_X$	$Y - M_Y$	$(X - M_X)^2$	$(Y - M_Y)^2$	$(X - M_X)(Y - M_Y)$
0	2	−6	−2	36	4	+12
10	6	+4	+2	16	4	+8
4	2	−2	−2	4	4	+4
8	4	+2	0	4	0	0
8	6	+2	+2	4	4	+4
				$SS_X = 64$	$SS_Y = 16$	$SP = +28$

that the points are clustered around a line that slopes up to the right. Second, the high value for the correlation (near 1.00) indicates that the points are very tightly clustered close to the line. Thus, the value of the correlation describes the relationship that exists in the data.

THE PEARSON CORRELATION AND z-SCORES

The Pearson correlation measures the relationship between an individual's location in the X distribution and his or her location in the Y distribution. For example, a positive correlation means that individuals who score high on X also tend to score high on Y. Similarly, a negative correlation indicates that individuals with high X scores tend to have low Y scores.

Recall from Chapter 5 that z-scores identify the exact location of each individual score within a distribution. With this in mind, each X value can be transformed into a z-score, z_X, using the mean and standard deviation for the set of Xs. Similarly, each Y score can be transformed into z_Y. If the X and Y values are viewed as a sample, the transformation is completed using the sample formula for z (Equation 5.3). If the X and Y values form a complete population, the z-scores are computed using Equation 5.1. After the transformation, the formula for the Pearson correlation can be expressed entirely in terms of z-scores.

$$\text{For a sample, } r = \frac{\Sigma z_X z_Y}{(n - 1)} \tag{15.4}$$

$$\text{For a population, } \rho = \frac{\Sigma z_X z_Y}{N} \tag{15.5}$$

Note that the population value is identified with a Greek letter, in this case the letter rho (ρ), which is the Greek equivalent of the letter r.

LEARNING CHECK

1. Describe what is measured by a Pearson correlation.
2. Can SP ever have a value less than zero?
3. Calculate the sum of products of deviations (SP) for the following set of scores. Use the definitional formula and then the computational formula. Verify that you get the same answer with both formulas.

X	Y
0	1
4	3
5	3
2	2
4	1

4. For the following data:
   a. Sketch a scatter plot and make an estimate of the Pearson correlation.
   b. Compute the Pearson correlation.

X	Y
2	6
1	5
3	3
0	7
4	4

ANSWERS

1. The Pearson correlation measures the degree and direction of the linear relationship between two variables.
2. Yes. *SP* can be positive, negative, or zero depending on the relationship between *X* and *Y*.
3. $SP = 5$
4. $r = -8/10 = -0.80$

15.3 USING AND INTERPRETING THE PEARSON CORRELATION

WHERE AND WHY CORRELATIONS ARE USED

Although correlations have a number of different applications, a few specific examples are presented next to give an indication of the value of this statistical measure.

1. **Prediction.** If two variables are known to be related in a systematic way, then it is possible to use one of the variables to make accurate predictions about the other. For example, when you applied for admission to college, you were required to submit a great deal of personal information, including your scores on the Scholastic Achievement Test (SAT). College officials want this information so that they can predict your chances of success in college. It has been demonstrated over several years that SAT scores and college grade point averages are correlated. Students who do well on the SAT tend to do well in college; students who have difficulty with the SAT tend to have difficulty in college. Based on this relationship, college admissions officers can make a prediction about the potential success of each applicant. You should note that this prediction is not perfectly accurate. Not everyone who does poorly on the

SAT has trouble in college. That is why you also submit letters of recommendation, high school grades, and other information with your application.

2. **Validity.** Suppose that a psychologist develops a new test for measuring intelligence. How could you show that this test truly measures what it claims; that is, how could you demonstrate the validity of the test? One common technique for demonstrating validity is to use a correlation. If the test actually measures intelligence, then the scores on the test should be related to other measures of intelligence—for example, standardized IQ tests, performance on learning tasks, problem-solving ability, and so on. The psychologist could measure the correlation between the new test and each of these other measures of intelligence to demonstrate that the new test is valid.
3. **Reliability.** In addition to evaluating the validity of a measurement procedure, correlations are used to determine reliability. A measurement procedure is considered reliable to the extent that it produces stable, consistent measurements. That is, a reliable measurement procedure produces the same (or nearly the same) scores when the same individuals are measured twice under the same conditions. For example, if your IQ was measured as 113 last week, you would expect to obtain nearly the same score if your IQ was measured again this week. One way to evaluate reliability is to use correlations to determine the relationship between two sets of measurements. When reliability is high, the correlation between two measurements should be strong and positive. Further discussion of the concept of reliability is presented in Box 15.2.
4. **Theory Verification.** Many psychological theories make specific predictions about the relationship between two variables. For example, a theory may predict a relationship between brain size and learning ability; a developmental theory may predict a relationship between the parents' IQs and the child's IQ; a social psychologist may have a theory predicting a relationship between personality type and behavior in a social situation. In each case, the prediction of the theory could be tested by determining the correlation between the two variables.

INTERPRETING CORRELATIONS

When you encounter correlations, there are four additional considerations that you should bear in mind:

1. Correlation simply describes a relationship between two variables. It does not explain why the two variables are related. Specifically, a correlation should not and cannot be interpreted as proof of a cause-and-effect relationship between the two variables.
2. The value of a correlation can be affected greatly by the range of scores represented in the data.
3. One or two extreme data points, often called *outliers,* can have a dramatic effect on the value of a correlation.
4. When judging how "good" a relationship is, it is tempting to focus on the numerical value of the correlation. For example, a correlation of +0.5 is halfway between 0 and 1.00 and, therefore, appears to represent a moderate degree of relationship. However, a correlation should not be interpreted as a proportion. Although a correlation of 1.00 does mean that there is a 100% perfectly predictable relationship between X and Y, a correlation of 0.5 does not mean that you can make predictions with 50% accuracy. To describe how accurately one variable predicts the other, you must square the correlation. Thus, a

BOX 15.2 RELIABILITY AND ERROR IN MEASUREMENT

The idea of reliability of measurement is tied directly to the notion that each individual measurement includes an element of error. Expressed as an equation,

$$\text{measured score} = \text{true score} + \text{error}$$

For example, if I try to measure your intelligence with an IQ test, the score that I get is determined partially by your actual level of intelligence (your true score) but it also is influenced by a variety of other factors such as your current mood, your level of fatigue, your general health, and so on. These other factors are lumped together as *error,* and are typically a part of any measurement.

It is generally assumed that the error component changes randomly from one measurement to the next and that this causes your score to change. For example, your IQ score is likely to be higher when you are well rested and feeling good compared to a measurement that is taken when you are tired and depressed. Although your actual intelligence hasn't changed, the error component causes your score to change from one measurement to another.

As long as the error component is relatively small, then your scores will be relatively consistent from one measurement to the next, and the measurements are said to be reliable. If you are feeling especially happy and well rested, it may affect your IQ score by a few points, but it is not going to boost your IQ from 110 to 170.

On the other hand, if the error component is relatively large, then you will find huge differences from one measurement to the next and the measurements are not reliable. Measurements of reaction time, for example, tend to be very unreliable. Suppose, for example, that you are seated at a desk with your finger on a button and a light bulb in front of you. Your job is to push the button as quickly as possible when the light goes on. On some trials, you are focused on the light with your finger tensed and ready to push. On other trials, you are distracted, or day dreaming, or blink when the light goes on so that time passes before you finally push the button. As a result, there is a huge error component to the measurement and your reaction time can change dramatically from one trial to the next. When measurements are unreliable you cannot trust any single measurement to provide an accurate indication of the individual's true score. To deal with this problem, researchers typically measure reaction time repeatedly and then average it over a large number of measurements.

Correlations can be used to help researchers measure and describe reliability. By taking two measurements for each individual, it is possible to compute the correlation between the first score and the second score. A strong, positive correlation indicates a good level of reliability: people who scored high on the first measurement also scored high on the second. A weak correlation indicates that there is not a consistent relationship between the first score and the second score; that is, a weak correlation indicates poor reliability.

correlation of $r = .5$ means that one variable *partially* predicts the other, but the predictable portion is only $r^2 = 0.5^2 = 0.25$ (or 25%) of the total variability.

We now discuss each of these four points in detail.

CORRELATION AND CAUSATION

One of the most common errors in interpreting correlations is to assume that a correlation necessarily implies a cause-and-effect relationship between the two variables. (Even Pearson blundered by asserting causation from correlational data [Blum, 1978].) We constantly are bombarded with reports of relationships: Cigarette smoking is related to heart disease; alcohol consumption is related to birth defects; carrot consumption is related to good eyesight. Do these relationships mean that cigarettes cause heart disease or carrots cause good eyesight? The answer is *no*. Although there may be a causal relationship, the simple existence of a correlation does not prove it. Earlier, for example, we discussed a study showing a relationship between high school grades and family income. However, this result does not mean that having a higher family income *causes* students to get better grades. For example, if mom gets an unexpected bonus at work, it is unlikely that her child's grades will also show a sudden increase. To establish a cause-and-effect relationship, it is necessary to conduct a true experiment (see p. 14) in which one variable is manipulated by a researcher and other variables are rigorously controlled. The fact that a correlation does not establish causation is demonstrated in the following example.

EXAMPLE 15.4

Suppose we select a variety of different cities and towns throughout the United States and measure the number of churches (X variable) and the number of serious crimes (Y variable) for each. A scatter plot showing hypothetical data for this study is presented in Figure 15.6. Notice that this scatter plot shows a strong, positive correlation between churches and crime. You also should note that these are realistic data. It is reasonable that small towns would have less crime and fewer churches and that large cities would have large values for both variables. Does this relationship mean that churches cause crime? Does it mean that crime causes churches? It should be clear that both answers are no. Although a strong correlation exists between number of churches and crime, the real cause of the relationship is the size of the population.

CORRELATION AND RESTRICTED RANGE

Whenever a correlation is computed from scores that do not represent the full range of possible values, you should be cautious in interpreting the correlation. Suppose, for example, that you are interested in the relationship between IQ and creativity. If you select a sample of your fellow college students, your data probably will represent only a limited range of IQ scores (most likely from 110 to 130). The correlation

FIGURE 15.6

Hypothetical data showing the logical relationship between the number of churches and the number of serious crimes for a sample of U.S. cities.

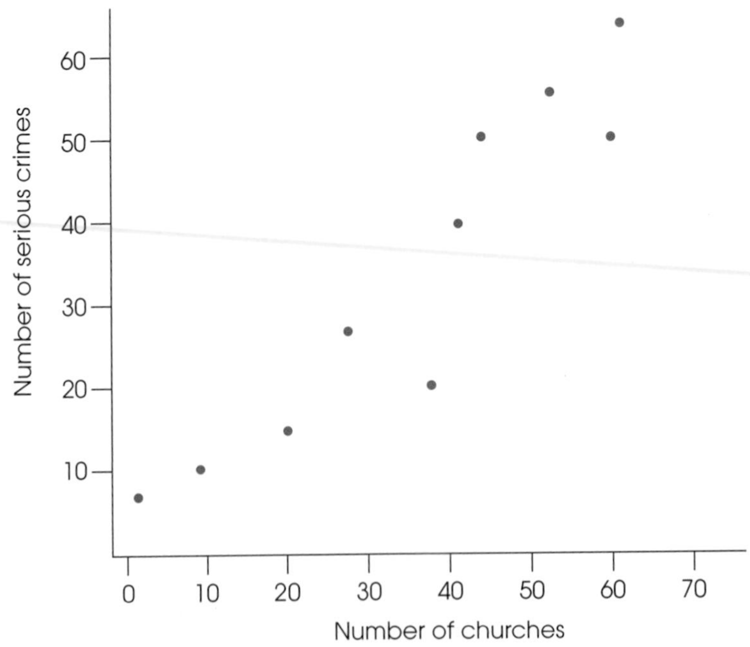

within this *restricted range* could be completely different from the correlation that would be obtained from a full range of IQ scores. For example, Figure 15.7 shows a strong positive relationship between X and Y when the entire range of scores is considered. However, this relationship is obscured when the data are limited to a restricted range.

To be safe, you should not generalize any correlation beyond the range of data represented in the sample. For a correlation to provide an accurate description for the general population, there should be a wide range of X and Y values in the data.

OUTLIERS

An outlier is an individual with X and/or Y values that are substantially different (larger or smaller) from the values obtained for the other individuals in the data set. The data point of a single outlier can have a dramatic influence on the value obtained for the correlation. This effect is illustrated in Figure 15.8. Figure 15.8(a) shows a set of $n = 5$ data points for which the correlation between the X and Y variables is nearly zero (actually $r = -0.08$). In Figure 15.8(b), one extreme data point (14, 12) has been added to the original data set. When this outlier is included in the analysis, a strong, positive correlation emerges (now $r = +\ 0.85$). Note that the single outlier drastically alters the value for the correlation and, thereby, can affect one's interpretation of the relationship between variables X and Y. Without the outlier, one would conclude there is no relationship between the two variables. With the extreme data point, $r = +0.85$, which implies a strong relationship with Y increasing consistently as X increases. The problem of outliers is a good reason for looking at a scatter plot, instead of simply basing your interpretation on the numerical value of the correlation. If you only "go by the numbers," you might overlook the fact that one extreme data point inflated the size of the correlation.

CORRELATION AND THE STRENGTH OF THE RELATIONSHIP

A correlation measures the degree of relationship between two variables on a scale from 0 to 1.00. Although this number provides a measure of the degree of relationship, many researchers prefer to square the correlation and use the resulting value to measure the strength of the relationship.

One of the common uses of correlation is for prediction. If two variables are correlated, you can use the value of one variable to predict the other. For example, college admissions officers do not just guess which applicants are likely to do well; they use other variables (SAT scores, high school grades, and so on) to predict which students are most likely to be successful. These predictions are based on correlations. By using

FIGURE 15.7
In this example, the full range of X and Y values shows a strong, positive correlation, but the restricted range of scores produces a correlation near zero.

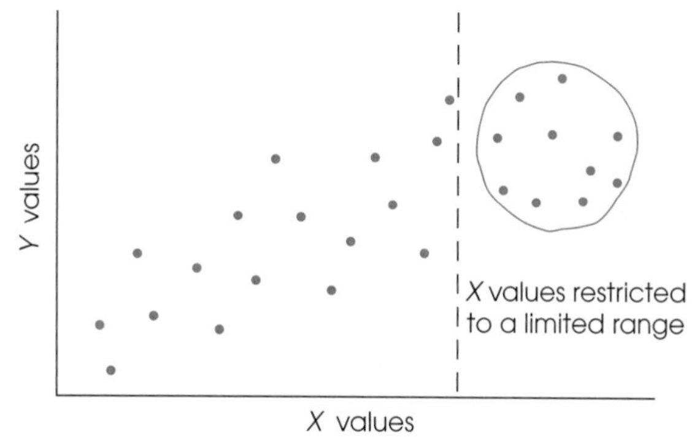

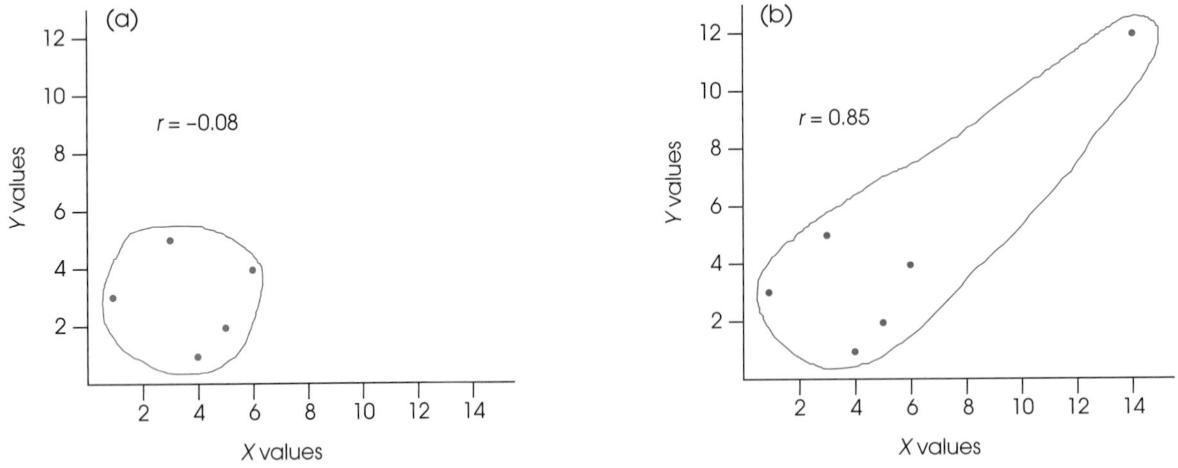

Original Data		
Subject	X	Y
A	1	3
B	3	5
C	6	4
D	4	1
E	5	2

Data with Outlier Included		
Subject	X	Y
A	1	3
B	3	5
C	6	4
D	4	1
E	5	2
F	14	12

FIGURE 15.8
A demonstration of how one extreme data point (an outlier) can influence the value of a correlation.

correlations, the admissions officers expect to make more accurate predictions than would be obtained by chance. In general, the squared correlation (r^2) measures the gain in accuracy that is obtained from using the correlation for prediction. The squared correlation measures the proportion of variability in the data that is explained by the relationship between X and Y. It is sometimes called the *coefficient of determination.*

DEFINITION

The value r^2 is called the **coefficient of determination** because it measures the proportion of variability in one variable that can be determined from the relationship with the other variable. A correlation of $r = 0.80$ (or -0.80), for example, means that $r^2 = 0.64$ (or 64%) of the variability in the Y scores can be predicted from the relationship with X.

In earlier chapters (see pp. 299, 328, and 361) we introduced r^2 as a method for measuring effect size for research studies where mean differences were used to compare treatments. Specifically, we measured how much of the variance in the scores was accounted for by the differences between treatments. In experimental terminology, r^2 measures how much of the variance in the dependent variable is accounted for by the independent variable. Now we are doing the same thing, except that there is no independent or dependent variable. Instead, we simply have two variables, X and Y, and we use r^2 to measure how much of the variance in one variable can be determined from its relationship with the other variable. The following example demonstrates this concept.

EXAMPLE 15.5 Figure 15.9 shows three sets of data representing different degrees of linear relationship. The first set of data [Figure 15.9(a)] shows the relationship between IQ and shoe size. In this case, the correlation is $r = 0$ (and $r^2 = 0$), and you have no ability to predict a person's IQ based on his or her shoe size. Knowing a person's shoe size provides no information (0%) about the person's IQ. In this case, shoe size provides no help explaining why different people have different IQs.

Now consider the data in Figure 15.9(b). These data show a moderate, positive correlation, $r = +0.60$, between IQ scores and college grade point averages (GPA). Students with high IQs tend to have higher grades than students with low IQs. From this relationship, it is possible to predict a student's GPA based on his or her IQ. However, you should realize that the prediction is not perfect. Although students with high IQs *tend* to have high GPAs, this is not always true. Thus, knowing a student's IQ provides some information about the student's grades, or knowing a student's grades provides some information about the student's IQ. In this case, IQ scores help explain the fact that different students have different GPAs. Specifically, you can say that *part* of the differences in GPA are accounted for by IQ. With a correlation of $r = +0.60$, we obtain $r^2 = 0.36$, which means that 36% of the variance in GPA can be explained by IQ.

Finally, consider the data in Figure 15.9(c). This time we show a perfect linear relationship ($r = +1.00$) between monthly salary and yearly salary for a group of college employees. With $r = 1.00$ and $r^2 = 1.00$, there is 100% predictability. If you know a person's monthly salary, you can predict perfectly the person's annual salary. If two people have different annual salaries, the difference can be completely explained (100%) by the difference in their monthly salaries.

Just as r^2 was used to evaluate effect size for mean differences in Chapters 9, 10, and 11, r^2 can now be used to evaluate the size or strength of the correlation. The same standards that were introduced in Table 9.3 (p. 299), apply to both uses of the r^2 measure. Specifically, an r^2 value of 0.01 indicates a small effect or a small correlation, an r^2 value of 0.09 indicates a medium correlation, and r^2 of 0.25 or larger indicates a large correlation.

More information about the coefficient of determination (r^2) is presented in Section 15.5 and in Chapter 16. For now, you should realize that whenever two variables are consistently related, it is possible to use one variable to predict values for the

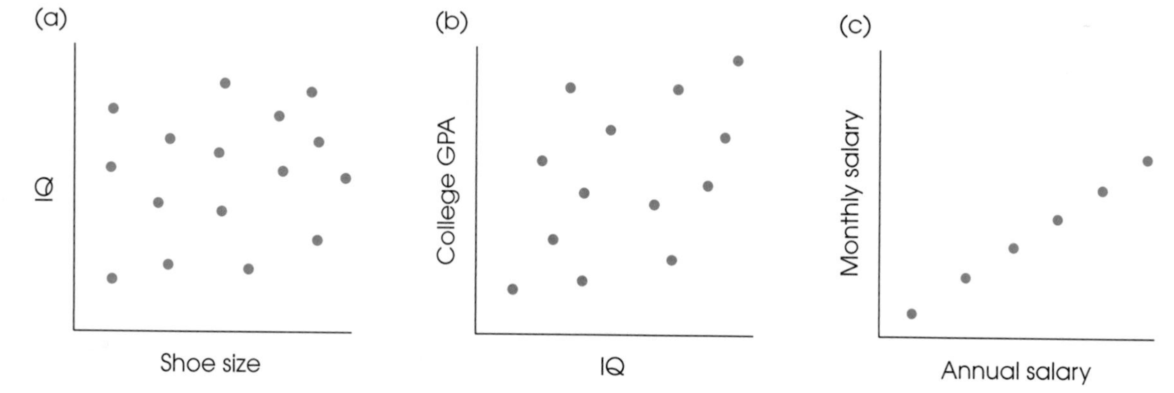

FIGURE 15.9
Three sets of data showing three different degrees of linear relationship.

second variable. One final comment concerning the interpretation of correlations is presented in Box 15.3.

BOX 15.3 REGRESSION TOWARD THE MEAN

Consider the following problem.

> Explain why the rookie of the year in major-league baseball usually does not perform as well in his second season.

Notice that this question does not appear to be statistical or mathematical in nature. However, the answer to the question is directly related to the statistical concepts of correlation and regression (Chapter 16). Specifically, there is a simple observation about correlations known as *regression toward the mean.*

DEFINITION When there is a less-than-perfect correlation between two variables, extreme scores (high or low) for one variable tend to be paired with the less extreme scores (more toward the mean) on the second variable. This fact is called **regression toward the mean.**

Figure 15.10 shows a scatter plot with a less-than-perfect correlation between two variables. The data points in this figure might represent batting averages for baseball rookies in 2010 (variable 1) and batting averages for the same players in 2011 (variable 2). Because the correlation is less than perfect, the highest scores on variable 1 are generally *not* the highest scores on variable 2. In baseball terms, the rookies who had the highest averages in 2010 do not have the highest averages in 2011.

Remember that a correlation does not explain *why* one variable is related to the other; it simply says that there is a relationship. The correlation cannot explain why the best rookie does not perform as well in his second year. But, because the correlation is not perfect, it is a statistical fact that extremely high scores in one year generally will *not* be paired with extremely high scores in the next year.

Regression toward the mean often poses a problem for interpreting experimental results. Suppose, for example, that you want to evaluate the effects of a special preschool program for disadvantaged children. You select a sample of children who score extremely low on an academic performance test. After participating in your preschool program, these children score significantly higher on the test. Why did their scores improve? One answer is that the special program helped. But an alternative answer is regression toward the mean. If there is a less-than-perfect correlation between scores on the first test and scores on the second test (which is usually the case), individuals with extremely low scores on test 1 will tend to have higher scores on test 2. It is a statistical fact of life, not necessarily the result of any special program.

Now try using the concept of regression toward the mean to explain the following phenomena:

1. You have a truly outstanding meal at a restaurant. However, when you go back with a group of friends, you find that the food is disappointing.
2. You have the highest score on exam I in your statistics class, but score only a little above average on exam II.

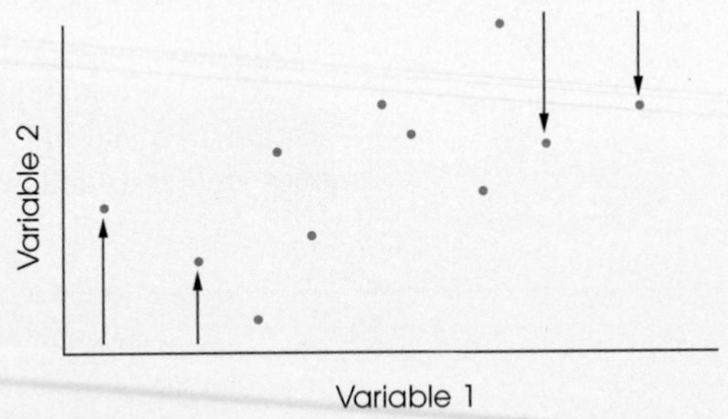

FIGURE 15.10

A demonstration of regression toward the mean. The figure shows a scatterplot for a set of data with a less-than-perfect correlation. Notice that the highest scores on variable 1 (extreme right-hand points) are not the highest scores on variable 2, but are displaced downward toward the mean. Also, the lowest scores on variable 1 (extreme left-hand points) are not the lowest scores on variable 2, but are displaced upward toward the mean.

LEARNING CHECK

1. A researcher finds a correlation of $r =$ (0.71 between the time spent playing video games each week and grade point average for a group of high school boys. This means that playing video games causes students to get lower grades. (True or false?)

2. A researcher finds a correlation of $r = 0.60$ between salary and the number of years of education for a group of 40-year-old men. How much of the variance in salary is explained by the years of education?

ANSWERS

1. False. You cannot conclude that there is a cause-and-effect relationship based on a correlation.

2. $r^2 = 0.36$, or 36%

15.4 HYPOTHESIS TESTS WITH THE PEARSON CORRELATION

The Pearson correlation is generally computed for sample data. As with most sample statistics, however, a sample correlation is often used to answer questions about the corresponding population correlation. For example, a psychologist would like to know whether there is a relationship between IQ and creativity. This is a general question concerning a population. To answer the question, a sample would be selected, and the sample data would be used to compute the correlation value. You should recognize this process as an example of inferential statistics: using samples to draw inferences about populations. In the past, we have been concerned primarily with using sample means as the basis for answering questions about population means. In this section, we examine the procedures for using a sample correlation as the basis for testing hypotheses about the corresponding population correlation.

THE HYPOTHESES

The basic question for this hypothesis test is whether a correlation exists in the population. The null hypothesis is "No. There is no correlation in the population," or "The population correlation is zero." The alternative hypothesis is "Yes. There is a real, nonzero correlation in the population." Because the population correlation is traditionally represented by ρ (the Greek letter rho), these hypotheses would be stated in symbols as

H_0: $\rho = 0$ (There is no population correlation.)

H_1: $\rho \neq 0$ (There is a real correlation.)

When there is a specific prediction about the direction of the correlation, it is possible to do a directional, or one-tailed, test. For example, if a researcher is predicting a positive relationship, the hypotheses would be

H_0: $\rho \leq 0$ (The population correlation is not positive.)

H_1: $\rho > 0$ (The population correlation is positive.)

The correlation from the sample data is used to evaluate the hypotheses. For the regular, nondirectional test, a sample correlation near zero provides support for H_0 and a sample value far from zero tends to refute H_0. For a directional test, a positive value for the sample correlation would tend to refute a null hypothesis stating that the population correlation is not positive.

Although sample correlations are used to test hypotheses about population correlations, you should keep in mind that samples are not expected to be identical to the populations from which they come; there is some discrepancy (sampling error) between a sample statistic and the corresponding population parameter. Specifically, you should always expect some error between a sample correlation and the population correlation it represents. One implication of this fact is that even when there is no correlation in the population ($\rho = 0$), you are still likely to obtain a nonzero value for the sample correlation. This is particularly true for small samples. Figure 15.11 illustrates how a small sample from a population with a near-zero correlation could result in a correlation that deviates from zero. The colored dots in the figure represent the entire population and the three circled dots represent a random sample. Note that the three sample points show a relatively good, positive correlation even through there is no linear trend ($\rho = 0$) for the population.

When you obtain a nonzero correlation for a sample, the purpose of the hypothesis test is to decide between the following two interpretations:

1. There is no correlation in the population ($\rho = 0$), and the sample value is the result of sampling error. Remember, a sample is not expected to be identical to the population. There always is some error between a sample statistic and the corresponding population parameter. This is the situation specified by H_0.
2. The nonzero sample correlation accurately represents a real, nonzero correlation in the population. This is the alternative stated in H_1.

The correlation from the sample helps to determine which of these two interpretations is more likely. A sample correlation near zero supports the conclusion that the population correlation is also zero. A sample correlation that is substantially different from zero supports the conclusion that there is a real, nonzero correlation in the population.

FIGURE 15.11

Scatterplot of a population of X and Y values with a near-zero correlation. However, a small sample of $n = 3$ data points from this population shows a relatively strong, positive correlation. Data points in the sample are circled.

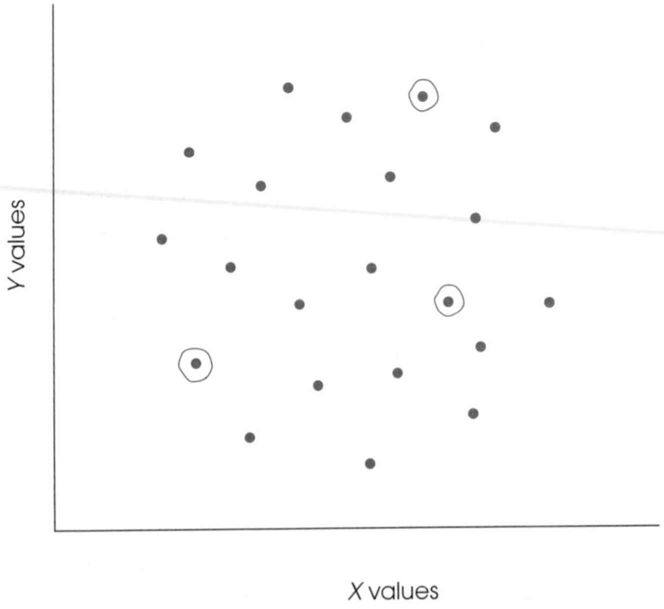

DEGREES OF FREEDOM FOR THE CORRELATION TEST

The hypothesis test for the Pearson correlation has degrees of freedom defined by $df = n - 2$. An intuitive explanation for this value is that a sample with only $n = 2$ data points has no degrees of freedom. Specifically, if there are only two points, they will fit perfectly on a straight line, and the sample produces a perfect correlation of $r = +1.00$ or $r = -1.00$. Because the first two points always produce a perfect correlation, the sample correlation is free to vary only when the data set contains more than two points. Thus, $df = n - 2$.

THE HYPOTHESIS TEST

Although it is possible to conduct the hypothesis test by computing either a t statistic or an F-ratio, the computations for evaluating r have already been completed and are summarized in Table B.6 in Appendix B. The table is based on the concept that a sample is expected to be representative of the population from which it was obtained. In particular, a sample correlation should be similar to the population correlation. If the population correlation is zero, as specified in the null hypothesis, then the sample correlation should be near zero. Thus, a sample correlation that is close to zero provides support for H_0 and a sample correlation that is far from zero contradicts the null hypothesis.

The table lists critical values in terms of degrees of freedom: $df = n - 2$. Remember to subtract 2 when using this table.

Table B.6 identifies exactly which sample correlations are likely to be obtained from a population with $\rho = 0$ and which values are very unlikely. To use the table, you need to know the sample size (n) and the alpha level. With a sample size of $n = 20$ and an alpha level of .05, for example, you locate $df = n - 2 = 18$ in the left-hand column and the value .05 for either one tail or two tails across the top of the table. For $df = 18$ and $\alpha = .05$ for a two-tailed test, the table shows a value of 0.444. Thus, if the null hypothesis is true and there is no correlation in the population, then the sample correlation should be near to zero. According to the table, the sample correlation should have a value between +0.444 and –0.444. If H_0 is true, it is very unlikely ($\alpha = .05$) to obtain a sample correlation outside this range. Therefore, a sample correlation beyond ±0.444 leads to rejecting the null hypothesis. The following examples demonstrate the use of the table.

EXAMPLE 15.6

A researcher is using a regular, two-tailed test with $\alpha = .05$ to determine whether a nonzero correlation exists in the population. A sample of $n = 30$ individuals is obtained. With $\alpha = .05$ and $n = 30$, the table lists a value of 0.361. Thus, the sample correlation (independent of sign) must have a value greater than or equal to 0.361 to reject H_0 and conclude that there is a significant correlation in the population. Any sample correlation between 0.361 and –0.361 is considered within the realm of sampling error and, therefore, is not significant.

EXAMPLE 15.7

This time the researcher is using a directional, one-tailed test to determine whether there is a positive correlation in the population.

H_0: $\rho \leq 0$ (There is not a positive correlation.)

H_1: $\rho > 0$ (There is a positive correlation.)

With $\alpha = .05$ and a sample of $n = 30$, the table lists a value of 0.306 for a one-tailed test. To reject H_0 and conclude that there is a significant positive correlation in the population, the sample correlation must be positive (as predicted) and have a value greater than or equal to 0.306.

IN THE LITERATURE
REPORTING CORRELATIONS

When correlations are computed, the results are reported using APA format. The statement should include the sample size, the calculated value for the correlation, whether it is a statistically significant relationship, the probability level, and the type of test used (one- or two-tailed). For example, a correlation might be reported as follows:

> A correlation for the data revealed a significant relationship between amount of education and annual income, $r = +0.65$, $n = 30$, $p < .01$, two tails.

Sometimes a study might look at several variables, and correlations between all possible variable pairings are computed. Suppose, for example, that a study measured people's annual income, amount of education, age, and intelligence. With four variables, there are six possible pairings leading to six different correlations. The results from multiple correlations are most easily reported in a table called a *correlation matrix,* using footnotes to indicate which correlations are significant. For example, the report might state:

> The analysis examined the relationships among income, amount of education, age, and intelligence for $n = 30$ participants. The correlations between pairs of variables are reported in Table 1. Significant correlations are noted in the table.

TABLE 1

Correlation matrix for income, amount of education, age, and intelligence

	Education	Age	IQ
Income	+.65*	+.41**	+.27
Education		+.11	+.38**
Age			−.02

$n = 30$
*$p < .01$, two tails
**$p < .05$, two tails

LEARNING CHECK

1. A researcher obtains a correlation of $r = -0.39$ for a sample of $n = 25$ individuals. Does this sample provide sufficient evidence to conclude that there is a significant, nonzero correlation in the population? Assume a two-tailed test with $\alpha = .05$.
2. For a sample of $n = 15$, how large a correlation is needed to conclude at the .05 level of significance that there is a nonzero correlation in the population? Assume a two-tailed test.
3. As sample size gets smaller, what happens to the magnitude of the correlation necessary for significance? Explain why this occurs.

ANSWERS

1. No. For $n = 25$, the critical value is $r = 0.396$. The sample value is not in the critical region.
2. For $n = 15$, $df = 13$ and the critical value is $r = 0.514$.
3. As the sample size gets smaller, the magnitude of the correlation needed for significance gets larger. With a small sample, it is easy to get a relatively large correlation just by chance. Therefore, a small sample requires a very large correlation before you can be confident there is a real (nonzero) relationship in the population.

PARTIAL CORRELATIONS

Occasionally a researcher may suspect that the relationship between two variables is being distorted by the influence of a third variable. Earlier in the chapter, for example, we found a strong positive relationship between the number of churches and the number of serious crimes for a sample of different towns and cities (see Example 15.4, p 522). However, it is unlikely that there is a direct relationship between churches and crime. Instead, both variables are influenced by population: Large cities have a lot of churches and high crime rates compared to smaller towns, which have fewer churches and less crime. If population were controlled, there probably would be no real correlation between churches and crime.

Fortunately, there is a statistical technique, known as *partial correlation,* that allows a researcher to measure the relationship between two variables while eliminating or holding constant the influence of a third variable. Thus, a researcher could use a partial correlation to examine the relationship between churches and crime without the risk that the relationship is distorted by the size of the population.

DEFINITION

A **partial correlation** measures the relationship between two variables while controlling the influence of a third variable by holding it constant.

In a situation with three variables, *X*, *Y*, and *Z*, it is possible to compute three individual Pearson correlations:

1. r_{XY} measuring the correlation between *X* and *Y*
2. r_{XZ} measuring the correlation between *X* and *Z*
3. r_{YZ} measuring the correlation between *Y* and *Z*

These three individual correlations can then be used to compute a partial correlation. For example, the partial correlation between *X* and *Y*, holding *Z* constant, is determined by the formula

$$r_{XY-Z} = \frac{r_{XY} - (r_{XZ}r_{YZ})}{\sqrt{(1-r_{XZ}^2)(1-r_{YZ}^2)}} \tag{15.6}$$

The following example demonstrates the calculation and interpretation of a partial correlation.

EXAMPLE 15.8

We begin with the hypothetical data shown in Table 15.2. These scores have been constructed to simulate the church/crime/population situation for a sample of $n = 15$ cities. The *X* variable represents the number of churches, *Y* represents the number of

TABLE 15.2

Hypothetical data showing the relationship between the number of churches, the number of crimes, and the population of a set of $n = 15$ cities.

Number of Churches (X)	Number of Crimes (Y)	Population (Z)
1	4	1
2	3	1
3	1	1
4	2	1
5	5	1
7	8	2
8	11	2
9	9	2
10	7	2
11	10	2
13	15	3
14	14	3
15	16	3
16	17	3
17	13	3

crimes, and Z represents the population for each city. For these scores, the individual Pearson correlations are all large and positive:

a. The correlation between churches and crime is $r_{XY} = 0.923$.

b. The correlation between churches and population is $r_{XZ} = 0.961$.

c. The correlation between crime and population is $r_{YZ} = 0.961$.

The data points for the 15 cities are shown in the scatter plot in Figure 15.12. Note that there are three categories for the size of the population (three values for Z) corresponding to small, medium, and large cities. Also note that the population variable, Z, separates the scores into three distinct groups: When $Z = 1$, the population is low and churches and crime (X and Y) are also low; when $Z = 2$, the population is moderate and churches and crime (X and Y) are also moderate; and when $Z = 3$, the population is large and churches and crime are both high. Thus, as the population increases from one city to another, the number of churches and crimes also increase, and the result is a strong positive correlation between churches and crime.

Within each of the three population categories, however, there is no linear relationship between churches and crime. Specifically, within each group, the population variable is constant and the five data points for X and Y form a circular pattern, indicating no consistent linear relationship. The partial correlation allows us to hold population constant across the entire sample and measure the underlying relationship between churches and crime without any influence from population. For these data, the partial correlation is

$$r_{XY-Z} = \frac{0.923 - 0.961(0.961)}{\sqrt{(1-0.961^2)(1-0.961^2)}}$$

$$= \frac{0}{0.076}$$

$$= 0$$

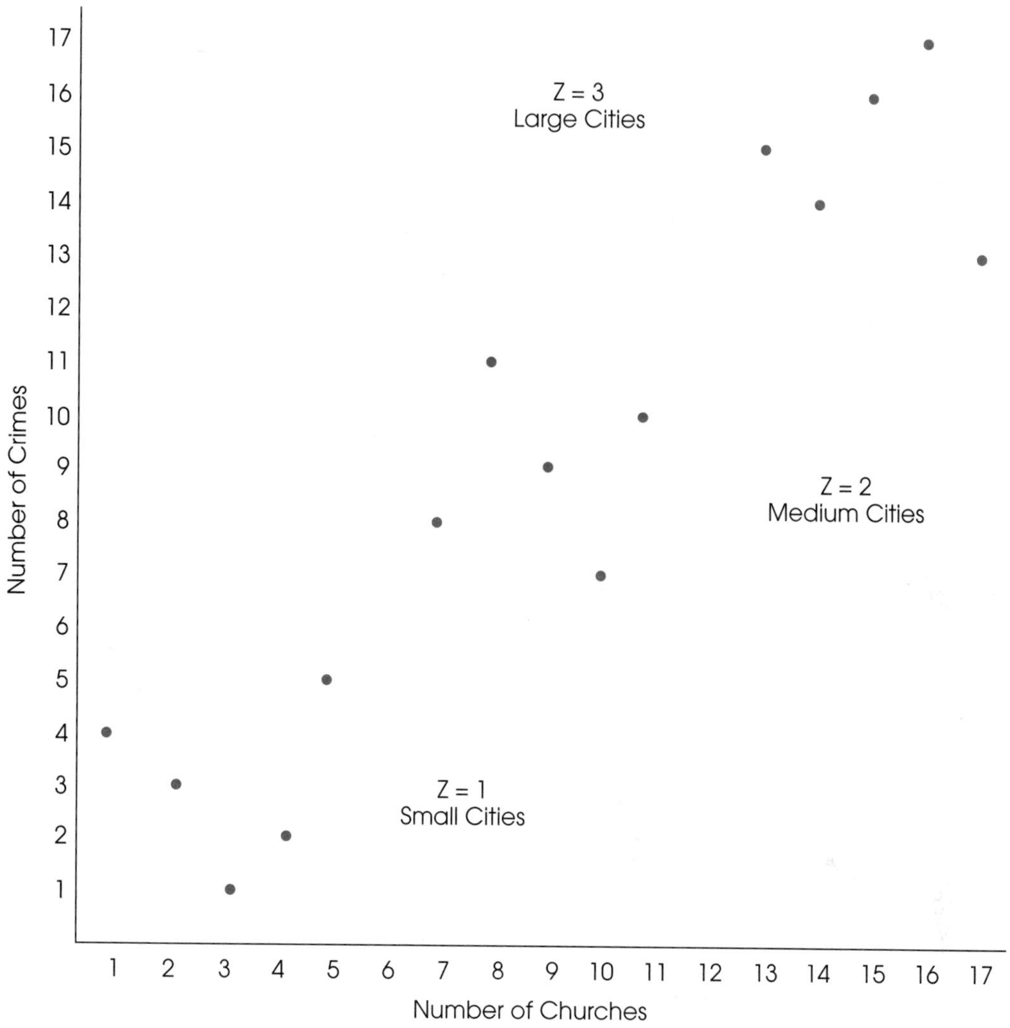

FIGURE 15.12

Hypothetical data showing the relationship between the number of churches and the number of crimes for three groups of cities. Those with small populations ($Z = 1$), those with medium populations ($Z = 2$), and those with large populations ($Z = 3$).

Thus, when the population differences are eliminated, there is no correlation remaining between churches and crime ($r = 0$).

In Example 15.8, the population differences, which correspond to the different values of the Z variable, were eliminated mathematically in the calculation of the partial correlation. However, it is possible to visualize how these differences are eliminated in the actual data. Looking at Figure 15.12, focus on the five points in the bottom left corner. These are the five cities with small populations, few churches, and little crime. The five points in the upper right corner represent the five cities with large populations, many churches, and a lot of crime. The partial correlation controls population size by mathematically equalizing the populations for all 15 cities. Population is increased for the five small cities. However, increasing the population also increases churches and crime. Similarly, population is decreased for the five large cities, which also decreases churches and crime. In Figure 15.12, imagine the five points in the bottom left moving up and to the right so that they overlap with the points in the center. At the same time, the five points in the upper right move down and to the left so that they also overlap the points in the center. When population is equalized, the resulting set of 15 cities is shown in Figure 15.13. Note that controlling the population appears to have eliminated the relationship between churches and crime. This appearance is verified by the correlation for the 15 data points in Figure 15.13, which is $r = 0$, exactly the same as the partial correlation.

In Example 15.8 we used a partial correlation to demonstrate that an apparent relationship between churches and crime was actually caused by the influence of a third variable, population. It also is possible to use partial correlations to demonstrate that a relationship is not caused by the influence of a third variable. As an example, consider research examining the relationship between exposure to sexual content on television and sexual behavior among adolescents (Collins et al., 2004). The study consisted of a survey of 1,792 adolescents, 12 to 17 years old, who reported their television viewing

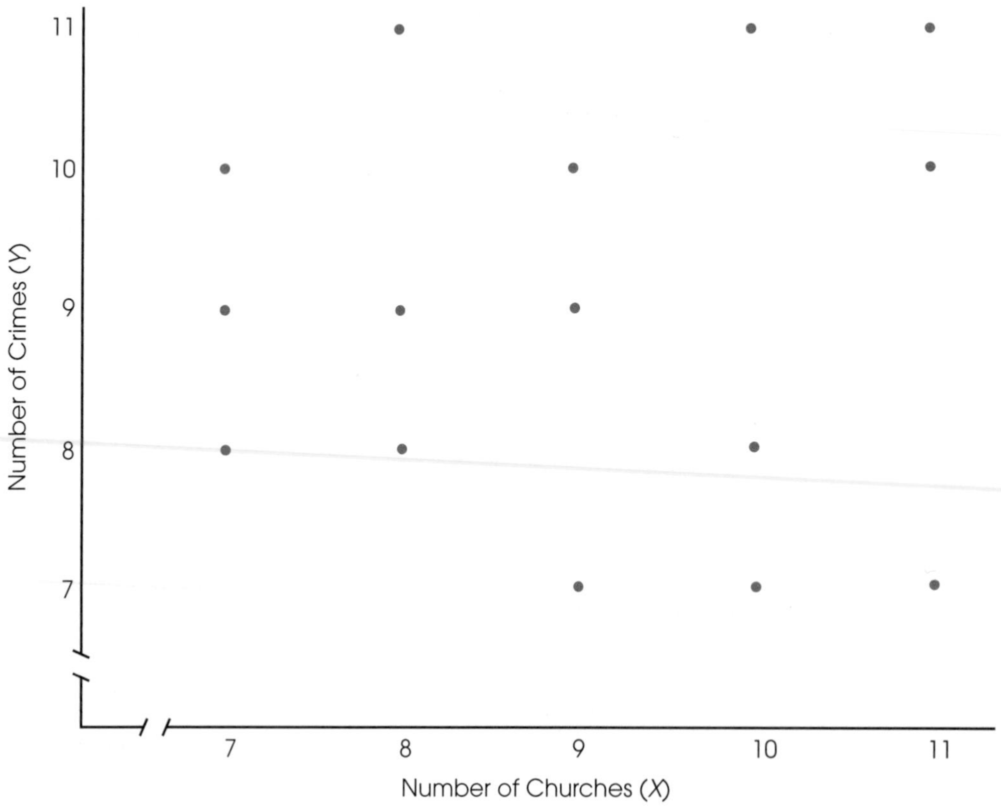

FIGURE 15.13

The relationship between the number of churches and the number of crimes for the same 15 cities shown in Figure 15.12 after the populations have been equalized.

habits and their sexual behaviors. The results showed a clear relationship between television viewing and behaviors. Specifically, the more sexual content the adolescents watched on television, the more likely they were to engage in sexual behaviors. One concern for the researchers was that the observed relationship may be influenced by the age of the participants. For example, as the adolescents mature from age 12 to age 17, they increasingly watch television programs with sexual content and they increase their own sexual behaviors. Although the viewing of sexual content on television and the participants' sexual behaviors are increasing together, the observed relationship may simply be the result of age differences. To address this problem, the researcher used a partial correlation technique to eliminate or hold constant the age variable. The results clearly showed that a relationship still exists between television sexual content and sexual behavior even after the influence of the participants' ages was accounted for.

Testing the significance of a partial correlation The statistical significance of a partial correlation is determined using the same procedure as is used to evaluate a regular Pearson correlation. Specifically, the partial correlation is compared with the critical values listed in Table B6. For a partial correlation, however, you must use $df = n - 3$ instead of the $n - 2$ value that is used for the Pearson correlation. A significant correlation means that it is very unlikely ($p < \alpha$) that the sample correlation would occur without a corresponding relationship in the population.

LEARNING CHECK

1. Sales figures show a positive relationship between temperature and ice cream consumption; as temperature increases, ice cream consumption also increases. Other research shows a positive relationship between temperature and crime rate (Cohn & Rotton, 2000). When the temperature increases, both ice cream consumption and crime rates tend to increase. As a result, there is a positive correlation between ice cream consumption and crime rate. However, what do you think is the true relationship between ice cream consumption and crime rate? Specifically, what value would you predict for the partial correlation between the two variables if temperature were held constant?

ANSWER

1. There should be no systematic relationship between ice cream consumption and crime rate. The partial correlation should be near zero.

15.5 ALTERNATIVES TO THE PEARSON CORRELATION

The Pearson correlation measures the degree of linear relationship between two variables when the data (X and Y values) consist of numerical scores from an interval or ratio scale of measurement. However, other correlations have been developed for nonlinear relationships and for other types of data. In this section we examine three additional correlations: the Spearman correlation, the point-biserial correlation, and the phi-coefficient. As you will see, all three can be viewed as special applications of the Pearson correlation.

THE SPEARMAN CORRELATION

When the Pearson correlation formula is used with data from an ordinal scale (ranks), the result is called the *Spearman correlation*. The Spearman correlation is used in two situations.

First, the Spearman correlation is used to measure the relationship between X and Y when both variables are measured on ordinal scales. Recall from Chapter 1 that an ordinal scale typically involves ranking individuals rather than obtaining numerical scores. Rank-order data are fairly common because they are often easier to obtain than interval or ratio scale data. For example, a teacher may feel confident about rank-ordering students' leadership abilities but would find it difficult to measure leadership on some other scale.

In addition to measuring relationships for ordinal data, the Spearman correlation can be used as a valuable alternative to the Pearson correlation, even when the original raw scores are on an interval or a ratio scale. As we have noted, the Pearson correlation measures the degree of *linear relationship* between two variables—that is, how well the data points fit on a straight line. However, a researcher often expects the data to show a consistently one-directional relationship but not necessarily a linear relationship. For example, Figure 15.14 shows the typical relationship between practice and performance. For nearly any skill, increasing amounts of practice tend to be associated with improvements in performance (the more you practice, the better you get). However, it is not a straight-line relationship. When you are first learning a new skill, practice produces large improvements in performance. After you have been performing a skill for several years, however, additional practice produces only minor changes in performance. Although there is a consistent relationship between the amount of practice and the quality of performance, it clearly is not linear. If the Pearson correlation were computed for these data, it would not produce a correlation of 1.00 because the data do not fit perfectly on a straight line. In a situation like this, the Spearman correlation can be used to measure the consistency of the relationship, independent of its form.

The reason that the Spearman correlation measures consistency, rather than form, comes from a simple observation: When two variables are consistently related, their ranks are linearly related. For example, a perfectly consistent positive relationship means that every time the X variable increases, the Y variable also increases. Thus, the smallest value of X is paired with the smallest value of Y, the second-smallest value of X is paired with the second smallest value of Y, and so on. Every time the rank for X goes up by 1 point, the rank for Y also goes up by 1 point. As a result, the ranks fit perfectly on a straight line. This phenomenon is demonstrated in the following example.

FIGURE 15.14

Hypothetical data showing the relationship between practice and performance. Although this relationship is not linear, there is a consistent positive relationship. An increase in performance tends to accompany an increase in practice.

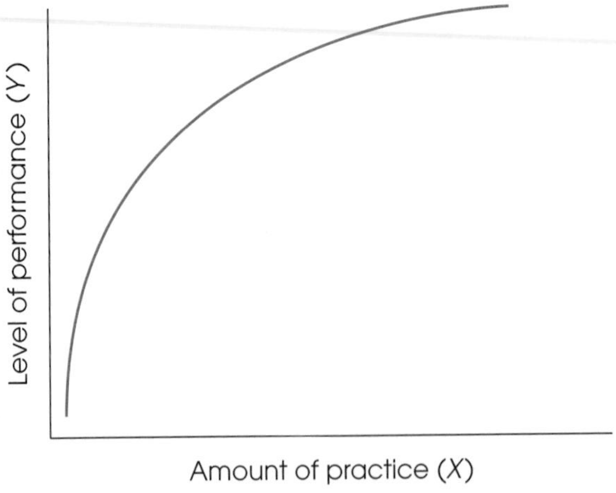

EXAMPLE 15.9 Table 15.3 presents X and Y scores for a sample of $n = 4$ people. Note that the data show a perfectly consistent relationship. Each increase in X is accompanied by an increase in Y. However the relationship is not linear, as can be seen in the graph of the data in Figure 15.15(a).

Next, we convert the scores to ranks. The lowest X is assigned a rank of 1, the next lowest a rank of 2, and so on. The Y scores are then ranked in the same way. The ranks are listed in Table 15.3 and shown in Figure 15.15(b). Note that the perfect consistency for the scores produces a perfect linear relationship for the ranks.

The preceding example demonstrates that a consistent relationship among scores produces a linear relationship when the scores are converted to ranks. Thus, if you want to measure the consistency of a relationship for a set of scores, you can simply convert the scores to ranks and then use the Pearson correlation formula to measure the linear relationship for the ranked data. The degree of linear relationship for the ranks provides a measure of the degree of consistency for the original scores.

TABLE 15.3

Scores and ranks for Example 15.9.

Person	X	Y	X−Rank	Y−Rank
A	4	9	3	3
B	2	2	1	1
C	10	10	4	4
D	3	8	2	2

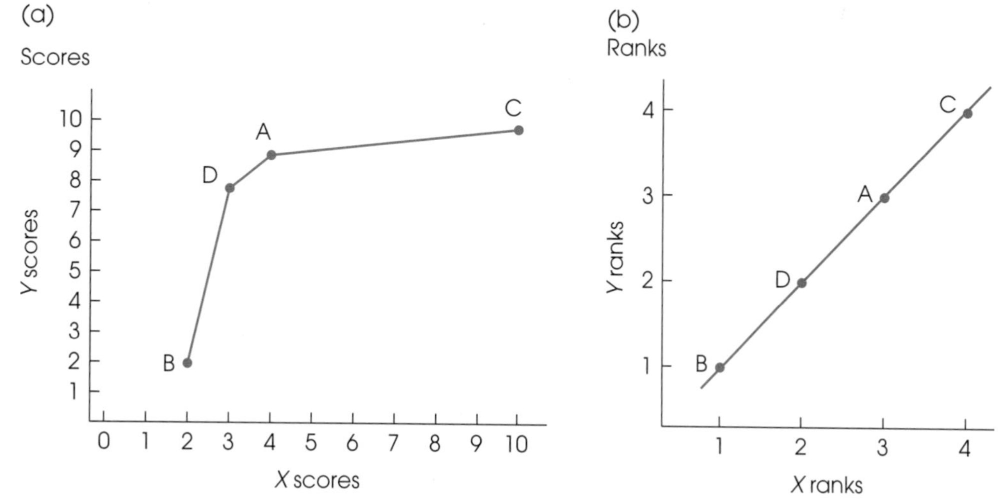

FIGURE 15.15

Scatter plots showing (a) the scores and (b) the ranks for the data in Example 15.9. Notice that there is a consistent, positive relationship between the X and Y scores, although it is not a linear relationship. Also notice that the scatter plot of the ranks shows a perfect linear relationship.

To summarize, the Spearman correlation measures the relationship between two variables when both are measured on ordinal scales (ranks). There are two general situations in which the Spearman correlation is used:

1. Spearman is used when the original data are ordinal; that is, when the *X* and *Y* values are ranks. In this case, you simply apply the Pearson correlation formula to the set of ranks.
2. Spearman is used when a researcher wants to measure the consistency of a relationship between *X* and *Y*, independent of the specific form of the relationship. In this case, the original scores are first converted to ranks, then the Pearson correlation formula is used with the ranks. Because the Pearson formula measures the degree to which the ranks fit on a straight line, it also measures the degree of consistency in the relationship for the original scores. Incidentally, when there is a consistently one-directional relationship between two variables, the relationship is said to be *monotonic*. Thus, the Spearman correlation measures the degree of monotonic relationship between two variables.

The word *monotonic* describes a sequence that is consistently increasing (or decreasing). Like the word *monotonous*, it means constant and unchanging.

In either case, the Spearman correlation is identified by the symbol r_S to differentiate it from the Pearson correlation. The complete process of computing the Spearman correlation, including ranking scores, is demonstrated in Example 15.10.

EXAMPLE 15.10 The following data show a nearly perfect monotonic relationship between *X* and *Y*. When *X* increases, *Y* tends to decrease, and there is only one reversal in this general trend. To compute the Spearman correlation, we first rank the *X* and *Y* values, and we then compute the Pearson correlation for the ranks.

We have listed the *X* values in order so that the trend is easier to recognize.

Original Data		Ranks		
X	*Y*	*X*	*Y*	*XY*
3	12	1	5	5
4	10	2	3	6
10	11	3	4	12
11	9	4	2	8
12	2	5	1	5
				$36 = \Sigma XY$

To compute the correlation, we need *SS* for *X*, *SS* for *Y*, and *SP*. Remember that all of these values are computed with the ranks, not the original scores. The *X* ranks are simply the integers 1, 2, 3, 4, and 5. These values have $\Sigma X = 15$ and $\Sigma X^2 = 55$. The *SS* for the *X* ranks is

$$SS_X = \Sigma X^2 - \frac{(\Sigma X)^2}{n} = 55 - \frac{(15)^2}{5} = 10$$

Note that the ranks for *Y* are identical to the ranks for *X*; that is, they are the integers 1, 2, 3, 4, and 5. Therefore, the *SS* for *Y* is identical to the *SS* for *X*:

$$SS_Y = 10$$

To compute the *SP* value, we need ΣX, ΣY, and ΣXY for the ranks. The *XY* values are listed in the table with the ranks, and we already have found that both the *X*s and the *Y*s have a sum of 15. Using these values, we obtain

$$SP = \Sigma XY - \frac{(\Sigma X)(\Sigma Y)}{n} = 36 - \frac{(15)(15)}{5} = -9$$

Finally, the Spearman correlation simply uses the Pearson formula for the ranks.

$$r_s = \frac{SP}{\sqrt{(SS_X)(SS_Y)}} = \frac{-9}{\sqrt{10(10)}} = -0.9$$

The Spearman correlation indicates that the data show a consistent (nearly perfect) negative trend.

RANKING TIED SCORES

When you are converting scores into ranks for the Spearman correlation, you may encounter two (or more) identical scores. Whenever two scores have exactly the same value, their ranks should also be the same. This is accomplished by the following procedure:

1. List the scores in order from smallest to largest. Include tied values in the list.
2. Assign a rank (first, second, etc.) to each position in the ordered list.
3. When two (or more) scores are tied, compute the mean of their ranked positions, and assign this mean value as the final rank for each score.

The process of finding ranks for tied scores is demonstrated here. These scores have been listed in order from smallest to largest.

Scores	Rank Position	Final Rank	
3	1	1.5	Mean of 1 and 2
3	2	1.5	
5	3	3	
6	4	5	Mean of 4, 5, and 6
6	5	5	
6	6	5	
12	7	7	

Note that this example has seven scores and uses all seven ranks. For $X = 12$, the largest score, the appropriate rank is 7. It cannot be given a rank of 6 because that rank has been used for the tied scores.

SPECIAL FORMULA FOR THE SPEARMAN CORRELATION

After the original *X* values and *Y* values have been ranked, the calculations necessary for *SS* and *SP* can be greatly simplified. First, you should note that the *X* ranks and the *Y* ranks are really just a set of integers: 1, 2, 3, 4, ... , *n*. To compute the mean for these integers, you can locate the midpoint of the series by $M = (n + 1)/2$. Similarly, the SS for this series of integers can be computed by

$$SS = \frac{n(n^2 - 1)}{12} \quad \text{(Try it out.)}$$

Also, because the X ranks and the Y ranks are the same values, the SS for X is identical to the SS for Y.

Because calculations with ranks can be simplified and because the Spearman correlation uses ranked data, these simplifications can be incorporated into the final calculations for the Spearman correlation. Instead of using the Pearson formula after ranking the data, you can put the ranks directly into a simplified formula:

$$r_S = 1 - \frac{6\Sigma D^2}{n(n^2 - 1)} \qquad (15.7)$$

Caution: In this formula, you compute the value of the fraction and then subtract from 1. The 1 is not part of the fraction.

where D is the difference between the X rank and the Y rank for each individual. This special formula produces the same result that would be obtained from the Pearson formula. However, note that this special formula can be used only after the scores have been converted to ranks and only when there are no ties among the ranks. If there are relatively few tied ranks, the formula still may be used, but it loses accuracy as the number of ties increases. The application of this formula is demonstrated in the following example.

EXAMPLE 15.11

To demonstrate the special formula for the Spearman correlation, we use the same data that were presented in Example 15.10. The ranks for these data are shown again here:

Ranks		Difference	
X	Y	D	D^2
1	5	4	16
2	3	1	1
3	4	1	1
4	2	−2	4
5	1	−4	16
			$38 = \Sigma D^2$

Using the special formula for the Spearman correlation, we obtain

$$r_S = 1 - \frac{6\Sigma D^2}{n(n^2 - 1)} = 1 - \frac{6(38)}{5(25 - 1)} = 1 - \frac{228}{120} = 1 - 1.90 = -0.90$$

This is exactly the same answer that we obtained in Example 15.10, using the Pearson formula on the ranks.

TESTING THE SIGNIFICANCE OF THE SPEARMAN CORRELATION

Testing a hypothesis for the Spearman correlation is similar to the procedure used for the Pearson r. The basic question is whether a correlation exists in the population. The sample correlation could be the result of chance, or perhaps it reflects an actual relationship between the variables in the population. For the Pearson correlation, the Greek letter rho (ρ) was used for the population correlation. For the Spearman, ρ_S is used for the population parameter. Note that this symbol is consistent with the sample statistic, r_S. The null hypothesis states that there is no correlation (no monotonic relationship) between the variables for the population, or, in symbols:

$$H_0: \quad \rho_S = 0 \qquad \text{(The population correlation is zero.)}$$

The alternative hypothesis predicts that a nonzero correlation exists in the population, which can be stated in symbols as

$$H_1: \quad \rho_S \neq 0 \qquad \text{(There is a real correlation.)}$$

To determine whether the Spearman correlation is statistically significant (that is, H_0 should be rejected), consult Table B.7. This table is similar to the one used to determine the significance of Pearson's r (Table B.6); however, the first column is sample size (n) rather than degrees of freedom. To use the table, line up the sample size in the first column with one of the alpha levels listed across the top. The values in the body of the table identify the magnitude of the Spearman correlation that is necessary to be significant. The table is built on the concept that a sample correlation should be representative of the corresponding population value. In particular, if the population correlation is $\rho_S = 0$ (as specified in H_0), then the sample correlation should be near zero. For each sample size and alpha level, the table identifies the minimum sample correlation that is significantly different from zero. The following example demonstrates the use of the table.

EXAMPLE 15.12

An industrial psychologist selects a sample of $n = 15$ employees. These employees are ranked in order of work productivity by their manager. They also are ranked by a peer. The Spearman correlation computed for these data revealed a correlation of $r_S = .60$. Using Table B.7 with $n = 15$ and $\alpha = .05$, a correlation of at least ± 0.45 is needed to reject H_0. The observed correlation for the sample easily surpasses this critical value. The correlation between manager and peer ratings is statistically significant.

LEARNING CHECK

1. Describe what is measured by a Spearman correlation, and explain how this correlation is different from the Pearson correlation.
2. If the following scores are converted into ranks, what rank will be assigned to the individuals who have scores of $X = 7$?

   Scores: 1, 1, 1, 3, 6, 7, 7, 8, 10
3. Rank the following scores and compute the Spearman correlation:

X	Y
2	7
12	38
9	6
10	19

ANSWERS

1. The Spearman correlation measures the consistency of the direction of the relationship between two variables. The Spearman correlation does not depend on the form of the relationship, whereas the Pearson correlation measures how well the data fit a linear form.
2. Both scores get a rank of 6.5 (the average of 6 and 7).
3. $r_S = 0.80$

THE POINT-BISERIAL CORRELATION AND MEASURING EFFECT SIZE WITH r^2

In Chapters 9, 10, and 11 we introduced r^2 as a measure of effect size that often accompanies a hypothesis test using the t statistic. The r^2 used to measure effect size and the r used to measure a correlation are directly related, and we now have an opportunity to demonstrate the relationship. Specifically, we compare the independent-measures t test (Chapter 10) and a special version of the Pearson correlation known as the *point-biserial correlation.*

The point-biserial correlation is used to measure the relationship between two variables in situations in which one variable consists of regular, numerical scores, but the second variable has only two values. A variable with only two values is called a *dichotomous variable* or a *binomial variable*. Some examples of dichotomous variables are

1. Male versus female
2. College graduate versus not a college graduate
3. First-born child versus later-born child
4. Success versus failure on a particular task
5. Older than 30 years versus younger than 30 years

It is customary to use the numerical values 0 and 1, but any two different numbers would work equally well and would not affect the value of the correlation.

To compute the point-biserial correlation, the dichotomous variable is first converted to numerical values by assigning a value of zero (0) to one category and a value of one (1) to the other category. Then the regular Pearson correlation formula is used with the converted data.

To demonstrate the point-biserial correlation and its association with the r^2 measure of effect size, we use the data from Example 10.1 (p. 326). The original example compared high school grades for two groups of students: one group who regularly watched Sesame Street as 5-year-old children and one who did not watch the program. The data from the independent-measures study are presented on the left side of Table 15.4. Notice that the data consist of two separate samples and the independent-measures t was used to determine whether there was a significant mean difference between the two populations represented by the samples.

On the right-hand side of Table 15.4, we have reorganized the data into a form that is suitable for a point-biserial correlation. Specifically, we used each student's high school grade as the X value and we have created a new variable, Y, to represent the group, or condition, for each student. In this case, we have used $Y = 1$ for students who watched Sesame Street and $Y = 0$ for students who did not watch the program.

When the data in Table 15.4 were originally presented in Chapter 10, we conducted an independent-measures t hypothesis test and obtained $t = 4.00$ with $df = 18$. We measured the size of the treatment effect by calculating r^2, the percentage of variance accounted for, and obtained $r^2 = 0.47$.

Calculating the point-biserial correlation for these data also produces a value for r. Specifically, the X scores produce $SS = 680$; the Y values produce $SS = 5.00$, and the

TABLE 15.4

The same data are organized in two different formats. On the left-hand side, the data appear as two separate samples appropriate for an independent-measures *t* hypothesis test. On the right-hand side, the same data are shown as a single sample, with two scores for each individual: the original high school grade and a dichotomous score (*Y*) that identifies the group in which the participant is located (Seasame Street = 1 and No-Sesame Street = 0). The data on the right are appropriate for a point-biserial correlation.

Data for the Independent-Measures *t* test. Two separate samples, each with $n = 10$ scores.

Average High School Grade			
Watched Seasame Street		Did Not Watch Sesame Street	
86	99	90	79
87	97	89	83
91	94	82	86
97	89	83	81
98	92	85	92
$n = 10$		$n = 10$	
$M = 93$		$M = 85$	
$SS = 200$		$SS = 160$	

Data for the Point-Biserial Correlation. Two scores, *X* and *Y* for each of the $n = 20$ participants.

Participant	Grade *X*	Group *Y*
A	86	1
B	87	1
C	91	1
D	97	1
E	98	1
F	99	1
G	97	1
H	94	1
I	89	1
J	92	1
K	90	0
L	89	0
M	82	0
N	83	0
O	85	0
P	79	0
Q	83	0
R	86	0
S	81	0
T	92	0

sum of the products of the *X* and *Y* deviations produces $SP = 40$. The point-biserial correlation is

$$r = \frac{SP}{\sqrt{(SS_X)(SS_Y)}} = \frac{40}{\sqrt{(680)(5)}} = \frac{40}{58.31} = 0.686$$

Notice that squaring the value of the point-biserial correlation produces $r^2 = (0.686)^2 = 0.47$, which is exactly the value of r^2 we obtained measuring effect size.

In some respects, the point-biserial correlation and the independent-measures hypothesis test are evaluating the same thing. Specifically, both are examining the relationship between the TV-viewing habits of 5-year-old children and their future academic performance in high school.

1. The correlation is measuring the *strength* of the relationship between the two variables. A large correlation (near 1.00 or –1.00) would indicate that there is a consistent, predictable relationship between high school grades and watching Sesame Street as a 5-year-old child. In particular, the value of r^2 measures how much of the variability in grades can be predicted by knowing whether the participants watched Sesame Street.
2. The *t* test evaluates the *significance* of the relationship. The hypothesis test determines whether the mean difference in grades between the two groups is greater than can be reasonably explained by chance alone.

As we noted in Chapter 10 (pp. 332–333), the outcome of the hypothesis test and the value of r^2 are often reported together. The t value measures statistical significance and r^2 measures the effect size. Also, as we noted in Chapter 10, the values for t and r^2 are directly related. In fact, either can be calculated from the other by the equations

$$r^2 = \frac{t^2}{t^2 + df} \quad \text{and} \quad t^2 = \frac{r^2}{\left(1 - r^2\right)/df}$$

where df is the degrees of freedom for the t statistic.

However, you should note that r^2 is determined entirely by the size of the correlation, whereas t is influenced by the size of the correlation and the size of the sample. For example, a correlation of $r = 0.30$ produces $r^2 = 0.09$ (9%) no matter how large the sample may be. On the other hand, a point-biserial correlation of $r = 0.30$ for a total sample of 10 people ($n = 5$ in each group) produces a nonsignificant value of $t = 0.889$. If the sample is increased to 50 people ($n = 25$ in each group), the same correlation produces a significant t value of $t = 2.18$. Although t and r are related, they are measuring different things.

POINT-BISERIAL CORRELATION, PARTIAL CORRELATION, AND EFFECT SIZE FOR THE REPEATED-MEASURES *t* TEST

In the previous section we demonstrated that the point-biserial correlation produces an r value that is directly related to the r^2 value used to measure effect size for the independent-measures t test. With one modification, this same process can be duplicated for the repeated-measures t test. The modification involves using a partial correlation (see pp. 531–535) to control for individual differences.

You should recall from Chapters 11 and 13 that one of the major distinctions between independent-measures and repeated-measures designs is that the repeated-measures designs eliminate the influence of individual differences. When computing a point-biserial correlation for repeated-measures data, we can use a partial correlation to eliminate individual differences once again.

The left-hand side of Table 15.5 shows data from a repeated-measures study comparing two treatments with a sample of $n = 4$ participants. Note that we have added a column of P values, or participant totals, showing the sum of the two scores for each participant. For example, participant A has scores of 3 and 5, which add to $P = 8$. The P values provide an indication of the individual differences. Participant A, for example, has consistently smaller scores and a smaller P value than all of the other participants. These data produce $t = 2.00$ with $df = 3$, which results in $r^2 = 4/(4 + 3) = 0.5714$ as the measure of effect size.

TABLE 15.5

The data on the left represent scores from a repeated-measures study comparing two treatments with a sample of $n = 4$ participants. The data on the right are the same scores in a format compatible with the point-biserial correlation. The P values in each set of data show the sum of the two scores for each participant and provide a measure of individual differences.

	Treatment		
Participant	I	II	P
A	3	5	8
B	4	14	18
C	5	7	12
D	4	6	10

Score (X)	Treatment (Y)	P
3	0	8
4	0	18
5	0	12
4	0	10
5	1	8
14	1	18
7	1	12
6	1	10

On the right-hand side of Table 15.5 we have reorganized the data into a format compatible with the point-biserial correlation. The individual scores, or X values are listed in the first column. The second column, or Y values, are numerical codes corresponding to the two treatment conditions: Treatment I = 0 and Treatment II = 1. The third column contains the P value for each individual, which measures the individual differences between participants. For these data, the partial correlation between X and Y, controlling for the P values, is

$$r_{XY\text{-}P} = 0.756$$

Note that this is a slightly modified point-biserial correlation. The modification is that we used a partial correlation to control the individual differences. However, squaring this correlation produces $r^2 = (0.756)^2 = 0.5715$, which is identical, within rounding error, to the r^2 value that measures effect size for the repeated-measures t test.

THE PHI-COEFFICIENT

When both variables (X and Y) measured for each individual are dichotomous, the correlation between the two variables is called the *phi-coefficient.* To compute phi (ϕ), you follow a two-step procedure:

1. Convert each of the dichotomous variables to numerical values by assigning a 0 to one category and a 1 to the other category for each of the variables.
2. Use the regular Pearson formula with the converted scores.

This process is demonstrated in the following example.

EXAMPLE 15.13

A researcher is interested in examining the relationship between birth-order position and personality. A random sample of $n = 8$ individuals is obtained, and each individual is classified in terms of birth-order position as first-born or only child versus later-born. Then each individual's personality is classified as either introvert or extrovert.

The original measurements are then converted to numerical values by the following assignments:

Birth Order	Personality
1st or only child = 0	Introvert = 0
Later-born child = 1	Extrovert = 1

The original data and the converted scores are as follows:

Original Data		Converted Scores	
Birth Order (X)	Personality (Y)	Birth Order (X)	Personality (Y)
1st	Introvert	0	0
3rd	Extrovert	1	1
Only	Extrovert	0	1
2nd	Extrovert	1	1
4th	Extrovert	1	1
2nd	Introvert	1	0
Only	Introvert	0	0
3rd	Extrovert	1	1

The Pearson correlation formula is then used with the converted data to compute the phi-coefficient.

Because the assignment of numerical values is arbitrary (either category could be designated 0 or 1), the sign of the resulting correlation is meaningless. As with most correlations, the *strength* of the relationship is best described by the value of r^2, the coefficient of determination, which measures how much of the variability in one variable is predicted or determined by the association with the second variable.

We also should note that although the phi-coefficient can be used to assess the relationship between two dichotomous variables, the more common statistical procedure is a chi-square statistic, which is examined in Chapter 17.

LEARNING CHECK

1. Define a *dichotomous* variable.
2. The following data represent job-related stress scores for a sample of $n = 8$ individuals. These people also are classified by salary level.
   a. Convert the data into a form suitable for the point-biserial correlation.
   b. Compute the point-biserial correlation for these data.

Salary More than $40,000	Salary Less than $40,000
8	4
6	2
5	1
3	3

3. A researcher would like to know whether there is a relationship between gender and manual dexterity for 3-year-old children. A sample of $n = 10$ boys and $n = 10$ girls is obtained and each child is given a manual-dexterity test. Five of the girls failed the test and only two of the boys failed. Describe how these data could be coded into a form suitable for computing a phi-coefficient to measure the strength of the relationship.

ANSWERS

1. A dichotomous variable has only two possible values.
2. a. Salary level is a dichotomous variable and can be coded as $Y = 1$ for individuals with salary more than $40,000 and $Y = 0$ for salary less than $40,000. The stress scores produce $SS_X = 36$, the salary codes produce $SS_Y = 2$, and $SP = 6$.
   b. The point-biserial correlation is 0.71.
3. Gender could be coded with male = 0 and female = 1. Manual dexterity could be coded with failure = 0 and success = 1. Eight boys would have scores of 0 and 1 and two would have scores of 0 and 0. Five girls would have scores of 1 and 1 and five would have scores of 1 and 0.

SUMMARY

1. A correlation measures the relationship between two variables, X and Y. The relationship is described by three characteristics:

   a. *Direction.* A relationship can be either positive or negative. A positive relationship means that X and Y vary in the same direction. A negative relationship means that X and Y vary in opposite directions. The sign of the correlation (+ or –) specifies the direction.

   b. *Form.* The most common form for a relationship is a straight line, which is measured by the Pearson correlation. Other correlations measure the consistency or strength of the relationship, independent of any specific form.

   c. *Strength or consistency.* The numerical value of the correlation measures the strength or consistency of the relationship. A correlation of 1.00 indicates a perfectly consistent relationship and 0.00 indicates no relationship at all. For the Pearson correlation, $r = 1.00$ (or -1.00) means that the data points fit perfectly on a straight line.

2. The most commonly used correlation is the Pearson correlation, which measures the degree of linear relationship. The Pearson correlation is identified by the letter r and is computed by

$$r = \frac{SP}{\sqrt{SS_X SS_Y}}$$

   In this formula, SP is the sum of products of deviations and can be calculated with either a definitional formula or a computational formula:

$$\text{definitional formula: } SP = \Sigma(X - M_X)(Y - M_Y)$$

$$\text{computational formula: } SP = \Sigma XY - \frac{\Sigma X \Sigma Y}{n}$$

3. A correlation between two variables should not be interpreted as implying a causal relationship. Simply because X and Y are related does not mean that X causes Y or that Y causes X.

4. To evaluate the strength of a relationship, you square the value of the correlation. The resulting value, r^2, is called the *coefficient of determination* because it measures the portion of the variability in one variable that can be predicted using the relationship with the second variable.

5. A partial correlation measures the linear relationship between two variables by eliminating the influence of a third variable by holding it constant.

6. The Spearman correlation (r_S) measures the consistency of direction in the relationship between X and Y—that is, the degree to which the relationship is one-directional, or monotonic. The Spearman correlation is computed by a two-stage process:

   a. Rank the X scores and the Y scores separately.

   b. Compute the Pearson correlation using the ranks.

7. The point-biserial correlation is used to measure the strength of the relationship when one of the two variables is dichotomous. The dichotomous variable is coded using values of 0 and 1, and the regular Pearson formula is applied. Squaring the point-biserial correlation produces the same r^2 value that is obtained to measure effect size for the independent-measures t test. When both variables, X and Y, are dichotomous, the phi-coefficient can be used to measure the strength of the relationship. Both variables are coded 0 and 1, and the Pearson formula is used to compute the correlation.

KEY TERMS

correlation (510)
positive correlation (512)
negative correlation (512)
perfect correlation (513)
Pearson correlation (514)
sum of products (*SP*) (515)
restricted range (522)
coefficient of determination (524)
regression toward the mean (526)
correlation matrix (530)
partial correlation (531)
Spearman correlation (535)
point-biserial correlation (542)
phi-coefficient (545)

RESOURCES

Book Companion Website: www.cengage.com/psychology/gravetter

You can find a tutorial quiz and other learning exercises for Chapter 15 on the book companion website. The website also provides access to two workshops entitled *Correlation* and *Bivariate Scatter Plots,* which include information on regression.

aplia

Improve your understanding of statistics with Aplia's auto-graded problem sets and immediate, detailed explanations for every question. To learn more, visit **www.aplia.com/statistics.**

CENGAGE brain .com

Log in to CengageBrain to access the resources your instructor requires. For this book, you can access:

Psychology CourseMate brings course concepts to life with interactive learning, study, and exam preparation tools that support the printed textbook. A textbook-specific website, Psychology CourseMate includes an integrated interactive eBook and other interactive learning tools including quizzes, flashcards, and more.

Visit www.cengagebrain.com to access your account and purchase materials.

SPSS

General instructions for using SPSS are presented in Appendix D. Following are detailed instructions for using SPSS to perform **The Pearson, Spearman, point-biserial, and partial correlations.** *Note:* We focus on the Pearson correlation and then describe how slight modifications to this procedure can be made to compute the Spearman, point-biserial, and partial correlations. Separate instructions for the **phi-coefficient** are presented at the end of this section.

Data Entry

The data are entered into two columns in the data editor, one for the X values (VAR00001) and one for the Y values (VAR00002), with the two scores for each individual in the same row.

Data Analysis

1. Click **Analyze** on the tool bar, select **Correlate,** and click on **Bivariate.**
2. One by one, move the labels for the two data columns into the **Variables** box. (Hightlight each label and click the arrow to move it into the box.)

3. The **Pearson** box should be checked but, at this point, you can switch to the Spearman correlation by clicking the appropriate box.
4. Click **OK.**

SPSS Output

We used SPSS to compute the correlation for the data in Example 15.3 and the output is shown in Figure 15.16. The program produces a correlation matrix showing all the possible correlations, including the correlation of X with X and the correlation of Y with Y (both are perfect correlations). You want the correlation of X and Y, which is contained in the upper right corner (or the lower left). The output includes the significance level (p value or alpha level) for the correlation.

To compute a partial correlation, click **Analyze** on the tool bar, select **Correlate,** and click on **Partial.** Move the column labels for the two variables to be correlated into the **Variables** box and move the column label for the variable to be held constant into the **Controlling for** box and click **OK.**

To compute the **Spearman** correlation, enter either the X and Y ranks or the X and Y scores into the first two columns. Then follow the same Data Analysis instructions that were presented for the Pearson correlation. At step 3 in the instructions, click on the **Spearman** box before the final OK. (*Note:* If you enter X and Y scores into the data editor, SPSS converts the scores to ranks before computing the Spearman correlation.)

To compute the **point-biserial** correlation, enter the scores (X values) in the first column and enter the numerical values (usually 0 and 1) for the dichotomous variable in the second column. Then, follow the same Data Analysis instructions that were presented for the Pearson correlation.

The **phi-coefficient** can also be computed by entering the complete string of 0s and 1s into two columns of the SPSS data editor, then following the same Data Analysis instructions that were presented for the Pearson correlation. However, this can be tedious, especially with a large set of scores. The following is an alternative procedure for computing the phi-coefficient with large data sets.

FIGURE 15.16

The SPSS output for the correlation in Example 15.3.

Correlations

		VAR00001	VAR00002
VAR00001	Pearson Correlation	1	.875
	Sig. (2-tailed)		.052
	N	5	5
VAR00002	Pearson Correlation	.875	1
	Sig. (2-tailed)	.052	
	N	5	5

Data Entry

1. Enter the values, 0, 0, 1, 1 (in order) into the first column of the SPSS data editor.
2. Enter the values 0, 1, 0, 1 (in order) into the second column.
3. Count the number of individuals in the sample who are classified with $X = 0$ and $Y = 0$. Enter this frequency in the top box in the third column of the data editor. Then, count how many have $X = 0$ and $Y = 1$ and enter the frequency in the second box of the third column. Continue with the number who have $X = 1$ and $Y = 0$, and finally the number who have $X = 1$ and $Y = 1$. You should end up with 4 values in column three.
4. Click **Data** on the Tool Bar at the top of the SPSS Data Editor page and select **Weight Cases** at the bottom of the list.
5. Click the circle labeled **Weight cases by,** and then highlight the label for the column containing your frequencies (VAR00003) on the left and move it into the **Frequency Variable** box by clicking on the arrow.
6. Click **OK**.
7. Click **Analyze** on the tool bar, select **Correlate,** and click on **Bivariate.**
8. One by one, move the labels for the two data columns containing the 0s and 1s (probably VAR00001 and VAR00002) into the **Variables** box. (Highlight each label and click the arrow to move it into the box.)
9. Verify that the **Pearson** box is checked.
10. Click **OK.**

SPSS Output

The program produces the same correlation matrix that was described for the Pearson correlation. Again, you want the correlation between *X* and *Y*, which is in the upper right corner (or lower left). Remember, with the phi-coefficient, the sign of the correlation is meaningless.

FOCUS ON PROBLEM SOLVING

1. A correlation always has a value from +1.00 to –1.00. If you obtain a correlation outside this range, then you have made a computational error.

2. When interpreting a correlation, do not confuse the sign (+ or –) with its numerical value. The sign and the numerical value must be considered separately. Remember that the sign indicates the direction of the relationship between *X* and *Y*. On the other hand, the numerical value reflects the strength of the relationship or how well the points approximate a linear (straight-line) relationship. Therefore, a correlation of –0.90 is as strong as a correlation of +0.90. The signs tell us that the first correlation is an inverse relationship.

3. Before you begin to calculate a correlation, sketch a scatter plot of the data and make an estimate of the correlation. (Is it positive or negative? Is it near 1 or near 0?) After computing the correlation, compare your final answer with your original estimate.

4. The definitional formula for the sum of products (*SP*) should be used only when you have a small set (*n*) of scores and the means for *X* and *Y* are both whole numbers. Otherwise, the computational formula produces quicker, easier, and more accurate results.

5. For computing a correlation, n is the number of individuals (and therefore the number of *pairs* of X and Y values).

DEMONSTRATION 15.1

CORRELATION

Calculate the Pearson correlation for the following data:

Person	X	Y	
A	0	4	$M_X = 4$ with $SS_X = 40$
B	2	1	$M_Y = 6$ with $SS_Y = 54$
C	8	10	$SP = 40$
D	6	9	
E	4	6	

STEP 1 **Sketch a scatter plot.** We have constructed a scatter plot for the data (Figure 15.17) and placed an envelope around the data points to make a preliminary estimate of the correlation. Note that the envelope is narrow and elongated. This indicates that the correlation is large—perhaps 0.80 to 0.90. Also, the correlation is positive because increases in X are generally accompanied by increases in Y.

STEP 2 **Compute the Pearson correlation.** For these data, the Pearson correlation is

$$r = \frac{SP}{\sqrt{SS_X SS_Y}} = \frac{40}{\sqrt{40(54)}} = \frac{40}{\sqrt{2160}} = \frac{40}{46.48} = 0.861$$

FIGURE 15.17

The scatter plot for the data of Demonstration 15.1. An envelope is drawn around the points to estimate the magnitude of the correlation. A line is drawn through the middle of the envelope.

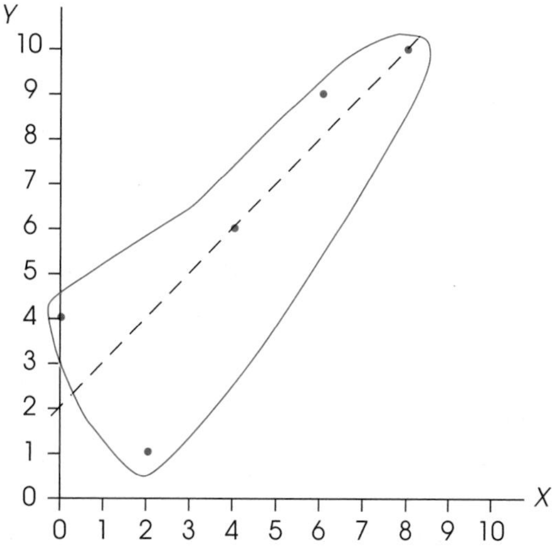

In step 1, our preliminary estimate for the correlation was between +0.80 and +0.90. The calculated correlation is consistent with this estimate.

STEP 3 **Evaluate the significance of the correlation.** The null hypothesis states that, for the population, there is no linear relationship between X and Y, and that the value obtained for the sample correlation is simply the result of sampling error. Specifically, H_0 says that the population correlation is zero ($\rho = 0$). With $n = 5$ pairs of X and Y values the test has $df = 3$. Table B.6 lists a critical value of 0.878 for a two-tailed test with $\alpha = .05$. Because our correlation is smaller than this value, we fail to reject the null hypothesis and conclude that the correlation is not significant.

PROBLEMS

1. What information is provided by the sign (+ or –) of the Pearson correlation?

2. What information is provided by the numerical value of the Pearson correlation?

3. Calculate *SP* (the sum of products of deviations) for the following scores. *Note:* Both means are whole numbers, so the definitional formula works well

X	Y
0	2
1	4
4	5
3	3
7	6

4. For the following scores,

X	Y
1	3
3	5
2	1
2	3

a. Sketch a scatter plot and estimate the Pearson correlation.
b. Compute the Pearson correlation.

5. For the following scores,

X	Y
7	6
9	6
6	3
12	5
9	6
5	4

a. Sketch a scatter plot showing the six data points.
b. Just looking at the scatter plot, estimate the value of the Pearson correlation.
c. Compute the Pearson correlation.

6. Calculate *SP* (the sum of products of deviations) for the following scores. *Note:* Both means are decimal values, so the computational formula works well.

X	Y
0	2
0	1
1	0
2	1
1	2
0	3

7. For the following scores,

X	Y
1	7
4	2
1	3
1	6
2	0
0	6
2	3
1	5

a. Sketch a scatter plot and estimate the Pearson correlation.
b. Compute the Pearson correlation.

8. For the following scores,

X	Y
1	6
4	1
1	4
1	3
3	1

a. Sketch a scatter plot and estimate the value of the Pearson correlation.
b. Compute the Pearson correlation.

9. With a small sample, a single point can have a large effect on the magnitude of the correlation. To create the following data, we started with the scores from problem 8 and changed the first X value from $X = 1$ to $X = 6$.

X	Y
6	6
4	1
1	4
1	3
3	1

a. Sketch a scatter plot and estimate the value of the Pearson correlation.
b. Compute the Pearson correlation.

10. Judge and Cable (2010) report the results of a study demonstrating a negative relationship between weight and income for a group of women professionals. Following are data similar to those obtained in the study. To simplify the weight variable, the women are classified into five categories that measure actual weight relative to height, from 1 = thinnest to 5 = heaviest. Income figures are annual income (in thousands), rounded to the nearest $1,000.
a. Calculate the Pearson correlation for these data.
b. Is the correlation statistically significant? Use a two-tailed test with $\alpha = .05$.

Weight (X)	Income (Y)
1	125
2	78
4	49
3	63
5	35
2	84
5	38
3	51
1	93
4	44

11. Correlation studies are often used to help determine whether certain characteristics are controlled more by genetic influences or by environmental influences. These studies often examine adopted children and compare their behaviors with the behaviors of their birth parents and their adoptive parents. One study examined how much time individuals spend watching TV (Plomin, Corley, DeFries, & Fulker, 1990). The following data are similar to the results obtained in the study.

Amount of Time Spent Watching TV

Adopted Children	Birth Parents	Adoptive Parents
2	0	1
3	3	4
6	4	2
1	1	0
3	1	0
0	2	3
5	3	2
2	1	3
5	3	3

a. Compute the correlation between the children and their birth parents.
b. Compute the correlation between the children and their adoptive parents.
c. Based on the two correlations, does TV watching appear to be inherited from the birth parents or is it learned from the adoptive parents?

12. For the following set of scores,

X	Y
6	4
3	1
5	0
6	7
4	2
6	4

a. Compute the Pearson correlation.
b. Add 2 points to each X value and compute the correlation for the modified scores. How does adding a constant to every score affect the value of the correlation?
c. Multiply each of the original X values by 2 and compute the correlation for the modified scores. How does multiplying each score by a constant affect the value of the correlation?

13. The researchers cited in the previous problem also examined the weight/salary relationship for men and found a positive relationship, suggesting that we have very different standards for men than for women (Judge & Cable, 2010). The following are data similar to those obtained for working men. Again, weight relative to height is coded in five categories from 1 = thinnest to 5 = heaviest. Income is recorded as thousands earned annually.

a. Calculate the Pearson correlation for these data.
b. Is the correlation statistically significant? Use a two-tailed test with $\alpha = .05$.

Weight (X)	Income (Y)
4	156
3	88
5	49
2	73
1	45
3	92
1	53
5	148

14. Identifying individuals with a high risk of Alzheimer's disease usually involves a long series of cognitive tests. However, researchers have developed a 7-Minute Screen, which is a quick and easy way to accomplish the same goal. The question is whether the 7-Minute Screen is as effective as the complete series of tests. To address this question, Ijuin et al. (2008) administered both tests to a group of patients and compared the results. The following data represent results similar to those obtained in the study.

Patient	7-Minute Screen	Cognitive Series
A	3	11
B	8	19
C	10	22
D	8	20
E	4	14
F	7	13
G	4	9
H	5	20
I	14	25

a. Compute the Pearson correlation to measure the degree of relationship between the two test scores.
b. Is the correlation statistically significant? Use a two-tailed test with $\alpha = .01$.
c. What percentage of variance for the cognitive scores is predicted from the 7-Minute Screen scores? (Compute the value of r^2.)

15. Assuming a two-tailed test with $\alpha = .05$, how large a correlation is needed to be statistically significant for each of the following samples?

a. A sample of $n = 8$
b. A sample of $n = 18$
c. A sample of $n = 28$

16. As we have noted in previous chapters, even a very small effect can be significant if the sample is large enough. For each of the following, determine how large a sample is necessary for the correlation to be significant. Assume a two-tailed test with $\alpha = .05$. (*Note:* The table does not list all the possible *df* values. Use the sample size corresponding to the appropriate *df* value that is listed in the table.)

a. A correlation of $r = 0.30$.
b. A correlation of $r = 0.25$.
c. A correlation of $r = 0.20$.

17. A researcher measures three variables, *X*, *Y*, and *Z*, for each individual in a sample of $n = 25$. The Pearson correlations for this sample are $r_{XY} = 0.8$, $r_{XZ} = 0.6$, and $r_{YZ} = 0.7$.

a. Find the partial correlation between *X* and *Y*, holding *Z* constant.
b. Find the partial correlation between *X* and *Z*, holding *Y* constant. (*Hint:* Simply switch the labels for the variables *Y* and *Z* to correspond with the labels in the equation.)

18. A researcher records the annual number of serious crimes and the amount spent on crime prevention for several small towns, medium cities, and large cities across the country. The resulting data show a strong positive correlation between the number of serious crimes and the amount spent on crime prevention. However, the researcher suspects that the positive correlation is actually caused by population; as population increases, both the amount spent on crime prevention and the number of crimes also increases. If population is controlled, there probably should be a negative correlation between the amount spent on crime prevention and the number of serious crimes. The following data show the pattern of results obtained. Note that the municipalities are coded in three categories. Use a partial correlation, holding population constant, to measure the true relationship between crime rate and the amount spent on prevention.

Number of Crimes	Amount for Prevention	Population Size
3	6	1
4	7	1
6	3	1
7	4	1
8	11	2
9	12	2
11	8	2
12	9	2
13	16	3
14	17	3
16	13	3
17	14	3

19. A common concern for students (and teachers) is the assignment of grades for essays or term papers. Because there are no absolute right or wrong answers, these grades must be based on a judgment of quality. To demonstrate that these judgments actually are reliable, an English instructor asked a colleague to rank-order a set of term papers. The ranks and the instructor's grades for these papers are as follows:

Rank	Grade
1	A
2	B
3	A
4	B
5	B
6	C
7	D
8	C
9	C
10	D
11	F

a. Compute the Spearman correlation for these data. (*Note:* You must convert the letter grades to ranks, using tied ranks to represent tied grades.)

b. Is the Spearman correlation statistically significant? Use a two-tailed test with $\alpha = .05$.

20. Problem 22 in Chapter 10 presented data showing that mature soccer players, who have a history of hitting soccer balls with their heads, had significantly lower cognitive scores than mature swimmers, who do not suffer repeated blows to the head. The independent-measures t test produced $t = 2.11$ with $df = 11$ and a value of $r^2 = 0.288$ (28.8%).

a. Convert the data from this problem into a form suitable for the point-biserial correlation (use 1 for the swimmers and 0 for the soccer players), and then compute the correlation.

b. Square the value of the point-biserial correlation to verify that you obtain the same r^2 value that was computed in Chapter 10.

21. Problem 12 presented data showing a negative relationship between weight and income for a sample of working women. However, weight was coded in five categories, which could be viewed as an ordinal scale rather than an interval or ratio scale. If so, a Spearman correlation is more appropriate than a Pearson correlation.

a. Convert the weights and the incomes into ranks and compute the Spearman correlation for the scores in problem 12.

b. Is the Spearman correlation large enough to be significant?

22. It appears that there is a significant relationship between cognitive ability and social status, at least for birds. Boogert, Reader, and Laland (2006) measured social status and individual learning ability for a group of starlings. The following data represent results similar to those obtained in the study. Because social status is an ordinal variable consisting of five ordered categories, the Spearman correlation is appropriate for these data. Convert the social status categories and the learning scores to ranks, and compute the Spearman correlation.

Subject	Social Status	Learning Score
A	1	3
B	3	10
C	2	7
D	3	11
E	5	19
F	4	17
G	5	17
H	2	4
I	4	12
J	2	3

23. Problem 14 in Chapter 10 described a study by Rozin, Bauer, and Cantanese (2003) comparing attitudes toward eating for male and female college students. The results showed that females are much more concerned about weight gain and other negative aspects of eating than are males. The following data represent the results from one measure of concern about weight gain.

Males	Females
22	54
44	57
39	32
27	53
35	49
19	41
	35
	36
	48

Convert the data into a form suitable for the point-biserial correlation and compute the correlation.

24. Studies have shown that people with high intelligence are generally more likely to volunteer as participants in research, but not for research that involves unusual experiences such as hypnosis. To examine this phenomenon, a researcher administers a questionnaire to a sample of college students. The survey asks for the student's grade point average (as a measure of intelligence) and whether the student would like to take part in a future study in which participants would be hypnotized. The results showed that 7 of the 10 lower-intelligence people were willing to participant but only 2 of the 10 higher-intelligence people were willing.

a. Convert the data to a form suitable for computing the phi-coefficient. (Code the two intelligence categories as 0 and 1 for the *X* variable, and code the willingness to participate as 0 and 1 for the *Y* variable.)

b. Compute the phi-coefficient for the data.

CHAPTER

16

Introduction to Regression

Tools You Will Need

The following items are considered essential background material for this chapter. If you doubt your knowledge of any of these items, you should review the appropriate chapter or section before proceeding.

- Sum of squares (*SS*) (Chapter 4)
  - Computational formula
  - Definitional formula
- *z*-scores (Chapter 5)
- Analysis of variance (Chapter 12)
  - *MS* values and *F*-ratios
- Pearson correlation (Chapter 15)
  - Sum of products (*SP*)

Preview

In Chapter 15, we noted that one common application of correlations is for purposes of prediction. Whenever there is a consistent relationship between two variables, it is possible to use the value of one variable to predict the value of another. Managers at the electric company, for example, can use the weather forecast to predict power demands for upcoming days. If exceptionally hot summer weather is forecast, they can anticipate an exceptionally high demand for electricity. In the field of psychology, a known relationship between certain personality characteristics and eating disorders can allow clinicians to predict that individuals who show specific characteristics are more likely to develop disorders. A common prediction that is especially relevant for college students (and potential college students) is based on the relationship between scores on aptitude tests (such as the SAT) and future grade point averages in college. Each year, SAT scores from thousands of high school students are used to help college admissions officers decide who should be admitted and who should not.

The Problem: The correlations introduced in Chapter 15 allow researchers to measure and describe relationships, and the hypothesis tests allow researchers to evaluate the significance of correlations. However, we now want to go one step further and actually use a correlation to make predictions.

The Solution: In this chapter we introduce some of the statistical techniques that are used to make predictions based on correlations. Whenever there is a linear relationship (Pearson correlation) between two variables, it is possible to compute an equation that provides a precise, mathematical description of the relationship. With the equation, it is possible to plug in the known value for one variable (for example, your SAT score), and then calculate a predicted value for the second variable (for example, your college grade point average). The general statistical process of finding and using a prediction equation is known as *regression*.

Beyond finding a prediction equation, however, it is reasonable to ask how good its predictions are. For example, I can make predictions about the outcome of a coin toss by simply guessing. However, my predictions are correct only about 50% of the time. In statistical terms, my predictions are not significantly better than chance. In the same way, it is appropriate to challenge the significance of any prediction equation. In this chapter we introduce the techniques that are used to find prediction equations, as well as the techniques that are used to determine whether their predictions are statistically significant. Incidentally, although there is some controversy about the practice of using SAT scores to predict college performance, there is a great deal of research showing that SAT scores really are valid and significant predictors (Camera & Echternacht, 2000; Geiser & Studley, 2002).

16.1 INTRODUCTION TO LINEAR EQUATIONS AND REGRESSION

In the previous chapter, we introduced the Pearson correlation as a technique for describing and measuring the linear relationship between two variables. Figure 16.1 presents hypothetical data showing the relationship between SAT scores and college grade point average (GPA). Note that the figure shows a good, but not perfect, positive relationship. Also note that we have drawn a line through the middle of the data points. This line serves several purposes:

1. The line makes the relationship between SAT scores and GPA easier to see.
2. The line identifies the center, or *central tendency,* of the relationship, just as the mean describes central tendency for a set of scores. Thus, the line provides a simplified description of the relationship. For example, if the data points were removed, the straight line would still give a general picture of the relationship between SAT scores and GPA.
3. Finally, the line can be used for prediction. The line establishes a precise, one-to-one relationship between each X value (SAT score) and a corresponding Y value (GPA). For example, an SAT score of 620 corresponds to a GPA of 3.25 (see Figure 16.1). Thus, the college admissions officers could use the straight-line

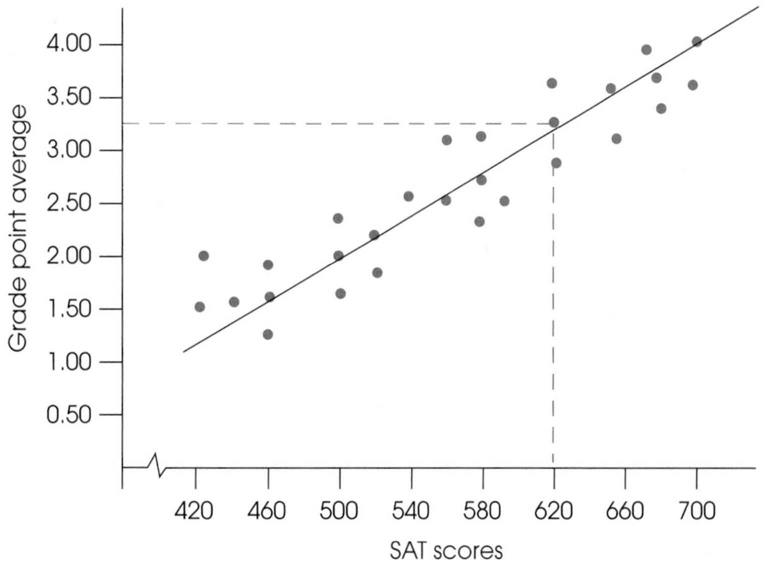

FIGURE 16.1
Hypothetical data showing the relationship between SAT scores and GPA with a regression line drawn through the data points. The regression line defines a precise, one-to-one relationship between each X value (SAT score) and its corresponding Y value (GPA).

relationship to predict that a student entering college with an SAT score of 620 should achieve a college GPA of approximately 3.25.

Our goal in this section is to develop a procedure that identifies and defines the straight line that provides the best fit for any specific set of data. This straight line does not have to be drawn on a graph; it can be presented in a simple equation. Thus, our goal is to find the equation for the line that best describes the relationship for a set of X and Y data.

LINEAR EQUATIONS

In general, a *linear relationship* between two variables X and Y can be expressed by the equation

$$Y = bX + a \tag{16.1}$$

where a and b are fixed constants.

For example, a local video store charges a membership fee of $5 per month, which allows you to rent videos and games for $2 each. With this information, the total cost for 1 month can be computed using a *linear equation* that describes the relationship between the total cost (Y) and the number of videos and games rented (X).

$$Y = 2X + 5$$

Note that a positive slope means that Y increases when X is increased, and a negative slope indicates that Y decreases when X is increased.

In the general linear equation, the value of b is called the *slope*. The slope determines how much the Y variable changes when X is increased by 1 point. For the video store example, the slope is $b = 2$ and indicates that your total cost increases by $2 for each video you rent. The value of a in the general equation is called the Y-*intercept* because it determines the value of Y when $X = 0$. (On a graph, the a value identifies the point where the line intercepts the Y-axis.) For the video store example, $a = 5$; there is a $5 membership charge even if you never rent a video.

Figure 16.2 shows the general relationship between the monthly cost and number of videos for the video store example. Notice that the relationship results in a straight

FIGURE 16.2

The relationship between total cost and number of videos rented each month. The video store charges a \$5 monthly membership fee and \$2 for each video or game rented. The relationship is described by a linear equation $Y = 2X + 5$ where Y is the total cost and X is the number of videos.

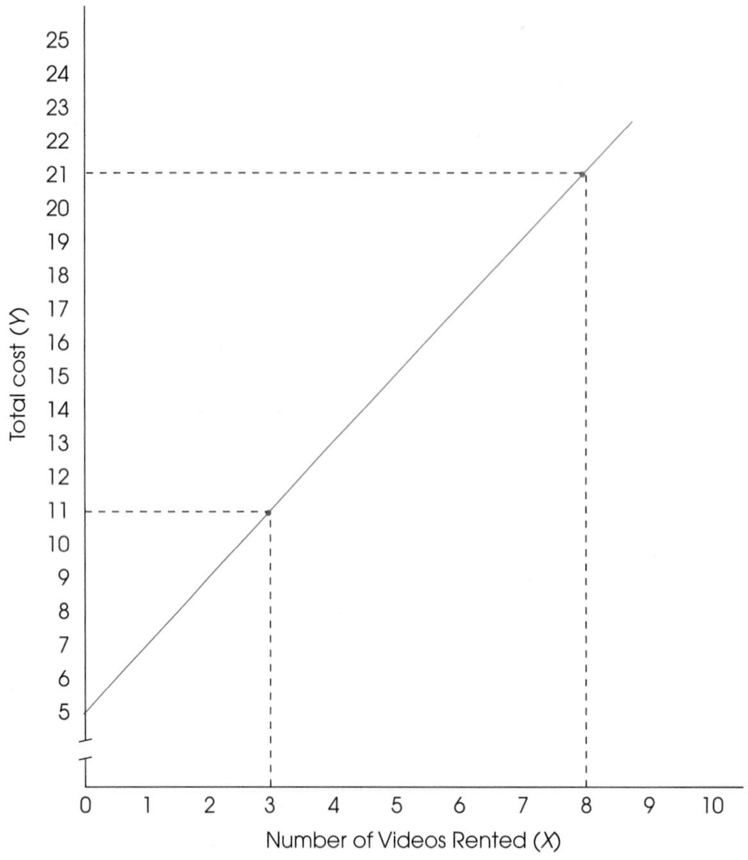

line. To obtain this graph, we picked any two values of X and then used the equation to compute the corresponding values for Y. For example,

when $X = 3$:	when $X = 8$:
$Y = bX + a$	$Y = bX + a$
$= \$2(3) + \$5$	$= \$2(8) + \$5$
$= \$6 + \$5$	$= \$16 + \$5$
$= \$11$	$= \$21$

When drawing a graph of a linear equation, it is wise to compute and plot at least three points to be certain that you have not made a mistake.

Next, these two points are plotted on the graph: one point at $X = 3$ and $Y = 11$, the other point at $X = 8$ and $Y = 21$. Because two points completely determine a straight line, we simply drew the line so that it passed through these two points.

LEARNING CHECK

1. A local gym charges a \$25 monthly membership fee plus \$2 per hour for aerobics classes. What is the linear equation that describes the relationship between the total monthly cost (Y) and the number of class hours each month (X)?

2. For the following linear equation, what happens to the value of Y each time X is increased by 1 point?

$$Y = -3X + 7$$

3. Use the linear equation $Y = 2X - 7$ to determine the value of Y for each of the following values of X: 1, 3, 5, 10.

4. If the slope constant (b) in a linear equation is positive, then a graph of the equation is a line tilted from lower left to upper right. (True or false?)

ANSWERS

1. $Y = 2X + 25$

2. The slope is -3, so Y decreases by 3 points each time X increases by 1 point.

3.

X	Y
1	−5
3	−1
5	3
10	13

4. True. A positive slope indicates that Y increases (goes up in the graph) when X increases (goes to the right in the graph).

REGRESSION

Because a straight line can be extremely useful for describing a relationship between two variables, a statistical technique has been developed that provides a standardized method for determining the best-fitting straight line for any set of data. The statistical procedure is *regression,* and the resulting straight line is called the *regression line.*

DEFINITION

The statistical technique for finding the best-fitting straight line for a set of data is called **regression,** and the resulting straight line is called the **regression line.**

The goal for regression is to find the best-fitting straight line for a set of data. To accomplish this goal, however, it is first necessary to define precisely what is meant by "best fit." For any particular set of data, it is possible to draw lots of different straight lines that all appear to pass through the center of the data points. Each of these lines can be defined by a linear equation of the form $Y = bX + a$ where b and a are constants that determine the slope and Y-intercept of the line, respectively. Each individual line has its own unique values for b and a. The problem is to find the specific line that provides the best fit to the actual data points.

THE LEAST-SQUARES SOLUTION

To determine how well a line fits the data points, the first step is to define mathematically the distance between the line and each data point. For every X value in the data, the linear equation determines a Y value on the line. This value is the predicted Y and is called $\hat{Y}$ ("Y hat"). The distance between this predicted value and the actual Y value in the data is determined by

$$\text{distance} = Y - \hat{Y}$$

Note that we simply are measuring the vertical distance between the actual data point (Y) and the predicted point on the line. This distance measures the error between the line and the actual data (Figure 16.3).

Because some of these distances are positive and some are negative, the next step is to square each distance to obtain a uniformly positive measure of error. Finally, to

FIGURE 16.3

The distance between the actual data point (Y) and the predicted point on the line ($\hat{Y}$) is defined as $Y - \hat{Y}$. The goal of regression is to find the equation for the line that minimizes these distances.

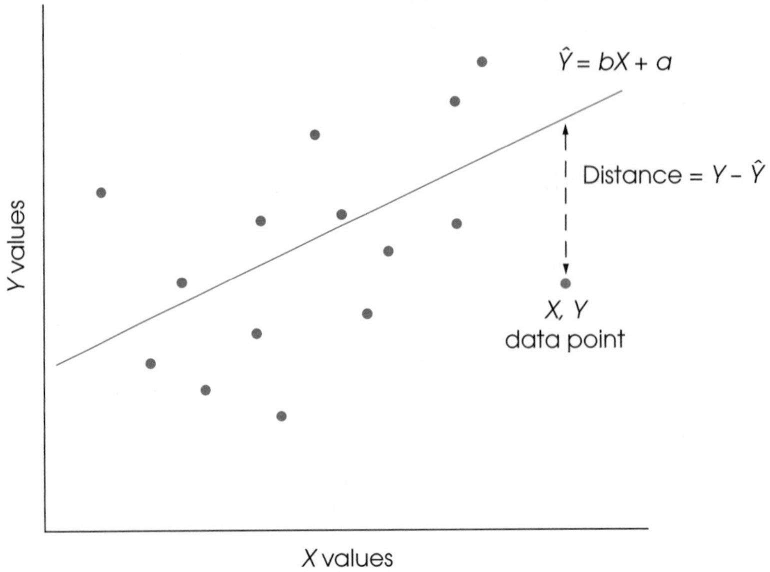

determine the total error between the line and the data, we add the squared errors for all of the data points. The result is a measure of overall squared error between the line and the data:

$$\text{total squared error} = \Sigma(Y - \hat{Y})^2$$

Now we can define the *best-fitting* line as the one that has the smallest total squared error. For obvious reasons, the resulting line is commonly called the *least-squared-error solution*. In symbols, we are looking for a linear equation of the form

$$\hat{Y} = bX + a$$

For each value of X in the data, this equation determines the point on the line ($\hat{Y}$) *that gives the best prediction of Y*. The problem is to find the specific values for a and b that make this the best-fitting line.

The calculations that are needed to find this equation require calculus and some sophisticated algebra, so we do not present the details of the solution. The results, however, are relatively straightforward, and the solutions for b and a are as follows:

$$b = \frac{SP}{SS_X} \qquad (16.2)$$

where SP is the sum of products and SS_X is the sum of squares for the X scores.

A commonly used alternative formula for the slope is based on the standard deviations for X and Y. The alternative formula is

$$b = r\frac{s_Y}{s_X} \qquad (16.3)$$

where s_Y is the standard deviation for the Y scores, s_X is the standard deviation for the X scores, and r is the Pearson correlation for X and Y. The value of the constant a in the equation is determined by

$$a = M_Y - bM_X \qquad (16.4)$$

Note that these formulas determine the linear equation that provides the best prediction of Y values. This equation is called the *regression equation for* Y.

DEFINITION

The **regression equation for Y** is the linear equation

$$\hat{Y} = bX + a \tag{16.5}$$

where the constant b is determined by Equation 16.2, or 16.3 and the constant a is determined by Equation 16.4. This equation results in the least squared error between the data points and the line.

EXAMPLE 16.1 The scores in the following table are used to demonstrate the calculation and use of the regression equation for predicting Y.

X	Y	$X - M_X$	$Y - M_Y$	$(X - M_X)^2$	$(Y - M_X)^2$	$(X - M_x)(Y - M_Y)$
2	3	−2	−5	4	25	10
6	11	2	3	4	9	6
0	6	−4	−2	16	4	8
4	6	0	−2	0	4	0
7	12	3	4	9	16	12
5	7	1	−1	1	1	−1
5	10	1	2	1	4	2
3	9	−1	1	1	1	−1
				$SS_X = 36$	$SS_Y = 64$	$SP = 36$

For these data, $\Sigma X = 32$, so $M_X = 4$. Also, $\Sigma Y = 64$, so $M_Y = 8$. These values have been used to compute the deviation scores for each X and Y value. The final three columns show the squared deviations for X and for Y, and the products of the deviation scores.

Our goal is to find the values for b and a in the regression equation. Using Equations 16.2 and 16.4, the solutions for b and a are

$$b = \frac{SP}{SS_X} = \frac{36}{36} = 1.00$$

$$a = M_Y - bM_X = 8 - 1(4) = 4.00$$

The resulting equation is

$$\hat{Y} = X + 4$$

The original data and the regression line are shown in Figure 16.4.

The regression line shown in Figure 16.4 demonstrates some simple and very predictable facts about regression. First, the calculation of the Y-intercept (Equation 16.4) ensures that the regression line passes through the point defined by the mean for X and the mean for Y. That is, the point identified by the coordinates M_X, M_Y will always be on the line. We have included the two means in Figure 16.4 to show that

FIGURE 16.4

The X and Y data points and the regression line for the $n = 8$ pairs of scores in Example 16.1.

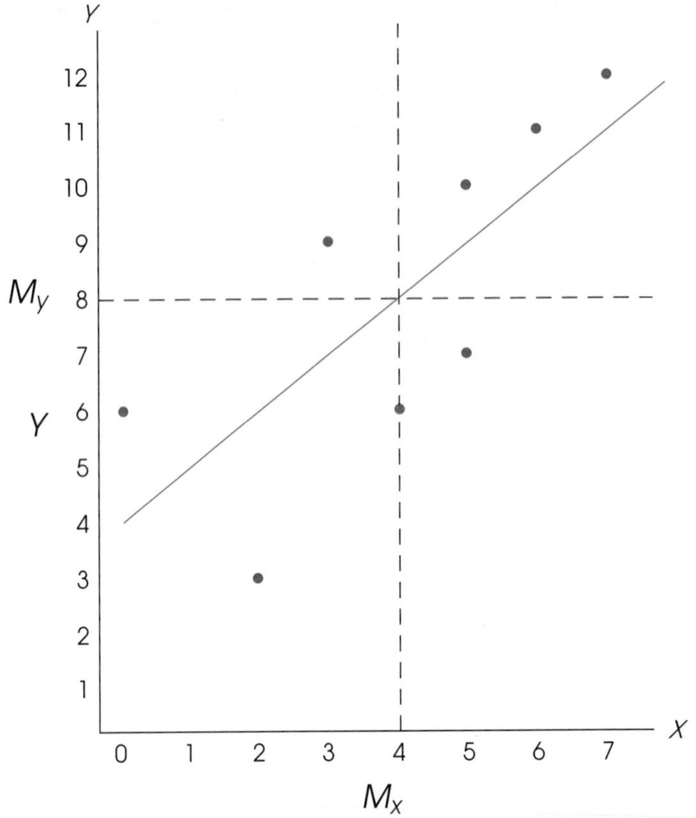

the point they define is on the regression line. Second, the sign of the correlation (+ or −) is the same as the sign of the slope of the regression line. Specifically, if the correlation is positive, then the slope is also positive and the regression line slopes up to the right. On the other hand, if the correlation is negative, then the slope is negative and the line slopes down to the right. A correlation of zero means that the slope is also zero and the regression equation produces a horizontal line that passes through the data at a level equal to the mean for the Y values. Note that the regression line in Figure 16.4 has a positive slope. One consequence of this fact is that all of the points on the line that are above the mean for X are also above the mean for Y. Similarly, all of the points below the mean for X are also below the mean for Y. Thus, every individual with a positive deviation for X is predicted to have a positive deviation for Y, and everyone with a negative deviation for X is predicted to have a negative deviation for Y.

USING THE REGRESSION EQUATION FOR PREDICTION

As we noted at the beginning of this section, one common use of regression equations is for prediction. For any given value of X, we can use the equation to compute a predicted value for Y. For the equation from Example 16.1, an individual with a score of $X = 1$ would be predicted to have a Y score of

$$\hat{Y} = X + 4 = 1 + 4 = 5$$

Although regression equations can be used for prediction, a few cautions should be considered whenever you are interpreting the predicted values:

1. The predicted value is not perfect (unless $r = +1.00$ or -1.00). If you examine Figure 16.4, it should be clear that the data points do not fit perfectly on the line. In general, there is some error between the predicted Y values (on the line) and the actual data. Although the amount of error varies from point to point, on average the errors are directly related to the magnitude of the correlation. With a correlation near 1.00 (or -1.00), the data points generally are clustered close to the line and the error is small. As the correlation gets nearer to zero, the points move away from the line and the magnitude of the error increases.
2. The regression equation should not be used to make predictions for X values that fall outside of the range of values covered by the original data. For Example 16.1, the X values ranged from $X = 0$ to $X = 7$, and the regression equation was calculated as the best-fitting line within this range. Because you have no information about the X-Y relationship outside this range, the equation should not be used to predict Y for any X value lower than 0 or greater than 7.

STANDARDIZED FORM OF THE REGRESSION EQUATIONS

So far we have presented the regression equation in terms of the original values, or raw scores, for X and Y. Occasionally, however, researchers standardize the scores by transforming the X and Y values into z-scores before finding the regression equation. The resulting equation is often called the standardized form of the regression equation and is greatly simplified compared to the raw-score version. The simplification comes from the fact that z-scores have standardized characteristics. Specifically, the mean for a set of z-scores is always zero and the standard deviation is always 1. As a result, the standardized form of the regression equation becomes

$$\hat{z}_Y = (\text{beta})z_X \tag{16.6}$$

First notice that we are now using the z-score for each X value (z_X) to predict the z-score for the corresponding Y value (z_Y). Also, note that the slope constant that was identified as b in the raw-score formula is now identified as beta. Because both sets of z-scores have a mean of zero, the constant a disappears from the regression equation. Finally, when one variable, X, is being used to predict a second variable, Y, the value of beta is equal to the Pearson correlation for X and Y. Thus, the standardized form of the regression equation can also be written as

$$\hat{z}_Y = rz_X \tag{16.7}$$

Because the process of transforming all of the original scores into z-scores can be tedious, researchers usually compute the raw-score version of the regression equation (Equation 16.5) instead of the standardized form. However, most computer programs report the value of beta as part of the output from linear regression, and you should understand what this value represents.

LEARNING CHECK

1. Sketch a scatter plot for the following data—that is, a graph showing the X, Y data points:

X	Y
1	4
3	9
5	8

a. Find the regression equation for predicting Y from X. Draw this line on your graph. Does it look like the best-fitting line?

b. Use the regression equation to find the predicted Y value corresponding to each X in the data.

ANSWERS **1. a.** $SS_X = 8$, $SP = 8$, $b = 1$, $a = 4$. The equation is $\hat{Y} = X + 4$.

b. The predicted Y values are 5, 7, and 9.

THE STANDARD ERROR OF ESTIMATE

It is possible to determine a regression equation for any set of data by simply using the formulas already presented. The linear equation you obtain is then used to generate predicted Y values for any known value of X. However, it should be clear that the accuracy of this prediction depends on how well the points on the line correspond to the actual data points—that is, the amount of error between the predicted values, $\hat{Y}$, and the actual scores, Y values. Figure 16.5 shows two different sets of data that have exactly the same regression equation. In one case, there is a perfect correlation ($r = +1$) between X and Y, so the linear equation fits the data perfectly. For the second set of data, the predicted Y values on the line only approximate the real data points.

A regression equation, by itself, allows you to make predictions, but it does not provide any information about the accuracy of the predictions. To measure the precision of the regression, it is customary to compute a *standard error of estimate.*

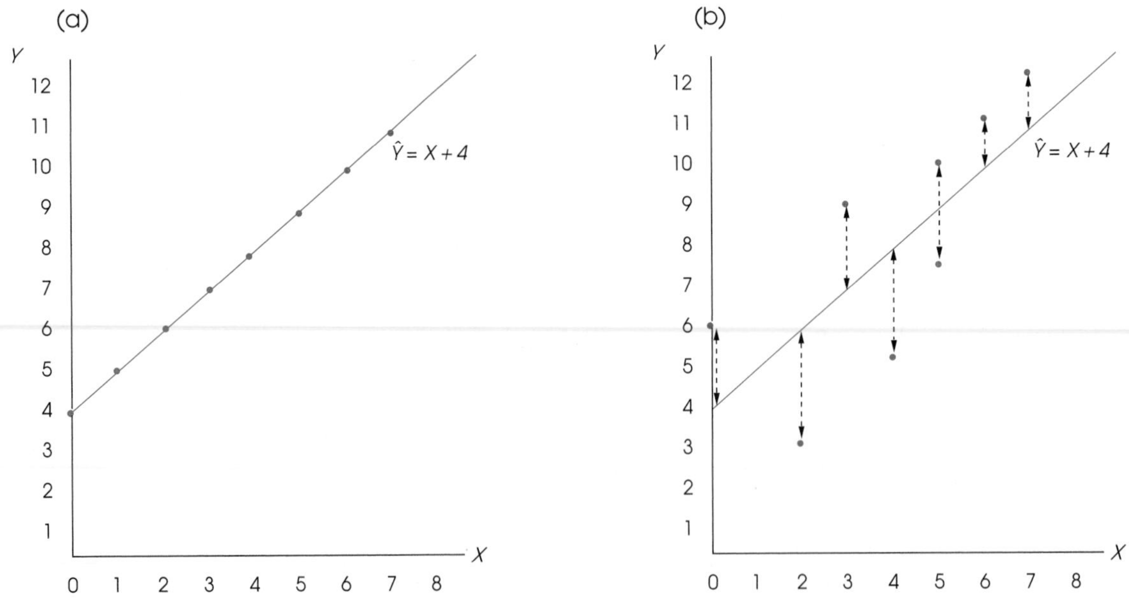

FIGURE 16.5

(a) A scatter plot showing data points that perfectly fit the regression line defined by the equation $\hat{Y} = X + 4$. Note that the correlation is $r = +1.00$. (b) A scatter plot for the data from Example 16.1. Notice that there is error between the actual data points and the predicted Y values of the regression line.

DEFINITION

The **standard error of estimate** gives a measure of the standard distance between the predicted Y values on the regression line and the actual Y values in the data.

Conceptually, the standard error of estimate is very much like a standard deviation: Both provide a measure of standard distance. Also, the calculation of the standard error of estimate is very similar to the calculation of standard deviation.

To calculate the standard error of estimate, we first find the sum of squared deviations (SS). Each deviation measures the distance between the actual Y value (from the data) and the predicted Y value (from the regression line). This sum of squares is commonly called SS_{residual} because it is based on the remaining distance between the actual Y scores and the predicted values.

$$SS_{\text{residual}} = \Sigma(Y - \hat{Y})^2 \qquad (16.8)$$

The obtained SS value is then divided by its degrees of freedom to obtain a measure of variance. This procedure should be very familiar:

$$\text{Variance} = \frac{SS}{df}$$

The degrees of freedom for the standard error of estimate are $df = n - 2$. The reason for having $n - 2$ degrees of freedom, rather than the customary $n - 1$, is that we now are measuring deviations from a line rather than deviations from a mean. To find the equation for the regression line, you must know the means for both the X and the Y scores. Specifying these two means places two restrictions on the variability of the data, with the result that the scores have only $n - 2$ degrees of freedom. (*Note*: the $df = n - 2$ for SS_{residual} is the same $df = n - 2$ that we encountered when testing the significance of the Pearson correlation on page 529.)

Recall that variance measures the average squared distance.

The final step in the calculation of the standard error of estimate is to take the square root of the variance to obtain a measure of standard distance. The final equation is

$$\text{standard error of estimate} = \sqrt{\frac{SS_{\text{residual}}}{df}} = \sqrt{\frac{\Sigma(Y - \hat{Y})^2}{n - 2}} \qquad (16.9)$$

The following example demonstrates the calculation of this standard error.

EXAMPLE 16.2

The same data that were used in Example 16.1 are used here to demonstrate the calculation of the standard error of estimate. These data have the regression equation

$$\hat{Y} = X + 4$$

Using this regression equation, we have computed the predicted Y value, the residual, and the squared residual for each individual, using the data from Example 16.1.

Data		Predicted Y Values	Residual	Squared Residual
X	Y	$\hat{Y} = X + 4$	$Y - \hat{Y}$	$(Y - \hat{Y})^2$
2	3	6	−3	9
6	11	10	1	1
0	6	4	2	4
4	6	8	−2	4
5	7	9	−2	4

(continued)

Data		Predicted Y Values	Residual	Squared Residual
X	Y	$\hat{Y} = X + 4$	$Y - \hat{Y}$	$(Y - \hat{Y})^2$
7	12	11	1	1
5	10	9	1	1
3	9	7	2	4
			0	$SS_{residual} = 28$

First note that the sum of the residuals is equal to zero. In other words, the sum of the distances above the line is equal to the sum of the distances below the line. This is true for any set of data and provides a way to check the accuracy of your calculations. The squared residuals are listed in the final column. For these data, the sum of the squared residuals is $SS_{residual} = 28$. With $n = 8$, the data have $df = n - 2 = 6$, so the standard error of estimate is

$$\text{standard error of estimate} = \sqrt{\frac{SS_{residual}}{df}} = \sqrt{\frac{28}{6}} = 2.16$$

Remember: The standard error of estimate provides a measure of how accurately the regression equation predicts the Y values. In this case, the standard distance between the actual data points and the regression line is measured by standard error of estimate = 2.16.

RELATIONSHIP BETWEEN THE STANDARD ERROR AND THE CORRELATION

It should be clear from Example 16.2 that the standard error of estimate is directly related to the magnitude of the correlation between X and Y. If the correlation is near 1.00 (or −1.00), then the data points are clustered close to the line, and the standard error of estimate is small. As the correlation gets nearer to zero, the data points become more widely scattered, the line provides less accurate predictions, and the standard error of estimate grows larger.

Earlier (p. 524), we observed that squaring the correlation provides a measure of the accuracy of prediction. The squared correlation, r^2, is called the coefficient of determination because it determines what proportion of the variability in Y is predicted by the relationship with X. Because r^2 measures the predicted portion of the variability in the Y scores, we can use the expression $(1 - r^2)$ to measure the unpredicted portion. Thus,

$$\text{predicted variability} = SS_{regression} = r^2 SS_Y \qquad (16.10)$$

$$\text{unpredicted variability} = SS_{residual} = (1 - r^2)SS_Y \qquad (16.11)$$

For example, if $r = 0.80$, then the *predicted variability* is $r^2 = 0.64$ (or 64%) of the total variability for the Y scores and the remaining 36% $(1 - r^2)$ is the *unpredicted variability*. Note that when $r = 1.00$, the prediction is perfect and there are no residuals. As the correlation approaches zero, the data points move farther off the line and the residuals grow larger. Using Equation 16.11 to compute $SS_{residual}$, the standard error of estimate can be computed as

$$\text{standard error of estimate} = \sqrt{\frac{SS_{residual}}{df}} = \sqrt{\frac{(1 - r^2)SS_Y}{n - 2}} \qquad (16.12)$$

Because it is usually much easier to compute the Pearson correlation than to compute the individual $(Y - \hat{Y})^2$ values, Equation 16.11 is usually the easiest way to compute SS_{residual}, and Equation 16.12 is usually the easiest way to compute the standard error of estimate for a regression equation. The following example demonstrates this new formula.

EXAMPLE 16.3

We use the same data used in Examples 16.1 and 16.2, which produced $SS_X = 36$, $SS_Y = 64$, and $SP = 36$. For these data, the Pearson correlation is

$$r = \frac{36}{\sqrt{36(64)}} = \frac{36}{48} = 0.75$$

With $SS_Y = 64$ and a correlation of $r = 0.75$, the predicted variability from the regression equation is

$$SS_{\text{regression}} = r^2 SS_Y = (0.75^2)(64) = 0.5625(64) = 36.00$$

Similarly, the unpredicted variability is

$$SS_{\text{residual}} = (1 - r^2)SS_Y = (1 - 0.75^2)(64) = 0.4375(64) = 28.00$$

Notice that the new formula for SS_{residual} produces exactly the same value that we obtained by adding the squared residuals in Example 16.2. Also note that this new formula is generally much easier to use because it requires only the correlation value (r) and the SS for Y. The primary point of this example, however, is that SS_{residual} and the standard error of estimate are closely related to the value of the correlation. With a large correlation (near +1.00 or −1.00), the data points are close to the regression line, and the standard error of estimate is small. As a correlation gets smaller (near zero), the data points move away from the regression line, and the standard error of estimate gets larger.

Because it is possible to have the same regression equation for several different sets of data, it is also important to consider r^2 and the standard error of estimate. The regression equation simply describes the best-fitting line and is used for making predictions. However, r^2 and the standard error of estimate indicate how accurate these predictions are.

LEARNING CHECK

1. Describe what is measured by the standard error of estimate for a regression equation.
2. As the numerical value of a correlation increases, what happens to the standard error of estimate?
3. A sample of $n = 6$ pairs of X and Y scores produces a correlation of $r = 0.80$ and $SS_Y = 100$. What is the standard error of estimate for the regression equation?

ANSWERS

1. The standard error of estimate measures the average, or standard, distance between the predicted Y values on the regression line and the actual Y values in the data.
2. A larger correlation means that the data points are clustered closer to the line, which means the standard error of estimate is smaller.
3. The standard error of estimate $= \sqrt{36/4} = 3$.

16.2 ANALYSIS OF REGRESSION: TESTING THE SIGNIFICANCE OF THE REGRESSION EQUATION

As we noted in Chapter 15, a sample correlation is expected to be representative of its population correlation. For example, if the population correlation is zero, then the sample correlation is expected to be near zero. Note that we do not expect the sample correlation to be exactly equal to zero. This is the general concept of *sampling error* that was introduced in Chapter 1 (p. 8). The principle of sampling error is that there is typically some discrepancy or error between the value obtained for a sample statistic and the corresponding population parameter. Thus, when there is no relationship whatsoever in the population, a correlation of $\rho = 0$, you are still likely to obtain a nonzero value for the sample correlation. In this situation, however, the sample correlation is caused by chance and a hypothesis test usually demonstrates that the correlation is not significant.

Whenever you obtain a nonzero value for a sample correlation, you also obtain real, numerical values for the regression equation. However, if there is no real relationship in the population, both the sample correlation and the regression equation are meaningless—they are simply the result of sampling error and should not be viewed as an indication of any relationship between X and Y. In the same way that we tested the significance of a Pearson correlation, we can test the significance of the regression equation. In fact, when a single variable, X, is being used to predict a single variable, Y, the two tests are equivalent. In each case, the purpose for the test is to determine whether the sample correlation represents a real relationship or is simply the result of sampling error. For both tests, the null hypothesis states that there is no relationship between the two variables in the population. A more specific null hypothesis for testing the significance of a regression equation is that the equation does not account for a significant proportion of the variance in the Y scores. An alternative version of H_0 states that the values of b or beta that are computed for the regression equation do not represent any real relationship between X and Y but rather are simply the result of chance or sampling error. In other words, the true population value of b or beta is zero.

The process of testing the significance of a regression equation is called *analysis of regression* and is very similar to the analysis of variance (ANOVA) presented in Chapter 12. As with ANOVA, the regression analysis uses an F-ratio to determine whether the variance predicted by the regression equation is significantly greater than would be expected if there were no relationship between X and Y. The F-ratio is a ratio of two variances, or mean square (MS) values, and each variance is obtained by dividing an SS value by its corresponding degrees of freedom. The numerator of the F-ratio is $MS_{\text{regression}}$, which is the variance in the Y scores that is predicted by the regression equation. This variance measures the systematic changes in Y that occur when the value of X increases or decreases. The denominator is MS_{residual}, which is the unpredicted variance in the Y scores. This variance measures the changes in Y that are independent of changes in X. The two MS value are defined as

$$MS_{\text{regression}} = \frac{SS_{\text{regression}}}{df_{\text{regression}}} \text{ with } df = 1 \quad \text{and} \quad MS_{\text{residual}} = \frac{SS_{\text{residual}}}{df_{\text{residual}}} \text{ with } df = n - 2$$

The F-ratio is

$$F = \frac{MS_{\text{regression}}}{MS_{\text{residual}}} \quad \text{with } df = 1, n - 2 \tag{16.13}$$

The complete analysis of *SS* and degrees of freedom is diagrammed in Figure 16.6. The analysis of regression procedure is demonstrated in the following example, using the same data that we used in Examples 16.1, 16.2, and 16.3.

EXAMPLE 16.4

The data consist of $n = 8$ pairs of scores with a correlation of $r = 0.75$ and $SS_Y = 64$. The null hypothesis either states that there is no relationship between *X* and *Y* in the population, or that the regression equation does not account for a significant portion of the variance for the *Y* scores.

The *F*-ratio for the analysis of regression has $df = 2, n - 2$. For these data, $df = 1, 6$. With $\alpha = .05$, the critical value is 5.99.

As noted in the previous section, the *SS* for the *Y* scores can be separated into two components: the predicted portion corresponding to r^2 and the unpredicted, or residual, portion corresponding to $(1-r^2)$. With $r = 0.75$, we obtain $r^2 = 0.5625$ and

$$\text{predicted variability} = SS_{\text{regression}} = 0.5625(64) = 36$$

$$\text{unpredicted variability} = SS_{\text{residual}} = (1 - 0.5625)(64) = 0.4375(64) = 28$$

Using these *SS* values and the corresponding *df* values, we calculate a variance, or *MS*, for each component. For these data the *MS* values are

$$MS_{\text{regression}} = \frac{SS_{\text{regression}}}{df_{\text{residual}}} = \frac{36}{1} = 36$$

$$MS_{\text{residual}} = \frac{SS_{\text{residual}}}{df_{\text{residual}}} = \frac{28}{6} = 4.67$$

Finally, the *F*-ratio for evaluating the significance of the regression equation is

$$F = \frac{MS_{\text{regression}}}{MS_{\text{residual}}} = \frac{36.00}{4.67} = 7.71$$

The *F*-ratio is in the critical region, so we reject the null hypothesis and conclude that the regression equation does account for a significant portion of the variance for the *Y* scores. The complete analysis of regression is summarized in Table 16.1, which is a common format for computer printouts of regression analysis.

FIGURE 16.6

The partitioning of *SS* and *df* for analysis of regression. The variability in the original *Y* scores (both SS_Y and df_Y) is partitioned into two components: (1) the variability that is explained by the regression equation, and (2) the residual variability.

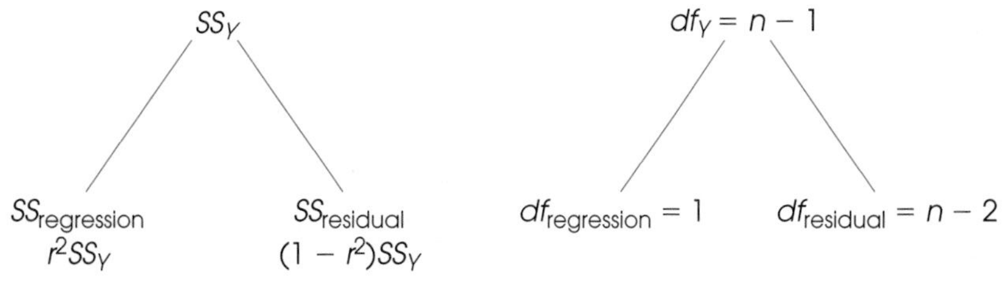

TABLE 16.1

A summary table showing the results of the analysis of regression in Example 16.4.

Source	*SS*	*df*	*MS*	*F*
Regression	36	1	36.60	7.71
Residual	28	6	4.67	
Total	64	7		

SIGNIFICANCE OF REGRESSION AND SIGNIFICANCE OF THE CORRELATION

As noted earlier, in situation with a single X variable and a single Y variable, testing the significance of the regression equation is equivalent to testing the significance of the Pearson correlation. Therefore, whenever the correlation between two variables is significant, you can conclude that the regression equation is also significant. Similarly, if a correlation is not significant, then the regression equation is also not significant. For the data in Example 16.3, we concluded that the regression equation is significant. This conclusion is perfectly consistent with the corresponding test for the significance of the Pearson correlation. For these data, the Pearson correlation is $r = 0.75$ with $n = 8$. Checking Table B.6 in Appendix B, you should find a critical value of 0.707. Our correlation exceeds this criterion, so we conclude that the correlation is also significant. In fact, the critical values listed in Table B.6 were developed using the F-ratio (Equation 16.13) from analysis of regression.

LEARNING CHECK

1. A set of $n = 18$ pairs of scores produces a Pearson correlation of $r = 0.60$ with $SS_Y = 100$. Find $SS_{\text{regression}}$ and SS_{residual} and compute the F-ratio to evaluate the significance of the regression equation of predicting Y.

ANSWER

1. $SS_{\text{regression}} = 36$ with df $= 1$. $SS_{\text{residual}} = 64$ with $df = 16$. $F = 9.00$. With $df = 1, 16$, the F-ratio is significant with either $\alpha = .05$ or $\alpha = .01$.

16.3 INTRODUCTION TO MULTIPLE REGRESSION WITH TWO PREDICTOR VARIABLES

Thus far, we have looked at regression in situations in which one variable is being used to predict a second variable. For example, IQ scores can be used to predict academic performance for a group of college students. However, a variable such as academic performance is usually related to a variety of other factors. For example, college GPA is probably related to motivation, self-esteem, SAT score, rank in high school graduating class, parents' highest level of education, and many other variables. In this case, it is possible to combine several predictor variables to obtain a more accurate prediction. For example, IQ predicts some of academic performance, but you can probably get a better prediction if you use IQ and SAT scores together. The process of using several predictor variables to help obtain more accurate predictions is called *multiple regression.*

Although it is possible to combine a large number of predictor variables in a single multiple-regression equation, we limit our discussion to the two-predictor case. There are two practical reasons for this limitation.

1. Multiple regression, even limited to two predictors, can be relatively complex. Although we present equations for the two-predictor case, the calculations are

usually performed by a computer, so there is not much point in developing a set of complex equations when people are going to use a computer instead.

2. Usually, different predictor variables are related to each other, which means that they are often measuring and predicting the same thing. Because the variables may overlap with each other, adding another predictor variable to a regression equation does not always add to the accuracy of prediction. This situation is shown in Figure 16.7. In the figure, IQ overlaps with academic performance, which means that part of academic performance can be predicted by IQ. In this example, IQ overlaps (predicts) 40% of the variance in academic performance (combine sections a and b in the figure). The figure also shows that SAT scores overlap with academic performance, which means that part of academic performance can be predicted by knowing SAT scores. Specifically, SAT scores overlap, or predict, 30% of the variance (combine sections b and c). Thus, using both IQ and SAT scores to predict academic performance should produce better predictions than would be obtained from IQ alone. However, there is also a lot of overlap between SAT scores and IQ. In particular, much of the prediction from SAT scores overlaps with the prediction from IQ (section b). As a result, adding SAT scores as a second predictor only adds a small amount to the variance already predicted by IQ (section c). Because variables tend to overlap in this way, adding new variables beyond the first one or two predictors often does not add significantly to the quality of the prediction.

REGRESSION EQUATIONS WITH TWO PREDICTORS

We identify the two predictor variables as X_1 and X_2. The variable we are trying to predict is identified as Y. Using this notation, the general form of the multiple regression equation with two predictors is

$$\hat{Y} = b_1X_1 + b_2X_2 + a \tag{16.14}$$

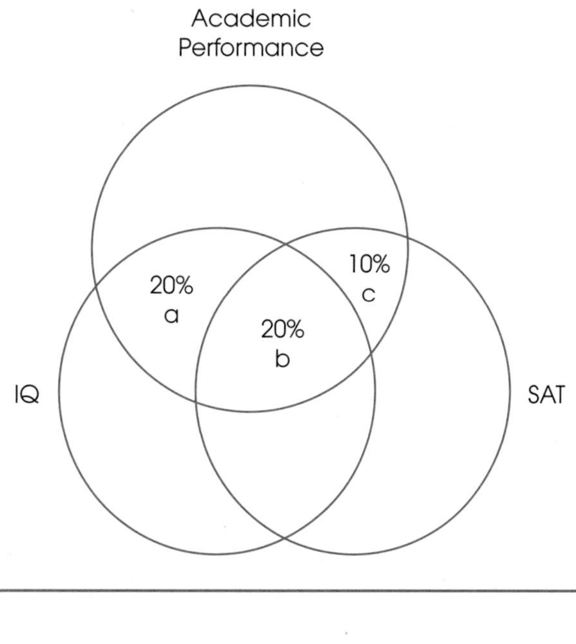

FIGURE 16.7
Predicting the variance in academic performance from IQ and SAT scores. The overlap between IQ and academic performance indicates that 40% of the variance in academic performance can be predicted from IQ scores. Similarly, 30% of the variance in academic performance can be predicted from SAT scores. However, IQ and SAT also overlap, so that SAT scores contribute an additional predication of only 10% beyond what is already predicted by IQ.

If all three variables, X_1, X_2, and Y, have been standardized by transformation into z-scores, then the standardized form of the multiple regression equation predicts the z-score for each Y value. The standardized form is

$$\hat{z}_Y = (\text{beta}_1)z_{X1} + (\text{beta}_2)z_{X2} \quad (16.15)$$

Researchers rarely transform raw X and Y scores into z-scores before finding a regression equation, however, the beta values are meaningful and are usually reported by computer programs conducting multiple regression. We return to the discussion of beta values later in this section.

The goal of the multiple-regression equation is to produce the most accurate estimated values for Y. As with the single-predictor regression, this goal is accomplished with a least-squared solution. First, we define "error" as the difference between the predicted Y value from the regression equation and the actual Y value for each individual. Each error is then squared to produce uniformly positive values, and then we add the squared errors. Finally, we calculate values for b_1, b_2, and a that produce the smallest possible sum of squared errors. The derivation of the final values is beyond the scope of this text, but the final equations are as follows:

$$b_1 = \frac{(SP_{X1Y})(SS_{X2}) - (SP_{X1X2})(SP_{X2Y})}{(SS_{X1})(SS_{X2}) - (SP_{X1X2})^2} \quad (16.16)$$

$$b_2 = \frac{(SP_{X2Y})(SS_{X1}) - (SP_{X1X2})(SP_{X1Y})}{(SS_{X1})(SS_{X2}) - (SP_{X1X2})^2} \quad (16.17)$$

$$a = M_Y - b_1M_{X1} - b_2M_{X2} \quad (16.18)$$

In these equations, you should recognize the following SS and SP values:

SS_{X1} is the sum of squared deviations for X_1

SS_{X2} is the sum of squared deviations for X_2

SP_{X1Y} is the sum of products of deviations for X_1 and Y

SP_{X2Y} is the sum of products of deviations for X_2 and Y

SP_{X1X2} is the sum of products of deviations for X_1 and X_2

Note: More detailed information about the calculation of SS is presented in Chapter 4 (pp. 111–112) and information concerning SP is in Chapter 15 (pp. 515–516). The following example demonstrates multiple regression with two predictor variables.

EXAMPLE 16.5

We use the data in Table 16.2 to demonstrate multiple regression. Note that each individual has a Y score and two X scores that are used as predictor variables. Also note that we have already computed the SS values for Y and for both of the X scores, as well as all of the SP values. These values are used to compute the coefficients, b_1 and b_2, and the constant, a, for the regression equation.

$$\hat{Y} = b_1X_1 + b_2X_2 + a$$

TABLE 16.2

Hypothetical data consisting of three scores for each person. Two of the scores, X_1 and X_2, are used to predict the Y score for each individual.

Person	Y	X_1	X_2	
A	11	4	10	$SP_{X1Y} = 54$
B	5	5	6	$SP_{X2Y} = 47$
C	7	3	7	$SP_{X1X2} = 42$
D	3	2	4	
E	4	1	3	
F	12	7	5	
G	10	8	8	
H	4	2	4	
I	8	7	10	
J	6	1	3	
	$M_Y = 7$	$M_{X1} = 4$	$M_{X2} = 6$	
	$SS_Y = 90$	$SS_{X1} = 62$	$SS_{X2} = 64$	

$$b_1 = \frac{(SP_{X1Y})(SS_{X2}) - (SP_{X1X2})(SP_{X2Y})}{(SS_{X1})(SS_{X2}) - (SP_{X1X2})^2} = \frac{(54)(64) - (42)(47)}{(62)(64) - (42)^2} = 0.672$$

$$b_2 = \frac{(SP_{X2Y})(SS_{X1}) - (SP_{X1X2})(SP_{X1Y})}{(SS_{X1})(SS_{X2}) - (SP_{X1X2})^2} = \frac{(47)(62) - (42)(54)}{(62)(64) - (42)^2} = 0.293$$

$$a = M_Y - b_1M_{X1} - b_2M_{X2} = 7 - 0.672(4) - 0.293(6) = 7 - 2.688 - 1.758 = 2.554$$

Thus, the final regression equation is,

$$\hat{Y} = 0.672X_1 + 0.293X_2 + 2.554$$

Example 16.5 also demonstrates that multiple regression can be a tedious process. As a result, multiple regression is usually conducted on a computer. To demonstrate this process, we used the SPSS computer program to perform a multiple regression on the data in Table 16.2 and the output from the program is shown in Figure 16.8. At this time, focus on the Coefficients Table at the bottom of the printout. The values in the first column of Unstandardized Coefficients include the constant, b_1 and b_2 for the regression equation. We discuss other portions of the SPSS output later in this chapter.

LEARNING CHECK

1. A researcher computes a multiple-regression equation for predicting annual income for 40-year-old men based on their level of education (X_1 = number of years after high school) and their social skills (X_2 = score from a self-report questionnaire). The regression equation is $\hat{Y} = 8.3X_1 + 2.1X_2 + 3.5$ and predicts income in thousands of dollars. Two individuals are selected from the sample. One has $X_1 = 0$ and $X_2 = 16$; the other has $X_1 = 3$ and $X_2 = 12$. Compute the predicted income for each.

ANSWER

1. The first man has a predicted income of $\hat{Y} = 37.1$ thousand dollars and the second has $\hat{Y} = 53.6$ thousand dollars.

Model Summary

Model	R	R Square	Adjusted R Square	Std. Error of the Estimate
1	.746[a]	.557	.430	2.38788

a. Predictors: (Constant), VAR00003, VAR00002

ANOVA[b]

Model		Sum of Squares	df	Mean Square	F	Sig.
1	Regression	50.086	2	25.043	4.392	.058[a]
	Residual	39.914	7	5.702		
	Total	90.000	9			

a. Predictors: (Constant), VAR00003, VAR00002
b. Dependent Variable: VAR00001

Coefficients[a]

		Unstandardized Coefficients		Standardized Coefficients		
Model		B	Std. Error	Beta	t	Sig.
1	(Constant)	2.552	1.944		1.313	.231
	VAR00002	.672	.407	.558	1.652	.142
	VAR00003	.293	.401	.247	.732	.488

a. Dependent Variable: VAR00001

FIGURE 16.8
The SPSS output for the multiple regression in Example 16.5.

R^2 AND RESIDUAL VARIANCE

In the same way that we computed an r^2 value to measure the percentage of variance accounted for with the single-predictor regression, it is possible to compute a corresponding percentage for multiple regression. For a multiple-regression equation, this percentage is identified by the symbol R^2. The value of R^2 describes the proportion of the total variability of the Y scores that is accounted for by the regression equation. In symbols,

$$R^2 = \frac{SS_{\text{regression}}}{SS_Y} \quad \text{or} \quad SS_{\text{regression}} = R^2 SS_Y$$

For a regression with two predictor variables, R^2 can be computed directly from the regression equation as follows:

$$R^2 = \frac{b_1 SP_{X1Y} + b_2 SP_{X2Y}}{SS_Y} \tag{16.19}$$

For the data in Table 16.2, we obtain a value of

$$R^2 = \frac{0.672(54) + 0.293(47)}{90} = \frac{50.059}{90} = 0.5562 \text{ (or } 55.62\%)$$

In the computer printout in Figure 16.8, the value of R^2 is reported in the Model Summary table at the top.

Thus, 55.6% of the variance for the Y scores can be predicted by the regression equation. For the data in Table 16.2, SSY = 90, so the predicted portion of the variability is

$$SS_{\text{regression}} = R^2 SS_Y = 0.5562(90) = 50.06$$

The unpredicted, or residual, variance is determined by $1 - R^2$. For the data in Table 16.2, this is

$$SS_{\text{residual}} = (1 - R^2)SS_Y = 0.4438(90) = 39.94$$

COMPUTING R^2 AND $1 - R^2$ FROM THE RESIDUALS

The value of R^2 and $1 - R^2$ can also be obtained by computing the residual, or difference between the predicted Y and the actual Y for each individual, then computing the sum of the squared residuals. The resulting value is SS_{residual} and measures the unpredicted portion of the variability of Y, which is equal to $(1 - R^2)SS_Y$. For the data in Table 16.2, we first use the multiple-regression equation to compute the predicted value of Y for each individual. The process of finding and squaring each residual is shown in Table 16.3.

Note that the sum of the squared residuals, the unpredicted portion of SS_Y, is 39.960. This value corresponds to 44.4% of the variability for the Y scores:

$$\frac{SS_{\text{residual}}}{SS_Y} = \frac{39.96}{90} = 0.444 \text{ (or } 44.4\%)$$

Because the unpredicted portion of the variability is $1 - R^2 = 44.4\%$, we conclude that the predicted portion is $R^2 = 55.6\%$. Note that this answer is within rounding error of $R^2 = 55.62\%$ that we obtained from equation 16.19.

TABLE 16.3

The predicted Y values and the residuals for the data in Table 16.2. The predicted Y values were obtained using the values of X_1 and X_2 in the multiple-regression equation for each individual.

Actual Y	Predicted Y ($\hat{Y}$)	Residual ($Y - \hat{Y}$)	Squared Residual $(Y - \hat{Y})^2$
11	8.17	2.83	8.010
5	7.67	−2.67	7.129
7	6.62	0.38	0.144
3	5.07	−2.07	4.285
4	4.10	−0.10	0.010
12	8.72	3.28	10.758
10	10.27	−0.27	0.073
4	5.07	−1.07	1.145
8	10.19	−2.19	4.796
6	4.10	1.90	3.610
			$39.960 = SS_{\text{residuals}}$

THE STANDARD ERROR OF ESTIMATE

On page 567, we defined the standard error of estimate for a linear regression equation as the standard distance between the regression line and the actual data points. In more general terms, the standard error of estimate can be defined as the standard distance between the predicted Y values (from the regression equation) and the actual Y values (in the data). The more general definition applies equally well to both linear and multiple regression.

To find the standard error of estimate for either linear regression or multiple regression, we begin with SS_{residual}. For linear regression with one predictor, $SS_{\text{residual}} = (1 - r^2)SS_Y$ and has $df = n - 2$. For multiple regression with two predictors, $SS_{\text{residual}} = (1 - R^2)SS_Y$ and has $df = n - 3$. In each case, we can use the SS and df values to compute a variance or MS_{residual}.

$$MS_{\text{residual}} = \frac{SS_{\text{residual}}}{df}$$

The variance, or MS value, is a measure of the average squared distance between the actual Y values and the predicted Y values. By simply taking the square root, we obtain a measure of standard deviation or standard distance. This standard distance for the residuals is the standard error of estimate. Thus, for both linear regression and multiple regression

$$\text{the standard error of estimate} = \sqrt{MS_{\text{residual}}}$$

In the computer printout in Figure 16.8, the standard error of estimate is reported in the Model Summary table at the top.

For either linear or multiple regression, you do not expect the predictions from the regression equation to be perfect. In general, there is some discrepancy between the predicted values of Y and the actual values. The standard error of estimate provides a measure of how much discrepancy, on average, there is between the $\hat{Y}$ values and the actual Y values.

TESTING THE SIGNIFICANCE OF THE MULTIPLE REGRESSION EQUATION: ANALYSIS OF REGRESSION

Just as we did with the single-predictor equation, we can evaluate the significance of a multiple-regression equation by computing an F-ratio to determine whether the equation predicts a significant portion of the variance for the Y scores. The total variability of the Y scores is partitioned into two components, $SS_{\text{regression}}$ and SS_{residual}. With two predictor variables, $SS_{\text{regression}}$ has $df = 2$, and SS_{residual} has $df = n - 3$. Therefore, the two MS values for the F-ratio are

$$MS_{\text{regression}} = \frac{SS_{\text{regression}}}{2} \qquad (16.20)$$

and

$$MS_{\text{residual}} = \frac{SS_{\text{residual}}}{n - 3} \qquad (16.21)$$

Because of rounding error, the value we obtain for SS_{residual} is slightly different from the value in Table 16.3.

The data for the $n = 10$ people in Table 16.2 have produced $R^2 = 0.5562$ (or 55.62%) and $SS_Y = 90$. Thus,

$$SS_{\text{regression}} = R^2 SS_Y = 0.556(90) = 50.06$$

$$SS_{\text{residual}} = (1 - R^2)SS_Y = 0.4438(90) = 39.94$$

Therefore, $$MS_{\text{regession}} = \frac{50.06}{2} = 25.03 \quad \text{and} \quad MS_{\text{residual}} = \frac{39.94}{7} = 5.71$$

and $$F = \frac{MS_{\text{regression}}}{MS_{\text{residual}}} = \frac{25.03}{5.71} = 4.38$$

With $df = 2, 7$, this F-ratio is not significant with $\alpha = .05$, so we cannot conclude that the regression equation accounts for a significant portion of the variance for the Y scores.

The analysis of regression is summarized in the following table, which is a common component of the output from most computer versions of multiple regression. In the computer printout in Figure 16.8, this summary table is reported in the ANOVA table in the center.

Source	*SS*	*df*	*MS*	*F*
Regression	50.06	2	25.03	4.38
Residual	39.94	7	5.71	
Total	90.00	9		

LEARNING CHECK

1. Data from a sample of $n = 15$ individuals are used to compute a multiple-regression equation with two predictor variables. The equation has $R^2 = 0.20$ and $SS_Y = 150$.
   a. Find SS_{residual} and compute the standard error of estimate for the regression equation.
   b. Find $SS_{\text{regression}}$ and compute the F-ratio to evaluate the significance of the regression equation.

ANSWER

1. **a.** $SS_{\text{residual}} = 120$. The standard error of estimate is $\sqrt{10} = 3.16$.
   b. $SS_{\text{regression}} = 30$ with $df = 2$. $SS_{\text{residual}} = 120$ with $df = 12$. $F = 1.50$. With $df = 2, 12$, the F-ratio is not significant.

16.4 EVALUATING THE CONTRIBUTION OF EACH PREDICTOR VARIABLE

In addition to evaluating the overall significance of the multiple-regression equation, researchers are often interested in the relative contribution of each of the two predictor variables. Is one of the predictors responsible for more of the prediction than the other? Unfortunately, the b values in the regression equation are influenced by a variety of other factors and do not address this issue. If b_1 is larger than b_2, it does not necessarily mean that X_1 is a better predictor than X_2. However, in the standardized form of the regression equation, the relative size of the beta values is an indication of the relative contribution of the two variables. For the data in Table 16.3, the standardized regression equation is

$$\hat{z}_Y = (\text{beta}_1)z_{X1} + (\text{beta}_2)z_{X2}$$
$$= 0.558z_{X1} + 0.247z_{X2}$$

For the SPSS printout in Figure 16.8, the beta values are shown in the Coefficients table.

In this case, the larger beta value for the X_1 predictor indicates that X_1 predicts more of the variance than does X_2. The signs of the beta values are also meaningful. In this example, both betas are positive, indicating the both X_1 and X_2 are positively related to Y.

Beyond judging the relative contribution for each of the predictor variables, it also is possible to evaluate the significance of each contribution. For example, does variable X_2 make a significant contribution beyond what is already predicted by variable X_1? The null hypothesis states that the multiple-regression equation (using X_2 in addition to X_1) is not any better than the simple regression equation using X_1 as a single predictor variable. An alternative view of the null hypothesis is that the b_2 (or beta$_2$) value in the equation is not significantly different from zero. To test this hypothesis, we first determine how much more variance is predicted using X_1 and X_2 together than is predicted using X_1 alone.

Earlier we found that the multiple regression equation with both X_1 and X_2 predicted $R^2 = 55.62\%$ of the variance for the Y scores. To determine how much is predicted by X_1 alone, we begin with the correlation between X_1 and Y, which is

$$r = \frac{SP_{X1Y}}{\sqrt{(SS_{X1})(SS_Y)}} = \frac{54}{\sqrt{(62)(90)}} = \frac{54}{74.70} = 0.7229$$

Squaring the correlation produces $r^2 = (0.7229)^2 = 0.5226$ or 52.26%. This means that the relationship with X_1 predicts 52.26% of the variance for the Y scores. Therefore, the additional contribution made by adding X_2 to the regression equation can be computed as

$$(\% \text{ with both } X_1 \text{ and } X_2) - (\% \text{ with } X_1 \text{ alone})$$

$$= 55.62\% - 52.26\%$$

$$= 3.36\%$$

Because $SS_Y = 90$, the additional variability from adding X_2 as a predictor amounts to

$$SS_{\text{additional}} = 3.36\% \text{ of } 90 = 0.0336(90) = 3.024$$

This SS value has $df = 1$, and can be used to compute an F-ratio evaluating the significance of the contribution of X_2. First,

$$MS_{\text{additional}} = \frac{SS_{\text{additional}}}{1} = \frac{3.024}{1} = 3.024$$

This MS value is evaluated by computing an F-ratio with the MS_{residual} value from the multiple regression as the denominator. (*Note:* This is the same denominator that was used in the F-ratio to evaluate the significance of the multiple-regression equation.) For these data, we obtain

$$F = \frac{MS_{\text{additional}}}{MS_{\text{residual}}} = \frac{3.024}{5.71} = 0.5296$$

With $df = 1, 7$, this F-ratio is not significant. Therefore, we conclude that adding X_2 to the regression equation does not significantly improve the prediction compared to using X_1 as a single predictor. The computer printout shown in Figure 16.8 reports a t statistic instead of an F-ratio to evaluate the contribution for each predictor variable. Each t value is simply the square root of the F-ratio and is reported in the right-hand side of the Coefficients table. Variable X_2, for example, is reported as VAR00003 in the table and has $t = 0.732$, which is within rounding error of the F-ratio we obtained; $\sqrt{F} = \sqrt{0.5296} = 0.728$.

MULTIPLE REGRESSION AND PARTIAL CORRELATIONS

In Chapter 15 we introduced *partial correlation* as a technique for measuring the relationship between two variables while eliminating the influence of a third variable. At that time, we noted that partial correlations serve two general purposes:

1. A partial correlation can demonstrate that an apparent relationship between two variables is actually caused by a third variable. Thus, there is no direct relationship between the original two variables.
2. Partial correlation can demonstrate that there is a relationship between two variables even after a third variable is controlled. Thus, there really is a relationship between the original two variables that is not being caused by a third variable.

Multiple regression provides an alternative procedure for accomplishing both of these goals. Specifically, the regression analysis evaluates the contribution of each predictor variable after the influence of the other predictor has been considered. Thus, you can determine whether each predictor variable contributes to the relationship by itself or simply duplicates the contribution already made by another variable.

SUMMARY

1. When there is a general linear relationship between two variables, X and Y, it is possible to construct a linear equation that allows you to predict the Y value corresponding to any known value of X.

$$\text{predicted } Y \text{ value} = \hat{Y} = bX + a$$

The technique for determining this equation is called regression. By using a *least-squares* method to minimize the error between the predicted Y values and the actual Y values, the best-fitting line is achieved when the linear equation has

$$b = \frac{SP}{SS_X} = r\frac{s_Y}{s_X} \quad \text{and} \quad a = M_Y - bM_X$$

2. The linear equation generated by regression (called the regression equation) can be used to compute a predicted Y value for any value of X. However, the prediction is not perfect, so for each Y value, there is a predicted portion and an unpredicted, or residual, portion. Overall, the predicted portion of the Y score variability is measured by r^2, and the residual portion is measured by $1 - r^2$.

$$\text{predicted variability} = SS_{\text{regression}} = r^2 SS_Y$$

$$\text{unpredicted variability} = SS_{\text{residual}} = (1 - r^2)SS_Y$$

3. The residual variability can be used to compute the standard error of estimate, which provides a measure of the standard distance (or error) between the predicted Y values on the line and the actual data points. The standard error of estimate is computed by

$$\text{standard error of estimate} = \sqrt{\frac{SS_{\text{residual}}}{n-2}} = \sqrt{MS_{\text{residual}}}$$

4. It is also possible to compute an F-ratio to evaluate the significance of the regression equation. The process is called analysis of regression and determines whether the equation predicts a significant portion of the variance for the Y scores. First a variance, or MS, value is computed for the predicted variability and the residual variability,

$$MS_{\text{regression}} = \frac{SS_{\text{regression}}}{df_{\text{regression}}} \qquad MS_{\text{residual}} = \frac{SS_{\text{residual}}}{df_{\text{residual}}}$$

where $df_{\text{regression}} = 1$ and $df_{\text{residual}} = n - 2$. Next, an F-ratio is computed to evaluate the significance of the regression equation.

$$F = \frac{MS_{\text{regression}}}{MS_{\text{residual}}} \quad \text{with } df = 1, n - 2$$

5. Multiple regression involves finding a regression equation with more than one predictor variable. With two predictors (X_1 and X_2), the equation becomes

$$\hat{Y} = b_1X_1 + b_2X_2 + a$$

with the values for b_1, b_2, and a computed using equations 16.16, 16.17, and 16.18.

6. For multiple regression, the value of R^2 describes the proportion of the total variability of the Y scores that is accounted for by the regression equation. With two predictor variables,

$$R^2 = \frac{b_1SP_{X1Y} + b_2SP_{X2Y}}{SS_Y}$$

Predicted variability $= SS_{\text{regression}} = R^2SS_Y$.
Unpredicted variability $= SS_{\text{residual}} = (1 - R^2)SS_Y$.

7. The residual variability for the multiple-regression equation can be used to compute a standard error of estimate, which provides a measure of the standard distance (or error) between the predicted Y values from the equation and the actual data points. For multiple regression with two predictors, the standard error of estimate is computed by

$$\text{standard error of estimate} = \sqrt{\frac{SS_{\text{residual}}}{n-3}} = \sqrt{MS_{\text{residual}}}$$

8. Evaluating the significance of the two-predictor multiple-regression equation involves computing an F-ratio that divides the $MS_{\text{regression}}$ (with $df = 2$) by the MS_{residual} (with $df = n - 3$). A significant F-ratio indicates that the regression equation accounts for a significant portion of the variance for the Y scores.

9. An F-ratio can also be used to determine whether a second predictor variable (X_2) significantly improves the prediction beyond what was already predicted by X_1. The numerator of the F-ratio measures the additional SS that is predicted by adding X_2 as a second predictor.

$$SS_{\text{additional}} = SS_{\text{regression with } X1 \text{ and } X2} - SS_{\text{regression with } X1 \text{ alone}}$$

This SS value has $df = 1$. The denominator of the F-ratio is the MS_{residual} from the two-predictor regression equation.

KEY TERMS

linear relationship (559)
linear equation (559)
slope (559)
Y-intercept (559)
regression (561)
regression line (561)
least-squared-error solution (562)
regression equation for Y (563)
standard error of estimate (567)
predicted variability ($SS_{\text{regression}}$) (568)
unpredicted variability (SS_{residual}) (568)
analysis of regression (570)
multiple regression (572)
partial correlation (581)

RESOURCES

Book Companion Website: www.cengage.com/psychology/gravetter

You can find a tutorial quiz and other learning exercises for Chapter 16 on the book companion website. The website also provides access to a workshop entitled *Correlation* that includes information on regression.

CENGAGE brain.com

Log in to CengageBrain to access the resources your instructor requires. For this book, you can access:

Psychology CourseMate brings course concepts to life with interactive learning, study, and exam preparation tools that support the printed textbook. A textbook-specific website, Psychology CourseMate includes an integrated interactive eBook and other interactive learning tools including quizzes, flashcards, and more.

Visit www.cengagebrain.com to access your account and purchase materials.

SPSS

General instructions for using SPSS are presented in Appendix D. Following are detailed instructions for using SPSS to perform the **Linear Regression** and **Multiple Regression** presented in this chapter.

Data Entry

With one predictor variable (X), you enter the X values in one column and the Y values in a second column of the SPSS data editor. With two predictors (X_1 and X_2), enter the X_1 values in one column, X_2 in a second column, and Y in a third column.

Data Analysis

1. Click **Analyze** on the tool bar, select **Regression,** and click on **Linear.**
2. In the left-hand box, highlight the column label for the Y values, then click the arrow to move the column label into the **Dependent Variable** box.
3. For one predictor variable, highlight the column label for the X values and click the arrow to move it into the **Independent Variable(s)** box. For two predictor variables, highlight the X_1 and X_2 column labels, one at a time, and click the arrow to move them into the **Independent Variable(s)** box.
4. Click **OK.**

SPSS Output

We used SPSS to perform multiple regression for the data in Example 16.4 and the output is shown in Figure 16.8 (p. 576). The Model Summary table presents the values for R, R^2, and the standard error of estimate. (*Note:* For a single predictor, R is simply the Pearson correlation between X and Y.) The ANOVA table presents the analysis of regression evaluating the significance of the regression equation, including the F-ratio and the level of significance (the p value or alpha level for the test). The **Coefficients** table summarizes both the unstandardized and the standardized coefficients for the regression equation. For one predictor, the table shows the values for the constant (a) and the coefficient (b). For two predictors, the table shows the constant (a) and the two coefficients (b_1 and b_2). The standardized coefficients are the beta values. For one predictor, beta is simply the Pearson correlation between X and Y. Finally, the table uses a t statistic to evaluate the significance of each predictor variable. For one predictor variable, this is identical to the significance of the regression equation and you should find that t is equal to the square root of the F-ratio from the analysis of regression. For two predictor variables, the t values measure the significance of the contribution of each variable beyond what is already predicted by the other variable.

FOCUS ON PROBLEM SOLVING

1. A basic understanding of the Pearson correlation, including the calculation of *SP* and *SS* values, is critical for understanding and computing regression equations.

2. You can calculate $SS_{residual}$ directly by finding the residual (the difference between the actual *Y* and the predicted *Y* for each individual), squaring the residuals, and adding the squared values. However, it usually is much easier to compute r^2 (or R^2) and then find $SS_{residual} = (1 - r^2)SS_Y$.

3. The *F*-ratio for analysis of regression is usually calculated using the actual $SS_{regression}$ and $SS_{residual}$. However, you can simply use r^2 (or R^2) in place of $SS_{regression}$ and you can use $1 - r^2$ or $(1 - R^2)$ in place of $SS_{residual}$. *Note:* You must still use the correct *df* value for the numerator and the denominator.

DEMONSTRATION 16.1

LINEAR REGRESSION

The following data are used to demonstrate the process of linear regression. The scores and summary statistics are as follows:

Person	*X*	*Y*
A	0	4
B	2	1
C	8	10
D	6	9
E	4	6

$M_X = 4$ with $SS_X = 40$
$M_Y = 6$ with $SS_Y = 54$
$SP = 40$

These data produce a Pearson correlation of $r = 0.861$.

STEP 1 **Compute the values for the regression equation.** The general form of the regression equation is

$$\hat{Y} = bX + a \qquad \text{where } b = \frac{SP}{SS_X} \qquad \text{and} \quad a = M_Y - bM_X$$

$$\text{For these data, } b = \frac{40}{40} = 1.00 \qquad \text{and} \qquad a = 6 - 1(4) = +2.00$$

Thus, the regression equation is $\hat{Y} = (1)X + 2.00$ or simply, $\hat{Y} = X + 2$.

STEP 2 **Evaluate the significance of the regression equation.** The null hypothesis states that the regression equation does not predict a significant portion of the variance for the *Y* scores. To conduct the test, the total variability for the *Y* scores, $SS_Y = 54$, is partitioned into the portion predicted by the regression equation and the residual portion.

$$SS_{regression} = r^2(SS_Y) = 0.741(54) = 40.01 \text{ with } df = 1$$

$$SS_{residual} = (1 - r^2)(SS_Y) = 0.259(54) = 13.99 \text{ with } df = n - 2 = 3$$

The two *MS* values (variances) for the *F*-ratio are

$$MS_{\text{regression}} = \frac{SS_{\text{regression}}}{df} = \frac{40.01}{1} = 40.01$$

$$MS_{\text{residual}} = \frac{SS_{\text{residual}}}{df} = \frac{13.99}{3} = 4.66$$

And the *F*-ratio is

$$F = \frac{MS_{\text{regression}}}{MS_{\text{residual}}} = \frac{40.01}{4.66} = 8.59$$

With $df = 1, 3$ and $\alpha = .05$, the critical value for the *F*-ratio is 10.13. Therefore, we fail to reject the null hypothesis and conclude that the regression equation does not predict a significant portion of the variance for the *Y* scores.

DEMONSTRATION 16.2

MULTIPLE REGRESSION

The following data are used to demonstrate the process of multiple regression. Note that there are two predictor variables, X_1 and X_2, that are used to compute a predicted *Y* score for each individual.

Person	X_1	X_2	Y
A	0	5	2
B	3	1	4
C	5	2	7
D	6	0	9
E	8	4	5
F	2	6	3
	$M_{X1} = 4$	$M_{X2} = 3$	$M_Y = 5$
	$SS_{X1} = 42$	$SS_{X2} = 28$	$SS_Y = 34$
	$SP_{X1Y} = 27$	$SP_{X2Y} = -24$	$SP_{X1X2} = -15$

STEP 1 **Compute the values for the multiple regression equation.** The general form of the multiple-regression equation is

$$\hat{Y} = b_1X_1 + b_2X_2 + a$$

The values for the multiple regression equation are

$$b_1 = \frac{(SP_{X1Y})(SS_{X2}) - (SP_{X1X2})(SP_{X2Y})}{(SS_{X1})(SS_{X2}) - (SP_{X1X2})^2} = \frac{(27)(28) - (-15)(-24)}{(42)(28) - (-15)^2} = 0.416$$

$$b_2 = \frac{(SP_{X2Y})(SS_{X1}) - (SP_{X1X2})(SP_{X1Y})}{(SS_{X1})(SS_{X2}) - (SP_{X1X2})^2} = \frac{(-24)(42) - (-15)(27)}{(42)(28) - (-15)^2} = -0.634$$

$$a = M_Y - b_1M_{X1} - b_2M_{X2} = 5 - 0.416(4) - -0.634(3) = 5 - 1.664 + 1.902 = 5.238$$

The multiple-regression equation is

$$\hat{Y} = 0.416X_1 - 0.634X_2 + 5.238$$

STEP 2 **Evaluate the significance of the regression equation.** The null hypothesis states that the regression equation does not predict a significant portion of the variance for the Y scores. To conduct the test, the total variability for the Y scores, $SS_Y = 34$, is partitioned into the portion predicted by the regression equation and the residual portion. To find each portion, we must first compute the value of R^2.

$$R^2 = \frac{b_1SP_{X1Y} + b_2SP_{X2Y}}{SS_Y}$$

$$\frac{(0.416)(27) + (-0.634)(-24)}{34} = 0.778 \text{ (or 77.8\%)}$$

Then, the two components for the F-ratio are

$$SS_{\text{regression}} = R^2(SS_Y) = 0.778(34) = 26.45 \text{ with } df = 2$$

$$SS_{\text{residual}} = (1 - R^2)(SS_Y) = 0.222(34) = 7.55 \text{ with } df = n - 3 = 3$$

The two MS values (variances) and the F-ratio are

$$MS_{\text{regression}} = \frac{SS_{\text{regression}}}{df} = \frac{26.45}{2} = 13.23$$

$$MS_{\text{residual}} = \frac{SS_{\text{residual}}}{df} = \frac{7.55}{3} = 2.52$$

$$F = \frac{MS_{\text{regression}}}{MS_{\text{residual}}} = \frac{13.23}{2.52} = 5.25$$

with $df = 2, 3$, the F-ratio is not significant.

PROBLEMS

1. Sketch a graph showing the line for the equation $Y = -2X + 4$. On the same graph, show the line for $Y = X - 4$.

2. A set of $n = 25$ pairs of scores (X and Y values) produces a regression equation of $\hat{Y} = 3X - 2$. Find the predicted Y value for each of the following X scores: 0, 1, 3, −2.

3. A set of $n = 20$ pairs of scores (X and Y values) has $SS_X = 16$, $SS_Y = 100$, and $SP = 32$. If the mean for the X values is $M_X = 6$ and the mean for the Y values is $M_Y = 20$.
   a. Calculate the Pearson correlation for the scores.
   b. Find the regression equation for predicting Y from the X values.

4. The regression equation is intended to be the "best fitting" straight line for a set of data. What is the criterion for "best fitting"?

5. Briefly explain what is measured by the standard error of estimate.

6. In general, how is the magnitude of the standard error of estimate related to the value of the correlation?

7. For the following set of data, find the linear regression equation for predicting Y from X:

X	Y
7	6
9	6
6	3
12	5
9	6
5	4

8. For the following data:
   a. Find the regression equation for predicting Y from X.
   b. Calculate the Pearson correlation for these data. Use r^2 and SS_Y to compute $SS_{residual}$ and the standard error of estimate for the equation.

X	Y
1	2
4	7
3	5
2	1
5	14
3	7

9. Does the regression equation from problem 8 account for a significant portion of the variance in the Y scores? Use $\alpha = .05$ to evaluate the F-ratio.

10. A professor obtains SAT scores and freshman grade point averages (GPAs) for a group of $n = 15$ college students. The SAT scores have a mean of $M = 580$ with $SS = 22{,}400$, and the GPAs have a mean of 3.10 with $SS = 1.26$, and $SP = 84$.
   a. Find the regression equation for predicting GPA from SAT scores.
   b. What percentage of the variance in GPAs is accounted for by the regression equation? (Compute the correlation, r, then find r^2.)
   c. Does the regression equation account for a significant portion of the variance in GPA? Use $\alpha = .05$ to evaluate the F-ratio.

11. Problem 12 in Chapter 15 examined the relationship between weight and income for a sample of $n = 10$ women. Weights were classified in five categories and had a mean of $M = 3$ with $SS = 20$. Income, measured in thousands, had a mean score of $M = 66$ with $SS = 7430$, and $SP = -359$.
   a. Find the regression equation for predicting income from weight. (Identify the income scores as X values and the weight scores as Y values.)
   b. What percentage of the variance in the income is accounted for by the regression equation? (Compute the correlation, r, then find r^2.)
   c. Does the regression equation account for a significant portion of the variance in income? Use $\alpha = .05$ to evaluate the F-ratio.

12. For the following scores,

X	Y
3	6
6	1
3	4
3	3
5	1

   a. Find the regression equation for predicting Y from X.
   b. Calculate the predicted Y value for each X.

13. Problem 14 in Chapter 15 described a study examining the effectiveness of a 7-Minute Screen test for Alzheimer's disease. The study evaluated the relationship between scores from the 7-Minute Screen and scores for the same patients from a set of cognitive exams that are typically used to test for Alzheimer's disease. For a sample of $n = 9$ patients, the scores for the 7-Minute Screen averaged $M = 7$ with $SS = 92$. The cognitive test scores averaged $M = 17$ with $SS = 236$. For these data, $SP = 127$.
   a. Find the regression equation for predicting the cognitive scores from the 7-Minute Screen score.
   b. What percentage of variance in the cognitive scores is accounted for by the regression equation?
   c. Does the regression equation account for a significant portion of the variance in the cognitive scores? Use $\alpha = .05$ to evaluate the F-ratio.

14. There appears to be some evidence suggesting that earlier retirement may lead to memory decline (Rohwedder & Willis, 2010). The researchers gave a memory test to men and women aged 60 to 64 years in several countries that have different retirement ages. For each country, the researchers recorded the average memory score and the percentage of individuals in the 60 to 64 age range who were retired. Note that a higher percentage retired indicates a younger retirement age for that country. The following data are similar to the results from the study. Use the data to find the regression equation for predicting memory scores from the percentage of people aged 60 to 64 who are retired.

Country	% Retired (*X*)	Memory Score (*Y*)
Sweden	39	9.3
U.S.A.	48	10.9
England	59	10.7
Germany	70	9.1
Spain	74	6.4
Netherlands	78	9.1
Italy	81	7.2
France	87	7.9
Belgium	88	8.5
Austria	91	9.0

15. The regression equation is computed for a set of $n = 18$ pairs of X and Y values with a correlation of $r = +80$ and $SS_Y = 100$.

a. Find the standard error of estimate for the regression equation.

b. How big would the standard error be if the sample size were $n = 38$?

16. A researcher obtained the following multiple-regression equation using two predictor variables: $\hat{Y} = 0.5X_1 + 4.5X_2 + 9.6$. Given that $SS_Y = 210$, the SP value for X_1 and Y is 40, and the SP value for X_2 and Y is 9, find R^2, the percentage of variance accounted for by the equation.

17. a. A researcher computes the regression equation for a sample of $n = 25$ pairs of scores, X and Y values. If an analysis of regression is used to test the significance of the equation, what are the df values for the F-ratio?

b. A researcher evaluating the significance of a regression equation obtains an F-ratio with $df = 1, 18$. How many pairs of scores, X and Y values, are in the sample?

18. For the following data:

a. Find the regression equation for predicting Y from X.

b. Use the regression equation to find a predicted Y for each X.

c. Find the difference between the actual Y value and the predicted Y value for each individual, square the differences, and add the squared values to obtain SS_{residual}.

d. Calculate the Pearson correlation for these data. Use r^2 and SS_Y to compute SS_{residual} with Equation 16.11. You should obtain the same value as in part c.

X	*Y*
7	16
5	2
6	1
3	2
4	9

19. A multiple-regression equation with two predictor variables produces $R^2 = .22$.

a. If $SS_Y = 20$ for a sample of $n = 18$ individuals, does the equation predict a significant portion of the variance for the Y scores? Test with $\alpha = .05$.

b. If $SS_Y = 20$ for a sample of $n = 8$ individuals, does the equation predict a significant portion of the variance for the Y scores? Test with $\alpha = .05$.

20. a. One set of 20 pairs of scores, X and Y values, produces a correlation of $r = 0.70$. If $SS_Y = 150$, find the standard error of estimate for the regression line.

b. A second set of 20 pairs of X and Y values produces of correlation of $r = 0.30$. If $SS_Y = 150$, find the standard error of estimate for the regression line.

21. In Chapter 15 (p. 531), we presented an example showing the general relationship among the number of churches, the number of serious crimes, and the population for a set of cities. At that time, we used a partial correlation to evaluate the relationship between churches and crime while controlling population. It is possible to use multiple regression to accomplish essentially the same purpose. For the following data,

Number of Churches (X_1)	Population (X_2)	Number of Crimes (Y)
1	1	4
2	1	1
3	1	2
4	1	3
5	1	5
7	2	8
8	2	11
9	2	9
10	2	7
11	2	10
13	3	15
14	3	14
15	3	16
16	3	17
17	3	13

a. Find the multiple regression equation for predicting the number of crimes using the number of churches and population as predictor variables.

b. Find the value of R^2 for the regression equation.

c. The correlation between the number of crimes and population is $r = 0.961$, which means that $r^2 = .924$ (92.4%) is the proportion of variance in the number of crimes that is predicted by population size. Does adding the number of churches as a second variable in the multiple regression equation add a significant amount to the prediction? Test with $\alpha = .05$.

22. Problem 11 in Chapter 15 examined the TV-viewing habits of adopted children in relation to their biological parents and their adoptive parents. The data are reproduced as follows. If both the biological and adoptive parents are used to predict the viewing habits of the children in a multiple-regression equation, what percentage of the variance in the children's scores would be accounted for? That is, compute R^2.

Amount of Time Spent Watching TV		
Adopted Children Y	Birth Parents X_1	Adoptive Parents X_2
2	0	1
3	3	4
6	4	2
1	1	0
3	1	0
0	2	3
5	3	2
2	1	3
5	3	3
$SS_Y = 32$	$SS_{X1} = 14$	$SS_{X2} = 16$

$SP_{X1X2} = 8$
$SP_{X1Y} = 15$
$SP_{X2Y} = 3$

23. For the data in problem 22, the correlation between the children's scores and the biological parents' scores is $r = 0.709$. Does adding the adoptive parents' scores as a second predictor significantly improve the ability to predict the children's scores? Use $\alpha = .05$ to evaluate the F-ratio.

24. For the following data, find the multiple-regression equation for predicting Y from X_1 and X_2.

X_1	X_2	Y
1	3	1
2	4	2
3	5	6
6	9	8
4	8	3
2	7	4
$M = 3$	$M = 6$	$M = 4$
$SS_{X1} = 16$	$SS_{X2} = 28$	$SS_Y = 34$

$SP_{X1X2} = 18$
$SP_{X1Y} = 19$
$SP_{X2Y} = 21$

25. A researcher evaluates the significance of a multiple-regression equation and obtains an F-ratio with $df = 2, 36$. How many participants were in the sample?

CHAPTER

17

The Chi-Square Statistic: Tests for Goodness of Fit and Independence

Tools You Will Need

The following items are considered essential background material for this chapter. If you doubt your knowledge of any of these items, you should review the appropriate chapter or section before proceeding.

- Proportions (math review, Appendix A)
- Frequency distributions (Chapter 2)

Preview

Loftus and Palmer (1974) conducted a classic experiment demonstrating how language can influence eyewitness memory. A sample of 150 students watched a film of an automobile accident. After watching the film, the students were separated into three groups. One group was asked, "About how fast were the cars going when they smashed into each other?" Another group received the same question except that the verb was changed to "hit" instead of "smashed into." A third group served as a control and was not asked any question about the speed of the two cars. A week later, the participants returned and were asked if they remembered seeing any broken glass in the accident. (There was no broken glass in the film.) Notice that the researchers are manipulating the form of the initial question and then measuring a yes/no response to a follow-up question 1 week later. Table 17.1 shows the structure of this design represented by a matrix with the independent variable (different groups) determining the rows of the matrix and the two categories for the dependent variable (yes/no) determining the columns. The number in each cell of the matrix is the frequency count showing how many participants are classified in that category. For example, of the 50 students who heard the word *smashed,* there were 16 (32%) who claimed to remember seeing broken glass even though there was none in the film. By comparison, only 7 of the 50 students (14%) who heard the word *hit* said they recalled seeing broken glass. The researchers would like to use these data to support the argument that a witness's "memory" can be influenced by the language used during questioning. If the two cars *smashed* into each other, then there must have been some broken glass.

The Problem: Although the Loftus and Palmer study involves an independent variable (the form of the question) and a dependent variable (memory for broken glass), you should realize that this study is different from any experiment we have considered in the past. Specifically, the Loftus and Palmer study does not produce a numerical score for each participant. Instead, each participant is simply classified into one of two categories (yes or no). The data consist of *frequencies* or *proportions* describing how many individuals are in each category. You should also note that Loftus and Palmer want to use a hypothesis test to evaluate the data. The null hypothesis would state that the form of the question has no effect on the memory of the witness. The hypothesis test would determine whether the sample data provide enough evidence to reject this null hypothesis.

Because there are no numerical scores, it is impossible to compute a mean or a variance for the sample data. Therefore, it is impossible to use any of the familiar hypothesis tests (such as a t test or analysis of variance [ANOVA]) to determine whether there is a significant difference between the treatment conditions. What is needed is a new hypothesis testing procedure that can be used with non-numerical data.

The Solution: In this chapter we introduce two hypothesis tests based on the *chi-square* statistic. Unlike earlier tests that require numerical scores (X values), the chi-square tests use sample frequencies and proportions to test hypothesis about the corresponding population values.

TABLE 17.1

A frequency distribution table showing the number of participants who answered either yes or no when asked whether they recalled seeing any broken glass 1 week after witnessing an automobile accident. Immediately after the accident, one group was asked how fast the cars were going when they smashed into each other. A second group was asked how fast the cars were going when they hit each other. A third group served as a control and was not asked about the speed of the cars.

		Response to the Question: Did You See Any Broken Glass?	
		Yes	No
Verb Used to Ask about the Speed of the Cars	Smashed into	16	34
	Hit	7	43
	Control (Not Asked)	6	44

17.1 PARAMETRIC AND NONPARAMETRIC STATISTICAL TESTS

All of the statistical tests that we have examined thus far are designed to test hypotheses about specific population parameters. For example, we used t tests to assess hypotheses about a population mean (μ) or mean difference ($\mu_1 - \mu_2$). In addition, these tests typically make assumptions about other population parameters. Recall that, for analysis of variance (ANOVA), the population distributions are assumed to be normal and homogeneity of variance is required. Because these tests all concern parameters and require assumptions about parameters, they are called *parametric tests*.

Another general characteristic of parametric tests is that they require a numerical score for each individual in the sample. The scores then are added, squared, averaged, and otherwise manipulated using basic arithmetic. In terms of measurement scales, parametric tests require data from an interval or a ratio scale (see Chapter 1).

Often, researchers are confronted with experimental situations that do not conform to the requirements of parametric tests. In these situations, it may not be appropriate to use a parametric test. Remember that when the assumptions of a test are violated, the test may lead to an erroneous interpretation of the data. Fortunately, there are several hypothesis-testing techniques that provide alternatives to parametric tests. These alternatives are called *nonparametric tests*.

In this chapter, we introduce two commonly used examples of nonparametric tests. Both tests are based on a statistic known as chi-square and both tests use sample data to evaluate hypotheses about the proportions or relationships that exist within populations. Note that the two chi-square tests, like most nonparametric tests, do not state hypotheses in terms of a specific parameter and they make few (if any) assumptions about the population distribution. For the latter reason, nonparametric tests sometimes are called *distribution-free tests*.

One of the most obvious differences between parametric and nonparametric tests is the type of data they use. All of the parametric tests that we have examined so far require numerical scores. For nonparametric tests, on the other hand, the participants are usually just classified into categories such as Democrat and Republican, or High, Medium, and Low IQ. Note that these classifications involve measurement on nominal or ordinal scales, and they do not produce numerical values that can be used to calculate means and variances. Instead, the data for many nonparametric tests are simply frequencies—for example, the number of Democrats and the number of Republicans in a sample of $n = 100$ registered voters.

Occasionally, you have a choice between using a parametric and a nonparametric test. Changing to a nonparametric test usually involves transforming the data from numerical scores to nonnumerical categories. For example, you could start with numerical scores measuring self-esteem and create three categories consisting of high, medium, and low self-esteem. In most situations, the parametric test is preferred because it is more likely to detect a real difference or a real relationship. However, there are situations for which transforming scores into categories might be a better choice.

1. Occasionally, it is simpler to obtain category measurements. For example, it is easier to classify students as high, medium, or low in leadership ability than to obtain a numerical score measuring each student's ability.
2. The original scores may violate some of the basic assumptions that underlie certain statistical procedures. For example, the t tests and ANOVA assume that the data come from normal distributions. Also, the independent-measures

tests assume that the different populations all have the same variance (the homogeneity-of-variance assumption). If a researcher suspects that the data do not satisfy these assumptions, it may be safer to transform the scores into categories and use a nonparametric test to evaluate the data.

3. The original scores may have unusually high variance. Variance is a major component of the standard error in the denominator of t statistics and the error term in the denominator of F-ratios. Thus, large variance can greatly reduce the likelihood that these parametric tests will find significant differences. Converting the scores to categories essentially eliminates the variance. For example, all individuals fit into three categories (high, medium, and low), no matter how variable the original scores are.
4. Occasionally, an experiment produces an undetermined, or infinite, score. For example, a rat may show no sign of solving a particular maze after hundreds of trials. This animal has an infinite, or undetermined, score. Although there is no absolute number that can be assigned, you can say that this rat is in the highest category, and then classify the other scores according to their numerical values.

17.2 THE CHI-SQUARE TEST FOR GOODNESS OF FIT

Parameters such as the mean and the standard deviation are the most common way to describe a population, but there are situations in which a researcher has questions about the proportions or relative frequencies for a distribution. For example,

How does the number of women lawyers compare with the number of men in the profession?

Of the two leading brands of cola, which is preferred by most Americans?

In the past 10 years, has there been a significant change in the proportion of college students who declare a business major?

The name of the test comes from the Greek letter χ (chi, pronounced "kye"), which is used to identify the test statistic.

Note that each of the preceding examples asks a question about proportions in the population. In particular, we are not measuring a numerical score for each individual. Instead, the individuals are simply classified into categories and we want to know what proportion of the population is in each category. The *chi-square test for goodness of fit* is specifically designed to answer this type of question. In general terms, this chi-square test uses the proportions obtained for sample data to test hypotheses about the corresponding proportions in the population.

DEFINITION

The **chi-square test for goodness of fit** uses sample data to test hypotheses about the shape or proportions of a population distribution. The test determines how well the obtained sample proportions fit the population proportions specified by the null hypothesis.

Recall from Chapter 2 that a frequency distribution is defined as a tabulation of the number of individuals located in each category of the scale of measurement. In a frequency distribution graph, the categories that make up the scale of measurement are listed on the X-axis. In a frequency distribution table, the categories are listed in the first column. With chi-square tests, however, it is customary to present the scale of measurement as a series of boxes, with each box corresponding to a separate category on the scale. The frequency corresponding to each category is simply presented as a number written inside the box. Figure 17.1 shows how a distribution of eye colors for a set of $n = 40$ students can be presented as a graph, a table, or a series of boxes. The scale of measurement for this example consists of four categories of eye color (blue, brown, green, other).

THE NULL HYPOTHESIS FOR THE GOODNESS-OF-FIT TEST

For the chi-square test of goodness of fit, the null hypothesis specifies the proportion (or percentage) of the population in each category. For example, a hypothesis might state that 50% of all lawyers are men and 50% are women. The simplest way of presenting this hypothesis is to put the hypothesized proportions in the series of boxes representing the scale of measurement:

	Men	Women
H_0:	50%	50%

Although it is conceivable that a researcher could choose any proportions for the null hypothesis, there usually is some well-defined rationale for stating a null hypothesis. Generally H_0 falls into one of the following categories:

1. **No Preference, Equal Proportions.** The null hypothesis often states that there is no preference among the different categories. In this case, H_0 states that the population is divided equally among the categories. For example, a hypothesis stating that there is no preference among the three leading brands of soft drinks would specify a population distribution as follows:

	Brand X	Brand Y	Brand Z
H_0:	$\frac{1}{3}$	$\frac{1}{3}$	$\frac{1}{3}$

(Preferences in the population are equally divided among the three soft drinks.)

The no-preference hypothesis is used in situations in which a researcher wants to determine whether there are any preferences among the categories, or whether the proportions differ from one category to another.

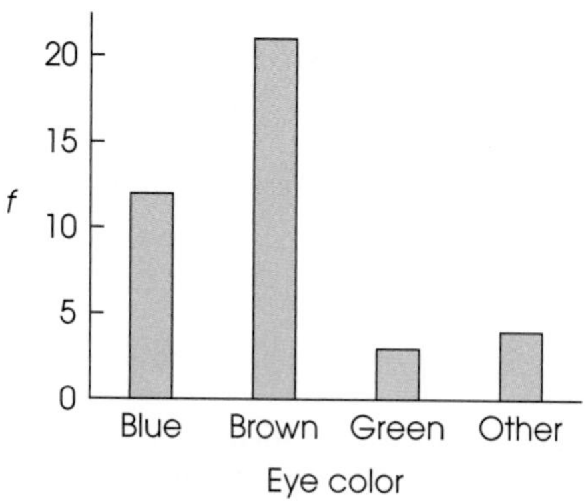

Eye color (X)	f
Blue	12
Brown	21
Green	3
Other	4

Blue	Brown	Green	Other
12	21	3	4

FIGURE 17.1

Distribution of eye colors for a sample of $n = 40$ individuals. The same frequency distribution is shown as a bar graph, as a table, and with the frequencies written in a series of boxes.

Because the null hypothesis for the goodness-of-fit test specifies an exact distribution for the population, the alternative hypothesis (H_1) simply states that the population distribution has a different shape from that specified in H_0. If the null hypothesis states that the population is equally divided among three categories, then the alternative hypothesis says that the population is not divided equally.

2. **No Difference from a Known Population.** The null hypothesis can state that the proportions for one population are not different from the proportions that are known to exist for another population. For example, suppose it is known that 28% of the licensed drivers in the state are younger than 30 years old and 72% are 30 or older. A researcher might wonder whether this same proportion holds for the distribution of speeding tickets. The null hypothesis would state that tickets are handed out equally across the population of drivers, so there is no difference between the age distribution for drivers and the age distribution for speeding tickets. Specifically, the null hypothesis would be

	Tickets Given to Drivers Younger Than 30	Tickets Given to Drivers 30 or Older
H_0:	28%	72%

(Proportions for the population of tickets are not different from proportions for drivers.)

The no-difference hypothesis is used when a specific population distribution is already known. For example, you may have a known distribution from an earlier time, and the question is whether there has been any change in the proportions. Or, you may have a known distribution for one population (drivers) and the question is whether a second population (speeding tickets) has the same proportions.

Again, the alternative hypothesis (H_1) simply states that the population proportions are not equal to the values specified by the null hypothesis. For this example, H_1 would state that the number of speeding tickets is disproportionately high for one age group and disproportionately low for the other.

THE DATA FOR THE GOODNESS-OF-FIT TEST

The data for a chi-square test are remarkably simple. There is no need to calculate a sample mean or SS; you just select a sample of n individuals and count how many are in each category. The resulting values are called observed frequencies. The symbol for observed frequency is f_o. For example, the following data represent observed frequencies for a sample of 40 college students. The students were classified into three categories based on the number of times they reported exercising each week.

No Exercise	1 Time a Week	More Than Once a Week
15	19	6

$n = 40$

Notice that each individual in the sample is classified into one and only one of the categories. Thus, the frequencies in this example represent three completely separate groups of students: 15 who do not exercise regularly, 19 who average once a week, and 6 who exercise more than once a week. Also note that the observed frequencies add up to the total sample size: $\Sigma f_o = n$. Finally, you should realize that we are not assigning individuals to categories. Instead, we are simply measuring individuals to determine the category in which they belong.

DEFINITION

The **observed frequency** is the number of individuals from the sample who are classified in a particular category. Each individual is counted in one and only one category.

EXPECTED FREQUENCIES

The general goal of the chi-square test for goodness of fit is to compare the data (the observed frequencies) with the null hypothesis. The problem is to determine how well the data fit the distribution specified in H_0—hence the name *goodness of fit*.

The first step in the chi-square test is to construct a hypothetical sample that represents how the sample distribution would look if it were in perfect agreement with the proportions stated in the null hypothesis. Suppose, for example, the null hypothesis states that the population is distributed in three categories with the following proportions:

	Category A	Category B	Category C
H_0:	25%	50%	25%

(The population is distributed across the three categories with 25% in category A, 50% in category B, and 25% in category C.)

If this hypothesis is correct, how would you expect a random sample of $n = 40$ individuals to be distributed among the three categories? It should be clear that your best strategy is to predict that 25% of the sample would be in category A, 50% would be in category B, and 25% would be in category C. To find the exact frequency expected for each category, multiply the sample size (n) by the proportion (or percentage) from the null hypothesis. For this example, you would expect

25% of 40 = 0.25(40) = 10 individuals in category A

50% of 40 = 0.50(40) = 20 individuals in category B

25% of 40 = 0.25(40) = 10 individuals in category C

The frequency values predicted from the null hypothesis are called *expected frequencies*. The symbol for expected frequency is f_e, and the expected frequency for each category is computed by

$$\text{expected frequency} = f_e = pn \qquad (17.1)$$

where p is the proportion stated in the null hypothesis and n is the sample size.

DEFINITION

The **expected frequency** for each category is the frequency value that is predicted from the proportions in the null hypothesis and the sample size (n). The expected frequencies define an ideal, *hypothetical* sample distribution that would be obtained if the sample proportions were in perfect agreement with the proportions specified in the null hypothesis.

Note that the no-preference null hypothesis always produces equal f_e values for all categories because the proportions (p) are the same for all categories. On the other hand, the no-difference null hypothesis typically does not produce equal values for the expected frequencies because the hypothesized proportions typically vary from one category to another. You also should note that the expected frequencies are calculated, hypothetical values and the numbers that you obtain may be decimals or fractions. The observed frequencies, on the other hand, always represent real individuals and always are whole numbers.

THE CHI-SQUARE STATISTIC

The general purpose of any hypothesis test is to determine whether the sample data support or refute a hypothesis about the population. In the chi-square test for goodness of fit, the sample is expressed as a set of observed frequencies (f_o values), and the null hypothesis is used to generate a set of expected frequencies (f_e values). The *chi-square statistic* simply measures how well the data (f_o) fit the hypothesis (f_e). The symbol for the chi-square statistic is χ^2. The formula for the chi-square statistic is

$$\text{chi-square} = \chi^2 = \Sigma \frac{(f_o - f_e)^2}{f_e} \qquad (17.2)$$

As the formula indicates, the value of chi-square is computed by the following steps:

1. Find the difference between f_o (the data) and f_e (the hypothesis) for each category.
2. Square the difference. This ensures that all values are positive.
3. Next, divide the squared difference by f_e.
4. Finally, add the values from all of the categories.

The first two steps determine the numerator of the chi-square statistic and should be easy to understand. Specifically, the numerator measures how much difference there is between the data (the f_o values) and the hypothesis (represented by the f_e values). The final step is also reasonable: we add the values to obtain the total discrepancy between the data and the hypothesis. Thus, a large value for chi-square indicates that the data do not fit the hypothesis, and leads us to reject the null hypothesis.

However, the third step, which determines the denominator of the chi-square statistic, is not so obvious. Why must we divide by f_e before we add the category values? The answer to this question is that the obtained discrepancy between f_o and f_e is viewed as *relatively* large or *relatively* small depending on the size of the expected frequency. This point is demonstrated in the following analogy.

Suppose that you were going to throw a party and you *expected* 1,000 people to show up. However, at the party you counted the number of guests and *observed* that 1,040 actually showed up. Forty more guests than expected are no major problem when all along you were planning for 1,000. There will still probably be enough beer and potato chips for everyone. On the other hand, suppose you had a party and you expected 10 people to attend but instead 50 actually showed up. Forty more guests in this case spell big trouble. How "significant" the discrepancy is depends in part on what you were originally expecting. With very large expected frequencies, allowances are made for more error between f_o and f_e. This is accomplished in the chi-square formula by dividing the squared discrepancy for each category, $(f_o - f_e)^2$, by its expected frequency.

THE CHI-SQUARE DISTRIBUTION AND DEGREES OF FREEDOM

It should be clear from the chi-square formula that the numerical value of chi-square is a measure of the discrepancy between the observed frequencies (data) and the expected frequencies (H_0). As usual, the sample data are not expected to provide a perfectly accurate representation of the population. In this case, the proportions or observed frequencies in the sample are not expected to be exactly equal to the proportions in the population. Thus, if there are small discrepancies between the f_o and f_e values, we obtain a small value for chi-square and we conclude that there is a good fit between the data and the hypothesis (fail to reject H_0). However, when there are large discrepancies between f_o and f_e, we obtain a large value for chi-square and conclude that the data do not fit the hypothesis (reject H_0). To decide whether a particular chi-square value is "large" or "small," we must refer to a *chi-square distribution.* This distribution is the set of chi-square values for all of the possible random samples when H_0 is true. Much like other distributions that we have examined (t distribution, F distribution), the chi-square distribution is a theoretical distribution with well-defined characteristics. Some of these characteristics are easy to infer from the chi-square formula.

1. The formula for chi-square involves adding squared values, so you can never obtain a negative value. Thus, all chi-square values are zero or larger.
2. When H_0 is true, you expect the data (f_o values) to be close to the hypothesis (f_e values). Thus, we expect chi-square values to be small when H_0 is true.

These two factors suggest that the typical chi-square distribution is positively skewed (Figure 17.2). Note that small values, near zero, are expected when H_0 is true and large values (in the right-hand tail) are very unlikely. Thus, unusually large values of chi-square form the critical region for the hypothesis test.

Although the typical chi-square distribution is positively skewed, there is one other factor that plays a role in the exact shape of the chi-square distribution—the number of categories. Recall that the chi-square formula requires that you add values from every category. The more categories you have, the more likely it is that you will obtain a large sum for the chi-square value. On average, chi-square is larger when you are adding values from 10 categories than when you are adding values from only 3 categories. As a result, there is a whole family of chi-square distributions, with the exact shape of each distribution determined by the number of categories used in the study. Technically, each specific chi-square distribution is identified by degrees of freedom (*df*) rather than the number of categories. For the goodness-of-fit test, the degrees of freedom are determined by

$$df = C - 1 \qquad (17.3)$$

Caution: The *df* for a chi-square test is *not* related to sample size (n), as it is in most other tests.

where C is the number of categories. A brief discussion of this *df* formula is presented in Box 17.1. Figure 17.3 shows the general relationship between *df* and the shape of the chi-square distribution. Note that the chi-square values tend to get larger (shift to the right) as the number of categories and the degrees of freedom increase.

FIGURE 17.2

Chi-square distributions are positively skewed. The critical region is placed in the extreme tail, which reflects large chi-square values.

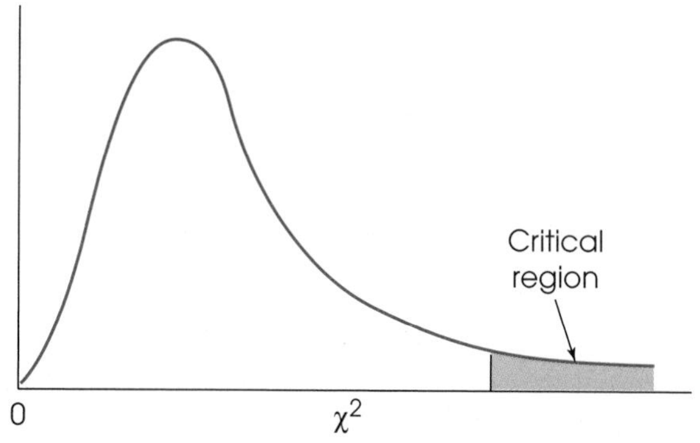

BOX 17.1 A CLOSER LOOK AT DEGREES OF FREEDOM

Degrees of freedom for the chi-square test literally measure the number of free choices that exist when you are determining the null hypothesis or the expected frequencies. For example, when you are classifying individuals into three categories, you have exactly two free choices in stating the null hypothesis. You may select any two proportions for the first two categories, but then the third proportion is determined. If you hypothesize 25% in the first category and 50% in the second category, then the third category must be 25% to account for 100% of the population.

Category A	Category B	Category C
10	20	?

In general, you are free to select proportions for all but one of the categories, but then the final proportion is determined by the fact that the entire set must total 100%. Thus, you have $C - 1$ free choices, where C is the number of categories: degrees of freedom, df, equal $C - 1$.

LOCATING THE CRITICAL REGION FOR A CHI-SQUARE TEST

Recall that a large value for the chi-square statistic indicates a big discrepancy between the data and the hypothesis, and suggests that we reject H_0. To determine whether a particular chi-square value is significantly large, you must consult the table entitled The Chi-Square Distribution (Appendix B). A portion of the chi-square table is shown in Table 17.2. The first column lists df values for the chi-square test, and the other column heads are proportions (alpha levels) in the extreme right-hand tail of the distribution. The numbers in the body of the table are the critical values of chi-square. The table shows, for example, that when the null hypothesis is true and $df = 3$, only 5% (.05) of the chi-square values are greater than 7.81, and only 1% (.01) are greater than 11.34. Thus, with $df = 3$, any chi-square value greater than 7.81 has a probability of $p < .05$, and any value greater than 11.34 has a probability of $p < .01$.

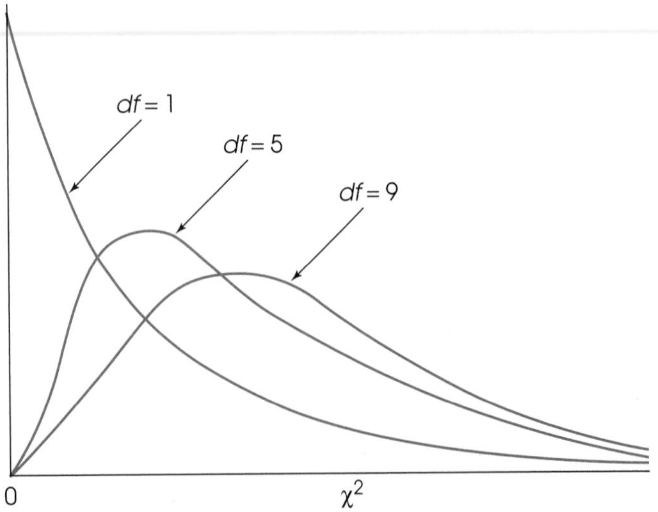

FIGURE 17.3
The shape of the chi-square distribution for different values of *df*. As the number of categories increases, the peak (mode) of the distribution has a larger chi-square value.

TABLE 17.2

A portion of the table of critical values for the chi-square distribution.

	Proportion in Critical Region				
df	0.10	0.05	0.025	0.01	0.005
1	2.71	3.84	5.02	6.63	7.88
2	4.61	5.99	7.38	9.21	10.60
3	6.25	7.81	9.35	11.34	12.84
4	7.78	9.49	11.14	13.28	14.86
5	9.24	11.07	12.83	15.09	16.75
6	10.64	12.59	14.45	16.81	18.55
7	12.02	14.07	16.01	18.48	20.28
8	13.36	15.51	17.53	20.09	21.96
9	14.68	16.92	19.02	21.67	23.59

EXAMPLE OF THE CHI-SQUARE TEST FOR GOODNESS OF FIT

We use the same step-by-step process for testing hypotheses with chi-square as we used for other hypothesis tests. In general, the steps consist of stating the hypotheses, locating the critical region, computing the test statistic, and making a decision about H_0. The following example demonstrates the complete process of hypothesis testing with the goodness-of-fit test.

EXAMPLE 17.1

A psychologist examining art appreciation selected an abstract painting that had no obvious top or bottom. Hangers were placed on the painting so that it could be hung with any one of the four sides at the top. The painting was shown to a sample of $n = 50$ participants, and each was asked to hang the painting in the orientation that looked correct. The following data indicate how many people chose each of the four sides to be placed at the top:

Top Up (Correct)	Bottom Up	Left Side Up	Right Side Up
18	17	7	8

The question for the hypothesis test is whether there are any preferences among the four possible orientations. Are any of the orientations selected more (or less) often than would be expected simply by chance?

STEP 1 State the hypotheses and select an alpha level. The hypotheses can be stated as follows:

H_0: In the general population, there is no preference for any specific orientation. Thus, the four possible orientations are selected equally often, and the population distribution has the following proportions:

Top Up (Correct)	Bottom Up	Left Side Up	Right Side Up
25%	25%	25%	25%

H_1: In the general population, one or more of the orientations is preferred over the others.

We use $\alpha = .05$.

STEP 2 Locate the critical region. For this example, the value for degrees of freedom is

$$df = C - 1 = 4 - 1 = 3$$

For $df = 3$ and $\alpha = .05$, the table of critical values for chi-square indicates that the critical χ^2 has a value of 7.81. The critical region is sketched in Figure 17.4.

STEP 3 Calculate the chi-square statistic. The calculation of chi-square is actually a two-stage process. First, you must compute the expected frequencies from H_0 and then calculate the value of the chi-square statistic. For this example, the null hypothesis specifies that one-quarter of the population ($p = 25\%$) will be in each of the four categories. According to this hypothesis, we should expect one-quarter of the sample to be in each category. With a sample of $n = 50$ individuals, the expected frequency for each category is

Expected frequencies are computed and may be decimal values. Observed frequencies are always whole numbers.

$$f_e = pn = \frac{1}{4}(50) = 12.5$$

The observed frequencies and the expected frequencies are presented in Table 17.3. Using these values, the chi-square statistic may now be calculated.

$$\chi^2 = \Sigma\frac{(f_o - f_e)^2}{f_e}$$

$$= \frac{(18-12.5)^2}{12.5} + \frac{(17-12.5)^2}{12.5} + \frac{(7-12.5)^2}{12.5} + \frac{(8-12.5)^2}{12.5}$$

$$= \frac{30.25}{12.5} + \frac{20.25}{12.5} + \frac{30.25}{12.5} + \frac{20.25}{12.5}$$

$$= 2.42 + 1.62 + 2.42 + 1.62$$

$$= 8.08$$

STEP 4 State a decision and a conclusion. The obtained chi-square value is in the critical region. Therefore, H_0 is rejected, and the researcher may conclude that the four orientations are not equally likely to be preferred. Instead, there are significant differences among the four orientations, with some selected more often and others less often than would be expected by chance.

FIGURE 17.4

For Example 17.1, the critical region begins at a chi-square value of 7.81.

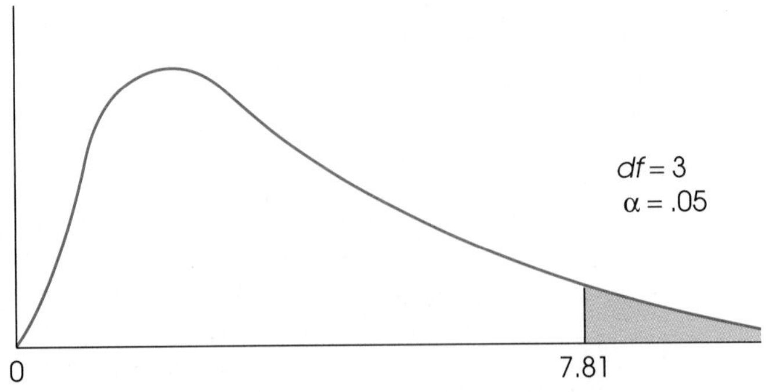

TABLE 17.3

The observed frequencies and the expected frequencies for the chi-square test in Example 17.1.

	Top Up (Correct)	Bottom Up	Left Side Up	Right Side Up
Observed Frequencies	18	17	7	8
Expected Frequencies	12.5	12.5	12.5	12.5

IN THE LITERATURE

REPORTING THE RESULTS FOR CHI-SQUARE

APA style specifies the format for reporting the chi-square statistic in scientific journals. For the results of Example 17.1, the report might state:

> The participants showed significant preferences among the four orientations for hanging the painting, $\chi^2(3, n = 50) = 8.08, p < .05$.

Note that the form of the report is similar to that of other statistical tests we have examined. Degrees of freedom are indicated in parentheses following the chi-square symbol. Also contained in the parentheses is the sample size (n). This additional information is important because the degrees of freedom value is based on the number of categories (C), not sample size. Next, the calculated value of chi-square is presented, followed by the probability that a Type I error has been committed. Because we obtained an extreme, very unlikely value for the chi-square statistic, the probability is reported as *less than* the alpha level. Additionally, the report may provide the observed frequencies (f_o) for each category. This information may be presented in a simple sentence or in a table.

GOODNESS OF FIT AND THE SINGLE-SAMPLE *t* TEST

We began this chapter with a general discussion of the difference between parametric tests and nonparametric tests. In this context, the chi-square test for goodness of fit is an example of a nonparametric test; that is, it makes no assumptions about the parameters of the population distribution, and it does not require data from an interval or ratio scale. In contrast, the single-sample t test introduced in Chapter 9 is an example of a parametric test: It assumes a normal population, it tests hypotheses about the population mean (a parameter), and it requires numerical scores that can be added, squared, divided, and so on.

Although the chi-square test and the single-sample t are clearly distinct, they are also very similar. In particular, both tests are intended to use the data from a single sample to test hypotheses about a single population.

The primary factor that determines whether you should use the chi-square test or the t test is the type of measurement that is obtained for each participant. If the sample data consist of numerical scores (from an interval or ratio scale), it is appropriate to compute a sample mean and use a t test to evaluate a hypothesis about the population mean. For example, a researcher could measure the IQ for each individual in a sample of registered voters. A t test could then be used to evaluate a hypothesis about the mean IQ for the entire population of registered voters. On the other hand, if the individuals in the sample are classified into nonnumerical categories (on a nominal or ordinal scale), then the researcher would use a chi-square test to evaluate a hypothesis about the population proportions. For example, a researcher could classify people according to gender by simply counting the number of males and females in a sample of registered voters. A chi-square test would then be appropriate to evaluate a hypothesis about the population proportions.

LEARNING CHECK

1. For a chi-square test, the observed frequencies are always whole numbers. (True or false?)
2. For a chi-square test, the expected frequencies are always whole numbers. (True or false?)
3. A researcher has developed three different designs for a computer keyboard. A sample of $n = 60$ participants is obtained, and each individual tests all three keyboards and identifies his or her favorite. The frequency distribution of preferences is as follows:

Design A	Design B	Design C	
23	12	25	$n = 60$

   a. What is the *df* value for the chi-square statistic?
   b. Assuming that the null hypothesis states that there are no preferences among the three designs, find the expected frequencies for the chi-square test.

ANSWERS

1. True. Observed frequencies are obtained by counting people in the sample.
2. False. Expected frequencies are computed and may be fractions or decimal values.
3. a. $df = 2$
   b. According to the null hypothesis one-third of the population would prefer each design. The expected frequencies should show one-third of the sample preferring each design. The expected frequencies are all 20.

17.3 THE CHI-SQUARE TEST FOR INDEPENDENCE

The chi-square statistic may also be used to test whether there is a relationship between two variables. In this situation, each individual in the sample is measured or classified on two separate variables. For example, a group of students could be classified in terms of personality (introvert, extrovert) and in terms of color preference (red, yellow, green, or blue). Usually, the data from this classification are presented in the form of a matrix, where the rows correspond to the categories of one variable and the columns correspond to the categories of the second variable. Table 17.4 presents hypothetical data for a sample of $n = 200$ students who have been classified by personality and color preference. The number in each box, or cell, of the matrix indicates the frequency, or number of individuals in that particular group. In Table 17.4, for example, there are 10 students who were classified as introverted and who selected red as their preferred color. To obtain these data, the researcher first selects a random sample of $n = 200$ students. Each student is then given a personality test and is asked to select a preferred color from among the four choices. Note that the classification is based on the measurements for each student; the researcher does not assign students to categories. Also, note that the data consist of frequencies, not scores, from a sample. The goal is to use the frequencies from the sample to test a hypothesis about the population frequency distribution. Specifically, are these data sufficient to conclude that there is a significant relationship between personality and color preference in the population of students?

You should realize that the color preference study shown in Table 17.3 is an example of nonexperimental research (Chapter 1, page 17). The researcher did not manipulate any variable and the participants were not randomly assigned to groups or

TABLE 17.4

Color preferences according to personality types.

	Red	Yellow	Green	Blue	
Introvert	10	3	15	22	50
Extrovert	90	17	25	18	150
	100	20	40	40	$n = 200$

treatment conditions. However, similar data are often obtained from true experiments. A good example is the study described in the Preview, in which Loftus and Palmer (1974) demonstrate how eyewitness memory can be influenced by the kinds of questions that witnesses are asked. In the study, a sample of 150 students watched a film of an automobile accident. After watching the film, the students were separated into three groups and questioned about the accident. The researchers manipulated the type of question each group was asked. One group was asked to estimate the speed of the cars when they "smashed into each other." Another group estimated speed when the cars "hit each other." A third group served as a control and was not asked any question about the speed of the two cars. A week later, the participants returned and were asked if they remembered seeing any broken glass in the accident. (There was no broken glass in the film.) The researchers recorded the number of Yes and No responses for each group (see Table 17.1, page 592). As with the color preference data, the researchers would like to use the frequencies from the sample to test a hypothesis about the corresponding frequency distribution in the population. In this case, the researchers would like to know whether the sample data provide enough evidence to conclude that there is a significant relationship between eyewitnesses' memories and the questions they were asked.

The procedure for using sample frequencies to evaluate hypotheses concerning relationships between variables involves another test using the chi-square statistic. In this situation, however, the test is called the *chi-square test for independence.*

DEFINITION

The **chi-square test for independence** uses the frequency data from a sample to evaluate the relationship between two variables in the population. Each individual in the sample is classified on both of the two variables, creating a two-dimensional frequency-distribution matrix. The frequency distribution for the sample is then used to test hypotheses about the corresponding frequency distribution for the population.

THE NULL HYPOTHESIS FOR THE CHI-SQUARE TEST FOR INDEPENDENCE

The null hypothesis for the chi-square test for independence states that the two variables being measured are independent; that is, for each individual, the value obtained for one variable is not related to (or influenced by) the value for the second variable. This general hypothesis can be expressed in two different conceptual forms, each viewing the data and the test from slightly different perspectives. The data in Table 17.4 describing color preference and personality are used to present both versions of the null hypothesis.

H_0 version 1 For this version of H_0, the data are viewed as a single sample with each individual measured on two variables. The goal of the chi-square test is to evaluate the relationship between the two variables. For the example we are considering, the goal is to determine whether there is a consistent, predictable relationship between personality and color preference. That is, if I know your personality, will it help me to predict your color preference? The null hypothesis states that there is no relationship. The alternative hypothesis, H_1, states that there is a relationship between the two variables.

H_0: For the general population of students, there is no relationship between color preference and personality.

This version of H_0 demonstrates the similarity between the chi-square test for independence and a correlation. In each case, the data consist of two measurements (*X* and *Y*) for each individual, and the goal is to evaluate the relationship between the two variables. The correlation, however, requires numerical scores for *X* and *Y*. The chi-square test, on the other hand, simply uses frequencies for individuals classified into categories.

H_0 version 2 For this version of H_0, the data are viewed as two (or more) separate samples representing two (or more) populations or treatment conditions. The goal of the chi-square test is to determine whether there are significant differences between the populations. For the example we are considering, the data in Table 17.4 would be viewed as a sample of $n = 50$ introverts (top row) and a separate sample of $n = 150$ extroverts (bottom row). The chi-square test determines whether the distribution of color preferences for introverts is significantly different from the distribution of color preferences for extroverts. From this perspective, the null hypothesis is stated as follows:

H_0: In the population of students, the proportions in the distribution of color preferences for introverts are not different from the proportions in the distribution of color preferences for extroverts. The two distributions have the same shape (same proportions).

This version of H_0 demonstrates the similarity between the chi-square test and an independent-measures *t* test (or ANOVA). In each case, the data consist of two (or more) separate samples that are being used to test for differences between two (or more) populations. The *t* test (or ANOVA) requires numerical scores to compute means and mean differences. However, the chi-square test simply uses frequencies for individuals classified into categories. The null hypothesis for the chi-square test states that the populations have the same proportions (same shape). The alternative hypothesis, H_1, simply states that the populations have different proportions. For the example we are considering, H_1 states that the shape of the distribution of color preferences for introverts is different from the shape of the distribution of color preferences for extroverts.

Equivalence of H_0 version 1 and H_0 version 2 Although we have presented two different statements of the null hypothesis, these two versions are equivalent. The first version of H_0 states that color preference is not related to personality. If this hypothesis is correct, then the distribution of color preferences should not depend on personality. In other words, the distribution of color preferences should have the same proportions for introverts and for extroverts, which is the second version of H_0.

For example, if we found that 60% of the introverts preferred red, then H_0 would predict that we also should find that 60% of the extroverts prefer red. In this case, knowing that an individual prefers red does not help you predict his or her personality. Note that finding the *same proportions* indicates *no relationship*.

On the other hand, if the proportions were different, it would suggest that there is a relationship. For example, if red is preferred by 60% of the extroverts but only 10% of the introverts, then there is a clear, predictable relationship between personality and color preference. (If I know your personality, then I can predict your color preference.) Thus, finding *different proportions* means that there is *a relationship* between the two variables.

DEFINITION

Two variables are **independent** when there is no consistent, predictable relationship between them. In this case, the frequency distribution for one variable is not related to (or dependent on) the categories of the second variable. As a result, when two variables are independent, the frequency distribution for one variable has the same shape (same proportions) for all categories of the second variable.

Thus, stating that there is no relationship between two variables (version 1 of H_0) is equivalent to stating that the distributions have equal proportions (version 2 of H_0).

OBSERVED AND EXPECTED FREQUENCIES

The chi-square test for independence uses the same basic logic that was used for the goodness-of-fit test. First, a sample is selected and each individual is classified or categorized. Because the test for independence considers two variables, every individual is classified on both variables, and the resulting frequency distribution is presented as a two-dimensional matrix (see Table 17.4). As before, the frequencies in the sample distribution are called *observed frequencies* and are identified by the symbol f_o.

The next step is to find the expected frequencies, or f_e values, for this chi-square test. As before, the *expected frequencies* define an ideal hypothetical distribution that is in perfect agreement with the null hypothesis. Once the expected frequencies are obtained, we compute a chi-square statistic to determine how well the data (observed frequencies) fit the null hypothesis (expected frequencies).

Although you can use either version of the null hypothesis to find the expected frequencies, the logic of the process is much easier when you use H_0 stated in terms of equal proportions. For the example we are considering, the null hypothesis states

H_0: The frequency distribution of color preference has the same shape (same proportions) for both categories of personality.

To find the expected frequencies, we first determine the overall distribution of color preferences and then apply this distribution to both categories of personality. Table 17.5 shows an empty matrix corresponding to the data from Table 17.4. Notice that the empty matrix includes all of the row totals and column totals from the original sample data. The row totals and column totals are essential for computing the expected frequencies.

The column totals for the matrix describe the overall distribution of color preferences. For these data, 100 people selected red as their preferred color. Because the total sample consists of 200 people, the proportion selecting red is 100 out of 200, or 50%. The complete set of color preference proportions is as follows:

100 out of 200 = 50% prefer red

20 out of 200 = 10% prefer yellow

40 out of 200 = 20% prefer green

40 out of 200 = 20% prefer blue

The row totals in the matrix define the two samples of personality types. For example, the matrix in Table 17.5 shows a total of 50 introverts (the top row) and a sample of 150 extroverts (the bottom row). According to the null hypothesis, both personality groups should have the same proportions for color preferences. To find the expected frequencies, we simply apply the overall distribution of color preferences to

TABLE 17.5

An empty frequency distribution matrix showing only the row totals and column totals. (These numbers describe the basic characteristics of the sample from Table 17.4.)

	Red	Yellow	Green	Blue	
Introvert					50
Extrovert					150
	100	20	40	40	

each sample. Beginning with the sample of 50 introverts in the top row, we obtain expected frequencies of

50% prefer red:	$f_e = 50\%$ of $50 = 0.50(50) = 25$
10% prefer yellow:	$f_e = 10\%$ of $50 = 0.10(50) = 5$
20% prefer green:	$f_e = 20\%$ of $50 = 0.20(50) = 10$
20% prefer blue:	$f_e = 20\%$ of $50 = 0.20(50) = 10$

Using exactly the same proportions for the sample of $n = 150$ extroverts in the bottom row, we obtain expected frequencies of

50% prefer red:	$f_e = 50\%$ of $150 = 0.50(50) = 75$
10% prefer yellow:	$f_e = 10\%$ of $150 = 0.10(50) = 15$
20% prefer green:	$f_e = 20\%$ of $150 = 0.20(50) = 30$
20% prefer blue:	$f_e = 20\%$ of $150 = 0.20(50) = 30$

The complete set of expected frequencies is shown in Table 17.6. Notice that the row totals and the column totals for the expected frequencies are the same as those for the original data (the observed frequencies) in Table 17.3.

A simple formula for determining expected frequencies Although expected frequencies are derived directly from the null hypothesis and the sample characteristics, it is not necessary to go through extensive calculations to find f_e values. In fact, there is a simple formula that determines f_e for any cell in the frequency distribution matrix:

$$f_e = \frac{f_c f_r}{n} \tag{17.4}$$

where f_c is the frequency total for the column (column total), f_r is the frequency total for the row (row total), and n is the number of individuals in the entire sample. To demonstrate this formula, we compute the expected frequency for introverts selecting yellow in Table 17.6. First, note that this cell is located in the top row and second column in the table. The column total is $f_c = 20$, the row total is $f_r = 50$, and the sample size is $n = 200$. Using these values in formula 17.4, we obtain

$$f_e = \frac{f_c f_r}{n} = \frac{20(50)}{200} = 5$$

TABLE 17.6

Expected frequencies corresponding to the data in Table 17.4. (This is the distribution predicted by the null hypothesis.)

	Red	Yellow	Green	Blue	
Introvert	25	5	10	10	50
Extrovert	75	15	30	30	150
	100	20	40	40	

This is identical to the expected frequency we obtained using percentages from the overall distribution.

THE CHI-SQUARE STATISTIC AND DEGREES OF FREEDOM

The chi-square test for independence uses exactly the same chi-square formula as the test for goodness of fit:

$$\chi^2 = \Sigma \frac{(f_o - f_e)^2}{f_e}$$

As before, the formula measures the discrepancy between the data (f_o values) and the hypothesis (f_e values). A large discrepancy produces a large value for chi-square and indicates that H_0 should be rejected. To determine whether a particular chi-square statistic is significantly large, you must first determine degrees of freedom (*df*) for the statistic and then consult the chi-square distribution in Appendix B. For the chi-square test of independence, degrees of freedom are based on the number of cells for which you can freely choose expected frequencies. Recall that the f_e values are partially determined by the sample size (n) and by the row totals and column totals from the original data. These various totals restrict your freedom in selecting expected frequencies. This point is illustrated in Table 17.7. Once three of the f_e values have been selected, all of the other f_e values in the table are also determined. For example, the bottom number in the first column must be 75 to produce a column total of 100. Similarly, the last number in the top row must be 10 to produce a row total of 50. In general, the row totals and the column totals restrict the final choices in each row and column. As a result, we may freely choose all but one f_e in each row and all but one f_e in each column. If R is the number of rows and C is the number of columns, and you remove the last column and the bottom row from the matrix, you are left with a smaller matrix that has $C - 1$ columns and $R - 1$ rows. The number of cells in the smaller matrix determines the *df* value. Thus, the total number of f_e values that you can freely choose is $(R - 1)(C - 1)$, and the degrees of freedom for the chi-square test of independence are given by the formula

$$df = (R - 1)(C - 1) \tag{17.5}$$

Also note that once you calculate the expected frequencies to fill the smaller matrix, the rest of the f_e values can be found by subtraction.

AN EXAMPLE OF THE CHI-SQUARE TEST FOR INDEPENDENCE

The following example demonstrates the complete hypothesis-testing procedure for the chi-square test for independence.

TABLE 17.7

Degrees of freedom and expected frequencies. (Once three values have been selected, all the remaining expected frequencies are determined by the row totals and the column totals. This example has only three free choices, so $df = 3$.)

Red	Yellow	Green	Blue	
25	5	10	?	50
?	?	?	?	150
100	20	40	40	

EXAMPLE 17.2 Research has demonstrated strong gender differences in teenagers' approaches to dealing with mental health issues (Chandra & Minkovitz, 2006). In a typical study, eighth-grade students are asked to report their willingness to use mental health services in the event they were experiencing emotional or other mental health problems. Typical data for a sample of $n = 150$ students are shown in Table 17.8. Do the data show a significant relationship between gender and willingness to seek mental health assistance?

STEP 1 State the hypotheses, and select a level of significance. According to the null hypothesis, the two variables are independent. This general hypothesis can be stated in two different ways:

Version 1

H_0: In the general population, there is no relationship between gender and willingness to use mental health services.

This version of H_0 emphasizes the similarity between the chi-square test and a correlation. The corresponding alternative hypothesis would state:

H_1: In the general population, there is a consistent, predictable relationship between gender and willingness to use mental health services.

Version 2

H_0: In the general population, the distribution of reported willingness to use mental health services has the same proportions for males and for females.

The corresponding alternative hypothesis would state:

H_1: In the general population, the distribution of reported willingness to use mental health services for males has proportions that are different from those in the distribution for females.

The second version of H_0 emphasizes the similarity between the chi-square test and the independent-measures *t* test.

Remember that the two versions for the hypotheses are equivalent. The choice between them is largely determined by how the researcher wants to describe the outcome. For example, a researcher may want to emphasize the *relationship* between variables or the *difference* between groups.

For this test, we use $\alpha = .05$.

STEP 2 Determine the degrees of freedom and locate the critical region. For the chi-square test for independence,

$$df = (R - 1)(C - 1) = (2 - 1)(3 - 1) = 2$$

With $df = 2$ and $\alpha = .05$, the critical value for chi-square is 5.99 (see Table B.8, p. 711).

TABLE 17.8

A frequency distribution showing willingness to use mental health services according to gender for a sample of $n = 150$ students.

	Willingness to Use Mental Health Services			
	Probably No	Maybe	Probably Yes	
Males	17	32	11	60
Females	13	43	34	90
	30	75	45	$n = 150$

STEP 3 Determine the expected frequencies, and compute the chi-square statistic. The following table shows an empty matrix with the same row totals and column totals as the original data. The expected frequencies must maintain the same row totals and column totals, and create an ideal frequency distribution that perfectly represents the null hypothesis. Specifically, the proportions for the group of 60 males must be the same as the proportions for the group of 90 females.

Willingness to Use Mental Health Services

	Probably No	Maybe	Probably Yes	
Males				60
Females				90
	30	75	45	$n = 150$

The column totals describe the overall distribution of willingness. These totals indicate that 30 out of 150 students reported that they would probably not use mental health services. This proportion corresponds to $\frac{30}{150}$, or 20% of the total sample. Similarly, $\frac{75}{150} = 50\%$ reported that they might use mental health services. Finally, $\frac{45}{150} = 30\%$ reported that they probably would use the services. The null hypothesis (version 2) states that these proportions are the same for males and females. Therefore, we simply apply the proportions to each group to obtain the expected frequencies. For the group of 60 males (top row), we obtain

20% of 60 = 12 males who would probably not seek services

50% of 60 = 30 males who might seek services

30% of 60 = 18 males who probably would seek services

For the group of 90 females (bottom row), we expect

20% of 90 = 18 females who would probably not seek services

50% of 90 = 45 females who may seek services

30% of 90 = 27 females who probably would seek services

These expected frequencies are summarized in Table 17.9.

The chi-square statistic is now used to measure the discrepancy between the data (the observed frequencies in Table 17.8) and the null hypothesis that was used to generate the expected frequencies in Table 17.9.

TABLE 17.9

The expected frequencies (f_e values) of willingness to use mental services is completely independent of gender.

Willingness to Use Mental Health Services

	Probably No	Maybe	Probably Yes	
Males	12	30	18	60
Females	18	45	27	90
	30	75	45	

$$\chi^2 = \frac{(17-12)^2}{12} + \frac{(32-30)^2}{30} - \frac{(11-18)^2}{18}$$

$$+ \frac{(13-18)^2}{18} + \frac{(43-45)^2}{45} + \frac{(34-27)^2}{27}$$

$$= 2.08 + 0.13 + 2.72 + 1.39 + 0.09 + 1.82$$

$$= 8.23$$

STEP 4 Make a decision regarding the null hypothesis and the outcome of the study. The obtained chi-square value exceeds the critical value (5.99). Therefore, the decision is to reject the null hypothesis. In the literature, this would be reported as a significant result with $\chi^2(2, n = 150) = 8.23$, $p < .05$. According to version 1 of H_0, this means that we have decided there is a significant relationship between gender and willingness to use mental health services. Expressed in terms of version 2 of H_0, the data show a significant difference between males' and females' attitudes toward using mental health services. To describe the details of the significant result, you must compare the original data (Table 17.8) with the expected frequencies in Table 17.9. Looking at the two tables, it should be clear that males were less willing to use mental health services and females were more willing than would be expected if the two variables were independent.

LEARNING CHECK

1. A researcher would like to know which factors are most important to people who are buying a new car. A sample of $n = 200$ customers between the ages of 20 and 29 are asked to identify the most important factor in the decision process: Performance, Reliability, or Style. The researcher would like to know whether there is a difference between the factors identified by women compared to those identified by men. The data are as follows:

	Observed Frequencies of Most Important factor According to Gender			
	Performance	Reliability	Style	Totals
Male	21	33	26	80
Female	19	67	34	120
Totals	40	100	60	

a. State the null hypotheses.

b. Determine the value for *df* for the chi-square test.

c. Compute the expected frequencies.

ANSWERS **1. a.** H_0: In the population, the distribution of preferred factors for men has the same proportions as the distribution for women.

b. $df = 2$

c. f_e values are as follows:

Expected Frequencies

	Performance	Reliability	Style
Male	16	40	24
Female	24	60	36

17.4 MEASURING EFFECT SIZE FOR THE CHI-SQUARE TEST FOR INDEPENDENCE

A hypothesis test, like the chi-square test for independence, evaluates the statistical significance of the results from a research study. Specifically, the intent of the test is to determine whether it is likely that the patterns or relationships observed in the sample data could have occurred without any corresponding patterns or relationships in the population. Tests of significance are influenced not only by the size or strength of the treatment effects but also by the size of the samples. As a result, even a small effect can be statistically significant if it is observed in a very large sample. Because a significant effect does not necessarily mean a large effect, it is generally recommended that the outcome of a hypothesis test be accompanied by a measure of the effect size. This general recommendation also applies to the chi-square test for independence.

THE PHI-COEFFICIENT AND CRAMÉR'S *V*

In Chapter 15 (p. 545), we introduced the *phi-coefficient* as a measure of correlation for data consisting of two dichotomous variables (both variables have exactly two values). This same situation exists when the data for a chi-square test for independence form a 2 × 2 matrix (again, each variable has exactly two values). In this case, it is possible to compute the correlation phi (ϕ) in addition to the chi-square hypothesis test for the same set of data. Because phi is a correlation, it measures the strength of the relationship, rather than the significance, and thus provides a measure of effect size. The value for the phi-coefficient can be computed directly from chi-square by the following formula:

Caution: The value of χ^2 is already a squared value. Do not square it again.

$$\phi = \sqrt{\frac{\chi^2}{n}} \qquad (17.6)$$

The value of the phi-coefficient is determined entirely by the *proportions* in the 2 × 2 data matrix and is completely independent of the absolute size of the frequencies. The chi-square value, however, is influenced by the proportions and by the size of the frequencies. This distinction is demonstrated in the following example.

EXAMPLE 17.3 The following data show a frequency distribution evaluating the relationship between gender and preference between two candidates for student president.

Candidate

	A	B
Male	5	10
Female	10	5

Note that the data show that males prefer candidate B by a 2-to-1 margin and females prefer candidate A by 2 to 1. Also note that the sample includes a total of 15 males and 15 females. We will not perform all the arithmetic here, but these data produce chi-square equal to 3.33 (which is not significant) and a phi-coefficient of 0.333.

Next we keep exactly the same proportions in the data, but double all of the frequencies. The resulting data are as follows:

	Candidate A	Candidate B
Male	10	20
Female	20	10

Once again, males prefer candidate B by 2 to 1 and females prefer candidate A by 2 to 1. However, the sample now contains 30 males and 30 females. For these new data, the value of chi-square is 6.66, twice as big as it was before (and now significant with $\alpha = .05$), but the value of the phi-coefficient is still 0.333.

Because the proportions are the same for the two samples, the value of the phi-coefficient is unchanged. However, the larger sample provides more convincing evidence than the smaller sample, so the larger sample is more likely to produce a significant result.

The interpretation of ϕ follows the same standards used to evaluate a correlation (Table 9.3, p. 299 shows the standards for squared correlations): a correlation of 0.10 is a small effect, 0.30 is a medium effect, and 0.50 is a large effect. Occasionally, the value of ϕ is squared (ϕ^2) and is reported as a percentage of variance accounted for, exactly the same as r^2.

When the chi-square test involves a matrix larger than 2×2, a modification of the phi-coefficient, known as *Cramér's* V, can be used to measure effect size.

$$V = \sqrt{\frac{\chi^2}{n(df^*)}} \tag{17.7}$$

Note that the formula for Cramér's V (17.7) is identical to the formula for the phi-coefficient (17.6) except for the addition of df^* in the denominator. The df^* value is *not* the same as the degrees of freedom for the chi-square test, but it is related. Recall that the chi-square test for independence has $df = (R - 1)(C - 1)$, where R is the number of rows in the table and C is the number of columns. For Cramér's V, the value of df^* is the smaller of either $(R - 1)$ or $(C - 1)$.

Cohen (1988) has also suggested standards for interpreting Cramér's V that are shown in Table 17.10. Note that when $df^* = 1$, as in a 2×2 matrix, the criteria for interpreting V are exactly the same as the criteria for interpreting a regular correlation or a phi-coefficient.

We will use the results from Example 17.2 (p. 610) to demonstrate the calculation of Cramér's V. The example evaluated the relationship between gender and willingness to use mental health services. There were two levels of gender and three levels of willingness producing a 2×3 table with a total of $n = 150$ participants. The data produced $\chi^2 = 8.23$. Using these values, we obtain

$$V = \sqrt{\frac{\chi^2}{n(df^*)}} = \sqrt{\frac{8.23}{150(1)}} = \sqrt{0.055} = 0.23$$

TABLE 17.10

Standards for interpreting Cramér's V as proposed by Cohen (1988).

	Small Effect	Medium Effect	Large Effect
For $df^* = 1$	0.10	0.30	0.50
For $df^* = 2$	0.07	0.21	0.35
For $df^* = 3$	0.06	0.17	0.29

According to Cohen's guidelines (see Table 17.10), this value indicates a small or medium relationship.

In a research report, the measure of effect size appears immediately after the results of the hypothesis test. For the study in Example 17.2, the results would be reported as follows:

> The results showed a significant difference between males' and females' attitudes toward using mental health services, $\chi^2(2, n = 50) = 8.23, p < .05, V = 0.23$.

17.5 ASSUMPTIONS AND RESTRICTIONS FOR CHI-SQUARE TESTS

To use a chi-square test for goodness of fit or a test of independence, several conditions must be satisfied. For any statistical test, violation of assumptions and restrictions casts doubt on the results. For example, the probability of committing a Type I error may be distorted when assumptions of statistical tests are not satisfied. Some important assumptions and restrictions for using chi-square tests are the following:

1. **Independence of Observations.** This is *not* to be confused with the concept of independence between *variables,* as seen in the chi-square test for independence (Section 17.3). One consequence of independent observations is that each observed frequency is generated by a different individual. A chi-square test would be inappropriate if a person could produce responses that can be classified in more than one category or contribute more than one frequency count to a single category. (See p. 254 for more information on independence.)
2. **Size of Expected Frequencies.** A chi-square test should not be performed when the expected frequency of any cell is less than 5. The chi-square statistic can be distorted when f_e is very small. Consider the chi-square computations for a single cell. Suppose that the cell has values of $f_e = 1$ and $f_o = 5$. Note that there is a 4-point difference between the observed and expected frequencies. However, the total contribution of this cell to the total chi-square value is

$$\text{cell} = \frac{(f_o - f_e)^2}{f_e} = \frac{(5 - 1)^2}{1} = \frac{4^2}{1} = 16$$

Now consider another instance, in which $f_e = 10$ and $f_o = 14$. The difference between the observed and the expected frequencies is still 4, but the contribution of this cell to the total chi-square value differs from that of the first case:

$$\text{cell} = \frac{(f_o - f_e)^2}{f_e} = \frac{(14 - 10)^2}{10} = \frac{4^2}{10} = 1.6$$

It should be clear that a small f_e value can have a great influence on the chi-square value. This problem becomes serious when f_e values are less than 5. When f_e is very small, what would otherwise be a minor discrepancy between f_o and f_e results in large chi-square values. The test is too sensitive when f_e values are extremely small. One way to avoid small expected frequencies is to use large samples.

LEARNING CHECK

1. A researcher completes a chi-square test for independence and obtains $\chi^2 = 6.2$ for a sample of $n = 40$ participants.
   a. If the frequency data formed a 2 × 2 matrix, what is the phi-coefficient for the test?
   b. If the frequency data formed a 3 × 3 matrix, what is Cramér's V for the test?
2. Explain why a very small value for an expected frequency can distort the results of a chi-square test.

ANSWERS

1. **a.** $\phi = 0.394$
   b. $V = 0.278$
2. With a very small value for an expected frequency, even a minor discrepancy between the observed frequency and the expected frequency can produce a large number that is added into the chi-square statistic. This inflates the value of chi-square and can distort the outcome of the test.

17.6 SPECIAL APPLICATIONS OF THE CHI-SQUARE TESTS

At the beginning of this chapter, we introduced the chi-square tests as examples of nonparametric tests. Although nonparametric tests serve a function that is uniquely their own, they also can be viewed as alternatives to the common parametric tests that were examined in earlier chapters. In general, nonparametric tests are used as substitutes for parametric tests in situations in which one of the following occurs:

1. The data do not meet the assumptions needed for a standard parametric test.
2. The data consist of nominal or ordinal measurements, so that it is impossible to compute standard descriptive statistics such as the mean and standard deviation.

In this section, we examine some of the relationships between chi-square tests and the parametric procedures for which they may be substituted.

CHI-SQUARE AND THE PEARSON CORRELATION

The chi-square test for independence and the Pearson correlation are both statistical techniques intended to evaluate the relationship between two variables. The type of data obtained in a research study determines which of these two statistical procedures is appropriate. Suppose, for example, that a researcher is interested in the relationship between self-esteem and academic performance for 10-year-old children. If the researcher obtained numerical scores for both variables, then the resulting data would be similar to the values shown in Table 17.11(a) and the researcher could use a Pearson correlation to evaluate the relationship. On the other hand, if both variables are classified into non-numerical categories as in Table 17.11(b), then the data consist of frequencies and the relationship could be evaluated with a chi-square test for independence.

TABLE 17.11

Two possible data structures for research studies examining the relationship between self-esteem and academic performance. In part (a) there are numerical scores for both variables and the data are suitable for a correlation. In part (b) both variables are classified into categories and the data are frequencies suitable for a chi-square test.

(a)

Participant	Self-Esteem X	Academic Performance Y
A	13	73
B	19	88
C	10	71
D	22	96
E	20	90
F	15	82
.	.	.
.	.	.
.	.	.

(b)

		Level of Self-Esteem			
		High	Medium	Low	
Academic Performance	High	17	32	11	60
	Low	13	43	34	90
		30	75	45	$n = 150$

CHI-SQUARE AND THE INDEPENDENT-MEASURES *t* AND ANOVA

Once again, consider a researcher investigating the relationship between self-esteem and academic performance for 10-year-old children. This time, suppose that the researcher measured academic performance by simply classifying individuals into two categories, high and low, and then obtained a numerical score for each individual's self-esteem. The resulting data would be similar to the scores in Table 17.12(a), and an independent-measures t test would be used to evaluate the mean difference between the two groups of scores. Alternatively, the researcher could measure self-esteem by classifying individuals into three categories: high, medium, and low. If a numerical score is then obtained for each individual's academic performance, the resulting data would look like the scores in Table 17.12(b), and an ANOVA would be used to evaluate the mean differences among the three groups. Finally, if both variables are classified into non-numerical categories, then the data would look like the scores shown earlier in Table 17.11(b) and a chi-square test for independence would be used to evaluate the difference between the two academic-performance groups or the differences among the three self-esteem groups.

The point of these examples is that the chi-square test for independence, the Pearson correlation, and tests for mean differences can all be used to evaluate the relationship between two variables. One main distinction among the different statistical procedures is the form of the data. However, another distinction is the fundamental purpose of these different statistics. The chi-square test and the tests for mean differences (t and ANOVA) evaluate the *significance* of the relationship; that is, they determine whether the relationship observed in the sample provides enough evidence to conclude that there is a corresponding relationship in the population. You can also evaluate the significance of a Pearson correlation, however, the main purpose of a correlation is to measure the *strength* of the relationship. In particular, squaring the correlation, r^2,

TABLE 17.12

Data appropriate for an independent-measures t test or an ANOVA. In part (a), self-esteem scores are obtained for two groups of students differing in level of academic performance. In part (b), academic performance scores are obtained for three groups of students differing in level of self-esteem.

(a) Self-esteem scores for two groups of students.

Academic Performance	
High	Low
17	13
21	15
16	14
24	20
18	17
15	14
19	12
20	19
18	16

(b) Academic performance scores for three groups of students.

Self-esteem		
High	Medium	Low
94	83	80
90	76	72
85	70	81
84	81	71
89	78	77
96	88	70
91	83	78
85	80	72
88	82	75

provides a measure of effect size, describing the proportion of variance in one variable that is accounted for by its relationship with the other variable.

THE MEDIAN TEST FOR INDEPENDENT SAMPLES

The *median test* provides a nonparametric alternative to the independent-measures t test (or ANOVA) to determine whether there are significant differences among two or more independent samples. The null hypothesis for the median test states that the different samples come from populations that share a common median (no differences). The alternative hypothesis states that the samples come from populations that are different and do not share a common median.

The median is the score that divides the population in half, with 50% scoring at or below the median.

The logic behind the median test is that whenever several different samples are selected from the same population distribution, roughly half of the scores in each sample should be above the population median and roughly half should be below. That is, all of the separate samples should be distributed around the same median. On the other hand, if the samples come from populations with different medians, then the scores in some samples will be consistently higher and the scores in other samples will be consistently lower.

The first step in conducting the median test is to combine all of the scores from the separate samples and then find the median for the combined group (see Chapter 3, page 83, for instructions for finding the median). Next, a matrix is constructed with a column for each of the separate samples and two rows: one for individuals with scores above the median and one for individuals with scores below the median. Finally, for each sample, count how many individuals scored above the combined median and how many scored below. These values are the observed frequencies that are entered in the matrix.

The frequency-distribution matrix is evaluated using a chi-square test for independence. The expected frequencies and a value for chi-square are computed exactly as described in Section 17.3. A significant value for chi-square indicates that the discrepancy between the individual sample distributions is greater than would be expected by chance.

The median test is demonstrated in the following example.

EXAMPLE 17.4

The following data represent self-esteem scores obtained from a sample of $n = 40$ children. The children are then separated into three groups based on their level of academic performance (high, medium, low). The median test evaluates whether there is a significant relationship between self-esteem and level of academic performance.

Self-Esteem Scores for Children at Three Levels of Academic Performance

High		Medium				Low	
22	14	22	13	24	20	11	19
19	18	18	22	10	16	13	15
12	21	19	15	14	19	20	16
20	18	11	18	11	10	10	18
23	20	12	19	15	12	15	11

The median for the combined group of $n = 40$ scores is $X = 17$ (exactly 20 scores are above this value and 20 are below). For the high performers, 8 out of 10 scores are above the median. For the medium performers, 9 out of 20 are above the median, and for the low performers, only 3 out of 10 are above the median. These observed frequencies are shown in the following matrix:

Academic Performance

	High	Medium	Low
Above Median	8	9	3
Below Median	2	11	7

The expected frequencies for this test are as follows:

Academic Performance

	High	Medium	Low
Above Median	5	10	5
Below Median	5	10	5

The chi-square statistic is

$$\chi^2 = \frac{9}{5} + \frac{9}{5} + \frac{1}{10} + \frac{1}{10} + \frac{4}{5} + \frac{4}{5} = 5.40$$

With $df = 2$ and $\alpha = .05$, the critical value for chi-square is 5.99. The obtained chi-square of 5.40 does not fall in the critical region, so we would fail to reject the null hypothesis. These data do not provide sufficient evidence to conclude that there are significant differences among the self-esteem distributions for these three groups of students.

A few words of caution are in order concerning the interpretation of the median test. First, the median test is *not* a test for mean differences. Remember: The mean for a distribution can be strongly affected by a few extreme scores. Therefore, the mean and the median for a distribution are not necessarily the same, and they may not even be related. The results from a median test *cannot* be interpreted as indicating that there is (or is not) a difference between means.

Second, you may have noted that the median test does not directly compare the median from one sample with the median from another. Thus, the median test is not a test for significant differences between medians. Instead, this test compares the distribution of scores for one sample to the distribution for another sample. If the samples are distributed evenly around a common point (the group median), then you can conclude that there is no significant difference. On the other hand, finding a significant difference simply indicates that the samples are not distributed evenly around the common median. Thus, the best interpretation of a significant result is that there is a *difference in the distributions* of the samples.

SUMMARY

1. Chi-square tests are nonparametric techniques that test hypotheses about the form of the entire frequency distribution. Two types of chi-square tests are the test for goodness of fit and the test for independence. The data for these tests consist of the frequency or number of individuals who are located in each category.

2. The test for goodness of fit compares the frequency distribution for a sample to the population distribution that is predicted by H_0. The test determines how well the observed frequencies (sample data) fit the expected frequencies (data predicted by H_0).

3. The expected frequencies for the goodness-of-fit test are determined by

$$\text{expected frequency} = f_e = pn$$

where p is the hypothesized proportion (according to H_0) of observations falling into a category and n is the size of the sample.

4. The chi-square statistic is computed by

$$\chi^2 = \Sigma\frac{(f_o - f_e)^2}{f_e}$$

where f_o is the observed frequency for a particular category and f_e is the expected frequency for that category. Large values for χ^2 indicate that there is a large discrepancy between the observed (f_o) and the expected (f_e) frequencies and may warrant rejection of the null hypothesis.

5. Degrees of freedom for the test for goodness of fit are

$$df = C - 1$$

where C is the number of categories in the variable. Degrees of freedom measure the number of categories for which f_e values can be freely chosen. As can be seen from the formula, all but the last f_e value to be determined are free to vary.

6. The chi-square distribution is positively skewed and begins at the value of zero. Its exact shape is determined by degrees of freedom.

7. The test for independence is used to assess the relationship between two variables. The null hypothesis states that the two variables in question are independent of each other. That is, the frequency distribution for one variable does not depend on the categories of the second variable. On the other hand, if a relationship does exist, then the form of the distribution for one variable depends on the categories of the other variable.

8. For the test for independence, the expected frequencies for H_0 can be directly calculated from the marginal frequency totals,

$$f_e = \frac{f_c f_r}{n}$$

where f_c is the total column frequency and f_r is the total row frequency for the cell in question.

9. Degrees of freedom for the test for independence are computed by

$$df = (R - 1)(C - 1)$$

where R is the number of row categories and C is the number of column categories.

10. For the test for independence, a large chi-square value means there is a large discrepancy between the f_o and f_e values. Rejecting H_0 in this test provides support for a relationship between the two variables.

11. Both chi-square tests (for goodness of fit and independence) are based on the assumption that each observation is independent of the others. That is, each observed frequency reflects a different individual, and no individual can produce a response that would be

classified in more than one category or more than one frequency in a single category.

12. The chi-square statistic is distorted when f_e values are very small. Chi-square tests, therefore, should not be performed when the expected frequency of any cell is less than 5.

13. The effect size for a chi-square test for independence is measured by computing a phi-coefficient for data that form a 2 × 2 matrix or computing Cramér's V for a matrix that is larger than 2 × 2.

$$\text{phi} = \sqrt{\frac{\chi^2}{n}} \qquad \text{Cramér's } V = \sqrt{\frac{\chi^2}{n(df^*)}}$$

where df^* is the smaller of $(R - 1)$ and $(C - 1)$. Both phi and Cramér's V are evaluated using the criteria in Table 17.10.

KEY TERMS

parametric test (593)
nonparametric test (593)
chi-square test for goodness-of-fit (594)
observed frequencies (597)
expected frequencies (597)
chi-square statistic (598)
chi-square distribution (599)
chi-square test for independence (605)
phi-coefficient (613)
Cramér's V (614)
median test (618)

RESOURCES

Book Companion Website: www.cengage.com/psychology/gravetter
You can find a tutorial quiz and other learning exercises for Chapter 17 on the book companion website. The website also provides access to a workshop entitled *Chi-Square* that reviews the chi-square tests presented in this chapter.

aplia

Improve your understanding of statistics with Aplia's auto-graded problem sets and immediate, detailed explanations for every question. To learn more, visit **www.aplia.com/statistics.**

CENGAGE brain.com

Log in to CengageBrain to access the resources your instructor requires. For this book, you can access:

Psychology CourseMate brings course concepts to life with interactive learning, study, and exam preparation tools that support the printed textbook. A textbook-specific website, Psychology CourseMate includes an integrated interactive eBook and other interactive learning tools including quizzes, flashcards, and more.

Visit www.cengagebrain.com to access your account and purchase materials.

SPSS

General instructions for using SPSS are presented in Appendix D. Following are detailed instructions for using SPSS to perform **The Chi-Square Tests for Goodness of Fit and for Independence** that are presented in this chapter.

The Chi-Square Test for Goodness of Fit

Data Entry

1. Enter the set of observed frequencies in the first column of the SPSS data editor. If there are four categories, for example, enter the four observed frequencies.
2. In the second column, enter the numbers 1, 2, 3, and so on, so that there is a number beside each of the observed frequencies in the first column.

Data Analysis

1. Click **Data** on the tool bar at the top of the page and select **weight cases** at the bottom of the list.
2. Click the **Weight cases by** circle, then highlight the label for the column containing the observed frequencies (VAR00001) on the left and move it into the **Frequency Variable** box by clicking on the arrow.
3. Click **OK.**
4. Click **Analyze** on the tool bar, select **Nonparametric Tests,** and click on **Chi-Square.**
5. Highlight the label for the column containing the digits 1, 2, 3, and move it into the Test Variables box by clicking on the arrow.
6. To specify the expected frequencies, you can either use the **all categories equal** option, which automatically computes expected frequencies, or you can enter your own values. To enter your own expected frequencies, click on the **values** option, and, one by one, enter the expected frequencies into the small box and click **Add** to add each new value to the bottom of the list.
7. Click **OK.**

SPSS Output

The program produces a table showing the complete set of observed and expected frequencies. A second table provides the value for the chi-square statistic, the degrees of freedom, and the level of significance (the p value, or alpha level, for the test).

The Chi-Square Test for Independence

Data Entry

1. Enter the complete set of observed frequencies in one column of the SPSS data editor (VAR00001).
2. In a second column, enter a number (1, 2, 3, etc.) that identifies the row corresponding to each observed frequency. For example, enter a 1 beside each observed frequency that came from the first row.
3. In a third column, enter a number (1, 2, 3, etc.) that identifies the column corresponding to each observed frequency. Each value from the first column gets a 1, and so on.

Data Analysis

1. Click **Data** on the tool bar at the top of the page and select **weight cases** at the bottom of the list.
2. Click the **Weight cases by** circle, then highlight the label for the column containing the observed frequencies (VAR00001) on the left and move it into the **Frequency Variable** box by clicking on the arrow.

3. Click **OK.**
4. Click **Analyze** on the tool bar at the top of the page, select **Descriptive Statistics,** and click on **Crosstabs.**
5. Highlight the label for the column containing the rows (VAR00002) and move it into the **Rows** box by clicking on the arrow.
6. Highlight the label for the column containing the columns (VAR00003) and move it into the **Columns** box by clicking on the arrow.
7. Click on **Statistics,** select **Chi-Square,** and click **Continue.**
8. Click **OK.**

SPSS Output

We used SPSS to conduct the chi-square test for independence for the data in Example 17.2, examining the relationship between gender and willingness to use mental health services, and the output is shown in Figure 17.5. The first table in the output simply lists the variables and is not shown in the figure. The **Crosstabulation** table simply shows the matrix of observed frequencies. The final table, labeled **Chi-Square Tests,** reports the results. Focus on the top row, the **Pearson Chi-Square,** which reports the calculated chi-square value, the degrees of freedom, and the level of significance (the *p* value, or the alpha level, for the test).

VAR00002*VAR00003 Crosstabulation

Count

		VAR00003			
		1.00	2.00	3.00	Total
VAR00002	1.00	17	32	11	60
	2.00	13	43	34	90
Total		30	75	45	150

Chi-Square Tests

	Value	df	Asymp.Sig. (2-sided)
Pearson Chi-Square	8.231[a]	2	.016
Likelihood Ratio	8.443	2	.015
Linear by Linear Association	8.109	1	.004
N of Valid Cases	150		

a. 0 cells (.0%) have expected count less than 5. The minimum expected count is 12.00.

FIGURE 17.5

The SPSS output for the chi-square test for independence in Example 17.2.

FOCUS ON PROBLEM SOLVING

1. The expected frequencies that you calculate must satisfy the constraints of the sample. For the goodness-of-fit test, $\Sigma f_e = \Sigma f_o = n$. For the test for independence, the row totals and column totals for the expected frequencies should be identical to the corresponding totals for the observed frequencies.
2. It is entirely possible to have fractional (decimal) values for expected frequencies. Observed frequencies, however, are always whole numbers.
3. Whenever $df = 1$, the difference between observed and expected frequencies $(f_o = f_e)$ is identical (the same value) for all cells. This makes the calculation of chi-square easier.
4. Although you are advised to compute expected frequencies for all categories (or cells), you should realize that it is not essential to calculate all f_e values separately. Remember that df for chi-square identifies the number of f_e values that are free to vary. Once you have calculated that number of f_e values, the remaining f_e values are determined. You can get these remaining values by subtracting the calculated f_e values from their corresponding row or column totals.
5. Remember that, unlike previous statistical tests, the degrees of freedom (df) for a chi-square test are *not* determined by the sample size (n). Be careful!

DEMONSTRATION 17.1

TEST FOR INDEPENDENCE

A manufacturer of watches would like to examine preferences for digital versus analog watches. A sample of $n = 200$ people is selected, and these individuals are classified by age and preference. The manufacturer would like to know whether there is a relationship between age and watch preference. The observed frequencies (f_o) are as follows:

	Digital	Analog	Undecided	Totals
Younger than 30	90	40	10	140
30 or Older	10	40	10	60
Column totals	100	80	20	$n = 200$

STEP 1 State the hypotheses, and select an alpha level.

The null hypothesis states that there is no relationship between the two variables.

H_0: Preference is independent of age. That is, the frequency distribution of preference has the same form for people younger than 30 as for people 30 or older.

The alternative hypothesis states that there is a relationship between the two variables.

H_1: Preference is related to age. That is, the type of watch preferred depends on a person's age.

We set alpha to $\alpha = .05$.

STEP 2 Locate the critical region.

Degrees of freedom for the chi-square test for independence are determined by

$$df = (C - 1)(R - 1)$$

For these data,

$$df = (3 - 1)(2 - 1) = 2(1) = 2$$

For $df = 2$ with $\alpha = .05$, the critical chi-square value is 5.99. Thus, our obtained chi-square must exceed 5.99 to be in the critical region and to reject H_0.

STEP 3 Compute the test statistic. Two calculations are required: finding the expected frequencies and calculating the chi-square statistic.

Expected frequencies, f_e. For the test for independence, the expected frequencies can be found using the column totals (f_c), the row totals (f_r), and the following formula:

$$f_e = \frac{f_c f_r}{n}$$

For people younger than 30, we obtain the following expected frequencies:

$$f_e = \frac{100(140)}{200} = \frac{14{,}000}{200} = 70 \text{ for digital}$$

$$f_e = \frac{80(140)}{200} = \frac{11{,}200}{200} = 56 \text{ for analog}$$

$$f_e = \frac{20(140)}{200} = \frac{2800}{200} = 14 \text{ for undecided}$$

For individuals 30 or older, the expected frequencies are as follows:

$$f_e = \frac{100(60)}{200} = \frac{6000}{200} = 30 \text{ for digital}$$

$$f_e = \frac{80(60)}{200} = \frac{4800}{200} = 24 \text{ for analog}$$

$$f_e = \frac{20(60)}{200} = \frac{1200}{200} = 6 \text{ for undecided}$$

The following table summarizes the expected frequencies:

	Digital	Analog	Undecided
Younger than 30	70	56	14
30 or Older	30	24	6

The chi-square statistic. The chi-square statistic is computed from the formula

$$\chi^2 = \Sigma \frac{(f_o - f_e)^2}{f_e}$$

The following table summarizes the calculations:

Cell	f_o	f_e	$(f_o - f_e)$	$(f_o - f_e)^2$	$(f_o - f_e)^2/f_e$
Younger than 30—digital	90	70	20	400	5.71
Younger than 30—analog	40	56	−16	256	4.57
Younger than 30—undecided	10	14	−4	16	1.14
30 or Older—digital	10	30	−20	400	13.33
30 or Older—analog	40	24	16	256	10.67
30 or Older—undecided	10	6	4	16	2.67

Finally, add the values in the last column to get the chi-square statistic.

$$\chi^2 = 5.71 + 4.57 + 1.14 + 13.33 + 10.67 + 2.67$$

$$= 38.09$$

STEP 4 Make a decision about H_0, and state the conclusion.

The chi-square value is in the critical region. Therefore, we reject the null hypothesis. There is a relationship between watch preference and age, $\chi^2(2, n = 200) = 38.09, p < .05$.

DEMONSTRATION 17.2

EFFECT SIZE WITH CRAMÉR'S *V*

Because the data matrix is larger than 2 × 2, we compute Cramér's *V* to measure effect size.

$$\text{Cramér's } V = \sqrt{\frac{\chi^2}{n(df^*)}} = \sqrt{\frac{38.09}{200(1)}} = \sqrt{0.19} = 0.436$$

PROBLEMS

1. Parametric tests (such as *t* or ANOVA) differ from nonparametric tests (such as chi-square) primarily in terms of the assumptions they require and the data they use. Explain these differences.
2. The student population at the state college consists of 55% females and 45% males.
   a. The college theater department recently staged a production of a modern musical. A researcher recorded the gender of each student entering the theater and found a total of 385 females and 215 males. Is the gender distribution for theater goers significantly different from the distribution for the general college? Test at the .05 level of significance.
   b. The same researcher also recorded the gender of each student watching a men's basketball game in the college gym and found a total of 83 females and

97 males. Is the gender distribution for basketball fans significantly different from the distribution for the general college? Test at the .05 level of significance.

3. A developmental psychologist would like to determine whether infants display any color preferences. A stimulus consisting of four color patches (red, green, blue, and yellow) is projected onto the ceiling above a crib. Infants are placed in the crib, one at a time, and the psychologist records how much time each infant spends looking at each of the four colors. The color that receives the most attention during a 100-second test period is identified as the preferred color for that infant. The preferred colors for a sample of 60 infants are shown in the following table:

Red	Green	Blue	Yellow
20	12	18	10

a. Do the data indicate any significant preferences among the four colors? Test at the .05 level of significance.
b. Write a sentence demonstrating how the outcome of the hypothesis test would appear in a research report.

4. Research has demonstrated that people tend to be attracted to others who are similar to themselves. One study demonstrated that individuals are disproportionately more likely to marry those with surnames that begin with the same last letter as their own (Jones, Pelham, Carvallo, & Mirenberg, 2004). The researchers began by looking at marriage records and recording the surname for each groom and the maiden name of each bride. From these records it is possible to calculate the probability of randomly matching a bride and a groom whose last names begin with the same letter. Suppose that this probability is only 6.5%. Next, a sample of $n = 200$ married couples is selected and the number who shared the same last initial at the time they were married is counted. The resulting observed frequencies are as follows:

Same Initial	Different Initials	
19	181	200

Do these data indicate that the number of couples with the same last initial is significantly different that would be expected if couples were matched randomly? Test with $\alpha = .05$.

5. To investigate the phenomenon of "home-team advantage," a researcher recorded the outcomes from 64 college football games on one Saturday in October. Of the 64 games, 42 were won by home teams. Does this result provide enough evidence to conclude that home teams win significantly more than would be expected by chance? Assume that winning and losing are equally likely events if there is no home-team advantage. Use $\alpha = .05$.

6. Data from the department of motor vehicles indicate that 80% of all licensed drivers are older than age 25.
a. In a sample of $n = 60$ people who recently received speeding tickets, 38 were older than 25 years and the other 22 were age 25 or younger. Is the age distribution for this sample significantly different from the distribution for the population of licensed drivers? Use $\alpha = .05$.
b. In a sample of $n = 60$ people who recently received parking tickets, 43 were older than 25 years and the other 17 were age 25 or younger. Is the age distribution for this sample significantly different from the distribution for the population of licensed drivers? Use $\alpha = .05$.

7. Suppose that the researcher from the previous problem repeated the study of married couples' initials using twice as many participants and obtaining observed frequencies that exactly double the original values. The resulting data are as follows:

Same Initial	Different Initials	
38	362	400

a. Use a chi-square test to determine whether the number of couples with the same last initial is significantly different than would be expected if couples were matched randomly. Test with $\alpha = .05$.
b. You should find that the data lead to rejecting the null hypothesis. However, in problem 6 the decision was fail to reject. How do you explain the fact that the two samples have the same proportions but lead to different conclusions?

8. A professor in the psychology department would like to determine whether there has been a significant change in grading practices over the years. It is known that the overall grade distribution for the department in 1985 had 14% As, 26% Bs, 31% Cs, 19% Ds, and 10% Fs. A sample of $n = 200$ psychology students from last semester produced the following grade distribution:

A	B	C	D	F
32	61	64	31	12

Do the data indicate a significant change in the grade distribution? Test at the .05 level of significance.

9. Automobile insurance is much more expensive for teenage drivers than for older drivers. To justify this cost difference, insurance companies claim that the younger drivers are much more likely to be involved in costly accidents. To test this claim, a researcher obtains information about registered drivers from the department of motor vehicles (DMV) and selects a sample of $n = 300$ accident reports from the police department. The DMV reports the percentage of registered drivers in each age category as follows: 16% are younger than age 20; 28% are 20 to 29 years old; and 56% are age 30 or older. The number of accident reports for each age group is as follows:

Under age 20	Age 20–29	Age 30 or older
68	92	140

a. Do the data indicate that the distribution of accidents for the three age groups is significantly different from the distribution of drivers? Test with $\alpha = .05$.
b. Write a sentence demonstrating how the outcome of the hypothesis test would appear in a research report.

10. In problem 11, a researcher asked college students to evaluate three new cell phone designs. However, the researcher suspects that college students may have criteria that are different from those used by older adults. To test this hypothesis, the researcher repeats the study using a sample of $n = 60$ older adults in addition to a sample of $n = 60$ students. The distribution of preference is as follows:

	Design 1	Design 2	Design 3	
Student	27	20	13	60
Older Adult	21	34	5	60
	48	54	18	

Do the data indicate that the distribution of preferences for older adults is significantly different from the distribution for college students? Test with $\alpha = .05$.

11. A communications company has developed three new designs for a cell phone. To evaluate consumer response, a sample of 120 college students is selected and each student is given all three phones to use for 1 week. At the end of the week, the students must identify which of the three designs they prefer. The distribution of preference is as follows:

Design 1	Design 2	Design 3
54	38	28

Do the results indicate any significant preferences among the three designs?

12. The color red is often associated with anger and male dominance. Based on this observation, Hill and Barton (2005) monitored the outcome of four combat sports (boxing, tae kwan do, Greco-Roman wrestling, and freestyle wrestling) during the 2004 Olympic games and found that participants wearing red outfits won significantly more often than those wearing blue.
a. In 50 wrestling matches involving red versus blue, suppose that the red outfit won 31 times and lost 19 times. Is this result sufficient to conclude that red wins significantly more than would be expected by chance? Test at the .05 level of significance.
b. In 100 matches, suppose red won 62 times and lost 38. Is this sufficient to conclude that red wins significantly more than would be expected by chance? Again, use $\alpha = .05$.
c. Note that the winning percentage for red uniforms in part a is identical to the percentage in part b (31 out of 50 is 62%, and 62 out of 100 is also 62%). Although the two samples have an identical winning percentage, one is significant and the other is not. Explain why the two samples lead to different conclusions.

13. Research suggests that romantic background music increases the likelihood that a woman will give her phone number to a man she has just met (Guéguen & Jacoby, 2010). In the study, women spent time in a waiting room with background music playing. In one condition, the music was a popular love song and for the other condition the music was a neutral song. The participant was then moved to another room in which she was instructed to discuss two food products with a young man. The men were part of the study and were selected because they had been rated as average in attractiveness. The experimenter returned to end the study and asked the pair to wait alone for a few minutes. During this time, the man used a scripted line to ask the woman for her phone number. The following table presents data similar to those obtained in the study, showing the number of women who did or did not give their numbers for each music condition.

	Phone Number	No Number	
Romantic Music	21	19	40
Neutral Music	9	31	40
	30	50	

Is there a significant difference between the two types of music? Test with $\alpha = .05$

14. Mulvihill, Obuseh, and Caldwell (2008) conducted a survey evaluating healthcare providers' perception of a new state children's insurance program. One question

asked the providers whether they viewed the reimbursement from the new insurance as higher, lower, or the same as private insurance. Another question assessed the providers' overall satisfaction with the new insurance. The following table presents observed frequencies similar to the study results.

	Satisfied	Not Satisfied	
Less Reimbursement	46	54	100
Same or More Reimbursement	42	18	60
	88	72	

Do the results indicate that the providers' satisfaction of the new program is related to their perception of the reimbursement rates? Test with $\alpha = .05$.

15. A local county is considering a budget proposal that would allocate extra funding toward the renovation of city parks. A survey is conducted to measure public opinion concerning the proposal. A total of 150 individuals respond to the survey: 50 who live within the city limits and 100 from the surrounding suburbs. The frequency distribution is as follows:

	Opinion		
	Favor	Oppose	
City	35	15	50
Suburb	55	45	100
	90	60	

a. Is there a significant difference in the distribution of opinions for city residents compared to those in the suburbs? Test at the .05 level of significance.

b. The relationship between home location and opinion can also be evaluated using the phi-coefficient. If the phi-coefficient were computed for these data, what value would be obtained for phi?

16. The data from problem 15 show no significant difference between the opinions for city residents and those who live in the suburbs. To construct the following data, we simply doubled the sample size from problem 15 so that all of the individual frequencies are twice as big. Notice that the sample *proportions* have not changed.

	Opinion		
	Favor	Oppose	
City	70	30	100
Suburb	110	90	200
	180	120	

a. Test for a significant difference between the city distribution and the suburb distribution using $\alpha = .05$. How does the decision compare with the decision in problem 14? You should find that a larger sample increases the likelihood of a significant result.

b. Compute the phi-coefficient for these data and compare it with the result from problem 15. You should find that the sample size has no effect on the strength of the relationship.

17. In the Preview for this chapter, we discussed a study investigating the relationship between memory for eyewitnesses and the questions they are asked (Loftus & Palmer, 1974). In the study, participants watched a film of an automobile accident and then were questioned about the accident. One group was asked how fast the cars were going when they "smashed into" each other. A second group was asked about the speed when the cars "hit" each other, and a third group was not asked any question about the speed of the cars. A week later, the participants returned to answer additional questions about the accident, including whether they recalled seeing any broken glass. Although there was no broken glass in the film, several students claimed to remember seeing it. The following table shows the frequency distribution of responses for each group.

		Response to the Question "Did You See Any Broken Glass?"	
		Yes	No
Verb Used to Ask About the Speed of the Cars	Smashed into	16	34
	Hit	7	43
	Control (not asked)	6	44

a. Does the proportion of participants who claim to remember broken glass differ significantly from group to group? Test with $\alpha = .05$.

b. Compute Cramérs *V* to measure the size of the treatment effect.

c. Describe how the phrasing of the question influenced the participants' memories.

d. Write a sentence demonstrating how the outcome of the hypothesis test and the measure of effect size would be reported in a journal article.

18. In a study investigating freshman weight gain, the researchers also looked at gender differences in weight (Kasparek, Corwin, Valois, Sargent, & Morris, 2008). Using self-reported heights and weights, they computed the body mass index (BMI) for each student. Based on the BMI scores, the students were classified as either desirable weight or overweight. When the students were further classified by gender, the researchers found results similar to the frequencies in the following table.

	Desirable Weight	Overweight
Males	74	46
Females	62	18

a. Do the data indicate that the proportion of overweight men is significantly different from the proportion of overweight women? Test with $\alpha = .05$.
b. Compute the phi-coefficient to measure the strength of the relationship.
c. Write a sentence demonstrating how the outcome of the hypothesis test and the measure of effect size would be reported in a journal article.

19. Research results suggest that IQ scores for boys are more variable than IQ scores for girls (Arden & Plomin, 2006). A typical study looking at 10-year-old children classifies participants by gender and by low, average, or high IQ. Following are hypothetical data representing the research results. Do the data indicate a significant difference between the frequency distributions for males and females? Test at the .05 level of significance and describe the difference.

	IQ			
	Low	Average	High	
Boys	18	42	20	80
Girls	12	54	14	80
				$n = 160$

20. A recent study indicates that people tend to select video game avatars with characteristics similar to those of their creators (Bélisle & Onur, 2010). Participants who had created avatars for a virtual community game completed a questionnaire about their personalities. An independent group of viewers examined the avatars and recorded their impressions of the avatars. One personality characteristic considered was introverted/extroverted. The following frequency distribution of personalities for participants and the avatars they created.

	Participant Personality		
	Introverted	Extroverted	
Introverted Avatar	22	23	45
Extroverted Avatar	16	39	55
	38	62	

a. Is there a significant relationship between the personalities of the participants and the personalities of their avatars? Test with $\alpha = .05$.
b. Compute the phi-coefficient to measure the size of the effect.

21. In a study similar to one conducted by Fallon and Rozin (1985), a psychologist prepared a set of silhouettes showing different female body shapes ranging from somewhat thin to somewhat heavy and asked a group of women to indicate which body figure they thought men would consider the most attractive. Then a group of men were shown the same set of profiles and asked which image they considered the most attractive. The following hypothetical data show the number of individuals who selected each of the four body image profiles.
a. Do the data indicate a significant difference between the actual preferences for the men and the preferences predicted by the women? Test at the .05 level of significance.
b. Compute the phi-coefficient to measure the strength of the relationship.

	Body Image Profiles				
	Somewhat Thin	Slightly Thin	Slightly Heavy	Somewhat Heavy	
Women	29	25	18	8	80
Men	11	15	22	12	60
	40	40	40	20	

22. Gender differences in dream content are well documented (see Winget & Kramer, 1979). Suppose a researcher studies aggression content in the dreams of men and women. Each participant reports his or her most recent dream. Then each dream is judged by a panel of experts to have low, medium, or high aggression content. The observed frequencies are shown in the following matrix:

		Aggression Content		
		Low	Medium	High
Gender	Female	18	4	2
	Male	4	17	15

Is there a relationship between gender and the aggression content of dreams? Test with $\alpha = .01$.

23. Research indicates that people who volunteer to participate in research studies tend to have higher intelligence than nonvolunteers. To test this phenomenon, a researcher obtains a sample of 200 high school students. The students are given a description of a psychological research study and asked whether they would volunteer to participate. The researcher also obtains an IQ score for each student and classifies the students into high, medium, and low IQ groups. Do the following data indicate a significant relationship between IQ and volunteering? Test at the .05 level of significance.

	IQ			
	High	Medium	Low	
Volunteer	43	73	34	150
Not Volunteer	7	27	16	50
	50	100	50	

24. Cialdini, Reno, and Kallgren (1990) examined how people conform to norms concerning littering. The researchers wanted to determine whether a person's tendency to litter depended on the amount of litter already in the area. People were handed a handbill as they entered an amusement park. The entrance area had already been prepared with either no litter, a small amount of litter, or a lot of litter lying on the ground. The people were observed to determine whether they dropped their handbills. The frequency data are as follows:

	Amount of Litter		
	None	Small Amount	Large Amount
Littering	17	28	49
Not Littering	73	62	41

a. Do the data indicate that people's tendency to litter depends on the amount of litter already on the ground? That is, is there a significant relationship between littering and the amount of existing litter? Test at the .05 level of significance.

b. Compute Cramér's V to measure the size of the treatment effect.

25. Although the phenomenon is not well understood, it appears that people born during the winter months are slightly more likely to develop schizophrenia than people born at other times (Bradbury & Miller, 1985). The following hypothetical data represent a sample of 50 individuals diagnosed with schizophrenia and a sample of 100 people with no psychotic diagnosis. Each individual is also classified according to season in which he or she was born. Do the data indicate a significant relationship between schizophrenia and the season of birth? Test at the .05 level of significance.

	Season of Birth				
	Summer	Fall	Winter	Spring	
No Disorder	26	24	22	28	100
Schizophrenia	9	11	18	12	50
	35	35	40	40	

CHAPTER

18

The Binomial Test

Tools You Will Need

The following items are considered essential background material for this chapter. If you doubt your knowledge of any of these items, you should review the appropriate chapter or section before proceeding.

- Binomial distribution (Chapter 6)
- *z*-score hypothesis tests (Chapter 8)
- Chi-square test for goodness of fit (Chapter 17)

Preview

In 1960, Gibson and Walk designed a classic piece of apparatus to test depth perception. Their device, called a *visual cliff*, consisted of a wide board with a deep drop (the cliff) to one side and a shallow drop on the other side. An infant was placed on the board and then observed to see whether he or she crawled off the shallow side or crawled off the cliff. Infants who moved to the deep side actually crawled onto a sheet of heavy glass, which prevented them from falling. Thus, the deep side only appeared to be a cliff—hence the name *visual cliff*.

Gibson and Walk reasoned that if infants are born with the ability to perceive depth, they would recognize the deep side and not crawl off the cliff. On the other hand, if depth perception is a skill that develops over time through learning and experience, then infants should not be able to perceive any difference between the shallow and the deep sides.

Out of 27 infants who moved off the board, only 3 ventured onto the deep side at any time during the experiment. The other 24 infants stayed exclusively on the shallow side. Gibson and Walk interpreted these data as convincing evidence that depth perception is innate. The infants showed a systematic preference for the shallow side.

The Problem: You should notice immediately that the data from this experiment are different from the data that we usually encounter. There are no scores. Gibson and Walk simply counted the number of infants who went off the deep side and the number who went to the shallow side. Still, we would like to use these data to make statistical decisions. Do these sample data provide sufficient evidence to make a confident conclusion about depth perception in the population? Suppose that 8 of the 27 infants had crawled to the deep side. Would you still be convinced that there is a significant preference for the shallow side? What about 12 out of 27?

The Solution: We are asking a question about statistical significance and need a hypothesis test to obtain an answer. The null hypothesis for the Gibson and Walk study would state that infants have no depth perception and cannot perceive a difference between the shallow and deep sides. In this case, their movement should be random with half going to either side. Notice that the data and the hypothesis both concern frequencies or proportions. This situation is perfect for the chi-square test introduced in Chapter 17, and a chi-square test can be used to evaluate the data. However, when individuals are classified into exactly two categories (for example, shallow and deep), a special statistical procedure exists. In this chapter, we introduce the *binomial test*, which is used to evaluate and interpret frequency data involving exactly two categories of classification.

18.1 OVERVIEW

Data with exactly two categories are also known as dichotomous data.

In Chapter 6, we introduced the concept of *binomial data*. You should recall that binomial data exist whenever a measurement procedure classifies individuals into exactly two distinct categories. For example, the outcomes from tossing a coin can be classified as heads and tails; people can be classified as male or female; plastic products can be classified as recyclable or non-recyclable. In general, binomial data exist when

1. The measurement scale consists of exactly two categories.
2. Each individual observation in a sample is classified in only one of the two categories.
3. The sample data consist of the frequency of, or number of individuals in, each category.

The traditional notation system for binomial data identifies the two categories as A and B and identifies the probability (or proportion) associated with each category as p and q, respectively. For example, a coin toss results in either heads (A) or tails (B), with probabilities $p = \frac{1}{2}$ and $q = \frac{1}{2}$.

In this chapter, we examine the statistical process of using binomial data for testing hypotheses about the values of p and q for the population. This type of hypothesis test is called a *binomial test.*

DEFINITION

A **binomial test** uses sample data to evaluate hypotheses about the values of p and q for a population consisting of binomial data.

Consider the following two situations:

1. In a sample of $n = 34$ color-blind students, 30 are male, and only 4 are female. Does this sample indicate that color blindness is significantly more common for males in the general population?
2. In 2005, only 10% of American families had incomes below the poverty level. This year, in a sample of 100 families, 19 were below the poverty level. Does this sample indicate that there has been a significant change in the population proportions?

Notice that both of these examples have binomial data (exactly two categories). Although the data are relatively simple, we are asking a statistical question about significance that is appropriate for a hypothesis test: Do the sample data provide sufficient evidence to make a conclusion about the population?

HYPOTHESES FOR THE BINOMIAL TEST

In the binomial test, the null hypothesis specifies exact values for the population proportions p and q. Theoretically, you could choose any proportions for H_0, but usually there is a clear reason for the values that are selected. The null hypothesis typically falls into one of the following two categories:

1. **Just Chance.** Often the null hypothesis states that the two outcomes, A and B, occur in the population with the proportions that would be predicted simply by chance. If you were tossing a coin, for example, the null hypothesis might specify $p(\text{heads}) = \frac{1}{2}$ and $p(\text{tails}) = \frac{1}{2}$. Notice that this hypothesis states the usual, chance proportions for a balanced coin. Also notice that it is not necessary to specify both proportions. Once the value of p is identified, the value of q is determined by $1 - p$. For the coin toss example, the null hypothesis would simply state

   $$H_0:\quad p = p(\text{heads}) = \frac{1}{2} \quad \text{(The coin is balanced.)}$$

   Similarly, if you were selecting cards from a deck and trying to predict the suit on each draw, the probability of predicting correctly would be $p = \frac{1}{4}$ for any given trial. (With four suits, you have a 1-out-of-4 chance of guessing correctly.) In this case, the null hypothesis would state

   $$H_0:\quad p = p(\text{guessing correctly}) = \frac{1}{4} \quad \text{(The outcome is simply the result of chance.)}$$

   In each case, the null hypothesis states that there is nothing unusual about the proportions in the population; that is, the outcomes are occurring by chance.

2. **No Change or No Difference.** Often you may know the proportions for one population and want to determine whether the same proportions apply to a different population. In this case, the null hypothesis would simply specify that there is no difference between the two populations. Suppose that national

statistics indicate that 1 out of 12 drivers will be involved in a traffic accident during the next year. Does this same proportion apply to 16-year-olds who are driving for the first time? According to the null hypothesis,

H_0: For 16-year-olds, $p = p(\text{accident}) = \frac{1}{12}$ (Not different from the general population)

Similarly, suppose that last year, 30% of the freshman class failed the college writing test. This year, the college is requiring all freshmen to take a writing course. Will the course have any effect on the number who fail the test? According to the null hypothesis,

H_0: For this year, $p = p(\text{fail}) = 30\%$ (Not different from last year's class)

THE DATA FOR THE BINOMIAL TEST

For the binomial test, a sample of n individuals is obtained and you simply count how many are classified in category A and how many are classified in category B. We focus attention on category A and use the symbol X to stand for the number of individuals classified in category A. Recall from Chapter 6 that X can have any value from 0 to n and that each value of X has a specific probability. The distribution of probabilities for each value of X is called the *binomial distribution.* Figure 18.1 shows an example of a binomial distribution for which X is the number of heads obtained in four tosses of a balanced coin.

THE TEST STATISTIC FOR THE BINOMIAL TEST

As we noted in Chapter 6, when the values pn and qn are both equal to or greater than 10, the binomial distribution approximates a normal distribution. This fact is important because it allows us to compute z-scores and use the unit normal table to answer probability questions about binomial events. In particular, when pn and qn are both at least 10, the binomial distribution has the following properties:

1. The shape of the distribution is approximately normal.
2. The mean of the distribution is $\mu = pn$.

FIGURE 18.1

A binomial distribution for the number of heads obtained in four tosses of a balanced coin.

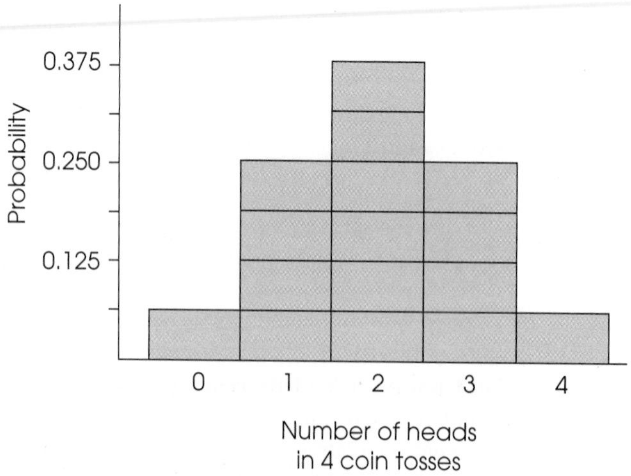

3. The standard deviation of the distribution is

$$\sigma = \sqrt{npq}$$

With these parameters in mind, it is possible to compute a z-score corresponding to each value of X in the binomial distribution.

$$z = \frac{X - \mu}{\sigma} = \frac{X - pn}{\sqrt{npq}} \quad \text{(See Equation 6.3.)} \tag{18.1}$$

This is the basic z-score formula that is used for the binomial test. However, the formula can be modified slightly to make it more compatible with the logic of the binomial hypothesis test. The modification consists of dividing both the numerator and the denominator of the z-score by n. (You should realize that dividing both the numerator and the denominator by the same value does not change the value of the z-score.) The resulting equation is

$$z = \frac{X/n - p}{\sqrt{pq/n}} \tag{18.2}$$

For the binomial test, the values in this formula are defined as follows:

1. X/n is the proportion of individuals in the sample who are classified in category A.
2. p is the hypothesized value (from H_0) for the proportion of individuals in the population who are classified in category A.
3. $\sqrt{pq/n}$ is the standard error for the sampling distribution of X/n and provides a measure of the standard distance between the sample statistic (X/n) and the population parameter (p).

Thus, the structure of the binomial z-score (Equation 18.2) can be expressed as

$$z = \frac{X/n - p}{\sqrt{pq/n}} = \frac{\begin{array}{c}\text{sample}\\ \text{proportion}\\ \text{(data)}\end{array} - \begin{array}{c}\text{hypothesized}\\ \text{population}\\ \text{proportion}\end{array}}{\text{standard error}}$$

The logic underlying the binomial test is exactly the same as we encountered with the original z-score hypothesis test in Chapter 8. The hypothesis test involves comparing the sample data with the hypothesis. If the data are consistent with the hypothesis, then we conclude that the hypothesis is reasonable. But if there is a big discrepancy between the data and the hypothesis, then we reject the hypothesis. The value of the standard error provides a benchmark for determining whether the discrepancy between the data and the hypothesis is more than would be expected by chance. The alpha level for the test provides a criterion for deciding whether the discrepancy is significant. The hypothesis-testing procedure is demonstrated in the following section.

LEARNING CHECK

1. In the Preview, we described a research study using a visual cliff. State the null hypothesis for this study in words and as a probability value (p) that an infant will crawl off the deep side.

2. If the visual cliff study had used a sample of $n = 15$ infants, would it be appropriate to use the normal approximation to the binomial distribution? Explain why or why not.

3. If the results from the visual cliff study showed that 9 out of 36 infants crawled off the deep side, what z-score value would be obtained using Equation 18.1?

ANSWERS

1. The null hypothesis states that the probability of choosing between the deep side and the shallow side is just chance: $p(\text{deep side}) = \frac{1}{2}$.

2. The normal approximation to the binomial distribution requires that both pn and qn are at least 10. With $n = 15$, $pn = qn = 7.5$. The normal approximation should not be used.

3. With $n = 36$ and $p = \frac{1}{2}$, the binomial distribution has $\mu = \frac{1}{2}(36) = 18$, and $\sigma = \sqrt{\left(\frac{1}{2}\right)\left(\frac{1}{2}\right)(36)} = \sqrt{9} = 3$. $X = 9$ corresponds $z = -9/3 = -3.00$

18.2 THE BINOMIAL TEST

The binomial test follows the same four-step procedure presented earlier with other examples for hypothesis testing. The four steps are summarized as follows.

STEP 1 *State the hypotheses.* In the binomial test, the null hypothesis specifies values for the population proportions p and q. Typically, H_0 specifies a value only for p, the proportion associated with category A. The value of q is directly determined from p by the relationship $q = 1 - p$. Finally, you should realize that the hypothesis, as always, addresses the probabilities or proportions for the *population*. Although we use a sample to test the hypothesis, the hypothesis itself always concerns a population.

STEP 2 *Locate the critical region.* When both values for pn and qn are greater than or equal to 10, then the z-scores defined by Equation 18.1 or 18.2 form an approximately normal distribution. Thus, the unit normal table can be used to find the boundaries for the critical region. With $\alpha = .05$, for example, you may recall that the critical region is defined as z-score values greater than $+1.96$ or less than -1.96.

STEP 3 *Compute the test statistic (z-score).* At this time, you obtain a sample of n individuals (or events) and count the number of times category A occurs in the sample. The number of occurrences of A in the sample is the X value for Equation 18.1 or 18.2. Because the two z-score equations are equivalent, you may use either one for the hypothesis test. Usually Equation 18.1 is easier to use because it involves larger numbers (fewer decimals) and it is less likely to be affected by rounding error.

STEP 4 *Make a decision.* If the z-score for the sample data is in the critical region, then you reject H_0 and conclude that the discrepancy between the sample proportions and the hypothesized population proportions is significantly greater than chance. That is, the data are not consistent with the null hypothesis, so H_0 must be wrong. On the other hand, if the z-score is not in the critical region, then you fail to reject H_0.

The following example demonstrates a complete binomial test.

EXAMPLE 18.1 In the Preview section, we described the *visual cliff* experiment designed to examine depth perception in infants. To summarize briefly, an infant is placed on a wide board that appears to have a deep drop on one side and a relatively shallow drop on the other. An infant who is able to perceive depth should avoid the deep side and move toward the shallow side. Without depth perception, the infant should show no preference between the two sides. Of the 27 infants in the experiment, 24 stayed exclusively on the shallow side and only 3 moved onto the deep side. The purpose of the hypothesis test is to determine whether these data demonstrate that infants have a significant preference for the shallow side.

This is a binomial hypothesis-testing situation. The two categories are

A = move onto the deep side

B = move onto the shallow side

STEP 1 The null hypothesis states that, for the general population of infants, there is no preference between the deep and the shallow sides; the direction of movement is determined by chance. In symbols,

$$H_0:\ p = p(\text{deep side}) = \frac{1}{2} \quad \left(\text{and } q = \frac{1}{2}\right)$$

$$H_1:\ p \neq \frac{1}{2} \quad (\text{There is a preference.})$$

We use $\alpha = .05$.

STEP 2 With a sample of $n = 27$, $pn = 13.5$ and $qn = 13.5$. Both values are greater than 10, so the distribution of z-scores is approximately normal. With $\alpha = .05$, the critical region is determined by boundaries of $z = \pm\ 1.96$.

STEP 3 For this experiment, the data consist of $X = 3$ out of $n = 27$. Using Equation 18.1, these data produce a z-score value of

$$z = \frac{X - pn}{\sqrt{npq}} = \frac{3 - 13.5}{\sqrt{27\left(\frac{1}{2}\right)\left(\frac{1}{2}\right)}} = \frac{-10.5}{2.60} = -4.04$$

To use Equation 18.2, you first compute the sample proportion, $X/n = 3/27 = 0.111$. The z-score is then

$$z = \frac{X/n - p}{\sqrt{pq/n}} = \frac{0.111 - 0.5}{\sqrt{\frac{1}{2}\left(\frac{1}{2}\right)/27}} = \frac{-0.389}{0.096} = -4.05$$

Within rounding error, the two equations produce the same result.

STEP 4 Because the data are in the critical region, our decision is to reject H_0. These data do provide sufficient evidence to conclude that there is a significant preference for the shallow side. Gibson and Walk (1960) interpreted these data as convincing evidence that depth perception is innate.

REAL LIMITS AND THE BINOMIAL TEST

In Chapter 6, we noted that a binomial distribution forms a discrete histogram (see Figure 18.1), whereas the normal distribution is a continuous curve. The difference between the two distributions was illustrated in Figure 6.18,

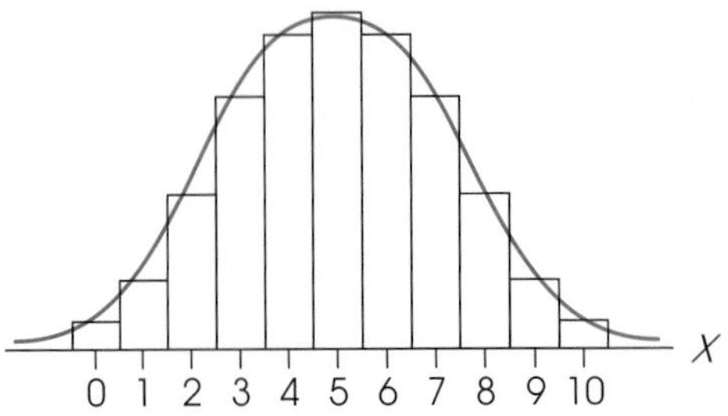

FIGURE 18.2

The relationship between the binomial distribution and the normal distribution. The binomial distribution is always a discrete histogram, and the normal distribution is a continuous, smooth curve. Each X value is represented by a bar in the histogram or a section of the normal distribution.

which is repeated here as Figure 18.2. In the figure, note that each score in the binomial distribution is represented by a bar in the histogram. For example, a score of $X = 6$ actually corresponds to a bar that reaches from a lower real limit of $X = 5.5$ to an upper real limit of 6.5.

When conducting a hypothesis test with the binomial distribution, the basic question is whether a specific score is located in the critical region. However, because each score actually corresponds to an interval, it is possible that part of the score is in the critical region and part is not. Fortunately, this is usually not an issue. When pn and qn are both equal to or greater than 10 (the criteria for using the normal approximation), each interval in the binomial distribution is extremely small and it is very unlikely that the interval overlaps the critical boundary. For example, the experiment in Example 18.1 produced a score of $X = 3$, and we computed a z-score of $z = -4.04$. Because this value is in the critical region, beyond $z = -1.96$, we rejected H_0. If we had used the real limit boundaries of $X = 2.5$ and $X = 3.5$, instead of $X = 3$, we would have obtained z-scores of

$$z = \frac{2.5 - 13.5}{2.60} = -4.23 \quad \text{and} \quad z = \frac{3.5 - 13.5}{2.60} = -3.85$$

Thus, a score of $X = 3$ actually corresponds to an interval of z-scores ranging from $z = -3.85$ to $z = -4.23$. However, this entire interval is in the critical region beyond $z = -1.96$, so the decision is still to reject H_0.

In most situations, if the whole number X value (in this case, $X = 3$) is in the critical region, then the entire interval is in the critical region and the correct decision is to reject H_0. The only exception to this general rule occurs when an X value produces a z-score that is barely past the boundary into the critical region. In this situation, you should compute the z-scores corresponding to both real limits to determine whether any part of the z-score interval is not located in the critical region. Suppose, for example, that the researchers in Example 18.1 found that 8 out of 27 infants in the visual cliff experiment moved onto the deep side. A score of $X = 8$ corresponds to

$$z = \frac{8 - 13.5}{2.60}$$

$$z = \frac{-5.5}{2.60}$$

$$= -2.12$$

Because this value is beyond the − 1.96 boundary, it appears that we should reject H_0. However, this z-score is only slightly beyond the critical boundary, so it would be wise to check both ends of the interval. For $X = 8$, the real-limit boundaries are 7.5 and 8.5, which correspond to z-scores of

$$z = \frac{7.5 - 13.5}{2.60} = -2.31 \qquad \text{and} \qquad z = \frac{8.5 - 13.5}{2.60} = -1.92$$

Thus, a score of $X = 8$ corresponds to an interval extending from $z = -1.92$ to $z = -2.31$. However, the critical boundary is $z = -1.96$, which means that part of the interval (and part of the score) is not in the critical region for $\alpha = .05$. Because $X = 8$ is not completely beyond the critical boundary, the probability of obtaining $X = 8$ is greater than $\alpha = .05$. Therefore, the correct decision is to fail to reject H_0.

In general, it is safe to conduct a binomial test using the whole-number value for X. However, if you obtain a z-score that is only slightly beyond the critical boundary, you also should compute the z-scores for both real limits. If any part of the z-score interval is not in the critical region, the correct decision is to fail to reject H_0.

IN THE LITERATURE

REPORTING THE RESULTS OF A BINOMIAL TEST

Reporting the results of the binomial test typically consists of describing the data and reporting the z-score value and the probability that the results are caused by chance. It is also helpful to note that a binomial test was used because z-scores are used in other hypothesis-testing situations (see, for example, Chapter 8). For Example 18.1, the report might state:

> Three out of 27 infants moved to the deep side of the visual cliff. A binomial test revealed that there is a significant preference for the shallow side of the cliff, $z = -4.04$, $p < .05$.

Once again, p is *less than* .05. We have rejected the null hypothesis because it is very unlikely, probability less than 5%, that these results are simply caused by chance.

ASSUMPTIONS FOR THE BINOMIAL TEST

The binomial test requires two very simple assumptions:

1. The sample must consist of *independent* observations (see Chapter 8, page 254).
2. The values for pn and qn must both be greater than or equal to 10 to justify using the unit normal table for determining the critical region.

LEARNING CHECK

1. For a binomial test, the null hypothesis always states that $p = 1/2$. (True or false?)
2. The makers of brand X beer claim that people like their beer more than the leading brand. The basis for this claim is an experiment in which 64 beer drinkers compared the two brands in a side-by-side taste test. In this sample, 40 preferred brand X, and 24 preferred the leading brand.
   - **a.** If you compute the z-score for $X = 40$, do these data support the claim that there is a significant preference? Test at the .05 level.
   - **b.** If you compute z-scores for the real limits for $X = 40$, do the data support the claim that there is a significant preference? Test at the .05 level.

ANSWERS

1. False.
2. a. H_0: $p = \frac{1}{2} = q$, $X = 38$, $\mu = 32$, $\sigma = 4$, $z = 2.00$, reject H_0. Conclude that there is a significant preference.
   b. The real limits of 39.5 and 40.5 correspond to z-scores of 1.88 and 2.13. The entire interval is not in the critical region so fail to reject H_0 and conclude that there is not a significant preference.

18.3 THE RELATIONSHIP BETWEEN CHI-SQUARE AND THE BINOMIAL TEST

You may have noticed that the binomial test evaluates the same basic hypotheses as the chi-square test for goodness of fit; that is, both tests evaluate how well the sample proportions fit a hypothesis about the population proportions. When an experiment produces binomial data, these two tests are equivalent, and either may be used. The relationship between the two tests can be expressed by the equation

$$\chi^2 = z^2$$

where χ^2 is the statistic from the chi-square test for goodness of fit and z is the z-score from the binomial test.

To demonstrate the relationship between the goodness-of-fit test and the binomial test, we reexamine the data from Example 18.1.

STEP 1 *Hypotheses.* In the visual cliff experiment from Example 18.1, the null hypothesis states that there is no preference between the shallow side and the deep side. For the binomial test, the null hypothesis states

$$H_0\text{: } p = p(\text{deep side}) = q = p(\text{shallow side}) = \frac{1}{2}$$

The chi-square test for goodness of fit would state the same hypothesis, specifying the population proportions as

	Shallow Side	Deep Side
H_0:	$\frac{1}{2}$	$\frac{1}{2}$

STEP 2 *Critical region.* For the binomial test, the critical region is located by using the unit normal table. With $\alpha = .05$, the critical region consists of any z-score value beyond ±1.96. The chi-square test would have $df = 1$, and with $\alpha = .05$, the critical region consists of chi-square values greater than 3.84. Notice that the basic relationship, $\chi^2 = z^2$, holds:

$$3.84 = (1.96)^2$$

STEP 3 *Test statistic.* For the binomial test (Example 18.1), we obtained a z-score of $z = -4.04$. For the chi-square test, the expected frequencies are

	Shallow Side	Deep Side
f_e	13.5	13.5

With observed frequencies of 24 and 3, respectively, the chi-square statistic is

$$\begin{aligned}\chi^2 &= \frac{(24 - 13.5)^2}{13.5} + \frac{(3 - 13.5)^2}{13.5} \\ &= \frac{(10.5)^2}{13.5} + \frac{(-10.5)^2}{13.5} \\ &= 8.167 + 8.167 \\ &= 16.33\end{aligned}$$

With a little rounding error, the values obtained for the z-score and chi-square are related by the equation

Caution: The χ^2 value is already squared. Do not square it again.

$$\chi^2 = z^2$$

$$16.33 = (-4.04)^2$$

STEP 4 *Decision.* Because the critical values for both tests are related by the equation $\chi^2 = z^2$ and the test statistics are related in the same way, these two tests *always* result in the same statistical conclusion.

18.4 THE SIGN TEST

Although the binomial test can be used in many different situations, there is one specific application that merits special attention. For a repeated-measures study that compares two conditions, it is often possible to use a binomial test to evaluate the results. You should recall that a repeated-measures study involves measuring each individual in two different treatment conditions or at two different points in time. When the measurements produce numerical scores, the researcher can simply subtract to determine the difference between the two scores and then evaluate the data using a repeated-measures t test (see Chapter 11). Occasionally, however, a researcher may record only the *direction* of the difference between the two observations. For example, a clinician may observe patients before therapy and after therapy and simply note whether each patient got better or worse. Note that there is no measurement of how much change occurred; the clinician is simply recording the direction of change. Also note that the direction of change is a binomial variable; that is, there are only two values. In this situation it is possible to use a binomial test to evaluate the data. Traditionally, the two possible directions of change are coded by signs, with a positive sign indicating an increase and a negative sign indicating a decrease. When the binomial test is applied to signed data, it is called a *sign test.*

An example of signed data is shown in Table 18.1. Notice that the data can be summarized by saying that seven out of eight patients showed a decrease in symptoms after therapy.

The null hypothesis for the sign test states that there is no difference between the two treatments. Therefore, any change in a participant's score is the result of chance. In terms of probabilities, this means that increases and decreases are equally likely, so

$$p = p(\text{increase}) = \frac{1}{2}$$

$$q = p(\text{decrease}) = \frac{1}{2}$$

A complete example of a sign test follows.

TABLE 18.1

Hypothetical data from a research study evaluating the effectiveness of a clinical therapy. For each patient, symptoms are assessed before and after treatment and the data record whether there is an increase or a decrease in symptoms following therapy.

Patient	Direction of Change After Treatment
A	− (decrease)
B	− (decrease)
C	− (decrease)
D	+ (increase)
E	− (decrease)
F	− (decrease)
G	− (decrease)
H	− (decrease)

EXAMPLE 18.2 A researcher testing the effectiveness of acupuncture for treating the symptoms of arthritis obtains a sample of 36 people who have been diagnosed with arthritis. Each person's pain level is measured before treatment starts, and measured again after 4 months of acupuncture treatment. For this sample, 25 people experienced a reduction in pain, and 11 people had more pain after treatment. Do these data indicate a significant treatment effect?

STEP 1 State the hypothesis. The null hypothesis states that acupuncture has no effect. Any change in the level of pain is caused by chance, so increases and decreases are equally likely. Expressed as probabilities, the hypotheses are

$$H_0\colon\ p = p(\text{increased pain}) = \frac{1}{2} \text{ and } q = p(\text{decreased pain}) = \frac{1}{2}$$

$$H_1\colon\ p \neq q \qquad \text{(Changes tend to be consistently in one direction.)}$$

Set $\alpha = .05$.

STEP 2 Locate the critical region. With $n = 36$ people, both pn and qn are greater than 10, so the normal approximation to the binomial distribution is appropriate. With $\alpha = .05$, the critical region consists of z-scores greater than $+1.96$ at one extreme and z-scores less than -1.96 at the other.

STEP 3 Compute the test statistic. For this sample we have $X = 25$ people with decreased pain. This score corresponds to a z-score of

$$z = \frac{X - pn}{\sqrt{npq}} = \frac{25 - 18}{\sqrt{36\left(\frac{1}{2}\right)\left(\frac{1}{2}\right)}} = \frac{7}{3} = 2.33$$

Because the z-score is only slightly beyond the 1.96 critical boundary, we consider the real limits for $X = 25$ to be certain that the entire interval is beyond the boundary. For $X = 25$, the real limits are 24.5 and 25.5, which correspond to z-scores of

$$z = \frac{24.5 - 18}{3} = 2.17 \qquad \text{and} \qquad z = \frac{25.5 - 18}{3} = 2.50$$

Thus, a score of $X = 25$ corresponds to an interval of z-scores ranging from $z = 2.17$ to $z = 2.50$. Note that this entire interval is beyond the 1.96 critical boundary.

STEP 4 Make a decision. Because the data are in the critical region, we reject H_0 and conclude that acupuncture treatment has a significant effect on arthritis pain, $z = 2.33, p < .05$.

ZERO DIFFERENCES IN THE SIGN TEST

You should notice that the null hypothesis in the sign test refers only to those individuals who show some difference between treatment 1 versus treatment 2. The null hypothesis states that if there is any change in an individual's score, then the probability of an increase is equal to the probability of a decrease. Stated in this form, the null hypothesis does not consider individuals who show zero difference between the two treatments. As a result, the usual recommendation is that these individuals be discarded from the data and the value of n be reduced accordingly. However, if the null hypothesis is interpreted more generally, it states that there is no difference between the two treatments. Phrased this way, it should be clear that individuals who show no difference actually are supporting the null hypothesis and should not be discarded. Therefore, an alternative approach to the sign test is to divide individuals who show zero differences equally between the positive and negative categories. (With an odd number of zero differences, discard one, and divide the rest evenly.) This alternative results in a more conservative test; that is, the test is more likely to fail to reject the null hypothesis.

EXAMPLE 18.3 It has been demonstrated that stress or exercise causes an increase in the concentration of certain chemicals in the brain called endorphins. Endorphins are similar to morphine and produce a generally relaxed feeling and a sense of well-being. The endorphins may explain the "high" experienced by long-distance runners. To demonstrate this phenomenon, a researcher tested pain tolerance for 40 athletes before and after they completed a mile run. Immediately after running, the ability to tolerate pain increased for 21 of the athletes, decreased for 12, and showed no change for the remaining 7.

Following the standard recommendation for handling zero differences, you would discard the 7 participants who showed no change and conduct a sign test with the remaining $n = 33$ athletes. With the more conservative approach, only 1 of the 7 who showed no difference would be discarded and the other 6 would be divided equally between the two categories. This would result in a total sample of $n = 39$ athletes with $21 + 3 = 24$ in the increased-tolerance category and $12 + 3 = 15$ in the decreased-tolerance category.

WHEN TO USE THE SIGN TEST

In many cases, data from a repeated-measures experiment can be evaluated using either a sign test or a repeated-measures t test. In general, you should use the t test whenever possible. Because the t test uses the actual difference scores (not just the signs), it makes maximum use of the available information and results in a more powerful test. However, there are some cases in which a t test cannot or should not be used, and in these situations, the sign test can be valuable. Four specific cases in which a t test is inappropriate or inconvenient are described below.

Before	After	Difference
20	23	+3
14	39	+25
27	Failed	+??
.	.	.
.	.	.
.	.	.

1. When you have infinite or undetermined scores, a t test is impossible, and the sign test is appropriate. Suppose, for example, that you are evaluating the effects of a sedative drug on problem-solving ability. A sample of rats is obtained, and each animal's performance is measured before and after receiving the drug. Hypothetical data are shown in the margin. Note that the third rat in this sample failed to solve the problem after receiving the drug. Because there is no score for this animal, it is impossible to compute a sample mean, an *SS*, or a t statistic. However, you could do a sign test because you know that the animal made more errors (an increase) after receiving the drug.
2. Often it is possible to describe the difference between two treatment conditions without precisely measuring a score in either condition. In a clinical setting, for example, a doctor can say whether a patient is improving, growing worse, or showing no change even though the patient's condition is not precisely measured by a score. In this situation, the data are sufficient for a sign test, but you could not compute a t statistic without individual scores.
3. Often a sign test is done as a preliminary check on an experiment before serious statistical analysis begins. For example, a researcher may predict that scores in treatment 2 should be consistently greater than scores in treatment 1. However, examination of the data after 1 week indicates that only 8 of 15 subjects showed the predicted increase. On the basis of these preliminary results, the researcher may choose to reevaluate the experiment before investing additional time.
4. Occasionally, the difference between treatments is not consistent across participants. This can create a very large variance for the difference scores. As we have noted in the past, large variance decreases the likelihood that a t test will produce a significant result. However, the sign test only considers the direction of each difference score and is not influenced by the variance of the scores.

LEARNING CHECK

1. A researcher used a chi-square test for goodness of fit to determine whether people had any preferences among three leading brands of potato chips. Could the researcher have used a binomial test instead of the chi-square test? Explain why or why not.
2. A researcher used a chi-square test to evaluate preferences between two logo designs for a minor-league hockey team. With a sample of $n = 100$ people, the researcher obtained a chi-square of 9.00. If a binomial test had been used instead of chi-square, what value would have been obtained for the z-score?
3. A developmental psychologist is using a behavior-modification program to help control the disruptive behavior of 40 children in a local school. After 1 month, 26 of the children have improved, 10 are worse, and 4 show no change in behavior. On the basis of these data, can the psychologist conclude that the program is working? Test at the .05 level.

ANSWERS

1. No, the binomial test cannot be used when there are three categories.
2. The z-score would be $\sqrt{9} = 3.00$.
3. Discarding the four participants who showed zero difference, $X = 26$ increases out of $n = 36$; $z = 2.67$; reject H_0; the program is working. If the four participants showing no change are divided between the two groups, then $X = 28$ out of $n = 40$; $z = 2.53$ and H_0 is still rejected.

SUMMARY

1. The binomial test is used with dichotomous data—that is, when each individual in the sample is classified in one of two categories. The two categories are identified as *A* and *B*, with probabilities of

$$p(A) = p \text{ and } p(B) = q$$

2. The binomial distribution gives the probability for each value of *X*, where *X* equals the number of occurrences of category *A* in a sample of *n* events. For example, *X* equals the number of heads in $n = 10$ tosses of a coin.

3. When *pn* and *qn* are both at least 10, then the binomial distribution is closely approximated by a normal distribution with

$$\mu = pn \qquad \sigma = \sqrt{npq}$$

By using this normal approximation, each value of *X* has a corresponding *z*-score:

$$z = \frac{X - \mu}{\sigma} = \frac{X - pn}{\sqrt{npq}} \quad \text{or} \quad z = \frac{X/n - p}{\sqrt{pq/n}}$$

4. The binomial test uses sample data to test hypotheses about the binomial proportions, *p* and *q*, for a population. The null hypothesis specifies *p* and *q*, and the binomial distribution (or the normal approximation) is used to determine the critical region.

5. Usually the *z*-score in a binomial test is computed using the whole-number *X* value from the sample. However, if the *z*-score is only marginally in the critical region, you should compute the *z*-scores corresponding to both real limits of the score. If either one of these real-limit *z*-scores is not in the critical region, then the correct decision is to fail to reject the null hypothesis.

6. One common use of the binomial distribution is for the sign test. This test evaluates the difference between two treatments using the data from a repeated measures design. The difference scores are coded as being either increases (+) or decreases (−). Without a consistent treatment effect, the increases and decreases should be mixed randomly, so the null hypothesis states that

$$p(\text{increase}) = \frac{1}{2} = p(\text{decrease})$$

With dichotomous data and hypothesized values for *p* and *q*, this is a binomial test.

KEY TERMS

binomial data (634)
binomial test (635)
binomial distribution (636)
sign test (643)

RESOURCES

Book Companion Website: www.cengage.com/psychology/gravetter

You can find a tutorial quiz and other learning exercises for Chapter 18 on the book companion website.

aplia

Improve your understanding of statistics with Aplia's auto-graded problem sets and immediate, detailed explanations for every question. To learn more, visit **www.aplia.com/statistics.**

CENGAGEbrain.com

Log in to CengageBrain to access the resources your instructor requires. For this book, you can access:

Psychology CourseMate brings course concepts to life with interactive learning, study, and exam preparation tools that support the printed textbook. A textbook-specific website, Psychology CourseMate includes an integrated interactive eBook and other interactive learning tools including quizzes, flashcards, and more.

Visit www.cengagebrain.com to access your account and purchase materials.

SPSS

General instructions for using SPSS are found in Appendix D. If you are testing a null hypothesis specifying that $p = q = \frac{1}{2}$, then you can use SPSS to perform The Binomial Test presented in this chapter. Following are detailed instructions for the test. For other versions of the null hypothesis, use the equivalent chi-square test for goodness of fit presented in Chapter 17 (p. 594). The chi-square test allows you to specify expected frequencies, which is equivalent to specifying values for p and q.

Data Entry

1. Enter the category labels A and B in the first column of the SPSS data editor.
2. In the second column, enter the frequencies obtained for the two binomial categories. For example, if 21 out of 25 people were classified in category A (and only 4 people in category B), you would enter the values 21 and 4 in the second column.

Data Analysis

1. Click **Data** on the tool bar at the top of the page and select **weight cases** at the bottom of the list.
2. Click the **Weight cases by** circle, then highlight the label for the column containing the frequencies for the two categories and move it into the **Frequency Variable** box by clicking on the arrow.
3. Click **OK.**
4. Click **Analyze** on the tool bar, select **Nonparametric Tests,** and click on **One Sample.**
5. Select **Automatically compare observed data to hypothesis**.
6. Click **RUN.**

SPSS Output

We used SPSS to analyze the data from Example 18.1 and the output is shown in Figure 18.3. The output reports the null hypothesis for the test and the level of significance, which is rounded to .000 for this example.

FIGURE 18.3

The SPSS output for the binomial test in Example 18.1.

Hypothesis Test Summary

Null Hypothesis	Test	Sig.	Decision
The categories defined by VAR00001 = A and B occur with probabilities 0.5 and 0.5.	One-Sample Binomial Test	.000	Reject the null hypothesis.

Asymptotic significances are displayed. The significance level is .05.

FOCUS ON PROBLEM SOLVING

1. For all binomial tests, the values of p and q must add up to 1.00 (or 100%).
2. Remember that both pn and qn must be at least 10 before you can use the normal distribution to determine critical values for a binomial test.

DEMONSTRATION 18.1

THE BINOMIAL TEST

The population of students in the psychology department at State College consists of 60% females and 40% males. Last semester, the Psychology of Gender course had a total of 36 students, of whom 26 were female and only 10 were male. Are the proportions of females and males in this class significantly different from what would be expected by chance from a population with 60% females and 40% males? Test at the .05 level of significance.

STEP 1 *State the hypotheses, and specify alpha.* The null hypothesis states that the male/female proportions for the class are not different from what is expected for a population with these proportions. In symbols,

$$H_0\text{:}\quad p = p(\text{female}) = 0.60 \text{ and } q = p(\text{male}) = 0.40$$

The alternative hypothesis is that the proportions for this class are different from what is expected for these population proportions.

$$H_1\text{:}\quad p \neq 0.60 \text{ (and } q \neq 0.40\text{)}$$

We set alpha at $\alpha = .05$.

STEP 2 *Locate the critical region.* Because pn and qn are both greater than 10, we can use the normal approximation to the binomial distribution. With $\alpha = .05$, the critical region is defined as a z-score value greater than -1.96 or less than -1.96.

STEP 3 *Calculate the test statistic.* The sample has 26 females out of 36 students, so the sample proportion is

$$\frac{X}{n} = \frac{26}{36} = 0.72$$

The corresponding z-score (using Equation 18.2) is

$$z = \frac{X/n - p}{\sqrt{pq/n}} = \frac{0.72 - 0.60}{\sqrt{\dfrac{0.60(0.40)}{36}}} = \frac{0.12}{0.0816} = 1.47$$

STEP 4 *Make a decision about H_0, and state a conclusion.* The obtained z-score is not in the critical region. Therefore, we fail to reject the null hypothesis. On the basis of these data, you conclude that the male/female proportions in the gender class are not significantly different from the proportions in the psychology department as a whole.

PROBLEMS

1. To investigate the phenomenon of "home team advantage," a researcher recorded the outcomes from 64 college football games on one Saturday in October. Of the 64 games, 42 were won by home teams. Does this result provide enough evidence to conclude that home teams win significantly more than would be expected by chance? Use a two-tailed test with $\alpha = .05$.

2. A researcher would like to determine whether people really can tell the difference between bottled water and tap water. Participants are asked to taste two unlabeled glasses of water, one bottled and one tap, and identify the one they thought tasted better. Out of 40 people in the sample, 28 picked the bottled water. Was the bottled water selected significantly more often than would be expected by chance? Use a two-tailed test with $\alpha = .05$.

3. Güven, Elaimis, Binokay, and Tan (2003) studied the distribution of paw preferences in rats using a computerized food-reaching test. For a sample of $n = 144$ rats, they found 104 right-handed animals. Is this significantly more than would be expected if right- and left-handed rats are equally common in the population? Use a two-tailed test with $\alpha = .01$.

4. During the 2004 Olympic Games, Hill and Barton (2005) monitored contests in four combat sports: Greco-Roman wrestling, freestyle wrestling, boxing, and tae kwon do. Half of the competitors were assigned red outfits and half were assigned blue. The results indicate that participants wearing red won significantly more contests. Suppose that a sample of $n = 100$ contests produced 60 winners wearing red and only 40 wearing blue.
   a. Is this enough evidence to justify a conclusion that wearing red produces significantly more wins than would be expected by chance? Use a two-tailed test with $\alpha = .05$.
   b. Because the outcome of the binomial test is a borderline z-score, use the real limits for $X = 60$ to determine if the entire z-score interval is located in the critical region. If any part of the interval is not in the critical region, the correct decision is to fail to reject the null hypothesis.

5. Problem 6 in Chapter 17 cited a study showing that people tend to choose partners who are similar to themselves. Jones, Pelham, Carvallo, & Mirenberg, (2004) demonstrated that people have a tendency to select marriage partners with surnames that begin with the same last letter as their own. The probability of randomly matching two last names beginning with the same letter is only $p = 0.065$ (6.5%). The researchers looked at marriage records and found that 38 out of 400 brides and grooms had surnames beginning with the same last letter. Is this significantly more than would be expected by chance? Use a two-tailed test with $\alpha = .05$.

6. Insurance companies charge young drivers more for automobile insurance because they tend to have more accidents than older drivers. To make this point, an insurance representative first determines that only 16% of licensed drivers are age 20 or younger. Because this age group makes up only 16% of the drivers, it is reasonable to predict that they should be involved in only 16% of the accidents. In a random sample of 100 accident reports, however, the representative finds 31 accidents that involved drivers who were 20 or younger. Is this sample sufficient to show that younger drivers have significantly more accidents than would be expected from the percentage of young drivers? Use a two-tailed test with $\alpha = .05$.

7. In 1985, only 8% of the students in the city school district were classified as being learning disabled. A school psychologist suspects that the proportion of learning-disabled children has changed dramatically over the years. To demonstrate this point, a random sample of $n = 300$ students is selected. In this sample there are 42 students who have been identified as learning-disabled. Is this sample sufficient to indicate that there has been a significant change in the proportion of learning-disabled students since 1985? Use the .05 level of significance.

8. In the Preview section for Chapter 17, we discussed a study by Loftus and Palmer (1974) examining how different phrasing of questions can influence eyewitness testimony. In the study, students watched a video of an automobile accident and then were questioned about what they had seen. One group of participants was asked to estimate the speed of the cars when they "smashed into" each other. Another group of was asked to estimate the speed of the cars when they "hit" each other. Suppose that the actual speed of the cars was 22 miles per hour.
   a. For the 50 people in the "smashed-into" group, assume that 32 overestimated the actual speed, 17 underestimated the speed, and 1 was exactly right. Is this result significantly different from what would be expected by chance? Use a two-tailed test with $\alpha = .05$.
   b. For the 50 people in the "hit" group, assume that 27 overestimated the actual speed, 22 underestimated the speed, 1 was exactly right. Again, use a two-tailed test with $\alpha = .05$ to determine whether this result significantly different from what would be expected by chance.

9. A recent survey of practicing psychotherapists revealed that 25% of the individuals responding agreed with the

statement, "Hypnosis can be used to recover accurate memories of past lives" (Yapko, 1994). A researcher would like to determine whether this same level of belief exists in the general population. A sample of 192 adults is surveyed and 65 believe that hypnosis can be used to recover accurate memories of past lives. Based on these data, can you conclude that beliefs held by the general population are significantly different from beliefs held by psychotherapists? Test with $\alpha = .05$.

10. In 2005, Fung et al. published a study reporting that patients prefer technical quality versus interpersonal skills when selecting a primary care physician. Participants were presented with report cards describing pairs of hypothetical physicians and were asked to select the one that they preferred. Suppose that this study is repeated with a sample of $n = 150$ participants, and the results show that physicians with greater technical skill are preferred by 92 participants and physicians with greater interpersonal skills are selected by 58. Are these results sufficient to conclude that there is a significant preference for technical skill?

11. Danner and Phillips (2008) report the results from a county-wide study showing that delaying high school start times by one hour significantly reduced the motor vehicle crash rate for teen drivers in the study. Suppose that the researchers monitored 500 student drivers for 1 year after the start time was delayed and found that 44 were involved in automobile accidents. Before delaying the start time, the accident rate was 12%. Use a binomial test to determine whether these results indicate a significant change in the accident rate following the change in school start time. Use a two-tailed test with $\alpha = .05$

12. In the Preview section for Chapter 11, we presented a study showing that swearing can help relieve pain (Stephens, Atkins, & Kingston, 2009). In the study, participants placed one hand in freezing cold water for as long as they could bear the pain. In one condition, they shouted a swear word over and over while the hand was in the water. In the other condition, they shouted a neutral word. Suppose that 18 of the 25 participants tolerated the pain longer while swearing than while shouting neutral words. Is this result significantly different from chance? Use a two-tailed test with $\alpha = .01$.

13. On a multiple-choice exam with 100 questions and 4 possible answers for each question, you get a score of $X = 32$. Is your score significantly better than would be expected by chance (by simply guessing for each question)? Use a two tailed test with $\alpha = .05$.

14. For each of the following, assume that a two-tailed test using the normal approximation to the binomial distribution with $\alpha = .05$ is being used to evaluate the significance of the result.

a. For a multiple-choice test with 48 questions, each with 4 possible answers, how many would you have to get right to do significantly better than chance? That is, what X value is needed to produce a z-score greater than 1.96?

b. How many would you need to get right on a multiple-choice test with 192 questions to be significantly better than chance?

Remember that each X value corresponds to an interval with real limits. Be sure that the entire interval is in the critical region.

15. Reed, Vernon, and Johnson (2004) examined the relationship between brain nerve conduction velocity and intelligence in normal adults. Brain nerve conduction velocity was measured three separate ways and nine different measures were used for intelligence. The researchers then correlated each of the three nerve velocity measures with each of the nine intelligence measures for a total of 27 separate correlations. Unfortunately, none of the correlations were significant.

a. For the 186 males in the study, however, 25 of the 27 correlations were positive. Is this significantly more than would be expected if positive and negative correlations were equally likely? Use a two-tailed test with $\alpha = .05$.

b. For the 201 females in the study, 20 of the 27 correlations were positive. Is this significantly more than would be expected if positive and negative correlations were equally likely? Use a two-tailed test with $\alpha = .05$.

16. For each of the following, assume that a two-tailed test using the normal approximation to the binomial distribution with $\alpha = .05$ is being used to evaluate the significance of the result.

a. For a true-false test with 20 questions, how many would you have to get right to do significantly better than chance? That is, what X value is needed to produce a z-score greater than 1.96?

b. How many would you need to get right on a 40-question true-false test?

c. How many would you need to get right on a 100-question true-false test?

Remember that each X value corresponds to an interval with real limits. Be sure that the entire interval is in the critical region.

17. Thirty percent of the students in the local elementary school are classified as only children (no siblings). However, in the special program for talented and gifted children, 43 out of 90 students are only children. Is the proportion of only children in the special program significantly different from the proportion for the school? Test at the .05 level of significance.

18. Stressful or traumatic experiences can often worsen other health-related problems such as asthma or rheumatoid arthritis. However, if patients are instructed to write about their stressful experiences, it can often lead to improvement in health (Smyth, Stone, Hurewitz, & Kaell, 1999). In a typical study, patients with asthma or arthritis are asked to write about the "most stressful event of your life." In a sample of $n = 112$ patients, suppose that 64 showed improvement in their symptoms, 12 showed no change, and 36 showed worsening symptoms.
   a. If the 12 patients showing no change are discarded, are these results sufficient to conclude that the writing had a significant effect? Use a two-tailed test with $\alpha = .05$.
   b. If the 12 patients who showed no change are split between the two groups, are the results sufficient to demonstrate a significant change? Use a two-tailed test with $\alpha = .05$.

19. Langewitz, Izakovic, and Wyler (2005) reported that self-hypnosis can significantly reduce hay-fever symptoms. Patients with moderate to severe allergic reactions were trained to focus their minds on specific locations where their allergies did not bother them, such as a beach or a ski resort. In a sample of 64 patients who received this training, suppose that 47 showed reduced allergic reactions and 17 showed an increase in allergic reactions. Are these results sufficient to conclude that the self-hypnosis has a significant effect? Use a two-tailed test with $\alpha = .05$.

20. The habituation technique is one method that is used to examine memory for infants. The procedure involves presenting a stimulus to an infant (usually projected on the ceiling above the crib) for a fixed time period and recording how long the infant spends looking at the stimulus. After a brief delay, the stimulus is presented again. If the infant spends less time looking at the stimulus during the second presentation, it is interpreted as indicating that the stimulus is remembered and, therefore, is less novel and less interesting than it was on the first presentation. This procedure is used with a sample of $n = 30$ 2-week-old infants. For this sample, 22 infants spent less time looking at the stimulus during the second presentation than during the first. Do these data indicate a significant difference? Test at the .01 level of significance.

21. In Problem 21 in Chapter 11, we described a study showing that students are likely to improve their test scores if they go back and change answers after reconsidering some of the questions on the exam (Johnston, 1975). In the study, one group of students was encouraged to reconsider each question and to change answers whenever they felt it was appropriate. The students were asked to record their original answers as well as the changes. For each student, the exam was graded based on the original answers and on the changed answers. For a group of $n = 40$ students, suppose that 29 had higher scores for the changed-answer version and only 11 had higher scores for the original-answer version. Is this result significantly different from chance? Use a two-tailed test with $\alpha = .01$.

22. Group-housed laying hens appear to prefer having more floor space than height in their cages. Albentosa and Cooper (2005) tested hens in groups of 10. The birds in each group were given free choice between a cage with a height of 38 cm (low) and a cage with a height of 45 cm (high). The results showed a tendency for the hens in each group to distribute themselves evenly between the two cages, showing no preference for either height. Suppose that a similar study tested a sample of $n = 80$ hens and found that 47 preferred the taller cage. Does this result indicate a significant preference? Use a two-tailed test with $\alpha = .05$.

23. Most children and adults are able to learn the meaning of new words by listening to sentences in which the words appear. Shulman and Guberman (2007) tested the ability of children to learn word meaning from syntactical cues for three groups: children with autism, children with specific language impairment (SLI), and children with typical language development (TLD). Although the researchers used relatively small samples, their results indicate that the children with TLD and those with autism were able to learn novel words using the syntactical cues in sentences. The children with SLI, on the other hand, experienced significantly more difficulty. Suppose that a similar study is conducted in which each child listens to a set of sentences containing a novel word and then is given a choice of three definitions for the word.
   a. If 25 out of 36 autistic children select the correct definition, is this significantly more than would be expected if they were simply guessing? Use a two-tailed test with $\alpha = .05$.
   b. If only 16 out of 36 children with SLI select the correct definition, is this significantly more than would be expected if they were simply guessing? Use a two-tailed test with $\alpha = .05$.

24. A researcher is testing the effectiveness of a skills-mastery imagery program for soccer players. A sample of $n = 25$ college varsity players is selected and each player is tested on a ball-handling obstacle course before beginning the imagery program and again after completing the 5-week program. Of the 25 players, 18 showed improved performance on the obstacle course after the imagery program and 7 were worse.

a. Is this result sufficient to conclude that there is a significant change in performance following the imagery program? Use a two-tailed test with $\alpha = .05$.

b. Because the outcome of the binomial test is a borderline z-score, use the real limits for $X = 18$ and verify that the entire z-score interval is located in the critical region.

25. Last year the college counseling center offered a workshop for students who claimed to suffer from extreme exam anxiety. Of the 45 students who attended the workshop, 31 had higher grade-point averages this semester than they did last year. Do these data indicate a significant difference from what would be expected by chance? Test at the .01 level of significance.

26. Trying to fight a drug-resistant bacteria, a researcher tries an experimental drug on infected subjects. Out of 70 monkeys, 42 showed improvement, 22 got worse, and 6 showed no change. Is this researcher working in the right direction? Is there a significant effect of the drug on the infection? Use a two-tailed test at the .05 level of significance.

27. Biofeedback training is often used to help people who suffer migraine headaches. A recent study found that 29 out of 50 participants reported a decrease in the frequency and severity of their headaches after receiving biofeedback training. Of the remaining participants in this study, 10 reported that their headaches were worse, and 11 reported no change.

a. Discard the zero-difference participants, and use a sign test with $\alpha = .05$ to determine whether the biofeedback produced a significant difference.

b. Divide the zero-difference participants between the two groups, and use a sign test to evaluate the effect of biofeedback training.

PART V

REVIEW

After completing this part, you should be able to calculate and interpret correlations, find linear regression equations, conduct the chi-square tests for goodness of fit and for independence, and do a binomial test.

The most commonly used correlation is the Pearson correlation, which measures the direction and degree of linear relationship between two variables (X and Y) that have been measured on interval or ratio scales (numerical scores). The regression equation determines the best fitting line to describe the relationship between X and Y, and to compute predicted Y values for each value of X. A partial correlation can be used to reveal the underlying relationship between X and Y when the influence of a third variable is eliminated.

The Pearson formula is also used in a variety of other situations to compute special correlations. The Spearman correlation uses the Pearson formula when X and Y are both measured on ordinal scales (ranks). The Spearman correlation measures the direction and the degree to which the relationship is consistently one directional. When one of the variables consists of numerical scores and the other has only two values, the two values of the dichotomous variable can be coded as 0 and 1, and the Pearson formula can be used to find the point-biserial correlation. The point-biserial correlation measures the strength of the relationship between X and Y, and can be squared to produce the same r^2 value that is used to measure effect size for the independent-measures t test. When both variables are dichotomous, they can both be coded as 0 and 1, and the Pearson formula can be used to find the phi-coefficient. As a correlation, the phi-coefficient measures the strength of the relationship and is often used as a measure of effect size to accompany a chi-square test for independence for a 2×2 data matrix.

The chi-square test for goodness of fit uses the frequency distribution from a sample to evaluate a hypothesis about the corresponding population distribution. The null hypothesis for the goodness-of-fit test typically falls into one of two categories:

1. Equal proportions: The null hypothesis states that the population is equally distributed across the set of categories.
2. No difference: The null hypothesis states that the distribution for one population is not different from the known distribution for another population.

The chi-square test for independence uses frequency data from a sample to evaluate a hypothesis about the relationship between two variables in the population. The null hypothesis for this test can be phrased two different ways:

1. No relationship: The null hypothesis states that there is no relationship between the two variables in the population.
2. No difference: One variable is viewed as defining a set of different populations. The null hypothesis states that the frequency distribution for the second variable has the same shape (same proportions) for all the different populations.

The binomial test uses the frequencies or proportions from a sample to test a hypothesis about the corresponding population proportions for a binomial variable in the population. Because the binomial distribution approximates the normal distribution when pn and qn are both at least 10, it uses z-scores and proportions from the unit normal table for the test.

REVIEW PROBLEMS

1. The following scores are related by the equation $Y = X^2$. Note that this is not a linear relationship, but every time X increases, Y also increases.

X	Y
2	4
4	16
6	36
8	64
10	100

   a. Compute the Pearson correlation between X and Y. You should find a positive, but not perfect, correlation.

   b. Convert the scores to ranks and compute the Spearman correlation. You should find a perfect, positive correlation.

2. It is well known that similarity in attitudes, beliefs, and interests plays an important role in interpersonal attraction (see Byrne, 1971, for example). Thus, correlations for attitudes between married couples should be strong. Suppose that a researcher developed a questionnaire that measures how liberal or conservative one's attitudes are. Low scores indicate that the person has liberal attitudes, whereas high scores indicate conservatism. The following hypothetical data are scores for married couples.

Couple	Wife	Husband
A	11	14
B	6	7
C	16	15
D	4	7
E	1	3
F	10	9
G	5	9
H	3	8

a. Compute the Pearson correlation for these data.
b. Find the regression equation for predicting the husband's score from the wife's.

3. A researcher is investigating the physical characteristics that influence whether a person's face is judged as beautiful. The researcher selects a photograph of a woman and then creates two modifications of the photo by (1) moving the eyes slightly farther apart and (2) moving the eyes slightly closer together. The original photograph and the two modifications are then shown to a sample of $n = 150$ college students, and each student is asked to select the "most beautiful" of the three faces. The distribution of responses was as follows:

Original Photo	Eyes Moved Apart	Eyes Moved Together
51	72	27

Do the data indicate any significant preferences among the three versions of the photograph? Test at the .05 level of significance.

4. Friedman and Rosenman (1974) have suggested that personality type is related to heart disease. Specifically, type A people, who are competitive, driven, pressured, and impatient, are more prone to heart disease. On the other hand, type B individuals, who are less competitive and more relaxed, are less likely to have heart disease. Suppose that an investigator would like to examine the relationship between personality type and disease. For a random sample of individuals, personality type is assessed with a standardized test. These individuals are then examined and categorized as to whether they have a heart disorder. The observed frequencies are as follows:

	No Heart Disease	Heart Disease	
Type A	32	18	50
Type B	128	22	150
	160	40	

a. Is there a relationship between personality and disorder? Test at the .05 level of significance.
b. Compute the phi-coefficient to measure the strength of the relationship.

5. One of the original methods for testing ESP (extrasensory perception) used Zener cards, which were designed specifically for the testing process. Each card shows one of five symbols (square, circle, star, wavy lines, cross). The person being tested must predict the symbol before the card is turned over. Chance performance on this task would produce 1 out of 5 (20%) correct predictions. Use a binomial test to determine whether 27 correct predictions out of 100 attempts is significantly different from chance performance? Use a two-tailed test with $\alpha = .05$.

CHAPTER

19

Choosing the Right Statistics

Tools You Will Need

This chapter provides an organized overview for most of the statistical procedures presented in this book. The following items are considered background material for this chapter. If you doubt your knowledge of any of these items, you should review the appropriate chapter or section before proceeding.

- Descriptive statistics
- Mean (Chapter 3)
- Standard deviation (Chapter 4)
- Correlation (Chapter 15)
- Inferential Statistics (Chapters 9, 10, 11, 12, 13, 14, 15, 16, 17, 18)

Preview

After students have completed a statistics course, they occasionally are confronted with situations in which they have to apply the statistics they have learned. For example, in the context of a research methods course, or while working as a research assistant, students are presented with the results from a study and asked to do the appropriate statistical analysis. The problem is that many of these students have no idea where to begin. Although they have learned the individual statistics, they cannot match the statistical procedures to a specific set of data. Our goal for this chapter is to provide some help with the problem.

We assume that you know (or can anticipate) what your data look like. Therefore, we begin by presenting some basic categories of data so you can find that one that matches your own data. For each data category, we then present the potential statistical procedures and identify the factors that determine which are appropriate for you based on the specific characteristics of your data.

19.1 THREE BASIC DATA STRUCTURES

Most research data can be classified in one of three basic categories.

Category 1: A single group of participants with one score per participant.

Category 2: A single group of participants with two (or more) variables measured for each participant.

Category 3: Two (or more) groups of scores with each score a measurement of the same variable.

In this section, we present examples of each structure. Once you match your own data to one of the examples, you can proceed to the section of the chapter in which we describe the statistical procedures that apply to that example.

SCALES OF MEASUREMENT

Before we begin discussion of the three categories of data, there is one other factor that differentiates data within each category and helps to determine which statistics are appropriate. In Chapter 1, we introduced four scales of measurement and noted that different measurement scales allow different kinds of mathematical manipulation, which result in different statistics. For most statistical applications, however, ratio and interval scales are equivalent so we group them together for the following review.

Ratio scales and **interval scales** produce numerical scores that are compatible with the full range of mathematical manipulation. Examples include measurements of height in inches, weight in pounds, the number of errors on a task, and IQ scores.

Ordinal scales consist of ranks or ordered categories. Examples include classifying cups of coffee as small, medium, and large or ranking job applicants as 1st, 2nd, and 3rd.

Nominal scales consist of named categories. Examples include gender (male/female), academic major, or occupation.

Within each category of data, we present examples representing these three measurement scales and discuss the statistics that apply to each.

CATEGORY 1: A SINGLE GROUP OF PARTICIPANTS WITH ONE SCORE PER PARTICIPANT

This type of data often exists in research studies that are conducted simply to describe individual variables as they exist naturally. For example, a recent news report stated that half of American teenagers, ages 12 through 17, send 50 or more text messages a day. To get this number, the researchers had to measure the number of text messages for each individual in a large sample of teenagers. The resulting data consist of one score per participant for a single group.

It is also possible that the data are a portion of the results from a larger study examining several variables. For example, a college administrator may conduct a survey to obtain information describing the eating, sleeping, and study habits of the college's students. Although several variables are being measured, the intent is to look at them one at a time. For example, the administrator will look at the number of hours each week that each student spends studying. These data consist of one score for each individual in a single group. The administrator will then shift attention to the number of hours per day that each student spends sleeping. Again, the data consist of one score for each person in a single group. The identifying feature for this type of research (and this type of data) is that there is no attempt to examine relationships between different variables. Instead, the goal is to describe individual variables, one at a time.

Table 19.1 presents three examples of data in this category. Note that the three data sets differ in terms of the scale of measurement used to obtain the scores. The first set (a) shows numerical scores measured on an interval or ratio scale. The second set (b) consists of ordinal, or rank ordered categories, and the third set shows nominal measurements. The statistics used for data in this category are discussed in Section 19.2.

CATEGORY 2: A SINGLE GROUP OF PARTICIPANTS WITH TWO (OR MORE) VARIABLES MEASURED FOR EACH PARTICIPANT

These research studies are specifically intended to examine relationships between variables. Note that different variables are being measured, so each participant has two or more scores, each representing a different variable. Typically, there is no attempt to manipulate or control the variables; they are simply observed and recorded as they exist naturally.

Although several variables may be measured, researchers usually select pairs of variables to evaluate specific relationships. Therefore, we present examples showing pairs of variables. Table 19.2 presents four examples of data in this category. Once again, the four data sets differ in terms of the scales of measurement that are used. The first set of data (a) shows numerical scores for each set of measurements. For the second set (b), we have ranked the scores from the first set and show the resulting ranks. The third data set (c) shows numerical scores for one variable and nominal scores for the second variable. In the fourth set (d), both scores are measured on a nominal scale

TABLE 19.1

Three examples of data with one score per participant for one group of participants.

(a) Number of Text Messages Sent in Past 24 Hours	(b) Rank in Class for High School Graduation	(c) Got a Flu Shot Last Season
X	X	X
6	23rd	No
13	18th	No
28	5th	Yes
11	38th	No
9	17th	Yes
31	42nd	No
18	32nd	No

TABLE 19.2

Examples of data with two scores for each participant for one group of participants.

(a) SAT Score (*X*) and College Freshman GPA (*Y*)		(b) Ranks for the Scores in Set (a)	
X	*Y*	*X*	*Y*
620	3.90	7	8
540	3.12	3	2
590	3.45	6	5
480	2.75	1	1
510	3.20	2	3
660	3.85	8	7
570	3.50	5	6
560	3.24	4	4

(c) Age (*X*) and Wrist Watch Preference (*Y*)		(d) Gender (*X*) and Academic Major (*Y*)	
X	*Y*	*X*	*Y*
27	digital	M	Sciences
43	analog	M	Humanities
19	digital	F	Arts
34	digital	M	Professions
37	digital	F	Professions
49	analog	F	Humanities
22	digital	F	Arts
65	analog	M	Sciences
46	digital	F	Humanities

of measurement. The appropriate statistical analyses for these data are discussed in Section 19.3.

CATEGORY 3: TWO OR MORE GROUPS OF SCORES WITH EACH SCORE A MEASUREMENT OF THE SAME VARIABLE

A second method for examining relationships between variables is to use the categories of one variable to define different groups and then measure a second variable to obtain a set of scores within each group. The first variable, defining the groups, usually falls into one of the following general categories:

a. Participant characteristic: For example, gender or age.

b. Time: For example, before versus after treatment.

c. Treatment conditions: For example, with caffeine versus without caffeine.

If the scores in one group are consistently different from the scores in another group, then the data indicate a relationship between variables. For example, if the performance scores for a group of females are consistently higher than the scores for a group of males, then there is a relationship between performance and gender.

Another factor that differentiates data sets in this category is the distinction between independent-measures and repeated-measures designs. Independent-measures designs were introduced in Chapters 10 and 12, and repeated-measures designs were presented in Chapters 11 and 13. You should recall that an *independent-measures design,* also known as a *between-subjects design,* requires a separate group of participants for each group of scores. For example, a study comparing scores for males with scores for females would require two groups of participants. On the other hand, a *repeated-measures design,* also known as a *within-subjects design,* obtains several groups of scores from the same group of participants. A common example of a repeated-measures design is a before/after study in which one group of individuals is measured before a treatment and then measured again after the treatment.

Examples of data sets in this category are presented in Table 19.3. The table includes a sampling of independent-measures and repeated-measures designs as well as examples representing measurements from several different scales of measurement. The appropriate statistical analyses for data in this category are discussed in Section 19.4.

19.2 STATISTICAL PROCEDURES FOR DATA FROM A SINGLE GROUP OF PARTICIPANTS WITH ONE SCORE PER PARTICIPANT

One feature of this data category is that the researcher typically does not want to examine a relationship between variables but rather simply intends to describe individual variables as they exist naturally. Therefore, the most commonly used statistical procedures for these data are descriptive statistics that are used to summarize and describe the group of scores.

We should note that the same descriptive statistics used to describe a single group are also used to describe groups of scores that are a part of more complex data sets. For example, a researcher may want to compare a set of scores for males with a set of scores

TABLE 19.3

Examples of data comparing two or more groups of scores with all scores measuring the same variable.

(a) Attractiveness Ratings for a Woman in a Photograph Shown on a Red or a White Background

White	Red
5	7
4	5
4	4
3	5
4	6
3	4
4	5

(b) Performance Scores Before and After 24 Hours of Sleep Deprivation

Participant	Before	After
A	9	7
B	7	6
C	7	5
D	8	8
E	5	4
F	9	8
G	8	5

(c) Success or Failure on a Task for Participants Working Alone or in a Group

Alone	Group
Fail	Succeed
Succeed	Succeed
Succeed	Succeed
Succeed	Succeed
Fail	Fail
Fail	Succeed
Succeed	Succeed
Fail	Succeed

(d) Amount of Time Spent on Facebook (Small, Medium, Large) for Students from Each High School Class

Freshman	Sophomore	Junior	Senior
med	small	med	large
small	large	large	med
small	med	large	med
med	med	large	large
small	med	med	large
large	large	med	large
med	large	small	med
small	med	large	large

for females (data from category 3). However, the statistics used to describe the group of males would be the same as the descriptive statistics that would be used if the males were the only group in the study.

SCORES FROM RATIO OR INTERVAL SCALES: NUMERICAL SCORES

When the data consist of numerical values from interval or ratio scales, there are several options for descriptive and inferential statistics. We consider the most likely statistics and mention some alternatives.

Descriptive Statistics The most often used descriptive statistics for numerical scores are the mean (Chapter 3) and the standard deviation (Chapter 4). If there are a few extreme scores or the distribution is strongly skewed, the median (Chapter 3) may be better than the mean as a measure of central tendency.

Inferential Statistics If there is a basis for a null hypothesis concerning the mean of the population from which the scores were obtained, a single-sample t test (Chapter 9) can be used to evaluate the hypothesis. Some potential sources for a null hypothesis are as follows:

1. If the scores are from a measurement scale with a well-defined neutral point, then the t test can be used to determine whether the sample mean is significantly different from (higher than or lower than) the neutral point. On a 7-point rating scale, for example, a score of $X = 4$ is often identified as neutral. The null hypothesis would state that the population mean is equal to (greater than or less than) $\mu = 4$.
2. If the mean is known for a comparison population, then the t test can be used to determine whether the sample mean is significantly different from (higher than or lower than) the known value. For example, it may be known that the average score on a standardized reading achievement test for children finishing first grade is $\mu = 20$. If the sample consists of test scores for first grade children who are all the only child in the household, the null hypothesis would state that the mean for children in this population is also equal to 20. The known mean could also be from an earlier time, for example 10 years ago. The hypothesis test would then determine whether a sample from today's population indicates a significant change in the mean during the past 10 years.

The single-sample t test evaluates the statistical significance of the results. A significant result means that the data are very unlikely ($p < \alpha$) to have been produced by random, chance factors. However, the test does not measure the size or strength of the effect. Therefore, a t test should be accompanied by a measure of effect size such as Cohen's d or the percentage of variance accounted for, r^2.

SCORES FROM ORDINAL SCALES: RANKS OR ORDERED CATEGORIES

Descriptive Statistics Occasionally, the original scores are measurements on an ordinal scale. It is also possible that the original numerical scores have been transformed into ranks or ordinal categories (for example, small, medium, and large). In either case, the median is appropriate for describing central tendency for ordinal measurements and proportions can be used to describe the distribution of individuals across categories. For example, a researcher might report that 60% of the students were in the high self-esteem category, 30% in the moderate self-esteem category, and only 10% in the low self-esteem category.

Inferential Statistics If there is a basis for a null hypothesis specifying the proportions in each ordinal category for the population from which the scores were obtained, then a chi-square test for goodness of fit (Chapter 17) can be used to evaluate the hypothesis. With only two categories, the binomial test (Chapter 18) also can be used. For example, it may be reasonable to hypothesize that the categories occur equally often (equal proportions) in the population and the test would determine whether the sample proportions are significantly different. If the original data were converted from numerical values into ordered categories using z-score values to define the category boundaries, then the null hypothesis could state that the population distribution is normal, using proportions obtained from the unit normal table. A chi-square test for goodness of fit would determine whether the shape of the sample distribution is significantly different from a normal distribution. For example, the null hypothesis would state that the distribution has the following proportions, which describe a normal distribution according to the unit normal table:

$z < -1.5$	$-1.5 < z < -0.5$	$-0.5 < z < 0.5$	$0.5 < z < 1.5$	$z > 1.50$
6.68%	24.17%	38.30%	24.17%	6.68%

SCORES FROM A NOMINAL SCALE

For these data, the scores simply indicate the nominal category for each individual. For example, individuals could be classified as male/female or grouped into different occupational categories.

Descriptive Statistics The only descriptive statistics available for these data are the mode (Chapter 3) for describing central tendency or using proportions (or percentages) to describe the distribution across categories.

Inferential Statistics If there is a basis for a null hypothesis specifying the proportions in each category for the population from which the scores were obtained, then a chi-square test for goodness of fit (Chapter 17) can be used to evaluate the hypothesis. With only two categories, the binomial test (Chapter 18) also can be used. For example, it may be reasonable to hypothesize that the categories occur equally often (equal proportions) in the population. If proportions are known for a comparison population or for a previous time, the null hypothesis could specify that the proportions are the same for the population from which the scores were obtained. For example, if it is known that 35% of the adults in the United States get a flu shot each season, then a researcher could select a sample of college students and count how many got a shot and how many did not [see the data in Table 19.1(c)]. The null hypothesis for a chi-square test or a binomial test would state that the distribution for college students is not different from the distribution for the general population. For the chi-square test

	Flu Shot	No Flu Shot
H_0:	35%	65%

For the binomial test, H_0: $p = p(\text{shot}) = 0.35$ and $q = p(\text{no shot}) = 0.65$

Figure 19.1 summarizes the statistical procedures used for data in category 1.

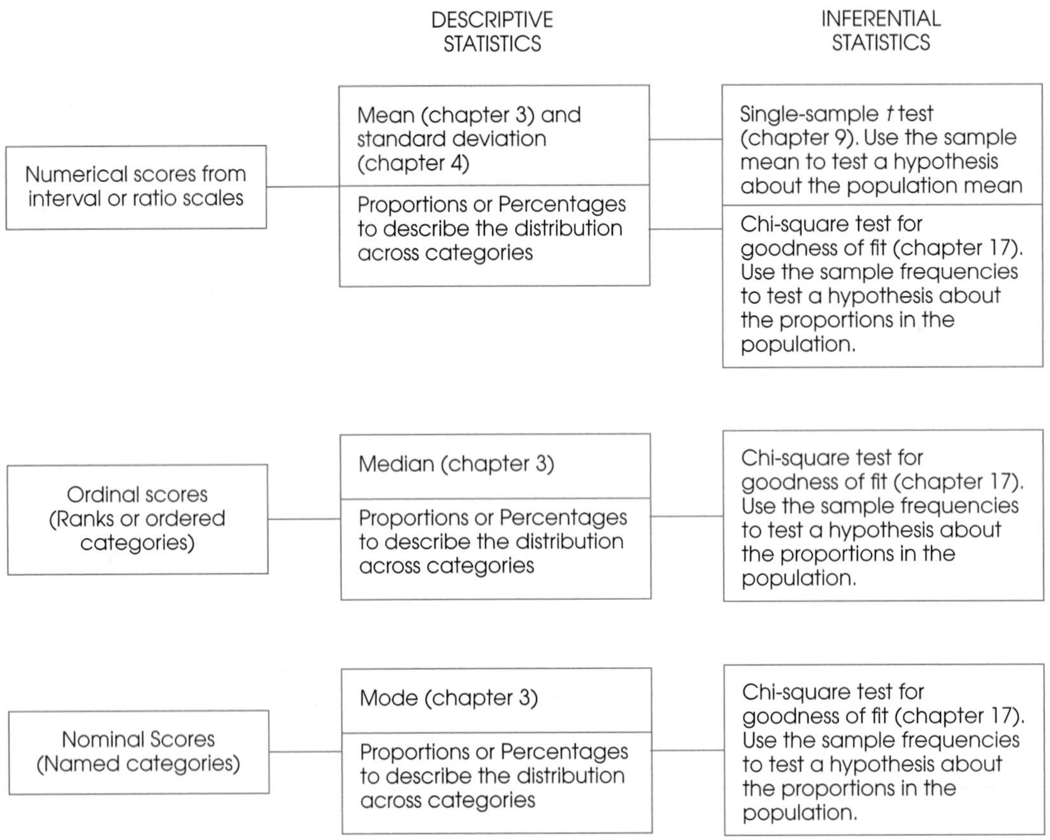

FIGURE 19.1

Statistics for Category 1 data. A single group of participants with one score per participant. The goal is to describe the variable as it exists naturally.

19.3 STATISTICAL PROCEDURES FOR DATA FROM A SINGLE GROUP OF PARTICIPANTS WITH TWO (OR MORE) VARIABLES MEASURED FOR EACH PARTICIPANT

The goal of the statistical analysis for data in this category is to describe and evaluate the relationships between variables, typically focusing on two variables at a time. With only two variables, the appropriate statistics are correlations (Chapter 15), linear regression (Chapter 16), and the chi-square test for independence (Chapter 17). With three or more variables, the applicable statistics are partial correlation (Chapter 15) and multiple regression (Chapter 16).

TWO NUMERICAL VARIABLES FROM INTERVAL OR RATIO SCALES

The Pearson correlation measures the degree and direction of linear relationship between the two variables (see Example 15.3 on p. 517). Linear regression determines the equation for the straight line that gives the best fit to the data points. For each X value in the data, the equation produces a predicted Y value on the line so that the squared distances between the actual Y values and the predicted Y values are minimized.

Descriptive Statistics The Pearson correlation serves as its own descriptive statistic. Specifically, the sign and magnitude of the correlation describe the linear relationship between the two variables. The squared correlation is often used to describe the strength of the relationship. The linear regression equation provides a mathematical description of the relationship between X values and Y. The slope constant describes the amount that Y changes each time the X value is increased by 1 point. The constant (Y intercept) value describes the value of Y when X is equal to zero.

Inferential Statistics The statistical significance of the Pearson correlation is evaluated by comparing the sample correlation with critical values listed in Table B6. A significant correlation means that it is very unlikely ($p < \alpha$) that the sample correlation would occur without a corresponding relationship in the population. Analysis of regression is a hypothesis-testing procedure that evaluates the significance of the regression equation. Statistical significance means that the equation predicts more of the variance in the Y scores than would be reasonable to expect if there were not a real underlying relationship between X and Y.

TWO ORDINAL VARIABLES (RANKS OR ORDERED CATEGORIES)

The Spearman correlation is used when both variables are measured on ordinal scales (ranks). If one or both variables consist of numerical scores from an interval or ratio scale, then the numerical values can be transformed to ranks and the Spearman correlation can be computed.

Descriptive Statistics The Spearman correlation describes the degree and direction of monotonic relationship; that is the degree to which the relationship is consistently one directional.

Inferential Statistics The statistical significance of the Spearman correlation is evaluated by comparing the sample correlation with critical values listed in Table B7. A significant correlation means that it is very unlikely ($p < \alpha$) that the sample correlation would occur without a corresponding relationship in the population.

ONE NUMERICAL VARIABLE AND ONE DICHOTOMOUS VARIABLE (A VARIABLE WITH EXACTLY 2 VALUES)

The point-biserial correlation measures the relationship between a numerical variable and a dichotomous variable. The two categories of the dichotomous variable are coded as numerical values, typically 0 and 1, to calculate the correlation.

Descriptive Statistics Because the point-biserial correlation uses arbitrary numerical codes, the direction of relationship is meaningless. However, the size of the correlation, or the squared correlation, describes the degree of relationship.

Inferential Statistics The data for a point-biserial correlation can be regrouped into a format suitable for an independent-measures t hypothesis test, or the t value can be computed directly from the point-biserial correlation (see the example on pages 542–544). The t value from the hypothesis test determines the significance of the relationship.

TWO DICHOTOMOUS VARIABLES

The phi-coefficient is used when both variables are dichotomous. For each variable, the two categories are numerically coded, typically as 0 and 1, to calculate the correlation.

Descriptive Statistics Because the phi-coefficient uses arbitrary numerical codes, the direction of relationship is meaningless. However, the size of the correlation, or the squared correlation, describes the degree of relationship.

Inferential Statistics The data from a phi-coefficient can be regrouped into a format suitable for a 2 × 2 chi-square test for independence, or the chi-square value can be computed directly from the phi-coefficient (see Example 17.3 on p. 613). The chi-square value determines the significance of the relationship.

TWO VARIABLES FROM ANY MEASUREMENT SCALES

The chi-square test for independence (Chapter 17) provides an alternative to correlations for evaluating the relationship between two variables. For the chi-square test, each of the two variables can be measured on any scale, provided that the number of categories is reasonably small. For numerical scores covering a wide range of value, the scores can be grouped into a smaller number of ordinal intervals. For example, IQ scores ranging from 93 to 137 could be grouped into three categories described as high, medium, and low IQ.

For the chi-square test, the two variables are used to create a matrix showing the frequency distribution for the data. The categories for one variable define the rows of the matrix and the categories of the second variable define the columns. Each cell of the matrix contains the frequency or number of individuals whose scores correspond to the row and column of the cell. For example, the gender and academic major scores in Table 19.2(d) could be reorganized in a matrix as follows:

	Arts	Humanities	Sciences	Professions
Female				
Male				

The value in each cell is the number of students with the gender and major identified by the cell's row and column. The null hypothesis for the chi-square test would state that there is no relationship between gender and academic major.

Descriptive Statistics The chi-square test is an inferential procedure that does not include the calculation of descriptive statistics. However, it is customary to describe the data by listing or showing the complete matrix of observed frequencies. Occasionally researchers describe the results by pointing out cells that have exceptionally large discrepancies. For example, in the Preview for Chapter 17 we described a study investigating eyewitness memory. Participants watched a video of an automobile accident and were questioned about what they saw. One group was asked to estimate the speed of the cars when they "smashed into" each other and another group was asked to estimate speed when the cars "hit" each other. A week later, they were asked additional questions, including whether they recalled seeing broken glass. Part of the description of the results focuses on cells reporting "Yes" responses. Specifically, the "smashed into" group had more than twice as many "Yes" responses than the "hit" group.

Inferential Statistics The chi-square test evaluates the significance of the relationship between the two variables. A significant result means that the distribution of frequencies in the data is very unlikely to occur ($p < \alpha$) if there is no underlying relationship between variables in the population. As with most hypothesis tests, a significant result does not provide information about the size or strength of the relationship. Therefore, either a phi-coefficient or Cramér's V is used to measure effect size.

THREE NUMERICAL VARIABLES FROM INTERVAL OR RATIO SCALES

To evaluate the relationship among three variables, the appropriate statistics are partial correlation (Chapter 15) and multiple regression (Chapter 16). A partial correlation measures the relationship between two variables while controlling the third variable. Multiple regression determines the linear equation that gives the best fit to the data points. For each pair of X values in the data, the equation produces a predicted Y value so that the squared distances between the actual Y values and the predicted Y values are minimized.

Descriptive Statistics A partial correlation describes the direction and degree of linear relationship between two variables while the influence of a third variable is controlled. This technique determines the degree to which the third variable is responsible for what appears to be a relationship between the first two. The multiple regression equation provides a mathematical description of the relationship between the two X values and Y. Each of the two slope constants describes the amount that Y changes each time the corresponding X value is increased by 1 point. The constant value describes the value of Y when both X values are equal to zero.

Inferential Statistics The statistical significance of a partial correlation is evaluated by comparing the sample correlation with critical values listed in Table B6 using $df = n - 3$ instead of the $n - 2$ value that is used for a routine Pearson correlation. A significant correlation means that it is very unlikely ($p < \alpha$) that the sample correlation would occur without a corresponding relationship in the population. Analysis of regression evaluates the significance of the multiple regression equation. Statistical significance means that the equation predicts more of the variance in the Y scores than would be reasonable to expect if there were not a real underlying relationship between the two Xs and Y.

THREE VARIABLES INCLUDING NUMERICAL VALUES AND DICHOTOMOUS VARIABLES

Partial correlation (Chapter 15) and multiple regression (Chapter 16) can also be used to evaluate the relationship among three variables, including one or more dichotomous variables. For each dichotomous variable, the two categories are numerically coded, typically as 0 and 1, before the partial correlation or multiple regression is done. The *descriptive statistics* and the *inferential statistics* for the two statistical procedures are identical to those for numerical scores except that direction of relationship (or sign of the slope constant) is meaningless for the dichotomous variables.

Figure 19.2 summarizes the statistical procedures used for data in category 2.

19.4 STATISTICAL PROCEDURES FOR DATA CONSISTING OF TWO (OR MORE) GROUPS OF SCORES WITH EACH SCORE A MEASUREMENT OF THE SAME VARIABLE

Data in this category includes single-factor and two-factor designs. In a single-factor study, the values of one variable are used to define different groups and a second variable (the dependent variable) is measured to obtain a set of scores in each group. For a two-factor design, two variables are used to construct a matrix with the values of one variable defining the rows and the values of the second variable defining the columns. A third variable (the dependent variable) is measured to obtain a set of scores in each cell of the matrix. To simplify discussion, we focus on single-factor designs now and address two-factor designs in a separate section at the end of this chapter.

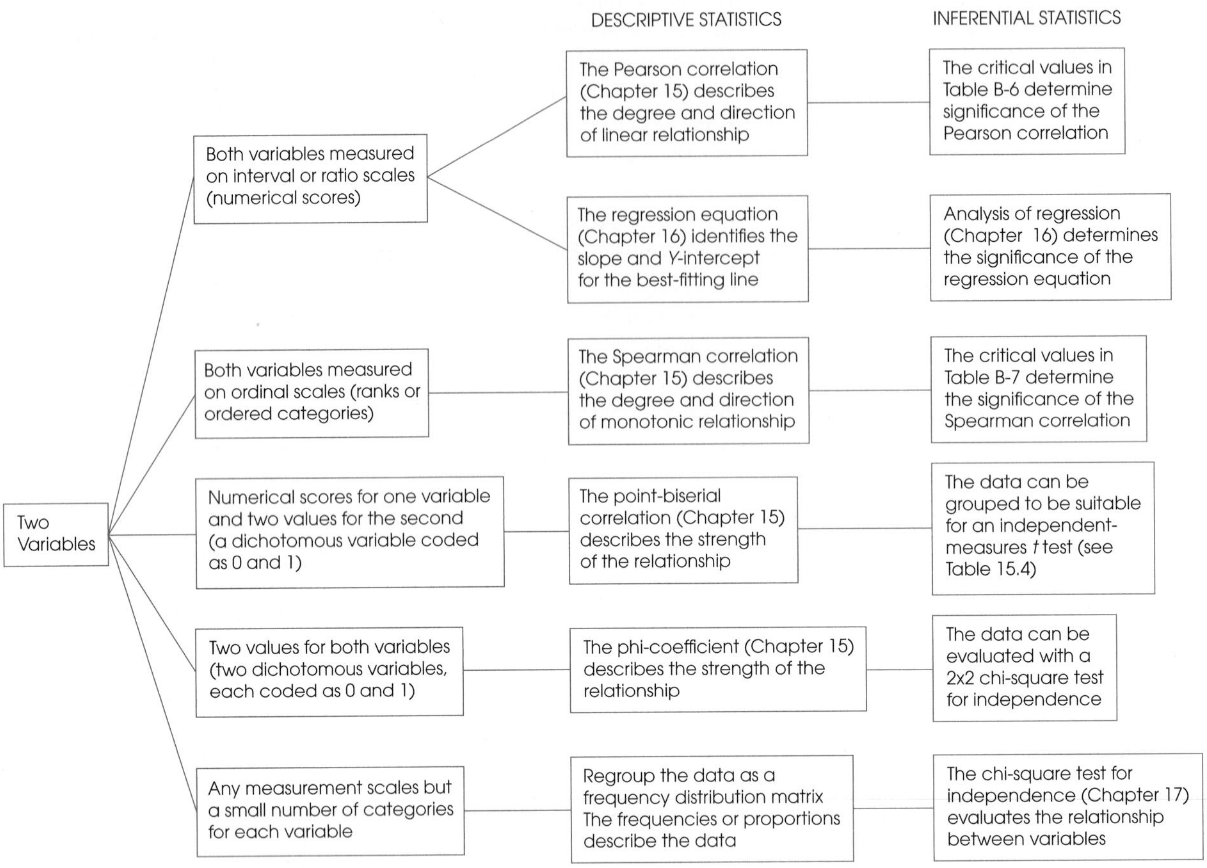

FIGURE 19.2

Statistics for Category 2 data. One group of participants with two (or more) variables measured for each participant. The goal is to describe and evaluate the relationship between variables.

The goal for a single-factor research design is to demonstrate a relationship between the two variables by showing consistent differences between groups. The scores in each group can be numerical values measured on interval or ratio scales, ordinal values (ranks), or simply categories on a nominal scale. The different measurement scales permit different types of mathematics and result in different statistical analyses.

SCORES FROM INTERVAL OR RATIO SCALES: NUMERICAL SCORES

Descriptive Statistics When the scores in each group are numerical values, the standard procedure is to compute the mean (Chapter 3) and the standard deviation (Chapter 4) as descriptive statistics to summarize and describe each group. For a repeated-measures study comparing exactly two groups, it also is common to compute the difference between the two scores for each participant and then report the mean and the standard deviation for the difference scores.

Inferential Statistics Analysis of variance (ANOVA) and *t* tests are used to evaluate the statistical significance of the mean differences between the groups of

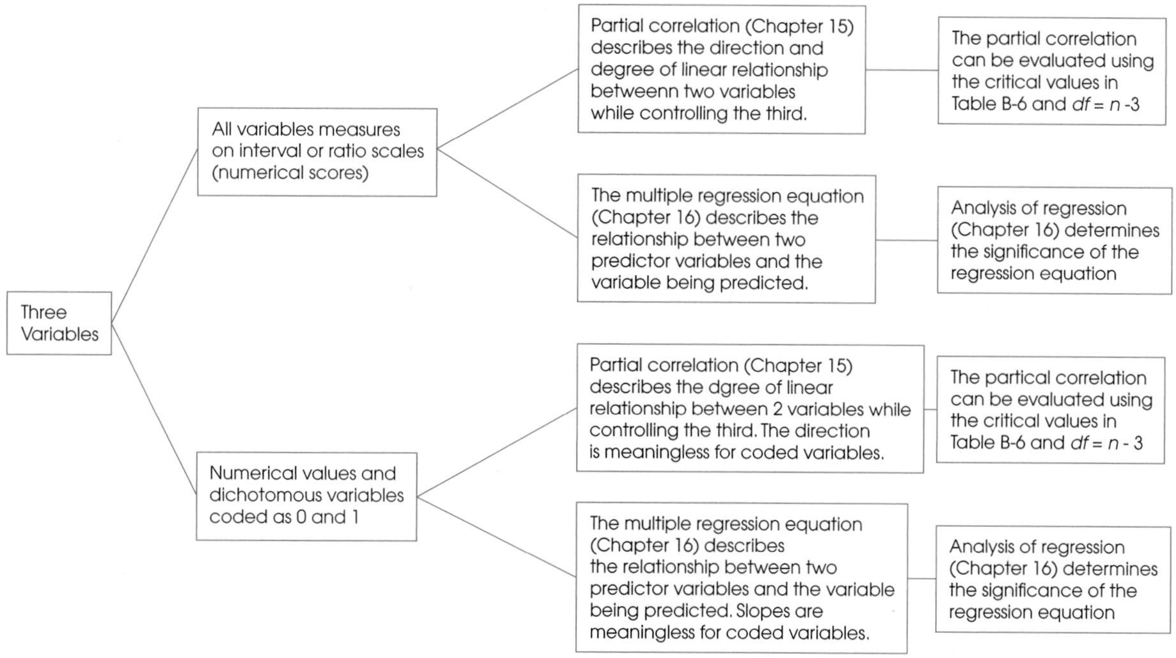

FIGURE 19.2—Cont'd

scores. With only two groups, the two tests are equivalent and either may be used. With more than two groups, mean differences are evaluated with an ANOVA. For independent-measures designs (between-subjects designs), the independent-measures *t* (Chapter 10) and independent-measures ANOVA (Chapter 12) are appropriate. For repeated-measures designs, the repeated-measures *t* (Chapter 11) and repeated-measures ANOVA (Chapter 13) are used. For all tests, a significant result indicates that the sample mean differences in the data are very unlikely ($p < \alpha$) to occur if there are not corresponding mean differences in the population. For an ANOVA comparing more than two means, a significant *F*-ratio indicates that post tests such as Scheffé or Tukey (Chapter 12) are necessary to determine exactly which sample means are significantly different. Significant results from a *t* test should be accompanied by a measure of effect size such as Cohen's *d* or r^2. For ANOVA, effect size is measured by computing the percentage of variance accounted for, η^2.

SCORES FROM ORDINAL SCALES: RANKS OR ORDERED CATEGORIES

For scores that are rank ordered, there are hypothesis tests developed specifically for ordinal data to determine whether there are significant differences in the ranks from one group to another. Also, if the scores are limited to a relatively small number of ordinal categories, then a chi-square test for independence can be used to determine whether there are significant differences in proportions from one group to another.

Descriptive Statistics Ordinal scores can be described by the set of ranks or ordinal categories within each group. For example, the ranks in one group may be consistently larger (or smaller) than ranks in another group. Or, the "large" ratings may be concentrated in one group and the "small" ratings in another.

Inferential Statistics Appendix E presents a set of hypothesis tests developed for evaluating differences between groups of ordinal data.

1. The Mann-Whitney *U* test evaluates the difference between two groups of scores from an independent-measures design. The scores are the ranks obtained by combining the two groups and rank ordering the entire set of participants from smallest to largest.
2. The Wilcoxon signed ranks test evaluates the difference between two groups of scores from a repeated-measures design. The scores are the ranks obtained by rank ordering the magnitude of the differences, independent of sign (+ or −).
3. The Kruskal-Wallis test evaluates differences between three or more groups from an independent-measures design. The scores are the ranks obtained by combining all of the groups and rank ordering the entire set of participants from smallest to largest.
4. The Friedman test evaluates differences among three or more groups from a repeated-measures design. The scores are the ranks obtained by rank ordering the scores for each participant. With three conditions, for example, each participant is measured three times and would receive ranks of 1, 2, and 3.

For all tests, a significant result indicates that the differences between groups are very unlikely ($p < \alpha$) to have occurred unless there are consistent differences in the population.

A chi-square test for independence (Chapter 17) can be used to evaluate differences between groups for an independent-measures design with a relatively small number of ordinal categories for the dependent variable. In this case, the data can be displayed as a frequency distribution matrix with the groups defining the rows and the ordinal categories defining the columns. For example, a researcher could group high school students by class (Freshman, Sophomore, Junior, Senior) and measure the amount of time each student spends on Facebook by classifying students into three ordinal categories (small, medium, large). An example of the resulting data is shown in Table 19.3(d). However, the same data could be regrouped into a frequency-distribution matrix as follows:

	Amount of Time Spent on Facebook		
	Small	Medium	Large
Freshman			
Sophomore			
Junior			
Senior			

The value in each cell is the number of students, with the high school class and amount of Facebook time identified by the cell's row and column. A chi-square test for independence would evaluate the differences between groups. A significant result indicates that the frequencies (proportions) in the sample data would be very unlikely ($p < \alpha$) to occur unless the proportions for the population distributions are different from one group to another.

SCORES FROM A NOMINAL SCALE

Descriptive Statistics As with ordinal data, data from nominal scales are usually described by the distribution of individuals across categories. For example, the scores in one group may be clustered in one category or set of categories and the scores in another group may be clustered in different categories.

Inferential Statistics With a relatively small number of nominal categories, the data can be displayed as a frequency-distribution matrix with the groups defining the rows and the nominal categories defining the columns. The number in each cell is the frequency, or number of individuals in the group, identified by the cell's row, with scores corresponding to the cell's column. For example, the data in Table 19.3(c) show success or failure on a task for participants who are working alone or working in a group. These data could be regrouped as follows:

	Success	Failure
Work Alone		
Work in a Group		

A chi-square test for independence (Chapter 17) can be used to evaluate differences between groups. A significant result indicates that the two sample distributions would be very unlikely ($p < \alpha$) to occur if the two population distributions have the same proportions (same shape).

TWO-FACTOR DESIGNS WITH SCORES FROM INTERVAL OR RATIO SCALES

Research designs with two independent (or quasi-independent) variables are known as two-factor designs. These designs can be presented as a matrix with the levels of one factor defining the rows and the levels of the second factor defining the columns. A third variable (the dependent variable) is measured to obtain a group of scores in each cell of the matrix (see Example 14.1 on page 477).

Descriptive Statistics When the scores in each group are numerical values, the standard procedure is to compute the mean (Chapter 3) and the standard deviation (Chapter 4) as descriptive statistics to summarize and describe each group.

Inferential Statistics A two-factor ANOVA is used to evaluate the significance of the mean differences between cells. The ANOVA separates the mean differences into three categories and conducts three separate hypothesis tests:

1. The main effect for factor *A* evaluates the overall mean differences for the first factor; that is, the mean differences between rows in the data matrix.
2. The main effect for factor *B* evaluates the overall mean differences for the second factor; that is, the mean differences between columns in the data matrix.
3. The interaction between factors evaluates the mean differences between cells that are not accounted for by the main effects.

For each test, a significant result indicates that the sample mean differences in the data are very unlikely ($p < \alpha$) to occur if there are not corresponding mean differences in the population. For each of the three tests, effect size is measured by computing the percentage of variance accounted for, η^2.

Figure 19.3 summarizes the statistical procedures used for data in category 3.

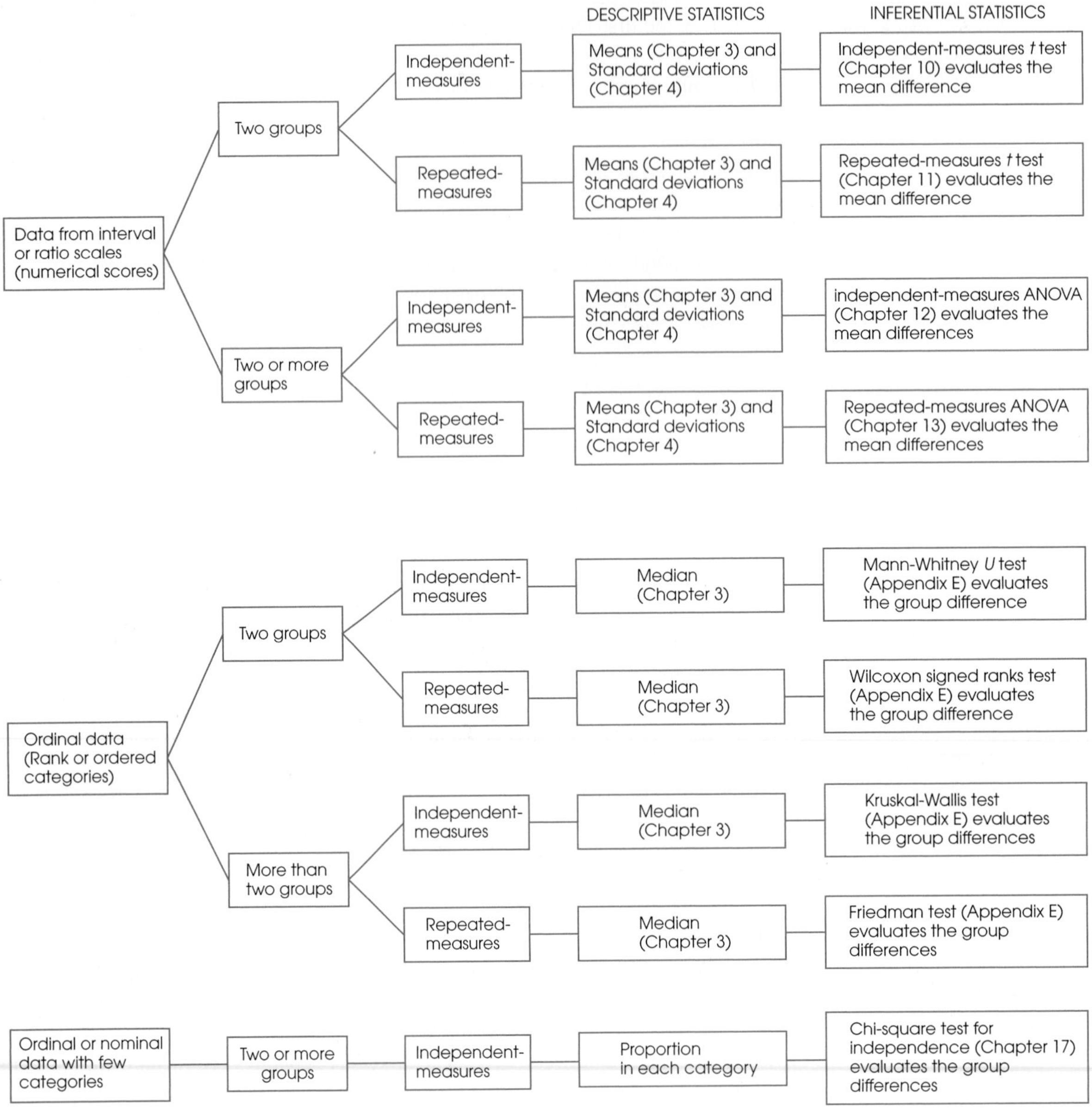

FIGURE 19.3

Statistics for Category 3 data. Two or more groups of scores with one score per participant. The goal is to describe and evaluate differences between groups of scores.

RESOURCES

Book Companion Website: www.cengage.com/psychology/gravettter

You can find a tutorial quiz and other learning exercises for Chapter 19 on the book companion website.

aplia

Improve your understanding of statistics with Aplia's auto-graded problem sets and immediate, detailed explanations for every question. To learn more, visit **www.aplia.com/statistics.**

CENGAGE **brain**.com

Log in to CengageBrain to access the resources your instructor requires. For this book, you can access:

Psychology CourseMate brings course concepts to life with interactive learning, study, and exam preparation tools that support the printed textbook. A textbook-specific website, Psychology CourseMate includes an integrated interactive eBook and other interactive learning tools including quizzes, flashcards, and more.

Visit www.cengagebrain.com to access your account and purchase materials.

PROBLEMS

Each problem describes a research situation and the data it produces. Identify the statistical procedures that are appropriate for the data. When possible, identify descriptive statistics, inferential statistics, and a measure of effect size.

1. Research suggests that the antioxidants in foods such as blueberries can reduce and even reverse age-related declines in cognitive functioning (Joseph et al., 1999). To test this phenomenon, a researcher selects a sample of $n = 25$ adults aged 70 to 75 and administers a cognitive function test to each participant. The participants then drink a blueberry supplement every day for 4 months before they are tested again. The researcher compares the scores before treatment with the scores after treatment to see if there is any change in cognitive function.

2. Recent budget cuts forced the city school district to increase class size in the elementary schools. To determine student reaction to the change, the district administered a survey to students asking whether the larger classes were "better, worse, or not different" from the classes the previous year. The results from the survey will be used to describe the students' attitude.

3. Last fall, the college introduced a peer-mentor program in which a sample of $n = 75$ freshmen was each assigned an upperclassman mentor. To evaluate the success of the program, the administration looked at the number of students who returned to the college to begin their second year. The data showed that 88% of the students in the peer-mentor program returned, compared to 72% for freshmen who were not in the program.

4. To examine the relationship between alcohol consumption and birth weight, a researcher selects a sample of $n = 20$ pregnant rats and mixes alcohol with their food for 2 weeks before the pups are born.

One newborn pup is randomly selected from each subject's litter and the average birth weight for the $n = 20$ pups is recorded. It is known that the average birth weight for regular rats (without exposure to alcohol) is $\mu = 5.6$ grams.

5. To examine the relationship between texting and driving skill, a researcher uses orange cones to set up a driving circuit in the high school parking lot. A group of students is then tested on the circuit, once while receiving and sending text messages and once without texting. For each student, the researcher records the number of orange cones hit while driving each circuit.

6. A researcher investigated different combinations of temperature and humidity to examine how heat affects performance. The researcher compared three temperature conditions (70°, 80°, and 90°) with a high humidity and a low humidity condition for each temperature. A separate group of participants was tested in each of the six different conditions. For each participant, the researcher recorded the number of errors on a problem-solving task. The researcher would like to know how different combinations of temperature and humidity influence performance.

7. There is some evidence indicating that people with visible tattoos are viewed more negatively than people without visible tattoos (Resenhoeft, Villa, & Wiseman, 2008). In a similar study, a researcher showed male college students photographs of women and asked the students to rate the attractiveness of each woman using a 7-point scale. One of the women was selected as the target. For one group of participants, the target was photographed with a large tattoo on her shoulder and for a second group her photograph showed no tattoo. The researcher plans to compare the target's ratings for the two groups to determine whether the tattoo had any effect on perceived attractiveness.

8. Childhood participation in sports, cultural groups, and youth groups appears to be related to improved self-esteem for adolescents (McGee, Williams, Howden-Chapman, Martin, & Kawachi, 2006). In a representative study, a researcher compares scores on a standardized self-esteem questionnaire for a sample of $n = 100$ adolescents with a history of group participation and a separate sample of $n = 100$ who have no history of group participation.

9. Hallam, Price, and Katsarou (2002) investigated the influence of background noise on classroom performance for children aged 10 to 12. In a similar study, students in one classroom worked on an arithmetic task with calming music in the background. Students in a second classroom heard aggressive, exciting music, and students in a third room had no music at all. The researchers measured the number of problems answered correctly for each student to determine whether the music conditions had any effect on performance.

10. A survey of female high school seniors includes one question asking for the amount of time spent on clothes, hair, and makeup each morning before school. The researcher plans to use the results as part of a general description of today's high school students.

11. A researcher is investigating the relationship between personality and birth order position. A sample of college students is classified into four birth-order categories (1st, 2nd, 3rd, 4th or later) and given a personality test that measures the degree of extroversion on a 50-point scale.

12. A researcher is investigating the relationship between personality and birth order position. A sample of college students is classified into four birth-order categories (1st, 2nd, 3rd, 4th or later) and classified as being either extroverted or introverted.

13. Brunt, Rhee, and Zhong (2008) surveyed 557 undergraduate college students to examine their weight status, health behaviors, and diet. In a similar study, researchers used body mass index (BMI) to classify a group of students into four categories: underweight, healthy weight, overweight, and obese. The students were also surveyed to determine the number of fatty and/or sugary snacks they eat each day. The researchers would like to use to data to determine whether there is a relationship between weight status and diet.

14. A researcher would like to determine whether infants, age 2 to 3 months, show any evidence of color preference. The babies are positioned in front of a screen on which a set of four colored patches is presented. The four colors are red, green, blue, and yellow. The researcher measures the amount of time each infant looks at each of the four colors during a 30 second test period. The color with the greatest time is identified as the preferred color for the child.

15. A researcher administers a survey to graduating seniors, asking them to rate their optimism about the current job market on a 7-point scale. The researcher plans to use the results as part of a description of today's graduating seniors.

16. Standardized measures seem to indicate that the average level of anxiety has increased gradually over the past 50 years (Twenge, 2000). In the 1950s, the average score on the Child Manifest Anxiety Scale was $\mu = 15.1$. A researcher administers the same test to a sample of $n = 50$ of today's children to determine whether there has been a significant change in the average anxiety level.

17. Belsky, Weinraub, Owen, and Kelly (2001) reported on the effects of preschool childcare on the development of young children. One result suggests that children who spend more time away from their mothers are more likely to show behavioral problems in kindergarten. Suppose that a kindergarten teacher is asked rank order the degree of disruptive behavior for the $n = 20$ children in the class.

a. Researchers then separate the students into two groups: children with a history of preschool and children with little or no experience in preschool. The researchers plan to compare the ranks for the two groups.

b. The researchers interview each child's parents to determine how much time the child spent in preschool. The children are then ranked according to the amount of preschool experience. The researchers plan to use the data to determine whether there is a relationship between preschool experience and disruptive behavior.

18. Research results indicate that physically attractive people are also perceived as being more intelligent (Eagly, Ashmore, Makhijani, & Longo, 1991). As a demonstration of this phenomenon, a researcher obtained a set of $n = 25$ photographs of male college students. The photographs were shown to a sample of female college students who used a 7-point scale to rate several characteristics, including intelligence and attractiveness, for the person in each photo. The average attractiveness rating and the average intelligence rating were computed for each photograph. The researcher plans to use the averages to determine whether there is relationship between perceived attractiveness and perceived intelligence.

19. Numerous studies have found that males report higher self-esteem than females, especially for adolescents (Kling, Hyde, Showers, & Buswell, 1999). A recent study found that males scored an average of 8 points higher than females on a standardized questionnaire measuring self-esteem. The researcher would like to know whether this is a significant difference.

20. Research has demonstrated that IQ scores have been increasing, generation by generation, for years (Flynn, 1999). A researcher would like to determine whether this trend can be described by a linear equation showing the relationship between age and IQ scores. The same IQ test is given to a sample of 100 adults who range in age from 20 to 85 years. The age and IQ score are recorded for each person.

21. A researcher is investigating the effectiveness of acupuncture treatment for chronic back pain. A sample of $n = 20$ participants is obtained from a pain clinic. Each individual rates the current level of pain and then begins a 6-week program of acupuncture treatment. At the end of the program, the pain level is rated again and the researcher records whether the pain has increased or decreased for each participant.

22. McGee and Shevlin (2009) found that an individual's sense of humor had a significant effect on how attractive the individual was perceived to be by others. In a similar study, female college students were given brief descriptions of three potential romantic partners. One was identified as the target and was described positively as being single, ambitious, and having good job prospects. For half of the participants, the description also said that he had a great sense of humor. For another half, it said that he has no sense of humor. After reading the three descriptions, the participants were asked to rank the three men 1st, 2nd, and 3rd in terms of attractiveness. For each of the two groups, the researchers recorded the number of times the target was placed in each ordinal position.

23. Research has shown that people are more likely to show dishonest and self-interested behaviors in darkness than in a well-lit environment (Zhong, Bohns, & Gino, 2010). In a related experiment, students were given a quiz and then asked to grade their own papers while the teacher read the correct answers. One group of students was tested in a well-lit room and another group was tested in a dimly-lit room. The researchers recorded the number of correct answers reported by each student to determine whether there was a significant difference between the two groups.

24. There is some evidence suggesting that you are likely to improve your test score if you rethink and change answers on a multiple-choice exam (Johnston, 1975). To examine this phenomenon, a teacher encouraged students to reconsider their answers before turning in exams. Students were asked to record their original answers and the changes that they made. When the exams were collected, the teacher found that 18 students improved their grades by changing answers and only 7 students had lower grades with the changes. The teacher would like to know if this is a statistically significant result.

25. A researcher is evaluating customer satisfaction with the service and coverage of three phone carriers. Each individual in a sample of $n = 25$ uses one carrier for 2 weeks, then switches to another for 2 weeks, and finally switches to the third for 2 weeks. Each participant then rates the three carriers.

a. Assume that each carrier was rated on a 10-point scale.
b. Assume that each participant ranked the three carriers 1st, 2nd and 3rd.
c. Assume the each participant simply identified the most preferred carrier of the three.

26. There is some research indicating that college students who use Facebook while studying tend to have lower grades than non-users (Kirschner & Karpinski, 2010). A representative study surveys students to determine the amount of Facebook use during the time they are studying or doing homework. Based on the amount of time spent on Facebook, students are classified into three groups (high, medium, and low time) and their grade point averages are recorded. The researcher would like to examine the relationship between grades and amount of time on Facebook.

27. To examine the effect of sleep deprivation on motor-skills performance, a sample of $n = 10$ participants was tested on a motor-skills task after 24 hours of sleep deprivation, tested again after 36 hours, and tested once more after 48 hours. The dependent variable is the number of errors made on the motor-skills task.

28. Ryan and Hemmes (2005) examined how homework assignments are related to learning. The participants were college students enrolled in a class with weekly homework assignments and quizzes. For some weeks, the homework was required and counted toward the student's grade. Other weeks, the homework was optional and did not count toward the student's grade. Predictably, most students completed the required homework assignments and did not do the optional assignments. For each student, the researchers recorded the average quiz grade for weeks with required homework and the average grade for weeks with optional homework to determine whether the grades were significantly higher when homework was required and actually done.

29. Ford and Torok (2008) found that motivational signs were effective in increasing physical activity on a college campus. In a similar study, researchers first counted the number of students and faculty who used the stairs and the number who used the elevators in a college building during a 30-minute observation period. The following week, signs such as "Step up to a healthier lifestyle" and "An average person burns 10 calories a minute walking up the stairs" were posted by the elevators and stairs and the researchers once again counted people to determine whether the signs had a significant effect on behavior.

APPENDIX A Basic Mathematics Review

Preview

Preview

This appendix reviews some of the basic math skills that are necessary for the statistical calculations presented in this book. Many students already will know some or all of this material. Others will need to do extensive work and review. To help you assess your own skills, we include a skills assessment exam here. You should allow approximately 30 minutes to complete the test. When you finish, grade your test using the answer key on page 697.

Notice that the test is divided into five sections. If you miss more than three questions in any section of the test, you probably need help in that area. Turn to the section of this appendix that corresponds to your problem area. In each section, you will find a general review, examples, and additional practice problems. After reviewing the appropriate section and doing the practice problems, turn to the end of the appendix. You will find another version of the skills assessment exam. If you still miss more than three questions in any section of the exam, continue studying. Get assistance from an instructor or a tutor if necessary. At the end of this appendix is a list of recommended books for individuals who need a more extensive review than can be provided here. We stress that mastering this material now will make the rest of the course much easier.

SKILLS ASSESSMENT PREVIEW EXAM

SECTION 1

(corresponding to Section A.1 of this appendix)

1. $3 + 2 \times 7 = ?$
2. $(3 + 2) \times 7 = ?$
3. $3 + 2^2 - 1 = ?$
4. $(3 + 2)^2 - 1 = ?$
5. $12/4 + 2 = ?$
6. $12/(4 + 2) = ?$
7. $12/(4 + 2)^2 = ?$
8. $2 \times (8 - 2^2) = ?$
9. $2 \times (8 - 2)^2 = ?$
10. $3 \times 2 + 8 - 1 \times 6 = ?$
11. $3 \times (2 + 8) - 1 \times 6 = ?$
12. $3 \times 2 + (8 - 1) \times 6 = ?$

SECTION 2

(corresponding to Section A.2 of this appendix)

1. The fraction $\frac{3}{4}$ corresponds to a percentage of __________.
2. Express 30% as a fraction.
3. Convert $\frac{12}{40}$ to a decimal.
4. $\frac{2}{13} + \frac{8}{13} = ?$
5. $1.375 + 0.25 = ?$
6. $\frac{2}{5} \times \frac{1}{4} = ?$
7. $\frac{1}{8} + \frac{2}{3} = ?$
8. $3.5 \times 0.4 = ?$
9. $\frac{1}{5} \div \frac{3}{4} = ?$
10. $3.75/0.5 = ?$
11. In a group of 80 students, 20% are psychology majors. How many psychology majors are in this group?
12. A company reports that two-fifths of its employees are women. If there are 90 employees, how many are women?

SECTION 3

(corresponding to Section A.3 of this appendix)

1. $3 + (-2) + (-1) + 4 = ?$
2. $6 - (-2) = ?$
3. $-2 - (-4) = ?$
4. $6 + (-1) - 3 - (-2) - (-5) = ?$
5. $4 \times (-3) = ?$
6. $-2 \times (-6) = ?$
7. $-3 \times 5 = ?$
8. $-2 \times (-4) \times (-3) = ?$
9. $12 \div (-3) = ?$
10. $-18 \div (-6) = ?$
11. $-16 \div 8 = ?$
12. $-100 \div (-4) = ?$

SECTION 4

(corresponding to Section A.4 of this appendix)

For each equation, find the value of X.

1. $X + 6 = 13$
2. $X - 14 = 15$
3. $5 = X - 4$
4. $3X = 12$
5. $72 = 3X$
6. $X/5 = 3$
7. $10 = X/8$
8. $3X + 5 = -4$
9. $24 = 2X + 2$
10. $(X + 3)/2 = 14$
11. $(X - 5)/3 = 2$
12. $17 = 4X - 11$

SECTION 5

(corresponding to Section A.5 of this appendix)

1. $4^3 = ?$
2. $\sqrt{25 - 9} = ?$
3. If $X = 2$ and $Y = 3$, then $XY^3 = ?$
4. If $X = 2$ and $Y = 3$, then $(X + Y)^2 = ?$
5. If $a = 3$ and $b = 2$, then $a^2 + b^2 = ?$
6. $(-3)^3 = ?$
7. $(-4)^4 = ?$
8. $\sqrt{4} \times 4 = ?$
9. $36/\sqrt{9} = ?$
10. $(9 + 2)2 = ?$
11. $5^2 + 2^3 = ?$
12. If $a = 3$ and $b = -1$, then $a^2b^3 = ?$

The answers to the skills assessment exam are at the end of the appendix (pages 697–698).

A.1 SYMBOLS AND NOTATION

Table A.1 presents the basic mathematical symbols that you should know, along with examples of their use. Statistical symbols and notation are introduced and explained throughout this book as they are needed. Notation for exponents and square roots is covered separately at the end of this appendix.

Parentheses are a useful notation because they specify and control the order of computations. Everything inside the parentheses is calculated first. For example,

$$(5 + 3) \times 2 = 8 \times 2 = 16$$

Changing the placement of the parentheses also changes the order of calculations. For example,

$$5 + (3 \times 2) = 5 + 6 = 11$$

ORDER OF OPERATIONS

Often a formula or a mathematical expression will involve several different arithmetic operations, such as adding, multiplying, squaring, and so on. When you encounter these situations, you must perform the different operations in the correct sequence. Following is a list of mathematical operations, showing the order in which they are to be performed.

1. Any calculation contained within parentheses is done first.
2. Squaring (or raising to other exponents) is done second.
3. Multiplying and/or dividing is done third. A series of multiplication and/or division operations should be done in order from left to right.
4. Adding and/or subtracting is done fourth.

The following examples demonstrate how this sequence of operations is applied in different situations.

To evaluate the expression

$$(3 + 1)^2 - 4 \times 7/2$$

first, perform the calculation within parentheses:

$$(4)^2 - 4 \times 7/2$$

Next, square the value as indicated:

$$16 - 4 \times 7/2$$

TABLE A.1

Symbol	Meaning	Example
$+$	Addition	$5 + 7 = 12$
$-$	Subtraction	$8 - 3 = 5$
$\times$, ( )	Multiplication	$3 \times 9 = 27$, $3(9) = 27$
$\div$, /	Division	$15 \div 3 = 5$, $15/3 = 5$, $\frac{15}{3} = 5$
$>$	Greater than	$20 > 10$
$<$	Less than	$7 < 11$
$\neq$	Not equal to	$5 \neq 6$

Then perform the multiplication and division:

$$16 - 14$$

Finally, do the subtraction:

$$16 - 14 = 2$$

A sequence of operations involving multiplication and division should be performed in order from left to right. For example, to compute $12/2 \times 3$, you divide 12 by 2 and then multiply the result by 3:

$$12/2 \times 3 = 6 \times 3 = 18$$

Notice that violating the left-to-right sequence can change the result. For this example, if you multiply before dividing, you will obtain

$$12/2 \times 3 = 12/6 = 2 \qquad \text{(This is wrong.)}$$

A sequence of operations involving only addition and subtraction can be performed in any order. For example, to compute $3 + 8 - 5$, you can add 3 and 8 and then subtract 5:

$$(3 + 8) - 5 = 11 - 5 = 6$$

or you can subtract 5 from 8 and then add the result to 3:

$$3 + (8 - 5) = 3 + 3 = 6$$

A mathematical expression or formula is simply a concise way to write a set of instructions. When you evaluate an expression by performing the calculation, you simply follow the instructions. For example, assume you are given these instructions:

1. First, add 3 and 8.
2. Next, square the result.
3. Next, multiply the resulting value by 6.
4. Finally, subtract 50 from the value you have obtained.

You can write these instructions as a mathematical expression.

1. The first step involves addition. Because addition is normally done last, use parentheses to give this operation priority in the sequence of calculations:

   $$(3 + 8)$$

2. The instruction to square a value is noted by using the exponent 2 beside the value to be squared:

   $$(3 + 8)^2$$

3. Because squaring has priority over multiplication, you can simply introduce the multiplication into the expression:

   $$6 \times (3 + 8)^2$$

4. Addition and subtraction are done last, so simply write in the requested subtraction:

$6 \times (3 + 8)^2 - 50$

To calculate the value of the expression, you work through the sequence of operations in the proper order:

$$\begin{aligned} 6 \times (3 + 8)^2 - 50 &= 6 \times (11)^2 - 50 \\ &= 6 \times (121) - 50 \\ &= 726 - 50 \\ &= 676 \end{aligned}$$

As a final note, you should realize that the operation of squaring (or raising to any exponent) applies only to the value that immediately precedes the exponent. For example,

$2 \times 3^2 = 2 \times 9 = 18$ (Only the 3 is squared.)

If the instructions require multiplying values and then squaring the product, you must use parentheses to give the multiplication priority over squaring. For example, to multiply 2 times 3 and then square the product, you would write

$(2 \times 3)^2 = (6)^2 = 36$

LEARNING CHECK

1. Evaluate each of the following expressions:

a. $4 \times 8/2^2$
b. $4 \times (8/2)^2$
c. $100 - 3 \times 12/(6 - 4)^2$
d. $(4 + 6) \times (3 - 1)^2$
e. $(8 - 2)/(9 - 8)^2$
f. $6 + (4 - 1)^2 - 3\_4^2$
g. $4 \times (8 - 3) + 8 - 3$

ANSWERS **1. a.** 8 **b.** 64 **c.** 91 **d.** 40 **e.** 6 **f.** −33 **g.** 25

A.2 PROPORTIONS: FRACTIONS, DECIMALS, AND PERCENTAGES

A proportion is a part of a whole and can be expressed as a fraction, a decimal, or a percentage. For example, in a class of 40 students, only 3 failed the final exam.

The proportion of the class that failed can be expressed as a fraction

$$\text{fraction} = \frac{3}{40}$$

or as a decimal value

$$\text{decimal} = 0.075$$

or as a percentage

$$\text{percentage} = 7.5\%$$

In a fraction, such as $\frac{3}{4}$, the bottom value (the denominator) indicates the number of equal pieces into which the whole is split. Here the "pie" is split into 4 equal pieces:

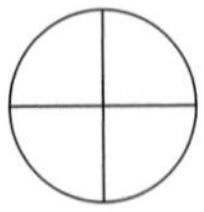

If the denominator has a larger value—say, 8—then each piece of the whole pie is smaller:

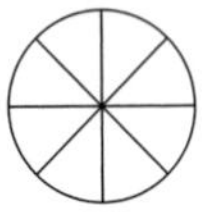

A larger denominator indicates a smaller fraction of the whole.

The value on top of the fraction (the numerator) indicates how many pieces of the whole are being considered. Thus, the fraction $\frac{3}{4}$ indicates that the whole is split evenly into 4 pieces and that 3 of them are being used:

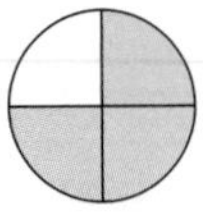

A fraction is simply a concise way of stating a proportion: "Three out of four" is equivalent to $\frac{3}{4}$. To convert the fraction to a decimal, you divide the numerator by the denominator:

$$\frac{3}{4} = 3 \div 4 = 0.75$$

To convert the decimal to a percentage, simply multiply by 100, and place a percent sign (%) after the answer:

$$0.75 \times 100 = 75\%$$

The U.S. money system is a convenient way of illustrating the relationship between fractions and decimals. "One quarter," for example, is one-fourth $\left(\frac{1}{4}\right)$ of a dollar, and its decimal equivalent is 0.25. Other familiar equivalencies are as follows:

	Dime	Quarter	50 Cents	75 Cents
Fraction	$\frac{1}{10}$	$\frac{1}{4}$	$\frac{1}{2}$	$\frac{3}{4}$
Decimal	0.10	0.25	0.50	0.75
Percentage	10%	25%	50%	75%

FRACTIONS

1. **Finding Equivalent Fractions.** The same proportional value can be expressed by many equivalent fractions. For example,

$$\frac{1}{2} = \frac{2}{4} = \frac{10}{20} = \frac{50}{100}$$

To create equivalent fractions, you can multiply the numerator and denominator by the same value. As long as both the numerator and the denominator of the fraction are multiplied by the same value, the new fraction will be equivalent to the original. For example,

$$\frac{3}{10} = \frac{9}{30}$$

because both the numerator and the denominator of the original fraction have been multiplied by 3. Dividing the numerator and denominator of a fraction by the same value will also result in an equivalent fraction. By using division, you can reduce a fraction to a simpler form. For example,

$$\frac{40}{100} = \frac{2}{5}$$

because both the numerator and the denominator of the original fraction have been divided by 20.

You can use these rules to find specific equivalent fractions. For example, find the fraction that has a denominator of 100 and is equivalent to $\frac{3}{4}$. That is,

$$\frac{3}{4} = \frac{?}{100}$$

Notice that the denominator of the original fraction must be multiplied by 25 to produce the denominator of the desired fraction. For the two fractions to be equal, both the numerator and the denominator must be multiplied by the same number. Therefore, we also multiply the top of the original fraction by 25 and obtain

$$\frac{3 \times 25}{4 \times 25} = \frac{75}{100}$$

2. **Multiplying Fractions.** To multiply two fractions, you first multiply the numerators and then multiply the denominators. For example,

$$\frac{3}{4} \times \frac{5}{7} = \frac{3 \times 5}{4 \times 7} = \frac{15}{28}$$

3. **Dividing Fractions.** To divide one fraction by another, you invert the second fraction and then multiply. For example,

$$\frac{1}{2} \div \frac{1}{4} = \frac{1}{2} \times \frac{4}{1} = \frac{1 \times 4}{2 \times 1} = \frac{4}{2} = \frac{2}{1} = 2$$

4. **Adding and Subtracting Fractions.** Fractions must have the same denominator before you can add or subtract them. If the two fractions already have a common denominator, you simply add (or subtract as the case may be) *only* the values in the numerators. For example,

$$\frac{2}{5} + \frac{1}{5} = \frac{3}{5}$$

Suppose you divided a pie into five equal pieces (fifths). If you first ate two-fifths of the pie and then another one-fifth, the total amount eaten would be three-fifths of the pie:

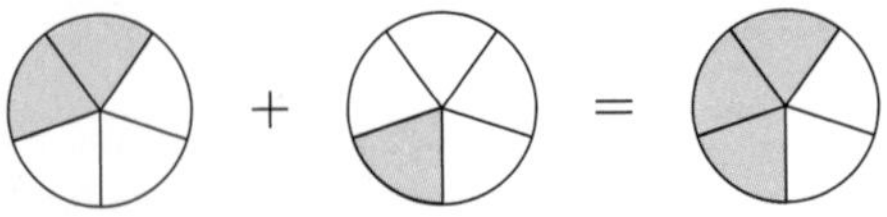

If the two fractions do not have the same denominator, you must first find equivalent fractions with a common denominator before you can add or subtract. The product of the two denominators will always work as a common denominator for equivalent fractions (although it may not be the lowest common denominator). For example,

$$\frac{2}{3} + \frac{1}{10} = ?$$

Because these two fractions have different denominators, it is necessary to convert each into an equivalent fraction and find a common denominator. We will use $3 \times 10 = 30$ as the common denominator. Thus, the equivalent fraction of each is

$$\frac{2}{3} = \frac{20}{30} \quad \text{and} \quad \frac{1}{10} = \frac{3}{30}$$

Now the two fractions can be added:

$$\frac{20}{30} + \frac{3}{30} = \frac{23}{30}$$

5. **Comparing the Size of Fractions.** When comparing the size of two fractions with the same denominator, the larger fraction will have the larger numerator. For example,

$$\frac{5}{8} > \frac{3}{8}$$

The denominators are the same, so the whole is partitioned into pieces of the same size. Five of these pieces are more than three of them:

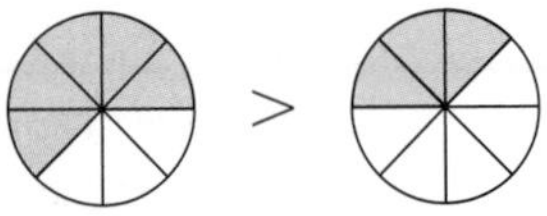

When two fractions have different denominators, you must first convert them to fractions with a common denominator to determine which is larger. Consider the following fractions:

$$\frac{3}{8} \quad \text{and} \quad \frac{7}{16}$$

If the numerator and denominator of $\frac{3}{8}$ are multiplied by 2, the resulting equivalent fraction will have a denominator of 16:

$$\frac{3}{8} = \frac{3 \times 2}{8 \times 2} = \frac{6}{16}$$

Now a comparison can be made between the two fractions:

$$\frac{6}{16} < \frac{7}{16}$$

Therefore,

$$\frac{3}{8} < \frac{7}{16}$$

DECIMALS

1. **Converting Decimals to Fractions.** Like a fraction, a decimal represents part of the whole. The first decimal place to the right of the decimal point indicates how many tenths are used. For example,

$$0.1 = \frac{1}{10} \qquad 0.7 = \frac{7}{10}$$

The next decimal place represents $\frac{1}{100}$, the next $\frac{1}{1000}$, the next $\frac{1}{10{,}000}$, and so on. To change a decimal to a fraction, just use the number without the decimal point for the numerator. Use the denominator that the last (on the right) decimal place represents. For example,

$$0.32 = \frac{32}{100} \qquad 0.5333 = \frac{5333}{10{,}000} \qquad 0.05 = \frac{5}{100} \qquad 0.001 = \frac{1}{1000}$$

2. **Adding and Subtracting Decimals.** To add and subtract decimals, the only rule is that you must keep the decimal points in a straight vertical line. For example,

$$\begin{array}{r} 0.27 \\ +1.326 \\ \hline 1.596 \end{array} \qquad \begin{array}{r} 3.595 \\ -0.67 \\ \hline 2.925 \end{array}$$

3. **Multiplying Decimals.** To multiply two decimal values, you first multiply the two numbers, ignoring the decimal points. Then you position the decimal point in the answer so that the number of digits to the right of the decimal point is equal to the total number of decimal places in the two numbers being multiplied. For example,

$$\begin{array}{rl} 1.73 & \text{(two decimal places)} \\ \times 0.251 & \text{(three decimal places)} \\ \hline 173 & \\ 865 & \\ 346 & \\ \hline 0.43423 & \text{(five decimal places)} \end{array} \qquad \begin{array}{rl} 0.25 & \text{(two decimal places)} \\ \times 0.005 & \text{(three decimal places)} \\ \hline 125 & \\ 00 & \\ 00 & \\ \hline 0.00125 & \text{(five decimal places)} \end{array}$$

4. **Dividing Decimals.** The simplest procedure for dividing decimals is based on the fact that dividing two numbers is identical to expressing them as a fraction:

$$0.25 \div 1.6 \text{ is identical to } \frac{0.25}{1.6}$$

You now can multiply both the numerator and the denominator of the fraction by 10, 100, 1000, or whatever number is necessary to remove the decimal places. Remember that multiplying both the numerator and the denominator of a fraction by the *same* value will create an equivalent fraction. Therefore,

$$\frac{0.25}{1.6} = \frac{0.25 \times 100}{1.6 \times 100} = \frac{25}{160} = \frac{5}{32}$$

The result is a division problem without any decimal places in the two numbers.

PERCENTAGES

1. **Converting a Percentage to a Fraction or a Decimal.** To convert a percentage to a fraction, remove the percent sign, place the number in the numerator, and use 100 for the denominator. For example,

$$52\% = \frac{52}{100} \qquad 5\% = \frac{5}{100}$$

To convert a percentage to a decimal, remove the percent sign and divide by 100, or simply move the decimal point two places to the left. For example,

$$83\% = 83. = 0.83$$

$$14.5\% = 14.5 = 0.145$$

$$5\% = 5. = 0.05$$

2. **Performing Arithmetic Operations with Percentages.** There are situations in which it is best to express percent values as decimals in order to perform certain arithmetic operations. For example, what is 45% of 60? This question may be stated as

$$45\% \times 60 = ?$$

The 45% should be converted to decimal form to find the solution to this question. Therefore,

$$0.45 \times 60 = 27$$

LEARNING CHECK

1. Convert $\frac{3}{25}$ to a decimal.
2. Convert $\frac{3}{8}$ to a percentage.
3. Next to each set of fractions, write "True" if they are equivalent and "False" if they are not:

   a. $\frac{3}{8} = \frac{9}{24}$ ______________ **b.** $\frac{7}{9} = \frac{17}{19}$ ______________

   c. $\frac{2}{7} = \frac{4}{14}$ ______________

4. Compute the following:

a. $\frac{1}{6} \times \frac{7}{10}$ **b.** $\frac{7}{8} - \frac{1}{2}$ **c.** $\frac{9}{10} \div \frac{2}{3}$ **d.** $\frac{7}{22} + \frac{2}{3}$

5. Identify the larger fraction of each pair:

a. $\frac{7}{10}, \frac{21}{100}$ **b.** $\frac{3}{4}, \frac{7}{12}$ **c.** $\frac{22}{3}, \frac{19}{3}$

6. Convert the following decimals into fractions:

a. 0.012 **b.** 0.77 **c.** 0.005

7. $2.59 \times 0.015 = ?$

8. $1.8 \div 0.02 = ?$

9. What is 28% of 45?

ANSWERS **1.** 0.12 **2.** 37.5% **3. a.** True **b.** False **c.** True

4. a. $\frac{7}{60}$ **b.** $\frac{3}{8}$ **c.** $\frac{27}{20}$ **d.** $\frac{65}{66}$ **5. a.** $\frac{7}{10}$ **b.** $\frac{3}{4}$ **c.** $\frac{22}{3}$

6. a. $\frac{12}{1000} = \frac{3}{250}$ **b.** $\frac{77}{100}$ **c.** $\frac{5}{1000} = \frac{1}{200}$ **7.** 0.03885 **8.** 90 **9.** 12.6

A.3 NEGATIVE NUMBERS

Negative numbers are used to represent values less than zero. Negative numbers may occur when you are measuring the difference between two scores. For example, a researcher may want to evaluate the effectiveness of a propaganda film by measuring people's attitudes with a test both before and after viewing the film:

	Before	After	Amount of Change
Person A	23	27	+4
Person B	18	15	−3
Person C	21	16	−5

Notice that the negative sign provides information about the direction of the difference: A plus sign indicates an increase in value, and a minus sign indicates a decrease.

Because negative numbers are frequently encountered, you should be comfortable working with these values. This section reviews basic arithmetic operations using negative numbers. You should also note that any number without a sign (+ or −) is assumed to be positive.

1. **Adding Negative Numbers.** When adding numbers that include negative values, simply interpret the negative sign as subtraction. For example,

$$3 + (-2) + 5 = 3 - 2 + 5 = 6$$

When adding a long string of numbers, it often is easier to add all the positive values to obtain the positive sum and then to add all of the negative values to obtain the negative sum. Finally, you subtract the negative sum from the positive sum. For example,

$$-1 + 3 + (-4) + 3 + (-6) + (-2)$$

positive sum = 6 negative sum = 13

Answer: $6 - 13 = -7$

2. **Subtracting Negative Numbers.** To subtract a negative number, change it to a positive number, and add. For example,

$$4 - (-3) = 4 + 3 = 7$$

This rule is easier to understand if you think of positive numbers as financial gains and negative numbers as financial losses. In this context, taking away a debt is equivalent to a financial gain. In mathematical terms, taking away a negative number is equivalent to adding a positive number. For example, suppose you are meeting a friend for lunch. You have \$7, but you owe your friend \$3. Thus, you really have only \$4 to spend for lunch. But your friend forgives (takes away) the \$3 debt. The result is that you now have \$7 to spend. Expressed as an equation,

$$\$4 \text{ minus a } \$3 \text{ debt} = \$7$$

$$4 - (-3) = 4 + 3 = 7$$

3. **Multiplying and Dividing Negative Numbers.** When the two numbers being multiplied (or divided) have the same sign, the result is a positive number. When the two numbers have different signs, the result is negative. For example,

$$3 \times (-2) = -6$$

$$-4 \times (-2) = +8$$

The first example is easy to explain by thinking of multiplication as repeated addition. In this case,

$$3 \times (-2) = (-2) + (-2) + (-2) = -6$$

You add three negative 2s, which results in a total of negative 6. In the second example, we are multiplying by a negative number. This amounts to repeated subtraction. That is,

$$\begin{aligned} -4 \times (-2) &= -(-2) - (-2) - (-2) - (-2) \\ &= 2 + 2 + 2 + 2 = 8 \end{aligned}$$

By using the same rule for both multiplication and division, we ensure that these two operations are compatible. For example,

$$-6 \div 3 = -2$$

which is compatible with

$$3 \times (-2) = -6$$

Also,

$$8 \div (-4) = -2$$

which is compatible with

$$-4 \times (-2) = +8$$

LEARNING CHECK

1. Complete the following calculations:
   a. $3 + (-8) + 5 + 7 + (-1) + (-3)$
   b. $5 - (-9) + 2 - (-3) - (-1)$
   c. $3 - 7 - (-21) + (-5) - (-9)$
   d. $4 - (-6) - 3 + 11 - 14$
   e. $9 + 8 - 2 - 1 - (-6)$
   f. $9 \times (-3)$
   g. $-7 \times (-4)$
   h. $-6 \times (-2) \times (-3)$
   i. $-12 \div (-3)$
   j. $18 \div (-6)$

ANSWERS **1. a.** 3 **b.** 20 **c.** 21 **d.** 4 **e.** 20
f. −27 **g.** 28 **h.** −36 **i.** 4 **j.** −3

A.4 BASIC ALGEBRA: SOLVING EQUATIONS

An equation is a mathematical statement that indicates two quantities are identical. For example,

$$12 = 8 + 4$$

Often an equation will contain an unknown (or variable) quantity that is identified with a letter or symbol, rather than a number. For example,

$$12 = 8 + X$$

In this event, your task is to find the value of X that makes the equation "true," or balanced. For this example, an X value of 4 will make a true equation. Finding the value of X is usually called *solving the equation.*

To solve an equation, there are two points to keep in mind:

1. Your goal is to have the unknown value (X) isolated on one side of the equation. This means that you need to remove all of the other numbers and symbols that appear on the same side of the equation as the X.
2. The equation remains balanced, provided you treat both sides exactly the same. For example, you could add 10 points to *both* sides, and the solution (the X value) for the equation would be unchanged.

FINDING THE SOLUTION FOR AN EQUATION

We will consider four basic types of equations and the operations needed to solve them.

1. **When X Has a Value Added to It.** An example of this type of equation is

$$X + 3 = 7$$

Your goal is to isolate X on one side of the equation. Thus, you must remove the $+3$ on the left-hand side. The solution is obtained by subtracting 3 from *both* sides of the equation:

$$X + 3 - 3 = 7 - 3$$

$$X = 4$$

The solution is $X = 4$. You should always check your solution by returning to the original equation and replacing X with the value you obtained for the solution. For this example,

$$X + 3 = 7$$

$$4 + 3 = 7$$

$$7 = 7$$

2. **When X Has a Value Subtracted From It.** An example of this type of equation is

$$X - 8 = 12$$

In this example, you must remove the -8 from the left-hand side. Thus, the solution is obtained by adding 8 to *both* sides of the equation:

$$X - 8 + 8 = 12 + 8$$

$$X = 20$$

Check the solution:

$$X - 8 = 12$$

$$20 - 8 = 12$$

$$12 = 12$$

3. **When X Is Multiplied by a Value.** An example of this type of equation is

$$4X = 24$$

In this instance, it is necessary to remove the 4 that is multiplied by X. This may be accomplished by dividing both sides of the equation by 4:

$$\frac{4X}{4} = \frac{24}{4}$$

$$X = 6$$

Check the solution:

$$4X = 24$$

$$4(6) = 24$$

$$24 = 24$$

4. **When X Is Divided by a Value.** An example of this type of equation is

$$\frac{X}{3} = 9$$

Now the X is divided by 3, so the solution is obtained by multiplying by 3. Multiplying both sides yields

$$3\left(\frac{X}{3}\right) = 9(3)$$

$$X = 27$$

For the check,

$$\frac{X}{3} = 9$$

$$\frac{27}{3} = 9$$

$$9 = 9$$

SOLUTIONS FOR MORE COMPLEX EQUATIONS

More complex equations can be solved by using a combination of the preceding simple operations. Remember that at each stage you are trying to isolate X on one side of the equation. For example,

$$3X + 7 = 22$$

$$3X + 7 - 7 = 22 - 7 \quad \text{(Remove +7 by subtracting 7 from both sides.)}$$

$$3X = 15$$

$$\frac{3X}{3} = \frac{15}{3} \quad \text{(Remove 3 by dividing both sides by 3.)}$$

$$X = 5$$

To check this solution, return to the original equation, and substitute 5 in place of X:

$$3X + 7 = 22$$

$$3(5) + 7 = 22$$

$$15 + 7 = 22$$

$$22 = 22$$

Following is another type of complex equation frequently encountered in statistics:

$$\frac{X + 3}{4} = 2$$

First, remove the 4 by multiplying both sides by 4:

$$4\left(\frac{X + 3}{4}\right) = 2(4)$$

$$X + 3 = 8$$

Now remove the +3 by subtracting 3 from both sides:

$$X + 3 - 3 = 8 - 3$$

$$X = 5$$

To check this solution, return to the original equation, and substitute 5 in place of X:

$$\frac{X+3}{4} = 2$$

$$\frac{5+3}{4} = 2$$

$$\frac{8}{4} = 2$$

$$2 = 2$$

LEARNING CHECK

1. Solve for X, and check the solutions:

a. $3X = 18$ **b.** $X + 7 = 9$ **c.** $X - 4 = 18$ **d.** $5X - 8 = 12$

e. $\frac{X}{9} = 5$ **f.** $\frac{X+1}{6} = 4$ **g.** $X + 2 = -5$ **h.** $\frac{X}{5} = -5$

i. $\frac{2X}{3} = 12$ **j.** $\frac{X}{3} + 1 = 3$

ANSWERS **1. a.** $X = 6$ **b.** $X = 2$ **c.** $X = 22$ **d.** $X = 4$ **e.** $X = 45$

f. $X = 23$ **g.** $X = -7$ **h.** $X = -25$ **i.** $X = 18$ **j.** $X = 6$

A.5 EXPONENTS AND SQUARE ROOTS

EXPONENTIAL NOTATION

A simplified notation is used whenever a number is being multiplied by itself. The notation consists of placing a value, called an *exponent,* on the right-hand side of and raised above another number, called a *base*. For example,

7^3 ← exponent
↑
base

The exponent indicates how many times the base is used as a factor in multiplication. Following are some examples:

$7^3 = 7(7)(7)$ (Read "7 cubed" or "7 raised to the third power")
$5^2 = 5(5)$ (Read "5 squared")
$2^5 = 2(2)(2)(2)(2)$ (Read "2 raised to the fifth power")

There are a few basic rules about exponents that you will need to know for this course. They are outlined here.

1. **Numbers Raised to One or Zero.** Any number raised to the first power equals itself. For example,

$$6^1 = 6$$

Any number (except zero) raised to the zero power equals 1. For example,

$$9^0 = 1$$

2. **Exponents for Multiple Terms**. The exponent applies only to the base that is just in front of it. For example,

$$XY^2 = XYY$$

$$a^2b^3 = aabbb$$

3. **Negative Bases Raised to an Exponent.** If a negative number is raised to a power, then the result will be positive for exponents that are even and negative for exponents that are odd. For example,

$$\begin{aligned}(-4)^3 &= -4(-4)(-4)\\ &= 16(-4)\\ &= -64\end{aligned}$$

and

$$\begin{aligned}(-3)^4 &= -3(-3)(-3)(-3)\\ &= 9(-3)(-3)\\ &= 9(9)\\ &= 81\end{aligned}$$

Note: The parentheses are used to ensure that the exponent applies to the entire negative number, including the sign. Without the parentheses there is some ambiguity as to how the exponent should be applied. For example, the expression -3^2 could have two interpretations:

$$-3^2 = (-3)(-3) = 9 \quad \text{or} \quad -3^2 = -(3)(3) = -9$$

4. **Exponents and Parentheses.** If an exponent is present outside of parentheses, then the computations within the parentheses are done first, and the exponential computation is done last:

$$(3 + 5)^2 = 8^2 = 64$$

Notice that the meaning of the expression is changed when each term in the parentheses is raised to the exponent individually:

$$3^2 + 5^2 = 9 + 25 = 34$$

Therefore,

$$X^2 + Y^2 \neq (X + Y)^2$$

5. **Fractions Raised to a Power.** If the numerator and denominator of a fraction are each raised to the same exponent, then the entire fraction can be raised to that exponent. That is,

$$\frac{a^2}{b^2} = \left(\frac{a}{b}\right)^2$$

For example,

$$\frac{3^2}{4^2} = \left(\frac{3}{4}\right)^2$$

$$\frac{9}{16} = \frac{3}{4}\left(\frac{3}{4}\right)$$

$$\frac{9}{16} = \frac{9}{16}$$

SQUARE ROOTS

The square root of a value equals a number that when multiplied by itself yields the original value. For example, the square root of 16 equals 4 because 4 times 4 equals 16. The symbol for the square root is called a *radical,* $\sqrt{}$. The square root is taken for the number under the radical. For example,

$$\sqrt{16} = 4$$

Finding the square root is the inverse of raising a number to the second power (squaring). Thus,

$$\sqrt{a^2} = a$$

For example,

$$\sqrt{3^2} = \sqrt{9} = 3$$

Also,

$$(\sqrt{b})^2 = b$$

For example,

$$(\sqrt{64})^2 = 8^2 = 64$$

Computations under the same radical are performed *before* the square root is taken. For example,

$$\sqrt{9 + 16} = \sqrt{25} = 5$$

Note that with addition (or subtraction), separate radicals yield a different result:

$$\sqrt{9} + \sqrt{16} = 3 + 4 = 7$$

Therefore,

$$\sqrt{X} + \sqrt{Y} \neq \sqrt{X + Y}$$

$$\sqrt{X} - \sqrt{Y} \neq \sqrt{X - Y}$$

If the numerator and denominator of a fraction each have a radical, then the entire fraction can be placed under a single radical:

$$\frac{\sqrt{16}}{\sqrt{4}} = \sqrt{\frac{16}{4}}$$

$$\frac{4}{2} = \sqrt{4}$$

$$2 = 2$$

Therefore,

$$\frac{\sqrt{X}}{\sqrt{Y}} = \sqrt{\frac{X}{Y}}$$

Also, if the square root of one number is multiplied by the square root of another number, then the same result would be obtained by taking the square root of the product of both numbers. For example,

$$\sqrt{9} \times \sqrt{16} = \sqrt{9 \times 16}$$

$$3 \times 4 = \sqrt{144}$$

$$12 = 12$$

Therefore,

$$\sqrt{a} \times \sqrt{b} = \sqrt{ab}$$

LEARNING CHECK

1. Perform the following computations:

a. $(-6)^3$

b. $(3 + 7)^2$

c. a^3b^2 when $a = 2$ and $b = -5$

d. a^4b^3 when $a = 2$ and $b = 3$

e. $(XY)^2$ when $X = 3$ and $Y = 5$

f. $X^2 + Y^2$ when $X = 3$ and $Y = 5$

g. $(X + Y)^2$ when $X = 3$ and $Y = 5$

h. $\sqrt{5 + 4}$

i. $(\sqrt{9})^2$

j. $\frac{\sqrt{16}}{\sqrt{4}}$

ANSWERS **1. a.** −216 **b.** 100 **c.** 200 **d.** 432 **e.** 225 **f.** 34 **g.** 64 **h.** 3 **i.** 9 **j.** 2

PROBLEMS FOR APPENDIX A Basic Mathematics Review

1. $50/(10 - 8) = ?$

2. $(2 + 3)^2 = ?$

3. $20/10 \times 3 = ?$

4. $12 - 4 \times 2 + 6/3 = ?$

5. $24/(12 - 4) + 2 \times (6 + 3) = ?$

6. Convert $\frac{7}{20}$ to a decimal.

7. Express $\frac{9}{25}$ as a percentage.

8. Convert 0.91 to a fraction.

9. Express 0.0031 as a fraction.

10. Next to each set of fractions, write "True" if they are equivalent and "False" if they are not:

a. $\frac{4}{1000} = \frac{2}{100}$ ____________

b. $\frac{5}{6} = \frac{52}{62}$ ____________

c. $\frac{1}{8} = \frac{7}{56}$ ____________

11. Perform the following calculations:

a. $\frac{4}{5} \times \frac{2}{3} = ?$ b. $\frac{7}{9} \div \frac{2}{3} = ?$

c. $\frac{3}{8} + \frac{1}{5} = ?$ d. $\frac{5}{18} - \frac{1}{6} = ?$

12. $2.51 \times 0.017 = ?$

13. $3.88 \times 0.0002 = ?$

14. $3.17 + 17.0132 = ?$

15. $5.55 + 10.7 + 0.711 + 3.33 + 0.031 = ?$

16. $2.04 \div 0.2 = ?$

17. $0.36 \div 0.4 = ?$

18. $5 + 3 - 6 - 4 + 3 = ?$

19. $9 - (-1) - 17 + 3 - (-4) + 5 = ?$

20. $5 + 3 - (-8) - (-1) + (-3) - 4 + 10 = ?$

21. $8 \times (-3) = ?$

22. $-22 \div (-2) = ?$

23. $-2(-4) \_ (-3) = ?$

24. $84 \div (-4) = ?$

Solve the equations in problems 25–32 for *X*.

25. $X - 7 = -2$

26. $9 = X + 3$

27. $\frac{X}{4} = 11$

28. $-3 = \frac{X}{3}$

29. $\frac{X + 3}{5} = 2$

30. $\frac{X + 1}{3} = -8$

31. $6X - 1 = 11$

32. $2X + 3 = -11$

33. $(-5)^2 = ?$

34. $(-5)^3 = ?$

35. If $a = 4$ and $b = 3$, then $a^2 + b^4 = ?$

36. If $a = -1$ and $b = 4$, then $(a + b)^2 = ?$

37. If $a = -1$ and $b = 5$, then $ab^2 = ?$

38. $\frac{18}{\sqrt{4}} = ?$

39. $\sqrt{\frac{20}{5}} = ?$

SKILLS ASSESSMENT FINAL EXAM

SECTION 1

1. $4 + 8/4 = ?$

2. $(4 + 8)/4 = ?$

3. $4 \times 3^2 = ?$

4. $(4 \times 3)^2 = ?$

5. $10/5 \times 2 = ?$

6. $10/(5 \times 2) = ?$

7. $40 - 10 \times 4/2 = ?$

8. $(5 - 1)^2/2 = ?$

9. $3 \times 6 - 3^2 = ?$

10. $2 \times (6 - 3)^2 = ?$

11. $4 \times 3 - 1 + 8 \times 2 = ?$

12. $4 \times (3 - 1 + 8) \times 2 = ?$

SECTION 2

1. Express $\frac{14}{80}$ as a decimal.

2. Convert $\frac{6}{25}$ to a percentage.

3. Convert 18% to a fraction.

4. $\frac{3}{5} \times \frac{2}{3} = ?$

5. $\frac{5}{24} + \frac{5}{6} = ?$

6. $\frac{7}{12} \div \frac{5}{6} = ?$

7. $\frac{5}{9} - \frac{1}{3} = ?$

8. $6.11 \times 0.22 = ?$

9. $0.18 \div 0.9 = ?$

10. $8.742 + 0.76 = ?$

11. In a statistics class of 72 students, three-eighths of the students received a B on the first test. How many Bs were earned?

12. What is 15% of 64?

SECTION 3

1. $3 - 1 - 3 + 5 - 2 + 6 = ?$

2. $-8 - (-6) = ?$

3. $2 - (-7) - 3 + (-11) - 20 = ?$

4. $-8 - 3 - (-1) - 2 - 1 = ?$

5. $8(-2) = ?$

6. $-7(-7) = ?$

7. $-3(-2)(-5) = ?$

8. $-3(5)(-3) = ?$

9. $-24 \div (-4) = ?$

10. $36 \div (-6) = ?$

11. $-56/7 = ?$

12. $-7/(-1) = ?$

SECTION 4

Solve for X.

1. $X + 5 = 12$

2. $X - 11 = 3$

3. $10 = X + 4$

4. $4X = 20$

5. $\frac{X}{2} = 15$

6. $18 = 9X$

7. $\frac{X}{5} = 35$

8. $2X + 8 = 4$

9. $\frac{X + 1}{3} = 6$

10. $4X + 3 = -13$

11. $\frac{X + 3}{3} = -7$

12. $23 = 2X - 5$

SECTION 5

1. $5^3 = ?$

2. $(-4)^3 = ?$

3. $(-2)^5 = ?$

4. $(-2)^6 = ?$

5. If $a = 4$ and $b = 2$, then $ab^2 = ?$

6. If $a = 4$ and $b = 2$, then $(a + b)^3 = ?$

7. If $a = 4$ and $b = 2$, then $a^2 + b^2 = ?$

8. $(11 + 4)^2 = ?$

9. $\sqrt{7^2} = ?$

10. If $a = 36$ and $b = 64$, then $\sqrt{a + b} = ?$

11. $\frac{25}{\sqrt{25}} = ? = ?$

12. If $a = -1$ and $b = 2$, then $a^3b^4 = ?$

ANSWER KEY Skills Assessment Exams

PREVIEW EXAM

SECTION 1

1. 17	**2.** 35	**3.** 6
4. 24	**5.** 5	**6.** 2
7. $\frac{1}{3}$	**8.** 8	**9.** 72
10. 8	**11.** 24	**12.** 48

SECTION 2

1. 75%	**2.** $\frac{30}{100}$, or $\frac{3}{10}$	**3.** 0.3
4. $\frac{10}{13}$	**5.** 1.625	**6.** $\frac{2}{20}$, or $\frac{1}{10}$
7. $\frac{19}{24}$	**8.** 1.4	**9.** $\frac{4}{15}$
10. 7.5	**11.** 16	**12.** 36

SECTION 3

1. 4	**2.** 8	**3.** 2
4. 9	**5.** −12	**6.** 12
7. −15	**8.** −24	**9.** −4
10. 3	**11.** −2	**12.** 25

FINAL EXAM

SECTION 1

1. 6	**2.** 3	**3.** 36
4. 144	**5.** 4	**6.** 1
7. 20	**8.** 8	**9.** 9
10. 18	**11.** 27	**12.** 80

SECTION 2

1. 0.175	**2.** 24%	**3.** $\frac{18}{100}$, or $\frac{9}{50}$
4. $\frac{6}{15}$, or $\frac{2}{5}$	**5.** $\frac{25}{24}$	**6.** $\frac{42}{60}$, or $\frac{7}{10}$
7. $\frac{2}{9}$	**8.** 1.3442	**9.** 0.2
10. 9.502	**11.** 27	**12.** 9.6

SECTION 3

1. 8	**2.** −2	**3.** −25
4. −13	**5.** −16	**6.** 49
7. −30	**8.** 45	**9.** 6
10. −6	**11.** −8	**12.** 7

PREVIEW EXAM

SECTION 4

1. $X = 7$	**2.** $X = 29$	**3.** $X = 9$
4. $X = 4$	**5.** $X = 24$	**6.** $X = 15$
7. $X = 80$	**8.** $X = -3$	**9.** $X = 11$
10. $X = 25$	**11.** $X = 11$	**12.** $X = 7$

SECTION 5

1. 64	**2.** 4	**3.** 54
4. 25	**5.** 13	**6.** −27
7. 256	**8.** 8	**9.** 12
10. 121	**11.** 33	**12.** −9

FINAL EXAM

SECTION 4

1. $X = 7$	**2.** $X = 14$	**3.** $X = 6$
4. $X = 5$	**5.** $X = 30$	**6.** $X = 2$
7. $X = 175$	**8.** $X = -2$	**9.** $X = 17$
10. $X = -4$	**11.** $X = -24$	**12.** $X = 14$

SECTION 5

1. 125	**2.** −64	**3.** −32
4. 64	**5.** 16	**6.** 216
7. 20	**8.** 225	**9.** 7
10. 10	**11.** 5	**12.** −16

SOLUTIONS TO SELECTED PROBLEMS FOR APPENDIX A Basic Mathematics Review

1. 25

5. 21

7. 36%

10. b. False

11. a. $\frac{8}{15}$ b. $\frac{21}{18}$ c. $\frac{23}{40}$

12. 0.04267

3. 6

6. 0.35

9. $\frac{31}{10{,}000}$

14. 20.1832

17. 0.9

21. −24

25. $X = 5$

30. $X = -25$

34. −125

37. −25

19. 5

22. 11

28. $X = -9$

31. $X = 2$

36. 9

39. 2

SUGGESTED REVIEW BOOKS

There are many basic mathematics books available if you need a more extensive review than this appendix can provide. Several are probably available in your library. The following books are but a few of the many that you may find helpful:

Gustafson, R. D., Karr, R., & Massey, M. (2011). *Beginning Algebra* (9th ed.). Belmont, CA: Brooks/Cole.

Lial, M. L., Salzman, S.A., & Hestwood, D.L. (2006). *Basic College Mathematics* (7th ed). Reading MA: Addison-Wesley.

McKeague, C. P. (2010). *Basic College Mathematics: A Text/Workbook.* (7th ed.). Belmont, CA: Brooks/Cole.

APPENDIX B Statistical Tables

TABLE B.1 THE UNIT NORMAL TABLE*

*Column A lists z-score values. A vertical line drawn through a normal distribution at a z-score location divides the distribution into two sections.
Column B identifies the proportion in the larger section, called the *body*.
Column C identifies the proportion in the smaller section, called the *tail*.
Column D identifies the proportion between the mean and the z-score.
Note: Because the normal distribution is symmetrical, the proportions for negative z-scores are the same as those for positive z-scores.

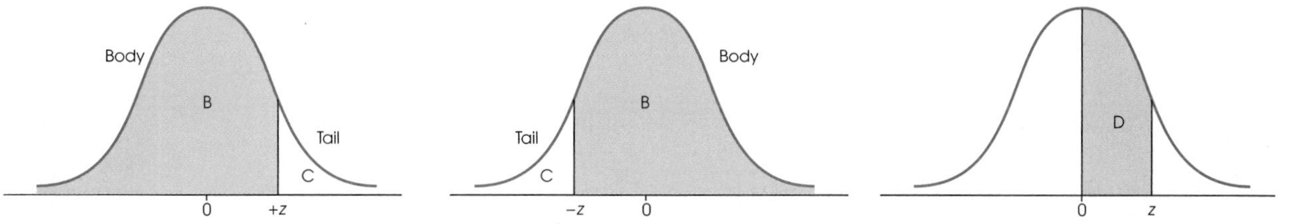

(A) z	(B) Proportion in Body	(C) Proportion in Tail	(D) Proportion Between Mean and z	(A) z	(B) Proportion in Body	(C) Proportion in Tail	(D) Proportion Between Mean and z
0.00	.5000	.5000	.0000	0.25	.5987	.4013	.0987
0.01	.5040	.4960	.0040	0.26	.6026	.3974	.1026
0.02	.5080	.4920	.0080	0.27	.6064	.3936	.1064
0.03	.5120	.4880	.0120	0.28	.6103	.3897	.1103
0.04	.5160	.4840	.0160	0.29	.6141	.3859	.1141
0.05	.5199	.4801	.0199	0.30	.6179	.3821	.1179
0.06	.5239	.4761	.0239	0.31	.6217	.3783	.1217
0.07	.5279	.4721	.0279	0.32	.6255	.3745	.1255
0.08	.5319	.4681	.0319	0.33	.6293	.3707	.1293
0.09	.5359	.4641	.0359	0.34	.6331	.3669	.1331
0.10	.5398	.4602	.0398	0.35	.6368	.3632	.1368
0.11	.5438	.4562	.0438	0.36	.6406	.3594	.1406
0.12	.5478	.4522	.0478	0.37	.6443	.3557	.1443
0.13	.5517	.4483	.0517	0.38	.6480	.3520	.1480
0.14	.5557	.4443	.0557	0.39	.6517	.3483	.1517
0.15	.5596	.4404	.0596	0.40	.6554	.3446	.1554
0.16	.5636	.4364	.0636	0.41	.6591	.3409	.1591
0.17	.5675	.4325	.0675	0.42	.6628	.3372	.1628
0.18	.5714	.4286	.0714	0.43	.6664	.3336	.1664
0.19	.5753	.4247	.0753	0.44	.6700	.3300	.1700
0.20	.5793	.4207	.0793	0.45	.6736	.3264	.1736
0.21	.5832	.4168	.0832	0.46	.6772	.3228	.1772
0.22	.5871	.4129	.0871	0.47	.6808	.3192	.1808
0.23	.5910	.4090	.0910	0.48	.6844	.3156	.1844
0.24	.5948	.4052	.0948	0.49	.6879	.3121	.1879

(A) z	(B) Proportion in Body	(C) Proportion in Tail	(D) Proportion Between Mean and z	(A) z	(B) Proportion in Body	(C) Proportion in Tail	(D) Proportion Between Mean and z
0.50	.6915	.3085	.1915	1.00	.8413	.1587	.3413
0.51	.6950	.3050	.1950	1.01	.8438	.1562	.3438
0.52	.6985	.3015	.1985	1.02	.8461	.1539	.3461
0.53	.7019	.2981	.2019	1.03	.8485	.1515	.3485
0.54	.7054	.2946	.2054	1.04	.8508	.1492	.3508
0.55	.7088	.2912	.2088	1.05	.8531	.1469	.3531
0.56	.7123	.2877	.2123	1.06	.8554	.1446	.3554
0.57	.7157	.2843	.2157	1.07	.8577	.1423	.3577
0.58	.7190	.2810	.2190	1.08	.8599	.1401	.3599
0.59	.7224	.2776	.2224	1.09	.8621	.1379	.3621
0.60	.7257	.2743	.2257	1.10	.8643	.1357	.3643
0.61	.7291	.2709	.2291	1.11	.8665	.1335	.3665
0.62	.7324	.2676	.2324	1.12	.8686	.1314	.3686
0.63	.7357	.2643	.2357	1.13	.8708	.1292	.3708
0.64	.7389	.2611	.2389	1.14	.8729	.1271	.3729
0.65	.7422	.2578	.2422	1.15	.8749	.1251	.3749
0.66	.7454	.2546	.2454	1.16	.8770	.1230	.3770
0.67	.7486	.2514	.2486	1.17	.8790	.1210	.3790
0.68	.7517	.2483	.2517	1.18	.8810	.1190	.3810
0.69	.7549	.2451	.2549	1.19	.8830	.1170	.3830
0.70	.7580	.2420	.2580	1.20	.8849	.1151	.3849
0.71	.7611	.2389	.2611	1.21	.8869	.1131	.3869
0.72	.7642	.2358	.2642	1.22	.8888	.1112	.3888
0.73	.7673	.2327	.2673	1.23	.8907	.1093	.3907
0.74	.7704	.2296	.2704	1.24	.8925	.1075	.3925
0.75	.7734	.2266	.2734	1.25	.8944	.1056	.3944
0.76	.7764	.2236	.2764	1.26	.8962	.1038	.3962
0.77	.7794	.2206	.2794	1.27	.8980	.1020	.3980
0.78	.7823	.2177	.2823	1.28	.8997	.1003	.3997
0.79	.7852	.2148	.2852	1.29	.9015	.0985	.4015
0.80	.7881	.2119	.2881	1.30	.9032	.0968	.4032
0.81	.7910	.2090	.2910	1.31	.9049	.0951	.4049
0.82	.7939	.2061	.2939	1.32	.9066	.0934	.4066
0.83	.7967	.2033	.2967	1.33	.9082	.0918	.4082
0.84	.7995	.2005	.2995	1.34	.9099	.0901	.4099
0.85	.8023	.1977	.3023	1.35	.9115	.0885	.4115
0.86	.8051	.1949	.3051	1.36	.9131	.0869	.4131
0.87	.8078	.1922	.3078	1.37	.9147	.0853	.4147
0.88	.8106	.1894	.3106	1.38	.9162	.0838	.4162
0.89	.8133	.1867	.3133	1.39	.9177	.0823	.4177
0.90	.8159	.1841	.3159	1.40	.9192	.0808	.4192
0.91	.8186	.1814	.3186	1.41	.9207	.0793	.4207
0.92	.8212	.1788	.3212	1.42	.9222	.0778	.4222
0.93	.8238	.1762	.3238	1.43	.9236	.0764	.4236
0.94	.8264	.1736	.3264	1.44	.9251	.0749	.4251
0.95	.8289	.1711	.3289	1.45	.9265	.0735	.4265
0.96	.8315	.1685	.3315	1.46	.9279	.0721	.4279
0.97	.8340	.1660	.3340	1.47	.9292	.0708	.4292
0.98	.8365	.1635	.3365	1.48	.9306	.0694	.4306
0.99	.8389	.1611	.3389	1.49	.9319	.0681	.4319

(A) z	(B) Proportion in Body	(C) Proportion in Tail	(D) Proportion Between Mean and z	(A) z	(B) Proportion in Body	(C) Proportion in Tail	(D) Proportion Between Mean and z
1.50	.9332	.0668	.4332	2.00	.9772	.0228	.4772
1.51	.9345	.0655	.4345	2.01	.9778	.0222	.4778
1.52	.9357	.0643	.4357	2.02	.9783	.0217	.4783
1.53	.9370	.0630	.4370	2.03	.9788	.0212	.4788
1.54	.9382	.0618	.4382	2.04	.9793	.0207	.4793
1.55	.9394	.0606	.4394	2.05	.9798	.0202	.4798
1.56	.9406	.0594	.4406	2.06	.9803	.0197	.4803
1.57	.9418	.0582	.4418	2.07	.9808	.0192	.4808
1.58	.9429	.0571	.4429	2.08	.9812	.0188	.4812
1.59	.9441	.0559	.4441	2.09	.9817	.0183	.4817
1.60	.9452	.0548	.4452	2.10	.9821	.0179	.4821
1.61	.9463	.0537	.4463	2.11	.9826	.0174	.4826
1.62	.9474	.0526	.4474	2.12	.9830	.0170	.4830
1.63	.9484	.0516	.4484	2.13	.9834	.0166	.4834
1.64	.9495	.0505	.4495	2.14	.9838	.0162	.4838
1.65	.9505	.0495	.4505	2.15	.9842	.0158	.4842
1.66	.9515	.0485	.4515	2.16	.9846	.0154	.4846
1.67	.9525	.0475	.4525	2.17	.9850	.0150	.4850
1.68	.9535	.0465	.4535	2.18	.9854	.0146	.4854
1.69	.9545	.0455	.4545	2.19	.9857	.0143	.4857
1.70	.9554	.0446	.4554	2.20	.9861	.0139	.4861
1.71	.9564	.0436	.4564	2.21	.9864	.0136	.4864
1.72	.9573	.0427	.4573	2.22	.9868	.0132	.4868
1.73	.9582	.0418	.4582	2.23	.9871	.0129	.4871
1.74	.9591	.0409	.4591	2.24	.9875	.0125	.4875
1.75	.9599	.0401	.4599	2.25	.9878	.0122	.4878
1.76	.9608	.0392	.4608	2.26	.9881	.0119	.4881
1.77	.9616	.0384	.4616	2.27	.9884	.0116	.4884
1.78	.9625	.0375	.4625	2.28	.9887	.0113	.4887
1.79	.9633	.0367	.4633	2.29	.9890	.0110	.4890
1.80	.9641	.0359	.4641	2.30	.9893	.0107	.4893
1.81	.9649	.0351	.4649	2.31	.9896	.0104	.4896
1.82	.9656	.0344	.4656	2.32	.9898	.0102	.4898
1.83	.9664	.0336	.4664	2.33	.9901	.0099	.4901
1.84	.9671	.0329	.4671	2.34	.9904	.0096	.4904
1.85	.9678	.0322	.4678	2.35	.9906	.0094	.4906
1.86	.9686	.0314	.4686	2.36	.9909	.0091	.4909
1.87	.9693	.0307	.4693	2.37	.9911	.0089	.4911
1.88	.9699	.0301	.4699	2.38	.9913	.0087	.4913
1.89	.9706	.0294	.4706	2.39	.9916	.0084	.4916
1.90	.9713	.0287	.4713	2.40	.9918	.0082	.4918
1.91	.9719	.0281	.4719	2.41	.9920	.0080	.4920
1.92	.9726	.0274	.4726	2.42	.9922	.0078	.4922
1.93	.9732	.0268	.4732	2.43	.9925	.0075	.4925
1.94	.9738	.0262	.4738	2.44	.9927	.0073	.4927
1.95	.9744	.0256	.4744	2.45	.9929	.0071	.4929
1.96	.9750	.0250	.4750	2.46	.9931	.0069	.4931
1.97	.9756	.0244	.4756	2.47	.9932	.0068	.4932
1.98	.9761	.0239	.4761	2.48	.9934	.0066	.4934
1.99	.9767	.0233	.4767	2.49	.9936	.0064	.4936

(A) z	(B) Proportion in Body	(C) Proportion in Tail	(D) Proportion Between Mean and z	(A) z	(B) Proportion in Body	(C) Proportion in Tail	(D) Proportion Between Mean and z
2.50	.9938	.0062	.4938	2.95	.9984	.0016	.4984
2.51	.9940	.0060	.4940	2.96	.9985	.0015	.4985
2.52	.9941	.0059	.4941	2.97	.9985	.0015	.4985
2.53	.9943	.0057	.4943	2.98	.9986	.0014	.4986
2.54	.9945	.0055	.4945	2.99	.9986	.0014	.4986
2.55	.9946	.0054	.4946	3.00	.9987	.0013	.4987
2.56	.9948	.0052	.4948	3.01	.9987	.0013	.4987
2.57	.9949	.0051	.4949	3.02	.9987	.0013	.4987
2.58	.9951	.0049	.4951	3.03	.9988	.0012	.4988
2.59	.9952	.0048	.4952	3.04	.9988	.0012	.4988
2.60	.9953	.0047	.4953	3.05	.9989	.0011	.4989
2.61	.9955	.0045	.4955	3.06	.9989	.0011	.4989
2.62	.9956	.0044	.4956	3.07	.9989	.0011	.4989
2.63	.9957	.0043	.4957	3.08	.9990	.0010	.4990
2.64	.9959	.0041	.4959	3.09	.9990	.0010	.4990
2.65	.9960	.0040	.4960	3.10	.9990	.0010	.4990
2.66	.9961	.0039	.4961	3.11	.9991	.0009	.4991
2.67	.9962	.0038	.4962	3.12	.9991	.0009	.4991
2.68	.9963	.0037	.4963	3.13	.9991	.0009	.4991
2.69	.9964	.0036	.4964	3.14	.9992	.0008	.4992
2.70	.9965	.0035	.4965	3.15	.9992	.0008	.4992
2.71	.9966	.0034	.4966	3.16	.9992	.0008	.4992
2.72	.9967	.0033	.4967	3.17	.9992	.0008	.4992
2.73	.9968	.0032	.4968	3.18	.9993	.0007	.4993
2.74	.9969	.0031	.4969	3.19	.9993	.0007	.4993
2.75	.9970	.0030	.4970	3.20	.9993	.0007	.4993
2.76	.9971	.0029	.4971	3.21	.9993	.0007	.4993
2.77	.9972	.0028	.4972	3.22	.9994	.0006	.4994
2.78	.9973	.0027	.4973	3.23	.9994	.0006	.4994
2.79	.9974	.0026	.4974	3.24	.9994	.0006	.4994
2.80	.9974	.0026	.4974	3.30	.9995	.0005	.4995
2.81	.9975	.0025	.4975	3.40	.9997	.0003	.4997
2.82	.9976	.0024	.4976	3.50	.9998	.0002	.4998
2.83	.9977	.0023	.4977	3.60	.9998	.0002	.4998
2.84	.9977	.0023	.4977	3.70	.9999	.0001	.4999
2.85	.9978	.0022	.4978	3.80	.99993	.00007	.49993
2.86	.9979	.0021	.4979	3.90	.99995	.00005	.49995
2.87	.9979	.0021	.4979	4.00	.99997	.00003	.49997
2.88	.9980	.0020	.4980				
2.89	.9981	.0019	.4981				
2.90	.9981	.0019	.4981				
2.91	.9982	.0018	.4982				
2.92	.9982	.0018	.4982				
2.93	.9983	.0017	.4983				
2.94	.9984	.0016	.4984				

TABLE B.2 THE *t* DISTRIBUTION

Table entries are values of *t* corresponding to proportions in one tail or in two tails combined.

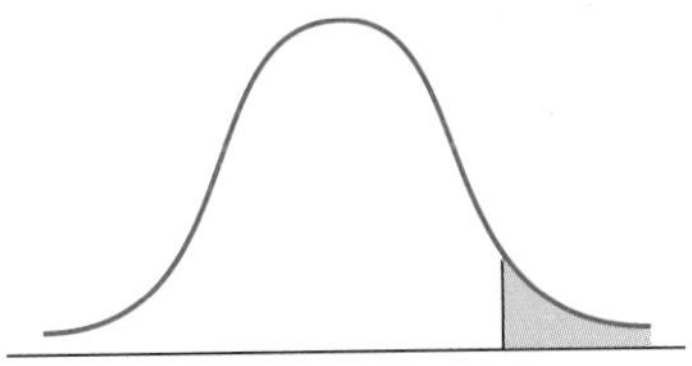

One tail
(either right or left)

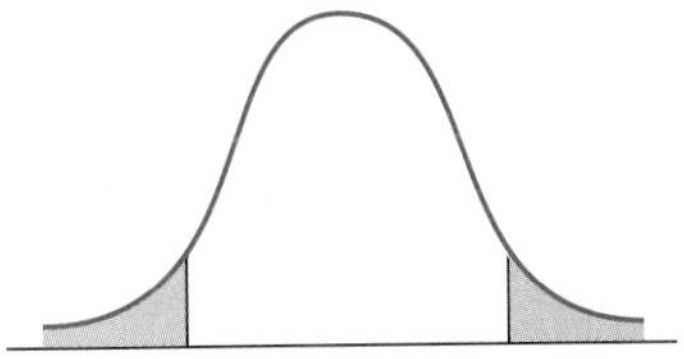

Two tails
combined

	Proportion in One Tail					
	0.25	0.10	0.05	0.025	0.01	0.005
	Proportion in Two Tails Combined					
df	0.50	0.20	0.10	0.05	0.02	0.01
1	1.000	3.078	6.314	12.706	31.821	63.657
2	0.816	1.886	2.920	4.303	6.965	9.925
3	0.765	1.638	2.353	3.182	4.541	5.841
4	0.741	1.533	2.132	2.776	3.747	4.604
5	0.727	1.476	2.015	2.571	3.365	4.032
6	0.718	1.440	1.943	2.447	3.143	3.707
7	0.711	1.415	1.895	2.365	2.998	3.499
8	0.706	1.397	1.860	2.306	2.896	3.355
9	0.703	1.383	1.833	2.262	2.821	3.250
10	0.700	1.372	1.812	2.228	2.764	3.169
11	0.697	1.363	1.796	2.201	2.718	3.106
12	0.695	1.356	1.782	2.179	2.681	3.055
13	0.694	1.350	1.771	2.160	2.650	3.012
14	0.692	1.345	1.761	2.145	2.624	2.977
15	0.691	1.341	1.753	2.131	2.602	2.947
16	0.690	1.337	1.746	2.120	2.583	2.921
17	0.689	1.333	1.740	2.110	2.567	2.898
18	0.688	1.330	1.734	2.101	2.552	2.878
19	0.688	1.328	1.729	2.093	2.539	2.861
20	0.687	1.325	1.725	2.086	2.528	2.845
21	0.686	1.323	1.721	2.080	2.518	2.831
22	0.686	1.321	1.717	2.074	2.508	2.819
23	0.685	1.319	1.714	2.069	2.500	2.807
24	0.685	1.318	1.711	2.064	2.492	2.797
25	0.684	1.316	1.708	2.060	2.485	2.787
26	0.684	1.315	1.706	2.056	2.479	2.779
27	0.684	1.314	1.703	2.052	2.473	2.771
28	0.683	1.313	1.701	2.048	2.467	2.763
29	0.683	1.311	1.699	2.045	2.462	2.756
30	0.683	1.310	1.697	2.042	2.457	2.750
40	0.681	1.303	1.684	2.021	2.423	2.704
60	0.679	1.296	1.671	2.000	2.390	2.660
120	0.677	1.289	1.658	1.980	2.358	2.617
∞	0.674	1.282	1.645	1.960	2.326	2.576

TABLE B.3 CRITICAL VALUES FOR THE *F*-MAX STATISTIC*

*The critical values for $\alpha = .05$ are in lightface type, and for $\alpha = .01$, they are in boldface type.

	k = Number of Samples										
$n - 1$	2	3	4	5	6	7	8	9	10	11	12
4	9.60	15.5	20.6	25.2	29.5	33.6	37.5	41.4	44.6	48.0	51.4
	23.2	**37.**	**49.**	**59.**	**69.**	**79.**	**89.**	**97.**	**106.**	**113.**	**120.**
5	7.15	10.8	13.7	16.3	18.7	20.8	22.9	24.7	26.5	28.2	29.9
	14.9	**22.**	**28.**	**33.**	**38.**	**42.**	**46.**	**50.**	**54.**	**57.**	**60.**
6	5.82	8.38	10.4	12.1	13.7	15.0	16.3	17.5	18.6	19.7	20.7
	11.1	**15.5**	**19.1**	**22.**	**25.**	**27.**	**30.**	**32.**	**34.**	**36.**	**37.**
7	4.99	6.94	8.44	9.70	10.8	11.8	12.7	13.5	14.3	15.1	15.8
	8.89	**12.1**	**14.5**	**16.5**	**18.4**	**20.**	**22.**	**23.**	**24.**	**26.**	**27.**
8	4.43	6.00	7.18	8.12	9.03	9.78	10.5	11.1	11.7	12.2	12.7
	7.50	**9.9**	**11.7**	**13.2**	**14.5**	**15.8**	**16.9**	**17.9**	**18.9**	**19.8**	**21.**
9	4.03	5.34	6.31	7.11	7.80	8.41	8.95	9.45	9.91	10.3	10.7
	6.54	**8.5**	**9.9**	**11.1**	**12.1**	**13.1**	**13.9**	**14.7**	**15.3**	**16.0**	**16.6**
10	3.72	4.85	5.67	6.34	6.92	7.42	7.87	8.28	8.66	9.01	9.34
	5.85	**7.4**	**8.6**	**9.6**	**10.4**	**11.1**	**11.8**	**12.4**	**12.9**	**13.4**	**13.9**
12	3.28	4.16	4.79	5.30	5.72	6.09	6.42	6.72	7.00	7.25	7.48
	4.91	**6.1**	**6.9**	**7.6**	**8.2**	**8.7**	**9.1**	**9.5**	**9.9**	**10.2**	**10.6**
15	2.86	3.54	4.01	4.37	4.68	4.95	5.19	5.40	5.59	5.77	5.93
	4.07	**4.9**	**5.5**	**6.0**	**6.4**	**6.7**	**7.1**	**7.3**	**7.5**	**7.8**	**8.0**
20	2.46	2.95	3.29	3.54	3.76	3.94	4.10	4.24	4.37	4.49	4.59
	3.32	**3.8**	**4.3**	**4.6**	**4.9**	**5.1**	**5.3**	**5.5**	**5.6**	**5.8**	**5.9**
30	2.07	2.40	2.61	2.78	2.91	3.02	3.12	3.21	3.29	3.36	3.39
	2.63	**3.0**	**3.3**	**3.5**	**3.6**	**3.7**	**3.8**	**3.9**	**4.0**	**4.1**	**4.2**
60	1.67	1.85	1.96	2.04	2.11	2.17	2.22	2.26	2.30	2.33	2.36
	1.96	**2.2**	**2.3**	**2.4**	**2.4**	**2.5**	**2.5**	**2.6**	**2.6**	**2.7**	**2.7**

Table 31 of E. Pearson and H.O. Hartley, Biometrika Tables for Statisticians, 2nd ed. New York: Cambridge University Press, 1958. Adapted and reprinted with permission of the Biometrika trustees.

TABLE B.4 THE *F* DISTRIBUTION*

*Table entries in lightface type are critical values for the .05 level of significance.
Boldface type values are for the .01 level of significance.

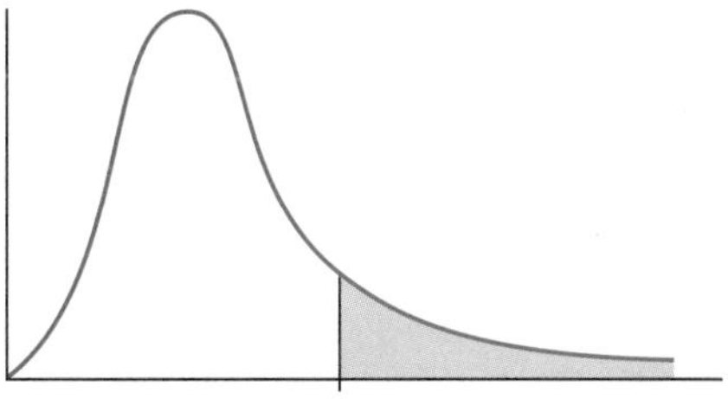

Critical
F

Degrees of Freedom: Denominator	Degrees of Freedom: Numerator														
	1	2	3	4	5	6	7	8	9	10	11	12	14	16	20
1	161	200	216	225	230	234	237	239	241	242	243	244	245	246	248
	4052	**4999**	**5403**	**5625**	**5764**	**5859**	**5928**	**5981**	**6022**	**6056**	**6082**	**6106**	**6142**	**6169**	**6208**
2	18.51	19.00	19.16	19.25	19.30	19.33	19.36	19.37	19.38	19.39	19.40	19.41	19.42	19.43	19.44
	98.49	**99.00**	**99.17**	**99.25**	**99.30**	**99.33**	**99.34**	**99.36**	**99.38**	**99.40**	**99.41**	**99.42**	**99.43**	**99.44**	**99.45**
3	10.13	9.55	9.28	9.12	9.01	8.94	8.88	8.84	8.81	8.78	8.76	8.74	8.71	8.69	8.66
	34.12	**30.92**	**29.46**	**28.71**	**28.24**	**27.91**	**27.67**	**27.49**	**27.34**	**27.23**	**27.13**	**27.05**	**26.92**	**26.83**	**26.69**
4	7.71	6.94	6.59	6.39	6.26	6.16	6.09	6.04	6.00	5.96	5.93	5.91	5.87	5.84	5.80
	21.20	**18.00**	**16.69**	**15.98**	**15.52**	**15.21**	**14.98**	**14.80**	**14.66**	**14.54**	**14.45**	**14.37**	**14.24**	**14.15**	**14.02**
5	6.61	5.79	5.41	5.19	5.05	4.95	4.88	4.82	4.78	4.74	4.70	4.68	4.64	4.60	4.56
	16.26	**13.27**	**12.06**	**11.39**	**10.97**	**10.67**	**10.45**	**10.27**	**10.15**	**10.05**	**9.96**	**9.89**	**9.77**	**9.68**	**9.55**
6	5.99	5.14	4.76	4.53	4.39	4.28	4.21	4.15	4.10	4.06	4.03	4.00	3.96	3.92	3.87
	13.74	**10.92**	**9.78**	**9.15**	**8.75**	**8.47**	**8.26**	**8.10**	**7.98**	**7.87**	**7.79**	**7.72**	**7.60**	**7.52**	**7.39**
7	5.59	4.74	4.35	4.12	3.97	3.87	3.79	3.73	3.68	3.63	3.60	3.57	3.52	3.49	3.44
	12.25	**9.55**	**8.45**	**7.85**	**7.46**	**7.19**	**7.00**	**6.84**	**6.71**	**6.62**	**6.54**	**6.47**	**6.35**	**6.27**	**6.15**
8	5.32	4.46	4.07	3.84	3.69	3.58	3.50	3.44	3.39	3.34	3.31	3.28	3.23	3.20	3.15
	11.26	**8.65**	**7.59**	**7.01**	**6.63**	**6.37**	**6.19**	**6.03**	**5.91**	**5.82**	**5.74**	**5.67**	**5.56**	**5.48**	**5.36**
9	5.12	4.26	3.86	3.63	3.48	3.37	3.29	3.23	3.18	3.13	3.10	3.07	3.02	2.98	2.93
	10.56	**8.02**	**6.99**	**6.42**	**6.06**	**5.80**	**5.62**	**5.47**	**5.35**	**5.26**	**5.18**	**5.11**	**5.00**	**4.92**	**4.80**
10	4.96	4.10	3.71	3.48	3.33	3.22	3.14	3.07	3.02	2.97	2.94	2.91	2.86	2.82	2.77
	10.04	**7.56**	**6.55**	**5.99**	**5.64**	**5.39**	**5.21**	**5.06**	**4.95**	**4.85**	**4.78**	**4.71**	**4.60**	**4.52**	**4.41**
11	4.84	3.98	3.59	3.36	3.20	3.09	3.01	2.95	2.90	2.86	2.82	2.79	2.74	2.70	2.65
	9.65	**7.20**	**6.22**	**5.67**	**5.32**	**5.07**	**4.88**	**4.74**	**4.63**	**4.54**	**4.46**	**4.40**	**4.29**	**4.21**	**4.10**
12	4.75	3.88	3.49	3.26	3.11	3.00	2.92	2.85	2.80	2.76	2.72	2.69	2.64	2.60	2.54
	9.33	**6.93**	**5.95**	**5.41**	**5.06**	**4.82**	**4.65**	**4.50**	**4.39**	**4.30**	**4.22**	**4.16**	**4.05**	**3.98**	**3.86**
13	4.67	3.80	3.41	3.18	3.02	2.92	2.84	2.77	2.72	2.67	2.63	2.60	2.55	2.51	2.46
	9.07	**6.70**	**5.74**	**5.20**	**4.86**	**4.62**	**4.44**	**4.30**	**4.19**	**4.10**	**4.02**	**3.96**	**3.85**	**3.78**	**3.67**
14	4.60	3.74	3.34	3.11	2.96	2.85	2.77	2.70	2.65	2.60	2.56	2.53	2.48	2.44	2.39
	8.86	**6.51**	**5.56**	**5.03**	**4.69**	**4.46**	**4.28**	**4.14**	**4.03**	**3.94**	**3.86**	**3.80**	**3.70**	**3.62**	**3.51**
15	4.54	3.68	3.29	3.06	2.90	2.79	2.70	2.64	2.59	2.55	2.51	2.48	2.43	2.39	2.33
	8.68	**6.36**	**5.42**	**4.89**	**4.56**	**4.32**	**4.14**	**4.00**	**3.89**	**3.80**	**3.73**	**3.67**	**3.56**	**3.48**	**3.36**
16	4.49	3.63	3.24	3.01	2.85	2.74	2.66	2.59	2.54	2.49	2.45	2.42	2.37	2.33	2.28
	8.53	**6.23**	**5.29**	**4.77**	**4.44**	**4.20**	**4.03**	**3.89**	**3.78**	**3.69**	**3.61**	**3.55**	**3.45**	**3.37**	**3.25**

TABLE B.4 (continued)

Degrees of Freedom: Denominator	Degrees of Freedom: Numerator														
	1	2	3	4	5	6	7	8	9	10	11	12	14	16	20
17	4.45	3.59	3.20	2.96	2.81	2.70	2.62	2.55	2.50	2.45	2.41	2.38	2.33	2.29	2.23
	8.40	**6.11**	**5.18**	**4.67**	**4.34**	**4.10**	**3.93**	**3.79**	**3.68**	**3.59**	**3.52**	**3.45**	**3.35**	**3.27**	**3.16**
18	4.41	3.55	3.16	2.93	2.77	2.66	2.58	2.51	2.46	2.41	2.37	2.34	2.29	2.25	2.19
	8.28	**6.01**	**5.09**	**4.58**	**4.25**	**4.01**	**3.85**	**3.71**	**3.60**	**3.51**	**3.44**	**3.37**	**3.27**	**3.19**	**3.07**
19	4.38	3.52	3.13	2.90	2.74	2.63	2.55	2.48	2.43	2.38	2.34	2.31	2.26	2.21	2.15
	8.18	**5.93**	**5.01**	**4.50**	**4.17**	**3.94**	**3.77**	**3.63**	**3.52**	**3.43**	**3.36**	**3.30**	**3.19**	**3.12**	**3.00**
20	4.35	3.49	3.10	2.87	2.71	2.60	2.52	2.45	2.40	2.35	2.31	2.28	2.23	2.18	2.12
	8.10	**5.85**	**4.94**	**4.43**	**4.10**	**3.87**	**3.71**	**3.56**	**3.45**	**3.37**	**3.30**	**3.23**	**3.13**	**3.05**	**2.94**
21	4.32	3.47	3.07	2.84	2.68	2.57	2.49	2.42	2.37	2.32	2.28	2.25	2.20	2.15	2.09
	8.02	**5.78**	**4.87**	**4.37**	**4.04**	**3.81**	**3.65**	**3.51**	**3.40**	**3.31**	**3.24**	**3.17**	**3.07**	**2.99**	**2.88**
22	4.30	3.44	3.05	2.82	2.66	2.55	2.47	2.40	2.35	2.30	2.26	2.23	2.18	2.13	2.07
	7.94	**5.72**	**4.82**	**4.31**	**3.99**	**3.76**	**3.59**	**3.45**	**3.35**	**3.26**	**3.18**	**3.12**	**3.02**	**2.94**	**2.83**
23	4.28	3.42	3.03	2.80	2.64	2.53	2.45	2.38	2.32	2.28	2.24	2.20	2.14	2.10	2.04
	7.88	**5.66**	**4.76**	**4.26**	**3.94**	**3.71**	**3.54**	**3.41**	**3.30**	**3.21**	**3.14**	**3.07**	**2.97**	**2.89**	**2.78**
24	4.26	3.40	3.01	2.78	2.62	2.51	2.43	2.36	2.30	2.26	2.22	2.18	2.13	2.09	2.02
	7.82	**5.61**	**4.72**	**4.22**	**3.90**	**3.67**	**3.50**	**3.36**	**3.25**	**3.17**	**3.09**	**3.03**	**2.93**	**2.85**	**2.74**
25	4.24	3.38	2.99	2.76	2.60	2.49	2.41	2.34	2.28	2.24	2.20	2.16	2.11	2.06	2.00
	7.77	**5.57**	**4.68**	**4.18**	**3.86**	**3.63**	**3.46**	**3.32**	**3.21**	**3.13**	**3.05**	**2.99**	**2.89**	**2.81**	**2.70**
26	4.22	3.37	2.98	2.74	2.59	2.47	2.39	2.32	2.27	2.22	2.18	2.15	2.10	2.05	1.99
	7.72	**5.53**	**4.64**	**4.14**	**3.82**	**3.59**	**3.42**	**3.29**	**3.17**	**3.09**	**3.02**	**2.96**	**2.86**	**2.77**	**2.66**
27	4.21	3.35	2.96	2.73	2.57	2.46	2.37	2.30	2.25	2.20	2.16	2.13	2.08	2.03	1.97
	7.68	**5.49**	**4.60**	**4.11**	**3.79**	**3.56**	**3.39**	**3.26**	**3.14**	**3.06**	**2.98**	**2.93**	**2.83**	**2.74**	**2.63**
28	4.20	3.34	2.95	2.71	2.56	2.44	2.36	2.29	2.24	2.19	2.15	2.12	2.06	2.02	1.96
	7.64	**5.45**	**4.57**	**4.07**	**3.76**	**3.53**	**3.36**	**3.23**	**3.11**	**3.03**	**2.95**	**2.90**	**2.80**	**2.71**	**2.60**
29	4.18	3.33	2.93	2.70	2.54	2.43	2.35	2.28	2.22	2.18	2.14	2.10	2.05	2.00	1.94
	7.60	**5.42**	**4.54**	**4.04**	**3.73**	**3.50**	**3.33**	**3.20**	**3.08**	**3.00**	**2.92**	**2.87**	**2.77**	**2.68**	**2.57**
30	4.17	3.32	2.92	2.69	2.53	2.42	2.34	2.27	2.21	2.16	2.12	2.09	2.04	1.99	1.93
	7.56	**5.39**	**4.51**	**4.02**	**3.70**	**3.47**	**3.30**	**3.17**	**3.06**	**2.98**	**2.90**	**2.84**	**2.74**	**2.66**	**2.55**
32	4.15	3.30	2.90	2.67	2.51	2.40	2.32	2.25	2.19	2.14	2.10	2.07	2.02	1.97	1.91
	7.50	**5.34**	**4.46**	**3.97**	**3.66**	**3.42**	**3.25**	**3.12**	**3.01**	**2.94**	**2.86**	**2.80**	**2.70**	**2.62**	**2.51**
34	4.13	3.28	2.88	2.65	2.49	2.38	2.30	2.23	2.17	2.12	2.08	2.05	2.00	1.95	1.89
	7.44	**5.29**	**4.42**	**3.93**	**3.61**	**3.38**	**3.21**	**3.08**	**2.97**	**2.89**	**2.82**	**2.76**	**2.66**	**2.58**	**2.47**
36	4.11	3.26	2.86	2.63	2.48	2.36	2.28	2.21	2.15	2.10	2.06	2.03	1.98	1.93	1.87
	7.39	**5.25**	**4.38**	**3.89**	**3.58**	**3.35**	**3.18**	**3.04**	**2.94**	**2.86**	**2.78**	**2.72**	**2.62**	**2.54**	**2.43**
38	4.10	3.25	2.85	2.62	2.46	2.35	2.26	2.19	2.14	2.09	2.05	2.02	1.96	1.92	1.85
	7.35	**5.21**	**4.34**	**3.86**	**3.54**	**3.32**	**3.15**	**3.02**	**2.91**	**2.82**	**2.75**	**2.69**	**2.59**	**2.51**	**2.40**
40	4.08	3.23	2.84	2.61	2.45	2.34	2.25	2.18	2.12	2.07	2.04	2.00	1.95	1.90	1.84
	7.31	**5.18**	**4.31**	**3.83**	**3.51**	**3.29**	**3.12**	**2.99**	**2.88**	**2.80**	**2.73**	**2.66**	**2.56**	**2.49**	**2.37**

TABLE B.4 (continued)

Degrees of Freedom: Denominator	Degrees of Freedom: Numerator 1	2	3	4	5	6	7	8	9	10	11	12	14	16	20
42	4.07	3.22	2.83	2.59	2.44	2.32	2.24	2.17	2.11	2.06	2.02	1.99	1.94	1.89	1.82
	7.27	**5.15**	**4.29**	**3.80**	**3.49**	**3.26**	**3.10**	**2.96**	**2.86**	**2.77**	**2.70**	**2.64**	**2.54**	**2.46**	**2.35**
44	4.06	3.21	2.82	2.58	2.43	2.31	2.23	2.16	2.10	2.05	2.01	1.98	1.92	1.88	1.81
	7.24	**5.12**	**4.26**	**3.78**	**3.46**	**3.24**	**3.07**	**2.94**	**2.84**	**2.75**	**2.68**	**2.62**	**2.52**	**2.44**	**2.32**
46	4.05	3.20	2.81	2.57	2.42	2.30	2.22	2.14	2.09	2.04	2.00	1.97	1.91	1.87	1.80
	7.21	**5.10**	**4.24**	**3.76**	**3.44**	**3.22**	**3.05**	**2.92**	**2.82**	**2.73**	**2.66**	**2.60**	**2.50**	**2.42**	**2.30**
48	4.04	3.19	2.80	2.56	2.41	2.30	2.21	2.14	2.08	2.03	1.99	1.96	1.90	1.86	1.79
	7.19	**5.08**	**4.22**	**3.74**	**3.42**	**3.20**	**3.04**	**2.90**	**2.80**	**2.71**	**2.64**	**2.58**	**2.48**	**2.40**	**2.28**
50	4.03	3.18	2.79	2.56	2.40	2.29	2.20	2.13	2.07	2.02	1.98	1.95	1.90	1.85	1.78
	7.17	**5.06**	**4.20**	**3.72**	**3.41**	**3.18**	**3.02**	**2.88**	**2.78**	**2.70**	**2.62**	**2.56**	**2.46**	**2.39**	**2.26**
55	4.02	3.17	2.78	2.54	2.38	2.27	2.18	2.11	2.05	2.00	1.97	1.93	1.88	1.83	1.76
	7.12	**5.01**	**4.16**	**3.68**	**3.37**	**3.15**	**2.98**	**2.85**	**2.75**	**2.66**	**2.59**	**2.53**	**2.43**	**2.35**	**2.23**
60	4.00	3.15	2.76	2.52	2.37	2.25	2.17	2.10	2.04	1.99	1.95	1.92	1.86	1.81	1.75
	7.08	**4.98**	**4.13**	**3.65**	**3.34**	**3.12**	**2.95**	**2.82**	**2.72**	**2.63**	**2.56**	**2.50**	**2.40**	**2.32**	**2.20**
65	3.99	3.14	2.75	2.51	2.36	2.24	2.15	2.08	2.02	1.98	1.94	1.90	1.85	1.80	1.73
	7.04	**4.95**	**4.10**	**3.62**	**3.31**	**3.09**	**2.93**	**2.79**	**2.70**	**2.61**	**2.54**	**2.47**	**2.37**	**2.30**	**2.18**
70	3.98	3.13	2.74	2.50	2.35	2.23	2.14	2.07	2.01	1.97	1.93	1.89	1.84	1.79	1.72
	7.01	**4.92**	**4.08**	**3.60**	**3.29**	**3.07**	**2.91**	**2.77**	**2.67**	**2.59**	**2.51**	**2.45**	**2.35**	**2.28**	**2.15**
80	3.96	3.11	2.72	2.48	2.33	2.21	2.12	2.05	1.99	1.95	1.91	1.88	1.82	1.77	1.70
	6.96	**4.88**	**4.04**	**3.56**	**3.25**	**3.04**	**2.87**	**2.74**	**2.64**	**2.55**	**2.48**	**2.41**	**2.32**	**2.24**	**2.11**
100	3.94	3.09	2.70	2.46	2.30	2.19	2.10	2.03	1.97	1.92	1.88	1.85	1.79	1.75	1.68
	6.90	**4.82**	**3.98**	**3.51**	**3.20**	**2.99**	**2.82**	**2.69**	**2.59**	**2.51**	**2.43**	**2.36**	**2.26**	**2.19**	**2.06**
125	3.92	3.07	2.68	2.44	2.29	2.17	2.08	2.01	1.95	1.90	1.86	1.83	1.77	1.72	1.65
	6.84	**4.78**	**3.94**	**3.47**	**3.17**	**2.95**	**2.79**	**2.65**	**2.56**	**2.47**	**2.40**	**2.33**	**2.23**	**2.15**	**2.03**
150	3.91	3.06	2.67	2.43	2.27	2.16	2.07	2.00	1.94	1.89	1.85	1.82	1.76	1.71	1.64
	6.81	**4.75**	**3.91**	**3.44**	**3.14**	**2.92**	**2.76**	**2.62**	**2.53**	**2.44**	**2.37**	**2.30**	**2.20**	**2.12**	**2.00**
200	3.89	3.04	2.65	2.41	2.26	2.14	2.05	1.98	1.92	1.87	1.83	1.80	1.74	1.69	1.62
	6.76	**4.71**	**3.88**	**3.41**	**3.11**	**2.90**	**2.73**	**2.60**	**2.50**	**2.41**	**2.34**	**2.28**	**2.17**	**2.09**	**1.97**
400	3.86	3.02	2.62	2.39	2.23	2.12	2.03	1.96	1.90	1.85	1.81	1.78	1.72	1.67	1.60
	6.70	**4.66**	**3.83**	**3.36**	**3.06**	**2.85**	**2.69**	**2.55**	**2.46**	**2.37**	**2.29**	**2.23**	**2.12**	**2.04**	**1.92**
1000	3.85	3.00	2.61	2.38	2.22	2.10	2.02	1.95	1.89	1.84	1.80	1.76	1.70	1.65	1.58
	6.66	**4.62**	**3.80**	**3.34**	**3.04**	**2.82**	**2.66**	**2.53**	**2.43**	**2.34**	**2.26**	**2.20**	**2.09**	**2.01**	**1.89**
∞	3.84	2.99	2.60	2.37	2.21	2.09	2.01	1.94	1.88	1.83	1.79	1.75	1.69	1.64	1.57
	6.64	**4.60**	**3.78**	**3.32**	**3.02**	**2.80**	**2.64**	**2.51**	**2.41**	**2.32**	**2.24**	**2.18**	**2.07**	**1.99**	**1.87**

TABLE B.5 THE STUDENTIZED RANGE STATISTIC (*q*)*

*The critical values for q corresponding to $\alpha = .05$ (lightface type) and $\alpha = .01$ (boldface type).

df for Error Term	*k* = Number of Treatments										
	2	3	4	5	6	7	8	9	10	11	12
5	3.64	4.60	5.22	5.67	6.03	6.33	6.58	6.80	6.99	7.17	7.32
	5.70	**6.98**	**7.80**	**8.42**	**8.91**	**9.32**	**9.67**	**9.97**	**10.24**	**10.48**	**10.70**
6	3.46	4.34	4.90	5.30	5.63	5.90	6.12	6.32	6.49	6.65	6.79
	5.24	**6.33**	**7.03**	**7.56**	**7.97**	**8.32**	**8.61**	**8.87**	**9.10**	**9.30**	**9.48**
7	3.34	4.16	4.68	5.06	5.36	5.61	5.82	6.00	6.16	6.30	6.43
	4.95	**5.92**	**6.54**	**7.01**	**7.37**	**7.68**	**7.94**	**8.17**	**8.37**	**8.55**	**8.71**
8	3.26	4.04	4.53	4.89	5.17	5.40	5.60	5.77	5.92	6.05	6.18
	4.75	**5.64**	**6.20**	**6.62**	**6.96**	**7.24**	**7.47**	**7.68**	**7.86**	**8.03**	**8.18**
9	3.20	3.95	4.41	4.76	5.02	5.24	5.43	5.59	5.74	5.87	5.98
	4.60	**5.43**	**5.96**	**6.35**	**6.66**	**6.91**	**7.13**	**7.33**	**7.49**	**7.65**	**7.78**
10	3.15	3.88	4.33	4.65	4.91	5.12	5.30	5.46	5.60	5.72	5.83
	4.48	**5.27**	**5.77**	**6.14**	**6.43**	**6.67**	**6.87**	**7.05**	**7.21**	**7.36**	**7.49**
11	3.11	3.82	4.26	4.57	4.82	5.03	5.20	5.35	5.49	5.61	5.71
	4.39	**5.15**	**5.62**	**5.97**	**6.25**	**6.48**	**6.67**	**6.84**	**6.99**	**7.13**	**7.25**
12	3.08	3.77	4.20	4.51	4.75	4.95	5.12	5.27	5.39	5.51	5.61
	4.32	**5.05**	**5.50**	**5.84**	**6.10**	**6.32**	**6.51**	**6.67**	**6.81**	**6.94**	**7.06**
13	3.06	3.73	4.15	4.45	4.69	4.88	5.05	5.19	5.32	5.43	5.53
	4.26	**4.96**	**5.40**	**5.73**	**5.98**	**6.19**	**6.37**	**6.53**	**6.67**	**6.79**	**6.90**
14	3.03	3.70	4.11	4.41	4.64	4.83	4.99	5.13	5.25	5.36	5.46
	4.21	**4.89**	**5.32**	**5.63**	**5.88**	**6.08**	**6.26**	**6.41**	**6.54**	**6.66**	**6.77**
15	3.01	3.67	4.08	4.37	4.59	4.78	4.94	5.08	5.20	5.31	5.40
	4.17	**4.84**	**5.25**	**5.56**	**5.80**	**5.99**	**6.16**	**6.31**	**6.44**	**6.55**	**6.66**
16	3.00	3.65	4.05	4.33	4.56	4.74	4.90	5.03	5.15	5.26	5.35
	4.13	**4.79**	**5.19**	**5.49**	**5.72**	**5.92**	**6.08**	**6.22**	**6.35**	**6.46**	**6.56**
17	2.98	3.63	4.02	4.30	4.52	4.70	4.86	4.99	5.11	5.21	5.31
	4.10	**4.74**	**5.14**	**5.43**	**5.66**	**5.85**	**6.01**	**6.15**	**6.27**	**6.38**	**6.48**
18	2.97	3.61	4.00	4.28	4.49	4.67	4.82	4.96	5.07	5.17	5.27
	4.07	**4.70**	**5.09**	**5.38**	**5.60**	**5.79**	**5.94**	**6.08**	**6.20**	**6.31**	**6.41**
19	2.96	3.59	3.98	4.25	4.47	4.65	4.79	4.92	5.04	5.14	5.23
	4.05	**4.67**	**5.05**	**5.33**	**5.55**	**5.73**	**5.89**	**6.02**	**6.14**	**6.25**	**6.34**
20	2.95	3.58	3.96	4.23	4.45	4.62	4.77	4.90	5.01	5.11	5.20
	4.02	**4.64**	**5.02**	**5.29**	**5.51**	**5.69**	**5.84**	**5.97**	**6.09**	**6.19**	**6.28**
24	2.92	3.53	3.90	4.17	4.37	4.54	4.68	4.81	4.92	5.01	5.10
	3.96	**4.55**	**4.91**	**5.17**	**5.37**	**5.54**	**5.69**	**5.81**	**5.92**	**6.02**	**6.11**
30	2.89	3.49	3.85	4.10	4.30	4.46	4.60	4.72	4.82	4.92	5.00
	3.89	**4.45**	**4.80**	**5.05**	**5.24**	**5.40**	**5.54**	**5.65**	**5.76**	**5.85**	**5.93**
40	2.86	3.44	3.79	4.04	4.23	4.39	4.52	4.63	4.73	4.82	4.90
	3.82	**4.37**	**4.70**	**4.93**	**5.11**	**5.26**	**5.39**	**5.50**	**5.60**	**5.69**	**5.76**
60	2.83	3.40	3.74	3.98	4.16	4.31	4.44	4.55	4.65	4.73	4.81
	3.76	**4.28**	**4.59**	**4.82**	**4.99**	**5.13**	**5.25**	**5.36**	**5.45**	**5.53**	**5.60**
120	2.80	3.36	3.68	3.92	4.10	4.24	4.36	4.47	4.56	4.64	4.71
	3.70	**4.20**	**4.50**	**4.71**	**4.87**	**5.01**	**5.12**	**5.21**	**5.30**	**5.37**	**5.44**
∞	2.77	3.31	3.63	3.86	4.03	4.17	4.28	4.39	4.47	4.55	4.62
	3.64	**4.12**	**4.40**	**4.60**	**4.76**	**4.88**	**4.99**	**5.08**	**5.16**	**5.23**	**5.29**

TABLE B.6 CRITICAL VALUES FOR THE PEARSON CORRELATION*

*To be significant, the sample correlation, r, must be greater than or equal to the critical value in the table.

	Level of Significance for One-Tailed Test			
	.05	.025	.01	.005
	Level of Significance for Two-Tailed Test			
$df = n - 2$	.10	.05	.02	.01
1	.988	.997	.9995	.9999
2	.900	.950	.980	.990
3	.805	.878	.934	.959
4	.729	.811	.882	.917
5	.669	.754	.833	.874
6	.622	.707	.789	.834
7	.582	.666	.750	.798
8	.549	.632	.716	.765
9	.521	.602	.685	.735
10	.497	.576	.658	.708
11	.476	.553	.634	.684
12	.458	.532	.612	.661
13	.441	.514	.592	.641
14	.426	.497	.574	.623
15	.412	.482	.558	.606
16	.400	.468	.542	.590
17	.389	.456	.528	.575
18	.378	.444	.516	.561
19	.369	.433	.503	.549
20	.360	.423	.492	.537
21	.352	.413	.482	.526
22	.344	.404	.472	.515
23	.337	.396	.462	.505
24	.330	.388	.453	.496
25	.323	.381	.445	.487
26	.317	.374	.437	.479
27	.311	.367	.430	.471
28	.306	.361	.423	.463
29	.301	.355	.416	.456
30	.296	.349	.409	.449
35	.275	.325	.381	.418
40	.257	.304	.358	.393
45	.243	.288	.338	.372
50	.231	.273	.322	.354
60	.211	.250	.295	.325
70	.195	.232	.274	.302
80	.183	.217	.256	.283
90	.173	.205	.242	.267
100	.164	.195	.230	.254

Table VI of R. A. Fisher and F. Yates, *Statistical Tables for Biological, Agricultural and Medical Research*, 6th ed. London: Longman Group Ltd., 1974 (previously published by Oliver and Boyd Ltd., Edinburgh).

TABLE B.7 CRITICAL VALUES FOR THE SPEARMAN CORRELATION*

*To be significant, the sample correlation, r_s, must be greater than or equal to the critical value in the table.

	Level of Significance for One-Tailed Test			
	.05	.025	.01	.005
	Level of Significance for Two-Tailed Test			
n	.10	.05	.02	.01
4	1.000			
5	0.900	1.000	1.000	
6	0.829	0.886	0.943	1.000
7	0.714	0.786	0.893	0.929
8	0.643	0.738	0.833	0.881
9	0.600	0.700	0.783	0.833
10	0.564	0.648	0.745	0.794
11	0.536	0.618	0.709	0.755
12	0.503	0.587	0.671	0.727
13	0.484	0.560	0.648	0.703
14	0.464	0.538	0.622	0.675
15	0.443	0.521	0.604	0.654
16	0.429	0.503	0.582	0.635
17	0.414	0.485	0.566	0.615
18	0.401	0.472	0.550	0.600
19	0.391	0.460	0.535	0.584
20	0.380	0.447	0.520	0.570
21	0.370	0.435	0.508	0.556
22	0.361	0.425	0.496	0.544
23	0.353	0.415	0.486	0.532
24	0.344	0.406	0.476	0.521
25	0.337	0.398	0.466	0.511
26	0.331	0.390	0.457	0.501
27	0.324	0.382	0.448	0.491
28	0.317	0.375	0.440	0.483
29	0.312	0.368	0.433	0.475
30	0.306	0.362	0.425	0.467
35	0.283	0.335	0.394	0.433
40	0.264	0.313	0.368	0.405
45	0.248	0.294	0.347	0.382
50	0.235	0.279	0.329	0.363
60	0.214	0.255	0.300	0.331
70	0.190	0.235	0.278	0.307
80	0.185	0.220	0.260	0.287
90	0.174	0.207	0.245	0.271
100	0.165	0.197	0.233	0.257

Zar, J. H. (1972). Significance testing of the Spearman rank correlation coefficient. *Journal of the American Statistical Association*, 67, 578–580. Reprinted with permission from the *Journal of the American Statistical Association*.

TABLE B.8 THE CHI-SQUARE DISTRIBUTION*

*The table entries are critical values of χ^2.

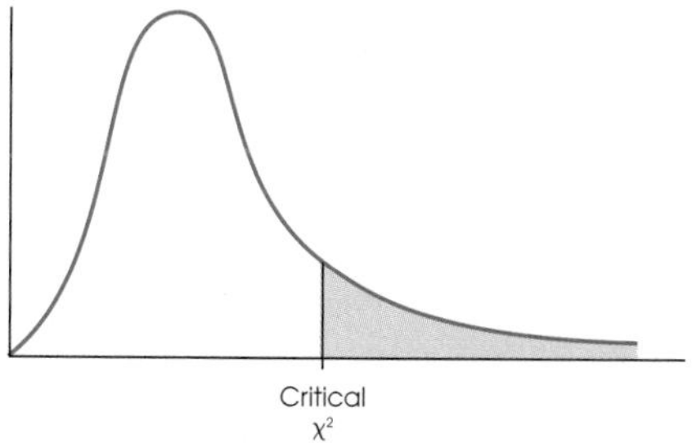

df	Proportion in Critical Region 0.10	0.05	0.025	0.01	0.005
1	2.71	3.84	5.02	6.63	7.88
2	4.61	5.99	7.38	9.21	10.60
3	6.25	7.81	9.35	11.34	12.84
4	7.78	9.49	11.14	13.28	14.86
5	9.24	11.07	12.83	15.09	16.75
6	10.64	12.59	14.45	16.81	18.55
7	12.02	14.07	16.01	18.48	20.28
8	13.36	15.51	17.53	20.09	21.96
9	14.68	16.92	19.02	21.67	23.59
10	15.99	18.31	20.48	23.21	25.19
11	17.28	19.68	21.92	24.72	26.76
12	18.55	21.03	23.34	26.22	28.30
13	19.81	22.36	24.74	27.69	29.82
14	21.06	23.68	26.12	29.14	31.32
15	22.31	25.00	27.49	30.58	32.80
16	23.54	26.30	28.85	32.00	34.27
17	24.77	27.59	30.19	33.41	35.72
18	25.99	28.87	31.53	34.81	37.16
19	27.20	30.14	32.85	36.19	38.58
20	28.41	31.41	34.17	37.57	40.00
21	29.62	32.67	35.48	38.93	41.40
22	30.81	33.92	36.78	40.29	42.80
23	32.01	35.17	38.08	41.64	44.18
24	33.20	36.42	39.36	42.98	45.56
25	34.38	37.65	40.65	44.31	46.93
26	35.56	38.89	41.92	45.64	48.29
27	36.74	40.11	43.19	46.96	49.64
28	37.92	41.34	44.46	48.28	50.99
29	39.09	42.56	45.72	49.59	52.34
30	40.26	43.77	46.98	50.89	53.67
40	51.81	55.76	59.34	63.69	66.77
50	63.17	67.50	71.42	76.15	79.49
60	74.40	79.08	83.30	88.38	91.95
70	85.53	90.53	95.02	100.42	104.22
80	96.58	101.88	106.63	112.33	116.32
90	107.56	113.14	118.14	124.12	128.30
100	118.50	124.34	129.56	135.81	140.17

Table 8 of E. Pearson and H. O. Hartley, *Biometrika Tables for Statisticians*, 3rd ed. New York: Cambridge University Press, 1966. Adapted and reprinted with permission of the Biometrika trustees.

TABLE B.9A CRITICAL VALUES OF THE MANN-WHITNEY U FOR $\alpha = .05$*

*Critical values are provided for a *one-tailed* test at $\alpha = .05$ (lightface type) and for a *two-tailed* test at $\alpha = .05$ (boldface type). To be significant for any given n_A and n_B, the obtained U must be *equal to* or *less than* the critical value in the table. Dashes (—) in the body of the table indicate that no decision is possible at the stated level of significance and values of n_A and n_B.

n_B \ n_A	1	2	3	4	5	6	7	8	9	10	11	12	13	14	15	16	17	18	19	20
1	—	—	—	—	—	—	—	—	—	—	—	—	—	—	—	—	—	—	0	0
	—	—	—	—	—	—	—	—	—	—	—	—	—	—	—	—	—	—	—	—
2	—	—	—	—	0	0	0	1	1	1	1	2	2	2	3	3	3	4	4	4
	—	—	—	—	—	—	—	**0**	**0**	**0**	**0**	**1**	**1**	**1**	**1**	**1**	**2**	**2**	**2**	**2**
3	—	—	0	0	1	2	2	3	3	4	5	5	6	7	7	8	9	9	10	11
	—	—	—	—	**0**	**1**	**1**	**2**	**2**	**3**	**3**	**4**	**4**	**5**	**5**	**6**	**6**	**7**	**7**	**8**
4	—	—	0	1	2	3	4	5	6	7	8	9	10	11	12	14	15	16	17	18
	—	—	—	**0**	**1**	**2**	**3**	**4**	**4**	**5**	**6**	**7**	**8**	**9**	**10**	**11**	**11**	**12**	**13**	**13**
5	—	0	1	2	4	5	6	8	9	11	12	13	15	16	18	19	20	22	23	25
	—	—	**0**	**1**	**2**	**3**	**5**	**6**	**7**	**8**	**9**	**11**	**12**	**13**	**14**	**15**	**17**	**18**	**19**	**20**
6	—	0	2	3	5	7	8	10	12	14	16	17	19	21	23	25	26	28	30	32
	—	—	**1**	**2**	**3**	**5**	**6**	**8**	**10**	**11**	**13**	**14**	**16**	**17**	**19**	**21**	**22**	**24**	**25**	**27**
7	—	0	2	4	6	8	11	13	15	17	19	21	24	26	28	30	33	35	37	39
	—	—	**1**	**3**	**5**	**6**	**8**	**10**	**12**	**14**	**16**	**18**	**20**	**22**	**24**	**26**	**28**	**30**	**32**	**34**
8	—	1	3	5	8	10	13	15	18	20	23	26	28	31	33	36	39	41	44	47
	—	**0**	**2**	**4**	**6**	**8**	**10**	**13**	**15**	**17**	**19**	**22**	**24**	**26**	**29**	**31**	**34**	**36**	**38**	**41**
9	—	1	3	6	9	12	15	18	21	24	27	30	33	36	39	42	45	48	51	54
	—	**0**	**2**	**4**	**7**	**10**	**12**	**15**	**17**	**20**	**23**	**26**	**28**	**31**	**34**	**37**	**39**	**42**	**45**	**48**
10	—	1	4	7	11	14	17	20	24	27	31	34	37	41	44	48	51	55	58	62
	—	**0**	**3**	**5**	**8**	**11**	**14**	**17**	**20**	**23**	**26**	**29**	**33**	**36**	**39**	**42**	**45**	**48**	**52**	**55**
11	—	1	5	8	12	16	19	23	27	31	34	38	42	46	50	54	57	61	65	69
	—	**0**	**3**	**6**	**9**	**13**	**16**	**19**	**23**	**26**	**30**	**33**	**37**	**40**	**44**	**47**	**51**	**55**	**58**	**62**
12	—	2	5	9	13	17	21	26	30	34	38	42	47	51	55	60	64	68	72	77
	—	**1**	**4**	**7**	**11**	**14**	**18**	**22**	**26**	**29**	**33**	**37**	**41**	**45**	**49**	**53**	**57**	**61**	**65**	**69**
13	—	2	6	10	15	19	24	28	33	37	42	47	51	56	61	65	79	75	80	84
	—	**1**	**4**	**8**	**12**	**16**	**20**	**24**	**28**	**33**	**37**	**41**	**45**	**50**	**54**	**59**	**63**	**67**	**72**	**76**
14	—	2	7	11	16	21	26	31	36	41	46	51	56	61	66	71	77	82	87	92
	—	**1**	**5**	**9**	**13**	**17**	**22**	**26**	**31**	**36**	**40**	**45**	**50**	**55**	**59**	**64**	**67**	**74**	**78**	**83**
15	—	3	7	12	18	23	28	33	39	44	50	55	61	66	72	77	83	88	94	100
	—	**1**	**5**	**10**	**14**	**19**	**24**	**29**	**34**	**39**	**44**	**49**	**54**	**59**	**64**	**70**	**75**	**80**	**85**	**90**
16	—	3	8	14	19	25	30	36	42	48	54	60	65	71	77	83	89	95	101	107
	—	**1**	**6**	**11**	**15**	**21**	**26**	**31**	**37**	**42**	**47**	**53**	**59**	**64**	**70**	**75**	**81**	**86**	**92**	**98**
17	—	3	9	15	20	26	33	39	45	51	57	64	70	77	83	89	96	102	109	115
	—	**2**	**6**	**11**	**17**	**22**	**28**	**34**	**39**	**45**	**51**	**57**	**63**	**67**	**75**	**81**	**87**	**93**	**99**	**105**
18	—	4	9	16	22	28	35	41	48	55	61	68	75	82	88	95	102	109	116	123
	—	**2**	**7**	**12**	**18**	**24**	**30**	**36**	**42**	**48**	**55**	**61**	**67**	**74**	**80**	**86**	**93**	**99**	**106**	**112**
19	0	4	10	17	23	30	37	44	51	58	65	72	80	87	94	101	109	116	123	130
	—	**2**	**7**	**13**	**19**	**25**	**32**	**38**	**45**	**52**	**58**	**65**	**72**	**78**	**85**	**92**	**99**	**106**	**113**	**119**
20	0	4	11	18	25	32	39	47	54	62	69	77	84	92	100	107	115	123	130	138
	—	**2**	**8**	**13**	**20**	**27**	**34**	**41**	**48**	**55**	**62**	**69**	**76**	**83**	**90**	**98**	**105**	**112**	**119**	**127**

TABLE B.9B CRITICAL VALUES OF THE MANN-WHITNEY *U* FOR $\alpha = .01$*

*Critical values are provided for a *one-tailed* test at $\alpha = .01$ (lightface type) and for a *two-tailed* test at $\alpha = .01$ (boldface type). To be significant for any given n_A and n_B, the obtained U must be *equal to* or *less than* the critical value in the table. Dashes (—) in the body of the table indicate that no decision is possible at the stated level of significance and values of n_A and n_B.

n_B \ n_A	1	2	3	4	5	6	7	8	9	10	11	12	13	14	15	16	17	18	19	20
1	—	—	—	—	—	—	—	—	—	—	—	—	—	—	—	—	—	—	—	—
2	—	—	—	—	—	—	—	—	—	—	—	—	0	0	0	0	0	0	1	1
	—	—	—	—	—	—	—	—	—	—	—	—	—	—	—	—	—	—	**0**	**0**
3	—	—	—	—	—	—	0	0	1	1	1	2	2	2	3	3	4	4	4	5
	—	—	—	—	—	—	—	—	**0**	**0**	**0**	**1**	**1**	**1**	**2**	**2**	**2**	**2**	**3**	**3**
4	—	—	—	—	0	1	1	2	3	3	4	5	5	6	7	7	8	9	9	10
	—	—	—	—	—	**0**	**0**	**1**	**1**	**2**	**2**	**3**	**3**	**4**	**5**	**5**	**6**	**6**	**7**	**8**
5	—	—	—	0	1	2	3	4	5	6	7	8	9	10	11	12	13	14	15	16
	—	—	—	—	**0**	**1**	**1**	**2**	**3**	**4**	**5**	**6**	**7**	**7**	**8**	**9**	**10**	**11**	**12**	**13**
6	—	—	—	1	2	3	4	6	7	8	9	11	12	13	15	16	18	19	20	22
	—	—	—	**0**	**1**	**2**	**3**	**4**	**5**	**6**	**7**	**9**	**10**	**11**	**12**	**13**	**15**	**16**	**17**	**18**
7	—	—	0	1	3	4	6	7	9	11	12	14	16	17	19	21	23	24	26	28
	—	—	—	0	1	3	4	6	7	9	10	12	13	15	16	18	19	21	22	**24**
8	—	—	0	2	4	6	7	9	11	13	15	17	20	22	24	26	28	30	32	34
	—	—	—	**1**	**2**	**4**	**6**	**7**	**9**	**11**	**13**	**15**	**17**	**18**	**20**	**22**	**24**	**26**	**28**	**30**
9	—	—	1	3	5	7	9	11	14	16	18	21	23	26	28	31	33	36	38	40
	—	—	**0**	**1**	**3**	**5**	**7**	**9**	**11**	**13**	**16**	**18**	**20**	**22**	**24**	**27**	**29**	**31**	**33**	**36**
10	—	—	1	3	6	8	11	13	16	19	22	24	27	30	33	36	38	41	44	47
	—	—	**0**	**2**	**4**	**6**	**9**	**11**	**13**	**16**	**18**	**21**	**24**	**26**	**29**	**31**	**34**	**37**	**39**	**42**
11	—	—	1	4	7	9	12	15	18	22	25	28	31	34	37	41	44	47	50	53
	—	—	**0**	**2**	**5**	**7**	**10**	**13**	**16**	**18**	**21**	**24**	**27**	**30**	**33**	**36**	**39**	**42**	**45**	**48**
12	—	—	2	5	8	11	14	17	21	24	28	31	35	38	42	46	49	53	56	60
	—	—	1	3	6	9	12	15	18	21	24	27	31	34	37	41	44	47	51	54
13	—	0	2	5	9	12	16	2	23	27	31	35	39	43	47	51	55	59	63	67
	—	—	**1**	**3**	**7**	**10**	**13**	**17**	**20**	**24**	**27**	**31**	**34**	**38**	**42**	**45**	**49**	**53**	**56**	**60**
14	—	0	2	6	10	13	17	22	26	30	34	38	43	47	51	56	60	65	69	73
	—	—	**1**	**4**	**7**	**11**	**15**	**18**	**22**	**26**	**30**	**34**	**38**	**42**	**46**	**50**	**54**	**58**	**63**	**67**
15	—	0	3	7	11	15	19	24	28	33	37	42	47	51	56	61	66	70	75	80
	—	—	**2**	**5**	**8**	**12**	**16**	**20**	**24**	**29**	**33**	**37**	**42**	**46**	**51**	**55**	**60**	**64**	**69**	**73**
16	—	0	3	7	12	16	21	26	31	36	41	46	51	56	61	66	71	76	82	87
	—	—	**2**	**5**	**9**	**13**	**18**	**22**	**27**	**31**	**36**	**41**	**45**	**50**	**55**	**60**	**65**	**70**	**74**	**79**
17	—	0	4	8	13	18	23	28	33	38	44	49	55	60	66	71	77	82	88	93
	—	—	**2**	**6**	**10**	**15**	**19**	**24**	**29**	**34**	**39**	**44**	**49**	**54**	**60**	**65**	**70**	**75**	**81**	**86**
18	—	0	4	9	14	19	24	30	36	41	47	53	59	65	70	76	82	88	94	100
	—	—	**2**	**6**	**11**	**16**	**21**	**26**	**31**	**37**	**42**	**47**	**53**	**58**	**64**	**70**	**75**	**81**	**87**	**92**
19	—	1	4	9	15	20	26	32	38	44	50	56	63	69	75	82	88	94	101	107
	—	**0**	**3**	**7**	**12**	**17**	**22**	**28**	**33**	**39**	**45**	**51**	**56**	**63**	**69**	**74**	**81**	**87**	**93**	**99**
20	—	1	5	10	16	22	28	34	40	47	53	60	67	73	80	87	93	100	107	114
	—	**0**	**3**	**8**	**13**	**18**	**24**	**30**	**36**	**42**	**48**	**54**	**60**	**67**	**73**	**79**	**86**	**92**	**99**	**105**

TABLE B.10 CRITICAL VALUES OF T FOR THE WILCOXON SIGNED-RANKS TEST*

*To be significant, the obtained *T* must be *equal to* or *less than* the critical value. Dashes (—) in the columns indicate that no decision is possible for the stated α and *n*.

	Level of Significance for One-Tailed Test			
	.05	.025	.01	.005
	Level of Significance for Two-Tailed Test			
n	.10	.05	.02	.01
5	0	—	—	—
6	2	0	—	—
7	3	2	0	—
8	5	3	1	0
9	8	5	3	1
10	10	8	5	3
11	13	10	7	5
12	17	13	9	7
13	21	17	12	9
14	25	21	15	12
15	30	25	19	15
16	35	29	23	19
17	41	34	27	23
18	47	40	32	27
19	53	46	37	32
20	60	52	43	37
21	67	58	49	42
22	75	65	55	48
23	83	73	62	54
24	91	81	69	61
25	100	89	76	68
26	110	98	84	75
27	119	107	92	83
28	130	116	101	91
29	140	126	110	100

	Level of Significance for One-Tailed Test			
	.05	.025	.01	.005
	Level of Significance for Two-Tailed Test			
n	.10	.05	.02	.01
30	151	137	120	109
31	163	147	130	118
32	175	159	140	128
33	187	170	151	138
34	200	182	162	148
35	213	195	173	159
36	227	208	185	171
37	241	221	198	182
38	256	235	211	194
39	271	249	224	207
40	286	264	238	220
41	302	279	252	233
42	319	294	266	247
43	336	310	281	261
44	353	327	296	276
45	371	343	312	291
46	389	361	328	307
47	407	378	345	322
48	426	396	362	339
49	446	415	379	355
50	466	434	397	373

Adapted from F. Wilcoxon, S. K. Katti, and R. A. Wilcox, *Critical Values and Probability Levels of the Wilcoxon Rank-Sum Test and the Wilcoxon Signed-Ranks Test*. Wayne, NJ: American Cyanamid Company, 1963. Adapted and reprinted with permission of the American Cyanamid Company.

APPENDIX C Solutions for Odd-Numbered Problems in the Text

Note: Many of the problems in the text require several stages of computation. At each stage there is an opportunity for rounding answers. Depending on the exact sequence of operations used to solve a problem, different individuals will round their answers at different times and in different ways. As a result, you may obtain answers that are slightly different from those presented here. To help minimize this problem, we have tried to include the numerical values obtained at different stages of complex problems rather than presenting a single final answer.

CHAPTER 1: INTRODUCTION TO STATISTICS

1. **a.** The population is the entire set of adolescent boys who are taking medication for depression.
b. The sample is the group of 30 boys who were tested in the study.

3. Descriptive statistics are used to simplify and summarize data. Inferential statistics use sample data to make general conclusions about populations.

5. A correlational study has only one group of individuals and measures two (or more) different variables for each individual. Other research methods evaluating relationships between variables compare two (or more) different groups of scores.

7. The independent variable is holding a pen in your teeth versus holding the pen in your lips. The dependent variable is the rating given to each cartoon.

9. **a.** This is a nonexperimental study. The researcher is simply observing, not manipulating, two variables.
b. This is an experiment. The researcher is manipulating the type of drink and should control other variables by beginning with equivalent groups of participants.

11. This is not an experiment because there is no manipulation. Instead, the study is comparing two preexisting groups (American and Canadian students).

13. **a.** continuous. Time is infinitely divisible.
b. discrete. Family size consists of whole-number categories that cannot be divided.
c. discrete. There are two separate and distinct categories (analog and digital).
d. continuous. The variable is knowledge of statistics, which is measured with quiz scores. It could be a 5-point quiz, a 10-point quiz, or a 50-point quiz, which indicates that knowledge can be divided indefinitely.

15. **a.** The independent variable is humorous versus nonhumorous.
b. The independent variable is measured on a nominal scale.
c. The dependent variable is the number of sentences recalled.
d. The dependent variable is measured on a ratio scale.

17. **a.** The independent variable is whether or not the motivational signs were posted, and the dependent variable is amount of use of the stairs.
b. Posting versus not posting is measured on a nominal scale.

19. **a.** $\Sigma X = 15$
b. $\Sigma X^2 = 65$
c. $\Sigma(X + 1) = 20$
d. $\Sigma(X + 1)^2 = 100$

21. **a.** $\Sigma X = 11$
b. $\Sigma Y = 25$
c. $\Sigma XY = 54$

23. **a.** $\Sigma X^2 = 30$
b. $(\Sigma X)^2 = 64$
c. $\Sigma(X - 2) = 0$
d. $\Sigma(X - 2)^2 = 14$

CHAPTER 2: **FREQUENCY DISTRIBUTIONS**

1.

X	*f*
10	3
9	6
8	4
7	2
6	3
5	1
4	1

3. a. $n = 12$
b. $\Sigma X = 40$
c. $\Sigma X^2 = 148$

5. a.

X	*f*
28-29	1
26-27	4
24-25	7
22-23	4
20-21	2
18-19	2
16-17	1
14-15	0
12-13	1
10-11	1
8-9	1

b.

X	*f*
25-29	8
20-24	10
15-19	3
10-14	2
5-9	1

7. a. 2 points wide and around 8 intervals
b. 5 points wide and around 12 intervals or 10 points wide and around 6 intervals
c. 10 points wide and around 9 intervals

9. A bar graph leaves a space between adjacent bars and is used with data from nominal or ordinal scales. In a histogram, adjacent bars touch at the real limits. Histograms are used to display data from interval or ratio scales.

11.

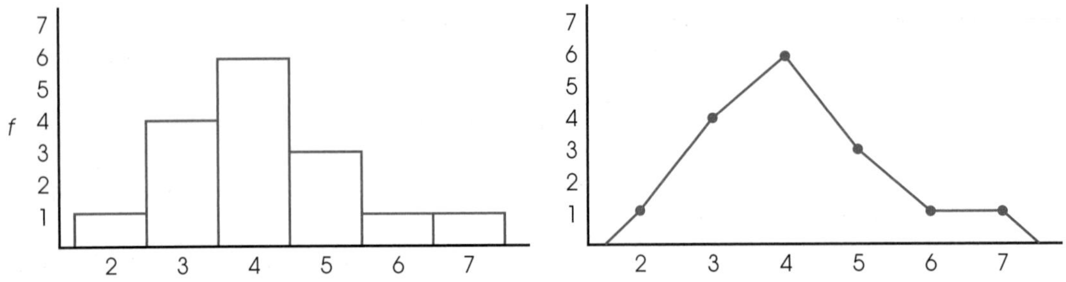

13. a. A bar graph should be used for measurements from an ordinal scale.
b.

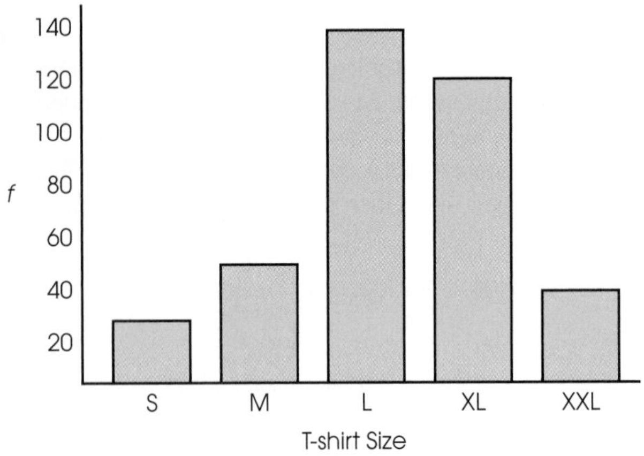

15. a.

X	*f*
9	1
8	1
7	4
6	5
5	7
4	2

b. positively skewed

17. a.

X	*f*
10	1
9	2
8	2
7	2
6	4
5	3
4	2
3	2
2	1

b.

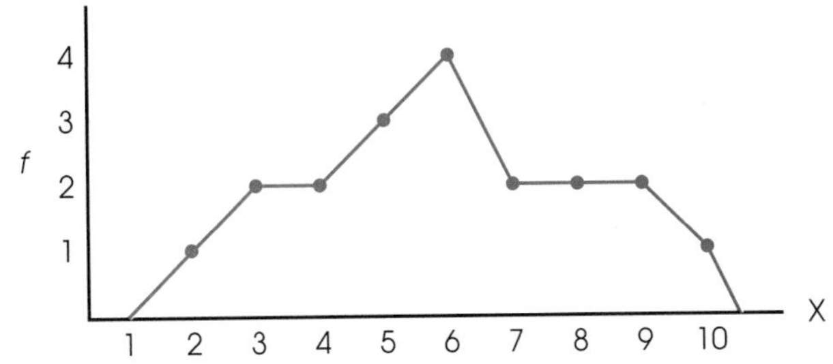

c. It is a fairly symmetrical distribution centered at $X = 6$. The scores are scattered across the scale.

19.

X	*f*	*cf*	*c%*
7	2	24	100
6	3	23	92
5	6	20	80
4	9	14	56
3	4	5	20
2	1	1	4

a. The percentile rank for $X = 2.5$ is 4%
b. The percentile rank for $X = 6.5$ is 92%
c. The 20th percentile is $X = 3.5$.
d. The 80th percentile is $X = 5.5$.

21.

X	*f*	*cf*	*c%*
10	2	50	100
9	5	48	96
8	8	43	86
7	15	35	70
6	10	20	40
5	6	10	20
4	4	4	8

a. The percentile rank for $X = 6$ is 30%.
b. The percentile rank for $X = 9$ is 91%.
c. The 25th percentile is $X = 5.75$.
d. The 90th percentile is $X = 8.9$.

23. a. The percentile rank for $X = 5$ is 8%.
b. The percentile rank for $X = 12$ is 85%.
c. The 25th percentile is $X = 7$.
d. The 70th percentile is $X = 10$.

25.

1	796
2	0841292035826
3	094862
4	543
5	3681
6	4

27.

2	80472
3	49069
4	543976
5	4319382
6	5505
7	24
8	1

CHAPTER 3: CENTRAL TENDENCY

1. The purpose of central tendency is to identify a single score that serves as the best representative for an entire distribution, usually a score from the center of the distribution.

3. The mean is $\frac{29}{10} = 2.9$, the median is 2.5, and the mode is 2.

5. The mean is $\frac{69}{12} = 5.75$, the median is 6, and the mode is 7.

7. a. Median = 2.83 (2.5 + 0.33)
b. Median = 3

9. $N = 25$

11. The original sample has $n = 5$ and $\Sigma X = 60$. The new sample has $n = 4$ and $\Sigma X = 52$. The new mean is $M = 13$.

13. After the score is removed, $n = 8$, $\Sigma X = 88$, and $M = 11$.

15. After the score is changed, $n = 7$, $\Sigma X = 49$, and $M = 7$.

17. The original sample has $n = 16$ and $\Sigma X = 320$. The new sample has $n = 15$ and $\Sigma X = 285$. The score that was removed must be $X = 35$.

19. a. The new mean is $\frac{75}{10} = 7.5$.

b. The new mean is (20 + 60)/10 = 8
c. The new mean is (30 + 40)/10 = 7

21. The median is used instead of the mean when there is a skewed distribution (a few extreme scores), an open-ended distribution, undetermined scores, or an ordinal scale.

23. a. Mode = 2
b. Median = 2
c. You cannot find the total number of fast-food visits (ΣX) for this sample.

25. a. For weekdays $M = 0.99$ inches and for weekend days is $M = 1.67$ inches.
b. There does appear to be more rain on weekend days than there is on weekdays.

CHAPTER 4: **VARIABILITY**

1. a. *SS* is the sum of squared deviation scores.
b. Variance is the mean squared deviation.
c. Standard deviation is the square root of the variance. It provides a measure of the standard distance from the mean.

3. Standard deviation and variance are measures of distance and are always greater than or equal to zero.

5. Without some correction, the sample variance underestimates the variance for the population. Changing the formula for sample variance (using $n - 1$ instead of N) is the necessary correction.

7. a. $s = 2$ is better (you are above the mean by 3 standard deviations).
b. $s = 10$ is better (you are below the mean by less than half a standard deviation).

9. a. The original mean is $M = 80$ and the standard deviation is $s = 8$.
b. The original mean is $M = 12$ and the standard deviation is $s = 3$.

11. a. The range is either 11 or 12, and the standard deviation is $\sigma = 4$.
b. After adding 2 points to each score, the range is still either 11 or 12, and the standard deviation is still $\sigma = 4$. Adding a constant to every score does not affect measures of variability.

13. For sample A the mean is $M = 4.50$, so the computational formula would be easier. For this sample, $SS = 25$. For sample B the mean is $M = 4$ and the definitional formula would be easier. For this sample, $SS = 42$.

15. a. The mean is $M = 4$ and the standard deviation is $s = \sqrt{9} = 3$.
b. The new mean is $M = 6$ and the new standard deviation is $\sqrt{49} = 7$.
c. Changing one score changes both the mean and the standard deviation.

17. $SS = 32$, the population variance is 4, and the standard deviation is 2.

19. $SS = 36$, the sample variance is 9, and the standard deviation is 3.

21. a.

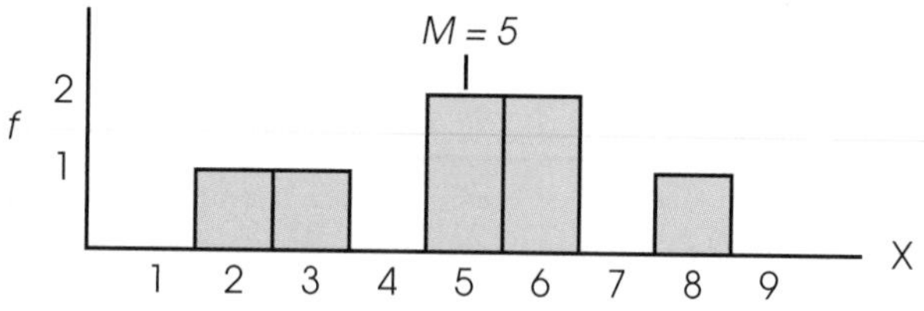

b. The mean is $\frac{35}{7} = 5$. The two scores of $X = 5$ are exactly equal to the mean. The scores $X = 2$ and $X = 8$ are farthest from the mean (3 points). The standard deviation should be between 0 and 3 points.
c. $SS = 24$, $s^2 = 4$, $s = 2$, which agrees with the estimate.

23. a. For the younger woman, the variance is $s^2 = 0.786$. For the older woman, the variance is $s^2 = 1.696$.
b. The variance for the younger woman is only half as large as for the older woman. The younger woman's scores are much more consistent.

SECTION I **REVIEW**

1. a. The goal for descriptive statistics is to simplify, organize, and summarize data so that it is easier for researchers to see patterns.
b. A frequency distribution provides an organized summary of the complete set of scores.
c. A measure of central tendency summarizes an entire set of scores with a single value that is representative of the whole set.
d. A measure of variability provides a single number that describes the differences that exist from one score to another.

2. a.

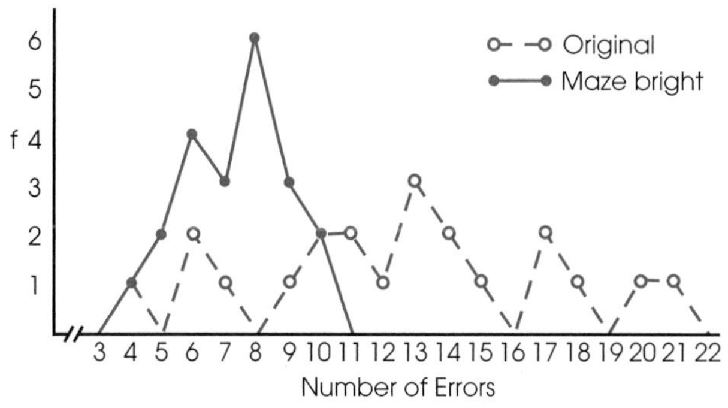

The original rats appear to make far more errors that the seventh-generation maze-bright rats

b. The original rats made an average of $M = 12.43$ errors compared to an average of only $M = 7.33$ for the maze-bright rats. On average, the original rats made far more errors.

c. For the original rats, $SS = 427.14$, the variance is $s^2 = 21.36$ and the standard deviation is $s = 4.62$. For the maze-bright rats, $SS = 54.67$, the variance is $s^2 = 2.73$ and the standard deviation is $s = 1.65$. The error scores for the original rats are much more spread out. The seventh generation rats are a much more homogeneous group.

CHAPTER 5: *z*-SCORES

1. The sign of the *z*-score tells whether the location is above (+) or below (−) the mean, and the magnitude tells the distance from the mean in terms of the number of standard deviations.

3. a. above the mean by 12 points
b. above the mean by 3 points
c. below the mean by 12 points
d. below the mean by 3 points

5.

X	z	X	z	X	z
45	0.71	51	1.57	41	0.14
30	−1.43	25	−2.14	38	−0.29

7. a.

X	z	X	z	X	z
44	0.50	50	1.25	52	1.50
34	−0.75	28	−1.50	64	3.00

b.

X	z	X	z	X	z
46	0.75	52	1.50	24	−2.00
38	−0.25	36	−0.50	50	1.25

9.

X	z	X	z	X	z
88	0.80	92	1.20	100	2.00
76	−0.40	74	−0.60	62	−1.80

11. a. $X = 41$
b. $X = 42$
c. $X = 43$
d. $X = 45$

13. $\sigma = 4$

15. $M = 50$

17. $\sigma = 4$

19. $\mu = 61$ and $\sigma = 3$. The distance between the two scores is 3 points which is equal to 1.0 standard deviation.

21. a. $\sigma = 4$
b. $\sigma = 8$

23. a. $X = 95$ ($z = -0.25$)
b. $X = 80$ ($z = -1.00$)
c. $X = 125$ ($z = 1.25$)
d. $X = 110$ ($z = 0.50$)

25. a. $\mu = 5$ and $\sigma = 4$
b. and **c.**

Original X	z-score	Transformed X
0	1.25	75
6	0.25	105
4	−0.25	95
3	−0.50	90
12	1.75	135

CHAPTER 6: **PROBABILITY**

1. a. $p = \frac{1}{50} = 0.02$
b. $p = \frac{10}{50} = 0.20$
c. $p = \frac{20}{50} = 0.40$

3. The two requirements for a random sample are: (1) each individual has an equal chance of being selected, and (2) if more than one individual is selected, the probabilities must stay constant for all selections.

5. a. tail to the right, $p = 0.0228$
b. tail to the right, $p = 0.2743$
c. tail to the left, $p = 0.0968$
d. tail to the left, $p = 0.3821$

7. a. $p(z > 0.25) = 0.4013$
b. $p(z > -0.75) = 0.7734$
c. $p(z < 1.20) = 0.8849$
d. $p(z < -1.20) = 0.1151$

9. a. $p = 0.1974$
b. $p = 0.9544$
c. $p = 0.4592$
d. $p = 0.4931$

11. a. $z = \pm 0.25$
b. $z = \pm 0.67$
c. $z = \pm 1.96$
d. $z = \pm 2.58$

13. a. tail to the right, $p = 0.4013$
b. tail to the left, $p = 0.3085$
c. tail to the right, $p = 0.0668$
d. tail to the left, $p = 0.1587$

15. a. $z = 2.00$, $p = 0.0228$
b. $z = 0.50$, $p = 0.3085$
c. $z = 1.28$, $X = 628$
d. $z = -0.25$, $X = 475$

17. a. $p(z > 1.50) = 0.0668$
b. $p(z < -2.00) = 0.0228$

19. a. $z = 0.60$, $p = 0.2743$
b. $z = -1.40$, $p = 0.0808$
c. $z = 0.84$, $X =$ \$206 or more

21. $p(X > 36) = p(z > 2.17) = 0.0150$ or 1.50%

23. a. $p = \frac{1}{2}$
b. $\mu = 20$
c. $\mu = \sqrt{10} = 3.16$ and for $X = 25.5$, $z = 1.74$, and $p = 0.0409$
d. For $X = 24.5$, $z = 1.42$, and $p = 0.0778$

25. a. With five options, $p = \frac{1}{5}$ for each trial, $\mu = 20$, and $\sigma = 4$; for $X = 20$, $z = \pm 0.13$ and $p = 0.1034$.
b. For $X = 30.5$, $z = 2.63$ and $p = 0.0043$.
c. $\mu = 40$ and $\sigma = 5.66$; for $X = 49.5$, $z = 1.68$ and $p = 0.0465$

27. a. With $n = 50$ and $p = q = \frac{1}{2}$, you may use the normal approximation with $\mu = 25$ and $\sigma = 3.54$. Using the upper real limit of 30.5, $p(X > 30.5) = p(z > 1.55) = 0.0606$.
b. The normal approximation has $\mu = 50$ and $\sigma = 5$. Using the upper real limit of 60.5, $p(X > 60.5) = p(z > 2.10) = 0.0179$.
c. Getting 60% heads with a balanced coin is an unusual event for a large sample. Although you might get 60% heads with a small sample, you should get very close to a 50-50 distribution as the sample gets larger. With a larger sample, it becomes very unlikely to get 60% heads.

CHAPTER 7: **THE DISTRIBUTION OF SAMPLE MEANS**

1. a. The distribution of sample means consists of the sample means for all the possible random samples of a specific size (n) from a specific population.
b. The expected value of M is the mean of the distribution of sample means (μ).
c. The standard error of M is the standard deviation of the distribution of sample means ($\sigma_M = \frac{\sigma}{\sqrt{n}}$).

3. a. The expected value is $\mu = 40$ and $\sigma_M = \frac{8}{\sqrt{4}} = 4$.
b. The expected value is $\mu = 40$ and $\sigma_M = \frac{8}{\sqrt{16}} = 2$.

5. a. Standard error $= \frac{30}{\sqrt{4}} = 15$ points
b. Standard error $= \frac{30}{\sqrt{25}} = 6$ points
c. Standard error $= \frac{30}{\sqrt{100}} = 3$ points

7. a. $n \geq 16$
b. $n \geq 100$
c. $n \geq 400$

9. a. $\sigma = 50$
b. $\sigma = 25$
c. $\sigma = 10$

11. a. $\sigma_M = 5$ points and $z = -1.00$
b. $\sigma_M = 10$ points and $z = -0.50$
c. $\sigma_M = 20$ points and $z = -0.25$

13. a. With a standard error of 4, $M = 33$ corresponds to $z = 0.75$, which is not extreme.

b With a standard error of 1, $M = 33$ corresponds to $z = 3.00$, which is extreme.

15. a. $z = 0.50$ and $p = 0.6915$
b. $\sigma_M = 5$, $z = 1.00$ and $p = 0.8413$
c. $\sigma_M = 2$, $z = 2.50$ and $p = 0.9938$

17. a. $z = \pm 0.50$ and $p = 0.3830$
b. $\sigma_M = 5$, $z = \pm 1.00$ and $p = 0.6826$
c. $\sigma_M = 2.5$, $z = \pm 2.00$ and $p = 0.9544$

19. a. $p(z < -0.50) = 0.3085$
b. $p(z < -1.00) = 0.1587$

21. a. With a standard error of 3.58 this sample mean corresponds to a z-score of $z = 1.28$. A z-score this large (or larger) has a probability of $p = 0.1003$.
b. A sample mean this large should occur only 1 out of 10 times. This is not a very representative sample.

23.

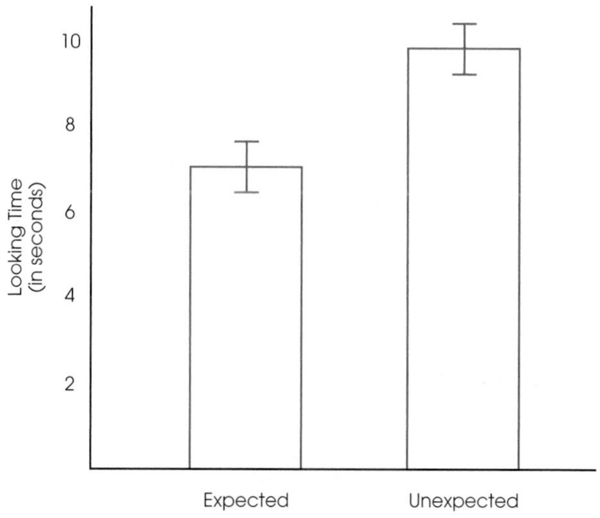

CHAPTER 8: **INTRODUCTION TO HYPOTHESIS TESTING**

1. a. $M - \mu$ measures the difference between the sample mean and the hypothesized population mean.
b. A sample mean is not expected to be identical to the population mean. The standard error measures how much difference, on average, is reasonable to expect between M and μ.

3. The alpha level is a small probability value that defines the concept of "very unlikely." The critical region consists of outcomes that are very unlikely to occur if the null hypothesis is true, where "very unlikely" is defined by the alpha level.

5. a. The null hypothesis states that the herb has no effect on memory scores.
b. H_0: $\mu = 80$ (even with the herbs, the mean is still 80). H_1: $\mu \neq 80$ (the mean has changed)
c. The critical region consists of z-scores beyond ± 1.96.
d. For these data, the standard error is 3 and $z = \frac{4}{3} = 1.33$.
e. Fail to reject the null hypothesis. The herbal supplements do not have a significant effect on memory scores.

7. a. H_0 $\mu = 80$. With $\sigma = 12$, the sample mean corresponds to $z = -\frac{4}{3} = -1.33$. This is not sufficient to reject the null hypothesis. You cannot conclude that the course has a significant effect.
b. H_0 $\mu = 80$. With $\sigma = 6$, the sample mean corresponds to $z = -\frac{4}{1.5} = -2.67$. This is sufficient to reject the null hypothesis and conclude that the course does have a significant effect.
c. There is a 4 point difference between the sample and the hypothesis. In part a, the standard error is 3 points and the 4-point difference is not significant. However, in part b, the standard error is only 1.5 points and the 4-point difference is now significantly more than is expected by chance. In general, a larger standard deviation produces a larger standard error, which reduces the likelihood of rejecting the null hypothesis.

9. a. With $\sigma = 18$, the standard error is 3, and $z = -\frac{8}{3} = -2.67$. Reject H_0.
b. With $\sigma = 30$, the standard error is 5, and $z = -\frac{8}{5} = -1.60$. Fail to reject H_0.
c. Larger variability reduces the likelihood of rejecting H_0.

11. a. With a 2-point treatment effect, for the z-score to be greater than 1.96, the standard error must be smaller than 1.02. The sample size must be greater than 96.12; a sample of $n = 97$ or larger is needed.
b. With a 1-point treatment effect, for the z-score to be greater than 1.96, the standard error must be smaller than 0.51. The sample size must be greater than 384.47; a sample of $n = 385$ or larger is needed.

13. a. H_0: $\mu = 4.9$ and the critical values are ± 1.96. The standard error is 0.21 and $z = -3.33$. Reject the null hypothesis.
b. Cohen's $d = \frac{0.7}{0.84} = 0.833$ or 83.3%
c. The results indicate that the presence of a tattoo has a significant effect on the judged attractiveness of a woman, $z = -3.33$, $p < .01$, $d = 0.833$.

15. a. H_0: $\mu \leq 50$ (endurance is not increased). The critical region consists of z-scores beyond $z = +1.65$.

For these data, $\sigma_M = 1.70$ and $z = 1.76$. Reject H_0 and conclude that endurance scores are significantly higher with the sports drink.

b. H_0: $\mu = 50$ (no change in endurance). The critical region consists of z-scores beyond $z = \pm 1.96$. Again, $\sigma_M = 1.70$ and $z = 1.76$. Fail to reject H_0 and conclude that the sports drink does not significantly affect endurance scores.

c. The two-tailed test requires a larger z-score for the sample to be in the critical region.

17. H_0: $\mu \leq 12$ (no increase during hot weather). H_1: $\mu > 12$ (there is an increase). The critical region consists of z-score values greater than +1.65. For these data, the standard error is 1.50, and $z = 2.33$ which is in the critical region so we reject the null hypothesis and conclude that there is a significant increase in the average number of hit players during hot weather.

19. a. With no treatment effect the distribution of sample means is centered at $\mu = 75$ with a standard error of 1.90 points. The critical boundary of $z = 1.96$ corresponds to a sample mean of $M = 78.72$. With a 4-point treatment effect, the distribution of sample means is centered at $\mu = 79$. In this distribution a mean of $M = 78.72$ corresponds to $z = -0.15$. The power for the test is the probability of obtaining a z-score greater than −0.15, which is $p = 0.5596$.

b. With a one-tailed test, critical boundary of $z = 1.65$ corresponds to a sample mean of $M = 78.14$. With a 4-point treatment effect, the distribution of sample means is centered at $\mu = 79$. In this distribution a mean of $M = 78.14$ corresponds to $z = -0.45$. The power for the test is the probability of obtaining a z-score greater than −0.45, which is $p = 0.6736$.

21. a. Increasing alpha increases power.

b. Changing from one- to two-tailed decreases power.

23. a. For a sample of $n = 16$ the standard error would be 5 points, and the critical boundary for $z = 1.96$ corresponds to a sample mean of $M = 89.8$. With a 12-point effect, the distribution of sample means would be centered at $\mu = 92$. In this distribution, the critical boundary of $M = 89.8$ corresponds to $z = -0.44$. The power for the test is $p(z > -0.44) = 0.6700$ or 67%.

b. For a sample of $n = 25$ the standard error would be 4 points, and the critical boundary for $z = 1.96$ corresponds to a sample mean of $M = 87.84$. With a 12-point effect, the distribution of sample means would be centered at $\mu = 92$. In this distribution, the critical boundary of $M = 87.84$ corresponds to $z = -1.04$. The power for the test is $p(z > -1.04) = 0.8508$ or 85.08%.

SECTION II **REVIEW**

1. a. $z = 1.50$

b. $X = 36$

c. If the entire population of X values is transformed into z-scores, the set of z-scores will have a mean of 0 and a standard deviation of 1.00.

d. The standard error is 4 points and $z = 0.50$.

e. The standard error is 2 points and $z = 1.00$.

2. a. $p(X > 40) = p(z > 0.36) = 0.3594$ or 35.94%.

b. $p(X < 10) = p(z < -1.79) = 0.0367$ or 3.67%.

c. The standard error is 2 points and $z = -2.50$. The probability is $p = 0.0062$.

3. a. The null hypothesis states that the overweight students are no different from the overall population, $\mu = 4.22$. The standard error is 0.10 and the z-score for this sample is $z = 2.60$. Reject the null hypothesis. The number of snacks eaten by overweight students is significantly different from the number for the general population.

b. The null hypothesis states that the healthy-weight students do not eat fewer snacks than the overall population, H_0: $\mu \geq 4.22$. The standard error is 0.12 and the z-score for this sample is $z = -1.75$. For a one-tailed test, the critical value is $z = -1.65$. Reject the null hypothesis. The number of snacks eaten by healthy-weight students is significantly less than the number for the general population.

CHAPTER 9: **INTRODUCTION TO THE *t* STATISTIC**

1. A z-score is used when the population standard deviation (or variance) is known. The t statistic is used when the population variance or standard deviation is unknown. The t statistic uses the sample variance or standard deviation in place of the unknown population values.

3. a. The sample variance is 16 and the estimated standard error is 2.
b. The sample variance is 54 and the estimated standard error is 3.
c. The sample variance is 12 and the estimated standard error is 1.

5. a. $t = \pm 2.571$
b. $t = \pm 2.201$
c. $t = \pm 2.069$

7. a. $M = 5$ and $s = \sqrt{20} = 4.47$
b. $s_M = 2$.

9. a. With $s = 9$, $s_M = 3$ and $t = -\frac{7}{3} = -2.33$. This is beyond the critical boundaries of ± 2.306, so we reject the null hypothesis and conclude that there is a significant treatment effect.
b. With $s = 15$, $s_M = 5$ and $t = -\frac{7}{5} = -1.40$. This value is not beyond the critical boundaries, so there is no significant effect.
c. As the sample variability increases, the likelihood of rejecting the null hypothesis decreases.

11. a. With a two tailed test, the critical boundaries are ± 2.306 and the obtained value of $t = \frac{3.3}{1.5} = 2.20$ is not sufficient to reject the null hypothesis.
b. For the one-tailed test the critical value is 1.860, so we reject the null hypothesis and conclude that participants significantly overestimated the number who noticed.

13. a. With $df = 15$, the critical values are ± 2.947. For these data, the sample variance is 16, the estimated standard error is 1, and $t = \frac{8.2}{1} = 8.20$. Reject the null hypothesis and conclude that there has been a significant change in the level of anxiety.
b. With $df = 15$, the t values for 90% confidence are ± 1.753, and the interval extends from 21.547 to 25.053.
c. The data indicate a significant change in the level of anxiety, $t(16) = 8.20$, $p < .01$, 95% CI [21.547, 25.053].

15. a. With $df = 63$, the critical values are ± 2.660 (using $df = 60$ in the table). For these data, the estimated standard error is 1.50, and $t = \frac{7}{1.50} = 4.67$. Reject the null hypothesis and conclude that there has been a significant change in the average IQ score.
b. Using $df = 60$, the t values for 80% confidence are ± 1.296, and the interval extends from 105.056 to 108.944.

17. a. The estimated standard error is 1.50, and $t = \frac{7.7}{1.50} = 5.13$. For a one-tailed test, the critical value is 2.602. Reject the null hypothesis, children with a history of day care have significantly more behavioral problems.
b. The percentage of variance accounted for is $r^2 = \frac{26.32}{41.32} = 0.637$ or 63.7%.
c. The results show that kindergarten children with a history of day care have significantly more behavioral problems than other kindergarten children, $t(15) = 5.13$, $p < .01$, $r^2 = 0.637$.

19. a. Cohen's $d = \frac{3}{6} = 0.50$. With $s = 6$, the estimated standard error is 1.2 and $t = \frac{3}{1.2} = 2.50$. $r^2 = \frac{6.25}{30.25} = 0.207$.
b. Cohen's $d = \frac{3}{15} = 0.20$. With $s = 15$, the estimated standard error is 3 and $t = \frac{3}{3} = 1.00$. $r^2 = \frac{1.00}{25.00} = 0.04$.
c. Measures of effect size tend to decrease as sample variance increases.

21. a. The estimated standard error is 0.20 and $t = \frac{2.2}{0.2} = 11.00$. The t value is well beyond the critical value of 2.492. Reject the null hypothesis.
b. Cohen's $d = \frac{2.2}{1} = 2.20$ and $r^2 = \frac{121}{145} = 0.8345$.

23. a. H_0: $\mu = 40$. With $df = 8$ the critical values are $t = \pm 2.306$. For these data, $M = 44$, $SS = 162$, $s^2 = 20.25$, the standard error is 1.50, and $t = 2.67$. Reject H_0 and conclude that depression for the elderly is significantly different from depression for the general population.
b. Cohen's $d = \frac{4}{4.5} = 0.889$.
c. The results indicate that depression scores for the elderly are significantly different from scores for the general population, $t(8) = 2.67$, $p < .05$, $d = 0.889$.

CHAPTER 10: THE *t* TEST FOR TWO INDEPENDENT SAMPLES

There are several possible solutions to the matchstick problem in the Chapter 10 Preview but all involve destroying two of the existing squares. One square is destroyed by removing two matchsticks from one of the corners and a second square is destroyed by removing one matchstick. The three removed matchsticks are then used to build a new square using a line that already exists in the figure as the fourth side. One solution is shown in the following figure. Arrows indicate the three matchsticks to be removed from the original pattern and their locations in the new pattern.

Original pattern with 5 squares

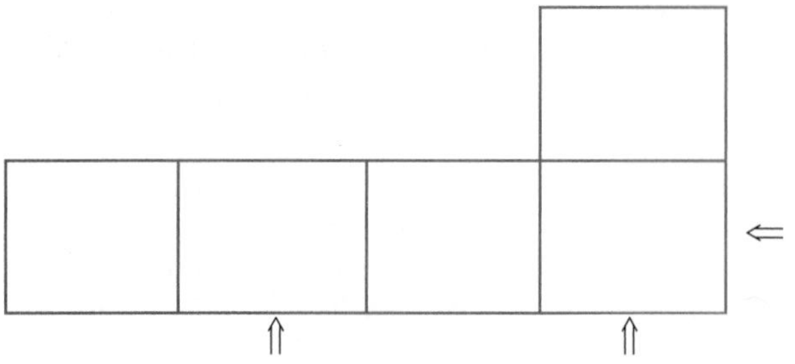

New pattern with 4 squares

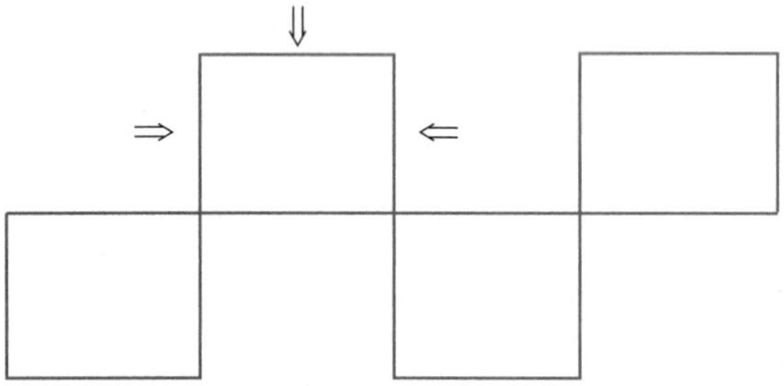

1. An independent-measures study uses a separate sample for each of the treatments or populations being compared.

3. **a.** The size of the two samples influences the magnitude of the estimated standard error in the denominator of the t statistic. As sample size increases, the value of t also increases (moves farther from zero), and the likelihood of rejecting H_0 also increases.
   b. The variability of the scores influences the estimated standard error in the denominator. As the variability of the scores increases, the value of t decreases (becomes closer to zero), and the likelihood of rejecting H_0 decreases.

5. **a.** The first sample has $s^2 = 12$ and the second has $s^2 = 8$. The pooled variance is $\frac{80}{8} = 10$ (halfway between).
   b. The first sample has $s^2 = 12$ and the second has $s^2 = 4$. The pooled variance is $\frac{80}{12} = 6.67$ (closer to the variance for the larger sample).

7. **a.** The pooled variance is 6 and the estimated standard error is 1.50.
   b. The pooled variance is 24 and the estimated standard error is 3.
   c. Larger variability produces a larger standard error.

9. **a.** The pooled variance is 90.
   b. The estimated standard error is 5.
   c. A mean difference of 10 points produces $t = 2.00$. With critical boundaries of ± 2.160, fail to reject H_0.
   d. A mean difference of 13 points produces $t = 2.60$. With critical boundaries of ± 2.160, reject H_0

11. **a.** The pooled variance is 60 and the estimated standard error is 5.
   b. The pooled variance is 240 and the estimated standard error is 10.
   c. Increasing the sample variance produces an increase in the standard error.

13. **a.** Using $df = 30$, because 34 is not listed in the table, and $\alpha = .05$, the critical region consists of t values beyond ± 2.042. The pooled variance is 81, the estimated standard error is 3, and $t(34) = \frac{7.6}{3} = 2.53$. The t statistic is in the critical region. Reject H_0 and conclude that there is a significant difference.
   b. For 90% confidence, the t values are ± 1.697 (using $df = 30$), and the interval extends from 2.509 to 12.691 points higher with the calming music.
   c. Classroom performance was significantly better with background music, $t(34) = 2.53$, $p < .05$, 95% CI [2.509, 12.691].

15. **a.** For the offensive linemen, the standard error is 0.97 and $t = 4.54$. For a one-tailed test with $df = 16$, the critical value is 2.583. Reject the null hypothesis. The offensive linemen are significantly above the criterion for BMI.
   b. For the defensive linemen, the standard error is 0.80 and $t = 2.375$. For a one-tailed test with $df = 18$, the critical value is 2.552. Fail to reject the null hypothesis. The defensive linemen are not significantly above the criterion for BMI.
   c. For the independent-measures t, the pooled variance is 14.01, the estimated standard error is 1.25, and $t(34) = 2.00$. For a two-tailed test using $df = 30$ (because 34 is not listed), the critical value is 2.750. Fail to reject the null hypothesis. There is no significant difference between the two groups.

17. **a.** The research prediction is that participants who hear the verb "smashed into" will estimate higher speeds than those who hear the verb "hit." For these data, the pooled variance is 33, the estimated standard error is 2.10, and $t(28) = 3.24$. With $df = 28$ and $\alpha = .01$, the critical value is $t = 2.467$. The sample mean difference is in the right direction and is large enough to be significant. Reject H_0.
   b. The estimated Cohen's $d = \frac{6.8}{\sqrt{33}} = 1.18$.
   c. The results show that participants who heard the verb "smashed into" estimated significantly higher speeds than those who heard the verb "hit," $t(28) = 3.24$, $p < .01$, $d = 1.18$.

19. a. The null hypothesis states that there is no difference between the two sets of instructions, H_0: $\mu_1 - \mu_2 = 0$. With $df = 6$ and $\alpha = .05$, the critical region consists of t values beyond ± 2.447. For the first set, $M = 6$ and $SS = 16$. For the second set, $M = 10$ with $SS = 32$. For these data, the pooled variance is 8, the estimated standard error is 2, and $t(6) = 2.00$. Fail to reject H_0. The data are not sufficient to conclude that there is a significant difference between the two sets of instructions.

b. For these data, the estimated $d = \frac{4}{\sqrt{8}} = 1.41$ (a very large effect) and $r^2 = \frac{4}{10} = 0.40$ (40%).

21. The humorous sentences produced a mean of $M = 4.25$ with $SS = 35$, and the non-humorous sentences had $M = 4.00$ with $SS = 26$. The pooled variance is 2.03, the estimated standard error is 0.504, and $t = 0.496$. With $df = 30$, the critical value is 2.042. Fail to reject the null hypothesis and conclude that there is no significant difference in memory for the two types of sentences.

23. a. The null hypothesis states that the lighting in the room does not affect behavior. For the well-lit room the mean is $M = 7.55$ with $SS = 42.22$. For the dimly-lit room, $M = 11.33$ with $SS = 38$. The pooled variance is 5.01, the standard error is 1.06, and $t(16) = 3.57$. With $df = 16$ the critical values are ± 2.921. Reject the null hypothesis and conclude that the lighting did have an effect on behavior.

b. $d = \frac{3.78}{2.24} = 1.69$.

CHAPTER 11: THE *t* TEST FOR TWO RELATED SAMPLES

1. a. This is an independent-measures experiment with two separate samples.

b. This is repeated-measures. The same individuals are measured twice.

c. This is repeated-measures. The same individuals are measured twice.

3. For a repeated-measures design the same subjects are used in both treatment conditions. In a matched-subjects design, two different sets of subjects are used. However, in a matched-subjects design, each subject in one condition is matched with respect to a specific variable with a subject in the second condition so that the two separate samples are equivalent with respect to the matching variable.

5. a. The standard deviation is 5 points and measures the average distance between an individual score and the sample mean.

b. The estimated standard error is 1.67 points and measures the average distance between a sample mean and the population mean.

7. a. The estimated standard error is 2 points and $t(8) = 1.50$. With a critical boundary of ± 2.306, fail to reject the null hypothesis.

b. With $M_D = 12$, $t(8) = 6.00$. With a critical boundary of ± 2.306, reject the null hypothesis.

c. The larger the mean difference, the greater the likelihood of finding a significant difference.

9. The sample variance is 9, the estimated standard error is 0.75, and $t(15) = 4.33$. With critical boundaries of ± 2.131, reject H_0

11. a. The null hypothesis says that there is no difference in judgments for smiling versus frowning. For these data, the sample variance is 6.25, the estimated standard error is 0.5, and $t = \frac{1.6}{0.5} = 3.20$. For a one-tailed test with $df = 24$, the critical value is 2.492. Reject the null hypothesis.

b. $r^2 = \frac{10.24}{34.24} = 0.299$ (29.9%)

c. The cartoons were rated significantly funnier when people held a pen in their teeth compared to holding a pen in their lips, $t(24) = 3.20$, $p < .01$, one tailed, $r^2 = 0.299$.

13. The null hypothesis states that there is no difference in the perceived intelligence between attractive and unattractive photos. For these data, the estimated standard error is 0.4 and $t = \frac{2.7}{0.4} = 6.75$. With $df = 24$, the critical value is 2.064. Reject the null hypothesis.

15. a. The difference scores are 3, 7, 3, and 3. $M_D = 4$.

b. $SS = 12$, sample variance is 4, and the estimated standard error is 1.

c. With $df = 3$ and $\alpha = .05$, the critical values are $t = \pm 3.182$. For these data, $t = 4.00$. Reject H_0. There is a significant treatment effect.

17. The null hypothesis states that the images have no effect on performance. For these data, the sample variance is 12.6, the estimated standard error is 1.45, and $t(5) = 2.97$. With $df = 5$ and $\alpha = .05$, the critical values are $t = \pm 2.571$. Reject the null hypothesis, the images have a significant effect.

19. a. The pooled variance is 6.4 and the estimated standard error is 1.46.

b. For the difference scores the variance is 24, the estimated standard error is 2.

21. a. The null hypothesis says that changing answers has no effect, H_0: $\mu_D = 0$. With $df = 8$ and $\alpha = .05$, the critical values are $t = \pm 2.306$. For these data, $M_D = 7$, $SS = 288$, the standard error is 2, and $t(8) = 3.50$. Reject H_0 and conclude that changing answers has a significant effect on exam performance.

b. For 95% confidence use $t = \pm 2.306$. The interval extends from 2.388 to 11.612.

c. Changing answers resulted in significantly higher exam scores, $t(8) = 3.50$, $p < .05$, 95% CI [2.388, 11.612].

23. The null hypothesis says that there is no difference between shots fired during versus between heart beats, H_0: $\mu_D = 0$. With $\alpha = .05$, the critical region consists of t values beyond ± 2.365. For these data, $M_D = 3$, $SS = 36$, $s^2 = 5.14$, the standard error is 0.80, and $t(7) = 3.75$. Reject H_0 and conclude that the timing of the shot has a significant effect on the marksmen's scores.

SECTION III **REVIEW**

1. a. For these data, the mean is $M = 23$ and the standard deviation is $s = 3$.

b. H_0: $\mu \leq 20$. With $df = 8$, the critical region consists of t values greater than 1.860. For these data, the standard error is 1, and $t(8) = 3.00$. Reject H_0 and conclude that participation in the interview significantly increases life satisfaction.

c. Cohen's $d = \frac{3}{3} = 1.00$.

d. The 90% confidence interval is $\mu = 23 \pm 1.86$ and extends from 21.14 to 24.86.

2. a. The pooled variance is 1.2, the standard error is 0.40, and $t(28) = \frac{0.7}{0.4} = 1.75$. With a critical value of 2.048, the decision is to fail to reject the null hypothesis.

b. For these data, $r^2 = \frac{3.06}{31.06} = 0.099$ or 9.9%.

c. The presence of a tattoo did not have a significant effect on the attractiveness ratings, $t(28) = 1.75$, $p > .05$, $r^2 = 0.099$.

3. a. The estimated standard error is 2.5 and $t(19) = 1.92$. With a critical value of 1.729, reject the null hypothesis and conclude that attention span is significantly longer with the medication.

b. The 80% confidence interval is $\mu_D = 4.8 \pm 1.328(2.5)$ and extends from 1.48 to 8.12.

CHAPTER 12: **INTRODUCTION TO ANALYSIS OF VARIANCE**

1. When there is no treatment effect, the numerator and the denominator of the F-ratio are both measuring the same sources of variability (random, unsystematic differences from sampling error). In this case, the F-ratio is balanced and should have a value near 1.00.

3. a. As the differences between sample means increase, $MS_{between}$ also increases, and the F-ratio increases.

b. Increases in sample variability cause MS_{within} to increase and, thereby, decrease the F-ratio.

5. a. Posttests are used to determine exactly which treatment conditions are significantly different.

b. If there are only two treatments, then there is no question as to which two treatments are different.

c. If the decision is to fail to reject H_0, then there are no significant differences.

7. a.

Source	SS	df	MS	
Between treatments	84	2	42	$F(2, 15) = 6.00$
Within treatments	105	15	7	
Total	189	17		

With $\alpha = .05$, the critical value is $F = 3.68$. Reject the null hypothesis and conclude that there are significant differences among the three treatments.

b. $\eta^2 = \frac{84}{189} = 0.444$.

c. Analysis of variance showed significant mean differences among the three treatments, $F(2, 15) = 6.00$, $p < .05$, $\eta^2 = 0.444$.

9. a. The sample variances are 4, 5, and 6.

b.

Source	SS	df	MS	
Between treatments	90	2	45	$F(2, 12) = 9.00$
Within treatments	60	12	5	
Total	150	14		

With $\alpha = .05$, the critical value is $F = 3.68$. Reject the null hypothesis and conclude that there are significant differences among the three treatments.

11. a.

Source	SS	df	MS	
Between treatments	70	2	35	$F(2, 12) = 17.50$
Within treatments	24	12	2	
Total	94	14		

With $\alpha = .05$, the critical value is $F = 3.68$. Reject the null hypothesis and conclude that there are significant differences among the three treatments.

b. $\eta^2 = \frac{70}{94} = 0.745$.

c. Analysis of variance showed significant mean differences in perfectionism related to parental criticism among the three groups of students, $F(2, 15) = 6.00, p < .05, \eta^2 = 0.745$.

13. a. $k = 3$ treatment conditions.

b. The study used a total of $N = 57$ participants.

15.

Source	SS	df	MS	
Between treatments	30	2	15	$F = 5$
Within treatments	63	21	3	
Total	93	23		

17.

Source	SS	df	MS	
Between treatments	20	2	10	$F = 2.50$
Within treatments	180	45	4	
Total	200	47		

19. a. The pooled variance is 6, the estimated standard error is 1.50 and $t(10) = 4.00$. With $df = 10$, the critical value is 2.228. Reject the null hypothesis.

b.

Source	SS	df	MS	
Between treatments	96	1	96	$F(1, 10) = 16$
Within treatments	60	10	6	
Total	156	11		

With $df = 1, 10$, the critical value is 4.96. Reject the null hypothesis. Note that $F = t^2$.

21. a.

Source	SS	df	MS	
Between treatments	252	2	126	$F(2, 15) = 19.30$
Within treatments	98	15	6.53	
Total	350	17		

With $df = 2, 15$ the critical value is 3.68. Reject the null hypothesis.

b. The percentage of variance explained by the mean differences is $\eta^2 = 0.72$ or 72%.

c. The analysis of variance shows significant differences in average brain size among the three groups of birds, $F(2, 15) = 19.30, p < .01, \eta^2 = 0.72$.

d. With $k = 3$ groups and $df = 15$, $q = 3.67$. The HSD = 3.83. The non-migrating birds are significantly different from either other group, but there is no significant difference between the short- and long-distance migrants.

23. a. The means and standard deviations are

Little	Moderate	Substantial
$M = 4.00$	$M = 5.00$	$M = 6.50$
$s = 2.11$	$s = 2.00$	$s = 1.51$

Source	SS	df	MS	
Between treatments	31.67	2	15.83	$F(2, 27) = 4.25$
Within treatments	100.50	27	3.72	
Total	132.17	29		

With $df = 2, 27$ the critical value is 3.35. Reject the null hypothesis.

b. $\eta^2 = \frac{31.67}{132.17} = 0.240$.

c. Tukey's HSD = 3.49(0.610) = 2.13 (using $df = 30$). The only significant mean difference is between those who watch little or no TV and those whose viewing is substantial.

CHAPTER 13: **REPEATED-MEASURES ANOVA**

1. For an independent measures design, the variability within treatments is the appropriate error term. For repeated measures, however, you must subtract out variability due to individual differences from the variability within treatments to obtain a measure of error.

3. a. A total of 30 participants is needed; three separate samples, each with $n = 10$. The F-ratio has $df = 2, 27$.

b. One sample of $n = 10$ is needed. The F-ratio has $df = 2, 18$.

5. a. 3 treatments
b. 16 participants

7.

Source	SS	df	MS	
Between treatments	28	2	14	$F(2, 10) = 7.78$
Within treatments	28	15		
Between subjects	10	5		
Error	18	10	1.8	
Total	56	17		

With $df = 2, 10$, the critical value is 4.10. Reject H_0. There are significant differences among the three treatments.

9. a. The null hypothesis states that there are no differences among the three treatments. With $df = 2, 8$, the critical value is 4.46.

Source	SS	df	MS	
Between treatments	70	2	35	$F(2, 8) = 35$
Within treatments	26	12		
Between subjects	18	4		
Error	8	8	1	
Total	96	14		

Reject H_0. There are significant differences among the three treatments.

b. For these data, $\eta^2 = \frac{70}{78} = 0.897$.

c. The analysis of variance shows significant mean differences among the three treatments, $F(2, 8) = 35.00, p < .05, \eta^2 = 0.897$.

11. The null hypothesis states that there are no differences among the three treatments, H_0: $\mu_1 = \mu_2 = \mu_3$. With $df = 2, 6$, the critical value is 5.14.

Source	SS	df	MS	
Between treatments	8	2	4	$F(2, 6) = 6.00$
Within treatments	94	9		
Between subjects	90	3		
Error	4	6	0.67	
Total	102	11		

Reject H_0. There are significant differences among the three treatments.

13. a. For the independent-measures ANOVA, we obtain:

Source	SS	df	MS	
Between treatments	48	2	24	$F(2, 15) = 3.46$
Within treatments	104	15	6.93	
Total	152	17		

With a critical value of 3.68 for $\alpha = .05$, fail to reject the null hypothesis.

b. For the repeated-measures ANOVA,

Source	SS	df	MS	
Between treatments	48	2	24	$F(2, 10) = 12.00$
Within treatments	104	15		
Between subjects	84	5		
Error	20	10	2	
Total	152	17		

With a critical value of 4.10 for $\alpha = .05$, reject the null hypothesis.

c. The repeated-measures ANOVA reduces the error variance by removing individual differences. This increases the likelihood that the ANOVA will find significant differences.

15.

Source	SS	df	MS	
Between treatments	2	1	2	$F(1, 24) = 4.00$
Within treatment	21	48		
Between subjects	9	24		
Error	12	24	0.5	
Total	23	49		

17.

Source	SS	df	MS	
Between treatments	54	3	18	$F(3, 33) = 6.00$
Within treatments	140	44		
Between subjects	41	11		
Error	99	33	3	
Total	194	47		

19. a. The null hypothesis states that there is no difference between the two treatments, H_0: $\mu_D = 0$. The critical region consists of t values beyond ± 3.182. The mean difference is $M_D = +4$. SS for the difference scores is 48, and $t(3) = 2.00$. Fail to reject H_0.

b. The null hypothesis states that there is no mean difference between treatments, H_0: $\mu_1 = \mu_2$. The critical value is $F = 10.13$.

Source	SS	df	MS	
Between treatments	32	1	32	$F(1, 3) = 4.00$
Within treatments	36	6		
Between subjects	12	3		
Error	24	3	8	
Total	68	7		

Fail to reject H_0. Note that $F = t^2$.

21. The means and standard deviations for the five delay periods are as follows:

1 month	6 months	1 year	2 years	5 years
$M = 866.67$	$M = 816.67$	$M = 766.67$	$M = 700.00$	$M = 583.33$
$S = 81.65$	$s = 81.65$	$s = 81.65$	$s = 70.71$	$s = 60.55$

Source	*SS*	*df*	*MS*	
Between treatments	291,333.3	4	72,833.3	$F(4, 20) = 56.75$
Within treatments	143,333.3	25		
Between subjects	117,666.7	5		
Error	25,666.7	20	1,283.3	
Total	434,666.7	29		

With $\alpha = .01$, the critical value is 4.43. There are significant differences.

CHAPTER 14: **TWO-FACTOR ANOVA**

1. a. In analysis of variance, an independent variable (or a quasi-independent variable) is called a *factor*.

b. The values of a factor that are used to create the different groups or treatment conditions are called the *levels* of the factor.

c. A research study with two independent (or quasi-independent) variables is called a *two-factor study*.

3. During the second stage of the two-factor ANOVA the mean differences between treatments are analyzed into differences from each of the two main effects and differences from the interaction.

5. a. $M = 10$

b. $M = 30$

c. $M = 50$

7. a. The scores in treatment 1 are consistently higher than the scores in treatment 2. There is a main effect for treatment.

b. The overall mean is around $M = 15$ for all three age groups. There is no main effect for age.

c. The two lines are not parallel. Instead, the difference between the treatments increases as the participants get older. Yes, there is an interaction.

9. a.

Source	*SS*	*df*	*MS*	
Between treatments	100	3		
A	10	1	10	$F(1,36) = 2$
B	90	1	90	$F(1,36) = 18.00$
A × B	0	1	0	$F(1,36) = 0$
Within treatments	180	36	5	
Total	280	39		

All *F*-ratios have $df = 1, 36$ and the critical value is $F = 4.11$. The main effect for factor B is significant, but factor A and the interaction are not.

b. For factor A, $\eta^2 = \frac{10}{190} = 0.053$, for factor B, $\eta^2 = \frac{90}{270} = 0.333$, and for the interaction, $\eta^2 = 0$.

11. a. $df = 1, 66$

b. $df = 2, 66$

c. $df = 2, 66$

13. a.

Source	*SS*	*df*	*MS*	
Between treatments	340	5		
Pouring	60	1	60	$F(1,54) = 10.00$
Temperature	280	2	140	$F(2,54) = 23.33$
Interaction	0	2	0	$F(2,42) = 0$
Within treatments	324	54	6	
Total	664	59		

b. Temperature and pouring method both have significant effects on the bubbles in the wine. However, the effects are independent, there is no interaction.

15.

Source	*SS*	*df*	*MS*	
Between treatments	144	8		
A	36	2	18	$F(2,72) = 6.00$
B	24	2	12	$F(2,72) = 4.00$
A × B	84	4	21	$F(4,72) = 7.00$
Within treatments	216	72	3	
Total	360	80		

17.

Source	*SS*	*df*	*MS*	
Between treatments	116	5		
A	28	1	28	$F(1,24) = 7.00$
B	64	2	32	$F(1,24) = 8.00$
A × B	24	2	12	$F(1,24) = 3.00$
Within treatments	240	60	4	
Total	356	65		

19. a.

Source	*SS*	*df*	*MS*	
Between treatments	360	5		
Gender	72	1	72	$F(1, 12) = 9.00$
Treatments	252	2	126	$F(1, 12) = 15.75$
Gender × treatment	36	2	18	$F(1, 12) = 2.25$
Within treatments	96	12	8	
Total	456	17		

With $df = 1, 12$, the critical value for the gender main effect is 4.75. The main effect for gender is significant. With $df = 2, 12$, the critical value for the treatment main effect and the interaction is 3.88. The main effect for treatments is significant but the interaction is not.

b. For treatment I, $F = 0$; for treatment II, $F = \frac{54}{8} = 6.75$; and for treatment III, $F = \frac{54}{8} = 6.75$. With $df = 1, 12$, the critical value for all three tests is 4.75. The results indicate a significant difference between males and females in treatments II and III, but not in treatment I.

21. a. The means for the six groups are as follows:

	Middle School	High School	College
Non-User	4.00	4.00	4.00
User	3.00	2.00	1.00

Source	*SS*	*df*	*MS*	
Between treatments	32	5		
Use	24	1	24	$F(1, 18) = 14.4$
School level	4	2	2	$F(2, 18) = 1.2$
Interaction	4	2	2	$F(2, 18) = 1.2$
Within treatments	30	18	1.67	
Total	62	23		

For $df = 1, 18$ the critical value is 4.41 and for $df = 2, 18$ it is 3.55. The main effect for Facebook use is significant but the other main effect and the interaction are not.

b. Grades are significantly lower for Facebook users. A difference exists for all three grade levels but appears to increase as the students get older although there is no significant interaction.

23. a.

Source	*SS*	*df*	*MS*	
Between treatments	216	3		
Self-esteem	96	1	96	$F(1, 20) = 22.33$
Audience	96	1	96	$F(1, 20) = 22.33$
Interaction	24	1	24	$F(1, 20) = 5.58$
Within treatments	86	20	4.3	
Total	300	23		

With $df = 1, 20$ the critical value is 4.35 for all three tests. Both main effects and the interaction are significant. Overall, there are fewer errors for the high self-esteem participants and for those working alone. The audience condition has very little effect on the high self-esteem participants but a very large effect on those with low self-esteem.

b. For both main effects, $\eta^2 = \frac{96}{182} = 0.527$. For the interaction, $\eta^2 = \frac{24}{110} = 0.218$.

SECTION IV **REVIEW**

1. a.

Source	*SS*	*df*	*MS*	
Between treatments	40	3	13.33	$F(3, 12) = 7.98$
Within treatments	20	12	1.67	
Total	60	15		

With $\alpha = .05$, the critical value is $F = 3.49$. Reject the null hypothesis.

b. $\eta^2 = \frac{40}{60} = 0.67$

c. The results show significant differences among the four levels of severity, $F(3, 12) = 7.98, p < .05, \eta^2 = 0.67$.

2. a. The null hypothesis states that there are no differences in quality of life among the three time periods.

Source	SS	df	MS	
Between treatments	56	2	28	$F(2, 6) = 10.49$
Within treatments	28	9		
Between subjects	12	3		
Error	16	6	2.67	
Total	84	11		

With $df = 2, 6$, the critical value is 5.14. Reject H_0.

b. For these data, $\eta^2 = \frac{56}{72} = 0.778$.

c. The results indicate significant changes in life satisfaction across the three time periods, $F(2, 6) = 10.49$, $p < .05$, $\eta^2 = 0.778$.

3. An interaction indicates that the effect of one factor depends on the levels of the other factor. Alternatively, it indicates that the main effects for one factor are not consistent across the levels of the other factor.

4.

Source	SS	df	MS	
Between treatments	148	3		
A (safety)	98	1	98	$F(1,28) = 13.52$
B (skill)	32	1	32	$F(1,28) = 4.41$
A × B	18	1	18	$F(1,28) = 2.48$
Within treatments	203	28	7.25	
Total	351	31		

All F-ratios have $df = 1, 28$ and the critical value is $F = 4.20$. With $\alpha = .05$ both main effects are significant but the interaction is not. Overall driving risk was significantly higher for those drivers who rated themselves as highly skilled compared to those with low ratings. Also, drivers rated low in safety had significantly more risk than those rated high.

CHAPTER 15: CORRELATION

1. A positive correlation indicates that X and Y change in the same direction: As X increases, Y also increases. A negative correlation indicates that X and Y tend to change in opposite directions: As X increases, Y decreases.

3. $SP = 15$

5. a. The scatter plot shows points widely scattered around a line sloping up to the right.

b. The correlation is small but positive; around 0.4 to 0.6.

c. For these scores, $SS_X = 32$, $SS_Y = 8$, and $SP = 8$. The correlation is $r = \frac{8}{16} = 0.50$.

7. a. The scatter plot shows points moderately scattered around a line sloping down to the right.

b. $SS_X = 10$, $SS_Y = 40$, and $SP = -13$. The correlation is $r = -\frac{13}{20} = -0.65$.

9. a. The scatter plot shows points clustered around a line sloping up to the right.

b. $SS_X = 18$, $SS_Y = 18$, and $SP = 5$. The correlation is $r = \frac{5}{18} = 0.278$.

11. a. For the children, $SS = 32$ and for the birth parents, $SS = 14$. $SP = 15$. The correlation is $r = 0.709$.

b. For the children, $SS = 32$ and for the adoptive parents $SS = 16$. $SP = 3$. The correlation is $r = 0.133$.

c. The children's behavior is strongly related to their birth parents and only weakly related to their adoptive parents. The data suggest that the behavior is inherited rather than learned.

13. a. For the men's weights, $SS = 18$ and for their incomes, $SS = 13{,}060$. $SP = 281$. The correlation is $r = 0.580$.

b. With $n = 8$, $df = 6$ and the critical value is 0.707. The correlation is not significant.

15. a. $r = 0.707$

b. $r = 0.468$

c. $r = 0.374$

17. a. $r_{XY\text{-}Z} = \frac{0.38}{0.57} = 0.667$

b. $r_{XZ\text{-}Y} = \frac{0.04}{0.428} = 0.093$

19. a. $r_S = +0.907$

b. With $n = 11$, the critical value is 0.618. The correlation is significant.

21. a. $r_S = -0.985$

b. For $n = 10$, the critical values are 0.648 and 0.794 for 5 and 0.1, respectively. The correlation is significant at either level.

23. Using the eating concern scores as the X variable and coding males as 1 and females as 0 for the Y variable produces $SS_X = 1875.6$, $SS_Y = 3.6$, and $SP = -50.4$. The point-biserial correlation is $r = -0.613$. (Reversing the codes for males and females will change the sign of the correlation.)

CHAPTER 16: INTRODUCTION TO REGRESSION

1.

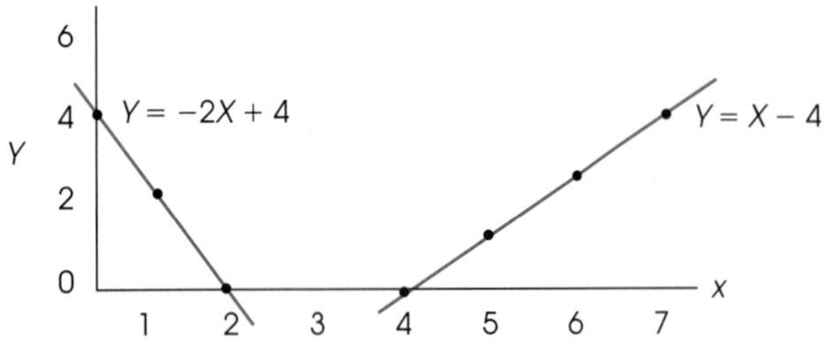

3. a. $r = 0.80$
b. $\hat{Y} = 2X + 8$

5. The standard error of estimate is a measure of the average distance between the predicted Y points from the regression equation and the actual Y points in the data.

7. $SS_X = 32$, $SS_Y = 8$, $SP = 8$. The regression equation is $\hat{Y} = X + 3$

9. $SS_{\text{regression}} = r^2 SS_Y = 90.02$ with $df = 1$. $MS_{\text{residual}} = \frac{18}{1} = 4.5$. $F = \frac{90.02}{4.5} = 20.00$. With $df = 1, 4$, the F-ratio is significant with $\alpha = .05$.

11. a. $SS_{\text{weight}} = 20$, $SS_{\text{income}} = 7430$, $SP = -359$. $\hat{Y} = -17.95X + 119.85$
b. $r = -0.931$ and $r^2 = 0.867$
c. $F = 52.15$ with $df = 1, 8$. The regression equation is significant with $\alpha = .05$ or $\alpha = .01$.

13. a. $\hat{Y} = 1.38X + 7.34$
b. $r^2 = 0.743$ or 74.3%
c. $F = 20.23$ with $df = 1, 7$. The equation accounts for a significant portion of the variance.

15. a. The standard error of estimate is $\sqrt{36/16} = 1.50$.
b. The standard error of estimate is $\sqrt{36/36} = 1.00$.

17. a. $df = 1, 23$
b. $n = 20$ pairs of scores

19. a. $F = \frac{2.2}{1.04} = 2.11$. With $df = 2, 15$, the critical value is 3.68. The equation does not account for a significant portion of the variance.
b. $F = \frac{2.2}{3.12} = 0.705$. The equation is not significant.

21. a. $SS_{\text{churches}} = 390$, $SS_{\text{population}} = 10$, and $SS_{\text{crime}} = 390$. SP for churches and population is 60, SP for churches and crime is 363, and SP for population and crime is 60. The regression equation is. $\hat{Y} = 0.1X_1 + 5.4X_2 - 2.7$.
b. $R^2 = 0.924$ or 92.4%
c. Population by itself predicts 92.4% of the variance. Nothing is gained by adding churches as a second variable.

23. Using the biological parents as a single predictor accounts for $r^2 = 0.503$ or 50.3% of the variance. The multiple regression equation accounts for $R^2 = 58.7\%$ (see problem 22). The extra variance predicted by adding the adoptive parents as a second predictor is $58.7 - 50.3 = 8.4\%$ and has $df = 1$. The residual from the multiple regression is $1 - R^2 = 41.3\%$ and has $df = 6$. The F-ratio is $8.4/(41.3/6) = 1.22$. With $df = 1, 6$ the F-ratio is not significant.

25. $n = 39$

CHAPTER 17: CHI-SQUARE TESTS

1. Nonparametric tests make few if any assumptions about the populations from which the data are obtained. For example, the populations do not need to form normal distributions, nor is it required that different populations in the same study have equal variances (homogeneity of variance assumption). Parametric tests require data measured on an interval or ratio scale. For nonparametric tests, any scale of measurement is acceptable.

3. a. The null hypothesis states that there is no preference among the four colors; $p = \frac{1}{4}$ for all categories. The expected frequencies are $f_e = 15$ for all categories, and chi-square $= 4.53$. With $df = 3$, the critical value is 7.81. Fail to reject H_0 and conclude that there are no significant preferences.
b. The results indicate that there are no significant preferences among the four colors, $\chi^2(3, N = 60) = 4.53$, $p > .05$.

5. The null hypothesis states that wins and loses are equally likely. With 64 games, the expected frequencies are 32 wins and 32 losses. With $df = 1$ the critical value is 3.84, and the data produce a chi-square of 6.25. Reject the null hypothesis and conclude that home team wins are significantly more common than would be expected by chance.

7. a. The null hypothesis states that couples with the same initial do not occur more often than would be expected by chance. For a sample of 400, the expected frequencies are 26 with the same initial and 374 with different initials. With $df = 1$ the critical value is 3.84, and the data produce a chi-square of 5.92. Reject the null hypothesis.

b. A larger sample should be more representative of the population. If the sample continues to be different from the hypothesis as the sample size increases, eventually the difference will be significant.

9. a. H_0 states that the distribution of automobile accidents is the same as the distribution of registered drivers: 16% under age 20, 28% age 20 to 29, and 56% age 30 or older. With $df = 2$, the critical value is 5.99. The expected frequencies for these three categories are 48, 84, and 168. Chi-square = 13.76. Reject H_0 and conclude that the distribution of automobile accidents is not identical to the distribution of registered drivers.

b. The chi-square test shows that the age distribution for people in automobile accidents is significantly different from the age distribution of licensed drivers, $\chi^2(3, N = 180) = 13.76, p < .05$.

11. The null hypothesis states that there are no preferences among the three designs; $p = \frac{1}{3}$ for all categories. With $df = 2$, the critical value is 5.99. The expected frequencies are $f_e = 40$ for all categories, and chi-square = 8.60. Reject H_0 and conclude that there are significant preferences.

13. The null hypothesis states that there is no relationship between the type of music and whether the women give their phone numbers. With $df = 1$, the critical value is 3.84. The expected frequencies are:

	Phone Number	No Number	
Romantic Music	15	25	40
Neutral Music	15	25	40
	30	50	

Chi-square = 7.68. Reject H_0.

15. a. The null hypothesis states that the distribution of opinions is the same for those who live in the city and those who live in the suburbs. For $df = 1$ and $\alpha = .05$, the critical value for chi-square is 3.84. The expected frequencies are:

	Favor	Oppose
City	30	20
Suburb	60	40

For these data, chi-square = 3.12. Fail to reject H_0 and conclude that opinions in the city are not different from those in the suburbs.

b. The phi coefficient is 0.144.

17. a. The null hypothesis states that the proportion who falsely recall seeing broken glass should be the same for all three groups. The expected frequency of saying yes is 9.67 for all groups, and the expected frequency for saying no is 40.33 for all groups. With $df = 2$, the critical value is 5.99. For these data, chi-square = 7.78. Reject the null hypothesis and conclude that the likelihood of recalling broken glass depends on the question that the participants were asked.

b. Cramérs $V = 0.228$.

c. Participants who were asked about the speed of the cars that "smashed into" each other were more than two times more likely to falsely recall seeing broken glass.

d. The results of the chi-square test indicate that the phrasing of the question had a significant effect on the participants' recall of the accident, $\chi^2(2, N = 150) = 7.78, p < .05, V = 0.228$.

19. The null hypothesis states that IQ and gender are independent. The distribution of IQ scores for boys should be the same as the distribution for girls. With $df = 2$ and and $\alpha = .05$, the critical value is 5.99. The expected frequencies are 15 low IQ, 48 medium, and 17 high for both boys and girls. For these data, chi-square is 3.76. Fail to reject the null hypothesis. These data do not provide evidence for a significant relationship between IQ and gender.

21. The null hypothesis states that there is no difference between the distribution of preferences predicted by women and the actual distribution for men. With $df = 3$ and $\alpha = .05$, the critical value is 7.81. The expected frequencies are:

	Somewhat Thin	Slightly Thin	Slightly Heavy	Somewhat Heavy
Women	22.9	22.9	22.9	11.4
Men	17.1	17.1	17.1	8.6

Chi-square = 9.13. Reject H_0 and conclude that there is a significant difference in the preferences predicted by women and the actual preferences expressed by men.

23. a. The null hypothesis states that there is no relationship between IQ and volunteering. With $df = 2$ and $\alpha = .05$, the critical value is 5.99. The expected frequencies are:

	High IQ	Medium IQ	Low IQ
Volunteer	37.5	75	37.5
Not Volunteer	12.5	25	12.5

The chi-square statistic is 4.75. Fail to reject H_0 with $\alpha = .05$ and $df = 2$.

25. The null hypothesis states that there is no relationship between the season of birth and schizophrenia. With $df = 3$ and $\alpha = .05$, the critical value is 7.81. The expected frequencies are:

	Summer	Fall	Winter	Spring
No Disorder	23.33	23.33	26.67	26.67
Schizophrenia	11.67	11.67	13.33	13.33

Chi-square = 3.62. Fail to reject H_0 and conclude that these data do not provide enough evidence to conclude that there is a significant relationship between the season of birth and schizophrenia.

CHAPTER 18: THE BINOMIAL TEST

1. H_0: p(home team win) = .50 (no preference). The critical boundaries are $z = \pm1.96$. With $X = 42$, $\mu = 32$, and $\sigma = 4$, we obtain $z = 2.50$. Reject H_0 and conclude that there is a significant difference. Home teams win significantly more than would be expected by chance.

3. H_0: $p = q = \frac{1}{2}$ (right and left are equally common). The critical boundaries are $z = \pm2.58$. With $X = 104$, $\mu = 72$, and $\sigma = 6$, we obtain $z = 5.33$. Reject H_0 and conclude that right- and left-handed rats are not equally common.

5. H_0: $p = 0.065$ (just chance). The critical boundaries are $z = \pm1.96$. With $X = 38$, $\mu = 26$, and $\sigma = 4.93$, we obtain $z = 2.43$. Reject H_0. The initials of spouses are significantly different from what would be expected by chance.

7. H_0: $p = .08$ (still 8% learning disabled). The critical boundaries are $z = \pm1.96$. With $X = 42$, $\mu = 24$, and $\sigma = 4.70$, we obtain $z = 3.83$. Reject H_0 and conclude that there has been a significant change in the proportion of students classified as learning disabled.

9. H_0: $p = .25$ (the general population has the same proportion of belief as the psychotherapists). The critical boundaries are $z = \pm1.96$. With $X = 65$, $\mu = 48$, and $\sigma = 6$, we obtain $z = 2.83$. Reject H_0 and conclude that the proportion of belief is significantly different for the general population and for psychotherapists.

11. H_0: p(accident) = 0.12 (no change). The critical boundaries are $z = \pm1.96$. With $X = 44$, $\mu = 60$, and $\sigma = 7.27$, we obtain $z = -2.20$. Reject H_0, there has been a significant change in the accident rate.

13. H_0: $p = \frac{1}{4} = p$(guessing correctly). The critical boundaries are $z = \pm1.96$. With $X = 32$, $\mu = 25$, and $\sigma = 4.33$, we obtain $z = 1.62$. Fail to reject H_0 and conclude that this level of performance is not significantly different from chance.

15. **a.** H_0: $p = q = \frac{1}{2}$ (positive and negative correlations are equally likely). The critical boundaries are $z = \pm1.96$. With $X = 25$, $\mu = 13.5$, and $\sigma = 2.60$, we obtain $z = 4.42$. Reject H_0, positive and negative correlations are not equally likely.
 b. The critical boundaries are $z = \pm1.96$. With $X = 20$, $\mu = 13.5$, and $\sigma = 2.60$, we obtain $z = 2.50$. Reject H_0, positive and negative correlations are not equally likely.

17. H_0: $p = .30$ and $q = .70$ (proportions for the special program are the same as in the population). The critical boundaries are $z = \pm1.96$. The binomial distribution has $\mu = 27$ and $\sigma = 4.35$. With $X = 43$ we obtain $z = 3.68$. Reject H_0 and conclude that there is a significant difference between special program students and the general population.

19. H_0: $p = \frac{1}{2} = p$(reduced reactions). The critical boundaries are $z = \pm1.96$. The binomial distribution has $\mu = 32$ and $\sigma = 4$. With $X = 47$ we obtain $z = 3.75$. Reject H_0 and conclude that there is evidence of significantly reduced allergic reactions.

21. H_0: $p = q = \frac{1}{2}$(higher and lower grades are equally likely). The critical boundaries are $z = \pm2.58$. The binomial distribution has $\mu = 20$ and $\sigma = 3.16$. With $X = 29$ we obtain $z = 2.85$. Reject H_0 and conclude that there are significantly more higher grades than would be expected by chance.

23. **a.** H_0: $p = \frac{1}{3}$ and $q = \frac{2}{3}$ (just guessing). The critical boundaries are $z = \pm1.96$. The binomial distribution has $\mu = 12$ and $\sigma = 2.83$. With $X = 25$ we obtain $z = 4.59$. Reject H_0 and conclude that the children with autism are performing significantly better than chance.
 b. H_0: $p = \frac{1}{3}$ and $q = \frac{2}{3}$ (just guessing). The critical boundaries are $z = \pm1.96$. The binomial distribution has $\mu = 12$ and $\sigma = 2.83$. With

$X = 16$ we obtain $z = 1.41$. Fail to reject H_0 and conclude that the children with SLI are not performing significantly better than chance.

25. H_0: $p = q = \frac{1}{2}$ (any change in grade point average is due to chance). The critical boundaries are $z = \pm 2.58$. The binomial distribution has $\mu = 22.5$ and $\sigma = 3.35$. With $X = 31$ we obtain $z = 2.54$. Fail to reject H_0 and conclude that there is no significant change in grade point average after the workshop.

27. a. H_0: $p = q = \frac{1}{2}$ (the training has no effect). The critical boundaries are $z = \pm 1.96$. Discarding the 11 people who showed no change, the binomial distribution has $\mu = 19.5$ and $\sigma = 3.12$. With $X = 29$ we obtain $z = 3.05$. Reject H_0 and conclude that biofeedback training has a significant effect.

b. Discarding only 1 participant and dividing the other 10 equally, the binomial distribution has $\mu = 24.5$ and $\sigma = 3.50$. With $X = 34$ we obtain $z = 2.71$. Reject H_0.

SECTION V **REVIEW**

1. a. $SS_X = 40$, $SS_Y = 5984$, $SP = 480$, and the Pearson correlation is $r = 0.981$.

b. The Spearman correlation is $r_S = 1.00$.

2. a. For these data, $SS_{\text{wife}} = 172$, $SS_{\text{husband}} = 106$, and $SP = 122$. The Pearson correlation is $r = 0.904$.

b. $b = \frac{122}{172} = 0.709$ and $a = 9 - 0.709(7) = 4.037$. $\hat{Y} = 0.709X + 4.037$.

3. The null hypothesis states that there is no preference among the three photographs; $p = \frac{1}{3}$ for all categories. The expected frequencies are $f_e = 50$ for all categories, and chi-square $= 20.28$. With $df = 2$, the critical value is 5.99. Reject H_0 and conclude that there are significant preferences

4. a. The null hypothesis states that there is no relationship between personality and heart disease. For $df = 1$ and $\alpha = .05$, the critical value for chi-square is 3.84. The expected frequencies are:

	No Disease	Heart Disease
Type A	40	10
Type B	120	30

For these data, chi-square $= 10.67$. Reject H_0 and conclude that there is a significant relationship between personality and heart disease.

b. $\varphi = 0.231$

5. H_0: $p = 0.20$ (correct predictions are just chance). The critical boundaries are $z = \pm 1.96$. With $X = 27$, $\mu = 20$, and $\sigma = 4$, we obtain $z = 1.75$. Fail to reject H_0 and conclude that this level of performance is not significantly better than chance.

CHAPTER 19: **CHOOSING THE RIGHT STATISTICS**

1. The mean and standard deviation could be used to describe the set of scores before treatment and the set of scores after treatment. Or a difference score could be computed for each participant and the results could be described with the mean and standard deviation for the set of difference scores. A repeated-measures t test would evaluate the significance of the mean difference and effect size would be measured by Cohen's d or r^2.

3. The data would form a 2×2 frequency distribution matrix and the proportion in each cell would describe the result. A chi-square test for independence would determine whether the proportions for the peer mentor group are significantly different from the proportions for other freshmen. Effect size would be measured with a phi-coefficient.

5. The mean and standard deviation could be used to describe the set of scores with texting and the set of scores without texting. Or a difference score could be computed for each participant and the results could be described with the mean and standard deviation for the set of difference scores. A repeated-measures t test would evaluate the significance of the mean difference and effect size would be measured by Cohen's d or r^2.

7. The mean and standard deviation could be used to describe the set of scores for each condition. An independent-measures t test would evaluate the significance of the mean difference, and effect size would be measured by Cohen's d or r^2.

9. The mean and standard deviation could be used to describe the set of scores for each condition. An independent-measures ANOVA would evaluate the significance of the mean differences and effect size would be measured by η^2.

11. The mean and standard deviation could be used to describe the set of scores for each of the four birth order groups. An independent-measures ANOVA would evaluate the significance of the mean differences and effect size would be measured by η^2.

13. The mean and standard deviation could be used to describe the set of scores for each of the four weight groups. An independent-measures ANOVA would evaluate the significance of the mean differences and effect size would be measured by η^2.

15. The mean and standard deviation rating could be used to describe the group. If the rating scale has a neutral point, a single-sample t test could be used to determine whether the mean optimism level is significantly different from neutral.

17. **a.** The data could be described by how the higher and lower ranks are clustered in the two groups. A Mann-Whitney test could determine whether there is a significant difference between the groups.
b. With two ordinal scores for each child, a Spearman correlation could measure and describe the relationship between variables. The significance of the correlation could be determined by comparing the sample value with the critical values listed in Table B7.

19. The mean and standard deviation could be used to describe the set of scores for each group. An independent-measures t test would evaluate the significance of the mean difference, and effect size would be measured by Cohen's d or r^2.

21. The proportion or percentage showing decreased pain could be used to describe the results. A binomial sign test would evaluate the significance of the treatment.

23. The mean and standard deviation could be used to describe the set of scores for each group. An independent-measures t test would evaluate the significance of the mean difference, and effect size would be measured by Cohen's d or r^2.

25. **a.** The mean and standard deviation could be used to describe the set of scores for each carrier. A repeated-measures ANOVA would evaluate the significance of the mean differences, and effect size would be measured by η^2.
b. The data would form a 3×3 frequency distribution matrix and the proportion in each cell would describe the results. A chi-square test for independence would determine whether the proportions of 1st-, 2nd-, and 3rd-place ratings are significantly different from one carrier to another. Effect size would be measured with Cramér's V. Alternatively, the data form three sets of scores, one for each phone. The scores are the rankings given by the participants. A Friedman test could evaluate the significance of the difference between carriers.
c. The three proportions would describe the relative preference for the carriers. A chi-square test for goodness of fit would determine whether there are significant preferences among the three carriers.

27. The mean and standard deviation could be used to describe the three deprivation conditions. A repeated-measures ANOVA would evaluate the significance of the mean differences, and effect size would be measured by η^2.

29. The data would form a 2×2 frequency distribution matrix, and the proportion in each cell would describe the results. A chi-square test for independence would determine whether the proportions using the stairs and elevators are significantly different from one condition to the other. Effect size would be measured with a phi-coefficient.

APPENDIX D

General Instructions for Using SPSS

The Statistical Package for the Social Sciences, commonly known as SPSS, is a computer program that performs statistical calculations, and is widely available on college campuses. Detailed instructions for using SPSS for specific statistical calculations (such as computing sample variance or performing an independent-measures *t* test) are presented at the end of the appropriate chapter in the text. Look for the SPSS logo in the Resources section at the end of each chapter. In this appendix, we provide a general overview of the SPSS program.

SPSS consists of two basic components: A data editor and a set of statistical commands. The **data editor** is a huge matrix of numbered rows and columns. To begin any analysis, you must type your data into the data editor. Typically, the scores are entered into columns of the editor. Before scores are entered, each of the columns is labeled "var." After scores are entered, the first column becomes VAR00001, the second column becomes VAR00002, and so on. To enter data into the editor, the **Data View** tab must be set at the bottom left of the screen. If you want to name a column (instead of using VAR00001), click on the **Variable View** tab at the bottom of the data editor. You will get a description of each variable in the editor, including a box for the name. You may type in a new name using up to 8 lowercase characters (no spaces, no hyphens). Click the **Data View** tab to go back to the data editor.

The **statistical commands** are listed in menus that are made available by clicking on **Analyze** in the tool bar at the top of the screen. When you select a statistical command, SPSS typically asks you to identify exactly where the scores are located and exactly what other options you want to use. This is accomplished by identifying the column(s) in the data editor that contain the needed information. Typically, you are presented with a display similar to the following figure. On the left is a box that lists all of the columns in the data editor that contain information. In this example, we have typed values into columns 1, 2, 3, and 4. On the right is an empty box that is waiting for you to identify the correct column. For example, suppose that you wanted to do a statistical calculation using the scores in column 3. You should highlight VAR00003 by clicking on it in the left-hand box, then click the arrow to move the column label into the right hand box. (If you make a mistake, you can highlight the variable in the right-hand box, which will reverse the arrow so that you can move the variable back to the left-hand box.)

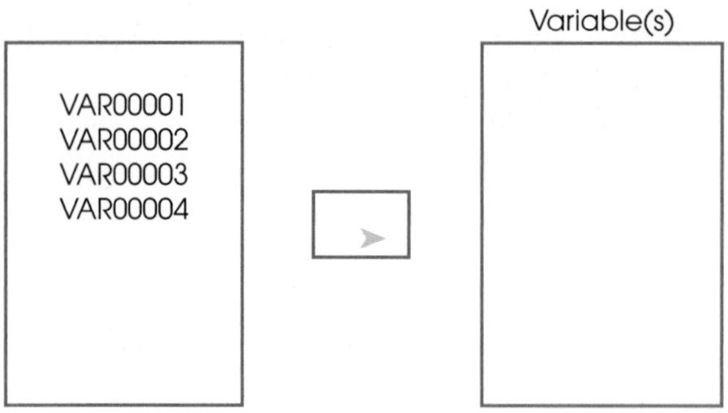

SPSS DATA FORMATS

The SPSS program uses two basic formats for entering scores into the data matrix. Each is described and demonstrated as follows:

1. The first format is used when the data consist of several scores (more than one) for each individual. This includes data from a repeated-measures study, in which each person is measured in all of the different treatment conditions, and data from a correlational study where there are two scores, *X* and *Y*, for each individual. Table D1 illustrates this kind of data and shows how the scores would appear in the SPSS data matrix. Note that the scores in the data matrix have exactly the same structure as the scores in the original data. Specifically, each row of the data matrix contains the scores for an individual participant, and each column contains the scores for one treatment condition.

TABLE D1

Data for a repeated-measures or correlational study with several scores for each individual. The left half of the table (a) shows the original data, with three scores for each person; and the right half (b) shows the scores as they would be entered into the SPSS data matrix. Note: SPSS automatically adds the two decimal points for each score. For example, you type in 10 and it appears as 10.00 in the matrix.

(a) Original data

	Treatments		
Person	I	II	III
A	10	14	19
B	9	11	15
C	12	15	22
D	7	10	18
E	13	18	20

(b) Data as entered into the SPSS data matrix

	VAR0001	VAR0002	VAR0003	var
1	10.00	14.00	19.00	
2	9.00	11.00	15.00	
3	12.00	15.00	22.00	
4	7.00	10.00	18.00	
5	13.00	18.00	20.00	

2. The second format is used for data from an independent-measures study using a separate group of participants for each treatment condition. This kind of data is entered into the data matrix in a *stacked* format. Instead of having the scores from different treatments in different columns, all of the scores from all of the treatment conditions are entered into a single column so that the scores from one treatment condition are literally stacked on top of the scores from another treatment condition. A code number is then entered into a second column beside each score to tell the computer which treatment condition corresponds to each score. For example, you could enter a value of 1 beside each score from treatment #1, enter a 2 beside each score from treatment #2, and so on. Table D2 illustrates this kind of data and shows how the scores would be entered into the SPSS data matrix.

TABLE D2

Data for an independent-measures study with a different group of participants in each treatment condition. The left half of the table shows the original data, with three separate groups, each with five participants, and the right half shows the scores as they would be entered into the SPSS data matrix. Note that the data matrix lists all 15 scores in the same column, then uses code numbers in a second column to indicate the treatment condition corresponding to each score.

(a) Original data

Treatments		
I	II	III
10	14	19
9	11	15
12	15	22
7	10	18
13	18	20

(b) Data as entered into the SPSS data matrix

	VAR0001	VAR0002	var
1	10.00	1.00	
2	9.00	1.00	
3	12.00	1.00	
4	7.00	1.00	
5	13.00	1.00	
6	14.00	2.00	
7	11.00	2.00	
8	15.00	2.00	
9	10.00	2.00	
10	18.00	2.00	
11	19.00	3.00	
12	15.00	3.00	
13	22.00	3.00	
14	18.00	3.00	
15	20.00	3.00	

APPENDIX E

Hypothesis Tests for Ordinal Data: Mann-Whitney, Wilcoxon, Kruskal-Wallis, and Friedman Tests

E.1 DATA FROM AN ORDINAL SCALE

Occasionally, a research study generates data that consist of measurements on an ordinal scale. Recall from Chapter 1 that an ordinal scale simply produces a *rank ordering* for the individuals being measured. For example, a kindergarten teacher may rank children in terms of their maturity, or a business manager may classify job applicants as outstanding, good, and average.

RANKING NUMERICAL SCORES

In addition to obtaining measurements from an ordinal scale, a researcher may begin with a set of numerical measurements and convert these scores into ranks. For example, if you had a listing of the actual heights for a group of individuals, you could arrange the numbers in order from greatest to least. This process converts data from an interval or a ratio scale into ordinal measurements. In Chapter 17 (page 593), we identify several reasons for converting numerical scores into nominal categories. These same reasons also provide justification for transforming scores into ranks. The following list should give you an idea of why there can be an advantage to using ranks instead of scores.

1. Ranks are simpler. If someone asks you how tall your sister is, you could reply with a specific numerical value, such as 5 feet $7\frac{3}{4}$ inches tall. Or you could answer, "She is a little taller than I am." For many situations, the relative answer would be better.
2. The original scores may violate some of the basic assumptions that underlie certain statistical procedures. For example, the *t* tests and ANOVA assume that the data come from normal distributions. Also, the independent-measures tests assume that the different populations all have the same variance (the homogeneity-of-variance assumption). If a researcher suspects that the data do not satisfy these assumptions, it may be safer to convert the scores to ranks and use a statistical technique designed for ranks.
3. The original scores may have unusually high variance. Variance is a major component of the standard error in the denominator of *t* statistics and the error term in the denominator of *F*-ratios. Thus, large variance can greatly reduce the likelihood that these parametric tests will find significant differences. Converting the scores to ranks essentially eliminates the variance. For example, 10 scores have ranks from 1 to 10 no matter how variable the original scores are.
4. Occasionally, an experiment produces an undetermined, or infinite, score. For example, a rat may show no sign of solving a particular maze after hundreds of trials. This animal has an infinite, or undetermined, score. Although there is no absolute score that can be assigned, you can say that this rat has the highest score for the sample and then rank the rest of the scores by their numerical values.

RANKING TIED SCORES

Whenever you are transforming numerical scores into ranks, you may find two or more scores that have exactly the same value. Because the scores are tied, the transformation process should produce ranks that are also tied. The procedure for converting tied scores into tied ranks was presented in Chapter 15 (page 539) when we introduced the Spearman correlation, and is repeated briefly here. First, you list the scores in order, including tied values. Second, you assign each position in the list a rank (1st, 2nd, and so on). Finally, for any scores that are tied, you compute the mean of the tied ranks, and use the mean value as the final rank. The following set of scores demonstrates this process for a set of $n = 8$ scores.

Original scores:	3	4	4	7	9	9	9	12
Position ranks:	1	2	3	4	5	6	7	8
Final ranks:	1	2.5	2.5	4	6	6	6	8

STATISTICS FOR ORDINAL DATA

You should recall from Chapter 1 that ordinal values tell you only the direction from one score to another, but provide no information about the distance between scores. Thus, you know that first place is better than second or third, but you do not know how much better. Because the concept of *distance* is not well defined with ordinal data, it generally is considered unwise to use traditional statistics such as t tests and analysis of variance with scores consisting of ranks or ordered categories. Therefore, statisticians have developed special techniques that are designed specifically for use with ordinal data.

In this chapter we introduce four hypothesis-testing procedures that are used with ordinal data. Each of the new tests can be viewed as an alternative for a commonly used parametric test. The four tests and the situations in which they are used are as follows:

1. The Mann-Whitney test uses data from two separate samples to evaluate the difference between two treatment conditions or two populations. The Mann-Whitney test can be viewed as an alternative to the independent-measures t hypothesis test introduced in Chapter 10.
2. The Wilcoxon test uses data from a repeated-measures design to evaluate the difference between two treatment conditions. This test is an alternative to the repeated-measures t test from Chapter 11.
3. The Kruskal-Wallis test uses data from three or more separate samples to evaluate the differences between three or more treatment conditions (or populations). The Kruskal-Wallis test is an alternative to the single-factor, independent-measures ANOVA introduced in Chapter 12.
4. The Friedman test uses data from a repeated-measures design to compare the differences between three or more treatment conditions. This test is an alternative to the repeated-measures ANOVA from Chapter 13.

In each case, you should realize that the new, ordinal-data tests are back-up procedures that are available in situations in which the standard, parametric tests cannot be used. In general, if the data are appropriate for an ANOVA or one of the t tests, then the standard test is preferred to its ordinal-data alternative.

E.2 THE MANN-WHITNEY *U*-TEST: AN ALTERNATIVE TO THE INDEPENDENT-MEASURES *t* TEST

Recall that a study using two separate samples is called an *independent-measures* study or a *between-subjects* study. The Mann-Whitney test is designed to use the data from two separate samples to evaluate the difference between two treatments (or two populations). The calculations for this test require that the individual scores in the two samples be rank-ordered. The mathematics of the Mann-Whitney test are based on the following simple observation:

> A real difference between the two treatments should cause the scores in one sample to be generally larger than the scores in the other sample. If the two samples are combined and all the scores are ranked, then the larger ranks should be concentrated in one sample and the smaller ranks should be concentrated in the other sample.

THE NULL HYPOTHESIS FOR THE MANN-WHITNEY TEST

Because the Mann-Whitney test compares two distributions (rather than two means), the hypotheses tend to be somewhat vague. We state the hypotheses in terms of a consistent, systematic difference between the two treatments being compared.

H_0: There is no difference between the two treatments. Therefore, there is no tendency for the ranks in one treatment condition to be systematically higher (or lower) than the ranks in the other treatment condition.

H_1: There is a difference between the two treatments. Therefore, the ranks in one treatment condition are systematically higher (or lower) than the ranks in the other treatment condition.

CALCULATING THE MANN-WHITNEY U

Again, we begin by combining all the individuals from the two samples and then rank ordering the entire set. If you have a numerical score for each individual, combine the two sets of scores and rank order them. The Mann-Whitney U is then computed as if the two samples were two teams of athletes competing in a sports event. Each individual in sample A (the A team) gets one point whenever he or she is ranked ahead of an individual from sample B. The total number of points accumulated for sample A is called U_A. In the same way, a U value, or team total, is computed for sample B. The final Mann-Whitney U is the smaller of these two values. This process is demonstrated in the following example.

EXAMPLE E.1

We begin with two separate samples with $n = 6$ scores in each.

Sample A (treatment 1):	27	2	9	48	6	15
Sample B (treatment 2):	71	63	18	68	94	8

Next, the two samples are combined, and all 12 scores are ranked.

Ranks for Sample A	7	1	4	8	2	5
Ranks for Sample B	11	9	6	10	12	3

Each individual in sample A is assigned 1 point for every score in sample B that has a higher rank. $U_A = 4 + 6 + 5 + 4 + 6 + 5 = 30$. Similarly, $U_B = 0 + 0 + 2 + 0 + 0 + 4 = 6$.

Thus, the Mann-Whitney U is 6. As a simple check on your arithmetic, note that $U_A + U_B = n_A n_B$. For these data, $30 + 6 = 6(6)$.

COMPUTING U FOR LARGE SAMPLES

Because the process of counting points to determine the Mann-Whitney U can be tedious, especially with large samples, there is a formula that will generate the U value for each sample. To use this formula, you combine the samples and rank-order all the individuals as before. Then you must find ΣR_A, which is the sum of the ranks for individuals in sample A, and the corresponding ΣR_B for sample B. The U value for each sample is then computed as follows: For sample A,

$$U_A = n_A n_B + \frac{n_A(n_A + 1)}{2} - \Sigma R_A$$

and for sample B,

$$U_B = n_A n_B + \frac{n_B(n_B + 1)}{2} - \Sigma R_B$$

These formulas are demonstrated using the data from Example E.1. For sample A, the sum of the ranks is

$$\Sigma R_A = 1 + 2 + 4 + 5 + 7 + 8 = 27$$

For sample B, the sum of the ranks is

$$\Sigma R_B = 3 + 6 + 9 + 10 + 11 + 12 = 51$$

By using the special formula, for sample A,

$$\begin{aligned} U_A &= n_A n_B + \frac{n_A(n_A + 1)}{2} - \Sigma R_A \\ &= 6(6) + \frac{6(7)}{2} - 27 \\ &= 36 + 21 - 27 \\ &= 30 \end{aligned}$$

For sample B,

$$\begin{aligned} U_B &= n_A n_B + \frac{n_B(n_B + 1)}{2} - \Sigma R_B \\ &= 6(6) + \frac{6(7)}{2} - 51 \\ &= 36 + 21 - 51 \\ &= 6 \end{aligned}$$

Notice that these are the same U values we obtained in Example E.1 using the counting method. The Mann-Whitney U value is the smaller of these two, $U = 6$

EVALUATING THE SIGNIFICANCE OF THE MANN-WHITNEY *U*

Table B9 in Appendix B lists critical value of U for $\alpha = .05$ and $\alpha = .01$. The null hypothesis is rejected when the sample data produce a U that is *less than or equal to* the table value.

In Example E.1 both samples have $n = 6$ scores, and the table shows a critical value of $U = 5$ for a two-tailed test with $\alpha = .05$. This means that a value of $U = 5$ or smaller is very unlikely to occur (probability less than .05) if the null hypothesis is true. The data actually produced $U = 6$, which is not in the critical region. Therefore, we fail to reject H_0 because the data do not provide enough evidence to conclude that there is a significant difference between the two treatments.

There are no strict rules for reporting the outcome of a Mann-Whitney U-test. However, APA guidelines suggest that the report include a summary of the data (including such information as the sample size and the sum of the ranks) and the obtained statistic and p value. For the study presented in Example E.1, the results could be reported as follows:

> The original scores were ranked ordered and a Mann-Whitney U-test was used to compare the ranks for the $n = 6$ participants in treatment A and the $n = 6$ participants in treatment B. The results indicate no significant difference between treatments, $U = 6, p > .05$, with the sum of the ranks equal to 27 for treatment A and 51 for treatment B.

NORMAL APPROXIMATION FOR THE MANN-WHITNEY *U*

When the two samples are both large (about $n = 20$) and the null hypothesis is true, the distribution of the Mann-Whitney U statistic tends to approximate a normal shape. In this case, the Mann-Whitney hypotheses can be evaluated using a z-score statistic and the unit normal distribution. The procedure for this normal approximation is as follows:

1. Find the U values for sample A and sample B as before. The Mann-Whitney U is the smaller of these two values.
2. When both samples are relatively large (around $n = 20$ or more), the distribution of the Mann-Whitney U statistic tends to form a normal distribution with

$$\mu = \frac{n_A n_B}{2} \quad \text{and} \quad \sigma = \sqrt{\frac{n_A n_B (n_A + n_B + 1)}{12}}$$

   The Mann-Whitney U obtained from the sample data can be located in this distribution using a z-score:

$$z = \frac{X - \mu}{\sigma} = \frac{U - \dfrac{n_A n_B}{2}}{\sqrt{\dfrac{n_A n_B (n_A + n_B + 1)}{12}}}$$

3. Use the unit normal table to establish the critical region for this z-score. For example, with $\alpha = .05$, the critical values would be ± 1.96.

Usually the normal approximation is used with samples of $n = 20$ or larger; however, we will demonstrate the formulas with the data that were used in Example E.1. This study compared two treatments, A and B, using a separate sample of $n = 6$ for each treatment. The data produced a value of $U = 6$. The z-score corresponding to $U = 6$ is

$$z = \frac{U - \dfrac{n_A n_B}{2}}{\sqrt{\dfrac{n_A n_B (n_A + n_B + 1)}{12}}}$$

$$= \frac{6 - \dfrac{6(6)}{2}}{\sqrt{\dfrac{6(6)(6 + 6 + 1)}{12}}}$$

$$= \frac{-12}{\sqrt{\dfrac{468}{12}}}$$

$$= -1.92$$

With $\alpha = .05$, the critical value is $z = \pm 1.96$. Our computed z-score, $z = -1.92$, is not in the critical region, so the decision is to fail to reject H_0. Note that we reached the same conclusion for the original test using the critical values in the Mann-Whitney U table.

E.3 THE WILCOXON SIGNED-RANKS TEST: AN ALTERNATIVE TO THE REPEATED-MEASURES t TEST

The Wilcoxon test is designed to evaluate the difference between two treatments, using the data from a repeated-measures experiment. Recall that a repeated-measures study involves only one sample, with each individual in the sample being measured twice. The difference between the two measurements for each individual is recorded as the score for that individual. The Wilcoxon test requires that the differences be rank-ordered from smallest to largest in terms of their absolute magnitude, without regard for sign or direction. For example, Table E.1 shows differences scores and ranks for a sample of $n = 8$ participants.

TABLE E.1

Ranking difference scores. Note that the differences are ranked by magnitude, independent of direction.

Participant	Difference from Treatment 1 to Treatment 2	Rank
A	+4	1
B	−14	5
C	+5	2
D	−20	7
E	−6	3
F	−16	6
G	−8	4
H	−24	8

ZERO DIFFERENCES AND TIED SCORES

For the Wilcoxon test, there are two possibilities for tied scores:

1. A participant may have the same score in treatment 1 and in treatment 2, resulting in a difference score of zero.
2. Two (or more) participants may have identical difference scores (ignoring the sign of the difference).

When the data include individuals with difference scores of zero, one strategy is to discard these individuals from the analysis and reduce the sample size (n). However, this procedure ignores the fact that a difference score of zero is evidence for retaining the null hypothesis. A better procedure is to divide the zero differences evenly between the positives and negatives. (With an odd number of zero differences, discard one and divide the rest evenly.) When there are ties among the difference scores, each of the tied scores should be assigned the average of the tied ranks. This procedure was presented in detail in an earlier section of this appendix (see page 742).

HYPOTHESES FOR THE WILCOXON TEST

The null hypothesis for the Wilcoxon test simply states that there is no consistent, systematic difference between the two treatments.

If the null hypothesis is true, any differences that exist in the sample data must be due to chance. Therefore, we would expect positive and negative differences to be intermixed evenly. On the other hand, a consistent difference between the two treatments should cause the scores in one treatment to be consistently larger than the scores in the other. This should produce difference scores that tend to be consistently positive or consistently negative. The Wilcoxon test uses the signs and the ranks of the difference scores to decide whether there is a significant difference between the two treatments.

H_0: There is no difference between the two treatments. Therefore, in the general population there is no tendency for the difference scores to be either systematically positive or systematically negative.

H_1: There is a difference between the two treatments. Therefore, in the general population the difference scores are systematically positive or systematically negative.

CALCULATION AND INTERPRETATION OF THE WILCOXON *T*

After ranking the absolute values of the difference scores, the ranks are separated into two groups: those associated with positive differences (increases) and those associated with negative differences (decreases). Next, the sum of the ranks is computed for each group. The smaller of the two sums is the test statistic for the Wilcoxon test and is identified by the letter *T*. For the difference scores in Table E.1, the positive differences have ranks of 1 and 2, which add to $\Sigma R = 3$ and the negative difference scores have ranks of 5, 7, 3, 6, 4, and 8, which add up to $\Sigma R = 33$. For these scores, $T = 3$.

Table B10 in Appendix B lists critical values of T for $\alpha = .05$ and $\alpha = .01$. The null hypothesis is rejected when the sample data produce a T that is *less than or equal to* the table value. With $n = 8$ and $\alpha = .05$ for a two-tailed test, the table lists a critical value of 3. For the data in Table E.1, we obtained $T = 3$ so we would reject the null hypothesis and conclude that there is a significant difference between the two treatments.

As with the Mann-Whitney *U*-test, there is no specified format for reporting the results of a Wilcoxon *T*-test. It is suggested, however, that the report include a summary of the data and the value obtained for the test statistic as well as the p value. If there are zero-difference scores in the data, it is also recommended that the report describe how they were treated. For the data in Table E.1, the report could be as follows:

> The eight participants were rank ordered by the magnitude of their difference scores and a Wilcoxon T was used to evaluate the significance of the difference between treatments. The results showed a significant difference, $T = 3$, $p < .05$, with the positive ranks totaling 3 and the negative ranks totaling 33.

NORMAL APPROXIMATION FOR THE WILCOXON *T*-TEST

When a sample is relatively large, the values for the Wilcoxon T statistic tend to form a normal distribution. In this situation, it is possible to perform the test using a z-score statistic and the normal distribution rather than looking up a T value in the Wilcoxon table. When the sample size is greater than 20, the normal approximation is very accurate and can be used. For samples larger than $n = 50$, the Wilcoxon table typically does not provide any critical values, so the normal approximation must be used. The procedure for the *normal approximation for the Wilcoxon* T is as follows:

1. Find the total for the positive ranks and the total for the negative ranks as before. The Wilcoxon T is the smaller of the two values.
2. With n greater than 20, the Wilcoxon T values form a normal distribution with a mean of

$$\mu = \frac{n(n + 1)}{4}$$

and a standard deviation of

$$\sigma = \sqrt{\frac{n(n+1)(2n+1)}{24}}$$

The Wilcoxon T from the sample data corresponds to a z-score in this distribution defined by

$$z = \frac{X - \mu}{\sigma} = \frac{T - \frac{n(n+1)}{4}}{\sqrt{\frac{n(n+1)(2n+1}{24}}}$$

3. The unit normal table is used to determine the critical region for the z-score. For example, the critical values are ±1.96 for $\alpha = .05$.

Although the normal approximation is intended for samples with at least $n = 20$ individuals, we will demonstrate the calculations with the data in Table E.1. These data have $n = 8$ and produced $T = 3$. Using the normal approximation, these values produce

$$\mu = \frac{n(n+1)}{4} = \frac{8(9)}{4} = 18$$

$$\sigma = \sqrt{\frac{n(n+1)(2n+1)}{24}} = \sqrt{\frac{8(9)(17)}{24}} = \sqrt{51} = 7.14$$

With these values, the obtained $T = 3$ corresponds to a z-score of

$$z = \frac{T - \mu}{\sigma} = \frac{3-18}{7.14} = \frac{-15}{7.14} = 2.10$$

With critical boundaries of ±1.96, the obtained z-score is close to the boundary, but it is enough to be significant at the .05 level. Note that this is exactly the same conclusion we reached using the Wilcoxon T table.

E.4 THE KRUSKAL-WALLIS TEST: AN ALTERNATIVE TO THE INDEPENDENT-MEASURES ANOVA

The *Kruskal-Wallis test* is used to evaluate differences among three or more treatment conditions (or populations) using ordinal data from an independent-measures design. You should recognize that this test is an alternative to the single-factor ANOVA introduced in Chapter 12. However, the ANOVA requires numerical scores that can be used to calculate means and variances. The Kruskal-Wallis test, on the other hand, simply requires that you are able to rank-order the individuals for the variable being measured. You also should recognize that the Kruskal-Wallis test is similar to the Mann-Whitney test introduced earlier in this chapter. However, the Mann-Whitney test is limited to comparing only two treatments, whereas the Kruskal-Wallis test is used to compare three or more treatments.

THE DATA FOR A KRUSKAL-WALLIS TEST

The Kruskal-Wallis test requires three or more separate samples. The samples can represent different treatment conditions or they can represent different preexisting populations. For example, a researcher may want to examine how social input affects creativity. Children are asked to draw pictures under three different conditions: (1) working alone without supervision, (2) working in groups where the children are encouraged to examine and criticize each other's work, and (3) working alone but with frequent supervision and comments from a teacher. Three separate samples are used to represent the three treatment conditions with $n = 6$ children in each condition. At the end of the study, the researcher collects the drawings from all 18 children and rank-orders the complete set of drawings in terms of creativity. The purpose for the study is to determine whether one treatment condition produces drawings that are ranked consistently higher (or lower) than another condition. Notice that the researcher does not need to determine an absolute creativity score for each painting. Instead, the data consist of relative measures; that is, the researcher must decide which painting shows the most creativity, which shows the second most creativity, and so on.

The creativity study that was just described is an example of a research study comparing different treatment conditions. It also is possible that the three groups could be defined by a subject variable so that the three samples represent different populations. For example, a researcher could obtain drawings from a sample of 5-year-old children, a sample of 6-year-old children, and a third sample of 7-year-old children. Again, the Kruskal-Wallis test would begin by rank-ordering all of the drawings to determine whether one age group showed significantly more (or less) creativity than another.

Finally, the Kruskal-Wallis test can be used if the original, numerical data are converted into ordinal values. The following example demonstrates how a set of numerical scores is transformed into ranks to be used in a Kruskal-Wallis analysis.

EXAMPLE E.2

Table E.2(a) shows the original data from an independent-measures study comparing three treatment conditions. To prepare the data for a Kruskal-Wallis test, the complete set of original scores is rank-ordered using the standard procedure for ranking tied scores. Each of the original scores is then replaced by its rank to create the transformed data in Table E.2(b) that are used for the Kruskal-Wallis test.

THE NULL HYPOTHESIS FOR THE KRUSKAL-WALLIS TEST

As with the other tests for ordinal data, the null hypothesis for the Kruskal-Wallis test tends to be somewhat vague. In general, the null hypothesis states that there are no differences among the treatments being compared. Somewhat more specifically, H_0 states that there is no tendency for the ranks in one treatment condition to be systematically higher (or lower) than the ranks in any other condition. Generally, we use the concept of "systematic differences" to phrase the statement of H_0 and H_1. Thus, the hypotheses for the Kruskal-Wallis test are phrased as follows:

H_0: There is no tendency for the ranks in any treatment condition to be systematically higher or lower than the ranks in any other treatment condition. There are no differences between treatments.

H_1: The ranks in at least one treatment condition are systematically higher (or lower) than the ranks in another treatment condition. There are differences between treatments.

TABLE E.2

Preparing a set of data for analysis using the Kruskal-Wallis test. The original data consisting of numerical scores are shown in table (a). The original scores are combined into one group and rank ordered using the standard procedure for ranking tied scores. The ranks are then substituted for the original scores to create the set of ordinal data shown in table (b).

(a) Original Numerical Scores

I	II	III	
14	2	26	$N = 15$
3	14	8	
21	9	14	
5	12	19	
16	5	20	
$n_1 = 5$	$n_2 = 5$	$n_3 = 5$	

(b) Ordinal Data (Ranks)

I	II	III	
9	1	15	$N = 15$
2	9	5	
14	6	9	
3.5	7	12	
11	3.5	13	
$T_1 = 39.5$	$T_2 = 26.5$	$T_3 = 54$	
$n_1 = 5$	$n_2 = 5$	$n_3 = 5$	

Table E.2(b) presents the notation that is used in the Kruskal-Wallis formula along with the ranks. The notation is relatively simple and involves the following values:

1. The ranks in each treatment are added to obtain a total or T value for that treatment condition. The T values are used in the Kruskal-Wallis formula.
2. The number of subjects in each treatment condition is identified by a lowercase n.
3. The total number of subjects in the entire study is identified by an uppercase N.

The Kruskal-Wallis formula produces a statistic that is usually identified with the letter H and has approximately the same distribution as chi-square, with degrees of freedom defined by the number of treatment conditions minus one. For the data in Table E.2(b), there are 3 treatment conditions, so the formula produces a chi-square value with $df = 2$. The formula for the Kruskal-Wallis statistic is

$$H = \frac{12}{N(N+1)}\left(\Sigma\frac{T^2}{n}\right) - 3(N+1)$$

Using the data in Table E.2(b), the Kruskal-Wallis formula produces a chi-square value of

$$\begin{aligned} H &= \frac{12}{15(16)}\left(\frac{39.5^2}{5} + \frac{26.5^2}{5} + \frac{54^2}{5}\right) - 3(16) \\ &= 0.05(312.05 + 140.45 + 583.2) - 48 \\ &= 0.05(1035.7) - 48 \\ &= 51.785 - 48 \\ &= 3.785 \end{aligned}$$

With $df = 2$, the chi-square table lists a critical value of 5.99 for $\alpha = .05$. Because the obtained chi-square value (3.785) is not greater than the critical value, our statistical decision is to fail to reject H_0. The data do not provide sufficient evidence to conclude that there are significant differences among the three treatments.

As with the Mann-Whitney and the Wilcoxon tests, there is no standard format for reporting the outcome of a Kruskal-Wallis test. However, the report should provide a summary of the data, the value obtained for the chi-square statistic, as well as the value of *df, N,* and the *p* value. For the Kruskal-Wallis test that we just completed, the results could be reported as follows:

> After ranking the individual scores, a Kruskal-Wallis test was used to evaluate differences among the three treatments. The outcome of the test indicated no significant differences among the treatment conditions, $H = 3.785$ (2, $N = 15$), $p > .05$.

There is one assumption for the Kruskal-Wallis test that is necessary to justify using the chi-square distribution to identify critical values for H. Specifically, each of the treatment conditions must contain at least five scores.

E.5 THE FRIEDMAN TEST: AN ALTERNATIVE TO THE REPEATED-MEASURES ANOVA

The *Friedman test* is used to evaluate the differences between three or more treatment conditions using data from a repeated-measures design. This test is an alternative to the repeated-measures ANOVA that was introduced in Chapter 13. However, the ANOVA requires numerical scores that can be used to compute means and variances. The Friedman test simply requires ordinal data. The Friedman test is also similar to the Wilcoxon test that was introduced earlier in this chapter. However, the Wilcoxon test is limited to comparing only two treatments, whereas the Friedman test is used to compare three or more treatments.

THE DATA FOR A FRIEDMAN TEST

The Friedman test requires only one sample, with each individual participating in all of the different treatment conditions. The treatment conditions must be rank-ordered for each individual participant. For example, a researcher could observe a group of children diagnosed with ADHD in three different environments: at home, at school, and during unstructured play time. For each child, the researcher observes the degree to which the disorder interferes with normal activity in each environment, and then ranks the three environments from most disruptive to least disruptive. In this case, the ranks are obtained by comparing the individual's behavior across the three conditions. It is also possible for each individual to produce his or her own rankings. For example, each individual could be asked to evaluate three different designs for a new smart phone. Each person practices with each phone and then ranks them, 1st, 2nd, and 3rd in terms of ease of use.

Finally, the Friedman test can be used if the original data consist of numerical scores. However, the scores must be converted to ranks before the Friedman test is used. The following example demonstrates how a set of numerical scores is transformed into ranks for the Friedman test.

EXAMPLE E.3

To demonstrate the Friedman test, we will use the same data that were used to introduce the repeated-measures ANOVA in Chapter 13 (see page 440–441). The data are reproduced in Table E.3(a) and consist of ratings of four television-viewing distances for a sample of $n = 5$ participants. To convert the data for the Friedman test, the four scores for each participant are replaced with ranks 1, 2, 3, and 4, corresponding to the size of the original scores. As usual, tied scores are assigned the mean of the tied ranks. The complete set of ranks is shown in part (b) of the table.

THE HYPOTHESES FOR THE FRIEDMAN TEST

In general terms, the null hypothesis for the Friedman test states that there are no differences between the treatment conditions being compared so the ranks in one treatment should not be systematically higher (or lower) than the ranks in any other treatment condition. Thus, the hypotheses for the Friedman test can be phrased as follows:

H_0: There is no difference between treatments. Thus, the ranks in one treatment condition are not systematically higher or lower than the ranks in any other treatment condition.

H_1: There are differences between treatments. Thus, the ranks in at least one treatment condition are systematically higher or lower than the ranks in another treatment condition.

NOTATION AND CALCULATION FOR THE FRIEDMAN TEST

The first step in the Friedman test is to compute the sum of the ranks for each treatment condition. The ΣR values are shown in Table E.3(b). In addition to the ΣR values, the calculations for the Friedman test require the number of individuals in the sample (n) and the number of treatment conditions (k). For the data in Table E.3(b), $n = 5$ and

TABLE E.3

Results from a repeated-measures study comparing four television-viewing distances. Part (a) shows the original rating score for each of the distances. In part (b), the four distances are rank-ordered according to the preferences for each participant. The original data appear in Table 13.2 (page 441) and were used to demonstrate the repeated-measures ANOVA.

(a) The original rating scores.

Person	9 Feet	12 Feet	15 Feet	18 Feet
A	3	4	7	6
B	0	3	6	3
C	2	1	5	4
D	0	1	4	3
E	0	1	3	4

(b) The ranks of the treatment conditions for each participant

Person	9 Feet	9 Feet	9 Feet	9 Feet
A	1	2	4	3
B	1	2.5	4	2.5
C	2	1	4	3
D	1	2	4	3
E	1	2	3	4
	$\Sigma R_1 = 6$	$\Sigma R_2 = 9.5$	$\Sigma R_3 = 19$	$\Sigma R_4 = 15.5$

$k = 4$. The Friedman test evaluates the differences between treatments by computing the following test statistic:

$$\chi_r^2 = \frac{12}{nk(k+1)} \Sigma R^2 - 3n(k+1)$$

Note that the statistic is identified as chi-square (χ^2) with a subscript r, and corresponds to a chi-square statistic for ranks. This chi-square statistic has degrees of freedom determined by $df = k - 1$, and is evaluated using the critical values in the chi-square distribution shown in Table B8 in Appendix B.

For the data in Table E.3(b), the statistic is

$$\begin{aligned}\chi_r^2 &= \frac{12}{5(4)(5)}(6^2 + 9.5^2 + 15.5^2 + 19^2) - 3(5)(5)\\ &= \frac{12}{100}(36 + 90.25 + 240.25 + 361) - 75\\ &= 0.12(727.5) - 75\\ &= 12.3\end{aligned}$$

With $df = k - 1 = 3$, the critical value of chi-square is 9.35. Therefore, the decision is to reject the null hypothesis and conclude that there are significant differences among the four treatment conditions.

As with most of the tests for ordinal data, there is no standard format for reporting the results from a Friedman test. However, the report should provide the value obtained for the chi-square statistic as well as the values for df, n, and p. For the data that were used to demonstrate the Friedman test, the results would be reported as follows:

> After ranking the original scores, a Friedman test was used to evaluate the differences among the four treatment conditions. The outcome indicated that there are significant differences, $\chi_r^2 = 12.3$ $(3, n = 5)$, $p < .05$.

References

Note: Numbers in **bold** type indicate the textbook page(s) on which each reference is mentioned.

Ackerman, P. L., & Beier, M. E. (2007). Further explorations of perceptual speed abilities in the context of assessment methods, cognitive abilities, and individual differences during skill acquisition. *Journal of Experimental Psychology: Applied, 13,* 249–272. **(p. 138)**

Albentosa, M. J., & Cooper, J. J. (2005). Testing resource value in group-housed animals: An investigation of cage height preference in laying hens. *Behavioural Processes, 70,* 113–121. **(p. 652)**

American Psychological Association (APA). (2010). *Publication manual of the American Psychological Association* (6th ed.) Washington, DC: Author. **(pp. 82, 93, 466)**

Anderson, D. R., Huston, A. C., Wright, J. C., & Collins, P. A. (1998). Initial findings on the long term impact of Sesame Street and educational television for children: The recontact study. In R. Noll and M. Price (Eds.), *A communication cornucopia: Markle Foundation essays on information policy* (pp. 279–296). Washington, DC: Brookings Institution. **(p. 326)**

Arden, R., & Plomin, R. (2006). Sex differences in variance of intelligence across childhood. *Personality and Individual Differences, 41,* 39–48. **(pp. 131, 630)**

Athos, E. A., Levinson, B., Kistler, A., Zemansky, J., Bostrom, A., Freimer, N., & Gitschier, J. (2007). Dichotomy and perceptual distortions in absolute pitch ability. *Proceedings of the National Academy of Science of the United States of America, 104,* 14795–14800. **(p. 88)**

Bartus, R. T. (1990). Drugs to treat age-related neurodegenerative problems: The final frontier of medical science? *Journal of the American Geriatrics Society, 38,* 680–695. **(pp. 235, 376)**

Bélisle, J., & Bodur, H. O. (2010). Avatars as information: Perception of consumers based on the avatars in virtual worlds. *Psychology & Marketing, 27,* 741–765. **(p. 630)**

Belsky, J., Weinraub, M., Owen, M., & Kelly, J. (2001). Quality of child care and problem behavior. In J. Belsky (Chair), *Early childcare and children's development prior to school entry.* Symposium conducted at the 2001 Biennial Meetings of the Society for Research in Child Development, Minneapolis, MN. **(pp. 313, 674)**

Blest, A. D. (1957). The functions of eyespot patterns in the Lepidoptera. *Behaviour, 11,* 209–255. **(p. 284)**

Blum, J. (1978). *Pseudoscience and mental ability: The origins and fallacies of the IQ controversy.* New York: Monthly Review Press. **(p. 521)**

Boogert, N. J., Reader, S. M., & Laland, K. N. (2006). The relation between social rank, neophobia and individual learning in starlings. *Behavioural Biology, 72,* 1229–1239. **(p. 555)**

Bradbury, T. N., & Miller, G. A. (1985). Season of birth in schizophrenia: A review of evidence, methodology, and etiology. *Psychological Bulletin, 98,* 569–594. **(p. 631)**

Broberg, A. G., Wessels, H., Lamb, M. E., & Hwang, C. P. (1997). Effects of day care on the development of cognitive abilities in 8-year-olds: A longitudinal study. *Development Psychology, 33,* 62–69. **(p. 313)**

Brunt, A., Rhee, Y., & Zhong, L. (2008). Differences in dietary patterns among college students according to body mass index. *Journal of American College Health. 56,* 629–634. **(pp. 278, 674)**

Byrne, D. (1971). *The attraction paradigm.* New York: Academic Press. **(p. 654)**

Camera, W. J., & Echternacht, G. (2000). *The SAT 1 and high school grades: Utility in predicting success in college* (College Board Report No. RN-10). New York: College Entrance Examination Board. **(p. 558)**

Candappa, R. (2000). *The little book of wrong shui.* Kansas City: Andrews McMeel Publishing. **(p. 4)**

Cerveny, R. S., & Balling, Jr., R. C. (1998). Weekly cycles of air pollutants, precipitation and tropical cyclones in the coastal NW Atlantic region. *Nature, 394,* 561–563. **(p. 102)**

Chandra, A., & Minkovitz, C. S. (2006). Stigma starts early: Gender differences in teen willingness to use mental health services. *Journal of Adolescent Health, 38,* 754.el–754.e8. **(p. 610)**

Cialdini, R. B., Reno, R. R., & Kallgren, C. A. (1990). A focus theory of normative conduct: Recycling the concept of norms to reduce littering in public places. *Journal of Personality and Social Psychology, 58,* 1015–1026. **(p. 631)**

Cohen, J. (1988). *Statistical power analysis for the behavioral sciences.* Hillsdale, NJ: Lawrence Erlbaum Associates. **(pp. 262, 263, 299)**

Cohn, E. J., & Rotton, J. (2000). Weather, disorderly conduct, and assaults: From social contact to social avoidance. *Environment and Behavior, 32,* 651–673. **(p. 535)**

Collins, R. L., Elliott, M. N., Berry, S. H., Kanouse, D. E., Kunkel, D., Hunter, S. B., & Miu, A. (2004). Watching sex on television predicts adolescent initiation of sexual behavior. *Pediatrics, 114,* e280–e289. **(pp. 326, 534)**

Cook, M. (1977). Gaze and mutual gaze in social encounters. *American Scientist, 65,* 328–333. **(p. 284)**

Cowles, M., & Davis, C. (1982). On the origins of the .05 level of statistical significance. *American Psychologist, 37,* 553–558. **(p. 246)**

Craik, F. I. M., & Lockhart, R. S. (1972). Levels of processing: A framework for memory research. *Journal of Verbal Learning and Verbal Behavior, 11,* 671–684. **(p. 386)**

Danner F., & Phillips B. (2008). Adolescent sleep, school start times, and teen motor vehicle crashes. *Journal of Clinical Sleep Medicine, 4,* 533–535. **(p. 651)**

Downs, D. S., & Abwender, D. (2002). Neuropsychological impairment in soccer athletes. *Journal of Sports Medicine and Physical Fitness, 42,* 103–107. **(pp. 349, 500)**

Eagly, A. H., Ashmore, R. D., Makhijani, M. G., & Longo, L. C. (1991). What is beautiful is good but . . . : meta-analytic review of research on the physical attractiveness stereotype. *Psychological Bulletin,110,* 109–128. **(pp. 376, 675)**

Elliot, A. J., Niesta, K., Greitemeyer, T., Lichtenfeld, S., Gramzow, R., Maier, M. A., & Liu, H. (2010). Red, rank, and romance in women viewing men. *Journal of Experimental Psychology: General, 139,* 399–417. **(p. 503)**

Elliot, A. J., & Niesta, D. (2008). Romantic red: Red enhances men's attraction to women. *Journal of Personality and Social Psychology, 95,* 1150–1164. **(pp. 359, 503)**

Fallon, A. E., & Rozin, P. (1985). Sex differences in perceptions of desirable body shape. *Journal of Abnormal Psychology, 94,* 102–105. **(p. 630)**

Flett, G. L., Goldstein, A., Wall, A., Hewitt, P. L., Wekerle, C., and Azzi, N. (2008). Perfectionism and binge drinking in Canadian students making the transition to university. *Journal of American College Health, 57,* 249–253. **(p. 429)**

Flynn, J. R. (1984). The mean IQ of Americans: Massive gains 1932 to 1978. *Psychological Bulletin. 95,* 29–51. **(p. 312)**

Flynn, J. R. (1999). Searching for justice: The discovery of IQ gains over time. *American Psychologist, 54,* 5–20. **(pp. 312, 675)**

Ford, A. M., & Torok, D. (2008). Motivational signage increases physical activity on a college campus. *Journal of American College Health, 57,* 242–244. **(pp. 35, 675)**

Fowler, J. H., & Christakis, N. A. (2008). Dynamic spread of happiness in a large social network: Longitudinal analysis over 20 years in the Framingham heart study. *British Medical Journal (Clinical Research ed.), 337,* pp a2338 (electronic publication). **(p. 68)**

Friedman, M., & Rosenman, R. H. (1974). *Type A behavior and your heart.* New York: Knopf. **(p. 655)**

Frieswijk, N., Buunk, B. P., Steverink, N., & Slaets, J. P. J. (2004). The effect of social comparison information on the life satisfaction of frail older persons. *Psychology and Aging, 19,* 183–190. **(p. 380)**

Fuchs, L. S., Fuchs, D., Craddock, C., Hollenbeck, K. N., Hamlett, C. L., and Schatschneider, C. (2008). Effects of small-group tutoring with and without validated classroom instruction on at-risk students' math problem solving: Are two tiers of prevention better than one? *Journal of Educational Psychology, 100,* 491–509. **(p. 502)**

Fung, C. H., Elliott, M. N., Hays, R. D., Kahn, K. L., Kanouse, D. E., McGlynn, E. A., Spranca, M. D., & Shekelle, P. G. (2005). Patient's preferences for technical versus interpersonal quality when selecting a primary care physician. *Health Services Research, 40,* 957–977. **(p. 651)**

Gibson, E. J., & Walk, R. D. (1960). The "visual cliff." *Scientific American, 202,* 64–71. **(p. 634)**

Gilovich, T., Medvec, V. H., & Savitsky, K. (2000). The spotlight effect in social judgment: An egocentric bias in estimates of the salience of one's own actions and appearance. *Journal of Personality and Social Psychology, 78,* 211–222. **(p. 311)**

Gintzler, A. R. (1980). Endorphin-mediated increases in pain threshold during pregnancy. *Science, 210,* 193–195. **(p. 463)**

Green, L., Fry, A. F., & Myerson, J. (1994). Discounting of delayed rewards: A lifespan comparison. *Psychological Science, 5,* 33–36. **(p. 434)**

International Journal of Neuroscience, 113, 1675–1689.

Guéguen, N., & Jacob, C. (2010). 'Love is in the air': Effects of songs with romantic lyrics on compliance with a courtship request. *Psychology of Music, 38,* 303–307. **(p. 628)**

Güven, M., Elaimis, D. D., Binokay, S., & Tan, O. (2003). Population-level right-paw preference in rats assessed by a new computerized food-reaching test. **(p. 650)**

Hallam, S., Price, J., & Katsarou, G. (2002). The effects of background music on primary school pupils, task